THE CRITICS' FILM GUIDE

CHRISTOPHER TOOKEY

Christopher Tookey has been Film and Video Critic (and occasional Theatre Critic) for the *Daily Mail* since 1993. He was TV Critic for the *Sunday Telegraph* and *Daily Telegraph* from 1987-90, Film Critic for the *Sunday Telegraph* from 1989-92, and Theatre Critic for the *Mail on Sunday* in 1993. He has written for numerous other publications, including the *Sunday Times, Observer, European, Books & Bookmen, Literary Review*, and (in the USA) *National Review*. A frequent broadcaster on TV and radio, he has been Film Critic for Radio 2's 'The Arts Programme' since 1994. He is Chairman of the British Film Critics' Circle.

As a book writer, lyricist and composer, he has had ten stage musicals produced professionally and written the theme music for three TV series. Between 1974 and 1982, he directed extensively in regional theatre, on the fringe and in the West End. From 1975 to 1989, he worked as a director and producer on hundreds of TV programmes, including the award-winning rock series, *Revolver*.

BOXTREE

First published in Great Britain in 1994 by Boxtree Limited

1 2 3 4 5 6 7 8 9 10

Designed by Design 23
Typeset by SX Composing, Essex
Printed and bound in England by Redwood Books, Trowbridge, Wiltshire, for

Boxtree Limited
Broadwall House
21 Broadwall
London SE1 9PL

A CIP catalogue entry for this book is available from the British Library.

ISBN 1 85283 415 3

Front cover design by Design 23

CONTENTS

INTRODUCTION

Burt Reynolds on people who criticize: 'Those who can – do. Those who can't – teach. Those who can't do either – review.'

'Absolutely disgusting'. Film criticism was born with those two words, about an otherwise forgotten picture called *May Irwin Kiss* in the *Chap Book* for 15 June 1896. The first regular film critic, Frank Woods, began reviewing for the *New York Dramatic Mirror* on 1 May 1909, for a salary of $20 a week.

Since then, there has been an extraordinary amount of good and bad writing about the movies. While I can't claim to have read it all, I hope that this volume will preserve some of the best, and show why critics are worth reading. At a time when newspapers and magazines are increasingly fearful of offending advertisers and interest groups, and are becoming part of conglomerates which include film-making interests, the employment of honest, incorruptible critics is a vital sign of a journal's health.

But what is a critic's job? No two people will come up with the same answer. In my view, good critics should do a number of things:

(1) offer a subjective response and analysis – the more intelligent, mature, tasteful and well-informed, the better;
(2) encourage creative and technical talent, and increase an audience's appreciation of that talent;
(3) understand what the film-makers are trying to achieve, and judge how well they have succeeded according to their own objectives;
(4) put films in their social and historical context;
(5) advise readers of movies which the critic may not personally like but which may well have an appeal or importance nonetheless;
(6) entertain readers who may rarely go to the cinema or rent a video, but do enjoy a good read.

Is there a difference between a critic and a mere reviewer? John Simon has defined the difference as being: 'a reviewer has opinions; a critic can back them up with reasons . . . At fewer than fifteen hundred words a critic is condemned to being a reviewer.' However, many columnists are placed in the position of performing both functions on the same page – writing an in-depth analysis of the week's main film, but having to deal with other releases in a few sentences.

And length isn't everything. Many of the best 'reviewers', such as James Agee, have been able to sum up a film brilliantly in a sentence, while some of those who have pontificated at length in *Cahiers du Cinéma* or the *Monthly Film Bulletin* have had little worthwhile to say. One of the most regrettable things about film criticism today is its long-windedness. A spell of reviewing might do some critics a lot of good.

An even more regrettable tendency on both sides of the Atlantic is to judge films according to how '—ist' they are – sexist, racist, elitist, populist, rightist or leftist. Good critics will see beyond such terms, or at any rate see that they are reductionist. Just because a film's racial assumptions are outmoded (as in *Gone With The Wind*) does not invalidate it as a work of art or entertainment; nor does the fact that a film has impeccable non-sexist credentials mean that it is any good.

While I have been researching this book I have often been asked what kind of film has been most consistently underrated by critics. The short answer is: entertainment movies as a whole, and 'genre' films, in particular. For years, thrillers and westerns were not taken seriously by 'important' critics, such as Bosley Crowther of the *New York Times* or Caroline (C.A.) Lejeune of the *Observer*, who favoured psychological studies, 'social issue' films or costume drama. Ironically, many of the pictures which they praised most highly are now forgotten: few of us now remember, or would want to, *The Searching Wind* (1946), *Gentleman's Agreement* (1947) or *The Rose Tattoo* (1958).

A breakthrough came with so-called 'auteur ' criticism in the 1950s, led by Frenchmen like Truffaut and Chabrol. They had been brought up on American thrillers, gangster movies and westerns, and were anxious to prove that directors such as Hitchcock and John Ford were important film-makers, pursuing personal visions through the thriller and western genres.

Unfortunately, the 'auteur' critics often overestimated the role of the director and downgraded the writers, studios, actors, producers and craftspeople who contributed. They also tended to overpraise movies by 'auteurs' (many quite unworthy of the name) while downgrading films which were obviously the product of commercial studios. Even today, influenced by that tradition, some influential critics have a knee-jerk reaction to any Hollywood blockbuster; if it isn't 'personal', they argue, how can it be any good?

The answer is, of course, that many of the best movies have been commercially motivated, and have sought to do little more than entertain. We may be more prepared nowadays to recognize the merits of a *Singin' in the Rain* or *Casablanca*; but many mere 'entertainment' films remain despised, especially if they fall into an unfashionable category like 'slasher movie' (Scorsese's *Cape Fear*), 'monster movie' (Spielberg's *Jurassic Park*) or 'action-movie' (Cameron's *True Lies*).

If this book has any impact, I hope it will be to make readers realize there is often more to entertainment or commercial movies than they might imagine, and that a film is not intrinsically better for being in a foreign language or designed for the 'art-house'.

My thanks to my researchers Beth Porter, Catherine Townsend and Robin Bridges; to the British Film Institute Library (with the hope that they may find larger and more hospitable premises and be able to show more consideration to those who need to use their unique but inadequate facilities); to all others involved in the preparation of this volume, especially Katy Carrington, Linda Wood, Susanna Wadeson and Krystyna Zukowska; to my fellow-critics, especially Alan Frank, for advice and access to material; to all those at the *Daily Mail, Sunday Telegraph, Daily Telegraph* and *New Era Television* who have helped and encouraged me – especially Richard Addis, Paul Dacre, Sir David English, Robin Esser, Rod Gilchrist, Miriam Gross, Max Hastings, Derwent May, John Underwood and Sir Peregrine Worsthorne; and – of course – to my wife Frances and son Daniel.

It is certain that somewhere along the three-year gestation period of this book, mistakes and odd omissions have been made, or quotations wrongly attributed, and I will be very pleased to set these right in a future edition, if you write to me, care of the publishers. I would also be interested to know if readers can inform me of appropriate critics' names, where only periodicals have been credited.

HOW THE FILMS IN THIS GUIDE WERE SELECTED

Since over 250,000 films have been released in the last 100 years, every film guide has to be selective, and there is always a trade-off between breadth and depth. Many film guides are excessively superficial, one-sided and exclude fine films out of editorial whim or absent-mindedness; this one has, at least, been selected according to objective, statistical criteria. It contains over 2,000 entries, and they were chosen for the following reasons:

Automatically included were over a thousand films which scored an average of 7 or more, according to the star systems in the various film guides (with 10 points awarded to a film which gained the maximum number of stars). Also included were 172 films to which I alone gave a score of 7 or more; 77 got in because they were 'so bad, they're good', and another 50 because they attracted entertainingly bad reviews; 66 were included because they were controversial on release; 25 because they were undeservedly panned; 17 because they were greatly underrated; 88 because they were overrated; around 200 because they were important for some other reason.

Those criteria excluded some films which are quite watchable, but a volume which included every movie which scored an average of 5 marks or more would have had to be at least three times the size of this one. I have, in fact, gathered together reviews of most of those films in my personal computer database and hope that at some future date I shall be able to release a more universal film guide, either in multi-volume form or on CD-ROM.

This book includes no documentaries (e.g. *Burden of Dreams*), compilations (e.g. *That's Entertainment!*) or concert movies (e.g. *Woodstock*). Films were also excluded if they were unable to gain a cinema release in the UK, though there are a few exceptions to this rule.

GUIDE TO THE GUIDE

TITLE. Films are listed alphabetically, ignoring the English article (The, A or An). The exceptions are films which are part of a well-known series, such as the *Bond* or *Star Wars* films, which are listed chronologically under 'B' for *Bond* and 'S' for *Star Wars*. All alternative titles have a cross-reference so that if you look up *EMPIRE STRIKES BACK, THE* alphabetically under 'E', you will be referred to *STAR WARS SERIES, THE*. All foreign titles are also cross-referenced so if you look up *À BOUT DE SOUFFLE*, you will be advised of its alternative English title, *BREATHLESS*.

Foreign titles are listed strictly alphabetically, so if you wish to look up *LA DOLCE VITA*, you will find it under 'L', rather than 'D'. Where a foreign title (such as *LA STRADA*) is much better known than the English equivalent (*THE ROAD*), that movie's main entry will be found under its foreign name. Otherwise, it will be found under its English title. Either way, there will be a cross-reference, so if you know either title you should find it.

The only time that a film is not cross-referenced is when the two alternative titles are next to each other: for instance, *BABETTE'S GASTEBUD* would follow its English title *BABETTE'S FEAST*, so it is not listed separately – merely in brackets under the more familiar English title.

Each film title is alphabeticized according to a word-by-word rather than letter-by-letter system. Therefore, a gap between words is treated as though it has priority over the letter 'A'. So *ABE LINCOLN IN ILLINOIS* precedes *ABEL GANCE'S BEETHOVEN*. An apostrophe in a title, e.g. 'I'M', takes priority over the letter 'A' also, but takes second place to a space. So I'M ALL RIGHT JACK follows I WAS A MALE WAR BRIDE but precedes IF . . .

Abbreviations are ordered strictly as spelled: e.g. DR STRANGELOVE will be found under DR, not DOCTOR.

Titles which include numbers are as though spelled out: e.g. '10' will be found as if spelled TEN.

The spelling of the country of origin is used, e.g. MY FAVORITE YEAR and not MY FAVOURITE YEAR. (The same goes for critical extracts, which are spelled as originally written.)

CT: These are my marks out of 10 for each film as follows – 9 or 10: a personal favourite of mine; 8: excellent; 7: very good; 6: entertaining; 5: entertaining and/or interesting if you're in the mood; 4: flawed but watchable; 3: seriously flawed; 2: worth avoiding; 1: dire. Please notice that these marks bear little or no relation to a film's importance. *Birth of a Nation* is a hugely significant film in the development of cinema, but because I don't consider it very enjoyable to a modern audience, I have given it only 5 marks. On the rare occasions when I haven't seen a film, I put a dash (–).

AV: This mark shows the current critical consensus about a film. It is an average of the scores in the most recent edition of numerous leading film guides, with marks of 1 to 10 being awarded according to the stars awarded in each guide. The books consulted include the most recent editions of *Roger Ebert's Video Companion; Elliot's Guide to Films on Video*; Jim Fredrickson and Steve Stewart's *Film Annual, 1993*; (Leslie) *Halliwell's Film Guide; Leonard Maltin's Movie and Video Guide*; Nick Martin and

Marsha Porter's *Video Movie Guide; Barry Norman's Good Night In Guide*; (with 10 points automatically awarded to any movie included in Norman's sister volume, *100 Best Films of the Century*); Derek Winnert's *Radio Times Film and Video Guide*; the Consumer Guide's *Rating The Movies;* Simon Rose's *One Essential Film Guide*, Jeff Rovin's *The Laserdisc Film Guide*; Stephen H. Scheuer's *Movies on TV, Video and cassette*; David Shipman's *The Good Film and Video Guide*; David Quinlan's *TV Times Film and Video Guide*; and the *Virgin Film Guide*. In addition, 10 points were awarded for each time a movie appeared in the following books: Neil Sinyard's *Classic Movies*, Allan Hunter's *Movie Classics*, Daniel & Susan Cohen's *500 Great Films*, and David Zinman's *50 Classic Motion Pictures*; 8 points were awarded to any film that appeared as 'recommended' in Tom Wiener's *Book of Video Lists*, and 10 to those he 'highly recommended'. 10 points were also awarded for each time a film appeared in one of *Sight & Sound*'s polls of the 10 best films of all time, or if it appeared in *Time Out*'s 1989 list of the 100 Best Films of all time. Where a film has been released too recently for an average to be made, I have estimated its critical reception and placed after it the suffix 'est' (for 'estimated').

ALTERNATIVE TITLES. These are in parentheses under the main title.

YEAR OF RELEASE. The year a film was first released to the public (which may not be the year it was made).

COUNTRY OF ORIGIN.

RUNNING TIME. Given in minutes, this figure is often debatable. Many films are cut for US release or TV, and different versions are often in circulation. Because films are shown in an imperceptibly speeded-up version on British TV, a 100-minute film will run only 96 minutes on the box.

COLOUR FORMAT

Colour is indicated by 'C' and black-and-white by 'BW'.

CATEGORY

This gives some indication as to the principal genre(s) of the film – e.g. THRILLER, COMEDY, HORROR, FAMILY. Where films have been included in the *Guide* because they are 'so bad, they're good', this is indicated under the abbreviation SO BAD. If it is a foreign-language film, it is called FOREIGN.

PRODUCTION CREDITS – DIRECTOR (D) AND WRITER (W).

LEADING CAST MEMBERS.

PLOT SYNOPSIS.

MY CRITICAL SUMMARY. The length of this depends on the importance of the film, and how far my analysis differs from the consensus. My summary will often include outstanding technical credits. Many guides spread the misapprehension that the only creative input to a film comes from the director or writer. This is often a long way from the truth.

WHAT THE CRITICS SAID. You may or may not agree with my opinion – but whatever your view of a film, you should find it represented in this section. I have tried to show how critical opinion has changed on each picture, and how wide that range of opinion is. Most entries are arranged under favourable (PRO), mixed (MIXED) or hostile (ANTI). I have chosen reviews to be as illuminating, witty and representative as possible. Just because critics are quoted under 'ANTI' does not mean that their entire review was hostile – merely that the most interesting, penetrative or typical thing they said happened to fall into that category. Contemporary reviews always precede later reviews.

Reviews from the London listing magazine *Time Out* are usually contemporary, as long as the films date from 1968 onwards. Pauline Kael's reviews are contemporary, as long as the movies date from 1967 or later (she was at the *New Yorker* from 1967 until 1991). Danny Peary's comments are mostly after the event, and from his *Guide for the Film Fanatic* (1986). Reviews accredited to Margulies and Rebello are from *Bad Movies We Love* (1993) by Edward Margulies and Stephen Rebello. Reviews by Harry and Michael Medved are from *The Golden Turkey Awards* (1980). Reviews from James R. Parish and Michael R. Pitts are from their series of volumes about the various genres: *The Great Combat Pictures, The Great Spy Pictures*, etc.

Much-quoted US contemporary critics include James Agee, who wrote for *Time* and *The Nation* during the 1940s; Judith Crist, a reviewer on the *New York Herald Times* and other publications from 1945; Bosley Crowther, who was the most influential critic in the USA during his tenure at the *New York Times* (1940-1967); Crowther's nearest present-day equivalent, Roger Ebert, of the *Chicago Sun-Times, New York Daily News*, etc., and the *Siskel and Ebert Show*. Otis Ferguson, critic for *The New Republic* from 1934 to 1941; Stanley Kauffmann, film critic for *The New Republic* since 1958; Dwight MacDonald, critic for many magazines from 1929 to 1966, notably *The New Yorker* and *Esquire*; Andrew Sarris, critic for the *Village Voice* and other journals since 1960; John Simon, the most acid of all critics, on magazines such as *Esquire, New York, The New Leader*, and (lately) the *National Review*; and Herb Sterne, who wrote for *Rob Wagner's Script* throughout the 1940s.

The most-quoted British critics include Richard Winnington, of the *News Chronicle*, Dilys Powell of the *Sunday Times*, Graham Greene of *The Spectator* and *Night and Day*, C.A. Lejeune of the *Observer* and A.E. Wilson of *The Star*. Other attributions without a newspaper, magazine or book title attached refer to film guides by writers such as Leslie Halliwell, Simon Rose and Leonard Maltin, Ronald Bergan and Robyn Karney (their *Foreign Film Guide* was especially valuable) and Alan Frank (very knowledgeable in the horror and science fiction fields).

Christopher Tookey,
London, 1994

SIGNS AND ABBREVIATIONS:

AAW	Academy Award Winner
AAN	Academy Award Nominee
AV	Average
BW	Black and white
C	Colour
CEA	Cinema Exhibitors' Association (UK)
D	Directed by
(est)	Estimated
F & F	*Films & Filming*
FOREIGN	Foreign-language
MFB	*Monthly Film Bulletin*
NBR	*US National Board of Review*
NFT	*National Film Theatre*
PM	*Pathescope Monthly*
SF	Science Fiction
S & S	*Sight & Sound*
SO BAD	So bad it's enjoyable
W	Written by
☆	Critically acclaimed
✓	Acclaimed by me
✗	Overrated by the critics
●	Dire

THE 200 BEST FILMS OF ALL TIME

	TITLE	DIRECTOR	DATE	AV
1	HIS GIRL FRIDAY	Howard Hawks	1940	10.00
2	SINGIN' IN THE RAIN	Gene Kelly; Stanley Donen	1952	9.90
3	CASABLANCA	Michael Curtiz	1942	9.89
3	SNOW WHITE AND THE SEVEN DWARFS	David Hand	1937	9.89
5	CITIZEN KANE	Orson Welles	1941	9.84
6	POTEMKIN	Sergei Eisenstein	1925	9.83
6	SULLIVAN'S TRAVELS	Preston Sturges	1941	9.83
8	DOUBLE INDEMNITY	Billy Wilder	1944	9.81
9	HIGH NOON	Fred Zinnemann	1952	9.80
10	THE GRAND ILLUSION	Jean Renoir	1937	9.79
11	THE GRAPES OF WRATH	John Ford	1940	9.78
12	ALL QUIET ON THE WESTERN FRONT	Lewis Milestone	1930	9.76
12	THE GENERAL	Buster Keaton; Clyde Bruckman	1926	9.76
14	THE THIRD MAN	Carol Reed	1949	9.74
15	THE ADVENTURES OF ROBIN HOOD	Michael Curtiz; William Keighley	1938	9.73
15	CHILDREN OF PARADISE	Marcel Carné	1945	9.73
17	BONNIE AND CLYDE	Arthur Penn	1967	9.71
17	THE LADY VANISHES	Alfred Hitchcock	1938	9.71
17	THE MALTESE FALCON	John Huston	1941	9.71
17	PINOCCHIO	Ben Sharpsteen; Hamilton Luske	1939	9.71
21	SEVEN SAMURAI	Akira Kurosawa	1954	9.70
22	IT'S A WONDERFUL LIFE	Frank Capra	1946	9.69
22	THE 39 STEPS	Alfred Hitchcock	1935	9.69
24	THE AFRICAN QUEEN	John Huston	1951	9.67
24	THE BICYCLE THIEVES	Vittorio de Sica	1949	9.67
24	GREAT EXPECTATIONS	David Lean	1946	9.67
24	TOKYO STORY	Yasujiro Ozu	1953	9.67
28	ALL ABOUT EVE	Joseph L. Mankiewicz	1950	9.65
29	GONE WITH THE WIND	Victor Fleming	1939	9.63
29	TOP HAT	Mark Sandrich	1935	9.63
31	MR. SMITH GOES TO WASHINGTON	Frank Capra	1939	9.62
32	SOME LIKE IT HOT	Billy Wilder	1959	9.61
33	ON THE WATERFRONT	Elia Kazan	1954	9.56
33	THE WIZARD OF OZ	Victor Fleming	1939	9.56
35	KING KONG	Merian C. Cooper; Ernest B. Schoedsack	1933	9.53
35	THE MAGNIFICENT AMBERSONS	Orson Welles	1942	9.53
35	STAGECOACH	John Ford	1939	9.53
38	THE BANK DICK	Edward Cline	1940	9.50
38	IT HAPPENED ONE NIGHT	Frank Capra	1934	9.50
38	LOVE ME TONIGHT	Rouben Mamoulian	1932	9.50
38	PSYCHO	Alfred Hitchcock	1960	9.50
42	RASHOMON	Akira Kurosawa	1950	9.47
43	OLIVER TWIST	David Lean	1948	9.46
43	REBECCA	Alfred Hitchcock	1940	9.46
43	THE SEVENTH SEAL	Ingmar Bergman	1956	9.46
43	SWING TIME	George Stevens	1936	9.46
47	THE LOST WEEKEND	Billy Wilder	1945	9.45
48	MR. DEEDS GOES TO TOWN	Frank Capra	1936	9.43
49	BRIEF ENCOUNTER	David Lean	1945	9.41
49	NORTH BY NORTHWEST	Alfred Hitchcock	1959	9.41
49	THE RULES OF THE GAME	Jean Renoir	1939	9.41
52	THE 400 BLOWS	François Truffaut	1958	9.40
52	HENRY V	Laurence Olivier	1944	9.40
54	SUNSET BOULEVARD	Billy Wilder	1950	9.39
55	THE BIG SLEEP	Howard Hawks	1946	9.38
55	8½	Federico Fellini	1963	9.38
55	THE GOLD RUSH	Charles Chaplin	1925	9.38
55	KIND HEARTS AND CORONETS	Robert Hamer	1949	9.38
55	TOUCH OF EVIL	Orson Welles	1958	9.38
60	I AM A FUGITIVE FROM A CHAIN GANG	Mervyn LeRoy	1932	9.33
60	LAWRENCE OF ARABIA	David Lean	1962	9.33
60	PATHS OF GLORY	Stanley Kubrick	1957	9.33
63	THE GODFATHER	Francis Ford Coppola	1972	9.32
64	THE LAVENDER HILL MOB	Charles Crichton	1951	9.31
64	M	Fritz Lang	1931	9.31
64	PYGMALION	Anthony Asquith	1938	9.31
64	WHITE HEAT	Raoul Walsh	1949	9.31
68	THE BAND WAGON	Vincente Minnelli	1953	9.27
69	THE SEARCHERS	John Ford	1956	9.26
70	DR STRANGELOVE	Stanley Kubrick	1964	9.25
70	2001: A SPACE ODYSSEY	Stanley Kubrick	1968	9.25
72	DESTRY RIDES AGAIN	George Marshall	1939	9.23
72	THE THIEF OF BAGHDAD	Ludwig Berger; Michael Powell; Tim Whelan, Zoltan Korda; William Cameron Menzies; Alexander Korda	1940	9.23
74	TROUBLE IN PARADISE	Ernst Lubitsch	1932	9.22
75	PATHER PANCHALI	Satyajit Ray	1955	9.21
75	THE PHILADELPHIA STORY	George Cukor	1940	9.21
75	THE RED SHOES	Michael Powell; Emeric Pressburger	1948	9.21
78	DUCK SOUP	Leo McCarey	1933	9.20
78	NIGHT OF THE HUNTER	Charles Laughton	1955	9.20
78	TO BE OR NOT TO BE	Ernst Lubitsch	1942	9.20
81	JAWS	Steven Spielberg	1975	9.18
81	MY DARLING CLEMENTINE	John Ford	1946	9.18
83	LOST HORIZON	Frank Capra	1937	9.17
84	CHINATOWN	Roman Polanski	1974	9.16
85	BAMBI	David Hand	1942	9.15
85	GREED	Erich von Stroheim	1923	9.15
87	THE BIG PARADE	King Vidor	1925	9.14
87	BRINGING UP BABY	Howard Hawks	1938	9.14
87	DUMBO	Ben Sharpsteen	1941	9.14
90	FROM HERE TO ETERNITY	Fred Zinnemann	1953	9.13
90	THE GRADUATE	Mike Nichols	1967	9.13
90	OH, MR PORTER!	Marcel Varnel	1937	9.13
90	A STAR IS BORN	George Cukor	1954	9.13
94	A STREETCAR NAMED DESIRE	Elia Kazan	1951	9.12
95	FANTASIA	Ben Sharpsteen	1940	9.11
96	WAGES OF FEAR	Henri-Georges Clouzot	1953	9.09
96	THE WORLD OF APU	Satyajit Ray	1958	9.09
98	BEAUTY AND THE BEAST	Gary Trousdale; Kirk Wise	1991	9.08
98	BLACK NARCISSUS	Michael Powell; Emeric Pressburger	1946	9.08
98	CYRANO DE BERGERAC	Jean-Paul Rappeneau	1990	9.08
98	DINNER AT EIGHT	George Cukor	1933	9.08
98	INTOLERANCE	D.W. Griffith	1916	9.08
98	A MATTER OF LIFE AND DEATH	Michael Powell; Emeric Pressburger	1946	9.08
98	THE PRISONER OF ZENDA	John Cromwell	1937	9.08
105	THE BRIDE OF FRANKENSTEIN	James Whale	1935	9.07
105	FANNY AND ALEXANDER	Ingmar Bergman	1982	9.07
105	WILD STRAWBERRIES	Ingmar Bergman	1957	9.07
108	BEAUTY AND THE BEAST	Jean Cocteau	1946	9.00
108	THE BRIDGE ON THE RIVER KWAI	David Lean	1957	9.00
108	THE CROWD	King Vidor	1928	9.00
108	DAY FOR NIGHT	François Truffaut	1973	9.00
108	42ND STREET	Lloyd Bacon	1933	9.00
108	THE KID BROTHER	Ted Wilde; J.A. Howe	1927	9.00
108	A MAN ESCAPED	Robert Bresson	1956	9.00
108	NAPOLÉON	Abel Gance	1927	9.00
108	NINOTCHKA	Ernst Lubitsch	1939	9.00
108	ODD MAN OUT	Carol Reed	1947	9.00
108	THE PASSION OF JOAN OF ARC	Carl Dreyer	1928	9.00
108	RIDE THE HIGH COUNTRY	Sam Peckinpah	1962	9.00
120	RAGING BULL	Martin Scorsese	1980	8.94
121	THE APARTMENT	Billy Wilder	1960	8.93
121	DANCES WITH WOLVES	Kevin Costner	1991	8.93
121	LAURA	Otto Preminger	1944	8.93
121	STRANGERS ON A TRAIN	Alfred Hitchcock	1951	8.93
125	HOW GREEN WAS MY VALLEY	John Ford	1941	8.92
125	HOWARDS END	James Ivory	1992	8.92
125	GENEVIEVE	Henry Cornelius	1953	8.92
125	HUD	Martin Ritt	1963	8.92
125	THE MAN IN THE WHITE SUIT	Alexander Mackendrick	1951	8.92
130	DODSWORTH	William Wyler	1936	8.91
130	SHADOW OF A DOUBT	Alfred Hitchcock	1943	8.91
132	AMARCORD	Federico Fellini	1973	8.89
133	THE DIARY OF A COUNTRY PRIEST	Robert Bresson	1950	8.88
134	12 ANGRY MEN	Sidney Lumet	1957	8.87
135	ALEXANDER NEVSKY	Sergei Eisenstein	1938	8.86
135	THE BLUE ANGEL	Josef von Sternberg	1930	8.86
135	GOODFELLAS	Martin Scorsese	1990	8.86
135	GREEN FOR DANGER	Sidney Gilliat	1946	8.86
135	THE LAST PICTURE SHOW	Peter Bogdanovich	1971	8.86
135	THE NAVIGATOR	Buster Keaton	1924	8.86
135	SANSHO THE BAILIFF	Kenji Mizoguchi	1954	8.86
142	THE ASPHALT JUNGLE	John Huston	1950	8.85
142	THE HUSTLER	Robert Rossen	1961	8.85
142	THE LETTER	William Wyler	1940	8.85
145	FOREIGN CORRESPONDENT	Alfred Hitchcock	1940	8.83
145	GOLD DIGGERS OF 1933	Mervyn LeRoy	1933	8.83
145	JULES AND JIM	François Truffaut	1961	8.83
145	THE THIN MAN	W.S. Van Dyke	1934	8.83

149	NASHVILLE	Robert Altman	1975	8.82
149	A NIGHT AT THE OPERA	Sam Wood	1935	8.82
149	REAR WINDOW	Alfred Hitchcock	1954	8.82
149	WAY OUT WEST	James Horne	1936	8.82
153	THE GODFATHER, PART II	Francis Ford Coppola	1974	8.81
153	MEET ME IN ST. LOUIS	Vincente Minnelli	1944	8.81
155	GUNGA DIN	George Stevens	1939	8.80
155	LE MILLION	René Clair	1930	8.80
155	THE LEOPARD	Luchino Visconti	1963	8.80
155	METROPOLIS	Fritz Lang	1926	8.80
155	MODERN TIMES	Charles Chaplin	1936	8.80
155	UMBERTO D	Vittorio de Sica	1962	8.80
155	THE WIND	Victor Sjöström	1927	8.80
162	DAVID COPPERFIELD	George Cukor	1934	8.79
162	SWEET SMELL OF SUCCESS	Alexander Mackendrick	1957	8.79
162	THE TREASURE OF THE SIERRA MADRE	John Huston	1948	8.79
165	E.T. THE EXTRA-TERRESTRIAL	Steven Spielberg	1980	8.78
166	THE DISCREET CHARM OF THE BOURGEOISIE	Luis Buñuel	1972	8.77
166	THE LADY EVE	Preston Sturges	1941	8.77
166	THE LIFE AND DEATH OF COLONEL BLIMP	Michael Powell; Emeric Pressburger	1943	8.77
166	THE MANCHURIAN CANDIDATE	John Frankenheimer	1962	8.77
170	ALL THE PRESIDENT'S MEN	Alan J. Pakula	1976	8.75
170	THE BEST YEARS OF OUR LIVES	William Wyler	1946	8.75
170	FRANKENSTEIN	James Whale	1931	8.75
170	FREEDOM FOR US	René Clair	1931	8.75
170	INVASION OF THE BODY SNATCHERS	Don Siegel	1956	8.75
170	ONE FLEW OVER THE CUCKOO'S NEST	Milos Forman	1975	8.75
170	THE RED BALLOON	Albert Lamorisse	1956	8.75
170	SHE DONE HIM WRONG	Lowell Sherman	1932	8.75
170	UNE PARTIE DE CAMPAGNE	Jean Renoir	1936	8.75
179	AND THEN THERE WERE NONE	René Clair	1945	8.73
179	RED RIVER	Howard Hawks	1948	8.73
181	JEUX INTERDITS	René Clément	1952	8.73
181	THE PLAYER	Robert Altman	1992	8.73
183	VERTIGO	Alfred Hitchcock	1958	8.72
184	A MAN FOR ALL SEASONS	Fred Zinnemann	1966	8.71
184	ONCE UPON A TIME IN AMERICA	Sergio Leone	1984	8.71
184	YANKEE DOODLE DANDY	Michael Curtiz	1942	8.71
187	IT'S A GIFT	Norman Z. McLeod	1934	8.70
188	L'AVVENTURA	Michelangelo Antonioni	1960	8.69
188	QUEEN CHRISTINA	Rouben Mamoulian	1933	8.69
188	ON THE TOWN	Gene Kelly; Stanley Donen	1949	8.69
188	RICHARD III	Laurence Olivier	1955	8.69
188	SCARFACE	Howard Hawks	1932	8.69
188	Z	Costa-Gavras	1968	8.69
194	BAD DAY AT BLACK ROCK	John Sturges	1955	8.67
194	CABARET	Bob Fosse	1972	8.67
194	CLOSE ENCOUNTERS OF THE THIRD KIND	Steven Spielberg	1977	8.67
194	THE CONVERSATION	Francis Ford Coppola	1974	8.67
194	THE GREAT ESCAPE	John Sturges	1963	8.67
194	LA STRADA	Federico Fellini	1954	8.67
194	ORPHEUS	Jean Cocteau	1950	8.67
194	THE PALM BEACH STORY	Preston Sturges	1942	8.67
194	SONS OF THE DESERT	William A. Seiter	1934	8.67
194	TOM JONES	Tony Richardson	1963	8.67
194	WHISKY GALORE	Alexander Mackendrick	1949	8.67

CHRISTOPHER TOOKEY'S 200 FAVOURITE FILMS OF ALL TIME

TITLE	YEAR	DIRECTOR
ADVENTURES OF ROBIN HOOD, THE	1938	Michael Curtiz; William Keighley
AFRICAN QUEEN, THE	1951	John Huston
AFTER HOURS	1985	Martin Scorsese
AGE OF INNOCENCE, THE	1993	Martin Scorsese
AIRPLANE!	1980	Zucker, Abrahams, Zucker,
ALIEN	1979	Ridley Scott
ALL ABOUT EVE	1950	Joseph L. Mankiewicz
AMERICAN WEREWOLF IN LONDON, AN	1981	John Landis
ANNIE HALL	1977	Woody Allen
APARTMENT, THE	1960	Billy Wilder
ARACHNAPHOBIA	1990	Frank Marshall
AWAKENINGS	1990	Penny Marshall
BABETTE'S FEAST	1987	Gabriel Axel
BACK TO THE FUTURE	1985	Robert Zemeckis
BAMBI	1942	David Hand
BAND WAGON, THE	1953	Vincente Minnelli
BEAUTY AND THE BEAST	1991	Gary Trousdale; Kirk Wise
BEGUILED, THE	1971	Don Siegel
BICYCLE THIEVES, THE	1949	Vittorio de Sica
BIG SLEEP, THE	1946	Howard Hawks
BLADE RUNNER (Director's Cut)	1992	Ridley Scott
BLAZING SADDLES	1974	Mel Brooks
BLUE KITE, THE	1992	Tian Zhuangzhuang
BLUE VELVET	1986	David Lynch
BONNIE AND CLYDE	1967	Arthur Penn
BRIEF ENCOUNTER	1945	David Lean
CABARET	1972	Bob Fosse
CAPE FEAR	1991	Martin Scorsese
CAROUSEL	1956	Henry King
CARRIE	1976	Brian de Palma
CASABLANCA	1942	Michael Curtiz
CAT AND THE CANARY, THE	1939	Elliott Nugent
CHARLEY VARRICK	1973	Don Siegel
CHINATOWN	1974	Roman Polanski
CITIZEN KANE	1941	Orson Welles
CLAIRE'S KNEE	1971	Eric Rohmer
CLOSE ENCOUNTERS OF THE THIRD KIND (Special Edition)	1980	Steven Spielberg
COMMITMENTS, THE	1991	Alan Parker
CRIES AND WHISPERS	1972	Ingmar Bergman
CRIMES AND MISDEMEANORS	1989	Woody Allen
CYRANO DE BERGERAC	1990	Jean-Paul Rappeneau
DANCES WITH WOLVES (Director's Cut)	1991	Kevin Costner
DEATH IN BRUNSWICK	1990	John Ruane
DELIVERANCE	1972	John Boorman
DEMOLITION MAN	1993	Marco Brambilla
DIE HARD	1988	John McTiernan
DON'T LOOK NOW	1973	Nicolas Roeg
DOUBLE INDEMNITY	1944	Billy Wilder
DUCK SOUP	1933	Leo McCarey
DUMBO	1941	Ben Sharpsteen
E.T. THE EXTRA-TERRESTRIAL	1980	Steven Spielberg
EDWARD SCISSORHANDS	1990	Tim Burton
FALLING DOWN	1993	Joel Schumacher
FANNY AND ALEXANDER	1982	Ingmar Bergman
FAREWELL MY LOVELY	1944	Edward Dmytryk
FIELD OF DREAMS	1989	Phil Alden Robinson
FLIRTING	1991	John McDuigan
FOLLOW THE FLEET	1936	Mark Sandrich
FOREIGN CORRESPONDENT	1940	Alfred Hitchcock
42ND STREET	1933	Lloyd Bacon
FOUR WEDDINGS AND A FUNERAL	1994	Mike Newell
GASLIGHT	1940	Thorold Dickinson
GENEVIEVE	1953	Henry Cornelius
GENTLEMEN PREFER BLONDES	1953	Howard Hawks
GIGI	1958	Vincente Minnelli
GOLD DIGGERS OF 1933	1933	Mervyn LeRoy
GONE WITH THE WIND	1939	Victor Fleming
GOODFELLAS	1990	Martin Scorsese
GRAND ILLUSION, THE	1937	Jean Renoir
GRAPES OF WRATH, THE	1940	John Ford
GREAT ESCAPE, THE	1963	John Sturges
GREAT EXPECTATIONS	1946	David Lean
GREGORY'S GIRL	1981	Bill Forsyth
GROUNDHOG DAY	1992	Harold Ramis
GUNGA DIN	1939	George Stevens
HANNAH AND HER SISTERS	1986	Woody Allen
HARD DAY'S NIGHT, A	1964	Richard Lester
HEAR MY SONG	1991	Peter Chelsom
HEAVEN'S GATE	1980	Michael Cimino
HEIRESS, THE	1949	William Wyler
HENRY V	1944	Laurence Olivier
HIGH NOON	1952	Fred Zinnemann
HIS GIRL FRIDAY	1940	Howard Hawks
HOMICIDE	1991	David Mamet
HOUSE OF ANGELS	1993	Colin Nutley
HOUSE OF GAMES	1987	David Mamet
HUSBANDS AND WIVES	1992	Woody Allen
I'M ALL RIGHT JACK	1959	John Boulting
IMPORTANCE OF BEING EARNEST, THE	1952	Anthony Asquith
INNOCENTS, THE	1960	Jack Clayton
IT'S A WONDERFUL LIFE	1946	Frank Capra
JACOB'S LADDER	1991	Adrian Lyne
JEAN DE FLORETTE	1986	Claude Berri
JESUS OF MONTREAL	1989	Denys Arcand

JU DOU	1991	Zhang Yimou, Zhang
JURASSIC PARK	1993	Steven Spielberg
KES	1969	Ken Loach
KILLING FIELDS, THE	1984	Roland Joffe
KIND HEARTS AND CORONETS	1949	Robert Hamer
KING AND I, THE	1956	Walter Lang
KING KONG	1933	Schoedsack Cooper
KING OF COMEDY, THE	1986	Martin Scorsese
LADY AND THE TRAMP	1955	Luske, Geronimi, Jackson
LADY VANISHES, THE	1938	Alfred Hitchcock
LAST SEDUCTION, THE	1993	John Dahl
LAVENDER HILL MOB, THE	1951	Charles Crichton
LETTER, THE	1940	William Wyler
LION KING, THE	1994	Roger Allers; Rob Minkoff
LOCAL HERO	1983	Bill Forsyth
LOVE ME TONIGHT	1932	Rouben Mamoulian
M	1931	Fritz Lang
MAGNIFICENT SEVEN, THE	1960	John Sturges
MALTESE FALCON, THE	1941	John Huston
MAN BITES DOG	1992	Belvaux, Bonzel, Poelevoorde
MAN ESCAPED, A	1956	Robert Bresson
MAN FOR ALL SEASONS, A	1966	Fred Zinnemann
MANHATTAN	1979	Woody Allen
MATTER OF LIFE AND DEATH, A	1946	Michael Powell; Emeric Pressburger
MIDNIGHT RUN	1988	Martin Brest
MIRACLE WORKER, THE	1962	Arthur Penn
MOVIE MOVIE	1978	Stanley Donen
MR. SMITH GOES TO WASHINGTON	1939	Frank Capra
MY FAIR LADY	1964	George Cukor
MY FAVORITE YEAR	1982	Richard Benjamin
NIGHT AT THE OPERA, A	1935	Sam Wood
NIGHT OF THE HUNTER	1955	Charles Laughton
NORTH BY NORTHWEST	1959	Alfred Hitchcock
NOTORIOUS	1946	Alfred Hitchcock
OKLAHOMA!	1955	Fred Zinnemann
ON THE WATERFRONT	1954	Elia Kazan
101 DALMATIANS	1961	Reitherman, Luske, Geronimi
PATHER PANCHALI	1955	Satyajit Ray
PHILADELPHIA STORY, THE	1940	George Cukor
PINOCCHIO	1939	Hamilton Sharpsteen, Ben Luske
PLAY MISTY FOR ME	1971	Clint Eastwood
PRIVATE LIFE OF HENRY VIII, THE	1933	Alexander Korda
PRODUCERS, THE	1968	Mel Brooks
PSYCHO	1960	Alfred Hitchcock
PULP FICTION	1994	Quentin Tarantino
QUEEN OF HEARTS	1989	Jon Amiel
RAIDERS OF THE LOST ARK	1981	Steven Spielberg
RAILWAY CHILDREN, THE	1970	Lionel Jeffries
REAR WINDOW	1954	Alfred Hitchcock
REBECCA	1940	Alfred Hitchcock
RIDE THE HIGH COUNTRY	1962	Sam Peckinpah
ROADHOUSE	1989	Rowdy Herrington
ROBOCOP	1987	Paul Verhoeven
ROMUALD AND JULIETTE	1989	Coline Serreau
SALVADOR	1986	Oliver Stone
SANSHO THE BAILIFF	1954	Kenji Mizoguchi
SCARLET PIMPERNEL, THE	1934	Harold Young
SCHINDLER'S LIST	1994	Steven Spielberg
SHADOW OF A DOUBT	1943	Alfred Hitchcock
SHADOWLANDS	1993	Richard Attenborough
SHOP AROUND THE CORNER, THE	1940	Ernst Lubitsch
SHORT CUTS	1993	Robert Altman
SHOW PEOPLE	1928	King Vidor
SILENCE OF THE LAMBS, THE	1991	Jonathan Demme
SILVERADO	1985	Lawrence Kasdan
SINGIN' IN THE RAIN	1952	Gene Kelly; Stanley Donen
SINGLES	1992	Cameron Crowe
SLEEPLESS IN SEATTLE	1993	Nora Ephron
SNOW WHITE AND THE SEVEN DWARFS	1937	David Hand
SOME LIKE IT HOT	1959	Billy Wilder
SOUND OF MUSIC, THE	1965	Robert Wise
SPARTACUS	1960	Stanley Kubrick
SPEED	1994	Jan de Bont
SPIRAL STAIRCASE, THE	1946	Robert Siodmak
STAGECOACH	1939	John Ford
STAR IS BORN, A	1954	George Cukor
STAR WARS	1977	George Lucas
STRICTLY BALLROOM	1992	Baz Luhrmann
SULLIVAN'S TRAVELS	1941	Preston Sturges
SUNSET BOULEVARD	1950	Billy Wilder
SWING TIME	1936	George Stevens
TALE OF THE FOX	1932	Wladyslaw Starewicz
TAXI DRIVER	1976	Martin Scorsese
TERMINATOR 2: JUDGMENT DAY	1991	James Cameron
THELMA & LOUISE	1991	Ridley Scott
THIRD MAN, THE	1949	Carol Reed
39 STEPS, THE	1935	Alfred Hitchcock
THIS IS SPINAL TAP	1984	Rob Reiner
TO BE OR NOT TO BE	1942	Ernst Lubitsch
TOKYO STORY	1953	Yasujiro Ozu
TOM JONES	1963	Tony Richardson
TOOTSIE	1982	Sydney Pollack
TOP HAT	1935	Mark Sandrich
TOTAL RECALL	1990	Paul Verhoeven
TOTO THE HERO	1991	Jaco van Dormael
TREMORS	1989	Ron Underwood
TROUBLE IN PARADISE	1932	Ernst Lubitsch
TRUE LIES	1994	James Cameron
12 ANGRY MEN	1957	Sidney Lumet
VANISHING, THE	1988	George Sluizer
VERTIGO	1958	Alfred Hitchcock
WAGES OF FEAR	1953	Henri-Georges Clouzot
WEST SIDE STORY	1961	Robert Wise; Jerome Robbins
WHO FRAMED ROGER RABBIT?	1988	Robert Zemeckis
WILD TARGET	1993	Pierre Salvadori
WORLD OF APU, THE	1958	Satyajit Ray
YOUNG AND THE DAMNED, THE	1950	Luis Buñuel

THE 50 BEST DIRECTORS OF ALL TIME

Calculated by the total score of their 4 top-scoring films. The number of their films to score over 7.00 is in the first column.

	DIRECTOR	scores over 7	av top 4
1.	Alfred Hitchcock	17	38.36
2.	Billy Wilder	10	38.26
3.	Frank Capra	11	38.24
4.	David Lean	11	37.87
5.	John Ford	17	37.75
6.	Howard Hawks	13	37.25
7.	John Huston	11	37.02
8.	Michael Powell	7	36.60
9.	Akira Kurosawa	10	36.31
10.	Michael Curtiz	10	36.29
11.	George Cukor	13	36.21
12.	Emeric Pressburger	5	36.14
13.	Ingmar Bergman	11	36.10
14.	Orson Welles	4	36.08
15.	Jean Renoir	6	35.85
15.	Preston Sturges	8	35.85
17.	Stanley Kubrick	7	35.83
18.	Ernst Lubitsch	9	35.82
19.	King Vidor	6	35.70
20.	Fred Zinnemann	6	35.54
21.	Carol Reed	7	35.40
22.	Francis Ford Coppola	4	35.21
23.	Sergei Eisenstein	5	35.20
24.	Buster Keaton	5	35.19
25.	Vittorio de Sica	6	35.17
26.	George Stevens	8	35.04
27.	William Wyler	14	35.01
28.	Elia Kazan	10	35.00
29.	François Truffaut	9	34.98
30.	Victor Fleming	5	34.96
31.	Alexander Mackendrick	4	34.84
32.	Stanley Donen	6	34.75
32.	Charles Chaplin	6	34.75
32.	Vincente Minnelli	8	34.75
35.	James Whale	5	34.70
36.	Steven Spielberg	6	34.69
37.	Federico Fellini	5	34.58
38.	Martin Scorsese	6	34.50
39.	Rouben Mamoulian	4	34.25
40.	Mervyn LeRoy	6	34.14
41.	Luis Buñuel	11	34.01
42.	Fritz Lang	9	33.80
43.	Sidney Lumet	8	33.77
44.	William Keighley	4	33.68
45.	Satyajit Ray	6	33.66
46.	Robert Bresson	5	33.63
47.	Woody Allen	7	33.26
48.	Leo McCarey	6	33.20

49.	Robert Altman	4	32.93
50.	Kenji Mizoguchi	4	32.91

NB To qualify for this list, a director must have made at least 3 films scoring over 7.00. Several famous directors do not qualify, e.g. Yasujiro Ozu (2 entries), Marcel Carné, Jean-Luc Godard and Laurence Olivier (3 entries each).

FILMS THAT WERE UNDERRATED ON RELEASE

TITLE	YEAR	AVE
ACE IN THE HOLE	1951	8.44
AIRPLANE!	1980	6.86
ALIEN	1979	7.23
APARTMENT, THE	1960	8.93
ARACHNAPHOBIA	1990	5.58
AVANTI!	1972	6.30
AWAKENINGS	1990	7.33
BEACHES	1988	5.33
BEAT THE DEVIL	1953	6.33
BEGUILED, THE	1971	6.64
BLADE RUNNER	1982	7.47
BLAZING SADDLES	1974	6.36
BLUE VELVET	1986	6.29
CAPE FEAR	1991	6.69
CARRIE	1976	6.21
CASABLANCA	1942	9.89
CHILDREN'S HOUR, THE	1961	6.00
CLIFFHANGER	1993	4.75
COOL RUNNINGS	1993	7.00
CURSE OF FRANKENSTEIN, THE	1957	5.56
CURSE OF THE WEREWOLF, THE	1961	5.14
DAWN OF THE DEAD	1979	7.17
DIE HARD	1988	7.71
DRACULA	1958	7.75
EDWARD SCISSORHANDS	1990	6.54
FISTFUL OF DOLLARS, A	1964	6.00
FLY, THE	1958	4.88
FRANKENSTEIN	1931	8.75
FRIDAY THE 13TH	1980	3.80
GENTLEMEN PREFER BLONDES	1953	6.62
GHOST	1990	6.75
GHOSTBUSTERS	1984	7.07
GIRL CAN'T HELP IT, THE	1956	6.00
HALLOWEEN	1978	6.93
HANS CHRISTIAN ANDERSEN	1952	5.45
HAROLD AND MAUDE	1971	7.09
HEAVEN'S GATE	1980	4.15
HIGH SOCIETY	1956	6.15
HOME ALONE	1990	5.77
HOOK	1992	5.09
HOUSE OF ANGELS	1993	6.50
HUSBANDS AND WIVES	1992	6.67
JACOB'S LADDER	1991	5.92
JASON AND THE ARGONAUTS	1963	6.50
KIND HEARTS AND CORONETS	1949	9.38
KINDERGARTEN COP	1990	5.18
LADY AND THE TRAMP	1955	7.73
LAST BOY SCOUT, THE	1991	5.00
MAD MAX	1979	6.67
MCCABE AND MRS. MILLER	1971	7.31
MIDNIGHT RUN	1988	7.42
MOVIE MOVIE	1978	6.90
MY DARLING CLEMENTINE	1946	9.18
NEW YORK, NEW YORK	1977	5.08
NIGHTMARE ALLEY	1947	7.20
NIGHTMARE ON ELM STREET, A	1984	5.58
OKLAHOMA!	1955	6.67
PARALLAX VIEW, THE	1974	7.08
PEEPING TOM	1959	6.86
PENNIES FROM HEAVEN	1981	5.58
PETULIA	1968	6.91
PLANES, TRAINS AND AUTOMOBILES	1987	5.85
PLANET OF THE APES	1968	6.92
POINT BLANK	1967	6.90
POSTMAN ALWAYS RINGS TWICE, THE	1946	7.92
PRODUCERS, THE	1968	7.08
QUEEN OF HEARTS	1989	7.23
RAMBO: FIRST BLOOD	1982	4.42
RIVER'S EDGE	1987	7.08
ROADHOUSE	1989	4.10
ROBIN HOOD: PRINCE OF THIEVES	1991	5.31
ROBOCOP 2	1990	3.90
SALVADOR	1986	7.15
SHADOW OF A DOUBT	1943	8.91
SHANGHAI GESTURE, THE	1941	4.14
SHOT IN THE DARK, A	1964	7.00
SILVERADO	1985	6.00
SINGIN' IN THE RAIN	1952	9.90
SLEEPLESS IN SEATTLE	1993	7.25
SOMETHING WILD	1986	6.50
SOUTH PACIFIC	1958	5.67
SPLASH!	1984	6.47
STAR!	1968	5.89
STAR WARS	1977	8.18
STARDUST MEMORIES	1980	5.00
SUPERMAN	1978	7.13
SWEET CHARITY	1969	6.67
SYLVIA SCARLETT	1935	6.00
TEN COMMANDMENTS, THE	1956	7.36
TERMINATOR, THE	1984	7.07
TERMINATOR 2: JUDGMENT DAY	1991	7.23
TO BE OR NOT TO BE	1942	9.20
TOTAL RECALL	1990	6.17
TREMORS	1989	6.64
TROUBLE WITH HARRY, THE	1955	6.50
UNFORGIVEN, THE	1960	6.22
WHATEVER HAPPENED TO BABY JANE?	1962	7.15
WHITE HEAT	1949	9.31
WIZARD OF OZ, THE	1939	9.56

FILMS THAT WERE OVERRATED ON RELEASE

TITLE	YEAR	DIRECTOR	AVE
ABRAHAM LINCOLN	1930	D.W. Griffith	5.13
ACCIDENT	1967	Joseph Losey	6.00
AFTER DARK, MY SWEET	1990	James Foley	5.10
ALEXANDER NEVSKY	1938	Sergei Eisenstein	8.86
ALICE'S RESTAURANT	1969	Arthur Penn	5.18
ALPHAVILLE	1965	Jean-Luc Godard	5.00
ANDREI RUBLEV	1966	Andrei Tarkovsky	8.10
BAD TIMING: A SENSUAL OBSESSION	1980	Nicolas Roeg	5.00
BARTON FINK	1991	Joel Coen	6.00
BATMAN	1989	Tim Burton	6.36
BELLE DE JOUR	1967	Luis Buñuel	8.29
BELLE EPOQUE	1993	Fernando Trueba	6.00
BILLY JACK	1971	Tom Laughlin	3.80
BIRTH OF A NATION, THE	1915	D.W. Griffith	8.55
BORN ON THE FOURTH OF JULY	1989	Oliver Stone	7.31
BOYS' TOWN	1938	Norman Taurog	5.80
BUGSY	1991	Barry Levinson	6.31
CAT ON A HOT TIN ROOF	1958	Richard Brooks	7.46
CLOCKWORK ORANGE, A	1971	Stanley Kubrick	8.00
CLOSE MY EYES	1991	Stephen Poliakoff	4.56
COLOR PURPLE, THE	1985	Steven Spielberg	6.92
CONFIDENTIAL REPORT	1955	Orson Welles	4.44
COOK, THE THIEF, HIS WIFE & HER LOVER, THE	1989	Peter Greenaway	6.77
COUP DE FOUDRE	1983	Diane Kurys	7.22
DAYS OF HEAVEN	1978	Terrence Malick	7.47
DEAD AGAIN	1991	Kenneth Branagh	5.50
DEATH IN VENICE	1971	Luchino Visconti	6.42
DERSU UZALA	1975	Akira Kurosawa	7.22
DISCREET CHARM OF THE BOURGEOISIE, THE	1972	Luis Buñuel	8.77
DO THE RIGHT THING	1989	Spike Lee	7.92
DOUBLE LIFE OF VERONIQUE, THE	1991	Krzysztof Kieślowski	5.88
DRAUGHTSMAN'S CONTRACT, THE	1982	Peter Greenaway	5.82
DROWNING BY NUMBERS	1991	Peter Greenaway	5.40
EASY RIDER	1969	Dennis Hopper	7.54
EDWARD II	1991	Derek Jarman	6.10
8½	1963	Federico Fellini	9.38
ENEMIES, A LOVE STORY	1989	Paul Mazursky	7.38
EXCALIBUR	1981	John Boorman	6.29
EXTERMINATING ANGEL, THE	1962	Bunuel, Luis	8.50
FREEDOM FOR US	1931	René Clair	8.75
GARDEN, THE	1990	Derek Jarman	4.60
GENTLEMAN'S AGREEMENT	1947	Elia Kazan	6.20
GIANT	1956	George Stevens	6.64
GODFATHER, PART II, THE	1974	Francis Ford Coppola	8.81
GOOD EARTH, THE	1937	Sidney Franklin	8.45

GREAT ZIEGFELD, THE	1936	Robert Z. Leonard	7.00
HARD BOILED	1992	John Woo	4.33
HIROSHIMA MON AMOUR	1959	Alain Resnais	7.27
L' AVVENTURA	1960	Michelangelo Antonioni	8.69
LA CHINOISE	1967	Jean-Luc Godard	7.00
LA TERRA TREMA	1948	Visconti, Luchino	7.71
LAST PICTURE SHOW, THE	1971	Peter Bogdanovich	8.86
LITTLE DORRIT	1988	Christine Edzard	7.27
LOLA MONTÈS	1955	Max Ophuls	6.88
M*A*S*H	1970	Robert Altman	8.07
MARTY	1955	Delbert Mann	8.45
MATADOR	1986	Pedro Almodovar	6.25
MIRACLE OF MORGAN'S CREEK, THE	1944	Preston Sturges	8.36
MISSION TO MOSCOW	1943	Michael Curtiz	5.67
MY BEAUTIFUL LAUNDRETTE	1985	Stephen Frears	6.40
NAKED	1993	Mike Leigh	7.67
NASHVILLE	1975	Robert Altman	8.82
NINOTCHKA	1939	Ernst Lubitsch	9.00
OH, WHAT A LOVELY WAR!	1969	Richard Attenborough	5.90
ON THE BEACH	1959	Stanley Kramer	5.89
OUT OF AFRICA	1985	Sidney Pollack	7.07
PARIS, TEXAS	1984	Wim Wenders	6.14
PETRIFIED FOREST, THE	1936	Archie Mayo	7.10
PIANO, THE	1993	Jane Campion	7.25
PINKY	1949	Elia Kazan	6.38
PLACE IN THE SUN, A	1951	George Stevens	6.33
PLOUGHMAN'S LUNCH, THE	1983	Richard Eyre	5.78
PROSPERO'S BOOKS	1991	Peter Greenaway	6.00
PROVIDENCE	1977	Alain Resnais	5.44
QUIET MAN, THE	1952	John Ford	7.93
SACRIFICE, THE	1986	Andrei Tarkovsky	6.44
SANTA SANGRE	1990	Alejander Jodorowsky	5.38
SHIP OF FOOLS	1965	Stanley Kramer	7.00
STRANGER THAN PARADISE	1984	Jim Jarmusch	6.40
THIS SPORTING LIFE	1963	Anderson, Lindsay7.18	
TRAVELLING PLAYERS, THE	1975	Theodor Angelopoulos	3.50
UNBEARABLE LIGHTNESS OF BEING, THE	1987	Philip Kaufman	6.83
UNMARRIED WOMAN, AN	1978	Paul Mazursky	7.33
VICTIM	1961	Basil Dearden	7.10
WEEKEND	1967	Jean-Luc Godard	7.82
WILD AT HEART	1990	David Lynch	5.75
WOMEN ON THE VERGE OF A NERVOUS BREAKDOWN	1988	Pedro Almodovar	6.23
ZELIG	1983	Woody Allen	6.40

THE WORST FILMS OF ALL TIME

ABIE'S IRISH ROSE	1946	A. Edward Sutherland
AIRPORT 77	1977	Jerry Jameson
AIRPORT 1979: THE CONCORDE	1979	David Lowell Rich
ALMOST AN ANGEL	1990	John Cornell
AMBUSHERS, THE	1967	Henry Levin
ASH WEDNESDAY	1973	Larry Peerce
BEST DEFENSE	1984	Willard Huyck
BILLY JACK	1971	Tom Laughlin
BLUE BIRD, THE	1976	George Cukor
BOLERO: AN ADVENTURE IN ECSTASY	1984	John Derek
BONFIRE OF THE VANITIES, THE	1990	Brian de Palma
BOOM!	1968	Joseph Losey
BULLSEYE!	1990	Michael Winner
CALIGULA	1979	Tinto Brass
CAN HIERONYMUS MERKIN EVER FORGET MERCY HUMPPE AND FIND TRUE HAPPINESS?	1969	Anthony Newley
CANDY	1968	Christian Marquand
DEATH SHIP	1980	Alvin Rakoff
DOCTOR DOLITTLE	1967	Richard Fleischer
DROP DEAD FRED	1991	Ate de Jong
1871	1989	Ken McMullen
ENCINO MAN	1992	Les Mayfield
GABLE AND LOMBARD	1976	Sidney J. Furie
GREEK TYCOON, THE	1978	J. Lee Thompson
HARLEY DAVIDSON AND THE MARLBORO MAN	1991	Simon Wincer
HOWARD THE DUCK	1986	Willard Huyck
HUDSON HAWK	1991	Michael Lehmann
HURRY SUNDOWN	1967	Otto Preminger
ISHTAR	1987	Elaine May
JAZZ SINGER, THE	1980	Richard Fleischer
LOST HORIZON	1972	Ross Hunter
LUCKY LADY	1975	Stanley Donen
MAGUS, THE	1968	Guy Green
MAN WITH THE GOLDEN GUN, THE	1994	Guy Hamilton
MISSOURI BREAKS, THE	1976	Arthur Penn
MOMENT BY MOMENT	1978	Jane Wagner
MUSIC LOVERS, THE	1970	Ken Russell
MYRA BRECKENRIDGE	1970	Michael Sarne
ORCA . . . KILLER WHALE	1977	Michael Anderson
PLACE FOR LOVERS, A	1969	Vittorio de Sica
REVOLUTION	1985	Hugh Hudson
SERGEANT PEPPER'S LONELY HEARTS CLUB BAND	1978	Michael Schultz
SHANGHAI SURPRISE	1986	Jim Goddard
SONG OF NORWAY	1970	Andrew L. Stone
TATTOO	1981	Bob Brooks
TEENAGERS FROM OUTER SPACE	1959	Tom Graeff
TERROR OF TINY TOWN	1938	Sam Newfield
TOYS	1992	Barry Levinson
TRIAL OF BILLY JACK, THE	1974	Frank Laughlin
WHERE THE BOYS ARE '84	1984	Hy Averback
XANADU	1980	Robert Greenwald

FILMS THAT ARE SO BAD, THEY'RE GOOD

ADVENTURERS, THE	1970	Lewis Gilbert
ADVENTURES OF ROBIN HOOD	1991	John Irvin
AGONY AND THE ECSTASY, THE	1965	Carol Reed
AIRPORT 75	1970	Jack Smight
ASSASSINATION OF TROTSKY, THE	1972	Joseph Losey
AT LONG LAST LOVE	1975	Peter Bogdanovitch
ATTACK OF THE 50 FT. WOMAN, THE	1958	Nathan Hertz
BEYOND THE VALLEY OF THE DOLLS	1970	Russ Meyer
BLONDE VENUS	1932	Josef von Sternberg
BRIDE OF THE MONSTER	1955	Edward D. Wood
BUSINESS AFFAIR, A	1994	Charlotte Brandstrom
CARPETBAGGERS, THE	1964	Edward Dmytryk
CAT-WOMEN OF THE MOON	1953	Arthur Milton
CHE!	1969	Richard Fleischer
COBRA WOMAN	1944	Robert Siodmak
CONQUEROR, THE	1956	Dick Powell
DESPERATE HOURS, THE	1987	Michael Cimino
DINOSAURUS!	1960	Irvin Yeaworth Jr.
DOUBLE X	1992	Shani S. Grewal
FEMALE ON THE BEACH	1955	Joseph Pevney
FIRE MAIDENS FROM OUTER SPACE	1956	Cy Roth
FOOD OF THE GODS, THE	1976	Bert I. Gordon
GIANT CLAW, THE	1957	Fred F. Sears
GIRL ON A MOTORCYCLE	1968	Jack Cardiff
GLEN OR GLENDA?	1953	Edward D. Wood
GODDESS, THE	1958	John Cromwell
GREATEST STORY EVER TOLD, THE	1956	George Stevens
GREEN BERETS, THE	1968	John Wayne; Ray Kellog; Mervyn Le Roy
GREEN SLIME, THE	1969	Kinji Fukasaku
HARRAD EXPERIMENT, THE	1973	Ted Post
HOMEBOY	1988	Michael Seresin
HORROR OF PARTY BEACH, THE	1964	Del Tenney
HOUSE OF THE SPIRITS, THE	1994	Bille August
INCHON	1981	Terence Young
JULIE	1956	Andrew Stone
JUPITER'S DARLING	1954	George Sidney
KICKBOXER	1989	Mark DiSalle; David Worth
KING RICHARD AND THE CRUSADERS	1954	David Butler
LEGEND OF LYLAH CLARE, THE	1968	Robert Aldrich
LONELY LADY, THE	1982	Peter Sasdy
MAME	1974	Gene Saks
MOMMIE DEAREST	1981	Frank Perry
MONSIGNOR	1982	Frank Perry
NIGHT OF THE GHOULS	1960	Edward D. Wood Jr
NORTH STAR, THE	1943	Lewis Milestone
ONE MILLION YEARS B.C.	1966	Don Chaffey
OSCAR, THE	1966	Russel Rouse
OTHER SIDE OF MIDNIGHT, THE	1975	Charles Jarrott
PASSENGER 57	1992	Kevin Hooks
PLAN NINE FROM OUTER SPACE	1959	Edward D. Wood Jr
POINT BREAK	1991	Kathryn Bigelow
POSEIDON ADVENTURE, THE	1972	Ronald Neame
QUEEN OF OUTER SPACE	1958	Edward Bernds
ROBOT MONSTER	1953	Philip Tucker
RUBY GENTRY	1952	King Vidor
SAMSON AND DELILAH	1949	Cecil B. DeMille
SANTA CLAUS CONQUERS THE MARTIANS	1964	Nicholas Webster
SHACK OUT ON 101	1955	Ed Dein

SHANGHAI GESTURE, THE	1941	Josef von Sternberg
SHINING THROUGH	1992	David Seltzer
SINCERELY YOURS	1955	Gordon Douglas
STAR IS BORN, A	1976	Frank Pierson
STAYING ALIVE	1983	Sylvester Stallone
STORY OF MANKIND, THE	1957	Irwin Allen
STUD, THE	1978	Quentin Masters
SWARM, THE	1978	Irwin Allen
SWINGER, THE	1966	George Sidney
TANK MALLING	1988	James Marcus
TARZAN, THE APE MAN	1981	John Derek
TORCH SONG	1953	Charles Walters
TWO MOON JUNCTION	1988	Zalman King
VALLEY OF THE DOLLS	1967	Mark Robson
WHEN DINOSAURS RULED THE EARTH	1970	Val Guest
WILD ORCHID	1989	Zalman King
YOUNGBLOOD HAWKE	1964	Delmer Daves
ZANDALEE	1991	Sam Pillsbury
ZEE AND CO	1971	Brian Hutton

FILMS THAT WERE PANNED BUT ARE NOW CONSIDERED CLASSICS

TITLE	YEAR	AVE
DUCK SOUP	1933	9.20
GENERAL, THE	1926	9.76
MAGNIFICENT AMBERSONS, THE	1942	9.53
MAN WHO SHOT LIBERTY VALANCE, THE	1962	6.80
NIGHT OF THE HUNTER	1955	9.20
NIGHT OF THE LIVING DEAD	1968	7.23
ONCE UPON A TIME IN THE WEST	1969	8.13
PEEPING TOM	1959	6.86
PSYCHO	1960	9.50
RIO BRAVO	1959	7.43
TOUCH OF EVIL	1958	9.38
VERTIGO	1958	8.72

THE MOST CONTROVERSIAL FILMS OF ALL TIME

TITLE	YEAR	AVE
ACCUSED, THE	1988	6.42
ANATOMY OF A MURDER, AN	1959	7.36
ANOTHER WOMAN	1988	5.73
APOCALYPSE NOW	1979	8.41
BABY OF MÂCON, THE	1993	3.33
BARBARELLA	1967	4.45
BIG SLEEP, THE	1946	9.38
BLOWUP	1966	7.33
BRING ME THE HEAD OF ALFREDO GARCIA	1974	4.82
BRITANNIA HOSPITAL	1982	4.11
CAPE FEAR	1991	6.69
CARNAL KNOWLEDGE	1971	6.08
CLOCKWORK ORANGE, A	1971	8.00
CONAN THE BARBARIAN	1981	4.73
DIRTY HARRY	1971	7.38
DO THE RIGHT THING	1989	7.92
DON'T LOOK NOW	1973	7.21
DRESSED TO KILL	1980	5.46
DUEL IN THE SUN	1946	5.85
EUREKA	1981	5.50
EXORCIST, THE	1973	7.80
FALLING DOWN	1993	6.57
FATAL ATTRACTION	1987	6.29
FOOLISH WIVES	1922	6.50
GOOD, THE BAD AND THE UGLY, THE	1966	6.92
GREED	1923	9.15
HEAVEN'S GATE	1980	4.15
HENRY: PORTRAIT OF A SERIAL KILLER	1986	6.83
INDECENT PROPOSAL	1992	4.88
INTOLERANCE	1916	9.08
LAST TANGO IN PARIS	1972	6.81
LAST TEMPTATION OF CHRIST, THE	1988	6.58
LAST YEAR AT MARIENBAD	1961	6.00
LONG DAY CLOSES, THE	1992	6.25
LONG GOODBYE, THE	1973	5.77
MAN WITH THE GOLDEN ARM, THE	1955	5.33
MIDNIGHT EXPRESS	1978	6.73
MISSISSIPPI BURNING	1988	6.75
MOMMIE DEAREST	1981	4.73
MONSIEUR VERDOUX	1947	7.30
MONTY PYTHON'S LIFE OF BRIAN	1979	6.85
NIGHT OF THE LIVING DEAD	1968	7.23
9½ WEEKS	1986	3.36
1900	1976	5.67
ONE-EYED JACKS	1961	6.50
PEEPING TOM	1959	6.86
PRETTY WOMAN	1990	6.77
PSYCHO	1960	9.50
PULP FICTION	1994	8.00
RESERVOIR DOGS	1992	7.30
RIVER'S EDGE	1987	7.08
ROSEMARY'S BABY	1968	8.13
SANTA SANGRE	1990	5.38
SATYRICON	1969	5.33
SEVEN BEAUTIES	1975	7.56
SHANGHAI GESTURE, THE	1941	4.14
SHINING, THE	1980	5.54
STRAW DOGS	1971	6.33
TELL ME THAT YOU LOVE ME, JUNIE MOON	1969	5.00
TEXAS CHAINSAW MASSACRE, THE	1974	4.90
THELMA & LOUISE	1991	7.92
TROPIC OF CANCER	1970	4.50
VERTIGO	1958	8.72
WEE WILLIE WINKIE	1937	6.22
WILD BUNCH, THE	1969	8.63
WILD ONE, THE	1954	6.90

THE 50 BEST FILMS MADE BY CRITICS

1	THE THIRD MAN	W Graham Greene
2	THE AFRICAN QUEEN	W James Agee
3	THE 400 BLOWS	W/D François Truffaut
4	THE AGE OF INNOCENCE	W Jay Cocks
5	THE SEARCHERS	W Frank S. Nugent
6	NIGHT OF THE HUNTER	W James Agee
7	DAY FOR NIGHT	W/D François Truffaut
8	LAST PICTURE SHOW, THE	D Peter Bogdanovich
9	JULES AND JIM	W/D François Truffaut
10	WEST SIDE STORY	Lyrics by Stephen Sondheim.
11	BREATHLESS	W/D Jean-Luc Godard
12	THE FALLEN IDOL	W Graham Greene
13	SHE WORE A YELLOW RIBBON	W Frank S. Nugent
14	THE QUIET MAN	W Frank S. Nugent
15	LA FEMME INFIDÈLE	W/D Claude Chabrol
16	SATURDAY NIGHT AND SUNDAY MORNING	D Karel Reisz
17	WEEKEND	W/D Jean-Luc Godard
18	THE BUTCHER	W/D Claude Chabrol
19	MISTER ROBERTS	W Frank S. Nugent
20	SHOOT THE PIANO PLAYER	W/D François Truffaut
21	IF . . .	D Lindsay Anderson
22	CLAIRE'S KNEE	W/D Eric Rohmer
23	SMALL CHANGE	W/D François Truffaut
24	LA BELLE NOISEUSE	D Jacques Rivette
25	GOLDFINGER	W Paul Dehn
26	PAPER MOON	W/D Peter Bogdanovich
27	SEVEN DAYS TO NOON	W Paul Dehn
28	FORT APACHE	W Frank S. Nugent
29	ANNE AND MURIEL	W/D François Truffaut
30	THE LAST HURRAH	W Frank S. Nugent
31	TARGETS	W/D Peter Bogdanovich
32	THE GREEN RAY	W/D Eric Rohmer
33	THE WILD CHILD	W/D François Truffaut
34	THE SPY WHO CAME IN FROM THE COLD	W Paul Dehn
35	THIS SPORTING LIFE	D Lindsay Anderson
36	STOLEN KISSES	W/D François Truffaut
37	THREE GODFATHERS	W Frank S. Nugent
38	MASK	D Peter Bogdanovich
39	LA CHINOISE	W/D Jean-Luc Godard
40	LES BICHES	W/D Claude Chabrol
41	THE STORY OF ADELE H	W/D François Truffaut
42	SUNDAY, BLOODY SUNDAY	W Penelope Gilliatt
43	O LUCKY MAN!	D Lindsay Anderson
44	WAGON MASTER	W Frank S. Nugent
45	GREMLINS II: THE NEW BATCH	D Joe Dante
46	FOUR ADVENTURES OF REINETTE & MIRABELLE	W/D Eric Rohmer
47	NORTHWEST FRONTIER	W Frank S. Nugent
48	BRIGHTON ROCK	W Graham Greene
49	MY NIGHT AT MAUD'S	W/D Eric Rohmer
50	GREMLINS	D Joe Dante

BEST BY GENRE

HORROR (ALL CRITICS)

1	KING KONG	1933	9.53
2	PSYCHO	1960	9.50
3	NIGHT OF THE HUNTER	1955	9.20
4	JAWS	1975	9.18
5	THE BRIDE OF FRANKENSTEIN	1935	9.07
6	FRANKENSTEIN	1931	8.75
7	INVASION OF THE BODY SNATCHERS	1956	8.75
8	LES DIABOLIQUES	1954	8.60
9	THE SPIRAL STAIRCASE	1946	8.60
10	THE HUNCHBACK OF NOTRE DAME	1939	8.53

HORROR (TOOKEY)

1	THE VANISHING	1988	10
2	NIGHT OF THE HUNTER	1955	9
3	PSYCHO	1960	9
4	BLUE VELVET	1986	9
5	THE CAT AND THE CANARY	1939	9
6	DELIVERANCE	1972	9
7	PLAY MISTY FOR ME	1971	9
8	THE INNOCENTS	1960	9
9	CAPE FEAR	1991	9
10	THE SILENCE OF THE LAMBS	1991	9

FANTASY (ALL CRITICS)

1	IT'S A WONDERFUL LIFE	1946	9.69
2	WIZARD OF OZ	1939	9.56
3	THE SEVENTH SEAL	1956	9.46
4	THE THIEF OF BAGHDAD	1940	9.23
5	LOST HORIZON	1937	9.17
6	A MATTER OF LIFE AND DEATH	1946	9.08
7	BEAUTY AND THE BEAST	1946	9.00
8	ORPHEUS	1950	8.67
9	HERE COMES MR. JORDAN	1941	8.64
10	FIELD OF DREAMS	1989	8.54

FANTASY (TOOKEY)

1	IT'S A WONDERFUL LIFE	1946	10
2	QUEEN OF HEARTS	1989	10
3	FIELD OF DREAMS	1989	10
4	EDWARD SCISSORHANDS	1990	9
5	TALE OF THE FOX	1932	9
6	LOCAL HERO	1983	9
7	GROUNDHOG DAY	1992	9
8	CAROUSEL	1956	8
9	THE FISHER KING	1991	8
10	ALL THAT JAZZ	1979	8

SCIENCE FICTION (ALL CRITICS)

1	DR STRANGELOVE	1964	9.25
2	2001: A SPACE ODYSSEY	1968	9.25
3	THE BRIDE OF FRANKENSTEIN	1935	9.07
4	THE MAN IN THE WHITE SUIT	1951	8.92
5	METROPOLIS	1926	8.80
6	E.T. THE EXTRA-TERRESTRIAL	1980	8.78
7	THE MANCHURIAN CANDIDATE	1962	8.77
8	FRANKENSTEIN	1931	8.75
9	INVASION OF THE BODY SNATCHERS	1956	8.75
10	CLOSE ENCOUNTERS OF THE THIRD KIND (SPECIAL EDITION)	1980	8.67

SCIENCE FICTION (TOOKEY)

1	E.T. THE EXTRA-TERRESTRIAL	1980	10
2	TERMINATOR 2: JUDGMENT DAY	1991	9
3	BLADE RUNNER (DIRECTOR'S CUT)	1992	9
4	JURASSIC PARK	1993	9
5	CLOSE ENCOUNTERS OF THE THIRD KIND (SPECIAL ADITION)	1980	9
6	STAR WARS	1977	9
7	ROBOCOP	1987	8
8	TOTAL RECALL	1990	8
9	DEMOLITION MAN	1993	8
10	STAR TREK VI: THE UNDISCOVERED COUNTRY	1991	8

WESTERN (ALL CRITICS)

1	HIGH NOON	1952	9.80
2	STAGECOACH	1939	9.53
3	THE SEARCHERS	1956	9.26
4	DESTRY RIDES AGAIN	1939	9.23
5	MY DARLING CLEMENTINE	1946	9.18
6	RIDE THE HIGH COUNTRY	1962	9.00
7	DANCES WITH WOLVES (DIRECTOR'S CUT)	1991	8.93
8	HUD	1963	8.92
9	WAY OUT WEST	1936	8.82
10	THE TREASURE OF THE SIERRA MADRE	1948	8.79

WESTERN (TOOKEY)

1	DANCES WITH WOLVES (DIRECTOR'S CUT)	1991	10
2	THE MAGNIFICENT SEVEN	1960	10
3	HIGH NOON	1952	9
4	STAGECOACH	1939	9
5	HEAVEN'S GATE	1980	9
6	THE BEGUILED	1971	9
7	BLAZING SADDLES	1974	9
8	WESTWORLD	1973	8
9	RIDE THE HIGH COUNTRY	1962	8
10	UNFORGIVEN	1992	8

THRILLER (ALL CRITICS)

1	DOUBLE INDEMNITY	1944	9.81
2	THE THIRD MAN	1949	9.74
3	THE LADY VANISHES	1938	9.71
4	BONNIE AND CLYDE	1967	9.71
5	THE MALTESE FALCON	1941	9.71
6	THE 39 STEPS	1935	9.69
7	RASHOMON	1950	9.47
8	REBECCA	1940	9.46
9	NORTH BY NORTHWEST	1959	9.41
10	TOUCH OF EVIL	1958	9.38
11	THE BIG SLEEP	1946	9.38

THRILLER (TOOKEY)

1	THE LADY VANISHES	1938	10
2	NORTH BY NORTHWEST	1959	10
3	REAR WINDOW	1954	10
4	SHADOW OF A DOUBT	1943	10
5	FOREIGN CORRESPONDENT	1940	10
6	PULP FICTION	1944	10
7	WILD TARGET	1993	10
8	DOUBLE INDEMNITY	1944	9
9	HOMICIDE	1991	9
10	WAGES OF FEAR	1953	9

WAR (ALL CRITICS)

1	CASABLANCA	1942	9.89
2	THE GRAND ILLUSION	1937	9.79
3	THE GENERAL	1926	9.76
4	ALL QUIET ON THE WESTERN FRONT	1930	9.76
5	THE AFRICAN QUEEN	1951	9.67
6	GONE WITH THE WIND	1939	9.63
7	HENRY V	1944	9.40
8	LAWRENCE OF ARABIA	1962	9.33
9	PATHS OF GLORY	1957	9.33
10	TO BE OR NOT TO BE	1942	9.20

WAR (TOOKEY)

1	CASABLANCA	1942	10
2	THE GREAT ESCAPE	1963	10
3	CYRANO DE BERGERAC	1990	10
4	SCHINDLER'S LIST	1994	9
5	GONE WITH THE WIND	1939	9
6	THE AFRICAN QUEEN	1951	9
7	THE GRAND ILLUSION	1937	9
8	TO BE OR NOT TO BE	1942	9
9	HENRY V	1944	9
10	THE KILLING FIELDS	1984	8

ACTION/ ADVENTURE (ALL CRITICS)

1	THE ADVENTURES OF ROBIN HOOD	1938	9.73
2	SEVEN SAMURAI	1954	9.70
3	THE AFRICAN QUEEN	1951	9.67
4	LAWRENCE OF ARABIA	1962	9.33
5	THE PRISONER OF ZENDA	1937	9.08
6	NAPOLÉON	1927	9.00
7	GUNGA DIN	1939	8.80
8	THE TREASURE OF THE SIERRA MADRE	1948	8.79
9	THE GREAT ESCAPE	1963	8.67
10	YOJIMBO	1961	8.60

ACTION/ ADVENTURE (TOOKEY)

1	THE ADVENTURES OF ROBIN HOOD	1938	10
2	THE GREAT ESCAPE	1963	10
3	THE MAGNIFICENT SEVEN	1960	10
4	DIE HARD	1988	9
5	THE AFRICAN QUEEN	1951	9
6	JURASSIC PARK	1993	9
7	RAIDERS OF THE LOST ARK	1981	9
8	DELIVERANCE	1972	9
9	STAR WARS	1977	9
10	SPEED	1994	9

MUSICAL (ALL CRITICS)

1 SINGIN' IN THE RAIN 1952 9.90
2 TOP HAT 1935 9.63
3 WIZARD OF OZ 1939 9.56
4 LOVE ME TONIGHT 1932 9.50
5 SWING TIME 1936 9.46
6 THE BAND WAGON 1953 9.27
7 A STAR IS BORN 1954 9.13
8 BEAUTY AND THE BEAST 1991 9.08
9 42ND STREET 1933 9.00
10 THE BLUE ANGEL 1930 8.86

MUSICAL (TOOKEY)

1 SINGIN' IN THE RAIN 1952 10
2 A STAR IS BORN 1954 10
3 THE BAND WAGON 1953 10
4 GIGI 1958 10
5 WEST SIDE STORY 1961 10
6 BEAUTY AND THE BEAST 1991 10
7 42ND STREET 1933 10
8 SWING TIME 1936 10
9 GOLD DIGGERS OF 1933 1933 10
10 TOP HAT 1935 10

ROMANTIC COMEDY (ALL CRITICS)

1 HIS GIRL FRIDAY 1940 10.00
2 THE LADY VANISHES 1938 9.71
3 SOME LIKE IT HOT 1959 9.61
4 IT HAPPENED ONE NIGHT 1934 9.50
5 LOVE ME TONIGHT 1932 9.50
6 THE RULES OF THE GAME 1939 9.41
7 THE PHILADELPHIA STORY 1940 9.21
8 TO BE OR NOT TO BE 1942 9.20
9 THE GRADUATE 1967 9.13
10 THE KID BROTHER 1927 9.00

ROMANTIC COMEDY (TOOKEY)

1 THE SHOP AROUND THE CORNER 1940 10
2 SINGLES 1992 10
3 THE APARTMENT 1960 10
4 FOUR WEDDINGS AND A FUNERAL 1994 10
5 FLIRTING 1991 10
6 GREGORY'S GIRL 1981 10
7 MANHATTAN 1979 10
8 STRICTLY BALLROOM 1992 10
9 THE LADY VANISHES 1938 10
10 HIS GIRL FRIDAY 1940 10

OTHER COMEDY (ALL CRITICS)

1 SULLIVAN'S TRAVELS 1941 9.83
2 THE GENERAL 1926 9.76
3 THE BANK DICK 1940 9.50
4 MR. DEEDS GOES TO TOWN 1936 9.43
5 THE GOLD RUSH 1925 9.38
6 KIND HEARTS AND CORONETS 1949 9.38
7 THE LAVENDER HILL MOB 1951 9.31
8 PYGMALION 1938 9.31
9 DR. STRANGELOVE 1964 9.25
10 DESTRY RIDES AGAIN 1939 9.23

OTHER COMEDY (TOOKEY)

1 THE LAVENDER HILL MOB 1951 10
2 KIND HEARTS AND CORONETS 1949 10
3 WILD TARGET 1993 10
4 MOVIE MOVIE 1978 10
5 CRIMES AND MISDEMEANORS 1989 10
6 WILD TARGET 1993 10
7 THIS IS SPINAL TAP 1984 10
8 HUSBANDS AND WIVES 1992 10
9 SULLIVAN'S TRAVELS 1941 10
10 GENEVIEVE 1953 10

ROMANTIC DRAMA (ALL CRITICS)

1 CASABLANCA 1942 9.89
2 CHILDREN OF PARADISE 1945 9.73
3 GREAT EXPECTATIONS 1946 9.67
4 GONE WITH THE WIND 1939 9.63
5 REBECCA 1940 9.46
6 BRIEF ENCOUNTER 1945 9.41
7 THE BIG PARADE 1925 9.14
8 FROM HERE TO ETERNITY 1953 9.13
9 BLACK NARCISSUS 1946 9.08
10 CYRANO DE BERGERAC 1990 9.08
11 A MATTER OF LIFE AND DEATH 1946 9.08

ROMANTIC DRAMA (TOOKEY)

1 CASABLANCA 1942 10
2 GREAT EXPECTATIONS 1946 10
3 THE AGE OF INNOCENCE 1993 10
4 CYRANO DE BERGERAC 1990 10
5 REBECCA 1940 9
6 GONE WITH THE WIND 1939 9
7 SHADOWLANDS 1993 9
8 BRIEF ENCOUNTER 1945 9
9 THE LETTER 1940 9
10 THE BIG PARADE 1925 8

OTHER DRAMA (ALL CRITICS)

1 CITIZEN KANE 1941 9.84
2 THE GRAPES OF WRATH 1940 9.78
3 THE BICYCLE THIEVES 1949 9.67
4 TOKYO STORY 1953 9.67
5 ALL ABOUT EVE 1950 9.65
6 MR. SMITH GOES TO WASHINGTON 1939 9.62
7 ON THE WATERFRONT 1954 9.56
8 THE MAGNIFICENT AMBERSONS 1942 9.53
9 OLIVER TWIST 1948 9.46
10 THE SEVENTH SEAL 1956 9.46

OTHER DRAMA (TOOKEY)

1 THE GRAPES OF WRATH 1940 10
2 CITIZEN KANE 1941 10
3 ON THE WATERFRONT 1954 10
4 TOKYO STORY 1953 10
5 GOODFELLAS 1990 10
6 BABETTE'S FEAST 1987 10
7 THE WORLD OF APU 1958 10
8 A MAN FOR ALL SEASONS 1966 10
9 JESUS OF MONTREAL 1989 9
10 SCHINDLER'S LIST 1994 9

CARTOONS (ALL CRITICS)

1 SNOW WHITE AND THE SEVEN DWARFS 1937 9.89
2 PINOCCHIO 1939 9.71
3 BAMBI 1942 9.15
4 DUMBO 1941 9.14
5 FANTASIA 1940 9.11
6 BEAUTY AND THE BEAST 1991 9.08
8 ALADDIN 1992 8.30
9 LADY AND THE TRAMP 1955 7.73
10 101 DALMATIANS 1961 7.56

CARTOONS (TOOKEY)

1 BEAUTY AND THE BEAST 1991 10
2 PINOCCHIO 1939 10
3 LADY AND THE TRAMP 1955 10
4 SNOW WHITE AND THE SEVEN DWARFS 1937 9
5 THE LION KING 1961 9
6 101 DALMATIANS 1961 9
7 BAMBI 1942 9
8 YELLOW SUBMARINE 1968 8
9 LITTLE MERMAID, THE 1989 8
10 FANTASIA 1940 8

FAMILY (ALL CRITICS)

1 SNOW WHITE AND THE SEVEN DWARFS 1937 9.89
2 PINOCCHIO 1939 9.71
3 THE THIEF OF BAGDAD 1940 9.23
4 BAMBI 1942 9.15
5 DUMBO 1941 9.14
6 FANTASIA 1940 9.11
7 BEAUTY AND THE BEAST 1991 9.08
8 MEET ME IN ST. LOUIS 1944 8.81
9 E.T. THE EXTRA-TERRESTRIAL 1980 8.78
10 RED BALLOON 1956 8.75

FAMILY (TOOKEY)

1 BEAUTY AND THE BEAST 1991 10
2 E.T. THE EXTRA-TERRESTRIAL 1980 10
3 PINOCCHIO 1939 10
4 LADY AND THE TRAMP 1955 10
5 WHO FRAMED ROGER RABBIT 1988 10
6 STAR WARS 1977 9
7 THE RAILWAY CHILDREN 1970 9
8 SNOW WHITE AND THE SEVEN DWARFS 1937 9
9 THE LION KING 1994 9
10 BAMBI 1942 9

FOREIGN LANGUAGE (ALL CRITICS)

1 POTEMKIN 1925 9.83
2 THE GRAND ILLUSION 1937 9.79
3 CHILDREN OF PARADISE 1945 9.73
4 SEVEN SAMURAI 1954 9.70
5 THE BICYCLE THIEVES 1949 9.67
5 TOKYO STORY 1953 9.67
7 RASHOMON 1950 9.47
8 THE SEVENTH SEAL 1956 9.46

9	THE RULES OF THE GAME	1939	9.41
10	THE 400 BLOWS	1958	9.40

FOREIGN LANGUAGE (TOOKEY)

1	TOKYO STORY	1953	10
2	BABETTE'S FEAST	1987	10
3	THE VANISHING	1988	10
4	THE WORLD OF APU	1958	10
5	CYRANO DE BERGERAC	1990	10
6	JESUS OF MONTREAL	1989	9
7	A MAN ESCAPED	1956	9
8	WAGES OF FEAR	1953	9
9	CLAIRE'S KNEE	1971	9
10	ROMUALD AND JULIETTE	1989	9

BRITISH (ALL CRITICS)

1	THE THIRD MAN	1949	9.74
2	THE LADY VANISHES	1938	9.71
3	THE 39 STEPS	1935	9.69
4	GREAT EXPECTATIONS	1946	9.67
4	THE AFRICAN QUEEN	1951	9.67
6	OLIVER TWIST	1948	9.46
7	BRIEF ENCOUNTER	1945	9.41
8	HENRY V	1944	9.40
9	KIND HEARTS AND CORONETS	1949	9.38
10	LAWRENCE OF ARABIA	1962	9.33

BRITISH (TOOKEY)

1	GREAT EXPECTATIONS	1946	10
2	THE LADY VANISHES	1938	10
3	THE LAVENDER HILL MOB	1951	10
4	KIND HEARTS AND CORONETS	1949	10
5	QUEEN OF HEARTS	1989	10
6	FOUR WEDDINGS AND A FUNERAL	1994	10
7	A HARD DAY'S NIGHT	1964	10
8	GREGORY'S GIRL	1981	10
9	A MAN FOR ALL SEASONS	1966	10
10	TOM JONES	1963	10

DIRECTORS INDEX

Aldrich, Robert
KISS ME DEADLY 1955
WHATEVER HAPPENED TO BABY JANE? 1962
FLIGHT OF THE PHOENIX 1965
THE DIRTY DOZEN 1967
THE LEGEND OF LYLAH CLARE 1968

Allen, Irwin
THE STORY OF MANKIND 1957
THE TOWERING INFERNO 1974
THE SWARM 1978

Allen, Lewis
THE UNINVITED 1944

Allen, Woody
TAKE THE MONEY AND RUN 1969
SLEEPER 1973
ANNIE HALL 1977
MANHATTAN 1979
STARDUST MEMORIES 1980
BROADWAY DANNY ROSE 1984
ZELIG 1985
HANNAH AND HER SISTERS 1986
RADIO DAYS 1987
ANOTHER WOMAN 1988
CRIMES AND MISDEMEANORS 1989
HUSBANDS AND WIVES 1992
MANHATTAN MURDER MYSTERY 1994

Allers, Roger
THE LION KING 1994

Almódovar, Pedro
MATADOR 1986
WOMEN ON THE VERGE OF A NERVOUS BREAKDOWN 1988

Altman, Robert
M*A*S*H 1970
MCCABE AND MRS MILLER 1971
THE LONG GOODBYE 1973
BUFFALO BILL AND THE INDIANS 1976
NASHVILLE 1975
A WEDDING 1978
POPEYE 1980
THE PLAYER 1992
SHORT CUTS 1993

Amelio, Gianni
THE STOLEN CHILDREN 1992

Amiel, Jon
QUEEN OF HEARTS 1989

Anderson, Lindsay
THIS SPORTING LIFE 1963
IF . . . 1969
O LUCKY MAN! 1973
BRITANNIA HOSPITAL 1982

Anderson, Michael
THE DAM BUSTERS 1954
AROUND THE WORLD IN 80 DAYS 1956
ORCA . . . KILLER WHALE 1977

Angelopoulos, Theodor
THE TRAVELLING PLAYERS 1975

Annakin, Ken
THE LONGEST DAY 1962

Antonioni, Michelangelo
L' AVVENTURA 1960
BLOWUP 1966

Apted, Michael
COAL MINER'S DAUGHTER 1980

Arcand, Denys
JESUS OF MONTREAL 1989

Armstrong, Gillian
MY BRILLIANT CAREER 1979

Arnold, Jack
THE MOUSE THAT ROARED 1959

Ashby, Hal
HAROLD AND MAUDE 1971
THE LAST DETAIL 1973
BOUND FOR GLORY 1976
COMING HOME 1978

Asquith, Anthony
PYGMALION 1938
THE WAY TO THE STARS 1945
THE WINSLOW BOY 1948
THE BROWNING VERSION 1951
THE IMPORTANCE OF BEING EARNEST 1952

Attenborough, Richard
OH, WHAT A LOVELY WAR! 1969
GANDHI 1982
SHADOWLANDS 1993

August, Bille
PELLE THE CONQUEROR 1987
THE BEST INTENTIONS 1992
THE HOUSE OF THE SPIRITS 1994

Autant-Lara, Claude
DEVIL IN THE FLESH 1946
KEEP AN EYE ON AMELIA 1949

Averback, Hy
WHERE THE BOYS ARE '84 1984

Avildsen, John G.
ROCKY 1976

Avnet, Jon
FRIED GREEN TOMATOES AT THE WHISTLE STOP CAFE 1992

Axel, Gabriel
BABETTE'S FEAST 1987

Babenco, Hector
PIXOTE 1980
KISS OF THE SPIDER WOMAN 1985

Bacon, Lloyd
FOOTLIGHT PARADE 1933
42ND STREET 1933
A SLIGHT CASE OF MURDER 1938

Badham, John
SATURDAY NIGHT FEVER 1977

Baker, Roy Ward
A NIGHT TO REMEMBER 1958

Ballard, Carroll
THE BLACK STALLION 1979

Barron, Steve
TEENAGE MUTANT NINJA TURTLES 1990

Barton, Charles T.
ABBOTT AND COSTELLO MEET FRANKENSTEIN 1948

Beatty, Warren
REDS 1981
DICK TRACY 1990

Becker, Harold
SEA OF LOVE 1989
MALICE 1993

Becker, Jacques
CASQUE D'OR 1952

Beineix, Jean-Jacques
DIVA 1981

Bellocchio, Marco
FIST IN HIS POCKET 1965

Belvaux, Rémy
MAN BITES DOG 1992

Benedek, Laslo
DEATH OF A SALESMAN 1951
THE WILD ONE 1954

Benjamin, Richard
MY FAVORITE YEAR 1982

Bennett, Compton
THE SEVENTH VEIL 1945

Benton, Robert
THE LATE SHOW 1977
KRAMER VS. KRAMER 1979

Beresford, Bruce
BREAKER MORANT 1979
DRIVING MISS DAISY 1989

Berger, Ludwig
THE THIEF OF BAGDAD 1940

Bergman, Andrew
FRESHMAN 1990

Bergman, Ingmar
SMILES OF A SUMMER NIGHT 1955
THE SEVENTH SEAL 1956
WILD STRAWBERRIES 1957
THE VIRGIN SPRING 1959
PERSONA 1966
THE PASSION OF ANNA 1969
CRIES AND WHISPERS 1972
SCENES FROM A MARRIAGE 1974
FACE TO FACE 1975
AUTUMN SONATA 1978
FANNY AND ALEXANDER 1982

Berkeley, Busby
FOOTLIGHT PARADE 1933
THE GANG'S ALL HERE 1943

Bernds, Edward
QUEEN OF OUTER SPACE 1958

Berri, Claude
JEAN DE FLORETTE 1986
MANON DES SOURCES 1986

Bertolucci, Bernardo
THE CONFORMIST 1969
LAST TANGO IN PARIS 1972
1900 1976
THE LAST EMPEROR 1987

Bigelow, Kathryn
POINT BREAK 1991

Blier, Bertrand
GET OUT YOUR HANDKERCHIEFS 1977

Blystone, Jack
OUR HOSPITALITY 1923

Boese, Carl
THE GOLEM 1920

Bogdanovich, Peter
TARGETS 1967
THE LAST PICTURE SHOW 1971
WHAT'S UP, DOC? 1972
PAPER MOON 1973
AT LONG LAST LOVE 1975
MASK 1985

Boleslawski, Richard
LES MISERABLES 1935

Bondarchuk, Sergei
WAR AND PEACE 1967

Bonzel, André
MAN BITES DOG 1992

Boorman, John
POINT BLANK 1967
DELIVERANCE 1972
EXORCIST II: THE HERETIC 1977
EXCALIBUR 1981
HOPE AND GLORY 1987

Borsos, Phillip
THE GREY FOX 1983

Borzage, Frank
A FAREWELL TO ARMS 1932
DESIRE 1936
THREE COMRADES 1938
THE MORTAL STORM 1940

Boulting, John
BRIGHTON ROCK 1947
SEVEN DAYS TO NOON 1950
I'M ALL RIGHT JACK 1959

Boulting, Roy
THUNDER ROCK 1942

Brambilla, Marco
DEMOLITION MAN 1993

Branagh, Kenneth
HENRY V 1989
DEAD AGAIN 1991
PETER'S FRIENDS 1992
MUCH ADO ABOUT NOTHING 1993

Brando, Marlon
ONE-EYED JACKS 1961

Brandstrom, Charlotte
A BUSINESS AFFAIR 1994

Brass, Tinto
CALIGULA 1979

Bresson, Robert
THE DIARY OF A COUNTRY PRIEST 1950
A MAN ESCAPED 1956
PICKPOCKET 1959
AU HAZARD BALTHAZAR 1966
LANCELOT OF THE LAKE 1974

Brest, Martin
BEVERLY HILLS COP 1984
MIDNIGHT RUN 1988

Bridges, James
THE PAPER CHASE 1973
THE CHINA SYNDROME 1979

Brooks, Bob
TATTOO 1981

Brooks, James L.
TERMS OF ENDEARMENT 1983
BROADCAST NEWS 1987

Brooks, Mel
THE PRODUCERS 1968
BLAZING SADDLES 1974
YOUNG FRANKENSTEIN 1974

Brooks, Richard
CAT ON A HOT TIN ROOF 1958
ELMER GANTRY 1960
THE PROFESSIONALS 1966
IN COLD BLOOD 1967

Brown, Clarence
ANNA KARENINA 1935
NATIONAL VELVET 1944
THE YEARLING 1946
INTRUDER IN THE DUST 1949

Browning, Tod
DRACULA 1931
FREAKS 1932

Bruckman, Clyde
THE GENERAL 1926

Buñuel, Luis
UN CHIEN ANDALOU 1928
L'AGE D'OR 1930
THE YOUNG AND THE DAMNED 1950

Crichton, Michael
WESTWORLD 1973
COMA 1978

Cromwell, John
OF HUMAN BONDAGE 1934
THE PRISONER OF ZENDA 1937
ABE LINCOLN IN ILLINOIS 1940
ANNA AND THE KING OF SIAM 1946

Cronenberg, David
THE FLY 1986
DEAD RINGERS 1988

Crosland, Alan
THE JAZZ SINGER 1927

Crowe, Cameron
SINGLES 1992

Cruze, John
IF I HAD A MILLION 1932

Cukor, George
ONE HOUR WITH YOU 1932
DINNER AT EIGHT 1933
LITTLE WOMEN 1933
DAVID COPPERFIELD 1934
SYLVIA SCARLETT 1935
CAMILLE 1936
HOLIDAY 1938
THE WOMEN 1939
THE PHILADELPHIA STORY 1940
GASLIGHT 1944
A DOUBLE LIFE 1947
ADAM'S RIB 1949
BORN YESTERDAY 1950
A STAR IS BORN 1954
MY FAIR LADY 1964
THE BLUE BIRD 1976

Cunningham, Sean S.
FRIDAY THE 13TH 1980

Curtiz, Michael
CAPTAIN BLOOD 1935
THE CHARGE OF THE LIGHT BRIGADE 1936
THE ADVENTURES OF ROBIN HOOD 1938
FOUR DAUGHTERS 1938
ANGELS WITH DIRTY FACES 1938
THE SEA HAWK 1940
YANKEE DOODLE DANDY 1942
CASABLANCA 1942
MISSION TO MOSCOW 1943
MILDRED PIERCE 1945
LIFE WITH FATHER 1947

Dahl, John
RED ROCK WEST 1993
THE LAST SEDUCTION 1993

Dante, Joe
GREMLINS 1984
GREMLINS II: THE NEW BATCH 1990
MATINEE 1992

Dassin, Jules
BRUTE FORCE 1947
THE NAKED CITY 1948
RIFIFI 1955
TOPKAPI 1964

Daves, Delmer
3:10 TO YUMA 1957
YOUNGBLOOD HAWKE 1964

Davies, Terence
DISTANT VOICES, STILL LIVES 1988
THE LONG DAY CLOSES 1992

Davis, Andrew
THE FUGITIVE 1993

De Bont, Jan
SPEED 1994

De Jong, Ate
DROP DEAD FRED 1991

De Mille, Cecil B.
SAMSON AND DELILAH 1949
THE TEN COMMANDMENTS 1956

De Palma, Brian
CARRIE 1976
DRESSED TO KILL 1980
THE UNTOUCHABLES 1987
CASUALTIES OF WAR 1989
THE BONFIRE OF THE VANITIES 1990

De Sica, Vittorio
SHOESHINE 1946
THE BICYCLE THIEVES 1949
MIRACLE IN MILAN 1951
TWO WOMEN 1961
UMBERTO D 1962
A PLACE FOR LOVERS 1969
THE GARDEN OF THE FINZI-CONTINIS 1970

Dearden, Basil
MY LEARNED FRIEND 1943
DEAD OF NIGHT 1945
THE BLUE LAMP 1949
THE LEAGUE OF GENTLEMEN 1960
VICTIM 1961

Dein, Ed
SHACK OUT ON 101 1955

Demme, Jonathan
MELVIN AND HOWARD 1981
SOMETHING WILD 1986
THE SILENCE OF THE LAMBS 1991
PHILADELPHIA 1993

Demy, Jacques
THE UMBRELLAS OF CHERBOURG 1964

Denis, Claire
CHOCOLAT 1988

Derek, John
TARZAN APE MAN 1981
BOLERO: AN ADVENTURE IN ECSTASY 1984

DeVito, Danny
THE WAR OF THE ROSES 1989

Dickinson, Thorold
GASLIGHT 1940

Dieterie, William
THE LAST FLIGHT 1931
A MIDSUMMER NIGHT'S DREAM 1935
THE STORY OF LOUIS PASTEUR 1936
THE LIFE OF EMILE ZOLA 1937
THE HUNCHBACK OF NOTRE DAME 1939
DR. EHRLICH'S MAGIC BULLET 1940
ALL THAT MONEY CAN BUY 1941
PORTRAIT OF JENNIE 1948

DiSalle, Mark
KICKBOXER 1989

Dmytryk, Edward
FAREWELL MY LOVELY 1944
CROSSFIRE 1947
THE CAINE MUTINY 1954

Donen, Stanley
ON THE TOWN 1949
SINGIN' IN THE RAIN 1952
SEVEN BRIDES FOR SEVEN BROTHERS 1954
FUNNY FACE 1957
PAJAMA GAME 1957
CHARADE 1963
LUCKY LADY 1975
MOVIE MOVIE 1978

Donner, Clive
WHAT'S NEW PUSSYCAT? 1965

Donner, Richard
THE OMEN 1976
SUPERMAN 1978
LETHAL WEAPON 1987

Donskoy, Mark
THE CHILDHOOD OF MAXIM GORKY 1938

Douglas, Gordon
THEM! 1954
SINCERELY YOURS 1955

Dovzhenko, Alexander
EARTH 1930

Dragoti, Stan
LOVE AT FIRST BITE 1979

Dreyer, Carl
THE PASSION OF JOAN OF ARC 1928

Garnett, Tay
THE POSTMAN ALWAYS RINGS TWICE 1946

Germi, Pietro
DIVORCE ITALIAN STYLE 1961

Geronimi, Clyde
PETER PAN 1953
LADY AND THE TRAMP 1955

Gibbons, Cedric
TARZAN AND HIS MATE 1934

Gilbert, Lewis
REACH FOR THE SKY 1956
ALFIE 1966
YOU ONLY LIVE TWICE 1967
THE ADVENTURERS 1970
THE SPY WHO LOVED ME 1977
MOONRAKER 1979

Gilliam, Terry
BRAZIL 1985
THE FISHER KING 1991

Gilliat, Sidney
GREEN FOR DANGER 1946
ONLY TWO CAN PLAY 1961

Glen, John
FOR YOUR EYES ONLY 1981
OCTOPUSSY 1983
A VIEW TO A KILL 1985
THE LIVING DAYLIGHTS 1987
LICENCE TO KILL 1989

Glenville, Peter
BECKET 1964

Godard, Jean-Luc
BREATHLESS 1959
ALPHAVILLE 1965
WEEKEND 1967
LA CHINOISE 1967

Goddard, Jim
SHANGHAI SURPRISE 1986

Goldstone, James
WHEN TIME RAN OUT . . . 1980

Gordon, Bert I.
THE FOOD OF THE GODS 1976
EMPIRE OF THE ANTS 1977

Gordon, Steve
ARTHUR 1981

Goren, Serif
YOL: THE WAY 1982

Goulding, Edmund
GRAND HOTEL 1932
DARK VICTORY 1939
THE OLD MAID 1939
NIGHTMARE ALLEY 1947

Graeff, Tom
TEENAGERS FROM OUTER SPACE 1959

Green, Alfred E.
THE JOLSON STORY 1946

Green, Guy
THE ANGRY SILENCE 1960
THE MAGUS 1968

Green, Joseph
THE BRAIN THAT WOULDN'T DIE 1963

Greenaway, Peter
THE DRAUGHTSMAN'S CONTRACT 1982
COOK THIEF, HIS WIFE & HER LOVER 1989
DROWNING BY NUMBERS 1988
PROSPERO'S BOOKS 1991
THE BABY OF MÂCON 1993

Greenwald, Robert
XANADU 1980

Grewal, Shani S.
DOUBLE X 1992

Griffith, D.W.
THE BIRTH OF A NATION 1915
INTOLERANCE 1916
ORPHANS OF THE STORM 1921
ABRAHAM LINCOLN 1930

Guest, Christopher
THE BIG PICTURE 1989

Guest, Val
THE DAY THE EARTH CAUGHT FIRE 1962
WHEN DINOSAURS RULED THE EARTH 1970

Guillermin, John
THE TOWERING INFERNO 1974

Hall, Alexander
HERE COMES MR. JORDAN 1941

Hallström, Lasse
MY LIFE AS A DOG 1985

Halperin, Victor
WHITE ZOMBIE 1932

Hamer, Robert
DEAD OF NIGHT 1945
IT ALWAYS RAINS ON SUNDAY 1947
KIND HEARTS AND CORONETS 1949

Hamilton, Guy
GOLDFINGER 1964
DIAMONDS ARE FOREVER 1971
LIVE AND LET DIE 1973
THE MAN WITH THE GOLDEN GUN 1974

Hand, David
SNOW WHITE AND THE SEVEN DWARFS 1937
BAMBI 1942

Hanson, Curtis
THE HAND THAT ROCKS THE CRADLE 1992

Hardy, Robin
THE WICKER MAN 1973
CLIFFHANGER 1993

Harvey, Anthony
THE LION IN WINTER 1968

Hathaway, Henry
LIVES OF A BENGAL LANCER 1934
HOUSE ON 92ND STREET 1945
KISS OF DEATH 1947
CALL NORTHSIDE 777 1948
NIAGARA 1952
TRUE GRIT 1969

Hawks, Howard
SCARFACE 1932
TWENTIETH CENTURY 1934
BRINGING UP BABY 1938
ONLY ANGELS HAVE WINGS 1939
HIS GIRL FRIDAY 1940
SERGEANT YORK 1941
BALL OF FIRE 1941
TO HAVE AND HAVE NOT 1944
THE BIG SLEEP 1946
RED RIVER 1948
I WAS A MALE WAR BRIDE 1949
GENTLEMEN PREFER BLONDES 1953
RIO BRAVO 1959

Hay, Will
MY LEARNED FRIEND 1943

Heckerling, Amy
LOOK WHO'S TALKING 1989

Heerman, Victor
ANIMAL CRACKERS 1930

Heisler, Stuart
THE GLASS KEY 1942

Herek, Stephen
BILL & TED'S EXCELLENT ADVENTURE 1988

Herrington, Rowdy
ROADHOUSE 1989

Hertz, Nathan
THE ATTACK OF THE 50 FOOT WOMAN 1958

Herzog, Werner
AGUIRRE, WRATH OF GOD 1972
FITZCARRALDO 1982

Hill, George Roy
BUTCH CASSIDY AND THE SUNDANCE KID 1969
THE STING 1973
THE WORLD ACCORDING TO GARP 1982

Kanin, Garson
BACHELOR MOTHER 1939
MY FAVORITE WIFE 1940

Kaplan, Jonathan
THE ACCUSED 1988

Kasdan, Lawrence
BODY HEAT 1981

Kasdan, Lawrence
THE BIG CHILL 1983
SILVERADO 1985
THE ACCIDENTAL TOURIST 1988
GRAND CANYON 1991

Kaufman, Philip
THE RIGHT STUFF 1983
THE UNBEARABLE LIGHTNESS OF BEING 1987

Kazan, Elia
A TREE GROWS IN BROOKLYN 1945
BOOMERANG! 1947
GENTLEMAN'S AGREEMENT 1947
PINKY 1949
PANIC IN THE STREETS 1950
A STREETCAR NAMED DESIRE 1951
VIVA ZAPATA! 1952
ON THE WATERFRONT 1954
EAST OF EDEN 1955
BABY DOLL 1956
A FACE IN THE CROWD 1957
AMERICA, AMERICA 1963

Keaton, Buster
OUR HOSPITALITY 1923
SHERLOCK JR. 1924
THE NAVIGATOR 1924
SEVEN CHANCES 1925
THE GENERAL 1926

Keighley, William
FOOTLIGHT PARADE 1933
G MEN 1935
THE ADVENTURES OF ROBIN HOOD 1938
THE MAN WHO CAME TO DINNER 1941

Kellog, Ray
THE GREEN BERETS 1968

Kelly, Gene
ON THE TOWN 1949
SINGIN' IN THE RAIN 1952

Kenton, Erle C.
THE ISLAND OF LOST SOULS 1933
THE GHOST OF FRANKENSTEIN 1941
HOUSE OF FRANKENSTEIN 1944
HOUSE OF DRACULA 1945

Kershner, Irvin
THE EMPIRE STRIKES BACK 1980
NEVER SAY NEVER AGAIN 1983
ROBOCOP 2 1990

Kieslowski, Krzysztof
A SHORT FILM ABOUT KILLING 1989
THE DOUBLE LIFE OF VERONIQUE 1991

King, Henry
THE SONG OF BERNADETTE 1943
TWELVE O'CLOCK HIGH 1949
THE GUNFIGHTER 1950
CAROUSEL 1956

King, Zalman
TWO MOON JUNCTION 1988
WILD ORCHID 1989

Kleiser, Randal
GREASE 1978

Kloves, Steve
THE FABULOUS BAKER BOYS 1989

Kobayashi, Masaki
KWAIDAN 1964

Korda, Alexander
MARIUS 1931
THE PRIVATE LIFE OF HENRY VIII 1933
REMBRANDT 1936
THE THIEF OF BAGDAD 1940

Korda, Zoltan
THE FOUR FEATHERS 1939
THE THIEF OF BAGDAD 1940

Koster, Henry
ONE HUNDRED MEN AND A GIRL 1937
HARVEY 1950

Kotcheff, Ted
RAMBO: FIRST BLOOD 1982

Kramer, Stanley
THE DEFIANT ONES 1958
ON THE BEACH 1959
INHERIT THE WIND 1960
JUDGMENT AT NUREMBURG 1961
SHIP OF FOOLS 1965
GUESS WHO'S COMING TO DINNER? 1967

Kubrick, Stanley
THE KILLING 1956
PATHS OF GLORY 1957
SPARTACUS 1960
DR STRANGELOVE 1964
2001: A SPACE ODYSSEY 1968
A CLOCKWORK ORANGE 1971
BARRY LYNDON 1975
THE SHINING 1980
FULL METAL JACKET 1987

Kurosawa, Akira
STRAY DOG 1949
RASHOMON 1950
IKIRU 1952
SEVEN SAMURAI 1954
THRONE OF BLOOD 1957
THE HIDDEN FORTRESS 1958
YOJIMBO 1961
DERSU UZALA 1975
KAGEMUSHA 1980
RAN 1985

Kurys, Diane
COUP DE FOUDRE 1983

La Cava, Gregory
MY MAN GODFREY 1936
STAGE DOOR 1937

Lamont, Charles
SALOME, WHERE SHE DANCED 1945

Lamorisse, Albert
THE RED BALLOON 1956

Landis, John
THE BLUES BROTHERS 1980
AN AMERICAN WEREWOLF IN LONDON 1981
TRADING PLACES 1983

Lanfield, Sidney
THE HOUND OF THE BASKERVILLES 1939

Lang, Fritz
DR. MABUSE, THE GAMBLER 1922
THE NIBELUNGEN 1924
METROPOLIS 1926
M 1931
THE TESTAMENT OF DR MABUSE 1932
FURY 1936
MAN HUNT 1941
THE WOMAN IN THE WINDOW 1944
SCARLET STREET 1945
THE BIG HEAT 1953
THOUSAND EYES OF DR. MABUSE 1960

Lang, Walter
THE KING AND I 1956

Laughlin, Frank
THE TRIAL OF BILLY JACK 1974

Laughlin, Tom
BILLY JACK 1971

Laughton, Charles
NIGHT OF THE HUNTER 1955

Launder Frank
THE HAPPIEST DAYS OF YOUR LIFE 1950

Le Roy, Mervyn
LITTLE CAESAR 1930
I AM A FUGITIVE FROM A CHAIN GANG 1932
GOLD DIGGERS OF 1933 1933
THEY WON'T FORGET 1937
RANDOM HARVEST 1942
MISTER ROBERTS 1956

Lean, David
IN WHICH WE SERVE 1942
THIS HAPPY BREED 1944
BLITHE SPIRIT 1945
BRIEF ENCOUNTER 1945
GREAT EXPECTATIONS 1946
OLIVER TWIST 1948
HOBSON'S CHOICE 1953
SUMMERTIME 1955
THE BRIDGE ON THE RIVER KWAI 1957
LAWRENCE OF ARABIA 1962
DOCTOR ZHIVAGO 1965
RYAN'S DAUGHTER 1970
A PASSAGE TO INDIA 1984

Leconte, Patrice
MONSIEUR HIRE 1989

Lee, Ang
THE WEDDING BANQUET 1993

Lee, Rowland V.
THE COUNT OF MONTE CRISTO 1934
SON OF FRANKENSTEIN 1939

Lee, Spike
DO THE RIGHT THING 1989
JUNGLE FEVER 1991
MALCOLM X 1992

Lehmann, Michael
HUDSON HAWK 1991

Leigh, Mike
LIFE IS SWEET 1990
NAKED 1993

Leisen, Mitchell
MIDNIGHT 1939
ARISE, MY LOVE 1940

Lelouch, Claude
A MAN AND A WOMAN 1966

Leonard, Robert Z.
THE GREAT ZIEGFELD 1936
PRIDE AND PREJUDICE 1940

Leone, Sergio
A FISTFUL OF DOLLARS 1964
THE GOOD, THE BAD AND THE UGLY 1966
ONCE UPON A TIME IN THE WEST 1969
ONCE UPON A TIME IN AMERICA 1984

Lester, Richard
A HARD DAY'S NIGHT 1964
THE KNACK AND HOW TO GET IT 1965
HELP! 1965
PETULIA 1968
THE THREE MUSKETEERS 1973
THE FOUR MUSKETEERS 1975
SUPERMAN II 1980
SUPERMAN III 1983

Levant, Brian
THE FLINTSTONES 1994

Levin, Henry
THE AMBUSHERS 1967

Levinson, Barry
DINER 1982
GOOD MORNING, VIETNAM 1987
RAIN MAN 1988
AVALON 1990
BUGSY 1991
TOYS 1992

Lewin, Albert
THE PICTURE OF DORIAN GRAY 1945

Lewis, Jerry
THE NUTTY PROFESSOR 1963

Littman, Lynne
TESTAMENT 1983

Litvak, Anatole
MAYERLING 1936
THE ROARING TWENTIES 1939
SORRY, WRONG NUMBER 1948
THE SNAKE PIT 1948

Lloyd, Frank
CAVALCADE 1933
MUTINY ON THE BOUNTY 1935

Loach, Ken
KES 1969
RAINING STONES 1993

Logan, Joshua
PICNIC 1955
BUS STOP 1956
SOUTH PACIFIC 1958
CAMELOT 1967

Losey, Joseph
THE SERVANT 1963
ACCIDENT 1967
BOOM! 1968
THE GO-BETWEEN 1971
THE ASSASSINATION OF TROTSKY 1972

Lounguine, Pavel
TAXI BLUES 1991

Lubitsch, Ernst
THE GOLEM 1920
THE SMILING LIEUTENANT 1931
ONE HOUR WITH YOU 1932
TROUBLE IN PARADISE 1932
IF I HAD A MILLION 1932
NINOTCHKA 1939
THE SHOP AROUND THE CORNER 1940
TO BE OR NOT TO BE 1942
HEAVEN CAN WAIT 1943

Lucas, George
AMERICAN GRAFFITI 1973
STAR WARS 1977

Luhrmann, Baz
STRICTLY BALLROOM 1992

Lumet, Sidney
12 ANGRY MEN 1957
LONG DAY'S JOURNEY INTO NIGHT 1962
FAIL SAFE 1964
THE PAWNBROKER 1965
THE DEADLY AFFAIR 1966
SERPICO 1973
DOG DAY AFTERNOON 1975
NETWORK 1976
THE VERDICT 1982

Luske, Hamilton
PINOCCHIO 1939
PETER PAN 1953
LADY AND THE TRAMP 1955
101 DALMATIANS 1961

Lynch, David
ERASERHEAD 1976
THE ELEPHANT MAN 1980
DUNE 1984
BLUE VELVET 1986
WILD AT HEART 1990

Lynch, Jennifer Chambers
BOXING HELENA 1993

Lyne, Adrian
9½ WEEKS 1986
FATAL ATTRACTION 1987
JACOB'S LADDER 1991
INDECENT PROPOSAL 1992

Lynn, Jonathan
MY COUSIN VINNY 1992

Mackendrick, Alexander
WHISKY GALORE 1949
THE MAN IN THE WHITE SUIT 1951
THE LADYKILLERS 1955
SWEET SMELL OF SUCCESS 1957

Mackenzie, John
THE LONG GOOD FRIDAY 1980

Malick, Terrence
DAYS OF HEAVEN 1978

Malle, Louis
LACOMBE LUCIEN 1974
ATLANTIC CITY USA 1981
AU REVOIR LES ENFANTS 1988
MILOU IN MAY 1989

Mamet, David
HOUSE OF GAMES 1987
HOMICIDE 1991

Mamoulian, Rouben
DR. JEKYLL AND MR. HYDE 1931
LOVE ME TONIGHT 1932
QUEEN CHRISTINA 1933
THE MARK OF ZORRO 1940

Mandoki, Luis
WHITE PALACE 1990

Mankiewicz, Joseph L.
GHOST AND MRS. MUIR 1947
A LETTER TO THREE WIVES 1949
ALL ABOUT EVE 1950
FIVE FINGERS 1952
JULIUS CAESAR 1953
GUYS AND DOLLS 1955
CLEOPATRA 1963
SLEUTH 1972

Mann, Anthony
WINCHESTER '73 1950
NAKED SPUR 1953
EL CID 1961

Mann, Delbert
MARTY 1955
SEPARATE TABLES 1958

Mann, Michael
MANHUNTER 1986

Marcus, James
TANK MALLING 1988

Marquand, Christian
CANDY 1968

Marquand, Richard
RETURN OF THE JEDI 1983

Marshall, Frank
ARACHNAPHOBIA 1990

Marshall, Garry
BEACHES 1988
PRETTY WOMAN 1990
FRANKIE & JOHNNY 1991

Marshall, George
DESTRY RIDES AGAIN 1939
GHOST BREAKERS 1940

Marshall, Penny
BIG 1988
AWAKENINGS 1990

Marton, Andrew
THE LONGEST DAY 1962

Masters, Quentin
THE STUD 1978

May, Elaine
ISHTAR 1987

Mayfield, Les
ENCINO MAN 1992

Mayo, Archie
THE PETRIFIED FOREST 1936

Mazursky, Paul
AN UNMARRIED WOMAN 1978
ENEMIES, A LOVE STORY 1989

McBride, Jim
BIG EASY 1987

McCarey, Leo
DUCK SOUP 1933
RUGGLES OF RED GAP 1935
MAKE WAY FOR TOMORROW 1937
THE AWFUL TRUTH 1937
LOVE AFFAIR 1939
GOING MY WAY 1944
THE BELLS OF ST. MARY'S 1945

McDuigan, John
FLIRTING 1991

McLeod, Norman Z.
MONKEY BUSINESS 1931
HORSE FEATHERS 1932
IF I HAD A MILLION 1932
IT'S A GIFT 1934
TOPPER 1937

McMullen, Ken
1871 1989

McNaughton, John
HENRY: PORTRAIT OF A SERIAL KILLER 1986

McTiernan, John
DIE HARD 1988
THE LAST ACTION HERO 1993

Medak, Peter
A DAY IN THE DEATH OF JOE EGG 1972

Megahy, Leslie
THE HOUR OF THE PIG 1994

Menzel, Jiri
CLOSELY OBSERVED TRAINS 1966

Menzies, William Cameron
THINGS TO COME 1936
THE THIEF OF BAGDAD 1940

Meyer, Nicholas
TIME AFTER TIME 1979
STAR TREK II: THE WRATH OF KHAN 1982
STAR TREK VI: THE UNDISCOVERED COUNTRY 1991

Meyer, Russ
BEYOND THE VALLEY OF THE DOLLS 1970

Milestone, Lewis
ALL QUIET ON THE WESTERN FRONT 1930
THE FRONT PAGE 1931
OF MICE AND MEN 1939
THE NORTH STAR 1943
A WALK IN THE SUN 1945

Milius, John
CONAN THE BARBARIAN 1981

Miller, George
MAD MAX 1979
MAD MAX II 1981
MAD MAX BEYOND THUNDERDOME 1985

Milton, Arthur
CAT-WOMEN OF THE MOON 1953

Minghella, Anthony
TRULY, MADLY, DEEPLY 1990

Minkoff, Rob
THE LION KING 1994

Minnelli, Vincente
MEET ME IN ST. LOUIS 1944
THE PIRATE 1948
FATHER OF THE BRIDE 1950
AN AMERICAN IN PARIS 1951
THE BAD AND THE BEAUTIFUL 1952
THE BAND WAGON 1953
LUST FOR LIFE 1956
GIGI 1958

Mizoguchi, Kenji
LIFE OF OHARU 1952
UGETSU MONOGATARI 1953
CHIKAMITSU MONOGATARI 1954
SANSHO THE BAILIFF 1954

Molinaro, Edouard
LA CAGE AUX FOLLES 1978

Monicelli, Mario
THE BIG DEAL ON MADONNA STREET 1958

Mulligan, Robert
TO KILL A MOCKINGBIRD 1962

Murnau, F. W.
NOSFERATU – EINE SYMPHONIE DES GRAUENS 1921
THE LAST LAUGH 1924
FAUST 1926
SUNRISE 1927

Murphy, Eddie
HARLEM NIGHTS 1989

Musker, John
THE LITTLE MERMAID 1989
ALADDIN 1992

Nair, Mira
SALAAM BOMBAY! 1988

BLACK NARCISSUS 1946
THE RED SHOES 1948
PEEPING TOM 1959

Preminger, Otto
LAURA 1944
THE MAN WITH THE GOLDEN ARM 1955
AN ANATOMY OF A MURDER 1959
ADVISE AND CONSENT 1962
HURRY SUNDOWN 1967
SKIDOO 1968
TELL ME THAT YOU LOVE ME, JUNIE MOON 1969

Pressburger, Emeric
THE LIFE AND DEATH OF COLONEL BLIMP 1943
I KNOW WHERE I'M GOING 1945
A MATTER OF LIFE AND DEATH 1946
BLACK NARCISSUS 1946
THE RED SHOES 1948

Pudovkin, D.I.
MOTHER 1926

Puenzo, Luis
THE OFFICIAL STORY 1985

Rademakers, Fons
THE ASSAULT 1986

Rafelson, Bob
FIVE EASY PIECES 1970
MOUNTAINS OF THE MOON 1989

Rakoff, Alvin
DEATH SHIP 1980

Ramis, Harold
GROUNDHOG DAY 1992

Rappeneau, Jean-Paul
CYRANO DE BERGERAC 1990

Rapper, Irving
NOW, VOYAGER 1942

Rash, Steve
THE BUDDY HOLLY STORY 1978

Ruane, John
DEATH IN BRUNSWICK 1990

Ray, Nicholas
REBEL WITHOUT A CAUSE 1955

Ray, Satyajit
PATHER PANCHALI 1955
APARAJITO 1956
THE WORLD OF APU 1958
KANCHENJUNGHA 1962
THE MUSIC ROOM 1963
DISTANT THUNDER 1973

Redford, Robert
ORDINARY PEOPLE 1980

Reed, Carol
THE STARS LOOK DOWN 1939
NIGHT TRAIN 1940
THE WAY AHEAD 1944
ODD MAN OUT 1947
THE FALLEN IDOL 1948
THE THIRD MAN 1949
THE AGONY AND THE ECSTASY 1965
OLIVER! 1968

Reed, Luther
HELL'S ANGELS 1930

Reeves, Michael
WITCHFINDER GENERAL 1968

Reiner, Rob
THIS IS SPINAL TAP 1984
WHEN HARRY MET SALLY . . . 1989
MISERY 1990
A FEW GOOD MEN 1992

Reinhardt, Max
A MIDSUMMER NIGHT'S DREAM 1935

Reisz, Karel
SATURDAY NIGHT AND SUNDAY MORNING 1960

Reitherman, Wolfgang
101 DALMATIANS 1961
THE JUNGLE BOOK 1967
THE ARISTOCATS 1970

Reitman, Ivan
GHOSTBUSTERS 1984
KINDERGARTEN COP 1990
DAVE 1993

Renoir, Jean
BOUDU SAVED FROM DROWNING 1932
THE CRIME OF MONSIEUR LANGE 1936
UNE PARTIE DE CAMPAGNE 1936
THE GRAND ILLUSION 1937
THE RULES OF THE GAME 1939
THE SOUTHERNER 1945
THE RIVER 1951

Resnais, Alain
HIROSHIMA MON AMOUR 1959
LAST YEAR AT MARIENBAD 1961
PROVIDENCE 1977

Reynolds, Kevin
ROBIN HOOD: PRINCE OF THIEVES 1991

Rich, David Lowell
AIRPORT 1979: THE CONCORDE 1979

Richards, Dick
FAREWELL, MY LOVELY 1975

Richardson, Tony
THE ENTERTAINER 1960
A TASTE OF HONEY 1961
THE LONELINESS OF THE LONG DISTANCE RUNNER 1962
TOM JONES 1963
CHARGE OF THE LIGHT BRIGADE 1968

Riesner, Charles
STEAMBOAT BILL, JR. 1928

Ritchie, Michael
SMILE 1975
THE BAD NEWS BEARS 1976

Ritt, Martin
HUD 1963
THE SPY WHO CAME IN FROM THE COLD 1965
SOUNDER 1972
THE FRONT 1976
NORMA RAE 1979

Rivette, Jacques
LA BELLE NOISEUSE 1992

Robbins, Jerome
WEST SIDE STORY 1961

Robbins, Tim
BOB ROBERTS 1992

Robert, Yves
THE GLORY OF MY FATHER 1991
MY MOTHER'S CASTLE 1991

Roberts, Stephen
IF I HAD A MILLION 1932

Robinson, Bruce
WITHNAIL AND I 1987

Robinson, Phil Alden
FIELD OF DREAMS 1989

Robson, Mark
CHAMPION 1949
VON RYAN'S EXPRESS 1965
VALLEY OF THE DOLLS 1967

Roeg, Nicolas
WALKABOUT 1970
DON'T LOOK NOW 1973
BAD TIMING: A SENSUAL OBSESSION 1980
EUREKA 1981
THE MAN WHO FELL TO EARTH 1987

Rohmer, Eric
MY NIGHT AT MAUD'S 1969
CLAIRE'S KNEE 1971
THE GREEN RAY 1986
4 ADVENTURES OF REINETTE & MIRABELLE 1986

Romero, George A.
NIGHT OF THE LIVING DEAD 1968
DAWN OF THE DEAD 1979

Rose, Bernard
CANDYMAN 1992

Sidney, George
SHOW BOAT 1951
SCARAMOUCHE 1952
KISS ME KATE 1953
JUPITER'S DARLING 1954
THE SWINGER 1966

Siegel, Don
INVASION OF THE BODY SNATCHERS 1956
THE BEGUILED 1971
DIRTY HARRY 1971
CHARLEY VARRICK 1973
THE SHOOTIST 1976

Silver, Joan Micklin
CROSSING DELANCEY 1988

Singleton, John
BOYZ ' N THE HOOD 1991

Siodmak, Robert
COBRA WOMAN 1944
PHANTOM LADY 1944
THE KILLERS 1946
THE SPIRAL STAIRCASE 1946
THE CRIMSON PIRATE 1952

Sirk, Douglas
WRITTEN ON THE WIND 1956

Sjostrom, Victor
THE WIND 1927

Skolimowski, Jerzy
DEEP END 1970
MOONLIGHTING 1982

Sluizer, George
THE VANISHING 1988

Smight, Jack
AIRPORT 75 1970

Soderbergh, Steven
SEX, LIES AND VIDEOTAPE 1989

Spielberg, Steven
DUEL 1971
JAWS 1975
CLOSE ENCOUNTERS OF THE THIRD KIND 1977
E.T. THE EXTRA-TERRESTRIAL 1980
RAIDERS OF THE LOST ARK 1981
INDIANA JONES AND THE TEMPLE OF DOOM 1984
THE COLOR PURPLE 1985
EMPIRE OF THE SUN 1987
INDIANA JONES AND THE LAST CRUSADE 1989
HOOK 1992
JURASSIC PARK 1993
SCHINDLER'S LIST 1993

Spottiswoode, Roger
UNDER FIRE 1983

Stallone, Sylvester
STAYING ALIVE 1983

Starewicz, Wladyslaw
TALE OF THE FOX 1932

Steinberg, Michael
THE WATERDANCE 1991

Stevens, George
ALICE ADAMS 1935
SWING TIME 1936
GUNGA DIN 1939
WOMAN OF THE YEAR 1941
THE TALK OF THE TOWN 1942
THE MORE THE MERRIER 1943
I REMEMBER MAMA 1948
A PLACE IN THE SUN 1951
SHANE 1953
GIANT 1956
THE GREATEST STORY EVER TOLD 1965

Stevenson, Robert
JANE EYRE 1944
DARBY O'GILL AND THE LITTLE PEOPLE 1959
MARY POPPINS 1964

Stillman, Whit
METROPOLITAN 1989

Stone, Andrew
JULIE 1956
SONG OF NORWAY 1970

Stone, Oliver
SALVADOR 1986
PLATOON 1986
TALK RADIO 1988
BORN ON THE FOURTH OF JULY 1989
THE DOORS 1991
JFK 1991

Strick, Joseph
TROPIC OF CANCER 1970

Sturges, John
BAD DAY AT BLACK ROCK 1955
GUNFIGHT AT THE O.K. CORRAL 1957
THE MAGNIFICENT SEVEN 1960
THE GREAT ESCAPE 1963

Sturges, Preston
THE GREAT MCGINTY 1940
CHRISTMAS IN JULY 1940
SULLIVAN'S TRAVELS 1941
THE LADY EVE 1941
THE PALM BEACH STORY 1942
THE MIRACLE OF MORGAN'S CREEK 1944
HAIL THE CONQUERING HERO 1944
UNFAITHFULLY YOURS 1948

Sturridge, Charles
A HANDFUL OF DUST 1988

Sutherland, A. Edward
ABIE'S IRISH ROSE 1946

Szabó, István
MEPHISTO 1981

Tacchella, Jean-Charles
COUSIN, COUSINE 1975

Tanner, Alain
JONAH – WHO WILL BE 25 IN THE YEAR 2000 1976

Tarantino, Quentin
RESERVOIR DOGS 1992
PULP FICTION 1994

Tarkovsky, Andrei
ANDREI RUBLEV 1966
SOLARIS 1972
MIRROR 1974
SACRIFICE 1986

Tashlin, Frank
THE GIRL CAN'T HELP IT 1956
WILL SUCCESS SPOIL ROCK HUNTER? 1957

Tati, Jacques
MONSIEUR HULOT'S HOLIDAY 1953

Taurog, Norman
IF I HAD A MILLION 1932
BOYS' TOWN 1938

Tavernier, Bertrand
LIFE AND NOTHING BUT 1989

Taviani, Paolo & Vittorio
PADRE PADRONE 1977
NIGHT OF THE SHOOTING STARS 1981

Taylor, Sam
SAFETY LAST 1923
FRESHMAN 1925

Tenney, Del
THE HORROR OF PARTY BEACH 1964

Teshigahara, Hiroshi
WOMAN IN THE DUNES 1964

Tetzlaf, Ted
THE WINDOW 1949

Thomas, Gerald
CARRY ON UP THE KHYBER 1968

Thompson, J. Lee
TIGER BAY 1959
NORTHWEST FRONTIER 1959
THE GUNS OF NAVARONE 1961
THE GREEK TYCOON 1978

Tornatore, Giuseppe
CINEMA PARADISO 1989

Tourneur, Jacques
CAT PEOPLE 1942
I WALKED WITH A ZOMBIE 1943
OUT OF THE PAST 1947

THE OLD DARK HOUSE 1932
THE INVISIBLE MAN 1933
THE BRIDE OF FRANKENSTEIN 1935
SHOW BOAT 1936

Whelan, Tim
THE THIEF OF BAGDAD 1940

Wicke, Bernhard
THE LONGEST DAY 1962

Widerberg, Bo
ELVIRA MADIGAN 1967

Wiene, Robert
THE CABINET OF DR CALIGARI 1919

Wilcox, Fred McLeod
FORBIDDEN PLANET 1956

Wilde, Ted
THE KID BROTHER 1927

Wilder, Billy
FIVE GRAVES TO CAIRO 1943
DOUBLE INDEMNITY 1944
THE LOST WEEKEND 1945
SUNSET BOULEVARD 1950
ACE IN THE HOLE 1951
STALAG 17 1953
THE SEVEN YEAR ITCH 1955
WITNESS FOR THE PROSECUTION 1957
SOME LIKE IT HOT 1959
APARTMENT 1960
ONE, TWO, THREE 1961
AVANTI! 1972

Wincer, Simon
HARLEY DAVIDSON & THE MARLBORO MAN 1991

Winner, Michael
DEATH WISH 1974
BULLSEYE! 1990

Wise, Kirk
BEAUTY AND THE BEAST 1991

Wise, Robert
THE SET UP 1949
THE DAY THE EARTH STOOD STILL 1951
WEST SIDE STORY 1961
THE SOUND OF MUSIC 1965
STAR! 1968
STAR TREK: THE MOTION PICTURE 1979

Woo, John
HARD BOILED 1992

Wood, Edward D.
GLEN OR GLENDA? 1953
BRIDE OF THE MONSTER 1955
PLAN NINE FROM OUTER SPACE 1959
NIGHT OF THE GHOULS 1960

Wood, Sam
A NIGHT AT THE OPERA 1935
A DAY AT THE RACES 1937
GOODBYE, MR. CHIPS 1939
KING'S ROW 1942

Worth, David
KICKBOXER 1989

Wyler, William
THESE THREE 1936
DODSWORTH 1936
DEAD END 1937
JEZEBEL 1938
WUTHERING HEIGHTS 1939
THE LETTER 1940
THE LITTLE FOXES 1941
MRS. MINIVER 1942
THE BEST YEARS OF OUR LIVES 1946
THE HEIRESS 1949
ROMAN HOLIDAY 1953
THE DESPERATE HOURS 1955
THE FRIENDLY PERSUASION 1956
BEN-HUR 1959
THE CHILDREN'S HOUR 1961
FUNNY GIRL 1968

Yates, Peter
BULLITT 1968
THE FRIENDS OF EDDIE COYLE 1973
BREAKING AWAY 1979
THE DRESSER 1983

Yeaworth Jr, Irvin
DINOSAURUS! 1960

Yimou, Zhang
RED SORGHUM 1987
JU DOU 1991
RAISE THE RED LANTERN 1992
THE STORY OF QIU JU 1993

Young, Harold
THE SCARLET PIMPERNEL 1934

Young, Terence
DR. NO 1962
FROM RUSSIA WITH LOVE 1963
THUNDERBALL 1965
WAIT UNTIL DARK 1967
INCHON 1981

Zaillian, Stephen
SEARCHING FOR BOBBY FISCHER 1993

Zanussi, Krzysztof
THE CONTRACT 1982

Zemeckis, Robert
BACK TO THE FUTURE 1985
WHO FRAMED ROGER RABBIT 1988
BACK TO THE FUTURE PART II 1989
BACK TO THE FUTURE PART III 1990
FORREST GUMP 1994

Zhuangzhuang, Tian
THE BLUE KITE 1992

Zinnemann, Fred
THE MEN 1950
HIGH NOON 1952
FROM HERE TO ETERNITY 1953
OKLAHOMA! 1955
NUN'S STORY 1959
SUNDOWNERS 1960
A MAN FOR ALL SEASONS 1966

Zucker, Abrahams, Zucker
AIRPLANE! 1980

Zucker, David
NAKED GUN 1988
NAKED GUN 2½ 1991

Zucker, Jerry
GHOST 1990

Zwick, Edward
GLORY 1989

À BOUT DE SOUFFLE: *see* BREATHLESS.

À NOUS LA LIBERTÉ: *see* FREEDOM FOR US.

AANSLAG, DER: *see* ASSAULT, THE.

ABBOTT AND COSTELLO MEET FRANKENSTEIN: *see* THE *FRANKENSTEIN* SERIES.

ABBOTT AND COSTELLO MEET THE GHOSTS: *see* THE *FRANKENSTEIN* SERIES.

ABE LINCOLN IN ILLINOIS CT: 5 AV: 7.38

(aka *Spirit of the People*)

1940 US 110 BW DRAMA/BIOPIC

D John Cromwell
W Grover Jones from Robert E. Sherwood's play

Raymond Massey ☆ AAN Ruth Gordon
Gene Lockhart Mary Howard Dorothy Tree

The life and times of a future American president (Raymond Massey).

Respectful, worthy, stiff account of the great man's early years. But Massey is splendid in the title role.

PRO:

'Fine direction of interesting subject . . . Outstanding entertainment.' *(The Cinema)*

'What counts here is the humanism of Lincoln . . . And, of course, the uncanny reincarnation of the character by Raymond Massey . . . a really miraculous job.' *(Herman G. Weinberg, S & S)*

'Massey is so good that it is difficult to remember him in his previous parts.' *(Documentary News Letter)*

MIXED:

'Faults there are – the opening is slow and a bit laboured; continuity is poor at times and the episodic treatment . . . seems deliberately unbalanced. But once the story gets firmly into its stride all weaknesses are forgotten. Much of its compelling interest comes from the magnificent acting of Raymond Massey.' *(MFB)*

'If you want attitudes, a five gallon hat, famous incidents, and One Nation Indivisible, they're all here. As a picture and as a whole, it just doesn't stick.' *(Otis Ferguson)*

ABEL GANCE'S BEETHOVEN CT: 5 AV: 7.00

(aka *Beethoven's Great Love; Beethoven; The Life and Loves of Beethoven; Un Grand Amour de Beethoven*)

1937 France 116/135 BW DRAMA/BIOPIC

D Abel Gance ☆
W Abel Gance

Harry Baur Annie Ducaux Jany Holt
Jean-Louis Barrault

The life of a composer (Harry Baur) battling against deafness.

There are the impressive visual touches you would expect from the director of *Napoleon* (1927), and great aural moments – such as the scene when our hero begins to lose his hearing – but in the main this is a plodding biopic which, though cut for foreign consumption (Jean-Louis Barrault, playing the composer's nephew, disappears entirely), still seems mighty long.

'Beautiful and moving . . . As in all Gance's films there are parts which are too long and often of very little interest while others are excellent. This film shows force in direction and the music and photography are excellent.' *(Moving Picture Daily)*

'Gance was not at his best with dialogue as this rather leaden biopic demonstrates.' *(Bergan & Karney)*

ABIE'S IRISH ROSE CT: 1 AV: 2.00

1946 US 96 BW COMEDY

D Edward A. Sutherland ●
W Anne Nichols ● from her own play

Joanne Dru Richard Norris Michael Chekhov
J.M. Kerrigan

Irish girl (Joanne Dru) marries Jewish boy (Richard Norris) with resulting clash of cultures.

Crude comedy teeming with racial stereotypes. It might be funny, if it weren't so boring.

PRO:

'Care is taken . . . to avert denominational resentment.' *(Motion Picture Herald, 1946)*

'A simple entertaining story, rich in humour and loving kindness which will make you laugh one minute and cry the rest; and there is quite a lot in it to make you think. The religious and political angle is tactfully approached and there is nothing to offend the most delicate susceptibility.' *(MFB, 1948)*

ANTI:

'Hum-drum story . . . May prove successful to unsophisticated patronage.' *(Today's Cinema)*

'The essence of film fare is obviously to entertain. This one doesn't.' *(Variety)*

'[It] was first made a long while ago. Not long enough, however. I can still remember it.' *(Sunday Times)*

ABOMINABLE DOCTOR PHIBES, THE

CT: 6 AV: 5.70

(aka *Dr Phibes; Doctor Phibes; The Abominable Dr Phibes*)

1971 GB 94 C HORROR/COMEDY

D Robert Fuest ✔
W James Whiton William Goldstein

Vincent Price ✔ Joseph Cotten Virginia North Terry-Thomas Hugh Griffith Peter Jeffrey

Musical genius (Vincent Price) wreaks spectacular vengeance on doctors he blames for death of his wife.

Entertainingly over-the-top comic-strip horror, with terrific Art Deco sets, ingenious murders, and one of Vincent Price's more eccentric performances (speaking and eating through a hole in his neck). Sample line . . . A police chief: 'A brass unicorn has been catapulted across a London street and impaled an eminent surgeon! Words fail me!'

ANTI:

'Anachronistic period horror musical camp fantasy is a fair description, loaded with comedic gore of the type that packs theatres and drives child psychologists up the walls.' *(Variety)*

MIXED:

'The beauties are considerable, albeit completely on the surface and lacking any but momentary satisfaction . . . But if the whole concoction doesn't hold together too well, there are a few scenes of rare imagination.' *(Richard Koszarski, Village Voice)*

PRO:

'To see [Price] in horror films is to witness a master at work. He is the thinking man's Boris Karloff.' *(Arthur Thirkell, Daily Mirror)*

'[Fuest's] light touch has been up to now disastrously hidden under a bushel and here it emerges to altogether appealing effect.' *(John Russell Taylor, The Times)*

'No film can be all bad which opens in a vast Art Deco chamber looking like a cross between the old Strand Palace lobby and the Finsbury Park Astoria.' *(Christopher Hudson, Spectator)*

'The sets are awful, the plot ludicrous and the dialogue inane – what more could a horror freak desire?' *(Motion Picture Guide)*

ABRAHAM LINCOLN

CT: 4 AV: 5.13

1930 US 80 BW DRAMA/BIOPIC

D D.W. Griffith ✗
W Stephen Vincent Benet Gerrit Lloyd

Walter Huston ☆ Una Merkel ● Edgar Dearing Russell Simpson Henry B. Walthall

The life of the US President (Walter Huston).

D.W. Griffith's first talkie is an amazingly dreary, static biopic, wildly overrated on release both because of the patriotic subject and the director's reputation. Walter Huston gives a solid performance, and the film is reasonably faithful to the facts; that's about the most that can be said for it. Sample dialogue . . . Abe: 'Every time I dream, your face gets mixed up in it.' Ann: 'Does it really, Abe? I know that's just flattery, but I love it.'

PRO:

'A startlingly superlative accomplishment.' *(Variety)*

'A treasure trove of magnificent moments.' *(MFB, 1973)*

'The early incidences of Lincoln's life and upbringing are truthfully portrayed and his pathetic romance with Ann Rutledge is sympathetically depicted.' *(National Board of Review)*

ANTI:

'The portrayal of Mrs Lincoln is more than a trifle too literal . . . There are moments too when the dialogue appears to be more than a trifle nearer this day than it should be.' *(Mordaunt Hall, New York Times)*

'It brings to us – with a curious finality of disappointment, a sentimental sense of the closing of a chapter – the impression of a director who has nowhere made a valid contact with the condition of the screen today.' *(C.A. Lejeune)*

'Static . . . No feeling for the movie medium.' *(Lewis Jacobs, The Rise of the American Film)*

'It is difficult to understand why contemporary critics were so impressed by this dull, episodic, overlong production . . . . Griffith appears to use Mrs Lincoln as a substitute for the Negro comic relief of many of his other productions . . . Nor does Una Merkel help; her portrayal of Ann Rutledge must qualify as the worst example of miscasting in the history of the cinema.' *(Anthony Slide, The Films of D.W. Griffith)*

ABYSS: SPECIAL EDITION, THE

CT: 7 AV: 5.18

1989/93 US 140 (original)/168 (special) C SF/ACTION

D James Cameron ✔
W James Cameron

Ed Harris ✔ Mary Elizabeth Mastrantonio ✔

Michael Biehn Leo Burmester Todd Graff
John Bedford Lloyd J.C. Quinn Kimberley Scott

Undersea oil-rig workers including a sparring husband and wife (Ed Harris, Mary Elizabeth Mastrantonio) investigate crashed nuclear submarine.

The principal weaknesses of the version released in 1989 – poorly delineated characters and a lame climax which looked like a rip-off of *Close Encounters* – are rectified in the 'special edition' which, though longer than the original, seems shorter because story and characters have not been sacrificed to thrills and special effects.

The 1993 special edition, though occasionally portentous, is a sci-fi spectacular on the scale of *2001*, with a fine central performance from Ed Harris. Unfortunately, the moralizing at the end does get ponderous, and Cameron seems undecided whether he is in favour of unilateral disarmament or The Ultimate Deterrent. You could interpret the peaceloving aliens' threat to engulf the world in tidal waves as being analogous to Reagan's Star Wars strategy – but probably he intended another anti-nuclear, end-the-Cold War message not dissimilar to the sci-fi classic, *The Day The Earth Stood Still* (1951).

ANTI:

'This quasi-religious sentimentality with which Cameron soaks the riggers' encounters with the aliens seems painfully artificial and laboured . . . The film unashamedly attempts to recreate the emotional awe evoked by the conclusion of *Close Encounters*, despite having skimped on the driven narrative structure which made that encounter so powerful.' *(Stephen Dark, Film Yearbook, 1989)*

MIXED:

'A first rate underwater suspenser with an otherworldly twist, *The Abyss* suffers from a payoff unworthy of its buildup.' *(Variety, 1989)*

PRO:

'For the most part, as exciting an undersea drama as one could imagine.' *(MFB, 1989)*

ACCIDENT

CT: 4 AV: 6.00

1967 GB 105 C DRAMA

D Joseph Losey ✗
W Harold Pinter ✗ from Nicholas Mosley's novel

Dirk Bogarde ☆ Stanley Baker ☆
Jacqueline Sassard Michael York ☆
Vivien Merchant Harold Pinter

Oxford tutor (Dirk Bogarde) unravels circumstances which led to death of an undergraduate.

There are strong performances by Dirk Bogarde and Stanley Baker; but 20 years on it all seems plodding, stagebound, talky and needlessly abstruse. Losey's few attempts to be cinematic look like amateurish attempts to come to terms with a zoom lens. Wildly overrated by critics who may not have been able to understand what it all meant, but knew that Pinter was a respected playwright.

PRO:

'A haunting study in relationships, with Harold Pinter's flair for spare, suggestive dialog getting full scope in an adaptation which stays remarkably faithful to the book.' *(Variety)*

'A film to watch with fascination and brood about afterward. And if ultimately we are left to question whether it is worth the brooding, at least we are left also with the satisfaction of having watched two master craftsmen at work.' *(Judith Crist)*

'Justly acclaimed as masterly in its exploration, through a dislocated time structure, of the turbulent emotions lying unspoken and unperceived beneath a calm surface . . . Brilliantly shot to accentuate the atmosphere of bewilderment and mystery . . . the accident is made to seem a key . . . In fact there is no mystery about [it]; it is a key to nothing . . . [The film] forces one to look and look again, to make connections where none are apparent . . . You have to do your share of the work . . . and [are] rewarded almost constantly by the moments of glittering illumination.' *(Tom Milne, S & S)*

'Everything is calm, unruffled, lacquered in a veneer of civilization, yet underneath it all, one gradually begins to realize, the characters are tearing each other emotionally to shreds.' *(MFB)*

ANTI:

'The whole thing is such a teapot tempest and it is so assiduously underplayed that it is neither strong drama nor stinging satire. It is just a sad little story of a wistful don.' *(Bosley Crowther)*

'Losey never acquired a technical expertise with the medium . . . Losey has sought to accentuate Pinter's bizarre elements by unbelievably slow cutting and self-important lingering shots, for instance, on the door that somebody has closed or an empty seat before somebody walks up to it.' *(Mike Sarne, F & F)*

'It is Harold Pinter's misfortune to be an unusually clever child . . . This former and, occasionally, present actor has worked out a three-part program for himself. (1) Use dialogue with cryptic laconism; make it mostly commonplaces but surround these with an indefinable, urking, omnipresent nastiness and have the most banal utterance bulge with an ill-concealed threat. (2) Stick in as many ugly jokes and befogging ambiguities as possible; even a sophomoric jape in a tart sauce of ambivalence strikes the gullible palate as haute cuisine. (3) When asked about your work, keep smilingly silent, or practice every form of put-down or put-on you can muster. (Being an actor helps.) You will thus shroud yourself in a tantalizing mystery and be a sort of intellectual Greta Garbo. With a measure of talent and mastery of this trio of tricks, you become the Kierkegaard of the kindergarten . . . After the process of Pinterization comes Loseyfying. The director decks out the picture with all kinds of arty gimmicks, such as, for example, a series of pointless zoomings out.' *(John Simon)*

ACCIDENTAL HERO: *see* HERO.

ACCIDENTAL TOURIST, THE AAN

CT: 8 AV: 7.00

1988 US 121 C DRAMA/COMEDY/ROMANCE

D Lawrence Kasdan ☆
W Frank Galati Lawrence Kasdan ☆ AAN
from Anne Tyler's novel

William Hurt ☆ Kathleen Turner ☆
Geena Davis ☆ AAW Amy Wright Bill Pullman
Ed Begley Jr

Uptight travel writer (William Hurt) deserted by his wife (Kathleen Turner) finds love with goofy dog-trainer (Geena Davis).

A gently amusing romantic comedy, subtly written and directed. It suffers from an infuriatingly passive hero (though the whole point is how he snaps himself out of this); but the spirit of Anne Tyler's quirky novel survives, thanks to Hurt's entertainingly introverted performance, Geena Davis's delightful turn as the girlfriend who re-inspires him with joie de vivre – and let's not forget the contribution of Bud, as Edward the dog.

ANTI:

'I found Tourist hell to sit through, but it has an audience appeal: it provides a new romantic myth of the eighties – a time of widespread remarriage and hoped-for rebirth. The film's gloominess doesn't keep it from being a crowd pleaser, because it leads to that final moment when Macon makes his choice – his "commitment". In the movie, as in the novel, he abandons his old emotional luggage. Essentially, this is a dating movie, like Claude Lelouch's *A Man and a Woman*, but for darker times, for times of lowered expectations.' *(Pauline Kael)*

'An incredibly lifeless and programmatic concoction, the most solemnly dull award-winner since *Chariots of Fire* . . . It would be an exaggeration to describe this film as having a plot. The development seems random, pointless. In the end, he picks one woman over the other, because "she's given me another chance to decide who I am – to step out of the Leary groove and stay out. It's a mistake," he declares, "to plan everything as if it were a business trip" – and this feeble insight is actually meant to constitute an epiphany, a profound moment of truth. It's almost embarrassing to sit in the theater and realize that one has been taken on so long a journey for so little. Macon is like nobody one has ever known, and the "lesson" he ultimately learns is one at which the filmmakers have been tiresomely hammering away since the opening frames.' *(Bruce Bawer, American Spectator)*

PRO:

'Smart, witty and sophisticated.' *(Brian D. Johnson, Maclean's)*

'Not melodrama, but mellow drama . . . It further expands Hollywood's rediscovery of lower-class lifestyles, and of a rarely-seen slice of America's middle classes – the quiet, melancholic, reclusive people, who contentedly dwell in dark brown homes, making me think sometimes of *Lake Wobegon Days*, Garrison Keillor's sadder (and even better-selling) evocation of another old-fangled, backwaterish, "woe-begone" America.' *(Raymond Durgnat, Film Review)*

ACCUSED, THE

CT: 6 AV: 6.42

1988 US 110 C DRAMA

D Jonathan Kaplan
W Tom Topor

Kelly McGillis Jodie Foster ☆AAW Bernie Coulson
Leo Rossi Ann Hearn.

Raped woman (Jodie Foster) and her lawyer (Kelly McGillis) prosecute those who looked on when she was assaulted.

Prurient scenes of sexual violence have disfigured many a Hollywood picture. But apart from a needlessly graphic portrayal of the rape at the end, *The Accused* avoids the obvious pitfalls, mainly thanks to Tom Topor's sensitive screenplay. The magic ingredient, however, is the leading actor. This is one of those rare 'social issues' pictures in which the central character really comes alive, and Jodie Foster's first Oscar for Best Actress was richly deserved.

ANTI:

'About as sophisticated as a mallet on the noggin . . . borderline sicko. Its aesthetic mindset is Liberal Tabloid.' *(Dave Penman, The Face)*

'For Jodie Foster . . . acting bad may be synonymous with bad acting . . . She's breezily over-emphatic, packaging herself as a babe in every sequence.' *(J. Hoberman, Village Voice)*

'Many women will be exceedingly troubled by Topor's use of a worse-case-scenario heroine-victim. We might well ask ourselves why the woman gang-banged had to be drunk and doped-up, and wearing a revealing blouse, a mini-skirt and heels, and a come-hither look. Foster even performs a sexy dance (first by herself, and later with a partner she voluntarily kisses) immediately before the attack. Doesn't the use of such a situation somehow imply that this is precisely the type of woman who gets gang-raped? And doesn't this invite the audience to think that such horrors only happen, after all, to bad girls, and not to them, or their wives and daughters?' *(Kathy Maio)*

'The filmmakers have taken all the intellectual and moral depth out of the issue they say they wanted to explore. Nor does the movie get at the real problem in rape trials – of convincing juries that the nice looking men sitting there at the defense table with their female attorneys could hurt anyone. These movie defendants look like the creeps that they are; the scuzziest among them has a red scorpion tattooed on his arm . . . By saving the visualization of the rape until the end of the movie, director Jonathan Kaplan (*Heart Like a Wheel, Project X*) and screenwriter Tom Topor (*Nuts*) pretend to the seriousness of a documentary while slyly milking the squalid incident as hard as any tabloid headline writer ever could.' *(Julie Salamon, Wall Street Journal)*

MIXED:

'The film, though it doesn't come across as a shrill tract in sexual politics, has a strong polemical bent. When you think about it afterward you're surprised to realize how effectively . . . the filmmakers have faked you into buying a nightmarish view of the relations between men and women – relations which, though the director and writer are both men, are observed entirely from the women's perspective. Men are . . . threatening figures who, whether friends or lovers or strangers, could at any moment turn into attackers. Every man, in short, is a potential rapist.' *(Bruce Bawer, American Spectator)*

PRO:

'Foster plays the girl without the slightest concession to easy sympathy . . . Hollywood stars of this calibre don't simply appear in movies, they embody them.' *(Alexander Walker, Evening Standard)*

'Another box-office winner which once again negotiates a fine line between social concern, feminism and exploitation.' *(MFB)*

'For the most part, a responsible social problem picture about the rights of women to go unmolested (no matter what provocation they offer).' *(Graham Fuller, Film Review)*

ACE IN THE HOLE

CT: 8 AV: 8.44

(aka *The Big Carnival*)

1951 US 111 BW DRAMA

D Billy Wilder ☆
W Billy Wilder Lesser Samuels Walter Newman ☆ AAN

Kirk Douglas ☆ Jan Sterling ☆ Bob Arthur Porter Hall ☆ Frank Cady Richard Benedict ☆

An unscrupulous journalist (Kirk Douglas) delays rescue of a cave-in victim (Richard Benedict).

Billy Wilder's mordant masterpiece was very unpopular on release. As Wilder says, 'Americans expected a cocktail and felt I was giving them a shot of vinegar instead'. Although often regarded as an attack on gutter journalists, it's just as cruelly accurate when satirizing the morbid mob psychology which creates the demand for gutter journalism.

ANTI:

'Douglas hams it up relentlessly. Perhaps that is not his fault; the whole story is treated as melodrama rather than as a study of human beings.' *(Dilys Powell)*

'Some people have tried to claim some sort of satirical brilliance for it, but it's really rather nasty, in a sociologically pushy way.' *(New Yorker, 1980)*

'A sordid and cynical drama . . . delivered with all the stinging impact of an angry slap in the face . . . But regrettably . . . Mr Wilder has let imagination so fully take command of his yarn that it presents not only a distortion of journalistic practice but something of a dramatic grotesque. Beyond any questions [he] has done a spectacular job of visioning the monstrous vulgarity of mob behavior as influenced by a weird catastrophe . . . [and] caught the ice-cold commercialism and the carnival atmosphere . . . [giving] us a masterly film . . . But for all its revelation of scene and character [it] is badly weakened by a poorly constructed plot which depends for its strength upon assumptions that are not only naive but absurd . . . [Finally] the whole yarn collapses limply and depressingly at the audience's feet.' *(Bosley Crowther)*

MIXED:

'Has the acidity and ruthlessness characteristic of [Wilder's] best work . . . Few . . . possibilities for irony, cruelty and horror are missed . . . Though the last reel is neither incredible nor sentimental, it lacks the strength and directness of the rest of the film. This apart, a notable achievement.' *(Gavin Lambert, MFB)*

'Absorbing in a nauseating kind of way.' *(Daily Graphic)*

PRO:

'As stimulating as black coffee.' *(Richard Mallett, Punch)*

'Hardly representative of a nation that celebrates Mother's Day and regards milk as a national beverage. But the social satirist must weary of big targets . . . Mr Wilder's detached observation . . . [has]that cold, brilliant artistry that makes [him] one of the few great contemporary directors.' *(Milton Shulman, Evening Standard)*

'The film's blackness is overwhelming and it can also be read as an allegory about Hollywood.' *(NFT Bulletin, 1984)*

'A savage poem on the eternal subject of man's inhumanity . . . It implies in its characters and crowds an impersonal callousness, crueller than conscious evil and awful in its detachment.' *(Time & Tide)*

'I think *Ace in the Hole* is one of Billy Wilder's best pictures. It was a hit in the rest of the world, but it wasn't doing well in the United States, so they changed the title to *The Big Carnival*. I think the reason it wasn't successful here was the newspapers. The unfavorable reviews of this movie about an unscrupulous newspaper reporter – based on a true incident, the Floyd Collins case, where a reporter actually kept a man down in a mine – were written by newspaper reporters. Critics love to criticize, but they don't like being criticized. Also, Billy Wilder was saying to Mr and Mrs Average, "This is you, the people who stop and stare at accidents."' *(Kirk Douglas)*

ACROSS THE PACIFIC CT; 6 AV: 6.60

1942 US 86/99 BW ACTION/ADVENTURE/WAR

D John Huston (after he had been called up for military service, direction was completed by Vincent Sherman)
W Richard Macauley from Robert Carson's serial *Aloha Means Goodbye*

Humphrey Bogart ☆ Sydney Greenstreet ☆ Mary Astor ☆ Sen Yung ☆ Monte Blue

Army officer (Bogart) tracks down Japanese spies, pre-Pearl Harbour.

Thrilling war adventure which is never remotely plausible, but has a star performance in the lead, great pace and enjoyable dialogue.

ANTI:

'A poor espionage film, without vigor or rhyme.' *(La Saison Cinématographique)*

PRO:

'Although picture does not quite hit the edge-of-seat tension engendered by *Maltese Falcon*, it's a breezy and fast-paced melodrama. Huston directs deftly from thrill-packed script.' *(Variety)*

'Clever direction and fine character-featuring lift this picture above the average espionage drama . . . Humphrey Bogart is an arresting hero.' *(CEA Film Report)*

'Like having a knife at your ribs for an hour and a half.' *(New York Times)*

ADAM'S RIB CT: 6 AV: 8.58

1949 US 103 BW COMEDY/ROMANCE

D George Cukor ☆
W Ruth Gordon Garson Kanin ☆ AAN

Spencer Tracy Katharine Hepburn ☆ Judy Holliday ☆ Tom Ewell ✔ David Wayne Jean Hagen

Married lawyers (Spencer Tracy, Katharine Hepburn) have a battle of the sexes as they prosecute and defend a dumb blonde (Judy Holliday) on trial for attempted murder.

Critically acclaimed, classy but dated. Katharine Hepburn is at her irascible best as the wife, but Judy Holliday steals the show as a murderess.

'The stars get a lot of fun out of it, and the danger of the joke failing to last has been cleverly lessened by thickening up the proceedings with a new straight-faced comedienne (Judy Holliday) who is magnificent as the husband-shooter.' *(Daily Mail)*

'My sole complaint is that the two stars behaved like a honeymoon couple when they must have been married for years.' *(Parry Miller, Evening Standard)*

'It isn't solid food but it certainly is meaty and juicy and comically nourishing.' *(Bosley Crowther)*

'Writers Ruth Gordon and Garson Kanin packed this comedy with the kind of running wit that will leave you breathless.' *(Fortnight)*

'Cukor has directed with a deliberate, polished theatricality which emphasizes the artificiality of the piece. The camera often remains anchored for quite an appreciable time so that the screen becomes simply a frame for the two stars, and theatricality is heightened by the device of a stage curtain, with the title "that evening", used to separate court and home scenes. Hepburn and Tracy are masters of the artificial comedy, but once or twice they seem to strain a little too hard after the light touch . . . The real discovery of the film is Judy Holliday. The part could have been quite ordinary, but she makes it both touching and comic: a remarkable performance.' *(BFI Bulletin, 1950)*

ADVENTURE, THE: *see* L'AVVENTURA.

ADVENTURERS, THE CT: 5 AV: 2.25

1970 US 163/171 C DRAMA/SO BAD

D Lewis Gilbert ●
W Michael Hastings Lewis Gilbert from Harold Robbins's novel ●

Bekim Fehmiu ● Charles Aznavour ● Alan Badel Candice Bergen ● Thommy Berggren Ernest Borgnine Rossano Brazzi Olivia de Havilland

Playboy (Bekim Fehmiu) tries to overthrow South American dictator (Alan Badel), finds love (Candice Bergen) but loses her when she turns lesbian.

Astonishingly squalid movie, so wretchedly acted and directed from a stupid script that it's funny.

'Vulgar, witless and dull . . . would soil the inside of a garbage can.' *(Rex Reed)*

'A classic monument to bad taste . . . profligate and squandered production opulence; inferior, imitative and curiously old-hat direction; banal, ludicrous dialog; sub-standard, lifeless and embarrassing acting; cornball music; indulgent, gratuitous and boring violence; and luridly non-erotic sex.' *(Variety)*

'A three-hour slog through every imaginable cliché of writing and direction. In addition to an abundance of flaccid sex and violence, it offers drugs, sadism, orchids, fireworks, orgies, lesbianism, a miscarriage, a private torture chamber, and the hell of several fashion shows with loud pop music accompaniment. This might well be described as the film with everything; trouble is, it is difficult to imagine anybody wanting any of it.' *(MFB)*

'Good actors like Borgnine and de Havilland approach the whole thing as if they would prefer to handle it with tongs.' *(Daily Sketch)*

'The film equivalent of a bad long read.' *(Shipman)*

ADVENTURES OF ROBIN HOOD, THE AAN

CT: 10 AV: 9.73

1938 US 104 C ACTION/ADVENTURE

D Michael Curtiz☆ William Keighley
W Seton I. Miller Norman Reilly Raine☆

Errol Flynn☆ Olivia de Havilland Basil Rathbone☆ Claude Rains☆ Patric Knowles Eugene Pallette☆ Alan Hale☆ Ian Hunter☆ Melville Cooper☆

Robin (Errol Flynn) swashbuckles his way to success, with help from Maid Marian (de Havilland) and his merry men.

Wonderful – widely, and rightly, considered to be the definitive swashbuckler. Not the least extraordinary aspect of this apparently seamless success was that it was the work of two very different directors: William Keighley and Michael Curtiz, who replaced Keighley during shooting, and shot virtually all the action sequences.

'Unfortunately, the action scenes were not effective, and I had to replace the director in mid-production, an unheard-of-event at that time. I felt that only Mike Curtiz could give the picture the color and scope it needed. The reason we hadn't used him in the first place was because Errol had begged us not to. He preferred the elegant and civilized William Keighley [who had directed him in *The Prince and The Pauper*].' *(Producer Hal B. Wallis)*

'There is no hint or trace of social, political or economic preachment. Sympathy is on the side of the poor.' *(William Weaver, Motion Picture Herald)*

'Such a film as this is payment in full for many dull hours of picture-going.' *(Frank Nugent, New York Times)*

'Story grand, acting superb, thrills spectacular and atmosphere picturesque.' *(Kine Weekly)*

'Errol Flynn is the embodiment of everything that Robin Hood should be . . . Production is on the grand scale but dramatic qualities and characterisation are never subordinated to mere spectacle.' *(MFB)*

'The whole thing has an air of being a costume party, a jolly and rather athletic one, with a lot of well-bred Englishmen playing at being in the greenwood. Their bright, fresh clothes, their house-party kind of conversation, the clean castles and neat forests might all have been something an affluent host arranged for the entertainment of summer guests . . . Except for some tedious and modernish love-making it keeps moving.' *(James Shelley Hamilton, National Board of Review)*

'[Its] excellence lies not just in Errol Flynn's athleticism, Basil Rathbone's dastardly villainy or de Havilland's demure heroine, but also in the rousing musical soundtrack . . . the sumptuous use of colour and the set design . . . The film set standards for adventure yarns that have never been surpassed.' *(Allan Hunter & Kenny Mathieson, Movie Classics, 1992)*

ADVENTURES OF ROBIN HOOD, THE

CT: 5 AV: 4.00

(aka *Robin Hood*)

1991 GB 104/116/150 C ACTION/ADVENTURE/SO BAD

D John Irvin
W Mark Allen Smith John McGrath

Patrick Bergin● Uma Thurman● Jurgen Prochnow Edward Fox●

Robin Hood (Patrick Bergin) takes on all-comers.

A misconceived British attempt to depict the legend of Robin Hood in social realist terms. More than once, it threatens to turn into agit-prop on the importance of defeating the Poll Tax. Director John Irvin does his best to bridge the conceptual chasm between romantic fantasy and muddy reality, but plunges straight down the abyss. Script and casting are about as medieval as a plastic bucket.

The one enjoyable aspect of the whole fiasco is the acting. It is hard to say who gives the worst performance: Patrick Bergin as a half-Irish Robin, the most wooden thing in Sherwood Forest? Uma Thurman as a transatlantic Maid Marian, equally treelike and reciting the lines with an icy contempt which would get her drummed out of the average school play? or Jurgen Prochnow's strangely-accented villain, a sort of Nazi Inspector Clouseau? All are unmemorable beside a kamikaze cameo appearance from Edward Fox. Shamelessly ham-acting his way through his one scene as Prince John, he adopts an astonishing vocal delivery which is one-third Edward VIII, one-third Vincent Price, and one-third Mr Spock from Star Trek.

PRO:

'A defiantly traditional movie and all the better for it . . . Not a moment too long, deftly paced and perfectly happy to be so knowing.' *(Chris Simpson, City Limits)*

PRO:

'A notable film about politics . . . It affirms the necessity of truth, liberalism, and come to that peace.' *(Dilys Powell)*

MIXED:

'Supremely ambivalent, a battle between fascinatingly real props and procedures and melodramatically unreal characters and situations.' *(Peter John Dyer)*

'Slightly stagey, corny and overheated . . . Plays like a good old-fashioned night at the theatre.' *(Winnert)*

ANTI:

'Intermittently well dialogued and too talky, and, strangely, arrested in its development and illogical . . . Disturbing is lack of sufficiently clear motivation for the nub of the action.' *(Variety)*

'Pure hokum.' *(John Simon, 1972)*

AFRICAN QUEEN, THE CT: 9 AV: 9.67

1951 GB 104 C ACTION/ADVENTURE/ROMANCE

D John Huston ☆ AAN
W James Agee from C.S. Forester's novel ☆ AAN

Humphrey Bogart ☆ AAW Katharine Hepburn ☆ AAN
Robert Morley Peter Bull Theodore Bikel
Walter Gotell

Mismatched couple – a missionary (Katharine Hepburn) and a hard-drinker (Humphrey Bogart) – find love as they sabotage a German gunboat prior to World War I.

An all-time-great blend of character comedy and adventure, with two of Hollywood's finest screen actors on top form.

ANTI:

'Entertaining but not entirely plausible or original. Miss Hepburn's prim missionary is too patly competent in adversity, the love affair is too predictable and too successful, the river cataracts are too tempestous, the Germans are too stupid, and the destruction of the gun-boat is too unlikely and too inevitable. So, however excellent the technique, however painstaking the execution, however well timed the laughs, the thrills, and the embraces, one's judgment in the end is 'So what?' *The African Queen* is a good picture in the sense that it will amuse almost anyone and irritate almost no one, but . . . in the sense of have a source or a purpose or a place in the records of our time, it is no picture at all.' *(Robert L. Hatch, Hollywood Reporter)*

'A picture in which two or three sequences were interesting; a few hundred feet were good color; all the rest was without taste and even without cinematic skill.' *(Gilbert Seldes, The Public Arts, 1956)*

MIXED:

'Katharine Hepburn and Humphrey Bogart come up with a couple of remarkable performances and it's fortunate . . . for the movie concentrates on them so single-mindedly that any conspicuous uncertainties in their acting would have left the whole thing high and dry . . . Never having read [the book] I can't say whether its climax was like the one tacked on to the film. The one here is wildly melodramatic, and quite at variance with the simplicity of the action that has led up to it.' *(John McCarten, New Yorker)*

PRO:

'Bogart's Allnutt is something quite new. He has chosen to play so many solemn neurotics that you might not suppose him capable of such kindly, likeable humanity.' *(Daily Telegraph)*

'Mr Huston is a great director; there is no other word for him . . . The blossoming of love . . . is handled with acute sensitiveness. Miss Hepburn . . . is extremely moving.' *(Virginia Graham)*

'Only once in a blue moon does a picture like this offer itself for our delight.' *(New York Daily News)*

'True comedy is always closely related to pain . . . In *The African Queen*, one of the richest comedies ever made, the central situation is essentially tragic.' *(Eugene Archer, Film Culture, 1959)*

AFTER DARK, MY SWEET CT: 4 AV: 5.10

1990 US 111 C THRILLER/ROMANCE

D James Foley ✗
W Bob Redlin ● from Jim Thompson's novel

Jason Patric ✗ Rocky Giordani Rachel Ward ●
Bruce Dern ✗ George Dickerson

A vagrant (Jason Patric) stumbles across – or, since he is being played by a method actor, mumbles across – a plot by an ex-cop (Bruce Dern) and a beautiful drunk (Rachel Ward) to kidnap a child.

Many critics adored the film noir atmosphere, but this overrated thriller is self-indulgently slow. The shambolic sreenplay by Bob Redlin does nothing to conceal novelist Jim Thompson's over-reliance on lazy plot contrivances. The kidnappers, for example, have an improbably cavalier approach to security, and there's the equally creaky device of a doctor who wanders into patients' houses without knocking.

Bruce Dern gives us his over-familiar grinning loony, while Jason Patric does a passable impersonation of Mickey Rourke in one of Bruce Willis's sweatier t-shirts. The thing which reduces the film to farce, however, is Rachel Ward's embarrassing attempt to play the femme fatale: her idea of how to play an alcoholic is to stand next to an empty wine bottle.

PRO:

'Confounds expectations with every twist and turn of its sinuous plot . . . [It] segues from a thriller to a profound psychosexual tragedy.' *(Robert Seidenberg, American Film)*

'A brisk, entertaining contemporary melodrama . . . Mr Foley is adroit at keeping everyting in scale. In a Foley film, people don't have thoughts too big to come out of their small, muddled brains. The performances here are exceptionally good.' *(Vincent Canby, New York Times)*

'It broods over the elements of threat, callousness, betrayal and cruelty to devastating effect . . . Very good indeed.' *(Brian Case, Time Out)*

'Not perfect. A bit slow and self-conscious in places . . . But no one could deny that the worm-in-the-bud, dark-toned sense of romantic doom that hangs around most Thompsons stories is well-sustained . . . Nothing in the film is better than the production design.' *(Derek Malcolm, Guardian)*

ANTI:

'Not best served by Jason Patric's unvarying croak, somnambulistic shamble and leaden scowl or by Rachel Ward's languidly graceless body language . . . The lack of chemistry at the film's centre leaves an exasperating void, despite all the visual appeal.' *(Philip Strick, S & S)*

'Rachel Ward . . . makes you wonder what a nice girl from the Home Counties is doing in these film noir latutides. She doesn't seem to know either.' *(Evening Standard)*

'Interesting at first, but eventually you catch on that it's heading absolutely nowhere – at 10 miles per hour, at that.' *(Maltin)*

AFTER HOURS CT: 9 AV: 6.53

1985 US 97 C COMEDY

D Martin Scorsese ☆
W Joseph Minion ✔

Griffin Dunne ☆ Rosanna Arquette ☆ Verna Bloom Thomas Chang Linda Fiorentino Teri Garr

Young man (Griffin Dunne) suffers a nightmarish series of accidents in New York.

The ultimate paranoid comedy, with an endearing performance by Griffin Dunne, a wonderfully loopy one by Rosanna Arquette, and some stunning visuals by Scorsese. Thelma Schoonmaker's editing is outstanding. Not everyone enjoys this, but almost everyone remembers it.

ANTI:

'The essentially episodic nature of the film, loosely threaded by visual in-jokes and character connections, does not exactly grip and the result is a few good laughs here and there but an overall uneven mix of farce and social comment.' *(Don Minifie, Films & Filming)*

'Where Scorsese usually creates an ambivalent sympathy for at least one of his characters, here it's difficult to find him in sympathy for any of them.' *(Don Watson, New Musical Express)*

'Rather draggy . . . Overrated.' *(Rose)*

MIXED:

'The cinema of paranoia and persecution reaches apogee . . . Anxiety-ridden picture would have be pretty funny if it didn't play like a confirmation c everyone's worst fears about contemporary urbar life.' *(Variety)*

'How much you enjoy this comic nightmare will depend on how closely you identify with Dunne - the only normal person in the picture!' *(Maltin)*

PRO:

'The best film in years . . . as if Fellini and Pinter collaborated to produce an absurdist nocturne.' *(Nigel Andrews, Financial Times)*

'At a certain highly enjoyable level, [it] is the yea best shaggy-dog story. But it is also a subtle exe in comedic and cinematic stylization . . . Scorses has told his tale at a pace just a little fizzier thar merely life-like . . . His splendid actors never pa to explain their strange behavior. The result is a delirious and challenging comedy, a postmoderr Ulysses in Nighttown.' *(Richard Schickel, Time)*

AGE D'OR, L':

see L'AGE D

AGE OF INNOCENCE, THE CT: 10 AV: 8

1993 US 139 C DRAMA/ROMANCE

D Martin Scorsese ☆
W Jay Cocks and Martin Scorsese ☆ AAN from Edith Wharton's novel

Daniel Day-Lewis ☆ Michelle Pfeiffer Winona Ryder ☆ AAN Geraldine Chaplin Mary Beth Hurt Miriam Margolyes Richard E. Grant Alec McCowen ✔

A cultivated conformist in 1870s New York socie (Daniel Day-Lewis) is on track for a highly suit marriage to a beautiful but apparently vapid ch bride (Winona Ryder); he becomes derailed by t of a scandalous countess (Michelle Pfeiffer).

Martin Scorsese interprets Edith Wharton's clas novel with passion and panache, helped by two astonishing performances by Daniel Day-Lewis Michelle Pfeiffer. The film takes Scorsese into a world of refinement already meticulously explo by Merchant Ivory. But he approaches it in a ve different spirit: with the sensuous romanticism Victor Fleming's *Gone With The Wind* and the colour sense of Powell and Pressburger's *The R Shoes*. It is appropriate that the editing, sensati throughout, is by Michael Powell's widow, Thel Schoonmaker.

The film begins at a performance of Gounod's c *Faust*, and is itself a Faustian tale: about a man sells his soul to, if not the Devil, at least to oth hellishly high expectations of him. Scorsese ke in suspense until the end as to whether Winon

Ryder – here the epitome of female fragrance – is an angel, a devious little devil, or a combination of the two.

It is also, in its own subtle way, a comedy. One great delight is seeing upper-class social mechanisms quietly at work: Alec McCowen and Richard E. Grant exude lubricious hypocrisy; Miriam Margolyes disrupts the best laid plans with massive, regal insensitivity; and Joanne Woodward pulls off the hardest task of all, with her studiously non-judgmental but cruelly omniscient role as narrator-cum-hostess.

A few may find Scorsese's camera tricks distracting, but it is these which help to make the film a personal – and honestly 20th-century – vision, not a mere reproduction of a literary work. Besides, they aren't just tricks; every camera move has its emotional justification, whether it be a long, voyeuristic tracking shot through overstuffed rooms, or sharp sideways glances at the opera.

Scorsese's film skilfully manages to be about a fetishistic love of possessions, without ever becoming fetishistic itself. He retains an amused, civilized detachment from the kind of American high society which has always mimicked European culture. As a result, he is able to demonstrate an ironic appreciation – as well as imply his condemnation – of a world where magnificent public facades conceal private vices. This is the clear-sighted film about the rich which Stanley Kubrick probably hoped he was making in *Barry Lyndon*, and there has been no more sympathetic study of a class in decline since Visconti's *The Leopard*.

ANTI:

'It's all capes and no fear.' *(Anonymous Hollywood studio mogul)*

'I assume . . . that Day-Lewis goes through the movie murmuring and making soft, uncertain gestures because Scorsese told him to . . . This keenly intelligent actor recites his lines as if they'd been learned by rote in a foreign language.' *(Stuart Klawans, New Republic)*

PRO:

'Everything here serves to express an erotic fervour, imprisoned by unbending social rituals designed to preserve the status quo in favour of a self-appointed aristocracy; as a result it's Scorsese's most poignantly moving film.' *(Geoff Andrew, Time Out)*

'If they gave Oscars for Best Food Preparation, this would be a shoo-in.' *(Angie Errigo, Empire)*

'I have seen love scenes in which naked bodies thrash in sweaty passion, but I have rarely seen them more passionate than in this movie, when everyone is wrapped in layers of Victorian repression. The big erotic moments take place in public among fully clothed people speaking in perfectly modulated phrases, and they are so filled with libido and terror that the characters scarcely survive them.' *(Roger Ebert)*

'Like *Raging Bull* with clean clothes, upholstered furniture and proper English. And good table manners . . . The two-hours-plus Innocence is implicitly stultifying and claustrophobic, because that's how the society he's examining is . . . A triumph for all concerned.' *(David Bartholomew, The Film Journal)*

AGONY AND THE ECSTASY, THE

CT: 5 AV: 4.75

1965 US 134/140 C DRAMA/BIOPIC/SO BAD

D Carol Reed ●
W Philip Dunne ● from Irving Stone's novel

Charlton Heston ● Rex Harrison Diana Cilento Harry Andrews ☆ Alberto Lupo Adolfo Celi Thomas Milian

Pope Julius II (Rex Harrison) gets Michelangelo (Charlton Heston) to paint the Sistine Chapel, and often wishes he hadn't.

Rubbish for the connoisseur. A handsome movie directed catatonically by Carol Reed. In an inspired piece of miscasting, Michelangelo (in real life, a homosexual dwarf) is played by that well known gay homunculus, Charlton Heston. As if to avenge himself upon the casting director, Heston overacts abominably. Rex Harrison enjoys himself as Pope Julius II, and gets the chance to deliver one of the immortal lines of world cinema: 'You dare to dicker with your pontiff?'

PRO:

'Harrison is outstanding as the Pope, from the moment of his striking entrance as a hooded soldier leading the suppression of a pocket of revolt, to his later scenes as an urbane, yet sensitive, pragmatic ruler of a worldly kingdom . . . Heston's Michelangelo is, in its way, also outstanding. Combination of austere garb, thinned face, short hair and beard, plus underplaying in early scenes, effectively submerge the Heston image fostered by his earlier epix.' *(Variety)*

ANTI:

'All agony, no ecstasy.' *(Judith Crist)*

'The major if not the only feeling aroused by this more than two-hour work is one of sympathy with the mounting impatience of the Pope . . . driven to annoyance, impatience, despair and finally to violent papal anger as the work goes on and on . . . Heston . . . is arrogant, agonized and cranky without a glimmer of ecstasy or warmth.' *(Bosley Crowther)*

'Made with numbing reverence and a stupendous soundtrack of choirs and symphonies . . . I'm sure that [Reed and Heston] are sincere in thinking they are conveying the essence of genius. But they have trusted themselves to an immensely commonplace script, which has just about as much insight into the workings of the creative impulse as a Los Angeles computer.' *(Robert Ottaway, Daily Sketch)*

AGUIRRE, WRATH OF GOD CT: 6 AV: 7.50

(aka *Aguirre, Der Zorn Gottes*)

1972 West Germany 95 C EPIC/ADVENTURE/ FOREIGN

D Werner Herzog ☆
W Werner Herzog

Klaus Kinski ☆ Ruy Guerra Helena Rojo Cecilia Rivera

A conquistador (Klaus Kinski) searches for El Dorado.

Klaus Kinski gives a memorable character study of a man obsessed with gold; the spectacular cinematography of the Peruvian Andes has a hallucinatory intensity; and the film works well enough as an epic boys' own adventure. However, the pace is terribly ponderous, as is the moralizing: Herzog seems to be trying to tell us something about the nature of fascism, but never makes his point clearly enough.

ANTI:

'Heavy heavy hangs the parable over our heads. Hitler and other dictators are being schematized for us . . . The film reveals nothing about power hunger or societal disease that we aren't aware of, but it so clearly thinks it does reveal something that it's somewhat maimed. This is a quality of some of the new German artists: they pound away at the horrors of dictatorship. Please – I'm not exactly advocating leniency toward fascism or the Nazi past: I note merely that lessons as elemental as those in Aguirre are familiar by now.' *(Stanley Kauffmann)*

MIXED:

'Herzog is more a poet than a storyteller, and Aguirre has a few lapses as a narrative that may throw people off. One of Aguirre's prisoners escapes and we never find out what happens to him. Having made the point that no one can open the captive Ursua's closed fist to discover what he is holding, we expect a fascinating revelation. It never comes. It's not a seamless film, not a particularly subtle one. But that is not the point. Herzog is not a director of nuance. His strokes are broad, his vision is grand, and in Aguirre his power is enormous.' *(David Ansen)*

PRO:

'Ingeniously combines Herzog's gift for deep irony, his strong social awareness, and his worthy ambition to fashion a whole new visual perspective on the world around us via mystical, evocative, yet oddly direct imagery. It is a brilliant cinematic achievement.' *(David Skerritt, Christian Science Monitor)*

'One of the great, mad, passionate, foolhardy masterpieces.' *(Roger Ebert)*

AI NO CORRIDA: *see* IN THE REALM OF THE SENSES.

AIRPLANE! CT: 9 AV: 6.85

1980 US 88 C COMEDY

D Jim Abrahams ✓ David Zucker ✓ Jerry Zucker ✓
W Jim Abrahams Jerry Zucker David Zucker ✓

Robert Hays ✓ Julie Hagerty ✓ Lloyd Bridges ✓ Peter Graves Leslie Nielsen ✓ Robert Stack

Ex-pilot (Robert Hays), emotionally crippled by fear of flying, has to land plane when pilots contract food poisoning.

Hilarious, best-ever spoof of the disaster genre, particularly of *Airport* (1970) and *Zero Hour* (1957). Note the throwaway visual gags going on in the background, and Elmer Bernstein's witty, deliberately over-melodramatic score.

ANTI:

'A series of dolefully unfunny, endlessly repetitive jokes.' *(Minty Clinch, Ms London)*

'Of course, I laughed a lot; seamy wise cracks aimed at the diaphragm kick hard . . . But the fact that I laughed at other people's pain and horror ended up by shaming me into not laughing.' *(David Hughes, Sunday Times)*

'It's compiled like a jokebook and has the kind of pacing that goes with a laugh track.' *(Pauline Kael)*

PRO:

'Has jokes – hilarious jokes – to spare. It's also clever and confident and furiously energetic.' *(Janet Maslin, New York Times)*

'A splendidly tacky, totally tasteless completely insignificant flight, a gooney bird of a movie that looks as if it could never get off the ground and then surprises and delights with its free-spirited aerobatics.' *(Richard Schickel, Time)*

'It keeps going, like a dervish with skids on.' *(Derek Malcolm, Guardian)*

'Proof that the cinema is alive and well and bursting with ingenuity.' *(David Hughes, Sunday Times)*

THE *AIRPORT* SERIES

AIRPORT AAN CT: 6 AV: 5.85

1970 US 137 C THRILLER

D George Seaton
W George Seaton from Arthur Hailey's novel AAN

Burt Lancaster Dean Martin Jean Seberg

Helen Hayes ☆ AAW Jacqueline Bisset
George Kennedy Maureen Stapleton ☆ AAN
Van Heflin ●

Plane is threatened by a mad bomber and a blizzard.

First and most gripping of a profitable series of airborne disaster movies, all of them inferior to this. It's well acted, especially by Helen Hayes (who won an Oscar); but the plot is terribly mechanical, and it's hard to care what happens to characters so cardboard that in a real air disaster they would merely blow away.

PRO:

'Airport, with its superb line-up of talent and already known title should give Universal one of its more popular films of the year . . . The one place it may find limited appeal will be on transoceanic flights.' *(Hollywood Reporter)*

'For sheer contentment there is nothing to beat the sight of constant catastrophe happening to others.' *(Alexander Walker, Evening Standard)*

ANTI:

'137 minutes of unadulterated trash.' *(Judith Crist)*

AIRPORT 75

CT: 5 AV: 3.55

(aka *Airport 1975*)

1970 US 106 C THRILLER/SO BAD

D Jack Smight ●
W Don Ingalls ●

Charlton Heston Karen Black ● George Kennedy
Efrem Zimbalist Jr Susan Clark Gloria Swanson
Sharon Gless Linda Blair Helen Reddy

Stewardess (Karen Black) has to land a disabled Boeing 747 after mid-air collision.

Not frightfully convincing. Charlton Heston does a one-man impersonation of the US cavalry – airborne. The greatest line is spoken by an airport attendant about Linda (*The Exorcist*) Blair who plays the film on a stretcher: 'The poor kid! She's in Washington and her kidney is in Los Angeles.' Also starring Helen Reddy as a singing nun. One of the most enjoyably rotten movies of all time.

PRO:

'It is much better put together [than the original]. And even though the involuntary laughter is never very far away, it does grip you by the seat of your unsuspecting pants . . . Yes, of course, it's total bunk. But . . . there's nothing like a good disaster to keep you going.' *(Derek Malcolm, Guardian)*

ANTI:

'Jack Smight's direction has the refreshing pace of a filmmaker who knows his plot can crash unless he hurries.' *(Variety)*

'A box of rotten candy for movie junkies and TV dipsos.' *(Pauline Kael, New Yorker)*

'Doesn't even have a wing and a prayer.' *(Paul D. Zimmerman, Newsweek)*

'American film making at its shabbiest, most unimaginative, most exploitative. Nothing about *Airport 1975* is good; no actor in the cast of dubious luminaries even tries to be . . . It is to be wished that everyone in the film would go away – violently.' *(Jay Cocks, Time)*

'The laughs start when Sister Reddy, guitar in hand, serenades the ailing Blair whom no one has told that patients in dire need of organs don't beam like contestants in a Junior Miss contest.' *(Margulies & Rebello)*

'Try not to see it on a plane because it might force you to walk out.' *(John Barbour, Los Angeles)*

AIRPORT 77

CT: 4 AV: 3.36

(aka *Airport III*)

1977 US 113 C THRILLER

D Jerry Jameson ●
W Michael Scheff ● David Spector ●

Jack Lemmon Lee Grant ● Brenda Vaccaro
Joseph Cotten Olivia de Havilland Darren McGavin

Hijacked plane crashes into oil-rig and settles on underwater sandbank.

Not as funny as its predecessor, nor as bad as its sequel.

'The story's formula banality is credible most of the time and there's some good actual US Navy search and rescue procedure interjected in the plot.' *(Variety)*

'Neither as riveting as it should be, nor as much fun as its absurd plotline would suggest.' *(Verina Glaessner, MFB)*

'Lee Grant's hilariously over-the-top performance is permanent evidence of the spontaneous laughter that is produced when the full weight and training of Method acting is brought to bear on a script that would hardly pass muster as a made-for-cable-TV movie.' *(Margulies & Rebello)*

AIRPORT 1979: THE CONCORDE

CT: 1 AV: 2.20

(aka *Airport '80: The Concorde*)

1979 US 123/142 (TV version) C THRILLER

D David Rich Lowell ●
W Eric Roth ●

Alain Delon Susan Blakely Robert Wagner
Sylvia Kristel George Kennedy Eddie Albert
Bibi Andersson John Davidson Martha Raye
Cicely Tyson Mercedes McCambridge

A Concorde has an eventful journey from Washington to Paris.

ANTI:

'The picture will meet with good results wherever its political sentiments find established adherents. Otherwise it's almost nil for general appeal.' *(Variety)*

MIXED:

'The constructed historical parallel – Templars = Nazi, Nevsky = Stalin – is labored but effectively driven home . . . The style of characterization throughout is operatic. One expects Nevsky to sing his unfailing orders. [The film] is primitive, patriotic propaganda – we are good, the enemy is bad . . . It has nothing whatever to do with revolutionary art. It is not proof of Eisenstein's resurgence but of his suppression.' *(Franz Hoellering, Nation)*

'Historical drama with a strong topical reference and notable as being Eisenstein's first full-scale sound film . . . In editing technique it cannot be said that the old Eisenstein is much in evidence . . . and some may find the slowness overdone . . . The characterization is simple but quite effective . . . On the whole . . . unquestionably interesting . . . perhaps not quite up to expectation.' *(MFB)*

PRO:

'Superb sequences of cinematic opera . . . pass from pastoral to lamentation and end in a triumphal cantata.' *(Georges Sadoul)*

'Cherkassov is memorable as Nevsky, but possibly the greatest contribution is Edouard Tiss's camera work. The great set scene is, of course, the final battle between the Russians and the Germans on the ice of Lake Peipus, enhanced by Prokofiev's dramatic music.' *(NFT Bulletin, 1975)*

'It's the union of Eisenstein's visual design and Prokofiev's aural design that makes Nevsky the mother of all montages.' *(Kathy Schulz Huffhines)*

'Crammed with tremendous images, focused on physical action, couched in black-and-white morality, Nevsky was nearly indistinguishable from a spectacle by De Mille or Curtiz, except for Eisenstein's discriminating taste and his supreme mastery of crowd scenes, and the absence of Errol Flynn.' *(Paul Rotha)*

'A masterpiece.' *(Maltin)*

ALFIE AAN — CT: 8 AV: 7.31

1966 GB 114 C COMEDY/DRAMA

D Lewis Gilbert
W Bill Naughton ☆ AAN

Michael Caine ☆ AAN Vivien Merchant ☆ AAN Shelley Winters Millicent Martin Julia Foster ☆ Jane Asher Shirley Anne Field Eleanor Bron Denholm Elliott

Womanizer (Michael Caine) in Swinging London gets his come-uppance.

A quintessential film of the Swinging 60s, in that it affects to condemn the pushy amorality of its hero but clearly adores him. Still, it is so well acted – especially by Michael Caine, Vivien Merchant and Julia Foster – that it is hard to take offence, easy to enjoy.

ANTI:

'[The] direction seems determined to beat the life and sparkle out of the film: at any rate it succeeds all too well in doing so.' *(The Times)*

'I must admit to a prejudice against films which begin with shots of a dog wandering through a deserted city at night . . . Caine did not manage to convey Alfie's supposedly irresistible charm.' *(Richard Roud, Guardian)*

'The characters are . . . fine. But how they are presented is disastrous . . . The stop-go policy of laugh-cry-laugh-cry . . . just doesn't work because the moods overlap, one feels emotionally cheated.' *(Isabel Quigly, Spectator)*

PRO:

'It adds up, beneath its surface of comic amorality, to a moral tract about egoism and spivvery.' *(Dilys Powell)*

'Tremendously exuberant and enjoyable . . . From Michael Caine . . . comes a performance of such king-sized stamina and tight packed skill that he makes all the other anti-heroes of the screen look like catchpenny bargains.' *(Alexander Walker, Evening Standard)*

ALICE ADAMS AAN — CT: 6 AV: 7.56

1935 US 99 BW DRAMA/ROMANCE

D George Stevens ☆
W Dorothy Yost Mortimer Offner Jane Murfin from Booth Tarkington's novel

Katharine Hepburn ☆ AAN Fred MacMurray ☆ Fred Stone Evelyn Venable Frank Albertson Ann Shoemaker

Aspirational small-town girl (Katharine Hepburn) falls in love.

This remake of a 1923 silent loses practically all the satirical edge of Booth Tarkington's novel and softens Hepburn's snobbishness to the point that she becomes quite endearing. What remains is a handsome, nostalgic vision of small-town America, an excellent performance by Hepburn, and some marvellous set-pieces, especially the dinner scene.

'Goes about slugging its points home by means of an assortment of devices that are only described with the beautiful economy of one word, which word is hokum.' *(Otis Ferguson)*

'A nice middle-class film, as trivial as a schoolgirl's diary, and just about as pathetically true.' *(C.A. Lejeune)*

'What was in 1922 a biting and observant novel emerges in 1935 as a bitingly satiric portrait of an era.' *(Time)*

'The young Hepburn was never better.' *(Shipman)*

ALICE DOESN'T LIVE HERE ANYMORE

CT: 8 AV: 8.23

1975 US 112 C DRAMA/ROMANCE

D Martin Scorsese ✓
W Robert Getchell ☆ AAN

Ellen Bursten ☆ AAW Alfred Lutter ☆
Kris Kristofferson Billy Green Bush
Diane Ladd ☆ AAN Lelia Goldoni Harvey Keitel ☆
Jodie Foster ☆

Widow (Ellen Bursten) and young son (Alfred Lutter) go in search of love and happiness.

Robert Getchell's lightweight story with feminist overtones but a soppy ending is given a hefty dose of realism by Scorsese's tough direction and a realistically nasty performance by Harvey Keitel. A young Jodie Foster makes an impact as the boyish girl who befriends the son, and Ellen Burstyn deserved her Oscar. It's an odd mixture of 70s road movie and 40s weepie, but it has a lot of charm.

ANTI:

'Takes a group of well cast film players and largely wastes them on a smaller-than-life film – one of those 'little people' dramas that make one despise little people . . . A distended bore.' *(Variety)*

'Labored, superficial and old hat beneath the trendy veneer.' *(John Simon)*

'Sways, with a good deal of cussing and swearing, between the gritty and the romantic . . . directed by Martin Scorsese, who made *Mean Streets*; it has the fluent playing of the earlier piece but not the jagged edges of character.' *(Dilys Powell)*

'It's a hip Doris Day film . . . Director and screenwriter . . . never allow her any success on the road . . . It's inevitable that she will sink back down into a complacent marriage before the film ends . . . When [it] isn't being repressive, it's camp. It likes women . . . but the women it likes are such harmless, cute kooks. What a relief! (They're no threat.)' *(James Monaco, American Film Now, 1979)*

PRO:

'An American odyssey, with women's lib overtones . . . With his stylistic exuberance at full stretch, Martin Scorsese creates an uncommon range and density of emotional life.' *(Tom Milne, S & S)*

'Full of funny malice and breakneck vitality.' *(New Yorker)*

'A tough weepie, redeemed by its picturesque locations and its eye for social detail.' *(Michael Billington, Illustrated London News)*

'Fine, moving, frequently hilarious tale . . . The geography is familiar and mostly flat . . . strewn with . . . the bright bright shiny artifacts of American's mobile optimism. The interior landscape . . . is something else again. It's a Krazy Kat world where it's difficult to tell the difference between night and day . . . The experience is scary but if you keep your wits about you, as Alice ultimately does, the chances are that things will work out . . . It's a comedy that creeps up on you . . . Miss Burstyn . . . is able to seem appealing, tough, intelligent, funny and bereft all at approximately the same moment . . . Mr Scorsese . . . [is] one of the best of the new American filmmakers.' *(Vincent Canby, New York Times)*

ALICE'S RESTAURANT

CT: 4 AV: 5.18

1969 US 110 C DRAMA

D Arthur Penn AAN
W Venable Herndon Arthur Penn

Arlo Guthrie Pat Quinn James Broderick
Michael McClanathan Geoff Outlaw Tina Chen

Folk-singer (Arlo Guthrie) drops out, has problems with the law and tries to avoid getting drafted for Vietnam.

Aimless, mostly tedious exercise in self-conscious hippiedom which received much better reviews than it deserved, because of anti-Vietnam sentiment. It does hold some interest because of its period setting and attitudes.

PRO:

'The film has the comic mood of the song, which is wry, light, staunch, and sweetly ironic about an America that rains blows on the heads of its dissenting young and also says that they can have the world.' *(Penelope Gilliatt)*

'The movie is never dull, and moves along at its own informal, quirky, personal pace. It is as likable as Arlo himself.' *(Dan Wakefield, Atlantic Monthly)*

'With a film as interesting and fine as [this] structural weaknesses, seen in proper perspective, simply become cinematic complexities to be cherished.' *(Vincent Canby, New York Times)*

ANTI:

'Arthur Penn, the director and co-scenarist, apparently cannot make up his mind whether he laughs with or laughs at the hippies and their world. Either attitude is possible; in the hands of a very great artist, which Penn emphatically is not, the two might perhaps coexist. Here, the warring attitudes produce fragmentation and nervous dishevelment. The breath is pummeled out of the spectator, and the meaning out of the film.' *(John Simon)*

'In a world nodding and bobbing with boring folk singers, Arlo bores his way to the top . . . Few [socially topical] reflections get into the film. One thinks fondly of the fierce and honest *Easy Rider*.' *(Gavin Millar, Listener)*

'Poor stuff, [Penn's] only really inadequate film . . . It's not so much that [he] aims high and falls short . . . it's that he aims everywhere . . . [He introduces] ambivalence and hopes it will be mistaken for significance instead of confusion.' *(Clive James, New Society)*

'As lacking in originality as the song: mild, well-meaning, aimless and as nourishing as a bag of stale popcorn.' *(Penelope Mortimer, Observer)*

'Somewhere along the way (or so it would seem from the film's seesawing uncertainties of tone), Arthur Penn appears to have sensed that all this is not really heaven, and that flower children, too, can be up-tight, have problems, destroy themselves, or reach thirty. This is the news that *Alice's Restaurant* brings, to which at least one possible response might be: So what?' *(William S. Pechter, Commentary)*

THE *ALIEN* SERIES

ALIEN CT: 8 AV: 7.23

1979 US/GB 124 C SF/HORROR

D Ridley Scott ☆
W Dan O'Bannon ✓ from O'Bannon and Ronald Shusett's story

Sigourney Weaver ✓ Tom Skerritt
Veronica Cartwright Harry Dean Stanton
John Hurt Ian Holm

A mutating alien murders the crew of a spacecraft, one by one.

A 50s pulp science-fiction plot, reminiscent of *The Thing* and *It! The Terror From Beyond Space*, is pressed into service once again . . . but to marvellous effect, thanks to a suspenseful script, atmospheric direction and (for the time) impressively gruesome special effects. Its central weakness is that there's no one to root for: the members of the crew are not deeply characterized or likeable. But they are convincingly blue-collar, like long-distance lorry-drivers. And there's a refreshing willingness to use the female lead (Sigourney Weaver) as the brave central protagonist, and not marginalize her – as a 50s movie would have done – as tedious love interest. The other way in which Alien broke new ground is that its imagery, which owes much to H.R. Giger's illustrations of books by H.P. Lovecraft, is sexual rather than hi-tech. Like most of the great horror movies, it was underrated and even vilified on release.

ANTI:

'Despite all its technical excellence, Alien is a horrid film, skilful and studied in its nastiness, and there is little the cast can do to mitigate its manipulative horror . . . Those with the stomach for indulgent nastiness may go and gibber.' *(Film Illustrated)*

'There is very little involvement with the characters themselves . . . A generally good cast in cardboard roles.' *(Variety)*

'Empty bag of tricks whose production values and expensive trickery cannot disguise imaginative poverty.' *(Time Out)*

'A sort of inverse relationship to *The Thing* invites unfavourable comparisons.' *(S & S)*

'The roles might have been written by a computer.' *(Vincent Canby, New York Times)*

'Just another bloodthirsty shocker, albeit with a classier production than most, and with an army of interesting special effects.' *(Cinefantastique)*

'Some people's idea of a good time.' *(Maltin)*

'Deeply dislikeable.' *(Shipman)*

MIXED:

'Alien has the usual number of inconsistencies, improbabilities and outright absurdities characteristic of the sci-fi and horror genres. What is interesting, though, is its hostile critical reception, despite the excellent visual values, direction that is no more hokey than usual in such films, dialogue that (when it is decipherable) is par for the course, and acting that is generally superior. What earmarks *Alien* as a probable audience hit and certifiable critical flop is merely that the horror is more horrible than usual.' *(John Simon)*

PRO:

'The heroine stands up to the image of male sexual aggression and comes through as the only survivor in a genre where men only reign supreme.' *(Martin Sutton, Orbis)*

'A *tour de force* of pure horror . . . The alien [is] an insane mesh of hungry teeth straight from the painting of Francis Bacon.' *(J.G. Ballard, American Film)*

ALIENS CT: 7 AV: 7.80

1986 US 137/154 (director's cut) C SF/HORROR

D James Cameron ☆
W James Cameron

Sigourney Weaver ☆ AAN Carrie Henn ☆
Michael Biehn Lance Henricksen Paul Reiser
Jenette Goldstein ☆

Futuristic marines investigate demise of a space colony and find themselves at risk from malevolent aliens.

Exemplary action movie starring Sigourney Weaver as the survivor from *Alien*, returning to wipe out the creatures which attacked her last crew. The special effects won an Oscar; and though the story-line is mechanical and the intention frankly exploitative, it certainly grips the attention. The director's cut has a clearer narrative, especially when it comes to Weaver's rescue of a small child (Carrie Henn), and the additions make more sense of the maternal symbolism which pervades the movie. It remains unusual for action movies in the way it makes use of strong female protagonists. The film was much better received than its predecessor, although some critics seemed to be wondering if Alien had not been underrated.

ANTI:

'*Alien*, with its horrible mutating creature (you never knew what form it would take), made you dread the scenes to come; it tied your innards in a knot. *Aliens* isn't that scary.' *(Pauline Kael)*

'Impression is of a film made by an expert craftsman, while Scott [director of *Alien*] clearly had something of the artist in him.' *(Variety)*

MIXED:

'The film suffers from a prolonged build-up which mistakes dragging things out for suspense, but after an initial encounter with the title character, Cameron switches to high gear and reverts back to the relentless action and suspense approach that helped make *The Terminator* such a massive hit. Cameron isn't as concerned with scares or atmosphere, the staples of traditional horror films, as he is with setting up difficult situations for his characters to get out of, leaving audiences deliciously on edge.' *(Dennis Fischer, Hollywood Reporter)*

'Weaver gives the movie a presence; without her it's a B picture that lacks the subplots and corny characters that can make B pictures amusing . . . [Even so] she's no more than a smart Rambo.' *(Pauline Kael)*

PRO:

'Cameron has shaped his film around the defiant intelligence and sensual athleticism of Weaver, and that's where *Aliens* works best. In a funny way, she's become an image ripped from today's statistics: the Single Parent Triumphant – if not absolutely Rampant.' *(Sheila Benson, Los Angeles Times)*

'The film has 300 per cent more action than its predecessor once it gets going and 100 per cent more logic.' *(Quinlan)*

ALIEN³ CT: 5 AV: 4.46

1992 US 115 C SF/HORROR

D David Fincher
W David Giler Walter Hill Larry Ferguson

Sigourney Weaver Charles S. Dutton
Charles Dance Paul McGann Brian Glover

The only human survivor of the past two films, Ripley (Sigourney Weaver) crashes on to a planet of male convicts-turned-religious-fanatics, and fears that the homicidal aliens have hitched a ride on her spacecraft.

Alien 3 was itself a monster: it lay semi-dormant in Hollywood for years, chewing up and spitting out no fewer than three directors and eight screenwriters. It emerged on screen with a serious identity problem. At some point, early in its gestation, its makers seemed to have thought of the enterprise not as a blatantly commercial enterprise, but as a Religious Parable. In earlier drafts of the script, this doubtless led to much musing on the nature of redemption and self-sacrifice. These religious aspects of the plot are carefully established on screen; but they are junked mid-way, never to return.

The monster has all the sadism of its predecessors, plus one extra personality defect: it doesn't tolerate personality. The two most interesting characters (Charles Dance and Brian Glover) are eviscerated early, and from then on the various victims are as hard to distinguish as red balls on a snooker table. American director David Fincher makes elementary errors: we see far too much of the alien, which isn't as scary as letting us see it in our imagination; he never allows us to understand the geography of the planet – crucial during the last half-hour, when the humans are trying to trap the alien. He might also have done something about the ending, a feeble echo of *Terminator 2*.

'The plot and dialogue are largely incomprehensible and the only action comes from interminable chases down dark tunnels as yet another prisoner has his sentence terminated prematurely. The best thing about it? There definitely won't be an *Alien 4*.' *(Rose)*

'In space no one can hear you snore.' *(Andy Klein, Los Angeles Reader)*

ALL ABOUT EVE AAW CT: 8 AV: 9.65

1950 US 138 BW DRAMA

D Joseph L. Mankiewicz ☆ AAW
W Joseph L. Mankiewicz ☆ AAW

Bette Davis ☆ AAN Anne Baxter ☆ AAN
George Sanders ☆ AAW Celeste Holm ☆ AAN
Gary Merrill Thelma Ritter AAN

Ambitious starlet (Anne Baxter) undermines ageing Broadway star (Bette Davis).

The storyline may be thin, and the characters merely stereotypes, but this is still a classic drama, thanks to witty dialogue and four sensational performances including an all-time-great exhibition of histrionics by Bette Davis. As a withering satire on theatrical luvvies, it has hardly dated at all.

The New York Film Critics and the British Film Academy voted it the Best Motion Picture of 1950. Mankiewicz won the Directors Guild Award as well as the New York Film Critics Award. Bette Davis won the New York Film Critics Award and the Cannes Film Festival Award for Best Female Performance of 1951.

ANTI:

'Plenty of surface cynicism, but no detachment, no

edge and no satire. Boiled down it is a plush backstage drama.' *(Richard Winnington)*

'It will leave nobody any wiser (or sadder) about the New York or any other stage.' *(Richard Winnington, S & S)*

'Mankiewicz only pretends to attack the theater and its milieux, but it's really a lovers' quarrel.' *(Jacques Doniol-Valcroze, Cahiers du Cinéma)*

'The dialogue and atmosphere are so peculiarly remote from life that they have sometimes been mistaken for art.' *(Pauline Kael)*

MIXED:

'A cynical story of the theatre which never moves beyond the modish. It is a very long piece (two hours and a-quarter) and it often seems long, though never when Bette Davis is on the screen; Miss Davis as the Broadway star, insolent, stormy, waspish and terrified of growing old, is magnificent. There is a beautifully modelled portrait, too, from Anne Baxter as the girl who sidles in, all heroine-worship and modest violetry, and schemes to supplant the established actress; and George Sanders is in form as that constant villain of films about stage or cinema, the critic. *All About Eve*, in short, is an accomplished piece of film-manufacture, a tale smartly written as well as smartly directed by Joseph Mankiewicz; it would be unfair not to point out that the dialogue is streets ahead of the twaddle usually spoken on the screen.' *(Dilys Powell)*

'A somewhat tedious film which happily boasts an extra-special performance by Bette Davis. Just to see her with a part that fits is reason enough for going . . . Unfortunately full of stereotypes, from the earnest playwright to the producer with a thick accent, the film is a half-successful attempt at defining Broadway and the legitimate stage to moviegoers.' *(Esquire)*

'So well and amusingly written that, in spite of its enormous length, the obvious artificiality of its plot, and the flagrant exaggeration of its only-too-wicked people, it never really flags.' *(James Monahan)*

PRO:

'The wittiest, the most devastating, the most adult and literate motion picture ever made that had anything to do with the New York stage.' *(Leo Mishkin)*

'A withering satire – witty, mature and worldly-wise . . . Obviously, Mr Mankiewicz, who wrote and directed it, had been sharpening his wits and his talents a long, long time for just this go.' *(Bosley Crowther, New York Times)*

'An example of the perfect screenplay . . . Few movies have such witty dialogue and such bright characters doing such terrible things to each other. And with that Bette Davis performance, the film has the very helpful quality of abrasiveness.' *(William Goldman, NFT Bulletin, 1984)*

'The whole atmosphere is deliberately theatrical: the gestures a little too studied, the settings a little too opulent, the emotions not quite sincere: everyone is playing a part. Eve begins by turning the artificiality to her own ends, but finally succumbs to it herself. When the film was released, it was criticised in some quarters as being too wordy, stagey and superficial. What was not realised was that the film aimed at exposing a group of shallow, egocentric people.' *(George Aachen)*

ALL QUIET ON THE WESTERN FRONT AAW

CT: 8 AV: 9.76

1930 US 152/140/121/105/100 BW WAR

D Lewis Milestone ☆ AAW
W Lewis Milestone Maxwell Anderson Del Andrews George Abbott ☆ AAN

Lew Ayres Louis Wolheim John Wray Raymond Griffith.

Enthusiastic young Germans are sent to their deaths in World War I.

One of the great anti-war films, directed by Lewis Milestone with nods in the direction of Eisenstein and Fritz Lang. It still dictates the way we see the 1914-18 war, and is all the more remarkable because we see the war from the viewpoint of German soldiers. Arthur Edeson's cinematography was Oscar-nominated, and the film itself was hugely acclaimed. Not only did it win the Best Picture Oscar, it was voted winner of the Photoplay Gold Medal for Best Film of the Year by the moviegoing public of America, the Film Daily poll of American film critics, the National Board of Review citation for Best Film of 1930, and the Picturegoer Seal of Merit for an Outstanding and Exceptional Motion Picture.

ANTI:

'I was hardly moved at all . . . I had read of the terrific realism of this film and didn't find it . . . One saw many men killed. After which they appeared to vanish. For the film does not show so much as a dead horse lying about. I suppose I expected to receive at least the impression of what must be the most sickening thing in war – its dreadful stench . . . My disappointment began as soon as I realised that the soldiers in the film were not young Germans torn from their homes, but admirable film actors magnificently entrenched in Hollywood.' *(James Agate, Tatler)*

'This is not true tragedy . . . Here death is terrible enough, but all that is lost is a rather sentimental undefined demonstration of youthfulness. The film deduces no considered or deepening reason why one should weep for it.' *(John Grierson, The Clarion)*

'The agony and the 'relief' are discharged with equal force and reach the same pitch, so that the experience is neutralized. The final experience is one of no experience.' *(Harry Alan Potamkin, New Masses)*

'There is much talk of the picture's realism, but I found the sets extremely artificial and the lighting very much in the overdramatic, glossy slick Hollywood manner.' *(Dwight Macdonald, 1933)*

PRO:

'Magnificent . . . No more terrific picture of war has been made . . . Sometimes one wishes there were not quite so much talk . . . But to say this is to find fault with one minute brush stroke in a huge and superb canvas.' *(James Shelley Hamilton, Cinema)*

'The most stupendous piece of peace propaganda that ever has been presented to the world . . . It does not preach; it does not plead . . . it is content to let us see war as it is and to let us make up our minds about it . . . The greatest motion picture ever made.' *(Wilford Beaton, Film Spectator)*

'A harrowing, gruesome, morbid tale of war, compelling in its realism, bigness and repulsiveness . . . Standout performances.' *(Variety)*

'Battle scenes have been represented in many a picture, but *All Quiet* surpasses them all in the stark horror and madness of the business of fighting.' *(Alexander Bakshy, Nation)*

'Above all, he liberated the camera from the trammels which sound had placed upon it, and set it roving over the battlefield, living in the trenches and in front of the guns with the soldiers. With a remarkable series of tracking shots along sandbag and body-strewn trenches, he showed that sound need not tie the film down to the confines of the stage.' *(Ray McDonald)*

ALL THAT JAZZ AAN

CT: 8 AV: 6.58

1979 US 123 C MUSICAL/ FANTASY

D Bob Fosse ☆ AAN
W Robert Alan Arthur Bob Fosse AAN

Roy Scheider ☆ AAN Jessica Lange
Ann Reinking ✓ Leland Palmer Cliff Gorman
John Lithgow Erzebet Foldi Ben Vereen

Joe Gideon, a Fosse-like director of stage musicals and films (Roy Scheider), dies of work, women and song.

Extraordinary, ambitious, fascinating attempt to make a musical comedy out of the most unpromising material: death and directorial egotism. Fosse's technically brilliant self-portrait is unflattering but strangely unrevealing: full of glitz and almost devoid of feeling. The film won Oscars for art direction, editing, musical adaptation and costume design. Giuseppe Rotunno's cinematography and Alan Heim's editing are outstanding.

'Self-important, egomaniacal, wonderfully choreographed, often compelling . . . The film's major flaw lies in its lack of real explanation of what, beyond ego, really motivates Gideon.' *(Variety)*

'An improbable mixture of crass gags, song 'n' dance routines and open heart surgery. Not for the squeamish.' *(Time Out)*

'High cholesterol hokum. Enjoyable, but probably not good for you.' *(Pauline Kael)*

'A vapid, vertiginous farrago, this, clearly derived from Fellini – call it *Beat Me, Daddy, 8½ to the Bar*. The film is both too close and not close enough to a rather sleazy reality that this kind of self-serving apotheosis makes grimier yet. But all the dancing and much of the acting (notably Roy Scheider's callow yet likable Joe), beautifully shot by Fellini's cameraman Giuseppe Rotunno and trickily edited by Alan Heim, exude a blend of titillation and hypnosis that is not without interest.' *(John Simon)*

'By the end I felt I'd learned a lot more about Bob Fosse than I actually cared to know.' *(Daily Mail)*

ALL THAT MONEY CAN BUY

CT: 8 AV: 8.44

(aka *The Devil and Daniel Webster; Daniel and the Devil; Here is a Man*)

1941 US 112/85 BW DRAMA/FANTASY

D William Dieterle ☆
W Dan Totheroh from Stephen Vincent Benet's story *The Devil and Daniel Webster* ☆

Walter Huston ☆ AAN James Craig ✓
Edward Arnold ☆ Anne Shirley Simone Simon ✓
Jane Darwell Gene Lockhart John Qualen
H.B. Warner

A poor farmer (James Craig) is tempted by the Devil (Walter Huston) but rescued by lawyer Daniel Webster (Edward Arnold).

Maybe it could have been done with a lighter touch; but tremendous performances, entertaining special effects and a great score (Bernard Herrmann's only Oscar-winner) combine with an ingenious script and stylish, expressionist direction to make this a minor classic – although it was a commercial flop on release.

ANTI:

'Oratory profoundly American and personalia foreign to British observer.' *(Today's Cinema)*

'Humourless and arty in the Germanic tradition.' *(Shipman)*

MIXED:

'Some of those in the movie industry who saw it restively called it a dog; but some of them cried it was another catapult hurling the cinema up to its glorious destiny. Well, it's interesting and charming and beguiling. It has integrity and only honest intentions, even in the moments when it fails.' *(Cecilia Ager)*

'Dan Totherot joined Benet in writing the screenplay. It is good writing, almost poetic in numerous passages. Particularly well handled are the time lapses under Dieterle's skilled direction. He does not hesitate to employ the artistic, even at sacrifice of pace . . . Perhaps there would be some benefit in eliminating nearly a reel from the finished picture, but this reviewer is glad he saw it exactly as it is.' *(Hollywood Reporter)*

PRO:

'Faces the hazard of being proclaimed an artistic triumph while faring in the field of commerce according to the state of the public's appetite for fantasy, allegory and symbolism at the moment and point of exhibition . . . The production abounds in entertainment value . . . it ranks with the finest productions Hollywood has made in point of artistic quality.' *(Moving Picture Herald)*

'A now classic movie, handsomely photographed and beautifully scored and one that stands the test of time almost as well as the masterly *Citizen Kane* made in the same year.' *(Roy Pickard, Dictionary of 1000 Best Films, 1971)*

ALL THE KING'S MEN AAW CT: 6 AV: 8.15

1949 US 109 BW DRAMA

D Robert Rossen ☆ AAN
W Robert Rossen from Robert Penn Warren's novel ☆ AAN

Broderick Crawford ☆ AAW John Derek
Joanne Dru ☆ John Ireland ☆
Mercedes McCambridge ☆ AAW Anne Seymour
Shepperd Strudwick

Power corrupts a small-town politician (Broderick Crawford).

One of the most famous films about American politics, full of authentic detail and flashy camerawork. Broderick Crawford gives a memorable portrayal of corruption (his character was based on southern senator Huey Long), and there are excellent supporting performances (especially from Mercedes McCambridge in her first screen role). Yet it's vaguely unsatisfactory and superficial, and eventually slides into melodrama.

PRO:

'Broderick Crawford as Willie gives one of the most colorful and sympathetic performances of his (or Hollywood's) career.' *(Esquire)*

'A smashing, dramatically-compelling piece of picture-making revolving around the political scene which reflects highest credit upon all concerned with its production.' *(Daily Variety)*

'Robert Rossen made one very extraordinarily fine picture, *All The King's Men*, a hard-hitting, muscular study of the rise of a demagogue that achieved its power through blunt statement and technical means that reveal him for what he was – another graduate of the Warner Brothers academy.' *(Richard Schickel, 1964)*

MIXED:

'It exposes political graft; it has a social conscience; it is not about boy-meets-girl; and that, apparently, is enough for some people. I cannot help feeling that it is not enough to present a character without working it out. Mr Crawford's playing gives the central figure the semblance of life; but Stark remains a superficial portrait, the stuff of pretentious half-educated fiction. And all round him characters are left hanging in air, going nowhere for nothing.' *(Dilys Powell)*

'More conspicuous for scope and worthiness of intention than for inspiration.' *(Gavin Lambert)*

'The picture bounces from raw-boned melodrama into dark psychological depths and thrashes around in those regions until it claws back to violence again. Consistency of structure – or of character revelation – is not in it. But it has a superb pictorialism which perpetually crackles and explodes.' *(Bosley Crowther)*

ANTI:

'The film is like one of those lifeless digests, designed for people who cannot spare the time to read whole books. Perhaps that accounts for its popularity.' *(Lindsay Anderson)*

ALL THE PRESIDENT'S MEN AAN CT: 8 AV: 8.75

1976 US 138 C THRILLER

D Alan J. Pakula ☆ AAN
W William Goldman from Carl Bernstein and Bob Woodward's book ☆

Dustin Hoffman ☆ Robert Redford ☆ Jack Warden
Martin Balsam Hal Holbrook ☆
Jason Robards ☆ AAW Jane Alexander ☆ AAN

Journalists (Dustin Hoffman, Robert Redford) discover the astonishing truth behind the Watergate break-in.

A riveting thriller of journalistic investigation, all the better for making it clear that the protagonists' motivation was professional, rather than political. The faint narcissism of the two stars only adds another layer to the characterization: Bernstein and Woodward were not shrinking violets either. Alan J. Pakula's direction effectively contrasts the lightness of the newspaper office with the shady nature of Nixonian politics. Jason Robards turns in an outstanding performance as *Washington Post* Editor Ben Bradlee.

MIXED:

'When the reporters' book about their Watergate investigation was bought for films, a lot of people said it couldn't be made into a film. Well, it couldn't. But on the way to an ultimately static and uncomfortable result, there's some passable acting, by Redford and Hoffman and others, and there's some pleasure in seeing again the defeat of – no calmer term will do – an attempted fascist coup. The trouble with the film is that it's inevitably off-center: the interest in the Woodward-Bernstein story is mostly in what they uncovered, not in the act of uncovering it.' *(Stanley Kauffmann)*

'An absorbing drama from the headlines which despite its many excellences would have been better with a more audible dialogue track, less murky photography and a clearer introduction of the characters concerned. The acting however is a treat.' *(Halliwell)*

'Would have been better with a more audible dialogue track, less murky photography and a clearer introduction of the characters concerned. The acting however is a treat.' *(Quinlan. Spot the similarity to Halliwell?)*

PRO:

'Spellbinding . . . the thinking man's *Jaws*.' *(New York Times)*

'The film is not about the fall of Nixon, or the disgrace of political aides, or the complicity of great departments. It is a stunningly well-made reconstruction of a hunt for facts. One may have qualms, as I have, and still admire the brilliance of the job done. I don't think anything as close to life – close in time, close in personalities – has been done in the cinema before.' *(Dilys Powell)*

'As a wag has suggested, the movie is admirable in never letting you forget who the real enemy was for Carl Bernstein and Bob Woodward: a composite of Walter Cronkite and the *New York Times*. Certainly our two journalist heroes never express the slightest concern for patriotism, justice, and similar niceties; getting the story and making it stick is all that matters – before, that is, the competition might get hold of it. These are not idealistic men, but they are bright, clever, and breathtakingly persistent.' *(John Simon)*

'It works as a detective thriller (even though everyone knows the ending), as a credible (if occasionally romanticized) primer on the prosaic fundamentals of big league investigative journalism, and best of all as a chilling tone poem that conveys the texture of the terror in our nation's capital during that long night when an aspiring fascist regime held our democracy under siege.' *(Frank Rich, New York Post)*

ALMOST AN ANGEL CT: 1 AV: 3.00

1990 US 95 C COMEDY/FANTASY

D John Cornell ●
W Paul Hogan ●

Paul Hogan Elias Koteas ☆ Linda Kozlowski
Charlton Heston Doreen Lang Joe Dallesandro

A supposedly lovable criminal (Paul Hogan) returns to earth as a trainee angel, and helps a dying paraplegic (Elias Koteas) and his bespectacled sister (Linda Kozlowski) to keep open a day-care centre for the local latch-key kids.

An Australian-American turkey with the charm of a funnel-web spider, the pace of a catatonic koala, and the wit of a dehydrated dingo. Hogan has only himself to blame, since he wrote and executive-produced it. John Cornell directs so unattractively that Miss Kozlowski looks no better even after she has removed her glasses. Proof that, though the Devil may have all the good tunes, God has some of the most nauseating movies.

'The movie's plot is not exactly sophisticated, and some of the sequences are so naive that they seem borrowed from old grade-B westerns . . . But the movie's low-key charm and good-will make up for a lot. And so does Hogan's natural, entertaining screen presence.' *(Roger Ebert)*

'No-effort vanity project with only Paul Hogan's easygoing charm to fill the space between the sprocket holes.' *(Variety)*

'This awful load of mush, written by Hogan, is so unbelievably sentimental they should be handing out sick bags to the audience.' *(Rose)*

'Almost a turkey.' *(Mark Kermode, Time Out)*

ALPHAVILLE CT: 4 AV: 5.00

(aka *Alphaville, Une Étrange Aventure de Lemmy Caution*)

1965 France 100 BW SF/THRILLER/FOREIGN

D Jean-Luc Godard ✗
W Jean-Luc Godard ✗

Eddie Constantine Anna Karina Akim Tamiroff
Howard Vernon Laszlo Szabo

Special agent (Eddie Constantine) travels through space to investigate the disappearance of a fellow agent (Akim Tamiroff).

Deadly dull picture of a dehumanized society. Godard's attempts to make political statements amount, as usual, to inane twaddle. It was voted Best Film at Berlin in 1965, and ludicrously overpraised by critics.

PRO:

'The first science-fiction film to offer the uneasy reminder that our own world is already more than halfway to science-fiction.' *(Tom Milne, MFB)*

'Makes no separation between fantasy and reality . . . Maybe, in this case, the term science fiction is no longer applicable; *Alphaville* is S-P, science poetry.' *(Carlos Clarens, An Illustrated History of the Horror Film, 1967)*

'Blends utopian satire, pop art, and comic book imagery to create the alienated landscape of [a] distant planet.' *(J.G. Ballard, American Film, 1987)*

'One of Godard's most sheerly enjoyable movies.' *(Tom Milne, Time Out)*

'Godard depicted the future in terms of film noir paranoia. In a soulless world taken over by technology, fascism rules over any emotion, any art. Detective-hero Caution stands in for Godard, representing the principles recognized as the caring, educated humanism of our day. Godard combines an Aldous Huxley-type presentiment to the then-new sociological perceptions of Marshall McLuhan.' *(Armond White)*

MIXED:

'Satiric, exciting and amusing up to a third or fourth reel point. Then it becomes repetitious, solemn, meandering and thin.' *(Bosley Crowther, New York Times)*

'Very old dramatic hat . . . [but] there is a connecting brilliance of style.' *(Dilys Powell)*

ANTI:

'A dry travesty . . . [The film], with its superior air of playful condescension toward its material, is fake intellectual satire for juvenile adults and adult juveniles. It is Glossy Entertainment: past, present and future.' *(Parker Tyler, Portfolio/Art News)*

'A tedious and erratic film that suffers badly from the director's failure to impose clarity of vision. Ideas swim about in there but remain undeveloped.' *(Elliot)*

'Has dated as badly as most of this director's output. His city of the future, boldly photographed by Raoul Coutard, consists of tacky Paris hotel rooms and impersonal glass skyscrapers; but most other devices are borrowed from Orwell's 1984 and the plot from pulp fiction.' *(Shipman)*

AMADEUS AAW — CT: 6 AV: 8.19

1984 US 158 C DRAMA

D Milos Forman ☆ AAW
W Peter Shaffer ☆ AAW from his own play

F. Murray Abraham ☆ AAW Tom Hulce ☆ AAN Elizabeth Berridge Simon Callow Roy Dotrice Christine Ebersole Jeffrey Jones ☆

Viennese court composer Salieri (F. Murray Abraham) envies talent of Mozart (Tom Hulce) and plots to kill him.

A film which, like Shaffer's play, is a shade ponderous, overlong and not altogether convincing when it depicts genius: Tom Hulce's Mozart is a posturing ninny. Its greatest strength is a wonderfully convincing portrait of envy, in the form of Salieri. Glorious to look at, and hear.

ANTI:

'The stature and power the work possessed onstage have been noticeably diminished, and Milos Forman's handling is perhaps too naturalistic for what was conceived as a highly stylized piece.' *(Variety)*

'Abraham [plays] Salieri without wit or subtlety.' *(Ms London)*

'Hulce's Mozart is so extraordinarily annoying, we can easily sympathise with Salieri.' *(Rose)*

MIXED:

'Hulce . . . gets better and better as the drama progresses . . . Not so great is Elizabeth Berridge – a large casting mistake . . . it's probably not her fault that she suggests her native Westchester far more often than 18th century Vienna . . . Forman . . . has preserved the fascinating heart of [the] play and made it available to millions . . . Well done.' *(Vincent Canby, New York Times)*

'The play was a much stronger piece about cancerous envy and gnawing mediocrity. Where the film does win hands down however is in the almost seamless thread of Mozart music and in Twyla Tharp's brilliant staging of the operatic excerpts.' *(Michael Billington, Guardian)*

'The rhetoric of the film's conception . . . has outstripped its execution . . . Forman has nevertheless turned this into a colourful and ornate piece of work . . . It is one of those films which combines a credulity about [great artists'] exciting or tormented lives with an inability to describe or measure their actual achievement. But at least the music is good.' *(Peter Ackroyd, Spectator)*

'Great to look at, and only the American accents jar the ear.' *(Halliwell)*

PRO:

'A magnificent film, full and tender and funny and charming – and, at the end, sad and angry too, because in the character of Salieri it has given us a way to understand not only greatness, but our own lack of it.' *(Roger Ebert)*

'Not, praise be, the sort of toe curling excess Ken Russell has more than once conjured from a composer's corpse and corpus . . . and I applaud its outfacing or outvoicing of that sanctified convention whereby only English actors are allowed to play cultivated Europeans.' *(John Coleman, New Statesman)*

AMARCORD AAW — CT: 8 AV: 8.89

1973 Italy/France 123 C DRAMA/FOREIGN

D Frederico Fellini ☆
W Frederico Fellini Tonino Guerra

Puppela Maggio Magali Noel Armando Brancia Ciccio Ingrassia

Frederico Fellini's reminiscences (the title means 'I remember') of growing up in the Italian provinces at the time of Mussolini.

No masterpiece of narrative structure – but its series

of fragmented episodes and images, mostly joyful but some melancholic, make this one of the most evocative autobiographical films ever made. There's a darker side too: it's a memorable portrait of a people's childlike submission to fascist authority.

'A rich surface texture and a sense of exuberant melancholia.' *(Michael Billington, Illustrated London News)*

'Peaks of invention separated by raucous valleys of low comedy.' *(S & S)*

'Witty, tender, humane, marvellously photographed.' *(Benny Green, Punch)*

'Fellini, the most honest and lovable faker who ever made a film, here presents a beautiful carnival show of the sacred things in his life.' *(Stanley Kauffmann)*

AMBUSHERS, THE — CT: 1 AV: 2.14

1967 US 101/102 C ACTION/ADVENTURE

D Henry Levin ●
W Herbert Baker

Dean Martin ● Senta Berger Janice Rule James Gregory Albert Salmi Kurt Kaznar

Matt Helm (Dean Martin) investigates the disappearance of a flying saucer.

The third Matt Helm spy spoof, and easily the worst of a horrible series. The others, if you're a masochist, are *The Silencers* (1966), *Murderer's Row* (1966) and *The Wrecking Crew* (1969). Sample dialogue . . . Matt's secretary, Lovey Cravesit, bringing him supplies: 'I think I've got everything you want.' Matt, as camera zooms in on her behind: 'Yeah!'

'Although visual aspects – the Oleg Cassini wardrobe and overall fashion supervision – are very good, pic at same time has that slap-dash quickie look.' *(Variety)*

'It belongs to the Playboy ethos of 'Look, but you can't touch' . . . full of phoney promises but no real action. The credit sequence of glamorous girls and sunny beaches is exactly like flicking through the pages of one of those glossy magazines, and the film never really develops beyond that.' *(F & F)*

'The makers . . . appear to be proceeding under the theory that off-color jokes, a leering star, and scantily clad females will make money at the box office. They may be right. But for someone who demands that the jokes be funny as well as dirty, that Martin give some semblance of an acting performance, and that a spy script (who stole the flying saucer?) be intelligent, *The Ambushers* hits a new low.' *(William Wolf, Cue)*

'Martin comes across as a male Mae West.' *(Art Murphy, Variety)*

'The sole distinction of this vomitous mess is that it just about reaches the nadir of witlessness, smirky sexiness and bad taste – and it's dull, dull, dull to boot.' *(Judith Crist)*

AMERICA, AMERICA AAN — CT: 5 AV: 7.17

(aka *The Anatolian Smile*)

1963 US 177 BW DRAMA/ADVENTURE

D Elia Kazan AAN
W Elia Kazan AAN

Stathis Giallellis ☆ Frank Wolff Harry Davis Linda Marsh ☆ Paul Mann ☆ Lou Antonio ☆

In 1896, a young Greek (Stathis Giallelis) tries to migrate to US.

Very long, rambling, hopelessly self-indulgent film cobbled together from family anecdotes. But as long you don't care about narrative drive and can tolerate the film's sentimental view of America, there are impressive moments.

'*America, America*, in my opinion the best film I ever made, was a total flop – total catastrophe. Nobody went to see the goddamn thing.' *(Elia Kazan)*

PRO:

'Heartfelt and heart-rending.' *(Maltin)*

MIXED:

'Elia Kazan's *America, America* manifests why he is an outstanding director. The chief flaw is a recurrent one in Kazan's work on film and stage: a defective sense of proportion. He does not know when to condense and move on; if he sinks his teeth in a scene or a sequence that he enjoys, the audience can just wait around and be damned to it until he has worried the material in every way his warm invention can think of.' *(Stanley Kauffmann)*

ANTI:

'Elia Kazan's *America, America* runs for three hours. It is a slow, a tedious picture. Partly the tedium results from Mr Kazan's screen style. He works methodically, filling his scenes with factitious detail and apparently uninterested in the wit and allusiveness of which the camera is capable. Every episode, almost every shot, has its own beginning, middle, and end, and the numberless playlets are cemented together into a strip which, after the first two hours, threatens to stretch grimly to eternity.' *(John Simon)*

'A massive piece of self-indulgence by a one-man band [Kazan], fascinating for his family circle but so poorly constructed as to be of very limited interest elsewhere.' *(Halliwell)*

AMERICAN FRIEND, THE CT: 5 AV: 6.73

(aka *Der Amerikanische Freund*)

1977 West Germany 127 C THRILLER

D Wim Wenders ☆
W Wim Wenders Fritz Müller-Scherz from Patricia Highsmith's novel *Ripley's Game*

Dennis Hopper Bruno Ganz ☆ Liza Kreuzer Gérard Blain Nicholas Ray Samuel Fuller Daniel Schmid

A picture-framer named Ripley (Bruno Ganz) becomes an assassin for the Mafia.

Directorially flashy, terminally modish destruction of a decent thriller. Wim Wenders loses the coherence of Patricia Highsmith's narrative, not to mention the suaveness of her central character, in pursuit of existential angst and a ponderous statement about the way American culture dominates Europe. Cult directors Sam Fuller and Nicholas Ray turn up as heavies, and add to the air of self-congratulation. Even so, the ingenious structure of Highsmith's story does shine through; and a few critics consider this to be a great film.

PRO:

'Ripley . . . becomes the quintessential Wenders hero, the loner travelling through alien lands in quest of himself, of friendship, of some meaning to life.' *(Tom Milne, Time Out)*

'One of the best thrillers for many a moon . . . Many of Wenders' scenes are reminiscent of Hitchcock at his best; there is no higher praise.' *(David Hughes, Western Mail)*

'The cinema's best Highsmith adaptation since Hitchcock's *Strangers on a Train*. Cavalier and casually funny, it is also a riveting film noir.' *(Tom Milne, Observer)*

'Riveting stuff, a superlative suspense thriller springing surprises right to the end.' *(Richard Barkley, Sunday Express)*

'Take it at a Hitchcockian level . . . . enjoy the grand camera work and evocation of mood . . . . After that you can start getting metaphysical about its meanings if you really want to.' *(Molly Plowright, Glasgow Herald)*

MIXED:

'There are times when the film comes near foundering as Wenders heaps metaphysical significance upon the perversely warm and trusting relationship growing between Hopper and Ganz.' *(Alan Brien, Sunday Times)*

'Wenders's unsettling compositions are neurotically beautiful visions of a disordered world, but the film doesn't have the nasty, pleasurable cleverness of a good thriller; dramatically, it's stagnant – inverted Wagenerianism.' *(Pauline Kael)*

AMERICAN GRAFFITI CT: 7 AV: 7.86

1973 US 109 C COMEDY/DRAMA/RITES-OF-PASSAGE

D George Lucas ☆
W George Lucas

Richard Dreyfuss ☆ Ron Howard Paul Le Mat Charles Martin Smith Cindy Williams Candy Clark ☆ AAN Harrison Ford

An eventful summer night in the lives of four American schoolfriends, 1962.

George Lucas's nostalgic evocation of teenagers growing up in middle America has a great soundtrack, and is beautifully designed and acted by a talented young cast, including Richard Dreyfuss, Harrison Ford, Ron Howard and Candy Clark. It seems almost churlish to point out that the plot is weak, the situations contrived, and the characters stereotypes.

'A most vivid recall of teenage attitudes and mores, told with outstanding empathy and compassion through an exceptionally talented cast . . . Design consultant Al Locatelli, art director Dennis Clark and set director Douglas Freeman have brilliantly reconstructed the fabric and texture of the time, while Walter Murch's outstanding sound collage – an unending stream of early rock platter hits – complements in the aural department.' *(Variety)*

'A small film, but with a rich ore of truth in it.' *(John Simon)*

'Lucas typically uses color and lighting effects to achieve a sense of immediate excitement, not to convey nuances of theme or feeling . . . [Lucas is guilty of] an artificially confining structure and unfelt manipulation of stereotyped characters.' *(James Bernardoni, The New Hollywood, 1991)*

AMERICAN IN PARIS, AN AAW CT: 6 AV: 8.12

1951 US 113 MUSICAL/ROMANCE

D Vincente Minnelli ☆ AAN
W Alan Jay Lerner ✗ AAW (music by George Gershwin ☆ lyrics by Ira Gershwin)

Gene Kelly ☆ Leslie Caron ☆ Oscar Levant ☆ Georges Guetary ☆ Nina Foch ☆ Eugene Borden

A US artist (Gene Kelly) patronized by rich woman (Nina Foch) falls instead for Parisian gamine (Leslie Caron).

The story is trite and predictable. The 'I Got Rhythm' number is given horribly twee treatment, and the final ballet is so tasteless that it puts some viewers' teeth on edge. But the performers are so outstanding, and the Gershwin score so imperishable that the film achieves a classic status.

'Too fancy and overblown.' *(Pauline Kael)*

'There are those who describe this [the final ballet] as vulgar or pretentious, forgetting that the story is about Kelly as a frustrated artist.' *(Geoff Andrew, Time Out)*

'[Kelly's] diversified dancing is as great as ever and his thesping is standout. But he reveals new talents in this one with his choreography. There's a lengthy ballet to the film's title song which is a masterpiece of design, lighting, costumes and colour photography. It's a unique blend of classical and modern dance with vaude-style tapping.' *(Variety)*

'A warm and witty and utterly believable story of the small-town American in big-time Paris. Gene Kelly, who has also provided dazzling choreography, and Leslie Caron, scintillating and fresh in her delightful film debut as the French dream-girl of every American boy, are the ultimate romantic leads; and Vincente Minnelli has directed with warmth and chic. This film should become a fixture on television, shown annually to refresh our hearts.' *(Judith Crist)*

AMERICAN WEREWOLF IN LONDON, AN

CT: 8 AV: 6.31

1981 US 97 C HORROR/COMEDY

D John Landis ☆
W John Landis ☆

David Naughton Jenny Agutter ✔ Griffin Dunne John Woodvine Brian Glover Frank Oz

Two American tourists in Britain (David Naughton, Griffin Dunne) get bitten on the Yorkshire moors, with unpleasant consequences.

Sophisticated, well-crafted venture by comedy director John Landis into the horror genre, with great, Oscar-winning special effects by Rick Baker, genuinely horrific moments and a surprisingly moving central performance by Jenny Agutter.

'The gear changes of tone and pace make for a very jerkily driven vehicle.' *(Sunday Times)*

'Seems curiously unfinished, as though Landis spent all his energy on spectacular set-pieces and then didn't want to bother with things like transitions, character development, or an ending.' *(Roger Ebert)*

'A clever mixture of comedy and horror which succeeds in being both funny and scary . . . Talents of special make-up effects designer Rick Baker are shown in full flower.' *(Variety)*

'This may be the most successful attempt to mix horror and comedy there has been.' *(Danny Peary)*

AMERIKANISCHE FREUND, DER: *see* AMERICAN FRIEND, THE.

ANATOMY OF A MURDER, AN AAN

CT: 6 AV: 7.36

1959 US 160 BW DRAMA

D Otto Preminger
W Wendell Mayes ☆ AAN

James Stewart ☆ AAN Lee Remick Ben Gazzara ✔ Arthur O'Connell ☆ AAN Eve Arden Kathryn Grant Joseph N. Welch ☆ George C. Scott ☆ AAN

Small-town attorney (James Stewart) defends army lieutenant (Ben Gazzara) on trial for murder.

Big, bulky courtroom drama thought racy and controversial in its time. Though overlong, it's neatly plotted; and the splendid cast sustains audience interest. Duke Ellington contributes a memorable score.

'Preminger purposely creates situations that flicker with uncertainty, that may be evaluated in different ways. Motives are mixed and dubious, and, therefore, sustain interest.' *(Variety)*

'The best courtroom melodrama this old judge has ever seen.' *(Bosley Crowther)*

'Sexploitation is one of Preminger's fortes and he handles easily the problem of how to put on the soundtrack talk of torn panties, spermatogenesis and vaginal examinations without anyone being able to prove it was done for pornographic purposes. Nor does character superficiality bother [him] . . . As a consequence, [the film] is a sure-fire box-officer. It is also an example of expert filmmaking . . . Its greatest cinematic virtue is its casting.' *(Henry Hart, Films in Review)*

'Preminger's undeniably entertaining courtroom melodrama is a . . . brilliantly and often wittily dialogued and ingeniously constructed; the attitude cynical, consciously disenchanted . . . Generally satisfying until the last half hour, when it becomes over concerned with the increasingly predictable mechanics of its detection and totally inadequate as drama of character.' *(MFB)*

'Far less confident in the law than most courtroom dramas, which makes one suspect that it was this probing cynicism rather than the 'daring' use of words that caused controversy at the time of release.' *(Geoff Andrew, Time Out)*

AND THEN THERE WERE NONE

CT: 8 AV: 8.73

(aka *Ten Little Niggers*)

1945 US 98 BW THRILLER

D René Clair ☆
W Dudley Nichols from Agatha Christie's novel ☆

Walter Huston ☆ Barry Fitzgerald ☆

Louis Hayward ☆ June Duprez Roland Young ☆
Richard Haydn ☆ C. Aubrey Smith
Judith Anderson Queenie Leonard Mischa Auer

Ten people are invited to an island house-party, where they are bumped off one by one.

A top-notch cast, clever script, efficient direction, and great cinematography by Lucien Andriot combine to make this a classic suspense thriller with darkly comic overtones. It all looks effortless, yet attempts to emulate it have often proved disastrous.

PRO:

'A smooth, cold, amusing show.' *(James Agee, Nation)*

'Rich in the elements which have made mystery melodramas popular, yet not in the precise form of any previously made.' *(Hollywood Reporter)*

'Full marks . . . for a most ingenious who-dun-it yarn and cordial praise for an intelligent treatment which so suavely blends drama with action and tones down the thrill at tense moments by touches of natural comedy. The portrayal, too, is first rate.' *(Today's Cinema)*

'Out of this lethal hocus-pocus, René Clair has produced an exciting film and has directed a splendid cast in it with humor and a light macabre touch.' *(Bosley Crowther, New York Times)*

'The most ingenious comedy-mystery by a director other than Hitchcock.' *(Gerald Mast, A Short History of the Movies)*

ANDALUSIAN DOG, AN: *see* UN CHIEN ANDALOU

ANDREI RUBLEV CT: 5 AV: 8.10

1966 USSR 146 (GB)/165 (US)/185 (USSR) C EPIC

D Andrei Tarkovsky ☆
W Andrei Mikhalkov Konchalovsky Andrei Tarkovsky

Anatoly Solonitsin Ivan Lapikov Nikolai Grinko
Nikolai Sergeyev

Eight fictitious episodes in the life of a real 15th century icon painter (Anatoly Solonitsin).

A memorable evocation of medieval life and a thoughtful analysis of the artist's place in society; but like all Tarkovsky's work it is stupefyingly slow.

'Better as kaleidoscope than insight.' *(Shipman)*

'The one indisputable masterpiece of the last decade.' *(Nigel Andrews, MFB)*

'Worthy of comparison with the best of Eisenstein's historical dramas.' *(Maltin)*

'Sweeping camera movement and stunning performances.' *(Scheuer)*

'With the exception of the great Eisenstein, I can't think of any film which has conveyed a feeling of the remote past with such utter conviction . . . a durable and unmistakable masterpiece.' *(Michael Billington, Illustrated London News)*

'Towering . . . one of world cinema's most enthralling films.' *(Geoff Brown, The Times)*

ANGEL AT MY TABLE, AN CT: 7 AV: 8.09

1990 NEW ZEALAND 158 C DRAMA/BIOPIC/RITES-OF-PASSAGE

D Jane Campion ☆
W Laura Jones from Janet Frame's autobiography

Kerry Fox ☆ Karen Fergusson Alexis Keogh
Melina Bernecker Glynis Angell

A portrait of writer Janet Frame (Kerry Fox), who spent eight years in a mental asylum, wrongly diagnosed as schizophrenic.

This tender, sensitive, realistic film was made as a three-part TV mini-series, and it all too often looks like one: at 158 minutes, its pace would have been helped by judicious cutting, and the budgetary constraints of TV seem to have inhibited Ms Campion from the imaginative framings which so skilfully reflected the heroine's insanity in her first film, *Sweetie*.

For all that, the film won the Grand Jury Prize at the Venice Film Festival and is no mean achievement. The childhood scenes have a wonderful freshness of observation; the asylum episode (the second) is harrowing and sad; it's only the third part, with its unconvincing love story, which stretches one's patience, and even here there is much to enjoy in the performance of the leading actress.

'Campion's previous film was burdened with precious camera work – high angles, low angles, weird vantage points. Not one bit of that is evident here. She was so concerned with her subject that she forgot about self-display and put her (considerable) pictorial skill at the service of Janet Frame. Oh, there are a couple of shots of a distant train chugging along past a sunset, but those are negligible if only because they are commonplace. Campion is so responsible to the currents of humanity in this story that she has found the exactly right general locus for her camera – close without close-ups. The camera is attentive, not intrusive.' *(Stanley Kauffmann)*

'An excruciating saga that Fox and Campion make both poetic and persuasive.' *(Bruce Williamson, Playboy)*

'An indisputable triumph.' *(George Perry, Sunday Times)*

ANGEL EXTERMINATADOR, EL: *see* EXTERMINATING ANGEL, THE.

ANGELS WITH DIRTY FACES

CT: 8 AV: 8.07

1938 US 97 BW DRAMA

D Michael Curtiz ☆ AAN
W John Wexley Warren Duff from Rowland Brown's story

James Cagney ☆ AAN Pat O'Brien ☆ Humphrey Bogart ☆ Ann Sheridan George Bancroft Billy Halop

Priest (Pat O'Brien) is disturbed to find gangster (James Cagney) worshipped as hero by Dead End Kids.

Classic gangster drama with a social conscience and strong moral. Craggy Pat O'Brien somehow manages to avoid seeming pious, as he shows his cocky childhood buddy on Death Row (James Cagney) why it's not such a great idea for the community that he's worshipped by the local youth. Cagney and O'Brien make a great screen partnership.

'Should do fair business, but the picture itself is no bonfire . . . In at least one instance the same set is used for two supposedly different locales.' *(Variety)*

'A rousing, bloody, brutal melodrama.' *(New York Mirror)*

'Standout gangster film that has often been copied but never equaled.' *(Danny Peary)*

'Has jokes and romance and a smashing last sequence on Death Row.' *(Pauline Kael)*

'A seminal movie . . . It combined gangster action with fashionable social conscience; it confirmed the Dead End Kids as stars; it provided archetypal roles for its three leading players and catapulted the female lead into stardom. It also showed the Warner style of film-making, all cheap sets and shadows, at its most effective.' *(Halliwell)*

ANGRY SILENCE, THE

CT: 7 AV: 6.63

1960 GB 95 BW DRAMA

D Guy Green ☆
W Bryan Forbes ☆ AAN from Richard Gregson and Michael Craig's story AAN

Richard Attenborough ☆ Pier Angeli Michael Craig ☆ Bernard Lee Alfred Burke Penelope Horner

Worker (Richard Attenborough) is spurned by workmates during industrial unrest.

Brave, sincere, very well acted drama about a subject which most other filmmakers assiduously steered clear of during the years when unions really did have too much power. Undeniably more interesting when it's in the workplace than when it's in the home – but even here the film is kept compelling by the two strong leading performances of Attenborough and Pier Angeli.

'Details the impact of industrial unrest on individuals, told with passion, integrity and guts, but without false theatrical gimmicks. Apart from the message, there is a solid core of entertainment produced by taut writing, deft direction and topnotch acting.' *(Variety)*

'A story with truth at its heart. And its subject is the new tyranny – I don't know what other name you can give to a system which destroys a man for honestly dissenting. After all, it is not so very different from the fine old ecclesiastical practice of excommunication. *The Angry Silence* was a brave film to make, and it has been bravely made – by people who care about the screen and care what they are saying on it. And one comes away reminded of that old thing about absolute power.' *(Dilys Powell)*

'Vastly entertaining as well as thought-provoking. Matter and manner are for once wholly in harmony.' *(Daily Mail)*

'A strange mixture of melodramatic union-bashing and sharp, penetrating observations on working-class life. The villains are phantoms of an ill-informed imagination, but Attenborough's lone wolf worker, holding out against an unofficial strike, is vivid and well thought out.' *(Robert Murphy, Time Out)*

'One of the great post-war films.' *(Quinlan)*

ANIMAL CRACKERS

CT: 8 AV: 7.25

1930 US 97/100 BW COMEDY

D Victor Heerman
W Morrie Ryskind from the musical play by Morrie Ryskind George S. Kaufman ☆ (music and lyrics by Bert Kalmar Harry Ruby ☆)

Groucho Marx ☆ Harpo Marx ☆ Chico Marx ☆ Zeppo Marx Lillian Roth Margaret Dumont Hal Thompson

An African explorer (Groucho Marx) attends society party in house where thieves plan to steal a valuable painting.

The Marx Brothers' second movie is one of their funniest. Forget the theatricality, bad puns and dull interludes and enjoy the classic scenes, especially those between Groucho and Margaret Dumont. Sample gag . . . Groucho: 'One morning I shot an elephant in my pajamas. How he got into my pajamas I'll never know.'

'Among the Marx boys there is no preference. Groucho shines; Harpo remains a pantomimic clown who ranks with the highest; Chico adds an unusual comedy sense to his dialog as well as business and piano playing; and Zeppo, if in on a split, is lucky.' *(Variety)*

'It is a nice change of pace watching Dumont play scenes with Harpo and Chico, and not just Groucho.' *(Danny Peary)*

'It looks stagey. But the film is too joyous for cavilling.' *(Pauline Kael)*

ANNA AND THE KING OF SIAM

CT: 6 AV: 7.00

1946 US 128 BW DRAMA/ROMANCE

D John Cromwell
W Talbot Jennings Sally Benson AAN from Margaret Landon's novel

Irene Dunne ☆ Rex Harrison ☆ Linda Darnell Lee J. Cobb Gale Sondergaard AAN

English widow (Irene Dunne) educates the Siamese court and the King himself (Rex Harrison).

Enjoyable escapism, though not up to the level of Rodgers and Hammerstein's musical remake. Post-war Hollywood's idea of a Siamese court is not entirely convincing and the pace drags at times, but the charm of the Dunne-Harrison team more than compensates. It's the kind of movie that you may start off finding laughable, but then find yourself surreptitiously shedding a tear over. Arthur Miller's cinematography won an Academy Award.

ANTI:

'A film that never touches the imagination, a film that leaves the mind uninformed and the memory unburdened. In endless glittering vistas of de luxe oriental suites, in conventional comedy and conventional pathos the spell of a unique human collision has been dispersed.' *(Richard Winnington)*

MIXED:

'I am not among those who take to Irene Dunne – as a rule she makes my skin crawl; nor do I wholly enjoy Rex Harrison's highly skilled, generally restrained horsing as the naively intelligent monarch whose good intentions enthrone him in a pratfall between his ancient and our modern world. There is indeed a good deal of high-polished and expensive cuteness about the whole production which stands, I suppose, as an apology for venturing to film a story that fits none of the formulas. But in spite of and through all this, the relationship between the rattled, irascible king and the English widow is often real, clear, and delightful, and occasionally very touching.' *(James Agee, Nation)*

'The harem is composed of starlets and the settings are risible, but if you think this all only bearable with music – it became, of course, *The King And I* – you are reckoning without the potent charm of Miss Dunne and the comic skill of Mr Harrison.' *(Shipman)*

PRO:

'Script builds fascinating adult interest without ever implying that relationship between teacher and pupil goes beyond the friendship stage.' *(Variety)*

'A delightful movie classic.' *(Judith Crist)*

ANNA KARENINA

CT: 6 AV: 7.00

1935 US 95 BW DRAMA/ROMANCE

D Clarence Brown ✗
W Clemence Dane Salka Viertel S.N. Behrman from Tolstoy's novel

Greta Garbo ☆ Fredric March Freddie Bartholomew Basil Rathbone ☆ Maureen O'Sullivan May Robson

Wife (Greta Garbo) of cold Russian aristocrat (Basil Rathbone) falls for young officer (Fredric March).

Garbo had already played this role in a previous film of the same story, called *Love* (1927), but here is the definitive tragic Garbo performance in a typically lavish MGM costume romance of the 30s. Freddie Bartholomew is hard to take as her would-be adorable son, but Basil Rathbone is on top villainous form as her husband. Although there's far too much dialogue and Clarence Brown's direction is no better than stolid, it is generally considered the best version of Tolstoy's classic novel.

'Miss Garbo, the first lady of the screen, sins, suffers and perishes illustriously in the new, ably produced and comparatively mature version of the Tolstoy classic . . . Samuel Goldwyn's screen edition of *Resurrection* last year discussed Tolstoy's theories of social reform, and now *Anna Karenina* widens the iris of the camera so as to link the plight of the lovers to the decadent and hypocritical society which doomed them. The photoplay is a dignified and effective drama which becomes significant because of that tragic, lonely and glamorous blend which is the Garbo personality.' *(Andre Sennwald, New York Times)*

'Cinch b.o. anywhere. In the foreign markets it should come close to establishing modern-day high.' *(Variety)*

'It reaches no great heights of tragedy or drama but rather moves forward relentlessly and a little coldly.' *(The Times)*

'Visually and emotionally the most rarefied of Garbo's 30s films, with William Daniels's radiant photography preventing decorative blossoms, vines, banquet tables and riding habits from congealing into the usual display of studio extravagance, and the dappled sunlight providing an ingenious background for Garbo's finely tortured passions.' *(Geoff Brown, Time Out)*

ANNE AND MURIEL

CT: 5 AV: 7.30

(aka *Two English Girls; Les Deux Anglaises et Le Continent*)

1971 France 108/132 C DRAMA/ROMANCE

D François Truffaut ☆
W François Truffaut Jean Grault from Henri Pierre Roche's novel

Jean-Pierre Léaud Kika Markham ✓

Stacey Tendeter ✔ Sylvia Marriott Marie Mansart Philippe Léotard Irene Tunch

Prior to World War I, a French writer (Jean-Pierre Léaud) falls for two English sisters (Kika Markham, Stacey Tendeter).

François Truffaut tries another triangular love story by the author of his previous success, *Jules et Jim* (1962), and strays into Eric Rohmer territory with this civilized, ironic but very static tale. The longer (132 minute) version released in 1984 is more satisfying than the 108 minute cut for American consumption. Nestor Almendros's cinematography is breathtaking, and makes interesting use of colour desaturation in an attempt to emulate early two-tone Technicolor.

'It's a tale of art born from emotional sacrifice as – all in love with one another and reluctant to cause hurt – the three withdraw from any final conflict or consummation of their feelings. As such, it's as much about what doesn't happen as about what does.' *(Geoff Andrew, Time Out)*

'Very civilized and rewarding.' *(Martin & Porter)*

'Despite much delicacy and wit, [it] is weighed down by the rather irritatingly oversensitive characters.' *(Bergan & Karney)*

'Lifeless.' *(Shipman)*

ANNÉE DERNIÈRE À MARIENBAD, L':

see LAST YEAR AT MARIENBAD.

ANNIE HALL AAW CT: 9 AV: 8.65

1977 US 93 C COMEDY/ROMANCE

D Woody Allen ☆ AAW
W Woody Allen Marshall Brickman ☆ AAW

Woody Allen ☆ AAN Diane Keaton ☆ AAW Tony Roberts Carol Kane Paul Simon Colleen Dewhurst

Angst-ridden Jewish comic (Woody Allen) wins then loses kooky girl from midwest (Diane Keaton).

Extremely charming period comedy, based on the stars' true-life romance. A memento to the self-indulgent anxieties of the 'me' generation in the 70s, it incurred some critical hostility on release; but it was a turning-point for Woody Allen, who began in this movie to turn away from one-liner gags and create characters who were three-dimensional, vulnerable and even likeable.

ANTI:

'The neurotic's version of *Abie's Irish Rose*.' *(Pauline Kael)*

'Everything we never wanted to know about Woody Allen's sex life and were afraid he'd tell us anyway . . . The jokes are tired and can often be seen dragging their feet towards us a mile off; when they finally arrive, we are more apt to commiserate than laugh . . . And then there is Diane Keaton's scandalous performance. Her work, if that is the word for it, always consists chiefly of a dithering, blithering, neurotic coming apart at the seams – an acting style that is really a nervous breakdown in slow motion – but it has never before been allowed such latitude.' *(John Simon)*

MIXED:

'If you can forgive the fact that it's a ragbag of half-digested intellectual ideas dressed up with trendy intellectual references, you should have a good laugh.' *(Nigel Floyd, Time Out)*

'[Allen's] direction has at last reached the level where it's unobtrusive.' *(Stanley Kauffmann)*

'The kindest thing one can say about the style is that it is eclectic.' *(Douglas Brode, 1985)*

PRO:

'Allen's most satisfying creation and our most gratifying comedic experience in recent years.' *(Judith Crist)*

'Bracingly adventuresome and unexpectedly successful, with laughs as satisfying as those in any of Allen's movies and a whole new staying power.' *(Janet Maslin, Newsweek)*

'A seriocomic meditation on the couple relationship that bears comparison with the best film on that subject, George Cukor's *Adam's Rib*.' *(James Bernardoni, The New Hollywood, 1991)*

'The film's priceless vignettes about the difficulties in chitchatting with strangers, the awkward moments in family visits, and the frequent breakdowns in communication and failures in intimacy, its reminiscences about the palpable horrors of growing up in Brooklyn, and its comic encounters with lobsters in the kitchen or spiders in the bathroom, all seem like snapshots from Allen and Keaton's own romance.' *(Les Keyser, Hollywood in the Seventies)*

ANOTHER WOMAN CT: 5 AV: 5.73

1988 US C DRAMA

D Woody Allen
W Woody Allen

Gena Rowlands ☆ Mia Farrow Ian Holm Blythe Danner Gene Hackman ☆ Martha Plimpton Betty Buckley John Houseman

Philosophy academic (Gena Rowlands) re-examines her life.

Woody Allen's version of Ingmar Bergman's *Wild Strawberries*. A well acted but emotionally self-indulgent film which attracts extremes of critical praise and opprobrium; it is Allen at his most introspective, depressed and Bergmanesque (he even uses Bergman's cinematographer, Sven Nykvist).

PRO:

'Brave, in many ways fascinating, and in all respects of a caliber rarely seen.' *(Variety)*

'Not only Allen's most wholly personal movie since *Stardust Memories* but arguably the most substantial achievement of his career.' *(Tim Pulleine, MFB)*

'A movie for sophisticates.' *(Alexander Walker, Evening Standard)*

'Searing, adult drama with a magnificent cast and many memorable moments.' *(Maltin)*

ANTI:

'... a line of dialogue sounds natural or true . . . as if Mr Allen were straining to achieve the kind of luminous poetic dialogue that goes most against his own iconoclastic, penetrating American sensibility.' *(Caryn James, New York Times)*

'Woody Allen is, for all his New York sophistication, just an old-fashioned guy when it comes to women. He tells us, through Marion's spontaneously ruined life, that a woman's existence must be based in emotion and not in the mind. Professional achievements are meaningless for a woman, he seems to be saying. If she is "afraid of the feelings she'd have for her baby" or rejects "intense [consuming] passion" for a man, then she is nothing.' *(Kathy Maio)*

'I didn't much care for *Wild Strawberries* the first time . . . Woody Allen's picture is meant to be about emotion, but it has no emotion. It's smooth and high-toned; it's polished in its nothingness . . . He doesn't place a high enough value on his own talents; he labors to be an artist like Bergman and turns into a pseud.' *(Pauline Kael)*

'More like a sixth-form essay on Great Art than an example of it.' *(Harlan Kennedy, Film Yearbook)*

'About as funny as a day in bed with the complete works of Schopenhauer.' *(Nigel Andrews, Financial Times)*

'A feel-good movie only in the sense that you feel much better when you stop watching it.' *(Rose)*

ANSIKTE MOT ANSIKTE: *see* FACE TO FACE.

APARAJITO: *see APU* TRILOGY.

APARTMENT, THE AAW CT: 10 AV: 8.93

1960 US 125 BW COMEDY/DRAMA/ROMANCE

D Billy Wilder ☆ AAW
W Billy Wilder I.A.L. Diamond ☆ AAW

Jack Lemmon ☆ AAN Shirley Maclaine ☆ AAN
Fred MacMurray ☆ Ray Walston Edie Adams
Jack Kruschen

Clerk (Jack Lemmon) lends apartment to boss (Fred MacMurray) for adulterous assignations, then falls in love with boss's girlfriend (Shirley Maclaine).

One of the cinema's comic masterpieces: so charming, brilliantly written and touchingly acted that it's hard to believe how many critics found it shockingly sleazy, cynical and amoral on release. Despite some very hostile reviews, it was voted the best picture of 1960 not only at the Oscars, but also by the Directors' Guild of America, the British Film Academy, and the annual poll of reviewers and writers of the US trade publication Film Daily.

ANTI:

'You don't get satire by treating the back alleys of infidelity with giggling facetiousness, periodically drenched by tears of bogus sentiment . . . As for Shirley Maclaine, it is tragic to see her great comic gifts butchered to prove that men are beasts and that she can also cry. A great disappointment.' *(Fred Majdalany, Daily Mail)*

'Without either style or taste, shifting gears between pathos and slapstick without any transition.' *(Dwight MacDonald)*

'Our hero is, in essence, little more than a climber who finds pimping the way to get ahead; the heroine is a tramp whom we are supposed to bleed for simply because her most recent and most permanent client refused to pay.' *(Judith Crist, New York Herald Tribune, 1965)*

'Billy Wilder directed this acrid story as if it were a comedy, which is a cheat, considering that it involves pimping and a suicide attempt and many shades of craven ethics.' *(New Yorker, 1980)*

PRO:

'Mr Lemmon, who has never given a bad performance, here surpasses his former best. He is at once wonderfully funny and immensely sympathetic, brazen and romantic, heroic and shy; were it for his performance alone, the picture would be well worth seeing. Yet his performance is not the only virtue of the film. There is also the screenplay . . . There are cynicism and bitterness in the writing; but there is also an extremely touching affirmation of the power of love and honesty . . . [The film] may be considered too long, sometimes too corny . . . Despite these faults, [it] remains original and amusing . . . a work of genuine talent and wit.' *(Richard Marek, McCalls Magazine)*

'I came out . . . bubbling over with recollection of the funniest moments – and they are legion – in a film I am convinced will be the comedy of the year. It is a masterpiece of fun and irony about the small men who make American big business . . . Mr Wilder has made a moral film that never moralises.' *(Alexander Walker, Evening Standard)*

'It's funny – and sad. It's ironic – and touching . . . The most delicately balanced tragi-comedy I've seen since Chaplin shut up shop . . . It's comedy that will make you cry . . . Underneath the astringent humour, this is essentially a serious film.' *(Margaret Hinxman, Daily Herald)*

APOCALYPSE NOW CT: 8 AV: 8.41

1979 US 153/141/139 C WAR

D Francis Ford Coppola ☆
W John Milius Francis Ford Coppola

Martin Sheen ☆ Marlon Brando ● Robert Duvall ☆ Frederic Forrest Dennis Hopper Harrison Ford

US captain (Martin Sheen) goes on mission to find colonel (Brando) who has deserted in Vietnam.

Francis Ford Coppola's extravagant drama about Vietnam is visually inspired and evidently sincere about the horrors of war, but almost ruined by its pretentious ending, built around a hopelessly self-indulgent performance by Marlon Brando.

'My film is not about Vietnam. It is Vietnam.' *(Francis Ford Coppola)*

PRO:

'Alternately a brilliant and bizarre film . . . It's the first film to directly excoriate US involvement in the Indochina war. Coppola virtually creates World War III onscreen. There are no models or miniatures, no tank work, nor process screens for the airborne sequences.' *(Variety)*

'Brilliant, beautiful, thought provoking and superbly acted, a horror movie and an adventure story, an important Vietnam War document . . . [which] pictures Vietnam as a nightmare that drove Americans crazy . . . [It] is a veritable acid trip, an LSD vision of Vietnam combat . . . [which] falters only when Sheen reaches the stronghold of Colonel Kurtz, in the final minutes of the drama . . . No matter that the film is marred by an inconclusive dramatic and emotional pay-off . . . [it] is exciting, ambitious, a near-great film.' *(Joseph Gelmis, Newsday)*

'An operatic examination of the deep-rooted evil in the human soul rather than a specific focus on the ideological contours of the Vietnam conflict . . . the film's real achievement lies in moments of hallucinatory carnage where the sensual delirium, horror and absurd beauty of wartime are disturbingly conveyed.' *(Allan Hunter & Kenny Mathieson, Movie Classics, 1992)*

MIXED:

'*Apocalypse Now*, despite Coppola's claims for its moral stature, despite its simplistic relation to Conrad's *Heart of Darkness*, is at its best in delivering the texture of the first freaked-out, pill-popping, rock-accompanied war . . . Where Coppola is short is in thought. He stumbles when he thinks, when he thinks he's thinking. In *Apocalypse Now*, the attempts to dramatize private moral agony and general moral abyss are disjointed, assumptive, weak . . . What moral insight is given into the Vietnam War? None.' *(Stanley Kauffmann)*

ANTI:

'Immature and pretentious. Even the notion that Conrad's *Heart of Darkness* could provide the basis for a large-scale attack on the Vietnam war, and modern warfare in general, is puerile and self-serving . . . When Willard, a burnt-out case to begin with (played stolidly by Martin Sheen), reaches Kurtz – a Brando who has become an obscene, secular Buddha with shaven head and ballooning midriff, whose voice emerges like the squeal of a mouse from a ridiculous mountain – two dullards confront each other over a thin gruel of pretentious platitudes or portentous understatement, and the film becomes worse than bad – abject.' *(John Simon)*

'A dumb movie that could only have been made by an intelligent and talented man . . . [who has] spectacularly overextended himself . . . [and] felt he was ready to make Citizen Kurtz . . . [It is] a director's movie that . . . resounding flops.' *(Richard T. Jameson, Seattle Weekly)*

'In the end, Coppola abruptly attempts to turn his film into a novel of ideas, in which one character (Willard) serves as a sounding board for the monologues of another character (Kurtz). The play of ideas, however, is distinctly lethargic, since Willard has become a nonentity and the ideas conveyed through Kurtz's monologues are obscure or pretentious or both.' *(James Bernardoni, The New Hollywood, 1991)*

APU SANSAR: *see* THE *APU* TRILOGY.

THE *APU* TRILOGY

PATHER PANCHALI CT: 9 AV: 9.21

1955 India 115 BW DRAMA/FOREIGN

D Satyajit Ray ☆
W Satyajit Ray from Bibhutbhusan Bandapaddhay's novel ☆

Kanu Bannerjee Karuna Bannerjee Uma Das Gupta Subir Bannerjee Chunibala

A small boy named Apu (Subir Bannerjee) grows up in Bengal.

Slow, episodic but riveting account of growing up in rural poverty. An outstandingly poetic, humane and humorous first feature by a writer-director who, though obviously a product of his own sub-continent, seemed to have more in common with humanistic western film-makers (such as Jean Renoir) than with the Indian movie industry. Though incredibly detailed, it deals with universal emotions and is undoubtedly a masterpiece. The music is by Ravi Shankar.

'It has been left to the Indian cinema to give us a picture of a childhood which preserves under the shadow of experience not only its innocence but its gaiety. Most films about children – I mean, of course, the serious films – deal with desperation: children troubled, neglected, terrified, children driven to flight, to crime, even to suicide. *Pather Panchali* (director, Satyajit Ray) is about children who, whatever misfortunes may envelop the lives around them, can still rely on love.' *(Dilys Powell)*

'Sombre but sincere . . . marks a notable advance in Indian film technique and approach.' *(Kinematograph Weekly)*

'A celebration of the utterly familiar, of the mysterious drone of life as it passes. In this, it is one of the beauties of our time.' *(Arlene Croce, Film Culture 1959)*

'No subsequent film could capture the lyricism of *Pather Panchali* which burst upon the cynical world of the 50s with such a sense of freshness and magic that Apu became part of our consciousness and we entered his world.' *(Brian Baxter, NFT Bulletin, 1974)*

'Beautiful, sometimes funny, and full of love, it brought a new vision of India to the screen.' *(Pauline Kael)*

APARAJITO CT: 6 AV: 8.36

(aka *The Unvanquished*)

1956 India 113 BW DRAMA/FOREIGN

D Satyajit Ray ☆
W Satyajit Ray from Bibhutbhusan Bandapaddhay's novel ☆

Pinaki Sen Gupt ☆ Karuna Bannerjee
Kanu Bannerjee Sumiran Ghosjal ☆

Apu (at first played by Pinaki Sen Gupta, then by Sumiran Ghosjal) grows up in Benares and studies for university.

The second part of Satyajit Ray's masterly trilogy is a slow but memorable study of a child growing away from his mother and rural background. Though the least gripping of the three films, it was voted Best Film at the Venice Film Festival.

'For the discriminating viewer, a must-see.' *(Scheuer)*

'A detailed and moving study of characters who are universally familiar despite an unusual background.' *(Halliwell)*

'The film chronicles the emergence of modern industrial India, showing it to be not a primitive society but a corrupted society. However, Apu himself embodies Ray's belief that individuals need not become corrupt.' *(Pauline Kael)*

WORLD OF APU, THE CT: 10 AV: 9.09

(aka *Apu Sansar*)

1958 India 106 BW DRAMA/FOREIGN

D Satyajit Ray ☆
W Satyajit Ray from Bibhutbhusan Bandapaddhay's novel ☆

Soumitra Chatterji ☆ Sharmila Tagore
Swapan Mukherji ☆

Apu (Soumitra Chatterji) marries, has a son, and struggles to be a writer.

The beautiful, touching final segment of the Apu trilogy is a tender but unsentimental love story with glorious performances. The social background is sketched in lightly but with great skill.

'One of the most vital and abundant movies ever made . . . [Ray] has superb control of his camera. His images are continuously beautiful but never obtrusive . . . there is nothing arty in his art . . . Ray's film has the generosity and the prodigal variety of genius.' *(Edward Harrison, Time, 1960)*

'Rich and contemplative, and a great, convincing affirmation.' *(Pauline Kael)*

'Ray has been criticized for failing to give a clear picture of the changing India. Here we see industrialization, get a quick view of a picket line, hear of strike-breaking, get a glimpse of a decrepit school where no education is possible and the back room of a factory where workers waste their lives 'labeling' for slave wages, and, of course, we see the poverty.' *(Danny Peary)*

'A slow, spiritual, beautifully acted Indian film that brings to a triumphant close one of the most impressive trilogies in the history of the cinema.' *(Roy Pickard 1971)*

ARACHNAPHOBIA CT: 8 AV: 5.58

1990 US 109 C HORROR/COMEDY

D Frank Marshall ✔
W Don Jakoby Wesley Strick ✔ from Don Jakoby's story Al Williams ✔

Jeff Daniels ☆ Harley Jane Kozak
John Goodman ☆ Julian Sands ● Stuart Pankin
Brian McNamara

Spiders threaten small American town.

Jeff Daniels plays a young doctor, scared of creepy-crawlies, who ends up having to protect his all-American family and town from – what else? – a plague of Venezuelan killer spiders. Like Roy Scheider in *Jaws*, he has to contend with local scepticism and complacency. Like Harrison Ford in *Raiders of the Lost Ark*, he is allowed to triumph only when he has come face to face with his phobia.

Formula stuff, perhaps, but both the two-legged and eight-legged supporting casts were terrific, especially

John Goodman as a pest exterminator with a lower IQ than his adversaries. The screenplay, by Don Jakoby (who co-wrote *Alien*) and Wesley Strick (who went on to write Scorsese's *Cape Fear*), wove a web of sophisticated variations around a pretty preposterous premise. Director Frank Marshall had been the second-unit director on *Raiders, Back To The Future* and *Who Framed Roger Rabbit?* His first solo effort was a top-class comic thriller, surprisingly unsuccessful at the box office (maybe people didn't understand the title) and underappreciated by critics who were too quick to dismiss it as a derivative, over-inflated B-movie.

ANTI:

'The arachnids are short on personality, and so is the movie. The script . . . has too many B-picture precursors, and the first-time director, Frank Marshall, is like a Boy Scout remaking *Jaws*.' *(Pauline Kael)*

'Suffers the dilemma of trying to live up to its horror image – without losing its juvenile audience. Something it fails significantly to achieve.' *(Brinley Hamer-Jones, Western Mail Weekender)*

'Standard monster insect fare.' *(Scheuer)*

PRO:

'Expertly blends horror and tongue-in-cheek comedy . . . Marshall has the directorial confidence to allow scripters plenty of screen time to develop characters more fully than usual in a horror film.' *(Variety)*

'Never goes over the edge into sheer disgusting horror. It maintains a certain humorous edge . . . This is the kind of movie where you squirm out of enjoyment, not terror.' *(Roger Ebert)*

'A genuinely scary and suspenseful thriller that has enough laughs to break the tension, if only to let him build it up all over again.' *(Marshall Julius, What's On in London)*

ARGENT DE POCHE, L': *see* SMALL CHANGE

ARISE, MY LOVE CT: 7 AV: 7.38

1940 US 113 BW DRAMA/COMEDY/WAR/ROMANCE

D Mitchell Leisen ☆
W Billy Wilder Charles Brackett ☆ from Benjamin Glazer and John S. Toldy's story AAW

Claudette Colbert ☆ Ray Milland ☆ Walter Abel ☆ Dennis O'Keefe George Zucco Dick Purcell

American reporter (Claudette Colbert) helps American aviator (Ray Milland) out of various scrapes.

Timely anti-isolationist propaganda film, adeptly mixing comedy, romance and thrills. Billy Wilder and Charles Brackett produced a typically intelligent script, although it was the original story which won an Academy Award. A forgotten classic, with fine Oscar-nominated photography by Charles Lang, music by Victor Young and art direction by Hans Dreier and Robert Usher.

MIXED:

'Romantic comedy at its most brilliant, scripted by Brackett and Wilder with a nice line in sexual innuendo and cynical irreverence. Inspiration flags latterly, though, as the groundwork is laid for a message to democracy.' *(Tom Milne, Time Out)*

'A slick combination of action, sentiment and comedy . . . The supporting cast are good when they are being funny, but embarrassing whenever they start to moralise.' *(Louis Macneice, Spectator)*

PRO:

'A film of absorbing romantic interest, proving that love will find a way through the hazards of air raids, torpedo attacks and enemy invasions.' *(Variety)*

'Claudette Colbert has never done better work . . . [She's] at her brilliant best . . . Brilliant domestic comedy.' *(Kine Weekly)*

'Finely artistic direction, beautiful backgrounds of French countryside. Outstanding general entertainment with assured two-star pull.' *(The Cinema)*

'[Milland and Colbert] give outstanding performances . . . Leisen has changed his tempo extremely well. As a rule farce and drama don't mix particularly well, but he has developed his theme with naturalness and conviction and what is more, has made the European background quite convincing . . . a lot must be said both on behalf of the cast and the skilfulness of the production.' *(Lionel Collier, Picturegoer)*

'First rate entertainment and good propaganda.' *(MFB)*

ARISTOCATS, THE CT: 7 AV: 5.80

1970 US 78 C CARTOON/COMEDY/ FAMILY

D Wolfgang Reitherman ✓
W Larry Clemmons and others

Voices: Phil Harris ☆ Eva Gabor ✓ Sterling Holloway ✓ Scatman Crothers ☆ Paul Winchell Hermione Baddeley ✓ Roddy Maude-Roxby ✓

Butler deliberately loses cats who may inherit his employer's fortune.

Warm, engaging and easy on the eye, this is the least scary and most undervalued of all the good Disney cartoons. Perhaps the romantic plot – an upper-class puss is booted out of her comfortable home, whereupon she falls for lovable alley-cat – is too close to *The Lady and the Tramp*, while the kidnapping of her feline family does bear a similarity to *101 Dalmatians*.

The storyline lacks the suspense and richness of the very best Disney: in order to eke it out to 79 minutes, the studio had to insert a lot of fairly irrelevant slapstick between the villainous butler and a couple of dogs. Although children may find the byplay amusing, adults would most likely prefer to be getting on with the main story. And the film was completed after the great storyteller Walt Disney's death, so perhaps there was a temptation for critics in 1970 to say that the studios could never be as good again.

Visually, however, *The Aristocats* bears comparison with Disney's masterpieces. The backgrounds of turn-of-the-century Paris are lovely, and the main characters skilfully animated, in a cross between traditional Disney cartoon and Art Nouveau posters. And there's just a hint of 60s psychedelia in the big production numbers.

Time has also been kind to the jazzy, musical comedy score, which must have sounded old-fashioned in 1970; at least one of the numbers, 'Everybody Wants To Be A Cat' sung by Scatman Crothers, can now be recognized as a classic, even though it was overlooked at that year's Oscars (as was the rest of the score).

But it's the voices which make this movie. Hermione Baddeley shines as a kindly and refined Madame, Roddy Maude-Roxby is all genial greed as Edgar the butler, and Eva Gabor is suitably seductive and exotic as the mother cat. Of the American contingent, Sterling Holloway (most familiar now as the voice of Winnie The Pooh) makes Rocquefort a delightfully cheesy mouse; and, as Thomas O'Malley the alley cat, Phil Harris adds to his triumphant Baloo the Bear from *The Jungle Book*.

ANTI:

'The Disney style of animation . . . is as old-fashioned and overdrawn as ever.' *(Nina Hibbin, Morning Star)*

MIXED:

'It's really quite good if you like this sort of thing . . . But save me from those dear little kittens and from a score which only just passes muster.' *(Derek Malcolm, Guardian)*

'Awfully coy in parts, but I shall take the children.' *(John Coleman, New Statesman)*

PRO:

'The technical details of the $4 million cartoon are marvellous to behold.' *(Variety)*

'Bless the Walt Disney Organization for *The Aristocats*, as funny, warm and sweet an animated cartoon package as ever gave a movie marquee a Christmas glow. . . . The real beauty of the picture, which is as amusing, smoothly machined and beautifully colored as any Disney should be, is in the characterizations, sustained within a sprightly but simple format.' *(New York Times)*

'For charm and style it approaches *101 Dalmatians* and I can think of no higher praise.' *(Felix Barker, Evening News)*

ARMOURED ATTACK: *see* NORTH STAR, THE.

AROUND THE WORLD IN EIGHTY DAYS

AAW CT: 7 AV: 6.85

1956 US 168/175 C COMEDY/ADVENTURE/EPIC

D Michael Anderson
W James Poe John Farrow S.J. Perelman AAW from Jules Verne's novel

David Niven ☆ Cantinflas ☆ Robert Newton ☆ Shirley Maclaine ✔ Charles Boyer Ronald Colman ☆ Noel Coward ☆ Buster Keaton ☆ Red Skelton ☆ Harcourt Williams ☆

Members of London club bet one of their number (David Niven) that he cannot circumnavigate the globe in 80 days.

An all-star, widescreen epic which suffers more than most films from being most familiar to modern audiences through television. Michael Anderson's direction is extremely plodding at times; but, at the very least, it's great fun, a miracle of production and a tribute to the energy of its short-lived producer Mike Todd. Actually, it's rather better than that, mainly thanks to the immense charm and comic timing of Niven – and, for once, the guest stars seize upon their cameo roles with zest.

ANTI:

'Michael Todd's "show", shorn of the ballyhoo and to critics not mollified by parties and sweetmeats, is a film like any other, only twice as long as most . . . The shots of trains and boats seem endless.' *(David Robinson)*

'What was breathtaking at the time seems generally slow and blunted in retrospect.' *(Halliwell)*

'Less a trip than a plod.' *(Shipman)*

PRO:

'Todd-AO system, here, for the first time, is properly used and fills the screen with wondrous effects. Images are extraordinarily sharp and depth of focus is striking in many scenes.' *(Variety)*

'David Niven as the imperturbable traveller could hardly be bettered . . . One feels like thanking Mr. Todd for bringing back into life . . . an extravagance, a bravura which has in it courage, imagination and something very like splendour.' *(Dilys Powell)*

'One of the reasons movies were invented. An exquisite travelogue, a true thriller – and a delight.' *(Judith Crist)*

ARSENIC AND OLD LACE CT: 7 AV: 7.92

1944 US 118 BW COMEDY

D Frank Capra ☆
W Julius J. Epstein Philip G. Epstein (assisted by Howard Lindsay, Russel Crouse) from Joseph Kesselring's play

Cary Grant Priscilla Lane Josephine Hull ☆ Jean Adair ☆ John Alexander ☆ Raymond Massey Jack Carson Peter Lorre Edward Everett Horton

Newlywed (Cary Grant) finds out his aunts are mass-murderers.

Black farce which some critics of the time found tasteless and cold-hearted. Many – though not all – found Cary Grant guilty of overacting (he is). The whole production is a bit stagey – but it's still funny, and much of the comic timing on display is razor-sharp.

ANTI:

'Under Capra's tutelage . . . no holds are barred in corning the comedic capers, and poor Cary Grant has been wheedled into providing a mugfest the likes of which hasn't affronted a camera since Wally Beery ceased delineating Swedish serving maids for dear old Essanay.' *(Herb Sterne)*

'Why Frank Capra chose or was chosen to direct *Arsenic and Old Lace* beats me. Here is a director with a feeling for romantic comedy, with skill in handling the emotions generated by groups of people and a talent for communicating the warmth of human relationship; why spend these gifts on a farce whose blood runs quite cold?' *(Dilys Powell)*

PRO:

'A madcap classic.' *(Scheuer)*

'Handsomely done and brilliantly acted, especially by Grant.' *(Shipman)*

'A model for stage play adaptation . . . The director coaxes some perfect if overstated performances from his star cast, and added his own flair for perpetuating a hubbub.' *(Halliwell)*

ARTHUR CT: 6 AV: 6.31

1981 US 117 C ROMANCE/COMEDY

D Steve Gordon
W Steve Gordon AAN

Dudley Moore ☆ AAN Liza Minnelli John Gielgud ☆ AAW Geraldine Fitzgerald Jill Eikenberry

Drunken playboy (Dudley Moore) propped up by butler (John Gielgud) has to choose between inheriting millions or marrying the shoplifter he loves (Liza Minnelli).

An enjoyable comedy thanks to a witty script, Gielgud's elegant performance, and a display of charm by Dudley Moore which compensates for the less savoury aspects of his character. The theme song by Burt Bacharach and Carole Bayer Sager won an Oscar – as did Gielgud. The film was a big hit. The sequel – *Arthur II: On The Rocks* (1988) – was much less entertaining.

PRO:

'Sparkling entertainment which attempts, with a large measure of success, to resurrect the amusingly artificial conventions of 1930s screwball romantic comedies.' *(Variety)*

'Gielgud may be the most poised and confident funnyman you'll ever see.' *(Pauline Kael)*

ANTI:

'Arthur may be the surprise hit of 1981, but to me he's a pain in the neck.' *(Margaret Hinxman, Daily Mail)*

'How can one applaud a movie which relies so heavily on the novelty value of Gielgud as a bitter butler pronouncing profanities in a posh accent?' *(Geoff Andrew, Time Out)*

ASANI SANKET: *see* DISTANT THUNDER.

ASH WEDNESDAY CT: 1 AV: 1.87

1973 US 99 C DRAMA

D Larry Peerce ●
W Jean Claude Tramont ● Elizabeth Taylor ● Henry Fonda Helmut Berger ● Keith Baxter Maurice Teynac Margaret Blye

Ageing US beauty (Elizabeth Taylor) rejuvenates herself with cosmetic surgery, leaves husband (Henry Fonda).

A tasteless turkey, with a deliriously bad script and Elizabeth Taylor hilariously self-indulgent throughout. The only tears this one jerks are of laughter. Sample dialogue . . . Elizabeth Taylor: 'Look at the stitches, Mark. Look at them! Count them! Every one of them was for you, so you could open your eyes again when you took me to bed. Look at these breasts! Aren't they beautiful? What more do you need?'

'A long-drawn-out ghoulish commercial for cosmetic surgery – made apparently for people who can't think of anything to do with their lives but go backwards.' *(Pauline Kael)*

'For the ultimate low I commend to you *Ash Wednesday*, directed by Larry Peerce, who has my vote for the most offensive young director in Hollywood today . . . The movie's main premise, voiced by Fonda, "We've both changed: we don't satisfy each other's needs any more," is never demonstrated or examined, and all the characters act to suit the whims of the plotting . . . So bad that even Liz Taylor's performance becomes almost inconspicuous in it. Fonda and Keith Baxter do act a bit, but only just, and Helmut Berger doesn't even try, which seems to come naturally to him.' *(John Simon)*

'Her pain is nothing compared to what the audience goes through.' *(Scheuer)*

ASHES AND DIAMONDS CT: 8 AV: 8.62

(aka *Popiol Y Diament*)

1959 Poland 104/109 BW DRAMA/FOREIGN

D Andrzej Wajda ☆
W Andrzej Wajda ☆ from Jerzy Andrzejewski's novel

Zbigniew Cybulski ☆ Ewa Krzyzanowska Adam Pawlikowski Bogumil Kobiela

After World War II, a Polish partisan (Zbigniew Cybulski) is confused by the need to carry on fighting in peacetime.

Third section of Wajda's 'war trilogy', the other parts being *A Generation* (1954) and *Kanal* (1957). Cybulski was hailed as the 'Polish James Dean' for his memorable portrait of a crazy, mixed up Partisan; but *Ashes and Diamonds* is more mature, interesting and incisive than Dean's pictures. This rebel has a cause; the trouble is that the cause keeps changing – and causes have unfortunate effects. Many consider the film a masterpiece, but it has a long dullish stretch in the middle.

'I cannot remember a film that better showed the dreadfulness of an impossible choice . . . The odd thing is this is a sensual and attractive and even at times a funny film . . . complex, tender, agonising; it makes a country's moral dilemma as personal as love and the pain of moral disillusionment . . . A human film, marvellously suprapolitical.' *(Isabel Quigly, Spectator)*

'Possibly the best film made since the war . . . A masterpiece.' *(New Statesman)*

'One of the most moving and impressive anti-political films ever made . . . Among the few real classics of the Western cinema.' *(Times Educational Supplement)*

'Thrilling to find a film so rich in texture, in meaning and poetry, so completely expressive of the mood of a generation . . . among the minor classics of the screen.' *(Financial Times)*

ASPHALT JUNGLE, THE CT: 8 AV: 8.85

1950 US 112 BW THRILLER

D John Huston ☆ AAN
W Ben Maddow John Huston ☆ AAN from W.R. Burnett's novel

Sterling Hayden ☆ Louis Calhern Sam Jaffe ☆ AAN James Whitmore Jean Hagen Marilyn Monroe ✔

Crooks (Sterling Hayden, Louis Calhern) execute jewellery heist.

John Huston's exciting thriller was among the first to see a robbery from the thieves' point of view. Sterling Hayden and Sam Jaffe stand out; a young Marilyn Monroe (in a small role) exudes star quality as a moll. Harold Rosson's atmospheric cinematography was nominated for an Oscar.

ANTI:

'That Asphalt Pavement thing is full of nasty, ugly people doing nasty things. I wouldn't walk across the room to see a thing like that.' *(Louis B. Mayer, head of the studio that made the film)*

'Stifles any spark of three-dimensional life . . . Huston and Maddow have assembled a gallery of types . . . It is disappointing that the resultant drama lacks depth of perception or scope of understanding.' *(Fortnight)*

MIXED:

'Everyone in the picture . . . gives an unimpeachable performance. If only it all weren't so corrupt.' *(Bosley Crowther)*

'Huston never lets himself go; there is no affection in his handling of the figures on the screen. Until he can achieve a warmer relation with the creatures of his cinema we cannot expect from him more than he has given us in *The Asphalt Jungle*: a brilliant, glacial thriller.' *(Dilys Powell)*

'The purpose of all this is obscure. Obviously Huston is giving us a view of the criminal as a human being lost in the concrete jungle, but he vitiates his detachment by a sentimentality that becomes positively mawkish in the long-drawn-out finale . . . Huston has preached a sermon without a text. But on the way he has given us some crisp characterisation delineated in exciting movie technique (seriously disrupted, incidentally, by pointless censor's cuts) and perhaps the best robbery ever staged in Hollywood. Only by Huston standards does this generally impressive film fall short.' *(Richard Winnington)*

PRO:

'A breathtaking and suspenseful screen story which literally has you rooting for the heavies. For sustained drama, few similar sequences pack the same taut excitement as that Huston achieves in the scene of the robbery.' *(Hollywood Reporter)*

'Has the authority of a blow in your solar plexus. It leaves you physically tired with sheer tension, participation and belief. It is the crime picture of the decade, and it may be the best one ever made . . . This picture drives home the corollary thought that criminals are also human beings.' *(Archer Winsten, New York Post)*

'John's pictures are usually grim . . . but always dramatic and exciting . . . This picture is packed with stand-out performances . . . There's a beautiful blonde, too, name of Marilyn Monroe, who plays Calhern's girl friend, and makes the most of her footage.' *(Liza Wilson, Photoplay)*

'A violent exhibition, dedicated to sluggings and large-scale jewel robberies, but Huston has made it a taut and engrossing melodrama.' *(Howard Barnes, New York Herald Tribune)*

ASSASSINATION OF TROTSKY, THE

CT: 5 AV: 3.44

1972 France/Italy 105 C DRAMA/BIOPIC/SO BAD

D Joseph Losey ●
W Nicholas Mosley ● Masolino d'Amico ●

Richard Burton ● Alain Delon ● Romy Schneider Valentina Cortese Luigi Vanucchi Giorgio Albertozzi

Russian revolutionary (Richard Burton) is murdered in exile.

A dire script plus director Joseph Losey at his most clumpingly banal, plus an out-of-control Richard Burton, add up to one of the worst biopics ever. It might have been merely boring, except that the assassination itself pushes the whole thing over into farce.

'Atrocious . . . tritely psychologized pretty pasteboard nonsense . . . About as lively as a Hollywood biography of the thirties.' *(Stanley Kauffmann)*

'Trotsky was an extremely public figure. Given the vast amount we know about him, it is inexcusable to present him as a foxy grandpa mouthing platitudes . . . We get lots of crazy acting and lots of the aimless camera movement which director Joseph Losey passes off as style.' *(Richard Schickel, Life)*

'Character assassination . . . has the faintly instructional air of a classroom filmstrip. By contrast, the movie assassination is staged like a scene out of some Hammer horror epic.' *(Jay Cocks, Time)*

'In time you give it up as a bad joke, and the murky solemnity of it all becomes rather funny . . . Another miserable Richard Burton performance . . . What a hopeless movie!' *(Gary Arnold, Washington Post)*

'A sorry mix of bad history and worse invention . . . Trotsky most of the way sounds like a pompous pedant . . . His assassin [Delon] in a trench coat and smoked glasses belongs to comic opera.' *(Charles Champlin, Los Angeles Times)*

'Not for anyone who knows, or cares, anything about Trotsky.' *(Pauline Kael, 1977)*

ASSAULT, THE AAW

CT: 6 AV: 7.18

(aka *Der Aanslag*)

1986 Netherlands 149 C DRAMA/FOREIGN

D Fons Rademakers ☆
W Gerard Soeteman from Harry Mulisch's novel

Derek de Lint Mac van Uchelen Monique van der Ven Huub van der Lubbe John Kraaykamp

An adult tries to repress his memories of World War II.

Though overlong, monotonous, and clumsily plotted, this critically acclaimed winner of the Academy Award for Best Foreign Film is a memorable and moving depiction of the horrors of war, and the legacy of war.

ANTI:

'Ponderous direction . . . simplistic use of actuality footage . . . indifferent music smeared across scenes like jam.' *(Geoff Brown, The Times)*

'A faithful adaptation . . . but jerks through the decades likes a car in the wrong gear.' *(Victoria Mather, Daily Telegraph)*

MIXED:

'At its best [it] achieves a breathless sense of personal fate hounded by the disasters of modern history . . . Rademakers is a powerful but clunky director. He indulges some terribly emphatic over-acting and he has a weakness for violent shocks . . . [but] this epic-length movie actually delivers on its Rashomon premise.' *(David Denby, New York Magazine)*

'Well sustained for much of the way, the film . . . begins to seem overdeliberate . . . All the same one keeps watching.' *(Tim Pulleine, Guardian)*

'Its episodic structure, rather heavy symbolism, and many coincidences, do not hinder the illumination of moral questions or its ability to move.' *(Bergan & Karney)*

PRO:

'Part gripping thriller, part indictment of those who would forget the past, and wholly watchable.' *(Halliwell)*

'Long, but suspenseful, with many thoughtful moments . . . not easy to forget.' *(Maltin)*

AT FIRST SIGHT: *see* COUP DE FOUDRE.

AT LONG LAST LOVE

CT: 5 AV: 2.67

1975 US 118 (original)/115 (re-edited) C MUSICAL/SO BAD

D Peter Bogdanovich ●
W Peter Bogdanovich ● (songs by Cole Porter)

Burt Reynolds ● Cybill Shepherd ● Eileen Brennan Madeleine Kahn Duilio del Prete ● John Hillerman Mildred Natwick

Bored millionaire (Burt Reynolds) falls in love with Broadway hoofer (Madeleine Kahn) and spoiled heiress (Cybill Shepherd).

This attempt at 30s sophistication must rank among the worst musicals of all time, and is certainly the worst-reviewed; but the sheer incompetence of the leading performances means that at least it is never boring.

'The one thing it proves is that I didn't know how to make a musical.' *(Peter Bogdanovich)*

PRO:

'*At Long Last Love* was not as bad as it was reviewed. I mean nothing could be that bad. What was reviewed was Cybill Shepherd and Peter Bogdanovich's relationship. You see, Peter has done something that all critics will never forgive him for doing. That is, stop being a critic, go make a film and have that, *The Last Picture Show*, become enormously successful. Well, what he did then was to go on talk shows and be rather arrogant and talk about how bad critics are. That was the final straw.' *(Burt Reynolds)*

ANTI:

'May be the worst movie musical of this – or any – decade . . . Sitting through this movie is like having someone at a fancy Parisian restaurant who neither speaks nor reads French read out stentoriously the entire long menu in his best Arkansas accent, and occasionally interrupt himself to chortle at his cleverness.' *(John Simon)*

'If this Peter Bogdanovich fiasco were any more of a dog, it would shed.' *(John Barbour, Los Angeles)*

'This is failure so dismal that it goes beyond failure. The musical is not trash, exactly. Its rottenness lies in the pretension and inflated ego behind its conception, in its pandering to film-buff nostalgia, and in some of the sorriest casting ever to sink a production.' *(Hollis Alpert, Saturday Review)*

'It just lies there and it dies there.' *(Variety)*

'The most perverse movie musical ever made . . . a colossal, overextravagant in-joke . . . Every time his stars open their mouths or shake their legs, they trample on Cole Porter's grave . . . When the leads break into song and dance at a night-club or a cotillion, the extras just stand there like goons, staring off into space; it's like watching a musical unfold within *The Night of the Living Dead*.' *(Frank Rich, New Times)*

'As for Burt Reynolds as a jaded millionaire playboy . . . there is in *Funny Lady* a buffalo named Charles, whom Billy Rose insists on displaying in a musical, where, on opening night, he creates havoc by improvising a one-buffalo stampede. Well, put a dinner jacket on Charles, and you've got Reynolds in *At Long Last Love*, except that he never musters enough animation for a stampede.' *(John Simon)*

'[Burt Reynolds] sings like Dean Martin with adenoids and dances like a drunk killing cockroaches.' *(John Barbour, Los Angeles)*

'Cybill Shepherd is a leading lady who can neither sing nor dance and who apparently thinks badinage is something you put on a small cut. *(Vincent Canby, New York Times)*

'Cybill Shepherd, Mr B's inamorata, plays a poor little snotty rich girl with a notion of sophistication that is underpassed only by her acting ability. (I will not even sully my pen by making it describe her singing and dancing.) If it weren't for an asinine superciliousness radiating from her, Miss Shepherd would actually be pitiable, rather like a kid from an orphanage trying to play Noel Coward. In fact, she comes across like one of those inanimate objects, say, a cupboard or a grandfather clock, which is made in certain humorous shorts to act, through trick photography, like people. Well, Bogdanovich is truly in love with Miss Shepherd, so one cannot call his slapping her into the lead of almost every one of his films the casting-couch approach; yet even those crude old-time producers who did have the crassness to use that method at least had the good sense to cast the girl, not the couch.' *(John Simon)*

'As for Shepherd's dancing, the best to be said is that it may not be recognizable as such: when this horsey ex-model starts prancing around, she tends to look as if she's fighting off a chronic case of trots.' *(Frank Rich, New Times)*

'Duilio Del Prete, an Italian discovery, sings as if he came to paint the mansion and stayed on to regale the company with wobbly impersonations of Louis Jordan and Maurice Chevalier.' *(Bruce Williamson, Playboy)*

'As a merry Italian Lothario, we get Duilio Del Prete, an Italian nonactor . . . Mr Del Prete might conceivably play a street arab, but in a sophicated role, with his thick accent and thin talent, he has as much charm as a broomstick with a smile painted on it.' *(John Simon)*

ATALANTE, L': *see* L'ATALANTE.

ATLANTIC CITY USA AAN CT: 7 AV: 8.08

(aka *Atlantic City*)

1981 Canada/France 105 C DRAMA/THRILLER

D Louis Malle ☆ AAN
W John Guare AAN

Burt Lancaster ☆ AAN Susan Sarandon ☆ AAN
Kate Reid Michel Piccoli Hollis McLaren
Robert Joy Al Waxman

Crooks congregate in Atlantic City, and one of them (Burt Lancaster) falls for a waitress (Susan Sarandon).

Superficially a gangster movie, but the thriller plot is very subsidiary. It's really more of a mood piece about American low-life, masterfully directed by Louis Malle, with his usual eye for the telling detail. Burt Lancaster and Susan Sarandon excel, especially together, so that the film also works as a character study.

'A genuinely watchable and intelligent film . . . Hardly the best Louis Malle ever, perhaps. But one of those movies made by a non-American in American [saying] a lot more about that country than the recent spate of myopic home-grown products.' *(Derek Malcolm, Guardian)*

'[Malle] delivers not only a riveting thriller . . . but also probes the rotten core of his chosen American scene with ironic Gallic perception.' *(Richard Barkley, Sunday Express)*

'A very funny, precise, ironic, deeply sad movie that escapes being aridly cynical or sentimentally patronising because of the way with which Malle and Guare observe the central characters.' *(Philip French, Observer)*

'Film is blessed with a spare, intriguing script by Yank John Guare, which always skirts impending clichés and predictability by finding unusual facets in his characters and their actions.' *(Variety)*

ATTACK OF THE 50 FT WOMAN, THE CT: 5 AV: 2.38

1958 US 66 BW SF/SO BAD

D Nathan Hertz ●
W Mark Hanna ●

Allison Hayes William Hudson Yvette Vickers Roy Gordon Ken Terrell

Hugely enlarged wife (Allison Hayes) wreaks vengeance on husband (William Hudson) and mistress (Yvette Vickers).

One of the great unintentional comedies – although the direction is pedestrian rather than awful, and the three leading performances aren't too bad for sci-fi films of the period. The special effects, however, are among the worst ever, and it doesn't help that the anti-heroine's height varies noticeably from shot to shot, rarely reaching the requisite fifty feet. The screenplay is a classic document of 50s male paranoia. The dialogue is, at best, corny and contains some magnificent scientific mumbo-jumbo ('There's not even a streptococcal infection to incite the inflammation of the lymph channels!'). At the other extreme, one medical specialist solemnly blames the leading lady's giantism on 'the supersonic age we live in'. Remade, too knowingly, in 1993.

ANTI:

'Feeble . . . the trick photography is weaker than the novelettish plot, while the standard of acting is weaker than either.' *(MFB)*

'Rather slow in pace, this science fiction thriller is for the most part ineffective. Acting, direction and effects offer little, and many things are left unexplained.' *(Motion Picture Exhibitor)*

PRO:

'A delightful romp through the nether reaches of the absurd.' *(Leonard Pinth Mandell, Fantastic Films)*

'This gloriously batty nonsense gets the production it deserves and a couple of deft performances – from Allison Hayes, William Hudson – it doesn't deserve.' *(Picturegoer)*

'Quite dotty in conception and execution, its straight-faced air of seriousness in all departments makes it a hugely entertaining minor genre entry.' *(Alan Frank)*

'Delirious pre-feminist horror movie . . . The special effects are dire but the film's psycho-pathology is fascinating, and the lines have to be heard to be believed.' *(David Pirie, Time Out)*

AU HAZARD BALTHAZAR CT: 7 AV: 7.40

(aka *Balthazar; Au Hasard Balthazar*)

1966 France/Sweden 95 BW DRAMA/FOREIGN

D Robert Bresson ☆
W Robert Bresson

Anne Wiazemsky François Lafarge Walter Green

The life and death of a donkey.

Though the story has obvious affinities with *Black Beauty*, this beautifully simple, poetic, brilliantly directed piece is more than a film for children or animal-lovers. Though obviously intended as a Christian parable, it can hardly fail to move the hardest atheistical heart. The hero's death is one of the most memorable in the whole of cinema. It won the special jury prize at the 1966 Venice Film Festival.

ANTI:

'A curious and disjointed piece . . . I am sure the film is meant to be highly significant but frankly I could not make head or tail of it.' *(Ann Pacey, Sun)*

'A bitter disappointment . . . The mule seems entirely incidental to a story so dark, glum, and confused that it was all I could do to follow it, never mind search for significance.' *(Alexander Walker, Evening Standard)*

'Considered a masterpiece by some; others may find it painstakingly tedious and offensively holy.' *(Pauline Kael)*

MIXED:

'Undoubtedly a superbly made film, possibly even a small misanthropic masterpiece and so I'm sorry to report that, while I admired it enormously, I also found it repugnant. Let me get this straight immediately, however . . . This is the real thing, an honestly made work of art, informed by a sense of style and by an intelligence all too rare in filmmaking . . . I respect M. Bresson's artistry but am appalled by his view of life.' *(Mordechai Richler, Spectator)*

PRO:

'This fine film views the wretched lives of the inhabitants of a French village with a sort of lyrical pessimism.' *(Patrick Gibbs, Daily Telegraph)*

'The donkey hero . . . is eminently viewable and

lovable . . . and reflects something of Christ's responsibility for the sins of man.' *(Cecil Wilson, Daily Mail)*

'It is not a film for the tired businessman or the tired anything . . . Does that mean there's no story? No, indeed, it does not . . . this one is loaded with plot . . . No, you won't be bored: at least you ought not.' *(Richard Roud, Guardian)*

'One of writer-director Robert Bresson's most enchanting and accessible works . . . a wonderful parable about the beauty of love and devotion and the willingness to please. It's a simple film that stirs the soul.' *(Scheuer)*

'The world in an hour and a half.' *(Jean-Luc Godard.)*

AU REVOIR LES ENFANTS AAN

CT: 7 AV: 8.09

1988 France 103 C DRAMA/RITES-OF-PASSAGE/WAR/FOREIGN

D Louis Malle ☆
W Louis Malle ☆ AAN

Gaspard Manesse Raphael Fejto Francine Racette Stanislas Carré de Malberg Philippe Morier-Genoud François Berleand

A small boy (Gaspard Manesse) befriends another (Raphael Fejto) but betrays him.

Louis Malle's richly observed, semi-autobiographical film about growing up in Nazi-occupied France. Some may find the plot thin and lacking in surprise, but it must still rank as one of the great rites-of-passage movies for its realistic, unsentimental view of childhood. It won the Golden Lion at the Venice Film Festival.

'I reinvented the past in the pursuit of a haunting and timeless truth.' *(Louis Malle)*

MIXED:

'Any film that leaves an audience this stunned is impossible to dismiss . . . And yet something is missing: the victimization of goodness, however powerful, is not the stuff of great tragedy, and the rest of [the film] is bottled up, anxious, pallid.' *(David Edelstein, Village Voice)*

'Sincere but curiously unemotional.' *(Virgin)*

PRO:

'Magnificently shot . . . and with astonishing performances from all the children [it] should be destined for major international success.' *(David Robinson, The Times)*

'Vivid and often witheringly funny, making all the more poignant . . . the gathering miasma of fear.' *(Nigel Andrews, Financial Times)*

'Deliberately understated . . . No swelling film score to tweak the heartstrings with artificial emotion. None is needed.' *(Victoria Mather, Daily Telegraph)*

'Full of surreal shafts of memory – stilt battles in the playground, prayer vigils in the dormitory, wild boars roaming the woods – Malle paints a yesterday full of pained rapport with today: an artist's sensibility written in the mirror of his boyhood.' *(Harlan Kennedy, Film Yearbook)*

'Malle never sentimentalises his material (neither boy is particularly lovable, nor is their friendship free of petty rivalries and cruelty). Instead, he creates an authentic mood of unspoken suspicions and everyday secrecy, drawing upon performances, decor, even nature itself to paint a wintry portrait of childhood on the brink of horrific discovery.' *(Geoff Andrew, Time Out)*

AUTUMN SONATA

CT: 5 AV: 7.00

1978 Sweden/West Germany/GB 97 C DRAMA/FOREIGN

D Ingmar Bergman ☆
W Ingmar Bergman ✗

Ingrid Bergman ☆ Liv Ullman ☆ Halvar Bjork

An unforgiving daughter (Liv Ullman) expresses resentment of her self-obsessed mother (Ingrid Bergman).

Harrowing, lacerating drama beautifully acted by the two principals and wonderfully photographed by Sven Nykvist. The script could have done with a bit more light and shade, though, and it would have been more cinematic if the leading characters could have revealed themselves more through action than words.

'Professional gloom.' *(Time)*

'Ingrid Bergman . . . is exalted in the hands of a master. So is the whole film. So, differently and gratefully, are we.' *(Stanley Kauffmann)*

'Ingmar Bergman understands the human heart: he doesn't like it. He says that *Autumn Sonata* is about "love . . . deformed love and love that is our sole chance of survival". I think it is about hate. And I find detestable its judgment of the mother for her decision to pursue a career. Nevertheless I find myself profoundly admiring the film: the best that Bergman has made or is likely to make. After all he cannot with greater skill, with more appalling assurance, go on saying that whatever is, is wrong.' *(Dilys Powell)*

'A chamber-work of almost Strindbergian intensity.' *(Bergan & Karney)*

AVALON

CT: 5 AV: 6.42

1990 US 128 C DRAMA

D Barry Levinson ☆
W Barry Levinson ✗ AAN

Armin Mueller-Stahl ☆ Elijah Wood Joan Plowright Elizabeth Perkins Aidan Quinn Israel Bubine ✗

A family saga covering four generations, a lament for the extended Jewish family, killed off – so Levinson argues – by prosperity, the move to suburbia, and television.

The third of this writer-director's pictures to be filmed in his home town of Baltimore (the others were *Diner* and *Tin Men*) is heavily autobiographical. It is glorious to look at, thanks to Allen Daviau's Oscar-nominated cinematography, and features a marvellous cast led by Armin Mueller-Stahl; but it's proof that if you don't have a good plot, you don't have anything. After more than two hours, most audiences will have formed their own opinion on why these extended families really break up: everyone just gets bored with all that incessant, pointless bickering. It divided the critics, some of whom loved it; others, like me, thought it rambling and sentimental.

PRO:

'Here's a gorgeous film with a spellbinding start . . . Levinson's . . . best.' *(Shaun Usher, Daily Mail)*

'A lengthy and leisurely epic . . . [which] epitomises the age-old struggle between defending one's national identity and the cultural assimilation that modern capitalism demands . . . Levinson manages to combine a cinematic sense of magic with a well-observed sense of reality.' *(Morning Star)*

'Masterpiece . . . heart-tugging . . . Armin Mueller-Stahl gives an unforgettable performance as the ultimate grandfather, whose honest values and love of family are slowly pushed out of fashion by something called progress.' *(Martin & Porter)*

ANTI:

'The affection and authenticity of this memoir are rich and appealing, but when someone slowly turns the pages of the family album, your interest tends to wane unless it happens to be your family.' *(Iain Johnstone, Sunday Times)*

'A lifeless experience devoid of a central conflict or purpose.' *(Variety)*

'An elegy to a mythical past. That's probably why people emerge from the theatre sniffling . . . There's a wide streak of fuddy-duddyism in Levinson's notion that the family used to be the bulwark of the nation's value system. It may seem unfair to say this, but at times the movie seems like a product of the cultural wing of the Republican Party – a lament for those bygone days when mothers stayed at home and watched over their children, and children obeyed their parents, and so on.' *(Pauline Kael)*

AVANTI! CT: 7 AV: 6.30

1972 US 144 C COMEDY

D Billy Wilder ☆
W Billy Wilder I.A.L. Diamond ☆ from Samuel Taylor's play

Jack Lemmon ✔ Juliet Mills ✔ Clive Revill Edward Andrews Gianfranco Barra Franco Angrisano

A stuffy American millionaire (Jack Lemmon) finds himself falling in love with his late father's hedonism, Italy and Juliet Mills.

Critics of the time underrated this movie because it had little importance and fell into no convenient genre ('black comedy' is probably the nearest classification). It is overlong and lacks pace, but in retrospect it looks like the last of writer/director Billy Wilder's really good films: witty, handsomely made and wonderfully acted.

ANTI:

'Flatter than a pizza . . . [with] all the air of a funeral.' *(Donald Mayerson, Cue)*

'Nothing to be cherished . . . Lovely Juliet Mills is forced to look like a stuffed pigeon.' *(Kathleen Carroll, New York Daily News)*

'Wilder, like Hitchcock, has doggedly refused to come to terms with contemporary issues.' *(Tony Rayns, S & S)*

'A romantic comedy that hardly fits the contemporary mood.' *(Derek Malcolm, Guardian)*

PRO:

'Wilder has recently bemoaned the fact that mass audiences do not like style any more, or wit or elegance. And that may account for the relative lack of success for . . . this . . . marvellous comedy . . . Because jokes and situations are actually allowed to develop and mature, people thought it slow.' *(NFT Bulletin, 1974)*

'A masterpiece . . . Wilder had fashioned a meticulous narrative of revelation and reversal, an epic survey of contrasting American and European values, and a moving elegy to the spirit and legacy of Lubitschian wit. Jack Lemmon gives the performance of his career – which is saying something.' *(NFT Bulletin, 1984)*

AWAKENINGS AAN CT: 8 AV: 7.33

1990 US 121 C DRAMA

D Penny Marshall ✔
W Steven Zaillian ✔ AAN from Oliver Sacks's book

Robert De Niro AAN Robin Williams ✔ Julie Kavner ✔ Ruth Nelson ✔ John Heard Penelope Ann Miller ✔ Alice Drummond Max Von Sydow

A neurologist (Robin Williams), himself emotionally crippled by shyness, becomes fascinated by some patients who appear catatonic but aren't. The fact that one of these 'living statues' is Robert De Niro is an early indication that Williams's attempts to revive at least one of them will meet with a measure of success.

This underrated – even patronized – film, set in

1969, was based on Oliver Sacks's 1973 book of case histories, which also formed the basis of a TV documentary and Harold Pinter's one-act play, *A Kind of Alaska*. Over the years, treatments of the idea had been turned down by most of the Hollywood film companies. Steven Zaillian's script – though much criticized by reviewers – was a verbally economical, splendidly visual example of Hollywood screenwriting at its best.

Robin Williams was impressive as a kind of white knight of the living dead, although his own escape from excessive rigidity was inevitably on a lower level of emotional intensity than De Niro's. De Niro's Oscar-nominated performance, a technical *tour de force*, was derided by some as a collection of tics and silly walks, and a cynical pursuit of his third Oscar (the previous two 'best actors', Dustin Hoffman and Daniel Day-Lewis, had both played people with handicaps). However, De Niro's was by no means a heartless or sentimentalized portrayal, and was also – according to Sacks himself – highly realistic.

My main quibble was that the sub-plot where he fell in love with a hospital visitor (Penelope Ann Miller) was handled with such conventional taste that it failed to carry conviction.

But it was refreshing to see a Hollywood movie which was thoughtful and unexploitative, which looked stylish, and was rich in visual imagery – the changing seasons and means of confinement are the dominant symbols – without sacrificing more populist elements such as emotional directness, humour and narrative drive. It left clinical questions unanswered, but then it never set out to be medical reportage. This was Hollywood drama, doing what it often does best: illuminating the extremes of human existence. The tragic and horrific aspects of the story were all there, though offset by delightful touches of irony and generosity of spirit. And the film was unusual for its positive portrayal of the 1960s, as a decade when a whole generation came to life and started expressing itself, before falling back into a state of apathy and inertia. Even if you don't share that view of the era, this is a magnificent, life-affirming film.

ANTI:

'The movie douses everything fiery. Everything is shaped for you to root for the resurrection, and then nothing much happens . . . The humanism is so pallid that the awakened patients don't seem very different from the way they were in their comatose states . . . Of course, we're affected by people coming to active life after decades of stillness – how could we not be? But this forced banalizing of our emotions is show-business shtick. The patients don't exist except as fodder for pathos.' *(Pauline Kael)*

'We are deep in *Rain Man* territory, a terrain notable for its squashiness . . . De Niro shakes his chassis to bits. Dramatically it's a twin tub with a big slot on top to pour in the caring.' *(Brian Case, Time Out)*

'Williams gives one of those 'please like me, I'm working very hard' genial, mannered performances that makes you want to cry with impatience. But mannered could only begin to describe the infusion of tics and tricks by De Niro's enactment of 'star' patient. It's like an acting thesis at Lee Strasberg Institute.' *(Virgin)*

PRO:

'De Niro's tendency to wander into physical artfulness is here held in check by a formidable discipline and his passage from catatonia . . . into palsied paranoia is frighteningly authentic. Robin Williams is also very fine . . . While lacking the accelerated impassioned narrative of *One Flew Over the Cuckoo's Nest*, Penny Marshall's impressive film offers its own kind of enlightenment and produces the theme of human communication back into the mean streets of mainstream cinema.' *(Evening Standard Magazine)*

'You can smell an Oscar nomination for Robert De Niro's portrayal of a statue . . . Bizarre, you may well think, but not as bizarre as the true story . . . Robin Williams is perfect . . . This sometimes funny, thought-provoking film . . . is a bit of a tearjerker.' *(Deborah Ward, The Voice)*

AWFUL TRUTH, THE AAN CT: 8 AV: 7.82

1937 US 90 BW COMEDY/ROMANCE

D Leo McCarey ☆ AAW
W Vina Delmar from Arthur Richman's play ☆ AAN

Cary Grant ☆ Irene Dunne ☆ AAN
Ralph Bellamy ☆ AAN Alexander D'Arcy
Cecil Cunningham Molly Lamont Esther Dale
Joyce Compton ✔

A husband (Cary Grant) and wife (Irene Dunne) who can't live with, or without each other, both think they want to divorce and remarry, but true love will always find a way . . .

One of the few 30s screwball comedies which remains charming and genuinely funny. The stage origins are obvious, and the film takes a while to get moving but there's an improvisational quality throughout (according to Ralph Bellamy, much of the dialogue was improvised). The scene where Dunne pretends to be Grant's ghastly sister to scare off his snobbish prospective in-laws is a classic, and the final scene still has a sexual charge.

'Fast, smart comedy that will please everywhere and do strong general biz.' *(Variety)*

'The funniest picture of the season.' *(Otis Ferguson)*

'A frothy bit of stuff that leaves no taste in the mouth and is easy on the stomach.' *(Marion Fraser, World Film News)*

B

BABETTE'S FEAST AAW CT: 10 AV: 8.50

(aka *Babette's Gaestebud*)

1987 Denmark 103 C DRAMA/COMEDY/FOREIGN

D Gabriel Axel ☆
W Gabriel Axel ☆ based on Karen Blixen's story

Stéphane Audran ☆ Jean-Philippe Lafont ✔ Gudmar Wivesson ✔ Jarl Kulle ✔ Bibi Andersson ✔ Bodil Kjer ✔ Birgitte Federspiel ✔

A French cook (Stéphane Audran), living in a small village on the Jutland peninsula, cooks a sumptuous meal for her Norwegian employers and their friends.

After a slow start, this develops into a gentle, delightful, wittily observed masterpiece which celebrates the joys of eating, drinking and cooking. All the performances are faultless – it's one of the greatest examples ever of ensemble acting – but Stéphane Audran is sublime.

'In all of movies there is no happier ending than this one: an artist achieving transcendence, her audience learning for the first (and possibly last) time the transforming power of art. And Axel is an altogether worthy saucier's apprentice. His orchestration of this perfect little parable matches her culinary skills in subtlety, verve, and perfect taste. From soup to cognac *Babette's Feast* is delicious, a meal memory will forever savor.' *(Richard Schickel)*

'A masterful, magical film that has us enraptured as we watch the suspicious villagers succumb to the delights of the 'pagan' feast. Trust me. It's brilliant.' *(Rose)*

'Axel shifts from past to present and between voice-over narrative and dialogue with considerable skill, casting a spell over the spectator with an entrancing bitter-sweet mix of comedy and deep poignancy.' *(Bergan & Karney)*

BABY DOLL CT: 6 AV: 7.33

1956 US 114 BW DRAMA/COMEDY

D Elia Kazan ☆
W Tennessee Williams ☆ AAN from his play *27 Wagonloads of Cotton*

Carroll Baker ☆ AAN Karl Malden ☆ Eli Wallach ☆ Mildred Dunnock ☆ Lonny Chapman Rip Torn ✔

A steamy situation develops between a child-bride (Carroll Baker), her thick husband (Karl Malden) and a male admirer (Eli Wallach).

Gripping southern drama with more than a hint of black comedy. Cleverly written, directed and acted for maximum sexual tension, it got itself condemned by America's Legion of Decency and therefore became a big hit. It's proof that one generation's near-pornography is the next's innocent amusement. Boris Kaufman's photography won an Oscar nomination, and Wallach and Torn made their big-screen debuts.

'Just possibly the dirtiest American-made picture that has ever been legally exhibited, with Priapean detail that might well have embarrassed Boccaccio.' *(Time)*

'Views southern pretensions with sardonic humor and builds an essentially minor story into a magnificently humorous study of the grotesque and decadent.' *(Hollis Alpert)*

'A film in which everything works: narration, casting, tempo, rhythm, dramatic tension.' *(Basil Wright, 1972)*

'*Baby Doll*, his [Kazan's] controversial spoof of sensuality, was a *tour de force*, a vehicle for its director rather than its performers and which, considered in that way, was eminently satisfying.' *(Richard Schickel, Movies, 1964)*

BABY OF MÂCON, THE CT: 2 AV: 3.33

1993 GB 122 C DRAMA

D Peter Greenaway ✗
W Peter Greenaway ●

Julia Ormond Ralph Fiennes Philip Stone Jonathan Lacey Don Henderson Celia Gregory

A beautiful male baby becomes revered in medieval times as a miracle-worker, and is exploited for gain by the Catholic Church and by a girl (Julia Ormond) wanting to make a fast franc out of claiming to be his virgin mother.

Peter Greenaway's defenders like to point out that he has a strong visual imagination. Certainly, his films look like Great Art. You could go through this film, and I imagine his admirers will do so, shrieking with approval: 'My dear – that shot is too, too Velasquez! Rembrandt would have LOVED those shadows!' The question arises as to where Eclectic Post-Modernism ends, and a lack of visual originality begins: his films are more an imitation of art than art themselves.

For here is one of the worst screenwriters in the world, with a cloth ear for dialogue, utter narrative incompetence, and no interest in character except as melodramatic mouthpieces. And, like the dreariest adolescent, he seems concerned to elicit no reaction from his audience except shock, disgust and admiration for his cleverness.

The most distasteful aspect of his gang-rape scene, for instance, is not that it is over-explicit, unhistorical, a slander on the Catholic Church and needlessly protracted, but that despite its excess it displays not the slightest interest in eliciting an emotional response from the audience. A film which deadens our response to such horror is doing no service to the director, still less to us.

A picture which is intended, if Greenaway's production notes are to be taken seriously, to be some kind of meditation upon the connection between greed and child abuse stands instead as a horrible example of audience abuse: an exercise in film-making decadence, the product of a barbaric, unfeeling aestheticism. Here is a man who delights in talking dirty and rubbing our noses in sexual humiliation. Watching this movie is about as pleasurable, and rewarding, as being subjected to a 120-minute dirty phone call.

PRO:

'Sumptuous . . . startling, brutal.' *(Alexander Walker, Evening Standard)*

'Breathtaking colour and splendour.' *(Sunday Express)*

MIXED:

'A nasty, weeping sore of a film, oozing as it is with all the director's usual obsessions, from bodily functions to death and decay . . . cruel, intoxicating offensive stuff, but so handsomely dressed . . . it could almost be seductive – which, of course, is the very point the director intends to make.' *(Phillipa Bloom, Empire)*

'A highly original, complex and difficult film packed with ugly and unpleasant images and incidents, though blessed by breathtakingly beautiful production, design and photography . . . It's claustrophobic, depressing, enormously intelligent and brilliantly filmic.' *(Winnert)*

ANTI:

'A sad decline not because of what it tries to encompass but because of the way it tries to do so . . . by handling that which consistently engages the curiosity without clarifying its true purpose . . . [it] turns out to be merely intellectually condescending, dramatically muddied and simply not good enough to pass muster from the considerably talented hands of Britain's most perversely brilliant filmmaker.' *(Derek Malcolm, Guardian)*

'Stultifyingly boring.' *(Stephen Amidon, Financial Times)*

'The critics finally joined the public in rubbishing Peter Greenaway, with the sexual excess, overwrought story and carcasses coming in for loads of abuse.' *(Empire)*

BACHELOR MOTHER CT: 6 AV: 7.10

1939 US 81 BW COMEDY

D Garson Kanin ☆
W Norman Krasna ☆ from Felix Jackson's story AAN

Ginger Rogers ☆ David Niven ☆ Charles Coburn ☆ Frank Albertson E.E. Clive Ernest Truex

Shop girl (Ginger Rogers) finds an abandoned baby and is mistaken for its mother.

Charming performances by Rogers and Niven and classic scene-stealing by Charles Coburn combine with Kanin's assured direction and an urbane, sometimes risqué script which surprisingly escaped censorship. Remade – badly – as *Bundle of Joy* (1956).

'Carries some rather spicy lines aimed at the adult trade, but broad enough in implication to catch the fancy of general audiences . . . a surprise laugh hit.' *(Variety)*

'An excellent comedy, beautifully done.' *(Richard Mallett, Punch)*

'This is the way farce should be handled, with just enough conviction to season its extravagances.' *(New York Times)*

'A hilarious, snappy, loose-jointed comedy in the best Hollywood tradition, but the script and direction by Kanin have an intelligence and a sense of irony which raise provocative question after provocative question – about the role of women as workers, mothers, and mistresses; about male hypocrisy.' *(Chris Auty, Time Out)*

BACK TO THE FUTURE CT: 8 AV: 7.27

1985 US 116 CSF/COMEDY/FAMILY

D Robert Zemeckis ✗
W Bob Gale Robert Zemeckis ☆

Michael J. Fox ☆ Christopher Lloyd ☆ Crispin Glover ☆ Lea Thompson ☆ Claudia Wells

Teenager (Michael J. Fox) travels back in time to make his father (Crispin Glover) less of a wimp.

Entertaining box-office smash for all the family, although its materialistic, yuppie values always looked suspect. Michael J. Fox's energy enables him not to be unduly overshadowed by Christopher Lloyd's entertainingly zany inventor; there's an affectionate evocation of the 1950s; and the ingenious plot makes lots of comic capital out of the Oedipal complications which ensue when the hero's mother falls in love with him back in the past. Within six months of its release, it had grossed over $200,000,000 at the domestic box-office. Both public and critics liked this film, with very few reservations.

'I swallowed all of this while I was watching it, even chewed it with gusto, but one hour later, eh!' *(Michael Dare, LA Weekly)*

'Accelerates with wit, ideas, and infectious wide-eyed wonder.' *(Variety)*

'Fun at the speed of light, a whiz-bang time-travel adventure likely to result in some decidedly high-octane box-office dollars.' *(Kirk Ellis, Hollywood Reporter)*

'A clever, generally engaging screwball comedy.' *(Pauline Kael)*

'The movie . . . resembles Capra's *It's a Wonderful Life* more than other, conventional time-travel movies. It's about a character who begins with one view of his life and reality, and is allowed, through magical intervention, to discover another. Steven Spielberg was the executive producer, and the movie's world view (smart kid in Yuppie suburb redefines reality for his parents) is part of the basic Spielberg approach. This time it comes with charm, brains, and a lot of laughter.' *(Roger Ebert)*

BACK TO THE FUTURE PART II

CT: 5 AV: 4.67

1989 US 107 C SF/COMEDY/FAMILY

D Robert Zemeckis
W Bob Gale

Michael J. Fox Christopher Lloyd Lea Thompson
Thomas F. Wilson Elizabeth Shue

Teenager (Michael J. Fox) travels forward in time to make his son less of a creep.

Despite ingenious special effects and flashes of wit, a grave disappointment. The time-travel plot is fiendishly complex and inventive; but there is too much of it, and the movie becomes bogged down in exposition – mainly delivered at the top of his voice by Doc (Christopher Lloyd). The movie will be incomprehensible to anyone who didn't see the original; the film has no proper ending; and not even Michael J. Fox's charm can conceal the crassly commercial nature of the enterprise. The critics were generally unimpressed.

PRO:

'Never degenerates into Spielbergian sentimentality: you can laugh, be thrilled and think without feeling embarrassed.' *(Geoff Andrew, Time Out)*

'Lacks the blend of nostalgic detail and bizarre family feeling that gave the first film heart as well as flash, but it replaces that with a plotline that never lets up, a wealth of interesting detail in all its time zones, and some mind-bending concepts.' *(Kim Newman, Film Yearbook)*

MIXED:

'Lacks the genuine power of the original film. The story of the 1985 film has real heart to it: if McFly didn't travel from 1985 to 1955 and arrange for his parents to have their first date, he might not even exist. The time travel in that film involved his own emotional confrontation with his own parents as teenagers. Part II, on the other hand, is mostly just zaniness and screwball jokes. But on that level, it's fun.' *(Roger Ebert)*

ANTI:

'Zemeckis' fascination with having characters interact at different ages of their lives hurts the film visually, and strains credibility past the breaking point, by forcing him to rely on some very cheesy makeup designs.' *(Variety)*

'Back to the bank would be more like it.' *(Michael J. Fox)*

BACK TO THE FUTURE PART III

CT: 5 AV: 7.25

1990 US 118 C SF/COMEDY/FAMILY/WESTERN

D Robert Zemeckis ☆
W Bob Gale

Michael J. Fox Christopher Lloyd ☆
Mary Steenburgen ☆ Thomas F. Wilson
Lea Thompson

Teenager (Michael J. Fox) travels back in time to rescue crazed scientist (Christopher Lloyd).

An amiable effort, spoofing classic westerns and giving Christopher Lloyd more to do than merely act the mad scientist (his scenes with Mary Steenburgen are the best in the film). It's a bit more enjoyable and a lot more comprehensible than *BTTF2*, but nowhere near as good as the original. Most of the inventiveness and originality which lay behind the first (and, despite its flaws, the second) have vanished: what we have here is a fairly unadventurous comedy western, an inferior version of *The Paleface* (1948).

The critics tended to overpraise it, not least because the copious allusions to old westerns – such as *El Dorado, A Fistful of Dollars* and *My Darling Clementine* – enabled them to display their own cinematic erudition. However, it's good-hearted with an excellent special-effects climax.

ANTI:

'Lacking both the mind-boggling timeshift complexities and frenetic pace of *Back to the Future II*, this final instalment in the series shows little real empathy for its Western setting and runs out of steam altogether in a railroad finale blueprinted in the Indiana Jones chases.' *(Graham Fuller, Film Yearbook)*

PRO:

'Recovers the style and wit and grandiose fantasy elements in the original. The simplicity of plot, and the wide expansiveness of its use of space, are a refreshing change from the convoluted, visually cramped and cluttered second part.' *(Variety)*

'Affectionate, innovative and vaguely lunatic. With Marty's experience of the past filtered through a lifetime of watching Westerns on TV, he struts around as as though he'd wandered onto the set of a Sergio Leone movie. Western conventions are gleefully challenged, and with the camera gliding and swooping over the action (though visual pyrotechnics never obscure the emotional core), Zemeckis and writer Bob Gale – insisting that this is the final outing – bring off an audacious marriage of genres to grand and enjoyable effect.' *(Colette Maude, Time Out)*

'The one thing that remains constant in all of the

Back to the Future movies, and which I especially like, is a sort of bittersweet, elegiac quality involving romance and time . . . In all of these stories, there is the realization that love depends entirely on time; lovers like to think their love is eternal, but do they ever realize it depends entirely on temporal coincidence?' *(Roger Ebert)*

BAD AND THE BEAUTIFUL, THE

CT: 6 AV: 8.09

1952 US 118 BW DRAMA

D Vincente Minnelli ☆
W Charles Schnee AAW

Kirk Douglas ☆ AAN Lana Turner Walter Pidgeon Dick Powell Barry Sullivan Gloria Grahame ☆ AAW Gilbert Roland Leo G. Carroll Vanessa Brown Paul Stewart

Four people remember a Hollywood producer (Kirk Douglas).

Vincente Minnelli's cynical film about Hollywood won five Oscars, including Best Screenplay, and was doubtless fascinating for Hollywood insiders, trying to guess who was meant to be whose real-life equivalent. In the cold light of today, however, the Oscar-winning screenplay looks patchy, episodic and glib; and it does suffer from a dearth of sympathetic characters.

'Exceptionally well written.' *(Variety)*

'Clever, sharply observed little scenes reflect the Hollywood surface: the egotistic babble at a party, the affectations of European directors, the sneak preview, the trying on of suits for catmen in a B picture.' *(MFB)*

'For all the cleverness of the apparatus, it lacks a central point of focus.' *(Penelope Houston)*

'Minnelli's direction of a script which tries a little too hard for bright sophistication . . . is brilliantly assured, clever and ingenious. Paradoxically, this ingenuity, with the deliberate pursuit of effects, seems to impose rather too much strain on the material; a story already involved becomes fragmentary and superficial.' *(BFI Bulletin)*

BAD DAY AT BLACK ROCK

CT: 8 AV: 8.67

1955 US 81 C WESTERN/THRILLER

D John Sturges ☆ AAN
W Millard Kaufman from Howard Brislin's story *Bad Time at Hondo* ☆ AAN

Spencer Tracy ☆ AAN Robert Ryan ☆ Anne Francis Dean Jagger Walter Brennan John Ericson Lee Marvin ✔ Ernest Borgnine ✔ Russell Collins Walter Sande

A one-armed stranger (Spencer Tracy) is greeted with hostility in a desert town.

This modern western is a tough drama about racism, directed by John Sturges at the top of his form and so brilliantly acted that it almost makes you forget how black-and-white is its view of humanity, There's plenty of sustained tension, and it's a welcome reminder that you don't need violence to make an effective thriller.

'One of the finest motion pictures ever made.' *(John O'Hara, Collier's Magazine)*

'The obvious picture of comparison is *High Noon*. Both are suspense thrillers with an evident moral, both center upon the behavior of a man isolated by mortal danger; both work toward a blazing climax through an atmosphere of hair-trigger calm. The new picture is the better by a variety of measurements . . . The conflict in *Bad Day at Black Rock* is less explicit, and the weight and determination of the opposing forces are less arbitrarily stated than the rather pat duel of *High Noon*. The suspense is therefore much tighter; it increases with the shifting and hardening resolution of the performers and is not a mechanical excitement keyed to the ticking of a clock.' *(Robert Hatch, Nation)*

'Eighty minutes of thrills with no more violence than a bad man having his head cuffed.' *(Harris Deans, Evening Standard)*

'An extraordinarily clever essay in suspense, clammily gripping, steamy with atmosphere.' *(Daily Mail)*

'*Bad Day at Black Rock* will be compared to *High Noon* – an honor in itself – for many reasons. It is not a traditional "head 'em off at the pass" Western, but a study of people caught in the grip of fear. The arrival of the stranger sends a tremor of panic through every man in town and each reacts in his own impulsive way. Also, the movie takes place within twenty-four hours. It has a dramatic unity, an economy of word and action, that is admirable in an age of flabby Hollywood epics that maunder on forever.' *(William K. Zinsser, New York Herald Tribune)*

'Though *Bad Day at Black Rock* is crudely melodramatic, it is a very superior piece of motion picture craftsmanship.' *(Pauline Kael)*

BAD GIRLS:

see LES BICHES.

BAD LIEUTENANT

CT: 5 AV: 5.18

1992 US 96 C DRAMA

D Abel Ferrara ✗
W Zöe Lund Abel Ferrara

Harvey Keitel ☆ Frankie Thorn Zöe Lund Anthony Ruggiero Eddie Daniels

A bad cop (Harvey Keitel) gets worse.

Sensational shocker tarted up as a no-holds-barred

character study. Plot and pacing leave much to be desired, but Harvey Keitel gives a courageously horrible performance.

PRO:

'Disturbing, raw film-making and award-winning acting.' *(Kim Newman, Empire)*

'Not a "dirty movie" . . . Takes spirituality and morality more seriously than most films do . . . Keitel gives one of the great screen performances of recent years.' *(Roger Ebert)*

'Film's frank treatment of drug addiction, obsessive sexuality and loss of religious faith spells instant controversy.' *(Variety)*

MIXED:

'*Bad Lieutenant* spells out its themes of hypocrisy and sexual obsession with the intensity of a nightmare. You won't be enlightened, but Keitel's performance has a snaky fascination.' *(Bruce Williamson, Playboy)*

'A serious film about the gnawing of conscience and the thirst for redemption, but the tone is so dispassionately vile it may leave viewers shaken or sick.' *(Richard Corliss, Time)*

ANTI:

'Shell out your seven bucks, and you'll get to see the ugly, particularly brutal rape of a nun. Also the buck-naked nun getting a pelvic exam. At this point, I turned to the person next to me, seeking comfort. Guess who God arranged to be sitting right beside me? That's right. The actress who played the nun. Not satisfied yet? Well, there are also shots of needles being shoved into veins . . . heads blown to smithereens . . . Keitel meeting, yes meeting, Jesus and calling him a rat – well, no, I will not repeat that foulness here. You'll notice I have not told you the story. That was God's ultimate punishment. With all this horror, things were not made even a little easier by having one to follow.' *(Rod Lurie, Los Angeles Magazine)*

'Keitel's sudden attack of conscience, when a raped nun refuses to condemn her attackers, comes out of left field and never convinces. Dramatically turgid, it's about as much fun as being whopped about the skull with a nightstick.' *(Rose)*

BAD NEWS BEARS, THE

CT: 7 AV: 6.27

1976 US 103 C COMEDY/FAMILY

D Michael Ritchie ✔
W Bill Lancaster ☆

Tatum O'Neal ☆ Walter Matthau ☆ Vic Morrow Alfred W. Lutter ☆ Joyce Van Patten Jackie Earle Haley ✔

A baseball coach (Walter Matthau) licks a baseball team of no-hopers into shape.

Engaging 'feelgood' baseball comedy for the whole family, with Matthau giving one of his funniest performances. Much imitated (as in *The Mighty Ducks*), but never bettered. The two sequels, however, really are bad news.

PRO:

Has the correct balance of warmth and empathy to make the gentle social commentary very effective.' *(Variety)*

'From Matthau he [Ritchie] gets one of his crustiest and unforcedly funniest performances, which does not let even such dazzling youngsters as Tatum O'Neal, Alfred W. Lutter, and Jackie Earle Haley steal the show. And Ritchie is marvelous at shooting action on the diamond, whether comic or tense. But he is most brilliant in moments of waiting, between plays or ploys, when people are nervously twitching or fidgeting, blinking or scratching themselves – when expectant emptiness begins to burst at the seams.' *(John Simon)*

'Amiably engrossing satire on the "win ethic" . . . consistently delights with its panoramic comic invention.' *(Paul Taylor, Time Out)*

BAD TIMING: A SENSUAL OBSESSION

CT: 2 AV: 5.00

1980 US 123 C DRAMA/THRILLER

D Nicholas Roeg ✗
W Yale Udoff ●

Theresa Russell ☆ Art Garfunkel ● Harvey Keitel ● Denholm Elliott Daniel Massey Dana Gillespie

Neurotic divorcee (Theresa Russell) has ill-fated affair with Viennese psychiatrist (Art Garfunkel).

Roeg's erotic thriller is distinguished by a strong central performance from Theresa Russell. However, Garfunkel and Keitel appear miscast; the excess of symbolism and narrative confusion leads to a suffocating atmosphere of pretentiousness; and it's all needlessly nasty. The British Film Critics' Circle voted Roeg director of the year for this; it was certainly the most directed film of the year.

PRO:

'Mesmerising melodrama.' *(Maltin)*

'Profoundly disturbing.' *(Scheuer)*

ANTI:

'Technically flashy, and teeming with degenerate chic, the downbeat tale is unrelieved by its tacked-on thriller ending, and deals purely in despair.' *(Variety)*

'The meretriciousness of the picture can be glimpsed through the battery of visual tricks.' *(Peter Ackroyd, Spectator)*

'It is plain that [Roeg] is deep into something . . . What it is, is less clear. Compulsive sadism? Infatuated passion? Irresistible necrophilia?

Existential exhibition? The mind watching this curious test-to-destruction movie doesn't boggle: it's bombarded, non-stop, by so much information about the characters that it becomes impossible to select what's significant.' *(Alexander Walker, Evening Standard)*

'What is most frightening about the film is that its camerawork, associative editing and narrative structure relentlessly reinforce and participate in this sensual obsession . . . from the opening images . . . to the closing moments of the film . . . compelling us in the audience to identify with this assault on the female victim . . . [making] some of us very uncomfortable to be drawn into a complicity with these male predators.' *(Susan Barker, Film Quarterly)*

'The folly of a talented man.' *(David Ansen, Newsweek)*

BAISERS VOLÉS: see STOLEN KISSES.

BAKER'S WIFE, THE CT: 6 AV: 8.00

(aka *La Femme du Boulanger*)

1938 France 110 BW ROMANCE/COMEDY/FOREIGN

D Marcel Pagnol ☆
W Marcel Pagnol from Jean Giono's novel *Jean Le Bleu*

Raimu ☆ Ginette Leclerc ☆ Charles Moulin ☆ Robert Vattier Robert Bassac

A baker (Raimu) can not bring himself to bake any more, when his wife (Ginette Leclerc) runs off with another man.

Sweet, sentimental tragi-comedy with a marvellous central performance.

'One of the minor tragedies of this war is that the French cannot spend more time making pictures like [this] uproariously spicy comedy.' *(Robert Joseph, Hollywood Spectator)*

'Almost as good as its ecstatic admirers say it is . . . featuring Raimu in a well-nigh perfect performance . . . Droll and merry, capitally acted and as French as *pâté de foie gras*.' *(Richard Sheridan Ames, Rob Wagner's Script)*

'Leisured of pace but bitingly satirical . . . The absolutely lifelike portraits of village cronies give a background of minute (albeit comic) realism both to the surface plot and to the withering attack on the Church.' *(Arthur Vesselo, MFB)*

'Raimu's baker is an acting classic – a true tragicomic hero – and it's easy to agree with Orson Welles, who cited this comedy as proof that "a story and an actor, both superb" can result in "a perfect movie" even if the direction and the editing are not "cinematic".' *(Pauline Kael)*

'Flagrantly unfashionable, but bursting with bucolic vigour and sly satirical wit.' *(Geoff Brown, Time Out)*

'This rather obvious and long-drawn-out joke is important because international critics hailed it as a work of art (which it isn't) and because it fixed an image of the naughty bucolic French.' *(Halliwell)*

BALL OF FIRE CT: 6 AV: 7.10

1941 US 111 BW COMEDY/ROMANCE

D Howard Hawks ☆
W Charles Brackett Billy Wilder ☆ from Billy Wilder's story Thomas Monroe AAN

Gary Cooper ☆ Barbara Stanwyck ☆ AAN Oscar Homolka ☆ Henry Travers S.Z. Sakall ☆ Tully Marshall Leonid Kinskey ☆ Dana Andrews Dan Duryea Allen Jenkins

Showgirl Sugarpuss O'Shea (Barbara Stanwyck) causes mayhem among seven professors, including Bertram Potts (Gary Cooper).

Update of *Snow White and the Seven Dwarfs*: very much a one-joke picture, lifted above the ordinary by charming performances by Cooper and Stanwyck.

ANTI:

'A funny enough idea, but it's spun to chiffon sheerness. Picture might have been more amusing if one could have seen the action distinctly. Gregg Toland's highly touted low-key photography is all very well for a *Kane* or *The Little Foxes*, but here it acts as a depressant.' *(Herb Sterne)*

'Rather shrill and tiresome.' *(Pauline Kael, 1982)*

PRO:

'A flashing, sudden St. Catherine's wheel of a film, a truly American compound of sentimentality, toughness, and crackle . . . Howard Hawks has directed the film with a faultless sense of timing, giving to the story, with its robust and picturesque dialogue, all the solidity necessary to carry its superstructure of fantasy.' *(Dilys Powell)*

'Cooper has never been more appealing and Stanwyck is an unbridled joy, vivacious, witty and bursting with zing.' *(Winnert)*

BALLAD OF A SOLDIER CT: 5 AV: 7.33

(aka *Ballada o Soldate*)

1959 USSR 89 BW ROMANCE/FOREIGN

D Grigori Chukrai
W Valentin Yezhov Grigori Chukrai AAN

Vladimir Ivashov ☆ Zhanna Prokhorenko Antonina Maximova Nicolai Kruchkov Yevgeny Urbaanskly

Young soldier (Vladimir Ivashov) takes a few days leave after fighting heroically in World War II.

Beautiful but heavily sentimental weepie which won

prizes at the Cannes and San Francisco Film Festivals. The director's woolly propagandizing for peace on earth is less interesting than his portrayal of 'ordinary' Russian life, which now comes across as highly idealized.

'Chukhrai's hero is upholding Humanism and Poetry – both with capital letters . . . and failing to appreciate he is not yet strong enough as an artist to put them honourably on the screen . . . If this is Left Wing cinema, I feel that one would almost prefer the Alamo style of treatment.' *(Robert Vas, S & S)*

'A profound and cumulative lament for the disorder, the grief and the frustration of people borne down upon by war . . . The tragedy of it is concealed by a gentle lyric quality.' *(Bosley Crowther)*

'Has a ballad-like simplicity both beautiful and moving . . . The lyric realism of the images is perfectly attuned to the emotional demands of the scenario . . . [Chukrai] may yet completely transform social realism and become a figure of real stature in the international cinema.' *(Richard Whitehall, F & F)*

'An engaging piece of hokum . . . A cut above the usual tractor-girl drama, for Chukrai . . . in a way that would delight John Ford . . . has redeemed it by grace and humour, notably so in the love scenes.' *(MFB)*

'Man is good! is the message . . . There is warmth in the very sadness of this film, for it is pervaded with progressive ideas and radiant with talent and love of man.' *(Newsreel)*

BALLADA O SOLDATE: *see* BALLAD OF A SOLDIER.

BALLON ROUGE, LE: *see* RED BALLOON, THE.

BALTHAZAR: *see* AU HAZARD BALTHAZAR.

BAMBI CT: 9 AV: 9.15

1942 US 72 C CARTOON/FAMILY

D David D. Hand ☆
W Perce Pearce Larry Morey from Felix Salten's book

Voices: Peter Behn Paula Winslowe Bobby Stewart Stan Alexander Cammie King

Baby deer grows up.

A classic horror film. It starts out cosy, cute and secure. Then, three quarters of an hour in, the unthinkable happens with the death of Bambi's mother; for the last 25 minutes, most children are in a state of traumatic shock.

It's surprising to look at Bambi with adult eyes and discover that this supposedly 'cute' cartoon paints so dark, visceral and elemental a picture. Probe beneath the storybook surface, and you can see many of the tough, cynical, survivalist attitudes which made the 1940s the heyday of film noir. It's a movie permeated with the sense of a dangerous world outside, of man's incomprehensible viciousness – though no human is ever seen in the film, only the effects of his destructive presence on the world around him. No picture has captured better, in the sense of making you actually feel, the randomness and desolation of bereavement.

The sexual stereotyping is of its day. The does are left to look after the children, bond with them, give everyday advice and protection. The stags are distant: their job is to gallop around in formation, look magnificent, fight and turn up in moments of crisis. A young stag's duty is to conform to society's expectations, compete for a mate, and procreate.

Ever since the film's first appearance in 1942, some critics have found the picture too anthropomorphic. True, Disney cut out many of the more bestial sides of Felix Salten's novel, which dealt as much with the predatory nature of animals within the forest as it did with the conflict between nature and man. But a modern audience expects a Disney forest to be twee-ridden as well as tree-ridden, and is more likely to admire how skilfully human and animal nature have been reconciled. Thumper the rabbit's natural characteristics are, for example, merged with an infant's voice, appearance and attitudes, to make one of Disney's most endearing characters. Everyone will identify with Bambi's tentative attempts to walk, make friends, conquer fear and loneliness. Not only are the early scenes amusing and 'cute': they bring back universal memories of growing up.

The film loses some of its oomph when its leading characters – Bambi, Thumper and Flower the skunk – discover sex and romance, and become (in their friend Owl's terms) 'twitterpated'. But in the later part of the film, there are marvellously stark set-pieces: Bambi's battle with another young stag for the deer Faline demonstrates that even a nice, peace-loving chap like Bambi has to struggle and fight for what he wants. 'Green' the film may be; hippie, it definitely isn't.

On visual grounds alone, Bambi would deserve to be considered a classic. To see it today, in another Golden Age of Disney animation, is to be reminded that Bambi remains a high-point in motion-picture technique and originality.

ANTI:

'Left at least one grown-up more than a little disappointed . . . Mr Disney has again revealed a discouraging tendency to trespass beyond the bounds of cartoon fantasy to the tight naturalism of magazine illustration. His painted forest is hardly to be distinguished from the real forest . . . The free and whimsical cartoon caricatures have made way for a closer resemblance to life, which the camera can show better. Mr Disney seems intent on moving from art to artiness.' *(New York Times)*

'Lacks the vitality of *Dumbo*, as it lacks the grandeur of *Pinocchio*, substituting for both a wistfulness which sometimes verges on the insipid . . . Those who remember the Schubert in *Fantasia* will know what I mean when I say that a good deal of this tale of a forest deer is in Disney's Ave Maria manner.' *(Dilys Powell)*

MIXED:

'A touching and beguiling thing, in the master's most felicitous style. Disney has sought after no new forms here, pursued no social allegory here. He is happy and relaxed with the things he does best – sketches of wild life, studies of young animals and their endearing ways . . . The later scenes are a little uneven in their draughtsmanship and invention. The Disney artists have not yet learnt how to give bone and muscle to a full-grown quadruped . . . But for sixty out of its seventy minutes *Bambi* is sheer enchantment.' *(C.A. Lejeune)*

'The color and the three-dimensional effect of the scenery are certainly up to standard, but the characterizations, on the other hand, are slightly sub.' *(David Lardner, New Yorker)*

PRO:

'Gem-like in its reflection of the color and movement of sylvan plant and animal life . . . The glow and texture of the Disney brush reach new heights, especially in the treatment of a summer thunderstorm and a raging snowstorm.' *(Variety)*

'Superb draughtsmanship and exquisite colouring lend depth, beauty . . . Typical comedy touches heighten drama of spectacular moments; delightful dialogue . . . tuneful songs . . . expert animation. Walt Disney's finest achievement.' *(Today's Cinema)*

'I think back to 1942 when we released that picture and there was a war on, and nobody cared much about the love life of a deer, and the bankers were on my back. It's pretty gratifying to know that Bambi finally made it.' *(Walt Disney)*

BAND WAGON, THE CT: 10 AV: 9.27

1953 US 112 C MUSICAL/ROMANCE

D Vincente Minnelli ☆
W Adolph Green Betty Comden ☆ AAN lyrics and music by Howard Dietz Arthur Schwartz ☆

Fred Astaire ☆ Jack Buchanan ☆ Cyd Charisse ☆ Oscar Levant ☆ Nanette Fabray

A fading Broadway hoofer (Fred Astaire) puts on a musical version of Faust *with a pretentious actor-manager (Jack Buchanan).*

Charming, elegant backstage musical with the mature Fred Astaire and Jack Buchanan at their best, a witty script, numerous great songs, plus the legs, sex appeal and dancing ability of Cyd Charisse. One of the best screen musicals ever.

ANTI:

'A bit noisy and eyestraining.' *(Evening News)*

'*The Band Wagon* might well have been a good film without [Fred Astaire and Jack Buchanan] . . . too long and too noisy . . . Now and then I sighed for the old black and white romances of Astaire and Rogers.' *(Brian Murtough, Daily Sketch))*

MIXED:

'Handsomely mounted musical with some high points of entertainment intermixed with much that just doesn't come off . . . Too many good tunes are thrown away in brief snatches . . . The story is weak . . . a disappointment in general.' *(Fortnight)*

'A good, lively musical, not quite as good as travellers' tales had led me to imagine, certainly not as good as the one and only *On the Town*, but good enough to enjoy all through. It has an exciting feeling for movement and rhythm, as indeed we should expect from its director, Vincente Minnelli, who has made some of the best musicals to come out of Hollywood in the last ten years. It has even an intelligent and amusing script.' *(Dilys Powell)*

PRO:

'Among the best entertainments of any year . . . a neat plot twist and reels of fresh ideas, brilliantly produced numbers and original songs and dances . . . [it] bounces along at a great rate – overflowing with mirth, melody and good humor. Best of all, perhaps, is the presence of the fabulous Jack Buchanan.' *(Jesse Zunser, Cue)*

'The best musical of the month, the year, the decade, or for all I know of all time.' *(Archer Winsten)*

'Witty, colorful and packed with inventive dance routines . . . Minnelli's best musical of the 1950s.' *(RAE Pickard, Dictionary of 1000 Best Films, 1971)*

'A supreme example of the standards reached by the Arthur Freed unit at MGM in the 1950s . . . Witty and sophisticated screen entertainment.' *(Allan Hunter & Kenny Mathieson, Movie Classics , 1992)*

BANK DICK, THE CT: 8 AV: 9.50

(aka *The Bank Detective*)

1940 US 74 BW COMEDY

D Edward Cline
W Mahatma Kane Jeeves ☆ (pseudonym for W.C. Fields)

W.C. Fields ☆ Franklin Pangborn Shemp Howard Jack Norton Grady Sutton Cora Witherspoon Una Merkel

Bank detective (W.C. Fields) foils a robbery and becomes a hero to all but his family.

Dismissed by *Variety* and some others on its release, this most subversive and anarchic of comedies displays W.C. Fields at his funniest.

MIXED:

'Adequate program supporter.' *(Variety)*

'When the man is funny he is terrific, but in between the high points . . . what is the audience doing? . . . The audience is asleep because this was never made as a picture. It is stiff and static and holds no interest outside of W.C. Fields – you don't care what happens to anyone else, you don't care what the outcome is; you forget immediately if there was any.' *(Otis Ferguson)*

'Fields is magnificently independent of the material which is foisted upon him. He seems to treat the poor story and thin situations which make up this film as he treats the characters in it, giving them now and again a nod of recognition, occasionally making an effort to placate them, but for the most part pushing them aside by the sheer force of his fruity, rotund personality.' *(The Times)*

PRO:

'Fields is a comedian of almost Shakespearean mould . . . one of those human balloons no amount of puncturing can deflate . . . [The film] contains more slapstick than usual, and the incidents are drastic, even in a world fit for Marx Brothers to live in.' *(William Whitebait, New Statesman)*

'Just about the most sardonic film ever made and a wonderfully acute travesty of all those pious pictures purporting to reveal life in a small American town.' *(John McCarten, New Yorker)*

'One of the great classics of American comedy.' *(Robert Lewis Taylor)*

'Especially [in] *The Bank Dick*, Fields, like the Marx Brothers and Mae West, was the foe of everything sentimental and nice. In an era of glamorized sentimentality and niceness, their essential vulgarity and comic crudeness were especially refreshing.' *(Gerald Mast, A Short History of the Movies, 1971)*

BARBARELLA CT: 6 AV: 4.45

1967 France/Italy 98 C SF/COMEDY

D Roger Vadim
W Terry Southern Roger Vadim from Jean-Claude Forest's book

Jane Fonda John Phillip Law Anita Pallenberg ✓ Milo O'Shea David Hemmings Marcel Marceau Ugo Tognazzi Claude Dauphin

41st-century sexpot (Jane Fonda) has accidents throughout the galaxy, most of which involve her losing articles of clothing.

Jane Fonda exudes bimbo sex appeal in Roger Vadim's erotic cult comedy. Impressive sets and enjoyably camp jokes compensate for the juvenile moments and the sick, sadistic undertones. The plot is weak; the climax is unsatisfactory; and contemporary critics savaged it – but it remains in the mind as almost the only 60s film which hinted at the dark side of permissiveness.

'If Homer and Lewis Carroll had read the Marquis de Sade and a little sci-fi, this is what they would have produced.' *(Roger Vadim)*

ANTI:

'A special kind of mess . . . All the gadgetry of science-fiction . . . is turned into all kinds of jokes, which are not jokes, but hard-breathing sadistic thrashings, mainly at the expense of Barbarella, and of women.' *(Renata Adler, New York Times)*

'Sad rather than De Sade.' *(Alexander Walker, Evening Standard)*

'Glossy science fiction trash, which appears to be *2001: A Space Odyssey* seen through the eyes of Helen Gurley Brown and photographed by Vogue.' *(Rex Reed)*

'A flaccid, jaded appeal to our baser appetites.' *(John Simon)*

'Unintentionally unamusing . . . Barbarella is a weak heroine in that her actions have little effect on what transpires at the end.' *(Danny Peary)*

PRO:

'Most of the film's hilarity springs from the contrast between Miss Fonda's wide-eyed innocence and the astonishingly nasty situations she gets in . . . I found the fantasy quite irresistible.' *(Ian Christie, Daily Express)*

'Comic-strip buffs, science-fiction fans and admirers of the human mammae will get a run for their money.' *(Time)*

'Jane Fonda, that well-known heavenly body, has furthered the cause of science by performing the first striptease in Space . . . The fact that the whole film is so outrageous that you find yourself chortling, cannot save it from turning out as a twisted tale which makes the activities of the Marquis de Sade look like good clean fun.' *(John Smith, Sunday Mirror)*

BARRY LYNDON AAN CT: 7 AV: 6.38

1975 GB 187 C DRAMA

D Stanley Kubrick ☆ AAN
W Stanley Kubrick AAN from W.M. Thackeray's novel

Ryan O'Neal ● Marisa Berenson ● Patrick Magee Hardy Kruger Steven Berkoff Gay Hamilton Marie Kean Leonard Rossiter ✓ Michael Hordern ✓

Life and times of an 18th-century social climber (Ryan O'Neal).

Gloriously beautiful film which is more watchable (on the big screen, at least) than contemporary critics suggested. It rightly won four technical Oscars, including one for John Alcott's breathtaking cinematography. Thackeray's wit – thanks to Michael

Hordern's voice-over – raises a smile here and there; but the two leads (O'Neal and Berenson) are not remotely up to the job; and Kubrick's anxiety to emphasize the cold, uncaring nature of 18th-century life becomes tiresome and monotonous. At over three hours, the film is much, much too long.

PRO:

'What he did for the future in *2001* . . . Stanley Kubrick in [this film] has done for the past. He has projected us into an era of amazing strangeness . . . A piece of cinema to marvel at.' *(Alexander Walker, Evening Standard)*

'Handsome, assured . . . so long and leisurely, so panoramic in its narrative scope that it's as much an environment as it is a conventional film. Its austerity of purpose defines it as a costume movie unlike any you've ever seen.' *(Vincent Canby, New York Times)*

MIXED:

'The candlelight photography is only one of many aspects of Kubrick's mastery of technique and historical accuracy, to which his humanism, alas, cannot hold a candle . . . Alas, poor Kubrick! He expects to beat all box-office records with this film. But how does one attract crowds with a humdrum story about unprepossessing characters played by mostly undistinguished actors? No stars, no sex, no violence, no rollicking *Tom Jones* humor. Are the masses to be brought in by their interest in neoclassical architecture?' *(John Simon)*

ANTI:

'All art and no matter: a series of still pictures which will please the retina while denying our hunger for drama. And far from re-creating another century it more accurately embalms it.' *(Michael Billington, Illustrated London News)*

'The motion picture equivalent of one of these very large, very expensive, very elegant and very dull books that exist solely to be seen on coffee tables.' *(Charles Champlin)*

'Rarely has a film taken so long to achieve so little . . . Kubrick's lack of concern with his protagonist is underscored by his casting of Ryan O'Neal as Barry. This lump, this noodle, is meant to embody youth and high spirits, daring and devilry, courage and susceptibility to the ways of cunning, all with a heart of at least some gold underneath, as shown by his love for his little son and his grief when the boy is killed . . . Nor was Kubrick much concerned about Lady Lyndon or he would not have cast the role with an egregiously untalented ex-model named Marisa Berenson.' *(Stanley Kauffmann)*

'A Snob's Progress. Thackeray satirised it. Kubrick tells it straight. And that certainly is unexpected. What can have attracted the director to the subject? . . . I came out of the cinema feeling respectful, exhausted, and distinctly dispirited.' *(Dilys Powell)*

BARTON FINK

CT: 5 AV: 6.00

1991 US 116 C COMEDY/DRAMA/THRILLER

D Joel Coen ☆
W Ethan Coen Joel Coen

John Turturro ☆ John Goodman ☆ Judy Davis ✓
Michael Lerner ☆ AAN John Mahoney
Tony Shalhoub Jon Polito

A would-be screenwriter (John Turturro) wrestles with a script for a wrestling movie.

Set in the 1940s, this overrated film is partly a malicious satire about Hollywood's timeless antipathy towards the creative spirit. The Coens' mogul, Jack Lipnick (Michael Lerner), is very funny: he could have come out of Kaufman and Hart's *Once in a Lifetime*. He terrorizes his sidekick (Jon Polito), protests over-loudly that he worships creativity, and drums into Fink the one vital ingredient of a wrestling movie: 'big men in tights, both physically and mentally'. Turturro is never better than when blinking with astonishment, a short-sighted Alice in Blunderland. His hair and glasses are modelled on the playwright George S. Kaufman, but he also looks a bit like Joel Coen.

The film pokes fun at left-wing writers. Fink's notion that he is equipped to write about 'the common man' is fantasy: commissioned to write a wrestling picture, he makes no attempt to research the subject but retires to agonize in his hotel room. If Lipnick, the mogul, is monstrous when pretending to be a father-figure, Fink is creepiest when patronizing neighbour Charlie as 'the common man'. Charlie turns out to be a very uncommon man, and that's the central sick joke of the picture.

Barton Fink has an intensely conservative message: self-expression may be harmless enough in Fink, who has to work up courage to kill a mosquito, but it's potentially horrific in the common man. The Coens question whether 'the pursuit of happiness' can really be what life is about. They lovingly inspect the individualistic maggot at the core of the American Dream.

It's a good idea and the film looks terrific, so why does *Barton Fink* ultimately fail? Mainly, it's because the Coens change their style of story-telling and their attitude towards their central character in mid-picture. For the first 80 minutes the plot is slow but conventional. Fink is progressively humanized – through his writer's block, through his ludicrous treatment by Hollywood, through his emotional bond with Charlie. He becomes less self-absorbed, mainly because he sees an awful example of artistic selfishness in fellow-writer W.P. Mayhew (John Mahoney), who combines the worst aspects of William Faulkner and F. Scott Fitzgerald. Fink even finds a motherly girlfriend (Judy Davis).

Unfortunately, logical plotting and character development fly out of the window as soon as Fink learns that Charlie may be dangerous. He reverts to typewriter: he does not bother to inform his family that Charlie may be coming to kill them; he doesn't help the police; he doesn't reveal the existence of a package which may contain a human head. At the end, we don't know if Barton has been crushed or helped by his experiences, or if the script he has written is any good. We don't know if his family is still alive. He may have a severed head in his hatbox, or not. Critics may find the denouement intriguing: audiences are likely to find it infuriating and pretentious.

The film is a stylistic triumph. Richard Hornung's costumes wittily emphasize the contrast between buttoned-up Barton and chaotic Charlie. The cinematography, by Briton Roger Deakins, is stunning. The sound is startling. The trouble is that style swamps content, and the Coens' detached, flippant approach to their subject and characters ends up looking suspiciously like an inability to think through story, ideas or character. The film won the Palme d'Or at the Cannes Film Festival, and the best actor award for Turturro.

PRO:

'Scene after scene is filled with a ferocious strength and humor.' *(Variety)*

'Works on numerous levels, thrilling the mind, ears and eyes, and racking the nerves.' *(Geoff Andrew, Time Out)*

MIXED:

'Before it turns obscure, it is a hilarious, sometimes over-the-top dark comedy about Hollywood.' *(Vincent Canby, New York Times)*

'Stimulating entertainment, as vigorously challenging and painfully funny as anything the Coens have done. But it's necessary to meet [them] halfway. If you don't [the film] is an empty exercise that will bore you breathless. If you do, it's a comic nightmare that will stir your imagination like no film in years.' *(Peter Travers, Rolling Stone)*

ANTI:

'Leaves one with a distinctly hollow defeatist sensation. It's . . . too vain about its own diabolical, sadistic showmanship and too detached from genuine, inconsolable suffering to earn Profundity Points for emotional integrity or illumination.' *(Gary Arnold, Washington Times)*

'Ludicrously over-praised by the artier critics . . . all style and no substance. Despite some tricksy camera shots, this weird film becomes pretentious and mightily dull. Fine, perhaps, for those who actually like watching wallpaper peel.' *(Rose)*

BASIC INSTINCT CT: 6 AV: 4.31

1992 US 128 C THRILLER/ROMANCE

D Paul Verhoeven
W Joe Eszterhas

Michael Douglas Sharon Stone ✔ George Dzundza Jeanne Tripplehorne Denis Arndt Leilani Sarelle Bruce A. Young Chelcie Ross

A deeply unheroic cop (Michael Douglas) falls for a suspected murderess (Sharon Stone) with sado-masochistic, bisexual and exhibitionistic tendencies.

In the 1960s, this might have been made as a cheap drive-in movie and called Killer Dykes Go Bananas. In the 90s, it cost tens of millions and came replete with flashy direction by Paul (*RoboCop*) Verhoeven, plus a couple of spectacular car chases. It's vapid, sleazy and unbelievable – but fun. Don't even bother to try to make sense of the villainess's tactics. A big hit despite being vilified by most critics.

PRO:

'Rivets attention through its sleek style, attractive cast doing and thinking kinky things, and story, which is as weirdly implausible as it is intensely visceral.' *(Variety)*

ANTI:

'Saddled with extremely unattractive characters, vile dialogue and sex that appeals only to your baser instincts.' *(Jami Bernard, New York Press)*

'An unfeeling house of cards which falls apart when the loopholes and logical flaws that sustain the ambiguous resolution come to light.' *(Kim Newman, S&S)*

'The assorted killer-bimbos on display do not suggest much in the way of field research. Predictably, the American gay "community" is steamed up about the film's depiction of not just one but three lesbian mass murderers. The fuss does seem out of proportion: the heterosexual "community" seems fairly relaxed, after all, when one of its members commits mass murder on screen.' *(Christopher Tookey, Sunday Telegraph)*

'Strip out the steamy sex and you're left with a confusing and rather nasty little thriller that would've died a death were it not for the suspiciously useful public protests. The plot's wildly implausible, as well as being identical to the one Eszterhas uses in most of his pics.' *(Rose)*

'The surprise ending is – there isn't a surprise.' *(Winnert)*

BATMAN CT: 5 AV: 6.36

1989 US 126 C SF/ACTION/ADVENTURE

D Tim Burton ✗
W Sam Hamm Warren Skaaren from Sam Hamm's story ●

Michael Keaton Jack Nicholson ✗ Kim Basinger Robert Wuhl Pat Hingle Billy Dee Williams Michael Gough Jack Palance Jerry Hall

Small boy is driven batty by the murder of his parents, and turns urban vigilante (Michael Keaton).

Great sets (Anton Furst's design rightly won an Oscar) are dwarfed by colossal pretentiousness. Many films trivialize, but *Batman* does the opposite: it seeks to elevate the trivial to the level of an epic. Director Burton treats the psychological motivation of Batman (Michael Keaton) with a reverence more usually devoted to the life of Christ. Gone is the camped crusader played in the original *Batman* TV series and movie by Adam West, not to mention his even more questionable sidekick Robin. Instead, our hero is a lonely, unquestionably heterosexual, emotionally disturbed multi-billionaire. In keeping with this dark interpretation, Michael Keaton and blonde but bland Kim Basinger (playing his girlfriend) act their pathetically underwritten parts with a praiseworthy attempt at realism.

Burton's downbeat approach has two disastrous consequences. One is that the film becomes bogged down as it raises (but conspicuously fails to answer) moral questions about how one man's terrorist can be another man's super-hero. The other unwanted side-effect is that it leads to a lot of awkward practical questions. How did Wayne enrich himself to so elaborate an extent, yet still find time to become an expert in martial arts, a skilled acrobat, a crack racing-driver and a fearless fighter-pilot? Who made all his idosyncratic gadgets, his car and his plane, and how did he keep their manufacture a secret? And why has Wayne waited more than twenty years before starting to fight back against the criminals of Gotham City? Don't expect the film to answer any of the above questions. It doesn't. The credibility of Batman's character is, as a result, nil; and there is a bat-shaped vacuum at the centre of the film.

Which brings us to the star of the show. For that is what the Joker (Jack Nicholson) undoubtedly is. Nicholson's performance has the unselfish, self-effacing quality of Sir Donald Wolfit upstaging a performance of *Hamlet* by riding a unicycle across the Niagara Falls in lurex hot pants. I rather enjoyed it. The trouble is that he is working in so different a style and on so different a scale from Keaton, that he utterly destroys the balance of the film. His performance is a brilliant disaster.

At least when Nicholson is on screen, Batman isn't a bore. Without him, the plotting is slow and over-reminiscent of the first *Superman* movie; the dialogue is banal when it is not being facetious; and there is a sadistic quality to the movie's delight in violence and destruction. The fact that so many people were fooled into paying to see such meretricious garbage was a horribly revealing comment on the power of hype.

PRO:

'To me, it's much bigger than a film – or an event. The world is in need of direction and help. Everyone's looking for the answers. So this can be a great educator. It's a film very much about good and evil, about two great things on this earth: love and fear. The only two emotions there are. You choose which one to be – good or evil. You choose love or fear. Everything else stems from fear – anger, hatred, jealousy, greed, which causes war, devastation, terrorism, everything that's happening in the rain forests, the way the earth is now. And when something like this happens, it's a real symbol that help is there – and that it's in yourself. If you love yourself, and give out that love, then you can get it back. You can change the earth with that.' *(Kim Basinger)*

'Tim Burton's powerfully glamorous comic-book epic, with sets angled and lighted like film noir, goes beyond pulp. It has a funky, nihilistic charge, and an eerie, poetic intensity . . . It's mean and anarchic and blissful.' *(Pauline Kael)*

'Sheer bliss for the nasty-minded child in all of us, Batman is easily better even than such first-class superhero movies as *Superman* or *Raiders of the Lost Ark*, with a background as interesting as its hero and a noirish nightmare style far removed from the colourful camp of the 1960s TV show . . . The film is full of imaginative violence, clever rethinkings of the origins of its familiar characters, astonishing sets and witty lines.' *(Kim Newman)*

'A profound fairy-tale.' *(Markus Natten, Film Yearbook)*

'What keeps the film arresting is the visual stylization. It was a shrewd choice for Burton to emulate the jarring angles and creepy lighting of film noir.' *(Variety)*

MIXED:

'Nice pictures, shame about the story. Blurring the boundary between goodie and baddie is one thing, but making the baddie so much more fun unbalances everything.' *(Rose)*

'A moderately entertaining fantasy, with good design, strong performances and a desperate need of a script doctor.' *(Adam Mars-Jones, Independent)*

ANTI:

'A hostile, mean-spirited movie about ugly, evil people, and it doesn't generate the liberating euphoria of the *Superman* or *Indiana Jones* pictures . . . A depressing experience.' *(Roger Ebert)*

'No matter how hard you try, superheroes and film noir don't go together; the very essence of noir is that there are no more heroes.' *(Roger Ebert, on the 1992 sequel* Batman Returns)

BATTAGLIA DI ALGERI, LA: *see* BATTLE OF ALGIERS, THE.

BATTLE OF ALGIERS, THE

AAN CT: 7 AV: 7.72

(aka *La Battaglia di Algeri*)

1965 Italy/Algeria 125 BW DRAMA/WAR/FOREIGN

D Gillo Pontecorvo ☆ AAN
W Franco Solinas ☆

Brahim Haggiag Jean Martin Yacef Saadi Tommaso Neri

Pseudo-documentary about French-Algerian conflict between 1954 and 1962.

Skilfully written and realistically directed anti-colonialist propaganda, with the none too hidden agenda of castigating America for its involvement in Vietnam. Harrowing details help to give it the power of documentary. Voted Best Film at the Venice Film Festival, 1966, but banned for some years in France.

'The film, ostensibly fair to both sides, is nevertheless on the side of the guerillas; and the presentation of the facts, as well as the incidents of battle, is masterly.' *(Shipman)*

'There's a minimum of verbal rhetoric; the urgent images and Ennio Morricone's thunderous score spell out the underlying political sympathies.' *(Tony Rayns, Time Out)*

'Pontecorvo's inflammatory passion works directly on your feelings. He's the most dangerous kind of Marxist, a Marxist poet.' *(Pauline Kael)*

BATTLE STRIPE: *see* MEN, THE.

BATTLESHIP POTEMKIN: *see* POTEMKIM.

BAWANG BIE JI: *see* L'AVVENTURA.

BEACHES

CT: 7 AV: 5.33

1988 US 124 C MUSICAL/DRAMA

D Garry Marshall
W Mary Agnes Donoghue

Bette Midler ✔ Barbara Hershey John Heard Spalding Gray Mayam Bialik ✔

A story of two women's unlikely friendship.

Critics were mostly dismissive, but it became a big hit. Yes, it's episodic, schmaltzy and a feminist update of a 'woman's picture', with the men little more than cardboard cut-outs. It's also a sanitized version of a more hard-hitting novel, with Barbara Hershey dying of one of those Hollywood diseases which leave you looking lovely until your final moments. But Midler is superb, as is the young actress who impersonates her as an 11-year-old (Mayam Bialik); the script is often witty; and director Garry Marshall's unashamed manipulation of the audience's emotions has a certain Gothic splendour.

ANTI:

'An all-girl *Love Story* . . . The director, Garry Marshall, shows no feeling for the material – not even false feeling . . . The picture is rich in worst moments. Everything to do with CC's work at "a little theatre on the West Side" qualifies. And then there's CC in a musical number from her hit show; the berserk staging is a stunner – I haven't seen anything like this since the "Satan's Alley" number in Stallone's *Staying Alive*.' *(Pauline Kael)*

'The Divine Miss M seems unable to share the camera with another woman. As with the 1988 comedy *Big Business*, in which she practically elbowed Lily Tomlin off the screen, Midler reduces Hershey to a cipher.' *(Brian D. Johnson, Maclean's)*

'Interminable melodrama . . . a trite, maudlin, terribly superficial effort of the sub-made-for-TV quality, an insult to anyone who has ever befriended another human being.' *(Virgin)*

'A gooey, unpleasant mess. Add an overdose of Midler and you're ready to part with your dinner.' *(Rose)*

MIXED:

'Corny, clichéd and dripping with sentiment, but it's still an absolute belter.' *(Pauline McLeod, Daily Mirror)*

'The two women's performances are wonderful, their chemistry is perfect, and the way their lives develop and intersect has a naturalness about it that is very engaging and, in the end, astonishingly tender. Hershey is lovelier and more simpatica than ever, and Midler is superlative at every turn – funny, touching, and in great voice. Yes, the film has major weaknesses, among them a maddening series of false endings, and a loud, idiotic rock song that almost ruins the film's moving climax. For all this, however, it's extremely gratifying to see a contemporary film that's set over a long period of time, and that regards friendship and its attendant responsibilities with sympathy and respect.' *(Bruce Bawer, American Spectator)*

PRO:

'It is well known that children are a mistake – especially in pictures – but the little girl who plays Miss Midler (a certain Mayim Bialik) is so like her in both her appearance and her behavior that her choice for the part seems almost miraculous and constitutes, as far as I know, the only instance in the history of the movie industry of witty casting.' *(Quentin Crisp, Christopher Street)*

'A heck of an entertaining – if corny – mainstream film; I enjoyed it . . . Great art? Get outta here. Artful daydream pushing all the right buttons? You bet.' *(Shaun Usher, Daily Mail)*

'To see devoted friendship between women portrayed in a positive light is so unusual in a modern-day

Hollywood movie that I can't help but recommend *Beaches* to other women.' *(Kathi Maio)*

BEAT THE DEVIL CT: 5 AV: 6.33

1953 GB 100 BW THRILLER/COMEDY

D John Huston
W Truman Capote John Huston

Humphrey Bogart Gina Lollobrigida Peter Lorre ☆ Robert Morley ☆ Jennifer Jones Edward Underdown Ivor Barnard Bernard Lee Marco Tulli

Various travellers in Africa have their eye on land which may contain uranium deposits.

Uneven, self-indulgent comedy spy thriller, with little or no suspense, and Bogart and Gina Lollobrigida struggling as the leads. The main amusement lies in the self-parodying supporting cast, especially Lorre and Morley. It has the air of an 'in joke', and audiences responded just as badly as the overwhelming majority of critics. Recently, the film has been rehabilitated and become something of a cult.

'John Huston and I were the only ones who really liked it.' *(Truman Capote)*

PRO:

'Delicious entertainment.' *(Sunday Chronicle)*

'Sharp, satiric . . . John Huston . . . has assembled the strongest bunch of characters we've seen on screen in a long time . . . Unadulterated joy . . . One of those pictures you want to see again.' *(News of the World)*

ANTI:

'When the director is John Huston . . . one naturally expects a good deal . . . I, for one, didn't get it . . . It's neither exciting nor (often) funny.' *(Campbell Dixon, Daily Telegraph)*

'The effect is that of a crime melodrama seized from time to time with the giggles and it is difficult to know when to tingle with suspense or merely titter.' *(Cecil Wilson, Daily Mail)*

'A satire of *The Maltese Falcon* . . . a parody within parody, a private joke, amusing to the initiated, incomprehensible to the uninformed. If the wit is introverted, the technique is haphazard, skirting the borderline of embarrassment, veering toward the irrational, and trailing off into trivia . . . An act of self-indulgence, harmless in itself but disturbing in its implications.' *(Eugene Archer, 1959)*

'Miss Lollobrigida was still having trouble with the English language; the rest of the cast were merely in trouble with the plot.' *(Elkan Allen, NFT Bulletin)*

'Only the phonies think it's funny. It's a mess.' *(Humphrey Bogart, actor)*

BEAU GESTE CT: 6 AV: 7.50

1939 US 120 BW ADVENTURE/WAR

D William A. Wellman ☆
W Robert Carson from P.C. Wren's novel

Gary Cooper Ray Milland Robert Preston Brian Donlevy ☆ AAN J. Carrol Naish ☆ Susan Hayward Heather Thatcher James Stephenson Donald O'Connor Broderick Crawford

Three English brothers join the Foreign Legion.

Most exciting version of this story, with Brian Donlevy at least as good as his predecessor Noah Beery in the villain's role. Gary Cooper makes a nicely understated (though far from English) romantic hero, and the lavish set pieces are expertly directed by William Wellman. The art direction was Oscar-nominated.

ANTI:

'A morbid picture . . . because the brutality has no relation whatever to the real world; it is uncritical daydreaming.' *(Graham Greene)*

'Will do nominal biz, but lacks punch for smash proportions.' *(Variety)*

'Cooper, horribly miscast as a dashing young British gallant – saying things like "You young pup!" to Ray Milland – was embarrassingly callow, almost simpering.' *(Pauline Kael)*

PRO:

'Its melodrama is sometimes grim but never harrowing, its pace is close to hectic and its suspense is constant.' *(Herbert Cohn, Brooklyn Daily Eagle)*

'A handsome treatment of a well-loved adventure tale.' *(New York Daily Mirror)*

'Boy's Own stuff, maybe, but fun.' *(Geoff Andrew, Time Out)*

BEAUTY AND THE BEAST CT: 8 AV: 9.00

(aka *La Belle et La Bête*)

1946 France 96/90/87 (US) BW FANTASY/FOREIGN

D Jean Cocteau ☆
W Jean Cocteau from Madame Leprince de Beaumont's story

Josette Day Jean Marais ☆ Mila Parléy Marcel André Nane Germon Michel Auclair

A girl (Josette Day) saves her merchant father's life by agreeing to be the prisoner of a hideous Beast (Jean Marais).

Visually imaginative, surrealistic but slow-moving fairy tale with Freudian overtones, about a young woman who is too attached to her father, but learns to love another. Although Josette Day looks mature for her role as the young innocent Beauty (she was, in fact, 32), she plays the part attractively. Jean Marais is superb as the Beast, managing to appear both fierce and vulnerable, but he is less confident as the foolish Avanant and seems incongruously effete as the prince into whom the Beast finally changes.

The film is not helped for English-speaking audiences by banal, simplistic subtitles. Cocteau's inexperience – this was only his second film as director, and his first full-length effort – shows in the more naturalistic scenes; but as the action moves to the Beast's castle, the film becomes quite magical.

ANTI:

'Less beautiful or terrifying than I had been led to expect.' *(Dilys Powell)*

'The Beast speaks French but his appearance reminded me at times of Rudyard Kipling, Lon Chaney, and an agreeable cat called Ralph that I used to own . . . There comes a time – and it comes pretty quickly – when the spectator feels an urge to creep quietly away and leave M. Cocteau gazing raptly into the mirror of his own ingenuity.' *(John McCarten, New Yorker)*

'Dull, sadistic and ponderous . . . One has the feeling that Jean Cocteau is trying to be too clever.' *(Kinematograph Weekly)*

PRO:

'Brilliantly imaginative treatment retains all the charming fantasy of original by means of finely pictorial photography, grandiose medieval settings and sumptuous costuming. Narrative possibly rather slow and outlandish . . . though beauty of photographic effects, and ingenuity and visual appeal of trick technical work are undeniable . . . Excellent direction in own stylized genre.' *(Today's Cinema)*

'A sensuously fascinating film, a fanciful poem in movement.' *(Bosley Crowther)*

'*Beauty and the Beast* requires complete submissiveness from its audience which is no easy demand to make. Yet it will be worth it, whether one's eye is drawn to the implications within the text or to the visual delights of its make-believe.' *(Stephen Belcher, NBR Magazine)*

'Jean Cocteau's direction, under daunting technical and personal conditions (he was afflicted by both eczema and jaundice during the shooting), is nothing short of marvelous. There are countless memorably staged and photographed shots: Beauty's slow-motion passage through the hall of candelabras; Beauty seeming to float, her legs immobile, down the hallway to her room; Beauty's first encounter with the Beast; the unforgettable shot of the shadow of the Beast's glove on Beauty's face; and the fireplace heads following the Merchant's every move.' *(Kenneth Von Gunden, The Great Fantasy Films)*

'A masterly creation, notable for the lack of artiness in its artistry, its recounting of the extraordinary in ordinary terms. Cocteau – painter, novelist, poet – used remarkable imagination, using a Vermeer-like approach to the everyday scenes in Beauty's home, a Gustave Doré ambiance in the dreamy surreal sequences in Beast's domain.' *(Judith Crist)*

BEAUTY AND THE BEAST AAN

CT: 10 AV: 9.08

1991 US 85 C CARTOON/MUSICAL/FAMILY

D Gary Trousdale Kirk Wise ☆
W Linda Woolverton ☆ music and lyrics by Alan Menken ☆ AAW Howard Ashman ☆.

Voices: Paige O'Hara Robby Benson Jerry Orbach Angela Lansbury Richard White David Ogden Stiers

Nice girl is kept prisoner by apparently nasty beast.

Terrific songs, funny jokes, superb animation and a touching story – cannily updated with a touch of feminism – make this a rare treat, which can be enjoyed by people of any age, and compares favourably in all departments with classic feature-length cartoons such as *Pinocchio* or *Lady and the Tramp*. I have a couple of minor quibbles: if our heroine is so bookish and intellectually superior, how come she's still only reading fairytales when she's grown up? And isn't our leading man more attractive as the Beast than he is at the end, transformed into an ultra-conventional Chippendale? But if you want to know why the enjoyable but flawed *Aladdin* became such a colossal hit in 1992/3, look no further than this, its immediate predecessor: a masterpiece.

MIXED:

'The first politically correct picture to come off the animators' drawing board.' *(Alexander Walker, Evening Standard)*

'The fable's play on the riddles of surface and depth make it the ideal vehicle for animation . . . If this is very much a film of good and bad bits, that is because of the way the armies of animators (some 600) have been marshalled . . . The music however is the film's most consistent feature, showing that [Ashman and Menken] have been studying their Sondheim.' *(Jonathan Romney, F & F)*

PRO:

'Ranks with the best of Disney's animated classics.' *(Variety)*

'It's got storytelling vigor and clarity, bright eclectic animation, and a frisky musical wit.' *(New Yorker)*

'A superior achievement, with a sexual sophistication and wit that are new to the Disney canon . . . Sullen, short-tempered and grotesque, the beast is the ultimate bad date, and audiences of all ages and genders will enjoy watching his comic struggle to turn into a gentleman . . . The film is swiftly paced and bursting with entertainment.' *(Kevin Lally, Film Journal)*

'Reaches back to an older and healthier Hollywood tradition in which the best writers, musicians and filmmakers are gathered for a project on the assumption that a family audience deserves great entertainment too.' *(Roger Ebert)*

'A lush, romantic cartoon in the grand manner, with a witty Broadway-level score and an effective combination of old-fashioned character animation and up-to-the-moment computer trickery. With a more grown-up storyline than most Disney cartoons and an unfashionable commitment to pure romance, this is a constant delight.' *(Empire)*

BECKET AAN CT: 5 AV: 7.17

1964 GB 148 C DRAMA/COSTUME

D Peter Glenville AAN
W Edward Anhalt ✔ AAW from Jean Anouilh's play

Peter O'Toole ☆ AAN Richard Burton ☆ AAN John Gielgud ☆ AAN Pamela Brown ☆ Donald Wolfit Martita Hunt Sian Phillips Paolo Stoppa

Henry II (Peter O'Toole) has problems with a turbulent Archbishop of Canterbury (Richard Burton).

There are tremendous sets and locations, great cinematography by Geoffrey Unsworth, and memorable performances not only by the two principals, but also by John Gielgud (as King Louis) and Pamela Brown (as Queen Eleanor of Aquitaine). And yet the end result is dull: the fault lies in the Oscar-winning screenplay which tends to reveal character through talk rather than action.

PRO:

'That rare thing, a spectacular of content and character, faithful to its source and a powerful and fascinating film in its own right.' *(Judith Crist)*

'A very fine, perhaps great, motion picture. It is costume drama but not routine, invigorated by story, substance, personality clash, bright dialog and religious interest.' *(Variety)*

'Magnificently acted.' *(Martin & Porter)*

ANTI:

'Handsome, respectable and boring.' *(John Simon)*

'The paucity of physical action causes good scenes to alternate with long stretches of tedium.' *(Halliwell)*

'The performances of Richard Burton and Peter O'Toole are strictly for their admirers.' *(Shipman)*

BEETHOVEN:

see ABEL GANCE'S BEETHOVEN.

BEETHOVEN'S GREAT LOVE:

see ABEL GANCE'S BEETHOVEN.

BEGUILED, THE CT: 9 AV: 6.64

1971 US 109 C WESTERN/THRILLER/HORROR

D Don Siegel ✔
W John B. Sherry Grimes Grice ✔ from Thomas Cullman's novel

Clint Eastwood ✔ Geraldine Page ✔ Elizabeth Hartman ✔ Jo Ann Harris Darleen Carr Mae Mercer

A wounded soldier (Clint Eastwood) hides out in a school full of frustrated women.

An odd, haunting, Gothic western which is one of the most stylish horror films of all time, thanks to Siegel's claustrophobic direction and Bruce Surtees's outstanding cinematography. It is an unusual – and, to some, off-putting – mixture of genres and far from being the kind of action western for which Eastwood was then renowned. In previous films, Eastwood had always played characters in control of themselves and all around them – icons of self-sufficient masculinity. It came as a shock to see him as a victim (although he was to take much the same role in two of his later films, *Play Misty For Me* and *Tightrope*). Eastwood carried off the role with impressive ease, but audiences expecting a straightforward western were disappointed and confused by a film full of dark emotions – notably revenge and sexual envy – unfamiliar in the western genre.

'I was terribly disappointed by the way *The Beguiled* was sold. I told the studio before I made it that it was a completely different kind of story, a psychological gothic horror film. Then they sold it as just another Clint Eastwood picture, me with a cheroot cigar and stubble beard, which was awfully unfair to both my regular audience and those who wanted something different. That sort of thing can kill you in this business.' *(Clint Eastwood)*

ANTI:

'A must for sadists and woman-haters . . . One of 1971's worst movies.' *(Judith Crist)*

'Doesn't come off, and cues laughter in all the wrong places.' *(Variety)*

'I was not beguiled, merely bothered and bewildered by this mawkish melodrama.' *(Virginia Dignam, Morning Star)*

'Siegel has endowed his characters with more density than depth and his plot with more perverse twists than profound turns. Perhaps the tortuousness of his subject has simply overloaded his style. Or perhaps, even more sadly, Siegel has finally made the kind of epic he always wanted to make.' *(Andrew Sarris, Village Voice)*

PRO:

'Somewhere around the middle . . . things take a very peculiar turn. Up till then it has been mainly a mood piece about war and its innocent victims, but suddenly it blooms orchid-like into a rarified piece of Southern Gothic – I am not sure that the change entirely works, but it does make for a remarkably beguiling film.' *(Tom Milne, The Times)*

'A Southern gothic horror story that is the most scarifying film since Rosemary birthed her satanic baby . . . Eastwood, working with Siegel for the third time, exudes a cool, threatening sexuality.' *(Time)*

'A tale bizarre enough for Buñuel . . . The whole thing is managed with great address, well-paced, with atmospheres and undertones vividly and economically suggested, and a balance held adroitly between horror and grand guignol scepticism.' *(Financial Times)*

'Feminists have attacked the film as being misogynistic and in Siegel's case it's probably true; but I think Eastwood was attracted to it because he believed the stupid, insensitive gigolo deserved his sorry end.' *(Danny Peary)*

BEIJO DA A MULHER ARANHA: *see* KISS OF THE SPIDER WOMAN.

BELLE DE JOUR CT: 5 AV: 8.29

1967 France/Italy 100 C DRAMA/FOREIGN

D Luis Buñuel ☆
W Luis Buñuel ✗ Jean-Claude Carrière from Joseph Kessel's novel ✗

Catherine Deneuve ☆ Michel Piccoli ☆
Françoise Fabian ☆ Francisco Rabal ●
Pierre Clémenti ● Genevieve Page ☆ Jean Sorel

A rich, sexually dissatisfied wife (Catherine Deneuve) moonlights, or rather daylights, as a prostitute.

Thanks to its eroticism, this is Buñuel's most commercially successful film. Catherine Deneuve is realistic and oddly touching as a woman frightened by her sexuality. The film has Buñuel's surreal trademarks and is generally considered a classic. But Deneuve's fantasies are poorly directed (notice, for example, the extraneous car in the background of the first shot, and the flat lighting throughout); the story descends into melodrama in the final 20 minutes; the female actors are very much better than the men; and Buñuel doesn't seem to know ultimately what he's trying to communicate. If all he's saying is that cold exteriors often hide dark passions, *Belle de Jour* is little more profound than the average novel by Jackie Collins.

'The screenplay . . . tries hard to be clever and profound, but succeeds mostly in being coy and portentous . . . Nevertheless, and almost sadly, the presence of a master is felt in the film. The rhythm of the writing, the color changes, acting tempos, camera angles, the whole editing – all this is perfect. There is not one extraneous shot, nor one that is missing. Disparate elements are embraced in a self-possessed, lucidly enchanting flow. A directorial cleverness, such as an unexpected high-angle-shot, calls no attention to itself; the whole construction is a model for student directors to learn from.' *(John Simon)*

'Oppressively powerful. Like being buried alive in Sarah Bernhardt's dressing room.' *(Wilfred Sheed)*

'Remarkably beautiful . . . Comments on our sexual fantasies and hang-ups are humorous and perceptive.' *(Scheuer)*

BELLE EPOQUE AAN CT: 4 AV: 8.00 (est)

1993 Spain 108 C COMEDY/FOREIGN

D Fernando Trueba ✗
W Rafael Azcona ✗

Fernando Fernán Gómez Jorge Sanz
Maribel Verdú Ariadna Gil Miriam Diaz-Aroca
Penélope Cruz

On the eve of the Spanish civil war, a handsome young army deserter (Jorge Sanz) takes refuge with an old artist (Fernando Fernán Gómez) and his four nubile daughters. One by one, despite having all the charisma of last week's paella, the deserter gets to bonk them all.

The film's assets are an attractive cast and some glorious scenery. Unfortunately, it suffers from an almost complete absence of jokes, or perceptive observations about its characters and historical setting. This creaky, utterly predictable sex comedy might really have been called 'Plenty of Sex, Please, I'm Spanish', and has been written by Rafael Azcona and directed by Fernando Trueba in a manner which suggests that neither has strayed inside a cinema for 30 years.

PRO:

'A big, bounteous basket of delights. A new, sun-filled film brims with the best kind of escapism: 108 minutes of free sexuality, pleasant comradeship, mature perceptions and complete tolerance. Even death, as treated here, is the result of comic eccentricity.' *(Stanley Kauffmann)*

'A very funny movie. Yes, really. For there's a little bit of Luis Buñuel nestled in the heart of every Spaniard, something at once black and farcical, and director Fernando Trueba is no exception. He also loves the sun-splashed romanticism of Jean Renoir; the film's cheerful look, its air of bemused wonder at the things people do when the time is right for frolic, is a homage to that most civilized of directors.' *(Richard Corliss, Time)*

'Celebrates sensuality and the human body. It is a reminder that sex can be kind and gentle, tender and beautiful. American films link "sex and violence" so compulsively that we can hardly imagine an attractive woman who isn't hiding an icepick behind her back.' *(Roger Ebert)*

ANTI:

'Though commendably literate, it is a by-the-numbers farce, as each of the daughters, with geometrical precision, gets involved with our wide-eyed Candide . . . The whole thing is simplistic even for farce, and unfortunately shows its origin in a number of dinner-table conversations among the director and his two scenarists, one of whom, Rafael Azcona, wrote some of the best Spanish films, including Carlos Saura's *The Garden of Delights*. *Belle Epoque* is not one of them.' *(John Simon)*

BELLE ET LA BÊTE, LA: *see* BEAUTY AND THE BEAST (1946).

BELLE NOISEUSE, LA: *see* LA BELLE NOISEUSE.

BEN-HUR AAN CT: 8 AV: 8.13
(aka *Ben Hur*)

1959 US 217 C EPIC

D William Wyler ✗ AAW action sequences by Andrew Marton ☆
W Karl Tunberg AAN assisted by S.N. Behrman Gore Vidal Christopher Fry

Charlton Heston AAW Haya Harareet Jack Hawkins Stephen Boyd Hugh Griffith AAW Sam Jaffe Martha Scott Cathy O'Donnell Finlay Currie

Charlton Heston bares his chest and his soul, as a persecuted Jew in the time of Christ.

Terminally turgid and tediously devout remake of the 1925 silent, but splendidly spectacular: worth watching for the chariot race, the sea battle and the kind of crowd scenes you don't often see any more. It swept the Oscars for its year.

'Loved Ben, hated Hur.' *(Anon)*

ANTI:

'Watching it was like waiting at a railroad crossing while an interminable freight train lumbers past, often stopping completely for a while . . . Wyler doesn't know how to handle crowds nor how to get a culminating rhythm by cutting. He tries to make up for this lack by huge sets and thousands of extras, but a Griffith can make a hundred into a crowd while a Wyler can reduce a thousand to a confused cocktail party.' *(Dwight MacDonald)*

'Seemingly endless.' *(Shipman)*

MIXED:

'A decent level of writing and a distinguished level of directing have done what can be done with the best-selling mixture of adventure story and New Testament borrowings. They can't give it an imaginative size to match its physical size. One can tolerate the second-rate if it escapes comparison with the first-rate; not when, as here, it constantly recalls the tremendous Christian myth. Beside the august simplicity of the Gospels on which it draws *Ben-Hur* dwindles to an oleograph. Nevertheless if we must have films of this kind, this is the one to have.' *(Dilys Powell)*

PRO:

'Not only is it not simple-minded, it is downright literate.' *(Saturday Review)*

'The most tasteful and visually exciting film spectacle yet produced by an American company.' *(Albert Johnson, Film Quarterly)*

'Stands as the superspectacular and most tasteful and intelligent Biblical-fiction film in Hollywood's history.' *(Judith Crist)*

BERLIN ALEXANDERPLATZ CT: 4 AV: 7.57

1980 West Germany 921/930 C EPIC/DRAMA/FOREIGN

D Rainer Werner Fassbinder ☆
W Rainer Werner Fassbinder from Alfred Doblin's novel

Gunter Lamprecht ☆ Gottfried John ☆ Barbara Sukowa ☆ Hanna Schuygulla ☆

A pimp (Guntar Lamprecht) is released from jail and takes to the Berlin streets in the late 20s.

A portrait of a city, in much the same way as James Joyce's *Ulysses* depicted Dublin. Made for German TV in 14 episodes, this is an epic in the Germanic style: it sees its characters virtually throughout as victims. Xaver Schwarzenberger's cinematography is excellent, however. It's a remake of Phil Jutzi's 1931 film, which had the not inconsiderable merit of running a mere two hours.

PRO:

'A Mt Everest of modern cinema . . . it is not at all an arcane or obscure experience . . . it surpasses just about everything that has been done in the cinema this past two decades . . . Lamprecht's Franz Biberkopf will be the measure by which all future screen acting will be judged, and Sukowa, Hanna Schygulla as Eva, and Gottfried John as Franz's nemesis Reinhold are not to be left behind. All in all, the ensemble of *Berlin Alexanderplatz* is as seamless an expression of life-giving art as has ever graced the screen.' *(Andrew Sarris, Village Voice)*

'Some marvellous performances . . . Some new faces deserve a wider audience if someone can devise a way of showing it.' *(John Gillett, Sunday Telegraph)*

'Despite its length, the film's sense of composition is

rich and the director commands our attention throughout.' *(Scheuer)*

ANTI:

'Remember the scene in *A Clockwork Orange* in which Malcolm McDowell's eyes are wired open and he is forced to watch movies? That's how we often felt when wading through the fifteen-and-a-half hours of Rainer Werner Fassbinder's magnum opus.' *(Martin & Porter)*

'I saw a couple of episodes and found them flatulent and awful.' *(Nigel Andrews, Financial Times)*

'Almost every scene goes on too long and the general feeling is of a fatal slackness which might be okay on the box but gives the impatient a hard time in the cinema.' *(Derek Malcolm, Guardian)*

'Pitched at a level of operatic caricature, full of Joycean devices and Günter Grass symbolism . . . as likely to hit home for Britons as the *Forsyte Saga* among the Eskimos.' *(Alan Brien, Sunday Times)*

BEST DEFENSE CT: 1 AV: 2.10

1984 US 94 C COMEDY

D Willard Huyck ●
W Gloria Katz Willard Huyck from Robert Grossbach's novel *Easy and Hard Ways Out* ●

Dudley Moore ● Eddie Murphy ● Kate Capshaw Michael Scalera George Dzundza

Adventures of an incompetent inventor of armaments (Dudley Moore) and the army officer who must use them in Kuwait (Eddie Murphy).

A stupid script is given squalid direction, and further undermined by two lousy central performances. An all-time low in Hollywood comedy.

'How did I get involved? The door opened, and four men came in carrying a cheque.' *(Eddie Murphy)*

'About as funny as gettting hi-jacked by a group of kamikaze terrorists.' *(Derek Malcolm, Guardian)*

'One of Dud's duds.' *(Quinlan)*

'Hideously unfunny . . . You think they've both [Eddie Murphy and Dudley Moore] made some dogs before. This is practically rabid.' *(Rose)*

'The best defence is simply not to watch.' *(Winnert)*

BEST INTENTIONS, THE CT: 5 AV: 7.17

(aka *Den Goda Viljan*)

1992 Sweden 180 C DRAMA/ROMANCE/FOREIGN

D Bille August ✗
W Ingmar Bergman ✗

Samuel Fröler Pernilla August ☆ Max Von Sydow ☆ Ghita Norby Lennart Hjulström Mona Malm

Written by Ingmar Bergman, the film fictionalizes the love affair and early marriage of his parents.

The wonder is that the warring couple ever stayed together long enough to have little Ingmar – and no wonder the child grew up depressed. Elegantly but statically directed by Bille August (whose *Pelle the Conqueror* was much more impressive), the film has Bergmanesque moments of beauty and well-acted scenes of raw emotion. But it is formless, bleak and emptily portentous, with many prophecies of doom by both grandparents which never come to anything. The plot is too thin to sustain three hours, and its pace and sense of direction are those of a snail in a Swedish snowstorm. Skilfully though Pernilla August plays Bergman's mother, it is hard to see what attracts her to his diffident, guilt-ridden father (Samuel Fröler), who aroused little emotion in me except antipathy and boredom. Originally a six-hour mini-series for Swedish TV, it won the Palme d'Or and Best Actress award at Cannes.

'The film is uniformly well acted, has a wonderful feeling for the distinct Scandinavian seasons, and re-creates social occasions with an acute moral edge.' *(Philip French, Observer)*

'Ingmar Bergman may have officially retired from film direction, but his genius marches on.' *(Geoff Brown, The Times)*

'Wonderful . . . The detail, both emotional and physical, reaches a rare depth.' *(Winnert)*

'With a running time of three hours, this weighty drama tests the most patient soul.' *(Colette Maude, Time Out)*

BEST MAN, THE CT: 7 AV: 7.33

1964 US 102 BW DRAMA/POLITICAL

D Franklin Schaffner ☆
W Gore Vidal ☆ from his own play

Henry Fonda ☆ Cliff Robertson ✔ Lee Tracy ☆ AAN Margaret Leighton Edie Adams Shelley Berman ☆ Kevin McCarthy Ann Sothern Mahalia Jackson

Two US presidential candidates (Henry Fonda, Cliff Robertson) try to gain support of dying president (Lee Tracy).

Brilliantly detailed, darkly humorous study of a fictitious American Presidential campaign, with Gore Vidal contributing an enjoyably cynical screenplay. The most underrated performance is by Cliff Robertson, who plays an eerie Nixon figure. Haskell Wexler's black-and-white photography has the look of documentary.

'Although not an especially fresh or profound piece of work, it is certainly a worthwhile, lucid and entertaining dramatization of a behind-the-scenes power struggle.' *(Variety)*

'Some of the wittiest lines since *Strangelove* . . . the acting fairly crackled with authenticity.' *(Isabel Quigly)*

'You are left gasping at its sheer professionalism.' *(Evening News)*

'Stands out as a caustic commentary on the facts of our political life, a film bristling with topicality and saved from cynicism by its integrity, for it pretends to be neither a panacea nor a speech-ridden preachment – simply a picture of practical politics.' *(Judith Crist)*

BEST YEARS OF OUR LIVES, THE AAW

CT: 6 AV: 8.75

1946 US 172 BW DRAMA/WAR

D William Wyler ☆ AAW
W Robert Sherwood ☆ AAW from Mackinlay Kantor's novel *Glory For Me*

Fredric March ☆ AAW Myrna Loy Teresa Wright Dana Andrews Virginia Mayo Cathy O'Donnell Hoagy Carmichael ☆ Harold Russell ☆ AAW Gladys George Roman Bohnen Ray Collins

Three servicemen return home after World War II.

Liberal and sincere movie, typical of the kind which sweeps the Oscars (it won seven) but looks pretty dated and manipulative in future years, when time has taken away its social relevance. It's still a very polished piece of film-making, with great cinematography by Gregg Toland (also responsible for *The Grapes of Wrath* and *Citizen Kane*).

ANTI:

'Strains too earnestly to be a cross-section of average existence . . . Wyler's direction and Sherwood's script are so cunning, one almost feels embarrassed . . . But the film lacks shape . . . Above all it commits the indefensible crime of running for nearly three hours. No piece of entertainment, however intelligent or thrilling or beautiful can justify so Wagnerian a length.' *(Tribune)*

MIXED:

'William Wyler has left nothing to the imagination . . . The direction is admirable and the acting restrained and intelligent, at times brilliant. Yet for all this, the film left me strangely unmoved.' *(Elizabeth Frank, News Chronicle)*

'Not a great picture; it's too schematic, and it drags on after you've got the points. However, episodes and details stand out and help to compensate for the soggy plot strands, and there's something absorbing about the banality of its large-scale good intentions; it's compulsively watchable.' *(Pauline Kael)*

'Perhaps the finest representation of Wyler's consummate, if impersonal, craftsmanship.' *(Allan Hunter & Kenny Mathieson, Movie Classics, 1992)*

'The business of the amputee is very moving but the rest is fake liberalism.' *(Shipman)*

PRO:

'A drama of our lives and times, produced, written, directed, and acted by men and women who wish us well. It is no olive branch or Christmas wreath they hold out to us. It is a hard-hitting challenge to think through our problems and do justice to our ideals. And not to fail our fallen.' *(Richard Griffith, NBR)*

'Easily the best film from Hollywood on the warrior's return.' *(Sunday Graphic)*

'One of the best pictures of our lives.' *(Variety)*

'Aesthetically and in its emotional feeling for people and their surroundings, Toland's work in this film makes me think of the photographs of Walker Evans.' *(James Agee)*

'This is a picture that no Englishman could have made, or would have made if he could. In its sentiment, its code of accepted behaviour, and its attitude toward a job of work done, it is wholly foreign to our temperament. It would be the greatest mistake to judge this clever and beautifully acted film by our own standards of decorum.' *(C.A. Lejeune, Observer)*

'The situations and even some of the characters now seem a little obvious but this was a superb example of high-quality film-making in the forties, with smiles and tears cunningly spaced, and a film which said what was needed on a vital subject.' *(Halliwell)*

BETWEEN US: *see* COUP DE FOUDRE.

BEVERLY HILLS COP

CT: 5 AV: 6.60

1984 US 105 C THRILLER/COMEDY

D Martin Brest ✔
W Daniel Petrie Jr ✗ AAN

Eddie Murphy ☆ Judge Reinhold ✔ John Ashton Lisa Eilbacher Ronny Cox Steven Berkoff James Russo Bronson Pichot ✔

Black cop from Detroit (Eddie Murphy) meets resentment from local police force when he hunts killers of murdered buddy in California.

Though the plot was far from original or inspired, and the language is relentlessly foul, this slick blend of comedy and thriller made a mega-star of Murphy, who successfully built upon his following from *48 HRS* (1982) and *Trading Places* (1983). The script had originally been designed as a vehicle for Sylvester Stallone. There were two inferior sequels.

MIXED:

'The film's only function is to provide Murphy with the opportunity to work a dozen or so variations on his familiar and oddly endearing routine.' *(Time)*

'Although Murphy is good, there's a nagging feeling that it should all be much funnier and sharper. Almost spoiled by the silly ending which has a couple of handguns that never run out of bullets triumphing over automatic weapons.' *(Rose)*

PRO:

'Dirtier and hotter than Harry, Eddie Murphy is also the funniest screen cop since the Keystones . . . Even when the plot misfires, Murphy comes out shooting from the funny bone – and it's bull's eyes all the way.' *(People)*

'*Beverly Hills Cop* fits the cool, fresh-mouthed, jiveass hipness of Murphy's screen persona like a crash helmet.' *(Rex Reed, New York Post)*

'This lickety-spit action comedy is distinguished by the wry, character-conscious direction of Martin Brest, who coaxes a silver-bullet performance from star Eddie Murphy that's practically criminal in it's accuracy.' *(Hollywood Reporter)*

BEYOND THE FOREST

CT: 5 AV: 3.80

1949 US 96 BW THRILLER/SO BAD

D King Vidor ●
W Lenore Coffee ● from Stuart Engstrand's novel

Bette Davis ● Joseph Cotten David Brian Ruth Roman Minor Watson Dona Drake Regis Toomey

Man-mad small-town wife (Bette Davis) plans to leave hubby (Joseph Cotten) for Chicago millionaire (David Brian).

This is the flop which finally caused Bette Davis to part company with Warner Brothers. Watch it, and you'll see why: the script is beyond the pale, and a forest of clichés, with Davis being forced to play a caricature of her former roles – which she does with manic intensity.

PRO:

'Gives Bette Davis a chance to portray the neurotic femme she does so well . . . King Vidor seldom falters in his direction.' *(Variety)*

'Essentially the screenplay is a monologue for the star.' *(Hollywood Reporter)*

'Bette Davis gives her usual competent performance.' *(Today's Cinema)*

ANTI:

'The dialogue . . . may not be the worst you ever heard, since much of it rises to the level of humdrum, but some of the lines delivered by Miss Davis are as eerie as any that have come out of Hollywood in years.' *(John McCarten, New Yorker)*

'Clearly NOT one of Miss Davis's best roles. She permits herself to indulge in a performance of leers, grimaces and body contortions which make the intent clear but the professional judgement behind them cloudy.' *(Motion Picture Herald)*

'Bette Davis (looks) like a Charles Addams cartoon of herself.' *(Gavin Lambert, MFB)*

'Consistently (though inadvertently) hilarious; there's not a single dull scene in this peerless piece of camp.' *(Pauline Kael, 1978)*

'Riotously miscast as trashy mantrap Rosa Moline, a milltown Emma Bovary, Davis runs rampant, tweezing her eyebrows, toying with her Morticia Addams wig, undulating her hips and breasts, shotgunning porcupines ("I don't like 'em," she snarls), and spitting out what would become her signature phrase, "What a dump!" . . . leaving no co-star or piece of scenery unchewed.' *(Margulies & Rebello)*

'A terrible movie.' *(Bette Davis)*

BEYOND THE VALLEY OF THE DOLLS

CT: 5 AV: 3.88

1970 US 109 C DRAMA/COMEDY/SO BAD

D Russ Meyer
W Roger Ebert

Dolly Read Cynthia Myers Marcia McBroom John La Zar Michael Blodgett Edy Williams

Female rock band hits high spots in LA, then goes to the bad.

Reasonably enjoyable spoof of soap opera, the world of Jacqueline Susann and exploitation films in general. Film critic Roger Ebert wrote the screenplay, which is lumbering, obvious and (by modern standards) tame. It's hard to work out just how much of the movie's badness is intentional.

ANTI:

'The plot defies both credibility and synopsis.' *(Mark Goodman, Time)*

'Two hours or so of flagrant titillation.' *(Araminta Wadworth, Times Educational Supplement)*

'The film, awful, stupid and preposterous as it is, is also weirdly funny and a real curio, rather like a Grandma Moses illustration for a work by the Marquis de Sade . . . Accuse it of vicious affectlessness, and its makers will plead, "Just good campy fun." Accuse it of sick jokes that stick in the craw, and the makers will declare condescendingly, "The laughter is meant to turn into shivers, that's what makes you aware of the underlying moral purpose." In other words, you can have it any way; something for everyone – campy intellectual, long-faced moralizer, or swinging voyeur. Clever, but not so clever as it is swinish.' *(John Simon)*

'Ebert's script is smug and vulgar, and full of violence-against-females scenes (which Meyer films seriously) of the type he has crusaded against as a critic.' *(Danny Peary)*

MIXED:

'Any movie that Jacqueline Susann thinks would damage her reputation as a writer cannot be all bad. [The film] isn't – which is not to say it is any good. It is to say that on the scale that measures the comparative values of incomparable things, for example termites vs tides, *Beyond the Valley* comes off with a lightly higher rating than [the original] novel and the movie that Mark Robson distilled from it, making tap water out of tap water, as it were.' (*Vincent Canby, New York Times*)

'A film whose total, idiotic monstrous badness raises it to the pitch of near-risible entertainment . . . the kind of movie that a maladroit Mack Sennett might have made if he had worked in a sex shop, not a fun factory.' (*Alexander Walker, Evening Standard*)

'An hilarious, bangabout farce which only a Neanderthal child could respond to with any seriousness . . . I hope Russ Meyer becomes a cult figure; he deserves a fate like that.' (*Christopher Hudson, Spectator*)

BICHES, LES: *see* LES BICHES.

BICYCLE THIEF: *see* BICYCLE THIEVES, THE.

BICYCLE THIEVES, THE AAW CT: 9 AV: 9.67

(aka *Bicycle Thief; Ladri di Biciclette*)

1949 Italy 90 BW DRAMA/FOREIGN

D Vittorio de Sica ☆
W Cesare Zavatini ☆ AAN

Lamberto Maggiorani ☆ Enzo Staiola ☆

Unemployed worker (Lamberto Maggiorani) and his small son (Enzo Staiola) search Rome for stolen bicycle.

Apparently naturalistic, but actually very tightly plotted drama, with much telling social criticism along the way. Wonderfully acted by non-professionals, and a landmark in realist cinema.

'My idea is to de-romanticize the cinema.' (*Vittorio de Sica*)

MIXED:

'Just misses being a masterpiece. Its tale is formless and ends inconclusively in mid-air . . . de Sica has managed to impart to the somewhat disjointed film a stature and significance far greater than the bare outline of its theme . . . There are moments that are almost unbearable painful; others in which interest is maintained, but largely drained by obvious picturemaking tricks and self-conscious artistry.' (*Cue*)

'Though a little long-winded, the picture must be seen.' (*Sunday Chronicle*)

PRO:

'A nice mixture of humour and pathos and there are many moments one will recall fondly and with a chuckle.' (*Sunday Dispatch*)

'Doing something which the cinema alone can do: describing for us the actions and the sufferings of the individual against the huge, indifferent movement of life. Its pity is touched with irony, but not with bitterness; and for once I can beg you not to miss a film which observes the human creature with nothing but sympathy, forgiveness and love.' (*Dilys Powell*)

'De Sica has taken an incident in the life of a poor workman, stripped it of all but the barest essentials, and told it with an unerring instinct for character, a sure eye for telling detail and a sympathy untouched by patronage or cheap sentimentality.' (*Campbell Dixon*)

'It takes its place among the great films of the present Italian renaissance. It is informed with an innate tenderness, an implicit irony of observation, that transforms its episodes into an entity, a study of humanity, a work of art.' (*Matthew Norgate*)

'Among the great films of all time. Few films have matched it for its integrity, its profound humanism, its social comment on employment and unemployment, its portrayal of simple human relationships, its use of non-actors, its wholly successful interpretation of real life on the screen with a minimum of contrivance and great subtle technical skill.' (*Paul Rotha & Richard Griffith, The Film Till Now, 1949*)

'Vittorio de Sica's neorealist masterpiece, about an impoverished young Roman's search for his stolen bicycle – an odyssey through the city's lower depths which becomes (without a trace of contrivance) the pursuit of a lost sense of manhood, one's soul – and, by extension, a defeated nation's quest for self-respect and self-reliance. One of the movies that shatters you, if you see it at a young, idealistic age.' (*Michael Wilmington*)

BIG CT: 8 AV: 7.07

1988 US 102 C COMEDY/FANTASY/ROMANCE

D Penny Marshall ☆
W Gary Ross Anne Spielberg ☆ AAN

Tom Hanks ☆ AAN Elizabeth Perkins ✔ John Heard Jared Rushton Robert Loggia ✔ David Moscow Mercedes Ruehl

13-year-old boy wishes he were big – and turns into a boy inside a man's body (Tom Hanks).

A number of 80s movies mysteriously seized upon the same theme: *Like Father Like Son* (1987), *18 Again* (1988), and *Vice Versa* (1988). This is easily the most entertaining of the bunch. Tom Hanks exploits his overgrown schoolboy appeal, and gives perhaps his most charming performance, with admirable support from Elizabeth Perkins as the career-woman attracted to him, and Robert Loggia as his boss. Director Penny Marshall turns in another thoroughly professional directorial job.

MIXED:

'A formula fantasy fim . . . Everything has a tepid inevitability, and even as you smile you may be groaning inwardly.' (*Pauline Kael*)

'Makes for an ending oozing with saccharine

sentiment, but until then Marshall, Hanks and his co-stars seldom put a foot wrong.' *(Geoff Andrew, Time Out)*

PRO:

'Unspools with enjoyable genuineness and ingenuity.' *(Variety)*

'One of the most delightful comedies in recent memory . . . Hanks, whose talents have rarely seemed more than modest, does an absolutely extraordinary job of convincing one that he is a boy in a man's body. His performance is at once tender and hilarious, full of perfect small touches (eg the tentative way he peeks into his underpants after looking in the bathroom mirror and seeing a grown-up); at every turn, the awkwardness, exuberance, and innocence of this boy-man feel exactly on target, never overdone or sentimentalized.' *(Bruce Bawer, American Spectator)*

'Charming fantasy tackles a rare modern-day subject – innocence – and pulls it off.' *(Maltin)*

BIG BUS, THE CT: 6 AV: 5.10

1976 US 88 C COMEDY

D James Frawley
W Fred Freeman Lawrence J. Cohen ✔

Joseph Bologna ✔ Stockard Channing ✔ John Beck René Auberjonois Ned Beatty Bob Dishy Jose Ferrer Ruth Gordon Larry Hagman Sally Kellerman Richard Mulligan Lynn Redgrave Murphy Dunne ☆

Various disasters befall a new high-speed bus.

This fast-moving parody of disaster movie clichés is very hit-and-miss (the script is a lot more inventive than the direction) but if you're in the mood it has moments of high comic lunacy. Joseph Bologna is amusing as the bus-driver, and Stockard Channing delightful as his bemused girlfriend; but the film is stolen by Murphy Dunne, as the cocktail pianist from Hell. Well worth catching, especially if you liked *Airplane!* and the *Naked Gun* movies.

ANTI:

'So self-conscious that it misses the comic mark.' *(Scheuer)*

'Film doesn't sustain its promising idea.' *(Maltin)*

'Rather feeble . . . with some good moments.' *(Halliwell)*

MIXED:

'For the first few minutes [it] gives every forced sign of being one more gag-stuffed, landbound contraption. Then . . . for three-quarters of an hour it is sparingly, achingly funny. Then it settles back down . . . and bumps along more or less predictably. But the glow of startled gratitude lasts for quite a while.' *(Richard Eder, New York Times)*

PRO:

'"You will how it is! Everything seems to be plain sailing. Then suddenly, out of the blue, disaster . . . We were the sort of homely ordinary passengers you'd meet on any journey: a nymphomaniac dress designer, a priest who has lost his faith, a poor soul who has only six months to live . . . Like I said: just folks. The driver was a charming young man . . . [who'd] once been accused of eating his passengers . . . Little did we all know that the master criminal had planted a bomb on the bus . . . It was a trip I'll always remember." And just by the way [the film] is the funniest spoof of disaster movies imaginable . . . Take my tip: queue up for the next ride.' *(Margaret Hinxman)*

'Not easy to ridicule the ridiculous so it is greatly to the credit of Jim Frawley's film that it brings off the awkward feat of making fun of a disaster film . . . It owes much to an exuberance and irreverence that rather recalls, without actually imitating, the farces of Mel Brooks, quite the best man for burlesque.' *(Patrick Gibbs, Daily Telegraph)*

'Nearly as funny as *Airplane!*' *(Winnert)*

'Infinitely funnier than *Airplane!*' *(Shipman)*

BIG CARNIVAL, THE: *see* ACE IN THE HOLE.

BIG CHILL, THE AAN CT: 7 AV: 6.87

1983 US 105 C DRAMA/COMEDY/ROMANCE

D Lawrence Kasdan ☆
W Barbara Benedek Lawrence Kasdan ☆ AAN

Tom Berenger ☆ Glenn Close ☆ AAN Jeff Goldblum ☆ William Hurt ☆ Kevin Kline ☆ Mary Kay Place Meg Tilly JoBeth Williams Don Galloway

Friends gather together after the death of a friend they knew at college.

This is a film which I used to think was great, mainly because it was about my own generation; on re-seeing, it becomes more and more inconsequential, superficial and unwilling to challenge the central complacency of its characters. It's still enjoyable, though, because of its gentle, ironic humour and an inspired cast. Widely castigated as a rip-off of John Sayles's *Return of the Secaucus Seven* (1980), it has a different, more yuppie tone: it's recognizably a forerunner of *Thirtysomething*, with most of that TV series' strengths and weaknesses.

Kevin Costner played the dead best friend, but his scenes (played in flashback) were cut from the film: the only shots that remain of him are the close-ups of him being dressed for the funeral, over the main titles. Kasdan made up for Costner's disappointment by casting him in *Silverado*.

'No mystery unfolds. The film is as disappointing as being alive . . . *The Big Chill* is an almost-perfect television play, it is very thoughtful but very slight. Without embarrassment, we can watch it with a cup of tea and a piece of toast beside us, while we file out toenails just as we do when listening to the depressing confidences of our friends . . . [The film] chooses to regard the sixties wistfully as a time of spiritual hope in which the young would suddenly bring peace to all mankind, when in fact they were all tottering about some campus or other weak with debauchery and senseless with drugs.' *(Quentin Crisp, Christopher Street)*

'Essentially an empty orgy of generational self-love and self-congratulation. There was little moral exploration in *The Big Chill*, little attempt to find meaning in the characters' metamorphoses from young rebels into upstanding citizens in their thirties . . . This shallow picture struck as forceful a note with baby boomers as *Easy Rider* had done fourteen years earlier; and if the earlier movie had seemed to reflect a romantic conceit that baby boomers were the first generation ever to go through puberty and have sex, so *The Big Chill* likewise seemed to reflect an equally romantic conceit that they were the first generation ever to settle down with marriages, houses, careers, and children of their own.' *(Bruce Bawer, American Spectator)*

'There's no pay-off and it doesn't lead anywhere.' *(Roger Ebert)*

'The picture offers the pleasures of the synthetic. It's overcontrolled, it's shallow, it's a series of contrivances. And whenever Kasdan tries for depth, the result is phony. But a lot of the time he manages to turn phoniness into wisecracking fun.' *(Pauline Kael)*

'The final impression is of a collage of small relishable moments.' *(Kim Newman)*

BIG DEAL ON MADONNA STREET, THE AAN

CT: 6 AV: 7.29

(aka *Persons Unknown; I Soliti Ignoti; The Usual Unidentified Thieves*)

1958 Italy 91 BW COMEDY/THRILLER/FOREIGN

D Mario Monicelli ✔
W Age Scarpelli Suso Cecchi d'Amico Mario Monicelli

Vittorio Gassman Renato Salvatori Rossana Rory Carla Gravina Claudia Cardinale Carlo Pisacane Tiberio Murgia Memmo Carotenuto Marcello Mastroianni

Incompetent crooks try to rob a pawn shop.

Deliberately ludicrous parody of *Rififi* and other heist thrillers. Despite a slow start and a half-hearted attempt to insert love interest, it was a hit in Italy and America thanks to a host of fine sight gags. It may be a one-joke picture, but the joke is explored to the full. Remade by Louis Malle, with a San Francisco setting, as *Crackers* (1984).

'The great coup is a hilarious take-off in which the pace and comic invention never falter. But the film takes too long getting there . . . Monicelli's otherwise crisp direction allows much of the romantic by-play to slow the action down. The performances, however, are masterly.' *(MFB)*

'A comic masterpiece, the funniest film . . . in many years . . . Every apparent climax is brilliantly topped by another.' *(Derek Hill, Tribune)*

'This delightful comedy of errors . . . is no less funny for being firmly rooted in social conditions of deprivation.' *(Bergan & Karney)*

'Film buffs think this among the funniest films ever made, and they're dead right.' *(Scheuer)*

BIG EASY, THE

CT: 7 AV: 7.07

1987 US 106 C THRILLER/ROMANCE/POLICE

D Jim McBride ✔
W Daniel Petrie Jr Jack Baran

Dennis Quaid ☆ Ellen Barkin ☆ Ned Beatty ✔ John Goodman ✔ Lisa Jane Persky Ebbe Roe Smith Charles Ludlam Jim Garrison

An assistant DA (Ellen Barkin) investigates corrupt cops in New Orleans and falls for one (Dennis Quaid).

Sexy and quirky, with some scenes good enough to evoke memories of previous sparring partners like Hepburn and Tracy, or Hepburn and Bogart in *The African Queen*. The two leading actors deserved a rather wittier script, and the plot is that of a pretty routine crime thriller; but director McBride compensates with plenty of local colour, and there are enjoyable supporting characters. Uneven, but well worth seeing.

ANTI:

'Hardly provides a realistic view of New Orleans, of the judicial system, or (I suspect) of the real nature of institutional corruption. When Remy gives his heartfelt climactic speech about the way corruption, er, corrupts, it seems more forced than forceful; certainly it is nowhere near as dramatically powerful a moment as the makers of this film seem to think it is.' *(Bruce Bawer, American Spectator)*

'Has an amateurish, B-movie droopiness.' *(Pauline Kael)*

MIXED:

'The copious literature that, as is customary before screenings, was handed to us by Columbia Pictures informed us that the film was made with the cooperation of the New Orleans police department. If this is true, then all its members are madmen as well as rogues. Every officer in sight, including Mr Quaid, is an extortionist and some are murderers, but more unsettling than any one instance of corruption over which we are allowed to gloat is the all-pervading contempt in which all policemen hold all civilians. It is this quality that makes *The Big Easy* so fascinating.' *(Quentin Crisp, Christopher Street)*

'The cooks did the best they could with ingredients that tasted good but were a little tough to chew.' *(Daily Variety)*

'Until conventional plot contrivances begin to spoil the fun, *The Big Easy* is a snappy, sassy battle of the sexes.' *(Variety)*

PRO:

'Barrels along with enough action, enough dizzy personalities and enough good humor that you sometimes forget it's often very predictable . . . Quaid is terrific, both tough and breezy. It's a wonderfully spicy comic performance.' *(Duane Byrge, Hollywood Reporter)*

'McBride deserves some credit for making a thriller that's more than a collection of sadistic poses (like most contemporary thrillers) and actually holds that there are legitimate concerns about personal honesty and integrity.' *(Henry Sheehan, LA Reader)*

BIG HEART, THE: *see* MIRACLE ON 34TH STREET.

BIG HEAT, THE   CT: 6 AV: 7.08

1953 US 90 BW THRILLER

D Fritz Lang ☆
W Sydney Boehm from William P. McGivern's novel

Glenn Ford ☆ Lee Marvin ☆ Gloria Grahame ☆ Alexander Scourby Jocelyn Brando

Cop (Glenn Ford) uses gangster's moll (Gloria Grahame) to crack a crime ring controlling a small American town.

Fritz Lang's highly efficient thriller was, at the time, the last word in cinematic violence. Now, it seems restrained – although the coffee-throwing scene still shocks. Lang shows his mastery of film noir technique, but the most memorable aspect is the acting. Glenn Ford is the determined cop, Lee Marvin the sadistic baddie, Gloria Grahame the definitive femme fatale who gets stranded in between.

ANTI:

'The main impression is of violence employed arbitrarily, mechanically and in the long run pointlessly.' *(Penelope Houston)*

PRO:

'Exciting, made with cold, savage skill, played for all it is worth.' *(Dilys Powell)*

'Lang's direction builds taut suspense, throwing unexpected, and believable, thrills at the audience.' *(Variety)*

'No matter about the implications of shady cops and political goons . . . the only concern of the film-makers is a tense and eventful crime show, and this they deliver in a fashion that keeps you tingling like a frequently struck gong.' *(Oscar Godbout, New York Times)*

'Lang made the film a classic of its kind through his strikingly unique style, so well suited to the night-world he took as his subject, and an ability to let us share the hero's gradual realization that under the surface of respectable American life, unfathomable corruption could lurk.' *(Douglas Brode, The Films of the Fifties, 1976)*

'The movie is all of a piece; it's designed in light and shadows, and its underworld atmosphere glistens with the possibilities of sadism – this is a definitive film noir.' *(Pauline Kael)*

BIG PARADE, THE   CT: 8 AV: 9.14

1925 US 115/128/150 BW (colour sequences)
WAR/ROMANCE/SILENT

D King Vidor ☆
W Laurence Stallings Harry Behn

John Gilbert Renée Adorée Hobart Bosworth Karl Dane George K. Arthur

A rich young man joins the army in World War I, is badly wounded but finds love.

The most commercially successful of all silents. Innovative and spectacular in its time, and realistically grim when depicting warfare; but to modern eyes there's too much sentimentality and melodrama in the acting and script.

PRO:

'It renews faith in the cinema form and creates an enthusiasm for its destiny. *The Big Parade* is a cinegraphically visualized result of a cinegraphically imagined thing, not a book in pictures or the picture of a book: the story and the picture are one and the same thing.' *(NBR, 1925)*

'Because it depicts death, mutilation, and separation in wartime, *The Big Parade* was advertised as an antiwar film. It is not; at least not in the manner in which later films would attack war as an institution. Jim loses a leg in the war, but he also finds a lover and himself in the process. The theme of the film is maturation through conflict and testing, with war representing the ultimate test. War is horrible, but inevitable, and the men who survive it fulfill the rites of passage.' *(Don K. Thompson, Magill's Survey of Cinema, Silent Films, 1982)*

MIXED:

'A romantic depiction of America's part in the World War . . . a superficial, if impressively executed, production.' *(Lewis Jacobs, 1939)*

'Does not wear well: the first half is heavily sentimental, showing the enlisting of sympathy of the American people for war; the second half, staged on the Western Front, lacks the intensity of feeling that inspired Milestone's *All Quiet on the Western Front*. This remains an impressive spectacle to which Vidor brought little save his showman's skill.' *(Charles Higham, Film Heritage, 1966)*

BIG PICTURE, THE

CT: 7 AV: 5.80

1989 US 100 C COMEDY

D Christopher Guest ✔

W Michael Varhol Christopher Guest Michael McKean ✔

Kevin Bacon ✔ Emily Longstreth J.T. Walsh ✔ Jennifer Jason Leigh ✔ Michael McKean Martin Short ✔ Kim Miyori Teri Hatcher

A nice but not terribly talented film student (Kevin Bacon) is discovered, corrupted and ditched by Hollywood, whereupon he learns not to compromise his ideals or betray his friends.

This was never going to reach a mass audience, as the anti-hero was not the kind of guy you could root for; but Christopher Guest's underrated comedy satirizes Hollywood with the same panache that his previous script for *This Is Spinal Tap* pilloried rock bands. Delights include the witty set designs; J.T. Walsh, playing a studio executive so untalented that he can actually destroy the talent of others with arbitrary and asinine suggestions; and Martin Short, richly comic as Bacon's flamboyantly insincere agent. In a tongue-in-cheek concession to Hollywood, Guest supplies his hero with a happy ending, but smartly ensures that the nepotism, malevolence and megalomania of other characters are even better rewarded.

MIXED:

'You keep rooting for this Hollywood sendup to make it, even as the bad ideas start gaining on the good . . . When Short is onscreen, a movie that provides only fitful laughter bubbles over into bliss.' *(Peter Travers, Rolling Stone)*

'The film's strengths are its comic vignettes . . . Less convincing however is the message that the way to success for aspirant directors is to stick to their principles.' *(Hugo Davenport, Daily Telegraph)*

'Has enough jaundiced sideswipes and lighter chuckles to see it through its slacker spells. Even so, an increasing sense of bittiness creeps in.' *(Nigel Floyd, Time Out)*

PRO:

'Jennifer Jason Leigh steals the picture as a film-school graduate who's now into "ham radio performance art". Dressed in black, her feet in out-size sneakers, her body in perpetual motion as if she couldn't express herself fast enough verbally, Leigh gives a performance that suggests pixies are dancing in her brain.' *(John Harkness, Film Yearbook)*

'A wonderfully funny film, universally well played . . . [It] manages to combine home truths, great warmth and superb characterisation.' *(Sue Heal, Today)*

BIG RED ONE, THE

CT: 6 AV: 7.08

1980 US 111 C WAR

D Samuel Fuller ☆

W Samuel Fuller ☆

Lee Marvin ☆ Mark Hamill Robert Carradine Bobby DiCicco Kelly Ward Stéphane Audran Serge Marquand

Five infantryman learn to survive during World War II.

There is nothing terribly original in the 'war is hell' approach to the subject matter. Still, this is one of the most realistic of all war films, and obviously a labour of love, as veteran writer-director Fuller tells the story of his own military unit (with Robert Carradine playing his alter ego). Marvin's performance, in particular, lingers in the memory.

ANTI:

'A film that comes close to being imbecile . . . Offensive propaganda – not so much for a vulgar brand of America *uber alles* as for a kind of hack Hollywood filmmaking apparently unaware that an armistice has been declared.' *(John Simon)*

MIXED:

'Like all Fuller movies, about an inch from cliché all the way.' *(Guardian)*

PRO:

'A terrific war yarn, a picture of palpable raw power which manages both intense intimacy and great scope at the same time.' *(Variety)*

'Cinema has changed since Fuller's heyday, and he has remained much the same: wild and obsessive, striving for clarity at the expense of subtlety . . . Fuller has more to say than many of today's filmmakers, but he has no interest in obscuring his ideas with new cinematic techniques; consequently, there are moments in *The Big Red One* that may seem awkward and simpleminded for a "modern" film.' *(Howard H. Prouty, Magill's American Film Guide, 1983)*

'Profoundly comprehends the effects war has on men.' *(Scheuer)*

BIG SLEEP, THE

CT: 9 AV: 9.38

1946 US 114 BW THRILLER

D Howard Hawks ☆

W William Faulkner Leigh Brackett Jules Furthman from Raymond Chandler's novel ☆

Humphrey Bogart ☆ Lauren Bacall ☆ John Ridgely Martha Vickers Dorothy Malone Regis Toomey Charles Waldron Charles D. Brown Elisha Cook Jr Louis Jean Heydt Bob Steele Peggy Knudsen Sonia Darrin

Private eye Philip Marlowe (Humphrey Bogart) is hired to protect one daughter (Martha Vickers) and falls for the other one (Lauren Bacall).

Howard Hawks's marvellous film of Raymond Chandler's classic thriller. Some contemporary critics complained of excessive violence; but most agreed with posterity that Bogart is at his best. American Puritanism meant that some of the novel's explicit decadence was deleted, but there are enough hints for the audience to supply the missing information. Famously, the plot is so complex that not even the writers knew why the chauffeur was killed, or who did it; but frankly, with a script this witty and full of suspense, does it matter? Remarkably, the film did not receive even one Oscar nomination.

ANTI:

'A Bogart beanfeast – or perhaps bloodbath is a more appropriate term.' *(Kine Weekly)*

'The cat's cradle of a plot is, of course, ridiculous.' *(Tribune)*

PRO:

'There is not a single person in the film to whom any reasonable sympathy could be extended in any circumstances by any normal person, and I have to admit that I enjoyed every minute of it.' *(Spectator)*

'A violent, smoky cocktail shaken together from most of the printable misdemeanors and some that aren't . . . The picture is often brutal and sometimes sinister . . . but I can't bring myself to mind this sort of viciousness, far less to feel that it shouldn't be shown.' *(James Agee, Nation)*

'Rumors around Hollywood had it that *The Big Sleep* needed a lot of patching via retakes and cutting, but it comes off as first-rate melodrama. After a rather slow-paced and talky start, the film builds up tension as the stack of corpses grows higher, and ends with a big wallop.' *(Daily Variety)*

'Screen mystifiers mystify me completely, even after they are supposedly solved in the climactic sequences, so don't expect a detailed account of the hectic goings-on from this page. However, it is possible to report that the occurrences are rapid and frenetic; that there is the standard and capable delineation of a shamus from Humphrey Bogart – and that this time Baby Bacall's projection of a torrid slacks damsel is intriguing.' *(Herb Sterne)*

'A bullet-riddled thriller in the *Laura* class.' *(Sunday Express)*

'Wit, excitement and glamour in generous doses.' *(Francis Wyndham)*

'The plot of the film is a model of the thriller equation, with three unknowns (the blackmailer, the murderer, the avenger), so simple and so subtle that at first all is beyond comprehension; in fact, on a second viewing there is nothing easier than the unravelling of this film.' *(Claude Chabrol, Cahiers du Cinéma, 1955)*

'A near-masterpiece . . . The plot is impossible to follow.' *(Scheuer)*

'The only filmed Chandler to achieve the pace, toughness and elegance of his books. Bogart and Bacall play with a silky smoothness of technique and an underlying tension that give their scenes together the tingle and sparkle of an electric current. The film offers wit, excitement and glamour in generous doses.' *(NFT Bulletin, 1984)*

BILL & TED'S EXCELLENT ADVENTURE

CT: 6 AV: 4.73

1988 US 89 C SF/COMEDY

D Stephen Herek
W Chris Matheson Edward Solomon

Keanu Reeves ✔ Alex Winter ✔ George Carlin Terry Camilleri Dan Shor Tony Steedman Clifford David Al Leong Jane Wiedlin

Two gormless Californian 15-year-olds (Keanu Reeves and Alex Winter) have problems with their history at school, until a 700-year-old helper (George Carlin) emerges from the future in a time-travelling phone-booth. For reasons which are at first mysterious, he offers them the chance to improve their marks by kidnapping famous figures from history.

A silly sci-fi comedy poorly reviewed by most critics except this one. Older audiences may be put off by the tone of the film, which is parochially American and relentlessly yobbish: Socrates proves himself to be a regular guy by liking baseball, Beethoven ingratiates himself by becoming a fan of Bon Jovi, Abe Lincoln's message to humanity is reduced to 'Be excellent to each other, and party on, dudes!' The picture may make you despair of history teaching in American schools, but it has a lot of energy, plenty of gags, and it's endearingly good-natured.

It built up a cult reputation among the young in the States and spawned a sequel, *Bill & Ted's Bogus Journey*, which was inferior despite lavish sets, slick direction by Peter Hewitt, and a few good moments when Bill and Ted meet up with Death.

ANTI:

'So witlessly executed that it barely makes it as a bad movie. Nothing more than a brain-dead *Back to the Future* rip-off . . . I have seen the future of American cinema, and it's a downer man.' *(Trevor Willsmer, Film Yearbook)*

'Silly enough to persuade me that *Uncle Buck* was written by Tolstoy.' *(Daily Mail)*

'Makes the Carry Ons seem like Oscar Wilde.' *(Tom Hutchinson, Mail on Sunday)*

'Juvenile tale for teens, with embarrassingly overstated clowns' performances by the talented Reeves and Winter, who both look as though they're playing down to the imagined audience . . . Don't trust anybody who tells you it's excellent.' *(Winnert)*

MIXED:

'Dopey, annoyingly amusing.' *(Sheila Johnson, Independent)*

'I wish my history lessons had been like this . . . [The film] is 90 minutes of total inanity, stuffed with bargain basement jokes and special effects and directed as if for a pop video try-out . . . Strangely delightful like the idiot doodlings with crayon or paint of one's youngest child.' *(Nigel Andrews, Financial Times)*

PRO:

'[A] frothy, cheerful little fantasy . . . [which] makes no attempt to make its fantasy believable, but it works because of its zippy pace, dippy valley-speak dialogue and likeable performances. More subtly, it is a neat satirical comment on America's habit of reprocessing other cultures in its own image.' *(Hugo Davenport, Daily Telegraph)*

'The world is divided into those who love and those who hate B & T. For those who have seen the light, this is witty, inventive, uproarious, indeed, most excellent stuff.' *(Rose)*

BILLY JACK CT: 2 AV: 3.80

1971 US 112 C DRAMA

D Tom Laughlin ●
W Tom Laughlin ●

Tom Laughlin Delores Taylor Bert Freed Clark Howat Julie Webb Ken Tobey Victor Izay

Vietnam veteran of mixed race (Tom Laughlin) does good in Arizona desert.

Anyone who sees the 70s as a Golden Age of American Cinema should be made to watch this embarrassingly inept product of 60s radicalism, fascinating now as a period piece. It was popular at the time with youthful audiences and overpraised by the more determinedly 'populist' critics, including Pauline Kael. Second in the *Billy Jack* series – the first was the even more awful *Born Losers* (1967) – its surprising success led to two dreary sequels, *The Trial of Billy Jack* (1974) and *Billy Jack Goes To Washington* (1977).

PRO:

'There's a sweet, naive feeling to the movie even when it's violent and melodramatic and atrocious, and when it's good it's good in an unorthodox, improvisatory style. This may be the first movie in which a rape victim talks about what happened to her in terms of a specific feminine anger at her violation.' *(Pauline Kael)*

'Appears to be a labor of love in which the plight of the American Indian is pinpointed.' *(Variety)*

'Here at last is an anti-drug, anti-war movie that shows both sides of the generation gap in uncompromising terms. Its message is about the hypocrisy of America, the stupidity and lies creeping out of Washington and the need for compassion and understanding between people if life is to survive on this planet . . . Its power is incomparable.' *(Rex Reed, New York Daily News)*

ANTI:

'If good intentions and sincerity were enough to make a good film [this] would be a very good film indeed . . . The plot, and there is a great deal of it, is unwound with all the humourless earnestness of a bible tract, and the heavy-handed characterisation makes for laughter where there should be sympathy . . . Then, too, the story falls down badly in the casting of Delores Taylor . . . [who], not to put too fine a point on it, photographs as so exceedingly mature that not only do her romantic moments in a close-up bring a tendency to mirth, but in her rape scene one's ungallant reaction is that it must have been even less fun for the boys than for herself.' *(Eric Braun, F & F)*

'Archetypal trash . . . The writing, directing, and acting are as amateurish as they are tendentious, and obviousness and preposterousness are made to go happily hand in hand.' *(John Simon)*

BILLY LIAR CT: 6 AV: 7.54

1963 GB 96 BW DRAMA/COMEDY

D John Schlesinger ☆
W Keith Waterhouse Willis Hall ☆ from their play based on Waterhouse's novel

Tom Courtenay ☆ Julie Christie ☆ Wilfred Pickles Mona Washbourne Ethel Griffies ☆ Finlay Currie Rodney Bewes Leonard Rossiter Helen Fraser

A bored, lazy young man (Tom Courtenay) can only escape from his drab existence through his imagination.

One of the most memorable films of the 60s, with Julie Christie making an enormous impression as Billy's fantasy woman: though onscreen for only 11 minutes, she immediately became an icon of the decade. The fantasy sequences lack wit and are by far the weakest aspect of the film. In retrospect, too, Billy is infuriatingly passive.

'Imaginative, fascinating.' *(Variety)*

'Schlesinger's direction, I am delighted to say, is rich in wit.' *(Dilys Powell)*

'[Of the central character, who wishes to be a scriptwriter] Are we to sympathise with this wanker?

If his writing is as barren as his imagination, he has no talent anyway. All he seems to do is upset friends and foes alike. To put it bluntly, Billy is one big pain in the ass. Maybe *Billy Liar* seemed a good idea on paper? Maybe it was meant to be a portrait of a schizophrenic? Who knows? Certainly any healthy male who turns down an opportunity to run off to London with the young Julie Christie must be off his chump.' *(Ken Russell, 1993)*

BIRDMAN OF ALCATRAZ, THE

CT: 6 AV: 7.72

(aka *Bird Man of Alcatraz*)

1962 US 147 DRAMA/BIOPIC

D John Frankenheimer ☆
W Guy Trosper from Thomas E. Gaddis's book

Burt Lancaster ☆ AAN Karl Malden
Thelma Ritter ☆ AAN Edmond O'Brien Betty Field ✔
Neville Brand ✔ Hugh Marlowe
Telly Savalas ☆ AAN James Westerfield

A murderer (Burt Lancaster) becomes a celebrated ornithologist while in prison.

Based on the true story of Robert Stroud, this prison drama is inevitably somewhat static, and isn't helped by a pedestrian script. Even so, it's a gripping character study, and gave Burt Lancaster one of his greatest roles. Thelma Ritter and Telly Savalas also won Oscar nominations, as did Burnett Guffey's cinematography.

'The screenplay's, and the film's, only real flaw is its dismissal of Stroud's background, leaving the audience to mull over psychological ramifications and expositional data by and large denied it.' *(Variety)*

'A tribute to the iconoclastic courage needed to break the mold of the normal prison film dramas. The direction and Mr Lancaster's acting are notable for realism, nuance and restraint.' *(A.H. Weiler, New York Times)*

'An impressive depiction of the despair and inhumanity of imprisonment.' *(Judith Crist)*

'Intelligent, affecting, clearly well-meaning as it drones on and on, upliftingly.' *(Pauline Kael)*

BIRDS, THE

CT: 6 AV: 7.38

1963 US 119 C SF/HORROR

D Alfred Hitchcock ☆
W Evan Hunter from Daphne du Maurier's story

Rod Tayler Tippi Hedren Jessica Tandy Suzanne Pleshette Ethel Griffies

In California, birds with a grouse go cuckoo and end up making the humans duck and quail.

Apart from *Psycho*, no film of Hitchcock's has generated such critical controversy. There is even a feminist analysis which argues that the birds represent masculine aggression, and that the entire film is about the male protagonist working out his Oedipal problems: a view which seems far-fetched, not least because the female protagonist is presented throughout the movie as more important.

The truth is that *The Birds* suffers from an abstruse and frustrating screenplay. The opening is too slow; the directorial tone shifts uncertainly between light romantic comedy and portentous allegory; the heroine is uninteresting, as is her relationship with her boyfriend; the end is inconclusive. Technically, too, the film has faults. The back-projection is poor, and the process photography is not much better. However, the editing, camera direction and Hitchcock's manipulation of the audiences' fears combine to make *The Birds* a memorable thriller. It still has the power to make audiences scream, which was probably the director's primary intention. It's far from a turkey and well worth watching for a lark.

ANTI:

'An unnecessary elaborate romantic plot has been cooked up and then left suspended.' *(Variety)*

'We must sit through half an hour of pachydermous flirtation between Rod and Tippi before the seagull attacks, and another fifteen minutes of tedium . . . before the birds attack again. If one adds later interrelations between mother, girl friend and a particularly repulsive child actress, about two-thirds of the film is devoted to extraneous matters. Poe would have been appalled.' *(Dwight MacDonald)*

'The dialogue is stupid, the characters insufficiently developed to rank as clichés, the story incohesive.' *(Stanley Kauffmann)*

'Fans hooked on Hitchcock may be dismayed to discover that, after 38 years and more than 40 films, dealing mainly in straightforward shockery, the Master has traded in his uncomplicated tenets of terror for a new outlook that is vaguely nouvelle vague . . . Why did the birds go to war? . . . Hitchcock does not tell, and the movie flaps to a plotless end.' *(Time)*

PRO:

'A major work of cinematic art.' *(Andrew Sarris)*

'Hitchcock's . . . vision of Judgment Day and certainly among the most incisive and frightening movies he has made. *Psycho*, everyone was heard saying, couldn't be topped. He has topped it. *The Birds* is, in every way, a bit more serious, more thoroughly conceived film; an excellent blending of character and incident, of atmosphere and terror. If he had never made another motion picture in his life, *The Birds* would place him securely among the giants of the cinema.' *(Peter Bogdanovich)*

'Hitchcock at his best. Full of subterranean hints as to the ways in which people cage each other, it's fierce and Freudian as well as great cinematic fun.' *(Tom Milne)*

'The genius of *The Birds* is that its violence is totally irrational and thus totally inescapable . . . The birds are an eruption from the deepest levels of the unconscious, a visible manifestation of the capacity for irrational violence that we rarely acknowledge.' *(John Thomas, Film Society Review)*

BIRDS OF A FEATHER: *see* LA CAGE AUX FOLLES.

BIRTH OF A NATION, THE CT: 4 AV: 8.54
(aka *The Clansman*)

1915 US 157 BW WAR/EPIC/SILENT

D D.W. Griffith ☆
W D.W. Griffith Frank E. Woods from Thomas Dixon Jr's novel *The Klansman*

Henry B. Walthall Mae Marsh Miriam Cooper Lillian Gish Robert Harron Wallace Reid Donald Crisp Joseph Henabery Raoul Walsh Eugene Pallettte Walter Long

Two families endure the American Civil War and its aftermath.

D.W. Griffith's 1915 film is one of the most important films of all time, but it's now rarely shown because of what might mildly be described as its political incorrectness. The portrayal of the Ku Klux Klan as heroic is bad enough; almost as offensive are some of the white actors' performances in blackface. All the acting now looks painfully old-fashioned, and the script is very badly structured (apparently it was made up from day to day during shooting), so for modern audiences the film is remarkably uninvolving – and, at times, almost unwatchable. Students of cinema, however, should see it, preferably alongside one of its immediate predecessors, in order to recognize how visually imaginative and technically innovative it was for its day.

PRO:

'Like writing history with lightning. And it's all true.' *(Woodrow Wilson)*

'An impressive new illustration of the scope of the motion picture camera.' *(New York Times)*

'An attempt to criticise [it] would be utter folly . . . Historically it is magnificent; it is a great, true, artistic photograph of the crisis of a great war . . . Griffith's technique stands alone . . . Stirring and strong as the action is, the little human and comedy touches . . . relieve the tension and make the atmosphere . . . far from gloomy . . . It is regrettable that the phrase "greatest picture ever produced" has been used so often . . . But, had the phrase never been used, now would be the time to use it.' *(George D. Proctor, Motion Picture News)*

'Parallel action to create exciting climaxes, cameras moved from long-distant panoramas to close-ups for details, careful selection of incident, rhythmical editing of sequences, all these contributed to a new language of screen storytelling and influenced the shape of films to come.' *(Liam O'Leary, The Silent Cinema, 1965)*

'*The Birth of a Nation* was produced as an answer to Italy's super film *Quo Vadis?* of 1912. It was decided that *The Birth of a Nation* was to be the world's greatest film, in twelve reels, with many thousands of extras. Financially, the picture was a success, although much was said at the time about it being anti-Negro propaganda. Nevertheless, propaganda or not, all America, and later the rest of the world, went to see it, and if it achieved nothing else, it certainly placed the cinema as an entertainment and as a provocator of argument on the same level as the theatre and the novel.' *(Paul Rotha, The Film Till Now, 1930)*

ANTI:

'An impressive film – if one can suspend one's brain-power right through its tortuous duration and believe that the freed Negro is inevitably a cross between an anarchist and an animal while the Southern woman is unimpeachably an angel in taffeta and human disguise. This theory is made especially hard to take when Southern sainthood is personified in the poisonous sweetness of Lillian Gish, every inch the smarmy charmer who'd get a monumental kick out of setting up a sub-human ex-slave on a sex assault charge.' *(Julie Burchill, Girls on Film)*

'The film is as dull as it is absurd, and its racial views were even then backward-looking.' *(Shipman)*

BITTER TEA OF GENERAL YEN, THE CT: 6 AV: 7.33

1933 US 89 BW DRAMA/ROMANCE

D Frank Capra ☆
W Edward Paramore from Grace Zaring Stone's story

Barbara Stanwyck ☆ Nils Asther Toshia Mori Walter Connolly Gavin Gordon Lucien Littlefield

Chinese warlord (Nils Asther) captures missionary (Barbara Stanwyck) and wants her to become his mistress.

Frank Capra's version of *Beauty and the Beast* was daring and erotic for its day. Its subject matter – miscegenation – got it banned in Great Britain and in the British Commonwealth countries, thus ensuring its commercial failure. It is, however, an enjoyable drama, sensitively directed; and Stanwyck's performance stands up extremely well.

'After the Chinese general goes on the make for the white girl the picture goes blah. That's before the film is even half way. Barbara Stanwyck is the white girl. Pleasant enough and for the first half where she repulses the Chinaman gathers some audience sympathy. Subsequently, where the photography attempts to simulate that the girl, in her dreams, loves the Chinese, the role fails her.' *(Variety)*

'One of the first movies ever to deal openly with interracial sexual attraction. But the daring of its theme is continually undercut by a one-sided view of Chinese wartime brutality and some racist dialogue ("You yellow swine!").' *(Roy Hemming, Entertainment Weekly, 1993)*

'*The Bitter Tea of General Yen* lost money . . . It was 30 years ahead of its proper time. Nor did it receive any Academy Award mentions. Damn those Academy voters! Couldn't they recognize a work of art when they saw one?' *(Frank Capra)*

BLACK NARCISSUS   CT: 8 AV: 9.08

1946 GB 100 C DRAMA/ROMANCE

D Michael Powell Emeric Pressburger ☆
W Michael Powell Emeric Pressburger ☆
from Rumer Godden's novel

Deborah Kerr ☆ David Farrar Sabu
Jean Simmons Kathleen Byron ☆ Flora Robson
Esmond Knight Jenny Laird May Hallatt
Judith Furse

Sexually frustrated nuns in the Himalayas start to question their vows of celibacy.

Powell and Pressburger deal with one of their favourite subjects, British emotional constipation, but in an unusual context. It's a film which could easily have become tasteless or merely hysterical (you only have to think of how Ken Russell approached a similar theme in *The Devils*), but wonderful acting (especially by Kerr and Byron) prevents the movie from straying into vulgarity. Whatever reservations there may be about the plausibility of the story, there can be none about the look of the film. Jack Cardiff's magnificent cinematography deservedly won an Oscar, as did Alfred Junge's art direction.

ANTI:

'It is all intended to be very "psychological", "atmospheric", "rueful" and "worldly-wise". I suspect that the worst faults lie in Rumer Godden's original novel; that Michael Powell and Emeric Pressburger were badly mistaken in trying to make a movie of it at all. There is some unusually good colour photography, and as movie-making some of it is intelligent and powerful. But the pervasive attitude in and toward the picture makes it as a whole tedious and vulgar.' *(James Agee, Nation)*

'Kerr gets only occasional opportunities to reveal her talents.' *(Variety)*

PRO:

'A strange tale, beautifully photographed . . . and splendidly produced. Primarily it is an adult movie, with a strong spiritual theme involving the Devil and all his works . . . It is a grim tale, ending in defeat . . . A pretty picture but not a pretty tale.' *(Fortnight)*

'The convent was really in Pinewood and this wonderful Powell/Pressberger film shows British studio movie-making at is postwar peak. The production team rarely used colour or music to such a dazzling effect.' *(Geoff Brown, Time Out)*

BLACK ORPHEUS AAW   CT: 5 AV: 7.45

(aka *Orfeu Negro*)

1959 France/Italy/Brazil 98 C DRAMA/FOREIGN

D Marcel Camus ☆
W Vinitius de Moraes

Breno Mello Marpessa Dawn Ademar da Silva
Lourdes de Oliviera

The legend of Orpheus and Eurydice updated and transferred to Brazil.

Exciting, colourful melodrama which won 50s audiences over with all the fun of the fair – or rather the Rio carnival. It was voted Best Foreign Film at the Oscars and won the Palme d'Or at the Cannes Film Festival. In retrospect, it's all a bit naive, and the acting is distinctly amateurish; but it is still like no other film, and does have a great score.

ANTI:

'Mysteriously won an Oscar over *The 400 Blows* . . . [It] so literally retells the Orpheus story that it has little real drama.' *(Derek Hill, Tribune)*

'In the long run, the adaptation of the classical myth to this very special and modern society becomes extravagant and strained . . . and we do not really accept any of it.' *(Guardian)*

'Many things in [it] . . . one must respond to and admire, but is its final effect of more than palpitating exercise?' *(William Whitebait, New Statesman)*

'Irritating and noisy.' *(Halliwell)*

PRO:

'For that feeling of going mad over dazzling carnival dancing and throbbing drums I recommend it.' *(Jympson Harman, Evening News)*

'The most exciting musical entertainment now to be seen in town, on or off the screen.' *(Leonard Mosley, Daily Express)*

'An intoxicating experience . . . a stroke of lyrical magic.' *(Alexander Walker, Evening Standard)*

'Although certain of the sentimental scenes seem rather dated, the relentless – almost abstract – onslaught of colour, noise and frenetic movement stands up very well.' *(Frances Dickinson, Time Out)*

BLACK SHACK ALLEY: *see* RUE CASES NÈGRES.

BLACK STALLION, THE CT: 7 AV: 7.77

1979 US 119 C DRAMA/FAMILY

D Carroll Ballard ✔
W Melissa Mathison Jeanne Rosenberg William Witliff ✔ from Walter Farley's novel

Kelly Reno Mickey Rooney ☆ AAN Teri Garr Clarence Muse Hoyt Axton

A shipwrecked boy (Kelly Reno) and stallion grow up to run victoriously at Santa Anita.

A classic family film, and a horse movie to rank alongside *National Velvet*. Co-writer Melissa Mathison's next success was *E.T.* The sequel, *The Black Stallion Returns* (1983), is disappointing.

'A perfect gem . . . Ballard's camera eye and powers of sequence composition are manifestly extraordinary.' *(Variety)*

'The film jettisons most of the cuteness implicit in its theme and handles the material with dream-like clarity. A magnificently well-crafted movie.' *(David Pirie, Time Out)*

'It may be the greatest children's movie ever made.' *(Pauline Kael)*

'Touching and beautifully photographed, if slightly overlong.' *(Virgin)*

BLADE RUNNER CT: 7 AV: 7.35

BLADE RUNNER (DIRECTOR'S CUT) CT: 9 AV: 7.47

1982/92 US 118 (original)/116 (director's cut) C SF/DRAMA

D Ridley Scott ☆
W Hampton Fancher David Peoples from Philip K. Dick's novel *Do Androids Dream of Electric Sheep?*

Harrison Ford Rutger Hauer ✔ Sean Young ✔ Daryl Hannah Edward James Olmos M. Emmet Walsh

A futuristic private eye (Harrison Ford) tracks down rebellious androids.

Blade Runner is now widely considered to be a classic, but on release it received miserable reviews – mainly protesting about how miserable it was – and recovered only half its production costs of $30 million.

One reason it failed on first release was that it confounded too many expectations. In 1982, audiences and critics expected Harrison Ford to be the action-hero he had been in *Star Wars* and *Raiders of the Lost Ark*. They were unprepared for him to be morally ambivalent. Variety complained that 'The villain here is so intriguing and charismatic that one almost comes to prefer him to the more stolid hero.' But that, of course, was the film-makers' intention.

The film also confused people by being very different from the book on which it is based, Philip K. Dick's *Do Androids Dream of Electric Sheep?* Where Dick's Earth is underpopulated, Scott's is teeming with low-life; where Dick's replicants are evil, Scott's are sympathetic; where Dick's story ends with the hero realizing that he himself is a replicant, Scott leaves the question open.

Audiences were unprepared, too, for the film's darkness of tone. A happy ending was imposed by Warner Brothers after disastrous previews – but that, as critics remarked at the time, seemed to belong to a different picture. Similarly, the last-minute addition of a Chandleresque voice-over (put in for the sake of clarity) was widely perceived as extraneous. The happy ending and narration have both vanished from the director's cut, and the film becomes all the more consistent – and no less clear – for their absence.

Critics and audiences alike were repelled by the film's vision of the future as a slum. More than any other sci-fi film, *Blade Runner* emphasizes the noise, lack of privacy and commercialism of the future, not to mention the gulf between the rich – living offworld or in hubristically vast buildings – and the poor, dwelling like rats in a sewer. In *Blade Runner*, the rich care so little about the world that they have turned it into an inhospitable ghetto. This point may have looked far-fetched in 1982: ten years on, you can walk around many inner cities (if you dare) and watch the vision becoming a reality.

Many were confused by the genre of the piece. The sombre, rain-drenched mood evokes film noir, but the film keeps subverting noir expectations. The leading lady, Rachael, appears at first to be a straightforward femme fatale (Joan Crawford would kill for those shoulder-pads) but she turns out to be the opposite: she saves our hero from death and gives him something to live for . . . herself.

Nor is the hero, despite his 40s trenchcoat, a conventional Bogart or Cagney-figure. He's flawed like one – a loner at odds with society – and he ends up finding a lingering nobility within himself. But the choice of William S. Burroughs's phrase 'Blade

Runner' as the film's title is a tip-off that he's more like a Burroughs anti-hero, at the mercy of mind-controlling forces and perhaps even programmed by them. One result of Scott's re-editing job is that, by the end, Deckard is unsure if he is himself a replicant. Certainly, his arch-rival seems able to see the fantasies inside his head.

A few feminist critics have tried to dismiss the film by placing it within the *Dirty Harry* genre, as a woman-hating exploitation movie. They point to scenes like the one where Deckard pursues a fetishistically clad female replicant and shoots her dead: 'That she falls among store dummies is indicative of the film's sexual politics' *(Leighton Grist, The Movie Book of Film Noir, 1992)*.

Such criticisms totally miss the ironic point: which is that most of the females in this film are not women but replicants, built by men to serve their needs. Deckard's shooting of the first female replicant is meant to be shocking: it's a first indication that he is not a straightforward hero. The audience is surprised to find itself rooting for her to escape. The juxtaposition of her with the dummies is meant to signify not that she is the same as them, but that she is very different.

The film is far from a conventional law-and-order thriller, with Deckard defending the male-dominated status quo: indeed, it emphasizes his insignificance and impotence in a city of towering, flame-spurting phallic symbols.

Nor is the film a straightforward SF monster movie. True, there are overtones of Frankenstein in the way Rutger Hauer's replicant destroys his creator, but the film's accusation is not that the creator meddled with nature, but that he failed to do so in a sensitive or sympathetic way. The film is far from anti-scientific: it captures more than any other movie a love of technology – which is why it has become so much more pertinent over the past decade, when so many more of us have become dependent upon machines and computers. The scene where Hauer allows Ford to live is, as the critic Danny Peary has written, 'the ultimate gesture in the SF cinema between machine and man. It gives hope that we can live in harmony.'

As for lack of characterization, the point about the people in *Blade Runner* (even the hero) is that they are dehumanized: therefore, the sets and outfits have to tell you more than the characters themselves are capable of doing. For example, Deckard's boss neither says nor does anything particularly evil, and yet he emanates it. The reason is that Scott has placed his HQ in Los Angeles' Union Station, an extravagant piece of neo-fascist architecture, and kits him out like Rod Steiger in *In The Heat of the Night*. Implanted subconsciously in the audience's mind is the perception that this movie is partly about racism.

The deliberate echoes of Fritz Lang's *M* and *Metropolis* in the design should have been, but weren't, enough to alert critics to the film's true genre: this is, above all, an expressionist drama. We witness the confusion of the city, the sudden elation of being above it all, the lack of privacy, the crude commercialism, the need to scrape a living; but these are not visual gimmicks or set dressing – they reflect what is happening inside the hero's mind.

This is not to say that the plotting is faultless. The script is confused over whether Deckard has to hunt down four replicants or five (one replicant disappeared during a final re-write, but no one seems to have told Deckard's boss). And, dramatic though the opening scene of a replicator-detector test is, it's gratuitous: presumably the Tyrell Corporation can recognize its own replicants visually, so why bother testing in such an elaborate way? Fortunately, such doubts arise only after the event. The opening scene still works dramatically, for it's full of suspense and sets up the central conflict: between men who act like androids and androids who feel like men.

Blade Runner is worth reseeing, preferably on a big screen and in Ridley Scott's revised version – not because the director's cut is very different from the original, but because it bears watching without the preconceptions almost everyone had in 1982. Of all the films ever released, it seems to me the most critically misunderstood. Cool and detached though the film is, it does have a heart. It's one of the few movies in any genre which communicates how it feels to be oppressed, and it's steeped in the anguished knowledge that we are all going to die. Like most good whines, it has improved with age.

ANTI:

'*Blade Runner* is a stunningly interesting visual achievement, but a failure as a story.' *(Roger Ebert)*

'Ridley Scott is unkindly revealed as a film-maker who creates static tableaux rather than moving pictures.' *(Tom Milne, MFB)*

'*Blade Runner*, like its setting, is a beautiful, deadly organism that devours life.' *(Richard Corliss, Time)*

'Gloomy futuristic thriller, looking like a firework display seen through thick fog, and for all the tiring tricks and expense adding up to little more than an updated Philip Marlowe case.' *(Halliwell)*

'It hasn't been thought out in human terms. If anybody comes around with a test to detect humanoids, maybe Ridley Scott and his associates should hide.' *(Pauline Kael)*

PRO:

'One of the best sci-fi films of all time.' *(Winnert)*

'Unforgettable look at a future where machines have a truer sense of soul than humans do.' *(Scheuer)*

BLAZING SADDLES CT: 9 AV: 6.36

1974 US 93 C COMEDY/WESTERN

D Mel Brooks ✔
W Norman Steinberg Mel Brooks Andrew Bergman Richard Pryor Alan Unger ✔
Cleavon Little Gene Wilder ✔ Slim Pickens Harvey Korman ✔ Madeline Kahn ☆ AAN Mel Brooks

A western town gets a new sheriff – and he's black (Cleavon Little).

Mel Brooks's crude but more hit-than-miss parody of the western was a huge popular success and has innumerable hilarious moments: it's one of the great modern screen comedies, in which Gene Wilder gives one of his most memorable performances. Critics of the time disagreed.

ANTI:

'I admit that the Press show audience were often convulsed with laughter; to sit frozen faced among them was a disconcerting experience.' *(Dilys Powell)*

'One suspects that the film's gradual disintegration derives not from the makers' inability to end it, so much as from their inability to stop laughing at their own jokes.' *(Jan Dawson)*

'No mention of *Blazing Saddles* can be brief enough. Mel Brooks's film, like his previous *The Producers* and *The Twelve Chairs*, is a model of how not to make a comedy. It is like playing tennis not only without a net but also without a court, and with twenty balls simultaneously. All kinds of gags – chiefly anachronisms, irrelevancies, reverse ethnic jokes, and out-and-out vulgarities – are thrown together pell-mell, batted about insanely in all directions, and usually beaten into the ground. With several gag writers huffing away full blast, it is no wonder that a few one-liners come off; what I found more amazing is that, in one of our better theaters, a civilized-looking audience laughed loudest and longest at a scene in which a bunch of cowboys sit around a campfire eating beans. One after another, they raise their backsides a bit and break wind, each a bit louder than his predecessor, the turn, in a continuous crescendo, coming back to each three times. If that is what makes audiences happiest, all hope for the future of the cinema is gone with the wind.' *(John Simon)*

'Essentially a raunchy, protracted version of a television comedy skit.' *(Variety)*

'The humor is crude, rude, obvious, repetitive, self-impressed. There are laughs, but not many compared to the number of jokes and sight gags. Brooks shows no fondness for the western genre – in fact, his awful ending sequence shows how deeply he wanted to get back to the present.' *(Danny Peary)*

PRO:

'Very often the film is too fast and furious for its own good . . . But goldarned if it doesn't work. Goldarned if the whole fool enterprise is not worth the attention of any moviegoer with a penchant for . . . "authentic" western gibberish.' *(Richard Schickel, Time)*

'Insane take-off in the classic Western . . . triggering laughs that measure a full ten on the Richter scale.' *(Newsweek)*

'None of Brooks's later films has topped this one for sheer belly-laughs.' *(Maltin)*

BLITHE SPIRIT

CT: 8 AV: 8.40

1945 GB 96 C COMEDY/FANTASY

D David Lean
W Noel Coward ☆ from his own play

Rex Harrison ☆ Kay Hammond ☆ Constance Cummings Margaret Rutherford ☆ Hugh Wakefield Joyce Carey Jacqueline Clark

Elvira (Kay Hammond), a mischievous ghost, returns to haunt her novelist ex-husband (Rex Harrison) and his new spouse (Constance Cummings).

Critics in 1945 were quick to point out that the film resembled a stage production, and argued that Rex Harrison strolled through the film with an insouciance that diminished the little suspense there is. However, this supernatural comedy has stood the test of time, thanks to the great Margaret Rutherford, at her best as an eccentric medium, and Kay Hammond's delightfully naughty Elvira. (And Harrison's much-criticized performance looks pretty good to me.) Director David Lean went on to direct more cinematic movies, but none with more wit and humour. The excellent special effects won Tom Howard an Academy Award. It's one of the best ghost movies of all time

'Personally I would have liked Mr Coward to start again from scratch and write his astringent joke as a film.' *(Dilys Powell)*

'Largely a photographed copy of the stage play . . . Rex Harrison repeats his stage performance, which is so flawless as to merit some critics' charge of under-acting.' *(Variety)*

'Whenever Margaret Rutherford is on screen, as the medium who starts and tries to control the trouble, the picture is wonderfully funny.' *(James Agee, Nation)*

'The theme may not be everybody's idea of a subject for comedy, nevertheless, it is so handled that it becomes a merry frolic and enjoyable light entertainment for those able to accept it in the right spirit, its appeal being strongest to sophisticated audiences . . . Witty dialogue, skilful direction and excellent acting are the film's strong points.' *(CEA Film Report)*

BLONDE BOMBSHELL: *see* BOMBSHELL.

BLONDE VENUS

CT: 5 AV: 5.50

1932 US 80/97 BW DRAMA/ROMANCE/SO BAD

D Josef von Sternberg
W Jules Furthman S.K. Lauren

Marlene Dietrich Herbert Marshall Cary Grant Dickie Moore Francis Sayles

A wife (Marlene Dietrich) turns cabaret performer and sinner in order to pay for her husband's medical treatment.

Wonderful tosh, well worth seeing for Dietrich's first entrance in a gorilla suit. One has the horrible feeling that von Sternberg meant at least some of it seriously.

'There is more pleasure for the eye in *Blonde Venus* than in a hundred of its fellows. But what does beauty ornament? The story of a wife who becomes a kept woman for the sake of her husband, and a prostitute for the sake of her child.' *(Forsyth Hardy, Cinema Quarterly)*

'Weak story, inept direction and generally sluggish.' *(Variety)*

'I thought the production dreadful and can see no reason why nearly all of the scenes should take place in grottoes.' *(James Agate, Tatler)*

'There is no possible excuse for *Blonde Venus*, except that it supports the incredibly accurate prediction made in this department some months ago that Marlene Dietrich was due to explode with a loud hollow pop . . . Miss Dietrich, of course, seems utterly disinterested [sic] in the difficult business at hand and ignores poor Herbert Marshall, a child actor, and the world in general in as complete an exhibition of somnambulance as any actress ever gave an enthusiastic, if misled, public.' *(Pare Lorentz, 1932)*

'His latest movie, *Blonde Venus*, is perhaps the worst ever made. In it all Sternberg's gifts have turned sour. The photography is definitely "arty" – a nauseating blend of hazy light, soft focus, over-blacks and over-whites, with each shot so obviously "composed" as to be painful. Sternberg's rhythm has declined to a senseless, see-saw pattern. And his kaleidoscopic cutting has reached such a point that the film is all pace and nothing else.' *(Dwight Macdonald)*

'It would be hard to imagine a sillier picture than this one.' *(Shipman)*

BLOOD SIMPLE CT: 5 AV: 7.15

1983 US 99 C THRILLER

D Joel Coen ☆
W Joel Coen Ethan Coen

John Getz Frances McDormand Dan Hedaya ☆
M. Emmet Walsh ☆ Samm-Art Williams
Tommy Rettig

Bar-owner (Dan Hedaya) hires private eye (M. Emmet Walsh) to discover if wife (Frances McDormand) is having an affair.

Low-budget thriller with overtones of black comedy and a nasty climax. Not even the fine performances from Walsh and Hedaya and the Coen Brothers' sophisticated visual style can quite conceal the callowness of the script; but it's an impressive debut.

'Aside from the subtle performances . . . the observant viewer will find a cornucopia of detail.' *(Variety)*

'Occasionally implausible, but otherwise terrifically stylish, exciting and black. A dazzlingly original debut.' *(Rose)*

'Coen doesn't know what to do with the actors (they give their words too much deliberation and weight), but he knows how to place the characters and the props in the film frame in a way that makes the audience feel knowing and in on the joke . . . The film provides a visually sophisticated form of gross-out humor; the material is thin, though, and there isn't enough suspense until about the last ten minutes, when the action is so grisly that it has a kick.' *(Pauline Kael)*

BLOWUP CT: 5 AV: 7.33

(aka *Blow Up; Blow-up; The Blow-up*)

1966 GB 111 C THRILLER

D Michelangelo Antonioni ☆ AAN
W Michelangelo Antonioni ✗ AAN

David Hemmings Vanessa Redgrave Sarah Miles

Randy, trendy photographer (David Hemmings) thinks he has photographed a murder, but can't be sure.

A film which, despite many intensely irritating characteristics including an inconclusive plot and enigmatic characters, sums up the spirit of the Swinging 60s. Antonioni's use of colour really is wonderful.

PRO:

'One of the finest, most intelligent, least hysterical expositions of the modern existential agony we have yet had on film.' *(Richard Schickel, Time)*

'[The subject is] illusion, reality, and the wavering line between them . . . Antonioni is sympathetic to the uninhibited young. He sees them as deprived of the beliefs which supported an earlier generation: religion, the stability of the family. That is why they try to empty themselves of everything which belongs to the past; they are engaged, he says, in a kind of self-liberation. He is fascinated, as again and again some fragment of the film shows, by the spectacle: by the fashions in decor (the hero excitedly buys an airplane propeller); by the casual, almost dispassionate sexual encounters; by the love-hate relationship between young photographer and young model (there is a scene in which the act of photography becomes curiously erotic). And he uses all these fragments of reality to create the idea of illusion.' *(Dilys Powell, Sunday Times)*

ANTI:

'Antonioni has always been a cold director . . . *Blow Up* is his coldest film to date . . . There's no one to identify with; nothing to follow through.' *(Nina Hibbin, Morning Star)*

'Another exercise in petrifying boredom from Italy's Nihilist director Michelangelo Antonioni . . . *Blow-Up* could have been an ingenious thriller, but it is ruined by Antonioni's inability to tell a story simply or with compassion and by his refusal to use movies as anything but an intellectual device to relieve his own frustrations.' *(Rex Reed)*

'Antonioni, like his fashion-photographer hero, is more interested in getting pretty pictures than in what they mean. But for reasons I can't quite fathom, what is taken to be shallow in his hero is taken to be profound in him.' *(Pauline Kael)*

BLUE ANGEL, THE

CT: 8 AV: 8.86

1930 Germany 95 BW DRAMA/MUSICAL/FOREIGN & ENGLISH

D Josef Von Sternberg ☆
W Robert Liebmann Karl Zuckmayer Karl Vollmoeller from Heinrich Mann's novel *Professor Unrath*

Emil Jannings ☆ Marlene Dietrich ☆ Kurt Gerron Hans Albers

An ageing schoolteacher (Emil Jannings) is enslaved by a cabaret singer (Marlene Dietrich).

Classic study of a decent man led to his doom by a femme fatale. Dietrich is at her sexiest, with just the right overtone of sadism: it isn't hard to see why the role made her an international star. Jannings's acting is a little exaggerated – he was, after all, from the silent era – but still touching. It was made, and remains available, in both German and English versions. It was remade – badly – in 1959.

'Marlene Dietrich . . . makes Reason totter on her throne. And unless she is very careful, Greta Garbo also. But I will not be unfaithful, leastwise in print. Therefore I will only say that on the fair Greta's behalf I strongly object to the arrival of this supremely capable, superbly fascinating and exquisitely lovely actress.' *(James Agate, Tatler)*

'Reeks with the atmosphere of decay and sexuality.' *(Scheuer)*

'At the time I thought the film was awful and vulgar and I was shocked by the whole thing. Remember, I was a well brought up German girl.' *(Marlene Dietrich)*

BLUE BIRD, THE

CT: 1 AV: 2.14

1976 US/USSR 88 C MUSICAL/FANTASY/FAMILY

D George Cukor ●
W Hugh Whitemore Alfred Hayes ●

Elizabeth Taylor ● Ava Gardner ● Jane Fonda ● Cicely Tyson Harry Andrews Will Geer George Cole Mona Washbourne Patsy Kensit Todd Lookinland ✔

Woodcutter's children (Todd Lookinland, Patsy Kensit) seek the blue bird of happiness.

Remake of the 1939 Shirley Temple film, and a massive flop. Less a blue bird than a red-faced turkey.

'If you have any naughty children you want to punish, take them to *The Blue Bird* and make them sit all the way through it.' *(William Wolf, Cue)*

'Senile and interminable.' *(Stephen Farber, New West)*

'The movie gives evidence of being heavily edited, probably in a Cuisinart . . . Elizabeth Taylor, Ava Gardner and Jane Fonda camp it up like movie queens on an overseas press junket.' *(Jay Cocks, Time)*

'A mixture of Soviet ineptitude and the American belief that the grotesque expenditure of dollars can set anything a-right.' *(Daily Express)*

'Patsy Kensit is a cute Mytyl, but not much of an actress . . . and further cursed with reminding one of Goldie Hawn – let us pray that she outgrows it.' *(John Simon)*

BLUE COLLAR

CT: 6 AV: 7.08

1978 US 114 C DRAMA

D Paul Schrader ☆
W Paul Schrader

Richard Pryor ✔ Yaphet Kotto ✔ Harvey Keitel ✔ Ed Begley Jr Harry Bellaver

Three factory-workers (Richard Pryor, Yaphet Kotto, Harvey Keitel) have problems with their corrupt Union and the Inland Revenue.

Tough, realistic drama, admirably cynical about both bosses and unions, and well acted. Paul Schrader's impressive directing debut.

'Jukebox Marxism.' *(Pauline Kael, New Yorker)*

'An artistic triumph . . . powerful, gritty.' *(Variety)*

'Two principal themes connect under the clanky plot. The first is the changed status of the American worker: from the poverty of poverty to the higher-paid poverty of inflicted consumerism. Where he used to struggle for bread and shelter, now he struggles – not much less painfully – for back taxes and braces for his daughter's teeth. The second theme, the changed relation with the union, the changed union . . . The leaders are drawn as liars, crooks, users of race prejudice, brutes and murderers. We see the services that the union provides for its members, and we see the tyrannies leveled in exchange.' *(Stanley Kauffmann)*

BLUE KITE, THE CT: 8 AV: 8.00 (est)

(aka *Lan Fengzheng*)

1992 Hong Kong/China 138 C DRAMA/FOREIGN

D Tian Zhuangzhuang ☆
W Tian Zhuangzhuang

Lu Liping ☆ Pu Quanxin Guo Baochang Zhang Wenyao Zhong Ping

Ordinary people try to cope under Chinese Communism through the 1950s and 1960s.

Seen through the eyes of a child, this grim epic is an utterly convincing, realistic, terrifying picture of a society where hypocrisy and fear rule absolutely, punctuated by outbreaks of mob violence. Remarkably for a film which expresses enormous rage at the abuse of power and grotesquely arbitrary changes of public policy, director Tian Zhuangzhuang treats everyone in the film with understanding and respect. The wonderfully fresh performances – especially those of Lu Liping as the boy's mother – never strike a false note.

Not surprisingly, the film ran into trouble with the current Chinese regime, who did their best to ensure that it would never be completed. Post-production had to take place abroad; and everyone who participated is to be congratulated for fearlessness, as well as for making one of the greatest pictures ever about how people survive under totalitarianism.

'In America they give Oscars . . . in China, detention sentences.' *(Nigel Andrews, Financial Times)*

'As warmly human as Chen Kaige's [*Farewell My Concubine*] is epic in quality. Ken Loach versus David Lean, in fact. It is on no account to be missed.' *(Derek Malcolm, Guardian)*

'An absolutely compelling social-realist drama . . . a sensitively detailed tale of the horrors of social and individual manipulation.' *(Jeff Sawtell, Morning Star)*

'The plot may sound like little more than anti-agitprop. And indeed *The Blue Kite* is by far the most excoriating depiction in Chinese film of Mao's ravages. But at its heart it is about domestic dreams, about a hope for better days that flies above the characters as brightly and vulnerably as Tietou's favorite blue kite.' *(Richard Corliss, Time)*

'Tian manages to express both sympathy and righteous anger without once falling prey to rhetorical bombast or lachrymose sentimentality. A masterly blending of the personal and the political. Olly Stone should look, learn, and hang his head in shame.' *(Geoff Andrew, Time Out)*

BLUE LAMP, THE CT: 6 AV: 6.60

1949 GB 84 BW THRILLER

D Basil Dearden ☆
W T.E.B. Clarke ☆

Jack Warner ☆ Jimmy Hanley ✔ Dirk Bogarde ✔ Robert Flemyng Bernard Lee Peggy Evans Patric Doonan

An affronted underworld helps police catch a young murderer (Dirk Bogarde) who has committed the sin of using a firearm against a police officer.

The famous police melodrama which inspired the long-running TV series, 'Dixon of Dock Green', is not the gritty crime thriller that it was considered to be in 1949 – indeed, it's rather quaint – but it is a stirring tribute to the old-fashioned British Bobby, with effective leading performances.

ANTI:

'The mixture of coyness, patronage and naive theatricality which has vitiated British films for the last ten years.' *(Gavin Lambert)*

MIXED:

'A soundly made crime thriller which would not be creating much of a stir if it were American.' *(Richard Mallett, Punch)*

PRO:

'The real hero of the piece . . . is the police force; and for once we are given an authentic police station; an accurate picture of the work of the man on the beat and the detective . . . With the exception of the murderer's girl, who is shown in a state of constant and, to my mind, implausible hysteria, the characters in the story are admirably observed . . . [It] has both the dramatic tension and the robust ironic humour which have made the reputation of the realistic British cinema.' *(Dilys Powell)*

'This film, for all its clever, unobtrusive realism, is not – nor does it try to be – a profound study of the life and work of the police. It is not so much a portrait as an advertising poster, but the remarkable thing is that the poster has been so well designed – and that no one designed it before.' *(James Monahan)*

'As entertainment the film is fine. T.E.B. Clarke's script is quite outstanding. It is sharply dramatic, well constructed, deeply sentimental and wryly funny. And it has the huge merit that it never gloats over the sadism and violence it must show. It would rather show a copper at supper with his old woman than a gunman strangling his gal.' *(Paul Holt)*

'It is not only foreigners who find the English policeman wonderful, and, in composing this tribute to him, the Ealing Studios are giving conscious expression to a general sentiment.' *(The Times)*

BLUE VELVET CT: 9 AV: 6.29

1986 US 120 C THRILLER/HORROR

D David Lynch ☆ AAN
W David Lynch

Kyle MacLachlan ✔ Isabella Rossellini ✔ Dennis Hopper ☆ Laura Dern Hope Lange Dean Stockwell Jack Nance Brad Dourif

An innocent young man (Kyle MacLachlan) discovers the dark underside of Middle America.

Blue Velvet is an odd, deliberately unpleasant film which arouses strong emotions for and against. Dennis Hopper's memorable portrayal of a sado-masochistic nutter is all the more disturbing because our young anti-hero finds himself turned on by his brand of sexual violence, and seduced away from his nice, apparently conventional girl-friend (Laura Dern). Just as disturbing for the audience is that Hopper's female 'victim' is a masochist. Isabella Rossellini's raw, painfully felt performance remains vastly underrated, perhaps out of political correctness: women are not supposed to get sexual satisfaction out of being humiliated.

Blue Velvet poses an unreal set of options for the hero – sweeteness and light on the one hand, darkness and depravity on the other – but the film is a refreshingly black corrective to the Spielbergian sentiment so prevalent in modern commercial cinema. And its visual style – a combination of garish 50s colours and the shadows of 40s film noir – remains unusual and arresting. The plot may be unclear, and the message facile, but even today the film packs a punch.

It joins a small but select number of horrific rites-of-passage movies, such as *River's Edge* and *Carrie*, underrated by critics (especially middle-aged ones) for the same reason: they were reviewed as though they were realistic, rather than expressionistic, works. Lynch's opening image – of insects and death lurking beneath the surface of bourgeois America – says it all: this is a very pessimistic, punk film which sees the adult world from an almost hysterically adolescent point of view – it makes poetic sense only if we see the whole picture as filtered through the distorting mind of its young hero.

PRO:

'Lynch uncovers the dark underside of the all-American town . . . in a film of rare power and poetry.' *(Christopher Bagley, Premiere)*

'A hilarious satire of small town life that also succeeds as a gripping mystery.' *(Caryn James, New York Times, 1990)*

'Possibly the only coming-of-age movie in which sex has the danger and heightened excitement of a horror picture.' *(Pauline Kael)*

ANTI:

What are we being told? That beneath the surface of Small Town, USA, passions run dark and dangerous? Don't stop the presses.' *(Roger Ebert)*

'The scene in which Frank smears his own mouth with lipstick and kisses Jeffrey with a kind of horrified and horrifying passion before brutally beating him . . . repeats the hysterical homophobia of *Dune* [also by Lynch]. Its point here seems to be the lumping together of bisexuality and sadomasochism as equal and equally loathsome components of the alternative to . . . "normal" sexual conventions.' *(Robin Wood, 1989)*

MIXED:

'*Blue Velvet* may be thought of as posing a question: namely, which is more desirable, to settle for a civilized life of vacuous, superficial cheer, or to allow oneself to sink into the pit of cruel, destructive sadomasochistic passion? Lynch leaves the impression that life presents us with only these two alternatives, and that one would have to be less than human not to choose the latter. The catch, needless to say, is that there are other alternatives. But the film's awful effectiveness lies in its ability to make us forget that – for the duration, at any rate.' *(Bruce Bawer, American Spectator)*

BLUES BROTHERS, THE CT: 5 AV: 5.25

1980 US 133 C COMEDY/MUSICAL

D John Landis
W Dan Aykroyd John Landis

John Belushi Dan Aykroyd Kathleen Freeman James Brown Henry Gibson Cab Calloway Carrie Fisher

Two brothers (Dan Aykroyd, John Belushi) try to collect money for their old orphanage, and aren't fussy about how they get it.

A flop on first release, this exercise in vehicular slapstick with soul music interludes has become one of the highest-grossing films in cinema history. Fast, frenetic and sometimes funny, it's the ideal comedy for anyone who thinks loud noises and car crashes are a hoot.

ANTI:

'There's not a soupçon of wit or ingenuity in this brainless exercise in overspending.' *(Daily Mail)*

MIXED:

'If Universal had made it 35 years earlier, *The Blues Brothers* might have been called *Abbott and Costello in Soul Town*. Level of inspiration is about the same now as then, the humor as basic, the enjoyment as fleeting.' *(Variety)*

'It meanders expensively like some pedigreed shaggy dog through 70s/80s American cinema and 50s/60s American rock, cocking its leg happily at every popular landmark on the way.' *(Paul Taylor, MFB)*

'There's . . . room, in the midst of the carnage and

mayhem, for a surprising amount of grace, humor and whimsy.' *(Roger Ebert)*

'A monument to waste, noise, and misplaced cool, but it does have its engagingly nutty moments.' *(Virgin)*

BOAT, THE CT: 6 AV: 7.40

(aka *Das Boot*)

1982 West Germany 150 C DRAMA/WAR

D Wolfgang Petersen ☆ AAN
W Wolfgang Petersen AAN

Jürgen Prochnow Herbert Grönemeyer Klaus Wennemann Hubertus Bengsch Martin Semmelrogge

A German U-boat operates during World War II.

Impressive, claustrophobic film, cleverly directed to communicate what it must be like cooped up in a submarine. The weakness is the predictable plot, which doesn't measure up to the films to which it's most often compared, *All Quiet On The Western Front* and *The Cruel Sea*. A big hit internationally, it launched Petersen on a Hollywood career. Oscar-nominated for its cinematography, editing, sound and sound editing.

'A technical marvel, *The Boat* is a breathtaking and powerful portrait of war and death.' *(Virgin)*

'If you want to experience the tedium of life in a German submarine, this is the movie that will give it to you.' *(Pauline Kael)*

BOB ROBERTS CT: 6 AV: 6.10

1923 US 104 C MUSICAL/DRAMA

D Tim Robbins ✗
W Tim Robbins ✗

Tim Robbins ☆ Giancarlo Esposito Ray Wise Brian Murray Gore Vidal ☆ Kelly Willis John Cusack Alan Rickman Susan Sarandon James Spader

Bob Roberts (Tim Robbins) is a right-wing country singer with high ambitions, and he isn't fussy about how he achieves them.

Tim Robbins's début as a writer-director (he also composed the songs) is an entertaining satire – done in fake-documentary style – on the American way of politics. The film's not the inspired hatchet-job on Ross Perot, still less the artistic masterpiece, which some critics claimed – it has more than a hint of left-wing complacency – but the odd well-aimed satirical shaft makes it worth seeing. Gore Vidal is excellent as Roberts's gentlemanly Democrat rival; and a host of politically correct stars put in an appearance, including James Spader and Susan Sarandon (the real-life Mrs Robbins) as a couple of splendidly mindless newsreaders.

PRO:

'Both a stimulating satire and a depressing commentary on the devolution of the US political system.' *(Variety)*

'A wickedly funny satire, *Bob Roberts* cuts to the bone of the American body politic with uncanny timing.' *(Brian D. Johnson, Maclean's)*

ANTI:

'Unfocused, silly, timid, tasteless, uninformed.' *(Ralph Novak, People Weekly)*

'The mentality that informs *Bob Roberts* is the spirit of 1968, which, for all its gallant attitudinizing, was not quite the equal of that of 1776 . . . Much of the film uses the possibly ingenious and certainly economical device of shooting itself through the eye of a documentarist's mostly hand-held camera. This saves a lot of money on elaborate camera set-ups, and allows all kinds of booboos to look like the realistic portrayal of chaos. The result, however, is a movie very hard to watch. Following that frantic hand-held camera, you feel chained into a canoe shooting a nasty set of falls, and this with a stomach already nauseated by the crude oversimplifications, the stretchings of credibility, the self-congratulatory smugness of sequence after sequence.' *(John Simon)*

'As the movie goes on, Robbins turns his anti-hero into a straw man, the embodiment of patriarchal/racist/sexist right-wing power tripping . . . What starts as razor-sharp satire gets ground down to a bludgeon of agitprop.' *(Ty Burr, Entertainment Weekly)*

BODY AND SOUL CT: 6 AV: 7.82

1947 US 104 BW DRAMA

D Robert Rossen ☆
W Abraham Polonsky ☆ AAN

John Garfield ☆ AAN Lilli Palmer Hazel Brooks Anne Revere William Conrad Joseph Pevney Canada Lee

The rise of a prize-fighter (John Garfield).

Powerful acting from Garfield, an intelligent left-wing script by Abraham Polonsky, and atmospheric camerawork by James Wong Howe contribute to a classic, showing the environmental forces which shape a man. If some of the movie seems clichéd today, at least this was the film which created the clichés. The final fight is among the finest ever on screen; and editors Francis Lyon and Robert Parrish rightly won an Oscar.

'*Body and Soul*, which gets very bitter and discreetly leftish about commercialism in prize fighting, is really nothing much, I suppose, when you get right down to it. But it was almost continuously interesting and exhilarating while I watched it, mainly because everyone had clearly decided to do every scene to a finish and because, barring a few letdowns, scene after scene came off that way.' *(James Agee)*

'Written with more integrity than usual . . . and James Wong Howe's shrewd camera elicits more frenzy from the championship bout than newsreels draw from the real thing.' *(Stephen Belcher, New Movies)*

'Betrays an unusual awareness of certain social problems and challenges anyone to disprove the contention that environment is the force that shapes a man.' *(Fortnight)*

'Garfield's bullish performance saves the movie from its stagy moments and episodic script.' *(Geoff Andrew, Time Out)*

BODY HEAT

CT: 8 AV: 7.23

1981 US 113 C THRILLER/ROMANCE

D Lawrence Kasdan ☆
W Lawrence Kasdan ☆

William Hurt ✔ Kathleen Turner ☆ Richard Crenna Ted Danson ✔

Steamy noir drama about a femme fatale (Kathleen Turner) and her bemused lawyer lover (William Hurt).

Lawrence Kasdan pinched, I mean adapted, much of the story-line from Billy Wilder's *Double Indemnity*; but the leading actors make it seem fresh. Kathleen Turner may evoke memories of Lauren Bacall, but she makes the role her own. It's easy to see why William Hurt gets hooked.

'Film noir, if it is to be successfully reworked, needs to be approached with a sense of analysis, rather than simple excess.' *(Steve Jenkins, MFB)*

'An engrossing, mightily stylish meller in which sex and crime walk hand in hand, just like in the old days. Working in the imposing shadow of the late James M. Cain, screenwriter Lawrence Kasdan makes an impressively confident directorial debut.' *(Variety)*

'In the beginning of the movie, Kasdam uses golds and pastels to convey a hard, pedestrian world, but as we approach the murder scene a haze sets in and the colors evaporate. The light of the crime is etched in blacks, whites, and grays, and the killing takes place in a parlous fog, where things come at you out of nowhere: trees, guns, police cars, fire. Then, after the deed is done, the colors return. Only they're different this time: everything acquires a tawny, corroded look, like cheese that's been left out too long.' *(Stephen Schiff, Boston Phoenix)*

'Over-derivative of 1940s melodramas at first, then goes off on its own path and scores.' *(Maltin)*

'A sexy movie with a plot that will keep you guessing until the end.' *(Scheuer)*

BOLERO: AN ADVENTURE IN ECSTASY

CT: 1 AV: 1.20

1984 US 104 C DRAMA/ROMANCE

D John Derek ●
W John Derek ●

Bo Derek ● George Kennedy Andrea Occhipinti Greg Bensen Ana Obregon

In the 1920s an heiress fresh out of English boarding school (Bo Derek!) sets about losing her virginity.

Probably the most pathetic film of all time – with an average of 1.20, it comes out as the lowest scoring picture in this book. Intended to be erotic, it verges on the emetic. Bo Derek's acting abilities are invisible to the naked eye, but Meryl Streep couldn't have done much with a script like this. It contains the immortal line . . . 'Do everything to me. Show me how I can do everything to you. Is there anything I can do for you so you can give ecstasy to me?'

'Totally bonkers from start to finish, [it] never quite lets up being totally mesmerising as well.' *(Nigel Andrews, Financial Times)*

'A film that could set [Bo Derek's] career back 100 years . . . I must have seen sillier, more boring films but I can't remember when.' *(Alan Frank, Daily Star)*

'The only ecstatic moment a filmgoer might derive will be at the discovery that it's over.' *(Philip Strick, MFB)*

'About as riveting as watching somebody lose their glasses.' (Rose)

'There is one unforgettable slow-motion sex scene in which a sheik licks honey off Bo's tummy and all this disgusting gooey stuff forms on his face and hangs from his nose.' *(Danny Peary)*

'Completely insufferable and a total embarrassment.' *(Menahem Golan, who commissioned it)*

BOMBSHELL

CT: 7 AV: 7.67

(aka *Blonde Bombshell*)

1933 US 91 BW COMEDY

D Victor Fleming ☆
W Jules Furthman John Lee Mahin ☆ from Caroline Francke and Mack Crane's play

Jean Harlow ☆ Lee Tracy Frank Morgan Franchot Tone Pat O'Brien Ivan Lebedeff Una Merkel C. Aubrey Smith

Adventures of a sexpot of the silver screen (Jean Harlow).

One of the wittiest and most penetrating satires on the Golden Age of Hollywood. Proof that Jean Harlow was a fine comedienne, as well as a sex symbol.

'Excellent satire, rapid, extremely ingenious and not without subtlety. In fact with a little more metaphysics it would make a suitable theme for Pirandello.' *(The Times)*

'This delicious tale . . . has the real stuff of popular entertainment.' *(Sunday Express)*

'Crackpot farce which even by today's standards moves at a fair clip and enabled the star to give her best comedy performance.' *(Halliwell)*

'Victor Fleming directed rather stridently and unimaginatively, but from an enjoyably snappy, rude script.' *(Pauline Kael)*

THE BOND SERIES

DR NO CT: 6 AV: 7.21

(aka *Doctor No*)

1962 GB 111 C ACTION/ADVENTURE

D Terence Young ☆
W Richard Maibaum Johanna Harwood Berkely Mather ☆ from Ian Fleming's novel

Sean Connery Ursula Andress Jack Lord Joseph Wiseman John Kitzmiller Bernard Lee Lois Maxwell Zena Marshall Eunice Gayson Anthony Dawson

British spy (Sean Connery) investigates the murder in Jamaica of another secret agent and his secretary.

Made on a lower budget than its successors, this action-packed adventure nevertheless laid down the template for all future Bond movies. Sean Connery bears little relation to Ian Fleming's Old Etonian creation, but he has a rugged virility which made him more attractive to a mass international audience. The gadgetry and special effects had not yet overwhelmed the narrative; by far the most special effect is the moment when Ursula Andress rises out of the ocean.

'An entertaining piece of tongue-in-cheek action hokum.' *(Variety)*

'Efficiency: perhaps that doesn't sound high praise . . . I mean it as high. The first of the James Bond films (I trust there will be others) has the air of knowing exactly what it is up to, and that has not been common in British thrillers since the day Hitchcock took himself off to America . . . [It is] all good and, I am glad to say, not quite clean fun.' *(Dilys Powell)*

FROM RUSSIA WITH LOVE CT: 7 AV: 7.54

1963 GB 110/118 C ACTION/ADVENTURE

D Terence Young ☆
W Richard Maibaum Johanna Harwood ☆ from Ian Fleming's novel

Sean Connery ☆ Robert Shaw ☆ Lotte Lenya ☆ Pedro Armendariz ☆ Daniela Bianchi Bernard Lee Lois Maxwell Eunice Gayson

A Russian spy (Daniela Bianchi) poses as a spy to entrap Bond (Sean Connery).

Which is the best Bond movie? Most critics are divided between this one and *Goldfinger* (though I have a soft spot for *You Only Live Twice*). Istanbul and Venice are the main backdrops here, and there are two terrific villains in Robert Shaw and Lotte Lenya. Connery is more self-assured than he was in *Dr No*.

ANTI:

'Slightly disappointing . . . The set-pieces – rough stuff on a train and in a gypsy camp – seem sparse and the pace drags too often.' *(Shipman)*

PRO:

'A preposterous, skillful slab of hardhitting, sexy hokum. After a slowish start, it is directed by Terence Young at zingy pace.' *(Variety)*

'Secret Agent 007 is very much with us again, and anyone who hasn't yet got to know him is urged to do so right away!' *(New York Times)*

'Fast, funny entertainment . . . (Bond's) further antics should provide a strong box office attraction as his movie fame grows and his appeal broadens.' *(Hollywood Reporter)*

GOLDFINGER CT: 8 AV: 7.54

1964 GB 112 C ACTION/ADVENTURE

D Guy Hamilton ☆
W Richard Maibaum Paul Dehn ☆ from Ian Fleming's novel

Sean Connery ☆ Honor Blackman Gert Frobe ☆ Harold Sakata Shirley Eaton Bernard Lee Lois Maxwell Desmond Llewellyn

Bond (Sean Connery) thwarts an attack on Fort Knox.

Often regarded as the best Bond film, with a great opening, a well-crafted plot, and an exciting finale as 007 saves the world from financial ruin. Gert Frobe shines as the would-be world dominator with an appetite for gold, and there's a classic heavy in Oddjob (Harold Sakata). Honor Blackman is suitably alluring as Pussy Galore (though her lesbianism is toned down from the novel). The gadgetry – as used here in the famous Aston Martin chase – is now coming into its own, but has not taken over. The sound effects won an Oscar.

'The third James Bond movie isn't up to the standards set by *Dr No* and *From Russia with Love* in my book, despite its providing the same old suavity, chit chat and bang-bang, the same old illicit amours and illegal intrigues, semisatiric deering-do, and perfection of lush production. The focus seems to have shifted from emphatic action and vicarious heroism to sex and sadism (watch luscious Shirley Eaton get literally gilded to death), which outweigh the good dirty fun that initially gave Bond his adult-comic-strip status with grown-ups.' *(Judith Crist)*

'There's not the least sign of staleness.' *(Variety)*

'A dazzling object lesson in the principle that nothing succeeds like excess.' *(Penelope Gilliatt)*

THUNDERBALL CT: 5 AV: 5.33

1965 GB 132 C ACTION/ADVENTURE

D Terence Young
W Richard Maibaum John Hopkins from Ian Fleming's novel

Sean Connery ☆ Adolfo Celi ☆ Claudine Auger Luciana Paluzzi Rik Van Nutter Bernard Lee Lois Maxwell Martine Beswick

Bond (Sean Connery) foils blackmailers threatening to drop a nuclear bomb on Miami.

Fourth of the Bond films and good dirty fun; but for the first time the characterization and plot seem subservient to the stuntwork and effects (which won an Oscar for John Stears). Still, the Bahamas locations are lovely, the story zips along, and there's a splendid villain in Adolo Celi. Sean Connery felt the film could have been better, and remade it in 1983 as *Never Say Never Again*. The most successful of all the Bonds – but that's probably because of its two predecessors.

'Terence Young takes advantage of every situation in his direction to maintain action at fever-pitch.' *(Variety)*

'It's a bird! It's a plane! It's a Super-Bond!' *(Hollywood Reporter)*

'The screenplay stands on tiptoe at the outermost edge of the suggestive and gazes yearningly down into the obscene.' *(John Simon)*

YOU ONLY LIVE TWICE CT: 8 AV: 6.00

1967 GB 117 C ACTION/ADVENTURE

D Lewis Gilbert
W Roald Dahl from Ian Fleming's novel

Sean Connery ☆ Tetsuro Tamba Akiko Wakabayashi Mie Hama Charles Gray ☆ Donald Pleasence ☆ Karin Dor Bernard Lee Lois Maxwell Desmond Llewellyn

Bond travels to Japan to scotch another attempt at world domination.

One of the least plausible but most ingenious Bond screenplays (by Roald Dahl) and one of the biggest budgets combine with Lewis Gilbert's direction (superb in the action sequences) to create a memorable adventure. By now, Sean Connery's performance has virtually nothing to do with Ian Fleming's creation, but he has a suaveness and finesse which enable him to deliver the smuttiest one-liners without giving offence. The special effects (especially the volcano that opens) are excellent, the girls gorgeous (though virtually indistinguishable from one another), the cinematography by Freddie Young spectacular, the sets by Ken Adam amazing, and John Barry's music outstanding.

'The gaggy screenplay for this instalment coarsens the style.' *(New Yorker)*

'Some of the inventions are knockouts, but it would never occur to you that the hero's more stunning technical escapes from trouble could have originated in the head of the character . . . The man in the film is beginning to seem oddly inert, his eyes glazed with gadgets, as if this were Christmas morning in a millionaire's house and he a spoiled and lonely child with little flair for fun.' *(Penelope Gilliatt)*

'Lewis Gilbert is a rather more humanistic director than his predecessors and he's a reasonably efficient traffic manager; he doesn't let the actors loiter on the sets too long.' *(Pauline Kael)*

'Scientifically the most ambitious, sexually the most routine, scenically one of the best.' *(New York Post)*

ON HER MAJESTY'S SECRET SERVICE CT: 6 AV: 6.50

1969 GB 140 C ACTION/ADVENTURE

D Peter Hunt ☆
W Richard Maibaum from Ian Fleming's novel

George Lazenby Diana Rigg Telly Savalas Ilse Steppat Gabriele Ferzetti Yuri Borienko Bernard Lee Lois Maxwell

Bond (George Lazenby) foils a master-criminal's plan to infect the world through beautiful women carrying a deadly virus – and gets married.

As though to compensate for the absent Connery, this is the most action-packed Bond film: the one in which the stunts become all-important. Which is just as well, since the sexual chemistry is signally lacking between Lazenby and his leading lady (Diana Rigg).

'Film of break-neck physical excitement and stunning visual attractions.' *(Variety)*

'An attempt, repeated and strenuous is made to substitute quantities of violence for quality.' *(New York Post)*

'The direction of Peter Hunt – an editor on earlier Bond films – brought a cutting-room crispness to every set-up, though even he was not able to truncate a film that feels as if it is ending four times before it actually does so.' *(Alexander Walker)*

'As Agent 007, Lazenby is about as animated as Westminster Abbey.' *(Scheuer)*

DIAMONDS ARE FOREVER CT: 5 AV: 5.62

1971 GB 119 C ACTION/ADVENTURE

D Guy Hamilton
W Richard Maibaum Tom Mankiewicz from Ian Fleming's novel

Sean Connery Jill St John Charles Gray ☆ Lana Wood Jimmy Dean Bruce Cabot Bernard Lee Lois Maxwell

Bond (Sean Connery) investigates diamond-smuggling and visits Amsterdam and Las Vegas.

Connery's back, and more sinful and sadistic than ever. The production values remain up to the highest standards. The smutty script is a letdown, though; there's more gratuitous violence; and campy humour is allowed for the first time seriously to diminish the sense of menace. Weakest of the Bond films up to then.

PRO:

'Bond looks better than ever, partly because Sean Connery has returned to play him. During Connery's one-picture absence, some fellow named Lazenby filled the role – the way concrete fills a hole.' *(Time)*

'Apart from a clumsy climax, a wry and exhilarating bit of entertainment.' *(Time Out)*

ANTI:

'It has been claimed that the plot is impossible to describe, but I think I could do it if I wanted to. I can't think why anyone would want to, though.' *(Roger Ebert)*

'Connery . . . looks a bit long in the tooth to be running around the world scaling buildings, racing cars and generally cutting up.' *(Newsweek)*

'Everything is played more for laughs instead of thrills and suspense. Also there is no real sense of menace in the film.' *(John Brosnan, James Bond in the Cinema, 1972)*

LIVE AND LET DIE CT: 6 AV: 5.18

1973 GB 121 C ACTION/ADVENTURE

D Guy Hamilton
W Tom Mankiewicz from Ian Fleming's novel

Roger Moore Yaphet Kotto Jane Seymour Clifton James ✔ Bernard Lee Lois Maxwell David Hedison Geoffrey Holder

Bond (Roger Moore) takes on a black master-criminal (Yaphet Kotto).

Number eight in the Bond series, and the first to star Roger Moore. The plot is thinner than in the very best Bonds, but the locations are suitably exotic; the set-pieces (especially the boat chase) are fine; and Moore's suave sexlessness is offset by some good jokes and lively supporting performances (notably from Clifton James as a southern sheriff). Paul McCartney's title song, superbly orchestrated by George Martin, is one of the catchiest of all Bond themes, and was nominated for an Oscar.

'The script reveals that plot lines have descended further to the level of the old Saturday afternoon serial.' *(Variety)*

'Roger Moore is a handsome, suave, somewhat phlegmatic James Bond – with a tendency to throw away his throw-away quips as the minor embarrasment that, alas, they usually are.' *(Roger Greenspun, New York Times)*

'From this point, the emphasis began to be towards comedy, an emphasis that benefited Moore, but which radically altered the whole Bond mystique.' *(Stephen Jay Rubin, The James Bond Films, 1983)*

'Connery could always talk up something warm with his Bond Girl; Moore inspected his playmates as if they were privates on parade.' *(Julie Burchill, Girls on Film)*

MAN WITH THE GOLDEN GUN, THE CT: 1 AV: 4.00

1974 GB 125 C ACTION/ADVENTURE

D Guy Hamilton ●
W Richard Maibaum Tom Mankiewicz ● from Ian Fleming's novel

Roger Moore Christopher Lee Britt Ekland Maud Adams Hervé Villechaize Richard Loo Clifton James

Bond (Roger Moore) takes on a master-assassin (Christopher Lee) with three nipples.

Slow, tired, unfunny Bond film, worst of the series. Christopher Lee tries to summon up some menace. Roger Moore looks understandably bored. Attempts to drag in kung fu sequences add to the general air of desperation.

'Screenwriters' mission this ninth time round was to give the James Bond character more maturity, fewer gadgetry gimmicks, and more humor. On the last item, they fumbled badly.' *(Variety)*

'The throbbing information that "the energy crisis is still with us" isn't what you need or want to learn from a James Bond picture . . . If you enjoyed the early Bond films as much as I did, you'd better skip this one.' *(Mora Sayre, New York Times)*

SPY WHO LOVED ME, THE CT: 5 AV: 6.07

1977 GB 125 C ACTION/ADVENTURE

D Lewis Gilbert
W Christopher Wood Richard Maibaum from Ian Fleming's novel

Roger Moore Barbara Bach Curt Jurgens Richard Kiel Caroline Munro Walter Gotell Bernard Lee Lois Maxwell Desmond Llewellyn George Baker Edward De Souza Sydney Tafler

British secret agent (Roger Moore) and Russian spy (Barbara Bach) hunt a shipping magnate with dreams of world domination (Curt Jurgens).

Richard Kiel as the villainous Jaws gets his teeth into the only decent role in this moderate adventure. Moore sleepwalks through the role of James Bond, as well he might, with a script like this.

'Moves along at a serviceable clip, but it seems half an hour too long.' *(Janet Maslin, New York Times)*

'The continual appeal of the Bond movies is a real phenomenon – particularly when you consider what a dated cultural artifact James Bond is. More than any other pop character, Agent 007 emblemized the romantic values of the now-distant Camelot era: Bond was a cool, handsome, intellectual bon vivant who did battle against evil international forces, and in our consciousness he was nothing if not a Hollywood stand-in for John Kennedy . . . Bond's lifestyle – his fondness for shapely women, designer clothes and mechanical gimcracks – came right out of the pages of *Playboy* magazine and not since the early 60s has *Playboy* correctly expressed the fantasy lives of mainstream American men.' *(Frank Rich, New York Times)*

'Seems to do nothing more than anthologize its forerunners.' *(Tim Pulleine, MFB)*

'You could believe that Connery was cunning and apt enough to think up the clever things he said, and execute the mighty maneuvers he undertook. Not so Roger Moore, who looks handsome enough to be the mold from which the world's most expensive clothing dummies are cast, but who has absolutely no way with an expression, let alone with a line. You might say that, as 007, he does justice only to the first two thirds of his role.' *(John Simon)*

MOONRAKER CT: 2 AV: 3.42

1979 GB 126 C ACTION/ADVENTURE

D Lewis Gilbert
W Christopher Wood ● from Ian Fleming's novel

Roger Moore Lois Chiles Michael Lonsdale Richard Kiel Bernard Lee Lois Maxwell Geoffrey Keen

Bond (Roger Moore) investigates a missing space shuttle.

The best part of this amazingly feeble Bond film (there are so few new ideas that they even have to bring back Richard Kiel from *The Spy Who Loved Me*) is the space battle at the end. It's not that it's a great sequence; but you know they're going to let you out of the cinema soon. Opinion is divided as to whether this or *The Man With The Golden Gun* is the worst of the series; this one has the feeblest villain.

'Conspicuously expensive production values but an unmistakably cut price plot.' *(S & S)*

'An exhausted movie. Roger Moore is dutiful and passive as Bond, his clothes are neatly pressed and he shows up for work, like an office manager who is turning into dead wood but hanging on to collect his pension. As the scientist-heroine, Lois Chiles is so enervated she barely reacts to the threat of the end of the world. Michael Lonsdale walks through impassively.' *(Pauline Kael)*

FOR YOUR EYES ONLY CT: 6 AV: 5.54

1981 GB 127 C ACTION/ADVENTURE

D John Glen ✔
W Richard Maibaum Michael G. Wilson

Roger Moore Carol Bouquet Topol Lynn-Holly Johnson Julian Glover Jill Bennett Jack Hedley Lois Maxwell Desmond Llewellyn Geoffrey Keen

Bond (Roger Moore) tries to find an anti-Polaris device before the KGB.

The first Bond film in which Ian Fleming is uncredited is, ironically, something of a return to form: the stunts and special effects are excellent, Moore tries a bit harder, and there's a more interesting (if asexual) heroine than usual in Carole Bouquet. Impressionist Janet Brown puts in a late appearance as Margaret Thatcher.

'One of the most thoroughly enjoyable of the 12 Bond pix.' *(Variety)*

'Pretty boring between the stunts, as if the director isn't interested in actors, and Broccoli forgot to commission a screenplay.' *(Observer)*

'Roger Moore fronts for a succession of stunt men with all the relaxed, lifelike charm of a foyer poster of himself.' *(Sunday Times)*

NEVER SAY NEVER AGAIN CT: 5 AV: 5.50

1983 GB 137 C ACTION/ADVENTURE

D Irvin Kershner
W Lorenzo Semple Jr from Ian Fleming's novel *Thunderball*

Sean Connery Klaus Maria Brandauer Max Von Sydow Barbara Carrera Kim Basinger Bernie Casey Alex McCowen Edward Fox Rowan Atkinson

Bond (Sean Connery) foils yet another attempt at world domination.

Not strictly speaking one of the Bond series, since it was not produced by Cubby Broccoli. After an absence of 12 years, Sean Connery dons his toupé again to play Secret Agent 007. As Q (Alec McCowen) says, 'Good to see you again, Mr Bond. Let's get back to some gratuitous sex and violence, I say'. Reasonably enjoyable and Klaus Maria Brandauer makes an excellent villain; but the plot is merely *Thunderball* revisited, a lot of the original enthusiasm has vanished, and it's much too long-winded.

'Time has caught up with Bond – and he's very much the better for wear. He combines the wry reserve of yesteryear with a hint of weariness that, in the context of the screenplay's insistence on adventure, is genuinely amusing.' *(Janet Maslin, New York Times)*

'Connery brings both a human quality and a real style back to the anachronistic Bond who now seems to have a place in the world rather than in a dinner-jacket commercial.' *(Sheila Benson, Los Angeles Times)*

'Well into his fifties, the thrill was indubitably gone – and so, sadly, was a great deal of Mr Connery's hair.' *(Julie Burchill, Girls on Film)*

OCTOPUSSY CT: 5 AV: 5.67

1983 GB 131 C ACTION/ADVENTURE

D John Glen ✔
W George MacDonald Fraser Richard Maibaum Michael G. Wilson

Roger Moore Maud Adams ● Louis Jourdan Kristina Wayborn Kabir Bedi Steven Berkoff ✔ Desmond Llewelyn Robert Brown Walter Gotell Geoffrey Keen Lois Maxwell

Bond (Roger Moore) prevents a Russian general (Steven Berkoff) from nuking a US army base.

Evidently influenced by the success of *Raiders of the Lost Ark*, John Glen directs at top speed and with his usual flair for action. The wildly implausible script contains some laugh-lines, and Steven Berkoff overacts entertainingly as a mad Russian general, but on the whole this is wearisome stuff.

'High points are the spectacular aerial stuntwork marking both the pre-credits teaser and the extremely dangerous-looking climax.' *(Variety)*

'As the films drift further and further into self-parody, no one seems to notice and no one (at any rate in box office terms) seems to mind.' *(Nick Roddick, MFB)*

'The Bond of *Octopussy* has ceased to be a vital part of the mainspring action, as he is in the classic Bond stories and films, and declined into the position of a hero who has to keep up with the action initiated by the villains and frustrate them turn-by-turn.' *(Roger Manvell, Magill's Cinema Annual)*

VIEW TO A KILL, A CT: 4 AV: 4.45

1985 GB 121/131 C ACTION/ADVENTURE

D John Glen
W Richard Maibaum Michael G. Wilson ●

Roger Moore Christopher Walken ✔ Grace Jones ✔ Tanya Roberts Patrick MacNee David Yip Fiona Fullerton Patrick Bauchau Alison Doody Desmond Llewelyn Robert Brown Lois Maxwell (bit part Dolph Lundgren)

Bond (Roger Moore) foils plan to establish a monopoly in world's microchips.

The seventh and last appearance of Roger Moore as 007 is enlivened by two entertaining villains in Christopher Walken and Grace Jones. Basically, it's one of the weaker Bonds, but there are two exciting sequences: the chase down the Eiffel Tower and the climax on the Golden Gate Bridge.

'The James Bond series has had its bummers, but nothing before in the class of this one.' *(New Yorker)*

'Everything about *A View To A Kill* . . . suggests that the creative juices have begun to run dry. The plot, at once simple-minded and hopelessly convoluted, seems to be held together by spit.' *(Arthur Knight, Hollywood Reporter)*

'[Moore] still has the suave and cool for the part, but on occasion he looks a bit old and his womanizing seems dated.' *(Variety)*

'Roger Moore as James Bond: not so much like a piece of plastic as something embalmed but moving.' *(Shipman)*

LIVING DAYLIGHTS, THE CT: 6 AV: 5.91

1987 GB 130 C ACTION/ADVENTURE

D John Glen
W Richard Maibaum Michael G. Wilson

Timothy Dalton Maryam d'Abo Jeroen Krabbé ✔ Joe Don Baker ✔ John Rhys-Davies Art Malik Desmond Llewelyn Robert Brown Geoffrey Keen Caroline Bliss John Terry Virginia Hey

Bond (Timothy Dalton) comes into conflict with a fake Soviet defector (Jeroen Krabbe) and a rogue arms dealer (Joe Don Baker).

More plot, less humour, fewer gadgets and a more athletic Bond: on the whole, it's an improvement. Caroline Bliss takes over from Lois Maxwell as Miss Moneypenny.

'Dalton, the fourth Bond, registers beautifully on all key counts of charm, machismo, sensitivity and technique.' *(Variety)*

'At 40, Dalton takes a bow as James Bond. Although he isn't as quick with the wisecracks as earlier incarnations of 007, there's plenty of great action, a delicious damsel in distress and some wonderful scenery. What more do you want from a Bond film?' *(Rose)*

LICENCE TO KILL CT: 7 AV: 6.17

1989 US 133 C ACTION/ADVENTURE

D John Glen ☆
W Michael G. Wilson Richard Maibaum

Timothy Dalton Carey Lowell Robert Davi ☆
Talisa Soto Anthony Zerbe Frank McRae
Everett McGill Wayne Newton Benicio del Toro
Desmond Llewelyn ☆ David Hedison
Robert Brown Caroline Bliss

Bond (Timothy Dalton) risks his bosses' disapproval to go in search of drug-dealer (Robert Davi) who maimed fellow secret agent.

Fast, frenetic, and among the most exciting Bond films. Q (Desmond Llewellyn) is drafted in to supply light relief, leaving Dalton free to take the plot seriously and be even more of an action man than previous Bonds. Unfortunately, he still lacks either the presence of Sean Connery or the charm of Roger Moore. When Dalton's on screen with the villain, it's the villain you watch. One other caveat: this is easily the most violent of the Bond pictures.

'Dalton plays 007 with a vigor and physicality that harks back to the earliest Bond pics, letting full-bloodied action speak louder than words. The thrills-and-spills chases are superbly orchestrated.' *(Variety)*

'Lowell makes a wonderfully sassy heroine, and although the plot's as ropey as ever, the stunts are great.' *(Rose)*

'A great idea, but a terrible movie . . . Bond wanders through the film killing almost everyone he meets in increasingly unpleasant ways. *Licence to Kill* becomes almost a Freddy Krueger splatter movie without the splatter. Despite the corpses, the action sequences are uninvolving . . . Alec Mills cinematography makes the least of every location, cruelly exposing the artificiality of the sets. John Glen's direction is so unimaginative that it is hard to believe he did such sterling work on *The Living Daylights* and *For Your Eyes Only*. Worst still is Michael Kamen's dismal score . . . Most worrying of all is Dalton's Bond, a lethargic and limited performance reminiscent of Moore at his worst . . . Most of Bond's distinguishing characteristics are gone. Displaying no signs of class or intellect, he has become a mere killing machine.' *(Trevor Willsmer, Film Yearbook)*

BONFIRE OF THE VANITIES, THE CT: 4 AV: 3.00

1990 US 125 C COMEDY

D Brian De Palma ●
W Michael Cristofer ● from Tom Wolfe's novel

Tom Hanks ● Bruce Willis ● Melanie Griffith
Morgan Freeman ● F. Murray Abraham
Saul Rubinek Robert Stephens

A Wall Street whizz-kid (Tom Hanks) gets his come-uppance; a sleazy journalist (Bruce Willis) doesn't.

Two miscast actors, a style-junkie director at his most vacuous and an adapter without an ounce of sensitivity to the original material combine to make one of the biggest critical and box-office fiascos in history. The British reviews were less hard on the film than the Americans were, and if you haven't read the novel, the movie is just about bearable; if you have, however, you soon realize how mind-bogglingly terrible the adaptation is. The screenplay even tries to be politically correct – one of the faults which the original author was lampooning. Morgan Freeman's final speech is Hollywood schmaltz at its most risible (sample line: 'Decency is what your grandmother taught you.'). The main amusement to be had is from watching Melanie Griffith's breasts, which change size quite dramatically and without warning (she had implants during shooting).

'About as socially incisive as a *Police Academy* entry.' *(Variety)*

'The picture grates on your nerves: you sit there listening to Melanie Griffith's metallic whine and you watch Bruce Willis fail at the simple task of playing a comic drunk. These are talented people – what's happened to them? . . . Whatever one's feelings about the Wolfe novel (I disliked it), it works. Michael Cristofer's thin script doesn't; it's as if he had been hired to make the worst adaptation that could be made.' *(Pauline Kael)*

'No one cast in this movie ever stood a chance; they all go down with the ship . . . A disaster . . . The comedy is staged by a man who seems to have lost his sense of humor.' *(David Ansen, Newsweek)*

'A pilot light of the inanities . . . In softening Wolfe's scathing satire, De Palma . . . has become one of the buffoons . . . scorned in the bestseller.' *(Washington Post)*

'Those who have read the book will be constantly distracted because they know so much more than the movie tells them.' *(New York Daily News)*

'All the casting stinks . . . De Palma gave in to Hollywood's nerves about race . . . thus robbing the film of most of its point.' *(Reggie Nadelson, Independent)*

BONNIE AND CLYDE AAN CT: 9 AV: 9.71

1967 US 111 C THRILLER/ROMANCE

D Arthur Penn ☆ AAN
W David Newman Robert Benton ☆ AAN

Warren Beatty ☆ AAN Faye Dunaway ☆ AAN
Estelle Parsons ☆ AAW Gene Hackman ☆ AAN
Michael J. Pollard ☆ AAN Denver Pyle
Gene Wilder ✓

Two bank-robbers (Faye Dunaway, Warren Beatty) and their friends operate during the Depression.

Arthur Penn's movie controversially asks audiences to identify with amoral but attractive outlaws, right up to their inevitable slaughter by the guns of a repressive society. Though a product of the rebellious 60s, the film is so well made that it stands up as a classic of the gangster genre. Burnett Guffey's cinematography won an Oscar.

'It is not just an exciting picture. It is part of a campaign to destroy the morals of Western youth.' *(V. Menshikov, Pravda)*

ANTI:

'Killings and the backdrop of the Depression are scarcely material for a bundle of laughs.' *(Variety)*

'The whole thing stinks in the manner of a carefully made-up, combed, and manicured corpse . . . What is basically wrong with the film is not so much violence as hero worship . . . To argue as they do that in periods of social injustice (which means anywhere this side of Utopia) the outlaw is clearly superior to the staid, plodding citizen is sentimental nonsense and moral truancy.' *(John Simon)*

'The killing doubtless falls into the category of rollicking family entertainment, to be enjoyed by all except vegetarians and other mean and ascetic spoilsports. Yes, I have to admit that it was this that brought the censor out in me . . . I found it obscene.' *(Sean Day-Lewis, Daily Telegraph)*

PRO:

'As Clyde [Beatty's] performance is a frighteningly well-observed study of a criminal lunatic and a chilling example of controlled violence . . . Probably [its] only weakness (or is it its strength?) is that you can come away with more than a passing affection for the two leading characters. I was angry with myself for not loathing them.' *(Clive Hirschhorn, Sunday Express)*

'The most significant film to come out of America since On the Waterfront over 10 years ago . . . A film from which we shall date reputations and innovations in the American cinema . . . It cries to be seen.' *(Alexander Walker, Evening Standard)*

'The film shakes you up and worries and excites and challenges you . . . haunts you for days.' *(Nina Hibbin, Morning Star)*

'*Bonnie and Clyde* was released a scant two months before the anti-war march on the Pentagon in October of 1967. It was Clyde's lack of focus as an outlaw that made him the darling of 1967, the bloodiness of his demise that made audiences somehow reach to him, puzzled at their reasons for doing so. If the Johnson government was the law, then increasing numbers of people knew they were outside it: outside its draft laws, outside the drug laws. For thousands, 1967 marked a watershed, marked their deepening sense of becoming outlaws.' *(Andrew Bergman, We're in the Money, 1971)*

BOOM! CT: 2 AV: 2.83

1968 GB 113 C DRAMA/ROMANCE

D Joseph Losey ●
W Tennessee Wiliams ● from his own play *The Milk Train Doesn't Stop Here Any More*

Elizabeth Taylor ● Richard Burton ●
Joanna Shimkus ✔ Noel Coward Michael Dunn.

On a Mediterranean island, a dying millionairess (Elizabeth Taylor) seduces an itinerant poet (Richard Burton) who just happens to be the angel of death.

Preposterous, pretentious and a first-class ticket to torpor, this vehicle for Elizabeth Taylor and Richard Burton attracted some of the most vitriolic reviews of all time. There are some good things: Douglas Slocombe's cinematography and the lovely Joanna Shimkus, to name but two – and Noel Coward livens it up whenever he's camping around as a male witch. But the dead hand of Joseph Losey ensures that the film ends up as one that could bore for Britain.

'It's a beautiful picture, the best ever made of one of my plays.' *(Tennessee Williams)*

'An ordeal in tedium.' *(Hollywood Reporter)*

'Noel Coward seems determined to end his career by making a public fool of himself.' *(Stanley Kauffmann, New Republic)*

'The once delightful Coward is now a mincing senior citizen of Leprechaunia, still aiming for rapid-fire repartee with one foot in his mausoleum and the other in his overdentured mouth . . . Joseph Losey, the director, strains desperately to inject a note of art, but keeps missing the vein, if this dressmaker's dummy of a film can be said to have one.' *(John Simon)*

'Let them [Taylor and Burton] by all means do their thing, but why film it and charge admission?" *(Wilfred Sheed, Esquire)*

'That title could not be more apt; it is precisely the sound of a bomb exploding.' *(Richard Schickel, Life)*

BOOMERANG! CT: 8 AV: 7.80

1947 US 88 BW THRILLER

D Elia Kazan ☆
W Richard Murphy ☆ AAN from Anthony Abbott's *Reader's Digest* article 'The Perfect Case'

Dana Andrews ☆ Jane Wyatt Lee J. Cobb ☆ Cara Williams Arthur Kennedy Sam Levene Taylor Holmes Robert Keith Ed Begley

A prosecutor (Dana Andrews) investigates a false confession to a murder, and uncovers small-town corruption.

Kazan's second film as director is a gripping thriller, based on a true story and innovative for its documentary style and use of locations. Once considered to be hard-hitting, it has been much imitated and therefore lost a lot of its impact. It remains a film of high quality, and contains one of Dana Andrews's finest performances.

'For the first time in many a moon we are treated to a picture that gives a good example of a typical small American city – the people, their way of living, their mode of government, the petty politics practised, the power of the press.' *(Frank Ward, NBR)*

'[The] script clarifies the community's characters, conflicts and issues in crisp journalistic fashion . . . The whole show ticks like an expensive watch.' *(Time)*

'Fast, authentic and magnificently acted . . . the highest type of documentary fiction, terse, vivid and understated, and its revelation of American politics is ruthless.' *(Daily Worker)*

'A study of integrity, beautifully developed by Dana Andrews against a background of political corruption and chicanery that is doubly shocking because of its documentary understatement . . . This is not the Lullaby of Democracy we normally receive from Hollywood; but a much prouder work, ruthless and mature.' *(Richard Winnington, News Chronicle)*

BOOT, DAS:

see BOAT, THE.

BORN ON THE FOURTH OF JULY AAN

CT: 5 AV: 7.30

1989 US 144 C WAR/DRAMA

D Oliver Stone ✗ AAW
W Oliver Stone Ron Kovic based on Kovic's true story AAN

Tom Cruise ☆ AAN Kyra Sedgwick Willem Dafoe Tom Berenger Raymond J. Barry Caroline Kava Jerry Levine Frank Whaley Jamie Talisman Bryan Larkin

A young, gung-ho soldier, Ron Kovic (Tom Cruise) has his spine shattered in Vietnam, and his faith in the war shattered when he returns home to a country which regards him and the war as embarrassments.

Widely acclaimed on its release as the 'definitive' movie about Vietnam, *Born on the Fourth of July* is a serious but very flawed attempt to come to terms with the Vietnam war. It is very overlong, and much of it is over-familiar. We've seen the torching of defenceless villages and the shooting of Americans by Americans, in *Casualties of War* and *Platoon*; veterans adjusting to life in a wheelchair in *Coming Home* and *The Deer Hunter*; and the thankless return to *America in First Blood, Welcome Home* and *In Country* . . . When all this is paraded before us yet again, it's hard not to feel Viet numb.

The two climaxes of the film are parochial, self-pitying and complacent. The first – Kovic's greatest moment of defiance – comes when he attends the 1972 Republican National Convention and rages against Nixon, Agnew and the rest. 'They have killed a whole generation of young Americans!' he cries, momentarily forgetting perhaps that only 50,000 Americans died, while Vietnamese casualties ran into millions.

The final, supposedly uplifting set-piece is our hero's arrival as a guest speaker at the 1976 Democrat Convention. Surrounded by cheering activists and attentive journalists, Kovic looks happy and relaxed for the first time, and concludes: 'Maybe we're home'. The implication is clear: Kovic's physical injuries may remain, but his mental wounds – and the country's – are being cleansed by the democratic process and media publicity, of which this movie is a part. Such cosy rhetoric may be comforting, not least for American Democrats; but, unfortunately, it was Democrat Presidents Kennedy and Johnson who instigated the Vietnam war, and a Republican (Nixon) who ended it.

Although the American public was lied to by governments of both parties, these were leaders freely elected under a democratic system; and the truth about the war was available from early on, if the American people and media had cared to examine it. Stone conspicuously avoids a far less palatable truth about Vietnam: that the American people itself was responsible for sending so many young Americans (a disproportionate number of whom were black), and innumerable Vietnamese, to a futile death.

PRO:

'A powerful, heartfelt scream of rage and despair, both shocking and human, in Stone's best style. Cruise gives a remarkably good performance in this masterpiece of modern cinema.' *(Rose)*

ANTI:

'Overblown right from the start . . . It's almost inconceivable that Ron Kovic was as innocent as the movie and the 1976 autobiography on which it's based make him out to be. Was this kid kept in a bubble? At some level, everybody knows about the ugliness of war . . . Ron seems to have blotted out everything that didn't conform to his priggish views . . . Oliver Stone, who wrote the script with Kovic, is committed to the idea of Ron's total naiveté. He's presented as a credulous boy whose country lied to him . . . Kovic's book is simple and explicit; he states his case in plain, angry words. Stone's movie yells at you for two hours and twenty-five minutes.' *(Pauline Kael)*

'Preachy through and through – suggesting that its success should be ascribed to America's need for . . . a new nostalgia, no longer for 1950s suburbia but rather for a time when it was possible to believe that waving banners, burning flags and getting oneself arrested would be enough to change the world.' *(James Park, Film Yearbook)*

BORN YESTERDAY AAN CT: 7 AV: 8.15

1950 US 103 BW COMEDY/ROMANCE

D George Cukor ☆ AAN
W Albert Mannheimer AAN from Garson Kanin's play

Judy Holliday ☆AAW Broderick Crawford
William Holden

Harry Brock (Broderick Crawford), a boorish businessman , employs a Washington journalist (William Holden) to teach his dumb-blonde mistress Billie Dawn (Judy Holliday) to hold her own in Political Society.

Classic comedy which won Judy Holliday the Best Actress Oscar over Bette Davis in *All About Eve* and Gloria Swanson in *Sunset Boulevard*. Holliday is entrancing. A highly intelligent stage actress despite her dumb-blonde image, she played the part of Billie Dawn for over 1,600 performances on Broadway. She perfected a high-pitched, Minnie Mouse voice for much of her dialogue, a harsh, Brooklyn squawk when aggrieved, and a deep, contralto growl for her final dismissal of Harry.
The card-playing set-piece, where Billie casually massacres Harry Brock at gin rummy, is a show-stopper.

The disappointing aspect is that, despite the setting, there's surprisingly little satire on Washington. Even William Holden's investigative journalist seems inhibited by fear of being branded Communist: the system's fine, he says – it's just that there are 'one or two rotten apples'. Even though the enemy is described as illegality and 'fascism', the film's defence of American democratic values and naive jingoism mark it out as very much a Cold War, defensive movie. There was an inferior, though watchable, remake in 1993.

'I could not catch more than two-thirds of what Judy Holliday said. I am prepared to accept that she gives a notable imitation of a Brooklyn accent, but to non-American ears reception is difficult.' *(Daily Mail)*

'More fun to watch than anything Hollywood has put out this year.' *(Fortnight)*

'Comes off almost as freshly on the screen as it did on the stage.' *(Newsweek)*

'Miss Holliday was one of the most touching American comic actresses. To any luck dealt out to her in the parts she played – diamonds, nice men, high living – she extends a powerful disbelief. Orchids and sequins obviously arouse in her a very strong suspicion that the orchidless and sequinless times must be just around the corner. Her assumption that her grand clothes are a disguise to fool no one and that she is obviously a down-and-out to anyone with eyesight is specifically her country's, and wonderfully funny. She shared it with Marilyn Monroe.' *(Penelope Gilliatt, 1970)*

'The second half is pretty dreary: the movie . . . turns into a civics lesson. Broderick Crawford is too heavy and mean to be funny, and Holden's role is colorless . . . The movie is visually dead.' *(Pauline Kael)*

'The scenes in which Holliday visits the historical monuments and becomes excited by what America stands for are like bad Frank Capra.' *(Danny Peary)*

BOUCHER, LE: *see* BUTCHER, THE.

BOUDU SAUVÉ DES EAUX: *see* BOUDU SAVED FROM DROWNING.

BOUDU SAVED FROM DROWNING CT: 5 AV: 7.63

(aka *Boudu Sauvé des Eaux*)

1932 France 87 BW COMEDY/FOREIGN

D Jean Renoir ☆
W Jean Renoir

Michel Simon ☆ Charles Grandval ☆
Marcelle Hainia Sverine Lerczinska Jean Dast
Jacques Becker

An ungrateful tramp (Michel Simon) who is saved from drowning disrupts the existence of those who rescued him.

Cheerfully anarchic and technically adventurous for its time (Renoir experiments successfully with deep-focus photography). Regrettably, the screenplay is low on laughs, and hasn't much depth: it comes across less like the profound social critique it's sometimes cracked up to be, than a facile and all too influential example of bad-tempered snobbery about the bourgeoisie. It was remade, half a century later, as *Down and Out in Beverly Hills* (1985).

'There is in it something of the charm of French impressionist painting . . . But the whole middle part . . . is posey and synthetic in almost silent slapstick style and runs on much longer than is needed.' *(Bosley Crowther, on first US release, 1967)*

'Simon will show you how he can raise the comic to the level of fable . . . Boudu was a hippie long before the word was invented.' *(François Truffaut introducing the Renoir Festival at the Maison de la Culture de Vidaubon, 1967)*

'In the thirty-three years it has taken to officially arrive in this country Boudu hasn't aged a day. Its joy is as infectious as ever, its anarchy still as cutting . . . and the free-and-easy techniques once described by Sadoul as "of very uneven quality" look not only completely masterly but impeccable modern . . . All the modern lightweight equipment in the world could hardly have improved [Renoir's] location shooting on the banks of the Marne . . . Simon's Boudu . . . [is] surely one of the cinema's great performances.' *(Tom Milne, MFB)*

'A devastating indictment of crass, middle-class values and conformism . . . [It] is a hymn to Eros.' *(Peter Cowie, F & F)*

'Renoir's most Buñuelesque movie remains as fresh and "scandalous" as it must have been in 1932, a delicious clash of manners between the unregenerate tramp with bizarre principles of his own and the ultra-proper middle-class household where the principles are showing signs of tarnish.' *(Tony Rayns, Time Out)*

BOXING HELENA CT: 5 AV: 3.50

1993 US C DRAMA/ROMANCE/HORROR

D Jennifer Chambers Lynch ●
W Jennifer Chambers Lynch ●

Julian Sands ● Sherilyn Fenn ● Bill Paxton ● Art Garfunkel ●

A surgeon (Julian Sands) seized with unrequited love for a hard-hearted bitch (Sherilyn Fenn) keeps her imprisoned at his home by cutting off her limbs.

This misogynistic sex fantasy was notorious even before it was completed. Madonna accepted the starring role, then decided she wouldn't be seen dead in it; Kim Basinger walked out during pre-production, got sued and was bankrupted by the producers. The film's notoriety can only increase, for it is certainly one of the worst ever made. Mostly it's just Boring Helena, but it also abounds in risible performances and treasurably bad dialogue. Sample: (Sands to the limbless Fenn) 'You don't know what you're saying! You're all messed up!'

The acting is disastrous. Sherilyn Fenn merely fails to breathe life into an unremittingly unpleasant character, but Bill Paxton as Helena's macho ex-lover is so ludicrously over the top that he seems to be going for the Worst Performance of All Time. Amazingly, this is not the worst performance even in the film, for Julian Sands plays the central role as though someone has anaesthetized him and he's about to throw up. Perhaps someone did, and perhaps he was – and who can blame him. For some unexplained reason, he plays most (though not quite all) of his scenes with cotton wool in his left ear: this is by far the most interesting aspect of his performance.

'The thesps give it all the overheated conviction they can muster.' *(Variety)*

'Most of it is so ponderously serious that it's laughable . . . Not only is the script unbelievably bad . . . some of the acting has to be seen to be believed.' *(Amanda Lipman, S & S)*

'Jennifer daughter of David Lynch proves she is her father's child in name only with this risible attempt at sexual allegory. The Best Bit: when you realize you haven't seen a worse film in your entire life.' *(Empire)*

BOY FRIEND, THE CT: 6 AV: 5.75

1971 US 108 C MUSICAL/COMEDY/ROMANCE

D Ken Russell
W Ken Russell from Sandy Wilson's musical (music & lyrics by Sandy Wilson ☆)

Twiggy ☆ Christopher Gable Max Adrian ☆ Tommy Tune ✔ Barbara Windsor Moyra Fraser Bryan Pringle Vladek Sheybal Antonia Ellis ☆ Glenda Jackson ☆

An impresario (Vladek Sheybal) watches a repertory production of The Boy Friend and imagines what he could do with it.

A truly bizarre musical, much slammed for its flashiness. It's a pity so much of the charm of Sandy Wilson's stage musical got lost; and even Ken Russell wasn't happy with it (see below). And yet . . . many of the numbers are fun, and Twiggy is engaging in the ingénue role. Russell's direction has an endearing affection for Hollywood musicals and third-rate provincial theatricals. This may well be rediscovered, and become a cult hit – especially if there ever turns out to be a copy of the original director's cut.

'The acting was too broad, the gags too laboured and the pacing too slow. I should have cut it during the script stage, but, determined to be faithful to the original show, I kept in EVERYTHING! It was left to MGM, who financed the film, to do the job for me. A gorilla in boxing gloves wielding a pair of garden shears could have done a better job.' *(Ken Russell, 1993)*

ANTI:

'What I find unbearable . . . is that his [Russell's] talent should be so destructive. His touring company becomes a collection of vulgar caricatures. What was indulgent becomes grotesque; directed in exaggeration, the players themselves are destroyed . . . Some of the best numbers are ruined by farcical business . . . The talent is there all right. But somehow it is an appalling talent.' *(Dilys Powell)*

'The glittering, joyless numbers keep coming at you: you never get any relief from Russell's supposed virtuosity.' *(Pauline Kael)*

'Bloated Busby Berkeley pastiches . . . clash horribly with Sandy Wilson's mock-Twenties score.' *(Tom Milne, Time Out)*

'Russell demoted the Sandy Wilson text to the status of a background event hammed up by a third-rate provincial company . . . and then proceeded to fill up the foreground with his own variety of cinematic virtuosity, crying "Bring on the fantasies" the way Berkeley was supposed to cry "Bring on the girls". as the principal girl was the non-singing, non-dancing Sixties ex-photographer's model, Twiggy, the approach had its handicap. Not so ruinous, though, as trying to stage the numbers on a screen nearly three times as broad as it was high, totally unsuitable for the spectacular multiplication of leggy females whom Berkeley contrived to replicate on the perfectly rectangular screen of his day so that six dames looked like fifty. Russell's effects worked exactly the other way round.' *(Alexander Walker)*

PRO:

'Delightful entertainment, novel and engaging.' *(Variety)*

'Ken Russell's best film.' *(Danny Peary)*

BOYS TOWN AAN CT: 4 AV: 5.08

1938 US 93 BW DRAMA

D Norman Taurog AAN
W Dore Schary Eleanore Griffin AAW

Spencer Tracy ☆ AAN Mickey Rooney (AAW for his 'significant contribution in bringing to the screen the spirit and personification of youth') Henry Hull Gene Reynolds Bob Watson

Father Flanagan (Spencer Tracy) tries to give orphans and delinquents a chance in life.

Tracy's quiet integrity and iron determination very nearly save this tearjerker from being too schmaltzy to bear. But Rooney's performance, acclaimed at the time, is cringemaking; and the whole film is ludicrously slushy, phoney and cliché-ridden for modern tastes. Hugely popular on release, the film rated 4th on The Film Daily annual poll of film critics. Tracy was also cited for Best Acting by the National Board of Review. As a result of this movie, the real-life Boys' Town charity became one of the world's wealthiest.

PRO:

'A production that should build goodwill for the whole industry.' *(Variety)*

'One of the finest pictures to come from Hollywood.' *(Photoplay)*

'[Rooney's] overpowering pathos . . . must be obvious to anybody who is not blind, deaf and dumb.' *(James Agate, Tatler)*

'Told with the utmost sincerity it clutches you right around the heart . . . Tracy . . . might just as well be given next year's Academy Award here and now . . . Rooney . . . cannot be praised enough for his grand performance.' *(Silver Screen)*

MIXED:

'Manages, in spite of the embarrassing sentimentality of its closing scenes, to be a constantly and frequently touching motion picture.' *(Frank S. Nugent, New York Times)*

ANTI:

'It is unfortunate that there seems to be no other way of conveying religious feeling than by the singing of the Ave Maria – at appropriate and inappropriate moments . . . And it is perhaps rather difficult to believe in the almost immediate and complete reform of all the inmates, however excellent the system.' *(MFB)*

BOYZ 'N THE HOOD CT: 7 AV: 7.08

1991 US 107 C DRAMA/RITES-OF-PASSAGE

D John Singleton ☆ AAN
W John Singleton AAN

Ice Cube Cuba Gooding Jr Morris Chestnut Larry Fishburne Nia Long Tyra Ferrell

Young Los Angeles blacks get caught up in violence and crime.

This promising debut by 23-year-old writer-director John Singleton was over-praised. It is too long and didactic, while some of the speeches by Lawrence Fishburne are politically naive. But the film is also perceptive, well-structured and makes you feel sympathy for the main characters. The central conclusion (that boys need responsible fathers) is surprisingly conservative from a young man: some may find it sexist, others sensible.

'An absorbing, smartly made dramatic encyclopedia of problems and ethics in the black community.' *(Variety)*

'Not only important, but also a joy to watch, because his camera is so confident and he wins such natural performances from his actors.' *(Roger Ebert)*

Conveys a vivid sense of the dangers, both physical and emotional, of day-to-day existence in this ravaged urban environment.' *(New Yorker)*

'If the coming-of-age story is in itself hardly original, and the speeches are sometimes a mite preachy, writer/director Singleton . . . mounts his arguments forcefully and clearly.' *(Geoff Andrew, Time Out)*

BRAIN THAT WOULDN'T DIE, THE CT: 1 AV: 1.40

(aka *The Head That Wouldn't Die*)

1963 US 81 BW HORROR/SF/SO BAD

D Joseph Green ●
W Rex Carlton Joseph Green ●

Herb (Jason) Evers Virginia Leith Adele Lamont Leslie Dabniel Paula Maurice

Mad scientist (Herb Evers) tries to transplant decapitated head of his girlfriend (Virginia Leith) on to a stripper with a beautiful body but scarred face (Adele Lamont).

A splendidly tasteless premise, owing much to *Frankenstein* and *Donovan's Brain*, is explored with minimum competence and maximum gore. Highlight: the moment when the girlfriend's head starts to object, and our hero puts tape over her mouth. Kurt, the mad doctor's crippled assistant, gets probably the worst line as he addresses the head: Paths of experimentation twist and turn through mountains of miscalculation and often lose themselves in errors and darkness. Behind that door is the sum total of Dr Cortner's mistakes. Other stupefyingly bad horror movies involving brains are *The Brain Eaters* (1958), *The Brain From Planet Arous* (1958) and *Brain Damage* (1988), but this is the most brainless of the four.

'Beware of shorter version, which eliminates most of the gore.' *(Maltin)*

'The title of this effort seems to be the production's most imaginative ingredient.' *(Parish & Pitts)*

'A great, absurd movie . . . it took three years to reach an appalled public.' *(Michael Weldon, The Psychotronic Encyclopaedia of Film)*

'Despite its crudity, shapeless, thin plot and smutty atmosphere, Brain possesses a kind of ripe ludicrousness that makes it almost watchable. But not quite.' *(Bill Warren, Keep Watching The Skies!)*

BRAM STOKER'S DRACULA

CT: 5 AV: 5.55

1992 US 123/130 C HORROR/ROMANCE

D Francis Ford Coppola
W James V. Hart

Gary Oldman ☆ Winona Ryder Anthony Hopkins ● Keanu Reeves ● Richard E. Grant Cary Elwes Bill Campbell Sadie Frost ✔ Tom Waits

Transylvanian count (Gary Oldman) runs amok in England.

A sometimes compulsive, occasionally silly mixture of talent and tackiness, verve and vulgarity. The film is beautifully designed and offers plenty of visual excitement, but it isn't remotely scary, and the confusingly complex story makes it difficult to sympathise with any of the characters. Despite the film's title, Coppola isn't true to the spirit of Stoker's original – he's more romantic, sexually explicit, and anxious to show that Dracula is rooted in Transylvania's real history. Coppola's Nietzschian superhero-cum-villain is recognizably from the same mould as Brando's mad colonel in *Apocalypse Now*.

The performances are variable. Gary Oldman is charismatic and almost unrecognizable as Count Dracula: critics were divided as to whether he was impressive or over the top. Anthony Hopkins's Van Helsing is prime ham whichever way you slice it. As the central pair of lovers Winona Ryder and (especially) Keanu Reeves seem strangulated by the need to speak in English accents.

PRO:

'To the director, the count is a restless spirit who has been condemned for too many years to internment in cruddy movies. This luscious film restores the creature's nobility and gives him peace.' *(Richard Corliss, Time)*

ANTI:

'The eye and the ear are dazzled, but the nose must be held.' *(John Simon)*

'You emerge from the vampire's feast hungry and disappointed.' *(Geoff Brown, Times)*

'Reeves . . . behaves like a quite nice high-school boy in the senior class production of *Dracula*. Ryder matches him perfectly.' *(Stanley Kauffmann)*

'I know there is a storyline buried somewhere in all the violence and weirdness, but God only knows where. And even if you can take all the gore, you still have to contend with surfer dude Keanu Reeves' British accent.' *(Rod Lurie, Los Angeles Magazine)*

'Seems to sum up what people want from cinema nowadays: style hinting at content but gradually drowning it out with pyrotechnics.' *(Derek Malcolm, Guardian)*

BRAZIL

CT: 7 AV: 6.87

1985 GB 142 C SF/COMEDY

D Terry Gilliam ☆
W Terry Gilliam Tom Stoppard Charles McKeown

Jonathan Pryce Robert De Niro Katherine Helmond Ian Holm ✔ Bob Hoskins Michael Palin ✔ Ian Richardson Peter Vaughan Kim Greist Jim Broadbent Derrick O'Connor Bryan Pringle Nigel Planer Gorden Kaye

Some time in the future, a clerk in the Ministry of Information (Jonathan Pryce) falls foul of the authorities.

Terry Gilliam's pessimistic view of the future veers between brilliance and self-indulgence; but there are moments which switch memorably from comedy to terror. The art direction is outstanding and has proved influential on films such as *Delicatessen* (1990). The plot is muddled and hard to follow, the second half drags, and the ending is off-puttingly grim; but this remains one of the most strikingly cinematic films of its decade.

Contemporary reviews were mixed, but critics rallied round Gilliam when he refused Universal's instruction to change his downbeat ending. Since then, the film has built up a cult following and even been hailed as a masterpiece.

'Walter Mitty meets Franz Kafka.' *(Terry Gilliam)*

PRO:

'A *tour de force* of visual and narrative imagination.' *(Brian Howell, F & F)*

'The most potent piece of political satire since *Dr Strangelove*.' *(Kenneth Turan, California Magazine)*

'A near-masterpiece. This is a remarkably clever and ambitious, humorous yet frightening, visually spectacular – every shot is bizarre and fascinating.' *(Danny Peary)*

'The outlines of *Brazil* are much the same as those of *1984*, but the approach is different. While Orwell's lean prose was translated, last year, into an equally lean and dour film, *Brazil* seems almost like a throwback to the psychedelic 1960s, to an anarchic vision in which the best way to improve things is to blow them up.' *(Roger Ebert)*

'It's like a stoned, slapstick 1984; a nightmare comedy in which the comedy is just an aspect of the nightmarishness.' *(Pauline Kael)*

'Though it keeps hitting you with sharp images – jab, jab, jab – you never feel fear, pity, compassion or love. Everything has the same weight. Compared to the emotionally polyphonic *Blade Runner* (another visually brilliant film) *Brazil* has all the tonal variation of a kazoo.' *(John Powers, LA Weekly)*

BREAKER MORANT CT: 6 AV: 7.33

1979 Australia 107 C WAR/DRAMA

D Bruce Beresford
W Bruce Beresford Jonathan Hardy David Stevens from Kenneth Ross's play ☆ AAN

Edward Woodward ☆ Jack Thompson ☆ John Waters Bryan Brown ☆ Rod Mullinar Lewis Fitz-Gerald Charles Tingwell Vincent Ball Frank Wilson Terence Donovan

Three Aussies (led by Edward Woodward) are prosecuted by the British during the Boer War, for murdering prisoners.

Bruce Beresford's involving, straightforward courtroom drama. As you might expect, the British Empire doesn't come out of it too well.

'As a sheer exercise in manipulation, it approaches the masterful and is extremely effective.' *(Variety)*

'Engages one's emotions more powerfully than many a film with closer attention to cinematic style.' *(Dilys Powell)*

'Traditional and well-made above all else, *Breaker Morant* stuns not with originality but with expertise, a brisk, bracing film. The dialogue has a sharpness, a toughness to it, the use of dramatic close-ups and quick cutting in the courtroom scenes is precise and effective, and the acting, especially Edward Woodward as the ironically fatalistic Morant, and Jack Thompson as the inexperienced but impassioned lawyer who defends him, is excellent. Beresford has also done the material the great service of not whitewashing it, not diluting its unpalatable edges.' *(Kenneth Turan)*

'It is impossible to suppress a feeling that the spirit of Stanley Kramer is abroad on the veldt.' *(Tim Pulleine, MFB)*

BREAKFAST AT TIFFANY'S CT: 6 AV: 7.62

1961 US 115 C ROMANCE/COMEDY

D Blake Edwards ✗
W George Axelrod ✗ AAN from Truman Capote's novel

Audrey Hepburn ☆ AAN George Peppard Patricia Neal Buddy Ebsen Martin Balsam John McGiver Mickey Rooney

Writer (George Peppard) befriends a quirky Manhattan party-girl (Audrey Hepburn).

On one level, a comic romance starring Audrey Hepburn at her most charming, with an Oscar-winning Henry Mancini score. On another level, an asexual, poorly paced travesty of Truman Capote's story. Watch out for Mickey Rooney's wildly racist caricature of a Japanese photographer who lives upstairs.

'The speciousness lies in sweetening the character of the heroine so that she can be played by Audrey Hepburn without in any way changing her motives or actions, which remain monstrously avaricious . . . The book observes the streak of cold brutality that is often present in the romantic; the film merely sees the vivacity and sweetness of Audrey Hepburn.' *(Penelope Gilliatt)*

'In the Holly Golightly of print I have never believed . . . she is a sentimental fantasy . . . In the cinema Miss Hepburn with her incomparable amalgam of high spirits and delicate sensibilities, discipline and spontaneity, bewitches one into acceptance.' *(Dilys Powell)*

'A bit too precious, pat and glossy for comfort, but enough of the original's charm and vigor have been retained.' *(Variety)*

'The pace is slow, the atmosphere is unconvincingly clean, and the sentimentality kills it.' *(Halliwell)*

BREAKFAST CLUB CT: 5 AV: 5.43

1985 US 97 C COMEDY/DRAMA

D John Hughes
W John Hughes

Emilio Estevez ☆ Judd Nelson Molly Ringwald ☆ Anthony Michael Hall Ally Sheedy ☆

Five high-school students find they have much in common.

It's not hard to see why this rites-of-passage film by John Hughes – a kind of *Big Chill* about 80s teenagers – made his name as a writer-director: it is perceptive, knowledgeable and touching up to a point, and the performances (especially by Molly Ringwald and Emilio Estevez) are realistic. Some viewers may have a problem with the bad language, but the big creative failure is Hughes's mechanical plotting which eventually makes the film over-predictable and less than truthful.

PRO:

'Terrific comedy.' *(Martin & Porter)*

'Hughes's reputation-maker is an agreeably modest, well acted and thoughtful teen comedy . . . This conversation piece is always riveting, sometimes charming, and occasionally moving.' *(Winnert)*

ANTI:

'With the exception of Sheedy, who's a marvellous comic sprite and transcends her role until she is jerked back into the script mechanics, the movie is about a bunch of stereotypes who complain that other people see them as stereotypes.' *(Pauline Kael)*

'When the causes of the Decline of Western Civilisation are finally writ, Hollywood will surely have to answer why it turned one of man's most significant art-forms over to the self-gratification of high-schoolers. Or does director John Hughes really believe, as he writes here, that "when you grow up, your heart dies." It may. But not unless the brain has already started to rot with films like this.' *(Variety)*

'*The Big Chill* served up again for the Simple-Minded set.' *(Anne Billson, Time Out)*

'Abysmal apologia for loutish teenage behaviour.' *(Halliwell)*

BREAKING AWAY AAN CT: 6 AV: 7.83

1979 US 101 C DRAMA/COMEDY/RITES-OF-PASSAGE

D Peter Yates ☆
W Steve Tesich ☆ AAW

Dennis Christopher ☆ Dennis Quaid ☆ Daniel Stern Jackie Earle Haley Barbara Barrie Paul Dooley ☆

An American adolescent (Dennis Christopher) dreams of being an Italian cyclist.

This jolly, warm-hearted picture has a tendency to ramble. But it rightly won critical acclaim and a big audience for its youthful cast, stirring story of an underdog, and honest picture of class conflict in small-town America.

'It is not devoid of pleasures . . . but it fatally lacks a clear purpose and identity.' *(Geoff Brown, MFB)*

'Though its plot wins no points for originality, Breaking Away is a thoroughly delightful light comedy.' *(Variety)*

'A sunny, goofy, intelligent little film.' *(Roger Ebert)*

'One of the outstanding aspects of Breaking Away [is] its sympathetic unstereotyped portrayal of middle-class parents.' *(James Bernardoni, The New Hollywood, 1991)*

BREATHLESS CT: 5 AV: 8.46

(aka *À Bout de Souffle*)

1959 France 90 BW THRILLER/FOREIGN

D Jean-Luc Godard ☆
W Jean-Luc Godard from François Truffaut's story ☆

Jean-Paul Belmondo ☆ Jean Seberg Daniel Boulanger Jean-Pierre Melville Jean-Luc Godard.

French car thief (Jean-Paul Belmondo) kills cop, goes on run with American girlfriend (Jean Seberg).

Godard's first feature, a celebration of amoral youth, won him Best Director at the 1960 Berlin Festival and is an archetypal film of the French New Wave. It's an attempt to emulate the simplicity and impact of American gangster movies, but using very different tricks, such as jump-cuts, location shooting and hand-held camerawork. Now the techniques are no longer fresh, and the superficiality of the characters (not to mention their profound unloveliness) is much more apparent, but there's an energy and excitement about the film which Godard all too rapidly lost.

PRO:

'The most original, insolently gifted and shattering work the young French directors have yet produced.' *(Penelope Gilliatt, Observer)*

'It has a great look of speed and technical fun about it, of enormous cinematic enjoyment.' *(Isabel Quigly, Spectator)*

'An existential masterpiece.' *(Danny Peary)*

'It is Michel's adoration of American archetypes – especially the model of manhood he distills from Humphrey Bogart iconography – that illustrates Godard's most profound insight. The distance between one's social condition and personal identity – a fit that no longer fits – defined a generation's unease and the disaffection of the modern era.' *(Armond White)*

MIXED:

'This French "New Wave" film defines the whole movement better than anything I have ever seen or read. With no plot to speak of, shot and put together unconventionally, with tremendous freedom, it seems to have adapted neo-realist method for the use of the young, rich, idle and socially unconscious.' *(Tribune)*

ANTI:

'A film all dressed up for rebellion but with no real tangible territory on which to stand and fight.' *(Peter John Dyer)*

'A film in the veins of which runs not the healthy turbulent blood of anarchy but the thin, grey fluid of nihilism.' *(The Times)*

'I don't know how this film – entirely without

scruple or morals – passed the censor. Perhaps he thinks it a work of art.' *(Edward Betts, People)*

'In a film which lays such claims to realism we at least ought to care – care, I mean, about the creatures of the screen: involved, one way or the other, in their destiny. The sentimental cinema of right and wrong, good and evil, is derided today; often rightly. What the sentimental cinema does is to simplify the underlying emotions and bring them naked to the surface – where they may die of exposure. All the same that is a way of trying to be truthful; the emotions, after all, exist. The new, unsentimental cinema looks only at the cold and brutal surface of life; and that is a way of telling lies.' *(Dilys Powell)*

BRIDE OF FRANKENSTEIN, THE: *see* THE *FRANKENSTEIN* SERIES.

BRIDE OF THE ATOM: *see* BRIDE OF THE MONSTER.

BRIDE OF THE MONSTER CT: 5 AV: 1.67

(aka *Bride of the Atom*)

1955 US 69 BW SF/HORROR/SO BAD

D Edward D. Wood ●
W Edward D. Wood Jr Alex Gordon ●

Bela Lugosi ● Tor Johnson ● Loretta King ● Tony McCoy ● Harvey Dunn ●

Mad scientist (Bela Lugosi) tries to create super-race.

As with all this legendary auteur's efforts, it's hard to know whether to laugh or cry at this hopelessly under-budgeted, ludicrously acted and misdirected attempt to make a sci-fi horror movie. The elementary continuity errors, unconvincing sets and set pieces such as Bela Lugosi's fight with a rubber octopus mean that this can take its place among Wood's – and the world's – worst films.

PRO:

'Uninhibited schoolboy style stuff, though some shots would probably give the youngsters too much of the horrors.' *(Today's Cinema)*

'Follows the conventional horror approaches – stormy nights, strange disappearances, machine-full laboratory and [the actors] do their best with it.' *(Daily Film Renter)*

'Film is not as terrible as *Plan 9 from Outer Space* – but what film is? There are enough campy elements to keep Wood fanatics pleased – and Lugosi's fight with a rubber octopus (for which Lugosi must wrap the tentacles around himself) is truly hilarious. Sadly, some of the dialogue involving police indicates that on occasion Wood intentionally tried to be funny.' *(Danny Peary)*

ANTI:

'Singularly crude and tasteless in presentation, this film represents horror fiction at its lowest level.' *(MFB)*

'Abysmally inept horror: likely candidate for worst film ever made. Produced on a shoestring budget of what must have been $0.30.' *(Castle of Frankenstein)*

'Harvey Dunn was a clown for children's parties, specializing in a bird act. So his police captain has a parakeet with him most of the time, sitting on his shoulder or walking around the desk. To say that this is distracting would imply that there was something to be distracted from. Still, the sight of a pudgy policeman playing with a little birdie in the middle of a movie called *Bride of the Monster* at least gives one pause.' *(Bill Warren, Keep Watching The Skies!)*

'Unbelievable rubbish, with production values that include an old photographic enlarger masquerading as an atomic-ray machine, and script and direction to match.' *(Alan Frank)*

BRIDGE ON THE RIVER KWAI, THE AAW CT: 8 AV: 9.00

1957 GB 161 C WAR/DRAMA

D David Lean ☆ AAW
W Pierre Boulle from his novel (actually the script was co-written by blacklisted writers Carl Foreman and Michael Wilson)AAW

Alec Guinness ☆AAW William Holden Jack Hawkins Sessue Hayakawa ☆ AAN James Donald Geoffrey Horne André Morell Percy Herbert

British prisoners of war in Burma are put to work building a bridge, while other British soldiers plot to blow it up.

David Lean's visually stunning direction and a tremendous performance by Alec Guinness make this one of the most memorable and stirring of all anti-war films. But later critics have been right to point out that the balance between the two plot-lines is all wrong: Lean allows Guinness to take over the show from co-star William Holden – or maybe Holden wasn't strong enough to carry the part. Jack Hildyard's cinematography and Malcolm Arnold's score rightly won Oscars.

ANTI:

'A huge, expensive chocolate box of a war picture. Inside it is perhaps a bitter and ironic idea; but it takes more than the word madness repeated three times at the end of the film to justify comparisons with *All Quiet on the Western Front*. They'll be saying that the new Jayne Mansfield is better than Lubitsch next.' *(Lindsay Anderson, New Statesman)*

'Hollywood's mercantile concepts rule the entire show . . . Lean to our regret and disappointment simply does not make [the grade].' *(George N. Fenin, Film Culture)*

PRO:

'A gripping drama. expertly put together and handled with skill in all departments . . . Guinness etches an unforgettable portrait of the typical British army officer, strict, didactic and serene in his adherence to the book.' *(Variety)*

'If ever there was a nearly perfect motion picture in every way this . . . is it.' *(James Powers, Hollywood Reporter)*

'As thrilling an adventure film as was ever made.' *(Jympson Harmon, Evening News)*

'Unique in its success on three levels: as a taut adventure-suspense story that sags not for a second in its two hours and forty minutes; as a psychological study of a variety of men in a noncombat war situation; and as a beautiful example of the perfections of every aspect of cinematic art.' *(Judith Crist)*

'Splendidly professional, finely directed and excitingly photographed . . . I have rarely seen, in a film of action, a better cast.' *(Dilys Powell)*

MIXED:

A huge, popular success but was too confused storywise ever to be a good picture.' *(Paul Rotha & Richard Griffith, The Film Till Now, 1960)*

'A classic example of a film that fudges the issues it raises.' *(Phil Hardy, Time Out)*

BRIEF ENCOUNTER CT: 9 AV: 9.41

1945 GB 86 BW DRAMA/ROMANCE

D David Lean ☆ AAN

W Noel Coward from his play *Still Life* ☆ AAN

Celia Johnson ☆ AAN Trevor Howard Joyce Carey Stanley Holloway Joyce Carey Cyril Raymond

A married woman (Celia Johnson) contemplates an affair.

At some point during the Swinging 60s, this terribly stiff-upper-lip, British film fell out of critical fashion. Today, it's back where it belongs. Not merely the best of David Lean's four films with Coward, this is one of the great tearjerkers of all time. It suggests that the most successful romantic films (such as this and *Casablanca*) see love from a wider perspective than the personal, and make the leading characters choose self-sacrifice. David Lean's atmospheric direction – which shows cinematic genius as it nears the almost wordless climax – still has the power to move. Celia Johnson and Trevor Howard's beautifully understated performances are heart-breaking. The film was banned by the Spanish authorities, on the grounds that it might incite Spaniards to commit adultery. There was a hugely ill-advised 1974 remake, starring Sophia Loren and Richard Burton.

ANTI:

'The story belongs to the stage not to the screen.' *(Daily Mirror)*

'I found it dreadfully damp.' *(Dilys Powell)*

'Throughout the film the sympathy is with reckless romance rather than dull domesticity. It appears to encourage illicit love – to argue in defence of the wife who might have been unfaithful if the opportunity hadn't been spoiled . . . That's why for the most part it looks like immoral propaganda.' *(Evening Standard)*

'There's not a breath of air in it. Coward's material is implicitly condescending, even while he's making the two heroic.' *(Pauline Kael, 70s)*

MIXED:

'The same story, with fancy variations, is told once or twice in every issue of every magazine for housewives – often with a certain amount of sincerity, almost never with enough insight, detachment, style, or moral courage to make it better than wretched. Here, I must grant, there are several tricks of over-artifice and some of ham. But because in this case the story is written, filmed, and acted with a good deal of the positive qualities I mentioned, the picture is both a pleasure to watch as a well-controlled piece of work, and deeply touching.' *(James Agee, Nation)*

PRO:

'This week I confess that for the first time I was really moved by Mr Coward. His characters are flesh and blood . . . sensationally portrayed and acutely observed. The only character who does not ring true, amusing as she may be, is the barmaid.' *(Joan Lester)*

'For Celia Johnson's acting and indeed, for every one of these sterling players, no praise can be too lavish . . . the most polished production and performances of the year.' *(Patrick Kirwan, Evening Standard)*

'I am rarely moved to tears at the cinema, and during *Brief Encounter* I found my handkerchief a sodden ball without having noticed that I was crying, because I was too absorbed in what I was seeing.' *(Daily Mail)*

'In the end, duty and responsibility triumph over sex. There is a whole unspoken world-view in the pressure of Alec's hand on Laura's shoulder, which is his only parting gesture – a value system centred on decency, restraint and self-sacrifice.' *(Jeffrey Richards, Daily Telegraph, 1987)*

BRIGHTON ROCK CT: 7 AV: 6.56

(aka *Young Scarface*)

1947 GB 92 BW THRILLER

D John Boulting ☆

W Graham Greene Terence Rattigan from Greene's novel

Richard Attenborough ✔ Hermione Baddeley ✔
Harcourt Williams ☆ William Hartnell
Alan Wheatley ✔ Carol Marsh Nigel Stock
Wylie Watson

Teenage hoodlum (Richard Attenborough) marries waitress (Carol Marsh) who can link him with a murder – a wife cannot give evidence against her husband – and then decides to kill her.

Heavy-handed but enjoyable attempt to emulate American gangster movies of the period. It was renamed *Young Scarface* for transatlantic audiences. To anyone whose knowledge of Sir Richard Attenborough's acting abilities is restricted to seeing him struggle with a Scottish accent in *Jurassic Park*, the film may come as a revelation: he's splendidly sinister as a juvenile delinquent gang-leader. This did not prevent his performance from being reviewed unkindly at the time.

ANTI:

'Mr Attenborough's Pinkie is about as close to the real thing as Donald Duck is to Greta Garbo.' *(Leonard Mosley, Daily Express)*

'Something more exciting might reasonably have been expected. Some of the blame goes to director John Boulting whose tempo is much too leisurely for this type of picture . . . It is difficult to believe that any gang which included William Hartnell could be led by Richard Attenborough.' *(Variety)*

'The film is slower, much less compelling and, if you get me, much less cinematic than the book, as a child's guide to which I hereby offer it.' *(Richard Winnington)*

MIXED:

'In the persons of William Hartnell, Wylie Watson, Harcourt Williams and Alan Wheatley there is a nice collection of gangsterdom and crookery and if the subject is hardly exhilarating the action always keeps you at the pitch of excitement.' *(A.E. Wilson)*

PRO:

'That the production and direction, by the Boulting brothers, is first-rate goes almost without saying. But what is particularly striking in this brilliant and horrible English piece is its handling of background . . . Shots of the real Brighton – the streets, the promenade, the Pavilion, the Lanes – are skilfully cut in to the fiction of murder; there is an acute feeling of actual place . . . It proceeds with the efficiency, the precision and the anxiety to please of a circular saw.' *(Dilys Powell)*

'One of the finest British thrillers ever.' *(Geoff Andrew, Time Out)*

BRING ME THE HEAD OF ALFREDO GARCIA

CT: 3 AV: 4.81

1974 US 112 C DRAMA/ACTION

D Sam Peckinpah ●
W Gordon Dawson Sam Peckinpah ●

Warren Oates ☆ Gig Young Emilio Fernandez
Isela Vega Robert Webber Helmut Dantine
Kris Kristofferson

A general (Emilio Fernandez) puts out a contract on the man who made his daughter pregnant. The job is sub-contracted to a loser pianist (Waren Oates).

Though vilified on release, this stupefyingly dull, inconsequential gorefest has recently been rediscovered by some as a masterpiece. The critics got it right the first time.

PRO:

'One of the cinema's most perversely intriguing experiences . . . Peckinpah creates a haunting vision of a loser's quest for love and meaning in a harsh, brutal world.' *(Virgin)*

'Some kind of bizarre masterpiece . . . asking us to see past the horror and the blood to the sad poem he's trying to write about the human condition.' *(Roger Ebert)*

ANTI:

'Few movies are as tedious. Bring me the head of the studio that released this one.' *(Gene Shalit, Ladies' Home Journal)*

'The only kind of analysis it really invites is psychoanalysis.' *(Joy Gould Boyum, Wall Street Journal)*

'An exercise in manic machismo . . . so witless you can't believe it was made by the man who directed *The Wild Bunch*.' *(Vincent Canby, New York Times)*

'An all-out preposterous horror . . . Peckinpah clearly doesn't lack talent; what he lacks is brains.' *(John Simon)*

BRINGING UP BABY

CT: 8 AV: 9.14

1938 US 102 BW COMEDY

D Howard Hawks ☆
W Dudley Nichols Hagar Wilde ☆

Katharine Hepburn ☆ Cary Grant ☆ May Robson ☆
Charlie Ruggles ☆ Walter Catlett ☆ Fritz Feld ☆
Jonathan Hale Barry Fitzgerald

A mild-mannered palaeontologist (Cary Grant) is harrassed by an impulsive heiress (Katharine Hepburn) and her pet leopard.

A flop despite favourable reviews, Howard Hawks's fast, furious update of restoration comedy is now recognized as a definitive screwball farce, thanks to witty dialogue, sharp direction and a cavalcade of funny performances. There's too much slapstick for my taste, and Hepburn borders on the irritating, but it's undoubtedly a classic. Peter Bogdanovich copied copiously from it in *What's Up, Doc?* (1972)

'Rather frantically funny, relying on improbable situations and slapstick. Mr Grant and Miss Hepburn when in doubt, fall flat on their faces, trip over logs, knock each other out . . . Once was enough!' *(Eileen Creelman, New York Sun)*

'Constructed for a maximum of laughs . . . Chief shortcoming is that too much time is consumed with the jail sequence.' *(Variety)*

'The kind of laugh show that should spread a grin on the faces of the exhibitors.' *(Motion Picture Daily)*

'I am happy to report that it is funny from the word go, that it has no other meaning to recommend it . . . and that I wouldn't swap it for practically any three things of the current season.' *(Otis Ferguson)*

'The Hawks world is almost exclusively a world of men . . . [He] reserves his women for comedies, but even the delightfully wacky *Bringing Up Baby* has a tough, antisentimental core. Hawks runs Katharine Hepburn through swamps, mud, and thickets in a romantic chase . . . that has more to do with a tame leopard and a lost dinosaur bone than with love.' *(Gerald Mast, A Short History of the Movies, 1971)*

The finest example of the screwball comedy genre . . . A particularly zany antidote to the gloom of the real world.' *(Allan Hunter & Kenny Mathieson, Movie Classics, 1992)*

BRITANNIA HOSPITAL CT: 6 AV: 4.11

1982 GB 116 C COMEDY

D Lindsay Anderson
W David Sherwin

Leonard Rossiter Graham Crowden
Malcolm McDowell Joan Plowright Robin Askwith
Peter Jeffrey

A run-down hospital prepares for a royal visit.

The third part of Anderson's triptych on post-war Britain – the others are *If* . . . (1968) and *O Lucky Man!* (1973) – is a lacerating satire on 70s Britain, which veers from Swiftian brilliance to Carry On awfulness. Its parade of grotesque caricatures is undoubtedly ugly; but it's a lot truer and funnier than reviews from offended liberal film critics might lead you to imagine. Released at the time of the Falklands War, its all-out, 'unpatriotic' attack on British society could hardly have been less suitably timed. Despite its excesses and commercial failure, this is the only British movie which gives even a hint of why Labour failed to get elected throughout the 1980s.

ANTI:

'Nearly two hours worth of gloom masquerading as a sense of humour.' *(Michael Wood, New Society)*

'It has all the intensity, along with the flailing incoherence, of a soapbox Jeremiah.' *(Richard Combs, MFB)*

'One can't help feeling that so much contempt on the director's part only hides a lack of commitment and focus.' *(Geoff Andrew, Time Out)*

'Having once created a general shambles, the film is at a loss to clean it up.' *(Margaret Hinxman, Daily Mail)*

PRO:

'A witty, unsparing exposé of British manners and mores.' *(Variety)*

'Mr Anderson's best film to date . . . immensely bracing.' *(Vincent Canby, New York Times)*

'The wit, intelligence and deceptive ease with which social satire is handled . . . is almost unknown in cinema outside . . . [of] Buñuel.' *(Clive Hodgson, F & F)*

'Demonstrates . . . that when a good director turns his hand to horror comedy he can do it with a great deal more panache than *Texas Chainsaw Massacre* or *Friday the 13th*.' *(David Robinson, The Times)*

'Cruel and unremitting in its attack, but it takes great courage to make it and show it – especially today.' *(David Lewin, Daily Mail)*

BROADCAST NEWS AAN CT: 5 AV: 7.14

1987 US 132 C COMEDY/DRAMA

D James L. Brooks ✗
W James L. Brooks ✗ AAN

William Hurt ☆ AAN Holly Hunter ☆ AAN
Albert Brooks ☆ AAN Jack Nicholson ☆ (cameo)
Joan Cusack

A producer (Holly Hunter) is torn romantically between an ethical news reporter (Albert Brooks) and a smooth presenter (William Hurt).

Charming, well-acted romantic comedy with some very funny sequences. However, the characters are never deeper than sitcom caricatures; for a film which sets out as if it intends to satirize journalistic ethics, it's woefully superficial – and there's a ridiculous, cop-out ending.

'Underpinning what is a charming, protean love-triangle is a serious statement about the function, value and direction of television news.' *(Steve Grant, Time Out)*

'The script of *Broadcast News* is a most rickety contraption indeed, and when in its final pages Jane must decide whether to love Tom or leave him, the whole fragile structure collapses. For neither choice is dramatically workable. If she chooses to go with Tom, she's opting for the predictable romantic-comedy ending, and making it obvious that her declared moral objections to him were just plot gimmickry, and the film's pretensions to seriousness precisely that – pretensions. If, on the other hand, she decides to reject his love because of that faked cutaway, such an inane attempt at a "serious" ending cannot but expose the real shallowness of the material . . . *Terms of Endearment* showed us, and *Broadcast News* reminds us, that James L. Brooks doesn't know the difference between persons and personifications, characters and caricatures, emotion and sentimentality.' *(Bruce Bawer, American Spectator)*

'Basically all it's saying is that beautiful, assured people have an edge over the rest of us, no matter how high our IQs are.' *(Pauline Kael)*

BROADWAY DANNY ROSE CT: 7 AV: 7.07

1984 US 84 BW COMEDY/ROMANCE

D Woody Allen ✔ AAN
W Woody Allen ✔ AAN

Woody Allen ✔ Mia Farrow ✔ Nick Apollo Forte Craig Vandenbergh Herb Reynolds

A loser agent in showbiz (Woody Allen) inadvertently gets on the wrong side of the Mafia.

Woody Allen gives one of his most appealing performances as a showbiz agent whose variety acts invariably walk out on him as soon as they achieve success. Mia Farrow is a revelation – and almost unrecognizable – in the role of a Mafia gangster's moll. The comedy is low-key but gradually sneaks up on you, with its endearing affection for the naff end of showbiz. Perhaps Woody Allen's most underrated film.

ANTI:

'We have the paradox of a nervous realist writing about a sentimental domain that no longer exists and dealing with it harshly.' *(Stanley Kauffmann)*

'Everything is half-cooked. We are never really frightened of the mobsters; we can't bring ourselves to love Miss Farrow; we are only mildly sorry for the hero . . . What he has given us is a sketchy chain of events leading to a half-hearted liaison between a helpless man and a not very likeable girl.' *(Quentin Crisp, Christopher Street)*

PRO:

'To the honor roll of artists who worked in miniature – Vermeer, Webern, Fabergé, the medieval philosophers who squeezed a chorus line of angels on to the head of a pin – add Woody Allen's name.' *(Richard Corliss, Time)*

'In Danny, Woody's classic schlemiel becomes a kind of saint, watching over his stable of lame acts like Francis over the animals.' *(Jack Kroll, Newsweek)*

'A joy. It heralds a return to his earlier style of verbal comedy joined with some action-slapstick humor, while at the same time retaining the serious thread that has run thorugh his more recent films.' *(Linda-Marie Delloff, The Christian Century)*

BRONENOSETS POTEMKIN: *see* POTEMKIN.

BROWNING VERSION, THE CT: 6 AV: 7.10

1951 GB 90 BW DRAMA

D Anthony Asquith
W Terence Rattigan from his own play

Michael Redgrave ☆ Jean Kent ● Nigel Patrick Wilfrid Hyde White Bill Travers Ronald Howard

Schoolmaster (Michael Redgrave) finds his life falling apart.

Restrained but profoundly moving film of the Rattigan play, in which Michael Redgrave gives one of his greatest screen performances. Unfortunately, there's a tacked-on, schmaltzy ending which belatedly diminishes the central character; the production looks cheap; and Jean Kent is out of her depth as his wife.

'Crammed with emotional incidents and has two noteworthy tear-jerker scenes.' *(Variety)*

'Redgrave puts an infinity of variation into gestures which are involuntary in the driven human being; and when at a touch of kindness control suddenly gives way the contrast with the hardness and tightness of the earlier scenes is heartbreaking.' *(Dilys Powell)*

'If the sustained anguish of the role does not allow Redgrave a great deal of room to move around in, it does give him a chance to show what he can do in tight corners, and that, it turns out, is considerable.' *(Pauline Kael, 70s)*

'In effect a re-run of *Goodbye Mr Chips* seen through dark-tinted glasses – which draws what little venom the original had by adding an absurdly sentimental coda.' *(Tom Milne, Time Out)*

BRUTE FORCE CT: 5 AV: 7.22

1947 US 96 BW DRAMA

D Jules Dassin ☆
W Richard Brooks ☆ from Robert Pattison's story

Burt Lancaster ☆ Hume Cronyn ☆ Charles Bickford Ella Raines Yvonne de Carlo

Prisoners plan a break-out.

This thriller is grittily directed by Jules Dassin, and was very violent for its time. Though primarily an action movie, it's clearly intended to be an allegory about fascism. Hume Cronyn gives a chilling portrayal of the sadistic chief guard. The tension is diffused by rather too many flashbacks, which help flesh out the characters but often seem like half-hearted attempts to attract female audiences.

'I was astounded to hear that some knowledgeable people think of *Brute Force*, a movie about men in a big jail, as a happy return to the melodramas of the early thirties. Maybe so, in some of the jab-paced, slickly sadistic action sequences. But there isn't a line in it, or a performance, or an idea, or an emotion, that belongs much later than 1915, and cheesy 1915 at that.' *(James Agee, Nation)*

'A showmanly mixture of gangster melodramatics, sociological exposition, and sex' *(Variety)*

'The kind of picture that is often called a man's picture; that is, fast, action-packed, pseudo-realistic.' *(Pauline Kael)*

BUDDY HOLLY STORY, THE CT: 6 AV: 7.13

1978 US 113 C MUSICAL/BIOPIC

D Steve Rash
W Robert Gitler

Gary Busey ☆ AAN Dan Stroud
Charles Martin Smith Bill Jordan Maria Richwine

Life and times of a 50s pop star (Gary Busey).

A spirited recreation of a formative period in rock and roll. Talented actor-singer Gary Busey gives the performance of a lifetime as Buddy Holly – which is just as well, for the pop star's life story is not exactly rich in dramatic conflict. Musical director Joe Renzetti won an Oscar.

'Smacks of realism in almost every respect.' *(Variety)*

'Streets ahead of most rock celluloid.' *(Chris Auty, Time Out)*

'Busey's moving rendition of True Love Ways is actually better than Holly's . . . Thanks to Busey, it's consistently entertaining.' *(Danny Peary)*

'A B-movie leavened by grade-A talent.' *(Les Keyser, Hollywood in the Seventies)*

BUFFALO BILL AND THE INDIANS
(OR SITTING BULL'S HISTORY LESSON)
CT: 4 AV: 4.82

1976 US 118 C WESTERN/BIOPIC

D Robert Altman
W Alan Rudolph Robert Altman from Arthur Kopit's play

Paul Newman Burt Lancaster Joel Grey Kevin McCarthy Geraldine Chaplin Harvey Keitel John Considine Denver Pyle

Life and times of William Cody (Paul Newman), from buffalo hunter to showbiz celebrity.

Vigorous though not terribly entertaining (and overlong) debunking of the western 'myth'. The controversy it aroused among critics makes it more interesting to read about, than to watch.

ANTI:

'The western is an enormously resilient form, but never has that resilience been tested quite so much as in this movie.' *(Arthur Knight)*

'Altman is an ideological fashion-monger. He exploits established anti-establishment modes. He relies on predecessors to stake out and illuminate the ground, then he rides in like a black-humor Buffalo Bill expecting the cheers of a hip gallery for his safely satirical derring-do . . . About twenty-five per cent of the dialogue is simply incomprehensible.' *(Stanley Kauffmann)*

'Shelley Duvall, an Altman regular, is rapidly becoming one of the most predictably smarmy screen presences around . . . What good is Altman's celebrated eight-track sound if all it conveys is a one-track mind?' *(John Simon)*

MIXED:

'That American history is the creation of flamboyant lies and showmanship strikes us at first as an amusing trifle and then quickly becomes an epigram shaggy-dogging its way across two hours of eccentric Altmanship.' *(Will Aitken, Take One)*

'Attacks both the myth of Buffalo Bill, and the entire apparatus of the show-business which sustained/sustains it . . . A film which tries to create its own history. Most critics thought the exercise too destructive, but the Wild West-as-circus was never to be quite the same again.' *(NFT Bulletin, 1984)*

BUGSY AAN CT: 4 AV: 6.31

1991 US 135 C DRAMA/ROMANCE

D Barry Levinson ✗ AAN
W James Toback ✗ AAN

Warren Beatty ✗ AAN Annette Bening Harvey Keitel ✗ AAN Ben Kingsley ✗ AAN Elliott Gould
Joe Mantegna Bebe Neuwirth

A gangster (Warren Beatty) has the idea of setting up a gambling empire.

Turgid, tedious tale with a questionable morality, unconvincing characters, and a bizarrely reverential attitude towards the creation of Las Vegas. The handsome production and big-name cast make the whole thing even more sleazy. It received 10 Oscar nominations, but won only for Dennis Gassner's art direction and Albert Wolsky's costume design. Most critics liked it.

PRO:

'Some regard the American Dream as an expression of our best vision of ourselves. Others, like the makers of the sleek, funny, vastly entertaining *Bugsy* take a less sentimental view . . . A smart, seductive portrait of both the man and his monument . . . Beatty . . . has found the role of his career.' *(Janet Maslin, New York Times)*

'Ethnically, Beatty would seem to be all wrong for

the part . . . but he's surprisingly persuasive . . . What's even more surprising are his moments of fury . . . [He] has never shown this sort of raw, savage energy on screen before . . . The film is also blessed with a wondrous supporting cast.' *(Kevin Lally, Film Journal)*

'The screenplay by James Toback is packed with vivid characters and startling incidents which, under the inspired direction of Barry Levinson, build to a breathtaking climax.' *(Guy Flatley, Cosmopolitan)*

'It would be easy to dismiss *Bugsy* as a phoney Hollywood movie. Beatty seems an unlikely choice to play a Jewish gangster. The script is riddled with the kind of clever dialogue that happens only in movies. And Oscar-winning film-maker Barry Levinson directs with a studied slickness. But *Bugsy*'s artifice has a seductive resonance. The film is, after all, about contrivance – about the folly of a man who lived and died for delusions of grandeur. The story is compelling. At times, it is wickedly funny. And Beatty gives the most intriguing and complex performance of his career.' *(Brian D. Johnson, Maclean's)*

MIXED:

'The love affair between gangland and Hollywood comes vividly to life . . . *Bugsy* seldom digs deep but utilizes plenty of glitz and wry humor to present some bad eggs sunny-side up.' *(Bruce Williamson, Playboy)*

'A smooth, safe portrait of a volatile, dangerous character. An absorbing narrative flow and a parade of colorful underworld characters vie for screen time with an unsatisfactory central romance.' *(Variety)*

'Resplendently produced, slickly accomplished, and dazzlingly hollow.' *(John Simon)*

ANTI:

'As scintillating as watching someone play the slots for a couple of hours.' *(Rose)*

BUGSY MALONE CT: 7 AV: 5.92

1976 GB 93 C MUSICAL/FAMILY

D Alan Parker ☆
W Alan Parker songs by Paul Williams AAN

Jodie Foster ☆ Scott Baio ☆ Florrie Dugger
John Cassisi Martin Lev Paul Murphy
Dexter Fletcher Bonnie Langford

Gang warfare, acted out by children.

Inventive pastiche of gangster movies, which points up the clichés of the genre and gently satirizes the childishness of gangster behaviour. Paul Williams's songs are catchy. However, the overtones of eroticism to which John Simon took violent exception (see below) are certainly there – especially in Jodie Foster's performance.

ANTI:

'The film's gimmick is to turn the kids into appallingly realistic scale models of full-grown brutes and trollops for the amusement of whom, I wonder? Pederasts and child molesters certainly, who may find something deliciously provocative about tots got up as delinquent adults; some backward children, no doubt, who think this film exalts them; and adults benighted enough to perceive this offal as a lovable masquerade . . . On top of its other troubles, *Bugsy* is a musical, with songs by Paul Williams, not one bar of which strikes me as music. Worse yet, the songs are dubbed in by adult voices, many if not all belonging to Williams himself. This makes the transitions from speech to song perfectly ludicrous, and has the further depressing effect of suggesting that the very mouths of these children have been violated.' *(John Simon)*

'The almost pornographic dislocation, which is the source of the film's possible appeal as a novelty, is never acknowledged, but the camera lingers on a gangster's pudgy, infantile fingers or a femme fatale's soft little belly pushing out of her tight satin dress, and it roves over the pubescent figures in the chorus line.' *(Pauline Kael)*

'All the pizazz in the world couldn't lift it above the level of empty camp.' *(Frank Rich, New York Post)*

PRO:

'A movie shaped by taste, wit, melody and infinite affection for its adult world scaled down to a child's playground. The film-makers gave the impression they had forgotten nothing of their own childhood.' *(Alexander Walker)*

'May be a kid's adventure, but it is an adult's joke, a reminiscent comment on all the gang wars of the Hollywood screen. The detail is a delight from the gestures of the quartet of singing and dancing hoods to the furniture, to all the tiny appurtenances of life in a world of gang-battles. Everything is followed through, nothing disturbs the affectionate reconstruction of a film fantasy which today, after the massacres and the bombs of real life, seems almost pacific. Is it followed through too devotedly? An adult's joke – the variations on it are numerous and ingenious, but it is a single joke; occasionally one feels a desire to beak out of even so witty a cage.' *(Dilys Powell)*

'In an uncanny way the movie works as a gangster movie and we remember that the old Bogart and Cagney classics had a childlike innocence too.' *(Roger Ebert)*

BUILD MY GALLOWS HIGH: *see* OUT OF THE PAST.

BULL DURHAM CT: 8 AV: 7.00

1988 US 108 C DRAMA/ROMANCE/COMEDY

D Ron Shelton ☆
W Ron Shelton ☆ AAN

Kevin Costner ☆ Susan Sarandon ☆

Tim Robbins ☆ Trey Wilson Robert Wuhl William O'Leary David Neidorf Danny Gans

Crash, a downwardly mobile baseball player now in minor leagues (Kevin Costner), is given the task of helping 'Nuke', a rising pitcher (Tim Robbins) with a talent for getting himself into trouble. Both battle for the affections of Annie, an eccentric baseball groupie (Susan Sarandon).

Intelligent romantic comedy with three unusual and engaging central characters. Robbins is convincingly thick as the young man with 'a million dollar arm and a five cent head'. Costner is attractively thoughtful as baseball's answer to Mike Brearley. And you have to warm to any woman who ties sportsmen to her bed and then makes them listen to poetry. 'A guy will listen to anything,' Sarandon observes perceptively, 'if he thinks it's foreplay'.

'A fanciful and funny bush league sports story where the only foul ball is its over-use of locker-room dialog.' *(Variety)*

'Has the kind of dizzying, off-center literacy that Preston Sturges's pictures had.' *(Pauline Kael)*

'Paradoxically, Shelton's intimate knowledge of baseball allows him to convey the feel of the game, its esoteric mythology and quirky superstitions, without losing sight of the real issue: will Annie and Crash get it together? . . . Marvellous stuff.' *(Nigel Floyd, Time Out)*

'Lovely, sassy, often sexy, romantic comedy. Sarandon's performance is so good, it soars out of the ball park completely.' *(Rose)*

BULLITT

CT: 6 AV: 7.71

1968 US 113 C THRILLER

D Peter Yates ☆
W Harry Kleiner Alan R. Trustman from Robert L. Pike's novel *Mute Witness*

Steve McQueen ☆ Jacqueline Bisset Don Gordon Robert Vaughn Robert Duvall

San Francisco cop (Steve McQueen) goes after killers.

Stylish cop thriller with an exciting (and much imitated) car chase. You can see why the movie confirmed Steve McQueen as a star, and established the Hollywood career of British director Peter Yates. But the script and characters now look terribly clichéd. Frank P. Keller's editing won an Oscar.

MIXED:

'Essentially one of those deadpan-cop-against-the-system clichés, with Steve McQueen single-handedly solving the puzzle that the screenplay presents to the audience half-solved from the start. But Yates added the garnish of not just one but two chases, one around departing aircraft at a jetport and other by car up and down San Francisco's hills, and did them with such style that you never notice, for example, how peculiarly empty the streets are as the cars career by.' *(Judith Crist)*

'A competent director (Peter Yates), working with competent technicians, gives a fairly dense texture to a vacuous script.' *(Pauline Kael)*

PRO:

'Conflict between police sleuthing and political expedience is the essence of *Bullitt*, an extremely well-made crime melodrama.' *(Variety)*

'A terrific movie, just right for Steve McQueen – fast, well-acted, written the way people talk.' *(Renata Adler, New York Times)*

'A curiously exhilarating mixture of reality and fantasy, so actual that at times one could almost swear that the fictional adventures must have been shot with concealed cameras.' *(Tom Milne, Observer)*

'Wyler's *Ben Hur* had the best chariot-race in the history of the cinema; Peter Yates's *Bullitt* has the best car chase, a lethal bounce over the hill-top streets of the city . . . Outside the work of Antonioni I haven't seen such effective narrative and emotional use of an urban background.' *(Dilys Powell)*

BULLSEYE!

CT: 1 AV: 2.00

1990 US 92/102 C COMEDY/THRILLER

D Michael Winner ●
W Leslie Bricusse Laurence Marks Maurice Gran ●

Michael Caine ● Roger Moore ● Sally Kirkland ● Deborah Barrymore Jenny Seagrove John Cleese Derren Nesbitt ●

Two confidence tricksters (Roger Moore, Michael Caine) impersonate nuclear scientists.

A masterpiece of its kind: impressively, magnificently, astonishingly lousy in an unprecedented multiplicity of ways. There is not a single passable performance. Few leading actors as feeble, lazy and self-indulgent as Michael Caine and Roger Moore in this could reasonably expect to work again. The screenplay appears to have been written by drunken caption-writers from the *Sun*. It is hard to know which scene is the most vulgar, juvenile and pathetic.

A memorable contribution is made by the make-up department, for the stunt-doubles' wigs in this movie strike a new low. Casting, too, plays an important part, since the doubles look nothing like the characters whom they're impersonating. The editor (Mr Winner himself) has also contributed, by cutting the film so that we are fully aware of this fact. The lighting cameraman manages the difficult task of making some delightful stately homes and a beautiful young actress, Deborah Barrymore (Roger Moore's daughter), look repulsive.

Winner's views on the elitism of other British producers are well known, and mainly sensible. It hardly helps his argument, however, that in this film he aims for the lowest common denominator and misses. This asinine, ugly, loutish piece of work is certainly not the future of British film: it is more like Ealing Comedy as reinterpreted by neolithic man.

'Wallowing in its excremental humour, *Bullseye!* is content to reinforce the crudest of racial and sexual stereotypes.' *(MFB)*

'No actor comes out unscathed from this stinker.' *(Wally Hammond, Time Out)*

'Some of it is nearly passable, but not quite, and Caine's American accent as the "bad" double is atrocious . . . Numbingly unfunny and occasionally unpalatable.' *(Quinlan)*

'Forget about hitting the bull's-eye. The darts are so off-target, the entire pub should be evacuated.' *(Rose)*

'Surprisingly entertaining.' *(Martin & Porter)*

BUONO, IL BRUTTO, IL CATTIVO, IL: *see* GOOD, THE BAD AND THE UGLY, THE.

BUS STOP CT: 6 AV: 7.18

(aka *The Wrong Kind of Girl*)

1956 US 96 C COMEDY/DRAMA

D Joshua Logan
W George Axelrod from William Inge's play

Don Murray AAN Marilyn Monroe ☆
Arthur O'Connell Betty Field Eilenne Heckart
Hope Lange

Lovesick cowboy (Don Murray) abducts chanteuse (Marilyn Monroe).

Slow-moving comedy drama, made immortal by Marilyn Monroe's sizzling performance.

'Monroe comes off acceptably, even though failing to maintain any kind of consistency in the southern accent.' *(Variety)*

'Marilyn Monroe has finally proved herself an actress . . . Mr Logan has got her to do a great deal more than wiggle and pout and pop her big eyes and play the synthetic vamp in this film. He has got her to be the beat-up B-girl of Mr Inge's play, even down to the Ozark accent and the look of pellagra about her skin . . . And, what's most important, he has got her to light the small flame of dignity that sputters pathetically in this chippie and to make a rather moving sort of her.' *(Bosley Crowther)*

'In *Bus Stop* she has a wonderful role, and she plays it with a mixture of humor and pain that is very touching.' *(William K. Zinsser, New York Herald Tribune)*

'Nothing can quite match its delicately balanced mixture of tender anguish and uproarious comedy; its particular appeal is that it treads the fine line between pathos and laughter and carries a bit of both throughout. It also offers what was probably Marilyn Monroe's best performance.' *(Judith Crist)*

BUSINESS AFFAIR, A CT: 5 AV: 3 (est)

1994 US 101 C ROMANCE/DRAMA/SO BAD

D Charlotte Brandstrom ●
W William Stadiem ●

Christopher Walken ● Carol Bouquet Jonathan Pryce ● Sheila Hancock Anna Manghan

Budding authoress (Carole Bouquet) leaves literary genius (Jonathan Pryce) for sexy publisher (Christopher Walken), then has second thoughts.

An indigestible Euro-pudding of massive proportions, and a misconceived attempt to update Barbara Skelton's books about her marriages to (according to her account) two of the most thoroughgoing male chauvinists ever to deface the London book scene, Cyril Connolly and Lord Weidenfeld. With astounding perversity, the producers have allowed the males' antediluvian attitudes to remain unchanged from 40 years ago; and yet our modern heroine makes no attempt to look around for more congenial company.

In a fatuous token gesture towards feminism, Ms Skelton's literary abilities have been upgraded: she has become a brilliant popular novelist. Unfortunately, she is played by the French actress Carole Bouquet, whose grasp of the English language makes Jean-Paul Gaultier look like Vladimir Nabokov.

No fewer than eight different types of European film funding were tapped for the filming of a screenplay which might charitably be described as moronic. Perhaps no one connected with financing the production could read English. Screenwriter William Stadiem's knowledge of the English literary scene seems limited to thumbing through remaindered copies of Barbara Taylor Bradford. The characters converse entirely in pulp clichés, except when embarking on wild flights of verbal fantasy. 'He is,' Ms Bouquet informs an understandably astonished Mr Pryce about the nimble-footed Mr Walken, 'the Nijinsky of cunnilingus.' It's the kind of film where a stern-faced doctor has to come on, grave-faced, and deliver lines like 'The fibroid mass was intrusive.'

My favourite moment came as Pryce entered one scene with a couple of fishing rods and an untypically jovial expression. 'I've decided the one thing that can save this marriage,' he announces, 'is a spot of salmon-fishing.' A whale of a bad movie, one to be savoured by gourmets of the grotesque.

PRO:

'A well-written romantic comedy with a gently feminist undertow . . . Greatly helped by Pryce's atypically unsympathetic performance and Walken's quirky humour and easy charm, writer William

Stadiem and director Charlotte Brandstrom get to the intellectual root, if not the emotional heart, of this ill-fated triangle of ambition and desire . . . Ultimately, its ambitions are, perhaps, slightly too modest to attract the thoughtful art house audience it is aimed at.' *(Nigel Floyd, Time Out)*

ANTI:

'Why? Why did Christopher Walken agree to do it? He's not a complete nutcase, is he? And Jonathan Pryce – what's the matter with him? He's not a beggar. So did they both read the script of *A Business Affair*, and think it was fine? . . . I expected *A Business Affair* to be bad. People had told me that. But I didn't expect to be howling with pained laughter.' *(William Leith, Mail on Sunday)*

'Bad beyond the power of criticism to invoke . . . The script has an unerring instinct for the clunky detail, with a Euro-production feel, as if processed by a committee of translators.' *(Quentin Curtis, Independent on Sunday)*

'An astonishingly absurd Euromess . . . often very funny, but probably accidentally.' *(George Perry, Sunday Times)*

BUTCH CASSIDY AND THE SUNDANCE KID AAN

CT: 6 AV: 8.38

1969 US 110 C WESTERN/COMEDY

D George Roy Hill ☆ AAN
W William Goldman ☆AAW

Robert Redford ☆ Paul Newman ☆ Katharine Ross Strother Martin

Two cheerful criminals (Robert Redford, Paul Newman) flout law and order in the wild west.

The ultimate in cute buddy-buddy movies, charmingly acted by Paul Newman and Robert Redford, pacily directed by George Roy Hill, and written by William Goldman with a fine sense of comedy and thrills, though absolutely none of period. Conrad Hall's cinematography won an Oscar, as did Burt Bacharach's song and score. Very much a product of the Swinging 60s, it now looks ponderously anarchic and morally fatuous – but it's undeniably well-produced.

PRO:

'The Western, that Hollywood archetype, has outlived its usefulness as a straight dramatic device in which good, dressed white, guns down evil, dressed in black. Instead screen-writer William Goldman and director George Roy Hill have turned out an anti-Western in much the way Arthur Penn treated *Bonnie and Clyde* as an anti-gangster movie. In *Butch Cassidy and the Sundance Kid*, the railroads [are] the villainous symbols of an increasingly impersonal, industralized and mercantile society. It is 1898; the century and frontier life are both ending, but Butch Cassidy and the Sundance Kid refuse to surrender to this changing America, holding up trains and banks as though the sheriff and the local posse were their only adversaries. Paul Newman as Butch, a man chasing a vision of total freedom, and Robert Redford as the Sundance Kid, a professional triggerman as out-of-date as a samurai warrior, play their doomed roles with all the charm of children dancing in a setting sun.' *(Paul D. Zimmerman, Newsweek)*

MIXED:

'One of the funniest if slightest Westerns of recent years. Unashamedly escapist, it rips off most of its plot (from pursuit to final shooot-out) and much of its visual style from Peckinpah's *The Wild Bunch*, and even parodies *Jules et Jim*. It's slightly the worse for some of the borrowings, but the script is often hilarious.' *(Rod McShane, Time Out)*

ANTI:

'*Bonnie and Clyde* rides again. The attempt is both very attentive to period flavor, and wildly "now." Thus we get the quasi-imperceptible switch of Conrad Hall's photography from the sepia tones of yesteryear to the artfully understated colors of just yesterday; the continual dependence of William Goldman's script on standing every possible western convention on its brainless head; the endless wisecracking of Paul Newman and Robert Redford in a language and humor that are half a century too early and half a continent too easterly for their historic time and place.' *(John Simon)*

'Too cute for words and overrated to high hell; a soap bubble weighed down with praise from average minds . . . Butch hasn't aged particularly well; today, it looks cloying and strained.' *(Virgin)*

BUTCHER, THE

CT: 6 AV: 7.78

(aka *Le Boucher*)

1969 France/Italy 93 C THRILLER/FOREIGN

D Claude Chabrol ☆
W Claude Chabrol ☆

Stéphane Audran Jean Yanne Antonio Passalia Mario Beccaria

A village schoolteacher (Stéphane Audran) suspects that the local butcher (Jean Yanne) is a serial killer.

Though there are some pleasantly Hitchcocky touches, it's all a bit plodding. Besides, this is not so much a suspense thriller (there's never much doubt as to the killer's identity) as a psychological study of sexual frustration. Unfortunately, the insights offered are not very convincing. Jean Rabier's cinematography is outstanding, however, and there's a good feeling for the Perigord countryside.

'For the first time in his career almost Chabrol has managed to present rounded characters with whom one is in full sympathy.' *(Richard Roud, Guardian)*

'Very little is missing here in terms of sheer

suspense. but trust Chabrol . . . to add resonant undertones from beginning to end . . . [and] never stoop to sermonizing.' *(Playboy)*

'A beautifully made suspense thriller in the tradition of Hitchcock. The French understand Hitchcock's genius far better than the Americans.' *(Michael Goodwin, Rolling Stone)*

'A compelling psychological thriller that occasionally gets bogged down and fails to reach the level of suspense that could have been achieved.' *(Virgin)*

C'ERA UNA VOLTA IL WEST: *see* ONCE UPON A TIME IN THE WEST.

CABARET AAN CT: 9 AV: 8.67

1972 US 123 C MUSICAL/DRAMA

D Bob Fosse ☆ AAW
W Jay Presson Allen ☆ AAN from Christopher Isherwood's novel *Goodbye To Berlin* music & lyrics by John Kander Fred Ebb ☆

Liza Minnelli ☆ AAW Joel Grey ☆ AAW Michael York ☆ Helmut Griem Fritz Wepper Marisa Berenson

On the eve of World War II, a young British man (Michael York) visits Berlin and becomes involved with an American night-club singer (Sally Bowles) and a rich German nobleman (Helmut Griem).

A directorial and choreographic *tour de force*. The film is a sophisticated restructuring of the Broadway original and departs radically from screen musical convention: the songs comment on, rather than arise out of, the story – the film is among the most Brechtian ever made. It is if anything more hard-hitting than the stage version; master of ceremonies Joel Grey contributes a memorable portrayal of evil. A few minor quibbles: Fosse resorts to vulgar overstatement on a few occasions; the subsidiary love story between Marisa Berenson and Fritz Wepper is dull; Michael York can do little with the annoyingly passive Isherwood character; and, although the film made Liza Minnelli a star, she is – strictly speaking – miscast, since she is so obviously talented that she would hardly stay long in a dive like the Kit Kat Club. The score features much of the best work of composer and lyricist, John Kander and Fred Ebb.

ANTI:

'The trouble with the film is that it pretends to say more than it does. The basic connection between the decadence of a sleazy Berlin nightclub in the early thirties and the rise of Nazism, though continually hinted at, and sometimes leeringly rubbed in, is never truly demonstrated . . . Is Nazism a product of the decadence, or is the decadence an attempt to escape from, and so a product of, Nazism? And was there no political-economic crisis that begat them both? It may be too much to ask a musical to be thoughtful and iluminating, but if it comports itself as if it were both those things, we do ask questions.' *(John Simon)*

'Fosse unfortunately feels the need to put the boot in with some crude cross-cutting (eg from a man being beaten up by Nazis in the street to the leering faces of the cabaret performers) which lands the film in a queasy morass of overstatement.' *(Tom Milne, Time Out)*

'The film's irredeemable disaster is its Sally Bowles: changing her into an American was bad enough; into Liza Minnelli, catastrophe. Miss Minnelli cannot act any part without calling attention to how hard she is working at it and how far she is from having worked it out. She cannot even move right – in this case, like a sexy cabaret artiste and thriving nymphomaniac; instead, she rattles around gawkily and disjointedly, like someone who never got over being unfeminine and unattractive.' *(John Simon)*

PRO:

'Literate, bawdy, sophisticated, sensual, cynical, heart-warming, and disturbingly thought-provoking.' *(Variety)*

'Miss Minnelli, daughter of Judy Garland, now and then reminds one of her mother – the voice not, perhaps, as pure, but the same attack, the same quality, when it is needed, of heartbreak. Here is an actress with a superlatively controlled body; with comedy; with a magical range of look and gesture and a gift for self-mockery. What is more, she has something which I have not so far detected in the work of the much-admired Barbra Streisand – pathos. Really, I think a star is born.' *(Dilys Powell)*

'We see the decadence as garish and sleazy; yet we also see the animal energy in it – everything seems to become sexualized. The movie does not exploit decadence; rather, it gives it its due . . . Minnelli has such gaiety and electricity that she becomes a star before our eyes.' *(Pauline Kael)*

'Performs a daring feat – it creates a frightening real world and uses music to convey the horror.' *(Phillip J. Kaplan, 1983)*

CABINET OF DR CALIGARI, THE CT: 5 AV: 7.66

(aka *Das Kabinett von Dr Caligari*)

1919 Germany 69/90 BW HORROR/SILENT

D Robert Wiene ☆
W Carl Mayer Hans Janowitz ☆

Werner Krauss ✗ Conrad Veidt ☆ Lil Dagover Friedrich Feher Hans von Twardowski

Mad doctor (Werner Krauss) uses his sleep-walking assistant (Conrad Veidt) to commit murder.

A film with creepy images which stay in the mind, and a highly original vision: it was the first to put the audience into the mind of a madman by showing his distorted viewpoint. The camera angles, stylized sets and lighting have all been imitated in countless later films. The acting, however, is primitive and the plot both confusing and monotonous, so that it's a classic which few people nowadays watch for enjoyment.

'This barbaric carnival . . . the destruction of the healthy human infancy of our art.' *(Sergei Eisenstein)*

'The first hundred shocks are the hardest.' *(New York Evening Post, 1924)*

'An intensely exciting and forceful picture. *Dr Caligari* is one of the few films that do not seriously date . . . qualities of inner rhythm, visual imagination and specific logic made it one of the great adventures of its time.' *(Sketch, 1948)*

'One of the most exciting and inspired horror movies ever made. The story is a classic sampling of expressionist paranoia . . . full of the gloom and fear that prevailed in Germany as it emerged from WW1.' *(David Pirie, Time Out)*

CABIRIA: *see* NIGHTS OF CABIRIA, THE

CADUTA DEGLI DEI, LA: *see* DAMNED, THE.

CAGE AUX FOLLES, THE: *see* LA CAGE AUX FOLLES

CAINE MUTINY, THE AAN CT: 6 AV: 7.33

1954 US 123 C DRAMA

D Edward Dmytryk
W Stanley Roberts ☆ AAN from Herman Wouk's novel

Humphrey Bogart ☆ AAN Jose Ferrer ✔ Van Johnson ✔ Fred MacMurray ✔ Robert Francis May Wynn Tom Tully ☆ AAN E.G. Marshall Lee Marvin Claude Akins

A naval captain (Humphrey Bogart) cracks up in peacetime and is court-martialled.

Stagey, turgid drama with little sense of the sea. Director Dmytryk bends over backwards to be fair to everyone, and the result is worthy but long-winded. However, the screenplay is well structured and never fails to grip, and the acting is more than competent; especially memorable is the courtroom scene where Bogart crumbles under interrogation from Jose Ferrer. Max Steiner's score was Oscar-nominated, as was the editing by William A. Lyon and Henry Batista.

'Scene after scene in the picture during the hour and one-half buildup to the court-martial stand out, either for high action, drama or the beauty and grace of ships making their way proudly through the seas.' *(Variety)*

Bogart takes this by no means easy part and wrings every drop of sourness and sadness from it.' *(Spectator)*

'Picture seems more concerned not to hurt the image of the Navy than to condemn Queeg, or to probe the military mentality and suggest that his phobias are not rare among military leaders.' *(Danny Peary)*

CALIFORNIA MAN: *see* ENCINO MAN.

CALIGULA CT: 1 AV: 1.60

1979 US/Italy 105/150/210 C DRAMA/ROMANCE

D Tinto Brass ● (principally) Giancalo Lui ● Bob Guccione ● (additional scenes)
W Bob Guccione ● from Gore Vidal's screenplay (who understandably had his name taken off the credits)

Malcolm McDowell ● John Gielgud Peter O'Toole ● Helen Mirren Teresa Ann Savoy John Steiner

Life and death of an unpleasant Roman emperor (Malcolm McDowell).

Perhaps the least erotic sex movie of all time, with writer/producer Bob Guccione (editor of *Penthouse*) trying to beef up its impact with disgustingly gratuitous violence and obvious, poorly shot inserts of copulation between the non-stars.

'Such established names as John Gielgud and Peter O'Toole will have to be seen to be believed. Malcolm McDowell as the sick and/or insane emperor runs the gamut of cardboard emotions from grand guignol to hapless pathos.' *(Variety)*

'A dreary shambles, directed by Brass *toto drosso con abandimento*.' *(Chris Peachment, Time Out)*

'Director Tinto Brass tries to create a surreal Felliniesque atmosphere, as was present in Fellini's *Satyricon*, but where Fellini was sublime and funny, Brass is ugly and raunchy. He's the type of guy who will have Caligula strip the clothes off his dead sister just so viewers can get one last glimpse of her crotch – making us share Caligula's necrophilia.' *(Danny Peary)*

'Mostly revolting except for admirers of the hard core and decapitation.' *(Winnert)*

'Far more Gore than Vidal.' *(Variety)*

CALL NORTHSIDE 777 CT: 6 AV: 7.14

1948 US 111 BW THRILLER
D Henry Hathaway
W Jerome Cady, Jay Dratler

James Stewart ☆ Lee J. Cobb Helen Walker Kazia Orzazweski ☆ Bety Garde Richard Conte

A dogged journalist (James Stewart) tries to clear an imprisoned man (Richard Conte) of murder.

Based on a true story and filmed in semi-documentary style (the authentic locations are in the polish district of Chicago), this solid thriller contains one of Stewart's finest performances –

undervalued by contemporary critics and audiences, because it was so much tougher and more abrasive than his usual roles. Two minor let-downs are a late descent into implausibility, and the fact that we know the killer's identity too soon.

'Has all the ingredients of a sock film but registers only with mild impact due to a lack of integration. Anong the film's principal drawbacks is James Stewart's jarring and unpersuasive performance in the key role.' *(Variety)*

'A most satisfying thriller, generously streaked with class." *(Daily Mail)*

'Absorbing, exciting, realistic.' *(Star)*

CAMELOT

CT: 6 AV: 4.45

1967 US 181 C MUSICAL/DRAMA

D Joshua Logan ●
W Alan Jay Lerner from T.H. White's novel *The Once and Future King* songs by Frederick Loewe, Alan Jay Lerner

Richard Harris Vanessa Redgrave David Hemmings Franco Nero Lionel Jeffries Laurence Naismith

Guenevere (Vanessa Redgrave) and Arthur (Richard Harris) have matrimonial problems.

All-American view of Arthurian legend, overlong, stodgily directed but with some indestructible, moving moments. The sumptuous art direction (which is breathtakingly vulgar at times) overshadows Lerner and Loewe's variable songs, and the acting is far superior to the singing (Vanessa Redgrave should either have been dubbed or replaced altogether). Towards the end, Richard Harris makes up for his vocal deficiencies and sporadic bouts of overacting and is genuinely touching as the medieval John F. Kennedy. A massive flop at the box office, but surprisingly watchable despite its obvious flaws.

ANTI:

'Three hours of unrelieved glossiness, meticulous inanity, desperate and charmless striving for charm. This film is the Platonic idea of boredom, roughly comparable to reading a three-volume novel in a language of which one knows only the alphabet . . . All the horses wear $6,000 suits of armor; this is helpful in that it enables us to distinguish them from Vanessa Redgrave, who has never been shot to look so equine before.' *(John Simon)*

'A gaudy, mawkish, pretentious, disorganized bore . . . Whatever meaning Lerner's book once had is defeated by one of the worst examples of screen direction in recent years and is crushed beneath gargantuan, tasteless production.' *(Robert Downing, Films in Review)*

'It's like a huge ruin that makes one wonder what the blueprints could possibly have indicated.' *(Pauline Kael)*

'One may wonder whether the fashion for musicals in which only the chorus can actually sing may be reaching its final stage.' *(MFB)*

'To take all three hours, one probably needs a fairly tireless addiction to knights, toy castles, rapt pauses and battlefield farewells.' *(Penelope Houston, Spectator)*

'The thing about this stupidly long extravaganza is that the intimate scenes are powerful enough to make one quite dread the songs.' *(John Coleman New Statesman)*

PRO:

'What gives *Camelot* special value is a central dramatic conflict that throbs with anguish and compassion.' *(Variety)*

'Looks simply ravishing.' *(Clive Hirschhorn, Sunday Express)*

'Both wonderful entertainment and memorable art. The cast is formidable . . . [It] misses corn by inches and those inches make it intensely moving and harrowing.' *(Celia Holt, Daily Telegraph)*

CAMILLE

CT: 7 AV: 8.25

1936 US 108 BW DRAMA/ROMANCE

D George Cukor ☆
W Zoe Akins Frances Marion James Hilton from Alexandre Dumas fils's novel and play *La Dame aux Camélias*

Greta Garbo ☆ Robert Taylor Lionel Barrymore Henry Daniell ☆, Elizabeth Allan Leonore Ulric Laura Hope Crews Rex O'Malley Jessie Ralph E.E. Clive

An innocent young man (Robert Taylor) falls for a dying courtesan (Greta Garbo).

One of the most unashamedly glamorous, romantic movies ever made, it also shows why Garbo was a star. She's totally miscast – never for one moment can one believe that her character is really a whore – and yet it's impossible to take one's eyes off her. Her magical performance (her most popular with the public) is really a triumph of the studio system, for Cukor's sensitive direction, Adrian's pale costumes and William Daniels's exquisite cinematography all helped to create the Garbo image – and it was studio head Irving Thalberg who ordered Cukor to reshoot the famous death scene shorter, and on a chaise-longue rather than a bed (it proved to be Thalberg's last film). Robert Taylor isn't in the same league as regards acting ability or charisma, but he is touchingly young and handsome. Henry Daniell is a tremendous villain.

'The surprise is to find a story that should by rights be old hat coming to such insistent life on the screen.' *(Otis Ferguson)*

'Robert Taylor plays with surprising assurance and ease . . . Garbo's impersonation of Marguerite Gautier is one of her best portraits.' *(Variety)*

'This production of *Camille* is, and not altogether because of the sumptuously human, moving performance of Miss Greta Garbo, a performance hardly equaled, never exceeded in the history of the screen.' *(NBR)*

'This is not death as mortals know it. This is but the conclusion of a romantic ritual.' *(Bosley Crowther)*

CAMPANADAS A MEDIANOCHE: *see* CHIMES AT MIDNIGHT.

CAN HIERONYMUS MERKIN EVER FORGET MERCY HUMPPE AND FIND TRUE HAPPINESS? CT: 1 AV: 2.33

1969 GB 117 C FANTASY/COMEDY

D Anthony Newley ●
W Herman Raucher Anthony Newley ●

Anthony Newley ● Joan Collins ● Milton Berle George Jessel Connie Kreski Bruce Forsyth Stubby Kaye Victor Spinetti Patricia Hayes

Singing star (Anthony Newley) has mid-life crisis, a bit like Fellini's but not as interesting.

Unintentionally horrifying ego-trip for its overconfident writer-star-director.

'Anthony Newley has now cornered the market on Hollywood-style pornography . . . he dances in the nude, performs cunnilingus on a naked girl underwater, sings a song called "What a Son of a Bitch I Am" and, for the crowning blow, actually allows a dirty old letch to run his hand up his own baby daughter's dress in a scene that has to win some kind of award for the penultimate in rotten bad taste . . . If I'd been Anthony Newley I would have opened it in Siberia during Christmas week and called it a day.' *(Rex Reed)*

'The kindest thing for all concerned would be that every available copy should be quietly and decently buried.' *(Michael Billington, Illustrated London News)*

'Obscure and pointless personal fantasy, financed at great expense by a major film company as a rather seedy monument to Anthony Newley's totally uninteresting sex life, and to the talent which he obviously thinks he possesses. The few mildly amusing moments are not provided by him.' *(Halliwell)*

CAN'T STOP THE MUSIC CT: 1 AV: 2.78

1980 US 117 C MUSICAL

D Nancy Walker ●
W Bronte Woodward Allan Carr ●

Valerie Perrine Steve Guttenberg ● June Havoc Barbara Rush Leigh Taylor-Young The Village People ● Tammy Grimes Bruce Jenner ●

A singing group (The Village People) is formed to perform the songs of an aspiring composer (Steve Guttenberg).

One of the tackiest acts in pop music have a fittingly atrocious memorial to their, er, talents. The number YMCA is a show-stopping piece of tasteless camp, but there are many more ghastly moments at which to cringe. Sample line . . . Model agency head (Tammy Grimes) eying male talent (Bruce Jenner): 'Fruit of the Loom is doing a big ad campaign, and something tells me you could really fit into a pair of jockey shorts.' A famous flop.

PRO:

'Choreographed with a showmanship that would not have shamed Busby Berkeley.' *(William Hall, Evening News)*

'Slicker and more sophisticated than *Grease* . . . the film will appeal to audiences who like their entertainment at full blast . . . As a frantic display of razzle-dazzle energy, the movie has merit.' *(Arthur Thirkell, Daily Mirror)*

ANTI:

'A forced marriage between the worst of sitcom plotting and the highest of high camp production numbers.' *(New West)*

'One doesn't watch *Can't Stop the Music*. One is attacked by it.' *(New England Entertainment Digest)*

'Producer Allan Carr's guiding principle seems to be: shoot everything that moves, throw it on the cutting room floor, give the editor a vacuum cleaner and hope that it will all work out. It doesn't.' *(Time)*

'This shamefully tacky musical extravaganza fails on every aesthetic level . . . Considering the low level of wit, perhaps The Village People should consider renaming themselves The Village Idiots.' *(Los Angeles Herald Examiner)*

'Could have been more aptly titled "Can't Stand The Music".' *(Margulies & Rebello)*

CANDY CT: 3 AV: 3.00
(aka *Candy Mountain*)

1968 US/France/Italy 124 COMEDY

D Christian Marquand ●
W Buck Henry ● from Terry Southern's novel

Ewa Aulin ● Richard Burton ● Marlon Brando ● James Coburn Walter Matthau Charles Aznavour John Huston Elsa Martinelli Ringo Starr ● John Astin

During the 60s, an 'innocent' nymphet (Ewa Aulin) is repeatedly deflowered.

Absolutely awful, self-indulgent, sniggering sex

comedy with a hopeless central actress and embarrassing cameo performances by (among others) Richard Burton, Marlon Brando and Ringo Starr. Marquand's direction grotesquely over-extends almost every scene; but even if the film had been cut to half its length (as it would have been by any competent director), it would still be lousy. Variety's review took charity to the point of insanity.

'A mixed bag of goodies . . . The continuing characters are excellent. Aulin's performance in the title role is a delight. John Astin plays both her straight father and her lecherous uncle, and he is terrific. Elsa Martinelli also is excellent as Aunt Livia . . . Ringo Starr, as the Mexican gardener, is very good.' *(Variety)*

'To merely call this repulsive, talentless little 42nd Street peep show the worst picture of the year would be philanthropic. Just call it the worst picture ever made.' *(Rex Reed)*

'If you know someone you want to start the new year as nauseated as possible, send him to see *Candy*. As an emetic, liquor is dandy, but *Candy* is quicker.' *(John Simon)*

'Like sitting through a two-hour cartoon in Playboy.' *(Scheuer)*

CANDYMAN CT: 8 AV: 6.00

1992 US 93 C HORROR

D Bernard Rose ✓
W Bernard Rose ☆ from Clive Barker's story *The Forbidden*

Virginia Madsen ✓ Tony Todd Xander Berkeley Kasi Lemmons Vanessa Williams DeJuan Guy

Academic (Virginia Madsen) investigates an urban myth.

A first-rate horror film and a welcome return to form for British director Bernard Rose after his awful *Chicago Joe and the Showgirl*. Clive Barker's original short story was about a female university academic investigating the 'urban myth' of a vicious murderer on a housing estate in England. The locale is shifted to a black-dominated housing project in Chicago, with frightening results. It's intelligent and gripping, it will make you jump, and Virginia Madsen is excellent in the leading role.

'Performances are unusually credible for this sort of fare.' *(Variety)*

'A horror thriller that operates several astute and imaginative levels above the general norm.' *(Gary Arnold, Washington Post)*

'Faithful, scary and visually imaginative . . . Rose stages the suspense and horror with skill and panache, making this one of the best sustained horror movies for some years.' *(Nigel Floyd, Time Out)*

'Elements of the plot may not hold up in the clear light of day, but that didn't bother me much. What I liked was a horror movie that was scaring me with ideas and gore, instead of simply with gore.' *(Roger Ebert)*

CAPE FEAR CT: 6 AV: 6.15

1961 US 106 BW THRILLER/HORROR

D J. Lee Thompson
W James R. Webb from John D. MacDonald's novel *The Executioners*

Robert Mitchum ☆ Gregory Peck Polly Bergen ✓ Martin Balsam Lori Martin Jack Kruschen Telly Savalas

The family of a lawyer (Gregory Peck) is threatened by a madman (Robert Mitchum).

Straightforward, unpretentious horror yarn with memorable performances (especially from Mitchum, reprising his *Night of the Hunter* role) and a fine Bernard Herrmann score (reused by Martin Scorsese in his 90s remake). Scorsese's film is flashier and has more psychological depth, but the original is more realistic and no less frightening.

PRO:

'Competent and visually polished.' *(Variety)*

'If director J. Lee Thompson isn't quite skilful enough to give the film its final touch of class (many of the shocks are just too planned), the relentlessness of the story and Mitchum's tangibly sordid presence guarantee the viewer's quivering attention.' *(David Thompson, Time Out)*

'Impeccable playing by the whole cast, and Thompson never lets up on the tension or the terror.' *(Winnert)*

ANTI:

'Unpleasant and drawn out supenser with characters of cardboard and situations from stock.' *(Halliwell)*

CAPE FEAR CT: 9 AV: 6.69

1991 US 123 C THRILLER/HORROR

D Martin Scorsese ✓
W Wesley Strick ✓ from John D. MacDonald's novel *The Executioners*

Robert De Niro ☆ Nick Nolte Jessica Lange Juliette Lewis ☆ Joe Don Baker Robert Mitchum ✓ Gregory Peck ✓ Martin Balsam Illeana Douglas ✓ Fred Dalton Thompson

A lawyer (Nick Nolte) and his family are threatened by a madman (Robert De Niro).

One of the most controversial films of recent years. Technically – as even Scorsese's most scathing critics admitted – his direction, Thelma Schoonmaker's editing and Freddie Francis's cinematography are spectacular. The film is an even more stunning succession of images and visual pyrotechnics than *GoodFellas*. Scorsese is a director who can turn a teddy-bear into a symbol of evil, and an ordinary staircase into a vision of Dante's Inferno.

There's an unforgettable shot, for example, of the villain (Robert De Niro) seducing the hero's daughter (Juliette Lewis) over her pink little bedroom phone: De Niro's silky, reasonable voice contrasts with the camera's serpentine slide past his hard, black, fetishistic body-building equipment to reveal the man himself. Only then do we find he's hanging upside down, like a tattooed, muscular bat. And the camera itself turns through 180 degrees, to show De Niro's unearthly grin, with gravity standing his hair on end, as if he's a demon from Struwwelpeter. Scorsese transforms a small, functional scene into a masterpiece of menace.

But the best thrillers are more than well-crafted: they bring us face to face with our deepest fears. De Niro's bogeyman, Max Cady, is a wonderfully complex nightmare figure, the unconscious wish-fulfilment of every main character. To his rape victim (Illeana Douglas), he's a piece of rough whom she picks up in a bar, to express her independence from the lover who's stood her up (Nick Nolte). She's turned on by Cady's boast that 'I'm just one hell of an animal'; she even giggles in bed when he handcuffs her. Cady is an embodiment of her sexual fantasies, taken just that one horrible step further into nightmare.

Cady appeals to the hero's 15-year-old daughter by voicing her adolescent sense of injustice. He echoes the marital resentments of his wife (Jessica Lange), with whom Cady shares a sense of betrayal and a history of mental illness. To our lawyer hero (Nick Nolte), Cady represents his own guilty conscience – Cady has a perfectly reasonable legal grievance against him. Cady is also an unpleasant reminder to our hero of his own violent side. From the start, Nolte is a mass of sublimated aggression: his squash defeat of his mistress is as violent in its way as Cady's rape of her, only a few scenes later. Nolte hires men to beat up Cady and – another hint of suppressed sadism – goes to watch. Under stress, Nolte even comes close to striking his wife and daughter. In the first *Cape Fear*, Gregory Peck played the hero as a pillar of family rectitude: Nolte is an altogether more flawed, Scorsesian and believable character.

Here, as in *Taxi Driver*, Scorsese is fascinated by the violence which exists below the surface of respectable society. The first attack we see in the picture is performed not by the psychopathic villain, but by Nolte on Cady – and the setting is highly significant. The 4th of July parade featuring soldiers carrying an American flag, is a reminder that America is a society founded not only on legal rights, but also on the threat of institutionalized violence.

This most Hobbesian of films also exploits our unconscious fears about the rule of law. Nolte's original betrayal of Cady, by not revealing the sexual past of his last rape victim, reflects our hero's belief that the law doesn't protect a promiscuous woman who has been raped. Nolte's girlfriend, the rape victim, knows for the same reason that the law won't protect her and refuses to press charges.

And it's a film which strikes to the heart of middle-class anxieties about materialism. Cady expresses Nolte's unconscious fear that he has lost his sense of values. 'I'm gonna teach you the meaning of commitment,' Cady tells him, in a friendly moment. 'You could say I'm here to save you.' Nolte and his family pass through a Hell where they are tested by fire and water, and end up baptized and 'born again'. It's a story of guilt and redemption. Scorsese once studied to become a Catholic priest, and his religious theme places *Cape Fear* in the mainstream of his work.

The acting throughout is of a high standard. Juliette Lewis is sensational in her one-take scene with De Niro in an empty theatre, and Robert De Niro makes seamless transitions from sly comedy to the grandest of grand guignol. It's not hard to see why De Niro likes appearing in Scorsese movies (*Cape Fear* is his seventh). He is wonderfully served by the visuals: one of the most terrifying shots is almost before he's had to start acting. Cady leaves jail with storm clouds and lightning flickering overhead, walks expressionlessly towards camera and never stops coming until his face is distorted by the anamorphic lens. You can actually feel the audience flinch and pull back.

The serious aspects of the film are, to some extent, victims of its success as a thriller: you can enjoy *Cape Fear* merely as the Rolls Royce of slasher movies, a two-hour anxiety attack, without bothering to look far into its murky depths. But that is only to say that it repays being seen more than once. *Cape Fear* is one of the most misjudged films in recent history.

ANTI:

'Everyone concerned with this repellent attempt to make a great deal of money out of a clumsy plunge into sexual pathology should be thoroughly ashamed of himself.' *(J. Hoberman, S&S)*

'A spectacularly bad movie for Scorsese to have made. I don't think he's a hack but it turned into a piece of hack work.' *(Pauline Kael)*

'Have our lives truly become so hollow that this kind of unapologetic bludgeoning of our sensibilities passes for jolly weekend entertainment?' *(Kenneth Turan, LA Times)*

'A disgrace, an ugly, incoherent, dishonest piece of work . . . What makes the long scene between Cady and Danielle so surpassingly ugly is that it turns the normal confused sexuality of a teenage girl into something unclean: As Danielle begins to respond to the advances of her would-be rapist, the movie unavoidably suggests that she, like the unfortunate Lori, is asking for it . . . The Christian implications that Scorsese lays on this elemental story actually serve to make the message more reactionary: Violence is no longer just a matter of survival – it's now the instrument of salvation.' *(Terrence Rafferty, New Yorker)*

'A slasher film by Martin Scorsese is still a slasher film.' *(Dave Kehr, Chicago Tribune)*

'Scorsese has done more than reshoot in colour; he has also taken away the comforting black and white nature of the characters . . . In the move away from the clear-cut morality of the earlier film, Scorsese muddies the waters of audience sympathy.' *(Iain Johnstone, Sunday Times)*

'The rape is dismissed in predictable misogynistic fashion – the woman was promiscuous and thus by implication deserved all she got. Instead we are invited to sympathize with Bowden [and] Cady [who] is presented as an illiterate working class man, victimized by and denied access to the corrupt and misogynistic mechanics of a legal system that could have saved him from imprisonment . . . At the same time the audience is invited to hate [him] for his class and smirk at his ridiculous middle-class affectation . . . [It's] a compelling and frightening film [which] should not be missed. But, unlike *Silence of the Lambs*, there is no safe Jodie Foster to hold your hand. There is no safety in this film at all.' *(Irene Coffey, Spare Rib)*

'The second half of [the film] lurches towards the ridiculous. Scorsese seems unsure of himself, despite the dazzling camerawork. The greatest horror . . . is the death of imagination brought about by its suffocating reliance on pastiche.' *(Angela McRobbie, F&F)*

PRO:

'History robbed Scorsese of the chance to be an auteur in the full oppositional sense of the term. So now, as compensation, he's gone back thirty years and inserted himself into a studio product . . . giving it the one thing it lacked in 1962 – a star performance by the director.' *(Stuart Klawans, Nation)*

'With its jagged editing style, breathless camera movement and especially its disturbing psychological currents, this popularly conceived chiller bears the distinctively volatile stamp of a master director . . . It truly does scare the bejeezus out of you.' *(Kevin Lally, Film Journal)*

'Sleight of hand of a high order and at carefully calculated moments, a blunt shocker . . . Stay away if you're squeamish but if you do you'll miss an essential work by one of our masters.' *(Vincent Canby, New York Times)*

CAPTAIN BLOOD CT: 7 AV: 7.54

1935 US 99/119 BW ACTION/ADVENTURE

D Michael Curtiz ☆
W Casey Robinson from Rafael Sabatini's novel

Errol Flynn ☆, Olivia de Havilland ✔
Basil Rathbone ☆, Lionel Atwill Guy Kibbee
Ross Alexander Henry Stephenson

British surgeon with unfortunate name of Blood (Errol Flynn) turns Caribbean pirate.

Magnificent swashbuckler well liked by critics and audiences. It made stars of Errol Flynn and teenage actress Olivia de Havilland (they went on to make seven more films together). Michael (*Casablanca*) Curtiz directs the mayhem with panache, and this remains probably the most exciting pirate movie of all time. The 119-minute version is greatly to be preferred.

'Romantic interest . . . [is] all too paltry.' *(Variety)*

'Magnificently photographed, lavishly produced, and directed with consummate skill.' *(Picturegoer)*

'A fine spirited mix-up with clothes and wigs which sometimes hark back to the sixteenth century and sometimes forward to the period of Wolfe . . . One is quite prepared for the culminating moment when the Union Jack breaks proudly, anachronistically forth at Peter Blood's masthead.' *(Graham Greene)*

CAPTAINS COURAGEOUS AAN CT: 7 AV: 7.76

1937 US 116 BW DRAMA/FAMILY

D Victor Fleming
W John Lee Mahin Marc Connelly Dale Van Every from Rudyard Kipling's novel ☆ AAN

Spencer Tracy ✗ AAW Lionel Barrymore
Freddie Bartholomew Mickey Rooney
Melvyn Douglas Charley Grapewin John Carradine
Leo G. Carroll

Spoiled rich kid (Freddie Bartholomew) is taught how to live his life by Portuguese fisherman (Spencer Tracy).

Highly successful, sentimental family film which inexplicably won an Oscar for Spencer Tracy, whose performance is far from his best. The MGM production values are excellent, and it manages to be entertaining and heart-warming. It was voted the third Best Film of 1937 (after *Zola* and *The Good Earth*) in the annual poll of US film critics conducted by the *Film Daily*. It also won the Photoplay Gold Medal Award as Best Picture of 1937, voted for by America's cinemagoing public.

'I used to pray that something would happen to halt production. I was positive I was doing the worst job of my life.' (Spencer Tracy)

'Another of those grand jobs of moviemaking we

have come to expect from Hollywood's most profligate studio.' *(Frank S. Nugent, New York Times)*

'*Captains Courageous* is as real and immediate as a documentary, yet stylishly and attractively photographed. Some of the process work is obvious, but few members of a 1937 audience would have detected it.' *(John Howard Reid)*

'The Kipling novel was reworked – sugared – by experienced hands.' *(Pauline Kael)*

CARMEN AAN CT: 6 AV: 7.11

1983 Spain 101 C MUSICAL/FOREIGN

D Carlos Saura ☆
W Carlos Saura Antonio Gades from Prosper Merimée's novel

Antonio Gades ☆ Laura Del Sol ☆ Paco de Lucia Christina Hoyos

An actress-dancer (Laura del Sol) falls in love with her choreographer (Antonio Gades) as they prepare a production of Carmen*; and life proceeds to imitate art.*

Passionate performances and fiery choreography (by Saura and Gades) combine to make this an unusually lively musical – principally indebted to Bizet (whose music propels the action), but with melodramatic overtones of *Blood Wedding* and *The Red Shoes*.

'Lacks the edge that would make it in any way compelling.' *(Jill Forbes, MFB)*

'An erotic roller-coaster of a movie, incorporating dance into its story more effectively than any movie I can remember.' *(Roger Ebert)*

'Visually exhilarating . . . Both a new kind of musical and marvellous cinema.' *(Nick Roddick, Time Out)*

CARNAL KNOWLEDGE CT: 5 AV: 6.08

1971 US 97 C DRAMA/COMEDY

D Mike Nichols
W Jules Feiffer

Jack Nicholson ☆ Art Garfunkel ☆ Candice Bergen Ann-Margret ☆ AAN Rita Moreno Carol Kane Cynthia O'Neal

A male chauvinist pig (Jack Nicholson) screws his way through life, from the late 40s to 1971. His college chum (Art Garfunkel) leads a less eventful but equally empty life.

Hip movie of its period, once thought witty and sexually daring: now it looks cold, unsympathetic and sneering, and the didactic script is further marred by gimmicky direction. Even though Nicholson and Garfunkel give outstanding performances, it's hard to care about anyone on screen (although Ann-Margret, as Nicholson's mistress, comes close). The film seems to promise a moment when Nicholson's eminently loathsome character will receive his come-uppance; but no such luck.

PRO:

'Controversial, painfully savage and perhaps the most important film to come out of Hollywood in the 1970s . . . The film is uneven and flawed because it dared to be so ugly, because life is not a thing of beauty or perfection, balance or fairness. *Carnal Knowledge* presents human existence as ravaged, painful and terribly difficult. It's damn near perfect.' *(Virgin)*

ANTI:

'A rather superficial and limited probe of American male sexual hypocrisies.' *(Variety)*

'A fine example of a film that combines delusions of grandeur with delusions of honesty . . . Jack Nicholson and Candice Bergen look like chaperones rather than freshmen . . . It is not merely a question of ages: Miss Bergen cannot act any age even though, with every new film, she tries harder, which does make her a *rara avis* among no-talent actresses. Nicholson . . . is less than ideal for a leading man: his somewhat whiny, high-pitched voice lacks range, and he tries to compensate with rant; he has moreover, a countrified, lower-class speech pattern that does not fit in here. He is also apt to overact.' *(John Simon)*

'Feiffer rigged the case and wrote a grimly purposeful tract on depersonalization and how we use each other as objects, and in the director Mike Nichols's cold, slick style, the movie is like a neon sign spelling out the soullessness of neon.' *(Pauline Kael)*

CARNIVAL IN FLANDERS CT: 5 AV: 7.17

(aka *La Kermesse Héroique*)

1935 France 115 BW COMEDY/FOREIGN

D Jacques Feyder ☆
W Charles Spaak Jacques Feyder ✗ from Spaak's novel

Françoise Rosay ☆ Louis Jouvet ☆ Jean Murat Alfred Adam André Alerme

Women in occupied Flanders during the 17th century make themselves available to the Spanish soldiers.

This bawdy sex comedy must have seemed daring at the time – and that presumably accounts for its commercial success, since it is far from hilarious and has many longueurs. But Harry Stradling's cinematography is superb; pictorially and atmospherically, it's a wonderful evocation of 17th-century life. It won Feyder the Best Director prize at the 1936 Venice Film Festival. The central argument – which seemed to be in favour of survival through collaboration – ensured that the film did not retain its popularity into the 40s, except with the Nazis.

'A mixture of gay absurdity and shrewd comment, selecting its own pitch and holding it.' *(Otis Ferguson)*

'Everything fits perfectly into the pattern of cultured and sophisticated entertainment. Nowhere is there a false touch.' *(The Times, 1952)*

'It's almost too close to perfect; it's so archly classic that it isn't really very funny.' *(Pauline Kael)*

CAROUSEL CT: 8 AV: 6.91

1956 US 128 C MUSICAL/DRAMA/FANTASY

D Henry King
W Phoebe and Harry Ephron from the musical based on Ferenc Molnar's play *Liliom* (songs by Richard Rodgers Oscar Hammerstein II ☆)

Gordon Macrae Shirley Jones ☆ Cameron Mitchell Gene Lockhart Barbara Ruick Robert Rounseville

A fairground barker (Gordon Macrae) does not respond well to the responsibilities of marriage.

Though schmaltzy at times and with a weakish storyline (mainly because the anti-hero is so unsympathetic), this remains one of the best screen musicals. Several production numbers – notably the ballet and 'June Is Busting Out All Over' – are classics; and the score is arguably the best that Rodgers and Hammerstein ever wrote. Gordon Macrae was a late replacement for Frank Sinatra, and he is vocally strong if a little too mature for the role. Shirley Jones is delightful as his wife.

ANTI:

'The melodies have all their clovered freshness still, but if film fans lick their lips over anything else about this movie version of the Broadway musical, it will be because they can't tell sweet from saccharine.' *(Time)*

'The story . . . does not stand up too well to the merciless glare of CinemaScope. Hollywood is never at ease in the celestial regions.' *(Fred Majdalany, Daily Mail)*

'Hollow and boring, a humourless whimsy in which even the songs seem an intrusion.' *(Halliwell)*

MIXED:

'Miss Jones's face makes the prettiest dumpling you ever saw. She acts with a simple sincerity that has the sweetness of new-mown hay . . . I hail Carousel as a fine musical . . . gloriously filmed . . . but I also sound a warning note. If you dislike sentiment and whimsy you may be in for some sticky moments . . . I squirmed a little myself at the Heaven episodes, but the sentiment I swallowed whole.' *(Harold Conway, Daily Sketch)*

'The tunes aren't bad, they hang about for a day or two . . . The triumph of [the film] is that it makes this trite nonsense tuneful and affecting.' *(William Whitebait, New Statesman)*

PRO:

'Under Henry King's direction, the grand score soars on . . . And Rod Alexander's dances have lusty vitality.' *(New York Times)*

'Pretty, high-coloured, ear-splitting, corny and enormous fun.' *(Isabel Quigly, Spectator)*

CARPETBAGGERS, THE CT: 5 AV: 5.00

1964 US 150 C DRAMA/SO BAD

D Edward Dmytryk ●
W John Michael Hayes from Harold Robbins's novel

George Peppard Carroll Baker Alan Ladd Martin Balsam ☆ Bob Cummings Martha Hyer Elizabeth Ashley Lew Ayres

Playboy (George Peppard) becomes megalomaniac tycoon.

Highly coloured, would-be sophisticated version of a Howard Hughes-type character. Harold Robbins trash, but the actors look as if they're enjoying themselves. It's a bit like have someone bash you over the head for two and a half hours with an airport novel.

PRO:

'A swift, irresistibly vulgar compilation of all the racy stories anyone has ever heard about wicked old Hollywood of the 20s and 30s.' *(Time)*

'A sex shocker by some of the film industry's most humourless executives . . . [It] was supposed to drain you of emotion (and so on) – but the only thing it drained me of in the smoke-filled cinema was air – not so much from smoke as laughing.' *(Robin Bean, S&S)*

ANTI:

'There is hardly a decent bone in its whole lascivious body.' *(Margaret Hinxman, Sun)*

'Sensational is the word for it. Trashy is another. You could also add three more – bad, bad, bad.' *(Leonard Mosley, Daily Express)*

CARRIE CT: 8 AV: 6.21

1976 US 98 C HORROR/RITES-OF-PASSAGE

D Brian De Palma ☆
W Laurence D. Cohen

Sissy Spacek ☆ AAN Piper Laurie ☆ AAN
Amy Irving ✔ William Katt ✔ John Travolta ✔
Nancy Allen ✔ P.J. Soles ✔ Betty Buckley ✔

Repressed, victimized teenage girl (Sissy Spacek) wreaks vengeance on her enemies.

A genre classic, mainly because the horror comes out of established character, and right up to the end we can empathize with the disturbed heroine: in this respect, it's not unlike Polanski's *Repulsion*. Sissy Spacek led a generally good cast with an outstanding psychological study.

Like many horror movies – *Psycho, Peeping Tom*, Scorsese's *Cape Fear* – *Carrie* was underrated on its release. De Palma's camera tricks were generally deemed gimmicky, whereas mostly they are very effective. The scene at the prom is an example, where an initially romantic camera movement around Carrie and her date builds up to a nightmarish speed. And the shock ending – though it has lost some of its impact through being much imitated – is a classic moment of cinema.

ANTI:

'These events aren't so much horrifying as downright silly.' *(Daily Express)*

'A piece of old-fashioned grand guignol lent a spurious contemporaneity by the use of up-to-date technique.' *(Financial Times)*

MIXED:

'Combining Gothic horror, offhand misogyny and an air of studied triviality, *Carrie* is De Palma's most enjoyable movie in a long while, and also his silliest.' *(Janet Maslin, Newsweek)*

'The big effects [are] drawn out to impossible lengths and shot with trashy blatancy . . . The performances are mostly humdrum or worse, except for that of Sissy Spacek in the lead: a touchingly unspoiled, intense and various creation.' *(John Simon)*

PRO:

'De Palma's ability to combine the romantic and the horrific has never been so pulverising.' *(David Pirie, Time Out)*

'A movie that marks the final emergence of yet another major young directorial talent.' *(Arthur Knight, Hollywood Reporter)*

'The best scary-funny movie since *Jaws* – a teasing, terrific, lyrical shocker, directed by Brian De Palma, who has the wickedest baroque sensibility at large in American movies.' *(Pauline Kael)*

'De Palma's interests – in satire, Hitchcockian horror and gothic romance – finally converge in a fully integrated, iconoclastic work.' *(Stephen Farber, New West)*

'Narrative development hasn't exactly been De Palma's strong point, but here he exhibits a gift for painting personalities; we didn't know De Palma, ordinarily so flashy on the surface, could go so deep.' *(Roger Ebert)*

CARRY ON UP THE KHYBER CT: 7 AV: 6.14

1968 GB 88 C COMEDY

D Gerald Thomas
W Talbot Rothwell ✔

Sidney James ☆ Kenneth Williams ☆ Charles Hawtrey Joan Sims Peter Butterworth Bernard Bresslaw ☆ Roy Castle Terry Scott Angela Douglas Cardew Robinson Julian Holloway Peter Gilmore

Plucky British soldiers repel Afghan tribesmen on the North-West Frontier.

The 'Carry On' films span 20 years from 1958 until 1978 – or 1992, if you include the ill-advised afterthought *Carry On Columbus*. This one is easily the funniest, and features plucky British soldiers repelling Afghan tribesmen on the North-Western Frontier.

There's more plot than usual, the production values are for once better than pathetic (it was shot on location in exotic Wales). Kenneth Williams is amusing as chief of the revolting tribesmen ('I am the Khasi . . .'), and Sidney James is at his most ebullient as the British governor, Sir Sidney Ruff-Diamond. The finale, where the stiff-upper-lip Brits continue to have dinner while they are under attack is a classic set-piece.

The 'Carry On' series was poorly received by most critics, and some of them really are terrible; the worst is probably *Carry On Emmanuelle* (1978). The other 11 which have entertainment value are *Cleo* (64), *Cowboy* (67), *Doctor* (68), *Don't Lose Your Head* (66), *Follow That Camel* (67), *Henry* (72), *Nurse* (59) *Screaming* (66), *Sergeant* (58), *Spying* (64) and *Teacher* (59).

MIXED:

'What I liked . . . was that it took advantage of the permissive society and made nonsense of the censorship . . . But it didn't have the inevitable rhythm of its predecessors.' *(Richard Roud, Daily Sketch)*

'Vulgar it certainly is, but the cast . . . bring considerable comic ability to their roles.' *(Daily Express)*

PRO:

'Performance of Sidney James . . . is a gem, impeccably timed, wily and always in character.' *(Variety)*

'Best of the series, full of outrageous double-meanings and visual foolery.' *(Arthur Thirkell, Daily Mirror)*

'The series reaches a new height of happy delirium.' *(John Russell Taylor, The Times)*

CASABLANCA AAW CT: 10 AV: 9.89

1942 US 102 BW DRAMA/ROMANCE/WAR

D Michael Curtiz ☆AAW
W Julius J. Epstein Philip G. Epstein Howard Koch ☆ AAW from Murray Burnett and Joan Alison's play *Everybody Comes To Rick's*

Casey Robinson wrote the flashback love story, the scene where Heinreid comes to Rick, and most of the final scene. Producer Hal Wallis wrote the final line – 'Louis, I think this is the beginning of a beautiful friendship.' Other contributors to the script included Albert Maltz, Aeneas Mackenzie and Wally Kline. Director Michael Curtiz and star Humphrey Bogart also had suggestions acted upon.

Humphrey Bogart ☆ AAN Ingrid Bergman ☆ Claude Rains ☆ AAN Paul Henreid Conrad Veidt ☆ Sydney Greenstreet Peter Lorre S.Z. Sakall Dooley Wilson ☆ Marcel Dalio ☆ Madeleine LeBeau Joy Page John Qualen Ludwig Stossel Leonid Kinskey Helmut Dantine Ilka Gruning

In North Africa during World War II, a café proprietor (Humphrey Bogart) abandons neutrality for the sake of an old flame (Ingrid Bergman).

Why have the critics always got *Casablanca* so wrong? One reason it has been underrated is that it was not made in the way that great pictures are meant to be made. It is eternal and uncomfortable proof that great films are often made not by auteurs, but by collaboration between craftsmen, at uncomfortable speed, within an authoritarian studio system, and with a cavalier attitude to creative talent (at least eight writers, and probably twelve, contributed to the final screenplay).

Another reason for its critical failure – it was not disliked, just damned with faint praise or patronized as mere 'entertainment' – is its unfashionable politics: it was, and remains, pro-war propaganda. The hero's transformation from disinterested isolationist into an American prepared to kill for the right cause may have been just about acceptable against Nazis. It became much less 'politically correct' during the Cold War, as the post-war liberal establishment argued that America had no right to police the world.

Although the film is often dismissed as romantic or sentimental, its romanticism is not the kind beloved of liberals. Bogart – like Celia Johnson in another unfashionable but well-loved film, *Brief Encounter* – comes to realize that romantic love and personal fulfilment are not enough. Both films end with acts of self-sacrifice. *Casablanca* is not conventionally romantic at all, and is profoundly antipathetic towards the kind of emotional self-indulgence which resulted in permissiveness and the 'me' generation.

The other reason why the film has never been intellectually fashionable is that the posher critics have always been notoriously incapable of distinguishing between sentiment and sentimentality (a legacy, perhaps, of having American cinema try to manipulate their sensitive emotions, week after week). *Casablanca* is the most shameless tear-jerker of all time. If you don't blub when Bergman and Bogart meet in Rick's Cafe and during the final airport scene, there must be something wrong with you. Whether you care to admit in print that you wept at some commercial Hollywood movie is another matter.

Casablanca is, as almost every non-critic knows instinctively, a masterpiece. The screenplay may be the result of last-minute rewrites and studio strife, but it ended up as a triumphant example of intricate plotting, subtle exposition and witty dialogue. It is high drama and not (as it's often accused of being) melodrama for the simple reason that all the big scenes of emotion are thoroughly motivated by the writers and beautifully underplayed by the actors. Bogart, Bergman and Rains all give Oscar-worthy performances (though none of them won, and Bergman wasn't even nominated). Michael Curtiz's direction is unobtrusively excellent, and Arthur Edeson's Oscar-nominated cinematography bettered even his work on trendier classics such as *All Quiet on the Western Front* and *The Maltese Falcon*. However many times you may have seen Casablanca on TV, it is still worth re-seeing on a big screen, for it is a high point in cinema.

'There is a great deal of corn there, more corn than the states of Kansas and Iowa combined. But when corn works, there's nothing better.' *(Julius J. Epstein, co-writer, 1992)*

'All I was trying to do was save it from being a flop.' *(Howard Koch, co-writer)*

'There was a whole group of people sitting around being terribly unhappy, not knowing what we were going to do the following day. Humphrey Bogart was extemely unhappy. He spent most of his time between takes arguing with director Mike Curtiz. Curtiz couldn't eat a lunch because he had to argue with Hal Wallis [the producer].' *(Ingrid Bergman)*

ANTI:

'Overrated.' *(Dilys Powell, in her review of To Have and Have Not, 1945)*

'If the history of France were written according to the American films devoted to it, our country would be described as peopled by imbeciles and Vichyites convinced of German victory. The French could become patriots but only out of love for a secret agent; in that case they were dragged into incredible adventures in which there were stupid Germans or romantic Italians. This curious historical conception inspired *Five Graves to Cairo* by the Austrian Billy Wilder and Michael Curtiz' *Casablanca*, which in 1942 won seven or eight Oscars. Such were the films that were set in Occupied France, and their ridiculousness prevented them from being shown here.' *(Georges Sadoul, Histoire d'un art: le cinéma, 1949)*

'*Casablanca* was in its time (1942), and looks now just like, a routine, surefire piece of commercial film-making. No pretensions to art, and precious few to originality. Warner Brothers going happily, uncomplicatedly through the motions, with all the usual people. The film takes place almost entirely in interiors, or at night, against backgrounds so simple and shadowy that they could be anywhere, any time. No director now would dare to do it that way. If you were making a film called *Casablanca* you would have to go to Casablanca, or somewhere that would pass for it, and then provide tangible evidence that you had been in the shape of picturesque detail, quite irrelevant to the story but obedient to the theory that part of the something-for-everybody ethos is vicarious travel for those who don't like the stars and find the story too difficult, or too dull, to follow.' *(Arkadin, S&S, 1968)*

'Gross sentimentality . . . schlock.' *(Derek Malcolm, Guardian, 1992)*

'The outdoor settings now look really cheesy. The streets of Casablanca were mostly refurbished sets for *The Desert Song*, we're told, and they look it . . . The deadest scenes in the story are in the flashback about the Paris romance: Humphrey Bogart simply doesn't convince as a man maddeningly in love.' *(Stanley Kauffmann, New Republic, 1992)*

MIXED:

'Ineffectual but a pleasure of sorts' *(New Republic)*

'Some of the characterizations are a bit on the overdone side.' *(Variety)*

'A busy film with bright lines, a perfunctory romance and a dim message.' *(C.A. Lejeune, Observer)*

'Apparently *Casablanca*, which I must say I liked, is working up a rather serious reputation as a fine melodrama. Why? It is obviously an improvement on one of the world's worst plays; but it is not such an improvement that that is not obvious . . . Curtiz still has a twenties director's correct feeling that everything, including the camera, should move; but camera should move for purposes other than those of a nautch-dancer, and Mr Curtiz's bit players and atmospheric scenes are not even alien corn.' *(James Agee, Nation)*

'The ending is satisfactory enough, if a bit hasty and arbitrary. Up to then it is superb melodrama, so expert that it almost gives the illusion of character creating events instead of a plot-spinner skillfully manipulating his puppets. That they never seem like puppets is due to the first-rate workmanship that a fine cast, fine direction, and a dramatic camera instinct put into the picture, with the anonymous help of the people who build the scenes and set the lights. And somehow there comes out of it a conviction that people, in these times, cannot run away from the decency that is in them, not even at Rick's, in *Casablanca*.' *(James Shelley Hamilton, New Movies)*

'The drama has all the subtlety of a three-alarm fire, but the blaze is attractive.' *(Herb Sterne)*

'A movie that demonstrates how entertaining a bad movie can be.' *(Pauline Kael, 70s)*

'If you analyse it, it's not a good movie, it's pure melodrama. For instance, Casablanca never was an escape route out of France during the war. It's absurd. They invented the whole thing – but with such panache and conviction that you really have to get down and think hard about it to say this is rubbish.' *(Barry Norman)*

'Excessively romantic . . . B picture values except for the superb cast.' *(David Shipman, 1984)*

PRO:

'Makes the spine tingle and the heart take a leap . . . one of the year's most exciting and trenchant films. It certainly won't make Vichy happy – but that's just another point for it.' *(Bosley Crowther, New York Tribune)*

'The atmosphere of uneasy distrustfulness makes a sharp background for swift action, the characterization is clear cut and credible and the strong cast drop into their places without even an audible click.' *(Manchester Guardian)*

'One of the most arresting instances of political melodrama seen for many a day . . . Bogart strides off with all the acting honours.' *(The Cinema)*

'The apotheosis of the Hollywood romantic melodrama, a kind of fearless and perfected make-believe that you probably couldn't get away with today. Singing the Marseillaise in the face of the snarling Gestapo men! As I am frequently told (as if it were somehow my fault), they don't make movies like that any more. It's true, they don't, and I explain sadly that it's because they don't make the world the way they used to, either. Romantic idealism doesn't come as easily as once it did.' *(Charles Champlin, 1992)*

'Succeeds as allegory, popular myth, clinical psychology or whatever, and as a superb romantic melodrama.' *(Richard Corliss, 1992)*

'The direction of Michael Curtiz is remarkable for being completely economical. He creates a picture we would be hard-pressed to improve, and does it without calling attention to the fact that it has been directed at all.' *(Roger Ebert, 1992)*

'The director's one enduring masterpiece is, of course, *Casablanca*, the happiest of happy accidents, and the most decisive exception to the auteur theory.' *(Andrew Sarris, The American Cinema, 1968)*

'Tension is what *Casablanca* is all about. The war-time tension of the setting, the tension of the plot, and especially the tension between the characters – not just tension in the broad sense or even tension between the principal figures in the action, but tension between just about every character in the script . . . Then you have inner tension in the characters themselves, particularly Bogart and Bergman of course, but even in minor figures like John Qualen and Dooley Wilson.' *(George Aachen)*

'Like an old-fashioned department store, it delivers the goods on every level.' *(Anthony Lane, Independent on Sunday 1992)*

CASE OF JONATHAN DREW, THE: *see* LODGER, THE.

CASQUE D'OR CT: 7 AV: 8.17
(aka *Le Casque d'Or; Golden Marie*)

1952 France 96 BW DRAMA/ROMANCE/FOREIGN

D Jacques Becker ☆
W Jacques Becker Jacques Companeez

Simone Signoret ☆ Serge Reggiani
Claude Dauphin Raymond Bussières

Tragic, turn-of-the-century romance in which a carpenter (Serge Reggiani) avenges the deceitful seduction of his lover (Simone Signoret), a gangster's moll.

Passionate, picturesque film of Parisian low-life, beautifully shot by Jean Renoir's former assistant and wonderfully acted by the leads. The title refers to Signoret's golden hair; she is at her most ripely sensual in this film.

MIXED:

'Brilliantly cast, excellently dressed, and directed . . . with strength and imagination . . . but the material lacks . . . deep emotional strength.' *(G. Bowman, Evening News)*

'The movie is beautifully made, yet there's something touristy about its view of low-life – "Look, they have feelings too".' *(Pauline Kael)*

PRO:

'Signoret is feminine allure incarnate . . . [the film] is beautifully acted and has been superbly directed.' *(Elspeth Grant, Daily Graphic)*

'Excellent . . . Brutal and squalid in its way and with a shocking finish, it yet keeps its distance and leaves one admiring but emotionally undisturbed.' *(Spectator)*

'Takes its place alongside *Le Jour Se Lève* among the masterpieces of the French cinema.' *(Karel Reisz)*

CASTLE OF DOOM: *see* VAMPYR.

CASUALTIES OF WAR CT: 5 AV: 5.36

1989 US 113 C WAR

D Brian De Palma ✗
W David Rabe from Daniel Lang's book

Michael J. Fox Sean Penn ☆ Don Harvey
John C. Reilly John Leguizamo Thuy Thu Le
Erik King Jack Gwaltney (cameo from Woody Harrelson)

A decent young soldier (Michael J. Fox) is appalled when other members of his squad kidnap a Vietnamese girl, rape her repeatedly, and finally murder her.

The best thing about this film, very overrated by some critics, are the bad guys: Sean Penn and his evil sidekicks are totally convincing. Deep in the jungle with this lot, however, an amiable light comedian like Michael J. Fox looks as incongruous as Bambi. The message of the movie is bizarre, when applied to the Vietnam experience. It proclaims that American values will prevail, as long as there is one good man who will stand up and be counted: Bambo will triumph over Rambo. At the end of the film, a Vietnamese girl even likens the Vietnam experience to a bad dream. 'It is over now, I think,' she says, with commendable forgiveness. So that's all right, then.

The movie seeks to focus our attention on the kidnap of one particular girl, which is fair enough; but it seems oddly uninterested in the fact that all around equally hideous events were happening, with no judicial comeback. The film never questions the morality of the Americans fighting in Vietnam, and goes through remarkable contortions to disguise the fact that the Americans lost. Brian De Palma is too skilful a director of action pictures to have made the worst film about Vietnam; but many will find it the most morally repugnant.

PRO:

'A powerful metaphor of the national shame that was America's orgy of destruction in Vietnam.' *(Variety)*

'A great, intense movie about war and rape . . . the culmination of his [De Palma's] best work. In essence, it's feminist.' *(Pauline Kael)*

ANTI:

'What's wrong with the film . . . is a certain coldness, which somehow distances our emotions. That and the fact that teenage idol Fox is essentially a dull actor who can't convey more than a small part of the horror of the situation he faces.' *(Derek Malcolm, Guardian)*

'The movie does not work. Its true story is too singular to serve as the basis for moral generalizations . . . It numbs the conscience instead of awakening it.' *(Richard Schickel, Time)*

'There are one or two moments that remind you this is a De Palma film, but quite a lot of it is so bombastic and pompous that it could almost have come from Richard Attenborough or David Puttnam.' *(Kim Newman, Film Yearbook)*

CAT AND THE CANARY, THE

CT: 9 AV: 7.30

1939 US 72 BW HORROR/COMEDY

D Elliott Nugent ☆
W Walter de Leon Lynn Starling ☆ ☆

Bob Hope ☆ Paulette Goddard ☆ Gale Sondergaard ☆ Douglass Montgomery John Beal George Zucco ☆ Nydia Westman ☆ Elizabeth Patterson John Wray

Grasping relatives assemble for the reading of a will.

Remake of Paul Leni's silent classic, and even more entertaining than the original. It was Bob Hope's first big hit in the cinema, the one which established his screen personality, and remains arguably his funniest film. It's an adroit mixture of shocks and comedy, with some classic Hope wisecracks 'Don't these big empty houses scare you? Not me, I used to be in vaudeville.' The picture benefits from a wonderful cast of character actors who all seem to have enjoyed themselves. The on-screen chemistry between Hope and Goddard led to them teaming up again for *The Ghost Breakers* (1940).

'The objective is carried out briskly and to our complete satisfaction.' *(New York Times)*

'The film keeps up the tension without descending to the sadism which is the usual stock-in-trade of the horrific.' *(Dilys Powell)*

'A perfect vehicle for Hope's bluff, cowardly persona. Predictable, but surprisingly atmospheric (Sondergaard helps no end) and often very funny.' *(Geoff Andrew, Time Out)*

CAT ON A HOT TIN ROOF AAW

CT: 5 AV: 7.46

1958 US 103/108 C DRAMA

D Richard Brooks ✗ AAN
W Richard Brooks James Poe ✗ AAN from Tennessee Williams's play

Paul Newman ☆ AAN Elizabeth Taylor ✗ AAN Burl Ives ☆ Jack Carson Judith Anderson Madeleine Sherwood

A family gathers round its wealthy father (Burl Ives) who is dying of cancer.

Hugely over-acclaimed, over-theatrical filming of Tennessee Williams's pompous melodrama, rendered even more absurd by the fact that no one dares to mention that one of the leading characters (Paul Newman) is homosexual. The performances were highly rated at the time, but now look stagey. William Daniels's cinematography was Oscar-nominated.

PRO:

'An intense, important motion picture. By no means is this a watered-down version, though "immature dependence" has replaced any hint of homosexuality. Motivations remain psychologically sound.' *(Variety)*

'One of the best presentations of neurotic family life in the Deep South . . . One gets a picture of the contemporary South that does not exist, really, but its images hold us constantly.' *(Albert Johnson, Film Quarterly)*

'They talk – my goodness how they talk! . . . but how magnificently they do it.' *(Nina Hibbin, Daily Worker)*

MIXED:

'The astonishing Liz puts up the performance of her career . . . but neither the author's technical brilliance nor the semi-happy ending can cleanse away an unsavoury taste.' *(Harold Conway, Daily Sketch)*

'Nothing would be nicer for me than to say that Elizabeth Taylor has made a success of her greatest chance . . . But she hasn't. Her Maggie is a pedigree kitten (and that's a long way from the alley-cat intended) . . . This is Newman's greatest performance.' *(Anthony Carthew, Daily Herald)*

'The acting is first-rate . . . Yet in spite of the acting and script . . . the film fails to carry conviction. The direction . . . never managed much more than a photographed stage play.' *(Isabel Quigly, Daily Mail)*

'Frequently errs on the side of overstatement and pretension, but still remains immensely enjoyable as a piece of cod-Freudian codswallop.' *(Geoff Andrew, Time Out)*

ANTI:

'Homosexuality has generally been regarded as a distasteful subject for the motion picture screen and all reference to it has therefore been eliminated . . . And while [it] is often biting and strongly acted, while it is noisy, virulent and violent, the hullaballoo much of the time seems directionless, like a hurricane without an eye . . . Even the plot has become rudderless . . . Our best contemporary playwright deserves better than this.' *(Hollis Alpert, Saturday Review)*

CAT PEOPLE

CT: 6 AV: 6.40

1942 US 73 BW HORROR

D Jacques Tourneur ☆
W De Witt Bodeen

Simone Simon Kent Smith Tom Conway Jane Randolph Jack Holt Alan Napier

Woman (Simone Simon) turns into cat when sexually excited.

Subtle, sinister movie horror notable for its look, its atmosphere, and the way it leaves so much – perhaps too much – to the audience's imagination. There are some classic sequences – notably the one at the swimming pool. But the script is a let-down: it takes ages to get going and is much too verbose (nor is Simon at her best when handling dialogue). The acting is only competent. Tourneur's feature début, and first of producer Val Lewton's influential horror films for RKO.

ANTI:

'A laboured and obvious attempt to induce shock. And Miss Simone's cuddly little tabby would barely frighten a mouse under a chair.' *(New York Times)*

'A questionable subject for screening. The narrative is obscure . . . Doubtful entertainment.' *(CEA Film Report)*

'Editing . . . is irritatingly inexpert and the direction . . . sloughs a number of the important dramatic points of the piece . . . Simone Simon essays Irena with a seemingly confused idea of what the part is about, and reads her dialogue in a language that sounds like anything but English.' *(Herb Sterne)*

MIXED:

'Simon only partly succeeds in interpreting the part of Irena, but lighting and camerawork and sound recording help to make her performance adequate.' *(MFB)*

PRO:

'A most sensitive handling of light and sound, including the score, builds up a supporting atmosphere of supernatural evil seldom achieved in these tales.' *(New Movies)*

'Bizarre . . . out-of-rut thriller for non-squeamish tastes . . . Clearly such a yarn is out for the thrill, entirely regardless of conviction . . . For those who care for this sort of thing, here is a decidedly juicy dish.' *(Today's Cinema)*

'[Lewton] revolutionized scare movies with suggestion, imaginative sound effects and camera angles, leaving everything to the fear-filled imagination.' *(Pauline Kael, 1968)*

CAT-WOMEN OF THE MOON CT: 6 AV: 2.14

(aka *Rocket to the Moon; Cat Women of the Moon*)

1953 US 64 BW SF/SO BAD

D Arthur Hilton ●
W Roy Hamilton ●

Sonny Tufts ● Victor Jory ● Marie Windsor ● William Phipps ● Douglas Fowley ●

A rocket-ship from Earth discovers feline females on the dark side of the moon.

A naive premise is turned by sublime incompetence into a nadir of screenwriting, direction and acting. Every expense is spared. The moment which sums up the film is when the crew-members solemnly prepare for landing, by strapping themselves into ordinary desk-chairs . . . on castors. Unbelievably, it attracted a favourable review in *Variety* and there was a remake, named *Missile to the Moon* (1958). It was slightly better, but not as funny.

PRO:

'Imaginatively conceived and produced science-fiction yarn. Enough novelty is inserted to attract both juve and adult spectators who lean towards this form of entertainment.' *(Variety)*

ANTI:

'Imagine . . . a moon that looks like a moth-eaten Nerf ball. Imagine a spaceship periscope left over from a submarine movie. Imagine a tin can rocketship, huge hairy spiders on strings, and a cardboard moon palace. Imagine it all in 3-D . . . It is breathtakingly bad.' *(Melanie Pitts, Village Voice)*

'Being hep cats as well as moon maidens, they try to get their hands on the visitors' rocket ship, hoping to come down here and hypnotize us all. Considering the delegation that went up, it's hard to imagine why.' *(Howard Thompson, New York Times)*

'Juvenile space fiction in which the moon is found to be inhabited by the Hollywood Cover Girls . . . Treatment and playing . . . are wholly lacking in verve.' *(MFB)*

'One of the most alarmingly awful films in the history of movies. While it's rarely dull, it is also so excruciatingly, stupidly bad as to plumb depths unheard of in science fiction films at that time.' *(Bill Warren, Keep Watching The Skies!)*

'So bad it looks like an unclaimed work by Edward D. Wood Jr.' *(Scheuer)*

CAVALCADE AAW CT: 5 AV: 7.11

1933 US 110 BW DRAMA

D Frank Lloyd ☆ AAW
W Reginald Berkeley from Noel Coward's play

Diana Wynyard ☆ AAN Clive Brook Ursula Jeans Herbert Mundin Una O'Connor Irene Browne Merle Tottenham Beryl Mercer Frank Lawton Billy Bevan

An upper-class English family lives through the first three decades of the 20th century.

Hugely popular and critically acclaimed at the time, *Cavalcade* now looks stagebound and predictable – and it helps if you're sympathetic to Coward's view of the lower classes as local colour/comic relief. For all that, it's stirring, on the grand scale, and has terrific set pieces. It was named Best Picture of 1933 by Mordaunt Hall in the *New York Times*, and in the *Film Daily* poll of US film critics. The action scenes are by William Cameron Menzies.

PRO:

'Greater even than *Birth of a Nation*.' *(Louella Parsons)*

'Dignified and beautiful spectacle that will demand respect.' *(Variety)*

MIXED:

'If there is anything that moves the ordinary American to uncontrollable tears, it is the plight – the constant plight – of dear old England . . . In picture form, *Cavalcade* is superlative newsreel, forcibly strengthened by factual scenes, good music, and wonderful photography. It is marred by pat and obvious dramatic climaxes, and by a conclusion which is anti-climactical and meaningless. And when one forgets the pace, the flow, and the really dignified and lovely quality of the picture – which is easier said than done – one can hear some very cheap theatrical observations from that choleric old empire-builder, Mr Coward.' *(Pare Lorentz, Vanity Fair, 1933)*

'An orgy of British self-congratulation . . . but Noel Coward knows plenty of tricks, and the performers know how to get the most out of his lines.' *(Pauline Kael)*

ANTI:

'Snobbery, sentimentality and jingoism run riot.' *(Tom Milne, Time Out)*

CELLO: *see* TRULY, MADLY, DEEPLY.

CÉSAR CT: 5 AV: 7.13

1936 France 125/160/170 BW DRAMA/COMEDY/FOREIGN

D Marcel Pagnol ☆
W Marcel Pagnol ☆

André Fouché Oran Demazis Pierre Fresnay Raimu Charpin Alida Rouffe

An 18-year-old (André Fouch) tries to reconcile his mother (Oran Demazis) and father (Pierre Fresnay), with the help of his bar-owning grandfather (Raimu).

This is best enjoyed as the third part of Marcel Pagnol's *Marius* trilogy – the first two are *Marius* (1931) and *Fanny* (1932). It's the only one to be directed by Pagnol himself, and he seems to be still learning his craft. The trilogy is a masterpiece of sentimental storytelling, with likeable characters and a splendid central performance by Raimu; this episode is a shade predictable and theatrical, and Raimu is too self-consciously lovable.

The film was not released in Britain until 1951. There was a 1938 American compression of the trilogy, *Port of the Seven Seas*; and a Broadway musical based on the whole trilogy, *Fanny*, was shot as a non-musical comedy (retaining the score as background music) in 1961. The latter is much better than the former.

ANTI:

'Spends too much time in long, heart-searching conversations . . . [which] reveal too obviously the theatrical origins of the story.' *(Milton Shulman, Evening Standard)*

MIXED:

'Anyone who did not know the two preceding films would miss much of the point . . . As a job of filmcraft it is quite rudimentary. All three films look like thinly adapted plays: all are static and wordy. In fact, they defy the rules of filmmaking . . . but is good to be reminded from time to time that art can be more than technique.' *(Manchester Guardian)*

PRO:

'When the screen closes one is filled with a feeling of regret that it is the end of the delightful [trilogy] . . . Note how everything in this amusing and affecting picture, so nobly acted, springs from normal human reactions to events.' *(Jympson Harman, Evening News)*

'The word masterpiece is tossed about so lightly in the film world that a critic develops an inhibition about ever using it at all. It is nevertheless unavoidable in [this] case . . . The acting . . . is way beyond anything normally encountered.' *(Fred Majdalany, Daily Mail)*

'Good enough to make you sadly wish there were more to come.' *(Roy Nash, News Chronicle)*

C'EST ARRIVÉ PRÈS DE CHEZ VOUS: *see* MAN BITES DOG.

CET OBSCUR OBJET DU DÉSIR: *see* THAT OBSCURE OBJECT OF DESIRE.

CHALAND QUI PASSE, LE: *see* L'ATALANTE.

CHAMBER OF HORRORS: *see* THE *FRANKENSTEIN* SERIES: HOUSE OF FRANKENSTEIN.

CHAMP, THE AAN CT: 5 AV: 6.44

D King Vidor ☆
W Leonard Praskins Frances Marion from story by Frances Marion AAW

Wallace Beery ☆ AAW Jackie Cooper ☆ Irene Rich Roscoe Ates Edward Brophy

A young boy (Jackie Cooper) is the only person who still has faith in his father (Wallace Beery), an ex-heavyweight boxing champ.

Two terrific leading performances and Vidor's almost documentary-style direction made this predictable father-son melodrama a very effective tearjerker in its day – and it still works, for all but the most cynical. It's a lot better than the two remakes, *The Clown* (1952) and Zeffirelli's prettified *The Champ* (1979).

PRO:

'A good picture, almost entirely by virtue of an

inspired performance by a boy, Jackie Cooper. There is none of the usual hammy quality of the average child actor in this kid.' *(Variety)*

ANTI:

'Rancid.' *(John Simon, 1979)*

'Soggy load of heart-breaking melodrama.' *(Pauline Kael)*

CHAMPION

CT: 5 AV: 7.33

1949 US 99 BW DRAMA

D Mark Robson ☆
W Carl Foreman ☆ AAN from Ring Lardner's story.

Kirk Douglas ☆ AAN Arthur Kennedy ☆ AAN Marilyn Maxwell Paul Stewart Ruth Roman Lola Albright Luis Van Rooten

A boxer (Kirk Douglas) fights his way to the top.

Carl Foreman's hostile, unromantic view of boxing has lost the shock value it had on release, but still impresses with its action sequences (for which editor Harry Gerstad won an Oscar and cinematographer Franz Planer was nominated). Kirk Douglas is unpleasant but charismatic; too bad the film-makers softened his character by making him love his ma. Dmitri Tiomkin contributes one of his best scores, for which he too received an Oscar nomination.

'Stark, realistic . . . Unrelenting pace is set by the opening sequence.' *(Variety)*

'Kirk Douglas, who has been edging himself rapidly up the stellar ladder, completes the climb with his performance of the Champion. Here is a vigorous, manly, exciting actor whose personality, torso, and skilful histrionic talent give his every second on the screen conviction and authority.' *(Hollywood Reporter)*

'Well directed by Mark Robson . . . A welcome fresh treatment of a dramatic subject that has become too stereotyped. In the leading role Kirk Douglas achieves mixed results.' *(Fortnight)*

CHARADE

CT: 5 AV: 7.83

1963 US 113 C THRILLER/COMEDY/ROMANCE

D Stanley Donen ☆
W Peter Stone from the short story *The Unsuspecting Wife* by Peter Stone Marc Behm

Cary Grant Audrey Hepburn ☆ Walter Matthau James Coburn ☆ George Kennedy Ned Glass Jacques Marin

A Parisienne (Audrey Hepburn) finds herself under threat when her husband is murdered.

A sub-Hitchcock chase thriller which also includes comedy and romance. Stanley Donen organizes the grossly implausible plot with panache, and dangles numerous red herrings before us with every appearance of enthusiasm. Cary Grant's presence invites unfavourable comparisons to *North by Northwest*, especially as he is starting to look old for his role; but the chic Paris settings, Hepburn's beauty, witty dialogue and some gripping action sequences (especially the rooftop fight) make it just about worth seeing. Contemporary critics thought it too violent; now it seems unnecessarily tame.

'One hesitates to be uncharitable to a film like *Charade*, which seeks only to provide a little innocent merriment and make a pot of money . . . Of itself, it is a stylish and amusing melodrama, but in the context of the bloodlust that seems unloosed in our land it is as sinister as the villains who stalk Miss Hepburn through the cobbled streets of Paris.' *(Arthur Knight)*

'A chic, sprightly, urbane chiller sparked by Audrey Hepburn at her loveliest and Cary Grant at his suavest. Maybe the plotting isn't perfect, but the blend of good humor and suspense is.' *(Judith Crist)*

'A debonair macabre thriller – romantic, scary, satisfying . . . As enjoyable in its way as The Big Sleep.' *(Pauline Kael)*

CHARGE OF THE LIGHT BRIGADE, THE

CT: 8 AV: 7.30

1936 US 115 BW WAR/CRIMEAN/ACTION-ADVENTURE

D Michael Curtiz ☆
W Michel Jacoby Rowland Leigh

Errol Flynn ☆ Olivia de Havilland Patric Knowles Donald Crisp C. Aubrey Smith David Niven Henry Stephenson Nigel Bruce C. Henry Gordon Spring Byington E.E. Clive Lumsden Hare Robert Barrat J. Carrol Naish

On the North West frontier, two brothers (Errol Flynn, Patric Knowles) fall out over a girl (Olivia de Havilland). Eventually, there's a cavalry charge in the Crimea.

Inaccurate historical romance which takes far too long to get going: the main romantic plot is tedious. The point of the film, however, is the final charge – breathtakingly photographed. It looks dangerous, and it was: many men and horses were injured, and it led to tougher rules on animal safety. Max Steiner was nominated for his score, his first for Warner Brothers.

'A virile and picturesque saga of blood and empire in India.' *(Frank S. Nugent, New York Times)*

'A travesty of history . . . As pure entertainment, however, it is a most superior slice of Hollywood hokum and the film which set the seal on Errol Flynn's superstardom.' *(Halliwell)*

'When the charge comes it is so spectacularly staged and choreographed that it takes over the movie, and is really all that one remembers.' *(Pauline Kael)*

'One of the most dynamic Hollywood films ever made. It is a straightforward and strikingly carried-off exercise in motion, culminating in the final, head-on charge, and, as such, for camerawork, cutting and over-all pace, ranks with some of the best things done in this field.' *(Ezra Goodman, The Fifty-Year Decline and Fall of Hollywood, 1961)*

CHARGE OF THE LIGHT BRIGADE

CT: 5 AV: 5.88

1968 GB 141 C WAR/DRAMA

D Tony Richardson
D Charles Wood

Trevor Howard ☆ John Gielgud ☆
David Hemmings Vanessa Redgrave Jill Bennett
Harry Andrews Peter Bowles Mark Burns

The reasons behind one of the biggest bungles in military history.

Vigorous de-bunking of the military mind, class snobbery and Victorian values. The performances at their best have a Hogarthian savagery, and Richard Williams's witty cartoons link the scenes economically, and call attention to the film's cartoonish qualities. But there's a smugness implicit throughout, an unwillingness to acknowledge even the possibility of military heroism – which, along with the lack of character development, leaves one less than impressed.

MIXED:

'Uneven but often brilliant.' *(Dilys Powell)*

'Almost all prelude and then almost no climax . . . The film is two hours of brilliant period reconstruction, with a devastating running comment on the class system and military castes of Victorian England which combined to produce history's greatest blunder. As such it is [Richardson's] surest, most incisive film to date and one that will bite deep into my memory . . . One can't help admiring the artistry and intelligence of the film – which make it all the more regrettable that everything travels towards the anticlimax at the end . . . It lives up to everything, except the title.' *(Alexander Walker, Evening Standard)*

'The colour photography . . . is astonishingly beautiful. Most of the actors give immaculate performances. The music . . . underlines the action without swamping it. And the battle scenes are violently spectacular . . . It is a beautiful production. But if its aim had been clearer . . . it could have been a great one.' *(Ian Christie, Daily Express)*

'High entertaining dudgeon, but it's approximately 114 years too late.' *(Vincent Canby, New York Times)*

ANTI:

'Almost as inexcusably muddled as the British commanders at Balaclava . . . David Hemmings, . . . besides being a mediocre actor, looks in long shots like something out of *Planet of the Apes*.' *(John Simon)*

'Richardson has at times lost sight of the story and allowed his characters to become ciphers illustrating his theme of military stupidity.' *(Felix Barker, Evening News)*

'A sumptuous bore . . . a colossal waste of everyone's time, including mine.' *(Rex Reed)*

CHARIOTS OF FIRE AAW

CT: 7 AV: 8.33

1981 GB 123 C DRAMA

D Hugh Hudson ☆ AAN
W Colin Welland ✗ AAW

Ben Cross ☆ Ian Charleson ☆ Ian Holm ☆
Nigel Havers ✓ Nicholas Farrell Cheryl Campbell
Alice Krige Lindsay Anderson John Gielgud
Nigel Davenport Patrick Magee

Two British athletes (Ian Charleson, Ben Cross) try to win gold medals at the 1924 Olympic Games.

Oscar-winning movie about the Olympic spirit, God and the class system. Although Colin Welland's script has little perceptive to say about anything and contains a fair number of anachronisms, it's a stirring tale. Vangelis's impressive score won an Oscar, as did the costume design. Ian Holm, who should have won an Oscar, didn't.

'Hudson's direction gets it all together with admirable assurance and narrative style.' *(Variety)*

'A piece of technological lyricism held together by the glue of simpleminded sentiment; basically, its appeal is in watching a couple of guys win races.' *(Pauline Kael)*

'A hymn to the human spirit as if scored by Barry Manilow.' *(Richard Corliss, Film Comment)*

'Gosh, aren't the British remarkable? They win Olympic races despite runing in slow motion, they castigate old conservatives while revelling in patriotic claptrap, they win Oscars galore while making crappy films. OK, so some of the acting's all right, but really this is an overblown piece of self-congratulatory emotional manipulation perfectly suited to Thatcherite liberals. Pap.' *(Geoff Andrew, Time Out)*

CHARLEY VARRICK

CT: 8 AV: 7.30

1973 US 111 C THRILLER/COMEDY

D Don Siegel ☆
W Howard Rodman Dean Reisner ✓
from John Reese's novel *The Looters*

Walter Matthau ☆ Joe Don Baker ✓ Felicia Farr
Andy Robinson John Vernon Sheree North ✓
Norman Fell Marjorie Bennett ✓ Don Siegel

A small-time crook (Walter Matthau) gets into trouble with the Mafia.

First-rate comedy thriller, very well-constructed with many a twist and lively characterization. Walter Matthau is a funny, likeable anti-hero. Joe Don Baker is chillingly believable as a Mafia hit-man. Ace action-director Don Siegel skates over the plot contrivances, as to the manner born; and the denouement is a delight.

'Noisy and brutal, with sentimental flourishes.' *(Pauline Kael)*

'A sometimes fuzzy melodrama, but so well put together that it merges a hardhitting actioner with a sock finale.' *(Variety)*

'More than adequate, simple-minded entertainment of the kind movies had better manage if they are to survive at all.' *(John Simon)*

'It proves there is nothing wrong with an auteur director that a good script can't cure.' *(Stanley Kauffmann)*

'The narrative line is clean and direct, the characterizations economical and functional, and the triumph of intelligence gloriously satisfying.' *(Andrew Sarris)*

CHARME DISCRET DE LA BOURGEOISIE, LE:

see DISCREET CHARM OF THE BOURGEOISIE, THE.

CHÂTEAU DE MA MÈRE, LE:

see MY MOTHER'S CASTLE.

CHE!

CT: 5 AV: 2.16

1969 US 94 C BIOPIC/SO BAD

D Richard Fleischer ●
W Michael Wilson Sy Bartlett ●

Omar Sharif ● Jack Palance ● Cesare Danova Robert Loggia Woody Strode Barbara Luna

The life and times of a revolutionary.

A biopic which takes inanity to the point of insanity. Sample lines . . . (1) Castro: 'Che, sometimes I just don't understand you.' (2) Che Guevara: 'I'm faced with enormous domestic problems!' (3) Che to his rebel army: 'The peasant is like a wild flower in the forest, and the revolutionary like a bee. Neither can survive or propagate without the other. There is one essential difference between us and the bees, however. In this hive, I will not tolerate drones!'

PRO:

'Fairly absorbing . . . a well-structured, well-directed effort. Palance and especially Sharif are forceful . . . a commendable undertaking reflecting a concern for topicality all too rare in Hollywood.' *(Kevin Thomas, LA Times)*

ANTI:

'Goes at the pace of a drugged ox . . . it hasn't an ounce of political or historical sense in its nut.' *(Penelope Gilliatt, New Yorker)*

'A libelous fiction . . . Jack Palance plays Castro like a comedy act on The Ed Sullivan Show . . . The direction is by Richard Fleischer; the history by Aesop.' *(Rex Reed)*

'As Castro, Jack Palance sporting a fake nose, outsize glasses, and a cigar, comes off as a bit of a fuddy-duddy revolutionist, sounding oddly like someone impersonating Jimmy Cagney.' *(New Films)*

'Palance's performance raises the possibility that his portrayal is meant as pure camp.' *(Tom Ramage, Boston After Dark)*

'Stinkeroo . . . All this movie inspires toward the Cuban Revolution is excruciating boredom, accompanied with nausea.' *(Roger Ebert)*

'Omar Sharif can no more interpret the fiery revolutionary than Elvis Presley could portray Lenin.' *(Sherwood Ross, Christian Century)*

'Actually seems to diminish the sum total of knowledge with which one enters the theater.' *(Vincent Canby, New York Times)*

'If anyone doubts Che's death he has only to look at the celluloid coffin that bears his name.' *(Time)*

CHIEN ANDALOU, UN:

see UN CHIEN ANDALOU.

CHIKAMITSU MONOGATARI

CT: 7 AV: 8.20

(aka *The Crucified Lovers*)

1954 Japan 110 BW DRAMA/ROMANCE/FOREIGN

D Kenji Mizoguchi ☆
W Yoshitaka Yoda

Kazuo Hasegawa ☆ Kyoko Kagawa ☆ Eitaro Shindo Sakae Ozawa Yoko Minamida

In 17th-century Kyoto, a scroll-maker (Kazuo Hasegawa) falls in love with his employer's wife (Kyoko Kagawa), and they try to escape together.

One of those rare costume dramas which have beauty and emotional impact. Kazuo Miyagawa's photography and Mizoguchi's mature direction (keeping much of the action distanced) are complemented by two moving lead performances.

'No one could fail to find in it unforgettable images or to be impressed by its moral beauty.' *(Philip French, Observer, 1977)*

'The film has a slow, remorseless pace but all the artifice of a lifetime's experience of filmmaking to help one get through it . . . an almost perfect vehicle for the director's ideas about the hardness of the individual spirit in the face of cruelty of fate and the necessity of love to redeem that spirit.' *(Derek Malcolm, Guardian, 1977)*

'He suggests great depths of eroticism by a glance or a flutter of a hand.' *(David Robinson, The Times, 1977)*

'A thing of atmospheric beauty, heavily shadowed by the lowering skies . . . [conveying] the tenderness behind the formality, the desperation at the heart of the transgression.' *(Patrick Gibbs, Daily Telegraph, 1977)*

'Period-style at its highest . . . its most painterly.' *(Joseph Anderson & Donald Richie, The Japanese Film, 1982)*

CHILDHOOD OF MAXIM GORKY, THE

CT: 6 AV: 7.16

(aka *Detstvo Gorkovo*)

1938(USSR)/1943(GB) USSR 99 BW BIOPIC/ DRAMA/FOREIGN

D Mark Donskoi ☆
W Mark Donskoi I. Grudzev ☆

Alexei Lyarsky ☆ Mark Troyanovski ☆ Varvara Massalitinova ☆

Poor, small-town childhood of a writer (Alexei Lyarsky) in Czarist Russia.

First part of Mark Donskoi's famous trilogy, based on Maxim Gorky's memoirs: the others are *My Apprenticeship* (aka *Out In The World*) and *My Universities*. This beautiful rites-of-passage film lacks a strong story and unsurprisingly romanticizes its hero's revolutionary leanings, but creates memorable characters in the young hero, his grandfather (Mark Troyanovski) and grandmother (Varvara Massalitinova).

'Remarkable realism, force and charm . . . A powerful cast.' *(MFB, 1943)*

'Has the substance of good literature.' *(The Times)*

'To an extraordinary degree [it has] the ability to communicate the poetic quality in human relationships and the inquiries of the human mind.' *(Sunday Times)*

'The most inspired screen projection of a major piece of writing I have yet seen, for [it] truly lights up and even extends the original [holding] you spellbound.' *(News Chronicle, 1945)*

'It's the expressiveness of the images of the Volga that stays with you.' *(Pauline Kael)*

CHILDREN OF PARADISE

CT: 6 AV: 9.73

(aka *Les Enfants du Paradis*)

1945 France 195 BW DRAMA/ROMANCE/EPIC

D Marcel Carné ☆
W Jacques Prévert ☆ AAN

Arletty ☆ Jean-Louis Barrault ☆ Pierre Brasseur ☆ Marcel Herrand ☆ Maria Casarès ☆ Louis Salon Pierre Renoir Gaston Modot Jane Marken

A mime (Jean-Louis Barrault) falls hopelessly in love with an enigmatic courtesan Garance (Arletty), with tragic but intensely romantic consequences.

Marcel Carné's classic tragic-romance, a lavish costume drama set in Paris during the 1840s, is a meditation on different sorts of love, most memorably the unreciprocated kind. I'm sorry to say that I've never found it very moving, or been able to take it totally seriously because I find Barrault so mannered, but that's probably my loss. It's bursting with life, magnificent visually and widely considered to be one of the finest films ever made.

ANTI:

'Downright dull.' *(Variety)*

PRO:

'Close to perfection of its kind and I very much like its kind – the highest kind of slum-glamor romanticism about theater people and criminals, done with strong poetic feeling, with rich theatricality, with a great delight and proficiency in style, and with a kind of sophistication which merely cleans and curbs, rather than killing or smirking behind the back of its more powerful and vulgar elements. All the characters are a little larger and a good deal more wonderful than life.' *(James Agee, Nation)*

'I don't believe a finer group of actors was ever assembled on film.' *(John Simon)*

'Succeeds in impaling the thrill and enthralment of the theater . . . The acting has a verve and style astounding to the eyes accustomed to the Hollywood variety.' *(Herb Sterne)*

'Probably the greatest literary-novelistic film of all time . . . Carné and Prévert use the theatre as the film's central metaphor . . . The title of the film itself is part of its theatre metaphor. The Paradise of the title is not a heavenly, metaphysical one, but an earthly one – it is the slang name for the second balcony, the highest, cheapest seats in the theatre, the seats where the masses sit . . . The chaotic, seething, energetic masses (the gods) in Paradise parallel the masses just outside the theatre on the teeming, vital, packed Boulevard du Temple, also known as the Street of Crime.' *(Gerald Mast, A Short History of the Movies, 1971)*

'The culmination of pre-war studio production expertise at it most lavish, most perfectly finished, most appealing to the emotions . . . Arletty's central performance places her alongside Vivien Leigh's Scarlett O'Hara in the pantheon of the screen's great romantic heroines.' *(Allan Hunter & Kenny Mathieson, Movie Classics, 1992)*

CHILDREN'S HOUR, THE CT: 7 AV: 6.00

(aka *Loudest Whisper, The*)

1961 US 108 BW DRAMA

D William Wyler ✔
W Lillian Hellman from her own play

Audrey Hepburn ✔ Shirley Maclaine ✔ James Garner Miriam Hopkins Fay Bainter ☆ AAN Karen Balkin

Two teachers (Audrey Hepburn and Shirley Maclaine) become the victims of malicious gossip.

William Wyler's remake of his own 1936 film, *These Three*, is more heavy-handed dramatically, but also more honest about its lesbian content. Maclaine's agonized performance is one of her best. Much maligned by the critics (because of its theme?), it's very moving. Franz Planer's cinematography was Oscar-nominated; and it's hard to see why Maclaine wasn't.

ANTI:

'All very exquisite, and dead as mutton.' *(Tom Milne, MFB)*

'Some Hollywood films give one the feeling that they must have been made entirely in the girls' powder room . . . The style of the film is so unfocused and characterless that the story emerges like a repertory melodrama.' *(Penelope Gilliatt, Observer)*

'How much more effective it would have been to let both girls live and leave the moral clear – that lesbianism is a form of love, that love is rare, and that people's private lives belong to themselves.' *(W.J. Weatherby, Guardian)*

'There were complaints at the time that the studio had hacked out the center of the film – which is a bit like saying that a corpse has had a vital organ removed.' *(Pauline Kael)*

MIXED:

'Has important things to say and it often says them with skill and effectiveness; but it also lapses now and then into a theatrical artificiality which, at several key moments, blows reality to smithereens . . . The movie's acting is its chief virtue.' *(Newsweek)*

PRO:

'Cinematic . . . and subtly atmospheric . . . [with] some of the most intelligent, sensitive and, in fact, awe-inspiring acting I have seen for a long time . . . especially that of Shirley Maclaine . . . She has just the right shade of ambiguity and the right murderous honesty . . . This is living, not just performing, a part.' *(Isabel Quigly, Spectator)*

CHIMES AT MIDNIGHT CT: 7 AV: 7.33

(aka *Falstaff; Campanadas a Medianoche*)

1966 Spain/Switzerland 119 BW DRAMA

D Orson Welles ☆
W Orson Welles from William Shakespeare's plays

Orson Welles ✔ Keith Baxter ☆ John Gielgud ☆ Margaret Rutherford ✔ Jeanne Moreau Norman Rodway Alan Webb ✔ Marina Vlady Tony Beckley Fernando Rey Ralph Richardson (narrator)

King Henry V discards his old buddy Falstaff (Orson Welles).

The fate of this movie, drawn from Shakespeare's history plays and now generally regarded as a near-masterpiece, is depressing testimony to the undue influence at one time of Bosley Crowther, the *New York Times* film critic. After he wrote a scathing review of it at the Cannes Film Festival, the film never received much distribution in the US; and it remains the least seen of Welles's better films. The badly-dubbed opening scenes are a defect; but the film is visually imaginative and well enough acted to justify most of the superlatives which critics now seem happy to heap on it.

ANTI:

'It is still every bit as difficult as I found it [at the Cannes Film Festival] to comprehend what several of the actors are saying, especially Mr Welles . . . [Welles] generally bluffs his way through [it] . . . making [Falstaff] a sort of Jackie Gleason getting off one of his homilies . . . It is a big, squashy, tatterdemalion show.' *(Bosley Crowther)*

'Ridiculous is the word for the whole enterprise – not funny and certainly not moving . . . John Gielgud . . . plays the aging warrior-king as a flabby, aging queen . . . What awful direction! . . . The camera work of Edmond Richard is arty to a fault, though the fault may as easily be Welles's. Thus there is a battle scene (effective but quite extraneous) that takes place in three different kinds of weather at once – sunny, overcast, and foggy – and with two kinds of ground – hard and dry for cavalry charges, and deeply muddy for footsoldiers to wallow and croak in.' *(John Simon)*

'Welles is probably the first actor in the history of the theater to appear too fat for the role.' *(Time)*

'He is simply too lazy – or perhaps too frightened – to take on the role as Shakespeare wrote it, not a jolly saloon-mural fat man, but a giant of slyness, wit, guile and vitality. But this ebullience, this radiant self-confident energy, would be too much work for Welles, who has let the muscles of his talent get flabby, so again he devises a way around the part. He erects a theory of Falstaff as sinning saint or somnolent pseudo-Hamlet which makes the character very much less trouble for him to play.' *(Stanley Kauffmann)*

PRO:

'Welles makes the vainglorious knight wonderfully human . . . [His] direction is not only fast-moving and full of dazzling shots; it captures all the dirt and squalor, the sweaty shirts and greasy hair of medieval England.' *(Felix Barker, Evening News)*

'The battle scenes are very painful to watch as battle scenes should be, chopped into bruising fragments by the editing as swords chop flesh . . . I suspect this is a film we shall return to with increasing admiration and affection.' *(John Coleman, New Statesman)*

'French critics . . . seemed to see . . . a paradigm of Welles' own career, a too early prodigy never finally accepted as an interpreter of his beloved Shakespeare, never a king but always a curiosity and sometimes a clown. Perhaps for this reason, several of my own French friends seemed uneasy with the film; they found it, they said, unnerving, rather painful. And yet others applauded the empty screen. Why? Partly I think, because of the sheer visual energy in any of Welles's pictures . . . But most of all the applause came for this giant of a man, astride the film like a dictator.' *(New Statesman)*

'A near-masterpiece. Welles's direction of the Battle of Shrewsbury is unlike anything he has ever done – indeed, unlike any battle ever done on the screen before. It ranks with the finest of Griffith, John Ford, Eisenstein, Kurosawa. The compositions suggest Uccello, and the chilling, ironic music is a death knell for all men in battle. The soldiers, plastered by the mud they fall in, are already monuments. It's the most brutally sombre battle ever filmed.' *(Pauline Kael)*

'The most deeply felt of all Welles's works; a film that is the product of pain itself, of Welles coming to grips with the realities of middle age, old age, and death.' *(Charles Higham, 1970)*

CHINA SYNDROME, THE   CT: 6 AV: 7.93

1979 US 123 C THRILLER

D James Bridges ☆
W Mike Gray T.S. Cook James Bridges AAN

Jane Fonda ☆ AAN Michael Douglas ✔
Jack Lemmon ☆ AAN Scott Brady Peter Donat
James Hampton

TV reporter and her cameraman (Jane Fonda, Michael Douglas) uncover worrying facts about a nuclear power plant.

Exciting thriller about a nuclear accident draws good performances from Michael Douglas, Jane Fonda and (best of all) Jack Lemmon. The release of the film luckily coincided with the Three Mile Island disaster, but now that the topicality has passed (or has it?) it remains a gripping, well constructed movie.

'A moderately compelling thriller about the potential perils of nuclear energy, whose major fault is an overweening sense of its own self-importance.' *(Variety)*

'A smashing thriller – the most exciting thriller I've seen since *Z*.' *(Stanley Kauffmann)*

'The performances are so good, and the screen so bombarded with both action and informative images . . . that it's only with considerable hindsight that one recovers sufficient breath to reproach the script with the occasional glib symmetry.' *(Jan Dawson, MFB)*

CHINATOWN AAN   CT: 8 AV: 9.16

1974 US 131 C THRILLER

D Roman Polanski ☆ AAN
W Robert Towne ☆ AAW

Jack Nicholson ☆ AAN Faye Dunaway ☆ AAN
John Huston ☆ Roman Polanski Perry Lopez
John Hillerman Darrell Zwerling Diane Ladd

Private detective (Jack Nicholson) uncovers a public and private scandal in 1937 Los Angeles.

Perhaps too self-consciously an American Myth, with self-conscious and draggy passages, but undoubtedly an all-time-great thriller about urban corruption. Jack Nicholson gives one of his best – and most self-effacing – performances. Faye Dunaway is excellent as the femme fatale, and John Huston is chilling as her dirty dad. There was belatedly a sequel, *The Two Jakes* (1990), but it suffered badly by comparison. Not surprisingly, John A. Alonso's cinematography and Jerry Goldsmith's score were Oscar-nominated.

ANTI:

'If *Chinatown* were shorter and less consciously paradigmatic, it would be a good sinister thriller. But Towne and Polanski are insufficiently innocent.' *(Stanley Kauffmann)*

'Pretentious melodrama which is basically no more serious than the Raymond Chandler mysteries from which it derives; the tragic ending is merely an irritation . . . Superficially, however, it is eminently watchable, with effective individual scenes and performances, and photography which is lovingly composed though tending to suggest period by use of an orange filter.' *(Halliwell)*

MIXED:

'The success of *Chinatown* – with its beautifully structured script and draggy, overdeliberate direction – represents something dialectically new: nostalgia (for the thirties) openly turned to rot, and the celebration of rot.' *(Pauline Kael)*

'What really brings the film into the 1970s is the loss of innocence that permeates its world: the boundaries between right and wrong have become hazy even in the good – or better – people, and the two genuine innocents of the film are both, in one way or another, victimized . . . Entirely new is the approach to violence. There is less of it than in the Marlovian heyday, and much less than in the Spillanian decadence; what there is of it, however, is more discriminating, disturbing, and real . . . The hold of the genre is so strong that, even with sensational plot twists kept at a minimum, there simply isn't room enough for full character development – for the richer humanity required by art.' *(John Simon)*

PRO:

'Richard Sylbert's production . . . hasn't missed a trick in recreating the period. And the most gratifying aspect is that the audience is never insulted by overemphasis on period. There's absolutely no offensive showoff of the nostalgia, the clothes, cars, houses, etc, are simply part of the scenes.' *(Variety)*

'[Nicholson] plays the detective as if he were anybody . . . Not good-looking, not seductive, merely nosey (in more senses than one); Nicholson breaks all the rules. But he is alive, he is real; one may not recognize but one remembers him.' *(Dilys Powell)*

'Satisfactory as a period piece, intriguing as a thriller, and highly provocative as social comment.' *(Richard Barkely, Sunday Express)*

'Comes as close to being a great thriller as makes no difference.' *(Margaret Hinxman, Sunday Telegraph)*

'Forget Hitchcock. We've got Polanski!' *(Tom Burke, Rolling Stone)*

'Takes the insidious growth of Los Angeles in the 30s as a metaphor for contemporary America.' *(NFT Bulletin, 1980)*

'A stunningly textured vision of individual naivety and the forms of wider evil and corruption attendant on the birth of a nation like America.' *(Allan Hunter & Kenny Mathieson, Movie Classics, 1992)*

CHINESE GIRL, THE: *see* LA CHINOISE.

CHINOISE, LA: *see* LA CHINOISE.

CHIOCARA, LA: *see* TWO WOMEN.

CHOCOLAT CT: 7 AV: 7.38

1988 France/Germany/Cameroon 105 C ROMANCE/FOREIGN

D Claire Denis ☆
W Claire Denis Jean-Pol Fargeau

Isaach De Bankol ☆ Giúlia Boschi François Cluzet Kenneth Cranham Mireille Perrier ☆ Emmet Judson Williamson Cécile Ducasse ☆ Jean-Claude Adelin

French woman (Mireille Perrier) recalls her colonial upbringing in French West Africa.

This extraordinarily talented, personal directorial debut shows a lovely pictorial sense, skill with actors (child-actress Cécile Ducasse is outstanding), and a profound understanding of racism and racial differences.

ANTI:

'Here was an ideal chance to make a film about colonialism in Africa . . . but *Chocolat* blew it . . . A boring story badly told.' *(Kay Holmes, Morning Star)*

MIXED:

'[The] script . . . is well-observed and has flashes of tenderness . . . A very assured piece of work and [Denis] manifestly knows what she is doing. But it seems not to occur to her to wonder why stereotypes arose in the first place. A stereotype is a way of understanding the world . . . [The] film acknowledges this only obliquely.' *(Adam Mars-Jones, Independent)*

'Over-generous, fictionalised and nostalgic, but it is also well observed and shot through with a dry sense of humour.' *(Jill Forbes, MFB)*

PRO:

'A unique portrait of a paternalistic colonial society in the grip of remorseless and unending change . . . [It] is as subtle and surprising as *White Mischief* was not and as generously leavened with humour as with a sense of time, place and particular circumstances.' *(Derek Malcolm, Guardian)*

'Following the plethora of British films about the declining days of empire, *Chocolat* is a delicate and affecting French variation on the same theme. By comparison with *The Kitchen Toto*, which it resembles in many ways, it is masterfully subtle and suggestive, and benefits from a non-judgmental approach to all its characters. Finally, Chocolat is just as it is titled – rich, sweet and surprisingly filling.' *(Kim Newman, Film Yearbook)*

CHRISTMAS CAROL, A: *see* SCROOGE.

CHRISTMAS IN JULY CT: 5 AV: 7.10

1940 US 70 BW COMEDY

D Preston Sturges ✗
W Preston Sturges ☆

Dick Powell ☆ Ellen Drew Ernest Truex
Al Bridge ☆ Raymond Walburn William Demarest

An ambitious clerk (Dick Powell) is tricked into believing he has won $25,000.

Good-natured comedy which modern critics, rediscovering Sturges as a Hollywood auteur, have elevated into some kind of masterpiece. It isn't, because there are dull patches, any satirical point gets lost along the way, and the plot is over-predictable – but it's reasonably good fun. Best aspects are the strong character performances,

Powell being winning as the non-winner, and an inventive custard-pie fight, using fish.

'Just about as cunning and carefree a comedy as any one could possibly preordain – the perfect restorative, in fact, for battered humors and jangled nerves. As a post-election job to national sanity, we recommend Christmas in July.' *(Bosley Crowther)*

'Mildly diverting . . . lacks both the overall spontaneity and entertainment impress of Sturges's first picture [The Great McGinty].' *(Variety)*

'Agreeable enough – it's rather sweet, actually – but it lacks the full-fledged Sturges lunacy.' *(Pauline Kael)*

'This satire on big business, advertising and the success ethic doesn't amount to much, but the Sturges stock company is rampant.' *(Tom Milne, Time Out)*

CINEMA PARADISO AAW — CT: 7 AV: 8.07

(aka *Nuovo Cinema Paradiso*)

1989 Italy/France 123/155 C DRAMA/FOREIGN

D Giuseppe Tornatore ☆
W Giuseppe Tornatore

Philippe Noiret ☆ Jacques Perrin
Salvatore Cascio ☆ Mario Leonardi Agnese Nano
Leopoldo Trieste Antonella Attili Enzo Cannavale
Isa Danieli Leo Gullotta Pupella Maggio

Heartwarming, tearduct-pummelling account of a Sicilian film director's childhood (Salvatore Cascio) and adolescence, when he learned about love and life from Alfredo (Philippe Noiret), the crusty old projectionist at his local cinema.

The picture works beautifully as a tribute to the innocence of childhood and the 'golden age of cinema'. There is wonderful detail in the director's observation, superb acting by Noiret, and a charming performance by the child-actor, Salvatore Cascio. The main defects are a soft centre and the fact that it runs badly out of steam towards the end.

It won the Special Jury Prize at the 1989 Cannes Film Festival and the 1990 Academy Award for Best Foreign Film. It became (until the release of *Cyrano de Bergerac*) the highest-grossing foreign language film ever in the UK. In the 90s, *Guardian* readers voted it the best movie of the 80s.

Four years after the initial release came a 155-minute 'special edition', no mere 'director's cut', or compendium of afterthoughts, but the cut which was originally released in Italy, with little commercial impact. It restores 50 minutes of footage, darkens the mood and fills out the unsatisfactory adult love-life of the central character. One of the leading actresses (Brigitte Fossey) didn't appear at all in the international version. The additions don't make it better, though: the strength of the film remains in the childhood sequences.

ANTI:

'Toto, adorable for three minutes, is encouraged to mug, mime, and make cute until I wanted to throttle the wee thing. What should be delicate and understated is almost always too explicit. Tornatore's rule of thumb seems to be: when in doubt, go for the obvious . . . [It] does have its moments (my eyes were occasionally moist) . . . If you have a tolerance for schmaltz, you should see [it] just for the potential movie, the one you invent in your head.' *(Georgia Brown, Village Voice)*

'Alfredo's mystical sagacity is implausible, and the infant Salvatore (Cascio) is too cutely precocious by half.' *(Geoff Andrew, Time Out)*

PRO:

'An eulogy to the romance of the imagination soaring on a thermal of childhood passions . . . The film shimmers with sentiment . . . Somewhere beneath the conventional character studies and cutesy tiddley-winking pranks, is a warning about letting go of your dreams.' *(Angus Wolfe Murray, Scotsman)*

'Movie lovers will lose their hearts to *Cinema Paradiso*, not out of nostalgia, but for Tornatore's vigorous demonstration of the enduring power of dreams.' *(Peter Travers)*

CITADEL, THE AAN — CT: 6 AV: 8.00

1938 GB 113 DRAMA

D King Vidor ☆ AAN
W Elizabeth Hill Ian Dalrymple Emlyn Williams Frank Wead ☆ AAN from A.J. Cronin's novel

Robert Donat ☆ Rosalind Russell ☆
Ralph Richardson ☆ Rex Harrison Emlyn Williams
Penelope Dudley Ward Francis L. Sullivan

Doctor (Robert Donat) works in slums of a mining town, loses idealism and moves to Mayfair, but pulls himself together in the end.

A.J. Cronin's moving tale is beautifully acted – not only by Donat, but also by Rosalind Russell as his wife, and Ralph Richardson as his close friend Denny. There is a great deal of moral earnestness on display, but it's tied to a narrative that's always interesting.

'*The Citadel* is far and away his [Vidor's] best film. In it he appears to have found a theme – the socializing and humanization of the medical profession – that has permitted a better coalescence of his gifts than previously . . . He has found himself after the almost self-imposed trivialities of straight commercial production.' *(Robert Stebbins, TAC)*

'Reveals him not as a man who has seen his day but as a director who will continue in the forefront of his contemporaries by the earnestness of his social outlook.' *(Lewis Jacobs)*

'Picture is studded with brilliant human and dramatic sequences.' *(Variety)*

'Here is a medical picture with no *Men in White* hokum, no hysterical, incredible melodrama, but with an honest story, honestly told. And that's a rare picture.' *(Pare Lorentz)*

CITIZEN KANE AAN CT: 10 AV: 9.84

1941 US 119 BW DRAMA

D Orson Welles ☆ AAN
W Herman J. Mankiewicz Orson Welles ☆ AAW

Orson Welles ☆ Joseph Cotten ☆ Dorothy Comingore ☆ Everett Sloane ☆ Ray Collins ☆ Paul Stewart ☆ Ruth Warrick ☆ Erskine Sanford ☆ Agnes Moorehead ☆ Harry Shannon ☆ George Coulouris ☆ William Alland ☆ Fortunio Bonanova ☆

A reporter tries to interpret the last words of a newspaper proprietor (Orson Welles).

Has the onerous reputation of being generally regarded as The Greatest Film Of All Time. More than 50 years after its release, and despite glaring faults (some of the matte shots are awful), *Citizen Kane* looks more impressive than ever. If Orson Welles's debut as a film director had been made today, it would still be innovative and exhilarating.

Over the decades, various attempts have been made, notably by the American critic Pauline Kael, to minimize Welles's contribution to the film. The screenplay, co-written by Welles (who initially claimed all the credit) and the more established writer Herman J. Mankiewicz, remains a witty lesson in how to depart from chronology without losing your audience. The way they borrowed from different genres (detective, newsreel, film noir and biopic) still seems daring.

Oscar-nominated Gregg Toland's stunning deep-focus, wide-angle photography, often from floor-level, may not have been Welles's idea: Toland had refined his technique through years of shooting every kind of film from horror to period drama, and many of his tricks are visible in his film of the year before, *The Grapes of Wrath*. However, Welles chose him and gave him his head. Never has a flat cinema screen looked more three-dimensional. Van Nest Polglase's art direction and Robert Wise's editing were also Oscar-nominated.

Welles was also bright enough to commission Bernard Herrmann's score (which was Oscar-nominated, and should have won). Indeed, the use of sound is masterly throughout: *Citizen Kane* is gripping and atmospheric even if you close your eyes – a legacy of Welles's radio background, and proof that cinema is not only about pictures.

The theme is still relevant: the corrupting nature of power, fame and worldly success. The hero is majestic in his hubris (even as an infant, Welles had staged Shakespearean tragedy in his playroom), and the 26-year-old Welles's portrayal of the man's disintegration is as charismatic as they come. It was a brave film in more ways than one. Much has been made of Kane's similarity to the powerful newspaper magnate, W. Randolph Hearst, whose reasonable hostility to the enterprise ensured its early commercial failure. One aspect which is often overlooked is that the film is also courageously autobiographical.

Like Kane, Welles had a wealthy father, but became the ward of another man. Welles even mischievously borrowed his guardian's name, Bernstein, and gave it to the manager of Kane's newspapers. Like Kane, Welles was rich and a media phenomenon by his mid-twenties. Welles's own life-story – early success followed by years of controversy, marital problems, reclusiveness and failure – is forecast in the film with startling accuracy. *Citizen Kane* is not just one of the all-time-greats: it's also among the most intensely personal films ever to emerge from Hollywood.

The kind of journalistic, exuberantly muckraking film which might be expected to appeal to journalists, *Citizen Kane* opened to overwhelmingly, though not universally, favourable reviews.

ANTI:

'Repulsive' *(Louella Parsons – but then she was one of Hearst's top columnists)*

'The closing scene shows the sleigh being thrown on a fire. The flames light up its name. The story significance is that the last thought of the doer of great things was of the sleigh he owned as a child, and that does not strike me as important enough to justify all the fuss and footage devoted to it . . . I was more bored than entertained.' *(Welford Beaton, Hollywood Spectator)*

'Well, dear readers, that's that. You know now that all the vulgar beef, beer and tobacco barons are vulgar because when they were about seven years of age somebody came and took away their skates . . . I thought the photography quite good, but nothing to write to Moscow about, the acting middling, and the whole thing a little dull . . . Mr Welles's high-brow direction is of that super-clever order which prevents you from seeing what that which is being directed is all about.' *(James Agate, Tatler)*

'Tinpot Freud, if not crackpot Freud.' *(Paul Rotha & Richard Griffith, The Film Till Now, 1949)*

'There is nothing about the work of Orson Welles to convince us that he has ever felt humility or love anywhere except in front of a mirror. The success of *Citizen Kane,* Welles's only unassailable achievement, stems in large part from the fact that the protagonist elicits mingled contempt and envy, feelings that Welles is perfectly equipped to dispense. The sentimental note in Kane, the quest for Rosebud, is much more of a useful narrative device than a convincing expression of fellow feeling.' *(John Simon, 1963)*

MIXED:

'A fascinating picture, but because of the congestion of technical stunts, it fails to move us.' *(Egon Larsen)*

'The fact that the picture contains no "heart" will prevent wide popularity. Its appeal will likely be greatest to craftsmen capable of appreciating its technique.' *(Herb Sterne)*

'Some of it is obvious but mighty little of it is crude or unskillful, and it is subtle where subtlety counts most powerfully. Above everything else it is full of young and vigorous energy. That must be why some people find it exhausting – some even tiresome. People who like a straightforward story with likeable people in it may find this picture confusing and unsympathetic, even cold and unpleasant. A psychological study of a very complicated man,told without signposts for the slow-witted or inattentive, is pretty much of a gamble. How it will fare will come out when the picture leaves the haunts of the highbrows and starts jogging through the second and third runs.' *(James Shelley Hamilton, NBR)*

PRO:

'Far and away the most surprising and cinematically exciting motion picture to have been seen here in many a moon. As a matter of fact, it comes close to being the most sensational film ever made in Hollywood.' *(Bosley Crowther)*

'Orson Welles with this one film establishes himself as the most exciting director now working.' *(Archer Winsten, Post)*

'Seeing it, it's as if you never really saw a movie before: no movie has ever grabbed you, pummelled you, socked you on the button with the vitality, the accuracy, the impact, the professional aim, that this one does.' *(Cecilia Ager, PM)*

'A few steps ahead of anything that has been made in pictures before.' *(Hollywood Reporter)*

'Probably the most exciting film that has come out of Hollywood for twenty-five years. I am not at all sure that it isn't the most exciting film that ever came out of anywhere.' *(C.A. Lejeune)*

'An adult film, technically and psychologically adult, recognising the ultimate obscurity in which every human life moves; one of the few, the very few films to present not an abstraction, but a man . . . There is no question here of experiment for experiment's sake; it is a question of a man with a problem of narrative to solve, using lighting setting, sound, camera angles and movement much as a genuine writer uses words, phrases, cadences, rhythms; using them with the ease and boldness and resource of one who controls and is not controlled by his medium . . . The camera moves, voices mingle and echo in caverns of space, with narrative purpose and not from exuberance; a face is shadowed not because it makes a beautiful individual shot, but because the character, the motives of the speaker are shadowed.' *(Dilys Powell)*

'Welles has shown Hollywood how to make movies . . . He has made the movies young again, by filling them with life.' *(Gilbert Seldes, Esquire)*

'So sharply does *Citizen Kane* veer from cinema cliché, it hardly seems like a movie.' *(Time)*

CITY LIGHTS

CT: 6 AV: 8.47

1931 US 87 BW COMEDY/SILENT (with music and effects)

D Charles Chaplin ☆
W Charles Chaplin

Charles Chaplin ☆ Virginia Cherrill Florence Lee Harry Myers

Tramp (Charles Chaplin) tries to gather together enough money to finance an eye operation for a blind flower-seller (Virginia Cherrill).

Chaplin wisely insisted on making silent (or in this case, almost silent) pictures well into the sound era: his little tramp could never have talked, or audiences would have seen his essential unreality. *City Lights* is often called Chaplin's best picture. The humorous sections, especially those where the tramp tries to extract money from a booze-sozzled millionaire, are funny; too much of the rest seems cloyingly sweet or melodramatic for modern tastes. The final scene, though, can still make audiences cry.

ANTI:

'It's not Chaplin's best picture, because he has sacrificed speed to pathos, and plenty of it.' *(Variety)*

'Even while laughing, one is aware of a faint and uneasy feeling that Chaplin has been pondering with more than a bit of solemnity on conventional story values, and it has led him further than ever into the realms of what is called pathetic.' *(NBR)*

PRO:

'Every second of *City Lights* provides something to engage the attention. Not a gesture is superfluous, and the fountain of laughter and tears bubbles continuously.' *(A. Jympson Harman)*

'At the end of *City Lights* the blind girl who has regained her sight, thanks to the Tramp, sees him for the first time. She has imagined and anticipated him as princely, to say the least; and it has never seriously occurred to him that he is inadequate. She recognizes who he must be by his shy, confident, shining joy as he comes silently toward her. And he recognizes himself, for the first time, through the terrible changes in her face. The camera just exchanges a few quiet close-ups of the emotions which shift and intensify in each face. It is enough to shrivel the heart to see, and it is the greatest piece of acting and the highest moment in movies.' *(James Agee, Life, 1949)*

'I have just seen *City Lights* again . . . I had

forgotten that the last scene of *City Lights* was so perfectly beautiful, in spite of a melodramatic situation which only by a miracle does not become ridiculous . . . it is unrivalled. Every picture, the entire cadence, even the light – everything in that scene is perfect, everything bears a rare and moving stamp, the hallmark of genius.' *(René Clair, Reflections on the Cinema, 1950)*

CITY OF HOPE CT: 5 AV: 7.60

1991 US 129 C DRAMA

D John Sayles ☆
W John Sayles ✗

Vincent Spano Joe Horton Tony Lo Bianco Barbara Williams John Sayles

The cocaine-sniffing son (Vincent Spano) of a rich builder (Tony Lo Bianco) tries to escape from his father's shadow but gets involved in a botched robbery. Meanwhile, a black community leader (Joe Morton) is placed in a moral quandary when two black youths claim that the white professor they have mugged was making homosexual advances to them: a claim which Morton guesses is false, but which he's unable to say is false because of his precarious position within the community.

John Sayle's ambitious study of urban America owes a lot to Tom Wolfe's *Bonfire of the Vanities* and the big ensemble films of Robert Altman. It suffers from lack of a sympathetic central character or a clear point of view. All the same, it's quite an achievement, notable for fluid camerawork and fine naturalistic performances from a huge cast.

'What a superb film these stories could make! And what a stately mess Sayles has made of them. The three dozen characters he spills on to the wide screen weave past one another, or arrantly collide, like sodden sparring partners. Talk like them too – Damon Runyon gonifs gone sourly self-conscious. Thanks to cinematographer Robert Richardson, the picture looks great. But it has a tin ear and a soft head. The complex evil of which a big city is capable deserves better than this *reductio ad urbem*.' *(Richard Corliss, Time)*

'A major film. suggesting that Sayles might become as significant a film-maker for the 90s as Altman was for the 70s.' *(Kim Newman, S&S)*

'Epic, masterly, urgent, adult and unforgettable.' *(Alexander Walker, Evening Standard)*

'Genuinely epic, politically astute, profoundly humanist and dramatically gripping.' *(Geoff Andrew, Time Out)*

'For much of the film, the restlessness of focus seems a liability. But when the camera stops long enough to put two characters together together one-on-one, dialog and emotional connection emerge.' *(Variety)*

'A splendidly confident dissection of a city's despair over its race clashes, its poor, its past and its future.' *(Winnert)*

CITY SLICKERS CT: 7 AV: 7.83

1991 US 112 C WESTERN/COMEDY

D Ron Underwood ☆
W Lowell Ganz Babaloo Mandel ☆

Billy Crystal ✓ Daniel Stern ✓ Bruno Kirby Patricia Wettig ✓ Helen Slater Jack Palance ☆ AAW Josh Mostel David Paymer Noble Willingham

Three men from the city go on a back-to-nature, cattle-driving holiday to 'find themselves'.

The same idea lay behind John Boorman's *Deliverance*, but here it's handled as comedy. Crystal's middle-age crisis speech to a schoolroom of perplexed nine-year-olds is a great moment in modern movies, and manages to make Jacques's 'Seven Ages of Man' speech in *As You Like It* seem comparatively optimistic.

The relationship between Crystal and his wife (Patricia Wettig, Nancy in *Thirtysomething*) is marvellously written and played, on a knife-edge between comedy and tragedy. The uneasy relationship between the three men is funnier but no less truthful.

Some of the humour is a bit broad – Stern's wife, for instance, is too monstrous to be wholly credible; the verbal wit of the first hour gradually gives way to rather less inspired visual gags; and the ending doesn't so much teeter on the edge of sentimentality, as plunge headlong into it. Still, this is an inventive, highly enjoyable variation on the buddy-buddy movie. The story could reasonably be accused of being 'mechanical', but only in the way that a Rolls Royce is mechanical: it's elegantly designed and immaculately crafted.

ANTI:

'You've seen it all before . . . Crystal's self-pitying character starts out promisingly . . . but the constant rapid-fire quips become increasingly predictable.' *(Colette Maude, Time Out)*

PRO:

'A deft blend of wry humour and warmth (albeit with a little too much *Thirtysomething*-esque angst for its own good).' *(Variety)*

'Combines an engrossing story with some wonderfully funny lines.' *(Rose)*

'A skewed, serio-comic remake of Howard Hawks's classic *Red River* in which the cattle drive becomes a two-week vacation . . . A friendly heartfelt celebration of friendship and community.' *(Virgin)*

CLAIRE'S KNEE CT: 9 AV: 7.67

(aka *Le Genou de Claire*)

1971 France 103 C ROMANCE/COMEDY/FOREIGN

D Eric Rohmer ☆
W Eric Rohmer ☆

Jean-Claude Brialy ☆ Béatrice Romand ☆ Aurora Cornu Laurence de Monaghan Michèle Montel Gérard Falconetti Fabrice Luchini

A diplomat (Jean-Claude Brialy) on the verge of marriage becomes obsessed with the knee of a girl he hardly knows.

A gentle but perceptive film about unrequited love, self-deception and the difference between love and erotic attraction. It's beautifully photographed by Nestor Almendros, on and around Lake Annecy in France. Béatrice Romand is wonderful as our anti-hero's gawky teenage admirer. Rohmer's warmth and wit are at their most appealing in this movie, which is one of my favourites – though it's very verbose, and not for anyone whose idea of a good movie involves car chases.

'To say his films are cool (one is always saying his films are cool) is dangerously near, in the present overheated cinematic climate, to implying that they have no excitement, which would be the opposite of the truth. They are full of the what-happens next element . . . The film remains the conversation piece which is the basis of the Rohmer cinema. One might say, though, that it is the conversation piece dramatised.' *(Dilys Powell)*

'Rohmer's quiet, complacent movie-novel game is pleasing.' *(Pauline Kael)*

'A sophisticated, literate gem . . . A film full of grace and gossamer joys.' *(Scheuer)*

CLANSMAN, THE: *see* BIRTH OF A NATION, THE.

CLEOPATRA CT: 6 AV: 5.00

1963 US 243/246 C DRAMA/EPIC/ROMANCE

D Joseph L. Mankiewicz
W Joseph L. Mankiewicz Ranald MacDougall Sidney Buchman from histories by Plutarch, Suetonius, Appian and C.M. Franzero's *The Life and Times of Cleopatra*

Elizabeth Taylor Richard Burton Rex Harrison Martin Landau Roddy McDowall Carroll O'Connor

Egyptian temptress (Elizabeth Taylor) causes problems for Ancient Rome.

Ludicrously over-the-top epic, even more unconsciously camp than DeMille's 1934 version. Dramatically, the film never recovers from the death of Julius Caesar (Rex Harrison). Richard Burton and Elizabeth Taylor aren't remotely convincing as Tony and Cleo, but the sets are great, if you get a kick out of Las Vegas decor. Sample line (as Cleo enters Rome): 'Nothing like this has come to Rome since Romulus and Remus!' Though savaged by the critics, its spectacle and surrounding publicity ensured that it was an enormous hit.

ANTI:

(Of its London premiere) 'Afterwards, I raced back to the Dorchester [Hotel] and just made it to the downstairs lavatory and vomited.' *(Elizabeth Taylor)*

'Elizabeth Taylor is the first Cleopatra to sail down the Nile to Las Vegas.' *(Anonymous)*

'A total failure . . . [Miss Taylor] remains resolutely suburban.' *(Richard Roud, Guardian)*

'Size, and nobody to support its weight: no great figures; no persuasive and commanding players. Wrong: one – Rex Harrison. But then, the Ides of March impend over the first half of *Cleopatra*, and Mr Harrison, of whom I have never felt fonder, is killed off before the interval . . . It is a fearful let-down when Elizabeth Taylor is unrolled from the famous carpet . . . It may be unfair to expect a range and power of voice which are not at her disposal. It is not unfair to expect a range of feeling . . . All through the first half one longs for Shaw, and all through the second one pines for Shakespeare.' *(Dilys Powell)*

PRO:

'A surpassing entertainment, one of the great epic films of our day . . . There may be those who find the length too tiring, the emphasis on Roman politics a bit too involved and tedious, the luxuriance too much. But . . . I don't see how you can fail to find this a generally brilliant, moving and satisfying film.' *(Bosley Crowther)*

CLIFFHANGER CT: 7 AV: 4.75

1993 US 112 C ACTION/ADVENTURE

D Renny Harlin ✔
W Michael France Sylvester Stallone

Sylvester Stallone John Lithgow ✔ Michael Rooker Janine Turner Leon Ralph Walte Caroline Goodall Craig Fairbass ●

Gabe (Sylvester Stallone), a mountain rescuer with forearms which would be the envy of Popeye, loses his confidence after one of his rescues goes terribly wrong. Encouraged by his rescue-pilot girlfriend (Janine Turner), Gabe goes up for one last rescue with his buddy (Michael Rooker). They have the bad luck to run into a merry band of international thieves and maniacs whose plane has crashed in the mountains.

Exciting action adventure, featuring Sylvester Stallone on peak form. The Finnish director Renny Harlin builds on his experience gained from *Die Hard 2*, skates cheerily over the logical crevasses and keeps the action sequences coming with an inventiveness rarely seen since the heyday of James Bond. His aerial shots have a balletic grace, and he makes the scenery (most of it filmed in the Italian Dolomites) look vertiginous.

The story may be rockier than the landscape, and John Lithgow's joyous performance as the villain reaches new heights of base camp. It would be easy to complain at the things which *Cliffhanger* lacks: profound characterization, sparkling dialogue, good supporting actors . . . Most of all, it lacks a sense of development. In the very best movies in the action-adventure genre, such as Hitchcock's *North by Northwest* or Zoltan Korda's *The Four Feathers*, there's a sense of the hero growing: because of his adventures, he ends the film a better man than he started. The way Gabe wins back his confidence and his girl isn't cumulative, and there's no sense of personal growth. He responds to every threat with such courage, athleticism and resourcefulness that we can't identify with his struggle, or really believe he ever lost his confidence in the first place. The film is, like *Raiders Of The Lost Ark*, as impersonal and amoral as a roller-coaster ride – but if you watch it in the right spirit, the film's calculated brainlessness is part of its charm.

ANTI:

'For its first ten minutes [it] gives the impression it's going to be a terrific action picture . . . From then on the film slides rapidly down the mountain with the inexorability of an avalanche.' *(Sean French, Observer)*

'If the special effects – digital erasing of guy-ropes from the picture; model photography that dovetails with location shots – are state of the art, the script is state of the Ark . . . In *Raising Cain* he [John Lithgow] was a killer with a multiple personality. That was better than here, where he hasn't even got one personality – just a strangled English accent and standard baddie-nage. Too slow and pudgy to be a top terrorist, he comes over as a testy don on a hiking holiday.' *(Quentin Curtis, Independent on Sunday)*

MIXED:

'*Cliffhanger* has exploding planes, avalanches, hungry wolves, panicked bats, frigid waters and lots of bodies falling, falling, falling. Everything but the abominable snowman dancing the watusi during a blizzard. Even with all this, you may find yourself missing the self-mocking playfulness that gives an Indiana Jones or an 007 epic added zing. Lithgow, who normally makes a sensationally over-the-top baddie, underplays here. It's like having to make do with Ethel Merman humming.' *(Tom Gliatto, People Weekly)*

'You worry about Sylvester Stallone. For most of *Cliffhanger* he runs around in a T shirt atop a mountain range in the snow. The absence of parka and mittens is, of course, dictated by the desire to show off his huge, ever straining biceps. Still, you hate to see a guy risking pneumonia for his art, so it's a relief when, a couple of shots after he has fought a subsidiary bad guy in an icy tarn, his shirt is shown to be miraculously dry. But we are not at *Cliffhanger* for realism; we're there for the cliffhanging, and there's plenty of it.' *(Richard Schickel, Time)*

PRO:

'True, there's not a moment in the plot that I could believe. That didn't bother me for an instant. *Cliffhanger* is a device to entertain us, and it works, especially during those moments when Stallone is hanging by his fingernails over a three-mile fall, and the bad guys are stomping on him.' *(Roger Ebert)*

'Any film which ends up with one of the heroes saying of the villain: "You'll find him four thousand feet below us and wearing a helicopter," gets my vote for action picture of the summer.' *(Sheridan Morley, Sunday Express)*

CLOCKWORK ORANGE, A AAW

CT: 8 AV: 8.00

1971 GB 136 C SF/DRAMA

D Stanley Kubrick ☆ AAN
W Stanley Kubrick ✗ AAN from Anthony Burgess's novel

Malcolm McDowell ☆ Michael Bates Adrienne Corri Patrick Magee Warren Clarke

A young thug (Malcolm McDowell) has his anti-social tendencies removed by the State.

One of the most controversial films of all time, mainly because of its obvious sympathy for a violent anti-hero. As the original author has pointed out, the film-makers did not set out to condone violence:

'*A Clockwork Orange* was an attempt to make a very Christian point about the importance of free will. If we are going to love mankind, we will have to love Alex as a not unrepresentative member of it. If anyone sees the movie as a bible of violence, he's got the wrong point.' *(Anthony Burgess)*

However, Burgess's original novel was considerably cheapened in Kubrick's adaptation, and loaded against conventional society:

'The picture plays with violence in an intellectually seductive way – Alex's victims are twisted and incapable of suffering. Kubrick carefully estranges us from these victims so that we can enjoy the rapes and beatings. Alex alone suffers. And how he suffers! He's a male Little Nell.' *(Pauline Kael)*

'Without exception, Kubrick makes Alex's victims more obnoxious than they are in the book (his treatment of women is insulting). Kubrick makes their abuse at Alex's hands more palatable by making them grotesque, mannered, snobbish figures. Kubrick uses other distancing devices: extreme wide angles, slow motion, fast motion, surreal background songs that counterpoint the violence.' *(Danny Peary)*

The result is a film which attacks state authority (even from liberal motives) while sympathizing with fascist-style brutality by the mob. Such attitudes make it a quintessentially 60s movie, and – despite its artistic merits – a hard one for modern audiences to enjoy. It was voted best film of 1971 by the New York critics.

PRO:

'An unpleasant but brilliant and provocative movie.' *(Newsday)*

'The belief that our children will reproduce ourselves is one that has kept the human race going. *A Clockwork Orange* not only intimated that henceforth we would bring forth monster-children only, but that the progeny in turn would be worse than unforgiving. Whether or not they were able to articulate their feelings, many left *A Clockwork Orange* with fear in their hearts that their offspring would up and murder them, too.' *(Alexander Walker)*

'Kubrick has pushed the unsettling powers of the cinema beyond the limits probed by Buñuel. For savagery of image dredged from the depths of the subconscious, Kubrick is the prince of darkness and the apostle of light.' *(David Annan, Movie Fantastic, 1975)*

'An explosive film, that might prove dangerous if it fell into the wrong hands, or minds. But, if one believes in the sovereignty of human choice, which is the film's main theme, then this is a risk that a liberal, civilized society should – and must – take.' *(Neil Sinyard, Classic Movies)*

ANTI:

'Each episode looks isolated, sealed off from the rest, making the film unduly episodic, and giving it an unpleasingly lurching and halting rhythm. The camera positions are amazingly predictable: for almost every entrance there is an establishing long shot with the new arrival entering from the back of the set. Accelerated and slow motion are used overabundantly. Field distortion by wide-angle lenses becomes wearying after a while; the lighting tends to be melodramatic and obvious. John Alcott's color cinematography is routine stuff, and John Barry's set design, though trying to be clever, is mostly derivative.' *(John Simon)*

'Very early there are hints of triteness and insecurity, and before half an hour is over it begins to slip into tedium.' *(Stanley Kauffmann)*

'In the name of free will, all self-expression becomes highly valued – even the freedom to commit atrocities.' *(Clayton Riley, New York Times)*

'Its very strong exploitative elements . . . savour of a gloating admiration for the very violence it professes to deprecate. A classic of the genre and an extremely unpleasant and unlikeable movie.' *(Alan Frank)*

CLOSE ENCOUNTERS OF THE THIRD KIND

CT: 8 AV: 8.61

CLOSE ENCOUNTERS (SPECIAL EDITION)

CT: 9 AV: 8.67

1977/80 US 135/132 (special) C SF/DRAMA

D Steven Spielberg ☆
W Steven Spielberg

Richard Dreyfuss François Truffaut Teri Garr Melinda Dillon Cary Guffey Bob Balaban Patrick McNamara Warren Kemmerling Roberts Blossom Philip Dodds

A repairman, Roy Neary (Richard Dreyfuss), becomes obsessed with the idea that aliens are about to land near a large mountain.

It's confused and confusing, lacks dramatic conflict, and has a tiresome hero. Much of the plotting doesn't bear close inspection – especially if you try and work out what on earth the aliens are hoping to achieve, or why our hero and heroine climb up Devil's Mountain when the base for the UFO landing is so clearly at its foot – and the characterizations are superficial in either version. Even so, this is a classic film because of its special effects, optimism and peculiarly childlike sense of wonder. It's also a memorable case study of obsession, and there's an obvious parallel between Neary's faith in his vision and the single-mindedness of a film-maker like Spielberg.

If you have a choice, see the Special Edition. Sixteen minutes of film have been removed from the original, seven minutes of unused footage reinstated, and six minutes of entirely new material inserted. Spielberg's revisions excise boring bits from the middle, make more sense of Neary's deteriorating relationship with his wife (Teri Garr) and take us inside the alien spacecraft at the end:

'The Special Edition would have been the first film had I two more months. I didn't have the time and so, as a result, the entire second act of the first film is for me very unsatisfying. Specifically, the pacing between Richard's story and the François Truffaut story, and the correlation, symbolically, that one has toward the other is much more deliberate in the Special Edition than it is in the original version.' *(Steven Spielberg)*

ANTI:

'The one salient feature of Spielberg's script is that it makes no sense whatever. This may have something to do with its having been shot over a period of three years and with five different cinematographers (sometimes the same car has different license plates). But it must have more to do with a basic contempt for consistency . . . Spielberg's UFOs, though meant to be manned by benevolent, superior creatures, play nasty practical jokes on mankind, and are criminally careless of human safety . . . Spielberg – which in German means toy mountain – may indeed have made the most monumental molehill in movie history, conveniently cone-shaped to serve as a dunce's cap for an extremely swelled head.' *(John Simon)*

'The human factor in Spielberg's screenplay is, well, boring. The basic difficulty is that there isn't any conflict.' *(Cinefantastique)*

'Spielberg's preoccupation, here and in his other big box-office movies, with childhood dreams of outer-space visitors and with preposterous, boyishly imagined fears of derring-do is so romantic and obsessive that it would have unsettled Rousseau. These are children's movies for grown-ups; and their well-nigh unparalleled popularity among baby-boomers makes it clear that baby boomers want children's movies.' *(Bruce Bawer, American Spectator)*

PRO:

'The Holy Grail of UFO movies.' *(Ed Naha, The Science Fictionary, 1980)*

'It has visionary magic and a childlike comic spirit, along with a love of surprises and a skeptical, let's-try-it-on spirit. It sends you out in a state of blissful satisfaction.' *(Pauline Kael)*

'The long, last, thrilling scene overpowers us because, given any reasonable chance to be overpowered by it, we want to be overpowered by it. The film does everything in idea and execution to make it possible. Outer-space creatures, if they ever come, may in fact prove to be malevolent, or stupider than we are. Those possibilities are not part of the faith. We need them to be benevolent and brighter, and that's what *Close Encounters* gives us . . . That finale doesn't bring us salvation – there is no hint of what will come out of the encounter – it brings us companionship.' *(Stanley Kauffmann)*

CLOSE MY EYES

CT: 5 AV: 4.56

1991 GB 107 C DRAMA/ROMANCE

D Stephen Poliakoff ✗
W Stephen Poliakoff ✗

Clive Owen Saskia Reeves ✓ Alan Rickman ☆
Lesley Sharp Niall Buggy Karl Johnson

A brother and sister (Clive Owen and Saskia Reeves) commit incest, as an antidote to the lack of feeling in Thatcher's Britain.

Unusually for a British film on a low budget (£1.28 million), *Close My Eyes* looks terrific. The glass-and-metal jungle of the Isle of Dogs (where the brother works, thanklessly, for a kind of architectural Greenpeace) is in danger of becoming a cliché; but no film has done more to capture the exotic richness of suburban Surrey. Sunshine during the shooting period has something to do with this, but so have lighting cameraman Witold Stock, production designer Luciana Arrighi, and location manager Angus More Gordon. Michael Gibbs's music is also highly atmospheric.

Poliakoff's screenplay shows his strengths – he excels at jagged emotions and people who say one thing and mean another. He is not so impressive at narrative twists, and there is a disastrous one at the end which is unnecessary and totally lacks conviction. Poliakoff's apocalyptic pronouncements, always a depressing feature of his work, are more than usually contrived: he is a writer incapable of depicting a sunny day without speculating on the greenhouse effect, or a pool without suggesting it might contain corpses. It almost goes without saying that a subsidiary character dies of AIDS.

The most surprising aspect of the film is that it is so (unconsciously) reactionary. Poliakoff exhibits near-hysteria about the new Docklands: his slimy property developers are crude enough caricatures to have been written by Howard Brenton. Unfortunately for Poliakoff's formulaic equation of enterprise with greed, he chooses to contrast the unplanned sprawl of Docklands with the lush gardens and quirky buildings of scenic Surrey. The irony which escapes him is that suburbia itself was largely unplanned and the work of property speculators.

Despite Poliakoff's best efforts, his film doesn't work as a parable about the demise of Thatcherite certainties and free enterprise, because he shows no sign of understanding either. All that comes across instead is a nostalgia for some mythical golden age of planning in the sexual, architectural and political areas. For reasons which remain abstruse, *Close My Eyes* received much critical acclaim, and won Best Picture of the Year at the Evening Standard Film Awards.

PRO:

'Should have a solid career ahead of it and is a major plus for all concerned.' *(Variety)*

'Reeves and Owen generate an impressive heat.' *(Hugo Davenport, Daily Telegraph)*

'A pleasure to watch.' *(Iain Johnstone, Sunday Times)*

'Poliakoff . . . has given his story a theatrical structure whose metaphors cluck a bit too heavily for the machinery not to seem overexposed. Yet the characters . . . are drawn with depth and subtlety.' *(Stephen Holden, New York Times)*

ANTI:

'Supremely confident in its absurdity . . . Just misses the boat for being good, gaudy trash on the order of films like *Valley of the Dolls* . . . Rickman . . . provides the only amusement here, with his overly precise, excruciating calibrated readings of the sorry dialogue.' *(David Noh, Film Journal)*

'Drags itself across the screen. After much huffing

and puffing, the script refuses to become the sum of its many, many scholarly observations about life, love, the universe. The lack of feeling is fatal.' *(John Lyttle, Independent)*

'Hysterical and dull, peopled by fashionable but inert characters given to boring introspection.' *(Halliwell)*

'Close them? It's only too easy. Quite how such an accomplished team of actors and technicians could have generated something so drab and long-winded out of such potentially sizzling material remains a mystery.' *(Rose)*

CLOSELY OBSERVED TRAINS AAW

CT: 7 AV: 7.25

(aka *Closely Watched Trains; Ostre Sledovane Vlaky*)

1966 Czechoslovakia 92 BW WAR/COMEDY/ FOREIGN

D Jiri Menzel ☆
W Jiri Menzel from Bohumil Hrabal's novel

Vaclav Neckar Jitka Bandova Vladimir Valenta Josef Somr

A young railway trainee (Vaclav Neckar) learns about life, love and premature ejaculation with the stationmaster's wife.

Writer-director Jiri Menzel's bitter-sweet 1966 comedy used World War II as the backdrop for a rites-of-passage film, and won the Oscar for Best Foreign Film – not least because it caught the optimism of the brief period in which it was made, Dubcek's Prague Spring. It's a slight film and its political aspect – when the hero is invited to join the resistance – almost gets lost in the parochial detail and personal (extremely personal) sides of the story, but it has great charm. Menzel also manages one of the most difficult tricks a director can bring off: a sudden darkening of tone towards the end, when heart-warming comedy turns into sombre tragedy. And the acting is superb throughout.

'Like Forman, Menzel seems incapable of being unkind to anybody.' *(Tom Milne)*

'A film where everything works, including that most dangerous of devices, the shift, at the last moment from comedy to tragedy . . . Tenderness mitigates the farcical, a certain seriousness gives an edge to the laughter, and a lyricism in the photography and editing poeticizes the foolishness.' (John Simon)

COAL MINER'S DAUGHTER AAN

CT: 6 AV: 7.79

1980 US 125 C DRAMA/BIOPIC/MUSIC

D Michael Apted ☆
W Tom Rickman ☆ AAN

Sissy Spacek ☆ Beverly D'Angelo ☆ Tommy Lee Jones ☆ Levon Helm Jennifer Beasley Phyllis Boyens

Country singer Loretta Lynn (Sissy Spacek) emerges from Kentucky to become a superstar.

Michael Apted's film may skate over the less savoury aspects of Lynn's later life – drugs, nervous breakdowns, etc – but as a rags-to-riches story it works beautifully, and Tom Rickman's script is perceptive about the effects of fame on an unsophisticated person. Spacek's gives an extraordinary, touching performance: she ages from 13 to 40, and does her own singing. Tommy Lee Jones and Beverly D'Angelo also impress, and Apted displays a great sense of period and place.

'A thoughtful, endearing film . . . mostly avoids the sudsy atmosphere common to many showbiz tales.' *(Variety)*

'Highly conventional stuff, but lovingly constructed to produce unremarkable but heart-warming entertainment.' *(Geoff Andrew, Time Out)*

'Mainly notable for its depiction of backwoods Kentucky.' *(Halliwell)*

COBRA WOMAN

CT: 6 AV: 4.50

1944 US 71 C ADVENTURE/SO BAD

D Robert Siodmak
W Richard Brooks Gene Lewis

Maria Montez ☆ Jon Hall ● Sabu Lon Chaney Jr Mary Nash Edgar Barrier Lois Collier

An innocent South Seas islander (Maria Montez) is abducted by her wicked twin (Maria Montez).

Hollywood hokum at its most heroically serious, and pleasingly ludicrous. A camp classic.

'Elaborately and colorfully mounted for maximum eye-appeal . . . Montez is decidedly shapely.' *(Variety)*

'Just watch Maria do her suggestive dance with a live cobra!' *(Winnert)*

'Easily the most spectacularly ridiculous, outrageously escapist yarn ever to emerge from Hollywood. If you're looking for glamour – iridescent, bewitching, fascinating – it's impossible to go futher than Maria Montez. Totally unreal, yet played with astonishing sincerity and conviction, her roles are brought to life by a unique talent that wipes the rest of the cast right off the map. Jon Hall is absolutely ludicrous. Poor old Jon is not helped by the fact that he shares many of his scenes with a chimpanzee who not only blatantly outshines him in star personality and acting ability but even outstrips him in rescuing the heroine at the climax! *Cobra Woman* fully deserves its front-running as one of America's favourite cult movies.' *(George Aachen)*

COEUR EN HIVER, UN: *see* HEART IN WINTER, A.

COLONEL BLIMP, *see* LIFE AND DEATH OF COLONEL BLIMP, THE.

COLOR OF MONEY CT: 6 AV: 6.29

1986 US 119 C DRAMA

D Martin Scorsese ☆
W Richard Price AAN based on characters created by Walter Tevis

Paul Newman ☆ AAN Tom Cruise
Mary Elizabeth Mastrantonio ☆ AAN Helen Shaver
Bill Cobbs John Turturro Elizabeth Bracco
Vito D'Ambrosio Forest Whitaker ✔

Fast Eddie Felson (Paul Newman), a former pool hustler, passes his skills on to a cocky kid (Tom Cruise).

Hugely successful sequel – 25 years on – to *The Hustler*, in which Paul Newman played the same disillusioned drifter and pool-player. This time round, under the assured and atmospheric direction of Martin Scorsese, Newman picked up an overdue Oscar. The film isn't nearly as good as *The Hustler* – there are too many clichés and the plot runs out of steam – but it's still stylish and gripping. There's a fine performance from Mary Elizabeth Mastrantonio as Cruise's girlfriend, discovering the effect she has on men. Good soundtrack, too.

'Another inside look at society's outsiders from Martin Scorsese . . . keenly observed and immaculately crafted.' *(Variety)*

'Scorsese's direction at its most downmarket and upbeat.' *(Sheila Johnson, Time Out)*

'Might have been a pop classic if it had stayed at the level of impudence that it reaches at its best. But about midway Fast Eddie has a crisis of identity or something, and when Eddie locks his jaw and sets forth to become a purified man of integrity, the joy goes out of Newman's performance, which (despite the efforts of a lot of good actors) is the only life in the movie.' *(Pauline Kael)*

COLOR OF POMEGRANATES: *see* COLOUR OF POMEGRANATES, THE.

COLOR PURPLE, THE AAN CT: 3 AV: 6.92

1985 US 152 C DRAMA

D Steven Spielberg ✗
W Menno Meyjes ✗ AAN from Alice Walker's novel

Whoopi Goldberg ✗ AAN Danny Glover
Margaret Avery ✗ AAN Oprah Winfrey ✗ AAN Willard Pugh Akosua Busia Desreta Jackson
Adolph Caesar Rae Dawn Chong Dana Ivey
Leonard Judison Larry Fishburne

A black woman (Whoopi Goldberg) frees herself from racist and male oppression.

Ghastly, overrated, bad-taste travesty of Alice Walker's female-chauvinist tract, leaving out the lesbianism and much else that was central to the book: about the only aspects which Spielberg preserves are the melodrama and the one-dimensional characterization. Quincy Jones contributes an over-emphatic, Oscar-nominated score which emphasizes the slushiness of Spielberg's approach. Transparently designed to win Oscars for political correctness, it was nominated for no fewer than 11 but didn't win one – and for once the Academy was dead right.

PRO:

'A fine attempt by Spielberg to break away from his usual happy alien pics.' *(Rose)*

'Due in no small measure to a superb cast spearheaded by Whoopi Goldberg, this is a powerful and honourable attempt to wrest an unusual book into the populist Hollywood mainstream.' *(Sheila Johnston, Time Out)*

ANTI:

'Marred in more than one place by overblown production that threatens to drown in its own emotions.' *(Variety)*

'Spielberg has chosen to elegize the story by romanticising it, swathing the characters in Norman Rockwell attitudes, a meddlesome symphonic score and a golden fairy dust that shines through the windows like God's blessing.' *(Richard Corliss, Life)*

COLOUR OF MONEY: *see* COLOR OF MONEY, THE.

COLOUR OF POMEGRANATES, THE CT: 5 AV: 7.80

(aka *Tsvet Granata; Nran Gouyne*)

1980 USSR 73 C DRAMA/FOREIGN/BIOPIC

D Sergei Paradjanov
W Sergei Paradjanov

Sofiko Chiaureli M. Aleksanian V. Galstian
G. Gegechkori, O. Minassian

The life of an 18th-century Armenian poet.

One of those films which critics acclaim, but leaves most audiences baffled. It is the exact opposite of the Soviet realism which has dominated that country's cinema – amazing and impressive as a succession of visual images, but very, very obscure as regards meaning.

'The film's specific range of Armenian/Georgian references inevitably puts the average Western viewer at a disadvantage. Much of the symbolism remains opaque . . . [His] achievement . . . is, in the fullest sense, extraordinary. It has the quality of a cinema without precedent.' *(Tony Rayns, MFB)*

'A masterpiece . . . incomparably beautiful images

and compositions, an endless cornucopia of artistic profusion.' *(Herbert Marshall, S & S)*

'If ever film were poem, it is *The Colour of Pomegranates* . . . It takes its structure from the most conventional of narrative modes, historical chronology . . . Nor does any shot succeed its forerunner in simple accordance with the precepts of classical (or modern) montage. They are, instead, laid out like so many Tarot cards, and in such a way that, were it not for the biographical continuity underpinning the film, they could quite conceivably be reshuffled and redealt at random to produce a different but no less viable fiction . . . As is the case with all great works of art, there is no alternative.' *(Gilbert Adair, S&S, 1983)*

'Eye-catching, even hypnotic and almost wholly obscure . . . A knowledge of the life of Sayat Nova may make it slightly less indecipherable, but the film is elusive in any circumstances.' *(Janet Maslin, New York Times, 1980)*

COLOUR PURPLE, THE: *see* COLOR PURPLE, THE.

COMA CT: 8 AV: 6.27

1978 US 113 C THRILLER

D Michael Crichton ✔
W Michael Crichton ✔ from Robin Cook's novel

Genevieve Bujold ☆ Michael Douglas Richard Widmark Elizabeth Ashley Rip Torn Lois Chiles Harry Rhodes

Woman doctor (Genevieve Bujold) investigates mysterious deaths during routine operations in her hospital.

A rarity: a feminist sci-fi thriller, which taps into many females' feelings that the medical profession is patronizing and male-dominated. Great atmosphere and suspense, neat plot, fine acting.

ANTI:

'A disgrace to the several physicians involved in it . . . Let's not bother with the holes in the plot. (Why didn't the maintenance man who knew the truth go to his boss or the police? Why didn't Bujold go to the police after she locked the killer in the refrigerator?) Let's disregard the ludicrous SF fantasy of the huge automated institute for the comatose. If this were just a schlock medical thriller, it might be worth pointing out its many flaws as entertainment, but it's not schlock – immediately. All these medical men got together to make it seem authentic, to make it seem as if such a moronic story actually could take place. What a great gift to give a public who are nervous enough about hospitals these days.' *(Stanley Kauffmann)*

PRO:

'A Nancy Drew-like murder mystery updated to the seventies . . . You'll have to suspend your disbelief at every turn, forgive a lot of the now trite dialogue relating to Bujold being a woman in a man's world, and even look the other way a couple of times when the mike slips into view. But the hospital atmosphere and operation-room scenes are very true to life. Bujold is an unusually appealing heroine and the film is a real nail-biter.' *(Danny Peary)*

'An extremely entertaining suspense thriller in the Hitchcock tradition.' *(Variety)*

COMING HOME AAN CT: 5 AV: 6.69

1978 US 128 C WAR/ROMANCE

D Hal Ashby ✗ AAN
W Waldo Salt Robert C. Jones ✗ AAW from Nancy Dowd's story

Jane Fonda ☆ AAW Jon Voight ☆ AAW Bruce Dern ☆ AAN Robert Carradine Penelope Milford

The wife (Jane Fonda) of a gung-ho army officer (Bruce Dern) finds love with an embittered, paraplegic war veteran (John Voight).

Jon Voight and Jane Fonda both won Oscars for their roles in what seemed at the time a hard-edged anti-Vietnam drama, but now looks more like an old-fashioned, soft-centred soap opera. Hal Ashby directs with little flair; it's the three leading actors who carry this one.

PRO:

'An excellent Hal Ashby film . . . has Jane Fonda in another memorable and moving performance; Jon Voight, back on the screen much more mature, assured and effective; Bruce Dern, continuing to forge new career dimension.' *(Variety)*

'Thanks to the performances, this is big emotional stuff, more rewarding than the similar *Born on the Fourth of July*.' *(Winnert)*

ANTI:

'Hal Ashby's direction . . . is stiff and unimaginative.' *(Stanley Kauffmann)*

'Splendid performances . . . cannot make up for a script in which preposterousness vies with tendentious banality . . . The film depends on facile sensationalism: the inept pleasuring by the husband; the fabulous loving of the paraplegic, who, with the mere help of a few pillows to prop him up, makes it good business to hire the handicapped; the gross paranoia of the husband, especially as portrayed by Dern, who has made creepiness bordering on craziness his stock in trade. Why couldn't the contest have been between personalities and ideologies rather than between glossy or grotesque oversimplifications?' *(John Simon)*

'There's a strong element of self-admiration in the film's anti-Vietnam attitude.' *(Pauline Kael)*

COMMITMENTS, THE CT: 8 AV: 6.92

1991 GB 116 C MUSICAL/COMEDY

D Alan Parker ☆
W Dick Clement Ian La Frenais from Roddy Doyle's novel

Robert Arkins ✔ Andrew Strong ✔
Michael Aherne ✔ Angeline Ball ✔ Maria Doyle ✔
Dave Finnegan ✔ Bronagh Gallagher ✔
Félim Gormley Glen Hansard Johnny Murphy ✔
Colm Meaney ✔ (cameo Alan Parker)

A Dublin soul band fights for success and survival.

An extremely funny, quirky, generous-spirited tale of working-class dreamers, in the tradition of *Billy Liar* and *Gregory's Girl*. It's about the huge gulf between ordinary people's dreams and reality, and how essential it is to have those dreams even in the face of near-certain defeat. Uproarious performances and terrific music contribute to director Alan Parker's finest achievement. Editor Gerry Hambling deservedly won an Oscar nomination.

'Fresh, well-executed and original . . . Pictorially, the film is full of variety and unexpected pleasures, and the complex editing work by Gerry Hambling is marvelously accomplished.' *(Variety)*

'The script precisely captures both the witty banter and the modest dreams of the streetwise kids . . . Parker never over-emphasises the unemployment and poverty, nor does he glamorize the band. The result is a gritty, naturalistic comedy blessed with a wry, affectionate eye for the absurdities of the band's various rivalries and ambitions; and the songs are matchless.' *(Geoff Andrew, Time Out)*

'A hilariously funny, richly humane, consistently truthful story . . . The movie pulsates with vitality, high spirits and the exhilarating feeling of people growing as they work together to transcend the seeming hopelessness of their surroundings.' *(Philip French, Observer)*

'More like a documentary than a feature film, except that the characters are more true to life.' *(Ken Russell, 1993)*

COMRADESHIP: *see* KAMERADSCHAFT.

CONAN THE BARBARIAN CT: 2 AV: 4.73

1981 US 129 C FANTASY/ACTION/ADVENTURE

D John Milius ●
W John Milius Oliver Stone ●

Arnold Schwarzenegger James Earl Jones ●
Max von Sydow Sandahl Bergman Ben Davidson

Nordic Barbarian (Arnold Schwarzenegger) teams up with Valeria, Queen of Thieves (Sandahl Bergman) to avenge the death of his parents at the hands of Thulsa Doom (James Earl Jones).

Panned on release, the reputations of Stone, Milius and Schwarzenegger have ensured some measure of upward re-evaluation – undeserved, in this case. Crudely scripted and directed in no particular style, this Nietschian fantasy has macho and fascistic overtones only too typical of the co-screenwriters. Basil Poledouris's music and an over-the-top performance by James Earl Jones add to the air of unclean pomposity. The sequel, *Conan the Destroyer* (1984), is worse.

PRO:

'*Conan the Barbarian* does for the heroic epic what *Star Wars* did for space fantasy and *Raiders of the Lost Ark* for Saturday serials. It revives a beloved genre in all its innocent pleasures on a spectacular scale and with sophisticated style.' *(Kevin Thomas, LA Times)*

'A remarkably well-made film which takes its hero and its subject-matter seriously – no tongue-in-cheekiness or condescending camping it up here.' *(Kenneth Von Gunden, Flights of Fancy: The Great Fantasy Films, 1989)*

ANTI:

'Has a heavy, murky, pig-iron quality; it's oppressive rather than heart-stirring.' *(Jack Kroll, Newsweek)*

'Instead of the giddy lift one sometimes gets from improbably heroic adventures, one gets a grim endorsement of the uses of primitive mysticism and brutality. *Conan* is a sort of psychopathic *Star Wars*, stupid and stupefying.' *(Richard Schickel, Time)*

'The dreary, uninvolving narrative lurches from brutal "realism" to cruddy oracular pomp to zippy fantasy to Christian and phallic symbolism. In brief, Milius worships force, but he doesn't have the consistency or skills to be a good fascist film-maker.' *(David Denby, New York)*

'When Conan and Doom meet at the top of the Mountain of Power, it was, for me, a rather unsettling image to see this Nordic superman confronting a black, and when Doom's head was sliced off and contemptuously thrown down the stairs by the muscular blond Conan, I found myself thinking that Leni Riefenstahl could have directed the scene, and that Goebbels might have applauded it.' *(Roger Ebert)*

CONFIDENTIAL REPORT CT: 4 AV: 4.44

(aka *Mr Arkadin*)

1955 Spain 99 BW DRAMA

D Orson Welles ✗
W Orson Welles ● from his own book

Orson Welles ● Robert Arden Paola Mori
Akim Tamiroff Grgoire Aslan Patricia Medina
Jack Watling Mischa Auer Michael Redgrave
Katina Paxinou Suzanne Flon Peter van Eyck

An amnesiac financier (Orson Welles) hires a researcher (Robert Arden) to investigate his past.

Idiotically overpraised, partly because of the writer-director's reputation and partly because of its superficial similarities to *Citizen Kane*, this is a total shambles, poorly acted (especially by Welles), full of irrelevant visual flourishes, and with an uninteresting plot.

PRO:

'A film that so outraged its European financiers that they sued Mr Welles for unprofessional conduct during its production. At about the same time, a group of highbrow French critics, writing in the influential little magazine *Cahiers du Cinéma*, cited it as one of the 12 best films ever made . . . It is, in turn, baffling, exciting, infuriating, original and obscure. It is also, from start to finish, the work of a man with an unmistakable genius for the film medium. In other words, it is typically Orson Welles.' *(Eugene Archer, New York Times, on the film's New York premiere, October, 1962)*

'Has much to fascinate the student of film manners . . . A second visit is almost essential.' *(Jympson Harman, Evening Standard)*

'Welles' best film since *The Magnificent Ambersons* . . . Given Welles' capabilities, it fascinates, stirs but disappoints. But disappointment with such thrills is worth half a dozen successes.' *(New Statesman)*

'Fortunately Welles has gone his own way, and what dazzling spectacle he provides here for those discerning moviegoers who have outgrown the tedious affections of realism.' *(Andrew Sarris, 1962)*

ANTI:

'The quality of the soundtrack is quite disastrous, but there is a certain grandeur about the carelessness of the film's construction which makes one forget everything except the immediacy of the moment.' *(Basil Wright, 1972)*

'There is, as one expects, evidence of a great deal of talent in this film – but it is a talent misapplied, destroying itself, even, in its wilful isolation from anything first-hand. A pity, when the talent itself is obviously so considerable.' *(MFB)*

'Tilted camera angles, heavy atmospheric shots, overlapping dialogue – all the trademarks are here, sometimes over-used to a hysterical degree, but they have little significance.' *(Gavin Lambert)*

'Frequently suggestive of self-parody.' *(Variety)*

CONFORMIST, THE   CT: 6 AV: 7.40

(aka *Il Conformista*)

1969 Italy/France/West Germany 108 C DRAMA/FOREIGN

D Bernardo Bertolucci ☆
W Bernardo Bertolucci from Alberto Moravia's novel

Jean-Louis Trintignant Stefania Sandrelli
Dominique Sanda Pierre Clementi
Gastone Moschin Enzo Tarascio Jose Quaglia

A repressed homosexual (Jean-Louis Trintignant) becomes involved in the Italian Fascist movement and is asked to assassinate his former professor.

A tense but over-protracted thriller which compensates for an emaciated, slow-moving plot with strong performances and a terrific sense of visual style (Vittorio Storaro's camerawork is among the best ever). The most impressive aspect is the way Bertolucci evokes a feeling of decadence and Fascism during the 1930s. Unfortunately, his Freudian link between sexual and political repression seems, to say the least, glib.

'Not only does the film analyze the roots of Fascism with X-ray intensity, a theme made popular recently in such films as *Z* and *Investigation of a Citizen above Suspicion*, but indeed, the film could almost be seen as a chamber music version of Visconti's operatic *The Damned*.' *(Independent Film Journal)*

'Here, as in all his best work, Bertolucci addresses the issue of duality – of both sexual and political conflict. Marcello's personal contradictions parallel those of the Italian government, with his own decline taking place at the same time as Mussolini's in 1943.' *(Virgin)*

'If the ideas don't touch the imagination, the film's sensuous texture does. It's a triumph of feeling and of style – lyrical, flowing, velvety style, so operatic that you come away with sequences in your head like arias.' *(Pauline Kael)*

CONQUEROR, THE   CT: 5 AV: 2.71

1956 US 112 C ACTION/ADVENTURE/ROMANCE/SO BAD

D Dick Powell ●
W Oscar Millard ●

John Wayne ● Susan Hayward ●
Pedro Armendariz Agnes Moorehead Thomas Gomez John Hoyt William Conrad Ted de Corsia Lee Van Cleef

The life and loves of Genghis Khan (John Wayne).

Magnificently ham-fisted attempt to portray the great eastern warrior in terms more suited to a western. Wayne is, to say the least, unconvincing; and the romantic scenes are ridiculous both intrinsically, and for the amount of time dedicated to them. Sample dialogue . . . Hayward (as she tries to kill Wayne): 'For me, there is no peace while you live, Mongol!' Wayne: 'Say . . . you're beautiful in your wrath!'

A macabre footnote is that most of the people connected with the movie died of cancer – which may be connected with the fact that the desert locations used on the film had recently been used for atom bomb tests.

PRO:

'The audience can sit back and thoroughly enjoy a huge, brawling, sex-and-sand actioner.' *(Variety)*

'Has touches of greatness.' *(Peter Baker, S&S)*

ANTI:

'A substandard horse opera . . . History has not been well served and neither has the popcorn public.' *(Robert Hatch, Nation)*

'Susan Hayward, cast as Mr Wayne's cutie, seems a rather odd Tartar, what with her red hair and fair skin. But then, Mr Wayne seems a rather odd Mongolian.' *(John McCarten, New Yorker)*

'John Wayne as Genghis Khan – history's most improbable piece of casting unless Mickey Rooney were to play Jesus in *King of Kings*.' *(Jack Smith, LA Times)*

'Wayne . . . portrays the great conqueror as a sort of cross between a square-shootin' sheriff and a Mongolian idiot. The idea is good for a couple of snickers, but after that it never Waynes but it bores. The terror of two continents takes almost two full hours to win one girl, so the script just skips the conquest of Asia. It apparently wasn't very important anyway.' *(Time)*

'A monument to bad taste . . . One of Wayne's worst . . . He . . . simply shuddered when anyone mentioned this film.' *(Alan G. Barbour, The Films of John Wayne)*

CONQUEROR WORM, THE: *see* WITCHFINDER-GENERAL.

CONTRACT, THE CT: 6 AV: 7.29

(aka *Kontrakt*)

1982 Poland 100/111 C COMEDY/FOREIGN

D Krzysztof Zanussi
W Krzysztof Zanussi

Maja Komorowska Tadeusz Lomnicki
Magda Jaroszowna Krzystof Kolberger
Nina Andrycz Leslie Caron

A Polish wedding goes horribly wrong. The guests decide to have the party anyway.

Comic ensemble piece, one of the few light-hearted films recently to have come out of Poland. In atmosphere and observation, it has some affinity with Milos Forman's Czech comedy, *The Firemen's Ball* (1967).

'Managed with much skill, only the satire is laid on too thickly and one looks in vain for one normal human being.' *(Patrick Gibbs, Daily Telegraph)*

'Virtuoso filmmaking.' *(J. Hoberman, Village Voice)*

'When not railroading us with messages and top-heavy emblems [it] is a tragicomedy both serious and scintillating.' *(Nigel Andrews, Financial Times)*

'Packed with incident and wit, yet grisly . . . and moral judgments are made upon both East and West.' *(Philip French, Observer)*

CONVERSATION, THE CT: 6 AV: 8.67

1974 US 113 C THRILLER/DRAMA

D Francis Ford Coppola ☆
W Francis Ford Coppola

Gene Hackman ☆ John Cazale Allen Garfield
Frederic Forrest Cindy Williams Michael Higgins
Elizabeth MacRae Teri Garr Harrison Ford
Mark Wheeler

Inquisitive bugger (Gene Hackman) believes he may have stumbled across an incriminating conversation.

Fine acting by Gene Hackman and flashy direction by Francis Ford Coppola enliven this paranoid thriller about an eavesdropping bugging expert. Very much a film of its Watergate period (though it was made before that famous burglary – it was obviously inspired by Antonioni's *Blow-Up* is gripping and technically brilliant. Somewhere along the line, though, the plot loses its way in a forest of repetition, and the hero's character becomes implausible (for a genius, he's awfully gullible). This may be why the film has always been more of a hit with critics than audiences.

'I had been terrified by the whole Orwellian dimension of electronic spying and the invasion of privacy when I started writing *The Conversation* five years ago. I realized a bugging expert was a special breed of man, not just a private eye playing with far-out gadgets.' *(Francis Ford Coppola, 1973)*

ANTI:

'Icy fascination soon succumbs to two forms of excess. One is Coppola's growing infatuation with the technical aspects of his subject, which drenches us with ever splashier aural effects, closely combined with scarcely less frantic visual hocus-pocus. The other is a mystery story that thickens into ever greater contrivance, improbability, and opacity, at the same time obliging the protagonist, a master wiretapper with an awakening conscience, to become progressively, not more human, as intended, but weirder and less believable. Gene Hackman heftily overplays both the character's quirkiness and emotional paralysis.' *(John Simon)*

'Coppola delves into pretentious fantasy (Harry's nightmares) when realism is the picture's strongest suit, and he temporarily turns the best wiretapper in the business into a foolish amateur (who allows a whore to spend the night although his precious tapes, which he knows people are after, are very accessible) for the sake of plot convenience.' *(Danny Peary)*

MIXED:

'A really superior new American thriller . . . A couple

of points in the plot . . . do not survive too close scrutiny, but the skill of Coppola . . . immunises you against its faults . . . Gene Hackman . . . is superb.' *(Clive Hirschhorn, Sunday Express)*

PRO:

'Hitchcockian thriller, first rate portrait of a distinctive modern villain and a bitter attack on American business values, all in one movie.' *(David Denby, S&S)*

'A film of enormous enterprise and tension . . . about moral paralysis . . . works as a psychological thriller to which Coppola has given a musical construction . . . Meticulously cast . . . Hackman . . . responds with the most sustained screen performance he has ever done.' *(Jay Cocks, Time)*

'With clinical precision and psychological insight, *The Conversation* sets the parameters of a world where conspiracies proliferate . . . in which there is no reliable basis for moral action.' *(Seth Cagin and Philip Dray, Hollywood Films of the 70s, 1984)*

COOK, THE THIEF, HIS WIFE AND HER LOVER, THE CT: 5 AV: 6.77

1989 GB/France 120 C DRAMA/COMEDY/HORROR

D Peter Greenaway ***X***
W Peter Greenaway ***X***

Richard Bohringer Michael Gambon Helen Mirren Alan Howard Tim Roth Ciaran Hinds Gary Olsen Ewan Steward Liz Smith

In a restaurant which looks like Hell, a thief (Michael Gambon) forces dog excrement down someone's throat. One of the thief's gang vomits mussels at the dinner table. A boy is forced to eat his own navel. A woman has a fork stuck through her cheek. The thief's wife (Helen Mirren) exhibits a taste for inter-course intercourse, is beaten up and talks of suffering sado-masochistic indignities. Her Lover (Alan Howard) proves, by coupling vigorously in a game cupboard, that he is game for anything. As a reward, he is choked to death on his own books, roasted and eaten.

Peter Greenaway's pretentious, dehumanized and disgusting film is obviously an allegory about something or other (capitalism? Thatcher's Britain? dodgy restaurants?). It tricked some critics into eulogies because it looks like a great film. The director's use of colour, attention to visual detail, and mastery of camera movement suggest an artist at the peak of his powers – but with nothing whatever to say.

Greenaway is often called 'cerebral', and he is certainly bleak and unemotional; but there's nothing brainy about the pseudo-poetic flights of fancy in this film. 'Eating black food is like consuming death,' says the Thief. To which the only possible reply is 'No, it's not.' There is also much half-baked nonsense – spoken, equally improbably, by the Thief – about the affinity between the excretory and sexual orifices. Greenaway's stupid script is almost saved by the performances. Helen Mirren copes wonderfully with some truly laughable lines. I shall long treasure the moment when she pleads with the Cook to do her Lover one last favour: 'This was his favourite restaurant. It's also mine. Cook Michael for me!'

The movie is also enlivened by Michael Gambon's energetic if one-dimensional performance as the Thief. It is a measure of Greenaway's failure, however, that he takes such delight in his anti-hero's monstrosity and shows so little sympathy for the other characters (this auteur's attitude towards the wife, in particular, is one of the most disgustingly sadistic prurience) that one may come away worrying not so much about capitalism, as about Mr Greenaway.

PRO:

'Visually astonishing . . . horrifying as well as funny . . . One of the ten best films of the 1980s.' *(Barry Norman)*

'Peter Greenaway's grim sense of humor and cheerful assault on all our sacred cows is evident in this new outing from the iconoclastic filmmaker.' *(Variety)*

'All artifice: splendid, meticulous, extravagant . . . Greenaway – inspired by Jacobean revenge plays and Dutch masters' paintings – stuffs the viewer with ripe images and raw language. He tests your appetite for intelligent sensation. For many it may be a daunting test, but it is worth taking. Elegant and rancid, this movie rates an X as in excellent.' *(Richard Corliss, Time)*

'Sex, murder, cannibalism and high fashion – it's all in there and more . . . quality erotica.' *(Jonathan Romney, Blitz)*

'A deliberate and thoughtful film in which the characters are believable and we care about them.' *(Roger Ebert)*

'Profound . . . a work so intelligent and powerful that it evokes our best emotions and least civil impulses.' *(Caryn James, New York Times)*

'[In] Peter Greenaway's brilliant, savage morality play . . . we are told . . . that within humankind's allegedly civilised breast beats sometimes the heart of a predatory beast or swine. Few films ever have served up humanity and its foibles with such infernal relish and poisonous panache. It's a feast for the eyes, a purge for the belly and a scourge for the soul . . . It will be a hard film for some to take . . . because Greenaway's juxtapositions are so extreme . . . Beneath all our . . . civilizations, the film suggests, lies a wormy layer of evil and lust and blood and shit.' *(Michael Wilmington, Isthmus)*

'Michael Gambon makes Bob Hoskins in *The Long Good Friday* look like an Avon lady.' *(Steve Grant, Time Out)*

MIXED:

'Beautifully art-directed, photographed, produced and acted, the film deals with the kind of subject-matter usually only found under the counter at your local video-nasty dealer. Guaranteed to offend everybody, it's compulsive and unforgettable, but you'd be hard-pressed to like the thing.' *(Kim Newman, Film Yearbook)*

ANTI:

'Greenaway's dialogue cannot sustain our interest, and his lack of humor is the film's biggest drawback. For a lover of games, the director is never remotely playful.' *(Virgin)*

'For a Jacobean-style drama about deadly emotions, the film lacks passion.' *(Geoff Andrew, Time Out)*

'Virtually every frame could be reproduced in a film journal and would look enticingly magnificent; but the magnificence gets more and more hollow as the film progresses. The actors seem deluded. Why did they want these roles? . . . These are vacuous parts. Gambon is surely one of the best actors now at work in Britain . . . but his role here has absolutely no growth or reward. His character merely repeats his coarseness and bullying over and over and over.' *(Stanley Kauffman)*

'What's offensive about [it] isn't its violence or its visceral shocks but the patrician arrogance, the smug aestheticism, the snobbishness that suffuses every frame.' *(Terrence Rafferty, New Yorker)*

'I have always considered the interior decorator one of the more sinister influences on modern life, particularly when, like Peter Greenaway, he sets himself up as a social-metaphysical moviemaker. *The Cook, the Thief, His Wife & Her Lover* is part post-modern vomitorium, part pseudo-Buñuelian existential parable, and altogether undesirable.' *(John Simon)*

COOL HAND LUKE

CT: 6 AV: 7.85

1967 US 126 C DRAMA

D Stuart Rosenberg ☆
W Donn Pearce Frank R Pierson AAN from Donn Pearce's novel

Paul Newman ☆ AAN George Kennedy ☆ AAW
Jo Van Fleet ☆ J.D. Cannon Lou Antonio
Robert Drivas Strother Martin ☆ Clifton James

A chain-gang prisoner (Paul Newman) becomes a hero to his fellow-prisoners when he won't submit to the bullying of the boss man (George Kennedy).

Earnest, critically acclaimed prison drama. It's over-familiar and heavy-going at times; Rosenberg's direction is needlessly flashy; and the religious allegory (Newman becomes a Christ-figure to his comrades) seems to be at the expense of character depth and leads to an atmosphere of pretentiousness. Even so, a well-made, grittily acted film.

ANTI:

'The contradictory behaviour, at once disciplined and anarchic, of the central figure seems unmotivated, and the final resort to private conversation with the Almighty is in the context pure enigma. Some good playing, especially from Paul Newman; but without psychological background it isn't enough to make the continuous savagery bearable.' *(Dilys Powell)*

'There is a lack of genuine development in the characters . . . Luke and the bosses remain precisely as they were given in the beginning. No one seems to learn anything from their repeated – and finally repetitious – conflicts.' *(Richard Schickel, Life)*

MIXED:

'Versatile and competent cast maintains interest throughout rambling exposition to a downbeat climax.' *(Variety)*

'An updating of the old chain gang movies, only now both inmates and warders are considerably more neurotic than they used to be. They remain entertaining, although you may wonder about the film's ultimate point.' *(Shipman)*

PRO:

'May have been the best American film of 1967 . . . saved from plummeting into cliché by freshly observed and overheard detail. It is a hairbreadth rescue, but it works in this sympathetic and, for the most part, unsentimental film. To the rescue comes, above all, an offbeat, ironic understatement laced with little jolts of eccentricity in both protagonist and plot.' *(John Simon)*

'Newman's Luke, the born loser who manages to become a hero to his fellows and their victim as well, is unforgettable, as are Jo Van Fleet's stunning portrait of his mother and George Kennedy's role as a fellow convict for which he was awarded a supporting-actor Oscar.' *(Judith Crist)*

COOL RUNNINGS

CT: 6 AV: 4.00 (est)

1993 US 99 C ACTION/COMEDY/FAMILY

D Jon Turteltaub ✔
W Lynn Siefert Tommy Swerdlow Michael Goldberg based on a story by Siefert and Michael Ritchie and on a true story

Doug E. Doug Rawle D. Lewis Malik Yoba
John Candy ✔

Four Jamaicans form themselves into a bobsled team for the 1988 Winter Olympics.

The Disney studios take an improbable real-life story, sanitize it (Rastafarianism has never looked so cute), and Americanize it (the whole team drinks Coke and learns the American work ethic). No matter that the climax is invented, the characters stereotyped, and the scenes where each lad learns more about himself hopelessly corny: the laughs keep coming, aided by one of John Candy's more restrained performances as their surly, has-been Olympian coach. The result is a deliriously enjoyable piece of feelgood hokum, which combines many of the best points of *A League of Their Own, The Bad News Bears* and *Downhill Racer*.

ANTI:

'A mass of clichés that only a tourist board could love . . . At its infrequent best, the movie works as acceptably unsophisticated kiddie fodder. At its worst, it borders on a minstrel show: *The Love Bug* with Herbie played by four Jamaican guys.' *(Ty Burr, Entertainment Weekly)*

'Director Turteltaub is happy to patronise both characters and audience with daft knockabout humour, tear-jerking sentiment and racial stereotyping that skates on very thin ice. The effectively understated Candy aside, it's downhill all the way.' *(Nigel Floyd, Time Out)*

MIXED:

'With adorably cute fluffiness . . . [it] tugs at your heartstrings . . . and smothers Jamaican culture in ersatz guava jelly . . . Engineered for maximum handkerchief wetness.' *(James Hannahan, Village Voice)*

'Plays upon the audience the way Heifetz played the violin . . . No good looking here for cinematic finesse.' *(Geoff Brown, Times)*

'Enormously mushy but very cute.' *(Angie Errigo, Today)*

COUNT OF MONTE CRISTO, THE

CT: 7 AV: 7.22

1934 US 114 BW ACTION/ADVENTURE

D Rowland V. Lee ☆
W Philip Dunne Dan Totheroh Rowland V. Lee from Alexandre Dumas's novel

Robert Donat ☆ Elissa Landi Louis Calhern Sidney Blackmer Raymond Walburn O.P. Heggie William Farnum

Unjustly imprisoned for 15 years, a French sailor (Robert Donat) seeks revenge on those who framed him.

Classic swashbuckler in which acting and dialogue are almost as impressive as the action. Immaculately produced for its period, and still the best version of the story.

MIXED:

'It is [when Edmond sets forth on his implacable quest] that the film fails, for as the Count, Mr Donat, hitherto persuasive enough, taxes our credulity . . . He is too jaunty . . . [and] we don't believe him.' *(Reynolds News)*

'The best thing about this somewhat grisly epic is the acting of Robert Donat.' *(Sunday Express)*

PRO:

'Accepts and translates Dumas's story without any sophistication or false shame . . . It is pure and innocent romanticism. But at the same time it is a clever story and the cleverness remains in the film.' *(Times)*

'A near-perfect blend of thrilling action and grand dialog.' *(Variety)*

COUP DE FOUDRE AAN

CT: 4 AV: 7.22

(aka *Entre Nous; At First Sight; Between Us*)

1983 France 111 C DRAMA/FOREIGN

D Diane Kurys ✗
W Diane Kurys Alain Le Henry ✗ from Kurys's book

Isabelle Huppert ☆ Miou-Miou ☆ Jean-Pierre Bacri Guy Marchand Robin Renucci Patrick Bauchau

Two women (Miou-Miou, Isabelle Huppert) leave their husbands, set up home together, and start up a dress shop.

A gentle little feminist film, full of nostalgia for the Lyons of the 1950s. The two leading performances are good, but the women are hero-worshipped rather than portrayed. The narrative structure is flaccid and episodic. The story is based on the life of the writer-director's mother, and hints of lesbianism are handled with an irritating coyness. As so often in films of this kind, the men are caricatures.

'An excellent examination of the bond of friendship.' *(Virgin)*

'The two women . . . are lighted and posed so that they are two heroic profiles, with taut neck tendons and beautiful chins. Kurys lets us see their self-preoccupation and their unresponsiveness to their children, but this is all pushed to the side; it isn't given any weight. The women are romanticized and politicized as soul mates.' *(Pauline Kael)*

COURT JESTER, THE

CT: 6 AV: 7.58

1955 US 101 C MUSICAL/COMEDY

D Norman Panama Melvin Frank ☆
W Norman Panama Melvyn Frank

Danny Kaye ☆ Glynis Johns Basil Rathbone ☆ Cecil Parker ✓ Mildred Natwick ☆ Angela Lansbury Edward Ashley

Mild-mannered medieval subject (Danny Kaye) poses as jester to defeat King Roderick (Cecil Parker) who has ousted the real royal family.

Danny Kaye is at his best in this much loved but heavy-handed spoof on medieval swashbucklers. Whether or not you appreciate him, the songs are jolly and the supporting cast performs wonders with some medieval jokes. Compared with Mel Brooks's

Robin Hood: Men In Tights (1994), it's a masterpiece.

ANTI:

'Desperately lively to little purpose.' *(Shipman)*

'Whether it's really watchable depends on what you feel about the charmless Kaye.' *(Geoff Andrew, Time Out)*

MIXED:

'For rather more than half its length [it] seemed to me the best Kaye comedy since his early masterpieces . . . During the remaining parts, I consoled myself gratefully with the thought that half a good Kaye picture is still better value than we are likely to find elsewhere.' *(Harold Conway, Daily Sketch)*

'Norman Panama and Melvyn Frank drag in virtually every time-honored, and timeworn, medieval drama cliché for Kaye and cast to re-play for laughs via not-so-subtle treatment.' *(Variety)*

PRO:

'Like all the best clowns, Kaye picks up a few simple jokes and begins to juggle them in the air with dizzying speed.' *(Alan Brien, Evening Standard)*

'Kaye has taken a running jump at the super spectacle screen epics of all time and reduced them to the nonsense they are.' *(Jympson Harman, Evening News)*

'One of [Kaye's] best – witty, tuneful, tasteful and quite often rollicking fun.' *(Leonard Mosley, Daily Express)*

'Medieval England [is] amusingly if not brilliantly parodied . . . Glorious nonsense . . . Kaye reassures us that he is still unique in the field of entertainment, a magical phenomenon weaving an irresistible spell.' *(Virginia Graham, Spectator)*

COUSIN, COUSINE AAN — CT: 7 AV: 6.44

1975 France 95 C COMEDY/ROMANCE/FOREIGN

D Jean-Charles Tacchella ☆
W Jean-Charles Tacchella ☆ AAN

Marie-France Pisier Marie-Christine Barrault ☆ AAN Victor Lanoux Guy Marchand Ginette Garcin

After a family wedding, various people have extra-marital affairs.

Escapist fantasy about adultery, entertaining thanks to a bright script and a delightful central performance from Barrault. It's only in retrospect that the morality (or lack of it) becomes troublesome.

'It is literate, expert, witty, and handsome, and it touches again the romantic strand without which the movies do not long endure.' *(Charles Champlin)*

'One of those rare delights you want to see again and again just to share the sheer joy of living, zest for love, genuine affection, all-too-human absurdity, and pure happiness of all those delicious people on screen.' *(Judith Crist)*

'Winning performances, well handled peripheral details and characters, all as tasty and insubstantial as a marshmallow.' *(Geoff Brown, Time Out)*

'The French as they fondly imagine they are – anti-bourgeois and managing their sex lives with acumen.' *(Shipman)*

'Rhythmless, mediocre . . . so pro-life that it treats sex like breakfast cereal. It features adultery without dirt – adultery as carefree nonconformity – and the way the chorus of understanding kids applauds the parents' displays of innocent happy sensuality, it could be the first Disney True Life Adventure about people.' *(Pauline Kael)*

COUSINS — CT: 7 AV: 6.08

1989 US 113 C COMEDY/ROMANCE

D Joel Schumacher
W Stephen Metcalfe

Ted Danson ✓ Isabella Rossellini ☆ Sean Young ✓ William Petersen ✓ Lloyd Bridges Norma Aleandro Keith Coogan Gine DeAngelis George Coe

Two couples meet at a wedding. The more boorish husband (William Petersen) and the more self-absorbed wife (Sean Young) fall in lust. The other husband and wife (Ted Danson, Isabella Rossellini) try not to fall in love.

An Americanization of the French romantic comedy *Cousin, Cousine*; this leads to a coarsening of the humour. But Ted Danson is immensely sympathetic as an unambitious Mr Niceguy sabotaged by sexual and emotional forces beyond his control – and Isabella Rossellini, the reluctant saboteuse, is wonderful: she has the same ability to radiate painful conflict between sense and sensuality which her mother, Ingrid Bergman, demonstrated in *Casablanca*. An enjoyable emotional wallow, especially if you agree with me that Miss Rossellini is gorgeous.

'Much less comic in tone [than its French inspiration] . . . actually a romantic study of the extended family, the individual options available within its framework, and the nature of personal commitment.' *(Dan Yakir, Film Journal)*

'A hearty comedy about the big A. I mean adultery . . . This is a laugh with rather than at the need for beauty and romance no matter how tasteless, even horrible, the results are . . . It's a will they/won't they movie. And when the tears start flowing, does the shlock get going? Yes, but in acceptable measures.' *(Richard North, New Musical Express)*

'"Ooh aah" we sigh as the toilet-tissue visuals plus

deodorant music combat the nasty odour of sexual duplicity . . . ludicrous and mildly entertaining at the same time.' *(Nigel Andrews, Financial Times)*

'In [the] wickedly tart script both partners have the personal depth of a marshmallow.' *(Mike Naughton, Morning Star)*

CRANES ARE FLYING, THE CT: 7 AV: 7.63

(aka *Letyat Zhuravli*)

1957 USSR 94 BW DRAMA/ROMANCE/FOREIGN

D Mikhail Kalatozov ☆
W Vikton Rozov from his own play

Tatiana Samoilova ☆ Alexei Batalov
Vasily Merkuryev Alexander Shvorin
Svetlana Kharitonova Konstantine Niktin

A girl (Tatiana Samoilova) can't believe that her fiancé (Alexei Batalov) has been killed in the Second World War. Emotionally numbed, she marries his cousin (Vasily Merkuryev) who raped her during an air-raid.

Why? That's the question which the film fails to answer convincingly. Never mind – Samoilova, the great-niece of Stanislavsky, was compared to Garbo and Audrey Hepburn after her moving performance and won a special award at Cannes. The film was also judged Best Picture, and it's certainly more realistic a wartime romance than its Hollywood counterparts.

'One of the most notable bits of true filmcraft I have seen since the war.' *(Jympson Harman, Evening News)*

'A masterly piece of filmmaking . . . that fascinates eye and mind.' *(Ivon Adams, Star)*

'Not a great film, though it may be an enduring one . . . A jagged, turbulent film, communicating its excitement in snatches, swept along by the sustaining emotional authority of Tatiana Samoilova's playing. A film, emphatically, to see.' *(Penelope Houston, Observer)*

'A warm and moving love story . . . [Samoilova] knocks the average Anglo-Saxon star right back into the arms of her press agent.' *(Robert Robinson, Sunday Graphic)*

'A simple, deeply moving story . . . For all its sadness this is not a tragic film . . . It is a wonderful film.' *(Nina Hibbin, Daily Worker)*

CRAWLING MONSTER, THE: *see* CREEPING TERROR, THE.

CRAWLING TERROR, THE: *see* CREEPING TERROR, THE.

CREEPING TERROR, THE CT: 1 AV: 1.60

(aka *The Crawling Monster; The Crawling Terror*)

1964 US 75 BW HORROR/SF/SO BAD

D John Sherwood ● (pseudonym for Art J. Nelson Jr)
W Arthur Ross ●

Vic Savage (pseudonym for Art J. Nelson Jr) ●
Shannon O'Neil William Thourlby Norman Boone
John Caresio Buddy Mize

An alien monster with an insatiable hunger disrupts a hootenanny, a fishing trip and a high school dance.

Unspeakably ridiculous attempt at horror sci-fi, with nothing beyond unintentional laughs to recommend it. The monster (actually one of a pair, but its twin is sensibly asleep for most of the movie) might have been more scary if it hadn't been quite clearly a carpet propelled by human feet. The voice-over narration helps to explain what is going on, and became necessary when the producers lost the soundtrack.

'An obscure little film featuring a carpet sample from outer space that devours the entire population of Lake Tahoe . . . If this ain't the worst, it's the next thing to it.' *(Harry and Michael Medved, Golden Turkey Awards, 1980)*

'Poor on every conceivable (and inconceivable) level.' *(Maltin)*

'There is a monumental monster that no one can forget (a bunch of guys huddled under a carpet) and a gut-wrenching finale in which a soldier pulls a pin out of a grenade and hangs onto it for 27 seconds before tossing it at the creature. The movie does, however, suggest the possibility that there is a limit to how bad a movie can be and still remain within the realm of unintentional entertainment.' *(Fangoria, 1983)*

'Undoubtedly one of the top five worst movies of all time.' *(Michael Weldon, The Psychotronic Encyclopaedia of Film)*

CRIES AND WHISPERS CT: 9 AV: 8.33

(aka *Viskingar Och Rop*)

1972 Sweden 91/94/106 C DRAMA/FOREIGN

D Ingmar Bergman ☆
W Ingmar Bergman

Ingrid Thulin ☆ Liv Ullmann ☆ Harriet Andersson ☆
Kari Sylwan Erland Josephson Georg Arlin
Henning Moritzen Anders Ek Rosanna Mariano

A woman (Harriet Andersson) dies of cancer, watched over by her two sisters (Ingrid Thulin, Liv Ullmann).

Visually beautiful, impeccably acted and emotionally gruelling, this is the hardest to watch of all great films, simply because it succeeds in making you share the characters' pain and grief, and there's no let-up. Sven Nykvist's stunning cinematography won an Oscar.

'Harrowing, spare and perceptive, but lacking the humour that helps to put life and death into perspective.' *(Michael Billington, Illustrated London News)*

'Images more beautiful than anything he [Bergman] has done before . . . the handling of colour is unforgettable. But is the whole film the masterpiece it has been called? Will its horror – for it is a film of horror – compose with time into a durable reflection of life? True that at the end Bergman lets himself come nearer than ever before to a kind of reconciliation with living. But I can't help suspecting that his women, monumental creatures, will stand outside the human race.' *(Dilys Powell)*

'Bergman keeps his pace slow, his drama intense, and uses music and color thematically – the result is that you're almost seduced into sleep, despite fine acting and the interesting subject.' *(Danny Peary)*

'Smooth and hypnotic; it has oracular power and the pull of a dream. Yet there's a 19th-century dullness at the heart of it.' *(Pauline Kael)*

'Cries is about bodies, female bodies, in extremity of pain, isolation or neglect.' *(Verina Glaessner, Time Out)*

'A powerful document about dying, and reactions to dying, made by a master.' *(Bergan & Karney)*

CRIME OF MONSIEUR LANGE, THE

CT: 7 AV: 7.29

(aka *La Crime de Monsieur Lange*)

1936/1965 France 85 BW COMEDY/THRILLER/ROMANCE/FOREIGN

D Jean Renoir ☆
W Jean Castanier Jean Renoir Jacques Prévert from a story by Castanier and Renoir

René Lefèvre Florelle Jules Berry Henri Guisol Marcel Levesque Odette Talazac

Employees of a publishing firm set up a collective when their boss (Jules Berry) goes missing, believed dead.

This could easily have been just an anti-capitalist tract. The film's central character is, after all, a dyed-in-the-wool villain, and the political message ('Workers, unite!') is very clear. What saves it is the richness of the characterization. Verbosely scripted and in some ways primitive (it was shot in only 25 days, and the sound quality is dire), this is one of Renoir's least known yet most charming films.

'It was made thirty years ago, but its appeal is undiminished. For reasons I cannot explain, it has not been shown here before. Don't let it escape you now.' *(Philip Oakes, Daily Telegraph, 1965)*

'[A] script that matches Renoir's immaculate direction.' *(Cecil Wilson, Daily Mail)*

'[A] gem . . . I can't think of a film that so overwhelmingly encapsulates an intelligent person's reasons for respecting la vie Parisienne.' *(John Coleman, New Statesman)*

'Electrifying. Renoir's realism matched with Prévert's poetic whimsy . . . A moving and delightful film.' *(Richard Roud, Guardian)*

'Is it a comedy, a thriller, a love story or a political documentary? . . . Renoir makes nonsense of pigeon holes.' *(Kenneth Tynan, Observer)*

'Renoir at his best, a marvelously moving, beautifully directed and acted celebration of romance, brotherhood, art, life, and the common French men and women who are guided by their hearts . . . Picture has wit, warmth, characters you care about. What is most remarkable is the picture's sexual maturity and frankness.' *(Danny Peary)*

CRIMES AND MISDEMEANORS

CT: 10 AV: 7.75

1989 US 104 C DRAMA/COMEDY

D Woody Allen ☆ AAN
W Woody Allen ☆ AAN

Caroline Aaron Alan Alda ☆ Woody Allen ☆ Claire Bloom Mia Farrow Joanna Gleason Anjelica Huston Martin Landau ☆ AAN Jenny Nichols Jerry Orbach Sam Waterston

A successful opthalmologist (Martin Landau) tries to get rid of a mistress (Anjelica Huston); an unsuccessful filmmaker (Woody Allen) tries to attract one (Mia Farrow).

The most successful marriage of Allen's comic one-liners with his pessimistic world-view. The two, interlinked stories centre on a basic question: why should we bother to behave morally in a universe where God may not exist, and where goodness is so rarely rewarded? Though dark in tone, the film has an ironic approach to the self-pity which has detracted from other serious Allen movies: it's highly entertaining, and contains some of Woody Allen's wittiest one-liners. It even leaves room for cautious optimism. Allen suggests that a cold universe is at least warmed by our capacity to love, however inadequate this may be.

The central metaphor concerns sight: the murderous Judah (Martin Landau) is an ophthalmologist, constantly worrying that (in the words of his father) 'the eyes of God are on us always'. Judah's friend and patient, the rabbi (Sam Waterston), rebukes him for not viewing the world correctly: 'You see it as harsh and empty of values'. The two imperfect seekers after truth, Clifford and

Halley (Allen and Farrow), both wear glasses. At the moment when Clifford finds that she has rejected him, she no longer wears them, evidently content to look elegant but to be short-sighted.

The other main theme of the film is a familiar one in the Woody Allen canon: the distance between movies and reality. Clifford is a fan of escapist pictures and doesn't like the ending of *Crimes and Misdemeanors* when Judah tells it to him as a possible plot. Clifford suggests that if the murderous adulterer turned himself in, instead of going free, this would add a tragic dimension. 'If you want a happy ending, you should go see a Hollywood movie,' snaps Judah.

ANTI:

'Allen's most fully orchestrated attempt yet at symbolism, wherein everybody in the picture makes constant references to eyes, blindness, vision, and the like . . . This pattern of symbolic references is grotesquely overdone and thoroughly mechanical, a textbook example of symbolism-by-the-textbook.' *(Bruce Bawer, American Spectator)*

'An extremely ambitious film, most akin perhaps to *Hannah and Her Sisters*, the narrative and tonal coherence of which it sadly lacks, though the assured direction and typically fine ensemble acting manage partly to conceal the seams. Dramatically, the film seldom fulfils its promise, and its pessimistic "moral" – that good and evil do not always meet with their just desserts – looks contrived and hollow.' *(Geoff Andrew, Time Out)*

'Allen's much admired doctor who cheats on the most basic human decencies is meant to be symptomatic of the Reagan eighties. He learns to live comfortably with his lack of conscience. (And we can feel morally superior to the "successful") . . . If Woody Allen were interested in drama (rather than pieties), he wouldn't make us reject the emotional plight of the doctor's mistress. The camera loiters on her rear end, as if to dehumanize her; she's presented as hulking and insistent, like the knife-wielder in *Fatal Attraction*. So the doctor's final acceptance of his crime against her has no horror. The film's emphasis is confusing: the spectator has more anxiety about the doctor's possibly revealing his crime to the authorities than about what he does to her.' *(Pauline Kael)*

'Allen's apparent new found esteem for Jehovah feels slick, insincere; though his message is presumably that, in order to behave decently, we must believe God's eyes are on us, he doesn't convince us for a minute that it's a lack of religious conviction that makes possible Judah and Clifford's ethical waverings. (He doesn't even convince us that this is what he believes.) *Crimes and Misdemeanors* pays homage to the Almighty, in short, in the same superficial way that earlier Allen films have paid homage to Bergman and Fellini.' *(Bruce Bawer, American Spectator)*

'Although some people's favourite Allen pic, this rather unsatisfying movie is really two films running side by side that have little to do with each other.' *(Rose)*

PRO:

'The first Woody Allen I've seen which attempted to deal with human nature beyond the level of a sophisticated gag.' *(Michael Radford, Film Yearbook)*

'Who else but Woody Allen could make a movie in which virtue is punished, evildoing is rewarded, and there is a lot of laughter – even subversive laughter at the most shocking times?' *(Roger Ebert)*

MIXED:

'If *Manhattan*, coming at the end of the 70s, was Woody Allen's summarizing comment on that decade's besetting sin of self-absorption, then this is his concluding unscientific postscript on the besetting sin of the 80s, which is greed. Sometimes the joins in the movie's carpentry are awkward, sometimes its mood swings are jarring. But they also stir us from our comfortable stupor and vilify a true moral, always acute and often hilarious, meditation on the psychological economy of the Reagan years.' *(Richard Schickel)*

CRIMES OF DR MABUSE, THE: *see* THE *DOCTOR MABUSE* SERIES (THE TESTAMENT OF DR MABUSE).

CRIMES OF PASSION   CT: 5 AV: 3.50

1984 US 107 C DRAMA

D Ken Russell
W Barry Sandler

Kathleen Turner ✔ Anthony Perkins
John Laughlin ● Annie Potts Bruce Davison
John G. Scanlon

A fashion designer (Kathleen Turner) works as hooker part-time.

It may be the sickest of all Ken Russell's masturbatory fantasies, but it's certainly cinematic. Kathleen Turner (brave woman) has never looked sexier, nor Anthony Perkins (as the man out to kill h er with an outsize sex aid) twitchier.

PRO:

'Dismissed in some quarters as yet another over-the-top foray by the courageous Ken, [it] deserves more consideration. It is a blistering, entertaining and cynical comment on sexism in America . . . A film with a hard-edged, perspicacious and witty outlook on its time.' *(George Perry, Sunday Times)*

MIXED:

'Turner throws herself headfirst into the film . . . a clever, daring, mad performance in a movie that is just as reckless.' *(Richard Corliss, Time)*

'Certainly misogynistic and extremely funny and

sexy in parts, too . . . How anyone could deny Russell's essential talent has always been beyond me, profligate as he often is.' *(Derek Malcolm, Guardian)*

ANTI:

'One of the silliest movies in a long time.' *(Roger Ebert)*

'[Russell] is back at his worst . . . The occasional insights of the script stand no chance at all enveloped as they are by his lurid imagination and enormous ego.' *(The Face)*

'For all their extravagance Ken Russell's films have never lacked exuberance or humour, which makes the flat, joyless tone of [this one] a surprise . . . [It] is best when it makes the least sense. All too often it becomes just lucid enough for the extreme tawdriness of the material to take over.' *(Janet Maslin, New York Times)*

CRIMSON PIRATE, THE CT: 7 AV: 7.10

1952 GB 104 C ACTION/ADVENTURE/FAMILY

D Robert Siodmak ☆
W Roland Kibbee

Burt Lancaster ☆ Nick Cravat Eva Bartok Torin Thatcher James Hayter Leslie Bradley Margot Grahame Noel Purcell Frederick Leister Eliot Makeham

A swashbuckling pirate (Burt Lancaster) pursues his vocation on the high seas.

Big, brash adventure with the athletic star performing his own stunts, and a pleasant sense of self-mockery. An all-time-great pirate movie.

'Though some of the stunts are ingenious the constant high spirits tend to become a little wearying.' *(Shipman)*

'Has the physical exuberance of the early Douglas Fairbanks Sr pictures . . . Siodmak's direction is lively; Roland Kibbee's script is bright and improvisatory (much of the film's wit derives from a series of casual anachronisms.' *(Pauline Kael)*

'A burlesque . . . with Lancaster poking fun at his own acrobatic ability, ably assisted by little Nick Cravat, in real life his former circus partner.' *(Quinlan)*

'Marvellous . . . It effortlessly merges thrills and spoofery to produce entertainment that really is, for once, suitable for "kids of all ages".' *(Geoff Andrew, Time Out)*

'CROCODILE' DUNDEE CT: 7 AV: 6.69

1986 Australia 102 C COMEDY/ROMANCE

D Peter Faiman
W Paul Hogan Ken Shadie John Cornell based on a story by Hogan

Paul Hogan ☆ Linda Kozlowski John Meillon Mark Blum Michael Lombard David Gulpilil Ritchie Singer

Aussie from the outback comes to terms with the concrete jungle of New York, and vice versa.

Immensely likeable Australian romantic comedy which merged the best aspects of *Romancing The Stone* and *Tarzan's New York Adventure*, and momentarily made a star out of Paul Hogan. The critics may have gaven it a mixed reception, but audiences loved it. The sequel (*Crocodile Dundee 2*) was a big disappointment.

'Not that funny, more chucklesome than hysteric-inducing, the pacing . . . is somewhat leisurely for a farce, and lacking point for satire.' *(Phillip Bergson, What's On)*

'Not all that funny nor all that original . . . but the vote for the movie [at the box office] is a vote for human beings . . . and for the special effects of a credible hero at large in a credibly unnerving environment.' *(Nigel Andrews, Financial Times)*

'The contrasts of the outback and modern New York provide some moments of refreshing comic genius.' *(Adrian Sibley, F&F)*

'Hogan's persona is the film's small secret. He is shrewd without being worldly, naive without being at all vulnerable . . . The film is . . . mildly but continuously entertaining. You would hardly think that was a trade secret, a magic ingredient, but it seems to be.' *(Adam Mars-Jones, Independent)*

'Should delight audiences hungry for hero figures.' *(Milton Shulman, Evening Standard)*

CROSSFIRE CT: 6 AV: 7.25

1947 US 86 BW THRILLER

D Edward Dmytryk ☆
W John Paxton from Richard Brooks's novel *The Brick Foxhole*

Robert Young ☆ Robert Mitchum ☆ Robert Ryan ☆ Gloria Grahame ☆ AAN Paul Kelly ☆ Sam Levene.

An anti-semitic soldier (Robert Ryan) is suspected of murdering a Jew in a New York hotel.

Acclaimed thriller about anti-semitism (it's against it). It's often called Dmytryk's best picture, and he makes the most of his small budget; but he settles on no consistent style. Some of it is stagey, some of it naturalistic, some of it expressionist and distorted, and there isn't always an easy transition between the various approaches. Still, there are gripping performances from the three Roberts (Ryan, Young and Mitchum).

ANTI:

'The direction of Edward Dmytryk . . . does little to alleviate the visually static nature of many scenes.' *(Blake Lucas, Film Noir: An Encyclopedic Reference to the American Style, 1979)*

MIXED:

'Very good and very heartening too, but I think the following qualifiers must be recognized: 1) In a way it is as embarrassing to see a movie Come Right Out Against anti-semitism as it would be to see a movie Come Right Out Against torturing children. 2) Few things pay off better in prestige and hard cash – granted you present it in an entertaining way – than safe fearlessness. 3) This film is not entirely fearless, even within its relatively safe terms.' *(James Agee)*

PRO:

'Murder story that holds its own with any on the basis of suspense and speed. The courage lies in motivating the murder with something that is dreadfully real and practially unmentionable in films unless in connection with the safely villainous Nazi – anti-semitism.' *(Richard Winnington)*

'An unqualified A for effort in bringing to the screen a frank and immediate demonstration of the brutality of religious bigotry . . . And an equally high mark for lacing this exceedingly thoughtful theme through a grimly absorbing melodrama.' *(Bosley Crowther)*

CROSSING DELANCEY CT: 8 AV: 6.15

1988 US 133 C DRAMA/ROMANCE

D Joan Micklin Silver ✔
W Susan Sandler from her own play

Amy Irving ☆ Peter Riegart ✔ Reizl Bozyk ✔ Jeroen Grabbé ✔ Sylvia Miles ✔ George Martin John Bedford Lloyd David Pierce

Literary-minded Jewish girl (Amy Irving) ignores local pickle-seller (Peter Riegart) in favour of pretentious Dutch writer (Jeroen Krabbé).

Charming romantic comedy which gave Amy Irving the best role of her career. The story proceeds along predictable lines, but characterization and dialogue are so sharp (even if the pickle-seller is idealized) that it's highly enjoyable.

ANTI:

'Precious, genteel comedy about Jewish social manners . . . The film's myopic world view is peopled with over-familiar stereotypes, such as Irving's mother, a sprightly middle-aged crone. A moral tale of passionless love, Micklin Silver's whimsical love story emerges as a twee, pallid imitation of a short story by Isaac Bashevis-Singer, displaying neither heart nor conviction.' *(Stephen Dark, Film Review)*

'An articulate young Jewish CUNY graduate selling pickles out of barrels on Delancey Street? Tell me another. Peter Riegart's Sam, moreover, is so down-to-earth and secure about his identity that he sometimes comes across as downright smug and self-satisfied. And Sandler gives him at least one line of dialogue – "What's wrong with my world? You think it's so small? You think it defines me?" – that should have gone unspoken; it makes Sam sound less like a Lower East Side pickle merchant than, well, a Dutch novelist.' *(Bruce Bawer, American Spectator)*

MIXED:

'A Jewish fairytale . . . that almost defies you not to believe it . . . Perhaps the film is not really hard-edged enough, but its muted drama is still extraordinarily effective . . . Much better than *Moonstruck*.' *(Derek Malcolm, Guardian)*

'Very schmaltzy but enjoyable.' *(John Mount, Girl About Town)*

'Silver's beautifully directed new ethnic comedy . . . asks you to believe that its attractive leading lady . . . has a problem finding a fellow. And if you believe that you'll believe anything . . . Riegert's performance is the shrewdest thing in the film – it's worth crossing Delancey to catch it.' *(Clive Hirschhorn, Sunday Express)*

PRO:

'Silver and Sandler manage to combine a down-to-earth, contemporary outlook with the dreaminess of a fairy tale. The film's style is deliberately broad, but the actors give it humour and delicacy. Amy Irving . . . gives Izzy a refreshing worldliness, a hint of disappointment and a hard-won wisdom that banish any trace of ingenuousness from the role.' *(New York Times)*

'Notable are the modest but deeply poignant images of the loneliness of a single woman's life in New York: grabbing dinner with girlfriends at a corner hot dog stand, jawing over coffee in a diner, haunting the take-out salad bar at the Korean delicatessen after work. I've complained previously about how few films manage to capture the feel of life in Manhattan; this ones does so, with astonishing sensitivity and without making a fuss about it. Likewise, while American films tend to be notoriously bad at capturing the way literary people look and talk and behave, this one does a pretty good job of it.' *(Bruce Bawer, American Spectator)*

CROWD, THE CT: 6 AV: 9.00

1928 US98 BW DRAMA/SILENT

D King Vidor ☆
W King Vidor John V.A. Weaver Harry Behn

James Murray Eleanor Boardman Bert Roach Estelle Clark

A working man (James Murray) struggles for survival in the big city, but gets little support from his wife (Eleanor Boardman).

A landmark in silent film: a film which paid attention to the common man without patronizing or (as in the case of Chaplin) sentimentalizing him. Though impressively realistic in many ways, the film failed to find an audience. Movie historians since have tended to blame the public for not being able to cope with reality; but the characters are dull, and the film is a little too relentlessly depressing.

ANTI:

'A drab actionless story of ungodly length and apparently telling nothing.' *(Variety)*

'It has the fundamental weakness of attempting to interest us in something inherently uninteresting. We are not interested in average things, whether animate or inanimate . . . What does anyone get from *The Crowd?* . . . It shows the crowd is too powerful to be combatted, and it breathes hopelessness and despair.' *(Film Spectator)*

'Vidor's theme was vast . . . a man's ineffectual struggle against the hostile indifference of the masses . . . The film should have been the spirit and the humanity of the crowd . . . Instead, it concentrated . . . on . . . a single individual . . . It should . . . have been called *The Man*.' *(Paul Rotha, The Film Till Now, 1930)*

PRO:

'No picture is perfect, but this comes as near to reproducing reality as anything you have ever witnessed. Yet it loses none of the suspense and thrills of a great picture because it is a real-life story. Take several handkerchiefs, because you will cry with laughter and weep with sympathy while viewing this unusual King Vidor production. Don't miss it.' *(Photoplay)*

'King Vidor's style as well as his spirit has displeased many. Certainly, *The Crowd* contains many useless, ugly, and heavy repetitions; Vidor cannot decide to choose; he puts everything in and no doubt he feels the need to explain, to clarify, to feel that everybody understands what he is showing. He piles details upon detail, which crush by their weight and reality.' *(Jean-Georges Auriol, Revue du Cinéma, 1929)*

'It failed, commercially, because people were too accustomed to the usual halcyon treatment of human life to stand it . . . It cut across Hollywood's world audiences like a whip. It hurt them.' *(John Grierson, 1932)*

'Film has marvellous visuals of New York. Sometimes it is portrayed as romantic (with amusement parks, streetcars, beaches, ferries, theaters); at other times it's frightening (with high buildings; fast, dizzy traffic; noise). Always it is extremely crowded . . . It's a test for Murray and Boardman to remain individuals in this depersonalized city.' *(Danny Peary)*

CRUCIFIED LOVERS, THE: *see* CHIKAMITSU MONOGATARI.

CRUEL SEA, THE CT: 6 AV: 7.62

1953 GB 120 BW WAR

D Charles Frend ☆
W Eric Ambler ☆ AAN from Nicholas Monsarrat's novel

Jack Hawkins ☆ Donald Sinden ☆ Stanley Baker ☆ John Stratton Denholm Elliott John Warner Bruce Seton Virginia McKenna Moira Lister June Thorburn

A British corvette patrols the North Atlantic in World War II.

Classic war movie with outstanding performances but a run-of-the-mill plot.

'A serious, authentic reconstruction . . . Production, despite its long running time, emerges as a picture of dramatic intensity.' *(Variety)*

'An unimpeachable testament to gallantry, but this drama of the tiny armed convoy escorts and their crews, most of whom were either enlisted or drafted landlubbers, is expert documentation rather than high film art.' *(A.H. Weiler, New York Times)*

'A story of lethal adventure, but first it is a story of character: the character of the captain, a professional sailor hardened by experience, of the lieutenant who learns devotion, the young volunteers who give their lives. It is finely acted . . . admirably directed, a film of a kind we make well in this country. It does Ealing credit.' *(Dilys Powell)*

CRYING GAME, THE AAN CT: 6 AV: 7.27

1992 GB 112 C THRILLER/DRAMA

D Neil Jordan ✗ AAN
W Neil Jordan ✗ AAW

Stephen Rea ☆ AAN Miranda Richardson ✗ Forest Whitaker Jim Broadbent Ralph Brown Adrian Dunbar Jaye Davidson ☆ AAN

An IRA terrorist (Stephen Rea) befriends a black British soldier (Forest Whitaker), then goes to London, where he falls for the soldier's lover (Jaye Davidson).

Neil Jordan's thriller with a sexual twist suffers from a slow, talky start and was more admired by Americans than the British, who found it unrealistically contrived and starry-eyed about the IRA; but Stephen Rea's central performance is funny and touching.

PRO:

'An astonishingly good and daring film that richly develops several intertwined thematic lines, *The Crying Game* takes giant risks that are stunningly rewarded.' *(Variety)*

'Jordan's deftly handled tale is a forceful and gripping one, a brilliantly controlled mixture of violence, harshness, sexuality, cynical humour and moments of surprising tenderness . . . The film really belongs to Davidson . . . Her performance, like the film, is a memorable triumph.' *(Rose Collis, Gay Times)*

'Richardson is, in conventional terms, the strongest character on screen, a truth that probably won't save [the film] from party-line feminist thinkers determined to be scandalised by the portrayal of Dil as black, exotic and alluring.' *(John Lyttle, Independent)*

ANTI:

'There's a problem not only in the clumsy structure, but in Jordan's determination to keep surprising us with twists.' *(Geoff Andrew, Time Out)*

'Why did Jordan cast American Forest Whitaker – who looks more like a sumo wrestler than a squaddie? . . . What about our boys? Brian Bovell or Gary McDonald would both have been excellent for this part . . . American audiences aren't all culturally dumb.' *(Tony Sewell, The Voice)*

'A bust in Britain but a phenomenal success in America, this confused film is part thriller, part romantic comedy. The middle section, with an IRA man seeking out the girlfriend of a dead squaddie, is touching and delightfully funny, sporting an incredible twist in the tale. The outer sections, involving the IRA, are tedious and in desperate need of a storyline to hold them together.' *(Rose)*

'Absolute twaddle . . . Neil Jordan, who wrote and directed, is a good film maker. *Company of Wolves* and *High Spirits* had much to commend them. But with *The Crying Game* nonetheless, he has gone Hollywood (probably without even knowing it).' *(Ken Russell, 1993)*

CURSE OF FRANKENSTEIN, THE

CT: 6 AV: 5.55

1957 GB 83 C HORROR/SF

D Terence Fisher ✓
W Jimmy Sangster ✓ from Mary Shelley's novel *Frankenstein*

Peter Cushing ☆ Christopher Lee ☆ Hazel Court Robert Urquhart Valerie Gaunt Melvyn Hayes

Scientist (Peter Cushing) creates monster (Christopher Lee).

One of the very few horror films to be made in colour, it shocked critics unused to seeing the colour of blood – although the graphic scenes which earned it condemnation are mild by modern standards. Panned on release for being gruesome and inferior to the 1931 *Frankenstein*, it was actually more faithful than that film to Mary Shelley's original, restored some dignity to the Monster despite an unimpressive make-up job, and featured a sensitive performance by Peter Cushing as the Baron. Equally underrated was Terence Fisher's direction (although his use of colour was more confident in the following year's Dracula). The sets and costumes – while tacky by modern standards – weren't bad, especially as they had to be assembled within a very low budget of $350,000. It grossed over $8 million worldwide, made stars of Cushing and Lee, and led to six sequels (starting with *The Revenge of Frankenstein*) and a whole range of films by Britain's Hammer Studios. Its critical stock has risen hugely.

ANTI:

'Among the half dozen most repulsive films I have encountered in the course of some 10,000 miles of film reviewing.' *(Observer)*

This is the ugh-est film I've ever seen.' *(Emery Pearce, Daily Herald)*

'It doesn't have sufficient tension or impact.' *(Harold Conway, Daily Sketch)*

MIXED:

'Routine horror picture, which makes no particular attempt to do anything more important than scare you with corpses and blood. The most familiar monster of science fiction . . . is just a big clumsy ruffian with a face that even a mother couldn't love and a cantankerous disposition . . . Cold-cuts for old timers who remember Boris Karloff . . . but it may titillate the blissful youngsters.' *(Bosley Crowther, New York Times)*

'A real "gruesome" for those who like shivering like a jelly at a children's party.' *(Evening Standard)*

PRO:

'Looks today like a colourful and witty fairy story, which is exactly what it always was.' *(David Pirie, A Heritage of Horror)*

CURSE OF THE WEREWOLF, THE

CT: 7 AV: 5.29

1961 GB 92 C HORROR/ROMANCE

D Terence Fisher ☆
W John Elder (Anthony Hinds) from Guy Endore's novel *The Werewolf of Paris*

Oliver Reed ✓ Cifford Evans Catherine Feller Yvonne Romain Anthony Dawson Richard Wordsworth Warren Mitchell Justin Walters ✓

A raped servant girl gives birth to a werewolf (Oliver Reed).

Both a horror story and an offbeat romance, with an exotic Spanish setting. It starts slowly and lacks the usual Hammer shocks or gallons of gore, but director Terence Fisher makes up for this with greater depth of characterization and attention to visual detail. Oliver Reed makes a splendid werewolf, helped by Roy Ashton's make-up effects. One of the most underrated Hammer films, and among the best werewolf movies of all time – though it might, of course, have been more frightening if the werewolf had changed into Oliver Reed.

'I consider it to be a tragic love story and not fundamentally a "horror" story.' *(Terence Fisher)*

ANTI:

'Excessively dull, tediously paced . . . poorly acted.' *(Hollywood Citizen News)*

Even by Hammer standards this is a singularly repellent job of slaughter-house horror . . . Surely the time has come when a film like this should be turned over to the alienists for comment; as entertainment its stolid acting, writing, presentation and direction could hardly be more preclusive.' *(MFB)*

'Serial-like, acting uneven, direction clumsy, but presentation lush . . . The picture . . . eschews blood and guts and delves into murky eugenics for its thrills . . . Oliver Reed grossly overacts . . . [It] will make the hard-boiled, let alone the squeamish, wince.' *(Josh Billings, Kine Weekly)*

MIXED:

'Dwells at extraordinary length, even for a horror picture, on expository background – on the vile heritage responsible for the genesis of the story's monster. But it is a credit to all concerned that this lengthy prolog sustains equal, if not greater, interest than the film's principal story which involves the personal plight of the wolfman himself.' *(Variety)*

PRO:

'Chills and horrors are made realistic, and running beneath the picture is an undercurrent of intelligence and insight.' *(Film Daily)*

'It has been done with a visual richness and theatrical care almost unique . . . Attempts to humanize, to give logic and motivation to what – to modern minds – is ludicrous, cruel, or incomprehensible . . . Presented with intelligence and sympathy, not horror for its own sake.' *(Hollywood Reporter)*

'Different from run-of-the-mill horror species . . . [It] unfolds against a rich period decor – some of the color photography is beautiful . . . [Its] Gothic type of narrative . . . is not uninteresting, if broadly acted . . . Don't go expecting early summer relaxation.' *(Howard Thompson, New York Times)*

'One of Hammer's best movies, often underrated because of its deliberate avoidance of the traditional blood and violence and shock moments.' *(Alan Frank)*

CYRANO DE BERGERAC CT: 10 AV: 9.08

1990 France 138 C ROMANCE/DRAMA/FOREIGN

D Jean-Paul Rappeneau ☆
W Jean-Paul Rappeneau Jean-Claude Carrière from Edmond Rostand's play

Gérard Depardieu ☆ Anne Brochet ☆ Vincent Perez ✓ Jacques Weber Roland Bertin Philippe Morier-Genoud Philippe Volter Pierre Maguelon

Poet-warrior with big nose (Gérard Depardieu) is shy.

To say that Gérard Depardieu rightly won the best actor award at Cannes for *Cyrano* is to be needlessly mealy-mouthed. This is one of the great performances of all time. Depardieu definitively captures Cyrano's self-loathing, his pathos and, above all, his panache. Depardieu's masculinity is reminiscent of Olivier in his prime; his swashbuckling is on a par with Errol Flynn's; and he miraculously combines all this with the more modern, anti-heroic, screen subtlety of a De Niro. On a screen filled with distractions – beautiful scenery, wonderfully detailed costumes, thousands of extras – it is hard to take your eyes off him. Depardieu alone would make the film worth seeing twice.

But as Roxane, the cousin who doesn't quite requite, Anne Brochet is a match for him. Even though the character might cruelly be summarized as an insensitive pseud infatuated with her illusions, she is still delightful: you can understand why Cyrano has fallen head-over-nose in love. The usually tedious role of Christian, Roxane's stupid paramour, is played with nobility by Vincent Perez. The villains have complexity and humanity. Even in the crowd scenes, everyone seems to know what he's doing.

The screenplay is (bravely) in verse, and a reminder of how elegant French can sound. Anthony Burgess's rhyming subtitles capture the meaning and spirit perfectly. Even the spelling mistakes in the subtitles (inexcusable in a film with such meticulous attention to detail in every other respect) are not too distracting.

This is a splendid, moving, lyrical romance, brilliantly filmed by director Jean-Paul Rappeneau, who also wrote the screenplay with Jean-Claude Carrière. It is not static, like so many adaptations of classic stage plays; the beauty of the lighting, the fluidity of the camerawork and the energy of the staging make it better than the best of Zeffirelli. It's a masterpiece, and on a scale which means that it should be enjoyed first on the big screen.

MIXED:

'The problem with this version is the axe with which director Rappaneau . . . approached the play. Everyone is too cowed to introduce an original idea. Likewise the production is too theatrical, yet not theatrical enough: stage hallmarks are . . . rife, yet the film lacks the sense of pacing that marks a good cinematic production. Still . . . Depardieu is excellent. And there is plenty of costly looking spectacle . . . Unlikely to be remembered long after it closes.' *(William Fisher, Screen International)*

'The English subtitles, in a rhyming translation by Anthony Burgess, are a distraction.' *(Halliwell)*

'Quite visceral and frequently inspired (vide the decision to stage the balcony scene during a mild rainstorm), faltering only a little during the finale, which is overextended.' *(Maltin)*

'Gérard Depardieu has, of course, the role of his career, and plays it to the hilt . . . However, in spite of the brilliant production and excellent portrayal, the film lacks tightness. It runs far too long . . . as if the filmmaker was so enchanted by the material he couldn't bear to discipline it. Nevertheless, if this isn't the ultimate *Cyrano*, it is a marvellous example of the artistic possibilities of the medium and, as such, merits respect and admiration.' *(Eva Kissin, Films in Review)*

PRO:

'*Cyrano*? Bravo!' *(Le Monde)*

'A near-perfect balance of verbal and visual flamboyance.' *(Variety)*

'Other actors have given more flamboyant interpretations of the role, but Depardieu is the definitive romantic Cyrano. He makes you ache with him. As an actor, he has found the confidence to do less. It's a towering performance, magnificent and moving, that does just what any honest telling of the Cyrano legend should strive to do: set us all dreaming.' *(Peter Travers, Rolling Stone)*

'[Gérard Depardieu's] performance is expansive, funny, gross, dainty, and always humane. It's a disciplined whirlwind of conflicting emotion that finds surprising new life in the theatrical antique . . . the definitive Cyrano, the Cyrano that will make all other actors hesitate before they take on the role.' *(Vincent Canby, New York Times)*

'Depardieu is perfect for the part, Fairbanks-like in the duelling sequences and eminently believable in the more emotional moments.' *(Rose)*

'The performance of a lifetime . . . a thundering success.' *(Geoff Brown, The Times)*

'Visually ravishing, sumptuous and altogether wonderful.' *(Scheuer)*

'An astonishingly lavish and gorgeous production: the reconstruction of the 17th-century theatre and the street scenes are superb.' *(Winnert)*

CZLOWIEK Z ZELAZA: *see* MAN OF IRON.

CZLOWIEK Z MARMUR: *see* MAN OF MARBLE.

D

DAHONG DENGLONG GAOGAO GUA: *see* RAISE THE RED LANTERN.

DAM BUSTERS, THE CT: 8 AV: 8.09

1954 GB 125 (102 in US) BW WAR

D Michael Anderson ✔
W R.C. Sheriff from books by Guy Gibson and Paul Brickhill

Michael Redgrave ☆ Richard Todd ✔ Basil Sydney Derek Farr

British scientist Barnes Wallis (Michael Redgrave) develops a bouncing bomb; Commander Guy Gibson (Richard Todd) uses it.

A magnificent war film, with fine leading performances, direction that cleverly builds up the tension, and a fascinating script based on true events. Eric Coates's famous 'Dam Busters' March' adds to the patriotic impact.

MIXED:

'Begins a little slowly . . . The success of the film, despite its length and tempo, is due partly to its epic subject . . . partly to skilful treatment. R.C. Sheriff's script avoids outmoded slang and the humour is dry and English.' (*Campbell Dixon, Daily Telegraph*)

'A good story [told] . . . with compelling conviction . . . a magnificently exciting picture . . . [It] doesn't entirely steer clear of facile sentiment and the ops-room cliché, but most of it is straightforward, honest and remarkably fresh.' (*Thomas Spencer, Daily Worker*)

PRO:

'A small slice of history, told with painstaking attention to detail and overflowing with the British quality of understatement.' (*Variety*)

'A triumph of stagecraft.' (*Reynolds News*)

'Understated British war epic with additional scientific interest and good acting and model work, not to mention a welcome lack of love interest.' (*Halliwell*)

'A decent, suspenseful film, infinitely better than most British war films of the period.' (*Shipman*)

DAMNED, THE CT: 2 AV: 5.55

(aka *Götterdammerung; La Caduta degli Dei*)

1969 West Germany/Italy 164 BW DRAMA/ FOREIGN

D Luchino Visconti ✗
W Nicola Badalucco Enrico Medioli Luchino Visconti ✗ AAN

Dirk Bogarde Ingrid Thulin Helmut Berger ● Renaud Verley Helmut Griem Ren Kolldehof Albrecht Schönhals Umberto Orsini

A family of munitions manufacturers is attracted to Nazism.

Camp, fetishistic, more than slightly silly cartoon of the Nazi era. Helmut Berger goes blatantly over the top. Bogarde looks embarassed, as well he may.

'This has got to be the most violent family since the Borgias. Screaming, yelling, scheming, and conniving over factory ownership is but part of it: they murder each other with no hesitation to achieve their ends, they have perverse sexual hang-ups, they are dope-fiends, and, in the film's most spectacular sequence, a mother amongst them sleeps with her son.' *(Variety)*

MIXED:

'Made with hatred recollected in something which isn't quite tranquillity . . . In a way I find it hateful; something of its theme has seeped through into its handling. All the same its images have been accompanying me for days.' *(Dilys Powell)*

ANTI:

'Grandiose, lurid, sluggish . . . Has all the disadvantages of a dubbed movie – everything sounds stilted and slightly off. The characters talk in a language that belongs to no period or country and sounds like translated subtitles.' *(Pauline Kael)*

'One is left lamenting that such a quondam master of realism as Visconti is making his films look like operas from which the score has been inexplicably removed.' *(MFB)*

'There is no more overblown, self-inflated and preposterous reputation in film than that of Luchino Visconti . . . *The Damned*, included in the ten-best Pantheon of both Vincent Canby and Judith Crist, is meant to be tragic and terrifying, but it emerges as the ludicrous flailings of puny puppets in inscrutable, wooden frenzies. "It's an object lesson, a morality tale, a tragedy of historic proportions!" shrieks the puppeteer, and all we see is the bashing together of stupid, wooden heads, while our notions of what it may all mean remain dim and unrewarding.' *(John Simon)*

'A ludicrously baroque and garish caricature of the 20th century's most tragic era.' *(Bergan & Karney)*

DANCES WITH WOLVES AAW CT: 9 AV: 8.86

DANCES WITH WOLVES: THE DIRECTOR'S CUT CT: 10 AV: 8.93

1991 US 180/232 (director's cut) C WESTERN/ EPIC

D Kevin Costner ☆ AAW
W Michael Blake ☆ AAW from his own novel

Kevin Costner ☆ AAN Mary McDonnell ✗ AAN
Graham Greene ☆ AAN Rodney A. Grant
Floyd Red Crow Westerman Tantoo Cardinal
Robert Pastorelli Charles Rocket Maury Chaykin
Jimmy Herman

A white soldier (Kevin Costner) stationed on the frontier of the Old West learns to love the Indians.

A good yarn. The epic set-pieces – such as the buffalo-hunt, the battles and the cross-country journeys – are magnificent. And, whenever the story seems to be lapsing into cliché, it always manages some clever inversion of our expectations.

Most praise was rightly showered on Costner, who co-produced, starred and made an outstanding directorial debut. But Australian cinematographer Dean Semler, who displayed his eye for lighting and landscape in *Mad Max Beyond Thunderdome* and *Young Guns*, surpassed himself with shots worthy of a David Lean epic. The film's loving attention to detail also reflected credit on production designer Jeffrey Beechcroft, costume designer Elsa Zamperelli, and Michael Blake for his well-researched screenplay.

To the great credit of Costner's team, however, they don't allow period authenticity to overwhelm the story. Nor do they allow their modern concerns – for the environment, and about the need to respect other cultures – to become preachy or anachronistic. They have been content to tell a simple tale which illuminates great truths, with a sincerity and humour which speedily involves the emotions of an audience.

The three-hour print feels longer than the four-hour version, the director's cut, which avoids the pro-Sioux sentimentality of the original, fills in holes in the plot, and makes more sense of the romantic interludes. Most crucially, the full version is sceptical about whether Costner can ever become, or truly wants to become, a true Indian – he never understands their marriage traditions, and even at the end we see him stopping a Sioux warrior from scalping a white officer. This makes much better sense of the ending, when Costner decides that his future lies in returning to white society.

Even in its shorter, more commercially viable form, the film was a handsome piece of story-telling, and one of the most impressive Oscar-winners of recent years. Revealed on the scale intended by its director, *Dances With Wolves* is much richer, more complex and sophisticated. It deserves to take its place among the classic westerns.

ANTI:

'This is a nature-boy movie, a kid's daydream of being an Indian. When Dunbar has become a Sioux named Dances with Wolves, he writes in his journal that he knows for the first time who he really is. Costner has feathers in his hair and feathers in his head. The movie – Costner's debut as a director – is childishly naive . . . There isn't even anything with narrative power or bite to it. This Western is like a New Age social-studies lesson. This epic was made by a bland megalomaniac. (The Indians should have named him Plays with Camera.) You look at that untroubled face and know he can make everything lightweight. How is he as a director? Well, he has moments of competence.' *(Pauline Kael)*

'Would be easier to love if screenwriter Blake had resisted the temptation to plug every positive stereotype about Native Americans. The characters, alternately stoic, are ecologically aware and brave. Even Hollywood Indians don't have to be like this.' *(Michael Dorris, Premiere)*

MIXED:

'Long, simplistic and lacking in irony, though not in pawky humor. The action set-pieces (two ambushes, two pitched battles, a grand buffalo hunt) are dynamically handled. But the picture lacks the visual and dramatic authority of the best westerns.' *(Philip French, Observer)*

PRO:

'A very fine film . . . an unashamed elegy for the way of life of the American Indians . . . In fact its portrayal of a Sioux tribe shows a reverence which at times comes perilously close to the myth of the Noble Savage.' *(Daily Telegraph)*

'A conservationist western? An eco-western? *Dances With Wolves* wears its New Age labels with pride and, more importantly, rises above them.' *(Neil Norman, Evening Standard)*

'Costner brings a rare degree of grace and feeling to this elegiac tale . . . From its three-hour length, which amazingly does not become tiresome, to its bold use of subtitled Lakota language (the Sioux tongue) for at least a third of the dialog, it's clear the filmmakers were proceeding without regard for the rules.' *(Variety)*

'An instant classic.' *(Tom Hutchinson, Mail on Sunday)*

DANGEROUS LIAISONS CT: 6 AV: 7.36

1988 US 120 C DRAMA

D Stephen Frears ✗
W Christopher Hampton ☆ AAW from the play by Hampton and the novel by Choderlos de Laclos

Glenn Close ☆ AAN John Malkovich
Michelle Pfeiffer ☆ AAN Swoosie Kurtz
Keanu Reeves ● Mildred Natwick Uma Thurman
Peter Capaldi

Two decadent aristocrats (John Malkovich, Glenn Close) plan to debauch various sexual innocents.

A handsome, enjoyable film with a moving performance by Pfeiffer, as the good wife who falls fatally for Malkovich. But something is missing: it lacks the power it had on the stage (with Alan Rickman and Lindsay Duncan stunning in the leading roles). The two leading actors here play their parts intelligently and make the most of every nuance; but they remain too modern, insufficiently French and aristocratic. Frears's direction reflects all those years he spent directing for television – you keep wishing the camera would pull back a little – but he's very sensitive to the human drama. Stuart Craig won an Oscar for his production design. George Fenton was nominated for his music.

ANTI:

'The two principal actors – Glenn Close and John Malkovich – are among the most decidedly contemporary, and decidedly American, in the business. Neither brings us anywhere near the heart of his character's particular darkness. Glenn Close, a wonderful actress, fakes her way through her part creditably enough. But Malkovich is awful: his delivery, his body language, everything down to the way he drops his two front teeth over his lower lip when he closes his mouth, says Off-Off-Broadway. His Vicomte simply oozes sleaze. And he's supposed to be sleazy. But he's also supposed to be able to fool lovely, intelligent, and refined young ladies into thinking that he isn't sleazy, and, beyond that, able to make them fall madly in love with him. Patently, the part calls for someone with great surface charm and attractiveness (it's the kind of role George Sanders used to play), but Malkovich is about as far as you can get, in the Screen Actors Guild directory, from charm and attractiveness, surface or otherwise.' *(Bruce Bawer, American Spectator)*

'A good but incompletely realized film . . . takes too long to catch fire and suffers from a deficient central performance . . . (Malkovich) lacks the devilish charm and seductiveness one senses Valmont would need.' *(Variety)*

'As for Valmont, he is portrayed by Mr John Malkovich as a leering satyr, launching himself at women with a vulgar abandon that would get him banned from every respectable drawing-room in the land. Valmont had his faults, certainly, but lack of savoir faire was not one of them.' *(Anne Billson, Film Review)*

PRO:

'A lavish costume drama prickling with wit, mischief and erotic intrigue.' *(Brian D. Johnson, Maclean's)*

'Beautifully acted (by Glenn Close in particular), elegantly phrased, carefully shot on location in an appropriate selection of chateaux, directed with a limpidly formalised serenity, it's a handsome and intelligent piece of work.' *(Tom Milne, MFB)*

'One of the least static costume films ever made, and what costumes! . . . This first-rate piece of work by the daring and agile director Stephen Frears is alive in a way that movies of classics rarely are. The paradisially beautiful Pfeiffer is wonderfully affecting as the pawn of the debauchers' final game.' *(Pauline Kael)*

'One of the film's enormous strengths is scriptwriter Christopher Hampton's decision to go back to the novel, and save only the best from his play.' *(Steve Grant, Time Out)*

'Directed with an elegance, wit and style, not seen in a long time from a British director.' *(Sandy Lieberson, Film Review)*

'Although modern accents intrude and it's a little hard to believe in Close as this all-powerful sexual being, Pfeiffer is painfully brilliant as the doomed Mme de Tourvel. Costume drama has rarely been so captivating.' *(Rose)*

DANTON

CT: 5 AV: 7.20

1982 France/Poland 136 C DRAMA/BIOPIC

D Andrzej Wajda ☆
W Jean-Claude Carrière Andrzej Wajda Agnieszka Holland Boleslaw Michalek Jacek Gasiorowski based on Stanislawa Przbyszewska's play

Gérard Depardieu Wojciech Pszoniak Patrice Chereau Angela Winkler Boguslaw Linda

A revolutionary (Gérard Depardieu) upbraids his colleagues for having forgotten their original purpose.

Epic costume drama with splendid set-pieces, obviously intending to draw parallels between 18th-century France and modern Poland. Marred by a talky script, too slow a pace, uninspired direction and some over-acting by Depardieu.

'The temptation to see it in terms of Solidarity is unavoidable.' *(Philip Strick, MFB)*

ANTI:

'By any reasonable standard, terrible.' *(New Yorker)*

'Long-winded, visually conventional.' *(Bergan & Karney)*

'Depardieu does his familiar Depardieu act, diminishing the man if not the film.' *(Shipman)*

MIXED:

'Beautifully crafted, intriguingly claustrophobic and pleasantly old-fashioned, its virtues outweigh the minuses of an overwordy script and sedate pacing.' *(Winnert)*

PRO:

'Wajda's magnificent film . . . compelling, fiercely intelligent.' *(Philip French, Observer)*

'The [Edinburgh Film] Festival reached its peak . . . with the showing of Wajda's exhilarating film . . . The swirling urgency and physical vigour of [his] direction puts flesh, bone and human faces on the arguments as the Revolution devours its children . . . Wajda's main and most marvellous achievement, however, has been to keep the scale of his theme to proportions which are always human and recognisable, and to create a kind of hectic intimacy through the deployment of his cameras and the organisation of his cast . . . An epic film without the vulgarity of epics.' *(Julie Davidson, Glasgow Herald)*

'Art of a high order precisely because it manages to convey its messages in so many ways . . . It is a mighty film in simple garb.' *(Ian Bell, Scotsman)*

DARBY O'GILL AND THE LITTLE PEOPLE

CT: 7 AV: 6.80

1959 US 93 C FAMILY/FANTASY

D Robert Stevenson ✔
W Lawrence E. Watkin from H.T. Kavanagh's stories

Albert Sharpe Janet Munro ✔ Sean Connery ✔ Jimmy O'Dea ☆ Janet Munro Kieron Moore ✔ Estelle Winwood Walter Fitzgerald Denis O'Dea J.G. Devlin Jack MacGowran

An Irish caretaker with the gift of the gab (Albert Sharpe) falls down a well, encounters the little people under their leader King Brian (Jimmy O'Dea) and is given three wishes.

One of Disney's lesser-known but finest live-action fantasies, with a quirky script, excellent special effects and endearing characters. Sean Connery is surprisingly good as a juvenile lead, and his female co-star Janet Munro is equally appealing. Some sequences – including the most exciting ones – are scary and unsuitable for small children, and it's all a bit relentlessly Oirish; but this is a minor masterpiece, waiting to be rediscovered. The catchy songs are by Oliver Wallace and Lawrence E. Watkin.

ANTI:

'The Irish much as the Americans like to see them, all fey and whimsical, full of talk about leprechauns and jolly little songs with opening lines like "Och, have you ever seen the seagulls a-flying o'er the heather?" . . . the whole thing is fatally lacking in lightness and charm; in fact a lot of it is just dull.' *(The Times)*

'A Disney whimsy . . . which may scare some of the children in the audience into fits.' *(Charles MacLaren, Time and Tide)*

PRO:

'Very entertaining in a sentimental but not too sticky way.' *(Derek Monsey, Sunday Express)*

'This wonderful tale is told with a brisk, imaginative pace, and the special effects – whereby Darby interacts with the tiny leprechauns – are marvelously executed, and sometimes frightening.' *(Virgin)*

'One of the best fantasies ever put on film.' *(Maltin)*

DARK VICTORY AAN

CT: 6 AV: 7.38

1939 US 106 BW DRAMA

D Edmund Goulding
W Casey Robinson from George Emerson Brewer Jr and Bertram Bloch's play

Bette Davis ☆ AAN George Brent ☆ Humphrey Bogart Geraldine Fitzgerald Ronald Reagan Henry Travers Cora Witherspoon Virginia Brissac Dorothy Peterson Charles Richman

A flighty heiress (Bette Davis) discovers she has a brain tumour, and comes down to earth.

Goulding's direction is no better than competent, but this remains a classic weepie, with Bette Davis at her most delightful wringing every ounce of tragedy out of the morbid, deliriously corny plot. Max Steiner's tearjerking score was Oscar-nominated.

'Presents Bette Davis in a powerful and impressive role.' *(Variety)*

'If this were an automobile, it would be a Rolls-Royce with the very best trimmings.' *(Time)*

'A completely cynical appraisal would dismiss it all as emotional flim-flam . . . but it is impossible to be that cynical about it.' *(Frank S. Nugent, New York Times)*

'Bette Davis is an actress of the wrong scale for this story. Her early scenes are brilliant: the head-strong girl sure of herself, sure of life, the hands madly fidgeting, the face blazing defiance. I have seen the film twice, and each time I found her performance at the climax heartrending. But the subject demanded something more, something that Miss Davis, with all her rare talent, was not born to give us. It demands acting on the grand scale. Her performance is not, and could never be, on the grand scale . . . And it seems to me that Edmund Goulding's direction, with all its feeling for the pathos of human life, the heroism of human death, is wanting in the visual imagination which might have made this picture grand as well as touching. For surely it is the essence of the cinema that it should make its points not only with words but also, indeed primarily, with pictures.' *(Dilys Powell)*

'A kitsch classic . . . a gooey collection of clichés, but Davis slams her way through them in her nerviest style.' *(Pauline Kael)*

DARLING AAN

CT: 5 AV: 7.00

1965 GB 128 BW DRAMA

D John Schlesinger ✗ AAN
W Frederic Raphael ✗ AAW from Raphael, Schlesinger and Joseph Janni's story

Laurence Harvey Dirk Bogarde Julie Christie ☆ AAW Roland Curram Jos-Luis de Vilallonga Alex Scott Basil Henson Helen Lindsay Pauline Yates Tyler Butterworth

An amoral young model (Julie Christie) sleeps her way to the top.

Still worth watching as a (perhaps the) quintessential film of the Swinging 60s, but its main strength is a rivetingly unpleasant but charismatic performance by Julie Christie. Weaknesses include Raphael's smug, patronizing attitude to all the characters, which becomes intensely irritating. Schlesinger's much-acclaimed direction now looks like a half-baked imitation of the French New Wave. The film as a whole appears as tacky and vacuous as its heroine.

PRO:

'The best, most impressive British film for years . . . It is not a pleasant picture – but it is a stunningly honest and uncompromising one, directed with integrity and taste.' *(Clive Hirschhorn, Sunday Express)*

'The fact that it now appears dated is a point in its favour. As a portrait of a swinger in the Swinging Sixties it is unique. Shallow relationships, bloated egos and cold-blooded betrayals are the order of the day in Frederic Raphael's tale of a shallow trendy of her times . . . *Darling* provides an A-Z of what fashionable, fun couples did at the time – such as booking into an hotel for an afternoon's illicit sex with a suitcase full of newspapers, skimming stones at Chelsea Reach, having an abortion, stealing food from Fortnum and Mason, joining an orgy, smoking pot, drowning your pet goldfish in gin and tonic and throwing it off Hammersmith Bridge in a matchbox. This was the sort of thing that trendy French directors had been making their mistresses do a decade earlier. So who wasn't influenced by the New Wave?' *(Ken Russell, 1993)*

ANTI:

'Raphael's script tramples its own studied issues (Third World poverty, corrupt Western values, jet-set alienation) under its equally studied Sophisticated Characterisation. Schlesinger's direction is a leaden rehash of ideas from Godard, Antonioni and Bergman, which nonetheless contrives to remain rooted in British theatre of the Royal Court school. Excruciatingly embarrassing at the time, it now looks grotesquely pretentious and pathetically out of touch with the realities of the life-styles that it purports to represent.' *(Tony Rayns, Time Out)*

'Silly and badly thought out . . . As empty of meaning and mind as the empty life it's exposing.' *(Pauline Kael)*

'Totally tiresome in retrospect.' *(Halliwell)*

DAS BOOT: *see* BOAT, THE.

DAS KABINETT VON DR CALIGARI: *see* THE CABINET OF DOCTOR CALIGARI.

DAS SCHRECKLICHE MADCHEN: *see* NASTY GIRL, THE.

DAS TESTAMENT DES DR MABUSE: *see* THE *DOCTOR MABUSE* SERIES (THE TESTAMENT OF DR MABUSE).

DAVE

CT: 7 AV: 7.00

1993 US 110 C COMEDY/DRAMA

D Ivan Reitman ✔
W Gary Ross ☆

Kevin Kline ☆ Sigourney Weaver ✔ Frank Langella ✔ Kevin Dunn ✔ Ben Kingsley Charles Grodin ✔

Warm, friendly Dave (Kevin Kline) is a lookalike for cold, calculating US President Bill Mitchell (also Kevin Kline), and when Bill keels over in flagrante with his blonde secretary the authorities conspire to have Dave stand in for him on a longer-term basis.

Comedic film-making at its most professional, and its generous-spirited populism is a welcome throwback to the days of Frank Capra's *Mr Smith Goes To Washington*. The production has the kind of gloss and apparently effortless pace which director Ivan Reitman brought to *Ghostbusters* and *Kindergarten Cop*. Gary Ross's inventive, intelligent script has the same humour and charm as his previous hit, *Big*.

As the less-than-outgoing president, Kevin Kline gives an acutely observed study of a cold, stiff politician; as Dave, he is maladroit, human and endearing: his performance is even cleverer, and much funnier, than the one in *A Fish Called Wanda* which won him an Oscar.

The rest of the cast lend outstanding support. Sigourney Weaver has the necessary dignity for a first lady, and shows unexpected sex appeal when she unbends; as Dave's over-ambitious, anti-democratic Chief of Staff, Frank Langella is a splendidly hissworthy villain; and, as Dave's accountant buddy, the magnificent Charles Grodin squeezes a laugh out of every moment he's on screen.

Additional piquancy comes from the fact that many of the subsidiary characters (politicans, TV pundits and the like) are played by themselves. Arnold Schwarzenegger puts in a brief appearance at a presidential photo-opportunity, and Oliver Stone pops up on telly to warn America that there are suspicious differences between the old President and the new. 'Don't you think you're being a little paranoid, Oliver?' smirks the interviewer.

The politics are, in fact, naive rather than paranoid: cutting the federal budget by 650 million dollars has never looked easier, nor has 'declaring war' on unemployment. But the film is so good-hearted that it's easy to be swept away by the prevailing breeze of cosy liberalism. The trouble with this kind of politics in practice is, of course, that you end up not with Dave as president, but with Jimmy Carter or Bill Clinton; still, if you're after undemanding entertainment, Dave's your man.

ANTI:

'Ivan Reitman, whose reputation for sparkling, sophisticated direction rests squarely on the shoulders of *Meatballs, Stripes, Ghostbusters, Legal Eagles*, and *Twins*, doesn't exactly expand his range with this slipshod series of sight gags and sophomoric skits.' *(Guy Flatley, Cosmopolitan)*

'By comparison *The Distinguished Gentleman* looks revolutionary . . . A gentle populist fable squarely in the tradition of Capra . . . [perpetrating the myth] that there's nothing fundamentally wrong with America, nothing that one good man couldn't put right.' *(Tom Charity, Time Out)*

PRO:

'Kline is at home in comedy. To the genuine president, he brings the right reminiscent air of Bush without *Saturday Night Live* imitation, the feeling that if he were stabbed and said "Ouch," the "Ouch" wouldn't quite be convincing. To Dave, the live-wire sub, he gives the familiar Klinian fizz, the feeling that he is basically a springy acrobat speaking his lines in between leaps and tumbles and that he may bounce off the walls at any moment.' *(Stanley Kauffmann)*

'A blissed-out satirical fantasy about the dawn of Clintonism . . . Kline plays President Mitchell as a hard-shelled aristocratic phony glued to his teleprompter. In other words, he's a broad projection of everything Americans rejected in George Bush. And Dave? He's the anti-Bush, the President as common man – industrious, compassionate, junk-food-loving. Like Tom Hanks in *Big* (cowritten by Gary Ross, who wrote this movie solo), he's a sweet-souled imposter who, because of his guileless nature, turns out to be far better at his job than the calculating adult he's impersonating. Dave incarnates the emotional quality that helped get Clinton elected – the sense that, after decades of corruption (Nixon), incompetence (Carter), and heartless media gamesmanship (Reagan/Bush), he was a leader who could reflect the better side of our natures.' *(Owen Gleiberman, Entertainment Weekly)*

'A dear and funny movie.' *(Richard Schickel, Time)*

'Reitman proves his comic credentials yet again.' *(Empire)*

'Surely Reitman has earned the right to grow a little, and that he does with [this] very likeable adult comedy . . . a Capraesque fairy tale.' *(Kevin Lally, Film Journal)*

DAVID COPPERFIELD AAN CT: 8 AV: 8.79

1934 US 132 BW DRAMA

D George Cukor ☆
W Howard Estabrook Hugh Walpole from Charles Dickens's novel

W.C. Fields ☆ Lionel Barrymore ☆ Maureen O'Sullivan Madge Evans, Edna May Oliver ☆ Lewis Stone Frank Lawton ☆ Freddie Bartholomew ✔ Elizabeth Allen Roland Young ☆ Jessie Ralph ☆ Basil Rathbone ☆

Young man (Freddie Bartholomew/Frank Lawton) in Victorian England becomes an author.

Filleted version of a classic, semi-autobiographical novel. Fields's famous performance as the feckless Micawber riled a few critics, who might have been happier with the actor originally cast, Charles Laughton, who resigned from the part after two days of shooting (someone on set said of him that 'he looked as though he were about to molest the child'); but to modern eyes, Fields is the best thing in the film. Production values and acting ability are high throughout (though Cukor's direction lacks the poetic intensity of David Lean's *Great Expectations*); the only regret is that, since so much of Dickens has been left out, it amounts to little more than an introduction to the story.

ANTI:

'[It] made me curse the name of Dickens and consign all his works to Hades. It is an extravagant exploitation of the famous novelist . . . [repeating] without stint all his habits of exaggeration, caricature, and journalese dialogue. Superbly photographed, magnificently mounted . . . it enjoys a lot of brilliant acting and suffers from a continuous over-emphasis . . . Never have I been so repelled by goodness in a film or so unattracted by badness.' *(Sydney W.Carroll, Sunday Times)*

MIXED:

'Nothing in the world is going to make me praise or even approve of the Micawber of Mr W.C. Fields. Here I only see a brilliant low comedian dressed up in Micawber's toggery and exciting laughter by bringing to Micawber the qualities of Fields, the famous low comedian . . . Apart from Micawber, I think the picture is a good one, and on the understanding that no first-class novel can ever make a first-class picture!' *(James Agate, Tatler)*

PRO:

'It is one of the ironies of the film world that it should have been left to Hollywood to produce the most English of films. [It] is a triumph, it is well cast, the photography is superb and there is nothing lacking in stage-craft . . . It may not satisfy all lovers of Dickens . . . but there is no mutilation and the true spirit of the book has been skilfully maintained throughout . . . A film everyone should see.' *(MFB)*

'Very long . . . but never boring, and it has the great

and unusual merit, for an adaptation, that to enjoy it you need not have read the book.' *(Daily Telegraph)*

'Though half the characters are absent, the whole spectacle of the book, Micawber always excepted, is conveyed.' *(James Agee)*

'Perhaps the finest casting of all time.' *(Basil Wright, 1972)*

'One of the best ensembles ever . . . unusually good production which will win general approval . . . Now and then they (the adapters) linger too elaborately in a scene and they put the play completely off the track in introducing the mechanically melodramatic shipwreck scene, which might easily have been left undone.' *(Variety)*

'The most profoundly satisfying screen manipulation of a great novel that the camera has ever given us.' *(Andre Sennwald, New York Times, 1935)*

'The casting was brilliant, the sets immaculate and the movie's spirit truly Dickensian.' *(Daniel and Susan Cohen, 500 Great Films, 1987)*

DAWN OF THE DEAD CT: 6 AV: 7.17

(aka *Zombies; Zombies: Dawn of the Dead)*

1979 US 127 C HORROR

D George A. Romero ✔
W George A. Romero ✔

Scott Reininger Ken Foree Gaylen Ross David Emge

Flesh-eating zombies terrorize America.

George A. Romero's tongue-in-cheek rip-off of his biggest success, *The Night of the Living Dead*, is repetitive, crudely acted and self-consciously repulsive, but fun if approached in the right, ghoulish spirit. And it's one of the most vicious satires ever on American materialism.

ANTI:

'Romero's script is banal when not incoherent – those who haven't seen *Night of the Living Dead* may have some difficulty deciphering exactly what's going on at the outset.' *(Variety)*

'One by one, heads splatter and drip in bright, gory reds. You're supposed to need a strong stomach to sit through this one, but it's so stupefyingly obvious and repetitive that you begin to laugh with relief that you're not being emotionally affected; it's just a gross-out.' *(Pauline Kael)*

'Seemingly endless horror comic with pretensions to be an allegory of something or other; occasionally laughable, otherwise sickening or boring.' *(Halliwell)*

'A dreadful, embarrassing picture by a director who should know better.' *(Danny Peary)*

PRO:

'One of the most gut-gripping fantasies of apocalyptic horror in recent years . . . A picture which keeps the pupils popping.' *(Sunday Times)*

'Extremely gory, graphic and gruesome. A director's *tour de force* that overcomes amateur performances and a repetitive script and splendidly avoids sheer sensationalism by treating the whole bloody business as a horror comic.' *(Alan Frank)*

'The horror/suspense content is brilliant enough to satisfy the most demanding fan, and the film uses superb locations like a huge shopping mall to further its Bosch-like vision of a society consumed by its own appetites.' *(David Pirie, Time Out)*

'Brilliantly crafted, funny, droll and savagely merciless in its satiric view of the American consumer society . . . It is not depraved, although some reviewers have seen it that way. It is about depravity. If you can see beyond the immediate impact of Romero's imagery, if you can experience the film as being more than just its violent extremes, a most unsettling thought may occur to you: the zombies in *Dawn of the Dead* are not the ones who are depraved. They are only acting according to their natures, and, gore dripping from their jaws, are blameless. The depravity is in the behavior of the healthy survivors, and the true immorality comes as two bands of human survivors fight each other for the shopping center: now look who's fighting over the bones! But *Dawn* is even more complicated than that, because the survivors have courage, too, and a certain nobility at times, and a sense of humor, and loneliness and dread, and are not altogether unlike ourselves. A-ha.' *(Roger Ebert)*

DAY AT THE RACES, A CT: 7 AV: 7.31

1937 US 109 BW COMEDY

D Sam Wood
W Robert Pirosh George Seaton George Oppenheimer from Pirosh and Seaton's story

Groucho Marx ☆ Chico Marx Harpo Marx Allan Jones Maureen O'Sullivan Margaret Dumont Leonard Ceeley

A hypochondriac socialite (Margaret Dumont) employs a horse doctor (Groucho Marx) to take over a sanitarium.

MGM executive producer Irving Thalberg (who died during production) made the Marx Brothers acceptable to a wider audience by interspersing their comic routines with romantic interludes, and improving the production values of their films. While his policy worked reasonably well on *A Night at the Opera*, this follow-up grinds to a halt too often. Still, there are great lines ('Either this man is dead or my watch has stopped'), funny routines, and the racecourse climax works beautifully.

'Surefire film fun and up to the usual parity of the

madcap Marxes, even though a bit hectic in striving for jolly moments and bright quips.' *(Variety)*

'The money is fairly splashed about; the capitalists have recognized the Marx Brothers; ballet sequences, sentimental songs, amber fountains, young lovers. Easily the best film to be seen in London, but all the same I feel a nostalgia for the old, cheap rickety sets.' *(Graham Greene)*

'It's not up to *Opera* or *Duck Soup*, but it's better than just about everything else they did.' *(Pauline Kael)*

DAY FOR NIGHT AAW CT: 8 AV: 9.00

(aka *La Nuit Américaine)*

1973 France/Italy 116 C COMEDY/FOREIGN

D François Truffaut ☆ AAN
W François Truffaut Jean-Louis Richard Suzanne Schiffman ☆ AAN

Jacqueline Bisset Valentina Cortese ☆ AAN Jean-Pierre Aumont Jean-Pierre Léaud Dani Alexandra Stewart (cameo by author Graham Greene, as insurance representative Henry Graham)

A film crew in Nice has problems.

A witty comedy which exposes the mechanics of film-making without scorning the process which can create cinematic magic. Many clichés are lovingly satirized, and there's a terrific performance by Valentina Cortese as the temperamental, alcoholic grande dame. Although Truffaut deals mainly in caricatures, they are presented so realistically and affectionately that an audience can hardly help but like them. Though it's all very lightweight, this remains one of the best films about films, and a valuable corrective to the all-enveloping cynicism of Robert Altman's *The Player*.

'True some of the jokes are old . . . But . . . it seems new-mined.' *(Patrick Gibbs, Daily Telegraph)*

'Any reader who chooses not to see this tribute to the cinema should stop reading this column . . . Truffaut has finished another movie dedicated to the increasingly dubious proposition that there is still a vast audience out there waiting to be seduced by the cinema. Raped, yes; brutalized, yes; massaged, yes; but seduced? We shall have to see.' *(Andrew Sarris, Village Voice)*

'If you want a film that will send you away . . . actually liking the people in it and chuckling retrospectively over two hours of blissful entertainment, then don't miss [it] . . . A work of love and craftsmanship.' *(Alexander Walker, Evening Standard)*

'The style and the language match perfectly . . . A lovely film, not to be missed.' *(Christopher Hudson, Spectator)*

'I thought I'd had my last dram of enjoyment out of the Pagliacci theme and studio magic, and Truffaut shows there's life in the old whirl yet.' *(Stanley Kauffmann)*

'Made with such dazzling craftsmanship and confidence that you can never quite believe Truffaut's point that directing a movie is a danger-fraught experience.' *(Michael Billington, Illustrated London News)*

'At the start the action on the screen may seem fragmentary, perhaps a shade puzzling. But then a film, any film, is composed of fragments; and by the end the pieces of the jigsaw have slipped easily into place. It has been a pleasure; one is sorry it is over and I at any rate came out feeling positively good-tempered myself.' *(Dilys Powell)*

'A love song to the cinema, not the cinéaste, and even when Gerrand is seen sleeping alone in his monastic bed, there is no suggestion of any moral superiority over his cast or crew.' *(Jan Dawson, S & S)*

'Less about moviemaking than about a way of facing the conundrum of human existence . . . I don't want to freight [it] with too much drug-store philosophy. It's such a buoyant, charming film though I fear that its wisdom . . . will be overlooked.' *(Vincent Canby, New York Times)*

DAY IN THE COUNTRY, A: *see* UNE PARTIE DE CAMPAGNE.

DAY OF WRATH CT: 8 AV: 8.33

(aka *Vreden's Dag)*

1943 Denmark 105 BW DRAMA/HORROR/ FOREIGN

D Carl Dreyer ☆
W Carl Dreyer Poul Knudsen Mogens Skot-Hansen from Hans Wiers Jenssen's play *Anne Pedersdotter*

Thorkild Roose Anna Svierkier Lisbeth Movin Preben Lerdoff Rye

Pastor (Thorkild Roose) cursed by a dying witch (Anna Svierkier) discovers that his wife (Lisbeth Movin) has been committing adultery with a younger man (Preben Lerdoff Rye).

A bright and breezy comedy . . . Only joking. This is a sombre, harrowing and at times horrific melodrama – ostensibly about 17th-century superstition and nastiness, but really about man's infinite capacity for evil and cruelty. It can also, more parochially, be seen as an allegory about the German occupation of Denmark. Though extremely slow, the piece is powerful and beautifully photographed: one of the cinema's dark masterpieces. Not surprisingly, audiences have never flocked to see it.

ANTI:

'The tax of [Dreyer's] slow and ponderous tempo

upon the average person's time is a rather presumptuous imposition for any motion-picture artist to make. Maybe the cultists can take it. But is it justified? Is it art?' *(Bosley Crowther, New York Times)*

'Close-ups . . . [are] so insistent, so deliberated and elaborated they defeat their own aim . . . I can see no justification for [seeing the witch tipped into the flames]. It does not increase our sense of pity or horror, rather it diminishes it . . . At no point does one feel inclined to laugh: one does often yawn . . . [It] is taken at a pace which would make a funeral march seem like a polka.' *(Life and Letters)*

'Technically, Dreyer's direction is slow and of the silent period, totally lacking any of the dynamic camera qualities that made *Jeanne d'Arc* such a graphic achievement. The acting is stilted and frozen, and one cannot help feeling that there existed no sympathy and understanding between Dreyer and his players. There was not a vestige of warmth or hope in the film, only the dominant theme that evil will ultimately triumph . . . Without question, Carl Dreyer is a film artist of immense skill and, compared with much that runs through the projectors, *Day of Wrath* has qualities of honesty of effort and a certain dignity, but I cannot find myself alongside the many international critics who claim the film as a masterpiece of cinema; in fact, I can find little justification as to why the film was made at all.' *(Paul Rotha & Richard Griffith, The Film Till Now, 1949)*

PRO:

'I don't think there is a single excess in word or lighting or motion, or a single excessive stopping-down of any of these. Dreyer appears to know and to care more about faces than anything else; it seems to me a sound preference; and since he is served at worst by very good actors and faces and at best by wonderful ones, the best things in this film are the close-ups . . . a quiet masterpiece.' *(James Agee, Nation)*

'Artistic camerawork and clever use of shadow. Commendable performances, settings and costumes.' *(Today's Cinema)*

'A masterpiece. *Day of Wrath* will ravage you with its power of horror and pity and will haunt you with its beauty.' *(Richard Winnington)*

'Absorbing to watch . . . heartrending.' *(Jane Lockheart, The Rotarian)*

'Completely realistic and convincing . . . Altogether this film strikes me as being one of the best ever made . . . superb in all departments.' *(John McCarten, New Yorker)*

'Goes apparently against the stream of filmmaking. It moves slowly, but at times with an almost unbearable intensity . . . it specializes in delay, the reflected emotion, the action off-stage. Not the methods our eyes and ears have grown used to. Nor are we accustomed to the degrees of visual beauty with which Dreyer alone . . . enriches his subjects . . . It moves, but never shocks . . . By its truthfulness and nobility of style, [it] leaves impressions, not of pain but of beauty.' *(Statesman)*

'The dreadful moment in *Day of Wrath* is, not the second when the witch is pitched face down into the bonfire, but a passage in which the action is hidden from us. It is the scene of the witch's questioning and torture: and Dreyer, who uses camera movement with such sinister meaning, allows us to look, not at the fleshy shapeless body of the old woman, but at the faces of her questioners: the camera pans over the group of figures, over the faces with their expressions of interest, curiosity, cruel patience; and the spectator is torn between his own hateful curiosity and a natural humane disgust at its object.' *(Dilys Powell)*

DAY THE EARTH CAUGHT FIRE, THE

CT: 7 AV: 6.71

1962 GB 99 BW SF/DRAMA

D Val Guest ☆
W Wolf Mankowitz Val Guest ☆

Edward Judd Janet Munro Leo McKern
Michael Goodliffe Bernard Braden

The possible end of the world, as seen from a London newspaper office.

Tense Science Fiction about the dangers of nuclear testing. The characterization is thin, the special effects aren't special, and the message has dated. But, thanks to the fact that it is set largely in the Daily Express's former building in Fleet Street, it is one of the most convincing movies with a newspaper background; Val Guest's direction makes excellent use of London locations, and even the studio sets looks real. Guest is at his best: he keeps the suspense going, and handles the love story between Judd and Munro with intelligence and – for the time – daring. For a British heroine of the 50s, Munro is amazingly sexy. The script is talky, but much of it is good talk; and the characters behave realistically throughout. There's a delightful supporting performance from Leo McKern as rumpled reporter Maguire. Critics are divided over whether the 'open' ending is chilling or a cop-out, but the film received almost unanimously rave reviews on release, since when it has fallen into obscurity.

ANTI:

'Here is a film touching on the major issue of our time, which apparently asks to be taken seriously. Yet instead of presenting a point of view and a defined attitude towards their theme, the authors have tricked it out with all manner of exploitable devices and cheap Shaftesbury Avenue giggles. As in *On the Beach*, good intentions are not enough.' *(MFB)*

'The plot gets lost in sub-plots, and vice versa. Then

again, the plots are such that they should get lost.' *(Don Willis, 1972)*

MIXED:

'Always sensational and sometimes silly, but it reminds the viewer perhaps salutarily, that with a little nuclear encouragement this really could be a cock-eyed world.' *(Time)*

'Laudable tract and a fairly taut thriller . . . The tract is often more impressive than the terror.' *(New York Times)*

PRO:

'Guest's direction is brisk and makes good use of newsreel sequences and special effects.' *(Variety)*

'Its premise is . . . so close to prevalent and widespread fears and worries that it is not so much science fiction as it is a dramatic and imaginative extension of the news . . . The movie achieves its impact because it was made not merely to entertain, but out of a sense of outrage. It will be compared to *On The Beach*. Good as that one was, *The Day the Earth Caught Fire* is better.' *(Hollis Alpert, Sunday Review)*

'Bless the British anyway. They have succeeded in making the first witty movie about the end of the world. They have managed, further, to do it with taste . . . The story is spiced with some funny secondary characters, and laced with satire on the hypocrisies of governments.' *(Newsweek)*

'Perhaps the reason that *The Day the Earth Caught Fire* has not been acknowledged as the near-classic it is, lies in the fact that it was made for adults, not children – and those who were children in the 1950s and early 60s are those who now determine which films do have classic status.' *(Bill Warren, Keep Watching The Skies!)*

DAY THE EARTH STOOD STILL, THE

CT: 6 AV: 7.67

1951 US 92 BW SF/DRAMA

D Robert Wise ☆
W Edmund H. North based on Harry Bates's story

Michael Rennie ☆ Patricia Neal ☆ Hugh Marlowe ☆ Sam Jaffe Billy Gray Frances Bavier

Klaatu (Michael Rennie), an austere extra-terrestrial, arrives on earth with a warning for humanity.

A grandiose, melodramatic title for a small-scale, thoughtful picture. Critics have always thought highly of this picture, a landmark of its time; but the special effects now look primitive and some of the acting (especially Marlowe's) stiff. The screenplay has also dated, mainly because of its tendency to lecture. Despite its ponderous pacifism, obviously designed with an eye to the Cold War between America and the Soviet Union, it's a grown-up drama which can still interest and entertain. Classic ingredients include impressive performances by Michael Rennie and Patricia Neal – while Bernard Herrmann adds to the supense with one of his most effective scores.

ANTI:

'Interrupts its wonders to lecture us on the dangers of international aggression and the duties of the interplanetary police; and gaiety is restored only by the idiocies of dialogue. Patricia Neal and Michael Rennie accept their situation with gravity, and Robert Wise has directed the story for far more than it is worth.' *(Dilys Powell)*

MIXED:

'The yarn is told interestingly enough and imbued with sufficient scientifiction lures and suspense so that only seldom does its moralistic wordiness get in the way . . . Robert Wise's direction permits the action to drag at times, but is also responsible for the suspense.' *(Variety)*

'Still by far the most ambitious of the recent scientific fantasies . . . The determination to take the subject seriously reduces the pace and vigour of the film as an adventure story, but it never rises to the level of its own pretensions.' *(MFB)*

'Remains not only a SF cinema classic, but one of the few really intelligent science fiction films.' *(James Van Hise, Films Fantastique)*.

'The Washington backgrounds are well used, especially in night sequences where stark side-lighting gives a hard-edged intensity to the white flying saucer squatting in the park. Klaatu's recipe for peace – a robot police force unsusceptible to corruption or scientific tampering – sounds alarmingly Fascist but whatever its political pedigree, *The Day the Earth Stood Still* remains one of the most entertaining excursions into SF attempted by Hollywood.' *(John Baxter, Science Fiction in the Cinema, 1970)*

PRO:

'Thoughtful rather than horrifying, with subtle antifascist hints scattered throughout.' *(Scheuer)*

'A very good movie, briskly paced, entertaining, a great deal of fun. In it, Robert Wise showed himself at his peak of ability. Scenes have vitality and movement. The cutting is extremely sharp. Except for Marlowe's, the performances are subtle and detailed. The point of each scene is admirably transmitted. The structure of the film is clean and uncluttered, and is eminently satisfactory for a thriller. (The movie was modeled on heroic-spy stories.) In its visual style, it lies between the mock documentaries and the films noir of its period.' *(Bill Warren, Keep Watching The Skies!)*

DAYBREAK

CT: 6 AV: 8.36

(aka *Le Jour se Lève)*

1939 France 95 BW DRAMA/FOREIGN

D Marcel Carné ☆
W Jacques Viot Jacques Prévert ☆

Jean Gabin ☆ Jules Berry Arletty
Jacqueline Laurent

A murderer (Jean Gabin), surrounded by the police after his crime of passion, has a series of flashbacks.

Highly acclaimed as an example of 'poetic realism', this film is much more poetic than realistic. Everything in it combines to create a mood of depression and despair and, although it contains Gabin's finest performance, it's so relentlessly dour and talky that it's hard to watch. But it caught the mood of its time: Paris was occupied and many French people must have felt like the hero – surrounded, with nowhere to turn. Whether the film's intentions were political or not, the Vichy government banned it.

MIXED:

'Brilliantly demonstrates the value in the cinema of narrative construction, shape, unity . . . Carné has not quite overcome the dangers in the cinema of long passages of dialogue, and there are scenes of entreaty and argument which remain static and therefore a shade tedious. Again, here and there, the characters would be the more effective for a trifle more explanation.' *(Dilys Powell)*

'Now, it seems hollow but with its lust and despair – or, if you like, love and desperation – the quintessential French movie of the time.' *(Shipman)*

'Not up to *Grande Illusion* or *La Kermesse Héroique, Daybreak* . . . is a worthy swansong. It has the same distinguishable Gallic qualities of artistic shrewdness and spiritual disenchantment that make most Hollywood pictures by comparison seem, for better or for worse, not quite grown up.' *(Time)*

PRO:

'Will make the more serious lovers of things cinematic bemoan the fact that the French film industry . . . is no more. A somber quiet study of murder . . . Jean Gabin adds another unforgettable portrait to his already worthy gallery.' *(Herb Sterne)*

'Superb direction, the film keeps its painful grip to the very last shot.' *(Campbell Dixon, Daily Telegraph)*

'The man walks about his room, moves a few things, lies on his bed, looks out of the window, chain-smokes . . . and one is genuinely interested in him all the time (remembering afterwards that there exist directors who contrive to be boring even when they use fifteen characters in a motor car chase crackling with revolver shots).' *(Richard Winnington)*

'Brilliant character study . . . a tragedy of stark passion, simple but extremely gripping . . . has all the hallmarks of the finest French technical qualities as well as unimpeachable cast. A really brilliant picture . . . Jean Gabin is excellent.' *(Kinematograph Weekly, 1944)*

'Beautifully made, sensitively acted.' *(Paul Rotha & Richard Griffith, The Film Till Now, 1949)*

'The last of Marcel Carné's prewar masterpieces, this melancholy film presented Jean Gabin with perhaps the finest role of his career . . . The despair and pessimism so prevalent in the French cinema of the 1930's was never more in evidence than in this bleak story of human tragedy.' *(R.A.E. Pickard, Dictionary of 1000 Best Films, 1971)*

'Marks a peak in that fruitful collaboration between Carné . . . and frequent screenwriter Jacques Prévert.' *(Allan Hunter & Kenny Mathieson, Movie Classics, 1992)*

DAYS OF HEAVEN

CT: 4 AV: 7.47

1978 US 95 C DRAMA

D Terrence Malick ☆
W Terrence Malick

Richard Gere Brooke Adams Sam Shepard
Linda Manz Bob Wilke Jackie Shultis
Stuart Margolin Timothy Scott Gene Bell
Doug Kershaw

Three migrants (Richard Gere, Brooke Adams, Linda Manz) go to work on a farm belonging to a farmer (Sam Shepard) with only a year to live. Adams marries him for his money.

Audiences stayed away from this beautiful, critically acclaimed film, Malick's follow-up to *Badlands* – and no wonder. Even Nestor Almendros's cinematography (which rightly won an Oscar) can't disguise the fact that the screenplay is sordid, depressing and leaves too many questions unanswered (why, for example, does Brooke Adams pretend to be Richard Gere's sister?). The characters are undeveloped, and the voice-over is irritating. Ennio Morricone's score, the sound and costume design were all Oscar-nominated.

PRO:

'To say the film is visually beautiful is not enough. The point is that in Terrence Malick's work the images are strictly linked to the nature of the subject and the development of its action. Obviously the opening black-and-white portraits and groups are necessary to the narrative. But the harvesting scenes – the movement of the figures, the plumes of dark smoke from the harvesting machine, the billowing plain – have a different significance. Their lovely calm intensifies the feeling of an interlude in paradise . . . *Days of Heaven* is superbly directed and acted; see it for a second time and its hold is still more relentless. Nevertheless it is a disquieting film. It may deal with a period over half a century ago; as it ends the First World War is with us. But it is evidence of the sentiments of today. It presents the restlessness, the anchorless mood of a world which has lost its book of rules.' *(Dilys Powell)*

'It's serious, yes, very solemn, but not depressing.' *(Roger Ebert)*

'Dramatically moving and technically breathtaking . . . filled with some offbeat touches, literary references and beautifully developed characters.' *(Variety)*

MIXED:

'As Bill, Richard Gere is out of place in his fancy 1970s haircut, trim clothes, actorish speech, and less than earthy performance . . . The closing sequences lapse into contrivance and utter inscrutability. Nevertheless, the visual splendor remains throughout.' *(John Simon)*

ANTI:

'When the director is weak, as Malick is here, he tends to lean more and more heavily on the good cinematographer's ability, and so swamps the film in pretty pictures. *Days of Heaven* is swamped . . . The story soon becomes background for the scenery.' *(Stanley Kauffmann)*

'The film is an empty Christmas tree: you can hang all your dumb metaphors on it.' *(Pauline Kael)*

'This is art for art's sake, too slow and studied . . . When the film finally becomes lively and exciting, Malick spoils it with a thoroughly depressing ending. No wonder his films don't make money.' *(Danny Peary)*

'Perhaps the purest example of the modernist aesthetic applied to film to come out of the New Hollywood era thus far. Malick at least had the courage of his (to my mind) misguided convictions: his near total indifference to the central realist task of creating meaning . . . Malick's modernism, interesting enough, manifests itself as a commitment to the aesthetic of the silent film: *Days of Heaven* has very little dialogue and features considerable emphasis on facial expressions, pantomimic gestures, sound effects, still-life shots of inanimate objects, and artfully composed tableaux. Malick . . . asserts his artistic presence but also distances audiences from involvement in his film.' *(James Bernardoni, The New Hollywood, 1991)*

DAYS OF WINE AND ROSES CT: 6 AV: 7.75

1962 US 117 BW DRAMA

D Blake Edwards ☆
W J.P. Miller from his own television play

Jack Lemmon ☆ AAN Lee Remick ☆ AAN
Charles Bickford ☆ Jack Klugman Alan Hewitt
Debbie Megowan Jack Albertson

PR man (Jack Lemmon) and wife (Lee Remick) turn to drink: one gets over it, the other doesn't.

Adapted from a TV play, this is a marvellously acted film which preaches the dangers of alcoholism. It's quite unlike any other movie directed by Blake Edwards, and is usually regarded as his best; however, he is more at ease with the humorous first half than he is with the second, which is saved only by the performances from descending into didactic melodrama. The title song (music by Henry Mancini, lyrics by Johnny Mercer) won an Oscar.

'Lemmon gives a dynamic and chilling performance. Scenes of his collapse, particularly in the violent ward, are brutally realistic and terrifying. Remick, too, is effective.' *(Variety)*

'The film's distinction is Jack Lemmon's outstanding performance as the alcoholic husband. A grim and graphic depiction of the tragedy of drink, the movie is for those who can take it straight.' *(Judith Crist)*

'Serious enough about its subject. The trouble for me is that I find the film less convincing in its serious than in its gay passages.' *(Dilys Powell)*

'You almost forget it's a Blake Edwards picture.' *(Trevor Johnston, Time Out)*

DEAD AGAIN CT: 4 AV: 5.50

1991 US 101 C THRILLER

D Kenneth Branagh ✗
W Scott Frank ✗

Kenneth Branagh ● Andy Garcia Derek Jacobi
Hanna Schygulla Emma Thompson ●
Robin Williams

A cynical, hard-bitten private detective (Kenneth Branagh, looking like a prep-school choirboy) falls for a beautiful amnesiac (Emma Thompson, equally grievously miscast). She has terrifying dreams of an actress who looks like Emma Thompson in one of Rita Hayworth's old wigs, being attacked by a scissors-wielding Kenneth Branagh, looking like Olivier in a silly beard. Gradually, with the help of a dodgy hypnotist (Derek Jacobi) and an even dodgier ex-shrink (Robin Williams), they discover they are reincarnations of a German composer (that's Branagh with beard) and his murdered wife (Thompson plus wig), who died in the 40s.

Stylish but preposterous Kenneth Branagh thriller, ludicrously overpraised by some critics – especially in America. It may look like a Hitchcock classic (*Spellbound*, to be precise) but suffers from disastrously miscast leads and a plot which makes no sense and cheats the audience. Unbelievably, the film-makers never bother to tell us why the beautiful amnesiac became traumatized. Nor does the German composer have any reason for acting so passively after his wife's death. The true murderer's identity may surprise some members of the audience, but only because it leaves him/her with no conceivable motive for acting the way he/she does for most of the film.

Branagh's decision to miscast himself and his real-life wife not once but twice renders the story even more nonsensical. For a start, it is incredible that no one notices the extraordinary resemblance between the modern couple and their historical predecessors: the physical similarity between the two couples makes the murderer's behaviour doubly incomprehensible. The casting looks like the vanity of an old-fashioned actor-manager, and transforms the film from being merely stupid and poorly made, into a colossally arrogant act of folly.

PRO:

'Branagh brings the same zest and bravura style to this actor's romp of a mystery-thriller as he did to *Henry V*.' *(Variety)*

'A big, convoluted, entertainingly dizzy romantic mystery melodrama. It is also another coup de cinema for Mr Branagh . . . Though . . . very much the work of a contemporary filmmaker, it's also a luxuriant evocation of the sort of overripe melodramas that Warner Brothers turned out forty years ago . . . Yet [it] doesn't reinvent a particular picture . . . Rather it recalls the tone of certain kinds of studio films of the 1940s and 50s, and the manner in which we used to respond to them . . . Mr Branagh doesn't exactly transform the absurdity of the story into great art . . . He recognizes them without condescension, turning out a most enjoyable and knowing homage . . . [It's] a lot of fun.' *(Vincent Canby, New York Times)*

'Hitchcockian is a cliché bandied about for everything from the pathological noodling of Brian De Palma to cheery thrillers like *Pacific Heights*. To his credit Branagh knows he is no Hitchcock . . . In fact, if anything, [he's] far too much of a chipper romantic. Yet what [he] lacks in neurotic intensity, he more than makes up for in sheer skill.' *(Mahahla Dargis, Village Voice)*

'A clever tale which possesses more than a hint of Hitchcock suspense . . . Dead good.' *(Karen Hockney, Sun)*

'A marvellous piece of pure cinema.' *(Martin & Porter)*

'A grandly entertaining thriller, with plenty of surprising twists.' *(Scheuer)*

'Romance with all the stops out . . . I am a particular pushover for movies like this, movies that could go on the same list with *Rebecca, Wuthering Heights* and *Vertigo*.' *(Roger Ebert)*

'Complex, intriguing.' *(Barry Norman)*

MIXED:

'The peculiar thing about [the film] is that it's not just the characters who feel they've seen everything before – so does the audience. Branagh has borrowed, quoted, and downright copied from the film noir oeuvre with varying degrees of subtlety . . . Each shot bears a reference – Hitchcock mainly – to traces of a former life . . . And though this is a classy pastiche of the genre . . . is it really anything more substantial than reconstituted film noir product?' *(Clare Bayley, What's On in London)*

ANTI:

'Sloppily constructed and cut, riddled with clichés and cant.' *(Geoff Andrew, Time Out)*

'Terrible . . . ghastly . . . dreadful.' *(Steven Keane, City Limits)*

'This ironic and openly melodramatic bow to Hitchcock, Welles and the film noir of old is too self-conscious by half and hasn't the cinematic know-how to get away with it.' *(Derek Malcolm, Guardian)*

'Branagh doesn't begin to fill the space he has claimed for himself in his dual role . . . It's a sad comment . . . that the film is stolen not by an actor but by a set.' *(Adam Mars-Jones, Independent)*

'Even if regarded as a charade, [the film] remains more risible than amusing.' *(Geoff Brown, S & S)*

DEAD CALM CT: 8 AV: 6.67

1988 Australia 96 C THRILLER/HORROR

D Phillip Noyce ✓
W Terry Hayes ✓

Nicole Kidman ✓ Sam Neill ✓ Billy Zane ✓

A sailing husband and wife (Sam Neill and Nicole Kidman), recovering from the death of their young son in a motor accident, have the bad luck to encounter a mysterious, drifting schooner carrying handsome Hughie (Billy Zane).

Although the plot never rises above the formulaic and there's a silly false ending, this is a superbly directed thriller with a trio of memorable performances and many scary moments. Orson Welles (who was trying to make this film but shelved it when his leading actor, Laurence Harvey, died) couldn't have done better. The film is mostly kept afloat by Miss Kidman, who makes her transition from weaker vessel to self-reliant shipmate very nearly believable. It's one of the few successful horror thrillers – another notable example being *The Silence of the Lambs* – to have a feminist subtext.

'Handsomely produced, inventively directed.' *(Variety)*

'Welles might have done more to play up the Pandora's Box of plot twists that follow; but the story keeps us guessing and gasping, and Dean Semler's photography is knockout.' *(Harlan Kennedy, Film Yearbook)*

'Time and again in the movie, the story would be over if someone – anyone – simply pulled the trigger. There is a moment when the wife temporarily has the upper hand against this madman who had assaulted and beaten her and left her husband to drown, and what does she do? She ties him up! And with the knot in front, too – where he can get at it. Later in the film, after he appears to be dead, he reappears, of course, and has to be fought a second time. And yet *Dead Calm* generates genuine tension because the story is so simple and the performances are so straightforward. This is not a gimmick film (unless you count the husband's method of escaping from the sinking ship), and Nicole Kidman and Billy Zane do generate real, palpable hatred in their scenes together.' *(Roger Ebert)*

DEAD END AAN CT: 5 AV: 7.58

1937 US 92 BW DRAMA/SOCIAL

D William Wyler ☆
W Lillian Hellman from Sidney Kingsley's play

Joel McCrea Sylvia Sidney Humphrey Bogart ☆ Wendy Barrie Claire Trevor AAN Allen Jenkins Marjorie Main ☆ James Burke Ward Bond The Dead End Kids (in their first film appearance)

On New York's east side, rich and poor live side by side.

Preachy social drama of the kind which dates rapidly – especially if it is as theatrical and setbound as this. However, Gregg Toland's Oscar-nominated cinematography is remarkable within those limitations; Bogart's performance is one of his best as a bad guy; and the Dead End Kids caught the imagination of audiences all over the world.

MIXED:

'*Dead End* was a serious and successful play on Broadway. It is equally serious and successful as a film. It is beautifully directed by William Wyler, who is not only one of the great directors, but one of the rare two or three whose sense of drama is as adult as his skill. It is profuse in human sympathy as it dives down into the tenements of East Side New York and discovers the teemingtragedy of the poor. Yet, and in spite of watching the film with eagerness and respect, I dislike it intensely and it won't do at all. It is aquarium stuff. It looks at people distantly, like fish, and its sympathy is cold with distance. It lacks gusto.' *(John Grierson, World Film News)*

'Tense and accurate transcription, but sordid and depressing.' *(Variety)*

PRO:

'*Dead End* stands as a beautiful document of a nearly vanished consciousness in America. The realism of its tenements was self-conscious, but the concern in the film with social issues was genuine.' *(Andrew Bergman, 1971)*

ANTI:

'A muscle-bound Goldwyn production with an inflated reputation . . . The Dead End Kids are about as menacingly streetwise as Shirley Temple in her naughtier moods . . . The basic mawkishness . . . keeps sticking in the craw.' *(Tom Milne, Time Out)*

DEAD OF NIGHT CT: 8 AV: 8.18

1945 GB 104 BW HORROR

D Basil Dearden Alberto Cavalcanti ☆ Robert Hamer ☆ Charles Crichton
W John V. Barnes Angus Macphail T.E.B. Clarke

Mervyn Johns ☆ Michael Redgrave ☆ Roland Culver ☆ Mary Merrall Judy Kelly Anthony Baird Sally Ann Howes ☆ Frederick Valk ☆ Googie Withers ☆ Ralph Michael Naunton Wayne Basil Radford Esmé Percy Miles Malleson Hartley Power Elizabeth Welch

An architect (Mervyn Johns) finds that a country house is inhabited by people from his nightmares.

Still the most highly regarded of all portmanteau horror films, and one which used some of the leading talents at Michael Balcon's Ealing Studios. Parts of it are very disappointing, and the comic relief has dated, but the best parts – notably the mirror sketch directed by Robert Hamer, and the story directed by Alberto Cavalcanti, in which ventriloquist Michael Redgrave is taken over by his own dummy – are among the most frightening sequences ever filmed. The final pay-off is a classic.

'Redgrave turns in a masterful piece of acting.' *(Variety)*

'A perfect piece of filmcraft, as thrilling and original as anything turned out by Hollywood.' *(Sunday Express)*

'Mr Balcon has made an excellent picture, one that in acting, direction and technique often reaches brilliance.' *(Sunday Pictorial)*

'Made with exceptional skill and wit; as intelligent light entertainment it could not be better, and its famous last shot, whether one has foreseen it or not, is one of the most successful blends of laughter, terror and outrage that I can remember.' *(James Agee, Nation)*

'A classic supernatural masterpiece . . . The Ventriloquist's Dummy is a genuinely terrifying experience, superbly directed and with a stunning performance by Redgrave as the demented ventriloquist.' *(Alan Frank)*

'Michael Redgrave's overpowering performance – a small work of art – lifts this five part English production above the elegant, sophisticated entertainment it aspired to be.' *(Pauline Kael)*

DEAD RINGERS CT:5 AV: 5.40

1988 Canada 115 HORROR

D David Cronenberg
W David Cronenberg Norman Snider from Barry Wood's book Twins

Jeremy Irons ☆ Genevieve Bujold
Heidi von Palleske Barbara Gordon
Shirley Douglas Stephen Lack Nick Nicholas
Lynne Cormack

Twin gynaecologists (Jeremy Irons) fall out over a woman (Genevieve Bujold).

Downbeat to the point of dullness, Cronenberg's film has a sinister atmosphere like no other film. Jeremy Irons's amazing double performance, though unrecognized at the Oscars, was widely credited with his winning of the Best Actor award for *Reversal of Fortune* (1990).

'The point about the film to me is that the twins need each other and they also need to establish their own identities. And these two things become confused.' *(David Cronenberg)*

ANTI:

'Imagistically reticent, even dull. And a fascinating subtext . . . never pushes through the unambitious teleplay visuals.' *(Nigel Andrews, Financial Times)*

'Downbeat and grisly.' *(Halliwell)*

MIXED:

'Powerfully made, although it fell apart in the third act.' *(Franc Roddam, Film Yearbook)*

'It's almost too rich in ideas for its own good: the sense of concentration and proportion isn't there. But it remains an astonishing, magnetic, devastating piece of work . . . the most romantic film of the year.' *(Dave Kehr, Chicago Tribune)*

PRO:

'Irons's delicately nuanced interactions with himself are even more of an acting *tour de force* than Bob Hoskins' manic intimacies with Roger Rabbit. He plays the twins not as diametrical opposites but as complementary partial personalities . . . [Some] will mistake the critique of misogyny for the thing itself.' *(Amy Taubin, Village Voice)*

'Clever, bright as a newly sterilised surgical instrument.' *(Derek Malcolm, Guardian)*

'The least bloody of all [Cronenberg's] movies, ironically and yet it is also his darkest and strangest.' *(Tom Hutchinson, Hampstead and Highgate Express)*

'Brilliant . . . I guarantee . . . that most women in the audience will sit with their legs tightly crossed throughout.' *(Suzanne Moore, New Statesman)*

'This chilling masterpiece is perhaps the greatest contemporary example of sustained intellectual dread . . . A powerful bleak vision.' *(Kim Newman, S & S, 1993)*

'Its disturbing impact derives from a laying bare of male fantasies in such a way that masculinity itself is revealed as fragile, unstable, even impossible.' *(Pam Cook, MFB)*

DEAD, THE CT: 6 AV: 7.38

1987 GB 83 C DRAMA

D John Huston ☆
W Tony Huston ☆ AAN from James Joyce's short story in *Dubliners*

Anjelica Huston ☆ Donal McCann ☆
Rachael Dowling Cathleen Delany Dan O'Herlihy
Helena Carroll Donal Donnelly

In 1904 Dublin, two sisters (Helena Carroll, Cathleen Delany) throw a dinner party for friends and relatives, including their favourite nephew (Donal McCann) and his wife (Anjelica Huston).

John Huston's final film is a family affair. His son Tony's screenplay is very faithful to the spirit of James Joyce's story, and the film captures its essence to a remarkable degree. Huston Senior reminds us of his talent for set-pieces in a marvellously choreographed party scene, but the central strength of the picture lies in the husband-wife relationship between Donal McCann and John's daughter Anjelica, whose monologue about a remembered love is very moving. Dorothy Jeakins was Oscar-nominated for her costume designs. It was acclaimed critically, though audiences did not respond so enthusiastically; the film is rather slow, sombre and lacking in story.

'A delicate coda in a minor key to an illustrious 46-year career.' *(Daily Variety)*

'A small masterpiece.' *(Brian Case, Time Out)*

'A great, warm, funny movie . . . Huston never before blended his actors so intuitively, so musically . . . suggests the Chekhov production of your dreams, or maybe one of Satyajit Ray's triumphs.' *(Pauline Kael)*

DEAD POETS SOCIETY AAN CT: 7 AV: 6.58

1989 US 129 C DRAMA

D Peter Weir ✔ AAN
W Tom Schulman ☆ AAW

Robin Williams ✔ AAN Robert Sean Leonard ✔
Ethan Hawke ✔ Josh Charles Gale Hansen

An eccentric but inspirational teacher of English (Robin Williams) at a conventional private school in Vermont, during the Eisenhower years, broadens his pupils' horizons with comic and tragic consequences, including the death of a star pupil.

Some critics found Peter Weir's film over-sentimental; one or two found it dangerously subversive. I thought it had charm, and was moved by its good-hearted liberalism. Refreshingly, the film avoids the Hollywood trap of the cop-out happy ending. It dares to be dark.

Tom Schulman's Oscar-winning screenplay paints the forces of reaction in melodramatic black and white, but succeeds in championing literature without seeming too pious. Williams is in his most restrained mode, and his self-discipline helps to elicit totally convincing performances from the then unknown teenagers, including Robert Sean Leonard and Ethan Hawke, playing his followers.

But the single most impressive aspect of Weir's film is the way it combines the intimate with the grand. Like David Lean, Weir has an eye for detailed human behaviour and a love of the larger landscape. His theme is timely, individualistic and universal: education should prepare children not just for a career, but for life.

ANTI:

'How callow, how sentimental, this film is about its subject! . . . In this age of sex, drugs, rock-and-roll, and other forms of instant gratification, 'seize the day' is among the last messages teenagers need to hear – which may be why *Dead Poets Society* is set not in an inner-city high school in 1989 (where a John Keating would merely be contributing to the reigning chaos) but in a stuffy late-fifties prep school, a numbingly reactionary environment in which teaching methods like Keating's can actually be made to seem plausible and sympathetic.' *(Bruce Bawer, American Spectator)*

'Don't be fooled, this is a dog of the first water. For a start, it really does believe that a group of rich teenagers standing on desks are making a significant statement against the dehumanizing process, and it claims to be a serious film while resorting to annoyingly hackneyed and manipulative plot-devices to beef up its slender storyline, uninvolving script and overwhelming pomposity . . . Its whole idea of high culture, rebellion and dehumanisation is essentially obvious, banal, patronising and trite . . . The worst kind of bad film, in that it gets treated seriously and respectfully while it force-feeds rubbish into your head. I'm giving it an 'F', and so will history.' *(Kim Newman, Film Yearbook)*

'Anomalous – a prestige picture. It's on the side of youth, rebellion, poetry, passion. And, like Weir's *Gallipoli*, it has a gold ribbon attached to it. But the film's perception of reality is the black and white of pulp fiction (without the visceral excitement). The picture doesn't rise to the level of tragedy, because it's unwilling to give us an antagonist who isn't hopelessly rigid. (Neil Perry gets all A's, so his father can't even have a rational objection to his extracurricular activities.) There's no other side to anything in this movie – Weir, it appears, is more interested in the elegiac than in the dramatic.' *(Pauline Kael)*

PRO:

'Story sings whenever Williams is onscreen. Screen belongs just as often to Leonard, who as Neil has a quality of darting confidence mixed with hesitancy. Hawke, as the painfully shy Todd, gives a haunting performance.' *(Variety)*

'Weir infuses the film with his customary mysticism, but, more importantly, draws sensitive performances from his largely inexperienced cast.' *(Colette Maude, Time Out)*

MIXED:

'Melodramatic but effective.' *(Scheuer)*

'Yes, it's sentimental. Yes, the story's a little obvious. But it's one of those rare, life-enhancing films that make you feel so much better about things, even if you can't later explain just why.' *(Rose)*

DEADLY THREE, THE: *see* ENTER THE DRAGON.

DEATH IN BRUNSWICK CT: 8 AV: 7.00

1990 Australia 109 C COMEDY

D John Ruane ✔
W John Ruane ✔

Sam Neill ✔ Zoe Carides John Clarke ✔
Yvonne Lawley ✔ Nico Lathouris
Nicholas Papademetriou Boris Brkic
Deborah Kennedy Doris Younane

Within a few days, a middle-aged mother's boy (Sam Neill) meets the slut of his dreams (Zoe Carides), kills a workmate, causes another man to be beheaded by Turks, and turns his mother into a vegetable.

Sam Neill showed surprising comic talent in John Ruane's amusingly black, anarchic comedy from Australia. I laughed uproariously. A huge hit in Australia but virtually ignored elsewhere, it is destined to be a cult classic.

'An unusual, intelligent black comedy. Some will find the film outrageous, but word-of-mouth should give the pic legs on the international art-house circuit.' *(Variety)*

'Likeably offbeat and often surprisingly dark comedy thriller, set amid a seldom acknowledged working class ethnic community.' *(Nigel Floyd, Time Out)*

'Violent, mocking, but often very funny.' *(Elliot)*

DEATH IN VENICE CT: 5 AV: 6.42

(aka *Morte a Venezia*)

1971 Italy/France 127 C DRAMA

D Luchino Visconti ✘
W Luchino Visconti Nicola Bandolucco from Thomas Mann's novella

Dirk Bogarde ☆ Björn Andresen Silvana Mangano Marisa Berensen Mark Burns

Ageing composer (Dirk Bogarde) fancies 14-year-old boy (Björn Andresen).

Dirk Bogarde gives one of his subtlest performances as a thinly disguised Mahler, in Visconti's gorgeous-looking film of Thomas Mann's novella. Homosexual obsession has seldom been more lovingly portrayed, nor Venice more beautifully photographed; but Visconti sinks faster than the city, when attempting to communicate the ideas in Mann's story. Piero Tosi's costume design was Oscar-nominated, and the film attracted rave reviews – although critical opinion has noticeably cooled over the years.

PRO:

'The film is for me preferable to the novella. In the past quarter of a century there have been films potentially more influential (not, of course, necessarily for good). I can think of none which has been more truly a work of art.' *(Dilys Powell)*

'The most deeply-felt of all Visconti's films.' *(Nina Hibbin, Morning Star)*

'To call it a story of homosexual attachment . . . is to lay too heavy a contemporary hand on its hidden chords . . . Bogarde makes every moment transmit its telepathic signal. His playing is minute and masterly.' *(Alexander Walker, Evening Standard)*

'The reconstruction of turn-of-the-century Venice . . . could hardly have been in more appropriate hands, and Visconti has done full justice to his task.' *(Philip Strick, S & S)*

'A major Visconti work, beyond doubt . . . The boy emerges as the very image of Mann's devising . . . His stillness . . . is the interior quiet of one who has been endowed with a secret mission, beyond his own comprehension. How Visconti managed it, by what Italian genius he drew from this kid's face and bearing so beautiful and sinister an implication is beyond credence.' *(Gordon Gow, F & F)*

'Visconti has opened up the relationship between the beautiful Polish boy . . . and the elderly musician in this exquisite version of Mann's novella, and perhaps the purity is partly gone . . . Bogarde is superb.' *(NFT Bulletin, 1974)*

'Just a love story or a portrait of an artist, his life and the quest for beauty and perfection?' *(Winnert)*

MIXED:

'Maybe a story as elusive as *Death in Venice* simply can't be filmed. Visconti has made a brave attempt, always sensitive to the original; but it's finally not quite the same thing.' *(David Wilson, MFB)*

'Meticulous if curiously de-energized . . . almost inanimate.' *(Arthur Knight, The Liveliest Art, 1978)*

'Lavish but quite vacuous.' *(Elliot)*

'Visually absorbing but lifeless.' *(Martin & Porter)*

'Camp and miscalculated from start to finish . . . a prime contender for the title Most Overrated Film Of All Time.' *(Time Out, 1985)*

'Dire . . . hollow, camped-up . . . Bogarde is more than a little mannered . . . Everything is slowed down to a funereal (some might claim magisterial) pace. Mann's metaphysical musings on art and beauty are jettisoned in favour of pathetic scenes of runny mascara, and the whole thing is so overblown as to become entirely risible.' *(Geoff Andrew, Time Out)*

DEATH OF A SALESMAN CT: 6 AV: 7.56

1951 US 112 BW DRAMA

D Laslo Benedek
W Stanley Roberts from Arthur Miller's play

Fredric March ✗ AAN Kevin McCarthy ☆ AAN Cameron Mitchell Mildred Dunnock ☆ AAN Howard Smith Royal Beal Jesse White

A salesman (Fredric March) loses his faith in the American Dream and himself.

Arthur Miller's play is transferred to celluloid from a Broadway production. March's performance will strike most modern viewers as theatrical – which is ironic, since he was the one movie star imported for the screen version. Even so, a fine ensemble cast ensures a powerful emotional experience. Franz Planer's cinematography and Alex North's music were both Oscar-nominated.

'Its time shifts with light, which were poetic in the theatre, seemed shabby in a medium that can dissolve time and space so easily.' *(Stanley Kauffmann)*

'Fredric March, in the part created on the New York stage by Lee J. Cobb, gives perhaps the greatest performance of his career.' *(Variety)*

'Fredric March gives an over-enthusiastic portrayal of disintegration, but the others are very fine.' *(Shipman)*

DEATH SHIP CT: 1 AV: 1.75

1980 Canada/GB 91 C HORROR

D Alvin Rakoff ●
W John Robins ●

George Kennedy Richard Crenna Nick Mancuso Sally Ann Howes Kate Reid, Victoria Burgoyne Jennifer McKinney Danny Higham Saul Rubineck

A bloodthirsty ship kills off its passengers.

The ultimate example of a lamebrain horror film where plot logic soon flies out of the window, and all the potential victims do their best to place themselves in maximum jeopardy for our sadistic enjoyment. Malevolent machinery can be frightening, as in Spielberg's *Duel* (1971), but here it's delightfully ridiculous.

'An hour and a half of short cuts and cut corners, of quick solutions made by fast buck artists . . . [It's] a shoddy film that mistakes mild repulsiveness for genuine horror, a twinge of disgust for the grimace of fear . . . Excrement is [its] reigning metaphor.' *(John Azzopardi, Cinefantastique)*

'A silly idea is carried to extremes and the result is laughable instead of exciting or scary.' *(Alan Frank)*

'The most horrifying aspect is the fact that the film was ever made.' *(Hollywood Reporter)*

'Bottom of the barrel. It should be bottom of the sea.' *(Winnert)*

DEATH WISH CT: 6 AV: 5.60

1974 US 94 C THRILLER/ACTION

D Michael Winner
W Wendell Mayes based on Brian Garfield's novel

Charles Bronson Hope Lange Vincent Gardenia Steven Keats William Redfield Stuart Maragolin

Vigilante (Charles Bronson) whose family is wrecked by a mugging 'cleans up' New York.

Thematically a companion-piece to *Dirty Harry* and *Taxi Driver*, this was very controversial on release, for the way it placed itself firmly on the side of the murderous anti-hero. Violent and simplistic it may be; but it communicates a sense of New York as a jungle and is brutally effective at what it sets out to do. Michael Winner's most competent film.

ANTI:

'Poisonous incitement to do-it-yourself law enforcement is the vulgar exploitation hook on which *Death Wish* is awkwardly hung.' *(Variety)*

'Objectionable vigilante trash from the objectionable Winner.' *(Geoff Andrew, Time Out)*

'Colorfully presented, but a violent, unpleasant movie.' *(Scheuer)*

'A one-man springclean with a sub-automatic machine gun. The savages are, inevitably, black – imagine *Birth of a Nation* with Bronx accents. These films are spectacularly successful; the audience stands up and cheers when Bronson, driven berserk beyond belief, blows another sewer-rat away. Though I know they are cheering the killing of a black rather than the killing of a killer.' *(Julie Burchill, Girls on Film)*

MIXED:

'A quasifascist advertisement for urban vigilantes, done up as a slick and exciting action movie; we like it even while we're turned off by the message.' *(Roger Ebert)*

'This urban version of *Walking Tall* transcends its violence to satisfy every base instinct that "we liberals" are heir to.' *(Judith Crist)*

'The script is tolerable, and the director, Michael Winner, is a fairly glib imitator of his betters.' *(Stanley Kauffmann)*

'Nice, simplistic, Nixonian stuff. The thing that annoyed the [New York] liberals was that the popular reaction in the film was translated into reality.' *(John Torode, Guardian)*

'Chilling but irresistible; a bastardization of the Brian Garfield novel, in which vigilantism as a deterrent to crime is not a solution but another problem.' *(Maltin)*

PRO:

'It soon becomes less of a morality tale than a crime thriller. Quite a good one too, but not as good as the book . . . The killings are, in fact, quick, clean and unconvincing . . . You can, in fact, keep your eyes wide open throughout this film without being shocked.' *(Kenneth Robinson, Spectator)*

DEEP END CT: 7 AV: 6.75

1970 US/West Germany 88 C DRAMA

D Jerzy Skolimowski
W Jerzy Skolimowski Jerzy Gruza Boleslaw Sulik

Jane Asher ✓ John Moulder-Brown Diana Dors ✓ Karl Michael Vogler Christopher Sandford

A 15-year-old (John Moulder-Brown) gets a job in a seedy London bath-house and falls for a fellow employee (Jane Asher).

A memorable study of obsessive adolescent love. Even though it has a sly sense of humour, the film is extremely depressing, with a very unswinging view of 60s London. It was therefore underrated; but Skolimowski makes great use of dingy colour, and Jane Asher confounds those who say she's just a pretty face. Diana Dors offers a wonderfully over-ripe portrayal of over-ripe, middle-aged sexuality.

MIXED:

'Often original and pertinent. But the totally unnecessary ending is just too much to swallow.' *(David Gillard, Daily Sketch)*

'Very Polish in style with lots of highly original comic invention. A comedy of the grotesque and absurd – a rompish, ribald view of worldliness through the eyes of an innocent. But it is far too lightweight to accommodate the sudden and unexpected tragic ending, which spoils everything by hinting at underlying meanings which simply don't exist.' *(Nina Hibbin, Morning Star)*

'Interestingly made but rather dreary.' *(Halliwell)*

PRO:

'Skolimowski keeps the film alive with quirky incidents.' *(Variety)*

'A study in the growth of obsession that is both funny and frighteningly exact.' *(Nigel Andrews, MFB)*

'The most extraordinary love scene I have ever witnessed on the screen . . . [in] a film of unusual quality . . . One of those surprises that make film reviewing such an exciting adventure.' *(Felix Barker, Evening News)*

DEER HUNTER, THE AAW CT: 6 AV: 7.93

1978 US 183 C WAR/ DRAMA

D Michael Cimino ☆ AAW
W Deric Washburn AAN

Robert De Niro ☆ AAN Christopher Walken ☆ AAW
John Cazale ☆ John Savage ☆ Meryl Streep AAN

Three friends from a Pennsylvanian steel town go to Vietnam.

Big, bold, butch movie by Michael Cimino set against the background of the Vietnam War. The macho overtones become wearisome; the view of the Viet Cong is insultingly racist; and the films says surprisingly little about the conflict – it also annoyed the Left by not being conventionally anti-war. Although it is wonderfully photographed by the Oscar-nominated Vilmos Zsigmond, its greatest strength lies in the leading performances of Robert De Niro, Christopher Walken, John Cazale and John Savage.

PRO:

'Intense, powerful and fascinating.' *(Variety)*

'One is grateful to the direction, at once sensitive and powerful, of Michael Cimino. And grateful for his splendid cast.' *(Dilys Powell)*

'One of the few great films of the decade.' *(Chris Auty, Time Out)*

ANTI:

'Its apologists insult the memory of every American who died in Vietnam.' *(John Pilger, New Statesman)*

'We are asked to believe that the VC or North Vietnamese would set up their torture camp in a fully exposed site on a riverbank policed by American helicopters; that they would torture the prisoners by, among other things, forcing them to play Russian roulette while heavy bets are placed on which player will survive. We are to swallow the assumptions that the captors are stupid enough to have no guards surrounding the shack where the game is played; that they would idiotically fall for Michael's scheme and allow a pistol to be loaded with three bullets instead of one; and that, even so, this would prove enough for the tortured and weakened Michael and Nick to kill off all their tormentors, despite the submachine guns trained on them. I am afraid that the preposterousness of all this outweighs its technical brilliance . . . For all its pretensions to something newer and better, this film is only an extension of the old Hollywood war-movie lie. The enemy is still bestial and stupid, and no match for our purity and heroism . . . The average moviegoer gets no antiwar message . . . He simply identifies himself with Michael – the best – and envisions himself as survivor and hero of the next war to come along.' *(John Simon)*

MIXED:

'The picture is about that perennial American preoccupation . . . with male friendship, seen as a finer and stronger thing than love between men and women. And it's about the other side of that coin, loneliness, the brooding cosmic solitude Americans have felt ever since they confronted the overpowering vastness of their continent . . . *The Deer Hunter* deals with an ethnic community largely untouched by the great social currents of the 1960s and is constructed quite deliberately to eliminate discussion of war-aims and the larger issues involved in the Vietnam conflict.' *(Philip French, Observer)*

'Although the direction is generally good and the acting always fine, the script flounders increasingly as it goes on.' *(Stanley Kauffmann)*

'It has no more moral intelligence than the Clint Eastwood action pictures, yet it's an astonishing piece of work, an uneasy mixture of violent pulp and grandiosity, with an enraptured view of common life – poetry of the commonplace.' *(Pauline Kael)*

DEFIANT ONES, THE AAN CT: 6 AV: 7.64

1958 US 96 BW DRAMA/THRILLER

D Stanley Kramer ☆ AAN
W Nathan E. Douglas Harold Jacob Smith ✗ AAW

Tony Curtis ☆ AAN Sidney Poitier ☆ AAN
Theodore Bikel ☆ AAN Cara Williams ☆ AAN
Charles McGraw ✓ Lon Chaney Jr ✓
King Donovan Claude Akins

Two escaped convicts of different races (Tony Curtis, Sidney Poitier), handcuffed together, grow to respect each other.

Rather an obvious metaphor for American race-relations, and the predictability of the message removes that element of surprise which a great thriller needs. The shackles of Stanley Kramer's liberalism often trip up the narrative just as it threatens to get going; but it's still a superior chase movie, thanks to the excellent acting and Sam Leavitt's photography.

PRO:

'The performances by Tony Curtis and Sidney Poitier are virtually flawless.' *(Variety)*

'Probably Kramer's best picture. The subject matter is relatively simple, though "powerful"; the action is exciting; the acting is good. But the singleness of purpose behind it all is a little offensive . . . Moviegoers with good memories amused themselves by pointing out that *The Defiant Ones* was *The Thirty-Nine Steps* in drag, and by noting that the episode about the farm woman was badly lifted from

La Grande Illusion – with the convenient substitution of Negro for Jew (a familiar device in Kramer productions).' *(Pauline Kael, 1965)*

MIXED:

'Today, the story may seem slick, its symbolism obvious, and its message a pat one. But thanks to fine performances by Sidiney Poitier and Tony Curtis (certainly the finest of Curtis's efforts), a taut script, and Kramer's direction, there is still power in the story of a Negro and a white man literally chained together as fugitives, totally interdependent for survival, and cogency in its conclusions.' *(Judith Crist)*

ANTI:

'Though we didn't know it at the time, this was the first of Stanley Kramer's Messages to the World, so sure of its intent that it appears not to mind the gaping holes in the plot.' *(Shipman)*

DELICATESSEN

CT: 6 AV: 7.36

1991 France 97 C SF/COMEDY/HORROR/FOREIGN

D Jean-Pierre Jeunet Marc Caro ☆
W Jean-Pierre Jeunet Marc Caro Gilles Adrien

Dominique Pinon Marie-Laure Dougnac Jean-Claude Dreyfus

A clown (Dominique Pinon) falls in love with the innocent, short-sighted daughter (Marie-Laure Dougnac) of a butcher (Jean-Claude Dreyfus) whose greatest delicacy is human flesh.

Bizarre, visually stunning. Although obvious influences include René Clair, Marcel Carné and (more recently) Terry Gilliam, David Lynch and the Coen brothers, first-time directors Jean-Pierre Jeunet and Marc Caro orchestrate the action and camera movements with their own style and panache. There is one extraordinary sequence where the rhythm of the butcher's love-making is gradually picked up by all the residents of a tenement block in their daily pursuits: a *tour de force* of shooting and editing.

The good aspects are so good that it seems churlish to point out that the plot is as structurally unsound as the tenement block. The background is needlessly confusing (why if it's the future, for example, are there only nostalgic black and white programmes on TV?). The motives of the characters are as foggy as the exteriors, and change without much reason. Ultimately the film is too clever by half: an empty exercise in style, directorial exhibitionism and intentional bad taste. Still, it's bloody good fun – and if these directors were to stumble across a decent screenplay, the results could be outstanding. Though it baffled many members of the public, the critics were quick to embrace it.

'Absurd, imaginative French-language fantasy that's ready-made for cult adoration. The style is kinetic, and the characters off-the-wall; the result is brilliant . . . The performers deserve special plaudits for adding an extra level of charm to the film, making it as special as it is (and qualifying it as the most endearing post-nuke fantasy ever) . . . [The film] firmly establishes Jeunet and Caro as talents of the first order . . . These are filmmakers who don't need either a multi-million dollar budget or Industrial Light and Magic's tricks to produce a fantasy masterwork.' *(Edmond Grant, Film Journal)*

'An impressive achievement and very funny.' *(Philip French, Observer)*

'Increasingly inventive as it progresses, Jeunet and Caro's fast, funny feature debut entertains from sinister start to frantic finish.' *(Geoff Andrew, Time Out)*

'Beautifully textured, cleverly scripted and eerily shot . . . a zany little film that should get terrific word of mouth.' *(Variety)*

'Not so much a story as a series of funny and clever gags, stunts and scenes . . . Still, it rattles along, and keeps boredom away by being busy and inventive.' *(Winnert)*

'At the very least, this is the most original and entertaining comedy about cannibalism made to date.' *(Scheuer)*

DELIVERANCE

CT: 9 AV: 8.29

1972 US 109 C THRILLER/ HORROR

D John Boorman ☆
W James Dickey ☆ from his novel

Jon Voight ☆ Burt Reynolds ✔ Ned Beatty ✔ Ronny Cox James Dickey Bill McKinney ✔ Herbert 'Cowboy' Coward ✔

Four businessmen go on the sort of canoe holiday you won't find at Thomas Cook's.

John Boorman's gripping, nightmarish movie is both repulsive and compulsive: thematically, a combination of *Lord of the Flies* and *Straw Dogs*. Jon Voight is excellent as the mild chap who learns to survive in the wild; and the movie helped make Burt Reynolds a star.

ANTI:

'There is fundamentally no view of the material. Just a lot of painful grasping and groping.' *(Stanley Kauffmann)*

'What is perhaps most acutely missing from the film is Dickey's poetry . . . Simpler things yet are gone, including the sense of unity between man and animals and nature – the profound underside of surface hostilities. Gone too is Ed's final, amoral victory; his ascent to true supermanhood for having been able to kill an inferior human being with impunity. The movie carefully avoids this ticklish central issue and substitutes a protagonist haunted by nightmares of retribution – the ultimate flattening compromise.' *(John Simon)*

'What makes for a pervading uneasiness is the implication of the story: the strongest shall survive. The values of Reynolds' character are repulsive; Ronny Cox is a cardboard-cutout as an intellectual type; Ned Beatty is the easy-going, middle-class figurehead patronized by both the "doers" and the "thinkers" of the world; leaving Voight apparently as the one to lead them out of travail. In the depiction of sudden, violent death, there is the rhapsodic wallowing in the deadly beauty of it all: protruding arrows, agonizing expiration, etc. It's the stuff of which slapdash oaters and crime programmers are made but the obvious ambitions of *Deliverance* are supposed to be on a higher plane.' *(Variety)*

MIXED:

'It is narrative drive that swings the film along. The story is simple to the point of obtuseness, and a ragbag of all the myths about maleness that an analyst's couch ever put up with. What a – er, rugged tale . . . Are city sportsmen really such goons and so alarmed about their manhood quotient? Never mind. [The film] is strongly made and a fine yarn as long as the story of the delivered ones isn't taken as metaphysically as the title suggest it should be.' *(Penelope Gilliatt, New Yorker)*

'Virtually an orgy of suspense . . . At times Dickey's dialogue is pretentiously poetic . . . [and in his appearance] as a surly small town sheriff . . . demonstrates that he knows little about acting. It's the sole mediocre performance in the film . . . Feminists are likely to sneer . . . because it features no women and seems to glorify masculinity. But such a simplistic approach overlooks the major theme.' *(Dennis Hunt, San Francisco Chronicle)*

PRO:

'[I was] completely absorbed and breathless, pressed back against my seat by the centrifugal velocity.' *(Joseph Gelmis, Newsday)*

'Ranks high indeed . . . Grit [your] teeth, hold tight and prepare for one hair-raising ride down the rapids.' *(William Wolf, Cue)*

'Boorman has retained the movie's tension . . . Dickey cannot resist crowding the dialogue with capsule messages such as "Sometimes you have to lose yourself before you can find anything".' *(Paul D. Zimmerman, Newsweek)*

'A cracking good story.' *(Derek Malcolm, Guardian)*

'Seeing [it] is like looking at a bright light. Long after it's extinguished, your retina holds the impression of it, your mind the memory.' *(Alexander Walker, Evening Standard)*

'If you go down to the woods today, you're sure of a big surprise. But believe me . . . [it's] no Teddy Bear's picnic.' *(Jack Tinker, Daily Mail)*

'On its allegorical level, *Deliverance* is not unlike that far less illustrious horror film, *Frogs*, in which the natural life of the forest, mutated by the endless flow of human wastes and poisons, finally loses its patience and cuts mankind down to size. Yet Boorman's film is vastly strengthened by its ambiguities . . . When the fighting stops, Boorman suggests, you still have to talk to people – so why fight in the first place? . . . Rich, meaty and unsettling.' *(Philip Strick, S & S)*

'A strong and exciting narrative and this and the setting form a lynch-pin for the deeper implications of the men's physical and spiritual journey of discovery. Boorman has made a disturbing movie – an examination of the men's strength (inner and physical) and, importantly, of their self-delusions. An ambitious, successful film.' *(NFT Bulletin)*

'A delirious expression of male sexual paranoia.' *(Martin Sutton, Orbis, 1984)*

'In some of our more terrifying dreams we may find ourselves thrust into an alien, hostile environment where we are at the mercy of strangers from another culture who want to kill us for reasons we can't comprehend. No film better captures the essence of this particular nightmare . . . Indeed, this film depicts the male's worst nightmare – having his masculinity threatened.' *(Danny Peary)*

'An odyssey through a land that is already dead, killed by civilisation and peopled by alien creatures rather than human beings . . . A haunting, nightmarish vision.' *(Tom Milne, Time Out)*

DEMOLITION MAN — CT: 8 AV: 6.00

1993 US 115 C ACTION/THRILLER/COMEDY/SF

D Marco Brambilla ✔
W Peter M. Lenkov Robert Reneau Daniel Waters ✔

Sylvester Stallone Wesley Snipes Sandra Bullock Lori Petty Nigel Hawthorne Melinda Dillon Benjamin Bratt

20th-century cop (Sylvester Stallone) hunts a 20th-century killer (Wesley Snipes) in the 21st century.

Sylvester Stallone has taken on many terrible enemies in his screen career: drugs barons, heavyweight boxing champions, the Viet Cong, the Red Army. Here, he gets the chance to weigh in against perhaps the most fearsome of them all, Political Correctness. The film depicts a future California where conventional morality, faddiness and political correctness have triumphed: among those things illegal are alcohol, caffeine, salt, chocolate, swearing, abortion, unlicenced pregnancy, kissing, and non-educational toys. As with the stultifyingly claustrophobic world created by Joe Dante in the *Gremlins* pictures, you can hardly wait for it all to be blown apart. Between them, Stallone and Snipes proceed to do just that.

It is both a compliment to and a criticism of the young director that the movie looks as if it could easily have been directed by Paul (*Total Recall*)

Verhoeven or James (*Terminator*) Cameron. Where he differs from those two is that he exhibits at all points a refreshing sense of humour, place and narrative. But the main strength is a screenplay which sustains the satire and energy of the premise.

The film is, of course, not in the least moving, and the characters are deliberately comic-strip. The final showdown, though neat structurally (it's a mirror image of the opening scene), lacks ingenuity and freshness. Nevertheless, its message is an intelligent one, and close to that of Anthony Burgess's A *Clockwork Orange*: it is that, by sanitizing the evil and violence that are in human nature, you risk building a world that's tedious, dehumanized and anti-libertarian. The film is, in fact, Hollywood's riposte to all those who would like to remove violence, bad language and anti-social tendencies from the movies. It also makes a more controversial point (especially in the conservative 90s): that crime is often a reaction by the underclass to social injustice.

As too often, producer Joel Silver caters cynically to redneck susceptibilities by lionizing guns and brute force, and prizing American guts over the rest of the world's intellect. Silver's movies are littered with sinister, foreign villains, usually played by English actors, such as Joss Ackland, Stuart Wilson and Alan Rickman. This is no exception. But whether or not one approves whole-heartedly of Silver, *Demolition Man* is one of his most entertaining films: a winning comedy which ranks it alongside *Blade Runner, Terminator 2* and *RoboCop* as among the best science fiction thrillers yet produced by Hollywood.

ANTI:

'Self-consciousness can be a heady, intoxicating thing in a film: with Godard, for instance, it is a means of grandstanding cinema's limitations, giving us a guided tour of its outer reaches. The self-consciousness of *Demolition Man*, though, is simply a way of grandstanding its own limitations, like the class nerd whose only means of ingratiating himself with the bunch is to point out his own inadequacies before anybody else can get round to it. In the long run, though, it never works, because the audience, given the go-ahead to treat everything as a joke, will always be one step ahead.' *(Tom Shone, British Premiere)*

'The action movie has entered its Rococo Phase. The genre is trapped in helplessly escalating spirals of bigger explosions, more ornate plotlines, and increasingly swollen macho. The stars rumble through the decadence like mastodons through a gaudy landfill, trumpeting louder and louder so as not to hear approaching extinction . . . *Demolition Man* turns into a two-headed monster, a witty Orwellian spoof and a brain-dead wrestling match.' *(Ty Burr, Entertainment Weekly)*

MIXED:

'Until it kicks into full-tilt destructo mode the picture is an intermittently amusing sci-fi satire . . . *Demolition Man* is as much a piece of cheese as the grade-B sci-fi movies of the 50s, which also satirized, with a kind of touching literal-mindedness, the brainy emasculation of the future. The main difference is that those films didn't climax with 45 minutes of smashing mayhem.' *(Owen Gleiberman, Entertainment Weekly)*

'The script's often sharp social satire is drowned out by the noise and confusion. It is also undercut by casting virtually all the psychopathically murderous criminals as minority-group members. A little political correctness in that matter would have prevented this movie from playing right into the dismissive hands of the forces it most wants to criticize.' *(Richard Schickel, Time)*

PRO:

'The most entertaining futuristic action film since the original *Terminator* . . . The movie has some fun with Bullock's malapropish use of late 20th-century slang ("Take this job and shovel it"). And the fight and chase scenes are staged with maximum energy and minimum gore. Stallone actually gets to act a little. Bullock is a lively, attractive presence. Snipes is in delightfully malevolent mode, flashing his expressive eyes and using all his athleticism in the fight scenes.' *(Ralph Novak, People Weekly)*

'Forget your preconceptions, but not your brain-cells and sense of irony.' *(Nigel Floyd, Time Out)*

DEN GODA VILJAN: *see* BEST INTENTIONS, THE.

DER AANSLAG: *see* ASSAULT, THE.

DER AMERIKANISCHE FREUND: *see* AMERICAN FRIEND, THE.

DER GOLEM, WIE ER IN DIE WELT KAM: *see* THE GOLEM: HOW HE CAME INTO THE WORLD.

DER HIMEL ÜBER BERLIN: *see WINGS Of DESIRE.*

DER LETZE MANN: *see* LAST LAUGH, THE.

DER STUDENT VON PRAG: *see* STUDENT OF PRAGUE, THE.

DER TRAUM DES ALLAN GRAY: *see* VAMPYR.

DERSU UZALA AAW CT: 5 AV: 7.22

1975 USSR/Japan 140 C DRAMA/EPIC/FOREIGN

D Akira Kurosawa ✗
W Akira Kurosawa Yuri Nagibin from Vladimir Arseniev's journals

Maxim Munzuk Yuri Solomin
Schemeiki Chokmorov Vladimir Klemena
Svetlana Danielchanka

A hunter (Maxim Munzuk) helps a young Russian officer (Yuri Solomin) make a topographical survey of some Russian forests in 1902.

Kurosawa's epic is about an apparently primitive man who's more in tune with his Siberian environment than the 'sophisticated' people who patronize him. The film exemplifies the weaknesses of Kurosawa's later output – a plodding pace, a facile environmentalism, and a tendency to lecture long after the point has been made – but it's wonderful to look at. One further caveat: it needs to be seen on the big screen.

PRO:

'Yes, I like it, and I know why . . . Kurosawa . . . has a deep respect for the dignity of the human being . . . A fine, caring film.' *(Margaret Hinxman)*

'Full of sequences of spectacular adventure, beautiful and threatening.' *(Alan Brien, Sunday Times)*

'Many people (I'm among them) believe it to be a masterpiece of modern cinema . . . You don't need to accept the whole of Kurosawa's philosophy to be moved and inspired by his vision.' *(Nina Hibbin, Morning Star)*

'Kurosawa is a calibre of filmmaker that speaks directly back to D.W. Griffith or John Ford . . . [The film] celebrates and at the same time regrets the passing of an age and certain kind of man.' *(Tom Hutchinson, Sunday Telegraph)*

'As intimate in relationships and details as it is grand in vistas and scope.' *(Martin & Porter)*

'At its least, this film is a good example of the Noble Savage syndrome but because of some exciting and haunting sequences (Dersu saving the captain from a tiger and from dying of exposure) many think it a masterpiece.' *(Shipman)*

'Many remarkable scenes in Kurosawa's best style, with exciting use of widescreen and stereo.' *(Winnert)*

MIXED:

'Pitched in an alien key, bearing little resemblance to his own Japanese classics . . . as if [Munzak and Kurosawa] were bent upon wooing us with quaintness, not to say cuteness . . . For a while this is tedious, but . . . enlivening incidents are frequent enough.' *(Gordon Gow, F & F)*

'Rescued from the reefs of sentimentality by direction as calmly matter-of-fact in its elegiacs as the best of John Ford . . . and by Munzak's marvellously apt performance.' *(Tom Milne, MFB)*

'The photography is superb but, like the expedition itself, the film moves along at a slow pace.' *(Ian Christie, Daily Express)*

ANTI:

'Plodding.' *(Halliwell)*

DESERTO ROSSO, IL: *see* RED DESERT, THE

DESIRE CT: 6 AV: 7.00

1936 US 89 BW ROMANCE/COMEDY

D Frank Borzage ☆
W Edwin Justus Mayer Waldemar Young Samuel Hoffenstein from Hans Szekeley and R.A. Stemmle's play

Marlene Dietrich ☆ Gary Cooper John Halliday ☆
William Frawley ✔ Ernest Cossart
Akim Tamiroff ✔ Alan Morbray Zeffie Tilbury

A jewel thief (Marlene Dietrich) uses an innocent young man (Gary Cooper) to smuggle her ill-gotten gains through customs.

Stylish Hollywood hokum of its period, very much in the style of its producer (Ernst Lubitsch). The Paramount art department is on top form, Dietrich is at her loveliest, and there are pleasantly playful love scenes between her and Cooper. However, the plot runs badly out of steam.

'It sparkles and twinkles . . . one of the engaging pictures of the season.' *(Frank S. Nugent, New York Times)*

'Brilliant treatment, superb staging and inspiring acting. Irresistible entertainment.' *(CEA Film Report)*

'Mr Lubitsch's picture is like – I almost said – a breath of spring.' *(Alistair Cooke, S & S, Spring 1936)*

'The direction is subtle and inspired . . . The love scenes are excellently handled and written.' *(Variety)*

'Dietrich, with her pencil-line arched eyebrows, as the most elegantly amusing international jewel-thief ever . . . Cooper is a bit coy and rambunctious in his Americanness, but wearing narrow-tailored suits and with his hair sleek he's the ideal Art Deco hero.' *(Pauline Kael)*

DESPERATE HOURS, THE CT: 6 AV: 6.40

1955 US 112 BW THRILLER

D William Wyler
W Joseph Hayes from his own play and novel

Fredric March ☆ Humphrey Bogart ☆ Martha Scott
Arthur Kennedy Gig Young Dewey Martin
Mary Murphy Robert Middleton Richard Eyer

Three convicts take over a house and hold a family hostage.

Stagey but suspenseful melodrama, with Bogart a marvellously malevolent bad guy.

PRO:

'Bogart gives a piteously horrible impression of the essential criminal.' *(Time)*

'Bogart . . . looks like an elderly, thin-lipped monkey, uses a voice of unvarying venom – and is right back at the top of the form that made him famous.' *(Daily Herald)*

'A solid, deliberate and long-drawn-out exercise in the mechanics of suspense.' *(Penelope Houston)*

ANTI:

'Maybe I'm getting too old to play hoodlums.' *(Humphrey Bogart, after attending a sneak preview)*

DESPERATE HOURS CT: 5 AV: 4.10

1990 US 107 C THRILLER/SO BAD

D Michael Cimino ●
W Lawrence Konner Mark Rosenthal Joseph Hayes ● from Joseph Hayes' novel

Mickey Rourke ● Anthony Hopkins ● Mimi Rogers ● Lindsay Crouse ● Kelly Lynch ● Elias Koteas

You remember William Wyler's claustrophobic thriller which starred Humphrey Bogart as a brilliant but psychotic escaped prisoner holding to ransom Fredric March's upper middle-class family? This is nothing like it.

Michael Cimino's unintentionally hilarious and therefore perversely entertaining remake of the Bogart classic is innocently unfettered by notions of taste, proportion or suspense, while the screenplay is so criminally inept that its improbabilities are too numerous to bother mentioning. Symptomatic of the film's problems is the fact that, instead of Bogie snarling silkily in a crumpled suit, we get Mickey Rourke as a nightmare in shining Armani.

Mumbling Mickey Rourke and Anthony Hopkins at his hammiest (and least convincingly American) are just the *hors d'oeuvres* in a banquet of bad acting. Mimi Rogers, as Hopkins's wife, weeps and gibbers so irritatingly that murdering her in the first reel would rank as mercy killing. Kelly Lynch plays a supposedly high-powered lawyer as though auditioning for the role of a deranged hooker in a John Waters movie; while as a super-aggressive female FBI agent, Lindsay Crouse gives a ludicrously deranged performance, like Hitler on acid. Towards the end, when someone tries to slow her down by shooting her in the leg, she abandons all restraint and gives us her Long John Silver.

This is one of those films which should never have been released, not even on parole. It's a danger to itself.

PRO:

'For those with eyes to see [it] carries the sign "Major Filmmaker at work". The male-powered *corrida* of the plot is irresistible, finely played by Rourke and Hopkins – [It] is an American fable vibrant with the great American ambiguities.' *(Nigel Andrews, Financial Times)*

'Mickey Rourke is chillingly persuasive as a raging homicidal psychopath, the best part he has had in years.' *(Bruce Williamson, Playboy)*

ANTI:

'[It] overestimates itself. It is, thank God, only a matter of a desperate 105 minutes.' *(Hugo Davenport, Daily Telegraph)*

'In a competitive Bad Actor act-off, Hopkins does his customary Richard Burton imitation while Rourke does his customary Marlon Brando imitation.' *(Margulies & Rebello)*

'Kelly Lynch, as a micro-skirted bimbo whose blouse keeps flapping open, is the cinema's least convincing lawyer since Cher in *Suspect*.' *(Rose)*

DESPERATELY SEEKING SUSAN CT: 7 AV: 6.43

1985 US 104 C COMEDY

D Susan Seidelman
W Leora Barish

Rosanna Arquette ☆ Madonna ✗ Aidan Quinn ✓ Mark Blum Robert Jo Laurie Metcalf ✓ Will Patton Steven Wright John Turturro

A housewife (Rosanna Arquette), bored with her humdrum bourgeois existence, investigates a mysterious personal ad.

It was Madonna who received all the publicity for her role as a sluttish drifter. The real star of Susan Seidelman's screwball comedy was Rosanna Arquette. Arquette displays comic gifts which she's never had a chance to use again, and the scenes where she finds 'liberation' as a magician's assistant have a uniquely crazy charm. There are charming supporting performances from Aidan Quinn, as the love interest, and Laurie Metcalf, as Arquette's horribly yuppie sister-in-law.

ANTI:

'Seidelman . . . wipes out her actors. All their responsiveness is cut off – there's nothing going on in them, no subtext – nothing. This flatness can make your jaw fall open, but it seems to be accepted by the audience as New Wave postmodernism.' *(Pauline Kael)*

PRO:

'Simple, easy entertainment, with a lively cast caught up in a silly situation.' *(Variety)*

'Done with real wit and verve.' *(Tom Hutchinson, Mail on Sunday)*

'Once upon a time, there was a pop singer on the verge of fame who starred in a quirky, fast-faced farce that was funny and fresh.' *(Rose)*

DESTRY RIDES AGAIN CT: 8 AV: 9.23

1939 US 94 BW WESTERN/COMEDY

D George Marshall ☆
W Felix Jackson Henry Myers Gertrude Purcell from Max Brand's novel

James Stewart ☆ Marlene Dietrich ☆ Mischa Auer Charles Winninger Brian Donlevy Allen Jenkins Warren Hymer Irene Hervey Una Merkel Tom Fadden

Peace-loving sheriff (James Stewart) is forced to sort out the bad guys.

James Stewart is delightful, and Marlene Dietrich gives one of her most flamboyant performances as Frenchy the saloon singer. Surprisingly, most critics hated it on release; perhaps they were confused as to whether the melodramatic elements were to be taken seriously, or maybe they were pre-judging it (Stewart was not yet a star, and Dietrich had recently appeared in a string of bad movies). Whatever the reason, they were dead wrong; it became a hit, and is now rightly considered among the best comedy westerns.

ANTI:

'Dietrich . . . is unable to triumph over her material, while James Stewart seems thoroughly at a loss . . . a failure [which] is the fault only of bad taste and a poor script.' *(New Statesman)*

'A rather tired Western with a rather tired Dietrich . . . there is no falling in love again, even if we wanted to.' *(Graham Greene, Spectator)*

PRO:

'Just plain, good entertainment, primed with action and laughs and human sentiment.' *(Variety)*

'The alternation of comedy, romance, rough stuff and song has terrific showmanship.' *(Kinematograph Weekly)*

'What is remarkable about the film is the way it combines humour, romance, suspense so seamlessly . . . Flawless performances, pacy direction and a snappy script place it head and shoulders above virtually any other spoof oater.' *(Geoff Andrew, Time Out)*

'James Stewart is charming and even a little bit sexy.' *(Pauline Kael)*

DET SJUNDE INSEGLET: *see* SEVENTH SEAL, THE.

DETSTVO GORKOVO: *see* CHILDHOOD OF MAXIM GORKY, THE.

DEUX OU TROIS CHOSES QUE JE SAIS D'ELLE: *see* TWO OR THREE THINGS I KNOW ABOUT HER.

DEVIL IN THE FLESH CT: 5 AV: 7.11

(aka *Le Diable au Corps*)

1946 France 110 BW DRAMA/ROMANCE/FOREIGN

D Claude Autant-Lara ☆
W Jean Aurenche Pierre Bost from Raymond Radiguet's novel

Gérard Philipe Micheline Presle ☆ Jean Debucourt Denise Grey Jacques Tati

A 17-year-old schoolboy (Gérard Philipe) has an affair with a married woman (Micheline Presle) during World War I.

One of the great doomed romances, considered very immoral in its day (many resented being asked to sympathize with an adulterous couple, cheating on a soldier who was away at the front). Banned in Canada and exhibited in New York only in expurgated form, the film became a *succès de scandale* and made Philipe a star. Beautifully acted, stylishly directed but too slowly paced, it's based on an autobiographical novel by Raymond Radiguet, who died at the age of 20. Worn out, I should imagine.

PRO:

'Tragic, tender, poignant . . . deeply affecting.' *(Elspeth Grant, Daily Graphic)*

'Brilliantly acted . . . the best French film for some time and one that should certainly not be missed.' *(Fred Majdalany, Daily Mail)*

'Beautifully presented and adapted.' *(Shipman)*

ANTI:

'Calf love can be very moving, but I did not find it so in [this film] . . . Jaubert gives an impression of precociousness rather than innocent youth.' *(Reynolds News)*

'Autant-Lara unfortunately overplays some of his stylistic devices (such as the slowed-down sound that announces each flashback), but for the main part he elicits sensitive performances from his leads, and the smoky atmosphere and sets evoke a unique period atmosphere.' *(David Thompson, Time Out)*

'This touching story now seems quite harmless, but it still works extremely well as drama.' *(Virgin)*

'Slow and dreary.' *(Halliwell)*

DEVILS, THE

CT: 4 AV: 5.17

1970 GB 111 C DRAMA

D Ken Russell ●
W Ken Russell ● from John Whiting's play and Aldous Huxley's book *The Devils of Loudoun*

Vanessa Redgrave Oliver Reed Dudley Sutton Max Adrian Gemma Jones Murray Melvin Michael Gothard Graham Armitage

In 17th-century France, a sexy priest (Oliver Reed) awakens forbidden passions in a humpbacked nun (Vanessa Redgrave).

Silly, sensationalist filming of a moderately serious play. Russell indulges his taste for sadism; Reed and Redgrave overact – forgivably, in view of the script. Derek Jarman's set designs are effective, though.

ANTI:

'As if the story weren't bizarre enough, Russell has spared nothing in hyping the historic events by stressing the grisly at the expense of dramatic unity.' *(Variety)*

'Russell's swirling multi-colored puddle . . . made me glad that both Huxley and Whiting are dead, so that they are spared this farrago of witless exhibitionism.' *(Stanley Kauffmann)*

'A garish glossary of sado-masochism . . . a taste for visual sensation that makes scene after scene look like the masturbatory fantasies of a Roman Catholic boyhood.' *(Alexander Walker, Evening Standard)*

'Ken Russell doesn't report hysteria, he markets it.' *(Pauline Kael, 1976)*

PRO:

'For once Russell's seemingly out-of-control, hallucinogenic style is appropriate for his subject matter.' *(Danny Peary)*

DIABOLICAL DR MABUSE, THE:

see THE *DOCTOR MABUSE* SERIES (THE THOUSAND EYES OF DOCTOR MABUSE).

DIABOLIQUE:

see LES DIABOLIQUES.

DIABOLIQUES, LES:

see LES DIABOLIQUES.

DIAL M FOR MURDER

CT: 6 AV: 6.15

1954 US 105 C THRILLER

D Alfred Hitchcock ✔
W Frederick Knott from his own play

Ray Milland John Williams ☆ Grace Kelly Robert Cummings Anthony Dawson Leo Britt Patrick Allen

A playboy (Ray Milland) devises an ingenious plan to murder his wife (Grace Kelly).

It isn't Hitchcock's most cinematic film, mainly because it's all on one set, and producer Jack Warner insisted that it be shot in 3-D, which necessitated static cameras. However, Hitchcock works round these limitations with typical ingenuity, creating an atmosphere of claustrophobia and rising suspense. Though the rest of the cast are uninspired, John Williams's performance as a suspicious police inspector is a delight.

ANTI:

'More of a filmed play than a motion picture.' *(Variety)*

'Those who like drawing-room murder and cold, literate, gentlemanly skulduggery will find this ingenious and almost entertaining . . . All this is related with Hitchcock's ghoulish chic but everyone in it seems to be walking around with tired blood.' *(Pauline Kael)*

MIXED:

'You won't believe that Milland is a tennis player, or that he chooses to kill gorgeous Kelly instead of Cummings, or that Kelly would be attracted to Cummings. Also you'll find that this adaptation of Frederick Knott's play is too stagy. But the intricate plot twists are a lot of fun and the sequence in which Dawson tries to strangle Kelly is superbly directed.' *(Danny Peary)*

'For a one-room film with a not very exciting cast the film holds its grip pretty well.' *(Halliwell)*

DIAMONDS ARE FOREVER:

see BOND SERIES.

DIARY OF A COUNTRY PRIEST, THE

CT: 8 AV: 8.88

(aka *Le Journal d'un Curé de Campagne*)

1950 France 120 BW DRAMA/FOREIGN

D Robert Bresson ☆
W Robert Bresson ☆ from Georges Bernanos's novel

Claude Laydu ☆ Jean Riveyre Armand Guibert, Nicole Ladmiral Nicole Maurey

A callow young curate dying of cancer (Claude Laydu) ponders his failures.

Evidence yet again of Bresson's doom-laden genius. This is a film in which everything is going on inside its hero's head, yet all is made abundantly clear to the audience. Through Bresson's artistry, a picture which sounds as if it must be static and depressing turns into an experience which is both moving and life-affirming. Claude Laydu had never acted before, but gives one of the great screen performances.

ANTI:

'An unrelievedly gloomy, abysmally slow, and philosophically pretentious picture. I should describe it as "fraught" – but I am not quite sure with what.' *(Paul Dehn, Sunday Chronicle)*

MIXED:

'Directed with brooding sincerity . . . this sombre work is dedicated exclusively to anguish, spiritual and physical, devoted entirely to loneliness and despair. Though impressive, it is, to my mind, too relentlessly gloomy, too shadowed and tortured to be effective . . . Laydu . . . gives a truly exquisite performance.' *(Virginia Graham, Spectator)*

PRO:

'Makes no concessions to an audience's desire for emotional comfort. There is nothing comfortable about the story of the young priest, dying of a terrible illness, who finds grace in the acceptance of pain, solitude and the injustice which the world has heaped on him. It never relents: its devotion is absolute. And yet it leaves one with a sense of triumph. I have seen numbers of films which claim to be religious. Many have seemed to me to degrade as well as sentimentalize religion; here is one for the austerest taste.' *(Dilys Powell)*

'Superb.' *(Manchester Guardian)*

'Surely the one great religious film of recent years.' *(Pauline Kael)*

'A quiet, exquisitely wrought expression of faith . . . the tribulations of the soul are dramatized with astonishing clarity.' *(Scheuer)*

DIARY OF A LOST GIRL CT: 6 AV: 7.25

(aka *Tagebuch einer Verlorenen*)

1929 Germany 99/104/110 BW DRAMA/SILENT/FOREIGN

D G.W. Pabst
W Rudolf Leonhardt from Margaret Böhme's novel

Louise Brooks ☆ Fritz Rasp Josef Ravensky

A young rape victim (Louise Brooks) has an illegitimate child and escapes from a reformatory.

Surprisingly seamy, sensationalist classic of the silent period. Director G.W. Pabst's treatment is heavy-handed and humourless for modern tastes, while the plot fizzles out rather than ends (according to some sources, half-way through the screenplay because of censorship); but Louise Brooks's luminous performance in the title role has lost none of its erotic intensity.

ANTI:

'However damning Pabst's indictment of the bourgeoisie as torn between powerless compassion, greed and scandal-lust, his alternatives – the brothel as the one place of true friendship, or the aristocratic father-figure who puts everything right in the end – smack very much of a cop-out, allowing him to both revel in decadence and enjoy the moral superiority of denouncing it.' *(Ruth Baumgarten, Time Out)*

MIXED:

'Certainly Margaret Böhme's popular romance did not seem ideal content for a Pabst film . . . If you are impersonal simply, you are going to get into trouble with the censor. That Pabst remained considerably so is perhaps borne out by the fact that the film we see is his minus several hundred metres. It is partly on this account that it does not cohere. However, though not good as a whole, indeed far from it, it does give us some of the finest work he has done . . . These astounding scenes [in the reformatory] . . . have all the epigrammatic wrath . . . that almost Delphic quality which Pabst alone possesses . . . There is life – mean, angry, consummately cruel, gay, endearing, triumphant. You either have to swallow it or get up and walk out . . . Pabst's camera is like a busy eye. It plucks at a million details . . . The film is important . . . The story is worthless.' *(Kenneth MacPherson, Close Up, 1929)*

PRO:

'[Pabst is] a remarkable director . . . [The film is] notable for the camerawork of Sepp Allgeier.' *(Paul Rotha, The Film Till Now, 1930)*

'Directed with Pabst's customary profound humanity . . . Brooks fully justifies her survival as a legend . . . whether [she] was a great actress of conscious imagination or one of those apparently passive beauties with a gift of transparency for the camera to her subconscious.' *(Freda Bruce Lockhart, Catholic Herald, 1982)*

'It's deceptive, because there is no moral triumph at the core of the film . . . It's [his] marvellous skill with composition that makes [it] so riveting, in spite of its heart of stone . . . Pabst photographs [Brooks] as if she were marble . . . Gruelling it may be; as film-making it's so accomplished it should leave you breathless.' *(Richard Cook, New Musical Express, 1982)*

'What lingers in the mind is the exquisite bob-haired Louise Brooks exerting her femme fatale fascination, continuing the impact she made in Pabst's *Pandora's Box* of the same year.' *(Bergan & Karney)*

DIARY OF OHARU: *see* LIFE OF OHARU.

DICK TRACY CT: 5 AV: 5.92

1990 US 103 C MUSICAL/COMEDY/THRILLER

D Warren Beatty
W Jim Cash Jack Epps Jr ● from Chester Gould's characters (songs by Stephen Sondheim)

Warren Beatty ● Charlie Korsmo ✔ Al Pacino ☆ AAN Glenne Headly ✔ Madonna ● William Forsythe Dustin Hoffman Charles Durning Mandy Patinkin Paul Sorvino Dick Van Dyke Kathy Bates James Caan Michael J. Pollard

A detective (Warren Beatty) wrestles with master-criminals and the problem of committing himself to the woman he loves (Glenne Headly).

Great visuals, shame about the script. Young Charlie

Korsmo, Glenne Headly and an unrecognizable Al Pacino do their best to give the dreary narrative some human interest and humour; but Warren Beatty gives a lacklustre performance in the lead. Beatty's girlfriend of the time, Madonna, isn't up to the job of being a *femme fatale*, or singing Stephen Sondheim's songs, which are far from his best – even though one, 'Sooner or Later', won an Oscar. Art direction and makeup both won Academy Awards; the costume design, sound and Vittorio Storaro's cinematography were all nominated.

PRO:

'A charming and beautifully designed work of American popular art.' *(David Denby, New York Magazine)*

'A grand exercise in cinema imagination and wit for their own sake.' *(Vincent Canby, New York Times)*

'Richard Sylbert's designs . . . are further evidence of the American man's persistent yearning for boyhood.' *(Stanley Kauffmann)*

ANTI:

'A major disappointment.' *(Variety)*

'As the visual novelty of Dick Tracy slowly wears off, it becomes clear that, for all its undeniable charm, the movie beneath its lacquered surface is hollow.' *(Brian D. Johnson, Maclean's)*

'Although there's a toughingly chivalrous, incorruptible quality about Beatty's Tracy, there is, disastrously, no passion in him, even in his feeling for Tess . . . [Beatty] could have made Tracy a suave Mike Hammer (troubled by his machismo) or a *jejune* Philip Marlowe; instead he made him a curiously limp dick.' *(Graham Fuller, Film Yearbook)*

DIE NIBELUNGEN: *see* NIBELUNGEN, THE.

DIE BLECHTROMMEL: *see* TIN DRUM, THE.

DIE EHE DER MARIA BRAUN: *see* MARRIAGE OF MARIA BRAUN, THE.

DIE HARD CT: 9 AV: 7.71

1988 US 132 C ACTION/ADVENTURE

D John McTiernan ✔
W Jeb Stuart Steven E. de Souza from Roderick Thorp's novel *Nothing Lasts Forever*

Bruce Willis ✔ Bonnie Bedelia Alan Rickman ✔ Alexander Godunov ✔ Reginald Veljohnson Paul Gleason De'voreaux White William Atherton Hart Bochner James Shigeta Robert Davi Grand L. Bush

An off-duty cop (Bruce Willis) wages a one-man war with terrorists who take over a high-rise building.

An all-time-great action thriller, with Willis ideally cast as a wise-cracking cop taking on terrorists inside a high-rise building (actually, it's the 20th Century Fox Building in Century City). Alan Rickman makes a superb, lip-curling villain. McTiernan handles the action sequences brilliantly.

ANTI:

'Rambo for snobs.' *(Jane Solanas, New Musical Express)*

'Bruce Willis in another one of those Hollywood action roles where the hero's shirt is ripped off in the first reel so you can see how much time he's been spending at the gym . . . The film-makers introduce a gratuitous and unnecessary additional character, the deputy police chief (Paul Gleason) . . . in the movie for only one purpose: to be consistently wrong at every step of the way, and to provide a phony counterpoint to Willis's progress . . . Without the deputy chief and all he represents, *Die Hard* would have been a more than passable thriller. With him, it's a mess.' *(Roger Ebert)*

'In the first half . . . Willis wears an undershirt. In the second half he gets rid of it. And that's pretty much it for his performance. Of course, an actor is hard pressed to create a characterization when all he has to play against is gunshots and explosions. Any actor deserves sympathy when his love interest is sequestered from him, his nemeses are without human interest, his potential allies are all idiots, and the only sensible figure on the scene (Reginald Veljohnson) is always a walkie-talkie away. Still, Willis' presence is whiny and self-involved, and it is a ludicrous error to have him stop to confess past insensitivities before effecting his wife's climactic rescue. That is not the dramatically opportune moment to go *Moonlighting*.' *(Richard Schickel, Time)*

'This kind of filmmaking turns the thrills. It does not allow for any interactions with the emotions or ideas in the movies. No time is allotted for that, only a moment precisely calibrated for you to react before the next gag appears on screen.' *(Henry Sheehan, LA Reader)*

MIXED:

'The filmmakers attempt to deflect the groans . . . from more sophisticated moviegoers by treating the whole picture as a joke, a ploy grown familiar from expensive action pix in recent years. This is just great for Willis, whose terrific sense of humor makes him a star as much as his broad shoulders do. But the effect ultimately lays bare the film's bedroom cynicism.' *(Kevin Thomas, LA Times)*

'Outrageous. It's violent, overdone, hokey, and unbelievable. It's also a lot of fun.' *(William Gibbons, Films in Review)*

'It is all preposterous, but mostly fun, and sometimes even exciting . . . Many of the best hated Nazis in American movies about World War II were played by Britishers (a phenomenon that could use some analyzing), and Rickman sneeringly carries on the tradition as Bruber. He is helped by his ability to contort his mouth in more ways than the average dentist is likely to have encountered, and by displaying the sinisterly bad teeth inhabiting so many British mouths. The film, effectively directed and well cast, contains only one poor performance, that of Hart Bochner, who greasily overacts a cowardly, coke-snorting, scheming colleague of Mrs McClane's. We also learn from *Die Hard* that younger terrorists tend to wear their hair long, that terrorist leaders and top Japanese executives have the same Savile Row tailors, and that one New York cop is worth about the whole Los Angeles department – this last, especially comforting news for us New Yorkers.' *(John Simon)*

'His (Bruce Willis) alienated New York cop . . . might be the most complex action-hero creation since *Dirty Harry* first loaded his Magnum . . . *Die Hard* occasionally lapses into something that looks like an episode of *McCloud*, but there's a lot of great gunplay, terrific explosions, and the swell spectacle of a particularly ugly Century City office building being reduced to rubble.' *(Jonathan Gold, LA Weekly)*

'Some fine gung-ho performances, particularly from snakelike Rickman . . . [The film] constantly promises to transcend its violence and become a witty thriller. But no sooner does hope flicker than we are again surrounded by splintering glass windows and machine-gunned Italian furniture.' *(Sue Heal, Today)*

PRO:

'Dazzling action thriller . . . Director McTiernan delivers one wide-screen jolt after another . . . on a sleek and dizzying ride that combines hard action with playful self-awareness. Though the stakes are high and the thrills are sometimes gruesome, it never takes itself too seriously or forgets the audience's thirst for entertainment.' *(Kevin Lally, Film Journal)*

'The myriad of shafts and machinery endemic to a high-tech building become the location for a cat and mouse game which makes Tom and Jerry look like lovers. McTiernan uses his wide screen and the location to good effect and Bruce Willis, in a role somewhere between Dirty Harry and Rambo, without the arrogance of either, manages to hold his own against all comers. The film also has the virtue of managing to avoid any racism and sexism.' *(Sheila Whitaker, London Film Festival Brochure)*

'A gung-ho, hammy, cliché-ridden thriller . . . and an absolute hoot!' *(Pauline McLeod, Daily Mirror)*

'The American public, powerless in the face of terrorism and angered by the humilating revelations of Irangate, is provided through *Die Hard* with a face-to-face battle between the might of the all-American hero and the cold-blooded valueless terrorists.' *(Stephen Dark, Film Review)*

'Situated somewhere between *The Towering Inferno* and *The Poseidon Adventure*, this is an inventively entertaining full-blooded all-action film mixed with a little acerbic wit and social commentary.' *(Jeff Sawtell, Morning Star)*

DIE HARD 2: DIE HARDER CT: 6 AV: 5.92

1990 US 120/124 C ACTION/ADVENTURE

D Renny Harlin ✓
W Steven E. de Souza Doug Richardson

Bruce Willis ✓ Bonnie Bedelia William Atherton Reginald Veljohnson Franco Nero William Sadler John Amos Dennis Franz Fred Dalton Thompson Tom Bower Sheila McCarthy Don Harvey Robert Patrick John Leguizamo Colm Meaney Robert Costanzo

Off-duty cop (Bruce Willis) fights terrorists who take over an airport.

Although it's not as fresh, logical or claustrophobic as its predecessor, it's just as exciting. Renny Harlin's action sequences have the bravura confidence of mid-period James Bond. And there's a delightfully outrageous plot-twist at the end, which revitalizes the film just as you think it's running out of steam.

The movie skilfully exploits the anxieties of a 90s audience. There is the fear of terrorism and drug-running. There's the fascination with, yet unease about, technology (Willis hates flying and doesn't know how to use a fax). And, underlying everything else, there's the little man's distrust of authority (despite his heroic deeds in the first movie, Willis still hasn't got promotion, and his only allies are a black engineer and an old janitor).

Willis is no Bond-style sophisticate. When he witnesses a fatal plane crash he roars like Bruce Springsteen in concert; and he is doggedly faithful to his wife Bonnie Bedelia. Although he has a healthy, post-Irangate suspicion of conspiracy in high places, he and his wife also mistrust the journalists who expose such abuses (the two reporters we see are as irresponsible as they are intrusive).

Willis has a chunky, working man's physique, but the magic of the movies enables him to kill trained, muscular mercenaries in unarmed combat. Though he is only an off-duty cop, he knows just what to do when trapped in a cockpit full of live grenades, and thinks nothing of being lowered by helicopter on to the wing of a moving aircraft. *Die Hard 2* creates a blue-collar fantasy world.

'Violence in films of this kind rarely seems violent to me, or how could so many machine guns fire at the hero without ever nicking him? People get killed, but the Angel of Death is always able to distinguish the subordinate actors from the stars.' *(Stanley Kauffmann, New Republic)*

ANTI:

'One might think a movie with a reported budget of $62 million would have had a few bucks to spend on a gaffe spotter. For instance, Willis, again playing cop John McClane, opens the film at Dulles International Airport. This is outside Washington, D.C., but not so far outside that the pay phones – prominent during one long scene – should be labeled Pacific Bell. Then there's the central plot: that terrorists seize Dulles so they can spring a Latin American drug lord from custody. The villains threaten to turn off all the guidance equipment so planes won't be able to land, will run out of fuel and crash. A fleet of airliners proceeds to meekly circle the field for two hours, even though dozens of alternate fields are within range of two hours' fuel.' *(Ralph Novak, People Weekly)*

MIXED:

'Lacks the inventiveness of the original but compensates with relentless action.' *(Variety)*

'Fast and exciting and with plenty of wry humour, this sequel would be as good as the original were it not for some wild implausibilities. Not least of them is the idea that a man with a handgun not only never runs out of bullets but is invincible against baddies who play dirty by using automatic weapons.' *(Rose)*

PRO:

'As unlikely as the Bond pictures and as much fun . . . terrific entertainment.' *(Roger Ebert)*

'A preposterous high adventure that gives hordes of thrill-hungry customers exactly what they want.' *(Bruce Williamson, Playboy)*

'We're talking action not art, and on that level Die *Hard 2* succeeds magnificently.' *(Dominic Wells, Time Out)*

DIE TAUSEND AUGEN DES DR MABUSE:

see THE *DOCTOR MABUSE* SERIES (THE THOUSAND EYES OF DOCTOR MABUSE).

DIMANCHE À LA CAMPAGNE, UN:

see SUNDAY IN THE COUNTRY.

DINER CT: 6 AV: 7.53

1982 US 110 C COMEDY/DRAMA

D Barry Levinson ☆
W Barry Levinson ☆ AAN

Steve Guttenberg Daniel Stern ☆ Mickey Rourke ☆ Kevin Bacon ☆ Timothy Daly ☆ Ellen Barkin ☆ Paul Reiser Kathryn Dowling Michael Tucker Jessica James Kelle Kipp

Young people congregate in a diner in the 1950s.

Talky but brightly observed movie about growing up in 50s America: it helped make the reputation of writer-director Barry Levinson, who went on to bigger but not always better things. Lively characters and some lovely comic performances.

MIXED:

'Female viewers seem to respond to this film more than men. Perhaps that's because they dated similar flawed, funny characters, while we men don't wish to identify with guys who have jerk streaks a mile long.' *(Danny Peary)*

'Not a lot to it, but the sense of period is acute, the script witty without falling into the crude pitfalls that beset other adolescent comedies, and the performances are spot-on.' *(Geoff Andrew, Time Out)*

PRO:

'Provides a look at middle-class relations between the sexes just before the sexual revolution, at a time when people still laughed (albeit uneasily) at the gulf between men and women, It isn't remarkable visually, but it features some of the best young actors in the country.' *(Pauline Kael)*

'An assured debut from Levinson, it's splendidly evocative and has extraordinarily naturalistic dialogue. Full of memorable moments, particularly the scenes with the popcorn in the cinema and in the strip joint when they decide the music isn't fast enough. Wise, witty and wonderful.' *(Rose)*

DINNER AT EIGHT CT: 8 AV: 9.08

1933 US 113 BW COMEDY/DRAMA

D George Cukor ☆
W Frances Marion Herman J. Mankiewicz Donald Ogden Stewart from George S. Kaufman and Edna Ferber's play

Marie Dressler ✔ John Barrymore Wallace Beery Jean Harlow ✔ Lionel Barrymore Lee Tracy Edmund Lowe Billie Burke Madge Evans Jean Hersholt

Sophisticated New Yorkers prepare for dinner.

Lovers of sparkling dialogue will adore this satirical comedy drama, given the full MGM production treatment. The Art Deco designs are wonderful (just get an eyeful of Jean Harlow's bedroom). George Cukor directs his all-star cast with theatrical panache. Harlow (as a gold-digger) and Marie Dressler (as a bitchy grand dame) are extremely funny. Less amusing is the fact that John Barrymore (playing a drunken has-been) effectively plays himself.

PRO:

'It lives up to every expectation . . . a fast-moving narrative . . . one that offers a greater variety of characterizations than have been witnessed in any other picture. Some are polished and others decidedly rough and ready . . . a grand evening.' *(Mordaunt Hall, New York Times)*

'A veritable screen banquet, a lavish splendid repast,

with every course representing infinite variety, faultlessly served by a colossal cast . . . Unique in the annals of entertainment in every respect . . . a great piece of work, and the cleverness of its construction, the comprehensiveness of its entertainment and the superb showmanship of its presentation are certain to meet with the rewards they merit at the box office.' *(Kinematograph Weekly)*

'The quintessential MGM movie: an all-star cast, impeccably directed, in a version of a popular Broadway play.' *(Shipman)*

MIXED:

'The story grips from beginning to end with never-relaxing tension, its sombre moments relieved by lighter touches into a fascinating mosaic for nearly two hours. Play is a more searching document than Grand Hotel but not quite its equal in dramatic vividness.' *(Variety)*

'The laughs are mainly at the expense of the nouveau riche couple, a comedy of manners in which Harlow reveals her natural gift for humour and Beery confirms his status as the definitive boor. But the film also reflects the vagaries of the 1930s social scene . . . Perfect viewing for a wet Saturday afternoon.' *(Martyn Auty, Time Out)*

ANTI:

'He set up his camera on a stage, and photographed *Dinner at Eight* just exactly as it appeared in the Music Box Theatre last year. You will get no atmospheric camera studies, no photomontage, no music, no outdoor scenes in this picture.' *(Pare Lorentz, Vanity Fair)*

'I never knew a greater bother about nothing . . . It is amusing to think that people accumulated round a dinner table are not all that they pretend, or all that they seem. But the detached particulars of each personal lie are, as in this case, only gossip. The *News of the World* will do as much for you, for tuppence. Creatively handled, the little personal lies might be built into one grand accumulate lie, commanding men's horror or anger or laughter, or only their pity. *Dinner at Eight* does not give you anything of the sort.' *(John Grierson, New Britain)*

DINOSAURUS! CT: 6 AV: 5.40

1960 US 85 C SF/HORROR/SO BAD

D Irvin Yeaworth Jr
W Jean Yeaworth Dan E. Weisburd

Ward Ramsey Paul Lukather Kristina Hanson Alan Roberts Gregg Martell

A caveman (Gregg Martell), Tyrannosaurus Rex and Brontosaurus are disturbed from hibernation on a tropical island.

A movie intended to be light-hearted fun for the family, but certainly not a spoof, has acquired a reputation as a cult film mainly because of its terrible animation and lamebrain plot. Though it could not remotely be described as good, it has a neanderthal charm all its own.

'Motion picture art hit rock bottom all over town yesterday . . . If ever there was a tired synthetic, plodding sample of movie junk, it's this "epic".' *(Howard Thompson, New York Times)*

'*Dinosaurus!* looks plodding and cheap; the stop-motion animation of the dinosaurs is among the worst ever done in an American sound film, further injuring the already crippled movie.' *(Bill Warren, Keep Watching The Skies!)*

'Presumably intended as a comedy . . . [it] has an intermittent charm. The acting is rigid and the line between the serious and the tongue-in-cheek none too well defined, the film just about gets by on its two main ideas – the caveman's amiability and the vegetarian monster's devotion to the small boy.' *(MFB)*

'Much of the comedy may be crude, but its charm ranges from [slapstick] to sophisticated satire.' *(Daily Variety)*

'An amusing romp . . . boasting good use of color, excellent animation and enough excitement to hold the audience's interest.' *(Parish & Pitts, The Great Science Fiction Pictures)*

'The funniest science-fiction movie ever made – unintentionally, that is . . . Side-splitting from beginning to end.' *(John Stanley, Revenge of the Creature Features Movie Guide)*

'Amusingly daft . . . Hard to dislike, easy to laugh at, possible to enjoy.' *(Winnert)*

DIRTY DOZEN, THE CT: 6 AV: 7.07

1967 US/Spain 149 C WAR/ACTION/ADVENTURE

D Robert Aldrich ☆
W Nunnally Johnson Lukas Heller from E.M. Nathanson's novel

Lee Marvin ☆ Ernest Borgnine Robert Ryan Charles Bronson ☆ Jim Brown John Cassavetes ☆ AAN George Kennedy Richard Jaeckel Trini Lopez Telly Savalas ☆ Ralph Meeker Clint Walker Robert Webber Donald Sutherland ✔

12 condemned soldier-prisoners are formed into a crack unit in World War II.

Though condemned by some critics for excessive violence, Robert Aldrich's brutal war picture was 1967's most popular film. It combines the usual war-is-hell clichés with the 60s convention whereby the enemies you really had to fear were the high-ups on your own side. Despite dull patches, the action sequences remain exciting and the whole thing is well acted. John Poyner's exceptionally noisy sound effects received an Academy Award. Though much imitated (by movies like *The Devil's Brigade* and *A*

Reason To Live, A Reason To Die), the basic plotline was borrowed from a 1964 Roger Corman movie, *The Secret Invasion*.

'*The Dirty Dozen* is the definitive enlisted man's picture. In its view World War II was a private affair in which officers were hypocritical, stupid or German, and only the dogfaced soldier was gutsy enough to be great. In this film, the lopsided interpretation works largely because of a fine case and a taut plot that closes the credibility gap . . . Director Robert Aldrich gets convincingly raw, tough performances in even the smallest roles.' *(Time)*

'*The Dirty Dozen* . . . is the beneficiary of extensive advance publicity and excitement and has a strong, virile cast to deliver both the brutalizing violence and grotesque comedy which will make it one of MGM's big money pictures of the year. It is overlong, uneven and frequently obscure, but will succeed by virtue of its sustained action, even though what it attempts to say, if anything, remains elusive.' *(Hollywood Reporter)*

'Lee Marvin is superb as the major who trains twelve convict-volunteers for a suicidal raid on German headquarters. It's rough, tough, sadistic, and brutal on an intellectual level and a he-man entertainment on the gut level.' *(Judith Crist)*

'Apart from the values of team spirit, cudgeled by Marvin into his dropout group, Aldrich appears to be anti-everything: anti-military, anti-establishment, anti-women, anti-religion, anti-life . . . Overriding such nihilism is the super-crudity of Aldrich's energy and his humour, sufficiently cynical to suggest that the whole thing is a game anyway.' *(Chris Peachment, Time Out)*

'Film is solidly directed and has a strange appeal; its oddest aspect (perhaps Aldrich sees the irony) is that these criminals are redeemed when they commit acts that are far more repugnant than the ones for which they were arrested.' *(Danny Peary)*

DIRTY HARRY

CT: 8 AV: 7.38

1971 US 103 C THRILLER

D Don Siegel
W Harry Julian Fink Rita M. Fink Dean Riesner from H.J. and R.M. Fink's story

Clint Eastwood ☆ Reni Santoni Harry Guardino Andy Robinson John Mitchum John Larch John Vernon Mae Mercer Lyn Edgington Ruth Kobart

A San Francisco police inspector (Clint Eastwood) isn't fussy about legal niceties as he sticks up for law and order.

Cop movies had become so stereotyped in their liberal responses that this tough, well-made, exciting thriller came as a welcome relief. The fact that it was little more than a western in modern dress did not save it from being hated by most critics. An enormous and well-deserved hit, it spawned four sequels (*Magnum Force, The Enforcer, Sudden Impact, The Dead Pool*) and innumerable imitations. Recent critics have been much more kindly disposed towards it.

ANTI:

'Two brilliant cinematographic moments in the film do little to compensate for the facile and far-fetched special pleading on which it is based.' *(Nina Hibbin, Morning Star)*

'The grim devotion to duty that has always been the badge of Siegel's constabulary is here, in Clint Eastwood's tough San Francisco plainclothesman, pushed beyond professionalism into a kind of iron-jawed self-parody . . . It is not the hard-hat sentiment that I find disturbing in all this so much as the dull-eyed insensitivity.' *(Roger Greenspun, New York Times)*

'You could drive a truck through the plotholes in *Dirty Harry*, which wouldn't be so serious were the film not a specious, phoney glorification of police and criminal brutality. Clint Eastwood in the title role is a superhero whose antics become almost satire. Strip away the philosophical garbage and all that's left is a well-made but shallow running and jumping meller.' *(Variety)*

'In *Dirty Harry* a raped and murdered body is a neat little sexual object, and orgies seen through windows are both reprehended and meant to turn you on. Violence is utterly brutal yet somehow fun. With the same dishonesty all liberals are shown as phonies or cowards, and their laws as affording protection to homicidal maniacs. The film's politics matches its aesthetics in doing violence to all – including to violence.' *(John Simon)*

'This right-wing fantasy about the San Francisco police force as a helpless group (emasculated by the unrealistic liberals) propagandizes for para-legal police power and vigilante justice . . . Harry's hippie adversary is pure evil: sniper, rapist, kidnapper, torturer, defiler of all human values. This monster – who wears a peace symbol – stands for everything the audience fears and loathes. The action genre has always had a fascist potential, and it surfaces in this movie.' *(Pauline Kael)*

MIXED:

'On the face of it . . . [the film] looks deeply reactionary. Actually [it] deserves better than instant dismissal as a piece of ambivalent law and order propaganda, since it recognises . . . that in the predatory world of big-city America, you can't send a puppy to chase wolves.' *(Derek Malcolm, Guardian)*

'Very violent and too long; it is also the best entertainment in this week's assortment, racy and holding.' *(John Coleman, New Statesman)*

'Uniformly unpleasant . . . The psychopath, played with gusto by Andy Robinson, is a truly horrific creation . . . Siegel is an expert . . . who moves things along with pace and tact . . . If he had used a better lead than Clint Eastwood . . . he would have made a film to remember.' *(Christopher Hudson, Spectator)*

PRO:

'A zinger of a crime movie, whatever you think of its politics.' *(David Ansen, Newsweek)*

'Directed by Don Siegel, the story is quite incredible and reasonably exciting. With policemen like Clint Eastwood and cowboys like John Wayne, civilization has nothing to fear.' *(Daily Express)*

As crackingly fast and exciting as anything Don Siegel has yet made.' *(Tom Milne, Observer)*

'Not a pretty movie, but a marvellously professional job of filmmaking . . . There is an elegant precision about the way [Siegel] charts his action which contrasts with the horror of what he is portraying . . . And the narrative rhythm is so right you barely have time to notice that the whole city seems to be policed almost single-handedly by Harry.' *(Margaret Hinxman, Sunday Telegraph)*

'It could be argued that the film is a bitterly anti-liberal tract that condones police violence and embraces a fascist mentality; yet Harry is typical of the Siegel loner, operating within his own moral code and growing anachronistic within a world that confuses him. Harry's climactic disposal of his police badge is evidence that his particular brand of individualistic endeavour has no place within the proper restraints of today's law-enforcement agencies. It's hardly a call-to-arms for would-be vigilantes.' *(Allan Hunter & Kenny Mathieson, Movie Classics, 1992)*

DISCREET CHARM OF THE BOURGEOISIE, THE AAW CT: 5 AV: 8.77

(aka *Le Charme Discret de la Bourgeoisie*)

1972 France/Spain/Italy 105 C COMEDY/DRAMA/FOREIGN

D Luis Buñuel ✗AAN
W Luis Buñuel Jean-Claude Carrière ✗ AAN

Fernando Rey Delphine Seyrig Stéphane Audran Bulle Ogier Jean-Pierre Cassel Paul Frankeur Julien Bertheau Claude Pieplu Michel Piccoli Muni

Posh people try to have dinner.

What's the most overrated film of all time? This would be my nominee. It's mildly enjoyable as a puzzle, and the most interesting aspect remains its structure, which is of dreams within dreams within dreams. It still has the power to surprise, and must have seemed innovative on the art-house circuit in 1972. However, uncertainty over whether events are real or merely dreamed has long been a commonplace of less intellectually respectable pictures in the horror genre.

The adjective most often applied to Buñuel's film is 'witty'. His running joke, though I've never heard it make an audience laugh, is that the central characters are always interrupted just as they are about to eat dinner. The gag soon becomes repetitious, however, as do the intrusions by subsidiary characters to tell us their dreams, which are all tiresomely inconsequential.

So where is all this alleged wit? Certainly not in the words. Writers such as Coward or Molière exposed the workings of the bourgeois mind via adazzling, epigrammatic facade. Although Buñuel and his co-writer Jean-Claude Carrière frame the action in scenes of drawing-room comedy, with consciously theatrical touches (painted backdrops and even, at one stage, an applauding audience), there is no verbal wit of the kind you get in genuine drawing-room comedy.

Nor does Buñuel reveal the inner core of his characters, except in the crudest way. All appear motivated by the seven deadly sins, or not at all. They have the same nihilistic hysteria as the scatalogical cartoons of Gerald Scarfe, whose fashionable heyday was around the same period.

Buñuel's middle classes are cardboard cut-outs of hypocrisy. They despise those who smoke marijuana as 'drug addicts' but smuggle heroin under cover of diplomatic immunity. They fraternize with the military, support dictatorships, shoot their enemies or make them 'disappear'. Buñuel's film might have some validity as a comment on Franco's Spain, from which Buñuel was a refugee, but *Discreet Charm* was widely construed as having a worldwide resonance.

Buñuel's film, though made by a man of 72, caught the mood of a younger generation overawed by Vance Packard's *Hidden Persuaders* and Wright Mills's *Power Elite* and eager to see Fascist values behind every capitalist establishment and middle-class facade. More than 20 years on, it looks like a ludicrously naive vision of the kind that motivated terrorist groups all over the world, from the Angry Brigade to the Manson family.

'The unique creation of a director who at 72 has never been more fully in control of his talents, as a filmmaker, a moralist, social critic and humorist . . . Don't miss it.' *(Vincent Canby, New York Times)*

'Masterpiece . . . the first great French film of the 70's . . . For all its mordancy [it] is surprisingly good-natured. The old hatreds have mellowed – the sadistic anarchist of *L'Age d'Or* has tempered to a savant entomologist.' *(Elliott Stein, Financial Times)*

'I haven't said what the film is about . . . I don't know. But I really don't care, either . . . A poem should not mean, but be . . . and if ever there was a film poem, this is it.' *(Richard Roud, Guardian)*

'A perfect synthesis of surreal wit and blistering social assault.' *(Jan Dawson, MFB)*

'Buñuel's savage and blisteringly funny demonstration of the power of appetite to exceed consumption, with six imperturbably elegant bourgeois surviving artistic and physical annihilation in their relentless pursuit of an elusive dinner.' *(S & S)*

'Fernando Rey unloading smuggled heroin from his diplomatic pouch is a hip reference to *The French Connection*, and much of the rest of the film works as a parody of icons and stances in modern cinema. Florence's neuroticism – as evidenced by her loathing of cellos and her "Euclid complex" – lampoons Ogier's role in *L'Amour Fou*; Audran's stiff elegance and country house hark back to *La Femme Infidèle*; while Seyrig's frozen, irrelevant smiles on every occasion are a comic variation of her ambiguous *Marienbad* expressions.' *(Jonathan Rosenbaum)*

'The piece slides with ease into fantasy and anarchy but some of the jokes are a trifle jaded.' *(Shipman)*

'A frequently hilarious, sometimes savage surrealist fable which makes all its points beautifully and then goes on twenty minutes too long.' *(Halliwell)*

DISTANT THUNDER

CT: 6 AV: 7.00

(aka *Asani Sanket*)

1973 India 100 C DRAMA/FOREIGN

D Satyajit Ray ☆
W Satyajit Ray from Bibhutibhusan Banerjee's novel

Soumitra Chatterjee ☆ Babita ☆ Romesh Mukherjee Chitra Banerjee Gobinda Chakravarti Sandhya Roy

Famine, exacerbated by World War II, strikes a Bengali village.

A touching but surprisingly amusing story based on a real-life famine which killed over five million in East Bengal in 1943. It's also a profound character study of its doctor hero (played by Soumitra Chatterjee, star of Ray's *The World of Apu*), who learns a great deal about himself and his wife – a lovely performance by Babita, a far cry from the idealized women in more traditional Indian cinema. Soumendu Ray's cinematography brilliantly combines the realistic with the lyrical. Winner of the Golden Bear award for Best Film at the Berlin Film Festival.

MIXED:

'The pain at the heart of the film, just as the hunger in the bellies of the people, is given almost a passive quality by the continuing beauty of the small world that is disintegrating . . . Ray doesn't handle some of the violence as confidently as he always handles the upset of the moral and social equilibrium. He occasionally lapses into cliché and bathos. But such flaws don't negate [his] achievement.' *(Alexander Walker, Evening Standard)*

'I don't know when I've been so moved by a picture that I knew was riddled with flaws. It must be that Ray's vision comes out of so much hurt and guilt and love that the feeling pours over all the cracks in *Distant Thunder* and fills them up.' *(Pauline Kael)*

PRO:

'Shot in brilliant colour, with a fine sense of psychological nuance . . . and a lyrical grasp of natural beauty in the midst of imminent apocalypse.' *(S & S)*

'Even in this isolated community there is scope for Ray's familiar comedy of manners.' *(Russell Davies, Observer)*

'A superb film.' *(Tom Milne, Time Out)*

'Often criticised for ignoring the bitter realities of his country, Ray here takes a more political line while retaining his gentle wit and humanism. The village movingly becomes a microcosm for the wider sufferings of India.' *(Bergan & Karney)*

DISTANT VOICES, STILL LIVES

CT: 5 AV: 6.50

1988 GB 84 C DRAMA/RITES-OF-PASSAGE

D Terence Davies ☆
W Terence Davies

Freda Dowie ✔ Pete Postlethwaite ✔
Angela Walsh Dean Williams Lorraine Ashbourne

A young boy grows up in a working-class environment with an abusive father (Pete Postlethwaite).

Slow, stylish, sentimental film about the writer-director's childhood, which appears on this evidence to have been highly melodramatic. Acclaimed as a masterpiece by the critics (the British ones voted it Best Film of the Year), but most members of the public seemed to find it a plotless bore. It's visually striking, very well acted, and makes pertinent use of popular songs (in a manner reminiscent of Dennis Potter). It was followed by the more optimistic but even less dramatically structured companion-piece, *The Long Day Closes*.

PRO:

'Nostalgia with the blinkers off. It understands that in family life everything is complicated, even a grown child's hatred for the ogre who sired him . . . [Davies] turns anecdote into artistry.' *(Richard Corliss, Time)*

'Ambitious, intelligent, profoundly moving, it thrills with a passion, integrity and imagination unseen in British cinema since Powell and Pressburger.' *(Geoff Andrew, Time Out)*

'A film about memory, but it's also a film about making a film about memory. Davies stuffs the movie with deliberately exposed pieces of grammar and homage. You're aware of the artifices of film lighting. You're aware that each crane-shot is a crane-shot. You're aware that a camera tracking from a wedding reception hall into a gulf of darkness then into a candlelit church then into more darkness and then along a terraced street is a geography-defying coup de cinema. And you're aware of the recurring door-frame motif, Searchers-style, distancing and contextualizing the memory of family or friends . . . *Distant Voices, Still Lives* is post-modernist cinema just as the Paris Pompidou Centre building is post-modernist architecture. The visual devices and creative "plumbing", far from being tucked away, are on open display.' *(Harlan Kennedy, Film Yearbook)*

'Pulls you into other people's lives in a way which few recent releases have achieved. A masterpiece.' *(John Marriott, Daily Mail)*

'About emotional resilience and shared feelings as much as it is about pain and darkness. The counter to the family's suffering is the strength its members draw from the humblest of resources: the popular songs they sing in the pub. Some of the most beautiful sequences in the film – without affectation or sentimentality – are those in which the camera simply dwells on faces, as people pour their hearts into some corny, long forgotten tune.' *(Stuart Klawans, Nation)*

'While its pacing and structure may exasperate some, should envelop receptive audiences with its special magic.' *(Variety)*

'A masterpiece that reinvents filmgoing itself. The awesome strength of *Distant Voices, Still Lives* as a whole is that it makes every moment necessary and indelible as well as beautiful. I have every reason to believe that years from now when practically all the other new movies playing are long forgotten, it will be remembered and treasured as one of the greatest of all English films.' *(Jonathan Rosenbaum)*

ANTI:

'What Rohmer might do if he were English, from a working-class background, and had less talent . . . *Distant Voices* is a lot of ponderous apparatus applied to trite material, not even seen in any rewardingly familiar way. In *Hamlet*, when Polonius holds forth rhetorically, the queen says, "More matter, with less art." Hear, hear.' *(Stanley Kaufmann, New Republic)*

'*Still Born*, more like. Life in the slums of Liverpool in the 50s, chock-full of drunken, abusive fathers, nobly suffering wives and tearful pub singalongs. Shot in an attractively stylised manner, this film is an inspiration to some and an over-praised, bum-numbing puzzle to rather more.' *(Rose)*

'This snapshot album of a film chronicles the fortunes of a family dominated by a near homicidal maniac. Someone told me that this monster of depravity, who sweeps the Christmas dinner off the table on to the floor, punches his wife in the face and wallops the kids for getting caught in an air raid, was actually the director's father. If this is so, and Mr Davies is trying to exorcise this brute from his psyche, then he should see an analyst, and not inflict his therapy on us. For much of the film Davies' camera is locked off, as in the very early days of the Biograph, where the camera stays clamped to its tripod on the station plafform, filming miles of empty track before the train finally comes into shot. I believe Mr Davies went to film school – presumably not for long.' *(Ken Russell, 1993)*

DIVA

CT: 6 AV: 7.15

1981 France 117/123 C THRILLER/ FOREIGN

D Jean-Jacques Beineix ☆
W Jean-Jacques Beineix Jean Van Hamme from Delacorta's novel

Frédéric Andrei Wilhelmenia Wiggins Fernandez Richard Bohringer Thuy An Luu Jacques Fabbri Chantal Deruaz Roland Bertin Gérard Damon Dominique Pinon Jean-Jacques Moreau

A postal messenger (Frédéric Andrei) is pursued by baddies who think he has an incriminating cassette tape.

Jean-Jacques Beineix's much imitated thriller is visually brilliant but irredeemably pretentious, and storywise a complete mess. It should be seen, if only because it is one of the most stylish and confident directorial debuts of all time and, for good and ill, the apotheosis of the movie as rock promo.

'The most exciting debut in years, it is unified by the extraordinary decor – colour supplement chic meets pop art surrealism – which creates a world of totally fantastic reality situated four-square in contemporary Paris.' *(Tom Milne, Time Out)*

'Outlandishly, ostentatiously dazzling, more so than any other recent thriller which hoped to knock us between the eyes – and with a humour seldom found in movies of this manner.' *(Shipman)*

'Goofy, glittering, dazzlingly stylish.' *(Danny Peary)*

'Nimble and pretty and lighter than air, *Diva* is a delicious little movie, and part of what one loves about it is its Frenchness. And in the end, when Jules admits to Cynthia that he has recorded her voice, he insists on playing the tape for her, and she is overwhelmed, enchanted, renewed: she has never heard her voice before. There are those, even among the film's admirers, who accuse *Diva* of being meaningless. And it's true that the movie pretends to meaninglessness, even mocks meaning. But there is meaning in it. Here, in this scene between the French boy and the American woman who has mastered so European an art form, here one catches the whiff of the olive branch. In its parade of American cars and rock 'n' roll thugs and pinball machines, *Diva* brings us news of America, the way *Breathless* did so many years ago. It lets us hear our voice.' *(Stephen Schiff)*

'A flashy package of ultra-chic designer images and

punk aesthetics of little meaning and less coherence.' *(Bergan & Karney)*

DIVORCE ITALIAN STYLE CT: 6 AV: 8.10

(aka *Divorzio all'Italiana*)

1961 Italy 104 BW COMEDY/FOREIGN

D Pietro Germi ☆ AAN
W Ennio de Concini Pietro Germi Alfredo Gianetti ☆ AAW

Marcello Mastroianni ☆ AAN Daniela Rocca ☆ Stefania Sandrelli ✓ Leopoldo Trieste ☆ Odoaldo Spadaro

A lazy Sicilian count (Marcello Mastroianni) takes steps to be rid of his annoying wife (Daniela Rocca), so that he can marry the girl next door (Stefania Sandrelli).

Dry, witty black comedy – an Italian equivalent to *Kind Hearts and Coronets* – with great sight-gags and Rocca hilarious as the kind of wife who might drive anyone to thoughts of murder. Mastroianni's deadpan performance won him awards from the Golden Globes and the British Film Academy.

'Mastroianni is uniformly marvelous, a perfect parody of a small-town smoothie . . . Germi . . . one of the least known, but one of the most talented of the major Italian directors, shows a flair for deadly fun that few of his rivals can rival.' *(Time)*

'I think you will enjoy this spicy, bawdy picture. I know I did.' *(William Hall, Evening News)*

'The film's greatest asset is its playing.' *(David Robinson, Financial Times)*

'Excellent satire on modern Italian manners and mores.' *(Scheuer)*

'Delightfully satirizes the Italian male and the country's laws on divorce and crime passionnel.' *(Bergan & Karney)*

DIVORZIO ALL'ITALIANA: *see* DIVORCE ITALIAN STYLE.

DO THE RIGHT THING CT: 5 AV: 7.92

1989 US 120 C DRAMA/COMEDY

D Spike Lee ✗
W Spike Lee ✗ AAN

Danny Aiello ☆ AAN Ossie Davis, Ruby Dee Richard Edson Giancarlo Esposito Spike Lee ✗ Bull Nunn John Turturro Rosie Perez

Italians who own a New York pizza parlour spark off a riot with local black youths.

Much overpraised by critics who wanted it to be a great film and elevated Spike Lee well beyond his capacities, into a cultural and political guru. Energetic and well photographed (by Ernest Dickerson) but shambolic as narrative, this is a film in which virtually every character from a racial minority, regardless of colour or creed, behaves like a jerk. The claim of Mr Lee and some critics that this was a work of social realism was absurd. The characters were didactic caricatures, and any film about black street life in 1989 which tried to get away without mentioning crack was plainly escapism. Lee was even confused about whether racial violence was to be condemned or condoned. At the end, he offered contradictory quotations from Martin Luther King and Malcolm X: a blatant cop-out.

'I'm not advocating violence. I'm saying I can understand it. If the people are frustrated and feel oppressed and feel this is the only way they can act, I understand.' *(Spike Lee)*

PRO:

'Funny, poignant and ultimately disquieting. Sure to be controversial and likely to be ranked as a landmark in black cinema . . . a provocative exploration of urban racial tensions that's as entertaining as it is disturbing . . . Displaying all the confidence and style of a veteran filmmaker, Lee spins out his cautionary tale of escalating anger . . . The last half-hour . . . is strong stuff indeed, echoing as it does the Howard Beach rampage, the killing by transit cops of [a] graffiti artist . . . But the first 90 minutes . . . offer the emotional and dramatic underpinnings which make it all so powerful. Perhaps Lee's most remarkable achievement is his evocation of daily life in a neighborhood which most white New Yorkers . . . would dismiss as beyond the pale.' *(Ed Kelleher, Film Journal)*

'I think the film is marked by extraordinary restraint and responsibility.' *(Paul Schrader, New York Times)*

'A comedy which lurches into tragedy, *Do the Right Thing* is also anti-racist agitprop and funky, galvanizing entertainment which, in its rap-acious rhythms and tumultuous urban panoramas, makes giddy viewing . . . Until the promised "kinder, gentler" America finally materializes, whatever needs to be done must, perforce, be the right thing. That's the realistic message of one of the most courageous movies of the 1980s.' *(Graham Fuller)*

'If the audience . . . cannot think or feel their way into Mookie's position . . . then [his] act of violence will seem rhetorical and contrived . . . but for any spectator who agrees to identify with [him] and his ethical crisis, the moment assumes a certain tragedy – not a tragic inevitability . . . but a tragic ethical impasse.' *(Jonathan Rosenbaum, Chicago Reader)*

'[Lee] gives a virtuoso performance, with all instruments played to near-perfection.' *(Lawrence Alster, F & F)*

'A virtual explosion of dissatisfaction, faded hope, and strained love.' *(Bruce Bibby, Premiere)*

'The most honest, complex and unblinking film I

have ever seen about the subject of racism.' *(Roger Ebert)*

'Lee's most complex, heartfelt and disturbing film to date . . . Editorialists will probably call Lee's film an incitement to riot. (Sure – and racism, as Reagan informed us, is caused by civil rights leaders.) Among more open-minded viewers, though, *Do the Right Thing* will be seen as an incitement to thought. I hope the sidewalks outside the movie theaters this summer will be filled with people arguing over the rights and wrongs of Mookie's actions and the meanings of the two texts – one by Dr King, the other by Malcolm X – that close the film.' *(Stuart Klawans, Nation)*

'Buzzes throughout with the sheer, edgy bravado that comes from living one's life on the streets. It looks, sounds and feels right: sure proof that Lee's virtuoso technique and righteous anger are tempered by real humanity.' *(Geoff Andrew, Time Out)*

MIXED:

'Spike Lee's both disturbing and disorganized, but he hereby earns points as a militant moviemaker who brightens his harangues with the soul of a born showman.' *(Bruce Williamson, Playboy)*

ANTI:

'What worries me is whites are going to look at this movie in an unthinking fashion and suddenly increase fear, hate, whatever for the black community.' *(Bronx State Supreme Court Judge Burton B. Roberts, New York Times)*

'The thinness of the characterization isn't a big problem for the first hour or so, while the tone is still light and comic . . . It's only later . . . that [Lee's] approach lets the audience down . . . Lee wants to . . . prove the inevitability of the race conflict in America and he can't do it because no filmmaker could: movies aren't very good at proving things . . . If you think . . . that not every individual is a racist . . . then you have to conclude that Spike Lee has taken a wild shot and missed the target . . . [The film] winds up bullying the audience – shouting at us rather than speaking to us.' *(Terrence Rafferty, New Yorker)*

DOCTOR DOLITTLE AAN CT: 2 AV: 3.00

1967 US 152 C MUSICAL/FANTASY/FAMILY

D Richard Fleischer ●
W Leslie Bricusse ● from the books by Hugh Lofting

Rex Harrison Samantha Eggar
Richard Attenborough ☆ William Dix Peter Bull
Anthony Newley

Wet vet (Rex Harrison) talks to animals.

This promising idea for a family musical is sabotaged from the outset, thanks to a script and songs by the dreaded Leslie Bricusse. The least bad song, 'Talk To The Animals', won an Oscar; and shamefully the picture was nominated for an Oscar as Best Film – almost certainly the worst movie ever to be so. The musical direction and (unbelievably) the music were also nominated. Robert Surtees's cinematography (rightly Oscar-nominated) is the one bright spot. Despite the strenuous efforts of Academy members, the movie did little at the box office, and nearly bankrupted Twentieth Century Fox.

PRO:

'Far and away the best children's film I have seen since *The Wizard of Oz*.' *(Nina Hibbin, Morning Star)*

'Fleischer's [direction is] spectacular yet subtle . . . The glory of this picture is that it is funny and fantastic without being foolish, fey without being twee, touching without being treacly.' *(Cecil Wilson, Daily Mail)*

MIXED:

'Only one lyric falls flat – a crassly commercial song sung by Mr Newley to a bunch of brown-skinned jungle kids . . . But . . . [the film is] directed with skill, ingenuity and above all kindliness.' *(Alexander Walker, Evening Standard)*

ANTI:

'Kids are not so dumb; I have yet to meet a single child who actually enjoyed *Dr Dolittle*.' *(Rex Reed, 1969)*

'Lumpish family spectacular with no imagination whatever, further handicapped by charmless performances and unsingable songs.' *(Halliwell)*

'Overlong and overproduced.' *(Judith Crist)*

'The acting is weak and any real script is nonexistent.' *(Martin & Porter)*

'One merit: if you have unruly children, it may put them to sleep.' *(Maltin)*

'The original idea was lovely, but somehow the film got blown out of all proportion.' *(Samantha Eggar, co-star)*

DOCTOR EHRLICH'S MAGIC BULLET

CT: 6 AV: 7.50

(aka *The Story of Dr Ehrlich's Magic Bullet; Dr Ehrlich's Magic Bullet*)

1940 US 103 BW DRAMA/BIOPIC

D William Dieterle ☆
W John Huston Heinz Herald Norman Burnside ☆ AAN

Edward G. Robinson ☆ Ruth Gordon
Otto Kruger ✔ Donald Crisp Maria Ouspenskaya
Montagu Love Sig Rumann Donald Meek
Albert Basserman ✔ Henry O' Neill

A German doctor (Edward G. Robinson) tries to find a cure for the disease that dare not speak its name (actually syphilis).

Edward G. Robinson gives one of his finest performances. Based on real life, it's in many ways just a typically polished studio biopic of its time, smoothly directed by William Dieterle, and with a conscientious screenplay by John Huston, Heinz Herald and Norman Burnside. It's also a landmark film in in the way it tries to make science comprehensible to a mass audience, and treats venereal disease in a grown-up manner.

'A splendid production, with much care and attention to detail.' *(Variety)*

'A superb motion picture.' *(Pare Lorentz)*

'Merits nothing but the sincerest praise.' *(Basil Wright, Spectator)*

'Worthy and sometimes engrossing.' *(Shipman)*

DOCTOR JEKYLL AND MR HYDE: *see* DR JEKYLL AND MR HYDE

DOCTOR MABUSE, KING OF CRIME: *see* THE *DOCTOR MABUSE* SERIES (DR MABUSE, THE GAMBLER).

THE *DOCTOR MABUSE* SERIES

DR MABUSE, THE GAMBLER

CT: 5 AV: 6.42

(aka *Doctor Mabuse: the Fatal Passion; The Fatal Passion of Doctor Mabuse; Doktor Mabuse, Der Spieler;* second half is also known as *Doctor Mabuse, King of Crime*)

1922 Germany 265 (Pt I 153; Pt II 112) BW SILENT/SF/THRILLER/FOREIGN

D Fritz Lang ☆
W Thea von Harbou Fritz Lang from Norbert Jacques's novel

Rudolph Klein-Rogge Paul Richter Alfred Abel Bernhard Goetzke Georg John Otto Wernicke

A criminal mastermind (Rudolph Klein-Rogge) dominates the underworld of Weimar Germany.

A silent classic which, though a seminal work of German expressionism and recognizably the work of a talented director, is hard to enjoy. The narrative is chaotic, hard to follow and more than a little ludicrous. One suspects its continuing high reputation may rely on critics who haven't had to sit through it.

PRO:

'Imaginative and chilling.' *(Neil Sinyard, Silent Movies)*

'Brilliantly directed, designed, photographed.' *(Maltin)*

'This trend-setting epic . . . not only works as a classic cops-and-robbers actioner, but it also serves as a fascinating expressionist portrait of the times in which it was made – the decadent German 1920s.' *(Scheuer)*

'Period document which provides penetrating insights into the economic, political, social and intellectual chaos of post-World War I Germany, together with the consequences – inflation and revolution plus sexual promiscuity, compulsive gambling and decadence, particularly in the upper classes.' *(Hoffman's Guide to SF, Horror and Fantasy Movies)*

MIXED:

'Lang has said that he intended the film as a kind of social criticism, and his sprawling plot does take glimpses of night-life decadence and themes like economic inflation in its stride. But overall the grasp of social reality is as shaky as the plotting, and the film's interest – certainly by comparison with the later *Testament of Dr Mabuse* – remains basically historical.' *(Tony Rayns, Time Out)*

'Although very few of the copies now circulating are anything like complete, they do make a long haul and one to be wholly recommended only to those with an unlimited taste for plots about plots, disguises, secret hide-outs, dropped notes, coincidences and cardboard characters, What social comment there was in Norbert Jacques's original story has been mislaid on its way to the screen.' *(Shipman)*

'A real wallow in German post-war depression . . . Fascinating scene by scene, but by now a slightly tiresome whole.' *(Halliwell)*

TESTAMENT OF DR MABUSE, THE

CT: 5 AV: 7.00

(aka *Last Will of Doctor Mabuse; The Crimes of Doctor Mabuse*)

1932 Germany 71/122 BW SILENT/THRILLER/FOREIGN/SF

D Fritz Lang ☆
W Fritz Lang Thea von Harbou based on characters from Norbert Jacques's novel

Rudolph Klein-Rogge Otto Wernicke Oskar Beregi Wera Liessem Gustav Diesel Karl Meixner Theodor Loos Klaus Pohl Camilla Spira Rudolph Schundler

A criminal mastermind (Rudolph Klein-Rogge), though in a lunatic asylum, spouts Nazi slogans and uses hypnotism to dominate the underworld of Weimar Germany.

More watchable than its predecessor, with a more comprehensible narrative, better pace and impressive set-pieces (a high-speed car chase at night, an underwater explosion) – but it's primitive by modern standards. Almost certainly intended as an allegory about the mind-control being exerted over Germany by Hitler, the film was unsurprisingly banned by Goebbels. Goebbels was, however, a fan of Lang's *Metropolis* and offered him the leadership of the German film industry. Lang took this invitation as his cue to make a precipitate, overnight disappearance from his fatherland.

PRO:

'Almost exemplary in its use of sound effect and dialogue. In its whole palpitating first reel, for example, not a word of dialogue is spoken, there is only action and sound effect, yet Hitchcock himself never made a more suspenseful and effective sequence.' *(John T. McManus, PM, 1943)*

'Haunting, suspenseful.' *(Virgin)*

'There is an atmosphere of evil, and it is curious to see the denizens of the underworld going about their dastardly business in spats and bowler hats.' *(Shipman)*

ANTI:

'Technically and directorially, the film is superior. The same can not be said of the manuscript by Thea von Harbou which becomes kitsch in the film's hypnotic scenes. The script makes too exaggerated a demand on the credulity of the public.' *(Der Kinematograph, Berlin)*

'Fast-moving penny dreadful, alleged by its director to be a denouncing of the doctrines of Hitler, but showing little evidence of being more than a very slick entertainment.' *(Halliwell)*

THOUSAND EYES OF DR MABUSE, THE

CT: 4 AV: 5.16

(aka *Eyes of Evil; The Secret of Dr Mabuse; The Diabolical Dr Mabuse; Die Tausend Augen des Dr Mabuse*)

1960 France/Italy/West Germany 103 BW SF/CRIME/THRILLER/FOREIGN

D Fritz Lang ☆
W Fritz Lang Jeinz Oskar Wuttig based on characters from Norbert Jacques's novel

Dawn Addams Peter Van Eyck Gert Frobe Wolfgang Priess Werner Peters

A Berlin police commissioner (Gert Frobe) fears that murders in a hotel may be the work of a man who thinks he is the reincarnation of Dr Mabuse.

One of the most belated sequels in movie history, a film whose reputation rests more on its director and predecessors, than on any merits of its own. A stylish enough thriller, and Lang's last film as director, but the plot is dull and the denouement unsurprising.

Further inferior German sequels followed the commercial success of *The Thousand Eyes of Doctor Mabuse: The Return of Dr Mabuse* (1961), a remake of *The Testament of Doctor Mabuse* (1962), *Scotland Yard Hunts Dr Mabuse* (1963), *Dr Mabuse's Rays of Death* (1964), *The Invisible Dr Mabuse* (1965) and *The Terror of Dr Mabuse* (1965).

PRO:

'Lang fills his eerie tale with a tightly controlled *mise-en-scène*, a world of hidden cameras, two-way mirrors and mistaken impressions . . . Pure cinema, using camera angle, shot composition, and lighting to achieve an overwhelming power.' *(Virgin)*

ANTI:

'Gets lost in stale criminal film gags and confused puzzle games. Mabuse's dangerous practices are reduced to underworld jokes . . . Even the excellent cast . . . cannot lift the story, which Fritz Lang directed with verve.' *(Frankfurter Allgemeine Zeitung, 1960)*

'Ignore the dopey romantic subplot.' *(Martin & Porter)*

DOCTOR MABUSE: THE FATAL PASSION:

see THE *DOCTOR MABUSE* SERIES (DR MABUSE, THE GAMBLER).

DOCTOR MABUSE, THE GAMBLER:

see THE *DOCTOR MABUSE* SERIES (DR MABUSE, THE GAMBLER).

DOCTOR NO:

see BOND SERIES (DR NO).

DOCTOR PHIBES RISES AGAIN:

see DR PHIBES RISES AGAIN.

DOCTOR PHIBES:

see ABOMINABLE DOCTOR PHIBES, THE.

DOCTOR STRANGELOVE:

see DR STRANGELOVE.

DOCTOR ZHIVAGO AAN

CT: 7 AV: 7.40

1965 US C DRAMA/EPIC/ROMANCE

D David Lean ☆ AAN
W Robert Bolt AAW from Boris Pasternak's novel

Omar Sharif Julie Christie ✔ Tom Courtenay ☆ AAN Rod Steiger ✔ Alec Guinness ✔ Ralph Richardson Rita Tushingham Geraldine Chaplin Siobhan McKenna Noel Willman Geoffrey Keen Adrienne Corri

A Moscow doctor (Omar Sharif) is separated from his true love (Julie Christie) by historical events beyond his control.

The story proceeds by fits and starts, and the historical background is confusing if you don't already know it. Those who have read the book also accuse the film of being a trivialization. But this remains one of the best cinematic epics, with generally strong performances (from Steiger and Courtenay, especially) and Julie Christie at her loveliest. The set-pieces are superbly photographed by Freddie Young (who rightly won an Oscar) – the real Russian Revolution probably looked unimpressive by comparison. And the love story between Julie Christie and Omar Sharif still jerks the tears, helped along by Maurice Jarre's Oscar-winning slushy score. The critics have always hated this film; but the public made it one of the most popular of all time.

PRO:

'The sweep and scope of the Russian Revolution . . . has been captured . . . frequently with soaring dramatic intensity . . . Sharif, largely through expressions of indignation, compassion and tenderness, makes the character very believable. Christie is outstanding in a sensitive, yet earthy and full-blooded portrayal.' *(Variety)*

'A majestic, magnificent picture of war and peace, on a national scale and scaled down to the personal. It has every element that makes a smash, long-run boxoffice hit.' *(Hollywood Reporter)*

MIXED:

'Robert Bolt, condensing and smoothing for the purposes of the screenplay, has caught something of the helplessness of the human creature in that storm in history . . . Lean contributes a few extraordinary moments: Zhivago's capture by the partisans; the fight in the cornfields and the machine gunning of the White Russians. Yet sometimes one can't help recalling *The Battleship Potemkin* or *Chapayev* and the recollection is not to the advantage of the new film . . . The individuals sometimes appear bloodless.' *(Dilys Powell)*

'David Lean's *Doctor Zhivago* does for snow what his *Lawrence of Arabia* did for sand.' *(John Simon)*

ANTI:

'It is all too bad to be true: that so much has come to so little, that tears must be prompted by dashed hopes instead of enduring drama.' *(Newsweek)*

'It isn't shoddy (except for the music); it isn't soap opera; it's stately, respectable, and dead. Neither the contemplative Zhivago nor the flow of events is intelligible, and what is worse, they seem unrelated to each other.' *(Pauline Kael)*

'A long haul along the road of synthetic lyricism.' *(MFB)*

'Visually impressive in a picture postcard sort of way. Otherwise an interminable emasculation of Pasternak's novel, seemingly trying to emulate *Gone with the Wind* in romantic vacuity . . . Steiger and Courtenay excepted, all the performances are very uncomfortable.' *(Tom Milne, Time Out)*

DODSWORTH CT: 8 AV: 8.91

1936 US 101 BW DRAMA/ROMANCE

D William Wyler ☆
W Sidney Howard from own play adapted from Sinclair Lewis's novel

Walter Huston ☆ Mary Astor ☆ Ruth Chatterton ☆ David Niven Paul Lukas Gregory Gaye Maria Ouspenskaya ☆ Odette Myrtil Spring Byington John Payne

Mid-West businessman (Walter Huston) takes his pretentious wife (Ruth Chatterton) to Europe, where he loses her.

It isn't hard to see why this drama failed at the box office: underneath the glossy production (art director Richard Day won an Oscar) it's a tough and realistic portrait of a failing marriage. Unconventionally, it had a businessman as the hero rather than the villain; and women did not do the lion's share of the suffering. William Wyler drew good performances from his cast and mainly concealed its stage origins. Walter Huston gave his finest performance on film. Rudolph Mat's cinematography was brilliantly innovative in its use of deep focus, years before *Citizen Kane*.

PRO:

'William Wyler has had the skill to execute it in cinematic terms, and a gifted cast has been able to bring the whole alive to our complete satisfaction.' *(New York Times)*

'A smoothly flowing narrative of substantial interest, well-defined performances and good talk.' *(New York Times)*

'An offering of dignity and compelling power to provide you with a treat you can rarely experience in a picture house.' *(Hollywood Spectator)*

'A superb motion picture and a golden borealis over the producer's name.' *(Variety)*

ANTI:

'[Of David Niven] In this picture we are privileged to see Mr Samuel Goldwyn's latest "discovery". All we can say about this actor is that he is tall, dark and not the slightest bit handsome.' *(Detroit Free Press)*

MIXED:

'No one, I think, will fail to enjoy it, in spite of its too limited and personal plot; the sense it leaves behind is of a very expensive, very contemporary Bond Street vacuum flask.' *(Graham Greene)*

'Don't talk to me about Dodsworth. I lost my goddamn shirt. I'm not saying it wasn't a fine picture. It was a great picture, but nobody wanted to see it. In droves.' *(Samuel Goldwyn)*

DOES, THE: *see* LES BICHES.

DOG DAY AFTERNOON AAN CT: 8 AV: 8.23

1975 US 130 C THRILLER

D Sidney Lumet ☆ AAN
W Frank Pierson AAW

Al Pacino ☆ AAN Chris Sarandon ☆ AAN
John Cazale ✔ Charles Durning ☆ Sully Boyar
James Broderick ✔ Carol Kane

A young man (Al Pacino) holds up a bank to pay for his boyfriend's sex-change operation.

Based on real events in 1972, this is a daring mixture of thriller and black comedy, with a sensationally good performance by Al Pacino. Director Sidney Lumet captures the edginess of the people involved and creates an atmosphere of heat and tension; the pity is that he allows the film to go on for too long, and become bogged down in verbiage. The film was quietly revolutionary in its portrayal of the hero's bisexuality. No attempt was made to explain or excuse it; it was simply accepted as a fact.

ANTI:

'A long, wearying case history of the beaten, sobbing, despairing and ultimately powerless anti-hero.' *(Karyn Kay, Jump Cut)*

'Carol Kane once again proves one of our screen's more untalented and graceless presences.' *(John Simon)*

PRO:

'A hilarious and moving story.' *(Variety)*

'The mask of frenetic cliché doesn't spoil moments of pure reporting on people in extremity.' *(New Yorker)*

'There is plenty of Lumet's vital best here in a film that at least glancingly captures the increasingly garish pathology of our urban life.' *(Jack Kroll)*

'Brisk, humorous and alive with urban energies and angers fretting through the 92 degrees heat.' *(S & S)*

'Full of galvanic mirth rooted in human desperation.' *(Michael Billington, Illustrated London News)*

MIXED:

'It is always hard to mix comedy and drama, and particularly when there is no clear moral attitude at work. It is impossible to tell whether these underprivileged and maladjusted veterans are ultimately treated with compassion or ridicule; whether homosexual marriage is accepted or made fun of; whether the law enforcers are viewed as put-upon befuddled creatures attempting to do their best, or brutish villains; whether hostages are little people doing their utmost in trying circumstances or a variety of buffoons and poltroons either lighting up indecently in the spotlight or just turning yellow.' *(John Simon)*

'When Cazale's body is wheeled past Pacino at the end and he looks at it numbly, what are we supposed to feel? Pathos? Society's triumph? Something else? I don't know. The facts of the dog day don't clarify Pacino's character – as hero or social victim or moral anarchist or psychic deviant or anything else – and the script is bound to the facts. No matter how good a film is segmentally, if we don't know how we're supposed to feel at the end, it can hardly be called satisfying. On the other and substantial hand, most of those segments are very good. If the whole is less than the sum of the parts, if there really is no sum of the parts, those parts are extraordinarily well made.' *(Stanley Kauffmann)*

DOKTOR MABUSE, DER SPIELER: *see* THE *DOCTOR MABUSE* SERIES (DR MABUSE, THE GAMBLER).

DOLCE VITA, LA: *see* LA DOLCE VITA.

DON'T LOOK NOW CT: 8 AV: 7.21

1973 GB/Italy 110 C THRILLER/HORROR

D Nicolas Roeg ☆
W Allan Scott Chris Bryant from Daphne du Maurier's story

Donald Sutherland ☆ Julie Christie ☆ Hilary Mason
Clelia Matania Massimo Serrato

A couple (Donald Sutherland and Julie Christie) whose daughter has drowned go to Venice, where the husband thinks he sees her.

Infuriatingly fragmented, enigmatic and pretentious; yet Nic Roeg's film is also one of the most atmospheric, frightening and memorable horror movies ever, and makes stunning use of its Venice locations. The film contains one of the longest, sexiest lovemaking scenes in cinematic history, and one of the nastiest shocks.

ANTI:

'Story is amazingly simple, but it comes across as perplexing because of Roeg's stylistic impositions. He uses bizarre angles, constantly cuts back and forth between present, past, and future, and stages conversations in which everyone seems out of sync with everyone else. All characters, including Sutherland and Christie, seem disoriented – what are they thinking? The battle between conventional religion and the occult doesn't matter much as far as Sutherland or Christie is concerned (only the priest seems shaken); in fact, I can't really figure out why it matters if the sister or Sutherland has extrasensory powers or if the daughter is sending warnings from the grave – certainly Sutherland would chase any small figure in a hooded red outfit (his daughter wore a red housecoat), regardless of what he'd been warned. All the occult stuff is creepy, yet it really doesn't tie together very well.' *(Danny Peary)*

'The genre can do without filmmakers who value intellectual process over dramatic reality – particularly when the intellectual process leads the viewer to confuse superficial emptiness with the transcendental kind.' *(Cinefantastique)*

'Full of grandly vacuous statements about life, death, love, art, religion, and whatnot (especially whatnot). There was . . . enough artsy crosscutting (particularly in the big sex scene) and flashing backward and forward to have Roeg arrested as a flasher. The shoddy underlying material, blown up, dragged out, worried to would-be metaphysical significance, became merely ludicrous, and, ipso facto, the delight of specialists in false profundity.' *(John Simon)*

MIXED:

'Begins brilliantly but loses its compulsive thread in a maze of gloomy canals.' *(Photoplay)*

'The fanciest, most carefully assembled enigma yet put on the screen. Nicolas Roeg is a chillingly chic director; the picture is an example of high-fashion gothic sensibility. It seems to say what Joseph Losey never dared to but what the audience for Losey's films was always responding to: that decay among the rich and beautiful is sexy. Using du Maurier as a base, Roeg comes closer to getting Borges on the screen than those who have tried it directly, but there's a distasteful clamminess about the picture. Roeg's style is in love with disintegration.' *(Pauline Kael)*

PRO:

'Du Maurier's story is faithfully followed: but the compass needle Roeg follows points to the more distant latitudes of the Argentinian writer Jorge Luis Borges – his symbols of symmetry and reflection, labyrinth and water throng the film . . . It reveals its meaning only at the moment one plunges through the trap door into the abyss of madness. *Don't Look Now* is Roeg's best film: what the story tells and what it intimates are so well balanced.' *(Alexander Walker)*

'The performances are right on the button; Donald Sutherland is (unusually) at his most subdued, top effectiveness as the materialist who ironically becomes the victim of his refusal to believe in the intangible, Julie Christie does her best work in ages as his wife, while a superbly-chosen cast of British and Italian supporting players etch a number of indelibly vivid portraits. Editing too is careful and painstaking (the classically brilliant and erotic love-making scene is merely one of several examples) and plays a vital role in setting the film's mood.' *(Variety)*

'A powerful and dazzling visual texture.' *(Penelope Houston)*

'Conceived in Roeg's usual imagistic style and predicated upon a series of ominous associations (water, darkness, red, shattering glass), it's hypnotically brilliant as it works remorselessly toward a sense of dislocation in time; an undermining of all the senses, in fact, perfectly exemplified by Sutherland's marvellously Hitchcockian walk through a dark alley where a banging shutter, a hoarse cry, a light extinguished at a window, all recur as in a dream, escalating into terror the second time round because a hint of something seen, a mere shadow, may have been the dead child.' *(Tom Milne, Time Out)*

DOOM OF DRACULA: *see* THE *FRANKENSTEIN* SERIES (HOUSE OF FRANKENSTEIN).

DOOMED: *see* IKURU.

DOORS, THE CT: 4 AV: 5.33

1991 US 141 C MUSICAL/BIOPIC

D Oliver Stone
W Oliver Stone J. Randal Johnson

Val Kilmer☆ Frank Whaley Kevin Dillon Meg Ryan Kyle MacLachlan Dennis Burkley Billy Idol Johnny Depp Josh Evans Michael Madsen (cameos by Eric Burdon Mimi Rogers Crispin Glover)

Life and death of Jim Morrison (Val Kilmer).

The Doors might more accurately be called The Bores. Having to sit all the way through it reminded me of arriving very late at a 60s student party full of people you didn't know, where everybody was drunk, stoned or being sick on the carpet. Despite the efforts of Val Kilmer, Morrison emerges not as Stone intends, a poetic, mystical leader of his generation, but as a pretentious prick in tight trousers.

Instead of character and insight, Stone provides monumental, rock-operatic set-pieces of how the Sixties might have been but weren't, and much heavy-handed, film-school symbolism. An Indian chief keeps appearing in Morrison's imagination, though whether he represents morality, our hero's instinctive feeling for the underprivileged, or his empathy for some mystical 'real' America is left up to us.

Stone is too intelligent to portray Morrison without irony, but too humourless to see his hero with any kind of proportion. Typical of Stone's selective vision is the way he excludes the Doors' biggest US hit, the wondrously meat-headed and distinctly unpoetic Morrison composition, 'Hello I Love You, Won't You Tell Me Your Name'. Worse still, Stone fails to provide us with any understanding of how this particular Door, the son of an admiral, came to be unhinged.

The title of the film itself is a misnomer, since the other members of the group are depicted with contempt. Meg Ryan is wasted as Pamela, Morrison's doll-like travelling companion, fellow-junkie and Doormat, who survived him for three years before succumbing to heroin. A big film, but a huge disappointment.

PRO:

'Oliver Stone's clamorous, reverential, much-larger-than-life portrait of the 60's most self-important rock band . . . [He] retains his ability to grab an audience by the throat and sustain that hold for hours, without interruption. And he has succeeded in raising the dead . . . Nowhere is . . . attention to detail more astonishing than in Mr Kilmer's performance which is so right it goes well beyond the uncanny.' *(Janet Maslin, New York Times)*

MIXED:

'Everything one expects from the filmmaker – intense, overblown, riveting, humorless, evocative, self-important and impossible to ignore.' *(Variety)*

'An Oliver Stone movie all the way, big and brave and foolish.' *(Robert Horton, Film Comment)*

ANTI:

'It is folly to lavish $40 million – that's $10 million a Door! – and 2 hr 15 min of your time – on a proposition – some guys can't handle fame – that was evident two decades ago. Maybe it was fun to bathe in decadence back then. But this is no time to wallow in that mire.' *(Richard Corliss, Time)*

DOUBLE, THE: *see* KAGENUSHA.

DOUBLE INDEMNITY AAN   CT: 9 AV: 9.81

1944 US 107 BW THRILLER/ROMANCE

D Billy Wilder ☆ AAN
W Billy Wilder Raymond Chandler ☆ AAN from James M. Cain's novel

Barbara Stanwyck ☆ AAN Fred MacMurray ☆ Edward G. Robinson ☆ Tom Powers Porter Hall Jean Heather Richard Gaines

A femme fatale (Barbara Stanwyck) lures an insurance agent (Fred MacMurray) into murder.

Billy Wilder's superb, clinically detached, suspenseful thriller has been much imitated (*Body Heat* is one example), but never surpassed. The performances of Fred MacMurray, Barbara Stanwyck and Edward G. Robinson are three-dimensional, with the two men being cast against type (MacMurray was usually a light comedian, while Robinson was normally the criminal); and the script, based on a James M. Cain novel, is an inspired collaboration by Billy Wilder and Raymond Chandler. In the original ending shot by Wilder, MacMurray was executed in the gas chamber in San Quentin. Thought to be too shocking, the scenes were cut from the release print – although Wilder claims they were among the best he ever directed. John Seitz's film noir cinematography and Miklos Rozsa's score were both Oscar-nominated.

ANTI:

'The picture never fully takes hold of its opportunities, such as they are, perhaps because those opportunities are appreciated chiefly as surfaces and atmospheres and as very tellable trash. It is proper enough, for instance, that Barbara Stanwyck should suggest a greatly coarsened Esquire drawing and that her affair with MacMurray should essentially be as sexless as it is loveless. Her icy hair and teeth and dresses are well worked out toward communicating this idea. But in Wilder's apparent desire to make it clear that nympholets are cold he has neglected to bring to life the sort of freezing rage of excitations which such a woman presumably inspires in such a fixer as Walter Neff; this sort of genre love scene ought to smell like the inside of an overwrought Electrolux. Wilder has not made much, either, of the tensions of the separateness of the lovers after the murder, or of the coldly nauseated despair and nostalgia which the murderer would feel.' *(James Agee)*

MIXED:

'A trifle long . . . but the realism never relaxes . . . Tough it certainly is . . . a cut above *The Postman* who rang rather too often for my taste.' *(William Whitebait, New Statesman)*

'Most of the high points . . . are visually presented: the killing in the car, the faking of evidence, the encounter with the only dangerous witness. Here and there an imaginative precision in detail bears witness to a good eye; the cigarette the wounded man takes from his pocket carries the moist stain of blood. Against this must be set occasional over-reliance on spoken narrative. The tale is told into a dictaphone by the murderer; a series of flashbacks takes us through the crime and its consequences. The device of the dictaphone is economically used. But the visual basis of the cinema must be jealously guarded; and at a time when film after film talks when it should act one is disinclined to forgive even the mild faults of narrative in *Double Indemnity*.' *(Dilys Powell)*

'There are no appealing characters in this melodrama in which a California femme fatale seduces an insurance salesman into helping her murder her older husband so she can collect on a double indemnity policy. Not even the murder victim or the insurance agent working to solve the case arouses any strong feelings of sympathy. The public went to see it anyhow back in wartime 1944, and it still holds up well today, when its coldly analytical approach is even more widely appreciated. The lack of passion extends to every element of the picture, including the love scenes between murder conspirators Barbara Stanwyck and Fred MacMurray, which are downright frosty.' *(Martin Quigley, Jr and Richard Gertner, 1970)*

PRO:

'Billy Wilder is, from beginning to end, the complete

master of his story, tells it with consummate economy and packs it with visual subtlety.' *(Richard Winnington)*

'Profoundly, intensely entertaining.' *(Richard Mallett, Punch)*

'The saga of chicanery and death is told with all the relish of a Hearst reporter, sans the sentimentality, and with considerably more art . . . *Double Indemnity* at no time makes compromise with an adult approach to drama. Both Wilder and Paramount are to be congratulated for having the courage to prepare and present such a photoplay.' *(Herb Sterne)*

'The greatness of this seedy masterpiece is that all three are real, little people fatally drawn into combat. If there's a better thriller, and a more penetrating study of greed within the genre, then its title escapes me.' *(NFT Bulletin)*

'Anyone who has read Chandler's novels and short stories recognizes the great ear he had for flip and mordant dialogue. Because of its brilliant script, fine characterizations, noir aesthetics and its sense of time and place, *Double Indemnity* has become one of the cornerstone films in any retrospective screening of films noir.' *(Robert Ottoson, A Reference Guide to the American Film Noir: 1940-58, 1981)*

DOUBLE LIFE, A

CT: 5 AV: 7.30

1947 US 103 BW DRAMA/THRILLER

D George Cukor AAN
W Ruth Gordon Garson Kanin AAN

Ronald Colman ☆ AAW Shelley Winters ☆ Signe Hasso ☆ Edmond O'Brien Millard Mitchell

Deranged actor (Ronald Colman) loses himself in the role of Othello, and carries it over into his offstage life.

This entertaining if far-fetched variation on *Jekyll and Hyde* won Colman an Oscar (even though his onstage performance as Othello looks embarrassing today). It also made a star of Shelley Winters (playing his blowsy waitress-victim). Director Cukor, who had been a theatre director himself, is more at ease within the theatre than when he ventures into the more realistic world outside. The same could be said of husband-and-wife writers, Garson Kanin and Ruth Gordon.

PRO:

'Reproduces the atmosphere of the theatre in a way that puts most backstage movies to shame. Its characters are recognizable stage folk – temperamental actors, harried directors, short-tempered stage managers and frantic publicists. When you watch the lengthy sequences from the last act of *Othello*, you have the conviction that this is a performance actually being witnessed by a live audience as well as by the camera. George Cukor deserves much credit for the effectiveness of the film, for his fluid staging neatly blends sharply detailed realism with hallucination. Milton Krasner's artful camera work is of tremendous assistance, as is Miklos Rozsa's score.' *(Fortnight)*

'Superb melodrama, suspenseful, excellently written, directed, acted. Highly recommended.' *(Scheuer)*

MIXED:

'One of the effects overdone is the exuberance of an audience aroused to a pitch of excitement only possible from "dress extras" rehearsed to applaud wildly, all together now! at an assistant director's signal. The second year of *Othello* on Broadway, with a promised third, must be looked upon as exuberance of another kind, since the theatre repudiates any such phenomenon. However, the picture's entertainment quotient is higher than average to the susceptible and overshadows these lapses.' *(Norbert Lusk, New Movies)*

'As a piece of film story-telling it is generally skilled. Yet the central situation is artificial.' *(Dilys Powell)*

'Colman is not at his best, and the role of Othello is so far out of his range that he's gentlemanly and dispassionate when he means to be fiery and hot.' *(Pauline Kael)*

'Despite a pleasant star performance remains unrewarding if taxing, and the entertainment value of the piece is on the thin side considering the mighty talents involved.' *(Halliwell)*

DOUBLE LIFE OF VÉRONIQUE, THE

CT: 4 AV: 5.88

(aka *La Double Vie De Véronique*)

1991 France/Poland 92/96 C DRAMA/FOREIGN

D Krzysztof Kieślowski ✗
W Krzysztof Kieślowski Krzysztof Piesewicz ●

Irène Jacob ✗ Halina Gryglaszewska Kalina Jedrusik Aleksander Bardini Wladyslaw Kowalski Jerzy Gudejko

Two identical young women – one Polish, one French – exist in different parts of Europe (both are played by Irène Jacob). Their relationship is never explained: perhaps they are twins, or the Polish one is being imagined by the other, or they reflect the fact that east and west are mirror images of each other. Who knows? Who cares?

Its publicity blurb described this as 'a simple and moving love story which transcends life itself'. Whatever that means. This is a horrible example of how low a talented director can sink, if he swallows certain film academics' insistence that a movie is merely a collection of signs and symbols: here there are signs and symbols galore, mainly on the theme of mirrors, glass and puppetry, but they fail to add up to a meaning or a comprehensible narrative. Still less do they offer insights or entertainment. The central performance by Irène Jacob (which won her Best Actress at Cannes) is, like the film itself, beautiful, moody, heavily romantic and empty. The film does have an excellent soundtrack and received reverential reviews because of the Polish director's previous work, notably his distinguished but dour *Dekalog*. Rambling, abstruse, pseudo-mystical and pointless, it exemplifies the deadly sterility of so much European art-house cinema.

PRO:

'Coherence is assured by Irène Jacob's luminous central performance, by Kieślowski's effortless control of mood, and by his subtle use of repeated motifs. Whether you swallow what seems to be Kieślowski's thesis (if we can recognize our affinities with some obscure soul-twin, we may learn from their suffering) comes down to a matter of faith; but there's no denying his compassion or ability to invest places, objects and passing moments with an almost luminous power.' *(Geoff Andrew, Time Out)*

'Mysterious and poetic.' *(Roger Ebert)*

MIXED:

'Kieślowski crafts a haunting atmosphere, preferring mood to meaning, emphasizing his charismatic leading lady over the plot. If it doesn't add up to much, Véronique casts a hypnotic spell all the same.' *(Video Magazine)*

'Despite pic's many-splendoured outbursts of filmic creativity and intense emotion, final result remains a head-scratching cipher with blurred edges.' *(Variety)*

DOUBLE, THE: *see* KAGEMUSHA.

DOUBLE X CT: 6 AV: 2.40

1992 GB 97 C THRILLER/SO BAD

D Shani S. Grewal ●
W Shani S. Grewal ●

Simon Ward ● William Katt Norman Wisdom ●
Bernard Hill ● Gemma Craven ●

Electronics genius (Norman Wisdom) seeks to escape clutches of evil gang.

Publicized as 'a tough, all-action British thriller', this brought Norman Wisdom out of movie retirement as Arthur Clutten – not, as you might imagine, a clottish glutton for punishment, but a criminal mastermind and electronics genius. One minor flaw in the movie is that our Norman is about as convincing a computer whizz as Russ Abbott would be, playing Indiana Jones. Clutten is trying to escape from 'The Organisation', a sinister if grievously undermanned band of criminals, consisting of an evil property developer (Simon Ward), an over-the-hill gangster's moll (Gemma Craven), and an over-the-top, sadistic Irish cripple (Bernard Hill). We are asked to believe that the forces of law and order are powerless against this terrible trio – frightened out of their collective wits, perhaps, by the acting.

Double X stands head-and-shoulders below all competitors for its kamikaze casting, deplorable direction, preposterous plot, abysmal acting, catatonic cinematography and pathetic production values. I shudder at the thought of what the out-takes must have been like, if indeed there were any out-takes. One can only await with eager pessimism the further work of its writer-producer-director, a gentleman calling himself Shani S. Grewal – which is, as the publicity blurb says, 'a name to remember'. Perhaps at last we have found a cinematic equivalent to the great poet William McGonagall, a world-class incompetent to rival Edward D. Wood Jr (1922-78), the legendary American auteur responsible for such cinematic horrors as *Plan 9 From Outer Space*. *Double X* marks a new low in British cinema, and I must confess that the masochist in me enjoyed every regrettable, mindboggling minute of it.

'An inept low-budget suspenser. Reliable cast is double-crossed by a laughable script and clumsy helming.' *(Variety)*

'Norman Wisdom's first film for 20 years is a giggle-free British thriller that makes the worst of his Pinewood comedies seem sophisticated masterpieces.' *(Tom Hutchinson, Mail on Sunday)*

'The name of the game here is don't try and teach an old dog new tricks.' *(Michael Darvell, What's On in London)*

'An unspeakable and amateurish affair which if nothing else shows what desperate straits the British film industry is in these days . . . Clueless . . . There is absolutely no level – not even in the realms of self-parody – on which the film works.' *(Steve Grant, Time Out)*

'The worst British film for decades. A truly dreadful amateurish shambles.' *(Alexander Walker)*

'Enjoyable only under the influence of a six-pack and a stiff vindaloo.' *(Sheila Johnston, Independent)*

'As the film's executive producer Noel Cronin says, "If you make a film of high quality with a low budget, it will make money". Daringly, however, he has avoided doing anything so obvious: instead, he has made a film of such baroque incompetence that it will make money by attracting the kind of audience which slows down to watch traffic accidents.' *(Christopher Tookey, Sunday Telegraph)*

'I suppose the team's next project will star Charlie Drake in a remake of *Die Hard* set in a bungalow in Clacton.' *(Sean French, Observer)*

'Suggests that the British film industry is bent on ritual suicide.' *(Halliwell)*

'Candidate for the funniest bad film ever. Lovers of all-time turkeys should seek it out.' *(Rose)*

DOWN WENT MCGINTY: *see* GREAT MCGINTY, THE.

DR CRIPPEN LEBT: *see* THE *DOCTOR MABUSE* SERIES (DR MABUSE, THE GAMBLER).

DR DOLITTLE/DR DOOLITTLE: *see* DOCTOR DOLITTLE.

DR EHRLICH'S MAGIC BULLET: *see* DOCTOR EHRLICH'S MAGIC BULLET.

DR JEKYLL AND MR HYDE CT: 8 AV: 8.50

1931 US 90 BW SF/HORROR

D Rouben Mamoulian ☆
W Samuel Hoffenstein Percy Heath ☆ from Robert Louis Stevenson's novel

Fredric March ☆ AAN Miriam Hopkins ✔
Rose Hobart Holmes Herbert Halliwell Hobbes
Edgar Norton

A doctor (Fredric March) accidentally turns himself into a homicidal maniac.

There had already been four previous attempts to film Robert Louis Stevenson's story, but this – the first talkie version – was easily the best, and is even today considered a classic of the horror and science fiction genres. The source of Dr Jekyll's psychosis in sexual frustration is made surprisingly clear: a reminder that this was made in the days before the puritanical Hays code. The main reasons this is a classic, though, are Mamoulian's innovative direction; Karl Struss's stunning cinematography; and Fredric March's central performance, which may today look over-the-top (especially thanks to some exaggerated make-up effects) but was deemed impressive and terrifying enough to win him an Academy Award. The critical response, though mixed, was unusually favourable for a horror film – perhaps because of the film's origins in an acknowledged literary classic.

ANTI:

'I should like to suggest that it should be made illegal to trot out any further version of this hackneyed story for another twenty years.' *(James Agate, Tatler)*

'A cheaply sensational affair compared to the silent Barrymore version. The brutal exaggeration of Hyde's makeup, physically so much more revolting than Barrymore's, spiritually so much less so, is a typical Mamoulian touch.' *(Dwight Macdonald)*

MIXED:

'In many passages it is an astonishingly fine bit of interpreting a classic, but as popular fare it loses in vital reaction. Camera trick of changing a central figure from the handsome Fredric March into the bestial, ape-like monster Mr Hyde, carries a terrific punch, but in each successive use of the device – and it is repeated four times – it weakens in hair-raising effect.' *(Variety)*

'The director, Rouben Mamoulian, rather overdoes the pseudo-science at the beginning, but at some levels this story seems to work in every version and this one, set in a mid-Victorian environment, suggests the lust that has to come out – and the attraction of the gutter.' *(Pauline Kael)*

PRO:

'A far more tense and shuddery affair than it was as John Barrymore's silent picture . . . Mr March's portrayal is something to arouse admiration, even taking into consideration the camera wizardry.' *(New York Times)*

'Mamoulian was known as an experimentalist and would introduce such ideas in *Dr Jekyll and Mr Hyde* as voice-over dialogue to reveal a character's thoughts, dissolves with one scene directly relating to the next and diagonal split-screens with the character in one shot indirectly interacting with the character in the other shot.' *(Donald F. Glut, Classic Movie Monsters, 1978)*

'Not only the most horrific but also much the best of the various versions.' *(Ivan Butler, Horror in the Cinema, 1967)*

DR MABUSE'S RAYS OF DEATH: *see* THE *DOCTOR MABUSE* SERIES (THE THOUSAND EYES OF DOCTOR MABUSE).

DR NO: *see BOND* SERIES.

DR PHIBES: *see* ABOMINABLE DOCTOR PHIBES, THE.

DR PHIBES RISES AGAIN CT: 7 AV: 5.50

1972 GB 89 C HORROR/COMEDY

D Robert Fuest
W Robert Fuest Robert Blees ✔

Vincent Price ☆ Robert Quarry ☆ Valli Kemp
Fiona Lewis Peter Cushing Beryl Reid Terry-Thomas Hugh Griffith Peter Jeffrey ☆ Gerald Sim
John Thaw John Cater Lewis Fiander.

Dr Phibes (Vincent Price) seeks the elixir of life to revive his dead wife.

Comic-strip horror which has to be approached in the right spirit if it is to be enjoyed: everything is hammy and over the top, and Vincent Price gives one of his most enjoyable performances, aided and abetted by an admirable British supporting cast. Brian Eatwell contributes splendid art direction.

ANTI:

'Dull, witless rehash of *The Abominable Doctor Phibes* . . . The same wasted opportunities with art deco sets, a scattering of pointless guest appearances, and only one death scene with balls (murder by scorpion). Pity it wasn't given to a director who could exploit the real possibilities.' *(Tony Rayns, Time Out)*

PRO:

'Vincent Price, as Phibes, delivers one of his priceless theatric performances, and Quarry is a properly ruthless rival who nearly matches Phibes in knowledge and cunning.' *(Variety)*

'It's refreshing to find a sequel that's better than its prototype. The return of the abominable Phibes, his pallor flushed with the success of his initial screen appearance, is accompanied both by a larger budget and, more to the point, by a greater display of confidence at all levels of the production.' *(Philip Strick, MFB)*

'Splendid sequel to *The Abominable Doctor Phibes* with a witty and inspired script whose absurdities are convincingly integrated into the story line and with a magnificently camp performance by Price.' *(Alan Frank)*

DR STRANGELOVE AAN CT: 7 AV: 9.25

(aka *Dr Strangelove or: How I Learned to Stop Worrying and Love the Bomb*)

1964 GB 94 BW COMEDY/WAR/SF

D Stanley Kubrick ☆ AAN
W Stanley Kubrick Terry Southern
Peter George ☆ AAN from Peter George's book *Red Alert*

Peter Sellers ✗ AAN George C. Scott ☆ Peter Bull
Sterling Hayden Keenan Wynn Slim Pickens
James Earl Jones Tracy Reed

A mad general (George C. Scott), helped by stupidity, malice and incompetence in high places, brings about the nuclear holocaust.

An undoubted landmark in cinema, this black comedy was immediately helped by those establishment voices which attacked it:

'No Communist could dream of a more effective anti-American film to spread abroad than this one. US officials, including the President, had better take a look . . . to see its effect on the national interest.' *(Chalmers Roberts, Washington Post)*

'[It] will harm America's reputation as a reliable ally.' *(Clare Boothe Luce, New York Herald Tribune)*

'I cannot abide [Kubrick's] blasts of derisions and mockery at everyone . . . [He] is saying that top-level scientists with their computers and their mechanical brains, the diplomats, the experts, the prime ministers, and even the president of the United States are all fuddy duddies or maniac monsters who are completely unable to control the bomb.' *(Bosley Crowther)*

The film received huge acclaim from most 60s critics, not least because it reinforced their view of military authority and the Cold War:

'A tragi-comic masterpiece – the first truly moral film of our time.' *(F & F)*

'The first American movie to speak truly for our generation.' *(Robert Brustein, New York Review of Books)*

'The mordant humor and Swiftian satire of *Dr Strangelove* . . . leaves certain hallowed local institutions (which were in dire need of unhallowing) reeling against the ropes.' *(Herman G. Weinberg)*

'One of the most cogent, comic and cruel movies to come along in many a year, and one of the best. Don't miss it – provided that you have the wit and stamina to withstand a savage satire on a number of our society's untouchables, the courage to hear a howl of outrage at the supersonic supersecurity idiocies of our time and the readiness to share Stanley Kubrick's realization that ironic laughter and ferocious caricature are the only possible responses of a sane man to the insanities of the international race toward nuclear self-destruction.' *(Judith Crist)*

'May be the best comedy since sound came to Hollywood, or if not that, the best of the postwar years. Respectable people have argued that it is an un-American film because of its refusal to accept at face value authority's claim to responsibility. But this is nonsense. In its rowdy questioning of verities it reasserts one of Americanism's oldest tenet – skepticism.' *(Richard Schickel)*

'*Dr Strangelove* is, first and foremost, absolutely unflinching: relentlessly perceptive of human beings to the point of inhumanity. In technique, it understates provocatively and comments by apposition. Kubrick's precise use of camera angles, his uncanny sense of lighting, his punctuation with close-ups and occasionally with zoom shots, all galvanize the picture into macabre yet witty reality.' *(Stanley Kauffman)*

'The most courageous film ever made . . . Its style is Juvenalian satire; this purpose, the evacuation of fear and anger through the acting out of frightful fantasies. Kubrick has flushed a monster from its psychic lair – the universal fear of nuclear accident – and then proceeded to feed and nourish it, letting it perform its worst before your eyes. The consequence of spectacle is . . . a temporary purgation; to witness the end of the world as a comic event is, indeed, to stop worrying and to love the bomb.' *(Robert Brustein, New York Review of Books)*

In retrospect, some of the satire seems not so much Juvenalian as juvenile. The phallic symbolism is especially crude. And, as Alan Frank has written:

'Kubrick's casting of Peter Sellers in three roles was more of a gimmick than dramatically satisfying since the actor was allowed to overact fatally in comparison with the rest of the cast. Seen now, the film is less impressive and much of the humour seems laid on too thickly and, in terms of its anti-nuclear message, *Fail Safe* makes the same points rather more chillingly.'

The screenplay is more like a series of revue sketches than a sustained and developing narrative:

'Artistically it cloaks its imperishable moments by untidy narrative and unattractively contrasty photography.' *(Halliwell)*

However, Kubrick's directorial skills are in evidence:

'Visually, it is always fascinating. Each of the three parallel stories is shot in its own camera style: the hazy, vibrating, incoherent battle footage of the assault or Burpleson Air Force Base; the quickly cut, intense close-ups of the bomber flight-deck, straining crew, endless instruments – especially the fragmented hysterically tense duel with the missile; the weird immense black steeple of the War Room shot with carefully composed static shots of eerie beauty.' *(Norman Kagan, The Cinema of Stanley Kubrick, 1972)*

At the end of a Cold War which did not end in nuclear conflagration, it may be tempting to regard it as a museum piece, or join Joan Didion in her lofty dismissal of the film:

'Seldom have we seen so much made over so little.'

But much of the black humour does work in the way that the contemporary critics described:

'What makes the picture so funny, terrifying and horribly believable is that everyone in the film really has learned to stop worrying, as smokers do about lung cancer after living with the statistics for a bit.' *(Penelope Gilliatt)*

However, audiences usually like someone to root for; and the absence of anyone along these lines may account for the film's being more popular with critics than with audiences. One of the most unusual aspects of the film, in fact, is its apparent detachment:

'*Dr Strangelove* has been made from the viewpoint of another race in another universe observing how mankind, its reflexes scored in its nervous system and its mind entangled in orthodoxies, insisted on destroying itself.' *(Stanley Kauffmann)*

In reality, though, the film was far from detached: part of its skill lay in making the audience feel morally superior to those it was watching:

'[It is] thoroughly irreverent about everything the establishment takes seriously . . . there are no rebels, only heroes; heroes of politics, warfare, science, all of them so repellent or, at best, nondescript, that the only rebels must be in the audience – amused, revolted, and ready to revolt.' *(John Simon)*

Beneath the surface of *Dr Strangelove* it is not difficult to see the modishness of 60s rebellion which – almost alone of contemporary critics – Pauline Kael found irritating (even though she went on to promulgate it, later in the 60s):

'*Dr Strangelove* opened a new movie era. It ridiculed everything and everybody it showed, but concealed its own liberal pieties.' *(Pauline Kael)*

DR ZHIVAGO: *see* DOCTOR ZHIVAGO.

DRACULA CT: 6 AV: 7.73

1931 US 84 BW HORROR

D Tod Browning
W Garrett Fort from Bram Stoker's novel

Bela Lugosi ☆ Helen Chandler David Manners
Dwight Frye ✔ Edward Van Sloan

Transylvanian vampire count (Bela Lugosi) rampages through England.

An important horror film because of its opening fifteen minutes, which establish a creepy atmosphere and have been imitated ad nauseam. From then on, however, it's downhill all the way: staginess and endless verbosity triumph over visual imagery, Lugosi (who had played the role on stage since 1927) becomes more hammy than frightening, and when the Count hits London the story becomes incomprehensible. Far too much of the exciting action takes place offscreen, and the climax is extraordinarily lame. A massive popular success despite these failings, it spawned innumerable imitations and sequels, including two from Universal: *Dracula's Daughter* (1936) and *Son of Dracula* (1943).

MIXED:

'An exciting melodrama, not as good as it ought to be but a cut above the ordinary trapdoor-and-winding-sheet mystery film.' *(Time)*

'What with Mr Browning's imaginative direction and Mr Lugosi's make-up and weird gestures, this picture succeeds to some extent in its grand guignol intentions.' *(New York Times)*

'Had the rest of the picture lived up to the first sequence in the ruined castle in Transylvania, *Dracula* would be acclaimed by public and critics. It would have been a horror and thrill classic long remembered; and a splendid example of true motion picture. However, after this grand introduction, Universal elected to desert the Bram Stoker novel and follow the stage play.' *(Hollywood Filmograph)*

'The mistiest parts are the best; when the lights go up, the interest goes down . . . The dialogue, even by former standards, is deadeningly slow, and long stretches never break away from the confines of the stage. Much of the camerawork is uninspired and static, though there is one travelling shot, through the Doctor's sanatorium grounds, which is remarkable for those days of enclosed booths. The sea journey to Whitby promises much, but then cuts straight to the finding of the dead crew. Almost every climax, in fact, is cut before it reaches its peak.' *(Ivan Butler, 1967)*

'There are various reasons why the film has lost some of its effectiveness today. Styles in acting and direction have undergone considerable alteration in the past thirty years and more. Much of the performances in *Dracula* today seem considerably overdone, a result of too literal transference from the stage, where broadness of performances is a necessity. The action seems somewhat static, more in keeping with stage production rather than the greater freedom of the film. In many portions the sound was faulty and the photography indistinct. Today the total lack of musical scoring creates an air of monotony, particularly in the opening scenes at Castle Dracula.' *(Drake Douglas)*

PRO:

'It'll chill you and fill you full of fears. You'll find it creepy and cruel and crazed. It is superbly photographed . . . Brrrrr! We enjoyed it!' *(New York Daily News)*

It is difficult to think of anybody who could quite match the performance in the vampire part of Bela Lugosi, even to the faint flavour of foreign speech that fits so neatly.' *(Variety)*

'Lugosi outdoes any of the performances of the undead count which we have seen him give on the stage. There are times when the force of the evil vampire seems to sweep from him beyond the confines of the screen and into the minds of the audience. His cruel smile – hypnotic glance – slow, stately tread, they make *Dracula*.' *(Hollywood Filmograph)*

'This horror classic has been much maligned in recent years by turncoats who somehow expect it to become more modern as years pass. Actually, it's great for its time and the first quarter-hour is still unsurpassed for sheer atmosphere. Flaws lie in its stagey adaptation, some dated techniques, but it's still entertaining. Stylized acting fits in remarkably well, malcontents notwithstanding.' *(Castle of Frankenstein)*

DRACULA

CT: 8 AV: 7.75

(aka *The Horror of Dracula*)

1958 GB 82 C HORROR

D Terence Fisher ☆
W Jimmy Sangster ☆ from Bram Stoker's novel ☆

Christopher Lee ☆ Peter Cushing ☆
Melissa Stribling Carol Marsh Michael Gough
John Van Eyssen Valerie Gaunt Miles Malleson

Transylvanian count (Christopher Lee) visits Britain.

Wonderfully stylish, colourful though hardly subtle version of the Dracula story, with two definitive performances by Christopher Lee as Dracula and Peter Cushing as his nemesis, Van Helsing. Director Terence Fisher shows himself here to be a master of colour, mood and editing. There are many classic moments, chief among them Dracula's first appearance, his attack on the vampire woman in his castle, and the climactic battle between Dracula and Van Helsing.

It was disliked intensely by most contemporary critics for its perverse eroticism (the young women seem to invite the Count's dental caresses, and Lucy's luring of the child suggests sexual abuse) and for its sadistic brutality (director Terence Fisher is at pains to emphasize the savagery of the Christians who wish to destroy Dracula). The use of colour was also much criticized: critics didn't like the sight of blood if it was red. The public on both sides of the Atlantic, however, responded to the merits of the film, or the sensations that it offered, and took it to its heart. This ground-breaking British horror film is now generally considered a masterpiece.

ANTI:

'A case of a good ghoul gone wrong . . . Instead of the vintage horror of old Transylvania, we have Dr Peter Cushing treating a case of galloping vampirism as if it were all part of the National Health Service.' *(Evening Standard)*

'The blood is too much like ketchup to be taken seriously, but Dracula disintegrating under our noses is something I draw the line at.' *(Isabel Quigly, Daily Mail)*

'Perhaps the constant hunt for hemoglobin is slowing our villain down for this time there are strong indications that the once gory plot is showing signs of anemia.' *(A.H. Weiler, New York Times)*

'Gore blimey! . . . a truly horrible Horror film . . . I'm sure that whoever said the film industry needed a shot in the arm did not expect to be taken quite so literally.' *(Anthony Carthew, Daily Herald)*

'One of the most revolting pictures I have seen for years.' *(Leonard Mosley, Daily Express)*

MIXED:

'It is so well made that it doesn't frighten . . . Probably the best acted, directed and photographed horror film yet made. But to be effective *Dracula* needs a certain amount of bad acting. Ham as well as blood is what he feeds on.' *(Ivon Adams, Morning Star)*

'Scriptwriter Jimmy Sangster concluded [Bram Stoker's novel] was old-fashioned, overlarded with symbols, and much too concerned with establishing the proper mood of terror and anguish . . . and to bury all the covert symbolism of the vampire the new Dracula substituted a blatant, almost athletic display of sadism and necrophilia – a young (physiognomically) uncadaverous vampire slobbering blood over the naked throats of his victims . . . It was most impressive in its physical aspects, in lushly colored sets and costumes and a distinct flair for period touches . . . And sometimes even a whiff of Gothic survives Terence Fisher's pedestrian direction.' *(Carlos Clarens, An Illustrated History of the Horror Film, 1967)*

PRO:

'Lotsatension and suspense.' *(Variety)*

'It's the only one that I've done that's ever been any good, in my opinion. It's the only one that remotely resembles the original book.' *(Christopher Lee)*

'Directed by Terence Fisher with immense flair for the blood-curdling shot, this Technicoloured nightmare should prove a real treat . . . The scenes are smoothly meshed, the dialogue crisp enough, the plotting done with a deft hand at creating a sense of mystery. Even the acting has style. Peter Cushing is coolly scientific as the medical hero who combats the century-old evils of Count Dracula, and Christopher Lee is a real fright as that royal fiend . . . The James Bernard score is monumentally sinister and the Jack Ashley photography full of foreboding atmosphere.' *(Film Bulletin)*

'Christopher Lee scores points by not looking too much a monster.' *(William Whitebait, New Statesman)*

'Picture has a lot of graphic violence, but it fits the subject rather than being exploitative. Other than the two leads, all the performances are forgettable. Cushing's well cast as Van Helsing, but in this film he's a little too humorless, as if his blood had already been drained. But Lee's madly inspired vampire is terrific: he's cruel, energetic, intelligent, tall and imposing.' *(Danny Peary)*

'The film is perhaps typified by its beautiful opening sequence in which Christopher Lee appears, a menacing shadow between pillars at the top of a staircase, then glides down the stairs in a prolonged take to reveal not the grotesque figure that Lugosi portrayed but, on the contrary, a crisply charming aristocrat.' *(David Pirie, Time Out)*

'Certainly Hammer's best film and probably the best in the post-war genre movie. The movie established Lee as the ideal screen Dracula and provided him with a worthy opponent in Cushing's Van Helsing. Sangster's script is spare and effective and wisely returns to Stoker's book rather than the stage play. The film gains immeasurably by its period setting and Bernard Robinson's Gothic sets, while Fisher's masterly direction sets a standard in Gothic horror as yet unmatched by any other director.' *(Alan Frank)*

DRAUGHTSMAN'S CONTRACT, THE

CT: 2 AV: 5.81

1982 GB 103 C DRAMA/THRILLER

D Peter Greenaway ✗
W Peter Greenaway ●

Anthony Higgins Janet Suzman
Anne Louise Lambert Hugh Fraser
Neil Cunningham Dave Hill David Gant
David Meyer Tony Meyer Nicholas Amer

In the 17th century, a lady (Janet Suzman) hires an artist (Anthony Higgins) to make drawings of her house, and rewards him with access to her bedchamber. Then there is a mysterious murder . . .

Peter Greenaway's first critical success made an impression because of the way it looked: elegant, formal, austere. Emperors' new clothes have never been worn with more confidence. But it is a murder mystery without a solution, an essay in precious pomposity with cardboard characters, abominable dialogue, and the pace of a drugged snail. It is familiarly known among Greenaway's detractors as *The Draughtsman's Con-Trick*; a more appropriate title, in view of its strenuous attempts to emulate Revenge Drama, might be *'Tis Pity He's a Bore*.

PRO:

'The film is about painting, and as paintings don't move, so the camera doesn't move.' *(Peter Greenaway)*

'An elegantly malevolent delight.' *(Stanley Kauffman)*

'What we have here is a tantalizing puzzle, wrapped in eroticism and presented with the utmost elegance. I have never seen a film quite like it.' *(Roger Ebert)*

'The visually splendid style of the film is matched by performances of enormous wit and that flair for period posturing that is one of the grace notes of British acting at its classiest.' *(Daily Mail)*

'Highly English, in both use of landscape and its deployment, albeit in period terms, of that most native of genres, the detective story.' *(Tim Pulleine)*

'Delicious thematic adumbrations peep up like moles surfacing on the immaculate Augustan lawns.' *(Nigel Andrews, Financial Times)*

'Best enjoyed as a sly piece of double bluff, a puzzle without a solution, an avant garde hoax in the spirit of Dada and the surrealists.' *(Observer)*

'Greenaway creates an imaginary world . . . which enables him to explore certain intellectual concepts. Behind all [his] works is a postmodernist sense that narrative structures of chronological succession and logical cause-and-effect are false to the essentially chaotic and problematic nature of subjective experience, and that the patterns we discern in experience are wholly illusory.' *(James Park, Learning to Dream, 1984)*

'A teasingly enigmatic elaboration of a 17th-century sexual conspiracy.' *(John Wyver, The Moving Image, 1989)*

'A film of great idiosyncrasy, imagination and visual panache ... [But] where is the density of detail, the crisp comedy, of his earlier films?' *(The Times)*

MIXED:

'A snappy cruel comedy ... Though hinting that any attempt to understand reality leads us to insoluble mysteries, Greenaway also insists that material power determine which interpretations of the world prevail at any given time ... Not a pleasant movie ... charged by a morbidity that verges on the misanthropic.' *(John Powers, LA Weekly)*

'The impeccable pictorial surface can't disguise a degree of academic dryness in the story's conception and execution. The piece becomes too fond of conversations which ... grow turgidly verbose ... A tale which slowly runs out of creative steam.' *(Douglas McVay, F & F)*

'Greenaway ... marvellously portrays the squalor of morals beneath an elegance of dress ... It is a chilly film engaging the mind and eye but not the heart, for Greenaway uses characters like pawns not people.' *(Mail on Sunday)*

ANTI:

'A load of posturing poo-poo.' *(Alan Parker, fellow director)*

'Perhaps the four-hour version which may one day become available is clearer.' *(Guardian)*

'So pretentious, hollow, and odious that it set my teeth on edge; I had the urge to throw something equally rotten back at the screen. It was an attempt at a bawdy, witty, nasty Restoration comedy bolstered with the savagery of Jacobean revenge tragedy. But the comedy was not witty enough, the tragedy was gratuitously grafted on, and the whole thing made no sense. An *olla podrida* of smuttiness, obscurantism, and self-congratulation?' *(John Simon)*

'The combination of pretension and theatrical posturing proves as depressing an experience as the cinema can provide. If you stay with it that long you'll find an undergraduate socialist comment at the end.' *(Shipman)*

DRESSED TO KILL

CT: 6 AV: 5.46

1980 US 100/105 C THRILLER

D Brian De Palma ✗
W Brian De Palma

Michael Caine Angie Dickinson Nancy Allen Keith Gordon Dennis Franz David Margulies Kenny Baker Brandon Maggart Susanna Clemm Fred Weber

Hooker (Nancy Allen) investigates knife-murder of randy houswife (Angie Dickinson).

Crude, pornographically violent, misogynistic and over-indebted to *Psycho*: Brian De Palma's psychological slasher movie is all of these. (The plot logic doesn't stand up to close examination either.) All the same, it's genuinely shocking, there are many sequences of great technical ingenuity and it can certainly make an audience scream.

ANTI:

'Sophomoric soft-core pornography, vulgar manipulation of the emotions for mere sensation, salacious but inept dialogue that is a cross between comic-strip Freudianism and sniggering double entendres, and a plot line so full of holes as to be at best a dotted line ... The murder scene is profoundly distasteful ... fashion-magazine chic à la Helmut Newton – perhaps the unholiest form of titillation. Claims by De Palmists notwithstanding, this is neither unblinking stoicism; nor, more preposterous yet, the meting out of poetic justice. It is moral aphasia, and something uglier still: the drawing out of murder into languorous, lascivious excitation.' *(John Simon)*

'By casting a halo of excitement around killing, a glow of degradation around living, and linking the two in a queasy, guilty partnership, De Palma is asking us to celebrate the joys of barbarism in a world already drunk on rape, torture, murder and war.' *(Sunday Times)*

PRO:

'De Palma's interests – in satire, Hitchcockian horror and gothic romance – finally converge in a fully integrated, iconoclastic work.' *(Stephen Farber, New West)*

'The only blacks we see in this movie find the very sight of an attractive white woman an inducement to rape. No doubt about it: in this movie, what women dream of is rape. Some will find that notion repugnant. People are going to be outraged that he has depicted female fantasies as being about rape; they are going to be outraged that he makes violence unutterably beautiful. But if this movie has a theme, it's that there's a vast difference between fantasy and reality, and hence a vast difference between the screen and real life. Dickinson and Allen both dream of violence, but that doesn't mean they welcome violence in their lives. And we may go to the movies to indulge our own naughty fantasies, but that doesn't mean we want to go home and enact them. In fact, the people who refuse to soften up and let themselves enjoy a dirty dream like this one – they, De Palma says, are the dangerous ones. Refuse fantasy, and you get twisted inside.' *(Stephen Schiff, Boston Phoenix)*

'The characters ... are not candidates for compassion or figures of raunchy fun. They are animated mannequins ... De Palma knows all about [camera tricks]. His camera glides down corridors and through rooms as elegantly as a downhill racer with murder on his mind . . . He builds up suspense through the use of the unsuspecting detail . . . [His films] have become exhibitions of a master puppeteer pulling high-tension strings.' *(Richard Corliss, Time)*

'Something of a technical exercise . . . an essay on the tracking shot, framed by a pair of dreams. Its major sequences are all variations on the idea of surveillance, and they all turn out to be elaborate little jokes on the audience's belief that it has been following the action; in this flashy, shameless thriller of sexual anxiety, the audience is always taken from behind . . . De Palma is so confident in this picture, and so determined to show us the errors of our perceptions, that he can repeat an effect and fool us the second time, too . . . [in a] relentless demonstration that we shouldn't trust what we see.' *(Terrence Rafferty, S & S)*

'As fascinating in its suggestiveness as it is infuriating in its incoherence, [the film] plays intricately throughout on doubles and on ambiguities of sexual identity . . . It seems extremely important that the film should produce as its male hero a gentle and feminine character who is excluded . . . from becoming the female hero's lover. The film, in other words, while built on the horrors arising from sexual difference, can see . . . no resolution of that difference except through castration . . . This may be why De Palma's habitual identification with women is accompanied, paradoxically, by an apparent animus against them.' *(Robin Wood, Hollywood From Vietnam to Reagan, 1986)*

'The first great film of the eighties.' *(David Denby)*

'De Palma goes right for the audience's jugular . . . it fully milks the boundaries of its "R" rating.' *(Variety)*

'De Palma earns the title of master, all right . . . but Hitch remains the grand master.' *(Roger Ebert)*

MIXED:

'Destined for controversy due to its frequent bloodletting, its porno-romantic situations, its depiction of a transsexual as a pathological murderer and of [extramarital] sex . . . [The] erotic expository opening is shortly followed by a magnificently conceived and executed [silent] sequence . . . The transsexual is seen by De Palma as an object of amusement and menace . . . Yet the director's point-of-view . . . [and] his combination of conflicting moods are all sewn together in a manner so compellingly cinematic that you easily forgive (or at least forget) the [implausibilities].' *(Jack Babuscio, Gay News)*

'The success of the film undoubtedly hangs around the highly charged erotic content that shadows every scene the way the maniac shadows his-her victims. And if Mr De Palma's direction is as subtle as a sledgehammer, I have to admit that it does make compulsive watching.' *(William Hall, Evening News)*

'It doesn't matter that the plot has more flaws than a second-hand suit and that the ending is something of a cheat. This is a masterly piece of filmmaking with the grip of a hangman's noose.' (Ian Christie, Daily Express)

DRESSER, THE AAN CT: 6 AV: 7.14

1983 GB 118 C DRAMA

D Peter Yates ☆ AAN
W Ronald Harwood AAN

Albert Finney, ☆ AAN Tom Courtenay ☆ AAN Edward Fox Zena Walker Eileen Atkins Michael Gough Betty Marsden Lockwood West

An old actor-manager (Albert Finney) poses problems for his faithful dresser (Tom Courtenay).

Ronald Harwood's play – transparently a study of Sir Donald Wolfit – is skilfully opened out by director Peter Yates, but it remains a miniaturistic character study. For the most part this looks more like a TV play than a film. But the moment when Finney stops a train through sheer force of personality is a classic in modern cinema.

ANTI:

'Pointless and repetitive.' *(Shipman)*

MIXED:

'A straightforward, barely opened-out transcription of [the] play . . . Albert Finney and Tom Courtenay dutifully chew up the scenery, unlike Peter Yates who fulfils his contract with a minimum of directorial mediation.' *(S & S)*

'It is British and therefore tells a tale not of effortless overnight success but of day by day humiliation and defeat. Everybody in the film is utterly ignoble . . . If you ever thought of taking up residence in the British Isles, let this picture be a warning to you. In that benighted region, you may discover eccentricity – even talent, stoicism – even courage, but you will find no happiness . . . *The Dresser* is a powerful film. I cannot quite bring myself to say that you will enjoy it. It is utterly joyless. I can only claim that it tells its grim tale with sparks of humor and in merciless detail.' *(Quentin Crisp, Christopher Street)*

'A strained film, but a valuable record of a play. The leading performances are too strident for the close-ups.' *(Halliwell)*

PRO:

'The performance of Courtenay . . . is a *tour de force*. Finney's perhaps is too relentless . . . but this is a minor criticism of a major triumph.' *(Margaret Hinxman, Daily Mail)*

'One of the best movies of the year. Glorious entertainment.' *(Dennis Cunningham, WCBS-TV)*

'Indisputably one of the best films ever made about theatre. It's funny, compassionate, compelling, and in its final moments pulls off an uncanny juxtaposition between the emotionally and physically crumbling Albert Finney and the character he's playing on stage for the 227th time, King Lear.' *(Variety)*

'The best sort of drama, fascinating us on the surface with color and humor and esoteric detail, and then revealing the truth underneath.' *(Roger Ebert)*

'Despite looking as if it's been adapted from a play, which it has, this is still wonderfully entertaining drama from two of the best troupers in the business.' *(Rose)*

DRIFTING WEEDS: *see* FLOATING WEEDS.

DRIVING MISS DAISY AAW CT: 5 AV: 6.77

1989 US 99 C DRAMA

D Bruce Beresford
W Alfred Uhry AAW from his own play

Morgan Freeman ☆ AAN Jessica Tandy ☆ AAW
Dan Aykroyd ✔ AAN Patti LuPone Esther Rolle

A rich, crotchety, prejudiced old lady (Jessica Tandy) – herself a potential target for bigotry, as a Jew in the Deep South – is initially unpleasant to, but ultimately finds friendship with, her poor, black chauffeur (Morgan Freeman).

And that's it, really. Director Bruce Beresford does a smooth job of handling the period detail – all soft-focus, blossom in bloom, and shiny antique cars. Jessica Tandy and Morgan Freeman's Oscar-nominated performances are similarly well-judged, and ignore excessive sentimentality. But there is no serious dramatic conflict, because the black chauffeur is too polite ever to put up much of a fight. The film sheds little light on the inter-racial realities of the period, and even less on those of the present day. Despite its liberal pretensions, the film obviously reflects a subconscious, nostalgic yearning for the days when blacks were dignified and knew their place, ghetto-blasters were the Ku Klux Klan, and crack was something caused by subsidence.

PRO:

'Miraculously affecting – and I mean miraculously; for though it moves modestly and unhurriedly from episode to episode, taking care that every word and gesture comes across as utterly natural and unmagnified, it packs an unprepared-for punch at the end that does seem rather magical. It's a textbook demonstration of the fact that, even in the most notoriously immoderate of all genres, less can be more, and that – given an honest, humane, and intelligent script, a company of dexterous and discerning actors, and a sensitive, compassionate director with a first-rate eye for illuminating detail – a film's paucity of incident can be more than compensated for by a credible and captivating richness of character.' *(Bruce Bawer, American Spectator)*

MIXED:

'The movie gives us an insight into the author's background that we didn't get from the play, but it's still a rigged view of the past. The black man is made upright, considerate, humane – he's made perfect – so that nothing will disturb our appreciation of the gentle, bittersweet reverie we're watching.' *(Pauline Kael)*

'Far too cosy to serve as an effective social or political metaphor; better to regard it as a solid ensemble piece.' *(Colette Maude, Time Out)*

ANTI:

'A film in which almost nothing happens: where the cops who approach a nigger with menace in their eyes drive away after merely letting drop a few racial aspersions; where nobody gets beaten up; where old age doesn't seem all that tough and where anything vicious that does happen – a Jewish Temple is fire-bombed – remains firmly off-screen.' *(James Park, Film Review)*

'*Driving Miss Daisy* gives us poor African-Americans propping up the lives of rich white folks, and calls it a healthy relationship. It romanticizes, rather than challenges, the racial power politics it presents. Hoke is Miss Daisy's "best friend" by the end of the movie, but theirs is never an alliance of mutual regard and support between two equals. Daisy is not even a friend Hoke would choose. She is a "friend" forced on him by the economic necessity of feeding his family. What kind of a friendship is that?' *(Kathy Maio)*

DROP DEAD FRED CT: 1 AV: 1.75

1991 US 99 C COMEDY

D Ate de Jong ●
W Carlos Davis Anthony Fingleton ●

Phoebe Cates Rik Mayall ● Marsha Mason
Tim Matheson Carrie Fisher Keith Charles
Bridget Fonda

A vacuous American (Phoebe Cates), who as a child had an imaginary friend, loses her husband, money, car and job. Her imaginary friend (Rik Mayall), who is for some reason English, returns to solve her problems.

Mayall at his least disciplined gives a laughter-freezing performance that makes one yearn for the sophistication of Pee Wee Herman. Too boring to entertain children, too infantile to amuse anyone older, this would-be comedy doesn't deserve any friends, imaginary or otherwise. Depressingly, it became popular in America, but then so has serial-killing.

PRO:

'All right, it's not *Thelma and Louise*, but come Labor Day I'll bet [this] will still be my second favorite good-time summer movie . . . Cates is both an adroit physical comic and an appealing straight woman to the carrot-haired, manic Mayall.' *(Amy Taubin, Village Voice)*

'A wild romp with stunning visual effects.' *(Martin & Porter)*

MIXED:

'An uneasy blend of Hollywood schmaltz and flashes of Mayall's undoubted gifts . . . Thank heaven for Carrie Fisher . . . [who] has cornered the market in the cynical, wise-cracking "friend of the heroine" . . . Her acerbic interjections become the only oases in an increasingly tedious exercise.' *(Western Mail)*

ANTI:

'This celebration of mental retardation is where the nadirs of two current Hollywood cycles – the regression to childhood/lifeswap movie and the ghost/revenant picture – intersect.' *(Philip French, Observer)*

'The British Film Industry deserves to die when it copies the Americans and tries to entice them into accepting its product by using a junior league star and setting the whole thing in Hollywood's back yard . . . This is *Viz* humour . . . [which] might have worked for Danny Kaye, although it's doubtful, using this script. Mayall will empty cinemas and destroy his film career even before it's started. His performance lacks charm, wit and style. Also, it's as funny as a kick in the pants.' *(Angus Wolfe Murray, Scotsman)*

'Harvey reimagined for the *Beetlejuice* generation, with strident sight gags standing in for magic and relentless obviousness overriding the disturbing ambiguity that might have made the film work.' *(Kim Newman, S & S)*

'Putrid . . . Recommended only for people who think nose-picking is funny.' *(Maltin)*

DROWNING BY NUMBERS CT: 3 AV: 5.40

1988 GB/Netherlands 112/121 C DRAMA

D Peter Greenaway ✗
W Peter Greenaway

Joan Plowright Juliet Stevenson Joely Richardson Bernard Hill Jason Edwards Bryan Pringle

Three women from different generations, all with the same christian name, drown unwanted husbands.

More pointless, pseudo-intellectual drivel from the critics' darling.

PRO:

'Greenaway . . . arranges the movie's images with a painter's eye. Using a special process to alter the color values in the processed film footage, he creates scenes of English countryside that look more like paintings than photography. Death lurks in the fertile landscape like an animate force, intimidating the men and intriguing the women. In the end, the story adds up to a feminist revenge fantasy, vicariously played out from a male point of view. All in all, it is great fun.' *(Brian D. Johnson, Maclean's)*

'Stunningly filmed and very entertaining.' *(Maltin)*

'Dense, and possibly meaningless, but great fun.' *(Scheuer)*

'Cynical black comedy, beautifully played and more accessible than this director's earlier work, although with some obsure formalism.' *(Halliwell)*

ANTI:

'My complaint is not that his cleverness gets tiresome (which it does) or that the human element is missing (which is irrelevant), but that if he is going to depend on ideas alone he will have to get some new ones!' *(Suzanne Moore, New Statesman)*

'Undeniably some of this is arresting to the eye, thanks to the luminous cinematography of Sacha Vierny, and to the ear as well, thanks to Michael Nyman's score . . . It is debatable, however, whether anything could adequately intimate the depths of tedium the film managed to plumb for at least one spectator.' *(Tim Pulleine)*

'So suffocatingly intent on High Art that we wonder why some accomplished actors consented to appear in it. What persuaded Joan Plowright and Juliet Stevenson and Bernard Hill to accept their roles? This self-adulating pussycat picture gives them and other actors plenty to do, but none of it is even vaguely related to character or story or credible feeling. The actors are all mobile mannequins, posing in different ways for Greenaway's exhibitionism.' *(Stanley Kauffmann)*

'What is it about Greenaway's films that makes the flesh crawl? I think it's his apparent loathing of the human race . . . I remember Michael Nyman, who composes most of Greenaway's film scores, telling me that he usually supplies the director with reams of music, not necessarily composed for any particular scene, which Greenaway cuts into arbitrary chunks according to his needs. It seems to me that Greenaway treats the human race in much the same way. And he is more interested in shit than soul.' *(Ken Russell, 1993)*

DRUGSTORE COWBOY CT: 6 AV: 7.17

1989 US 100 C DRAMA/ROMANCE

D Gus Van Sant ✗
W Gus Van Sant Daniel Yost from James Fogle's novel

Matt Dillon ☆ Kelly Lynch James Remar

James Le Gros Heather Graham
William S. Burroughs

Four junkies rob pharmacies across the United States.

Gus Van Sant's low-budget film was a surprise hit in the USA; but it's more successful as a dark caper movie than it is in the final, didactic half-hour. Although Gus Van Sant's film gets admirably close to capturing the single-mindedness, superstitiousness and stupidity of junkie life, the four anti-heroes are far too pretty to be convincing as long-term addicts. Our hero is rehabilitated with unlikely ease, and the reasons for his transformation are vague. Though more successful than most other films about drug culture, the movie still romanticizes and trivializes its subject-matter. The critics liked it, though.

PRO:

'No previous drug-themed film has the honesty or originality . . . Pic addresses the fact that people take drugs because they enjoy them.' *(Variety)*

'Keeps you laughing because it's so nonjudgmental. Van Sant is half in and half out of the desire of adolescents to remain kids forever.' *(Pauline Kael)*

'Half road-movie, half outlaw-comedy, *Drugstore Cowboy* shares the Beat anomie of a Jim Jarmusch film (or a Robert Frank photograph): no matter how bloodied or beaten up he gets, Bob [Dillon's character] is almost nonchalant when he's on the job. Like Jarmusch, Van Sant recognizes that the splendid isolation of the existential desperado frequently borders on the banal, the farcical and the tragic.' *(Graham Fuller, Film Yearbook)*

ANTI:

'Once Bob returns to Portland the whole contraption falls apart. His transformation doesn't convince for a second. Nor does his explanation help matters much: as he tells Dianne, he was so freaked out by Nadine's death that he vowed he'd kick the habit if only God or the Devil or Whoever Was Up There helped him get safely through the ordeal of disposing of her body . . . Bob doesn't quit drugs because he comes to realize that it's wrong for him to be robbing pharmacies, sponging on society, getting cops shot up, breaking his poor mother's heart, and so forth; nor does he quit because he wants to do himself a favour. Rather, he quits because of an asinine superstition. (As he puts it "I like drugs. I like the whole life-style. But it just didn't work out.") His reversal is thus both dramatically inert and ethically meaningless.' *(Bruce Bawer, American Spectator)*

'Rather thoughtless and unenlightening.' *(MFB)*

DU RIFIFI CHEZ LES HOMMES: *see* RIFIFI.

DUCK SOUP CT: 8 AV: 9.29

1933 US 70/72 BW COMEDY

D Leo McCarey ☆
W Bert Kalmar Harry Ruby Arthur Sheekman Nat Perrin

Groucho Marx ☆ Chico Marx ☆ Harpo Marx ☆ Zeppo Marx Raquel Torres Louis Calhern Margaret Dumont Verna Hillie Leonid Kinskey Edgar Kennedy

President of a Ruritanian State (Groucho Marx) goes to war because he's been called an upstart and he's paid a month's advance rent on a battlefield.

Contemporary critics took *Duck Soup* to task for its satirical intent, which at this remove is virtually invisible to the naked eye. A penetrating satire on diplomacy and war, *Duck Soup* ain't; but posterity has recognized this as the fastest, most anarchic and probably the funniest of all the Marx Brothers' movies – without the romantic interludes which slowed down (but increased the commercial success of) the Brothers' later movies. The mirror sequence remains hilarious, as do the exchanges between Groucho and Margaret Dumont. A comedy classic.

ANTI:

'A production in which the bludgeon is employed more often than the gimlet . . . [It] is for the most part extremely noisy without being nearly as mirthful as their other films.' *(Mordaunt Hall, New York Times)*

'It is sad to have to express disappointment with that foolish fraternity, the Marx Brothers, but . . . I found [the film] very much below the average of inane insanity or insane inanity that we expect from them . . . [It] flags. One reason, I fancy, is that it has a plot.' *(F.V. Lucas, Punch)*

'The rest of the cast are atmospheric stooges . . . Concentration is on straight fun-making and girl glamour is absent.' *(McCarthy, Motion Picture Herald)*

MIXED:

'The morose Marxes . . . dart about [in] adventures . . . properly madcap and completely cockeyed, and there is much work that is hilariously and crazily funny. Nevertheless it is my fear that American experts at satirical fare are not at their best when mocking the frailties of dictatorship. Perhaps they are not bitter enough.' *(Richard Watts Jr, New York Herald Tribune)*

'The laughs come often, too often sometimes, which has always been the case with Marx talkers, although in this instance more care appears to have been taken with the timing, since the step-on gags don't occur as frequently in the past.' *(Variety)*

PRO:

'Superb Marx Brothers movie . . . Beautifully put together and containing not only all the usual visual gags and wisecracks but also a large element of satire.' *(R.A.E. Pickard, Dictionary of 1000 Best Films, 1971)*

'Short, swift, and polished . . . The famous sequence of Harpo and Chico as spies impersonating Groucho in itself justifies seeing the film. There's not a dud moment anywhere.' *(NFT Bulletin, 1984)*

'A breathtakingly funny and imaginative spoof of war movie heroics . . . Totally irreverent towards patriotism, religion (a song proclaims "We Got Guns, They Got Guns, All God's Children Got Guns"), diplomacy, courtroom justice, and anything even vaguely respectable . . . A masterpiece.' *(Geoff Andrew, Time Out)*

DUEL CT: 6 AV: 7.64

1971 US 90 C THRILLER

D Steven Spielberg ☆
W Richard Matheson

Dennis Weaver Jacqueline Scott Eddie Firestone Lou Frizzell

Travelling salesman (Weaver) is stalked by homicidal petrol-tanker.

Don't expect any explanation of what the villain is up to. This is a technical exercise – originally made for TV but later granted cinema release – where Spielberg honed those suspense skills he was to use even more effectively on *Jaws, Raiders* and *Jurassic Park*.

'Mr Spielberg comes from television (*Duel* was made for television); he is only twenty-five. No prophesies; but somehow I fancy this is another name to look out for.' *(Dilys Powell)*

'The truck becomes alternately wolf, shark, tank, or prehistoric monster; it has a set of strategies from patient waiting to sudden strikes.' *(Michael Pye and Lynda Myles, The Movie Brats, 1979)*

'Established its director's reputation and is typical of his later work, being clever in an elementary way and without any intellectual substance.' *(Shipman)*

DUEL IN THE SUN CT: 5 AV: 5.85

1946 US 136/138 C WESTERN/EPIC/ROMANCE/SO BAD

D King Vidor (uncredited directors included Joseph Von Sternberg, William Dieterle, B. Reeves Eason, and producer David O. Selznick)
W David O. Selznick Oliver H.P. Garrett from Niven Busch's novel

Jennifer Jones ☆ AAN Joseph Cotten Gregory Peck ☆ Lionel Barrymore Lillian Gish ☆ AAN Walter Huston Herbert Marshall Charles Bickford Tilly Losch

Jealousy over half-breed girl (Jennifer Jones) causes trouble between two brothers: one good, one bad (Joseph Cotten and Gregory Peck).

Vulgar, melodramatic and overblown, this lurid western romance was producer David O. Selznick's attempt to follow up *Gone with the Wind* – though much less successful artistically and commercially, it has a certain bizarre appeal. The fact that Jennifer Jones is about as half-bred as the Queen mother, and Peck as lively as the average coffee-table only adds to the fun.

The Legion of Decency demanded retakes of some romantic scenes; it was denounced from the pulpit by Catholics and Protestants; local censorship boards in Memphis, Tennessee and Hartford, Connecticut were among those to forbid the film from being shown in their cities. It received one of the biggest publicity campaigns in American film history and grossed over $17 million.

PRO:

'In the bold sweep of its drama, the strength of its characterisation, its integrity, the steady progress towards a moving climax, and its pictorial beauty (from which, however, I except displays of blood and the tomato purée effect of its too vivid sunsets), I rate it very highly.' *(A.E. Wilson)*

'As sexual melodrama with a spectacular background it is in its way remarkable.' *(New Statesman)*

'A knowing blend of oats and aphrodisiac.' *(Time)*

'A lavish, sensual spectacle, so heightened it becomes a cartoon of passion.' *(Pauline Kael, 70s)*

MIXED:

'A lot of this makes for flamboyant action and a sweeping panorama of the great Southwest – and a lot more makes for sexy pulp writing that should have stayed on the wrong side of the railroad tracks.' *(Newsweek)*

'Visually [it] is magnificent. Morally it is ignoble. I don't mean that I mind the recurrent rape scenes which have earned [it] the nickname Lust in the Dust. I mean that for me a heroine who spends most of the picture on her back or grovelling on her belly is revolting . . . [Her] behaviour seems to me a conclusive argument for chastity.' *(Helen Fletcher, Time & Tide)*

'Either you love it or you loathe it. It is grim, gory and gaudy . . . [but] don't let's put on our prunes and prism faces . . . Probably life was not very prim in Texas at the turn of the century [and it's] not meant to be *Little Women*. Still, how much better [it] would have been if Selznick had stuck to the book.' *(Sunday Chronicle)*

'In the midst of all this din and Technicolor glare, the quiet, gentle performance of Lillian Gish is a particularly exquisite thing. The writing of this character, like that of all the others, is never very clear, but Miss Gish surmounts this lack with a fragile and tender performance which culminates in a death scene as lovely, as touching, as the one she played once before for director King Vidor in *La Boheme*. Lionel Barrymore, sheared of his more exasperating mannerisms, is exceptionally good as the overbearing cattle baron, and Walter Huston is excellent, too, in the flashy role of the revivalist.' *(Herb Sterne)*

'A razzmatazz of thunderous naivety simmering into a kind of majestic dottiness.' *(Basil Wright, 1972)*

'A top-heavy piece of deep purple, laughable at times, which quite overpowered some likely action aspects.' *(Walter Clapham; The Movie Treasury of Western Movies, 1974)*

ANTI:

'The biggest and emptiest thing since the Grand Canyon . . . At no time does this highly touted picture have validity – either in plot, development, characterization or performance. The whole absurdly overblown emotional steam bath is frequently and comically reminiscent of the 1890 school of panting passion and asthmatic melodrama. Its pop-eyed, hard-breathing innuendoes are aimed directly and without subterfuge at the peanut-munching, gum-chewing level of movie-goers – and will undoubtedly pay off heavily in proportion.' *(Jesse Zunser, Cue)*

'In recent years Selznick has come to confuse extravagance with quality and no matter what subject he selects to film, it is couched in terms of the Ringling Brothers and staged to suit the visual requirements of the type of amphitheater Vespasian most admired and the intellectual and emotional level of the subscribers to the *New York Mirror*. Gone with the wind are the days when Selznick was content to sponsor such normal-length and intelligently entertaining productions as *A Bill of Divorcement, What Price Hollywood?* and *Nothing Sacred*. Today, it would appear, he is not interested in filming any story that does not permit him, one way or another, to burn down the city of Atlanta . . . There are times when the photoplay courts interest. There are times when it courts disdainful laughter.' *(Herb Sterne)*

'The most dangerous film so far released this year . . . All set for popular success, a film to stir brooding ideas of violence in the hearts of too many people packed under our wet, grey skies.' *(Tribune)*

'The whole thing fluctuates between the repellent and the ridiculous.' *(Stephen Watts, Sunday Express)*

'How dreary to see something so absolutely certain of itself, that it has the inspiration of a sucked orange . . . I'm hanged if I can see why this kind of thing should be dressed up with a portentous opening commentary spoken with no pictures at the opening as if we are going to be told a fable which holds the secrets of life.' *(Geoffrey Bell, Spectator)*

'Cornographic.' *(Daily Mail)*

DUMBO

CT: 10 AV: 9.14

1941 US 64 C CARTOON/MUSICAL/FAMILY

D Ben Sharpsteen ☆
W Joe Grant Dick Huemer from Helen Aberson and Harold Pearl's book

Voices: Edward Brophy Herman Bing Verna Felton Sterling Holloway Cliff Edwards

Small elephant with big ears makes good.

The ever-delightful Disney tear-jerker looks better and better through the years (not least because, at 65 minutes, it doesn't outstay its welcome). And even if the crows who sing 'When I See An Elephant Fly' are politically incorrect racial caricatures, they're jolly entertaining. All the songs are tuneful; the animation is stunning – especially during the drunk sequence – and the story is guaranteed to touch anyone over the age of two. It's also a film with ideals: it celebrates the family, looks for the good in people, and shows sympathy for those different from oneself. A classic cartoon.

'There's a pleasant little story, plenty of pathos mixed in with the large doses of humor, a number of appealing new animal characters, lots of good music, and the usual Disney skilfulness in technique. Defects are some decidedly slow spots and that the film is somewhat episodic in nature.' *(Variety)*

'*Dumbo* is the nicest, kindest Disney yet. It has the most heart, taste, beauty, compassion, skill, restraint . . . It's got ideals: it venerates mother love; it believes people are essentially good; it preaches sympathy, not derision, for Nature's slip-ups. It does its good and noble and utterly enjoyable job with more camera angles than Citizen Kane, with every bit as much subtle, and also obvious, suggestion.' *(Cecilia Ager, PM)*

'The most genial, the most endearing, the most completely precious cartoon film ever to emerge from the magical brushes of Walt Disney's wonder-working artists.' *(Bosley Crowther)*

'Every time that you think the Disney studio can't do any more because they have done everything, they turn around and do it again, the new and never dreamed of, the thing lovely and touching and gay.' *(Otis Ferguson)*

'Of all the joyous presents which have come from the Disney plant, this feature-length three-ring circus is the best yet . . . The reality Dumbo possesses is remarkable. He is a pathetic little fella, with all the whimsey, pathos, hopes and fears that Chaplin implants in his tramp figure. Like the chap with the derby, cane, and shuffling gait, Dumbo is a misfit, a target for jibes and assorted misfortunes . . .

It is suggested that you watch for such innovations as the successful psychological use of color, the superb cutting and "angles", and the amusing satire on "abstract" films (so dear to the hearts of devotees of *l'art moderne de cinéma*) – the Pink Elephant Ballet.' *(Herb Sterne)*

'A spectacular success . . . stands up well on purely technical grounds despite a slightly dated overall effect . . . Happily, [it] has one of the best stories Disney has used and the characterisation is faultless . . . Dumbo . . . is a masterpiece of character establishment . . . There are, of course, sentimental moments . . . but they are executed with . . . delicacy and good taste . . . a close second [to *Bambi*].' *(F & F, 1962)*

'The least pretentious as well the least costly of Disney's animated features . . . *Dumbo* carried far less cultural weight than the major Disney films that had preceded it, and the artists seemed grateful to be relieved of the burden. Their work recaptured some of the freshness, exuberance and innocence of the short cartoons as well as their pure and simple fun . . . There was one distasteful moment in the film. The crows who teach Dumbo to fly are too obviously Negro caricatures.' *(Richard Schickel, 1968)*

DUNE

CT: 4 AV: 3.58

1984 US 140 C SF/EPIC

D David Lynch
D David Lynch ● from Frank Herbert's novel

Francesca Annis Jose Ferrer Sian Phillips Brad Dourif Dean Stockwell Freddie Jones Linda Hunt Kenneth McMillan Richard Jordan Kyle MacLachlan Silvana Mangano Jürgen Prochnow Max Von Sydow Sting

Frank Herbert's hit fantasy novel brought to the screen by cult director David Lynch. The result is visually impressive and full of wonderful special effects – but don't expect to be able to follow the plot: the important information is all on the cutting-room floor. A massive flop.

PRO:

'A gorgeous intergalactic pantomime.' *(Victor Davis, Daily Express)*

'Lynch has made . . . an almost mythic, semi-religious fable with a true sense of grandeur, the like of which the screen has not felt since the heady days of *The Ten Commandments, Spartacus* and *Ben-Hur*.' *(Tony Sloman, F & F)*

ANTI:

'There are things in Heaven and on Earth that passeth all understanding and [this[high, wide and handsome tale of dark deeds . . . is one of them.' *(William Russell, Glasgow Herald)*

'Several of the characters are psychic, which puts them in the unique position of being able to understand what goes on in the movie.' *(Janet Maslin, New York Times)*

'The most obscenely homophobic film I have ever seen, managing to associate with homosexuality in a single scene physical grossness, moral depravity, violence and disease. It shows no real interest in its land, young lovers or its last-minute divine revelation, all its energies being devoted to the expression of physical and sexual disgust.' *(Robin Wood, Hollywood From Vietnam to Reagan, 1986)*

'Reckoned to be the most expensive film ever made. It is also the worst . . . [It] has you peering at your watch and longing for it to end.' *(Sun)*

'A real mess, an incomprehensible, ugly, unstructured, pointless excursion into the murkier realms of one of the most confusing screenplays of all time.' *(Roger Ebert)*

'I don't ever want to compromise again like I did on *Dune*. The whole experience was a disaster. I was lying to myself the whole way through.' *(David Lynch)*

E.T. THE EXTRA-TERRESTRIAL AAN

CT: 10 AV: 8.78

1980 US 115 C SF/FAMILY/DRAMA

D Steven Spielberg ☆ AAN
W Melissa Mathison ☆ AAN

Dee Wallace Henry Thomas ☆ Peter Coyote Robert MacNaughton Drew Barrymore K.C. Martel Sean Frye

An alien befriends a small boy (Henry Thomas).

E.T. was one of the most successful films of all time at the box office: it grossed over $700 million worldwide, to say nothing of merchandizing spin-offs. Many have tried to explain its success in terms of its being an updated *Lassie* film. Really, it's a new twist on *The Wizard of Oz* and looks forward to a more candid statement of its theme in another big hit of the 80s, *Home Alone*. Just like Dorothy, E.T. knows there is no place like home. Elliott (who comes from a broken one) has to learn this for himself, just like Kevin in *Home Alone*.

The film is often seen as a byword for cosiness, but some critics noticed a dark subtext. On its release an American columnist, George F. Will, fulminated against it for promoting 'subversive' ideas, namely: 'Children are people. Adults are not. Science is sinister.' Others agreed. Censors in Sweden, Finland and Norway ruled that *E.T.* was unfit for child audiences because 'the film portrays adults as enemies of children'. Although the Scandinavian censors overreacted, they were quicker than most critics to spot that Spielberg's film portrays grown-ups in a very unflattering light. As Danny Peary noticed in 1993, 'Peter Coyote's scientist tells Elliott that he's been dreaming of meeting an alien since he was Elliott's age. But his motives have changed: boys want to play with aliens, adults want to experiment on them. *E.T.* celebrates children.'

The main point about the film is that it never fails to work emotionally, however mawkish people may claim to have found it in retrospect. Henry Thomas delivers a fine performance as the little boy, and Spielberg's style of shooting (mostly from Thomas's eye level) encourages us to see E.T. from his point of view. The special effects, including E.T. himself, are stupendous. The shot when Elliott and E.T. take flight and fly across the moon is one of the great moments in cinema. So I have no problem siding with those original critics who regarded *E.T.* not merely as an exercise in marketing, but as a work of cinematic genius.

ANTI:

'Mawkish.' *(Elliot)*

'In reducing the unknowable to the easily lovable, the film sacrifices a little too much truth in favour of its huge emotional punch . . . The first half contains a couple of comedy sequences as vulgar as a Brooke Bond TV chimps commercial.' *(David Pirie, Time Out)*

'There are overdone embarrassments: when E.T. gets slapsticky drunk, and the hysterical scene in which Elliott lets loose the frogs intended for classroom dissection because they remind him of his new friend.' *(Tom Hutchinson, Mail on Sunday)*

'John Williams's music [is] far too pompous in the circumstances.' *(David Hughes, Sunday Times)*

'For some reason this thin little tale was extremely popular . . . The concept and the humour are simplistic; its only ingredient above the elementary is the final chase and the best of that is taken from *The Great Escape* and *Miracolo a Milano*.' *(Shipman)*

PRO:

'*E.T.* equals B.O . . . The best Disney film Disney never made.' *(Variety)*

'Should make truckloads of money.' *(Time)*

'Spielberg manipulates our emotions with supreme skill and never puts a foot wrong.' *(Ivor Davis, Daily Express)*

'With its Nativity-like opening and its final revelation, the plot of *E.T.* has parallels with religious mythology that help to explain its electric effect on audiences.' *(David Pirie, Time Out)*

[E.T. is] very much every child's wish-fulfilment dream: a real friend, intensified in this case because the boy's father has left his wife and kids to go off with another woman.' *(Richard Roud, Guardian)*

'The film captures the whole gamut of childhood experience, fear of losing one's parents, homesickness, instinctive identification with the unprotected, and the unique relationship children have with their pets.' *(Judith M. Kass, Magill's Cinema Annual, 1983)*

'It's significant that Spielberg conceived his story when he himself was lonely. Because the visitor who becomes pal to this boy who misses his father is much like Robert Louis Stevenson's "imaginary playmate" – I've long thought that E.T. is the ideal friend for all kids (especially those without two parents) who wish their stuffed animals would hug them back.' *(Danny Peary, Alternate Oscars, 1993)*

'The film's overwhelming emotional appeal lies in the opportunity it affords the audience to participate in . . . genuinely child-like love, an experience heightened by the drama of the creature's "death" and resurrection. The alien Other of paranoid 1950s science fiction has thus become man's best friend and the Christ figure rolled into one, the feel-good Spielbergian theology of space as heaven sending us out of the cinema reassured by its notion of the great nuclear family in the sky.' *(Allan Hunter, Movie Classics, 1992)*

'*E.T.* achieves its almost hypnotic hold through the . . . subtly manipulative play of light, which Spielberg and his cinematographer, Allen Daviau, orchestrate like symphonic motifs: the lush darkness of the forest contrasts with the flat brightness of the suburban community; a kind of holy back light bathes Elliott and the E.T. whereas Elliott's family – his mother, little sister and older brother – are viewed in natural, all-around light; the black silhouettes of the advancing government forces suddenly blaze into clinical fluorescence after they find E.T. in his hideaway.' *(Charles Michener and Katrine Ames, Newsweek)*

'A miracle movie, and one that confirms Spielberg as a master storyteller of his medium.' *(Richard Corliss, Life)*

'As an originator of movie magic, director Steven Spielberg has no equal. *Jaws, Close Encounters of the Third Kind*, and *Raiders of the Lost Ark* were merely foretastes of the spell-binding artistry he brings to his most personal film . . . Pure enchantment of the kind I never dared hope to see on the screen again.' *(Margaret Hinxman, Daily Mail)*

EARTH CT: 6 AV: 8.44

(aka *Soil; Zemlya*)

1930 USSR 63 BW DRAMA/FOREIGN/SILENT

D Alexander Dovzhenko ☆
W Alexander Dovzhenko

Semyon Svashenko Stephen Shkurat
Mikola Nademsky Yelena Maximova

Peasants form a collective in a Ukrainian village, despite the opposition of reactionary landowners.

Sincere, earnest, almost plotless film which was effective propaganda in favour of collectivization. It shows a sensuous link between peasants and the soil (one of the most famous scenes is of couples embracing on the ground), and a symbiotic relationship between man and machine (in a scene cut from all foreign prints until 1958, peasants cool the engine of a tractor with their own urine). Hopelessly optimistic and romantic, of course, but hailed as a masterpiece of realism by those unrealistic about Communism. In the 50s, it was voted one of the 10 greatest films of all time by an international group of critics.

'A picture for film-goers who are prepared to take their cinema as seriously as Tolstoy took the novel.' *(James Agate, Tatler)*

'A meditative film . . . not of strict Communist ideology . . . An original and beautiful film.' *(H.P.J. Marshall, Close Up)*

'Confirms that the late Dovzhenko was possessed of one of the cinema's most intensely poetic visions.' *(Derek Hill, Screen, on first British showing of original version, 1962)*

'Perhaps the most beautiful film ever made in the Soviet Union . . . It is a true song of the earth.' *(Guardian)*

'One of the supreme masterpieces of Soviet cinema . . . Using choreographed images, counterpoints, juxtapositions and a final long elaborate parallel montage, Dovzhenko has created an indelible image of a rural paradise earned by the blood of the peasants.' *(Bergan & Karney)*

'The specific subject is collectivization, but Dovzhenko's masterwork is a passionate lyric on the continuity of man, death, and nature. The theme is perhaps most startlingly expressed in a sequence about a man who has just celebrated the arrival of a tractor. He starts to dance – for sheer love of life – on his way home, and as he dances in the middle of the moonlit road he is suddenly struck by a bullet.' *(Pauline Kael)*

'Film celebrates life, and though it expresses grief for the recent dead, it is more concerned with rebirth than with inevitable death.' *(Danny Peary)*

'Though increasingly an absentee from Ten Best lists, a very great film indeed.' *(Geoff Andrew, Time Out)*

EARTH'S FINAL FURY: *see* WHEN TIME RAN OUT.

EAST OF EDEN CT: 6 AV: 7.76

1955 US 114 C DRAMA

D Elia Kazan ✗ AAN
W Paul Osborn ✗ from John Steinbeck's novel

Raymond Massey ☆ James Dean ✗ AAN
Jo Van Fleet ☆ AAW Julie Harris Richard Davalos
Burl Ives Albert Dekker

Cain (James Dean) and Abel (Richard Davalos) are alive and well, and living on a lettuce farm in California.

Stodgy melodrama which remains interesting for its romantic view of the mixed-up kid (it was largely thanks to this and *Rebel Without a Cause* that the astonishingly mannered Dean became a teen icon). The confrontations between Massey and Dean are still effective, and Jo Van Fleet deserved her Oscar; but Kazan's directing style changes arbitrarily from scene to scene. Leonard Rosenman's score is over-emphatic and adds to the sense that this is melodrama.

'A *tour de force* for the director's penchant for hard-hitting forays with life.' *(Variety)*

'The first distinguished production in Cinemascope, and will be remembered as such by future motion picture historians. Kazan used the wide screen functionally, panning horizontally, tilting to emphasize distorted relationships, experimenting with soft-focus lenses and unusual lighting and shadow effects, and constantly employing inventive devices to keep his camera moving and the viewer's attention directed to the appropriate section of the screen. The result is a widescreen film which moves smoothly and dramatically, and expresses its symbolic theme in visual terms. Although the film is marred by Kazan's habit of over-statement and his exaggerated emphasis on violence, the extremes seem appropriate to the Cain-Abel conflict which motivates the plot.' *(Eugene Archer, Film Culture)*

MIXED:

'Amazingly high-strung, feverishly poetic . . . It's like seeing a series of teasers: violent moments and charged scenes without much coherence.' *(Pauline Kael)*

ANTI:

'Long-winded and bloated with biblical allegory.' *(Geoff Andrew, Time Out)*

EASTER PARADE CT: 7 AV: 7.69

1948 US 109 C MUSICAL/COMEDY

D Charles Walters
W Sidney Sheldon Frances Goodrich Albert Hackett

Fred Astaire ☆ Judy Garland ☆ Ann Miller ☆ Peter Lawford ● Clinton Sundberg Jules Munshin

A song-and-dance act (Fred Astaire and Ann Miller) splits up, and he has to find a new partner (Judy Garland).

Fred Astaire and Judy Garland combine in an enjoyable if lightweight vehicle which might have been made for their talents, but wasn't: Astaire stepped in at the last moment, to replace an injured Gene Kelly. The story is extremely weak, and Peter Lawford could profitably have been excised (his scenes are feeble, and he struggles when singing 'A Fella with an Umbrella'). But the Astaire-Garland duet, 'A Couple of Swells', is a high point in musical cinema – as are Astaire's solo spots 'Stepping Out with my Baby' and 'Drum Crazy'. Roger Edens and Johnny Green won the Oscar for musical direction.

'The important thing is that Fred Astaire is back, with Irving Berlin calling the tunes.' *(Newsweek)*

'Fred Astaire, Judy Garland, Ann Miller, and several of Irving Berlin's old songs ought to add up to something better than this; but much of it is painless and some of it – chiefly Astaire – is pretty good.' *(James Agee, Nation)*

'Who cares for the triteness of such a fable when the wistful Astaire is on hand to delight us with the miraculous neatness and finish of his dancing and when spirited Miss Garland is ready to drop into song even in the depths of sorrow and to confide to a sympathetic barman the extent of her heartbreak?' *(A.E. Wilson)*

'One of MGM's brightest, cheeriest musicals.' *(Danny Peary)*

EASY RIDER CT: 5 AV: 7.53

1969 US 94 C DRAMA

D Dennis Hopper ✗
W Peter Fonda Dennis Hopper Terry Southern ●

Peter Fonda ✗ Dennis Hopper ✗ Jack Nicholson ☆ AAN Antonio Mendoza Phil Spector Mac Mashourian

Bikers (Peter Fonda, Dennis Hopper) cross America to find freedom.

A fatuous film about sexist drug-dealers, replete with narcissism and fashionable hippie paranoia. It has dated horribly, except for Jack Nicholson's amiably crazed performance. Its imitation of the French New Wave, and anti-establishment posturing, made it a favourite with critics and youth audiences alike. Audiences today may be amused as well as shocked that the foolish and incoherent script actually won an Oscar nomination (it's almost as bad as the script for *The Piano*, which won in 1994).

PRO:

'The definitive youth odyssey of the 1960s. *Easy Rider* is an excruciating look at where this country is today. It's about as horrifying an indictment of America as I've ever seen in any medium, and certainly a bold, courageous statement of life seldom matched in motion pictures . . . Nothing looks set-up. Nothing looks rehearsed. Peter Fonda and Dennis Hopper can be proud of a movie which, in all of its hysteria and venom, looks not so much photographed as actually lived.' *(Rex Reed)*

'It isn't the miraculous playing by Jack Nicholson of an idiosyncratic character which makes this the key to the film, though Mr Nicholson, an actor whom I don't remember seeing before, looks and sounds like one of heaven's gifts to the screen. The point is that suddenly, after all the underground cinema and all the cinema letting itself go in conventional ridicule of the hippies, here is a piece which shows with infectious sympathy the grounds of their rebellion. *Easy Rider* is truly a film of protest.' *(Dilys Powell)*

'Ninety-four minutes of what it is like to swing, to watch, to be fond, to hold opinions and to get killed in America at this moment.' *(Penelope Gilliatt)*

ANTI:

'The presentation is one-sided. Hippies are basically free, good, and love mankind and life; the others are envious, hateful, murderous slaves. That Wyatt and Billy have scarcely more conversation than do their motorcycles, that they live by dope-smuggling, and are hooked on the stuff, that their relationships with girls are trivial if not meaningless, that their freedom is considered a noble end in itself rather than the road to anarchy, is all meant to be swallowed like a happy-pill without questioning. The fact that the commune, unversed in agriculture, may face starvation is not meant to throw doubt on its sanity, George's ideas about the Venutians are not intended to invalidate the wisdom of his pronouncements. And when Wyatt finally concedes, "We blew it!" we are left unenlightened about what, when, how, and by whose fault.' *(John Simon)*

'These were characters that baby boomers could "identify with." They were "free." They'd "dropped out" of a corrupt society, a plastic society. Yet what did they have to offer in its place? "Do your own thing," they said. Yet in these movies, and others like them, they all were doing exactly the same thing – goofing off, abusing controlled substances, wandering aimlessly across America . . . Pictures like *Easy Rider* didn't encourage independence on the part of their young viewers; they fostered imitation. They provided baby boomers with a dress code, a vocabulary, a primer of attitudes. And their arrival marked the beginnings of something else, too: a new, distinctly baby boomer attitude toward movies. For *Easy Rider* and its ilk weren't primarily out to entertain: weak on story and character and dialogue, they sought rather to embody the vapid slogans of Youth Culture, to epitomize the politically correct generational attitudes.' *(Bruce Bawer, American Spectator)*

EDGE OF THE CITY CT: 5 AV: 6.88

(aka *A Man is Ten Feet Tall*)

1957 US 85 BW DRAMA

D Martin Ritt
W Robert Alan Arthur ☆ from his play

Sidney Poitier ☆ John Cassavetes ☆ Jack Warden Kathleen Maguire Ruby Dee Robert Simon Ruth White

Down at the New York docks, a black foreman (Sidney Poitier) stands up for a white man (John Cassavetes) bullied by a union racketeer (Jack Warden).

Black and white in more senses than one, Martin Ritt's directorial debut is transparently an attempt to emulate the success of *On The Waterfront* (1954), with Sidney Poitier cast as the courageous man standing out against the system. It's powerful, well acted and makes good use of authentic locations; but the plot holds few surprises.

'Courageous, thought-provoking and exciting.' *(Variety)*

'Ritt . . . sustains the tension with great skill but can't resist clinching the case with gratuitous violence, and the author . . . works with such precision that he reduces his subject to pat melodrama.' *(Pauline Kael)*

EDWARD II CT: 5 AV: 6.10

1991 GB 90 C DRAMA

D Derek Jarman ✗
W Derek Jarman Stephen McBride Ken Butler ● from Christopher Marlowe's play

Steven Waddington Andrew Tiernan Tilda Swinton Nigel Terry

Edward II (Steven Waddington) and his lover, Piers Gaveston (Andrew Tiernan), fall victim to a homophobic society.

Visually, it's Derek Jarman's most accomplished effort since *Caravaggio*, and one can only admire his ability to make the most of a tiny budget. It's also the best-structured of his films – thanks to the merits of Christopher Marlowe's play. As an adaptation of Marlowe, however, it's a travesty. The dialogue is a disjointed, shambolic mixture of Elizabethan and modern. This kind of technique can be interesting in the hands of a Steven Berkoff (he used it to great effect in his play *East*), but in Jarman's it seems to be just an excuse for sloppy verse speaking, and lots of swear-words to shock the straights.

In Jarman's version, Edward's fatal flaw is that he refuses to desert his old friends (in ironic counterpoint to Kenneth Branagh's Henry V). In Marlowe's play, of course, Edward's flaw is his self-indulgent refusal to place public duty above personal inclination. Those parts of the text which conflict with Jarman's distortion are obliterated, and new scenes inserted – notably, ones where Edward's wife Isabella (Tilda Swinton) shows herself to be a nymphomaniac killer-vampire, and Mortimer (Nigel Terry) becomes a sado-masochist cavorting with lesbians.

There are half-baked attempts to draw parallels between those who rebelled against Edward II and those who imposed Clause 28, with scenes of riot police attacking gay demonstrators, lining them up against a wall and shooting them: events which have happened only in Jarman's imagination, and which have no reference whatever to 14th-century England.

There's even a new happy ending, with Edward escaping the notorious red-hot poker because his would-be assassin falls in love with him. Young Prince Edward celebrates dad's lucky escape by dressing up in high heels, lipstick and ear-rings. Marlowe (though himself a homosexual) didn't write any of this, and history shows that Edward III was almost offensively heterosexual, with seven sons and five daughters.

In his published screenplay of the film, Jarman admits that his aim was to 'make a film of a gay love affair and get it commissioned'. The method he hit upon was to 'find a dusty old play and violate it'. He has certainly done that. But what a pity that his film should end up looking more like a labour of hatred than of love. As usual with Jarman's films, he found a receptive audience in the critics; but the public stayed away.

PRO:

'Invested with a powerful contemporary resonance.' *(Stephen Holden, New York Times)*

'Through the miracle of cinema, two sensibilities and centuries become wondrously fused. Bold passionate and savagely beautiful, this is one of the best British films for some time.' *(Geoff Brown, The Times)*

'Jarman is back on form in vivid, spectacular fashion . . . The movie becomes a dark, intensely played eulogy to a gay relationship battling against prejudice and medieval retribution.' *(Sue Heal, Today)*

'Excites through its sheer guts and combativeness. Despite the visual lyricism, the film is raw and angry.' *(Wally Hammond, Time Out)*

'By mixing old (Marlowe's text) and new (actors in modern fashions, scenes of gay protests, Annie Lennox singing Cole Porter), Jarman has made a movie that speaks eloquently – and loudly – about the love that once dared not speak its name. The film is obviously not for everyone (Jesse Helms, this means you), but it sure makes history seem relevant.' *(Leah Rozen, People Weekly)*

'Grabs Christopher Marlowe's sixteenth century play by the throat and heaves it kicking and screaming into the 1990s.' *(Martin & Porter)*

MIXED:

'Provocative and challenging . . . likely will be the director's most commercial production to date . . . Jarman fails to make the film accessible to heterosexual male audiences. Pic seems to be provoking straight viewers.' *(Variety)*

'All Jarman's artistic choices seem designed to cement modern parallels. Yet his approach begs many questions. "Then as now" only works up to a point, and to transform Marlowe's work into a denunciation of contemporary "homophobia" is to ignore not only the political context of the period, but also a good deal of the play itself . . . This said, Jarman has made a film which weaves its own peculiar . . . visual and emotional magic.' *(Hugo Davenport, Daily Telegraph)*

'Only occasionally does Jarman's whimsy seem indulgent. For the most part, these touches illuminate the story and keep it interesting to modern audiences. Traditionalists, of course, will fret, but Jarman has done a fine job of serving both his audience and his material.' *(M. Faust, Video Magazine)*

ANTI:

'Marlowe's play, while never a masterpiece, was always more than a tale of gay persecution. In giving one dimension of the work new life, Jarman allows the rest to look even more moribund than usual . . . At its worst [the film] looks like an act of jaded restlessness by an artist who cannot find quite enough in this ancient artwork creatively to subvert.' *(Nigel Andrews, Financial Times)*

'Seeks to reclaim English history for the OutRage campaign and present homosexuality as the driving force behind social repression in modern as well as medieval England . . . The movie possesses a strong streak of wishful martyrdom . . . The movie testifies more to Jarman's strengths (public provocation) and weaknesses (indiscriminate puerility) than any film he has ever made.' *(Alexander Walker, Evening Standard)*

'Unfortunately, the two male leads are so tiresomely portrayed, you end up sympathising with their oppressors.' *(Rose)*

EDWARD SCISSORHANDS CT: 9 AV: 6.53

1990 US 98 C SF/FANTASY

D Tim Burton ✔
W Caroline Thompson ✔

Johnny Depp ✔ Winona Ryder ✔ Dianne Wiest ✔ Anthony Michael Hall Alan Arkin ✔ Kathy Baker ✔, Vincent Price

An old inventor (Vincent Price) dies as he is about to fit hands to his finest creation: a real, live boy called Edward (Johnny Depp). A kindly Avon Lady (Dianne Wiest) takes Edward down to her neighbourhood, where he wins popularity through his talent for topiary, hair-cutting and dog-grooming. The tone darkens as he allows himself to become exploited by her teenage daughter Kim (Winona Ryder) and her yob boyfriend (Anthony Michael Hall). Edward's nonconformity becomes a threat, and his scissors are no longer seen as creative tools, but as weapons.

Several dozen cuts above the Hollywood average: the story is a weird but wonderful mix of American suburban comedy and Gothic romance – a bit like *Happy Days*, re-written by Roald Dahl. There are delightful performances from Johnny Depp and Dianne Wiest, and anyone who enjoys character acting will enjoy Alan Arkin as the well-meaning, blue-collar Mr Boggs, and Kathy Baker as the neighbourhood man-eater in man-made fibres. There's a deliberate lack of depth to these characters: they have the kind of simplicity you find in fairy tales. And yet they're convincing: Winona Ryder's teenager is lovable in her adolescent weakness, and touching when she realizes the extent of her awfulness. The scene where she dances in the snow is one of the most magical moments in cinema.

The film is plainly an allegory; and like all the richest allegories, you will find your own meaning. On one level, it's about handicap: Edward is both handicapped and 'special', like an autistic child with miraculous drawing ability. Edward also represents the artist, tolerated and celebrated by 'normal' people – but only as long as he is not unduly threatening. Others may spot the affinity which Edward has with Christ – there are hints at the end that he has the power to control the weather and that he's immortal. All in all, it's a highly original, modern fairy-tale about the eternal gulf between conformism and creativity.

Pedants should give the film a wide berth. Its tone is deliberately unrealistic in the juxtaposition of suburban normality next to Gothic horror, and in the conscious use of anachronism (colour television, aerobics and videotape are all around, even though the setting seems to be the late 50s). Cinastes, however, should enjoy the film's wealth of cinematic allusions (which range from *The 5000 Fingers of Dr T* to *Nightmare On Elm Street*, the slasher movie in which Johnny Depp had his first role). And lovers of legend will have a fine time spotting influences which range from *Beauty and the Beast* to *Struwwelpeter*.

There was evidence of director Tim Burton's visual flair in his three previous films, *Pee-wee's Big Adventure, Beetlejuice* and *Batman*. Here, he had reason to thank his co-screenwriter, Caroline Thompson (who wrote a deceptively simple script which would be enjoyable without subtitles in any country), and a superb design team. *Edward Scissorhands* attracted mixed reviews and didn't set the box office on fire either, but posterity may recognize it for what it was: a fantastic achievement.

MIXED:

'[Burton] has fashioned a topiaristic diversion, eye-catching, ingenious, but . . . ultimately of no great concern.' *(Philip Strick, S & S)*

'A visual treat . . . but it remains curiously hollow.' *(Colette Maude, Time Out)*

'We don't want to see the conventional "dark side" of these people: it's a betrayal of the film's comic spirit – the material turns into cheesy plot-centered melodrama. Johnny Depp's Edward is an emasculated Tim Burton. Edward isn't angry even when he's mistreated; his scissor hands have no relation to his mild, angelic nature . . . It could have used more interaction between the inventor and Edward, and some suggestion of what the boy was intended for. (With those whirling, rhythmic shears, he should have become a film editor.)' *(Pauline Kael)*

'All of Burton's movies look great. *Pee-wee's Big Adventure* was an unalloyed visual delight, and so was *Beetlejuice*. And *Batman* gave us a Gotham City that was one of the most original and atmospheric places I've seen in the movies. But shouldn't there be something more? Some attempt to make the characters more than caricatures? All of the central characters in a Burton film – Pee-wee, the demon Betelgeuse, Batman, the Joker, or Edward Scissorhands – exist in personality vacuums; they're self-contained oddities with no connection to the real world. It's saying something about a director's work when the most well-rounded and socialized hero in any of his films is Pee-wee Herman.' *(Roger Ebert)*

'Like a great chef concocting an exquisite peanut butter and jelly sandwich, Mr Burton invests awe-inspiring ingenuity into the process of reinventing something very small . . . a tale of misunderstood gentleness and stifled creativity, of civilization's power to corrupt innocence, of a heedless beauty and a kindhearted beast . . . [It] reveals proudly adolescent lessons for us all.' *(Janet Maslin, New York Times)*

'This imaginative modern fairy tale has some truly weird designs, but it's hard to get involved with the characters. Like Burton's *Batman* films, your view probably depends on whether you love his amazing visual style or whether you prefer a strong story.' *(Rose)*

'A mean-spirited, violent ending irrevocably mars what might have been a charming fantasy.' *(Martin & Porter)*

PRO:

'A delightful and delicate comic fable.' *(Variety)*

'Simply the best film for years . . . magic.' *(Sun)*

'Funny and touching.' *(Company)*

'Edward is an archetypal misunderstood teenager . . . Johnny Depp's performance . . . [is] of a calibre little seen since the days of silent film . . . There are a few weaknesses, notably a bald stab at upbeat lyricism near the end that rings briefly false. And since despite its virtually unceasing humor, the film never deviates from its essentially tragic trajectory, an inevitable predictability gradually lessens its power throughout. None of this diminishes . . . the magnitude of its achievement.' *(Myron Meisel, Film Journal)*

'A fairy tale mix of *Charles Addams, Frankenstein, Pinocchio* and *I Love Lucy*, this offbeat offering . . . emerges as a triumphantly strange picture.' *(Kim Newman, Empire)*

EHE DER MARIA BRAUN, DIE: *see* MARRIAGE OF MARIA BRAUN, THE.

8½ AAW

CT: 6 AV: 9.38

(aka *Otto e Mezzo*)

1963 Italy 138 BW DRAMA/FOREIGN

D Federico Fellini ☆ AAN
W Federico Fellini Tullio Pinelli Ennio Flaiano Brunello Rondi AAN based on Federico Fellini and Ennio Flaiano's story

Marcello Mastroianni ☆ Claudia Cardinale Anouk Aimée Sandra Milo Rossella Falk

Barbara Steele Mario Pisu Guido Alberti Madeleine LeBeau Jean Rougeul

A womanizing film-maker (Marcello Mastroianni) suffers a creative block.

A self-obsessed art-house movie or a brilliant, autobiographical study of a creative talent in crisis? A bit of both, really; Fellini's quasi-autobiographical movie takes self-flagellation to the point of self-abuse. Many other auteurs have tried to repeat the formula (Woody Allen in *Stardust Memories*, Bob Fosse in *All That Jazz*, and Paul Mazursky in *Alex in Wonderland*) for much the same reason that cabaret singers are drawn to singing 'My Way'. Fellini's film remains the best of the bunch, not least because he retains a sense of humour about his self-absorption and has himself played by Marcello Mastroianni, an actor of enormous, self-mocking charm.

Although the look of the piece has dated and the pace is over-indulgent, there is plenty to admire in Fellini's virtuoso use of fantasy sequences, his unromantic attitude towards film-making, and his honesty about his own sexual selfishness.

PRO:

'A film only an exceptional personality like Fellini could have considered . . . the film fresco is majestic, fascinating and complex.' *(Il Messagero)*

'An important film in Fellini's career and an important film for the Italian cinema.' *(Alberto Moravia, Express)*

'Nothing like *8½* has ever been done before in the cinema. The only work I can think of that has the same grim comic capacity for self-exposure is Evelyn Waugh's *The Ordeal of Gilbert Pinfold*. *8½* a rueful account of a peculiarly contemporary kind of man, imaginative, openly greedy, riddled with the bullet holes of his self-accusations, and almost dying of neurotic sloth.' *(Penelope Gilliatt)*

'Everything that [Pietro] Gherardi [the designer] touches in *8½*, from a railroad station to a concrete garden seat in which a short-legged monk sits and swings his feet, creates a world that, in pure romantic process, has been seized, fondled, and given back to us in revised, personal form. No one who has seen *8½* could ever mistake one minute of it – hardly one frame – for any other film.' *(Stanley Kauffmann)*

'A complex, stimulating, adventurous masterpiece.' *(Scheuer)*

'One of the most intensely personal statements ever made on celluloid.' *(Maltin)*

MIXED:

'The whole may add up to a magnificent folly, but it is too singular, too candid, too vividly and insistently alive to be judged as being in any way diminishing.' *(Peter John Dyer, MFB)*

'Often slow, flabby and repetitive. But between the damp patches there are plenty of brisk amusing ones . . . It is all a good deal jollier than that macabre museum piece among cinematic bores *La Dolce Vita*.' *(Isabel Quigley, Spectator)*

'The surface is particularly glittering . . . But behind this surface the symbolism runs a danger of becoming bloodless, repetitive and naive. The repetition of motif emotionally enervates the spectator.' *(James Price, London Magazine)*

'The let-down of the ending and the general emptiness of the film's philosophy are in part compensated for by some fascinating moments . . . In the end [its] greatest achievement is the dazzling photography.' *(The Times)*

'Some of it is fascinating, some not worth the trouble of sorting out.' *(Halliwell)*

ANTI:

'We emphatically reject any attempts to present the decision of the international jury of the third Moscow Film Festival [which had awarded it Best Foreign Film] as a positive appraisal by the Soviet public of . . . *8½*.' *(Alexander Romanov, USSR State Committee for Cinematography)*

'Fellini's intellectualizing is not even like dogs dancing; it is not done well, nor does it surprise us that it is done at all. It merely palls on us, and finally appals us.' *(John Simon)*

EIGHT MEN OUT

CT: 5 AV: 6.15

1988 US 119 C DRAMA

D John Sayles
W John Sayles

John Cusack Clifton James Michael Lerner Christopher Lloyd Charlie Sheen David Strathairn D.B. Sweeney John Sayles Nancy Travis (cameo Studs Turkel)

In 1919, members of a baseball team take bribes to lose the World Series.

Well acted but overlong drama which could have done with a few more narrative surprises, less chat and greater depth of character. The attention evidently lavished on accurate sets might also have been spent on removing some obvious anachronisms from the dialogue. Sayles is on top form when showing the social and economic reasons behind the scandal; he's on less certain ground when he seems to argue that the poor aren't to blame for taking bribes – it's the rich who are responsible for tempting them.

'Where Sayles succeeds triumphantly is in creating a period atmosphere where this clash between sporting ideals and the greed of the high rollers seems utterly convincing. It's a dark film.' *(William Parente, Scotsman)*

'The problem with the film is that Sayles the screenwriter is at the mercy of Sayles the director

. . . [It] is a textbook exercise in confusion . . . The design . . . appears to have been bought wholesale from a Ralph Lauren boutique.' *(Victoria Mather, Daily Telegraph)*

'Handsomely crafted, but the period atmosphere encourages . . . Sayles to deal in broad strokes . . . One longs for a few surprises, the filmic equivalent of a sudden steal or a game-saving catch . . . The film's most lively and engrossing moments occur on the field . . . Here drama is truly expressed in action . . . Sayles may be growing as a filmmaker . . . but his screenplay here lacks texture and shading . . . [It] just misses the big league.' *(Kevin Lally, Film Journal)*

'The script is so scrupulous in painting in individual motivations for the characters that clutter the piece and makes this a brave effort, characterized by colourful performances, that never quite cracks it.' *(James Park, Film Yearbook)*

1871 CT: 1 AV: 2.33

1989 GB 100 C DRAMA

D Ken McMullen ●
W Terry James James Leahy Ken McMullen ●

Roshan Seth John Lynch Timothy Spall
Alexandre de Sousa Maria de Medeiros
Ann Padrao Jack Klaff Jacqueline Dankworth ✓

The fall of the Paris Commune, which was accompanied by ten times the bloodshed of the 1789 Terror.

The subject is fascinating; but director Ken McMullen and his co-screenwriters haven't a clue how to illuminate the issues. Not even the powerful singing of Cleo Laine's daughter, Jackie Dankworth, can rescue agit-prop in which she is saddled with having to play The Marxist Conscience Of The French Nation. The film as a whole looks like some unperformable Brecht play, mounted by the amateur dramatic branch of Militant Tendency. The setting is cheapskate, the dialogue risible and the anti-Thatcher, pro-IRA message so crude, that Channel Four (who commissioned it) might have been well advised to cut their losses, add a laughtrack and try to pass it off as as the latest offering by the National Theatre of Brent.

PRO:

'It looks a treat and its emphasis on theatricality and polemical flourish has considerable fascination.' *(Derek Malcolm, Guardian)*

'Has all the elements of terrific television: romance, revolution, murder, a good cast and top-notch production values.' *(Variety)*

MIXED:

'A grand, ambitious, three-act, sub-Brechtian affair, which exhibits the McMullen trademarks: a painterly eye, an unashamed taste for Big Ideas and allusive puns, and a tendency to lapse into obscurity and pretentiousness.' *(Wally Hammond, Time Out)*

'Spends 100 minutes trying to turn a feeble Brechtian burlesque about the days of the Paris Commune into incendiary satire. Jolly photography; pretty pantomime-style sets; but an infantile script and a tendency to stoke the story's dying flames with endless renditions of the Internationale.' *(Nigel Andrews, Financial Times)*

'A clever but cold film which will afford some pleasure and insights for upmarket audiences.' *(Winnert)*

ANTI:

'Ghastly. I walk out after about half an hour, and I'm not the first to do so.' *(Bruce Bawer, American Spectator)*

'Another melancholy example of rigid radicalism lacking mainstream and popular sophistication.' *(Raymond Durgnat, S & S)*

EINE STADT SUCHT EINEN MÖRDER: *see* M.

EL ANGEL EXTERMINADOR: *see* EXTERMINATING ANGEL, THE.

EL CID CT: 8 AV: 6.00

1961 US/Spain 184 C DRAMA/EPIC/ROMANCE/WAR

D Anthony Mann ✓
W Philip Yordan Fredric M. Frank

Sophia Loren Charlton Heston John Fraser
Raf Vallone Genevieve Page ✓ Gary Raymond
Herbert Lom Massimo Serato Douglas Wilmer
Frank Thring

Charlton Heston battles the Moors and finds Sophia Loren extremely more-ish.

Handsome epic with splendid scenery, lavish costumes and a surprisingly intelligent script. There's also a great final battle scene, though it is a long time coming. It received Oscar nominations for Best Colour Art Direction, Scoring of a Dramatic Picture, and song (The Falcon and the Dove).

ANTI:

'The dramatics in it explode with all the force of a panful of popcorn . . . Mann's direction is slow, stately, and confused, while Miss Loren and Heston spend much of the picture simply glaring at each other.' *(Newsweek)*

MIXED:

'*El Cid* is a fast-action, color-rich, corpse-strewn battle picture . . . The one reservation is that the action engages the eye rather than the mind.' *(New York Times)*

'Only the human drama is still and dull in this narrative.' *(Newsweek)*

'Endless glum epic with splendid action sequences as befits the high budget.' *(Halliwell)*

PRO:

'Creates respect for its sheer picture-making skills.' *(Variety)*

'A dazzler. A historical epic jam-crammed with castles and crowds and battles galore and enough jousts and tournaments and armored extras to satisfy the most ardent medievalist among us.' *(Judith Crist)*

EL NORTE CT: 5 AV: 7.58

(aka *The North*)

1983 US/GB 141 C DRAMA

D Gregory Nava ●
W Gregory Nava Anna Thomas ✗ AAN

Zaide Silvia Gutierrez David Villalpando
Ernesto Gomez Cruz Alicia del Lago

After a massacre of their family, a Guatemalan brother and sister (David Villalpando, Zaide Silvia Gutierrez) leave for the 'land of opportunity' and become part of the hispanic cheap labour-force in Los Angeles.

Typical of the kind of 'art' movie which attracts favourable criticism but not audiences. The subject-matter is interesting, but the screenplay doesn't dramatize it in an appealing way: the downbeat message is made relentlessly clear, and the characters throughout are heading for disaster. However, Nava's directing style moves easily between realism and surrealism, and there are moments of comic and compassionate relief.

PRO:

'Not a documentary, neither does it have any ideological point of view. It presents the facts with heightened realism and total absorption almost to the point of melodrama.' *(Virginia Dignam, Morning Star)*

'A truly absorbing primitive film holding attention all the way.' *(Freda Bruce Lockhart, Catholic Herald)*

'Although the story lapses sometimes into soap-operatics, it is remarkable for its insights into human-smuggling, the exploitation of illegal immigrant labour, and for its evocation of the fears of having absolutely no idea of what is going to happen to you next.' *(Paul Jackson, Western Mail)*

'An effective and moving drama.' *(Virgin)*

MIXED:

'You really get to love these two characters who (naively, it turns out) try to see the silver linings in the dark clouds, have hope where there is none, find humor in their confusing lifestyle. Exceptional film is marred by an ending that is overly depressing. The characters are already defeated – there is no need to destroy them.' *(Danny Peary)*

'Although occasionally mushy, this is a stark, moving look at the reality of the American dream and the strength of the human spirit.' *(Rose)*

ANTI:

'Like many another American "art" movie, this is by turns schematic, over-simplistic, cunning, studied, rhetorical, naive and self-conscious; but for once it's not pretentious.' *(Shipman)*

'Uninspired, but the subject has so much resonance that the picture doesn't leave you feeling quite as empty as an ordinary mediocre movie does.' *(Pauline Kael)*

ELEPHANT MAN, THE AAN CT: 7 AV: 6.93

1980 US 118/125 BW DRAMA

D David Lynch ☆ AAN
W Christopher De Vore Eric Bergren David Lynch from *The Elephant Man, A Study in Human Dignity* by Ashley Montagu and *The Elephant Man and Other Reminiscences* by Sir Frederick Treves

John Hurt ☆ AAN Anthony Hopkins ☆
John Gielgud ✔ Anne Bancroft Freddie Jones
Wendy Hiller Michael Elphick Hannah Gordon

A doctor (Anthony Hopkins) saves a deformed man (John Hurt) from the indignity of appearing in a fairground freak show.

A very moving movie, based on truth, directed with surprising restraint and humanity by David Lynch. The performances of Hurt, Hopkins and Gielgud are all terrific, as is Freddie Francis's black-and-white cinematography. Extraordinarily, Francis wasn't Oscar-nominated; but the music (John Morris), editing (Anne V. Coates), art direction (Stuart Craig, Bob Cartwright, Hugh Scaife), and costume design (Patricia Norris) were all recognized. It won Best Film at the BAFTA Awards – also best actor (John Hurt) and production design.

ANTI:

'The story, which needs tact and taste in the telling, was, unfortunately produced by Mel Brooks, not known for either . . . Wild elephants shouldn't drag you to this one.' *(John Simon)*

PRO:

'If there's a wrong note in this unique movie – in performance, production design, cinematography or anywhere else – I must have missed it.' *(Paul Taylor, Time Out)*

'Perhaps the most beautiful example of black-and-white cinematography in about 15 years.' *(Pauline Kael)*

'In an age of horror movies this is a film which takes

the material of horror and translates it into loving kindness.' *(Dilys Powell, Punch)*

'The facts have been changed around to make them more dramatic but the film remains sufficiently sober and compassionate to impress.' *(Shipman)*

ELMER GANTRY AAN CT: 6 AV: 8.00

1960 US 146 C DRAMA

D Richard Brooks
W Richard Brooks ✗ AAW from Sinclair Lewis's novel

Burt Lancaster ☆ AAW Jean Simmons ☆
Shirley Jones ☆ AAW Arthur Kennedy Dean Jagger
Edward Andrews Patti Page John McIntire

An unprincipled con-man (Burt Lancaster) realizes the business potential of an evangelist (Jean Simmons) in the 1920s.

An enjoyable adaptation of Sinclair Lewis's novel (or to be more accurate, the first part of it), inspired by the life of Aimee Semple Macpherson. The target looks obvious now, and the last 30 minutes look like a hurried attempt to build to a big finish and tie up the loose ends. The characters are superficial – even at the end it's impossible to know if Sister Sharon (Jean Simmons) is sincere or a charlatan – but fine performances go a long way to compensate.

'One wonders why Brooks, and producer Bernard Smith, went to so much trouble over such superficially handled material. After all, the real drama about a corrupt revivalist is more in the lives he affects than in the greeds and elusions of the man himself. Sinclair Lewis evaded these real issues and was content merely to expose a crude and obvious fraud. Brooks repeats this mistake.' *(Colton Washburn, Films in Review)*

'[Lancaster] acts with such broad and eloquent flourish that a finely balanced, more subdued performance by Jean Simmons as Sister Sharon seems pale by comparison.' *(Variety)*

'When Lancaster plays a kinetic, broadly exaggerated character like the lecher Gantry, you can't take your eyes off him; and Simmons is one of the most quietly commanding actresses Hollywood has ever trashed.' *(Pauline Kael)*

'Sister Sharon is beautifully realized by Jean Simmons, but even more triumphant is the throbbing vitality of time and place that is recreated.' *(Judith Crist)*

ELVIRA MADIGAN CT: 5 AV: 6.70

1967 Sweden 90 C ROMANCE/DRAMA/FOREIGN

D Bo Widerberg ✗
W Bo Widerberg

Thommy Berggren Pia Degermark

Count (Thommy Berggren) deserts Swedish army to be with his new love (Pia Degermark).

Based on a real double suicide in 1889, this remains a picturesque example of the Laura Ashley School of Film-Making, and its portrait of doomed romantic love will strike a responsive chord in adolescents of all ages. I loved it when I was 17, but now have less sympathy for the hero, who seems to have deserted his wife and two children without the least sign of remorse, and who appears constitutionally idle. His tightrope-walker girlfriend is pretty but vacuous, and equally lacking in resource. Their joint suicide at the end comes not a moment too soon.

Nor has the look of the film aged well. Some of Jorgen Persson's much-acclaimed camerawork is wobbly, and not so much soft-focus as out of focus; the symbolism (with red wine, for example, serving as a reminder of mortality) is crass; and its monotonously lyrical visual style – much imitated by advertisers – gives it the coyness of a commercial for condoms. The use of Mozart's Piano Concerto 21 on the soundtrack serves only to emphasize the appalling and unbridgeable artistic gulf between Mozart and Bo Widerberg.

PRO:

'One of the most beautiful films I have ever seen.' *(John Russell Taylor, The Times)*

'Of its rare kind, it is very nearly perfection.' *(Alexander Walker, Evening Standard)*

'Highly recommended for its striking color photography and for the [performances].' *(Thomas Quinn Curtiss, International Herald Tribune)*

'A production of exquisite beauty, with color so ravishing that it brings a lump to the throat.' *(Nina Hibbin, Morning Star)*

'One of the most exquisite, romantic movies ever made.' *(Scheuer)*

MIXED:

'An exceptional piece of film-making. At the same time, we do sense a certain hollowness at its centre, a hollowness typical of most exercises in colour . . . you remain troubled . . . by its simplification of character.' *(Eric Rhode, Listener)*

'More like a visit to an art gallery than a cinema.' *(Clive Hirschhorn, Sunday Express)*

ANTI:

'Too often resembles a shampoo commercial.' *(Maltin)*

EMPIRE DES SENS, L': *see* IN THE REALM OF THE SENSES.

EMPIRE OF THE ANTS CT: 1 AV: 1.57

1977 US 89 C HORROR

D Bert I. Gordon ☆
W Jack Turley ● from H.G. Wells's story

Joan Collins ● Robert Lansing John David Carson
Albert Salmi Jacqueline Scott

Oversized ants terrorize Florida.

This so much resembles a B-feature from the 1950s that it's a shock to realize it was made in 1977. Dreadfully unconvincing from start to finish, and the script is a joke.

PRO:

'An above-average effort . . . Periodic moments of good special effects are separated by reels of dramatic banality as players flounder in flimsy dialog and under sluggish direction.' *(Variety)*

MIXED:

'Filled with silly dialogue . . . The performances range from the acceptable to the self-conscious . . . Passable summer fare.' *(Ron Pennington, Hollywood Reporter)*

'It could be worse.' *(Halliwell)*

ANTI:

'Routine mutant picture.' *(John Pym, MFB)*

'"Have you ever taken a close look at what the ant is all about?" a voice harangues us in the opening minutes of this flat-footed piece of stupidity . . . Thanks to Gordon's special effects, a close look reveals that the ant is really an incredibly hairy octopus and about as frightening as a muppet.' *(Geoff Brown, Time Out)*

'Ludicrous Big-Bug flick in which the unstoppable Collins hit another low point of her career.' *(Scheuer)*

'H.G. Wells must somersault in his grave every time somebody watches this insulting adaptation.' *(Martin & Porter)*

'Tackily made and boring, but funny if you're in the mood to scoff.' *(Winnert)*

EMPIRE OF THE PASSIONS: *see* IN THE REALM OF THE SENSES.

EMPIRE OF THE SENSES: *see* IN THE REALM OF THE SENSES.

EMPIRE OF THE SUN CT: 5 AV: 5.79

1987 US 152 C WAR/DRAMA

D Steven Spielberg ●
W Tom Stoppard ● from J.G. Ballard's autobiographical novel

Christian Bale ☆ John Malkovich
Miranda Richardson Nigel Havers Joe Pantoliano
Leslie Phillips Masato Ibu Emily Richard
Rupert Frazer

A spoilt expatriate 11-year-old (Christian Bale) is taken prisoner by the Japanese after the fall of Shanghai, and learns to survive.

A travesty of J.G. Ballard's astonishing, poetic novel. In going for epic grandeur and that glossy Hollywood look, Spielberg completely misses the darker depths which presumably attracted him in the first place: the boy he presents us with is not a child clawing towards survival but a sunny Californian kid, so full of joy and wonder that you keep expecting E.T. to appear and whisk him away on a bicycle. It's a pity Spielberg couldn't have brought the same sensitivity to this that he did seven years later, to *Schindler's List*. Allen Daviau's Oscar-nominated cinematography is simply too beautiful. John Williams's lush score is a still more terrible error of taste: the last word in vacuity. You're much more likely to enjoy this if you haven't read the book.

PRO:

'A masterpiece of popular cinema.' *(MFB)*

'Intelligent and thought-provoking movie about the loss of childhood innocence through the horrors of war. Bale, as the boy, gives an extraordinarily believable performance.' *(Halliwell)*

'Visually stunning, emotionally thrilling, with outstanding acting, it's filming on the grandest scale.' *(Winnert)*

ANTI:

'Spielberg appears to be more interested in lighting surfaces in pretty ways than in exploring the ugly depths of the material; to him, the way the light reflects off of the suitcase that Jim throws into the water in the film's last shot would seem to be more important than his reason for throwing it. Another shot – of Jim standing behind the barbed wire of the camp – looks just like a Ralph Lauren ad in *GQ*. To look at these images is to recognize that Spielberg has absolutely no comprehension of the life they are supposed to represent.' *(Bruce Bawer, American Spectator)*

'A combination of craftsmanship and almost unbelievable tastelessness. Every time Spielberg makes a humanist statement, he falls flat on his face – not just because his statements are so naive, but because they go against the grain of Ballard's material.' *(Pauline Kael)*

EMPIRE STRIKES BACK, THE: *see* THE *STAR WARS* SERIES.

ENCHANTED APRIL CT: 6 AV: 6.71

1991 GB 95/101 C COMEDY

D Mike Newell ☆
W Peter Barnes ✗ AAN

Miranda Richardson ☆ Joan Plowright ☆ AAN
Alfred Molina Josie Lawrence ☆ Polly Walker
Michael Kitchen Jim Broadbent

Two bored wives (Joely Lawrence, Miranda Richardson) take a vacation from dismal post-World

War I London and their no less dismal husbands – a boring solicitor (Alfred Molina) and a philandering author (Jim Broadbent). They rent a small medieval castle in Italy with two other women, a harridan (Joan Plowright) and a society beauty (Polly Walker). In the unaccustomed warmth, all four women blossom.

Playwright Peter Barnes's over-theatrical adaptation dwells fatally long on the London section of Elizabeth von Arnim's novel, has a leaden sense of humour, and fails to make sense of why the two female principals eventually get back together with their husbands. The end result is ponderous and insubstantial when compared with cinematic predecessors such as Bergman's *Smiles of a Summer Night*; while its facile, Forsterian affection for things Italian is strictly for those who feel in need of a *Where Angels Fear To Re-Tread*. And yet it's easy to see what made this a hit in America: it has elegance, and the quality of the acting makes you sympathise with the female characters. The movie itself is enjoyable as a surrogate summer holiday, and the blinkered conservatism becomes part of its charm.

ANTI:

'Doesn't spring many surprises. Strong cast's reliable playing is undercut by a script that dawdles over well-trod territory.' *(Variety)*

'Newell does manage to draw out fine performances (although Lawrence does struggle with an impossibly simplistic role), but this is a sentimental journey you'd be wise to avoid.' *(Colette Maude, Time Out)*

'Twittery tedium that mostly comes across as mediocre Masterpiece Theatre.' *(Joanne Kaufman, People Weekly)*

MIXED:

'Everyone – especially Joan Plowright and Miranda Richardson – acts beautifully, and the screenplay by that fine playwright-scenarist Peter Barnes (*The Ruling Class*, etc) is particularly distinguished. One's two minor regrets are that the film ends somewhat abruptly, and that the men in it are a bit too unprepossessing. Yet how much superior this film is to another period piece, the vastly overrated adaptation of *Howards End*.' *(John Simon)*

PRO:

'It is a privilege to be in the company of these four women. Like the actresses in *Howards End*, the quartet in *Enchanted April* summon bygone graces and glamour. In a raucous movie summer, this is a film for those who appreciate wisteria and sunshine, and a recollection of a time when women and movies could be purveyors of enchantment.' *(Richard Corliss, Time)*

'Less ambitious than Forster's tales, *Enchanted April* is a delightful fable without a mean moment in it.' *(M. Faust, Video Magazine)*

EN PASSION: *see* PASSION OF ANNA, THE.

ENCINO MAN CT: 1 AV: 2.63

(aka *California Man*)

1992 US 88 C COMEDY

D Les Mayfield ☆
W Shawn Schepps

Sean Astin Brendan Fraser Pauly Shore ●
Megan Ward

High school students (Sean Astin, Pauly Shore) revive frozen caveman (Brendan Fraser) who adapts surprisingly well to Californian lifestyle.

Not a bad idea for a comedy, but a truly horrible script aimed at the lowest common denominator, and a cringe-makingly ingratiating performance by Pauly Shore make this an emetic experience to remember.

PRO:

'Far better than the critics allowed, this patchily amusing sub-*Bill & Ted* comedy could entertain.' *(Rose)*

ANTI:

'Mindless would-be comedy . . . insulting even within its own no-effort parameters.' *(Variety)*

'Depressingly witless.' *(Tom Charity, Time Out)*

'Less funny than your own funeral.' *(Washington Post)*

ENEMIES, A LOVE STORY CT: 5 AV: 7.38

1989 US 120 C DRAMA/ROMANCE

D Paul Mazursky ✗
W Roger L. Simon Paul Mazursky ✗ from Isaac Bashevis Singer's novel

Anjelica Huston ☆ AAN Ron Silver ☆
Lena Olin ☆ AAN Margaret Sophie Stein
Judith Malina Alan King Rita Karin Phil Leeds

A Jew (Ron Silver) who escaped the Holocaust goes to New York, and ends up married to three women (Anjelica Huston, Lena Olin and Margaret Sophie Stein).

An ambitious tragi-comedy which doesn't quite deliver. The script is noticeably short on laughs; but there is a good sense of period and of the dislocation in Jewish lives caused by the war, and the performances are outstanding. The central problem is a failure to involve the audience. The hero is a weak man (and is played by Silver, a not especially charismatic actor), and he cannot blame his indecisiveness on the Holocaust. It's hard to sympathize with the women when they are so obsessed with a man who constantly takes a path of least resistance. Audiences stayed away, but most critics (especially Jewish ones) loved it.

PRO:

'Hauntingly, mordantly amusing, deliciously sexy.' *(Variety)*

'A beautifully shaped film, with a rare sense of story, character, and place (and an entirely appropriate musical score by Maurice Jarre); the consistent matter-of-factness with which it contemplates Herman's increasingly outrageous situation is perfect, as is its scrupulously sustained balance of gentleness and irony. And while all the actors are fine, Miss Huston's wise, droll, and thoroughly authentic performance is a standout; the surgical precision and seeming effortlessness with which she delineates this complex, singular woman are breathtaking.' *(Bruce Bawer, American Spectator)*

'Mazursky's robust, mesmeric film of the Isaac Bashevis Singer novel defies categorization as it glides brazenly from tragedy to farce, from lyrical romance to raw sexplay, in an effort to rattle us and force us to rethink our own moral judgments. While in no way shifting guilt from perpetrator to victim, the movie does ask us to consider the possibility that not every survivor of Nazi barbarism qualifies for instant sainthood . . . *Enemies, A Love Story* is packed with challenge and exhilaration – a raucous, poignant, deeply resonant entertainment.' *(Guy Flatley, Cosmopolitan)*

'It's not a perfect film, it's better than that: it's a moving and thought-provoking one.' *(Raymond Durgnat, Film Yearbook)*

'Amid glowing local color just right for title period, Mazursky sets forth a tender modern folk tale that ultimately hails the indomitability of women as well as the sexual preoccupation of men. And the women in this case – Huston and Olin in particular – embody guilty pleasures that any philanderer might connive to keep.' *(Bruce Williamson, Playboy)*

'Conveys emotion without manipulation, sensitively distilling despair and self-hatred, but lifting the mood with dark humour . . . Period is beautifully evoked in subdued tones and subtly lit interiors.' *(Colette Maude, Time Out)*

'A moving, often wryly funny film with some wonderful acting.' *(Rose)*

MIXED:

'It may be that, in the novel, Singer can make the bizarre and violent fluctuations of Masha's behavior, which drag Herman partially along, believable; in Roger L. Simon and Paul Mazursky's screenplay, they are a capricious mixture of the willful and woeful, more arbitrary than fateful. Perhaps part of the problem is that, despite canny casting, a certain imbalance obtains. The simply competent and earthy Yadwiga of Margaret Sophie Stein and the cynically brooding Tamara of Anjelica Huston cannot quite compete – perhaps nobody could – with Lena Olin's dazzlingly sensual Masha.' *(John Simon)*

ANTI:

'Mazursky miscast badly . . . in choosing Silver to play the lead role. A distinguished Broadway actor and effective character player in such films as *Best Friends* and *Silkwood*, Silver seems strikingly insubstantial in a role that a Hoffman or a De Niro or a Kline could have turned into award fodder. Silver seems nothing like the sexual magnet the character is supposed to be, has difficulty pulling off the vulnerable scenes where he has nightmares about his wartime experiences and – especially when Huston is on-screen with him – has a hard time competing with his female co-stars.' *(Ralph Novak, People Weekly)*

'Silver's portrayal of the befuddled Herman is amusing, but the man is so unsympathetic that it is difficult to understand why any of the women are attracted to him.' *(Maclean's)*

'Rushed in its telling . . . and lacking conviction.' *(Halliwell)*

ENEMIES OF THE PUBLIC: *see* PUBLIC ENEMY, THE.

ENFANT SAUVAGE, L': *see* WILD CHILD, THE.

ENFANTS DU PARADIS, LES: *see* CHILDREN OF PARADISE.

ENTER THE DRAGON

CT: 7 AV: 6.64

(aka *The Deadly Three*)

1973 US/Hong Kong 99 C THRILLER/ACTION

D Robert Clouse
W Michael Allin

Bruce Lee ☆ John Saxon Jim Kelly Shih Kien Bob Wall Anna Capri Angela Mao Ying Betty Chung Geoffrey Weeks Yang Sze

Kung fu master (Bruce Lee) arrives on an island ruled by a criminal mastermind (Shih Kien).

A simple-minded plot, reminiscent of an early Bond movie, is the exceedingly slim pretext for stunning action sequences which have never been equalled for athleticism and speed.

ANTI:

'A sorry mixture of James Bond and Fu Manchu . . . Worth seeing for Lee, but still unforgivably wasteful of his talents.' *(Time Out)*

PRO:

'A good-natured example of the pleasures of schlock art . . . It could be billed as the movie with a thousand climaxes. But it's not all schlock: the slender, swift Bruce Lee was the Fred Astaire of martial arts, and many of the fights which could be merely brutal come across as lightning-fast choreography.' *(Pauline Kael)*

'Lee socks over a performance seldom equalled in action.' *(Variety)*

'Arguably the most entertaining, colorful and spectacular kung fu film ever made . . . The story is on a comic-book level; but the production values are high, the action is nonstop and consistently exciting; and the atmosphere is rich.' *(Danny Peary)*

ENTERTAINER, THE

CT: 5 AV: 7.36

1960 GB 96/104 BW DRAMA

D Tony Richardson
W John Osborne Nigel Kneale from John Osborne's play

Laurence Olivier ☆ AAN Brenda de Banzie Joan Plowright Roger Livesey Alan Bates Daniel Massey Albert Finney Miriam Karlin Shirley Ann Field Thora Hird

A clapped-out seaside entertainer (Laurence Olivier) regales us with his failures.

Tony Richardson's film of a successful play makes the most of the setting, an out-of-season seaside resort. Although the play had pretensions to being a portrait of England, it works best on a much smaller scale, as a character study of a failed, dead-behind-the-eyes vaudevillian. Laurence Olivier is stagey but memorably horrific as a personification of seedy self-disgust. A marvellous supporting cast includes Olivier's future wife, Joan Plowright, playing the entertainer's daughter.

MIXED:

'Raw, but vital stuff, which you'll either like or loathe.' *(Variety)*

'The film errs in many ways, and at times the editing is glaringly poor, but Olivier's performance gives it venomous excitement.' *(Pauline Kael)*

'Too many words, too many tantrums, too much kitchen-sink mentality; yet there are moments when this looks like a good film.' *(Robert Murphy, Time Out)*

'A harrowing embodiment of the divided, decaying spirit of England at midcentury. The greatest classical actor of our time was never more low-down and poetic, more brilliant and blatant, more graceful and crude, more eruptive and restrained than in this modern role.' *(Michael Sragow)*

'Twenty-nine years after seeing the film, his grotesque smile and dead eyes remain vivid in the memory.' *(Quinlan)*

ANTI:

'No amount of deafening sound effects and speciously busy cutting can remove one's feeling that behind this distracting facade of heightened realism lurks a basic lack of confidence.' *(Peter John Dyer)*

'Is *The Entertainer* still considered as wonderful as it was in 1960? This tears-of-a-clown piece about a down-at-the-heels vaudeville comic, Archie Rice, has always struck me as dull, facile, and stagy, the protagonist's seedy pathos as ultimately pointless; Olivier's spirited performance seems wasted on the one-note script.' *(Bruce Bawer, American Spectator)*

ENTRE NOUS: *see* COUP DE FOUDRE.

ERASERHEAD

CT: 5 AV: 6.11

1976 US 89 BW HORROR

D David Lynch
W David Lynch

Jack Nance Charlotte Stewart Allen Joseph Jeanne Bates Judith Roberts Laurel Near V. Phipps-Wilson Jack Fisk

Young man (John Nance) marries girlfriend (Charlotte Stewart) when she announces her pregnancy, then finds himself fathering a monster.

Weird, unpleasant film with horrible special effects, an expressionist shooting style, and a memorably twisted outlook on sexuality and parenthood. The lack of a coherent storyline makes it boring at time – but it's not a film you forget in a hurry.

PRO:

'This nightmare comedie noire [featuring the presence of] a bizarre baby . . . whose head and neck resemble those of a shaved Bedlington terrior . . . [and which] tilts the film towards macabre genius . . . is a surrealist coup de cinéma.' *(Nigel Andrews, Financial Times)*

'An astonishing achievement . . . Shows what can be done by determination and boundless imagination . . . Lynch has done a magnificent job of rubbing our noses in the decay around us.' *(Eric Braun, F & F)*

MIXED:

'Looking on the bright side it has the atmosphere of a German expressionist film, the tedium of a Warhol epic and the obscene symbolism of an early Buñuel satire.' *(Nicholas Wapshott, Scotsman)*

'Like taking a day-trip to Dante's Inferno . . . more a nightmare than a dream and not recommended to the squeamish.' *(Virginia Dignam, Morning Star)*

ANTI:

'A murkily pretentious shocker . . . Not . . . particularly horrifying . . . merely interminable.' *(Tom Buckley, New York Times)*

'It's about a man's deepseated fear of his own sexuality, his hatred of women and the terrors created by the thought of procreation . . . It is said in California . . . audiences attend screenings dressed as their favourite *Eraserhead* characters. I do not find this encouraging news.' *(Philip French, Observer)*

'A least Buñuel and Dali didn't take so long about their nonsense.' *(Halliwell)*

ET, THE EXTRA-TERRESTRIAL: *see* E.T. THE EXTRA-TERRESTRIAL.

EUREKA CT: 5 AV: 5.50

1981 (released 1985) US 129 C DRAMA

D Nicholas Roeg ✗
W Paul Mayersberg ● from Marshall Houts's book *Who Killed Sir Harry Oakes?*

Gene Hackman ☆ Theresa Russell ☆ Rutger Hauer Jane Lapotaire Ed Lauter Mickey Rourke Joe Pesci Helena Kallianiotes

The world of a very rich man (Gene Hackman) crumbles as hoods close in on him.

Pretentious, overheated, overpraised melodrama with an awful script. Based on a true story, it is partially redeemed by stunning images and powerful performances from Hackman and Russell. This is the closest that Roeg has got to creating *Citizen Kane*; but it ain't that close. Sample line . . . Whorehouse madam: 'Tonight, I took a bath, maybe because of you . . . My Jack had all the nuggets we needed right between his legs . . . With you, gold is everything. We had a crock of gold between us: his cock and my crack! Then, one morning . . . Jack was dead, dead inside me, dead in bed. That must have been when I started to smell bad.'

PRO:

'A spellbinder . . . Murder and mystery in a modern-day Aeschylean dynasty; and a film that fissures into new cinematic forms before your very eyes. Dazzling.' *(Nigel Andrews, Financial Times)*

'A film of such intimidating complexity and sophistication as to shame the customary brief of the moviemaker . . . A drama on the scale of the planets themselves.' *(Richard Cook, New Musical Express)*

'A profoundly unsettling, provocative film, brilliantly realised.' *(Elissa Van Poznak, Girl About Town)*

ANTI:

'A Roeg elephant film.' *(Variety)*

'The script seems very, very confused.' *(Derek Elley, F & F)*

'I've a feeling it will become a cult movie, but no one will convince me that it isn't just the poshest kind of tosh.' *(Margaret Hinxman, Daily Mail)*

EUROPA, EUROPA CT: 6 AV: 7.75

1991 France/Germany 115 C DRAMA/WAR/FOREIGN

D Agnieszka Holland ✗
W Agnieszka Holland Paul Hengge from Solomon Perel's book *Memoires*

Marco Hofschneider Julie Delpy Andre Wilms Solomon Perel Aschley Wanninger Ren Hofschneider

A Jewish teenager (Marco Hofschneider) survives the Second World War by becoming a member first of Stalin's Komsomol, then of the Hitler Youth.

Some American critics hailed this as one of the best movies of its year. Some Germans dismissed it as an insulting trivialization of history (and the German committee responsible for such matters refused to nominate it for the Best Foreign Film Oscar). It's an amazing true story, clearly told, with deliciously ironic moments. The high point of absurdity comes when our hero's attempt to desert to the Russians is misinterpreted by his own side as a charge against an enemy position, and he becomes a German war hero. There's pathos, too, in his tentative romance with a young Nazi blonde (Julie Delpy, who confirms the promise that she showed in *Voyager*).

The Polish director Agnieszka Holland cleverly uses the symbol of water to emphasize that our essentially innocent young hero is being re-baptized throughout the picture. The bathing images mean also that he is at his most naked and defenceless when unnerving things happen to him. She skilfully leads up the final *deus ex machina* coincidence which saves his life, by constantly raining things upon him from out of the sky: sweets from Stalin, bombs from the Americans, and finally a cleansing cloudburst.

There is much to admire in her direction, and the story never fails to grip. Yet it doesn't fully engage the emotions. The young leading actor, Marco Hofschneider, lacks depth and variety, and the picaresque narrative means that no one else has time to develop. But the basic flaw is the same one which renders Bernstein's musical version of *Candide* unsatisfying. The central character is essentially passive: he survives through luck, rather than skill or exceptional resilience. He also lacks internal life: even his dream sequences emphasize the grotesque nature of his situation, when they might more usefully have expressed his unexpressed feelings about being among enemies, or his agony at losing his identity. The director appears detached from her subject, so that the result is entertaining but oddly trivial: the stuff of which TV mini-series, not great films, are made.

ANTI:

'I walked out of the cinema feeling short-changed. The film is a ripping good yarn, but it lacks intellectual and moral rigour.' *(Vanessa Letts, Spectator)*

MIXED:

'Flawed, certainly; something goes seriously awry after the first third . . . And there are times when the implied horror of the situation disintegrates into mere dazed bewilderment; but perhaps that, too, is truthful. [The] images rise up like so many beautiful, paint-daubed canvases . . . This is an absorbing film, and an important one.' *(Nigella Lawson, Daily Telegraph)*

PRO:

'The farce of it all is poignantly edged . . . Holland . . . offers history not only with the understanding of hindsight but with the smack of immediacy.' *(David Hughes, Mail on Sunday)*

'A compelling story told with intelligence and wit.' *(Virgin)*

'Filled with suspense and touches of humor, pic brings a fresh approach to familiar themes and should find an appreciative arthouse audience in many parts of the world.' *(Variety)*

'Exciting, rousing and emotional . . . If this were fiction you wouldn't believe it.' *(Winnert)*

EVERGREEN CT: 7 AV: 6.63

1934 GB 90 BW MUSICAL/DRAMA

D Victor Saville
W Emlyn Williams Marjorie Gaffney from Benn W. Levy's play

Jessie Matthews ☆ Sonnie Hale Betty Balfour Barry Mackay Ivor McLaren Hartley Power

A star's daughter (Jessie Matthews) impersonates her own mother, in order to find fame and fortune.

An untypically sophisticated British screen musical of the period, and everlasting proof of Jessie Matthews's talent as a dancer. There are moments in this when she is stunning, giving you the kind of frisson which Garland or Astaire gave you at their best. She is helped by a Rodgers and Hart score, including 'Over my Shoulder' and 'Dancing on the Ceiling', which compensates for the fragile storyline. After this, Matthews – with characteristically foolish self-destructiveness – turned down the chance to become Fred Astaire's dancing partner in Hollywood and change the course of musical comedy history.

MIXED:

'The technique of this production, its presentation, everywhere rises above the material it is handling, but the last dance-ensemble is an anti-climax which is apt to upset one's final impressions of the rest of the picture.' *(MFB)*

'[Matthews's] movement and poise . . . is enchanting . . . The chance to end up on a really dramatic note is missed for the sake of a shoddy production number that nobody has had the courage to scrap.' *(Observer)*

'Not the biting wit of Lubitsch, but something silly and sweet.' *(Penelope Gilliatt, New Yorker, 1973)*

PRO:

'Jessie Matthews . . . will entrench herself in the hearts of American moviegoers with this film . . . A merry and interesting story.' *(Photoplay)*

EXCALIBUR CT: 4 AV: 6.28

1981 US 140 C FANTASY/DRAMA

D John Boorman ✗
W Rospo Pallenberg John Boorman ● from Thomas Mallory's *Morte D'Arthur*

Nigel Terry Nicol Williamson ● Nicholas Clay Helen Mirren Cherie Lunghi Paul Geoffrey Robert Addie Gabriel Byrne Liam Neeson Corin Redgrave

The life of King Arthur (Nigel Terry).

This Arthurian claptrap by British director John Boorman did well at the box office, and looks magnificent. (Alex Thomson's photography was Oscar-nominated.) It's also ridiculously overblown, humourless and pretentious, with a script which veers crazily between mysticism, heroic seriousness, Jungian psychology and high camp. Nicol Williamson's performance as Merlin (in which his accent changes from shot to shot) is perhaps the most ludicrously undisciplined ever on screen.

PRO:

'Exquisite, a near-perfect blend of action, romance, fantasy and philosphy, finely acted and beautifully filmed.' *(Variety)*

'The imagery is impassioned and has a hypnotic quality. The film is like Flaubert's more exotic fantasies – one lush, enraptured scene after another. As Merlin, Nicol Williamson (who affects a touch of the gaelic and makes wonderful lilting and growling sounds) is the presiding spirit; he stands in for Jung, and he informs us of the meaning of what we're seeing.' *(Pauline Kael)*

'The handsomest film since . . . *Days of Heaven* and it is as alive to the subtle textures of earth, water and sky . . . Love [it] or hate it, but give Boorman credit for the loopy grandeur of his imagery and imaginings, for the sweet smell of excess, for his heroic gamble that a movie can dare to trip over its pretensions – and still fly.' *(Richard Corliss, Time)*

MIXED:

'All's not well in Camelot . . . Boorman's telling of the Arthurian legend [is] a long meandering, often spectacular, but finally flawed epic . . . Williamson's Merlin is a hoot – often unintentionally . . . but in trying to construct an adult epic from the involved and mythological tale, Boorman has lost most of the magic.' *(Arthur Thirkell, Daily Mirror)*

'Visually . . . often stunning, but the dialogue never rises to the level of Boorman's visual and philosophical ambitions . . . It is almost impossible to describe how Nicol Williamson reads his lines . . . It's the quirkiest rendition imaginable.' *(Richard Roud, Guardian)*

ANTI:

'Overlong and incoherent.' *(Geoff Andrew, Time Out)*

THE *EXORCIST* SERIES

EXORCIST, THE CT: 7 AV: 7.80

1973 US 122 C HORROR

D William Friedkin ✔ AAN
W William Peter Blatty AAN from his own novel

Ellen Burstyn Max Von Sydow ✔ Jason Miller Linda Blair Lee J. Cobb Kitty Winn Jack McGowran

Demon possesses 12-year-old girl (Linda Blair).

A horror film which revolutionized the genre – for good and ill – with its spectacularly unpleasant effects. The script is pretentious, confused and lacks human sympathy, but that didn't prevent it from winning an Academy Award. The film works because it is a vicarious roller-coaster ride for the audience, and a professional piece of manipulative film-making. Many found it terrifying.

'I just throw everything at the audience and give them a real thrill. That's what they want. They don't want to go into a theater and treat it like a book. They don't even read books!' *(William Peter Blatty)*

ANTI:

'I hated it . . . For the first time I believe a film should be banned . . . [It] is unpleasant and nasty without the saving grace of having some artistic merit.' *(Paula James, Daily Mirror)*

'All I can say after squirming through this sickening excess of blood, vomiting, lewd language and gruesome Satanic phenomena is that I hope never again to have to see anything half so hateful.' *(Cecil Wilson, Daily Mail)*

'Vile and brutalizing.' *(Jay Cocks, Time)*

'One could wish that Ellen Burstyn exuded more glamour and magnetism as a supposed movie star . . . [and] that Friedkin had succeeded in imaginatively recreating the book as often as he perfunctorily referred to it. Nonetheless . . . the book is there on the screen in all its inexhaustible ghoulishness . . . On another deeper level, it is a thoroughly evil film.' *(Andrew Sarris, Village Voice)*

'It is Friedkin's ruthless and calculated decision to devote himself to mechanics rather than meaning that finally pushes [the film] past the point of shallowness and into an area of narcissistic arrogance which, while sometimes entertaining, even amusing . . . is finally more morally than physically disgusting.' *(Jon Landau, Rolling Stone)*

'Paranormal garbage . . . scabrousness, goose pimples and moral uplift . . . a ten million-dollar movie that will increase the birthrate of suckers from one to a hundred per minute.' *(John Simon)*

'The demonic possession of a child, treated with shallow seriousness. The picture is designed to scare people, and it does so by mechanical means: levitations, swivelling heads, vomit being spewed in people's faces. A viewer can become glumly anesthetized by the brackish color and the senseless ugliness of the conception. Neither the producer-writer, William Peter Blatty, nor the director, William Friedkin, shows any feeling for the little girl's helplessness and suffering, or for her mother's.' *(Pauline Kael)*

MIXED:

'Nothing but a superior shocker. A very well-made horror movie with pretensions to something better (or certainly deeper) that never does more than stick its nose out, then hastily withdraw. For . . . it does nothing but exhibit the physical state. Though posing as a serious film, it has hardly six lines of serious dialogue about the inner life of the afflicted.' *(Alexander Walker, Evening Standard)*

'An old-fashioned horror movie: fine when it sticks to the horrors but seized by paralysis of the pretentious when it gets serious.' *(Richard Combs, S & S)*

'No more nor less than a blood and thunder horror movie, foundering heavily on the rocks of pretension.' *(Tom Milne)*

'It exploits the subject of diabolic possession without telling you anything about it . . . just a stylistic exercise.' *(Michael Billington, Illustrated London News)*

'All *The Exorcist* does is take its audience for a ride, spewing it out the other end, shaken up but none the wiser.' *(Chris Peachment, Time Out)*

PRO:

'As an engine of manipulation, *The Exorcist* succeeds magnificently . . . It is violently effective . . . [it] is a catalogue of devices that work.' *(James Monaco, American Film Now, 1979)*

'Startling, terrifying and downright superb.' *(LA Times)*

'The well cast film makes credible in powerful laymen's terms the rare phenomenon of diabolic possession . . . The climactic sequences assault the senses and the intellect with pure cinematic terror.' *(Variety)*

'An extremely powerful film which relentlessly batters the eyes and ears. It is high class horror.' *(Sunday Mirror)*

'A superior horror story very ably directed.' *(Spectator)*

'I felt that it was one of the best films of all time because it achieved everything it set out to accomplish.' *(Bizarre)*

'Special effects make-up by Dick Smith and Rick Baker revolutionized the horror genre – you'll feel sorry for Blair. Friedkin's direction is solid – I particularly like the way he refrigerated Blair's room so that steam pours out of everyone's mouth . . .

Blatty's script is flimsy and often stupid – he allows the Devil to provide most of his humor. I think the most interesting aspect of the picture is that it conveys a fear that is rarely dealt with: Regan doesn't have those around her turn into monsters (a basic primal fear) but becomes a monster herself. Not since Pinocchio grew donkey ears and a tail has a child become so bestial. Significantly we aren't scared of this child – as we are in several child-as-monster films – but sympathize, even identify, with her.' *(Danny Peary)*

'A masterwork of the genre.' *(Alan Frank)*

'One of the best movies of its type ever made . . . [but] are people so numb they need movies of this intensity in order to feel anything at all?' *(Roger Ebert)*

EXORCIST II: THE HERETIC CT: 1 AV: 2.11

1977 US 110/117 (on video) C HORROR/SO BAD

D John Boorman ●
W William Goodhart ●

Richard Burton ● Linda Blair Louise Fletcher Kitty Winn Max Von Sydow Paul Henreid James Earl Jones Ned Beatty

Priest (Richard Burton) tries to exorcize young girl (Linda Blair).

Despite fine special effects, this is a hopelessly confused and confusing sequel. The attempts to delve into mysticism are laughably pretentious, and Richard Burton's performance must be one of the worst and hammiest ever committed to celluloid. Sample line of Burton dialogue: 'Evil is a spiritual being, alive and living, perverted and perverting, weaving its way insidiously into the very fabric of life!'

PRO:

'The theme is attacked with engaging intensity, and Boorman brings off more than one visual coup (notably the ingenious locust photography in the African sequences. Dennis Wheatley fans, at least, will love it.' *(David Pirie, Time Out)*

'Boorman [rejects] the vulgar, sensational approach . . . mixing terror with compassion.' *(Virginia Dignam, Morning Star)*

MIXED:

'Boorman . . . has put some genuine effort into it – it shows thought and care and more than a touch of originality. [He] takes some interesting chances and even if none of them really pay [sic] off, he deserves a little credit for trying to bring something other than mindless mimicry to a sequel . . . People are coming to see a version of Friedkin's crude suspense mechanism . . . but they're not getting it. Instead . . . Boorman is serving up a blend of H.P. Lovecraft, Vincente Minnelli and Luis Buñuel . . . As a sequel . . . it's an obvious flop, but as continuation of the concerns that have governed Boorman's art, [it] has to be counted as a quasi success . . . an intriguing, if not memorable experience.' *(Dave Kehr, Chicago Reader)*

'This picture has a visionary crazy grandeur (like that of Fritz Lang's loony *Metropolis*). Some of its telepathic sequences are golden-toned and lyrical, and the film has a swirling, hallucinogenic, apocalyptic quality; it might have been a horror classic if it had had a simpler, less ritzy script . . . But it's winged camp – a horror fairy tale gone wild, another in the long history of moviemakers' king-size follies. There's enough visual magic in it for a dozen good movies; what it lacks is judgment.' *(Pauline Kael)*

'In the teeth of Boorman's admirers who are now joining ranks to defend the film, I should say at once that it seems to matter very little how it ends since it is almost incomprehensible to follow . . . Indeed it would be unviewable were it not for William A. Fraker's assured and decisive camerawork.' *(Margaret Tarratt, F & F)*

ANTI:

'Not as good as *The Exorcist*. It isn't even close. Gone now is the simple clash between Good and Evil, replaced by some goofy trasnscendental spiritualism.' *(Variety)*

'Explosive editing, not much suspense and a waste of Burton's excellent performance. Much as I loathed [the original] *Exorcist*, at least it seemed to know what it was trying to do.' *(Margaret Hinxman, Daily Mail)*

'Richard Burton . . . [is attacked] by a swarm of locusts. He deserves all he gets, believe me.' *(Ian Christie, Daily Express)*

'An almost total disappointment – muddled, confused, atrociously acted and laughably written.' *(John McCarty, Cinefantastique)*

'It's all too ludicrous to frighten and the only time you're likely to hide your head will be in shame for watching it.' *(Jack Lewis, Daily Mirror)*

'The director, John Boorman, just doesn't know where to stop in his quest to shock.' *(News of the World)*

'There is a very strong probability that *Exorcist II* is the stupidest major movie ever made. I hate to sound that categorical, because it may send collectors of imbecilities scurrying off in droves to see this execrable product; but, then, I suppose, collectors of imbecilities are the fitting audience for this film, and they deserve each other.' *(John Simon)*

'A commercial disaster, it was released in two versions and is unintelligible in either.' *(Halliwell)*

EXORCIST III: THE LEGION, THE

CT: 4 AV: 4.20

1990 US 109 C HORROR

D William Peter Blatty
W William Peter Blatty

George C. Scott Ed Flanders Brad Dourif Jason Miller Nicol Williamson Scott Wilson Nancy Fish George Dienzo Don Gordon

Veteran cop (George C. Scott) investigates mysterious killings.

It begins admirably, with a malevolent atmosphere and well-timed backchat between George C. Scott and Ed Flanders (as a witty priest); but as more and more of the cast lose their heads – quite literally – the plot gets sillier and sillier. As horror, the film fails to deliver many shocks, since the nastiest action takes place offscreen: instead, we are treated to much vacuous philosophizing about evil, and some ludicrously self-indulgent overacting. A final showdown, guest-starring Nicol Williamson as an excitable exorcist, is crudely tacked on, to supply more in the way of gore, but frankly it's just a bloody bore.

'A restrained, haunting chiller which stimulates the adrenaline and intellect alike.' *(Mark Kermode, Time Out)*

'Intriguing, but rather passé twenty years down the line.' *(Rose)*

'Begins well but grows more absurd and confusing until it self-destructs.' *(Maltin)*

EXTERMINATING ANGEL, THE

CT: 5 AV: 8.50

(aka *El Angel Exterminador*)

1962 Mexico 95 BW DRAMA/COMEDY/FOREIGN

D Luis Buñuel ✗
W Luis Buñuel Luis Alcoriza from José Bergamin's play *Los Naufragos de la Calle de la Providentia*

Silvia Pinal Jacqueline Andere José Baviera Augusto Benedico Luis Beristain Antonio Bravo Claudio Brook Cesar del Campo Lucy Gallardo

Guests at a dinner party are too lazy to leave.

One of Buñuel's unfunny, plodding satires on the bourgeoisie, with the characters gradually reverting to bestiality and cannibalism. Even *The Discreet Charm of the Bourgoisie* did it better. *Lord of the Flies* did it a lot better. Adored by critics, who found it wittily surreal and evidently felt superior to the characters portrayed here with such unconscious complacency.

PRO:

'An extraordinarily powerful and imaginative piece, sometimes obscure, often deliberately shocking, but composed with a mordant wit and a tough intellectual energy that make it richly rewarding.' *(James Breen, Spectator)*

'No matter if the allegory is not fully worked out, at least the situation is wonderfully worked up and the conclusion could hardly be more amusing or more wicked.' *(Patrick Gibbs, Daily Telegraph)*

'I found it fascinating, frightening, faintly horrific, and absolutely engrossing.' *(Ann Pacey, Sun)*

'One of the greatest masterworks of a giant of cinema.' *(Virgin)*

'Wry assault on bourgeois manners.' *(Maltin)*

'A banquet of Buñuelian surrealism.' *(Scheuer)*

MIXED:

'Fascinating surrealist fantasia on themes elaborated with even more panache in *The Discreet Charm of the Bourgeoisie*. Nevertheless, one of the director's key films.' *(Halliwell)*

'Clumsily acted – his films often are, partly because this master has habitually had to work in a hurry with tenth-string casts – but it is hallucinatorily funny and very much his own.' *(Penelope Gilliatt)*

ANTI:

'An unsound and unsightly mixture of spurious allegory and genuine craziness.' *(John Simon)*

EYES WITHOUT A FACE

CT: 6 AV: 6.43

(aka *Les Yeux sans Visage; Horror Chamber of Dr Faustus*)

1959 France/Italy 90 BW HORROR/FOREIGN

D Georges Franju ☆
W Jean Redon from his novel

Pierre Brasseur Alida Valli Edith Scob François Gurin

A surgeon (Pierre Brasseur) tries to graft the faces of kidnapped women on to his daughter (Edith Scob), grotesquely deformed after a car crash.

Despite a naive plot and melodramatic moments, rightly famous as one of the most stylish, poetic horror films ever made. The final sequence, when the daughter rebels against her fatther, is unforgettable. The magnificent cinematography is by Eugene Schuftan.

'Unpleasant horror film which its director seems to have made as a joke; the years have made it a cult.' *(Halliwell)*

'Franju, despite the crass American release title [*Horror Chamber of Dr Faustus*], managed to evolve a style that was both elegant and expressionistic, pure and magical.' *(Scheuer)*

'Perhaps the most austerely elegant horror film ever made.' *(Pauline Kael)*

'Illuminated throughout by Franju's unique sense of poetry – nowhere more evident than in the final shot of Scob wandering free through the night, her mask discarded but her face seen only by the dogs at her feet, and the dove on her shoulder – it's a marvellous movie in the fullest sense.' *(Tom Milne, Time Out)*

FABULOUS BAKER BOYS, THE

CT: 7 AV: 6.46

1989 US 113 C MUSICAL/ROMANCE

D Steve Kloves
W Steve Kloves

Jeff Bridges ✓ Michelle Pfeiffer ☆ AAN
Beau Bridges ✓ Ellie Raab Jennifer Tilly

Two brothers (Jeff and Beau Bridges) who play dire cocktail-piano duets in cheesy Seattle bars find that their act no longer goes down a storm, or even a light breeze. Together, they audition 37 girl singers, not one of whom can carry a tune without dropping it. The 38th, a hard-bitten escort called Susie Diamond (Michelle Pfeiffer) turns up an hour and a half late. 'Punctuality!' Frank admonishes her. 'First rule of show business!' Susie looks around at the dive where they're auditioning. 'This is show business?' she rasps. No sooner has Frank grown accustomed to her face than there's a small hotel where they start having feelings and makin' whoopee; no longer strangers in the night, they do the act their way; she goes up, up and away, and the party's over.

The film's 20 minutes too long and doesn't have a lot of point – unless it's to prove the old adage that he who lays the Pfeiffer mauls the tune. But the actors keep the whole thing afloat with their charm; and the leading lady's rendition of 'Makin' Whoopee' is, er, memorable. Michael Ballhaus's cinematography was Oscar-nominated, as were the editing and original score.

'Pfeiffer's good-bad Susie recalls the grinning infectiousness of Carole Lombard, the radiance of the very young Lauren Bacall, and Pfeiffer herself in other movies. By ordinary-movie standards, the pacing here could be snappier at times – more decisive – but it's a piece with the bluesiness . . . The choice of songs, their placement, and the sound mix itself are extraordinary – so subtle they make fun of any fears of kitschy emotions. And there's a thrill in watching the three actors, because they seem perfect at what they're doing – newly minted icons.' *(Pauline Kael)*

'Pfeiffer is an absolute revelation when singing "Makin' Whoopee", convincingly striding through the picture as if aware that she's on her way to a somewhere that the Baker Boys haven't got a chance of gettting to.' *(Kim Newman, Film Yearbook)*

'Snappy dialogue and snazzy performances elevate routine plot of musician finding himself. The lounge act's got a lot of pep, and surprising class . . . Kloves' dialogue is crisp as bacon on the griddle and his direction never falters. There are a few slow patches, but not so many as to diminish interest . . . The Bridges brothers are at their peak . . . [The film] lives up to its title.' *(Bruce Feld, Film Journal)*

'[Pfeiffer's] jaw-dropping rendition of "Makin' Whoopee" on the piano top is one of the highlights of 80's cinema.' *(Rose)*

FACE IN THE CROWD, A

CT: 6 AV: 7.64

1957 US 126 BW DRAMA

D Elia Kazan ☆
W Budd Schulberg from his short story *The Arkansas Traveler*

Andy Griffith ☆ Patricia Neal ☆ Anthony Franciosa
Walter Matthau ☆ Lee Remick ☆ Percy Waram
Rod Brasfield Charles Irving Howard Smith
Paul McGrath

Reporter (Patricia Neal) helps a philosophizing, guiter-playing hillbilly (Andy Griffith) to stardom, whereupon he becomes a right-wing demagogue.

Despite wonderful performances, the film degenerates into liberal finger-wagging. A forerunner to *Bob Roberts* (1992), which suffered from many of the same faults.

PRO:

'A devastating commentary on hero-worship and success cults in America.' *(Variety)*

'Savagery, bitterness, cutting humour.' *(Penelope Houston)*

'One of the few genuinely political assaults the cinema has made . . . It savages. It explodes: it is the guided missile.' *(Dilys Powell)*

'The script . . . has brilliant satiric detail and the film overall may be the best made about the abuse of power by the media.' *(Shipman)*

'Brilliantly cinematic melodrama of its time which only flags in the last lap and paints a luridly entertaining picture of modern show business.' *(Halliwell)*

ANTI:

'Exhibits a tough-minded approach to the problems of mass culture and the facile manipulation of public opinion. If Kazan and Schulberg had been content to make their case by implication, it might have been a completely sophisticated piece of movie-making. Instead, everything is elaborately spelled out, and the film degenerates into preposterous liberal propaganda.' *(Andrew Sarris)*

'Some exciting scenes in the first half, but the later developments are frenetic, and by the end the film is a loud and discordant mess.' *(Pauline Kael, 70s)*

'The ordinary "little people" are presented as being

so gullible that what starts out as a seemingly liberal tract rapidly becomes a smug, cynical exercise in misanthropy.' *(Geoff Andrew, Time Out)*

FACE, THE: *see* MAGICIAN, THE.

FACE TO FACE CT: 6 AV: 7.75

(aka *Ansikte Mot Ansikte*)

1975 Sweden 136 C DRAMA/FOREIGN

D Ingmar Bergman ☆ AAN
W Ingmar Bergman

Liv Ullmann ☆ AAN Erland Josephson
Gunnar Björnstrand Aino Taube-Henrikson
Karl Sylwan Sif Ruud

Psychiatrist (Liv Ullmann) suffers nervous breakdown.

Originally filmed as a four-part series for Swedish TV, this must be one of the most disturbing and gruelling portraits of a crack-up ever to reach the screen. Intense but very, very slow.

'Takes us into the heart's depths so that we can better understand its heights . . . Despite storyline deletions . . . the travail is magnificently worth it.' *(Tom Hutchinson, Sunday Telegraph)*

'Curiously hopeful for a Bergman film.' *(Margaret Hinxman, Daily Mail)*

'Bergman directs it as an intellectual exercise, the suspense being in teasing out what it means.' *(Kenneth Baily, Sunday People)*

'A devastating masterpiece . . . featuring one of the most remarkable acting performances in modern cinema.' *(Scheuer)*

'Too long.' *(Halliwell)*

FAHRENHEIT 451 CT: 5 AV: 6.50

1966 GB 112 C SF/DRAMA

D François Truffaut
W François Truffaut Jean-Louis Richard from Ray Bradbury's novel

Oskar Werner ☆ Julie Christie Cyril Cusack Anton Diffring Jeremy Spenser Ann Bell

In a future state, books are burned.

The finale is memorable, there are pleasant touches of humour, and it looks good (the talented cinematographer was Nicolas Roeg); but the dystopic vision of the future is too low-key to be frightening, the pace drags, and it's hard to care about the characters. Critical opinion has always been divided.

PRO:

'Rises like Everest, crystal-pure and shiny, towering above the hills of mediocrity and trash the movies have turned out lately to become (in my opinion) one of the most interesting films of the decade.' *(Rex Reed)*

'There may be other ways of putting Bradbury on film, but there can be none better than this.' *(MFB)*

'Thoughtfully directed . . . there is adequate evidence of light touches to bring welcome and needed relief to a sombre and scarifying subject.' *(Variety)*

ANTI:

'He barely dramatizes the material at all, and though there are charming, childlike moments, the performers seem listless, and the whole enterprise is a little drab.' *(Pauline Kael)*

'We are left only with a beautiful and slightly hysterical Julie Christie, a deadpan Oskar Werner, and an obvious language difficulty between an American science-fictioner, a French-speaking director, and a made-in-England movie.' *(Judith Crist)*

'Truffaut . . . is out of his milieu. His strength is in the presentation of character which has been deformed by circumstances. Here he has taken on characters which have no depth; he has worked with a screenplay which allows him only the most obvious of comments on a flat regimented community. He has taken on a plot which needs emphasis, climax, above all speed. And he doesn't show the pace for it.' *(Dilys Powell)*

FAIL SAFE CT: 7 AV: 7.09

(aka *Fail-Safe*)

1964 US 112 BW SF/THRILLER

D Sidney Lumet ☆
W Walter Bernstein

Henry Fonda ☆ Dan O'Herlihy Walter Matthau ☆
Frank Overton ☆ Edward Binns Fritz Weaver
Larry Hagman ☆

A computer malfunction endangers the safety of the world.

Expertly made cold-war thriller which had the ring of truth, and was undeservedly eclipsed on release by *Dr Strangelove*, which approached an identical theme in a more comedic manner. Excellent performances by Henry Fonda (as the US President), Walter Matthau, Frank Overton and Larry Hagman; but the whole cast is convincing.

MIXED:

'May be remembered . . . as the film there seemed little point in making after *Dr Strangelove* . . . On its own level it is not bad . . . Some of the acting . . . is overdone with only . . . Fonda . . . happily transcending the script and . . . Lumet's over-emphatic direction. But the plot is holding.' *(The Times)*

'It seems fair to propose that a robot wrote its dialogue. Most that disappoints comes down to a matter of feeble or portentous words.' *(John Coleman, New Statesman)*

'The script is half-baked but its heart is in the right place and well directed.' *(Shipman)*

PRO:

'A gripping narrative realistically and almost frighteningly told.' *(Variety)*

'Brilliantly made, totally credible, and very disturbing.' *(F & F)*

'Though I relished the wit and audacity of *Dr Strangelove*, I never felt personally threatened; *Fail Safe* . . . makes the logic of catastrophe seem much more intimate and irrefutable. Step by plausible step, we are drawn into an apocalyptic experience.' *(Kenneth Tynan, 1968)*

'Brilliant, numbing look at the implications of the computers and transistors, the buttons and little red lights that man has created for self-defence . . . Over-dramatised it may be but in this nuclear vale of tears, memorable is a better word.' *(Ann Pacey, Sun)*

'This thriller is a chiller and you will not warm up again for a long time after it is over . . . Fonda [performs] with a magisterial calm that is deeply moving . . . Brrr! Will someone please turn up the central heating?' *(Leonard Mosley, Daily Express)*

'A devastating film . . . Brilliantly made, totally credible and very disturbing . . . [Lumet] has chosen the most important universal subject and has done complete justice to it.' *(Robin Bean, S & S)*

'*Dr Strangelove* without the laughs . . . tight, tense, terrifying and entirely convincing.' *(NFT Bulletin, 1984)*

Bleak and bitter science fiction that packs a strong charge of credibility and is a far more sober indictment of nuclear politics than the sometimes overrated *Dr Strangelove*.' *(Alan Frank)*

FALLEN IDOL, THE   CT: 8   AV: 8.20

(aka *The Lost Illusion*)

1948 GB 94 BW DRAMA/THRILLER

D Carol Reed ☆
W Graham Greene ☆ AAN from his story *The Basement Room*

Ralph Richardson ☆ Michèle Morgan Bobby Henrey ☆ Sonia Dresdel Jack Hawkins

A boy (Bobby Henrey) tries to protect the butler he idolizes (Ralph Richardson) from being accused of murder.

Carol Reed's moving film from Graham Greene's story views the adult world through a child's eyes. It also works as a tense thriller. Ralph Richardson turns in one of his finest screen performances. All in all, a masterly chamber-piece, directed with taste and economy.

PRO:

'A fine sensitive story, a brilliant child star and a polished cast . . . a satisfying piece of intelligent entertainment.' *(Variety)*

'A short story has become a film which is compact without loss of variety in pace or shape.' *(Dilys Powell)*

'A near-perfect piece of small-scale cinema, built up from clever nuances of acting and cinematic technique.' *(Halliwell)*

ANTI:

'It's too deliberate and hushed to be much fun . . . you wait an extra beat between the low-key lines of dialogue.' *(Pauline Kael)*

FALLING DOWN   CT: 9   AV: 6.57

1993 US 115 C THRILLER/COMEDY

D Joel Schumacher ✔
W Ebbe Roe Smith ✔

Michael Douglas ✔ Robert Duvall ✔ Barbara Hershey Rachel Ticotin ✔ Tuesday Weld Frederic Forrest ✔ Lois Smith

A white, middle-class, unemployed defence worker (played by Michael Douglas) cracks under the strain of urban living. Seemingly sane and starting out with nothing more lethal in his briefcase than a packed lunch, he abandons his car in a traffic jam and sets out on an innocent stroll across Los Angeles, to his daughter's birthday party. On the way, he accumulates a baseball bat, a switchblade, machine-guns and a bazooka from fellow city-dwellers intent on giving him a hard time. He finds a sense of liberation in a violent rampage – wrecking a convenience store, stabbing a mugger, shooting up a fast-food joint. Everyman turns into Everymonster.

Rarely, perhaps never, has a movie inspired more hatred. The excellent script for this unsettling, paranoid black comedy was rejected by every major Hollywood studio, including the one that finally made it (Rupert Murdoch's Twentieth Century Fox).

The patriotic symbolism which surrounds Douglas's character – coupled with his nickname, D-FENS – is a hint that he symbolizes America itself: uncertain of its role in the world, unsure why it isn't obeyed more readily, and only certain of respect when it starts threatening violent recriminations. It was easier when you could blame everything on the Commies. Now he and his country have become the bad guy in so many people's eyes, and neither of them can understand why.

The film is often funny and always gripping; and Robert Duvall's character (he's the cop trailing Douglas) is a reminder of the film's central message, that patience is a virtue. Despite moments of crudeness and overstatement, it's a landmark film of the 1990s.

'A lot of people are angry out there now. They've worked hard all their lives, they've got nothing to show for it and they don't know who to be angry at.' *(Michael Douglas)*

'So-called politically correct movies are fairytales. This movie shows the way things really are, not the way they should be . . . We've kind of swept this accumulating white rage under some big carpet, some terrible Astroturf, for twelve years.' *(Director Joel Schumacher)*

ANTI:

'Clearly an attempt to exploit the frustrations of riot-weary, white Los Angeles.' *(Gene Siskel, Chicago Tribune)*

'The last thing Los Angeles, or any other urban center, needs is a movie that feeds the paranoia of one demographic group's anxieties, connects all the emotional dots and seems to conclude that even though violence is wrong, it's an understandable response.' *(Jack Matthews, Newsday)*

'Crude, shrewd, dangerous and morally stupid.' *(Time)*

'Nasty in the way it manipulates one's darkest feelings.' *(Vincent Canby, New York Times)*

'[The leading character is a] devastating stereotyping of defense workers'. *(America's National Center for Career Change)*

'The social critique here isn't very incisive. And it gets more forced and didactic.' *(Georgia Brown, Village Voice)*

MIXED:

'Douglas and Schumacher . . . clearly . . . wanted to make a *Taxi Driver* for the 90s, to update the toll of urban stress on the working man's psyche. To this end [it] is paced and shot idiosyncratically, cleverly scripted and structured . . . and wonderfully lit . . . Yet its driving force is the same old shameless Hollywood formula: horror pic meets action pic meets urban-anxiety thriller. Added to this is a level of product placement (masquerading as irony) which would shame even Nike . . . Robert Duvall walks away with the film [and] runs a by-the-numbers thriller inside out.' *(Cynthia Rose, S & S)*

'A dangerous film. But it is also a grim state of the nation report that rings truer than . . . any inspirational message from Bill Clinton . . . [It is] a film about rage, not violence . . . It is perceptive, not exploitative.' *(Alexander Walker, Evening Standard)*

PRO:

'An immensely entertaining action thriller.' *(Alan Frank, Daily Star)*

'So many movies have told so many sentimental lies over the years and tacked on so many happy endings, that any kind of opposing proposition comes as a rude shock to a generation substantially weaned on large doses of comforting pap . . . *Driving Miss Daisy* it very definitely is not.' *(Derek Malcolm, Guardian)*

'Riveting satirical thriller . . . a fable of protest, a howl of rage.' *(Philip French, Observer)*

'A thunderously good story, ably directed.' *(Empire)*

FALSTAFF: *see* CHIMES AT MIDNIGHT.

FAMILY PLOT

CT: 6 AV: 6.27

1976 US 120/126 C THRILLER/COMEDY

D Alfred Hitchcock ✗
W Ernest Lehman from Victor Canning's novel *The Rainbird Pattern*

Karen Black Bruce Dern Barbara Harris
William Devane Ed Lauter Cathleen Nesbitt
Katherine Helmond Warren J. Kemmerling

A fake medium (Barbara Harris) and her cab-driver boyfriend (Bruce Dern) get mixed up with more professional villains.

Enjoyable, though very slight and quite unbelievable, Hitchcock thriller with a few good ideas. The master's last film, but no masterpiece.

PRO:

'Hitchcock has never made a strategically wittier film, or a fonder; and this in his seventy-seventh year.' *(Penelope Gilliatt, New Yorker)*

'It is atmospheric, characterful, precisely paced, intricately plotted, exciting and suspenseful, beautifully acted and, perhaps more than anything else, amusing.' *(Charles Champlin, LA Times)*

'Witty screenplay . . . is a model of construction, and the cast is uniformly superb.' *(Variety)*

ANTI:

'A laborious piece of crinkum-crankum.' *(Stanley Kauffmann)*

'Given the script Hitchcock had to work with this time around, however, we should be grateful for small favors . . . Lehman's contribution here, adapted from a novel by Victor Canning, is shoddy and, at times, downright sleazy.' *(Frank Rich, New York Post)*

'Close your eyes during the opening credits of *Family Plot*. Then try to keep them open for the next two hours. Then close them through the final credits. Now tell me: who directed the film? If you say Alfred Hitchcock, it can only be because you spotted his familiar silhouette in one of the scenes, and not because *Family Plot* has any of the skillful storytelling or moral ambiguity associated with the Master of Suspense. To call this "a Hitchcock film" is to be an accessory to false advertising. *Family Plot* should be reported to the Consumer Protection Agency.' *(Richard Corliss)*

'Anyone who says that Hitchcock's last film [*Family Plot*] was a masterpiece is a fool. The man has clearly lost his sense of timing, of cinema. He's 75!

You can't be a genius forever.' *(Brian De Palma, 1976)*

'[As Lumley, Bruce Dern's] mugging now reaches a new low: even if Lumley is not meant to be brilliant, neither need he be a cretin whose facial muscles carry like a Shriners' convention . . . Nothing can explain or excuse the frenzied overacting [by Barbara Harris] throughout, except the mistaken notion that an electric blender can whip up comedy even when it has nothing inside it.' *(John Simon)*

'One senses that Hitchcock deliberately avoided those aspects of the original material (Victor Canning's thriller *The Rainbird Pattern*) that might have engaged deeper levels of his creative personality; In the book, for example, the Barbara Harris character is abruptly and brutally murdered by the other couple: one can imagine a more centrally, intensely, and disturbingly Hitchcockian film that took that as its source of inspiration.' *(Robin Wood, Hitchcock's Films Revisited, 1989)*

FANNY AND ALEXANDER AAW

CT: 9 AV: 9.07

(aka *Fanny och Alexander*)

1982 Sweden/France/West Germany 188/197/420 (TV version) C DRAMA/FOREIGN

D Ingmar Bergman ☆ AAN
W Ingman Bergman ☆ AAN

Gunn Wålgren Ewa Fröling Jarl Kulle
Erland Josephson, Allan Edwall Börje Ahlstedt
Mona Malm Gunner Björnstrand Jan Malmsjö
Pernilla Allwin Lena Olin

Two years in the life of a well-to-do Swedish family.

Bergman's most accessible film is notable for the lack of that bleak pessimism which is usually considered his hallmark. It is essentially a fantasy childhood, a celebration of idealized family life, a piece of Dickensian escapism – and none the worse for that. Long, even in its shortened form, but very charming. Sven Nykvist's Oscar-winning cinematography is among the most ravishing ever committed to celluloid. The art direction and costumes also won Academy awards.

MIXED:

'The conventionality of the thinking in the film is rather shocking. It's as if Bergman's neuroses had been tormenting him for so long that he cut them off and went sprinting back to Victorian health and domesticity.' *(Pauline Kael)*

'It is a movie that rambles and there is the occasional jolt of dislocation – it has been cut to 197 minutes – in its coverage of Bergman's childhood memories and cinematic obsessions. But the greatness is to make his particular our universal. The Ekdahl family is a family to which we would all like to belong.' *(Tom Hutchinson, Mail on Sunday)*

PRO:

'In a way, *Fanny and Alexander* represents a conciliatory move by Bergman toward the appetites of the new movie audience: it is airy and bawdy in its first part, spooky and magical towards the end. It means to send viewers away happy and a bit misty-eyed.' *(Richard Corliss)*

'A sure fire attraction for all discriminating film buffs and admirers of Bergman . . . the product of a mind mellowed in autumn mists and fruitfulness . . . Christmas is so Christmassy you can smell the port wine and cigars; death is terrifying but the memory of it is made less cruel by the certainty that the departed can return . . . Like the early *David Copperfield* (which it so much resembles) *Fanny and Alexander* can be relished as a laughter and tears good read but can also be returned to and enjoyed in different ways at different times and for different reasons.' *(Screen International)*

'The whole world of the imaginative child is so brilliantly summoned up . . . If this is really Bergman's farewell to the big screen, one could hardly imagine a valediction more decisively forbidding mourning.' *(John Russell Taylor, F & F)*

'Let us enjoy on a big screen this wonderful family history. The key word here is enjoy for Bergman's image as a purveyor of gaunt and intensive films is thoroughly demolished by the delicacy and beauty of this masterpiece.' *(William Goldman, NFT Bulletin)*

'Ingmar Bergman has said of his *Fanny and Alexander* that it is the sum total of his life as a film-maker. One could say also that it is a distillation of his own life and, for those of us who up to this splendid moment have not liked his work, have even shrunk from it, an explanation, an apologia.' *(Dilys Powell)*

'Cinema at its most magnificent.' *(The Times)*

'He couldn't have produced a more magical valedictory.' *(Daily Mail)*

'Glowing, magnificent, enchanting.' *(Philip French, Observer)*

FANTASIA

CT: 8 AV: 9.11

1940 US 135 C CARTOON/FAMILY

D Ben Sharpsteen
W Lee Blair Elmer Plummer Phil Dike
Sylvia Moberly-Holland and others

Deems Taylor Leopold Stokowski The Philadelphia Symphony Orchestra

A selection of classical music is illustrated in cartoon form.

Banal kitsch or a cartoon masterpiece? Actually it's both, but discerning audiences will continue to revel in the good bits (especially The Nutcracker, The Sorcerer's Apprentice and The Dance of the Hours), while enjoying a cringe at what the Disney animators did to Beethoven's Pastorale. There's no doubting the ambition, or the technical ingenuity: multiplane cameras, showing degrees of depth in animation, were used here for the first time. Walt Disney and Leopold Stokowski both received special awards for the film at the Oscars.

The film was re-released in a new print in 1990. At a cost of hundreds of thousands of dollars a black 'piccaninny centaurette' seen polishing the hooves of a preening blonde was removed. Gone too were her servile role and the bows decorating her 1940s hairstyle. The changes were in the cause of erasing racial stereotyping in an American culture that had by then fully embraced such political correctness. 'Tampering with *Fantasia* is astonishing over-sensitivity,' commented cartoon historian John Cawley at the time. 'This black character is clearly a caricature and should be accepted as part of American history.' Quite right.

PRO:

'Screen poetry.' *(Motion Picture Herald)*

'A masterpiece of filmcraft. Its colour photography is the best ever.' *(Daily Mail)*

'Walt Disney, the screen's greatest genius, ascends to new heights in his creation of *Fantasia*. In all its aspects it is an extraordinary accomplishment . . . For its entire length *Fantasia* thrilled me, moved me profoundly, which makes it, for me, superb entertainment.' *(Welford Beaton, Hollywood Spectator)*

'Motion picture history was made last night [by *Fantasia* which] dumps conventional formulas overboard and reveals the scope of films for imaginative excursion . . . *Fantasia* . . . is simply terrific.' *(Bosley Crowther)*

'A remarkably bold experiment and still, some thirty years later, the most ambitious animated cartoon ever made.' *(R.A.E. Pickard, Dictionary of 1000 Best Films, 1971)*

MIXED:

'*Fantasia* may have its faults (it is too long and some of it is too loud, for one thing), and it will no doubt be improved upon next time it is done, but to Walt Disney now should go fresh laurels for giving us a new artistic experience of great beauty – another milestone in the motion picture.' *(Philip T. Hartung, The Commonweal)*

'A courageous and distinguished production . . . [but] Disney is attempting the impossible. There are times when his breaking down of music into animated art strikes me as definitely pretentious . . . The images on the screen are not apt to match with your reactions to the score.' *(Howard Barnes, New York Herald Tribune)*

'A promising monstrosity and an experiment containing many lessons. There is enough in it to make up for the shocks one suffers. And to be shocked in these times of blood and tears by a handling of the problem of art is in itself an experience of temporary relief . . . Yet to have the Pastoral Symphony interrupted by applause for sugar-sweet centaurettes is painful . . . In technical respects the film is of unsurpassed quality . . . Everywhere one notices great progress. *Fantasia* in spite of its shortcomings . . . is a work of promise.' *(Franz Hoellering, Nation)*

'Dull as it is towards the end, ridiculous as it is in the bend of the knee before Art, it is one of the strange and beautiful things that have happened in the world.' *(Otis Ferguson)*

'Disney sometimes at his worst, often at his very best; and the best is on a level which no cinematographic designer has reached. It takes two hours, but somehow or other you will have to find the time.' *(Dilys Powell)*

'Even in the most pretentious of *Fantasia*'s sequences there is an eclecticism, a reaching out beyond the studio's standard style that is most welcome. The massive renderings of the earth in upheaval in "The Rite of Spring" and the battle of the dinosaurs that follows do have a certain rude power one might not have thought the animated film capable of attempting, however flawed the results.' *(Richard Schickel)*

ANTI:

'Beethoven's "Pastoral Symphony" shows Disney at his abysmal worst . . . I found all this part of the picture quite embarrassingly common . . . To help it to succeed I make one or two suggestions: 1. Shorten it by the better part of an hour; at present it runs two hours and twenty minutes. 2. Delete the compère, conferencier, announcer, or whatever he is called. His material is dull and redundant, and his dress-suit is awful. 3. Do away with the interval. 4. Delete the lecture on the sound track. 5. Build up with a good news picture and a good gangster short.' *(James Agate, Tatler)*

'I saw the film with George Balanchine in a Hollywood studio at Christmas time, 1939. I remember someone offering me a score and, when I said I had my own, the someone saying, "But it is all changed." It was indeed. The instrumentation [of The Rite of Spring] had been improved by such stunts as having the horns play their glissandi an octave higher in the "Danse de la Terre." The order of the pieces had been shuffled, too, and the most difficult of them eliminated – though this did not save the musical performance, which was execrable. I will say nothing about the visual complement, as I do not wish to criticize an unresisting imbecility.' *(Igor Stravinsky)*

'An attempt at academicism by a half-educated man. As such, it was highly praised by the half-educated.' *(Paul Rotha & Richard Griffith The Film Till Now, 1949)*

'The only composer to suffer serious vandalism is poor old Beethoven, whose pastoral Symphony is set to a grotesquely kitsch "classical" vision of courtship between centaurs and centauresses reminiscent of My Little Pony.' *(Hugo Davenport, Daily Telegraph)*

'Probably the worst thing in the film is its conclusion, in which the terrors of "A Night on Bald Mountain" – bats and gargoyles and devils and the other creatures of the gothic demonology engage in a black mass – are dispelled by the coming of dawn and a procession of the churchly singing the "Ave Maria" . . . In itself, the idea of this juxtaposition is not offensive, but as the climax of the film it seems insincere – a conventionalized invocation of religiosity, an arbitrary resort to a surefire sentiment, rather like the placement of a brassy patriotic number at the end of a musical review. The execution of the sequence is arty, the musical arrangement throbs with false emotion achieved through an excess of stringed instruments and a lush choral setting of Schubert's song, which is, of course, intended for a solo voice.' *(Richard Schickel)*

'People who remember *Fantasia* with simple wonder may find themselves wincing at the tattiness of what they see . . . *Fantasia* is a series of classical music videos from the Stone Age of animation technology, and in many ways it has not worn well.' *(Adam Mars-Jones, Independent, 1991)*

'Oh, *Fantasia*! Well, we made it and I don't regret it. But if we had it to do all over again, I don't think we'd do it.' *(Walt Disney, 1961)*

FAREWELL MY CONCUBINE AAN

CT: 7 AV: 7.75

(aka *Bawang Bie Ji*)

1993 Hong Kong/China 156 C DRAMA/EPIC/FOREIGN

D Chen Kaige ☆
W Chen Kaige from Lilian Lee's novel

Leslie Cheung ☆ Zhang Fengwi ☆ Gong Li ☆ Lu Qi

Visually magnificent epic which tries to tell the history of 20th-century China via three characters: a female impersonator at the Chinese Opera (Leslie Cheung), his more masculine co-star (Zhang Fengwi) and the latter's ex-prostitute wife (Gong Li).

It is hard to sympathize with the characters' enthusiasm for China's operatic tradition; the characters age inconsistently, and the plot progresses by equally arbitrary leaps and bounds. It's particularly hard to see why the final, climactic catharsis occurs precisely when it does, and not years earlier (if it needed to happen at all: it doesn't in the book). But it is easy to forgive the flaws in a film which attempts so much, and looks so gorgeous. The director of photography, Gu Changwei, also responsible for *Ju Dou* and *Raise The Red Lantern*, is undoubtedly one of the most spectacular practitioners of his art in the world. Shared the Palme d'Or at Cannes with *The Piano*.

'Portrays political trauma with a vividness and candor unprecedented in Chinese cinema . . . Despite a fine performance from Gong Li, who plays the prostitute-bride, her character seems unduly vilified. And, as the melodrama forges stoically through the decades, its lack of humor or irony seems forbidding. But Cheung is superb as the story's sexually ambiguous hero. And writer-director Chen Kaige has created a drama of undeniable power. A daring affront to the Chinese status quo, *Farewell My Concubine* is not just a story about the struggle for artistic freedom but a triumph of it.' *(Brian D. Johnson, Maclean's)*

'Chen's visually spectacular epic is sumptuous in every respect. This is marvellous movie-making, enthralling, intelligent and headily rhapsodic.' *(Geoff Andrew, Time Out)*

'Begins very strongly and ends equally powerfully, but has a long, sagging middle, where it . . . turns pretty soapy . . . It does, however, pick up tremendous power when the three principals fall victim to the Cultural Revolution. The manner in which the Red Guards, hardly more than children, manage to make three adults go morally to pieces is depicted with sickening authenticity.' *(John Simon, National Review)*

FAREWELL MY LOVELY

CT: 9 AV: 8.58

(aka *Murder, My Sweet*)

1944 US 95 BW THRILLER

D Edward Dmytryk ☆
W John Paxton from Raymond Chandler's novel

Dick Powell ☆ Claire Trevor Anne Shirley Mike Mazurki ☆ Otto Kruger ☆ Miles Mander Douglas Walton Ralf Harolde Don Douglas Esther Howard

Private eye (Dick Powell) tries to find missing girlfriend (Claire Trevor) of ex-convict Moose Malloy (Mike Mazurki).

A marvellous example of film noir: the most visually stylish of all the films of Raymond Chandler's novels and very faithful to the original text. Dick Powell (better known as a light tenor in Busby Berkeley musicals) makes a surprisingly effective Philip Marlowe, and the supporting cast is flawless.

MIXED:

'*Farewell, My Lovely*, as Raymond Chandler wrote it, combined about equal parts of poetic talent, arrested adolescent prurience, and the sort of self-pity which, rejoicing in all that is hardest-boiled, turns the two former faculties toward melodramatic, pretentiously unpretentious examination of big cities and their inhabitants. The picture preserves most of the faults and virtues of the book.' *(James Agee, Nation)*

'Some of the poetry . . . has been lost in the passage

from one medium to another. The story has a different finish. But whatever has been subtracted, a brilliantly hard, fast film comes out at the end . . . The quality is in the sense of movement, the subtly handled lighting, the multiplication of the tiny narrative touches and revelations of character in action. Dick Powell sitting in his office at night, high above the restless neon lights, and the stiffening of his face as he sees, intermittently reflected in the window, the gigantic moron standing silent behind him; the eye's passage along a shaft of light to the twining hands of the dancer, crudely haloed in the vulgar darkness of the road-house; the shabby ferocity of the bar-room behind the half-extinguished electric sign, and the meaningless spaces of the millionaire's house with its mausoleum echoes – these are the moments, these the shots which give the film an imaginative excitement not met with in this genre since *The Maltese Falcon*.' *(Dilys Powell)*

'Serviceable but not inspired.' *(Shipman)*

PRO:

'Director Edward Dmytryk explored the full vocabulary of film to convey the descent of private eye Marlowe into the nether world of homicide, blackmail, charlatanism, thievery, sadistic violence, sexual enslavement, and above all else, Mystery. The film's dream and drug sequences . . . were especially effective in the visualization of Marlowe's confused and paranoic state of mind. One of the refreshing aspects of *Murder, My Sweet* was its notable lack of clean-living, soft-spoken heroes and heroines.' *(Richard B. Jewell & Vernon Harbin, The RKO Story, 1982)*

'Unquestionably one of the best private eye films ever made.' *(Stephen Pendo, Raymond Chandler on Screen, 1976)*

FAREWELL, MY LOVELY CT: 8 AV: 6.91

1975 US 95 C THRILLER

D Dick Richards ☆
W David Zelag Goodman from Raymond Chandler's novel

Robert Mitchum ☆ Charlotte Rampling ✔ John Ireland Sylvia Miles Jack O'Halloran ✔ Anthony Zerbe Harry Dean Stanton Jim Thompson John O'Leary Kate Murtagh Sylvester Stallone

Private eye (Robert Mitchum) tries to find missing girlfriend (Charlotte Rampling) of ex-convict Moose Malloy (Jack O'Halloran).

Not quite up to the Dick Powell version of 1944, and Mitchum finally got to play Philip Marlowe too late in life; but his performance, Dick Richards's direction and Chandler's classic one-liners splendidly evoke a mythical Los Angeles of the 1940s. Charlotte Rampling is well cast as the *femme fatale*. Watch out for Sylvester Stallone as one of the baddies.

ANTI:

'Lethargic, vaguely campy . . . Fails to generate much suspense or excitement.' *(Variety)*

MIXED:

'Charlotte Rampling [is] a poor actress who mistakes creepiness for sensuality . . . Then there is Robert Mitchum, looking more than ever like a bloodhound that has seen too many horrible truths to stir so much as a jowl, and reading lines with his customary incertitude whenever they come in bunches bigger than five or contain words with more syllables than two. But he certainly looks and growls his part.' *(John Simon)*

PRO:

'A moody, bluesy, boozy recreation of Marlowe's tacky, neon-flashed Los Angeles of the early forties.' *(Judith Crist)*

'A delicious remake with a nice, smoky 1940s atmosphere.' *(Michael Billington, Illustrated London News)*

'Angelo Graham's art direction is a triumph.' *(Roger Ebert)*

'*Farewell, My Lovely* stands out as the excellent "Marlowe" film. Its few faults are far outweighed by its many virtues, and it certainly comes close to realizing Richards' goal of creating "the basic classic detective movie".' *(Stephen Pendo, Raymond Chandler on Screen, 1976)*

FAREWELL TO ARMS, A AAN CT: 8 AV: 6.73

1932 US 78 BW DRAMA/ROMANCE/WAR

D Frank Borzage
W Benjamin Glazer Oliver H.P Garrett from Ernest Hemingway's novel

Gary Cooper ✔ Helen Hayes ☆ Adolphe Menjou Mary Philips Jack La Rue Blanche Frederici Henry Armetta

In World War I, a nurse (Helen Hayes) and wounded ambulance driver (Gary Cooper) fall in love, with unforeseen consequences.

A cleverly filleted version of Hemingway's novel; the 1957 remake runs almost double the length of this and includes more of the book, but it isn't as touching. Borzage's sense of pace and expressionistic style are well suited to the material, and the lead performances make this one of the screen's most moving love stories. It was voted number 4 on the National Board of Review list of Exceptional American Films of the year. It won Oscars for cinematography (Charles Lang) and sound recording, and was nominated for art direction (by Hans Dreier and Roland Anderson).

ANTI:

'Bravely as it is produced for the most part, there is too much sentiment and not enough strength in the pictorial conception . . . Several of the strong dramatic incidents of the novel are not included in the film, obviously because the producers did not wish to offend Italians.' *(Mordaunt Hall, New York Times)*

MIXED:

'There's enough emotional gloss on this picture to hide its lack of argument . . . [Hayes] is not a very deep actress, but a tricky one, and her mannerisms are deliberate enough to be taken for the grand style.' *(Observer)*

PRO:

'Corking femme film fare at any angle or price.' *(Variety)*

'Borzage's direction was never more dramatically fluid and inventive. Not only does he set his camera in motion for dramatic effect as it traverses marble-floored hospital corridors (and even for one memorable sequence assumes a first person viewpoint), but this probing camera can also be pointedly witty while it explores the mean furnishings of Catherine's room as she writes of their charms to her lover.' *(John Howard Reid)*

FAT CITY — CT: 6 AV: 7.18

1972 US 96 C DRAMA

D John Huston ☆
W Leonard Gardner from his novel

Stacy Keach Jeff Bridges ☆ Susan Tyrrell AAN Candy Clark Nicholas Colasanto Art Aragon Curtis Cokes Sixto Rodriguez Billy Walker Wayne Mahan

Two boxers struggle to make a living: one is on his way up (Jeff Bridges), the other is in decline (Stacy Keach).

John Huston was a boxer in his youth, and it shows in this truthful, gripping, atmospheric movie, well shot in the cinema verité style by Conrad Hall. Bridges is outstanding, and the film's quite moving about the minimal expectations of its characters. The big drawbacks are the disjointed plot and its consistently depressing tone.

PRO:

'A brilliant and loving portrait of a world of illusions without hope, stunningly shot to look like a blues for the American Dream.' *(S & S)*

'Hailed at the Cannes Festival . . . as John Huston's best film for years, [it] is just that.' *(Michael McNay, Guardian)*

'A lean, compassionate, detailed, raucous, sad, strong look at some losers and survivors on the side streets of small-city Middle America.' *(LA Times)*

'The real point of the film is its loving . . . exploration of this shadowy half-world . . . It is never depressing to see a superlatively good film, whatever it may happen to be about . . . There is a lot of humour in [it] and above all there is a warm, completely unsentimental humanity which makes us understand these characters and even find them attractive.' *(John Russell Taylor, The Times)*

'Ranks among [Huston's] most sincere attempts to introduce us sympathetically to a seedy world of persistent hope and resisted disillusion . . . It is acted with great depth and sincerity of feeling.' *(Eric Shorter, Daily Telegraph)*

MIXED:

'A modest success that the esthetic poverty of the season has elevated into a major triumph.' *(Village Voice)*

ANTI:

'The critically acclaimed *Fat City* is supposed to mark the return of John Huston to his former mastery. Although I have some doubts about his former mastery, they are as nothing to my doubts about this film . . . At least as released, the film is sadly disjointed . . . Stacy Keach does not convince me that he is a working-class semi-derelict: he has a certain softness and gentility built into his appearance, manner, and speech that is too civilized for Tully. As for Susan Tyrrell, her Oma is no performance at all, merely a self-disembowelment with the performer spewing up her inner chaos, guts and all, untransformed by art or even self-control, for the delectation of idiotic viewers and reviewers who cannot tell the difference between creation of a character and embarrassing, unwholesome self-display.' *(John Simon)*

FATAL ATTRACTION AAN — CT: 7 AV: 6.29

1987 US 119 C THRILLER/ROMANCE/HORROR

D Adrian Lyne ☆ AAN
W James Dearden ✔ AAN

Michael Douglas ☆ Glenn Close ☆ AAN Anne Archer AAN Ellen Hamilton Latzen Stuart Pankin Ellen Foley Fred Gwynne

A married man (Michael Douglas) has an affair with a career-woman (Glenn Close) who turns out to be unbalanced and over-possessive.

Though basically a rehash of a superior film about male paranoia, *Play Misty For Me* (1971), it is undeniably gripping, thanks to a well-constructed screenplay, stylish direction and two strong leading performances. Widely interpreted as a drama which warned surreptitiously of Aids, it was also criticized by feminists as hostile towards career women.

The original ending had Douglas put in jail for murdering Close (who had in fact committed suicide in such a way as to implicate him); this was too dark for preview audiences, and became changed to a much more conventional (and far too predictable) slasher climax. A huge hit.

ANTI:

'Touches on something deeper than men's fear of

feminism: their fear of women, their fear of women's emotions, of women's hanging on to them. *Fatal Attraction* doesn't treat the dreaded passionate woman as a theme; she's merely a monster in a monster flick.' *(Pauline Kael)*

'A predictable dog's dinner of Pavlovian thriller clichés, this will appeal strongly to those who think women should be kept on a short leash.' *(Nigel Floyd, Time Out)*

MIXED:

'Alex is a figure designed to send men rushing off to their shrinks, aquiver with sexual paranoia . . . What Freddy or Jason is to horny teens, Alex may become to the yuppie male contemplating an extramarital fling. [She] makes a smashingly depraved villain . . . Lyne is a slick technician who will sacrifice anything for an effect . . . [As an ex-ad man] he knows how to sell a product, in this case fear and loathing . . . But in the course of getting the audience to squirm and writhe, he dispenses with whatever psychological nuance might have made James Dearden's story something more than mere exploitation . . . [Lansing] and her cohorts have made . . . the *Reefer Madness* of adultery.' *(David Ansen, Newsweek)*

'*Play Psycho For Me* might be an apt subtitle . . . The woman is so unstable that the feminist point about men thinking they can have their crumpet and eat it, is lost. Yet, though the role is psychologically unfocused, the portrayal . . . by the riveting Glenn Close is of utter conviction . . . In fact, there is not false note in any of the performances . . . Surprisingly, Adrian Lyne . . . also shows subtlety for most of the time . . . The problem begins when [he] steps deeper into Grand Guignol territory where fear is signalled by screeching stabbing music and dramatic camera angles. A more restrained approach could have been more effective.' *(Ronald Bergan, F & F)*

'A film more about style than substance, which implies culture through arias from *Madame Butterfly*, defines taste as luxury and glitz, telegraphs exactly what it intends to do without subtlety or suspense, and plunders shamelessly from other films, most notably a climax borrowed from *Les Diaboliques*.' *(Allan Hunter & Kenny Mathieson, Movie Classics, 1992)*

'An outrageous melodrama. It sacrifices probability to spectacular effects quite shamelessly. How could a woman, sophisticated, well dressed (only her hair is raving), and sane enough to hold a job in a publishing firm fall apart completely after one mad weekend with an unknown man . . . It is marvelously prepared for the screen. There is always a hint of danger – a knife lying at the edge of the frame, seen by an audience seconds before the participants in the battle notice it, or some sign, which its occupants have not yet understood, that Miss Close is in the house. Mr Hitchcock couldn't have done better. In the way in which it plucks at the nerves of the audience, *Fatal Attraction* is almost a masterpiece.' *(Quentin Crisp, Christopher Street)*

PRO:

'Electrifying thriller . . . a terrific suspense film grounded in recognizable human behavior . . . [It] is much more provocative and disturbing than the average thriller because it shrewdly taps into the audience's conflicting feelings about fidelity, sexual attraction and responsibility . . . Dearden's screenplay is somewhat derivative of . . . *Play Misty For Me*, but finds added complexity . . . Lyne's direction is in the Hitchcock mode – providing sudden jolts that heighten our anticipation of unpleasant things to come and create a powerful sense of dread during even the most mundane moments . . . Lyne generates suspense from an accumulation of neutral images – a faucet running, a pot boiling over . . . Close, who's always had a fairly prim image . . . leaves all that behind with a sensual, high-voltage performance to remember . . . [The film] should shake up audiences.' *(Kevin Lally, Film Journal)*

FATAL PASSION OF DOCTOR MABUSE, THE:

see THE *DOCTOR MABUSE* SERIES (DR MABUSE, THE GAMBLER).

FATHER AND MASTER:

see PADRE PADRONE.

FATHER OF THE BRIDE

CT: 8 AV: 7.55

1950 US 93 BW COMEDY

D Vincente Minnelli ☆
W Frances Goodrich Albert Hackett from Edward Streeter's novel

Spencer Tracy ☆ Elizabeth Taylor ☆ Joan Bennett Don Taylor Billie Burke Leo G. Carroll Moroni Olsen Melville Cooper Taylor Holmes

A father (Spencer Tracy) worries about the impending marriage of his daughter (Elizabeth Taylor).

Tracy gives one of his most charming comic performances in this slice of American middle-class family life. Elizabeth Taylor plays the 18-year-old daughter beautifully, and Vincente Minnelli directs with his usual finesse. Pleasantly remade with Steve Martin in 1991.

PRO:

'Minnelli's direction is deft and sharp, and in the hands of a veteran acting company, *Father of the Bride* registers some good laughs and sustains an infectious spirit of fun-poking.' *(Fortnight)*

'The film is full of ironic observation: the man who can't sleep slamming down the glass of water on the bedside table in the hope of making a fellow-sufferer of his wife. Vincente Minnelli has directed brilliantly, turning what might have been farce into the best of comedy. But amidst so much excellence Spencer Tracy is still outstanding; this is his best playing for years.' *(Dilys Powell)*

ANTI:

'Since the plot consists simply of outlining the difficulties of putting on a wedding, including, of course, the damnable expense of it all, it grows a little tiresome after a half hour or so.' *(John McCarten, New Yorker)*

'The lead character in a wedding is not the blushing bride or her stammering groom. The star of a wedding is the patriarch who pays for it all, the dad in the act of marrying off "daddy's little girl". At least that's Hollywood's view of weddings, and has been for forty years. *Father of the Bride*, Vincente Minnelli's 1950 smash sentimental comedy, made no bones about it. The bride may have been played by none other than Elizabeth Taylor, and her mom played by the exquisite Joan Bennett, but their parts were merely support player filler and their lives were but the setting for the real star, the title character, Stanley T. Banks, played with comic brilliance by Spencer Tracy.' *(Kathy Maio, 1991)*

'Within its own terms the picture is sensitive and very well done, but it's also tiresomely fraudulent – an idealization of a safe, sheltered existence, the good life according to MGM: 24 carat complacency.' *(Pauline Kael, 1980)*

FAUST CT: 5 AV: 7.16

1926 Germany 100/136 BW DRAMA/FANTASY/ SILENT/FOREIGN

D F.W. Murnau ☆
W Hans Kyser

Emil Jannings ☆ Gosta Ekman Camilla Horn Yvette Guilbert William Dieterle

Professor (Gosta Ekman) sells soul in exchange for youth.

F.W. Murnau's silent classic from 1926 features huge, romantic sets, great chiascuro cinematography, and a magnificently hammy performance by Emil Jannings as Mephistopheles. A must-see for film buffs, but the sad truth is that vast stretches of it are boring.

PRO:

'The mounting is a triumph of film technique . . . remarkably well-played . . . A fine rendering of a great story . . . Jannings gives a magnificent performance.' *(Bioscope, 1927)*

'A consummate example of German craftsmanship . . . the work . . . of an artist, working with sincerity among harmonious surroundings . . . showed [Murnau] to have a very sensitive knowledge of the resources of the cinema . . . [Among] Jannings' best work.' *(Paul Rotha, The Film Till Now, 1930)*

'Splendid . . . a production of note for the fine treatment that must have been accorded in its preparation.' *(Pathescope Monthly, 1933)*

'The best of many silent versions.' *(Halliwell)*

'Features imaginative sets and Carl Hoffman's sublime photography; Jannings, as Mephistopheles, is brilliant.' *(Scheuer)*

MIXED:

'Illustrates once more, in forcible fashion, the artistic supremacy of the Germans in motion picture production . . . Jannings is one of the very few film stars of repute who has never made a bad picture . . . and his rendering of the devil is a sheer joy to watch. He is the incarnation of all evil – his every action spiced with wicked and malicious humour . . . The only poor scene in the whole picture is a totally unnecessary one at the end [in which Faust] ascends to Paradise, in what appears to be a sort of heavenly escalator. The crudity of the effect, coming after so much really clever camera work, is like a cold shock.' *(Picturegoer, 1927)*

'Visually extraordinary but dismally uneven in terms of its dramatic impact.' *(Geoff Andrew, Time Out)*

FELLINI SATYRICON: *see* SATYRICON.

FELLOW TRAVELLER CT: 7 AV: 6.22

1989 GB 97 C THRILLER/ROMANCE

D Philip Saville ✔
W Michael Eaton ✔

Ron Silver ☆ Imogen Stubbs Hart Bochner ✔ Daniel J. Travanti Katherine Borowitz Julian Fellowes Richard Wilson Doreen Mantle David O'Hara

Asa (Ron Silver), a blacklisted Hollywood screenwriter, escapes to England in the 1950s, and survives through hackwork on TV scripts for Robin Hood. *He is shocked when he hears that his best friend, handsome screenstar Clifford Byrne (Hart Bochner), has committed suicide in his Los Angeles swimming pool. Asa pieces together the explanation in England via a series of* Citizen Kane*-style flashbacks, meetings with Clifford's ex-girlfriend (Imogen Stubbs), and a final confrontation with his psycho-therapist (Daniel J. Travanti). As in all the best thrillers, there is a final twist.*

A bleaker, more grown-up film on the same theme as Martin Ritt's 1976 movie about McCarthyism, *The Front*. The background is well-researched; and the story (though fictitious) has the ring of truth. Also, its politic approach is more sophisticated than one might expect, and lapses only occasionally into 80s-style conspiracy theory.

Most importantly, the film has a heart as well as a head – thanks, in no small measure, to the leading American actors. Hart Bochner excels as a flawed screen idol from the Golden Age; Daniel J. Travanti is all hooded eyes and watchfulness as the questionable psychiatrist; and Ron Silver is genuinely moving as an open-hearted, Yank compelled to live in the repressed, careful Britain of the 1950s – a country so quaintly parochial in its paranoia that a BBC director's whispered talk of 'defecting to the other side' means merely that he is thinking of taking a job in commercial TV.

The film's central weakness commercially, but its main interest artistically, lies in the complexity of Michael Eaton's screenplay. For better or worse, there's a strong Dennis Potter influence. There are stylized flashbacks to a traumatic, sexual episode in Asa's childhood (heigh ho). Instead of Potteresque popular songs, we are given extracts from the episode of *Robin Hood* which Asa is writing. These, like Potter songs, act as ironic commentary on the main themes of the film: betrayal, revenge, and heroism. This may sound alarmingly pretentious; but the *Robin Hood* extracts are actually great fun, and Philip Saville directs with a cineaste's love of pastiche. Almost every scene contains references to a different kind of cinema: film noir, Ealing comedy, Hitchcock, Cagney . . . Some may find the film confusing, over-elaborate and self-indulgent, but I found it refreshing, ingenious and enjoyable.

ANTI:

'As often happens with British films, the impression is that no one involved in the production had the conviction or authority or bloody-mindedness to insist on throwing out the bits that didn't work, and that consequently the whole adds up to less than the sum of its parts.' *(William Parente, Scotsman)*

PRO:

'Thought-provoking, entertaining and visually pleasurable . . . one of the most original and impressive British films of the 80s.' *(MFB)*

'One of the most politically sophisticated, visually imaginative British pictures of the past decade.' *(Philip French, Observer)*

'An intriguing mix of character study, docu-drama and multi-media fantasy.' *(Kim Newman, Film Review)*

'Wittily scripted, punchy and continually self-doubting, [it] deals as wryly with the big issues of suppression and censorship as it does with personal repressions and self censorship as people's lives fall apart.' *(Amanda Lipman, The Face)*

'Thanks to the capable direction . . . it looks like a film and benefits from luxuriant locations.' *(Michael Eaton, What's On in London)*

FEMALE ON THE BEACH CT: 5 AV: 4.83

1955 US 97 BW DRAMA/SO BAD

D Joseph Pevney
W Robert Hill Richard Alan Simmons ●

Joan Crawford ● Jeff Chandler Jan Sterling Cecil Kellaway Natalie Schafer Charles Drake

A wealthy widow (Joan Crawford) falls for a young beach bum (Jeff Chandler) who may be about to kill her.

A camp classic, with Crawford wildly out of control and a memorably daft screenplay. Sample line, Crawford to her lover's inquiry if he should make the coffee: 'If you don't, I'll beat you.'

'Will not disappoint [Crawford] admirers . . . Extreme ferocity is once again the keynote of her characterisation . . . The more tender moments . . . are less convincing . . . The first hour . . . with its bored, impatient, rancid mood and its exasperated love-hate scenes, is by far the best.' *(MFB)*

'Connoisseurs may appreciate the ecstasy of ill-humour to which [Crawford] now devotes herself . . . A glimmer lights those saurian eyes.' *(Sunday Times)*

'Slow and old-fashioned mystery thriller . . . Miss Crawford and Mr Chandler labor grimly toward a storm-lashed climactic scene. Their progress is rendered no more fetching by the inanities of a hackneyed script and the artificiality and pretentiousness of Miss Crawford's acting style. At the end, the guilty party is revealed in a ridiculous way.' *(Bosley Crowther)*

'Hot, heavy – and very tacky . . . Outrageously trashy script is crammed with sexual double entendres. A must for Crawford fans – but don't expect anything resembling a good movie.' *(Maltin)*

FEMME DU BOULANGER, LA: *see* BAKER'S WIFE, THE

FEMME INFIDÈLE, LA: *see* LA FEMME INFIDÈLE

FEW GOOD MEN, A AAN CT: 5 AV: 7.22

1992 US 138 C DRAMA

D Rob Reiner
W Aaron Sorkin

Tom Cruise Jack Nicholson ☆ AAN Demi Moore Kevin Bacon ✔ Kiefer Sutherland Kevin Pollak James Marshall J.T. Walsh Christopher Guest J.A. Preston Matt Craven Wolfgang Bodison

A courtroom drama about bullying within the US marines.

Jack Nicholson is always excellent when playing an obsessive, and here gives a chilling portrait of a blinkered military type. The weaknesses are two bland performances from Demi Moore and Tom Cruise, as (respectively) a Lieutenant Commander and a brilliant lawyer. And Aaron Sorkin's screenplay, though clever for much of its length, spoils it all with an unconvincing and contrived climax. Robert Leighton's editing was Oscar-nominated.

'A big-time, mainstream Hollywood movie *par excellence*.' *(Variety)*

'A slick, entertaining, flashily-acted courtroom drama replete with all the standard ingredients.' *(Philip French, Observer)*

'One of the best, all-round Hollywood entertainments for years . . . Despite only having three scenes, Jack [Nicholson] dominates the film.' *(Rose)*

'The intellectual cut-and-thrust of the courtroom is largely absent here, and the denouement seems slick, arbitrary and derived from the *Captain Queeg* catalogue. Even worse, Cruise is cast as the dilettante Navy lawyer with a brilliant legal brain, and jives about in much the same manner as he did in *Top Gun*.' *(Brian Case, Time Out)*

FIDDLER ON THE ROOF AAN CT: 8 AV: 6.79

1971 US 180 C MUSICAL

D Norman Jewison AAN
W Joseph Stein from musical based on Sholem Aleichem's stories (music and lyrics by Jerry Bock, Sheldon Harnick ☆)

Topol ☆ AAN Norma Crane Leonard Frey AAN Molly Picon Paul Mann Rosalind Harris Michele Marsh Neva Small Paul Michael Glaser Raymond Lovelock

Jews struggle to survive in Czarist Russia, and one Jewish father (Topol) strives to sustain his family traditions.

Director Norman Jewison isn't renowned for his lightness of touch, and the all-conquering Broadway musical looks lumbering on the big screen. But fine songs, a charismatic perfomance by Topol and a warm-hearted story add up to great entertainment on the grand scale. Oswald Morris's cinematography and John Williams's musical direction won Oscars.

ANTI:

'Most of the time, the picture seems attenuated and flat, because it's a complicated, tricked-up story that needed a steady pace and strong characterizations to work – neither of which it has . . . Its boxoffice possibilities look slim.' *(Hollywood Reporter)*

'Jewison hasn't so much directed a film as prepared a product for world consumption.' *(Stanley Kauffmann)*

'Very hard to take with the film sitting up and practically slobbering in its eagerness to prove how loveable it is.' *(Tom Milne, Time Out)*

'Self-conscious, grittily realistic adaptation of the stage musical, with slow and heavy patches in its grossly overlong celebration of a vanished way of life.' *(Halliwell)*

PRO:

'Sentimental in a theatrical way, romantic in the old-fashioned way, nostalgic of immigration days, affirmative of human decency, loyalty, bravery and folk humor . . . A powerhouse attraction.' *(Variety)*

FIELD OF DREAMS AAN CT: 10 AV: 8.54

1989 US 106 C FANTASY/DRAMA

D Phil Alden Robinson ☆
W Phil Alden Robinson ☆ AAN from W.P. Kinsella's novel *Shoeless Joe*

Kevin Costner ✔ Amy Madigan ✔ James Earl Jones ✔ Timothy Busfield Ray Liotta Burt Lancaster ✔ Gaby Hoffmann Frank Whaley Dwier Brown

A 36-year-old farmer in Iowa (Kevin Costner) appears a contented family man. But he has nagging regrets: he never got on with his dead father; he has not achieved his ambitions; and 60s idealism has given way to narrower concerns. Suddenly, he hears a mysterious voice, telling him to plough up a cornfield and turn it into a baseball park. Sceptical at first, he becomes obsessed with following his dream – or delusion.

Ignore anyone who tells you that *Field of Dreams* is about baseball: it is no more about baseball than *Harvey* was about rabbits. Baseball is just a metaphor for personal achievement, reconciliation, and a less mean-spirited society. The story is about exorcising the ghosts, or regrets, from one's past.

Most of the major studios turned down the screenplay; and it certainly strays close to being fey, whimsical and pseudo-religious. Perhaps the film's greatest achievement is that the acting – and not just Costner's – is so realistic that the audience becomes as caught up as the characters in solving the mystery.

If Gabriel García Marquez had written *Field of Dreams*, intellectuals might be hailing it as magic realism. Just because it is a Hollywood project which moves at a decent pace, is humorous and entertaining, and made millions at the box office does not make it any less successful as a modern ghost story. This is an offbeat, lyrical, moving film, on a par with Frank Capra's *It's a Wonderful Life*. James Horner's score was Oscar-nominated.

ANTI:

'Ray runs around the country (and into the past) carrying out the orders of the Great Whisperer in the sky. He doesn't give any thought to the farm, though it's about to be lost and he and his family ruined. Brainless Ray doesn't have to do much of anything except smile at Shoeless Joe and crinkle his shiny eyes. He's like a flower child who thinks that if you remain a child you'll wind up as William Blake ... Baseball here is a metaphor for the "old" American values – conformist values ... Is the movie saying no more than that if you challenge your parents' values you may regret it later? Not exactly, because the religiose context gives Ray's spiritual distress a cautionary impact. The movie is pretty close to saying: Don't challenge your parents' values, because if you do you'll be sorry. It's saying: Play ball.' *(Pauline Kael)*

'Amy Madigan is irritatingly complacent and compliant as Costner's wife. In particular, the attempt to give the film an edge by having her champion the writings of Jones – he plays a J.D. Salinger-like writer who, though he's lost his faith in himself, articulated the dreams of the 1960s – against her book-burning neighbours, is distressingly weak.' *(Phil Hardy, Film Yearbook)*

MIXED:

'Alternately affecting and affected ... In spite of a script hobbled with cloying aphorisms and shameless sentimentality, *Field of Dreams* sustains a dreamy mood in which the idea of baseball is distilled to its purest essence: a game that stands for unsullied innocence in a cruel, imperfect world.' *(Variety)*

PRO:

'Robinson has embellished Kinsella's novel to examine the ideological conflict between the 60s and the 80s; together with moments of dry humour and fine performances, the political element lends the film gravity sufficient to counterbalance any sense of whimsy. Pure magic.' *(Colette Maude, Time Out)*

'Unless you're wholly immune to whimsy, it is also a magical, heart-warming tale which not only grips totally but is even surprisingly believable.' *(Rose)*

FIENDS, THE: *see* LES DIABOLIQUES.

FIRE MAIDENS FROM OUTER SPACE

CT: 5 AV: 1.71

(aka *Fire Maidens of Outer Space*)

1956 GB 80 BW SF/SO BAD

D Cy Roth ●
W Cy Roth ●

Susan Shaw ● Anthony Dexter ● Harry Fowler Sidney Tafler Owen Berry Paul Carpenter

Astronauts find scantily clad girls on one of Jupiter's moons.

The only controversy about this film (apart from whether the Fire Maidens are from or of outer space) is whether the movie is merely one of the worst films ever made, or bad enough to be funny. I incline towards the latter, but to sit through the whole film is a long haul.

PRO:

'Plenty of good-natured fooling ... Camerawork and technical effects are good.' *(Today's Cinema)*

'Its story far exceeds the bounds of credibility but tongue-in-cheek presentation partly disarms criticism ... More a folk dance display than an outer space thriller.' *(Kine Weekly)*

'Supremely daft ... very entertaining.' *(Quinlan)*

'Hysterically awful ... Truly one of the worst films ever made and consequently great fun.' *(Winnert)*

'You haven't lived until you've seen the *Fire Maidens* perform their ritual dance to "Stranger in Paradise".' *(Maltin)*

ANTI:

'A film that I nominate as the stupidest ever.' *(Picturegoer)*

'Even the most dedicated connoisseurs of the artless are likely to find this British attempt at science fiction something of a strain on their patience. The gyrations of the ladies from Jupiter around their sacrificial fires introduce an unintentionally comic note to the proceedings.' *(MFB)*

'Dull, silly, phony and preposterous. Usually when a film is as absurd as this, at least it's lively, but *Fire Maidens* is a crashing bore.' *(Bill Mitchell, Keep Watching The Skies!)*

'A kindergarten pageant would probably have a bigger budget.' *(Scheuer)*

'The creature ... looks as though it has mange and sounds as if it suffers from gas pains.' *(Parish & Pitts, The Great Science Fiction Pictures)*

'A ridiculous monster, less than amateur ritual dancing and even worse acting, it's easy to figure out the rest. Receiving less than limited theatrical release, this turkey pops up from time to time on the late-late-late show, promptly putting anybody with insomnia right to sleep.' *(Eric L. Hoffman, Monsters of the Movies magazine, 1975)*

'A strong contender for the title of worst movie ever made, with diaphonously clad English gals striking embarrassed poses against cardboard sets. Must be seen to be believed.' *(Halliwell)*

FIRE OVER ENGLAND

CT: 8 AV: 6.56

1937 GB 92 BW DRAMA/ACTION/ADVENTURE

D William K. Howard
W Clemence Dane Sergei Nolbandov from A.E.W. Mason's novel

Flora Robson ✔ Laurence Olivier ✔ Leslie Banks Vivien Leigh Raymond Massey ✔ Tamara Desni Morton Selten Lyn Harding James Mason ✔

Elizabeth I (Flora Robson) resists the Spanish Armada, with the help of a young man (Laurence

Olivier) avenging his father's death at the hands of the Spanish Inquisition.

Jolly swashbuckler, jolly well acted – especially by Robson, in her love scenes with Leicester (Leslie Banks). Lavishly produced by British standards, though an obviously stretched budget doesn't help the disappointingly staged climax.

ANTI:

'[Producer] Pommer and Howard have done one remarkable thing: they have caught the very spirit of an English schoolmistress's vision of history.' *(Graham Greene)*

MIXED:

'Flora Robson is an unusually talented artist, but the character is a bit too much for her . . . The film is a ponderous, slow-moving unfoldment . . . The cutting . . . is erratic, hampers cumulative impact. Carefully produced, always literate, the production arouses admiration though never dramatic tenseness.' *(Herb Sterne)*

'For the less critical majority, who, in a cinema's inky privacy are willing to shed a patriotic tear . . . [the film] will provide a cordial orgy of heart swellings . . . [Olivier and Leigh] play the young lovers with great style, efficiency and beauty . . . The sea fights are less spectacular than they might have been, but less obviously faked than usual . . . With any luck at all, [it] should retrieve some of the money the British film industry has, on the whole so deservedly, been losing.' *(New Statesman)*

'Swashbuckling nonsense, but with a fine spirit.' *(Pauline Kael)*

PRO:

'Even if [it] did not have much more to recommend it, the characterization of the queen in itself would make it worthwhile. But it has much more . . . Howard's direction is masterful throughout, as telling in intimate scenes as in his handling of great mass effects . . . An outstanding feature . . . is the superb camera work . . . Visually the picture is one of the most beautiful ever brought to the screen.' *(Welford Beaton, Hollywood Spectator)*

'Handsomely mounted and forcefully dramatic . . . It holds a succession of brilliantly played scenes, a wealth of choice diction, pointed excerpts from English history and a series of impressive tableaux.' *(Variety)*

FIRST BLOOD: *see* RAMBO: FIRST BLOOD.

FISH CALLED WANDA, A CT: 6 AV: 7.71

1988 US 108 C COMEDY

D Charles Crichton ✓ AAN
W John Cleese Charles Crichton ✓ AAN

John Cleese ✓ Jamie Lee Curtis ✓ Kevin Kline ☆ AAW Michael Palin Maria Aitken Tom Georgeson Patricia Hayes Geoffrey Palmer Peter Jonfield

Strait-laced English barrister (John Cleese) is lured into a life of crime.

Mean-spirited, cruel but (sporadically) very funny comedy which won international success by telling everyone what hell it is to be English. Though almost 80, Charles Crichton directs with pace and panache; the performances (especially Kevin Kline's) are funny; and several set-pieces – notably the one where Cleese is caught with more than his trousers down – are bliss.

ANTI:

'Some of it is wickedly witty, some of it is mutinously mean-spirited. All of it sees only greed, lust and incompetence as our prime movers . . . Cleese's cinema of cruelty can be abominably funny, but sourness sets in.' *(Tom Hutchinson, Mail on Sunday)*

'A very nasty film. It is brutal, lustful, sadistic – in short, it has all the elements of comedy. Look at *Rambo*.' *(John Cleese, actor/writer)*

MIXED:

'The film is not poor; but it's only a pretty good farce, not a high-level manic assault on all that the audience holds dear . . . The picture owes much to its director, Charles Crichton, now 78, who . . . was known for his editing and his work with actors; both those qualities shine here. He has given Curtis sharp timing, and he has repaid Cleese's confidence by getting a first-class performance of the barrister from him. Because it happens to be a straight performance in a farce, it's been undervalued. Cleese doesn't give us a cartoon in human form, as he so often did, but a credible man, credibly-stripped naked – figuratively and literally – à la Feydeau. That is, the suppressed secret self comically overpowers the public self.' *(Stanley Kauffmann)*

'That it isn't quite as hilarious as you hope for is in part due to the over-obvious attempt to internationalise it. Nonetheless, it's one of the funniest comedies in recent years.' *(Rose)*

PRO:

'[Charles Crichton's] ability to build up a comic sequence and leave it just at the right moment is still as strong as ever.' *(John Marriott, Daily Mail)*

'To the Pythons' anarchy and perception of the *Alice in Wonderland* surreality lurking in English life and society, Crichton adds discipline, story-telling skill and a standard of filmcraft almost extinct today.' *(David Robinson, The Times)*

'The basic plot could have come from any "commercial" British film of the past 40 years – it is John Cleese's cynicism, wit and irreverence that provides the magic ingredient . . . By no means insignificant too is the way that Cleese has refined his own screen persona, recognizing the potential for comic pathos in his gallery of pompous, impatient and physically inept heroes. He gives Leach (as well as the best lines) a vulnerability which is the stuff of all good comedy, and there is a genuinely touching quality about his scenes with Wanda. One can almost feel the audience willing him to break out of his straitjacket of Englishness. It's a fine piece of character writing: Cleese understands not only what is funny but also what is right for his character, a sureness of touch matched only by Woody Allen amongst current film comedy actors.' *(Adrian Hodges, Film Yearbook)*

'A hilarious fusion of old-time cosiness and modern cynicism, English eccentricity and US pizzazz . . . Ealing director Crichton performs the trick of a lifetime – a hit comeback at 78. Wandaful!' *(Winnert)*

FISHER KING, THE CT: 8 AV: 6.67

1991 US 135 C FANTASY/ROMANCE/DRAMA/ COMEDY

D Terry Gilliam ☆
W Richard LaGravenese ☆ AAN
Robin Williams ☆ AAN Jeff Bridges ☆
Amanda Plummer ☆ Mercedes Ruehl ☆ AAW
Michael Jeter Ted Ross

An arrogant radio talk-show host (Jeff Bridges) who has hit the booze and the gutter, is saved from some punks with a nasty penchant for setting fire to the homeless, by a smiley but smelly vagrant (Robin Williams) who, in return, requests help on his quest for the Holy Grail.

This 90s parable about a selfish individualist learning to care may be overextended, uneven and sentimental about homelessness – but its successes far outweigh its failures. Passionate and imaginative, it's an extraordinary achievement by one of cinema's most gifted originals. Director Terry Gilliam illustrates and bridges the chasm between Bridges's reality and Williams's fantasies. Grand Central Station turns into a gigantic ballroom, Central Park a Forest of Arden. The whole of Manhattan becomes an island of enchanted castles and damn fools in distress. The film is, quite literally, elemental: Gilliam builds the film's symbolic structure on fire, water and air. He is helped by a quartet of outstanding performances from Jeff Bridges, Robin Williams, Amanda Plummer and Mercedes Ruehl (the only one who won an Oscar). Mel Bourne's production design and George Fenton's music were Oscar-nominated.

ANTI:

'One of the most nonsensical, pretentious, mawkishly cloying movies I have ever had to retch through . . . Any film that hinges on whether Bridges can cast off convention and spend a (platonic) night lying naked with Willams on a Central Park lawn as both gaze at the moon is, at best, wholly frail; at worst, a bitter chalice, dregs from the first sip.' *(John Simon)*

'A peculiarly irritating failure – a leaden piece of uplift.' *(Pauline Kael)*

'The direction of the film is exaggeratedly coy, arch, limpingly lyrical, sweatingly unusual. In other words, it's by Terry Gilliam . . . whose work has become increasingly cute . . . Gilliam is precisely the worst director in the world for Williams, who needs guidance, not abetment, and who, electrically gifted though he is, here merely carries on. Bridges has a different kind of self-indulgence. He thinks that merely by hulking around, he is a presence. He isn't.' *(Stanley Kauffmann)*

'The film's moral is bizarre: for two guys to achieve sanity and humanity, they should get naked together some night in Central Park. What if moviegoers take this advice to heart? They could get a stern lesson, and it wouldn't be applied with a ruler.' *(Richard Corliss, Time)*

'The sagacity of the saga is diminished by screenwriter Richard LaGravenese's naively sentimental approach to homelessness and insanity. Madness in this film can be cured just by knowing that someone cares about you, and homelessness is not a social problem, but a picturesque way that individuals have of coping with personal tragedy. I have a horrible suspicion that one reason for the film's success in the US is that its audiences feel that by attending the film they have "done their bit" for people whom they would cheerfully step over on the street.' *(Christopher Tookey, Sunday Telegraph)*

MIXED:

'A giant dumpster of a movie that contains some gems amid the jumble.' *(Brian D. Johnson, Maclean's)*

'The movie is riddled with surrealistic sequences. Some, such as commuters in Grand Central Station breaking into a mass waltz, offer compensatory grace while crippling the pace. Others, such as a specter Williams keeps seeing of a fiery fiend mounted on a huge charger, are silly – the specter looks more like a flaming mulberry bush riding a horse than a symbol of terror. Still others, such as Williams's penchant for running around Central Park naked, are embarrassing. (Williams, for the record, is amazingly hairy; any more furry and he'd be hunted for his pelt.)' *(Ralph Novak, People Weekly)*

'A disorganized, rambling and eccentric movie that contains some moments of truth, some moments of humor, and many moments of digression.' *(Roger Ebert)*

'Despite being hopelessly self-indulgent in places, it's so weird, inventive and imaginative that you're rarely bored and end up feeling all's right with the world after all.' *(Rose)*

PRO:

'Has all the ingredients of a major critical and commercial event: two actors at the top of their form, and a compelling, well-directed and well-produced story.' *(Variety)*

'A dense, astonishing comedy about love, loss and redemption . . . Like *Brazil* and previous Gilliam works, *Fisher King* bypasses easy formula moviemaking to score as a bold, unique and exhilarating cinematic trip.' *(Bruce Williamson, Playboy)*

'Scary, touching, often hilarious, this modern fairytale is surprisingly enchanting.' *(Geoff Andrew, Time Out)*

FIST IN HIS POCKET CT: 6 AV: 7.00

(aka *Fists in the Pocket; I Pugni in Tasca*)

1965 Italy 113 BW DRAMA/COMEDY/FOREIGN

D Marco Bellocchio ☆
W Marco Bellochio ☆

Lou Castel ☆ Paola Pitagora Liliona Gerace Marino Masé

Young man (Lou Castel) murders the more dependent members of his family – one is blind, two are epileptic, another is insane – to help his 'normal' brother (Marino Masé) escape the responsibility of looking after them.

Like an incredibly dark soap opera: a stylish, savage, anarchic parody of Italian bourgeois life, with a riveting performance from the leading man.

'There have been few debuts as exciting as this in recent years.' *(Tom Milne, MFB)*

'A remarkable first feature, it is notable for its intensity, claustrophobic atmosphere, and a powerful performance from Castel.' *(Bergan & Karney)*

'A grim, frequently grotesque study of rampant psychopathology. A morbidly fascinating drama.' *(Scheuer)*

'The family as a divisive force has seldom been better explored.' *(Shipman)*

FISTFUL OF DOLLARS, A CT: 6 AV: 6.00

(aka *per Un Pugno di Dollari*)

1964 Italy/Germany/Spain 100 C WESTERN

D Sergio Leone ☆
W Sergio Leone Duccio Tessari Victor A. Catena G. Schock from Akira Kurosawa's film *Yojimbo*

Clint Eastwood ☆ Marianne Koch Gian Maria Volonté Pepe Calvo Wolfgang Lukschy

A stranger arrives in a Mexican border town, and he doesn't seem to have a sunny disposition.

A charismatic young Clint Eastwood impersonates *The Man With No Name* – and precious little dialogue – in Sergio Leone's violent, influential, spaghetti western. Loathed by the critics, loved by the masses. Leone made two sequels, *For A Few Dollars More* and *The Good, The Bad And The Ugly*.

'[*The Man With No Name* is] the kind of anti-hero who does what everybody would secretly like to do . . . a kind of Bogart in the saddle – who is not afraid to be himself, good or bad.' *(Clint Eastwood)*

ANTI:

'Eastwood, the sometime star of television's *Rawhide*, is certainly not paid by the word. In *Fistful* he hardly talks at all. Doesn't shave, either. Just drawls orders. Sometimes the bad guys drawl back. Just as tersely. Trouble is, after they stop talking, their lips keep moving. That's because the picture is dubbed. Like the villains, it was shot Spain. Pity it wasn't buried there.' *(The Times)*

'A straining-hard-to-be-off-beat almost pop Western; not bad enough to be bad or good enough to be good.' *(New York Daily News)*

'The calculated sadism of the film would be offensive were it not for the neutralizing laughter aroused by the ludicrousness of the whole exercise.' *(Observer)*

'I feel definitely queasy about [it] . . . the most unnecessarily violent film I can remember. Apologists . . . claim it is a satire . . . Well, if you can get any fun out of [it] you had better read some other critic . . . If this is parody it needs to be a good deal lighter on the trigger.' *(Felix Barker, Evening News)*

MIXED:

'Just another Western tale of the stranger in town. But it is the fancy trimmings that make it. We have seen it all before . . . What we have not seen is [the presentation] in such vicious, violent and visually dramatic terms.' *(Cecil Wilson, Daily Mail)*

'While the picture lacks the subtler characterizations of its prototypes it does have fully as much gore as usual . . . Eastwood as the stranger, makes full use of his one expression, dangles a cheroot from the corner of his mouth, and, with two sequels already on the way, is obviously going to replace the ageing John Wayne. It is obvious, too, that the American Western is not dead; it has merely gone to Italy.' *(Saturday Review)*

PRO:

'A major candidate to be the sleeper of the year . . . This is a hard-hitting item, ably directed, splendidly lensed, neatly acted, which has all the ingredients wanted by action fans and then some.' *(Variety)*

'A cruel but memorable picture.' *(Daily Mail)*

'Once in a great while a western comes along that breaks new ground and becomes a classic of the genre . . . This year *A Fistful of Dollars* is the feature that dares to be different. It may well be the first western since *The Great Train Robbery* without a subplot.' *(Time)*

'Eastwood's taciturn presence, although haunted and laconic, was central to Leone's reinvention of the Western. This reworking of Kurosawa's *Yojimbo* is less of a bravura attack on Hollywood conventions than its successors, but the elements are all in place.' *(Elkan Allan, NFT Bulletin)*

'[Leone's] fresh approach comprised pushing the genre into an operatic sense of overstatement . . . the film adopted a baroque approach that became synonymous with what was tagged the spaghetti western . . . and the film was further distinguished by a style that detailed violence in brutal, lingering close-ups and orchestrated endlessly drawn-out ritualistic confrontations to the memorably shrieking accompaniment of Ennio Morricone's music. The result made Eastwood a star, revolutionized the western and led to a slew of generally inferior imitations.' *(Allan Hunter & Kenny Mathieson, Movie Classics, 1992)*

FISTS IN THE POCKET: *see* FIST IN HIS POCKET.

FITZCARRALDO CT: 4 AV: 7.31

1982 West Germany 158 C DRAMA//ADVENTURE/FOREIGN

D Werner Herzog ☆
W Werner Herzog

Klaus Kinski Claudia Cardinale José Lewgoy Miguel Angel Fuentes Paul Hittscher Huerequeque Enrique Bohorquez

At the turn of the century, an eccentric Irishman (Klaus Kinski) tries to build an opera house in the Peruvian jungle.

Initially impressive, then terribly turgid. Frankly, the documentary about the making of the movie (*Burden of Dreams*) is more gripping – and Herzog makes a more interesting anti-hero. Even so, *Fitzcarraldo* won Herzog the Best Director prize at the Cannes Film Festival.

PRO:

'It hasn't the neat, well-combed appearance of a comparable David Lean epic, but a straggly, unkempt craziness that is exactly right.' *(David Castell, Sunday Telegraph)*

'Herzog has dispensed with all illusion . . . Everything that appears to happen has actually happened (bar fatalities) . . . [It is] a triumph, founded in part on the untiring assistance of the enigmatic Indians . . . and actors, above all the gloriously mad-looking Klaus Kinski (his hair expressing everything).' *(Sue Lermon, Times Educational Supplement)*

'The centrepiece of the film, the transporting of the entire ship by a pulley system . . . is almost as dramatic, enthralling and heart-stopping on screen as it must have been in real life. Herzog is clearly another alias for Fitzcarraldo, and it is difficult to decide how far the film is an allegory of its own making.' *(Alan Brien, Sunday Times)*

MIXED:

'[The hero] seems meant to be a lovable loser, but it's hard to know quite what Kinski's Fitzcarraldo is because he's not like anyone else in the world – except maybe Bette Davis playing Rutger Hauer.' *(Pauline Kael)*

'Operatic excess is both the subject and the keynote.' *(Paul Taylor, Time Out)*

'Slow but awe-inspiring.' *(Danny Peary)*

FIVE EASY PIECES AAN CT: 7 AV: 8.57

1970 US 98 C DRAMA

D Bob Rafelson ☆
W Adrien Joyce AAN from Joyce and Rafelson's story

Jack Nicholson ☆ AAN Karen Black AAN Billy 'Green' Bush Fannie Flagg Sally Struthers Marlena MacGuire Richard Stahl

A redneck drifter (Jack Nicholson) turns out to be an alienated middle-class lad with a background of classical music.

One of those American road movies which doesn't have a lot to say, but leaves you with pleasant memories and some sense of what America is about. Nicholson, as a middle-class drop-out who finds most women as easy to play on as any piano, emerges from this film a great leading actor. The scene where he tries to order a meal in a café is a classic.

ANTI:

'The very title, *Five Easy Pieces*, strikes me as a bit of attitudinizing. It refers primarily to the pieces of piano music performed at various times in the film (two Chopins, two Mozarts, one Bach), although I cannot affirm that they are really easy pieces. A parallel is presumably intended with the five women with whom we see Bobby making out: Rayette, two small-town hookers, one pickup in Los Angeles, and Catherine. Yet what is this analogy saying? Something about a parallel between music and sex, art and life? Something about everything in life being, or seeming, too easy for the disaffected person? Bobby himself does not play more than two of those piano pieces, however, and Tita finds one of the others anything but easy going. We are meant to feel some grand assertion or irony lurking in the title, if we could only seize it; but here as elsewhere the film fails to deliver. Pretentious, too, is the color cinematography by Laszlo Kovacs . . . The film certainly keeps the senses occupied as we watch and listen. I only wish it could make a deeper kind of sense.' *(John Simon)*

MIXED:

'There are blurred passages in *Five Easy Pieces* – for instance in the relationship with the married pair, friends at the oilfields. But there are none in Mr Nicholson's performance.' *(Dilys Powell)*

PRO:

'It would be impossible to over-praise the simplicity and deep, intrinsic wisdom of Jack Nicholson's performance. He is the great white hope among the current group of screen actors and this is the first film he has yet had the good fortune to appear in that has used all of his intelligence and artistry to the fullest of their capabilities . . . *Five Easy Pieces* is that rarest event in the cinema – a movie in which absolutely nothing ever goes wrong. It breaks new ground in American films by photographing and communicating the messages inside the human heart and relating them to life in the style of art. It is the movie of 1970 to see if you are even remotely interested in the medium.'*(Rex Reed)*

'A masterpiece of heartbreaking intensity . . . Robert Eroica Dupea is one of the most unforgettable characters in American movies.' *(Roger Ebert)*

'Less a story and more a collection of incidents and character studies, all of which inform each other and extend our understanding of Nicholson's mode of survival: flight.' *(Phil Hardy, Time Out)*

FIVE FINGERS

CT: 7 AV: 7.44

1952 US 108 BW THRILLER

D Joseph L. Mankiewicz ☆ AAN
W Michael Wilson ☆ AAN from L.C. Moyzisch's book *Operation Cicero*

James Mason ☆ Danielle Darrieux ✔
Michael Rennie Walter Hampden Oscar Karlweis
Herbert Berghof

An Albanian valet (James Mason) at the British embassy in Turkey passes secrets to the Germans in World War II, under the codename Cicero.

Witty, cleverly plotted spy thriller, based on a true story. Mason endows an underwritten part with considerable depth; Danielle Darrieux also impresses as the woman who causes his downfall.

ANTI:

'Something seems missing – maybe from the character of Cicero himself; we don't have much involvement with him, or with anybody else.' *(Pauline Kael)*

MIXED:

'Good, if somewhat overlong . . . The script runs to considerable dialog in the first portions. However, pace quickens and becomes a sock suspense drama, tight and tingling, when the story gets down too cases.' *(Variety)*

PRO:

'One of the highest, fastest and most absorbing spy melodramas since Hitchcock crossed the Atlantic.' *(Arthur Knight)*

'Civilized suspense entertainment with all talents contributing nicely.' *(Halliwell)*

'An irresistible treat.' *(Tom Milne, Time Out)*

FIVE GRAVES TO CAIRO

CT: 8 AV: 7.70

1943 US 96 BW WAR/THRILLER

D Billy Wilder ☆
W Charles Brackett Billy Wilder ☆ from Lajos Biro's play *Hotel Imperial*

Franchot Tone Anne Baxter Akim Tamiroff
Erich von Stroheim ☆ Peter Van Eyck
Fortunio Bonanova Konstanti Shayne

British spies attempt to disrupt Rommel's North African campaign.

Billy Wilder's wartime thriller suffers from a slow start and an untypically weak, sentimental ending, but along the way it benefits from sparkling dialogue, ingenious plot twists, and Erich von Stroheim as Rommel.

'Crackling dialog and fine scripting . . . Camerawork of John Seitz is outstanding, as is the film editing by Dennis Harrison. Use of sound effects, indicating superb recording, especially during the running gunfight, also is topflight.' *(Variety)*

'An unusually intriguing thrilldrama. Atmospherically directed by Billy Wilder, and produced with considerable discrimination by Charles Brackett, the film is founded on a well-contrived script written by the pair – which makes the production something in the nature of a two-man triumph for the versatile team . . . *Five Graves to Cairo* is sparkling and exciting melodramatic fare, garnished with witty and observant dialogue. The ending is weak and mawkish, but the reels that precede it are eminently enjoyable.' *(Herb Sterne)*

'von Stroheim has all the other movie Huns backed completely off the screen.' *(Variety)*

'A fabulous film fable, but it has been executed with enough finesse to make it a rather exciting pipe dream.' *(Howard Barnes, New York Herald Tribune)*

'Ingeniously plotted . . . [Wilder] must have had something a little grander in mind; the cleverness lacks luster.' *(Pauline Kael)*

FLAME OVER INDIA: *see* NORTHWEST FRONTIER.

FLIGHT OF THE PHOENIX CT: 6 AV: 7.11

1965 US 149 C DRAMA/ACTION/ADVENTURE

D Robert Aldrich ☆
W Lukas Heller from Elleston Trevor's novel

James Stewart ✔ Richard Attenborough ✔ Peter Finch Hardy Kruger ✔ Ernest Borgnine Ian Bannen AAN Ronald Fraser Christian Marquand Dan Duryea George Kennedy

Passengers from a crashed cargo-plane try to survive in the desert.

Orthodox, overlong disaster-movie, made memorable by three fine performances from Stewart (as the pilot), Attenborough (as the drunken navigator) and Kruger (as the guy to get them out of this mess).

'An often-fascinating and superlative piece of film-making highlighted by standout performances and touches that show this producer-director at his best.' *(Variety)*

'What takes the film right out of the rut is the gradual emergence of the group's saviour: a youthful German designer of model aircraft (Kruger), who develops a strain of pure Nazi fanaticism in his determination to prove that he can build a plane that will fly from bits of the wreck. He does it, too, although his only previous experience has been in toy-making; and in doing so, he raises questions about leadership (democratic/dictatorial) and the survival of the fittest.' *(Tom Milne, Time Out)*

'A sweat-and-survival story distinguished by fascinating character studies, high drama, and an exhilarating resolution.' *(Judith Crist)*

FLINTSTONES, THE CT: 8 AV: 4 (est)

1994 US 92 C COMEDY/FAMILY

D Brian Levant ✔
W Tom S. Parker Jim Jennewein Steven E. de Souza based on the animated series by Hanna-Barbera

John Goodman ☆ Elizabeth Perkins Rick Moranis Rosie O'Donnell Kyle MacLachlan Halle Berry Elizabeth Taylor

A ruthless yuppie, Cliff Vandercave (Kyle MacLachlan) wants modern technology to replace the workers in the Bedrock quarry. He then aims to embezzle funds and fly off to Rocapulco with his sexy secretary, called – naturally – Sharon Stone (Halle Berry), and blame everything on his new Vice-President, poor old Fred Flintstone (John Goodman).

Forget the hype. Forget the fact that more writers contributed to the script (at least 32) than it took to sign the American Declaration of Independence. The important thing about *The Flintstones* is that it is fun. And spectacular. The dinosaurs are of *Jurassic Park* quality; the puppetry is as sophisticated as in the best Muppet movies; the integration of live action with special effects is as sensational as in *Who Framed Roger Rabbit*. All this is hardly surprising, since many people involved in the making of those blockbusters were also involved in this. As a feat of modern technology, *The Flintstones* makes *Star Wars* look prehistoric.

The actors are perfect for their parts. John Goodman was born to play Fred – loud-mouthed, lumpen but lovable. Rick Moranis personifies the nerdish resilience of Barney Rubble, while Elizabeth Perkins and Rosie O'Donnell expertly capture the mannerisms of Wilma and Betty.

Director Brian Levant and executive producer Steven Spielberg evidently understand the appeal of *The Flintstones*. It isn't really set in the past at all – although the action is supposedly in the Stone Age, dinosaurs (which died out millions of years previously) are still around. And it's a Stone Age where TV, the gramophone, credit cards and, of course, rock music exist. *The Flintstones* is in fact, set in an alternate form of the present, a kind of Greenpeace Garden of Eden, where humans have found low-tech solutions to thoroughly modern problems. A garbage disposal system is an ancestor of the pig sitting open-mouthed underneath your kitchen sink; a shower is a mammoth squirting water over you; an alarm call is a pulley system that drops a rock on your head.

The wittiest touches are in these visual gags; but the dialogue is amusing too. When Fred and Wilma are trying to convince Fred's mother-in-law (played by Elizabeth Taylor, no less) that Fred is a good provider, she rasps: 'What has he ever provided for you except shade?' Later, she moans about how disappointed she is in Wilma: 'When I think of all the sacrifices your father made for you – lambs, oxen, your brother Jerry . . .'

The original TV series has been cleverly updated for the 90s. Some of the best visual jokes come as proletarian Fred and Wilma turn bourgeois, trapped by material success into buying ridiculous fashions, a jacuzzi, and exercising with a personal fitness trainer. *The Flintstones* is hardly a socialist tract; but it does satirize materialism, and upholds traditional values, such as friendship, family life and (more surprisingly) working-class solidarity at a time of technological and financial uncertainty. These Flintstones are recognizably from the Clintstone era.

The film rises high above that run of movies which tried to capitalize on nostalgia for old TV series. There is something in this for every age group. The American critics gave *The Flintstones* a drubbing, and after the press screening their British counterparts looked pretty Yabba-Dabba-doomladen too. No one is going to pretend it's great art, but I thoroughly enjoyed it.

ANTI:

'Yabba dabba dud.' *(New York Daily Post)*

'Yabba dabba don't.' *(USA Today)*

'Initially at least, the novelty of seeing a cartoon world cloned in three-dimensional flesh is startling, like virtual reality. But, oddly enough, the live-action Flintstones seems less real than the cartoon. Although the actors are well cast, their characters are still replicas, like animatronic figures in a theme-park ride . . . And once the novelty of Virtual Bedrock starts to wear off, the problem with the film becomes apparent: it isn't funny. Despite brainstorming by some 30 writers, the script is lifeless and flat . . . Yabba-Dabba-Doodoo.' *(Brian D. Johnson, Maclean's)*

'Leaves you fidgety and dissatisfied, as if you had just spent 92 minutes taking apart a pile of pebbles, stone by stone, and then built another identical one two feet away.' *(Tom Gliatto, People Weekly)*

'There isn't, of course, a single thought in its silly head.' *(Derek Malcolm, Guardian)*

'Loudness is too often confused with humour . . . Relentlessly, boomingly cute and obvious . . . Pitifully bereft of wit . . . When a pterodactyl doing what pigeons are famed for doing gets the biggest laugh, you know you're in trouble. Yabba Dabba Poo!' *(Angie Errigo, Empire)*

MIXED:

'If "The Flintstones" had been able to devise a story as interesting as its production values, it would have been some kind of wonderful. This is a great-looking movie, a triumph of set design and special effects, creating a fantasy world halfway between suburbia and a prehistoric cartoon. The frame is filled with delightful and inventive notions, all based on the idea that modern America might somehow be reconstructed out of rocks. Just watching it is fun. Following the plot is not so much fun . . . The story is confusing, not very funny, and kind of odd, given the target audience of younger children and their families. Do kids really care much about office politics, embezzlement, marital problems, difficulties with adoption, aptitude exams and mothers-in-law?' (Roger Ebert)

'A big, shiny package of comic nostalgia, as much a theme park as a movie. Does it say something about the infantilization of American cinema that an absurdly literal-minded big-budget version of a goofy cartoon series is now our idea of a major motion-picture event? You bet it does. That said, I had a good time at *The Flintstones*. The movie has been made with affection and occasional slivers of wit, and it tickled my memories of the show's weirdly earthbound charm.' *(Owen Gleiberman, Entertainment Weekly)*

PRO:

'All tread a nice, comically persuasive line between caricature and naturalism under Brian Levant's direction. And while more than 30 writers worked on the screenplay and untold numbers labored to re-create the ambiance and effects that the animators once tossed off with a few squiggles of their pencils, *The Flintstones* doesn't feel overcalculated, over-produced or overthought.' *(Richard Schickel, Time)*

'What makes "The Flintstones" work on so many levels is the adoration the creative teams have brought to the project. It all comes together for a laugh-filled 92 minutes.' *(John Larsen, Hollywood Hotline)*

FLIRTING

CT: 10 AV: 7.90

1991 Australia 100 C COMEDY/ROMANCE/RITES-OF-PASSAGE

D John Duigan ✓
W John Duigan ✓

Noah Taylor ✓ Thandie Newton ✓ Nicole Kidman Bartholomew Rose Felix Nobis

First love between pupils at neighbouring Australian boarding schools. The boy (Noah Taylor) is white, and the girl (Thandie Newton) is black. The reason they're attracted to each other is mainly that they're outsiders.

John Duigan's charming sequel to the critically acclaimed *The Year My Voice Broke* features the same remarkable young actor, Noah Taylor, and is even better. It evokes the ethos of single-sex education in 1965 with hilarious accuracy, and anyone who attended an English public school around that time will find the setting horribly familiar. You can almost smell the acne cream, sweaty socks and football boots. The story meanders, but the script is so full of human sympathy and wit that this hardly matters. There haven't been many more perceptive films about adolescence.

'Duigan's ability to summon up the past with conviction, get good performances from his cast and to apply a sense of humour as well as a feeling of horror at what Australians did to their young circa 1965, makes the film universal in its appeal.' *(Derek Malcolm, Guardian)*

'One of those rare movies with characters I cared about intensely. I didn't simply observe them on the screen; I got involved with their decisions and hoped they made the right ones.' *(Roger Ebert)*

'Maintains a delicate balance between wry satire, childish laughter, and dark, brooding malevolence . . . Electrifying and heartbreaking.' *(Mark Kermode, Time Out)*

FLOATING WEEDS CT: 8 AV: 8.40

(aka *Drifting Weeds; Ukigusa*)

1959 Japan 119 C DRAMA/FOREIGN

D Yasujiro Ozu ☆
W Yasujiro Ozu Kogo Noda

Ganjiro Nakamura Haruko Sugimura Machiko Kyo Ayako Wakao Hiroshi Kawaguchi

The leader of a theatrical troupe (Ganjiro Nakamura) meets an old mistress (Haruko Sugimura) and makes his current lover (Machiko Kyo) jealous.

Ozu's remake of his own *A Story of Floating Weeds* (1934) is, like most of his work, straightforward, civilized and touching. There are untypical touches of humour in the theatrical scenes, and it is notably beautiful: cinematography is by one of Japan's finest, Kazuo Miyagawa, who only worked with Ozu this once. It's also rather long-winded.

'The mood is the late Ozu mood: immaculately serene, quietly poignant; the color work is magnificent.' *(Michael Wilmington, LA Times)*

'Ozu [is] perhaps the most accessible and surely one of the most enjoyable Japanese directors for Western audiences . . . In the humor or sadness or generic truth of its vignettes . . . the cinema of Ozu provides the justification for its gentle and unassuming forms.' *(Roger Greenspun, New York Times)*

'Filled with the most arrant propaganda for the left-wing theater . . . Kabuki fans of Japan severely attacked the film for its anti-Kabuki stand.' *(Joseph Anderson & Donald Richie, The Japanese Film, 1982)*

'The re-make gains enormously from the playing of Ganjiro Nakamura and Machiko Kyo and the stunning colour photography of the great Kazuo Miyagawa . . . the small alterations made by Ozu in this version, strengthening the end and introducing a different flavour to the scenes of the troupe at work.' *(Elkan Allan, NFT Bulletin)*

'One of Yasujiro Ozu's best . . . Lightly comic and magnificently photographed by the master Kazuo Miyagawa.' *(Scheuer)*

'Powerful drama is meticulously directed, solidly acted.' *(Maltin)*

FLY, THE CT: 6 AV: 5.50

1958 US 94 C SF/HORROR

D Kurt Neumann
W James Clavell from George Langelaan's short story

David Hedison Patricia Owens Herbert Marshall Vincent Price ☆

Mad scientist (David Hedison) turns into angry insect.

Banned on release, this shocker was a big hit with the public and has become more critically respectable over the years. The special effects were gruesome and shocking in their day, but now look faintly ludicrous, and the acting – by the leads in particular – suffers by comparison with Jeff Goldblum and Geena Davis in David Cronenberg's gory remake. But the narrative is gripping, with unusually feminist overtones for its period – the wife who starts as helpless becomes progressively more empowered as her husband becomes disabled and confined to his laboratory.

ANTI:

'A degrading business.' *(Charles Maclaren, Time & Tide)*

'Plush horror has arrived; in other words a monstrosity has achieved a kind of respectability, which is hardly a pretty thought . . . From this to exhibiting two-headed babies or bearded ladies seems a very short step.' *(Isabel Quigly, Spectator)*

'One may wonder what all the fuss has been about . . . [The film is] only mildly disturbing . . . As science-fiction it is bosh . . . and doesn't shock.' *(William Whitebait, New Statesman)*

'The early sequences of this film have great mystery and tension, and the situation is ingeniously built up. But the film soon becomes as nauseating as its bare outline suggests; even the moments which in healthier pictures might provoke a laugh through sheer absurdity offer little relief. The horror is set among scenes of dogged respectability, matched by empty but determinedly genteel performances.' *(MFB)*

'Morally repugnant.' *(Richard Hodgens, Focus on the Science Fiction Film)*

'This is probably the most ludicrous, and certainly one of the most revolting science-horror films ever perpetrated.' *(Ivan Butler, Horror in the Cinema)*

'Tacky . . . the draggy direction is by Kurt Neumann.' *(Pauline Kael)*

PRO:

'Making brilliant use of camera and soundtrack, it proves that intelligent production pays off even when you're trying something as unintelligent as deliberately scaring people out of their wits.' *(Frank Jackson, Reynolds News)*

'One of the better, more restrained entries of the "shock" school . . . A quiet, uncluttered and even unpretentious picture, building up almost unbearable tension by simple suggestion.' *(Howard Thompson, New York Times)*

'A high budget, beautifully and expensively mounted exploitation picture . . . One strong factor of the picture is its unusual believability.' *(Variety)*

'Ludicrous stuff, of course, but Price lends his own inimitable and delightful brand of bravura to the role of Hedison's concerned brother, while James (*Shogun*) Clavell's script successfully treads a fine line between black comedy and po-faced seriousness.' *(Geoff Andrew, Time Out)*

'The scene in which Owens pulls off her husband's head and sees his fly head – and he looks at her image with a fly's vision, seeing numerous images of her screaming face – is shocking, one of the greatest moments in horror movies.' *(Danny Peary)*

FLY, THE CT: 6 AV: 6.85

1986 US 100 C SF/HORROR

D David Cronenberg ☆
W Charles Edward Pogue David Cronenberg

Jeff Goldblum ✔ Geena Davis ✔ John Getz Joy Boushel Les Carlson (cameo: David Cronenberg as the gynaecologist)

Another scientific experiment goes wrong – and even more gruesomely.

David Cronenberg's initially gripping, ultimately revolting remake of the 1958 cult film succeeds in everything it sets out to do, but it's nasty and sadistic. Jeff Goldblum and Geena Davis hold their own with remarkably realistic performances among the Oscar-winning make-up and special effects. Critical reaction was mixed, but generally favourable. The film grossed almost $35 million in its first nine weeks at the domestic box-office, and led to an inferior sequel, *The Fly II* (1989) with Eric Stoltz.

ANTI:

'The sympathy from the early going is squandered on sensationalism late on . . . *The Fly* is too trapped by its desire to shock to be truly affecting.' *(Daily Variety)*

MIXED:

'One does not have to be totally warped to appreciate this film, but it does take a particular sensibility to embrace it.' *(Variety)*

'Cronenberg wants to drive you to revulsion; that's his aim. And if the movie has a power, it's simply in our somewhat prurient fixation on watching a man rot until finally he's pleading for a *coup de grace*. So, despite Goldblum's terrific performance and despite the graceful teamwork between him and Geena Davis, moviegoers may not feel that they're having such a great time.' *(Pauline Kael)*

PRO:

'What makes the story more than just a gore-fest of corroded limbs and inside-out baboons is the touching relationship between Brundle and journalist Veronica Quaife (Davis) and their respective attitudes to the "disease", which is representative of any modern scourge of the flesh, from cancer and Aids to plain old age. Full stomachs may heave at the film's high yuck factor and Grand Guignol climax, but the poignancy is that of a *Love Story* for the 80s, with real raw meat on it.' *(Anne Billson, Time Out)*

'Unfolds with such eerie grandeur that it will leave you stoked with a creepy high for hours after you've left the theater . . . He's spun a tale that peeks into the darkest corners of our wildest dreams.' *(Patrick Goldstein, LA Times)*

'Cronenberg has layered the story with so many possible interpretations and resonances that one's head swims. The megalomania followed by deterioration precisely depicts the psychology of the heavy coke abuser – as well as bringing to mind James Mason's terrifying response to cortisone in Nicholas Ray's great 1956 drug film, *Bigger Than Life*. Goldblum's decay also plays on our fears of cancer, cells running amok within, eating us up. As one colleague has suggested, the fear may be even more specifically that of Aids; Veronica is penalized for having slept with Brundle before his sickness was evident. An innocent act of love may cause her destruction as well.' *(Andy Klein, Los Angeles Reader)*

'By far the best Davis performance to date has been in *The Fly*. She's only off-screen in four scenes of Cronenberg's shocker, and during the rest she has to evolve through three phases. One, brash scepticism. (After all, she's a working newswoman, with a raincoat, a tape-recorder and a hardboiled smile; so what's this stuff about "teleportation"?) Two, growing love and empathy as crazy Jeff gropes towards a place in scientific history. Three, grief and horror as the boyfriend grows hairs, sheds ears, throws up over the doughnuts and behaves in ways that would make any less lovestruck woman reach for the Mafu spray . . . She wins by never letting go of the character's master-key; which is that love and revulsion are locked inextricably in battle right to the end.' *(Harlan Kennedy, Film Yearbook)*

'The transformations are gross, but terrifically done. A contender for best horror pic of the 80s.' *(Rose)*

FLYING DOWN TO RIO CT: 7 AV: 6.50

1933 US 89 BW MUSICAL/COMEDY

D Thornton Freeland
W Cyril Hume H.W. Hannemann Erwin Gelsey from Anne Caldwell's play from Louis Brock's story

Dolores del Rio Gene Raymond Raul Roulien Ginger Rogers ☆ Fred Astaire ☆ Blanche Frederici Walter Walker Franklin Pangborn Eric Blore

A band leader (Gene Raymond) and a Brazilian millionaire (Raul Roulien) both have eyes for a sultry South American heiress (Dolores del Rio).

Not a great film musical, and the central plot is eminently forgettable; but it deserves a place in screen history for its ridiculous airborne finale, naive period charm, wonderful Art Deco sets, and (best of all) Fred Astaire and Ginger Rogers dancing together for the first time. If you've ever wondered what star quality is, just watch these two perform everyone else off the screen.

MIXED:

'One of those bright, efficiently produced comedies with a little of everything – love, spectacle, dancing, crooning and all the other ingredients recommended by the screen's Mrs Beetons. It only wanted wit and taste to be first-rate.' *(Daily Telegraph)*

PRO:

'An ambitious show . . . The tunes are good, the dancing is good, the whole show has a picturesque pep. But I must not deceive you about its novelty. It is based on an old and secret formula, which I now publish for the first time: Girls, girls, girls, girls, girls, girls, girls.' *(Sunday Graphic)*

'Its main point is the screen promise of Fred Astaire . . . The others are all hoofers after him.' *(Variety)*

FOLLOW THE FLEET CT: 9 AV: 7.64

1936 US 110 BW MUSICAL/COMEDY/ROMANCE

D Mark Sandrich ✓
W Dwight Taylor Allan Scott from Hubert Osborne's play *Shore Leave*

Fred Astaire ☆ Ginger Rogers ☆ Randolph Scott Harriet Hilliard Astrid Allwyn Harry Beresford Russell Hicks Brooks Benedict Ray Mayer Lucille Ball

Sailors on shore leave (Randolph Scott, Fred Astaire) romance two girl singers (Ginger Rogers, Harriet Hilliard).

A dull script with poorly integrated songs can't disguise the talents of Fred and Ginger, which have never been equalled. The Irving Berlin numbers are imperishable, and the dancing is out of this world. The routine to 'Let's Face The Music and Dance' must be one of the most romantic dance numbers in screen history.

MIXED:

'Some of the material appears contrived, especially the introduction of the dance numbers . . . The songs are good . . . but none of them is sensational. Something will have to be done about stories for these two . . . General appeal: Excellent.' *(Era)*

'The running time is way overboard . . . Dialogue is good and can be depended upon for laughs, with the Astaire-Rogers dancing sure to do the rest. But cutting it would have helped a lot more.' *(Variety)*

'If I say this is below *Top Hat* standard I am neither being hard on two of my screen favourites nor putting you off a very pleasant entertainment. Anyway, how could any sensible person do anything but go and see a Fred Astaire picture?' *(Sunday Express)*

PRO:

'Let me confess that I used not to like Fred Astaire . . . [He] has won me over. His dancing has always been brilliant, and now he has learned to act . . . The dancing . . . is well up to standard. That, my dear fans, is all ye know on earth and all ye need to know.' *(Daily Telegraph)*

FOOD OF THE GODS, THE CT: 5 AV: 2.22

1976 US 88 C SF/HORROR/SO BAD

D Bert I. Gordon
W Bert I. Gordon from H.G. Wells's story

Marjoe Gortner Pamela Franklin Ida Lupino Ralph Meeker John McLiam

Weird diet causes chickens, rats, insects, etc to attack humans.

God-awful. Dud director Bert I. Gordon remakes his film of 11 years previously, *Village of the Giants*, and this time it's so bad it's hilarious. The classic dialogue exchange occurs as Ida Lupino rushes screaming out of her farm. 'Rats! Awful giant rats,' she screeches. 'But we're looking for Mr Skinner,' says someone. Poor Pamela Franklin gets lumbered with the worst line of all, when asked by an industrialist why she works for him. 'Well,' she tells him, 'jobs for female bacteriologists are just not that easy to find.'

MIXED:

'Fair-to-middling . . . Not for the squeamish.' *(Maltin)*

'Patently atrocious . . . The rat sequences are pretty horrible, but hardly as horrible as the worms – rats are better actors . . . For all its overt badness it is nevertheless thoroughly entertaining.' *(Julian Fox, F & F)*

'A welter of poor characterization, inept plotting and truly awful special effects. You can, however, see Ida Lupino attacked by a giant worm.' *(Alan Frank)*

ANTI:

'Since the opening scene is one of American football, the philosophies of H.G. Wells seem somewhat remote, particularly when the script ploughs ahead with some abysmally flat and inane dialogue.' *(Films Illustrated)*

'I wish I hadn't seen the movie, so I could avoid it like the plague.' *(John Simon)*

'More plot holes than any movie in recent memory, and enough dopey lines to make a Saturday night audience howl in all the wrong places.' *(David Sterritt, Christian Science Monitor)*

'Giant rats appear. They are the size of Great Danes, with intestinal-looking yards of pink tail . . . [and] weigh 150 pounds each. They are a lot more interesting than the trailer couple's discussion of marriage.' *(Penelope Gilliatt, New Yorker)*

'The process work is so crude that anyone over five could see that the wasps were animations, the rooster a large-scale dummy and the rodents were plain ordinary rodents swarming amid doll-sized VW's, campers and cottages . . . Not only sick, but sickening.' *(Arthur Knight, Hollywood Reporter)*

'A ridiculous script, bad camerawork . . . poor acting, nonexistent direction and laughable special effects.' *(Harry and Michael Medved, Golden Turkey Awards, 1980)*

FOOLISH WIVES CT: 4 AV: 6.50

1922 US 84/107/115/210/408 BW DRAMA/SILENT

D Erich von Stroheim
W Erich von Stroheim

Erich von Stroheim ☆ Mae Busch ☆ Maud George Cesare Gravina

A fake Russian count (Erich von Stroheim) preys on rich women in Monte Carlo.

Tatty old melodrama – though it is hardly fair to judge it now, since most prints that exist are a fraction of the film which von Stroheim made. Controversial with the critics, but a hit with the American public, who evidently enjoyed seeing European decadence at a safe distance.

ANTI:

'Obviously intended to be a sensational sex melodrama, *Foolish Wives* is at the same time frankly salacious.' *(Variety)*

'[von Stroheim] has made a photoplay that is unfit for the family to see; that is an insult to American ideals and womanhood . . . an insult to every American in the audience. Consider: an American, of sufficient prestige and importance to be selected by the President of the United States as a special envoy in charge of a vitally important mission to the Prince of Monaco, is depicted as a man who does not know how to enter a room or wear a formal dress! . . . It is not a picture that will do you any good. It is not good, wholesome entertainment. It is not artistically great. It is real nothing.' *(Photoplay, 1922)*

'A thick mixture of fetishistic sophistication and sentimentality. It's just about impossible to sort out one's responses. Has any other filmmaker made carnal desire so revolting?' *(Pauline Kael)*

MIXED:

'The settings . . . are as rich and splendid as one who thinks of Monte Carlo can imagine . . . It possesses [its essential dramatic quality] because, most importantly, it is largely composed of dynamic, expressive motion pictures. Mr von Stroheim . . . has a keen sense of the dramatic and a pictorial point of view . . . [The story] is not pleasant. In many places it is decidedly repulsive. It is what is generally called "continental", and as such is exceedingly well done. But whether you like that kind of a story is . . . another question.' *(New York Times)*

'Still has a certain power but you must be prepared for some rather ripe melodrama.' *(Shipman)*

PRO:

'*Foolish Wives*, which bored the mobocracy and brought ridicule from the brilliant critical brethren, was in reality a very superior piece of photoplay craftsmanship, original in ideas and treatment and deserving of higher rating than *Orphans of the Story, Loves of Pharoah, The Storm* and other second-class material which however brought forth applause and bravos from both screen public and scribes.' *(Tamar Lane, 1923)*

FOOTLIGHT PARADE CT: 8 AV: 7.92

1933 US 102 BW MUSICAL

D Lloyd Bacon William Keighley Busby Berkeley ☆
W Manuel Seff James Seymour

James Cagney ☆ Joan Blondell Ruby Keeler Dick Powell Guy Kibbee Ruth Donnelly Claire Dodd Hugh Herbert Frank McHugh

A theatrical producer (James Cagney) has big ideas during the Depression.

Forget the thin, episodic plot and just enjoy James Cagney's acting, singing and dancing. Director-choreographer Busby Berkeley contributes some of his most memorable production numbers: 'Honeymoon Hotel', 'Shanghai Lil', and (best of all) 'By a Waterfall', which is virtually a definition of kitsch.

MIXED:

'[Cagney's] song-and-dance number in the closing minutes . . . is almost the sole compensation for a dull and turgid musical film.' *(ADS, New York Times)*

'Very reminiscent of other song and dance spectacles and the story is accountable for much repetition. Spectacular scenes are novel, including an original water ballet.' *(MFB)*

PRO:

'This is mammoth, terrific, dazzling – a wilful whirl of pulchritude, with thousands of girls bathing and swimming under water . . . And James Cagney lashing them to work . . . I warn you to wait for the end of the picture. All the big stuff is saved for the climax.' *(Sunday Express)*

'An amazing cultural index of the depression . . . one of the greatest of the Berkeley extravaganzas.' *(Virgin)*

FOR YOUR EYES ONLY: *see* BOND SERIES.

FORBIDDEN GAMES: *see* JEUX INTERDITS.

FORBIDDEN PLANET

CT: 5 AV: 7.38

1956 US 98 C SF/DRAMA

D Fred McLeod Wilcox ✗
W Cyril Hume

Walter Pidgeon Anne Francis ● Leslie Nielsen ● Warren Stevens Jack Kelly

Commander Adams (Leslie Nielsen) and his crew land on a planet under the control of a mysterious inventor Morbius (Walter Pidgeon) and his nubile daughter Alta (Anne Francis).

This sci-fi version of *The Tempest* is entertaining, and the art direction, cinematography and special effects are impressive. Its Shakespearean origins and Freudian subtext have endeared it to intellectuals and cultists. However, the script is illogical and often fatuous, while a lot of the acting is either dull or atrocious. Robby the Robot – the film's equivalent of Caliban – may be one of the more endearing non-human characters in science fiction, but he is far too peripheral to the plot (Robby went on to star in his own film, *The Invisible Boy*, in 1957). Some contemporary critics were sufficiently confused by it to hail it as a comedy, and a few have (I think wrongly) elevated it into the pantheon of all-time-great science-fiction films.

PRO:

'It offers some of the most amusing creatures conceived since the *Keystone Cops* . . . If you've got an ounce of taste for crazy humor, you'll have a barrel of fun.' *(New York Times)*

'During the first ten minutes of this film it is pleasantly obvious that there is to be no allegorical finger-shaking, but science-fiction in the best strip-cartoon tradition . . . delightful hokum.' *(F & F)*

'I haven't enjoyed a science-fiction so much since *Them!* Ingenious, inventive, spectacular – *Forbidden Planet* has another distinction. It is the first Freudian space-film; and to all the Beasts and Creatures we can now add the Thing from the Id.' *(Dilys Powell)*

'Imaginative gadgets galore, plus plenty of suspense and thrills, make the production a top offer in the space travel category.' *(Variety)*

'An ingenious script, excellent special effects and photography, and superior acting (with the exception of Francis), make it an endearing winner.' *(Geoff Andrew, Time Out)*

'Elaborate beyond the dreams of SF fans, *Forbidden Planet* was and still is the most remarkable of SF films, the ultimate recreation of the future, a studio-bound extravaganza where every shot is taken under artificial light and on a sound stage. The system begun by George Pal had reached its logical conclusion; everything was false, everything controlled. Reality was not permitted to intrude on this totally manufactured, totally believable world.' *(John Baxter, Science Fiction in the Cinema)*

ANTI:

'It's a pity they didn't lift some of Shakespeare's dialogue: its hard to believe you're in the heavens when the diction of the hero (Leslie Nielsen) and his spaceshipmates flattens you down to Kansas.' *(Pauline Kael, 1977)*

'Since the old man has a daughter, some have seen this as a reworking of *The Tempest*, conferring a respectability it little deserves. The art direction isn't bad.' *(Shipman)*

'Cyril Hume wrote a very trite, juvenile script, in which the Freudian-incestuous elements are toned down so that we never understand the exact nature of the rivalry between Adams and Morbius for Alta. Direction by Fred Wilcox lacks excitement, the acting is stiff, and the crew-cutted, always snickering, obedient, white, WASPish soldiers are more fitting for the dull Eisenhower Era than the 23rd century. How can Adams be a near-genius and not know what id means? How can Morbius be so scholarly and have such an ignorant (and lazy) daughter? Why doesn't he punch out Doc (Warren Stevens) for his supposedly flattering remarks about his daughter? Why does the Id Monster sabotage the ship when Morbius wants the crew to leave the planet?' *(Danny Peary)*

FOREIGN CORRESPONDENT

CT: 10 AV: 8.83

1940 US 120 BW THRILLER

D Alfred Hitchcock ☆
W Charles Bennett Joan Harrison James Hilton Robert Benchley ☆ from Vincent Sheean's memoirs *Personal History*

Joel McCrea Laraine Day Herbert Marshall ☆ George Sanders ☆ Albert Basserman ☆ Robert Benchley ☆ Edmund Gwenn ☆ Eduardo Ciannelli ☆ Martin Kosleck Harry Davenport ☆

An American correspondent in Europe (Joel McCrae) gets mixed up in espionage.

In other hands, this might have been a run-of-the-mill chase thriller. In Hitchcock's, an already witty, inventive script became a classic, despite a lacklustre performance by the leading man (Gary Cooper had turned the role down, and later admitted he had made a mistake in doing so). Designed as an anti-Nazi propaganda piece to entice America into World War II, the film was admired by Goebbels himself as a masterpiece of enemy propaganda.

ANTI:

'A masterpiece of propaganda, a first class production which no doubt will make a certain impression upon the broad masses of the people in enemy countries.' *(Joseph Goebbels)*

PRO:

'Romantic spy melodrama of urgent and exciting topicality. Story gripping, direction brilliant, acting outstanding and thrills vividly spectacularly realistic. Appeal universal.' *(Kine Weekly)*

'Whether you like thrillers or not, Hitchcock has a genius for filmmaking . . . [This] is the best that Hitchcock has ever done and . . . very much more than a thriller . . . It is a message to the States . . . Neither a warlike nor a political piece of propaganda; it stimulates thought and its message should strike home.' *(Documentary News Letter)*

'Vivid story . . . achieves particularly gripping panorama of espionage intrigue, colourful yet plausible heroics, and thrilling suspense . . . Masterly direction, brilliant stellar portrayal, forceful all-round support, admirable general production qualities. First class melodramatic entertainment.' *(The Cinema)*

'Alfred Hitchcock . . . has packed about as much romantic action, melodramatic hullaballoo, comical diversion and illusion of momentous consequence as the liveliest imagination could conceive . . . Never . . . has Mr Hitchcock let his flip fancy roam with such wild and reckless abandon as he does in the present case . . . It does make for some oddly exciting and highly improbably shenanigans. Improbable? Well, after all no one expects probability in a Hitchcock picture . . . Usually he manages to keep things moving with such fascinating rapidity that he never goes over the edge, but this time he comes perilously close . . . The cast is uniformly good, especially in the minor roles, and some of the photographic sequences are excellent.' *(Bosley Crowther)*

'The most excitingly shot and edited picture of the year.' *(Basil Wright)*

'Easily one of the year's finest pictures.' *(Time)*

'It should not be missed by anyone who cherishes the sheer sorcery of the medium . . . This juxtaposition of outright melodramatics with deadly serious propaganda is eminently satisfactory . . . Hitchcock uses camera tricks, cinematic rhythm and crescendo to make his points.' *(Howard Barnes, New York Herald Tribune)*

'Hitchcock is smart. When he has a chase it is, like the March Hare's butter, the best: the chase of chases . . . This is genuine Hitchcock, the kind of chiaroscuro of sinister and jolly which Hitchcock handles better than any other living director . . . The dialogue is amusing throughout. There are one or two moments when the tension of the plot is allowed to slacken more, perhaps, than it need. But with so much that is brilliant . . . I scarcely noticed the blemishes. This film is worth fifty *Rebeccas*.' *(Dilys Powell)*

'A splendid Hitchcock movie . . . fast, exciting, very imaginative and strongly reminiscent of his British thrillers . . . a magnificently handled assassination scene in pouring rain. Edmund Gwenn in a minor role . . . out-acted everyone inthe picture.' *(R.A.E. Pickard, Dictionary of 1000 Best Films, 1971)*

'So amusing . . . so breathlessly paced and so broad in scope and sweep . . . that it's easy to miss the serious issues moving beneath the surface.' *(Elkan Allan, NFT Bulletin)*

FORREST GUMP CT: 7 AV: 6.00 (est)

1994 US 142 C COMEDY/DRAMA

D Robert Zemeckis ☆
W Eric Roth from Winston Groom's novel
Tom Hanks ☆ Gary Sinise ☆ Robin Wright
Sally Field Mykelti Williamson

A simpleton (Tom Hanks) prospers through the last four decades of the 20th century, thanks to luck, the ability to run fast, and an intuitive sense of right and wrong.

The surprise smash-hit of 1994, *Forrest Gump* is a 90s update of the American Dream. The hero is the kind of good – if slightly scrambled – egg who would never say anything hurtful and would only resort to violence to protect a woman or his country. He's a regular sort of guy, except of course that he's abnormal. He is also beautifully acted. Hanks does more than reprise his overgrown child routine from *Big*; he adds a meticulous Southern accent and an adult compassion and sensitivity which makes this probably the finest performance he has given. Almost as good in a supporting role is Gary Sinise, playing the crippled army lieutenant who becomes Gump's greatest friend; he lends a pain and reality to a yarn which is constantly in danger of drowning in schmaltz.

The whole film is superbly made. Director Robert Zemeckis follows up his special effects success with *Who Framed Roger Rabbit* to bring off new technological miracles, enabling Gump to hold conversations with three US Presidents and John Lennon. Woody Allen did the same sort of thing in *Zelig*, but here it's more technologically ambitious, and funnier. Just as effective, though not as ostentatious, is the mastery which goes into a classic opening shot, of a symbolic feather being blown – just like our hero – this way and that. And gone are the days when an actor playing an amputee had to tuck one leg up behind him, Long John Silver-style; now, the missing limbs can be deleted electronically.

The film's greatest strength is the shrewd way it reinvigorates old-fashioned moral values. Our hero may not know much, but he knows how to love, thanks to a caring mother (a single parent, played with all the emotional stops out by Sally Field, who may remember ruefully that in *Punchline* she got to play Hanks's girlfriend). Forrest's childhood sweetheart (Robin Wright) has no such luck, having suffered at the hands of an abusive father. Her only good fortune is that she keeps being saved by Gump, and gets to die from one of those Hollywood illnesses which leave you looking radiantly beautiful even on your death-bed.

So why, although I greatly admired the film, did it leave a nasty taste in my mouth? For a start, *Forrest Gump* is roughly as truthful about the world of intellectual handicap as *The Little Mermaid* was about fish. The real-life handicapped may be excused a hollow laugh at Gump's rise to riches; in the real America, a bonanza for a man with his learning difficulties would be a low-paid job with inadequate health insurance. In the original novel, Gump's mother tells him: 'Being an idiot is no box of chocolates'. In the movie, this becomes: 'My mother used to say life is like a box of chocolates: you never know what you're gonna get.' Rather different: sweeter, less truthful.

It is disturbing to note that Gump only escapes the real fate of his intellectual equals, not through superior moral values or abilities, but through corruption and deceit. His mother prostitutes herself in order to bribe her son's way into a 'normal' school. Later, he lies to the public in order to earn the $25,000 which are to turn him into a millionaire. He becomes rich, not as most high-achievers do – through skill, intellect or imagination – but thanks to Acts of God (or screenwriter); Gump's shrimping boat is the only one not to be destroyed in a hurricane, and he absent-mindedly invests in a fruit company, only to discover that he has become a founding father of Apple Computers.

On close inspection, Gump's much-acclaimed moral values look equally suspect. His short hair and 50s dress-sense mark him out from the start as a conservative conformist, rather like the Michael Douglas character who ran amok in *Falling Down*. Forrest's success in the army is based on blinkered obedience to orders (his superiors', and his girl-friend's). On the one occasion he seems about to come out with a political opinion, at an Anti-Vietnam peace rally, the microphone fortuitously goes dead on him.

The only way we can discover what he really stands for is by examining his polar opposite – his childhood sweetheart, whose troubled background makes her fall prey to hippiedom, the Peace Movement, the Black Panthers, drugs, casual sex and (although the word isn't mentioned) AIDS. She sums up the rebelliousness of the baby-boom generation; too late in life, she comes to embrace the more conservative, steadfast values of Gump.

This does not strike me as a very useful, or honest way of portraying recent American history. After all, those who opposed the war in Vietnam had a point. And if life is really like a box of chocolates, it's better to be critical enough to examine the writing on the inside of its lid. The ingredients in this movie have a distinct aftertaste of fudge.

Forrest Gump's admirers have likened him to Candide; but he is much more candied, and less candid. Voltaire's hero was a satire on the simplistic notion that cheerfulness and stoicism are enough in the face of the world's cruelties. And by the end, Voltaire's central character abandoned his foolish belief that all is for the best in this best of all possible worlds. In *Gump*, however, the idiot hero comes out a winner, simply by luck and spouting the same Christmas-cracker platitudes that he did at the start. And America applauds him for it.

The film preaches that anyone can survive disaster with the right attitude – a philosophy that does not exactly bode well for, say, the homeless or disabled. Political problems are real and complex, not ones which can be solved by Gumpist methods – throwing windfall profits around or simply running away. People in the underclass aren't always there because they needed a more positive outlook – or more Southern courtesy, or stronger family values.

That is why the film left me not merely cold, but chilled. The movie's success offers a harrowing insight into how adult Americans see themselves. Forrest is clearly meant to represent all that's best in the States. And yet the central image is of running – a running away from reality.

'I imagined Norman Rockwell painting the baby boomers.' *(Robert Zemeckis)*

PRO:

'Like a dream of reconciliation for our society. What a magical movie.' *(Roger Ebert)*

'Hanks holds it together because he is working to discover Forrest's inner adult – the mature man under his infantile guilelessness. This effort pays off magnificently in Forrest's climactic declaration of love. Hanks' tone is both operatic and judicious; he makes passionate sentiment seem the highest form of common sense. Other stars attract audiences by saving the world or stopping a runaway bus. A Hanks movie deals with more mundane imperatives: doing your job, staying alive, getting the girl. Simple things seem unattainable; when attained, they feel sublime.' *(Richard Corliss, Time)*

'A complex human comedy that is heartwarming to the max, both curiously offbeat and oddly disarming.' *(Bruce Williamson, Playboy)*

MIXED:

'A sort of updated, hip version of a Frank Capra movie. Capra's heroes were no great shakes in the brains department either, but at least they didn't make the point that being slow-witted was a big social and moral advantage. The good news is that the central Frank Capra message is in this movie too – that character and courage can prevail over all obstacles. The wonder is that a hip, hilarious movie has been made without bitterness or cynicism about good behavior in awful times. It's almost enough to make you forget the message about the great value of being blank and dumb.' *(John Leo, U.S. News & World Report)*

ANTI:

'The narrative is so programmed it is like watching software. *Forrest Gump* is a medley of sound bites –

clever, cute, amusing, silly, sentimental – and irritatingly phoney . . . Zemeckis sets about healing wounds with an Oliver-Stone-lite version of the modern American tragedy. Through Gump's uncomprehending eyes – shades of Dustin Hoffman's autistic hero in *Rain Man* – he renders it meaningless. As an exercise in high-powered manipulation, the movie works: audiences may find it irresistible. But *Forrest Gump* is, quite literally – to quote Shakespeare – "a tale told by an idiot, full of sound and fury, signifying nothing."' *(Brian D. Johnson, Maclean's)*

'If he [Gump] represents America, then America is not so amiable an idiot as we'd like to think. It (he) is an idiot who keeps himself pure by bullying others: beating up anyone who touches the object of his love, while making the love object feel bad for wanting what Forrest himself won't give. It's remarkable how Forrest's innocence keeps exploding into violence; how he feels that sex must be performed carefully (since it's basically grotesque and tawdry); how he can find his ideal only in someone who is thoroughly unworthy and must be made to suffer, again and again. I believe this Forrest, this America, will be recognizable to foreign audiences. It's not much different from the America they will recognize in *True Lies*.' *(Stuart Klawans, Nation)*

'A tale told by an idiot, full of saccharin and sentimentality, signifying a new low in American film-making.' *(Quentin Curtis, Independent on Sunday)*

FORT APACHE

CT: 6 AV: 7.31

1948 US 127 BW WESTERN

D John Ford ☆
W Frank S. Nugent from James Warner Bellah's story *Massacre*

Henry Fonda ☆ John Wayne ☆ Shirley Temple ● John Agar Pedro Armendariz Ward Bond Irene Rich George O'Brien Anna Lee Dick Foran Victor McLaglan Guy Kibbee

An inflexible military man (Henry Fonda) clashes with wiser heads (John Wayne, mostly) on how to deal with Indians.

Vintage John Ford western, with the usual ingredients: broad comedy, spectacular scenery, pioneering sentiment. Henry Fonda stars as a thinly disguised General Custer, John Wayne as his more level-headed junior officer. Shirley Temple is badly miscast as the love interest. This is the first of Ford's celebrated 'cavalry trilogy', the other parts being *She Wore a Yellow Ribbon* and *Rio Grande*.

MIXED:

'Shirley Temple and her husband, Jon Agar, handle the love interest as if they were sharing a soda-fountain special, and there is enough Irish comedy to make me wish Cromwell had done a more thorough job . . . However, John Ford directed it, and the Indian parleys and fights and a good deal of the camera work which sneaks by as incidental are somewhere near worth enduring the rest for.' *(James Agee, Nation)*

PRO:

'Mass action, humorous byplay in the western cavalry outpost, deadly supense and romance are masterfully combined.' *(Variety)*

'There is a oneness about the cavalry, a wholeness that makes the sacrifice of individuality worthwhile. The men are not even remembered by their names except for Thursday, who is remembered as something he was not. Never again is Ford so sure about the sacrifice of the individual.' *(J.A. Place, The Western Films of John Ford, 1975)*

'The whole picture is bathed in a special form of patriotic sentimentality: scenes are held so that we cannot fail to appreciate the beauty of the American West.' *(Paulien Kael, 1976)*

48 HRS

CT: 6 AV: 6.71

1982 US 96 ACTION/ADVENTURE

D Walter Hill ☆
W Roger Spottiswoode Walter Hill Larry Gross Steven E. de Souza

Nick Nolte ☆ Eddie Murphy ☆ Annette O'Toole ✓ Frank McRae James Remar David Patrick Kelly Sonny Landham Brion James Jonathan Banks

A white racist cop (Nick Nolte) and a black criminal (Eddie Murphy) are forced to work together.

Exciting buddy-buddy thriller, efficiently directed by Walter Hill: fast-moving, action-packed, and with enjoyable comic relief (especially when Murphy enters a bar full of red-necks). But the language is relentlessly foul, and there's a nasty appetite for violence: its influence has not been wholesome, nor has its encouragement of black racism towards whites. And the belated sequel, *Another 48 HRS* (1990), was lousy.

PRO:

'Violent, profane, and funny, this San Francisco-set police thriller has been furnished with up-to-the-minute urban slang and tough talk that leap out of the characters' mouths with the speed of a comic's patter . . . Its slightly slapdash style feels right for a milieu in which hardbitten cops and killers live violently, crazily, at the edge of crack-up or death.' *(David Denby, New York Magazine)*

'Mad-dog killers, mindless hookers, and all, *48 HRS* is paradoxically a sweet and sentimental entertainment . . . It is a movie to make the motor of the mind idle away for a pleasant 90 minutes or so.' *(Andrew Sarris, Village Voice)*

'We haven't had an action film with this much

charisma generated by a team of leading men in a long time.' *(Scheuer)*

MIXED:

'Its killers are no more than killing machines. And its hookers are too pretty for director Walter Hill's night-time San Francisco and the raw language that goes along with it. Yet, we say somewhat sheepishly, *48 HRS* is fun – a lightning-quick romp through the clichés of renegade-cop drama.' *(Alex Keneas, Newsday)*

ANTI:

'Like one of those new glues that are propped up near the cash register at the hardware store: it promises to bond two entirely incompatible substances forever. And . . . you know what will happen even as you shell out your cash; the job is going to fall apart the minute you look at it too hard.' *(Richard Schickel, Time)*

'You're probably meant to think this paranoid fantasy of race relations is what the TV shows with black and white buddies don't have the guts to let you see. It's as false as they are, but in a hip way. It's like *The French Connection, Dirty Harry* and *Butch Cassidy* all put in a compactor and pressed into cartoon form.' *(Pauline Kael)*

FORTY-EIGHT HOURS (1942): *see* WENT THE DAY WELL?

49TH PARALLEL AAN CT: 6 AV: 7.50

(aka *The Invaders*)

1941 GB 105 BW WAR/ADVENTURE

D Michael Powell ☆
W Emeric Pressburger Rodney Ackland AAN from Emeric Pressburger's story AAW

Eric Portman ☆ Laurence Olivier ✔ Anton Walbrook ☆ Leslie Howard ☆ Raymond Massey ☆ Glynis Johns Niall MacGinnis Finlay Currie Raymond Lovell John Chandos

U-boat commander (Eric Portman) stranded in Canada with some of his men encounters various people who teach him lessons about peace, democracy, freedom, etc.

Preachy, picaresque wartime melodrama by Powell and Pressburger, making the most of a strong cast.

PRO:

'An important and effective propaganda picture.' *(Variety)*

'An admirable piece of work from every point of view.' *(MFB)*

'The thing which makes this picture remarkable is its extraordinary fairness. To show the Nazis as unalloyed gangsters was never good enough. The philosophy of gangsterism is grabbing for one's self. The philosophy of Nazism is grabbing on behalf of a nation, which is not less base, but has this difference, that in pursuit of this vile doctrine there is scope in the individual Nazi for loyalty, purpose, tenacity and courage.' *(James Agate)*

'One of the best-made films ever produced in this country. It is, moreover, one of the few films of a purely episodic nature which has ever come off . . . Howard's portrayal of the dilettante is bound to cause a certain amount of heartburn.' *(Documentary News Letter)*

MIXED:

'The innately peaceful countryside, splendidly photographed . . . is Democracy's trump card, and its half-dozen invaders are made to look like cobras in a Surrey garden . . . [The film] doesn't go with a bang . . . and it isn't single-minded enough to be continuously exciting. However [it is] a thrilling adventure.' *(William Whitebait, New Statesman)*

'Some of the plotting and characterization look rather rusty at this remove, but the sense of landscape and figures passing through it remains authoritatively dynamic.' *(Tony Rayns, Time Out)*

42ND STREET AAN CT: 10 AV: 9.00

1933 US 89 BW MUSICAL/COMEDY

D Lloyd Bacon ☆
W James Seymour Rian James from Bradford Ropes's novel

Warner Baxter ☆ Ruby Keeler ☆ Bebe Daniels ☆ George Brent Una Merkel Guy Kibbee Dick Powell Ginger Rogers ☆ Ned Sparks ☆ George E. Stone Allen Jenkins

Understudy (Ruby Keeler) goes on Broadway stage and saves the day.

Arguably the greatest, and certainly the archetype, of all backstage musicals. Two charming production numbers early on ('Young and Healthy' and 'You're Getting To Be A Habit With Me') prevent the story becoming bogged down in talk. Worth waiting for are two of Harry Warren and Al Dubin's best songs: 'Shuffle Off To Buffalo' and the title number, both given the full treatment by choreographer Busby Berkeley. Dick Powell and Ruby Keeler are the romantic interest; but Warner Baxter has most of the classic lines, and is surprisingly moving as the Broadway producer ruthlessly determined to put on a show.

ANTI:

'Too lavish.' *(New York World Telegram)*

'Busby Berkeley has gone to a lot of ineffectual bother about his intricate formations.' *(Newsweek)*

PRO:

'The singing cinema comes into its own once again . . . We're offered a comprehensive study of theatrical life, replete with the vernacular of the stage world; the customers, the cues, the lingo, the laughs, the songs, the sorrows; action every minute, packed into a full picture at a breath-taking pace.' *(New York Daily News)*

'Everything about the production rings true. It's as authentic to the initiate as the novitiate.' *(Variety)*

'Brisk and alert.' *(New York Herald Tribune)*

'Brings musical back with a great big bang.' *(New York American)*

'Has the extraordinary quality of completely epitomizing the musical styles of its time, yet doing it with such verve and skill . . . The cast, perhaps more than any other factor, introduces the dated element: Ruby Keeler's stiff, unexpressive tap and flat notes are not easy to accept today; nor is Dick Powell's aggressively juvenile manner and the heavy mugging of Ned Sparks.' *(Karel Reisz, NFT Programme Notes)*

'The clichés are performed with great zest, the atmosphere is convincing, and the numbers when they come are dazzlers.' *(Halliwell)*

'The story has been copied a hundred times since, but never has the backstage atmosphere been so honestly and felicitously caught.' *(John Huntley, 1966)*

'Berkeley's wizardry with the camera created some of the screen's most amazing musical numbers to date and ushered in a new era. The outrageous extravaganzas he whipped up could never have originated on a theatre stage. But they were glorious fun.' *(John Kobal, Gotta Sing, Gotta Dance, 1972)*

'A special sense of modernity . . . an acid edge to the dialogue . . . an excitement about show business.' *(Journal of Popular Film, 1975)*

'The darkness of *42nd Street* is amplified by its careful juxtapositions of success and failure . . . Berkeley's mobile camera never rests long enough on one face to establish its distinctiveness, but draws all the characters momentarily into a quasi-democratic anonymity.' *(John Belton, Movie, 1977)*

FOUNTAINHEAD, THE CT: 5 AV: 5.00

1949 US 114 BW DRAMA/SO BAD

D King Vidor
W Ayn Rand ● from her own novel

Patricia Neal Gary Cooper Raymond Massey Kent Smith Robert Douglas Henry Hull Ray Collins

Principled architect (Gary Cooper) falls foul of press baron (Raymond Massey).

Ayn Rand's deeply felt tribute to individualism comes across as entertainingly silly melodrama on the screen, thanks to hammy performances, heavy-handed phallic symbolism, and Rand's over-ripe dialogue. Sample . . . Patricia Neal: 'I had a statue which I found in Europe – a statue of a god. I was in love with it. But I broke it. I threw it down the airshaft so that I wouldn't have to love it.' Robert Burks's cinematography is excellent.

PRO:

'If you like deep thinking, hidden meanings, plus pure modern architecture, then this is something for which you have been waiting a long time.' *(Screenland)*

ANTI:

'A long-winded complicated preachment on the rights of the individual in society . . . has been put on the screen with more fervor than compelling conviction . . . Wordy, uninvolving and pretentious . . . And a more curious lot of high-priced twaddle we haven't seen for a long time . . . A picture you don't have to see to disbelieve.' *(Bosley Crowther)*

'The garrulous script which Ayn Rand did from her novel calls for a great deal of posturing by the cast and King Vidor's direction permits much over-acting where underplaying might have helped . . . Gary Cooper has an uneasy time in the miscasting as the plot's hero . . . Raymond Massey is allowed to be too flamboyant as the publisher.' *(Variety)*

'These irritating characters . . . talk a lot of hooey dialogue which, like themselves, never existed outside the pages of an American best-seller.' *(Jympson Harman, Evening News)*

'It didn't seem to matter . . . that the architect was finally acquitted on the strength of his own defense that the ideas of an individual are personal property and must not be tampered with by others. An interesting theory. If they practised it in films they'd never make any.' *(Peter Barker, Sunday Pictorial)*

'A pretentious film in which Gary and Raymond look at a loss – but not for words.' *(Daily Graphic)*

'Even Gary Cooper could not save this pretentious nonsense from boredom and baloney.' *(People)*

'The idea is good; the dialogue is often atrocious.' *(Sunday Dispatch)*

'Lays on the expressionist symbolism with a "free enterprise" trowel.' *(Tony Rayns, Time Out, 1980)*

'Patricia Neal strides around in jodhpurs to denote her independence and Robert Douglas sports a cigarette-holder to indicate his decadence.' *(Shipman)*

'An extravaganza of romantic, right-wing camp.' *(Pauline Kael)*

FOUR ADVENTURES OF REINETTE & MIRABELLE CT: 7 AV: 6.57

(aka *Quatre Aventures de Reinette et Mirabelle*)

1986 France 95 C COMEDY/FOREIGN

D Eric Rohmer ☆
W Eric Rohmer ☆

Joëlle Miquel ✔ Jessica Forde ✔

Philippe Laudenbach Yasmine Haury Marie Rivière Béatrice Romand

Two contrasting girls (Joëlle Miquel, Jessica Forde) become flatmates in Paris.

Attractive, sympathetic character study of youth with this veteran director's usual wit and wisdom, and two lovely central performances. Some may find it too slow and lacking in plot, but it is rewarding if you have the patience. One of the best films to have evolved from actors' improvisation.

MIXED:

'A film of great delicacy and charm, but distinctly fragile by comparison with the best of Rohmer . . . If it is amazing that [he] should have made a film that could easily pass for a first feature by a highly promising twenty-year-old, it is equally amazing that he should also have contrived to underpin it with his usual complex, if largely subterranean, moral basis.' *(Tom Milne, MFB)*

PRO:

'Blithe, affectionate, enjoyable.' *(Leilah Farrah, F & F)*

'Remarkable chiefly for its air of breezily insolent spontaneity.' *(Tom Milne, S & S)*

'As casual as the movie's interactions are, they all raise issues of charity and honesty and situational ethics . . . What's truly extraordinary is how fresh [the] adventures seem to be. [The film] isn't slight, it has the callowness of youth.' *(J. Hoberman, Village Voice)*

'Unpredictable, exhilarating, full of life and light . . . Rohmer's best film in years.' *(Philip French, Observer)*

'A clever and lively character study of youth and people's foibles.' *(Winnert)*

'Filled with wisdom, idealism and beauty. One of director Rohmer's best.' *(Scheuer)*

FOUR DAUGHTERS AAN CT: 6 AV: 7.63

1938 US 90 BW ROMANCE/DRAMA

D Michael Curtiz ☆ AAN

W Julius Epstein Lenore Coffee ☆ AAN from Fannie Hurst's novel *Sister Act*

Claude Rains ☆ John Garfield ☆ AAN Priscilla Lane Rosemary Lane Lola Lane Gale Page Jeffrey Lynn Frank McHugh May Robson ☆ Dick Foran

A small-town family is disrupted by the arrival of a handsome, cynical stranger (John Garfield).

An oddity. Mainly it's heart-warming Americana with a charming, though prettified, view of family life – shades of *Meet Me In St Louis* (1944) – but there's also something much darker in Garfield's performance, which has overtones of Uncle Charlie in Hitchcock's *Shadow of a Doubt* (1943) and which shows a blistering working-class resentment of the lives enjoyed by the central family. The whole thing doesn't quite hang together; but it's never less than interesting, and the two leading male performances are exceptional.

PRO:

'It may be sentimental, but it's grand cinema.' *(New York Times)*

'It simply, yet powerfully, brings into focus a panorama of natural but startling events.' *(Motion Picture Herald)*

MIXED:

'Curtiz's direction is both affectionate and knowing. Claude Rains is irresistibly persuasive and attractive as the father . . . Garfield plays with such tight-lipped force he threatens to throw the picture out of focus by drawing too much interest.' *(Variety)*

'The director is afraid of his theme; he is apt to take refuge in conventional humour, in the pretence, for example, that grown men and ageing spinsters like nothing better than a good swing on the garden gate . . . We are beginning to abandon our hopes of the film when [along comes] John Garfield, who may prove an acquisition to the screen . . . His is a career to be watched.' *(New Statesman)*

FOUR FEATHERS, THE CT: 8 AV: 8.36

1939 GB 130 C WAR/ACTION/ADVENTURE

D Zoltan Korda ☆

W R.C. Sherriff Lajos Biro Arthur Wimperis based on A.E.W. Mason's novel

John Clements ☆ Ralph Richardson ☆ C. Aubrey Smith ☆ June Duprez ● Allen Jeayes Jack Allen Donald Gray Henry Oscar John Laurie

A young officer accused of cowardice (John Clements) wins back his self-respect through a series of improbable heroics during Kitchener's Egyptian campaign: it's a Boy's Own cartoon about a Boy's Own Khartoum.

The scenes in England are painfully stagebound, and the performances range from the delightfully theatrical (Ralph Richardson) to the desperately wooden (June Duprez). The film is jingoistic and dated in its casual dismissal of Africans as 'fuzzy-wuzzies', while the leading characters' preoccupation with gentlemanly behaviour is sometimes unintentionally comic. But it's a marvellous piece of storytelling, not without irony about militaristic values, and a stirring example of the action-adventure genre before it sacrificed humanity in pursuit of special effects. The battle sequences, among the first of their kind in colour, remain thrilling, and it's by far the best of the four versions of A.E.W. Mason's story.

MIXED:

'A terribly silly story . . . that unashamedly glorifies war as a romantic adventure. The film is marked, however, by some fine location (Sudan) photography by Osmond Borradaile and is worthy of mention . . . because of one memorable scene in which Ralph Richardson goes blind through sunstroke and finds himself alone in the desert with only his dead comrades and vultures for company.' *(R.A.E. Pickard, Dictionary of 1000 Best Films, 1971)*

PRO:

'Would be worth anyone's time and money if only for the scenes in which Lord Kitchener's gunboats are hauled up the cataracts of the Nile . . . Offers pleasant glimpses of English country life; Ralph Richardson in one of his ablest performances; and C. Aubrey Smith, delightful in comedy that supplements the major narrative gracefully.' *(Richard Sheridan Ames, Rob Wagner's Script)*

'The news this morning – is that Alexander Korda has re-taken the Sudan. In fact, Mr Korda, the Kipling of the kinema, has retaken the already twice-filmed *Four Feathers* . . . and a fine, stirring, gorgeously Technicolored, explosively cinematic job he has made of it, too . . . A fifth feather – for Mr Korda's cap . . . the biggest and best show in town.' *(Bosley Crowther)*

'The highest possible praise is due to Alexander Korda . . . and his brother Zoltan . . . They have succeeded in striking the right national note of the moment. Primarily, however, it is important as a film, and from that standpoint, it is without doubt a British achievement . . . superbly photographed . . . Certain scenes will remain unforgettable . . . Do not, I beg you, miss this film – it is tremendous and so far must rank as our finest and most successful British film.' *(Catholic Film News)*

'It cannot fail to be one of the best films of the year . . . even the richest of the ham goes smoothly down, savoured with humour and satire.' *(Graham Greene)*

'This grand Victorian adventure yarn is the zenith of the 1930's imperial adventure cycle. The cast is perfect, the colour glows, the battle scenes are stunning.' *(Philip French, NFT Bulletin, 1984)*

FOUR HORSEMEN OF THE APOCALYPSE, THE

CT: 5 AV: 7.00

1921 US 150 BW WAR/DRAMA/ROMANCE/EPIC/SILENT

D Rex Ingram ☆
W June Mathis from Vicente Blasco Ibañez's novel

Rudolph Valentino ☆ Alice Terry Nigel de Brulier Alan Hale Jean Hersholt Wallace Beery

An Argentinian young man (Rudolph Valentino) fights for France during World War I.

A silent classic, now very dated, and so long that it's virtually unwatchable. It's less of a war film than a love story, played out against a background of war; it's hardly the ringing anti-war statement which some claim it to be. In its opening section, the film gives the best hint to modern audiences of why Valentino became a star. Remade (badly) in 1961.

PRO:

'An exceptionally well done adaptation of a novel, and an extraordinary motion picture work to boot.' *(New York Times)*.

'A production of many nuances, shadings so artistic and skillful as to intrigue the mind of the spectator.' *(Variety)*

'A living breathing answer to those who still refuse to take motion pictures seriously. Its production lifts the silent drama to an artistic plane that it has never touched before.' *(Robert Sherwood, Life)*

'A blend of exotic settings, striking composition, dramatic lighting, and colourful if sordid atmosphere.' *(Lewis Jacobs)*

'Interesting and sufficiently away from the conventional story of the screen to give it a distinctive value of its own . . . Ingram is to be credited with a good job of directing. The cast is well-chosen, with an attractive boy, Rudolph Valentino.' *(Burns Mantle, Photoplay)*

'Extremely accomplished . . . It was exactly what the public wanted to see about the war.' *(Paul Rotha, The Film Till Now, 1949)*

'Not only was it marvellously effective in its appeal to the eye, but the logical and dramatic unfolding of the basic story was a striking revelation of the valuable service that an expert scenario-writer may render, now and then, to the professional writer of novels. For the many outrages that fictionists have received at the hands of the film-makers some atonement is offered at times, and *The Four Horsemen* as a photoplay proves that the pot may be unjust in calling the kettle black.' *(Edward S. Van Zile, The Marvel – The Movie, 1923)*

'Probably Rex Ingram's most distinguished work in the cinema, the pronounced pictorialism which later degenerated into a mere prettiness was here at its most controlled and concise.' *(Albert Johnson, Film Quarterly, 1959)*

MIXED:

'Achieves distinction through its sheer bulk . . . Skillful as the producer has been in evoking the old war mood in us, the picture as a whole shares most of the defects of [the] novel. It is . . . too prolix . . . Also it lacks an absorbing human story to pull it together.' *(Exceptional Photoplays)*

400 BLOWS, THE

CT: 8 AV: 9.40

(aka *Les Quatre Cents Coups*)

1958 France 94 BW DRAMA/FOREIGN

D François Truffaut ☆
W François Truffaut ☆ AAN

Jean-Pierre Léaud ☆ Claire Maurier Albert Rémy Guy Decombie Patrick Auffray Georges Flament

A neglected 12-year-old (Jean-Pierre Léaud) turns to crime.

François Truffaut's first, semi-autobiographical film was a touching rites-of-passage movie which, despite not having much in the way of plot, won him the Best Director prize at the 1959 Cannes Festival, and the New York Film Critics' award for best foreign film. It teems with a sense of Paris street-life and has an acute sense of the agonies of puberty; it made a child star out of Jean-Pierre Léaud; and it's one of the best films to have come out of the French New Wave.

MIXED:

'Seriously marred by a certain amateurishness in direction and by the sort of overinsistence (due to over-youthful anger, perhaps) on a pathetic theme which stiffens the audience's resistance . . . but the obvious flaws matter much less and the merits much more.' *(Guardian)*

PRO:

'One of the most beautiful films that I have ever seen.' *(Akira Kurosawa)*

'I have never been so moved at the cinema.' *(Jean Cocteau)*

'The first masterpiece of the New Wave.' *(Jonas Mekas, Film Culture)*

'*Les 400 Coups* is not a masterpiece. So much the better for François Truffaut! In the first place the word has been so debased that it finally becomes meaningless. Next, and above all, with a masterpiece in his pocket at twenty-seven Truffaut would really have something to worry about – he would have to spend his life trying to shed the burden. *Les 400 Coups* is better than a masterpiece. Together with *Hiroshima Mon Amour*, it is one of the two most original films made in France since the war.' *(Fereydoun Hoveyda, Cahiers du Cinéma)*

'The narrative is boldly fluent. Sympathetic, amused, reminded, occasionally puzzled, you are carried along with it. I don't think you will get away before the end.' *(Dilys Powell)*

'In every frame . . . Truffaut's force and intelligence are felt. He has a remarkable control of his medium and of himself.' *(Time)*

'Stylistically Truffaut has a marvellous command . . . The images effortlessly carry the narrative . . . The cinema achieves one of its pure moments of catharsis.' *(David Robinson, Financial Times)*

'Time will tell how much Truffaut has to say; in the meantime he, and this movie, bear watching.' *(Playboy)*

'A masterly and moving story . . . [The final freeze-frame is] a tremendous full-stop to a record of childhood unsurpassed by any other I have seen.' *(Alexander Walker, Evening Standard)*

'A perfect short story of puberty . . . all the rapt qualities of adventure and instinct.' *(New Statesman, 1961)*

'One of the greatest movies ever made.' *(Rex Reed)*

'The central artistic idea is freedom, both in human relationships and in film technique . . . *The 400 Blows* ranges from sentimental travelling shots of Antoine's tear-stained face, underscored by Jean Constantin's lush music; to improvised, candid comic scenes in the schoolroom, echoing Vigo's candid work with school children; to a *cinéma verité* interview between Antoine and a prying social worker; to agonizingly long, subjective travelling shots as Antoine escapes the reform school and races toward the sea.' *(Gerald Mast, A Short History of the Movies, 1971)*

'Although the film is relatively simple, Truffaut effectively uses cinematic technique to express the conflict between a spontaneous individual and a restrictive society . . . There is continual motion . . . enhanced by a flow of lyrical music, but also periodically interrupted by static scenes in confining places.' *(Marsha Kinder & Beverle Houston, Close-Up, A Critical Perspective on Film)*

FOUR WEDDINGS AND A FUNERAL

CT: 10 AV: 7 (est)

1994 GB 116 C COMEDY/ROMANCE

D Mike Newell ☆
W Richard Curtis ☆

Hugh Grant ☆ Andie MacDowell Kristin Scott Thomas ✔ Simon Callow ☆ James Fleet ☆ John Hannah ☆ Corin Redgrave Charlotte Coleman

A young Englishman (Hugh Grant) falls in love at first sight with an American (Andie MacDowell) and spends the rest of the movie trying to get together with her on a permanent basis.

The film may sound predictable, and ultimately it is. But it's brilliantly structured as a series of surprises, and incorporates more sub-plots even than two of the other great comedy scripts of recent years: *Parenthood* and *Singles*. It's written with both verbal and visual wit, and superbly acted by a virtually all-British cast (the casting director, Michelle Guish, deserved her own Oscar). I particularly liked James Fleet's engagingly cloddish Tom, the seventh-richest man in England – but in this film, even Simon Callow gives a good performance. It's directed by Mike Newell with the pace and eye for comic detail which he first showed on Jack Rosenthal's TV film, *Ready When You Are Mr McGill*.

Grant extracts every ounce of laughter and pathos from his role as a young man who's always late or making gaffes, and has a phobia about matrimony, concealed under an attractive veneer of self-mockery. American critics have likened him to Cary Grant, David Niven, even (a bit more disturbingly) a grown up Macaulay Culkin. His timing is a joy to behold; perhaps the best thing about him is that he manages to be cute without appearing narcissistic.

The film also made a transatlantic star out of Rowan Atkinson, who does a short revue sketch early on, as a nervous priest conducting his first marriage ceremony. Strictly speaking, it's irrelevant to the plot: it's the equivalent of those speciality acts which used to bring pre-war musical comedies to a halt, while someone juggled or did farmyard impressions. Its justification is that it's extremely funny, and adds to the gentle bonhomie of a film which all through takes a generous-spirited view of human failings.

The whole film has an underlying liberalism which stops it from being the conservative, middle-class escapism which some accused it of being. It recognizes – and condones – the fact that some people decide to have children together but not marry; it makes abundant use of four-letter expletives (to thankfully comic effect); and it suggests that a longstanding 'gay' couple may have just as rewarding and profound an emotional relationship as a heterosexual one. All these attitudes may be a far cry from Ealing days, but they do reflect the central Ealing ideal: that we should celebrate our differences, and then appreciate our underlying similarities.

In the same way, the inclusion of a deaf character – the hero's brother (David Bower) – is not just a 'politically correct' sop to a minority group, or a plea for easy sympathy. Sign-language leads to some of the film's funniest moments, and is brilliantly used to trigger the denouement.

Even the pathetic scenes are carried off with panache. So often in comedies these seem sentimental and included to give a spurious depth, or an opportunity for an actor to show off. But John Hannah's funeral oration is wonderfully written and performed, as is the scene where the delectable Kristin Scott Thomas reveals her unrequited passion for another character. The ease with which Curtis moves from comedy to pathos reminded me, I kid you not, of Chekhov.

The film is very commercial – there's a scene with the obligatory American guest-star Andie MacDowell (who is the one weak acting link) trying on wedding dresses which has a clear affinity with Julia Roberts's equivalent scene in *Pretty Woman* – and it has obviously been made with an eye to a transatlantic audience. Why else would the very first wedding invitation carry the gratuitous information that Somerset is in England? But frankly, who cares? *Four Weddings and a Funeral* is one of the great romantic comedies of all time, and is the funniest British comedy since *The Lavender Hill Mob*.

ANTI:

'A smarmy little fable about the magic of true love . . . It would help if there were a single spark of chemistry between the two leads. Andie MacDowell looks ravishing enough for anyone to be smitten at first sight, but as a light comedienne she is disastrous. Her idea of sprightly repartee is to pronounce every syllable, and she can't quite hide the furrow of perplexity around her eyes – she doesn't seem to grasp her own witticisms . . . She is not helped, either, by having to pretend that she has fallen for someone who looks like a chipmunk.' *(Caren Myers, S & S)*

MIXED:

'Broadly directed by Mike Newell (*Enchanted April*), the comedy bubbles along on a pink-champagne froth of wonderfully silly moments. It features a collection of English twits worthy of Monty Python. Rowan Atkinson delivers a priceless cameo as a minister with stage fright. And out of the blue, an achingly sad funeral scene provides an oasis of dramatic relief. The movie is weakened by a slapdash script with a lot of poorly sketched female characters – as a romance, *Four Weddings* has the makeshift quality of a bad marriage. But there is more than enough laughter to make it worth enduring.' *(Brian D. Johnson, Maclean's)*

'It amuses because of Curtis's snare-drum dialogue; because of Newell's spirited directing, which exploits various British types – of persons and settings; and because of Grant. He juggles his comic troubles with polish and dispatch, but he is also an absolute virtuoso of embarrassment, and he is frequently embarrassed in this nuptial odyssey . . . There's one sheer disaster – Simon Callow as an engulfingly convivial partygoer. Callow behaves like a great actor showing us his frolicsome side. He isn't and doesn't.' *(Stanley Kauffmann)*

'A British romantic comedy with not much inside its pretty head but the spinning out of an ancient Hollywood riddle: how long will it take the two leading characters to realize that they are destined to be together? . . . The movie strains a bit to prove it's all a lark, but because the mood is cunningly sunny, and the cast is so relaxed in its empyrean of casual sex and restorative love, you can bet the sterling silverware that America will give a warm reception to [it].' *(Richard Schickel, Time)*

PRO:

'Like Kenneth Branagh's *Peter's Friends*, this film forms a community that eventually envelops us. Also like that film, it's about how a homosexual character becomes a focus for much of what is best among the other characters, who are mostly straight; the gay man in both films is a center of good feeling, and helps create a sense of family. By the end of the movie, you find yourself reacting to the weddings, and the funeral, almost as you do at real events involving people you didn't know very well, but liked, and wanted to know better.' *(Roger Ebert)*

'Truly beguiling.' *(Variety)*

'Elegant, festive and very, very funny.' *(New York Times)*

'Laughter. Tears. Sex. Tragedy. Farce. You just can't weave all those elusive threads into one celluloid bundle – a rule to which this British comedy-drama proves a triumphantly untidy exception . . . sweet, reflective, shamelessly romantic.' *(Guy Flatley, Cosmopolitan)*

'Weddings have rarely been choreographed so appealingly as they are in this creation from writer Richard Curtis and director Mike Newell (who also presided over the nascent sensuality and lush scenery of *Enchanted April*). And Grant is the rare actor who can mix the characteristics of sex appeal and ambivalence in believable, rather than irritating, proportions. His slightly stuttering, desperately charming, deeply self-conscious, and therefore peculiarly English character puts his fear of the dangers (and pleasures) of commitment in keen relief. I'd prefer it if Charles' American object of desire weren't played by MacDowell in her usual soft-boned manner, which mistakes languor for acting (that the fourth wedding stumbles is not unconnected to her lack of magnetism). But as an object of desire she'll do, if only to motor *Four Weddings* to the inevitable conclusion for which any winter-ravaged soul might devoutly wish.' *(Lisa Schwarzbaum, Entertainment Weekly)*

'It will almost certainly make you shed tears of sympathy as well as laughter – and it ends with a record number of happy endings: I counted seven. If anyone inquires if you wish to see it, the only sensible response is "I do".' *(Christopher Tookey, Daily Mail)*

THE *FRANKENSTEIN* SERIES

FRANKENSTEIN CT: 8 AV: 8.75

1931 US 71 BW HORROR/SF

D James Whale ☆
W John L. Balderston Garrett Fort Francis Edward Faragoh based on Mary Shelley's novel

Colin Clive ● Mae Clarke John Boles
Boris Karloff ☆ Edward Van Sloan Dwight Frye

Scientist (Colin Clive) creates life (Boris Karloff) but accidentally gives it a murderer's brain.

Critics are divided as to whether this, or its more lighthearted sequel *The Bride of Frankenstein*, is the best *Frankenstein* movie. I favour this one, even though it suffers from the director's lack of interest in his romantic leads and his willingness to let Colin Clive ham abominably. This is, after all, the movie which was the blueprint for all future versions, and it is all the more eerily effective for being played straight. Karloff's sensitive performance, surely one of the greatest on celluloid, lingers in the mind – as does the magical look of the whole film. The Gothic atmosphere is beautifully established, while the sets, props and make-up are first-rate.

The original reviews were mixed and betrayed a patronizing attitude towards horror films and their likely audience. Certainly, they showed little appreciation that the film would become one of the most famous and influential of all time.

MIXED:

'Anything but a classic in filmcraft. As a rather crudely constructed blood curdler which will thrill those who find their pleasure in things morbid and humble.' *(Bioscope)*

'Of its type, it is very good – if you like thrillers, pure and simple, such as are solely designed to make your flesh creep. Personally, I do not, and even in the well designed and produced goose-flesh sequences of this film I feel that over-emphasis and over-elaboration simply lead to an artificiality which renders them nugatory . . . The legend has been very much contorted, but Boris Karloff certainly gives us an amazing performance as the monster.' *(Picturegoer)*

'*Frankenstein* is the sensation of the day. It is not . . . the best film in London; but it will make more money than any of them . . . In [the film] we advance majestically from the sevenpenny novelette to the penny blood. It sets out to scare you to death and it succeeds. This may or may not be an important thing to do . . . There is no use my saying that its direction is comical, its general level of acting atrocious, its romantic relief a last word in infantile imagining: when Frankenstein's monster is upon you, tearing and rending, and growling and whining, the yokel in you will rise and acclaim and tell me to take my criticism to the devil . . . This only proves . . . only the idea matters . . . What does it matter if it is presented idiotically, if the imagination that went to its making is the imagination of a rabbit: it is sensational enough in itself to emerge from any directorial murdering . . . When the bats fly low and night's in the sky, Universal Studios are at their best.' *(John Grierson, Everyman)*

'The only obvious ways in which the film dates are in quality of photography and in (relative) brevity for the subject matter . . . A subject of this kind could only gain any real value by being treated in psychological detail and the film's comparative shortness contributes to making it superficial.' *(MFB, 1938)*

'A stark, gloomy film, unrelieved by comedy or music . . . Never was Karloff more impressive . . . Pierce's conception and realization in makeup remain unsurpassed . . . There is little gruesomeness . . . Its terror is cold, chilling the marrow but never arousing malaise . . . Whale's direction, perfectly assured in the more fantastic scenes, falters in the brief romantic interludes, which were obviously of little interest to him.' *(Carlos Clarens, An Illustrated History of the Horror Film, 1967)*

PRO:

'One of the finest picture jobs I ever saw on the screen . . . As a horrifier it is a tremendous success, but I doubt very much if it will be equally successful as a financial venture . . . Boris Karloff is horrible in his role as the Monster, which merely is another way of saying that he is perfect – so perfect that I hope I never again will see anything like him . . . From a purely cinematic standpoint Whale and Fort did a brilliant piece of work. If your tastes run to the morbid you will enjoy *Frankenstein*. If, however, you have a healthy outloook on life you had better stay away from it.' *(Hollywood Spectator)*

'Frankenstein looks like a Dracula plus, touching a new peak in horror plays and handled in production with supreme craftsmanship.' *(Variety)*

'It is naturally a morbid, gruesome affair, but it is something to keep the spectator awake, for during its most spine-chilling periods it exacts attention . . . No matter what one may say about the melodramatic ideas here, there is no denying that it is far and away the most effective thing of its kind. Beside it *Dracula* is tame.' *(New York Times)*

'*Frankenstein* is a thriller, make no mistake. Women come out trembling, men exhausted.' *(Motion Picture Herald)*

'Probably the most famous of all horror films, and one of the best.' *(Pauline Kael, 70s)*

'The film's great imaginative coup is to show the monster "growing up" in all too human terms. First he is the innocent baby, reaching up to grasp the sunlight that filters through the skylight. Then the joyous child, playing at throwing flowers with a little girl whom he delightedly imagines to be another flower. And finally, as he finds himself progressively misjudged by the society that created him, the savage killer as whom he has been typecast.' *(Tom Milne, Time Out)*

'What's most interesting is that Whale seems to go along with Shelley's controversial belief that Frankenstein's sin is not that he defies God by creating life but that once he becomes a creator he both emulates God and competes with him for sovereignty . . . Frankenstein's real crimes are against society. He has withdrawn into self-imposed isolation (itself a perversion) and become an elitist, while the Monster seeks love, companionship, and camaraderie with the masses. Even worse is how Frankenstein neglects his fatherly obligations and abandons his "son", leaving the creature to make its way in a world repulsed by grotesquery. Consequently, the Monster-child ends up murdering everyone who rejects him.' *(Danny Peary)*

BRIDE OF FRANKENSTEIN, THE

CT: 7 AV: 9.07

1935 US 75/80/85/90 BW HORROR/COMEDY/SF
D James Whale ☆
W John L. Balderstone William Hurlbut ☆

Boris Karloff ☆ Colin Clive Ernest Thesiger ☆ Valerie Hobson E.E. Clive ☆ Dwight Frye O.P. Heggie Una O'Connor Elsa Lanchester ☆ Gavin Gordon Douglas Walton

Dr Pretorius (Ernest Thesiger) blackmails Baron von Frankenstein (Colin Clive) into resuscitating his monster (Boris Karloff) and making him a bride (Elsa Lanchester).

Much admired on release for its production values, monster and sense of humour, this is now generally considered the finest of all the *Frankenstein* movies. Boris Karloff is moving as the monster, and James Whale directs this sequel to his 1930 original with panache. Although some of the sequences have been parodied so often (most effectively by Mel Brooks in *Young Frankenstein* (1975)) that they have lost a lot of their impact, most of the humour is intentional. The big problem is that – because the monster is so sympathetic, and so much of it is camp – the film isn't nearly as horrific or frightening as it seemed in the 1930s.

ANTI:

'An unconvincing sequel . . . It gives a strong cast little scope for real acting, being, in the main a rehash of the salient points of the original. There are several moments of sheer horror, but also quite a number of banal ones and it can only be wholeheartedly recommended to those who put thrills and chills before plausibility.' *(John Gammie, Film Weekly)*

MIXED:

'Has to contend with all the difficulties which inevitably confront sequels and it is by no means completely successful in overcoming them. Though there are moments of real horror there are others when the thrills fail to thrill. The Monster is less terrifying, partly because the dawning in him of human qualities arouses sympathy for him . . . The technical side . . . is extraordinarily good and there are some extremely effective episodes, while the eerie and fantastic nature of the theme is emphasized by the excellence of the acting.' *(MFB)*

'Startlingly good in its primitive way . . . the screen's sophisticated masterpiece of black comedy.' *(Halliwell)*

'What distinguishes the film is less its horror content, which is admittedly low, than the macabre humour and sense of parody.' *(Geoff Andrew, Time Out)*

'While this is a major genre film, it is by no means the classic it is claimed to be. By infusing the movie with his own quirky sense of humour, Whale undermines the horror to its detriment. The failure is particularly noticeable in the character of Dr Pretorious, who takes the central role from Colin Clive as Frankenstein, and appears often to be in an entirely different picture . . . The monster is too sympathetic and Karloff himself is quoted as saying that it was a mistake to let it speak: "If the Monster has any impact or charm, it was because he was inarticulate".' *(Alan Frank)*

PRO:

'John Mescall at the camera managed to create a large number of unusual camera angles and process shots which help the film tremendously. It is this excellent camerawork coupled with an eerie but lingering musical score by Franz Waxman (one of Hitler's gifts to Hollywood) that gives a great deal of the film its real horror.' *(Variety)*

'Karloff's make-up should not be permitted to pass from the screen. The Monster should become an institution, like Charlie Chan.' *(New York Times)*

'A great deal of art has gone into it, but it is the kind of art that gives the healthy feeling of men with their sleeves rolled up and working, worrying only about how to put the thing over in the best manner of the medium – no time for nonsense and attitudes and long hair.' *(Otis Ferguson)*

'An extraordinary film, with sharp humour, macabre extravagance, and a narrative that proceeds at a fast, efficient pace.' *(Gavin Lambert, 1948)*

'This caricature by very knowing people is a macabre comedy classic.' *(Pauline Kael)*

'Indescribably witty, stylish and grotesque; nothing like it has ever been made since.' *(Scheuer)*

'Eye-filling sequel to *Frankenstein* is even better, with rich vein of dry wit running through the chills . . . Pastoral interlude with blind hermit and final, riotous creation scene are highlights of this truly classic movie.' *(Maltin)*

'Pretorius . . . is a wonderful cartoon condensation of all mad scientists, past and present. The most fabulous element of all is the moment of the creation of the She-Monster, a riotous display of unusual camera angles, fast editing, and electrical effects that reaches its climax with the unveiling of the Bride, scored by Waxman with a cacophony of bells . . . Lanchester . . . is a truly fantastic apparition. With Karloff, she manages to communicate . . . a delicate suggestion of both the wedding bed and the grave.' *(Carlos Clarens, An Illustrated History of the Horror Film, 1967)*

A brilliant parody, full of wit and dry humor and containing also a number of genuinely horrific scenes.' *(R.A.E. Pickard, Dictionary of 1000 Best Films, 1971)*

SON OF FRANKENSTEIN CT: 6 AV: 6.70

1939 US 95 BW HORROR/SF

D Rowland V. Lee
W Willis Cooper

Basil Rathbone ☆ Boris Karloff ☆ Bela Lugosi ☆ Lionel Atwill ☆ Josephine Hutchinson ● Donnie Dunagan Emma Dunn ●

Frankenstein's son (Basil Rathbone) resurrects father's monster (Boris Karloff) with help from a broken-necked shepherd (Bela Lugosi).

Handsomely mounted horror, played fairly straight: no longer very scary, but with splendidly Gothic atmosphere and sets, and an eerie Frank Skinner score. The leading actors are excellent, especially Basil Rathbone who is a great improvement on Colin Clive. But the two female performances are weak, and Karloff – in his third and final appearance as the monster – hasn't enough to do. The biggest problem is that the narrative is not as strong as its two immediate predecessors, *Frankenstein* and *The Bride of Frankenstein.*

PRO:

'No use beating around the razzberry bush: if Universal's *Son of Frankenstein* . . . isn't the silliest picture ever make, it's a sequel to the silliest picture ever made, which is even sillier. But its silliness is deliberate – a very shrewd silliness, perpetrated by a good director in the best traditions of cinematic horror, so that even when you laugh at its nonsense you may be struck with the notion that perhaps that's as good a way of enjoying oneself at a movie as any.' *(New York Times)*

'The slickness of production gives a kind of refinement to the horrific moments and a subtlety to the suspense.' *(Film Weekly)*

'The set, shot in a style reminiscent of the German Expressionist classics, is superb – a labyrynthine castle of gloomy shadows.' *(Geoff Andrew, Time Out)*

ANTI:

'Karloff's monster becomes a sort of zombie and only reveals a little of the impulse towards humanity that flickered through *Frankenstein* (1931) and flared up in *The Bride of Frankenstein* (1935) in two brief moments: once,unforgettably, when he discovers Lugosi's body and throws back his head to howl in grief; and once, more sentimentally, when Frankenstein's small son disarms him by showing no fear. The unmistakable shift is from monster as victim to monster as demon.' *(Phil Hardy, Horror: The Aurum Film Encyclopaedia)*

'The least stirring of the first three *Frankenstein* series films; relying too much on visual aesthetics rather than gripping and graphic elements.' *(Parish & Pitts, The Great Science Fiction Pictures)*

GHOST OF FRANKENSTEIN, THE

CT: 5 AV: 4.86

1941 US 68 BW HORROR/SF

D Erle C. Kenton ✔
W Scott Darling ● from Eric Taylor's story

Cedric Hardwicke ☆ Ralph Bellamy Lionel Atwill ☆ Bela Lugosi ☆ Evelyn Ankers Lon Chaney Jr ● Dwight Frye

Frankenstein's second son (Cedric Hardwicke) resurrects Dad's Monster (Lon Chaney Jr).

Lon Chaney Jr is not as subtle or pathetic as Boris Karloff was in the role of the Monster, but Bela Lugosi (reprising his role of Ygor from *Son of Frankenstein*), Lionel Atwill and Cedric Hardwicke (as bickering scientists) offer compensations. Direction and production values are fine: the problem is the stale and predictable script.

ANTI:

'The rot set in with this flatly-paced potboiler, which had none of the literary mood or cinematic interest of *Bride* or *Son* which preceded it, and suffered from from a particularly idiotic script.' *(Halliwell)*

MIXED:

'No masterpiece but better than its reputation.' *(Tom Milne, Time Out)*

PRO:

'Sadly underrated . . . the best of the Universal series after *Bride of Frankenstein*. Director Erle C. Kenton . . . creates some really chilling moments, especially when Ygor is reborn within the Creature.' *(Quinlan)*

'Luckily Bela Lugosi is back as Ygor, the supporting cast is good, the music score is first-rate, and there are enough dynamic set-pieces to liven up the story.' *(Martin & Porter)*

FRANKENSTEIN MEETS THE WOLFMAN

CT: 5 AV: 5.67

1943 US 72 BW HORROR/SF

D Roy William Neill ☆
W Curt Siodmak

Lon Chaney Jr Ilona Massey Patric Knowles Lionel Atwill Bela Lugosi Maria Ouspenskaya

Graverobbers accidentally revive a werewolf (Lon Chaney Jr), who goes on to resurrect a weakened Monster (Bela Lugosi).

A sequel not only to *The Ghost of Frankenstein* but also to *The Wolfman* (1941), this offered World War II audiences two monsters for the price of one. The film is not helped by the fact that Lugosi was ill, and several of his scenes (even in close-up) are obviously played by a double (stuntman Eddie Parker). But Lon Chaney Jr made a big impression again as Lawrence Talbot, a man wishing to be put out of his misery at being a werewolf. The film benefits from a fast pace and atmospheric direction which almost conceal the gaping holes in the plot.

PRO:

'The producers have spent time and money on the production and have gone to considerable trouble to give it the proper atmospheric touches that seem to delight the horrror addicts.' *(Kate Cameron, New York Daily News)*

'A creepy affair in grand style.' *(Variety)*

'Slick, atmospheric, fast-paced fun.' *(Maltin)*

MIXED:

'Competently directed (especially the beginning) but basically an unimaginative rehash, the film is definitively sunk by Lugosi's performance.' *(Phil Hardy, Horror: The Aurum Film Encyclopaedia)*

'Fast-paced and quite atmospheric in its own tacky way, but definitely sabotaged by Lugosi as the monster; at last getting to play the role he missed out on in 1931, he gives a performance of excruciatingly embarrassing inadequacy.' *(Tom Milne, Time Out)*

HOUSE OF FRANKENSTEIN

CT: 5 AV: 5.25

(aka *Doom of Dracula; Chamber of Horrors*)

1944 US 71 BW HORROR/SF

D Erle C. Kenton
W Edward T. Lowe Curt Siodmak

Boris Karloff ☆ Lon Chaney Jr John Carradine ☆ J. Carrol Naish George Zucco ✔ Anne Gwynne Peter Coe Lionel Atwill ✔ Elena Verdugo Sig Rumann ✔

A doctor (Boris Karloff) and a hunchback (J. Carrol Naish) try to emulate Frankenstein.

In order to revive audiences' flagging interest in the series, Universal threw in a mad scientist, a hunchback and no few than three monsters. The result is a mess, but an entertaining one. Karloff turns in one of his best performances.

'Chiller-diller meller.' *(Variety)*

'Absurdly indigestible but surprisingly watchable, thanks to classy camerawork from George Robinson, with Carradine making – all too briefly – a superb Dracula.' *(Tom Milne, Time Out)*

'So much is going on that nothing is developed and the whole film degenerates into an absurd montage of sketches.' *(Phil Hardy, Horror: The Aurum Film Encyclopaedia)*

HOUSE OF DRACULA

CT: 4 AV: 4.00

1945 US 67 BW HORROR/SF

D Erle C. Kenton
W Edward T. Lowe from George Bricker and Dwight V. Babcock's story

Lon Chaney Jr John Carradine Martha O'Driscoll Lionel Atwill Jane Adams Onslow Stevens Ludwig Stossel Glenn Strange Skelton Knaggs Joseph E. Bernard

A kindly doctor (Onslow Stevens) tries to cure Dracula (John Carradine), a werewolf (Lon Chaney Jr) and his pretty but hunchbacked assistant (Jane Adams) of their afflictions.

This sequel has a less confused script than the previous *House of Frankenstein* but shows unmistakable signs of its low budget, notably the fact that the climax has been lifted complete from *Ghost of Frankenstein* (1942). Unsurprisingly, this was the final film in Universal's *Frankenstein* series, although Lon Chaney Jr reprised his *Wolfman* role in *Abbott and Costello Meet Frankenstein* (1948).

'Upholds traditions of company's past offerings in this field . . . picture as a whole shall please horror addicts.' *(Variety)*

'Agreeably looney fun if you don't expect too much.' *(Tom Milne, Time Out)*

'Mind-boggling . . . has to be seen to be believed.' *(Halliwell)*

ABBOTT AND COSTELLO MEET FRANKENSTEIN CT: 6 AV: 7.27

(aka *Meet the Ghosts; Abbott and Costello Meet the Ghosts*)

1948 US 83/92 BW COMEDY/HORROR/SF

D Charles T. Barton
W Robert Lees Frederic I. Rinaldo John Grant ☆

Bud Abbott ☆ Lou Costello ☆ Lon Chaney Jr ☆ Bela Lugosi ☆ Glenn Strange Lenore Aubert Jane Randolph Frank Ferguson Charles Bradstreet Howard Negley

Porters (Bud Abbott and Lou Costello) deliver crates to a wax museum, unaware that they contain Count Dracula (Bela Lugosi) and Frankenstein's monster (Glenn Strange).

Amusing horror spoof which adroitly mixes scares and laughs. It's the funniest of Abbott and Costello's comedies (which is not saying much). Lon Chaney Jr plays a friendly werewolf, Bela Lugosi a less friendly Dr Frankenstein, and Vincent Price's voice puts in a non-corporeal appearance at the end, as the Invisible Man.

'Plenty of thrills and chills if you are unsophisticated enough to enjoy them.' *(Lionel Collier, Picturegoer)*

'It's amazing how few contemporary critics appreciated Abbott and Costello. They were generally dismissed with a sneer . . . *Meet Frankenstein* restored Abbott and Costello's flagging careers, putting them right back with the top ten money-making stars.' *(John Howard Reid)*

'One of the film's chief assets is that the horror sequences are played completely straight, leaving the comedy to the comedians . . . *Meet Frankenstein* is the best satire on horror movies ever made.' *(Jim Mulholland, The Abbott and Costello Book, 1975)*

FRANKIE AND JOHNNY CT: 8 AV: 6.23

1991 US 118 C DRAMA/ROMANCE

D Garry Marshall ✔
W Terrence McNally

Al Pacino ✔ Michelle Pfeiffer ✔ Hector Elizondo ✔ Nathan Lane Kate Nelligan ✔ Jane Morris Greg Lewis

A divorced ex-convict (Al Pacino) goes in romantic pursuit of a waitress who's disillusioned with men (Michelle Pfeiffer).

Pacino and Pfeiffer both excel in Garry Marshall's romantic comedy, which offers wise insights into urban loneliness, and is surprisingly realistic about how difficult it can be for two middle-aged, lonely people to sink their differences and lower their defences. Very underrated. A real tear-jerker.

ANTI:

'A lot of padding around a thin, predictable story. However, no padding hides the fact that we're dealing here with an updated version of Paddy Chayefsky – two Little People who are Lonely. Chayefsky at least could be true to his territory. McNally's handicap in writing about this world – he often writes about other sorts of people – is that he can't be true to it. He keeps intruding McNally smarts into a hash-house milieu. Frankie and Johnny exchange high-gloss repartee. And how many waitresses in diners refer to Marcel Marceau and Captain Ahab?' *(Stanley Kauffmann)*

'Johnny ought to be played by a younger and less well-known actor than Pacino. There is something a bit top-heavy about the star's presence and performance. Johnny, now with a prison past, broods a bit too much; when, with supposed lightheartedness but actual dogged determination, he showers Frankie with amorous declarations and advances, it begins to look more like harassment than whimsy and young love. The gaze with which Pacino fixes the object of his desire is perilously close to that with which a Rod Steiger or Anthony Hopkins mesmerizes his intended victim; and the growls with which Pacino registers passion are not that far removed from those with which the cavemen in *The Quest for Fire* approached their females from the rear.' *(John Simon)*

'Severely damaged by the decision to cast attractive stars.' *(Winnert)*

MIXED:

'A superior sitcom pilot, with lots of brisk banter and a wacky supporting cast.' *(Richard Corliss, Time)*

'Slick but diverting . . . the star wattage is blinding.

Pfeiffer and Pacino as two lonely working-class singles? You may have trouble suspending your disbelief, but this pairing of box office names does spark the kind of romantic chemistry of which hits are made.' *(Kevin Lally, Film Journal)*

PRO:

'A potentially grim tale of two lonely losers that turns out to be the best comedy of the year, the best love story, and maybe the best movie, period. Judging from the groans heard when it was announced that Michelle Pfeiffer would tackle the unsuitable role of the drab, depressed waitress played onstage by Kathy Bates, a miracle has taken place. For never has this Garbo of the nineties been more profoundly plausible.' *(Guy Flatley, Cosmopolitan)*

'Pfeiffer . . . delivers her most compelling performance to date. Eight years after *Scarface*, she is back on screen with Pacino, but on different terms. She is tougher; he is sweeter. Together, Pfeiffer and Pacino are dynamite – and both should get Oscar nominations . . . *Frankie and Johnny* is about facing middle-age with a lack of self-esteem and a fear of growing old alone. But the movie is much lighter in tone than in content. With a mushy sound track and a side order of slick images, Marshall serves it sunny-side up. He directs the movie as an easy-listening love story in which nothing really bad is going to happen. Ideal fare for a first date, a last date or a lonely Saturday night, it is the kind of movie that shows Hollywood at its best.' *(Brian D. Johnson, Maclean's)*

'A pleasing, old-fashioned starry romance from the director of *Pretty Woman*. The kiss in front of the truck is corny but inspired.' *(Rose)*

FRATERNALLY YOURS: *see* SONS OF THE DESERT.

FREAKS CT: 5 AV: 7.18

1932 US 64 BW HORROR

D Tod Browning ☆
W Willis Goldbeck Leon Gordon from Tod Robbins's story *Spurs*

Olga Baclanova Leila Hyams Wallace Ford Harry and Daisy Earles Johnny Eck (who had half a torso) Randion (known as the Living Torso) the Siamese twins Daisy and Violet Hilton Roscoe Ates Edward Brophy Henry Victor (the strong man)

Circus freaks avenge themselves on an able-bodied trapeze artist (Olga Baclanova) who marries a circus midget (Harry Earles) for his money, then poisons him.

MGM executive Irving Thalberg told director Tod Browning 'I want something that out-horrors *Frankenstein*.' When he got it, he didn't know what to do with it. This legendary exercise in bad taste, using cast-members with real and horrific disabilities, is a cinematic curiosity – so you would expect it to be riveting. Oddly, it's a bit dull. Its most dramatic scenes are let down by a banal script and amateurish acting; and the undoubted compassion which Browning shows is offset by his equally obvious voyeurism.

PRO:

'For pure sensationalism *Freaks* tops any picture yet produced.' *(Louella Parsons)*

'I still guarantee it to turn the strongest stomach and chill the strongest spine.' *(Daily Mail)*

'Does not merit that reputation for cruelty accorded it . . . What I found touching was the human beings' prodigious capacity for adaptation . . . [It] is a very honest film that can be seen with more pleasure than horror.' *(Jean Douchet, Cahiers du Cinéma, 1962)*

'An anti-horror movie. Browning's profound sympathy for his monsters nullifies any potential feelings of disgust . . . There is no hint of fetish or sexual obsession in the film . . . Love of money, not sexual perversion is the root of evil . . . *Freaks* is anti-shock . . . [The film] represents the best in man: his humility and tolerance . . . a challenge to the tradition that beauty is goodness and ugliness evil.' *(Paul Mayersberg, Movie Magazine)*

'Excellent at times and horrible, in the strict meaning of the word, at others. There are a few moments of comedy, but these are more than balanced by tragedy. Through long periods the story drags itself along and there is one of the most profound anti-climaxes of them all to form the ending. Yet . . . [it] is not a picture to be easily forgotten . . . [for] the underlying sense of horror, the love of the macabre.' *(New York Times)*

'Superb and unique . . . Although using real freaks, Browning's treatment is never voyeuristic or condescending, but sympathetic in such a way that after a few minutes we almost cease to perceive them as in any way abnormal.' *(Geoff Andrew, Time Out)*

MIXED:

'Either too horrible or not sufficiently so.' *(Variety)*

'It triumphs at once over your nausea; it also triumphs very quickly over your sense of what is curious.' *(Observer)*

'It would be foolish to suggest that the effect *Freaks* has on one is entirely the result of its qualities as a work of art.' *(The Times)*

ANTI:

'Freaks are people, individuals. The movie does not understand this and represents tham as a homogenized collection of semi-imbeciles.' *(Films in Review)*

'Better as a *cause célèbre* than as a horror film.

Usually regarded as his [Tod Browning's] masterpiece, it is more unpleasant than genuinely atmospheric.' *(Alan Frank)*

'Strident and silly.' *(Halliwell)*

'Though this circus story, directed by Tod Browning, is superficially sympathetic to the maimed and the mindless that it features, it uses images of physical deformity for their enormous potential of horror, and at the end, when the pinheads and the armless and legless creatures scurry about to revenge themselves on a normal woman (Olga Baclanova), the film becomes a true nightmare. If this film were a silent it might be harder to shake off, but the naive, sentimental talk helps us keep our distance.' *(Pauline Kael)*

FREEDOM FOR US CT: 5 AV: 8.75

(aka *À Nous la Liberté*)

1931 France 95/104 BW COMEDY/FOREIGN

D René Clair ☆
W René Clair

Raymond Cordy Henri Marchand Rolla France Paul Olivier

Factory owner (Raymond Cordy) escapes blackmail because of his criminal past, by taking up life as a vagabond.

Hailed as a masterpiece in its day, for the fluidity and elegance of Georges Prinal's camerawork, Lazare Meerson's imaginative sets and Georges Auric's impressive score (one of the earliest to be written specifically for the cinema). Nowadays, it does not raise as many laughs and is valued mainly as a precursor of Chaplin's *Modern Times* (1936), which did the same thing better. Clair's left-wing satire suffers from a script which becomes increasingly obvious and didactic.

'I was close to the extreme left . . . I wanted to attack the Machine, which led men into starvation instead of adding to their happiness.' *(René Clair)*

PRO:

'Easily understandable even to those who don't understand French.' *(Variety)*

'A comedy with a sardonic tilt at modern industrial conditions . . . A satire on mass production, full of biting comment and brilliantly manipulated slapstick.' *(News Chronicle, 1953)*

'Remains the rhythmic compact and altogether delightful work which we knew and applauded years ago.' *(Catholic Herald, 1953)*

'[Its] fresh charm . . . is not diminished at all by the slightness of its story and the sentimental inconsistencies of Clair's world . . . Emile and Louis are the cousins of Laurel and Hardy, innocents abroad, truly lovable, not for their malicious scheming, but because they are inclined to take nothing with undue seriousness and to treat most things they touch as toys.' *(John Pym, MFB, 1977)*

'A delightful romp.' *(Scheuer)*

'Classic satire on machinery and industrialisation . . . Arguably, Clair's masterpiece.' *(Maltin)*

MIXED:

'In terms of film flair, a revelation, though the plot has its tedious turns.' *(Halliwell)*

'He demonstrates that sound pictures can be as fluid as silents were, and the picture is rightly considered a classic. Yet it isn't as entertaining as his earlier (silent) *The Italian Straw Hat* or his later *Le Million*; the scenario (which he wrote) turns a little too carefree and ironic – the film grows dull.' *(Pauline Kael)*

ANTI:

'This director is somewhat of a god over here. Taking that into consideration, the reception by the press was mild. And René Clair himself admitted that the picture was not what he had hoped. There is no getting away from the fact that despite many charming moments and excellent directorial ideas, the whole picture is cold . . . and then, surprisingly enough, I found the film amateurish from a technical angle . . . Clair's directorial lapses went so far as to take the edge off a large proportion of his best humorous conceptions.' *(C. Hooper Trask, New York Times)*

FRENCH CONNECTION, THE AAW

CT: 8 AV: 8.21

1971 US 104 C THRILLER

D William Friedkin ☆ AAW
W Ernest Tidyman ☆ AAW from Robin Moore's book

Gene Hackman ☆ AAW Roy Scheider ☆ AAN Fernando Rey ☆ Tony Lo Bianco Frederic de Pasquale Bill Hickman Ann Rebbot Harold Gary Arlene Farber

Cop (Gene Hackman) tries to break a drugs ring.

Excellent thriller, convincingly acted (especially by Hackman), with an authentically sleazy New York atmosphere. Owen Roizman's colour cinematography, rightly Oscar-nominated, is wonderfully grim. Even the chase – the one under the elevated railway – manages to be original, though it's been so often imitated that inevitably it lacks the impact which it had on release. The sequel, wittily entitled *French Connection II*, was a disappointment.

ANTI:

'Typical of what might be called the New Brutality, a genre that serves up violence in loving detail: not just with a dab or two of ketchup, but also with a large amount of relish. Violent beatings and deaths are not only made extremely graphic, they are also treated with a nasty sense of fun. Thus a Marseilles murderer breaks off and munches on a bit of the baguette his dead victim has dropped, then tosses the rest jauntily back on the bloody corpse. And the blood-drenched victims of a fatal car crash are repeatedly scrutinized, almost anatomized, even though they are irrelevant to the main plot.' *(John Simon)*

'Lacks the stylish dramatics of *Dirty Harry* (1971), and the harshness with which Doyle and Russo treat even petty criminals makes it a far cry from a compassionate human-interest drama like *Serpico* (1973). Also, the scenes of violence in the *French Connection* have an unusually stark, brutal quality.' *(Robert Bookbinder, The Films of the Seventies, 1982)*

PRO:

'The actors who play the cops are so well cast that they seem to have grown up next door to the precinct house.' *(Time)*

'Gene Hackman, savage exasperated gestures and the mad ill-assembled features of a puppet carved from packing-case wood, gives a performance of devoted, inexorable vindictiveness.' *(Dilys Powell)*

'Popeye is insanely callous, a shrewd bully . . . The movie presents him as the most ruthlessly lawless of characters and yet – here is where the basic amorality comes through – shows that this is the kind of man it takes to get the job done. It's the vicious bastard who gets the results. Popeye . . . is a cop the way the movie Patton was a general.' *(Pauline Kael, The New Yorker)*

'He is a sardonic, hard-driving cop, a police character audiences had seldom seen before. Given to excesses he stops at nothing to get the job done . . . In fact, Popeye, pressured by a self-imposed mission in life, is almost an anti-hero. He is driven, obscene, brutal. And he is a racist. He cracks jokes about blacks who "pick their toes", has a kinky interest in girls who wear boots, and lives in a chaotic apartment. His redeeming feature is his incorruptibility.' *(David Zinman, 1986)*

FRENZY

CT: 7 AV: 6.92

1972 GB 116 C THRILLER

D Alfred Hitchcock
W Anthony Shaffer ✔ from Arthur LaBern's novel *Goodbye Piccadilly, Farewell Leicester Square*

Jon Finch Barry Foster ☆ Barbara Leigh-Hunt Anna Massey Alec McCowen ☆ Vivien Merchant ☆ Billie Whitelaw Clive Swift Bernard Cribbins Michael Bates

An innocent man (Jon Finch) is accused of sex murders in 70s London.

A favourite theme for Hitchcock, and a late return to form. Barry Foster is memorable as the real psychopath, but Alec McCowen and Vivien Merchant steal the picture as a cop and his wife, with the kind of 'normal' marriage which might drive anyone into a frenzy.

ANTI:

'Hitchcock's most stodgy piece since *Dial M For Murder* and possibly his least interesting film from any period.' *(William S. Pechter)*

PRO:

'A psychological thriller that ranks among his very best and shows the 72-year-old director in triumphant command of his unmatched artistic powers.' *(Newsweek)*

'Hitchcock seems to delight in making us aware of his craftsmanship – technique is flaunted the way it was in *Blowup, Persona*, and *2001*. And Hitchcock treats the audience as his intellectual equal; even when he's being coyly deceptive, he's really saying, "The others may not catch on to this, but I'm sure you will!"' *(Hollywood Reporter)*

'Were Hitchcock less evident throughout the film *Frenzy* would be as unbearable as it probably sounds when I report that the killer has to break the fingers of the corpse. Yet it is something more than just bearable because never for a minute does one feel the absence of the storyteller, raising his eyebrows in mock woe.' *(Vincent Canby, New York Times)*

'What is so curious about this effort is that while it freely, and offensively, takes advantage of recent permissiveness, it also portrays the English as stifled by sexual inhibition. An unmarried couple has to bribe the desk clerk at the Coburg Hotel, Bayswater, to hire a double room.' *(Listener)*

'It is . . . Hitchcock's far-from-simple art that makes the film work so splendidly . . . So sure is the style that there is never a frenetic moment, the enthrallment is accomplished with care to its totality. *Frenzy* is a complete entertainment for the viewer – and a total triumph for its creator.' *(Judith Crist, New York Magazine)*

'One might be tempted to see it as a surreptitious attack (under cover of a "thriller" plot structure) on the institution of marriage itself . . . The film's crucial thematic opposition is between characters who never come together until the very end of the film; Inspector Oxford (Alec McCowen) and Bob Rusk (Barry Foster): an opposition that can stand as part paradigm, part parody, of the Hitchcock view of life. The hilarious scenes of the Oxfords' domestic life, beautifully played by Alec McCowen and Vivien Merchant, are based on the notion that a "successful" marriage is built on the negative and repressive virtues of forbearance and endurance . . . Against this concept of "normality" is set, characteristically, the uncontrollable drive of a sexual psychopath. Oxford and Rusk are the two sides of the Hitchcock coin, archetypally confronting each other at the film's climax.' *(Robin Wood, Hitchcock's Films Revisited, 1989)*

FRESHMAN, THE

CT: 8 AV: 7.00

1925 US 75 BW COMEDY/SILENT

D Fred Newmeyer Sam Taylor
W Sam Taylor Ted Wilde Tim Whelan John Grey

Harold Lloyd ☆ Jobyna Ralston Brooks Benedict

College student (Harold Lloyd) unexpectedly becomes a football star.

The most commercially successful comedy of the silent era, though not the best. There are enjoyable set-pieces, however, and a tremendous finale at a football game.

MIXED:

'A laugh getter, but that is all that may be said of it . . . In story . . . it's the poorest devised of its kind ever put on . . . The entire fault is that Lloyd as a freshman at college has been over-boobed, made the boobiest sort of a booby boob, and in that they overdid it.' *(Variety)*

'Possibly Mr Lloyd was too well aware of the reliability of his material. He did not seem to strive as usual for novelty. It would be madness to say that *The Freshman* is not funny. Mr Lloyd could be funny playing an undisturbed mummy. Simply this: *The Freshman* is not so funny as earlier of the comedian's adventures.' *(Time)*

'It is a story which deserved more gentle handling, but there's no gainsaying that the buffoonery gained its end in its popular appeal.' *(New York Times)*

'A football game at the conclusion . . . atones for many dreary moments at the start.' *(Robert E. Sherwood, Life)*

PRO:

'Tops Lloyd's previous best for real laughs and pathos. Sets a new standard for well placed gags beautifully timed to collect 100% guffaws.' *(Film Daily)*

'It's the finest picture that Harold Lloyd has made because . . . it is more than just a series of gags. The gags are there, of course, and some of them are the funniest that Lloyd has ever presented; but there is a spirit back of the picture that makes it something greater than just an extraordinarily funny comedy . . . Lloyd can . . . make even a censor laugh. And what greater praise can there be than that?' *(Photoplay)*

FRESHMAN, THE

CT: 5 AV: 7.15

1990 US 102 C COMEDY

D Andrew Bergman
W Andrew Bergman

Marlon Brando ✗ Matthew Broderick Bruno Kirby Penelope Ann Miller Frank Whaley Jon Polito Paul Benedict B.D. Wong Maximilian Schell Richard Gant Pamela Payton-Wright Kenneth Welsh

Innocent film student (Matthew Broderick) gets caught up with the Mafia.

Writer-director Andrew Bergman's screenplay has several funny ideas (notably an obnoxious gourmet dining club which feeds off endangered species), but he doesn't string them together in a way which makes them credible: the denouement is, to put it politely, preposterous. The big let-down (though many critics don't agree with me) is Marlon Brando, who parodies himself as the Godfather but forgets that comedy should be played at a pace above that expected in a funeral parlour. Whenever Brando's whale-like presence fills the screen, the film grinds to a halt and smacks not of freshness, but of stale, starry self-satisfaction.

'Brando's sublime comedy performance elevates *The Freshman* from screwball comedy to a quirky niche in film history – among films that comment on cult movies.' *(Variety)*

'An eccentric and charming farce that includes a few really zany, hilarious moments. At least one is priceless: the sight of the portly, stately star waltzing on ice skates . . . No true Brando fan would miss this . . . Would [the film] be delightful without Brando? It's doubtful.' *(Georgia Brown, Village Voice)*

'Although the film itself is a bit too uneven to be first rate, it does provide the notoriously bumptious Brando with the opportunity to have some wicked fun with his own legend . . . . Bergman has fashioned a script of admirable pace and wit. The film contains many fine comic set pieces, not least of which involves an attempt to place a seat belt on a giant lizard.' *(Stephen Amidon, Financial Times)*

'There are two rare beasts on show . . . the Komodo dragon . . . and Marlon Brando . . . For some time now Brando has been too eccentric a talent to carry a film, but still being well able to knock one off-balance with a rampaging cameo . . . But audiences will prefer to remember him in earlier days, when he was perhaps no more comfortable, but put his dissatisfaction to better use.' *(Adam Mars-Jones, Independent)*

FRIDAY THE 13TH

CT: 6 AV: 3.80

1980 US 95 C HORROR

D Sean S. Cunningham
W Victor Miller

Betsy Palmer Adrienne King Jeannine Taylor Robbi Morgan Kevin Bacon Harry Crosby

Mass-killer terrorizes six teenage counsellors, about to open a summer camp.

Formulaic horror flick whose goriness, lack of

concern for its characters, and almost total unoriginality predictably incurred the wrath of critics. However, the director's skilful recycling of his betters' ideas (especially John Carpenter's and Brian De Palma's) – not to mention generous lashings of teenage sex – made it a massive hit for Paramount, and spawned numerous, much more wearisome sequels.

ANTI:

'Low budget in the worst sense – with no apparent talent or intelligence to offset its technical inadequacies . . . Cunningham telegraphs the six murders too far ahead to keep anyone in even vague suspense, and without building a modicum of tension in between.' *(Variety)*

'A tame, poorly plotted serving of schlock, less horrific for its ketchup-smeared murders than for the bare-faced fashion in which it tries and fails to rip off Carpenter's *Halloween* in matters of style and construction.' *(Tim Pulleine, Time Out)*

'By the end, the sight of a girl with an axe sticking out of her forehead hardly generates a ripple of concern. Even in spine-chillers, there is a law of diminishing returns.' *(Margaret Hinxman, Daily Mail)*

MIXED:

'The film is skillfully enough made by director Sean Cunningham that you'll be scared out of your wits waiting for each counselor to meet his or her ghastly end. The only thing to question is your own reason for sitting through entertainment with gratuitous sex and violence and teenagers who are portrayed as oversexed, insensitive clowns ideal for slaughter.' *(Danny Peary)*

PRO:

'Horribly well told, with all the ingredients of a classic spine-chiller.' *(Daily Star)*

'A taut, modest and extremely well-made film about a repulsive but fascinating business.' *(Felix Barker, Evening News)*

'Though I don't like violence, it had some of the most creative killings ever on screen.' *(Michael Eisner, then a Paramount executive, later at Disney)*

FRIED GREEN TOMATOES AT THE WHISTLE CAFÉ CT: 8 AV: 6.69

1992 US 130 C DRAMA

D Jon Avnet
W Fannie Flagg Carol Sobieski ☆ AAN from Flagg's novel

Kathy Bates Jessica Tandy ☆ AAN
Mary Stuart Masterson Mary Louise Parker
Nick Searcy Gailard Sartain Stan Shaw
Cicely Tyson Gary Basaraba Chris O'Donnell
Richard Riehle Grace Zabriskie

In the Deep South, an old woman (Jessica Tandy) befriends a lumpish housewife (Kathy Bates) and tells her how Idgie (Mary Stuart Masterson) saved Ruth (Mary Louise Parker) from a wife-beating husband, set up a home and business with her, and was put on trial for the husband's murder. The story, which is plainly autobiographical, changes Bates's life.

Excellent performances, an unpredictable script and a spirit of warm-heartedness compensate for lapses into soapiness. The view of women is grossly sentimental: almost every female on display is a long-suffering, secular saint. The men are as stereotypical a bunch as the women are in most movies, and a strong argument against heterosexuality. The good news is that the screenplay, adapted from Fannie Flagg's novel by Flagg herself and the director, is never less than entertaining and full of surprises. Fortunately, too, the more grimly feminist, 'consciousness-raising' and Flagg-waving aspects of the piece are amusingly and lightly played. One of the most original and touching films of 1991, it is a less violent but secretly more radical *Thelma and Louise*.

ANTI:

'It's utterly incomprehensible that Evelyn would find Ninny's elaborate tales compelling, let alone inspirational. The script plods. Tandy looks as though she'd rather be elsewhere. The desire is understandable.' *(Joanne Kaufman, People Weekly)*

'The screenplay . . . trades heavily on routine Southernness – the wistfulness, the special friendliness, the special hates. No doubt these are precise – Flagg is from Alabama – but the milieu, overused, is wearing away into cliché (*Steel Magnolias, The Miss Firecracker Contest*, innumerable others). Scented angst is a Southern growth industry. The second trouble is the script's implicit cowardice. Every attribute of the story of these two young women implies a lesbian attachment. For that lesbian love, Masterson rescues Parker, and that love warms their subsequent lives. That love also helps to explain (not justify) the battering by Parker's husband, who presumably senses it. But the screenplay omits any mention of this implied component.' *(Stanley Kauffmann)*

PRO:

'Unabashedly sentimental, often humorous, occasionally outlandish but always fascinating. In other words, it's a lot like real life.' *(April P. Bernard, Video Magazine)*

'Absorbing and life-afirming.' *(Variety)*

FRIENDLY PERSUASION, THE

CT: 6 AV: 8.00

1956 US 139 C DRAMA

D William Wyler
W Michael Wilson ☆ AAN uncredited because of Hollywood blacklist from Jessamyn West's stories

Gary Cooper Dorothy McGuire Marjorie Main Anthony Perkins ☆ AAN Richard Eyer Phyllis Love Robert Middleton Mark Richman Walter Catlett Richard Hale

Quaker family wonders what do at outbreak of American Civil War.

Old-fashioned, sentimental movie with its heart in the right place and an effective mix of comedy and drama, suspense and action. Competent rather than exciting.

'Something quite rare in recent screen history: a family picture (in the sense that it is about a family and also that both in suitability and appeal it is for the family) which is absolutely first-rate in quality. William Wyler's sure-handed direction consistently illuminates it with a humor, a gentle charm and a feeling for fundamental values that are rare indeed.' *(Moira Walsh)*

'Quiet dignity and charm.' *(Robert Kennedy, Daily Worker)*

'A slow-moving drama laced with comedy . . . the story is sincerely told, and well acted – but goes on for far too long . . . Beautifully made, but rather dull.' *(Reg Whitely, Daily Mirror)*

FRIENDS OF EDDIE COYLE, THE

CT: 6 AV: 7.13

1973 US 102 C DRAMA

D Peter Yates ☆
W Paul Monash from George V. Higgins's novel

Robert Mitchum ☆ Peter Boyle Richard Jordan Steven Keats Alex Rocco Joe Santos Mitchell Ryal Helene Carroll

Gangster (Robert Mitchum) who has turned police informer is hunted by former associates.

Yates's film of George V. Higgins's excellent novel about Boston low-life is remarkable for a first-rate performance by Robert Mitchum. This is more of a character study than an an action film, but it's a good one.

'A very fine film about real people.' *(Variety)*

'Rather accomplished.' *(John Simon)*

'There is more than mere looks to Robert Mitchum's performance . . . Strong, realistic and totally absorbing.' *(Richard Schickel, Time)*

'An unobtrusive director, Yates has few peers in stage-managing the suspense that explodes into action . . . Among the current breed of thrillers, [it] is in a class apart.' *(Margaret Hinxman, Sunday Telegraph)*

FROM HERE TO ETERNITY AAW

CT: 8 AV: 9.13

1953 US 118 BW DRAMA/WAR/ROMANCE

D Fred Zinneman ☆ AAW
W Daniel Taradash AAW from James Jones's novel

Burt Lancaster ☆ AAN Deborah Kerr AAN Montgomery Clift ☆ AAN Frank Sinatra ☆ AAW Donna Reed AAW Ernest Borgnine Philip Ober Jack Warden Mickey Shaughnessy Harry Bellaver

Life in a Honolulu barracks in the lead-up to Pearl Harbor.

Superior military soap opera with excellent performances, especially from Frank Sinatra. Burt Lancaster and Deborah Kerr's seashore embrace, as waves and war crashed around them, is no longer very sultry or shocking; and Zinnemann's direction is workmanlike, rather than inspired, and uncharacteristically brutal. The script inevitably reduces the bawdiness of the original novel, but remains pretty hard-hitting about military life, and does a good job of reducing the story to such a manageable length. Burnett Guffey's photography and William Lyon's editing won Oscars; George Duning's music was nominated.

PRO:

'In all respects a magnificent motion picture and a masterful job of moviemaking: in production, direction, performance, photography, editing and effective dramatic condensation . . . a remarkable achievement . . . [which] bristles with vivid images and unforgettable moments . . . In all probability, the finest picture of the year.' *(Jesse Zunser, Cue)*

'A lot will hate this film, all the more for its honesty.' *(Stanley Baron, News Chronicle)*

'Zinnemann, directing finely, has drawn extraordinary performances from his players, Burt Lancaster, Montgomery Clift, Deborah Kerr, Donna Reed and Frank Sinatra, the last three appearing quite transformed and Sinatra in particular acting with great ease and fluency.' *(Dilys Powell)*

MIXED:

'How often have you been disappointed in a film because you heard too much about it before you saw it? . . . This raw slice of life in the American Army is certainly a heavyweight, spectacular film – grim, gripping and beautifully produced. But [its] appeal is almost exclusively American and not by any means is it the picture of the year for British audiences . . . An outsize he man's picture.' *(Reg Whitely, Daily Mirror)*

ANTI:

'A lugubrious and lengthy preamble to the Pearl Harbor debacle, and seemed to us to be most aptly named.' *(Screencomber, Shell Magazine)*

'The worst piece of propaganda for the American way of life in khaki that I have ever witnessed.' *(Roy Nunn, Daily Sketch)*

'I could fill a whole examination paper explaining why this high-class obsession with sex stuff doesn't stand up to logical analysis and why it is a bad thing just when too many Britons are sneering at Americans. It is a pity because the picture has been admirably made and acted.' *(Jympson Harmon, Evening News)*

'The book protests against torture, but in spite of the protest it is in essence a glorification of toughness for its own sake; the real hero is a generic one, the hard wearing, ferocious enlisted man. But there is a redeeming feature, a feeling of loyalty between soldiers: and this, as well as the more hideous cruelties, has vanished in the film. What is left is a story of a savagery alleviated but, oddly enough, more pointless; a good deal of love-making, both amateur and professional; and an indictment of American civilisation with which since it is made by Americans, it is not my business to quarrel but which seems to me unfairly and inopportunely to put a weapon in the hands of America's enemies.' *(Dilys Powell)*

'This is not a theme which one would expect Zinnemann to approach in the hopeful, sympathetic mood of his earlier films; but neither could one expect the negative shrug of indifference with which he seems to have surrendered to its hysteria.' *(Karel Reisz, S & S)*

FROM RUSSIA WITH LOVE: *see BOND* SERIES.

FRONT, THE

CT: 6 AV: 7.00

1976 US 95 C DRAMA/COMEDY

D Martin Ritt
W Walter Bernstein

Woody Allen Zero Mostel ✔ Herschel Bernardi Michael Murphy Andrea Marcovicci Lloyd Gough Remak Ramsay ✔

During the Communist witch-hunts of the 50s, a talentless bookmaker (Woody Allen) stands in for a blacklisted writer (Michael Murphy).

Martin Ritt's picture, written by a writer (Walter Bernstein) who was himself blacklisted, tries to mix genuine anguish about McCarthyism with a lightweight comedy plot. Allen's performance came in for much criticism; actually, he's quite impressive – but miscast. It's impossible for the audience to accept that his character is really a useless writer because we're so used to Woody Allen playing variations on himself. Much of *The Front* works – the fate of Zero Mostel's character is quite moving – but in the end it's superficial and oddly apolitical. There's something complacent about a film which simply takes for granted the moral superiority of American socialists over those who (equally sincerely) thought they were following a dead-end, dangerous ideology.

PRO:

'A light comedy forged out of dark and authentic pain.' *(Frank Rich, New York Post)*

'The quiet but acid laughter in *The Front* is a humane and cleansing exorcism of a frightening moment of our time.' *(Jack Kroll, Newsweeek)*

'Full of laughs, full of tears . . . It doesn't tell you how bigotry gets a hold on this country from time to time, but what it does, which more serious discussions never quite seem to do is make you sense how it would feel to be played with by jackals.' *(Robert Hatch, Nation)*

'It catches the anguish of America's creative community with wit and feeling.' *(Sunday Express)*

ANTI:

'The pacing is off, the sequences don't flow, and the film seems sterile, unpopulated and flat.' *(Pauline Kael)*

'Allen makes it difficult for the people around him to work because they are trying to act and he is doing his night-club stuff . . . Hearing Mostel speak these days is like having him fall on you, repeatedly.' *(Stanley Kauffmann)*

'All façade, posturing, clichés, and cutenesses; it might as well have been made by people whose information about McCarthyism came from a couple of magazine articles, and their knowledge of human beings from Earl Wilson's column . . . It is not comedy that the film exudes but a self-serving smugness: anyone who was blacklisted was *ipso facto* a hell of a guy, manifestly superior to anyone who did not make this honor roll . . . I am sorry to have to say the obvious, but however vicious blacklisting was, and however hell its consequences were, it did not, as the film implies, confer a badge of honor. To have been a Communist or Communist-sympathizer is not an automatic guarantee of moral and intellectual superiority, yet that is what the film would have us believe by making all characters at the center or right of center fools or scoundrels or both.' *(John Simon)*

'Thin and schematic . . . There is, in the end, something held back about *The Front*, some strange refusal to really dig into and turn over very rich historical and psychological soil. The result is a film unworthy of its excellent inentions.' *(Richard Shickel, Time)*

'Its suggestion that each individual can buck the brutality of political oppression by standing up against the bullies lies squarely in the great reactionary tradition: "a man's gotta do what a man's gotta do" replaces political analysis, and turns the film into an empty monument to the senility of American liberalism.' *(Scott Meek, Time Out)*

FRONT PAGE, THE AAN CT: 8 AV: 8.40

1931 US 101 BW COMEDY

D Milestone, Lewis ☆AAN
W Bartlett Cormack Ben Hecht (uncredited) Charles Lederer ☆ from Hecht and Charles MacArthur's play

Adolphe Menjou ☆ AAN Pat O'Brien
Edward Everett Horton ✔ Walter Catlett ✔
George E. Stone Mae Clarke Slim Summerville
Matt Moore Frank McHugh ✔

An editor (Adolphe Menjou) keeps his star reported (Pat O'Brien) working on the eve of his wedding, while his bride-to-be waits.

You really have to have experienced the static nature of most early talkies to realize quite how revolutionary this film is: it's a forerunner of modern cinematic practice in the way the action is kept moving, with snappy editing, and dialogue delivered at speed and on the run. It's all been done better since (notably in one of the remakes, *His Girl Friday*), but that should take nothing away from Milestone's mile stone.

ANTI:

'No journalist can view without disgust, bordering on nausea, the screen version of that gross libel on his profession, *The Front Page* . . . The thinly veiled foul language, the brutal handling of women, the coarse cynicism over scruples of honour, the callous mentality that plays poker and shouts bawdy jests within hearing of the prison death-cell, these, and a hundred other barbaran vulgarities are not characteristic of journalism in any country known to civilisation.' *(G A. Atkinson, Daily Telegraph)*

MIXED:

'Realism run riot. By those who can understand its crude American sang, *The Front Page* will be accepted as an arresting technical achievement . . . As a realistic study of political corruption in what is presumably Chicago, *The Front Page* is the most sensational of talking pictures. Whether it will be regarded by British filmgoers as entertainment is another matter.' *Daily Mail)*

'It is astonishing with what zest and care the makers of American films will pillory their own institutions. Judged by this film it would be impossible to find a more placid cynical and unscrupulous set of men than the newspaper staff of the Chicago Press or a darker revelation of the workings of American justice.' *(The Times)*

PRO:

'A very entertaining picture. Action is here all of the time, even with and during the dialog . . . Milestone's big idea seems to have been to keep it moving, and he does.' *(Variety)*

'The most rip-roaring movie that ever came out of Hollywood.' *(Pare Lorentz)*

'He has, and probably quite wisely, gone in for entertainment above everything – if he had handled his material with a solemn regard for its significance in American life the result would have been shocking and almost unbearable.' *(James Shelley Hamilton, NBR, 1931)*

'There has seldom been a darker or more powerful revelation of the workings of American justice and of the yellow press.' *(The Times, 1937)*

'A robust film if not a great one. *The Front Page* excelled most of the talkies of its day by sheer treatment. The speedy delivery of lines and business and the reemphasis upon cutting as a prime structural element – dialogue is clipped, curt, direct, faster than normal, as are the players gestures and movements – made the film a model of mobility for confused directors who did not know yet how to handle sound.' *(Lewis Jacobs, 1939)*

FUGITIVE, THE AAN CT: 6 AV: 7.50

1993 US 127 C THRILLER

D Davis, Andrew ☆
W David Twohy

Harrison Ford ☆, Tommy Lee Jones ☆ AAW
Jeroen Krabbe Joe Pantoliano

Richard Kimble, a brilliant surgeon (Harrison Ford) is found guilty of murder, but goes on the run and tries to prove his innocence.

The second-biggest hit of 1993, after *Jurassic Park*. Too much of *The Fugitive* imitates other films, and some of the situations hover perilously near cliché: I've lost count of the number of times I've seen a hero shake off pursuers in a street carnival. It would be more surprising if he'd got caught. But director Andrew Davis ensures that the action sequences are impressive – notably an exciting train crash, a chase through sewers and a 100-foot dive from the top of a dam. Ford plays Kimble as the kind of hero who can survive such a dive and a swim through a raging torrent without getting his hair wet. Though understandably anxious to clear his name, he still finds time to drop in at his old hospital, and correct the mis-diagnosis of a little black boy.

The plot is barely worth following. It's hard to understand why cop Tommy Lee Jones, who realizes Kimble's possible innocence from an early stage, doesn't tip off his fellow law-enforcers that Kimble is behaving as though genuinely trying to clear his name: this might have deterred the local constabulary from taking pot-shots at him whenever he appears. It's childishly obvious who the principal villain is going to be, and his motive for behaving the way he does once our hero has escaped is, to put it mildly, opaque. Still, the chase movie has proved a successful standby over the years, and this one is helped by two strong central performances. Cinematography, music, editing and sound were all Oscar-nominated.

ANTI:

'Most of this gargantuan screenplay by Jeb Stuart and David Twohy, derived from TV antecedents, is a patchwork of familiar stuff newly touched up, like old stock-company scenery repainted for a new show . . . The credits say that the director was Andrew Lewis; it could have been any one of twenty professionals.' *(Stanley Kauffmann)*

PRO:

'Let me commend the filmmakers on several things. First, they have come up with some unusual locations: the inside of a large drainage pipe, various parts of a vast city hospital, and Chicago's boisterous Saint Patrick's Day parade. Here and there, as usual with this genre, the film strains credibility, but less so than most. Next, although the plot is properly convoluted, even someone as unsleuthy as I was able, for once, to keep up with the proceedings. The pace, though taut, stops short of being relentless. Furthermore, the casting is expert: everyone looks right for his or her part.' *(John Simon)*

'Nothing in the cinematic past of stalwart but stolid Harrison Ford prepared me for the immensely affecting grief, rage, fear, and bravery with which he imbues the character of Dr. Richard Kimble . . . No less stunning is the magnetic menace of Tommy Lee Jones.' *(Guy Flatley, Cosmopolitan)*

'The movie further establishes Davis as the best of current action directors. After last year's *Under Siege*, it shows him able to deliver thrills and suspense on a mass audience level, while making the absurdities of the plot somehow feel convincing. An early sequence, involving the hero's escape from a bus-train crash, is one of the most sensational action scenes in recent film history. *(Roger Ebert)*

FULL METAL JACKET CT: 6 AV: 7.15

1987 GB 116 C WAR

D Kubrick, Stanley ☆
W Stanley Kubrick Michael Herr
Gustave Hasford AAN from Hasford's novel *The Short Timers*

Matthew Modine Adam Baldwin Vincent D'Onofrio R. Lee Ermey Dorian Harewood Arlis Howard Kevyn Major Howard Ed O'Ross

Soldiers are trained and then sent to Vietnam.

Broken-backed film, with the message not only that war is hell, but training for war is hell. Much of the first half had been seen before – notably in *The Boys in Company C* (1978), where the sadistic army officer was played by the same actor, Lee Ermey. The most common criticism of the film was that the two halves have little to do with each other, with a new location and a seemingly different set of characters brought in midway; but the film does have an integrity. It traces the odyssey of the central character Joker (Matthew Modine) towards self-knowledge. And both sections emphasize the same fundamental point – that in time of war, intelligence and sensitivity are of less use than brutality and the will to survive.

ANTI:

'He's a great film maker, but I don't like training films. I got the first part in five minutes and if it wasn't Kubrick, I'd have left after 10.' *(Sam Fuller, director)*

'Short on logic, continuity and closure. Its tone is unsentimental to a fault. Its characters remain nondescript or cartoonish . . . and they lack coherent motivation. . . . *Full Metal Jacket* makes few concessions to our conventional gratification. It shocks us, alienates us, angers us and (it must be said) occasionally bores us with shapeless scenes.' *(John Powers, LA Weekly)*

MIXED:

'Kubrick plainly wants it to be assumed that the story he tells of these particular Marines is in some way representative of the military experience; for him to conclude the first section of the film the way he does, however, is to suggest that his film presents an exaggerated, even a romantic, view of its subject. How many Marines, after all, kill their drill inspectors and then commit suicide? . . . Much of the latter section of the film, in fact, is unsatisfying. We're constantly waiting for a plot to develop, and waiting as well for some indication of how the second part of the movie is supposed to tie in with the first part. (We might as well be waiting for Godot.) . . . On the night I saw it, the audience began murmuring with surprise when the closing credits began rolling. "Is that it?" one voice cried out. In a way, I suppose it was a tribute to Kubrick's artistry that they wanted more; the film had, after all, been visually striking, and at times quite gripping. But in the end it added up to little more than an assortment of memorable images and forgettable platitudes.' *(Bruce Bawer, American Spectator)*

'Sometimes unpleasant and often wrongheaded, but it's more than once indelible and hardly ever boring.' *(J. Hoberman, Village Voice)*

'Fails only by the standards the director demands be set for him. By normal movie standards, with whatever reservations one may entertain, the film is a technical knockout.' *(Richard Corliss, Time)*

PRO:

'Intense, schematic, superbly made Vietnam War drama . . . While it doesn't develop a particularly strong narrative line, script is loaded with vivid, outrageously vulgar military vernacular that contributes heavily to the film's power. Performances by the all-male cast (save for a couple of Vietnamese hookers) are also exceptional.' *(Variety)*

FUNNY FACE

CT: 8 AV: 7.85

1957 US 103 C MUSICAL/ROMANCE

D Donen, Stanley ☆
W Leonard Gershe Michael

Audrey Hepburn ✔ Fred Astaire Kay Thompson ✔ Michel Auclair Robert Flemyng Dovima Virginia Gibson Suzy Parker Sunny Harnett Don Powell O'Ross

A photographer (Fred Astaire) transforms a bookish girl (Audrey Hepburn) into a fashion model, and falls in love with her.

Delightful, lightweight, colourful musical with Audrey Hepburn at her most gamine, and the glorious Fred Astaire – who looks too old for the part, but wins through on sheer charm. The targets for satire – Left Bank philosophers and high fashion – are dated, and the basic story is so feeble that it would be turned down by any women's magazine; but the Gershwin songs have stood the test of time, and Stanley Donen directs with great style.

PRO:

'A scrumptiously delicious and filling musical with real gleam from all sides . . . a truly beguiling color production that makes the scenic most of some Paris backgrounds.' *(New York Times)*

'A musical that really sings . . . it has a wit, a zip and a charm, rarely touched since *On The Town*.' *(Philip Oakes, Evening Standard)*

'The story is slight, lightly romantic and entertainingly written.' *(MFB)*

MIXED:

'Hepburn . . . has never seemed to me to be the exceptional actress acclaimed by other people . . . She can dance and she can sing a bit . . . Her figure is ungainly, painfully scrawny. Her feet are too long. She has a jaw-line like the front end of a ski . . . Now Hollywood has found out in 1957 what London knew eight years ago . . . [she is] a song and dance girl . . . In many respects [this] is the best musical film for many a moon . . . I do wish, though, that at 56, Fred Astaire would stop running off with the girl at the end.' *(Jympson Harman, Evening New)*

'The clothes are dazzling, and she [Hepburn] wears them, as she wears her role, with a charm and a wistful composure which add greatly to the pleasures of this gay and lively musical. And yet they leave me in a difficulty I often find where caterpillar-into-butterfly films are concerned . . . To me Miss Hepburn, fetching as she is in her modish wardrobe, looks still more fetching when she first appears in her Greenwich Village outfit of sack-tunic over black sweater and skirt, black woollen stockings and clumping shoes. But then perhaps I am prejudiced by my vague longing to see, once in a while, a film in which the model girl throws up evening dresses, mushroom hats and all in order to become, not for love but for literature, an assistant in a bookshop.' *(Dilys Powell)*

FUNNY GIRL AAN

CT: 7 AV: 7.00

1968 US 169 C MUSICAL/BIOPIC

D Wyler, William
W Isobel Lennart from Jule Styne, Bob Merrill & Lennart's musical

Barbra Streisand ☆ AAW Omar Sharif Kay Medford ✔ AAN Anne Francis Walter Pidgeon Lee Allen Mae Questel Gerald Mohr Frank Faylen Mittie Lawrence

The rise to fame of comedienne Fanny Brice (Barbra Streisand).

The power of Streisand's performance helped to distract attention away from the film itself, which is a compendium of showbiz clichés and suffers from a dearth of good songs. Although Wyler is credited with the direction (it's his only musical), Herbert Ross directed the songs and Streisand was widely rumoured to have directed the dialogue herself. Oscar nominations went to photographer Harry Stradling, musical director Walter Scharf and the title song.

'The charismatic ingredients of the smash musical, the star's inspired song-styling . . . casting of Omar Sharif . . . combine into one of the more important roadshow film musicals . . . The face-value unreality of the suave confidence-man falling for the ungainly comedienne is overcome by their personal performances . . . It is to the credit of all concerned that the romance remains thoroughly believeable.' *(Variety)*

'People are always asking me for a definition of star quality. Barbra has defined it for generations to come . . . Unfortuately, Streisand is the only thing extraordinary about *Funny Girl*. The rest of the movie is chopped liver.' *(Rex Reed)*

'[Streisand's is] the most accomplished, original and enjoyable musical-comedy performance that has ever been captured on film.' *(Newsweek)*

'She's a clown and a tragedienne, a combination of gamine and galumpher, that contemporary enigma, the beautiful ugly who defies classic form. She is, in effect, a startling piece of pop art with a glittering potential for permanence. So revel in her film debut and her Oscar-winning impersonation of the immortal Fanny Brice.' *(Judith Crist)*

FURY CT: 8 AV: 8.09

1936 US 94 BW DRAMA/THRILLER

D Fritz Lang ☆
W Bartlett Cormack Fritz Lang from Norman Krasna's story *Mob Rule*

Spencer Tracy Sylvia Sidney Walter Abel Edward Ellis Walter Brennan Bruce Cabot George Walcott Frank Albertson Arthur Stonee Morgan Wallace

Stranger in town (Spencer Tracy) becomes innocent target of a lynch mob.

Lang returns tothe 'hounded man' theme of his greatest film, *M* (1931). The use of a white actor in what pretty clearly is meant to be a metaphor for the plight of the black man makes it seem coy to modern audiences, and the film becomes progressively more unlikely and artificial; but it's still a powerful dramatic piece, with an exceptional star performance.

MIXED:

Lynching is the subject . . . and you actually smell the burning flesh. It's really as savage and convincing and as good as that . . . a film that will haunt your dreams for many a night and make the ordinary Hollywood thing seem tamer than a vacation postcard, but there are a lot of ifs barring [it] being the great picture it might have been, and not even Spencer Tracy's fine electrically charged acting convinced me that a man so starkly burned to death could manage, by a simple miracle in the scenario, to come back to life . . . [it] is still an exceptional film.' *(Kenneth Fearing, The New Masses)*

'One's principal criticism . . . is that lengthy court-room scenes . . . are never good film material . . . [It] had certain faults, but . . . since the screen began to talk, no other serious film except *The Front Page* has so clearly shown that here is a new art and what this new art can do.' *(John Marks, S & S)*

'For half its length a powerful and documented piece of fiction about a lynching, and for the remaining half a desperate attempt to make love, lynching and the Hays Office come out even.'*(Otis Ferguson)*

'Powerful drama which become artificial in its latter stages but remains its director's best American film.' *(Halliwell)*

'Too Germanic, or just manic, for conviction – especially the second half.' *(Shipman)*

PRO:

'Astonishing, the only film I know to which I have wanted to attach the epithet of great.' *(Graham Greene)*

'The finest original drama the screen has provided this year. The theme is mob violence, its approach is coldly judicial, its treatment as relentless and unsparing as the lynching it portrays . . . This has been a completely enthusiastic report, and such was our intention. Hollywood rarely bothers with themes bearing any relation to significant aspects of contemporary life. When it does, in most cases, its approach is timid, uncertain or misdirected. Fury is direct, forthright and vehement. That it is brilliantly executed as well makes it all the more notable.' *(Frank S. Nugent, New York Times)*

'Short of a miracle it will remain the best film of the year.' *(Alistair Cooke, S & S)*

'The surface of American life has been runned away. Fury gets down to the bones of the thing and shows them what they are.' *(C. A. Lejeune)*

'Everyday events and people suddenly took on tremendous and horrifying proportion; even the most insignificant details had a pointed meaning.' *(Lewis Jacobs)*

G

G.I. JOE, WAR CORRESPONDENT: *see* STORY OF G.I. JOE, THE.

'G' MEN CT: 6 AV: 7.67

1935 US 85 BW THRILLER

D William Keighley ☆
W Seton I. Miller ☆ from Gregory Rogers's novel *Public Enemy No. 1*

James Cagney ☆ Ann Dvorak Margaret Lindsay Robert Armstrong Barton MacLane Lloyd Nolan William Harrigan Edward Pawley Russell Hopton Noel Madison

Lawyer (James Cagney) joins FBI to avenge death of friend.

Pressure from America's Legion of Decency and Production Code Authority meant that Cagney was, for once, on the side of right; but he's as violent and vengeful as ever in this red-blooded thriller, an exciting one of its kind.

MIXED:

'This is red hot off the front page. But beyond that it has nothing but a weak scenario along hackneyed lines.' *(Variety)*

PRO:

'The headiest dose of gunplay that Hollywood has unleashed in recent months.' *(Andre Sennwald, New York Times)*

'One of the fastest melodramas ever made.' *(New York Sun)*

'It is not violence alone which is in the air; there is also a skilfully contrived and well-maintained suspense, and throughout a feeling of respect for the men who are paid to die in the execution of necessary work.' *(The Times)*

'Not for the kiddies, but see it if your nerves are good.' *(Photoplay)*

'As simplistic and powerful as a tabloid headline.' *(Geoff Andrew, Time Out)*

GABLE AND LOMBARD CT: 1 AV: 1.71

1976 US 131 C DRAMA/ROMANCE/BIOPIC

D Sidney J. Furie ●
W Barry Sandler ●

Jill Clayburgh James Brolin ● Allen Garfield Red Buttons Melanie Mayron Joanne Linville

The love story of Clark Gable (James Brolin) and Carole Lombard (Jill Clayburgh).

Perhaps the most tasteless Hollywood biopic of all time, inadequately acted by all except Clayburgh and Allen Garfield, who does a passable impersonation of Louis B. Mayer. Brolin is way out of his depth, and the script sinks him.

PRO:

'A film with many major assets, not the least of which is the stunning and smashing perfomance of Jill Clayburgh as Carole Lombard. James Brolin manages excellently to project the necessary Clark Gable attributes while adding his own individuality to the characterization . . . Barry Sandler's original screenplay conveys the excitement and fun of an era when everyone seemed to enjoy themselves in the profession of making pictures.' *(Variety)*

ANTI:

'A limply raunchy, meaningless movie with nothing to say about the movies, about love, or about stardom. The moviemakers couldn't come up with any subject but the sex drive of its hero and heroine, who keep hopping on each other like deranged rabbits. One of the most famous quotes in Hollywood history is Lombard's "My God, you know I love Pa [Gable], but I can't say he's a hell of a lay".' *(Pauline Kael)*

'There is Barry Sandler's attitudinizing, bottomlessly inane and illiterate screenplay, always unfunny except when it tries to be moving . . . Sidney J. Furie's direction . . . does not miss a single cliché, and almost manages the unlikely feat of concocting a few new ones singlehandedly . . . There is the abysmal performance by James Brolin as Gable, who may not have been a great actor, but who was charming, sexy, and shrewd. Brolin comes out lumpish, loutish, and faintly imbecile . . . Jill Clayburgh . . . has neither the looks nor the voice of the late star, but manages, except in a few totally reprehensible scenes, to remain a woman and an actress. There are even a few moments when she ennobles her material, an accomplishment that makes crossing the Alps with a Carthaginian army complete with elephants seem like child's play in comparison.' *(John Simon)*

'An uneven combination of smut and sentimentality.' *(Les Keyser, Hollywood in the Seventies)*

'Low point: Carole Lombard licks Clark Gable on the ear and presents the King with an extra-large, knitted "cock-sock" to keep him warm at nights.' *(Harry & Michael Medved)*

GALLIPOLI CT: 7 AV: 7.57

1981 Australia 110 C WAR

D Peter Weir
W David Williamson

Mark Lee Mel Gibson ✔ Bill Hunter Robert Grubb Tim McKenzie Bill Kerr ✔

Two athletes (Mark Lee, Mel Gibson) join the army in 1915; one dies in the Dardanelles.

Handsomely produced and emotive anti-war drama which achieved international success and sent director Weir to Hollywood. The narrative is broken-backed, runs out of steam in the middle, and treats the British too much as caricature villains, while Mark Lee is dull in a role which treats him as a candidate for canonization; but Gibson is strong as the more abrasive of the two.

'[We are] encouraged to wonder at the indifference to danger exhibited by the Australian soldiers precariously dug into a cliffside while Turkish shells perpetually explode on the beach below – a beach on which they find time both to work and play. Weir states the case for innocence, but leaves matters there; his film strenuously avoids argument in favour of the creation of mood.' *(John Pym, MFB).*

'Highly entertaining drama on a number of levels.' *(Variety)*

'One of the most powerful cinematic examinations of the futility and tragic cost of war.' *(Virgin)*

'The central section devoted to training in Egypt sags badly through its crass buddy antics and its crude caricatures of wogs and pommies.' *(Tom Milne, Time Out)*

GAMMA SANGO UCHU DAISAKUSEN: *see* GREEN SLIME, THE.

GANDHI AAW — CT: 6 AV: 8.25

1982 GB 187 C DRAMA/EPIC/BIOPIC

D Richard Attenborough ✗ AAW
W John Briley AAW

Ben Kingsley ☆ AAW Candice Bergen Edward Fox John Gielgud Trevor Howard John Mills Martin Sheen Rohini Hattangady Ian Charleson Athol Fugard Saeed Jaffrey Geraldine James Amrish Puri Richard Griffiths Nigel Hawthorne Bernard Hepton Michael Hordern Om Puri Richard Vernon Daniel Day-Lewis

Life of a lawyer turned leader (Ben Kingsley).

Big, earnest, conventional epic with some dull moments, and a tendency to ignore Gandhi's misjudgments: you may look in vain for his instruction to Indians to support the Japanese during World War II. Still, there's a real love of India and sympathy for its hero. Although the crowd scenes (always Attenborough's strong point) need a big screen to be fully appreciated, Ben Kingsley's wonderfully convincing central performance (in which he ages over 50 years) emerges just as strongly on TV. Oscars were won by Stuart Craig for art direction, John Mollo and Bhanu Athalya for costume design, and John Bloom for editing.

ANTI:

'A laboriously illustrated textbook.' *(Vincent Canby)*

'Nearly everyone appeared freshly washed, and wore a pretty little sari with a fringe on the top. Gandhi looks as if it's been made for the Indian tourist board. The screen teems with bright-eyed children in Persil white. Venerable gentlemen with silver beards meditate quietly, as brutal red-faced British troops march up and down, barking orders and barking mad.' *(Ken Russell, 1993)*

MIXED:

'Kingsley is impressive; the picture isn't.' *(Pauline Kael)*

'The remarkable things about the film are first, that it was made at all in an age which regards inspirational epics as very old hat; and secondly, that it has brought into life so splendid a leading performance. Beside these factors the sluggish pace and the air of schoolbook history seem comparatively unimportant.' *(Halliwell)*

PRO:

'Bold, sweeping, brutal; tender, loving and inspiring.' *(Variety)*

'It reminds us that we are, after all, human, and thus capable of the most extraordinary and wonderful achievements, simply through the use of our imagination, our will, and our sense of right.' *(Roger Ebert)*

GANG WAR: *see* ODD MAN OUT.

GANG'S ALL HERE, THE — CT: 6 AV: 5.88

(aka *The Girls He Left Behind*)

1943 US 103 C MUSICAL

D Busby Berkeley ✓
W Walter Bullock (music and lyrics by Leo Robin and Harry Warren

Alice Faye ☆ Carmen Miranda ☆ Charlotte Greenwood Eugene Pallette Edward Everett Horton Phil Baker Sheila Ryan James Ellison

Nightclub artistes put on a charity show, while a soldier (James Ellison) has to choose between his rich fiancé (Sheila Ryan) and a sexy nightclub singer (Alice Faye).

Amazing campy musical, with virtually no plot, garish designs (Oscar-nominated!), and some of the most hilariously tasteless production numbers in history. 'The Lady in the Tutti Frutti Hat', featuring Carmen Miranda and giant bananas rising to salute her, is worth the price of admission on its own (it also got the film banned in her native Brazil).

PRO:

'Sumptuous is the word for *The Gang's All Here*. Nothing quite so lavishly routined for a maximum of stunning effects or so vividly splashed with the magnificences of Technicolor has ever been offered in a screen song and dance spectacle. The ending is sheer camera magic, a kaleidoscopic creation by Busby Berkeley.' *(Hollywood Reporter)*

'Mainly made up of Busby Berkeley's paroxysmic production numbers, which amuse me a good deal.' *(James Agee)*

MIXED:

'A weak script is somewhat relegated by the flock of tuneful numbers that frequently punctuate the picture. Alice Faye has never been screened more fetchingly.' *(Variety)*

'This picture contains some of the worst yet most inspired, colorful and extravagant musical numbers in cinema history. They boggle the mind.' *(Danny Peary)*

'Those who consider Berkeley a master consider this film his masterpiece. It is his maddest film.' *(Pauline Kael)*

'Like a male hairdresser's acid trip.' *(Virgin)*

GARDEN OF THE FINZI-CONTINIS, THE

AAW CT: 7 AV: 8.50

(aka *The Garden of Finzi-Continis; Il Giardino dei Finzi-Contini*)

1970 Italy/West Germany 90 C DRAMA/ROMANCE

D Vittorio De Sica ☆
W Tullio Pinelli Valeno Zurlini Franco Brusati Vittorio Bonicelli Ugo Pirro AAN from Giorgio Bassani's novel

Dominique Sanda ☆ Lino Capolicchio Helmut Berger Fabio Testi Romolo Valli Raffaele Curi Camillo Angelini-Rota Katina Viglietti Inna Alexeieff Barbara Pilavin

An aristocratic-Jewish family in Ferrara cannot believe that they are threatened by the rise of Fascism; how wrong they are.

Leisurely, luxurious, lovely film, a far cry from *The Bicycle Thieves* and the neo-realism which made De Sica famous. Though much criticized for its opulence, the director was surely right to emphasize the heights from which the family were to fall. The main problem is the predictability of the plot. It won Best Film at Berlin, 1971.

ANTI:

'De Sica . . . opts for an all embracing tenderness and humanity that more or less misfires . . . It's all very chic and that's one's objection . . . Dominique Sanda . . . makes [the] film worth visiting.' *(Mark Le Fanu, Spectator)*

'Given the faults of the screenplay, the principal actors do about all they can with their material . . . The film . . . leaves a curiously muted, unsatisfying impression, as though those responsible were within reach of something really distinguished and just did not know quite how to grasp it.' *(John Russell Taylor, The Times)*

'There has been much praise for the film's lush, dreamy photography, but the subject matter calls for something far less romantic.' *(Danny Peary)*

'Formally beautiful, sometimes moving, it's ultimately rather hollow.' *(Tom Milne, Time Out)*

PRO:

'I lived through the period. The same feelings I experienced in life I transposed to the picture: that is the definition of the artist.' *(Vittorio De Sica)*

'This extraordinary film, with its melancholy glamour, is perhaps the only one that records the halfhearted anti-Jewish measures of the Mussolini period.' *(Pauline Kael)*

'In presenting the garden to us, De Sica uses an interesting visual strategy; he never completely orients us visually, and so we don't know its overall size and shape. Therefore, visually, we can't count on it: we don't know when it will give out. It's an uneasy feeling to be inside an undefined space, especially if you may need to hide or run, and that's exactly the feeling De Sica gets.' *(Roger Ebert)*

GARDEN, THE

CT: 1 AV: 4.60

1990 GB 90 C DRAMA

D Derek Jarman ●
W Derek Jarman ●

Kevin Collins Roger Cook Jody Graber Pete Lee-Wilson Philip Macdonald Johnny Mills Tilda Swinton

Film-maker Derek Jarman (Derek Jarman) dreams that his garden is the Garden of Gethsemane.

Massively overrated on release. The setting of *The Garden* is Jarman's own cottage and garden, very handy for the scenic delights of Dungeness Power Station. He has captured the essence of the environment, in a succession of astonishingly ugly, garish and vulgar images, shot jerkily and lit abominably. The film takes the form of a vacuous and seemingly never-ending nightmare. 'I want to share this emptiness with you . . .' begins the narration, unpromisingly and only too accurately. 'I offer you a journey without direction.' The director himself appears early on, and falls asleep. It is not long before members of his audience have joined him.

Various old friends look in on Derek's Cocteau party. There's Tilda Swinton, who crops up in a variety of guises: a madonna with child, an enigmatic beachcomber, a waitress, a chicken-plucker . . . The same two expressions (enigmatic and anguished) suffice for all. An over made-up woman comes on and mimes very badly to a camp song from *Funny Face*. There is an embarrassingly limp revue sketch about Judas and credit cards.

Romping in the seaside shrubbery are two tattooed gays (Kevin Collins and Johnny Mills) who look as if they were drummed out of The Krays for gorse acting. They kiss, cuddle and moon around with flowers: for this, they are sentenced to undergo the sufferings of Christ. They are gagged, tarred and feathered by police, whipped by giggling psychotics in Santa costumes, kissed by drag queens. They end up crucified: though by whom or what, I'm not sure – the Church's attitude to homosexuality, Clause 28, Aids, police brutality, or simply the lack of a competent script.

The film raises, according to the publicity blurb, 'important ecological issues'. It's true that I did catch myself wondering why the planet's resources were being wasted on making such self-pitying, self-sanctifying garbage. Sitting through its 92 minutes is like having to watch a nine-hour home video. The last words on the credits say 'Made in England'. Where else?

PRO:

'Matchless . . . Jarman is in a class of his own as a poet of the cinema.' *(Derek Malcolm, Guardian)*

'Touching, intense, sometimes unexpectedly amusing, sometimes agonising, and always achingly sincere.' *(Tony Rayns, Time Out)*

'A requiem for a life, filled with the knowledge of love and innocence debased by decadence, brutalised by ego, martyred by intolerance. The joy of homosexual passion is equated with Christ's agony. Each suffer and die for what they believe . . . The spectre of Aids spins in the wind . . . Is this Jarman's swansong? If so, he's saying, sorry it wasn't better, stay in love, listen to Jesus.' *(Angus Wolfe Murray, Scotsman)*

'A wonderful film which measures mortality with intelligence and beauty.' *(Philip Blinko, What's On in London)*

'Vibrant and poetical allegory about Aids and mortality in this tour-de-force example of independent film-making.' *(Scheuer)*

'Brave and provocative . . . a rich tapestry of painterly images and sounds, and an eye-opening journey of moods from horror to humour. Through it all Jarman speaks clearly of his own feelings and gay injustice.' *(Winnert)*

MIXED:

'A graphic look at homosexual discrimination laden with campy gestures, music and religious dream sequences . . . Jarman forfeits the standard storyline for a panoply of images.' *(Variety)*

'Much of [its] elusive and elegiac power . . . derives from its extraordinary setting . . . in the shadow of Dungeness nuclear power station . . . The movie is presented as a dream . . . [Jarman's] players inhabit the real world and at the same time act out biblical roles . . . [Though] Jarman sinks into something perilously close to sentimentality, at its best [it's] a hard, cold and haunting confrontation with mortality.' *(Margaret Walters)*

'A collage of playlets . . . "The whole morality thing is topsy-turvy," [Jarman] says vaguely; but it has to be better than the monochrome moral vision into which his work has dwindled.' *(Anthony Lane, Sunday Independent)*

'I thought it was all interesting, thank you, but a little outré for my simple tastes.' *(Sue Heal, Today)*

'Most likely to find favour with those who share the director's preoccupations or who can admire his visual flair.' *(Halliwell)*

GASLIGHT CT: 9 AV: 8.13

(aka *Angel Street*)

1940 GB 88 BW THRILLER

D Thorold Dickinson ☆
W A.R. Rawlinson Bridget Boland from Patrick Hamilton's play

Anton Walbrook ☆ Diana Wynyard ☆
Frank Pettingell ☆ Cathleen Cordell
Robert Newton Jimmy Hanley

In Victorian times, a woman (Diana Wynyard) begins to wonder if she's going insane – or being driven mad on purpose?

Splendidly creepy suspense thriller. MGM tried to destroy the negative of this film when they remade it in 1944, but it has survived; many critics think it the better of the two versions.

MIXED:

'For one who has seen the stage play, much of the tension is destroyed by the insistence on explaining everything rather than hinting at it; what is more, the broadening of the scene seems to me to lessen the excitement . . . Diana Wynyard is unsuited to the part of the terrified wife . . . but Anton Walbrook is sinisterly effective, the atmosphere of Victorian discipline and well-ordered discomfort is most skilfully conveyed, and the film as a whole is highly creditable to British production.' *(Dilys Powell)*

PRO:

'A nice gooey, creepy, murky plot of steps in the dark and strangling hands and the cold, calculating eye of insanity . . . The skill is in the camera of an ample, spectacled young Englishman called Thorold Dickinson.' *(Paul Holt, Daily Express)*

'Irreproachable acting . . . smooth, inventive direction . . . [an] outstanding picture.' *(Sunday Dispatch)*

'Most of the stuff we have seen lately fails to qualify as diversion because it does not divert. *Gaslight* does.' *(Campbell Dixon, Daily Telegraph)*

'The electric sense of tension and mid-Victorian atmosphere are entirely cinematic.' *(Sequence, 1950)*

'Lurking menace hangs in the air like a fog and Wynyard suffers exquisitely as she struggles to keep dementia at bay.' *(Nigel Floyd, Time Out)*

'What this version lacks in budget, compared to the MGM version, it more than makes up for in electrifying atmosphere, delicious performances, and a succinctly conveyed sense of madness and evil lurking beneath the surface of the ordinary.' *(Maltin)*

GASLIGHT CT: 6 AV: 6.83

(aka *The Murder in Thornton Square*)

1944 US 114 BW THRILLER

D George Cukor ☆
W John Van Druten Walter Reisch John L. Balderston ☆ AAN from Patrick Hamilton's play

Charles Boyer ☆ AAN Ingrid Bergman ☆ AAW Joseph Cotten Dame May Whitty Barbara Everest Angela Lansbury ☆ AAN Edmund Breon Halliwell Hobbes

Remake of the 1940 film.

Expensive production can't disguise that this version lacks a clear sense of period and the Englishness that lay at the heart of the previous version; but the performances are fine, and the narrative is gripping. Joseph Ruttenberg's cinematography was nominated for an Oscar, and the art direction (by Cedric Gibbons and William Ferrari) won.

MIXED:

'Handsomely mounted, spiritedly performed, *Gaslight* is deft entertainment. If it never lashes the spectator to the convulsive state of jitters engendered by the stage play, mark that down to the physical disqualifications of the two central performers. Ingrid Bergman has a robustious quality that implies her quite capable, if ever really tired of Charles Boyer's iniquities, of launching a haymaker destined to knock the actor right into the middle of what is frequently termed next week.' *(Herb Sterne)*

PRO:

'Cannot fail to hold the spectator engrossed. The climax achieves the ultimate in terror and excitement.' *(Film Bulletin)*

'A gem of suspense and a high-class "meller", distinctly out of the ordinary . . . the film is a spell-binder.' *(Film Daily)*

'A faithful adaptation, conspicuously notable for fine performances of the stars and the screenplay.' *(Variety)*

'Good scary fun all the way.' *(Pauline Kael)*

GATTOPARDO, IL: *see* LEOPARD, THE.

GAY DIVORCEE, THE AAN CT: 8 AV: 7.91

(aka *The Gay Divorce*)

1934 US 107 BW MUSICAL

D Mark Sandrich
W George Marion Jr Dorothy Yost Edward Kaufman from Dwight Taylor's play and Samuel Hoffenstein, Kenneth Webb, Cole Porter's musical play ☆

Fred Astaire ☆ Ginger Rogers ☆ Alice Brady Edward Everett Horton Erik Rhodes Eric Blore Lillian Miles Charles Coleman William Austin Betty Grable

An American hoofer (Fred Astaire) falls for a woman (Ginger Rogers) who is on the verge of divorce.

Astaire and Rogers at their best in a flimsy farce: their second film and first major success. It features a superb ballad, 'Night and Day', and one of the great production numbers, 'The Continental' (expertly choreographed by Dave Gould), which won the Oscar for Best Song. Also nominated were the score, sound and art direction.

ANTI:

'The trouble is that the director does not realize that it is possible to have too much even of a good thing, and the song "The Continental" is repeated over and over again and illustrated by every possible combination between camera angles and chorus work.' *(The Times)*

MIXED:

'The plot is trivial French farce (about mistaken identities), but the dances are among the wittiest and the most lyrical expressions of American romanticism on the screen.' *(Pauline Kael)*

PRO:

'This is the best musical – Now how often have I said that this year? . . . Fred Astaire is no great actor, but what an artist he is on his feet! He says more with those two tantalising hoofs of his than any one else in the picture.' *(Edward Betts, Sunday Express)*

'Here is a musical done with wit and style.' *(Daily Telegraph)*

'All through the picture there's charm, romance, gaiety and eclat.' *(Variety)*

GENERAL, THE CT: 8 AV: 9.76

1926 US 80 BW COMEDY/SILENT

D Buster Keaton Clyde Bruckman ☆
W Al Boasberg Charles Smith

Buster Keaton ☆ Marion Mack Glen Cavander Charles Smith James Farley

In the American Civil War, a confederate train-

driver (Buster Keaton) has his train and girlfriend (Marion Mack) stolen by Union soldiers.

Buster Keaton, deadpan King of the Sight-Gag, is on top form as he tries to win back his train and his girl. After a slow start, it gathers pace to become among the best of all comedy silents, and the most lavishly produced. The period detail is extraordinary. Even more extraordinary was the hostile reception it ran into from critics on release. In a 1972 poll taken by *Sight & Sound* magazine, *The General* was voted one of the 10 greatest films of all time.

ANTI:

'Long and tedious – the least funny thing Buster Keaton has ever done.' *(New York Herald Tribune)*

'Slow, very slow . . . Pull yourself together, Buster.' *(Daily Mirror)*

'A one-man show, a mistake in a picture lasting an hour.' *(Norbert Lusk, Picture/Play Charm)*

'Buster Keaton shows signs of vaulting ambition . . . he appears to be attempting to enter the epic class. That he fails to get across is due to the scantiness of his material as compared with the length of his film; he has also displayed woefully bad judgment in deciding just where and when to stop . . . Many of his gags at the end of the picture are in such gruesomely bad taste that the sympathetic spectator is inclined to look the other way. *The General* has some grand scenes . . . and the ingenuity displayed by . . . Keaton in keeping these . . . tedious chases alive is little short of incredible. In spite of its pretentious proportions, *The General* is not nearly so good as Raymond Griffith's Civil War comedy *Hands Up*.' *(Robert E. Sherwood, Life)*

MIXED:

'The production itself is singularly well mounted, but the fun is not exactly plentiful. This is by no means so good as Mr Keaton's previous efforts. Here he is more the acrobat than the clown, and his vehicle might be described as a mixture of cast iron and jelly.' *(Mordaunt Hall, New York Times)*

PRO:

'When asked why *The General* gave a more convincing picture of the Civil War than *Gone with the Wind*, Keaton replied, "Well, you see they based their film on the novel. I went back to the history books".' *(Eric Rhode, Encounter, 1967)*

'Keaton at his best.' *(Paul Rotha & Richard Griffith, The Film Till Now, 1930)*

'The first, probably the greatest comic epic in film form . . . The great question [it] poses in the course of its narrative is how to perform heroic action in a universe that is not heroic . . . That heroism occurs as an accident in *The General* is at the center of its moral thrust . . . Buster's character exposes the folly of the accidents of heroism . . . The gallant and romantic are explicitly burlesqued in the film's final sequence . . . Buster heroically draws his sword only to see the blade fall off, leaving a stubby handle in his upstretched hand . . . The thing that distinguishes *The General* is that the senseless object, the huge infernal machine of this film, is war . . . This antiheroic comic epic must necessarily become an antiwar story, too, for the military heroism *The General* consistently debunks is the Circe that turns men into murdering and destructive swine . . . With its mixture of burlesque and grimness . . . [it] is the spiritual ancestor of that recent mixture of laughs and war horrors, *Doctor Strangelove*.' *(Gerald Mast, A Short History of the Movies, 1971)*

'The best train film ever made, with seven of the eight reels devoted to the train chase. The film is fast, ingenious and packed with impeccably timed visual gags.' *(R.A.E. Pickard, Dictionary of 1000 Best Films, 1971)*

'Not only one of Keaton's greatest, but also one of the funniest films ever made . . . with enough gags to fill a dozen modern comedies.' *(Elkan Allan, NFT Bulletin)*

'Masterly silent comedy . . . directed by Buster Keaton, an artist whose ill-deserved but unavoidable decline during the sound era has since been substantially countered by a great resurgence in critical admiration . . . [The films] provides ample evidence of his uniquely lugubrious comic persona, spellbinding physical agility and clinical filmmaking control . . . Keaton's art . . . comes across as effortless.' *(Allan Hunter & Kenny Mathieson, Movie Classics, 1992)*

GENEVIEVE CT: 10 AV: 8.92

1953 GB 86 C COMEDY/ROAD

D Henry Cornelius ☆
W William Rose ☆ AAN

Dinah Sheridan ☆ John Gregson ☆ Kay Kendall ☆ Kenneth More ☆ Geoffrey Keen ☆ Joyce Grenfell ☆ Reginald Beckwith ☆ Arthur Wontner

Two rivals (Kenneth More, John Gregson) compete in the London to Brighton veteran car race.

Classic, cosy, utterly charming British comedy which seems effortless but is a masterpiece of craftsmanship and gentle wit. It made stars of Kenneth More and Kay Kendall, but is immaculately acted throughout. Larry Adler's theme music is irritatingly catchy; it was credited on American prints and at the Oscar nominations to Muir Mathieson, since Adler was blacklisted.

'This lively comedy . . . is extremely funny . . . perfectly served by Kenneth More and Kay Kendall. [The] direction is crisp and well-paced . . . and the harmonica score by Larry Adler, novel and effective . . . One of the best things to have happened to British films over the last five years.' *(Gavin Lambert, MFB)*

'It is a pleasure to be able to acclaim a home-made comedy which fulfils completely the possibilities of its conception; which is beyond reproach in its acting and direction.' *(Fred Majdalany, Daily Mail)*

'Perfect fare for the present season, containing ingredients of all our national characteristics – endurance, eccentricity, charm and perfidy.' *(Virginia Graham, Spectator)*

'Rarely has a starring foursome been so consistently good.' *(Variety)*

'The perennial genre of middle-class comedy, essentially suburban and always respectable and conformist, could boast Cornelius's Genevieve as its proudest example.' *(Paul Rotha & Richard Griffith, The Film Till Now, 1960)*

'William Rose's script is constantly imaginative and witty – and it sees its two lead couples as sexual beings, which, as critic Richard Winnington pointed out, was unprecedented at the time. As members of the new, postwar affluent generation, Dinah Sheridan and John Gregson are good, and Kay Kendall and Kenneth More are even better, revealing their comic gifts for the first time.' *(NFT Bulletin, 1984)*

'Everything about this movie seems to go right, and it looks relaxed and effortless.' *(Pauline Kael)*

'As smooth as custard.' *(Variety)*

GENOU DE CLAIRE, LE: *see* CLAIRE'S KNEE.

GENTLEMAN'S AGREEMENT AAN

CT: 4 AV: 6.20

1947 US 118 BW DRAMA

D Elia Kazan ✗ AAW
W Moss Hart AAN from Laura Z. Hobson's novel

Gregory Peck AAN Dorothy McGuire AAN John Garfield ☆ Celeste Holm ☆ AAW Anne Revere ☆ AAN June Havoc Albert Dekker Jane Wyatt Dean Stockwell

A journalist (Gregory Peck) pretends to be Jewish in order to investigate racial discrimination.

Elia Kazan's well-intentioned but facile tract against anti-Semitism won The New York Film Critics' Best Picture and Best Director awards, then went on to win three Oscars, including Best Film. (Harmon James's editing was Oscar-nominated.) Once considered courageous and powerful, now it looks terribly slow, preachy and melodramatic. More evidence, if any were needed, that the 'socially important' picture of today is the deservedly forgotten film of tomorrow.

PRO:

'Here is an important picture. With a rare combination of passion and truth it focuses and turns to the light, in a succession of salient episodes, most of those common or garden aspects of anti-Semitism practiced in America today. Not by violent and dreadful people like Hitler and his gang, but by nice, very nice, people. Let me suggest by people like you and me . . . Darryl F. Zanuck has done a service to his company, to the screen, and to the American spirit in producing this sane, this responsible, this telling analysis of intolerance. He need not fear how our democracy will stand before the world if we are represented abroad by a picture such as this courageous producer has given us here.' *(Mary Britton Miller, New Movies)*

'The second film this year to speak out against a subject heretofore taboo in films: anti-Semitism. *Crossfire*, which put across its message in terms of melodrama, was a forceful document, sickening in its implications. The present film is equally forceful and even more frank. It is films like these two, which treat important themes in adult, cogent fashion, that make one realize what a powerful social force films could be.' *(Fortnight)*

'It tackles a difficult problem of the day with courage and understanding . . . The direction is taut, the sequence of events linked together with skill and dramatic cohesion.' *(MFB)*

'Here is Hollywood at its courageous best, entering bravely into the arena of religious intolerance and emerging from it with a motion picture of which the entire industry may be proud . . . Kazan's direction is expert, firm and true . . . He has drawn from his principals superlative performances.' *(Red Kann, Motion Picture Herald)*

'It is not difficult to comprehend the picture's enthusiastic reception in America . . . Peck turns in a flawless performance.' *(Today's Cinema)*

MIXED:

'A sizzling film. But the weaknesses of the original are also apparent in the film – the most obvious of which is the limited and specialized area observed. Although the hero of the story is apparently assigned to write a definitive article on anti-Semitism in the United States, it is evident that his explorations are narrowly confined to the upper-class social and professional level to which he is immediately exposed. And his discoveries are chiefly in the nature of petty bourgeois rebuffs, with no inquiry into the devious cultural mores from which they spring. Likewise it is amazing that the writer who undertakes this probe should be so astonished to discover that anti-Semitism is cruel. Assuming that he is a journalist of some perception and scope, his imagination should have fathomed most of these sudden shocks long since. And although the role is crisply and agreeably play by Gregory Peck, it is, in a careful analysis, an extraordinarily naive role.' *(Bosley Crowther, New York Times)*

'Though *Gentleman's Agreement* earned three Oscars as the best picture of the year, I found it a less exciting movie than *Crossfire* or *Boomerang* (also directed by Kazan): it yawns through whole patches. Its prominent virtue is to arraign the *laissez faire* of sympathetic Gentiles.' *(Richard Winnington)*

ANTI:

'A prettified series of clichés.' *(Elia Kazan, Kazan on Kazan, 1973)*

'A third-rate film . . . hailed as a masterpiece simply because it was about anti-Semitism.' *(Dilys Powell)*

'Sam Goldwyn's famous dictum against message pictures ("Messages are for Western Union!") was never more true. The players are forced to cope with a lot of naive, simplistic preaching without any help from the photographer, the director or the music department. Kazan's direction is clumsy and maladroit. Even a skilled actor would have difficulties with such impossible dialogue, but Peck's amateurishly mannered performance with its wearisome tricks of delivery and inflection, makes it seem even more unrealistic. Of all the Academy Award-winners for Best Motion Picture, the one that has dated most and seems in retrospect to have been least justified is *Gentleman's Agreement*.' *(George Aachen)*

'A talky, static affair that never generates much excitement. Be warned! The glum, humorless Peck is in every scene bar one – though he does not hold the monopoly on strained acting. True, he has a trencherman's share of stilted dialogue, but Anne Revere can do little better with hers and even John Garfield wears a general air of defeat. The one really powerful scene is the confrontation between Peck and the hotel manager, superbly played by a smiling, refusing-to-be-drawn Roy Roberts. The film's valid points are obscured, disguised and disfigured by being tied to a conventional dime-a-dozen romance that is unconscionably joined to a flag-waving jingoism that must surely be as tiresome to native Americans as embarrassingly laughable to everyone else. Kazan's dated technique with each scene faded in and out, its scrupulously uninspired staging and pedestrian compositions, makes *Gentleman's Agreement* look like a museum piece.' *(John Howard Reid)*

GENTLEMEN PREFER BLONDES

CT: 8 AV: 6.62

1953 US 91 C MUSICAL/COMEDY/ROMANCE

D Howard Hawks ✔
W Charles Lederer from Anita Loos and Joseph Fields's play

Jane Russell ☆ Marilyn Monroe ☆
Charles Coburn ✔ Elliott Reid Tommy Noonan
George 'Foghorn' Winslow Marcel Dalio
Taylor Holmes Norma Varden Howard Wendell

Gold-digger (Marilyn Monroe) and golden-hearted friend (Jane Russell) visit Paris.

Vulgar, gaudy, thoroughly enjoyable musical, the magnetic Marilyn Monroe and the equally voluptuous Jane Russell play fast and Anita Loos. Highlight: Monroe cooing 'Diamonds Are A Girl's Best Friend'. The cynicism of the original novel remains intact. There was an inferior sequel, *Gentlemen Marry Brunettes* (1955).

ANTI:

'A pointer to worse American film [to come] . . . A little of Anita Loos' sharp comedy survives in the dialogue . . . Otherwise this is a dull piece of calculated vulgarity.' *(Thomas Spencer, Daily Worker)*

MIXED:

'The picture, not content with good-enough, broadens an already broad theme, thereby coming too close to burlesque for constant satisfaction. But when you come right down to it, what more can you want than Marilyn Monroe under constant command to be sexy and Jane Russell trying to get her traditional share of the attention . . . As entertainment, *Gentlemen Prefer Blondes* is gay visually and kinetically, comparatively philosophical in its songs, and perhaps slightly heavy-handed in its preoccupation with that one method a girl uses to procure more "best friends".' *(Archer Winsten, New York Post)*

'Has some good lines and songs and in its brash overblown way is not bad fun.' *(Manchester Guardian)*

'Compromised by the casting of Marilyn Monroe, by the abandonment of the 20s period and the incongruous up-to-date streamlining, by inflating some bright, witty songs into lavish production numbers, and by tamely ending the whole thing by letting two true loves conventionally come true. There is, too, a lack of grasp in Howard Hawks' handling, which is scrappy and uninventive. The plot and continuity of the second half is so disjointed that one feels it must, for some reason, have been decided to finish the film in a hurry. It just stops.' *(BFI Bulletin)*

PRO:

'Singing, dancing or just staring at diamonds, these girls are irresistible and their musical is as lively as a string of firecrackers on the Fourth of July . . . As usual, Miss Monroe looks as though she would glow in the dark, and her version of the baby-faced blonde whose eyes open for diamonds and close for kisses is always amusing as well as alluring. Miss Russell is a Juno with nylon trimmings and she has the knack of snapping out gags with dead-pan sarcasm.' *(Otis L. Guernsey Jr, New York Herald Tribune)*

GESTAPO: *see* NIGHT TRAIN.

GET OUT YOUR HANDKERCHIEFS AAW

CT: 5 AV: 7.50

(aka *Préparez Vos Mouchoirs*)

1977 France/Belgium 109 C COMEDY/FOREIGN

D Bertrand Blier ✗
W Bertrand Blier

Gérard Depardieu ☆ Patrick Dewaere ☆
Carole Laure Riton Michel Serrault Eléonore Hirt
Sylvie Joly

Husband (Gérard Depardieu) tries to make his wife (Carole Laure) less frigid by finding her a lover.

Offbeat black comedy, not very funny but a good deal more enjoyable than Blier's previous film along the same lines, *Les Valseuses (Going Places)*. Depardieu and Dewaere continue their partnership from that film, and work well together. Despite critical acclaim for the film's eagerness to tackle taboo topics, it's all oddly pointless, unless it is to show the dislocation between sex and emotion; and there's something unpleasantly creepy about the denouement, where the wife finds sexual fulfilment with a 13-year-old.

PRO:

'An inspired attack on "real life" melodramas of the soppy kind capped by *Kramer vs Kramer* . . . The movie firmly puts the boot into mainstream French comedy, substituting absurd and amiable bad taste for the intellectual rigor mortis of which Parisians are so proud. An erratic, often hilarious movie.' *(Chris Auty, Time Out)*

'A beguiling French comedy, saucy and witty, but at heart naughty: amorous flim-flam . . . Tongue-in-cheek, [Blier] makes what is potentially distasteful entirely edible.' *(Richard Barkley, Sunday Express)*

'Often a film of originality beggars synopsis . . . [giving] no adequate idea of the qualities invoked, the emotions touched. Such a picture is . . . Blier's soft, discursive tale . . . [which] has a splendidly poetic sensuality all of its own . . . I do urge you to make a date with [this] mischievously funny film.' *(David Castell, Sunday Telegraph)*

'Flagrantly funny in a slangy, buoyant, unpredictable way. Feelings are expressed that hadn't come out in movies before, yet it's all reassuringly quiet.' *(Pauline Kael)*

MIXED:

'Neither as ribald nor as funny as it sets out to be, the film has a great deal of old-fashioned charm.' *(Bergan & Karney)*

ANTI:

'The young woman knits, and occasionally faints. How she eventually gets a child . . . is more baleful and alarming than entertaining.' *(Virginia Dignam, Morning Star)*

GHOST AAN

CT: 7 AV: 6.75

1990 US 127 C DRAMA/COMEDY/THRILLER

D Jerry Zucker
W Bruce Joel Rubin ☆ AAW

Patrick Swayze Demi Moore
Whoopi Goldberg ☆ AAW Tony Goldwyn ✓
Rick Aviles Vincent Schiavelli Stanley Lawrence
Christopher J. Keene Susan Breslau
Martina Degnan

A young man (Patrick Swayze) comes back from the dead to protect his girlfriend (Demi Moore), whose life is in danger. Because he can't warn her himself, he has to use a medium (Whoopi Goldberg) who thinks she's a fake, but isn't.

With the help of Whoopi Goldberg's Oscar-winning performance as a medium, *Ghost* succeeds in blending low comedy with high romance, ghost story with urban thriller.

Patrick Swayze has precisely the comic timing of a corpse, and it isn't hard to see that a skilful light comedian such as Tom Hanks or (in the old days) Cary Grant would have wrung many more laughs from the screenplay. However, Swayze's athleticism and reputation as an action-picture star, to say nothing of his sex appeal, add greatly to the thriller and romance elements, and make his frustration at being only a ghost – and therefore unable either to kiss or hit people on the mouth – that much more frustrating for him, and entertaining for the audience.

Mixed in with some yuppie conservatism is just enough watered-down feminism and liberalism to make it up-to-date. Over the course of the movie, Swayze learns that when he was alive he failed to appreciate his love for his girlfriend, and hers for him. He also learns tolerance towards a black con-woman for whom initially he feels only contempt. It is this growth of awareness and tolerance – more than any particular heroism or superior moral worth – which enables this rich young man to enter the kingdom of heaven, without having to pass through the eye of any proverbial needle. His final glitzy ascent to the angels certainly gives a whole new meaning to the phrase 'upward mobility'.

It's a highly enjoyable movie, and one which makes you feel – quite literally – glad to be alive. It was nominated for best score and editing.

ANTI:

'Wants justice and retribution (heaven for yuppies, hell for muggers).' *(Judith Williamson, Guardian)*

MIXED:

'Delivers the elements a *Dirty Dancing* audience presumably hungers for.' *(Variety)*

'Has . . . little to say about the difficulty of letting go when someone has died . . . It's mixture of special effects, scams, comedy and broken hearts makes [it] messy and over long. But Goldberg's vitality and

Moore's magical vulnerability also make it entertaining and occasionally delightful.' *(Ann Totterdell, Financial Times)*

'Essentially simple fantasy fare imbued with impressive special effects . . . [Its] major strength is unabashed warmth and sympathy for its neatly fleshed out characters, who manipulate our emotions without the standard overt cynicism . . . A superbly crafted balancing act of great flair.' *(Sue Heal, Today)*

'Current Hollywood thinking extends into the next world but not far . . . *Ghost* is nothing if not earnest. It's also eccentric enough to remain interesting even when the ghost story isn't easy to believe . . . [and] veers repeatedly from the somber to the broadly comic . . . Fortunately the third of the film's stars is Whoopi Goldberg, the one performer here who seems to have a clear idea of what she's up to . . . [The film] is too slow moving . . . and a few of its special effects look incongruously silly.' *(Janet Maslin, New York Times)*

'A sweet, almost alarmingly wholesome entertainment . . . The comedy is left to Whoopi Goldberg – who is well qualified to look after it . . . After [Swayze] is dead, [Moore] only has to act as if she can't see him, which must be easier than acting as if his facial expressions were ripe harvests of emotion.' *(Adam Mars-Jones, Independent)*

'Tony Goldwyn . . . plays *Ghost*'s lead heavy, Carl Brunner, and he's great in the part. Goldwyn makes it clear that Carl's villainy is a just a Gucci-shod baby step past normal yuppie greed and selfishness. And his panic when he realizes how messy clean, white-collar crimes can get is just standard yuppie work stress turned up several notches.' *(Kathy Maio)*

GHOST AND MRS. MUIR, THE

CT: 6 AV: 7.00

1947 US 104 BW COMEDY/FANTASY/ROMANCE

D Joseph L. Mankiewicz
W Philip Dunne from R.A. Dick's novel

Gene Tierney ☆ Rex Harrison ☆ George Sanders Edna Best Vanessa Brown Anna Lee Robert Coote Natalie Wood Isobel Elsom

A ghostly sea captain (Rex Harrison) dictates his memoirs to a widow (Gene Tierney) who falls in love with him.

Charming comedy-drama, elevated above whimsy by two leading actors on top form. Charles Lang Jr's lyrical cinematogaphy was Oscar-nominated, and Bernard Herrmann's appropriately haunting score should have been.

ANTI:

'I found my laughter glands completely unruffled . . . This production needs showmanship and a better brand of dialogue.' *(News of the World)*

'What I cannot understand is why anyone decided to make a film in which the hero can do nothing but haunt and the heroine has nothing to do but sip hot milk.' *(Sunday Graphic)*

MIXED:

'A fanciful and amusing yarn . . . A witty and entertaining piece with unconscious comedy supplied by Hollywood's idea of authentic London setting.' *(Daily Mirror)*

PRO:

'A jolly caper, gently humorous and often sparkling.' *(New York Times)*

'Delightful and entertaining in a simple way.' *(People)*

'A not-at-all disagreeable piece of whimsy.' *(News Chronicle)*

'Tierney gives what undeniably is her best performance to date. It's warmly human and the out-of-this-world romance pulls audience sympathy with an infectious tug that never slackens. In his role as the lusty, seafaring shade, Rex Harrison commands the strongest attention.' *(Variety)*

GHOST BREAKERS

CT: 8 AV: 7.11

1940 US 82 BW HORROR/COMEDY

D George Marshall ☆
W Paul Dickey Walter de Leon from Paul Dickey and Charles W. Goddard's play ☆

Bob Hope ☆ Paulette Goddard ☆ Paul Lukas Willie Best ☆ Richard Carlson Lloyd Corrigan ☆ Anthony Quinn Noble Johnson Pedro de Cordoba

A girl (Paulette Goddard) inherits a spooky castle in the West Indies.

Follow-up to *The Cat and the Canary*, and on the same high level. It's played less broadly for laughs, however, and Bob Hope plays a slightly different kind of hero: less cowardly and given to slapstick (Willie Best gets to do most of the physical comedy). The romantic side of the story is also well done: Paulette Goddard is an attractive, spirited heroine, while Hope was never more flatteringly photographed. An immaculate, tasteful production generally, and Ernst Toch's score adds to the mood. The story had already been made twice, in 1914 and 1922: it was remade in 1953 as *Scared Stiff*. This is the version to see.

'If you liked *The Cat and the Canary* you will appreciate the thrills and humour in this one.' *(Picturegoer)*

'Bob Hope can joke, apparently, even with a risen corpse.' *(MFB)*

'Paramount has found the fabled formula for making audiences shriek with laughter and fright at one and the same time.' *(New York Times)*

'One of Hope's finest comedies . . . Although the

general situation is much the same as in *The Cat and the Canary*, it works better here because the film provides thrills as well as laughs, thanks to Marshall's deft and delicate direction, Charles Lang Jr's shadowy camerawork, and Hans Dreier's authentically Gothic art direction.' *(Geoff Andrew, Time Out)*

GHOST OF FRANKENSTEIN, THE: *see* THE *FRANKENSTEIN* SERIES.

GHOSTBUSTERS CT: 7 AV: 7.06

1984 US 105 C COMEDY/HORROR

D Ivan Reitman ✔
W Dan Aykroyd Harold Ramis

Bill Murray ☆ Dan Aykroyd Harold Ramis Sigourney Weaver Rick Moranis Annie Potts William Atherton Ernie Hudson

A team of drop-out parapsychologists fight a plague of ghosts in New York City.

Fun for almost all the family (but not the very young, who will find it frightening). Sophisticates will enjoy moments of surreal humour, such as the moment Sigourney Weaver is revealed as the owner of a haunted refrigerator. The leading actors are funny as the misunderstood academics who save Manhattan from supernatural invasion – though there's an oafishness about them which is at times unappealing, and only Murray's character is properly characterized. (Ernie Hudson, the one black ghostbuster, is given virtually nothing to do.) The special effects are loud, spectacular, and sometimes scary. Some of them are also witty. Mixed reviews did not prevent this from being a massive hit, which gave rise to a vastly inferior, even more raucous sequel.

ANTI:

'It raised ne'er a smile as far as I was concerned, but children may well enjoy [it].' *(William Russell, Glasgow Herald)*

'Spectacular but suspenseless, loud but laughless . . . [It] could have left out the guests, the ghosts, and the gizmos and given Murray the whole gameshow.' *(Nigel Andrews, Financial Times)*

'Murray is the film's comic mechanism: the more supernatural the situation, the more jaded his reaction. But nobody else has much in the way of material, and since there's almost no give-and-take among the three men, Murray's lines fall on dead air. The film cost roughly $32 million, and the producer-director Ivan Reitman may have been overwhelmed by the scale of the sets and special effects; his work here is amateurish, with kid's-movie pacing. Audiences respond to the picture, though, and their laughter helps to fill the dead spots.' *(Pauline Kael)*

MIXED:

'Only intermittently impressive.' *(Variety)*

'However good an idea it may have been to unleash Mr Murray in an *Exorcist*-like setting, this film hasn't gotten very far past the idea stage. Its jokes, characters and story lines are as wispy as the ghosts themselves, and a good deal less substantial. (The ghosts, incidentally, are very winning.)' *(Janet Maslin, New York Times)*

PRO:

'The film's mood of compulsive irony is personified by Bill Murray's role as ringleader . . . neatly partnered by Ackroyd and Ramis . . . a team functioning with practised and enjoyable ease . . . [The film] is a great, goofy, gorgeous treat that deserves to be savoured for a long, long time.' *(Philip Strick, F & F)*

'One of those rare movies where the original, fragile comic vision has survived a multimillion-dollar production.' *(Roger Ebert)*

'Reitman shows greater flair at controlling the anarchic comic rhythms of the *National Lampoon/Saturday Night Live* crowd than most of the directors who have attempted that hopeless task, and the effects are truly astonishing.' *(Mike Bygrave, Time Out)*

GI JOE, WAR CORRESPONDENT: *see* STORY OF G.I. JOE, THE.

GIANT AAN CT: 4 AV: 6.64

1956 US 197 C WESTERN/DRAMA

D George Stevens ✗ AAW
W Fred Guiol Ivan Moffat ✗ AAN from Edna Ferber's novel

Elizabeth Taylor Rock Hudson AAN James Dean ● AAN Carroll Baker Jane Withers Chill Wills Mercedes McCambridge AAN Sal Mineo Dennis Hopper Judith Evelyn

Tale of two rival oil families.

Plodding, uninspired, overpraised soap opera now remembered principally for James Dean's last performance, which may strike modern audiences as hopelessly mannered and self-indulgent (Hudson and Taylor are much more impressive). The film is on a grand scale and picked up a large number of Oscar nominations – for Dmitri Tiomkin's music, Boris Leven's art direction and the editing by William Hornbeck, Philip W. Anderson and Fred Bohanan. George Stevens picked up the Best Director award, but his handling of the performers is uncertain; more worthy recipients might have been cinematographers William C. Mellor and Edwin DuPar.

PRO:

'A long, sprawling and tremendously vivid and

engrossing movie that spouts a tawdry tragedy. The picture flows fascinatingly.' *(New York Times)*

'In spite of the good acting throughout *Giant*, it is really producer-director Stevens' picture. His is the triumph in correlating all the departments in this enormous film and capturing this portrait of time and place.' *(Philip T. Hartung, The Commonweal)*

'[Dean] has caught the Texas accent to nasal perfection, and has mastered the lock-hipped, high-heeled stagger of the wrangler . . . The actor is able to press an amazing variety of subtleties into the mood of the moment, to achieve what is certainly the finest piece of atmospheric acting seen on screen since Marlon Brando and Red Steiger did their "brother scene" in *On the Waterfront*.' *(Time)*

'Some may find here a chunk of social history – the effect of oil on Texan society . . . There has been a shot at incorporating another aspect of social history, the segregation of the Mexican Indians. I think the shot misses: individually striking, the passages dealing with the racial problem, at any rate the later ones, are not integrated with the film – they make the effect of being stuck in for the sake of progressive sentiment . . . Yet the film is an astonishing achievement, evoking the ochre plains alive with cattle, the ruined earth belching oil, the millionaires' palaces and the secret human lives. *Giant* is heroic, a film of creative size . . . and Mr Stevens has elicited splendid acting performances . . . Dean's mumbling, awkward, shifty, watchful, secretly amorous boy seems to me miraculous; and though his performance as the adolescent grown into a drunken, egomaniac tycoon has the air of incompleteness the quality of an extraordinary talent is still there.' *(Dilys Powell)*

ANTI:

'An example of commercial filmmaking straining for prestige, and the performers can't blink an eye without announcing that they're acting – and acting, what's more, to live up to the scale of the production.' *(Pauline Kael)*

'Strives so hard for Serious Statements that it ends up as a long yawn.' *(Geoff Andrew, Time Out)*

GIANT CLAW, THE CT: 5 AV: 2.60

1957 US 76 BW HORROR/SO BAD

D Fred F. Sears ●
W Samuel Newman Paul Gangelin
Jeff Morrow Mara Corday Morris Ankrum

Big bird terrorizes New York.

No, not Big Bird from *Sesame Street*, but one of the most ridiculous special effects creations in Hollywood history. Without this improbable monster from outer space, this would be no more than another lousy B-movie: with him, it achieves a kind of weird greatness. Its bad-tempered exploits include kidnapping a train and eating a carload of teenagers. They probably died laughing. The film includes footage from another turkey, *Earth Versus the Flying Saucers*.

PRO:

'Well-constructed with stock shots integrated with the special effects to create the impression of a huge creature in combat with planes.' *(James Powers, Hollywood Reporter)*

'Nature red in beak and claw . . . Sears has taken pains to lend the whole thing an aura of conviction and the pseudo-scientific and aviation jargon has an authentic ring.' *(Daily Film Renter)*

'A sense of good-humoured cynicism distinguishes [it]. It is impossible to believe that Morrow and Corday are not to a great extent enjoying the absurdity of the story. The pseudo-documentary approach and the special effects – mostly superimpositions – are better than usual.' *(MFB)*

ANTI:

'Tired of too tame, too phoney monsters? Well, for sheer nerve, see this one.' *(Picturegoer)*

'Of all SF and monster movies of the 1950s, *The Giant Claw* is by all odds the funniest . . . I don't recall any film, not even *Monster From The Ocean Floor* or *From Hell It Came* or *Monstroid*, in which the menace is so pitifully inept. The bird has a round, heavy body and disproportionate feet (the giant claws), with turkey tail feathers on its wings. The long, gangly neck is ribbed like an accordion, and the giant beak has snaggly teeth. The staring, glassy eyes express a comically overstressed malevolence, and the head has a topping of tiny feathers . . . The sight of this pathetic horror has been known to bring strong men to their knees shrieking with laughter.' *(Bill Warren, Keep Watching The Skies!)*

GIARDINO DEI FINZI-CONTINI, IL: *see* GARDEN OF THE FINZI-CONTINIS, THE

GIGI AAW CT: 10 AV: 8.54

1958 US 119 C MUSICAL/ROMANCE

D Vincente Minnelli ☆ AAW
W Alan Jay Lerner ☆ AAW (music by Frederick Loewe ☆) from Anita Loos's play and Colette's novel

Leslie Caron ☆ (singing voice dubbed by Betty Wand ✔) Louis Jourdan ☆
Maurice Chevalier ☆ Hermione Gingold ☆
Isabel Jeans Jacques Bergerac Eva Gabor
John Abbott

A young, gawky, illegitimate Parisian girl (Leslie Caron) grows into a beautiful woman.

Lerner and Loewe's musical, written directly for the screen (and incorporating songs rejected from *My Fair Lady*), captures the charm and sexiness of the Colette novel, and is helped along by Minnelli's confident direction, Beaton's elegant design, and faultless performances; Leslie Caron, Maurice Chevalier and Hermione Gingold are enchanting. The songs, which failed to impress some critics of the time, have worn wonderfully well. The whole film is up to the standard of Lerner and Loewe's finest work, and ranks alongside their *My Fair Lady* as one of the great movie musicals. It won nine Oscars, including cinematography (Joseph Ruttenberg), editing (Adrienne Fazan), score (André Previn), title song, costume design (Cecil Beaton) and art direction (William A. Horning, Preston Ames, Henry Grace, Keogh Gleason).

ANTI:

'It's like a meal consisting of cheesecake, and one quickly longs for something solid and vulgar to weigh things down. No doubt inspired by the finicky, claustrophobic sets and bric-a-brac, the cast tries (with unfortunate success) to be more French than the French, especially Chevalier.' *(Geoff Brown, Time Out)*

'Caron – never the most effortless of waifs – had played the role of Gigi in the London production of the straight stage play and here leads the cast . . . in a contest to see who can be the most French. The winner is Chevalier, in a performance that makes one feel as if you're gagging on pastry.' *(Virgin)*

PRO:

'Consistently pleasant, but . . . the real star is Cecil Beaton, who designed the costumes and scenery. When the story ambles, and the songs don't quite soar, the clothes and settings continue to enchant.' *(Stanley Kauffmann)*

'One of the most tasteful and elegant musicals that MGM has ever turned out. Nor does it lag too far behind musically.' *(Variety)*

'Nine songs, sentimental and sardonic and high-spirited, illustrate, decorate, amplify and develop the plot. Nobody would claim that they have the musicianly interest of Bernstein's work in *West Side Story*. But they have the trick of singing in one's head without driving one off it which marks the good popular tune. I find them captivating. And they draw life from the film as well as giving life to it. Gigi's puzzled schoolgirl complaint that the Parisians spend all their time making love is much funnier if the singer is scurrying through a city where even the public statues are athletically engaged in amorous exercises; just as the fashionable young man's "She Is Not Thinking Of Me" is much more pointed when part of it comes over as unspoken thought, delivered with lips sealed and eyes irritably following the suspect hilarity of a mistress . . . Gigi strikes me as one of the half-dozen best screen musicals ever made.' *(Dilys Powell)*

'There won't be much point in anybody trying to produce a film of *My Fair Lady* for a while, because Arthur Freed has virtually done it with *Gigi*.' *(New York Times)*

'A lively score . . . and some high-style sets and costumes . . . lend a bright and colorful glow even to the slow stretches between musical numbers . . . Songs, enchantment and charm to spare.' *(Newsweek)*

'The kind of film that makes you wonder why they still try to do musicals on stage . . . Caron rises touchingly and masterfully to an occasion sewn stitch by stitch to her measurements . . . Minnelli . . . surpasses himself.' *(Fred Majdalany, Daily Mail)*

'Fizzes with every traditional French virtue . . . An absolute joy.' *(Paul Dehn, News Chronicle)*

'Has the sureness expected when a group of the most sophisticated talents are able to work together on material entirely suited to them.' *(Penelope Houston)*

GILDA

CT: 6 AV: 7.23

1946 US 110 BW THRILLER

D Charles Vidor ☆
W Marion Parsonnet from E.A. Ellington's story

Rita Hayworth ☆ Glenn Ford George Macready ☆ Steve Geray ☆ Joseph Calleia ☆ Joe Sawyer Gerald Mohr Ludwig Donath Saul Martell

A gambler (Glenn Ford) is employed to run a casino, but finds that his boss's new wife (Rita Hayworth) is an old flame.

Rita Hayworth as she should be remembered: the ultimate 40s femme fatale, in this most stylized example of Hollywood 'film noir', brilliantly shot by Rudolph Maté (this is his finest work as cinematographer). George Macready is icily effective as Gilda's sinister husband; but Glenn Ford lacks any likeable qualities as the unlucky anti-hero; his misogyny looks especially creepy today. The storyline becomes abstruse, and the ending is a let-down. But the film's worth seeing for Hayworth at her most radiantly erotic. She later accused the film of wrecking her private life: 'Every man I've known has fallen in love with Gilda and wakened with me.'

PRO:

'For director Charles Vidor, *Gilda* is an abiding masterpiece. Never again would he have the opportunity to work without financial or artistic restraint on a moody Gothic piece that was obviously so closely attuned to his brilliant – but extremely circumscribed – abilities. *Gilda* is directed with a pace and a style . . . a precision and an atmosphere totally alien to the mainstream Hollywood film. It is a land of intense shadows where there is no past, only the enigmatic characters of the present whose relationships are veiled by hinted innuendoes and unexplainable motivations. There's a surface story of course, but the film is least interesting when the plot gains control. The characters are at their most fascinating when they're at their most enigmatic.' *(George Aachen)*

'High in atmosphere thanks to Rudy Maté's skilfully shadowy and markedly contrasty photography, *Gilda* is a connoisseur's delight, with clever film editing that sometimes breaks all the rules effectively (eg jump-cutting to reverse angles on the wrong side of the screen; breaking up rapid tracking shots instead of using one continuous take) and at least one camera angle (Macready standing by a bed on which Rita is reclining) that must surely take its place as the most unusual set-up ever attempted in a mainstream film (the opening shot with the camera panning up through the sidewalk is rather dramatic too).' *(John H. Reid, Memorable Films of the Forties)*

ANTI:

'To worshippers of Miss Hayworth "Gilda" will be the feast of a lifetime, to those who don't wear her sort of Bobby-sox it will look like one of the worst films within recent memory. From a quick promising opening the film settles into an intractable obscurity of narrative through which as in a fog three characters bite off at each other words of hate. The producers seem to have shared our ennui, for the film collapses several times [only] to shake itself wearily into a fresh start.' *(Richard Winnington)*

'Overlong, silly and confusing, and Ford gives an uninteresting performance.' *(Danny Peary)*

MIXED:

'When things get trite and frequently far-fetched, somehow, at the drop of a shoulder strap, there is always Rita Hayworth to excite the filmgoer. When story interest lags, she's certain to shrug a bare shoulder, toss her tawny hair in an intimately revealing closeup, or saunter teasingly through the celluloid. She dissipates the theories, if any, that sex has its shortcomings as a popular commodity.' *(Variety)*

'The plot snakes away into extravagant and barely understandable complications: international cartels, tungsten, Nazis, secret police, philosophical lavatory attendants and a gambling-joint proprietor (nicely played by a new face, George Macready) with sword-stick and Mephistopheles cloak. I should perhaps put down in favour Miss Hayworth's rendering of "Put the Blame on Mame, Boys", and Saul Martell's appearance, cut too short for my taste, as a small bearded gambler.' *(Dilys Powell)*

'All will revel in Rita Hayworth's sultry beauty, and admire Glenn Ford's acting and the film's magnificent Buenos Aires sets and background. But not all will find things to admire in its hard to follow and often cheaply melodramatic and theatrical story . . . Its whole approach to its subject is miserably wrong. Not until its final scene does one begin to feel the least bit of sympathy for hero or heroine and no picture yet was very successful in which romantic leads were so badly written that audiences didn't feel one emotion or another for them.' *(Hollywood Review)*

GINGER AND FRED   CT: 8 AV: 6.50

(aka *Ginger & Fred*)

1986 Italy/France/West Germany 126 C DRAMA/FOREIGN

D Frederico Fellini
W Federico Fellini Tonino Guerra Tullio Pinelli

Giulietta Masina ☆ Marcello Mastroianni ☆
Franco Fabrizi Frederick von Ledenburg
Augusto Poderosi

Two aged entertainers (Marcello Mastroianni, Giulietta Masina), who used to tour with their homage to Astaire and Rogers, are reunited to appear on a TV show of astounding vulgarity.

Fellini attacks the commercialism and sensationalism of modern Italian television, in this satire which looks more and more relevant to other countries; it looks horribly like the kind of asinine extravaganza which Jonathan Ross might present in Britain. But more important than the film's cultural commentary is its nostalgic yet regretful atmosphere and two miraculous, touching performances by Masina (Fellini's wife) and Mastroianni. Perhaps it is a bit self-pitying, but so is *8½*. Underrated by contemporary critics, it's more charming, likeable and wise than most of this director's 'masterpieces'.

ANTI:

'I fear that Fellini's admirers are going to be . . . disappointed . . . Within this two-hour satire on Italian commercial television there are about 20 minutes of the purest and best Fellini . . . The trouble with [his] satire is that it is either too much like the real thing to be funny, or too broadly comic to be really amusing.' *(Richard Roud, Guardian)*

'Fellini never seems to know where he's going in this movie, and when he gets there, he seems puzzled by his destination.' *(Roger Ebert)*

'A cranky, wobbling movie. Fellini appears to be condemning TV for being a green slime that's absorbing everything, and denouncing it, too, for passing him by.' *(Pauline Kael)*

MIXED:

'The performances, especially Miss Masina's, are both a delight and a relief, but the parts are underwritten.' *(Patrick Gibbs, Daily Telegraph)*

'Fellini satirizes TV, and the cult of instant celebrity, in this relaxed and amusing film . . . The targets are a bit obvious and the pace a bit leisurely, but the climactic sequence is fun, and the two stars are wonderful to watch, as always.' *(Maltin)*

'Fellini doesn't have a lot to say; but it amounts to considerably more than his usual marginal doodlings, and it is irresistibly charming.' *(Chris Peachment, Time Out)*

GIRL CAN'T HELP IT, THE CT: 7 AV: 6.00

1956 US 99 C MUSICAL/COMEDY

D Frank Tashlin ☆
W Frank Tashlin Herbert Baker from Garson Kanin's story *Do Re Mi*

Tom Ewell ☆ Jayne Mansfield ☆
Edmond O'Brien ☆ Henry Jones John Emery
Julie London Ray Anthony Fats Domino
Little Richard The Platters

Press agent (Tom Ewell) launches talentless but buxom blonde (Jayne Mansfield) on path to stardom.

The plot is not dissimilar to *Born Yesterday*, with a gangster's moll falling for her Svengali, but the treatment is very different. This is *the* great 50s rock'n'roll musical with 17 numbers from artistes such as Fats Domino, Gene Vincent and Little Richard. Some of the humour is crude and sexist at the expense of Jayne Mansfield, but she rises above it with considerable charm. A lot of it really is funny; Ewell and O'Brien are expert comedians, and Tashlin directs with a fine sense of pace.

ANTI:

'I approached it in friendship ever on the side of the socially underprivileged; but . . . I recoiled pretty sharply as it bit me . . . Cheaply pre-fabricated and carelessly assembled . . . this is Hollywood on its knees.' *(Lindsay Anderson, New Statesman)*

PRO:

'An hilarious comedy with a beat.' *(Variety)*

'Basically a slipway for launching Miss Jayne Mansfield as a duplicate Miss Marilyn Monroe.' *(Technology)*

'One of the funnier of recent musicals . . . highly diverting.' *(Fred Majdalany)*

'Tashlin has referred to the breast fetish as the immaturity of the American male and uses the topic as source of comedy . . . Mansfield's role becomes a parody of herself.' *(Linda Obalil, NFT Programme notes)*

GIRL ON A MOTORCYCLE CT: 6 AV: 3.50

(aka *Naked under Leather; La Motocyclette*)

1968 GB/France 91 C DRAMA/ROMANCE

D Jack Cardiff
W Ronald Duncan from André Pieyre de Mandiargues's novel *La Motocyclette*

Marianne Faithfull Alain Delon Roger Mutton
Marius Goring Catherine Jourdan

A married woman (Marianne Faithfull) rides on her motorcycle to her college don lover (Alain Delon).

Blissfully silly soft porn, with the assets of the leading actress's beauty and Cardiff's cinematography. But the things which make it a camp classic are its unashamed leather fetishism and hilariously pretentious dialogue. Some samples:

Faithfull: 'A twist of the throttle and I obliterate this muck and turn myself on.' To Delon, eyeing her in black leather: 'Skin me.'

Delon (to Faithfull): 'Your body is like a violin in a velvet case.'

Faithfull (in a voice-over monologue): 'I was an adulterous teenage bride . . . Why did I marry him? Was it because I was a masochist? . . . You're a sadist, my darling, a magnificent sadist bastard!'

Delon to Faithfull: 'Your toes are like tombstones.'

Delon (I think): 'All of us are lemmings on the way to the cemetery.'

MIXED:

'The ride gets a bit long and the film lacks a true erotic flair. But it is well lensed and has a shattering finale.' *(Variety)*

'Very prettily photographed . . . Otherwise, it is slow, ponderous, pretentious and often unconsciously funny.' *(Ann Pacey, Sun)*

'Visually pleased as I was by [Faithfull's] journey, I felt untroubled by its abrupt ending.' *(Sean Day-Lewis, Sunday Telegraph)*

'A collector's item for motor-sex-leather-rose petal fans, as Mr Cardiff becomes a sort of D.H. Lawrence of the Harley-Davidson.' *(Renata Adler, New York Times)*

'Wonderfully schlocky piece for leather fetishists.' *(Winnert)*

ANTI:

'Memorably absurd dialogue.' *(John Russell Taylor, The Times)*

'The picture is almost a disaster . . . The dialogue . . . is dreadful . . . [It's] a good romantic drama, providing earplugs are worn.' *(News of the World)*

'An incredibly plotless and ill-conceived piece of sub-porn claptrap, existing only as a long series of colour supplement photographs.' *(Halliwell)*

'One of the dullest and most pointless films ever made . . . The sudden end is meant to shock but instead comes as a blessed relief.' *(Elliot)*

GIRL WAS YOUNG, A/THE: *see* YOUNG AND INNOCENT.

see YOUNG AND INNOCENT.

GIRLS HE LEFT BEHIND, THE: *see* GANG'S ALL HERE, THE.

GIRLS IN UNIFORM: *see* MÄDCHEN IN UNIFORM.

GLASS KEY, THE CT: 6 AV: 6.88

1942 US 85 BW THRILLER

D Stuart Heisler ☆
W Jonathan Latimer ✔ from Dashiell Hammett's novel

Alan Ladd ☆ Veronica Lake ☆ Brian Donlevy Bonita Granville Richard Denning Joseph Calleia William Bendix ✔

A politician (Brian Donlevy) asks a henchman (Alan Ladd) to clear him of murder.

Superior remake of the 1935 film by Frank Tuttle, with more developed characters than exist in Hammett's original novel. Later critics have liked to point out Ladd's sexual ambivalence: he seems more drawn to Donlevy than the official *femme fatale* (Veronica Lake). And there are erotic undercurrents to the beating which William Bendix administers to Ladd, one of the most memorably violent in screen history (Bendix did, in fact, knock Ladd unconscious at one point, and the blow remains in the film). *The Glass Key* stands out as one of director Heisler's best films, but credit may be due mainly to cinematographer Theodor Sparkuhl, who provides it with all the necessary film noir lighting and atmosphere.

'An entertaining whodunit with sufficient political and racketeer angles to make it good entertainment for general audiences.' *(Variety)*

'Depicts the world of the criminal, ignoring for the most part the legal authorities. This in turn leads into the sort of violence and brutality usually associated with the film noir, which certainly makes it a precursor to the more morbid films of the mid- and late forties. Much of the violence here is performed by Bendix, who bounces Alan Ladd around like a rubber ball . . . The film contains numerous other examples of the new-found brutality of forties films.' *(Robert Ottoson, A Reference Guide to the Film Noir: 1940-58, 1981)*

'Donlevy, a very uneven actor, gives one of his most indifferent performances throughout. At its best, it is superficial, often it is merely mechanical. No wonder the film loses direction and credibility and flounders in most of his scenes.' *(George Aachen)*

'Hammett fans hated our version of their favorite author's classic. Others never liked the original version with George Raft and felt we'd accomplished an improvement on the story. Either way, it all came off for me as a humdrum affair.' *(Veronica Lake, 1971)*

GLEN OR GLENDA? CT: 5 AV: 2.50

(aka *I Led Two Lives; I Changed My Sex; He or She; The Transvestite*)

1953 US 65 BW DRAMA

D Edward D. Wood Jr ●
W Edward D. Wood Jr ●

Daniel Davis ● (Edward D. Wood Jr) Dolores Fuller ● Tommy Haynes ● Bela Lugosi ● Lyle Talbot ● Timothy Farrell ●

A transvestite (Daniel Davis) has designs on his fiance's angora sweater.

This endearing apologia for transvestism marks Edward D. Wood Jr as a true auteur, and a fearlessly radical one at that. Particularly notable are the crazy lurches between lecturing his audience and wacky fantasy sequences.

'Though opening credits warn of film's stark realism, director Edward Wood Jr's use of stock footage, cheap sets, perfunctory visuals and recited-lecture dialog gives the picture a phony quality. What distinguishes it from other low-budget efforts are the occasional mad flights of fancy. Most involve a weird scientist, delightfully played by Bela Lugosi in eye-popping fashion. Also out of the ordinary is a suggestive (but far from pornographic) sequence of women writhing in their sexy undies, laden with bondage overtones, as well as a surrealist nightmare scene.' *(Variety)*

'Wood was more critical of America's government . . . and military strategy . . . than any other Hollywood establishment director of the period dared to be . . . One must be impressed by this film for the very reason that it takes a stand on a subject that surely was in 1953 not even acceptable enough too be considered controversial. Moreover, Wood dares to incorporate footage that was obviously influenced by surrealists and experimental filmmakers. No matter that this footage is absolutely ridiculous, it shows Wood had an imagination.' *(Danny Peary, 1988)*

'Incredible film by the incomparably inept Edward D. Wood Jr.' *(Martin & Porter)*

'Hilariously inept . . . candidate for worst-ever film.' *(Winnert)*

'The main story – a documentary-style look at the problems of transvestites – is a masquerade of good intentions shot with all the panache of an Indian restaurant commercial . . . When dressed to kill, [the hero] looks like a straggler from the Monty Python lumberjack song . . . but see for yourself, it's a film that defies description.' *(Chris Peachment, Time Out)*

'A deeply moving plea for human understanding,

years ahead of its time.' *(Tony Rayns, Time Out, 1979)*

GLENGARRY GLEN ROSS CT: 7 AV: 6.50

1992 US 100 DRAMA

D James Foley
W David Mamet ✔ from his play

Al Pacino ☆ AAN Jack Lemmon ☆ Alec Baldwin ✔ Ed Harris ✔ Alan Arkin ✔ Kevin Spacey ✔ Jonathan Pryce

Real-estate salesmen compete for survival.

David Mamet's study of salesmen under pressure, cleverly adapted from his own stage play, is a memorable metaphor for the free market rat-race. Although it was even better on stage, this must be one of the most brilliantly acted films of all time. Jack Lemmon and Al Pacino have never been better – which is saying a lot – but others in the cast with less to do (especially Arkin and Harris) are on their level. There's a lot of bad language, but for once it's artistically justified.

ANTI:

'The theatrical roots show rather clearly . . . A superb cast acts out one of David Mamet's major works but it doesn't quite all come together here as it did onstage.' *(Variety)*

'Gains nothing by the transfer from stage to screen.' *(Brian Case, Time Out)*

'Tepid stuff, which gets stuck as a feeble whodunit and lets down its two wonderful stars.' *(Winnert)*

MIXED:

'Boasts several fine performances but lacks the sting of the Broadway production . . . [whose] idiosyncratic perspective, machine-gun dialogue and vicious humour are easily recognizable as the work of this extraordinary writer . . . Foley's movie . . . earnestly recreates the world of Mamet without completely inhabiting it . . . The film's most pleasant surprise is Arkin, who fits snugly into the Mamet school of dialogue.' *(Ed Kelleher, Film Journal)*

PRO:

'Mamet's pungent chronicle . . . makes one of the great ensemble films of the decade . . . Brilliantly written and acted.' *(Empire)*

'Mamet's dialogue has a kind of logic, a cadence, that allows people to arrive in triumph at the ends of sentences we could not possibly have imagined. There is great energy in it. You can see the joy with which these actors get their teeth into these great lines, after living through movies in which flat dialogue serves only to advance the story.' *(Roger Ebert)*

GLOIRE DE MON PÈRE, LA: *see* MY FATHER'S GLORY.

GLORY CT: 8 AV: 8.21

1989 US 122 C WAR

D Edward Zwick ✔
W Kevin Jarre from the books *Lay This Laurel* by Lincoln Kirsten and *One Gallant Rush* by Peter Burchard and the letters of Robert Gould Shaw

Matthew Broderick ✔ Denzel Washington ☆ AAW Cary Elwes Morgan Freeman ☆ Jihmi Kennedy André Braugher Alan North Jay O. Saunders Richard Riehle Peter Michael Goetz Donovant Leitch

The story of America's first black regiment to bear arms in the American Civil War. Under white officers and a callow young colonel, the black soldiers have to fight not only the opposing Confederates, but also the prejudices of their own side.

That cherishable rarity: a war film which neither diminishes the heroism of soldiers, nor tries to glamorize warfare. James Horner's pompous, obtrusive score is a disastrous error of taste; the screenplay is efficient, rather than inspired; and you'd never guess from the upbeat ending that US regiments remained racially segregated until the Korean War, almost a hundred years later.

Despite these flaws, the film succeeds in being moving, entertaining and a stirring achievement on an epic scale. Veteran British cinematographer Freddie Francis deservedly won an Oscar; and director Edward Zwick, best known for TV's *thirtysomething*, shows he can handle action scenes as well as liberal angst (here embodied in the regiment's young, white commanding officer, Matthew Broderick: a sensitive and critically underrated performance). Steven Rosenblum was deservedly Oscar-nominated for his editing (the battle scenes are especially effective), as was Norman Garwood for his production design.

ANTI:

'The film's worst failing is that Shaw – thanks, largely, to Broderick's lack of range, presence, and moral weight – never grows as a character; and the film itself, excessively mindful of its Good Intentions, too often shares his empty earnestness. The film's other major roles, by contrast, are remarkably well served by the performers. Schematically routine though their parts may be, Washington, Braugher, Kennedy and (especially) Freeman all turn in riveting, beautifully shaped performances, lending depth and nuance to characters that might easily have been rendered as caricatures.' *(Bruce Bawer, American Spectator)*

MIXED:

'Why does the top billing in this movie go to a white

actor? I ask, not to be perverse, but because I consider this primarily a story about a black experience and do not know why it has to be seen largely through white eyes . . . *Glory* is a strong and valuable film no matter whose eyes it is seen through. But there is still, I suspect, another and quite different film to be made from this same material.' *(Roger Ebert)*

PRO:

'As the small, sad-faced Shaw, who saw Hell at Antietam and is determined to prepare his men for what's ahead, Matthew Broderick shows us the misery of a softhearted commanding officer. His Shaw is not a natural hero; he has to work at it. Even Broderick's drawbacks (the flat tone of his voice, his relative inexpressiveness) seem to help here. Shaw is decent, uncertain of himself – a worrier. It's a lovely performance, as remote and touching as a daguerreotype . . . The movie is terribly literal-minded, with evenhanded pacing, and this fastidiousness mutes it emotionally. *Glory* isn't a great film, but it's a good film on a great subject.' *(Pauline Kael)*

'A stirring and long overdue tribute . . . Has the sweep and magnificence of a Tolstoy battle tale or a John Ford saga of American history.' *(Variety)*

GODDESS, THE   CT: 5 AV: 6.37

1958 US 105 BW DRAMA/SO BAD

D John Cromwell
W Paddy Chayevsky ● AAN

Kim Stanley ☆ Lloyd Bridges ☆ Steven Hill Betty Lou Holland Patty Duke

Unhappy country girl (Patty Duke) turns into Hollywood sex goddess (Kim Stanley) but still cannot find happiness.

Relentlessly vicious indictment of the Hollywood star system and especially the Marilyn Monroe cult, written – at times over-written – by that self-appointed scourge of the media, Paddy Chayevsky. Kim Stanley doesn't quite have the looks of which sex goddesses are made, but gives a powerful performance in her big-screen début. Lloyd Bridges is fine in the Joe DiMaggio role of the sports star husband (though here he's a boxer, not a baseball star). The amazingly unsubtle script, which for some reason was Oscar-nominated, is the thing which makes this film a camp classic.

PRO:

'A dissection carried out . . . with an unhurried carefulness and the ability to cut clean and deep.' *(The Times)*

'A chilling picture but a compelling one, and Miss Stanley's electric performance is enough to set the town alight.' *(Star)*

'An idol of the world who is completely impossible . . . and who is completely worthless to be anything but a movie star.' [said] David O. Selznick about the heroine . . . [who] is played by Kim Stanley in a screen début of startling virtuosity which dominates the film . . . only too believable in her self-destructive obsession with stardom.' *(NFT Bulletin)*

MIXED:

'One of the best things about this film is that it has been made. It is episodic, unevenly directed, and could be too long – but it has an intensity, an authenticity and a vitality which, in the final count, dwarf all the weaknesses.' *(Paul Rotha, S & S)*

'Kim Stanley cannot look sixteen years old, but this stage actress can catch perfectly the tone of the girl's snobbish, aggrieved, defensive chatter – and as the mother driven half-crazy by a crying baby, as the incalculable, savagely egoistic wife, as the star, hands and voice shaking with drink and hysteria, she unerringly shades the picture in; almost clinical though it is she makes its central figure seem somehow defenceless and pitiful. She is surrounded by performers of extraordinary quality: performers from the New York theatre, performers from Hollywood, faces one knows, faces one doesn't know . . . A complete success? No, but a bold adventure – and uncomfortable, disturbing though *The Goddess* is, one looks forward with excitement to seeing it again.' *(Dilys Powell)*

'Savage attack on the Marilyn Monroe cult, a bit lachrymose and compromised by miscasting, but with interesting detail.' *(Halliwell)*

ANTI:

'Pretentious . . . shrill, verbose, theatrical and steeped in a sort of hysterical gloom.' *(Fred Majdalany, Daily Mail)*

'Terribly wordy. If snails could stutter they would go about this pace.' *(Jympson Harman, Evening News)*

'Preposterously overwrought and – this is vintage Paddy Chayevsky, after all – overwritten account of the Price of Fame. It's guaranteed to give you giggles from the dialogue alone.' *(Margulies & Rebello)*

'The film takes a psychiatric and sociological view of her career: she's a pathetic creature who has been deceived by false values and is destroyed by the Bitch-goddess Success. Chayevsky is so concerned with the heroine's pitifully unformed character that he fails to suggest what would make her stand out from all the other poor, deceived girls – what would make her a star. This is a conscientious, ambitious bad movie, with Chayevsky's famous ear for dialogue in full cauliflower.' *(Pauline Kael, 70s)*

GODFATHER, THE AAW CT: 7 AV: 9.32

1972 US 175 C THRILLER/DRAMA

D Francis Ford Coppola ☆ AAN
W Mario Puzo Francis Ford Coppola ✗ AAW from Mario Puzo's novel
Marlon Brando ✗ AAW Al Pacino ☆ AAN
James Caan ☆ AAN Richard Castellano
Robert Duvall ☆ AAN Sterling Hayden John Marley
Richard Conte Diane Keaton Al Lettieri

The son (Al Pacino) of a gangster boss (Marlon Brando) takes over.

A landmark in 70s cinema, if only because it proved that a movie of this weight could be a huge hit. It's certainly a bravura piece of direction with a superb performance by Pacino, a memorably hammy one by Brando, and brilliantly staged set pieces – but those critics who think it a great film seem to have confused detail and length with depth. As a parable about American free enterprise, it's facile and vacuous; and as insight into organized crime, it is extremely dubious. No wonder members of the Mafia loved it; it ends up celebrating the mob as a model of family life and corporate loyalty.

PRO:

'The greatest gangster picture ever made.' *(Pauline Kael)*

'I don't think the film is about the Mafia at all. I think it is about the corporate mind. In a way, the Mafia is the best example of capitalists we have. Don Corleone is just any ordinary American business magnate who is trying to do the best he can for the group he represents and for his family.' *(Marlon Brando)*

'One of the most brutal and moving chronicles of American life ever designed within the limits of popular entertainment.' *(Vincent Canby, New York Times)*

'With its attention to period . . . and its sureness in every detail, *The Godfather* shows there is still life in the massive production engineering that made Hollywood studios the wonder of the entertainment world in their great days.' *(Alexander Walker, Evening Standard)*

'Brando, perhaps America's greatest actor, in his finest role to date.' *(Ivor David, Daily Telegraph)*

'[It] looked like an action saga. It wasn't. It was really a film about relationships and connections: between men and women, between fathers and sons, between business and personal lives. Vito's tragedy is that he separates them: Michael's, that he can't . . . We can see why Brando was essential to *The Godfather*. No other actor . . . carries with him such a weight of personal myth . . . [It is] the most significant American film since *Citizen Kane*.' *(James Monaco, American Film Now, 1979)*

'A watershed film . . . Hollywood's requiem for the American dream.' *(Seth Cagin & Philip Dray, Hollywood Films of the 70s, 1984)*

MIXED:

'Though the performance looks all surface with its mask-like make-up, half-strangulated vocal delivery and physical intimations of old age, it has a core of iron underneath that never wavers . . . Nowhere else does the film measure up to the social and political significance with which Brando miraculously invests his part.' *(Derek Malcolm, Guardian)*

'*The Godfather* lost voltage the moment Marlon Brando wasn't on the screen.' *(Axel Madsen, The New Hollywood, 1975)*

ANTI:

'The basic dishonesty of the film lies in showing the Mafia mostly in extremes of heroic violence or sweet family life. Even the scenes of intimidation are grand and spectacular. Missing is the banality of evil: the cheap, ugly, racketeering that is the mainstay of organized crime . . . The acting is predominantly good, with the exception of the highly touted and critically acclaimed performance of Marlon Brando in the title part. Brando has a weak, gray voice, a poor ear for accents, and an unrivaled capacity for hamming things up by sheer underacting – in particular by unconscionably drawn-out pauses.' *(John Simon)*

'Most of the time he sounds like he has a mouth full of wet toilet paper.' *(Rex Reed)*

'The immorality lies in his presentation of murderers as delightful family men – the criminal is the salt of the earth – and to our shame we rub it into the wounds of our Watergate-world mortality and even ask for more.' *(Judith Crist)*

'They have put pudding in Brando's cheeks and dirtied his teeth, he speaks hoarsely and moves stiffly, and these combined mechanics are hailed as great acting . . . Like star, like film, the keynote is inflation. *The Godfather* was made from a big bestseller, a lot of money was spent on it, and it runs over three hours. Therefore, it's important.' *(Stanley Kauffmann)*

GODFATHER PART II, THE AAW CT: 5 AV: 8.81

1974 US 163/170 C THRILLER/DRAMA

D Francis Ford Coppola ☆ AAW
W Francis Ford Coppola Mario Puzo ●

Robert De Niro ☆ AAW Al Pacino ✗ AAN
Lee Strasberg ☆ AAN Michael V. Gazzo AAN
Talia Shire ☆ AAN Diane Keaton ● John Cazale
Robert Duvall ✓

More Mafia family life.

Coppola's sequel to *The Godfather* is just as atmospheric and spectacularly directed (especially in some set pieces). It is also better acted, and benefits from the absence of the mannered Marlon Brando. But there's a hopelessly disorganized plot, with narrative leaps and loose ends galore. Morally, it seems even more questionable than its predecessor: ever anxious to gather sympathy for the Mob, it suggests that they are just pursuing the American Dream by somewhat unconventional means. Symptomatic of the film's contempt for reality is the fact that the ship on which young Vito Corleone is supposed to be arriving in New York from Sicily sails south past the Statue of Liberty, and is therefore quite clearly leaving. Critics generally adored the film. It was the first ever sequel to win the Oscar for Best Picture. The score, by Nino Rota and Carmine Coppola (Francis's father), also won an Oscar.

PRO:

'Pays a great deal more attention to the parallelism between the Family business and business at large. What's good for the Corleones is good for America . . . It's important that Coppola doesn't take a liberal, accusative attitude here. We're all part of the same hypocrisy . . . As a cinaste Coppola can hold his own against any rivals. He takes real chances, artistically, and he succeeds.' *(James Monaco, American Film Now, 1979)*

'An epic vision of the corruption of America.' *(Pauline Kael)*

'An excellent epochal drama in its own right.' *(Variety)*

'One of the great films of the 70s.' *(Winnert)*

MIXED:

'An improvement on the original . . . since it doesn't have to cope with the distraction of Marlon Brando's heavy make-up job, and because Coppola has evidently taken the opportunity of a second chance to re-stage certain sequences even better than the first time round . . . One can ask . . . questions about holes and inconsistencies in the plot, but for the most part one is too busy relishing individual sequences and performances to bother.' *(MFB)*

'This successor to a blockbuster has better performances, more imaginative use of period décor, sharper photography, and less lurid violence. but it has nothing to say about the Corleone family and America that wasn't already evident in Part I.' *(S & S)*

'More subtle in its effects than Part I and less strident about its meanings, yet without that unity of effect and meaning which made *The Conversation* a more provocative and cohesive work . . . While the first Godfather gathered up all its elements in a continuous narrative sweep, the magisterial pace of the sequel . . . begins to flag about halfway through, regaining its strength only through isolated episodes. But the performances establish continuities of their own, and the acting throughout sustains a much higher level of assurance.' *(Jonathan Rosenbaum, S & S)*

'The mood is quite different from that of its predecessor. This is a much colder film, with austere aspirations – not fully realized – to transcend its melodramatic origins and to become an authentic tragedy . . . [It] also has a stronger moral dimension.' *(Richard Schickel, Time)*

'Better than its predecessor, though this is lukewarm praise at best . . . Coppola is getting to be a more competent director: a scene here is allowed more leisure and breathing space, is less like a guided missile trained with dumb, mechanical determinism to explode on a specific target . . . Granted, Coppola still goes in for repeating his fancy effects: there is far too much backlighting to reveal altogether any too stark silhouettes, and much too much interior underlighting to make rich mafiosi look like troglodytes in hiding . . . The moral defects are undeniable and repugnant . . . but the movie is well put together and steadily watchable.' *(John Simon)*

'[Coppola's] style tends to be rather ponderous, which isn't like him at all . . . remorselessly protracted, dwelling lugubriously upon the central figure of Michael . . . But a performance that nearly justifies the time is the first ever cinema appearance of Lee Strasberg . . . This is quiet greatness. Its like is rare. How I wish it could have had a worthier vehicle.' *(Gordon Gow, F & F)*

ANTI:

'If you're Italian or Sicilian and a fully paid up member of the Mafia then [this] is your sort of film, bambino. If you don't fit into the above categories, then this sprawling . . . extravaganza may strike you as more of an endurance test than compulsive entertainment . . . This *Godfather* is rather like a Grandfather. Sedate, with one or two colourful recollections of the good old days related between siesta snoozes.' *(Arthur Thirkell, Daily Mirror)*

'Rarely has so much screen time been spent on inflated clichés, so much portentousness lavished on the banal. When you add the facts that some of the cast are inadequate, that the structure is rickety, and that the ironies are juvenile, you are left with a vastly bloated mediocrity . . . [Coppola] seems locked here by past success to the manner of that success: arbitrarily dim, irrelevant "Old Master" lighting; impersonal, bland, Hollywood-studio camera style; dubious casting.' *(Stanley Kauffmann)*

'The supremely untalented Diane Keaton, as Kay, is worse yet in Part II, but one of her big scenes has been mercifully cut from the released version, and the other is so bad that it is deliciously giggle-provoking.' *(John Simon)*

'Pacino is a brooding bore. His character does not develop logically from the person he played in the original, but is a caricature of a crime boss. All the major scenes seem unreal, calculated for audience response. Phoniest of all is his break-up with Diane Keaton, which looks over-rehearsed, like a scene for an acting class . . . The scene in which the senator (G.D. Spradin) is found in a brothel with a hooker he brutally killed is similar to numerous sequences in exploitation films of the era and is included for no reason other than sensationalism.' *(Danny Peary)*

GODFATHER PART III, THE CT: 4 AV: 6.50

1990 US 161 C THRILLER/DRAMA

D Francis Ford Coppola ✗
W Mario Puzo Francis Ford Coppola

Al Pacino Diane Keaton Talia Shire Andy Garcia Eli Wallach Joe Mantegna George Hamilton Bridget Fonda Sofia Coppola ● Raf Vallone Franc D'Ambrosio

It tells no fewer than four stories: first, the ill-fated struggle of Michael Corleone (Al Pacino) to find redemption after a life of crime, corruption and fratricide; second, the burgeoning love affair between Michael's daughter (Sofia Coppola) and Michael's nephew Vincent (Andy Garcia); third, Vincent's rise to the top; and fourth, accounting irregularities at the Vatican Bank, which culminate in the assassination of Pope John Paul I.

Plotwise, the most grandiose of the *Godfather* trilogy. One unwelcome by-product of its complexity is that the film takes a long first hour to establish storylines and characters, most of whom are underwritten. Another side-effect is that the Vatican plot (which might have made a film in itself) remains skimped and incomprehensible throughout. The two strands which involve Vincent are diminished by the fact that he is never more than an amoral, violent hood, whose loyalty to Michael seems to be an excuse for killing anyone standing in the way of his own ambitions. The trilogy's glorification of Latin machismo continues.

The love story is further undermined by the performance of Coppola's own daughter. Sofia Coppola was given a rough time by the American critics, who probably hadn't forgiven her for co-perpetrating the dreadful middle section of *New York Stories*. She lends the role of Michael Corleone's daughter a certain adolescent gawkiness, but the flatness of her delivery suggests that she shares Arnold Schwarzenegger's dialogue coach. A more basic reason why her role has all the allure of stale pizza is that it is grievously undercharacterized. We never know how she feels about being a Mafia princess, still less what she sees in the appalling Vincent. Francis Ford Coppola has likened her ultimate, tragic fate to that of Lear's Cordelia, but at least Cordelia has the guts to stand up to her father in the opening scene: this character seems passive throughout, and it would be hard to care about her, whoever was in the role.

Only the first of the film's four stories is remotely gripping – partly because Pacino is always watchable, but mainly because this is the only aspect of the film which appears to interest the director. The climax of the movie – Michael's loss of a child – mirrors Coppola's experience (his own son died in a boating accident). Coppola's self-identification with the role is reflected not only in his casting of his daughter, but also in the fact that Michael's sister is played by Coppola's sister, Talia Shire (who really can act).

The result is a film which is so over-indulgent towards Pacino's agonized quest for respectability, that it ends up as a barely concealed celebration of middle-aged self-pity and egomania. At any moment, there's the horrible possibility that Al Pacino may start singing 'My Way'.

The reality of Mafia 'business' – based as it is on protection racketeering, pimping and crooked casinos – is fudged. The distinction between honest and dishonest is elided, with even legitimate investment portrayed as a cross between gambling and mortal combat ('Finance is a gamble, it's knowing when to pull the trigger' says a minor character shortly to perish for mixing metaphors). And the 60s-generation cynicism about political hierarchies – that they are as corrupt as any Mafia – is as omnipresent and unconvincing as ever.

The Godfather is too handsomely mounted to be a bad film (Alex Tavoularis's art direction and Gordon Willis's photography were both Oscar-nominated), but it is over-ambitious, under-involving and unpleasantly infatuated with the testosterone-crazed characters it half-heartedly affects to deprecate. Despite moments of grandeur, its style looked old-fashioned and its morality facile after Martin Scorsese's *GoodFellas*.

PRO:

'Locates an emotional gravity rare in American movies. The film is a slow fuse with a big bang – one that echoes through every family whose own tragedy is an aching for things past and loved ones lost.' *(Richard Corliss, Time)*

'Visually, this is the most gorgeous of the three *Godfathers*; Willis and production designer Dean Tavoularis have outdone themselves. And it's loaded with fascinating moments: Garcia's magnetic psychopathology, Pacino's weary pursuit of grace, Eli Wallach's angelic duplicities as Don Altobello, and, especially, that climactic opera house set-piece, with its bravura echoes of Visconti's *Senso* and Hitchcock's second *The Man Who Knew Too Much*.' *(Michael Wilmington, LA Times)*

MIXED:

'While certain flaws may prevent it from being regarded as the full equal of its predecessors . . . it nonetheless matches them in narrative intensity, epic scope, sociopolitical analysis, physical beauty and deep feeling for its characters and milieu.' *(Variety)*

'This engrossing movie is conceived and executed on a grand scale . . . Oddly enough, Michael seems to shrink in stature as the picture proceeds and the Lear-like tragedy at which Coppola aims is not realised.' *(Philip French, Observer)*

'Despite lacking the crispness of the brilliant originals and having a plot with a few loose ends, this is a severely underrated sequel. As a portrayal of repentance, salvation and spiritual decay, it remains very powerful. Had Winona Ryder played Mary instead of the dreadful Sofia Coppola, then it would have been a masterpiece.' *(Rose)*

ANTI:

'A confusing and disjointed film. It is said that Coppola was rewriting it as he went along, and indeed it lacks the confident forward sweep of a film that knows where it's going. Some of the dialogue scenes, especially in the beginning, sound vaguely awkward; the answers do not fit the questions, and conversations seem to have been rewritten in the editing room.' *(Roger Ebert)*

'The picture isn't just unpolished and weakly scored; it lacks coherence. The internal force has vanished from his work, but you still expect some narrative flow, instead, he reaches for awesomeness. Trying to make a masterpiece, he resorts to operatic pyrotechnics that don't come out of anything . . . But the illusion never takes hold. Where are the scenes in which Michael would recognize that Vincent has the steel and cunning to hold power? Michael seems to turn his empire over to a loyal bodyguard. The movie appears to be saying that Michael recognizes that in this depraved world Vincent, with his killer instincts, is the man for the job – the man that Michael now thinks he never was. Maybe that's too self-serving for Coppola to make it more explicit. *Godfather III* looks like a *Godfather* movie, but it's not about revenge and it's not about passion and power and survival. It's about a battered movie-maker's king-size depression.' *(Pauline Kael)*

GODS MUST BE CRAZY, THE

CT: 8 AV: 6.27

1980 South Africa 109 C COMEDY

D Jamie Uys
W Jamie Uys

Marius Weyers Sandra Prinsloo N!xau ✔
Louw Verwey Michael Thys Jamie Uys

Bushman (N!xau) finds a Coca-Cola bottle and, when it causes tribal dissension, tries to throw it off the edge of the world.

The politically correct and terminally humourless have always disliked this film as being racially patronizing; however, its portrayal of simple tribesmen, corrupt black bureaucrats and incompetent freedom fighters is balanced by its satirical view of white people. It's hard to resist the suspicion that this film's severest critics had a knee-jerk reaction to a film that was made by a white South African, for the central character (played by a non-professional) is highly sympathetic and far from patronized. The film's main justification is that, despite low production values and some crass over-acting, it's very funny. This cannot, unfortunately, be said of the sequel, *The Gods Must Be Crazy II* (1989), a film of such mammoth incompetence that it suggests this one was just a lucky aberration.

ANTI:

'Offensively racist and too gormless even for the kids at whom it is evidently aimed.' *(Sheila Johnston, Time Out)*

'A witless film of dumb car chases, unconvincing incidents, banal voice-overs and amateur camerawork and acting. The film-makers must have been crazy to produce this inept, offensive nonsense.' *(Winnert)*

'One for the Race Relations Board.' *(Halliwell)*

PRO:

'N!xau, because he approaches Western society without preconceptions, and bases all of his actions on logical conclusions, brings into relief a lot of the little tics and assumptions of everyday life. I think that reveals the thought that went into this movie: it might be easy to make a farce about screwball happenings in the desert, but it's a lot harder to create a funny interaction between nature and human nature. This movie's a nice little treasure.' *(Roger Ebert)*

'Film's main virtues are its striking widescreen visuals of unusual locations, and the sheer educational value of its narration.' *(Variety)*

'A hoot . . . brilliantly funny.' *(Virgin)*

'Has the production values of an episode of *Daktari* and features actors who can't act. Yet it is wonderfully, screamingly, tearfully funny. It begins slowly but will soon have you clutching your sides to stop the pain. The scene with the Landrover and the tree is a classic.' *(Rose)*

GOING MY WAY AAW

CT: 6 AV: 7.50

1944 US 126 BW COMEDY/MUSICAL

D Leo McCarey ☆ AAW
W Frank Butler Frank Cavett Leo McCarey AAW from Leo McCarey's story AAW

Bing Crosby ☆ AAW Barry Fitzgerald ☆ (AAW Best Supporting Actor, AAN Best Actor) Rise Stevens Frank McHugh James Brown Gene Lockhart Jean Heather Porter Hall

A new priest (Bing Crosby) rescues an ailing church and its old, stubborn curate (Barry Fitzgerald).

One of the most popular films of the 40s, it's good-hearted, entertaining, beautifully acted; and Leo McCarey's skilful direction keeps it, for the most part, from degenerating into schmaltz. It still has a lot of charm, although its view of human nature seems unduly sunny, and there is a distinct lack of dramatic tension: on a fundamental level, it fails to give evil its due. Its worst sin is that it was later recycled to produce such abominations as *Sister Act I* and *II*. Leroy Stone's editing and Lionel Lindon's photography were Oscar-nominated, and the song 'Swingin' On a Star' (music and lyrics by James Van Heusen and Johnny Burke) was voted Best Song.

PRO:

'[Catch] a wonderful Irishman named Barry Fitzgerald. His performance is one of the half-dozen finer things seen in motion pictures.' *(Life)*

'Barry Fitzgerald gives a truly brilliant performance every foot of the way . . . he is a joy.' *(Hollywood Reporter)*

'McCarey, a director of remarkable ability which he obstinately lavishes on second-rate material, wrings genuine pathos from the tritest situations; again and again the timing of a gesture, a scrap of dialogue, insists on admiration. Bing Crosby, by a performance both sincere and endearing, once again shows what a good actor he can be. But the star of the film is Barry Fitzgerald, who as the ageing, querulous, eccentric priest gives an impression of life and character rare on the screen.' *(Dilys Powell)*

MIXED:

'Its Hibernian humor and drama stroke the heartstrings with frankness, skill and an unashamed schmaltz that should rocket the reels into one of the biggest box-office bonanzas of all time.' *(Herb Sterne)*

'Its rather makeshift narrative is enlivened by good will and good humor, and two fine actors make the whole thing bubble with human interest.' *(James Shelley Hamilton, New Movies)*

'I should not feel safe in recommending it to anyone but a simple-hearted sentimentalist with a taste for light music.' *(Richard Mallett, Punch)*

'A rather saccharine story about priests, has a gentle, engaging performance by Bing Crosby, a very full and fine one by Barry Fitzgerald, and a general leisure and appreciation of character which I think highly of. It would have a little more stature as a "religious" film if it dared suggest that evil is anything worse than a bad cold and that lack of self-knowledge can be not merely cute and inconvenient but also dangerous to oneself and to others.' *(James Agee, Nation)*

GOLD DIGGERS OF 1933 CT: 10 AV: 8.83

1933 US 96 BW MUSICAL/COMEDY/ROMANCE

D Mervyn LeRoy
W Erwin Gelsey James Seymour David Boehm Ben Markson from Avery Hopwood's play

Warren William Joan Blondell ✓ Aline MacMahon ☆ Ruby Keeler ✓ Dick Powell ✓ Guy Kibbee Ned Sparks Ginger Rogers ✓ Clarence Nordstrom

Songwriter (Dick Powell) from wealthy family wishes to marry a chorus-girl (Ruby Keeler); his family tries to stop him.

Though hurriedly produced by Warner Brothers in only 45 days to cash in on the unexpected success of *42nd Street*, this is one of the all-time-great musicals. Even the plot holds up well, thanks to a romantic partnership (Powell and Keeler) with charm, and comic support from Joan Blondell, Aline MacMahon and Ginger Rogers. Admittedly, the Depression theme gets lost as the main plot takes over; when it surfaces belatedly and bizarrely in the final number, 'Forgotten Man', it seems to spring from nowhere. But there are classic ingredients, especially Busby Berkeley's elaborately vulgar, unforgettable stagings of Al Dubin and Harry Warren's terrific songs. It received only one Oscar nomination, for Best Sound. There were two sequels (*Gold Diggers of 1935* and *1937*), both vastly inferior to this one but watchable for the production numbers.

'The film's superiority to *42nd Street* lies in the greater romantic interest with a multitude of amorous complications.' *(Variety)*

'Imaginatively staged, breezy show with a story of no greater consequence than is to be found in this type of picture . . . More than once the audience applauded the excellent camera work and the artistry of the scenic effects.' *(New York Times)*

'If you thought *42nd Street* was good, you have a date with any theatre showing this one . . . Music, ensemble numbers, and acting . . . are splendid.' *(Photoplay)*

'It's a funny, good-natured backstage musical, and a Depression period piece as well. It was directed by the not conspicuously talented Mervyn LeRoy and it is memorable chiefly because the choreographer, Busby Berkeley, created a mad geometry of patterned chorines . . . The innocent vulgarity of the big numbers is charming and uproarious, and aesthetically preferable to the pretentious ballet finales of fifties musicals like *An American in Paris*.' *(Pauline Kael)*

'Just as the numbers in *42nd Street* progressively grew beyond the boundaries of a theatre stage, in *Gold Diggers of 1933* Busby Berkeley disbands an attempt to formulate a theatre style for more than a few minutes at the beginnings and ends of numbers . . . Berkeley and his disciples do not pretend to be filming theatre: they give us the cinematic equivalent of what theatre does.' *(Ethan Mordden, The Hollywood Musical)*

GOLD RUSH, THE CT: 8 AV: 9.38

1925/1942 (sound) US 142 (silent)/72 (sound)
BW COMEDY/SILENT

D Charles Chaplin ☆
W Charles Chaplin

Charles Chaplin ☆ Georgia Hale Mack Swain
Tom Murray Betty Morrissey

A poor prospector has poor prospects, but suddenly strikes it rich.

One of Chaplin's most successful movies. The comic set-pieces (including the dance of the bread-rolls and Charlie eating his boot and laces) show his talents to the full: it's the glutinous sentimentality in between which is hard to take. In 1958, an international jury voted the silent version the second-greatest film of all time (after Eisenstein's *Potemkin*); but some modern critics feel Chaplin is too strained in his attempts to ingratiate himself. The truncated sound version issued in 1942 is to be avoided.

PRO:

'A distinct triumph for Charlie Chaplin from both the artistic and commercial standpoints. Billed as a dramatic comedy, the story carries more of a plot than the rule with the star's former offerings.' *(Variety)*

'Chaplin's jokes have an unmistakable quality of personal fancy . . . [and he] uses gags to help him through the deliberate ironic or pathetic situations which have become more frequent in his comedies . . . *The Gold Rush* has some of his most ambitious – and most successful – scenes of this sort, but he seems to be afraid of losing touch with his popular audience by venturing upon these scenes without . . . breaking them up with gags . . . It may be that . . . *The Gold Rush* . . . represents the height of his achievement. He could scarcely do better . . . than . . . the opening.' *(Edmund Wilson, New Republic)*

'The greatest film author in the world . . . is Charlie Chaplin. But very few people suspect this. Even among the most fervent admirers of his acting, few are sufficiently aware that in a big film like *The Gold Rush* as well as a little sketch like *The Pilgrim*, his skill in dramatic construction more than equals his comic inventiveness.' *(René Clair, 1950)*

'The individual sequences . . . are rich in Chaplin's comic ingenuity and his ability to render the pathos of the tramp's disappointment . . . The film's theme is its consistent indictment of what the pursuit of the material does to the human animal; as in Greed it makes him an inhuman animal . . . The quest for gold perverts all human relationships in the film . . . perverts both love and friendship.' *(Gerald Mast, A Short History of the Movies, 1971)*

'Chaplin's greatest silent film, a masterly combination of pathos, humor and tragedy . . . After *City Lights* this is the funniest and saddest of all Chaplin's comedies.' *(R.A.E Pickard, Dictionary of 1000 Best Films, 1971)*

'A joyful highpoint in [Chaplin's] art . . . one of the highest-grossing of all silent films.' *(Allan Hunter & Kenny Mathieson, Movie Classics, 1992)*

'Extraordinarily sweet and graceful.' *(Pauline Kael)*

ANTI:

'Mercifully, it lacks the pretentious moralizing of his later work, and is far more professionally put together. But for all its relative dramatic coherence, it's still hard to see how it was ever taken as a masterpiece.' *(Geoff Andrew, Time Out)*

GOLDEN AGE, THE: *see* L'AGE D'OR.

GOLDEN MARIE: *see* CASQUE D'OR.

GOLDFINGER: *see BOND* SERIES.

GOLEM: HOW HE CAME INTO THE WORLD, THE CT: 6 AV: 8.00

(aka *Der Golem, Wie Er in Die Welt Kam*)

1920 Germany 97 BW HORROR/SILENT

D Paul Wegener Carl Boese (supervizing director)
Ernst Lubitsch ☆
W Paul Wegener Henrik Galeen

Paul Wegener Albert Steinrück Ernst Deutsch
Lyda Salmonova Hanns Sturm

Clay statue comes to life and terrorizes Prague.

Wegener had already filmed this story twice, and here it's third time lucky: a masterpiece of German Expressionism and one of the most memorable and influential silents, with marvellous sets and enjoyably stylized performances. There is also an interesting racial and political subtext: the monster is brought to life by a Jewish Rabbi in order to protect his people from a pogrom. That said, the plot is heavy going; and it contains few terrors for a modern audience.

'A masterpiece . . . presented with a sweep and a sincerity of purpose that thrills and amazes. It is racially Jewish; artistically international. A picture that is a credit to the screen.' *(Photoplay)*

'It will doubtless be disconcerting to some; it will be said that the photoplay does not develop climactically, and in places its lack of direction does leave the mind somewhat at sea, but this is not to say that it is ever dull, for one cannot lose interest in a world so strangely engrossing and with such power as The Golem has in many of its scenes.' *(New York Times)*

'The picture marked a decisive step forward in German, as well as world, cinema, blending all the resources of acting, set design, photography and direction into a wonderfully orchestrated piece of film which did not rely on ostentatious expense to achieve its effects. [Hanns] Poelzig's set of old Prague creates a sense of claustrophobia and instability with its oblique and jagged lines, while [Karl] Freund's virtuoso lighting weaves its own magic spells with dancing lights, deep shadows and ghostly impositions.' *(Phil Hardy, The Horror Film Encyclopaedia)*

'Classic German monster movie . . . containing many of the elements of plot, cinematography and design later incorporated in genre films, particularly those made in America by German emigrés such as Freund and Ulmer. Karloff's creature in the 1931 Frankenstein can be traced back to Wegener's Golem. The movie looks better than its content.' *(Alan Frank)*

GOLEM, WIE ER IN DIE WELT KAM, DER:

see GOLEM: HOW HE CAME INTO THE WORLD, THE.

GONE WITH THE WIND AAW CT: 9 AV: 9.63

1939 US 211/220/222/240 C DRAMA/ROMANCE/WAR/EPIC

D Victor Fleming ☆ AAW (uncredited: George Cukor, Sam Wood, William Cameron Menzies, Sidney Franklin)
W Sidney Howard AAW and others from Margaret Mitchell's novel

Clark Gable ☆ AAN Vivien Leigh ☆ AAW Olivia de Havilland ☆ AAN Leslie Howard Thomas Mitchell Barbara O'Neil Hattie McDaniel ☆ AAW Butterfly McQueen ☆ Victor Jory

A Southern belle, Scarlett O'Hara (Vivien Leigh), is attracted to a Southern gentleman (Leslie Howard), but he marries another (Olivia de Havilland); Scarlett marries twice, and is eventually tamed by a gambler (Clark Gable), who then deserts her.

A tremendous epic with inspired set-pieces (such as the burning of Atlanta, and the pull-back to reveal the carnage at the railway station). It's also one of the great love stories, especially refreshing because it does not have a cop-out happy ending and offers a complex picture of a self-destructive anti-heroine: Vivien Leigh gives one of the great performances on celluloid.

It's been criticized over the years for racism and sexism; but it's a film of its time, and describes rather than prescribes (unlike, say, *Birth of a Nation*). The Civil War is merely a backdrop, and although the detail is well observed, there's little attempt to take a political stance on the conflict.

Gone with the Wind is above all wonderful entertainment, handsomely produced, and another of those classics, like *Casablanca*, which proves that some of the best films are born out of collaboration and chaos. It was, of course, one of the biggest hits in screen history; and, despite a few longueurs and an uncharismatic performance by Leslie Howard, it's as enjoyable now as it ever was.

Not surprisingly, it won nine Oscars including best cinematography (Ernest Haller, Ray Rennahan), art direction (Lyle Wheeler) and editing (Hal C. Kern, James E. Newcom), plus a special award for production design (William Cameron Menzies). Max Steiner was nominated for his brilliant score, which even without the pictures can still make grown men cry. Gable should have won, too.

'Forget it, Louis. No civil war picture ever made a nickel.' *(MGM executive Irving Thalberg to Louis B. Mayer, 1936)*

ANTI:

'History has rarely been told with even an approximation of truth in Hollywood, because the few men in control there have no interest in the real forces behind historical movements and the new forces that every new epoch sets into motion. *Gone with the Wind* deserves our attention because it is an overinflated example of the usual, the false movie approach to history. Selznick's four-hour feature represents all Hollywood might do, and, unfortunately, most of what it usually does. In every foot of it is inscribed the tragic gap between possibility and achievement.' *(Lincoln Kirstein, Films)*

'Shakespeare's *The Taming of the Shrew* seems to have got mixed up with one of the novels of Ethel M. Dell . . . "Where shall I go? What shall I do?" says Scarlett O'Hara at the end of *Gone with the Wind*, and receives from Rhett Butler the reply: "Frankly, my dear, I don't care a damn!" The trouble with this film, which lasts four hours, is that for the last hour and a half nobody in the audience has been caring what happens to anybody . . . Since the Civil War is not the theme, what is? I can only suggest the minxishness of minxes. Indeed, Scarlett is so declared a baggage that I come away feeling that I have spent a long afternoon in the cloakroom at a literary Waterloo Station.' *(James Agate, Tatler)*

'Miss Leigh gave a performance compact of vivacity, coquettishness and rigid egoism, extremely clever and well-trained and almost entirely without interest.' *(Dilys Powell, in a review which led MGM to ban her for a year from all of their pictures)*

'Reduced the gigantic panorama of history to a painted backcloth for the cavortings of a group of vulgar little egoists.' *(Dilys Powell, unrepentant in 1945)*

'It does not seem to me the greatest film ever made . . . It lacks – shall we say? – heart, the high, noble memorable emotion one associates with great drama . . . [It] suits our wartime mood. It is a prodigal film, generous to overflowing with facile events.' *(C.A. Lejeune, Observer, 1942)*

'Ponderous trash.' *(Val Lewton)*

'The film succeeded admirably in continuing the

popular Southern myth the South had in fact won an ideological war, that, indeed, although the Negroes had been set free they still remained inescapably fettered as historic inferiors to the white race, socially, politically and economically.' *(Peter Noble, The Negro in Films, 1969)*

'It cannot be a coincidence that while the Second World War was wreaking havoc, America made its second Civil War epic. It was Griffith over again, except this time the excuse was more expensive – three years, thirteen writers and four million dollars to create three and three-quarter hours of the most boring celluloid ever to be shown on the screen . . . America was saying through Hollywood, its translator, "We've had our war. Leave us alone".' *(Julie Burchill, Girls on Film)*

'I'll let you in on a secret: *GWTW* is a piece of crap. It wouldn't outgross *Grumpy Old Men* in today's market. Hey, it couldn't even get made today. It's a four hour soap. Every scene is rushed, and something momentous just has to happen every three minutes. It's exhausting and phony.' *(Rod Lurie, LA Magazine, 1994)*

MIXED:

'A major event in the history of the industry but only a minor achievement in motion picture art . . . One admires an excellent cast and a hundred technical details, but one's heart seldom beats faster. While one waits to be carried away, critical thoughts have time to develop.' *(Franz Hoellering, Nation)*

'Faults could be found if one were looking at this film merely as a motion picture of Georgia in the war and reconstruction days; that it leaves too many important things untouched, that it has no historical perspective, that it provides no ethical or social comment on its characters or events, finally that it is still a novel more than it is a motion picture. But none of those things were intended, or really to be expected. It is enough that Margaret Mitchell's novel should have been put on the screen so satisfyingly for its millions of readers.' *(James Shelley Hamilton, NBR)*

'Has little dramatic pattern but which is yet unerring in its cumulative emotional effect . . . There will be some who will doubt the timeliness of showing in films hundreds of wounded soldiers in simulated agony, especially the scene of the amputation of a leg without an anaesthetic.' *(Seton Margrave, Daily Mail)*

'Not a great film in the true sense of the word, but undeniably a great piece of filmmaking and a monument to the skill of the technicians and actors associated with its production.' *(R.A.E Pickard, Dictionary of 1000 Best Films, 1971)*

'It's inevitably racist, alarmingly sexist (Scarlett's submissive smile after marital rape), nostalgically reactionary (wistful for a vanished, supposedly more elegant and honourable past), and often supremely entertaining.' *(Geoff Andrew, Time Out)*

PRO:

'The film has arrived at last, and we cannot get over the shock of not being disappointed; we had almost been looking forward to that.' *(Frank S. Nugent, New York Times)*

'One of the truly great films.' *(Variety)*

'Superbly comprehensive canvas embraces enchanting romance, thwarted love, heroic sacrifice and brutal savagery . . . enhanced by lovely Technicolor. Narration reaches rare heights of emotional intensity . . . Brilliant direction, flawless leading portrayal, dynamic support, wholly admirable production quality.' *(Today's Cinema on the 1947 re-issue)*

'No problem in summing up my feelings about this indelible legend of a film. Simply it's been part of my life for over 40 years. I can't count the number of times I have seen it. Always the emotional charge is as strong as ever, but I keep discovering new pleasures. Only recently did I realise how witty it is! It really isn't an epic. What sustains it is the truth and vividness of the relationships. Conceived in chaos, it emerges remarkably as a completely integrated masterpiece (I use the word advisedly), under the no doubt tyrannical guidance of David O. Selznick.' *(Margaret Hinxman, NFT Bulletin, 1984)*

GOOD EARTH, THE AAN CT: 5 AV: 8.45

1937 US 138 BW DRAMA/EPIC

D Sidney Franklin ✗

W Talbot Jennings Tess Schlesinger Claudine West from Owen and Donald Davis's play from Pearl S. Buck's novel

Paul Muni ✗ Luise Rainer ✗ AAW Walter Connolly Tilly Losch Jessie Ralph Charley Grapewin Keye Luke Harold Huber

A Chinese peasant (Paul Muni) becomes wealthy but loses his patient, selfless wife (Luise Rainer).

Three years in the making and with two changes of director (the original one, George Hill, shot location footage in China but committed suicide in 1934; his replacement, Victor Fleming, fell ill and had to be hospitalized), this epic was a big, prestigious hit of its day, but has dated badly. The direction is pedestrian, at best; while the performances of Muni and Rainer, thought moving at the time, are jarringly unconvincing – as a few critics pointed out even on release.

The scenes which work best are the sacking of the palace, and the plague of locusts (the matte work here now looks primitive, but was outstanding for its time). The film was voted Number 2 in the Film Daily annual poll of US film critics (*The Life of Emile Zola* was first). Karl Freund won an Oscar for his cinematography. Executive producer Irving

Thalberg died during production, and studio chief Louis B. Mayer put his name on the credits as a tribute: the only time it ever appeared on a film.

'Who wants to see a film about Chinese farmers?' *(Louis B. Mayer to Irving Thalberg; see also Thalberg to Mayer, warning him off Gone With The Wind)*

PRO:

'Performances, direction and photography are of a uniform excellence, and have been fused perfectly into a dignified, beautiful, but soberly dramatic production.' *(New York Times)*

'A classic . . . Rainer is overwhelming.' *(Virgin)*

ANTI:

'I did not feel that Mr and Mrs Chang, or whatever they are called, were remotely Chinese. I thought that Chang was just my old friend Mr Paul Muni giving an extremely good performance of what a very clever modern film actor thinks a Chinaman should be. And I also thought that Mrs Chang was just my young friend Miss Luise Rainer giving an exquisite rendering of what my clever Austrian actress imagines a Chinese peasant woman to be like . . . To tell the truth, of which I am horribly ashamed, I found the whole film a little pretentious and rather boring.' *(James Agate, Tatler)*

'Prestigious boredom, and it goes on for a very long time.' *(Pauline Kael, 1977)*

'The days are long since past when western actors, their eyes perfunctorily taped, were acceptable as orientals. The farce is compounded when, as here, such players are mixed with the genuine articles . . . All told, *The Good Earth* is a dated hodgepodge of a picture. Its dated acting styles and conventions are as unacceptable to a 1990 audience as its naive and laughable simplistic philosophy.' *(John Howard Reid)*

GOOD FELLAS: see GOODFELLAS.

GOOD MORNING, VIETNAM

CT: 6 AV: 6.67

1987 US 120 C COMEDY/WAR

D Barry Levinson
W Mitch Markowitz

Robin Williams ☆ AAN Forest Whitaker Tung Thanh Tran Bruno Kirby ✔ Chintara Sukapatana Robert Wuhl J.T. Walsh Noble Willingham Richard Edson Juney Smith Richard Portnow

An off-the-wall disc jockey (Robin Williams) upsets the American hierarchy in Vietnam.

As a vehicle for the improvisatory and imitative talents of Robin Williams, Levinson's film works well. Also in its favour is an attempt to show the Vietnamese in a reasonably rounded manner, neither as villains nor victims. However, the story is thin, contrived and sentimental; Williams is a good deal more convincing as the cool, wisecracking comic of the first part than the warmer, wiser humanitarian at the end.

PRO:

'Those who confuse solemnity with seriousness, preferring carefully researched filmic treatises on the Vietnam War done from the vantage of the British Museum, might find this Buena Vista release flip, raw and not necessarily in lock-step with their own apprehensions of military stereotypes. Nevertheless, it's just plain funny, and Williams' potshots rattle off faster than an M-16.' *(Duane Byrne, Hollywood Reporter)*

'Williams kicks the movie up to the sublimely ridiculous, hot-wires it into realms of quick-witted chaos. He gives a fine, freezingly cheery hello and goodbye to the hell of war and the purgatory of radio.' *(Michael Wilmington, Los Angeles Times)*

'At last, the great monologist gets to play – a great monologist . . . You may be all the way home before you realize you may have seen not just the comedy (and the comic performance) of the year, but just possibly the most insinuatingly truthful movie yet about Viet Nam.' *(Richard Schickel, Time)*

MIXED

'Offering only hackneyed insights into the war, the film makes for stodgy drama. But Williams's manic monologues behind the mike are worth anyone's money.' *(Geoff Andrew, Time Out)*

ANTI:

'Williams is a totally self-contained character, and despite numerous topical references, his comedy turns in on itself rather than opening on the scene outside . . . At a time when the world is truly in transition, it is a bit shameful to reduce the events of Vietnam to a few good jokes.' *(Daily Variety)*

'When Cronauer is forced to confront the relative pettiness of his clashes with Army brass on a scale of napalm and civil war, the film owns up – he's shallow and he knows it . . . There are more important questions than "But is it funny?" Even in comedy.' *(LA Reader)*

'Neither Williams' innocence nor his embitterment rings true.' *(Ralph Novak, People Weekly)*

GOOD, THE BAD AND THE UGLY, THE

CT: 5 AV: 6.92

(aka *Il Buono, Il Brutto, Il Cattivo*)

1966 Italy 161 C WESTERN/EPIC

D Sergio Leone ✗
W Luciano Vincenzoni Sergio Leone from Agenore Incrocci, Furio Scarpelli, Vincenzoni and Leone's story

Clint Eastwood Eli Wallach Lee Van Cleef

Aldo Giuffré Chelo Alonso Mario Brega Luigi Pistilli Rada Rassimov

Three unprepossessing characters search for stolen Confederate gold during the American Civil War.

Stylish spaghetti western on a grand scale, with Eastwood perfecting his impersonation of a waxwork Gary Cooper, Eli Wallach over-acting manfully to compensate, and Ennio Morricone contributing one of his most memorable scores. It's much admired by its fans; but to others (including me), it's pretentious, intolerably slow, and boring.

PRO:

'The definitive spaghetti western . . . A stunning, panoramic view of the west . . . This is Leone's most violent film, but also his most compassionate.' *(Virgin)*

'Exceptional, extremely exciting, extravagant and funny . . . Long film has an imaginative storyline, elaborate set pieces (some employing hundreds of extras), several terrific shoot-outs, much humor (built around the Eastwood-Wallach relationship), striking cinematography by Tonino Delli Colli, and Ennio Morricone's best score. Film has vague anti-war theme and, like all Leone's works, points out that America was civilized by men who killed for profit.' *(Danny Peary)*

'Delights through its subversive, operatic parody of genre conventions, undercutting heroism by means of black comedy and over-the-top compositions, all deep focus and zooms . . . Enormous fun.' *(Geoff Andrew, Time Out)*

MIXED:

'A sharp, cynical Continental Western which would have been a good deal more enjoyable if it hadn't been so determined to rise above its stylistic station . . . All the characters are strictly two-dimensional, but Clint Eastwood and Lee Van Cleef are impressively impassive, while Eli Wallach has a high old time sneering and grimacing in a valiant attempt to make a lovable rogue out of the double-crossing Tuco.' *(MFB)*

'Sergio Leone's comic, cynical, inexplicably moving epic spaghetti western, in which all human motivation has been reduced to greed.' *(Dave Kehr)*

ANTI:

'A curious amalgam of the visually striking, the dramatically feeble and the offensively sadistic.' *(Variety)*

'Zane Grey meets the Marquis de Sade . . . [It] must be the most expensive, pious and repellent movie in the history of its peculiar genre.' *(New York Times)*

'Crammed with sadism and a distaste for human values that would make the ordinary misanthrope seem like Pollyanna, their only possible excuse for existence is that [movies such as this] make money. Somehow, that isn't enough.' *(Arthur Knight, Saturday Review)*

'This 161-minute mess is strictly for viewers with a lust for gory garbage.' *(Judith Crist)*

GOODBYE, COLUMBUS CT: 7 AV: 6.63

1969 US 105 C COMEDY/ROMANCE

D Larry Peerce ☆
W Arnold Schulman ☆ AAN from Philip Roth's novella

Richard Benjamin ☆ Ali MacGraw ☆ Jack Klugman Nan Martin Michael Meyers Lori Shelle

Witty little comedy about a romance between an awkward, impoverished young man (Richard Benjamin) and a Jewish princess (Ali MacGraw).

Slight, witty, well-observed little tale, very sympathetically acted by Benjamin, and a telling satire on American materialism and snobbery. Critically underrated by comparison with *The Graduate* (1967), to which it is vastly superior. The Jewish wedding is a marvellous set-piece; Jack Klugman is terrific as MacGraw's father; and even the ex-model MacGraw (in her début) seems able to act, an impression which had to be revised in the light of her subsequent screen appearances.

PRO:

'A joy . . . castwise the feature excels . . . several outstanding sequences.' *(Variety)*

'Benjamin's scenes with Ali MacGraw are finely detailed and nice to watch; the reactions of the two mesh as if the characters were really in love – at least for a summer.' *(Penelope Gilliatt)*

'The picture of the family is extremely funny and sometimes likeable . . . And the acting all through is exceptionally skilled; one notes Richard Benjamin as the young man and as the girl Ali MacGraw, an elegant and gifted newcomer who handles the smart dialogue with flawless rhythm and timing. But in the end one recognises *Goodbye, Columbus* as an acid film, its transition from the impudent comedy of the start to the recriminations of the close tellingly managed by the director; in fact an attacking film, with conformity to the rules of getting on and settling down as the target. I think it is quite good enough to set beside *The Graduate*.' *(Dilys Powell)*

'Miss MacGraw, and for this Peerce may deserve some directorial credit, gives a delicately balanced performance, her Brenda emerging tough and unfeeling at times, tomboyish and silly at others, considerably yet not repellently narcissistic all along. There is inchoate feeling and vestigial thought, and also, at the right moments, something touching and pitiable. It is a graceful, nicely shaded piece of acting, enhanced by the fact that it comes from a young woman not merely lovely, but actually gifted with a kind of thinking man's loveliness.' *(John Simon)*

GOODBYE GIRL, THE AAN CT: 8 AV: 7.00

1977 US 110 C COMEDY/ROMANCE

D Herbert Ross
W Neil Simon ☆ AAN

Richard Dreyfuss ☆ AAW Marsha Mason ☆ AAN Quinn Cummings ☆ AAN Paul Benedict Barbara Rhodes Theresa Merritt Michael Shawn

A loser in love (Marsha Mason) who's also a single mother, falls for an equally difficult, and much more egocentric actor (Richard Dreyfuss).

Richard Dreyfuss is at his most charming in Neil Simon's best screen comedy. For once the one-liners come credibly out of all the characters' mouths, even that of the obligatory cute kid (beautifully played by Quinn Cummings). The most refreshing aspect is the heroine, who is believably over-sensitive and abrasive – so much so that it's hard at first to see why Dreyfuss takes a fancy to her. There are many funny moments – the gay, off-Broadway production of *Richard III* is a particular delight – and it's the kind of movie which can be guaranteed to leave almost anyone with a warm glow.

ANTI:

'[Simon] invents an absolutely incredible character hangup for his heroine – something about the courage to say goodbye in order to say hello again, and if I've got it wrong, it doesn't matter – but it's only an attempt to paste some disguise of depth on one more boy-meets-girl polka.' *(Stanley Kauffmann)*

'Simon's idea of depth is to tug at your heartstrings, and Marsha Mason's chin keeps quivering – her face is either squinched up to cry or crinkled up to laugh. This may be the bravest, teariest, most crumpled-face perfomance since the days of Janet Gaynor.' *(Pauline Kael)*

MIXED:

'Virtually none of the film's comedy stems from what the characters are supposed to be about. The ambitious young actor falls in love like a lamb, which makes the goodbye girl, who does worry a mite overmuch (but only a mite), no longer as cold, or ungiving, or a saboteur of relationships. Everything glibly ends well, and the jokes are mostly set pieces . . . The fun – good or bad – is extraneous, adventitious; some of it, moreover, is as hoary as passers-by getting into the act when lovers squabble in the street. Still, good performances, especially from Dreyfuss and little Quinn Cummings; serviceable, unpretentious direction from Herbert Ross; and, of course, some undeniably droll gags from Neil Simon do add up to a tolerable movie. But it could have been so much more.' *(John Simon)*

'A very moderate script aided by excellent acting.' *(Halliwell)*

PRO:

'Performances by Dreyfuss, Mason and Cummings are all great, and the many supporting bits are filled admirably.' *(Variety)*

'He [Dreyfuss] gets the girl in the end, but he gets the audience first.' *(Time)*

'Charmingly, abrasively funny, perfectly setting the manic rhythm for Simon's confrontational comedy.' *(Newsweek)*

'A funny movie with its heart finally in the right place.' *(Roger Ebert)*

GOODBYE, MR CHIPS AAW CT: 8 AV: 8.29

1939 GB 114 BW DRAMA

D Sam Wood ☆ AAN
W R.C. Sherriff Claudine West Eric Maschwitz Sidney Franklin ☆ AAN from James Hilton's novella

Robert Donat ☆ AAW Greer Garson ☆ AAN Terry Kilburn John Mills ☆ Paul Henreid Judith Furse Lyn Harding Milton Rosmer Frederick Leister Louise Hampton

The life of a British schoolmaster (Robert Donat).

Donat gives one of the most moving of all screen performances in this study of an old-fashioned man with unfashionable notions of duty, but Greer Garson and John Mills offer notable support. The production values may not be up to Hollywood standards, but Alfred Junge's art direction works wonders within the budget, helped immeasurably by Freddie Young's brilliant cinematography (which should have been Oscar-nominated, as the editing and sound were). It was voted Best Picture of 1939 in the *Film Daily* annual poll of US film critics, and should not be confused with the schmaltzy remake of 1968, with songs by the dreaded Leslie Bricusse.

MIXED:

'The novel became an American best seller when that old sentimentalist Alexander Woollcott touted it on the radio . . . It's an ingratiating, bitter-sweet record of a good life, though the movie clogs the nose more than necessary.' *(Pauline Kael)*

'The movie always was a museum piece, and – if you are in the right mood – a deeply affecting one.' *(Adrian Turner, Time Out)*

PRO:

'Mr Donat gives a beautiful performance in a part which must be the envy of every actor; beginning as the eager idealistic boy, he passes through the hesitations of middle age and the confidence of the man sure of affection to the obstinate benevolence of age with a delicate certainty. Greer Garson as the wife has a charm which almost persuades me that little boys are to be won over with a slice of cake and a crack about the lex Canuleia. If, in fact, we must have a sentimental film about the English public school system, this is probably the film to have.' *(Dilys Powell)*

'The whole picture has an assurance, bears a glow of popularity like the face of a successful candidate on election day. And it is wrong to despise popularity in the cinema.' *(Graham Greene)*

'Charming, quaintly sophisticated.' *(Variety)*

'Not again this year, and perhaps not for any other, does your reviewer expect to endorse so wholeheartedly a film which . . . will be treasured until their dying day by [patrons of all ages] . . . Apart from its cinematic cunning, notable production, direction, and the overwhelmingly beautiful performance given by [Donat, the film] . . . is an elegiac, atmospheric vignette.' *(Richard Sheridan Ames, Rob Wagner's Script)*

GOODFELLAS AAN CT: 10 AV: 8.86

1990 US 146 C DRAMA/BIOPIC

D Martin Scorsese ☆
W Martin Scorsese Nicholas Pileggi ☆ AAN from Nicholas Pileggi's novel *Wiseguy*

Robert De Niro ☆ Ray Liotta ☆ Joe Pesci ☆ AAW Lorraine Bracco ☆ AAN Paul Sorvino Frank Sivero Tony Darrow Mike Starr Frank Vincent Chuck Low

Thirty years in the career of real-life gangster Henry Hill (Ray Liotta), who descends into a self-made hell and the FBI's witness protection programme, accompanied by his wife (Lorraine Bracco), a nice Jewish girl seduced by wealth and the glamour of gangsterism.

The trouble with most gangster movies, from *Public Enemy* to *The Godfather*, is that, even though the film-makers dutifully ensure that their anti-heroes meet a nasty end, they usually glamorize the lifestyle, loyalty and competence of the criminal fraternity so much that any final come-uppance fails to outweigh the gangsters' overall attractiveness. Scorsese avoids this trap by constantly revealing the skull behind the smile. Seldom has violence been portrayed less glamorously, or with more moral effectiveness. Whether it's the slaying of a dying, defenceless rival in a car boot, or the shooting of a harmless waiter, there's never any doubt that violence is repellent: the work of inadequate, scared men.

And yet, Scorsese's anti-heroes make us care. Dangerous psychopath though Joe Pesci's character is, we are still shocked when he is gunned down. We sense Lorraine Bracco's fear of De Niro. We feel Liotta's panic when the FBI is on to him. We even share De Niro's sense of betrayal when Liotta testifies against him. All this is a tribute to magnificent acting, but also to Scorsese's direction, which constantly changes our viewpoint with consummate ease.

Technically, too, Scorsese manages some startling effects: there is one masterly steadicam shot, as Liotta leads the woman he is trying to impress (Bracco) into a nightclub by a side entrance. Another *tour de force* is the scene in a diner where Liotta realizes that De Niro is out to kill him, and the back-projection enlarges subliminally, to give the effect of Liotta's world closing in. Every shot shows a director at the height of his powers, with the entire vocabulary of film at his fingertips.

But the main reason why this is more than just another study of the Mafia is that Scorsese depicts criminality as being a temptation for all of us. His portrayal of Ms Bracco's seduction, in particular, is a memorable study of how anyone might be enticed into criminality. Some critics objected that there was little depth or complexity in Scorsese's characterization; but in doing so they missed the point. In other movies, such as *Raging Bull* and *Taxi Driver*, Scorsese chose to investigate an individual's psychology. In this film, he is doing something different: portraying a whole society of people who lack depth, who simply don't see any problem with what they're doing.

GoodFellas is full of detailed observation, humour and realism; but it's also a parable, a reminder that Scorsese once intended to become a priest. It's a sustained attack not only on gangsterism, but also on the three big, post-Marxist 'isms': opportunism, conformism and materialism. It's timely, horrible and devastating, the greatest of all gangster movies. Thelma Schoonmaker's editing was nominated for an Oscar; it remains a mystery as to why Michael Ballhaus's cinematography was ignored, and even more unfathomable is the reasoning as to why Scorsese wasn't nominated for Best Director.

ANTI:

'There can be few doubts over Martin Scorsese's flair as a director . . . but in moral terms, is it right that at a time when violence of all kinds is destroying whole generations, an auteur of [his] stature should dedicate a film to humanising the gangster?' *(John Francis Lane, Screen International)*

'A mite oppressive and certainly too long.' *(Quinlan)*

MIXED:

'Simultaneously fascinating and repellent . . . colorful but dramatically unsatisfying . . . One of the film's major flaws is that De Niro, with his menacing charm, always seems more interesting than Liotta, but he isn't given enough screen time to explore the relationship fully in his supporting role.' *(Variety)*

'Martin Scorsese's *GoodFellas* has a lift. It's about being a guy and guys getting high on being a guy.

The movie is about being cock of the walk, with banners flying and crowds cheering. Is it a great movie? I don't think so. But it's a triumphant piece of filmmaking – journalism presented with the brio of drama . . . The picture has scope rather than depth. We see Henry Hill only from the outside, and he has been made to seem slightly cut off from the mob life. He has been turned into a retread of the anxious, dutiful Harvey Keitel character in *Mean Streets*, when he needs to be a rat and the motor of the movie. *GoodFellas* is like the Howard Hawks *Scarface* without Scarface. Will the lift of the moviemaking still carry some people aloft? Maybe, because watching the movie is like getting strung out on pure sensation.' *(Pauline Kael)*

PRO:

'Quick-witted, supremely ambiguous . . . unsettling. Some of Mr Scorsese's most triumphant scenes depict the characters' most vicious behavior . . . This particular underside of life is quite different from the ants-in-the-crabgrass universe of David Lynch . . . Mr Scorsese invests his characters' savagery with a giddy, invigorating energy. The scariest thing about *GoodFellas* is its sheer entertainment value, which is so disorientedly high.' *(Janet Maslin, New York Times)*

'Arguably the apex of Scorsese's most open ethnic productions . . . Even at a cursory glance Scorsese's ethnic films . . . share a common attitude, an intensely contradictory ambivalence. It is a love/hate relationship . . . best summarized in the song at the end [of the film], Sid Vicious's version of . . . "My Way". Scorsese is drawn to tradition but he also questions it with the brutal aplomb of a punk.' *(Karen Jaehne, Film Quarterly)*

'Isn't a myth-making movie, like *The Godfather*. It's about ordinary people who get trapped inside the hermetic world of the mob, whose values get worn away because they never meet anyone to disagree with them.' *(Roger Ebert)*

'Rethinks the gangster in symbolic terms. Liotta escorts Lorraine Bracco through the underbelly of the Copacabana, up through the kitchen, and into the dining room, where they are seated at a front-row table. It's nothing less than the odyssey of the American mobster from underworld to ringside seat.' *(Carrie Rickey, Philadelphia Inquirer)*

'Rather than make facile condemnations of evil, Scorsese does something more important, trickier – and, in the end, far more moral. He takes us right into the criminal mind, into the wise guy life – a life of amorality, corruption, easy violence, and sudden death. He and his brilliant cast show us why killers kill, thieves steal, pushers push, rats squeal. He shows us why the Mafia has long been one of the most profitable American business entities, and – the core of his vision – exactly why young guys from poor city neighborhoods might make membership in organized crime their highest aspiration. He shows us the exhilaration of crime and also its consequences.' *(Michael Wilmington, Isthmus)*

GOSPEL ACCORDING TO SAINT MATTHEW, THE

CT: 5 AV: 7.90

(aka *Il Vangelo Secondo Matteo*)

1964 Italy/France 142 BW DRAMA/BIOPIC/ FOREIGN

D Pier Paolo Pasolini ☆
W Pier Paolo Pasolini from *The Gospel According to St. Matthew*

Enrique Irazoqui Margherita Caruso Susanna Pasolini Marcello Morante Mario Socrate Settimo Di Porto Otello Sestili Ferruccio Nuzzo Giacomo Morante Alfonso Gatto

The story of Christ in the words of the Gospel itself.

Desperately slow, soporific exercise in cinematic 'realism', much acclaimed on release – probably because its gritty, documentary style departed so completely from hokey, Hollywood treatments of the same story. Pasolini's Marxism diminishes Christ by trying to portray him as a revolutionary, motivated primarily by fury at social injustices; and the acting (by non-professionals) is variable. Winner of the Special Jury Prize at Venice, 1964.

PRO:

'Pasolini has chipped away the encrustations of time and given us the story as it was written in the first place . . . No one, whatever his faith or lack of faith, can fail to be touch by its grim and glorious sense of the life and the times of a Jesus who is here truly, agonizingly, a living Christ.' *(Richard Schickel, Life)*

'A splendid, severe astonishment.' *(Dilys Powell)*

'Pasolini's use of music, from Bach to Billie Holliday, is astounding.' *(Geoff Andrew, Time Out)*

ANTI:

'I could hardly wait for that loathsome prissy young man to get crucified.' *(Pauline Kael)*

GOTTERDAMMERUNG: *see* DAMNED, THE.

GRADUATE, THE AAN CT: 6 AV: 9.13
1967 US 105 C COMEDY/DRAMA/ROMANCE

D Mike Nichols ☆
W Calder Willingham Buck Henry AAN from Charles Webb's novel

Anne Bancroft ☆ AAN Dustin Hoffman ☆ AAW
Katharine Ross ✗ AAN William Daniels
Murray Hamilton Elizabeth Wilson Brian Avery
Walter Brooke Norman Fell Elizabeth Fraser

A graduate (Dustin Hoffman) feels alienated from his parents' expectations; he has an affair with a middle-aged neighbour (Anne Bancroft), then decides he prefers her daughter (Katharine Ross).

Acclaimed on release as the definitive statement about the generation gap, this now looks like a fairly tame sex comedy with a facile view of the older, wealth-creating generation, a misogynistic view of middle-aged sexuality, and a highly unconvincing ending. It's still notable, however, for Dustin Hoffman's funniest screen performance, Anne Bancroft's sex appeal (which totally overpowers her daughter's), and Simon and Garfunkel's (over-repetitive) score. Robert Surtees's photography was Oscar-nominated.

PRO:

'A milestone in American film history.' *(Stanley Kauffmann)*

'Marks the coming of age of the American cinema. Rarely has a film contained so much deadpan humour with such bitingly serious undertones.' *(Robin Turner, Daily Express)*

'Immensely funny . . . The story fixes your eye to the screen like a keyhole.' *(Robert Ottaway, Daily Sketch)*

'All who see it, whatever their age, will follow the education of the young hero with a sympathy that will make them forget that much of the time he behaves like a bit of a dope. Bristles with wit and irony.' *(Dick Richards, Sunday Mirror)*

'It is Dustin Hoffman . . . who turns Benjamin into an endearing, enduring hero. He never seems sure of what his voice, eyes or hands are doing, or whose orders they are following. He wears the world like a new pair of shoes. He nods his head whenever he doesn't quite know what he means, which is often. He is wrenchingly simple and vividly intelligent, even with his self-doubts, and his bumbling seduction scenes with the wife of his father's law partner . . . are as funny as anything ever committed to film.' *(Newsweek)*

'A peach of a comedy . . . It is all treated with an unblushing directness that not long ago would have frozen the blue pencil in the censors' hands.' *(Cecil Wilson, Daily Mail)*

'The roaring success of Mike Nichols' *The Graduate* is hardly surprising – he has built it on the dependable formula of Restoration comedy. Still, the spice of the piece, the source of its tension and laughter, is the confrontation of jaded maturity with the demanding innocence of youth. "Never trust anyone over 30" is a slogan that could have served the Restoration as well as it does our own time, and Nichols makes the old formula seem as topical as mini-skirts.' *(Robert Hatch, Nation)*

'Nichols is a brilliant director of actors. The seduction scenes in *The Graduate* have some of the mordant high style of *Bringing up Baby*; and some of its lucid precision.' *(Mike Wilmington, 1972)*

'A witty, often very funny film reflecting a wide range of attitudes, but saving most of its satirical comment for the social habits of the American middle class.' *(R.A.E. Pickard, Dictionary of 1000 Best Films, 1971)*

'Nichols consistently shoots from [Benjamin's] point of view, often distorting the image to formally italicize the protagonist's growing alienation.' *(Allan Hunter & Kenny Mathieson, Movie Classics, 1992)*

'Owed much of its enormous box-office success to its ability to catch the flavour of the time, both in its sexual frankness and in the theme of youthful rebellion that permeated America during the 1960s.' *(Peter Waymark, The Times, 1984)*

'It's a lovely case of Holden Caulfield going on to face life in black-comedy terms. Revel in it.' *(Judith Crist)*

MIXED:

'Sophisticated sex comedy . . . not so much a story as the witty way it is told that makes this such an amusingly saucy film and it introduces an interestingly new young male star . . . [It] does sag a bit towards the end.' *(Kinematograph Weekly)*

'Not a faultless film by any means. Some of it is melodramatic, some of it is ludicrous, some of it is over-played and riotous, but most of it riveting and poignant and dreadfully memorable.' *(Polly Devlin, Evening Standard)*

'The director is at his worst when the eclecticism of his visual style gets out of hand. The opening sequence of bobbing, tracking, lurching heads in nightmarishly mobile close-ups looks like an "homage" to Fellini's *8½*. A rain-drenched Anne Bancroft splattered against a starkly white wall evokes images in *La Notte*. The languorous lyricism of Ben at Berkeley seems derivative of Varda's *Le Bonheur* and even some of John Korty's landscape work in the same region. Still, I was with *The Graduate* all the way because I responded fully to its romantic feelings.' *(Andrew Sarris)*

'Served adults a digestible paraphrase of the cultural insurgency then gripping the country, while it offered youth an agreeable story of adolescent malaise relinquished by love . . . Became the third top-grossing film in Hollywood's history . . . and this may be its most legitimate claim to film history, for it alerted Hollywood executives . . . that their future lay with the youth market. *(Seth Cagin & Philip Dray, Hollywood Films of the 70s, 1984)*

ANTI:

'The movie's principal weaknesses are oversimplification, overelaboration, inconsistency, eclecticism, obviousness, pretentiousness, and, especially in the penultimate section, sketchiness . . . There is a line where satire ends and oafishness begins, and *The Graduate* keeps crossing it as if it had diplomatic immunity . . . Inconsistency is at the very core of the film . . . The supreme inconsistency is . . . in the basic impossibility of accepting the sudden change of Candide into an amalgam of Romeo, Don Quixote, and Lochinvar . . . For supreme pretentiousness, we get a protracted shot of Ben crucified against the plate glass of the choir loft at Elaine's wedding.' *(John Simon)*

'The darkening mood of the film's last half [has] no organic connection with character or situation. The true tensions generated by the generation gap are thus avoided and, along with them, the deepest comic possibilities as well. It's a shame – they were halfway to something wonderful when they skidded on a patch of greasy kid stuff.' *(Richard Schickel, Life)*

'The boy's interruption of the daughter's wedding . . . is exciting, it is funny, but it has little to do with what has gone before, with the worried youth in a cocktails-and-swimming-pool society, with the farcical acquisition of experience and the jealous paramour. Why, anyway, does the daughter let herself be hustled into marriage with the wrong boy? One needs a bit more explanation, especially since despite the shifts in mood up to this point the action has generally proceeded from character.' *(Dilys Powell)*

'Even the "happy" ending is shot in such a way that we are patently meant to feel that the young couple's future is hopelessly overshadowed by – what? Incest? The primal curse? Anyway, whatever it is, it must be something quite reassuringly nasty. A film for parents, then, reinforcing all their stuffiest received ideas about the rights and wrongs of youth.' *(John Russell Taylor, The Times)*

'Ben may be a self-centered, sleazy little twerp, but he is also the undisputed hero of this movie. When he and Mrs Robinson declare war, there is no doubt who will win. When he made off with the beautiful Katharine Ross, right under the nose of her furious mother, Young Benjamin won the admiration of a generation. Mrs R loses everything she cares about to that callous Graduate; her marriage, her daughter, and her dignified upper-middle-class social standing. And she, we know, deserves to suffer. To wear jungle print lingerie, to still want sex (especially with a younger man) at her age is a violation of nature, as defined by Hollywood.' *(Kathy Maio, 1991)*

'In 1967, every teenager I knew went to see it at least once and talked about nothing else for weeks. And it was an entertaining picture. But what inspired such extraordinary enthusiasm on the part of these teens? Mostly this: *The Graduate* made a hero of someone close to their own age – a rare thing for an American movie to do in those days – and made dolts of the grown-ups. The movie laughed at the whole idea of being a grown-up (a responsible one, anyway), laughed at the whole idea of making a career, of becoming a useful part of The System . . . Like Benjamin – and like most young people raised in peace and comfort and abundance – these baby boomers believed fervently in their own importance, believed in their superiority to the bourgeois moralities which had helped make that peace and comfort and abundance possible, and believed, too, that the movies should reflect their own ready-made, glibly seditious attitudes about life, love, and the world around them. Never mind that those attitudes were jejune and narcissistic, and that these kids didn't really know a damn thing about the world around them: *The Graduate* made money.' *(Bruce Bawer, American Spectator)*

GRAND AMOUR DE BEETHOVEN, UN: *see* ABEL GANCE'S BEETHOVEN.

GRAND CANYON CT: 8 AV: 6.00

1991 US 134 C DRAMA

D Lawrence Kasdan ✓
W Lawrence Kasdan Meg Kasdan ✓ AAN

Danny Glover ✓ Kevin Kline ✓ Steve Martin ☆
Mary McDonnell ✓ Mary-Louise Parker ✓
Alfre Woodard

An immigration lawyer (Kevin Kline) finds his liberal principles under strain and his life in danger, when his car expires in downtown Los Angeles and he's terrorized by black youths; fortunately for his own and the film's political correctness, he is saved by a mechanic who happens to be black (Danny Glover).

Lawrence Kasdan's perceptive analysis of a multi-racial society losing its self-control courageously steps into territory traditionally occupied by black film-makers (there are deliberate echoes here of John Singleton's *Boyz 'N' The Hood* and Spike Lee's *Do The Right Thing*) and by independent film-makers of a left-wing persuasion, such as John Sayles. Though not without faults, it was the most ambitious and socially alert film to have emerged from a major Hollywood studio in years.

It departs from Hollywood orthodoxy – and follows the tradition of Kasdan's *The Big Chill* and *Silverado* – by having not one hero but five interconnected ones. The screenplay, by Lawrence Kasdan and Meg Kasdan, his wife of 20 years, is at its most truthful about male-female relationships: their portrait of the central marriage is particularly moving. They also make intelligent use of ironic juxtaposition: the two contrasting dreams of Kline and his wife; the two educational driving scenes (one where Kline teaches his son how to survive Los Angeles traffic, the other where Steve Martin gives Kline a lesson on survival in the film industry); and two final scenes involving cops (one where Glover's gang-member nephew tries to escape from them, the other where Miss Parker finds a potential Mr Right in police uniform). To retain so intricate a structure while making an audience care about all the leading characters is fine screenwriting.

All five leading performances were worthy of an Oscar nomination, but the revelation is Steve Martin. He revels in the unsympathetic side of the film producer, but also manages to suggest a sharp intelligence and a resilient personality. One moment he angrily denounces his own movies for encouraging the 'dehumanizing rage which has swept across this country like a pestilence': the next, he denies responsibility and claims that he is simply an artist reflecting society as it is and 'helping us vent our rage'. The result is as spiky, self-contradictory and memorable an anti-hero as anyone you might find in George Bernard Shaw.

Like Woody Allen's *Crimes and Misdemeanours*, the film is an attempt to work out why – in an apparently Godless universe – people are under any obligation to behave decently towards each other. Kasdan contrasts the size of the Grand Canyon with the triviality of the individual and asks why if the individual is so unimportant and ephemeral, why bother to behave morally? He also uses the Grand Canyon to symbolize the chasm between poor and rich, black and white. Left-wingers criticized him for lamenting the hugeness of the abyss without putting forward proposals to bridge it, and it's true that Kasdan shies away from expressing a political opinion or apportioning blame.

However, his point is a perfectly reasonable if conservative one, that some such chasm will always exist, and we'd better learn to live with it. As in the case of another, angrier social commentator, Charles Dickens (who, faced with the crisis in American cities, might have had some pithy comments on the grotesque subservience of Congress to the Gun Lobby), Kasdan's conclusion is the apparently anodyne but actually rather profound one: that society will be a better place only if the individuals inside it learn to behave better.

ANTI:

'Danny Glover plays the tower-of-strength character, the mechanic, and fills it perfectly. Kevin Kline, the lawyer, once again maneuvers his way through a part rather than acting it; he suggests a revue performer who has been given serious things to do. Mary McDonnell and Mary-Louise Parker, as his wife and mistress, are undistinguished and, except for age, almost indistinguishable. Steve Martin, the producer, is, in his post-*Roxanne* days, much like his pre-*Roxanne* days: unbearable.' *(Stanley Kauffmann)*

'A feel-good movie only in the sense that it makes you feel good that you don't live in Los Angeles. Not only is the place incredibly violent (we are treated to one of the most horrible mugging scenes in the movies), but it's full of liberal forty-something do-gooders who never stop talking about how awful it is. The film's unstructured, haphazard and pretentious, with lots of slo-mo shots and time-lapse photography. A short of *LA Story* without the jokes.' *(Rose)*

MIXED:

'If this disaster-packed arable often smacks of melodramatic contrivance, it does at least benefit from solid performances and direction, and a leavening line in sardonic humour.' *(Geoff Andrew, Time Out)*

PRO:

'It is hard to think of another American movie that has so directly, even naively, confronted the basic source of our existential unease.' *(Richard Schickel, Time)*

'Honesty is all through *Grand Canyon* . . . In a time when our cities are wounded, movies like *Grand Canyon* can help to heal.' *(Elliot)*

'As a study of survival strategies in a disintegrating metropolis, pic brings a welcome seriousness and maturity to subject matter too often treated with flippancy and mindless romanticism.' *(Variety)*

GRAND CHEMIN, LE: *see* LE GRAND CHEMIN.

GRAND HIGHWAY, THE: *see* LE GRAND CHEMIN.

GRAND HOTEL AAW — CT: 6 AV: 8.31

1932 US 115 BW DRAMA

D Edmund Goulding ☆
W William A. Drake from Vicki Baum's play

Greta Garbo ☆ John Barrymore ☆
Joan Crawford ☆ Wallace Beery
Lionel Barrymore ☆ Jean Hersholt Robert McWade
Purnell Pratt Ferdinand Gottschalk Rafaela Ottiano

Events befalling the inmates of a Berlin hotel 'where nothing ever happens'.

Interesting both as melodramatic entertainment, and as a chance to see so many stars from the Golden Age of Hollywood. Lionel Barrymore is, for him, understated as the dying bookkeeper, and the young Joan Crawford is surprisingly fresh and charming. Garbo's mannered, theatrical style wears less well, but her star quality is incandescent. Director Edmund Goulding handles the numerous plot-strands with skill, and the production design is opulent without being vulgar. The film topped the 1932 *Film Daily* poll of the US's film critics by a commanding 296 votes compared to *The Champ*'s 214 in second place.

'Better than just a good transcription of the Vicki Baum stage play. Story is many angled in characters and incidents.' *(Variety)*

'Erratically acted by the male stars, but Garbo and especially Crawford, who was never more appealing, glow – as Hollywood stars once did.' *(Danny Peary)*

'Still entertaining because of . . . the personalities involved in the omnibus story. As a secretary in the hotel, there is a startlingly sexy minx named Joan Crawford, who bears only a slight resemblance to the later zombie of that name.' *(Pauline Kael)*

'What a pleasure it is to see sexual attraction handled realistically and (unlike today's so-called "liberated" offerings) with such subtlety, delicacy and sophistication!' *(John Howard Reid)*

GRAND ILLUSION, THE AAN CT: 9 AV: 9.79

(aka *La Grande Illusion*)

1937 France 94/117 BW WAR/FOREIGN

D Jean Renoir ☆
W Jean Renoir Charles Spaak ☆

Pierre Fresnay ☆ Erich von Stroheim ☆
Jean Gabin ☆ Julien Carette Marcel Dalio
Gaston Modot Jean Dasté Dita Parlo

A French officer (Pierre Fresnay) sacrifices his life for two soldiers he doesn't greatly like (Jean Gabin, Marcel Dalio), who want to escape from a prisoner-of-war camp (run by Erich von Stroheim).

Highly intelligent anti-war film which points up the futility of nationalism and argues for men of peace to unite against warmongers. It was a timely, though as it turned out ineffectual, message. Not surprisingly, the film was banned by Goebbels in Germany; and when Vienna was invaded, the Nazis took it off in mid-reel. On a more philosophical level, the film also takes a beady-eyed view of the possibility of true 'escape'; it's clear that the French soldiers will never escape their class background. Some may find the film too talky and cerebral, but it repays patience. Its humanity and technical excellence (Christian Matras's deep-focus photography is especially effective) make this a classic. Despite pressure from Hitler on Mussolini, it won a prize at Venice for the best artistic ensemble.

'The story is true. It was told to me by my friends in the war . . . notably by Pinsard who flew fighter planes. I was in the reconnaissance squadron. He saved my life many times when the German fighters became too persistent. He himself was shot down seven times. His escapes are the basis for the story.' *(Jean Renoir)*

'Artistically masterful.' *(Variety)*

'Justifies the reports, and in addition, has the virtue of shocking timeliness with respect to current war threat . . . It does not preach; it shows. The film's performances are flawless . . . Their admirable restraint is matched by abilities to give full meaning to their roles . . . and a happy conjunction of significant subject matter, a director equal to his task, and actors equal to theirs. A masterpiece is the inevitable result. English sub-titles . . . [are] too few in number . . . My only objection is that in a picture of such absorbing interest, it is annoying to miss a single word.' *(Archer Winston, New York Post)*

'Like most of Jean Renoir's films, *Grand Illusion* is an example of . . . intensive cinema . . . What, asks Renoir, is the experience of a man in modern war?' *(Richard Griffith, Nation)*

'The film was about the First World War, but the ideas in it were dangerously appropriate to the next. Wars, it said, are run for an elite. They will always be against the interests of most of the men who fight them. The flag is a remote symbol, and military honor is bunk; it is class, not honor, that unites the French and German officers in the film.' *(Penelope Gilliatt)*

'A film about World War One made on the brink of World War Two, is a milestone masterpiece, a war movie without a single battle scene. Above all, it is concerned with the illusions of elitism and of nationalism, the artificial boundaries man creates for his legal and illegal killings, the stupidities of the bigotries and class barriers that lead men to destroy each other . . . . Perhaps the ultimate film about war.' *(Judith Crist)*

'Indisputably a classic of the screen. A big theme: war and man's fundamental humanity to man, against a background which protests the very opposite. Renoir directs his prisoner-of-war story with a masterly blend of humour and suspense – and the acting is memorable.' *(NFT Bulletin, 1974)*

'One of the true masterpieces of the screen.' *(Pauline Kael)*

'A powerful attack on the stupidity and spiritual waste of war . . . A profound, almost great film dominated by the intellectual arguments of its script. It stands with Milestone's *All Quiet on the Western Front* and Kubrick's *Paths of Glory* as one of the most important antiwar films ever made.' *(R.A.E Pickard, Dictionary of 1000 Best Films, 1971)*

'With the exception of Dovzhenko's *Arsenal*, the most telling shaft which the cinema has ever directed against the institution of war . . . It touched upon the possibility that there is some perversity in the nature of man which is drawn to the unreasonable and profitless destruction which is brought by war . . . Today its argument, besides being profuse and rambling is wide of the mark . . . *La Grande Illusion* expressed itself entirely through dialogue and the actors who spoke it. Very accomplished actors they were, Stroheim, Gabin, and Fresnay, but their methods were of the theatre, all except Stroheim, whose vivid presence dominated and somewhat outbalanced the film.' *(Paul Rotha & Richard Griffith The Film Till Now, 1949)*

GRANDE ILLUSION, LA: *see* GRAND ILLUSION, THE.

GRAPES OF WRATH, THE AAN

CT: 10 AV: 9.78

1940 US 128 BW DRAMA

D John Ford ☆ AAW
W Nunnally Johnson ☆ AAN from John Steinbeck's novel

Henry Fonda ☆ AAN Jane Darwell ☆ AAW
John Carradine ☆ Charley Grapewin
Dorris Bowdon Russell Simpson Zeffie Tilbury
O.Z. Whitehead John Qualen Eddie Quillan
Grant Mitchell

In the 30s, Oklahoma farmers trek westwards for a better life.

Not many films look good more than 50 years after they are made, but this one does. It is usually recognized as John Ford's greatest film, and is certainly among the most moving of all time. The film version makes the end of Steinbeck's story less depressing, but still packs a mighty punch. Wonderful performances flourish under Ford's stirring direction. Robert Simpson's editing was Oscar-nominated, but not Toland's brilliant photography.

ANTI:

'It is a pity that Ford's sense of environment has not come through as well as his sense of people. The opening of the picture is greatly weakened because he has given us no feeling of the country or of the people's background. Where are the vast stretches of the Dustbowl and the tiny houses as lonely as ships at sea? Where is the dust? . . . The work of director, writer and camera could have been considerably enhanced by a good musical score. Alfred Newman has provided little more than fitful accompaniment.' *(Edwin Locke, Films)*

MIXED:

'Ford has handled the whole story as one never expected to find an American picture handled, using now wonderful pictorial effects of dark and candlelight, now the light of day falling coldly, precisely on the disgraces of starvation and misery . . . It is only towards the end of the picture, where Steinbeck's tale is not followed to its bitter conclusion, that Ford's grasp weakens . . . There is a softening here, due, I think, partly to the fact that Ma Joad (a finely natural performance by Jane Darwell) does not occupy the central position she holds in the book, and her tenacity and heroism do not therefore emerge as forcibly. The passages, too, in the Government camp, where for a time the Joads are received as men, with human respect, are robbed of some of their sharpness by a reshaping of the original story. But the film remains a terrific denunciation, a terrific manifesto.' *(Dilys Powell)*

PRO:

'A genuinely great motion picture which makes one proud to have even a small share of the affairs of the cinema.' *(Howard Barnes, New York Herald Tribune)*

'The most mature motion picture that has ever been made, in feeling, in purpose, and in the use of the medium.' *(Otis Ferguson)*

'Probably the greatest picture that has so far come from Hollywood.' *(Seton Margrave, Daily Mail)*

'It is, as it was bound to be, a singularly cheerless story. But it is gripping and powerful as well as a biting commentary upon a question which is left unsolved.' *(News Chronicle)*

'The actors . . . combine an exact observation of types with a sustained and powerful expression of their emotions.' *(The Times)*

'Ford always looks at his subject with the eye of a romantic. He looks beyond the immediate, the realistic, to the mystery of the solitary human soul. Even *The Grapes of Wrath* – that terrible indictment of gimcrack civilization – even *The Grapes of Wrath*, with its emphasis on individual heroism, was a romantic picture. No matter how much it insisted that it spoke for the masses, it spoke in those terms of pity and love which it is fashionable nowadays to reject. And pictorially it was romantic: in its tender emphasis on the solitary figure, the head and shoulders silhouetted against light. the features touched gently and lovingly by a shadow.' *(Dilys Powell, 1946)*

'One of the most outspoken and perhaps only truly socialistic film of the American cinema.' *(R.A.E Pickard, Dictionary of 1000 Best Films, 1971)*

'This brilliant and courageous achievement, by which Ford is best known, while it made necessary changes in plot and prudent concessions to political prejudice, preserved the essence of Steinbeck's monumental epic of agricultural mass-migration. For the first time, millions of Americans saw their faces, and their fate, on the entertainment screen . . . If the actors occasionally looked like actors, even without make-up, if the carefully filtered skies and landscapes were reminiscent of the familiar skies and landscapes of the studios, this was perhaps inevitable . . . What mattered, what matters today, is that Ford succeeded in producing a noble picture of emotional and social significance to every American. It understates the case to say also that *The Grapes of Wrath* contributed vitally to the political education of American voters.' *(Paul Rotha & Richard Griffith, The Film Till Now, 1949)*

GREASE CT: 6 AV: 5.08

1978 US 110 C MUSICAL/ROMANCE

D Randal Kleiser
W Bronte Woodard from Jim Jacobs and Warren Casey's stage musical

Olivia Newton-John ☆ John Travolta ☆ Stockard Channing ✔ Eve Arden Sid Caesar Frankie Avalon ✔ Joan Blondell Edd Byrnes

At high school during the 50s, a nice girl (Olivia Newton-John) learns how to attract boys (especially John Travolta).

Trite musical based (loosely) on a Broadway hit. Most of the best numbers are out of period, but Patricia Birch's choreography, a cheerful spirit, the star power of John Travolta (who had just had a hit with *Saturday Night Fever*), and the squeaky-clean Olivia Newton-John understandably made it a big hit. Miss Newton-John's transformation at the end into a mean dude is among the least convincing in screen history. Best performance (some would say, the only one) is from Stockard Channing as the naughtiest girl in the school. *Grease 2*, the inevitable sequel, is gross.

ANTI:

'A bogus, clumsily jointed pastiche of late fiftes high school musicals, studded with leftovers from *West Side Story* and *Rebel Without a Cause*.' *(Pauline Kael)*

'Its flashy opportunism (nostalgia pitched squarely at an audience too young to even recall the era) quickly becomes very irritating.' *(Rod McShane, Time Out)*

'A frantic musical, submerged in synthetic rock music . . . Travolta . . . has perfected the knack of imitating himself.' *(Nicholas Wapshott, Scotsman)*

'Witty or satiric it is not.' *(Shipman)*

MIXED:

'At its best [it] is mildly diverting. At its worst it is a mish-mash of memories.' *(Madeleine Harmsworth, Sunday Mirror)*

PRO:

'I went . . . expecting – almost intending – to hate it. To my complete surprise I enjoyed every minute of it. Well, nearly every minute . . . [It] remains as wonderfully innocent as the Garden of Eden. This film is the kind of film they used to make before they started making the kind of film that stopped me going to films.' *(Richard Boston, New Statesman)*

'Slick as a ducktail hairdo. *Grease* has got it, from the outstanding animated titles of John Wilson all the way through to the rousing finale as John Travolta and Olivia Newton-John ride off into pre-Vietnam era teenage happiness.' *(Variety)*

GREAT DICTATOR, THE CT: 5 AV: 7.75

1940 US 129 BW COMEDY

D Charles Chaplin ☆
W Charles Chaplin ✗ AAN

Charles Chaplin ☆ AAN Paulette Goddard Jack Oakie ☆ AAN Reginald Gardiner Henry Daniell Billy Gilbert Maurice Moscovich

A Jewish barber is confused with a Great Dictator, Adenoid Hynkel of Tomania.

Charlie Chaplin's first full talkie is a crude satire on Hitler and Mussolini. The final six-minute tirade on peace and serenity is a major embarrassment, but Chaplin is excellent in his two roles. Jack Oakie is entertainingly weird as Benzino Napaloni, the neighbouring dictator of Bacteria. Meredith Wilson's music was Oscar-nominated.

PRO:

'For this film he takes on more than a mimed representation of common humanity – he states, and accepts the responsibility of being one of humanity's best and most widely-known representatives.' *(Basil Wright)*

'You must go back to *Intolerance* for another motion picture that is so completely one man's personal expression of his attitude on something about which he feels deeply and passionately . . . It is not only the climax of Chaplin, so far, but a resumé of Chaplin's whole growth, in his picture-making and in the evolution of his social conscience.' *(James Shelley Hamilton, NBR)*

MIXED:

'How superbly he does the things which lie within the compass of his comic genius! . . . [But the] finale is so blatantly out of harmony with what has gone before as to nullify much of the effectiveness of the previous two hours.' *(Dilys Powell)*

ANTI:

'I find it difficult to understand how after five years of Hitler terror (and in the year XV of Mussolini's regime) the sensitive creator of *The Gold Rush* and *Modern Times* could still have considered Fascists and Fascism as something funny. At any rate the fact remains that in the last phase of his production Chaplin failed to translate Nazi violence and persecution into satire.' *(Rudolf Arnheim, Films)*

'[Chaplin] is not a good preacher. Indeed, he is frighteningly bad.' *(John O'Hara)*

GREAT ESCAPE, THE CT: 10 AV: 8.67

1963 US 163 C WAR/THRILLER/ACTION/ADVENTURE

D John Sturges ✔
W James Clavell W.R. Burnett ☆ from Paul Brickhill's book

Steve McQueen ☆ James Garner ☆ Richard Attenborough ☆ James Donald Charles Bronson Donald Pleasence ☆ James Coburn David McCallum Gordon Jackson John Leyton Hannes Messemer

Prisoners plan a mass break-out from a prisoner-of-war camp.

Based on an improbable true story, this is one of the most exciting action adventures ever made, helped along by Elmer Bernstein's stirring score, Daniel Fapp's excellent cinematography, a very strong cast, and a screenplay which skilfully mixes in character and comedy. It took a far more upbeat approach than most prisoner-of-war pictures of the time, such as *Stalag 17* (1953) and *King Rat* (1965), but still managed to generate suspense and pathos (Donald Pleasence is especially memorable as the prisoner losing his sight). The most interesting character in the film – and the key to its commercial success – is Hilts (Steve McQueen), a 60s anti-hero transported to a 1940s setting. Oddly enough, he doesn't jar, and gives the more orthodox heroes an additional, almost pathetic, dimension as the last of a dying breed.

MIXED:

'Everything has been done for authenticity of detail and yet the vital element has still eluded the unit. As a comedy with loosely drawn overtones the film does well enough – it's often funny and once or twice exciting – but there's a desperate lack of involvement . . . It's not just that the soggier clichés are handled soggily . . . but that the characterizations are pattern-moulded from a whole decade of Prisoner of War pictures . . . Only Hannes Messemer's subtle Commandant has an essential conflict between humanity and duty and is . . . the best performance in the film . . . *The Great Escape* isn't really . . . bad . . . just disappointing.' *(Richard Whitehall, F & F)*

'Early scenes . . . are played largely for laughs, occasionally at the expense of reality, and there are times when authority seems so lenient that the inmates almost appear to be running the asylum.' *(Variety)*

PRO:

'A great adventure picture, tense with excitement, rich in character, leavened with humor, novel in setting and premise . . . should be one of the year's biggest box office pictures . . . Sturges and his writers have admirably recreated the spirit of these men. Heroism of men armed only with their wits and courage is not blinkered, although it is often offhand or underplayed with humor . . . Humor may seems a dangerous commodity to mix with death but it is in the temper of the men, and true and accurate . . . McQueen, with his unique capacity for projecting both spitting meanness and easy charm, continues his steady, unwavering climb to the highest stardom . . . [The] plot is superb, Elmer Bernstein's music has the throb of excitement.' *(James Powers, Hollywood Reporter)*

'Direction exciting. Photography brilliant. A magnificently-made drama of suspense, adventure and excitement blazes forth . . . Sturges shows a command of visual and narrative values that throb with excitement.' *(Mandel Herbstman, Film Daily)*

'The picture is long . . . but it speaks very well for its intensive quality . . . that time passes quickly . . . a crackling screenplay . . . an outstanding picture.' *(Motion Picture Herald)*

'A first-rate adventure film fascinating in its detail, suspenseful in its plot, stirring in its climax and excellent in performance.' *(Judith Crist, New York Herald Tribune)*.

'It presents a picture of men in an almost Arthurian idyll . . . It looks backward since it is not touched by the popular themes of the Sixties – angst, alienation, malaise or anomie to name a few – but its universality makes it more timely than the work of hangers-on turning out feeble copies of Godard, and just as timeless as the best work of Godard himself. The utter fascination which attends the adventure stems from the juxtaposition of the differing personalities of the men as the plot progresses, and from the almost dreamlike beauty of many of the scenes themselves.' *(Leon Lewis & W.D. Sherman, 1967)*

GREAT EXPECTATIONS AAN

CT: 10 AV: 9.67

1946 GB 118 BW DRAMA/ROMANCE/RITES-OF-PASSAGE

D David Lean ☆ AAN
W Ronald Neame David Lean Kay Walsh Cecil McGivern Anthony Havelock-Allan ☆ AAN from Charles Dickens's novel

John Mills ☆ Finlay Currie ☆ Martita Hunt ☆ Bernard Miles Valerie Hobson Jean Simmons ☆ Alec Guinness Francis L. Sullivan Anthony Wager Ivor Barnard Freda Jackson Hay Petrie O.B. Clarence George Hayes Torin Thatcher

An orphan (Anthony Wager) grows into a snob (John Mills) before learning the error of his ways.

David Lean's masterly, atmospheric adaptation of the Dickens classic, which captures a vast panorama of Victorian life and is, in its first part, the greatest rites-of-passage story ever written. The childhood scenes in this film reflect this; they are, pictorially and emotionally, stunning. The film, like the book, loses some of its power towards the middle, and inevitably details from the original have been lost (especially the extent to which Orlick is Pip's evil alter ego); but the essence and spirit of the novel remain.

Miraculously, Lean and his Oscar-winning photographer (Guy Green) and art director (John

Bryan) manage to communicate the poetic nature of Dickens's writing in visual terms (admittedly, they are helped by the great Victorian's fertile visual imagination; the book is full of lighting and staging clues). Particularly notable is the supporting cast: Martita Hunt as Miss Havisham, Bernard Miles as Joe Gargery, Finlay Currie as Magwitch, Alec Guinness as Herbert Pocket. It is impossible to read the book now without thinking of those actors, and it is a tribute to them that Dickens isn't diminished by this.

ANTI:

'This is not art; this is nonsense.' *(Observer)*

'So particular have the producers been to avoid offending any Dickensian and every character is drawn so precise that many of them are puppets. That's the great fault of the film. It is beautiful but lacks heart. It evokes admiration but no feeling.' *(Variety)*

'Confession coming up: I have never read [the book] . . . which is why perhaps I found this undoubtedly worthy film version just a little unconvincing and rather smacking of melodrama rather than drama . . . Perhaps it all boils down to the fact that I'm a jaundiced, carping type given to thinking that film stars should put in a full-time job.' *(News of the World)*

'Mills . . . plays his role very tentatively – almost as if he were trying out for it. Jean Simmons is the young girl, Estella, and then Valerie Hobson takes over the part, though it's inconceivable that one could grow into the other, and despite Hobson's dignity and beauty something seems to be lost.' *(Pauline Kael)*

MIXED:

'I wish that the Dickens illustrations had been studied still more faithfully and imaginatively – that the whole tone of the film had had a kind of india-ink darkness, psychologically as well as visually: for it seems to me they had hold of a story much more cruel and mysterious than the one that got told . . . It is depressing to realize how many people feel that *Great Expectations* is about as good a job as the screen can do; how can people who believe that, think they really know or care much of anything about movies? But that is the prevailing taste, and I will admit that in its relatively mild terms this is a very good and enjoyable piece of work.' *(James Agee, Nation)*

'Exciting, humane, full of dramatic visual moments; it has shape and size; it has a subject. But it is still permissible to say that the film could have been richer with a bolder handling of Dickens's secondary characters; there was room, even in two hours, for more of the arabesques of minor characters.' *(Dilys Powell)*

'Lean's *Great Expectations* was a handsome version of Dickens, except that it blurred and minimised the most meaningful protagonist, Magwitch. It revealed Lean, however, as a brilliant technician, sensitive and serious about cinema, probably the most skilful of all the young British directors, obviously waiting for real material of contemporary importance to come into his hands.' *(Paul Rotha & Richard Griffith, The Film Till Now, 1949)*

PRO:

'Superlative British screen achievement . . . Delightful backgrounds of Old London . . . and lovely camerawork brilliantly recapture atmosphere of Dickens era . . . Many touches of unaffected comedy. Superb production qualities . . . Story powerful . . . direction polished . . . acting brilliant.' *(Today's Cinema)*

'The best, I think, of Dickens' novels comes to the screen with all the magical thrill it gave you on the first reading. A lavish, unostentatious film, romantic, exciting and English to the core. It will have, I venture to prophecy, the best of all Box-office worlds.' *(Richard Winnington)*

'A truly great picture and all should see it. Not even the most discerning lovers of Dickensian lore should find fault with it . . . I just can't help it if I sound over-enthusiastic.' *(Evening Standard)*

'Lean's triumph lies in the manner in which he catches the subtleties both of atmosphere and character and keeps the serial moving on the twin but different levels of excitement and personality.' *(The Times)*

'A film classic. It is a complete triumph for all concerned, and a milestone in the progress of British films. Absorbing story, a score of memorable characters, humour, sentiment, charm, moments of intense excitement, atmosphere, taste, pictorial beauty – there is not much else a motion picture can have and *Great Expectations* has the lot . . . Dickens, I feel certain, would have loved it.' *(Fred Majdalany, Daily Mail)*

'This film of a great novel misses nothing of its essential spirit, its mystery, its drama, its vigorous life, its beauty, and its rich humour and sentiment. The film is a triumph of British film-making, exploiting some of the hitherto untapped riches of the English scene.' *(A.E. Wilson)*

'Fulfills all expectations . . . The elaborate and exquisitely proportioned panorama is quickened by a galaxy of delightful and faithfully vivified Dickensian characters . . . The intricate plot . . . has been unfolded with crystal clarity, the suspense built with sensitive modulation of blood-and-thunder in the restrained contemporary key, and the happy ending comes as a natural and welcome resolution . . . Lean has directed with fine originality, blending comedy, romance and Gothic horror with ease . . . Certain . . . to become a classic of the screen.' *(Charles Faber, Hollywood Review)*

GREAT MCGINTY, THE CT: 6 AV: 7.36

(aka *Down Went McGinty*)

1940 US 83 BW COMEDY/DRAMA

D Preston Sturges ☆
W Preston Sturges ☆ AAN

Brian Donlevy ☆ Akim Tamiroff ☆ Muriel Angelus Louis Jean Heydt Arthur Hoyt Libby Taylor Thurston Hall Allyn Joslyn William Demarest

Crooked but dim politician (Brian Donlevy) rises to the top, though not for long.

Sturges, a successful screenwriter (he had written *Easy Living* and *Diamond Jim*), here makes his directorial début. He takes a more cynical view than usual of the American political system, and the result is very different than Frank Capra's pictures on the same subject: bleaker, more biting and brutally honest about smoke-filled room corruption. Akim Tarmiroff is especially impressive as the political boss who takes Donlevy under his wing. The film launched Sturges on a meteoric, though short-lived, directorial career.

'Sturges' story departs radically from accepted formula. His main character . . . creates more interest than sympathy.' *(Variety)*

'The tough dialogue is matched by short, snappy scenes; the picture seems to have wasted no time, no money.' *(Gilbert Seldes)*

'A director as adroit and inventive as any in the business . . . It starts like a five-alarm fire and never slackens pace for one moment until its unexpected conclusion.' *(Pare Lorentz)*

Sturges takes the success ethic and throws it in the face of the audience.' *(James Orsini)*

'This is his first directing job and where has he been all our lives? He has that sense of the incongruous which makes some of the best gaiety.' *(Otis Ferguson)*

'Capra with the gloves off.' *(Raymond Gurgnat)*

GREAT TRAIN ROBBERY, THE CT: 5 AV: 8.17

1903 US 10 BW ACTION/ADVENTURE/SILENT

D Edwin S. Porter ☆
W Edwin S. Porter

Marie Murray Broncho Billy Anderson George Barnes

Thieves rob a train.

Though a mere ten minutes long and containing only 14 scenes, this is generally regarded as the first narrative film. Primitive though it is, the exterior shooting is quite adventurous; and it is still possible to imagine its impact on audiences of the time.

'From laboratory examination of some of the popular films of . . . Méliès . . . I came to the conclusion that a picture telling a story in continuity form might draw the customers back to the theatres.' *(Edwin S. Porter, 1904)*

'Whilst the picture was shown, our nerves were sorely tried. The scene where the lady [is] robbed . . . is a triumph. The whole film is highly sensational and we can recommend any exhibitor looking for a film which will make the audience hold their breath, purchase this film.' *(Optical Lantern and Cinematograph Journal, 1904)*

'During the years 1902 to 1906, he [Porter] discovered the principle of editing *(The Life of an American Fireman)* and developed its methods to include direct story construction *(The Great Train Robbery)*, contrast construction *(The Ex-Convict)*, and parallel construction *(The Kleptomaniac)*. In these years also he reached out daringly for new social subject matter *(White Caps, The Miller's Daughter)*, explored more carefully the use of camera devices *(Dream of a Rarebit Fiend)*, and enlarged the scale of production *(Uncle Tom's Cabin)*.' *(Lewis Jacobs, 1939)*

'The success of this film was too overwhelming to be long ignored. It established the single reel as the standard length for American films (between eight and twelve minutes of film). It set both the fashion and the pattern for Western films. And it inspired other directors to join Porter in exploring the implications of his disjunctive style of editing, his free juggling of time and space. Their cameras were no longer confined to the studio: scenes taken on location were combined with shots staged against painted sets. And all were assembled and given their final form at the cutting bench, generally by the director himself.' *(Arthur Knight, 1957)*

'Some of [*The Great Train Robbery*] is quite ordinary. The interior scenes are shot in conventional stage fashion. The actors move right to left or left to right. Their gestures are theatrical. But once Porter is out of doors, we are almost in a modern picture. People move toward the camera and away from it. The camera itself rides on the top of a train as the bandits fight for control of the engine. When the train is stopped, and the passengers pile out and line up to be robbed, one makes a break – directly toward the camera – and is shot dead. Through the window of the railroad station, Porter managed to create the illusion of a train coming to a stop, and, through the open door of the express car, a moving landscape. In two pan shots, he carried his bandits down off the engine and across the woods. For a flip to excitement after the last scene of the story, Porter added a close-up of a bandit who aimed his pistol at the camera and pulled the trigger.' *(Kenneth Macgowan, 1965)*

GREAT ZIEGFELD, THE AAW CT: 5 AV: 7.00

1936 US 179 BW MUSICAL/BIOPIC

D Robert Z. Leonard ✗ AAN
W William Anthony McGuire AAN

William Powell Luise Rainer ● AAW Myrna Loy Frank Morgan Reginald Owen Nat Pendleton Virginia Bruce Ray Bolger ☆ Fanny Brice ☆ Robert Greig

Rise of a Broadway impresario (William Powell).

One of the worst movies ever to win an Oscar for Best Picture. William Anthony McGuire's Oscar-nominated screenplay is so shambolic that it's an hour before the first number, whereupon we are treated to six in succession! Luise Rainer gives such a gross display of over-acting that it's a shock to realize the New York Film Critics voted hers the Best Feminine Performance of 1936 (she also won the Oscar). Characteristic of Robert Z. Leonard's generally botched direction is the fact that he cuts Fanny Brice off in the middle of one of the strongest numbers, 'My Man'. It's watchable for the spectacular vulgarity of the production numbers and the genuine splendour of the finale; but the story (which is transparently a whitewash job on an unpleasant man) requires one finger on the fast-forward button. Seymour Felix's dance direction won an Oscar; the art direction by Cedric Gibbons, Eddie Imazu and Edwin B. Willis was nominated.

PRO:

'The last gasp in filmusical entertainment . . . Among a riot of song and dance, Seymour Felix's dances and ensembles stand out for imagination and comprehensive execution. William Powell's Ziggy is excellent. He endows the impersonation with all the qualities of a great entrepreneur and sentimentalist.' *(Variety)*

ANTI:

'This huge inflated gas-blown object bobs into the critical view as irrelevantly as an airship advertising somebody's toothpaste at a south coast resort. It lasts three hours. That is its only claim to special attention.' *(Graham Greene)*

'Everything should have been tightened . . . [by] boiling down the script, saving a line here, combining two scenes into one.' *(Otis Ferguson)*

GREATEST SHOW ON EARTH, THE AAW CT: 6 AV: 6.55

1952 US 153 C DRAMA/EPIC/FAMILY

D Cecil B. DeMille ☆ AAN
W Fredric M. Frank Theodore St. John Frank Cavett Barre Lyndon from Frank, St. John and Cavett's story AAW

Betty Hutton Charlton Heston Cornel Wilde James Stewart ☆ Dorothy Lamour Gloria Grahame Lyle Bettger Henry Wilcoxon

Trials and tribulations under the big top.

Big, brash circus melodrama which would be ideal family entertainment if it weren't so terribly long. The portrayal of circus life is splendidly authentic, and makes up for the soap-operatic excesses of the plot. James Stewart carries off the most mawkish and clichéd part (the clown with a past) with great charm; and the acting generally isn't as bad as recent film guides have claimed. Anne Bauchens's editing was Oscar-nominated. Sample line . . . elephant man (Lyle Bettger) to elephant girl (Gloria Grahame): 'Your hair is too red, your legs are too thin, you have lips like a cat but (thumping his heart) you make a fire, here!'

ANTI:

'DeMille's directorial ability is sufficiently skilful for him to have put the circus on the screen with ever intensified tempo. But he has to add love interest – and schmaltz it all up.' *(Films in Review)*

'Mawkish, trite . . . Life under this particular big top is . . . awesomely clean and awesomely melodramatic; Stewart isn't just a clown – he's a doctor who's disguised himself as a clown.' *(Pauline Kael)*

'Moribund circus drama with bad acting, stilted production, an irrelevant train crash climax and a few genuinely spectacular and enjoyable moments.' *(Halliwell)*

'The plot creaks worse than all the tent-poles in a gale – and the level of playing does little to help.' *(Shipman)*

PRO:

'Here, against the background of a circus, all the faults that caused such critical mutterings about *Samson and Delilah* are converted into positive virtues. Here it's right for DeMille to be vulgar, obvious, gaudy, for what else is a circus? In this film any other approach would produce the same pretentiousness that vitiated his earlier epics.' *(Saturday Review)*

'This film glorification of the circus would appear that one, far-off, divine event to which the whole creation of Cecil B. DeMille supremely moved.' *(Bosley Crowther)*

'This lavish, colorful, glittering classic remains an all-time bonanza "for children of all ages".' *(Judith Crist)*

MIXED:

'Not a film for those who shrink from noise and ostentation. It aims to be noisy and ostentatious, and the severest critic could not say it had failed . . . Not for delicate tastes; even so good an actor as James Stewart, who plays the sad good-hearted clown, is overwhelmed in the uproar. But though one may dislike DeMille's work one cannot disregard it. For forty years DeMille has been insisting that film direction is simply a form of showmanship, and that the cinema is simply a form of circus. His influence towards loudness, extravagance and violence may well linger after the work of many an artist on the screen has been forgotten.' *(Dilys Powell)*

GREATEST STORY EVER TOLD, THE

CT: 5 AV: 4.75

1965 US 127/147/197/225/238/260 C EPIC/BIOPIC/DRAMA/SO BAD

D George Stevens ●
W James Lee Barrett George Stevens ●

Max Von Sydow ☆ Charlton Heston Sidney Poitier Dorothy McGuire Claude Rains ✔ Jose Ferrer David McCallum Donald Pleasence Carroll Baker Pat Boone Gary Raymond Roddy McDowall Shelley Winters John Wayne ● Van Heflin Sal Mineo Ed Wynn Telly Savalas Angela Lansbury

The life of Christ (Max Von Sydow).

Despite the avalanche of critical contumely, this is an entertaining bad film – with Max Von Sydow giving an extraordinarily dignified, yet passionate, performance in the midst of much directorial and scenic vulgarity. The best parts of it are early on, featuring Claude Rains, and were directed by David Lean; but all through there are splendid moments, thanks to the Oscar-nominated cinematography by William C. Mellor and Loyal Griggs, and the delightfully tasteless art direction by Richard Day and William Creber. There is fun to be had from spotting guest stars in hilariously inapposite roles – most famously, John Wayne popping up to say one line as the centurion at the Crucifixion. The very loud but otherwise undistinguished score by Alfred Newman was nominated for an Oscar.

'Who but an audience of diplomats could sit through this thing? As the picture ponderously unrolled, it was mainly irritation that kept me awake.' *(Shana Alexander, Life)*

'If the subject matter weren't sacred in the original, we would be responding to the picture in the most charitable way possible by laughing at it from start to finish; this Christian mercy being denied us, we can only sit and sullenly marvel at the energy for which, for more than four hours, the note of serene vulgarity is triumphantly sustained.' *(Brendan Gill, New Yorker)*

'God is unlucky in *The Greatest Story Ever Told*. His only begotten son turns out to be a bore . . . George Stevens' direction is plodding and repetitious: whenever he has what he thinks is a fine shot, he is sure to repeat it several times; his groupings are studiedly picturesque, and a sequence like Christ's temptation in the wilderness is ludicrous throughout. Or take the scene in which the evils of everyday life are depicted in newsreel style with grainy photography, absurd in Cinerama and color. Here a robbery, there a rape, yonder a murder – all taking place side by side along the main street, for Christ to look at, suffer and do nothing about. It is sheer nonsense. As for pacing, the picture does not let you forget a single one of its four hours for a moment.' *(John Simon)*

'A Hollywood Reverential, a film so in awe of its subject that it dares approach it only in the most traditional terms at a slow and solemn pace.' *(Judith Crist)*

'George Stevens was once described as a water buffalo of film art. What this film more precisely suggests is a dinosaur.' *(MFB)*

'No more than three minutes of this new film have elapsed before we suspect that Stevens' name and fame have been purchased by the Hallmark Greeting Card Company and that what we are looking at is really a lengthy catalogue of Christmas cards for 1965 – for those Who Care Enough to Send the Very Best. All the side lighting (dawn or sunset), back lighting (halo effects), picturesque groupings, and soda-fountain colors seem inspired by the soggiest nineteenth-century religious chromos; any self-respecting Victorian household would have been proud, sir, to hang any still from this film in its parlor.' *(Stanley Kauffmann, 1965)*

GREED

CT: 5 AV: 9.15

1923 US 110 BW DRAMA/SILENT

D Erich von Stroheim ✗
W Erich von Stroheim from Frank Norris's novel *McTeague*

Gibson Gowland ☆ ZaSu Pitts Jean Hersholt ☆ Chester Conklin Dale Fuller

A dentist (Gibson Gowland) marries but runs foul of a rival (Jean Hersholt) for the attractions of his wife (ZaSu Pitts).

The original version of this is said to have lasted anything between 7 and 10 hours, which MGM proceeded to cut in ways of which von Stroheim disapproved. Even in its current, heavily edited version, it can be appreciated as a masterpiece of the silent screen; and it certainly has one of the most memorable final scenes in movie history. But acting styles have changed, and although the three leading performances still have a crude, melodramatic impact, they are not well served by a poorly paced narrative and many unexplained leaps of character. The relentless moralizing is wearisome, as is the reduction of almost the whole of human motivation to just one of the seven deadly sins.

PRO:

'A picture of undeniable power. Erich von Stroheim has let himself go and has produced a picture which . . . represents a logical development in [his] work. [He] is one of the great stylists of the screen . . . and . . . he has given us an example of realism at its starkest . . . undoubtedly one of the most uncompromising films ever shown . . . There have already been many critiques of its brutality, its stark realism, its sordidness. But . . . it was never intended to be a pleasant picture . . . Lest it be considered that so far this review has been propaganda rather that criticism, we hasten to add that *Greed* is not our idea of a perfect picture . . . But it is entirely to [von Stroheim's] credit that he has preferred to do some pioneer work.' *(Exceptional Photoplays)*

'In *Greed* he ripped the last shreds of respectability off the body of man as an animal and cried: "For shame!" The spectacle he revealed was shameful enough, but the disclosure only made him enemies and his eventual social ostracism was sealed with the mutilation of this film – a mutilation that endeavored to lessen the shock of this whining, pitiful creature that God was supposed to have created in his own image, and which Stroheim revealed so mercilessly under his microscope.' *(Herman G. Weinberg, 1936)*

'That von Stroheim had been a careful student of Griffith is evident throughout. The use of large close-ups, details, camera angles, dramatic lighting and composition, the iris-out, the mask-in – all stemmed from Griffith. Even more suggestive of the Griffith influence were the symbolism, the style of acting, the characterizations themselves. A person's rough treatment of a bird or cat, so familiar in Griffith's films, was used here to indicate that person's character. At the wedding we see a large close-up of Jean Hersholt's hands, clasped behind his back in jealousy. This was reminiscent of Griffith's close-up of hands clasped in anguish at the trial in *Intolerance*. The fragility and innocence of ZaSu Pitts, her fluttering delicacy, were all very close to the traits of the Griffith heroines in the Lillian Gish school.' *(Lewis Jacobs, 1939)*

'Still a film of tremendous visceral power, its final desperate scenes . . . a searing indictment of human avarice.' *(Allan Hunter & Kenny Mathieson, Movie Classics, 1992)*

MIXED:

'Ferocity, brutality, muscle, vulgarity, cruelty, naked realism and sheer genius are to be found – great hunks of them . . . It is a terribly powerful picture – and an important one. There are two defects in *Greed* – one of which is almost fatal. In the first place, von Stroheim has chosen to be symbolic at intervals, and has inserted some very bad handcoloring to emphasize the goldenness of gold. This detracts greatly from the realism of the picture. In the second place, von Stroheim has been, as usual, so extravagant with his footage that *Greed* in its final form is merely a series of remnants. It has been cut to pieces – so that entire sequences and important charaters have been left out. Thus the story has a choppy quality; many of its developments are abrupt. We see Trina in one instant the tremulous young bride, and in the next the hard, haggard, scheming shrew of several years later. The intervening stages in her spiritual decay are not shown, although von Stroheim undoubtedly included them originally. This is von Stroheim's own fault . . . He is badly in need of a stopwatch.' *(Robert E. Sherwood, 1925)*

ANTI:

'The New York critics acclaimed it as a masterpiece. *Greed* is sordid. *Greed* is depressing. *Greed* is brutal. *Greed* is shocking. It reeks with good acting and wonderful direction . . . Von Stroheim has emphasized every detail . . . until it becomes almost repulsive. It is the realism of vulgarity to the nth degree and if that is art, von Stroheim has provided a masterpiece. This is not one of *Photoplay*'s six best, and it is given a place on this page only because of its news value.' *(James R. Quirk, Photoplay, 1925)*

'The fact that *Greed*, in its original form, was twenty reels in length . . . indicates neither the mind of a genius nor a great film director . . . His obvious incapability to express his ideas adequately in ten thousand feet of film shows clearly his lack of understanding of the resources of the medium . . . [His] greatest faults are his love of excess and his failure to express his mind filmically . . . [His] best work is to be seen in small pieces.' *(Paul Rotha & Richard Griffith, The Film Till Now, 1949)*

'When ten years later I saw the film myself, it was like seeing a corpse in a graveyard.' *(Erich von Stroheim)*

GREEK TYCOON, THE

CT: 1 AV: 2.38

1978 US 106 C DRAMA/ROMANCE

D J. Lee Thompson ●
W Mort Fine ●

Anthony Quinn Jacqueline Bisset ● Raf Vallone Edward Albert James Franciscus Camilla Sparv

A shipping magnate (Anthony Quinn) attracts a dead president's wife (Jacqueline Bisset).

Repellent exploitation piece based on the real-life Onassis-Kennedy marriage, it reduces potentially interesting characters to soapy sterotypes. The script is pathetic. Bisset's non-acting doesn't help.

PRO:

'It has the ring of truth about it, largely due to the forceful, sensitive approach of Anthony Quinn . . . Bisset is almost adequate.' *(Ian Christie, Daily Express)*

'Oddly tender if titillating.' *(Richard Barkley, Sunday Express)*

MIXED:

'Trashy, opulent, vulgar, racy . . . Quinn is fabulous . . . As Liz Cassidy, Bisset capitalizes on her looks, but her accent seems off for the part, and much of her acting is just posing.' *(Variety)*

tubby, tattooed Frenchman with a criminal record and big nose (Gérard Depardieu). They marry in haste, hate at leisure, and fall in love.

Lightweight stuff, but miraculously acted and ably directed by Peter Weir. Ever since *Picnic at Hanging Rock*, Weir has seemed able to find fresh ways of seeing old places. Here, he portrays Manhattan with energy and originality, as an exotic jungle: his film opens with a youthful Afro-Caribbean drummer, crucial scenes take place in a cafe called the Afrika, and MacDowell's conservatory is a small rainforest in itself.

Green Card is essentially a throwback to the innocence of Rock Hudson and Doris Day movies. Its greatest failing is that the director and actor seem undecided over whether Depardieu's character (an avant-garde composer) is a poseur, or not. Even so, Depardieu comes across as the most lovable alien since E.T.

MIXED:

'Despite its pleasing light tone, many of the gags shoot wide of the mark while the wafer-thin plot threatens to break under the weight of Depardieu's heavy-handed comic turn.' *(Rose)*

'The threadbare screenplay and Weir's weak direction are barely able to hold things together. Much of the dialogue is insipid, and the action is driven by absurd behavior to the point that one can only feel exasperated by it all . . . Depardieu's performance is a redeeming factor.' *(Virgin)*

PRO:

'Although a thin premise endangers its credibility at times, *Green Card* is a genial, nicely played romance.' *(Variety)*

'Weir is good with his actors and good, too, at putting a slight spin on some of the obligatory scenes. When Depardieu meets MacDowell's parents, for example, the scene doesn't develop along standard lines of outrage and bluster. Instead, Conrad McLaren, as her father, grasps the situation instantly, and proves to be a good judge of character. I also liked the scene where Depardieu goes to a party and meets MacDowell's friends. Of course, they are snotty, and, of course, it is mentioned that Depardieu is a composer, and, of course, there is a piano there, and Depardieu is asked to play one of his compositions. But what happens then is perhaps the best scene in the movie.' *(Roger Ebert)*

'In terms of the genre's conventions, Weir likens this film to "a light meal". It's one to savour.' *(Colette Maude, Time Out)*

GREEN FOR DANGER

CT: 8 AV: 8.86

1946 GB 93 BW THRILLER/COMEDY

D Sidney Gilliat ☆
W Sidney Gilliat Claude Gurney ☆ from Christianne Brand's novel

Alastair Sim ☆ Sally Gray ☆ Trevor Howard ☆ Rosamund John ☆ Leo Genn ☆ Megs Jenkins ☆ Moore Marriott ☆ Judy Campbell ☆ Ronald Adam

An eccentric detective (Alastair Sim) investigates a double murder in a hospital during World War II.

Sim at his incomparable best is ably supported by a fine cast in this adroit comedy-thriller, with the clever script and light touch expected from this undervalued writer-director. Wilkie Cooper contributes apposite cinematography, which skilfully strikes a balance between the comic and the sinister.

ANTI:

'Gilliat and Launder [producer], one-time masters of suspense, are losing their touch. The plot is too laboriously constructed, and the reason for the murders appears too incredible.' *(Variety)*

'If my not knowing who was the murderer in [it] speaks ill for my intelligence, my not caring who was the murderer speaks ill for the intelligence of the director.' *(Helen Fletcher, Sunday Graphic)*

'Much overrated. The mystery is satisfactory, but the proceedings are surprisingly somber – in fact, the supposedly witty Cockrill (a poorly conceived character) seems to be in the wrong film. They should have lightened it all up, and Cockrill should have been more like Clouseau. Picture's one major advantage is that you forget who the murderer is from one viewing to the next.' *(Danny Peary)*

PRO:

'First-class middlebrow entertainment.' *(Daily Mail)*

'Nothing of importance, but mystery well sustained, narratively nicely compact in the manner we have learned these last years to expect of our native cinema.' *(Dilys Powell)*

'A British film once more shows itself superior to the Hollywood productions . . . Launder and Gilliat have told an exciting story excitingly.' *(The Times)*

'First-rate British crime thriller . . . Expert script . . . Delightful light comedy . . . Story gripping . . . Direction finely balanced . . . Acting admirable.' *(Today's Cinema)*

'The British have sent over a humdinger of a baffler . . . Once again the director/producer combination of Sidney Gilliat and Frank Launder have laid deftly humorous hands on the subject of murder. And, while they manage to keep the spectator chuckling most of the time, they never for a moment lose sight of a mystery film's prime purpose . . . to intrigue and startle . . . What more could one ask? . . . [It] will give the aisleside sleuths a better workout than they have had for months.' *(New York Times)*

'Slick, witty and consistently entertaining.' *(Daily Telegraph)*

GREEN RAY, THE CT: 6 AV: 7.22

(aka *Summer; Le Rayon Vert*)

1986 France 98 C ROMANCE/FOREIGN

D Eric Rohmer ☆
W Eric Rohmer Marie Rivière from Jules Verne's novel

Marie Rivière ☆ Lisa Heredia Béatrice Romand Vincent Gautier Eric Hamm Rosette Vanessa Leleu Irène Skobline Carita

A secretary (Marie Rivière) finds love while on holiday.

Some people find the anti-heroine annoying; for much of the film, she's discontented, self-centred and hard to please. If you have the patience, however, Rohmer's usual magic works its effect, and Rivière's improvized performance takes on a certain charm. It's one of the most perceptive films about that peculiar form of loneliness: being on your own in a crowd.

'Another delightful comedy . . . the word, quite bluntly, is masterpiece.' *(Geoff Andrew, Time Out)*

'A great film.' *(Terrence Rafferty)*

'A must for Rohmer fans and for anyone who's ever expected life to deliver more than it does.' *(Scheuer)*

GREEN SLIME, THE CT: 5 AV: 2.20

(aka *Gamma Sango Uchu Daisakusen*)

1969 US/Japan 88/99 C SF/HORROR/SO BAD

D Kinji Fukasaku ●
W Charles Sinclair ● William Finger ● Tom Rowe ●

Richard Jaeckel ● Robert Horton ● Luciana Paluzzi ●

Unlikely aliens attack space station.

A poor film with a negligible plot, amateurish acting and some of the most ridiculous monsters in screen history: uncredited midgets in slime suits. The most memorable aspect was its eye-catchingly illiterate ad campaign. Green posters proclaimed 'The Green Slime Are Coming!' then 'The Green Slime Are Here!'

PRO:

'Quite an entertaining piece of science-fiction, this has enough excitement and active monsters to offset its unconvincing plot . . . The green slime monsters, waddling about on stumpy legs and thrashing their tentacles, are not quite as terrifying as they might have been and are played for more than they are worth.' *(Kine Weekly)*

'Japanese expertise in animation and special effects gives gloss to the roughly-hewn plot . . . Smashing Bug Eyed Monster thrills and excellent special effects. Good value for the fans of this type of pseudo-scientific hokum.' *(Marjorie Bilbow, Today's Cinema)*

MIXED:

'The acting is stiff, the better not to snigger when delivering the lines . . . Fortunately a good trash film is almost everyone's secret vice.' *(John Mahoney, Hollywood Reporter)*

'Opens promisingly, keeps it up for about half an hour, but then fades badly. There is a quiet, tingling efficiency about those early scenes and very little nonsense . . . And the plot isn't half bad for this kind of operation . . . [It] simply runs downhill like a tedious game of hide and seek. The dialogue is wooden, so is most of the acting . . . green corn.' *(Howard Thompson, New York Times)*

'Junior league science-fiction . . . certainly schoolboy stuff. Most of this space opera aspect is well-enough done and the first appearance of the green slime looks promising, but the transformation of the lurid jelly into stock monsters is something of a let-down . . . and Luciana Paluzzi's presence as a most unlikely space station doctor is mere decoration.' *(MFB)*

ANTI:

'Looking like a paperback version of *2001* with papier-mâché models of space craft and warty green space monsters that are all too palpably little men in rubberized monkey suits, the whole thing would be laughably naive if caught at a Saturday matinee. The laughter stops, though, when one realizes that it comes from the once mighty Metro.' *(Arthur Knight, Saturday Review)*

'The one eyed creatures with stiff tentacles multiplied when shot! What should astronauts Richard Jaeckel and Robert Horton do? Fight over Luciana Paluzzi in her fetching minidress.' *(Michael Weldon, The Psychotronic Encyclopaedia of Film)*

'The monster itself ranks with *The Creeping Terror* and *Robot Monster* as filmdom's shoddiest lurking fiends.' *(Scheuer)*

GREGORY'S GIRL CT: 10 AV: 6.92

1981 GB 91 C COMEDY/RITES-OF-PASSAGE/ ROMANCE

D Bill Forsyth ✔
W Bill Forsyth ☆

Gordon John Sinclair ☆ Dee Hepburn Jake D'Arcy Clare Grogan Robert Buchanan Billy Greenlees Alan Love Caroline Guthrie

An awkward schoolboy adolescent (Gordon John Sinclair) becomes comically infatuated with a female football-player (Dee Hepburn).

A uniquely charming comedy on an ultra-low budget by Scottish writer-director Bill Forsyth, with a hilarious performance by Sinclair. All about the pain of adolescence, it's cruel and kind, knowing and innocent, realistic but magical at the same time.

'Delightfully gentle, quirky, droll, and daft.' *(Kathy Schulz Huffhines)*

'[Forsyth's] friendly, unmalicious approach recalls that of René Clair.' *(Variety)*

'Charming, innocent, very funny . . . The movie contains so much wisdom about being alive and teen-aged and vulnerable that maybe it would even be painful for a teenager to see it; it's not much help, when you're suffering from those feelings of low self-esteem and an absolutely hopeless crush, to realize that not only are you in pain and suffering an emotional turmoil, but you're not even unique.' *(Roger Ebert)*

'Every so often there is a slight attack of the cutes.' *(Shipman)*

GREMLINS

CT: 7 AV: 6.54

1984 US 106/111 C COMEDY/HORROR

D Joe Dante ☆
W Chris Columbus ☆

Zach Galligan Hoyt Axton Phoebe Cates Frances Lee McCain Polly Holiday Scott Brady Glynn Turman Corey Feldman Dick Miller Keye Luke Judge Reinhold

Nasty little varmints disturb the complacency of Middle America, run amok, and meet wonderfully grisly ends.

Joe Dante's witty comedy-horror film starts slowly and is too scary for the young, but it's great fun for teenagers upwards – especially if they are cine-literate enough to catch some of the subversive allusions to old movies. A massive hit – though not with the critics, who found it hard to categorize.

'Film buffs could spend a year trying to find all the in-jokes.' *(Rose)*

'The whole movie is a sly series of send-ups, inspired by movie scenes so basic they reside permanently in our subconscious. The opening scene, for example, involves a visit to your basic Mysterious Little Shop in Chinatown, where, as we all know, the ordinary rules of the visible universe cease to operate and magic is a reality. Later on, after a kid's father buys him a cute little gremlin in Chinatown, we have a new version of your basic Puppy for Christmas Scene. Then there are such basic movie characters as the Zany Inventor, the Blustering Sheriff, the Clean-Cut Kid, the Cute Girlfriend, and, of course, the Old Bag.' *(Roger Ebert)*

'One person calls it '*E.T.* with teeth'. You could also say it's *The Texas Chainsaw Massacre* with Muppets. Then again it's also *Invasion of the Body Snatchers* set in a back lot town of Frank Capra's *It's a Wonderful Life*. In fact, for all the hundreds of movie references one could conjure up to describe the film, no one is likely to confuse *Gremlins* with any other movie.' *(David Ansen, Newsweek)*

ANTI:

'The humans are little more than dress-extras for the mechanics.' *(Variety)*

'Comic horror film starts out in friendly spirits with references to *It's a Wonderful Life* and *The Wizard of Oz*, as well as projecting innocent, family and smalltown life found in the Andy Hardy series, but it degenerates into meanness. Not only is the violence vicious and cruel, but Galligan's girlfriend, Phoebe Cates, tells a nauseating story about why she hates Christmas: her father got stuck in the chimney and died. Is this supposed to be tongue-in-cheek?' *(Danny Peary)*

MIXED:

'Though sloppily plotted and stickily whimsical in parts, *Gremlins* is kept afloat by its splendid special effects and set pieces.' *(Anne Billson, Time Out)*

'The movie never comes together, but Dante is a genuine eccentric talent with a flair for malice, and it's certainly clear why Spielberg, whose production company made the film, believes in him – there are some crack sequences. At one point the lewd hipster dragons take over the town movie theatre, where *Snow White and the Seven Dwarfs* is playing; they pad up and down the aisles, eating, laughing, tearing up the place. And when the Seven Dwarfs on the screen start to sing "Heigh-Ho," they join in the singing. In their enthusiasm, they spin around on the projectors, and rip the screen to shreds. It's a delirious, kitschy travesty – a kiddy matinee in Hell.' *(Pauline Kael)*

GREMLINS 2: THE NEW BATCH

CT: 8 AV: 6.58

1990 US 105/7 C HORROR/FAMILY/COMEDY

D Joe Dante ☆
W Charlie Haas ✔

Zach Galligan Phoebe Cates John Glover ✔ Robert Prosky Robert Picardo Christopher Lee Haviland Morris Dick Miller Paul Bartel Kathleen Freeman Henry Gibson

Nasty little varmints trash a New York skyscraper.

Even more entertaining than the original. Where the first film was over-laborious in building up an image of small-town America for its anti-heroes to destroy, this picture quickly and gleefully establishes the environment which is to become Joe Dante's inferno: a horrible New York office building incorporating an offensive conglomeration of cable TV stations, and – more improbably – a grisly genetic laboratory under the direction of the sinister Dr Catheter (who else but Christopher Lee?).

The owner of this Tower of Babble is Daniel Cramp (John Glover), a nightmarish amalgamation of Donald Trump and Ted Turner. It is Cramp who happily claims responsibility for transmitting a new, improved version of *Casablanca*: 'in colour, and with a happier ending'. It is he too, presumably, who is responsible for soothing public address announcements throughout the building which end in 'Have a powerful day!' and talking lavatory doors which say 'Hey, pal, I sure hope you washed those hands!' You can't wait for the gremlins to strike.

The satire on modern New York life is spot-on. There's the casual rudeness and relentless vulgarity; the female workaholic who even attempts seduction in business jargon; the endless quest for new restaurants with an ethnic theme, culminating here in an only slightly far-fetched Canadian restaurant 'where they clean the fish right at your table', and where for dessert they serve a gigantic chocolate moose.

The heroes (Zach Galligan and Phoebe Cates) are no more interesting than they were in the first movie, but the real stars are the gremlins themselves: now too familiar to be scary, perhaps, but funnier and more varied than before. My favourite is the one which drinks brain hormone, undergoes a Jekyll and Hyde transformation, and turns into a loathsomely pretentious cross between William Buckley and Lloyd Grossman.

There are cinematic sideswipes galore at targets from Busby Berkeley to Batman. The speed, intricacy and sheer number of the sight-gags is reminiscent of the best silent comedies. It's much too knowing and grown-up for the teenage market at which the first *Gremlins* was aimed, but I laughed and laughed. It received mixed reviews.

ANTI:

'A chaotic affair which eschews narrative coherence for rapid-fire sight-gags and self-referential silliness.' *(Mark Kermode, Time Out)*

MIXED:

'The first *Gremlins*, in 1984, was a meditation on movie myths – on Christmas, small towns, and things that will jump up and scare you. It was a superior B movie and a lot of fun. *Gremlins 2* is a meditation on sequels, and like most sequels, it's a faded imitation of the original. Yes, it has some big laughs, and yes, some of the special effects are fun, but the movie has too many gremlins and not enough story line.' *(Roger Ebert)*

PRO:

'An hilarious sequel featuring equal parts creature slapstick and satirical barbs for adults.' *(Variety)*

'A post-modern assault on contemporary cinema.' *(John Harkness, Film Review)*

'One of those rare sequels that's more out-and-out enjoyable than the original. Whereas the first was a horror film that was funny, this one goes all out for the laughs.' *(Rose)*

GREY FOX, THE   CT: 6 AV: 7.33

1983 Canada 92 C ACTION/ADVENTURE/ WESTERN/BIOPIC

D Phillip Borsos ☆
W John Hunter

Richard Farnsworth ☆ Jackie Burroughs
Wayne Robson Ken Pogue Timothy Webber
Gary Reineke

In 1901, stagecoach bandit Bill Miner (Richard Farnsworth) emerges from 33 years in jail, is inspired by seeing Edwin S. Porter's film The Great Train Robbery *and changes to robbing trains.*

Richard Farnsworth gives a marvellous performance in this little-seen western, notable for the fine work of British cinematographer Frank Tidy. Documentary film-maker Phillip Borsos works hard and effectively at creating an authentic turn-of-the-century setting for his real-life anti-hero. The film's morality may not stand close scrutiny, and it's all paced too lackadaisically, but it's pleasantly rewarding.

'Graceful, stunningly-photographed.' *(Variety)*

'Farnsworth is one of those unstudied, graceful, absolutely natural actors who has spent a lifetime behaving exactly as he feels. I think he is incapable of a false or a dishonest moment. He makes Miner so proud, so vulnerable, such a noble rascal, that the whole movie becomes just a little more complex because he's in it.' *(Roger Ebert)*

'Superb, quirky, true-life Western is a little-known delight, with the laid-back performance of the mature Farnsworth a particular joy.' *(Rose)*

GRIFTERS, THE   CT: 6 AV: 7.38

1990 US 110/119 C THRILLER

D Stephen Frears ✗
W Donald Westlake AAN from Jim Thompson's novel

Anjelica Huston ☆ AAN John Cusack ☆
Annette Bening ☆ AAN Pat Hingle ☆ Henry Jones
Stephen Tobolowsky J.T. Walsh Charles Napier

A study of three con-artists: ice-maiden mother (Anjelica Huston), her confused son (John Cusack) and his sexpot girlfriend (Annette Bening). Huston is torn between maternal inclinations and her desperation to escape the Mob, Cusack between the urge to go straight and his talent for criminality, Bening between her desire for Cusack and her natural greed and immorality. All three pride themselves on being survivors. Only one makes it to the end.

A critically acclaimed, modern film noir; but, despite Stephen Frears's sensitive direction, the first half of the movie drags. It's hard to care about any of the characters in this tale of three confidence tricksters – even though they are beautifully acted. However, the skilfully plotted screenplay does take the thriller genre into darker, more Oedipal areas than usual; the violence is, for once, realistic in its effects; and the grim ending certainly packs a punch.

'Bening's two-faced little-girl quality is dazzling – just what film noir thrives on. When Moira blames Lilly for Roy's rejecting her proposition and turns treacherous, Bening makes the shift convincing; she's a stunning actress and superb wiggler. And film noir is enriched by two competing femmes fatales . . . But by the end of *The Grifters* (which Scorsese produced) Lilly's ruthless amorality is shocking – it has weight – and I think that's because Anjelica Huston is willing to be taken as monstrous; she contains this possibility as part of what she is. And when Lilly shows her willingness to do anything to survive she's a great character.' *(Pauline Kael)*

'By the end, when Roy and his mother are facing each other in their last desperate confrontation, the full horror of their lives is laid bare. Why do confidence operators do what they do? Why do they need to win our love and trust, and then betray us? In *The Grifters,* it's pretty clear that they're locked into an old pattern of trust and betrayal that goes back to childhood, and that they're trying to get even. Poor Roy. He thinks he wants to be a great con man, and all he really wants is to find just one person he can safely love, one person who isn't trying to con him.' *(Roger Ebert)*

'The performances are stunning, particularly the gorgeous Bening as the girl who never uses cash when her body will do, and Hingle as one of the nastiest hoods yet seen on the screen.' *(Rose)*

'Bleakly invigorating.' *(Halliwell)*

GROUNDHOG DAY CT: 9 AV: 6.56

1992 US 103 C ROMANCE/FANTASY/COMEDY

D Harold Ramis ✔
W Danny Rubin Harold Ramis ✔

Bill Murray ✔ Andie MacDowell Chris Elliott
Stephen Tobolowsky ✔ Brian Doyle-Murray
Marita Geraghty

A TV weatherman (Bill Murray) has to relive the same day over and over again, in his least favourite small town in America, on the occasion of the festival he most hates – one on which he has to hand over weather-forecasting duties, because of a local superstition, to an overgrown, underground squirrel. He is cursed – or blessed – with reliving this most demeaning day of his year until he gets it right.

Groundhog Day poses a question we all ask ourselves. What would I do if I had my life to live over again? I know I'd do things differently, but would I do them any better? The anti-hero of this movie reverts initially to the traditional pursuits of younger men. Since he doesn't have to care about consequences, he drinks heavily, drives like a maniac, pursues meaningless sex. Growing up a little, he tries to impress the woman he fancies (Andie MacDowell) by pretending they have a lot in common. Maturing still further, he realizes that to win her he must actually improve himself – in his case, by finding new skills (he turns into a demon piano-player) and developing something he has previously found anathema: community spirit.

The resulting film of self-redemption owes something to Dickens's novel *A Christmas Carol*, but more to Frank Capra's masterpiece, *It's A Wonderful Life*. In both films, the hero begins with so self-centred and restricted a view of his universe that he contemplates suicide. In both, he learns through supernatural intervention that he is part of a wider community, and he comes to appreciate small-town American values. There are, however, dissimilarities. The outcome of *It's A Wonderful Life* is, in a way, pessimistic: its hero, played by James Stewart, has to learn that his own thwarted personal ambitions are relatively unimportant, and he needs to sacrifice them for the good of his family and community. In *Groundhog Day*, the message is more upbeat: by improving yourself, you may learn that family and community are more important than career, but there's no reason why you shouldn't have your career as well.

All this may sound over-optimistic, and perhaps it is. Americans like to see life as a series of opportunities; Europeans tend to be more cynical and fatalistic. Murray's character is so entertaining when sneering at small-town Americana, popular taste and pushy life-insurance salesmen that it's almost a disappointment when he turns into a nice guy who might have voted for A Better Tomorrow With President Clinton. Murray's at his funniest, like his spiritual ancestor W.C.Fields, when being a curmudgeon.

But at least Murray has learned to mellow convincingly. At the end of a not dissimilar process in a Hollywood update of *A Christmas Carol, Scrooged* (1988), he seemed to be sneering at the sentimentality of the script. Maturity has turned Murray into a much more sympathetic comedian. So why was *Groundhog Day* such a success? Not even excellent performances by Murray could make hits out of his previous two movies, *Quick Change* and *What About Bob?* The answer, as so often, lies in the script. Given the highly restrictive premise, the film might have turned out over-repetitive and mechanical but it didn't: a tribute to writer Danny Rubin and his co-writer and director, Harold Ramis.

The film is, like a previous 'surprise' hit, *Ghost*, a very clever mixture of genres. Some American critics dismissed *Groundhog Day* as just another time travel picture, like *Back To The Future* or *The Terminator*. But the picture is completely uninterested in the logic or mechanism of time travel. *Groundhog Day* is more like those rather dated J.B. Priestley plays *(Dangerous Corner, I Have Been Here Before)* where time repeats itself without explanation.

It is also a middle-aged romantic comedy, like the underrated *Frankie and Johnny*, where both members of the duo bring their own hopes and insecurities to the party – and a middle-age crisis movie. The Bill Murray we see in the opening scenes is old before his time. He has forgotten how to enjoy himself: he even turns down a date with Andie MacDowell to read a book. As in Spielberg's *Hook*, he has to find the child – or at least the optimistic young man – within himself.

But the aspect which makes *Groundhog Day* so original and such a huge success is that this is a computer-age comedy. The American critics failed to notice something that will be obvious to most young moviegoers: Murray's character lives his new life just like the hero of an interactive adventure in a computer game. If he dies, he can always go back and make another choice; and he can use knowledge gained beforehand to make more informed choices next time. This was certainly the most ingenious comedy of 1993, and among the funniest and most heart-warming.

ANTI:

'Why should poor Rita be forced to relive this miserable day just to give Phil a chance to evolve from crafty Casanova into selfless swain? Though snooty Phil may not be missed back in the real world, why should Rita and Larry, the cameraman, be trapped in the same nightmare? Why should Rita be educating Phil? Compared to this, *Back to the Future*, which also cheated, was as pure as this movie's artificial snow . . . Groundhogwash.' *(John Simon)*

'The script is illogical and annoying and you don't know why this is happening to Murray.' *(Winnert)*

MIXED:

'The situation is ripe with comic potential but script provides more chuckles than belly-laughs. Some sequences are crisply paced and comically terse, some ramble and others just plain don't work.' *(Variety)*

'Most of the big laughs come in the first part of the movie, when Murray's Phil is only slightly less cantankerous than Phil, the scene-stealing groundhog himself. The late surge of Capraesque altruism is occasionally a bit much, but the Murray-MacDowell explosion of wit and charm sweeps everything before it.' *(Andrew Sarris, New York Observer)*

PRO:

'Lovable and sweet.' *(Roger Ebert)*

'Ramis directs this surreal suburban fantasy with an admirably light touch, revelling in its absurd repetitions, surprising us with narrative ellipses, and allowing Murray ample space to indulge his special mix of sarcasm and smarm. But this is first and foremost a comedy of ideas, on which score it never falters.' *(Geoff Andrew, Time Out)*

GUESS WHO'S COMING TO DINNER? AAN

CT: 4 AV: 5.92

1967 US 112 C DRAMA/COMEDY

D Stanley Kramer ✗ AAN
W William Rose ✗ AAW

Spencer Tracy ☆ AAN Katharine Hepburn ☆ AAW Sidney Poitier Katharine Houghton Cecil Kellaway ☆ AAN Beah Richards ☆ AAN Roy E. Glenn Sr

A rich husband and wife (Spencer Tracy, Katharine Hepburn) who consider themselves liberals are unnerved when their daughter (Katharine Houghton) brings home a black fiancé (Sidney Poitier).

Typically didactic, plodding, wet-liberal tract by Stanley Kramer. The situation is so phoney and grotesquely loaded in favour of the black boyfriend that there's never the slightest suspense; and one can't help wondering whether it might all be different if the young man were not so painfully personable and polite. It's a little sad that the last Tracy-Hepburn movie should also be their worst, but their performances are far better than the material. Frank de Vol's musical direction was Oscar-nominated.

PRO:

'It's entertaining and its heart is in the right place.' *(Winnert)*

MIXED:

'Looked at coolly the central problem is too smoothly solved by a series of private talks between the characters, who withdraw in pairs into studies or on to terraces, and a final speech from the girl's father (yes, Spencer Tracy); the structure is that of a stage play rather than a film. But William Rose's script has a sense of character, a feeling for comedy of situation and for natural-sounding dialogue and a wit which carry you along unprotesting. Anyhow, who wants to bother about structure when such a cast is on the screen?' *(Dilys Powell)*

'The problem picture that isn't really, since everyone is so nice and the prospective bridegroom is so eligible. It looks like a photographed play, but isn't based on one; the set is unconvincing; but the acting is a dream.' *(Halliwell)*

ANTI:

'*Abie's Irish Rose* in blackface.' *(Reporter)*

'Mendacious and sanctimonious drivel.' *(John Simon)*

'A load of embarrassing rubbish. In the circumstances there is little that director Stanley Kramer can do but see that his camera plod from room to room and make the most of people sitting down and getting up again.' *(Penelope Mortimer)*

'Since Stanley Kramer's direction doesn't help much to resolve their dilemma, the actors are left looking wooden and uneasy . . . Everybody's caught up in a kind of integrated drawing-room comedy, and unable to decide whether there's anything funny in it or not.' *(Ann Birstein, Vogue)*

'What Rose and Kramer have done is to create a number of elaborate Aunt Sallies, arrange them in attractive patterns, and dispose of them with the flick of a feather.' *(Basil Wright, 1972)*

'The film's ultimate thesis – that interracial marriage among the rich and successful is permissible, providing the couple leaves for Africa by midnight – is ludicrously condescending and offensive.' *(Judith Crist)*

GUNFIGHT AT THE O.K. CORRAL

CT: 7 AV: 7.00

1957 US 122 C WESTERN

D John Sturges ✔
W Leon Uris based on George Scullin's article *The Killer*

Burt Lancaster ☆ Kirk Douglas ☆ Rhonda Fleming Jo Van Fleet ✔ John Ireland ✔ Lee Van Cleef ✔

Wyatt Earp (Burt Lancaster) and Doc Holliday (Kirk Douglas) clean up Dodge City.

Reasonably impressive and spectacular, with solid characterization, an exceptional supporting cast, and wonderful photography by Charles Lang Jr; but somehow it doesn't quite take off like John Ford's *My Darling Clementine*, which covered virtually the same events, and it's a shade overlong. It received Oscar nominations for best editing (Warren Low) and sound (George Dutton). Sturges made a sequel, *Hour of the Gun* (1967), but it wasn't as enjoyable.

'An absorbing yarn . . . Both stars are excellently cast.' *(Variety)*

'A multileveled, gritty, often funny, beautifully paced film.' *(Judith Crist)*

'Carefully and lavishly mounted, but overlong and overwrought.' *(John Cutts)*

GUNFIGHTER, THE

CT: 6 AV: 7.60

1950 US 84 BW WESTERN

D Henry King ☆
W William Bowers William Sellers Nunnally Johnson André De Toth from Bowers's story

Gregory Peck ☆ Helen Westcott Millard Mitchell Jean Parker Karl Malden Skip Homeier

Ageing gunfighter (Gregory Peck) rides into town to see the wife and child he abandoned, but finds there's no such thing as retirement for a killer; it's kill or be killed.

Driven by character rather than action, *The Gunfighter* was not a hit in 1950. But it's gained in critical respectability over the years, as one of those adult westerns which paints an authentic picture of the 19th century west, and a burgeoning small-town community. Gregory Peck underacts effectively.

ANTI:

'Neither particularly exciting nor particularly moving . . . [because] Gregory Peck arouses no very profound sympathy for the central character; but more, I believe, because the director, Henry King, has not himself felt strongly about his material.' *(Dilys Powell)*

PRO:

'There's never a sag or an off moment in the footage . . . Peck perfectly portrays the title role . . . He gives it great sympathy and a type of rugged individualism that makes it real.' *(Variety)*

'Preserves throughout a respectable level of intelligence and invention.' *(Lindsay Anderson)*

'All the old stock characters are there – the ace gunman, the cowboys, the bar flies, the gamblers, the saloon girls, and so on. But from them Henry King and his screenwriters have made a different kind of Western, a film of character.' *(Matthew Norgate)*

'Not merely a good western, a good film.' *(Richard Mallett, Punch)*

'The movie is done in cold, quiet tones of gray, and every object in it – faces, clothing, a table, the hero's heavy moustache – is given an air of uncompromising authenticity, suggesting those dim photographs of the nineteenth-century west.' *(Robert Warshow, The Immediate Experience)*

'A taut, suspenseful script directed with style and photographed with just the right drab, realistic atmosphere; and acted by a group of players who are as natural, as weary, as vengeful, as cocky, as friendly, as indignant, as cowardly and as idly curious as the script requires them to be . . . King was at his best – his tautest, his most interesting, his most stylish, his most craftsmanlike, his most articulate, his most powerful – with a moderate the show in New York with 'Sit Down, You're Rocking The Boat'. Still, nothing can obscure the humour of Damon Runyon's low-life characters, much less the wit and melodic invention of Frank Loesser's songs. Harry Stradling's cinematography, the musical direction by Cyril Mockridge and Jay Blackton, and art direction by Joseph Wright were all Oscar-nominated.

PRO:

'A bangup filmusical in the topdrawer Goldwyn manner . . . Casting is good all the way.' *(Variety)*

'Relaxed and caressing, the dialogue sequences serve as a kind of foreplay, enhancing not merely the exquisite eruptions of pleasure aroused by the musical numbers, but the genuine lyricism of the romance . . . Inspired casting here, with Brando and Simmons – a Method counterbalance to the more traditional showbiz coupling of Sinatra and Blaine – lending an emotional depth rare in musicals.' *(Tom Milne, Time Out)*

MIXED:

'Mr Brando does very nicely as a musical-comedy hero, but then, once again, he should never do anything very nicely. He is a tiger as an actor and he should behave as a tiger.' *(The Times)*

'One of the principals in the show is Marlon Brando, who, though eminently plausible as a big-shot gambler – he sloughs off the Runyon bad-baby-talk a lot of the time, and sounds like a human being – sings through a rather unyielding set of sinuses.' *(New Yorker)*

ANTI:

'Extended and rather tedious.' *(Pauline Kael)*

'The two major flaws . . . are Oliver Smith's sets and Frank Sinatra's performance. Samuel Goldwyn, Joseph Mankiewicz, and Mr Smith apparently couldn't make up their minds whether the scenery should be realistic or stylized. As a result, they have the disadvantages of both, and these disadvantages work against the very special nature of Runyonesque story-telling.' *(Stephen Sondheim, Films in Review)*

HAIL THE CONQUERING HERO

CT: 6 AV: 8.58

1944 US 101 BW COMEDY/WAR

D Preston Sturges ✗
W Preston Sturges ☆ AAN

Eddie Bracken ☆ Ella Raines Bill Edwards Raymond Walburn ☆ William Demarest ☆ Franklin Pangborn ☆ Jimmie Dundee Georgia Caine Alan Bridge ☆ James Damore Freddie Steele

A smalltown boy (Eddie Bracken) goes home during wartime and is lauded as a military hero; he is afraid to tell his family that the marines turned him down because of chronic hay fever.

Preston Sturges's talented repertory company of character actors is seen to good effect in this satirical comedy which debunked patriotic humbug, military pretensions, and the American propensity for hero-worship. It would have been daring at any time, but was especially courageous during the war. It's fast-paced and full of snappy dialogue, but the plot is over-contrived; there's something sneery about Sturges's attitude toward the gullible townsfolk; and the targets have inevitably dated.

PRO:

'All the other films of this dynamic director, from *The Great McGinty* to *The Miracle of Morgan's Creek*, seem to be practice exercises for this latest release of his, which has the vitalizing, seasoned sureness of a creative hand with all its tools in order and sharpened to their utmost effectiveness, applied to the execution of a design that mind and feeling have plotted for all the highest values within its scope.' *(James Shelley Hamilton, New Movies)*

'First rate entertainment . . . not to be missed.' *(Richard Mallett, Punch)*

'One of the happiest, heartiest comedies in a twelvemonth.' *(Otis Guernsey Jr)*

'The energy, the verbal density, the rush of Americana and the congestion seen periodically in *The Miracle of Morgan's Creek* stagger the senses.' *(James Ursini)*

'He uses verbal as well as visual slapstick, and his comic timing is so quirkily effective that the dialogue keeps popping off like a string of firecrackers.' *(Pauline Kael, 1977)*

MIXED:

'Sturges' genius for reflective and satirical high jinks should not be permitted to gravitate to a thematic groove. His gifts are too great to permit needless repetition and such withdrawals as are here to be detected.' *(Herb Sterne)*

'Now that Sturges is being compared, I am told, with people like Voltaire . . . I think there is some point in putting on the brakes. Most certainly Sturges has fine comic and satiric gifts, and knows how to tell more truth than that when he thinks it expedient; but he seldom does. This film has enough themes for half a dozen first-rate American satires – the crippling myth of the dead heroic father, the gentle tyranny of the widowed mother, the predicament of the only child, the questionable nature of most heroism, the political function of returning soldiers, these are just a few; I suppose in a sense the whole story is a sort of *Coriolanus* on all fours. But not one of these themes is honored by more attention than you get from an incontinent barber in a railway terminal.' *(James Agee)*

HALLOWEEN

CT: 8 AV: 6.93

1978 US 91 C HORROR

D John Carpenter ☆
W John Carpenter Debra Hill

Donald Pleasence Jamie Lee Curtis ✓ P.J. Soles Nancy Loomis Tony Moran

Psychotic killer stalks small Illinois town.

John Carpenter's expertly made horror movie, in which Jamie Lee Curtis (daughter of Janet Leigh, the actress who met a grisly end in *Psycho*) made her screen début as the obligatory female adolescent under threat from a psychopathic killer. Despite superficial characters and little in the way of plot logic, it's a trailblazing slasher movie, much imitated in the various ways it builds up suspense: its success paved the way for four inferior sequels.

ANTI:

'After a promising opening, *Halloween* becomes just another maniac-on-the-loose*suspenser.*' *(Variety)*

'John Carpenter . . . has a visual sense of menace, but he isn't very gifted with actors, and he doesn't seem to have any feeling at all for motivation or for plot logic. An escaped lunatic wielding a kitchen knife stalks people in a small Midwestern town, and that's about it. There's no indication of why he selects any particular target; he's the bogeyman – pure evil – and he wants to kill. The film is largely just a matter of the camera tracking subjectively, from the mad killer's point of view, leading you to expect something awful to happen. But the camera also tracks subjectively when he isn't around at all; in fact, there's so much subjective tracking you begin to think everybody in the movie has his own camera.' *(Pauline Kael)*

'It's regrettable that even this film – like its many inferior imitators – thrives upon the deaths of sexually promiscuous, half-dressed young women.' *(Danny Peary)*

MIXED:

'Carpenter is young, clever and outspoken and . . . takes the old formula clichés of Hollywood, then shows that there is still plenty of life in old tricks and old actors. It is an engaging thriller . . . but it does not hold the attention . . . It sets out to frighten and does it well. Few filmmakers can say that they so easily match their goals to their abilities.' *(Nicholas Wapshott, Scotsman)*

'Carpenter . . . has already proved he can make silk purses from sow's ear budgets. This time he's also saddled himself with a sow's ear script . . . written by himself. But [he] is a dashing . . . stylist and his visual style does much to redeem this Z-movie tale.' *(Nigel Andrews, Financial Times)*

PRO:

'An instant shlock horror classic.' *(Tom Allen, Village Voice)*

'A horror movie in the classic tradition. It relies almost entirely on suspense, on the anticipation of something terrible . . . Mr Carpenter doesn't waste time on purposeless characterization or explanation . . . Analysis has no place here. The point of the movie is to cause us as much distress as possible in the safety of our theater seats . . . The screenplay . . . is simple. But not simple-minded . . . and is sometimes even funny.' *(Vincent Canby, New York Times)*

'My favourite in this week of thrills . . . with [Carpenter's] marvellous control of mood, he makes each ordinary everyday situation seem just out of true . . . For sheer filmcraft and real escalating terror you can't beat this one.' *(Molly Plowright, Glasgow Herald)*

'The cold sweat in the palm of my hands never had time to warm up.' *(Tom Hutchinson, Sunday Telegraph)*

'A superb essay in Hitchcockian suspense . . . Rarely have the remoter corners of the screen been used to such good effect as shifting volumes of darkness and light reveal the presence of a sinister something.' *(Tom Milne, Time Out)*

'I don't think the intriguing Michael is evil, just insane. There's that six-year-old inside a man's body, and everything he does – including his murders – is part of a mischievous game. He could kill his victims quickly, but he prefers to hide behind bushes and in closets, peer into windows, scare them, tease them with loud noises or, as in the case of Loomis, play tricks with her car door. Before he attacks Soles, he stands in the bedroom doorway with a sheet over his body and glasses on his covered face. In his never ending struggle with Curtis (who became a cult favorite from her début effort) he pretends to be dead several times, only to rise and resume his attack. Interestingly, he never attacks children, his peers. I am not as sold on the picture as are its many cultists, but I agree that it's the scariest horror film since *Psycho* and the most imaginatively directed.' *(Danny Peary)*

HAMLET AAW CT: 5 AV: 8.33

1948 GB 155 BW DRAMA

D Laurence Olivier ☆ AAN
W Alan Dent from William Shakespeare's play

Laurence Olivier ☆ AAW Eileen Herlie ☆
Basil Sydney ☆ Jean Simmons ☆ AAN
Norman Wooland Felix Aylmer ☆ Terence Morgan
Stanley Holloway John Laurie Esmond Knight
Anthony Quayle Niall MacGinnis Patrick Troughton

Gloomy Dane (Laurence Olivier) believes his stepfather killed his father.

A severely pruned version of Shakespeare's tragedy: Olivier excises Rosencrantz and Guildenstern, and interprets the play as being 'the tragedy of a man who couldn't make up his mind'. Olivier's directorial attempts to make the film more cinematic are more distracting than effective, and his performance hasn't stood the test of time – he seems bent at times on putting the 'ham' back into Hamlet. A far more moving performance comes from Jean Simmons as Ophelia. The art direction and costume design won Oscars; William Walton's score was nominated.

PRO:

'Restores something which had long vanished from the play: sympathy with its hero; that awed and loving pity, by evoking which the tragedian gives his audience some touch of the divine, making them at once judge as men and understand as gods.' *(Dilys Powell)*

'Be you 9 or 90, a PhD or just plain Joe, *Hamlet* is the movie of the year.' *(Washington Times)*

'Seems designed to make the Bard coherent and captivating to the average moviegoer. The wondrous thing is that the film actually does so without seriously compromising the play; and Olivier's vigorous, athletic Hamlet – a Dane as full of life as he is haunted by death – is well-nigh unforgettable. (One can hardly believe he was over forty at the time.)' *(Bruce Bawer, American Spectator)*

'The most exciting and most alive production of *Hamlet* you will ever see on the screen.' *(Pauline Kael)*

ANTI:

'Olivier has made in *Hamlet* no contribution to the evolution of the cinema or to appreciation of Shakespeare. The insuperably difficult task of transposing a great tragedy, depicted in sublime and intricate flights of verbal shades of meaning, into a medium predominately visual has been essayed. It must be said that in all its boldness the attempt has failed. It is precisely when Olivier is most enthusiastically cinemising that we lose contact with tragedy and pathos and become conscious of ingenuity and technique; the assertive lighting, the glossy art photography, the pointless meanderings of the camera, the self-conscious decor inhibit a full surrender . . . Critical reception of "Hamlet" has staggered me. The word genius has been plentifully applied to Olivier, the producer and director. I stake all my instincts for cinemaphotography that this is nonsense. If he intends to go on making Shakespearean films let him discover a director with something new to say in cinema terms, for Olivier clearly does not know how to make a film flow visually.' *(Richard Winnington)*

HAND THAT ROCKS THE CRADLE, THE

CT: 7 AV: 5.92

1992 US 110 C THRILLER/HORROR

D Curtis Hanson
W Amanda Silver ✔

Annabella Sciorra ✔ Rebecca De Mornay ☆
Matt McCoy Ernie Hudson Julianne Moore
Madeleine Zima John de Lancie

Nanny from hell (Rebecca De Mornay) disrupts the lives of a nice young couple (Annabella Sciorra, Matt McCoy), who really ought to have checked those references.

In a genre which constantly exploits the vulnerability of women, this film features two unusually strong central performances from the leading actresses, a pattern soon to be repeated in the not dissimilar *Single White Female*. But the most refreshing aspect of this thriller, which could easily have been just another mindless slasher film (and degenerates into just that during the last few minutes), is the way that first-time screenwriter Amanda Silver takes the trouble to establish a credible motive for her villainess (Rebecca De Mornay). Audiences even come to enjoy a sneaking respect for her single-mindedness as she terrorizes her decently liberal, Volvo-driving, Gilbert and Sullivan-loving employers.

Beneath its unpretentious facade, the film also has a clever symbolic structure which amusingly sees the menace in ordinary domestic equipment such as bedside radios, baby alarms and breast pumps. It also shows a sophisticated understanding of middle-class mothers' worst fears in the 1990s.

'Crackpot hybrid of *The Nanny, Rebecca* and *Fatal Attraction* . . . [Director Curtis Hanson] is to Hitchcock what Mountain Dew is to Moet.' *(Margulies & Rebello, Bad Movies We Love)*

'Its moral is simple: women beware and guard your family with your life . . . a wearisome formula . . . If the good woman/bad woman paradigm seems depressingly out of date, it is equalled by the racist Uncle Tom treatment of Solomon's character . . . [who is] presented as the kind of faithful servant that Bill Robinson might have portrayed in the 30s . . . [It] is calculated not so much to set biological alarm clocks ringing, but to set the clocks back.' *(Lizzie Francke, S & S)*

'As the film progresses, malicious schemes and loony excesses are combined, with Hanson's self-conscious direction rendering one particularly sensational murder even more implausible. Subtler and more involving are sequences which show the splendidly unnerving De Mornay in coercive, threatening mood.' *(Colette Maude, Time Out)*

'De Mornay is superb as the virginal-looking incarnation of evil, rightfully getting her big break after years of second-string roles. But Sciorra's family is so perfect they're sickening, while the tension is thrown out of the window by some daft *Fatal Attraction*-type silliness in the final confrontation scenes.' *(Rose)*

'Terrific thriller . . . full of suspense.' *(Daily Express)*

'Fine performances and a refusal to pander to the audience's grosser instincts raise this a notch or two above the norm.' *(Variety)*

'A rabble-rousing hit, so adept is the movie at exploiting the sinister potential in ordinary domestic surroundings.' *(Gary Arnold, Washington Times)*

'A flawed but pretty robust exercise in horror suspense that will have young parents calling their babysitters as soon as the movie lets out.' *(Ed Kelleher, Film Journal)*

HANDFUL OF DUST, A

CT: 5 AV: 7.18

1988 GB 118 C DRAMA/ROMANCE

D Charles Sturridge
W Charles Sturridge Tim Sullivan Derek Granger from Evelyn Waugh's novel

James Wilby Kristin Scott Thomas ☆
Rupert Graves ✔ Anjelica Huston Judi Dench
Alec Guinness Beatie Edney Graham Crowden
Stephen Fry

An aristocrat (James Wilby) is cuckolded by his wife (Kristin Scott Thomas).

Charles Sturridge's screen version of Evelyn Waugh's masterpiece is handsome but thin, and entirely misses the satirical point of the original. Kristin Scott Thomas and Rupert Graves play together well as the two lovers, but they unbalance the audience sympathies, which Waugh certainly intended to be with the wronged husband (nor does it help that he is played by Wilby as an ineffectual wimp). The decision to stage the piece glossily but prosaically, in the style of 'masterpiece theatre', means that the surreal climax in the jungle – an English vision of hell – has nothing to do with what has gone before. Jane Robinson's costume designs were Oscar-nominated.

PRO:

'Shrewdly characterised, nicely acted and elegantly shot in period . . . Kristin Scott Thomas . . . hardly puts a foot wrong throughout.' *(Derek Malcolm, Guardian)*

'Sturridge's own adaptation sticks limpet-like to the text . . . and the dialogue . . . achieves remarkable comic heights . . . [His] direction takes the early scenes along at a cracking pace, which helps make the longueurs in the jungle all the more effective . . . Sturridge's vision of the Wavian world strikes me as admirably accomplished.' *(Hugh Montgomery-Massingberd, Daily Telegraph)*

'British film-making at its finest. It looks good, the characters are well-acted and the script keeps you gripped.' *(Rose)*

MIXED:

'Technically, *A Handful of Dust* cannot be faulted. Where the film disaappoints is the story, which though it ably highlights the vacuous atitudes of the English upper classes, is essentially slight.' *(Variety)*

ANTI:

'The nearest thing to an artistic incubus I have ever seen. You cannot say it is good. You cannot say it is bad. It has no independent life of its own; it merely plants itself on Waugh's novel and sets about sucking its soul.' *(Nigel Andrews, Financial Times)*

'The film's Beaver (Rupert Graves) and Brenda (Kristin Scott Thomas) are so attractive, and its Tony (James Wilby) so hollow a vessel (why does this vapid and incompetent actor keep getting cast in lead roles?), that, in the earlier sequences at any rate, Brenda's infidelity seems perfectly understandable, and for a good portion of the film one actually finds oneself applauding Brenda and Beaver's romance – a response utterly at odds with Waugh's intentions. That this romance is meant to symbolize the amorality and irresponsibility into which men and women descend when they lose their respect for faith and tradition is thoroughly obscured.' *(Bruce Bawer, American Spectator)*

HANDS OF ORLAC, THE: *see* MAD LOVE.

HANNAH AND HER SISTERS AAN

CT: 9 AV: 8.53

1986 US 106 C DRAMA/COMEDY/ROMANCE

D Woody Allen ☆ AAN
W Woody Allen ☆ AAW

Woody Allen ☆ Michael Caine ☆ AAW Mia Farrow ☆ Carrie Fisher ✔ Barbara Hershey ☆ Lloyd Nolan Maureen O'Sullivan Daniel Stern Max Von Sydow Dianne Wiest ☆ AAW Sam Waterston Tony Roberts Bobby Short Julie Kavner J.T. Walsh John Turturro

Three sisters have romantic problems.

One of the best Woody Allen films – mature, funny, charming, moving – with a splendid array of sympathetic performances. Michael Caine and Dianne Wiest won Oscars, as did Allen's screenplay: Woody's own performance may well be his best. Carlo de Palma's outstanding cinematography sees New York in soft colours: a departure from the starker vision of Allen's usual cameraman, Gordon Willis, but it suits the warmer, kindlier vision of Allen's script. Susan E. Morse's Oscar-nominated editing is unobtrusively excellent.

MIXED:

'The script gives the impression that Allen, who wrote it, keeps notes . . . Allen, much like Neil Simon in method if not tone, deals in recognition. We spot the hang-ups as we spot the locales.' *(Stanley Kauffmann)*

'A minor, agreeably skillful movie . . . It's likeable, but you wish there were more to like . . . The willed sterility of his style is terrifying to think about; the picture is all tasteful touches, and there's an element of cultural self-approval in its tone, and a trace of smugness in its narrow concern for family and friends. He uses style to blot out the rest of New York City. It's a form of repression, and, from the look of the movie, repression is what's romantic to him.' *(Pauline Kael)*

PRO:

'A beguiling new comedy.' *(Richard Corliss, Time)*

'Allen's most ambitious work.' *(Brian D. Johnson, Maclean's)*

'One of Woody Allen's great films.' *(Variety)*

'Flat-out wonderful . . . Anyone bemoaning the disappearance of adult matter from the movies need look no farther.' *(David Ansen, Newsweek)*

'Comes down on the side of the best things in life: the primacy of love and feeling, qualified hope, and the fragility of it all.' *(Chris Peachment, Time Out)*

'A great film, rich and complex . . . Allen sees comedy and drama not in his old fashion, as separate moods, but as inextricably mixed. With laughter growing out of the painful incongruities and humiliations of life, and pain falling helplessly and brutally from pleasure. The two theatrical masks have joined into one, with an immense gain in power.' *(David Denby, New York)*

HANS CHRISTIAN ANDERSEN

CT: 8 AV: 5.45

1952 US 112 C MUSICAL/ROMANCE/FAMILY/BIOPIC

D Charles Vidor
W Moss Hart (music & lyrics by Frank Loesser ☆)

Danny Kaye ☆ Zizi Jeanmaire Farley Granger John Qualen Joey Walsh

A cobbler (Danny Kaye) makes a name for himself with fairtytales for children.

Though savaged by some critics for being old-fashioned, historically inauthentic and sentimental, this was one of my favourite films as a child. Danny Kaye's talents are obvious, and the eight songs by Frank Loesser amount to one of the outstanding movie soundtracks of all time. Harry Stradling's photography and Walter Scharf's musical direction were Oscar-nominated, and Richard Day's art direction should have been. The one song to be nominated – 'Thumbelina' – was probably the weakest number in the show. A great family musical, and still underrated.

ANTI:

'Lavish, cloying, pseudo-whimsical monstrosity.' *(Pauline Kael)*

'The accent is on whimsy and chocolate-box colours.' *(Thomas Spencer, Daily Worker)*

'Hollywood has gone simple and innocent on us . . . Frank Loesser's solid and catchy music sometimes makes the film nearly tolerable.' *(Richard Winnington, News Chronicle)*

MIXED:

'Mr Goldwyn has . . . publicly disclaimed even the mistiest resemblance between his hero in fact and his hero in Technicolor fiction. "Look," he seems to say, "no Hans!" . . . There is no question of serious dishonesty. The film is quite obviously a fairy tale . . . the perfect picture for your family Christmas outing.' *(Paul Dehn, Sunday Chronicle)*

'Ideal children's entertainment with some spectacular fantasy scenes – adults may become impatient with the excessive amount of sweetness and light.' *(Scheuer)*

PRO:

'Danny Kaye's triumphant switch to a gentle straight character part is the highlight, together with some delightful and elaborate ballet scenes.' *(Jympson Harman, Evening News)*

'The music is exceptionably hummable.' *(Manchester Guardian)*

'Pleasant spectacle for children of all ages.' *(Judith Crist)*

'This movie should be mandatory viewing for viewing for every child, or anyone who's been a child.' *(Susan Sackett, Box Office Hits, 1990)*

HAPPIEST DAYS OF YOUR LIFE, THE

CT: 8 AV: 8.25

1950 GB 81 BW COMEDY

D Frank Launder ☆
W Frank Launder John Dighton from Dighton's play

Alastair Sim ☆ Margaret Rutherford ☆ Joyce Grenfell ☆ Richard Wattis ☆ Edward Rigby ☆ Guy Middleton ☆ Muriel Aked ☆ John Bentley Bernadette O'Farrell.

A bureaucratic bungle means that a boys' school (headmaster Alastair Sim) is billeted on a girl's school (headmistress Margaret Rutherford).

Frank Launder 'opens out' the action, which in the stage version is confined to the teachers' common room, with often hilarious results. This is a classic English farce, with many of the best character actors in the world on top form. The indomitable Margaret Rutherford, all British bulldog spirit, repeats her stage success, but Alastair Sim's doleful dithering and evasive expressions ensure that the film is never merely a vehicle for her talents.

'The pace never lets up and one hilarious farcical incident only ends to give place to another . . . There is no shortage of laughs, but the joke is a little too protracted and wears thin before the end.' *(Variety)*

'The duel between Miss Rutherford and Mr Sim – she bluff and soldierly, he with a sinuous crushed charm – is a confrontation or long drawn-out skirmish that should not be missed.' *(William Whitebait)*

'The best mixed comedy pairing since Groucho Marx and Margaret Dumont.' *(Sunday Chronicle)*

'Absolutely first-rate fun.' *(Richard Mallet, Punch)*

'Launder couldn't have knocked another laugh out of the situation if he'd used a hockey stick.' *(Sunday Express)*

HARD BOILED

CT: 3 AV: 4.33

(aka *Lat Sau San Tam*)

1992 Hong Kong 126/132 C ACTION/ADVENTURE/FOREIGN

D John Woo ✗
W Barry Wong ●

Chow Yun Fat Tony Leung Mo Shun Kwan John Woo (cameo role as barman)

A cop (played by Chow Yun Fat, an actor who has three expressions: pained, more pained and utterly contorted with pain) spends two hours six minutes bringing a gang of gun-runners to a grisly end. In doing so, he befriends an undercover cop (Tony Leung), wins back the affections of his cop girl-friend, and rescues a roomful of babies.

Woo's films are blood-splattered thrillers, saturated with somersaulting stuntmen. The dialogue veers between cameraderie and camp, the comic-strip and the confessional. The soundtrack is to be measured not so much in decibels, as in megatons. Those admiring critics who describe Woo's violence as having a balletic grace are correct, but isn't there something distasteful, even obscene, about being asked to admire the athletic grace with which men kill and die? It's as if an art critic were to show us moving pictures of a concentration camp and invite us to admire the wonderful slimness of the inhabitants.

To describe Mr Woo as 'the Mozart of mayhem' (as BBC2's *Moving Pictures* did in 1993) is amusingly alliterative, but culturally crapulent. Mozart was a master of subtlety, aural beauty, variations on a theme: Mr Woo's films are an exercise in crudeness and monotony. In most action pictures, a delight in destruction and death forms a part of the appeal: in Mr Woo's, it seems to be the whole point. There's something fascistic about the way the people in this film are reduced to so many indistinguishable bodies, to be hacked, bludgeoned, exploded or incinerated for our entertainment. Woo is flippantly cynical and camp at the same time as ogling it: he's the Busby Berkeley of bloodshed.

The influence of this High Priest of Oriental Overkill can be seen all too clearly on recent western culture: on *Reservoir Dogs* and *True Romance* (especially in the scenes where all the gangsters pull guns on each other simultaneously), on the *Lethal Weapon* trilogy, and and on the films of James Cameron. The irony is that Woo himself is not an originator. Though following in the footsteps of kung-fu film-makers such as Bruce Lee, he was even more influenced by the west – by Jean-Pierre Melville's austere, European imitations of the American gangster film (such as *Le Samourai*): art-house thrillers with the plot, morality and characterization surgically removed. Woo's camera techniques and special effect trademarks are just as clearly indebted to Martin Scorsese and Walter Hill.

Woo's publicity material quoted Sam Raimi, director of *The Evil Dead*, as saying 'John Woo is to action what Hitchcock is to suspense'. If only he were. Hitchcock used suspense – and action – not just to titillate, but as a way of sustaining his audience's interest in stories which were – it's increasingly realized – exploring the darkest fears of 20th-century man. It was this tapping into the depths of the human psyche which made Hitchcock not only popular, but also a film-maker of power and importance.

Woo's films have no depth, no humanity, no light and shade, no point except to make money. Without even Pol Pot's pretence of a political purpose, they reduce the cinema screen to a killing field. Although they may arouse the admiration of some critics and film-makers who see only their craft, their excesses are more likely to rouse audiences to incredulous laughter; I fear, however, that even as we laugh we are being desensitized into coldness and callousness. Woo may well be as hard boiled as his heroes. But the ideas in his films are poached; his morality is over-easy; he leaves most of his characters fried and his audiences' brains scrambled. Mr Woo isn't God, Mozart or Hitchcock: he represents cinema at its most decadent and pernicious. He is the bore of gore.

'John Woo is the most exciting director to emerge in action cinema since Sergio Leone.' *(Quentin Tarantino)*

'John Woo is God.' *(Select)*

'More exciting than a dozen *Die Hards*.' *(Empire)*

'Gob smacking mayhem and outrageous massacres choreographed into a ballistic ballet . . . Only global thermonuclear annihilation would make for a higher body count. Hold on to your seats!' *(Premiere UK)*

'Anyone who saw *The Killer* will have a fair idea what to expect, from the intense male bonding to the hyper-kinetic editing style. What's new here is a rich vein of anarchic humour . . . and a bluesy back-beat of philosophical musings on a cop's sad lot.' *(Tony Rayns, Time Out)*

HARD DAY'S NIGHT, A   CT: 10 AV: 8.36

1964 GB 85 BW MUSICAL/COMEDY

D Richard Lester ☆
W Alun Owen ☆ AAN

John Lennon Paul McCartney George Harrison Ringo Starr ☆ Wilfrid Brambell Norman Rossington Victor Spinetti John Junkin Deryck Guyler Anna Quayle

Thirty-six hours in the life of a very successful group.

A none-too-realistic portrait of a rock band on the road; *This is Spinal Tap* is closer to the truth. But Dick Lester's flashy, gimmicky camera-work (the cinematographer was Gilbert Taylor) and scriptwriter Alun Owen's image-building of the Fab Four as the boys next door still works like a dream: this is a dream of the 60s as they never were, but as we would have liked them to have been. Endlessly eclectic, Lester's directing has the homespun energy that one associates with the French New Wave at its best, without the slightest element of Gallic pretention. The songs are wonderfully melodic and energetic; even though there's no dancing or lavish production, this must rank as one of the greatest musicals of all time. George Martin was nominated for an Oscar, but oddly none of the songs was. The film was shot in seven weeks, for around half a million dollars; it made a handsome profit.

ANTI:

'It is so rough and grainy, so choppy and new wave in its editing, so obtrusively hand-held in its camerawork that by the end more than a little dazzled and deafened one may find oneself thinking back nostalgically to the good old straightforward days of *Orchestra Wives* . . . The main trouble is . . . that there are too many bright ideas flung at us one after the other with no spacing and hardly any quiet patches for us to get our breath back before the next outburst; the whole film is oddly unremitting in its attack, and consequently muffs a number of its potentially most telling effects.' *(The Times)*

'At times the straining after a laugh at all costs is too hard.' *(Cecil Wilson, Daily Mail)*

MIXED:

'We're not very good, but we had a good producer.' *(Paul McCartney to Princess Margaret at the London premiere)*

'This is a comedy without one twinge of pity for human beings, particularly the old . . . *A Hard Day's Night* is brilliant, fast, funny and distinctly frightening.' *(Anne Scott-James, Daily Mail)*

'They can't sing nearly as well as they can't act, but they are themselves and that is enough.' *(New York Herald Tribune)*

'Instead of the raw excuse for Beatle-song which I had expected, here was a sharply professional piece, directed with great dash by Richard Lester, boldly photographed by Gilbert Taylor, smartly edited by John Jympson – and acted, as well as thrummed and bawled, with the most likeable aplomb by the Sacred Four. Deafening, of course. But it really is restoring to find in the British cinema, apt to waver between devoted amateurism and mad polish, the seeming spontaneity of this exercise in anarchy. I hope it isn't blasphemous to say I was reminded for a second or two of the Marx Brothers . . . I won't recommend *A Hard Day's Night* to the public for Palestrina. But if you can stand the racket it is very funny.' *(Dilys Powell)*

'No attempt has been made to build them up as Oliviers. They are at their best when the film has an off-the-cuff spontaneity But they emerge as individual characters and, carefully handled, may well develop the kind of cinematic zaniness that has not been seen since the Marx Brothers in their prime.' *(Variety)*

PRO:

'We had expected a show of monotonous and noisy songs and provocatve gags inder the label "Young people letting off steam". On the contrary, it is one of the most interesting music films of recent times.' *(Polityka, Poland's most serious political weekly)*

'The Beatles are a mixture of all the old-time slapstick comedians with a dash of up-to-date slickness. They are unique.' *(New York Daily News)*

'A fine conglomeration of madcap clowning . . . with such a dazzling use of camera that it tickles the intellect and electrifies the nerves.' *(Bosley Crowther)*

'Has no plot. What it has instead, which is plenty, is invention, good looks, and a lot of larky character. The narrative is simply a day in the Beatles' lives, and their situation when you think about it is pure comedy: four highly characterized people caught in a series of intensely public dilemmas but always remaining untouched by them, like Keaton, because they carry their private world around everywhere. Whether they are in a train carriage or at a press conference or in a television studio, the Beatles are always really living in a capsule of Liverpool . . . Ringo emerges as a born actor. He is like a silent comedian, speechless and chronically underprivileged, a boy who is already ageless with a mournful, loose mouth, like a Labrador's carrying a bird.' *(Penelope Gilliatt)*

'Director Richard Lester offers us camera work of fantastic charm, pacing and gaggery of the Mack Sennett and Marx Brothers schools, songs that improve in context, and probing portraits of four very likable young men. Aging squares and young swingers alike should put this 1964 film on their never-miss lists.' *(Judith Crist)*

'You'll see traces of Fellini, Berkeley, Antonioni, Sennett, Chaplin, Keaton. One scene will be abstract, the next absurd, the next realistic; he [Lester] moves from fantasy to cinema vérité . . . Alun Owen's imaginative, semi-plotless script, full of non-sequiturs, is the perfect vehicle for Lester's mad method.' *(Danny Peary)*

The *Citizen Kane* of Jukebox movies.' *(Andrew Sarris)*

HARLEM NIGHTS CT: 1 AV: 3.30

1989 US 106 C THRILLER/COMEDY

D Eddie Murphy ●
W Eddie Murphy ●

Eddie Murphy ● Richard Pryor ● Redd Foxx Danny Aiello Michael Lerner Della Reese Berlinda Tolbert Stan Shaw Jasmine Guy Vic Polizos (cameo Arsenio Hall)

An illegal club (run by Richard Pryor and Eddie Murphy) is threatened by rival gangsters (led by Michael Lerner).

The most hideous indictment of the Hollywood star system since Barbra Streisand's *Yentl*. The opening titles say it all: Paramount pictures have made 'in association with Eddie Murphy Productions' a 'film by Eddie Murphy, starring Eddie Murphy, executive produced by Eddie Murphy, written and directed by . . . Eddie Murphy.' The picture which follows is the equivalent of vanity publishing: a lame-brain rip-off of 1930s gangster films, and an embarrassing failure in virtually every department. The plot is risible, the execution without wit. The language is that of the gutter, and an extremely filthy, modern gutter at that. As if to compensate for being so up-to-the-moment verbally, the film's morality – in particular, its attitude towards women – is neanderthal. All complaints should be addressed to Eddie Murphy.

PRO:

'We found it enjoyable. Not only has . . . Murphy created an old-fashioned melodrama that save for the continuous profanity, could just as easily have starred Humphrey Bogart and James Cagney in the Thirties, but he has given fine roles to some of the entertainment industry's finest black performers.' *(Martin & Porter)*

ANTI:

'Overdone, too rarely funny, and, worst of all, boring.' *(Variety)*

'There is not an original idea in the movie from one end to the other . . . The dialogue is distractingly contemporary . . . If he [Murphy] wants to realize his potential, he needs to work with a better writer and director than himself.' *(Roger Ebert)*

'Doesn't so much climax as go prematurely limp.' *(Mark Kermode, Time Out)*

'This is the kind of movie that makes racism seem respectable. All the black characters are pimps, prostitutes, liars, cheats or murderers. And they're the good guys; none more so than Eddie Murphy, who proves it by shooting the foot off the madam of his brothel and murdering the girl he sleeps with. All women are "bitches" or "property" to be abused, insulted, tortured or killed by him. Misogyny doesn't even begin to describe the pure hatred this film expresses towards women. Why one of the few black stars with the muscle to bankroll any film he wants should make a movie that portrays blacks in such a low light is almost as much of a mystery as why the black press, which so vociferously protested a white director's version of *The Color Purple*, praised Murphy's portrayal of a "strong black leading man".' *(Trevor Willsmer, Film Review)*

'Nastily violent, sleazy and lamentably unfunny.' *(Rose)*

HARLEY DAVIDSON AND THE MARLBORO MAN CT: 1 AV: 2.11

1991 US 98 C ACTION/ADVENTURE

D Simon Wincer ●
W Don Michael Paul ●
Mickey Rourke ● Don Johnson ● Chelsea Field
Daniel Baldwin Giancarlo Esposito

Two bikers (Mickey Rourke, Don Johnson) rob a bank to save their favourite bar from redevelopment.

It was always going to be difficult to do something more horrific than *Homeboy*, weedier than *Wild Orchid*, more desperate than *The Desperate Hours*, but somehow in this movie Rourke pulls it off. With teeth like Bugs Bunny's, and a spiky haircut which makes him resemble a hedgehog undergoing electroconvulsive therapy, he plays a biker so brain-damaged that he thinks he's his own bike and has to wander round with his name on his back so he won't forget it. His best friend (Don Johnson) models himself on the cowboy on the cigarette poster, has a girlfriend called Virginia Slim, and is a king-sized drag.

The film should carry a government health warning. It contains all the most tasteless ingredients of the buddy-buddy genre – gratuitous topless nudity, impassive villains in black leather coats, poolroom brawls, bimbos ogling the heroes – and slaps them in front of us with the bored contempt of a waitress in a fast-food joint.

Sample Rourke monologue: 'If there is a God, I'd like to meet the dude, I'd like to go hang out with him.' Sample dialogue . . . Rourke (picking up female hitch-hiker): 'Where you headin?' She: 'Nowhere special.' Rourke: 'C'mon. I'll take you there.'

'A quite enjoyable instance of the good-bad movie. However, the dialogue might have been written by a computer programmed with back numbers of *Mad Magazine* . . . To be taken with at least a kilo of salt.' *(Tim Pulleine, Guardian)*

'Bone-headed.' *(Variety)*

'Messrs Rourke and Johnson must have been out of their heads when they agreed to appear in [this] . . . dire rubbish that gets physically painful to watch within five minutes . . . On the positive side? One or two nice views of Vegas.' *(Philip Blinko, What's On in London)*

'This disastrous modern Western veers between camp pastiche and po-faced machismo . . . Utter rubbish and badly dressed at that.' *(Mark Kermode, Time Out)*

'"No company has approved, sponsored or endorsed the title or the content of this film" say the pre-titles. Nor does this critic.' *(Hugo Davenport, Daily Telegraph)*

'Like *Easy* Rider restaged for an actor's retirement benefit.' *(Nigel Andrews, Financial Times)*

'The plot holds water like a leaking bucket, the script stinks, the acting would make a forest of Redwoods appear animated, and Rourke and Johnson have all the buddy allure of Godzilla taking tea with the Archbishop of Canterbury. If you know anyone who has recently had all their brain cells destroyed in a terrible accident shepherd them into this orbit.' *(Sue Heal, Today)*

'Imagine how your bum feels after sitting on a motorbike for twenty-four hours. Now imagine that feeling all over your body and you get a fair idea of the appeal of this Mickey Rourke biker pic.' *(Rose)*

'High concept meets rock bottom.' *(Margulies & Rebello)*

HAROLD AND MAUDE CT: 8 AV: 7.09

1971 US 92 C COMEDY

D Hal Ashby ☆
W Colin Higgins ✔

Bud Cort ☆ Ruth Gordon ☆ Vivian Pickles ☆
Cyril Cusack Charles Tyner Ellen Geer
Eric Christmas

Death-obsessed 20-year-old (Bud Cort) finds love with 79-year-old hippie (Ruth Gordon).

One of the funniest – and sickest – of all black comedies, with three great performances: the other one is from Vivian Pickles as Cort's mother. The 'do your own thing' message and some of the philosophizing has dated, but it's still very amusing. Critically mauled on release, it's built up a cult reputation.

ANTI:

'Has all the fun and gaiety of a burning orphanage . . . One thing that can be said about Ashby – he begins the film in a gross and macabre manner, and never once deviates from the concept. That's style for you.' *(Variety)*

'A two-joke comedy that is funny at first but . . . becomes unbearable through repetition.' *(Alexander Walker, Evening Standard)*

'[After a superbly grisly beginning] the film gets very sticky indeed.' *(Tom Milne, The Times)*

'Cort and Gordon are so aggressive, so creepy and offputting that they are obviously made for each other.' *(Vincent Canby, New York Times)*

MIXED:

'A rose et noir comedy and . . . I found myself relishing the noir and resisting the rose . . . It's a disappointment because it's main message . . . is so easy.' *(George Melly, Observer)*

'The black humour . . . is very amusing and Vivian Pickles . . . is sheer delight. But when [Harold] takes up with [Maude] . . . embarrassment sets in.' *(Nina Hibbin, Morning Star)*

'Bud Cort and Ruth Gordon are marvellously funny, and if the lyricism is a bit overdone in parts, it's still worth seeing for Harold's outstandingly realistic harikiri.' *(NFT Bulletin, 1984)*

'Often hilarious black comedy for those who can stand it; the epitome of bad taste, splashed around with wit and vigour, it became a minor cult.' *(Halliwell)*

PRO:

'It appears to be about redemption . . . Courageously Harold and Maude are not only misfits in temperament but misfits in age. That's what really worries the film's critics . . . the implication that an 18-year-old boy might actually go to bed with an octogenarian woman . . . It is a rich, inventive, outrageous, funny and uplifting film. I won't hear a word against it.' *(Margaret Hinxman, Sunday Telegraph)*

'A sick comedy all right – but if you go along with the spirit of this farce, it's one of the most inventive American comedy films in years.' *(Scheuer)*

HARRAD EXPERIMENT, THE

CT: 5 AV: 3.83

1973 US 97 C DRAMA/SO BAD

D Ted Post
W Michael Werner Ted Cassidy ● from Robert H. Rimmer's novel

James Whitmore ● Tippi Hedren ● Don Johnson Laurie Walters Robert Middleton Melanie Griffith

College professors (James Whitmore, Tippi Hedren) encourage student self-expression through sex and nudity.

Hilariously naive drama, obviously made to titillate. Unintentionally, it offers many comic insights into the seriousness of 60s sexual liberationists. This is the film during which leading man Don Johnson first encountered his co-star Tippi Hedren's 14-year-old daughter, Melanie Griffith; the rest is Hollywood history. Don't miss the horrific theme song.

'Highly erotic [but] no porno movie.' *(Donald J. Mayerson, Cue)*

'Not much new . . . Instead of honestly exploring the effect of simultaneous relationships on idealistic college students . . . the movie cops out for traditional morality . . . Post's direction is clean and controlled but too listless to give the movie energy.' *(Alan R. Howard, Hollywood Reporter)*

'The kind of movie in which never does flesh touch flesh without a choir of dulcet strings on the soundtrack to sanctify the meeting . . . But into any bowl of mush a little sweetener may fall. The goodness in this case comes . . . from the [teachers who] are so uncommonly, solemnly, unintentionally funny that they almost justify seeing [the film].' *(Roger Greenspun, New York Times)*

'The nudity is never offensive. What is offensive is the movie's appalling lack of intelligence.' *(Kathleen Carroll, LA Times)*

'A silly . . . badly directed . . . tickle and tease movie [which proves] actors become completely uninteresting without any clothes on.' *(Judith Crist, New York Magazine)*

'The cast is terribly earnest which probably may be explained by the fact that they hadn't seen the movie.' *(John L. Wasserman, San Francisco Chronicle)*

'So low-keyed that it almost fails to register at all; interest is kept alive, though, by its sheer silliness.' *(Geoff Brown, MFB)*

'Ludicrously sober-sided amalgam of nude yoga and extra-curricular groping, which should set sex educational theory back ten years.' *(S & S)*

'Gidget meets Masters and Johnson.' *(David Pirie, Time Out)*

HARVEY CT: 5 AV: 7.69

1950 US 104 BW COMEDY/FAMILY

D Henry Koster ☆
W Mary Chase Oscar Brodney from Chase's play

James Stewart ✗ AAN Josephine Hull ✗ AAW
Peggy Dow Charles Drake Cecil Kellaway
Victoria Home Jesse White William Lynn
Wallace Ford Nana Bryant

A sweet-natured alcoholic (James Stewart) imagines that he has been befriended by a 6 foot 4 inch tall rabbit named Harvey; his sister (Josephine Hull) decides that he, and if necessary Harvey, should be committed to a lunatic asylum.

Many find this delightful, but I find it much too studied in its whimsicality; the two central performances, though acclaimed at the time, look forced and theatrical today (and Stewart is clearly too young for the role). The view of alcoholism and mental illness as cosily charming is downright bizarre.

PRO:

'Continually springs chuckles, often hilarity, as the footage unfolds.' *(Variety)*

'The lovable animal who charmed so many theatre audiences for so long, has arrived on the screen with whimsy in full bloom . . . Pixyish as it all is, some reviewers didn't even see the rabbit.' *(Fortnight)*

'Although Stewart lacks the precision timing and the delicately deranged humor that Frank Fay brought to the original Elwood, his amiable, gregarious eccentric is a very satisfactory substitute.' *(Newsweek)*

MIXED:

'Gets underway slowly, hampered by an over-stagey performance from Josephine Hull, and a mannered one from James Stewart . . . Harvey himself scarcely begins to exist for the audience until the last few minutes.' *(MFB)*

'Charming, lightweight stuff so long as you can take Stewart's ingenuousness, but it does wear thin.' *(Geoff Andrew, Time Out)*

HE OR SHE: *see* GLEN OR GLENDA?

HEAD THAT WOULDN'T DIE, THE: *see* THE BRAIN THAT WOULDN'T DIE.

HEAR MY SONG CT: 9 AV: 7.36

1991 GB 113 C COMEDY/MUSICAL/ROMANCE

D Peter Chelsom ☆
W Peter Chelsom Adrian Dunbar ✓

Ned Beatty ☆ Adrian Dunbar ☆ Shirley Anne Field
Tara Fitzgerald ☆ William Hootkins Harold Berens
David McCallum James Nesbitt

A young Irishman (Adrian Dunbar), in an attempt to re-open his crumbling Liverpool club, hunts for Josef Locke (Ned Beatty), the popular Irish tenor whose real-life skirmishes with the tax authorities led to a precipitate departure from these shores.

A seemingly simple comedy with an ingenious dramatic structure (notice the way our hero's failings, and his quest, reflect those of Locke himself). But there's still time for illogical but charming touches, like the attempt to stop a cow from falling down a well. The final set-piece is wonderfully staged, and the whole of Peter Chelsom's film has a rare emotional warmth and sense of joy.

ANTI:

'Shameless stabs at cockle-warming charm make for ingratiating whimsy . . . The climax is cringingly contrived, the characters are insufficiently credible or sympathetic to make us care, the comedy is soggy sub-Forsyth fare. Of the conceit that modern audiences would rave to the dated strains of Locke's chirpy operetta, the less said the better.' *(Geoff Andrew, Time Out)*

'Far from making an innovative contribution to British cinema, *Hear My Song* relies for the most part on nostalgia, whimsy and sleight of hand.' *(Tom Charity, S & S)*

MIXED:

'Comedy is a tricky business and there are lots of ways to go wrong . . . Chelsom . . . takes a whimsical conceit and sells it so hard that it loses most of its fragile charm . . . The movie keeps looking back at us to make sure we're still with it, still responding to its relentless quirkiness. This sort of thing is annoying but [the film] is so brazenly, childishly eager to please that it's impossible to stay angry for long. On its own terms, the story is well constructed; the movie wraps everything up in a grand, silly climax . . . You can't say [the filmmakers] don't have the courage of their elfinness.' *(Terrence Rafferty, New Yorker)*

PRO:

'Deserves a rousing cheer . . . For here is a British film without so much as a flutter of Edwardian white linen, nor yet any trace of the draggy, doom-laden didacticism that too often passes for seriousness in British films set in the present.' *(Hugo Davenport, Daily Telegraph)*

'Sharp little British comedy . . . [is] a continual delight, smartly performed and written . . . A wonderfully ripe yet relaxed shaggy dog story, deftly directed . . . Chelsom . . . captures much of the winsome, leanly comic observation of Bill Forsyth's early films and harks back even further to the heyday of Ealing . . . Not the least of the film's pleasures are seemingly incidental: the stunning Irish countryside vistas – they're like a tonic –

beautifully photographed by Sue Gibson.' *(David Bartholomew, Film Journal)*

'A romantic comedy of great charm . . . Within five minutes the movie has created the sense of a tight-knit community, and within half an hour it has created the considerable miracle of making us care whether Micky can find Josef Locke . . . *Hear My Song* is the very soul of a great small film.' *(Roger Ebert)*

HEART IN WINTER, A CT: 6 AV: 7.33

(aka *Un Coeur en Hiver*)

1992 France 101 C DRAMA/ROMANCE/FOREIGN

D Claude Sautet ☆
W Claude Sautet Jacques Fieschi Jerome Tonnerre

Daniel Auteuil ☆ Emmanuelle Béart ☆
André Dussollier ☆ Elizabeth Bourgine
Brigitte Catillon Maurice Garrel Myriam Boyer
Stanislas Carré de Malberg Jean-Luc Bideau

A violin-maker (Daniel Auteuil) and his business partner (André Dussilier) fall out over a violinist (Emmanuelle Béart), who turns out to be so repressed that she can express emotion only through music.

Claude Sautet's attractive if protracted story of an eternal triangle, with three outstandingly sensitive performances.

'French film-making at its finest . . . Emmanuelle Béart's performance is immaculate.' *(Alexander Walker, Evening Standard)*

'Directed with mannered, well, Frenchness . . . The best bit: . . . when he rejects her – the clot! – at the end.' *(Empire)*

'Impeccably crafted . . . [it] offers a sterling cast and in-depth characterizations . . . Benefitting from a taut script, Sautet draws excellent performances from his actors in a hand-in-glove fit . . . This is masterful storytelling.' *(Liza Bear, Film Journal)*

'Sautet and his excellent trio of leads manage to convey complex emotional nuances without resorting to explicit dialogue, plot contrivance, or hackneyed visual metaphor.' *(Geoff Andrew, Time Out)*

'A complex and adult relationship drama of a level and kind seen too infrequently.' *(Winnert)*

HEARTLAND CT: 5 AV: 7.18

1979 US 96 C WESTERN/DRAMA

D Richard Pearce ☆
W Beth Ferris from Elinore Randall Stewart's books and papers

Rip Torn ✓ Conchata Ferrell ☆ Barry Primus
Lilia Skala Megan Folson Amy Wright
Jerry Hardin Mary Boylan Jeff Boschee
Robert Overholzer

Around 1910 in Wyoming, a poor woman (Conchata Ferrell) becomes housekeeper to a laconic Scottish rancher (Rip Torn).

An authentic-looking, elemental, de-mythologizing western, based on the real life of a settler named Elinore Randall Stewart, and splendidly shot by cameraman Fred Murphy, with Montana standing in for Wyoming. Director Richard Pearce treats it all in documentary style, and is well served by two convincing performances from the leads. The big problem is that the narrative is dour and predictable; and while you end up respecting the characters, it's hard really to like them.

PRO:

'Never betrays, in its high visual and narrative quality, the absurdly small budget on which it was made . . . [It] is finely and feelingly played by Rip Torn and Conchata Ferrell, an actress who embodies the quality of tough, cheerful resilience that alone could have survived this way of life.' *(David Robinson, The Times)*

'A word of praise for [its] reality and sense of hardship which your average western scrupulously avoids.' *(Eric Shorter, Daily Telegraph)*

'Earthy, unglamorous but always fascinating.' *(Ivan Waterman, News of the World)*

'A big, robust, joyous movie about people who make other movie heroes look tentative . . . Everything in this movie affirms life. Perhaps that is why *Heartland* can also be so unblinking in its consideration of death.' *(Roger Ebert)*

ANTI:

'Self-consciously arty . . . and simple to a fault . . . The reserved manner of these characters is annoying – the picture cries out for emotion and words. What's most disappointing is that there are no surprises; it's like a PBS program that you watch for about twenty minutes before flipping the channel.' *(Danny Peary)*

HEAVEN CAN WAIT AAN CT: 6 AV: 7.90

1943 US 112 C COMEDY/FANTASY

D Ernst Lubitsch ☆ AAN
W Samson Raphaelson from Ladislaus Bus-Fekete's play *Birthdays*

Gene Tierney Don Ameche ☆ Charles Coburn ☆
Marjorie Main ☆ Laird Cregar ☆ Spring Byington
Allyn Joslyn ☆ Eugene Pallette Signe Hasso
Louis Calhern

A New York dandy (Don Ameche) imagines his sexual indiscretions during the gay 1890s qualify him for Hell, but fails to impress Satan (Laird Cregar) with his reminiscences of a mis-spent life.

Endearing fantasy featuring Don Ameche's finest performance – though he had to wait another 50 years to win an Academy Award, for *Cocoon*. It's beautifully designed – Hell is a knockout – and colourfully photographed (cameraman Edward Cronjager was Oscar-nominated). The dialogue is witty, and Samson Raphaelson's urbane script shows little signs of its origins as a Hungarian play. Lubitsch is strong on period detail, and doesn't allow the element of social satire to interfere with the fun and good humour.

MIXED:

'Not up to his [Lubitsch's] best; nothing has been, for nearly twenty years. Its real matrix, for that matter, is the sort of smirking, "civilized", Central European puff paste with which the Theater Guild used to claim to bring vitality to the American stage. But it looks like a jewel against the wood-silk and cellophane which passes for a moving picture now that Hollywood has come of age.' *(James Agee, Nation)*

'Might all be a trifle unedifying but for the charm and the understanding of her man that Gene Tierney brings to the part of the wife.' *(Manchester Guardian)*

'Ameche is short on charm and too hapless for the role; he can't get any real chemistry cooking with Tierney.' *(Virgin)*

PRO:

'A return to the better, individual Lubitsch; not quite his best, perhaps, but near it . . . [It] has unusual wit and charm. It has Technicolor, too, wisely and not too gloriously used.' *(William Whitebait, New Statesman)*

'The best picture [Lubitsch] has made for a considerable time . . . Ameche is excellent.' *(Lionel Williams, Evening Standard)*

'Disarmingly light in tone but in fact quite astute in its social and sexual satire.' *(Martyn Auty, Time Out)*

HEAVEN'S GATE

CT: 9 AV: 4.15

1980 US 149/219 C WESTERN/EPIC

D Michael Cimino ✔

W Michael Cimino

Kris Kristofferson Christopher Walken John Hurt Isabelle Huppert Sam Waterston Jeff Bridges Joseph Cotten Roseanne Vela Ronnie Hawkins Geoffrey Lewis

Immigrants and capitalists clash on the American frontier; a lawman (Kris Kristofferson), a whore (Isabelle Huppert) and a gunfighter (Christopher Walken) form a romantic triangle.

A massive critical and commercial flop which sank an entire studio (United Artists) and dealt writer-director Michael Cimino's reputation a blow from which it has never recovered. It also illustrates how powerful a single critic can be; it was Vincent Canby's attack on it in the *New York Times* which made the studio cut it down to 149 minutes – in which form it was incomprehensible – and re-release it to the public, whereupon it earned an even worse set of reviews.

Protests by the American Humane Association and the Humane Society of the US caused wide-scale picketing of the film in the US. Animal rights protesters let off stink bombs at the film's West End premiere. The British censor called for cuts in the cock-fighting scenes and deleted scenes in which horses were made to fall in a way that might have caused them suffering.

Two years on, a fuller, 219-minute version (not unlike the version slated by Canby) was released in Britain to a rapturous reception from the critics, several of whom hailed it as a masterpiece. The truth is somewhere in between: its politics do savour of Hollywood Marxism; the story and characters are too thin to sustain its length; and the dialogue is occasionally bathetic. Sample line . . . Kris Kristofferson to Isabelle Huppert, after she has been gang-raped, seen her attackers shot and knifed, driven a carriage across a range war, killing several people, has had the carriage shot from under her, ridden horseback to a burnt-out house in the middle of a gun battle and found her lover smothered in blood: 'Are you all right, dear?'

At the same time, the period detail is unmatched; there's a sweep and a scale which is very impressive; and Cimino paints a mainly convincing picture of the birth of a nation. It is a great western, and not only in terms of its scale; by the end, it's very moving.

ANTI:

'You might suspect Mr Cimino sold his soul to the devil to obtain the success of *The Deer Hunter* and the devil has just come round to collect . . . Mr Cimino has written his own screenplay, whose awfulness has been considerably inflated by the director's wholly unwarranted respect for it.' *(Vincent Canby, New York Times)*

'Hollywood Marxism: the poor are better than the rich because they are more photogenic.' *(Richard Corliss, Time)*

'I am a little surprised that many of the same critics who lionized . . . *The Deer Hunter* have now thrown [Cimino] to the wolves with equal enthusiasm . . . I was never taken in . . . Hence, the stupidity and incoherence of [this film] came as no surprise.' *(Andrew Sarris, Village Voice)*

'An epic vision isn't worth much if you can't tell a story . . . Obviously the film is too long; what's more puzzling is that all the really crucial scenes seem to be missing.' *(David Ansen, Newsweek)*

'An all-out disaster . . . had the movie been filmed entirely in Russian without English subtitles it might have made more sense than it does in its present state.' *(Kathleen Carroll, New York Daily News)*

'The movie is almost totally devoid of narrative

drive. Even the most dramatic highlights suffer from a lack of logic. One night, during the climactic battle, the settlers are laid out wan and wounded in a barn. But the next morning they seem to have mustered the superhuman strength to construct a sturdy "Trojan horse" to repel their enemy . . . Isabelle Huppert, a fine actress . . . seems altogether too frail and winsome to be the madame of a frontier brothel . . . I suppose what is really so unacceptable is the cost: 50 million dollars give or take a million.' *(Margaret Hinxman, Daily Mail)*

'So confusing, so overlong at over three-and-a-half hours and so ponderous that it fails to work on almost every level.' *(Variety)*

'The most scandalous cinematic waste I have ever seen, and remember, I've seen *Paint Your Wagon*.' *(Roger Ebert)*

'I don't understand what it's about.' *(Kris Kristofferson at US premiere)*

'Characters and story were sacrificed to the filmmaker's love of visual effect and production for their own sakes. The "look" of the thing subsumed the sense of the thing and implied a callous or uncaring quality about characters for whom the audience was asked to care more than the film seemed to.' *(Stephen Bach, executive producer, Final Cut, 1985)*

'Michael Cimino made this gigantic film without an emotional or intellectual centre. He gave himself a brilliant narrative on a plate and then stubbornly refused to use it. It starts with two characters, one of whom is brilliant at college but can't cope with the outside world, the other of whom scrapes by at college and then gets out to find life is an oyster. It's a wonderful structure, which gets lost under the mound of detail. I remember arriving on the set when they were shooting a scene that in the script was described as "Averell passes the cockfight on the way to the bar." When I got there, they were on the third week of shooting the cockfight, which really says it all.' *(John Hurt)*

MIXED:

'Cimino is wonderful with the scenery of Montana, but lost among the actors. The handling of the dalogue is lethargic and muted, the quality of the script pathetic.' *(Victor Davis, Daily Express)*

'Far from an unqualified disappointment. The desiccated tones of Vilmos Zsigmond's photography are exactly right.' *(The Times)*

'Cimino's folly turned out to be neither the all-eclipsing masterwork he clearly intended nor the irredeemable turkey his critics dismissed. It is a triumph of style over context: marvelous set pieces, millions of authentic looking extras and a real sense of small bloody struggles in a big country . . . without at any stage making one interested in the people who participate in them.' *(Film Year Book)*

PRO:

'Cimino is shouldering the weight of Hollywood's collective guilt at over-budgeted films. *Heaven's Gate* does have considerable merits.' *(David Lewin, Daily Mail)*

'Not merely a fascinating Western but quite possibly the greatest American movie of the last 10 years . . . a masterpiece.' *(Nigel Andrews, Financial Times)*

'The cinematic equivalent of a leper or rabid dog; it also happens to be one of the most challenging American films in recent years – deeply flawed, heavily cut, but possessing a strange and terrible beauty . . . the *Barry Lyndon* of the American West . . . Cimino's epic vision . . . recalls Griffith . . . epic grandeur, an elusive and subjective quality, but [the film] bursts with it.' *(Adrian Turner, F & F)*

'The full version, I can assure you, is quite an experience – an extraordinary attempt to make a major American movie at a time when only the minors hold sway.' *(Derek Malcom, Guardian, 1982)*

'I hope this masterpiece will now get the support it deserves.' *(Philip French, S & S, 1982)*

'One emerges from the complete [film] dubious perhaps, about its intellectual worth, but dazzled and moved by cinema's magnetic power.' *(Geoff Brown, The Times, 1982)*

'I've just had the rare pleasure of seeing Cimino's master work as the director originally conceived it – all 3 hours. It bears cruelly little resemblance to the wreck of a movie I reviewed then . . . Relationships and incidents in the plot which made no sense when I first saw it now fall naturally into place.' *(Margaret Hinxman, Daily Mail, 1982)*

'The film is about loss in national as well as personal terms, its distinction lying in the way it counterpoints and connects the two . . . I think [it] rivals [*Birth of a Nation*], not only in sweep and ambition, but in realization . . . Among the supreme achievements of the Hollywood cinema.' *(Robin Wood, Hollywood From Vietnam to Reagan, 1986)*

HEIRESS, THE AAN — CT: 9 AV: 8.50

1949 US 115 BW DRAMA/ROMANCE

D William Wyler ☆ AAN
W Ruth Goetz Augustus Goetz from their play and Henry James's novel *Washington Square*

Olivia de Havilland ☆ AAW Montgomery Clift Ralph Richardson ☆ AAN Miriam Hopkins ☆ Vanessa Brown Mona Freeman Ray Collins Betty Linley Selena Royle Paul Lees

An unscrupulous gold-digger (Montgomery Clift) pursues a plain, lonely heiress (Olivia de Havilland).

William Wyler's immaculately stylish, deeply felt drama – based on Henry James's novel *Washington Square* – won de Havilland a well-deserved Academy

Award; but just as worth watching is Ralph Richardson as her authoritarian father. Clift was much criticized as lacking malevolence, but in retrospect it can be seen that he skilfully understates his character, allowing Wyler's clever direction (emphasizing his dislocation from those around him, and the shadows whenever he is around) to hint at his evil intentions. Critical accusations of directorial superficiality are likewise misdirected. The themes of the book are well explored throughout; and Wyler gets exceptional performances from his cast.

The excellent, Oscar-winning score is by Aaron Copland. The film has very high production values: the art and costume design won Oscars, while the cinematography (by Leo Tover, though very much in the style of Wyler's first-choice cameraman, Gregg Toland) was nominated.

ANTI:

'A sadly wasted opportunity. Ruth and Augustus Goetz, using their play as a foundation for the script, make no attempt to replace those overtones of feeling which they had sacrificed for broader theatrical effects. Rather, they simplify still further, to make of James' tragi-comedy only a polished period piece . . . Wyler has directed with the same faultless eye for externals. The photography (Leo Tover) makes great play with deep focus, with a camera whose movements become stylized, mechanical and obtrusive through their very meticulous care. Wyler, too, seems to accept the softening of the central situation, the film's fundamental fault: he has allowed *The Heiress* to assume a prettiness, an exhibition of the art director's skill, which can only detract from a story which not only has no need for such devices, but positively rejects them.' *(Penelope Houston, S & S)*

'So faithful to its mores that it is a museum piece.' *(Variety)*

PRO:

'Wyler is that rarest of craftsmen who can take such a drama as this, already completely fulfilled in theatre terms, and convert it to film.' *(Hermine Rich Isaacs, Films in Review)*

'There are few better films around these days than this one.' *(Fortnight)*

'At first the period settings and clothes may make the movie seem a little heavy and stagey, but then Wyler's mastery of the psychological nuances can have you drawing deep breaths. It's a peerless, super-controlled movie.' *(Pauline Kael)*

HELL'S ANGELS

CT: 5 AV: 7.33

1930 US 135 BW & C WAR/DRAMA

D Howard Hughes Marshall Neilan Luther Reed
W Howard Estabrook Harry Behn Joseph Moncure March

Ben Lyon James Hall Jean Harlow ●
John Darrow Lucien Prival Frank Clark
Roy Wilson Douglas Gilmore Jane Winton
Evelyn Hall

Two World War I pilots, who are also brothers (Ben Lyon, James Hall), love the same woman (Jean Harlow).

Great flying sequences, rarely if ever surpassed, can not disguise the foolish feebleness of the story-line; and although 18-year-old Jean Harlow had unmistakable potential as a sex bomb, it is horribly apparent that she hadn't yet learned to act. Made originally as a silent, it coincided with the coming of sound; Hughes fired the leading lady (Greta Nissen, a Norwegian) and cast Harlow. The cinematographers, Tony Gaudio, Harry Perry and E. Burton Steene, were Oscar-nominated.

'The photography is brilliant, many of the scenes are exceedingly beautiful, and the narrative is firm and swift, the only flaw in it being a strange suggestion that one of the German officers, because he had been an Oxford undergraduate and had a personal affection for England, deliberately dropped his bombs where they might fall harmlessly.' *(The Times)*

'Amazing pictures of aerial warfare . . . The height of dramatic sensation is reached by the truly wonderful picture of an airship coming down in flames . . . gigantic in its dramatic thrill. The connecting story is weak and trivial, but the aeroplanes are quite sufficient in themselves to assure the success of a remarkable picture.' *(Bioscope)*

'Only in spots is it great, notably in the immensity and daring of its flying stuff.' *(Photoplay)*

'Minus blue nose interference, it can't miss, but it's up to the brim with sex.' *(Variety)*

'It is not great, but it is as lavish as an eight-ring circus, and when you leave the theatre you will know you have seen a movie and not a tinny reproduction of a stage show.' *(Pare Lorentz)*

HELP!

CT: 7 AV: 6.67

1965 GB 92 C MUSICAL/COMEDY

D Richard Lester ☆
W Marc Behm Charles Wood from Behm's story

John Lennon Paul McCartney Ringo Starr
George Harrison Leo McKern Eleanor Bron
Victor Spinetti Roy Kinnear John Bluthal
Patrick Cargill

A mysterious religious sect (under Leo McKern) tries to get hold of one of one of Ringo's rings, in order to perform a sacrifice.

The screenplay is not on the level of its predecessor, *A Hard Day's Night*, but it has a daft charm. The quality of the songs – shot with an imagination that enables them to stand up today as rock videos – means that it's still highly enjoyable. Once again, none of the classic Lennon-McCartney songs was considered worthy of an Oscar nomination.

PRO:

'Another zany entertainment designed to delight those with a penchant for primitive sight and sound gags and subtle satire, and a feeling for the frenetic comedy of the non-sequitur and the pure pleasure of an inspired antic camera. Is *Help!* as good as *A Hard Day's Night*? I for one liked it even better.' *(Judith Crist, New York Herald Tribune)*

'The action is fast, the gags funny and the colour exceptionally good . . . It is a very funny film.' *(Kate Cameron, New York Daily News)*

MIXED:

'Put beside *A Hard Day's Night*, also by the same hand, *Help!* is ambitious; some of the spontaneity has gone. All the same, an advance. Cinema of exhaustion: one comes out battered by uproar, by the quickness demanded of the eye, by the athletic non-sequiturs of Marc Behm's and Charles Wood's screenplay and Ray Simm's sets – but dazzled too.' *(Dilys Powell)*

'The simple good spirits that pervaded *A Hard Day's Night* are now often smothered as if everybody is desperately trying to outsmart themselves and be ultra-clever-clever. Nevertheless, *Help!* is a good, nimble romp with both giggles and belly-laughs.' *(Variety)*

'The kindest way to describe it with malice towards none and charity for all is to label it 90 crowded minutes of good, clean insanity.' *(Bosley Crowther)*

ANTI:

'Where the first film was a highly-personalised piece of surrealism woven around their special talents, the second one reduces them to robots – agreeable as ever, but robots all the same – in a great beanfeast of gimmickry and gadgetry.' *(Cecil Wilson, Daily Mail)*

'I have to say my sides remained unsplit. I did not find myself rolling in the aisle.' *(Donald Zec, Daily Mirror)*

'This was the last feature film the Beatles ever made. I don't wonder. What a wasted opportunity. And yet, back in the Sixties, they seemed funny, didn't they? And wasn't Dick Lester supposed to be a whizz kid? Maybe these harmless romps were "innocent", but compared with the ribaldry and raw energy of *The Commitments* words like "commercial", "mindless" and "phoney" spring to mind.' *(Ken Russell, 1993)*

HENRY: PORTRAIT OF A SERIAL KILLER

CT: 8 AV: 6.83

1986 US 83 C THRILLER/ROMANCE/HORROR

D John McNaughton ☆
W John McNaughton Richard Fire
Michael Rooker ☆ Tom Towles Tracy Arnold
Mary Demas Anne Bartoletti

A serial killer (Michael Rooker) finds new friends.

Grim, depressing, horrific film, made on a shoestring, which scratches the greasy, malodorous underbelly of American life. Despite the title, there's little close-up analysis of why anyone becomes a serial killer; but writer-director John McNaughton and his cast depict the spiritual poverty of the characters' lives with grisly authenticity. Michael Rooker, as Henry, is unforgettable: a nightmare made flesh.

For all its notoriety, the film goes out of its way to de-glamorize violence. Rarely has murder looked nastier or more pointless. The two serial killers on display are sleazebags: some attempt is made to explain, but none to excuse, their crimes. The one sympathetic figure is Otis's self-destructive sister Becky (poignantly played by Tracy Arnold), who befriends Henry with gruesome results.

The film is deliberately as bleak, inexorable and desensitized as its 'hero'. Its most horrible sequence (a multiple murder on video) reminds the audience of its own voyeurism, and the love story skilfully subverts the Hollywood orthodoxy that Love Conquers All.

ANTI:

'The film it most resembles is Leonard Kastle's *The Honeymoon Killers*, which enjoyed a comparable cult success in 1970. Like that picture, Henry is a deliberately affectless treatment of gruesome true-crime material . . . Sure it's compelling; the nature of the material guarantees that. But it doesn't seem to be telling us much more than that the world is a scary place and murder is ugly. We knew those things. The most sickening murder takes place in an upper-middle-class house; we see the grim-faced Henry and the obscenely whooping Otis eliminate an entire family in their cozy living room. Is the movie also telling us that happy bourgeois homeowners should be more suspicious of lower-class beer-drinking men? Henry, both hip and deeply conservative, is consistent only in its bad faith. It's tabloid chic.' *(Terrence Rafferty, New Yorker)*

MIXED:

'At the Telluride Festival, where I saw it in September 1989, some said the film was too violent and disgusting to be endured. Others said it was justified because of its uncompromising honesty in a world where most horror films cheapen death by trivializing it. The division seemed to be between those who felt the film did its job brilliantly, and those who felt its job should not have been done at all.' *(Roger Ebert)*

'Rooker is perfect in the title role, but the acting of his co-stars is flat, the sick humor only occasionally hits the target.' *(Scheuer)*

PRO:

'Hard-driving, riveting . . . Film uses two strategies to keep audiences off balance. First is the use of violence, which starts off subtly but finally moves to a gory extreme. Early killings are shown in flashback where we only see bodies as grotesque still lives. The second tactic is the use of Becky to humanize Henry. Low budget pic looks surprisingly good, capturing the gritty feel of the characters' lives. Thesping is solid.' *(Variety)*

'An arresting example of low-budget American filmmaking . . . a raw-edged essay in nihilism, relating a chronicle of horrific abnormality in a manner deceptively matter of fact.' *(Tim Pulleine, Guardian)*

'A film of clutching terror that's meant to heighten our awareness instead of dulling it . . . [It] gives off a dark chill that follows you all the way home.' *(Peter Travers, Rolling Stone)*

'The avoidance of didacticism make it intellectually refreshing and provocative . . . The film encourages us to identify with [Henry], in the sense of seeing the world though his eyes . . . [which] is what makes the film so powerful and disturbing.' *(Geoff Andrew, Time Out)*

'Henry is not only the killer on the screen; he is the killer inside us . . . The film is more than a moralistic put-down of audience taste . . . not a condemnation so much as a restless examination . . . Dark and terrifying.' *(Henry Sheehan, LA Reader)*

'Exceptionally well-acted and shot for a zero-budget movie, and resolutely unexploitative in its approach.' *(Kim Newman, S & S)*

HENRY V AAN CT: 9 AV: 9.40

1944 GB 137 C WAR/DRAMA

D Laurence Olivier ☆ (AAW – special award)
W Laurence Olivier Alan Dent from Shakespeare's play

Laurence Olivier ☆ AAN Robert Newton ☆ Leslie Banks ☆ Esmond Knight ☆ Renée Asherson ☆ George Robey Leo Genn ☆ Ernest Thesiger Ivy St. Helier Ralph Truman Harcourt Williams Max Adrian Valentine Dyall Felix Aylmer John Laurie

An English prince (Laurence Olivier) grows into a warlike king.

Unashamed, war-mongering propaganda, and probably the greatest example of filmed Shakespeare. The visual style is deliberately heightened and unrealistic to match the poetic intensity of the speech, and Olivier's daring conception (this was his first attempt at directing) is wonderfully served by William Walton's Oscar-nominated music. The Battle of Agincourt is a thrilling action-scene, and Olivier's Crispin Day speech beforehand must be among the most stirring, unforgettable orations ever. Robert Krasker was responsible for the photography, and the Oscar-nominated art direction is by Paul Sheriff and Carmen Dillon.

MIXED:

'An ambitious, artistic and thoughtful film that has in it many moments of thrilling beauty . . . some of the finest scenes the motion picture has yet given us . . . There are . . . times when it stumbles somewhat confusedly, losing valuable ground on the perilous ascent to greatness . . . A noble experiment.' *(Diana Webber, Sound)*

'One of my dearest wishes [is to get a] film that has unity and sureness, one that never stumbles in confusion as this enormously expensive production does half the time.' *(Richard Winnington, News Chronicle)*

'Fussy, stately, stylized, and almost too richly hued, it hovers awfully close (in tone and aspect) to Michael Powell and Emeric Pressburger's luxuriant, borderline-campy *The Red Shoes* (1948) and *The Life and Death of Colonel Blimp* (1943), but is saved by its intelligence, its patent earnestness of intent, and its director's manifest reverence for the text at hand.' *(Bruce Bawer, American Spectator, 1989)*

PRO:

'What I like about [it] is that it gives Shakespeare back to the groundlings.' *(Helen Fletcher, Sunday Graphic)*

'Stunningly brilliant.' *(New York Times)*

'England has sent a superlative motion picture to these shores.' *(New York Herald Tribune)*

'One of the really great achievements in the history of the screen.' *(Journal American)*

'I am not a Tory, a monarchist, a Catholic, a medievalist, an Englishman, or, despite all the good that it engenders, a lover of war: but the beauty and power of this traditional exercise was such that, watching it, I wished I was, thought I was, and was proud of it. I was persuaded, and in part still am, that every time and place has since been in decline, save one, in which one Englishman used language better than anyone has before or since, or ever shall; and that nearly the best that our time can say for itself is that some of us are still capable of paying homage to the fact.' *(James Agee, Nation)*

'The story was told, the characters were presented, in terms, not only of movement and dialogue, but of colour; colour gave edge to excitement, pointed contrast, accentuated rhythm. The dark Rembrandtesque tones of Olivier's face, turning his eyes as he thinks, deepened the mood of his great soliloquy in the camp at night. The brilliant blues and yellows and scarlets of the morning French army heightened the sense of relief from vigil, the sense of released action and fulfilled expectation. And all through this brilliant film the colour of the dresses against the soft neutral shades of the architectural background was so handled as to direct the spectator's attention; to guide his eye; in fact to narrate as the cinema should narrate.' *(Dilys Powell, 1946)*

'Britain was under attack, and his film caught the mood of the moment. It was – and remains – a heart-lifting triumph; it has bright colors, trick perspectives, and the enormous charm of childhood tales of chivalry. Olivier (he was thirty-six) brings a playful, bashful glamour to the role. His voice rings out thrillingly; you carry the sound with you forever.' *(Pauline Kael)*

HENRY V

CT: 6 AV: 8.00

1989 GB 89 C WAR/DRAMA

D Kenneth Branagh ✗ AAN
W Kenneth Branagh from William Shakespeare's play

Kenneth Branagh ✗ AAN Derek Jacobi ✓
Simon Shepherd James Larkin Brian Blessed
James Simmons Paul Gregory Charles Kay
Alec McCowen Edward Jewesbury Ian Holm
Michael Williams Geoffrey Hutchings
Robert Stephens Judi Dench Paul Scofield
Harold Innocent Emma Thompson
Geraldine McEwan Richard Briers

An English prince (Kenneth Branagh) grows into a warlike king.

Branagh wisely builds on the performance which Director, Adrian Noble elicited from him at the Royal Shakespeare Company. His Henry is charming in his self-doubt, convincingly torn between personal feelings and principle, and rousing in his long speeches to the troops. Whether Branagh has the charisma for the part is another matter. Look at him and Olivier side by side, and there's no doubt which is the more photogenic. Unfair, I know, but there it is.

Henry V is like a glorious series of auditions for acting awards. First prize for declamatory verse-speaking goes to Derek Jacobi (Prologue). Most touching performance in a cameo role? That's Judi Dench (Mistress Quickly). Prize for wearing the most repulsive character make-up is shared equally between Richard Briers (Bardolph) and Robert Stephens (Pistol).

The big casting error is Emma Thompson, too sophisticated and mature by a decade to get away with playing Princess Katherine on screen. The comic scene between her and Geraldine McEwen is also far too long. These are areas in which Branagh might have taken advice from Shakespeare's King, and not allowed private emotions to dominate.

Branagh's directorial line is very different from Olivier's gung-ho, wartime approach. In keeping with post-war conventions, Branagh's production emphasizes the horror and futility of war, although Shakespeare probably had a more bellicose, propagandist objective when he wrote the piece. In keeping with this 'realistic' aproach to the play, Branagh adopts a visual style which might be described as early Terry Gilliam. These are the filthy, rain-swept Middle Ages of *Jabberwocky* and *Monty Python and the Holy Grail*, accompanied by the kind of Shakespearian acting which Peter Hall and John Barton introduced to Britain in the 1950s: mud-on-the-boots realism. Olivier's more stylized vision of the play, based on medieval illustrations, belongs to another world, and a more imaginative era in British cinema.

The opening of Branagh's film is, however, an improvement on Olivier's, since it creates a cinematic rather than theatrical expectation in the audience. Derek Jacobi, as the Prologue, lights a match ('O! For a muse of fire!'), strolls in modern dress through a deserted film studio and introduces the action by swinging open two gigantic doors. Unfortunately, this visual and stylistic daring is never matched in the rest of the film.

The success of the prologue makes me doubt whether Branagh was correct to aim for realism, especially with limited resources. He simply did not have a big enough budget to film a decent battle-scene; and so the one which has to serve as his climax (with loads of close-ups and slow motion) is unimpressive and uninformative. Elsewhere in the picture, there was all too obviously little money for sets; as a result, too many scenes are shot in a cramped, televisual way.

Branagh's main failure, however, is as an adapter. He has gone for realism, but retained the device of Derek Jacobi as a visible narrator: essentially an anti-realistic, distancing device. He is also fatally more interested in performances than in cinema. Mistress Quickly's account of Falstaff's death is delivered with skill and sincerity by Judi Dench; but it is irrelevant to the narrative and fundamentally non-cinematic. A cinema audience wants to see and experience events, not have them recounted at second hand. The moments following her speech, where she uses touch and facial expression, are cinematically more effective in communicating emotion than the whole of her long speech immediately before.

I like to think that Shakespeare, had he re-written *Henry V* for the screen, would have changed much more than Branagh has dared to do. He might have filled some gaping holes in the narrative, and been more ruthless about excising sub-plots (the one concerning MacMorris, played by Branagh's old buddy John Sessions, makes no sense at all). *Henry V* can most safely be recommended as a movie for those who prefer theatrical posturing to cinema. Phyllis Dalton won an Oscar for her costume design.

'The more I thought about it, the more convinced I became that here was a play to be reclaimed from jingoism and its World War Two associations.' *(Kenneth Branagh)*

PRO:

'A stirring, gritty and enjoyable pic which offers a plethora of fine performances from some of the UK's brightest talents.' *(Variety)*

'There's a psychotic intensity in Branagh's performance that keeps us, and his courtiers, on edge. His voice is steely, and he speaks low and naturally, rather than mellifluously, like Olivier. And his filmmaking mirrors his performance: there's a nervous, edgy momentum to the camera movement, editing, and music.' *(Joseph Gelmis)*

MIXED:

'The potato-faced Branagh's performance as the snotty tearaway turned militarist monarch is adequate.' *(Kim Newman, Film Yearbook)*

'Despite budgetary limitations which occasionally make the army look like an amateur soccer side struck by illness, this is a courageous and largely successful adaptation, excellently acted, bringing out Shakespeare's ambiguous feelings about patriotism and war.' *(Rose)*

'For the first reel or two I was unimpressed. Unflattering lighting made Branagh look more like Pinocchio than a monarch, and there was a jarring transition from the narrator on a windswept Beachy Head to a studio set purporting to be a castle in Southampton. There was also too much of Falstaff (as was the case in Olivier's version), for his sentimental death means nothing if you are not familiar with *Henry IV, Part 1*. Everyone is weeping and wailing for the passing of a tedious old fart the audience knows nothing about. However, there is a bonus in Branagh's version with the inclusion of an exciting scene where traitors are unmasked and summarily dealt with. That was omitted from Larry's scenario, possibly because the idea of an Englishman betraying his country in the last war was, if not unthinkable, certainly not to be encouraged.' *(Ken Russell, 1993)*

ANTI:

'He doesn't indicate why the French lost at Agincourt . . . doesn't show that the French and their horses were fatally encumbered by their armor and chain mail and other trappings; when the arrows hit . . . the riders fell into the water and mud, and were too weighed down to get up. They were massacred while they struggled like beetles on their backs. As Branagh stages the battle, with the two sides engaged in hand-to-hand combat, there's no way to understand why the English rather than the French won (except that God is with them).' *(Pauline Kael)*

'The film's visual tedium, vulgarity and musical mediocrity would be more bearable if Branagh himself were a more persuasive lead actor.' *(MFB)*

'Branagh's camera concentrates so intensely on Branagh that the drama, as such, suffers. Henry's Big Speeches, after all, are intended not just as histrionics but as calls to action; yet when Branagh cuts to the faces of his listeners at Harfleur or Agincourt, the tattered extras don't seem to have been told how to react: the expressions on their faces seem to be saying, variously, "What an actor!" "What a time to make a speech!" and "Gee, why's he speaking in iambic pentameter?" Yes, when the speeches are over the soldiers behave as if somebody's lit a fire under them, and proceed to fight heroically; but one misses a sense of vital connection between them and their king. Branagh appears, in short, to see Shakespeare less as drama than as an occasion for dazzling solo turns.' *(Bruce Bawer, American Spectator)*

HERE COMES MR. JORDAN AAN

CT: 5 AV: 8.64

1941 US 93 BW COMEDY/FANTASY

D Alexander Hall ☆ AAN
W Seton I. Miller Sidney Buchman (AAN for story and screenplay) from Harry Segall's play *Halfway to Heaven*

Robert Montgomery ✗ AAN Evelyn Keyes
Rita Johnson Claude Rains ☆
James Gleason ☆ AAN Edward Everett Horton ☆
John Emery Donald MacBride ☆ Halliwell Hobbes
Don Costello

Boxer (Robert Montgomery) who dies as a result of a heavenly clerical error returns to Earth with his Guardian Angel, Mr Jordan (Claude Rains).

A twee fantasy whose mawkishness hasn't worn well, though the film achieved popularity thanks to its cosy view of the afterlife at a time when millions were dying in war. Montgomery seems ill-at-ease, and who can blame him; there's too much chat, and not enough humour. Joseph Walker's cinematography was Oscar-nominated. Warren Beatty's 1978 remake, *Heaven Can Wait*, was no better.

PRO:

'Montgomery's portrayal is a highlight in a group of excellent performances.' *(Variety)*

'Only curmudgeons will not like [it] . . . Not that the curmudgeons couldn't make a couple of telling points against this scatterbrained fantasy . . . The plot, even in terms of fantasy, is pretty hard to swallow, the boy-gets-girl theme is too toilsomely pursued, and there is a touch too much metaphysical gab. But the hell with that, as Ernest Hemingway would say. *Here Comes Mr. Jordan* is one of the brightest comedies of the year, and you'd do well to see it.' *(Russell Maloney, New Yorker)*

ANTI:

'There appear to be certain kinds of fantasy to which the American genius is in general so ill-suited that it handles them with extreme clumsiness. This is a case in point.' *(MFB)*

'Nothing to make a song about. There are some genuine flashes of eerie comedy; but the authors seem to have taken *Outward Bound* and the *Topper* series, and to have tried hard to roll them into one.' *(William Whitebait, New Statesman)*

'The slickly hammy Rains gives Mr Jordan a sinister

gloss, as if he were involved in some heavenly racket, like smuggling Chinese . . . There's too much metaphysical gabbing and a labored boy-gets-girl romance, but audiences loved this chunk of whimsey.' *(Pauline Kael)*

HERO CT: 8 AV: 6.22

(aka *Accidental Hero*)

1992 US 116 C DRAMA/COMEDY

D Stephen Frears
W David Webb Peoples ✓ from Laura Ziskin and Alvin Sargent's story

Dustin Hoffman ● Andy Garcia ✓ Geena Davis ✓ Joan Cusack Kevin J. O'Connor Maury Chaykin Chevy Chase ✓

A petty criminal (Dustin Hoffman) behaves heroically in saving people from a crashed aeroplane, but a vagrant (Andy Garcia) claims the credit, and is turned into a media superstar by a journalist survivor from the crash (Geena Davis).

Stephen Frears's sharp satire on the media shows the gap between truth and the public's perception of it, and the extent to which people live up or down to their image. Neither critics nor public sufficiently appreciated David Webb Peoples's excellent, bitter-sweet screenplay, which had many of Billy Wilder's strengths (notably his wit and scepticism) without his bleak cynicism about human nature.

The biggest problem is Dustin Hoffman, who overacts his sleaziness at first (but is at least entertaining while doing so), then goes to the opposite extreme, playing for schmaltz to an unnecessary and counter-productive extent. With a different star, this could have been a classic; even so, it's very enjoyable.

'The movie cries out for an editor who could get it down to around ninety-five minutes, which is about where the material belongs, and leave out the dumb stuff and the false sentiment, and make it tough and witty.' *(Roger Ebert)*

'*Hero* is peppered with occasional gems but has to sift through a lot of wreckage to find them . . . Action tilts too heavily toward Hoffman, who simply mucks it up, seemingly playing a bad version of Razzo Rizzo had he survived events in *Midnight Cowboy*.' *(Variety)*

'It's moving, absorbing and beautifully-acted. keeping us dying to know what's going to happen next. It starts brilliantly and just gets better as it goes along. With the exception of Davis's squirm-inducing onion-peeling scene, this is quite simply one of the greatest films of the past decade, whatever anyone else might tell you.' *(Rose)*

HIDDEN FORTRESS, THE CT: 8 AV: 7.78

(aka *Kakushi Toride No San-akunin; The Wild Flight; Three Bad Men in a Hidden Fortress*)

1958 Japan 126/139 BW ADVENTURE/ACTION/ FOREIGN

D Akira Kurosawa ☆
W Ryuzo Kikushima Hideo Oguni Shinobu Hashimoto Akira Kurosawa

Toshiro Mifune ☆ Misa Uehara ✓ Minoru Chiaki ✓ Kamatari Fujiwara ✓ Susumu Fujita Takashi Shimura Eiko Miyoshi

In medieval Japan, a beautiful princess (Misa Uehara) tries to escape an army with orders to execute her; she does so with the help of a general (Toshiro Mifune) and two squabbling farmers (Minoru Chiaki, Kamatari Fujiwara).

Exciting and humorous, this has proved a highly influential picture; its impact can be seen on Sergio Leone's spaghetti westerns, and George Lucas has admitted that *The Hidden Fortress* was the inspiration behind *Star Wars*. There's more than a touch of R2D2 and See-Threepio (not to mention *Waiting For Godot*) in the relationship between the two cowardly farmers. But the influences are not all one way, from east to west; the scenic splendour owes no little amount to the great westerns of John Ford. The film shows off to the full Kurosawa's talent for action and scenic composition, and is adorned with excellent performances. The film won him Best Director at Berlin, in 1959.

'It would be wrong to pretend [it] is entirely a Japanese Western . . . What [it] really resembles is a filmed version of the *Iliad* or the *Chanson de Roland* made by someone who believes in them.' *(Anthony Hartley, Guardian)*

'Splendidly scenic adventure, barbarically staged duels.' *(Alexander Walker, Evening Standard)*

'Restates and enlarges, in more than "aspect ratio" terms, virtually every feature of the so-called entertainment film, as we know it, from the Fairbanks genre to *Treasure of the Sierra Madre*, while incorporating vestiges of the older Soviet masters and a host of samurai films.' *(Vernon Young, Hudson Review)*

'Kurosawa has made better movies, but never one more filled with humor and energy. His story isn't made into a dirge about honor and violence, but into a celebration of high spirits . . . There are close scrapes, double-crosses, cases of mistaken identity, and a thrilling lance-fight between Mifune and that other great Japanese star, Susumu Fujita. An overnight stop in a rowdy frontier town will remind you of the saloon planet in *Star Wars*.' *(Roger Ebert)*

HIGH NOON AAN CT: 9 AV: 9.80

1952 US 85 BW WESTERN/THRILLER

D Fred Zinnemann ☆ AAN
W Carl Foreman ✓ AAN from John W. Cunningham's story *The Tin Star*

Gary Cooper ☆ AAW Grace Kelly Thomas Mitchell Lloyd Bridges ✓ Katy Jurado ✓ Otto Kruger Lon Chaney Jr Henry Morgan Ian MacDonald Eve McVeagh

A marshall (Gary Cooper) who wishes only to leave town and start a peaceful life on a ranch with his new Quaker bride (Grace Kelly) gets no support from the local citizens as he awaits the arrival of killers swearing vengeance.

Now, it's the most critically acclaimed western of all time; but contemporary reviewers were less impressed. Many wondered how a town of pioneer frontiersmen had suddenly turned into a community of cowards; John Wayne and Howard Hawks's *Rio Bravo* (1959) was in part an attempt to counterbalance this 'unAmerican' image. The truth was, of course, that the film was a metaphor for the the craven way that Hollywood and America as a whole had bowed to the demands of the House Un-American Activities Committee (which later repaid the non-compliment by blacklisting writer Carl Foreman). The failure of the writer to explain how the characters had ended up so pusillanimous is the film's one real weakness.

The film's greatest strength, simplicity, was mistakenly construed as triteness. At 51 years old, Cooper was deemed insufficiently romantic a lead – whereas his haggard, leathery countenance actually helps to give weight to his lonely stand; this is his finest performance. Grace Kelly, in her first starring role is colourless as Cooper's pacifist bride, but Katy Jurado is excellent as the marshal's ex-girlfriend. Zinnemann's direction is a masterpiece of economy, and his greatest talent – drawing performances from actors – is obvious throughout.

Floyd Crosby's high-contrast cinematography (borrowing copiously from film noir) is outstanding, as is the Oscar-winning ballad by Dimitri Tiomkin (properly called 'High Noon', it's better known as 'Do Not Forsake Me'). The Oscar-winning editing by Elmo Williams and Harry Gerstad is unsurpassed in the creation of suspense; and, although *High Noon* is a great western, it is equally effective as a thriller.

ANTI:

'The western form is used for a sneak civics lesson . . . Its insights are primer sociology, and the demonstration of the town's cowardice is Q.E.D.' *(Pauline Kael)*

MIXED:

'Allowing for the triteness and the monotonous ageing Cooper . . . there is some fine tension and consistently high craftsmanship.' *(News Chronicle)*

'I would not claim any particular originality for [it] . . . but the producer and director . . . put [it] nearly into the classic class.' *(Jympson Harmon, Evening News)*

'The director permits his cameraman a few rather mannered shots of the excellent 1870 frontier-town set, and he is a little too fond of moments so "pregnant with meaning" that all motion is suspended; otherwise his work is impressively unpretentious. The dialogue is sensible; the music, primarily a lugubrious ballad, is appropriate and only occasionally takes the action over from the performers – a vice now most common in Hollywood. Those, then, are the excellences of *High Noon*, and they are sufficient to make the picture celebrated. But they are all technical. For a movie to be really superior, its content must be taken seriously, and on the level of ideas *High Noon* presents another face.' *(Robert L. Hatch, Reporter)*

'A neat, well-finished and literate piece of work, though its limitations are more conventional than most.' *(Gavin Lambert, S & S)*

PRO:

'A western to challenge *Stagecoach* for the all-time championship.' *(Bosley Crowther)*

'Few recent Westerns have gotten so much tension and excitement into the classic struggle between good and evil.' *(Life)*

'This is one of the finest westerns ever made . . . Here is no slapdash head 'em off at the pass gun-galloper, or cowhand-guns-rustler oats opera. With Gary Cooper in the key role, [it] is a dynamic drama of character, brilliantly told within the framework of one terrifying Sunday morning . . . This is explosive drama . . . a perfect picture of a live action story. The direction . . . and the screenplay . . . combine to make a taut, penetrating, psychological drama of character and communal responsibility.' *(Jesse Zunser, Cue)*

'More richly endowed that the average [Western] with suspense, atmosphere, skilful construction and a persistent impression that thoughtful and gifted brains had conspired together to make it.' *(Hollis Alpert, Saturday Review)*

'An exceptionally good Western: a dramatic, threatening start which does not wait for the credits to clear off the screen; a steady increase of alarm . . . and an exciting burst of action at the end . . . Fred Zinnemann . . . has given the film remarkable tension.' *(Dilys Powell)*

HIGH PLAINS DRIFTER CT: 5 AV: 5.42

1972 US 105 C WESTERN

D Clint Eastwood
W Ernest Tidyman

Clint Eastwood Verna Bloom Marianna Hill Mitch Ryan Jack Cring

Man with no name (Clint Eastwood) takes revenge on crooked law-enforcers.

Eastwood's second film as director and star is a slow, stylish revenge western in the tradition of Sergio Leone. It has a hard, cold approach to the genre and a very tough hero. Eastwood's direction borders on the pretentious and narcissistic; but this remains one of the most creepily atmospheric and offbeat of all 70s westerns, with an especially memorable ending.

ANTI:

'I suppose you could call it a supernatural Western, except that there is nothing natural about it and it certainly isn't super.' *(Ian Christie, Daily Express)*

'Ritualized violence and plodding symbolism make for heavy going.' *(S & S)*

'Rarely are humble Westerns permitted to drift around on such a highfalutin plane. That, however, is small comfort as this cold, gory and overthought movie unfolds.' *(Richard Schickel)*

'As a pasta-parable it drowns in its own ketchup.' *(Tom Hutchinson, Sunday Telegraph)*

MIXED:

'Eastwood rather overdoes his personal mystique . . . A shade self-conscious and pretentious . . . but enough of his old master Don Siegel's influence has rubbed off to make him an effective and promising commercial director.' *(The Times)*

'Shows [Eastwood] to be a genuinely talented filmmaker but a very suspect moralist . . . Not at all a likeable film, but an impressive one.' *(George Melly, Observer)*

'The scene is stunningly set, the characters well-observed in one-dimensional terms. And Eastwood plays the avenger as if born to it, a Dirty Harry unshackled by silly liberal laws. It all works well which is why one resents it so much.' *(Derek Malcolm, Guardian)*

'As a piece of storytelling . . . [it's] a mess, but tempers its savagery with a nice offhand wit and offers, in Billy Curtis, the novelty of a midget sheriff.' *(Cecil Wilson, Daily Mail)*

PRO:

'A stylized, allegorical Western of much chilling paranoid atmosphere and considerable sardonic humor.' *(LA Times)*

'A unique genre movie whose supernatural quality pervaded the atmosphere from the start . . . An off-beat, exciting and often exhilarating piece of work.' *(Alan Frank)*

HIGH SIERRA

CT: 6 AV: 7.25

1941 US 96 BW THRILLER/DRAMA

D Raoul Walsh ☆
W John Huston W.R. Burnett from Burnett's novel

Ida Lupino ☆ Humphrey Bogart ☆ Alan Curtis Arthur Kennedy Joan Leslie Henry Hull Barton MacLane Henry Travers Elisabeth Risdon Cornel Wilde

Ageing gangster (Humphrey Bogart) wants to pull off one last robbery before retirement, but things go wrong.

Dated, often dull, gangster thriller which was one of the last in the popular gangster genre. It remains watchable thanks to Walsh's smart direction and two fine performances by Ida Lupino and (especially) Humphrey Bogart. He fleshes out a screenplay by John Huston which crassly plays for audience sympathy by supplying the anti-hero with a crippled girl and a stray dog to show his softer side. Somehow, Bogart (made up to look like famous gangster John Dillinger) manages to make 'Mad Dog' Roy Earle believable and sympathetic; this is the role which allowed Bogie to cross over from playing bad guys (as in *The Petrified Forest*) to tough guys with a soul (as in *Casablanca*).

ANTI:

'A film that is weighted down by too much extraneous story and production matter . . . Suffers from slowness, Raoul Walsh's direction evidently being unable to overcome the screenplay plotting.' *(Variety)*

MIXED:

'So nearly a very good film that I came away in a state of exasperation . . . There were, it is true, brilliant sequences: the flight after the robbery across the white, blinding desert flats, the last chase up the mountain road and the siege amidst the rocks; but the story did not move with the inexorable swiftness of its car chases, and Bogart, always a good actor, seemed to be insisting that he was a good guy and not a pathological guy. All the same, for those whose tastes lie the Dillinger way this is a film worth having a look at.' *(Dilys Powell)*

PRO:

'Like it or not, I'll be damned if you leave before the end, or go to sleep.' *(Otis Ferguson)*

'As gangster pictures go, this one has everything – speed, excitement, suspense, and that ennobling suggestion of futility which makes for irony and poetry.' *(New York Times)*

'Humphrey Bogart was the perfect choice to play the role. Always a fine actor, he is particularly splendid as a farm boy turned outlaw, who is shocked and hurt when newspapers refer to him as a mad dog.' *(New York Herald Tribune)*

HIGH SOCIETY CT: 7 AV: 6.15

1956 US 107 C MUSICAL/ROMANCE

D Charles Walters
W John Patrick (music and lyrics by Cole Porter ☆)

Grace Kelly Bing Crosby ☆ Frank Sinatra ☆
Celeste Holm John Lund Louis Armstrong

A rich girl (Grace Kelly) has second thoughts on the eve of her wedding.

A generally unfavourable press for this musical remake of *The Philadelphia Story* pointed out that the film lacked genuine sophistication, and that Grace Kelly (in her last screen role) lacked the sparkle of Katharine Hepburn. However, production values were high; the other stars – especially Frank Sinatra, Bing Crosby and Celeste Holm – were on top form; and the new version had the inestimable advantage of some of Cole Porter's wittiest lyrics and catchiest tunes. As so often, one of the weaker songs, 'True Love', was nominated for the Oscar.

ANTI:

'As flimsy as a gossip columnist's word . . . it misses the snap and the crackle that its un-musical predecessor had . . . There are moments of amusement . . . However, there do come tedious stretches . . . due mainly to slow direction and the mildness of Miss Kelly in the pivotal role.' *(Bosley Crowther, New York Times)*

'Quite misses the earlier film's sophisticated charm . . . Grace Kelly gives a slightly strained performance with some unsuccessful sorties into the Hepburn territory.' *(MFB)*

'The principals perform, most of the time, with a kind of glum cheeriness.' *(Hollis Alpert)*

'Simply not *Top Drawer*.' *(Time)*

PRO:

'Dazzling musical version of *The Philadelphia Story* . . . Delightfully and disarmingly inconsequential, cleverly interweaves crisp humour with charming sentiment and polished dialogue firmly binds the two extremes . . . Great cast, smart cracks, neat romantic touches.' *(Josh Billings, Kine Weekly)*

'The plot is on the slender side – indeed . . . almost nothing happens at all . . . [But there are] such charming performances, such delightful musical numbers, and such amusing dialogue that everything else may be forgiven and forgotten . . . What a lineup for the marquee! . . . An exceptional product of outstanding box office appeal.' *(Daily Film Renter)*

'Thin in substance [the original] was given theatrical force and wit by [Hepburn's] virtuoso acting. This time around it may lack Hepburn but it has been recharged with a large battery of potential assets . . . By far [the film's] most exhilarating moments are provided by Crosby and Armstrong in a bouncy riotous duet called "Now You Has Jazz".' *(Motion Picture Herald)*

HIMMEL ÜBER BERLIN, DER: *see* WINGS OF DESIRE.

HIROSHIMA MON AMOUR CT: 4 AV: 7.27

(aka *Twenty-four Hour Love Affair*)

1959 France/Japan 91 BW DRAMA/ROMANCE/FOREIGN

D Alain Resnais ☆
W Marguerite Duras ✗ AAN

Emmanuelle Riva ☆ Eiji Okada Stella Dassas
Pierre Barbaud Bernard Fresson

A French actress (Emmanuelle Riva) wishes to break off her affair with a married Japanese architect (Eiji Okada) because it reminds her of a forbidden love affair with a German soldier during World War II.

Resnais's first feature was overrated because of its fashionable, anti-Bomb message and tricksy way of telling an essentially simple story (which continues to earn it undeserved comparisons with *Citizen Kane*). The extent to which Resnais innovated by using flashbacks in a subjective rather than chronological order has been exaggerated; directors such as Sjöberg, Cocteau and Buñuel had been using the technique for decades. Any film in which the heroine is merely named 'She' is likely to have pretentious overtones, and this one certainly does; worse still, the hero – though known as 'Hiroshima' and presumably symbolizing Japan – is a cypher, merely a sounding-board for the heroine's thoughts, which are supremely uninteresting. The insensitivity of Resnais and Duras towards the oriental side of the love affair ensured that the film was much more acclaimed in the west than in Japan, where it failed under the less politically ambitious title *Twenty-Four Hour Love Affair*.

PRO:

'A savage experience; but not a savage film. For all its reminders of cruelty and callousness, *Hiroshima Mon Amour* is full of pity and this complex work sends one away reflecting that hatred is a kind of murder.' *(Dilys Powell)*

'A difficult film, especially if one does not understand French . . . But its demands are commensurate with its rewards. To the list of revolutionary films of the last twenty years . . . one must now add [this one].' *(Richard Roud, Film)*

'A breathtaking film that, like so many great works of art, can never be entirely appreciated or understood. *Hiroshima Mon Amour* must be felt . . . and the feelings it evokes defy understanding or explanation.' *(Virgin)*

MIXED:

'An important film, superb in parts, irritating and disturbing in others.' *(Jean de Baroncelli, Le Monde)*

'The unfolding of the screenplay is primarily by means of dialogue, but dialogue of a caliber and pace which makes it the essence of action . . . The picture never loses the impetus provided by a flying start, while its comedy and action sequences are so deftly interspersed that it stands on its own feet as a film as modern as tomorrow despite its basis in the Chicago newspaper days of the riotous 1920s.' *(Walter Selden, Motion Picture Herald)*

'The strength of this delightful entertainment lies in its blend of piquant characterisation, slick dialogue and sparkling comedy events treading on the heels of simple emotion . . . put over at a tremendous pace, just clicking along with scarcely a pause.' *(Today's Cinema)*

'Explodes into the decorous quiet of the modern cinema like a high-powered shrieking bomb.' *(The Times)*

'A crackling, ingenious, and a most bewilderingly lively film . . . as devastatingly slick as a new streamlined locomotive and immeasurably noisier.' *(Manchester Guardian)*

'A *tour de force* of choreographed action: bravado posturings with body, lucid Cubistic composing with natty lapels and hat brims, as well as a very stylized discourse of short replies based on the idea of topping, out-maneuvering the other person with wit, cynicism, and verbal bravado. A line is never allowed to reverberate but is quickly attached to another, funnier line in a very underrated comedy that champions the sardonic and quick-witted over the plodding, sober citizens.' *(Manny Farber, Negative Space, 1969)*

'Presents a more open and tolerant range of sexual values than one might expect; its irreverence occasionally borders on the risqué, particularly for a film made under the Hays Code.' *(Tom Powers, Jump Cut)*

'[Russell] does not become an imitation male; she remains true to the two sides – feminine and professional – of her nature, and as such promises to exercise a healthy influence on the hard-boiled, all-male world of criminal reporting. It is as a news reporter rather than as wife and mother, that she discovers her true womanliness, which is to say, simply, herself.' *(Molly Haskell, From Reverence to Rape)*

'This peculiarly American genre of verbal slapstick was admired throughout the world for its vitality and freshness, and envied because of its freedom from certain kinds of political censorship. (If you didn't – and still rarely do – see corrupt politicians, a venal press, shocking prison conditions, and crooked cops in European films, it's not because Europe doesn't have them.) The target in all these impudent, irreverent comedies was always Amercia itself; perhaps no other country could so freely criticize and satirize itself. Ironically, this freedom was lost not because of governmental pressure but because of box-office pressure – the fear of giving offense. Even those marvelous character actors, with their idiosyncrasies of accent and appearance, their *ideés fixes*, are gone – one is not supposed to make fun of people.' *(Pauline Kael, 1970)*

HISTOIRE D'ADÈLE H, L': *see* STORY OF ADÈLE H, THE.

see STORY OF ADÈLE H, THE.

HISTORIA OFFICIAL, LA: *see* OFFICIAL STORY, THE.

HOBSON'S CHOICE

CT: 7 AV: 7.41

1953 GB 107 BW COMEDY/DRAMA

D David Lean ☆
W Norman Spencer Wynard Browne from Harold Brighouse's play

Charles Laughton ☆ Brenda de Banzie ☆ John Mills ☆ Richard Wattis Helen Haye Daphne Anderson Prunella Scales

An authoritarian Lancastrian father (Charles Laughton) gets his come-uppance at the hands of his daughter (Brenda de Banzie) and her mild-mannered husband (John Mills).

David Lean's touching film of Harold Brighouse's comedy-drama about Lancashire life in the 1890s is, at the very least, a silver oldie. Strong performances by Charles Laughton, John Mills and Brenda de Banzie almost conceal the fact that the film peaks at the end of the second act, and loses impetus in the last half hour.

'If I have a grumble about this beautifully directed film it is, curiously, that David Lean does not seem to coax from [the actors] the best . . . performances . . . What Mr Lean superbly furnishes is the high visual finish.' *(Philip Hope-Wallace, Observer)*

'A wealth of charm, humor and fine characterization.' *(Variety)*

'Something of a triumph . . . Lean . . . has done nothing better since *Great Expectations* . . . Laughton . . . has a field day . . . Newcomer Brenda de Banzie gives a surprisingly mature and rounded performance . . . Difficult to see how a better job could have been made of it.' *(Screencombers, Shell Magazine)*

'Lean creates humorous cadenzas by linking his camera movements and the soundtrack music. The wonderfully zesty performers – at times, Mills suggests Chaplin – give the material (which had been filmed twice before) a vaudevillian lift. Seeing this double bill, you realize what a shame it is that Lean has never directed a full-fledged musical comedy.' *(Michael Sragow)*

'It was useless reducing Laughton in size, as Hollywood tried to do by making him support younger and better-looking stars. Laughton does not support other players. He crushes them out. Laughton supporting Abbott and Costello or Rita Hayworth is like a whale supporting goldfish . . . David Lean, not the most spectacular but probably the most sensitive of British directors, has recognised this. There is no supporting nonsense about Laughton's Henry Hobson . . . [It] is a good film . . . constructed to measure. The measure of Charles Laughton.' *(Picture Post)*

HOLIDAY

CT: 7 AV: 8.22

1938 US 93 BW COMEDY/ROMANCE

D George Cukor ☆
W Donald Ogden Stewart Sidney Buchman ☆ from Philip Barry's play

Katharine Hepburn ☆ Cary Grant ☆ Doris Nolan Lew Ayres ☆ Edward Everett Horton ☆ Henry Kolker Ruth Donnelly ☆

A rich, stuffy family is disrupted by the arrival of a suitor (Cary Grant) who's a social dropout.

Cary Grant makes a surprising amount out of an underwritten role, investing it with vitality and charm. Katharine Hepburn is at her most tomboyish and free-spirited in this justly celebrated romantic comedy, which is talky and predictable but thoroughly entertaining. The message – that riches are futile – struck a chord in the Depression, but now seems a shade facile. Though screwball, the film as a whole is anything but escapist; running through it is a dark subtext about infidelity, alcoholism and self-destructive behaviour. Surprisingly, the only Oscar nomination received was for the art direction, by Stephen Goosson and Lionel Banks.

ANTI:

'A neat and sometimes elegant job, but under its surface of too much brightness and too many words it seems so deadly bored and weary. Hell, save your money and yawn at home.' *(Otis Ferguson)*

'One of those rather trying films which seem to have become part of Hollywood's permanent repertoire . . . [It] would be a very much more enjoyable film were it not for the ill-digested philosophical background which attempts to relate the unimportant doings of unimportant people to the extraordinary thesis that we must all be free to live without reference to money, provided that we live in the way we prefer in a state of considerable luxury, presumably on an unearned income.' *(Basil Wright, Spectator)*

PRO:

'Excellent entertainment, but it is a more than usually half-hearted specimen of Hollywood's new idealism. Capra and Cukor are no more capable than the business-men whom they ridicule of seeing business as a vital social activity.' *(Peter Galway, New Statesman)*

'The acting is superb and so is the direction.' *(Kinematograph Weekly)*

'Corking comedy.' *(Variety)*

'Played with the greatest cheerfulness and a winning skill.' *(Arthur Pollock, Brooklyn Daily Eagle)*

HOME ALONE

CT: 8 AV: 5.77

1990 US 102 C COMEDY/FAMILY

D Chris Columbus ✔
W John Hughes ✔

Macaulay Culkin ☆ Joe Pesci ☆ Daniel Stern ☆ John Heard Catherine O'Hara ✔ Roberts Blossom Gerry Bamman John Candy ✔ Kieran Culkin

An eight-year-old (Macaulay Culkin), inadvertently left at home while his parents spend Christmas abroad, outwits burglars.

John Hughes's best, as well as most successful, film: a family comedy featuring a shrewd mixture of slapstick and sentiment about the importance of family life. Macaulay Culkin is thoroughly engaging – much more so than in the sequel – and this tale of childish wish-fulfilment will entertain adults as well as their offspring. Most critics found it excessively violent and unbelievable; audiences loved it.

ANTI:

'The story is so implausible that it makes it hard for us to really care about the plight of the kid.' *(Roger Ebert)*

'Slapstick always flirts with sadism; in this film one is left with a nasty suspicion that it may have overstepped the mark.' *(Hugo Davenport, Daily Telegraph)*

'What charm there is swiftly evaporates into glossy shlock which finally brought out the bah humbug in Yours Truly.' *(Sue Heal, Today)*

'The basic idea is promising enough . . . Yet Hughes and Columbus stomp all over the scenario in hob-nailed boots . . . Fast-food American family entertainment made to order with relish but without finesse.' *(Geoff Brown, The Times)*

'What is astonishing is that a cute family comedy which takes over an hour really to get going should have provoked such an enthusiastic response and gained such a phenomenal word-of-mouth reputation.' *(MFB)*

MIXED:

'It is one of the ugliest-looking movies I've seen in a long time and has a grossly sentimental ending that would make a camel sick . . . It does miss many chances, but when it is good it is very good indeed.' *(Derek Malcolm, Guardian)*

'Sturdy, undemanding entertainment.' *(Kevin Jackson, Independent)*

PRO:

'A first-rate production in which every element contributes to the overall smartly realised tone.' *(Variety)*

'For someone of [Culkin's] years to exude as much acting talent as he clearly possesses, is nothing less than amazing.' *(Jeremy Clarke, What's On in London)*

HOMEBOY CT: 5 AV: 3.71

1988 US 116 C DRAMA/ROMANCE/SO BAD

D Michael Seresin
W Eddie Cook ● from Mickey Rourke's story ●

Mickey Rourke ● Christopher Walken ●
Debra Feuer Thomas Quinn Kevin Conway
Anthony Alda Jon Polito Bill Slayton David Taylor
Joseph Ragno

Brain-damaged, whisky-sodden fighter (Mickey Rourke) is lured into criminality by crook (Christopher Walken) but chooses instead to use the purse from his last fight, in which he knows he will probably die, to help repair the merry-go-round of the woman he loves (played by Rourke's real-life wife at the time, Debra Feuer).

The film looks good – as you might expect from a director, Michael Seresin, whose credits as a cameraman include Alan Parker's *Angel Heart*. But – although the director makes a valiant attempt to engage our affections by showing us (through blurred images and slowed-down sound) how dimly Johnny perceives the world – it's hard to feel sympathy for a drunken moron whose principal leisure interests are spitting, kicking passing cars and gratuitously attacking fellow-boxers after the bell.

Rourke's performance is a classic stinker: an unconsciously ridiculous parody of method acting. He out-mumbles Sylvester Stallone; his lopsided, vacant expression could pass as a vicious send-up of Dustin Hoffman in *Midnight Cowboy*; while his shuffling gait evokes not so much pathos as fond memories of Richard Dreyfuss's camp, off-off-Broadway *Richard III* in Neil Simon's more intentional comedy about egotistical actors, *The Goodbye Girl*.

Rourke's excesses might not matter so much, if the rest of his performance didn't render the plot nonsensical. The star's evident pride in his own boxing ability and physique (he used to be a boxer in his youth) ensures that this character – exaggeratedly unable to stand, talk, think, hear or see straight – becomes transformed in the ring, as it were miraculously, into a mean fighting machine who can take on the best. There have been dozens of boxing melodramas in cinematic history, but *Homeboy* is right up there among the very worst.

Sample dialogue . . . 'I was found in a mailbox, but I've tried to better myself over the years.' *(Christopher Walken)*

PRO:

'Forget *Rocky*, this is the real thing.' *(Jon Brett, Sun)*

MIXED:

'The actor's obvious identification with Johnny occasionally slides into pure self-indulgence . . . Rourke's mannerisms . . . only just skirt parody. He nevertheless has the screen presence to make his boxer unexpectedly convincing, even touching.' *(Margaret Walters, Listener)*

'Very well made, with fine, quirky performances by the leads, but so unrelentingly grim that it can scarcely be called entertainment.' *(Maltin)*

ANTI:

'*Homeboy* is to entertainment what the rail strike is to travel.' *(Clive Hirschhorn, Sunday Express)*

'As substantial as air pie.' *(Marshall Julius, What's On in London)*

'Rourke is a wonderful actor in the right film . . . [But] a gifted actor fooling around with his talent is one thing. A gifted actor who does not seem to realize he is fooling around is another.' *(Nigel Andrews, Financial Times)*

'Rourke, who was once a boxer, developed his own storyline for *Homeboy*, and shamelessly uses the film as an excuse to show off his Method mumbling. Unfortunately, this kind of dogged sluggishness also characterizes the laughably simplistic exposition.' *(Kim Newman, Film Yearbook)*

'A grindingly tedious totter through life's bargain basement.' *(Sue Heal, Today)*

'*Raging Bull* without horns, wallowing dully in the clichés of movieland gutter romanticism.' *(Variety)*

'The two men seem in competition to see who can turn in the more bizarre, mannered performance.' *(Winnert)*

'Sentimental and self-indulgent, with snot added.' *(Brian Case, Time Out)*

HOMICIDE CT: 9 AV: 7.10

1991 US 102 C THRILLER/COMEDY

D David Mamet ✔
W David Mamet ☆ from William Caunitz's novel *Suspects*

Joe Mantegna ☆ William H. Macy
Natalija Nogulich Ving Rhames
Vincent Guastaferro Rebecca Pidgeon

A Jewish cop (Joe Mantegna) is forced to choose between upholding the law and his racial roots.

No one writes dialogue better than David Mamet, and his direction has a documentary edge which stops the film from becoming too stylized or (in lighter moments) Runyonesque. The double-twist at the end of this highly intelligent mystery is a master-stroke, which causes one to look back on the entire film in a new light. It also changes the genre of the picture from cop-thriller to the darkest of black comedies.

Even though it's ingenious, intelligent and full of suspense, this is one thriller which is never likely to please the masses: it makes the audience work too hard. But it's far from 'intellectual', in the sense of being detached or clinical: the central character, brilliantly played by Mantegna, is portrayed with passion and pathos. Mamet is writing from the heart about his own Jewish roots, and gives the piece a much wider resonance; he poses the central problem of pursuing a 'liberal' American foreign policy – trying to be disinterested but not alienated in a world of warring interest-groups. The outstanding cinematography is by Roger Deakins.

ANTI:

'A genre picture with delusions of grandeur . . . The funereal pace and the melancholy, reflective tone seem intended to mask the story's essential recklessness and irresponsibility, and perhaps also to conceal the trite cop-movie mechanics of its construction.' *(Terrence Rafferty, New Yorker)*

'The transitions are sometimes abrupt and unconvincing, despite Mantegna's intensity. We can see how bigotry drives him away from his adoptive police family toward his own people, but not how his new militancy escalates so steeply.' *(Brian Case, Time Out)*

MIXED:

'One of the most intelligent thrillers of the year, but also a little problematical as an entity . . . Its disadvantage is that this story . . . has a conspiracy plot that isn't as convincing as the thesis behind the film.' *(Derek Malcolm, Guardian)*

'A little too over-plotted and sometimes on the sluggish side, [the film] is nevertheless an authentic, thoughtful film that delivers far more than your average cop thriller.' *(James Cameron-Wilson, What's On in London)*

PRO:

'Often brilliant, always compelling . . . Mantegna's performance in the central role is his strongest to date . . . [The film] is packed with the kind of raw, powerful dialogue we expect from [Mamet].' *(Bruce Feld, Film Journal)*

'Mamet controls the complexity of this scudding script, switching and changing direction, whenever the plot demands, never losing his balance . . . Mantegna . . . brings trust and authority to Bob Gold that elevates the film beyond its peak of tension to a higher plain of deftly-written, superbly-performed neo-thriller entertainment.' *(Angus Wolfe Murray, Scotsman)*

HOMME ÉCHAPPÉ, UN: *see* MAN ESCAPED, A.

HOMME ET UNE FEMME, UN: *see* MAN AND A WOMAN, A.

HONG GAOLIANG: *see* RED SORGHUM.

HOOK CT: 6 AV: 5.09

1992 US 135 C FANTASY/COMEDY/ADVENTURE/ FAMILY

D Steven Spielberg
W James V. Hart Malia Scotch Marmo after J.M. Barrie's novel

Dustin Hoffman ✔ Robin Williams ☆
Julia Roberts ● Bob Hoskins Maggie Smith
Caroline Goodall Charlie Korsmo ✔ Amber Scott
Laurel Cronin Phil Collins Arthur Malet
Glenn Close (cameo as a bearded pirate)

Peter Banning (Robin Williams), an American attorney turned corporate pirate, can't find time for his children (Charlie Korsmo and Amber Scott) and sees no irony in accusing them of childishness. He doesn't believe his wife's 92-year-old grandmother Wendy (Maggie Smith) when she assures him that he used to be Peter Pan. He treats a visit from Tinkerbell (Julia Roberts) as a hallucination, and a return to Neverland as an inconvenience. Not even the abduction of his children by Captain Hook (Dustin Hoffman) and his scurvy sidekick Smee (Bob Hoskins) can shake Peter's scepticism. Only with difficulty does he regain his imagination and conquer his fear of flying.

A big hit despite the critics, Spielberg's sequel to *Peter Pan* has obvious faults: tasteless concessions to skateboarding and rap, mermaids that look like My Little Ponies, and gross overlength. But it's still a marvellous family film, with first-rate special effects and performances. Robin Williams has precisely the driving, egomaniacal but mischievous quality which makes him believable as a grown-up Peter Pan. Dustin Hoffman is splendidly Old Etonian as Hook.

Behind the film's highly-coloured facade, too, lies a Barrie-esque darkness: Spielberg flagellates himself and his generation for 60s selfishness and 80s careerism. The whole film could be seen as the nightmare of a middle-aged divorcé whose children are being brought up by another man. It is a patently sincere celebration of fatherhood.

The accusation that Never-Neverland looks like a theme park is fair, but hardly a criticism: most children and adults enjoy Disneyland, and the movie is no more garish than *The Wizard of Oz*, a great children's film which has been rendered critically respectable by age. Spielberg's first and last shots – and a few in the middle – are of children open-mouthed with wonder. His film is dedicated to achieving that generous-spirited end. He succeeds.

ANTI:

'[Spielberg] has reduced one of the greatest plays in the English language to a Disneyland nightmare . . . set in some Pirates of the Caribbean theme park and peopled with waxwork characters . . . You will learn a lot more about Peter Pan from his statue in Kensington Gardens than from this horrendous Hollywood extravaganza.' *(Sheridan Morley, Sunday Express)*

'By the time this overstuffed epic comes to its conclusion, you feel like you've been watching the dance of an 800 lb elf.' *(Newsweek)*

'*Peter Pan* has been mugged.' *(Tom Hutchinson, Mail on Sunday)*

'Over-dressed, over-decorated, above all overlong – I thought I'd been sent to Everland.' *(Alexander Walker, Evening Standard)*

'Children . . . unacquainted with Barrie's play will be puzzled and, if they can read, will ask their parents what the four women listed in the cast as prostitutes are for. Adolescents will find it patronising (the film's adults are allowed real weapons but the kids can only fight with Bugsy Malone ammunition such as fruit, eggs and paint). Grown-ups will be bored, embarrassed and, if British, annoyed to find their childhood dreams so thoroughly colonised by Hollywood.' *(Philip French, Observer)*

'You're almost certain . . . to be repelled by the way overt sex has been injected into the . . . story . . . The only members of the cast who seem truly innocent are the 4- and 5-year-olds . . . Why can't the Americans leave us alone?' *(Vanessa Letts, Spectator)*

'Neither a hit nor a miss but a mess . . . repetitive, careless and cold.' *(Ian Lyness, Daily Express)*

'What is happening to the art of storytelling? It is, I suggest, being swamped by a visual literalism . . . which doesn't so much liberate our imaginations as circumscribe them . . . The movie seems less a child's fantasy than a set-decorator's dream . . . Story is less interesting than style . . . emotional effects matter less [than] special effects.' *(Michael Billington, Guardian)*

'Nothing works, but [Spielberg] keep throwing even more elaborate illusions at us and [the film] becomes so cluttered and so frenzied that it's nearly unwatchable . . . The Neverland of *Hook* feels joyless and claustrophobic, and its oppressiveness is disheartening, not only because it violates the expansive spirit of Barrie's story, but also because it betrays a profound weariness in Spielberg's attitude toward his art and his audience.' *(Terence Rafferty, New Yorker)*

PRO:

'I didn't know how awful it was supposed to be . . . [The critics] must have hearts of stone. [It] was magical . . . I admire the way Spielberg has developed the tale . . . Like all good storytellers [his] strength is the way he makes preposterous fantasy not only unpreposterous but desirable . . . [He] is the Andrew Lloyd Webber of the movies – an artist of great skill who understands popular taste.' *(Heather Welford, Guardian)*

'If ever a filmmaker was born to make a big-screen version of *Peter Pan*, it's Steven Spielberg . . . [He] returns full-throttle to the fantasy realm that has made him America's most successful movie magician.' *(Kevin Lally, Film Journal)*

'Spielberg scores again . . . With magnificent Disneyland sets, Dustin Hoffman romps around parodying Terry-Thomas.' *(Jeff Sawtell, Morning Star)*

MIXED:

'Cost a mint and it shows . . . the film is too much, yet the charm of the Barrie original has not been entirely lost. [It] has a hugely funny bravura performance by Dustin Hoffman . . . [who] preens, walks with a dainty step, loses his temper easily and tries very hard to be bad . . . Yet *Hook* is overwhelmed by a screenplay heavy with complicated exposition . . . Less a sequel to *Peter Pan* than a variation on it.' *(Vincent Canby, New York Times)*

'The critics who savaged it missed the point. This is panto on film, and jolly good fun it is too. Yes, it's too long. Yes, the plot's confusing. Yes, Roberts looks decidedly out of place as Tinkerbell. And yes, it's icky that The Lost Boys have been turned into the Politically Correct Benetton Boys (at least there aren't any girls!). But there's enough of the Spielberg magic and humour to keep the eye and the brain engaged and happy, with Hoffman and Hoskins a wonderful music-hall double-act.' *(Rose)*

HOPE AND GLORY AAN CT: 6 AV: 7.85

1987 GB 113 C WAR/COMEDY

D John Boorman ☆ AAN
W John Boorman AAN

Sebastian Rice-Edwards ☆ Geraldine Muir Sarah Miles David Hayman Sammi Davis Derrick O'Connor Susan Wooldridge Jean-Marc Barr Ian Bannen

A nine-year-old boy (Sebastian Rice-Edwards) finds that life during the Blitz is a lot of fun.

Boorman's unreliable memoir is noticeably lacking in narrative structure, which makes the film flag long before its end, but it works beautifully as a (mainly comic) montage of memorable moments. As so often in Boorman films, some performances are a matter of taste; both Sarah Miles and Ian Bannen are allowed to overact. Visually, however, it's a joy – thanks to Philippe Rousselot's photography and Don Dossett's art direction (both Oscar-nominated). Along with *Deliverance*, it's Boorman's most poetic film.

MIXED:

'A film of often startling details, put together with sharp psychological nuance . . . Boorman seldom strays very far from the mystical . . . and mixes comic imagery with stony realism, which keeps one constantly, and refreshingly, off-balance (this is no Mrs Miniver) . . . This powerfully visual level of poetic observation is, unfortunately, not sustained, and the film slows down a great deal when it moves . . . [to the] grandfather's riverside country house . . . Part of the problem here is that Ian Bannen . . . chews the scenery . . . The other performances, however, are superb.' *(David Bartholomew, Film Journal)*

PRO:

'Like *Empire of the Sun*, the film is episodic; but unlike Spielberg's movie, Boorman's is scaled to the perceptions of a child. It has an honesty, a modesty that *Empire* sorely lacks; Boorman doesn't strain after epic effects, doesn't engage in pointless displays of cinematographic brilliance. Most importantly, he coaxes from Edwards a performance of subtlety and coherence, with the result that we feel throughout the film as if we truly know and care about this boy. If the bombastic *Empire of the Sun* leaves one cold, one is surprised to find oneself being intensely moved by the simplest events and the smallest gestures in *Hope and Glory*.' *(Bruce Bawer, American Spectator)*

'The subversive thesis of John Boorman's *Hope and Glory* is this: war is a lark.' *(David Ansen)*

'A spellbinding evocation of family life in wartime suburban Britain, as seen through the eyes of a 9-year-old. Often funny, occasionally sad, but always with the ring of truth, there has never been better portrayal of life on the home front.' *(Rose)*

'We had to wait for *Hope and Glory* for a film on the Blitz that is free of propaganda and phoney heroics. What's more, it is a personal view – the view of an imaginative film-maker who was there.' *(Ken Russell, 1993)*

'An enormous success in England, where every frame must have its special memories for British audiences. Through American eyes, it is a more universal film, not so much about war as about memory. When we are young, what happens is not nearly as important as what we think happens. Perhaps that's true even when we are not so young.' *(Roger Ebert)*

HORI, MA PANENKO: *see* FIREMEN'S BALL, THE.

HORROR OF PARTY BEACH, THE

CT: 5 AV: 1.80

1964 US 72 BW HORROR/MUSICAL/SO BAD

D Del Tenney ●
W Richard L. Hilliard ●

John Scott ● Alice Lyon ● Allen Laurel ●
Marilyn Clark ● Eulabelle Moore ●

The dumping offshore of radio-active waste causes homicidal monsters to attack Connecticut teenagers.

Hilariously bad beach movie with silly monsters, abysmal music and a total absence of creative talent. Memorable aspects include a classic, stereotypical black maid (Eulabelle Moore) who, naturally, gets frightened out of whatever senses she had. It also contains the classic line (spoken by a doctor): 'It's a giant protozoa!' The intellectual level of the movie can best be gauged by close study of the lyrics for the movie's big number, 'The Zombie Stomp': 'Oh, everybody do the zombie stomp! / Doo-doo-doo-doop. / Just land your foot down with a bump! / Doo-doo-doo-doop. / Baby, baby, don't you care? / Something here looking kinda weird. / Honey, I'm no Frankenstein. / Oh yeah, baby, really I feel fine.'

'A radio-active vampire-zombie-sex-maniac would be disturbing enough, but musical numbers like "The Zombie Stomp" by the Del-Aires push this Twentieth Century-Fox release over the bottom as the worst movie of the last twelve months.' *(Newsweek)*

'Which is more horrible – the monsters, or the rock 'n' roll? The most curious aspect . . . is why, after the first couple of homicides, the rest of the victims linger around the disaster area, waiting for the worst. Audiences lured into the theater may ask themselves the same thing.' *(Eugene Archer, New York Times)*

'I've never seen such a bandy-legged monster in my life . . . Boredom is abject and total . . . 72 minutes (which felt to me like 72 centuries) . . . not only dreary but half-witted.' *(Raymond Durgnat, F & F)*

'There have been some comical monsters in previous horrific B pictures, but nothing quite so hilariously ridiculous as this assembly of sea-born brutes. Their rig-out is so phoney as to become almost fascinating, particularly a cluster of what looks like sausages in their mouths. The standard of acting is incredibly weak – including the most expressionless and inanimate heroine of all time.' *(MFB)*

'Dig that cat out there on the jetty. He's real cool. Looks like a stalk of asparagus with an artichoke heart for a head. Marinated by radio-active waste, maybe. And there's more where he came from. Crazy? Let's dance.' *(Time)*

'The amateur is evident in every phase of this would be horror film and this applies especially to the lack of imagination in the presentation of the creatures and in the acting generally. Mediocre fare for the very easily pleased.' *(Kine Weekly)*

'Crudely contrived and staged ghouls-and-guys-and-girls "shocker" pepped up with teenage cavorting and pop songs. Feeble . . . The construction of the sea-beasts would hardly scare a kiddy finding them floating in the bath . . . The actors put up a slightly less animated show than the monsters.' *(Daily Cinema)*

'One of the WORST movies of that or any other year, managing . . . to merge bad rock 'n' roll with atrocious acting, inept direction, and ludicrous fish monsters . . . a movie that will long be remembered by monster fans of a masochistic bent.' *(Jason Thomas, The Monster Times)*

'If you don't understand what's happening, newspaper headlines (MONSTERS STRIKE!, MONSTERS STRIKE AGAIN!, and MASS MURDER AT SLUMBER PARTY!) are shown to keep you informed.' *(Michael Weldon, Psychotronic Encyclopaedia of Film)*

'Billed as "the first horror musical" by its producers, who evidently never saw Liberace in *Sincerely Yours.*' *(Maltin)*

HORSE FEATHERS

CT: 7 AV: 8.58

1932 US 69 BW COMEDY

D Norman Z. McLeod
W Bert Kalmar Harry Ruby S.J. Perelman Will B. Johnstone ☆ (music and lyrics by Kalmar and Ruby)

Groucho Marx ☆ Harpo Marx Chico Marx ☆ Zeppo Marx Thelma Todd ☆ David Landau Florine McKinney Jim Pierce Nat Pendleton Reginald Barlow

College president (Groucho Marx) tries to reinforce his football team with two professional players, but accidentally recruits a bootlegger (Chico) and a dog-catcher (Harpo).

A surreal plot and innumerable wisecracks are run through at breakneck speed, despite one of Harpo's more boring harp solos. Groucho and Chico are on top form, and there is the bonus of Thelma Todd, one of Hollywood's most attractive comediennes. Sample line . . . Groucho: 'You have the brain of a four-year-old child, and I'll bet he was glad to get rid of it.'

ANTI:

'The Marx Brothers have lacked from the beginning a scenario-writer with sufficient imagination to create for them a realistic background to throw up their unique idiocy, and a director with sufficient power to shape their wildness into a wild logic. This film does not reveal the discovery of either . . . The madness lacks method and the picture a plan. Pity, but 'tis true.' *(Forsyth Hardy, Cinema Quarterly)*

PRO:

'It is quite possible to mistake the Marx Brothers for human beings. They are half human and half wild creatures, not unlike ourselves in their desires but with few of the repressions which hold society together, existing in a kind of happy void . . . [The film] is very funny, though not quite the funniest film that [they] have made.' *(The Times)*

'If you want to forget your troubles and you yearn for a long laugh, a howl and a yelp, see [the brothers as] through nine long reels and Thelma Todd's bedroom they race and tear, dripping wisecracks as they go.' *(Photoplay)*

'The current Marx comedy is the funniest talkie since the last Marx comedy, and the record it establishes is not likely to be disturbed until the next Marx comedy comes along. As for comparison, I was too busy having a good time to make any.' *(Philip K. Scheuer)*

HOUND OF THE BASKERVILLES, THE

CT: 8 AV: 7.09

1939 US 80 BW THRILLER

D Sidney Lanfield
W Ernest Pascal from Arthur Conan Doyle's novel

Basil Rathbone ☆ Richard Greene ☆ Wendy Barrie Nigel Bruce Lionel Atwill John Carradine Barlowe Borland

A private detective (Basil Rathbone) investigates the appearance of a supernatural dog on Dartmoor.

Basil Rathbone and Nigel Bruce are the definitive Sherlock Holmes and Dr Watson, and this is the first of 14 Holmes films they made. Though not the paciest of thrillers and rather studio bound, it remains a charming, spooky period piece and the most acclaimed version of this particular story (though some recent critics favour Terence Fisher's 1958 production, starring Peter Cushing). Peverell Marley's photography is outstanding.

'A startling mystery-chiller developed along logical lines without resorting to implausible situations and over-theatrics.' *(Variety)*

'It's fairly good fun and like old times to be seeing Sherlock again.' *(New York Times)*

'Rathbone gives a most efffective characterization of Sherlock Holmes, which will be relished by mystery lovers.' *(Variety)*

'Set completely in period, the picture was diabolically menacing, more so than any other Holmes film, past or present. It was powerfully cloaked with a consistently oppressive atmosphere of deep brooding and Gothic foreboding all the way from Baker Street in the opening reels to Dartmoor and Baskerville Hall later on, then finally to the classic finale that saw Holmes and Watson out on the fog-shrouded moors of Grimpen Mire stalking the legendary Hound with pistol, lantern and stealth.' *(Ron Haydock, Deerstalker! Holmes and Watson on Screen, 1978)*

'A little too measured in its pacing and never quite makes the most of its excitement potential . . . [It] also suffered from a surprising lack of background music.' *(William K. Everson, The Detective in Hollywood, 1972)*

HOUNDS OF ZAROFF, THE: *see* MOST DANGEROUS GAME, THE.

HOUR OF THE PIG, THE CT: 7 AV: 6 (est)

1994 GB C THRILLER/COMEDY

D Leslie Megahey ✔
W Leslie Megahey ✔

Colin Firth ✔ Jim Carter ✔ Harriet Walter
Ian Holm ✔ Donald Pleasence ✔ Michael Gough
Nicol Williamson Sophie Dix ✔

An idealistic, progressive Parisian lawyer (Colin Firth) comes – with his cynical clerk (Jim Carter) – to uphold law and order in a Godforsaken village in medieval France. Firth's inexperience leads to one of his first clients (Harriet Walter) being hanged as a witch, and then he suffers the indignity of having to defend a pig accused of murder. The rural idyll he anticipated looks more and more like a hell of superstition, racism and ignorance.

Leslie Megahey's medieval thriller has an unusual plot, an atmosphere and a bawdy vigour all its own. The plot is of secondary importance; Megahey is more interested in exploring the darkly comic implications of his story, based on real-life cases of animals being prosecuted in the Middle Ages, and the link between superstition and fear of the unknown. Even so, he sensibly takes the trouble to scatter enough reddish herrings – about mysterious strangers, Satanic cults, manhunts, etc – to hold any audience gripped.

The cast includes some fine character actors: Ian Holm as a randy priest, Donald Pleasence as a smug prosecutor, Michael Gough as an irascible judge, and Nicol Williamson as the sinister lord of the manor. Firth and Carter play off each other well, and Sophie Dix makes an impression as a randy serving wench.

'Neither stolid nor melodramatic [it] is a period tale like no other . . . The screenplay, relishing the absurdity of [the story] adopts a knowing tone without becoming anachronistic; so while the piece is convincingly in period, certain episodes are in the key of black comedy . . . The blend and range of moods may not appeal to everyone, but this variety gives the film real freshness.' *(Mansel Stimpson, What's On in London)*

'Thoroughly modern in outlook . . . refreshingly irreverent in tone, and remarkably accomplished in execution. It's hot to trot, as they surely didn't say in the Middle Ages.' *(Trevor Johnston, Time Out)*

'[It] isn't a total porker, but its good intentions have resulted in something not quite kosher . . . It comes unstuck, largely because Megahey can't decide whether to do *The Name of the Rose* or *It Shouldn't Happen to a Serf*.' *(Jonathan Romney, Guardian)*

HOUSE OF ANGELS CT: 9 AV: 5 (est)

1993 Sweden 126 C COMEDY/FOREIGN

D Colin Nutley ✔
W Colin Nutley ✔

Helena Bergström ☆ Rikard Wolff ✔
Sven Wollter ✔ Reine Brynolfsson ✔
Ernst Gunther ✔

A stuffy Swedish village is appalled by the arrival of a new, decadent lady of the manor (Helena Bergström) and her bisexual, biker boyfriend (Rikard Wolff).

House of Angels is best classified as a comedy. But it's a long way from Mel Brooks or *Airplane!* The humour arises from character, situation and observation, rather than gags, pastiche or slapstick. It's firmly in the British tradition of *Whisky Galore, Local Hero* and *Hear My Song*. The film is also made in a quite different way than the Americans would. It's slower – but, for once, slowness is a virtue. It reflects the pace of rural life, and leaves room for an important player in the drama: the landscape. There is the same lyrical feeling for the Swedish countryside that Claude Berri showed for Provence in *Jean de Florette* (another, more tragic film about an outsider's effect on a closed community).

Just as importantly, the leisurely pace gives room for the subsidiary characters to develop. Each is given the chance to come to life and then change as a result of the narrative, so that by the end you feel that the people existed both before and after the film. Nutley may be as beady-eyed about human frailty as Mike Leigh, but he neatly avoids Leigh's vice of patronizing his characters: his affection for nonconformists and conformists alike is reminiscent of another great Scandinavian film, *Babette's Feast*.

Nutley even manages to breathe new life into that most hackneyed comic figure: the rural vicar. At first Reine Brynolfsson seems to be be playing a caricature pastor: lacking in weight, easily pushed around, his religious duties confined to entertaining the ladies' sewing circle with sub-Barry Manilow songs at the piano. Increasingly, he comes into his own, so that by the end he really is trying – in his own bungling fashion – to be God's representative on earth. The role is charmingly played, but also exquisitely written.

The performances are enchanting, but Ernst Gunther as Gottfried, the fat old villager who befriends the couple, is especially subtle and funny. Rikard Wolff also shines as the heroine's leather-clad boyfriend: he makes the most of a part which starts out as cartoonish (with overtones of Tim Curry in *The Rocky Horror Picture Show*) but ends up surprisingly sympathetic. However, the film's central figure is Helena Bergström. The film would collapse as fast as a ten-ton soufflé if she didn't manage to combine pluck with pathos, shrewdness with silliness, verve with vulnerability.

The two city-dwellers' rebelliousness may be skin-deep, and the scene where their friends try to win over the villagers too tame; but these are minor reservations. The important thing is that Nutley doesn't fudge the incompatibility of the townies with the villagers, or try to make out that his heroine has all the answers, or provide a 'cop-out' happy ending: his point is that conservatives and anarchists should tolerate each other's tastes, differences and inadequacies, and then life can go on . . .

There will always be critics who accuse any film which contains emotion and brings a tear to one's eye of being 'sentimental', but there is no sense here of the film makers prettifying or infantilizing the real world: Nutley's film acknowledges the existence of bigotry, racism, pornography, avarice, ecological vandalism, adultery and bad performance art. At the same time, he suggests, in the best Dickensian tradition, that there is potential for good in human nature – forgiveness, tolerance, friendship and love of community, among other qualities. *House of Angels* is a rarity in modern cinema – a delightful, uplifting, humane entertainment – and it was sadly underrated by many critics.

ANTI:

'What a craven film this is! Zac is a crossdresser and, presumably, bisexual, who has a casually carnal, nonexclusive relationship with Fanny. When Marten, against his parents' orders, is enticed to the Zander farm to fix the windows, he seems about to be seduced first by Fanny, then by Zac. But none of this is followed through; like so much else, it is just left there, leeringly dangling . . . Most disappointing, though, is Helena Bergström, Sweden's alleged heartthrob, in whom I find nothing appealing. Her acting is mostly long, pseudo-sincere, blue-eyed stares, which the director holds endlessly; her looks, compared to those of the great Swedish actresses of yesteryear, are paltry; her cantilevered mouth with the rows of carnivorous teeth could scare small children. Let me add that the comic climax, involving questions of Fanny's paternity, is as lackluster as the rest of the movie. Yet the New York theater audience I saw it with seems to have had a whopping good time, and applauded lustily. That way there was at least something lusty about the evening.' *(John Simon)*

'A minor, overlong comedy drama only rarely sparks into something funny, touching or revealing. The charming Bergström is the film's major asset, but British director Nutley isn't nearly incisive enough.' *(Winnert)*

MIXED:

'Feather-weight fluff about an airhead, given some additional buoyancy by Bergström.' *(Bruce Williamson, Playboy)*

PRO:

'Perceptive warm-hearted comedy.' *(Hugo Davenport, Daily Telegraph)*

'Deeply enjoyable.' *(Rachel Simpson, Daily Express)*

'Warm, witty and wonderful.' *(Helen Renshaw, Today)*

'Beautifully played . . . a film with warmth and humour.' *(Derek Malcolm, Guardian)*

HOUSE OF DRACULA:

see THE *FRANKENSTEIN* SERIES.

HOUSE OF FRANKENSTEIN:

see THE *FRANKENSTEIN* SERIES.

HOUSE OF GAMES

CT: 9 AV: 7.14

1987 US 102 C THRILLER/ROMANCE

D David Mamet ☆
W David Mamet ☆

Lindsay Crouse ✓ Joe Mantegna ☆ Mike Nusbaum Lilia Skala J.T. Walsh Willo Hausman Karen Kohlhaas

A female psychiatrist (Linday Crouse) tries to work out what makes professional con-men tick. As she becomes emotionally involved with the king of them all (Joe Mantegna) she discovers that she too has a talent for deceit.

Playwright David Mamet makes a spectacular début as writer-director. It's several films in one. Like an Agatha Christie or a Hitchcock thriller, it keeps you guessing up to the end. Yet it also has a documentary realism: the various scams and rackets seem carefully researched, and have the ring of truth. On a deeper level, it's a black comedy about the war between the sexes. Can a woman ever really know a man, and vice versa? A brilliantly original film.

ANTI:

'Highly praised, yet I must admit to being underawed by its elaborate scam-ology, schematic structure, pseudo-noir stylization and unremitting coldness.' *(Graham Fuller, Film Yearbook)*

MIXED:

'Cold and stagey at the start, we become just as fascinated as her by this unknown world where nothing is as it seems. Mesmerising on first viewing, it fails to grip a second time when you know the surprises in store.' *(Rose)*

PRO:

'Remember *The Sting*? Well, this is twice as ingenious.' *(Shaun Usher, Daily Mail)*

'A riveting psychological thriller with a devastating

ace in the hole . . . Mamet's directing début is an engrossing study of the subtly corrupt art of the scam . . . deserves to play to a full house.' *(Nigel Floyd, New Musical Express)*

'An outrageously ambitious blend of psychology and the world of the confidence trickster, with a plot so relentlessly inventive as to be compelling in spite of its bitter tone.' *(William Parente, Scotsman)*

'Masterful directorial bow by . . . Mamet is a haunting brew of dark comedy and enveloping dread . . . Sure to be one of the most talked-about films of the year, it is also among the best.' *(Ed Kelleher, Film Journal)*

'Mamet has become a highly significant film-maker – an ace who uses a joker to win us round to some very profound ideas.' *(Mail on Sunday)*

HOUSE OF THE SPIRITS, THE

CT: 5 AV: 4.0 (est)

1994 Germany 138 C DRAMA/SO BAD

D Bille August ●
W Bille August ●

Jeremy Irons ● Meryl Streep ● Winona Ryder ● Glenn Close ● Antonio Banderas Vanessa Redgrave Armin Mueller-Stahl

Epic family saga set against social and political upheavals in Chile.

There may have been more colossal flops in the history of cinema, but few have threatened to destroy so many reputations at once. The movie version of Isabel Allende's novel is a kind of all-star, showbiz equivalent to the Somme. First – and most – over the top is Jeremy Irons, splendidly suicidal as a whip-brandishing South American patriarch. Invited to act an age range of about fifty years, he opts early on for a hilarious wig that makes him look like Mahatma Gandhi with a Kevin Keegan perm. His choice of accent is equally perplexing: a cross between a Robert Maxwell growl and Winston Churchill mumbling a cover version of 'I Was Born Under A Wandering Star'.

As Irons's wife, Meryl Streep, whom the more ageist among you may consider an unlikely teenager, skips around the set in a manner disturbingly reminiscent of Bette Davis in *Whatever Happened To Baby Jane*. Sometimes Streep's character refuses to speak to her husband for years on end, possibly in an attempt to show how right Meryl would have been for Holly Hunter's role in *The Piano*. After giving birth to Winona Ryder, Streep settles for a beatifically smug expression reminiscent of an ex-hooker accepting an Oscar for humanitarian achievement.

Glenn Close, as Irons's repressed, lesbian, moustacheoed sister, gives us a cross between Mrs Danvers from *Rebecca* and the late Sir Gerald Nabarro. I remain uncertain as to whether she's funniest when she's spelling out her carnal longings in the confessional to a badly dubbed priest, or when playing a ghost like a Victorian commode on castors.

Winona Ryder simpers sickeningly throughout like a hormonally-rampant Anne of Green Gables, while the older actresses sing her praises through gritted teeth. 'She's so brave, strong, true to her feelings,' sighs Meryl Streep, in that section of the movie where she has inexplicably opted to impersonate a spaced-out Californian Est therapist. As Winona's philosopher-peasant lover Pedro, Antonio Banderas wanders around looking vaguely Hispanic, revolutionary and unintentionally comic, a kind of Gaucho Marx.

Possibly the funniest performance is given by the actor playing Irons's bastard son. I shall not be so unkind as to identify him. He is not named in any of the publicity material, and it is as though, somewhere during the making of the film, there was a crisis of confidence about whether he was up to the job: is he, well . . . nasty enough? So not only does the poor chap have to be incestuous, a paedophile, a sneak, a sadist and wear a scar on his face: he even has to join the Fascist army and shoot up the ranks in time to torture his half-sister – though, frankly, he can't be much of a torturer, since his idea of interrogating her is to shine a light into her face . . . while she's wearing a blindfold.

Much of the blame for this 25 million-dollar fiasco must be laid at the door of the acclaimed Danish director Bille August, who confirms what I had suspected from his previous work, *Pelle The Conqueror* and *The Best Intentions*: namely that he has absolutely no sense of humour. This is the kind of movie which could only have been saved from total critical disaster had it been in some abstruse dialect of Finnish. In English, its idiocy is stupefyingly obvious.

August's less than august adaptation and direction are no more lumberingly ludicrous than in the scene where Streep's mother and father (Vanessa Redgrave and Armin Mueller-Stahl) meet a grisly end in a car whose brakes have been sabotaged so that it crashes into an oncoming train. So anxious is August to spin out the drama that he makes Mueller-Stahl notice the brakes have gone at least 250 yards before the railway track, giving him plenty of opportunity to steer his vehicle easily out of harm's way.

The most pitiful casualty of this whole sorry business is Isabel Allende's much-praised 'magic realist' novel. Under the wintry hand of August and stripped of most of its flowery verbiage, it stands revealed as embarrassing tosh, the silliest kind of soap opera, in which the world is portrayed in black and white, men are cardboard cut-outs, women are ethereal creatures born to suffer nobly, and such stunning insights are offered as 'Dying is just a change, like being born' – that's Meryl again: it's no wonder that part of her research for the role included ringing up Shirley Maclaine for a natter.

The politics of the film are those of a David Hare heroine haranguing a defenceless kindergarten; yet the film does not even have the courage of its pseudo-revolutionary convictions. The one conclusion drawn from the previous two and a half hours by our narrator (that's Winona, now happily recovered from torture) is that we should bear no hard feelings: 'To me, life is my daughter, Pedro, the light, the day, this very moment, the memories, the future.' The overall effect of the film is like having to sit through the First World War, as narrated by Claire Rayner. The American critics were remarkably kind; their British cousins, less so.

PRO:

'The thing works in its goofy way, mainly because Bille August (of *Pelle The Conqueror*) is a man of apparently dauntless conviction. He has written and directed every scene with serene authority, somehow compelling your belief in what he's doing through his own sublime self-confidence . . . The result is not epic cinema as David Lean defined it but as Bette Davis used to play it at Warner Bros – where history was a branch of melodrama and the subtler emotions were Xed out on the second-draft screenplay.' *(Richard Schickel, Time)*

'The movie works on a certain level simply because it tells an interesting story. The characters are clearly drawn, the story provides ironic justice, and the locations establish a certain reality. The cluttered city homes of the rich families, where every surface is lined with expensive bric-a-brac, speak eloquently for their materialistic values and traditions.' *(Roger Ebert)*

'In her inspired, astonishing performance, Close provides a tantalizing hint of the power of the book – and an appreciation of how rare and fortunate it is when art is truly touched by spirit.' *(Lisa Schwarzbaum, People Weekly)*

MIXED:

'Not so bad. As a family melodrama, it tells an engaging story climaxing in political upheaval. The images are lovely, the performances enjoyable. But the slow pace, August's workmanlike script and his static tableau-style photography suck the Latin lifeblood from Allende's tale. On-screen, *The House of the Spirits* preserves the original architecture while leaving behind the magic and the realism.' *(Brian D. Johnson, Maclean's)*

ANTI:

'A turkey. Irons [sounds] as if he were speaking with a mouth full of flapjack . . . The film has still to be rated . . . but it's best described as D for duff.' *(Hugo Davenport, Daily Telegraph)*

'This adaptation of Isabel Allende's epic of love, loss, redemption and spiritualism has removed all the juice from the best-selling 1985 novel, leaving a hacienda-high pile of pulp . . . Those who have not read the fanciful, ironic *The House of the Spirits* will be baffled by the movie, which frequently leaves relationships and motivations unexplained. Those who have read the novel will probably be annoyed by the liberties the screenwriters have taken.' *(Joanne Kaufman, People Weekly)*

'August's dialogue and direction are often awkward, at times laughable, as if his cool Scandinavian blood and Allende's Latin passions were intrinsically out of sync.' *(Bruce Williamson, Playboy)*

'August's first work outside Scandinavia. Written large, if invisibly, across the screen is the injunction, "August go home!" He needs to work where he understands what he's doing and really wants to do it . . . Rarely does a picture with such a promising list of names turn out to be such a misery.' *(Stanley Kauffmann)*

'Half the things that happen would be rejected as too phony by the writing staff of Melrose Place . . . Of course, all would have been forgiven if *House of the Spirits* had any artistic quality. But no such luck . . . I really couldn't figure out exactly what kind of accent Jeremy Irons was trying to conjure up. I suppose a Chilean one, whatever that sounds like. Nevertheless, he was so clearly struggling with it that it seems his entire dialogue was dubbed – by Kevin Costner.' *(Rod Lurie, Los Angeles Magazine, 1994)*

'Magic realism on screen is always good for a nervous laugh, and there are moments when the romanticism of Isabel Allende's novel sweeps the adaptation into triteness, turning lushness into slush.' *(Quentin Curtis, Independent on Sunday)*

'August plods through his own unwieldy, literal script without betraying any sensitivity to the material and coaxes an excruciating performance from Irons.' *(Tom Charity, Time Out)*

HOUSE ON 92ND STREET CT: 6 AV: 8.40

1945 US 88 BW DRAMA/SPY/WAR

D Henry Hathaway ☆
W Barre Lyndon Charles G. Booth John Monks Jr ☆ from Booth's story AAW

William Eythe Lloyd Nolan Signe Hasso ✔ Gene Lockhart Leo G. Carroll ☆ Lydia St. Clair Reed Hadley

A Federal investigator (Lloyd Nolan) investigates a Nazi spy-ring, with the help of a double-agent (William Eythe).

A melodrama presented unusually in the style of a 'March of Time' documentary, incorporating newsreel footage and actual spying locations. Made with the co-operation of the FBI (Edgar J. Hoover himself appears to introduce the movie), it tries to impress with up-to-date spying techniques; not surprisingly, many will strike a modern audience as laughably primitive. Even so, this is a fast, exciting thriller of its period.

MIXED:

'It is a pity that a film which takes such pains to sustain an atmosphere of accuracy and suspense should sound such a falsely theatrical note.' *(The Times)*

'Semi-fictional telescoping of several FBI espionage jobs . . . Convincing inadvertent suggestion that the FBI functions efficiently less through intelligence than through doggedness plus scientific equipment. Extensive and gratifying use of actual-spot shooting and reenactment. Effective pseudo-naturalistic performances by Lydia St. Clair, Gene Lockhart, William Eythe, and others, none of whom, however, manage to suggest how spies, counterspies, and traitors who look and act like that are not identifiable to those interested at five hundred paces. Unpersuasive, often skilled, generally enjoyable.' *(James Agee, Nation)*

PRO:

'One I can recommend . . . so factual is the direction, so natural the acting . . . that it gives new life to an old theme.' *(Standard)*

'Unreservedly commended as a Grade A spy thriller . . . A few months back there was a complaint that Britain had been slighted over her share in the invention [of the atom bomb] by this film . . . No one who enjoys this picture, as I did, could possibly share this asinine view.' *(Daily Herald)*

'One of the best thrillers that Hollywood ever made.' *(Quinlan)*

HOW GREEN WAS MY VALLEY AAN

CT: 8 AV: 8.92

1941 US 118 BW DRAMA/RITES-OF-PASSAGE

D John Ford ☆ AAW
W Philip Dunne ☆ AAN based on Richard Llewellyn's novel

Walter Pidgeon Maureen O'Hara Donald Crisp ☆ AAW Anna Lee Roddy McDowall John Loder Sara Allgood ☆ AAN Barry Fitzgerald Patric Knowles Morton Lowry

Nostalgic recollection of a childhood in a Welsh mining community.

Film buffs have never quite forgiven John Ford's picture for beating *Citizen Kane* to the Best Film Oscar for 1941. It is very conventional, a shade prettified, and the Welsh accents are sometimes wildly offbeam. It also contains more than a slight element of Hollywood schmaltz. But it's handsomely produced and movingly acted. Like Ford's masterpiece, *The Grapes of Wrath*, this is a song of praise to the common man; and it remains impossible to watch without shedding a tear. Oscars went to Arthur Miller (photography), Richard Day, Nathan Juran and Thomas Little (art direction). Nominated were Alfred Newman (music), E.H. Hansen (sound) and editor James B. Clark.

ANTI:

'Deserves the Guggenheim medal for the phoniest film of the year.' *(William Whitebait, New Statesman)*

MIXED:

'Something of the salt and wildness of the people about whom Richard Llewellyn wrote is gone. The rooms in which they live are too spacious and smooth; the line of slatey grey houses by the pithead is too cosy; the emotions of the characters themselves have been tamed . . . But the John Ford quality is not absent; the sympathy with men and women living simply and passionately, the essential faith in simple human beings. And, as always, he has communicated his feeling to his cast.' *(Dilys Powell)*

PRO:

'The same sort of solid enjoyment, enrichment and communication between authors and audience that comes from reading a good book . . . The film is conceived and executed with dignity, honesty, thoroughness and superlative competence. It is a full-bodied work. It has stature and completeness; a maximum of cinematic skill, the minimum of movie trickery.' *(Cecilia Ager, PM)*

'Looked at coldly – as coldly as one can with a picture so warm with humanness and its laughter and tears – the superlative thing about [It] is its technical style, the perfection of cinematic narrative that it achieves.' *(James Shelley Hamilton, NBR)*

'A motion picture of great poetic charm and dignity, a picture rich in visual fabrication and in the vigor of its imagery and one which may truly be regarded as an outstanding film of the year.' *(Bosley Crowther)*

'Replete with much human interest, romance, conflict and almost every other human emotion.' *(Variety)*

'One of the most meritorious motion pictures to hit the screen . . . John Ford has endowed the treatment with idyllic grandeur. His work has a deep, poetic cadence and, for the first time in his long and representative career, the director has captured the basic nature of all true art, the poignancy of humanity. With infinite pity he reveals the aspirations, the struggles, the small triumphs and harrowing defeats of Little People, and his personal concern with the fates of his characters breeds a lyricism that is all too rare in an era of the machine-made photoplay.' *(Herb Sterne)*

HOWARD THE DUCK

CT: 1 AV: 1.80

(aka *Howard, A New Breed of Hero*)

1986 US 111 C SF/COMEDY/COMIC STRIP

D Willard Huyck ●
W Willard Huyck Gloria Katz ● (character Steve Gerber, comic strip)

Lea Thompson Jeffrey Jones Tim Robbins Paul Guilfoyle

Big duck from another planet saves Earth from invading creatures from another dimension.

A disastrous, big-budget attempt to adapt the US

comic strip *Howard The Duck* to the big screen. Known in the movie biz as *Howard The Turkey*, it's only slightly more animated than Monty Python's dead parrot. It cost about $50 million and lost $35 million.

PRO:

'Howard's pop-cult standing isn't lost here, for he offers a wry view of contemporary America . . . It's a pleasant-enough spoof for 45 minutes or so. Suddenly we're into a different film . . . devoted to truly magnificent visual tricks . . . equal to anything in [Lucas's] *Star Wars*.' *(Caryn James, New York Times)*

ANTI:

'Watching an actor waddle around in the unimpressive costume (eight players are credited with the part), you don't know if you're at a movie or a shopping mall opening.' *(Scot Haller, People Weekly)*

'Too scuzzy to beguile children, too infantile to appeal to adults . . . When the filmmakers grow tired of fowl puns – about an hour after the audience does – they switch to space opera, and Howard battles a scientist (Jeffrey Jones, funny against all odds) whose body is invaded by a giant lobster-scorpion space troll. Moviegoers who are in search of a porno *Zoo Parade* may enjoy the bedroom tryst in which Howard's human sweetie (Lea Thompson) discovers a condom in his wallet, snuggles up and asks, "You think I might find love in the animal kingdom?" More fastidious viewers are advised to purchase a *Daffy Duck* videocassette.' *(Richard Corliss, Time)*

'A fantasy with nowhere to go . . . That this expensive curate's egg is not intended solely for a *Care Bears* audience soon becomes clear with the scenes of sex 'n' violence . . . The scene where the heroine takes [Howard] to bed and engages in double-entendre banter, is undeniably perverse and salacious, less because it hints at bestiality than at sexual congress with a marketing gimmick.' *(Richard Combs, MFB)*

'It is hard to understand how a film as bad as this ever reached the screen. If there was ever a case for studio executives committing hari kari, this was surely it.' *(Rose)*

HOWARDS END AAN   CT: 7 AV: 8.92

1992 GB 140 C DRAMA/ROMANCE

D James Ivory ☆ AAN
W Ruth Prawer Jhabvala ✗ AAW from E.M. Forster's novel

Anthony Hopkins ☆ Vanessa Redgrave ✗ AAN
Helena Bonham Carter ☆ Emma Thompson ☆ AAW
James Wilby Samuel West ✓ Jemma Redgrave
Nicola Duffett ✓ Prunella Scales Simon Callow

An emancipated, educated woman (Emma Thompson) is wooed by a businessman (Anthony Hopkins) who has robbed her of an inheritance.

This classy Merchant Ivory film faithfully reproduces Forster's skilful narrative surprises and the dramatic conflict between the caring, artistic Schlegels and the mean-minded, acquisitive Wilcoxes. *Howards End* is beautifully mounted, impeccably acted and demonstrates Ivory's unrivalled talent for expressing people's character through their possessions. Special credit, too, to the exquisite Oscar-winning design by Luciana Arrighi, Jenny Beavan and John Bright. The inspired cinematography by Tony Pierce-Roberts was Oscar-nominated, as were Sheena Napier's costumes and Richard Robbins's music.

Unfortunately, as in *The Bostonians*, director Ivory is over-indulgent to Vanessa Redgrave (I know she's a great actress, but the plot acquires momentum only after her character has died). Screenwriter Ruth Prawer Jhabvala fails yet again to be sufficiently ruthless with her source material: the opening 45 minutes could usefully have been compressed into 30, and she never addresses the central mystery of Forster's novel: why a generous-spirited, artistic 'new woman' such as Margaret Schlegel chooses to marry a mean, boring old hypocrite like Wilcox – even if he is played by the admirable Anthony Hopkins.

The screenplay falls short of the novel by failing to make us care enough about the two Schlegel girls, even though they are played with attractive sensitivity by Helena Bonham Carter and Emma Thompson. And there's an unconscious snobbery in Forster which dates and diminishes even his best work. The working-class hero of his sub-plot, Leonard Bast (splendidly interpreted by Samuel West as an explosive mixture of pride and deference), lacks the vibrancy which H.G. Wells or Arnold Bennett would have given him and seems to be deemed interesting by Forster only because of his literary leanings, while Bast's wife (played by another promising newcomer, Nicola Duffett) disappears much too abruptly when Forster – like Henry Wilcox – has no further use for her.

ANTI:

'Tasteful, lugubrious costume piece . . . As usual the cast is impressive, which only goes to show how unimportant acting can be . . . I'm sorry to say that just about everything is missing from this grating, oppressive movie. It just left me feeling pissed with the careless rich.' *(Georgia Brown, Village Voice)*

'The only way Ruth Prawer Jhabvala's overlong screenplay can incorporate all the incident is by having more black-outs than a convention of epileptics.' *(Mark Sanderson, Time Out)*

'Nothing more than a Mills and Boon period melodrama for the literary set. Vanessa Redgrave . . . is irritating beyond belief . . . too mannered, too intense and the acting style she employs here badly clashes with the more naturalistic performances of her co-stars.' *(Gay Times)*

'The success of a film like *Howards End* at the Oscars, BAFTA and elsewhere is depressing. Is this how the British cinema will end? Not with a bang, but a genteel whimper in full period costume.' *(Ken Russell, 1993)*

MIXED:

'Overlong screenplay . . . director James Ivory – the Laura Ashley of the lens – ensures throughout that *Howards End* is an extremely desirable residence . . . All the performances – except James Wilby's twitching baddy – are impeccable, but top honours go to Thompson who . . . manages to make Margaret's saintliness actually seem seductive.' *(Time Out)*

PRO:

Amost compelling drama, perhaps the best film made during the 30-year partnership of Ismail Merchant and James Ivory.' *(Variety)*

'So captivatingly exquisite in every detail . . . Performances are exemplary. Anthony Hopkins is simply masterful.' *(David McGillvray, What's On)*

'Exquisitely rendered . . . their best film yet . . . It begins as a witty comedy of manners, then evolves into a tragedy of clashing classes, before fading out on an evanescent note of renewal and hope. The challenge was to be more than merely faithful to the Forster masterwork – to convey not just its thematic sweep, but also its poetic subtlety. The filmmakers have succeeded with surpassing style and grace.' *(Michael Sauter, Film Journal)*

'At last an E.M. Forster adaptation that not only has the pretty frocks, meadows and steam trains, but a cracking good story.' *(Rose)*

HUD CT: 8 AV: 8.92

1963 US 112 BW WESTERN/DRAMA

D Martin Ritt ☆ AAN
W Irving Ravetch Harriet Frank ☆ AAN from Larry McMurtry's novel *Horseman Pass By*

Paul Newman ☆ AAN Patricia Neal ☆ AAW
Melvyn Douglas ☆ AAW Brandon de Wilde
Whit Bissell

A rancher's hedonistic son (Paul Newman) wishes to sell off a herd that may have foot-and-mouth disease; his father (Melvyn Douglas) has scruples and prefers to have them slaughtered.

Less a conventional western than a blistering study of American materialism, all the more powerful for being personified so charismatically by Paul Newman. Martin Ritt's superb character study is enriched by Patricia Neal's longsuffering housekeeper and Brandon de Wilde's hero-worshipping nephew. James Wong Howe's cinematography rightly won an Oscar.

'While it looks like a modern western and is an outdoor drama indeed, *Hud* is as wide and profound a contemplation of the human condition as one of the New England plays of Eugene O'Neill . . . The striking, important thing about it is the clarity with which it unreels. The sureness and integrity of it are as crystal clear as the plot is spare.' *(Bosley Crowther, New York Times)*

'*Hud* is a provocative picture with a shock for audiences who have been conditioned like laboratory mice to expect the customary bad-guy-is-really-good-guy reward in the last reel of a western . . . The point of the picture is as dry and nihilistic as a Panhandle dust storm. Once, when Douglas is berating his son, de Wilde asks: 'Why pick on Hud, Grandpa? Nearly everybody around town is like him".' *(Time)*

'Casting Newman as a mean materialist is like writing a manifesto against the banking system while juggling your investments to make a fortune.' *(Pauline Kael)*

'*Hud* looms as a landmark film that established the triumphant anti-hero in our movie mythology and provided as well an uncompromising view of the amoral men among us.' *(Judith Crist)*

HUDSON HAWK CT: 1 AV: 2.43

1991 US 100 C THRILLER/COMEDY

D Michael Lehmann ●
W Steven E. de Souza Daniel Waters ● from Bruce Willis's story ●

Bruce Willis ● Danny Aiello Andie MacDowell
Richard E. Grant ● Sandra Bernhard ●
Donald Burton James Coburn

Cat burglar (Bruce Willis) trying to go straight is lured back to using his skills.

Anyone who thinks it's easy to make tongue-in-cheek action movies should be forced to suffer this in its entirety. It's a miserable fiasco, and as horrible a commentary on the banality of Mr Willis's psyche, as *Harlem Nights* was on Eddie Murphy's. The plot is pathetic, the characters puerile, the performances (notably by Richard E. Grant and Sandra Bernhard as the villains) toe-curlingly abysmal.

PRO:

'Fans of Bruce Willis's wisecracking comedy style will enjoy.' *(Martin & Porter)*

MIXED:

'This quirkily amusing piece of vanity film-making is essentially a ludicrously expensive cult movie.' *(Nigel Floyd, Time Out)*

'Blissfully incoherent, with some good action scenes, but nothing to hang them on except a steady stream of Willis wisecracks, only some of which are funny.' *(Maltin)*

ANTI:

'Its utter failure can only be explained by some form

of madness having overcome the people involved in its making.' *(Philip French, Observer)*

'Ever wondered what a *Three Stooges* short would look like with a $40 million budget? Then meet *Hudson Hawk*, a relentlessly annoying clay duck that crash-lands in a sea of wretched excess and silliness.' *(Variety)*

HUE AND CRY

CT: 6 AV: 7.00

(aka *Shoot to Kill*)

1946 GB 82 BW COMEDY/CRIME

D Charles Crichton ☆
W T.E.B. Clarke

Alastair Sim ☆ Jack Warner Harry Fowler Valerie White Frederick Piper

A writer of detective stories (Alastair Sim) and a gang of Cockney children unmask a criminal plot.

This lesser known Ealing comedy is a gently amusing, modestly exciting family film set in blitzed London, photographed with great flair by Douglas Slocombe. It's pacily directed by Charles Crichton, who went on to direct his masterpiece, *The Lavender Hill Mob*, five years later. The children's performances are generally fine, but the piece is lifted into the realms of the sublime by Alastair Sim as a mild-mannered man catapulted into a situation more dangerous than anything he has previously imagined.

ANTI:

'Harry Fowler . . . fails to make the main character credible. And everything depends on believing in him . . . . Crichton has been conscientious, but queer camera angles and shadows can add little thrill when the original material lacks it.' *(Variety)*

PRO:

'Refreshing, bloodtingling and disarming.' *(Richard Winnington)*

'Goes with a swing . . . at once serious enough to be exciting and ironic enough to be funny . . . Occasionally I felt that the timing of action would have been the better for tightening; with a little more precision in direction, passages good as they are might have become first-rate. Charles Crichton's direction of the playing, however, is remarkable.' *(Dilys Powell)*

'What a piece of fun it is! What splendidly preposterous nonsense!' *(C.A. Lejeune)*

'It is a spirited adventure with a mostly juvenile cast which races along at topspeed from one dashing exploit to another and ends with a scene tough enough to set the blood of the chilliest person tingling.' *(A.E. Wilson)*

HUNCHBACK OF NOTRE DAME, THE

CT: 8 AV: 8.53

1939 US 117 BW DRAMA/COSTUME/ROMANCE/HORROR

D William Dieterle ☆
W Sonya Levien Bruno Frank ☆ from Victor Hugo's novel

Charles Laughton ☆ Maureen O'Hara ☆ Cedric Hardwicke ☆ Edmond O'Brien ☆ Thomas Mitchell ☆ Harry Davenport ☆ Walter Hampden Alan Marshal George Zucco Katharine Alexander Fritz Leiber Rod La Rocque

Hunchback (Charles Laughton) saves gypsy girl (Maureen O' Hara) from medieval Parisian mob.

Charles Laughton has a swinging time as perhaps the most likeable monster in cinematic history. Maureen O'Hara looks beautiful and is even more touching than Laughton, who plays a little too much for audience sympathy. Director William Dieterle splendidly evokes the Middle Ages, and Alfred Newman's score deserved its Oscar. Sets, costumes and acting all gell to make this one of the few remakes to surpass the original (a 1923 silent starring Lon Chaney).

ANTI:

'We prefer to cover our eyes when a monstrosity appears, even when we know he's a synthetic monster, compounded of sponge rubber, greasepaint and artifice. Horror films have their following, but children should not be among them. The Music Hall is no place for youngsters this week. Take warning!' *(New York Times)*

'In characters that call for fine diction and fine acting he [Laughton] has made such an impression on the public that it seems a pity he should have taken this excursion into the grotesque. His make-up . . . is yet not repellent enough to give the character its full measure of pathos.' *(Daily Mail)*

MIXED:

'A super thriller-chiller [but it] has its shortcomings. The elaborate sets and wide production sweep overshadows to a great extent the detailed dramatic motivation of the Victor Hugo tale.' *(Variety)*

PRO:

'It exceeds in sheer magnificence any similar film in history. Sets are vast and rich in detail, crowds are immense, and camera uses of both are versatile, varied and veracious.' *(Motion Picture Herald)*

'The art direction and cinematography represent Hollywood at its best and Dieterle's direction gives a harrowing picture of the squalor and cruelty of the Middle Ages. [Percy] Westmore's make-up is as impressive as Chaney's was in the 1923 version.' *(Alan Frank)*

'Although Laughton doesn't attempt the acrobatics

that Lon Chaney performed in the silent version, his hunchback comes across as one of the cinema's most impressive "grotesque" characterisations. Dieterle directs in a way that reminds you of his background as actor/director in the German expressionist cinema: the visuals here impressively recall earlier movies from *Metropolis* (the crowds) to *The Last Laugh* (tracking shots through the shadows). Richly entertaining.' *(Tony Rayns, Time Out)*

HUNDRED MEN AND A GIRL, A: *see* ONE HUNDRED MEN AND A GIRL.

HURRY SUNDOWN CT: 1 AV: 1.88

1967 US 146 C DRAMA

D Otto Preminger ●
W Thomas C. Ryan Horton Foote ● from K.B. Gliden's novel

Michael Caine ● Jane Fonda ● Robert Hooks
John Phillip Law ● Diahann Carroll
Faye Dunaway ● Burgess Meredith

In 1946, a grasping Southern landowner (Michael Caine with an indescribable accent) will stop at nothing to dispossess his black smallholders.

Perhaps the worst-reviewed film of all time. Although *At Long Last Love* must run it close, the extra ingredients of racial offensiveness and juvenile smut give this one the edge. Contains Michael Caine's worst performance outside a Michael Winner film.

PRO:

'An outstanding, tasteful, but hard-hitting, and handsomely-produced film . . . Told with a depth and frankness, the story develops its theme in a welcome, straightforward way that is neither propaganda nor mere exploitation material . . . Michael Caine leads the stars, and delivers an excellent performance.' *(Variety)*

ANTI:

'To criticize it would be like tripping a dwarf.' *(Wilfrid Sheed, Esquire)*

'Otto Preminger's worst, a hopelessly corny, clichéd soap opera . . . Preminger's taste is atrocious. His idea of erotic symbolism is Jane Fonda caressing Michael Caine's saxophone. Like the film, the scene is decidedly off-key.' *(William Wolf, Cue)*

'Critic Wilfrid Sheed wrote recently in *Esquire* that "no movie is ever so bad that you can't find some virtue in it." He must not have seen *Hurry Sundown* . . . Nobody has accused Otto [Preminger] of any particularly noticeable talents in recent years, but this time the Big O (as he is called by his co-workers) has pulled out all the stops in supreme bad taste . . . A slimy, crawling, pitiful obscenity.' *(Rex Reed)*

'An execrable film. Indeed, it is very possibly the worst major production to come out of Hollywood in the 1960s. This statement takes in a lot of territory, but there is a special kind of unredeemed awfulness about the movie that narrows the competition to a very few films . . . Reduction of difficult issues to a discussional level approximating that which obtains in Rex Morgan, MD . . . Much sexual activity presented with such determined bad taste and insensate boorishness that one does not know whether to avert one's eyes or join the adolescent hooting emanating from the balcony.' *(Richard Schickel, Life)*

'A terrible movie . . . meretricious nonsense from start to finish.' *(Brendan Gill, New Yorker)*

'A pantomime version of Greek tragedy.' *(MFB)*

'Crummy, monumentally tasteless . . . Otto Preminger apparently was out of town when the civil-rights movement started and still hasn't checked back in. Nobody told him that the old prewar collection of pickaninnies, Uncle Toms, Uncle Remuses and Little Black Sambos just doesn't stand up any more as a sociological cross section of the black community in the South.' *(Paul D. Zimmerman, Newsweek)*

'Sheer pulp fiction . . . It is a massive mishmash of stereotyped Southern characters and hackneyed melodramatic incidents . . . Totally flimsy in texture and dramatically beyond belief . . . Stereotypes are lifted from the bottom of the Southern cracker barrel . . . An offense to intelligence.' *(Bosley Crowther)*

'I'm sure that Mr Preminger didn't aim at boring viewers or making them laugh at the wrong times, but he's doing just that . . . Dreary, old-fashioned script . . . I doubt if even the scenes in bad taste and those relying on sex symbols to make their point will hold the restless audience.' *(Philip T. Hartung, Commonweal)*

'Superficial and patronizing in its treatment of racial attitudes and tensions, this melodramatic depiction of life in a small Southern town during the 1940s is also frequently prurient and demeaning in its approach to sex.' *(National Catholic Office of Motion Pictures)*

'The cartooning and patronizing of the blacks on hand makes intolerance of everyone and everything involved in this mess a virtue. Although we originally cited this offensively vulgar trash as the worst film of 1967, Preminger's brew of slickness, soap and slobbery in fact ranks with the worst films of all times.' *(Judith Crist)*

HUSBANDS AND WIVES CT: 10 AV: 6.67

1992 US 108 C COMEDY/DRAMA

D Woody Allen ✔
W Woody Allen ☆ AAN

Woody Allen ✔ Judy Davis ☆ AAN Sydney Pollack ☆ Liam Neeson ✔ Mia Farrow Juliette Lewis Lysette Anthony ✔ Blythe Danner

Two middle-aged couples split up; one of them gets back together again.

Strongly disliked by some critics for its bleakness and scrappy visual style, Woody Allen's 'feelbad' movie about marriage is among his sharpest and wittiest. His rough, documentary-style camerawork – a new stylistic departure for him – is designed to be disturbing, to make the audience feel intrusive into his characters' private lives; and the parallels with Allen's private tribulations are painfully apparent. It's a dark, sad but also very funny analysis of modern relationships, with two wonderful central performances by Sydney Pollack and Judy Davis. For the way it combines humour and seriousness and avoids his usual faults of self-pity and pretentious superficiality, this one is right up there among Allen's best work.

ANTI:

'Depressing and disappointing . . . with a heavily autobiographical slant that looks embarrassing in the wake of Allen's family troubles. The characters are boring and unattractive, some seem dragged in simply to poke fun at them, and it's all filmed in an ugly semi-documentary style with hand-held camera, zoom shots and jump cutting . . . How can a film-maker who's produced films of such great beauty have come up with something so scrappy and disjointed?' *(Winnert)*

'Woody must have let one of his kids operate the camera. What other explanation can there be for the extraordinary nausea-inducing, swaying picture? This is yet another Allen pic spent in the company of navel-grazing, angst-ridden, middle-class New Yorkers. Only the astounding performance of Davis marks it out from the others.' *(Rose)*

PRO:

'So vividly drawn are all the characters that one becomes wholly caught up in their tangled whirl of emotional/psychological confusion: though not consistently hilarious, the film is engrossing from start to finish. If the use of handheld camera is occasionally overdone, Allen's decision to shoot and structure his study of mid-life crisis in the style of fly-on-the-wall documentary pays dividends. With excellent performances (Davis and Pollack in particular), it's his finest film since *Hannah and Her Sisters*.' *(Geoff Andrew, Time Out)*

'Beneath the urgency of all the older characters – both men, both women, and even the older dating partners they experiment with – is the realization that life is short, that time is running out, that life sells you a romantic illusion and neglects to tell you that you can't have it, because when you take any illusion and make it flesh, its hair begins to fall out, and it has BO, and it asks you what your sign is. True love involves loving one another's imperfections, which are the parts that tend to endure. Woody Allen's character discovers that in *Husbands and Wives*, although perhaps not in time to help its creator.' *(Roger Ebert)*

'Wonderfully funny, tender and wise.' *(Mail on Sunday)*

'One of Woody Allen's best films to date, combining some of his finest serious writing about relationships, in the style of *Hannah and Her Sisters*, with humor that's all the more effective thanks to its dark, edgy subtext.' *(Virgin)*

HUSTLER, THE AAN CT: 6 AV: 8.85

1961 US 134 BW DRAMA

D Robert Rossen AAN
W Robert Rossen Sidney Carroll AAN from Walter Tevis's novel

Paul Newman ☆ AAN Jackie Gleason ☆ AAN George C. Scott ☆ AAN Piper Laurie ☆ AAN Myron McCormick

An up-and-coming pool hustler (Paul Newman) takes on the unbeatable Minnesota Fats (Jackie Gleason).

The story is predictable, the dialogue overblown and the film could have done with 30 minutes taken out of the middle; the memorable aspect of this movie is the acting – that, and the dark, sleazy claustrophobia of the pool-hall. Newman had to wait 25 years before he won an Oscar for his character (which he reprised in Martin Scorsese's *The Color of Money*), but the film picked up Oscars for cinematography (Eugene Shfftan) and art direction (Harry Horner, Gene Callahan). The film was virtually remade as *The Cincinnati Kid* (1965), with Steve McQueen as a young poker-player. Though much acclaimed in recent film guides, the contemporary critical response was less enthusiastic.

'Belongs to that school of screen realism that allows impressive performances but defeats the basic goal of pure entertainment.' *(Variety)*

'The picture is swollen with windy thoughts and murky notions of perversions . . . but it has strength and conviction, and Newman give a fine, emotional performance.' *(Pauline Kael)*

'Plumbs the unsuspected depths of depravity to which, apparently it is possibleto sink by way of billiards. After seeing this film I should not be surprised to learn that the Vice Squad was investigating ping-pong or that to help addicts get off the hook somebody had formed Golfers Anonymous.' *(Thomas Wiseman, Sunday Express)*

'A hateful film, dredged of any glimpse of spiritual light. But its power is undeniable.' *(Felix Barker, Evening News)*

'It's the sort of film that proves the wilful idiocy of that line about the irrelevance of content strongly plugged by *Cahiers du Cinéma* and their English adherents: shot with immense technical confidence, it still has to deal in humanity and, at a crucial point, it fumbles.' *(John Coleman, New Statesman)*

'Repeated viewings of the movie serve to underline the slickness of the story's resolution which seems more and more to indicate that there's nothing like the loss of a loved one to improve your pool game.' *(Judith Crist)*

I

I AM A FUGITIVE FROM A CHAIN GANG

AAN CT: 8 AV: 9.33

1932 US 90 BW DRAMA

D Mervyn LeRoy ☆
W Sheridan Gibney Brown Holmes
Robert E. Burns ☆

Paul Muni ☆ AAN Glenda Farrell Helen Vinson
Preston Foster Allen Jenkins
Edward J. Macnamara Berton Churchill

Prison turns an innocent man (Paul Muni) into a savage criminal.

Paul Muni gives his most powerful performance in this prison movie milestone, one of Mervyn LeRoy's finest. It's all the more powerful if you realize it's based on the true story of Robert Elliot Burns, who in 1920 stole $5.29 to buy food. He was sent to a Georgia chain gang, escaping two years later. The film was banned in Georgia and the state filed a libel suit against Warner Brothers (though it never came to anything). Drastic reforms of the US penal system followed the film's release. It can still shock, although the supporting performances look awfully one-dimensional. Sol Polito's cinematography is outstanding.

ANTI:

'I quarrel with the production not because it is savage and horrible, but because each step in an inevitable tragedy is taken clumsily, and because each character responsible for the hero's doom is shown more as a caricature than as a person.' *(Pare Lorentz, Vanity Fair)*

PRO:

'A picture with guts.' *(Variety)*

'The American motion picture comes into its estate as a medium for expressing the forces of social behaviour and corrective social thought . . . To be enthusiastically commended for its courage, artistic sincerity, dramatic vigor, high entertainment concept, and social message – the last a word we don't like, but have in all conscience to use.' *(Wilton A. Barrett, NBR)*

'Muni's captivating performance is nothing short of a masterpiece of acting. This marvelous actor, whose 1930s heyday on the screen established the benchmark for acting excellence, stripped away his own identity to assume that of the victim.' *(Baseline)*

I CHANGED MY SEX: *see* GLEN OR GLENDA?

I KNOW WHERE I'M GOING CT: 8 AV: 8.00

1945 GB 91 BW DRAMA/COMEDY/ROMANCE

D Michael Powell Emeric Pressburger ☆
W Michael Powell Emeric Pressburger ☆

Wendy Hiller ☆ Roger Livesey ☆ Pamela Brown
Nancy Price Finlay Currie John Laurie
George Carney Walter Hudd Petula Clark

A young naval officer (Roger Livesey) saves a headstrong girl (Wendy Hiller) from a potentially disastrous marriage.

Quirky Powell and Pressburger film, a Scottish romance starring Wendy Hiller at her most radiant and enchanting. The scenery of the Hebrides is equally lovingly photographed, by Erwin Hillier. The script has great charm; it's a pity, though, that the plot is so slight and predictable.

MIXED:

'Very pleasant . . . Some of this story is told, and charactered with slickness and whimsy as well as genuine lightness; I kept realizing, as I watched and enjoyed it, how shallow and shabby it would probably seem in print. But there are engaging performances by Miss Hiller and Roger Livesey; the sensitive photography and the intelligent if not very imaginative use of sound do more than enough to make eloquent the influence of place on people; and the whole thing is undertaken with a kind of taste and modesty whose absence did much to harm Messrs. Powell and Pressburger's *Stairway to Heaven* and *Black Narcissus*. Theirs is a gentle sort of talent at last, but at times they know very well how to use it, without much concession to their liabilities – inordinate ambition, bumptiousness, and a general unevenness of judgment.' *(James Agee, Nation)*

PRO:

'Continuously fresh and interesting, intelligently written and played, and full of beautiful photography.' *(Richard Mallett, Punch)*

'Communicates an overpowering sense of place . . . The stark sudden hills, the dark waters, the island seen through veils of spray and mist – landscape and seascape here are handled as if they had personalities of their own; one feels the presence of wind and shore in a manner for which I can think of no English parallel except in Brian Desmond Hurst's early film of Synge's *Riders to the Sea*. The shots of the furious sea, the sullen curtain of the approaching storm, the whirlpool in whose gulf the little boat which plies between the islands is nearly lost, are as good as anything of their kind I can remember. And over and above the feeling of the physical setting there persists the feeling of a way of life too, remote and self-contained.' *(Dilys Powell)*

'The most magical romantic comedy ever made in

England. If we hadn't read the credits, we could be forgiven for imagining the hand of a great American director, such as Preston Sturges or Billy Wilder, to be at work here, so sure is the style, so witty the telling of the tale. See this film and weep. You will never see its like again.' *(Ken Russell, 1993)*

'The film's lilting look at the Scottish landscape and people presaged *Local Hero* by forty years.' *(Carrie Rickey)*

I LED TWO LIVES: *see* GLEN OR GLENDA?

I NEVER SANG FOR MY FATHER

CT: 6 AV: 7.20

1970 US 92 C DRAMA

D Gilbert Cates ☆
W Robert Anderson ☆ AAN

Melvyn Douglas ☆ AAN Gene Hackman ☆ AAN Dorothy Stickney Estelle Parsons ☆ Elizabeth Hubbard

A middle-aged widower (Gene Hackman) has plans to remarry, but his father (Melvyn Douglas) has other ideas.

Slow, stagey drama, sensitively directed and superbly acted. Though the screenplay strays into Arthur Miller/Eugene O'Neill territory, it avoids histrionics and contains notably realistic dialogue. However, it lacks a lightness of touch; many episodes of the TV sitcom *Steptoe and Son* made the same points more entertainingly.

PRO:

'It seeks honest and painful answers to the questions of where responsibility to one's parents ends and commitment to oneself begins. These problems are universal, but seldom explored on the screen.' *(Rex Reed)*

'Not often nowadays is one allowed to become gradually, rightfully engaged with characters drawn with such subtlety, with such an accurate weight of life and experience behind their every reaction . . . A distinguished achievement.' *(Derek Prouse, Sunday Times)*

'A jewel of a film . . . No tricks or showing off . . . just a highly intelligent interpretation of a universal and very human theme.' *(Nina Hibbin, Morning Star)*

ANTI:

'Distended and lacking clear point of view . . . Given all the acting talent, the direction, writing and pacing are dreary.' *(Variety)*

'Glum's the word! . . . [The film] misses the intensity and insights that have transformed Arthur Miller's very similar themes into high tragedy . . . In simplifying and concentrating the anguish of several lifetimes into a few fraught days the film tends to take on the one-damn-thing-after-another momentum of a geriatric soap-opera.' *(Margaret Hinxman, Sunday Telegraph)*

I PUGNI IN TASCA: *see* FIST IN HIS POCKET.

I REMEMBER MAMA

CT: 5 AV: 7.45

1948 US 134 BW DRAMA

D George Stevens ☆
W DeWitt Bodeen from John Van Druten's play and Kathryn Forbes's book *Mama's Bank Account*

Irene Dunne ☆ AAN Barbara Bel Geddes ☆ AAN Oscar Homolka ☆ AAN Edgar Bergen ☆ Philip Dorn ☆ Ellen Corby ☆ AAN Cedric Hardwicke Barbara O'Neil Rudy Vallee

An author (Barbara Bel Geddes) remembers her Norwegian-American mother (Irene Dunne).

It's more likely that Grandma will recall this nostalgic, weepie example of mom-worship. A strong ensemble works wonders with the virtually plotless material; George Stevens's direction is strong on detail and warming the heart, but allows scenes to run on for too long.

'Frequently sentimental but never hokey.' *(Variety)*

'Mild but generally gratifying "family" movie.' *(James Agee)*

'There is not much to describe in the way of plot, for *Mama* is merely a set of loosely connected reminiscences about a San Francisco family's domestic crises and humors, and an affectionate portrait of the matriarch of the family. This altogether delightful material has been adapted for filming with conspicuous skill. Carefully avoiding either mawkishness or bathos, George Stevens, executive producer and director, staged it like a man who must have had a mother himself.' *(Fortnight)*

I SOLITI IGNOTI: *see* BIG DEAL ON MADONNA STREET.

I WALKED WITH A ZOMBIE

CT: 6 AV: 7.00

1943 US 69 BW HORROR/ZOMBIE

D Jacques Tourneur ✓
W Curt Siodmak

Frances Dee James Ellison Tom Conway Christine Gordon Edith Barrett James Bell Sir Lancelot

Nurse (Frances Dee) encounters voodoo and zombies in West Indies.

Haunting horror full of suspense and threat, with a plot exhumed from a most unlikely classic: it's *Jane Eyre*, transported to the West Indies. Director Jacques Tourneur skilfully avoids the ludicrous, sensibly avoids pouring scorn on the black characters' religious beliefs, and makes the most of his exotic setting: this is one of the most picturesque of all horror films.

ANTI:

'Fails to measure up to the horrific title. Film contains some terrifying passages, but is overcrowded with trite dialog and ponderous acting.' *(Variety)*

PRO:

'A nightmarishly beautiful tone poem of voodoo drums, dark moonlight and somnambulist ladies in floating white, brought to perfection by Tourneur's direction, Roy Hunt's photography and Ardel Wray's dialogue.' *(Focus on Film)*

'It is Tourneur's caressingly evocative direction, superbly backed by Roy Hunt's cinematographic images, that makes sheer magic of the film's brooding journey into fear by way of voodoo drums, gleaming moonlight, somnambulistic ladies in fluttering white, and dark, silent, undead sentries.' *(Tom Milne, Time Out)*

'The lyrical quality of the long silent passages – Dee and Gordon's nocturnal walk through the mysterious woods, Ellison carrying Gordon toward the ocean while a giant zombie (Darby Jones) follows – the shadows, the lighting, the music, the exotic settings contribute to making this one of the masterpieces of the genre.' *(Danny Peary)*

I WAS A MALE WAR BRIDE CT: 5 AV: 7.22

(aka *You Can't Sleep Here*)

1949 US 105 BW COMEDY

D Howard Hawks ✗
W Charles Lederer Hagar Wilde Leonard Spigelgass from Henri Rochard's novel

Cary Grant ✗ Ann Sheridan ✗ Marion Marshall Randy Stuart Eugene Gericke

A French officer (Cary Grant) has to dress up as a woman to get round American red-tape and marry the girl of his dreams (Ann Sheridan).

It's hard to see why this draggy comedy has acquired a reputation as one of the better screwball farces of the 40s. In undercharacterized leading roles, Ann Sheridan lacks charm, and Grant seems embarrassed. Howard Hawks directs without his usual pace and polish.

PRO:

'Manages to lollop along laughably through a series of situations that might have seemed a shade too risqué and too antique had a lesser artist [than Grant] been involved . . . Miss Sheridan is at all times an agreeable Amazon.' *(Daily Graphic)*

'It is excellent light entertainment but it is not likely to appeal to the prudish and some discretion should be exercised in booking it.' *(CEA Film Report)*

MIXED:

'[The] prelude, despite its coarseness and sparse supply of gags is easily the best section of a thoroughly blowsy version of the sort of thing Hollywood used to do so well.' *(Richard Winnington, News Chronicle)*

'Hackneyed situations, slapstick, impersonations, and risqué lines are all there, and it is due to [Grant and Sheridan] more than to Hawks' rather slapdash handling, that a number of scenes, at least, reappear polished and still funny . . . The camera looks down every derelict Strasse rather wistfully – almost half-expecting to see Dietrich rounding the corner. One cannot help wishing she had.' *(MFB)*

ANTI:

'The whole thing is one of those awful transvestite jokes that never has the grace to go off-color; it all stays at the chortling, wholesome-family-picture level.' *(Pauline Kael)*

I'M ALL RIGHT JACK CT: 8 AV: 7.75

(aka *I'm Alright Jack*)

1959 GB 104 BW COMEDY

D John Boulting
W Frank Harvey John Boulting ☆ from Alan Hackney's novel *Private Life*

Ian Carmichael Peter Sellers ☆ Terry-Thomas Richard Attenborough Irene Handl Liz Fraser Dennis Price John le Mesurier Milles Malleson Margaret Rutherford

A graduate (Ian Carmichael) gaining work experience on the shop floor inadvertently starts a union dispute.

The Boulting Brothers' trenchant satire on industrial relations features many of the familiar British stars of the era, including a delightfully shifty Richard Attenborough, as one of the bosses; but Peter Sellers steals the show with his restrained, wonderfully observed performance as Union organizer Fred Kite. Sellers originally turned down the role as not funny enough.

'The one really funny film satire of . . . labor-management conflicts.' *(Pauline Kael)*

'The film . . . hits out all round . . . Though the workers are shown as lazy and truculent they are not scoundrels; dishonesty is left to the employers. Why then does one feel that *I'm All Right, Jack* is a satire chiefly at the expense of the unions? I fancy that an outstanding comic portrait by Peter Sellers is largely responsible. The employers are parodied; Peter Sellers's shop steward, unblinking, self-important, weighing out his half-educated phrases, is acted . . . Mr Sellers's Fred Kite . . . with his moments of deflation and even pathos gets as near life as you are likely to see in a farcical comedy in the cinema. One can be grateful to the Boulting Brothers for letting that happen. And one can be grateful for their nerve in daring to joke about that sacred institution, trade unionism.' *(Dilys Powell)*

'With a lesser actor, Mr Kite would have been a crass caricature, but Sellers makes him credible – funny, outrageous, pathetic and sympathetic by turns.' *(Ken Russell, 1993)*

I'M GONNA GIT YOU, SUCKA

CT: 7 AV: 5.82

1988 US 89 C COMEDY

D Keenen Ivory Wayans ✔
W Keenen Ivory Wayans

Keenen Ivory Wayans ✔ Bernie Casey Antonio Fargas Steve James Issac Hayes Jim Brown Ja'Net DuBois

Naive young black, Jack Spade (Keenen Ivory Wayans), seeks to avenge the death of his brother, who OGd: that is, dropped dead in the street from wearing too many gold chains.

Does for black exploitation movies (such as *Shaft* and *Superfly*) what Mel Brooks's *Blazing Saddles* did for westerns. The production is knowingly tacky – with, for example, stuntmen look nothing like the stars for whom they double. The gags are many and inventive; and the movie works as a satire on all movies which glorify violence. Underrated – its array of gags is very nearly on a par with *Airplane!* – and great fun.

'I wanted to make a movie that was as funny as *Hollywood Shuffle* or *School Daze*, but I wanted it to be a movie that will take me out of the art houses and into the mainstream . . . As black filmmakers in the 80s we have to prove that we're financially viable.' *(Keenen Ivory Wayans)*

MIXED:

'Has moments of brilliance but doesn't hang together . . . It sounds reasonable when Wayans, co-author of Robert Townsend's *Hollywood Shuffle* and Eddie Murphy's *Raw*, says . . . that he's always wanted to make an affectionate parody of the black exploitation films he saw while growing up. But when you think about it, it's an odd idea; however straight [the originals] may have been played, the element of self-parody was always perilously close to the surface . . . Sadly, much of the movie drags, leaving viewers with far too much time to ponder its deficiencies. Comedy is hard, and *I'm Gonna Git You, Sucka* just isn't bad enough.' *(Maitland McDonagh, Film Journal)*

'Sporadic, but often very funny shafting of the blacksploitation movie of the early 1970s. Aiming at the same audience as *Hollywood Shuffle*, the film lacks Robert Townsend's sure touch and runs out of steam too soon, but it has more than enough great moments to make up for its failings.' *(Trevor Willsmer, Film Review)*

'Antonio Fargas . . . [and] other veteran comedians who are able to rise above the muddled plot perform admirably . . . but there's also some embarrassingly poor acting.' *(Donald Suggs, Village Voice)*

'Wayans has a field day . . . [with this] good-natured sporadically funny bid to mock absurd racial stereotypes in order to destroy them.' *(Sheila Johnston, Independent)*

'The good ideas run out about half an hour before the movie does.' *(Rose)*

PRO:

'An engaging spoof . . . Plenty of cinematic in jokes and some splendid parodies of black stereotypes keep it bubbling to the end.' *(Hugo Davenport, Daily Telegraph)*

'[Wayans] has a nice sense of the absurd, skill at sight gags, and creditable irreverence and the sense to keep his film to a tight 87 minutes.' *(David Robinson, Times)*

I'M NO ANGEL

CT: 8 AV: 8.25

1933 US 88 BW COMEDY

D Wesley Ruggles
W Mae West Harlan Thompson ☆

Mae West ☆ Cary Grant Gregory Ratoff Edward Arnold Ralf Harolde Kent Taylor Gertrude Michael

A carnival entertainer (Mae West) turns society dame and has handsome young men (particularly Cary Grant) in her sights.

Campy, vampy entertainment with Mae West at her snappiest, slinging out the one-liners and double entendres in fine style.

'A rapid-fire entertainment, with shameless but thoroughly contagious humor . . . Miss West plays her part with . . . brightness and naturalness . . . She is a remarkable wit, after her fashion.' *(Mordaunt Hall, New York Times)*

'There is no story . . . It simply sets put to show you how a circus gal climbs to diamond-tiara and sable status by showering her favours on any men who can pay high enough for them . . . You will get at least half a dozen major laughs out of it. Then there are dull stretches, too; and you may find, as I did, that the fun begins to pall towards the end.' *(Sunday Express)*

'Mae paddles her way across the scenes, steering herself with her hips.' *(Welford Beaton, Hollywood Spectator)*

'After Mae West's sexual antics . . . censorship becomes negligible.' *(Paul Rotha, S & S)*

'Arguably West's best film, certainly one of her funniest.' *(Pauline Kael)*

IF . . .

CT: 8 AV: 7.71

1969 GB 107/111 C (BW sequences) DRAMA/ RITES-OF-PASSAGE

D Lindsay Anderson ☆
W David Sherwin

Malcolm McDowell David Wood Richard Warwick Robert Swann Christine Noonan Peter Jeffrey Arthur Lowe Graham Crowden Hugh Thomas

Schoolboys rebel against the authoritarianism of an English public school.

Heavily influenced by Jean Vigo's *Zéro de Conduite*, Lindsay Anderson's film is a high point of 60s cinema. The changes from colour to monochrome, and naturalism to surrealism, are distracting, and the politics are simplistic; but the film caught the 60s spirit of revolt like no other. I particularly enjoyed it, since the school being satirized was very recognizably Tonbridge, which both the writer David Sherwin and I attended. (The film was shot at Anderson's Alma Mater, Cheltenham). Malcolm McDowell leads the rebels against the Establishment.

ANTI:

'They loved it at the Cannes Festival, though. And the comment made to me by an approving Swedish female may, for all I know, typify the universal reception. Looking me straight in the eye, she said brightly, "It certainly makes one understand why the English are so arrogant and stupid." I consoled myself with the belief that she had Mr Lindsay Anderson in mind.' *(Vernon Young)*

'It does suggest that the only way to deal with a corrupt or a decadent society is to wipe it out. That brings up the old question: which came first, the hen or the egg, men or society? And if we destroy society shouldn't we find ourselves re-inventing it?' *(Dilys Powell)*

'Combines a cold and queasy view of youth with a romantic view of violence.' *(New Yorker)*

'Brilliantly captures the sadistic side of the public school system . . . But fantasy has its rules, and you break them at your peril. By resurrecting the padre in the office of the headmaster, and making him exact an apology from the offenders for killing him, Anderson is guilty of cheating. It profoundly diminishes the impact of his message.' *(Ken Russell, 1993)*

MIXED:

'The funny or cruel scenes work very handily; it is only the apocryphal and apocalyptic material that fails to persuade. Yet the film is never uninteresting, seldom unspirited, and there is some sort of intelligence even in its miscalculations.' *(John Simon)*

PRO:

'The general effect is to make you rock with laughter and then send you away for some very serious thinking.' *(Cecil Wilson, Daily Mail)*

'Has a topical revolutionary fervour, fine direction and an insight into the elitist traditions of British public schools.' *(Alexander Walker, Evening Standard)*

'The school . . . is the perfect metaphor for the established system all but a few of us continue to accept.' *(David Wilson)*

'*If* . . . reminds me of a hornet. According to aerodynamic theory, any creature so woefully misdesigned is not supposed to be able to fly at all, and according to such theories of movie construction as I hold, a mixture of film moods and methods like *If* . . . shouldn't be able to get off the ground either. But it does – angry, tough, and full of sting. A public school boy himself, Mr Anderson has obviously thought hard about what happens when unformed adolescents come into conflict with rigidly formed institutions. The result is that his film is felt.' *(Richard Schickel)*

IF I HAD A MILLION

CT: 6 AV: 7.22

1932 US 88 BW COMEDY

D Ernst Lubitsch Norman Taurog Stephen Roberts Norman Z. McLeod John Cruze William A. Seiter H. Bruce Humberstone
W Claude Binyon Whitney Bolton Malcolm Stuart Boylan John Bright Sidney Buchman Lester Cole Isabel Dawn Boyce DeGaw Walter de Leon Oliver H.P. Garrett Harvey Gates Grover Jones Ernst Lubitsch Lawton Mackaill Joseph L. Mankiewicz William Slavens McNutt Seton I. Miller Tiffany Thayer

W.C. Fields ☆ Charles Laughton ☆ May Robson Richard Bennett Alison Skipworth Gary Cooper Wynne Gibson George Raft Jack Oakie Frances Dee

A millionaire (Richard Bennett) gives a million dollars to various strangers, who react in extraordinary ways.

Chaotic, uneven, episodic comedy, worth watching for the hilarious episode starring W.C. Fields getting his own back against road-hogs. The Charles Laughton section pleased audiences at the time (it is said to have been directed by Lubitsch) but seems much weaker now.

ANTI:

'Develops an obvious idea in an obvious way.' *(Time)*

PRO:

'[An] exceedingly novel and entertaining picture. It touches, too, on all the emotions: pathos, drama, tragedy and satire . . . Laughton's *pièce de résistance . . . is as clever as anything he has done.' (Lionel Collier, Picturegoer)*

'Slickly turned out and well-balanced, none of the

episodes falling below a high standard of technical accomplishment.' *(Campbell Nairne, Cinema Quarterly)*

'Out of this Jack Horner pie [Paramount] have pulled a perfectly grand picture . . . a smooth and expert picture. Don't miss it.' *(Photoplay)*

IKIRU CT: 5 AV: 7.50

(aka *Living; To Live; Doomed*)

1952 Japan 143 BW DRAMA/FOREIGN

D Akira Kurosawa ☆
W Akira Kurosawa Hideo Oguni Shinobu Hashimoto

Takashi Shimura ☆ Nobuo Kaneko Kyoko Seki Miki Odagiri Kamatari Fujiwara Makoto Koburi

A minor bureaucrat (Takashi Shimura) learns that he is about to die, and tries to give a meaning to his life.

Touching little story, too doom-laden for most tastes. Shimura is wonderful in the leading role.

ANTI:

'Whether there is a deficiency in the central performance of this story, or whether the awakening and change of direction by the principal character is too arbitrary, I am not sure: but I am conscious of . . . a certain lack of conviction in the total effect.' *(Lindsay Anderson, S & S, 1957)*

MIXED:

'Extremely uneven – there are slick and sentimental passages and some that are impenetrable. But there are also emotional revelations and there's a superb sequence – almost an epiphany – when the dying man, who has accomplished what he hoped to, sits in a swing in the snow and hums a little song.' *(Pauline Kael)*

PRO:

'Dwarfs the major works of the world's best directors . . . [It] gets its gentle tweezers into your conscience, into all the dusty corners you though so peculiarly your own, and begs you to look at yourself . . . Every aspect of [it] is universal . . . I can see no flaws in this film . . . revolutionary in construction and often in technique; yet these values never dominate or distract. [It] probes deeper and with more humanity than the cinema has ever done before. I cannot visualise anything more perfect.' *(Derek Hill, Tribune, 1959)*

'It is worth travelling a long way to see it . . . Underneath [its stoic surface] is a great rage about death, the rage that is one of the deepest sources of art.' *(Penelope Gilliatt, Observer, 1963)*

'Although the movement of Ikiru is extremely low key, the overall emotional impact is quite powerful, with the character of Kanji serving as a metaphor for human individuality in postwar Japan. Though Japanese culture is Kurosawa's main target, this theme easily becomes a universal one.' *(Baseline)*

IL BUONO, IL BRUTTO, IL CATTIVO: *see* GOOD, THE BAD AND THE UGLY, THE.

IL CONFORMISTA: *see* CONFORMIST, THE.

IL DESERTO ROSSO: *see* RED DESERT, THE

IL GATTOPARDO: *see* LEOPARD, THE.

IL LADRO DI BAMBINI: *see* STOLEN CHILDREN, THE.

IL PORTIERE DI NOTTE: *see* NIGHT PORTER, THE

IL VANGELO SECONDO MATTEO: *see* GOSPEL ACCORDING TO SAINT MATTHEW, THE.

IMMORTAL BATTALION, THE: *see* WAY AHEAD, THE.

IMPORTANCE OF BEING EARNEST, THE CT: 8 AV: 7.40

1952 GB 95 C COMEDY/ROMANCE

D Anthony Asquith
W Anthony Asquith from Oscar Wilde's play

Michael Redgrave ☆ Michael Denison ☆ Edith Evans ☆ Margaret Rutherford ☆ Joan Greenwood ☆ Miles Malleson ☆ Dorothy Tutin ☆ Walter Hudd

Two young men (Michael Redgrave, Michael Denison) encounter numerous obstructions on the path to true love.

Anthony Asquith's film is a classic, not by virtue of any visual genius, but because of an array of comedy character-acting which has never been equalled. It helps, of course, that this is the wittiest play ever written.

ANTI:

'A more positive decision on style should have been taken. A film of this kind must be either an adaptation or a piece of filmed theatre. This one, being partially both, is not wholly either.' *(Gavin Lambert)*

'Asquith was trying to persuade me this week that . . . [this] is a film. I hope to see the day when [he] will retract that opinion . . . He should not be deceiving himself about photographed stage plays.' *(Jympson Harman, Evening News)*

MIXED:

'Very well made . . . Asquith has deliberately emphasised the artificiality by presenting it as a play

. . . The wit, after a too deliberate start, glitters like a chandelier.' *(Campbell Dixon, Daily Telegraph)*

'Disappointingly stagey . . . As a record of a theatrical performance, however, it is valuable.' *(Halliwell)*

PRO:

'All the charm and glossy humor of Oscar Wilde's classic emerges faithfully.' *(Variety)*

'The Oscar Wilde play is unlikely ever to be staged with a more impeccable array of performers. Wilde's play is probably the most perfect British comedy since the restoration.' *(Scheuer)*

IN COLD BLOOD CT: 6 AV: 7.27

1967 US 134 BW THRILLER/BIOPIC

D Richard Brooks ☆ AAN
W Richard Brooks AAN from Truman Capote's book

Robert Blake Scott Wilson John Forsythe
Paul Stewart Gerald S. O'Loughlin Jeff Corey

Two young men (Robert Blake and Scott Wilson) murder an innocent family and are put on trial.

Richard Brooks's film of Truman Capote's 'documentary novel' about a famous murder was once considered the ultimate in screen violence: nowadays, it looks relatively restrained. It switches genre with ease between being a road movie, a thriller, a psychological investigation into the mentality of two murderers, and finally an indictment of the Death Penalty. At no point does it fail to grip, and it's helped considerably by Conrad Hall's cinematography and Quincy Jones's score (both Oscar-nominated).

Less successful is Brooks's shifting point of view. He wishes us to feel for the murderers and for their victims, so that one moment we are wanting revenge on the killers, the next moment demanding mercy for them. In its way, the movie epitomizes the strengths and weaknesses of the 60s. In being so studiously non-judgmental, it deepens our understanding of an apparently motiveless act. But in trying to make us see things from every point of view, it fails to develop a coherent moral standpoint of its own.

PRO:

'It's not exactly my book but it's a hell of a movie.' *(Truman Capote)*

'Probing, sensitive, tasteful, balanced and supenseful.' *(Variety)*

'Not the unnecessary study in horror which some people have feared. It is glacial; but it is salutary; it is moral.' *(Dilys Powell)*

'One of the best true-crime films of the cinema.' *(Judith Crist)*

ANTI:

'Continually shifts its ground: now it is full of compassion for the victims, now for the murderers; now it makes you root for a speedy come-uppance, now for mercy and abolition of capital punishment . . . Complexity is one thing, inconsistency another.' *(John Simon)*

'The first half of the film looks promising; the second half becomes boring. The trouble is that Brooks has focused almost entirely on the killers and their sick minds and childhood dreams. Consequently the movie is motivated by the kind of facile Freudianism that is supposed to have gone out in the Forties . . . The whiplash documentary style of much of the photography clashes with the tired German expressionism of dreams and hallucinations, and the mixture is a bit dishonest besides, in that it places an aura of subjectivity around the killers and around no one else. In the book the dead and even the detectives were allowed the dignity of their own dreams and reveries.' *(Andrew Sarris, Confessions of a Cultist, 1970)*

'Unnecessarily complicated as narrative, and uncompromisingly brutal in treatment, this well-meaning film is hard to take in many ways.' *(Halliwell)*

IN THE HEAT OF THE NIGHT AAW CT: 7 AV: 8.23

1967 US 109 C THRILLER

D Norman Jewison ☆ AAN
W Sterling Silliphant ☆ AAW

Sidney Poitier ☆ Rod Steiger ☆ AAW Lee Grant ☆
Warren Oates Quentin Dean William Schallert
Scott Wilson

A black detective (Sidney Poitier) tries to help a redneck southern sheriff (Rod Steiger) solve a murder in Mississippi.

An enjoyable enough thriller and superbly photographed, but overrated on release because of its civil rights message. The plot is disappointing, but the developing relationship between the two leads is well written and amusingly played. Hal Ashby's editing won an Oscar, as did the sound crew. Poitier appeared in a couple of inferior sequels, *They Call Me Mister Tibbs* and *The Organization*.

MIXED:

'A very nice film and a very good film and yes, I think it's good to see a black man and a white man working together . . . but it's not going to take the tension out of New York City; its not going to stop the riots in Chicago.' *(Rod Steiger)*

'The plot itself is so full of holes that it will scarcely bear examination, and the fact that this does not disturb one in the least during the film is in itself a tribute to the skill of the writing and to the firm control of Norman Jewison's direction . . . A murder mystery seldom gives rise to such a splendidly integrated entertaining and disturbing film.' *(MFB)*

'Looking back, I see that most of the truth in this movie was in Steiger's performance and in Haskell Wexler's really masterful camera work, which definitively captured the look of the American small town today – neon and false fronts over decay . . . So if it wasn't the best American film of the year, as I said it was, it was at least an honorable and craftsmanlike little movie in which at least a couple of the craftsmen quite transcended the natural limits of their material. Considering the way things have been going, that's rather good going.' *(Richard Schickel, Life, 1972)*

PRO:

'An American movie of great distinction . . . Sidney Poitier adds a new dimension to the Noble Negro he has been portraying recently, providing a streak of bigotry and tension that gives superb complement to Steiger. Theirs is a remarkable duet.' *(Judith Crist, NBC-TV Today Show)*

'A film that is as fresh as this one deserves to be seen by fresh eyes and savored by fresh minds.' *(Joseph Morgenstern, Newsweek)*

'Beyond the taut thriller elements, Jewison brings truth to the thesis that despite ignorance and prejudice and mistrust men can reach understanding and even affection through common cause.' *(Judith Crist)*

'Fast and enjoyable, with Poitier's color used for comedy. He's like a black Sherlock Holmes in a *Tom-and-Jerry* cartoon of reversals. For once it's funny (instead of embarrassing) that he's superior to everybody else.' *(Pauline Kael)*

IN THE LINE OF FIRE CT: 9 AV: 6.25

1993 US 125 C THRILLER

D Wolfgang Petersen ☆
W Jeff Maguire ☆ AAN

Clint Eastwood ☆ John Malkovich ☆ AAN
Rene Russo ✔ Dylan McDermott ✔ Gary Cole

Presidential bodyguard (Clint Eastwood) has to protect his boss from an expert assassin (John Malkovich).

At an age when most actors are resigned to playing character parts, Clint Eastwood remains at his most compulsively watchable. And director Wolfgang Petersen (who first showed his talent with *Das Boot*) produces a blend of excitement and comedy, suspense and romance, which bears comparison with the best of Hitchcock.

Jeff Maguire's screenplay takes pains to supply Malkovich's hit-man with a believable motive and background, and Petersen's direction skilfully concentrates on the minutiae of his preparation. The result is the most chilling picture of a professional assassin since *The Day of the Jackal*. Even the inevitable romantic sub-plot fleshes out the characters much beyond the usual dimensions: it's superbly played by Eastwood and Rene Russo, as a more mature Benedick and Beatrice. Eastwood is both funny and irritating as he needles his fellow FBI agent (Russo) for being feminist 'window-dressing'.

MIXED:

'Although the script is generally credible (the film is the first to have the co-operation of the usually arcane Secret Service), the dialogue is occasionally over-the-top. "Well, Abe," Horrigan says to the Lincoln Memorial statue, "Damn, I wish I could have been there for you, pal." The film also tastelessly exploits Kennedy's memory: Horrigan, it is revealed, once pretended that one of the president's mistresses was in fact his girlfriend in order to protect the boss's reputation. And . . . a painfully unimaginative love interest is superimposed on the psychological drama.' *(Scott Steele, Maclean's)*

'Though the movie is engrossing, it lacks something: fire, weirdness, originality. The director, Wolfgang Petersen (*Das Boot*), knows how to cobble a scene together, but he's not exactly a wizard at pace. At times, Petersen seems to be aping the sleek existential doom of Oliver Stone's *JFK*, but that was a dazzling labyrinth of a movie, one willing to open raw wounds. *In the Line of Fire* is just a moody popcorn thriller, and, what's more, it seems almost completely derived from other popcorn thrillers.' *(Owen Gleiberman, Entertainment Weekly)*

'Malkovich . . . always seems effete even when he's playing a manic killer. There is much ponderous palaver about the whole thing being a game and about the supposed similarities between Eastwood and Malkovich.' *(Ralph Novak, People Weekly)*

'The movie can exasperate when it embraces – and this is the last time we'll point this out, Hollywood, so listen up – the cockamamie conventions of the thriller genre: the buddy-partner who announces his retirement, then dies violently; the smart female officer who's around for window dressing and romantic relief; the pot-bellied villain who is more athletic than the slim, trim hero; and the mandatory climactic chase, in which the bad guy loads his gun, the good guy careers across town, and the moviegoer checks his watch.' *(Richard Corliss, Time)*

PRO:

'Once again demonstrates Eastwood's power to enlarge a film through his persona . . . his role here, as a Lord Jim of the Secret Service, overflows its original dimensions and involves more elements than may have been bargained for. His guilt – at failing to save a president who (he thinks) might have greatly benefited America's future – becomes symbolic of a vague, oppressive national guilt.' *(Stanley Kauffmann)*

'John Malkovich . . . [is] the most delicious villain since Hannibal Lecter.' *(Rod Lurie, LA Magazine)*

'No new heights are scaled in the film, but neither does the tension ever sloppily subside. The overconscientious and aging Horrigan is hampered by colleagues and superiors, there are costly rivalries between members of the Secret Service and the CIA, there is a series of well-staged ancillary killings and many a rousing foot chase, always more rewarding than car chases.' *(John Simon)*

'Builds meticulously to a heart-stopping climax; creates at least three strong, believable characters (four if you count Dylan McDermott's wimpish rookie agent); gives a twist to the classic American theme of second chances; and is salted with wit.' *(Quentin Curtis, Independent on Sunday)*

'Respects the audience by taking itself seriously, but through Frank's wry humour and Booth's black wit In *The Line of Fire* is far more amusing than recent comedy-thrillers. A lovely scene where Frank and a female Secret Service colleagure (Rene Russo) make their amorous way towards a hotel bed discarding handcuffs, guns and blackjacks along with their clothes, is funnier than anything in a *Naked Gun* parody, yet also oddly tender and romantic.' *(Philip French, Observer)*

IN THE NAME OF THE FATHER AAN

CT: 7 AV: 8.50

1994 US 135 C DRAMA

D Jim Sheridan ☆ AAN
W Terry George Jim Sheridan ✗ AAN

Daniel Day-Lewis ☆ AAN Pete Postlethwaite ☆ AAN
Emma Thompson ✗ AAN Don Baker ✓
Corin Redgrave John Lynch

After an IRA bombing, several innocent Irish people are picked on as scapegoats.

Jim Sheridan's docu-drama about the Guildford Four is not pro-IRA. The horrific bombing at Guildford is the first event we see, and it haunts the rest of the picture. The one, self-confessed bomber (a chilling performance by Don Baker) is portrayed not as a freedom-fighter, but as a gangster. The moral centre of the movie is Giuseppe Conlon (Pete Postlethwaite), a non-political Catholic with no sympathy for bombers. The film is partly the story of how he changes from well-meaning naivety – 'Sure an' I'm almost visitin' here meself,' he tells his wife and daughters perkily on their first prison visit – into a grimly determined campaigner. Perhaps the screenplay goes overboard in suggesting he is some kind of secular saint (if he was that good a father, how come his son Gerry was such a mess?), but Postlethwaite plays him so beautifully that he is a character whom any audience will take to its heart.

The star of the show, however, is Giuseppe's son Gerry (Daniel Day-Lewis). Little attempt is made to whitewash him; and Day-Lewis gives a breathtaking performance. He starts out a shambling oaf, a petty thief and liar, with a crooked grin and a refusal to look anyone in the eye. He passes through a 'hard-man' flirtation in prison with the IRA, mainly in rebellion against his father's pacifism: 'You're better off being guilty,' he exclaims bitterly. 'At least you get some respect.' And he ends up a more self-aware, educated man than if he had never gone to prison.

Jim Sheridan's film lives up technically to the two magnificent central performances: Peter Biziou's cinematography and Gerry Hambling's editing put it on the same level as the glossiest Hollywood feature. It is gripping, splendidly made and succeeds triumphantly as fiction.

But this is not fiction: it is that hybrid known as faction, and it is riddled with intentional inaccuracies. The Conlons are shown sharing a cell for years, when often they were not even in the same prison. That could be considered dramatic licence, especially in a film whose central theme is the development of a father-son relationship – but it made me wonder if Conlon *père et fils* ended up quite as close and sympathetic to one another as they do here.

Just as questionable, and far more significant, is the change whereby the entire campaign to get them released is personified by one woman, the Conlons' solicitor Gareth Pierce – played most unconvincingly by Emma Thompson as a kind of dotty aunt. This seems at first a harmless simplification, until you realise that it gives an entirely misleading impression: that the whole of the legal, political and media establishment was against the Guildford Four. Tell that to Lord Devlin, Lord Scarman, Robert Kee and Yorkshire TV.

The final courtroom showdown, in which Thompson – miraculously transformed for the occasion into a hot-shot barrister – produces startling new evidence not only over-dramatizes the truth: it is so stagey that it borders on the risible. The unfortunate effect is to make you question how much of what has gone before has been just as much of a fantasy.

Easily the most misleading aspect of Sheridan's movie lies not in its narrative simplifications, but in its portrayal of the Irish as second-class British citizens. 'All second class passengers boarding now!' booms the tannoy as Gerry Conlon leaves Ireland for the mainland, just to emphasize the point. Inside prison, the people immediately sympathetic to the Conlons are black: the implication, especially for the American audience at whom this film is primarily aimed, is that the Ulster problem is an issue of Civil Rights, and about fighting back against racist, patriarchal oppression.

Now this may mirror the Conlons' developing father-son relationship very neatly; but it bears precious little relation to the reality of the Northern Ireland situation. This is not – if one is to use the family analogy – a case of a heavy-handed Victorian father exerting arbitrary power over long suffering sons and daughters. It is much more a problem of warring brothers and sisters, with the 'fatherland' more than willing to hand over power were the siblings to behave in a more sensible and civilized fashion.

Where the film is so unjust to the vast majority of the British public, is that it is shown throughout as people calling for the heads of the Guildford Four. Yet most Britons did not want scapegoats for the Guildford bombing: they wanted the real bombers caught. The miscarriage of justice in the case came about not primarily because of British racism or imperialism, but because of the eagerness of the police and judiciary to rely on flawed forensic evidence (which, to do them justice, they may not have realized was inconclusive) and to ignore evidence which did not fit in with their preconceived ideas: presumably the police regarded Gerry Conlon's alibi, a vagrant named Charlie Burke, as an unreliable witness and leapt to the presumptuous conclusion that a court would think the same.

In taking a much more simplistic attitude, the film-makers are guilty of the same crimes which they attempt to pin on the British Establishment: namely, knee-jerk racism and the invention of scapegoats. For the purposes of this film, virtually all the guilt is laid on one senior English policeman, Robert Dixon. But he is a fictitious creation, who works very well as a melodramatic stereotype: an obsessive, avenging fury, like Javert pursuing the innocent Valjean in *Les Misérables*. His surname is presumably a satirical comment about how far the police sometimes fall short of their kindly P.C.Dixon image. But the film might have been more realistic had the forces of law and order been shown to be misguided, rather than malicious.

'Faction' is a dangerous form of screen drama, not least when dramatic distortions can easily be made – as here – to serve the purposes of republican propaganda, or even bomb-planting extremists.

PRO:

'The barrister who works furiously for the innocent prisoners' release is Emma Thompson. The screenplay never tells us who engaged her to fight the cause she is steeped in or whether it's *pro bono*, but we're so glad she is doing it that we don't care. The courtroom speech in which she presents the suppressed evidence is magnificent.' *(Stanley Kauffmann)*

'Sobering and brutal.' *(Rod Lurie, LA Magazine)*

MIXED:

'Some of the weaknesses of script and structure are obscured by the power of Day-Lewis' performance; he proves here once again that he is one of the most talented and interesting actors of his generation.' *(Roger Ebert)*

'Sheridan doesn't get into the ugly complexities of the Irish troubles – the tangled hatred between Catholics and Protestants. Yet he does something almost as revealing when he introduces Joe McAndrew (Don Baker), an ice-blooded IRA leader who, in prison, carries on his anti-British war with a meticulous ruthlessness that seems practically psychotic. When Gerry comes eye-to-eye with McAndrew, who's presented as a false, evil patriarch, he finally confronts the full force of the hatred that has been tearing his homeland apart. And only when he accepts the love of his own father do those same forces stop tearing at him. In the end, Gerry triumphs over injustice – but, even more stirringly, over the troubles in his own soul.' *(Owen Gleiberman, Entertainment Weekly)*

ANTI:

'The truth was sickening enough and needed no embroidery.' *(George Perry, Sunday Times)*

IN THE REALM OF THE SENSES

CT: 5 AV: 6.86

(aka *Ai No Corrida; Empire of the Passions; Empire of the Senses; L'Empire des Sens*)

1976 Japan 105 C DRAMA/ROMANCE/FOREIGN

D Nagisa Oshima ✗
W D Nagisa Oshima

Tatsuya Fuji ● Eiko Matsuda ☆ Aoi Nakajima Maika Seri Taiji Tonoyama Hiroko Fuji Naomi Shiraishi Kyoko Okada Kikuhei Matsunoya Yasuko Matsui

The story is of an obsessive, adulterous affair between a married Japanese inn-keeper (Tatsuya Fuji) and a young prostitute (Eiko Matsuda) with a friendly but unhygienic approach to food preparation. One particular trick she does with an egg gives new meaning to the phrase 'getting laid'. Their relationship takes on increasingly sado-masochistic overtones until in the end – by mutual agreement – she strangles him. The final scene, where she hacks off his genitalia as a memento, is guaranteed to make any man wince.

In The Realm of the Senses has spent most of its existence in the realm of the censors. Not surprisingly: the sex scenes are as explicit as in any hardcore porn movie, and constitute much of the film. The film rises above the pornographic norm only in the exoticism of the setting, and in Miss Matsuda's memorable portrayal of doomed sexual obsession. It resembles the worst pornography in that all other characterization is at a minimum. The leading man looks uncomfortable throughout and has an unfortunate tendency to snigger at inopportune moments: he might make a passable Demon King in panto, but here he fails to rise to the occasion, except in the most basic possible way.

Because the film is based on reality and set in 1936, a time of increasing Japanese militarism, critics have been quick to see it as an anti-nationalistic metaphor. As if to encourage this view, the director includes a shot of our hero walking to his final, fatal sex session, and encountering Japanese infantrymen marching in the opposite direction, presumably into China.

Such critics see the central love affair as a symbolic revolt against the taboos of a repressive society. This interpretation ignores the inconvenient fact that the happy couple are regarded with great tolerance by most of those around them, and even inspire some onlookers to join in. Nor do the hero or heroine suggest by a single word or facial expression that they have the least interest in politics. They have more pressing concerns.

The film's 'sexual politics' have also been commended, perhaps because the woman is usually on top (both mentally and geographically), and the man ends up castrated. One problem with this feminist interpretation is that the heroine is clearly shown as becoming more and more deranged. In one sequence (previously unseen in this country), she even initiates child sexual abuse – although fortunately, in the one moment of restraint during the whole picture, it is not fully enacted for our edification.

Unfortunately for the feminist interpretation, too, this is one of the more spectacularly phallocentric movies of our time. The heroine is obsessed with the man's penis, treating it as a wild beast, tamable only through death. It is no accident that the red of her clothing resembles the cloak of a matador, or that the gruesome climax resembles the moment when a matador cuts the ears and tail from a dead bull. Indeed, the film's original Japanese title, *Ai No Corrida*, means 'Love's Bullfight'. I suppose you could say it's a cock and bull story.

Basically the film is little more than erotica. All kinds of intellectual pretensions have been read into it by people who should know better and who argue that *In The Realm of The Senses* is great art not because it is, but because they disapprove of censoring erotic films. Still, I doubt whether the film will deprave or corrupt anyone over 18: it is much more likely to titillate, and then to bore.

PRO:

'By the final sequence, we are all implicated in the continuing social system which makes such love impossible. It is not de Sade, but the censor in all of us who ultimately wields the knife.' *(Jan Dawson, MFB)*

'Pretty explicit stuff . . . [It] is a colourful, claustrophobic film that deserves an audience if only to confront the idea that it is OK to have violence in the cinema but not sexual relations between consenting adults.' *(Sue Heal, Today, 1991)*

ANTI:

'An Oriental Elvira Madigan undressed, exalted for some by its closeups of screwing.' *(Stanley Kauffmann)*

'The few moments of genuine artistic and cinematic beauty are eclipsed by poorly-lit scenes shot in cramped paper-walled rooms with the wavering sub-titles . . . mocking in their banality. Shades of *Carry on Up the Kawasaki* . . . You can almost hear Sid James cackling . . . Instead of a plot, there is a cliché . . . The story thickens to the consistency of consommé . . . It is not art, it is anaesthetic.' *(Derek Bateman, Glasgow Herald, 1980)*

'I was distinctly unsettled . . . Actually watching people having sex can be quite interesting. Nevertheless, I feel that Oshima's film is aesthetically a failure and morally degraded, partly because it raises questions that have nothing to do with the theme of sexual obsession that the film explores so uncompromisingly . . . Somehow [the film] violates the privacy both of the audience and the actors.' *(Sean French, New Statesman and Society, 1991)*

IN THE WOODS: *see* RASHOMON.

IN WHICH WE SERVE AAN   CT: 8   AV: 8.50

1942 GB 115 BW WAR/DRAMA

D Noel Coward AAW ('for outstanding production achievement') David Lean ☆
W Noel Coward ☆ AAN

Noel Coward ☆ Bernard Miles ☆ John Mills ☆ Kay Walsh Joyce Carey Michael Wilding James Donald Celia Johnson ☆

Survivors of a German torpedo attack recall their lost ship.

One of those war films which can still bring a lump to the throat. This was Coward's finest hour as a screen actor, playing a character closely modelled on his friend Lord Mountbatten, in a film based on the exploits of his ship *HMS Kelly*. And it was the first film to be directed by David Lean (until then an editor). The underlying message is that even the class-ridden British can band together in time of war: what a shame that peacetime films never seem to reflect the same positive spirit. Voted best picture of the year by the New York Film Critics.

'One of the screen's proudest achievements at any time and in any country.' *(Newsweek)*

'The surprising thing about [it] is not that Coward ventured it . . . but that he has been technically elastic enough to strip the green carnation from his lapel, toss aside his Savile Row raiment, and convincingly work up a proletarian sweat that to the eyes and olfactory organs seems as authentic an article as that distilled by such practiced literary ditch-diggers as Steinbeck and Odets.' *(Herb Sterne, Rob Wagner's Script)*

'The finest war drama produced yet and because of the strength of its understatement and recognition occasionally of human weakness is propaganda of the very best sort. It should be seen by all.' *(MFB)*

'Never at any time has there been a reconstruction of human experience which could touch the savage grandeur and compassion of his production.' *(Howard Barnes, New York Herald Tribune)*

'Like a hymn to human nobility, staunchness, friendship and love.' *(Guardian)*

'We must recognize the technical skill, the command of the medium which has gone to its making. The authority with which the complex strands of the narrative are handled, the mastery of simple, unemphatic dialogue, the easy unobtrusive use of camera angle and movement – all are here. And the acting was pretty near faultless . . . *In Which We Serve* took a handful of typically British men and women and made from their stories, ordinary enough in themselves, a distillation of national character.' *(Dilys Powell)*

INCHON   CT: 5 AV: 2.50

1981 US/Korea 140/105 C WAR/SO BAD

D Terence Young
W Robin Moore Laird Koenig ●

Laurence Olivier ● Jacqueline Bisset ● Ben Gazzara Richard Roundtree David Janssen Toshiro Mifune Rex Reed ●

General MacArthur (Laurence Olivier), aided and abetted by God, wins the Korean War.

This $46,000,000 turkey was co-financed by a Japanese newspaper publisher (Mitsuharu Ishii) and – though this was only belatedly made known – by Reverend Sun Myung Moon of the Unification Church (more usually known as The Moonies). Although director Terence Young and cinematographer Bruce Surtees handle the battle scenes with reasonable competence, they can't do much about the ludicrously simple-minded, anti-Communist script – and someone might have done something about the elementary continuity errors which make Laurence Olivier's trousers change colour from shot to shot, and Richard Roundtree come back to life unscathed after a deadly explosion.

Olivier tries to render himself unrecognizable under a ton of make-up in arguably his most demeaning screen performance (and there are plenty to choose from). He was paid $1.25 million, but surely the man had some pride? At the other end of the acting profession, film critic Rex Reed continues his kamikaze on-screen career: his previous film was another disaster, *Myra Breckenridge* (1970). He would be ill-advised to give up his day job.

'The most blatant anti-Communist war movie since *The Green Berets* . . . An ear-shattering B-movie with ambitions . . . [which] only Olivier . . . comes near to realising . . . [He] brings out [MacArthur's] character and mannerisms brilliantly.' *(Alexander Walker Evening Standard)*

'Hysterical . . . The most expensive B-movie ever made . . . Olivier sends up the film and his employers with such zest – and so politely – that there must have been no way he could be decently restrained.' *(Vincent Canby, New York Times)*

'All plot digressions are simply window-dressing to the film's focus on the brutally invading North Koreans and the big-scalecounter-attack by the good guys. No speaking roles are given to the Communists, for example.' *(Variety)*

'The movie attributes the "winning" of the Korean War to an act of God. It may take more than that to foist this wreck off on the American public.' *(J. Hoberman, Village Voice)*

'As military spectacles go, one of the sorriest in military history . . . One has not seen a heroine's hairdo stay so splendidly in place, no matter what her travail, since the 1940s.' *(Richard Schickel, Time)*

'A near total loss as well as a laugh.' *(Bruce Williamson, Playboy)*

'The worst movie ever made, a turkey the size of Godzilla . . . Actually *Inchon* isn't really a film, it's a grotesque footnote in movie history.' *(Jack Kroll, Newsweek)*

'Quite possibly the worst movie ever made . . . stupefyingly incompetent.' *(Peter Rainer, Los Angeles Herald Examiner)*

'It's a terrible movie.' *(Inchon's distributors, MGM/UA)*

INDECENT PROPOSAL   CT: 5 AV: 4.88

1992 US 117 C DRAMA

D Adrian Lyne
W Amy Holden Jones

Robert Redford Demi Moore Woody Harrelson Oliver Platt Seymour Cassell Billy Connolly Billy Bob Thornton Rip Taylor

A millionaire (Robert Redford) pays a million bucks for one night with a nice, impoverished suburban wife (Demi Moore).

The stuff of which fantasies are made, and a big hit. The film's marketing strategy suggested that this was a 'woman's picture', but really it's centred on husband Woody Harrelson's guilt and jealousy. Becoming a pimp is, according to the filmmakers, much more of a big deal for a guy than becoming a whore is for a woman. Demi, though portrayed initially as an intelligent career woman, takes to prostitution like a duck to orange sauce. By the end, she's such a little fluffy-head that Redford has to fool her into going back to Woody. It's an interesting view of the female sex – but not one that any thinking woman is likely to feel happy about.

The movie is, like so many of British director Adrian Lyne's essays in misogyny – from *Fatal Attraction* to *9½ Weeks* – a glorification of masculine domination, with the equation between financial power and virility stressed to unintentionally comic effect. Redford's neo-classical mansion, all vertical lines and towering columns, is a massive display of phallic super-confidence. Towards the end, Woody is allowed to rise erect from his limp, crumpled, horizontal position. He shows he has regained his masculinity and thus his renewed right to Demi (ludicrously, he wows his female architecture students at the same time) by standing and rhapsodizing about the spires of Barcelona.

The predictably happy ending is reached by a patently phoney plot device. Redford's character is, for 99% of the movie, a Mephistophelean figure. All we know about him is that he is motivated by power, sexual attraction, and ruthless acquisitiveness. At the last moment, this wolf in chic clothing turns into Mother Teresa – for no better reason than that the Cinemagoing Audience and Popular Morality demand it. It's too sudden, and laughably unconvincing. Besides, the movie's imagery is geared to precisely the opposite conclusion. Moore looks gawky and adolescent when she's with Harrelson: with Redford, she looks like a million dollars. Lyne's direction lingers so seductively over her life with Redford that there's no question about it: wealth can buy happiness.

This underlying philosophy is hammered home in the final image. The climactic moment between Moore and Harrelson takes place on a pier: in other words, at the same time as they're playing a romantic reconciliation, the subliminal message is that the wife has been tricked into sacrificing life in the fast lane for a dead end existence. There's no doubt that *Indecent Proposal* will find an audience for its celebration of American materialism and financial power. It is a memorable exercise in Hollywood hypocrisy.

'What *(Pretty Woman, The Crying Game)* and *Indecent Proposal* all do brilliantly is to allow the audience to be voyeurs while acceptable people do unacceptable things. We might not admit we'd be intrigued by the idea of sleeping with a hooker, or accepting a million bucks for a night of sex, or accepting Jaye Davidson on rather unexpected terms. But we ARE intrigued by movies in which the plots somewhat plausibly present Richard Gere, Demi Moore or Stephen Rea with such a choice.' *(Roger Ebert)*

'The moral underpinning of the film is weakened by the fact that the millionaire in question is Redford and not, say, Danny DeVito.' *(Rose)*

'*Honeymoon in Vegas* without the laughs.' *(Quinlan)*

'Great hook, crap movie.' *(Trevor Johnson, Time Out)*

INDIANA JONES SERIES

RAIDERS OF THE LOST ARK AAN

CT: 9 AV: 8.06

1981 US 115 C ACTION/ADVENTURE

D Steven Spielberg ☆ AAN
W Lawrence Kasdan ✔ from George Lucas and Philip Kaufman's story

Harrison Ford Karen Allen Paul Freeman John Rhys-Davies Denholm Elliott Alfred Molina Anthony Higgins

Archaeologist (Harrison Ford) searches for the Ark of the Covenant.

Steven Spielberg's tribute to Boy's Own adventure is one of the most exciting action movies ever made, even if it never quite lives up to its opening sequence. Harrison Ford is very nearly credible as the world's most macho archaeologist; and despite its furious pace the movie is not without wit and charm. Audiences quite rightly ignored the more curmudgeonly critics and made this one of the top 10 moneymakers of all time. It won Oscars for art direction (Norman Reynolds, Leslie Dilley, Michael Ford), editing (Michael Hahn), visual effects, sound, and sound effects editing, and received nominations for cinematography (Douglas Slocombe) and score (John Williams).

ANTI:

'Children may well enjoy its simple-mindedness, untroubled by the fact that it looks so shoddy and uninventive.' *(Observer)*

'Both *de trop* and not enough.' *(S & S)*

'Kinesthetically, the film gets to you, but there's no exhilaration, and no surge of feeling at the end. It seems to be edited for the maximum number of showings per day.' *(Pauline Kael)*

'In the New Hollywood, the "fun" of Hawks's adventure films has been reduced to a matter of special effects and a frantic montage taking center stage from a hero who is mostly lacking in moral dimensions and is not required to take decisive action (or, indeed, any action: Jones passively sits out the climax of the film) . . . [It is] characterized by narrative incoherence; a *mise-en-scène* that highlights special effects and is fractured by a supercharged editing pattern, and an emphasis on action totally devoid of a moral dimension.' *(James Bernardoni, The New Hollywood, 1991)*

PRO:

'If George Lucas were to say that he could make a terrific entertainment out of Chairman Mao's *Little Red Book*, at this point I'd be inclined to believe him.' *(Hollywood Reporter)*

'An out-of-body experience, a movie of glorious imagination and breakneck speed that grabs you in the first shot, hurtles you through a series of incredible adventures, and deposits you back in reality two hours later – breathless, dizzy, rung-out, and with a silly grin on your face.' *(Roger Ebert)*

INDIANA JONES AND THE TEMPLE OF DOOM CT: 6 AV: 5.71

1984 US 118 C ACTION/ADVENTURE/FAMILY

D Steven Spielberg
W Willard Huyck Gloria Katz from George Lucas's story

Harrison Ford Kate Capshaw Ke Huy Quan Amrish Puri Roshan Seth Philip Stone David Yip

The world's most athletic archaeologist (Harrison Ford) searches for a scared stone in 1935.

Prequel to *The Raiders of the Lost Ark*. The attitude of the film towards the Indian characters is patronizing; and the heroine (Kate Capshaw, later to become Mrs Spielberg) is a pain. But the film is exciting, amusing and moves at a whip-cracking pace; though the weakest of the three *Indiana Jones* movies, it's still enjoyable. It won an Oscar for best visual effects, and was nominated for John Williams's score.

PRO:

'One of the most sheerly pleasurable comedies ever made.' *(Pauline Kael)*

'One of the most relentlessly nonstop action pictures ever made, with a virtuoso series of climactic sequences that must last an hour and never stop for a second. It's a roller-coaster ride, a visual extravaganza, a technical triumph, and a whole lot of fun . . . The most cheerfully exciting, bizarre, goofy, romantic adventure movie since *Raiders*, and it is high praise to say that it's not so much a sequel as an equal.' *(Roger Ebert)*

ANTI:

'A thin, arch, graceless affair.' *(Observer)*

'A two-hour series of none too carefully linked chase sequences . . . sitting on the edge of your seat gives you a sore bum but also a numb brain.' *(Guardian)*

'Spielberg has gone to such lengths to avoid boredom that he has leaped squarely into the opposite trap: this movie has such unrelenting action that it jackhammers you into a punch-drunk stupor.' *(Jack Kroll, Newsweek)*

'Exhausting and numbing.' *(Variety)*

'An astonishing violation of the trust people have in Spielberg's and Lucas's essentially good-natured approach to movies primarily intended for kids.' *(Ralph Novak, People)*

INDIANA JONES AND THE LAST CRUSADE CT: 7 AV: 6.91

1989 US 127 C ACTION/ADVENTURE/FAMILY

D Steven Spielberg ☆
W Jeffrey Boam from George Lucas and Menno Meyjes' story

Harrison Ford ✔ Sean Connery ☆ Denholm Elliott ☆ Alison Doody John Rhys-Davies Julian Glover River Phoenix Michael Byrne Kevork Malikyan Robert Eddison Richard Young Alexei Sayle

Archaeologist (Harrison Ford) searches for father (Sean Connery) kidnapped by Nazis while hunting Holy Grail.

Inevitably, this third in a series lacks the freshness of the first, *Raiders of the Lost Ark*, but director Spielberg shows a surer touch than he did on *Indiana Jones and the Temple of Doom*; and there's wit even in the action sequences. This time, Spielberg makes proper use of Denholm Elliott's comic gifts; and Harrison Ford succeeds in the difficult task of sending up the genre, while playing his own character for real. 'Nazis!' he snarls. 'I hate these guys!' The principal delight, though, is Sean Connery as Jones's bookish father: a performance which brings humanity to what might otherwise have been a coldly mechanical exercise. It won an Oscar for sound effects editing, and was nominated for best score and sound.

ANTI:

'One might justifiably be disturbed by Spielberg's consistently glib appropriation of profound religious images and ideas.' *(Bruce Bawer, American Spectator)*

'Steven Spielberg returns to the gentler adventure style of the first Indy production but, unfortunately, we've seen much of it before.' *(Bart Mills, Film Yearbook)*

MIXED:

'The Connery-Ford clowning distracts us from the doldrums of punches and chases and plot explication. The movie isn't bad; most of it is enjoyable. But it's familiar and repetitive – it's a rehash . . . Great Spielberg action is so brilliant it spooks you; it makes you want to cheer – you leave the theatre laughing at your own excitement. Here Indy punches out so many people that you weary of the amplified sound of fist against flesh.' *(Pauline Kael)*

PRO:

'Rollicking good fun, packed with great action sequences, villainous Nazis, great locations and wonderful bantering dialogue between Dad and Junior.' *(Rose)*

'Works thanks to some splendid set pieces and the genial interplay between Ford and Connery.' *(Halliwell)*

INFERNO: EIN SPIEL UM MENSCHEN UNSERER ZEIT: *see* THE *DOCTOR MABUSE* SERIES (DOCTOR MABUSE, THE GAMBLER).

INFORMER, THE AAN CT: 5 AV: 8.25

1935 US 91 BW DRAMA

D John Ford ✗ AAW
W Dudley Nichols ✗ AAW from Liam O'Flaherty's novel

Victor McLaglen ✗ AAW Preston Foster ● Una O'Connor ● Heather Angel Joseph Sawyer Wallace Ford J.M. Kerrigan Margot Grahame

A Dublin drunk (Victor McLaglen) betrays his best friend (Wallace Ford) to the authorities during the Sinn Fein rebellion of 1922.

Highly acclaimed classic – voted Best Film by the New York film critics – but it now looks terribly thin and over-simplified. Much of the acting seems either dull or (in the case of McLaglen) hammy; the screenplay is terribly verbose and almost every point is laboured. Max Steiner inexplicably won an Oscar for a score which is ridiculously over-emphatic. The best aspect is the look of the film. Joseph August's cinematography expresses the anti-hero's feelings and fright in a style reminiscent of Fritz Lang's masterpiece, *M* (1931); George Hively's skilful editing was Oscar-nominated; and the art direction by Van Nest Polglase also adds to the atmosphere. But it's all awfully arty. Remade (unsuccessfully) by Jules Dassin with a black cast, as *Up Tight* (1968).

PRO:

'At last this season is privileged to view a Hollywood product which for sustained brilliance of technical accomplishment can bear comparison with the best recent importations from other lands . . . The greatest importance of the films consists in its experimentation with the means of rendering subjective moods and states of mind on the screen . . . Mr. Ford has striven to integrate all the newer resources of the media and restore to it that identity which it has tended to lose since the introduction of sound What is most significant of all perhaps is Mr. Ford's rediscovery of the uses of silence . . . The best film that has come out of Hollywood in a very long time.' *(William Troy, Nation)*

'Among the best five pictures since the coming of sound.' *(Baltimore Sun)*

'Forcefully and intelligently written, directed and acted.' *(Variety)*

'A deeply moving performance from Victor McLaglen as the slow-witted informer Gypo Nolan and some inspired direction from Ford, although Van Nest Polgase (sets), Joseph August (camera work) and Max Steiner (music) all contribute equally to the film's success.' *(R.A.E. Pickard, Dictionary of 1000 Best Films, 1971)*

ANTI:

'Its persistent inadequacies make it more disappointing than many pictures with much less to recommend them . . . the result partly of bad casting, partly of a bad plot treatment. Margot Grahame has a weak part . . . and fits it; Heather Angel is a personal nonentity; the rebel leader (Preston Foster) is hollow . . . while Una O'Connor as the mother is a constant irritation . . . Whole organic stretches are made flabby or . . . actually distressing . . . [by] an elaborately cued and infirm musical score and the device of squeezing to the last drop of meaning or sentiment out of a ten-minute sequence by hanging on to it for a quarter of an hour . . . But any one of the ham touches would be negligible . . . if the central part had been sure of conception and if McLaglen had been all the way up to it . . . he simply does not carry the thing along.' *(Otis Ferguson, New Republic)*

'The power of Liam O'Flaherty's story was dissipated in a welter of camera pictorialism so studiously artistic as to betray Ford's . . . ardent desire to have the screen acquire prestige through reduplication of the effects of more traditionally respectable media. Only in one sequence, the night in the brothel, did his direction bring out the Dostoievskian implication of the narrative and its characters. For the rest, this famous film's reputation . . . rests mainly on a self-conscious and basically false use of the camera.' *(Paul Rotha & Richard Griffith, The Film Till Now, 1949)*

'Heavy-handed, humourless and patronising art film.' *(Tom Charity, Time Out)*

INHERIT THE WIND CT: 6 AV: 7.57

1960 US 127 BW DRAMA

D Stanley Kramer
W Nathan E. Douglas Harold Jacob Smith AAN from the play by Jerome Lawrence and Robert E. Lee

Spencer Tracy ☆ AAN Fredric March ☆ Dick York Gene Kelly Florence Eldridge Elliott Reid Harry Morgan

A schoolmaster is prosecuted for teaching Darwinian evolution; fortunately he has Clarence Darrow (Spencer Tracy) to defend him.

Well acted courtroom drama based on a true story,

much too long-winded and easily diverted into subplots, but reasonably absorbing as courtroom drama. Kramer skilfully cranks up the tension and the heat, but it's an actors' piece – at its best when Spencer Tracy and Fredric March are sparring (this was the only film they made together). The worst aspect is the facile, cop-out ending, which tries to establish the film's Christian credentials by belittling the great humanist journalist H.L. Mencken (impersonated, none too convincingly, by Gene Kelly). Ernest Laszlo's photography and Fredric Knudtson's editing were Oscar-nominated. Remade as a TV movie in 1988.

'The film got extravagant reviews, but it died at the box office. United Artists said this was just a silly story about two old men, so they didn't distribute it properly. Then the fundamentalists called me the anti-Christ, so there were some local problems in booking the film, too. It just died.' *(Stanley Kramer)*

PRO:

'Rousing and fascinating.' *(Variety)*

ANTI:

'There's an old show business proverb about it being unwise to try to burlesque burlesque. This film emerges as a case in point because, true or not, the ludicrous travesty into which the trial develops does largely blur the edge of the drama.' *(Fred Majdalany, Daily Mail)*

'I walked out . . . because I was bored.' *(Clancy Sigal, Time & Tide)*

'The famous Monkey Trial is a bit of a trial . . . I felt I'd been watching a circus rather than a supremely important test-case for free speech . . . Kelly, brilliant though he is, looks as though he's going to break into a dance routine at any moment.' *(Edward Betts, People)*

'A very crude piece of work, totally lacking in subtlety; what is meant to be a courtroom drama of ideas comes out as a caricature of a drama of ideas, and, maddeningly, while watching we can't be sure what is based on historical fact and what is invention.' *(Pauline Kael)*

INNOCENT MOVES: *see* SEARCHING FOR BOBBY FISCHER.

INNOCENT, THE

CT: 6 AV: 7.57

(aka *The Intruder; L'Innocente*)

1976 Italy 112 C DRAMA/FOREIGN

D Luchino Visconti ☆
W Suso Cecchi d'Amico Luchino Visconti Enrico Medioli from Gabriel D'Annunzio's novel *L'Innocente*

Giancarlo Giannini Laura Antonelli ✔
Jennifer O'Neill Didier Haudepin Marc Porel

A womanizing Sicilian aristocrat (Giancarlo Giannini) is upset when he finds that his wife (Laura Antonelli) is having an affair.

Visconti's last film is at its best in the lighter first half, but remains watchable for its elegance and a delightful performance from Laura Antonelli. The pan-and-scan video version is to be avoided, since it destroys Visconti's visual composition.

ANTI:

'A tasteful, undisturbing, sumptuously outfitted story . . . all surface, all visuals. It's a pity Visconti was a Red. If he had stayed an unreconstructed aristo, without formal social conscience, he might have made better, more ironic films . . . [The film] lacking a true moral centre, collapses into the easiest effect of all, elegant despair. It's also very long.' *(Clancy Sigal, Spectator)*

'The subtitles are shameful: "I'm perspired," "I thought of a catastrophy".' *(John Coleman, New Statesman)*

'In the second half, the picture runs out of steam and turns into a ponderous melodrama. Giannini is far from ideally cast, but he seems acceptable until he remembers to act; toward the end he's all over the place acting.' *(Pauline Kael)*

PRO:

'In its subtle fashion, [it] is as much of a political document as any of the strident American films of the past ten years. But it is infinitely more beguiling as a work of cinema.' *(Margaret Hinxman, Daily Mail)*

'An extraordinarily elegant last film . . . full of small, intimate scenes that look grandiose on the surface but actually push our understanding of the characters further forward.' *(Derek Malcolm, Guardian)*

'The sets are breathtaking and the costumes out of this world . . . Theatrical? Of course, it all is, and I can't imagine any Visconti stage production exceeding the beauty of this movie. How heartbreaking to think we'll never see a new Visconti again.' *(Molly Plowright, Glasgow Herald)*

'A worthy finale to a distinguished career.' *(Tony Rayns, Time Out)*

INNOCENTS, THE

CT: 9 AV: 8.22

(aka *The Turn of the Screw*)

1960 GB 99 BW HORROR

D Jack Clayton ✔
W William Archibald Truman Capote John Mortimer ☆ from Henry James's novel *The Turn of the Screw*

Deborah Kerr ☆ Martin Stephens ✔
Pamela Franklin ✔ Megs Jenkins
Michael Redgrave ☆ Peter Wyngarde
Clytie Jessop Isla Cameron

A Victorian housekeeper (Deborah Kerr) begins to wonder if the two children in her charge (Martin Stephens and Pamela Franklin) are as innocent and straightforward as they seem.

This masterpiece by that underrated British director Jack Clayton is probably the best filmed ghost story of all time, thanks to Freddie Francis's eerie photography, a sensuous atmosphere of threat, and fine performances all round. Despite excellent notices, it was not a hit at the box office.

'Catches an eerie, spine-chilling mood right from the start and never lets up on its grim, evil theme.' *(Variety)*

'A magnificent film, but I hope you've got strong nerves.' *(News of the World)*

'A spine-chiller of distinction.' *(Daily Worker)*

'With Freddie Francis's black-and-white photography it is not a question so much of beautiful shots as of a correlation of beauties. The park which on the clearest day is faintly unclear, as if it breathed mist; the vast solitary house with its long shadowed passages and the darkness pressing against the glass of the conservatory – the setting in which the governess and the two innocent-seeming, guilty-knowing children play out their story is exquisite, but the exquisiteness is to the point; the rose-petals incontinently fall, a beetle hangs from the lips of the sylvan statue, everything minutely threatens.' *(Dilys Powell)*

'One of the most elegantly beautiful ghost movies ever made. It features a scary, intense performance by Deborah Kerr, as the governess who sees demonic spectres and forces one of her two charges – the little boy Miles (Martin Stephens) – to confront them. Both Kerr and Michael Redgrave, as the gentleman who hires her, have just the right note of suppressed hysteria in their voices. The settings – the house, the park, the lake – are magnificent, and the script by William Archibald, Truman Capote, and John Mortimer offers the pleasures of literacy. The filmmakers concentrate on the virtuoso possibilities in the material, and the beauty of the images raises our terror to a higher plane than the simple fears of most ghost stories. There are great sequences (like one in a schoolroom) that work on the viewer's imagination and remain teasingly ambiguous.' *(Pauline Kael)*

'Extremely impressive . . . with Kerr perfectly cast as the prim, repressed Victorian governess who begins to worry that her young wards may be possessed by evil spirits of dead servants. No shock tactics here, just the careful creation of sinister atmosphere through decor, Freddie Francis' haunting camerawork, and evocative acting. Kerr, especially, is excellent: rarely was her air of struggling to veil growing hysteria under a civilised facade so appropriately deployed.' *(Geoff Andrew, Time Out)*

INTOLERANCE

CT: 5 AV: 9.08

1916 US 115 BW DRAMA/SILENT

D D.W. Griffith ☆
W D.W. Griffith

Mae Marsh Lillian Gish Constance Talmadge Robert Harron Elmo Lincoln Eugene Pallette

Four stories from history show the evil of intolerance.

It received very mixed reviews on its release in 1916, flopped at the box office, and was described by D.W. Griffith as 'my greatest failure' (though actually his worst films were all talkies). Now, of course, this long, earnest, visually impressive film drawing together is considered a classic, mainly by film buffs. Ordinary mortals, however, may notice that a lot of it is extremely ponderous, pretentious and hard going.

PRO:

'Here is a joy-ride through history; a Cook's tour of the ages; a college education crammed into a night. It is the most incredible experiment in story-telling that has ever been tried . . . The finest individual acting accomplishments are Mae Marsh's . . . Mr Bitzer's photography, devoid of anything sensational, flows like the transparent, limpid style of a finished writer . . . It is without tricks and without imperfections . . . Profoundest of the symbols is the Rocking Cradle.' *(Julian Johnson, Photoplay)*

'It is easy enough, as you catch your breath at the conclusion of *Intolerance* to indulge in trite superlatives. Film reviewing has been over-superlatived. But this new Griffith spectacle marks a milepost in the progress of the film. It reveals something of the future of the spectacle, something of the power to create pictures of tremendous sweeping beauty, drama and imagination . . . [It] is the screening of an idea. That alone places it as an advance.' *(Frederick James Smith, New York Dramatic Mirror)*

'The only film fugue.' *(Terry Ramsaye)*

'In *Intolerance* Griffith's genius reached its fullest expression.' *(Lillian Gish, actress)*

'At a date when few other directors even bothered to move the camera or show a face in close-up, Griffith sent his brilliant and fearless cameraman Billy Bitzer up in a balloon, pioneered the process shot, showed the ceiling of the Medici throne-room 20 years before *Citizen Kane* and – for his sins – found the time to invent false eyelashes.' *(David Ekserdjian, Independent, 1988)*

'Some aspects of [Griffith's] work are so daring that they discourage any attempt at imitation. Who, for example, would have the courage to tackle a design as vast as that of *Intolerance*? Four actions, placed in four different historical epochs, their four themes interwoven, unrolling side by side to the final simultaneous dnouement. In this way his chariots raced to the destruction of Babylon at the same time as the train swept the characters of the present day story through the plains of America, each of these actions progressing at an equal speed toward its appointed end. I have seen at that moment an average cinema public bursting into applause, so perfect was the rhythm and so triumphantly had that unbelievable hazardous conception been executed.' *(René Clair, 1950)*

'By now Griffith was working in terms of symphonic proportions and the result is a monument to his unbounded ambitions . . . The creative sweep of the work made people think in terms of Shakespeare and Beethoven . . . the film was really ahead of its time.' *(Liam O'Leary, The Silent Cinema, 1965)*

'The crowd scenes are brilliantly managed and so are the close-ups. The social message is laid on somewhat heavily, but the mark of an outstanding personality is on every frame.' *(Anthony Burgess, NFT Bulletin, 1984)*

'Has never been equalled for sheer spectacle – or cinematic daring.' *(Kevin Brownlow, London Film Festival Programme, 1988)*

MIXED:

'The second drama, built around the story of the Saviour at Nazareth, is nothing less than a cheap effort by a showman to get pictures out of a subject on which he ought not to have trespassed; and the third episode, which has to rake up the Massacre of St Bartholomew for a picture-palace holiday, is in itself an unconscious example of intolerance . . . [The] Babylonian episode and the new York "crook" drama provide a splendid picture entertainment. As for the rest, Mr Griffith might wisely employ an American phrase, "cut that stuff", and apply it to his picture show. What is left will be well worth paying to see.' *(Daily Mail)*

'Was and still is the greatest spectacular film. Its ingredients . . . have been at the back of every American producer's mind ever since [and] are indirectly responsible for the many imitations – *The Ten Commandments, Noah's Ark . . . Sodom and Gomorrah*, all of which failed because they lacked the fierce intensity of purpose and skill of Griffith. *Intolerance* had the makings of a great film, but failed because of its own immensity . . . the theme at once becomes superficial.' *(Paul Rotha & Richard Griffith, The Film Till Now, 1930)*

'Perhaps the greatest movie ever made and the greatest folly in movie history. It is charged with visionary excitement about the power of movies to combine music, dance, narrative, drama, painting, and photography – to do alone what all the other arts together had done. In this extravaganza one can see the source of most of the major traditions of the screen – the methods of Eisenstein and von Stroheim, the Germans and the Scandinavians, and, when it's bad, DeMille. It combines extraordinary lyric passages, realism, and psychological details with nonsense, vulgarity, and painful sentimentality.' *(Pauline Kael)*

ANTI:

'A pictorial epileptic fit.' *(Anonymous critic)*

'Hard to follow.' *(Variety)*

'The settings of ancient Babylon, wonderfully spectacular though they be, are a very grave travesty of good taste and understanding. I am convinced Babylon never looked like that.' *(Daily Mail, 1922)*

'To crosscut, as Griffith did, from the Siege of Babylon and/or the Massacre of the Huguenots to a speeding train pursued by motorists trying to secure a last-minute pardon from the governor was neither relative nor ironic – it was just damned silly! From *Intolerance*, which is simply the most egregious of his presentations, we can define D.W. Griffith as a Hollywood Faustus who, with no philosophy and no ideas, with bad taste and a middle-class apprehension of history, nonetheless establishes a magical point of departure, not only for the puerile Cecil B. DeMilles who have followed in his piously florid steps, but also for whatever newly equipped visionaries are now fighting, with batallions of experts in their laboratories and on their sets.' *(Vernon Young)*

INTRUDER IN THE DUST CT: 7 AV: 8.27

1949 US 87 BW DRAMA

D Clarence Brown ☆
W Ben Maddow from William Faulkner's novel

Juano Hernandez ✔ Elizabeth Patterson
David Brian Claude Jarman Jr Porter Hall
Will Geer

An obstinate old black man (Juano Hernandez) is accused of shooting a white man, and is threatened with lynching.

Gripping drama: a subtle, tasteful adaptation of William Faulkner novel's about racial injustice in the southern states. Robert Surtees contributes some of his best cinematography, and director Brown makes good use of authentic locations.

PRO:

'All in all, I think it is a good movie.' *(William Faulkner, at the movie's premiere)*

'Of all the recent films dealing with the colour question, Mr Brown's is the most pitiless in its exposure of the abominable savagery to which deep-rooted racial prejudice has given rise in some parts of the United States.' *(Elspeth Grant)*

'Should hold any audience in its spell from beginning to end, clearly deserves to be a notable success.' *(Showman's Trade Review)*

'An example of gripping film craftsmanship.' *(News of the World)*

'The first honestly worked out "racial" film I have seen.' *(Richard Winnington)*

'Beautifully made . . . all the acting is first-rate.' *(Richard Nash, Star)*

MIXED:

'Given depth and fascination principally by its presentation of Lucas the Negro, not a wholly sympathetic character . . . Brown directs . . . in a deliberate, rather mannered style (less mannered, however, than Faulkner's prose).' *(Gavin Lambert, MFB)*

'At the very end, a false note is struck by Chick's uncle (David Brian): "It will be all right, as long as some of us are willing to fight – even one of us," and the ultimate cliché, "Lucas wasn't in trouble; we were in trouble." It's the movie that gets in trouble. But Juano Hernandez's Lucas has the intensity and humor to transcend these Northern liberal platitudes.' *(Pauline Kael)*

INVADERS, THE: *see* FORTY-NINTH PARALLEL.

INVASION OF THE BODY SNATCHERS

CT: 8 AV: 8.75

1956 US 80 BW SF/HORROR

D Don Siegel ☆
W Daniel Mainwaring ☆ from Jack Finney's novel *The Body Snatchers*

Kevin McCarthy ☆ Dana Wynter ☆ Larry Gates King Donovan ☆ Carolyn Jones Virginia Christine Sam Peckinpah

Invaders from space take over the bodies of human beings.

Don Siegel's masterly sci-fi horror film is one of the most frightening, paranoid movies ever made. Siegel keeps his characters moving, hiding, suspicious . . . and heightens it all with sharp editing and shadowy lighting. The acting, though it was never going to win any Oscars and McCarthy overacts towards the end, is above-average for sci-fi of the period; and the script is intelligent. It was probably intended to be a timely allegory about America in the mid-50s, but it can be interpreted as either anti-McCarthyite (as it usually is) or anti-Communist. Whatever the film's politics, its artistic qualities enable it to be just as powerful and gripping today. Philip Kaufman remade the film (reasonably well) in 1978.

'Occasionally difficult to follow due to the strangeness of its scientific premise. Action nevertheless is increasingly exciting.' *(Variety)*

'An expert and off-beat science fiction thriller . . . Strongly sustained narrative style, accurate observation of behaviour and a high technical efficiency . . . In the main, this is a persuasive thriller, with excellent atmospheric lighting in the night scenes and a commendably concessionless ending.' *(MFB)*

'Seminal genre movie burdened with a catchpenny title, which excels in every department and is Siegel's best film. Its impact belies its low budget and, while analogies can be – and frequently are – drawn with Cold War hysteria and McCarthyism . . . The movie succeeds as a near-perfect piece of sheer science fiction entertainment.' *(Alan Frank)*

'A beautifully controlled work of hysteria.' *(Scheuer)*

'An intensely realistic drama of everyday people defending everyday values against inhuman invasion, done with a great deal of human feeling. Indeed it is the humanity of the drama that is its greatest strength, and it is this, too, that makes the story play so well.' *(Chris Steinbrunner and Burt Goldblatt, Cinema of the Fantastic, 1972)*

INVISIBLE MAN, THE

CT: 7 AV: 8.33

1933 US 71 BW SF/HORROR

D James Whale ☆
W R.C. Sherriff Philip Wylie ☆ (the latter uncredited) from H.G. Wells's novel

Claude Rains ☆ Gloria Stuart E.E. Clive ☆ William Harrigan Henry Travers Una O'Connor ☆ Forrester Harvey Dudley Digges Holmes Herbert

Scientist (Claude Rains) becomes invisible; increasingly crazed, he terrorizes the world.

James Whale's sense of humour is well suited to the early part of the film. The entertainment value is greatly enhanced by John P. Fulton's witty special effects, using piano wires and travelling mattes, which were outstanding for 1933. The film was a big hit, and made Rains a star. The critics, too, were impressed. Wells admired the film, but objected to the fact that his hero had been made into a madman.

'Well made and full of intentional and unintentional laughs. Should do well.' *(Variety)*

'Photographic magic abounds in the production . . . The story makes such superb cinematic material that one wonders that Hollywood did not film it sooner.' *(New York Times)*

'Taken either as a technical exercise or as a profoundly moving retelling of the Frankenstein fable, it is one of the most rewarding of recent films.' *(William Troy)*

ISHTAR

CT: 1 AV: 3.00

1987 US 107 C COMEDY

D Elaine May ●
W Elaine May ●

Warren Beatty ● Dustin Hoffman ● Isabelle Adjani Charles Grodin Jack Weston Tess Harper

Two talentless songwriters (Dustin Hoffman, Warren Beatty) are advised by their agent to get lost, so they go to Morocco and become involved in a revolution.

An attempt to make a Hope-and-Crosby-type comedy founders on the charmlessness of its two stars, both horrendously miscast. Perhaps audiences didn't realise that the songs by Paul Williams were meant to be bad, but they knew a rotten script when they heard one.

PRO:

'I don't mind saying that I like the movie. I don't think it's great, but I'm not sorry I made it.' *(Dustin Hoffman)*

'Deserves a kinder look; director Elaine May is a true original, and she coaxes performances of real, touching humour from the unlikely pairing of Dustin Hoffman and Warren Beatty.' *(Quinlan)*

'Had it taken people unawares, people might quite have liked May's amiable tale.' *(Winnert)*

ANTI:

'This isn't as bad as everyone says. But it is still appalling.' *(Rose)*

'[It's] not as bad as they said it was. It's worse.' *(Tom Hutchinson, Mail on Sunday)*

'One can't help but wonder whether the camel was the only blind creature who had something to do with this picture.' *(Variety)*

'May's . . . script has more than a passing resemblance to that camel, whirling in a double darkness with Beatty and Hoffman on its back, anxious to reach the oasis of comedy but having no idea of which direction to choose . . . It's like a *Road To* film with two dull Bob Hopes who think they're Bing Crosby.' *(Adam Mars-Jones, Independent)*

'It isn't dislikable, but it has no comic energy. May's directing is limp, passive; she doesn't do the obvious, but sometimes she doesn't do anything else, either. And when Beatty and Hoffman play small-timers it's a reverse conceit, a form of affectation.' *(Pauline Kael)*

'There's not much to show for the money. [Had it been made with a more modest budget] it would have been dismissed as an inexpert knockabout comedy that needed more work on the script.' *(David Robinson, Times)*

'A truly dreadful film, a lifeless, massive, lumbering exercise in failed comedy . . . It's not funny, it's not smart, and it's interesting only in the way a traffic accident is interesting.' *(Roger Ebert)*

ISLAND OF LOST SOULS, THE

CT: 6 AV: 7.12

1933 US 72 BW SF/HORROR

D Erle C. Kenton ✓
W Waldemar Young Philip Wylie based on H.G. Wells's book *The Island of Dr Moreau*

Charles Laughton ☆ Bela Lugosi Richard Arlen Kathleen Burke Leila Hyams

Mad scientist (Charles Laughton) experiments with turning animals into humans.

Remarkably powerful horror film with sadistic-erotic overtones, featuring a marvellously malign performance by Charles Laughton as the ultimate mad scientist, and wonderful cinematography by Karl Struss. The film can be seen as an allegory against imperialism or against a boss class. Its dark tone and subject-matter did not endear it to critics or the public. It was banned in many Mid-western states of America, Great Britain and New Zealand, and had to wait 21 years before gaining a release in Britian.

'While the action is not designed to appeal to other than the credulous, there are undoubtedly some horror sequences which are unrivaled. Those studies of a galaxy of Dr Moreau's 50-50 man and beast creations, as an example, will pique any type of mentality.' *(Variety)*

'A gripping, uncompromising tale whose entire appearance conveys gloom and misery . . . a maturity and harshness rarely found in fantasy films.' *(Photon)*

'Some parts are colourlessly acted, and stock situations creep in, but the impression of a spine chilling and truly "fantastic" reality remains to stamp this as a first class horror film.' *(MFB)*

'Anticipates *King Kong* (1933) in its embodiment of the underground spirit of revolt, a spirit extremely timely in its appeal to victims of the Depression years, who not only resented their material deprivations but were all too willing to blame a system which appeared to thrive on an arbitrary suspension of the individual's inalienable right to the pursuit of happiness. The delirious final revolt here, with the master dragged away to the "house of pain" in which he created his subservient brutes, echoes the wilder excesses of the French Revolution.' *(Phil Hardy, The Horror Film Encyclopaedia)*

IT ALWAYS RAINS ON SUNDAY

CT: 5 AV: 7.00

1947 GB 92 BW DRAMA

D Robert Hamer
W Angus Macphail Robert Hamer Henry Cornelius

Googie Withers John McCallum Jack Warner Edward Chapman Susan Shaw Sydney Tafler

A convict (John McCallum) seeks refuge with an old girlfriend (Googie Withers), now married but discontented.

A surprisingly grim, ungenerous film to have come from Ealing Studios – the nearest they ever got to film noir. Though the Bethnal Green setting is well observed, some of the supporting Cockney acting is strained and unconvincing. Any episode of *EastEnders* does this kind of thing rather better.

'Has the persuasiveness of an exciting story professionally told.' *(Dilys Powell)*

'There is no false sentiment, no romanticising in this picture. The guilty get what they deserve, justice is served and the honest folk go back to their work after the thrills and heat of the chase has disturbed their lives.' *(A.E. Wilson)*

'Influential slumland melodrama, now dated – the stuff of every other television play – but at the time electrifyingly vivid and very well done.' *(Halliwell)*

IT HAPPENED ONE NIGHT AAW

CT: 8 AV: 9.50

1934 US 105 BW COMEDY/ROMANCE

D Frank Capra ☆ AAW
W Robert Riskin ☆ AAW from Samuel Hopkins Adams's story *Night Bus*

Clark Gable ☆ AAW Claudette Colbert ☆ AAW
Walter Connolly Roscoe Karns Alan Hale
Ward Bond Jameson Thomas Arthur Hoyt

A cynical reporter (Clark Gable) falls for a runaway heiress (Claudette Colbert).

Simple, predictable and slightly corny, but still a delightful comedy romance. The studio thought of this as a pot-boiler (it was taken on by Columbia only after MGM had passed on it), and the female lead was turned down by Miriam Hopkins, Constance Bennett and Margaret Sullavan; but the touch of Frank Capra (and, just as importantly, his writer Robert Riskin) transformed a simple idea into a multiple Oscar-winner.

Clark Gable and Claudette Colbert are marvellous as the tough reporter and spoiled runaway heiress who can't stand each other. They manage to suggest a surprising amount of erotic tension, while keeping their banter bright and breezy, not sleazy. It was so popular that the famous scene where Gable removes his shirt and revealed no vest resulted in a worldwide slump in singlets. It also started the vogue for screwball comedy which lasted through the rest of the 30s.

MIXED:

'Entertaining [but] to claim any significance for the picture . . . would of course be a mistake.' *(Nation)*

PRO:

'Better than it has any right to be – better acted, better directed, better written . . . The cast was particularly sound from top to bottom. Claudette Colbert sensed what was required of her, and did it very well, though I do not care for her much as a person.' *(Otis Ferguson, New Republic)*

'Diverting.' *(Newsweek)*

'The film is conceived in a delightful vein of mingled romance and high comedy, and never departs from this vein for a single instant. It is brilliantly directed by Mr Frank Capra.' *(James Agate, Tatler)*

'For freshness of treatment and humor of presentation, we have had nothing to equal it in a long time.' *(Robert Forsythe, New Masses)*

'One of the few potential classics of the recent cinema . . . Although neither Miss Colbert nor Mr Gable demonstrated any particular comic talent before this picture, their playing here is at every step exactly in tune with the mood of the occasion.' *(William Troy, Nation)*

'Here, so much was pure Capra – the infectious good spirits of the entire busload of people singing "The Daring Young Man on the Flying Trapeze", the neatness of the hitch-hike episode when Claudette hitched her skirt after Cable's thumb had failed to stop a car; the "Walls of Jericho" situation; and finally, the wildly comic wedding, which was satirical slapstick put over with superb discretion. I put this as Capra's best picture ever – and I know all about Mr Deeds. It contains Gable's most likeable performance and Colbert's most bewitching. Bob Riskin never wrote a tighter, more appealing script.' *(Leonard Wallace, Picturegoer)*

'In the mid-30s, the Colbert and the Gable of this film became Americans' idealized view of themselves – breezy, likable, sexy, gallant, and maybe just a little harebrained. (It was the *Annie Hall* of its day – before the invention of anxiety.)' *(Pauline Kael)*

IT'S A GIFT

CT: 7 AV: 8.70

1934 US 73 BW COMEDY

D Norman Z. McLeod
W Jack Cunningham from a story by Charles Bogle (pseudonym for W.C. Fields)

W.C. Fields ☆ Kathleen Howard Jean Rouverol
Julian Madison Tommy Bupp Baby LeRoy

A curmudgeon (W.C. Fields) is increasingly irritated by small-town American life.

More a collection of old comedy routines than a narrative; three scenes are from the 1925 *Ziegfeld Follies*, two are from a play *The Comic Supplement*, and the whole film is basically a remake of a 1925 Fields silent, *It's The Old Army Game*. Production values are far from high, but Fields is at his funniest and the sight-gags are hilarious, so who cares?

MIXED:

'No plot, no suspense; rather coarse-grained in spots,

but packing a load of belly-laughs for people who like that sort of humor.' *(Variety)*

'Quite good holiday entertainment. I wish I could say more . . . We laughed very loudly indeed at times . . . but there were dull patches, and after a while the fun seemed very definitely to pall. One felt at the end that one had had enough of Mr Fields for quite a long time to come.' *(Punch)*

PRO:

'Fields gave me more laughs in this preposterous comedy than I have enjoyed since my last quota film, and that was pretty funny. Don't ask me what he does, how he does it or why . . . To see [him] . . . is to realise what a genius this old trouper has for pantomime.' *(Edward Betts, Sunday Express)*

'If there is a funnier comedian anywhere on the screen, stage or air, I have yet to see him.' *(Daily Telegraph)*

'Fiendishly funny and incisive.' *(James Agee, Life, 1949)*

'An enormously amusing succession of rough and ready gags.' *(Literary Digest)*

'Enshrines some of his [Fields's] very best languid loathing of family life.' *(Penelope Gilliatt)*

'Possibly the finest, funniest movie W.C. Fields ever made, this grand, side-splitting, rollicking spoof of middle-class marriage and mainstream ambitions is one of the screen's greatest comedies.' *(Baseline)*

IT'S A WONDERFUL LIFE AAN

CT: 10 AV: 9.68

1946 US 129 BW DRAMA/FANTASY

D Frank Capra ☆ AAN
W Frances Goodrich ☆ Albert Hackett ☆ Frank Capra ☆ Jo Swerling ☆ from Philip Van Doren Stern's story *The Greatest Gift*

James Stewart ☆ AAN Henry Travers ☆ Donna Reed Lionel Barrymore Thomas Mitchell Beulah Bondi Frank Faylen Gloria Grahame H.B. Warner Samuel S. Hinds Ward Bond Frank Albertson Mary Treen

Clarence, an angel (Henry Travers), shows a man on the verge of suicide, George Bailey (James Stewart), the value of his life.

And a wonderful movie, a charming and heartwarming variation on the story of *A Christmas Carol*. Despite its obvious quality, the original reviews were very mixed. Fantasy films were not taken particularly seriously in the 1940s; and the consensus was that this was a picture which sugarcoated reality. Bosley Crowther in the New *York Times* led the attack, calling it 'a figment of simple Pollyanna platitudes'. Surprisingly in view of its lukewarm reviews, the film won Capra the Foreign Correspondents' Golden Globe Award as Best Director; and was nominated at the Academy Awards for Best Picture. James Stewart was disappointed when the public at large, however, seemed to agree with the more carping critics:

'It didn't do well at all. I don't think it was the type of story people wanted right after the war. They wanted a war-related story or a pure slapstick, Red Skelton-type of comedy. Our movie just got lost.'

On its first release, the film ended up half a million dollars in the red. Since then, thanks to television, it has become of the best-loved films of all time.

Many critics have missed the heart of this movie. Though often thought of as sentimental and upbeat, the reason it is so profoundly moving is that – like *Casablanca* and many other classics – it ventures into the heart of darkness and despair. Far less sentimental than it's portrayed, the film is, stylistically, one of the high points of film noir.

James Stewart uses all his skill, integrity and acting range to play the central figure, who is at first – let us not forget – depressed, full of self-pity and contemplating suicide. Like a character in one of Warner Brothers' darkest gangster films, George Bailey is trapped inside a nightmare. Far from being the 'nice' small-town folk perceived by the original critics, George's fellow citizens are threatening to ruin him by drawing their money out of the very institution which George has been using to give them a decent life. Two 40s critics, Paul Rotha and Richard Griffith, went so far as to describe the film as 'a vivid portrayal of dog-eat-dog methods in small-town business'. As in many a gangster movie, the only person who understands the hero is the principal villain, Potter, who tempts him – diabolically, but sensibly – with security and a high salary.

Nor is the ending as upbeat as commonly supposed. As one recent critic has perceived, by the end:

'Poor George has been sandbagged, this time by Clarence, for good. He has been revealed as the only glue holding the town of Bedford Falls together, and the guardian of the lives of a number of people who would otherwise be dead. George now cheerfully accepts his imprisonment. Yet despite the warm and uplifting ending, nothing has really changed. George will pinch pennies for the rest of his life, bludgeoned into accepting his lot in life as inevitable and unavoidable. Mr. Potter and others like him will continue to oppose George and make his life difficult (Potter apparently even gets to keep the $8,000 Uncle Billy thoughtlessly gave him by accident!).' *(Kenneth Von Gunden, Flights of Fancy, 1989)*

It's A Wonderful Life is, in fact, a deeply ironic title. The film is all about middle-aged, middle-class self-sacrifice and counting one's – very limited – blessings: our hero regrets, but comes to terms with, the fact that he has had to give up his hopes of escape and self-improvement for the sake of his family and local community. The result is a long way from facile, sugar-coated fantasy, and one of Frank Capra's (and Hollywood's) finest films.

ANTI:

'The weakness of this picture, from this reviewer's point of view, is the sentimentality of it – its illusory concept of life. Mr Capra's nice people are charming, his small town is quite a beguiling place, and his pattern for solving problems is most optimistic and facile. But somehow they all resemble theatrical attitudes rather than average realities.' *(Bosley Crowther)*

'So mincing as to border on baby talk . . . Henry Travers, God help him, has the job of portraying Mr Stewart's guardian angel. It must have taken a lot out of him.' *(New Yorker)*

'In its own slurpy, bittersweet way, the picture is well done. But it's fairly humorless, and, what with all the hero's virtuous suffering, it didn't catch on with the public. Capra takes a serious tone here though there's no basis for the seriousness; this is doggerel trying to pass as art.' *(Pauline Kael)*

MIXED:

'Sentimental, but so expertly written, directed, and acted that you want to believe it.' *(Newsweek)*

'Hollywood's Horatio Alger fights with more cinematic knowhow and zeal than any other director to convince movie audiences that American life is exactly like the *Saturday Evening Post* covers of Norman Rockwell.' *(New Republic)*

'Often warm, human and likable, but it's as false as a scenario, shrewdly contrived to "please" an audience, can make it. It is not wrong in itself to try to "please" an audience, but to do it in terms that are not related to the world of reality but to those of daydreams and wishful thinking is wrong. When it is all over, it hasn't proved a thing – it has, in effect, only said: "Wouldn't it be nice if the world were full of the milk of human kindness?" My only answer to that is – it certainly would.' *(Herman G. Weinberg)*

'One of the most efficient sentimental pieces since *A Christmas Carol*. Often, in its pile-driving emotional exuberance, it outrages and insults, or at least accosts without introduction, the cooler and more responsible parts of the mind; it is nevertheless recommended.' *(James Agee, Nation)*

'Capra, in fact, shrinks, as Ford and Wyler have shrunk, from pursuing the inquiry into human nature; so far as the easy superficial goodness, but no farther. And while that is enough to start with, as the years go by one begins to ask, from the experienced and the serious artist in the cinema, for something more.' *(Dilys Powell)*

PRO:

'It is either magnificent hocus-pocus, smacking faintly of James Thurber and Thornton Wilder, or else just hocus-pocus. But it is vastly amusing . . . What the moral is, I have no idea.' *(Evening Standard)*

'A grand and heart-warming film, as American as apple pie – overflowing with bright comedy, gentle humor, chuckling homey philosophies and poignant drama . . . Aside from the obvious moralizing, *It's a Wonderful Life* is excellent drama, fine comedy, filled with the warm and sympathetic directorial touch of Capra and the catalytic ingratiating performance of Stewart.' *(Cue)*

'A masterful edifice of comedy and sentiment.' *(Life)*

'Capra's finest film and could lay claim to being one of the best movies ever made . . . The ending is a real tearjerker and, if you don't agree with Capra that life is really like this, then you might go along with his sentiment that it ought to be.' *(Quinlan)*

'I thought it was the greatest film I ever made. Better yet, I thought it was the greatest film anybody ever made. It wasn't made for the oh-so-bored critics or the oh-so-jaded literati. It was my kind of film for my kind of people.' *(Frank Capra)*

IVAN THE TERRIBLE (PARTS I & II)

CT: 6 AV: 8.62

(aka *Ivan Groznyi*)

1942/1946 USSR 188 BW (colour in part II)
DRAMA/BIOPIC/FOREIGN

D Sergei M. Eisenstein ✗
W Sergei M. Eisenstein

Nikolai Cherkassov ● Ludmilla Tselikovskaya
Serafina Birman Mikhail Nazvanov
Pavel Kadochnikov Andrei Abrikosov

Life and times of a Czar (Nikolai Cherkassov).

Eisenstein shot this film without a script, and it shows more clearly than any other 'classic' the limitations of the auteur theory. Though pictorially splendid, the film's a mess – clumsily acted and edited, with a narrative that is excruciatingly slow. Part II, which deals with attempts to unseat the great dictator, was suppressed until three years after the death of Josef Stalin; and Eisenstein never got round to his threatened Part III. Still, Prokofiev's score is fab.

PRO:

'One of the greatest historical film spectaculars by one of the greatest of filmmakers.' *(Judith Crist)*

'Film spectacle of the highest order.' *(Maltin)*

'Probably the most enjoyable of all Eisenstein's films . . . Cherkassov's contorted performance as Ivan, absurdly stylised as it is, beautifully expresses the conscience of the state torn between absolutism and factionalism, while managing a miraculous integration with a superbly operatic visual style.' *(Rod McShane, Time Out)*

MIXED:

'Pitiful to think of beside his finest work, but I was fascinated by his experiments in rigidity and religiosity.' *(James Agee, Nation)*

ANTI:

'Nikolai Cherkassov's performance – or, rather, his appearance – in the Ivan role is mainly a matter of his posing in grotesque get-ups and attitudes. The indication is that he is supposed to represent a lonely and angry man. He appears to be more of a mad one with a peculiarly pointed head.' *(Bosley Crowther)*

'A motionless motion picture. In some scenes only the slow movement of the eyeballs gives evidence of life.' *(Virginia Wright, LA Daily News)*

'Over-long and ponderous.' *(Variety)*

'A series of dramatic tableaux with rather choppy continuity and a minimum of subtlety in the characterization.' *(Newsweek)*

'Demoded, primitive acting that combines the weighty drama of early opera with the first rushes of *The Great Train Robbery*.' *(Shirley O'Hara, New Republic)*

'Slow-paced to the point of discomfort . . . The film appears to be more a curiosity than anything else, filled with plots rather than plot, done in a style that is supposedly monumental, and containing much rolling of eyes by leading Soviet actors.' *(Saturday Review)*

'Every frame in it looks great – it's a brilliant collection of stills – but as a movie, it's static, grandiose, and frequently ludicrous, with elaborately angled, overcomposed photography, and overwrought, eyeball-rolling performers slipping in and out of the walls, dragging their shadows behind them.' *(Pauline Kael)*

J

J.F.K.: *see* JFK.

JACOB'S LADDER CT: 8 AV: 5.92

1991 US 113 C WAR/DRAMA/HORROR

D Adrian Lyne ✔
W Bruce Joel Rubin ✔

Tim Robbins ☆ Elizabeth Pena Danny Aiello
Matt Craven Macaulay Culkin

A Vietnam veteran (Tim Robbins) starts having nightmare hallucinations and tries to discover why.

Adrian Lyne is at his flashiest directing this hugely underrated psychological thriller by Bruce Joel Rubin (who also wrote *Ghost*). It's one of the most frightening films of recent years, and one of the most stimulating; it makes the audience work hard to understand it, which is probably why it wasn't a hit (though the critics' notices can't have helped). Some reviewers found the final twist a let-down; I thought it brilliantly original. And yes, that is Macaulay Culkin as Robbins's son.

ANTI:

'Dull, unimaginative and pretentious.' *(Variety)*

'Much of [it] is so wrapped up in its own cleverness that there is little way in for an audience.' *(Geoff Brown, The Times)*

'The audience is whirled through the doors of perception at a giddy pace . . . But while the script takes on a whole range of mystical ideas, it reflects an outdated theology where the female characters are concerned.' *(Lizzie Francke, City Limits)*

'Oh no . . . another dose of the Dreaded Nam Flashback Disease . . . Nasty things happen willy-nilly, but they could just as well be happening nilly-willy.' *(Anne Billson, New Statesman & Society)*

'Exceedingly silly on every level, particularly in its supernatural dabblings.' *(Halliwell)*

'Intriguing for the first half but by the time you find out what's going on you may no longer care.' *(Scheuer)*

MIXED:

'Builds interestingly but collapses in its last third.' *(Kim Newman, S & S)*

'It was [once] rejected by every major studio and it's easy to see why . . . Despite its confusing structure and numerous loose ends [it] succeeds in terms of sheer audacity of idea and power of image.' *(Hugo Davenport, Daily Telegraph)*

'Enters into the hallucinations of a desperate mind, and lives there. It evokes a paranoid-schizophrenic state as effectively as any film I have ever seen. Despite an ending that is intended as victorious, the movie is a thoroughly painful and depressing experience – but, it must be said, one that has been powerfully written, directed, and acted.' *(Roger Ebert)*

'Creepy dream sequences and a script from *Ghost* writer Rubin still can't prevent the feeling that we're somehow having our legs pulled.' *(Rose)*

PRO:

'Superb . . . brilliant . . . Definitely one of the best of the year.' *(Daily Express)*

'Messy and maddening though some of it is, [it's] also an extraordinary, truly scary film . . . What makes the movie run is Lyne's giddyingly, unsettling direction . . . Genuinely disturbing stuff.' *(Steve Grant, Time Out)*

JALSAGHAR: *see* MUSIC ROOM, THE.

JANE EYRE CT: 6 AV: 7.46

1944 US 96 BW DRAMA/ROMANCE

D Robert Stevenson ☆
W Aldous Huxley Robert Stevenson
John Houseman from Charlotte Bronte's novel

Joan Fontaine Orson Welles ● Margaret O'Brien
Henry Daniell John Sutton Agnes Moorehead
Elizabeth Taylor

A governess (Joan Fontaine) falls for her mysterious employer (Orson Welles).

Best of the screen versions of Charlotte Bronte's romantic novel, with a handsome, Gothic production, a memorable score by Bernard Herrmann, and loads of atmosphere – George Barnes's deep-focus photography is obviously influenced by the work of Gregg Toland who shot *Citizen Kane*. Unfortunately, Stevenson directs at too slow a pace, and the cast is variable. Joan Fontaine is disappointingly bland, and appears content to reprise her role from *Rebecca*. Orson Welles looks the part and has the required intensity, but often seems rushed, mannered or over-the-top. Watch out for a youthful Elizabeth Taylor in one of her earliest screen roles, as the neglected child.

PRO:

'As intense on celluloid as it is on the printed page.' *(Variety)*

'Orson Welles is a strong, fantastic Rochester – the right vein exactly.' *(Manchester Guardian)*

'There is no disputing this is an "arty" hit. It is production achievement all the way, the kind that rears its beautiful head for Academy Award nomination – in production finesse, directorial fine points, characterizations supreme.' *(Hollywood Motion Picture Review)*

MIXED:

'There's electricity enough in Orson Welles' looks and presence . . . He gives a fine performance as Rochester, the only fault of which is that it leaves to Joan Fontaine little more than the role of a spectator.' *(New Statesman)*

'[Welles's] Rochester has the studied arrogance, the restless moods of a medieval king carrying his own soul to a halberd and demanding that everybody look at it. We only wish that he spoke more clearly; he so mumbles and macerates his words that half the time we are unable to tell what he was talking about.' *(Bosley Crowther)*

'The filmic transcription of the Charlotte Bronte novel should prove a satisfaction even to the more rabid devotees of the Victorian scrivener . . . Joan Fontaine . . . mirrors the text as flawlessly as one could expect or wish, and her performance, at all times, is a gracious and moving thing . . . Orson Welles's Rochester is obviously the product of faulty casting. The actor, feeling his inadequacies in a romantic role, has italicized the macabre measures of the character, and fashioned a performance so completely operatic that the spectator is continuously amazed that dialogue, rather than a Verdi aria, escapes from his lips.' *(Herb Sterne)*

ANTI:

'A careful and tame production, a sadly vanilla-flavoured Joan Fontaine, and Welles treating himself to road-operatic sculpturings of body, cloak, and diction, his eyes glinting in the Rembrandt gloom, at every chance, like side-orders of jelly. It is possible to enjoy his performance as dead-pan period parody; I imagine he did. I might have more if I hadn't wanted, instead, to see a good performance.' *(James Agee, Nation)*

'*Jane Eyre* is not innocent of monotony, with its unrelieved Gothic settings and types. Even the heroine herself is conceived as an angelic, edgeless character, an Agnes Wickfield; Joan Fontaine who plays the part, affects the coiffure of Charlotte Bronte but in other respects might be giving a performance as Norma Shearer.' *(Dilys Powell)*

JASON AND THE ARGONAUTS

CT: 7 AV: 6.50

1963 GB 103 C FANTASY/ADVENTURE/FAMILY

D Don Chaffey ☆
W Jan Read Beverly Cross ✔

Todd Armstrong Honor Blackman Ned MacGinnis Andrew Faulds Nancy Kovack

Jason (Todd Armstrong) travels in search of the Golden Fleece and comes up against various monsters.

A terrific adventure for all ages, featuring harpies, a seven-headed hydra, duelling skeletons and other phenomena. It boasts some of the greatest stop-motion animation in screen history (by courtesy of Ray Harryhausen) and a surprisingly intelligent script. Almost universally panned on release, it is now recognized as a classic of its kind.

ANTI:

'The straight story of Jason's exploits, told with magic and imagination and a minimum of studio trickery might have been delightful.' *(Time)*

'Strictly hot weather entertainment, suitable for keeping the children off the streets, perhaps, but hardly to be taken seriously by anybody beyond the age of puberty.' *(Leo Mishkin, New York Morning Telegraph)*

'Absurd, unwieldy . . . no worse, but certainly no better, than most of its kind.' *(Howard Thompson, New York Times)*

MIXED:

'Rather gruesome . . . Still, it is modestly literate and intelligently acted and has some capacity to stir youngsters' imagination in a constructive sense.' *(Moira Walsh, America)*

PRO:

'A splendidly spectacular treatment, rich in mythical monsters, trick camera effects and muscle-flexing men.' *(Daily Herald)*

'A colorful cast perform with zeal.' *(Variety)*

JAWS AAN

CT: 8 AV: 9.18

1975 US 125 C ACTION/ADVENTURE/HORROR

D Steven Spielberg ☆
W Peter Benchley Carl Gottlieb from Benchley's novel ☆

Roy Scheider ☆ Robert Shaw ✗
Richard Dreyfuss ☆ Lorraine Gary
Murray Hamilton Carl Gottlieb

Murderous shark terrorizes Long Island resort.

A ripping yarn. Rumour has it that the movie was rescued by Verna Fields in the cutting room; but there had to be something for her to her to rescue, so don't believe those who argue that Spielberg was just lucky. The opening sequence is a classic of cinema, as are several other moments (such as the one where the camera dollies in on Scheider while zooming out at the same time: a wonderful way of evoking Scheider's horror at seeing the disappearance of a child under the waves). John Williams's Oscar-winning score is among his best. The performances are above average, although Robert Shaw goes over the top and the shark itself is not altogether convincing. There are longueurs in the script; but Spielberg – still in his twenties when he made this – shows his talent for creating suspense, delivering shocks, defusing situations through humour, and building up to a great climax.

ANTI:

'The ads show a gaping shark's mouth. If sharks can yawn, that's presumably what this one was doing. It's certainly what I was doing all through this picture . . . The direction is by Steven Spielberg, who did the unbearable *Sugarland Express*. At least here he has shucked most of his arty mannerisms and has progressed almost to the level of a stock director of the 30s – say, Roy del Ruth.' *(Stanley Kauffmann)*

'The argument is ridiculous on its face; it suggests that the only way to stop people from swimming in shark infested waters is to close the beaches. I can think of a much easier way: simply tell people there's a shark out there.' *(Dan Rottenberg, Chicago Magazine)*

'Suspense is used to titillate and manipulate the audience rather than highlight character development and thematic concern . . . In the shark hunt section of his film, Spielberg fails to convey the Hawksian sense of men becoming more truly human in the process of engaging in a dangerous, perhaps foolhardy, adventure. As a consequence of that fundamental failure, the second half of *Jaws* plays as merely the rendering of the hunt by three men for a preposterously destructive sea monster.' *(James Bernardoni, The New Hollywood, 1991)*

MIXED:

'If you think about Jaws for more than 45 seconds, you will recognize it as nonsense, but it's the sort of nonsense that can be a good deal of fun if you like to have the wits scared out of you at irregular intervals.' *(New York Times)*

'A perfectly acceptable and sometimes genuinely exciting entry in the disaster stakes . . . The sense of edgy unease is beautifully transmitted in a series of tiny, throwaway moments . . . Spielberg almost manages to invest the shark . . . with the quality of a Jungian archetype. His good work, unfortunately, is partially undone by a script straining to become Herman Melville and ending the portentous profundities attached to Robert Shaw's Quint . . . by projecting him . . . into the jaws of his own unconvincing, mechanical Moby Dick.' *(MFB)*

'The whole film is very educational . . . To be fair to this film, and I can't see why I should be, it is an improvement on [the] book.' *(Kenneth Robinson, Spectator)*

'The word went around that [it] was a vagina dentata movie symbolizing the psychological violence of the devouring vagina and the threatened male . . . I . . . feel it is a really important film with interest especially for feminists . . . Analysis of the imagery . . . reflects the underlying or unconscious workings of ideology, which can be defined as the unconscious set of ideas that cultural products made by the dominant class, reflect and reproduce.' *(Griselda Pollock, Spare Rib)*

'The perfect movie for anyone with a larger-than-life castration complex.' *(Woman's Wear Daily)*

'Maybe it's just a monster movie reminiscent of all those 50s sci-fi films, but it's at least endowed with intelligent characterisation, a lack of sentimentality (in contrast to, say, *E.T.*) and it really is frightening.' *(Geoff Andrew, Time Out)*

PRO:

'One of the better films I have seen' *(Fidel Castro)*

'An $8 million dollar film of consummate suspense, tension and terror.' *(Variety)*

'Would someone pass me a drink because I need one very badly and very quickly. And no, I won't go for a swim right now . . . The first hour is sheer palm-sweating suspense.' *(William Hall, Evening News)*

'You need a strong stomach to sit through the film. It clenches you in its ferocious teeth from the second it opens and never lets up.' *(Daily Express)*

'A writer friend says: "I don't know what all the fuss is about. I wasn't frightened" . . . and neither was the man under my seat.' *(Roderick Mann, Sunday Express)*

'The best nature-retribution film since *The Birds*.' *(Danny Peary)*

'Depicts the extraordinary potency of capitalist greed . . . The shark in the water brings out the shark in members of the business community . . . Though its crisp cinematic values and emotional manipulativeness lifted it to blockbusterdom, the film aligns itself with the 70's Hollywood satirization of traditional movie heroism.' *(Seth Cagin & Philip Dray, Hollywood Films of the 70s, 1984)*

'Both a critique of and a triumph for uninhibited commercialism, the film drops topically disquieting post-Watergate markers of political cover-up before veering into reassuringly conventional adventure. The direction is the most efficient manipulation of an audience since *Psycho*.' *(Elkan Allan, NFT Bulletin)*

'An ingenious mixture of *The Creature From the Black Lagoon* and *Moby Dick*, with the actors taking back seats to the special effects, direction and, especially, Verna Fields's superb editing.' *(Alan Frank)*

'One hell of a good story, brilliantly told.' *(Roger Ebert)*

JAZZ SINGER, THE

CT: 5 AV: 6.00

1927 US 88 C MUSICAL/DRAMA

D Alan Crosland
W Alfred A. Cohn AAN from Samson Raphaelson's play

Al Jolson ☆ Mary McAvoy Warner Oland Eugenie Besserer William Demarest Otto Lederer

Cantor's son (Al Jolson) tries to make it in showbiz.

The first talkie – primitive, of course, but it began to show what was possible. Al Jolson shows why he was magnetic on stage, and the story is heart-tugging enough for it to have been remade twice, in 1953 and 1980. It won a special Academy Award for Warner Brothers, as 'the pioneer outstanding talking picture'.

ANTI:

'In its present stage of development the sounds we hear are a faint parody of the human voice. They seem incapable of the fine shades on which a beautiful style of speaking depends . . . The special subtlety of acting which is peculiar to the film has been sacrificed, we feel, to a poor imitation of the stage.' *(The Times)*

MIXED:

'Hebrew racial and religious propaganda of the most macabre kind, with the general air of making a determined effort to turn the cinema into a cinemagogue . . . *The Jazz Singer* is an impressive panorama of American Judaism . . . Discriminating folks are likely to find this strange film both interesting and instructive, though it is difficult to accept its basic assumption that jazz is a form of distorted prayer, wrung from distressed Judaism in the social chaos of modern America.' *(Daily Express)*

PRO:

'Definitely establishes the fact that talking pictures are imminent. Everyone in Hollywood can rise up and declare that they are not, and it will not alter the fact. If I were an actor with a squeaky voice I would worry.' *(Welford Beaton, Film Spectator)*

'Undoubtedly the best thing Vitaphone has ever put on the screen. The combination of the religious heart interest story and Jolson's singing 'Kol Nidre' in a synagog while his father is dying and two 'Mammy' lyrics as his mother stands in the wings of the theatre, and later as she sits in the front row, carry abundant power and appeal.' *(Variety)*

'A beautiful period piece, extravagantly sentimental . . . yet entirely compelling in its own conviction.' *(NFT, 1969)*

JAZZ SINGER, THE

CT: 5 AV: 2.89

1980 US 115 C MUSICAL/SO BAD

D Richard Fleischer ●
W Herbert Baker Stephen H. Foreman ●

Neil Diamond ● Laurence Olivier ● Lucie Arnaz Catlin Adams Sully Boyar

Young singer (Neil Diamond) defies dad (Laurence Olivier) by making it big in the record industry and living with a shiksa (Lucie Arnaz).

Wildly dated story is insufficiently updated and comes replete with all the expected clichés, delivered at full throttle by Olivier. Diamond is no gem as an actor.

PRO:

'Clearly a winner . . . The movie unashamedly pulls out all the stops with only the briefest of nods to modern sophistication, despite its contemporary setting.' *(Daily Mail)*

MIXED:

'While [it] breaks no barriers and will win no laurels, it will give great pleasure to many people.' *(Madeleine Harmsworth, Sunday Mirror)*

'Lucie Arnaz . . . plainly has in her the makings of a first rate romantic comedy actress . . . The movie is a mess, but it has its moments when the schmaltz isn't dripping off the screen and the clichés tripping off the tongue.' *(Stan Gebler Davis, New Standard)*

'Tepid, dull and mawkish, despite a really excellent performance from Diamond.' *(Elliot)*

ANTI:

'Diamond is unique among pop stars in that he projects not a scintilla of sexual danger . . . The movie plods along earnestly, endlessly – schmaltz in time . . . [It's] like eating your mother's chicken soup when you're not sick.' *(Richard Corliss, Time)*

'Diamond makes an inauspicious acting début and is thrown into total shadow by Olivier's outrageous hamming . . . Diamond . . . walks like a man waiting for the stitches to come out.' *(David Castell, Sunday Telegraph)*

'What is jazz to Neil Diamond and what is Neil Diamond to jazz? Old title has nothing to do with music on display here and would seem meaningless to modern audiences.' *(Variety)*

'Makes not one bit of sense . . . This movie has nothing but foolishness to carry it along.' *(New York Times)*

'Quick, name the pop singer who made the biggest fool out of himself when he unwisely tried his hand at making movies. If you answered, "Roger Daltrey in *Lisztomania*," "Paul Simon in *One-Trick Pony*," or "Madonna in *Who's That Girl?*" then you've never seen the third version of *The Jazz Singer*, which makes Neil Diamond the all-time champ chump . . . [But] it took the participation of a full-blown hamola like Olivier to turn this dross into a Bad Movie We Love.' *(Margulies & Rebello)*

'Impossibly dated, but Fleischer's film ploughs on regardless.' *(Winnert)*

'Trash.' *(Laurence Olivier)*

JEAN DE FLORETTE

CT: 9 AV: 8.50

1986 France/Italy 114/122 BW DRAMA/FOREIGN

D Claude Berri ☆
W Claude Berri Gérard Brach from Marcel Pagnol's novel *L'Eau des Collines*

Yves Montand ☆ Gérard Depardieu ☆ Daniel Auteuil ☆ Elisabeth Depardieu Ernestine Mazurowna

Hunchback (Gérard Depardieu) moves with family from town to Provençal countryside, but fails to make a living because local peasants (Yves Montand, Daniel Auteuil) cut off his water supply.

Elemental tragi-comedy, set in beautiful surroundings and featuring three marvellous performances.

Best seen as the first half of a double-bill; the sequel is *Manon des Sources*. A masterpiece of modern French cinema.

ANTI:

'The director, Claude Berri, who did the adaptation with Gérard Brach, aimed for fidelity to the novel; he said that it was his task to give the material "a cinematic rhythm", but "there was no need for imagination." That's what he thinks.' *(Pauline Kael)*

MIXED:

'Why is all this so intensely enjoyable? The people are convincing but not particularly clever, nice or interesting . . . There is no attempt to hide the brutishness and boredom of rural life. The answer lies chiefly in the skilfully written narrative . . . Afterwards the story fades and the atmosphere remains, so that it seems a good film, not a great one.' *(Mark Amory, Sunday Telegraph)*

PRO:

'The time is some sixty years ago. The place is equally distant; primitive Provence in the south of France. And the questions are: why do the machinations of these villains grip us so vividly? Why does the fate of Jean and his family move us so deeply? Above all, by what means does this cruel tale of victimization – there is probably no other great movie that so relentlessly documents the meanness of the human spirit in action – manage to release in us, of all ironies, such a spirit of joyous welcome? Partly it is a matter of emotional scale. This is not a movie of halfway measures. The wicked are irredeemably wicked. The good are unalterably good. And both qualities are played full-out.' *(Richard Schickel)*

'The telling of the story is superbly structured, expounding complex relationships without difficulty, giving a sense of time measured in seasons and generations without recourse to tricks or tedium.' *(William Parente, Scotsman)*

'Berri has made a beautiful and surprisingly humorous film, handling theme and narrative with economy and delicacy . . . [The film] shouldn't be missed.' *(Hilary Mantel, Spectator)*

JENNIE: *see* PORTRAIT OF JENNIE.

JESUS OF MONTREAL CT: 9 AV: 8.45

(aka *Jésus de Montréal*)

1989 Canada/France 120 C DRAMA/FOREIGN

D Denys Arcand ✔
W Denys Arcand ✔

Lothaire Bluteau ☆ Catherine Wilkening Johanne-Marie Tremblay Rémy Girard Robert Lepage Gilles Pelletier Yves Jacques

In Montreal a young, fringe-theatre actor called Daniel (Lothaire Bluteau) is invited to update the local Passion Play, and recruits four other actors to work with him. The controversial results appeal to critics and public, but scandalise the Church. Daniel soon finds his own life and that of Christ's running on parallel lines. For our part, we observe that a modern Christ would find survival today as hard as it ever was in Roman times.

Denys Arcand's project miraculously avoids the obvious pitfalls, only one of which is blasphemy. Although the film has much to say about morality and the role of the artist in society, there is a refreshing absence of portentous philosophizing. Thanks to some excellent performances, the characters all have a life of their own, and never appear driven by the exigencies of plot.

The parallels with Jesus are witty, rather than tendentious. For instance, the tempting of Christ in the wilderness is echoed by a showbiz solicitor tempting Daniel with commercial success, as they look down from a skyscraper over prosperous Montreal. Instead of the expulsion of moneylenders from the temple, Daniel disrupts some exploitative, contemptuous auditions for a beer commercial in his own 'temple', namely a theatre. And so on.

Jesus of Montreal tries to be tragedy, comedy and moral satire, and miraculously succeeds at all three. It is also accessible enough to straddle the difficult divide between art-house and popular cinema.

ANTI:

'Saying that capitalism is nasty and that Christ was a closet Marxist seems a little obvious. Likewise, the suggestion that if He came back today He would be given just as hard a time as He was then.' *(Suzanne Moore, New Statesman)*

'In drawing parallels between Daniel and Jesus, Arcand paints himself into a corner. The too-literal quality of these comparisons, as well as the sometimes over-scholarly (rather than dramatic) tone, diminishes the film's overall impact. As a result, the final resurrection sequence, which should be extraordinarily powerful, is instead cold and clinical.' *(Baseline)*

PRO:

'The film offers so much to both theologian and cinema-goer in its clever satire on the commercialisation of religion, art and human feeling that it would be a sin to miss it.' *(Trevor Willsmer, Film Yearbook)*

'Arcand is a master of tone, a sympathetic director of actors, and an unsanctimonious moralist, who locates his fable within a well-observed society.' *(Philip French, Observer)*

'Arcand doesn't force the parallels, and his screenplay is not simply an updated paraphrase of the New Testament. It's an original and uncompromising attempt to explore what really might happen if the spirit of Jesus were to walk among us in these timid and materialistic times.' *(Roger Ebert)*

JEUX INTERDITS AAW CT: 8 AV: 8.73

(aka *Les Jeux Interdits; Forbidden Games; The Secret Game*)

1952 France 84 BW WAR/DRAMA/FOREIGN

D René Clément ☆
W Jean Aurenche Pierre Bost René Clément from François Boyer's story AAN

Brigitte Fossey ☆ Georges Poujouly ☆ Amédée Jacques Marin Suzanne Courtal

An orphaned refugee (Brigitte Fossey) makes friends with a peasant boy (Georges Poujouly), early in the Second World War.

The anti-war message now seems 'vieux chapeau', and the contrast between childish innocence and adult corruption is too schematic to be convincing: it just looks naive and sentimental. Still, the performances are very touching, and this remains one of the most charming films ever made about childhood. Winner of the main prize at the Venice Film Festival.

MIXED:

'A touching little tale . . . Though a bit too concerned with the trappings of death for my taste, it is beautifully done . . . an experience to remember.' *(Roy Nash, Star)*

'Certainly one of the greatest examples of motion picture craft seen in post-war years . . . A too-boisterous comedy scene in the graveyard, out of key with the rest of the picture, is the only flaw in this screen masterpiece.' *(Jympson Harman, Evening News)*

'Seemed a masterpiece at the time and is full of marvellous moments but no longer holds up as a whole.' *(Halliwell)*

PRO:

'A sad, sad film that, even this early in 1953 I predict will be among the ten best of the year.' *(Leonard Mosley, Daily Express)*

'A truly imposing achievement of blending several seemingly unrelated elements into a totally meaningful whole.' *(John Simon, 1967)*

'Clément's method of presentation – a series of harsh contrasts, with on the one side the intuitive, lyric understanding between the two children and on the other the ludicrous comedy of the quarrelsome, ignorant peasant adults – is perhaps unfair to the adults. But it's an act of kindness to the audience: without this element of gross caricature, we might dissolve in tears.' *(Pauline Kael)*

JEZEBEL AAN CT: 8 AV: 8.00

1938 US 104 BW DRAMA

D William Wyler
W Clements Ripley Abem Finkel John Huston

Bette Davis ☆ AAW Henry Fonda George Brent Margaret Lindsay Donald Crisp Fay Bainter ☆ AAW Spring Byington Eddie Anderson

Unconventional, impetuous southern belle (Bette Davis) loses the man she loves (Henry Fonda) when she wears red at a ball.

The plot is ridiculous, and the characters melodramatic; but there are some extraordinary cinematic moments – none more so than the ball itself – and Davis gives one of the all-time-great movie performances, probably out of pique at not being offered the similar role of Scarlett in *Gone with the Wind*. Wyler shows that he is as adept at intimate, emotional scenes as he is at massive set-pieces. It's schlock, but on such a grand scale that it's terrific entertainment. Max Steiner's score won an Oscar nomination, as did Ernest Haller's photography.

ANTI:

'Just misses sock proportions. That's due to an anti-climactic development on the one hand, and a somewhat static character study of the Dixie vixen, on the other.' *(Variety)*

'The film's action is all implausible . . . and the idea that Jezebel should have such an abrupt change of heart in the last reel flies in the face of logic.' *(Baseline)*

MIXED:

'The material was already dated but was brought out of mothballs and refurbished because of the popularity of the novel *Gone with the Wind*, which the production beat to the screen; without the zing Davis gave it, it would have looked very mossy indeed.' *(Pauline Kael, 1968)*

'Would have been considerably more effective . . . if its heroine had remained unregenerate to the end. Miss Davis can be malignant when she chooses, and it is a shame to temper that gift for feminine spite . . . It is still an interesting film, though . . . colorful, generally well-performed and admirably directed . . . But . . . it needs a deal more character-shading than the author has given it.' *(Frank S. Nugent, New York Times)*

'A strong and fascinating effort and a triumph for

Miss Davis . . . Although the picture is rather slow in starting, it is always interesting once the character played by Bette Davis is properly established . . . But a little too gloomy to be widely popular, perhaps.' *(Film Weekly)*

'A thought-provoking and stimulating picture, but some film-goers may find the Southern dialect difficult to follow.' *(MFB)*

PRO:

'Far from the usual romantic southern tale. It is a penetrating study of character in a setting whose conventional surface handsomeness does not nullify its essential truth and solidity. As in any good movie its excellences came from many sources – good plotting and writing, a director and photographer who know how to make the thing flow along with dramatic pictorial effect, and a cast that makes its story a record of living people. It has enough romantic glamor to interest those who look only upon the surface, enough substance to satisfy those who like the surface to be a truthful expression of depths beneath, and – finally – the ultimate satisfaction of the demands of justice which art can supply though life so seldom does.' *(James Shelley Hamilton, NBR)*

'An example of the rarest sort of movie, that which tries to present a genuine picture of a complex individual character . . . A decorative film; but its most decorative moments reinforce the drama . . . Mr Fonda cannot put much life into the hero.' *(New Statesman)*

'[Davis's] best performance in one of the year's finest pictures . . . Wyler has molded an active, brilliant, often shocking story which implies much it does not say.' *(Photoplay)*

'Never before has Bette so triumphantly proved her point that a woman's face can be appealing and moving even when not preserved in peach-like perfection. Never again can her claim be denied that it is possible on the screen for acting to transmute personality.' *(Freda Bruce Lockhart, Catholic Herald)*

JFK AAN — CT: 8 AV: 7.54

1991 US 188 C DRAMA/THRILLER

D Oliver Stone ☆ AAN
W Oliver Stone Zachary Sklar AAN

Kevin Costner Sissy Spacek Joe Pesci ✓ Tommy Lee Jones ☆ AAN Gary Oldman ✓ Jay O. Saunders Michael Rooker Laurie Metcalf Gary Grubbs John Candy Jack Lemmon Walter Matthau Ed Asner Donald Sutherland Kevin Bacon ✓ Brian Doyle-Murray (cameo Jim Garrison, playing Earl Warren)

New Orleans District Attorney Jim Garrison refuses to believe that the assassination of President Kennedy was the work of a lone gunman (Gary Oldman).

The most lavish drama documentary of all time, and the ultimate Oliver Stone movie: portentous, enormous (over three hours) and obsessive about the 60s. Stone's thesis is that Kennedy's assassination in 1963 was not the act of a lone gunman, but a well-organized coup d'état by people within the American government.

The hero of the film is real-life New Orleans District Attorney Jim Garrison; Stone treats Garrison less as a man than as a peg on whom to hang the research of the past 29 years. This makes for a certain lack of realism: in the movie, he's one lone figure against a disbelieving world, whereas of course there has never been any shortage of conpiracy theorists.

Stone's lack of interest in his official hero (Stone's real hero is Kennedy) is painfully manifest. The Garrison of the film is too flawless to be credible: recognizably a leading man borrowed from a Frank Capra movie. Kevin Costner resists the temptation to play the role with a Jimmy Stewart accent, and reprises the decent but dull performance he gave as Eliot Ness investigating the Mob in *The Untouchables*. Even so, the final court-room summing-up – where Costner sobs as he talks of messages of support from 'the people' but conspicuously fails to make a case against the man he has put on trial for assassinating the President – is risible.

Garrison's domestic scenes are a compendium of clichés, and Stone inadvertently suggests that Garrison may have started the investigation simply to escape from his nagging wife (Sissy Spacek). They are further embarrassing proof that Stone can't write for women: Spacek joins a long list of illustrious actresses who have been weighed down and sunk by Stone.

Another off-putting aspect is that the film is like the swimming pool at a Democrat convention, full of well-known liberals with tiny parts: Jack Lemmon, Walter Matthau, Ed Asner and John Candy all turn up so briefly that the film sometimes seems like an Oliver Stone re-make of *Around The World In Eighty Days*. The only actors who make much impact are Gary Oldman as Lee Harvey Oswald, Joe Pesci as the bewigged, right-wing homosexual David Ferrie, and Kevin Bacon, who plays a flamboyant amalgamation of several real New Orleans rent-boys caught up in the CIA's anti-Castro activities.

Any notion of documentary realism is further undermined by the director's love of heavy-handed imagery: Stone marches to the crash of symbols. The most grotesque example of this occurs when an entirely fictitious 'deep throat' from the military establishment, played by Donald Sutherland, button-holes Garrison and talks to him openly in front of various symbolic Washington landmarks, at a time when (if Stone's thesis is remotely correct) the security services would have had Garrison under round-the-clock surveillance.

Stone spoils his thesis mainly by overstating it. His argument that Kennedy planned to decrease military involvement in Vietnam relies on highly selective use of the available evidence. Stone produces no evidence at all to support his claim that the assassinations of Martin Luther King and Robert Kennedy were part of the same illiberal master-scheme, nor does he offer proof (although Costner states it categorically) that Lyndon Johnson or Edgar J. Hoover were involved.

Stone does build a coherent thesis about how and why Oswald might have been chosen to be the fall-guy; and he demonstrates that the assassination was executed with military precision – but this need not mean, as he seems to think it does, that it was planned by the US military. Stone also produces evidence of a cover-up by the security establishment, but this is hardly conclusive proof that they were responsible for the assassination. Indeed, it seems inconceivable that any conspiracy which allegedly involved politicians, the Pentagon, the CIA, the FBI, the Mafia and armaments manufacturers would have held together for three weeks, let alone three decades.

JFK is over-ambitious, built on dodgy foundations and more than slightly cracked, but – like all magnificent follies – it deserves to be seen, not demolished. Stone organizes a vast amount of exposition so skilfully that Costner's detective-work is never less than fascinating. The film is impressively shot and edited (both departments won Oscars): Stone is ingenious at integrating new with documentary footage. *JFK* is extremely enjoyable as a paranoid thriller and, though too flawed to be a great movie, is certainly a big, bold, belligerent one.

PRO:

'Electric muckraking filmmaking.' *(Variety)*

'For sheer gall and raw filmmaking skill, if for no other reason, Oliver Stone's audacious reopening of the Kennedy assassination was the year's best film.' *(Roger Ebert)*

'Makes its troubling points forcefully, and at the very least persuades that a single assassin could not have done it all. That it turns Jim Garrison into a much more appetizing figure than he seems to have been or be strikes me as a footling misdemeanor.' *(John Simon)*

'The perfect example of why movies were invented: it shocks and challenges.' *(Scheuer)*

MIXED:

'Whatever its flaws – Stone is surely guilty of reshaping some facts to fit his thesis – this is a challenging, eerily plausible, excitingly cinematic probing of our dark past. Thanks to filmdom's magnificent muckraker we're beginning to see the light. Now it's up to our leaders to unseal those "national security" documents that tell the true truth.' *(Guy Flatley, Cosmopolitan)*

'One of the worst great movies ever made.' *(Norman Mailer, Vanity Fair)*

'First, *JFK* is a fine piece of film-making. Second, it is a passionate work in an art that is mostly treated as an industry. Third, it distorts facts in the assassination theory it presents. Fourth, it strongly underscores our incomplete knowledge about the assassination and possible conspiracy. (Let's all check this in 2029.) Fifth, although the proof that Kennedy was killed because of the war is very slim, the film is one more outcry against the waste and horror of Vietnam. As with a prism, we can rotate this set of elements so that we are looking at only one of them at a time. But even while we are looking at only one of them, all the other elements are true.' *(Robert Brustein, New Republic)*

'Courageous, gripping, reckless . . . the culmination or apotheosis of the paranoid political thriller.' *(Philip French, Observer)*

'Full of startling scenes and bravura acting: as dramatic moviemaking, it's superb. Not to be mistaken for a documentary, however, despite its sanctimonious attitude towards the truth.' *(Maltin)*

ANTI:

'Shortchanges the audience and at the end plays like a bait-and-switch scam.' *(Vincent Canby, New York Times)*

'A grand and bland docudrama packed with more celebrity cameos than a Muppet movie, more expository dialogue than a Church of Scientology training film, more types of montage than you'd get from Eisenstein with a bad case of the hiccups, more fake actualities footage than in a year's worth of America's Most Wanted – but shot for the widest screen, and lit like a dream. Bigger, better, more: if gonzo commitment were the only requirement, then *JFK* would be the *Intolerance* of the conspiracy-theory genre, if not its *Oberammergau* Passion Play. As the story's wooden Jesus we have Kevin Costner.' *(Stuart Klawans, Nation)*

'To cite just two problems with Stone's speculations: Earl Warren, the liberal former Chief Justice of the Supreme Court, had been under attack for years by arch conservatives: how did he then become their pawn? More specifically, *JFK* ignores the plain fact that Oswald owned the 6.5mm Mannlicher-Carcano rifle found at the assassination site and established by ballistics tests as the weapon that killed Kennedy and wounded Texas Gov John Connally Jr . . . One critic has lauded Stone for "tenaciously seeking higher truth" despite his guile. That seems like commending a rogue cop for planting evidence on an unpopular suspect. That's not the way malefactors are called to account, not in this republic. In the end, Stone's *JFK* emerges less as the voice of the auteur in pursuit of truth than the cry of the demagogue demanding that his deuces be declared wild.' *(Mark Goodman, People Weekly)*

JOHNNY BELINDA AAN CT: 6 AV: 7.72

1948 US 103 BW DRAMA

D Jean Negulesco ☆ AAN
W Irmgard Von Cube Allen Vincent AAN from Elmer Harris's play

Jane Wyman ☆ AAW Lew Ayres ☆ Charles Bickford ☆ Agnes Moorehead ☆ Stephen McNally Jan Sterling

A doctor (Lew Ayres) is suspected of raping the deaf-mute girl (Jane Wyman) to whom he has been tending.

Four strong central performances – especially Wyman's – lend integrity to what might easily have been just another tearjerker. Ted McCord's superb photography and Max Steiner's score were Oscar-nominated. 'A story that could easily have become a display of scenery-chewing theatrics. It has its theatrics but they spring from a rather earnest development of story fundamentals, tastefully handled.' *(Variety)*

'Beautifully written . . . Negulesco has not permitted sentiment to get the better of him and has managed to inspire all his cast to do rather better than they have ever done before . . . particularly . . . Jane Wyman.' *(Sunday Graphic)*

'Hollywood has tried something dangerously different here, and succeeded in making a powerful and sensitive job of it.' *(Observer)*

'A sea of my special dark red roses for Jane Wyman. I can think of no other actress more deserving of this year's Oscar Award.' *(Ewart Hodgson, News of the World)*

'Why is [it] such an exceptional piece of filmcraft? Because it's a story that for human understanding and sweet simplicity must rival the best; because the director . . . apparently knows how to make cynical young moderns weep . . . Because of these things, but mainly because of Jane Wyman.' *(W.A. Wilcox, Sunday Dispatch)*

'This Jerry Wald production might have been as exasperating as the Broadway play by Elmer Harris that it's based on, but the director, Jean Negulesco, managed to provide an atmosphere in which the hokey, tearjerking elements are used for more than mere pathos – an example of technique over subject matter.' *(Pauline Kael)*

JOHNNY IN THE CLOUDS: *see* WAY TO THE STARS, THE.

JOLSON STORY, THE CT: 6 AV: 7.00

1946 US 129 C MUSICAL/BIOPIC

D Alfred E. Green ☆
W Stephen Longstreet

Larry Parks ☆ AAN William Demarest ☆ AAN Evelyn Keyes ☆ Ludwig Donath ☆ Tamara Shayne ☆ Scotty Beckett ☆ Bill Goodwin John Alexander

Life of Al Jolson.

Though one of the best backstage biopics, that's because it's a cavalcade of great songs and performances; it bears practically no relation to Jolson's real life. Larry Parks is splendid in the title role, and Al himself does the singing. Hugely popular in its day. Cinematographer Joseph Walker and editor William Lyon were nominated for Oscars; musical director Morris Stoloff won one for his scoring. There was an inferior sequel, also starring Larry Parks: *Jolson Sings Again* (1949).

ANTI:

'The purpose of these dehydrated biographies would seem to be the dishing up of old numbers, and foremost among the old numbers I don't want to hear are those of Al Jolson, even if Larry Parks has been coached by the maestro himself to emulate every jerk and muffled sob while the maestro's voice records on the sound track.' *(Richard Winnington)*

MIXED:

'I have nothing in the world against this picture except that at least half of it seemed to me enormously tiresome. The other half of it is pleasant enough, but no more.' *(James Agee, Nation)*

'This romantic, sentimental fabrication of Al Jolson's life . . . makes an entertaining show, tuneful, clean and mildly informative, long on footage and deep in hokum but stamped with the image of its hero.' *(Arthur Beach, New Movies)*

PRO:

'Showmanship at its best.' *(Fortnight)*

'Larry Parks is a prettier Al than Al. He is also an astonishingly capable mimic. And consanguine with his image is the great Jolson voice, a voice whose dynamics seem to have lost nothing through the withering years. Mr Parks' skill and the magic of movie technique have made possible an astounding fusion of two people to create a memorable portrait. Even Al Jolson should be pleased with *The Jolson Story*.' *(Arthur Beach, New Movies)*

JONAH – WHO WILL BE 25 IN THE YEAR 2000 CT: 5 AV: 7.29

(aka *Jonas Qui Aura 25 Ans en L'an 2000*)

1976 Switzerland/France 116 C DRAMA/COMEDY

D Alain Tanner
W John Berger Alain Tanner

Jean-Luc Bideau Myriam Boyer Jacques Denis Rufus Miou-Miou ✔

Various French people ponder the future of Marxism.

A mildly interesting period piece. Not as dreary as it sounds, because the characters are painted with more depth than their tiresomely naive dialectical discussion really warrants. Miou-Miou, as a grocery clerk, is quite endearing. The black-and-white sections are almost as arbitrary as in Lindsay Anderson's *If . . .*, and far more irritating.

'If you want to see a film with more thought behind it about the way the world is going, then you should certainly head for [this], certainly the most important political film in town.' *(Derek Malcolm, Guardian)*

'Despite its silly title [it] largely succeeds.' *(Clancy Sigal, Spectator)*

'Impossible to pin down a film of so many crosscurrents, but its prevailing unity would seem to be atmospheric, its concern to trap a contemporary manic-depressive mood, at best poised somewhere between private angers about what we are doing to our world and optimism that . . . something better may yet emerge.' *(John Coleman, New Statesman)*

'This film, a play of ideas with the laconic irony of Renoir's *Boudu Saved from Drowning* and Buñuel's *The Discreet Charm of the Bourgeoisie*, stays suspended in the air, spinning – a marvellous toy, weightless, yet precise and controlled. The director, Alain Tanner, and his co-writer, John Berger, are willing to entertain possibilities for social rebirth even if they're cracked or pickled. It's a romantic, mystic, Utopian comedy – an Easter fable, with a dialectical bunny.' *(Pauline Kael)*

JOUR SE LÈVE, LE: *see* DAYBREAK.

JOURNAL D'UN CURÉ DE CAMPAGNE, LE: *see* DIARY OF A COUNTRY PRIEST, THE.

JOY LUCK CLUB, THE CT: 6 AV: 8.00 (est)

1993 US 134 C DRAMA

D Wayne Wang
W Amy Tan Ronald Bass from Amy Tan's novel

Ming-Na Wen Tamlyn Tomita Lauren Tom Rosalind Chao Kieu Chinh Tsai Chin France Nuyen Lisa Lu Andrew McCarthy

Chinese-American women swop hard-luck stories.

A sweet, well-acted weepie which is slow at the start and threatens at times to be the oriental equivalent to that Monty Python sketch about northerners insisting they were born and brought up in an eggbox in the middle of a motorway. Superior soap opera, really, and it's a pity that men are portrayed as such a relentlessly bad lot.

PRO:

'Glorious . . . A story of eternal longing, of hope everlasting, that impels us to seek a better tomorrow despite the devastation of today's frustrations.' *(Hollywood Hotline)*

'Believable, involving and subtle, with only the occasional swell of Rachel Portman's lachrymose music to remind you that your heart is being tugged remorselessly.' *(Marcus Berkmann, Daily Mail)*

'So cleverly constructed that we're not aware of its complexity, as we see some of these characters at two or three different times in their lives, trying to survive not only hard times in wartime China, but also the subservient role of women in their traditional society. The movie was described as a "four-hankie weeper", but every tear is earned.' *(Roger Ebert)*

MIXED:

'Thirteen dramas into two and a half hours means about ten minutes per sob story, and it must take a person very loose in his or her lachrymal glands to allow them to be jerked at such record speed, and with such frequency . . . On the other hand, most of the performances are extremely appealing, and some of the humor provides welcome leavening. Yet even the humor tends to leave a sudsy taste in your mouth. Wayne Wang has directed stylishly, and Amir Mokri's camera can wax duly poetic. And yes, it is nice to see Chinese-Americans achieve their embourgeoisement: what could be more middle-class than this movie?' *(John Simon, National Review)*

'The pacing is languorous, occasionally laborious. It is like watching a large family open their Christmas presents one at time. But under the assured hand of director-producer Wayne Wang, the movie takes on a crystalline beauty. The images are static yet haunting. The actual stories, meanwhile, have cumulative power . . . There are some cloying aspects to the dovetailed symmetry of the eight lives. All the women are beautiful, successful and affluent, a fact that is simply taken for granted. And all their men are stupid, evil or, at the very least, unfaithful. Still, the movie's directness is refreshing.' *(Brian D. Johnson, Maclean's)*

JU DOU AAN CT: 8 AV: 8.00

1991 China/Japan 93 C DRAMA/ROMANCE/FOREIGN

D Zhang Yimou ☆
W Liu Heng from own story *Fuxi Fuxi*

Li Wei Gong Li Li Baotian Zhang Yi Zheng Jian

In the 1920s, a young wife (Gong Li) purchased by an impotent, sadistic old husband (Li Wei), the owner of a rural dye-works, who has already tortured two previous wives to death for not bearing a son. She ensures her own survival when she gives birth to a boy by her secret lover (Li Baotian), the husband's adopted nephew; but the old husband turns the child against them, with results reminiscent of classical Greek tragedy.

The memorable aspects of the picture are not its storyline, which verges on melodrama, nor the acting – although Gong Li is the kind of seductive leading lady anyone might be willing to dye for. The most impressive elements are its mood of claustrophobic evil, sensuous feeling for texture, and remarkable beauty. I have never seen a director use colour – in lighting, fabric, scenery and camera-filters – to more dramatic effect. This is among the most ravishingly beautiful films ever made.

The film was directed by the 40 year-old Zhang Yimou, whose previous picture was the much-praised *Red Sorghum*. Here, the dye-works setting is an ironic reference to the fact that Zhang spent seven years labouring in a textile mill during the Cultural Revolution, when he and his family were persecuted for their 'bad class background'. Under the current regime, he has had to make his film with finance from Japan and post-produce it overseas, so that the negative is beyond the reach of the Chinese Film Bureau.

Ju Dou was rightly nominated for an Oscar as best Foreign Film, despite protests from the Chinese authorities, who have banned it. For some reason, they seemed offended by a film which portrays China as a repressive society run by malevolent old men, demanding hypocritical subservience from its citizens, and corrupting its youth with lies about the past. I can't think why.

'A film where the images do the talking, and almost everything they have to say is deeply cautionary. The result is neither a melodrama aspiring to the status of classical tragedy, nor a tragedy vitiated by elements of vulgar melodrama, but another of Zhang's quasi-authentic but modern-spirited folk tales, completely acceptable as a closed narrative for its own sake but also open to a wide variety of interpretations . . . [its] relevance is timeless.' *(Nigel Floyd)*

'A gripping yarn, splendidly arrayed and universally well acted.' *(Sue Heal, Today)*

'Beautifully photographed and extremely well directed, [it] is a reference to the stifling claustrophobia of tradition that has continued to permeate China, even to the extent of poisoning the mind of the youth during the Cultural Revolution.' *(Jeff Sawtell, Morning Star)*

'Appealed to me for two reasons. First, because of its unabashed, lurid melodrama, in which the days are filled with scheming and the nights with passion and violence. Second, because of its visual beauty. When the Technicolor company abandoned its classic three-strip process for reproducing color on film, two of its factories were closed down, but the third was packed up and sold to China, and that is why the bright colors in the vats of the textile mill will remind you of a brilliance not seen in Hollywood films since the golden age of the MGM musicals. Not that this story would have been very easily set to music.' *(Roger Ebert)*

'The "Fifth Generation" filmmakers began a new wave in Chinese cinema by emphasizing the visual and aural qualities of film rather than traditional dramatic and literary elements. *Ju Dou* is no exception to this trend.' *(Baseline)*

JUDGMENT AT NUREMBURG

CT: 5 AV: 7.17

1961 US 178/190 BW DRAMA/WAR

D Stanley Kramer AAN
W Abby Mann AAW from his play

Spencer Tracy ☆ AAN Marlene Dietrich
Burt Lancaster Richard Widmark ✓
Maximilian Schell ☆ AAW Judy Garland ☆ AAN
Montgomery Clift ☆ AAN William Shatner
Edward Binns Werner Klemperer

Members of the German judiciary are tried in 1948 for crimes against humanity.

Trying trial melodrama, turgid and bleak but with some searing moments. Based on a much shorter TV play from 1959, it suffers from a slow pace and gimmicky camerawork, obviously designed to conceal the static nature of the legal proceedings. Burt Lancaster is miscast (he was a late replacement for Laurence Olivier). But it was a big popular success – outside Germany. Photographer Ernest Laszlo won an Oscar – as did screenwriter Abby Mann, who accepted his award modestly 'on behalf of all intellectuals'.

'It never did three cents' business in Germany. It played so many empty houses it just stopped. People asked how could I, an American, try to rekindle German guilt? Well, I said that it would indeed have been better if the Germans had made it, but the fact is they didn't. So I did.' *(Stanley Kramer)*

ANTI:

'An all-star concentration-camp drama, with special guest-victim appearances.' *(Gavin Lambert)*

'Some believe that by tackling such themes Kramer earns at least partial remission from criticism. How much? 20% off for effort?' *(Stanley Kauffmann)*

'The film indicts all Germany for putting expediency, the desire for national unity and strength, above justice: now and then *Judgment at Nuremberg* has a single-minded ferocity of condemnation which I can't help finding a bit repellent.' *(Dilys Powell)*

'An intrepid indictment not of authoritarianism in the abstract, not of the trials themselves, not of the various moral and legal issues involved, but of Nazi war atrocities, about which there would have seemed already to be some consensus.' *(Joan Didion, Slouching Towards Bethlehem, 1968)*

'Another distinguishing mark of top directors is the absence of camera moves. Undiguised camera tricks are the mark of the beginners who fall in love with bizarre camera angles and hand-held moving camera shots. Wrong. Fall in love with your actors. All else is machinery, and directors' vanity . . . If they notice your "show off" camera, the mood goes out the window. Stanley Kramer's 360-degree pan in the courtroom of *Judgment at Nuremburg* served only to distract attention from his tense drama.' *(Frank Capra, 1971)*

MIXED:

'Interminable, heavy-going . . . All good stuff, but too much of it.' *(Halliwell)*

JULES AND JIM CT: 6 AV: 8.83

(aka *Jules et Jim*)

1961 France 105 BW DRAMA/ROMANCE/FOREIGN

D François Truffaut
W François Truffaut Jean Gruault from Henri-Pierre Roché's novel

Oskar Werner Jeanne Moreau Henri Serre
Marie Dubois Vanna Urbino Sabine Haudepin

A friendship between an Austrian and a Frenchman (Oskar Werner and Henri Serre) is tested over the early decades of the century by their love of the same woman (Jeanne Moreau).

At the start of the 60s, Moreau's heroine seemed like a force of nature and the height of sexual sophistication. Now, she looks in need of psychiatric counselling, and the heroes' dogged worship of her appears tiresomely masochistic. The relationship between the two men – one active, the other passive – also seems naive in retrospect. The film is endearingly the work of a young man: full of hurried panning shots and flashy freeze-frames. But Truffaut's visual vitality jars with his plodding, repetitive storyline and old-fashioned use of a narrator to tell us what his characters are thinking. Remade in 1980 by Paul Mazurski, as *Willie and Phil*.

ANTI:

'Moreau is miscast and inscrutable to the point of emptiness . . . It is . . . impossible not to be irritated by the character she is trying to depict.' *(Burgo Partridge)*

MIXED:

'Trails off a bit toward the end, but over three-quarters of the distance it is one of the most exciting and likeable films so far produced by the new French school of cinema. The performances are superb . . . It bubbles up like the spring of life itself.' *(Time)*

'Not a complete delight, but it does have numerous delights and surprises, due to the whimsical manner in which Truffaut tells a basically sad tale . . . Truffaut is an important French talent . . . [whose] errors derive from intelligence and enthusiasm, and never from lack of taste.' *(Hollis Alpert, Saturday Review)*

PRO:

'Stylistically . . . often breathtaking. Truffaut approaches the cinema with adoration . . . The nouvelle vague has no more dedicated director . . . The only way to approach [the film is] – to marvel, to cherish and to applaud decidedly more than half; to boo now and again and even yawn and fidget . . . and to realize that *The 400 Blows* still remains his best film.' *(Derek Hill, Financial Times)*

'The sense is of a director intoxicated with the pleasure of making films.' *(Penelope Houston, MFB)*

'A film about the impossibility of individual freedom.' *(Dilys Powell)*

'The beauty, the real wisdom, of *Jules and Jim* is that the disillusionment of its characters – their painfully protracted awareness of failure – doesn't diminish the value of their moral experiment.' *(Terrence Rafferty)*

'A movie milestone. This 1961 French new wave work offers an intriguing story of triangular relationships, fascinating performances by Oskar Werner, Jeanne Moreau, and Henri Serre and a feast of cinematic techniqes that changed the style of movies to come. You owe yourself the viewing – and the chance of sharing a moviemaker's absolute delight in his art.' *(Judith Crist)*

'The film's style reinforces this idea of the elusiveness of freedom . . . As in *400 Blows*, camera movement captures the exhilaration of free motion . . . sweeping across landscapes . . . As almost surrealistic contrast . . . come the war scenes, given exaggerated realism by Truffaut's use of documentary footage from World War I which forces our recognition of the bizarre contrast life offers.' *(Marsha Kinder & Beverle Houston, Close-Up, A Critical Perspective on Film, 1972)*

'Another study of the relationship of love and life. Catherine refuses to live any longer than she can love, feel, respond freely, act impulsively . . . The same impulsiveness later drives both her and Jim off a pier to their deaths. Truffaut establishes Catherine as a pure spirit, an incarnation of the goddess of love . . . But the pure spirit . . . has difficulties surviving in the real world . . . permanent love and human reality are mutually exclusive.' *(Gerald Mast, A Short History of the Movies, 1971)*

'Nostalgic study of deep and lasting friendship . . . A stylish, dazzlingly conceived picture . . . and containing some of Truffaut's most triumphant scenes . . . Hauntingly scored by Georges Delarue.' *(R.A.E. Pickard, Dictionary of 1000 Best Films, 1971)*

'One of Truffaut's most lyrical works . . . [he] and his cameraman Raoul Coutard use an endless variety of visual devices to reveal the shifting emotional patterns of the trio, in a blend of comedy and tragedy backed by the lovely ensemble playing of the three leads.' *(NFT Bulletin, 1975)*

'This vital, mature and cinematically inventive chronicle . . . is the most exquisite demonstration of the way in which its late director . . . carried the torch for the particularly Gallic lyricism which fired the earlier work of Jean Renoir and Jean Vigo.' *(Allan Hunter & Kenny Mathieson, Movie Classics, 1992)*

JULES ET JIM: *see* JULES AND JIM.

JULIE CT: 6 AV: 4.29

1956 US 97 BW THRILLER/SO BAD

D Andrew Stone
W Andrew Stone ✗ AAN

Doris Day Louis Jourdan Barry Sullivan Frank Lovejoy John Gallaudet Harlan Warde

Air stewardess (Doris Day) finds she's married a murderer (Louis Jourdan).

Enjoyably silly thriller. The inexplicably Oscar-nominated screenplay which combines dotty dialogue with a potty plot. Doris finds her husband's a killer in reel one, but illogically does little about it for ages. The climax, when she single-handedly brings a plane into San Francisco Airport, is a camp sequence worthy of the *Airport* series.

'Produced by Doris Day's own company, [it] provides the actress with something of a field day. The first part . . . is all hysterics, chases and pursuits . . . The climax finds an apparently nerveless heroine calmly assuming command of [an] airliner. This . . . is melodrama of the most extravagant kind, made no less unlikely by a script which never balks at stating the obvious in the most obvious way. The final sequence is mildly gripping and some of the dialogue reaches a fine pitch of banality.' *(MFB)*

'It will have audiences as tense and scared as those bewildered plane passengers who suddenly have Doris Day wished on them as their L-plate pilot.' *(Frank Jackson, Reynolds News)*

'In its efforts to out-Hitch Mr Hitchcock [it] may be said to go off at half-cock.' *(Cecil Wilson, Daily Mail)*

'A farrago of impossible nonsense.' *(Leonard Mosley, Daily Express)*

'I must have seen absurder dramas, but at the moment I can't remember one . . . I enjoyed every moment of the hokum.' *(Harold Conway, Daily Sketch)*

'*Julie* may hold the record for the number of times the microphone boom bobs into frame or casts a shadow.' *(Margulies & Rebello)*

'Too often unintentionally funny.' *(Maltin)*

JULIUS CAESAR AAN CT: 5 AV: 7.29

1953 US 121 BW DRAMA

D Joseph L. Mankiewicz
W Joseph L. Mankiewicz from Shakespeare's play

John Gielgud ☆ James Mason ☆ Marlon Brando ☆ AAN Greer Garson Deborah Kerr Louis Calhern ✓ Edmond O'Brien ✓

A Roman leader (Louis Calhern) is assassinated.

Solid but stolid production, with Brando surprisingly effective as Mark Anthony. The art direction by Cedric Gibbons and Edward Carfagno won an Oscar; also nominated were Joseph Ruttenberg's cinematography and Miklos Rosza's score.

'It's not in color because I've never seen a good, serious, dramatic movie in color, except maybe *Gone with the Wind*. You can't get drama and make people real in color. This is a picture of mood, of violence, of real people – their ambitions, their dreams. People dream in black and white. They don't dream in Technicolor.' *(Joseph L. Mankiewicz)*

PRO:

'Clearly presented, and excellently acted . . . Any fears about Brando appearing in Shakespeare are dispelled by his compelling portrayal as the revengeful Mark Antony, in which he turns in the performance of his career. His interpretation of the famous funeral oration will be a conversation piece. The entire speech takes on a new light as voiced by Brando.' *(Variety)*

'Standing head and shoulders above all is Marlon Brando as Mark Antony, delivering his eulogy over the body of Caesar. Here is an impassioned bit of acting, one of the most gripping, fiery scenes the screen has offered. Brando makes his Antony a brooding inexorable force of vengeance that calculatingly and impersonally plays upon the emotions of the mob to achieve his desired result.' *(Hollywood Reporter)*

'Marlon Brando, word-perfect and seemingly quite at home with the poetic diction required of him, makes Mark Antony an arrestingly dynamic figure – a subtle compound of heroic integrity and serpentine cunning.' *(The Cinema)*

ANTI:

'Mr Brando looks magnificent, moves powerfully and carries a sense of strength and fire. But his voice is not trained to the Shakespearean volume, his enunciation seems to me often imperfect, and in the funeral speech, though the power is there, the orator's emotional cunning is wanting: one feels that it is creditable in Mr Brando to have managed so well, but never that he is in absolute intellectual command . . . Gielgud gives the character of Cassius an extraordinary grandeur: a schemer, but a heroic schemer, teased by his own talents, helplessly watching the destruction of his plans by the figure he has elevated to carry them out. Willy-nilly Cassius it is who dominates the film; this is a performance to be seen again and again.' *(Dilys Powell)*

'Straightforward, rather leaden.' *(Halliwell)*

JUNGFRAUKALLAN: *see* VIRGIN SPRING, THE.

JUNGLE BOOK, THE CT: 6 AV: 7.30

1967 US 64 C CARTOON/MUSICAL/FAMILY

D Wolfgang Reitherman ☆
W Larry Clemmons Ralph Wright Ken Anderson Vance Gerry from Rudyard Kipling's stories (songs by Richard and Robert Sherman, Terry Gilkyson ☆)

Voices: Phil Harris ✔ Sebastian Cabot George Sanders Louis Prima ✔ Sterling Holloway

A small boy grows up in the jungle.

Disney's engaging cartoon is only loosely adapted from Kipling's *Just So* stories. Some of the characters (notably the Liverpudlian vultures) seem coarse and out of place. The ending, too, seems unduly schmaltzy and out of keeping with the rest of the film. But most of the time it is bounding with energy, sight gags and good humour. At least two of the songs – 'The Bare Necessities' (which was Oscar-nominated) and 'I Want To Be Like You' – are classics. It was the last cartoon which Disney himself completed, but it has a high-spiritedness as youthful as in his first animated features.

ANTI:

'I don't know, fellows. I guess I'm getting too old for animation.' *(Walt Disney, upon seeing some rushes)*

PRO:

'Ideal for the children . . . this glowing little picture should be grand fun for all ages . . . Simple, uncluttered, straight-forward fun.' *(New York Times)*

'Has a gaiety and a lack of pretentiousness absent from Disney animated features since *Dumbo*.' *(Richard Schickel)*

'If you are not a parent and feel embarrassed going alone, then borrow or hire a child to go with you. I'll guarantee that you'll both enjoy it enormously.' *(Ian Christie, Daily Express)*

'Only distantly related to Kipling, but pure enjoyable Disney – with a deftness in animated line and quip not surpassed since the dazzling *101 Dalmatians* . . . There, I think that solves the problem of the Christmas treat.' *(Evening Standard)*

MIXED:

'I suppose I should mind that Kipling has been mangled where he isn't ignored completely. But I honestly don't . . . Kiplingers, stay away! Disneyites, fall to!' *(Margaret Hinxman, Sunday Telegraph)*

'Patchily successful but no classic.' *(Halliwell)*

'The settings, which might have been magical, are insipid.' *(Shipman)*

JUNGLE FEVER CT: 6 AV: 6.23

1991 US 132 C DRAMA

D Spike Lee
W Spike Lee

Wesley Snipes ✔ Annabella Sciorra ✔ Spike Lee Anthony Quinn Ossie Davis Ruby Dee Samuel L. Jackson John Turturro ✔ Frank Vincent Tyra Ferrell Halle Berry Tim Robbins

Married black architect (Wesley Snipes) has affair with white Italian-American secretary (Annabella Sciorra).

Spike Lee's lively film about inter-racial relationships contains good performances from Annabella Sciorra and Wesley Snipes, and one taboo-breaking scene where black women discuss their men's preference for girls with lighter skin. But writer-director Spike Lee's own attitudes are hard to fathom, and smack of black racism. Lee argues that the central characters relationship is doomed, since they made love only out of curiosity. It's clear to the audience, though, that the relationship fails because of Flipper's [Wesley Snipes] reluctance to see it in anything but racial terms.

Lee's sub-plot takes a more orthodox, liberal line. Angie's longtime boyfriend Paulie (sensitively played by John Turturro) braves a racist attack and his ham-acting, Italian-American father (Anthony Quinn), in order to date a beautiful, black girl: a relationship which looks distinctly more hopeful. It is typical of Lee (he did the same in *Do The Right Thing*) to argue vigorously in two contradictory directions.

As if these stories were not sufficiently ambitious, there's a further, didactic, anti-drugs sub-plot – of little relevance to the movie's sexual theme – in which Flipper's crack-head brother (Samuel L. Jackson) begs and steals from his family in order to finance his habit. This results in a nightmarish scene where Flipper visits a crack-den to reason with him: unfortunately, there is never any suspense about the outcome of their discussion, so that the scene (though visually memorable) is dramatically redundant.

Depressingly, this is yet another film in which a black film-maker condemns drug abuse but refuses to side with law and order: in both films, the drug-abuser is gunned down by an irate, black man of an older generation. Are black film-makers really so prejudiced against the law that they see salvation only through vigilantes? And, for a film-maker so conspicuously determined to give a positive image of 'black culture', Lee seems over-pessimistic – both about the depths of white prejudice, and about black people's ability to overcome it. At the end, he even hints that Flipper's daughter may be condemned by her blackness to a future of drug abuse and prostitution. Lee seems undecided as usual about whether blacks can save themselves through upward mobility, or are condemned by cultural differences to form a lawless underclass.

The film has many of Lee's other weaknesses: it's overlong, the use of music is obtrusive, and odd moments of Brechtian alienation can't disguise the fact that Lee's style has become conventional since the joyful innovation of *She's Gotta Have It*. But it's splendidly acted by most of the cast, thoughtful as well as confused, and some scenes (especially the one where black women discuss their menfolk) stray commendably near to telling unpalatable truths.

PRO:

'An inspired and very welcome return to form.' *(Empire)*

MIXED:

'Given the violent emotions triggered in others, it would have helped to see more of Flipper Purify and Angie Tucci's feelings about each other as the surrounding fireworks go off.' *(Variety)*

'A thoughtful provocative and deeply-felt movie, its effect is sadly muffled by the over-emphasis on the drug subplot.' *(Rose)*

ANTI:

'If this is the fever, man, hand us the antidote.' *(Quinlan)*

JUPITER'S DARLING CT: 6 AV: 5.00

1954 US 96 C MUSICAL/ROMANCE/SO BAD

D George Sidney
W Dorothy Kingsley from Robert E. Sherwood's *The Road to Rome*

Esther Williams Howard Keel George Sanders Marge and Gower Champion Richard Haydn William Demarest

Hannibal (Howard Keel) falls in love with the Roman dictator's fiancée (Esther Williams).

Esther Williams swims, Howard Keel sings, in this amiably elephantine musical about Hannibal's sack of Rome. Understandably a flop at the box office (the score is terrible, and the story little better), the movie contains many endearingly eccentric moments. The scene where Marge and Gower Champion prance with pachyderms is some kind of weird classic, as is Esther's kitsch underwater ballet. George Sanders appears to have his tongue in both cheeks as the hen-pecked dictator. Has to be seen to be disbelieved.

ANTI:

'If *Jupiter's Darling* had been my first picture, there wouldn't have been a second.' *(Esther Williams)*

MIXED:

'Esther Williams' pictures are generally just so much water over the dame. This one tries to be different. Esther . . . even tries to act – a spectacle almost as alarming as that of the Burmese fish that climbs trees . . . And in case Esther isn't enough, there is a herd of elephants painted blue, green, yellow, lavender and gamboge.' *(Time)*

'As a takeoff, with satirical treatment, on costume actioners, *Jupiter's Darling* is a fairly entertaining, although a hit-and-miss, affair.' *(Variety)*

'An abortive attempt to make an amphibious musical out of Hannibal's conquest of Rome . . . [It] starts off well enough . . . but from the moment Esther Williams dives into her first pool, what promise there was goes with her.' *(Saturday Review of Literature)*

PRO:

'An inconsequential and quite engaging musical. The flippant dialogue of the opening scenes establishes a frivolous tone which later and more spectacular episodes scarcely sustain, and the direction is a little over-weighty, but the film has assets to fall back on in the form of Howard Keel . . . and Esther Williams.' *(MFB)*

'This latest extravaganza . . . has just about everything it takes . . . The crazy story is unfolded against a background of immense magnificence . . . Screwy it may be: but I guarantee the audience will go for it in a big way.' *(Peter Burnup, News of the World)*

'A splendid example of the higher lunacy . . . the gall is enough to be divided into three parts.' *(Halliwell)*

JURASSIC PARK CT: 9 AV: 7.71

1993 US 126 C ACTION/ADVENTURE/SF/FAMILY

D Steven Spielberg ☆
W Michael Crichton from his novel

Sam Neill Laura Dern Jeff Goldblum ✔ Richard Attenborough ● Samuel L. Jackson Bob Peck Martin Ferrero

A dinosaur expert (Sam Neill) and his botanist girlfriend (Laura Dern) are invited to a secret theme park, built on an island by Hammond, a Scottish entrepreneur (Richard Attenborough).

In terms of box office receipts, *Jurassic Park* is the most successful film of all time. It is also – along with *King Kong* – the best monster movie, if you can ignore the indistinct soundtrack, a dismal performance by Richard Attenborough, and some gaping holes in the plot (what happens to the sick triceratops? where do all the other people on the island go?).

As in Spielberg's *Close Encounters*, the special effects are unforgettable. As in his *Indiana Jones* films, the building of suspense is masterful and the action scenes are heart-stopping. But there are new Spielbergian strengths on display: a dryer sense of humour, an absence of sentimentality.

Particularly admirable is the cinematic skill with which Spielberg makes clear – through images of Sam Neill and the children nearly being killed by a falling car, an electrified perimeter fence, a failed computer system – that the real monster of his movie is not any dinosaur, but a modern technology that is out of human control.

Where *Jurassic Park* is superior to all Spielberg's previous adventures (and on a par with Hitchcock's *North by Northwest*) is that he takes the time to show how adventure can change people: Sam Neill's workaholic learns that he has unsuspected paternal feelings, while Hammond (Richard Attenborough) discovers the perils of even benevolent totalitarianism.

Jurassic Park is also a Film of Ideas. Spielberg may have simplified Michael Crichton's novel in order to work within the action-adventure genre, but he retains its most interesting concepts: about dinosaurs having much in common with birds, about scientific research falling into the hands of irresponsible commerce, about Chaos Theory (which holds that life is too complicated ever to be totally controlled).

Released in a year when the old world order all too visibly disintegrated in Yugoslavia and the Soviet Union, a film which explained Chaos Theory in terms that even a child could understand was extraordinarily well-timed.

On its release, however, most critics were dismissive of the plot and performances. Many considered that Spielberg had trivialized the ideas in Crichton's novel. Attenborough's role, in particular, had been softened from the book. Most thought this was an example of Spielbergian sentimentality, although one critic demurred:

'Spielberg has interestingly avoided making just another Mad Scientist movie. The genetic engineers in this film are mere subordinates of Hammond, and he's a fundamentally well-meaning man whose aim is not to dominate the world, or even make a lot of money, but to entertain: he's a flea-circus proprietor who's bitten off more than he can chew. It would be easy to be cruel about Attenborough's performance – his Scottish accent comes and goes – but he endows the character with a warmth and visionary enthusiasm that make his character's folly even more chilling.' *(Christopher Tookey, Daily Mail)*

ANTI:

'One-dimensional and even clunky in story and characterization . . . The monsters are far more convincing than the human characters.' *(Variety)*

'With state-of-the-art computer-generated effects, the creatures here are so good you hardly care what the rest of the film is like. Unfortunately, Spielberg seems to share the disinterest.' *(Dominic Wells, Time Out)*

'If you ask Steven Spielberg for bread, will he give you a stone? Yes – and then he'll sell you a T-shirt reading, "Stones Taste Great!" . . . *Jurassic Park* really is a hell of a piece of work, judged on a purely neurological level. Steven Spielberg wants you to jump, and you do. I suppose he could get an audience to wiggle its ears on cue. But this is all autonomic activity. The forebrain has nothing to do . . . (The) kid actors are so creepily vapid they must have bar codes printed on their skulls.' *(Stuart Klawans, Nation)*

'An eye-popper. What popped my eyes most was the stamina of a 9-year-old boy. In less than twenty-four hours, he is pinned beneath an overturned car, slides down a cliff, is pinned again under a car, cowers beneath a stampede of prehistoric animals, is blown off a fence when 10,000 volts suddenly electrify it, eats a huge meal and dodges two gigantic predatory beasts in a hotel kitchen. His 12-year-old sister shares most of these adventures. Next to the deeds of these two children, the special effects in the film don't stack up.' *(Stanley Kauffmann)*

'Has there ever been a director as unable as Spielberg to tackle the relationships of grown human beings? . . . The real problem with Spielberg is that, for all his technical cleverness, he keeps falling back on the same tricks. If in *Jaws* it was effective to start with someone being devoured by an invisible killer, that's the way to begin *Jurassic Park*; if in *Close Encounters of the Third Kind* it proved impressive to pan across a row of awestruck faces gazing at a phenomenon withheld from the camera for as long as possible, that shot goes straight into the new film. And once more John Williams has written redundantly overexplanatory background music that refuses to stay in the background.' *(John Simon)*

'Excuse me if I've lost my mind, but: (1) Aren't we missing an ending? Don't we still have a gaggle of evil dinosaurs, some of whom may be able to fly off their island? (2) Was there anyone on the planet who thought Spielberg would kill off any of the kids? (3) Weren't some of those dinos taken out of storage from Spielberg's *Gremlins* lot? (4) What the heck was Jeff Goldblum there for – was Spielberg just setting him up on a blind date with Laura Dern? (5) Is Spielberg trying to start a bed-wetting epidemic among kiddies across the world? (6) Hey, who forgot the story?' *(Rob Lurie, LA Magazine)*

'Michael Crichton's novel has been clumsily condensed and his nastier characters unnecessarily whitewashed.' *(Virgin)*

PRO:

'It's the dinosaurs you're really interested in, and they don't disappoint . . . they are quite astonishingly realistic.' *(Mark Salisbury, Empire)*

'You can ignore the plot, such as it is, since not much of it makes any sort of sense you can grasp . . . The dinosaurs themselves, of course, are the real stars, and they're marvellous.' *(Quinlan)*

'This is a monster movie. So how are they? Amazing

. . . Spielberg loves to mix wonder with horror, and he has fun creating a living Museum of Natural Fantasy. Then he scares you witless. Here come a nosy tyrannosaur and a fan-faced, bilious dilophosaur. Nastiest of all are the velociraptors, smart, relentless punks in packs – Saurz N the Hood. They have a special appetite for kids, just like the great white shark in the movie that made Spielberg's rep. Now it has some worthy successors: primeval creatures with personality and a lot of bite. *Jurassic Park* is the true *Jaws II* . . . Perhaps *Schindler's List*, the Nazi-era drama he has already completed shooting for Christmas release, will satisfy those who want Spielberg to enter an auteur rehab clinic. But no film could be more personal to him than this one. With its next-generation effects and its age-old story line, this is a movie whose subject is its process, a movie about all the complexities of fabricating entertainment in the microchip age. It's a movie in love with technology (as Spielberg is), yet afraid of being carried away by it (as he is).' *(Richard Corliss, Time)*

KABINETT VON DR CALIGARI, DAS: *see* THE CABINET OF DOCTOR CALIGARI.

KAGEMUSHA AAN   CT: 6 AV: 8.00

(aka *The Double; Shadow Warrior*)

1980 Japan 160/179 C COSTUME/EPIC/FOREIGN

D Akira Kurosawa ☆
W Akira Kurosawa Masato Ide

Tatsuya Nakadai Tsutomu Yamazaki Kenichi Hagiwara Kohta Yui Shuji Otaki Hideo Murata Daisuke Ryu Kaori Momoi

A thief (Tatsuya Nakadai) takes over from his double, a 16th-century warlord who has been killed in battle, and comes to take on his predecessor's attributes.

Big, bold, beautiful film with epic battle scenes. It is also much too long and lacks warmth; it's one of those classic films which many people find boring, but are ashamed to admit the fact. Though it won the Palme d'Or at Cannes, the less intellectually respectable Ivan Reitman's *Dave* covers the same ground more entertainingly and in equal depth.

PRO:

'Magnificent . . . Kurosawa doesn't engage the simple emotions as readily as some directors . . . but he beguiles the mind and senses as richly as any.' *(Nigel Andrews, Financial Times)*

'If Kagemusha belongs to any film genre, it most resembles the medieval costume epics Hollywood used to love, marzipan movies like *Ivanhoe* and *Knights of the Round Table*. What Kurosawa has achieved is what Bresson tried and failed to do in his *Lancelot of the Lake*: to probe more deeply into the nature of such spectacles, which depend so heavily on ritualistic forms and the play of appearances. Kagemusha is a film about the power of images and appearances; it takes place in a historical setting, but implicitly it is also a film about the cinema itself.' *(Morris Dickstein)*

'There are great images in this film: of a breathless courier clattering down countless steps, of men passing in front of a blood-red sunset, of a dying horse on a battlefield. But Kurosawa's last image – of the dying kagemusha floating in the sea, swept by tidal currents past the fallen standard of the Takeda clan – summarizes everything: ideas and men are carried along heedlessly by the currents of time, and historical meaning seems to emerge when both happen to be swept in the same way at the same time.' *(Roger Ebert)*

MIXED:

'There are plenty of things wrong – or perhaps not quite right enough . . . But look at [the film] beside all but the merest handful of the year's best movies, and it seems like a giant among the puniest of minnows. A great director is a great director, even when not at his absolute peak.' *(Derek Malcolm, Guardian)*

ANTI:

'I found it Kurosawa's weakest film in years – one of the very few that could be called boring.' *(Richard Roud, Guardian)*

'Ultimately rather empty and tedious; it could easily have been cut by almost an hour.' *(Geoff Andrew, Time Out)*

KAKUSHI TORIDE NO SAN-AKUNIN: *see* HIDDEN FORTRESS, THE.

KAMERADSCHAFT   CT: 5 AV: 7.25

(aka *Comradeship; La Tragédie de la Mine*)

1931 Germany/France 78/92 BW DRAMA/THRILLER/FOREIGN

D G.W. Pabst ☆
W Karl Otten Peter Martin Lampel Ladislas Vajda

Fritz Kampers Gustav Püttjer Alexander Granach Andrée Ducret Georges Charlia Ernst Busch

Frenchmen and Germans work together to save French miners after a pit disaster.

Film which interestingly mixes Socialist realism with German expressionism, still packs an emotional punch, and is generally hailed as a classic. Fritz Arno Wagner's photography is outstanding, as is the art direction. However, the film is naively sentimental and propagandistic; and its pacifist message looks unconvincing, in the light of Hitler's rise during the same decade. Modern audiences are likely to find it plodding and dull.

PRO:

'Every reel is packed with human interest.' *(George Blaisdell, International Photographer)*

'An extraordinary cinematic treat . . . We may have some directors who are capable of duplicating the terrific power that Pabst puts into [the film], but we lack producers big enough to allow them to prove it . . . [There are] several striking examples of filmic motion in static scenes . . . Not a word is spoken, yet the scene makes a powerful appeal to our emotions.' *(Welford Beaton, Hollywood Spectator)*

'Pabst plays on all our emotions . . . Only occasionally does lack of knowledge of the language hinder understanding, though this is now to a great extent counteracted by the inclusion of sub-titles . . . This is [a film] most people would wish to see and [which] would hold masses enthralled.' *(Bioscope)*

'Brilliantly staged, riveting.' *(Scheuer)*

'The story development is slow, but the concept is so strong, and the strong sense of cross-cultural cameraderie so stirring that the film remains impressive.' *(Martin & Porter)*

'Pabst's film, unashamedly propaganda, retains its freshness and its ability to create audience tension.' *(Shipman)*

'The absolute high-point of German socialist film-making of its period.' *(Tony Rayns, Time Out)*

MIXED:

'The film, of course, is admirable in many ways, but it did not succeed in removing from my mind that Pabst, though an honest fellow, is dull.' *(James Agate, Tatler)*

KANAL CT: 5 AV: 7.18

(aka *They Loved Life*)

1956 Poland 91/97 BW DRAMA/WAR/FOREIGN

D Andrzej Wajda
W Jerzy Izewska from Jerzy Stawinski's novel *Kloakerne*

Teresa Izewska Tadeusz Janczar Emil Kariewicz Wienczyslaw Glinski Vladek Sheybal Teresa Berezowska

Polish partisans hide from the Nazis during the 1944 Warsaw uprising.

Gruelling, stiflingly claustrophobic drama which suffers from pretentious references to Dante's *Inferno*, an unremittingly bleak storyline, and an absence of interesting characters (though their situation certainly holds the interest). The second part of Wajda's wartime trilogy, it comes between *A Generation* and *Ashes and Diamonds*. Won the Special Jury Prize at Cannes.

'It dwells rather too much on the details of the horror, but the point is truly made: that in this kind of final degradation many men become beasts but only a few become heroes.' *(Anthony Carthew, Daily Herald)*

'Take a strong stomach with you.' *(Ronald Higham, Daily Sketch)*

'An exquisitely filmed and deeply moving account of the last days of the Warsaw uprising.' *(Nina Hibbin, Daily Worker)*

'Has the claustrophobic intensity and steadily mounting suspense of the best Fifties war films. Wajda's partisans wander through the city's dank underground, while gunfire rakes the sunlit streets above; freedom seems a chimera to which they desperately cling.' *(Michael Wilmington)*

KEEP AN EYE ON AMELIA CT: 6 AV: 8.00

(aka *Occupe-toi D'Amlie; Oh, Amelia!*)

1949 France 80 BW COMEDY/FOREIGN

D Claude Autant-Lara
W Jean Aurenche Pierre Bost from Georges Feydeau's play

Danielle Darrieux ☆ Jean Desailly ☆ Bourvil Carette Grégoire Aslan

A French cocotte (Danielle Darrieux) has two lovers already but agrees to undergo a mock marriage ceremony with a young man (Jean Desailly) who needs to appear married in order to secure an inheritance from his uncle.

Frenetic Feydeau farce, typically contrived but amusingly acted and directed. Autant-Lara emphasizes its theatricality by setting it in a playhouse, but then moves between this and more naturalistic locations. Mildly saucy, but banned in some parts of Britain and attacked by some US critics as being lewd and immoral.

'This typical boulevard farce . . . has allowed Autant-Lara to give a virtuoso performance . . . The construction, the fluency and the pace are all dazzlingly assured.' *(MFB)*

'Most people, I think, could see it with considerable enjoyment even twice on the same evening.' *(Richard Mallett, Punch)*

'A cheerful and not awfully indelicate French bedroom farce, the staginess of which is cleverly dodged by leaving it on the stage.' *(The Times)*

'Autant-Lara . . . has treated it with much skilful imagination . . . The attempt is valiant, ingenious, and, at times, funny . . . Yet, when all is said and done, the material remains too intractable.' *(Manchester Guardian)*

'Feydeau filmed, and triumphantly.' *(Shipman)*

KERMESSE HÉROÏQUE, LA: *see* CARNIVAL IN FLANDERS.

KES CT: 8 AV: 7.00

1969 GB 109 C DRAMA/RITES-OF-PASSAGE/FAMILY

D Ken Loach ☆
W Barry Hines Ken Loach Tony Garnett from Barry Hines's novel *A Kestrel for a Knave*

David Bradley ☆ Lynne Perrie Colin Welland ✓ Freddie Fletcher Brian Glover ✓

A small boy (David Bradley) in a north Yorkshire town befriends a kestrel.

Funny, enchanting, and ultimately rather depressing. Barry Hines's story has the effect of marrying Loach's left-wing ideology and documentary realism to a humanity and humour which anyone can share. David Bradley is moving as the young boy, and there are very funny cameos as his schoolmasters from then unknowns Brian Glover and Colin Welland. The football game, in particular, remains a classic. Far superior to most 'boy and his pet' movies, this is one of the few British masterpieces never to have made much impact in the United States, where audiences seem to have found the accents impenetrable.

'There emerges a most discouraging picture of life in the industrial north . . . Infinitely sad in its total implications, it is also immensely funny in much of its detail.' *(Brenda Davies)*

'Particularly to be admired is the way in which the dialogue has been kept flowing, as if it were always spontaneous.' *(Dilys Powell)*

'Remarkable . . . wonderfully entertaining, and warm and restorative as a hotpot . . . Directed . . . with . . . insight and patience.' *(Robert Ottaway, Daily Sketch)*

KEY LARGO CT: 6 AV: 7.69

1948 US 101 BW THRILLER

D John Huston ☆
W John Huston Richard Brooks from Maxwell Anderson's play

Humphrey Bogart ☆ Edward G. Robinson ☆
Lauren Bacall Claire Trevor ☆ AAW
Lionel Barrymore ☆ Thomas Gomez

A World War II veteran (Humphrey Bogart) arrives in a hotel and find that it has been taken over by mobsters (under the leadership of Edward G. Robinson).

Melodrama which works as a thriller, thanks to the performances (though some, especially Barrymore's, border on the hammy) and some tense set-pieces. Unfortunately, it has pretensions as a metaphor for American society, with Roosevelt's New Deal being hi-jacked by gangsters because of public apathy. This social dimension can have been none too convincing at the time, and now looks painfully dated. *Die Hard*, built around a similar narrative premise, is more entertaining.

ANTI:

'A completely empty, synthetic work.' *(Gavin Lambert)*

MIXED:

'Some of the points Huston wanted most to make were cut out of the picture after he finished it, and I rather doubt anyhow whether gangsters can be made to represent all that he meant them to – practically everything that is wrong with post-war America; so the picture is weak in the way it was obviously intended to be strongest. Even as a study of character under stress it is sometimes stagey and once or twice next door to hammy; and nearly all of it has the smell of the studio and of intelligent but elaborate and compromised artifice. But it is exceedingly well acted, and as picture-making most of it is as well worth watching as anything you will see this year. Huston manages kinds of vitality, insight and continuance within each shot and from one shot to the next which are the most inventive and original, the most exciting and the hardest to analyze, in contemporary movies. Everything that he achieves visually is so revealing of character, atmosphere, emotion, idea, that its visual rightness and beauty, and the freshness and originality themselves, generally overtake one as afterthoughts.' *(James Agee)*

'The picture rambles endlessly – and unavoidably – and is not very exciting. There are, though, some quite effective scenes. Besides Robinson, who is in top form, Barrymore excels himself, and Thomas Gomez and Claire Trevor impress favorably.' *(Fortnight)*

'Huston fills the rancid atmosphere of the setting – a hotel in the Florida Keys – with suspense, ambiguous motives, and some hilariously hammy bits, and the cast all go at it as if the nonsense about gangsters and human dignity were high drama.' *(Pauline Kael)*

PRO:

'A moody and intense gangster drama – a sweeping, exciting narrative that carries the spectator along in a fascinated manner from its provocative opening to its suspenseful conclusion.' *(Hollywood Reporter)*

'A unique masterpiece, presenting the old criminal world of America pitted against post-World War II optimism. It's really a confrontation of ideologies and psychologies, expertly drawn on a common level of understanding. With expert casting, a wonderful script, and taut direction, this John Huston film is a suspenseful and entertaining film classic.' *(Baseline)*

KICKBOXER CT: 6 AV: 3.78

1989 US 97/103 C ACTION/ADVENTURE/SO BAD

D Mark DiSalle David Worth
W Glenn Bruce from Mark DiSalle and Jean Claude Van Damme's story

Jean-Claude Van Damme Dennis Alexio
Dennis Chan Tong Po Haskell Anderson
Rochelle Ashana Steve Lee Richard Foo Ricky Lui

Kickboxer with Belgian accent (Jean-Claude Van Damme) avenges American brother's defeat in ring at hands of villainous Thai.

It's hard to know what is most sickening: the brutality, the racism or the sentimentality. Enjoyable as a treasure trove of martial arts clichés, this is a trash collector's item. (*AWOL* is the other Van Damme film which is so desperate that it's entertaining.)

'Macho nonsense full of cliché characters and risible dialog. There is no denying, though, that the fight scenes – choreographed by Van Damme – are well handled.' *(Variety)*

'A laughably stupid film, but certainly an accomplished little piece of action exploitation.' *(Kim Newman, Film Review)*

'[Van Damme's] character is a sensitive kind of guy who likes children, flowers, and little white bunnies; on occasion he cries, which probably makes it all right for him to ram his opponent's teeth down his windpipe and slice through his face with cut glass . . . [The film] affords considerable amusement, not much of it intentional, which prevents it from being totally objectionable.' *(Sheila Johnston, Independent)*

'Mr Van Damme is a sensational discovery, combining the balletic grace of Mikhail Baryshnikov with the acting ability of a turnip.' *(Christopher Tookey, Sunday Telegraph)*

'The usual limb-flailing Oriental potted philosophy that has them queuing round the block at the late-night Gaumont. Need I say more? Okay – it stinks.' *(Sue Heal, Today)*

'Elder brother Eric built like a cross between an Oxo cube and a piledriver, gets his back broken . . . [His] problems are as nothing to those of the script, however, which is dead from the neck up.' *(Hugo Davenport, Daily Telegraph)*

'Thailand and its people simply serve as a beautiful and submissive backdrop to the offensive racist nonsense.' *(Mike Naughton, Morning Star)*

'Don't see it for psychological complexity, social comment, acting, plot or humour; go, if you must, just for kicks.' *(Tom Charity, Time Out)*

'Violent stuff, but those who like this sort of thing probably won't mind the quality of the acting or the plot.' *(Rose)*

'*The Karate Kid* for sadistic adults . . . completely unconvincing.' *(Quinlan)*

KID, THE

CT: 7 AV: 8.10

1921 US 52 BW COMEDY/SILENT

D Charles Chaplin ☆
W Charles Chaplin

Charles Chaplin ☆ Jackie Coogan ☆
Edna Purviance Carl Miller Granville Redmond
Lita Grey

A five-year-old (Jackie Coogan), growing up in destitution, fears he will be sent to an orphanage.

Pretty much the usual mixture of slapstick and sentiment, with rather too much of the latter. Even so, Chaplin's most autobiographical film (his first feature-length work) is among his most touching, thanks to Coogan's natural performance which triumphs over the maudlin material. It made Coogan the biggest child star of the 1920s.

ANTI:

'The blemish on *The Kid* is the same that has marred many of Chaplin's other pictures – vulgarity, or coarseness.' *(New York Times)*

PRO:

'In this, Chaplin is less of the buffoon and more of the actor. But his comedy is all there and there is not a dull moment.' *(Variety)*

'The nicest thing about *The Kid* is its freshness. Such naiveté – and I don't mean only the child's – amazes us. I do not think a film like that has ever been made in France. We are too cultured . . . No wonder the American film, crude and simple as it is, is so often a favourite with the most advanced of our literary men – precisely because it is not contaminated with literature.' *(René Clair)*

'The most enchantingly Victorian of Chaplin's features, and perhaps because of the way his sentimentality (which was often awkward, and even mawkish, later) fits the subject, this film seems remarkably innocent and pure.' *(Pauline Kael)*

KID BROTHER, THE

CT: 8 AV: 9.00

1927 US 82 BW COMEDY/ROMANCE/SILENT

D Ted Wilde J.A. Howe Lewis Milestone ☆
W John Grey Lex Neal Howard Green from John Grey, Tom Crizer, Ted Wilde's story

Harold Lloyd ☆ Jobyna Ralston Walter James
Leo Willis Olin Francis

Puny but intelligent country boy (Harold Lloyd) is cured of his inferiority complex by love.

One of the funniest silent comedies, with a succession of sight-gags, splendidly integrated with thrills and character development. Lloyd's country bumpkin has a lot of charm, too.

'We place it well below *The Freshman* . . . and a thousand miles ahead of *For Heaven's Sake* . . . [It] is full of snappy gags . . . The bespectacled Lloyd gives a human, mellow performance . . . Hand it to Harold.. [he] never mixed a pleasanter blend of laughter and pathos.' *(Photoplay)*

'About as gaggy a picture as he has ever done. It is just a series of gags . . . some funny and others funnier.' *(Variety)*

'Eventful and hilarious . . . Mr Lloyd displays no little ingenuity, none of his gags being inspired by any other comedian . . . literally made the audience rock with glee . . . You might go to see [this film] insisting that you would never laugh aloud, but it is questionable whether you would live in silence for longer than one or two sequences.' *(Mordaunt Hall, New York Times)*

'One of Lloyd's most disarming films . . . The film

takes pains in establishing mood and characterization . . . and recreates quite lovingly the milieu of country life . . . and Lloyd lives up to his reputation as the biggest laugh-getter of all the great comedians. He may not have a very complicated statement to get across but his is more charming than Keaton and less pretentious than Chaplin . . . The film remains a lovely Lloydian allegory on the rewards of virtue.' *(Richard Koszarski, Film Comment, 1971)*

'Delicate country settings give the film an unexpected lyrical feeling, but the mood changes at the quite ferocious climax when Harold is forced to tackle the villain . . . [and] a truly heroic battle takes place complicated by the presence of a monkey.' *(Elkan Allan, NFT Bulletin)*

'One of Lloyd's true masterpieces . . . No synopsis can describe the warmth, perception, and charm of the interactions between the characters, not to mention the endless flow of hysterical sight-gags.' *(Scheuer)*

KILLERS, THE CT: 8 AV: 8.44

1946 US 105 BW DRAMA/THRILLER

D Robert Siodmak ☆ AAN
W Anthony Veiller AAN (and John Huston, uncredited) from Ernest Hemingway's story

Burt Lancaster Edmond O'Brien Ava Gardner Albert Dekker Sam Levene William Conrad Charles McGraw

A gangster (Burt Lancaster) waits to be assassinated.

Remarkable, tense, film noir melodrama. There are plenty of twists in Ernest Hemingway's storyline; and Burt Lancaster, Edmond O'Brien and Ava Gardner give solid performances. Miklos Rozsa's Oscar-nominated score later became famous through the *Dragnet* television series. Arthur Hilton's editing was also nominated.

ANTI:

'[After the opening sequence] the film rockets away into a superficial narrative of violence . . . never anything beyond the facts of brutality, never any attempt to look beneath for the true pitiful springs of action.' *(Dilys Powell)*

MIXED:

'There is a good strident journalistic feeling for tension, noise, sentiment, and jazzed-up realism . . . There is nothing unique or even valuable about the picture, but energy combined with attention to form and detail doesn't turn up every day; neither does good entertainment.' *(James Agee, Nation)*

PRO:

'Seldom does a melodrama maintain the high tension that distnguishes this one.' *(Variety)*

Tough, rough and sordid, the film never compromises with its subject matter.' *(Herb Sterne)*

'A prime example of post-war pessimism and fatalism.' *(Tony Rayns, Time Out)*

KILLING FIELDS, THE AAN CT: 8 AV: 7.80

1984 GB 141 C WAR/DRAMA

D Roland Joffe ☆ AAN
W Bruce Robinson ☆ AAN based on Sidney Schanberg's article *The Death and Life of Dith Pran*

Sam Waterston AAN Haing S. Ngor ☆ AAW John Malkovich Julian Sands Craig T. Nelson Spalding Gray Bill Paterson

The harrowing true-life story of an American war correspondent, Sidney Schanberg, and his Cambodian translator, Dith Pran.

A great achievement for producer David Puttnam, writer Bruce Robinson, and particularly first-time British director Roland Joffe: it's visually spectacular, splendidly acted and a film which really brings to life the horrors of Cambodia. One regrettable error of taste is the mawkish use of John Lennon's song 'Imagine' over the final moments. There are also structural problems in the narrative, arising from repeated half-hearted attempts to build the story around Schanberg, when all the most interesting things happen to Pran (an amazing, Oscar-winning screen début by a doctor who himself escaped from Cambodia, Haing S. Ngor). But, quibbles aside, this is a magnificent, involving film. Chris Menges's cienematography deservedly won an Oscar, as did Jim Clark's editing.

ANTI:

'Some critics have complained that the occasionally breathtaking spectacle . . . obscures the savagery. I disagree . . . However, I think the makers of [the film] were wrong, both artistically and politically, in the way they present Sydney Schanberg as a self-centred, arrogant prig.' *(Richard West, Spectator)*

'It's written like a TV docudrama and it bogs down in the crosscutting between Pran's experiences of the atrocities in Cambodia and Schanberg's guilt and misery in various settings in the US. At times, it's almost as if Cambodia only existed to make Waterston's Schanberg suffer and soliloquize, endlessly asking, "Did I do what was right?".' *(Pauline Kael)*

MIXED:

'My only real criticism was the strange musical score from Mike Oldfield, which ranged from biblical to a poor Vangelis take off. I found it out of keeping with the style of the film . . . This apart, I thoroughly recommend [it].' *(Nine to Five)*

'Because of the overall aesthetic, which does not go in for nuances of character, performances are basically functional. Fortunately, Haing S. Ngor is . . . naturally sympathetic.' *(Variety)*

'Although moving and well-made, the relationship between the two leads still lacks the essential spark.' *(Rose)*

PRO:

'Movie making at its best and further evidence, if this were needed, that the British film industry is making a long overdue comeback . . . [It] is a film moving in its intimacy, and yet powerful in the impact it makes with the wide political issues.' *(The Voice)*

'As a human story, this is a compelling one. As a Hollywood story, it obviously will not do because the last half of the movie is essentially Dith Pran's story, told from his point of view. Hollywood convention has it that the American should fight his way back into the occupied country (accompanied by renegade Green Berets and Hell's Angels, and Rambo, if possible), blast his way into a prison camp, and save his buddy . . . By telling his [Pran's] story, and by respecting it, *The Killing Fields* becomes a film of an altogether higher order than the Hollywood revenge thrillers.' *(Roger Ebert)*

'Brilliantly filmed . . . leaves one reeling despite its comparatively happy ending.' *(Halliwell)*

KILLING, THE

CT: 6 AV: 7.10

1956 US 83 BW THRILLER

D Stanley Kubrick ☆
W Stanley Kubrick from Lionel White's novel *Clean Break*

Sterling Hayden Marie Windsor Jay C. Flippen Elisha Cook Jr Coleen Gray Vince Edwards Ted de Corsia Joe Sawyer Tim Carey

The story of a racetrack robbery.

Heist movie flawed by some major implausibilities – would, for example, a professsional hit-man really fire in full view of the police, without any plan for a getaway route? Still, it's exciting, competently acted and stylishly directed by Kubrick, who was only 27. Thematically and stylistically, it has much in common with Quentin Tarantino's later *Reservoir Dogs*.

MIXED:

'Though *The Killing* is composed of familiar ingredients and it calls for further explanations, it evolves as a fairly diverting melodrama.' *(New York Times)*

'The visual authority of *The Killing* consistently dominates a flawed script.' *(Arlene Croce, Film Culture)*

PRO:

'An excellent portrait of a crime, unusually taut, keenly directed and acted, and with a sharp, leanly written script.' *(New York Herald Tribune)*

'Sturdy fare for the action market, where it can be exploited for better than average returns.' *(Variety)*

'The camera watches the whole shoddy show with the keen eye of a terrier stalking a pack of rats.' *(Time)*

'An expert suspense film, with fast incisive cutting, a nervous edged style, and furtive little touches of character.' *(Pauline Kael, 1965)*

'Characteristically Kubrick in both its mechanistic coldness and its vision of human endeaviour undone by greed and deceit, this noir-ish heist movie is nevertheless far nore satisfying than most if his later work, due both to a lack of bombastic pretensions and to the style fitting the subject-matter.' *(Geoff Andrew, Time Out)*

KIND HEARTS AND CORONETS

CT: 10 AV: 9.38

1949 GB 106 BW COMEDY

D Robert Hamer ☆
W Robert Hamer John Dighton from Roy Horniman's novel *Israel Rank*

Alec Guinness Dennis Price Valerie Hobson Joan Greenwood Miles Malleson

In Edwardian times, a young man (Dennis Price) conducts a one-man crusade against the English aristocracy.

Most sophisticated and delightful of all British film comedies, and welcome proof that dialogue containing words of more than one syllable can have a place in the cinema. Dennis Price, Alec Guinness and Joan Greenwood – in an outrageously sexy performance – all contribute greatly to the fun, which centres on that most gentlemanly of English sports, murder in pursuit of a title. On its release, the critics were only partially impressed. Since, it has rightly been elevated to classic status.

Robert Hamer (on his intentions): 'Firstly, that of making a film not noticeably similar to any previously made in the English language. Secondly, that of using this English language, which I love, in a more varied and interesting way. Thirdly, that of making a picture which paid no regard whatever to established, although not practised, moral conventions.'

ANTI:

'Not the best [of Balcon's] films. It is clever. It has some exquisitely timed comic moments. But it fails to be a consistently entertaining whole.' *(Leonard Mosley, Daily Express)*

'While [Guinness] uses as many wigs and costumes as . . . a quick change artist, he never seems to be anything more than an actor who has overextended his lines. Since Mr Guinness is a man of merit, this is most unfortunate.' *(John McCarten, New Yorker)*

MIXED:

'Story . . . may appear to be banal. But translation to

a screen comedy has been effected with a mature wit.' *(Variety)*

'I presume to praise [the film] but upon what grounds I am unable to decide . . . [It] sags once only (and then curiously in a trial scene) but elsewhere it is as taut, glittering and quilted as the suffragette's balloon.' *(Sunday Chronicle)*

'[Dennis Price's] performance as Louis comes as a surprising revelation. Without being quite the master of technique which the part really demands (his impersonation of the Bishop of Matabele is, one feels, a bit of a struggle), he plays smoothly within his range and gives a performane of style and considerable malicious humour. Only Valerie Hobson, as the lovely widow of poor Henry D'Ascoyne, fails to make anything of her opportunities . . . Miss Hobson plays without any apparent consciousness of the implications of her lines, and succeeds in making Mrs D'Ascoyne as boring on the screen as she would be in life. The film in general lacks a visual style equal to its script. Not that it is often anything but attractive in appearance; the sets are mostly charming, the costumes exuberantly decorative, and the photography delicately sensitive to the period elegances of each. But visual flow, expressiveness of cutting set-up, seem largely absent. As a result, certain dialogue sequences become tedious to watch; and the important trial scene in the House of Lords (prefaced by an inexcusable stock-shot of the Houses of Parliament) is assembled without any particular logic or emphasis. This is a limitation, and the film suffers from it.' *(Lindsay Anderson)*

'A brilliant misfire for the reason that its plentiful wit is literary and practically never pictorial.' *(Richard Winnington)*

'Has not the warmth of *Passport to Pimlico* and *Whisky Galore* and I admit that the joke wears thin and rough during the last third . . . But this story . . . is told with an acid irony which I should until today have thought impossible in the British cinema: not since Guitry's *Le Roman d'un Tricheur* have we encountered so impudent and at the same time so well-bred a disregard of the moral convention. The screenplay, by John Dighton and Robert Hamer, is for the first hour brilliantly funny; and Mr Hamer, who directs also, has enjoined on his players a nonchalance which delicately sharpens the joke.' *(Dilys Powell)*

'Witty, genteel black comedy well set in the stately Edwardian era and quite deserving of its reputation for wit and style; yet the effect is curiously muffled and several opportunities are missed.' *(Halliwell)*

PRO:

'An extremely good comedy . . . Watch out for that Mr Guinness.' *(Sunday Dispatch)*

'Strikes a new and rare note as a satirical comment on the early Edwardian scene and the art of murder. Imagine Jane Austen writing at a later period than her own, suddenly becoming as wickedly witty as Oscar Wilde and you have some idea of the felicitious fun. Alas! for the elusiveness of that jade Perfection. Towards the end the film sadly loses its sense of fun in the prolonged and mainly serious trial scene. It fortunately manages to retain its wit in a finale which it would be a shame to disclose. This lapse is the only flaw in a script by Robert Hamer (who also directed) and John Dighton which ranks among the best-written that have graced British films.' *(A. Jympson Harman)*

'He [Balcon] describes it as his most daring experiment in that line of film. I should rather describe it as the most gaily cynical, the wittiest and most ingeniously satirical film comedy that London has seen for many a day.' *(A.E. Wilson)*

'Enlivened with cynicism, loaded with dramatic irony and shot through with a suspicion of social satire.' *(Daily Telegraph)*

'A theme which was, broadly speaking, very close to that of Verdoux and a marvellous elegance of form allowed scope for ambivalence. All very amusing. Meanwhile the film has been crushed by its own success as comedy . . . What it was all about in fact was . . . one of the cruellest and most savage attacks made on our society and its structures because it brings into question the very right to exist.' *(Pierre Kast, Cahiers du Cinéma)*

'A film which can be seen and seen again with undiminished pleasure.' *(Basil Wright, 1972)*

'Remains perhaps the most remarkable offering to emerge from Ealing Films . . . Its Wildean verbal wit and poised visual humour achieved a rare piquancy and Guinness's performance as all eight upper-class victims offered an exercise in comic observation to savour.' *(Allan Hunter & Kenny Mathieson, Movie Classics, 1992)*

'If one could view only one movie as an example of British film comedy at its best, this would be the movie to see; for rollicking black humor and satirical pokes at the English upper crust, nothing else comes close.' *(Baseline)*

KIND OF LOVING, A   CT: 6 AV: 7.40

1962 GB 112 BW DRAMA

D John Schlesinger ☆
W Keith Waterhouse Willis Hall from Stan Barstow's novel

Alan Bates ☆ June Ritchie ☆ Thora Hird ☆ Bert Palmer ☆ Gwen Nelson ☆ Malcolm Patton Leonard Rossiter James Bolam

A young, northern draughtsman (Alan Bates) woos, then weds, but has to live with his mother-in-law (Thora Hird) as well as his wife (June Ritchie).

This sympathetic portrait of young lust growing into

an unhappy marriage was strong stuff in its day. Now it looks dour, laborious and a bit hackneyed, but the honest, realistic performances still have an impact; Schlesinger's first feature is certainly a landmark British film of the 60s.

ANTI:

'Another *Room at the Top* or another *Saturday Night and Sunday Morning*, and that is just what is the matter with it. Though it has humour, feeling and a dozen very good performances, it goes out on a limb that is already creaking with other people's weight. The sad thing is that, with just an ounce more courage, it could have been a genuine, affronting original . . . for its real theme is not social discontent, like the other two, but the misogyny that has been simmering under the surface of half the interesting plays and films in England since 1956.' *(Penelope Gilliatt, Observer)*

'The trouble is that in avoiding whimsy its realism has remained so flat, so literal and so entirely without fireworks that it is just a little dull.' *(Isabel Quigly, Spectator)*

MIXED:

'The film, after the first lightly sketched encounters is glum and minatory – intentionally; one mustn't complain because the piece is what it means to be. Permissible to remark that it borrows from the documentary field a way of going on after the point has been made; but not permissible to go on oneself. Enough to find a new director and be thankful.' *(Dilys Powell)*

'An old story, but sensitively handled.' *(Scheuer)*

PRO:

'You will be shocked by this highly moral film only if you are shocked by life.' *(Evening Standard)*

'A deadly accurate piece of eavesdropping on life.' *(Thomas Wiseman, Sunday Express)*

KINDERGARTEN COP CT: 7 AV: 5.18

1990 US 107/111 C COMEDY/THRILLER/ROMANCE

D Ivan Reitman ✓

W Murray Salem Herschel Weingrod Timothy Harris

Arnold Schwarzenegger Penelope Ann Miller ✓ Pamela Reed ✓ Linda Hunt Richard Tyson Carroll Baker Cathy Moriarty Jayne Brook Richard Portnow Christian Cousins Joseph Cousins

A violent, obsessive, loner cop (Arnold Schwarzenegger), apparently without a private life or a personal identity beyond the need to catch criminals in the most brutal way possible, finds himself having to work undercover as a kindergarten teacher, trying to trace and protect the ex-wife and son of a vicious drug-dealer (Richard Tyson). Arnie finds that six-year-olds are even more of a challenge than murderers, and becomes dimly aware that a pretty schoolteacher (Penelope Ann Miller) is falling for him.

Predictably but undeservedly, *Kindergarten Cop* met with a patronizing critical response. True, like Arnold Schwarzenegger's breakthrough movie *The Terminator, Kindergarten Cop* has to work round its star's robotic delivery of lines and physical woodenness.

Even so, it is an ambitious and remarkably skilful movie. One strength is its fresh use of hitherto clichéd cinematic symbols. Toys and pets are traditionally used by film-makers to denote innocence and affection. Here, they are used in a variety of interesting ways. One of the mothers showers the kindergarten with toys and a pet pony: the audience subliminally appreciates that, for her, the giving of toys is a way to give herself status (her husband left her for another man). We learn that one of the children uses home-made toys as a psychological defence, 'to keep the bad people away': toys here are a symbol of deep psychological damage, and a strong hint that the boy's father may be the villain.

When the children stand up to tell teacher Schwarzenegger about their fathers, there in the background is another toy (an inflatable tyrannosaurus rex) symbolizing both the comic insights which Schwarzenegger is gaining into the kids' home lives, and the real-life monster who is stalking one of the children. The villain resorts to violence when baulked from buying one of those expensive toys where the racing-cars go round on rails, in endless circles: a coldly mechanical symbol of his obsessive determination to win back his son. The 'toys' of the villain's mother are more sinister – drugs and a rectal thermometer. A cuddly but distinctly phallic pet ferret comes to represent the masculine bond between Arnie and the villain's small son.

Naturally, the average movie audience is not going to recognize such symbols for what they are. Director Ivan Reitman's skill is such, however, that he still makes the audience respond to them on a subconscious level, and – independently of dialogue or subtext – elicits the mood and emotions which he wants.

Another unlikely aspect of *Kindergarten Cop* is that it has several pertinent things to say about child abuse. At first sight, the subject is contained within a minor, emotive sub-plot. Schwarzenegger discovers that one of the fathers is assaulting his small son, beats the father up, and is reprimanded – gently – by the diminutive headmistress (Linda Hunt).

But in fact the whole film is about child abuse. The villain initially appears to be a run-of-the-mill, motiveless psychopath – the kind all too common in the laziest action thrillers.Gradually, though, we appreciate the family background to his sadism: he has a creepily protective mother (Carroll Baker);

strong hints are dropped that he was a child abuser; then we discover that his mother abused him. Significantly, the final threat to Schwarzenegger's life (traditionally the job of the senior villain) is posed not by the villain himself, but by the villain's mother. Without a hint of didacticism, the film portrays clearly – though almost subliminally – the cyclical nature of child abuse.

The other praiseworthy aspect of the film is its daring mixture of genres: it's a comedy celebrating family values, a buddy-buddy cop movie, a love story, and a thriller which keeps you guessing. Despite occasional forays into schmaltz and over-obvious humour, *Kindergarten Cop* was an achievement. It deserved to be a hit, and was.

ANTI:

'A mish-mash of violence, psycho-drama and lukewarm kiddie comedy.' *(Variety)*

'Full of clumsy contrivance . . . Reitman builds the film around a series of one-liners [which] works well enough at the beginning . . . But things take a sentimental turn for the worse . . . Through the flimsiness, there are occasional intimations of something darker in the film's obsession with the nuclear family.' *(Mark Kermode, MFB)*

'The trouble with comedy thrillers is that while they are sometimes funny, they rarely thrill . . . Reitman should never have been allowed near the genre after *Legal Eagles* . . . That the film works at all is down to Big Arnie.' *(Tom Charity, Time Out)*

'Whatever the mood – sentimental, rude, blood-spattered, Reitman knows how to bludgeon a scene to the ground . . . Very much a film in the current Hollywood mode: strident, tethered to a formula, a star vehicle derailed by nasty hands.' *(Geoff Brown, The Times)*

'An intriguing idea is thrown away on a script that's flabby and badly in need of toning up.' *(Rose)*

'An undercurrent of brutality and objectionable morality.' *(Halliwell)*

'Offers a few easy laughs but little else.' *(Elliot)*

PRO:

'An example of a film that actually lives up to its clever trailer, combing elements of both sides of Arnold Schwarzenegger's personality – the comic and the adventurous – in this engaging holiday treat . . . The scenes of [him] in the classroom are among his most hilarious ever . . . The only drawback is that once the action leaves the classroom, the story becomes mired in a race to see who will discover the mother and son first . . . What places the film a cut above other commercial comedies is its strong cast, down to the smallest roles.' *(Nancy Kolomitz, Film Journal)*

'Big Arnie again demonstrates his ability to transcend the hardware movies for which he is best known . . . and [he] is never afraid to raise laughter at his own expense.' *(Kirsty McNeill, City Limits)*

KING AND I, THE AAN — CT: 9 AV: 7.54

1956 US 133 C MUSICAL

D Walter Lang ☆ AAN
W Ernest Lehman from Richard Rodgers and Oscar Hammerstein II's musical ☆

Deborah Kerr AAN (songs dubbed by Marni Nixon) Yul Brynner ☆ AAW Rita Moreno Martin Benson Alan Mowbray Terry Saunders

A prim governess (Deborah Kerr) tries to educate the children of the King of Thailand (Yul Brynner).

Thrilling, picturesque musical, based on a story previously filmed as *Anna and the King of Siam*. It is adorned with an all-time-great performance by Yul Brynner, and one of Rodgers and Hammerstein's finest scores. Great pieces of staging include 'Shall We Dance', 'The March of the Siamese Children', and 'The Little House of Uncle Thomas'. The colonial and racial overtones may make modern viewers queasy, but they are handled with considerable tact. It deservedly won Oscars for art direction, Irene Sharaff's costumes, Alfred Newman and Ken Darby's scoring. Leon Shamroy's photography was nominated.

ANTI:

'Gaiety has something of a struggle to survive.' *(Penelope Houston)*

'Opulent in lush detail but quite lacking in style.' *(Halliwell)*

MIXED:

'It is not to decry the pretty and touching performance of Deborah Kerr as the governess if I say that Yul Brynner dominates the screen . . . I am glad to say – for the whole story, with its air of Western patronage strikes me as a bit of a cheek – he is the one we look at, like, respect . . . In spite of a good deal of Surbiton-Oriental in the palace backgrounds there is an effect of brilliance, splendour and size not all attributable to the new 55mm CinemaScope.' *(Dilys Powell)*

'Full of pageantry, whimsy and song . . . Once you've got on the basic joke, though . . . you may find this quaint view of the East just a trifle too extensive. At any rate, it's all pretty harmless.' *(John McCarten, New Yorker)*

'Poor songs ("Hello Young Lovers", "Getting To Know You"), fair choreography, poor script, nice photography.' *(Geoff Andrew, Time Out)*

PRO:

'Pictorially exquisite, musically exciting, and dramatically satisfying.' *(Variety)*

'Brought the screen's wedding of romance, drama and music to the highest point in cinema history.' *(Harold Conway, Daily Sketch)*

'[In comparison with *Oklahoma!*] it is better directed – more shapely and distinguished, visually more satisfying and aurally at least as good . . . Nor does the film . . . sag at all.' *(Isabel Quigly, Spectator)*

'The film has Yul Brynner in his greatest performance (and the one that launched his career), his portrait of the king, a creation of overpowering magnetism in its combination of complex intelligence and simple primitivism, a portrait complemented by Deborah Kerr's as the genteel, stubborn and shyly warm Anna.' *(Judith Crist)*

KING KONG CT: 8 AV: 9.53

1933 US 100 BW HORROR/ROMANCE

D Merian C. Cooper Ernest B. Schoedsack ☆
W James Creelman Ruth Rose from Edgar Wallace's story ☆

Robert Armstrong ☆ Fay Wray ☆ Bruce Cabot Frank Reicher Sam Hardy

Gigantic amorous ape terrorizes New York.

An exciting story, with a climax which will be familiar even to those who haven't seen the whole film. It suffers from a slow beginning, several lapses in plot logic and human characters with nowhere near the impact of its monster; but Kong the ape is a classic movie underdog because he suffers (as a refugee, as an unrequited lover, and as a one-time god reduced to the indignity of being an exhibit), and fights back against insuperable odds.

It has great resonance as a modern myth, though critics have been divided over whether it is about a country boy being destroyed by the city; an attack on 'bring 'em back alive' game hunting; or a sick white fantasy about negro lust for white women. Danny Peary (see below) comes up with the most ingenious interpretation of the movie – as a trip through Denham's (Robert Armstrong) subconscious – but there is no evidence that the film-makers themselves ever had this idea consciously.

ANTI:

'There is not in the whole of *King Kong* . . . one single moment which makes my blood run cold. It is just amusing nonsense punctuated by such reflections as why, if the natives want to keep the monster on the other side of that wall, they should have built a door big enough to let him through. And why he doesn't climb it, anyhow. On the night I saw this film there was a great deal of laughter provoked by palpable absurdity.' *(James Agate, Tatler)*

'The scenario writers sought to unite two rather widely separated traditions of the popular cinema – thriller and sentimental romance. The only difference was that they failed to realize that such a union was possible only by straining our powers of credulity and perhaps also one or two fundamental laws of nature. For if the love that Kong felt for the heroine was sacred, it suggests a weakness that hardly fits in with his other actions; and if it was . . . merely profane, it proposes problems to the imagination that are not the less real for being crude.' *(William Troy, Nation)*

'The masterstroke was, of course, to delay the great ape's entrance by a shipboard sequence of such humorous banality and risible dialogue that Kong can emerge unchallenged as the most fully realized character in the film.' *(Wally Hammond, Time Out)*

MIXED:

'Highly imaginative and super-goofy . . . It takes a couple of reels for Kong to be believed, and until then it doesn't grip. But after the audience becomes used to the machine-like movements and other mechanical flaws in the gigantic animals on view, and become accustomed to the phoney atmosphere, they may commence to feel the power.' *(Variety)*

'There is something about Miss Wray that appeals to movie monsters . . . . Never, though, has this fatal lure of hers led into such predicaments . . . In the end, of course, she is rescued and married off to Mr Bruce Cabot, the juvenile, but I should like to know more about what sort of wives women who have been scared by giant apes make . . . There has . . . been nothing like [*King Kong*] . . . The picture emerges as an interesting and effective stunt, produced with considerable imagination.' *(Richard Watts Jr, New York Herald Tribune)*

'*King Kong*, if not a film either for children or the sophisticated, is an astonishing technical *tour de force* and it marks a distinct advance on anything in the same tradition which has yet been attempted.' *(The Times)*

PRO:

'The most spectacular film since the talkies and a masterpiece of technical ingenuity that marks a milestone in the development of the screen.' *(Picturegoer)*

'A sensational thrilling flight of fancy, an unforgettable picture, a living monument to the story-telling genius of Edgar Wallace and a sterling tribute to the brilliance of the Radio stars, directors and technicians.' *(Kine Weekly)*

'From the moment the *Venture* leaves port we are on a journey through Denham's subconscious. Skull (as in cerebral) Island's expressionistic landscape – fertile, overgrown, reptile-infested, cave-filled – is Denham's fantasized sexual terrain. And Kong is a manifestation of Denham's subconscious. Denham conjures up Kong as a surrogate to battle Driscoll for Ann's love and to perform "sexually" (their trip up the world's largest phallic symbol) with her when he has never been willing (or able) to have a sexual encounter himself. Although young and virile, Denham has traveled the world with an all-male crew to avoid intimate liaisons. Kong is Denham's female-lusting side – his alter ego . . . When Kong breaks the chains, Denham can no longer control his sexual urges toward Ann; significantly, we never see them together until Kong is dead. Denham's famous words "It was beauty killed the beast" make sense if he's referring to the bestial side of himself.' *(Danny Peary)*

'The first *King Kong* is still simply the best monster film ever; an island of exotic make-believe, lapped on all sides by absurdity but whose characters keep their feet dry by a steadfast and resolutely unfacetious approach to their material.' *(Financial Times, 1976)*

'A taut and exciting script and stunning special effects which have still to be surpassed make this the definitive monster movie. The climax is an acknowledged milestone in cinema history. Max Steiner's eerie score and first-rate editing contribute to a picture that is well-nigh faultless, including as it does moments of comedy, tension, terror and pathos. The 1976 remake shows how to do it all wrong.' *(Alan Frank)*

KING OF COMEDY, THE CT: 9 AV: 7.47

1982 US 109 C COMEDY/DRAMA

D Martin Scorsese ☆
W Paul D. Zimmermann ✔

Robert De Niro ☆ Jerry Lewis ☆ Diahnne Abbott Sandra Bernhard (cameos: Martin Scorsese, Catherine Scorsese, Liza Minnelli, Victor Borge, Tony Randall)

A would-be comedian (Robert De Niro) decides to crash into show business by kidnapping the host of a chat show (Jerry Lewis).

Director Martin Scorsese investigates the sinister side of showbiz celebrity. Robert De Niro is at his best as menacing would-be megastar Rupert Pupkin, and Jerry Lewis gives the performance of his life as the nasty comedian who has Pupkin as his biggest and most threatening fan. A movie that's one of a kind (although it has obvious thematic connections with *Taxi Driver*), it's too dark to have found favour with a mass audience; but it is a masterpiece of cinematic black comedy.

ANTI:

'Scorsese, must have decided to give us the cold creeps; the shots are held so long that we look for more in them than is there. Scorsese designs his own form of alienation in this mistimed, empty movie, which seems to teeter between jokiness and hate. It's *The Day of the Locust* in the age of television, but with a druggy vacuousness that suggests the Warhol productions of the 60s.' *(Pauline Kael)*

MIXED:

'This is a very frightening film, and in retrospect nothing about it seems funny at all.' *(Variety)*

'A long, sprawling self-indulgent showbiz fantasy that could do with some trimming. But it does have some genuinely funny moments.' *(Arthur Thirkell, Daily Mirror)*

'One of the most arid, painful, wounded movies I've ever seen. It's hard to believe Scorsese made it; instead of the big-city life, the violence and sexuality of his movies like *Taxi Driver* and *Mean Streets*, what we have here is an agonizing portrait of lonely, angry people with their emotions all tightly bottled up . . . *The King of Comedy* is not, you may already have guessed, a fun movie. It is also not a bad movie. It is frustrating to watch, unpleasant to remember, and, in its own way, quite effective.' *(Roger Ebert)*

PRO:

'Unquestionably one of the films of the year.' *(Guardian)*

'The combination of [De Niro and Lewis] is remarkable . . . [making] the film's sympathies quite complex . . . I presume Paul Zimmermann did not have to resort to Pupkin's tactics to interest Scorsese in his script . . . It is the most inventive comedy screenplay for some time. Scorsese directs with insolent ease.' *(Neil Sinyard, Sunday Telegraph)*

'De Niro's performance . . . was as perfect a piece of acting as you will see . . . The [character's name] has already entered the sub-culture of media gossip. Only the other day I heard Andrew Neil . . . described as "the Rupert Pupkin of journalism".' *(Julie Davidson, Glasgow Herald)*

'A frighteningly realistic satire on the world of entertainment, it is extremely funny, provided you like your comedy black, with no milk or sugar. What an actor Lewis turns out to be.' *(Rose)*

'Amusing, underplayed farce with a tragic lining.' *(Halliwell)*

KING RICHARD AND THE CRUSADERS CT: 6 AV: 4.00

1954 US 113 C WAR/ADVENTURE/SO BAD

D David Butler ●
W John Twist from Sir Walter Scott's novel *The Talisman*

Rex Harrison Virginia Mayo George Sanders Laurence Harvey ● Robert Douglas

During the Crusades, Saladin (Rex Harrison) visits England and is smitten by love of an English lady named Edith (Virginia Mayo).

The battles and other action sequences are the best part of this much maligned swashbuckler, which was surely never meant to be taken seriously. Rex Harrison (wildly miscast) and George Sanders camp it up with gusto, and the screenplay contains numerous classic, good/bad lines. Sample . . . Lady Edith (Virginia Mayo) to Richard the Lionheart

(George Sanders): 'War! War! That's all you think of, Dick Plantaganet! You burner! You pillager!'

'A hundred and thirteen minutes of *King Richard and the Crusaders* got me exactly nowhere. Don't ask me what it was all about.' *(Philip Hamburger, New Yorker)*

'Richard conducts himself with a stupidity so immense as to be truly royal . . . Laurence Harvey plays a Scottish knight who demonstrates his manly qualities by bellowing every speech, including his professions of love, at the very top of the decibel range.' *(Lee Rogow, Saturday Review)*

'Do not adjust your set – the sound you hear is Sir Walter Scott turning in his grave.' *(Sunday Express)*

'Director David Butler shows us why the Crusades never really amounted to much.' *(Time)*

'With all the sound and fury and show of pageantry, the actor in this epic who steals the scene, for my money, is a Great Dane dog.' *(Erskine Johnson, Los Angeles Daily News)*

'Ineptly written and cast, with poor production values.' *(Halliwell)*

KING'S ROW AAN — CT: 6 AV: 8.30

1942 US 127 BW DRAMA

D Sam Wood ☆ AAN
W Casey Robinson from Henry Bellamann's novel

Ann Sheridan Robert Cummings Ronald Reagan Claude Rains Betty Field Charles Coburn Judith Anderson Nancy Coleman

The story of a small American town at the turn of the century.

Superior, All-American soap opera, in which Ronald Reagan has his legs amputated but is right as rain thanks to the wonders of modern psychiatry. The over-the-top musical accompaniment will alert you as to when you're expected to cry. Subtle, it ain't; enjoyable, it is. James Wong Howe's cinematography was Oscar-nominated.

ANTI:

'A veritable Mount Rushmore of emotional and physical cripples.' *(Paul Kerr, Time Out)*

MIXED:

'Half masterpiece, half junk.' *(James Agate)*

'In the last third concessions are made to sentiment which wholly alter the mood of the piece; psychiatry becomes the answer to all evils (including the loss of a couple of legs), and the young doctor, after curing his patient, largely by a Henley recitation, finishes in a long shot running uphill towards a substitute love. But this cannot erase the quality of the earlier sequences with their tragic tension and their bold yet subtle handling of psychological obscurities. The acting throughout is notable. Betty Field, as the terrified victim of heredity, gives her best performance so far, and as the defeated daughter of repression, Nancy Coleman offers a sketch which might have come from an Orson Welles film. Robert Cummings and Ronald Reagan, not as a rule my favourite actors, are admirable here, and there is the usual sound playing from Ann Sheridan.' *(Dilys Powell)*

'A cozy little chamber of horrors. Shudder fans and those with a recherché sense of humor may find it worth their time.' *(Herb Sterne)*

'Will give you that rare glow from seeing a job done crisply, competently, and with confidence . . . Of course, every movie has its faults; in the case of *King's Row*, the worst fault is the musical background, which telegraphs all the punches.' *(Russell Maloney, New Yorker)*

PRO:

'An atmospheric story, steadily engrossing and plausible.' *(Variety)*

'Penetrating dissection of a small town's pervasive evil, superbly produced.' *(Scheuer)*

'Reagan's finest performance.' *(Maltin)*

KISS ME DEADLY — CT: 5 AV: 7.42

1955 US 105 BW THRILLER

D Robert Aldrich
W A.I. Bezzerides from Mickey Spillane's novel

Ralph Meeker Albert Dekker Cloris Leachman Maxine Cooper Gaby Rodgers Paul Stewart Jack Elam Jack Lambert

Private detective Mike Hammer (Ralph Meeker) foils criminals trying to steal a suitcase containing something extremely dangerous.

Extremely brutal thriller conceived and shot in very noir terms; this is one of those films where everyone is on the make, and no one is motivated by honour or principle – not even the 'hero', who's virtually a psychopath, and barely bothers to question people before starting to beat them up. Ernest Laszlo's cinematography is the best aspect. Reviewed as a straightforward pulp thriller in Britain and America, it gained a cult following as a result of French critics, who interpreted it as a metaphor for the Atomic Age, as Spillane meddles with forces greater than he can understand. So this is the film is to blame for the fashionable, but ultimately boring, nihilism associated with so many French new wave thrillers.

PRO:

'Here it is, the crime film of tomorrow, liberated from everything and especially from itself.' *(Claude Chabrol, Cahiers du Cinéma)*

'Like *Gun Crazy, Kiss Me Deadly* seems to be one of those films that get better as the years go by. The screenwriter, A.I. Bezzerides, transformed Spillane's book so that the film takes on a partial anti-Spillane quality.' *(Robert Ottoson, A Reference Guide to the American Film Noir: 1940-58)*

'[The picture] was passed aside as confused by American critics, but Europeans quickly pounced upon it as political, and allegorical, with a Pandora's box sought after by various forces . . . standing in for the secret of atomic power.' *(Don Miller, Focus on Film, 1975)*

MIXED:

'Distinguished from its predecessors by an extraordinary arty style – bold, formalised low-key effects, tilted shots, extreme close-ups, complicated long takes, sometimes *outré* compositions . . . [A curious] meeting of art and pulp.' *(Gavin Lambert)*

ANTI:

'A series of amorous dames, murder-minded plug-uglies and dangerous adventures that offer excitement but have little clarity to let the viewer know what's going on.' *(Variety)*

'Curiously arty and excruciatingly boring.' *(Halliwell)*

KISS ME KATE

CT: 8 AV: 7.69

1953 US 109 C MUSICAL/COMEDY/ROMANCE

D George Sidney ☆
W Dorothy Kingsley from Cole Porter ☆, Samuel Spewack and Bella Spewack's musical

Howard Keel ☆ Kathryn Grayson ☆ Ann Miller ☆ Keenan Wynn Bobby Van James Whitmore ✔ Tommy Rall Bob Fosse ✔

A couple of actors (Kathryn Grayson, Howard Keel) quarrel while performing Shakespeare's The Taming of the Shrew.

Cole Porter's best musical is given such a lively, colourful production that it's possible to overlook the gags which don't work and the inadequate acting of Kathryn Grayson (her claim that she belongs in the theatre can usually raise a titter). Highlights include Ann Miller's spirited hoofing, Keenan Wynn and James Whitmore singing the point number 'Brush Up Your Shakespeare', and the spectacular dancing in 'From This Moment On', featuring a youthfully athletic Bob Fosse. If you wonder why things keep being thrown at you, that's because the movie was originally made in 3-D. André Previn and Saul Chaplin were Oscar-nominated for Best Scoring of a Dramatic Picture; and it's the Porter score which makes this a minor classic.

ANTI:

'The script ever was and it seems ever will be rotten and only two of [the] tunes . . . are up to standard.' *(Virginia Graham, Spectator)*

'All the fun is at two or three removes from life and so lacks the ability to renew and refresh itself.' *(Thomas Spencer, Daily Worker)*

'Grayson's trilling is something to contend with, and so is her busy, amateurish performance, and there's a lot of badly placed rambunctious comedy from just about everybody.' *(Pauline Kael)*

MIXED:

'Forget two things – an extremely messy, lumbering start and the constant jump of on-stage to backstage continuity of the plot – and you'll find a movie version that does Cole Porter's grand Broadway musical full justice . . . The prankish spirit of the original is here, so are most of the dazzling Porter tunes . . . along with a splendid color production.' *(New York Times)*

'It's entertaining all right – until you get fed up with those 3-D glasses.' *(Reg Whitley, Daily Mirror)*

PRO:

'Brilliant.' *(Quinlan)*

KISS OF DEATH

CT: 6 AV: 7.09

1947 US 98 BW THRILLER

D Henry Hathaway ✔
W Ben Hecht Charles Lederer from Eleazar Lipsky's story AAN

Victor Mature Richard Widmark ☆ AAN Brian Donlevy Karl Malden ✔ Mildred Dunnock Coleen Gray ✔

An ex-gangster (Victor Mature) agrees to work as a police informer, for the sake of his children, whose mother has committted suicide.

Dark thriller, notable for its believable characters, and a very scary – if exaggerated – performance from Richard Widmark as a sadistic criminal. The let-down is Mature, who's sympathetic enough (and won respectable reviews at the time) but stolid compared with the supporting cast. The use of authentic New York locations was nothing new – Twentieth Century-Fox had already used them on films such as *The House on 92nd Street, Boomerang!* and *13 Rue Madeleine* – but here they are used (and lit) especially effectively in what we now know as the noir style by cinematographer Norbert Brodine. The script is unusually intelligent for the genre, although there are major improbabilities – surely our hero would have been informed of his wife's death when it happened? and given Widmark's obviously psychotic manner, would any jury on earth have let him back on the streets? Remade (badly, as a western) under the title *The Fiend Who Walked the West* (1958).

PRO:

'An underworld film which does not depend on violence, gunplay or noise for intensity and excitement. Enormously effective in giving credence to the tale of its characters are authentic backgrounds of New York and vicinity.' *(NBR)*

'One of the best things that is happening in Hollywood is the tendency to move out of the studio – to base fictional pictures on fact, and to shoot them not in painted studio sets, but in actual places.' *(James Agee)*

'It is a welcome change to find in this film as evil, convincing and hearty a villain as anything that ever came out of Frankenstein's laboratory. For in Richard Widmark Hollywood has produced a killer who is happy in his work.' *(Evening Standard)*

'A tense, terrifying New York crime melodrama, with an unusually authentic seamy atmosphere.' *(Pauline Kael)*

'It is unlikely that Henry Hathaway had heard of film noir at the time he made this film, and yet to some degree he must have been under the influence of the films that composed the genre, or under the general influences of the wartime atmosphere that produced them.' *(Eileen Bowser, Film Notes, 1969)*

MIXED:

'Moments of good drama.' *(Sunday Dispatch)*

'It only needed a better player in [Mature's] role to turn this well-directed and exciting film into a film to remember.' *(Manchester Guardian)*

KISS OF THE SPIDER WOMAN AAN

CT: 6 AV: 7.14

(aka *Beijo Da a Mulher Aranha*)

1985 US/Brazil 119 C DRAMA/ROMANCE

D Hector Babenco ☆ AAN
W Leonard Schrader ☆ AAN from Manuel Puig's novel

William Hurt ☆ AAW Raul Julia ✔ Sonia Braga José Lewgoy Milton Goncalves

A friendship develops in a South American prison between a revolutionary (Raul Julia) and an effeminate homosexual (William Hurt).

William Hurt gives one of his best performances in a role originally intended for Burt Lancaster (who was unable to play it because of a heart attack). But Raul Julia's quieter acting is also excellent in this highly unusual drama which cleverly mixes realism with fantasy sequences. The (partly sexual) fantasies seem rather tame, and and the film's view of revolutionary politics is romantic, but the narrative is sufficiently absorbing to allow one to suspend one's disbelief – at least for the duration.

ANTI:

'A slack piece of moviemaking, and as sentimental as the 40s screen romances that Molina is infatuated with.' *(Pauline Kael)*

MIXED:

'Little more than a gigantic duet for two, with some mesmeric mystery and fantasy sequences thrown in . . . Hurt's movie stories [are shown] as if Fritz Lang had been let loose on a French Resistance pastiche.' *(Nigel Andrews, Financial Times)*

PRO:

'A film of insights and surprises.' *(Roger Ebert)*

'Hurt's performance is stunning, brilliant and definitely Oscar material.' *(Pauline McLeod, Daily Mirror)*

'Brilliant performances make the movie a completely compelling experience.' *(Alan Frank, Star)*

'Funny, scary, original and thought-provoking . . . One of the great movies of the 80s.' *(Rose)*

KLUTE

CT: 6 AV: 8.24

1971 US 108/114 C THRILLER/ROMANCE

D Alan J. Pakula ☆
W Andy Lewis Dave Lewis ✗ AAN

Jane Fonda ☆ AAW Donald Sutherland Charles Cioffi Roy Scheider Jean Stapleton Rita Gam

A private eye (Donald Sutherland) investigating the disappearance of a scientist, becomes involved with a call-girl (Jane Fonda).

Pakula's flawed thriller starts as a straightforward detective story; but, along the way, the emphasis switches to character and the developing relationship between Sutherland and Jane Fonda. There's far too much exposition, and it is clear that no one connected with the movie had much interest in the thriller aspect, since the plot is predictable and the woman-in-peril climax is poorly handled. (It's surely a mistake that we see Fonda from the killer's point-of-view, rather than vice versa, when we have been made to sympathize with her so strongly.) It's most interesting as a snapshot of a 'modern' woman circa 1970, strong and vulnerable at the same time; this is probably Fonda's finest performance.

ANTI:

'Skilled but over fussy direction . . . With her Methody fidgets, [Fonda] is pretty glum company. So is Mr Sutherland.' *(Cecil Wilson, Daily Mail)*

MIXED:

'The actual intentions of *Klute* are not all that easy to spot, though I think they have more to do with its intellectual aspirations than with its thriller plot. For this is a thriller in which even the climactic terror . . . seems more like inter-personal relations than climactic terror, and the psychopathic killer, hooked on self-analysis, keeps a wire recording of his latest murder, as if to carry his guilt around in his pocket.' *(Roger Greenspun, New York Times)*

'It is an angular film – stronger on mood and characterization than plot, brighter in its modern visual dynamics than in its dramatic resolution.' *(Larry Cohen, Hollywood Reporter)*

'It lacks the punch a thriller needs, and its melodramatic ending is typically unconvincing. The appeal lies in the richness of detail about a stratum of life and in Miss Fonda's perceptive performance.' *(William Wolf, Cue)*

PRO:

'Jane Fonda, as Bree, is as irresistible as a surfy beach in July: her performance washes over you like a tartly cooling, drolly buffeting liquid benediction, bringing wave after wave of unpredictable, exhilarating delight. There is a perfect blend here of shrewdness, acerbity, toughness, anxiety, and vulnerability. A quintessential feminity is caught in transition between a badly dented girlishness and a nascent womanliness as innocent of its past as a buttefly of its larva . . . Truly this is one of our most valuable, loveliest young actresses – very possibly the most accomplished of them all . . . What a malodorous actor Sutherland has rapidly become: when he is not insanely overacting, as in *Alex in Wonderland* or *Act of the Heart*, he is equally maniacally underacting.' *(John Simon)*

'What makes *Klute* a superior film is its understanding of the psychosexual basis of so much of the present unhappiness in America, and its insistence that there are some normal people left.' *(Jonathan Stutz)*

'A cute psycho-thriller . . . Brevity makes it sound . . . Slickly directed.' *(Gavin Millar, Listener)*

'First-rate.' *(Jeremy Kingston, Punch)*

'Sharp, slick thriller about murder, perversion, paranoia, prostitution and a lot of other wonderful things about life in New York City.' *(Jay Cocks, Time)*

'I am convinced this is a work of great moral earnestness!' *(Richard Schickel, Life)*

KNACK . . . AND HOW TO GET IT, THE

CT: 6 AV: 7.00

1965 GB 84 BW COMEDY

D Richard Lester ☆
W Charles Wood from Ann Jellicoe's play

Michael Crawford ☆ Ray Brooks ☆ Rita Tushingham ☆ Donal Donnelly

A womanizer (Ray Brooks) teaches his shy young landlord (Michael Crawford) how to attract women; but a waif-like girl (Rita Tushingham) comes between them.

A celebration of youth and the Swinging 60s, presented in quick-fire fashion by Dick Lester. Frenetic fun in its day, now very much a period piece.

ANTI:

'Too clever for its own good.' *(Time)*

'The jokes whiz by so fast that the ingenuity becomes exhausting. The gags don't go anywhere. Lester gets caught up in surface agitation and loses track of what it's all for . . . The film's spirit is too anarchistically chic and on the side of larky youth. It's a fashionable, professionally youthful treatment of 60s underground attitudes; the content seems to be the same as the content of TV commercials, and by the time you're outside the theatre, you've already forgotten the movie.' *(Pauline Kael)*

MIXED:

'Attractiveness is really Mr Lester's trump card – his film is so remarkably likeable that you overlook practically all its limitations until afterwards.' *(Isabel Quigly, Spectator)*

PRO:

'Miss Tushingham's performance in particular shows a natural gaiety. The whole film has the anarchic quality modish today and at all times appealing to a new generation understandably bent on overturning the ideas which have hardened in the minds of their elders.' *(Dilys Powell)*

'A bold and jaunty comic moustache drawn blithely across the British Way of Sex.' *(Philip Oakes, Daily Telegraph)*

KNIFE IN THE WATER AAN

CT: 5 AV: 7.54

(aka *Noz W Wodzie*)

1962 Poland 94 BW DRAMA/FOREIGN

D Roman Polanski ☆
W Roman Polanski Jerzy Skolimowski Jakub Goldberg

Leon Niemczyk Jolanta Umecka Zygmunt Malanowicz

A husband and wife (Leon Niemczyk, Jolanta Umecka) picks up a hitchhiking student (Zygmunt Malanowicz) and invite him to share a weekend on their yacht.

Sinister, cruel film about sexual rivalry and the generation gap. All three actors are impressive – even though Polanski decided to use his own voice to re-dub the inexperienced Malanowicz. As so often in his later oeuvre, Polanski takes delight in showing bourgeois conformism disrupted by an attractive, sinister and sexual outside force – which may be one reason why it now seems a bit slow and predictable. It turned out to be his only Polish feature; it won an award at the Venice Film Festival and a Foreign Oscar nomination, and launched Polanski in the west.

PRO:

'Even if it means staying up until 11 pm and going home to Pinner in a taxi, do not miss [it].' *(Felix Barker, Evening News)*

'An exceptional work, funny, acute and dazzling in its mastery of the medium.' *(Scene)*

'There is little doubt why it won the International Critics' Prize at Venice . . . the taut detailed direction is masterly. The acting is impeccable. Yet the chance of seeing this at your local cinema is small.' *(J. Lewis, Sunday Citizen)*

MIXED:

'Psychological suspense in excelsis. This obviously chic-in-its-time film becomes more interesting in retrospect, whereby the filmmaker's inventiveness and camera technique outweigh his flawed realism, his tendency to tedium, and his superficial characterizations.' *(Judith Crist)*

KONTRAKT: *see* CONTRACT, THE.

KRAMER VS. KRAMER AAW CT: 7 AV: 8.36

1979 US 105 C DRAMA

D Robert Benton ☆ AAW
W Robert Benton ☆ AAW from Avery Corman's novel

Dustin Hoffman ☆ AAW Meryl Streep ✗ AAW
Jane Alexander ☆ AAN Justin Henry ☆ AAN
Howard Duff George Coe

An advertising executive (Dustin Hoffman) is deserted by his wife (Meryl Streep) and becomes a single parent.

An old-fashioned weepie, but with an Oscar-winning twist in the sexual role-reversal. Very well acted by Dustin Hoffman as the father, Justin Henry as the son, and Jane Alexander as the new woman in Hoffman's life. Meryl Streep has the tiresome role of the wife who's trying to 'find herself'. Hard to take seriously at the time, her character now looks incredibly tiresome. Nestor Almendros and Jerry Greenberg were Oscar-nominated for their cinematography and editing, respectively.

ANTI:

'Pastel colours, a cute kid and a good script make this one of the most undeserved successes of the year: wall-to-wall sentiment.' *(Time Out)*

MIXED:

'Benton's direction . . . is as solid as his writing and thinking are unreliable. Well beyond his work on *Bad Company* and *The Late Show*, Benton displays a true sense of pacing and framing, of camera placement and movement, as well as of working with actors and allowing them (especially young Justin Henry) to feel their way into a scene.' *(John Simon)*

'Essentially a television movie raised into the feature category by the excellence of its execution . . . As soapy as a washer full of Tide but so well done that we can overlook director Benton's manipulations of our emotions and let our feelings flow.' *(Baseline)*

PRO:

'*Kramer vs. Kramer* may not be what is termed in contemporary usage an "event" movie. It has no earthquakes, no towering infernos, no colossal meteorites on a collision course with old Manhattan. What this Stanley R. Jaffe production does have is wisdom, insight, compassion, and an extraordinary sensitivity to present-day problems and pain.' *(Hollywood Reporter)*

'Powerhouse drama . . . a perceptive, touching intelligent film about one of the raw sores of contemporary America, the dissolution of the family unit . . . *Kramer* is about people, not abstract stereotypes.' *(Variety)*

KROTKI FILM O ZABIJANIU: *see* SHORT FILM ABOUT KILLING, A.

KUMONOSU JO: *see* THRONE OF BLOOD.

KWAIDAN AAN CT: 5 AV: 7.33

1964 Japan 125/164 C HORROR/FOREIGN

D Masaki Kobayashi ☆
W Yoko Mizuki from Lafcadio Hearn's stories

Rentaro Mikuni Michiyo Aratama
Misako Watanabe Katsuo Nakamura
Ganjiro Nakamura Takashi Shimura Keiko Kishi
Tatsuya Nakadai

A collection of short ghost stories.

A feast for the eyes and ears: director Masaki Kobayashi makes stunning use of colour and an appropriately haunting soundtrack. The film's production values and sense of composition won it a jury prize at the Cannes Film Festival and an Oscar nomination for Best Foreign Film. However, the pacing is unendurably slow,and it's hardly frightening at all. It needs to be watched in widescreen. In the shorter, 125-minute version designed for US consumption, the second story (featuring Kishi and Nakadai) has been deleted.

PRO:

'Filmed in exquisite colour and told without any compromises to foreign tastes.' *(Alexander Walker, Evening Standard)*

'All three stories are weird and wonderful . . . The film casts its own exotic and highly colourful spell.' *(Michael Billington, The Times)*

'The really ravishing colour often looks as though it had been lovingly hand-painted by an old master. Even when the action gets dull (which is rare) one can still feast one's eyes on such delicacies as the shades of green [of a rich robe against the luxuriant forest].' *(Tom Milne, Financial Times)*

ANTI:

'So determinedly aesthetic in . . . design and style that horror frissons hardly get a look in.' *(Tony Rayns, Time Out)*

L

L'AGE D'OR CT: 4 AV: 7.80

(aka *The Golden Age*)

1930 France 63 BW FANTASY/FOREIGN

D Luis Buñuel ✗
W Luis Buñuel Salvador Dali ✗

Lya Lys Gaston Modot Max Ernst Pierre Prévert Caridad de Laberdesque Lionel Salem Madame Noizet José Llorens Jacques Brunius

Two bourgeois lovers (Lya Lys and Gaston Modot) constantly find that their lovemaking is being interrupted.

Once-daring avant-garde film full of surreal, sexual and anti-clerical images. Audiences pelted the screen with ink and stink-bombs at its first Paris screening and got it banned in France until 1979, so of course it has been hailed as a classic. Actually, it's pretty puerile.

'It is LOVE that brings about the transition from pessimism to action: Love, denounced in the bourgeois demonology as the root of all evil. For love demands the sacrifice of every other value: status, family, and honor.' *(Buñuel & Dali, in the programme which accompanied the first screening of the film)*

PRO:

'[It] is not aimed at the mind or the heart, it hits you in the solar plexus.' *(Henry Miller)*

'Drew a sell-out crowd . . . but disappointment was in the air . . . The film is still an eye-opener [and Buñuel and Dali] have packed just about every surrealist symbol they could think of into this rebellious epic . . . [But] since the filmmakers are catholic in their protest, indiscriminately opposing all forms of social conventions . . . it is difficult to take offence . . . The film's outstanding quality is not its defiance . . . but its wit, which is savage, scabrous and frequently hilarious.' *(Eugene Archer, New York Times, first US public review of 1964 New York Film Festival showing)*

'Retains its ability to enrage and infuriate 50 years after.' *(Philip French, Observer, 1980)*

'Should be studied by any serious student of cinema. The film is a surreal inquiry into the traditions and standards of modern culture that have kept true passion and instinct from being expressed freely.' *(Baseline)*

ANTI:

'[It] is extremely rarely screened . . . [so] the ICA is to be congratulated for giving us a chance to say what a load of cobblers it is . . . The film belongs to history, not large art . . . this is surrealism at its worst, cheaply blasphemous and boring to boot.' *(John Coleman, New Statesman)*

L'ALBERO DEGLI ZOCCOLI: *see* TREE OF WOODEN CLOGS, THE.

L'ANNÉE DERNIÈRE À MARIENBAD: *see* LAST YEAR AT MARIENBAD.

L'ARGENT DE POCHE: *see* SMALL CHANGE.

L'ATALANTE CT: 5 AV: 8.50

(aka *Le Chaland Qui Passe*)

1934 France 89 BW ROMANCE/DRAMA/FOREIGN

D Jean Vigo ☆
W Jean Vigo Albert Riéra from a scenario by René de Guichen

Michel Simon ☆ Jean Dasté Dita Parlo Gilles Margaritis Louis Lefebvre Fanny Clair Raphaël Diligent Maurice Gilles René Bleck Charles Goldblatt

The callow captain of a barge (Jean Dasté) and his new wife (Dita Parlo), a naive village girl, are passionately in love; but he is so wrapped up in his work that he fails to respond to her dreams of visiting Paris. She abandons ship, and he goes (at one point, literally) in Seine. Finally, with the help of his eccentric, tattooed first mate (Michel Simon), he wins her back.

Jean Vigo's feature-length début turned out to be his last film: he died of septicaemia three weeks after the film's release, at the age of only 28. Though usually described as a classic, it displeased its original exhibitors and has never been a box office success. The novelettish slightness of the plot is the film's greatest defect; there are dull patches; and the two central actors are a shade over-dramatic for modern tastes. However, Michel Simon contributes a splendidly anarchic performance; and, even today, the look of the film has an astonishing freshness and imagination.

The most innovative and influential aspect of Vigo's film is his reconciliation of two apparently incompatible styles: social realism and bawdy comedy on the one hand, surrealism and a dreamlike sensuality on the other. The shot which encapsulates the spirit of the film is one early on when the heroine, as incandescent as an angel in her white wedding-dress, walks along the grimy, grey roof of the barge.

PRO:

'The best French movie since the best of René Clair . . . Once in a while the picture breaks free into Vigo's half mad, strangely majestic kind of poetry.

The bridal procession from church to barge, which opens the film, is a great passage, forlorn, pitiful, cruelly funny, and freezingly sinister; Dita Parlo (the bride) is the fullest embodiment of sub-articulate that I have seen; the trinket salesman with whom she flirts is an astonishing cross-breed of slapstick with a kind of jailbird Ariel; and Michel Simon, as a pre-mental old man, is even more wonderfully realized as a poetic figure, a twentieth-century Caliban.' *(James Agee, Nation)*

'The singular talent – for once I think I may say genius – of the film lies in its translation into visual images of the mysterious and terrible and piteous undertones of even the simplest human life. And when I say visual images I do not mean that Vigo went outside the realistic for illustration; the poetry of this interpretation of life is conveyed without any recourse to extravagant symbolism . . . And everywhere the sad poetry of the river, the canal, the anchorage, the port, with the smoke of railway sidings, the tracery of bridges and cranes, the coldness and strangeness of unknown faces. There has come no artist in the cinema to fill the blank left when Vigo died.' *(Dilys Powell, 1943)*

'One of the most purely cinematic films ever made, surrealistic poetry in a realistic structure with astonishing images . . . Almost every moment in the film is charged with imaginative visual sequences created out of the bric-à-brac of every day life.' *(NFT Bulletin, 1975)*

'I discovered Jean Vigo through a 30-second clip during a film quiz in a Poitiers cinema and thought it the most cinematic 30 seconds I had ever seen. A few weeks later I saw the whole film and decided it was certainly the greatest film ever made. It still is . . . The most profoundly lyrical, surrealistic and erotic minutes in the cinema.' *(Ken Wlaschin, 1984)*

'*L'Atalante* shows how hopelessly, wonderfully unsuited he was to popular moviemaking. His storytelling is still casual, almost perfunctory: the narrative will slow to a languorous drift, then abruptly begin chugging forward, then stop to give us a long look at some unanticipated marvel off in the distance, then lurch irritably ahead again. And his approach to composition and editing is so personal that audiences expecting an ordinary movie might become disoriented: shots are taken from unexpected angles, are held longer than usual, are juxtaposed with other shots in unprecedented ways. Vigo was helplessly original; he seems at times to be speaking a different language from other filmmakers.' *(Terrence Rafferty)*

ANTI:

'Confused story . . . 12-year-old production betrays its age by poor camera work and dated technical qualities in general, markedly episodic treatment making scanty entertainment contribution in welter of candid sex-play, impoverished drama and interpolated hearty comedy, merging into confected happy ending. Melodramatic leading portrayal, involved direction, diverting though stereotyped comedy relief.' *(Today's Cinema, 1946)*

'One of those classics which no longer provide the authentic thrill; its lack of incident and plot lead quickly to boredom.' *(Halliwell)*

L'AVVENTURA   CT: 5 AV: 8.69

(aka *The Adventure*)

1960 Italy/France 145 BW DRAMA/FOREIGN

D Michelangelo Antonioni ☆
W Michelangelo Antonioni Elio Bartolini Tonino Guerra from Michelangelo Antonioni's story

Monica Vitti Gabriele Ferzetti Lea Massari Dominique Blanchar James Addams

A woman (Lea Massari) disappears on a Mediterranean cruise, and is searched for by her lover (Gabriele Ferzetti) and best friend (Monica Vitti), who in turn become lovers.

The film most often hailed as Antonioni's masterpiece is incredibly slow and contemptuous of narrative development: we never do find out what happened to the missing woman. He uses his thrillerish set-up to examine the angst, non-communication and joyless sexuality of his central couple, which he explores mainly in visual terms.

Many critics found – or said they found – the resulting film rewarding. It received the special Jury Prize at the Cannes Film Festival, even though (or because?) it had been booed and hissed at its first screening. It later received a much coveted 'condemned' rating from America's National League of Decency. Over 30 years later, its studied coldness and artiness are merely tiresome; increasingly, it looks like an exercise in style and minimalism, with nothing significant to say.

PRO:

'A film of complete maturity, sincerity and creative intuition.' *(Peter John Dyer, MFB)*

'The first time one simply watched, ravished. The second time – perhaps the second time – there will be a chance to analyse, to mark the elements of the bold freehand style. Anyhow, one tries. One drags one's eyes away from the screen and makes, as one thinks, notes. But at the end of nearly two and a half hours there is nothing on the paper but a straggle in which a few words recur. "Landscape," they say; "architecture"; "figures" . . . complex, difficult, splendid.' *(Dilys Powell)*

'Stylised, but beautifully untricksy. It has got polish, it gleams with intelligence, but is never glossy . . . [I] found it one of the most satisfying films I ever saw.' *(Isabel Quigly, Spectator)*

'Masterpiece is the only word to describe *L'Avventura*, one of the very few films which achieve in cinematic terms the subtlety and complexity of a good novel . . . Like all great art it is sometimes difficult because it probes boldly into uncharted regions of the human heart, but it never indulges in cold, intellectual meanings . . . for its own sake . . . Complex without being complicated.' *(The Times)*

'Studied, perceptive film about empty relationships in an unfeeling world.' *(Scheuer)*

'As with all Antonioni, the cinematography and composition are unsurpassed. He scatters his existential characters over the landscape, brilliantly emphasizing empty space over the trappings of plot.' *(Virgin)*

'Seen again it seems complex yet not obscure and certainly not slow despite its lack of action.' *(Brian Baxter, NFT Bulletin, 1974)*

ANTI:

'A nightmarish masterpiece of tedium.' *(Time)*

'It leaves me cold . . . It has a drifting, restless quality which, divorced from the general depth of emotion, leaves me irritated and bored; and the beauty of the camerawork is no compensation.' *(Nina Hibbin, Daily Worker)*

'A difficult, slow-paced film, marked by uneven acting and stolid characters.' *(Judith Crist)*

'Aimless, overlong parable with lots of vague significance . . . It made its director a hero of the highbrows.' *(Halliwell)*

'If it once seemed the ultimate in arty, intellectually chic movie-making, the film now looks all too studied and remote a portrait of emotional sterility.' *(Geoff Andrew, Time Out)*

L'EMPIRE DES SENS: *see* IN THE REALM OF THE SENSES.

L'ENFANT SAUVAGE: *see* WILD CHILD, THE.

L'HISTOIRE D'ADÈLE H: *see* STORY OF ADELE H, THE.

L'INNOCENTE: *see* INNOCENT, THE.

LA BELLE ET LA BÊTE: *see* BEAUTY AND THE BEAST (1946).

LA BELLE NOISEUSE CT: 5 AV: 7.63

1992 France 240 C DRAMA/FOREIGN

D Jacques Rivette ***X***
W Pascal Bontizar Christine Laurent based on Balzac's novella

Michel Piccoli ☆ Jane Birkin ☆ Emmanuelle Béart ☆ David Bursztein Marianne Denicourt Gilles Arabona Bernard Dufour

An artist (Michel Piccoli), who has suffered a creative block for 10 years, paints a young woman (Emmanuelle Béart) in the nude, and her husband (David Bursztein) becomes envious of their relationship.

It's sensitively acted by Michel Piccoli as an old artist struggling with powers which are failing (or, by the look of his paintings, failed). Jane Birkin gives a lovely, self-effacing, understated performance as his long suffering wife and ex-model, and the beautiful Emmanuelle Béart shines as the model who's replaced her. The film shows a loving appreciation of Provençal light, and is director Jacques Rivette's prettiest since *Celine and Julie Go Boating* in 1974.

It also has the reverential, quasi-mystical approach to artistic creation which always seems to go down well with critics. I found it unnecessarily protracted, self-conscious and – despite its length – a good deal sketchier than the Balzac novella on which it's based. It is, in fact, just the kind of deadly conventional, decorative, romanticized art-house film that the 64-year-old director used to rail against in the *Cahiers du Cinéma* during the 50s and 60s.

There is a shorter – but still long – version of the film called *La Belle Noiseuse – Divertimento*. Clocking in at 126 minutes, this shortens the painting process and therefore slightly diminishes one's understanding of the relationship between artist and model. Instead, there's more emphasis on the painter's wife.

PRO:

'The best film of the year . . . magnificent performances . . . a classic of cinema . . . Both the length and the seriousness of purpose make this a demanding film, but it amply rewards the spectator who makes the effort.' *(Mansel Stimpson, What's On in London)*

'The film's director, Jacques Rivette, takes a brilliant risk, showing the pencil drawings, charcoals and watercolor washes in great detail. The camera regards the artist's hand for minutes at a time, which may sound boring, but when the process of art and the process of life come into such a fascinating conflict, it is more thrilling than a car chase. At four hours, *La Belle Noiseuse* is not one second too long.' *(Roger Ebert)*

'Perhaps the most meticulous and seductive depiction of the hard work of making art.' *(Richard Corliss, Time)*

'Occasionally a movie defies all conventions, takes risks that almost knock the breath from you and emerges as a masterpiece that haunts the memory. [This] is an exceptionally fine film . . . [that] must be seen.' *(Sue Heal, Today)*

MIXED:

'To enjoy [it] you need a strong interest . . . in the psychological complexities of making art . . . and the physical processes of painting. You will also need stamina . . . The weakness is in the drawing and paintings themselves . . . [whose] images are not strong enough to carry the weight attributed to them. We never see the final picture, which, after four hours, is galling, even if arguably unnecessary.' *(Hugo Davenport, Daily Telegraph)*

LA CADUTA DEGLI DEI: *see* DAMNED, THE.

LA CAGE AUX FOLLES CT: 7 AV: 7.17
(aka *Birds of a Feather)*

1978 France/Italy 91 BW COMEDY/FOREIGN

D Edouard Molinaro ☆ AAN
W Marcello Danon Edouard Molinaro
Francis Véber Jean Poiret ☆ AAN from Poiret's play

Ugo Tognazzi ☆ Michel Serrault ☆ Michel Galabru
Claire Maurier Rémi Laurent Benny Luke
Carmen Scarpitta Luisa Maneri

A gay nightclub owner (Ugo Tognazzi) and his transvestite 'wife' (Michel Serrault) try to act straight for the sake of Tognazzi's son, who's bringing home his fiancée and her puritanical parents.

Stereotypes abound in this risqué boulevard farce with a winning performance by Michel Serrault and a couple of very, very funny set-pieces, as Tognazzi tries to teach Serrault how to act macho, and they try to hold a respectable dinner party. Piero Tosi and Ambra Danon were Oscar-nominated for their outrageous costume designs. It spawned two dismally unfunny sequels and a successful Broadway musical.

'Let me recommend [this] wickedly funny Franco-Italian comedy . . . Hilarious.' *(Felix Barker, Evening News)*

'Continuously inventive and funny.' *(Alan Brien, Sunday Times)*

'Hilarious comedy full of double-entendres, double-takes and guffaws.' *(Virginia Dignam, Morning Star)*

LA CHINOISE CT: 5 AV: 7.00
(aka *La Chinoise, Ou Plutôt La Chinoise; The Chinese Girl)*

1967 France 90 C DRAMA/FOREIGN

D Jean-Luc Godard ✗
W Jean-Luc Godard ✗

Anne Wiazemsky Francis Jeanson
Jean-Pierre Léaud Juliet Berto

Five French students who think they are Maoists discuss the potential impact of Mao's Cultural Revolution upon the West.

Rambling, politically ill-informed posturing by the director as well as the characters – wildly overrated on release. However, it is fascinating as an insight into the naivety that helped to inspire the riots of May 1968. Winner of the Special Jury Prize at Venice in 1967.

PRO:

'Godard's best film since *Breathless* . . . What [he] has caught, in absolutely pure, flat beautiful photography, is the look of these young people who are so caught up in the vocabulary of the class struggle of a class to which they do not belong – the look of hurt and intelligence and gentleness quite at odds with what they are saying.' *(Renata Adler, New York Times)*

'A movie masterpiece . . . Made . . . before the disturbance of May, 1968 . . . In retrospect [it] looks prophetic . . . Simultaneously sad and funny . . . Cross-cut with swift visual and aural references: it moves more like a comic strip than a drama.' *(Michael McNay, Guardian)*

'Brilliant.' *(Tom Milne, Observer)*

'The most dazzling of Godard's revolutionary sermons . . . manages to be occasionally witty about the pretentious of its young people.' *(Margaret Hinxman, Sunday Telegraph)*

'Like a speed-freak's anticipatory vision of the political horrors to come; it's amazing.' *(Pauline Kael)*

'An artistic watershed for Godard, [since which he has rejected] completely that technical virtuosity associated with Coutard which make *La Chinoise* a joy to look at.' *(Michael Garnham, New Statesman)*

'Enigmatic, infuriating, thought-provoking and, at times, deeply disturbing.' *(Virginia Dignam, Morning Star)*

ANTI:

'Either *La Chinoise* is fundamentally serious or it is an inconsequential divertissement on a serious theme. If the latter, it is irresponsible; if the former, it is glib.' *(Stanley Kauffmann)*

'*La Chinoise*, already hailed by Renata Adler, Pauline Kael, Richard Schickel, Joseph Morgenstern, and Andrew Sarris, among others, as a major film, is, in my opinion, a piece of mitigated trash. There is the excellent color photography of Raoul Coutard, and Francis Jeanson comes in briefly to talk a little sense. For the rest, Godard, his material, his pretentiousness and undisciplined garrulity, are boring when not exasperating. 'It is fiction," says the heroine about her experience, "but it has brought me closer to reality." Godard himself does not so much confuse fiction and reality as totally lack a sense of either: he cannot create a believable fiction and he firmly believes that whatever floats into his head or camera is *ipso facto* real. So he wallows in a no-man's-land between meaningful fiction and digested reality, a Disneyland for those who want to escape from both art and life.' *(John Simon)*

LA CIOCIARA: *see* TWO WOMEN.

LA CRIME DE MONSIEUR LANGE: *see* CRIME OF MONSIEUR LANGE, THE.

LA DOLCE VITA

CT: 4 AV: 7.64

(aka *The Sweet Life)*

1960 Italy/France 173 BW DRAMA/FOREIGN

D Federico Fellini ✗ AAN
W Federico Fellini Ennio Flaiano Tullio Pinelli Brunello Rondi ✗ AAN from Fellini, Flaiano and Pinelli's story

Marcello Mastroianni Anita Ekberg Anouk Aimée Yvonne Furneaux Magali Noël Alain Cuny Nadia Gray Lex Barker Annibale Ninchi Walter Santesso

Rambling account of one man's progress through a corrupt society.

Daring, sexy and sophisticated in 1960, this has not worn well; it now looks suspiciously like voyeurism, under the guise of moralizing; the narrative is disorganized; and the quality of acting is not high.

PRO:

'An awesome picture, licentious in content but moral and vastly sophisticated in its attitude and what it says.' *(Bosley Crowther)*

'One of the few films that one feels can be seen with increasing enjoyment a second or third time.' *(Paul V. Backley, New York Herald Tribune)*

'Its personification of various familiar symbols – love, death, purity, sin, reason and so on – never succeeds in reflecting human values or creating intellectual excitement . . . Its actual significance rests in the way its (albeit specious) social attack has stirred the imagination of other Italian film-makers, as well as public interest in their work.' *(Robert Vas, MFB)*

'Panorama of a man's progress through a corrupt society . . . Fellini has not forced his material into a neat shape. He uses it in huge, bold chapters, each chapter independent enough to make a film on its own.' *(Dilys Powell)*

'A classic film that blends vision, humor, darkness, nobility, and tawdriness to form a total cinematic experience. In its own way, the film is just as much a breakthrough as *Citizen Kane*.' *(Baseline)*

ANTI:

'A marathon self-indulgent wallow with a wagging finger never far away.' *(Halliwell)*

LA FEMME DU BOULANGER: *see* BAKER'S WIFE, THE.

LA FEMME INFIDÈLE

CT: 6 AV: 7.86

(aka *The Unfaithful Wife)*

1968 France/Italy 98 C THRILLER/COMEDY

D Claude Chabrol ☆
W Claude Chabrol

Stéphane Audran ☆ Michel Bouquet ☆ Maurice Ronet Serge Bento Michel Duchaussoy Guy Marly Stéphane Di Napoli Louise Chevalier Louise Rioton Henri Marteau

A husband (Michel Bouquet) wins the admiration of his wife (Stéphane Audran) when he murders her lover (Maurice Ronet).

Slick thriller with a jaundiced view of the middle class and two immaculate performances from Audran and Bouquet discovering murky depths to their psyches. Obviously influenced by Buñuel and Hitchcock, it also looks forward to the works of David Lynch in its offbeat cynicism about supposedly respectable folk.

PRO:

'On any level, this bizarre murder framed by whiskies emerges as Chabrol's most flawless work to date.' *(Jan Dawson, MFB)*

'Chabrol succeeds in making his fairly standard characters interesting in their minor quirks, the slightly raveled texture of their lives, the urbane banalities they bandy about, which seem somehow to debouch on malfeasance and crime . . . He has directed with assurance, indeed finesse, restraining even that ostentatious interior decorator who lurks in his indecorous interior.' *(John Simon)*

'Almost a Buñuel-like black comedy, spare and quiet, with immaculateperformances.' *(Halliwell)*

MIXED:

'An exquisitely detailed, impeccably acted, stunningly directed suspense story about adultery and passion among the bourgeoisie. Yet there isn't a breath of life in it. You observe Michel Bouquet's foxy little performance as the cuckold, the glossy beauty of Stéphane Audran (she looks like a rich, chic Jeanne Hébuterne) as the wife, and Maurice Ronet's assured professionalism as the seducer, and you see the points being made about the hidden violence of overcivilized people. But the expertise is so tired, so masterly and perfectly slick, that the film looks as if Chabrol polished it until he ran out of spit.' *(Pauline Kael)*

LA GLOIRE DE MON PÉRE: *see* MY FATHER'S GLORY.

LA GRANDE ILLUSION: *see* GRAND ILLUSION, THE.

LA HISTORIA OFICIAL: *see* OFFICIAL STORY, THE.

LA KERMESSE HÉROÏQUE: *see* CARNIVAL IN FLANDERS.

LA MOTOCYCLETTE: *see* GIRL ON A MOTORCYCLE.

LA NOTTE DI SAN LORENZO: *see* NIGHT OF THE SHOOTING STARS.

LA NUIT AMÉRICAINE: *see* DAY FOR NIGHT.

LA PASSION DE JEANNE D'ARC: *see* PASSION OF JOAN OF ARC, THE.

LA RÈGLE DU JEU: *see* RULES OF THE GAME, THE.

LA RONDE AAW CT: 6 AV: 7.83

1950 France 100 BW DRAMA/ROMANCE/FOREIGN

D Max Ophuls ☆
W Max Ophuls Jacques Natanson ☆ AAN from Arthur Schnitzler's play *Der Reigen*

Anton Walbrook ☆ Simone Signoret ☆ Gérard Philipe Serge Reggiani Simone Simon Daniel Gélin Danielle Darrieux Fernand Gravet Odette Joyeux Jean-Louis Barrault Isa Miranda

The merry-go-round of love in 19th-century Vienna.

Understated, ironic, sexy French filming of Arthur Schnitzler's play, with Simone Signoret outstanding, and Anton Walbrook giving an urbane commentary on the vagaries of love. The women seem more in tune with their emotions than the men, who see love in terms of sex and power. Because of weaker performances towards the end, and the repetitive format, the film wilts just as it reaches its climax. The New York State censorship board judged it to be 'immoral' and banned it for four years; but it won Best Screenplay at the Venice Film Festival, Best Film at BAFTA, and was nominated for two Academy Awards: Best Screenplay and Best Art Direction. Remade, without any charm, by Roger Vadim as *Circle of Love* (1964). Temistocles Lopez made a bisexual variation, for the post-Aids era, in *Chains of Desire* (1992). Ophuls's version remains easily the best.

ANTI:

'A film that drags on and on by what seems like geometric progression.' *(John Simon, 1968)*

PRO:

'One of the most civilized films to have come from Europe in a long time.' *(Gavin Lambert, MFB)*

'Consistently charming, witty, and delightful to watch. Occasionally it inquires into the less dignified twists of the pursuit of love, and draws from them a comedy which would be impossible save to a director and players of exceptional brilliance.' *(Dilys Powell)*

'Superb, stylized comedy with a fine cast, subtle jokes, rich decor and fluent direction; not to mention a haunting theme tune.' *(Halliwell)*

LA STRADA AAW CT: 8 AV: 8.67

(aka *Road, The*)

1954 Italy 94 BW DRAMA/FOREIGN

D Federico Fellini ☆
W Federico Fellini Tullio Pinelli Ennio Flaiano from Fellini and Pinelli's story

Anthony Quinn ☆ Giulietta Masina ✗ Richard Basehart ☆ Aldo Silvani Marcella Rovera Livia Venturini

A peasant girl (Giulietta Masina) falls in love with a brutish circus strong-man (Anthony Quinn).

Fellini's Oscar-winning road movie. Despite much pathos and depressing neo-realist settings, the script has many touches of humour and romance. It's lovely to look at (cinematography is by Otello Martelli) and to hear: Nino Rota adorns the movie with one of his most haunting scores. Giulietta Masina's performance is a little too winsomely Chaplinesque for some tastes, incluing mine.

ANTI:

'Grim to a degree . . . In directing this piece of vagabondage, Fellini spares the audience nothing in the way of bestiality and degradation; this is realism crowing on a dung-hill.' *(The Times)*

'It is on the portrait of the girl that the film depends. Giulietta Masina plays her with an urchin cut, a tomboy walk and four expressions; interest, injury, gratification, ecstasy. It is an effective performance. But pathos, I take it, is intended, and I have difficulty in finding pathos in a performance so reminiscent of Harpo Marx . . . Continental audiences, especially intellectual ones, find in the circus a mystical significance which escapes me.' *(Dilys Powell)*

PRO:

'A gloomy picture? By no means unrelievedly . . . Masina [is] a rainbow . . . bent perfectly between the setting's sunlight and the story's showers.' *(Paul Dehn, News Chronicle)*

'[Its] real enchantment stems from Giulietta Masina . . . whose gauche sadness and naive wonder . . . should be chalked up as the performance of the year.' *(Milton Shulman, Sunday Express)*

'Brilliant and bizarre . . . Unquestionably the work of a . . . genius.' *(Alan Brien, Evening Standard)*

'A road down which all who love the cinema should stray.' *(Spectator)*

'Its sombre imagery haunts me still.' *(Daily Telegraph)*

'The theme of Frederico Fellini's spiritual fable is that everyone has a purpose in the universe. It is acted out by three symbolic characters. Giulietta Masina is the waif Gelsomina (soul, innocence, spirit, dreams); Anthony Quinn is the strong man Zampano (brute physical strength, man as animal); Richard Basehart is an artist-fool (mind). Though the background of the film is neo-realist poverty, it is transformed by the romanticism of the conception.' *(Pauline Kael)*

'Led the way out of the neo-realist dead end and into baroque romanticism. It's a film of disarming simplicity . . . Richly symbolic and compassionate, this tale of interdependence and half-articulate feelings still has terrific force.' *(NFT Bulletin, 1984)*

'Giulietta Masina . . . is to Anna Magnani as a sun beam is to a pack horse.' *(Gerald Mast, A Short History of the Movies, 1971)*

'It is Quinn's performance that holds up best, because it is the simplest. Zampano is not much more intelligent than Gelsomina. Life has made him a brute and an outcast, with one dumb trick (breaking a chain by expanding his chest muscles), and a memorized line of patter that was perhaps supplied to him by a circus owner years before. His tragedy is that he loves Gelsomina and does not know it, and that is the central tragedy for many of Fellini's characters: they are always turning away from the warmth and safety of those who understand them, to seek restlessly in the barren world.' *(Roger Ebert, 1994)*

LA TERRA TREMA   CT: 4 AV: 7.71

1948 Italy 160 BW DRAMA/FOREIGN

D Luchino Visconti ☆
W Luchino Visconti from Giovanni Verga's novel *I Malavoglia*

Antonio Arcidiacono. Narrators: Luchino Visconti, Antonio Pietrangeli

A Sicilian fisherman (Antonio Arcidiacono) and his family scrape an existence, despite exploitation by fish wholesalers and boat owners.

Documentary drama shot on location in Aci Trezza, Sicily. It does a good job of romanticizing reality and the struggles of its characters, but the absence of a gripping narrative is noticeable. It won a special prize at the Venice Film Festival, supposedly for its 'choral qualities and style', but actually – according to some eye-witnesses – for its politics. On release, it was a commercial disaster – not least because Italians found the characters' accents incomprehensible – and narration had to be added on later.

PRO:

'Visconti has fashioned a massive four-square chronicle, austere and formal in design . . . a classic of neo-realism, and a remarkably original one.' *(Peter John Dwyer, Observer)*

'Magnificent . . . for two pins I would call it great . . . Visconti's ways with this story is original and extraordinary . . . [preserving] a formal, almost mandarin style of composition and movement, marvellously controlled . . . Its aestheticism gives [it] is a quality of refinement . . . and [it] is saved from preciousness by . . . unsparing integrity.' *(Lindsay Anderson, New Statesman)*

MIXED:

'Luchino Visconti's neorealist tragedy, set among the exploited Sicilian fishermen, is long and full of political clichés, and yet in its solemnity and beauty it achieves a true epic vision. The film is lyrical yet austere, and it's beautifully proportioned. It may be the best boring movie ever made: although you might have to get up and stretch a few times, you're not likely to want to leave.' *(Pauline Kael)*

ANTI:

'Made by the Communists and meant to rouse the Italian rich to action on behalf of the poorest fishermen . . . It had dragged out its interminably sordid shots for nearly three hours when many of the critics became thoroughly bored with it. Then the communists who packed the cinema began cheering.' *(Daily Express, Venice Film Festival Report)*

LA TRAGÉDIE DE LA MINE: *see* KAMERADSCHAFT.

LA VIE ET RIEN D'AUTRE: *see* LIFE AND NOTHING BUT.

LACOMBE LUCIEN AAN   CT: 6 AV: 7.71

1974 France/Italy/West Germany 141 C DRAMA/WAR

D Louis Malle ☆
W Louis Malle Patrick Modiano

Pierre Blaise Aurore Clément Holger Lowenadier Thérèse Gieshe Stéphane Bouy Loumi Iacabesco

Turned down by the French Resistance, a young peasant (Pierre Blaise) joins the Gestapo instead.

A rarity – a French film which acknowledges the existence of collaboration with the Nazis during World War II. It aroused some anger in its homeland, and Malle went to America as a result. Audiences tend to get the point very early on – about how easy it is to drift unthinkingly towards evil –

and the length (not to mention the blank central character) becomes wearisome.

PRO:

'Subtle, intelligent.' *(Jay Cocks, Time)*

'A fascinating experience.' *(Richard Barkley, Sunday Express)*

'One of [Malle's] best.' *(Nouvel Observateur)*

'Malle's film is a long, close look at the banality of evil; it is – not incidentally – one of the least banal movies ever made.' *(Pauline Kael)*

MIXED:

'There are some good moments, because of one good performance, but the character exploration rarely deepens . . . and the iron-fisted irony rarely relents.' *(Stanley Kauffmann)*

ANTI:

'Very boring.' *(Dilys Powell)*

LADRI DI BICICLETTE: *see* BICYCLE THIEVES, THE.

LADRO DI BAMBINI, IL: *see* STOLEN CHILDREN, THE.

LADY AND THE TRAMP CT: 10 AV: 7.73

1955 US 76 C CARTOON/FAMILY

D Hamilton Luske Clyde Geronimi Wilfred Jackson ✔
W Erdman Penner Joe Rinaldi Ralph Wright Don DaGradi ✔ based on Ward Greene's story (music and lyrics by Peggy Lee and Sonny Burke ☆)

Voices: Peggy Lee ☆ Larry Roberts (as Tramp) ✔ Barbara Luddy (Lady) Bill Thompson Bill Baucon Stan Freberg (Beaver) ☆ Verna Felton

Upmarket but misunderstood spaniel meets mongrel and overcomes obstacles to happiness.

Perfection of its kind. A cartoon classic which received undeservedly poor reviews. The characters and animation are charming – the Italian restaurant sequence is a classic; there's a suspense-packed ending; and the dog characters are endearingly doggy, as well as anthropomorphic. The Disney Studio's first feature in CinemaScope, it is best appreciated in widescreen.

ANTI:

'As with many of Disney's less bearable efforts there are usually one or two passages which remind me of his earlier brilliance.' *(Fred Majdalany, Daily Mail)*

'Offers nothing revolutionary . . . Mr Disney's sentimentality . . . has the quality of half-set junket.' *(Paul Dehn, Sunday Chronicle)*

'Not the best [Disney] has done in this line. It is a coyly romantic story, done with animals. The sentimentality is mighty . . . Unfortunately and surprisingly the artists' work is below par . . . But there are some charming things . . . Peggy Lee . . . [does] the niftiest song in the film.' *(Bosley Crowther)*

'As cute as it sounds, with inspiration particularly lacking in the settings.' *(Shipman)*

MIXED:

'One does not need to be a psychiatrist to recognize the sentimentalist, the satirist, and the sadist in Walt Disney. [This film] is a fusion of these elements . . . I found the sentimentality . . . nauseating . . . The sadism is . . . puzzling . . . But there can be no doubt about the success of the satirist . . . Disney's dog-opera gloriously takes the mickey out of horse-operas and soap-operas of all time . . . I love it for its debunking of stale screen conventions.' *(Jympson Harman, Evening News)*

'The animation is not that ambitious and there are few surprises in the storyline, but the central relationship between Lady and Tramp is sweet. The Italian dinner (behind the restaurant) is probably one of the cinema's most romantic courtship scenes.' *(Danny Peary)*

PRO:

'Easily outstrips the average conventional film in laughs, human interest and suspense . . . The musical score, like the draughtsmanship, is superb.' *(Josh Billings, Kine Weekly)*

'A delight for the juveniles and lots of fun for adults.' *(Variety)*

LADY EVE, THE CT: 6 AV: 8.77

1941 US 97 BW COMEDY/ROMANCE

D Preston Sturges ☆
W Preston Sturges from Monckton Hoffe's story AAN *The Faithful Heart*

Barbara Stanwyck ☆ Henry Fonda Charles Coburn Eugene Pallette William Demarest Eric Blore

A con-woman (Barbara Stanwyck) tries to lure a young millionaire scientist (Henry Fonda) to his financial doom, but instead they fall in love.

One of writer-director's most famous (and best reviewed) comedies, this is a witty, hard-edged romance which mainly stands the test of time. Much of the comedy which arises from the central relationship is funny, and Stanwyck is irresistible; Sturges was right to insist that she be allowed to play the part, despite Paramount's preference for Madeleine Carroll or Paulette Goddard. The two things which let it down are a weakish ending, and the fact (though some critics would dispute this) that Henry Fonda is not really cut out to be a slapstick comedian; all his physical comedy routines look contrived and awkward. A classic comedy of its period, it was remade, not very well, as a musical, *The Birds and the Bees* (1956).

'Neither very big nor very flashy, but the best fun in months.' *(Otis Ferguson)*

'Has a sustained comic flavour and an individual treatment that are rarely found in Hollywood's antic concoctions.' *(New York Herald Tribune)*

'Outstanding is Sturges's flair for a mobile camera, for smoothly flowing visual motion to give emphasis to spoken lines.' *(Welford Beaton, Hollywood Spectator)*

'Has not merely verbal wit, but cinematographic wit; while the dialogue fizzes and crackles, the story is told with a lively understanding of what the camera, and the camera alone, can do.' *(Dilys Powell)*

'As gay, as debonair as anything that's ever been run though a projector.' *(Herb Sterne, Rob Wagner's Script)*

'[He] . . . is apparently called in Hollywood the streamlined Lubitsch. This needn't put you off because if he goes on producing films as lively as this one he will one day come to be known as Preston Sturges . . . It is drastically funny.' *(William Whitebait, New Statesman)*

'A more charming or distinguished gem of nonsense has not occurred since *It Happened One Night*.' *(New York Times)*

'A mixture of visual and verbal slapstick, of high artifice and pratfalls . . . it represents the dizzy high point of Sturges's writing.' *(Pauline Kael, 1977)*

'[Sturges's] greatest film . . . has nothing to recommend it but perfection.' *(Richard Corliss Hollywood Screen Writers, 1970)*

'Screwball comedy . . . is an original American contribution to the arts, and *The Lady Eve* . . . is perhaps the most accomplished of the lot.' *(David Denby, Premiere, 1991)*

LADY FOR A DAY AAN CT: 7 AV: 8.14

1933 US 95 BW COMEDY

D Frank Capra ☆ AAN
W Robert Riskin ☆ AAN from Damon Runyon's story *Madame La Gimp*

May Robson ☆ AAN Warren William Guy Kibbee Glenda Farrell Ned Sparks ✔ Jean Parker

Racketeer (Warren William) helps an apple seller (May Robson) to deceive her visiting daughter (Jean Parker), who thinks she is rich.

Social realism, this ain't. Some may find the sentimentality hard to take in these, more cynical times; others may find, to their surprise, that this little fantasy generates laughs and jerks the tears just as effectively now as it did in 1933. Credit is due to Robert Riskin, who wrote a wonderfully witty adaptation of Damon Runyon's story. Remade by Capra (not so convincingly) as *Pocketful of Miracles* (1961). David Burton also made a reasonably enjoyable sequel, *Lady By Choice* (1934), co-starring May Robson with Carole Lombard.

MIXED:

'May Robson uses the cheapest tricks in the actor's bag . . . Warren William is a lightweight with little charm, and Ned Sparks is an old-time comedian who can't deliver a line without winking broadly at the audiences and falling down a flight of stairs . . . [but it's] an amusing, sentimental tale.' *(Pare Lorentz, Vanity Fair, 1933)*

PRO:

'It's Hans Christian Andersen stuff written by a hard-boiled journalist and transferred to the screen by trick-wise Hollywoodites. While not stinting a full measure of credit to director Frank Capra, it seems as if the spotlight of recognition ought to play rather strongly on scriptwriter Robert Riskin.' *(Variety)*

'A merry tale with touches of sentiment . . . Miss Robson is splendid.' *(Bosley Crowther, New York Times)*

'A film full of hearty laughs, full of real humanity and sentiment that is never overdone . . . The whole picture overflows with little gems of character-drawing.' *(Sunday Express)*

LADY VANISHES, THE CT: 10 AV: 9.71

1938 GB 97 BW THRILLER/ROMANCE/COMEDY

D Alfred Hitchcock ☆
W Sidney Gilliat Frank Launder ☆ from Ethel Lina White's novel *The Wheel Spins*

Margaret Lockwood ☆ Michael Redgrave ☆ Dame May Whitty ☆ Paul Lukas Basil Radford ☆ Naunton Wayne ☆ Catherine Lacey Cecil Parker Linden Travers Googie Withers Mary Clare Margaretta Scott

A young woman (Margaret Lockwood) believes that an old woman (Dame May Whitty) has gone missing on a transcontinental train, but only one man (Michael Redgrave) believes her.

There are a few dodgy model-shots and some unconvincing back-projection – this is, after all, a low-budget British movie – but they are easy to overlook, for in every other way this film is perfection. A fascinating story, witty dialogue, top-notch performances and brilliant direction (skilfully merging three genres – comedy, thriller and romance) make this many people's favourite movie. Orson Welles is reputed to have seen it 11 times, James Thurber 13. On the strength of *The Lady Vanishes*, New York film critics voted Hitchcock best director of 1938; and he moved to the US in 1939. There was an abysmal remake in 1979, which showed just how hard it is to make this kind of nonsense credible.

MIXED:

'Sometimes eerie and eventually melodramatic, but

it's all so well done as to make for intense interest. It flits from one set of characters to another and becomes slightly difficult to follow, but finally all joins up.' *(Variety)*

PRO:

'An excellent picture in which suspense and comedy are cleverly mixed.' *(Evening Standard)*

'If it were not so brilliant a melodrama, we should class it as a brilliant comedy . . . When your sides are not aching from laughter, your brain is throbbing in its attempts to outguess the director. Hitch occasionally relents with his rib-tickling, but his professional honor would not brook your catching up with the plot . . . We cannot conceal our admiration for the way in which Mr Hitchcock and his staff have pieced it together . . . The man is diabolical; his film is devilishly clever. His casts are always neglected by reviewers, which isn't fair, especially since he has so perfect a one here.' *(Frank S. Nugent, New York Times)*

'Diabolically suspenseful, impishly humorous, breath-taking and vigorous.' *(New York World Telegram)*

'Alfred Hitchcock has directed . . . with all his individual expertness of touch . . . an out of the ordinary and exciting thriller. With polished restraint [Paul Lukas] conveys the head foreign agent . . . The supporting players do fine work.' *(MFB)*

'Espionage romance, brilliant directed . . . All the rich entertainment content . . . of *The 39 Steps*. Suspense, fear, mystery and surprise . . . are whipped into crisp concerted action by subtle, but by no means highbrow treatment. Great as the mystery aspect of the drama is, it is not, however greater than its comic relief and it is because of its perfect balance and sustained verve that it can claim universal appeal . . . The direction . . . amounts to genius . . . Another irresistible attribute is smart yet natural dialogue . . . Refreshingly English . . . Great story, brilliant direction, big thrills, delightful romance, marvellous comedy, cast value, feminine angle, exciting staging and provocative title.' *(Kine Weekly)*

'Ingenious, lightweight, fast-moving . . . ranking . . . as one of the best of Alfred Hitchcock's prewar thrillers. Basil Radford and Naunton Wayne add considerably to the film's entertainment value.' *(R.A.E. Pickard, Dictionary of 1000 Best Films, 1971)*

'The energy that fuels this film is the energy of the chase; what makes it unusual is that both the pursuer and the pursued are women. The young heroine becomes investigator and encounters a series of deceptions and disguises in her attempt to find the missing, apparently helpless, old lady who has been kidnapped on the train. Hitchcock also uses comedy sequences to comment on Englishness and stoicism faced with the exoticism of the snowscapes.' *(NFT Bulletin, 1984)*

LADYKILLERS, THE

CT: 7 AV: 8.46

1955 GB 90/97 C COMEDY/THRILLER

D Alexander Mackendrick ☆
W William Rose ☆ AAN

Alec Guinness ☆ Katie Johnson ☆ Peter Sellers Cecil Parker Herbert Lom Danny Green Jack Warner Frankie Howerd Kenneth Connor

Criminals receive their come-uppance at the hands of an innocent old lady (Katie Johnson).

Highly praised black comedy which would have been helped by wittier dialogue. Even so, it's entertaining and satisfying as the crooks gradually come to grief. Alec Guinness gives one of his most sinister (though not funniest) performances; despite all the famous character actors, the film is effortlessly stolen by Katie Johnson as his landlady nemesis (the role won her a British Film Academy Award). Last of the Ealing Studios' comedy films.

PRO:

'The acting is triumphant. As the Professor, brains of the conspirators, Alec Guinness gives – I will make the claim high – the best of his comic performances I have seen: shabby-sinister, teetering on the edge of mania, yet in its lightning changes from urbane to savage cunning gloriously funny.' *(Dilys Powell)*

'A film which has made me laugh more frequently, and more heartily, than any this year . . . It has a script with excellent ideas; it is very well directed . . . and it is brilliantly acted.' *(Julian Lynne, Tribune)*

'Aside from Scotch whisky, Mr Alec Guinness is the best export to America we have got.' *(Leonard Mosley, Daily Express)*

'A finely wrought image of terminal stasis, national, political (Charles Barr suggests the gang as the first post-war Labour government), and/or creative (the house as Ealing, Johnson as Balcon???).' *(Paul Taylor, Time Out)*

MIXED:

'An amusing piece of hokum, being a parody of American gangsterdom interwoven with whimsy and exaggeration that makes it more of a macabre farce . . . Guinness tends to overact.' *(Variety)*

'No one could call [it] socially-minded . . . A richly comic situation has been invented and developed – and some people feel that the entertainment would be better without the darkening of the story and final holocaust. Yet it is surely the very fact that murder is beyond a joke which gives the film its full flavour.' *(Times Educational Supplement)*

ANTI:

'Overrated comedy in poor colour; those who made it quite clearly think it funnier than it is.' *(Halliwell)*

LAN FENGZHENG: *see* BLUE KITE, THE.

LANCELOT OF THE LAKE CT: 4 AV: 7.25

(aka *Lancelot du Lac*)

1974 France 85 C DRAMA/FOREIGN

D Robert Bresson ✗
W Robert Bresson ✗

Luc Simon Laura Duke Condominas
Humbert Balsan Vladimir Antolek-Oresek
Patrick Bernhard Arthur de Montalambert

Knights who have despaired of their quest for the Holy Grail return to a disintegrating Arthurian court.

Austere (i.e. extremely low-budget) account of the well-known legend, stressing the bleakness of an existence without spiritual beliefs. Wildly overrated, turgid film with minimal charcterization and unintentionally funny special effects. Monty Python did the debunking job more entertainingly.

'A film I will return to because it lives and breathes in its own world like few others.' *(Guardian)*

'Comes nearest to vindicating the Bresson technique: and to substantiating the high claim once made by Jean-Luc Godard for [his] status in cinema history. "Bresson," he wrote, "is the French cinema, as Dostoievsky is the Russian novel and Mozart is German music".' *(Financial Times)*

'The Arthurian legend stripped bare, spotlighting the characters' cruelty, pride, and the aching need for human affection . . . Stunningly beautiful, mesmerising, exhausting, uplifting, amazing – all the things you could possibly expect from a masterpiece.' *(Geoff Brown, Time Out)*

LAST ACTION HERO, THE CT: 5 AV: 4.83

1993 US 122 C ACTION/ADVENTURE/COMEDY

D John McTiernan
W Shane Black, David Arnott

Arnold Schwarzenegger Austin O'Brien
Mercedes Ruehl F. Murray Abraham Art Carney
Anthony Quinn Charles Dance

Danny (Austin O'Brien) is an 11-year-old New Yorker with an unhealthy predilection for action movies. A friendly, old projectionist gives him a magic ticket which transports him into the world of Jack Slater (Arnold Schwarzenegger), the violent hero of four action-movies, imaginatively entitled Jack Slater I, II, III and IV.

A Schwarzenegger film which flopped critically and at the box office; though it isn't great, it is underrated. There are funny moments, and it's hard to dislike a film which suffers from that rare disease in Hollywood, a surfeit of ideas. The best sequences (such as the Schwarzenegger Hamlet) offer tantalizing glimpses of the film it might have been.

The movie is beset, however, by disastrous misjudgments of tone. The relationship between the boy and the projectionist is meant to be charming, like the one in *Cinema Paradiso*. Instead, the old man comes across as criminally irresponsible. What's he doing, showing this kid a diet of violent films for which he's too young, then ensuring with a special late-night screening that the boy will be on his own on the New York streets after 1 a.m.?

The kid is odious too, never sparing a thought for his mother who doesn't know where he is, and must be worrying herself stupid. Danny's enthusiasm for bad action-movies also has the unfortunate effect of making the audience start blaming him for the fact that trash like *Jack Slater IV* ever gets made.

The film also fails as satire. Its idea of a telling jibe at Hollywood is to show a police precinct so over-glamorized that it looks like the lobby of a hotel, yet no action picture I have seen has ever gone in for that kind of glamorization. Meanwhile, it conveniently ignores the real accusations against the Hollywood action film industry – of sadism, racism, sexism, contempt for human values and helping to create a generation with the attention-span of a gnat.

The film-within-a-film, *Jack Slater IV*, is not only terrible, but terribly unconvincing. Its opening scene, between a Mafioso (Anthony Quinn) and his evil hit-man (Charles Dance) is too slow and boring to elicit the enthusiastic response we see from our one-child audience. Its unimaginative chases and inept contrivances are presumably, and patronizingly, meant to keep us entertained; instead, they leave us sceptical as to whether so incompetent an action-series could have proved more long-lived than the *Die Hard* or *Lethal Weapon* sagas.

It's even hard to see what *kind* of film *Jack Slater IV* is meant to be. Sometimes it seems just to be an inane action movie; at others, it's clearly a spoof of one – with steam coming out of an irate policeman's ears, a cartoon cat rescuing Jack Slater, the baddie clicking his fingers and his Rottweilers forming themselves into a canine pyramid. Such moments may get a laugh, but they leave the audience confused: why doesn't our movie-literate-brat hero realize that he's not (as he keeps on saying he is) in a terrific action movie, but in a really rotten comedy?

Just as puzzling are the sequences where the action returns to 'reality': why does director John McTiernan carry on shooting in exactly the same, lamebrain style? And isn't it a mistake to have the brat's 'real' mother played by so well-known an actress as the Oscar-winning Mercedes Ruehl? *En passant*, we are asked to believe that a cinema near Times Square has booted out the Hollywood hits and the pornographers, to make way for Ingmar Bergman's *The Seventh Seal*: this, in order to facilitate a gag which will amuse only film-buffs, as Death (an uncredited Ian McKellen) is released from the screen to stalk the streets of Manhattan.

I imagine that in some earlier draft of the screenplay Danny grew in wisdom as the film progressed, while Jack Slater came to terms with the fact that he was a fictional character. Unfortunately, both points are lost in the final product. The charm of most Schwarzenegger films is that they pretend to be dumb, but in reality are extremely sophisticated. This movie thinks it's clever, but is actually incredibly dumb.

'A joyless, soulless machine of a movie.' *(Variety)*

'A noisy monstrosity.' *(Hollywood Reporter)*

'A movie reeking of tunnel vision, insularity, smugness, cynicism and virulent, self-serving commercialism.' *(Montreal Gazette)*

'Plays more like a bright idea than like a movie that was thought through.' *(Roger Ebert)*

LAST BOY SCOUT, THE CT: 7 AV: 5.00

1991 US 101/107 C ACTION/ADVENTURE

D Tony Scott ✔
D Shane Black ☆

Bruce Willis ✔ Damon Wayans Chelsea Field Noble Willingham Taylor Negron Danielle Harris Halle Berry Bruce McGill Chelcie Ross

Football player (Damon Wayans) hires clapped-out private eye (Bruce Willis) to protect stripper girl-friend.

Violent, foul-mouthed but wittily scripted action-comedy which reinvigorated the flagging career of Bruce Willis. It's the most accomplished and exciting film yet by Ridley Scott's young brother Tony, whose direction here is fast and humorous. Inspired editing transforms the mayhem into flashy, pop art. Shane Black's script reputedly earned him $1.75 million; and, for finding new twists to the worn-out buddy-buddy genre and writing dialogue much sparkier than the average, he deserved it.

ANTI:

'A sort of poor man's *The Big Sleep*, but here all the questions are answered by another car chase, smashing someone in the face or shooting someone in the forehead.' *(Variety)*

'Oft-told, nasty tale . . . The pyrotechnics are obvious and the acting is uniformly awful.' *(Scheuer)*

MIXED:

'Should satisfy anyone who has a craving for death and violence . . . [It] may not win any awards for originality and while most of the characters are as stereotyped as the story is predictable, Black writes one-liners like nobody else in the business.' *(Marshall Julius, What's On in London)*

'Tripe, but top-class, highly enjoyable tripe, which like all good tripe intriguingly reflects the culture which produced it.' *(Sheila Johnston, Independent)*

'Reprehensible bilge, of course, otherwise a shamelessly enjoyable night out for the boys.' *(Trevor Johnson, City Limits)*

'To give it a negative review would be dishonest. To be positive is to seem to approve of its sickness.' *(Roger Ebert)*

PRO:

'Willis is back doing what he does best . . . What sets the film apart . . . is the crackling wit of [the] script.' *(Hugo Davenport, Daily Telegraph)*

LAST DETAIL, THE CT: 6 AV: 7.57

1973 US 104 C DRAMA

D Hal Ashby
W Robert Towne AAN from Darryl Ponicsan's novel

Jack Nicholson ☆ AAN Otis Young Randy Quaid ☆ AAN Clifton James Carol Kane Nancy Allen Gilda Radner Luana Anders Michael Moriarty

Two old salts (Jack Nicholson, Otis Young) escorting a young sailor (Randy Quaid) to jail plan to give him the time of his life.

Jack Nicholson had one of his most showy roles in this tough, bawdy drama. Even though his character doesn't really develop – he just reveals himself to us – he is wonderfully funny and realistic. This is just as well, since Hal Ashby directs without much flair. There is a very 70s determination to focus on the sleaziness of everything, a lot of foul language, and an underlying yobbisness in its outlook; but Towne's script shows a moving humanity towards the kleptomaniac, beautifully played by Randy Quaid, who seems to grow up before our eyes.

PRO:

'Salty, bawdy, hilarious and very touching.' *(Variety)*

'Beautiful, disturbing and compassionate . . . Pity, horror and shame at the inhumanities of society – those are the themes of *The Last Detail*, those and the redeeming desire of ordinary men to redress the balance. The playing of the three principals, subtly heightening reality, is beyond praise; and the entire film with its tiny details of behaviour, its shifts of mood and the swift leaps, like the movements of memory itself, from scene to scene belongs to the class of cinema which, from *Easy Rider* to *Steelyard Blues* and *The King of Marvin Gardens*, has been changing the face of the American screen.' *(Dilys Powell)*

MIXED:

'Distinguished by the fine performances of Nicholson and Quaid, and by remarkably well-orchestrated profane dialogue. It's often very funny. It's programmed to wrench your heart, though – it's about the blasted lives of people who discover their humanity too late.' *(Pauline Kael)*

ANTI:

'Too schematic in its rote ups and downs, too predictable in its calculated alternation of drama and farce, and too whorish in its playing to the gallery . . . Ashby's direction is plodding, always settling for the obvious shot and betraying not a hint of a personal vision . . . One cannot get around the feeling that the basic pigment of all Nicholson performances is an impasto of smugness.' *(John Simon)*

'The criticism of modern America hits out at all too easy targets in a vague and muffled manner . . . The overlay of bleak cynicism barely conceals a troubled – and, dare one say, sometimes misogynist – sentimentality about what it means to be men together.' *(Geoff Andrew, Time Out)*

LAST EMPEROR, THE AAW CT: 6 AV: 8.21

1987 Italy/Hong Kong/GB 160 C DRAMA/EPIC/BIOPIC

D Bernardo Bertolucci ☆ AAW
W Mark Peploe Bernardo Bertolucci ✗ AAW

John Lone (Pu Yi as a man) Joan Chen ✓ Peter O'Toole Ying Ruocheng Richard Vuu (Pu Yi, age 3) Tijger Tsou (Pu Yi, age 8) Wu Tao (Pu Yi, age 15)

The life of China's last Emperor, Pu Yi (John Lone).

A gorgeous spectacle – but very tedious and much too long. One of the biggest problems is endemic to the material; the central character is passive and therefore unsympathetic, while the story of his life lacks any conventional dramatic structure. There is something comic about his passivity, yet the screenplay and direction never betrays enough sense of humour to explore this; it is too busy pointing out the constricting, imprisoning nature of privilege (a point made quite exquisitely within seconds of the start). The political stance of the film is, in fact, worryingly blinkered. It must be one of the few films ever to take a sympathetic view of Communist brainwashing; the Emperor's demotion to being a gardener is depicted as a terrific idea. Would Bertolucci like it if someone tried to 're-educate' him out of his beliefs? Other faults are the hurried narrative of the second half, and a tendency to ignore aspects of the real Emperor's personality (such as his sadistic and homosexual tendencies) which don't fit in with the film-makers' thesis. Vittorio Storaro's breathtaking cinematography well deserved its Academy Award – and the film also won Oscars for score, editing, art direction, costumes and sound. Despite its nine Oscars, it failed to make much of an impression at the box office.

PRO:

'A spectacular saga on the grand scale . . . The tragic and occasionally humorous life of [Yi] is chronicled with detached bewilderment, but also sympathy.' *(Mary Dejevsky, The Times)*

'One soon gets used to English as the film's vernacular. When O'Toole . . . speaks it, enunciating as if to the deaf, it even sounds foreign: but his wily, cadaverous charm dominates the screen.' *(Richard Mayne, Sunday Telegraph)*

MIXED:

'If spectacle finally triumphs over sympathy, it is not without a decent struggle.' *(Brian Case, Time Out)*

'A film of unique, quite unsurpassed visual splendor, *The Last Emperor* makes for a fascinating trip to another world, but for the most part proves remote and untouchable.' *(Variety)*

'A lavish spectacle which caught the imagination of audiences, though many found the compression of 60 years of Chinese politics baffling.' *(Halliwell)*

'Terrific camerawork and art direction, pretty good performances, but oh so hellishly overlong.' *(Rose)*

ANTI:

'Like opium smoke its gorgeous, narcotic images . . . float on . . . bewitching the senses and befuddling the mind . . . but where, one keeps wondering, is it all going?' *(Nigel Andrews, Financial Times)*

'The movie doesn't have the juicy absurdity that seems to pour right out of the historical story. And it suppresses the drama. But it has pictorial grace and a dull fascination. Bertolucci presents Pu Yi (John Lone) as a man without will or backbone who lives his life as spectacle – who watches his life go by. And so we're given a historical pageant without a protagonist. There's an idea here, but it's a dippy idea – it results in a passive movie.' *(Pauline Kael)*

LAST FLIGHT, THE CT: 6 AV: 7.20

1931 US 80 BW COMEDY

D William Dieterle ☆
W John Monk Saunders ✗ from his novel *Single Lady*

Richard Barthelmess ☆ Helen Chandler ☆ David Manners John Mack Brown Elliott Nugent ☆ Walter Byron

Four ex-pilot invalids meet a rich girl (Helen Chandler) in a Paris bar, after World War I.

Offbeat, mildly interesting, very well-acted evocation of the 'Jazz Age' mentality and the so-called 'lost generation'. But it suffers from sub-Scott Fitzgerald characters and a sub-Hemingway storyline (it is, in fact, suspiciously similar to his *The Sun Also Rises*).

ANTI:

'Has an appeal no doubt for aviation enthusiasts, but hardly much attraction for the romantic. Handicapped by a series of platitudinous sub-titles, an otherwise sincere film is spun in mediocre stuff.' *(Mordaunt Hall, New York Times)*

MIXED:

'There is an unusual theme and an understanding of human psychology in this picture which have not, perhaps, been given their true value.' *(Lionel Collier, Picturegoer)*

'One can now see exactly why the film was passed over in embarrassed silence in 1931. It must have seemed quite bizarre in relation to the ordinary commercial cinema of that period. There is no conventional story [so that] even after Antonioni . . . the film's object and method still seem startlingly modern . . . [It] survives very largely on [the] script.' *(David Robinson, Financial Times, 1968)*

PRO:

'If the crowd can understand that girl character in this picture the film is an undoubted grosser.' *(Variety)*

'A narrative as tight and spare as a Racine tragedy . . . unique in Hollywood of that time in its persistent, calculated understatement.' *(Tom Milne, 1975)*

LAST HURRAH, THE CT: 6 AV: 7.30

1958 US 125 BW DRAMA

D John Ford ✗
W Frank S. Nugent from Edwin O'Connor's novel (loosely based on life of James Curley, mayor of Boston)

Spencer Tracy ☆ Dianne Foster Jeffrey Hunter Pat O'Brien ☆ Basil Rathbone ☆ Donald Crisp ☆ James Gleason ☆ Anna Lee Edmund Lowe John Carradine ☆ Jane Darwell Wallace Ford Ricardo Cortez ☆ Wallace Ford ☆ Frank McHugh ☆ Edward Brophy ☆

A feisty politician (Spencer Tray) fights his last campaign.

Tracy is at his best, and well matched by an illustrious supporting cast. Unfortunately, the script is a compendium of clichés; and Ford's direction goes overboard with Irish-American sentimentality and the somewhat brutish sense of humour which often marred his work.

ANTI:

'One of John Ford's weakest films.' *(Virgin)*

'John Ford turned into a sentimental faker whenever he got near the Blarney stone, and Edwin O'Connor's novel about the final campaign and last days of Frank Skeffington, an old-style Boston mayor (Spencer Tracy), gave him an opportunity he couldn't resist. The subject is richly comic, and the picture has its moments despite the sprightly foolery, but Skeffington is so full of the milk of human kindness that he almost moos.' *(Pauline Kael)*

MIXED:

'I would like to be able to say [it] gets three cheers from me, for it has one of my favourite actors . . . and is made by one of the greatest of filmmakers . . . But from time to time . . . the film sags, the Ford fury abates and the Ford fun fails.' *(Ivon Adams, Star)*

'Tracy's performance . . . [is] a lesson in screen acting . . . [The film] is slow and loaded with sentiment, but carried by its star.' *(Peter Brinson, Financial Times)*

PRO:

'Fits Tracy like a glove, or at least a knuckleduster.' *(Fred Majdalany, Daily Mail)*

'Edwin O' Connor's novel has been transmuted to the screen in slick style. Spencer Tracy makes the most of the meaty role . . . A series of memorable scenes.' *(Variety)*

'Outstanding camerawork by Charles Lawton, and a rich gallery of performances in which Hollywood veterans and Ford's stock company are well to the fore.' *(Tom Milne, Time Out)*

LAST LAUGH, THE CT: 8 AV: 8.22

(aka *Der Letze Mann; The Least of Men*)

1924 Germany 73 BW DRAMA/SILENT/FOREIGN

D F.W. Murnau ☆
W Carl Mayer

Emil Jannings ☆ Max Hiller Maly Delschaft Hans Unterkirchen Emilie Kurz

A proud doorman (Emil Jannings) struggles to keep his self-respect as he is demoted to lavatory attendant at a luxury hotel.

This silent classic made history by being told entirely in pictures, without any title cards. Karl Freund's camerawork is outstanding. Poorly remade in Germany, in 1955.

'A marvellous picture – marvellous in its simplicity, its economy of effect, its expressiveness, and its dramatic power.' *(Life)*

'First appropriately named *The Least of Men* [it] is one of the most important pictures yet to be observed on any screen . . . Its expressionism is that of the rational world, conveyed in terms of everyday objects. It raises no barriers of doubtful meaning. Essentially it is a picture of thought . . . [It] is a perfect photoplay.' *(Exceptional Photoplays)*

'The old fellow is superbly done by Emil Jannings, who comes mighty near being the most eloquent cinema actor of any land. Actually, [the film] has more to recommend it than fine acting. It is a superb adventure into new phases of film direction. We have never seen the camera made so pliable to moods and moments.' *(Will Hays Jr, New Yorker)*

'A masterpiece of silent storytelling, a milestone in the fluid use of the camera and in the total "silence" of the film. The only title card used introduces the controversial epilogue – and it is up to you to determine whether it is a dream sequence, a catering to popular taste, or a satire on the Hollywood ending. In any case, it explains the change of title for this portrait of a man in a materialistic society that values the uniform above the individual who wears it.' *(Judith Crist)*

'Murnau makes a film of mythic resonance from almost nothing – and sends up rotten the happy resolution that the studio, UFA, insisted be grafted on.' *(Steve Grant, Time Out)*

LAST OF THE MOHICANS, THE

CT: 7 AV: 6.00

1992 US 122 C ACTION/ADVENTURE/ROMANCE

D Michael Mann ☆
W Michael Mann Christopher Crowe from James Fenimore Cooper's novel

Daniel Day-Lewis ☆ Madeleine Stowe ✔
Russell Means Eric Schweig Jodhi May
Steven Waddington Wes Studi Maurice Roeves

Frontiersman (Daniel Day-Lewis) rescues British officer's daughters (Madeleine Stowe, Jodhi May) from Indians.

Director Michael Mann created TV's *Miami Vice*, so it's no surprise that this contains violence and bloodshed. It also has pace, excitement and – more surprisingly – beauty. Dante Spinotti's lighting and cinematography are best appreciated on the big screen, but are sensational even on TV. Daniel Day-Lewis is outstanding as the virile but sensitive hero. It's good to see an action picture which is acted with depth, and where the baddies (here, the Huron Indians) are given grievances to motivate their viciousness. Despite moments when the plot could be clearer, this is a first-rate action adventure. Winner of an Oscar for best sound.

'There is grace and poetry and action and suspense and that clumsily named but oh so rare thing called historical verisimilitude about a film that restores to the screen what it used to do best: grandeur of scale, intimacy of people, generosity of emotion, a subtext of saga and legend. Oh hell, what's the word for it? Yes, epic.' *(Alexander Walker, Evening Standard)*

'Day-Lewis is exactly right – sinewy, laconic, watchful. Above posing or bluster, he radiates the aura of a free spirit. You accept that he can hit an elusive target at a quarter-mile, read the significance of a scrap of moss scraped from a rock, influence men with a look or a couple of words.' *(Shaun Usher, Daily Mail)*

'May be the only war film more popular with women than men. The romance between English lady Stowe and the wild, frequently topless, fur trader Day-Lewis struck some as wonderful, others as ridiculous and stilted. Although the battle scenes are among the best put on film, it's dashed difficult to know what's going on for much of the time. The music is wholly inappropriate and the scalpings horrendously realistic.' *(Rose)*

LAST PICTURE SHOW, THE AAN

CT: 5 AV: 8.86

1971 US 118 BW DRAMA/RITES-OF-PASSAGE

D Peter Bogdanovich ✗ AAN
W Larry McMurtry Peter Bogdanovich

Timothy Bottoms ✗ Jeff Bridges ☆ AAN
Cybill Shepherd ● Ben Johnson AAW
Cloris Leachman ✗ AAW Ellen Burstyn AAN
Clu Gulager ✗ Randy Quaid

Adolescent angst in a dying small town, in the early 1950s.

Critically acclaimed but terribly derivative film which seems to lack any real feeling for the characters, some of whom are not well acted. It all seems like an academic exercise in various old-fashioned directing styles, although Robert Surtees's Oscar-nominated cinematography is undeniably atmospheric. There was a belated sequel, *Texasville* (1990), which lacked all sense of style and was even more miserable.

'Held particular interest for me because the closing down of the small-time movie theater was kind of a metaphor for the continuing isolation of the world, but specifically America, the closing in of the country, and new ideas.' *(Peter Bogdanovich, Reel Conversations, 1991)*

'Where McMurtry saw Hollywood as the provider of false dreams and images of behaviour, Bogdanovich is celebrating a golden age of the movies at the point where it was about to give way to television.' *(Philip French, S & S)*

PRO:

'The most important work by a young American director since *Citizen Kane*.' *(Paul D. Zimmerman)*

'What I find extraordinary in the film is its power to suggest not only the social background but the situations and the unspoken desires of its characters . . . I do not propose to put the film, as I believe some American critics have put it, on the level of achievement of a *Citizen Kane*. But *The Last Picture Show* is certainly worth anybody's money.' *(Dilys Powell)*

'Bogdanovich has achieved a tactile sense of time and place . . . [and] he has made ennui fascinating.

Together that is enough to herald him as possibly the most exciting new director in America today.' *(Stefan Kanter, Time)*

'This amusing and beautifully acted film brings to life realistically the mood of the early 50s in America.' *(Arthur Thirkell, Daily Mirror)*

'What shines through *The Last Picture Show* is not so much the heroism of the characters as their capacity for survival . . . It is to Bogdanovich's credit and profit that he had managed at one and the same time to turn out an extraordinarily good movie and a refreshing affirmation of the life force of our civilization.' *(Andrew Sarris, Village Voice)*

MIXED:

'Its shallow overview of town life is dangerously close to TV, and especially to the "Peyton Place" series. The movie suggests what TV soap opera would be if it looked at ordinary experience in a non-exploitative way, if it had observation and humor.' *(Pauline Kael)*

'So many things in it are so good that I wish I liked it more.' *(Stanley Kauffmann)*

ANTI:

'Bogdanovich's direction is sheer derivativeness. To put it bluntly, it is *cinematheque* direction. A John Ford shot is followed by a George Stevens one; a Welles shot by one out of Raoul Walsh. Even if every sequence is not so patently copied as the funeral is from *Shane*, the feeling is unmistakable that one is watching a film directed not by a young director in 1971, but by a conclave of the bigger Hollywood directors circa 1941. This gives the film visual authenticity, but of what kind? Imagine a present-day composer writing like Haydn, a painter working in the exact style of Vermeer. At best, such men are epigones; at worst, forgers. At its most successful, *The Last Picture Show* rises to the heights of pastiche . . . The acting is far from consistently good. Aside from Cloris Leachman and Randy Quaid's unpleasant work, there are Clu Gulager's Abilene, Timothy and Sam Bottoms's Sonny and Billy, and Cybill Shepherd's Jacy to leave one unmoved. Miss Shepherd is a model (though how, with that dubious figure, I can't imagine) whose face Bogdanovich found on a magazine cover. Although her face is absolutely right for Jacy, nothing else is.' *(John Simon)*

'One stopped constantly to admire the justness of a period detail, the skill with which the look of a Fifties movie as seen now on the late late show was recreated, the grace of an homage to this or that old Hollywood master. And each time we stepped back to admire, the film died a little.' *(David Robinson, The Times)*

LAST SEDUCTION, THE

CT: 8 AV: 6(est)

1993 US 110 C THRILLER/ROMANCE

D John Dahl ☆
W Steve Baranczik ☆

Linda Fiorentino ☆ Bill Pullman ✔ Peter Berg ✔ J.T. Walsh ✔

Insurance saleswoman Bridget (Linda Fiorentino) persuades creepy doctor husband (Bill Pullman) to pull off a drugs deal, then runs off with the cash. She hides out under an assumed name, and takes up with a likeable young insurance adjustor (Peter Berg).

Fiorentino makes a great *femme fatale*. She goes through the movie having sex standing up in alleyways, messing with men's minds, murdering the odd guy, absent-mindedly stubbing out cigarettes in pies from grandma. She has the abilities of a corporate high-flyer and the scruples of a ten-dollar hooker. The role could easily have been a misogynistic fantasy-woman; Fiorentino makes you believe in her, even recognize her as a mildly exaggerated version of career-women you know.

Director John Dahl directed and wrote another recent exercise in film noir, the ingeniously plotted *Red Rock West*; and this is even more enjoyable. Mainly, this is because of a top-quality script by first-time writer Steve Baranczik – masterfully crafted with lots of sparky lines and black comedy. If some of the supporting characters seem drawn from stock, that is probably just to make the audience feel at home. There's freshness and ingenuity on display as well, and the final twist works like a bad dream.

'Nothing is ever what it seems in this gloriously evil world.' *(Premiere)*

'Breathtaking, ball-breaking.' *(ID)*

'Gleefully amoral.' *(Geoff Andrew, Time Out)*

'An extremely entertaining film, with excellent supporting performances, a music score from Joseph Vitarelli that is two steps beyond the average, and the sense that here is a director glorying in his material without camping it up. We know he's joking but he keeps an admirably straight face throughout.' *(Derek Malcolm, Guardian)*

'Well-placed, cleverly written and quite diabolical.' *(David Stratton)*

LAST TANGO IN PARIS

CT: 5 AV: 6.81

(aka *Ultimo Tango a Parigi*)

1972 France/Italy/US 129 C DRAMA/ROMANCE

D Bernardo Bertolucci ✗ AAN
W Bernardo Bertolucci Franco Arcalli from Bertolucci's story

Marlon Brando ✗ AAN Maria Schneider ✔ Jean-Pierre Léaud Massimo Girotti Maria Michi

Veronica Lazare   Gitt Magrini   Darling Legitmus   Catherine Sola   Mauro Marchetti

Paul (Marlon Brando), a middle-aged American widower, and a French girl (Maria Schneider) have a sexual liaison.

Paul may wonder why his wife committed suicide; my guess is that she was bored to death. This wildly overpraised film (almost any film that runs into censorship problems gets overpraised) has powerful moments; but Brando's performance is tiresomely mannered rather than savagely passionate – it's the kind of bad acting which Mickey Rourke has drifted into, rather earlier in his career. Schneider is a good deal more convincing, but got indifferent reviews; of course, she didn't have a reputation as a great actress. Not even Vittorio Storare's camerawork can save this one. It's pretentious, salacious, sexist and soporific.

PRO:

'Bertolucci and Brando have altered the face of an art form.' *(Pauline Kael, New Yorker)*

'An intense meditation on the realization of mortality.' *(S & S)*

'As he did previously in *The Conformist*, Bernardo Bertolucci finds sexual behavior symptomatic of the situation of society. In *The Conformist*, sexual anxieties and frustrations seemed to be the makings of a fascist. In *Last Tango*, a kind of sexual abandonment seems to characterize lives (or at least a life) that have ceased to have real meaning.' *(Charles Champlin, LA Times)*

'One of the great emotional experiences of our time. It's a movie that exists so resolutely on the level of emotion, indeed, that possibly only Marlon Brando, of all living actors, could have played its lead. Who else can act so brutally and imply such vulnerability and need?' *(Roger Ebert)*

MIXED:

'An uneven, convoluted, certainly dispute-provoking study of sexual passion in which Marlon Brando gives a truly remarkable performance.' *(Variety)*

'The film is Brando, and he provides not only the most satisfying and complete characterization since his *Streetcar, On the Waterfront*, and *One-Eyed Jacks* performances, but also two sequences of such power, of such piercing emotional intensity and perception, that he brings an aura of greatness to the entire film. It is, alas, only an aura, for the film is all machismo filled with such detestation of and contempt for women that its universality is limited; its plot detailing and mechanics tend to the pop and the slick and the self-indulgent, marred by the contrivances of theatricals that replace the insights of drama, and so the artistry is flawed.' *(Judith Crist, New York)*

ANTI:

'A deeply corrupting film. It corrupts and wastes the talents of the undoubtedly gifted people who produced it. It corrupts the film industry which puts it out as entertainment. And it corrupts and coarsens the sensibilities of all of us, not because we are shocked by it but because we are not. We are being led, more and more, to take for granted things which ought to sicken us . . . If the censor lets this one through, he might as well give up altogether . . . Any community which cannot, or will not, show its disapproval of a film like *Last Tango In Paris* deserves to be called decadent.' *(Anthony Lejeune, Daily Mail)*

'I cannot regard it as a landmark in cinema. Reviewers, especially those who have to see all the rubbish and not just that selected to show to the critics, have been subjected to a barrage of over-exposed erotica for ages now; it's merely that the prestigious Marlon Brando doesn't happen to be the star performer and the films are blatant porn instead of serious works of cinema . . . Brando has always been a supremely inventive actor in the tawdriest of films and people in the business ought to be able to tell the difference between the skill of the actor and the range of the role.' *(Margaret Hinxman, Sunday Telegraph)*

'True that by force of personality Brando compels one to watch him with deep curiosity. Even in the improbable turnabout of the last minutes with the savagery transmuted into romantic pursuit ("I love you") he still persuades. But if the couple remain unknown not merely to one another but to you and me, if the script, if the whole film declines to involve us, we are thrown back not on interest in human beings but on inquisitiveness about sexual practices. And again I find myself asking what the fuss is about. After all, the cinema has before now offered a variety of vicarious experiences. A more stirring display of sodomy was seen in Bergman's *The Silence*, and a more ferocious one in John Boorman's *Deliverance. Flesh* and *Trash* are more explicit about sex than *Last Tango In Paris*. And I am driven to conclude that the fuss is about manufactured characters, about a false situation, about a piece of fake brilliantly executed, indeed, but still a piece of fake.' *(Dilys Powell)*

'One of the silliest and most boring films ever made.' *(Marcus Berkmann, Daily Mail, 1993)*

LAST TEMPTATION OF CHRIST, THE

CT: 5   AV: 6.58

1988   US/Canada   163   C   DRAMA/BIOPIC

D Martin Scorsese ✗ AAN
W Paul Schrader   from Nikos Kazantzakis's novel

Willem Dafoe   Harvey Keitel   Barbara Hershey   Harry Dean Stanton   David Bowie

Life and times of a Saviour (Willem Dafoe).

Despite the religious controversy which it aroused,

this is neither irreligious nor shockingly salacious. It is, in fact, Scorsese's most boring film, more tedium than Te Deum. He is evidently inhibited by his high subject-matter and low budget; he is not helped by a script of painful banality.

PRO:

'A film of challenging ideas and not salacious provocations.' *(Variety)*

'Arguably the most powerful and intelligent film so far made on the life of Christ.' *(Sue Heal, Today)*

'A stunning film . . . A major work . . . By far the boldest reinterpretation of Christ I have ever seen . . . It adds a dimension to divinity that ecclesiastical authority will deny to its own loss and not Jesus Christ's.' *(Alexander Walker, Evening Standard)*

'One of the most intense and moving religious pictures made in America. It's not an assault upon Christian values or beliefs as its detractors claim, but an attempt to reconcile them with the attitudes and anxieties felt most keenly by unbelievers . . . Part of what fascinated him [Scorsese] here was the possible similarities between Christ's apostles and the rootless urban loners of his other movies . . . Few American films in the last decade have argued so exquisitely and so powerfully for the vitality of Christ's principles in the modern world . . . And none has been more completely misunderstood and despicably treated by the very people . . . who should have been . . . sympathetic to its aims.' *(Michael Wilmington, Isthmus)*

'Among those who do not already have rigid views on the subject, this film is likely to inspire more serious thought on the nature of Jesus than any other ever made.' *(Roger Ebert)*

MIXED:

'At times moving, often overwrought and at least forty minutes too long.' *(Bob Thomas, Associated Press)*

'Christ's temptations in the desert are shown with a worrying literalness that some will read more as Disney silliness than Pasolinian simplicity . . . The piece is not so well sustained in the concluding dream sequence . . . but, above all, Scorsese has succeeded magnificently in bringing a Christ to the screen who lives as a man of this world.' *(David Thompson, F & F)*

'Though "How are you feeling?" must have been asked of Lazarus, raised from the grave, such banality jars. But those are fleeting irritations . . . Mainly it is enthralling.' *(Shaun Usher, Daily Mail)*

ANTI:

'A Lite Jesus – a timid, snivelling, banal, seedy-looking, not particularly bright Saviour who's utterly without majesty or depth or what junior high school teachers used to call "Leadership qualities". There's no sense of profound love or goodness here, no sense of a huge soul in torment. There's not even any warmth . . . When he's with Mary Magdalene (who is played by the lovely and gifted, but ever-spacey, Barbara Hershey), the two of them look and behave like one of those aging flower-child couples who live in Topanga Canyon, drive around in pick-up trucks, and analyze each other in pop-psych fashion ("You were hanging on to your mother," Mary Magdalene tells Christ, "Then you were hanging on to me, now you're hanging on to God."). You get the feeling that Dafoe and Hershey's way of getting into the characters was to decide that Christ and Mary Magdalene must have been pretty much like George Harrison and Mia Farrow after a visit to their Indian guru . . . Overacted throughout. Dafoe and Hershey in particular seem incapable of saying hello without putting on an intense Actors Studio expression.' *(Bruce Bawer, American Spectator)*

'Desperately silly and utterly Californian, featuring that uniquely American deity Gahd, with whom many of us will be familiar from earlier attempts at Biblical representation . . . If Christ, when he returns to judge the living and the dead, also sets up as a film critic, I don't see much hope for Martin Scorsese.' *(Alice Thomas Ellis, Daily Telegraph)*

'The filmmakers are struggling to rationalize a Jesus who reflects their own self-conscious anxieties and pretensions. They want him to be more human, more culpable, more like them . . . The curse of wishy-washy holiness makes Dafoe look like a downright stupid performance.' *(Gary Arnold, The Connection)*

'The dream-on-the-cross sequence, featuring Jesus making love with Mary Magdalene, which brought down the first God-squad thunderbolts, is the crucial anti-climax. The concept is dazzling: the execution is banal. The climactic revelation of "Christ the human being", dreaming of the companionship of sex, marriage and the family, comes over less as a powerful humanist apocalypse than as an abruptly collapsed passion play. The scenery totters, the illusion falters.' *(Harlan Kennedy, Film Yearbook)*

LAST WILL OF DOCTOR MABUSE, THE:

see THE *DOCTOR MABUSE* SERIES (THE TESTAMENT OF DR MABUSE).

LAST YEAR AT MARIENBAD

CT: 2 AV: 6.00

(aka *Last Year in Marienbad; L'Année Dernière à Marienbad*)

1961 France/Italy 94 BW DRAMA/ROMANCE/ FOREIGN

D Alain Resnais ***X***
W Alain Robbe-Grillet ***X*** AAN

Delphine Seyrig Giorgio Albertazzi Sacha Pitoëff Françoise Bertin Luce Garcia-Ville Héléna Kornel

The story, if you can call it that, consists mainly of a monologue by 'X' (Giorgio Albertazzi), a man with

the charisma of a speak-your-weight machine, who may or may not have met 'A' (Delphine Seyrig) a year before in Marienbad, or Frederiksbad, or more likely Writingsbad. Mme Seyrig wanders about the marbled halls and formal gardens, as gorgeous and vapid as a Vogue model out of her skull on glue. Now and again there wanders across frame 'M' (Sacha Pitoff), who may be her husband or even the Devil, but mainly looks as if he regrets failing his audition to butler for the Munsters.

An art-house 'classic' that looks elegant and has a dreamlike atmosphere, but is devoid of drama, characterization or discernible point. This staggeringly pretentious film has, over the years, brought the worst out of many normally intelligent people. It won top prize at the 1961 Venice Film Festival, shared the André Bazin Gold Medal given by the International Federation of Film Critics, and won the French film critics' Méliès award as best picture of the year. It packed out cinemas in Paris and New York, and even won an Oscar nomination for its screenplay (perhaps the most bizarre nomination in the Oscar's chequered history).

British critics and audiences have always been more sceptical. I would like to think well of writer Alain Robbe-Grillet and director Alain Resnais, so perhaps they made the film with the intention of exposing the pretentiousness of pseudo-intellectuals. In keeping with this thesis, I couldn't help noticing that the topiary in the formal gardens is mainly in the shape of dunces' hats and (if you'll pardon my French) balls.

PRO:

'A truly extraordinary French film . . . an experience full of beauty and mood.' *(Bosley Crowther)*

'A work of art.' *(Dwight MacDonald, Esquire)*

'Marvelously fascinating . . . a ritualized, almost lifeless experience.' *(Hollis Alpert, Saturday Review)*

'It will appeal most to those who appreciate form, intellectual ideas presented with regard to its style, as in the best of Cocteau, as against commonplace attempts at realism.' *(The Times)*

'Compresses and realigns conventional treatment of time, making a looping bow of past and future and knotting it down on the present. Leaving relationships vague, carefully avoiding the usual structure of cause and effect, it tries to force the audience to interpret the story for themselves.' *(Time)*

'Represents in moviemaking what Les Demoiselles d'Avignon of Picasso does in the history of painting. It is the first cubist film.' *(Jean de Baroncelli)*

'Clearly the film's creators know exactly what they wanted to do and have done it with complete success. Whether one responds to the result is entirely a matter of temperament.' *(John Russell Taylor, MFB)*

MIXED:

'Both brilliant and banal, soaringly poetic and tiresomely talky, mature and sophomoric, photographically lovely as a symphony in celluloid, but dramatically as dizzying and monotonously repetitious as a carousel. Its murky, shallow, "ultra-civilized" love-story-triangle has been devitalized to the point of dramatic anaemia . . . The snail-like pace of the film's emotions – vicariously felt, dialoguishly dissected and almost yak-yakked to death – becomes altogether exhausting.' *(Jesse Zunser, Cue)*

ANTI:

'Elaborate, ponderous and meaningless.' *(Newsweek)*

'So basically sterile and emotionally frustrating that interest drains long before France's young New Wave director concludes his camera explorations . . . There are interminable views of ornate halls and formal gardens. People in elegant dinner dress stand frozen into stylized patterns against the baroque trappings . . . Repetitious and meaningless.' *(Margaret Harford, LA Times)*

'I got one clear impression . . . of Resnais and Robbe-Grillet grinning wickedly at each other above the heads of a trustful public that was flogging its poor little brain into some notion of what in hell the picture is all about.' *(Robert Hatch, Nation)*

'So repetitious, slow-moving and difficult to understand that it made me drowsy . . . I think it's a lot of pseudo-artistic HOOEY.' *(Hazel Flynn, Hollywood Citizen-News)*

'Historians of the future who are concerned with the Decline of the West would do well to glance at this so-called motion picture, and to ponder the reasons for the fatuous things that are currently being said in its praise . . . The narration is nothing but adolescently grandiloquent gabble . . . Resnais, and his publicity-agented claque, have uttered the usual rationalizations for the ineptitudes and incompetence of the film.' *(Louise Corbin, Films in Review)*

'Highbrow camp . . . not the most artistic film I know but it is the most self-consciously artistic film I know.' *(Parker Tyler, Film Culture)*

LAT SAU SAN TAM: *see* HARD BOILED.

LATE SHOW, THE CT: 8 AV: 7.50

1977 US 94 C THRILLER/ COMEDY

D Robert Benton ☆
W Robert Benton ☆ AAN

Art Carney ☆ Lily Tomlin ☆ Bill Macy
Eugene Roche Joanna Cassidy John Considine
Ruth Nelson John Davey Howard Duff

An ageing private detective (Art Carney) attempts to trace the killer of his partner. He is hindered and helped by a hippie (Lily Tomlin) whose cat he is trying to find.

Successful attempt to update the Chandler-Hammett school of crime thriller to the 1970s, cleverly mingling comedy with film noir. Tomlin and Carney play the unlikely investigating team with humour and sympathy; and there are freshly written supporting roles.

MIXED:

'Both performances are knockout . . . Top-heavy plot unwinds with the usual potboiler ingredients – blackmail, murder, philandering wives and double-cross.' *(Variety)*

'Though its plotting is somewhat rudimentary and its illogic gigantic, it has oodles of atmosphere, oddball characters, snappy dialogue, affectionate allusions, and a likable way of not taking itself seriously. Lily Tomlin, whom I have never previously liked, is totally winning as an absurd, aging hippie with solid instincts well hidden under layers of bizarre clothing, parlance, and behavior . . . And then there is Art Carney. This basic nonactor tries very hard, and manages to avoid obvious errors, but still fails to convince me. It may be that he is a little too successful at being as common as dirt even while he thinks he is charmingly matter-of-fact; whatever it is, Carney always makes me feel slightly unclean just watching him.' *(John Simon)*

PRO:

'[A] funny, touching pastiche about times and people out of joint.' *(David Robinson, The Times)*

'Ira [is] played with conviction and taciturn wit by Art Carney . . . Tomlin is also a delight . . . The film . . . is full of small surprises . . . I was very sorry when it ended.' *(Ian Christie, Daily Express)*

'A film so engagingly claustrophobic that it suggests something no less pleasurable and odd than an American continuation of the Ealing Comedy tradition.' *(Russell Davies, Observer)*

'One of the few comprehensible motion pictures with which Robert Altman [producer] has yet been involved.' *(Parish & Pitts)*

LAURA

CT: 6 AV: 8.93

1944 US 85 BW THRILLER

D Otto Preminger ☆ AAN
W Jay Dratler Samuel Hoffenstein Elizabeth Reinhardt Ring Lardner Jr Jerry Cady ☆ AAN from Vera Caspary's novel

Gene Tierney ✔ Dana Andrews Clifton Webb ☆ AAN Vincent Price ✔ Judith Anderson ✔ Dorothy Adams James Flavin Slyde Fillmore Ralph Dunn Grant Mitchell

A detective (Dana Andrews) investigates the death of a beautiful woman, and finds himself increasingly intrigued by her.

Stagey by modern standards, but still a classic black-and-white murder mystery. The atmosphere is a mixture of drawing-room comedy and murder mystery. The ultimate film noir, it crackles with character conflict, romance and necrophilia. The most memorable character is the acerbic journalist Waldo Lydecker, played by stage actor Clifton Webb (and clearly inspired by columnist Alexander Woolcott).

It had one of the most troubled production histories in Hollywood history. Both the director, Rouben Mamoulian, and the cinematographer, Lucien Ballard, were fired during shooting by the head of Twentieth Century-Fox, Darryl F. Zanuck. Producer Otto Preminger was put in Mamoulian's place, and – though unpopular with most of the cast – never directed anything better. Joseph La Shelle's wonderful noir photography rightly won an Oscar; the art direction of Lye R. Wheeler and Leland Fuller was nominated. David Raksin's haunting theme tune was shamefully overlooked.

MIXED:

'Though it is not in the class of *The Maltese Falcon* or *Double Indemnity*, shows throughout a nice sense of straightforward cinema technique.' *(Dilys Powell)*

PRO:

'Situations neatly dovetail and are always credible. Developments, surprising as they come, are logical. The dialog is honest, real and adult.' *(Variety)*

'Contrived with care, mood and style.' *(Herb Sterne, Rob Wagner's Script)*

'One of the best thrillers ever made . . . witty without being forced, laconic without a lot of hammy biting on the bullet.' *(Campbell Dixon, Daily Telegraph)*

'A crime story connoisseur's dish which has much to sell as absorbing entertainment.' *(Daily Variety)*

'Everything happens as if the characters had been created before the plot (it usually happened the other way round, of course), as if they themselves were constructing the plot, transposing it on to a level to which it never aspired . . . Here was the proof that thrillers can also be beautiful and profound, that it is a question of style and conviction . . . Nonetheless [it] is still far from exemplary, since its success postulates a pre-existing detective story plot that fits in with the filmmaker's purpose . . . demands of the filmmaker a vision that can be integrated into a given thriller theme.' *(Claude Chabrol, Cahiers du Cinéma, 1955)*

'Established many of the tenets of film noir in its atmospheric, heavily-lit camerawork, use of flashbacks, haunting theme song . . . and ability to examine an elusive central figure through the testimony and shifting perspectives of a host of vividly etched secondary characters.' *(Allan Hunter & Kenny Mathieson, Movie Classics, 1992)*

'Everybody's favourite chic murder mystery.' *(Pauline Kael, 1977)*

LAVENDER HILL MOB, THE CT: 10 AV: 9.31

1951 GB 78 BW COMEDY/THRILLER

D Charles Crichton ☆
W T.E.B. Clarke ☆ AAW

Alec Guinness ☆ AAN Stanley Holloway ☆
Sidney James ✔ Alfie Bass ✔ Marjorie Fielding
Edie Martin John Gregson Gibb McLaughlin

Bullion robbers (Alec Guinness, Stanley Holloway) plan the perfect crime.

Perfection. Brilliantly written, directed and acted, this must surely rank among the funniest films of all time. It's also an effective little thriller. Anarchic in spirit (we sympathize with Guinness's criminality because he's such an underdog), this harmless Ealing comedy was banned in Hungary, Czechoslovakia and (by an obscure arm of the British government, the Native Film Censorship Board) in Northern Rhodesia. According to Hansard, the British minister concerned, one John Profumo, told the Commons: 'the film was declared unsuitable for African audiences because it contained scenes judged likely to encourage disrespect of law and order'. Hansard records that this announcement was greeted with laughter. Watch out for bit-part player Audrey Hepburn in the opening scene.

ANTI:

'Being an Ealing film it suffers from a congenital inability to leave well alone and carries a certain air of parochial smugness.' *(Richard Winnington, News Chronicle)*

'Comedy flounders into farce and a delightful idea has not worked out quite as it should have.' *(Sunday Times)*

MIXED:

'A work comparable with the best that has come before . . . the effects are almost always successful and the theme round which the film was made is certainly rich enough . . . Not all the links in the chain of fantasy are as convincing as they should be, but the joke has enough vitality . . . to make such frailties seem unimportant.' *(Manchester Guardian)*

PRO:

'Ealing clicks with another comedy winner.' *(Variety)*

'Whatever your views on larceny, I'm sure you will enjoy.' *(John McCarten, New Yorker)*

'For 80 minutes one never stops chuckling . . . As exciting as any gangster film. Despite the constant laughter, the tension never slackens.' *(Evening Standard)*

'An irresistibly funny film – to date, the comedy of the year.' *(Fred Majdalany, Daily Mail)*

'How proud we ought to be of Ealing Studios! . . . It not only gives us fun, it gives us folklore . . . Outrageous comedy . . . I can hardly think of a single improvement to this very happy, very native picture.' *(Observer)*

'Classic comedy caper . . . Alec Guinness . . . is the personification of Ealing's gentle breed of pin-striped anarchists . . . One of the best Ealing comedies.' *(Elkan Allan, NFT Bulletin, 1951)*

'A minor classic, a charmer.' *(Pauline Kael)*

'Amusing situations and dialogue are well paced and sustained throughout: the climax is delightful.' *(MFB)*

'The funniest thing in chases since the days of the Keystone cop.' *(Daily Express)*

'A bright, amusing little Ealing comedy . . . Witty, imaginative, very British and completely original. Especially memorable is the inspired climax in which Alec Guinness broadcasts misleading instructions to pursuing police cars.' *(R.A.E. Pickard, Dictionary of 1000 Best Films, 1971)*

LAWRENCE OF ARABIA AAW CT: 8 AV: 9.33

1962 GB 216/222 C DRAMA/WAR/EPIC/ADVENTURE/BIOPIC

D David Lean ☆ AAW
W Robert Bolt AAN based on *Seven Pillars of Wisdom* by T.E. Lawrence

Peter O'Toole ☆ AAN Alec Guinness AAN
Anthony Quinn Omar Sharif AAN Jose Ferrer
Arthur Kennedy Jack Hawkins

Life and death of a war hero (Peter O'Toole).

The first half is a splendid adventure, and Freddie Young's masterly cinematography gives a wonderful sense of the desert. Maurice Jarre's best score also contributes to the grandeur. It seems almost churlish to point out that the narrative is confused, and the politics incomprehensible. The second half, which tries to portray the man in decline, is stodgy and superficial, despite the best efforts of O'Toole (who is far too obviously made up). Despite all these failings, a hammy performance by Anthony Quinn, and a reluctance to be explicit about Lawrence's homosexuality, it remains an all-enveloping cinematic experience, like *2001* or *Close Encounters*. This flawed masterpiece is even more impressive in the 216-minute 'director's cut', released in 1989.

'Only one thing made me stick it out, and that was David Lean. Of all the principals, only he and I were in Jordan for the entire ten months. He carried the tripod, I the camera. After a horrible day I would see him sitting outside his tent, smoking a cigarette. I thought if he could do it, I could bloody well do it too.' *(Peter O'Toole)*

ANTI:

'Just a huge thundering camel-opera.' *(Variety)*

'I should not have recognised my brother.' *(Professor Arnold Lawrence, T.E.'s brother)*

'History is put through the mangle and comes out tattered, torn and largely unrecognisable . . . If Lawrence was corny, naively romantic and absurd, then I congratulate Mr O'Toole on a masterly portrait.' *(Cassandra, Daily Mirror)*

MIXED:

'The only criticism I might level at the film is that it has taken the evaluation of the Arabs by Lawrence without question . . . Purely on artistic merits, however, this is a great film.' *(Nate Wheeler, Scene)*

'The first half gave the sense of expanse; adventure was there, the desert was there. But when it came to the second half with the disintegration into failure one felt the need of a sharper analysis of character. The depths were lacking.' *(Dilys Powell)*

'More Arabia than Lawrence . . . The screenplay . . . uses a remarkable economy of dialogue; perhaps it is too economical, for the actors have the difficult task of developing depth to characters against the enormous and emotionally exhausting desert background, a task made none the easier if they are lost for words . . . There are several historical inaccuracies . . . But no one has claimed Lawrence of Arabia to be documentary; it is the work of artists and as such seeks truth more through poetry than through fact . . . On the level of cinematic spectacle, *Lawrence of Arabia* makes films about Jesus Christ seem as empty as a used can of beer in the desert. And as small.' *(Peter Barker, F & F)*

'Fails to give an acceptable interpretation of Lawrence, or to keep its action intelligible, but it is one of the most literate and tasteful and exciting of expensive spectacles.' *(Pauline Kael)*

'As an abbreviated history of the part the Arab nation played in the Great War, the film is simple but effective. In its effort to portray the complex man at the heart of the conflict, it comes a cropper.' *(Ken Russell, 1993)*

PRO:

'Authentic desert locations, a stellar cast and an intriguing subject combine to put this into the blockbuster league.' *(Variety)*

'Here is an epic with intellect behind it, an unforgettable display of action staged with artistry. A momentous story told with moral force . . . A revolutionary film in possessing an epic hero whom it doesn't hero-worship.' *(Alexander Walker, Evening Standard)*

'The direction of David Lean is masterly.' *(Thomas Wiseman, Sunday Express)*

'Thank not only David Lean but also Peter O'Toole [in] the performance of the year and I only hope [he] can equal it in his subsequent career . . . [The film] made me proud of the cinema as a medium of entertainment.' *(Daily Express)*

'A landmark in the history of cinema . . . [The] central performance is great enough to rank with Massalitinova in the Gorki films or Stroheim in *Grand Illusion*.' *(David Robinson, Financial Times)*

'Sets a new standard for the spectacular, for beyond being an absorbing and exotic adventure story it provides a subtle exploration of the eternal enigma of one of the most intriguing of our century's heroes.' *(Judith Crist)*

'Cinema's best epic. If Ingmar Bergman is the cinema's finest exponent of the close-up, David Lean is the master of the long-shot. There's a scene with O'Toole riding a camel which any ordinary director would have shot from an angle without any extras in the background, but Lean has an entire army in the shot! The pains he takes are extraordinary. And Robert Bolt's script is just wonderful.' *(William Goldman, NFT Bulletin, 1984)*

'An intelligent and stirring epic [which] demonstrates [Lean's] expansive pictorialism tempered by a resonant psychological insight into the complex motivations of enigmatic English soldier and scholar T.E. Lawrence . . . [it] literally turns the genre inside-out, with its underlying impulse, a challenging interior odyssey.' *(Allan Hunter & Kenny Mathieson, Movie Classics, 1992)*

'Now more breathtaking than ever . . . a stirring and spectacularly beautiful epic.' *(New York Times on the director's cut)*

LE BALLON ROUGE: *see* RED BALLOON, THE.

LE BOUCHER: *see* BUTCHER, THE.

LE CASQUE D'OR: *see* CASQUE D'OR.

LE CHALAND QUI PASSE: *see* L' ATALANTE.

LE CHARME DISCRET DE LA BOURGEOISIE: *see* DISCREET CHARM OF THE BOURGEOISIE, THE.

LE CHÂTEAU DE MA MÈRE: *see* MY MOTHER'S CASTLE.

LE DIABLE AU CORPS: *see* DEVIL IN THE FLESH.

LE GENOU DE CLAIRE: *see* CLAIRE'S KNEE.

LE GRAND CHEMIN CT: 6 AV: 7.14

(aka *The Grand Highway*)

1987 France 107 C DRAMA/FOREIGN

D Jean-Loup Hubert
W Jean-Loup Hubert

Anémone ☆ Richard Bohringer ☆ Antoine Hubert ☆

Vanessa Guedi ☆ Christine Pascal Raoul Billerey Pascale Roberts Marie Matheron Daniel Railet

A small boy (Antoine Hubert) is dumped on a squabbling couple (Richard Bohringer, Anémone) while his mother goes into hospital to have a baby.

Sparky performances from the two children and mature, sensitive ones from the adults make this rites-of-passage film a delight, even though it's too easy to predict the direction of the narrative. Remade – quite well – as *Paradise* (1991), starring Melanie Griffith and Don Johnson.

'[The] characters are funny, passionate, pitiful and frustrating; they could be the people next door.' *(Stephanie Calman, Sunday Express)*

'The considerable charm of the two juvenile stars . . . provides much of the substance for this film.' *(Kay Holms, Morning Star)*

'Charming, undemanding . . . [it] contains a wonderful performance from [Guedi] and a gorgeous lazy, hazy background of French village life.' *(Sue Heal, Today)*

'The squabbling couple won French Oscars and richly deserve them – Anémone for her sassy walk and prissy ways, Bohringer for his rough, bawdy tenderness. The sense of a childhood summer is sensitively conveyed.' *(Brian Case, Time Out)*

LE JOUR SE LÈVE: *see* DAYBREAK.

LE JOURNAL D'UN CURÉ DE CAMPAGNE: *see* DIARY OF A COUNTRY PRIEST.

LE LOCATAIRE: *see* TENANT, THE.

LE MILLION

CT: 8 AV: 8.80

(aka *The Million*)

1930 France 89 BW MUSICAL/COMEDY/FOREIGN

D René Clair ☆
W René Clair from Georges Berr and Marcel Guillemaud's musical play

Annabella René Lefèvre Paul Ollivier Louis Allibert Constantin Stroesco Odette Talazac

Poor artist (René Lefèvre) loses winning lottery ticket and scours Paris to find it.

Dated but delightful escapism which made Clair's international reputation. The musical numbers are beautifully integrated into the plot – which may not seem unusual now, but certainly was in 1930. The film's success proved influential on the course of the modern musical; and the chase sequence in the opera house was imitated by the Marx Brothers in *A Night At The Opera*.

'I wanted an atmosphere of foolishness . . . We put gauze between the actors and the sets, which created an illusion of unreality.' *(René Clair)*

'From every point of view one of the two best films I have ever seen. What the other one is I have no notion; I merely put that in for safety . . . The story is pure nightmare, and its whole point lies in character-drawing, the wealth of burlesque, and the amazing pictoriality throughout. There is not a single shot in the whole film which might not have proceeded from the brush of a modern French master. The music is delicious, and the acting throughout as good as you will see in any theatre in Paris.' *(James Agate, Tatler)*

'A good musical farce that ought to do well everywhere . . . It has speed, laughs, splendid photography and a good cast.' *(Variety)*

'You remember *Sous les Toits de Paris* – well, this is better still . . . Closely blending light opera, drama, comedy and slapstick, it is almost impossible to classify this comedy . . . A picture which will rank with the best talkies of our time.' *(Harold J. Salemson, Rob Wagner's Script)*

'A gorgeous burlesque on all other musical farces, but adept and hilarious in its own right . . . Please bring René Clair to America to teach some of our directors.' *(Photoplay)*

'How good [it] is! How gay and how fresh! . . . Clair's fun is inexhaustible. One can abandon oneself to laughter without fearing the flatness that follows laughter in other people's comedies.' *(Helen Fletcher, Time & Tide, 1945)*

'The only thing about this film that can be said to date is the length of the dresses.' *(William Whitebait, New Statesman, 1945)*

'René Clair at his exquisite best; no one else has ever been able to make a comedy move with such delicate inevitability . . . Lyrical, choreographic, giddy – it's the best French musical of its period.' *(Pauline Kael, 1978)*

LE NOTTI DI CABIRIA: *see* NIGHTS OF CABIRIA, THE.

LE QUAI DES BRUMES: *see* PORT OF SHADOWS.

LE RETOUR DE MARTIN GUERRE: *see* RETURN OF MARTIN GUERRE, THE.

LE RAYON VERT: *see* GREEN RAY, THE.

LE SALAIRE DE LA PEUR: *see* WAGES OF FEAR.

LE TESTAMENT D'ORPHÉE: *see* TESTAMENT OF ORPHEUS, THE.

LE WEEKEND: *see* WEEKEND.

LEAGUE OF GENTLEMEN, THE

CT: 6 AV: 7.30

1960 GB 116 BW COMEDY/THRILLER

D Basil Dearden
W Bryan Forbes from John Boland's novel

Jack Hawkins ☆ Nigel Patrick ☆ Roger Livesey Richard Attenborough Bryan Forbes Kieron Moore Robert Coote Terence Alexander Melissa Stribling Norman Bird ☆

Ex-army colonel (Jack Hawkins) persuades and, where persuasion fails, blackmails former colleagues into helping him pull off a bank robbery.

After a slow start, this develops into a likeable caper movie, with many thrills, amusing characterizations, and a suitably commanding performance by Jack Hawkins. It was actor Bryan Forbes's breakthrough as a screenwriter; and it's a pity he couldn't think of a less conventional ending. Oliver Reed has a cameo appearance as, believe it or not, a ballet dancer.

ANTI:

'Much of the pleasure of the film comes from watching the intricate strategy of crime carried out like a military exercise . . . The morality of all this is a different matter.' *(The Times)*

'Its brisk, lively script avoids the obvious. While snickering behind its back, it tells an exciting story that could be taken quite seriously . . . The picture takes a while to warm up and, at the end, the script is too clever for its own good.' *(Margaret Hinxman, Daily Herald)*

PRO:

'A smooth piece of teamwork . . . It takes time to get under way, but once the gang is formed, the situations pile up to an exciting and funny finale. Dearden's direction is sure, and Arthur Ibbetson has turned in some excellent camerawork.' *(Variety)*

'Give us more films like [this] . . . and more people will go to the pictures . . . A dashing, spirited affair which puts British pictures on the up-beat.' *(Edward Betts, People)*

LEAST OF MEN, THE: *see* LAST LAUGH, THE.

LEGEND OF LYLAH CLARE, THE

CT: 5 AV: 3.85

1968 US 130 C THRILLER/SO BAD

D Robert Aldrich ●
W Hugo Butler Jean Rouverol ● from Robert Thom and Edward de Blasio's TV play

Peter Finch Kim Novak ● Ernest Borgnine ● Michael Murphy Valentina Cortese Rossella Falk Coral Browne George Kennedy

A Hollywood Svengali (Peter Finch) falls in love with his Trilby (Kim Novak), whom he has fashioned to resemble his dead wife (also Kim Novak).

Gloriously awful, transcendentally trashy melodrama, not helped by a dreadful double performance by Kim Novak. Peter Finch does his best to make it all serious, but even back in the 60s audiences hooted their derision. Sample line . . . 'I'll rummage through your soul like a pickpocket through a stolen purse.'

PRO:

'Kim Novak brings off her dual role as Elsa-Lylah well. Peter Finch is very good as the director who's her doing and undoing, and there's a very amusing and talented performance by Ernest Borgnine as a studio boss.' *(Variety)*

ANTI:

'Heavy-handed camp . . . Maybe an amusing macabre pastiche could have been made of it if the director, Robert Aldrich, hadn't been so clumsy . . . Ernest Borgnine . . . has rarely been worse – he demonstrates his shouting range.' *(Pauline Kael)*

'One way of dealing with Kim Novak's acting is to pretend that it was meant to be that way . . . Instead of being outrageously funny [the film] is merely outrageously silly.' *(Time)*

'It took a minor effort on my part not to flee from the screening room.' *(Hollis Alpert, Saturday Review)*

'It is not merely awful: it is grandly, toweringly, amazingly so . . . I laughed myself silly.' *(Richard Schickel, Life)*

'Not funny exactly . . . but it is kind of fun to watch.' *(Renata Adler, New York Times)*

'Supremely vulgar . . . Necrophilia, cancer, cripples, French critics, lesbianism, ignorant producers, nepotism, abortion, "film-artists", Italian studs and TV are the tasty elements Aldrich ghoulishly (and a little masochistically) juggles into a film-fan's delight, a side-splitting charade of satire, sarcasm and sheer perverse affection.' *(Paul Taylor, Time Out)*

'This Hollywood hothouse melodrama directed by Robert ("Over the top? Never heard of it.") Aldrich is a laugh-till-you-ache classic.' *(Margulies & Rebello)*

'About as schmaltzy and wonderful and well acted and cliché-ridden and stereotype-filled a piece of contrived entertainment as ever kept you enthralled and didn't make you feel foolish an hour later.' *(Judith Crist)*

LENNY AAN   CT: 5 AV: 7.73

1974 US 111 BW DRAMA/BIOPIC

D Bob Fosse ✗ AAN
W Julian Barry ✗ AAN from his play

Dustin Hoffman ☆ AAN Valerie Perrine ☆ AAN Jan Miner Stanley Beck Gary Morton

Life and times of a social satirist (Dustin Hoffman).

Deeply disappointing biopic, despite two powerful performances in the leads, and Bruce Surtees's Oscar-nominated photography. Director Fosse does his best to give it some life but ends up being obnoxiously tricksy, and Julian Barry's script is nowhere near adequate. It even suggests, inadvertently, that Bruce didn't have a sense of humour. He fails to raise a laugh, on or off stage; and without the odd chuckle or comedic insight, his life story is unilluminating, unconvincing and deeply depressing.

PRO:

'Lenny Bruce was one of the precursors of social upheaval, and like most pioneers, he got clobbered for his foresight. Bob Fosse's remarkable film version of Julian Barry's legit play, *Lenny*, stars Dustin Hoffman in an outstanding performance.' *(Variety)*

ANTI:

'For audiences who want to believe that Lenny Bruce was a saintly gadfly who was martyred for living before his time . . . Hoffman makes a serious, honorable try, but his Lenny is a nice boy. Lenny Bruce was uncompromisingly not nice; the movie turns a teasing, seductive hipster into a putz.' *(Pauline Kael)*

'A mess . . . Fosse and [screenwriter Julian] Barry never figured out for themselves how this nothingy little comic grew into a heroic figure and, rightly or wrongly, a legend; they further becloud the issue with "arty" fragmentation and time shifts.' *(John Simon)*

'The wildness of Bruce's sex life is only sketched . . . His decline into drugs is shown but not motivated or dramatized, as is his decline into legal boringness . . . As authentic and significant as he was, the Bruce aggrandizement, the glib comparisons with Voltaire and Swift, the effort to make him a figure of continuing importance seem to me foolish.' *(Stanley Kauffmann)*

'Has all the faults of the Hollywood biopic . . . The monochrome photography and pseudo-documentary interpolations can't conceal the basic Harold Robbins material . . . Bruce emerges quite unfairly as little more than a tiresome, self-obsessed trouper.' *(David Pirie, Time Out)*

'Filmically extremely clever, emotionally hollow.' *(Halliwell)*

LEOPARD, THE   CT: 7 AV: 8.80

(aka *Il Gattopardo*)

1963 Italy/France/USA 165/205 C DRAMA/EPIC/FOREIGN

D Luchino Visconti ☆
W Luchino Visconti Suso Cecchi D'Amico Pasquale Festa Campanile Enrico Medioli Massimo Franciosa from Giuseppe Tomasi de Lampedusa's novel

Burt Lancaster ☆ Claudia Cardinale Alain Delon Paolo Stoppa Serge Reggiani Romolo Valli

An Italian aristocrat (Burt Lancaster) can't cope with the rise of the bourgeoisie in the 1860s.

Visconti's sumptuous 19th-century epic wonderfully evokes the time of Garibaldi, and the emotions of being part of a declining aristocracy. Lancaster, though not well dubbed, gives a memorable character portrait (based, so he said, on Visconti himself). The set-pieces – whether battles, dinners or balls – are all magnificently photographed by Giuseppe Rotunno. Nino Rota's score is one of his best. Avoid the badly dubbed 165-minute version, which also suffers from poor colour. Winner of the Palme d'Or as Best Film at Cannes, it also received an Oscar nomination for Best Costume Design.

MIXED:

'I commend this film for its ravishing colour and picture of how Sicilian aristocrats lived in 1860 . . . But I am disappointed in the film. Burt Lancaster's performance is worthy but stiff, dignified but a little dull.' *(Alexander Walker, Evening Standard)*

'Fascinating, moving and satisfying . . . If it hadn't been for some glaring faults, I mightn't have been half so conscious of its virtues.' *(Leonard Mosley, Daily Express)*

'[The] three leading actors . . . are superb . . . One can only hope that, before it's too late, someone will point out to the distributors that the scenes which are not "essential to the plot" are crucial to the meaning. If they fear a flop with the whole picture, they will do no better with half of it . . . Should only a mutilated version appear, it will be every critic's duty to tell his public that the masterpiece, which they would be paying to see, has been degraded to a series of pretty but meaningless scenes.' *(Ian Cameron, Spectator)*

'The color and scenery and evocations of mid-nineteenth-century Sicily are beautiful but the 165-minute film itself is a tedious, disjointed, ultimately stultifying series of scenes and performances. It fails either as an epic view of history, a consideration of social change (the passing of the privileged class) or a character study.' *(Judith Crist)*

PRO:

'From John Huston to Sam Peckinpah, Lancaster has collaborated with some of the most adventurous, "masculine" American directors, and in recent years he's won thunderous acclaim for his work in Louis Malle's *Atlantic City* and Lamont Johnson's *Cattle Annie and Little Britches*. Still, few of the characters he's portrayed have released everything that's in him (not even his showboat turns in *Elmer Gantry* and *The Rainmaker*). Astonishingly, the one moviemaker who fully realized Lancaster's complexity on film was an equally complicated, superficially opposite personality – the homosexual Marxist aristocrat Luchino Visconti. In *The Leopard*, Lancaster channels his animal grace and exploits a quality that Norman Mailer once alluded to: his ability to suggest self-creation. This extraordinary movie is, along with Lawrence of Arabia, the most successful cinematic attempt to interpret spectacular historical events through one person's consciousness. The vividness and poignance and odd, lush urgency of *The Leopard* stem from its intensely mixed feelings about the death of the feudal ruling class.' *(Michael Sragow)*

LES BICHES

CT: 5 AV: 7.00

(aka *The Does; Bad Girls*)

1968 France/Italy 99/104 C DRAMA/FOREIGN

D Claude Chabrol ☆
W Claude Chabrol ✗

Stéphane Audran ☆ Jacqueline Sassard ●
Jean-Louis Trintignant

Rich bisexual (Stéphane Audran) seduces artist (Jacqueline Sassard) and architect (Jean-Louis Trintignant).

A once-fashionable, callous little suspense drama which restored Chabrol to critical favour, but now looks overrated and (like much of Chabrol's work) very sub-Hitchcock. Strengths include Stéphane Audran's cool performance – which won her the Best Actress award at the Berlin Festival – and a well-established atmosphere of lust. However, the plot isn't up to much; nor is it helped by Jacqueline Sassard's inadequate performance.

PRO:

'Confirms a talent at least as awe-inspiring as that of his peers. It is, I think, one of the most beautifully composed films I have seen: nothing is superfluous, nothing mis-paced, no detail extraneous.' *(Margaret Hinxman, Sunday Telegraph)*

'Unquestionably this very accomplished film-maker's best for some time . . . Audran . . . is superb . . . There's form and content in this one, in spite of its tendency to play games with both us and its characters on occasion.' *(Derek Malcolm, Guardian)*

'Delirious, decadent, but ultimately delightful.' *(Andrew Sarris)*

'Exquisite masterly study of sexual domination.' *(Scheuer)*

'Fascinating and well-detailed character study with more depth than at first appears.' *(Halliwell)*

'Impeccably performed, often bizarrely funny, the film winds, with brilliant clarity, through a maze of shadowy emotions to a splendidly Grand-Guignolesque ending.' *(Tom Milne, Time Out)*

MIXED:

'Languorous exercise in classy eroticism; very little of anything goes on.' *(Pauline Kael)*

ANTI:

'As stupid, ugly and mean-spirited a film as you can find this side of Godard and that side of Losey . . . You can almost see tubes attached to the heels of all the characters, through which the meaning has been sucked out of them and Chabrol pumped in.' *(John Simon)*

LES DIABOLIQUES

CT: 7 AV: 8.60

(aka *The Fiends; Diabolique*)

1954 France 114 BW THRILLER/HORROR/FOREIGN

D Henri-Georges Clouzot ☆
W Henri-Georges Clouzot Jérôme Geronimi ☆ from Pierre Boileau and Thomas Narcejac's novel *The Woman Who Was*

Simone Signoret ✔ Véra Clouzot Charles Vanel
Paul Meurisse Thérèse Dorny

The wife (Véra Clouzot) and mistress (Simone Signoret) of a cruel headmaster (Paul Meurisse) conspire to murder him, but no sooner have they done so than the body vanishes.

Classic, horrific thriller with a plot twist that caught a 50s audience unawares. Much imitated – most notoriously in *Fatal Attraction* – the film is not so shocking now, but it's still gripping, strong on atmosphere and unsettlingly misanthropic. Technically, it's superb: expertly directed for suspense by Henri-Georges (*Wages of Fear*) Clouzot. This is one of the few horror films to have impressed critics on release – possibly because it was made in French. At any rate, it shared the New York Film Critics' Award for Best Foreign Film with Vittorio De Sica's *Umberto D*. Authors Pierre Boileau and Thomas Narcejac went on to write another suspense thriller, *D'Entre Les Mortes*, which Hitchcock filmed as *Vertigo* (1958).

MIXED:

'Scary, but so calculatedly sensational that it's rather revolting.' *(New Yorker, 1978)*

'If crawling flesh is your idea of delight, then your pleasure is secured by a calculated sequence of incidents, tricks, stratagems, each of which holds its surprise.' *(Dilys Powell)*

PRO:

'It depends very much on the intimate details of the seedy, fourth-rate school, with its inadequate education and uneatable food, its general smell of unwashed children, hatred and petty perversions.' *(Basil Wright, 1972)*

'Slow to start and shabby-looking as befits its grubby school setting, it gathers momentum with the murder and turns the screw with fine professionalism.' *(Halliwell)*

'Excellent, scary . . . edge-of-the-seat excitement.' *(Scheuer)*

'Classic chiller . . . a must.' *(Maltin)*

'The last 15 minutes are as suspenseful as anything ever put on film.' *(Virgin)*

'I sought only to amuse myself and the little child who sleeps in all our hearts – the child who hides her head under the bed-covers and begs, "Daddy, Daddy, frighten me."' (Henri-Georges Clouzot)

LES ENFANTS DU PARADIS: *see* CHILDREN OF PARADISE.

LES JEUX INTERDITS: *see* JEUX INTERDITS.

LES MISERABLES AAN CT: 8 AV: 8.44

1935 US 109 BW DRAMA

D Richard Boleslawski ✗
W W.P. Lipscomb from Victor Hugo's novel

Fredric March ✗ Charles Laughton ☆
Cedric Hardwicke ● Rochelle Hudson
Marilyn Knowlden Frances Drake

Reformed criminal (Fredric March) is pursued by implacable police officer (Charles Laughton).

Best of the many film versions of Victor Hugo's classic novel, but that isn't saying much. The adaptation is reasonably faithful to the classic novel, but changes the ending so that the hero doesn't die. Charles Laughton (who does die, and in grand style) steals the picture as the villain of the piece, tormented by repressed sexuality (there are hints of homosexuality, sadism and paedophilia). March won critical acclaim, but is a lot more sympathetic and believable in the first part of the movie than he is after his spiritual re-birth. Cedric Hardwicke (as a bishop) is insufferably priggish, and Alfred Newman's pompous score doesn't help. Richard Boleslawski's direction is painfully slow at first, and doesn't extend to helping the child-actors; the outstanding, Oscar-nominated cinematography is by Gregg Toland. Barbara McLean's editing, especially impressive in the Barricades sequences, was also nominated.

ANTI:

'Not too happy in its choice of principal players, nor convincing in its atmosphere . . . In trying to achieve the impossible, that of condensing Victor Hugo's mammoth novel . . . without obscuring its message and its moral, the picture becomes one of rather aimless misery . . . and consequently fails to secure a firm emotional grip on the audience . . . Everything is hurried over and the important incidents are inadequately stressed . . . The direction improves enormously with the riots and scenes on the barricades . . . For the most part both direction and dialogue are naive.' *(Kine Weekly)*

PRO:

'Magnificent entertainment.' *(James Agate, Tatler)*

'Will satisfy the most exacting Victor Hugo followers, and at the same time please those looking only for entertainment.' *(Variety)*

'Unbelievably thrilling in all the departments of its manufacture . . . a memorable experience in the cinema.' *(New York Times)*

'A superlative effort, a thrilling, powerful, poignant picture.' *(New York Evening Post)*

'Deserving of rank among the cinema's finest achievements.' *(New York World Telegram)*

'A close-knit and powerful screen recountal of the immortal Victor Hugo classic . . . Vivid portrayals . . . Director Richard Boleslawski [was] almost invariably faithful to Hugo . . . And after watching the film trace through 35 years of Valjean's tragic life, you rejoice over the happy ending.' *(Photoplay)*

LES PARAPLUIES DE CHERBOURG: *see* UMBRELLAS OF CHERBOURG, THE.

LES PORTES DE LA NUIT: *see* GATES OF NIGHT, THE.

LES QUATRE CENTS COUPS: *see* 400 BLOWS, THE.

LES VACANCES DE MONSIEUR HULOT: *see* MONSIEUR HULOT'S HOLIDAY.

LES YEUX SANS VISAGE: *see* EYES WITHOUT A FACE.

LETHAL WEAPON CT: 7 AV: 6.77

1987 US 110 C ACTION/ADVENTURE

D Richard Donner ✓
W Shane Black ✓

Mel Gibson ☆ Danny Glover ☆ Gary Busey Mitchell Ryan Tom Atkins Darlene Love

Mel Gibson is a crazed LA cop who has lost his sense of self-preservation after the death of his family, Danny Glover his cautious sidekick.

First and best of the popular action series, but certainly not an instructional film about correct police procedure. Fast and furious fun for the lads.

ANTI:

'Style masquerading as content.' *(Pauline Kael)*

'Extremely violent.' *(Halliwell)*

MIXED:

'A film teetering on the brink of absurdity when it gets serious, but thanks to its unrelenting energy and insistent drive, it never quite fails.' *(Variety)*

'*Lethal Weapon* comes by its R rating honestly. Its opening scene has nudity and virtually every other scene has street-corner language and graphic violence . . . The plot is nothing new, either: two LA cops as unlike as they can be take on a bunch of big-time heroin dealers. And yet, if none of that bothers you, you will find that *Lethal Weapon* is a movie that really moves. Mel Gibson and Danny Glover as the cops are excellent . . . Their chemistry – and their rapid-fire dialogue – are the film's prime appeal.' *(TV Guide, US)*

'Packing some hard action scenes and boasting some traditional buddybanter, *Lethal Weapon* hits all the right marks; in fact, there's hardly a genre mark it doesn't nail . . . Screenwriter Shane Black obviously knows his way around the LA cop story beat, and has intelligently woven classic noir themes and ingredients into *Lethal Weapon*. It's a murky and dazzling milieu . . . [However, the] atmosphere, the buddy-stuff and the flashy setting don't make up for the fact the main story is too distanced throughout much of the movie . . . Far too often lame expository scenes serve to advance the plot or explain the back story.' *(Duane Byrge, Hollywood Reporter)*

PRO:

'In a sense, a movie like *Lethal Weapon* isn't about violence at all. It's about movement, and timing, the choreography of bodies and weapons in time and space . . . In a movie with the energy of this one, we're exhilarated by the sheer freedom of movement; the violence becomes surrealistic and less important than the movie's underlying energy level.' *(Roger Ebert)*

'It's a big, shallow, flashy, buddy-buddy cop thriller; it attacks you like a stereophonic steamroller, flattening everything behind it. Snatches of *Hustle* (1975), *Magnum Force* (1973) and *48 HRS.* (1982) float above this plot like scum on a polluted lake, and the holes in logic and mindless climax are (or should be) embarrassing. Director Richard Donner puts it into bright jazzy overdrive, and the cinematography . . . and music . . . are just right . . . And, at center, is the first big juicy mythic-hero part Gibson has had since *Mad Max*.' *(Michael Wilmington, LA Times)*

'A cracking thriller.' *(Rose)*

LETTER, THE AAN CT: 9 AV: 8.85

1940 US 95 BW ROMANCE/THRILLER

D William Wyler ☆ AAN
W Howard Koch from W. Somerset Maugham's novel

Bette Davis ☆ AAN Herbert Marshall James Stephenson ☆ AAN Sen Yung Frieda Inescort Gale Sondergaard

Murderous adultress (Bette Davis) attempts to evade legal penalties by pleading self-defence.

Bette Davis at her best in this tale of steamy passion and intrigue among Malayan rubber-planters. Somerset Maugham's story survives the Hollywood studio treatment intact (except for a bowdlerized ending), and all concerned were at the height of their powers: from director William Wyler through to composer Max Steiner, who contributed one of his most haunting scores, which was Oscar-nominated along with Tony Gaudio's cinematography and George Amy and Warren Low's editing. An all-time-great. Sample line . . . 'Yes, I killed him. And I'm glad, I tell you. Glad, glad, glad!'

MIXED:

'Never has [the play] been done with greater production values, a better all-round cast or finer direction. Its defect is its grimness.' *(Variety)*

'Very good . . . Tempo on slow side partly due to preponderance of dialogue over action . . . Strong climax intensified by drama of aftermath. Effective dialogue gains from natural delivery . . . Freedom from melodramatics . . . Exquisitely expressive photography.' *(Today's Cinema)*

PRO:

'Though tragedy stalks through this film, its handling is such as to prevent it from being wholly unrelieved . . . due mainly to the beauty of the photography . . . Bette Davis gives a very striking performance.' *(MFB)*

'The writing is taut and spare throughout . . . the unravelling of Maugham's story is masterly and the presentation visual and cinematic.' *(James Agate)*

'Sex melodrama brilliantly adapted from Somerset Maugham's famous play. Story arresting . . . Bette Davis's performance magnificent . . . at the top of her form . . . Direction faultless and atmosphere both colourful and convincing.' *(Kine Weekly)*

'Intelligently adapted from Maugham's story, the film grips from the famous opening sequence in the Singapore plantation with . . . Bette Davis emptying her revolver into her lover under the shimmering night. The *mise en scène*, photographed in torrid dark images by Tony Gaudio is made up of exotic details . . . Max Steiner's score conveys the anguish of the heroine as she lies and lies, pretending to her interlocutors that she killed only to save herself from rape.' *(NFT Bulletin, 1974)*

'Davis gives what is very likely the best study of female sexual hypocrisy in film history. Cold and proper, she yet manages to suggest the passion of a woman who'd kill a man for trying to leave her.' *(Pauline Kael)*

'A superbly crafted melodrama, even if it never manages to top the moody montage with which it opens.' *(Tom Milne, Time Out)*

LETTER FROM AN UNKNOWN WOMAN

CT: 8 AV: 8.60

1948 US 89 BW DRAMA/ROMANCE

D Max Ophuls ☆
W Howard Koch from Stefan Zweig's novel *Brief Einer Unbekannten*

Joan Fontaine Louis Jourdan Mady Christians Art Smith Marcel Journet

A young woman (Joan Fontaine) falls in love with the concert pianist next door (Louis Jourdan).

One of the great 'woman's films', exquisitely produced, and so magically directed by Max Ophuls that the flaws in the plot matter only in retrospect. Joan Fontaine is the romantic heroine made to suffer at her lover's piano-playing hands.

MIXED:

'One of those old-fashioned, sentimental, lavender-cased pieces which have no particular resemblance to life, but which once had a great vogue in the theatre. It belongs to the *East Lynne* era, when women were gentle creatures, ruled by sentiment, easily seduced and betrayed, but, through it all, bravely loyal . . . It is questionable how much popular interest a film like this can have today.' *(Fortnight)*

'A good film . . . novelettish enough, but that skilful director Max Opals [sic] has adorned it tastefully.' *(Manchester Guardian)*

'Story unfolds in flashback, a device that makes plot a bit difficult to follow at times, but Max Ophuls's direction holds it together. He doesn't rush his direction, adopting a leisurely pace that permits best use of the story. Film is endowed with little touches that give it warmth and heart while the tragic tale is being unfolded.' *(Variety)*

PRO:

'Admirably directed in the romantic manner.' *(Joan Lester, Reynolds News)*

'It is fascinating to watch the sure, deft means by which Ophuls sidetracks seemingly inevitable clichés and holds on to a shadowy, tender mood, half buried in the past. Here is a fragile filmic charm that is not often or easily accomplished.' *(Richard Winnington)*

'Film narrative of a most skilled order.' *(William Whitebait)*

'Probably the toniest "woman's picture" ever made.' *(Pauline Kael, 70s)*

'A film full of snow, sleigh bells, lights gleaming in ornamental gardens and trysts at night.' *(Charles Higham, 1972)*

'Of all the cinema's fables of doomed love, none is more piercing than this.' *(Tony Rayns, Time Out)*

LETTER TO THREE WIVES, A AAN

CT: 7 AV: 7.73

1949 US 102 BW DRAMA/COMEDY

D Joseph L. Mankiewicz ☆ AAW
W Joseph L. Mankiewicz Vera Caspary ☆ AAW from John Klempner's novel *A Letter to Five Wives*

Jeanne Crain ☆ Ann Sothern ☆ Linda Darnell ☆ Kirk Douglas ☆ Paul Douglas ☆ Celeste Holm ☆ (voice only)

Three women (Jeanne Crain, Ann Sothern, Linda Darnell) receive letters from the same woman (Celeste Holm) saying that she has run off with one of their husbands; they (and we) have to guess which.

Clever, though contrived, exploration of female unease and jealousies lurking behind calm, prosperous facades. All the acting is superb, but the two leading men stand out. Mankiewicz's script may be full of talk, but it's witty, enjoyable talk; and his direction is more visual than usual, thanks to Arthur Miller's photography.

MIXED:

'Bitter and truthful without risking the complete reality of the Italian pictures.' *(Kenneth MacGowan, Script)*

'A mere shadow of those acid Hollywood comedies of the Thirties, but it had a supply of ironies and made a certain alkaline comment on present-day American customs and manners. It was in general over-written and under-directed – the laughs being predominantly verbal and the structure literary.' *(Richard Winnington, S & S, 1951)*

PRO:

'Replete with sharp dialogue. He aims barbed darts at the country's favourite institutions, and makes them score with telling effect.' *(Variety)*

'[Mankiewicz] has accomplished the rare feat of making a very contrived drama seem a very convincing one, and of making his characters seem thoroughly real.' *(Fortnight)*

'Mankiewicz's dialogue is sharp, piquant, and witty. His direction too is taut and moving. The selection of Holm as narrator of the film, the vixen Addie Ross, was a stroke of genius on Mankiewicz's part; she had the perfect voice for such an off-camera role, sweet and sour, kind and bitchy.' *(Baseline)*

LETYAT ZHURAVLI: *see* CRANES ARE FLYING, THE.

LETZE MANN, DER: *see* LAST LAUGH, THE.

LIBELED LADY CT: 6 AV: 8.20

1936 US 98 BW COMEDY/ROMANCE

D Jack Conway ☆
W Maurine Watkins Howard Emmett Rogers George Oppenheimer from Wallace Sullivan's story

William Powell Myrna Loy Jean Harlow Spencer Tracy Walter Connolly Charley Grapewin Cora Witherspoon E.E. Clive Bunny Beatty Otto Yamaoka

An heiress (Myrna Loy) sues a newspaper; its editor (Spencer Tracy) takes steps to make her drop the suit.

Ingeniously plotted comedy with hit-and-miss gags delivered at a furious pace by talented character actors.

MIXED:

'Even though *Libeled Lady* goes overboard on plot and its pace sags badly in several spots, Metro has brought in a sockeroo of a comedy.' *(Variety)*

'Enjoyable, but it's rather charmless. It's constructed like a 70s sit-com, and it has the same kind of forced atmosphere of hilarity; it looks and sounds factory-made. The stars (and the supporting players, too) do their patented characters – the ones they'd invented some years earlier. (Almost nothing seems to be happening for the first time.)' *(Pauline Kael)*

PRO:

'Handsomely mounted and produced, lavishly costumed, cleverly written and artfully directed, *Libeled Lady* is entirely worthy of the noble comedians who head its cast.' *(Bland Johaneson, New York Daily Mirror)*

'If you like sparkling comedy, breath-taking action and four stars all in one picture, then pay [it] a visit . . . [It's] one of the gayest and snappiest comedies that Hollywood has sent us.' *(Daily Sketch)*

'A succession of crazy situations and slapstick scenes in which Powell seems to have persuaded the director to stand by while he enjoyed himself with the assistance and often at the expense of his three co-stars . . . Almost as full of laughter and amusement as a film can comfortably be.' *(MFB)*

'A delightful piece of irresponsible fooling, original in idea and brilliantly characterized and directed . . . The comedy is fast and furious, and includes some slapstick sequences which are hilariously funny.' *(Lionel Collier, Picturegoer)*

LICENCE TO KILL: *see BOND* SERIES.

LIFE AND DEATH OF COLONEL BLIMP, THE CT: 8 AV: 8.77

(aka *Colonel Blimp)*

1943 GB 163 C DRAMA/WAR/COMEDY

D Michael Powell Emeric Pressburger ☆
W Michael Powell Emeric Pressburger ☆

Roger Livesey ☆ Deborah Kerr ✔ Anton Walbrook ✔ Roland Culver James McKechnie Albert Lieven Arthur Wontner David Hutcheson Ursula Jeans John Laurie

A rigid British soldier (played with enormous sympathy by Roger Livesey) fights for King, Country and Deborah Kerr across four decades – only to find his sense of honour and fair play being overtaken by history.

A film which Winston Churchill hated (and banned from export) but which, thanks to the skill of its writer-directors, Michael Powell and Emeric Pressburger and its sheer good humour, has become a comic classic. The story rambles a bit, but there are solid performances all round, not least by Kerr in a multiplicity of roles, and Anton Walbrook as Blimp's German friend (an unexpected character to find in a wartime film). There are many funny moments, though not every critic has cared for the final descent into farce, and some feel the character in the film is a 'whitewash' on cartoonist David Low's more offensive original. The unforeseen irony is that decades after this film, which even then had the air of an affectionate funeral oration, the Blimps of this world still go from strength to strength.

MIXED:

'David Low's lovingly malicious archetype – and by implication, every Tory – has been relieved of all selfish motives for his actions and of nearly all dangerousness or even obstructiveness in those actions. This is annoying, and worse; but at the same time the movie's characterization of an innocent, brave, honorable, and stupid man is, within its own limits, so persuasive and so endearing, and so rare to movies, that I am at least as grateful as I am annoyed . . . There is nothing brilliant about the picture, but it is perceptive, witty, and sweet-tempered, and it shows a continuous feeling for the charm and illuminating power of mannerism, speech, and gesture used semi-ritually, rather than purely realistically, which owes a good deal to Lubitsch in the good second-best of his comedies.' *(James Agee, Nation)*

'The role of Candy is spasmodically well acted by Roger Livesey, who looks a little too mature in the scenes of his younger days and a bit too virile at the finish. More generous praise should go to Anton Walbrook.' *(Variety)*

'But for a final descent into clumsy farce, [this] would have been a remarkable film.' *(Elliot)*

PRO:

'Like the conversation of a clever and plausible talker with the gift of the gab; that is to say, it holds the attention, it is interlarded with excellent jokes, it has patches of feeling and patches of making do, and it goes on for a long time . . . There are passages of enchanting satire, and the acting is generally first-rate. Roger Livesey, whose make-up in the later sequences is brilliant, gives the hero exactly the right air of devil-may-care rigidity.' *(Dilys Powell)*

'A truly superb film . . . Roger Livesey is excellent in the title role. Deborah Kerr portrays the four women in his life across four decades with charm and insight.' *(Martin & Porter)*

'No one else has so well captured English romanticism banked down beneath emotional reticence.' *(Chris Peachment, Time Out, 1985)*

LIFE AND LOVES OF BEETHOVEN, THE:

see ABEL GANCE'S BEETHOVEN.

LIFE AND NOTHING BUT   CT: 7   AV: 7.50

(aka *La Vie et Rien d'Autre)*

1989 France 134 C DRAMA/WAR

D Bertrand Tavernier ☆
W Bertrand Tavernier Jean Cosmos

Philippe Noiret ☆ Sabine Azéma Pascale Vignal Maurice Barrier François Perrot Jean-Pol Dubois Daniel Russo Michel Duchaussoy Arlette Gilbert Louis Lyonnet

Counterpointed with the search by two women (Sabine Azéma, Pascale Vignal) through mud and debris for their husband and fiancé, missing after World War I, are the near-farcical attempts by a French major (Philippe Noiret) to please his superiors, and find an unknown soldier (any unknown French soldier will do) to bury beneath the Arc de Triomphe.

Where most pictures about the futility of war concentrate on wartime itself, this one concentrates on the messy aftermath of the First World War, when almost 350,000 French soldiers were still missing in action. On a more intimate level, the film is a delicately understated love story between the grizzled major (Philippe Noiret) and the more elegant of the two women (Sabine Azéma). Here again, Tavernier dares to avoid the obvious; and perhaps the most startling aspect of the film lies in his John Ford-like ability to express deeply personal emotions through use of landscape and wide shots. *Life And Nothing But* may be a little too leisurely for its own good; but it's arguably Tavernier's masterpiece.

ANTI:

'Often wanders too far from the essentials of its plot and can't avoid a certain ponderousness of expression.' *(Derek Malcolm, Guardian)*

PRO:

'A remarkably intelligent contribution to a genre . . . which had seemed pretty much played out . . . It is an extraordinary achievement to have found a new path through such a thicket of images and archetypes . . . The emotional plot of the film . . . has in truth its fair share of the novelettish . . . What saves the film from its faults is the subtle strangeness of its atmosphere, helped by a succession of displaced settings.' *(Adam Mars-Jones, Independent)*

'Fascinating . . . classic film-making in the *Jean de Florette* tradition.' *(Alexander Walker, Evening Standard)*

'All the best anti-war movies take place after the battle has ended, and this ranks alongside *J'accuse, La Grande Illusion* and *Paths of Glory* as one of the very best of them all, as well as providing all the proof you'll ever need that Philippe Noiret is the greatest actor in continental cinema.' *(Trevor Willsmer, Film Yearbook)*

'From such muddy, grey-toned misty material, Tavernier has crafted a magnificent piece of work, so clear of sentiment, so rich in irony, enormously enhanced by Noiret's sensitive portrayal of an old soldier.' *(Angus Wolfe Murray, Scotsman Weekend)*

LIFE IS SWEET CT: 6 AV: 6.55

1990 GB 102 C COMEDY/DRAMA

D Mike Leigh ☆
W Mike Leigh ✗

Alison Steadman ☆ Jim Broadbent ☆ Claire Skinner ☆ Jane Horrocks ☆ Stephen Rea Timothy Spall David Thewlis

A family survives in the London suburbs.

The most compassionate of Mike Leigh's vivisections of family life. Superior acting by Alison Steadman, Jim Broadbent and Jane Horrocks – plus a hilariously gross performance by Timothy Spall – make this well worth catching. The big weakness is the lack of story; the whole film is dedicated to the setting up of the characters. Named Best Picture of the year by the US National Society of Film Critics.

PRO:

'Neither as grotesque as the Simpsons nor (despite the title) as cloying as the Cosbys, this is one family worth visiting.' *(Michael Faust, Video Magazine)*

'Leigh refuses to sneer at the forced optimism of working people. Some observers – the ones who can afford to – might say that Nicola's family is rotten with denial. To Leigh, they're just trying to get through the day; and though he might not approve of all their methods, he won't judge them, either. That's why this "comedy" (as a valorous distributor calls it) plays so lightly, while touching on such terrible pain.' *(Stuart Klawans, Nation)*

'A winsome, offbeat, ironically titled comedy of people whose big dreams are often dashed at gale force . . . The strength of *Life is Sweet* lies not in its hyperrealistic dialogue, slender plot and sometimes inconsistent tone but in its flavorsome and in some cases touchingly valiant characters.' *(Joanne Kaufman, People Weekly)*

'By the end of *Life is Sweet* we are treading close to the stuff of life itself – to the way we all struggle and make do, compromise some of our dreams and insist on the others. Watching this movie made me realize how boring and thin many movies are; how they substitute plots for the fascinations of life.' *(Roger Ebert)*

MIXED:

'Although it's clear that Leigh has a warm spot for these losers, his wry view of the sweet life in English is unlikely to bring on a rush of immigration.' *(Bruce Williamson, Playboy)*

'Not every character rings true. With [Spall's] Aubrey, Leigh's gift for sociological caricature leads him astray into grating fantasy . . . but in the bulk of [the film] affection shines through the comic portrait of working class suburbia on the march.' *(Geoff Brown, The Times)*

'Despite two performances of insufficient conviction (Spall and Horrocks), the film is magnificent, mixing enormous fun with sad, serious subjects: the enterprise rip-off, adolescent despair, parents' lost dreams for their children, role-playing, the gutsy optimism of decent, ordinary humanity (represented by Broadbent and Steadman in two stunningly unflashy performances.' *(Steve Grant, Time Out)*

ANTI:

'Praised in some quarters as Leigh's best film . . . From where I sat it went absolutely nowhere in record time . . . [It] has some passable satire on the paucity of working class aspirations – if you like your black comedy looking down from a very great height.' *(Sue Heal, Today)*

'Starting hilariously and movingly, the film gets bogged down and never recovers. Leigh's skill with actors counts for naught when the structure of the film is so lopsided.' *(Rose)*

LIFE OF BRIAN: *see* MONTY PYTHON'S LIFE OF BRIAN.

LIFE OF EMILE ZOLA, THE AAW CT: 7 AV: 7.45

1937 US 123 BW DRAMA/BIOPIC

D William Dieterle ☆ AAN
W Norman Reilly Raine Heinz Herald Geza Herczeg ☆ AAW from Heinz Herald and Geza Herczeg's story AAN

Paul Muni ☆ AAN Joseph Schildkraut ☆ AAW Gale Sondergaard Donald Crisp Dickie Moore Louis Calhern

Famous French novelist (Paul Muni) is unjustly banished when he springs to the defence of Alfred Dreyfus (Joseph Schildkraut), a Jewish officer accused of betraying military secrets.

Muni delivers the most impassioned performance of his career in this gripping true-life story. The Warner production values are here at their peak (Max Steiner's score and Anton Grot's art direction were Oscar-nominated); and although the word 'Jew' is never used, the message on anti-Semitism is clear. Dieterle's direction is visually imaginative, maintains suspense, and draws splendid performances from his cast. Winner of the New York Film Critics' and the American National Critics' awards as Best Motion Picture of 1937.

PRO:

'A vibrant, tense and emotional story . . . finely made.' *(Variety)*

'Along with Louis Pasteur, it ought to start a new category – the Warner crusading films, costume division.' *(Otis Ferguson)*

'With *The Life of Emile Zola* the Warner Brothers inaugurate a new era in the film industry. For the first time a commercial producer has given us a film with a broad political idea. It is a dignified and stirring motion picture.' *(Peter Ellis, New Masses)*

'A grave story told with great dignity and superbly played and produced.' *(Pare Lorentz)*

'Rich, dignified, honest and strong, it is at once the finest historical film ever made and the greatest screen biography.' *(New York Times)*

'It is great because it has captured the throb of human experience in a memorable biography, beautifully filmed and magnificently acted.' *(New York Herald Tribune)*

'Other films like *Lost Horizon* have been as big in scale; but none has been more weighty in theme and sincere at heart.' *(John Grierson, World Film News)*

MIXED:

'Plodding briefly, inaccurately and somewhat risibly through Zola's early career, this solemn biopic improves no end when it gets to its main course: an account of the Dreyfus affair and how the now prosperously ageing Zola rediscovered his youthful ideals in an impassioned fight for justice. Carefully mounted, well directed and acted, but basically the sort of well-meaning pap out of which Oscars are made.' *(Tom Milne, Time Out)*

LIFE OF OHARU CT: 5 AV: 7.43

(aka *Saikaku Ichidai Onna; Life of O-haru; Diary of Oharu)*

1952 Japan 118/146 BW DRAMA/FOREIGN

D Kenji Mizoguchi ☆
W Yoshikata Yoda Kenji Mizoguchi from Saikaku Ibara's novel *Koshuku Ichidai Onna*

Kinuyo Tanaka ☆ Tsukie Matsura Ichiro Sugai Toshiro Mifune Toshiaki Konoe Hisako Yamane Jukichi Uno

A woman at the imperial court of 17th-century Japan declines to a life of prostitution.

A film that's always been popular with feminists because of its repeatedly victimized central character (beautifully played, but with remarkably few concessions to the fact that she is supposed to age 30 years). It's beautiful to look at, but relentlessly downbeat.

'Tanaka acts with an exactitude of tone bordering on the occidental, for its naturalness, simplicity and intimacy . . . Certain scenes are theatrically inspired . . . [and] demand from the viewer participation in ritual which is shocking for Westerners.' *(Monique Tosello, Institut des Hautes Études Cinématographique)*

'From the first frame to the last, one is aware of sublime directional purpose. To understand the full meaning of a Mizoguchi film is to understand the art of direction as a manner of looking at the world rather than as a means of changing it . . . With [his] first tracking shot . . . weaving and bobbing across a licentious world to a religious temple, we are in the presence of an awesome parable of womankind.' *(Andrew Sarris, Village Voice, 1964)*

'Oharu combines the form of the picaresque novel with much of the social analysis common to Mizoguchi's "contemporary" geisha films. Above all, it is a materialist analysis – a depiction of woman treated, traded, valued, degraded, and discarded as material object.' *(Jonathan Rosenbaum, MFB, 1975)*

'By turns brutal and elegiac.' *(Shipman)*

LIFE WITH FATHER CT: 5 AV: 7.30

1947 US 118 C DRAMA

D Michael Curtiz
W Donald Ogden Stewart from Howard Lindsay and Russel Crouse's play and Clarence Day Jr's book

William Powell ☆ AAN Irene Dunne ☆ Edmund Gwenn ZaSu Pitts Martin Milner Jimmy London Elizabeth Taylor

Portrait of a marriage between a Victorian sexist (William Powell) and his longsuffering wife (Irene Dunne).

Those personifications of 40s charm, William Powell and Irene Dunne, star in an endearing, eccentric comedy handsomely directed by Michael Curtiz and written by one of Hollywood's finest screenwriters, Donald Ogden Stewart (whose career was cruelly curtailed when he was blacklisted). Today, it looks stagey, and the eccentricities seem forced, but it remains a mildly enjoyable period-piece. The photography by Peverell Marley and William V. Skall, score by Max Steiner, and art direction by Robert Haas were all Oscar-nominated.

PRO:

'An example of Hollywood craftsmanship at its very finest . . . A vast improvement over the play . . . [because] Father Day has been humanized . . . Powell is just wonderful.' *(Hollywood Reporter)*

'Curtiz has captured the style and tempo of the original stories and the stage production and has added new values to every chuckle and sentimental touch in the play.' *(Fortnight)*

MIXED:

'Nothing more than a string of domestic incidents, but it is alive with small-scale drama . . . It is one of the most diverting screen comedies of the year.' *(A.E. Wilson, Star)*

'Rich, careful, rather heavily proficient. Fun, I suppose; but I can't really enjoy laughing at tyrants, least of all tyrants who are forgiven because of their innocence. William Powell acts, rather than is, Father rather well, but it's strictly an impersonation. Irene Dunne is painfully miscast as Mother; she would probably keep her tongue in her cheek uttering the Seven Last Words.' *(James Agee)*

ANTI:

'The director, Michael Curtiz, seems to be totally out of his element in this careful, deadly version of the celebrated, long-running Broadway comedy – a piece of starched Americana.' *(Pauline Kael)*

LIFEBOAT CT: 6 AV: 7.36

1944 US 96 BW WAR/DRAMA

D Alfred Hitchcock ☆ AAN

W Jo Swerling from John Steinbeck's story AAN

Tallulah Bankhead ☆ Walter Slezak ☆ Henry Hull John Hodiak Canada Lee Hume Cronyn Heather Angel Mary Anderson William Bendix

Survivors of a torpedoed passenger ship share a lifeboat with the U-boat commander responsible (Walter Slezak).

A skilful piece of craftsmanship and wartime propaganda by Alfred Hitchcock, miraculous for the way it changes the audience's point of view, sometimes even within the same shot. As an allegory about the nature of Fascism, however, it seems more than a little contrived . . . and confused. It works best as a simple demonstration of the fact that the allies must set aside their petty differences if they are to overcome their common enemy. Glen MacWilliams's photography – inventive within a tightly confined space – was Oscar-nominated.

PRO:

'A film that can well be compared with the best the screen has ever offered, the work has the advantage of the discriminating production guidance of Kenneth Macgowan, Alfred Hitchcock's sensitive and restrained direction, a literate and literary original by John Steinbeck, an incisively dramatic screenplay by Jo Swerling, and acting performances that both individually and collectively, are just about precisely right.' *(Herb Sterne)*

'Hitchcock has piloted the piece skillfully, ingenuously developing suspense and action.' *(Variety)*

'By paralleling the Nazi captain and the American self-made millionaire, it suggests that fascism is an extension rather than an opposite of capitalist democracy. That is again, however, too simple a formula for this extremely complex work, one of the guiding principles of which seems to be that every position, once established, is elsewhere qualified or contradicted. The Nazi is also paralleled, even more explicitly, with the Communist stoker.' *(Robin Wood, Hitchcock's Films Revisited, 1989)*

MIXED:

'As allegory, the film is nicely knit, extensively shaded and detailed, and often fascinating. But the allegory itself is always too carefully slide-ruled . . . Though every performance has, within the limits which seem so arduously and coldly set, fine spirit and propriety, only William Bendix occasionally transcends those limits and becomes an immediate human being. The handling of the cinematic problems is extremely astute, in spite of a smell of studio about most of it . . . What disturbs me is the question whether Hitchcock . . . has at last become so engrossed in the solution of pure problems of technique that he has lost some of his sensitiveness toward the purely human aspects of what he is doing.' *(James Agee)*

'Ham-handed, wartime Hitchcock, highly regarded by many, and a big hit. John Steinbeck and Jo Swerling concocted the symbol-laden script about the ordeal of a group of survivors of a torpedoed ship; the script's chief virtue is that it provides a raucous opportunity for Tallulah Bankhead to strut her comic sexiness. The picture made her, for the first time, a popular movie star.' *(Pauline Kael)*

LILIES OF THE FIELD CT: 6 AV: 7.22

1963 US 94 BW DRAMA

D Ralph Nelson

W James Poe ☆ AAN from William E. Barrett's novel

Sidney Poitier ☆ AAW Lilia Skala ☆ AAN Lisa Mann Isa Crino Stanley Adams

An odd job man (Sidney Poitier) helps build a chapel in Arizona for German-speaking nuns.

Small-scale film which is only too evidently aimed at debunking the idea that black people are idle and unreliable, but it's less earnest and sanctimonious than it sounds; it's a gentle funny, 'feelgood' movie. Poitier was the first black actor ever to win an Oscar. Ernest Haller's photography was Oscar-nominated.

ANTI:

'Astutely made, it goes for laughs rather than religious or colour-bar nonsense. I found it steadily hateful and condescending.' *(John Coleman, New Statesman)*

'An irritating piece of whimsy.' *(Nina Hibbin, Daily Worker)*

PRO:

'The screenplay . . . has rare humour and the performances have real charm. A modest film, but good.' *(Philip Oakes, Sunday Telegraph)*

'Sweet and gentle.' *(Judith Crist)*

LIMELIGHT CT: 5 AV: 6.91

1952 US 144 BW DRAMA/ ROMANCE

D Charles Chaplin ***X***

W Charles Chaplin

Charles Chaplin Claire Bloom ☆ Buster Keaton Sydney Chaplin Nigel Bruce

A clapped-out comedian (Charlie Chaplin) is inspired to a final triumph by a young ballerina (Claire Bloom) whom he has saved from suicide.

Shamelessly schmaltzy, talky, self-indulgent but occasionally effective tearjerker with an authentic feel for the music hall stage. Chaplin won an Academy Award, but only for the music. Claire Bloom, then only 19, is quite magical; and there is a chance to enjoy Chaplin and Buster Keaton together as a double-act on piano and violin.

ANTI:

'Overwritten, underdirected, slowly paced, monotonously photographed, fumblingly cut – and oh so dreary . . . The whole gorgeous potentiality breaks down, washes away in a welter of tears, archness, smut, coincidental meetings, Pagliacci closeups, and in talk, talk, talk.' *(Vernon Young)*

'From the first reel of [*Limelight*] it is perfectly clear that Chaplin now wants to talk, that he loves to talk, that in this film he intends to do little but talk. Where a development in the story line might easily be conveyed by a small visual effect, he prefers to make a speech about it. Where the 1917 music-hall background obviously opens the door to extensive onstage pantomime, he prefers to stand still and sing a song. This is not a compromise between the old and the new, an adjustment to inevitable and necessary change; it is a disturbing rejection of the nature of the medium itself.' *(Walter Kerr, Theatre Arts)*

'His exhortations about life, courage, consciousness and "truth" are set in a self-pitying, self-glorifying story . . . Surely the richest hunk of self-gratification since Huck and Tom attended their own funeral.' *(Pauline Kael)*

PRO:

'The whole film is deeply felt . . . Chaplin wants to express what he feels about living, about growing old, about loneliness, about youth drawn to death and age clinging to life . . . Every time you begin to think he is moralizing too much or relying too much on some mannerism, a monotonously repeated shake of the head perhaps, in the delivery of an emotional passage, at that moment he breaks clear into irony or self-denigration . . . One of the great works of the cinema.' *(Dilys Powell)*

LION IN WINTER, THE AAN CT: 6 AV: 7.77

1968 GB 68 134 DRAMA

D Anthony Harvey AAN
W James Goldman ✗ AAW from his play

Katharine Hepburn ☆ AAW Peter O'Toole ☆ AAN
Jane Merrow John Castle Anthony Hopkins
Timothy Dalton Nigel Tery

Bickering at the court of King Henry II (Peter O'Toole).

Patently a film of a stage play, this hit historical movie won Hepburn her third Oscar, as an acerbic Eleanor of Aquitaine. Peter O'Toole acts King Henry II with his usual passion, and ages up with conviction. James Goldman's sparkling if anachronistic dialogue and John Barry's pompous score also won Academy Awards. It divided critics in a big way. It's quite entertaining, but much of it seems pseudo-poetic and pseudo-intellectual, with a tenuous grasp of Plantagenet politics. Sample line . . . Eleanor of Aquitaine: 'Henry's bed is his province. He can people it with sheep for all I care – as I believe on occasion he does.'

PRO:

'A film for people who love the beauty of language and marvel at the poetry words can become when they are molded together by a real craftsman instead of a hack. The year is 1183, but the impact is now.' *(Rex Reed)*

'A remarkable achievement, a bustling recreation of history's squalors and splendours . . . It has a sense of size not common in the British cinema.' *(Dilys Powell)*

'An intense, fierce, personal drama put across by outstanding performances of Peter O'Toole and Katharine Hepburn.' *(Variety)*

ANTI:

'The hoked-up filmization of an already insufferably coy and phony play . . . [The writing is] pseudoliterate hack work . . . Add to this the weightily inept direction of Anthony Harvey (remembered – would that he were not – for Dutchman), which mistakes boom-and-zoom-happy camera histrionics for liveliness and imagination. A typical sequence has Henry rattling up to the battlements of Chinon Castle, only to crumple there as the camera rises and rises to show us the king pitifully small from its eagle's-eye view. Simultaneously, John Barry's abominable score (a kind of Roseland Ballroom version of the Te Deum, complete with heavenly choir) soars to a pious crescendo, completing the image of man's puniness, especially when he gets involved in a film like this one . . . The New York Film Critics' Circle recently picked *The Lion in Winter* as Best Picture . . . Ratings, it would seem, are needed less by films than by film critics. Any critic voting for *The Lion in Winter* should be given a rating of X, meaning "not recommended as reviewer for any film aimed at the 'over-sixteen' audience".' *(John Simon)*

'Named best picture of the year by the New York Film Critics the first time I participated in that group's balloting, a choice that so offended some of us that we briefly resigned – an action that led to reform of the group's voting procedures. I still think this was a wretched movie – a pseudo-intellectual pseudo-epic that, I must say, still angers me.' *(Richard Schickel, Life, 1972)*

'On the Broadway stage this play seemed to be an entertaining melodrama about the Plantagenets as a family of monsters playing Freudian games of sex and power, but it was brought to the screen as if it were poetic drama of a very high order, and the point of view is too limited and anachronistic to justify all this howling and sobbing and carrying on.' *(Pauline Kael)*

LION KING, THE CT: 9 AV: 8.00 (est)

1994 US 87 C CARTOON/FAMILY

D Roger Allers Rob Minkoff
W Irene Mecchi Jonathan Roberts Linda Woolverton (music and lyrics by Elton John and Tim Rice)

Voices: Jonathan Taylor Thomas Matthew Broderick James Earl Jones Jeremy Irons ☆ Moira Kelly Niketa Calame Ernie Sabella Whoopi Goldberg Cheech Marin Jim Cummings Rowan Atkinson ☆

A lion cub grows up in a dangerous world.

Despite accusations of Political Incorrectness, this roaring success managed to recover its costs of 40 million dollars in its first weekend, and broke the $100 million barrier in under a fortnight. So it's easy to forget that it started as an underdog – Disney's first film to come up from nothing. Unlike every other feature-length success by the studio, it is not based on an established fairy tale, fable or children's book. Instead, the Disney team has tried to produce a late 20th-century myth of its own.

By far the most important contributor to the screenplay, which was worked on by at least 20 American writers, is an uncredited Englishman – one William Shakespeare. For a start, there's an indecisive, Hamlet-style hero exhorted by the ghost of his murdered father to take revenge on the wicked uncle who has usurped the throne. The villain bears a striking resemblance to Iago in *Othello*, as he skilfully exploits the fears of the hero. And the young lion king makes unsuitable friends but learns his royal duty in much the same way as Prince Hal does in Shakespeare's History Plays. It may seem far-fetched or even pretentious to draw such parallels; but, like all the great Disney cartoons, it teaches eternal truths about life and adult responsibility.

It is also very funny. The script is the wittiest ever written for a Disney cartoon, full of wisecracks and quick-fire gags. There may be no single figure as entertaining as Robin Williams's genie in *Aladdin*, but the jokes are shared out liberally among a terrific cast. Best of all are the two British actors. Jeremy Irons, who voices wicked Uncle Scar, hams it up royally and comes across as sly, smarmy and oddly likeable in his despicability. 'Are you weird?' our young hero asks him at one point. 'You have no idea,' drawls Irons, in a deliberate echo of his Oscar-winning performance as Claus von Bulow. The Disney animators have wittily used Irons's own facial expressions to add visual nuances to a sensational voice-over *tour de force*; here's the outstanding Disney villain since Cruella De Vil, way back in *101 Dalmatians*. Also excellent is Rowan Atkinson as Zazu, the Lion King's hornbill major domo.

The film has all that late 20th-century sophistication which made *Beauty and the Beast* and *Aladdin* so enjoyable. The ecological message is cleverly balanced; it does not disguise the fact that lions eat antelopes and zebra, but points out that there is a balance to nature, a circle of life, that is disrupted at every creature's peril. The animals are as anthropomorphic as in any Disney cartoon, but more knowingly so.

Artistically, the animators have departed from the Disney norm and gone primitive. *Bambi* used more delicate, Oriental-style backgrounds; *The Lion King* goes for strong shapes and lurid colours, which are exactly right for the African subject-matter. There is marvellous detail in the half-human, half-animal mannerisms of what is as lively a collection of characters as ever graced a cartoon. The wildebeest stampede and the Nuremberg-rally march past Uncle Scar by the hyenas are great set-pieces of modern cinema.

The film predictably came under fire in America from the Politically Correct lobby. Gay pressure groups objected that Uncle Scar was obviously homosexual – which seems a shade fanciful, since his sexuality is left unclear (if anything, one suspects it might involve doing things too kinky to mention with his goose-stepping hyena friends). Ethnic groups objected that the three hyena muggers (led by Whoopi Goldberg) were racial stereotypes – but ignore the fact that two of the most sympathetic characters are played by black actors, James Earl Jones and Robert Guillaume.

More damagingly, a few American parents objected that some passages (notably the first hyena attack and the wildebeest stampede) were too frightening for young children. In fact, the scenes are rather less upsetting than the Wicked Queen's death in *Snow White*, or the shooting of Bambi's mother. Even small children enjoy being pleasurably scared – as long as there is a reassuring grown-up voice to explain things, and an unscary life to return to, afterwards.

My one big reservation lies in the film's lack of quality as a musical. The songs in *Beauty and The Beast* and *The Jungle Book* remain far superior. Composer/orchestrator Hans Zimmer does wonders in arranging Elton John's score, to make it sound more African; but he can't disguise the fact that it is melodically undistinguished. Tim Rice's lyrics are even more of a disappointment. Not one of them carries the story forward – even with the advantage of rhyme – they are much less witty than the script. Fortunately, in the context of such outstanding entertainment, these are minor irritations.

'Primal Disney returns with a growl . . . Not since *Bambi* has so much been at stake in a Disney tale. There are kingdoms to be sundered, deaths to be atoned for. The father of a prince is killed, and his conniving uncle seizes the throne; driven from the kingdom, the lad leads a carefree life until the father's ghost instructs him to seek honorable revenge. Put it another way: a boy leaves home, escapes responsibility with some genially irresponsible friends, then returns to face society's obligations. *The Lion King* is a mix of two masterpieces cribbed for cartoons and brought ferociously up to date. On the grasslands of Africa, Huck Finn meets Hamlet.' *(Richard Corliss, Time)*

'This isn't the mindless romp with cute animals that the ads might lead you to expect. Although the movie may be frightening and depressing to the very young, I think it's positive that *The Lion King* deals with real issues. By processing life's realities in stories, children can prepare themselves for more difficult lessons later on. The saga of Simba, which in its deeply buried origins owes something to Greek tragedy and certainly to *Hamlet*, is a learning experience as well as an entertainment.' *(Roger Ebert)*

'Stunning motion picture entertainment and easily one of the best pictures of the year. Buoyed by brilliant songs from the team of Elton John and Tim Rice and a stirring score by Hans Zimmer, *The Lion King* tells its somewhat ordinary coming-of-age tale in an extraordinary way . . . The film's finale . . . is perhaps *The Lion King*'s only disappointment – and a minor one at that. The film seems to end too suddenly, too easily. Compared to the GRAND finales of *The Little Mermaid, Aladdin,* and *Beauty and the Beast, The Lion King*'s climax is rather tame. But it doesn't really matter. By the time *The Lion King* comes to an end, no audience in the world will feel they haven't been entertained.' *(Hollywood Hotline)*

'The themes – death, loss, the eternal cycle of growing up – couldn't be more mature, yet something about animation is ideally suited to these deep-dish Jungian fables. While a live-action film can tell us that a son is following in his father's footsteps, the wondrous exactitude of drawn images makes the repetition startlingly romantic. *The Lion King*, like *Bambi*, is a rapturous piece of storybook mythmaking: Joseph Campbell for kids . . . The most poignant element in the story is that, even after he has become a physically mature lion, Simba remains a youth inside. He has to will himself to face his enemies, to replace his father in the circle of life. When he does, *The Lion King*, more than any of the recent wave of Disney animated features, has the resonance to stand not just as a terrific cartoon but as an emotionally pungent movie.' *(Owen Glieberman, Entertainment Weekly)*

LITTLE BIG MAN CT: 6 AV: 7.47

1970 US 147 C WESTERN/WAR

D Arthur Penn
W Calder Willingham from Thomas Berger's novel

Dustin Hoffman ☆ Martin Balsam Faye Dunaway Chief Dan George Richard Mulligan

A 121-year-old man (Dustin Hoffman) claims to be the only survivor of the massacre at the Little Big Horn.

Hoffman is impressive, as is Chief Dan George, in this quirky, anti-war western which suffers from narrative leaps, an unhistorical approach to the Indians, and odd jolts between humour and seriousness. Our hero seems to be more a victim and witness of history, than to have much effect upon it (though perhaps that's partly the point). The overriding purpose of this long, rambling movie seems to be as a tract against genocide and imperialism. The film-makers evidently felt this to be relevant to the Vietnam conflict of the time; whether you agree may depend on your politics.

PRO:

'A tangy and, I think, unique film with American verve, about some of the things American verve has done.' *(Stanley Kauffmann)*

'The Indians in *Little Big Man* are neither murderous savages in the old style nor noble savages in the new style. Early in the narrative Jack explains that the name Cheyenne means "human being", and from then on the Cheyenne refer to themselves as "human beings" in the dialogue. Penn thinks the Cheyenne are human beings too: he makes them a part of the human comedy.' *(Colin Westerbeck Jr, Commonweal)*

'An endlessly entertaining attempt to spin an epic in the form of a yarn. It mostly works. When it doesn't – when there's a failure of tone or an overdrawn caricature – it regroups cheerfully and plunges ahead. We're disposed to go along; all good storytellers tell stretchers once in a while, and circle back to be sure we got the good parts.' *(Roger Ebert)*

MIXED:

'There are moments of vivid, almost scarring, visual loveliness, usually at times when the idyllic life of an Indian camp is about to be raped and destroyed by the US Cavalry. Thus it is a somewhat tendentious loveliness, but no matter. Particularly handsome are the views of such a camp from across a river; the framing effect of the water and the general composition of the shots are admirable. In one remarkable sequence the cavalry is first heard but not seen, and then, ever so slowly, eerily, chillingly, beautifully emerges from the mists. At other times, Harry Stradling Jr's color cinematography is merely ordinary, especially in the indoor scenes . . . Most of the scenes involving Custer strain too hard to be swingingly anti-militaristic, and end up being sweatily unfunny. Still, in a poor field of contenders, *Little Big Man* is several arrowheads ahead.' *(John Simon)*

'Penn himself has expressed doubt about the conviction of the Indian way of life he has created; and in the scenes of Jack's first arrival in the Cheyenne camp there is little to distinguish this set of Indians from that of an average Western. But in more special circumstances, Penn's individuality flourishes; in the desolate poetry of the snowbound reservation on the riverbank, where Jack quietly accepts both family and tribal obligations.' *(MFB)*

'A hip epic, with an amiable first hour. Then the massacres and messages take over.' *(Pauline Kael)*

ANTI:

'What starts as an elegy for lost values winds up as an exercise in white self-hatred, and although it may seem incongruous to say so, I can't help feeling that Penn's movie is another victim of the war in Vietnam.' *(David Denby, Atlantic Monthly)*

LITTLE CAESAR

CT: 7 AV: 8.21

1930 US 80 BW THRILLER

D Mervyn LeRoy ☆
W Robert N. Lee Francis Edward Faragoh AAN Darryl F. Zanuck (uncredited) Robert Lord from W.R. Burnett's novel

Edward G. Robinson ☆ Douglas Fairbanks Jr Glenda Farrell William Collier Jr Stanley Fields Sidney Blackmer

Rise and fall of a Chicago gangster (Edward G. Robinson).

This early talkie that founded the gangster genre is primitive and static by modern standards, but Edward G. Robinson gives one of his greatest performances as a thinly disguised Al Capone.

ANTI:

'Edward G. Robinson's Rico is one of the major prototypes of the movie gangster, but Mervyn LeRoy's direction is sluggish, and the actors seem to be transfixed by the microphone.' *(Pauline Kael)*

PRO:

'I should not hesitate to call *Little Caesar* the most successful talkie that has yet been made in this country.' *(Dwight Macdonald)*

'One of the best gangster pictures yet turned out ... a swell picture.' *(Variety)*

'The production is ordinary and would rank as just one more gangster film but for ... The excellence of [the] credible and compact story ... [and] Robinson's wonderfully effective performance.' *(Mordaunt Hall, New York Times)*

'It has irony and grim humor and a real sense of excitement and its significance does not get in the way of the melodrama.' *(Richard Dana Skinner)*

'I know the general cry is that we have had too many gangster pictures, but when we get one like [this] all the others fade into the background ... At times there is a satirical touch which helps soften the grimness and the tragedy ... There is no attempt to ennoble the gangster or have a death-bed repentance ... [All the cast] are overtopped by ... Robinson.' *(Lionel Collier, Picturegoer)*

'Powerful story ... Convincing portrayals. Realistic atmosphere and appealing, if slight, love interest ... First rate photography and recording.' *(Bioscope)*

LITTLE DORRIT

CT: 4 AV: 7.27

1988 GB 360/Pt I 176; Pt II 181 C DRAMA

D Christine Edzard ✗
W Christine Edzard ✗ AAN from Charles Dickens's novel

Derek Jacobi ☆ Alec Guinness ☆ AAN Roshan Seth Sarah Pickering Miriam Margolyes ☆ Cyril Cusack Max Wall Eleanor Bron Michael Elphick Joan Greenwood Patricia Hayes Robert Morley Bill Fraser Sophie Ward John Savident

A seamstress (Sarah Pickering) whose father (Alec Guinness) is confined to a debtor's prison enlists the aid of a businessman (Derek Jacobi) to get him out. The first half is seen through the eyes of Arthur Clennam, the second through the eyes of Little Dorrit herself.

It is a sign of Dickens's resilience and suitability for the cinema that *Little Dorrit* survives the dead hand of writer-director Christine Edzard, who seems far more interested in costumes than character. Several figures spring to life regardless, thanks to the efforts of (notably) Alec Guinness and Miriam Margolyes. However, the monotonous shooting style and laborious pace does diminish the impact of the book. One has only to compare the painfully inadequate, Schools Broadcasting style adopted here with David Lean's *Great Expectations* to feel regret that real writing and directing talent was not devoted to the project. Even so, it was over-praised and won the Los Angeles Film Critics' Association 1988 Award for Best Picture.

PRO:

'A remarkable achievement.' *(Variety)*

'So filled with characters, so rich in incident, that it has the expansive, luxurious feel of a Victorian novel.' *(Roger Ebert)*

'There are 242 actors, extras excluded, in this enthralling film version of the Charles Dickens novel. Not one gives a weak performance ... As the self-deluding old Dorrit, Alec Guinness gives the performance of his life, capturing the character's comic and tragic dimensions with magisterial subtlety. Cheers also to the hilarious Miriam Margolyes as the fat, flirtatious Flora Finching, Roshan Seth as the rent collector Pancks, Max Wall as the venomous steward Flintwinch and Eleanor Bron as the scheming Mrs Merdle, wife of the financial whiz who brings so many to ruin. There are more acting triumphs here than you can shake an Oscar at. Each actor goes beyond the exquisite period details to cut to the soul of the character. Dickens is superlatively served. Ditto the audience.' *(Peter Travers, People Weekly)*

'Besides the excitement of the story, the chief delight of this epic production lies in the superb performances . . . Impressive camera-work and Verdi's music help make the six hours roll by far too quickly.' *(Mark Sanderson, Time Out)*

'A great screen adaptation, as well as a cautionary fable for Mrs Thatcher's England.' *(Graham Fuller, Film Yearbook)*

MIXED:

'Lacks the gusto and dramatic sweep of both Dickens's novels and the best of the films based on them . . . Yet, finally, it is the brilliant acting that remains memorable about Little Dorrit. It stands above the movie's faults and murky atmosphere like an isolated streetlamp in a foggy London night.' *(John Bemrose, Maclean's)*

'The camerawork is slightly static, which does not make for the breadth and fluidity of a film made for the big screen, but this does not mitigate against the intensity of the interior shots . . . There is no sentimentality about the script and no cynicism either.' *(Virginia Dignam, Morning Star)*

ANTI:

'Part I [is] an experience so excruciating that wild Dickensian orphans would not drag me back into a cinema for Part II . . . Wit is on a power-cut. And the sets and lighting have to be seen to be pitied . . . The only way you can tell if it is morning, afternoon or early evening, is if the uniformly flat lighting . . . gives a token twitch of dimness, brightness or colour. By contrast, you can tell if it is night by the fact that you can scarcely see anything at all. (Eat a carrot beforehand.) . . . Only . . . Derek Jacobi . . . creates a seam of gold in a movie that is elsewhere sadly un-alchemised, a ten-ton block of cinematic lead.' *(Nigel Andrews, Financial Times)*

'Many of the scenes are beautiful and moving . . . [But the device of filming some scenes twice from slightly different angles] leads the film into some unprofitable repetition, and the gain in understanding is slight, because subliminal . . . There are also some alarming misjudgments [eg in inventing some scenes and quoting from other Dickens novels] . . . The most serious weakness arises from the wholesale removal of the Blandois-Rigaud element.' *(Adolph Wood, Times Literary Supplement)*

'Low-budget production is painstakingly slow-moving: viewers will either adore this or despise it . . . Second half of saga unfortunately insists on recreating almost the entire first half scene for scene before moving forward. As in first part, there are several good performances (notably Guinness's) but screenplay is inadequate.' *(Maltin)*

LITTLE FOXES, THE AAN   CT: 8 AV: 8.45

1941 US 116 BW DRAMA

D William Wyler ☆ AAN
W Lillian Hellman AAN with Arthur Kober, Dorothy Parker, Alan Campbell from Lillian Hellman's play

Bette Davis ☆ AAN Herbert Marshall Teresa Wright ☆ AAN Dan Duryea Charles Dingle Patricia Collinge ☆ AAN Richard Carlson

A Southern belle (Bette Davis) has plans to get rich quick.

Superb post-American Civil War drama with a strong story, memorable characters, wonderful cinematography by Gregg Toland, and sensitive direction by Wyler, but no one with whom to empathize. In the Broadway production, Tallulah Bankhead went for much greater warmth than Bette Davis, and was more sympathetic; Davis, by contrast, is all cold, avaricious ambition. Meredith Willson's romantic music, Stephen Goosson's art direction and Daniel Mandell's editing were Oscar-nominated.

PRO:

'One of the really beautiful jobs in the whole range of movie making.' *(Otis Ferguson)*

'No one knows better than Wyler when to shift the camera's point of view, when to cut, or how to relate the characters in one shot to those in the next . . . You never have to wonder where you are in a Wyler picture.' *(Arthur Knight)*

'It is a performance picture, a prestige picture, a women's picture, an artistic triumph, masterpiece and . . . a box office picture by reason of all these things at the expense of none of them. It is, in any case, a Bette Davis picture.' *(William Weaver, Motion Picture Herald)*

'Very good . . . The camera itself contributes enormously to this drama of rasping ambition and family breakdown . . . [It] enlarges, surprises, follows through shut doors, splits up a moment into its component parts . . . Davis . . . gives her best and most terrifying performance.' *(William Whitebait, New Statesman)*

'A strong, dramatic, grim story, well produced with careful attention to period detail, excellently directed and admirably acted. Bette Davis is superb.' *(MFB)*

'Translated to the screen with all its viciousness intact and with such extra-added virulence as the relentless camera of . . . Wyler and the tensile acting of Bette Davis could impart . . . [It] will not increase your admiration of mankind. It is cold and cynical. But it is a very exciting picture to watch . . . especially if you enjoy expert stabbing-in-the-back.' *(Bosley Crowther)*

'Davis, spraying the charm of arsenic over everyone.' *(Alexander Walker, Evening Standard, 1982)*

LITTLE MERMAID, THE CT: 8 AV: 7.29

1989 US 83 C CARTOON/ROMANCE/MUSICAL/FAMILY

D John Musker Ron Clements ☆
W John Musker Ron Clements from Hans Christian Andersen's story (music and lyrics by Alan Menken and Howard Ashman ☆)

Voices: Jodi Benson ☆ (Ariel) René Auberjonois ☆ (Sebastian) Pat Carroll ☆ (Ursula) Christopher Daniel Barnes Paddi Edwards Buddy Hackett Jason Marin Kenneth Mars Edie McClurg Will Ryan Ben Wright Samuel E. Wright

Mermaid princess longs to marry a landlubber.

A fine cartoon – partly because the animation ranges from the cuteness of *Bambi* to the ferocity of *Fantasia*. Another reason is the characterization: Ursula the Sea Witch is the most splendidly repulsive Disney villain since Cruella de Vil in *101 Dalmatians*. Even the heroine's range of facial expression is enchanting, far superior, in fact, to the blandness of *Snow White* and *The Sleeping Beauty*.

Other important ingredients are a catchy, Oscar-winning score and witty lyrics. The songs may be Broadway pastiche, but they advance the action, enlarge character, and here inspire some of the best visual gags ever seen in a Disney cartoon – or any screen musical.

A few elements of Hans Andersen's fairytale have been lost. In the original, the little mermaid sacrifices her tongue to the Sea Witch in order to gain legs, only to lose out to a princess with no such social handicap. The little mermaid then nobly refuses to stab the prince, and thereby win back her old life. The prophecies of her father, the Sea King, are proved true: she suffers agonies (every step she takes on dry land feels like treading on sharp knives); and she loses her lover, her family and her life.

In Disney's more upbeat version, the mermaid's teenage rebellion is crowned with success: she wins her prince and regains her voice – while her father learns not to stand in the way of young people's aspirations. The cartoon ends up, indeed, with the opposite message to Andersen's original: it is a homage to adolescent love, the 'can-do' culture and upward mobility. But then different nations and generations have always reinterpreted fairytales to suit their prejudices.

In common with other Disneyfied fairytales, there's something odd to British ears about medieval princes talking with American accents; and there's plenty for any agonized liberal to question in the movie's value system. The film deals ebulliently in racial stereotypes and retains all the snobbery and sexism of Andersen's original (the little mermaid's one aim is to catch her prince). But it's easy to be humourless about such matters: this was Disney's best new full-length cartoon in 30 years, and paved the way for an even finer film, *Beauty and the Beast*.

ANTI:

'I wish I could be more enthusiastic about [it]. It's a terribly well-behaved Disney cartoon, with pleasingly animated drawings in bright primary colours . . . But there's something fundamentally wrong with the whole confection: it's almost offensively inoffensive . . . [Disney's] successors seem to have taken a step backwards.' *(Iain Johnstone, Sunday Times)*

'Skilfully adhering to [Disney's] first principles . . . to deliver a basinful of kitsch . . . as if what was intended was a kind of Busby Berkeley water musical mixed with treacle.' *(Derek Malcolm, Guardian)*

'Disney-style kitsch. It's technologically sophisticated, but with just about all the simpering old Disney values in place.' *(Pauline Kael)*

MIXED:

'Clements has stated that fairy tales are great movie sources because of their ability 'to instill hope'. Of course, if they don't, he might have added, you can always pervert them to blunt their true poetry and make them over into merchandised musical lollipops . . . This said, the Disney version is an occasionally entertaining job, even if it does have trouble padding its thin story line to feature length . . . Sebastian is the film's Jiminy Cricket, its saving grace and only memorable character. The heroine . . . is a simpering implausibility . . . Andersen's mermaid yearns to become human as much to attain an immortal soul as to marry the prince. This movie doesn't know soles from souls.' *(Elliott Stein, Village Voice)*

'Sebastian saves the day, almost, before a tidal rush of Disney sentiment washes everything in pastel shades, and squeezeheart melodies swamp the soundtrack and every throat fills like a sink.' *(Angus Wolfe Murray, Scotsman Weekend)*

'Its animation stands up well – even if the characterisation doesn't.' *(Brinley Hamer-Jones, Western Mail)*

'Bright and busy enough to keep children amused; but sterner adults may find the old fairy-tale magic squeezed out by the film's synthetic mixture of styles.' *(Geoff Brown, The Times)*

PRO:

'Full of wit and colour and mercifully schmaltz-free: the best paint-and-brush show the studio has given us since *The Jungle Book*.' *(Harlan Kennedy, Film Yearbook)*

'Disney is almost back on top form with this Hans Christian Andersen story about the mermaid who wants to be human. The animation's great, the characters are fun and the songs are pretty.' *(Rose)*

'Here at last, once again, is the kind of liberating, original, joyful Disney animation that we remember from *Snow White, Pinocchio,* and the other first-generation classics. There has been a notion in recent years that animated films are only for kids.

But why? The artistry of animation has a clarity and a force that can appeal to everyone, if only it isn't shackled to a dim-witted story. *The Little Mermaid* has music and laughter and visual delight for everyone.' *(Roger Ebert)*

LITTLE WOMEN AAN

CT: 8 AV: 8.15

1933 US 115 BW DRAMA/ROMANCE/FAMILY

D George Cukor ☆ AAN
W Sarah Y. Mason Victor Heerman ☆ AAW from Louisa May Alcott's novel

Katharine Hepburn ☆ Joan Bennett ✔ Frances Dee ✔ Jean Parker Paul Lukas Spring Byington Edna May Oliver ✔ Douglass Montgomery ✔ Henry Stephenson

Four New England sisters grow up in post-Civil War America.

Handsomely produced costume drama with a plethora of strong female roles, expertly directed by George Cukor. Some of the acting (including Hepburn's) may be over-emphatic and theatrical for modern tastes, but overall this is the most endearing of the various versions. Despite a few sugary moments, the sisters are intensely sympathetic, especially Hepburn's tomboyish Jo; and Edna May Oliver contributes a welcome touch of vinegar as nasty Aunt March. Its ability to provoke tears and laughter made it Number five on *Film Daily*'s annual poll of the US film critics.

MIXED:

'There are small flaws – a few naive and cloying scenes, some obvious dramatic contrivances – but it's a lovely, graceful film, and surprisingly faithful to the atmosphere, the Victorian sentiments, and the Victorian strengths of the Louisa May Alcott novel.' *(Pauline Kael)*

PRO:

'If to put a book on the screen with all the effectiveness that sympathy and good taste and careful artifice can devise is to make a fine motion picture, then Little Women is a fine picture . . . Without being intended as an historical film it does really record, with surprising faithfullness, a period in America that many people think was most characteristically and ideally American. Here the simple sturdy virtues live as we like to think they lived in earlier times.' *(James Shelley Hamilton, NBR)*

'One of the most satisfactory pictures I have ever seen.' *(E.V. Lucas, Punch)*

'A reminder that emotions and vitality and truth can be evoked from lavender and lace as well as from machine guns and precision dances.' *(Thornton Delehanty, New York Post)*

LIVE AND LET DIE: *see BOND* SERIES.

LIVES OF A BENGAL LANCER AAN

CT: 7 AV: 8.40

1934 US 119 BW ACTION/ADVENTURE

D Henry Hathaway ☆ AAN
W Waldemar Young John Balderston Achmed Abdullah Grover Jones William Slavens McNutt ☆ AAN from Major Francis Yeats-Brown's novel

Gary Cooper ☆ Franchot Tone ☆ C. Aubrey Smith Richard Cromwell Sir Guy Standing ☆ Monte Blue Douglas Dumbrille ☆

The British put down an uprising on the Indian frontier.

Rousing adventure with a witty script, deft characterization, splendid baddies, exciting action sequences and a fine sense of the British Raj. Gary Cooper gives one of his strongest performances, though Tone has most of the best lines. Second only to *David Copperfield* in the *Film Daily* 1935 poll of the US film critics. Ellsworth Hoagland's editing and the art direction of Hans Dreier and Roland Anderson were Oscar-nominated. Assistant directors Clem Beauchamp and Paul Wing won Academy Awards for second-unit direction, although it is in fact rather too easy to see where Hathaway's work ends and theirs begins.

MIXED:

'We're supposed to feel pride in the imperial British gallantry of the Lancers (as they put down an uprising on the Indian frontier), and at some level we do, despite our more knowledgeable, disgusted selves. The adolescent boys' fantasy atmosphere is very powerful; the director, Henry Hathaway, gives us an empathic identification with all the high-minded stuff that's going on inside Cooper and his buddy, Franchot Tone. At the same time, part of the picture's romantic charge is its underlying homoeroticism, which comes out in Cooper and Tone's comic camaraderie. And the film works on an adolescent's fear of showing cowardice by supplying a weakling character (Richard Cromwell). But if the movie is morally repugnant, it's also a terrific piece of Hollywood Victoriana.' *(Pauline Kael)*

PRO:

'The poverty of this story is redeemed by the brilliance of its photography, direction, and acting.' *(James Agate, Tatler)*

'A splendid achievement . . . Aided in the preservation of the grand spirit of the original story by a great all-star cast, flawless down to the last member, and authentic settings, the producer has turned out a magnificent piece of entertainment. The film, a credit to the industry and Paramount, its sponsors, is a box-office certainty.' *(Kine Weekly)*

'In every respect a great picture . . . It may not be

Yeats-Brown, but it is magnificent.' *(Edward Betts, Era)*

'One of the most magnificently entertaining pictures ever made. It has spectacle, action, self-sacrificing heroism, pathos, lively humour – everything a picture can have except love.' *(Daily Telegraph)*

LIVING DAYLIGHTS, THE: *see* BOND SERIES.

LIVING: *see* IKIRU.

LOCAL HERO

CT: 9 AV: 8.53

1983 GB 111 C COMEDY/FANTASY

D Bill Forsyth ☆
W Bill Forsyth ☆

Burt Lancaster ☆ Peter Riegert ✓ Denis Lawson ☆ Peter Capaldi ✓ Fulton Mackay ✓ Jenny Seagrove Norman Chancer Rikki Fulton Alex Norton Jennifer Black John Gordon Sinclair

A brash American businessman (Burt Lancaster) wishes to buy a beautiful Scottish island to drill for oil there, and sends a minion called MacIntyre (Peter Riegert) to do the deal.

Odd, eccentric, very charming film full of quirky characters and apparently inconsequential detail. Some may find it too slow and whimsical, and it's not entirely original – influences obviously include Mackendrick's *Whiskey Galore* and Powell and Pressburger's *I Know Where I'm Going*. But it has a pictorial and verbal magic all its own.

And *Local Hero* has a serious point – about how money and power, though eminently attractive, are less important than other, less easily measurable aspects of life. The thing that makes it refreshingly different from a Hollywood film is that the characters are constantly surprising; by the end, it's even impossible to know how MacIntyre is going to behave – so infected has he become by the island he was sent to destroy. *Local Hero* thumbs its nose at Thatcherism and Reaganite economics, in the most delightful and inoffensive way possible. It's a masterpiece of character-driven comedy.

ANTI:

'To begin with it looks like another heart-winner . . . Alas, the pace of the film slows and despite touches of magic here and there, invention also grinds to a halt. Every situation seems contrived, and there is a superabundance of calculatedly cute characters.' *(Madeleine Harmsworth, Sunday Mirror)*

'At once the most subtle and intricate and the most frustrating of Forsyth's films . . . The pace becomes not so much mystical-hypnotic as just snail's pace slow . . . As played by gnomic and long-faced Peter Riegert [the hero] is a hole in the screen. And some sequences and characters seem to have stuck to the movie like otiose barnacles . . . The film freshens up at last when Lancaster helicopters in . . . and sets about trying to rescue both the deal and the movie. But by then it's already clear that a thumbnail verdict . . . is impossible. It's both a sterling advance and a perplexing hiccup in Forsyth's career.' *(Nigel Andrews, Financial Times)*

'Not really funny enough for its great length.' *(Halliwell)*

MIXED:

'A tartan encounter of the Ealing kind and many elements make up its fabric: charm, wit, fantasy, drama . . . What the film lacks is tension – a sense of urgency that we should want to know what is going to happen next. Not an unqualified delight, but there is enough to make it an experience which charms as it entertains.' *(Tom Hutchinson, Mail on Sunday)*

PRO:

'A director with a comic vision of his own – a way of seeing the world that is funny or odd down to its roots – comes along perhaps once in a decade. Bill Forsyth, the young Scottish writer-director, may be one of those talents.' *(David Denby)*

'Utterly delightful, magical comedy.' *(Rose)*

'Charming, whimsical, and nearly perfect, *Local Hero* proves again that you don't need a lot of money to make a good film.' *(Baseline)*

LOCATAIRE, LE: *see* TENANT, THE.

LODGER, THE

CT: 7 AV: 6.88

(aka *A Story of the London Fog; The Case of Jonathan Drew)*

1926 GB 84 BW THRILLER/ SILENT

D Alfred Hitchcock ☆
W Eliot Stannard Alfred Hitchcock

Ivor Novello June Marie Ault Arthur Chesney Malcolm Keen

A detective (Malcolm Keen) accuses a lodger (Ivor Novello) of murder.

Hitchcock's silent thriller brilliantly conjures up an atmosphere of threat and terror in the London fog. Influenced by German Expressionism, Hitchcock foreshadows the Fritz Lang masterpiece *M* (1931) in the mob's hunt for Novello. One of Hitchcock's favourite themes – the man unjustly accused – is established here, as is his taste for making cameo appearances in his own films.

'The first time I exercised my style . . . You might almost say it was my first picture.' *(Alfred Hitchcock, 1966)*

MIXED:

'The best thing about the picture is that despite its outrageous crudities, it somehow does manage to suggest that in its script form it probably had literary and dramatic excellence. And the worst thing about it is that the studio was not equal to developing its artistic merit on the screen.' *(Variety)*

PRO:

'[Possibly] the finest British production ever made.' *(Bioscope)*

'One of the first real landmarks in the coming advance of British pictures.' *(Kinematograph)*

'As an essay in film technique it ranks with the best films ever made.' *(Evening News)*

'The experienced audience which viewed the film were gripped from the start and hardly dared to breathe until the conclusion.' *(Daily Express)*

'The first "real" Hitchcock, and a landmark in the British silent period . . . It is, in fact, the treatment rather than the story which is memorable. The atmosphere is heavily Germanic, full of heavily symbolic shadows and chiaroscuro lighting effects . . . The film encountered some resistance from renters on its first appearance, and now seems tame, but there is no denying its historical importance.' *(Ivan Butler, Cinema in Britain, 1973)*

'Strangely enough, Hitchcock blends expressionism (low-key lighting, distorted mirror reflections) with realism, documenting the gathering, reporting, and dissemination to the hysterical populace of news of the Avenger's latest murder. Here, as later with his incorporation of montage and *mise-en-scène* into a single visual aesthetic, Hitchcock reveals an interest in synthesizing disparate styles.' *(John Belton, Cinema Stylists, 1983)*

'The first time in British film history that the director received an even greater press than his stars.' *(Donald Spoto, The Art of Alfred Hitchcock, 1976)*

LOLA MONTÈS CT: 5 AV: 6.88

(aka *The Sins of Lola Montès*)

1955 France/Germany 90/110/140 C DRAMA/ BIOPIC

D Max Ophuls ***X***
W Max Ophuls Jacques Natanson Franz Geiger Annette Wademant from Cecil Saint-Laurent's unpublished novel *La Vie Extraordinaire de Lola Montès*

Martine Carol ● Peter Ustinov Anton Walbrook Ivan Desny Will Quadflieg Oskar Werner Lise Delamare Henri Guisol Paulette Dubost Hélèna Manson

A circus performer (Martine Carol) remembers that she used to be very attractive to men.

It isn't hard to see why Ophuls's last film has been overpraised by critics: it is visually magnificent and makes inspired use of colour, widescreen and mobile camerawork. This is also a very romantic view of life: at any moment, one half expects the heroine to launch into 'Je Ne Regrette Rien'. However, it is let down by a dire script, a turgid pace, and a plainly inadequate leading actress. The film was made in three versions: English, French and German.

PRO:

'The greatest film of all time.' *(Andrew Sarris, 1963)*

'An extraordinary movie . . . It is not only Ophuls's last film . . . but it is also an eye-expanding summation of the lush, romantic style . . . A visibly dazzling ironic commentary on celebrity.' *(Vincent Canby, New York Times)*

'It is, as near as dammit, a masterpiece.' *(Tom Milne, Observer)*

'The lush colour, elaborate camera movement, sensuous music and highly decorative style makes a dazzling backdrop . . . [for] this reactionary material . . . given revolutionary treatment by Ophuls.' *(Virginia Dignam, Morning Star)*

'Certainly director Max Ophuls's greatest achievement . . . Along with Michael Powell's *Black Narcissus*, this is one of the most gorgeous films ever shot in color.' *(Virgin)*

MIXED:

'Reservations about the . . . coldness of decor now make me drop it down a notch or two from the very summit of greatness.' *(Andrew Sarris, 1969)*

'If you want to know what form can really do for content, rush along.' *(Derek Malcolm, Guardian, 1978)*

'The film is famous for its elaborate tracking shots [which are] justly renowned for their visual complexity, but their self-conscious artificiality is unfortunately emblematic of the movie's comic opera shallowness.' *(Matthew Hoffman, Sunday Times)*

'Ophuls hoped to illuminate the dangers of fame but the script and Martine Carol's poor performance make the film virtually pointless, if sometimes as dazzlingly done as we expect of this director.' *(Shipman)*

ANTI:

'In this [reshaped] form, the picture is bound artistically to fall to pieces. Some of the transitions in the narrative are impossibly abrupt; and inevitably the film has neither coherence, shape nor consistency of approach. Some of the circus material is finely atmospheric, but haphazardly attached to the end of the picture, its mood seems entirely out of keeping with the earlier scenes . . . [which] Martine Carrol's performance is not sufficiently vital or interesting to hold together.' *(Philip Hope-Wallace, MFB)*

'A masterpiece for chambermaids, especially those of the Austro-Hungarian sort, and for all those who share that worthy profession's legacy of dime-store romanticism . . . [It] sinks under the combined ballast of banality, sentimentality and pointlessness.' *(John Simon)*

'Disappointing – poorly acted and too shallow for its melancholy tone and its rich decor and elaborate structure.' *(Pauline Kael)*

LONELINESS OF THE LONG DISTANCE RUNNER, THE CT: 6 AV: 7.45

1962 GB 104 BW DRAMA

D Tony Richardson ☆
W Alan Sillitoe from his novel

Tom Courtenay ☆ Michael Redgrave James Fox Avis Bunnage Alec McCowen James Bolam Julia Foster

A Borstal boy (Tom Courtenay) with a talent for long-distance running rebels against the system.

A landmark British film, thanks to Tom Courtenay's riveting performance. The class conflict and authoritarian system are drawn very crudely, however; it is Courtenay's performance rather than anything in the script which makes us care about him.

MIXED:

'Riveting . . . fueled mainly on the power of the original story and the brilliance of Tom Courtenay's performance, thorough and physical . . . Romanticism blurs the story's edge from time to time . . . and there are too many styles . . . But it's still a good film.' *(P. Williams, Sunday Telegraph)*

'The hero is too palpably prolier-than-thou, his case is too obviously rigged. Fortunately, actor Courtenay is excellent . . . His eyes are as dark and empty as broken windows in an abandoned mill.' *(Time)*

PRO:

'It is Tom Courtenay who fills the whole affair with life: the shuttered, the truculent or the steely face, the shambler in the fumy city, the runner pounding with delighted flailing arms though the frosty morning woods, he is the young anarchist of our day. And it is in his most fightable moods that one feels most sharply for him. That seems to me the unique achievement of the film. The rebel against the world (I don't mean the psychological, James Dean rebel; I mean the social outlaw) has become familiar on the screen: familiar but not, to me at any rate, welcome. *The Loneliness of the Long Distance Runner* makes him a sympathetic figure. For the first time in the cinema one is persuaded to experience his defiance. It is not a matter of pity. One looks at the hopeless layabout of *Accatone* and pities him. One looks at Colin Smith and understands him.' *(Dilys Powell)*

'Sillitoe and Richardson observe [their] character and his peculiarly self-conscious relationship with society, with exceptional sympathy and intelligence . . . If for no other reason, the film would be important for the screen début of Tom Courtenay . . . This is as near as could be, a perfect performance, accurate and integrated . . . The main complaint against the film is that the director does not in the end repose enough confidence in this performance.' *(David Robinson, Financial Times)*

LONELY LADY, THE CT: 5 AV: 1.70

1982 US 92 C DRAMA/SO BAD

D Peter Sasdy ●
W John Kershaw Shawn Randall ● from Harold Robbins's novel

Pia Zadora ● Lloyd Bochner ● Bibi Besch ● Ray Liotta ● Lou Hirsch

A writer graduate (Pia Zadora) is undeterred from a Hollywood career, even after being raped in Beverly Hills with a garden hose.

Trashy film from a Harold Robbins novel about an innocent abroad in the wicked movie capital. Presumably this was a vanity project for the film's star – though how she kept any self-confidence, let alone vanity, after seeing herself in this horror is anyone's guess. The actors seem to be indulging in a perverse competition to give the worst performance of all time; and the atrocious script gives them every help. Sample dialogue . . . Hospital orderly to Pia Zadora's mother: 'She was suffering from paranoia and hallucinations, induced by tranquillizers, cocaine, amphetamines, alcohol . . .' Mother (Bibi Besch): 'She's always been difficult.'

'Pia Zadora manages to play her part better than expected, even if she does begin as a kind of "Miss Piggy made flesh." . . . A low-budget peep show of the high life.' *(Phillip Bergson, What's On in London)*

'The year's best bad film . . . Miss Pia Zadora . . . has a real life rich husband who wants to make her a star . . . Croesus would not have enough in his coffers to do the job.' *(William Russell, Glasgow Herald)*

'A new low for truthfulness in advertising . . . since the shower sex scene plastered all over the ad never actually materialises.' *(Cynthia Rose, New Musical Express)*

'You've got to say this much for Miss Zadora: she's got spunk . . . A badly acted, slovenly looking movie that isn't even much fun.' *(Janet Maslin, New York Times)*

'Risible concoction designed to show off the non-talents of a non-star in a film financed by her husband.' *(Halliwell)*

'Feast of Stone Age performances and Neanderthal dialog.' *(Scheuer)*

'Flaccid direction, a dire script, and some extremely poor acting add up to a miserable experience that only scores as kitsch entertainment to be laughed at.' *(Winnert)*

'Nothing like as lonely as the few lost souls watching this Zadora turkey.' *(Rose)*

LONG DAY CLOSES, THE CT: 6 AV: 6.25

1992 GB 83 C DRAMA

D Terence Davies ✗
W Terence Davies

Majorie Yates Leigh McCormack ☆
Anthony Watson Nicholas Lamont Ayse Owens

A boy grows up in 50s Liverpool.

A marvellous and infuriating film about childhood happiness, in the same tradition as John Boorman's wartime reminiscence, *Hope and Glory*. There are moments when it resembles an inordinately extended Hovis commercial: there's the same use of desaturated colour, evocative music (Davies's love of popular song as a substitute for dialogue is second only to Dennis Potter's), and a relentlessly glamorous view of the northern working class as a repository of warmth and kindness. Superficially, Davies's nostalgic view of 50s Liverpool appears as inert, complacent and class-ridden as Merchant-Ivory at their worst.

The film only really makes sense and delivers a powerful emotional impact if you're aware of Davies's cinematic past. It's not merely a successor but also an antidote to Davies's previous, critically applauded film, *Distant Voices Still Lives*, set during the 40s when his monstrous father was still alive and kicking hell out of his family. Together, the two films form adramatically contrasting diptych of pain and contentment.

Technically, the film is a triumph. Christopher Hobbs works wonders on a small budget: his exterior street set is a delightful tribute to both the reality of Liverpool and the stagey glamour of those American musicals which Davies so obviously admires. The film is often magical, and Davies's best in terms of craft: every shot seems meticulously planned. It's also a fine example of an apparently parochial film which has something universal to say about the human condition.

The aspect which prevents it from being a masterpiece is the same that prevents it from being a popular success – namely, the absence of narrative or character development. There is hardly any drama: although a few authority figures mete out 'justice' from on high, the only real conflict is between the mood of this film and the nightmarish world of its predecessor. The film lacks a protagonist: the central boy (though beautifully played by Leigh McCormack) does not develop, initiate anything or do much beyond look contented. The reels of the film could be reassembled in a different order, and make just as much sense. I can't help feeling this is a defect, for film is a narrative rather than a static medium.

PRO:

'A technically elaborate, dryly witty mood piece.' *(Variety)*

'A warm and oddly moving experience.' *(Empire)*

'Davies's best film yet.' *(Raymond Durgnat, S & S)*

MIXED:

'Undeniably evocative – at least until you remember *Cinema Paradiso* and how much better that Italian movie dealt with film and family nostalgia.' *(Sheridan Morley, Sunday Express)*

ANTI:

'Appallingly dull . . . There is no story here . . . Lurking in every scene our hero drifts through the film with corpse-like detachment. We do not like him and we do not dislike him, for he is nothing more, when it comes down to it, than a vessel.' *(Vanessa Letts, Spectator)*

'Offers nothing for the film-going public to connect with. It is a film which seems designed to appeal exclusively to critics . . . In spite of departing from virtually every cinematic convention [it] somehow manages to be depressingly predictable.' *(Toby Young, Guardian)*

'A perfect example of what is wrong with the British film industry. Ostensibly about a working-class childhood in 50's Liverpool, there's nothing so vulgar as a story, just a series of pretty pictures. These include a two-minute shot of sunlight playing on a carpet! Indescribably boring to everyone but insomniacs, who should rush out and rent the tape immediately.' *(Rose)*

LONG DAY'S JOURNEY INTO NIGHT CT: 6 AV: 8.40

1962 US 136/174 BW DRAMA

D Sidney Lumet ☆
W Eugene O'Neill

Ralph Richardson ☆ Katharine Hepburn ☆ AAN
Jason Robards Jr Dean Stockwell ☆ Jeanne Barr

Recriminations abound in the home of a washed-up actor (Ralph Richardson), his dope-fiend wife (Katharine Hepburn) and their two sons, an alcoholic (Jason Robards Jr) and a TB patient (Dean Stockwell), who is obviously based on Eugene O'Neill.

Very theatrical filming of O'Neill's lumbering drama, amply redeemed by powerful performances, especially by Richardson and Hepburn.

PRO:

'Lumet illuminates the play line by line, and gives it all the impact of a live performance.' *(Brenda Davies)*

'The best film ever made from an O'Neill play (and it's O'Neill's greatest play).' *(Pauline Kael)*

'An unrelenting, shattering film.' *(Scheuer)*

ANTI:

'A very great play has been not translated to the screen but reverently put behind glass – it matter little whether the plate glass around the stuffed fauna of museums or the glass of lenses encasing live theatre in inanimate images.' *(John Simon, Private Screenings, 1967)*

'*Long Day's Journey into Night* is filled with talk. It is great talk; but it is talk for the stage, not for the screen. As a result, Lumet is obliged to move his camera meaninglessly around the performers as they discourse within the confinement of the original stage setting.' *(Edward Murray, The Cinematic Imagination, 1972)*

LONG GOOD FRIDAY, THE CT: 6 AV: 7.79

1980 GB 118 C THRILLER

D John Mackenzie
W Barrie Keefe ☆

Bob Hoskins ☆ Helen Mirren Eddie Constantine Dave King Bryan Marshall George Coulouris

A gangland boss (Bob Hopkins) finds his organization under threat from the IRA.

Violent and melodramatic; but Barry Keefe's realistic dialogue holds up well, John Mackenzie's direction is cinematic given the budgetary constraints, and Hoskins's performance is Cagneyesque in its commitment and aggression.

'What we wanted to make was a really British gangster film. There've been a lot of attempts, but they usually end up as impersonations of American films.' *(Bob Hoskins)*

PRO:

'Three rousing cheers for . . . a cracking British thriller . . . Don't be put off by the beginning . . . which is fragmented and somewhat confusing. All the pieces eventually fit together and the result is ingenious, imaginative and tremendously exciting.' *(Ian Christie, Daily Express)*

'Two great benefits, a tough salty script . . . and a stand-out performance by the squat, strutting, vivid-tongued Bob Hoskins.' *(John Coleman)*

'I have rarely seen a movie character so completely alive. Shand is an evil, cruel, sadistic man. But he's a mass of contradictions, and there are times when we understand him so completely we almost feel affectionate. He's such a character, such an overcompensating Cockney, sensitive to the slightest affront, able to strike fear in the hearts of killers, but a pushover when his mistress raises her voice to him. Shand is played by a compact, muscular actor named Bob Hoskins, in the most-praised film performance of the year from England. Hoskins has the energy and the freshness of a younger Michael Caine, if not the good looks.' *(Roger Ebert)*

MIXED:

'Entertaining, if alarming . . . A wry wit illuminates the darker moments, although the film runs into its own clichés.' *(Tom Hutchinson, Now)*

'John Mackenzie's hot on fireworks and atmosphere, but a bit of a damp squib when it comes to storytelling.' *(Ken Russell, 1993)*

LONG GOODBYE, THE CT: 5 AV: 5.77

1973 US 111 C THRILLER

D Robert Altman
W Leigh Brackett from Raymond Chandler's novel

Elliott Gould ● Nina Van Pallandt Sterling Hayden Mark Rydell Henry Gibson David Arkin Jim Bouton Warren Berlinger

Private detective Philip Marlowe (Elliott Gould) investigates murder.

Some think that Robert Altman's jokey updating of Raymond Chandler to the 1970s is a great thriller; I thought it a great mistake. A companion-piece to Altman's *Buffalo Bill and the Indians,* which debunked the Western, this is an attempt to do the same to the thriller. Whether you love or hate it will depend on whether you warm to Elliott Gould as a private eye; if not, you'll find it brutal and boring. A youthful Arnold Schwarzenegger has a tiny role (he's billed as Arnold Strong).

'I'm really crazy about *The Long Goodbye*, and I'm really upset it didn't do well. We wanted a big, big hit, and I needed that to re-establish myself as a commercial entity. They made the mistake of opening it in Los Angeles and it was destroyed in the papers. It's an art film that should have opened in New York.' *(Elliott Gould)*

PRO:

'What Altman has cleverly done is turn [Chandler] upside down . . . Here he spends his whole time being put down until the very end, when he does the putting . . . It's a beautifully made film, with a prowling camera often edging away from the subject . . . and a towering performance . . . by Sterling Hayden.' *(Gavin Millar, Listener)*

'By updating Marlowe and his world he has demonstrated how American movies have changed and for the worse . . . Altman's direction is quite dazzling in its controlled irony . . . It doesn't diminish the original at all; on the contrary, it gives it another unexpected dimension.' *(George Melly, Observer)*

'Cameraman Vilmos Zsigmond turns the bleak contemporary landscape of LA into a city of hidden menace.' *(Margaret Hinxman, Sunday Telegraph)*

'A knockout of a movie. Altman tells a detective story all right, but he does it though a spree – a high-flying rap on Chandler and the movies and LA.' *(Pauline Kael)*

'Along with *Chinatown* the definitive private-eye and LA movie . . . proceeds to relocate the 40's film noir and the Chandler ethos in a 70's setting – the seductive Malibu colony and the Ocean seen, not as paradise, but as the edge of the world.' *(NFT Bulletin, 1980)*

'Suceeded in capturing Chandler's bleak vision of the great nowhere city.' *(Rob Reiner, Orbis, 1984)*

MIXED:

'A thoroughly entertaining movie, very funny in spots . . . [But] at a story point when conventional private eye movies should be setting everything straight, in exposition that may not be comprehensible to anyone who isn't following the film with a score [it] erupts with violence and ends in a mood of moral confusion that sends you out of the theater wondering not what happened but why it did.' *(Vincent Canby, New York Times)*

ANTI:

'My complaint against Robert Altman's film is . . . against an intrusively up-to-date jokeyness. A thriller, unless it is a comedy-thriller, and this isn't, is the better for taking its thrills seriously. This Marlowe kills – and goes off capering.' *(Dilys Powell)*

'A heartless picture.' *(Philip French, S & S)*

'[Looks] like a very late American imitation of a French imitation of earlier American films.' *(Michael Wood, New Society)*

'Elliott Gould has none of the characteristics of the tough, canny sleuth: his face and expressions, slack and self-indulgent, do not betray any signs of quick and sharp thinking – or, for that matter, of any other kind.' *(John Simon)*

'This Marlowe is an untidy, unshaven, semi-literate dimwit slob who could not locate a missing skyscraper and who would be refused service at a hot dog stand.' *(Charles Champlin)*

'A spit in the eye to a great writer.' *(Michael Billington, Illustrated London News)*

'The dialogue limps along on the crutches of profanity and adolescent wisecracks.' *(Charles Gregory, S & S)*

'Ugly, boring travesty.' *(Halliwell)*

LONG VOYAGE HOME, THE AAN

CT: 6 AV: 7.70

1940 US 104 BW WAR/DRAMA

D John Ford ☆
W Dudley Nichols ✗ AAN from Eugene O'Neill's plays *The Moon of the Caribbees, In the Zone, Bound East for Cardiff, The Long Voyage Home*

John Wayne Thomas Mitchell Ward Bond Ian Hunter Barry Fitzgerald Wilfrid Lawson Mildred Natwick ☆ John Qualen Arthur Shields Joe Sawyer

Adventures of merchant seamen aboard a freighter towards the start of World War II.

A curate's egg. Gregg Toland's Oscar-nominated camerawork is excellent, and John Ford shows many of his strengths as a director, brilliantly creating the atmosphere of shipboard life; but the cast-members have a distracting multitude of accents (John Wayne is especially hard to swallow as a Swedish farm-lad), and the screenplay ranges from moments of great power to romantic banalities about the sea. Richard Hageman's score and Sherman Todd's editing were Oscar-nominated.

'Grim and sombre are the appropriate adjectives to describe this relentlessly realistic picture . . . The director allows practically no relief, and only the slightest touch of comedy.' *(MFB)*

'One goes to see [it] because it is John Ford's, and one enjoys, and one is disappointed by John Ford. The faults are fairly obvious. He makes no fresh discovery of the human struggle . . . and [the] story is not particularly well managed . . . The photography, mostly in a dark key, compels the eye throughout, yet splendid as it is, we felt at times the straining after lustrous or murky effects.' *(William Whitebait, New Statesman)*

'Stagey-looking but dramatically interesting amalgam of four one-act plays by Eugene O'Neill, with talent abounding.' *(Halliwell)*

'One of the finest of all movies that deal with life at sea.' *(Pauline Kael, 70s)*

'Gripping, dramatic, often beautiful.' *(Scheuer)*

LONGEST DAY, THE AAN

CT: 7 AV: 7.15

1962 US 180 BW WAR/EPIC

D Andrew Marton Ken Annakin Bernhard Wicki
W Cornelius Ryan Romain Gary James Jones David Pursall Jack Seddon from Cornelius Ryan's novel

John Wayne Robert Mitchum Henry Fonda Robert Ryan Rod Steiger Robert Wagner Stuart Whitman Steve Forrest Fabian Richard Todd Richard Burton Paul Anka Sean Connery Peter Lawford

And an enormously long film, about the Normandy landings in June 1944.

Spectacular combat movie with a gung-ho attitude to war and a dated obsession with national stereotypes, but a proper respect for the courageous men involved. The emphasis is on the Americans, but a few British actors (notably Sean Connery and Richard Burton) are allowed a look-in from time to time. An Oscar-winner for cinematography (by Jean Bourgoin, Henri Persin and Walter Wottitz) and special effects; the art direction and editing were nominated.

PRO:

'I award a 21-gun salute to producer Darryl Zanuck.' *(Daily Mirror)*

'A remarkably good film . . . I don't mean to be beastly to our Allies when I say we honestly are not on the screen long enough.' *(Leonard Mosley, Daily Express)*

MIXED:

'Oh, what a lovely bore.' *(Penelope Mortimer, Observer, 1969)*

'The screenplay succeeds best in its historic viewpoint and scope, which mitigate the talkiness, the technical crudities and the soft pedaling of the horrors of killing and dying.' *(Judith Crist)*

LOOK WHO'S TALKING CT: 7 AV: 5.45

1989 US 96 C COMEDY

D Amy Heckerling
W Amy Heckerling

John Travolta Kirstie Alley Olympia Dukakis George Segal Abe Vigoda Bruce Willis (voice) Twink Caplan Joy Boushel Don S. Davis

Mikey, a sweet-looking baby with the plug-ugly voice of Bruce Willis, delivers a wisecracking commentary on his working mother Mollie (Kirstie Alley) as she seeks a remotely functional daddy for her child.

Since the three principal candidates for fathering Mr Willis are a middle-aged businessman (George Segal) with a wife, children and severe personality problems ('I'm going through a selfish phase right now'), a toupee-wearing accountant whose idea of seductive dinner conversation is to discuss constipation, and a youthful, charming, handsome, sexy babysitter (John Travolta), who is in his spare time the only helpful, English-speaking cab-driver in New York, it isn't hard to predict the winner.

Although this is a one-joke picture without much wit, depth or complexity, the babies are cute; there are many gentle laughs along the way; and the leading characters are heartwarming. Some radical feminists and male fellow-travellers found the implication that children need a father as well as a mother offensive, but then you can't always please everyone. Amiable, unpretentious entertainment.

ANTI:

'One of those rare films that induces instant and squirm-inducing hatred in the viewer . . . Inexcusable tripe . . . The thing I really hate most about the movie is its sneaky insistence – along with a whole slew of recent American pictures from *Parenthood* through *Fatal Attraction* to *Child's Play* – that men should go to work, women should stay at home, babies should puke up and that they should all arrange themselves in an unreal 1950s sitcom family unit for the betterment of God and country.' *(Kim Newman, Film Yearbook)*

'Heckerling, although I'm sure she'd deny the intention, has created the most outrageous piece of "Right-to-Life" propaganda you are likely to see on your neighborhood screen. This cutesy gimmick flick actually goes a step beyond the standard right-wing diatribe. Operation Rescue and friends would have you believe that a zygote is a baby. Amy Heckerling encourages you to identify the sperm as a baby. What else are we to think when the voice of the ringleader sperm (Willis) has the same voice as the fetus, and later on, the same voice as the preverbal, postbirth baby boy?' *(Kathi Maio)*

'Carelessly put together, ugly to look at and mawkish and stupid in turn.' *(Derek Malcolm, Guardian)*

'The novelty of the baby's growling voice-over wears off swiftly; thereafter the film settles down into a fairly gooey love story, and the jokes, alternating between dirty nappies and adult foibles, thin out.' *(Daily Telegraph)*

MIXED:

'This fairly unlikely idea for a movie turns into a warm and lovable comedy – although I still don't think it needed the voice-over from the baby.' *(Roger Ebert)*

'A comedy with one eye in its head. It is almost enough. Until it palls, the results are amusing and often hilarious.' *(Alexander Walker, Evening Standard)*

'An unpretentious, sweet-spirited little comedy . . . The film is not a side-splitter but it kept me amused and happy from start to finish.' *(Shaun Usher, Daily Mail)*

LOS OLVIDADOS: *see* YOUNG AND THE DAMNED, THE.

LOST HORIZON AAN CT: 8 AV: 9.17

1937 US 118 (1937)/109 (1943 re-release)/130 (1979 version) BW DRAMA/FANTASY

D Frank Capra ☆
W Robert Riskin from James Hilton's novel

Ronald Colman ☆ H.B. Warner ☆ AAN Thomas Mitchell ☆ Edward Everett Horton ☆ Sam Jaffe ☆ Isabel Jewell Jane Wyatt Margo John Howard

A western man (Ronald Colman) encounters an alien civilization and discovers the deficiencies of his own.

The sets are Hollywood kitsch – which did not prevent art director Stephen Goosson from winning an Oscar – and the philosophical discussions are tiresomely long-winded, but Frank Capra's parable remains pictorially impressive, movingly sincere in its message, and one of the great fantasies of the 30s. Luminous performances by Ronald Colman,

Sam Jaffe, H.B. Warner and Jane Wyatt are augmented by Joseph Walker's black-and-white photography, Ern Westmore's make-up and Dimitri Tiomkin's tremendous score. The excellent, Oscar-winning editing is by Gene Havlick and Gene Milford. Despite some scathing reviews, it was ranked Number 4 on the annual *Film Daily* poll of US film critics (after *The Life of Emile Zola, The Good Earth* and *Captains Courageous*).

ANTI:

'A very long picture . . . and a very dull one once the opening scenes are over . . . If the long, dull ethical sequences had been cut to the bone there would have been plenty of room for the real story: the shock of western crudity and injustice on a man returned from a more gentle and beautiful way of life.' *(Graham Greene)*

'A brilliant beginning and a great deal of wonderful photography throughout do not conceal the fact that the message of the movie is shamefully soft and false.' *(Mark Van Doren, Nation)*

'Longish and wearisome on the screen. I thought the old lama would go on talking forever. Ronald Colman is quite businesslike, [but] somehow I couldn't quite see him turning into a lama before our eyes.' *(John Mosher, New Yorker)*

'Frank Capra, from all evidence we have been able to gather, is solely responsible for *Lost Horizon*, having supervised every stage of its vast production. And great must the blame be. After *Mr Deeds Goes to Town*, the all-pervasive triteness of *Lost Horizon* is a disagreeable shock . . . One is reminded of a British critic's comment on Mary of Scotland "the inaccuracies must have involved tremendous research".' *(Robert Stebbins, New Theatre)*

'The master's hand was not steady on the throttle because in diving off the deep end he . . . landed on the horns of a dilemma and laid a pretty terrific egg.' *(Otis Ferguson, New Republic)*

MIXED:

'The best film I've seen for ages, but will somebody please tell me how they got the grand piano along a footpath on which only one person can walk at a time with rope and pickaxe and with a sheer drop of three thousand feet or so?' *(James Agate)*

'If the design has a look of Ziegfeld, that's Hollywood.' *(Halliwell)*

PRO:

'Director Capra . . . devised one of the most magnificent sets in cinema history. He had the good judgment to leave the story almost exactly as it was written and the skill to match Hilton's verbal talent with pictorial subtlety.' *(Time)*

'A grand adventure film, magnificently staged, beautifully photographed and capitally played.' *(Frank S. Nugent, New York Times)*

'One of the most impressive of all Thirties films, a splendid fantasy which, physically and emotionally, lets out all the stops.' *(John Baxter, 1968)*

LOST HORIZON

CT: 1 AV: 2.25

1972 US 143 C MUSICAL/ROMANCE/FANTASY

D Charles Jarrott ●
W Larry Kramer ● (music and lyrics by Burt Bacharach and Hal David ●)

Peter Finch ● Liv Ullmann ● James Shigeta
Charles Boyer Bobby Van George Kennedy
Michael York ● Olivia Hussey ● John Gielgud

Man (Peter Finch) discovers lost kingdom of Shangri-La, only to discover that it's full of people singing ghastly songs by Bacharach and David.

One of the world's worst musicals. It's hard to know which is worse: the songs or Stanley Kramer's ponderous script, which shows his customary insensitivity to language. Sample line . . . Peter Finch: 'I am desperately trying to keep my emotional feelings and my spiritual needs from clobbering each other to death.'

PRO:

'Total delight . . . This really is a marvelous film. It's entertaining . . . awe-inspiring . . . Rarely have I experienced such an abundance of actual pleasure in an actor's performance [Peter Finch's]. Here is a film with something for everyone. Even the most hard-hearted cynic who steadfastly refused to melt at *The Sound of Music* had better stock up plentifully with Kleenex before venturing forth this time . . . A beautiful film full of beautiful moments. Who said that remakes are only shadows?' *(Julian Fox, F & F)*

'Superbly mounted.' *(Variety)*

ANTI:

'Must have arrived in garbage rather than film cans . . . Makes *The Sound of Music* look like *La Règle du Jeu* . . . Not only Hunter's [producer] films are synthetic; so, too, are his name (really Martin Fuss), his hair, and, as far as I can glean from one conversation, his mind.' *(John Simon)*

'The narrative has no energy, and the pauses for the pedagogic songs are so awkward that you feel the director's wheelchair needs oiling.' *(Pauline Kael)*

'Worst Movie of the Year.' *(Esquire)*

'Fatuous and tasteless . . . could stand (or leap) as a concise definition of camp.' *(Jay Cocks, Time)*

'Totally unmemorable . . . Without redeeming feature in either its direction, scenario, acting, sets, music, choreography, or photography, it can't even be enjoyed as camp.' *(Joy Gould Boyum, Wall Street Journal)*

'Atrocious . . . lame-brained . . . Some $6 million was spent on this worst-of-worst remake.' *(William Wolf, Cue)*

'As uplifting as a whalebone bra – and just as dated.

There are . . . a dozen songs by Burt Bacharach and Hal David, which are so pitifully pedestrian it's doubtful that they'd sound good even if the actors could sing, which they can't. One lavish production number, "Living Together, Growing Together", may indeed be the silliest choreography ever put on film. The set for Shangri-La resembles the valley of the Jolly Green Giant – a fitting showcase for a film that is so much spinach.' *(Arthur Cooper, Newsweek)*

'Trash . . . an empty, wooden-headed musical . . . that should be frozen, like a chow mein TV dinner. I have never understood why anyone would want to improve old movies by remaking them. The result is almost always disastrous, and in this case, it's even worse than that . . . Its dance numbers are like half-time at the Super Bowl. The songs are dreadful . . . The dialogue is dumbfoundedly simple-minded. The costumes would embarrass Yvonne De Carlo. The photography would be laughed off the screen at campfire briefings for the National Forestry Service convention at Knott's Berry Farm.' *(Rex Reed, New York Daily News)*

'Mawkish songs . . . Costuming that could kindly be called comic . . . A vision of Shangri-La . . . that would embarrass a junior high film class . . . The simplemindedness of *Lost Horizon* suggests that only Ross Hunter would remake a 1937 movie into a 1932 one.' *(Judith Crist)*

'Dreadfully old-fashioned in the rigid handling of song and dance routines . . . One major trouble is that few of this cast can sing, and the songs have lyrics of awful banality and tunes to match.' *(Patrick Gibbs, Daily Telegraph)*

'Immensely silly . . . simple-minded.' *(Bruce Williamson, Playboy)*

'Cumbersome, unlyrical and tedious . . . a flat-footed disappointment.' *(Charles Champlin, LA Times)*

'Any Ten Worst list would have to start with Columbia's *Lost Horizon*.' *(John Barbour, Los Angeles)*

"Lost" is right.' *(Maltin)*

'I'm ashamed about *Lost Horizon*, but I stayed in a big rented house in Hollywood and the film was full of famous actors and how could we know what it was going to be like? I had fun and now I'm paying for it.' *(Liv Ullmann)*

LOST ILLUSION, THE: *see* FALLEN IDOL, THE.

LOST WEEKEND, THE AAW CT: 7 AV: 9.45

1945 US 101 BW DRAMA

D Billy Wilder ☆ AAW

W Charles Brackett Billy Wilder ☆ AAW from Charles R. Jackson's novel

Ray Milland ☆ AAW Jane Wyman Philip Terry Doris Dowling Frank Faylen ☆ Howard da Silva ☆

A writer (Ray Milland) spends an alcoholic weekend.

Billy Wilder's gruelling drama has Oscar-nominated cinematography by John F. Seitz, fine editing by Doane Herrison, and a great score by Miklos Rozsa. Ray Milland gives a sterling performance – although it might have been better if we knew more about the reasons for the anti-hero's alcoholism. As it is, the leading character's redemption in the final reel seems a tad sudden and improbable. Among the film's incidental pleasures are its poetic evocation of 40s New York. The American liquor industry offered Paramount $5 million for the negative of the film, in order to destroy it.

ANTI:

'In many ways a disappointing adaptation which failed to transmit to the screen the subtleties of the original. Much admired by the aesthetes, it caused a sensation because of its subject of a pernicious alcoholic, but it was not a step forward for Brackett and Wilder.' *(Paul Rotha & Richard Griffith, The Film Till Now, 1949)*

'There is very little appreciation . . . of the many and subtle moods possible in drunkenness; almost no registration of the workings of the several minds inside a drinker's brain; hardly a trace of the narcissism and self-deceit which are so indispensable or of the self-loathing and self-pity which are so invariable; hardly a hint, except through abrupt action, of the desperation of thirst; no hint at all of the many colorings possible in the desperation. The hangovers lack the weakness, sickness, and horrible distortions of time-sense which they need.' *(James Agee)*

MIXED:

'It's not a very likeable film, charting as it does the physical and spiritual collapse of a human being. Milland is brilliant, at once charming and pathetic and he is well supported by a fine cast, the use of New York backgrounds and a literate version of Charles Jackson's novel.' *(NFT Bulletin, 1975)*

PRO:

'The plight of the alcoholic may not seem one of the most important of world's problems, but there are plenty of people who have encountered it, and here it is presented not only with surprising force and understanding, but with expert cinematic skill.' *(James Shelley Hamilton, New Movies)*

'Packed with drama . . . Okay for those who like their drama neat!' *(Daily Mirror)*

'A new kind of dramatic triangle – boy, girl and bottle . . . Wilder keeps a businesslike eye upon entertainment values . . . The film is rich in cinematic ingenuities.' *(The Times)*

'An almost clinical study of an alcoholic . . . Were anyone but Ray Milland playing this part it might easily have turned out an utterly unsympathetic character . . . yet . . . [he] is made a sympathetic and even pitiable person . . . Ray Milland has illuminated the presentation of such a character with countless bits of expression, voice and gesture that convince as both outer and inner truth.' *(James Shelley Hamilton, New Movies)*

'There are times when the observer suffers almost as does the screen character, and the final fadeout left this spectator exhausted. In addition, I was parched, and forthwith hiked from the Paramount projection room to Lucey's across the street, where I promptly downed several double shots of bourbon, happy in the realization that, unlike Jackson's protagonist, I wasn't a rye man, so that it can't happen here.' *(Herb Sterne)*

'I undershtand that liquor interesh; innerish; intereshtsh are rather worried about thish film. Thatsh tough.' *(James Agee)*

'Most to be admired are its impressions of bare dreadful truth: the real crowds in the real streets as the hero-victim lugs his typewriter to the pawnshop, the trains screaming overhead, the awful night as he makes his escape from the alcoholics' ward.' *(Dilys Powell)*

'The director's first study in moral deformity, and, all things considered, probably his finest achievement. It is free alike from his habitual melodramatic contrivance and excess, and from a masochistic immersion in the hero's weakness. It approaches as close as Wilder has ever come to compassion.' *(Joel Greenberg, Film Journal (Australia)*, 1957)

LOUDEST WHISPER, THE: *see* CHILDREN'S HOUR, THE.

LOVE AFFAIR AAN CT: 8 AV: 8.29

1939 US 87 BW COMEDY/ROMANCE

D Leo McCarey ☆
W Delmer Daves Donald Ogden Stewart from McCarey, Daves and Mildred Cram's story AAN

Irene Dunne ☆ AAN Charles Boyer ☆
Maria Ouspenskaya ☆ AAN Lee Bowman Astrid Allwyn Maurice Moscovich Scotty Beckett

A European playboy (Charles Boyer) and a New York girl enjoy a shipboard romance, but an accident keeps them apart on dry land.

A famous romantic movie, later remade (very unevenly) as *An Affair To Remember*. That remake – dry and witty at sea, hopelessly wet on land – is the weepie remembered affectionately by the female characters in *Sleepless in Seattle. Love Affair* is much less broken-backed, and immaculately acted throughout.

PRO:

'Production is of grade A quality.' *(Variety)*

'McCarey brought off one of the most difficult things you can attempt with film. He created a mood, rather than a story; he kept it alive by expert interpolations; he provided comedy when he needed comedy and poignancy when he needed substance; and he did it with the minimum of effort.' *(Pare Lorentz)*

'In a sense the film is a triumph of indirection, for it does one thing while seeming to do another. Its immediate effect is comedy; its afterglow is that of a bitter-sweet romance. A less capable director, with a less competent cast, must have erred one way or the other – either on the side of treacle or on that of whimsy. Mr McCarey has balanced his ingredients skillfully and has merged them, as is clear in retrospect, into a glowing and memorable picture.' *(Frank S. Nugent, New York Times)*

MIXED:

'Clichés of situation and attitude are lifted almost beyond recognition by a morning freshness of eye for each small thing around.' *(Otis Ferguson)*

'It is only in the last reel that he finds out and so, after an agony of suspense, true love triumphs. Sloppy, yes, but it gets you, because there is a lot of delightful humour cunningly mixed up with the sentiment and because Dunne and Boyer pour out such quantities of charm that it is impossible to resist them.' *(Alan Page, S & S)*

LOVE AT FIRST BITE CT: 7 AV: 5.91

1979 US 96 C COMEDY/HORROR

D Stan Dragoti ✔
W Robert Kaufman ✔

George Hamilton ☆ Susan Saint James Richard Benjamin Dick Shawn Isabel Sanford Arte Johnson

Dracula (George Hamilton) tries to find love in New York.

Funniest of all spoof vampire films, as George Hamilton (who is a comic revelation) discovers that 70s Manhattan is more than a match for him. The gags may be hit-and-miss, but an awful lot hit the mark, and there's genuine affection for the vampire genre. Typical of the care taken is that William Tuttle, the original make-up artist for Bela Lugosi in 1934, was hired to do a parody of his own work, for George Hamilton.

MIXED:

'A good film to arrive 30 minutes late for: a Dracula burlesque in which lively middle and end portions make up for a sloppy, sophomoric beginning.' *(Nigel Andrews, Financial Times)*

'A rowdy burlesque of the Dracula movies, set in Manhattan, with dilapidated stuffed bats and a large assortment of gags; some of them are funny in a low-grade, moldy way, and some are even stupidly racist, but many are weirdly hip, with a true flaky wit. The scriptwriter, Robert Kaufman, will never be called a man of fine discrimination: he takes equal – almost obscene – relish in them all. Yet it's this relish – which the director, Stan Dragoti, seems to share – that fuels the movie, and, except for a wearying chase sequence toward the end, it bumps along entertainingly.' *(Pauline Kael)*

PRO:

'Peppered with good gags and stylish performances.' *(Films Illustrated)*

'It's a fun notion and George Hamilton makes it work.' *(Variety)*

'We are supposed to laugh at it, and we do, we do . . . The result is a joy.' *(David Hughes, Western Mail)*

'An amiable send-up . . . [whose] daftness is admirably sustained.' *(Richard Barkley, Sunday Express)*

LOVE ME TONIGHT CT: 9 AV: 9.50

(aka *Mariez-moi Ce Soir!)*

1932 US 104 BW MUSICAL/COMEDY/ROMANCE

D Rouben Mamoulian ☆
W Samuel Hoffenstein Waldemar Young George Marion Jr ☆ from Leopold Marchand and Paul Armont's play *Tailor in the Chateau* (music and lyrics by Richard Rodgus ☆ and Lorenz Hart ☆)

Maurice Chevalier ☆ Jeanette MacDonald ☆
Myrna Loy ☆ C. Aubrey Smith ☆
Elizabeth Patterson Ethel Griffies
Blanche Frederici Joseph Cawthorn
Charles Butterworth ☆ Charles Ruggles ☆

A Parisian tailor (Maurice Chevalier) goes among the aristocracy to collect a debt, is mistaken for a nobleman, and finds love with a princess (Jeanette MacDonald).

A charming period piece, with a surprisingly sharp edge (this was made before the Hays Code imposed a silence about all things sexual). Needless to say, the plot is negligible; but the Rodgers and Hart songs include 'Isn't It Romantic?' and 'Lover (When You Need Me)'. Mamoulian's direction is startlingly good; and there are delightful performances from the leads – with Myrna Loy memorable as a nymphomaniac countess.

MIXED:

'While Mamoulian has an excellent sense of pictorial development and detail, he has not quite the same delivery of touch as Lubitsch and is apt at times to mistake coarseness for wit. However, this airy little confection has many good points.' *(Picturegoer)*

PRO:

'Mr Mamoulian never neglects the opportunity . . . to make the most of a camera . . . [He] is at the height of his form.' *(Mordaunt Hall, New York Times)*

'Mamoulian . . . was not content to imitate [Clair and Murnau]. He simply applied the fundamental principle used by them and with the aid of a pleasant story, a good musician, a talented cast, and about a million dollars, he has done what someone in Hollywood should have done long ago: he has illustrated a musical score . . . Once under way, [he] never lets go . . . He has conceived and produced a fortunate, charming musical picture.' *(Pare Lorentz, Vanity Fair)*

'A musical frolic, whimsical in its aim and delicately carried out in its pattern.' *(Variety)*

'Gay, charming, witty, it is everything that the Lubitsch musicals should have been but never were.' *(John Baxter, 1968)*

'Has that infectious spontaneity that distinguishes the American musical at its best, and rarely makes the mistake of taking its romantic setting too seriously.' *(Peter Cowie, 1969)*

'Mamoulian . . . brought his own original style to the film, particularly in his use of sound and rhythmic dialogue.' *(R.A.E. Pickard, Dictionary of 1000 Best Films, 1971)*

'That rich amalgam of filmic invention, witty decoration and those wonderful Rodgers and Hart songs . . . Lovely comedy playing from Myrna Loy and Charles Ruggles.' *(NFT Bulletin, 1974)*

'Eternally fresh . . . The musical source of the film derives from the success of the team of Jeanette MacDonald and Maurice Chevalier.' *(Paddy Whannel, Movie)*

LOVE STORY AAN CT: 5 AV: 4.69

1970 US 100 C DRAMA/ROMANCE

D Arthur Hiller ✗ AAN
W Erich Segal ● AAN from his novelette ● AAN

Ali MacGraw ● AAN Ryan O'Neal ● AAN
Ray Milland John Marley ☆ AAN Katherine Balfour

A young man and woman from different ends of society (Ryan O'Neal and Ali MacGraw) fall in love, but the woman dies.

Loved by the public for its efficient narrative which moved millions to tears (a rarity in movies by the end of the 60s), but loathed by the critics – and it isn't hard to see why. O'Neal and MacGraw give facile, shallow performances which give little clue as to why they love each other, let alone why we should care about them. The disease which afflicts MacGraw's character is ludicrously unconvincing, and O'Neal's reactions are so wooden as to be embarrassing. Yet there must have been something about this story which made audiences identify with it: perhaps it was because these two young people were so reassuringly, even boringly, conventional, at a time when traditional moral values had been so long under attack. Sample of the characters' pretentious, self-aggrandizing self-pity . . . Ryan

O'Neal: 'She loved Mozart and Bach, the Beatles, and me.' Francis Lai's schmaltzy score won an Oscar. The sequel was *Oliver's Story* (1978).

PRO:

'An excellent film . . . generally successful on all artistic levels.' *(Variety)*

'Ali MacGraw promises to become the closest thing to a movie star of the 40s . . . When a Radcliffe girl chooses to die on-screen, the Academy Awards can be heard softly rustling like Kleenexes in the background . . . Ryan O'Neal gives the character of the neon scion a warmth and vulnerability.' *(Time)*

'There's nothing contemptible about being moved to joy by a musical, to terror by a thriller, to excitement by a Western. Why shouldn't we get a little misty during a story about young lovers separated by death? Hiller earns our emotional response because of the way he's directed the movie. The Segal book was so patently contrived to force those tears, and moved toward that object with such humorless determination, that it must have actually disgusted a lot of readers. The movie is mostly about life, however, and not death. And because Hiller makes the lovers into individuals, of course we're moved by the film's conclusion. Why not?' *(Roger Ebert)*

MIXED:

'Ryan O'Neal seems absolutely right in every way as Oliver, but Ali MacGraw looks too old for her role and has to work overhard at being Jenny and very young. Moreover, she looks considerably less good than in *Goodbye, Columbus*, or is photographed considerably less well. In fact, Dick Kratina's work is unusual in this day of almost invariably competent color cinematography. His hues manage to be predominantly sickly: the Harvard Yard, for instance, comes out an unwholesome purplish shade, as though it, too, were dying of leukemia.' *(John Simon)*

ANTI:

'Bypassed the brain and assaulted the tear-ducts.' *(Newsweek)*

'*Camille* with bullshit . . . Every element of reality that might grate against the mood has been screened out of the finished commercial for love – every one, that is, except the solid bourgeois necessity of money.' *(Alexander Walker, Evening Standard)*

'Very much [an] exploitation movie, cashing in on crying the way other movies cash in on sex.' *(Newsweek)*

'A lying, thoughtless and evasive piece of nonsense . . . A slum, for the film, is a nice flat you rent at $82.50 a month. Poverty is when you both have to work. A tragedy is a painless disease.' *(James Fenton, New Statesman)*

'One of the most ineptly made of all the lump-and-phlegm hits . . . Those who are susceptible to this sort of movie may not even notice that Ali MacGraw is horribly smug and smirky, though if you share my impulses, whenever she gets facetious you'll probably want to wham her one.' *(Pauline Kael)*

LOVERS AND OTHER STRANGERS

CT: 7 AV: 7.70

1970 US 104 C COMEDY

D Cy Howard
W Renée Taylor Joseph Bologna David Zelag Goodman ☆ AAN from Bologna and Taylor's play

Bonnie Bedelia Michael Brandon Gig Young ☆ Anne Jackson ☆ Beatrice Arthur ☆ Robert Dishy Harry Guardino Cloris Leachman Anne Meara Marian Hailey ☆ Richard Castellano ☆ AAN Diane Keaton

A couple (Michael Brandon, Bonnie Bedelia) who have been living together for 18 months decide to marry; but the news brings various skeletons rattling out of the family closet.

Sly, acerbic image of marital problems at the turn of the 60s: now a period piece, but enlivened by wonderful character performances and a script which cleverly interweaves the plot-lines. The song 'For All We Know' (music by Fred Karlin, lyrics by Robb Wilson and Arthur James) won an Oscar. Diane Keaton makes her début.

ANTI:

'I wish I could like [this] raucous, unblushing slab of bad taste, as much as everyone laughing around me obviously did.' *(Felix Barker, Evening News)*

MIXED:

'Some of the interwoven stories are very amusing and even rather wise . . . but some . . . are grossly overplayed.' *(Nina Hibbin, Morning Star)*

PRO:

'An extremely engaging comedy.' *(Gillian Hartnoll)*

'Distinguished by some fine acting . . . Not the least of the film's attractions is that it has intelligently taken advantage of the new freedom of discourse in the American cinema.' *(Richard Roud, Guardian)*

'Vividly real, genuinely funny.' *(Maltin)*

LOWER DEPTHS, THE: *see* LES BAS-FONDS.

LUCKY LADY

CT: 1 AV: 2.25

1975 US 118 C COMEDY

D Stanley Donen ●
W Willard Huyck Gloria Katz ●

Liza Minnelli ● Gene Hackman Burt Reynolds ● Michael Hordern Geoffrey Lewis

In 1930, a cabaret singer (Liza Minnelli) becomes involved in smuggling liquor.

Charmless, lazily written comedy with no jokes. Despite the stars, deservedly a flop.

'Forced hokum.' *(Variety)*

'It sports its calculations on its sleeve like rhinestones.' *(S & S)*

'[Of Liza Minnelli] Age cannot wither, nor make-up stale, her infinite sameness . . . [Burt Reynolds's] face looks like an armored car made, inexplicably, out of meat.' *(John Simon)*

'A manic mess that tries to be all things to all people and ends up offering nothing to anyone.' *(Frank Rich)*

'A big expensive movie for people who don't mind being treated like hicks: the audience is expected to shudder with delight every time it hears an obscenity or sees a big movie star grin.' *(Pauline Kael)*

'None of it holds the interest for a single moment.' *(Halliwell)*

LULU: *see* PANDORA'S BOX.

LUST FOR LIFE CT: 7 AV: 7.22

1956 US 122 C DRAMA/BIOPIC

D Vincente Minnelli ☆
W Norman Corwin from Irving Stone's novel AAN

Kirk Douglas ☆ AAN Anthony Quinn ☆ AAW
James Donald Pamela Brown Everett Sloane
Lionel Jeffries

The life of Vincent Van Gogh (Kirk Douglas).

CinemaScope and a plodding narrative detract from this otherwise enjoyable – and surprisingly accurate – Hollywood biopic. Anthony Quinn steals the show in his eight minutes as Gauguin; but, in a much more demanding role, Douglas does capture the intensity and passion which go to make a great artist. The hot, garish colours were deliberately chosen by director Minnelli, who chose the outmoded Ansco process rather than conventional Eastmancolor, because it gave an impression closer to Van Gogh's paintings.

ANTI:

'Unexciting. It misses out in conveying the color and excitement of the original Irving Stone novel . . . The measure of sympathy that should be engendered for the genius who was to turn insane is not realized.' *(Variety)*

'No doubt it would take little short of genius to turn the life of Van Gogh into an altogether adequate film; and genius is, unsurprisingly, absent from [the film], just as it was absent from the biographical novel whence the film derives.' *(Manchester Guardian)*

'On the one hand it strikes one as being sober, painstaking, thoughtful and worthy. But on the other hand it remains not an awfully good film.' *(Derek Granger, Financial Times)*

'What dates it is that Minnelli, following the dramatic conventions of his period, lays everything out for us, and, desperate not to be cheap or overblown, he's somewhat pedestrian.' *(Pauline Kael)*

'Uninspiring . . . It simply doesn't fall into a classic category.' *(Halliwell)*

PRO:

'Two hours of quite shattering and exciting entertainment.' *(Alan Dent, Illustrated London News)*

'Pictorial perfection . . . I warn you it's a long film. Some will find it slow. But its acting is superb.' *(Peter Burnup, News of the World)*

'Superb.' *(Scheuer)*

'Brilliant.' *(Maltin)*

M

M CT: 9 AV: 9.31
(aka *Eine Stadt Sucht Einen Mörder; Mörder Unter Uns*)

1931 Germany 99/118 BW THRILLER/FOREIGN

D Fritz Lang ☆
W Fritz Lang Thea von Harbou Paul Falkenberg Adolf Jansen Karl Vash from Egon Jacobson's article

Peter Lorre ☆ Otto Wernicke Gustaf Gründgens Theo Lingen Theodor Loos Inge Landgut

The underworld of a German city comes together to catch a child-murderer (Peter Lorre).

Seminal chase movie, often imitated but never surpassed for fear and excitement. Much of this is down to the subtle gradations of Peter Lorre's performance; but Fritz Lang proves himself a virtuoso behind the camera in his first sound movie. Sound is, in fact, used very cleverly throughout – especially in the murder sequences, where almost everything is left to the viewer's imagination. Based on the real-life story of a manhunt for a child-murderer in Dusseldorf.

ANTI:

'It is remarkable how Fritz Lang's instinct runs to bigger ideas than any other director; but it is just as remarkable how little he ever makes of them . . . By its subject-matter the film is unusual in all conscience, but I doubt if, on examination, it proves to be anything more than a plain thriller . . . If we look behind to the theme itself, we find that Lang's inspiration is only second-rate . . . It may possibly be asked if the whole idea of the film is not a little perverse: if anything is to be gained by creating sympathy for such a character . . . Lang has, as usual, peeped into his big subject and been satisfied with a glimpse.' *(John Grierson, Everyman)*

'It is said that Lang searches endlessly for suitable film material . . . His failure to find important stories, or to bring them to the screen importantly, may perhaps reflect a good deal more than his fear of the commercial market . . . To attempt to express the dislocations of this age of anxiety in terms of melodrama is an interesting and thoughtful idea, but it needs a deeper approach than Lang has ever brought to it, even in *M* . . . His films, for all their painstaking craftsmanship, are apt to emerge as melodramas thinly tied to current events. Their topicality seems to have a commercial rather than a philosophic origin.' *(Paul Rotha & Richard Griffith, The Film Till Now, 1949)*

PRO:

'If you like grim realism, superbly done, here it is . . . Not a melodrama; it is a tense, serious treatment of a horror theme . . . Not for children.' *(Photoplay)*

'Not only an overwhelming horror tale, but . . . one of the most poignantly pathetic documents of humanity ever filmed . . . it manages to be at the same time so sympathetic and understanding a study of a savage, pathological killer that it becomes a genuine tragedy as well as an essay in savagery. It strikes terror in the heart . . . and still succeeds in extending the borderline of human sympathy almost beyond breaking point . . . All combined into a great whole by the brilliant direction of Fritz Lang and the superb acting of Peter Lorre. *M* is one of the great motion pictures.' *(Richard Watts Jr, New York Herald Tribune)*

'Such are the tact and the genius with which Fritz Lang has handled it that the result is something at once more significant than either the horror story . . . or the so-called psychological document . . . The result is . . . a film which answers most of the demands of classical tragedy . . . The flawless acting of Peter Lorre . . . [is] such as we are accustomed to only in the great classic dramas when they are played by great tragic actors . . . *M* . . . confirms our belief in the continued vitality of the tragic emotion . . . Fritz Lang and Peter Lorre are better artists in their fields than most of those who have sought to revive tragedy in our time.' *(William Troy, Nation)*

'A movie . . . which, along with its esoteric technical innovations, also is a beautifully balanced melodrama.' *(Pare Lorentz, Vanity Fair)*

'Like Hitchcock, Lang effectively uses the visual resources of the silent cinema to present his view of society. He makes particularly effective use of recurring imagery . . . Throughout *M* there is a pattern of entrapment that particularly threatens Becker and the children, thereby linking them as victims of the orderly society.' *(Marsha Kinder & Beverle Houston Close-Up, A Critical Perspective on Film, 1972)*

'Not being shown what the child murderer (Peter Lorre) does to his poor victims in Fritz Lang's *M* is far more effective than the slow-motion pyrotechnics of Mr Peckinpah's type of violence; so much more horrific too, since our imagination . . . can conjure up unspeakable, unspecific terrors no camera can equal.' *(Peter Bogdanovich Picture Shows, 1975)*

'His portrait of a character in torment – "Who knows what it's like to be me?" he demands climactically, insisting that "Nobody can be punished for something he can't help" – is a pathological study that has not been equaled.' *(Judith Crist)*

M*A*S*H AAN CT: 5 AV: 8.07

1970 US 116 C WAR/COMEDY

D Robert Altman ✗ AAN
W Ring Lardner Jr AAW from Richard Hooker's book

Donald Sutherland Elliott Gould Sally Kellerman AAN Tom Skerritt Robert Duvall John Schuck Roger Bowen René Auberjonois Fred Williamson Bud Cort Jo Ann Pflug Gary Burghoff

Combat surgeons (Donald Sutherland, Elliott Gould) operate close to the front during the Korean War.

Robert Altman's black comedy about the Korean War is thought a classic by many, and certainly spawned a classic TV series. It was designed to be a veiled comment on Vietnam, and there is much jokey emphasis on the horrors of war and its pointlessness – neatly sidestepping the real context, which was the Korean War. I never liked it: its humour is brutish, its attitude to its characters (who never develop) self-consciously cool, glib and unfeeling. And far from being sincerely anti-war, it shows its heroes (Donald Sutherland and Elliott Gould) enjoying an oafishly good time. Named Best Film of 1970 by US National Society of Film Critics.

PRO:

'Most of it is totally ridiculous, yet the style of its zany good nature is so relentless in its insanity that I found myself laughing more hysterically than I've laughed at any Hollywood comedy since *Some Like It Hot*.' *(Rex Reed)*

'Bloody funny. A hyper-acute wiretap on mankind's death wish.' *(Joseph Morgenstern)*

'One of the best and funniest movies I've seen in years . . . You should go to *M*A*S*H* forewarned that its humor is not, as they say, in good taste. That is because war is not in good taste either . . . I have nothing but awed admiration for the way Altman has managed what is obviously a precarious project, one which could have gone all black on him. Or, more likely, have been betrayed by a lack of courage on his part. The thing has a loose, improvisational quality about it – as if his actors were encouraged to be as inventive as possible. But it is never slack, careless or indulgent of their whims or the director's. Every scene is both tight in execution and rich in detail. All concerned are sure about what they are doing, what they mean to say . . . *M*A*S*H* challenges us as few comedies – few movies of any kind – challenge us.' *(Richard Schickel, Life)*

'The laughter is blood-soaked and the comedy cloaks a bitter and terrible truth.' *(Judith Crist)*

MIXED:

'In its fast-cutting, modern style notably well and wittily made . . . I hope nobody will tell me . . . that *M*A*S*H* is anti-war. The two surgeons (played with audacious and infectious enjoyment by Donald Sutherland and Elliott Gould) who complete the disruption of camp discipline are not only thoroughly decent chaps beneath their levity, they are having the hell of a good time.' *(Dilys Powell)*

'Stomach-churning, gory, often tasteless, but frequently funny.' *(Variety)*

'The whole picture becomes a little too cute, too desperately calculating, and, finally, old hat and trivial . . . [But] I recommend *M*A*S*H* to those who can enjoy it without expecting a political satire or devastating anti-war black comedy. The film is no more anti-war than it is anti-surgery, but it is rich in irreverent laughs.' *(John Simon)*

ANTI:

'Its cynical stance often rings hollow; its targets – military decorum, religious platitudes and sexual hypocrisy – are too easy, and there's little of the director's muted, unsentimental humanism in evidence.' *(Geoff Andrew, Time Out)*

'Altman's attitude toward his characters is notably lacking in a spirit of generosity, and his treatment of them is at once insufferably glib and sentimental in an archly hip way. His film does not convey a sense of his characters moving toward anything, let alone salvation: the favored ones are saved from the beginning, and those out of favor remain so at the end . . . [It's] a film in which smugness frequently stands in for true humor.' *(James Bernardoni, The New Hollywood, 1991)*

MA NUIT CHEZ MAUD: *see* MY NIGHT AT MAUD'S.

MAD LOVE CT: 6 AV: 6.67

(aka *The Hands of Orlac)*

1935 US 84 BW HORROR/SF

D Karl Freund
W P.J. Wolfson Guy Endore John L. Balderston from Maurice Renard's novel *Les Mains d'Orlac*

Peter Lorre ☆ Frances Drake Colin Clive ● Ted Healy Edward Brophy Isabel Jewell

Mad doctor (Peter Lorre) gives concert pianist (Colin Clive) the hands of a killer, with gripping results.

Forget the dull script and Colin Clive's below-par performance: this one is a classic because of Peter Lorre's memorably bonkers performance in the lead. Karl Freund showed he was a great cinematographer on *The Golem* (1920) and *Dracula* (1931). His direction – both of this and *The Mummy* (1932) – shows a less certain hand as regards style and pace, although Gregg Toland's cinematography is excellent. Most contemporary reviews centred, understandably, on Lorre in his first American movie.

PRO:

'[Lorre is a] one-man chamber of horrors.' *(New York Herald Tribune)*.

'The usual Gothic motifs – dismemberment, murder, madness, and the threat of rape – all played out in semi-serious fashion with some delirious set-pieces . . . Great fun.' *(Geoff Andrew, Time Out)*

MIXED:

'An interesting but pretty trivial adventure in Grand Guignol horror . . . But Mr Lorre, with his gift for supplementing a remarkable physical appearance with his acute perception of the mechanics of insanity, cuts deeply into the darkness of the morbid brain.' *(New York Times)*

'The results in screen potency are disappointing . . . will probably do fair biz.' *(Variety)*

'Absurd Grand Guignol done with great style which somehow does not communicate itself in viewer interest, only in cold admiration.' *(Halliwell)*

'Freund's direction is disappointingly static, but the film has a distinctive Grand Guignol style, and it's of considerable visual and historical interest.' *(Pauline Kael)*

MAD MAX SERIES

MAD MAX — CT: 6 AV: 6.67

1979 Australia 79 C SF/ACTION/ADVENTURE

D George Miller ☆
W George Miller James McCausland

Mel Gibson ✔ Joanne Samuel Hugh Keays-Byrne Steve Bisley Roger Ward Tim Burns

Futuristic ex-cop (Mel Gibson) avenges death of his family at the hands of psychotic bikers.

A brutal, revenge western with sci-fi trappings, excitingly directed by George Miller, and much imitated. Influences on it are clearly Orwell's *1984* and Michael Winner's *Death Wish* movies; and it's a memorably cynical vision of a future society where humans have become as dehumanized as the machines on which they are dependent. (The idea arose from the violence which occurred in Australia when petrol rationing was imposed in the 1970s.) Miller's shooting style – especially his use of low, fast tracking shots and shock edits – is ideally suited to his material, even though there are a few rough edges. Subtlety is not its strong point: the stunts are. The film became Australia's biggest grossing feature film of all time. Contemporary critics could not, with a few exceptions, see past the violence.

ANTI:

'Really an excuse for everyone to get into leather, drag on a few chains and act like Marlon Brando on Valium.' *(Spectator)*

'Hell, we are told, is other people, but I would particularise it and say it is this picture . . . [George Miller's] heroes are indistinguishable from his villains . . . I suppose the nearest approach to a human being is Max . . . but I could do without him, too.' *(Daily Mail)*

'The stunt work and editing are proficient but not remarkable and the news that this commonplace movie is the most successful ever made in Australia is neither good nor altogether surprising.' *(Philip French, Observer)*

'A genuinely sick film . . . The fact that [it] is brilliantly made means the horror is all the more chillingly realistic.' *(Madeleine Harmsworth, Sunday Mirror)*

'Flimsy plot line . . . provides an adequate framework for some vivid chase-and-crash sequences across the unpopulated outback and a heavy dose of sadism with obvious homosexual overtones . . . [The film] is ugly and incoherent, and aimed, probably accurately, at the most uncritical moviegoers.' *(Tom Buckley, New York Times)*

'Outdirties Harry . . . Essentially an exploitation picture which revels in graphic violence.' *(Rob Reiner, Orbis, 1984)*

MIXED:

'The tone sometimes wavers into self-parody, and there are occasional crude patches, but overall this edge-of-seat revenge movie marks the most exciting début from an Australian director since Peter Weir.' *(David Pirie, Time Out)*

'An intermittently successful mining of the kinetic excitement of moving cars and cycles.' *(Donald C. Willis, Horror and Science Films III, 1984)*

'Less interesting as a story about people than as a marriage between a filmmaker's machines (his camera, editing tools) and the motor-powered machines (cars, motorcycles) that he films.' *(Danny Peary, 1981)*

PRO:

'Miller . . . shows he knows what cinema is all about.' *(Variety)*

'A winner, an exploitation film able to compete with the fastest and roughest productions of American International or Roger Corman's New World Pictures . . . Mel Gibson [is] a personable new star.' *(The Times)*

MAD MAX II — CT: 7 AV: 7.21

(aka *The Road Warrior)*

1981 Australia 97 C SF/ACTION/ADVENTURE

D George Miller ☆
W George Miller Terry Hayes Brian Hannant

Mel Gibson ✔ Bruce Spence ✔ Mike Preston Emil Minty Max Phipps Vernon Wells Kjell Nilsson

Mad Max (Mel Gibson) joins a commune which comes under attack from marauders.

First-rate action picture, best of the series, with a bigger budget, terrific costume designs by Norma Moriceau, a little more characterization and even more brilliantly orchestrated action sequences. Mad Max regains a little of the optimism he lost when his wife and children were killed in the first movie and becomes more of a mythic figure, like The Man With No Name in Sergio Leone's westerns. Critical reaction was warmer than for the previous picture, although it was still widely dismissed.

ANTI:

'Essentially just another display of vehicles smashing into each other.'*(David McGillivray, MFB)*

'Miller's attempt to tap into the universal concept of the hero (as enunciated by Jung and explicated by Joseph Campbell in *The Hero with a Thousand Faces*) makes the film joyless. He consciously uses his hero . . . as an icon; that's enough to squeeze the juice out of any actor, and Max seems bland and apathetic. There are perhaps 10 minutes of spectacular imagery, and if you think of George Miller as one of the kinetic moviemakers, such as John Carpenter and George A. Romero, he's a giant, but he's pushing for more and he apparently doesn't see the limitations of the kind of material he's working with. For all its huffing and puffing, this is a sappy sentimental movie.' *(Pauline Kael)*

MIXED:

'The sequel is as brash, bloody and brutal as its predecessor. It's not my kind of movie, but I can see why so many fans find it compellingly watchable.' *(Daily Mail)*

'Though the film can't quite sustain its length, it's kept alive by its humour and the sheer energy of its visuals. In fact, Miller's choreography of his innumerable vehicles is so extraordinary that it makes Spielberg's *Raiders of the Lost Ark* look like a kid fooling with Dinky toys.' *(David Pirie, Time Out)*

PRO:

'Very fine stunt work and special effects. Director Miller keeps the pic moving with cyclonic force, photography by Dean Semler is first class, editing is supertight, and Brian May's music is stirring.' *(Variety)*

'An epic action film, maybe the first great one since *The Wild Bunch*. Only one factor seriously compromises *The Road Warrior*'s claim to a place of honor up there with *Seven Samurai* and *The Wild Bunch*: it's populated with caricatures and character types rather than great flesh and blood characters. But they're vivid caricatures, strong and distinctively etched types. Mel Gibson's Max has darkened into a much more compelling fellow than he was in the earlier film.' *(Richard T. Jameson)*

'The special effects and stunts in this movie are spectacular; *The Road Warrior* goes on a short list with *Bullitt, The French Connection*, and the truck chase in *Raiders of the Lost Ark* as among the great chase films of modern years. What is the point of the movie? Everyone is free to interpret the action, I suppose, but I prefer to avoid thinking about the implications of gasoline shortages and the collapse of Western civilization, and to experience the movie instead as pure sensation. The filmmakers have imagined a fictional world. It operates according to its special rules and values, and we experience it. The experience is frightening, sometimes disgusting, and (if the truth be told) exhilarating. This is very skillful filmmaking, and *The Road Warrior* is a movie like no other.' *(Roger Ebert)*

MAD MAX BEYOND THUNDERDOME

CT: 6 AV: 6.15

1985 Australia 115 C SF/ACTION/ADVENTURE

D George Miller George Ogilvie ✓
W Terry Hayes George Miller

Mel Gibson ✓ Tina Turner ✓ Angelo Rossitto Helen Buday Bruce Spence ✓ Adam Cockburn Frank Thring Paul Larsson

Mad Max (Mel Gibson) is challenged to gladiatorial combat.

Max continues his development into mythic heroism. There are not quite such fearsome villains or as many bright ideas as previously; the plot gets bogged down as Max tries to help a tribe of children; and Gibson's character (no longer so strongly nihilistic) is in danger of being overshadowed by Tina Turner. However, the production design remains terrific; the dialogue is funnier; and the climactic duel and chase are wonderfully staged and shot.

ANTI:

'If ever there was a film that proved there is only a finite number of plots to be had, this is it; and although *Mad Max Beyond Thunderdome* is long on effects and set-pieces, it is short on the smaller incidents that make the difference in any story.' *(Richard Combs, MFB)*

'More violent futuristic rubbish.' *(Halliwell)*

MIXED:

'If the thrills and special effects lack a little of the punch of *Mad Max 2*, there's still enough imagination, wit and ingenuity to put recent Spielberg to shame.' *(Don Atyeo, Time Out)*

'An ambitious attempt to broaden, and soften, the Max persona is intriguing, if not wholly successful. A few more gratuitous car smashes wouldn't have gone amiss while Turner comes close to stealing the movie from Mel.' *(Rose)*

PRO:

'*Mad Max Three* places us more firmly within its

apocalyptic postnuclear world than ever before . . . The fight between Mad Max and Master-Blaster is one of the great creative action scenes in the movies . . . This is a movie that strains at the leash of the possible, a movie of great visionary wonders.' *(Roger Ebert)*

MÄDCHEN IN UNIFORM CT: 6 AV: 7.75

(aka *Girls in Uniform; Maedchen in Uniform)*

1931 Germany 91/110 BW DRAMA/ROMANCE/FOREIGN

D Leontine Sagan
W Christa Winsloe F.D. Andam from Winsloe's play *Gestern und Heute*

Emilia Unda Dorothea Wieck ☆ Hedwig Schlichter Hertha Thiele Ellen Schwannecke

Schoolgirl (Hertha Thiele) with a crush on a teacher (Dorothea Wieck) is driven to suicide.

Anti-authoritarian film often hailed as a classic; it was certainly brave in the context of Weimar Germany. It's all very sombre and symbolic, but remains one of the most sensitive films ever made about lesbianism, mainly because of Weick's performance, which is far from weak. Remade less successfully in 1958, with Romy Schneider and Lilli Palmer.

'Deserves every good thing said about it as a work of delicacy and beauty; but to save his life this reviewer could not detect the slightly decayed salacity that many critics averred it expounded . . . [It] does not propagandize . . . The appeal is made only to the heart.' *(José Rodriguez, Rob Wagner's Script)*

'Beautifully directed, beautifully written, and acted to a degree that approaches perfection.' *(Harry Evans, Life)*

'Many flashes of great beauty and fine acting.' *(Time & Tide)*

'An unusual and remarkable picture.' *(A.T. Borthwick, News Chronicle)*

'A film of such power and beauty . . . . It is life captured an transformed into shadows.' *(Ewart Hodgson, Daily Express)*

'A delicate understanding of adolescence . . . a triumph of naturalism.' *(Dudley Leslie, Sunday Dispatch)*

'The miracle of this film is the acting of Dorothea Wieck.' *(S.R. Littlewood, Sunday Referee)*

'[The film] is so revolutionary that it is only recently, with the women's movement's rediscovery and championing of the film, that the most clear and obvious implications of its narrative have been acknowledged and discussed . . . since its central message . . . presents a tremendous threat to the status quo . . . The modern feminist concept "the personal is political" is at the heart of [the film] . . . a moving, sensual affirmation of lesbian and feminist values.' *(Penny Ware, The Leveller, 1981)*

'At once a strident warning against the consequences of Hitler's regime and the first truly radical lesbian film.' *(Time Out, 1981)*

MAGNIFICENT AMBERSONS, THE AAN CT: 8 AV: 9.53

1942 US 88 BW DRAMA

D Orson Welles ☆
W Orson Welles from Booth Tarkington's novel

Joseph Cotten ☆ Dolores Costello ☆ Agnes Moorehead ☆ AAN Tim Holt ☆ Anne Baxter ☆ Ray Collins ☆ Richard Bennett ☆ Erskine Sanford Donald Dillaway

A proud family suffers several blows to its reputation.

Welles's drama exposing snobbery and selfishness in small-town America was generally, though not universally, panned on release, since when it has come to be considered a masterpiece. *A Sight & Sound* poll of 1972 voted *The Magnificent Ambersons* into eighth position in its list of Best Films of All Time. Welles's evocation of a gas-lit era is superb, as is the performance of Agnes Moorehead and Stanley Cortez's Oscar-nominated cinematography. But I find myself unmoved by it, and can't help wondering why Welles lavished such care upon remaking such a dull, small-scale story (it had previously been filmed in 1925, under the title *Pampered Youth*). The ending is notably weak, having been tacked on by the studio while Welles was away in South America.

ANTI:

'With a world in flames, nations shattered, populations in rags, with massacres and bombings, Welles devotes 9,000 feet of film to a spoiled brat who grows up as a spoiled, spiteful young man . . . . It piles on a tale of woe, but without once striking at least a true chord of sentimentality.' *(Life)*

'Lacked the roots in community life which were the strength of the Booth Tarkington novel (Welles states that scenes indicating the growth of an industrial community were excised by the studio, but they do not seem to be organically missing) and, in spite of moments of skill and intensity, was essentially a literary film. Its great central set . . . limited and retarded the action.' *(Paul Rotha & Richard Griffith, The Film Till Now, 1949)*

MIXED:

'I found three-quarters of the picture very interesting, but it seemed to me to become dull towards the close.' *(News of the World)*

'An exceptionally well-made film, dealing with a subject scarcely worth the attention which has been lavished upon it.' *(Thomas M. Pryor, New York Times)*

'Once again the overwhelming apparatus of chiaroscuro, vast menacing close-ups, brilliant elaboration of setting is brought into action. But the theme (from a Booth Tarkington novel) is banal and silly; a technique apt to some murky masterpiece is lavished on trivialities about a spoilt son who wrecks his mother's life.' *(Dilys Powell)*

'The same wilful mixture of sheer crudity and inspired experiment, deliberate entanglement of plot, unorthodox and ingenious direction and bizarre and exciting photography [as *Citizen Kane*] . . . [Welles] has already made a place for himself in the cinematic world which can only be compared with Berlioz in the history of music.' *(Manchester Guardian)*

'Recently I saw his second film again, *The Magnificent Ambersons*, and was struck even more strongly with its split – between the touching Midwestern story that Welles understands well and the impasto of inappropriate expressionistic chiaroscuro that he laid on it.' *(Stanley Kauffmann, 1977)*

PRO:

'If there are fewer tricks than in *Citizen Kane* the magic is more assured . . . Agnes Moorehead especially gives a remarkably fine performance.' *(William Whitebait, New Statesman)*

'The current film is more compact than *Citizen Kane*, its investigations of rhythmics more successful, and there is a taut, emotional quality which his début effort lamentably lacked. There is less of the arrogantly cerebral, more of the fluently human note in this brooding study of a wealthy home which houses a family of strangers. The speech of the people is flavorsomely idiomatic, and the evocations of the ponderous architecture, the heavy hangings, the bulky furnishings of gas-lighted America are as important and as articulate as the actors. Snobbery is satirized with marked skill, stupidities admirably ridiculed, and a dour, ominous threat of inevitable catastrophe is projected by the leitmotif of low-key camerawork . . . *The Magnificent Ambersons* is sinister, disturbing; as pungent, as stimulating, as Pernod.' *(Herb Sterne)*

'More seasoned, more satisfying and yet more revolutionary than *Citizen Kane*.' *(PM)*

'Overshadowed by *Citizen Kane* . . . but a remarkable film by any standards and containing some of Welles' most imaginative work eg the . . . sleigh ride . . . and the famous ball sequence in the Amberson mansion.' *(R.A.E. Pickard, Dictionary of 1000 Best Films, 1971)*

'Flawed as it is by the recutting of the studio, it is an even more daring and imaginative work [than *Citizen Kane*].' *(Peter Bogdanovich, 1975)*

'Even in this truncated form it's amazing and memorable.' *(Pauline Kael, 1977)*

MAGNIFICENT SEVEN, THE

CT: 10 AV: 8.00

1960 US 138 C WESTERN/ACTION/ADVENTURE

D John Sturges ☆
W William Roberts ✓

Yul Brynner ✓ Eli Wallach ✓ Steve McQueen ✓ Robert Vaughn ✓ James Coburn ✓ Brad Dexter Charles Bronson ✓ Horst Buchholz

Mexican peasants hire seven American gunslingers for protection.

Fine action western – not as highly acclaimed as the film it copied, Kurosawa's *The Seven Samurai*, but pacier, more accessible, and even better acted. Elmer Bernstein was Oscar-nominated for perhaps the greatest of all western themes. There were three lesser sequels – *Return of the Magnificent Seven* (1966), *Guns of the Magnificent Seven* (1969) and *The Magnificent Seven Ride!* (1972).

ANTI:

'Routine, with the characters of the gunmen too conventional to give [the actors] any chances.' *(Patrick Gibbs, Daily Telegraph)*

'After a spirited start this version . . . gets little further than splendid looks . . . Mexican poses, and too much thoughtful talk. I found the gunmen's quiet moments trying; and violence tended to be whipped into the serio-comic.' *(William Whitebait, New Statesman)*

'[It] isn't quite as awful as you might expect . . . But if you're an admirer of Kurosawa, stay away. it's not worth the anguish of watching Sturges muff scene after scene . . . Morally, too, the film is now far less acceptable, with worried introspection substituted for compassion.' *(Derek Hill, Tribune)*

MIXED:

'Several cuts above the average Western, but not in the same class [as *The Seven Samurai*].' *(Felix Barker, Evening News)*

'All too often . . . the psychological sophistication of [some] scenes . . . seems to pull against the drift of the form . . . As expositors of the code that makes the Western hero tick, [Sturges and Roberts] are well equipped to write a thesis, but by attributing the same perception to their characters they vitiate the film, for it is part of the essence of the epic hero that he should not be able to hear himself ticking.' *(Penelope Gilliatt, Observer)*

'[In comparison with Kurosawa's work, this is] undoubtedly the lesser film: it is less rich, for instance in characterisation . . . Its story is less closely woven and its dialogue is marred, here and there, by some high falutin' nonsense. Still, it makes a fine film.' *(Guardian)*

'Until the women and children arrive on the scene about two-thirds of the way through, *The*

Magnificent Seven is a rip-roaring rootin' tootin' western with lots of bite and tang and old-fashioned abandon. The last third is downhill, a long and cluttered anti-climax.' *(Variety)*

'Good action scenes, but the rest is verbose and often pretentious.' *(Halliwell)*

PRO:

'All right, it isn't a masterpiece as *The Seven Samurai* is a masterpiece. But it stirs, it moves ... It is a real film.' *(Dilys Powell)*

'An interesting example of international cross fertilization in film ... Americanizing a familiar and formal Oriental theme seems to be the first conscious formalizing of the Western as a classic movie form. This has not numbed or blunted the action; on the contrary, by discarding the surprise element in the plot [the moviemakers] have both dignified it and enabled themselves to give the individual incidents and characterizations more finish.' *(Paul V. Beckley, New York Herald Tribune)*

MAGUS, THE

CT: 1 AV: 1.60

1968 GB 116 C DRAMA

D Guy Green ●
W John Fowles ● from his novel

Michael Caine ● Anthony Quinn ● Candice Bergen ● Anna Karina Paul Stassino Julian Glover George Pastell

Schoolteacher (Michael Caine) arrives on Greek island and meets a tiresome old mystic (Anthony Quinn). After that, things get a bit confused.

A hot contender for the title 'Most Pretentious Movie Of All Time'. The two leading performances are laughable, but the film is too boring and incomprehensible to be fun. The once-fashionable novelist John Fowles has only himself to blame for the pitiful job of adaptation.

MIXED:

'It has much of the fascination of a Chinese puzzle, but it would have been infinitely more enthralling if it hadn't been quite so flatly acted and directed.' *(Michael Billington, Illustrated London News)*

'Esoteric, talky, slowly-developing, sensitively-executed and somewhat dull ... Michael Caine stars, in one of his better performances.' *(Variety)*

ANTI:

'Faintly ludicrous some of the time and painfully unexciting all of the time.' *(MFB)*

'A pretty good example of how not to turn a book into a movie ... This may not be the most misguided movie ever made ... but it's in there pitching ... The less said the better about Michael Caine's dreary, sloth-eyed, totally insincere work as the hero of the piece, but I would like to raise one question: Why is it that the men with the worst physiques in films continually appear in more than half the footage in each of their successive pictures wearing little more than a smile? ... Not that male nudity is likely to offend female moviegoers. Quite the contrary. But I can't imagine any female who prefers her movie's hero with a flat tire around his middle. Things are tough enough at home.' *(Rex Reed)*

'There's enough incoherence pretending to be enigma, sex play and chat about existentialism and self-discovery to make teenagers think they're having an experience; for grown-ups, it's an ordeal.' *(Judith Crist)*

'Guy Green, the director, succeeds in making sententiousness visual as well as aural, and multivalence as fascinating as the multiplication table. Billy Williams's color photography seems always overgrown with a thin film of greenish algae, and John Dankworth's score is banal. Anthony Quinn and Michael Caine are out of place in a film emphasizing (however ineptly) the cerebral and spiritual, and Candice Bergen cannot act. Which leaves us with Anna Karina, and any film in which she can walk off with the acting honors is in serious trouble.' *(John Simon)*

'A thundering, baffling bore ... [A] humourless and undramatic exercise in the occult, the macabre and the downright absurd.' *(Cecil Wilson, Daily Mail)*

'One of the basic faults, perhaps, is that Mr Fowles has been conned into changing the whole shape of his main character in order to identify him most improbably with Michael Caine ... The original Nicholas Urfe was believable enough to carry a very long, very complicated and often rather silly story. This one cannot carry a single scene with conviction ... Quite remarkably bad on any level.' *(Penelope Mortimer, Observer)*

'This weird story might have come alive if it had been done in a suitably weird style. Guy Green's competent but flat direction and Michael Caine's none-too-competent and flat acting make it a very dead piece of nonsense.' *(Nina Hibbin, Morning Star)*

MAJOR BARBARA

CT: 6 AV: 8.00

1941 GB 121 BW DRAMA/COMEDY

D Gabriel Pascal, Harold French, David Lean (uncredited)
W Anatole de Grunwald George Bernard Shaw from Shaw's play

Wendy Hiller ☆ Rex Harrison ☆ Robert Morley ☆ Emlyn Williams Robert Newton ☆ Sybil Thorndike Deborah Kerr ☆ David Tree Penelope Dudley Ward Marie Lohr ☆

A classics professor (Rex Harrison) woos a Socialist major in the Salvation Army (Wendy Hiller), who is

rebelling against her arms manufacturer father (Robert Morley).

Slow, talky filming of Shaw's social comedy. His central message – that it is better to give jobs, rather than charity, to the poor – remains topical, and if the script drags at times, there is plenty to enjoy in the performances. Morley (who was only 32 and had to age upwards) is especially impressive, as was Deborah Kerr in her screen début.

PRO:

'Perhaps the best characterisation is given . . . by Robert Newton . . . Excellent little vignettes of East End and West End life bring out all the subtleties and satire of which Shaw is capable . . . A memorable film.' *(MFB)*

'Despite the faults of casting and cutting . . . [the film] is still first-rate entertainment. Shaw's ebullience seems to provide an unslackening fount of energy . . . His people are outspoken as no one else is in films except the Marx Brothers. Wit, too, for once takes the place of wise-cracking.' *(William Whitebait, New Statesman and Nation)*

MIXED:

'Hiller . . . does much to carry the story along through some rather dull and weighty passages.' *(Variety)*

'It is sad about Major Barbara. It is an extremely well-made film, technically comparable to any from any country . . . It is also full of humour, but the one amazing thing is that basically the film is about nothing at all . . . Possibly everyone is over-estimating Mr Shaw's film. Maybe it is not the deep social document that it is supposed to be . . . It is a pity. It is more than a pity. It is a bloody shame.' *(Documentary NewsLetter)*

'Terrible, but bearable; there's a fascination to its clunkiness. Shaw had allowed Pygmalion to be cut and adapted for the screen, and it was a great success, but he got stubborn on this one and hung on to his dialogue; Gabriel Pascal, who had produced *Pygmalion*, had also been spoiled by its success and decided to direct this time. Their failings were compounded: the actors posture and talk, and the movie goes on and on until whatever it's meant to be about no longer seems to matter. It's too cheerful to be really boring, however.' *(Pauline Kael)*

MAKE WAY FOR TOMORROW

CT: 8 AV: 7.43

1937 US 91 BW DRAMA

D Leo McCarey ☆
W Vina Delmar from Josephine Lawrence's novel *The Years Are So Long* and Helen Leary and Nolan Leary's play

Victor Moore Beulah Bondi Thomas Mitchell Fay Bainter Porter Hall Barbara Read

An elderly couple (Victor Moore, Beulah Bondi) find themselves in financial trouble, but their children will not help them.

Touching drama, and a rarity – since it is about old people adapting to their obsolescence, a largely taboo subject in Hollywood movies. Thematically, it has much in common with Ozu's *Tokyo Story*, and it is very nearly as impressive.

ANTI:

'Had a devastating effect at the time but now seems oversimplified and exaggerated.' *(Halliwell)*

MIXED:

'A tearjerker, obviously grooved for femme fans.' *(Variety)*

PRO:

'The most brilliantly directed and acted film of the year.' *(John Grierson)*

'A sense of misery and inhumanity is left vibrating in the nerves.' *(Graham Greene)*

'We have not seen for a long time such a demonstration of what directorial control can mean to the art of acting.' *(John Grierson, World Film News)*

'Sensitive . . . beautifully done.' *(Maltin)*

'An unrecognized classic.' *(Scheuer)*

MALCOLM X

CT: 5 AV: 7.00

1992 US 201 C BIOPIC/DRAMA

D Spike Lee ✗
W Arnold Perl Spike Lee from *The Autobiography of Malcolm X* as told to Alex Haley

Denzel Washington ☆ AAN Angela Bassett Albert Hall Al Freeman Jr ✓ Delroy Lindo Spike Lee Theresa Randle Kate Vernon

Life and times of a black activist (Denzel Washington).

Terribly long, this seems at times to be more of a history lesson than a film – and the opening footage of Rodney King being beaten up by Los Angeles police smacks of sensationalist opportunism. Fortunately, Denzel Washington maintains audience interest with a powerful performance, and the first half of the movie (which isn't afraid to portray the black power leader as an unscrupulous criminal) is entertaining: it's only towards the end that the tone becomes so soupily reverential that it fails to convince. Ruth Carter was Oscar-nominated for her costumes.

PRO:

'One of the great screen biographies, celebrating the whole sweep of an American life that began in sorrow and bottomed out on the streets and in prison, before its hero reinvented himself. Watching the film, I understood more clearly how we do have the power to change our own lives, how fate doesn't deal all of the cards. The film is inspirational and educational – and it is also entertaining, as movies must be before they can be anything else.' *(Roger Ebert)*

'Although the movie feels long, it's never boring. One comes away from *Malcolm X* with the feeling of having witnessed more than just a dramatized story – indeed of having experienced a complex, meaningful, and powerful life.' *(Baseline)*

MIXED:

'The central factor in the film is, has to be, Denzel Washington's performance as Malcolm. Lean and supple, he moves through the story from ignorance to purpose like a man both obedient and grateful to fate. Himself the son of a Pentecostal minister, Washington understands what public speech means in a black mouth to black ears – as much communion through music as thematic charge. A last implication of reserve is missing in Washington, of untapped energy, but he has everything else.' *(Stanley Kauffmann)*

'Always watchable even if one can't call it memorable.' *(Derek Malcolm, Guardian)*

'A sprawling, sometimes awkward epic, marred by touches of self-indulgence. But it is a passionate, inspirational and beautifully acted piece of work.' *(Brian D. Johnson, Maclean's)*

'Although Lee has not turned out a hagiography, neither has he gone into the particularly spiky aspects of Malcolm's history: his negotiations on behalf of Elijah Muhammad with the KKK, his excursions into homosexuality and male hustling, and the NoI's anti-Semitism, which he espoused . . . I do not think that *Malcolm X* is a totally honest movie – if it were, it would offend almost everybody – but it is a genuine piece of filmmaking, with a savvily paced story, bustling and bristling atmosphere, security of technical execution, and devilishly good acting.' *(John Simon)*

'Lee sketches Malcolm's life colorfully, if by the numbers. But he falls victim to the danger of movie biography: he elevates Malcolm's importance until the vital historical context is obscured . . . So stately, reverent and academic, so suitable for the Oscars with which Hollywood rewards high-minded mediocrity.' *(Richard Corliss, Time)*

ANTI:

'Disappointingly sluggish and conventional.' *(Variety)*

'Spike Lee was right when he told kids to play hooky and see *Malcolm X*. With this picture, he's turned the movie theater into a classroom.' *(Stuart Klawans, Nation)*

'The corruption at the heart of Malcolm's legend is that he looked bigger than life because he always lived in small, cultish worlds, and always stood next to small people. He screamed at whites, but he had no idea of how to work with them to get things done. King was the man who had to get things done . . . Lee's film, as beautifully executed as it is, refuses to ask questions about Malcolm's legend. A quick look behind the legend, however, shows that Malcolm's real story was, in truth, tragedy. And the understanding of this grim truth would have helped the film better achieve the racial protest it is obviously after. Malcolm was hurt badly by oppression early in his childhood . . . But his compensations for the hurt only extended the hurt. And the tragedy was the life that this extraordinary man felt that he needed to live, that Malcolm Little had to become Malcolm X, had to be a criminal, then a racial ideologue, and finally a martyr for an indefinable cause. Black nationalism is a tragedy of white racism, and can sometimes be as ruinous as the racism itself.' *(Shelby Steele, New Republic)*

'There is not one sympathetic white character in the film, and Lee presents Malcolm's approving response to the murder of President Kennedy without even a hint of reproof . . . Lee lets his reverence for Malcolm sterilize the facts. There is no allusion, for instance, to the more extreme views of the Black Muslims. And Lee ignores the animosity between Malcolm and Martin Luther King Jr, other than having Malcolm blast "chicken-pecking Uncle Toms" less militant than he. Lee's lionization of a man with such a debatable social legacy raises more questions than it answers.' *Ralph Novak, People Weekly)*

MALICE

CT: 7 AV: 6.50

1993 US 111 C THRILLER

D Harold Becker ✔
W Aaron Sorkin Scott Frank ✔

Bill Pullman ✔ Nicole Kidman ✔ Alec Baldwin ✔ Anne Bancroft George C. Scott Bebe Neuwirth

A husband and wife (Bill Pullman and Nicole Kidman) hope to start a family in their newly bought Victorian home, and welcome in a charming but sinister lodger (Alec Baldwin). Oh yes, and there's a serial rapist-killer on the loose.

A cracking melodrama. Be warned by the message on the poster: 'See it before someone tells you the secret!' It starts as if it is a conventional woman-in-peril thriller, but then embarks on a switchback-ride of unexpected twists and turns, which leave the audience guessing until the final seconds.

There will be those who find the denouement as sick as it is unlikely, but few will deny that the saga is performed with panache. Nicole Kidman was the best feature of *Dead Calm* and *Billy Bathgate*, and more than confirms her promise. She is ably supported by Alec Baldwin, always at his best when playing slightly creepy characters, as he did in *Miami Blues*. Bill Pullman, fresh from playing the hapless sap in *Sleepless in Seattle*, *Singles* and

Sommersby, gets a chance to play a more intriguing role (hero? villain? wimp?), and does so impeccably.

The fact that a film is cast with the best actors for the parts, rather than with big stars, is often a clue that the producers have confidence in the screenplay – and here their trust is amply justified. The script is brilliantly structured. Becker's workmanlike direction lacks the visual pyrotechnics which a Brian De Palma would have brought to it, but he skilfully juggles with audience expectations, gradually darkening the film's tone until it emerges as fully-fledged film noir.

ANTI:

'Overplotted and underdirected . . . The greatest suspense arises from wondering if anyone will ever say or do anything remotely plausible.' *(Ralph Novak, People Weekly)*

'Do the creators of mainstream thrillers realize that, more and more often, audiences are laughing at the contrivances they're being asked to swallow? . . . The plot . . . is (to paraphrase Winston Churchill) an implausibility wrapped around a contrivance inside an enigma. The enigma is how this script, cowritten by *A Few Good Men*'s Aaron Sorkin, ever got sold.' *(Owen Gleiberman, Entertainment Weekly)*

MIXED:

'Things are not quite what they seem. Or possibly they are. Or something. [*Malice*], in short, is an exercise in piling up the red herrings and almost amusing enough to make the slog of following its twists seem worthwhile . . . Becker . . . makes it a diverting enough ride for those happy to tolerate the preposterous neatness of its plot.' *(Kevin Jackson, Independent)*

'Absurd but entertaining.' *(Hugo Davenport, Daily Telegraph)*

'It's hard to say what's more ridiculous, the serial-killer subplot that disappears mid-movie or the big twist that isn't shocking so much as . . . icky . . . Authentically bad, *Malice* is one of those rental treats that makes you realize you don't have to like a movie to enjoy it.' *(Ty Burr, Entertainment Weekly)*

PRO:

'Even if you've guessed whodunwhat, this is a clever wind-up right through to the final ironic revelation.' *(Angie Errigo, Today)*

'There is, of course, a bottom line to all thrillers. Did it shock you? Did it scare you? Judging from the butter stains all over my new silk shirt, I'd say Malice achieves its every intent.' *(Rod Lurie, LA Magazine)*

MALTESE FALCON, THE AAN CT: 9 AV: 9.71

1941 US 101 BW THRILLER

D John Huston ☆
W John Huston ☆ AAN from Dashiell Hammett's novel

Humphrey Bogart ☆ Mary Astor ☆ Sydney Greenstreet ☆ Peter Lorre ☆ Elisha Cook Jr Barton MacLane Lee Patrick Gladys George

Private eye Sam Spade (Humphrey Bogart) suffers the death of his partner, which seems to have something to do with a missing statuette.

Unbelievably in view of its assured style, this masterpiece of film noir was John Huston's directorial début. Not only is it one of his best (and most meticulously planned) films, it's one of the finest crime thrillers ever made – thanks in no small measure to Arthur Edeson's brilliant photography. The script cleverly captures the sardonic humour of Hammett's novel, and Huston is well served by a marvellous cast, with Sydney Greenstreet an especially sinister villain. Bogart and Astor make one of the screen's great film noir romantic pairings. It's a remake of a 1931 version, which isn't bad either, though it's been forgotten.

MIXED:

'Such a delirium of fibbing and killing and passion that we spectators, humdrum at heart after all, are never quite entirely sure what is happening, or that it makes any sense or is ever made tidy by logic. The delirium is sufficient, however, and somehow the effect is nicely refreshing, the wilder the better.' *(John Mosher, New Yorker)*

'This Dashiell Hammett melodrama had been filmed twice before, and had nothing in particular to say, but it was immediately clear that Huston was a greatly gifted director. His success in evoking the semi-civilised Hammett world . . . was largely a matter of camera placement and of the use of light and of inanimate objects.' *(Paul Rotha & Richard Griffith, The Film Till Now, 1949)*

'*The Maltese Falcon* is his [John Huston's] first movie, and though it leaves a few loose threads ungathered at its finish, it's good enough to make the next John Huston picture something to look forward to.' *(Louise Levitas, PM)*

PRO:

'Has nearly everything a mystery should have . . . [It] is rich in sardonic revelation and belongs to the vintage period of American gangsterdom.' *(William Whitebait, New Statesman)*

'Brilliant characterization, resourceful direction and imaginative camerawork . . . Bogart is brilliant as the unethical Spade.' *(Kine Weekly)*

'The story is strong of itself with an unusual ending and fine acting, but it is the treatment which makes it the best thriller so far this year.' *(Evelyn Russell, S & S)*

'The trick which Mr Huston has pulled is a combination of American ruggedness with the suavity of the English crime school – a blend of mind and muscle – plus a slight touch of pathos.' *(New York Times)*

'Has nearly everything a mystery film should have.' *(New Statesman)*

'The most interesting and imaginative detective film to come out of America, or anywhere else, since the first *Thin Man*, another Hammett story. Bogart is as good as he can be. The defensive, admiring and calculating stare on his first encounter with the beauty, the physical self-confidence he puts into their later meetings, his resentful, implacable rejection of her appeal at the last – who could do these scenes better, or as well?' *(Dilys Powell)*

'The melodramatic plot . . . is both suspenseful and satirical, and the technique, while not adventurous, extends each ingredient to its fullest cinematic effect . . . Huston's clever, brilliantly acted adaptation . . . established him as a director of much creative promise.' *(Eugene Archer, Film Culture, 1959)*

MAMA THERE'S A MAN IN YOUR BED:

SEE ROMUALD AND JULIETTE.

MAME CT: 5 AV: 2.22

1974 US 131 C MUSICAL/SO BAD

D Gene Saks ●
W Paul Zandel from Jerome Lawrence, Jerry Herman and Robert E. Lee's play from Patrick Dennis's book

Lucille Ball ● Beatrice Arthur ☆ Robert Preston Bruce Davison Jane Connell Joyce Van Patten John McGiver

In 1928, a 10-year-old boy goes to live with his mad but entertaining aunt (Lucille Ball).

An over-produced disaster. Lucille Ball gives one of the worst performances in musical screen history, being far too old for the role and unable to sing or dance. It's unintentionally funny, but also a bit sad.

'Do you have to bring that picture up? I wish to God I could bring it up! It was the worst mistake of my professional life. I wasn't completely well when I took it on, and, looking back, I may not have been right for it in the first place. But *Mame* was a great character and I wanted to play her. As it happened, no one wanted to see her – at least not with Lucy.' *(Lucille Ball)*

PRO:

'Lavishly costumed . . . smartly choreographed.' *(Variety)*

'A must for lovers of high camp.' *(Quinlan)*

MIXED:

'Inept in most departments but with occasional show-stopping moments.' *(Halliwell)*

'The production values are first class.' *(Scheuer)*

ANTI:

'It makes one realize afresh the parlous state of the Hollywood musical, fighting to survive against misplaced superstars and elephantine budgets matched with miniscule imagination.' *(Geoff Brown)*

'The cast seem to have been handpicked for their tone deafness, and Lucille Ball's close-ups are shot blatantly out of focus.' *(S & S)*

'So terrible it isn't boring; you can get fixated staring at it and wondering what Lucille Ball thought she was doing. When that sound comes out – it's somewhere between a bark, a croak, and a quaver – does she think she's singing? When she throws up her arms, in their red giant-bat-wing sleeves, and cries out "Listen, everybody!" does she really think she's a fun person?' *(Pauline Kael, 1977)*

MAN AND A WOMAN, A AAW CT: 5 AV: 6.67

(aka *Un Homme et Une Femme*)

1966 France 102 C/BW DRAMA/ROMANCE/ FOREIGN

D Claude Lelouch ✗
W Claude Lelouch Pierre Uytterhoeven

Anouk Aimée Jean-Louis Trintignant Pierre Barouh Valerie Lagrange Simone Paris

A racing-driver (Jean-Louis Trintignant) and a widow (Anouk Aimée) fall in love, while the soundrack goes yubba-dubba-dub, yubba-dubba-dub.

Slick, lyrical romance which was a popular dating movie in the 60s. Now it looks suspiciously like a commercial for hairspray. The changes from colour to black and white are irksome, as is the repetitive music.

PRO:

'Extraordinary . . . In the wrong hands, bungling Hollywood hands, this could be awful – trite, novelettish, embarrassing. But the ground is prepared with tender delicacy by Lelouch and by two exquisite performances from [Aimée and Trintignant].' *(Felix Barker, Evening News)*

'Technically the film is expressive and all of a piece, as only a movie written and shot by one man ever can be . . . Some of the photography is riskily pretty . . . but it struck me as genuinely lyrical.' *(Penelope Gilliatt, Observer)*

MIXED:

'A slick item with all the Hollywood ingredients.' *(John Simon)*

'When in doubt, Lelouch's motto seems to be, use a colour filter or insert lyrical shots of dogs and horse; when in real doubt, use both.' *(Tom Milne, MFB)*

'Lelouch . . . tries to make a lot out of a little. He has a dashing way of mixing together thought and reality, past and present and all kinds of contrasting styles and techniques . . . But most of it is terribly premeditated and schemed for – an ad-man's chic and seductive colour-supplement propaganda for life, rather than a suggestion of life itself.' *(Nina Hibbin, Morning Star)*

MAN BITES DOG CT: 8 AV: 5.40

(aka *C'est Arrivé Prés De Chez Vous*)

1992 Belgium 96 BW COMEDY/FOREIGN

D Rémy Belvaux André Bonzel Benoît Poelvoorde
W Rémy Belvaux André Bonzel Benoît Poelvoorde Vincent Tavier

Benoît Poelvoorde ✔ Jacqueline Poelvoorde-Pappaert Nelly Pappaert Jenny Drye Malou Madou Willy Vandenbroeck

The story of an increasingly desensitized documentary film crew as it follows a serial killer.

This blackest of black comedies is strictly for those with a strong stomach and a sense of humour. You could see it as a satire on the myth of 'journalistic objectivity', but it's also about the way TV and film can glorify the least deserving subject, and the way exposure to violence can deaden anyone's sensibilities; is it implicitly suggesting that a diet of violent movies may be doing the same to us? Many people took exception to the movie's jokey callousness, without realizing that it was precisely this emotional dislocation which the film is criticizing. The rape scene is shockingly realistic – but artistically justified. It's certainly very un-erotic. An interesting movie, and one of a kind.

ANTI:

'After the savagery of *Reservoir Dogs* . . . you should be well tuned for the hilarious horrors of [this] comic meditation on the conspiracy between media and that which it records – a kind of *Medium Cool* on absurdist drugs . . . Its locations are astonishing visually but its attitudes are horrific socially. Friends tell me I've missed the point of its deadpan humour. I think I may well be happy to have done so.' *(Tom Hutchinson, Hampstead & Highgate Express)*

'The earth-shattering idea here is that the media aid and abet bad behavior . . . Although it tries awfully hard to shock, [it's] finally more tedious than outrageous . . . Sometimes it works, sure. But I'm a vegetarian, I break down at the sight of a bloody steak.' *(Manohla Dargis, Village Voice)*

'A macabre send-up . . . [whose] conceit is funny at first, but over an hour and a half the joke becomes laboured. Boredom soon inures one to the impact of the various frights and shocks . . . The Belgians . . . might conclude that they would be better off as a nation forgetting about the movie business and sticking to making chocolate truffles.' *(Vanessa Letts, Spectator)*

PRO:

'This ferocious black comedy . . . does not involve Roddy McDowall striking back at Lassie . . . It is carefully shaped to draw us in and repel us, to make us laugh and wipe the smiles off our faces. The most horrendous scenes are calculated to force us into asking ourselves how we can bear to watch such things.' *(Philip French, Observer)*

'Raw gore on a rock-bottom budget . . . But then, who said screen violence was supposed to be palatable? . . . There are issues being addressed here which are of relevance to everyone in our television-based culture.' *(Anne Billson, Sunday Telegraph)*

'Terribly knowing, almost unnervingly realistic.' *(Marshall Julius, What's On in London)*

'Shocking less for its full-frontal murders . . . than for its own refusal to be shocked . . . for this black comedy about brutalisation is also about the voyeur implications of film-watching.' *(Nigel Andrews, Financial Times)*

'As an exploration of voyeurism, it's one of the most resonant, caustic contributions to cinema of violence since *Peeping Tom*.' *(Geoff Andrew, Time Out)*

MAN ESCAPED, A CT: 9 AV: 9.00

(aka *Un Hommé Echappé; Un Condamné à Mort S'est Échappé*)

1956 France 102 BW THRILLER/FOREIGN

D Robert Bresson ☆
W Robert Bresson from André Devigny's articles

François Leterrier Charles LeClainche Roland Monod Maurice Beerblock Jacques Ertaud Roger Treheme

A French resistance fighter (François Leterrier) tries to escape from prison. It takes him two months of hard work.

Bresson's film is such a *tour de force* in its use of camera-angles and sound that its main strength can easily be overlooked: it's a masterpiece of story-telling, one of the most gripping movies ever made. It's an antidote to modern American cinema, arousing such terror with the sound of a squeaky bicycle that it has no need for violence or sensationalism. It's also an antidote to the literary traditions of British moviemaking: there's no philosophizing here about freedom, resilience and the human spirit. There's no need: they pervade every frame.

It is a welcome reminder that it is possible to be cinematic within a very small physical area. Bresson's hero constantly looks out of his cell window, yet we never see the panorama which he does: a flagrant violation of cinematic convention, where such a shot is traditionally followed by a cut to wherever the person is looking. No less daringly, Bresson operates without recourse to that mechanism which film students learn is indispensable to story-telling: the 'establishing shot'. In ignoring this convention, he not only creates a sense of claustrophobia: he also concentrates our attention on essentials.

The characters are treated with equal ruthlessness. We hardly see the face of a German guard: when we do, it is either out of focus in long shot, or fleetingly a fragment of face. The oppressors are effectively and poetically dehumanized by the director, without their having to resort to sadistic or melodramatic acts. Every episode of violence occurs offscreen, and yet it's more shocking than the most explicitly photographed carnage.

Although the acting in the film is entirely by non-professionals, *A Man Escaped* is so well acted that it makes other escape movies seem mannered. The prisoners seem to share an almost tangible fatigue – which Bresson actually achieved by browbeating his cast with endless repetition and retakes of each scene. Never mind: the end justified the moans.

MIXED:

'Bresson's camera hovers about the central character, never seeing more of the visual world than is necessary . . . Since the audience sees even less than the hero, its sense of hearing is intensified by recurring off-screen noises . . . Bresson's emphasis on off-screen sounds and the limited range of his camera represents a new approach to the problems of subjective cinema in the age of the talking film . . . This path to intense drama has it hazards . . . It is almost impossible to generate any emotional power within the limits of Bresson's technique . . . Part of the reason that [the film] does not rise to the exultant pitch of Mozart's Mass in C Minor [on the soundtrack] is that Jost, the priest, and the old man all seem more recognizable than [the hero.]' *(Andrew Sarris, Film Culture)*

PRO:

'Grim, realistic but inspiring and hypnotic story [which] achieves a truth to life which, in spite of its grim surroundings, is still lit with hope and faith in mankind. For this reason the film never becomes depressing. Without sex, romance, humor or any of the usual ingredients it still supplies gripping entertainment.' *(Daily Film Renter)*

'Underplayed throughout, the climax will root you to your seat.' *(Sunday Express)*

'Bresson is perhaps the most individual artist working in the cinema . . . A major work of one of the most remarkable – and certainly the purest – of the cinema's living artists.' (MFB)

MAN FOR ALL SEASONS, A AAW

CT: 10 AV: 8.71

1966 GB 120 C DRAMA/BIOPIC

D Fred Zinnemann ☆ AAW
W Robert Bolt ☆ AAW from his play

Paul Scofield ☆ AAW Wendy Hiller ☆ AAN Robert Shaw ☆ AAN Orson Welles ☆ Leo McKern ☆ Susannah York Vanessa Redgrave John Hurt ☆ Nigel Davenport Corin Redgrave Cyril Luckham

The Lord Chancellor of England, Sir Thomas More (Paul Scofield), is torn between his loyalty to Roman Catholicism and his loyalty to King Henry VIII (Robert Shaw).

A good stage play becomes a wonderful film, thanks to excellent casting, stunning performances even in minor roles, unfussy direction and lovely photography (for which Ted Moore won an Oscar). One of the classic history films, and – contrary to some critics' beliefs – it does illuminate the issues of its time.

ANTI:

'Flattened-out, oversimplified, and uncinematic . . . The outdoor scenes always have that feel of, "Oh yes, that was thrown in to make it more of a movie!" about them, and Zinnemann's direction is decent but plodding.' *(John Simon)*

'On the whole, Zinnemann's visual style is recessive in that everyone is always seen at a safe distance. I don't like this style particularly. It's safe, tactful, and tentative for a director who doesn't want to get too involved with his characters. Yet it is probably wise for this project. Scofield and Bolt don't really take close-ups. They lack feeling and empathy. Scofield is a virtuoso on the stage, the dry inflections of his voice can ripple across the footlights with layers and layers of expressive irony and biting cynicism. When you look at his face on the screen, however, you get a guilty desire to look somewhere else.' *(Andrew Sarris, 1970)*

'Agonisingly respectable . . . Orson Welles alone relieves the boredom in a marvellous cameo as Cardinal Wolsey. If only they'd let him loose with the whole sorry history.' *(Tom Charity, Time Out)*

MIXED:

'Tasteful and moderately enjoyable. The weakness is that though Bolt's dialogue is crisp, lucid, and well-spoken, his presentation of More's martyrdom is so one-sided we don't even get to understand that side. More is the only man of honor in the movie, and he's got all the good lines; he's the kind of hero we used to read about in biographies of great men written for 12-year-olds, and Scofield is so refined, so controlled, so dignified, so obviously "subtle" he's like a man of conscience in a school play.' *(Pauline Kael)*

PRO:

'Excellent, handsome and stirring.' *(Variety)*

'[Zinnemann] has crystallized the essence of this drama in such pictorial terms as to render even its abstractions vibrant . . . Mr Scofield is brilliant . . . *A Man for All Seasons* is a picture that inspires admiration, courage and thought.' *(New York Times)*

'Quite simply, it is riches for the eye and ear.' *(Vernon Young)*

'Sumptuous to look at, intelligent to listen to and acted superbly well. It was the first film to give Scofield the chance this great actor deserved, and for that we should also be grateful.' *(Brian Baxter, NFT Bulletin)*

'The film makes fine use of the river by day or by night, still or trembling with reflections. The colour all through is exquisite, and the design of costumes and sets beguiles. But it is in the conflict of character and the victory – if having your head cut off is a victory – of conscience that the heart of the film lies. Here the playing is all-important – and Fred Zinnemann has always been a sympathetic director of players.' *(Dilys Powell)*

'Mr Scofield is brilliant in his exercise of temperance and restraint, of disciplined wisdom and humor, as he variously confronts his restless King or Cardinal Wolsey, who is played by Orson Welles with subtle, startling glints of poisonous evil that, in this day, are extraordinary for him.' *(Bosley Crowther)*

'Apart from [Paul] Scofield, I think one should pick out from the very good cast John Hurt as Rich, and Orson Welles appearing briefly as Cardinal Wolsey, a puckered, cantankerous clever face drooping over red robes like a deep imprint in sealing wax.' *(Observer)*

MAN HUNT

CT: 6 AV: 7.13

1941 US 105 BW THRILLER

D Fritz Lang
W Dudley Nichols from Geoffrey Household's novel *Rogue Male*

Walter Pidgeon ☆ Joan Bennett George Sanders ☆ John Carradine Roddy McDowall Ludwig Stossel Heather Thatcher Frederic Worlock Roger Imhof Egon Brecher

A big game hunter (Walter Pidgeon) stalks Hitler.

The big problem here is that everyone knows one aspect of the outcome: our hero never does shoot the Führer. Despite this, a rather confusing plot, and some painfully inauthentic British backgrounds, this is a gripping yarn – superior to that film on a similar theme, *Day Of The Jackal*. Lang and his cinematographer Arthur Miller make effective use of unusual camera angles and low-key lighting.

PRO:

'In its manipulation of these dark and intent forces on a checkerboard, it manages to take your breath away.' *(Otis Ferguson)*

'The very quintessence of rousing spine-chilling adventure . . . and a breathless testimony to the British bulldog spirit . . . Star, title, and exploitation values are colossal.' *(Kine Weekly)*

'The players never fail to make it both a vastly compelling entertainment and an arresting evaluation of a lot of ideas which most of us are considering at the moment.' *(Howard Barnes, New York Herald Tribune)*

'With Lang, everything is played out and knitted together at the heart of a highly moral universe.' *(François Truffaut, Cahiers du Cinéma, 1954)*

MIXED:

'It's a film everyone except a Nazi will enjoy, though in fact the promise of the beginning is never fulfilled . . . A pity . . . that the content of this film shouldn't be a little more original.' *(William Whitebait, New Statesman)*

'Lang's direction maintains excellent suspense in the first half, but yarn hits the skids for the second section to wind up with a series of overdrawn and inconclusive sequences.' *(Variety)*

MAN IN THE WHITE SUIT, THE

CT: 8 AV: 8.92

1951 GB 85 BW COMEDY/SF

D Alexander Mackendrick ☆
W John Dighton Alexander Mackendrick Roger MacDougall ☆ AAN from MacDougall's novel

Alec Guinness ☆ Joan Greenwood ☆ Cecil Parker ☆ Vida Hope Ernest Thesiger ☆ Michael Gough Howard Marion Crawford Miles Malleson George Benson ☆ Edie Martin ☆

A chemist (Alec Guinness) discovers a cloth that appears dirt-repellent and indestructible.

A classic in several genres – science fiction, Ealing comedy and social satire. Like another great British comedy, *I'm All Right Jack*, it satirizes both sides of industry for caring little or nothing about the consumer, and puts its finger on one of the weaknesses which crippled the British economy for decades after the Second World War. Alec Guinness gives one of his brightest and most energetic performances, while Joan Greenwood is as delightfully feline here as she was in *Kind Hearts in Coronets* and *The Importance of Being Earnest*. Mackendrick's pacy direction was well served by Douglas Slocombe's excellent cinematography. Reviews on both sides of the Atlantic were overwhelmingly favourable, and the few dissenting voices – on release and since – have tended to focus on an ending which some see as an anti-climax.

MIXED:

'The early reaches of the film . . . are full of that innocent nonsense, boyish knockabout, facetiousness and general air of undergraduate high spirits which (rather than wit) characterise the Ealing comedies. But the climax of the picture fails to reach the promised height, chiefly, I think, because it lacks the quality of surprise . . . Guinness . . . seems for once below par, relying on a scissors-and-paste composition of tricks that have worked before and now begin to be just a little too easily recognizable. In the circumstances, the Chaplinesque ending seems unfortunate, as it suggests an unfavourable comparison.' *(Fred Majdalany, Daily Mail)*

'A witty farce that, unfortunately, pulls its punches at the end, neatly restoring the status quo by having the fabric ultimately prove to be a little flawed.' *(Elliot)*

'The plot is a variation on an old theme, but it comes out with a nice fresh coat of paint.' *(Variety)*

PRO:

'Must be this reviewer's personal yardstick of comic perfection. Being the funniest picture he has seen in the last 10 years, it has to outrank the faded "greats" of the distant past, which makes it the funniest ever.' *(New York Post)*

'A delightful treat of unbridled fancy which made us laugh loud and long.' *(New York Daily Mirror)*

'The combination of an ingenious idea, a bright, funny and imaginative script, skilful playing and perceptive brisk direction has resulted once more in a really satisfying Ealing comedy.' *(Richard Mallett, Punch)*

'Comedy though it is, [the film] deals with a serious subject: the artist (for a scientist is a kind of artist) who prefers his work above all things, even love: above in this case even the enchanting Joan Greenwood. That the film manages almost without pause until a faintly disappointing end to be both funny and touching is partly due to this serious core: contrary to popular belief, the best comedy is about something, not about nothing.' *(Dilys Powell)*

'Guinness's bland monomaniacal scientist is beautifully matched by Joan Greenwood, who is all guile and scorn and perversity, without any real aim or purpose.' *(Pauline Kael)*

'Directed with a deft touch by Alexander Mackendrick, this deadly satire by Roger MacDougall had one of the most inventive film scores ever by Ben Frankel. Taking the original sounds of liquids bubbling away in beakers and cunningly mixing them with bassoons and a rhythm section, Frankel concocted an unforgettably witty jazz samba that in its day became a hit single.' *(Ken Russell, 1993)*

MAN IS TEN FEET TALL, A: *see* EDGE OF THE CITY.

MAN OF IRON AAN — CT: 8 AV: 7.56

(aka *Czlowiek Z Zelaza*)

1980 Poland 140 BW/C DRAMA

D Andrzej Wajda ☆
W Aleksander Ścibor-Rylski ☆

Jerzy Radziwilowicz Krystyna Janda
Marian Opania Irena Byrska Boguslaw Linda
Wieslawa Kosmalska

The Solidarity campaign of 1980 is seen through the eyes of a strike leader (Jerzy Radziwilowicz), who is the steely son of Wajda's Man of Marble *(see below).*

Sequel to *Man of Marble*, although it's perfectly comprehensible in its own right. The action revolves around a journalist (Marian Opania) who is sent to smear the strike leader, and the question of media ethics looms large. Wajda makes impressive use of documentary footage to generate excitement and realism, and not surprisingly won the Palme d'Or at the Cannes Film Festival. Lech Walesa makes a brief appearance as himself.

ANTI:

'Lauded more for its subject and its "heroic" anti-authoritarian stance than for its merits as a piece of cinema. These seem to me to be almost nil.' *(Nigel Andrews, Financial Times)*

MIXED:

'Exactly the same two techniques – the use of a character who is a journalist, and the juxtaposition of a fictional story with actual events – were used by Haskell Wexler in *Medium Cool*, the film about the 1968 Democratic convention demonstrations in Chicago. The approach leaves some ragged edges, but when you are filming at the cutting edge of history you can't stop for rewrites.' *(Roger Ebert)*

PRO:

'Not so much a sequel to . . . *Man of Marble* as a completion of it . . . And apart from its obvious documentary and political importance, it is also a great film. If any film deserves to win the Golden Palm, this one does.' *(Richard Roud, Guardian)*

'It is heroic film-making and anything less than the Palme d'Or would have been an insult.' *(David Castell, Sunday Telegraph)*

MAN OF MARBLE — CT: 8 AV: 8.13

(aka *Czlowiek Z Marmur*)

1978 Poland 165 C DRAMA/FOREIGN

D Andrzej Wajda ☆
W Aleksander Ścibor-Rylski

Jerzy Radziwilowicz Michael Tarkowski
Krystyna Zachwatowicz Piotr Cieślak
Wieslaw Wójcik Krystyna Janda Tadeusz Lomnicki

A young film-maker (Krystyna Janda) makes a documentary about a record-breaking bricklayer (Jerzy Radziwilowicz) who ran foul of the Polish communist system.

Savage indictment of Polish communism, using more-or-less the structure of *Citizen Kane*. Along with the propaganda, however, there is a well-told story with rounded characters.

PRO:

'Rich, energetic, superbly acted.' *(Richard Schickel, Time)*

'[The story is] beautifully fleshed-out in Wajda's brisk movie.' *(Allan Prior, Daily Mail)*

'An impassioned attempt by Poland's foremost director to make the audience confront and better understand his country's recent past . . . That [it] got made, and made without seeming compromise, is an added personal accomplishment in a major film by a major filmmaker.' *(David Castell, Sunday Telegraph)*

'Monumentally ambitious; it borrows the structures of *Citizen Kane* and then uses them to evoke the entire history of Poland since 1950. To Americans, of course, the dissection of a society is probably not as thrilling as the dissection of a great man. We're all individualists here, all intoxicated by the belief that men create history and bend the world to their wills; the theology of individual ambition has become our state religion. But in Eastern Europe, the state itself is the dominant religion. The state bends men to its will, creates personalities in its own image, and, when that image changes, destroys those who can't change with it. In the Poland that Wajda paints, one must be as canny as a con man to survive; one must watch for signals, for shifts in tone and emphasis; one must endorse the right propaganda. Public life comes to seem an endless game of cat and mouse, and woe to the innocent peasant who, like Birkut, becomes a pawn without even knowing he's playing.' *(Stephen Schiff)*

ANTI:

'Politically and ideologically he is not on our side. He has taken the position, often found among artists, of a "neutral judge" of history and today's times – believing that he has the right . . . to apply the gauge of humanism and morals to all the problems of the world and that he doesn't need Marxism nor any other philosophical-social system to do it.' *(Confidential report by the Polish censor on director Wajda, 1976)*

MAN OF THE WEST

CT: 5 AV: 6.00

1958 US 100 C WESTERN

D Anthony Mann
W Reginald Rose from Will C. Brown's novel *The Border Jumpers*

Gary Cooper Julie London Lee J. Cobb
Arthur O'Connell Jack Lord John Dehner

Gunman trying to go straight (Gary Cooper) agrees to help rob a bank.

Slow, set-bound western with too much talk, and Gary Cooper much too old for the leading role (as Lee J. Cobb's nephew!). Though a flop on release, it was rediscovered by the French critics – who regarded Anthony Mann as an important auteur – and now has cult appeal as a kind of minimalist, elemental western with morally equivocal characters. However, if you like that sort of thing, you're probably better off watching Clint Eastwood's *Unforgiven* (1992).

PRO:

'With Anthony Mann one rediscovers the Western, as one discovers arithmetic in an elementary maths class . . . [It] is the most intelligent of films and at the same time the most simple . . . Mann is returning to the basic truths.' *(Jean-Luc Godard, Cahiers du Cinéma)*

'Mann's last western, and his most disturbing foray into the genre.' *(Virgin)*

'Tense, claustrophobic . . . a minor classic.' *(Martin & Porter)*

'In contrast to the Westerns he (director Anthony Mann) made with James Stewart . . . *Man of the West* is a far more desperate film . . . The result is Mann's most powerful film, a movie whose characters are stripped of all but their elemental natures.' *(Phil Hardy, The Film Encyclopedia: The Western, 1983)*

ANTI:

'One of the nastiest Westerns I've seen for a long time . . . Arthur O'Connell plays a frightened cardsharper as if he thought he had the comedy part. He hasn't.' *(Anthony Carthew, Daily Herald)*

'A real shocker . . . Why so long-headed a guy as Gary Cooper gets himself let in for this sort of stuff I wouldn't know.' *(Edward Betts, The People)*

'Cooper rides through it all with a face as expressive as ancient granite. It is a sad thing to say, but at 57, age is beginning implacably to wear him down.' *(Derek Monsey, Sunday Express)*

'Westerns aren't what they used to be.' *(Charles Maclaren, Time & Tide)*

MAN WHO CAME TO DINNER, THE

CT: 6 AV: 8.36

1941 US 112 BW COMEDY

D William Keighley
W Julius J. Epstein Philip G. Epstein from George S. Kaufman and Moss Hart's play

Monty Woolley ☆ Bette Davis ☆ Ann Sheridan
Jimmy Durante ☆ Reginald Gardiner ☆
Billie Burke ☆ Richard Travis Grant Mitchell

An intellectual New Yorker (Monty Woolley) is forced by injury to spend time with a Middle American family he despises, and is further affronted when his secretary (Bette Davis) falls in love with a resident of Ohio.

Stagey comedy which satirizes prominent people of the time. (The central character is based on columnist Alexander Woolcott, while Gardiner spoofs Noel Coward.) Many of the references have inevitably dated, but there's still entertainment to be had from the 'fish out of water' situation and some delightfully malicious repartee.

ANTI:

'The play, however, was built on topical jokes and a series of vaudeville turns, and in this version the jokes are flat and the turns seemed forced and not very funny.' *(Pauline Kael)*

MIXED:

'The niftiest comedy of 1942 . . . Unquestionably the most vicious but hilarious cat-clawing exhibition ever put on the screen, a deliciously wicked character portrait and a helter-skelter satire, withal . . . [It] is a bit too long and internally complex for 100 per cent comprehension, considering the speed at which it clips. But . . . you're sure to get your money's worth.' *(Bosley Crowther)*

PRO:

'Two hours is a long stretch for wise-cracking round one man in a bathchair, but the situation holds, even for those who have seen the play.' *(William Whitebait, New Statesman)*

MAN WHO FELL TO EARTH, THE

CT: 5 AV: 7.20

1976 GB 117/120/125/140 C SF/DRAMA

D Nicolas Roeg ✗
W Paul Mayersberg from Walter Tevis's novel

David Bowie Rip Torn Buck Henry Candy Clark Bernie Casey

An alien (David Bowie) tries to colonize Earth, but with little success.

Critically acclaimed and a cult classic, this is an intriguing but abstruse – and ultimately depressing – film about an extra-terrestrial who, like Dorothy in *The Wizard of Oz* or another later alien, E.T., can't get home. Although the film looks good, it is often arty for its own sake, needlessly puzzling, and loses its central theme in a fog of pretentiousness. To confuse matters further, the film's US distributor has released the film in four different cuts: 117, 120, 125 and the original length, 140 minutes. Reviewers have always been divided as to the merits of the film, and its extraordinarily passive leading performance.

PRO:

'One of the most interesting science-fiction films of recent years . . . The focal point of the interest, to fascinate even non-sci-fi enthusiasts, is the casting of rock star David Bowie in the title role. His impersonation of the extraplanetary visitor goes beyond the physical to a magnetism of personality and persona that is remarkable.' *(Saturday Review)*

'Roeg, often using a dazzling technical skill, jettisons narrative in favour of thematic juxtapositions, working best when exploring the clichés of social and cultural ritual.' *(Chris Peachment, Time Out)*

'Highly original, fabulously photographed.' *(Maltin)*

'Has suspense, intrigue, romance of a sort, even humor. The sci-fi effects are absolutely beautiful.' *(Scheuer)*

ANTI:

'An extremely photogenic mess.' *(Jonathan Rosenbaum, MFB)*

'Produces puzzlement without involvement, and hence, fantasies without feelings.' *(Village Voice)*

'Once you have pierced through its glittering veneer, you find only another glittering veneer underneath.' *(Michael Billington, Illustrated London News)*

'There is a punch line, but it takes forever and great expectations slump away.' *(Charles Champlin, LA News)*

'You feel finally that all that has been achieved has been to impose an aura of mystery and enigma where essentially there is none; to turn a simple tale into the sort of accumulation of sensations that has become fashionable.' *(David Robinson, The Times)*

'Although Roeg and his screenwriter, Paul Mayersberg, pack in layers of tragic political allegory, none of the layers is very strong, or even very clear. The plot, about big-business machinations, is so uninvolving that one watches Bowie traipsing around – looking like Katharine Hepburn in her transvestite role in Sylvia Scarlett – and either tunes out or allows the film, with its perverse pathos, to become a sci-fi framework for a sex-role-confusion fantasy. The wilted stranger can be said to represent everyone who feels misunderstood, everyone who feels sexually immature or "different", everyone who has lost his way, and so the film is a gigantic launching pad for anything that viewers want to drift to.' *(Pauline Kael)*

'I defy anyone to come up with a coherent synopsis of this film, let alone an explication of the individual scenes and resolution of the inconsistencies, contradictions, and preposterous non sequiturs that litter it . . . How does the CIA profit from meaningless defenestrations? Why is our hero's attempt to return to outer space foiled? What, if any, is the meaning of the closing scenes? The point of all this is ambiguity, contradiction, or fuzziness for its own sake.' *(John Simon)*

MAN WHO KNEW TOO MUCH, THE

CT: 8 AV: 6.92

1934 GB 75/84 BW THRILLER

D Alfred Hitchcock ☆
W A.R. Rawlinson Charles Bennett D.B. Wyndham-Lewis Emlyn Williams Edwin Greenwood from Bennett and Wyndham-Lewis's story

Leslie Banks ☆ Edna Best Pierre Fresnay Nova Pilbeam Frank Vosper Peter Lorre ☆

A spy (Pierre Fresnay) is murdered in Switzerland, and a young girl (Nova Pilbeam) kidnapped. The girl's parents (Leslie Banks, Edna Best) try to track her down in London and foil the assassination of a diplomat at London's Royal Albert Hall.

First of two attempts by Hitchcock to film the same story (the other, made in 1956, starred Doris Day). This is better and faster, even though Edna Best is not altogether convincing as an action-woman, and the linkage between set-pieces is somewhat tenuous. As so often in Hitchcock films, the use of back projection stands out a mile – look at those Swiss mountains and weep – but the narrative excitement, witty settings, and a good villain (Peter Lorre in his first English-speaking role) carry the audience onwards to the perfectly staged climax. Hitchcock was still much influenced by German expressionism (it was after seeing *M* that he cast Lorre), and at this stage in his career it made for an interesting juxtaposition with his British wit and obvious liking for American gangster films. A minor classic.

MIXED:

'All very stagey by modern standards, but much more fun than the expensive remake.' *(Halliwell)*

PRO:

'A natural and easy production that runs smoothly and has the hallmark of sincerity.' *(Variety)*

'Now at last he has thrown critics and intellectuals overboard with one of his incomparable rude gestures, and gone in for making pictures for the people . . . For my own part, I am very happy about *The Man Who Knew Too Much*. It seems to me, because of its very recklessness, its blank refusal to indulge in subtleties, to be the most promising work that Hitchcock has produced since *Blackmail*, and quite possibly the best picture he has ever made.' *(C.A. Lejeune)*

'The balance between character and dramatic incident in the economic, unpretentious earlier film makes for a far better thriller [than the remake].' *(Philip French, The Observer, 1984)*

'The film's mainstay is its refined sense of the incongruous.' *(Peter John Dyer, 1964)*

'There's warmth and humor in the script that's jam-packed with sinister characters and nerve-tweaking devices; the acting is dandy from the leads on down.' *(Judith Crist)*

MAN WHO SHOT LIBERTY VALANCE, THE

CT: 5 AV: 6.80

1962 US 122 BW WESTERN

D John Ford
W James Warner Bellah Willis Goldbeck

James Stewart ☆ John Wayne Lee Marvin Vera Miles Edmond O'Brien Jeanette Nolan Andy Devine Woody Strode John Carradine Strother Martin Lee Van Cleef John Qualen

Lawyer (James Stewart) is made sheriff of a town terrorized by a mean hombre (Lee Marvin).

This stolid, plodding, predictable western, full of stereotypical characters, is only too obviously an allegory about the bringing of literacy, law and order (in the person of Stewart) to the Old West (personified by Wayne). It was unenthusiastically received on release, especially in America, but is now considered a classic by many. Edith Head was Oscar-nominated for her costume design.

MIXED:

'[This] basically honest, rugged and mature saga has been sapped of a great deal of effect by an obvious, overlong and garrulous anticlimax.' *(A.H. Weiler, New York Times)*

'Plain, substantial, wholesome fare, an uninspired but yeoman John Ford western. It's a bit on the murky and windy side in production and procedure, but it does boast the yeoman services of James Stewart and John Wayne as solid types with good sound feelings for Vera Miles, a yeoman-type heroine.' *(Judith Crist)*

PRO:

'Typical in its gusto and its excitement and also in its suggestion of self-mockery . . . can be fully enjoyed by the sophisticates . . . and by simpler folk . . . Take it as you will, this is a most capable and likeable film.' *(Guardian)*

'John Ford . . . is back on form doing what he does best.' *(Nina Hibbin, Daily Worker)*

'As a maker of westerns, John Ford is a die-hard traditionalist. Not for him the new-fangled approach . . . The pleasure of going to a John Ford film is the pleasure of going to a party and seeing lots of familiar faces . . . With such characters the outcome is pre-determined . . . Mr Stewart ends up ambassador . . . Whereas Mr Wayne just ends up dead.' *(Thomas Wiseman, Sunday Express)*

'A classic western. The definitive one, too, but not, I fear the last one.' *(Leonard Mosley, Daily Express)*

'The old master of the western [Ford] can fill the legends of the frontier with a romantic feeling which nobody else can quite command.' *(Dilys Powell)*

'[Ford's] most important film of the Sixties . . . he seems to be making his final statement on the western . . . It is perhaps the most mournful, tragic film Ford has made.' *(Peter Bogdanovich, John Ford, 1968)*

'The entire film, including the irony that the vicious villain bears the name of Liberty, is an allegorical study of the bringing of democracy and civilization to the Old West, an allegory of liberty as opposed to license . . . When the film makes its points with story, characterization, or images . . . it is effective;

when [it] stops for a discussion of political or emotional issues, it is not.' *(Gerald Mast, A Short History of the Movies, 1971)*

'In what is essentially a re-appraisal of *Stagecoach*, Ford shows western morality finally destroyed by democracy, with literacy as its most insidious weapon.' *(Elkan Allan, NFT Bulletin)*

'One of the great westerns.' *(Pauline Kael)*

MAN WHO WOULD BE KING, THE

CT: 7 AV: 7.71

1975 US 129 C ACTION/ADVENTURE

D John Huston ☆
W John Huston Gladys Hill ☆ AAN from Rudyard Kipling's story

Sean Connery ✔ Michael Caine ✔ Christopher Plummer Saeed Jaffrey ✔ Shakira Caine Jack May

Two con-men (Michael Caine, Sean Connery) persuade Indian tribe in 1880s that they are royal.

Jolly Kipling parable against get-rich-quick imperialism, ably directed by John Huston. He had originally wanted to make it with his friend Humphrey Bogart and Clark Gable, but Caine and Connery fill in admirably. Huston allows his admiration for the two anti-heroes' resourcefulness to cloud the morality of his tale, and turns it into a male bonding buddy-buddy movie. Still, it's a good one.

PRO:

'Has just enough romantic nonsense in it to enchant the child in each of us.' *(New York Times)*

'Huston has now made a good picture – not up to the level of his early best but with sweep and guts and with nicely overblown cinematic eloquence.' *(Stanley Kauffmann)*

'Huston's best film in twenty-three years, or since *The African Queen*.' *(John Simon)*

'Swashbuckling adventure, pure and simple, from the hand of a master. It's unabashed and thrilling and fun.' *(Roger Ebert)*

MIXED:

'As long as [Kipling, played by Christopher Plummer] is on hand to lend an air of how two British con men nearly conquered the never-never highlands of Kafirstan, the movie is an engaging realization of Kipling's wonderful schoolboy tale. But once the caper itself takes over, the movie loses its way, meandering uncertainly from high, bloody adventure to Stingmanship, British style, between the two con men to intimations of what Kipling's story really was – a satirical *tour-de-force* of British imperialism at its most horrific and absurd.' *(Newsweek)*

MAN WITH THE GOLDEN ARM, THE

CT: 5 AV: 5.33

1955 US 119 BW DRAMA

D Otto Preminger
W Walter Newman Lewis Meltzer from Nelson Algren's novel

Frank Sinatra ☆ AAN Kim Novak Eleanor Parker ● Darren McGavin Arnold Stang Robert Strauss

Chicago poker-player (Frank Sinatra) tries to kick his drugs habit.

The intelligentsia rushed to the film's defence when it was threatened with censorship (the Motion Picture Association of America wouldn't give it a certificate); but it was hardly worth the effort. Apart from Sinatra's performance and Elmer Bernstein's jazzy, Oscar-nominated score, there's isn't a lot to recommend it. The tone is sensationalist throughout, and the happy ending is obvious Hollywood hokum; it may have passed for realism in 1955 but it won't do now.

PRO:

'A gripping, fascinating film, expertly produced and directed.' *(Variety)*

'A harsh, uncompromising film and Mr Preminger . . . has managed to make even the black and white of the photography seem angry . . . [He] is so successful . . . that it is a physical relief to come out into the open air.' *(The Times)*

'Its once daring story of the gifted poker dealer, Frank Sinatra, trying to fight the drug habit and other monkeys on his back, may seem ordinary today. But beyond plot, it still provides excellent performances (Sinatra, Eleanor Parker, Darren McGavin) and a situation gritty with truth, glistening with cinematic effectiveness.' *(Judith Crist)*

MIXED:

'The best thing [Sinatra] has ever done . . . And the film is extremely well made. Yet I disliked it more than any picture I have seen for months . . . [It] just isn't my idea of entertainment. It is too sordid, too painful.' *(Richard Nash, Star)*

'Sinatra, always a good actor, excels himself – until the climax . . . [where] it failed: the writhings and the sobs were too mechanical, the cure too slick . . . and we are reduced to conventional Hollywood melodrama.' *(Harold Conway, Daily Sketch)*

'Effective, but in a garish, hyperbolic, and dated way.' *(Pauline Kael)*

ANTI:

'Nothing very surprising or exciting . . . a pretty plain and unimaginative look-see at a lower depths character.' *(Bosley Crowther)*

'In spite of some clever observation, there is about

the film's setting and characters something consciously picturesque, something at once calculating, immoral and cheap.' *(BFI Bulletin)*

'Lacks the serious realism which alone make its treatment on the screen valuable or indeed tolerable. Despite some appealing work by Frank Sinatra and Kim Novak, I just wasn't touched.' *(T. Spender, Daily Worker)*

'The script is inexcusably clumsy, the sets are unbelievable, and the casting is ridiculous. I do not see how Preminger will ever live down casting Eleanor Parker as the malingering wife . . . While it's true no normal person would be enticed into taking dope by seeing this picture, I am not so sure abnormal people may not have come away subconsciously and very complicatedly intrigued . . . As for the happy ending – in the book the addict commits suicide – Sinatra cures himself in a factually impossible way. And there should at least have been mention of the terrible truth that less than two per cent of those "cured", even with medical help, stay that way.' *(Diana Willing, Films in Review)*

MAN WITH THE GOLDEN GUN, THE: *see BOND* SERIES.

MANCHURIAN CANDIDATE, THE

CT: 8 AV: 8.77

1962 US 126 BW SF/THRILLER

D John Frankenheimer ☆
W George Axelrod from Richard Condon's novel

Frank Sinatra ☆ Janet Leigh Laurence Harvey ✔
Angela Lansbury ☆ AAN Henry Silva
James Gregory ☆

US ex-soldier (Frank Sinatra) realizes that a fellow-veteran (Laurence Harvey) has been brainwashed to become an assassin.

Classic conspiracy-thriller, with splendid characters and an extremely gripping plot. Harvey (obliged by his robotic character to underact, for once) is chilling; but Lansbury steals the picture as a mother-monster with White House ambitions. Frankenheimer and Axelrod combine several genres in an interesting and innovative way: noir thriller (with Sinatra as Bogartian hero), science fiction and political satire. Ferris Webster's editing was Oscar-nominated.

'It was devised as a satire on the whole idea of fanaticism, the far Right and the far Left being exactly the same thing, and the idiocy of it.' *(John Frankenheimer)*

'*The Manchurian Candidate*? Satire closes on Saturday night. Political satire starts dead. The movie went from failure to classic without passing through success.' *(George Axelrod)*

ANTI:

'It tries so hard to be different that it fails to be itself.' *(Time)*

MIXED:

'Watching [it] . . . gave me a curious sense of *déjà vu* . . . This was . . . our old childhood friend, the insidious Dr Fu Manchu . . . This film is enormously effective . . . Without question, it is the best-told story of the year. Without question it is also the most irresponsible.' *(Arthur Knight, Saturday Review)*

PRO:

'The unAmerican film of the year.' *(Penelope Houston)*

'As perfect a shibboleth picture as could be imagined.' *(New York Post)*

'Fiendishly clever spy thriller.' *(Alexander Walker, Evening Standard)*

'As an insolent, heartless thriller *The Manchurian Candidate* . . . can be recommended.' *(Dilys Powell)*

'Final evidence that Frankenheimer is one of the most spectacularly-gifted of contemporary American directors . . . No synopsis could convey the extraordinary assortment of humour, tension, excitement, and continual fascination in this magnificent banquet. I can only urge you to gorge yourself as swiftly as possible.' *(Derek Hill, Financial Times)*

'The most sophisticated political satire ever to come out of Hollywood.' *(Pauline Kael)*

'Fiendishly intelligent political thriller, wittily adapted by George Axelrod from Richard Condon's ingenious novel, that mocks both right and left . . . A sophisticated affair, simultaneously exploiting and satirising American paranoia on the eve of the Kennedy assassination.' *(Philip French, NFT Bulletin, 1984)*

MANHATTAN

CT: 10 AV: 8.33

1979 US 96 BW COMEDY/DRAMA/ROMANCE

D Woody Allen ☆
W Woody Allen Marshall Brickman ☆ AAN

Woody Allen Diane Keaton ☆ Michael Murphy
Mariel Hemingway ☆ AAN Meryl Streep Anne Byrne

A middle-aged comedy writer (Woody Allen) recovers from a failed marriage by having affairs with two women: a pretentious narcissist (Diane Keaton) and a precocious teenager (Mariel Hemingway).

Maybe it is narcissistic, and stylistically it isn't perfect: the story is shot a little too dramatically to generate the laughter its jokes deserve. But this is among the funniest, most intelligent and grown-up of all romantic comedies. Allen's direction is better than ever: note his (and cinematographer Gordon Willis's) inventive framing of shots, and the way he uses car and driving imagery throughout. The stars are the city, the Gershwin score, and Woody Allen himself, in that order.

'I've integrated things more . . . It's like a mixture of what I was trying to do with *Annie Hall* and *Interiors*.' *(Woody Allen)*

PRO:

'The only truly great American movie of the 1970s.' *(Andrew Sarris)*

'A prismatic portrait of a time and place that may be studied decades hence to see what kind of people we were.' *(Frank Rich, Time)*

'Allen's nostalgia isn't nostalgic, it's the ironic fist in the velvet glove.' *(Jack Kroll, Newsweek)*

'[Love] is an element which relaxes Mr Allen's fast frenzied style. And now I do laugh – laugh at the comedy which I think is natural to Woody Allen: dialogue-comedy . . . A film dazzlingly funny, true, touching.' *(Dilys Powell)*

ANTI:

'What's missing under Allen's highly saleable self-deprecation, is any true sense of dissatisfaction. Allen's mode, because it lacks valid critical or satirical edge (which Jules Feiffer, at his best, still has), is basically a version of self-love. And self-love, wrapped in awareness, is the prime marketable product these days. In Allen's hands, realism has turned from compassionate criticism to stroking. What George M. Cohan did with the Stars and Stripes in 1919, Allen is doing with neurosis in 1979: waving it, telling us that as long as we're proud of it, we're all pretty damned OK. That's the real romance of *Manhattan*.' *(Stanley Kauffmann)*

'A profoundly and multifariously dishonest picture . . . As in *Annie Hall*, there is again, and still more strongly, the implication that women are wicked or boring and can be redeemed solely through loving Woody Allen, the only decent male on the scene. Yet even this unappetizingly smug self-exaltation is not the ultimate moral (and intellectual) failure of the film. Most irresponsible is the implication that a thoroughly decent man of forty-two can find fulfillment in love and sex only with a seventeen-year-old girl. Mind you, it is neither Tracy's age nor the difference in ages between Tracy and Isaac – not even the underlying real-life nexus between Allen and Hemingway – that bothers me: if Humbert Humbert and Lolita could have found happiness together, I would have been all for it. What I deplore is the notion that maturing corrupts people, and that only being as privilegedly childlike as Isaac and Tracy (though even she may be corrupted by six months in swinging London) can truly love. If there is anything our era does not need – on screen or elsewhere – it is a paean to immaturity, an attempt to pass off infantilism as the sole protector of our amatory relationships.' *(John Simon)*

'Rather squalid . . . The last 30 minutes aren't bad.' *(Shipman)*

MANHATTAN MURDER MYSTERY

CT: 7 AV: 6.50

1994 US C COMEDY/THRILLER

D Woody Allen ☆
W Woody Allen Marshall Brickman ☆

Woody Allen Diane Keaton ☆ Jerry Adler
Alan Alda ✔ Anjelica Huston ✔

The marriage of a film buff and budding restaurateur (Woody Allen and Diane Keaton) comes under stress when she becomes obsessed with the idea that the man in the next door apartment (Jerry Adler) has murdered his wife. The one person who's sympathetic is a divorced playwright (Alan Alda) who has the ulterior motive of fancying Keaton. Meanwhile, Allen is getting the come-hither from a predatory film critic-turned-authoress (Anjelica Huston).

Woody Allen revisits familiar *Manhattan* territory but reworks it self-mockingly as a light-hearted caper. Yes, you may yawn, but haven't we been here before? Aren't Woody's characters always obsessed with food and films? Isn't Alda just reprising good-natured characters he's played before? Aren't the main couple just Annie Hall and Alvy Singer 20 years on, turned into a softer version of the warring Sydney Pollack and Judy Davis in Allen's *Husbands and Wives*?

The answer is yes, yes and yes. And there's more bad news. Allen persists with the nervy, spying camerawork from *Husbands and Wives*, but this time it's ill-suited to the script, which is very much an update of elegant caper movies like *The Thin Man*. And the endless allusions to old films – from *Double Indemnity, Rear Window* and *The Lady From Shanghai* through to Bob Hope comedies – become tiresome: it is as though Allen hopes allusions give an illusion of wit.

But the saving graces are considerable. Diane Keaton has drive and effervescence in the leading role: she's become less mannered over the years, and takes the chance to show she is more of a comedienne than Mia Farrow ever was. Allen seems happy to leave centre-stage to Keaton, except for a few moments when he can indulge his near-forgotten talent for neurotic slapstick.

Most of all, the movie works because Allen has made himself a master of narrative structure. He and his co-writer Marshall Brickman (who last worked together on *Manhattan*) cleverly set up an atmosphere of normality (normal for a Woody Allen film, that is) and proceed to subvert it, in much the way that Hitchcock used to. Even though Allen lacks Hitchcock's directorial flair for suspense, he does enough to keep his audience entertained and guessing. The final half-hour, as the whole idiotic plot gathers momentum and the four experienced leading actors start working together as a crazed comedy team – is terrifically enjoyable.

ANTI:

'If ever a picture seemed improvised, slapped together, disrespectful of the demands of the medium, this is it . . . The slovenliness and cynicism in scene after scene knows no limits or shame . . . Visual excitement has never been Allen's strong suit, and it isn't here either . . . Miss Keaton would be all right for her part if she were willing to settle for clothes and a hairstyle befitting her weight and age. As for Allen . . . he has the face of a middle-aged imp, a too-rumpled Rumpelstiltskin – a nerdy, over-age gnome impossible to warm to. There is amusing ugliness: think of Groucho Mark, of Buster Keaton. And there is the other kind: this.' *(John Simon)*

'Second-string material, a comedy of loose connections in which Woody, Diane Keaton, Alan Alda and company look less like real people than like performers over-working to revive a stiff.' *(Bruce Williamson, Playboy)*

'The picture's one big drawback . . . is Allen's performance. He cannot act. He never could act. There's no sign, at this late date, that he ever will be able to act.' *(Stanley Kauffmann, The New Republic)*

'[Allen] rather overdoes the clumsy schlemiel act.' *(George Perry, Sunday Times)*

MIXED:

'Given his recent circumstances, the distracted, unpolished air of this movie is understandable. It may even be that an air of modest amiability is – for him, for now – the right stance. But he has taught his devotees to expect more, and, perhaps cruelly, we continue to do so.' *(Richard Schickel, Time)*

'A lovely little film, sharp and light as a cheese soufflé . . . Keaton – whom I have always hated – is a treat . . . [The film] has Whodunits Disease; not Whodunit as in murder mystery, but as in Whodunit first. Call them homages, call them rip-offs – but I'm sick of going to the cinema clutching my Halliwell as though I was a tourist doing Italian churches with a Baedeker . . . You'll laugh at this one. You'll fall in love with Diane Keaton at long last. You'll have fun rubber-necking for Soon-Yi in the crowd scenes (she's not there). But also you might just think – what did they make films about, before they made films about films?' *(Julie Burchill, Sunday Times)*

PRO:

'Allen's most enjoyable movie since his segment in 1989's anthology film *New York Stories*, not least because it marks the return of Keaton as his leading lady . . . Dialogue is deft, funny, close to perfect.' *(Tom Gliatto, People Weekly)*

'Terrifically entertaining, a lighthearted escapade that offers comic relief – from both the soap opera of Allen's life and the intensifying moral angst of his recent work . . . It is a joy to watch Keaton and Allen together again, stepping back into their soft-shoe repartee without missing a beat, overlapping each other's sentences with the familiarity of Ginger Rogers and Fred Astaire. And Keaton's spunky, vivacious spirit is a refreshing change from the querulous, nattering whine that Farrow had adopted like a speech impediment.' *(Brian D. Johnson, Maclean's)*

'It isn't the very best Allen but, slight as it is, it is certainly both civilised filmmaking and a consistent pleasure to watch. There are no pretensions at all . . . He knows exactly what he is doing and how to do it. Of how many writer/directors can you say that?' *(Derek Malcolm, Guardian)*

MANHUNTER CT: 6 AV: 6.75

1986 US 115/120 C THRILLER

D Michael Mann ✗
W Michael Mann from Thomas Harris's novel *Red Dragon*

William Petersen ✔ Kim Greist Joan Allen Brian Cox ✔ Dennis Farina Stephen Lang Tom Noonan Patricia Charbonneau

Cop (William Peterson) who thinks like a serial killer tracks one down.

Interesting atmosphere but ultimately too clinical thriller, Brian Cox is a chilling Hannibal Lecter. Often, but erroneously, described as superior to the second film based on a Thomas Harris novel – *Silence of the Lambs*.

'Splendidly stylish and oppressive . . . Functions both as a disturbing examination of voyeurism, and as an often almost unbearably grim suspenser.' *(Geoff Andrew, Time Out)*

'This is the Hannibal Lecter film you should see, a chilling thriller that gets a good grip early on and refuses to let go until the end credits have finished.' *(Rose)*

MANON DES SOURCES CT: 8 AV: 7.93

(aka *Manon of the Springs)*

1986 France 113 C DRAMA/FOREIGN

D Claude Berri ☆
W Claude Berri Gérard Brach ✔ from Marcel Pagnol's novel *L'Eau des Collines*

Yves Montand ☆ Daniel Auteuil ☆ Emmanuelle Béart ✔ Hippolyte Girardot Margarite Lozano Gabriel Bacquier

Ugly peasant (Daniel Auteuil) falls for beautiful shepherdess (Emmanuelle Béart) whose father he and his uncle (Yves Montand) drove to an early death ten years earlier.

Sequel to *Jean de Florette*, this shares with that

picture an eye for the Provence countryside and two marvellous performances. Where Depardieu dominated the first film, Auteuil and Montand come into their own here, and both are marvellous – this may be Montand's finest role. To understand the full impact of the ending, it's a good idea to see the films in order. Critics mostly saw this as a pretty, nostalgic period-piece; but it has a contemporary resonance, in its message that prosperity isn't everything.

MIXED:

'[Montand's] work and Berri's lavish recreation of a vanished Provençal past are the true pleasures of [the film] and not its essentially lightweight attempt to achieve the stature of Greek tragedy or the deep personal warmth of Pagnol himself.' *(Derek Malcolm, Guardian)*

'I perceive little merit beyond Bruno Nuytten's photography.' *(Philip French, Observer)*

'For sheer pleasure this week, go and see [it] . . . In the last resort, Pagnol's story may have Dickensian implausibility: but Berri, his team and his landscapes play it to the hilt.' *(Richard Mayne, Sunday Telegraph)*

PRO:

'Berri has found his true talent with Pagnol, and made an extraordinarily satisfying work. It has the mark of a classic; you feel that it has always existed.' *(David Robinson, The Times)*

'If at all possible, this is almost better than the earlier film, becoming almost heart-stoppingly unbearable when Montand realises the true enormity of his crime.' *(Rose)*

MARIEZ-MOI CE SOIR!: *see* LOVE ME TONIGHT.

MARIUS CT: 6 AV: 7.13

(aka *Fanny)*

1931 France 125 BW DRAMA/FOREIGN

D Alexander Korda ●
W Marcel Pagnol from his play

Raimu ☆, Orane Demazis Pierre Fresnay Fernand Charpin Alida Rouffe Robert Vattier Paul Dulla

Lad (Pierre Fresnay) works in a Marseilles bar for his father Csar (Raimu) and loves local girl Fanny (Orane Demazis), but longs to go to sea.

This warm, exuberant tale suffers from stodgy direction by Korda and a lacklustre performance by Fresnay, but the rich cast of supporting characters goes a long way to compensate. The first part of Pagnol's famous trilogy, it was followed by *Fanny and César*. Originally denied a UK certificate, it was finally released in 1949

MIXED:

'Pagnol at it again: unmarried pregnancy. Some nice moments and some very nice acting, but much too wordy, slow and smug.' *(James Agee, Nation)*

PRO:

'A far cry from the fluffy, musical comedy screen efforts New York audiences have come to expect from that corner of the amusement world . . . Although all the players are first class, special praise is due M. Raimu.' *(New York Times)*

'Its belated appearance could not have been made at a time when it is more likely to be appreciated . . . The warmth and wisdom of [script and direction]; the feeling for the sea . . . but above all, the irreplaceable Raimu . . . [make] the film . . . exuberantly alive. Only Orane Demazis as Fanny suffers from the passage of time . . . a pity, for she acts well.' *(Margaret Hinxman, Time & Tide)*

'It passes the test of time so well that it remains a "must" for the connoisseur. But you're not a connoisseur? You're a low-brow? . . . Don't worry. You can have a brow at ground level and still appreciate [it].' *(Peter Burnup, Sunday Record)*

MARK OF ZORRO, THE CT: 6 AV: 7.56

1940 US 94 BW ACTION/ADVENTURE

D Rouben Mamoulian ☆
W John Tainton Foote Garrett Fort Bess Meredyth from Johnston McCulley's novel *The Curse of Capistrano*

Tyrone Power Basil Rathbone ☆ J. Edward Bromberg ☆ Linda Darnell Eugene Pallette

Returning to California from Spain, young man (Tyrone Power) discovers that his father has been replaced as Alcalde of Los Angeles, and the area is being ruled tyrannically.

The legend of *Robin Hood* rides again. After a slow start, this develops into a superb swashbuckler with great action-sequences. Power is weak in the role played in the 1920 silent version by Fairbanks, but Mamoulian's pictorial flair more than compensates – and Basil Rathbone is marvellous as the Sheriff of Nottingham-style villain. Alfred Newman's score was Oscar-nominated.

'Despite its obvious formula . . . picture holds plenty of entertainment.' *(Variety)*

'Tyrone Power is no Douglas Fairbanks . . . [He] rather overdoes the swishing and his swash is more beautiful than bold. Neither does he vault about with the athletic ease of a proper Zorro . . . But, for all that . . . Mamoulian has kept the picture in the spirit of romantic make believe . . . Mostly, it bounds along at a lively, exciting clip . . . And it has the proper look of spectacle. All right, then, we accede. Sergeant, turn out the guard!' *(Bosley Crowther)*

'Good entertainment . . . It is all nonsense, of

course, but it has the tonic qualities of some fancy long drink, iced and exotic with a dash of cointreau and a cherry . . . And the sun goes on shining and the air is full of hats. A good time, in fact, was had by all.' *(Louis MacNeice, Spectator)*

MARRIAGE OF MARIA BRAUN, THE

CT: 5 AV: 7.27

(aka *Die Ehe Der Maria Braun)*

1979 West Germany 119/120 C DRAMA/FOREIGN

D Rainer Werner Fassbinder
W Peter Märthesheimer Pea Fröhlich Rainer Werner Fassbinder from Fassbinder's idea

Hanna Schygulla ☆ Klaus Löwitsch Ivan Desny Gottfried John Günther Lamprecht Gisela Uhlen

Woman (Hanna Schygulla) schemes her way through life, first in order to survive, then for the sake of her imprisoned husband, but she is ultimately outwitted by men.

Fassbinder's most popular film is still not easily comprehensible; nor are his characters. It is an ironic parable partly about Germany, partly about the battle between the sexes. He certainly has a memorable heroine: the kind of strong, suffering character who appeared in Douglas Sirk's 'women's pictures', and used to be played by Joan Crawford. But this film lacks Hollywood's straightforward passion – deliberately so, since Fassbinder's heroine has had areas of her personality and morality deadened by her experience of war. The director evidently means to identify his alienated heroine with his country; whether you think he succeeds will depend on how far you can go along with his bleak, camp view of human nature. The film is the first in Fassbinder's trilogy about women in post-war Germany, which also includes *Veronika Voss* (1982) and *Lola* (1981).

'The tragedy [Fassbinder] presents is Maria's loss of "femaleness" – sympathy, intuition, empathy . . . and its replacement by "maleness" – a tough cynical competitiveness that leads to self-destruction . . . [His] tragedy has nothing to do with any predestined failure, and everything to do with the woman's success.' *(Tom Noonan, Film Quarterly)*

'[Its] narrative . . . clearly owes much to the tradition of the classical Hollywood melodrama with its central theme of the "irreconcilable" opposition for women between love and career . . . As in his earlier melodramas . . . Fassbinder uses the conventions of the genre to subvert the audience's expectations.' *(Sheila Johnston, Arnofilm)*

'Beautifully, unsparingly ironic . . . One of the most fascinating movies to emerge from West Germany for a long time . . . In a way it's Germany's own self-portrait . . . It can also be absurdly funny.' *(Molly Plowright, Glasgow Herald)*

'To watch this film of Fassbinder's is to realize how carelessly most movies are visualized. There is not a dull shot, not one that fails to catch the eye, provoke the intellect, and remind us what an invigoratingly participatory experience the watching of a film can be.' *(Richard T. Jameson)*

'A movie dripping with period detail, with the costumes and decor he was famous for, with the elegant decadence his characters will sell their souls for in a late-1940s economy without chic retail goods.' *(Roger Ebert)*

MARTY AAW

CT: 5 AV: 8.45

1955 US 91 BW DRAMA

D Delbert Mann ☆ AAW
W Paddy Chayefsky ✗ AAW from his television play

Ernest Borgnine ☆ AAW Betsy Blair ✗ AAN Esther Minciotti Joe Mantell ☆ AAN Jerry Paris

Ugly butcher (Ernest Borgnine) from the Bronx is attracted to plain schoolteacher (Betsy Blair).

Based on a TV play which had starred Rod Steiger, this won the Palme d'Or at Cannes and became a surprise hit in the cinema – mainly because, at the time, it seemed like a breath of fresh, realistic air in a Hollywood dominated by more conventional, beautiful romances. It's expertly put together – Joseph LaShelle's cinematography and the art direction by Edward S. Haworth and Walter Simonds won Oscar nominations – but to modern eyes the treatment of the relationship appears predictable and sentimental; Chayefsky's 'realistic' dialogue – using much repetition – appears mannered; and the women are poorly, patronizingly written.

PRO:

'Warm, human, sometimes sentimental and an enjoyable experience.' *(Variety)*

'As played with enormous skill by Ernest Borgnine, Marty develops rapidly into an utterly believable person.' *(John McCarten, New Yorker)*

'A television play has been transmuted into the best film to come from America in a long time . . . played entirely by character actors, each one hand-picked and perfect in his role.' *(Alan Brien, Evening Standard)*

'If there is a sentimentality . . . it is because life itself can so often become sentimental.' *(Maurice Wiltshire, Daily Mail)*

'Structurally and indeed emotionally there is nothing very novel here . . . But I . . . praise it (with only the faintest of damns) because Delbert Mann has seen fit to direct it as though he were a De Sica.' *(Paul Dehn, News Chronicle)*

ANTI:

'You have to have considerable tolerance to make it through Chayefsky's repetitive dialogue, his insistence on the humanity of "little" people, and his attempt to create poetry out of humble, drab conversations.' *(Pauline Kael)*

MARY POPPINS AAN CT: 5 AV: 7.58

1964 US 139 C MUSICAL/PART CARTOON/FAMILY

D Robert Stevenson AAN
W Bill Walsh Don DaGradi AAN from P.L. Travers's books (music and lyrics by Richard M. Sherman, Robert B. Sherman ☆)

Julie Andrews AAW Dick Van Dyke ●
David Tomlinson Glynis Johns Ed Wynn
Elsa Lanchester Arthur Treacher
Hermione Baddeley

A governess (Julie Andrews) takes charge of two children in 1910 London, and turns out to have magical powers.

I loved the original book so much as a child that I cringed when I saw this Disneyfied version of it. Even more embarrassing than the cuteness is Dick Van Dyke's cockney accent, the most diabolical ever preserved on celluloid. Although Julie Andrews is fresh, lovely and technically proficient, she's too young for the role (her Oscar was clearly a way of compensating her for losing the leading role in *My Fair Lady*); the supporting characters are unmemorable; and the once magical special effects now look primitive, compared to *Who Framed Roger Rabbit*. Despite all those reservations, this is a much-loved musical; some of the songs are catchy; and most kids love it. It won Oscars for Best Song ('Chim-Chim-Cheree'), original musical score, editing and visual effects. Also nominated were Edward Colman's cinematography, the costume design, art direction, adapted musical score, and sound.

PRO:

'If filmed straight, one imagines it could have been drearily old-fashioned, sloppily sentimental. But Disney chose to do it as a musical: and the result is quite astonishing. It somehow manages to combine charm, pace and humour in a way that is completely engrossing: it is a film one could happily sit through again with or without an audience because there is so much to delight the eye.' *(F & F)*

'Delightful . . . [It] is sentimental and whimsical – two adjectives often used to condemn. It is also funny, warm hearted, tuneful gay and very attractive to look at. It think it is an enchanting film, one of Disney's very best.' *(Iain Crawford, Sunday Express)*

'[Andrews] glows like a tree full of twinkling stars . . . She sings like a lark and charmed her way into my heart.' *(News of the World)*

'A likable piece of entertainment, and in its musical numbers, especially the picnic that takes place inside Dick Van Dyke's sidewalk painting and the chimney-sweep dance, it is rather more than merely likable. Indeed, these sequences have a cinematic excitement entirely missing from most film musicals of recent years and far in advance – as the whole film is – of something like *The Sound of Music*, to which it is superior musically, directorially, thespically and even intellectually.' *(Richard Schickel)*

'When a list of the greatest children's movies ever made is assembled, this film will probably tie for top spot with *The Wizard of Oz*.' *(Baseline)*

MIXED:

'A noisy medley of clashing colours, derivative songs, cartoon animals and three-dimensional supporting performers . . . [But] I cannot endorse the premature put-down that appeared last Sunday in *The Observer*'s Back Page, "Disney has added sugar, coyness and prettiness and taken out all the toughness and wit." . . . When I want my wit tough, I go to Dashiell Hammett, not P.L. Travers.' *(Kenneth Tynan, Observer)*

ANTI:

'I have never been able to think of the popular success *Mary Poppins* without shrinking.' *(Dilys Powell)*

MASK CT: 6 AV: 7.07

1985 US 120 C DRAMA

D Peter Bogdanovich ☆
W Anna Hamilton Phelan from her true story of Rocky Dennis

Cher ☆ Sam Elliott Eric Stoltz ☆ Estelle Getty
Richard Dysart Laura Dern

An unconventional mother (Cher) protects her deformed son (Eric Stoltz).

Based on a true story, this has the smell of reality about it, and considerable emotional power. Cher is so lovely to look at that she makes her unattractive lifestyle – hanging around with bikers, taking drugs, casual promiscuity – seem like a set of lovable character quirks. She is redeemed by the love of her son. This is a movie which ought to be clichéd, but isn't; Stoltz, in his screen début, is as outstanding here as he was later in *The Waterdance*.

'Anyone looking for a good uplifting cry should be well satisfied.' *(Variety)*

'Has revived Bogdanovich's fortunes . . . A tremendously moving and uplifting tale . . . At times the film teeters on the brink of pathos but it never topples over, remaining full of genuine compassion and vividly evoking a sense of community. The performances, too, are of a high calibre, especially Cher . . . and newcomer Eric Stoltz.' *(Adrian Turner, Hampstead & Highgate Express)*

'That Bogdanovich has succeeded [in convincingly painting a latter-day saint] against the odds is due, in large measure to Cher and Eric Stoltz . . . It is quite an achievement.' *(Minty Clinch, Ms London)*

'Bogdanovich and Phelan . . . have sentimentalised

the story, but not trivialised it . . . The film is a worthy memorial to a very brave boy . . . It could have been exploitative, but it is not.' *(William Russell, Glasgow Herald)*

'A wonderful movie, a story of high spirits and hope and courage.' *(Roger Ebert)*

MASK, THE

CT: 8 AV: 5 (est)

1994 US 100 C COMEDY

D Charles Russell ✓
W Mike Werb

Jim Carrey ✓ Cameron Diaz ✓ Richard Jeni
Peter Riegert Amy Yasbeck Peter Greene
Max ✓ (as Milo the dog)

Nice nerd Stanley Ipkiss (Jim Carrey) discovers a magic mask that releases his Id and gives him Superheroic powers.

It's difficult to identify with a superhero. Batman, as played by Michael Keaton, was too mysterious, too psychotic and lived in too grand a house. Warren Beatty's Dick Tracy was as cool, smooth and hard as a brilliantined door-knob. And Superman's dad was Marlon Brando. When transformed by his mask, Stanley Ipkiss doesn't set about righting society's wrongs. First, he pays off a few petty scores, gets rich quick and romances the girl of his dreams (Cameron Diaz). This may not be the stuff of which superheroes are traditionally made; but hey, wouldn't most of us be tempted to do the same? Stanley's wild alter ego gives anyone watching him a vicarious release, a rush of adrenaline. He is the incarnation of uninhibited Fun.

There are probably only two actors who could have played the larger-than-life, rip-roaring, multi-voiced Ipkiss: Robin Williams and Jim Carrey. If Williams had played it, we'd have to have put up with lots of schmaltz, so it's just as well they got Carrey, whose personality seems sharper, more cynical. But the thing that most people will be talking about when they leave the cinema are the special effects. These are laugh-out-loud funny, transforming human beings – and Stanley's dog – into live-action versions of Tex Avery cartoons (he's the man who created Daffy Duck and Bugs Bunny). *The Mask* is as revolutionary in its effects as *Terminator 2* or *Who Framed Roger Rabbit?* Along with Greg Cannom's Oscar-worthy make-up and some witty art direction, they show Hollywood technology at its most inventive.

The story begins as implausible and stereotypical. The view of women is on the same juvenile level as *Wayne's World*, and you may – like me – wonder why Stanley's Jack Russell terrior loves him so much when he never gets taken out for a walk. But just as we are starting to yawn and think we have seen it all before, there is the first in a series of neat, cynical twists – including a lovely one which makes us hastily revise our opinion of who the *femme fatale* is in this movie. Before the first half-hour is over, *The Mask* is looking fast, slick and entertaining enough to have been directed by Spielberg, or Robert (*Back To The Future*) Zemeckis. Terrific entertainment.

ANTI:

'Pretty thin stuff . . . a rattletrap Jekyll-and-Hyde farce that surrounds Carrey with a nothing plot and a cast of supporting ciphers (generic thug, generic cop, generic sexpot, etc.).' *(Owen Gleiberman, Entertainment Weekly)*

'That wide, mirthless grin and that arch, knowingly fatuous delivery grow tiring. After a while he comes across as Paul Lynde in a cobra head. And it's no help that this character seems to be a direct descendent of Jack Nicholson's candy-suited Joker and Michael Keaton's leering vaudevillian Beetlejuice.' *(Tom Gliatto, People Weekly)*

MIXED:

'An exceedingly silly fantasy adventure, but it hits the mark with its inventiveness and energy. Much of the latter comes from Carrey, who seems to have found a role perfect for his schizoid schtick . . . Tellingly, though, Carrey seems less comfortable out of the extensive Mask makeup. Perhaps he merely plays the doltish Stanley too convincingly: the character is truly uninteresting.' *(Joe Chidley, Maclean's)*

PRO:

'A perfect vehicle for the talents of Jim Carrey, who underwhelmed me with *Ace Ventura, Pet Detective)* but here seems to have found a story and character that work together with manic energy . . . Cameron Diaz is a true discovery in the film, a genuine sex bomb with a gorgeous face, a wonderful smile, and a gift for comic timing.' *(Roger Ebert)*

'Hip, flip and fly.' *(Tom Charity, Time Out)*

MASQUE OF THE RED DEATH, THE

CT: 7 AV: 6.78

1964 GB 86/89 C HORROR

D Roger Corman ✓
W Charles Beaumont R.Wright Campbell ✓ from Edgar Allan Poe's stories *The Masque of the Red Death* and *Hop-Frog or the Eight Chained Orang-outangs*

Vincent Price Hazel Court Jane Asher
David Weston Patrick Magee Nigel Green
Skip Martin Gaye Brown

Sadistic Satanist prince (Vincent Price) in medieval Italy tries to avoid plague and convert a Christian villager (Jane Asher) to his beliefs.

After a dodgy first scene, Nicolas Roeg's cinematography helps to make this one of the most pictorially exquisite of Corman's films. It has a more intelligent script than usual, cleverly merging two of Poe's stories and exploring the things which might drive a man towards Satanism – mainly, the feeling that a God which would allow plagues to destroy innocent people can't be worth worshipping. Vincent Price's performance keeps the pace going and neatly avoids pretentiousness. The plot is abstruse at times, not helped by the fact that the British censor cut out some black magic sequences. Many consider this Corman's best film; it would make an interesting double bill with Bergman's *The Seventh Seal*, many of whose themes it shares.

MIXED:

'The plot is a bit rickety . . . but much of the film has distinct style . . . [and] does supply some mildly amiable chills – and not too many laughs in the wrong places.' *(Dick Richards, Daily Mirror)*

'Dusts off a trifling Poe classic and adapts it to fit the collected smirks of Vincent Price.' *(Time)*

'Price presides magisterially over the doubtful goings-on . . . Hazel Court gets her throat torn out by a falcon as a little light relief, and only a certain absence of urgency prevents this from ranking with the best of Mr Corman's fantasies.' *(The Times)*

PRO:

'Unquestionably Roger Corman's best film to date.' *(MFB)*

'Corman's first British picture creates a powerful atmosphere of terror and evil; and Price, abandoning his tongue-in-cheek approach, gives a commanding performance.' *(Alan Frank)*

MATADOR

CT: 5 AV: 6.25

1986 Spain 102 C DRAMA/COMEDY/ROMANCE/FOREIGN

D Pedro Almódovar ✗
W Pedro Almódovar ✗

Nacho Martinez Assumpta Serna Eva Cobo Antonio Banderas Bibi Andersson

An everyday tale of two serial killers: one, an ex-matador (Nacho Martinez) who misses the excitement of killing and now gets it by murdering women; the other, a female lawyer (Assumpta Serna) who gets her kicks by stabbing lovers at the moment of orgasm.

Wildly overpraised by many critics, who hailed it either as a masterpiece of black comedy or as steamily sensuous, Pedro Almódovar's *Matador* is silly, psychologically unconvincing and crudely trivializes the connection between sex and violence. Its exploitation of serial killing seems all the more facile and sensationalistic if you compare it to the chilling *Henry: Portrait of a Serial Killer*. Apart from a few moments of eroticism, it's a dreary piece of camp by one of Europe's most overrated directors.

PRO:

'Fiercely funny, executed in a reckless, raucous rage by the most wantonly gifted new filmmaker on the international scene. Almódovar relishes mocking his country's sacred cows. But his ridicule resonates beyond the sex-death obsessions of the bullring. Almódovar assaults the emotions. He makes of passion a bleeding art.' *(Peter Travers, People Weekly)*

'The images are sumptuously sick and funny, with hair ornaments used as daggers, tall women in swirling cloaks, and love rites performed on the matador's hot-pink cape spread fanlike on the floor. This trashiness has its own poetry and bravura.' *(Pauline Kael)*

MIXED:

'It's all well done . . . Any one sequence, seen in isolation, would show the hand of a filmmaker with control and personality. But, assembled, *Matador* is a series of tugs and countertugs that leaves us muddled and remote.' *(Stanley Kauffmann, New Republic)*

'A mess of ludicrously contrived eroticism, pretentious dialogue, and reprehensibly voyeuristic sensationalism. Almódovar's silly, cod-philosophical whodunit impresses only for its bravado.' *(Geoff Andrew, Time Out)*

ANTI:

'Picador, and leave.' *(Christopher Tookey, Sunday Telegraph)*

MATEWAN

CT: 6 AV: 7.62

1987 US 133 C DRAMA

D John Sayles
W John Sayles

Chris Cooper ☆ Will Oldham ☆ Mary McDonnell Bob Gunton James Earl Jones ☆ Kevin Tighe Ken Jenkins Jace Alexander, John Sayles David Strathairn Gordon Clappe Bob Gunton

In 1920, a young man (Chris Cooper) organizes striking miners in West Virginia.

A good, solid film of its kind, with strong characters well played, and excellent, Oscar-nominated cinematography by Haskell Wexler. The view of unionism as a force for good may strike some people nowadays as blinkered and naive, but it's convincing enough within this historical context. Sayles's intention is clearly to remind modern audiences of the people who built trade unions, not those who corrupted them.

PRO:

'When [the inevitable bloody showdown] arrives Sayles ensures that it is felt as a genuine terror and regret rather than release or relish.' *(Ian Penman, The Face)*

'Important . . . because it acts in a way cinema rarely does. Plot, theme and characterisations go hand in hand, ideas and action flow naturally . . . The only crime about the film is that it has taken so long to reach us. Essential.' *(New Musical Express)*

'Doing wonders on a budget of just $4m, Sayles creates a truly exciting film, full of fascinating detail, characters, and a tense story to match. A remarkably fine, stirring movie which neither preaches nor patronises.' *(Rose)*

MIXED:

'Has real virtues and deserves an audience, though between the sombreness of its story and the worthiness of its politics there isn't quite enough fully realised drama.' *(Adam Mars-Jones, Independent)*

MATINEE   CT: 7 AV: 5.83

1992 US 99 C COMEDY

D Joe Dante
W Charlie Haas Jerico Stone Ed Naha

John Goodman ☆ Cathy Moriarty ✓ Simon Fenton Omri Katz Lisa Jakub Dick Miller John Sayles

Lawrence Woolsey (John Goodman), a producer of cheap horror flicks, frightens a Florida town at the time of the Cuban Missile Crisis.

The best things about *Matinee* are the films-within-a-film: there's a priceless parody of a Disney 60s comedy in 'The Shook Up Shopping Cart'. And Woolsey's horror film, 'Mant' ('Half man, half ant – all horror!'), is wonderfully ludicrous: lit in the style of the time and acted with hilarious solemnity, it's the best film parody since Stanley Donen's *Movie Movie*.

Dante has shot the main part of the film with an equally sharp eye, catching the cheap colours and plastic surfaces of 60s life to perfection. As in *Gremlins*, he paces the action with great skill, and takes an anarchic delight in blowing apart small-town American life. The central kids are somewhat under-characterized; but the writers, Charlie Haas (*Gremlins 2*), Jerico Stone (*My Stepmother is an Alien*) and Ed Naha (*Honey, I Shrunk The Kids*) have come up with lines for them which are funny and in character.

There's more potential in this idea than Dante explores. There's something quite moving about Woolsey's father-son relationship with his young fan Gene: it's like a skewed version of the one between the child and the projectionist in *Cinema Paradiso*. It's the awakening within Woolsey of a sense of parental responsibility that makes him finally propose marriage to his longsuffering girlfriend (played by the splendid Cathy Moriarty), and we needed to see more of it.

Dante neatly isolates the peculiar appeal of horror films, and action films in general, particularly for adolescents. He argues that they need to be scared – but in a safe way – at an age where they are starting to lose their innocence and ignorance of the world around them. Such an argument won't convince everyone, but it's a legitimate point of view and expressed with great charm.

MIXED:

'A pretty entertaining sitcom prank that works as long as you're willing to suspend the adult view.' *(Jonathan Romney, New Statesman & Society)*

'Goodman's performance and the excerpts from the film are hilariously accurate. But the rest is depressingly bland.' *(Rose)*

'An okay film geared towards buffs that should have been much better.' *(Variety)*

'Sweet-natured film, full of nostalgia and in-jokes for film buffs, but a little slow (and soft) until it gets rolling.' *(Maltin)*

PRO:

'Manages to combine A-bombs with B-movies and stirrings of adolescent lust to emerge as a charming and funny movie . . . The film brims over with beautifully observed detail, features fine performances and is very funny.' *(Helen Renshaw, Today)*

'A delightful comedy and one of the most charming movies in a long time.' *(Roger Ebert)*

MATTER OF LIFE AND DEATH, A   CT: 8 AV: 9.08

(aka *Stairway to Heaven*)

1946 GB 104 BW/C FANTASY/ROMANCE/DRAMA

D Michael Powell Emeric Pressburger ☆
W Michael Powell Emeric Pressburger ☆

David Niven ☆ Roger Livesey ☆ Kim Hunter ☆ Marius Goring ☆ Raymond Massey ☆ Abraham Sofaer ☆

A pilot (David Niven) bails out of his plane and finds himself in Heaven.

Weird but wonderful, with likeable characters, great cinematography by Jack Cardiff and excellent production design by Hein Heckroth. Niven gives one of his best performances as the doomed airman putting a bold face on disaster; good support, too, from Kim Hunter, Roger Livesey and the rest of the cast; but it's the wit, visual flair and sheer style of the production which makes this a classic. It was oddly unappreciated in Britain on release. Some critics – inexplicably – found it anti-British.

ANTI:

'The striving to appear intellectual is much too apparent . . . Action gives way to talk, some of it flat and dreary.' *(Variety)*

'It is hard to grasp why *A Matter of Life and Death* became the choice for Britain's first Royal Command Film Performance. The film has technical originality and a firmer narrative shape than anything we have seen from Michael Powell and Emeric Pressburger who wrote, produced and directed it. But it is even further away from the essential realism and the true business of the British movie than their two recent films, *I Know Where I'm Going* and *Canterbury Tales* . . . [Heaven is] an illimitable Wembley stadium, surrounded by tinkly music and mists, from which all men of insight, if they were ever careless enough to get there, would quickly blaspheme their way out.' *(Richard Winnington)*

'Visual narrative, cinematic sense; there is no denying the quality of the film in excitement, tension, pictorial shock. The quality of its imagination is another matter . . . From the beginning the situation is melodramatic rather than dramatic or poetic; the characters – David Niven's handsome, well-spoken young airman, Kim Hunter's pleasant, competent girl – are the characters of journalism and the novelette. And the central problem emerges as trivial . . . Platitudes about freedom and brotherhood, however ably delivered, won't turn a trivial story into a valid theme for treatment so spectacular . . . An audacious, sometimes beautiful, but basically sensational film about nothing.' *(Dilys Powell)*

'The concept and indeed the execution are grandiose but the views expressed are so trite that you are unlikely even to award the thing the marks it deserves for audacity.' *(Shipman)*

PRO:

'Powell and Pressburger [are] . . . a couple of men who know cinema well and are willing to experiment . . . Daring in production and satire [and] beautifully executed . . . this film is a delight from start to finish . . . Done with imagination and ingenuity; and it is full of adult surprises.' *(Philip T. Hartung, Commonweal)*

'Brilliant production qualities unmatched to date in purely cinematic innovation, masterly use of colour and remarkable blend of inventiveness and artistry . . . Early scenes somewhat jejeune in exchange of soulful romantic passages between doomed airman and pretty girl, but in general narration embraces charming romance, delightful whimsy, astringent political satire and grim operation drama. Story provocative . . . Direction masterly . . . Acting delightful.' *(Today's Cinema)*

'Brilliantly conceived phantasmagoria, deftly executed in Technicolor . . . David Niven has never done a better job and its blend of ethereal fantasy and down-to-earth pathology and romance is superb. Outstanding British picture, a film which deserves, nay demands, universal success.' *(Kine Weekly)*

'Not only fulfils [Powell and Pressburger's] brief of promoting greater understanding between the two nations concerned [UK & US], but is also an impassioned assertion of eternal love, a statement of faith in the individual and a visual *tour de force* as well.' *(Allan Hunter & Kenny Mathieson, 1992)*

MAY FOOLS: *see* MILOU IN MAI.

MAYERLING CT: 6 AV: 7.40

1936 US 96 BW ROMANCE/DRAMA/FOREIGN

D Anatole Litvak
W Joseph Kessel Irma Von Cube from Claude Anet's novel *Idyl's End*

Charles Boyer ☆ Danielle Darrieux ☆ Suzy Prim Jean Dax Gabrielle Dorziat Jean Debucourt Marthe Regnier

Heir to Austrian Empire (Charles Boyer) has doomed love affair with a 17-year-old aristocrat (Danielle Darrieux).

Darrieux is so gorgeous that it's easy to see why the prince is willing to give up an empire for her. Based on a true story, but immaculately produced in high romantic style. An international hit. There was a very boring remake in 1968, starring Omar Sharif and Catherine Deneuve.

MIXED:

'Technically the direction is sometimes mannered, particularly in its use of the superimposition and the long (and not very significant) dissolve.' *(A. Vesselo, MFB)*

PRO:

'One of the greatest love stories ever brought to the screen.' *(Virgin)*

'An amazingly good film. The acting is superb and the story is very interesting.' *(Somerset Maugham, Contemporary Interview)*

'One of the most memorable of all French romantic movies. (Several less effective versions followed.) Anatole Litvak directed with far more delicacy than he showed in his later work.' *(Pauline Kael)*

MCCABE & MRS. MILLER CT: 6 AV: 7.31

1971 US 120 C WESTERN/ROMANCE

D Robert Altman ☆
W Robert Altman Brian McKay from Edmund Naughton's novel *McCabe*

Warren Beatty Julie Christie ✗ AAN René Auberjonois Hugh Millais Shelley Duvall John Schuck Keith Carradine

A gambler (Warren Beatty) sets up a brothel in a northwest mining town.

Robert Altman's cheekily anti-heroic dissection of western frontier myth was a flop when first released in 1971, but has become more respected with the years. It's not quite a masterpiece. The soundtrack of Leonard Cohen songs gives the movie a dated air, and slows the action at times to a suicidal standstill; nor have I much enthusiasm for Warren Beatty's performance as McCabe. As usual, Beatty plays a cocky schmuck; and, whenever called upon to register much in the way of emotion, he simply turns his back to camera. Still, the movie has a refreshingly realistic angle on the wild west; it looks terrific; and there's a memorable closing sequence in the snow, when the cowardly McCabe silently stalks the killers who have been hired to get him.

PRO:

'*McCabe & Mrs. Miller* is organic because its central theme – the dilemma of the individual seeking community while retaining individuality – is present in every sequence, virtually every frame, of the film.' *(James Bernardoni, The New Hollywood, 1991)*

'One of best films of the early Seventies.' *(Danny Peary)*

'A beautiful pipe dream of a movie: Robert Altman's fleeting vision of what frontier life might have been.' *(Pauline Kael)*

MIXED:

'Suffers from Altman's taste for verbal obfuscation and it also suffers from the drip of Leonard Cohen's weary religious allegories on the music track . . . But it does have a slow, bitter distinction and an unstressed compassion which grows on you.' *(Gavin Millar, Listener)*

'The mixture doesn't fizz and is no more intoxicating than cream soda. Why? Too much McCabe and far too little Mrs Miller . . . The characters are never fully developed and the result of trying to tell too many stories is often utter confusion. But the stark, winterland settings are superb.' *(Arthur Thirkell, Daily Mirror)*

'Visually . . . [it] is superb. It has a real feel of time and place. But the story . . . is monumentally tedious to follow. It is like reading a novel minus half its pages, the ones in which the interesting things happen.' *(Richard Barkley, Sunday Express)*

ANTI:

'Christie . . . trailing about the worst Cockney accent in film history, doesn't get even vaguely under the skin of the part . . . Beatty doesn't seem quite sure what he is . . . The story is disjointed to the point of incoherence.' *(Felix Barker, Evening News)*

'Altman often seems to be trying to make his movie worse than it actually is. Working on impulses that seem more self-destructive than artistic, [he] insists on slicking up this straightforward saga with a barrage of stylistic fillips . . . that badly undercut the action . . . Beatty seems in danger, once again, of changing into a lump.' *(Jay Cocks, Time)*

'The plot should . . . rise to the excitement of a showdown; under Robert Altman's direction it is a slowdown, a kind of low-comedy *High Noon* finish where – this is the twist – all are losers. The movie is remarkably pretentious, its basic unit being neither a scene nor a shot, but a heavy hint or an arch symbol. Half the dialogue is delivered *sotto voce* out of the corners of people's mouths in a remote corner of the screen, or entirely off it; some of the sights are similarly relegated to the farthest crannies of the frame. The moviegoer now risks hurtling over the edge of his seat while straining to the utmost his eyes and ears (Julie Christie's accent is an additional burden on the latter) – rather as if he were a solitary sentinel on a foggy battlefield, with the enemy apt to strike anywhere, any moment . . . The poor continuity is given conclusive disruption by the constantly recurring balladeering of Leonard Cohen, the Rod McKuen of the pseudoliterate.' *(John Simon)*

MEAN STREETS

CT: 7 AV: 7.93

1973 US 110 C DRAMA

D Martin Scorsese ☆
W Martin Scorsese Mardik Martin

Harvey Keitel ☆ Robert De Niro ☆ David Proval
Amy Robinson Cesare Danova Richard Romanus

A young man (Harvey Keitel) grows up in the gangster-dominated world of Little Italy.

Critically acclaimed and sporadically impressive early Scorsese, with loads of atmosphere and good performances from young Robert De Niro and Harvey Keitel as young Italian-Americans on the make in New York. Its style is obviously indebted to Italian neo-realism, and the film has often been compared to Fellini's *I Vitelloni*. The lack of narrative progression may prevent it from being a truly great film, but it's still impressive.

ANTI:

'What may well prove the year's most overrated film . . . largely child's play – and rather sloppily written, improvised, acted, photographed and edited child's play at that . . . Comparisons to Fellini's masterpiece, *I Vitelloni*, glibly enunciated by certain critics, are otiose: not only do Fellini's characters exude a comic-pathetic humanity that Scorsese's never achieve, also there is organization in Fellini's film, so that events build toward climaxes and resolutions, however wan they may be – whereas *Mean Streets* merely slaps an arbitrary and unenlightening ending on ramblings that could go on forever, and indeed seem to do so.' *(John Simon)*

'Lacks a sense of story and structure . . . Unless a film-maker respects the needs of his audience, he can't complain if that audience fails to show up.' *(Variety)*

PRO:

'Extraordinarily rich and distinguished on many levels.' *(Joseph Gelmis)*

'Martin Scorsese's *Mean Streets* isn't so much a gangster movie as a perceptive, sympathetic, finally tragic story about how it is to grow up in a gangster environment . . . He shot on location in Little Italy, where he was born and where he seems to know every nuance of architecture and personality, and his story isn't built like a conventional drama: it emerges from the daily lives of the characters. They hang out. They go to the movies. They eat, they drink, they get in sudden fights that end as quickly as a summer storm. Scorsese photographs them with fiercely driven visual style. We never have the sense of a scene being set up and then played out; his characters hurry to their dooms while the camera tries to keep pace. There's an improvisational feel even in scenes that we know, because of their structure, couldn't have been improvised.' *(Roger Ebert)*

'A true original, and a triumph of personal filmmaking. This picture about the experience of growing up in New York's Little Italy has an unsettling, episodic rhythm and it's dizzyingly sensual. The director, Martin Scorsese, shows us a thicker-textured rot than we have ever had in an American movie, and a riper sense of evil.' *(Pauline Kael)*

'A terrifically well-made film, sharply photographed, and crisply edited, with the usual assured visual flair Scorsese puts into all of his films. Virtually plotless, *Mean Streets* offers a series of vignettes detailing life in Little Italy. The natural progression of the situations is so lifelike that no plot is necessary, and the characters are so realistic that the film is fascinating.' *(Baseline)*

MEDITERRANEO AAW CT: 7 AV: 6.14

(aka *Mediterranean*)

1991 Italy 92 C WAR/COMEDY/ROMANCE

D Gabriele Salvatores ☆
W Vincenzo Monteleone

Diego Abatantuono Claudio Bigagli Giuseppe Cederna Claudio Bisio Gigio Alberti Ugo Conti

A platoon of hopeless Italian misfits arrives on an Aegean island to keep it safe for fascism and ends up going native in spectacular style.

If you've ever wondered why the Italian army got such a bad reputation, see *Mediterraneo*. It's a novelty to see a movie in which the British are the enemy, but this isn't a conventional war film in any sense. There are no baddies. No one behaves with the slightest heroism or dies in action – the one mortality is a donkey, shot because it fails to give the right password.

Most Oscar-winning films have pretensions to realism, depth or social significance, but this is the exception. It's an exercise in escapism and wish-fulfilment: War re-imagined as a Club Med holiday. If any other nation had made *Mediterraneo*, the film might reasonably have been accused of racism. The cast seems drawn from stock: the cowardly deserter, the untrustworthy Turk, the tart with the heart of gold . . . But it's an enjoyable, lightweight comedy with a seductive delight in its own hedonism. If you're in search of a 'feelgood' movie with the warmth of Aegean sunshine, it can be highly recommended.

ANTI:

'A thin and obvious piece, with a simple-minded sense of humour . . . It's got little in the way of real guts, intelligence, sense of adventure or charisma.' *(Winnert)*

'The two female characters are little more than walking dolls with coy expressions. They are pretty but vacuous, much like the film itself.' *(Baseline)*

PRO:

'Sly and seductive.' *(New York Post)*

'A charming comedy.' *(New York Times)*

'Lyrical, warm-hearted and wonderfully touching.' *(Sheridan Morley, Sunday Express)*

MEDIUM COOL CT: 6 AV: 7.78

1969 US 111 C DRAMA

D Haskell Wexler ☆
W Haskell Wexler from Jack Couffer's novel *The Concrete Wilderness*

Robert Foster Verna Bloom Peter Bonerz Marianna Hill Harold Blankenship Sid McCoy Christine Bergstrom Robert McAndrew William Sickinger Beverly Younger

A TV cameraman (Robert Foster) strives to remain detached from the current events he is covering – which include the 1968 riot at the Democrat Convention in Chicago.

An interesting rarity, fuelled by resentment of the war in Vietnam. Wexler, a great cinematographer here making a Godard-influenced directorial début, is guilty of heavy-handedness and an assumption that there's only one side to each political question; but his sincerity and anger shine through. Paramount were so nervous of the movie's politics that they left it on the shelf for a year, until *Easy Rider* made it obvious there was a market for counter-cultural films. It was given an 18 certificate, supposedly because of nudity, but more probably because of its inflammatory political content.

ANTI:

'Buildup . . . frequently is confusing and motives difficult to fathom.' *(Variety)*

PRO:

'A deeply moving questioning of America's violence and voyeurism.' *(Jan Dawson)*

'A staggering and illuminating film that has hit me like a jolt of electro-shock therapy in a season of psychological placebos . . . It's that miraculous circumstance seldom seen in American movies – the truth on film.' *(Rex Reed)*

'I can't think of any film that tells one more about

the texture of American life today.' *(Michael Billington, Illustrated London News)*

'A landmark in the new American cinema . . . A Hollywood film for the first time faces up to the wretchednesses beneath our prosperity; dares to give us a political America, and one whose politics are not suffused with health.' *(John Simon)*

MEET JOHN DOE

CT: 5 AV: 7.25

1941 US 123/135 BW DRAMA/SOCIAL

D Frank Capra ☆
W Robert Riskin from Robert Presnell and Richard Connell's story *The Life and Death of John Doe* AAN

Gary Cooper Barbara Stanwyck ☆ Edward Arnold ☆ Walter Brennan James Gleason Spring Byington Gene Lockhart

Reporter (Barbara Stanwyck) concocts letter from 'John Doe' complaining about politicians who ignore the homeless, and threatening to jump off a building on Christmas Eve. She then hires an ex-baseball player (Gary Cooper) to impersonate her creation.

Much acclaimed, but the most tedious and didactic of all Capra's social films. Capra and Riskin were concerned to warn Americans about Fascist forces in their midst, but this purpose leads them into some uncharacteristic miscalculations. Their view of ordinary Americans seems patronizing, and Cooper's character comes across as a sanctimonious bore. And the tone is too dark and realistic for the obviously artificial plot.

PRO:

'Capra is as skilled as ever in keeping things moving along briskly and dramatically – though here and there are some pretty long speeches which for all his artful manipulation have something of the effect of a set aria in an opera. He is still gifted in making characters, particularly background characters, vivid and alive – though there is a reporter in this picture who appears to perform on the principle that tripping over a spitoon is always funny. Sentimentalities are neatly balanced with sharp commentaries on sentimentality.' *(James Shelley Hamilton, NBR)*

'By long odds the best thing Capra has done; it raises him to greater heights, gives him new importance, gives the screen new dignity. There is a lesson in *Meet John Doe* as universal as humanity itself, a lesson driven home by great screen writing, great direction, great acting. For two hours it will hold you in its grip, thrill you with its power, melt you with its humanness, leave you speechless when it ends. It is one of the greatest arguments for right living ever presented by any medium. And still it is superb entertainment.' *(Welford Beaton, Hollywood Spectator)*

'A superbly produced, wonderfully acted, beautifully written motion picture based on the simple theme that everything would be sweetness and light if we would make an effort to know one another better. It comes at a time when the country is hungry for such homely, down-to-earth sentiment.' *(Harry Evans, Family Circle)*

ANTI:

'The synthetic fabric of the story is the weakness.' *(Variety)*

'Frank Capra and Robert Riskin have provided an "inspirational" anthem, aimed at the more emotional members of the country's corn belt. Its rhythms proffer the intellectual stimulus of an Aimee Semple McPherson camp meeting, plus the added delights of such civilized bons mots as one encounters at a gathering of the International Ladies Garment Workers' Union. All stops are pulled out in sentimentalizing the bucolic viewpoint, and the considerable din fondly hopes to be mistaken for a sublime orchestration of democracy.' *(Herb Sterne)*

'For the sake of a happy ending that would keep Gary Cooper alive, the meanings were so distorted that the original authors sued . . . It starts out in the confident Capra manner, but with a darker tone; by the end, you feel puzzled and cheated.' *(Pauline Kael, 1978)*

MEET ME IN ST. LOUIS

CT: 8 AV: 8.81

1944 US 113 C MUSICAL/FAMILY/ROMANCE

D Vincente Minnelli ☆
W Irving Brecher Fred Finklehoffe ☆ AAN from Sally Benson's stories

Judy Garland ☆ Margaret O'Brien ☆ Leon Ames June Lockhart Harry Davenport Marjorie Main Mary Astor ☆ Lucille Bremer Tom Drake Joan Carroll Hank Daniels

Around the time of the 1904 World's Fair, a prosperous St. Louis businessman and his wife (Leon Ames and Mary Astor) try to cope with four daughters (Judy Garland, Lucille Bremer, Joan Carroll, and Margaret O'Brien), and a son (Hank Daniels).

Charming, lyrical musical about an idealized American family life. There are a few defects: there isn't much story, the dark mischief represented – brilliantly – by Margaret O'Brien rather shows up the artificiality of her surroundings, and Tom Drake doesn't seem a worthy suitor for Judy Garland, a fact which weakens the ending. Contemporary critics found plenty to sneer at; but the public took this movie to its heart, and rightly so. Minnelli's directorial talents are in full bloom; the score is delightful; MGM's production values are superb; and Garland is at her loveliest and most talented. George Folsey's cinematography was Oscar-nominated, as was 'The Trolley Song' (music and lyrics by Ralph Blane and Hugh Martin).

MIXED:

'Most of its rather pretty new and old tunes are sung in an up-to-date chromium-and-glucose style which bitterly imposes on one's ability to believe that the year is 1903; and most of its sets and costumes and colors and characters are too perfectly waxen to belong to that or any other year. Indeed, this habit of sumptuous idealization seriously reduces the value even of the few scenes on which I chiefly base my liking for the picture; but at the same time, and for that matter nearly all the time, it gives you, for once, something most unusually pretty to watch.' *(James Agee)*

'Judy Garland's singing slips easily and naturally into this rosy scene which for all its charm began to pall on me after just about one hour and twenty minutes.' *(Richard Winnington)*

PRO:

'Wholesome in story, colorful both in background and its literal Technicolor, and as American as the World's Series.' *(Variety)*

'The sets and Technicolor photography set a captivating mood, and director Vincente Minnelli has paced the piece for a leisurely and wholly encompassing charm. The costumes, by Irene Sharaff, are wonderfully decorative, and aid to provide a pleasure no other musical film has so successfully managed since *Cover Girl* . . . Judy Garland, both pert and pretty, again proves that she is a persuasive performer, as well as one of the screen's top purveyors of popular tunes . . . Mary Astor, one of the most lovely ladies to face a camera, is excellent as usual.' *(Herb Sterne)*

'A family group framed in velvet and tinsel . . . It has everything a romantic musical should have.' *(Dilys Powell, 1955)*

'In *Meet Me in St. Louis* we can for the first time see Minnelli's talents whole, or nearly whole (there is still almost no real dance for him to cope with). And it is here that we begin to appreciate the secret of his special way with musicals . . . *Meet Me in St. Louis* is conceived and directed as a coherent drama, a story about believable people in a believable situation. The musical episodes are all judged from the outset according to their power to advance the story, epitomize a situation, intensify a moon; they all have to have their dramatic raison d'être.' *(John Russell Taylor & Arthur Jackson, 1971)*

'Some friends who joined me not long ago in watching *Meet Me in St. Louis* . . . said they weren't sure it was the kind of movie they'd want little girls exposed to, because the lives of the two ingenues (Judy Garland and Lucille Bremer) revolve around finding men to marry. (Would they hesitate before handing their daughters Jane Austen?)' *(Steve Vineberg, 90s)*

MEET THE GHOSTS: *see* THE *FRANKENSTEIN* SERIES (ABBOTT AND COSTELLO MEET FRANKENSTEIN).

MEET WHIPLASH WILLIE: *see* FORTUNE COOKIE, THE.

MELVIN AND HOWARD CT: 6 AV: 7.75

1981 US 95 C COMEDY/DRAMA

D Jonathan Demme
W Bo Goldman ☆ AAW

Paul LeMat ✔ Jason Robards Jr ☆ AAN
Mary Steenburgen ☆ AAW Dabney Coleman
Gloria Grahame Michael J. Pollard
Pamela Reed ✔ Elizabeth Cheshire

Milkman Melvin Dummar (Paul LeMat) is kind to a hobo (Jason Robards Jr) in the Nevada desert, and disbelieves him when he says he is Howard Hughes. Eight years later, on Hughes's death, the milkman finds he has been left $156 million.

Offbeat, downbeat comedy based on a true story – if you can believe Melvin Dummar. It doesn't much matter whether we do or not, because the title of this movie is misleading. It's far more about Melvin, and ordinary people like him, than it is about Howard Hughes. This is a gentle, meandering, ironic tour of a side of American life not often encountered; and the film-makers' achievement is that they view it with compassion and don't patronize their characters, all of whom are well played. Mary Steenburgen is outstanding as Dummar's go-go dancer wife.

ANTI:

'Never quite lives up to its satiric or dramatic potential, suffering from a somewhat sidelong approach to Melvin's odyssey that renders the film more engaging than truly compelling.' *(Virgin)*

PRO:

'A pungent fable about the elusiveness of the American Dream . . . Exemplary for its rare concentration on the quality, or lack of it, in Middle American life, and incisive, if indirect, examination of the no-win syndrome for contemporary proletariat.' *(Variety)*

'A marvellous story and [the film] makes the most of it . . . highly recommended.' *(John du Pré, Sunday People)*

'I got the greatest sheer enjoyment out of [it] because of its narrative, visual qualities, and because of the unsolved puzzle we are left to take home with us.' *(Peter Clayton, Sunday Telegraph)*

'An almost flawless act of sympathetic imagination. Demme and Goldman have entered into the soul of American blue-collar suckerdom; they have taken for their hero a chucklehead who is hooked on TV game shows, and they have made us understand how it was that when something big – something legendary – touched his life, nobody could believe it . . . When Robards' Howard Hughes responds to Melvin's amiable prodding and begins to enjoy himself on a simple level and sings "Bye, Bye, Blackbird", it's a great moment. Hughes' eyes are an old man's eyes – faded into the past, shiny and glazed by recollections – yet intense. You feel that his grungy paranoia has melted away, that he has been healed . . . This picture has the same beautiful dippy warmth as its characters; it's what might have happened if Jean Renoir had directed a comedy script by Preston Sturges.' *(Pauline Kael)*

'It shows the flip side of Gary Gilmore's Utah. It is a world of mobile homes, Pop Tarts, dust, kids, and dreams of glory. It's pretty clear how this movie got made. The producers started with the notion that the story of the mysterious Hughes will might make a good courtroom thriller. Well, maybe it would have. But my hunch is that when they met Dummar, they had the good sense to realize that they could get a better – and certainly a funnier – story out of what happened to him between the day he met Hughes and the day the will was discovered. Dummar is the kind of guy who thinks they oughta make a movie out of his life. This time, he was right.' *(Roger Ebert)*

MEN, THE

CT: 6 AV: 7.82

(aka *Battle Stripe)*

1950 US 85 BW WAR/DRAMA

D Fred Zinnemann ☆
W Carl Foreman AAN

Marlon Brando ☆ Teresa Wright ☆ Everett Sloane ☆ Jack Webb Howard St. John Richard Erdman Arthur Jurado

War veteran paraplegics struggle to come to terms with their condition.

Brando gives his first, and one of his most memorable, screen performances as a young man confined to a wheelchair by war injuries. Zinnemann supplies his usual expert direction and prevents producer Stanley Kramer and writer Carl Foreman from becoming too mawkish or didactically melodramatic. The film's main fault is its conventional 'good taste'. Its reluctance to be sexually or politically controversial now looks dated, compared with a movie such as *The Waterdance*, which covers much of the same ground more honestly.

PRO:

'Don't be misled into feeling that to see this film is merely a duty; it is, simply, an experience worth having.' *(Richard Mallett, Punch)*

'A remarkable film which explores the relationships of a number of human beings living in circumstances of unusual tension and stress, while affording a dramatically realistic view of the mechanics of their existence. Most of the men are played by actual paraplegics and the film is dedicated to them.' *(Richard Winnington)*

'As the paralysed soldier, a newcomer from the stage, Marlon Brando, gives a strong and penetrating account of an isolated, bitter and savage man gradually being reconciled to his own tragedy.' *(Dilys Powell)*

'Marlon Brando is going to make a stir. He has an urgency about his acting. A brooding young man with puzzled eyes, he opens his mouth as though he has difficulty in forcing his thoughts into the open. So that when his words come the spontaneity is complete.' *(Daily Herald)*

MIXED:

'As a bold, brave motion picture, *The Men* is to be applauded; but it would be a mistake to imagine that noble intentions and the courage to speak in hitherto unmentionable medical jargon necessarily makes great films . . . Does underline the essential weakness in his [producer Kramer's] work: a certain lack of warmth and depth which is perhaps the inevitable result of veering too sharply from the sentimentality which many film-makers administer in large overdoses . . . Marlon Brando, as the tortured hero, is quite the most tremendous, if unlikeable, newcomer of the year.' *(Margaret Hinxman)*

'Conventional melodramatic banalities mar the Carl Foreman script, but it's an economical, vivid narrative.' *(Pauline Kael)*

ANTI:

'Once or twice the facts are, I think, unfairly stated. It is not the practice in civilized society to pause with the restaurant fork half-way to the mouth in order to stare lengthily at the wheel-chair which has just come in; and I doubt whether on her wedding night a young woman who had up to that moment shown nothing but understanding of the sick man's nervous miseries would have made such a fuss about the champagne spilt on the carpet. Indeed the girl's character and feelings are all through only superficially explored. But my lukewarmness has other causes. The film seems to me to be a result of the half-baked theory that an art which is adult has to deal with problems. *The Men* is all problem; the problem quite overshadows the people.' *(Dilys Powell)*

'Although Stanley Kramer's typically soapy production focuses on Brando's tempestuous relationship (wrecked by his feelings of shame and inadequacy) with devoted fiancée Teresa Wright (all syrupy sincerity), the film timidly skirts problems of sexual frustration and impotence. It also almost totally ignores the causes of the paraplegics' disabilities: not one of them ever expresses regret at having ruined life and limb for Uncle Sam.' *(Geoff Andrew, Time Out)*

MEPHISTO AAW CT: 8 AV: 8.00

1981 Hungary 135/144/160 C DRAMA/WAR/FOREIGN

D István Szabó ☆
W István Szabó Péter Dobai from Klaus Mann's novel

Klaus Maria Brandauer ☆ Krystyna Janda Ildikó Bánsági Karin Boyd Rolf Hoppe Christine Harbot György Cserhalmi

An actor (Klaus Maria Brandauer) sells his soul to the Devil (or, in this case, the Nazis) for worldly rewards.

A superbly directed drama, magically photographed by Lajos Koltai. Klaus Maria Brandauer, as Hendrik Hofgen, gives one of the great acting performances. His character is based on novelist Klaus Mann's brother-in-law, Gustaf Grundgens, who had been famous for his performance as Mephistopheles.

MIXED:

'Hofgen . . . seems too small for the epic scale of the attack. The picture is like *Citizen Kane* with somebody like John Dean at its center. The film is gripping but its stern air of rectitude produces discomfort; essentially Szabó seems to be condemning Hofgen for being an actor.' *(Pauline Kael)*

PRO:

'The screen's quintessential portrait of the artist as weak-willed, slimy opportunist, prostituting, corrupting, and destroying himself by inches as he toadies to a fascist regime. In Brandauer's hands Grundgens has posthumously won an evil immortality. Not that Hendrik is unattractive or unsympathetic. One of the great qualities of Szabó's film is that it makes us see the sympathetic side of Hendrik – his attempts to use his influence to help his friends, to administer "justly" as part of a fascist bureaucracy – and the real power and brilliance of his acting. He isn't an easy target for ridicule or contempt. To a degree, we can follow the justifications and sophistries he falls into – that he must preserve his art in the face of everything; that it can stay untouched by the bloodshed and chaos around him.' *(Michael Wilmington)*

'To watch a clever rogue played by [this] actor with the power of an Olivier in his prime, is to be totally ingested into the hideous ambiguities of daily survival in Nazi Germany.' *(Alexander Walker, Evening Standard)*

'Seldom has a film owed so much to a central bravado performance as [this].' *(Patrick Gibbs, Daily Telegraph)*

'A totally convincing study of the devastating moral compromises made by one weak man in politically trying times . . . What is most remarkable . . . is the rigour with which it develops all aspects of its protagonist's personality, however unpleasant, while at the same time maintaining audience identification . . . A very major work – totally absorbing, intellectually challenging, stunningly photographed, and with a superb central performance.' *(Jack Babuscio, Gay News)*

'A companion film to Fassbinder's *The Marriage of Maria Braun*. The Szabó film shows a man compromising his way to the top by lying to himself and everybody else, and throwing aside all moral standards. It ends as World War II is under way. The Fassbinder film begins after the destruction of the war, showing a woman clawing her way out of the rubble and repeating the same process of compromise, lies, and unquestioning materialism. Both the man in the Szabó film and the woman in the Fassbinder film maintain one love affair all through everything, using their love (he for a black woman, she for a convict) as a sort of token contempt for a society whose corrupt values they otherwise completely accept. The fact that they can still love, of course, makes it impossible for them to quite deceive themselves. That is the price they pay for their deals with the devil.' *(Roger Ebert)*

METROPOLIS CT: 6 AV: 8.80

1926/1984 Germany 120/83 BW SF/SILENT/FOREIGN

D Fritz Lang ☆
W Thea von Harbou

Alfred Abel Gustav Fröhlich Brigitte Helm Rudolf Klein-Rogge Fritz Rasp

Tyrannical industrialist (Alfred Abel) plots to incite riots so that he can crush the workers' rebelliousness, but reckons without his son (Gustav Fröhlich) who has fallen in love with one of them (Brigitte Helm).

The movie for which Fritz Lang will be longest remembered is a seminal science fiction film, despite a nonsensical narrative, static camerawork, a suspiciously fascistic message, strip-cartoon characters, and outrageous overacting. It has always attracted a mixed response, but few would deny its visual splendours. It mixes futuristic science fiction with Gothic horror, with remarkable results. Though it is not fashionable to say so, the 1984 version with a crass rock soundtrack by Giorgio Moroder cuts out most of the longueurs and is clearer – you can always turn the sound down,

ANTI:

'Quite the silliest film.' *(H.G. Wells, who took exception to the notion that machinery would enslave humans, rather than set them free)*

MIXED:

'The film has a remarkable pictorial power, and, in spite of its occasional solemnities, is one which will repay study by those who are interested in the development of a separate cinematographic technique. When it imitates the stage it often fails; but, when it remains on its own territory, it proves how wide are the boundaries of that territory and how little they have hitherto been explored.' *(The Times)*

'So grandiose a theme as that which *Metropolis* attempts to develop demanded, of course, something of the epic scale. The cinema, even here at its best, and full as it is of invention and thrill, is still only at the mental age of seventeen. It is still – quite rightly – far more concerned with its medium than with what its medium may most magnificently express . . . Yet *Metropolis* is the by far the most nearly adult picture we have seen. There are moments when it touches real greatness.' *(Spectator)*

'Although Carl Freund, the camera man for *The Last Laugh* and *Variety*, has worked here in the same capacity, *Metropolis* lacks cinematic subtlety. It is only in the shots of machinery in motion and in the surge of the revolutionists that it is dynamic. The camera is too often immobile, the technique that of the stylized theater. Yet here for the first time the chill mechanized world of the future, which only barely revealed itself in *RUR*, has been given reality.' *(Nation)*

'One of the last examples of the imaginative – but often monstrous – grandeur of the golden period of the German film, *Metropolis* is a spectacular example of expressionist design (grouped human beings are used architecturally), with moments of almost incredible beauty and power (the visionary sequence about the Tower of Babel), absurd ineptitudes (the lovesick hero in his preposterous knickerbockers), and oddities that defy analysis (the robot vamp's bizarre, lewd wink). It's a wonderful, stupefying folly.' *(Pauline Kael)*

'A feeble ending, but the best bits are thrilling and the political allegory is still powerful.' *(Winnert)*

PRO:

'One of the great achievements in the silent era, a work so audacious in its vision and so angry in its message that it is, if anything, more powerful today than when it was made.' *(Roger Ebert)*

'Long before René Clair and Charlie Chaplin satirized the assembly line in *Nous La Libert* and *Modern Times*, Lang's film dramatized the condition of workers bound to the machine and warned of future discontent and revolution.' *(Morris Dickstein)*

'The creation of the robot Maria is a classic sequence and one which inspired Frankenstein and subsequent monster movies, and the film remains one of the great examples of German expressionism.' *(Alan Frank)*

METROPOLITAN CT: 8 AV: 7.25

1989 US 98 C DRAMA/COMEDY/SOCIAL

D Whit Stillman ☆
W Whit Stillman ☆ AAN

Carolyn Farina Edward Clements Christopher Eigeman ☆ Taylor Nichols Allison Rutledge-Parisi Dylan Hundley Elizabeth Thompson

Young Tom Townsend (Edward Clements), a soggy socialist in a rented tuxedo, becomes involved with a brat-pack of Manhattan socialites.

Produced on a shoestring (and it sometimes shows in the sound quality), this satire on youthful arrogance and social hypocrisy is astute and affectionate. First-time writer-director Whit Stillman successfully updates Jane Austen-style romance and places it in Manhattan. The quality and charm of its ensemble playing puts it on a level with Woody Allen's *Hannah and Her Sisters*.

Hardly any of the actors had appeared before on film; but there isn't a single bad performance. As the girl whom Tom learns to love, Carolyn Farina is enchanting; and Christopher Eigeman is no less impressive – so much so that his departure before the end severely weakens the climax.

MIXED:

'For two-thirds of its running time [the film] scarcely puts a foot wrong, but then its most intriguing character . . . waves goodbye and the story peters out.' *(Anne Billson, Sunday Correspondent)*

'Less satisfying in content than in form. While Stillman doesn't sentimentalize his characters, he also doesn't put them in situations that disturb their cultivated ennui.' *(Amy Taubin, Village Voice)*

PRO:

'A cast of attractive young newcomers plays out this ironic, arch, gently mocking and refreshingly original comedy with confident style.' *(David Robinson, The Times)*

'There are few things less enthralling than the prospect of a Park Avenue after-party in the company of New York débutantes and their escorts . . . Despite expectations, it's worth dusting off the dinner jacket to accept an invitation. [Stillman's] screenplay is a lesson in tact, wit and modesty.' *(Angus Wolfe Murray, Scotsman)*

'That rarity, a literate comedy of drawing-room manners which is at once civilized and very funny.' *(Geoff Andrew, Time Out)*

'Stillman . . . has made a film F. Scott Fitzgerald might have been comfortable with, a film about people covering their own insecurities with a facade of social ease. And he has written wonderful dialogue, words in which the characters discuss ideas and feelings instead of simply marching through plot points as most Hollywood characters do. Not very much happens in *Metropolitan*, and yet everything that happens is felt deeply, because the characters in this movie are still too young to have perfected their defenses against life. They care very much about what others think of them, their feelings are easily hurt, their love affairs are really forms of asking for acceptance.' *(Roger Ebert)*

MIDNIGHT CT: 7 AV: 8.13

1939 US 94 BW COMEDY

D Mitchell Leisen ☆
W Billy Wilder Charles Brackett ☆ from Edwin Justus Mayer and Franz Shulz's story

Claudette Colbert ☆ Don Ameche
John Barrymore ☆ Francis Lederer Mary Astor
Elaine Barrie Hedda Hopper Rex O'Malley

Showgirl (Claudette Colbert) is hired to pose as a countess.

Colbert is at her most delightful in this sparkling comedy, arguably Leisen's best film, with a pleasantly acerbic screenplay. The plot takes a bit of swallowing, though.

MIXED:

'Direction . . . is generally satisfactory, although picture is slow in getting under way and has several spots that could be tightened. Editing shows sketchiness in several instances.' *(Variety)*

PRO:

'It has the elements of an American *Régle de Jeu*.' *(John Gillett)*

'Just about the best light comedy ever caught by the camera.' *(Motion Picture Daily)*

'Leisen's masterpiece, one of the best comedies of the Thirties.' *(John Baxter, 1968)*

'One of the authentic delights of the Thirties.' *(New Yorker, 1976)*

'Scintillating.' *(Scheuer)*

MIDNIGHT COWBOY AAW CT: 7 AV: 8.38

1969 US 113 C DRAMA

D John Schlesinger ✗ AAW
W Waldo Salt from James Leo Herlihy's novel

Jon Voight ☆ AAN Dustin Hoffman ☆ AAN
Sylvia Miles AAN John McGiver Barnard Hughes
Ruth White Jennifer Salt Bob Balaban
Paul Morrissey Brenda Vaccaro

A naive gigolo from Texas (Jon Voight), trying to survive in New York, is befriended by a street-smart layabout (Dustin Hoffman).

There are two great leading performances in John Schlesinger's hard-edged buddy-buddy picture. New York is filmed with a fresh eye; and I remember as a teenager being impressed by its apparently realistic view of America, which was suitably jaundiced for the Vietnam era.

Two and a half decades on, its weaknesses are obvious: the crudeness of its politics, the hatred of women, the exaggeration of how awful America is . . . We are given precious little explanation of why Joe Buck is the way he is. There are flashbacks from his old life which make little sense, and certainly don't constitute an explanation. And the burgeoning friendship between Joe and Rizzo looks like a plot device, rather than something which springs from either character, unless it is to be explained by a homosexual attraction that is never stated.

PRO:

'Almost all of the Joe-Ratso interplay (parts of it, apparently, based on improvisations) is delightful and affecting. This is due in large measure to extremely winning performances by Jon Voight and Dustin Hoffman, the former accomplishing the difficult task of reconciling militant stupidity with charm, the latter able to turn scrounging into a gallant, Robin-Hoodish activity.' *(John Simon)*

'A good deal besides cleverness, a great deal of good feeling and perception and purposeful dexterity.' *(Stanley Kauffmann)*

'Very funny, very sad, and very true.' *(Derek Malcolm, Guardian)*

'Emotionally shattering.' *(Maltin)*

'English director John Schlesinger had an unerring eye for capturing the grime and slime and reality of New York.' *(Baseline)*

MIXED:

'Sometimes amusing but essentially sordid.' *(Variety)*

'Schlesinger sometimes seems less interested in Buck and Rizzo than in himself, covering his film with a haze of stylistic tics and baroque decorations . . . Still, no amount of obfuscation can obscure the film's vaulting performances.' *(Time)*

'If only Schlesinger's directorial self-discipline had matched his luminous sense of scene and his extraordinary skill in handling actors, this would have been a far more considerable film.' *(Arthur Schlesinger Jr)*

'Schlesinger keeps pounding away at America, determined to expose how horrible the people are – he dehumanizes the people Joe Buck and Ratso are part of. If he could extend the same sympathy to the other Americans that he extends to them, the picture might make better sense. His spray of venom is just about overpowering, yet the two actors and the simple *Of Mice and Men* kind of relationship at the heart of the story save the picture.' *(Pauline Kael)*

ANTI:

'So long as Schlesinger handles the fantastic within

the styles of documentary realism his touch remains convincing. His grip loosens, though, when he tries to enact the cowboy's dreams and memories. He becomes derivative, a mini-Fellini.' *(Eric Rhode, Listener)*

'I might have been more touched by [Voight's and Hoffman's] plight if it had been more simply presented.' *(Felix Barker, Evening News)*

'Worse yet is the glib exploitation of America the all-purpose bogey as the cause of Joe's downfall: the mass media with their mendacious siren songs; the suspiciousness and lovelessness rampant in the land; the cruel socioeconomic gap between haves and have-nots; the maniacal, dehumanizing pursuit of money and success; etc, etc. But aside from the fact that these are commonplaces and remain so in the film, no matter how gussied up with superficial cleverness, there is no clear demonstration of how the society affects Joe Buck, of how his individual guilt is begotten by the community. If, indeed, there is any guilt at all. Rather, Joe is shown as the victim of the most prodigious streak of bad luck since Pauline of the Episodic Perils.' *(John Simon)*

'It doesn't work. One could accept mutually exploitative, explicitly stated faggery . . . To what, though, can we attribute the pretty impulse that overtakes them, converting them from a pair of dreary louts . . . into tender comrades? . . . Only as a fake, I fear. Or as the act of desperate movie-makers copping a plea.' *(Richard Schickel, Life)*

'Whatever was intended . . . I would classify this as a homosexual fantasy.' *(Alan Brien, Sunday Times)*

'Indulges in bland satire, fashionable flashiness, and a sodden sentimentality that never admits either to its homosexual elements or to the basic misogyny of its stance. Add to that a glamorisation of poverty and an ending that makes *Love Story* seem restrained, and you have a fairly characteristic example of Schlesinger's shallow talent.' *(Geoff Andrew, Time Out)*

MIDNIGHT EXPRESS CT: 5 AV: 6.73

1978 GB/US 120 C DRAMA

D Alan Parker ☆ AAN
W Oliver Stone ✗ AAW from Billy Hayes and William Hoffer's book

Brad Davis ☆ John Hurt ☆ AAN Randy Quaid Irene Miracle Bo Hopkins

American student (Brad Davis) ends up in a Turkish prison for smuggling drugs.

Gruelling, xenophobic prison drama with a typically melodramatic script from Oliver Stone which falsifies events by whitewashing the hero and turning the Turks into melodramatic villains. But there is no doubt about its impact on the unsophisticated, thanks to Alan Parker's emphatic direction, and strong performances from Brad Davis and John Hurt. Giorgio Moroder's score won an Oscar. Gerry Hambling's editing was nominated.

'I doubt whether it will be shown in Turkey.' *(Alan Marshall, producer)*

PRO:

'A brilliantly made, stomach-turning, frighteningly true tale . . . It pulls no punches.' *(Margaret Hinxman, Daily Mail)*

'Riveting from the word go. The acting is superb, the direction is excellent, and Moroder's score is exhilarating.' *(Virgin)*

MIXED:

'Panders to its audience's worst instincts magnificently.' *(Tony Rayns, Time Out)*

ANTI:

'The story is exploited only on the level of a shocker of torture, degradation and eventual revenge . . . though its factual origins tend to earn it unmerited critical reverence in some quarters.' *(David Robinson, The Times)*

'Except for a faint sensation of queasiness, it left me untouched . . . An unpleasant piece of work, of dubious intent.' *(John Coleman, New Statesman)*

'Acceptance of the film depends a lot on forgetting several things: he was smuggling hash; Turkey is entitled to its laws . . . Nor can an American expect to be treated with kid gloves everywhere.' *(Variety)*

'It is rather like being hit in the gut until you no longer feel a thing.' *(Derek Malcolm, Guardian)*

'Rushes from torment to torment, treating Billy's ordeals hypnotically in soft colors – muted squalor – with a disco beat in the background. The prison itself is more like a brothel than a prison. All of this is packaged as social protest.' *(Pauline Kael)*

'One of the ugliest sado-masochistic trips, with heavy homosexual overtones, that our thoroughly nasty movie age has yet produced.' *(Richard Schickel, Time)*

MIDNIGHT RUN CT: 8 AV: 7.42

1988 US 126 C COMEDY/ACTION/ADVENTURE

D Martin Brest ✓
W George Gallo ✓

Robert De Niro Charles Grodin ✓ Yaphet Kotto John Ashton Dennis Farina Joe Pantoliano

A bounty hunter (Robert De Niro) tries to escort an embezzler (Charles Grodin) across America, pursued by a rival bounty hunter, the Mob and the FBI.

Wonderfully funny, inventive, characterful chase thriller, with De Niro mostly playing second fiddle to a likeable, shifty performance by Charles Grodin. Slightly underrated on release, but increasingly acknowledged as a classic of its genre. Avoid the bowdlerized TV version.

ANTI:

'Dresses up a number of popular plot forms from an earlier era in more fashionable guise, but today's styles are hardly flattering to these worthy if worn clichés. George Gallo's highly buffed but derivative screenplay routinely ignores basic credibility . . . The story lurches from one arbitrary setup to another . . . undermined by the inherent phoniness of the whole. If anything, the degree of craftsmanship on display only underscores the barren narrative rather than distracting from it.' *(Myron Meisel, Film Journal)*

'The fact that subconsciously one longs for a more exotic comic tone, some divergent strain to unsettle the blandly steamrolling pace . . . says something about its limitations.' *(Richard Combs, MFB)*

'De Niro's performance style is more suited to Scorsese's coldly rational direction than Brest's heavy-handed, action-oriented camera work, leaving only Grodin's self-consciously prickly wimp to inject some fresh bile into the tepid narrative.' *(Stephen Dark, Film Review)*

MIXED:

'*Midnight Run* is two films. One is a succession of bright, razor-edge, nutty dialogues between two men. The other is the plot that keeps them together, which is stale and full of boring violent-comic action.' *(Stanley Kauffmann, New Republic)*

'Fun until the movie turns into ever more relentless car chases and helicopter shootouts, whereupon most of the charm gets lost. Nevertheless, the De Niro/Grodin relationship holds the interest even in the later, hokier sections of the movie . . . There they are, then, this not-so-wild boar and this not altogether cuddly teddy bear, always figuratively and often literally handcuffed together, making funny conversation or dropping even funnier throwaway lines. Suddenly the subtext dawns on us: De Niro is the goy and Grodin the Jew; they must make a go of it if the social fabric is not to rip. An interesting idea, but underdeveloped.' *(John Simon)*

PRO:

'Thoroughly enjoyable . . . Above all, the casting feels effortlessly right and the performances have unflagging spontaneity and attack, with Grodin quite unfazed by the competition from De Niro . . . There is no denying that while it is on the screen, it pulls off the trick of taking you out of yourself.' *(Tim Pulleine, F & F)*

'The appeal . . . is not in the extended stunt sequences but in the interaction between [De Niro and Grodin] . . . Very funny.' *(Jon Silberg, American Film)*

'Brest has made one of the best pictures of the summer by letting character dictate the action. No stunts are thrown in just for effect. The acting, even in the tiniest roles, is terrific. Grodin is a whiny wonder, especially when he's bitching about De Niro's smoking ("It'll kill you") or companionability ("You have two forms of expression: silence and rage"). One of the film's delights is watching the duo's mutual exasperation grow into grudging affection.' *(Peter Travers, People Weekly)*

'A buddy movie brim full of thrills, spills and honestly affecting pathos. Producer-director Martin Brest, who kept the pedal to the metal for *Beverly Hills Cop*, gets top mileage from George Gallo's taut, sophisticated screenplay . . . Grodin is the perfect straight man for De Niro, whose remarkable range as an actor allows him to switch instantly from knockabout farce to moments of painful insight or an emotionally wrenching encounter with his ex-wife and the daughter he scarcely knows. The last great screen actor who could work such magic without skipping a beat was Spencer Tracy.' *(Bruce Williamson, Playboy)*

'One of the most entertaining, best executed, original road pictures ever.' *(Variety)*

MIDSUMMER NIGHT'S DREAM, A AAN

CT: 7 AV: 6.64

1935 US 117/133 BW COMEDY/ ROMANCE

D Max Reinhardt William Dieterle ✓
W Charles Kenyon Mary C. McCall Jr from Shakespeare's play

James Cagney ☆ Mickey Rooney ☆ Dick Powell ● Jean Muir Ross Alexander ● Olivia de Havilland Joe E. Brown ✓ Victor Jory ☆ Hugh Herbert ● Arthur Treacher Frank McHugh Anita Louise Ian Hunter

Fairies sort out humans' problems – and some of their own – in a wood near Athens.

Much of it, especially the Busby Berkeley-style fairy-dancing routines, is kitsch and many of the actors – especially Dick Powell – look out of their depth. And yet this Hollywood extravaganza has a charm all its own. James Cagney is splendid as Bottom, as is Victor Jory as Oberon, and Mickey Rooney makes a memorably mischievous Puck (although some find him wearisome by the end).

Most of all, though, it's a treat for the eyes. The special effects and sets (by Arnold Grot) are wonderful; it is beautifully photographed by Hal Mohr, Fred Jackman, Byron Haskin and H.F. Koenekamp (who won an Oscar). Editor Ralph Dawson also won an Academy Award. Its technical excellence and intellectual pretensions won it tenth place on the *Film Daily* annual poll of US film critics.

PRO:

'You must see it if you want to be in a position to argue about the future of the film!' *(Picturegoer)*

MIXED:

'As was to be expected, Shakespeare's *A Midsummer Night's Dream* was turned into a Reinhardt's

Midsummer Nightmare. Never before has there been such leafery and greenage, such scampage and boundery. Chief bounders were Lysander and Demetrius, for Mr Dick Powell and Mr Ross Alexander would have been better employed in some American college film. Chief lady bounders were Hermia and Helena. To put it shortly, there wasn't an ounce of Shakespearean breeding among the quartet. Alone, Mr Hunter, as Theseus, spoke his lines beautifully and with a sense of poetry. The best part of the show was the fooling of the Athenian workmen, which is Hollywood-proof . . . Mr James Cagney's Bottom, though too young, seemed to me superb, and for once the metamorphosis was made credible. The man's an actor! Puck, in England generally played by a widower, has been wisely entrusted to Master Mickey Rooney. This Puck is not a fairy but a laughing, roguish boy, the wrong thing, but exquisite.' *(James Agate, Tatler)*

ANTI:

'Its worst contradiction lies in the way Warners first ordered up a whole batch of foreign and high-sounding names to handle music, dances, general production – and then handed them empty vessels for actors.' *(Otis Ferguson)*

'The selection of Dick Powell to play Lysander was unfortunate. He never seems to catch the spirit of the play or role. And Mickey Rooney, as Puck, is so intent on being cute that he becomes almost annoying.' *(Variety)*

MILDRED PIERCE AAN CT: 8 AV: 8.36

1945 US 111 BW DRAMA

D Michael Curtiz ☆
W Ranald MacDougall AAN from James M. Cain's novel

Joan Crawford ☆ AAW Ann Blyth ☆ AAN Zachary Scott Eve Arden ☆ AAN Jack Carson

After the breakdown of her marriage, a mother of two makes her way as a restauranteur, meets an attractive playboy (Zachary Scott) but once again bites off more than she can chew.

Wildly over-the-top, highly enjoyable soap opera. Joan Crawford made her triumphant comeback with a role that had been turned down by Bette Davis, Barbara Stanwyck and Ann Sheridan. Ann Blyth is equally terrific as Crawford's spoiled daughter. Curtiz directs with his usual unobtrusive skill, and cinematographer Ernest Haller won an Oscar.

MIXED:

'So they gave Joan Crawford an Academy Award for her performance in Mildred Pierce. Well, Miss Crawford has more on the ball than most of the elegant types who pose on the screen as dramatic actresses; and I suppose it is possible to admire her exhibition, through the trying circumstances of this film, of iron-faced imperturbability. Myself, I found the range of expression with which she greeted divorce, death, remarriage, financial ruin and murder so delicate as to approximate to indifference.' *(Dilys Powell)*

'From these first shots it is immediately obvious that Mildred Pierce is to be different – blacker, more pessimistic – than the average representative of the war years' most popular genre: the woman's picture. Designed as morale builders for the lonely females left working on the home front, this group of films invariably featured noble heroines enduring great hardship and strife to eventually win security and happiness (ie Love). While in some ways following the pattern (certainly Mildred is inflicted with sufficient suffering), Mildred Pierce perverts the comforting fantasy by exposing Work, Success, Marriage and even Mother Love as false, unrewarding ideals.' *(John Davis, The Velvet Light Trap, 1972)*

PRO:

'Nasty, gratifying version of the James Cain novel about suburban grass-widowhood and the power of the native passion for money and all that money can buy . . . John McManus of PM and doubtless many others regard the film as a bad advertisement for this country abroad. As movies go, it is one of the few anywhere near honest ones.' *(James Agee)*

'Miss Crawford shows an increasingly mature and subtle technique in her acting and insight into character. Jack Carson plays an earthy real estate agent with style and force. Zachary Scott does a fine job with the broken-down socialite. And Ann Blyth interprets the role of the nasty daughter with a brattishness that would get up anyone's dander. The production of this study in fulsome maternalism is smooth and handsome and very movie-wise.' *(New Movies)*

'*Mildred Pierce* has everything. A great star name in her most dazzling brilliance, a screenplay that bares emotion and then turns the screws on it, direction that never once fails to wring you limp and a production that not only welds these creative elements superbly together but is breathlessly beautiful on the physical side.' *(Hollywood Review)*

MILLER'S CROSSING CT: 7 AV: 7.31

1990 US 115 C THRILLER

D Joel Coen ☆
W Joel Coen Ethan Coen ✗

Gabriel Byrne Marcia Gay Harden John Turturro ☆ Jon Polito ☆ J.E. Freeman Albert Finney ☆ Steve Buscemi Mike Starr

In 1929, an Irish gangster (Gabriel Byrne) walks a perilous path between two warring camps of Irish and Italian hoods. He has compromised his livelihood, not to mention his life, by indulging a passion for the moll (Marcia Gay Harden) of his Irish employer (Albert Finney), and by not

executing her obnoxious kid brother (John Turturro) on behalf of Italian godfather (Jon Polito).

A confident, polished tribute to the gangster movies of the 30s and 40s. Lovers of the genre will admire the stylish set pieces, and the picture's elegant if labyrinthine structure. The movie suffers from having no likeable characters. In the leading role, Gabriel Byrne's motivation and morality are mysterious to the point of invisibility. The most charismatic character (the Irish boss played, with weight and depth, by Albert Finney) disappears for much of the movie. The picture ends up being stolen by two excellent supporting actors, John Turturro and Jon Polito.

The film never rises above the level of affectionate pastiche. The audience's feelings of *déjà-vu* mount as the beatings inflicted on the hero become over-repetitive and have little effect on his gaunt good looks; while the Coen brothers' glorification of amoral gangsterism and violence seems particularly old-fashioned, after Martin Scorsese's *GoodFellas*.

One unwelcome legacy of the Coen brothers' roots in alternative cinema is that there is much pretentiously symbolic nonsense about hats. The central visual image is an empty old hat travelling in whatever direction the wind blows; and this might act as a somewhat brutal summary of the film-makers' deficiencies.

ANTI:

'So clever about its sources, which are categorical but unacknowledged, that it has little life of its own. The plot proceeds loosely . . . but is overlaid with materials taken from two Dashiell Hammett novels . . . All too symptomatic of the movie's essential corniness is the presence of Danny Boy on the soundtrack.' *(Gary Giddins, Village Voice)*

'This doesn't look like a gangster movie, it looks like a commercial intended to look like a gangster movie. Everything is too designed. That goes for the plot and the dialogue, too. The dialogue is well-written, but it is indeed written. We admire the prose rather than the message. People make threats, and we think about how elegantly the threats are worded.' *(Roger Ebert)*

MIXED:

'A triumph of style over substance.' *(New York Times)*

PRO:

'Substance is here in spades, along with the twisted, brilliantly controlled style on which filmmakers Joel and Ethan Coen made a name.' *(Variety)*

'[It revels] in fast, sharp, humorous dialogue and Byzantine plotting . . . The brothers' richest, most sophisticated entertainment so far.' *(Geoff Andrew, Time Out)*

'Stylish, moody, wonderfully atmospheric. Little is what it seems in this complex, witty and hypnotically mesmerising cinematic *tour-de-force*. Superb performances and tough, if slightly cartoonish, action make this one of the greatest gangster movies ever.' *(Rose)*

'*Miller's Crossing* tackles big issues – the nature of love, loyalty, friendship, and responsibility – without putting any of them in the foreground. Never does the film resort to didacticism. Still more surprising, the Coens resisted the Hollywood dictum that the protagonist must be sympathetic (that is, better than the rest of us – no messy moral complexities allowed).' *(Baseline)*

MILLION, LE/THE: *see* LE MILLION.

MILOU IN MAY

CT: 6 AV: 7.13

(aka *Milou en Mai; May Fools*)

1989 France/Italy 105/108 C COMEDY/DRAMA/FOREIGN

D Louis Malle ☆
W Louis Malle Jean-Claude Carrière

Michel Piccoli ☆ Miou-Miou ☆ Michel Duchaussoy Dominique Blanc Harriet Walter Bruno Carette François Berléand Martine Gautier Paulette Dubost

A wealthy, haut-bourgeois family gathers together in provincial France after the death of the matriarch in 1968. In their different ways, they dabble in the permissiveness and trendiness of the age, but then – when informed erroneously that the revolution has begun – they realise that they themselves may be among its first targets. Panic ensues.

Ultimately, it doesn't quite compare with the film it most resembles, Jean Renoir's *Rules of the Game* (1939). There is not much in the way of a story, nor does it come to a great, decisive climax; but Louis Malle's charming, civilized satire on bourgeois hypocrisy and the fashionable leftism of the 1960s is lovely to look at and features a marvellous ensemble of actors. Despite an appearance of gentleness, Malle touches on the darker sides of life. Sado-masochism, paedophilia, lesbianism and adultery all crop up, and are dealt with in a way which manages to be inoffensive but honest.

ANTI:

'Cloying and precious and convinced too mightily of its own charm to be engaging . . . The viewer's patience, already wearing thin, gives out, finally and completely, with the whole hoary back-to-nature episode, which is both unbelievable and unfunny.' *(Baseline)*

'Falls for the conventional wisdom that lesbians are only waiting for a good man to rescue them.' *(Bergan & Karney)*

MIXED:

'Convivial but . . . conventional . . . Much of Malle's humour springs from the ironic juxtaposition of events within the film frame.' *(Sheila Johnston, Independent)*

PRO:

'A film of Chekhovian generosity that never strays into sentimentality or cynicism.' *(Philip French, Observer)*

'Delightful, sentimental . . . perceptively characterised, wittily observed, often very funny and spiced with sharp, sly black humour.' *(Richard Blaine, Today)*

'Watching [it] is like stumbling on water in the desert . . . This is a realistic period comedy assailed by the stings and arrows of surrealism . . . Malle uses incongruous details to make plausibility piquant . . . . In Malle the ordinary is never ordinary.' *(Nigel Andrews, Financial Times)*

'I think perhaps Malle is gently trying to make a movie about imperfect but interesting people, the goodness of whose souls is tested by the coincidence of a public and private crisis at the same time. No great lessons are learned, no great statements made, but by the end of the film, we have spent some interesting time with these people and know them better.' *(Roger Ebert)*

MIRACLE IN MILAN

CT: 5 AV: 7.00

(aka *Miracolo a Milano*)

1951 Italy 101 BW DRAMA/FANTASY/FOREIGN

D Vittorio De Sica ☆
W Cesare Zavattini Vittorio De Sica Suso Cecchi D'Amico Mario Chiari Adolfo Franci from Zavattini's story *Toto Il Buono*

Branduani Gianni Francesco Golisano Paolo Stoppa Emma Gramatica Guglielmo Barnabo Brunella ovo Anna Carena Alba Arnova Flora Cambi Virgilio Riento

Shantytown Italians battle against an uncaring oilman, with angelic assistance.

Vittorio De Sica's heartwarming fantasy is also a harsh condemnation of the way displaced Europeans were treated after World War II. There are many beautiful and touching moments, but his view of Capitalism is one-dimensional and old-fashioned; and modern audiences may find the central character, Toto the Good (Francesco Golisano) mawkish rather than Chaplinesque.

PRO:

'A naive morality fantasy with a beautiful sense of fun . . . In cold print it may seem embarrassingly mawkish, but on the warm screen it takes on an irresistible child-like magic.' *(Daily Mail)*

'This film would make you feel good in Esperanto.' *(Sunday Graphic)*

'An unlikely fable which manages to avoid all the obvious pitfalls and sends one out of the cinema in a warm glow.' *(Halliwell)*

'The failure of innocence here is touchingly absurd; the film is stylized poetry, and it is like nothing else that De Sica ever did.' *(Pauline Kael)*

MIXED:

'De Sica's kindly irony and humane pathos have more than a touch of Chaplin . . . There is a slipping away into pessimism here which [he] must master if it is not to destroy his work. Nevertheless, at least half of the picture is its brilliant filmmaking.' *(Daily Worker)*

'My enthusiasm is tempered by only two doubts. The extravagant fantasy of the second part of the story, when the natural is ousted by the supernatural, seems to me not entirely successful in persuading. And the satire on big business seems to me old hat. The fat financier with topper, fur collar and a palace with flunkeys was already a familiar symbol in the twenties; his revival here is crude and unworthy of De Sica's great talent.' *(Dilys Powell)*

MIRACLE OF MORGAN'S CREEK, THE

CT: 5 AV: 8.36

1944 US 99 BW COMEDY

D Preston Sturges ✗
W Preston Sturges ✗ AAN

Betty Hutton ☆ Eddie Bracken William Demarest Diana Lynn Brian Donlevy

An unmarried mother-to-be (Betty Hutton) can't recall the name of the man responsible for her current condition.

This Preston Sturges comedy was highly acclaimed on release for daring to make fun of the Hays Office, and is still usually hailed as a comedy classic. It was risqué for its time, but now it looks coy, the gags have not worn well, the characters are stereotypes, and the heroine's treatment of her suitor (Eddie Bracken) is needlessly cruel.

PRO:

'Not only Preston Sturges's major cinematic effort, but it is also one of my favourite motion pictures. It is so brilliant and blithe . . . The comedy spins like a pinwheel, races like a high-powered launch, and on occasion capers like a kitten on a catnap jag. Certain of my confêreres have seriously informed me: (a) The work lacks good taste (b) It is an insult to American Womanhood (c) It is a subversive gnawing at the very roots of Democracy. Still, I am afraid, I found it one of the wittiest and most enjoyable celluloid strips ever to run through a projection machine.' *(Herb Sterne)*

'This film moves in a fantastic and irreverent whirl of slapstick, nonsense, farce, sentiment, satire, romance, melodrama – is there any ingredient of dramatic entertainment except maybe tragedy and grand opera that hasn't been tossed into it?' *(NBR)*

'With his usual skill in reconciling farce and sentiment . . . Sturges brings off a wild brilliant finish. Like all his films this one is fresh as paint.' *(William Whitebait, New Statesman)*

'Bad taste, or no bad taste, I thoroughly enjoyed it.' *(Richard Mallett, Punch)*

'Brilliant . . . But [it makes] a statement that human beings are dopes . . . This is, of course, the essence of what passes for philosophy in Hollywood, but no one before has ever articulated it so boldly, perhaps because no one else had the talent to sugarcoat the pill and get away with it.' *(Paul Rotha & Richard Griffith, The Film Till Now, 1949)*

'The miracle of *The Miracle of Morgan's Creek* is how the film ever got made in the first place. This onslaught against American morals in small towns, against the wartime romances of servicemen, against just about everything that the country held sacred during World War II was reckless, exaggerated, and very funny. Sturges was at his irreverent best.' *(Baseline)*

MIXED:

'Some of the comedy situations lack punch, and the picture is slow to get rolling, but ultimately picks up smart pace and winds up quite strongly.' *(Variety)*

'Sturges holds his characters, and the people they comically represent, and their predicament, and his audience, and the best potentialities of his own work, essentially in contempt . . . Cynicism, which gives the film much of its virtue, also has it by the throat . . . I suspect that Sturges feels that conscience and comedy are incompatible. It would be hard for a man of talent to make a more self-destructive mistake.' *(James Agee, Nation)*

'Is it vulgar? Yes, in parts. Is it funny? Again, in parts. Is the acting good? Excellent, though the chief roles are in the hands of players not pleasing to my taste. Eddie Bracken in particular is first-rate. The technique of the piece is astonishing in its speed and panache; and if I have to choose between *The Miracle of Morgan's Creek* and the usual glycerine, give me Sturges.' *(Dilys Powell)*

MIRACLE ON 34TH STREET AAN

CT: 6 AV: 7.77

(aka *The Big Heart*)

1947 US 96 BW DRAMA/COMEDY/FANTASY

D George Seaton
W George Seaton ☆ AAW from Valentine Davies's story AAW

Edmund Gwenn ☆ AAW Natalie Wood ☆ Maureen O'Hara ☆ John Payne ☆ Gene Lockhart ☆ Porter Hall ☆

A man who believes himself to be Santa Claus (Edmund Gwenn) is put on trial, and has to prove his sanity.

Neat little parable about the way materialism, career and the pursuit of power have taken over, even during the season of goodwill. Despite the odd dull patch, it is a guaranteed tearjerker – mainly because all the actors play the fantasy as if it is for real.

MIXED:

'Clever, and pleased with itself.' *(James Agee)*

PRO:

'Altogether wholesome, stimulating and enjoyable.' *(Motion Picture Herald)*

'It's as entertaining and appealing a film as has appeared in many a day, done without the hint of cuteness, the actuality of its New York settings and the logic of its approach making heretofore legendary figures like Santa Claus and Mr Macy and Mr Gimbel as real as any of us.' *(New Movies)*

'One of the finest pictures of the season, with a tender story, charmingly told, of Santa Claus on trial. This movie, which will be known in the industry as a "sleeper" because it cost comparatively little and will be shown without advance fanfare, has a warmly human feeling and a simplicity of treatment that will please every member of the family.' *(Fortnight)*

'It is fantastic and it is Dickensian in sentiment, but the fantasy is perfectly sustained and the sentiment is so tempered with humour and satire that it never cloys. The result is a joyous piece of make-believe, a picture of continuous delight.' *(A.E. Wilson)*

'Christmas has been profiled in dozens of films but seldom, if ever, has the Yuletide been so wonderfully presented . . . Gwenn gives one of the most charming, endearing performances in the history of film.' *(Baseline)*

MIRACLE WORKER, THE

CT: 9 AV: 8.20

1962 US 106 BW DRAMA

D Arthur Penn ☆ AAN
W William Gibson ☆ AAN from his play and Helen Keller's book *The Story of My Life*

Anne Bancroft ☆ AAW Patty Duke ☆ AAW Victor Jory Inga Swenson Andrew Prine Beah Richards

Tutor (Anne Bancroft) teaches Helen Keller to communicate, even though Helen can neither see nor hear.

Profoundly moving film, based on real life, and wonderfully acted – on a visceral, not melodramatic, level – by the two leads. Especially interesting now, since it flies in the face of almost every modern theory of education. Today, a teacher who carried on like Anne Bancroft would probably be prosecuted for child abuse. Penn, Bancroft and Duke had all worked together on this as a Broadway play; but it succeeds as a film, mainly thanks to Ernest Caparros's artful camerawork, Laurence Rosenthal's score, and Aram Avakian's editing.

ANTI:

'Why . . . did I find . . . [this film] so dispiriting? . . . Gibson's error is not to rely on the strength of his central story. He follows too closely the old adage that conflict is the stuff of drama . . . As a result of the emphasis on clashes of character, the film always seems to be shouting at the top of its voice.' *(Patrick Gibbs, Daily Telegraph)*

'A moving real-life story is given hysterical treatment and the good scenes have a hard task winning through; in any case a documentary might have been more persuasive.' *(Halliwell)*

MIXED:

'Penn . . . is in the opening scenes especially, too loud and savage . . . These, however, are small details and they cannot mar the splendour and the beauty of the battle waged by Annie to establish communication . . . It is Miss Bancroft . . . who uplifts and upholds the film.' *(The Times)*

'Truffaut's *The Wild Child* is a more beautifully conceived picture on the same theme, but even with its imperfections and staginess this early Penn film is extraordinary.' *(Pauline Kael)*

PRO:

'Incomparably the best of the new films . . . And incomparably the best performance – or double performance . . . It is, in every sense of the word, sensational.' *(Sunday Telegraph)*

'Flawless . . . fine direction.' *(Scheuer)*

MIRACOLO A MILANO: *see* MIRACLE IN MILAN.

MIRROR

CT: 4 AV: 7.00

(aka *Zerkalo; A White White Boy . . .)*

1974 USSR 102 C/BW DRAMA/WAR/FOREIGN

D Andrei Tarkovsky
W Andrei Tarkovsky Aleksandr Misharin

Innokenti Smoktunovsky Margarita Terekhova L. Tarkovskaya Philip Yankovsky Ignat Daniltsev Anatoli Solonitsin

Andrei Tarkovsky's reflective essay about Russian childhood, based on his own boyhood during World War II.

Not exactly strong on narrative drive, and needlessly abstruse; it's best appreciated as a succession of images.

PRO:

'The Soviet critics judged the film obscure, incomprehensible and too long for the masses . . . It is a picture of air, water and fire, a feverish meditation of an artist at the turning point of his life, difficult, certainly, but rich, sensual and beautiful.' *(Alain Remond, Télérama)*

'Maybe it is a masterpiece; certainly it is a work of outstanding imagination and originality . . . Tarkovsky is artist enough to support the bravura scheme of the picture.' *(David Castell, Sunday Telegraph)*

'Doubtless sensing an individual force running counter to the collective will, Russian bureaucrats denied it foreign distribution and refused it entry to any film festival. To see it at last is a time for celebration and to realise what fools those bureaucrats were . . . It is a film to see again and again, cinema against which others will be gauged.' *(Tom Hutchinson, Now)*

'First it seems obscure, gnomic, perversely inaccessible; next illuminating, masterly, classic; finally obvious, familiar and traditional . . . Its oddities of vision, repetitions of incident, elisions of time, parallels of people and places, clearly stem from a highly personal determination to present it as it is . . . The nearest thing in the cinema to an epic poem.' *(Alan Brien, Sunday Times)*

'While difficult to understand, there can be no doubt as to the film's artistic worth or Tarkovsky's genius. It is a dazzlingly beautiful film.' *(Nicholas Wapshott, The Times)*

'You may – probably will – lose your bearing . . . on a first viewing. But don't be deterred. Just open your eyes to [the] images, your mind to [the] mazy, spell-casting storytelling, and your heart to a film that captures all the two-edged, beckon-and-repel fascination of the past.' *(Nigel Andrews, Financial Times)*

'See it above all for a series of images of such luminous beauty that they will make your heart burst.' *(Chris Peachment, Time Out)*

ANTI:

'Intensely personal and somewhat impenetrable.' *(Bergan & Karney)*

MISERABLES, LES: *see* LES MISERABLES.

MISERY

CT: 8 AV: 6.75

1990 US 90 C THRILLER/HORROR

D Rob Reiner ✔
W William Goldman ☆ from Stephen King's novel

James Caan ✔ Kathy Bates ☆ AAW Richard Farnsworth ✔ Frances Sternhagen ✔ Lauren Bacall

A romantic novelist (James Caan) is held captive by the female fan of his nightmares (Kathy Bates).

Kathy Bates won an Oscar for an acting *tour de force*, brilliantly and unpredictably changing mood from maternity nurse to tongue-tied girlfriend, adoring fan to scorned wife, nun to nutter. Some called the film misogynistic, but the 'normal' women are sympathetically portrayed by Lauren Bacall and Frances Sternhagen: the film really exploits that fear of dependency upon others which is one of the horrors of old age. At the same time, Rob Reiner's film is a masterly study of masculinity under siege.

For light relief, there's a charming sub-plot as the local sheriff and his wife (beautifully played by Richard Farnsworth and Frances Sternhagen) try to find the novelist. William Goldman's meticulously crafted screenplay steers a confident path between domestic comedy and Grand Guignol. He understands the great lesson of Hitchcock's successes: that suspense and black comedy need to exist side by side, to be truly gripping.

Although the film has obvious similarities to *Whatever Happened To Baby Jane?*, it rises above pastiche in every area. Kathy Bates was rightly praised: one false note, and a chilling film would have become a preposterous one. But Caan is no less outstanding as a writer who has secretly despised his public for years, and now finds his public gaining its revenge. The ironic point that both Annie and the novelist hero are split personalities is established visually, when the camera cuts from her (lit from the right) to him (lit from the left), so that their two half-faces for a split second seem to be one: a technique borrowed from Ingmar Bergman's *Persona*, no less.

A further ironic point – that Annie's mania is fed not by horror videos or vicious thrillers, but by slushy romance and Liberace records – is also made rather effectively.

ANTI:

'It is as if Reiner and Goldman are slumming in a genre that does not suit them. For a while, they get the better of it; eventually, however, it gets the better of them. By the end of the movie, they are wielding the blunt instrument of cliché with senseless abandon . . . And there is something distasteful about a movie that makes a plump, sweet-faced, sexually repressed woman the target of so much scorn.' *(Brian D. Johnson, Maclean's)*

'Stretched as it is over 105 minutes, the plot of this movie wears thinner and thinner until holes start popping out all over . . . The graphically violent final fight is clumsily staged, and there's a silly epilogue that recalls the laziest cheapo chillers.' *(Ralph Novak, People Weekly)*

MIXED:

'Very obvious and very commercial.' *(Variety)*

'Wonderfully acted horror comedy . . . suffers from pedestrian direction, and a predictable plot that collapses into Grand Guignol.' *(Scheuer)*

'Extremely well acted, but the suspense ebbs and flows.' *(Maltin)*

'It does not illuminate, challenge, or inspire, but it works.' *(Roger Ebert)*

PRO:

'William Goldman's intelligent script operates both as psycho-thriller and as sly comment on the sort of celebrity which can enshrine and – in this case literally – imprison the object of devotion.' *(Colette Maude, Time Out)*

'This astonishing film is a taut, darkly comic thriller and a post-modernist examination of the relationship between writer and reader, detached producer and vulnerable consumer, artist and critic.' *(Philip French, Observer)*

'Places ironic literary intelligence in conflict with the whacked-out innocence of fandom, and has a smart subtext of class warfare about it too. The actors are supported by the best kind of writerly craft and directorial technique, the kind that refuses to call attention to itself, never gets caught straining for scares or laughs. Popular moviemaking – elegantly economical, artlessly artful – doesn't get much better than this.' *(Richard Schickel, Time)*

MISFITS, THE

CT: 5 AV: 6.36

1961 US 124 BW DRAMA/WESTERN

D John Huston
W Arthur Miller

Clark Gable Marilyn Monroe Montgomery Clift Eli Wallach Thelma Ritter Kevin McCarthy

Young, idealistic stripper (Marilyn Monroe) takes up with old, matter-of-fact cowboy (Clark Gable), but it is not a relationship made in heaven.

A modern western and battle of the sexes, which sadly turned out to be the last film of Clark Gable and Marilyn Monroe. The film's reasonably effective when depicting the decline of the Old West mystique, and Gable endows his disillusioned cowpoke with considerable depth. Monroe seems much less confident, and seems to be having to spout lines which reflect her real-life husband Arthur Miller's disappointment in her. Huston's treatment of her, though par for the course in a Marilyn Monroe sex comedy, smacks of sexism in a drama such as this. Generally, he seems less than inspired by Miller's turgid, talky script, and it's hard to blame him.

ANTI:

'The greatest disappointment in the film is director John Huston; he is the one who should have made the camera do its work.' *(Gerald Weales, Reporter, 1961)*

'Burdened by a pretentious, muddled, and schmaltzy Arthur Miller screenplay.' *(Judith Crist)*

MIXED:

'Mr Huston's direction is dynamic, inventive and colorful. But the picture just doesn't come off.' *(New York Times)*

'Huston's direction is his best in years . . . Too bad that his camera occasionally peers lubriciously down the girl's bodice or elsewhere to remind us that Roslyn is really Marilyn Monroe.' *(New Republic)*

PRO:

'In this era when sex and violence are so exploited that our sensibilities are in danger of being dulled, here is a film in which both elements are as forceful as in life but never exploited for themselves. Here Miss Monroe is magic but not a living pin-up dangled in skin-tight satin before our eyes . . . And can anyone deny that in this film these performers are at their best? You forget they are performing and feel that they are.' *(Paul V. Beckley, New York Herald Tribune)*

'Gable has never done anything better on the screen, nor has Miss Monroe. Gable's acting is vibrant and lusty, hers true to the character . . . The screen vibrates with emotion during the latter part of the film, as Marilyn and Gable engage in one of those battles of the sexes that seem eternal in their constant eruption. It is a poignant conflict between a man and a woman in love, with each trying to maintain individual characteristics and preserve a fundamental way of life.' *(Kate Cameron, New York Daily News)*

'It is perfectly obvious that, in writing with this desperate perception about an impossible golden girl, Arthur Miller was writing about his wife. But art is often semi-autobiographical, especially about love, and the fact that the associations here are gossip-reporters' property is no reason to belittle the film. With reservations about some ineptly overcharged lines, *The Misfits* is a sad, beguiling allegory made with unmistakable truth of feeling; if it weren't, the caustic comedy of Thelma Ritter's performance and the hard violence of the mustang sequences could scarcely be accommodated so smoothly.' *(Penelope Gilliatt)*

'The theme with its implications of an essentially male savagery suits Mr Huston, and he has drawn extraordinary qualities from all his chief players; in particular, from Miss Monroe a kind of incandescence and from Clark Gable a masculine power, controlled, a shade rueful, which comes across in the cinema with physical force; one is glad to think that the last Gable performance should have been among the best. But the director has dealt successfully, too, with Mr Miller's suggestions of an uneasy society; the characters are in flight from some feared regimentation, and one perceives their anxieties not only in the half-spoken confidences but in the fluid, erratic movement of figures and crowds. And there perhaps we have it, the peculiar source of pleasure; *The Misfits* moves – peering and withdrawing, settling intently on some luminous close up, following the restlessness of bystanders, always using distance and change to hint or emphasise a mood or a feeling. It is, as I say, a film.' *(Dilys Powell)*

MISSING AAN

CT: 6 AV: 7.54

1982 US 122 C THRILLER

D Costa-Gavras ☆
W Costa-Gavras Donald Stewart ☆ AAW from Thomas Hauser's book *The Execution of Charles Horman*

Jack Lemmon ☆ AAN Sissy Spacek ☆ AAN Melanie Mayron John Shea Charles Cioffi David Clennon Richard Venture Jerry Hardin Richard Bradford Joe Regalbuto

A middle-aged, middle American father (Jack Lemmon) searches for his son, a writer who disappeared in South America (obviously Chile) after a coup.

Gripping, well acted drama. The relationship between Lemmon's conservative middle-American and his counter-cultural daughter-in-law (Sissy Spacek) is particularly moving; and their attempts to find out the truth are involving. If it doesn't quite deliver, it's because we can see where the narrative is heading, much too early on.

ANTI:

'Provocation and entertainment prove to be uneasy allies.' *(Tom Milne, MFB)*

'[Lemmon's and Spacek's] star presence and characterisations still interfere with the film's investigative thrust . . . For all their subtle performances, their scenes and attitudes seem too neat for the prickly surroundings.' *(Geoff Brown, The Times)*

MIXED:

'Demonstrates Costa-Gavras's ability to grab you unawares by the lapels and drag you through the labyrinth of intrigue and paranoia that lies beyond the more acceptable corridors of power . . . There is a certain shiftiness in [his] manipulation of his material . . . But the movie raises major issues in a usefully provocative way.' *(Philip French, Observer)*

'Much has already been written about the bravery of *Missing*, which dares, we are told, to make a specific attack on American policies in Chile during and after the Allende regime. I wish the movie had been even braver – brave enough to risk a clear, unequivocal, uncompromised statement of its beliefs, instead of losing itself in a cluttered mishmash of stylistic excesses. This movie might have really been powerful, if it could have gotten out of its own way.' *(Roger Ebert)*

'Costa-Gavras's antipathy to Americans appears to be so deep-seated that he can't create American characters. The only real filmmaking is in the backgrounds: in the anxious, ominous atmosphere of a city under martial law – the sirens, the tanks, the helicopters, the feeling of abnormal silences and of random terror.' *(Pauline Kael)*

PRO:

'The truth of *Missing* is not in its proven facts but in the way it dramatizes the sometimes unbridgeable gulf that separates us, the governed, and those who govern us in what are supposed to be our own best interests.' *(Vincent Canby, New York Times)*

'Lemmon applies to his dramatic *tour de force* much the same technique that serves him so well in comedy . . . A gruelling personal drama.' *(Cecil Wilson, Daily Mail)*

'Works, because of Costa-Gavras's convincing direction and Lemmon's emphatic performance.' *(Maltin)*

'Compelling, powerful and intense.' *(Scheuer)*

MISSION, THE AAN CT: 8 AV: 6.00

1985 GB 120/125 C DRAMA/WAR

D Roland Joffe ☆ AAN
W Robert Bolt

Robert De Niro Jeremy Irons ✔ Ray McAnally ☆
Liam Neeson Aidan Quinn Ronald Pickup
Cherie Lunghi Chuck Low

A pacifist Jesuit priest (Jeremy Irons) and a warlike one (Robert De Niro) unite with South American natives against greedy colonialists, and the closure by papal order of their mission to South America.

It's a shade over-earnest and under-involving; the script dawdles and loses its way in the middle; and there are times when the differing styles of the two leading actors jar (allowing Ray McAnally to steal the show as a worldly cardinal). However, Roland Joffe's epic is visually sumptuous (Chris Menges's splendid cinematography won an Oscar), always intelligent (the script is by Robert Bolt), and works to an exciting and stirring climax. There is also one of the all-time-great soundtracks, by Ennio Morricone (it was Oscar-nominated). Academy Award nominations also went to Jim Clark's editing, Stuart Craig's art direction, Jack Stephens's sound, and Enrico Sabbatini's costumes. It won the Palme d'Or at Cannes.

ANTI:

'De Niro gives a bland, uninteresting performance. The fundamental problem is that the script is cardboard thin, pinning labels on its characters and arbitrarily shoving them into various stances to make plot points.' *(Variety)*

'Father Gabriel [Irons] is not by today's movie definitions a man of action and this story clearly needs one . . . De Niro as Mendoza looks set to fill the bill . . . [He] does his very intense and committed best with a real non-starter of a role . . . [disappearing] into an intense and silent meaninglessness . . . The final act verges quite closely on the embarrassing . . . Robert Bolt's screenplay does not choose to reveal what we should make of these events.' *(Ann Lloyd, F & F)*

'It is a measure of the film's disorganization that at the end, when it is crucial that we understand who the Indians are fighting, and how the battle is going, mere chaos takes over the screen, and the actors stagger out of clouds of smoke as if they're looking for directions.' *(Roger Ebert)*

MIXED:

'Technically it's superb . . . It seems churlish to say it's not much more than spectacle, but for all my determination to like it, for all its magnificence, it struck me as empty and inert . . . Bolt's script always pulls back before it gets in too deep. We're left with a simple black and white conflict, an uplifting story about two good guys . . . who are destroyed – though not in spirit . . . Oddly some of the best scenes . . . are also the corniest.' *(Margaret Walters, Listener)*

'Plenty of flaws, but also . . . a considerable feat of filmmaking . . . Joffe is a class director . . . McAnally . . . is magnificent . . . The film is epic in scale, totally sincere in its intentions and full of a sense of horror at the ways the Indians were eventually betrayed. But it does tend to want to be all things to all men.' *(Derek Malcolm, Guardian)*

'A real work of art photographed with wonderful color consistency in a pinkish golden light. Its only fault was that Mr Irons was nowhere seen to be deteriorating from religious zeal into absolute madness. There was, after all, no sane need for him to persuade the women and children of an entire tribe to sacrifice themselves for You Know Who. His own martyrdom would surely have been enough to satisfy even the most devout Christian.' *(Quentin Crisp, Christopher Street)*

'Sincere to the point of boredom . . . short on plot development, long on superb photography.' *(Halliwell)*

'Despite the excellence of the acting, the script never fleshes out the characters enough to make us care. Lovely waterfalls, though.' *(Rose)*

PRO:

'A triumphant success . . . a unique film that is a feast for the eyes and fodder for the mind . . . Bolt's lucid script brings pathos and drama to the complexities of church and empire . . . Thank goodness films like this are still made.' *(Ian Johnstone, Sunday Times)*

'Lives up to the high standards [of] *The Killing Fields* . . . The care with which Joffe builds up the details of his story and the excellence of his actors should ensure that this excellent film reaches a large audience.' *(Jim Hickey, Scotsman)*

'Superbly directed, photographed and acted . . . capable of gripping, uplifting and stimulating audiences everywhere.' *(Philip French, Observer)*

'Powerful . . . contains quietly brilliant performances by the leads, hypnotic cinematography, and an evocative score.' *(Scheuer)*

MISSION TO MOSCOW CT: 4 AV: 5.67

1943 US 112 BW DRAMA/WAR

D Michael Curtiz
W Howard Koch from Joseph E. Davies's book

Walter Huston Ann Harding Oscar Homolka
George Tobias Gene Lockhart Eleanor Parker
Richard Travis Helmut Dantine Manart Kippen

Life and times of Joseph Davies (Walter Huston), US ambassador in Moscow from 1936 to 1938.

This pro-Soviet film, made at a time when the USA and the Soviet Union were allies, is a fascinating period piece. Manart Kippen does his best to portray Uncle Joe Stalin as a philanthropist, and Warner Brothers portray his purges as a necessary means of preserving Soviet national security. It's not altogether convincing. Not surprisingly, the film later became an embarrassment to the studio; and scriptwriter Howard Koch fell foul of the House UnAmerican Activities Committee. The art direction was Oscar-nominated.

PRO:

'A magnificent, informative and truly epochal screen document that every American owes himself the privilege of seeing. It answers so many questions that have been only partly answered before about an ally who is fighting our fight against a common enemy. And the answers are tremendously conclusive and of vital importance to us all . . . If *Mission to Moscow* on the screen is the enormous commercial success it should be, that success will be undebatable proof that motion pictures have come of age. Here is the most adult document of its kind ever turned out in Hollywood.' *(Hollywood Reporter)*

'Its admirable aim is . . . to overcome any latent suspicions America may have of its Russian ally.' *(The Times)*

'It is, politically, the most important film ever made.' *(Campbell Dixon, Daily Telegraph)*

'Attains the appearance of being actual documentary . . . Actual fact and represented fact have been blended with complete success. The result is an astonishing piece of filmmaking.' *(Manchester Guardian)*

'Sincere, emphatic, overlong and on the whole realistic.' *(William Whitebait, New Statesman)*

'Its general effect is to show everything about Russia in the best possible light and to create sympathetic understanding of a great ally . . . As a forerunner of serious films about contemporary history – a kind of thing fraught with danger and difficulty – it is an extremely important picture.' *(New Movies)*

'Film is of a highly intellectual nature, requiring constant attention and thought if it is to be fully appreciated.' *(Variety)*

ANTI:

'A mishmash: of Stalinism with New Dealism with Hollywoodism with opportunism with shaky experimentalism with mesmerism with onanism, all mosaicked into a remarkable portrait of what the makers of the film think the Soviet Union is like – a great glad two-million-dollar bowl of canned borscht, eminently approvable by the Institute of Good Housekeeping.' *(James Agee)*

'Comrade Jack L. Warner raises a loving cup of borscht to Soviet ideology . . . The Warner Brothers studio obviously feels about our Russian brethren as Bill Saroyan does about all Mankind, and it scrubs, fumigates and polishes them quite beyond nature and recognition for their appearance in this photoplay. Truth is bound, gagged and sterilized, and the complete composure with which one is expected to believe that the only fundamental difference between the peoples of the USA and the USSR is that one prefers jitterbug Terpsichore while the other relishes the kazotsky is a smugly cynical and idiotic computation of the reasoning powers of the average American citizen . . . The depiction of the purge trials is as tricky a whitewash job as has occurred since Sam Clemens penned Tom Sawyer, and there is more than hint and rumor that the Ogpu is really nothing more frightening than a frat organization.' *(Herb Sterne)*

MISSISSIPPI BURNING AAN CT: 7 AV: 6.75

1988 US 127 C THRILLER

D Alan Parker AAN
W Chris Gerolmo

Gene Hackman ☆ AAN Willem Dafoe ✔
Frances McDormand ☆ AAN Brad Dourif
R. Lee Ermey Gailard Sartain Stephen Tobolowsky
Michael Rooker

FBI men (Gene Hackman, Willem Dafoe) investigate the deaths of three civil rights workers in the south, in 1964.

Peter Biziou's Academy Award-winning photography, Gerry Hambling's Oscar-nominated editing and Parker's pacy direction combine with some excellent performances (especially Hackman's) to make a very exciting thriller, which may have been controversial with critics for departing from the documentary truth, but certainly pleased audiences.

ANTI:

'I am not just filled with sorrow. I am angry, too . . . So much talent in the making of [the film]. My anger? That the white-dominated . . . story . . . almost ignores the black-dominated civil rights movement . . . The blacks in the film are down-trodden, cringing, lacking in courage . . . [The film] typifies the white, well-meaning liberal approach to the life and death struggles against apartheid and for civil rights.' *(Mikki Doyle, Independent)*

'Another example of quasi-leftist sensationalism . . . Here we have a film about the civil rights movement in which the heroes are not just white men, but white FBI men with Rambotic pretensions. What [the film] lacks in black characters, it makes up for in white self-congratulation.' *(J. Hoberman, Village Voice)*

'The director Alan Parker likes to operate in a wildly melodramatic universe of his own creation. In *Mississippi Burning*, which is set during the Freedom Summer of 1964, he treats Southerners the way he treated the Turks ten years ago in *Midnight Express*. And he twists facts here as he did there, with the same apparent objective: to come up with garish forms of violence. The entire movie hinges on the ploy that the FBI couldn't stop the KKK from its terrorism against blacks until it swung over to vigilante tactics. And we're put in the position of applauding the FBI's dirtiest forms of intimidation. This cheap gimmick undercuts the whole civil-rights subject; it validates the terrorist methods of the Klan . . . Parker is a slicker – a man with talent and technique but without a sustaining sensibility. Each time I heard the pulsating music start working me up for the next bout of violence, I dreaded what was coming. The manipulation got to me, all right, but the only emotion I felt was hatred of the movie.' *(Pauline Kael)*

MIXED:

'Shows a director more anxious to concuss us with hyperbole than to let truth do its unharassed work . . . However, there is fine photography, and a superb central performance from Hackman.' *(Nigel Andrews, Financial Times)*

PRO:

'The historical "inaccuracies" provoked complaints from several quarters – the blacks should not have been shown as largely passive, and FBI officers just didn't behave that way. But . . . Parker has made a film that's much more interesting than what some critics seemed to be demanding – an account of how grass-roots radicalism transformed the situation of blacks in the 1960s. *Mississippi Burning* brings out precisely the imperviousness of a Southern community to change – the intractability of economic and social oppression . . . The crime is solved – the Deputy and his co-conspirators all receive jail sentences – and the cops reach some degree of mutual understanding, but there's no sense of triumph, no sense that racism has been dispersed.' *(James Park, Film Yearbook)*

'McDormand's face as moral battleground is the film's most compelling sight. She knows she's being soft-soaped, but she also knows Hackman genuinely admires her, and she's not indifferent to his good opinion. Watching her sort out her feelings and decide in favor of conscience over caution saves the film from its retreat to the simplistic.' *(Jay Carr, Boston Globe)*

'A strong, stirring film . . . [which] could have been very different in the hands of a black director . . . but it would have been hard pressed to be more damning of bigotry. I was left full of fury at the hatred of those who share the colour of my skin. Lord knows how a black person feels on seeing it.' *(Sue Heal, Today)*

'No other movie I've seen captures so forcefully the look, the feel, the very smell of racism. We can feel how sexy their hatred feels to the racists in this movie, how it replaces other entertainments, how it compensates for their sense of worthlessness. And we can feel something breaking free, the fresh air rushing in, when the back of that racism is broken.' *(Roger Ebert)*

MISSOURI BREAKS, THE CT: 1 AV: 2.92

1976 US 126 C WESTERN

D Arthur Penn ●
W Thomas McGuane

Marlon Brando Jack Nicholson Randy Quaid Harry Dean Stanton Frederic Forrest Kathleen Lloyd

A hired gun (Marlon Brando) and a horse thief (Jack Nicholson) battle it out with the locals for control of the territory.

Brando and Nicholson should have been a winning combination but weren't, in this surprisingly poor and incoherent western directed by Arthur Penn (of *Bonnie and Clyde* fame).

PRO:

'It is typical of the film's richness and ambiguity that the title has about five possible punning meanings.' *(Michael Billington, Illustrated London News)*

'The picture belongs to Brando. The crazy daring, the reckless bravado of his work simply overpowers everything else on the screen. You groan, you shake your head, you laugh wildly at each new lunacy, but you cannot help being fascinated by the man. In the gloomy middle years of his career, he used to demonstrate his contempt for the medium by giving the smallest part of his talents. Now he has apparently decided to give too much, to parody himself. His work in *The Missouri Breaks* is not so much a performance as it is a finger thrust joyously upward by an actor who has survived everything, including his own self-destructive impulses.' *(Time)*

ANTI:

'Penn is doing his number, Brando his, Nicholson his . . . Maybe the whole thing is just one big joke.' *(Variety)*

'Although listed as the director, Mr Penn finds himself perched on Brando's knee and manipulated as shamelessly as Edgar Bergen used to waggle Charlie McCarthy.' *(Benny Green, Punch)*

'Marlon Brando at 52 has the sloppy belly of a 62-year-old, the white hair of a 72-year-old, and the total lack of discipline of a precocious 12-year-old.' *(Sun)*

'If Brando hates acting, why doesn't he quit? If McGuane is going to set the film-writing profession to rights, why doesn't he learn how? If Penn's culture-vulture flabbiness is going to keep creeping, why doesn't he try some spiritual rigor?' *(Stanley Kauffmann)*

'Nothing more than the self-conscious cleverness of some merry prankster with a blanket of scorn for all who don't share his flippancy.' *(William S. Pechter)*

'The Western is losing something, is forgetting something. It grows more violent: that, though I shall always detest the savage handling of the horses, one has to accept. My complaint is that the violence has gone cold. And now I reflect on that missing attendant at the cradle of Mr Penn's film, and it seems to me that the gift denied is the gift of warmth, that what has been lost is the generosity of passion. Respectfully one watches the camerawork, the composition; one follows the players. But one simply cannot feel for them.' *(Dilys Powell)*

'What really hurts, though, is the dialogue. It is all studied quirkiness, self-congratulatory cuteness and insipid pseudopregnancy. No one ever talked like this in the West, East, North, or South . . . Utterly lamentable, too, is Brando's performance, even more slatternly and self-indulgent than his bloated physique. Starting with a correspondence-school brogue and bits of mannerism left over from his garish performance in *The Nightcomers*, he adds to them an effeteness and smarminess . . . Kathleen Lloyd as Jane Braxton . . . turns what needed to be only a badly written lost soul into a full-fledged driveling idiot. At UCLA, she won the 1969 Hugh O'Brian Acting Award, which, I assume, is given annually for the best impersonation of Hugh O'Brian trying to act.' *(John Simon)*

'A picture of which it might be said they shouldn't make 'em like that any more.' *(Robert Hatch, Nation)*

'I wrote it as . . . an ensemble movie about a little gang of outlaws who outlived their time. Then, all of a sudden, this star casting came in, and it went from being prospectively a very interesting genre movie to this kind of monster.' *(Thomas McGuane)*

MISTER AND MRS BRIDGE: *see* MR. AND MRS. BRIDGE.

MISTER ARKADIN: *see* CONFIDENTIAL REPORT.

MISTER BLANDINGS BUILDS HIS DREAM HOUSE: *see* MR. BLANDINGS BUILDS HIS DREAM HOUSE.

MISTER DEEDS GOES TO TOWN: *see* MR. DEEDS GOES TO TOWN.

MISTER HULOT'S HOLIDAY: *see* MONSIEUR HULOT'S HOLIDAY.

MISTER ROBERTS AAN   CT: 5 AV: 7.77

1956 US 123 C COMEDY/WAR/DRAMA

D John Ford (replaced during production), Mervyn LeRoy, Joshua Logan (uncredited)
W Joshua Logan Frank S. Nugent from Logan and Thomas Heggen's play and Heggen's novel

Henry Fonda ☆ James Cagney ☆ Jack Lemmon ☆ AAW William Powell ☆ Ward Bond Betsy Palmer Philip Carey Nick Adams Harry Carey Jr Ken Curtis

Men await military action on a cargo ship during World War II.

Hit comedy whose talkiness betrays its origins as a Broadway play. The acting is superb, but the mixture of comedy, sentiment and drama now looks artificial; and there are long dull patches. Director John Ford and Fonda rowed on set, even to the point of having a fist-fight; so Ford was replaced (feigning illness) and Mervyn LeRoy took over after a brief stint by the original stage director, Joshua Logan. There was an inferior sequel, *Ensign Pulver* (1964), which did *not* feature Jack Lemmon in the role which had brought him his first Oscar.

MIXED:

'Never once gives the feeling of being at sea . . . But, considered as a slapstick version of *The Caine Mutiny*, it succeeds in being enormously funny. The raucous and bawdy comedy is well laced with satirical wit and the four leading actors give expert and lively performances.' *(Alan Brien, Evening Standard)*

'You can call it crude, leering, bombastic, over-sentimental . . . But the fact remains that this lusty cruise . . . has tremendous gusto.' *(Roy Nash, Star)*

ANTI:

'I thought its seriousness as ham-fisted as its fun was deafeningly objectionable.' *(Paul Dehn, News Chronicle)*

'Mr Cagney throughout looks like a fat boy, there are

really no other words for it, decked out in fancy dress and pretending to be grown up. Never has Mr Cagney been so unsure of himself or been seen to such little advantage.' *(The Times)*

'A variation on the theme of *The Caine Mutiny*, without the characterisation and story value of that film, and with the ultimate acts of mutiny taking a more schoolboyish form. The presence of Henry Fonda and William Powell lends a certain amount of dignity to otherwise barren proceedings, but even they cannot save the banality of an ending which without warning winds up what has been a sort of perverted farce in a deluge of sentiment.' *(Daily Mail)*

'The comic and heroic spirit went out of the famous stage success . . . when the play was transferred to the screen; it's a miserable piece of moviemaking – poorly paced and tearjerking.' *(Pauline Kael)*

MISTER SKEFFINGTON: *see* MR. SKEFFINGTON.

MISTER SMITH GOES TO WASHINGTON: *see* MR. SMITH GOES TO WASHINGTON.

MIT LIV SOM HUND: *see* MY LIFE AS A DOG.

MODERN TIMES CT: 5 AV: 8.80

1936 US 87 BW COMEDY/ROMANCE/MAINLY SILENT

D Charles Chaplin ☆
W Charles Chaplin

Charles Chaplin Paulette Goddard
Henry Bergman Tiny Sandford Chester Conklin
Hank Mann Louis Natheaux Stanley Blystone
Allan Garcia Sammy Stein

An assembly-line worker (Charles Chaplin) is driven to distraction by his job.

A historical curiosity: a silent movie made well after the coming of talkies. The part of the film which still works is Charlie Chaplin's slapstick satire on assembly-line manufacture, although a lot of this was borrowed from René Clair's 1931 film, *Freedom For Us (À Nous La Libert)*. Although Chaplin and Paulette Goddard play the sentimental sequences to the hilt, these don't really fit in with the rest of the picture. The film's final speech, calling for peace and understanding, is embarrassing in its banality – Chaplin at his worst. The film was successful in the US, but was banned as Communist propaganda in Fascist Italy and in Nazi Germany.

'I give the talkies six months more, at the most a year. Then they're done.' *(Charles Chaplin, 1931)*

PRO:

'If you have tears, prepare to shed them; Charlie Chaplin is on the side of the angels . . . For the first time an American film was daring to challenge the superiority of an industrial civilization based upon the creed of men who sit at flat-topped desks and . . . demand more speed from tortured employees . . . Chaplin's methods are too kindly for great satire, but . . . he has made high humor out of material which is fundamentally tragic . . . But the hilarity is never an opiate . . . If I make it seem ponderous and social rather than hilarious it is because I came away stunned at the thought that such a film had been made and was being distributed . . . It is not social document, it is not a revolutionary tract, it is one of the funniest of all of Chaplin's films, but it is certainly no comfort to the enemy . . . Not so much a fine motion picture as an historical event.' *(Robert Forsythe [aka Kyle Crichton], The New Masses)*

'Wholesomely funny.' *(Variety)*

'The picture is about the social disorders of the 30s, and there are clashes between the unemployed and the police, and a gag about a Communist demonstration, yet it's one of the happiest and most lighthearted of the Chaplin pictures – partly because his new leading lady, Paulette Goddard, playing a character listed as "a Gamin", has a beautiful grin and a bouncy, outgoing personality. And with the use of more sound, Chaplin seems to drop some of his pathos; this picture doesn't pull at your heartstrings – it has the spirit of a good vaudeville show, and the tramp doesn't lose out at the end (he gets his gamin).' *(Pauline Kael)*

MIXED:

'In my view it is much less good than either *The Gold Rush* or *City Lights*, because I happen to like the pathetic side of Charlie better than the clowning. If this sounds ungracious on the part of one who, twice at least during *Modern Times*, laughed till the tears ran down his face, I cannot help it. The trouble with the present film, if there be any trouble, is that the story is weak, and that we really care very little what becomes of the tramp, whereas in *City Lights* we cared enormously . . . However, there are comic inventions in this film which transcend anything that Chaplin has ever given us.' *(James Agate, Tatler)*

'Positively, there are many superb gags and enough of Chaplin's brilliant dance and mime to make any film distinguished. Negatively, it is disconnected and, in its overtone, sad, sentimental and defeatist . . . His sympathies are fiercely against exploitation, but he proves himself the loosest of thinkers. His hatred of capitalist machinery and organization gets mixed up with the anarchist's hatred of all machinery and organization together . . . [His] usual collection of stock characters and sentimentalities . . . look somewhat mannered . . . His maintenance of pure mime with background music seems equally old-fashioned and uninspired . . . Avoiding the possibilities of sound . . . he merely demonstrates that he has lost interest in the technique of his art. He has . . . discovered nothing and created nothing

... He is out-of-date.' *(John Grierson, World Film News)*

ANTI:

'Disconnected comedy stuff ... Chaplin himself is not dated, never will be; he is a reservoir of humor, master of an infinite array of dodges ... not only a touching character but a first class buffoon ... But this does not make him a first class picture maker ... and I'll take bets that if he keeps on refusing to learn any more than he learned when movies themselves were just learning, each successive picture he makes will seem, on release, to fall short of what went before.' *(Otis Ferguson, New Republic)*

MOMENT BY MOMENT CT: 5 AV: 2.00

1978 US 105 C DRAMA/ROMANCE

D Jane Wagner ●
W Jane Wagner ●

John Travolta ● Lily Tomlin ● Andra Akers
Bert Kramer Shelley R. Bonus Debra Feuer

Rich Beverly Hills socialite (Lily Tomlin) falls for nubile young beach bum (John Travolta).

Dreadfully maudlin, ultra-Californian romance between the unlikely pair of Lily Tomlin (surprisingly dull) and John Travolta (unsurprisingly narcissistic). Audiences wisely stayed away in droves from this dreary attempt at sexual role-reversal, and Travolta's career took years to recover. The screenplay is so banal and humourless that the movie ends up working rather well – if unintentionally – as a satire on spoiled Californians.

Sample dialogue ... John Travolta (whose character's name is Strip) is naked in the bathtub with Lily Tomlin.
Travolta: 'I love you. Do you love me?'
Tomlin: 'Strip ...'
Travolta: 'You don't love me?'
Tomlin: 'Oh, Strip ...'
Travolta: 'I'm not good enough for you, is that it?'
Tomlin: 'Strip! This is ridiculous! Oh, Strip!'
Travolta: 'When you're ready to admit you love me, you can have me, but not until.'
Tomlin: 'Strip!'

'The first half hour of the pic, with this unusual courtship, is appealing, and only makes what follows more of a let-down ... Not helping matters is Wagner's banal script, which has cliché piled atop cliché, and dialog that evokes embarrassing laughter.' *(Variety)*

'An awful movie, but it may someday occupy a hallowed place in the pantheon of high camp.' *(Frank Rich, Time)*

'When John Travolta walks, the pavements are made out of pillows; his smile stretches from one side of the screen to the other; his teeth gleam like isotopes; the most inconsequential words come out of his mouth like crystallised fruit. Lily Tomlin is, in the face of such provocation, a model of restraint ... [She] is however not easily outperformed. Her trick is impassivity. Beside Travolta, she is a statue next to an eel ... Travolta or Tomlin, alone, could rescue [the film] from both its plot and its dialogue. Together they are unbearable.' *(Peter Ackroyd, Spectator)*

'A lot of soul searching, breast-beating, and crocodile tears are shed before an unconvincing solution is reached.' *(Virginia Dignam, Morning Star)*

'Just a terrible mess. Sooner or later, dear John is going to have to prove he can act.' *(News of the World)*

'Little more than an animated snapshot of its leading man, baring body and soul to various effect ... Truly terrible.' *(Gilbert Adair, MFB)*

'With totally unsympathetic characters set against a background of shrink-riddled, over-privileged Marin County society, and accompanied by some of the worst easy-listening Muzak LA could dredge up. Yuk.' *(Time Out)*

'Written and directed by Tomlin's friend Wagner, who deservedly took the flak for the clichéd script and risible dialogue.' *(Winnert)*

'*Moment by Moment* – that was the first time I heard the words, "Your career is over".' *(John Travolta)*

MOMMIE DEAREST CT: 6 AV: 4.73

(aka *Mommy Dearest*)

1981 US 129 C DRAMA/BIOPIC/SO BAD

D Frank Perry ●
W Frank Yablans Frank Perry Tracy Hotchner Robert Getchell from Christina Crawford's biography

Faye Dunaway ☆ Diana Scarwid Steve Forrest
Howard da Silva Mara Hobel ✔ Rutanya Alda ✔

Film star Joan Crawford (Faye Dunaway) and her adopted daughter Christina (Diana Scarwid) fail to get on.

There shouldn't be anything funny about child abuse, but there is in this entertaining, over-the-top melodrama, with Faye Dunaway alternately frightening and funny as the Hollywood Mother From Hell. It would be horrific if one took it seriously, but most people can't, because the script and direction are so patently trashy and give no real insight into why Crawford behaved the way she did (if, indeed, her daughter's account can be fully believed).

Sample lines ... Dunaway (cutting off daughter's hair): 'I'd rather you go bald to school than looking like a tramp!' Dunaway (wrecking daughter's closet): 'No wire hangers!'

'A wonderful performance by Faye Dunaway.' *(Sue Carroll, News of the World)*

'Dunaway does not chew scenery. Dunaway starts neatly at each corner of the set in every scene and swallows it whole, co-stars and all.' *(Variety)*

'Let us not mince words . . . This is a film patronised primarily . . . by homosexuals . . . Of course, many audiences might have preferred to see Stanley Baxter rather than Faye Dunaway in the central role . . . The paradox: this is a serious film, in no way designed to be funny; and yet it reduces audiences to hysteria.' *(Peter Ackroyd, Spectator)*

'Forget about *Aladdin* and *Puss in Boots*. [This is] the real pantomime . . . because . . . [it] has a wicked witch for everyone to hiss and boo. And to laugh at as well.' *(Sun)*

'Through the intensity of her performance, Faye Dunaway is able to show the flapper turning into stone . . . [She] seizes on every opportunity to suggest the sources of Crawford's pent-up fury . . . But the movie disintegrates messily when she starts to abuse her adopted children, failing to provide any coherent explanation of the incendiary subject of her child beating. The big scenes are hideous.' *(Michael Sragow, Rolling Stone)*

'Could have been – had it been cleverer – a melodrama about melodrama. But, alas . . . [it] piles agony upon agony until you laugh rather than scream . . . In the end one merely feels one has seen a rather bad Joan Crawford movie which happens to be about Joan Crawford.' *(Derek Malcolm, Guardian)*

'Faye Dunaway, in the role she was born to play . . . instantly installed herself as the all-time Contessa of Camp . . . It's anybody's call whether Crawford's supposed to be insane, or whether Dunaway perhaps just went bonkers playing her.' *(Margulies & Rebello)*

'A faithful adaptation of Christina's book . . . The only notable deviation . . . is rolling Crawford's various lovers into one composite man . . . a serious weakness, undermining the basis of [her] insecurity and removing a major reason for her outlandish behaviour . . . If the film fails, it is not because of Dunaway's superb performance but because . . . [it lapses] too easily into melodrama . . . The book struck a few false notes and unfortunately the film strikes more.' *(Sally Hibbin, F & F)*

'An absolute hoot.' *(NFT Bulletin, 1984)*

MONA LISA CT: 5 AV: 6.79

1986 GB 104 C THRILLER

D Neil Jordan ✗
W Neil Jordan David Leland

Bob Hoskins ☆ AAN Cathy Tyson Michael Caine ✓ Robbie Coltrane ✓ Clarke Peters Kate Hardie Zoe Nathenson Sammi Davis

Short, white, ex-convict George (Bob Hoskins) falls for the tall, black call-girl (Cathy Tyson) whom he's chauffeuring.

An immature, exploitative but critically acclaimed movie by Neil Jordan, which always seems about to take the lid off the sordid nature of the London underworld, but ends up merely glamorizing it. The movie found an audience because of the salacious subject-matter, and Bob Hoskins's very likeable, bull-necked performance. Cathy Tyson does her best with her role, but it's grievously underwritten – just another male fantasy-woman. (Virtually the same character turns up again, with a twist, in Jordan's later film, *The Crying Game*.) Michael Caine is effectively threatening in what might easily have been a clichéd cameo, but it's no surprise when he turns out to be Mr Big.

PRO:

'A pic that skilfully combines comedy and thriller, romance and sleaze.' *(Variety)*

'A film to see again, with the certainty that each viewing will add something new.' *(MFB)*

'A wonderful achievement, a dark film with a generous heart in the shape of an extraordinarily touching performance from Hoskins.' *(Richard Rayner, Time Out)*

'In movies, a stupid hero can be irritating and finally unbearable. But Hoskins, who is short, barrel-chested, and balding, with a pugnacious nose and a small mouth that can turn into an oval of rage, has played men of ordinary, or less than ordinary, intelligence without losing the audience for an instant. Utterly decisive in action, Hoskins becomes not merely the hero of his movies but an actor who is loved by the camera – loved, that is, the way Humphrey Bogart and James Cagney were loved – as a possibility of honor and courage.' *(David Denby)*

'The movie is lurid in a beautiful way . . . Jordan shows a gift for making the emotional atmosphere visual, and vice versa. And the way he uses baroque touches and the clichés of old thrillers they become part of a fluid, enjoyable texture, a melodramatic impasto with an expressive power of its own – a romanticism that pulls you along.' *(Pauline Kael)*

MIXED:

'Though Cathy Tyson manages to make Simone convincingly ambiguous, she is hardly as mesmerizing or mysterious as Jordan seems to think she is. Yet if we are more interested in George than in Simone it is less because of Tyson's deficiencies (it would, after all, take a Garbo to give this part everything it calls for) than because of Bob Hoskins's depth and intensity: he's simply so good an actor, so good at making credible both the violence and sweetness submerged beneath George's banal surface, that Tyson seems bland and one-dimensional by comparison. Robbie Coltrane, for his part, manages in his handful of scenes to turn his ficelle of a character into someone funny and touching, while Michael Caine is wasted as Denny – he isn't on screen very much, and his character is a shallow piece of business, the usual slimily elegant underworld bigshot. Indeed – despite its taut and witty script, its excellent pacing, and Hoskins's powerful acting – Mona Lisa is itself, in reality, a shallow piece of business; and Jordan's attempt to pass it off as something more is the film's ultimate deception.' *(Bruce Bawer, American Spectator)*

MONKEY BUSINESS CT: 8 AV: 7.44

1931 US 77 BW COMEDY

D Norman Z. McLeod
W Arthur Sheekman from S.J. Perelman, W.B. Johnstone and Roland Pertwee's story

Groucho Marx ☆ Harpo Marx ☆ Chico Marx ☆ Zeppo Marx Thelma Todd Tom Kennedy Ruth Hall Rockliffe Fellowes Harry Woods Ben Taggart

Four stowaways on a luxury liner get involved in gang warfare.

The shipboard sequences are among the funniest in any Marx Brothers movie, and the scene where all four pretend to be Maurice Chevalier in order to get off the liner is hilarious. The fun runs out once the Brothers are ashore, but the earlier parts of the film are not to be missed.

MIXED:

'You must possess a keen sense of the ridiculous if you are to appreciate [the Marx Brothers] at all. Personally, I find them generally very amusing, but less so in this picture than in their previous nonsensical knockabouts . . . The trouble with the picture is that some of their gags are beginning to wear thin . . . However, there are plenty of laughs for those who, as I have said, really appreciate nonsense.' *(Lionel Collier, Picturegoer)*

'Whether it is really as funny as *Animal Crackers* is a matter of opinion. Suffice it to say that few persons will be able to . . . keep a straight face . . . Chico goes from the ridiculous to the sublime when he plays the piano, as likewise does Harpo when he plays harp accompaniment.' *(Mordaunt Hall, New York Times)*

'No attempt had been made as in the later films to restrain [the Marx Brothers'] antics or to give their films great box-office appeal by introducing a straightforward boy-meets-girl romance.' *(MFB)*

PRO:

'It is composed of equal parts of absolute rot, silliness, insanity and nonsense, and is one of the funniest things I ever saw . . . McLeod keeps the thing moving at a terrific rate. I would guess that there will not be a moment while the picture is running that there will not be laughter coming from the audience . . . Don't miss [it].' *(Welford Beaton, Hollywood Spectator)*

MONSIEUR HIRE CT: 5 AV: 7.44

1989 France 81/97 C THRILLER/ROMANCE/ FOREIGN

D Patrice Leconte ✗
W Patrice Leconte Patrick Dewolf from Georges Simenon's novel *Les Fiançailles de Monsieur Hire*

Michel Blanc ☆ Sandrine Bonnaire Luc Thuillier André Wilms Eric Berenger

Middle-aged voyeur (Michel Blanc) chooses a new victim (Sandrine Bonnaire).

This hugely acclaimed film plays skilfully with the audience's expectations: our view of the sinister Monsieur Hire and his beautiful female 'victim' shifts inexorably, until the little man becomes sympathetic, and his erstwhile victim reveals herself as a predator. Directed as a cynical, Hitchcock-style thriller by a Chabrol or a Truffaut, the story might have held the attention. Mistakenly, director Patrice Leconte tries to create a heavily symbolic, psychological drama for the art-house. The two principals act well, and there is plenty of sexual tension (particularly, during one scene at a boxing match); but, for the most part, the story is told too slowly and the characters are too superficially drawn to sustain the interest.

PRO:

'Brilliantly conceived, admirably acted, and staged with stunning confidence.' *(Tom Milne, MFB)*

'A classic psychological thriller made with all the subtlety, elegance and skill which have placed the French at the head of the field in this genre.' *(Daily Telegraph)*

'For all its concentration on character, the film is remarkably successful as a mystery, and though the press kit warns the unwary reviewer not to give away the plot, I found the entire parade of reversals and twists so consistently surprising and pleasurable, that I am going to refrain from any further description of the plot altogether. Yet, these twists are, to use a sadly overworked word, organic, rather than mechanical. Like Hire's own stubbornly individual traits, they grow out of a faith in human possibilities that, no matter how unhappily stunted, form the essence of Monsieur Hire's convictions. And it is that faith that makes this film a lofty and brilliant work.' *(Henry Sheehan)*

'Has the disturbed sexuality and cold sensuality that was Simenon's hallmark . . . The film's timelessness is complimented by the lovely Bonnaire's style and simplicity . . . [The] film has a disquieting sense of desire that borders on the carnal.' *(Kim Shelley, New Musical Express)*

'Goes way beyond *Blue Velvet* in exploring "the dark side of the moon" of human nature, its mixtures of obstinacy and masochism, self-destruction and chilly shame . . . Simenon understands, from inside and "in the round", the spider-dances of intimacy, the strange moves between a man made passive by years of suspicion and despair, and a young girl with a peasant's silent, cautious, active strength . . . Leconte's short movie feels more like three hours, not because it drags, but because its reticence sets one thinking fast. It's part of a new idiom in French cinema. Leconte, like Beineix and Carax, tells the story less through a dramatic continuity, a flow of actions and declarations, than by a jigsaw of moments, making suggestions pictorially.' *(Raymond Durgnat, Film Review)*

MIXED:

'It's a great film to look at, stylish and inventive, full of the standard stuff . . . but also smart framing and some lurid greens and purples . . . But you just can't respect a film that so completely backs out of all its commitments. It's a *tour de force* in a vacuum: all dressed up and no place to go.' *(Julie Phillips, Village Voice)*

ANTI:

'The film does not withstand too close an examination of its supposed depths and insights.' *(Bergan & Karney)*

MONSIEUR HULOT'S HOLIDAY

CT: 6 AV: 7.69

(aka *Les Vacances de Monsieur Hulot; Mr. Hulot's Holiday)*

1953 France 91 BW COMEDY/FOREIGN

D Jacques Tati ☆
W Jacques Tati Henri Marquet

Jacques Tati ☆ Nathalie Pascaud Michèle Rolla Louis Perrault André Dubois Valentine Camax

A bachelor on holiday (Jacques Tati) proves accident-prone.

This collection of physical gags is Tati's funniest and tells more of a story than his latter films, although some of the jokes fizzle out. There is something missing – Tati's humour is all detached observation, and contains very little human warmth – but many of the deadpan routines are still hilarious. Winner of the Palme d'Or at Cannes.

PRO:

'There are . . . certain films which not only seem universally enjoyable, but probably yield their fullest flavour when seen in familiar company – and [this] is one of them.' *(Times Educational Supplement)*

'Had me laughing out loud with more enjoyment than any other comedy film this year.' *(Daily Express)*

'Chaos, glorious and unconfined, with France's best clown at the centre of it.' *(S. Baron, News Chronicle)*

'Incomparable clowning . . . And room for sentiment. I laughed from beginning to end. But when I came out into the street I felt I had been in warm-hearted company, and the tears in my eyes were not all tears of laughter.' *(Dilys Powell)*

'People are at their most desperate when they are working at enjoying themselves; it is Jacques Tati's peculiar comic triumph to have caught the ghastliness of a summer vacation at the beach. Fortunately, his technique is light and dry slapstick; the chronicle of human foibles and frustrations never sinks to the moist or the lovable. As director, co-author, and star, Tati is sparse, eccentric, quick. It is not until afterward – with the sweet, nostalgic music lingering – that these misadventures may take on a certain depth and poignancy.' *(Pauline Kael)*

MIXED:

'The casual, amateurish air of his films clearly adds to their appeal; it also appears to explain their defects.' *(Penelope Houston, MFB)*

'Despite lame endings to some of the jokes, this is a film to set the world laughing, Hulot himself being an unforgettable character and some of the timing magnificent.' *(Halliwell)*

MONSIEUR VERDOUX

CT: 5 AV: 7.30

1947 US 125 BW COMEDY

D Charles Chaplin ✗
W Charles Chaplin ✗ AAN

Charles Chaplin ✗ Martha Raye ✓ Isobel Elsom Marilyn Nash William Frawley Mady Correll

A modern Bluebeard (Charles Chaplin) murders rich widows for their money but feels no remorse, since he needs the money to support his crippled wife (Mady Correll).

Monsieur Verdoux still has the power to divide critics. It has less of the glutinous sentimentality which mars so many of Chaplin's films; but some scenes with the crippled wife are hard to watch. Although some of the low comedy with Martha Raye is amusing, much of the humour – especially some unfunny slapstick – has dated, and the didactically anti-capitalist, anti-war message is so crassly expressed as to be embarrassing. Personally embroiled at the time of its release in a much-publicized paternity case, Chaplin generated little public sympathy for a character with a cavalier approach to conventional morality. Though much praised by some critics (especially on the Left) it was a flop.

'In April of 1947, *Monsieur Verdoux* had its New York premiere – a sickening evening. Chaplin's awareness of his atrocious publicity resulting from a paternity case, as well as his much misunderstood political statements, prepared him somewhat for the at times frightening reception of some organized, hostile members of the audience. Insane booing greeted such lines as "Millions are starving and unemployed." Agonized groans greeted Verdoux's reply to his child who asks him what sort of man Santa Claus is: "Very kind – to the rich." . . . Charlie once told me of a terrifying, recurrent nightmare from which he suffered all his life. He'd be performing a comedy act in front of a large audience, and no one would be laughing. His nightmare had become a reality. "They couldn't take it, could they?" he kept repeating. "I kicked them in the balls. I hit them where it hurt".' *(Robert Lewis)*

'The cleverest and most brilliant film I have yet made.' *(Charles Chaplin)*

PRO:

'One of the best movies ever made, easily the most exciting and most beautiful since *Modern Times*. I will add that I think most of the press on the picture, and on Chaplin, is beyond disgrace . . . I love and revere the film as deeply as any I have seen . . . Chaplin's performance is the best piece of playing I have seen.' *(James Agee)*

'The most exciting thing that has happened to the screen for years; very probably it is his greatest film. Go for yourself and see a film that is refreshing in its moral courage and pacifist assertion of human dignity. And then, as I will do, go again.' *(Richard Winnington)*

'The most grown-up film ever to have come out of America. One comes away after the excitement and the belly laughs, feeling what a strength it is to have a genius like Charlie Chaplin lined up in the struggle for a better life.' *(Gabriel, Daily Worker)*

'His most serious and totally successful. In its social purpose it is bolder and more incisive than anything he has yet made . . . Not just a funny story about a murderer but a witty travesty on an unethical business-minded society.' *(Lewis Jacobs, Cinema)*

'There is a bitterness in [it] which makes a comparison possible with Voltaire, or better still with Swift.' *(Further Education)*

'Both the best example of the use of parable and the most significant [film] to launch an offensive on society that [has] been made in recent years.' *(Pierre Kast, Cahiers du Cinéma, 1951)*

'Whatever the reasons for its initial failure, Chaplin's Bluebeard story is ours to revel in for the sheer brilliance of performance, the cinematic excellence of his direction and the simplicity that shines in all its latter-day naiveté.' *(Judith Crist, New York Herald Tribune)*

MIXED:

'There are in *Monsieur Verdoux* one or two dull passages and one or two moments of incongruous sentiment. The rest is written and played with an incomparable sense of irony, of drama and of character; of character which, developing with the plot, attains at the last the dignity of pathos.' *(Dilys Powell)*

ANTI:

'With all my admiration for Charlie's courage and my enthusiasm for a remarkable picture, I for my part do not feel that he has quite managed to get away with it . . . He has reserved until his final sequences the expression of that savage and passionate indignation that should in one way or another have been animating every stroke of his sardonic little parable.' *(Mary Britton Miller, New Movies)*

'Chaplin has attempted to underscore his story with a message, which is a dubious one at best. *Monsieur Verdoux* gets out of hand at the end, when the little Bluebeard arraigns society at large for the sinister life it has forced him to lead. Chaplin's social thinking is confused here, and the audience goes away confused, not to say baffled.' *(Fortnight)*

'The film itself, by breaking Chaplin's aesthetic contract with his audience in a number of ways (especially by presenting a new central persona different in class and interests from the familiar Charlie) . . . undercut Chaplin's star image.' *(Charles J. Maland, Chaplin and American Culture)*

'Even today *Monsieur Verdoux* will seem a failure to anyone who has taken half a dozen lessons in film technique. Things were much worse, however, back in 1947 when Chaplin was squeezed between the patrons of Hollywood illusionism on the one hand and the partisans of Italian neorealism on the other. *Verdoux* is neither slick enough for the dream merchants nor sincere enough for the humanists, and this is not necessarily all to the good as Agee seemed to suggest. Indeed, the opening exposition involving the family of a Verdoux victim is about as bad as anything I have ever seen in the professional cinema. Yet after repeated reviewings, the badness seems not only integral to Chaplin's conception but decidedly Brechtian in the bargain.' *(Andrew Sarris, Confessions of a Cultist, 1970)*

MONSIGNOR

CT: 5 AV: 2.27

1982 US 121 C DRAMA/SO BAD

D Frank Perry ●
W Abraham Polonsky Wendell Mayes ● from Jack Alain Leger's novel

Christopher Reeve ● Genevieve Bujold ● Fernando Rey Jason Miller Joe Cortese Adolfo Celi Leonardo Cimino

A dodgy priest (Christopher Reeve) manoeuvres his way up the Roman Catholic hierarchy.

Schlockmeister Frank Yablans had already produced *The Other Side of Midnight* (1977) and *Mommie Dearest* (1981). With this unintentionally hilarious hokum, he showed that he was none the wiser. The deadly serious attempts to shock us are all risible; and the dialogue – from two of Hollywood's previously most respected screenwriters – is diabolical. Best watched on video, where one can fast-forward through the many boring bits.

Sample lines . . . Genevieve Bujold, stripping off to seduce cardinal (Christopher Reeve): 'God gave me a strange gift. He made me attract love affairs that quickly become disasters. That's why I decided to become a nun. But, here I am, ready for another disaster. I'll have some champagne.' Later . . . Bujold to Reeve: 'I was free with you and let you into my life, and you betrayed me. It's not love you betrayed – it's me! Clara! God can't forgive you. Only I can forgive you. And I never will. Never!'

MIXED:

'A long film which sags under the weight of its tremendous ambitions . . . However, clever casting and acting rescue many an embarrassing moment.' *(Michael Wigan, Scotsman)*

ANTI:

'Lots of potential for a rare, absorbing, behind-the-scenes look at the Vatican is totally blown . . . The self-serious $12 million pic teeters on the brink of being an all-out hoot through much of its running time . . . It's amazing that neither Abraham Polonsky nor Wendell Mayes, both outstanding screenwriters, didn't spot the most gaping fundamental flaw here, namely the lack of any convincing explanation why Reeve's character became a priest in the first place.' *(Variety)*

'Concerned Americans of every religion are trying to fight this movie by laughing it off the screen. But what I want to know is: where's the Legion of Decency when we really need it?' *(Time)*

'Perry lays a heavy hand on [it] but with the script at his disposal he can't be entirely blamed for the fact that the film is impossible to take seriously.' *(Ian Christie, Daily Express)*

'Guaranteed to appeal not so much to the faithful as to the gullible.' *(Virginia Dignam, Morning Star)*

'A 20-Hail Mary slice of epic schlock.' *(Chris Peachment, Time Out)*

'Preposterous . . . surprisingly dull for a film about sex and politics in high places.' *(Scheuer)*

'Grows more ridiculous as it goes along – with unintentional comedy on a grand scale – culminating in an astonishing final shot involving the Pope. Another camp classic from the producer and director of *Mommie Dearest*.' *(Maltin)*

MONSTERS FROM THE MOON: *see* ROBOT MONSTER.

MONTY PYTHON'S LIFE OF BRIAN

CT: 7 AV: 6.85

(aka *Life of Brian)*

1979 GB 94 C COMEDY

D Terry Jones
W Graham Chapman John Cleese Terry Gilliam Eric Idle Terry Jones Michael Palin

Graham Chapman John Cleese Terry Gilliam Eric Idle Terry Jones Michael Palin Sue Jones-Davies Spike Milligan

The life of Brian Cohen (Graham Chapman) mistakenly hailed as a Saviour.

Unjustly castigated as blasphemous when it came out, this tale of a reluctant Messiah (not the real one) begins with a very funny half-hour, then fizzles out badly towards the end. Even so, it's the best of the Python films. The message of the movie, which is about the futility and hypocrisy of religious intolerance, remains only too topical. Effective use is made of Tunisian locations.

ANTI:

'Although [it] tries hard to be outrageous, it's just a silly burlesque – tasteless but harmless, repetitive and dumb.' *(David Denby, New York Magazine)*

'In the face of such an onslaught of bad taste, criticism seems irrelevant.' *(Halliwell)*

MIXED:

'The old jokes, if not the best, seem to be the most successful; and the Monty Python team have never been known to leave a dead horse unflogged . . . The whole film is really an excuse for some relentlessly comic sketches, as though it were a kind of human strip cartoon . . . The visual humour which made [the TV series] so successful is almost entirely missing . . . and the only blasphemy it commits is against the late Cecil B. DeMille.' *(Peter Ackroyd, Spectator)*

PRO:

'The most consistently funny, sharply satiric, coherent and inventive of this team's comedies . . . See it!' *(Jack Babuscio, Gay News)*

'Hilarious, outrageous and the best Monty Python film so far.' *(Margaret Forwood, Sun)*

MOONLIGHTING

CT: 6 AV: 7.25

1982 GB 97 C DRAMA

D Jerzy Skolimowski
W Jerzy Skolimowski Boleslaw Sulik Barrie Vince Danuta Witold Stok

Jeremy Irons ☆ Eugene Lipinski Jiri Stanislav

Eugeniusz Haczkiewicz Dorothy Zienciowska Edward Arthur Denis Holmes Renu Setna David Calder

Polish workers arrive in London to renovate a house for their boss, but while they are away, martial law is declared in Poland.

It starts out as comedy, poking fun at the unintelligent workers, encouraging us to side with their more sophisticated foreman. But slowly (a little too slowly) it turns into a grim political allegory, with Irons becoming a totalitarian boss and destroying his workers' freedoms. The film is saved from being too simplistically anti-Communist by its equivocal view of life in London, and by Irons's subtly modulated performance.

PRO:

'A film more pertinent to a political crisis well outside our reach but thank God not outside our ken, it would be hard to imagine . . . Be proud [it] was made in Britain: it does more for Solidarity than a dozen demos.' *(Alexander Walker, Evening Standard)*

'Irons . . . shows what a fine actor he can be . . . in this quicksilver, tiny scale, haunting parable.' *(Richard Barkley, Sunday Express)*

'In its own way, this response to the crushing of Solidarity is as powerful as Andrzej Wajda's *Man of Iron*. It also is more fun.' *(Roger Ebert)*

MIXED:

'Inventive, though anecdotal.' *(Variety)*

ANTI:

'There is a rough and ready improvisational look . . . which works for rather than against it, but [the film] has been overwrought into a political parable about the recent events in Poland and the suppression of Solidarity. An extremist reaction . . . This film . . . is a way of averting attention from the real political truths of the Polish situation and the wholesale decline of capitalism in the West.' *(Virginia Dignam, Morning Star)*

'A box-office flop in the United States, and it's easy to see why. At a time when the West was eager to sentimentalize Solidarity Skolimowski showed a bunch of apparently bumbling workers led to disaster by an angst-riddled betrayer who wins no redemption. Nor did he give American audiences the easy satisfactions of, say, *Moscow on the Hudson*, which suggested that, despite everything, the West really is the Free World. For all the wit and grace of this movie (and of all his best work), Jerzy Skolimowski knows there are no Free Worlds to be found.' *(John Powers)*

MOONRAKER: *see BOND* SERIES.

MOONSTRUCK AAN   CT: 5 AV: 8.00

1987 US 102 C COMEDY/ROMANCE

D Norman Jewison ✗ AAN
W John Patrick Shanley ✗ AAW

Cher ☆ AAW Nicolas Cage ● Vincent Gardenia ☆ AAN Olympia Dukakis ☆ AAW Danny Aiello Julie Bovasso ✓ John Mahoney Louis Guss Feodor Chaliapin Anita Gillette Joe Grifasi Robin Bartlett Helen Hanft

Italian-American woman (Cher) finds love.

Romantic comedy of Italian-American life which did well at the box office and struck many as immensely charming. Some of the sentiment and philosophizing is hard to take, however, and the stereotypical characters seem lazily written, if energetically performed. Norman Jewison's direction is too heavy-handed for so frothy a story, and I could never work out why Cher wanted hammy Nicolas Cage in the same room, let alone as her lover – but what the hell, it's harmless entertainment.

PRO:

'A gem, light as a soufflé and every line a bullseye.' *(Sue Heal, Today)*

'The most beguiling comedy of sexual manners for ages.' *(Tom Hutchinson, Mail on Sunday)*

'The most enchanting quality about *Moonstruck* is the hardest to describe, and that is the movie's tone. Reviews of the movie tend to make it sound like a madcap ethnic comedy, and that it is. But there is something more here, a certain bittersweet yearning that comes across as ineffably romantic, and a certain magical quality that is reflected in the film's title.' *(Roger Ebert)*

'Cher is devastatingly funny and sinuous and beautiful . . . Cage is a wonderful romantic clown: he can look stupefied while he smolders . . . The picture is slender, but it's an original: its mockery is a giddy homage to our desire for grand passion.' *(Pauline Kael)*

'An utter charmer of a movie. Wit and wisdom shine out from this beautifully written and acted tale of love and family as the characters, so we're to believe, are driven by the influence of the moon.' *(Rose)*

MIXED:

'Warm to the point of turning gooey.' *(Richard Mayne, Sunday Telegraph)*

'Performances aside it is strictly a walk through New York sentimental comedy in which both script and situations have been set by computer.' *(John Marriott, Daily Mail)*

ANTI:

'An odd good line, one or two scenes involving

Olympia Dukakis, can't disguise the basic "happy families" sentimentality. And the narrative is not sufficiently tight for farce. It is fashioned in an overwrought Hollywood manner.' *(Michael Wigan, Scotsman)*

MÖRDER UNTER UNS: *see* M.

MORE THE MERRIER, THE AAN

CT: 6 AV: 7.56

1943 US 104 BW COMEDY/WAR

D George Stevens ☆ AAN
W Robert Russell Frank Ross Richard Flournoy Lewis R. Foster ☆ AAN from Ross and Russell's story AAN

Jean Arthur ☆ AAN Joel McCrea ☆ Charles Coburn ☆ AAW Richard Gaines Bruce Bennett

The housing shortage in wartime Washington makes a young woman (Jean Arthur) share her apartment with two men (Joel McCrea, Charles Coburn) who decide she is about to marry the wrong man.

Charming romantic comedy, marred for some by Jean Arthur's overacting. She's noticeably better when unbending towards Joel McCrea than early on, when playing the prim control-freak. The plot eventually runs out of steam, but there are many enjoyable set-pieces along the way. McCrea gives a fine, unselfish performance – arguably his best. Remade, not nearly so effectively, as *Walk Don't Run* (1966).

ANTI:

'A tired soufflé . . . Every good moment frazzles or drowns. The most flagrant example is Jean Arthur, whose mugging and whinnying seemed to me as redundant and, at length, as uningratiating, as if a particularly cute monkey, instead of merely holding out his hat for a penny which I might gladly have made a quarter, insisted that he was working his way through Harvard.' *(James Agee)*

PRO:

'A sparkling and effervescing piece of entertainment.' *(Variety)*

'The events have considerable charm, due chiefly to the talents of sandpaper-voiced Jean Arthur, and the antics of rotund Charles Coburn, who pulls every conceivable comedic trick from the bag of his many years experience in the theater.' *(Herb Sterne)*

'The gayest comedy that has come from Hollywood in a long time. It has no more substance than a watermelon, but is equally delectable.' *(Howard Barnes, New York Herald Tribune)*

MOROCCO

CT: 6 AV: 7.20

1930 US 90 BW DRAMA/ROMANCE

D Josef von Sternberg ☆ AAN
W Jules Furthman from Benno Vigny's novel *Amy Jolly*

Gary Cooper Marlene Dietrich ☆ AAN Adolphe Menjou Ullrich Haupt Juliette Compton Francis McDonald Albert Conti

A cabaret singer (Marlene Dietrich) has to choose between the wealthy man she likes (Adolphe Menjou) and the Foreign Legionnaire (Gary Cooper) she loves.

This kind of over-glamorous, high romance looks a bit ridiculous; and feminists might reasonably object to the extent that even this strong woman's fate is to follow her man. Slow and dated though it is, the film still packs a punch and has an erotic charge because of Dietrich, beautifully photographed by Lee Garmes (who was nominated for an Oscar, as was art director Hans Dreier). The film made Dietrich a star in America.

ANTI:

'Miss Dietrich bears a resemblance to Greta Garbo, but her acting hardly rivals that of the Swedish star . . . One might be justified in presuming that if she had been given more rein by Mr von Sternberg her work might have been more satisfactory, for her gamut of emotions here consists only of gazing intently, smiling and looking languid . . . handicapped, like the other players by the economy in dialogue, which results in many an uncomfortable pause.' *(New York Times)*

'Marlene Dietrich has little opportunities in her first American talker. There's nothing to the picture, except what Josef von Sternberg gives it in direction, and that's giving it more than it's got.' *(Variety)*

MIXED:

'Picturesque . . . . slight story . . . What is obviously a subtle study of opposing characters is here treated by . . . von Sternberg with considerable originality and a sincere feeling for the cinematic qualities as represented pictorially. The action at times is slow . . . Dietrich gives a performance of singular charm.' *(Bioscope)*

'Perhaps Josef von Sternberg's most effective piece of romantic mythmaking. It's enchantingly silly, full of soulful grand passions, drifting cigarette smoke, and a few too many pictorial shots of the Foreign Legion marching this way and that.' *(Pauline Kael)*

PRO:

'I am almost inclined now to place von Sternberg at the top of the list of American directors who have made notable contributions to the screen . . . [He] has taken this ordinary motion picture story and tells it across a glamorous background . . . making it a pulsing, moving drama of a great romance that will awaken the enthusiasm of the most blasé audience. He is helped by some superb performances, but he is entitled to some of the credit for them . . . He reveals himself as a master at uniting all the elements of his creation into a perfect whole.' *(Welford Beaton, Film Spectator)*

'Von Sternberg has introduced a thrilling new talkie technique. Hot stuff, this. Don't miss.' *(Photoplay)*

'A cinematic pattern, brilliant, profuse, subtle, and at almost every turn inventive.' *(Wilson A. Barrett)*

'A definite step forward in the art of motion pictures.' *(NBR)*

'The plotting and acting are in exactly the same expressionist register as everything else. Here, the highly nuanced portraits of men and a woman caught between the codes they live by, and their deepest, secret impulses, remain very moving and 100% modern.' *(Tony Rayns, Time Out)*

MORTAL STORM, THE

CT: 5 AV: 7.25

1940 US 100 BW DRAMA

D Frank Borzage ☆
W Claudine West Anderson Ellis George Froeschel from Phyllis Bottome's novel

Margaret Sullavan Robert Young James Stewart Frank Morgan Robert Stack Bonita Granville Irene Rich Maria Ouspenskaya

The rise of Nazism causes the breakup of a German family.

Earnest melodrama, propagandistic in tone (it was made before the US entered World War II). It suffers from unconvincing studio sets and doesn't illuminate the causes of Nazism; but the story is reasonably involving, as is the final escape. After seeing this movie, Goebbels banned all MGM films throughout German territories.

MIXED:

'Directed with skill and discretion, and acted sensitively and intelligently. But it is acted. The members of the cast never quite get under the skin of their parts. Neither the dialogue nor the action burns or sears.' *(MFB)*

'There is no use mincing words about it: [the film] falls definitely into the category of blistering anti-Nazi propaganda . . . As [such] it is a trumpet call to resistance, but as theatrical entertainment it is grim and depressing.' *(Bosley Crowther)*

'Here is a purely sentimental approach to Nazism . . . The finale is tragic, and there is a good deal of synthetic snow. So much for the worst that can be said about [it]. The curious thing is that with all its bogus trappings it almost comes near to genuine tragedy . . . largely due to Borzage's brilliance as a director . . . To the most hackneyed scenes he brings a freshness of eye and a great mastery of technique.' *(Basil Wright, Spectator)*

PRO:

'Gripping story . . . Brilliant portraiture, vivid dialogue, and finely composed succession of emotional domestic incident, combine to assert searing indictment of Hitler regime . . . Unreservedly recommended.' *(The Cinema)*

'So moving and shows so realistic an understanding of the growth of the Nazi "new world" that I recommend all except twitterers to go at once and see it.' *(William Whitebait, New Statesman)*

MORTE A VENEZIA: *see* DEATH IN VENICE.

MOST DANGEROUS GAME, THE

CT: 6 AV: 6.33

(aka *The Hounds of Zaroff*)

1932 US 63 BW HORROR/THRILLER

D Ernest B. Schoedsack Irving Pichel ☆
W James Creelman from Richard Connell's story ☆

Leslie Banks ☆ Joel McCrea Fay Wray Robert Armstrong Noble Johnson

Mad hunter (Leslie Banks) shipwrecks people to provide human prey.

Although this early talkie is a classic thriller with one of the most exciting chase sequences ever (beautifully scored by Max Steiner), it is not all that frightening. Audiences nowadays are more likely to appreciate Henry Gerrard's cinematography, and art direction which – though criticized on release as unrealistic – is clearly meant to evoke a nightmare. Leslie Banks dominates the film with a memorable performance. The director Schoedsack, producer Cooper and two of the cast (Robert Armstrong and Fay Wray) went on the following year to make arguably the greatest monster movie of all time, *King Kong*.

ANTI:

'Fantastic would-be thriller whose efforts at horrifying are not very effective . . . Although the swamp and jungle setting serve . . . they're frequently obviously phoney . . . With McCrea and Robert Armstrong (as a booze-guzzling simpleton) miscasting is evident.' *(Variety)*

PRO:

'The whole thing is most colourful, and Zaroff's human hunt is finely directed; thrilling and bizarre in turns. The interest is exceptionally well held, and the thrills, while occasionally forced by artificiality, are much more realistic than the majority seen in this picture's prototypes.' *(Picturegoer)*

'Vivid adaptation . . . Cleverly directed sequences of thrilling and exciting incident developed with maximum suspense values and enthrallingly eerie atmosphere . . . Staged with superlative skill and unusual conviction . . . Finely acted . . . Outstanding entertainment of its type.' *(The Cinema Supplement)*

'Through the imaginative fashion in which it has been produced, together with its effective staging and a noteworthy performance by Leslie Banks, the fantastic theme . . . makes a highly satisfactory melodrama. It has the much-desired virtue of originality, which, in no small measure, compensates for some of its gruesome ideas and its weird plot.' *(Mordaunt Hall, New York Times)*

'Still one of the best and most literate movies from the great days of horror, it is particularly effective in its measured graduation from words to action with the long, ferocious, beautifully choreographed hunt sequence, in which the human prey wins the day by drawing on all his reserves of animal cunning.' *(Tom Milne, Time Out)*

MOTHER CT: 6 AV: 7.14

(aka *Mat)*

1926 USSR 90 BW DRAMA/SILENT/FOREIGN

D Vsevolod Pudovkin ☆
W N. Zarkhi Vsevolod Pudovkin from Maxim Gorky's novel

Vera Baranovskaya ☆ A.P. Khristiakov Nikolai Batalov Ivan Kovel-Samborski Anna Zemtsova Vsevolod Pudovkin

A mother (Vera Baranovskaya) betrays her son (Nikolai Batalov), leader of an illegal strike, to the police but eventually learns to love Communism.

Classic Soviet propaganda-piece, with mother and son symbolizing the masses who eventually rose up against the Tsar. Montage is used skilfully to establish character; Baranovskaya is moving; and many sequences are the equal of anything produced by Eisenstein. It was banned in New York on release, but is undoubtedly a highlight of silent cinema.

'In [the film] we discovered the scientific method of the decomposition of a scene into its ingredients, the choice of the most powerful and suggestive, and the rebuilding of the scene by filmic representation on the screen . . . Without hesitation, I place it amongst the finest works in the history of the cinema.' *(Paul Rotha, The Film Till Now, 1929)*

'To Pudovkin the most important element is the story. His attitude to his subject is personal and emotional, not detached or intellectual.' *(Thorold Dickinson, Soviet Cinema)*

'For those who wish to idealise the restricted art of the silent film – cut off in its prime by the devastating intrusion of sound – *Mother* is as good an example as any of the high degree of imaginative expression which could be achieved by the moving picture alone . . . This film holds its own against time.' *(Roger Manvell, S & S, 1950)*

'Pudovkin proceeded from the whole to its parts, expressing the general through the particular. thus the attention given to the everyday, the ordinary, in people . . . Nilovna typified many people who were downtrodden and humiliated . . . The film broke ground hitherto untouched by the cinema born of the revolution.' *(Neya Zorkaya, Soviet Cinema, 1989)*

'Frequently selected by critics as one of the greatest films of all time, Pudovkin's masterpiece . . . is not overtly political; it gives an epic sense of . . . revolution through the emotions of the participants, and sweeps one along by its fervor and a brilliant and varied use of the medium.' *(Pauline Kael)*

MOTOCYCLETTE, LA: *see* GIRL ON A MOTORCYCLE.

MOULIN ROUGE AAN CT: 5 AV: 7.18

1952 GB 119/123 C DRAMA/ROMANCE/BIOPIC

D John Huston AAN
W Anthony Veiller John Huston from Pierre La Mure's novel

Jose Ferrer ☆ AAN Colette Marchand ☆ AAN Suzanne Flon Zsa Zsa Gabor Katherine Kath Claude Nollier Muriel Smith Georges Lannes Christopher Lee

A deformed artist, Toulouse Lautrec (Jose Ferrer), becomes increasingly bitter when he is rejected by women.

A film which contains a *tour de force* performance by Ferrer, marvellously evokes Montmartre in the Naughty Nineties, and makes wonderful use of colour. It won Oscars for art direction and costume design, and was nominated for its editing, although Oswald Morris's cinematography was inexplicably ignored. The big problem is the script, a mass of banalities and anachronisms, which portrays Lautrec's life as a downward spiral and therefore becomes increasingly depressing.

PRO:

'Bizarre and colorful . . . Huston hired *Life* photographer Eliot Elisofon as a color consultant who steered away from the usual unsubtle Technicolor lighting . . . Sometimes he used a rainbow of spotlights, like paints on an artist's palette, to tint every rainbow and highlight.' *(Life)*

'Beautifully patterned compositions conveying sentiments, moods and atmosphere . . . the eyes are played upon with colors and forms and compositions in a pattern as calculated as a musical score . . . keyed, indeed, to the plot.' *(New York Times)*

'In *Moulin Rouge* color was used, it was arbitrarily changed to create effects, it was taken away from realism, and the effect was pure magic; within this magic a cold, ferocious dislike of humanity suffused the screen, reflecting the hatred Toulouse Lautrec might have felt for the world, preventing us from having the faintest sympathy with him. It was a masterpiece of sculpture at the top of a glacier, and the great popular success it achieved is a tribute to

Huston's uncanny skill as much as to Jose Ferrer's technical brilliance in the lead. The odor of sexuality which occasionally came from the screen was a secondary item; the shooting of every scene to expose the vanity or the ugliness or the absurdity of the people involved was carried to the exact point at which a spectator might derive some pleasure from thinking himself superior to the unfortunates on the screen. The picture lacked all the elements of greatness – and was a triumph.' *(Gilbert Seldes, The Public Arts, 1956)*

ANTI:

'Not only is the story which has been imposed on Lautrec's life a mosaic of stock stuff about the artist of fiction, it is told in language of almost unrelieved banality . . . For a film such as *Moulin Rouge* literary talent is needed; at any rate a feeling for language which would save Lautrec's mistress from leaving him with the words "So long, Toulouse," and a knowledge which would shrink from showing the bearded stranger who buys a picture thrusting into the dealer's hand a visiting card: "Milan IV. King of Serbia".' *(Dilys Powell)*

'Pretty heavy going . . . reeks of sentimentalized invention.' *(Newsweek)*

MOUNTAINS OF THE MOON CT: 6 AV: 7.38

1989 US 135 C DRAMA/EPIC

D Bob Rafelson
W William Harrison Bob Rafelson from William Harrison's story *Burton and Speke*

Patrick Bergin ✔ Iain Glen ✔ Richard E. Grant Fiona Shaw ✔ John Savident James Villiers Adrian Rawlins Peter Vaughan ✔ Delroy Lindo Bernard Hill

An epic tale of two Victorian explorers, Sir Richard Burton (Patrick Bergin) and John Hanning Speke (Iain Glen), their search for the source of the Nile, and the pressures which soured their friendship and led to Speke's death.

Rafelson has always been attracted by outsider, maverick heroes (notably, Jack Nicholson in *Five Easy Pieces*); and in Burton, he has chosen one of the great mavericks in history. Bergin rises to the challenge with a performance that is complex, convincing and charismatic. Even more impressive is Iain Glen, playing the flawed, tormented Speke, a social misfit despite having been born into the English establishment. Also outstanding are Fiona Shaw, sharply intelligent as Burton's adoring Isabel, and Peter Vaughan, often cast as the heavy, but here roguishly sympathetic as Burton's loyal patron, Lord Houghton.

For all the film's virtues, it becomes bogged down in the middle, and for minutes at a time the audience is left wondering what new direction the film is exploring, never mind the characters. Burton, too, is problematic as the conduit for the audience's sympathy. Behind his 'action man' facade, he is an inaccessible, enigmatic, scholarly figure, with few of the moral certainties which propel more conventional superheroes, such as *Indiana Jones*. And, despite Glen's subtle and powerful performance, Speke is a character to whom it is difficult to warm.

Rafelson's movie takes some liberties with history – overstressing Burton's Irishness and glossing over the less savoury aspects of the great man's sexuality. Even so, this is a more truthful movie than most epics: it does justice to Burton's sensitivity towards indigenous cultures, and to the extraordinary bravery of Victorian explorers. And Roger Deakins's landscape photography has a magnificence rarely seen in the cinema since *Lawrence of Arabia*.

MIXED:

'A hybrid, a mini-series-like exotic adventure crossed with intimations of "modern" psychology . . . Vivid details here and there are not enough to sustain the over-generous length.' *(Tim Pulleine, Film Review)*

'Despite longueurs, this handsome epic has a spark of intelligence and a pleasing wit.' *(Nigel Floyd, Time Out)*

PRO:

'Somehow it conveys, as few movies ever have, the miserable realities that underlay the 19th century's heroic age of exploration.' *(Richard Schickel, Time)*

'Worth seeing principally because it is a real film by a director who understands the true nature of cinema as a visual medium.' *(Derek Malcolm, Guardian)*

'Provides deeply felt performances and refreshing, offbeat humor.' *(Variety)*

'Completely absorbing. It tells its story soberly and intelligently and with quiet style. It doesn't manufacture false thrills or phony excitement. It's the kind of movie that sends you away from the screen filled with curiosity to know more about this man Burton. Why, you ask yourself, has such an oversized character become almost forgotten? The movie is about the unquenchable compulsion of some men to see what is beyond the horizon, and about the hunger for glory. It is about stubbornness and pride. It is about a friendship that would have been infinitely less painful if the friends had not both been bullheaded and flawed. It is a tribute to this movie that, at the end, neither the filmmakers nor their audience have much interest in whether anyone found the source of the Nile.' *(Roger Ebert)*

MOUSE THAT ROARED, THE

CT: 6 AV: 6.55

1959 GB 85 C SF/COMEDY

D Jack Arnold
W Roger MacDougall Stanley Mann from Leonard Wibberley's novel *The Wrath of the Grapes*

Peter Sellers ☆ Jean Seberg David Kossoff William Hartnell Leo McKern Macdonald Parke

A tiny duchy declares war on America, with a view to winning aid after defeat and propping up its ailing economy.

A bright, though now dated, satirical idea is given adequate production, although director Arnold (an American veteran of the sci-fi genre) seems more at home with set-pieces than performances, and directs the comedy with a heavy hand. Though Peter Sellers was praised by the *New York Times* and the film introduced him to US audiences, he is not on his best form and is disappointingly muted in three roles, the Grand Duchess Gloriana, the prime minister and the field marshal. Although the narrative loses its way and runs out of steam, the film remains an endearing, enjoyable entertainment. The film did better in the US than in the UK and gave rise to an inferior sequel, *The Mouse on the Moon*.

PRO:

'Mr Sellers is the dominant performer and is most persistent in the role of the horn-rimmed-spectacled Field Marshal who is carried away by zeal.' *(Bosley Crowther)*

'There are a few occasions when *The Mouse That Roared* gets oversmart, but on the whole it keeps its slight amusing idea bubbling happily in the realms of straightforward comedy . . . The sight of the completely deserted city is an awesome one and owes considerably to Jack Arnold's direction, and remarkable artwork and lensing.' *(Variety)*

'The mouse restores to comedy its tonic purpose of puncturing political and militaristic shibboleths, and exposing to healthy laughter some of the more ridiculous aspects of these over-cautious times.' *(Saturday Reviews)*

'This charming movie is the sort a group of very talented friends might make on weekends, an easygoing fairy tale that succeeds by not pushing too hard.' *(Newsweek)*

'In a comic strip sort of way, the picture is pretty good.' *(Jack Moffitt, Hollywood Reporter)*

'Loads of satiric fun.' *(Scheuer)*

MIXED:

'A fairly witty example of a rare film form: political burlesque. It keeps the show bouncing along despite a director . . . and a star . . . who have not mastered the light-fantastic style that supports this sort of flimsy British whimsy.' *(Time)*

'The picture, after a fairly amusing start, runs down badly.' *(John McCarten, New Yorker)*

'Almost capsized by a superstructure of plot confusion and badly insufficient philosophical ballast.' *(MFB)*

'The script veers wildly between satire and slapstick.' *(Tom Milne, Time Out)*

'The film abandons its small, amusing idea and goes off on a wearying tangent about a scientist with a big bomb and an ingenue-daughter, but it was hugely and inexplicably popular.' *(Pauline Kael)*

'Its success wasn't really so inexplicable: it was a moderately funny, modest little picture about something very unusual. That it didn't answer the questions it raised is of little importance. It was a surprise.' *(Bill Mitchell, Keep Watching The Skies!)*

MOVIE MOVIE

CT: 10 AV: 6.90

1978 US 106 C (partly in BW) COMEDY/MUSICAL

D Stanley Donen
W Larry Gelbart Sheldon Keller

George C. Scott ☆ Trish Van Devere Red Buttons Eli Wallach Jocelyn Brando Barry Bostwick Art Carney Harry Hamlin Ann Reinking Michael Kidd (introduction by George Burns)

A sharp but affectionate parody of the sort of double bill around in the 1930s. The first half's a boxing melodrama ('Dynamite Hands'), the second a backstage musical ('Baxter's Beauties of 1933').

A box office flop, but a very funny film. Both halves use roughly the same casts and the same sets, not too subtly rearranged. George C. Scott is hilarious as boxing trainer 'Gloves' Mulloy and Broadway producer 'Spats' Baxter, he who perishes on stage uttering the immortal line: 'That's show business: one moment you're in the wings, the next you're wearing them.' It's high time this film was rediscovered and celebrated.

ANTI:

'Awful awful.' *(Variety)*

'Camp, which has to do with a switch of vision from one era to another, cannot be created, and where it is, as this and previous attempts testify it is immediately swallowed in its own idiocy.' *(Richard Combs, MFB)*

'Full of "in" jokes that must have wowed them in the film schools.' *(Stanley Kauffmann)*

MIXED:

'The oddest piece of encrusted flotsam yet washed to shore on the cinema's Nostalgia Wave . . . No over-abundance of artistic complexity . . . and a surprising amount of sheer charm. [It] may be froth, but it is high calibre froth.' *(Nigel Andrews, Financial Times)*

'Though [it is] a fluent entertainment, [it] never

quite works out . . . Donen's pastiche is not always spot on . . . Still I shouldn't be churlish. If you go in the right mood, you'll probably come out in a better one.' *(Derek Malcolm, Guardian)*

'Too tame and too dependent on mismatched metaphors, and the second "feature" sags, but it's generally friendly and enjoyable.' *(Pauline Kael)*

PRO:

'Poking fun at Hollywood has been done many times, but never so hilariously or with such affectionate charm . . . The dialogue is a knockout.' *(Arthur Thirkell, Daily Mirror)*

'A wicked send up . . . but affectionate enough to be forgiven . . . one of the funniest films around.' *(Margaret Forward, Sun)*

'They just don't make movies like this anymore, says master comic George Burns . . . And he's right . . . All the clichés are there lovingly and funnily satirised. *Movie, Movie* is superb, superb.' *(Ivan Waterman, News of the World)*

'Superb comic performances throughout make this a comic treat-treat.' *(Scheuer)*

'The threadbare settings for both films are a clever blend of parody and affection, whilst Donen and his cast clearly had a ball.' *(Elkan Allan, NFT Bulletin)*

MR. AND MRS. BRIDGE CT: 8 AV: 6.82

1990 US 127 C DRAMA

D James Ivory ☆
W Ruth Prawer Jhabvala from Evan S. Connell Jr's novels

Paul Newman ☆ Joanne Woodward ☆ AAN
Blythe Danner ☆ Simon Callow Kyra Sedgwick ☆
Robert Sean Leonard Margaret Welsh
Austin Pendleton

At the turn of the 1930s, a wife and mother (Joanne Woodward) has an insensitive husband.

Another exploration by Merchant-Ivory of E.M. Forster's favourite theme, 'Only Connect'. Though set in Kansas, the film's analysis of non-communication between husband and wife, parents and children, could apply to modern middle-class families from Bombay to Beckenham.

It is chiefly memorable for three great performances. One of Broadway's leading stage actresses, Blythe Danner, is tragic as Grace, the heroine's bridge partner who slips into alcoholism and insanity. Paul Newman succeeds in capturing Mr Bridge's intolerance, cruelty and philistinism while making us fully aware of his good points: a sense of duty and responsibility, and his love of wife and family.

The revelation, however, is Newman's wife Joanne Woodward, who plays Mrs Bridge with minute and devastating observation, making it movingly clear that beneath her foolishness and insularity lies a core of kindness, innocence and self-sacrifice.

ANTI:

'As social comment (comedy?) it is flattened by Paul Newman's performance. The realisation of his role does not go beyond the simplest mannerisms, allowing Joanne Woodward the unhappy task of exposing her husband's limitations with her own extraordinary interpretation.' *(Angus Wolfe Murray, Scotsman)*

'A plethora of intriguing but undeveloped, half-baked story threads make for a frustrating and unsatisfying experience.' *(Maltin)*

PRO:

'Affecting . . . Kyra Sedgwick is smashing.' *(Variety)*

'Observes with great care and an almost frightening detachment the precise ways in which an emotionally paralyzed couple gets through life together . . . Much is made of the excesses and silliness of the Sixties, but it is because of that liberating decade that Mr Bridge and his world will never quite exist again, and it is worth remembering that the young people of the 1960s were the children of parents who were often very much like the Bridges: parents who were playing out some ideal role of probity and respectability, and who were so wary of their own feelings that they disciplined their children for having feelings at all.' *(Roger Ebert)*

'Woodward's portrayal . . . is quite simply superb . . . But the film's outstanding strengths are . . . in Ivory's exact capturing of an age that saw a new generation break away from its parents' mores and women move painfully out of the neatly dusted parlour.' *(Sue Heal, Today)*

'Brilliantly written and acted, and immensely watchable.' *(MFB)*

'There is an old-fashioned episodic structure to [this] piquantly tasteful [film] reminiscent of those family sagas of the 1930s and 1940s.' *(George Perry, Sunday Times)*

'So what happens? Not much. But then that's just the point of the film . . . What fills the screen is not heightened melodrama, but a series of stark, sometimes painfully poignant vignettes that reflect the oppressive stasis of their lives. Still, boring lives don't necessarily make for boring films, and the cumulative impact onscreen is anything but.' *(Baseline)*

MR. ARKADIN: *see* CONFIDENTIAL REPORT.

MR. BLANDINGS BUILDS HIS DREAM HOUSE CT: 6 AV: 7.92

1948 US 84 BW COMEDY

D H.C. Potter ☆
W Norman Panama Melvin Frank ☆ from Eric Hodgins's novel

Cary Grant ☆ Myrna Loy ☆ Melvyn Douglas ☆ Reginald Denny ☆ Sharyn Moffett Connie Marshall Louise Beavers Harry Shannon Ian Wolfe Tito Vuolo

A man (Cary Grant) has problems making an ideal home.

Sweet, gentle, amiable comedy lifted to near-classic status by the leading performances.

ANTI:

'Eric Hodgins' novel . . . reads a lot funnier than they filmed . . . Script gets completely out of hand when unnecessary jealousy twist is introduced, neither advancing the story nor adding laughs.' *(Variety)*

'"Mr. Dreamings Builds his Bland House" would be a more accurate title.' *(Geoff Brown, Time Out)*

MIXED:

'A bull's-eye for middle-class middle-brows. For the low and the high not hard to take and just as easy to let alone.' *(James Agee, Nation)*

PRO:

'This is one of those American domestic comedies which purr their way into your affection like a tabby scrounging a sauce of milk. It is all so true, so recognisable, and everybody is going to love it – except, I fear, the estate men and the builders.' *(Jympson Harman, Evening News)*

'It is so long since there has been a really sparkling comedy . . . One is these days unused to brilliance . . . This is a delicious film which I can, and do, recommend without reservation.' *(Elspeth Grant, Daily Graphic)*

'It is long since I have seen a film so rich in continuous fun. And the beauty of it is that the laughter springs not from nonsense and wild absurdity but from an agonising experience which many house-hunters and home-builders have unhappily shared. Cary Grant – agitated, bewildered, exasperated and finally overwhelmed – gives a performance of comic perfection. Myrna Loy, looking more attractive than ever, is enchantingly feminine and unhelpful.' *(A.E. Wilson, Star)*

'I loved it. That was really a pleasure to make.' *(H.C. Potter, 1973)*

MR DEEDS GOES TO TOWN AAN

CT: 8 AV: 9.43

1936 US 115 BW COMEDY

D Frank Capra ☆ AAW
W Robert Riskin ☆ AAN from Clarence Budington Kelland's story *Opera Hat*

Gary Cooper ☆ AAN Jean Arthur Raymond Walburn Lionel Stander Walter Catlett ☆ George Bancroft ☆ Douglas Dumbrille ☆ H.B. Warner Ruth Donnelly Margaret Seddon ☆ Margaret McWade ☆

A reporter (Jean Arthur) sets out to investigate a man (Gary Cooper) who gives away $20 million inheritance and is suspected of being mad.

Delightful, if dawdling, comedy with one of Gary Cooper's most charismatic performances. Some of the social philosophizing seems dated and naive (it has much to say about the redistribution of wealth, nothing about its creation), and the dialogue could have used some pruning, but it's all fundamentally good-hearted. There is some evidence of the film's low budget, but this certainly deserves to be ranked among Capra's classics. The courtroom climax, in particular, is beautifully written and directed. It was voted Best Motion Picture of 1936 by the New York Film Critics and the US's National Board of Review.

ANTI:

'I have a feeling he's on his way out. He's started to make pictures about themes instead of people.' *(Alastair Cooke)*

MIXED:

'The farce is good-humored and the trouping and production workmanlike, but there are some lapses in midriff that cause considerable uncertainty . . . Audience credulity, despite the general lightness of the theme, becomes strained.' *(Variety)*

'Frank Capra-style folk humor is better in slightly shorter doses (this runs almost two hours and the pace could be quicker), but there's no use fighting one's enjoyment of this homey fantasy demonstrating the triumph of small-town values over big-city cynicism.' *(Pauline Kael)*

PRO:

'Everywhere the picture goes, from the endearing to the absurd, the accompanying business is carried through with perfect zip and relish.' *(Otis Ferguson)*

'A comedy quite unmatched on the screen.' *(Graham Greene)*

'Frank Capra has made an excellent job of a good story . . . Exaggeration has been carefully avoided. Gary Cooper . . . never becomes a simpleton or a buffoon and the gradual ripening of Jean Arthur's affection is excellently done . . . The only time [it] seems to flag is during the trial scene, when the final denouement is obvious . . . The film is excellent entertainment value, is full of laughs and of a good deal more for those who have eyes to see and ears to hear.' *(MFB)*

'Astounds with its unexpected warmth and indubitable sincerity of purpose . . . For the first time in the movies we have been given a sympathetic, credible portrait of a worker, speaking the language of workers, saying the things workers all over the country say . . . For Hollywood *Mr. Deeds* is a tremendous advance.' *(Robert Stebbins, aka Sidney Meyers, New Theatre)*

MR. HULOT'S HOLIDAY: *see* MONSIEUR HULOT'S HOLIDAY.

MR. SKEFFINGTON CT: 7 AV: 6.56

1944 US 116/127/146 BW DRAMA/ROMANCE

D Vincent Sherman ✔
W Julius J. Epstein Philip G. Epstein from 'Elizabeth''s novel

Bette Davis ☆ AAN Claude Rains ☆ AAN Walter Abel Richard Waring George Coulouris John Alexander Jerome Cowan

A selfish beauty (Bette Davis) marries a Jewish stockbroker (Claude Rains) for money and has affairs, but goes back to him when she has lost her looks through diphtheria; fortunately, he has been blinded in a concentration camp, so he still thinks she is beautiful.

Majestically acted, grand soap opera, with its eyes firmly fixed on a middle-aged, female audience. The more one thinks about it, the more alarming its outlook on relationships becomes; better to concentrate on the high production values and the two stars. It's jolly long, but guiltily enjoyable.

ANTI:

'A faithful regard for Miss Bette Davis makes me regret to state that in the 116 minutes running time of this film I was never remotely interested in her goings-on . . . A film without sufficient insight to atone for its lack of movement, its refutation of all that has ever been meant by cinema.' *(Richard Winnington, News Chronicle)*

'Another of those pictures in which Bette Davis demonstrates the horrors of egocentricity on a marathonic scale; it takes her just short of thirty years' living and two and a half hours' playing time to learn, from her patient husband (Claude Rains), that "a woman is beautiful only when she is loved" and to prove this to an audience which, I fear, will be made up mainly of unloved and not easily lovable women. Miss Davis, director Vincent Sherman, and several others put a great deal of hard work and some that is good into this show, and there are some expert bits of middle-teens and 1920s New York atmosphere. But essentially Mr. Skeffington is just a super soap opera, or an endless woman's-page meditation on What to Do When Beauty Fades. The implied advice is dismaying: hang on to your husband, who alone will stand by you then, and count yourself blessed if, like Mr Rains in his old age, he is blinded.' *(James Agee, Nation)*

'A piece of slick nonsense.' *(Simon Harcourt-Smith, Daily Mail)*

MIXED:

'To call the film a good one would be to exaggerate; but entertaining and interesting, I insist, it is.' *(Richard Mallett, Punch)*

PRO:

'Not only another triumph for the Warner star [Davis] but also a picture of terrific strength.' *(Variety)*

'Sherman takes these rich raw materials and handles them with directorial inventiveness, a sure knowledge of camera-placing and a nice appreciation of how to get he most colour into his lighting.' *(MFB)*

'Impeccably designed, overlong soap opera . . . Davis gives a powerhouse performance.' *(Scheuer)*

'Bette Davis at her considerable best.' *(Shipman)*

MR. SMITH GOES TO WASHINGTON AAN CT: 9 AV: 9.62

1939 US 125 BW DRAMA

D Frank Capra ☆ AAN
W Sidney Buchman ☆ AAN from Lewis R. Foster's novel *The Gentleman from Montana* AAW

James Stewart ☆ AAN Jean Arthur Claude Rains AAN Harry Carey ☆ AAN Edward Arnold Guy Kibbee Thomas Mitchell Eugene Pallette Beulah Bondi

A young senator (James Stewart) exposes political corruption in high places.

Frank Capra's tale of honesty, integrity and small-town values triumphing over corruption is a great emotional experience – and very nearly perfect. The only major fault is that the pace sags around the middle, when there's too much talk. James Stewart exudes simple idealism like no other actor; as a result, this is a genuinely inspiring movie. The whole film is beautifully acted, and Capra shows his directorial talent most obviously in the way he uses faces to tell his story. It was voted the second-best picture of 1939 (*Goodbye, Mr. Chips* was first) in *Film Daily*'s annual poll of US film critics, and was Oscar-nominated for art direction, editing, score and sound.

ANTI:

'I feel that to show this film in foreign countries will do inestimable harm to American prestige all over the world.' *(Joseph P. Kennedy, American ambassador to Great Britain and father of John)*

'Now and again you hear it said that foreign countries interpret life in America from what they see in American-made pictures. They're going to get a fine idea of the United States Senate when they take a squint at *Mr. Smith Goes to Washington*. They're going to get the idea that we reach into jails for our Senators and into the insane asylum for our reformers.' *(John M. Cummings, Philadelphia Inquirer)*

'Clumsy and irritating.' *(Otis Ferguson)*

'Capra played safe, played demagogue, and fought straw bosses.' *(Jay Leyda, Direction)*

'Succeeded commercially, but the picture has more of the heartfelt in it than is good for the stomach, and it goes on for over two hours . . . No one else can balance the ups and downs of wistful sentiment and corny humor the way Capra can – but if anyone else should learn to, kill him.' *(Pauline Kael)*

PRO:

'The great American picture.' *(Billboard)*

'Frank Capra has another smash hit . . . Stewart turns in the finest performance of his career.' *(Hollywood Reporter)*

'[Capra] has paced it beautifully and held it in perfect balance . . . James Stewart is a joy for this season, if not forever. He has too many good scenes, but we like to remember the way his voice cracked when he got up to read his bill.' *(New York Times)*

'It says all the things about America that have been crying out to be said again – and says them beautifully.' *(Philip Scheuer, LA Times)*

'For the first time the screen has become eloquent in relation to the significance of our times.' *(M.B. Spokane, Washington Spokesman Review)*

'*Mr. Smith* presents one of those dazzling simple revelations of human values in which Mr Capra excels.' *(C.A. Lejeune, London Observer)*

'Very good, beautifully done and extremely entertaining; long, but worth the time it takes.' *(Richard Mallett, Punch)*

'"Frank Capra attacks democracy", I saw one critic wrote . . . The truth is that democracy can stand any attack upon its weaknesses.' *(H. Swaffer, Daily Herald)*

'When Jimmy Stewart walked the halls of the Capitol building, I walked with him. When he stood in awe of that great man at the Lincoln Memorial, I bowed my head too. When he stood in the Senate chamber and refused to knuckle under to the vested interests, I began to realize, through the power of motion pictures, one man can make a difference.' *(Ronald Reagan)*

MRS. DOUBTFIRE

CT: 7 AV: 6.50

1993 US 121 C COMEDY

D Chris Columbus
W Randi Mayem Singer Leslie Dixon from Anne Fine's novel

Robin Williams ☆ Sally Field Pierce Brosnan ☆ Harvey Fierstein

Daniel Hilliard (Robin Williams) is an actor who loves his three kids more than he does his career-woman wife (Sally Field). When she finally cracks, he finds that he has access to his children on only one day a week. Convinced that this isn't enough, he gets his make-up artist brother (Harvey Fierstein) to disguise him as a 60-year-old Scottish housekeeper, Mrs Doubtfire: the answer to his wife's childcare dreams. The new arrangement works out well. Not only does Daniel learn things about his wife which he could never have discovered otherwise: he becomes tidier, more responsible, less selfish. But he finds himself increasingly jealous of his wife's new, rich, handsome boyfriend (Pierce Brosnan).

A variation on *The Marriage of Figaro*, with Williams doubling up as resourceful servant and suspicious husband. Schmaltz and Robin Williams are no strangers to each other; and one has to be prepared for scenes of stomach-turning sentimentality. Fortunately, such moments are offset by many more moments of ribaldry and wit, especially when Williams is scoring points off his wife's new boyfriend, Stu. 'Stu?' muses Mrs Doubtfire, thin-lipped. 'That's more of a thick soup than a name.' Besides, much of Williams's schmaltziness is in character: Daniel is meant to be difficult to live with – why else would his wife ditch someone so funny and talented? His biggest failing is that he wears his heart not so much on, as oozing all over his sleeve: he's so super-sensitive to his own and his children's feelings that he fails to be the least bit attentive to his wife.

The supporting actors have to play second fiddle, but when you're on the screen with Paganini, that's only to be expected. Chris Columbus directs with the same skill he showed on *Home Alone*; the screenplay, by Randi Mayem Singer and Leslie Dixon, is well-crafted – even if they do seem to think that Scotland is a part of England. The film is overlong, but that is because Williams embellishes every joke and set-piece with virtuoso bits of comic business, and – as producer – allows himself to do so.

There is no denying the man's talent. The role is tailor-made for a genius of mimicry, and Williams shows himself to be the natural heir of Peter Sellers – with the additional skill of being able to improvise his own material. This is one of the most constantly inventive, scintillating star performances ever in a screen comedy.

ANTI:

'Sometimes Williams attacks so hard with his comic artillery that you just want to hide under a rock . . . Even while we admire William's artistry . . . it is hard not to groan at the uses to which [the character] is put . . . The film positively drips with pleas for family togetherness.' *(Geoff Brown, The Times)*

'Regresses into the old story about a man who loves not wisely but too well. Personally, I'd strangle these kids before hugging them.' *(Derek Malcolm, Guardian)*

'A load of old tosh . . . A ridiculous piece of turbocharged nonsense . . . You get a Norman Wisdom kind of feeling, but worse, because you feel terribly manipulated – mauled, practically . . . It ends up insulting your intelligence. And I thought I liked films which insult my intelligence.' *(William Leith, Mail on Sunday)*

'A really wholesome movie about a man in a bra; it's like watching a John Waters movie rewritten by John Hughes.' *(Libby Gelman-Waxner, Premiere)*

'Maybe in another age one wouldn't worry about the mental-health implications of a scene in which a boy walks into the bathroom and discovers that his middle-aged nanny is actually his father in drag – but it's not my fault Freud was born, is it? *Mrs. Doubtfire* disposes of such issues as if they were so many Huggies: the boy cringes, a bit, but then all is well. That's because this family-oriented comedy – directed by that expert in holiday custard, Chris Columbus (*Home Alone*) – is determined to be warm-hearted and sweet, no matter how recklessly implausible it has to be.' *(Tom Gliatto, People Weekly)*

'What's really unpersuasive about *Mrs. Doubtfire* – not to say draggy – is its nondrag sequences. The children are goody-goodies, without mischief or quirks, and their father's relationship with them is unclouded by even minor impatience, let alone major outrage. The script . . . presents ideal fatherhood as a form of saintliness . . . Daniel Hilliard, of whom we see entirely too much, is winsome, childlike, too good for this world, the kind of wimped-out modern male Williams ought to be satirizing, not celebrating.' *(Richard Schickel, Time)*

MIXED:

'The film is best in its farce mode but goes limp when it attempts a *Kramer Vs. Kramer* plea on behalf of custody-denied fathers.' *(George Perry, Sunday Times)*

'Williams, wearing half a ton of prosthetic makeup, gives an inspired comic performance. Unfortunately, he outclasses the movie he's in . . . The casting of Sally Field doesn't help. Her Miranda is such a rancorous shrew that it's no fun watching *Mrs. Doubtfire* win her over; if anything, we want to see Daniel steal the kids for good.' *(Owen Gleiberman, Entertainment Weekly)*

'Highly reminiscent of *Tootsie* (1982), in which Dustin Hoffman's character masquerades as a woman to get a part in a TV soap opera. In both films, the impostor turns into a kindly mother figure for an unsuspecting woman, setting the stage for a climactic revelation. *Tootsie* is a better movie, with a more sophisticated, adult wit. But *Mrs. Doubtfire* works as formula farce, an antic comedy for adults and children that finds the daffiest common denominator. It is hilarious.' *(Brian D. Johnson, Maclean's)*

MRS. MINIVER AAW   CT: 6 AV: 7.17

1942 US 134 BW WAR/DRAMA

D William Wyler ☆ AAW
W Arthur Wimperis George Froeschel James Hilton Claudine West from Jan Struther's novel

Greer Garson ✗ AAW Walter Pidgeon ☆ AAN Teresa Wright ☆ AAW Dame May Whitty ☆ AAN Henry Travers ☆ AAN Reginald Owen Miles Mander Henry Wilcoxon Richard Ney

A normal English family helps defeat the Germans on the home front.

Rather wonderful, old-fashioned soap opera with a quaint notion of English village life. Everyone's frightfully pleasant and common-sensical and brave – they attend flower shows between air raids. It's easy to laugh at now; but it was a hugely important film of its day, enabling ordinary Americans to empathasize with people on the other side of the Atlantic. It undoubtedly helped increase enthusiasm for US entry into World War II (which had occurred just before the film's release). Cinematographer Joseph Ruttenberg won an Oscar; editor Harold F. Kress was nominated.

Garson (who was 34 when the film was made) resisted playing the lead which brought her stardom, because she feared that having a grown-up son on screen (played by 27-year-old Richard Ney) would make her look old. Norma Shearer and Ann Harding had turned down the part for the same reason. MGM chief Louis B. Mayer finally convinced Garson, who later – in real life – married her screen son Ney, although Mayer persuaded them to postpone their nuptuals until the movie had finished its first run. There is a persistent but untrue story that Greer Garson's acceptance speech at the Academy Awards lasted 55 minutes; it actually lasted about five and a half. It just felt like 55 minutes.

ANTI:

'Hollywooden . . . Greer Garson is insufferably genteel.' *(Shipman)*

'Generally offensive . . . Shamelessly, it ends with the heroic characters singing "Onward Christian Soldiers" in a partially destroyed church . . . One of the most scandalously smug of all Academy Award winners.' *(Pauline Kael)*

'When released it proved a beacon of morale despite its false sentiment, absurd rural types and melodramatic situations. It is therefore beyond criticism, except that some of the people involved should have known better.' *(Halliwell)*

MIXED:

'Has been translated from an artfully cosy column in *The Times* to the screen without any great loss of credibility . . . [Garson's] performance is charming, though years too young for the part . . . An English company with equally sentimental material would have made a dreadful mess of it.' *(New Statesman)*

'In America, William Wyler's *Mrs. Miniver* was considered the best dramatic film with a war background. But in Europe, even though it arrived preceded by considerable fame based mostly on the usual shower of Oscars, the movie had only a good commercial success. In truth, the excessive melodrama of the subject and a tiresome rhetoric could not be compensated for on the artistic plane by the convincing interpretations of Greer Garson and Walter Pidgeon.' *(Lino Lionello Ghirardini, 1965)*

PRO:

'That almost impossible feat, a war picture that photographs the inner meaning, instead of the outward realism of World War II.' *(Time)*

'The screen at the peak of its eloquence; a portrait of the war, which, without showing a flag or uttering a word of hate, graphically reveals the horror of it . . . As long as our memories last, [it] will be, to us, high on the list of the greatest achievements of the screen.' *(Welford Beaton, Hollywood Spectator)*

'Tender, genuine, eloquently presented, this MGM photoplay will do more to arouse Americans to their duty than an assortment of parades, and all the lugubrious ballads composed by Mr Irving Berlin. The exaltation burrows deep into the heart of the spectator and persists long after one has left the theater . . . *Mrs. Miniver* is an emotional experience. You owe it to yourself to see it, not only as a picture patron, but also as a human being.' *(Herb Sterne)*

'MGM has had the inspiration to shake the Minivers out of their peace-time routine to show you how they must be now . . . Their life still has an imperturbable dignity . . . Their insistence on the niceties is as funny as it is heroic.' *(Louise Levitas, PM)*

'An everlasting milestone in film history. Ladies and gentlemen, pray pay due tribute to the film itself, to the incomparable acting of the stars . . . and to [the director]' *(News of the World, 1948)*

MUCH ADO ABOUT NOTHING

CT: 7 AV: 6.43

1993 GB 110 C COMEDY/ROMANCE

D Kenneth Branagh
W Kenneth Branagh from Shakespeare's play

Kenneth Branagh ☆ Michael Keaton
Robert Sean Leonard ● Keanu Reeves ●
Emma Thompson ☆ Denzel Washington ☆
Richard Briers ☆ Kate Beckinsale Brian Blessed
Ben Elton Phyllida Law Imelda Staunton

A man (Kenneth Branagh) and a woman (Emma Thompson) bicker but are obviously made for each other, and are brought together by friends.

Emma Thompson makes a wonderfully witty Beatrice: her sharp tongue is evidently the product of a clear intelligence and a deeper vulnerability. As Benedick, Branagh has an easy informality in his monologues and makes his moments of romantic confusion seem spontaneous and comic. On a par with their excellence is Richard Briers as Leonato.

There's rather too much forced, theatrical joviality, led inevitably by that genial giant, Brian Blessed; and the American actors mostly struggle. Lords and servants mingle on equal terms, in a way that they never have in any society known to man, still less 16th-century man. The impression is less of high society, than of the Renaissance Theatre Company having fun on their summer hols.

Fortunately, Branagh does so many things right that his errors pale into relative insignificance. He has done a fine job of opening out the action, and it is no mean achievement to produce a Shakespearean comedy so that it will make a modern audience laugh. Both as director and adapter, he has shown sensitivity to the varying moods of the piece, emphasizing the romance, absurdity and joys of young love.

His enthusiasm swings you effortlessly past the dodgy points in Shakespeare's plot. Why, for example, doesn't the servant Margaret simply own up to the fact that it was her, not Hero, bonking with Borachio in Hero's bedroom? and why does Don John risk his newly found respectability on an easily disprovable slander? The director even succeeds in making us care a little whether that quintessential prig, Claudio, and the hopelessly wimpish Hero (prettily played by newcomer Kate Beckinsale) end up together. Branagh stresses the pair's painful immaturity, and the sincerity of Claudio's penance.

Most of all, though, the film is full of gusto and good humour. Even if you notice the irritations, it should win you over with its clarity and its delight in Shakespeare's words, wit and generosity of spirit. It's a joy to watch, and a breath of fresh Tuscan air.

ANTI:

'Such is the lack of crackle between Ken and Em that they might as well be tucked up in separate beds drinking a cup of cocoa. In terms of sexual electricity, these two are the filmic equivalents of John and Norma Major . . . This is a film in which the most exciting visual element is the bad-tooth make-up affected by Michael Keaton in his role as Dogberry, the comic-relief constable. It is as though Branagh has responded to accusations that British films are not visual by assuming that a nice Tuscan landscape in every frame will convey instant eye-appeal. Up to a point, Lord Kenneth: but it ends up looking like a shoddily photographed film against a nice Tuscan landscape.' *(Anne Billson, Sunday Telegraph)*

'More Tuscan-holiday romp than romantic-Sicilian idyll, this is Benedick's Chums.' *(Philip French, Observer)*

'Particularly disastrous is Michael Keaton as the comical constable, Dogberry, with a portrayal that smacks of a cross between the enunciation of Popeye and the slapstick moves of Moe Howard of the Three Stooges.' *(Robert S. Rothenberg, USA Today)*

'American actors will never equal British ones in Shakespeare, at the very least because they have not the right language. British English has a melody; American English has not. More precisely, British English is like classical music; American English is like a marching band . . . Though the American contingent was obviously brought in with an eye on the box office, the result, I repeat, is that the humblest Briton outshines the most stellar Yankee. Thus Hero, played by a mere Oxford student on temporary leave – the enormously personable and spirited Kate Beckinsale – totally overshadows her Claudio, even though he is the best of the Americans. It makes you wonder why she would be so upset to be ditched by such an insignificant popinjay, an obvious upstart trying to marry above his station.' *(John Simon)*

'The popularizing on display in *Much Ado* is the sort that insults the populace . . . Branagh, having made the potentially interesting decision to center his interpretation on the idea of female hostility and resilience, has so muddled it in the execution that despite the film's energy and commotion we are left at the end with little clue as to the cumulative significance of the action.' *(Richard Ryan, Commentary)*

MIXED:

'Kenneth Branagh and Emma Thompson are everything you could hope for . . . But now, as this review threatens to dissolve into gurglings of pleasure, I must bring up the unpleasant subject of Branagh's visual style. He hasn't got one . . . In defense of Branagh, I can say that his is a robust bad taste. If the good can't keep it in check, he might develop into the Bob Fosse of Shakespearean directors – which would be better than a lot of other possibilities. But . . . *Much Ado* . . . at its best reaches a level beyond criticism. It makes you marvel anew at Shakespeare.' *(Stuart Klawans, Nation)*

'Maybe the plot's a bit creaky, but it is a few hundred years old.' *(Rose)*

'Rowdy, high-spirited, and remarkably fast-paced; this exhilaration brings vigor to the Bard's text, though the poetry sometimes gets lost in the shenanigans.' *(Maltin)*

PRO:

'Branagh . . . performs a masterstroke of casting, playing British character acting and verbal wit off against American emotional power.' *(Quentin Curtis, Independent on Sunday)*

'Spirited, winningly acted . . . continuously enjoyable from its action-filled opening to the dazzling final shot.' *(Variety)*

'The skirmish of will and wit between Benedick (Branagh, never so charming a screen presence) and Beatrice (his wife Emma Thompson, here tart and intense) plays like a prime episode of *Cheers*. The characters' passions seem not revived but experienced afresh.' *(Richard Corliss, Time)*

'A ravishing entertainment.' *(Vincent Canby, New York Times)*

'As for Thompson . . . I'll try to restrain myself. She has elegance. She has the finest command of inflection and style. She has spirit and soul. She is the first film actress since Katharine Hepburn to make intelligence sexy . . . One doesn't often cry for pleasure at a film. It happened here.' *(Stanley Kauffmann)*

MUMMY, THE

CT: 5 AV: 6.75

1932 US 72 BW HORROR

D Karl Freund ☆
W John L. Balderston from Nina Wilcox Putnam and Richard Schayer's story

Boris Karloff Zita Johann David Manners Edward Van Sloan A.S. Byron Bramwell Fletcher Noble Johnson Leonard Mudie Katherine Byron Eddie Kane

Ancient Egyptian high priest (Boris Karloff) is revived and seeks reincarnation of former girl-friend (Zita Johann).

Classic horror film which goes for a weird atmosphere rather than shocks, and is a triumph of the cinematographer's art. Director Freund had previously photographed three great silents, *Der Golem, The Last Laugh* and *Metropolis*, and the original *Dracula*. Here, he collaborates effectively with cameraman Charles Stumar. Despite the film's visual strengths, modern audiences may find it slow-moving; and the performances are stiff and unconvincing. It was Karloff's first starring role.

MIXED:

'Most of [the film] is costume melodrama for the children . . . Karloff acts with the restraint natural to a man whose face is hidden behind synthetic wrinkles . . . The photography is superior to the dialogue.' *(New York Times)*

'A novel theme, and although wildly incredible has good suspense value of a somewhat grim order . . . An exceptionally good piece of camera technique.' *(Lionel Collier, Picturegoer)*

PRO:

'Beggars description. It is one of the most unusual talkies ever produced.' *(LA Times)*

'Serious and impressive treatment of macabre theme results in absorbing sequence of startling and awe-inspiring incident depicted in pictorially fine and emotionally compelling fashion . . . Brilliantly conceived reconstruction of ancient Egyptian life . . .

Excellent acting dominated by Boris Karloff.' *(The Cinema Supplement)*

'No other horror film has ever achieved so many emotional effects by lighting; this inexpensively made film has a languorous, poetic feeling, and the eroticism that lives on under Karloff's wrinkled parchment skin is like a bad dream of undying love.' *(Pauline Kael)*

MURDER, MY SWEET: *see* FAREWELL MY LOVELY (1944).

MUSIC BOX, THE CT: 8 AV: 6.17

1989 US 120/126 C THRILLER

D Costa-Gavras ✔
W Joe Eszterhas ✔

Jessica Lange ☆ AAN Armin Mueller-Stahl ✔ Frederic Forrest ✔ Donald Moffat Lukas Haas Cheryl Lynne Bruce Mari Töröcsik J.S. Block Sol Frieder

A lawyer (Jessica Lange) defends her Hungarian-born father (Armin Mueller-Stahl), now a proud American citizen, against charges of horrible war crimes committed 50 years before. As the story unfolds, she increasingly doubts his innocence.

A first-rate thriller, although some people complain about the film's detachment from its subject-matter. For once, the fate of six million Jews is the background, rather than the main issue. This is as much a film about children and parents, innocence and ignorance, as it is about war crimes.

Costa-Gavras's direction is taut, teasing and has none of the didacticism which coarsened his otherwise excellent work on *Z* and *Missing*. Joe Eszterhas's absorbing, masterfully plotted screenplay is at least the equal of his previous success, *Jagged Edge*, although he is guilty of underwriting for the father (we never really discover what motivated him). Jessica Lange deserved her Oscar nomination as leading actress. Although the film is over two hours long, the pace and suspense never flag. Winner of the Golden Bear at the Berlin Film Festival.

ANTI:

'This film seems to exist for one dubious purpose: to snag an Oscar nomination for Jessica Lange . . . [Eszterhas's] potboiler . . . has merely recycled the courtroom theatrics of . . . *Jagged Edge* and slapped on a Holocaust theme. Real-life tragedy has been used to hype cheap melodrama. It's more than offensive; it's vile.' *(Peter Travers, Rolling Stone)*

'Eszterhas uses historical crimes very astutely, but he forces them into an entertainment package alongside old-Hollywood devices. The final plot developments (after the music box makes it appearance) are over-extended, and they feel fake. The focus of the material goes wrong: what we're watching is suddenly too much about Ann's suffering – movie-star suffering.' *(Pauline Kael)*

'What could have been a cracking political thriller becomes a high-gloss melodrama instead, plodding and far-fetched.' *(Maltin)*

'Disappointingly pat: it's a structured whodunit when it would have been far richer as a whydunit.' *(Peter Rainer, American Film)*

PRO:

'Vintage Costa-Gavras and, as such, one of the classier and more politically resonant of the year's outings . . . A picture which abides with enduring human values and courses with dramatic tension.' *(Ed Kelleher, Film Journal)*

'As courtroom drama, it is artfully constructed . . . Like Pandora's Box, it disgorges monstrous secrets, but does not leave behind the hope offered in the original myth . . . This is a drama of cool, detached power, directed with consummate skill and played by a uniformly well-chosen cast.' *(Hugo Davenport, Daily Telegraph)*

'Harrowing, uncomfortable, but totally compelling.' *(Pauline McLeod, Daily Mirror)*

'As Ann, Lange gives her most powerful performance since playing the title role in *Frances* (1982) . . . German-born actor Mueller-Stahl portrays Mike as a chilling enigma. Mueller-Stahl, whose own father was executed by the Nazis for desertion on the last day of the war, seems to bring extraordinary commitment to the character. Costa-Gavras skilfully avoids conventional perceptions of heroism and villainy. As Jack, the crusading federal prosecutor – and the heroine's courtroom adversary – a hard-boiled Frederic Forrest occupies what would normally be the villain's role. But because of the ambiguity surrounding Mike's innocence, and the horror of the crimes he is alleged to have committed, nothing is as simple as it appears. Like Ann, the audience is torn by wildly conflicting sympathies. And the movie makes it clear that no courtroom triumph of good over evil can erase the tragedy of the Holocaust.' *(Maclean's)*

MUSIC LOVERS, THE CT: 2 AV: 3.88

1970 GB 122 C DRAMA/ROMANCE/BIOPIC

D Ken Russell ●
W Melvyn Bragg ● from C.D. Bowen and Barbara Von Meck's book *Beloved Friend*

Richard Chamberlain ● Glenda Jackson ● Christopher Gable Max Adrian Maureen Pryor Andrew Faulds

Gay composer Tchaikowsky (Richard Chamberlain) gets married, mad, moribund.

Lamentably crude, risible melodrama by Ken Russell, sex-obsessed and only vaguely based on the poor chap's real life. Though critics tended to attack

Russell, at least part of the blame for this fatuous film should be laid on at the door of his supremely untalented screenwriter, Melvyn Bragg (responsible for the equally naff script for *Jesus Christ Superstar*).

MIXED:

'Frequently dramatically and visually stunning but more often tedious and grotesque.' *(Variety)*

'Don't ask Russell for subtlety or historical accuracy, but there's energy, vulgarity and visual splendour in spades.' *(Winnert)*

ANTI:

'Awful . . . the worst experience I ever had in a cinema.' *(Gary Arnold, Washington Post)*

'Libellous not only to the composer but to his music.' *(Roger Ebert)*

'Tchaikowsky has been made the excuse for a crude melodrama about sex.' *(Konstantin Bazarov)*

'The characters slide in and out of fantasies that seem not so much theirs as Russell's . . . When the facts were falsified in the old Hollywood bios, it was to soften and simplify, to please the audience. Russell makes everything frenzied and violent and sadistic, as a form of stimulus for the audience, and possibly even more for himself. The film is homoerotic in style, and yet in dramatic content it's bizarrely anti-homosexual.' *(Pauline Kael)*

'I have seen sufficient of this film to predict that some fans of the Master may well come away intent upon strangling Mr Russell with a necklace of piano wire.' *(Donald Zec, Daily Mirror)*

'At no point did I find myself moved or even touched. This had nothing to do with the [excellent] performances . . . but a lot to do with what makes Russell tick . . . The sex act . . . moves him into genuine creative horror.' *(George Melly, Observer)*

'Russell overdoes it with phallic symbols and homoerotic references that are embarrassing to watch.' *(Martin & Porter)*

MUSIC MAN, THE AAN CT: 6 AV: 7.47

1962 US 151 C MUSICAL

D Morton da Costa ☆
W Marion Hargrove from Meredith Willson and Franklyn Lacey's musical (music and lyrics by Meredith Willson) ☆

Robert Preston ☆ Shirley Jones ☆ Buddy Hackett Hermione Gingold ☆ Pert Kelton Paul Ford Ronnie Howard ☆ (later to become director Ron Howard)

A confidence trickster (Robert Preston) plans to make money out of a small town by starting up a boys' band and embezzling the funds.

After a slow start, this develops into a big, bold musical with a terrific central performance, which Preston had already played with success on Broadway. Onna White's choreography is lively, and musical director Ray Heindorf won an Oscar.

PRO:

'A triumph, perhaps a classic, of corn, smalltown nostalgia, and American love of a parade.' *(Variety)*

'Mr Preston makes the film . . . The calculated folksiness of the sentiment is likeable. The high spirits of music and lyrics are infectious. Once or twice amidst all those trombones tromboning I fancied I heard the sound of ears splitting. But I don't think one should complain if a big, brassy, enthusiastic evening is big, brassy and enthusiastic.' *(Dilys Powell)*

'Shirley Jones . . . is happily back in a milieu of her own, musical romance. She is lovely to look at, sings like a flesh-and-blood angel, and carries conviction in every gesture. She is the best singing actress of the screen in her own category, practically the only operetta singer we have.' *(Hollywood Reporter)*

'The little boy with the stammer and the bashful ways is a small gem as impersonated by Ronny Howard. He stays safely away from precociousness in all his scenes.' *(Variety)*

'This is one of those triumphs that only a veteran performer can have; Preston's years of experience and his love of performing come together joyously.' *(Pauline Kael)*

MIXED:

'Reasonably cinematic, thoroughly invigorating . . . Splendid period "feel", standout performances, slight sag in second half.' *(Halliwell)*

'Overlong and overproduced it may be, but this lavish helping of nostalgic Americana still provides top quality family entertainment.' *(Judith Crist)*

MUSIC ROOM, THE CT: 5 AV: 7.00

(aka *Jalsaghar*)

1958 India 95 BW DRAMA/FOREIGN

D Satyajit Ray ☆
W Satyajit Ray from Tarashanka Banerjee's novel

Chabi Biswas Padma Devi Pinaki Sen Gupta Tulsi Lahari Kali Sarkar Ganga Pada Basu Akhtari Bai Salamat Khan Roshan Kumari Pratap Mukhopdhya

A reactionary, aristocratic connoisseur of music (Chabi Biswas) uses the last of his money to stage a musical evening.

Ray's love of music comes through in this poorly constructed, slow-paced drama which weaves its own spell – but only for the patient. The theme of a declining aristocracy was one to which Ray returned, most memorably in *The Chess Players* (1977).

PRO:

'Wonderfully evocative . . . Slow, rapt and hypnotic,

it is – given some appreciation of Indian music – a remarkable experience.' *(Tom Milne, Time Out)*

'A beautiful, heartfelt tribute to the joy of music.' *(Scheuer)*

MIXED:

'A great, flawed, maddening film – hard to take, but probably impossible to forget. It's often crude and it's poorly constructed, but it's a great experience.' *(Pauline Kael)*

'If I would not rate it quite so high as Ray's Apu Trilogy that is not because of any relative demerit in the quality of its direction, but because the subject itself is smaller and more esoteric; as a work of art it is entirely valid and complete but it does not have quite [sufficient] universal application.' *(Manchester Guardian)*

'I could write volumes about [it] if I had space, so puzzled, indeed foxed, am I by the director's attitude to his fairly ludicrous hero and situation and the whole, slow, gorgeous nonsense.' *(Isabel Quigly, Spectator)*

ANTI:

'[This] Indian legend . . . got me – I must honestly say – giggling quite early on, because I suddenly envisaged none other than Peter Sellers as playing the principal character.' *(Alan Dent, Sunday Telegraph)*

'A deeply felt, extremely tedious film.' *(Stanley Kauffmann)*

MUTINY ON THE BOUNTY AAW

CT: 8 AV: 8.57

1935 US 135 BW DRAMA/ADVENTURE

D Frank Lloyd ☆ AAN
W Talbot Jennings Jules Furthman Carey Wilson ☆ AAN from Charles Nordhoff and James Norman Hall's novels *Mutiny on the Bounty* and *Men Against the Sea*

Charles Laughton ☆ AAN Clark Gable ☆ AAN Franchot Tone ☆ AAN Herbert Mundin Eddie Quillan Dudley Digges Donald Crisp Henry Stephenson Francis Lister Spring Byington

A sailor (Clark Gable) leads a mutiny against a tyrannical captain (Charles Laughton).

A rousing adventure with one of the great screen villains in Laughton's Captain Bligh (who in real life was nothing like the monster pictured here, but never mind). There are longueurs in the narrative, but for the most part it remains highly entertaining. Director Frank Lloyd must be the most unjustly forgotten film-maker in Hollywood history, even though he won Best Director at the Academy Awards on two occasions, for *The Divine Lady* and *Cavalcade*. This, arguably his finest film, is a production triumph in all departments, and was voted Best Picture of 1936 in the *Film Daily* poll of US film critics. Herbert Stothart won an Oscar for his score; Margaret Booth was nominated for her editing.

'Look, Irving. I'm a realistic kind of actor. I've never played in a costume picture in my life. Now you want me to wear a pigtail and velvet knee pants and shoes with silver buckles! The audience will laugh me off the screen. And I'll be damned if I'll shave off my moustache just because the British navy didn't allow them. This moustache has been damned lucky for me.' *(Clark Gable, explaining to Irving Thalberg why he didn't want to play Fletcher Christian)*

ANTI:

'Mr Thalberg's production . . . has brought up the old question as to how far the novelist, playwright, or film director has an obligation to respect the facts of history . . . Personally, I think he should . . . Few will deny that [this film] is magnificent entertainment. To keep Mr Charles Laughton in the foreground, Mr Frank Lloyd has put Bligh instead of Edwards in command of HMS Pandora, which was sent in search of the mutineers . . . I cannot help feeling that if Mr Thalberg had [read existing documentary material] he would have given us a fairer portrait of the man who came to be known as Breadfruit Bligh.' *(Owen Rutter, The Era)*

'Seemed at the time like the pinnacle of Hollywood's achievement but can now be seen to be slackly told.' *(Halliwell)*

MIXED:

'Laughton . . . is as good as he has ever been, and never relaxes his grip on the part, to which he fits himself perfectly. Clark Gable, too . . . gives an acceptable performance . . . In many ways a film above the average, if not in every degree successful . . . Not for the unduly sensitive and certainly not for children.' *(MFB)*

'There is no real reason why this – or any – film should last two hours and thirteen minutes . . . In the midst of that gripping sea story, magnificently done, there are idyllic moments on Tahiti . . . It is not entertainment for children, but it is a powerful melodrama, brilliantly done.' *(Sunday Express)*

'The director, Frank Lloyd, goes after "human interest" details in a broad, conventional manner, and some of the bits of business of the minor characters are tediously simpleminded. But for the kind of big budget, studio controlled romantic adventure that this is, it's very well done.' *(Pauline Kael)*

PRO:

'Hollywood at its very best.' *(Variety)*

'Incidents are made vivid in terms of the medium – the swish and pistol crack of the lash, the sweating lean bodies, the terrible labour, and the ominous judgment from the quarterdeck.' *(Otis Ferguson)*

'It is a remarkable tribute to the film that one does not sigh for what is omitted . . . [The character of Bligh] gives Mr Laughton an opportunity to make a refined and dreadful study of perversion.' *(The Times)*

'The scenes on board ship have the very tang, bite, and almost smell of life as one imagines it was then led at sea, and I cannot imagine two hours of grander entertainment.' *(James Agate, Tatler)*

MY BEAUTIFUL LAUNDRETTE

CT: 4 AV: 6.40

1985 GB 93/97 C DRAMA/ROMANCE

D Stephen Frears ✗
W Hanif Kureishi ✗ AAN

Daniel Day-Lewis ☆ Saeed Jaffrey Roshan Seth Gordon Warnecke ● Shirley Anne Field Rita Wolf

Gay ex-National Front bovver boy (Daniel Day-Lewis) befriends Asian lad (Gordon Warnecke) and helps him open a laundrette.

Hugely praised for daring to depict Pakistani immigrant businessmen as rapacious. Kureishi, being of Pakistani stock himself, was allowed to do this; and, in common with most British films of the period, such greed was ascribed to the evil influence of Prime Minister Margaret Thatcher. It was also fashionable because it told a gay love story (although critics kindly ignored the fact that one of the leading actors, Gordon Warnecke, gave an embarrassingly feeble performance). Daniel Day-Lewis was outstanding and managed to conceal that his character was extraordinarily unrealistic. Stephen Frears's direction was, as ever, competent but utterly lacking in any style personal to himself. The seeds of Kureishi's subsequent, disastrous decline are already evident – especially his political naivety and lack of interest in narrative structure.

PRO:

'Every frame brims with energy and immigrant sass, mocking the lethargy of the dough-faced English, dancing circles around their twee little comedies and chortling like crazy over those overstuffed epics about the Raj. If this film has a flaw, it's that it has too many characters, too many stories, and too much sympathy to fit gracefully into ninety-seven minutes. And that's as it should be. For *My Beautiful Laundrette* is that rarest of things – a movie about now.' *(John Powers)*

'Has many virtues: wit, intelligence, perceptiveness, an exquisite tone, a well-paced narrative, a gallery of vivid and variegated characters, an excellent ensemble of players.' *(Bruce Bawer, American Spectator)*

'Had [it] been written by anybody but . . . Mr Kureishi . . . it would possibly seem racist . . . It's his comic paradox that his upperclass Pakistani immigrants have become the exploiters in a land that once exploited them . . . A fascinating, eccentric, very personal movie.' *(Vincent Canby, New York Times)*

'It's an enormous pleasure to see a movie that's really about something, and that doesn't lay on any syrupy coating to make the subject go down easily.' *(Pauline Kael)*

'Ground-breaking, extraordinarily intriguing and undoubtedly controversial . . . What it says about racial issues and attitudes is pretty important. But this is the absolute opposite of a tract.' *(Derek Malcolm, Guardian)*

'A morality tale for the times, dense in its multiple layers.' *(David Robinson, The Times)*

'Perceptive and revealing . . . about life in Britain today . . . Economically directed . . . [It] is full of choice paradoxes, removing it from sociological tract into the realms of persuasive drama.' *(Iain Johnstone, Sunday Times)*

'The strength of the film is its vision – cutting, compassionate and sometimes hilarious – of what it means to be Asian, and British, in Thatcher's Britain.' *(Richard Rayner, Time Out)*

MIXED:

'Some wish fulfilment here, some stilted acting and direction too, but Hanif Kureishi's script has some comic lines and a civilised, albeit unflattering, view of the go-getting Pakistanis.' *(Shipman)*

ANTI:

'Begs more questions than a Home Secretary explaining MI5 . . . Not brave, just British. With this sort of stuff we kid no-one but ourselves.' *(Ian Bell, Scotsman)*

'Fashionable enough to get critical acclaim . . . this soft-centred anecdote was a bit of a puzzle to those neither Asian nor homosexual.' *(Halliwell)*

MY BRILLIANT CAREER

CT: 6 AV: 7.18

1979 Australia 101 C DRAMA

D Gillian Armstrong ✓
W Eleanor Witcombe from Miles Franklin's novel

Judy Davis ☆ Sam Neill Wendy Hughes Robert Grubb Max Cullen Patricia Kennedy Aileen Britton Peter Whitford Carole Skinner Alan Hopgood

A young Australian woman (Judy Davis) rebels against her backwoods upbringing and becomes a writer.

Polished, sensitive but slow movie about a woman's cultural awakening in the early 1900s. The only character in the movie who isn't a stereotype is the heroine, beautifully played by Judy Davis, and the film is guilty of taking her rather too seriously on her own estimation. Still, it struck a chord with feminists and launched the international careers of its talented stars, Judy Davis and Sam Neill, and its director.

PRO:

'Confidently and assuredly directed . . . beautifully acted, glorious to look at, and heavily evocative of a period gone forever . . . A welcome treat for jaded cinemagoers.' *(Clive Hirschhorn, Sunday Express)*

'Gill Armstrong directs with mesmeric skill.' *(Virginia Dignam, Morning Star)*

'Beautiful to look at. It was filmed on location in the outback, in warm natural colors, and the costumes and settings meticulously establish the period. But Judy Davis's performance establishes it even more, because she creates a complicated character so naturally that we feel the conflicts instead of having to understand them intellectually. This is the best kind of movie of ideas, in which the movie supplies the people and emotions and *we* come up with the conclusions.' *(Roger Ebert)*

MIXED:

'The film resists [forcing a moral], dividing its sympathies equally and honestly. Mistakes are made. At least twice too often the camera makes pretty pictures of a landscape which needs no framing; some lines are said with more than merited relish. Quibbles, though, are silenced by the main attraction: a performance by Judy Davis . . . which ought to still complaints that Australian films are ill served by their actors.' *(David Wilson, New Statesman)*

'From the evidence of the film, the book, which was written by a 16-year-old girl under the name Miles Franklin, is a gothic feminist fantasy: feisty Cinderella wins Prince Charming but turns him down and goes off to fulfill herself. Though the movie doesn't go any deeper into the material than this sort of feminine self-infatuation, Sybylla is treated as if she were a precursor of the new woman: a model of the woman who resists conventional blandishments.' *(Pauline Kael)*

MY COUSIN VINNY CT: 7 AV: 5.77

1992 US 119 C COMEDY

D Jonathan Lynn ✔
W Dale Launer ✔

Joe Pesci ✔ Ralph Macchio ✔
Marisa Tomei ☆ AAW Mitchell Whitfield ✔
Fred Gwynne ✔ Lane Smith Austin Pendleton

An unconventional lawyer from Brooklyn (Joe Pesci), who's qualified in middle age after six trial runs, finds his first case is in the deep south defending his cousin on a murder charge.

Pesci is fast and funny, even though at first his character appears implausibly naive. He is supported by a marvellous cast, especially Ralph Macchio, Mitchell Whitfield and distinguished old-timer Fred Gwynne, whose range of reactions as a southern judge will be a revelation to those who remember him only as TV's Herman Munster. The film is stolen, however, by a delightful newcomer, Marisa Tomei. Actually, she made her début in the Stallone vehicle, Oscar, but let's draw a veil over that. Though ten years too young to play Pesci's fiancée, she gives a startling and hilarious performance.

The true hero of the piece, however, is writer Dale Launer, whose credits include *Ruthless People, Blind Date* and *Dirty Rotten Scoundrels*. After a sticky start, this develops into a very funny script which Jonathan Lynn, no mean writer himself, directs with pace and more sophistication than he showed in *Nuns on the Run*.

ANTI:

'The bits and pieces never quite add up. Somewhere during the film's making I suspect that half the script was mysteriously lost down a street grating.' *(Nigel Andrews, Financial Times)*

'Part of the problem with [the film] is that the comic elements haven't been properly worked out . . . Similarly scant attention has been played to the plot . . . None of this would matter much if [the film] had any pep, but [Lynn's direction] is so lacklustre it doesn't take off until the last 30 minutes . . . Tomei is the best comic turn in the movie, but her scenes with Pesci never catch fire.' *(Toby Young, Guardian)*

'We never feel much for, or about, the two accused prisoners. Macchio, who has been effective in movies like *The Karate Kid* and *Crossroads*, is used here essentially as a foil. He and Whitfield sit at the defense table and look worried, and that's about that.' *(Roger Ebert)*

'A boring, unsubtle situation comedy written and directed with clumsy hands, with hardworking performances finally turning it round for an entertaining climactic half hour.' *(Winnert)*

'Enormously overlong.' *(Quinlan)*

'Promising opening is sadly wasted by the hackneyed script and dumb dialogue.' *(Elliot)*

MIXED:

'As an actor, Pesci plays only variations on New Jersey machismo . . . but he alone cannot fill a comedy. Luckily [Launer] provides some fine routines for the supporting cast . . . It's a small, surprisingly gentle affair, prone to fits and starts, but fun.' *(Wally Hammond, Time Out)*

PRO:

'Let's hear it for the traditional, well-crafted, character-based comic screenplay that turns its back on pastiche, the easy-option bane of pop culture . . . There aren't many of these screenplays around, and most of them seem to have been written by Dale Launer . . . [His] latest [has] Jonathan Lynn . . . directing ably enough to wipe out memories of his execrable *Nuns on the Run*.' *(Anne Billson, New Statesman & Society)*

'As presiding judge on this page, I hereby sentence anyone with a taste for being taken out of themselves, to 119 minutes of the most effective courtroom comedy in recent times.' *(Shaun Usher, Daily Mail)*

'Although the film's a mite draggy in a couple of places, Pesci is brilliant in his first leading role. Despite this, he's almost acted off the screen by Tomei as his fiery, gum-chewing, wise-cracking girlfriend in one of the most electrifying comedy performances in years.' *(Rose)*

MY DARLING CLEMENTINE CT: 8 AV: 9.18

1946 US 98 B WESTERN

D John Ford ☆
W Samuel G. Engel Winston Miller from Stuart N. Lake's book *Wyatt Earp, Frontier Marshal*

Henry Fonda ☆ Walter Brennan ☆ Victor Mature ☆ Linda Darnell Cathy Downs Tim Holt Ward Bond Alan Mowbray ☆ John Ireland Jane Darwell

Wyatt Earp (Henry Fonda) cleans up the Clanton Gang.

John Ford's memorable, cinematic, much imitated movie. Because it was romantic rather than realistic, it was underrated on release; now it can be appreciated as a mythic masterpiece. Henry Fonda, Victor Mature and Walter Brennan are all much better than OK in the corral – though the film is let down by the female casting.

ANTI:

'A dazzling example of how not to make a Western.' *(Manny Farber, New Republic)*

'A most ordinary Western . . . a horse opera for the carriage trade.' *(News Chronicle)*

MIXED:

'A skilled romantic essay in riding and shooting, but not what one looks for from the director of *Grapes of Wrath* and *The Long Voyage Home*.' *(Dilys Powell)*

'Burdened by hackneyed characters and a scattered screenplay . . . this western, it must immediately be understood, is in no-wise another *Stage Coach*. However, it does have Ford's trenchant touch in building individual scenes, its scenic attractions are many, and there is a really rousing action climax which rates high amongst such things. The plot, unfortunately, is no better than the film's title.' *(Herb Sterne)*

'Melodrama or not, it was an eloquent and convincing account of the folkways of the cattle country in a period of growth, settlement, and economic transition. Ford has rarely surpassed his camerawork and his invention of action than in this recent film . . . For sheer inventiveness of camera placement and camera angle, it has no match in recent years. It is a throwback to an almost-forgotten cinematic tradition . . . It is perhaps significant that [its] technique . . . becomes, as it were, over-ripe. The camera dwells too longingly on this desert land inhabited by peasants; its eye is pictorial, romantic rather than realistic . . . There can be no question of Ford's enormous talent for the medium, or of his drive to explore and disclose life as it is actually lived. It is equally clear that he needs the collaboration . . . of a temperament less sentimental than his own. Without it, his command of the film medium is apt to be put to the service of confused thinking.' *(Paul Rotha & Richard Griffith, 1949)*

PRO:

'Ford is a man who has a way with a Western like nobody in the picture trade. Seven years ago his classic *Stagecoach* snuggled very close to fine art in this genre. And now, by George, he's almost matched it with *My Darling Clementine*. Not quite, it is true – for this picture . . . is a little too burdened with the conventions of Western fiction to place it on a par . . . But a dynamic composition of Western legend and scenery is still achieved. And the rich flavor of frontiering wafts in overpowering redolence from the screen.' *(Bosley Crowther)*

'A sustained and complex work of the imagination . . . Its qualities derive from Mr Ford's affection for the portrait he is drawing – the portrait of the Old West. It is a mixed portrait, half-truth, half folklore, but fact or fancy, it is the West as Americans still feel it in their bones.' *(Richard Griffith, New Movies)*

'The gentlemen are perfect. Their humors are earthy. Their activities are taut. The morality rate is simply terrific. And the picture goes off with several bangs.' *(New York Times)*

'A smooth and superior motion picture, wild and woolly Western though it certainly is.' *(New York Herald Tribune)*

'Having assembled all the elements of a conventional Western in *My Darling Clementine*, John Ford as director proceeds to make an excellent film out of his material, using the formula technique to say something about pioneer days in Arizona. What he has done bespeaks his artistry, his humor and his understanding of human nature.' *(Christian Science Monitor)*

'An inconsequent narrative artistically photographed in terms of period and occupational mannerisms, and in places stunningly acted, showed Ford at his visual best and suggested a latent charm he has nowhere else freely expressed.' *(Vernon Young)*

'Do you prefer [your Westerns] with punch and realism, dust you can almost smell and parched heat you can almost feel? . . . [Then this film] is your meat. It is mine.' *(Reynolds News)*

'The director . . . cuts another notch on his revolver . . . With the exception of *The Ox-Bow Incident*, the best Western yet.' *(Evening Standard)*

'Considerable care has gone to its period reconstruction, but the view is a poetic one.' *(Lindsay Anderson)*

MY FAIR LADY AAW CT: 9 AV: 7.71

1964 US 175 C MUSICAL/ROMANCE

D George Cukor AAW
W Alan Jay Lerner ☆ AAN from Lerner and Frederick Loewe's musical play ☆ and George Bernard Shaw's play *Pygmalion*

Audrey Hepburn (singing voice dubbed by Marni Nixon ☆) Rex Harrison ☆ AAW Stanley Holloway ☆ AAN Wilfrid Hyde-White ☆ Gladys Cooper AAN Jeremy Brett Theodore Bikel Isobel Elsom Mona Washbourne John Alderson

A linguistics professor (Rex Harrison) teaches a flower-girl (Audrey Hepburn) to speak 'correctly', but treats her insensitively as she falls in love with him.

The title is a pun on the cockney pronunciation of 'Mayfair Lady'; and Audrey Hepburn (in the role made famous by Julie Andrews) is miscast as a flower-girl – she always looks more like a society lady. Still, Rex Harrison and Stanley Holloway effect the transition from stage to screen with aplomb, making the most of Lerner and Loewe's witty, melodic songs and Shaw's original dialogue. Though unpopular with critics for its stiffness, staginess and failure to cast its Broadway star, Miss Andrews, this remains one of the most entertaining, touching and glamorous of movie musicals. A pity, though, about the odd Americanisms in Alan Jay Lerner's otherwise splendid lyrics. Why, for instance, didn't anyone tell him that English women wear wedding rings, not bands?

The film won seven Oscars, including awards for André Previn (scoring), Cecil Beaton (costumes), George R. Groves (sound) and Harry Stradling (photography). William Ziegler was nominated for his editing.

ANTI:

'With so much capital invested, *My Fair Lady* has been approached so reverently that transference has degenerated into transcription. This property has not been so much adapted as elegantly embalmed.' *(Andrew Sarris)*

MIXED:

'There are times when the fantastication of the Edwardian costumes is overpowering: in the Ascot scene, for instance. On the stage and against Oliver Smith's setting Mr Beaton's design in black and white had a concentrated and concentrating elegance; they pointed the fun. On the screen they knock your eye out, and uncomfortably . . . There is too much of a lot of things, and not only in the Ascot scene: too great a blare of the opening music; too unnerving a clarity of faces in a make-up which ranges from Higgins's tan (disconcerting in so indoor a character) to the curious lilac of Mrs Pierce (discreetly played by Mona Washbourne). And yet *My Fair Lady* persists in being extraordinarily enjoyable . . . The ballroom scene glows and the Covent Garden Opera House interior glitters, and there is a beautiful moment when the early moming flowers in the Market are uncovered.' *(Dilys Powell)*

'Careful, cold transcription of a stage success; cinematically quite uninventive when compared with *Pygmalion*, but a pretty good entertainment.' *(Halliwell)*

PRO:

'The clothes are gorgeous, the colours are gorgeous, Audrey Hepburn is gorgeous. And what does it all add up to? It adds up to a costly and lavish reconstruction of the stage musical with very few cinematic tricks added . . . So was it all worth it? Yes, I believe so.' *(Ann Pacey, Sun)*

'If there was disappointment among the devotees of the original stage version when it was decided to pass over Julie Andrews, they will be mollified when they see Audrey Hepburn in her place. She has caught and sharpened marvellously the picture of [Eliza].' *(Alex Faulkner, Daily Telegraph)*

'[It] must be unique among screen musicals in that most of the action is confined to one house, and much of it to one room; the measure of its success is that we never feel the smallest twinge of claustrophobia.' *(Kenneth Tynan, Observer)*

'Audrey Hepburn, given the thankless task of replacing Julie Andrews in the role she created, proved herself a satisfying and breath-takingly beautiful Eliza. And now one can only repeat that the very few flaws are minor ones and that the film is not only a loverly thing in itself but an outstanding example of moving a classic from stage to screen with integrity.' *(Judith Crist)*

MY FATHER'S GLORY CT: 4 AV: 7.56

(aka *La Gloire De Mon Père)*

1991 France 105 C DRAMA/FOREIGN

D Yves Robert ✗
W Yves Robert Jérôme Tonnerre ✗ from Marcel Pagnol's autobiogrpahy

Philippe Caubère Nathalie Roussel Didier Pain Thérèse Liotard Julian Ciamaca Yves Robert

Nostalgic memoirs of a Provence childhood.

Dark forebodings are roused by the opening music, so sweet and lush it made me long for the astringent atonality of Mantovani. The music is father to the film: a sentimental ramble through a boy's memories of childhood, shared with relations so wholesome they make the Von Trapps look like the Manson family. It's about the gentle pain of growing up: you know the kind of thing. An alternative, if racist, title might be My Life As A Frog.

It's narrated by the boy as a grown-up, and weighed down with kilos of faux-naif irony. 'Germs were a novelty then, as Pasteur had only just discovered them' is the kind of witticism which presumably had audiences rolling in the Ile de France.

Symptomatic of the film's attention to period but inattention to authenticity, is a park scene where all the ladies carry identical white parasols, evidently bought as a job-lot by an over-assiduous props-person. Every woman throughout the film is beautiful and crisply laundered, as though auditioning for the front picture on a box of Quality Street – with the exception of a schoolma'am and a comic maid, who are of course plain. Acting is of a Gallic exuberance which will be familiar to anyone who has suffered an amateur production of Molière.

The central character, the schoolmaster father (Philippe Caubère), is intended to be lovable but is merely smug, a soggier version of Mr. Chips. The boy (played mainly by Julien Ciamaca) is, how do you say, un petit pain. The touching scene where he donates his sailor-suit to a grateful peasant boy should have you blinking back tears of either nostalgia or rage.

This complacent, oddly loathsome film was manufactured by Yves Robert with an astute eye to the petit-bourgeois market, from an autobiographical work by Marcel Pagnol, who also wrote *Jean de Florette* and *Manon des Sources*. The setting – rural Provence – may be the same; but the quality is as different as Hirondelle is from Domaine de Trevallon. Many people will find it light and refreshing: for me, the memory evoked was of that grimmest of childhood experiences, flat Lucozade.

PRO:

'The wry commentary . . . keeps the film from becoming insipid or unduly sentimental.' *(Philip French, Observer)*

'*My Father's Glory* was released first, before *My Mother's Castle*, the continuation. That is the best way to see them – the first film about memory becoming a memory itself, to be reawakened by the second. What is surprising about the two films is the way they creep up on you emotionally, until at the end of the second one, when we discover the meaning of the movie's title, there is a deeply moving moment of truth and insight.' *(Roger Ebert)*

'Story-telling, and film-making, of the first order.' *(Maltin)*

'Poignant, observant and enchanting.' *(Scheuer)*

'Unforgettable.' *(Martin & Porter)*

MIXED:

'All as predictable as summer ending. I don't want to draw blood from [the] movie, because it has none. As a time-passer, it's very pleasant.' *(Tom Hutchinson, Mail on Sunday)*

ANTI:

'For the seriously sleep-deprived . . . Robert opts for gilded insipidity . . . Ten for scenery, two for drama and characterisation.' *(Nigel Andrews, Financial Times)*

MY FAVORITE WIFE CT: 6 AV: 7.64

1940 US 88 BWCOMEDY

D Garson Kanin ☆

W Sam Spewack Bella Spewack from Leo McCarey, Sam Spewack and Bella Spewack's story AAN

Cary Grant ☆ Irene Dunne ☆ Randolph Scott Gail Patrick Ann Shoemaker Donald MacBride

A respectable man (Cary Grant) discovers that he has inadvertently become a bigamist, and has two wives staying in different rooms at a hotel.

A screwball comedy which has retained its charm, thanks to two apparently effortless leading performances. Roy Webb's score and the art direction by Van Nest Polglase and Mark-Lee Kirk were Oscar-nominated.

'One of those comedies with a glow on it.' *(Otis Ferguson)*

'It must be admitted that . . . this situation is more amusing than shocking. This is partly due to clever direction and partly to skilful acting . . . The dialogue is smart and telling, and the settings lavish and in keeping.' *(MFB)*

'This is briefly to report the discovery of . . . a little island of joy [at Radio City Music Hall] . . . Let's hoist a flag and claim it for King Comus, for this is the sort of refuge we all can find pleasure in these days – a frankly fanciful farce, a rondo of refined ribaldries and an altogether delightful picture.' *(Bosley Crowther)*

'The supporting players maintain the comedy in the mood set by the principals . . . The [press] audience . . . was swept with laughter punctuated by titters at the frequent lines of double meaning.' *(James D. Ivers, Motion Picture Herald)*

'A well-worn situation gets its brightest treatment in this light star vehicle.' *(Halliwell)*

MY FAVORITE YEAR CT: 9 AV: 7.20

1982 US 92 C COMEDY/ROMANCE

D Richard Benjamin

W Norman Steinberg Dennis Palumbo ✔

Peter O'Toole ☆ AAW Mark Linn-Baker ✔ Jessica Harper ✔ Joseph Bologna ☆ Bill Macy Lainie Kazan ✔ Anne DeSalvo Lou Jacobi ✔

A young man (Mark Linn-Baker) who is an aspirant

writer on a comedy show is assigned to keep control of alcoholic guest star Alan Swann (Peter O'Toole).

Based on a real story of how a youthful Mel Brooks was assigned to care for Errol Flynn when he guested on *The Sid Caesar Show*, this is a richly rewarding comic fantasy, with hilarious performances from O'Toole and Joseph Bologna (as the Caesar figure), and charming ones from Linn-Baker and Jessica Harper (as his girlfriend). The background of live TV in the 1950s is portrayed in loving detail; and although the romantic sub-plot is sketchy, it adds to the prevailing atmosphere of good humour. Director Richard Benjamin, himself a talented actor, shows his love of actors by giving them all a chance to shine – which they do. O'Toole has never been better.

MIXED:

'O'Toole . . . is very funny. Like many drunks, he is also alarming . . . The film aspires to be something more than a comedy of alcoholic manners . . . Benjamin directs with more efficiency than feeling. But Joseph Bologna . . . will delight anyone who remembers Sid Caesar.' *(Alexander Walker, Evening Standard)*

'Not a perfect movie. I could have done without the entire romantic subplot between Benjy and KC. But I liked the movie's ability to move from one unexpected comic situation to another. That produces one of the best scenes, when Benjy takes Swann home to Brooklyn to meet his mother and weird Uncle Morty (Lainie Kazan and Lou Jacobi in hilarious performances). There is, to be sure, a force running through the movie's disorganization, and that force is O'Toole's charisma. He is so completely charming, so doomed, so funny, and so pathetically invincible as Swann that this movie succeeds despite its occasional unnecessary scenes.' *(Roger Ebert)*

PRO:

'A field-day for a wonderful bunch of actors.' *(Variety)*

'An engagingly barmy comedy . . . Despite the rollicking comedy and wisecracking dialogue, it is for the affectionate reconciliation of the private man and the public image that [the film] is to be cherished.' *(David Castell, Sunday Telegraph)*

'Most of the comedy emanates from Peter O'Toole . . . [who] is by turns charming, scathing, flamboyant and devastating.' *(Paul Jackson, Western Mail)*

'O'Toole is simply astounding. Ravaged and liquefied as Swann is, he still has his feelers out – he's always aware of the impression he's making; even when Swann is drunk, he's acting a great actor drunk.' *(Pauline Kael)*

MY LEARNED FRIEND CT: 6 AV: 7.50

1943 GB 76 BW COMEDY

D Basil Dearden, Will Hay ☆
W John Dighton Angus Macphail ☆

Will Hay ☆ Claude Hulbert ☆ Mervyn Johns ☆ Ernest Thesiger Charles Victor Lloyd Pearson Maudie Edwards

A criminal is determined to murder everyone connected with his trial, leaving his incompetent barrister (Will Hay) until last. The barrister tries to warn his fellow-victims, with little success.

Very British black comedy, with a famous climax on the clockface of Big Ben.

'[Macphail and Dighton] have written a wealth of craziness into this screenplay which emerges as a farce in the best and most violent tradition . . . Hay and Hulbert rush through their parts in rollicking irresponsibility which infects the whole cast.' *(MFB)*

'Crazy comedy extravaganza . . . The quips outnumber the stunts, but happily the co-stars are equally effective with both mediums. All told, good wholesome fun . . . [Hay and Hulbert] work hard, improvise cleverly and register in contrast as well as in concert.' *(Kine Weekly)*

'Sure fire comedy hit [which] perpetrates a further mix-up of slapstick and thrill . . . Considerable fun.' *(Today's Cinema)*

'Slightly desperate but surprisingly funny.' *(Tom Milne, Time Out)*

MY LEFT FOOT AAN CT: 7 AV: 8.31

1989 GB 103 C DRAMA/BIOPIC

D Jim Sheridan ☆ AAN
W Shane Connaughton Jim Sheridan ☆ AAN from Christy Brown's book

Daniel Day-Lewis ☆ AAW Ray McAnally ☆ Brenda Fricker ☆ AAW Ruth McCabe Fiona Shaw Eanna MacLiam Alison Whelan Declan Croghan Hugh O'Conor Cyril Cusack Adrian Dunbar

Biopic of the able Irish writer and artist, Christy Brown, whose cerebral palsy meant that he had to communicate via the aforementioned organ.

Moving, absorbing, far from depressing, and praiseworthy for the way it addresses the fact that the disabled have sexual feelings too. The objects of Christy's lust – his speech therapist and a nurse – are caricatures by comparison with Christy's parents, exquisitely played by Brenda Fricker and Ray McAnally. But the film works magnificently as a parental love story.

In one of the great screen performances, Daniel Day-Lewis makes Christy emerge as frustrated, devious and totally unsentimentalized, with the result that you sympathize with him all the more.

The restaurant scene where he expresses his feelings of frustration is extremely moving. 13-year-old Hugh O'Conor (the child star in *Lamb*) is no less effective as the young Christy.

ANTI:

'A zest-free experience . . . Day-Lewis gets to drool, suffer from cerebral palsy and do an Irish accent – all at the same time. No wonder he got the Best Actor Oscar – and no wonder they never gave it to Cary Grant, who throughout his career made the mistake of making screen acting look effortless . . . It's nothing but a social-realist soap opera that could barely pass muster as an American how-I-triumphed-over-my-disease TV Movie of the Week . . . In some ways, Christy's handicap is almost passed over. There is a tendency to concentrate on the end results of his achievements at the expense of what were, one assumes, arduous learning processes . . . This has a diminishing effect on Christy's character and is an insult to us, the audience – he is presented as not so much a human being who has surmounted incredible odds as a chair-bound superhero. But this is no superman or saint; Christy was extraordinary precisely because he was an ordinary, everyday man afflicted with an ordinary, everyday handicap. And there is considerable cowardice in the happy-ever-after ending which freeze-frames the artist-writer and his wife-to-be with a celebratory bottle of champagne – conveniently ignoring the hardships of his later life and its premature end.' *(Anne Billson, Film Review)*

MIXED:

'Not particularly cinematic, but boasting superb performances and a moving story.' *(Colin Vaines, Film Yearbook)*

'A gloriously rounded film without a duff performance in it . . . Day-Lewis is superb, but I had the uneasy feeling I was watching the wheelchair equivalent of a white man blacking up as Othello.' *(Sue Heal, Today)*

'Pedestrian narrative, relying on cinematic clichés, but enlivened by the intensity of Day-Lewis's performance and some good ensemble acting.' *(Halliwell)*

'While the idea might sound depressing, this turns out to be a remarkably joyous and witty film, superbly acted by the entire cast. It has its sentimental moments, to be sure, but the overall experience is wonderfully uplifting.' *(Rose)*

PRO:

'Warm, romantic and moving.' *(Variety)*

'This is not the namby-pamby inspirational porridge that most Hollywood films about the disabled . . . are cooked up to be . . . Sheridan's direction is unwaveringly on-target, consistently capturing both intelligence and emotion. And there's a bevy of powerhouse performances . . . most of all, Day-Lewis [in] a rare, incredibly subtle sometimes savagely humorous performance – and a courageous one.' *(David Bartholomew, Film Journal)*

'The strength of the screenplay is that it shows how everyone who helped Christy Brown on also held him back.' *(Adam Mars-Jones, Independent)*

'Moving and effective . . . Day-Lewis's uncannily accurate portrayal . . . deserves the highest praise . . . Brenda Fricker is superb.' *(Hugo Davenport, Daily Telegraph)*

'The greatness of Day-Lewis's performance is that he pulls you inside Christy Brown's frustration and rage (and his bottomless thirst) . . . Sheridan and Connaughton know that their story is not the making of an artistic genius: it's the release of an imprisoned comic spirit. What makes Christy Brown such a zesty subject for a movie is that, with all his physical handicaps, he became a traveller, a pub crawler, a husband, a joker. He became a literary lion and made a pile of money; *Down All the Days*, a best-seller, was published in fifteen countries. The movie may tear you apart, but it's the story of a triumphantly tough guy who lived it up.' *(Pauline Kael)*

MY LIFE AS A DOG   CT: 7 AV: 7.27

(aka *Mit Liv Som Hund)*

1985 Sweden 101 C COMEDY/DRAMA/FOREIGN

D Lasse Hallström ☆ AAN
W Lasse Hallström Reidar Jönsson Brasse Brannström Per Berglund ☆ AAN from Reidar Jönsson's autobiographical novel

Anton Glanzelius ✔ Manfred Serner Anki Lidén Tomas von Brömssen Melinda Kinnaman Ing-Marie Carlsson

A Swedish boy (Anton Glanzelius) grows up in the 1950s.

A delightfully quirky tragi-comedy. Lasse Hallström contributes subtly humorous direction (rather in the mould of Bill Forsyth) and 12-year-old Anton Glanzelius is touching without being soppy.

ANTI:

'There's only one combination in the movies that's worse than children and dogs, and that's children, dogs and glassblowing . . . [Young Ingemar's] Mama starts coughing up blood, as well she might, seeing she has to tolerate [his] cutely maladjusted antics day in day out . . . [Then he's] shipped off to the country to stay with jolly pipe-sucking Uncle Morbror, which is presumably Swedish for "man with a pipe stuck in his mouth".' *(Jonathan Romney, New Musical Express)*

MIXED:

'We must never forget that [Sweden] let the pop group Abba loose on the world. Some of this shame must attach to . . . Hallström, who made *Abba – The Movie*. I hope he gave the money to a good charity.

By way of a final atonement, we are now asked to accept [this film]. It will do as well as any other apology.' *(William Green, Sunday Today)*

PRO:

'How has Swedish director Lasse Hallström remembered so precisely that knife edge between pain and delight that is childhood? In *My Life as a Dog* he has caught it all, in a sterling film whose style sits between the light moments of his compatriot, Ingmar Bergman, and the darker moments of François Truffaut's childhood films. With freshness in such short supply that it's nearly endangered, *My Life as a Dog* should be cherished.' *(Sheila Benson)*

'The virtue of [the film] is its lack of sentimentality.' *(Victoria Mather, Daily Telegraph)*

'By turns painful and funny, the film manages to achieve genuine charm.' *(Halliwell)*

'Full of oddball humour, the impish Glanzelius convinces as a real human being having to grow up all too quickly.' *(Rose)*

MY MAN GODFREY CT: 6 AV: 8.64

1936 US 94 BW COMEDY

D Gregory La Cava ☆ AAN
W Morrie Ryskind Eric Hatch Gregory La Cava ☆ AAN from Eric Hatch's story *1101 Park Avenue*

Carole Lombard ☆ AAN William Powell ☆ AAN Alice Brady ☆ AAN Mischa Auer ☆ AAN Eugene Pallette Gail Patrick Alan Mowbray Jean Dixon Pat Flaherty Robert Light

A rich but eccentric family hires a tramp (William Powell) to be their butler.

Carole Lombard excels as an eccentric rich girl in this enjoyable screwball comedy, Gregory La Cava's directorial début. The plot is wildly improbable; and it's hard to swallow suave William Powell as a down-and-out. The message – that the rich are foolish and the poor wise – was understandably popular with audiences during the Depression; now, it looks a good deal less convincing. Charles D. Hall's art direction offers some of the most sublime Art Deco sets of the 1930s.

MIXED:

'*My Man Godfrey*, for three-quarters of its way, is acutely funny. But the film does not maintain quite so high a standard . . . nor does "the social conscience" remain agreeably implicit.' *(Graham Greene)*

'Starts out with a promising satiric idea and winds up in box-office romance, but it's likable and well-paced even at its silliest.' *(Pauline Kael)*

PRO:

'One of the smartest, most amusing comedies of the season . . . The script sparkles with witty speeches and the only weakness of the picture is its failure to space laughter, many lines being lost to the audience . . . William Powell and Carole Lombard seldom appeared to better advantage.' *(Welford Beaton, Hollywood Spectator)*

'Smart comedy of manners . . . exceptional quality of the humour. The stale wisecrack gives place to ludicrous buffoonery, which is all the better for being directed at a certain social type. The film is often reminiscent of the Marx Brothers . . . Into this charade the whole cast enters with terrific gusto. Carole Lombard gives a grand performance . . . William Powell is superb . . . Gregory La Cava's direction is more than equal to the job.' *(MFB)*

'The daffiest comedy of the year . . . There may be a sober moment or two in the picture; there may be a few lines of the script that do not pack a laugh. Somehow we cannot remember them. It's nonsense, of course, but it's something to relish on a damp September morning . . . An exuberantly funny picture.' *(Frank S. Nugent, New York Times)*

MY MOTHER'S CASTLE CT: 5 AV: 7.22

(aka *Le Château De Ma Mère*)

1991 France 98 C DRAMA/BIOPIC/FOREIGN

D Yves Robert
W Jérôme Tonnere Yves Robert from Marcel Pagnol's autobiography

Philippe Caubère Nathalie Roussel Didier Pain Thérèse Liotard Julien Ciamaca Victorien Delamare Joris Molinas

A paean to Provence – with our young hero (Julien Ciamaca), later to grow into the French film-maker Marcel Pagnol, discovering female perversity in the form of Isabella, a character modelled – but not well enough – on Dickens's Estella in Great Expectations.

An improvement on the picture to which it is a sequel, *My Father's Glory*, but only just. The second half of the film benefits, unlike its predecessor, from a modest amount of dramatic tension, and it's possible to keep one's eyes open in the hope that Marcel's pompous father (Philippe Caubère) might lose his job as a teacher. At the end, glad tidings of disasters which befall the characters in later life inject a welcome note of realism into the greetings-card soppiness of the previous two hours.

But it's still one of those films where you can't see the woods for the twee. Unwisely, the director Yves Robert includes some frames from one of Pagnol's own films, which reveal the spinelessness of everything else we are watching. This is the kind of picture where poverty is dismissed with a shrug of the shoulders, and Marcel's dying mother (Nathalie Roussel) looks so robust that she might be auditioning for the Ali McGraw role in *Love Story*. Strictly for devotees of the Laura Ashley school of film-making.

PRO:

'It is likely that no one, not even Pagnol, had a childhood quite this perfect, and yet all happy childhoods grow happier in memory, and it is the nature of film that we can share some of Pagnol's happiness.' *(Roger Ebert)*

'While the sequel isn't quite the equal of the original installment, it is a sheer delight.' *(Baseline)*

'Exquisite.' *(Martin & Porter)*

ANTI:

'Some of these European filmmakers . . . ought to be told that setting out to make a "charming" film is a thoroughly bad idea . . . It tends to lead to films like this, when scarcely a received idea about bourgeois childhood is left undisturbed . . . A series of important confrontations take place which deeply affect the boy hero and turn him into a whimsical, rose tinted git for the rest of his life.' *(Colin Donald, Scotsman)*

'If this film has a tougher edge than *My Father's Glory*, it's entirely involuntary.' *(Sheila Johnston, Independent)*

'On the Richter scale of boredom Robert's [previous film] was awarded eight out of 10. His continuing tribute to petty bourgeois proprieties gains a seven.' *(Jeff Sawtell, Morning Star)*

MY NIGHT AT MAUD'S AAN CT: 5 AV: 6.56

(aka *Ma Nuit Chez Maud; My Night with Maud*)

1969 France 110 BW DRAMA/ROMANCE

D Eric Rohmer ✗
W Eric Rohmer ✗ AAN

Jean-Louis Trintignant Françoise Fabian ☆
Marie-Christine Barrault Antoine Vitez
Leonide Kogan Anne Dubot Guy Leger
Marie Becker Marie-Claude Rauzier

Divorcée Maud (Françoise Fabian) tries to seduce a young man (Jean-Louis Trintignant), who is saving himself for the right girl (Marie-Christine Barrault), whom he dare not approach.

I'm one of the few who doesn't consider Eric Rohmer's austere moral comedy to be one of this writer-director's best. The leading character, an earnest Catholic engineer and chauvinist prig, is less enjoyably hypocritical than most of Rohmer's anti-heroes, and his philosophizing about Pascal and predestination is tedious. Rohmer's women, as usual, are fascinating – none more so than Françoise Fabian as she tries to lure Trintignant from the straight and narrow. The film might have been more entertaining had she succeeded.

PRO:

'For intellectuals, especially those with good French; since next to nothing happens . . . And since the players never stop talking the film has no business to be for people who like the cinema. But it qualifies. The interweaving of characters and the flowing sequence of the talk create in themselves a kind of movement, a kind of action. The talk is mesmerising.' *(Dilys Powell)*

'It looks as sharp, as witty and as dry – in the Martini sense – as it sounds, nothing flashy about the photography, nothing frenzied about the direction. Classic is the only word, if that still means restrained, economical and serene.' *(Richard Roud, Guardian)*

'The most remarkable element . . . is the Christianity, or maybe the daring required to present it as such a fact of some people's lives . . . Acted with hair-trigger sensitivity by everyone, this sport disturbs received ideas, and is consistently humorous to boot.' *(John Coleman, New Statesman)*

'A satire on the modern demi-intellectual's insistence on analyzing everything to death and you do not begin to laugh at until after you have left the theater when the lovely absurdity of the whole enterprise begins ticking like a time bomb in your brain.' *(Richard Schickel)*

'Marvelously witty and civilized.' *(Scheuer)*

'Tantalizingly witty, beautifully shot.' *(Virgin)*

MIXED:

'A non-French and not over-literary audience could rather easily be intimidated by [the film] with its lengthy debates on religion and morality, and its dialogue quotations from Pascal . . . Without being over-Philistine about it, it must make those of us who are not quite *au fait* with this tradition a little uneasy in our approach . . . That much admitted, it would be a pity if the rest of us were deterred . . . from enjoying a quiet, intelligent, literate and above all civilised comedy of manners.' *(David Robinson, Financial Times)*

ANTI:

'An intellectual exercise in which two men and a divorced woman sit around and discuss religion, sex, politics, and the boring philosophy of Pascal. An almost totally conversational movie, *Maud* is a great success in Paris, where they like things talky, but I found it as stimulating to the demands of American cinema as the sight of a dead mule.' *(Rex Reed)*

MYRA BRECKENRIDGE CT: 1 AV: 2.33

1970 US 94 C COMEDY

D Michael Sarne ●
W Michael Sarne David Giler ● from Gore Vidal's novel

Mae West ● Raquel Welch ● Rex Reed ●
John Huston ● Jim Backus John Carradine
Andy Devine Farrah Fawcett ●

Homosexual movie-buff (played by real-life film reviewer Rex Reed) has operation to turn himself into a woman (Raquel Welch), then decides to avenge himself on the American male.

This almost entirely unfunny and pretentious attempt by the untalented director and pop-singer Michael Sarne to film Gore Vidal's satirical novel received perhaps the worst reviews of all time. They were fully deserved. The general atmosphere of self-satisfied sleaze is moved into the realm of horror by the sight of Mae West, overmade-up, nearing eighty and looking like an animatronic corpse.

Sample line from the screenplay by Mike Sarne and David Giler . . . Myra (Raquel Welch): 'My goal is the destruction of the last vestigial traces of traditional manhood in order to realign the sexes, while preparing humanity for its next stage.'

PRO:

'Nowhere near as bad as its reputation . . . It's West's show, and here she is, an octogenarian hilariously sending herself up and still being funny about sex. A camp, silly, outrageous movie.' *(Winnert)*

ANTI:

'About as funny as a child molester.' *(Time)*

'I still can't believe I saw this freak show, a self-consciously mod, disjointed patchwork of leers, vulgarity, and general ineptness.' *(William Wolf, Cue)*

'The most flamboyant elaboration ever of the silliest, most meandering and sickest of nocturnal, sex-sprung fantasies . . . repulsively neurotic.' *(Winifred Blevins, Los Angeles Herald-Examiner)*

'Gore Vidal's smart, initially funny but finally nauseating little novel, a satire on the battle of the sexes, the dominant female and the Hollywood myth, has been turned into a film which can't manage the smartness but diligently preserves the nausea.' *(Dilys Powell)*

'The film looks like an abandoned battlefield after a lot of studio forces tussled and nobody won . . . Myra isn't even good opportunism.' *(Stanley Kauffmann, New Republic)*

'A horrifying movie . . . An entirely incompetent, impotent attempt at exploitation by an industry that knew once, at the very least, how to make a dishonest buck . . . Unprecedented unpleasantness.' *(Newsweek)*

'The only redeeming thought is that Myra is evidently aimed at the jaded and spent over-35s. Someone may have judged that a younger generation is happy to leave this sort of putrescence to their elders. I hope so.' *(Charles Champlin, LA Times)*

'A junk film . . . Satirizes nothing except, perhaps, the desperate lengths to which today's moviemakers will go to try to be different and dirty . . . unpleasant . . . dumb . . . inane.' *(Vincent Canby, New York Times)*

'Muddled and boringly smutty . . . Stay home!' *(Francis Russell, National Review)*

'Something is being ridiculed . . . the people who swallow the picture perhaps.' *(Penelope Gilliatt, New Yorker)*

'Myra Breckinridge collapses like a tired smirking elephant with no place to go.' *(Howard Thompson, New York Times)*

'A further minor though distinct horror is the presence of Rex Reed in the role of Myron. I had hoped that this campy butterfly and self-styled critic – who was cast, I am told, so as to make certain things about Myron obvious without the script's having to spell them out – would at least be able to portray himself on screen so that, on the strength of his success, we would be rid of him as a writer. No such luck. Reed's movements resemble Birnam's toward Dunsinane, his lines dribble from his mouth like moist mashed-potato mix, and his facial play is a permanent pudgy pout. In short, his acting is on a par with his writing . . . Still another dimension in horror is the casting and display of Mae West, fully clothed and perfectly mummified, as a nonstop sex talker and performer, playing endless sexual prologues and epilogues with young men who allegedly service and even desire her. These scenes are exquisitely stomach-turning.' *(John Simon)*

N

NAKED

CT: 5 AV: 7.67

1993 GB 126 C DRAMA

D Mike Leigh ✗
W Mike Leigh ✗

David Thewlis ☆ Lesley Sharp Katrin Cartlidge Greg Cruttwell Claire Skinner Peter Wight

A young man Johnny (David Thewlis) rapes a woman in a Manchester alley, then steals a car. In London, he finds the flat of an old girlfriend (Lesley Sharp) whom he ditched, has sadistic sex with her flatmate, a spaced-out Goth with understandably low self-esteem (Katrin Cartlidge), wanders the streets and encounter various other nocturnal deadbeats.

Naked was Britain's big success at the 1993 Cannes Film Festival: it won the best actor prize for David Thewlis, and Mike Leigh carried off the award for best director. And it's easy to see the film's appeal for foreigners and international jurors: it would make the most wretched political refugee grateful not to live in Britain.

Some critics commended *Naked* for being so perceptive about homelessness – odd, since Leigh doesn't explore this social problem at any point. Johnny may or may not be homeless: we never find out. When he leaves his hometown or his girlfriend's London flat, these are conscious choices, not forced on him by an uncaring family, society or government. The Scottish couple he meets may be homeless (although she says she has some money), but there's no attempt to discover why. The film adopts a distanced, even condescending, approach to them: they are just caricatures for the Mike Leigh cartoon gallery: we're even invited to laugh at the boy's nervous tic.

Leigh draws a portentous parallel between our wandering hero and Ulysses, even though there is nothing obviously brave, adventurous or grand about him. Johnny is fond of the grandiose: statements about the end of the world, God as sadist, and the like. These are presumably intended to be meaningful, rather than (as I found them) pretentious and self-pitying.

Johnny is played with commitment and charisma by Thewlis, but to a dispassionate observer he comes across, not as the publicity blurb suggests, the ultimate anti-hero of the 90s, but as an arrogant, half-educated nitwit with nothing more to recommend him than an acid tongue. Has his moral sense been dulled by his upbringing, class, or the State of Modern Britain? It's hard to tell, and harder to care.

Leigh directs with more visual ambition than usual. The exterior night sequences have the nightmarish intensity of film noir. But the memorable scenes remain the TV-style ones, where Leigh plonks down a camera and cross-cuts between his actors. When he does try to be artistic, his visuals often distract from, rather than add to, our understanding. Witness, for example, the lengthiest conversation in the film, between Johnny and the security man: here we are, getting to the nub of Johnny's philosophy, and Leigh as director chooses this of all moments to distance his audience by placing the characters in longshot and silhouette. Why? It makes a pretty picture, but the result is to alienate us from Johnny's apocalyptic disgust: the opposite dramatic effect to the one which – if the rest of the film is any guide – Leigh intends.

Leigh has certainly succeeded in creating a mood piece which expresses an alienation, despair and anger about Britain (or western man, or human nature, or something). But it gives little reason for us to share his mood. Still less does it illuminate for us why his characters are so amoral, vicious and vacuous. It's the kind of suicidal depression made celluloid which seems less in need of criticism than a course of psychiatric therapy.

PRO:

'Dwarfs everything the director has yet done.' *(Variety)*

'A vision of modern chaos with insights that will stay with you a long time.' *(Angie Errigo, Today)*

'A painful movie to watch. But it is also exhilarating, as all good movies are, because we are watching the director and actors venturing beyond any conventional idea of what a modern movie can be about. Here there is no plot, no characters to identify with, no hope. But there is care: the filmmakers care enough about these people to observe them very closely, to note how they look and sound and what they feel.' *(Roger Ebert)*

ANTI:

'Full of apocalyptic self-consciousness and cackhanded class comedy.' *(Nigel Andrews, Financial Times)*

'Thewlis is an impressive ranter, but director Mike Leigh sees Johnny less as a human being than as a mouthpiece.' *(Owen Gleiberman, Entertainment Weekly)*

'It would be hard to imagine a film much sourer than *Naked*, but sourness is not a fault, merely a characteristic. Hollowness, now, self-indulgence, a sort of gloating emotional ugliness – those are faults . . . *Naked* certainly doesn't show women the way they are, unless women are inert masochists who may or may not even notice they've been raped.' *(Adam Mars-Jones, Independent)*

'How can I possibly recommend [it] . . . You won't enjoy it. It won't teach you anything, not unless your address is somewhere in Cloud Cuckoo Land . . . There was a time when we used to laugh at Leigh's work. Not any more. *Naked* is desperate stuff.' *(Anne Billson, Sunday Telegraph)*

NAKED CITY, THE CT: 6 AV: 8.00

1948 US 96 BW THRILLER
D Jules Dassin
W Malvin Wald Albert Maltz from Wald's story AAN

Barry Fitzgerald ✗ Don Taylor ✗ Howard Duff Dorothy Hart Ted de Corsia Adelaide Klein House Jameson Anne Sargent Grover Burgess Tom Pedi

Homicide detectives (Barry Fitzgerald, Don Taylor) track down murderer in New York.

Moderately enjoyable thriller. It's been influential because of the way it used authentic locations, and William Daniels's cinematography and Paul Weatherwax's editing both won Oscars. But the story and acting aren't at all convincing.

PRO:

'Perhaps nothing makes more satisfactory movie entertainment than a good manhunt – and *The Naked City* is a first-rate one, climaxed by a hair-raising chase in the superstructure of Williamsburg Bridge. But *The Naked City* is more than an expert hunt. Filmed in the streets of New York, in actual apartments, offices and police stations, with real citizens peopling its scenes, it is an example of the documentary technique skillfully adapted to a fictional narrative. The gloss of studio sets is missing, well replaced by the actual settings.' *(Fortnight)*

'A boldly fashioned yarn about eastside, westside, about Broadway, the elevated . . . the homicide squad running down infinitesimal clues, roundup of suspects, all the details that goes with great crime-reporting . . . In this pic there are no props. A Manhattan police station scene was photographed in the police station . . . Barry Fitzgerald . . . in playing the police lieutenant of the homicide squad, strides through the role with tongue in cheek.' *(Variety)*

MIXED:

'Photographed by William Daniels – who shot *Greed* – with a lovely eye for space, size and light. A visually majestic finish. Otherwise, mawkish and naive.' *(James Agee, Nation)*

ANTI:

'The deficiencies of the picture are too obvious. Its overly melodramatic sequences are laid on a framework of documentary reality that makes them even more naked than the title. Some of them are the thin stupidity of the young detective in trying to make the arrest of a murderer by himself when 18,000 men were available on the nearest telephone; the implausibility of Barry Fitzgerald as a detective lieutenant; the cop-and-robber formula of shooting the criminal down from the stark heights of a superstructure on the Williamsburg Bridge (with some good photography as an offset); the assumption that a dead body floats during its first day in the river.' *(Paul J. Kern, New Movies)*

'No more than a conventional "slice of life" – a routine and unrevealing episode in the everyday business of the cops.' *(Bosley Crowther)*

NAKED GUN: FROM THE FILES OF POLICE SQUAD!, THE CT: 8 AV: 6.31

1988 US 85 C COMEDY
D David Zucker ✓
W Jerry Zucker Jim Abrahams David Zucker Pat Proft

Leslie Nielsen ✓ Priscilla Presley Ricardo Montalban George Kennedy O.J. Simpson Susan Beaubian Nancy Marchand Raye Birk Jeannette Charles

The worst cop in the world (Leslie Nielsen) discovers a plot to assassinate the Queen of England (Jeanette Charles).

Gags galore from the makers of *Airplane*. Like the TV show, *Police Squad*, which spawned this, the jokes range from the stupid to the sublime, and back again. Leslie Nielsen is magnificently bland and straight-faced. Like Basil Fawlty, he sees himself as a sane, world-weary man in a world of lunatics. Yet the reality is that he's a bumbling lecher and mass murderer. The whole *Naked Gun* series spoofs the Nietschian Superman ideology of the modern cop thriller: Drebin is more of a threat to order and society than any criminal or terrorist could ever be. Drebin is an anti-anti-hero, a truly Dirty Harry. Instead of representing some personal, higher standard of Justice, Values, or Protection, he is what our system of justice often seems to be – incompetent, stupid and sadistic.

ANTI:

'A sorry spoof of cops-and-killers movies . . . Despite some boffos, little of it works.' *(Bruce Williamson, Playboy)*

'A picture in thrall to its own silliness . . . The stretch marks show, in a plethora of chase scenes and bathroom humor that makes *The Naked Gun* seem like *Police Academy* with a brain. Well, maybe three brains . . . A movie made for a VCR Saturday night. They supply the jokes; you bring the microwave popcorn and modest expectations.' *(Richard Corliss, Time)*

MIXED:

'You laugh, and then you laugh at yourself for laughing. Some of the jokes are incredibly stupid.' *(Roger Ebert)*

PRO:

'Crass, broad, irreverent, wacky fun – and absolutely hilarious from beginning to end.' *(Variety)*

'If contemporary films use crime as an excuse to depict the human condition in extremis, then *Naked Gun* goes even further: it revels in tearing up the social contract between the state and governed, as well as between film and its audience . . . [The film] relies not on what we would like the world to be, but on our fearful suspicions of what it actually is. Random violence and stupidity can be and are visited upon the innocent by both criminals and the police. Perhaps that's why it has to be a comedy.' *(Steven Milulan, LA Weekly)*

'Never gumming up the works with restraint or refinement, director David Zucker keeps *Gun* completely cocked and going off in all the right, slam-bang directions. It's no mean trick to make slapstick work this well.' *(Hollywood Reporter)*

'In the years since he first played Drebin, Nielsen has deepened the role, made it more subtle, more universal, more paramount . . . Now, when Drebin bangs into a trash can, or crosses his eyes and falls over his foot, or plunges his hand into a tropical fish tank, or sets fire to an apartment while trying to light a match, one can sense profound world-weariness, an overpowering Angst.' *(Michael Wilmington, LA Times)*

NAKED GUN 2½: THE SMELL OF FEAR

CT: 7 AV: 5.33

1991 US 85 C COMEDY/SEQUEL

D David Zucker ✔
W David Zucker Pat Proft ✔

Leslie Nielsen ✔ Priscilla Presley George Kennedy O.J. Simpson Robert Goulet Richard Griffiths

The world's worst police lieutenant (Leslie Nielsen) uncovers a plot to assassinate an expert in solar energy (Richard Griffiths).

Either inspired or depressed by the success of his brother's film *Ghost*, writer-director David Zucker came up with this seriously funny comedy. Nielsen again plays Lieutenant Frank Drebin and shows himself the greatest master of stonefaced slapstick since Keaton (that's Buster, not Diane).

ANTI:

'At least two-and-a-half times less funny than its hilarious progenitor.' *(Variety)*

'Third-rate slapstick all the way. It's not cred and there are no shocks in it.' *(Nick James, City Limits)*

MIXED:

'Zucker goes for the jugular of other movies with glee . . . Such is the famine in film fun that we wolf back the hamburger when we would prefer prime steak.' *(Tom Hutchinson, Mail on Sunday)*

'An appealing rag-bag of the ribald and the ridiculous, showing only the slightest signs of running out of steam.' *(Philip Strick, S & S)*

PRO:

'The summer is saved . . . Drebin is back . . . The enthusiastic Zucker, Zucker and Abrahams style of parody is too rarely seen to prompt much headshaking about gags that don't work. The entire film is justified by those . . . that do.' *(Vincent Canby, New York Times)*

'The genius of Nielsen's performance is that . . . [he] plays Drebin as a straight arrow who's finally letting go giving in to his repressed impulses . . . This avuncular upholder of public good is profoundly crazy . . . [Nielsen] turns this rather alarming character into a sweet, ebullient lunatic.' *(Terence Rafferty, New Yorker)*

NAKED GUN 33⅓: THE FINAL INSULT

CT: 6 AV: 5 (est)

1994 US 75 C COMEDY/SEQUEL

D Peter Segal
W Pat Proft David Zucker Robert LoCash

Leslie Nielsen ✔ Priscilla Presley George Kennedy O.J. Simpson Fred Ward Anna Nicole Smith Kathleen Freeman Ellen Greene

A terrorist (Fred Ward) wants to blow up the Academy Awards.

Who doesn't, at times? This film is astonishingly funny for a second sequel. The movie parodies are as lovingly done as ever. Some are old hat but witty (satires on *The Untouchables, Thelma & Louise*, even *The Great Escape*). Others are up-to-date but less witty (sideswipes at *Jurassic Park* and *The Crying Game*). Best of all, during the Oscars' climax, there is a fictitious, but by no means improbable, Richard Attenborough musical celebrating the life of Mother Teresa. This *Naked Gun* is inevitably less fresh than the first two. A few of the gags misfire, as usual, but director Peter Segal hardly gives us time to notice. A lot of it is puerile. But it's still pretty funny.

ANTI:

'Has a sluggish, one-gag-at-a-time rhythm, and it aims at too many soft targets. Aside from the Oscar sequence, the movie's big satirical coup is a send-up of . . . prison-escape pictures (yawn) . . . The *Airplane!* style, in all its antic, hellzapoppin glory, has become rather predictable, like *Mad* magazine just when you've started to outgrow it.' *(Owen Gleiberman, Entertainment Weekly)*

MIXED:

'Kicks off with a double whammy – Zucker/ Abrahams do De Palma doing Eisenstein . . . There are a few belly laughs to be found in the set pieces . . . [but] Drebin might as well stick to his retirement plans.' *(Lizzie Francke, S & S)*

PRO:

'This movie is harmless fun defined.' *(Ralph Novak, People Weekly)*

'It occurred to me, watching the film, that what Leslie Nielsen and Priscilla Presley do here is not easy, and is done well. It would be fatal to the movie if either one ever betrayed the slightest suggestion that they know funny things are going on. They play everything on a level of seriousness that would be appropriate, say, for a 1960s TV cop drama. Their timing is impeccable. And they provide the sure, strong center around which the madness revolves.' *(Roger Ebert)*

NAKED SPUR, THE CT: 7 AV: 6.67

1953 US 91 C WESTERN

D Anthony Mann ☆
W Sam Rolfe Harold Jack Bloom ☆ AAN

James Stewart Janet Leigh Robert Ryan Ralph Meeker Millard Mitchell

Bounty-hunters pursue a man (Robert Ryan) with a price on his head, and his girlfriend (Janet Leigh) on his mind.

Big, action-packed western with greed as the spur. Anthony Mann directs a strong cast led by James Stewart, and a fine script which undoubtedly had a hefty, though uncredited, influence on *The Outlaw Josey Wales*. Cinematographer William Mellor shows a good eye for the Rockies scenery.

'A pleasant routine Western.' *(Sunday Graphic)*

'Taut outdoor melodrama made to order for the western action addict who likes rugged dramatics delivered without dilution.' *(Variety)*

'Has a really good adventure story to tell – one at which an intelligent adolescent would not scoff.' *(Manchester Guardian)*

'A first-class film.' *(Jympson Harman, Evening News)*

'One of the best westerns ever made.' *(Maltin)*

NAKED UNDER LEATHER: *see* GIRL ON A MOTORCYCLE

NAPOLÉON CT: 6 AV: 9.00

1927 France 140/240/378 BW (with colour sequences) EPIC/ACTION/DRAMA/SILENT/FOREIGN

D Abel Gance ☆
W Abel Gance

Albert Dieudonné Wladimir Roudenko Gina Manès Nicolas Koline Annabella Antonin Artaud Edmond Van Daële

Life and times of a French leader (Albert Dieudonné).

Like many, I first saw Napoléon in Kevin Brownlow's reconstituted 1981 version, with a live orchestra performing Carl Davis's score, and it was as impressive as it was overlong. Gance has a simplistic view of Bonaparte as a man of destiny; contemporary critical accusations of fascistic intent have some merit. However, its cinematic boldness – especially its use of split-screen, colour and moving camera – remains extraordinary. It was well worth reconstituting.

ANTI:

'This is not cinema. This turns its back on cinema. Better go and see *The Ingenue*, an American film about the amazon in love, whose finale is a discreet kiss, because it is at least light, fresh, full of rhythmical images, and made with an intuition that is authentically cinematic.' *(Luis Buñuel)*

'By turns dazzling and intensely irritating . . . One cannot possibly approve of it . . . One has no right to let French people, or foreigners for that matter, believe that Napoleon was a kind of Douglas Fairbanks holding out single-handed against a hundred armed opponents, leaping through the window and into the saddle . . . I . . . hope that Abel Gance will . . . never forget that by making light of the history of yesterday he is, without realising it, helping to write the history of tomorrow!' *(Emile Vuillermoz, Le Temps)*

'Tediously cumbersome and hopelessly overweighted with symbolic reference.' *(Paul Rotha, The Film Till Now, 1930)*

MIXED:

'Not only false but dangerous, and it deserves to be condemned without leave to appeal. . . . [Gance] reconstructs for us . . . a Bonaparte for budding fascists . . . In cinematographic terms, Napoleon is a bad film because it is only a succession of images, [but it] has given Abel Gance the opportunity to make use of his unquestionably original talents and these have brought about an enrichment of the domain of photogenics, a significant improvement of the apparatus, in short a major step forward for cinematography. It is an important moment in the history of the technical development of a mode of expression which will be the art of the future.' *(Léon Muoussinac, L'Humanité)*

'The greatest and certainly the most profound fascist film in the history of the cinema.' *(Peter Pappas, Cinéaste , 1981)*

PRO:

'A sublime opera of images.' *(Le Havre Libre, 1982)*

'One of the greatest films ever made . . . superbly reconstructed.' *(Scheuer)*

NARROW MARGIN, THE CT: 6 AV: 7.44

1952 US 71 BW THRILLER/POLICE/TRAIN

D Richard Fleischer ☆
W Earl Fenton from Martin Goldsmith and Jack Leonard's story AAN

Charles McGraw ☆ Marie Windsor ☆ Jacqueline White Gordon Gebert Queenie Leonard David Clarke Peter Virgo Don Beddoe Paul Maxey Harry Harvey

Cop (Charles McGraw) escorts gangster's widow (Marie Windsor) to testify before a grand jury.

Classic B-movie train thriller, with low production values but a story that still excites. There was a competent, colour remake by Peter Hyams in 1990, starring Gene Hackman and Anne Archer.

ANTI:

'One of those gangster pictures in which probability is thrown right overboard for the sake of dramatic effect . . . The direction is slick enough but the complications of the plot leave an alarming impression of fecklessness and irresponsibility on the part of the Law.' *(Elizabeth Frank, News Chronicle)*

PRO:

'Manages to be much more entertaining than many a fanfared epic . . . As slick and effective as a stiletto and does its chilling work just as efficiently.' *(Roy Nash, Star)*

'This picture knows just where and how fast it is going . . . An admirable illustration of swift, taut film-making.' *(Milton Shulman, Evening Standard)*

'[It] is almost a model of electric tension that, at least technically, nudges some of the screen's thriller milestones . . . By staging the incidents in a simple, chilling crescendo and by substituting an eagle camera eye for the usual musical background, Mr Fleischer has projected a superbly menacing frame for the action.' *(Howard Thompson, New York Times)*

NASHVILLE AAN CT: 5 AV: 8.82

1975 US 161 C DRAMA/COMEDY/MUSICAL

D Robert Altman ✗ AAN
W Joan Tewkesbury ✗

Ronee Blakley AAN Lily Tomlin AAN David Arkin Barbara Baxley Ned Beatty Karen Black Timothy Brown Keith Carradine Geraldine Chaplin Robert DoQui Shelley Duvall

A populist political campaign organizes a country-and-western concert to raise funds.

Altman at his smuggest and most chaotic. Hugely over-rated – mostly by critics of like-minded political views. Keith Carradine's song 'I'm Easy' won an Oscar.

PRO:

'A gigantic parody . . . crammed with samples taken from every level of Nashville society, revealed in affectionate detail bordering on caricature in a manner that would surely delight Norman Rockwell.' *(Philip Strick)*

'The sound, the images have the veracity of life. Was it really two hours and forty minutes? It seemed to me rather a short film.' *(Dilys Powell)*

'A wonderful mosaic which yields up greater riches with successive viewings . . . Immensely, exhilaratingly enjoyable.' *(Tom Milne, Time Out)*

'The funniest epic vision of America ever to reach the screen.' *(Pauline Kael)*

'This is a film about America. It deals with our myths, our hunger, our ambitions, and our sense of self. It knows how we talk and how we behave, and it doesn't flatter us but it does love us.' *(Roger Ebert)*

'One of Altman's best films, free of the rambling insider fooling that sometimes mars entire chunks of every second or third picture. When he navigates to defined goals, however, the results are superb.' *(Variety)*

'Immensely, exhilaratingly enjoyable.' *(Tom Milne, Time Out, 1989)*

MIXED:

'In Nashville, the sum of the parts is, unfortunately, greater than the whole, but, bit by bit, they are mostly well worth attending to.' *(John Simon)*

'A generally entertaining, conventionally critical look at Americana.' *(Stanley Kauffmann)*

'The actors are well chosen and their characters make strong initial impressions, but few are developed sufficiently.' *(Danny Peary)*

ANTI:

'A film in which virtually every aspect of directorial style has nothing to do with the communication of coherent meaning, everything to do with the creation and maintenance of the impression that something – anything – is happening, moving or changing. *Nashville* may also be the ultimate tribal comedy, a film in which twenty-odd characters react – or fail to react – to a series of situations that are strung together like beads on a string. It is just barely possible that Altman had parody in mind, that he directed *Nashville* as he did to show that, ultimately, the premises and aesthetics of television will lead a television-pervaded culture into a meaningless box without exits and without windows on to the real world. But if Altman constructed the elaborate box called *Nashville* only to demonstrate that television-saturated audiences live in a box and probably like it in there, then he has created a nasty, mean-spirited work that has little to do with the expansive, liberating ends of art.' *(James Bernardoni, The New Hollywood, 1991)*

'Wildly over-praised Altman, with all the defects we once looked on as marks of healthy ambitiousness: terrible construction, messy editing, leering jokes at its own characters, unending pomposity.' *(Time Out, 1980)*

NASTY GIRL, THE AAN CT: 7 AV: 7.75

(aka *Das Schreckliche Mädchen*)

1990 Germany 90 C FOREIGN/DRAMA

D Michael Verhoeven ☆
W Michael Verhoeven ☆

Lena Stolze ☆ Monika Baumgartner Michael Gahr Fred Stillkrauth Elisabeth Bertram Robert Giggenbach Karin Thaler Hans-Reinhard Müller

A young German historian (Lena Stolze) tries to discover what really went on in her home town during the Third Reich. At every turn, she encounters obstruction, litigation and violence, and comes to realize that the attitudes which led to fascism still persist.

The story is based on real-life events which happened to Anja Rosmus in the German town of Passau; and it's exquisitely acted (particularly by Lena Stolze). Michael Verhoeven writes and directs with flair and originality. The setting up of the situation, however, is slow and pedantic, and the plotting none too skilful. The stylized form of presentation, too, is too clever-clever: the use of deliberately unconvincing back-projection seems to be either a jokey reference to cheapskate TV documentary or a neo-Brechtian technique of distancing and universalizing the story. Unfortunately, the main effect will be to alienate the potential audience from this interesting film.

ANTI:

'It's the film's style that I object to. The story itself is fascinating, but the style seems to add another tone, a level of irony that is somehow confusing: Does Verhoeven see this as quite the cheery romp he pretends, or is there a sly edge to his method? As a rule, I welcome stylistic experiments – most movies are much too straightforward – but this time I'm not sure the movie's odd tone adds anything. Realism might have worked better.' *(Roger Ebert)*

PRO:

'Presented in something like cabaret style . . . [The] deadpan approach . . . is far more effective than the melodrama or shock-horror sermonising over Hitler's people.' *(Shaun Usher, Daily Mail)*

'[A] comparative rarity: an art-house film that bites . . . This is rumbustious film-making.' *(Geoff Brown, The Times)*

'The style more than the story delights . . . Character and action are artificialised to match the surreal kilter of the decor . . . Everything good agitprop should be: witty, intelligent, ill-behaved and scalding to the touch.' *(Nigel Andrews, Financial Times)*

NATIONAL VELVET CT: 8 AV: 7.23

1944 US 125 C DRAMA/FAMILY

D Clarence Brown
W Theodore Reeves Helen Deutsch from Enid Bagnold's novel

Mickey Rooney Donald Crisp Elizabeth Taylor ☆ Anne Revere Angela Lansbury Juanita Quigley Jackie 'Butch' Jenkins Reginald Owen Terry Kilburn Alec Craig

A girl wins a horse in a village lottery and is determined to enter him for the Grand National.

Classic family movie which doesn't exactly dwell on the practicalities of racing a horse in the Grand National, but works extremely well as sentimental escapism. Elizabeth Taylor is captivating.

ANTI:

'What I did find disturbing was the mentality of [the] heroine. As played by little Elizabeth Taylor, with quite remarkable virtuosity, she is a pathological case . . . An odd mixture of good and bad, of realism and Hollywood hokum.' *(Campbell Dixon, Daily Telegraph)*

MIXED:

'I wouldn't say she [Elizabeth Taylor] is particularly gifted as an actress. She seems, rather, to turn things off and on, much as she is told, with perhaps a fair amount of natural grace and of a natural-born female's sleepwalking sort of guile, but without much, if any, of an artist's intuition, perception, or resource. She strikes me, however, if I may resort to conservative statement, as being rapturously beautiful. I think she also has a talent, of a sort, in the particular things she can turn on: which are most conspicuously a mock-pastoral kind of simplicity, and two or three speeds of semi-hysterical emotion, such as ecstasy, an odd sort of pre-specific erotic sentience, and the anguish of overstrained hope, imagination, and faith. Since these are precisely the things she needs for her role in *National Velvet* . . . I think that she and the picture are wonderful, and I hardly know or care whether she can act or not.' *(James Agee)*

'An excellent motion picture, albeit several servings too lavish on the side of saccharine . . . Elizabeth Taylor proves quite miraculous as the mite heroine. The child has an earnestness absolutely encompassing, gentian eyes . . . and an honesty of approach which places her apart from other under-age Thespians . . . Jackie Jenkins, I have it on irrefutable report, is "a love," "a darling" and "a true depiction of the American urchin." Be that as it may, like Margaret O'Brien on the same lot, the acting of Master Jenkins imparts to me a frenzied desire to throw up.' *(Herb Sterne)*

PRO:

'Oddly enough the mental flora of [Bagnold's story] translates well into American.' *(Time & Tide)*

'Maybe the film should have been made here, but I doubt if it would have been more enjoyable.' *(P.L. Mannock, Daily Herald)*

'Here is a story of open air and of family life quite remarkable for its freshness, simplicity and gentleness . . . Rooney exploits his charm and his crinkled grin as efficiently as ever.'(MFB)

'One of the most likable movies of all time.' *(Pauline Kael)*

NATTVARDSGÄSTERNA: *see* WINTER LIGHT.

NAVIGATOR, THE CT: 8 AV: 8.86

1924 US 63 BW COMEDY/SILENT

D Buster Keaton ✓ Donald Crisp ✓
W Jean Havez Clyde Bruckman J.A. Mitchell

Buster Keaton ☆ Kathryn McGuire
Frederick Vroom Noble Johnson Clarence Burton

A millionaire (Buster Keaton) and his girl (Kathryn McGuire) cope with being the only people aboard an ocean liner.

One of the funniest silent comedies, with a multitude of slapstick sight-gags and Keaton on top form.

MIXED:

'Now and again the Keaton eyes evince a suggestion of life, but his lips barely budge. To have a contrast . . . we had only to look at those watching this picture. Mouths were wide open in explosions of laughter . . . While there is no denying the jocular and farcical action of this picture, there are stretches which should be cut, as some of the humor is just a bit overdone.' *(Mordaunt Hall, New York Times)*

'Spotty. That is to say it's both commonplace and novel, with the latter sufficient to make the picture a laughgetter . . . The actual story carries little weight.' *(Variety)*

PRO:

'Six reels – and funny practically every inch of the way . . . Studded with hilarious moments and a hundred and one adroit gags. Keaton was never funnier than in *The Navigator* and he has a pretty foil in Kathryn McGuire. Its a picture you'll enjoy. *(Photoplay)*

'Comic invention is not what it was. And if you don't believe me you should see *The Navigator* . . . Them wuz the days, my chickadees.' *(Elspeth Grant, Graphic, 1950)*

NÉRAN GOUYNE: *see* COLOUR OF POMEGRANATES, THE.

NETWORK AAN CT: 6 AV: 8.27

1976 US 120 C DRAMA

D Sidney Lumet ✗ AAN
W Paddy Chayefsky ✗ AAW

Faye Dunaway ☆ AAW William Holden ☆ AAN
Peter Finch ☆ AAW Robert Duvall Wesley Addy
Ned Beatty ☆ AAN Arthur Burghardt Bill Burrows
Beatrice Straight ☆ AAW John Carpenter
Jordan Charney

A news commentator (Peter Finch) becomes an embarrassment to his TV station.

An incoherent, bad-tempered, middle-aged crisis movie masquerading as a blistering satire on TV culture. The power of Peter Finch's performance and the lustre of the supporting cast go a long way to compensate. But Chayefsky's analysis of what is wrong with modern society and its media is disappointingly facile. Owen Roizman's cinematography was Oscar-nominated.

PRO:

'Absurdly plausible and outrageously provocative . . . Sidney Lumet's direction is outstanding.' *(Variety)*

'[Of the leading actors] All of them shine with the feeling that they know they are working for a director who understands actors, that they have relied on him, and that he has come through for them. As they have for him. They are all exceptionally good.' *(Stanley Kauffmann)*

'Here is a film to restore one's faith in the ability of the cinema to entertain and stimulate . . . No praise is too high for [the] witty screenplay.' *(Arthur Thirkell, Daily Mirror)*

'Chayefsky's script is written in vitriol . . . But it is . . . Lumet who makes the whole nightmare bore into our minds with such compulsive insistence . . . Tremendously exciting.' *(Felix Barker, Evening News)*

MIXED:

'We are asked to laugh at, be moved by, or get angry about such a long list of subjects: sexism and ageism and revolutionary ripoffs and upper-middle-class anomie and capitalist exploitation and Neilsen ratings and psychics and that perennial standby, the failure to communicate. Paddy Chayefsky's script isn't a bad one, but he finally loses control of it. There's just too much he wanted to say.' *(Roger Ebert)*

ANTI:

'What makes *Network* such a repulsive movie . . . is its combination of nasty-mindedness and hypocrisy. The shallow jibes aimed at television, even if they contain a good measure of truth, are top-heavy with leaden sarcasm, and rather unseemly coming from the commercial product of a movie industry hardly in the position to cast stones at TV. There is no vileness attributed to television here of which the movies have not shown themselves capable, yet they never muckrake in their own house . . . Purporting to dispense wittily devastating inside information, this crude film really panders to whatever is smug and pseudosophisticated in an audience of self-appointed insiders; their smart-alecky laughter was not an inspiriting thing to hear.' *(John Simon)*

'The cast of this messianic farce . . . all take turns yelling at us soulless masses.' *(Pauline Kael)*

'Too much of this film has the hectoring stridency of tabloid headlines.' *(Michael Billington, Illustrated London News)*

'Lumet's direction does nothing to contain the sprawl, and most of the interest comes in watching such a lavishly mounted vehicle leaving the rails so spectacularly.' *(Chris Peachment, Time Out)*

NEVER GIVE A SUCKER AN EVEN BREAK

CT: 6 AV: 7.10

(aka *What a Man*)

1941 US 70 BW COMEDY

D Edward Cline
W John T. Neville, Prescott Chaplin from Otis Criblecoblis's story (pseudonym for W.C. Fields)

W.C. Fields ☆ Gloria Jean Leon Errol Billy Lenhart Kenneth Brown Anne Nagel Franklin Pangborn Mona Barrie Margaret Dumont Susan Miller

Scriptwriter (W.C.Fields) pitches movie idea to a Hollywood studio, then undergoes a series of improbable adventures.

Chaotic collection of sketches, built around the star's persona. Totally lacking in discipline, often extremely funny, this was his last starring role in a film. Sample line . . . 'She drove me to drink – that's the one thing I'm indebted to her for.'

MIXED:

'We are not yet quite sure that this latest opus is even a movie – no such harum-scarum collection of song, slapstick and thumbnail sketches has defied dramatic law in recent history. We are more certain that at its worst the film is extravagantly bad, no less that William Claude [Fields] is wonderful.' *(New York Times)*

Fields improvises . . . running the scale from whimsy to whamstick. [The film] is therefore, as good as he is . . . Cline directed the enterprise precisely as if it were in fact a Sennett comedy.' *(William R. Weaver)*

'Although the film has amusing moments, there is so little coherence that interest wanes . . . But it is primarily a Fields film and enjoyment will largely depend on how much you appreciate his particular line.' *(MFB)*

'A hodge-podge of razzle-dazzle episodes, tied together in disjointed fashion but with sufficient laugh content for the comedian's fans.' *(Variety)*

'Has no plot and needs one . . . A maelstrom of slapstick, song, blackout episodes, old gags, new gags, confusion. That much of it is truly comic is testimony to the fact that Comedian Fields is one of the funniest men on earth . . . Fields is a beautifully timed exhibit of mock pomposity, puzzled ineffectualness, subtle understatement and true-blue nonchalance. *(James Agee, Time)*

PRO:

'Main situation has novelty as well as genuine hilarity . . . Slick direction, irresistible stellar drolleries, piquant supporting portrayal, lively atmosphere . . . The bulbous nosed Fields is heard to hilarious advantage in this characteristically crazy concoction.' *(Today's Cinema)*

NEVER SAY NEVER AGAIN:

see BOND SERIES.

NEW YORK, NEW YORK

CT: 7 AV: 5.08

1977 US 153 C MUSICAL/ROMANCE

D Martin Scorsese ✔
W Earl Mac Rauch Mardik Martin

Robert De Niro ☆ Liza Minnelli Lionel Stander Barry Primus Larry Kert Mary Kay Place George Memmoli Murray Moston Georgie Auld Dick Miller Leonard Gaines

A marriage sours between a sax player (Robert De Niro) and a big-band singer (Liza Minnelli).

Scorsese's big band-era musical is short on plot and human sympathy, and Robert De Niro acts Liza Minnelli off the screen. However, Minnelli comes into her own during the singing sequences, and is better than the savage reviews of her performance might suggest. It's beautifully photographed by Laszlo Kovacs and wittily designed in a deliberately old-fashioned way by Boris Leven. In years to come, this film may be appreciated on its own terms; on release it was gravely underrated by the critics, who spotted all the cinematic clichés and conventions without (in the main) realizing that Scorsese was subverting rather than trying to imitate them.

Scorsese on what he intended the film to be: 'A movie called *New York, New York* shot entirely in Los Angeles . . . a fantasy of New York . . . I tried to fuse whatever was a fantasy – the movies I grew up with as a kid – with the reality I experienced myself.'

ANTI:

'Occasionally repellent but mostly tedious and trite . . . Liza Minnelli, difficult to like at best, comes out looking like a giant rodent en route to a costume ball . . . Charm. This picture, faults and all, might have been pleasant if it had some. De Niro doesn't sell it. Minnelli doesn't have it. Scorsese doesn't comprehend it. So NY, NY is NG, NG.' *(Stanley Kauffmann)*

'The film, aside from being terrible in every way, makes no basic sense . . . No one has bothered to make the characters the least bit believable and sympathetic . . . The person who comes off least well here is Martin Scorsese, whose directorial vision seems to be no greater than that of a man driving through a downpour without turning on his windscreen wipers.' *(John Simon)*

'De Niro and Minnelli . . . are even more incompatible professionally than the characters they play. They don't mix well enough to combust.' *(Russell Davies, Observer)*

'Ends on a dying fall that is positively Chekhovian, still not able to make up its mind whether it was a musical romance or a drama about musicians . . . a sort of *The Way We Were* with songs . . . So much talent. So much misjudgment.' *(Julian Fox, F & F)*

'A clever recreation of the big band era, hampered by gross overlength, unattractive characters and a pessimistic plot.' *(Halliwell)*

MIXED:

'A mess. Nevertheless it is a splendid mess, like some early Orson Welles thrillers, which anyone with any addiction to the cinema will find little difficulty and much enjoyment in gulping down.' *(Alan Brien, Sunday Times)*

'Minnelli seems somewhat dazed – openmouthed and vacuous, and unpleasantly overripe. She pushes her scenes; in her hyper way, she's as false as Julie Andrews. Her two big numbers ('But the World Turns Round' and the title song) are, however, in their own wildly hysterical show-biz terms, smashing.' *(Pauline Kael)*

'Not just a socking good musical, it is also a haunting, sometimes cruel, love story that at the end dares to differ from the time-honoured Hollywood romance . . . If the film has a fault it is that De Niro upstages everyone.' *(Margaret Hinxman, Daily Mail)*

'[Scorsese] is relatively successful . . . There is an imbalance in the structure which loses sight of the character played by De Niro in the second half, so that the emotional drive . . . is weakened.' *(David Overbury, Orbis, 1984)*

'Why did it fail? I don't know. Of course, the only real thing in it was the actors. The snow, the trees, the sets – they just seemed too fake for that kind of realistic story. I would have taken a more realistic approach.' *(Larry Kert)*

PRO:

'A razor-sharp dissection of the conventions of both meeting-cute romances and rags-to-riches biopics, as it charts the traumatic love affair . . . On an emotional level, the film is a powerhouse, offering some of the most painfully convincing rows ever shot; as a depiction of changes in American music and the entertainment world, it is accurate and evocative; and as a commentary on showbiz films, it's a stunner.' *(Geoff Andrew, Time Out)*

NIAGARA

CT: 7 AV: 6.73

1952 US 89 C THRILLER/SUSPENSE

D Henry Hathaway ☆
W Charles Brackett Walter Reisch, Richard Breen

Marilyn Monroe ✗ Joseph Cotten ✗ Jean Peters Casey Adams Denis O'Dea Richard Allan Don Wilson Lurene Tuttle Russell Collins Will Wright

Adulterous wife (Marilyn Monroe) plots to murder her Korean war veteran husband (Joseph Cotten) on a visit to Niagara.

Battle-of-the-sexes film noir, which attempts to place the audience firmly on the side of the man. The camera ranges lasciviously over Monroe's body in her first starring film part and emphasizes her natural attractions, but she seems uneasy with the dialogue, and perhaps with playing such a dyed-in-the-wool villain. The plot descends into melodrama, but on the whole it's great fun.

PRO:

'The story is most imaginatively treated, the production values are excellent.' *(CEA Film Report)*

'A masterly example of fluid screen narrative.' *(Charles Higham)*

'Obviously ignoring the idea that there are Seven Wonders of the World, Twentieth Century-Fox has discovered two more and enhanced them with Technicolor . . . Seen from any angle, the Falls and Miss Monroe leave little to be desired by any reasonably attentive audience.' *(A.H. Weiler, New York Times)*

'Spectacle is the main attraction, but the script by Walter Reisch and Richard Breen is a steady, stable combination of menace and comedy relief . . . Miss Monroe plays the kind of wife whose dress, in the words of the script, is cut so low you can see her knees. The dress is red; the actress has very nice knees, and under Hathaway's direction she gives the kind of serpentine performance that makes the audience hate her while admiring her, which is proper for the story.' *(Otis L. Guernsey Jr, New York Herald Tribune)*

MIXED:

'Moves from hilarity to hilarious melodrama . . . I approached this richly idiotic film with caution but, as time went on, abandoned myself to an enjoyment which I hope was shared by the rest of the audience. At any rate I thought I noticed the hint of a cheer at Marilyn Monroe's later appearances. But that, of course, may have been for the story.' *(Dilys Powell)*

'This isn't a good movie but it's compellingly tawdry and nasty . . . the only movie that explored the mean, unsavoury potential of Marilyn Monroe's cuddly, infantile perversity.' *(Pauline Kael, 70s)*

ANTI:

'Morbid, clichéd.' *(Variety)*

'It would have turned out a much better picture if James Mason had played the husband as I wanted. He has that intensity, that neurotic edge. He was all set to do it, but his daughter Portland said she was sick of seeing him die in his pictures.' *(Henry Hathaway)*

NIBELUNGEN, THE CT: 6 AV: 7.50

1924 Germany BW SILENT/FOREIGN/MUSICAL/FANTASY/EPIC
Part I: 'Siegfried' 115m; Part II: 'Kriemheld's Revenge' 125m

D Fritz Lang ☆
W Thea von Harbou

Paul Richter Marguerite Schon Theodor Loos Hannah Ralph Rudolph Klein-Rogge

Mythic adventures of Siegfried (Paul Richter) and Brunhild (Hannah Ralph).

One of the most imaginative films of the silent period, with magnificent sets, a 70-foot dragon, a superb battle climax, and oodles of romantic atmosphere compensating for the simplistic characterization.

'A colossal and amazing achievement in film stagecraft and a triumph for the German magicians who work their arts at the UFA Studio.' *(Photoplay)*

'A magnificent piece of work that is not staled by age . . . A picture that can grin at Father Time.' *(Mordaunt Hall, New York Times)*

'A very beautiful production. It shows what marvellous things the cinematograph can achieve in the hands of an artist.' *(The Times)*

'The use of tone, of sharp black and clear white and clean silver, here and throughout, is very accomplished and lovely.' *(Iris Barry, Spectator)*

'It is really not necessary to quote the recognition accorded this film by Reich Propaganda Minister Dr Goebbels . . . Dr Goebbels pointed to this picture as a model of a film which concerned matters "non-topical and non-contemporary" being more direct in stirring the spirit of our time than the "modern films" manufactured quickly for profit, an observation which must make everybody happy who seriously cares about the German film and its future.' *(Der Kinematograph, 1933)*

NIGHT AT THE OPERA, A CT: 8 AV: 8.82

1935 US 96 BW COMEDY/ROMANCE/MUSICAL

D Sam Wood ☆
W George S. Kaufman Morrie Ryskind Al Boasberg Bert Kalmar Harry Ruby from James Kevin McGuinness's story

Groucho Marx ☆ Chico Marx ☆ Harpo Marx ☆ Kitty Carlisle Allan Jones Walter Woolf King Margaret Dumont

A crooked promoter, Otis B. Driftwood (Groucho Marx), attempts to con a multi-millionairess (Margaret Dumont) into investing in an opera company.

The Marx Brothers' biggest hit is not the best of their 13 films, mainly because of the irrelevant romantic interest dragged in by MGM executive Irving Thalberg to give the picture some feminine appeal. Even so, the plethora of one-liners and sight-gags make this one of the funniest screen comedies, and the stateroom scene is one of the most uproarious in screen history.

ANTI:

'A perfect example of the degenerate geniality of the Jewish race.' *(Tevere, anti-semitic newspaper, 1938)*

MIXED:

'The film, an incongruous mixture of quality musical and conventional gags, is, with all its expensive embellishments, a little too wide of both marks, the high and the low brow, to be other than a speculative booking proposition.' *(Kine Weekly)*

'Corking comedy . . . [but] songs in a Marx picture are generally at a disadvantage because they're more or less interruptions, the customers awaiting the next laugh.' *(Variety)*

PRO:

'Perfectly done.' *(Daily Mail)*

'Hilariously funny, the Marxian recipe rings the bell again with its topnotch punch features . . . Bang-up entertainment for all tastes.' *(Hollywood Reporter)*

'Tie the roof on tight when this one opens.' *(Motion Picture Daily)*

'There is nothing persuasive about the Marx Brothers. Nothing in their stories, their acrobatics, nor even their musical abilities, could cajole you into loving that pop-eyed trip against your will. They are like tripe or creme de menthe, the murder game or Hitler. You take them, or you don't take them. Personally, I take them, and, as the man says today so simply and elliptically, how.' *(Guardian)*

NIGHT OF SAN LORENZO, THE: *see* NIGHT OF THE SHOOTING STARS.

NIGHT OF THE GHOULS CT: 5 AV: 2.17

(aka *Revenge of the Dead*)

1960 US 75 BW HORROR/SO BAD

D Edward D. Wood Jr ●
W Edward D. Wood Jr ●

Duke Moore ● Kenne Duncan ● Paul Marco ● Tor Johnson ● John Carpenter ● Valda Hansen ● Criswell ●

Crooked medium (Kenne Duncan) accidentally revives corpses.

Not many writer-directors who had made a film as incompetent as *Plan 9 From Outer Space* (1958) would have the confidence to rework the same ideas in a later film; but Edward D. Wood was no ordinary auteur. This attempt to make a zombie picture is not as hilariously abysmal as his masterwork, but it confirms Wood as a man totally lacking in sophistication, irony or cinematic skill. It was so bad that it was not released.

'More blood and brutality than supernatural terror, this takes an idea brimming over with opportunities for terrifying special effects and squanders it in sock-it-to-them-hard sadism and gore.' *(Marjorie Bilbow, Screen International, 1978)*

'A muddled mixture of artiness and amateurishness in which the characters are too risibly sketchy for belief.' *(Tom Milne, MFB, 1978)*

'Aficionados of the work of the totally inept Wood may enjoy this, since it has all the hallmarks of his movies: bad acting, irrelevant voice-over and hopeless direction.' *(Halliwell)*

'Features god-awful acting, direction, music, dialogue, costumes, sets, props, lighting, pacing and camera work. But that won't be enough to satisfy hardcore Wood fanatics, who have the right to expect much worse . . . Alas, the picture hasn't the inspired madness of Woods classics.' *(Danny Peary)*

NIGHT OF THE HUNTER, THE CT: 9 AV: 9.20

1955 US 93 BW THRILLER/HORROR

D Charles Laughton ☆
W James Agee from Davis Grubb's novel ✓

Robert Mitchum ☆ Shelley Winters Lillian Gish ✓ Don Beddoe Evelyn Varden Peter Graves James Gleason

An evil preacher (Robert Mitchum) searches for hidden money.

It's partly a religious and political allegory about the importance of recognizing false prophets, and wolves in sheep's clothing. It's also one of the most frightening thrillers ever, although evil does get its come-uppance finally at the hands of a sweet old lady (Lillian Gish) and two resilient children. Charles Laughton's mastery of montage, water imagery, distorting lenses and chiaroscuro lighting makes this an incredible achievement for a first-time director: probably the most stunning debut since *Citizen Kane*, although Laughton's artistic, expressionist approach was out of fashion at the time of release. Mitchum gives probably his finest screen performance. A disgracefully hostile critical reception, coupled with box-office failure, meant that Laughton was never able to direct another film.

ANTI:

'Mitchum can't carry this story . . . It should have been a sinister film, but mainly it was grin-ister.' *(Harris Deans, Evening Standard)*

'Macabre thriller corroded by dank symbolism . . . Robert Mitchum gives an eerie, fascinating performance . . . but the crux of the play is frequently obscured by pretentious direction and photography. Confused and far from pleasant, it's unlikely to intrigue or grip other than longhaired boys and girls . . . Too clever by half.' *(Josh Billings, Kine Weekly)*

'No credit to Hollywood . . . Just another of those films which keep the youngsters out of the cinemas. It's a horrible yarn . . . Robert Mitchum overplays . . . Shelley Winters is his stupid wife and Lillian Gish the only decent adult character in this extremely morbid story. A repulsive picture.' *(Reg Whitley, Daily Mirror)*

'None the less interesting for being a failure . . . Too often the effect is funny rather than frightening . . . For once child actors disappoint and fail to communicate emotion.' *(The Times)*

'A fairly eclectic item that is alternately really artistic and dismally arty, with the latter . . . alas predominating . . . Mr Laughton all too frequently becomes fearfully entangled with dreary allegory . . . . . Uneven though it may be . . . [it] fails honorably.' *(John McCarten, New Yorker)*

'Mitchum intermittently shows some depth in his interpretation of the preacher but in instances where he's crazed with lust for the money, there's barely adequate conviction. *(Variety)*

'Ideas are original but they are also so heavily macabre that I found myself laughing in the wrong places. Shelley Winters . . . ends up . . . at the bottom of the river with her throat slit. Since she had previously gone around saying things like my whole body is just a-quivering with cleanliness I was rather glad.' *(Daily Herald)*

'Shelley Winters is unequal to the part of the widow, and the preacher surely should have been played not by Robert Mitchum but by Charles Laughton who instead directs: only Lillian Gish has the right feeling. All the same this murky film . . . is neither boring nor risible.' *(Dilys Powell)*

PRO:

'There are definite flaws but these are faults of the large reach, rather than the small grasp. Where [it] does succeed – is in its sensitivity, its imaginative and often poetic photography, its haunting musical score, its skillful blending of hymns and especially in its gripping, nervewracking narrative power . . . An important and memorable achievement.' *(Charlotte Speicher, Library Journal)*

'One of the most frightening movies ever made.' *(Pauline Kael, 1968)*

'Laughton's deliberately old-fashioned direction throws up a startling array of images: an amalgam of Mark Twain-like exteriors (idyllic riverside life) and expressionist interiors, full of moody nighttime shadows. The style reaches its pitch in the extraordinary moonlight flight of the two children downriver, gliding silently in the distance, watched over by animals seen in huge close-up, filling up the foreground of the screen.' *(Chris Peachment, Time Out)*

'We knew when we saw the first rushes that we were part of something classic and timeless. *Night of the Hunter* is probably the most thoughtful and reserved performance I ever gave. The studio released the film very quietly, and the public seemed to ignore it. I believe Charles Laughton had been "named" by someone and was therefore blacklisted. A decade later, both in Europe and the US, the film was finally recognized as a unique poetic achievement.' *(Shelley Winters)*

NIGHT OF THE LIVING DEAD

CT: 7 AV: 7.23

1968 US 96 BW HORROR

D George A. Romero ✓
W John A. Russo

Judith O'Dea Duane Jones Karl Hardman Keith Wayne Russell Streiner

Zombies terrorize American town.

The acting is amateurish, the budget miniscule, and the special effects extremely dodgy. The script is, at best, on the level of a horror comic-strip. And the shock value it had in 1968 has diminished, as we're used to seeing far gorier things than this. Even so, Romero's direction manages to create an atmosphere of suspense and terror which elevates this to the status of a cult classic. Its huge popularity with the public (though certainly not with critics – or the *Readers Digest*, which denounced it roundly) led to countless, even bloodier rip-offs. Romero remade his own picture in colour, in 1990, but it lacks the power of the original. A much better film is his belated sequel, *Dawn of the Dead* (1979).

ANTI:

'This film casts serious aspersions on the integrity of its makers, distrib Walter Reade, the film industry as a whole and exhibs who book the pic, as well as raising doubts about the future of the regional cinema movement and the moral health of filmgoers who cheerfully opt for unrelieved sadism . . . Amateurism of the first order.' *(Variety)*

'Romero appears incapable of contriving a single graceful set-up, and his cast is uniformly poor . . . John A. Russo's screenplay is a model of verbal banality and suggests a total antipathy for his characters.' *(Variety)*

'There is no doubt that the scenario and acting . . . are abominable, and that the 90 minutes of black-and-white storyline are crammed with gratuitous gore.' *(Parish & Pitts, The Great Science Fiction Pictures)*

PRO:

'With its radical rewriting of a genre in which good had always triumphed over evil, Romero's first feature shattered the conventions of horror and paved the way for the subversive visions of directors like David Cronenberg, Tobe Hooper and Sam Raimi.' *(Nigel Floyd, Time Out)*

'Pessimistic and unsentimental, the film works on basic fears: monsters that wont go away, darkness, claustrophobia.' *(Danny Peary)*

'Romero . . . was injecting an explicitness into the on-screen gore whilst encouraging a more serious interpretation of the story as symbolic of its times in depicting traditional American values under siege from strange, rapacious forces.' *(Allan Hunter & Kenny Mathieson, Movie Classics, 1992)*

'One of the most gruesomely terrifying movies ever made – and when you leave the theatre you may wish you could forget the whole horrible experience.' *(Pauline Kael)*

'One of the cinema's most unsettling visions of the collapse of civilization.' *(Elkan Allan, NFT Bulletin)*

NIGHT OF THE SHOOTING STARS

CT: 6 AV: 6.78

(aka *The Night of San Lorenzo; La Notte di San Lorenzo*)

1981 Italy 107 C WAR/FOREIGN

D Paolo Taviani Vittorio Taviani ☆
W Vittorio Taviani Paolo Taviani Giuliani G. De Negri Tonino Guerra

Omero Antonutti Margarita Lozano Claudio Bigagli Massimo Bonetti Norma Martelli Enrica Maria Modugno

During World War II, inhabitants of a Tuscan village await liberation by the Americans.

Slow-moving, schmaltzy but often magical evocation of a wartime childhood.

ANTI:

'That these past splendours and miseries are supposed to be mediated through the memory of a grown woman, then a little girl, rather dubiously explains some sentimental excesses.' *(John Coleman, New Statesman)*

'I found this would-be Tuscan *Iliad* a bit conventional.' *(Alexander Walker, Standard)*

PRO:

'Without pretension the Tavianis counter-cut a movie equal parts Proust and Gramsci . . . [It] would be unbearably depressing were it not for Rosanna's state of youthful grace.' *(Carrie Rickey, Village Voice)*

'The movie is not like anything else – the Taviani brothers' pleasure in the great collection of stories they're telling makes it euphoric. It's as if they had invented a new form. In its feeling and completeness, *Shooting Stars* may be close to the rank of Jean Renoir's bafflingly beautiful *Grand Illusion*.' *(Pauline Kael)*

NIGHT PORTER, THE — CT: 5 AV: 3.14

(aka *Il Portiere di Notte)*

1973 Italy/US 118 C DRAMA

D Liliana Cavani
W Liliana Cavani Italo Moscati

Dirk Bogarde Charlotte Rampling Philippe Leroy Gabriele Ferzetti Isa Miranda

The night porter in a hotel (Dirk Bogarde) comes face to face with a woman (Charlotte Rampling) he sexually exploited when commandant of a concentration camp – and they rekindle their affair.

Tacky, pretentious exercise in sado-masochism – a kind of *9½ Weeks* for fascists – somewhat redeemed by Bogarde's performance, which is better than the piece deserves.

PRO:

'The most harrowing and honest film that has yet been made about the legacy of Nazi crime and punishment. It is also the film that confirms Dirk Bogarde as one of the supreme screen actors.' *(Margaret Hinxman, Daily Mail)*

'One of the most interesting and controversial films that I have encountered in many a long day's march to the cinema.' *(Felix Barker, Evening News)*

'Superbly played and involving mystery, excitement, tension . . . A relationship is revealed, continuing into the post-war world, between torturer and tortured, between sadistic Nazi guard and helpless prisoner. It has an initial suggestion of the vicious, nevertheless it develops into a passion which is self-sacrificing and tragic. I can't see in the scenes of love, even of love shall I say a bit bent, anything to which film enthusiasts have not been acclimatised. The relationship, the general situation would be immediately accepted if it occurred in a novel.' *(Dilys Powell)*

ANTI:

'Next Tango in Vienna . . . Maybe I missed subtleties the first time round that, on a second viewing, will jump out and cosh me. But I doubt it at the moment . . . Degradation without illumination doesn't invite interest after the curiosity has been satisfied; it just breeds disgust.' *(Alexander Walker, Evening Standard)*

'Its claim to be saying something important is offensive, but the picture is too crudely trumped up to be a serious insult.' *(Pauline Kael)*

'A downright deplorable film, with no cinematic skill or grace to excuse it; the visuals are as loathsome as the sound is indecipherable, and the sheer pointlessness of it is insulting.' *(Halliwell)*

NIGHT TO REMEMBER, A — CT: 6 AV: 7.64

1958 GB 123 BW THRILLER

D Roy Ward Baker
W Eric Ambler from Walter Lord's book

Kenneth More Ronald Allen Robert Ayres Honor Blackman Anthony Bushell John Cairney Jill Dixon Jane Downs David McCallum Kenneth Griffith Michael Bryant

The sinking of the Titanic in 1912.

Pretty much what you'd expect, with Kenneth More on the bridge and a host of British character actors panicking, keeping a stiff upper lip, etc. The model shots are poor by modern standards, and the film is rather studio-bound, but it's enjoyable for all that – well-researched, competently written, and so realistically photographed by Geoffrey Unsworth that few who watch it will remain un-gripped.

MIXED:

'The makers seem to have been afraid to adopt a point of view which could give the film meaning . . . The result is a worthy, long-drawn-out documentary with noticeably more honesty about human nature than most films, but little shape or style.' *(Kenneth Cavander, MFB)*

'Occasionally repetitive and a little tedious. However, it has that rare quality of integrity.' *(Nina Hibbin, Daily Worker)*

PRO:

'As a feat of reconstruction this is a brilliant film, and by reconstruction I do not mean simply the rebuilding of the physical setting from boiler-room to deck, from cabin to smoking-room – though the work of the art director, Alex Vetchinsky, and the technicians concerned must be recognised as extraordinary. I mean the fitting together of the incidents, the fragments of talk, which Mr Lord's researches among survivors and contemporary reports have recovered for us . . . There has been no attempt to dress up the tragedy. The recorded cowardice is here as well as the recorded bravery . . . And the social climate is here. In the confusion of catastrophe the steerage passengers were almost forgotten. Those who managed to reach the boat deck got there, most of them by luck or pugnacity; it was their place to be saved last (if at all). The odious distinction belongs to the end of an age. Other aspects, too, of the story, are part of an end: the dissolution of a kind of confidence, a kind of optimism, the end of absolute faith in absolute safety.' *(Dilys Powell)*

'It is a kind of impressionist staged documentary, making its effect through a fragmentary collection of reconstructed incidents . . . The staging is exemplary.' *(David Robinson, Financial Times)*

'The retelling of an oft-told tragic story is done with such precision, such expertise , and such finesse that it's a movie not to miss.' *(Judith Crist)*

NIGHT TRAIN TO MUNICH CT: 7 AV: 7.40

(aka *Night Train; Gestapo*)

1940 GB 93 BW THRILLER/COMEDY

D Carol Reed ☆
W Sidney Gilliat Frank Launder ☆ from Gordon Wellesley's story *Report on a Fugitive* AAN

Margaret Lockwood Rex Harrison Paul Henreid Basil Radford Naunton Wayne James Harcourt Felix Aylmer Wyndham Goldie

British spy (Rex Harrison) has to rescue Czech scientist and his daughter (Margaret Lockwood) kidnapped by the Nazis.

Popular comedy thriller of its day, beautifully photographed by Otto Kanturek, with a climactic cable-car shoot-out which, even though it has been much imitated, still excites. Writers Launder and Gilliatt were obviously trying to repeat the success of their *The Lady Vanishes* – along with Margaret Lockwood and the train setting, Basil Radford and Naunton Wayne get a chance to reprise their character roles. This isn't in the same league, mainly because Reed lacks Hitchcock's wickedly black sense of humour and is heavy-handed when it comes to comedy direction, but it's pretty entertaining.

ANTI:

'[Its] chief fault . . . is that it tries to join two worlds: Hitler's Europe . . . and the jaunty return of those two brilliant cricket-talking buffoons, Wayne and Radford . . . This gradation from fact to make-believe, [the film] achieves successfully, but slowly, how slowly!' *(William Whitebait, New Statesman)*

MIXED:

'This holding story has abundance of thrills and maintains suspense to the last minute . . . The director has done a skilful piece of work, though possibly his interest in English types causes him to dwell on their delineation a shade long, and to slow down the pace thereby.' *(MFB)*

PRO:

'A very nice triumph of skill and maturity in films, and thus a pleasure to have.' *(Otis Ferguson)*

'Really good fun . . . Harrison is all that could be desired as a secret service agent.' *(Lionel Collier, Picturegoer)*

'Directed not by the fabulous Hitchcock . . . but by a brilliant newcomer . . . The swiftest and most harrowing thriller to come out of England since the Hitchcock work . . . Wittily written and spare as a coded message.' *(New York Times)*

NIGHTMARE ALLEY CT: 6 AV: 7.20

1947 US 112 BW HORROR/DRAMA

D Edmund Goulding ☆
W Jules Furthman ☆ from William Lindsay Gresham's novel

Tyrone Power ☆ Coleen Gray Joan Blondell Taylor Holmes ☆ Helen Walker Mike Mazurki ✔ Ian Keith

A fake mindreader (Tyrone Power) receives a horrific come-uppance.

This sinister drama which teeters on the edge of being a full-blown horror film offers a profoundly misanthropic view of post-war society. Its portrait of Americans as depressed, isolated, desperate and resentful is the opposite of Capra-esque. It wasn't a hit. Critics and audiences found it hard to accept the dashing Power in an anti-heroic role. Nor did they respond positively to the film's sleazy atmosphere; but the strangeness of the tale, Lee Garmes's noir shooting style, and the overall quality of the acting add up to one of the most unusual dramas of the 40s.

ANTI:

'Looks like real meat at first but turns out to be the usual canned stuff.' *(Time & Tide)*

'The far from extensive acting range of Tyrone Power is hardly equal to the demand of [the film] . . . The moral and social lifting of the story and its characters has deprived the film of any probability . . . I wonder why film companies buy books just to alter them out of recognition even if they are as in this case, no masterpieces.' *(Daily Worker)*

'Power is insufficiently dynamic.' *(Shipman)*

MIXED:

'The picture goes careful just short of all that might have made it very interesting . . . Even so, two or three sharply comic and cynical scenes make it worth seeing – Power's wrangle over "God" with his wonderfully stupid but not-that-stupid wife (Coleen Gray), a scene which has some of the hard, gay audacity of *Monsieur Verdoux*; and every scene in which Taylor Holmes impersonates a sceptical but vulnerable industrialist.' *(James Agee, Nation)*

'A brilliant, disturbing book has made an average innocuous, not wholly intelligible film, reasonably well acted.' *(Campbell Dixon, Daily Telegraph)*

PRO:

'A harsh, brutal story told with the sharp clarity of an etching.' *(Variety)*

'Another vivid acting performance by Tyrone Power.' *(Star)*

'Tyrone [Power] could never forget the dashing of his hopes in his favorite role of the geek in the film *Nightmare Alley* – which he would say had been his only chance of a real performance. He had begged to play the part, and his performance was magnificent. But the film was, for its day, powerfully realistic and violent in its climax. The studio was almost loath to show its most glamorous star in such a role, and the film was slipped out as a second-feature release, unnoticed.' *(Linda Christian)*

NIGHTMARE ON ELM STREET, A

CT: 6 AV: 5.58

1984 US 91 C HORROR

D Wes Craven ✔
W Wes Craven ✔

John Saxon Ronee Blakley Heather Langenkamp Amanda Wyss Nick Corri Robert Englund Johnny Depp

A mysterious slasher (Robert Englund) haunts the dreams of teenagers, and kills them.

The basic idea has a universal appeal – you have to stay awake in order to ward off demons which await you when you sleep – and it was the idea, rather than the repetitive execution, which made this a hit and spawned four sequels. Even so, Freddy Krueger (Robert Englund) is a genuinely scary figure, the kind who might have been in *Struwwelpeter*, and Wes Craven's direction builds up the suspense and delivers the requisite shocks, blood and guts, before a disappointingly anti-climactic ending. Four inferior sequels have tarnished the image of what was, in fact, an ingenious and original horror movie.

ANTI:

'The monster . . . wears a lot of masks that are about as scary as those worn by extremely small trick-or-treaters on Halloween.' *(Vincent Canby, New York Times)*

'Nasty little piece of shlock horror . . . The acting is universally bad . . . The script lacks imagination and fails to tell a "horrifying story" although mercifully it does provide a few unexpected laughs . . . What is frightening . . . is that there is an au[...] brand of mindless rubbish.' *(Curtis [...] Films & Filming)*

'What have we done to deserve this? [...] *Listener)*

PRO:

'A highly imaginative horror film that provides the requisite shocks to keep fans of the genre happy.' *(Variety)*

'An admirably crafted piece of horrific nonsense . . . calculated to make even the most blasé viewer hold on to his seat.' *(Keith Nurse, Daily Telegraph)*

'Usually I take copious notes . . . but during [this film] I chewed the pen with my eyes shut most of the time. It is a shocker . . . And before you see [it] I would strongly advise a valium sandwich.' *(Adela Lithman, Daily Express)*

NIGHTS OF CABIRIA, THE AAW

CT: 5 AV: 7.60

(aka *Le Notti di Cabiria; Cabiria*)

1957 Italy/France 110 BW DRAMA/ROMANCE/FOREIGN

D Federico Fellini ✗
W Federico Fellini Enio Flaiano Tullio Pinelli

Giulietta Masina François Perier Amedeo Nazzari Aldo Silvani Franca Marzi Dorian Gray Mario Passante

A Roman prostitute (Giulietta Masina) dreams of a more respectable life.

For some, this is Fellini's finest film. For others, including myself, it's sentimental, schlocky soap opera with painfully thin characterization. How much you enjoy it may depend upon how sympathetic you find Giulietta Masina, who strives a little too hard to be ingratiating as the tart with a heart, and ends up sugary-sweet. The story was later translated to New York, and became the musical *Sweet Charity*.

PRO:

'I welcome [Masina as] an artist who can fairly be described as Chaplinesque.' *(Peter Baker, F & F)*

'Stylistically the whole film with its dejected setting and its riotously fluent movement is brilliant. And the acting is superb . . . What Fellini and Masina give us is not a realistic portrait, not a piece of romanticizing either; it is the essence of the immortally hopeful, eternally cheated, indestructible human sparrow.' *(Dilys Powell)*

MIXED:

'Fellini's stimulating powers of observation again provide several outstanding sequences in an otherwise uncomfortable work . . . Masina brings [Cabiria] vividly to life, often striking a vein of true pathos.' *(MFB)*

...ching . . . But there are two weaknesses . . . It ...s a sordid atmosphere and there is something elusive and insufficient about the character of the heroine . . . [The film] is too long for the little it has to tell.' *(Bosley Crowther)*

ANTI:

'Any nobility in the original conception slowly suffocates in an atmosphere of subjective indulgence bordering dangerously on self-pity.' *(Peter John Dyer)*

9½ WEEKS CT: 2 AV: 3.36

1986 US 113/117 C DRAMA/ROMANCE

D Adrian Lyne
W Patricia Knop Zalman King Sarah Kernochan from Elizabeth McNeill's novel

Mickey Rourke Kim Basinger Margaret Whitton David Margulies Christine Baranski

A Wall Street financier (Mickey Rourke) has a steamy affair with an employee of an art gallery (Kim Basinger).

Designer porn for the jaded 80s, with Mickey Rourke as the man with the designs, and Kim Basinger as the porn. Lyne directs as if advertising something, possibly himself. Any serious intentions are left on the cutting-room floor.

PRO:

'I . . . came away surprised by how thoughtful the movie is, how clearly it sees exactly what really happens between its characters . . . What makes the movie fascinating [is] not that it shows these two people entering a bizarre sexual relationship, but because it shows the woman deciding for herself what she will, and will not, agree to.' *(Roger Ebert)*

MIXED:

'Lyne . . . is here superbly served both by his cast and by his designer and cinematographer . . . With a deeper examination of the darker areas hinted at in the relationship, [it] could have emerged as the searing document I suspect it aimed at being, but within its limits, it is not to be dismissed . . . Neither sexploitation nor soft porn, it is a genuinely adult attempt at a study of erotic obsession.' *(David Butler)*

'What matter that [it] debases women . . . when boredom is kept so effortlessly at bay? . . . Ms Basinger squirms as realistically as she can. Her success is limited by her talent.' *(Minty Clinch, Midweek)*

ANTI:

'It's *The Story of O* as it might look if conceived as a two-hour television commercial . . . Characters blended into the décor so completely that they take on the properties of animated products, no more or less important than exquisitely photographed strawberries . . . Mr Rourke and Miss Basinger move though the movie like robots.' *(Vincent Canby, New York Times)*

'Keeps drifting off into static, shiny attempts to make the ultimate perfume ad . . . almost completely boring.' *(David Denby, New York Magazine)*

'The virtual absence of anything happening between them – like plausible attraction, amazing sex or, God forbid, good dialogue – leaves one great hole on the screen for two hours.' *(Variety)*

'A two-hour commercial for weird sex with lots of bad ideas for the sexually adventurous.' *(Winnert)*

'It only seems that long.' *(Rose)*

1900 CT: 4 AV: 5.67

(aka *Novecento*)

1976 Italy/France/West Germany 243/311/320 C DRAMA/EPIC/FOREIGN

D Bernardo Bertolucci
W Franco Arcalli Bernardo Bertolucci

Burt Lancaster Romolo Valli Anna-Maria Gherardi Laura Betti Robert De Niro Paolo Pavesi Dominique Sanda Sterling Hayden Gérard Depardieu Roberto Maccanti Stejania Sandrelli Donald Sutherland

Epic about an Italian family (a microcosm of all Italy) surviving under fascism and communism.

Bertolucci's visual flair, Vittorio Storaro's glorious photography and occasional powerful moments can not compensate for soapy characterization, extremely dubious politics (sexual and otherwise), and an almost total absence of plot. It is also ludicrously overlong and boring.

PRO:

'A masterpiece, a true and rare marriage between the art film and popular cinema.' *(Richard Roud, Guardian)*

'A flawed masterpiece . . . A fanfare if you like, for the uncommon man.' *(Tom Hutchinson, Sunday Telegraph)*

'Bertolucci's heroically ambitious enterprise is almost always a stunning assault upon the eyes.' *(Alan Brien, Sunday Times)*

'Bertolucci has been criticised for his theatricality and exaggerated use of high contrast, but by these means he deliberately reminds the spectators that they are viewing not history itself, but an act of historical interpretation. A Marxist interpretation.' *(Virginia Dignam, Morning Star)*

'[The] almost religious division of [the world into good and evil] gives the film the strength and simplicity of a medieval passion play or a primitive icon. It is a deeply felt and absorbing epic, an instant history lesson and required viewing in the study of . . . Italian communism.' *(Joan Juliet Buck, Observer Magazine)*

ANTI:

'On the surface Bertolucci seeks to make a big popular historical movie that out-Hollywoods *Gone with the Wind* . . . But . . . he also wants the depth of a 19th-century novel and the grandeur of an opera by Verdi . . . None of these ambitions is achieved.' *(Philip French, Observer)*

'Whether one takes the two-part movie as a glamorous epic or as a lengthy advertisement for the Italian communist party, it still looks like a major catastrophe.' *(Tony Rayns, Time Out)*

'One of the most unsatisfactory and disappointing epics I've ever looked forward to seeing . . . Irredeemably shallow and perfunctory.' *(Derek Malcolm, Guardian)*

'Scales new heights of dreadfulness in film . . . When the film was over, I felt that we ought to be shown the menu on the back of which the script was outlined at the very first lunch of director and producer.' *(Stanley Kauffmann)*

NINOTCHKA AAN — CT: 5 AV: 9.00

1939 US 108/110 BW COMEDY

D Ernst Lubitsch ✗
W Charles Brackett Billy Wilder Walter Reisch ✗ AAN from story by Melchior Lengyel AAN

Greta Garbo ✗ AAN Melvyn Douglas Sig Rumann ✗ Alexander Granach ✗ Felix Bressart ✗ Ina Claire ✓ Bela Lugosi

A French playboy (Melvyn Douglas) falls in love with a Russian Communist (Garbo).

So high is the reputation of this film that it comes as a shock actually to see it and observe that (a) this supposedly sophisticated comedy is in fact patronizing and oafish in the way it scores points off the Soviets; (b) Garbo has no gift for comedy; (c) she looks as if she would be more at home jumping Becher's Brook; (d) most of the other performances, with the exception of Melvyn Douglas and Ina Claire, look like exercises in coarse acting; and (e) it's 20 minutes too long. Later re-made as the *Musical Silk Stockings*, with Fred Astaire and Cyd Charisse.

PRO:

'Smart sophisticated comedy satirising all things Russian. The communist and . . . the old nobility alike are the victims of its biting wit . . . Greta Garbo and her producer Ernst Lubitsch have, with all their subtlety, the common touch. The humour is marvellous. And is it timely? . . . Topnotchka . . . [Garbo's] performance is a revelation . . . Politically it's marvellous anti-Soviet propaganda . . . The rest is a delightful satire on the frailties of human nature and feminine in particular . . . Comic story, great comic twists, brilliant character parodies, elegant atmosphere, smart finale, good title, and the box office allure of Garbo.' *(Kine Weekly)*

'Whether or not Greta Garbo is a good actress I have no idea, but I am sure she is a great actress.' *(Dilys Powell, Sunday Times)*

'High calibre entertainment for adult audiences.' *(Variety)*

'What gives *Ninotchka* its distinction as a comedy is not its fairly cut and dried sequence of events, but the gaiety and impishness of its social satire.' *(Allen Bishop, Theater Arts)*

'Hilarious and humane satire on cold-war machinations.' *(Peter Bogdanovich, Picture Shows, 1975)*

MIXED:

'Strikes a wrong note occasionally – nothing serious, but a thing for example like the movie-German accent of a Soviet envoy, or like the weight of too much stationary conversation. But the story gets there, its people are real enough, it has an overall radiance of pleasant but knowing wit.' *(Otis Ferguson, 1939)*

ANTI:

'Garbo in *Ninotchka* gives no performance at all. For half an hour she is glum in the stereotyped Garbo fashion. And then she is supposed to laugh and doesn't . . . It is mirthless laughter, like the yawning of a horse. Look closely into this simulation and you will perceive that the simulator is not amused. Then she has a long and totally unfunny drunken scene, after which she spends the rest of the time looking like Norma Shearer's mother! In my view this is the worst performance I have ever seen Garbo give, and it is made to seem all the worse by the brilliant acting of Ina Claire, who sounds all the notes of polished comedy . . . Instead of being the major plum in the pudding, Garbo's performance is the one piece of suet in an otherwise entirely delectable dish.' *(James Agate, Tatler)*

NORA INU: *see* STRAY DOG.

NORMA RAE AAN — CT: 6 AV: 7.20

1979 US 114 C DRAMA

D Martin Ritt ☆
W Irving Ravetch Harriet Frank Jr ✗ AAN

Sally Field ☆ AAW Beau Bridges Ron Leibman Pat Hingle Barbara Baxley

Southern woman (Sally Field) becomes militant union organizer.

Good-natured, pro-union, mildly feminist tract about a woman 'finding herself' in her thirties. Maybe it could have been harder-edged and less politically one-sided, but Field's heartfelt performance makes it reasonably involving. The song 'It Goes Like It Goes' (music by David Shire, lyrics by Norman Gimbel) won a Oscar.

PRO:

'The film of his [Martin Ritt's] career . . . His best

strength, as always, is his work with actors.' *(Stanley Kauffmann)*

'Sally Field's sheer warmth of heart heats every scene . . . to blood temperature and makes sure a didactic story gets its due as a human one, too.' *(Alexander Walker, Evening Standard)*

MIXED:

'[Fields] is unbelievable, but terrific nevertheless, utterly watchable from first moment to last.' *(Richard Barkley, Sunday Express)*

ANTI:

'A big question-mark hangs over this film, and sometimes it threatens to fall down and give the movie concussion . . . Ritt tends to fall into positions of reverence when dealing with any persecuted group . . . But it's less his pie-eyed championing of the downtrodden that troubles one than the fact that he keeps having to . . . reach back into the past . . . to find them. It's a sort of *nostalgie de la souffrance*.' *(Nigel Andrews, Financial Times)*

NORTE, EL: *see* EL NORTE.

NORTH BY NORTHWEST CT: 10 AV: 9.41

1959 US 136 C ACTION/ADVENTURE/COMEDY

D Alfred Hitchcock ☆
W Ernest Lehman ☆

Cary Grant ☆ Eva Marie Saint James Mason Jessie Royce Landis Adam Williams Leo G. Carroll Martin Landau

A businessman (Cary Grant) is mistaken for a spy, and is understandably perturbed when people keep trying to kill him.

Hitchcock's masterly action-adventure includes the famous scenes of Cary Grant being chased by the crop-spraying aircraft and hanging off Mount Rushmore. The whole film's worth rewatching, if only to marvel at its wit, sophistication, and the wickedly ingenious ways Hitchcock gets us on the side of his complacent hero and then makes us suffer alongside him. For its mixture of humour and thrills, it has rarely been matched.

ANTI:

'Hitchcock in his late middle-age is becoming prolix. It is hard to believe that a director so green-fingered at making a plot sprout should be so butterfingered in the business of pruning . . . [It] huffs and puffs to its predictable close. Longwindedly.' *(Paul Dehn, News Chronicle)*

'Hitchcock has a lot in common with the late Cecil B. DeMille. Though he has too much levity and cynicism to bother with DeMille's Messages, the maestri are alike in their technical mastery . . . Mr Hitchcock's puppets walk and talk in a bright Charlie McCarthy fashion: they are jerked this way and that at the master's whim. But outside the great wide VistaVision Never Never Land they have no life to lose.' *(Daily Telegraph)*

MIXED:

'A real shaggy dog spy story . . . [which] taken seriously makes no sense whatsoever. This is fortunate because, taken seriously, its implications about the heroine's morals, the methods of American intelligence agencies and sundry other matters are alarming to say the least. It is amazing, nevertheless, how entertaining the picture is.' *(Moira Walsh, America)*

PRO:

'That master magician has done it again . . . [The Mt. Rushmore] scene alone is worth the money.' *(Peter Burnup, News of the World)*

'It is only when you adopt the basic premise that Cary Grant could not possibly come to harm that the tongue in Hitchcock's cheek becomes plainly visible.' *(Hollis Alpert, Saturday Review)*

'In the past one has occasionally felt that the director was losing, in the hugeness and wealth of the United States, his own sharp self. Not this time. The crimson-lined hotels, the trains full of lollers in armchairs, the empty, whistling, ochre plains – in *North by Northwest* he has taken pleasure in filling the screen with the extravagance of America, but he has used the extravagance without ever subordinating to it his own wicked ingenuity.' *(Dilys Powell)*

'[Most action sequences aim for] no effect beyond a purely physical titillation. In *North by Northwest* the crop-dusting sequence has essential relevance to the film's development. The complacent, self-confident Cary Grant character is shown here exposed in open country, away from the false security of office and cocktail bar, exposed to the menacing and the unpredictable. The man, who behaved earlier as if nobody mattered except himself, is here reduced to running for his life, scurrying for cover like a terrified rabbit; he is reminded – and we, who found him smart and attractive in his accustomed milieu, are reminded – of his personal insignificance in a vast, potentially inimical universe. The sequence marks a crucial stage in the evolution of the character and his relationships, and, through that, of the themes of the whole film. If the character were not attractive, for all his shortcomings, our response would be merely sadistic, we would delight in the spectacle of an unpleasant man getting his deserts; but we have become sufficiently identified with him for our suspense to be characterized by a tension between conflicting reactions to his predicament.' *(Robin Wood, Hitchcock's Films Revisited, 1989)*

NORTH STAR, THE CT: 5 AV: 4.71

(aka *Armored Attack*)

1943 US 105/82 (1957 version) BW WAR

D Lewis Milestone
W Lillian Hellman ● AAN

Anne Baxter ● Farley Granger ● Jane Withers
Dana Andrews ● Walter Huston Erich von Stroheim

Russian villagers defend themselves against the Nazis.

Hilariously terrible old wartime propaganda, politically correct before the concept had even been formulated; it's designed to show what nice chaps our allies the Russians are. In an excess of fellow-travelling zeal, Lillian Hellman's ghastly script was Oscar-nominated; slightly more comprehensible were nominations for cinematographer James Wong Howe, art directors Perry Ferguson amd Howard Bristol, and composer Aaron Copland. Copland's horrendous collaboration with Ira Gershwin on a would-be stirring song 'We're The Younger Generation and the Future of the Nation' is not to be missed. A shorter version, entitled 'Armored Attack' and with pro-Russian sentiment removed, was released in 1957.

PRO:

'A happily timed and splendid tribute . . . lavish thrills of spectacle, deep emotion, splendid acting.' *(Ivor Montagu, Daily Worker)*

MIXED:

'Effectively sets the hope and gaiety of the younger Russians against the dark realities of the Nazi invasion . . . At least it can be said [it] did not fail ignobly.' *(The Times)*

ANTI:

'Should have been first rate, but isn't . . . The emotional impact is negligible. We watch the film with polite attention because it is technically well made and the subject commands our respect . . . [But] we just don't believe it.' *(Campbell Dixon, Daily Telegraph)*

'Ersatz Russian.' *(Sunday Times)*

'Unrealism . . . Russians don't look or talk or work or fight like this . . . [The film] is sentimental and out of date; though, of course, it means well.' *(New Statesman)*

'Putting American villagers into Russian costumes and calling them by Russian names is never going to deceive this old bird.' *(James Agate)*

'Looks and feels like a European movie, except that it has no intellect.' *(Shipman)*

NORTH, THE: *see* EL NORTE.

NORTHWEST FRONTIER CT: 8 AV: 6.57

(aka *Flame Over India*)

1959 GB 129 C ACTION/ADVENTURE/FAMILY

D J. Lee Thompson ☆
W Robin Estridge ☆ from Frank Nugent's screenplay based on Patrick Ford and Will Price's story

Kenneth More Lauren Bacall ✓ Herbert Lom ✓
Ursula Jeans Wilfrid Hyde-White I.S. Johar ✓
Eugene Deckers Ian Hunter

English officer (Kenneth More) escorts young Indian prince on a dangerous train journey.

Exciting action yarn and one of the best to be set on a train, with Kenneth More giving a typically energetic, stiff upper lip performance. Bacall, Lom and Johar lend admirable support, and the top-notch cinematography is by Geoffrey Unsworth.

ANTI:

'Seems to have borrowed its eccentric engine from *The General*, its hazardous expedition from *Stagecoach* and its background of tribal violence from *The Drum*.' *(Penelope Houston)*

MIXED:

'Should have been twenty minutes shorter. What makes it drag is the dialogue, which contains every cliché in the phrase-book . . . On the other hand, the moments of suspense are better done than . . . Hitchcock [though] they are nothing like as clever, and the characters caught up in them are nothing like as interesting and sympathetic . . . *Northwest Frontier* is, indeed, a triumph of direction and editing.' *(David Sylvester, New Statesman)*

PRO:

'Surprising: but then Mr Lee Thompson's films are all surprises, for they vary so much in atmosphere and milieu, and even in style and attitude . . . [This] is a surprise because it is a full-scale expensive adventure film, like a Western . . . only an Eastern Western; and because its hero is quite unlike the heroes that tend to interest Mr Lee Thompson.' *(Isabel Quigly, Spectator)*

'Thompson seems to flourish in the change of air [from his usual intimate items] and piles excitement on excitement . . . what the script boys call a "cliff-hanger" . . . The suspense is tremendous.' *(Charles MacLaren, Time & Tide)*

'A perceptive screenplay and J. Lee Thompson's shrewd direction save the 130-minute film from the Eastern-Western stereotype and give remarkable sense of time and place and situation.' *(Judith Crist)*

NORTHWEST PASSAGE: PART 1, ROGERS' RANGERS CT: 6 AV: 7.70

1939 US 125 C WESTERN/ADVENTURE

D King Vidor ☆
W Laurence Stallings Talbot Jennings from Kenneth Robert's novel

Spencer Tracy ☆ Robert Young ☆ Ruth Hussey Walter Brennan Nat Pendleton Robert Barrat Lumsden Hare Donald MacBride

A band of settlers (led by Spencer Tracy) make parts of North America safe from Indians.

An odd title for a film which has nothing to do with the Northwest Passage. It's an exciting action epic of its era, much praised for Tracy's performance and its Technicolor cinematography, but now hard to watch. It suffers more than most westerns from its dated, frankly racist attitude towards Indians. Part Two was never made. Maybe they would have found the Northwest Passage in that one.

PRO:

'A robust adventure with a full measure of somber realism . . . Short on dialogue, long on Technicolor photography . . . No one can leave the theatre unimpressed.' *(Ted Magee, Picture Play)*

'Combines the thrills of warfare and exploration with quite exceptional force . . . What surprises is the touch of reality . . . Mr Tracy is as impressive as ever.' *(William Whitebait, New Statesman)*

ANTI:

'A story which ought to be epic, but which ends up as a first-class presentation of a serial from the *Boys' Own Paper* of the Eighties or Nineties . . . [The film] has a number of major defects. In the first place, it has nothing whatever to do with the North-West Passage . . . In the second place, its moral and dramatic values [fall below other treatments]. And in the third place, it is at least thirty minutes too long.' *(Basil Wright, Spectator)*

'Lurid dialogue, forcefully delivered and occasionally lightened by laconic comment, outlines plot which, however, lacks emotional impetus, being solely dependent upon action and movement . . . [The] finest Technicolor seen to date . . . Honors really [go] to the crowd players who work magnificently throughout.' *(Today's Cinema)*

NOSFERATU – EINE SYMPHONIE DES GRAUENS CT: 6 AV: 8.20

(aka *Nosferatu*)

1921 Germany 63/72 BW HORROR/SILENT

D F.W. Murnau ☆
W Henrik Galeen

Max Schreck ☆ Gustav von Wangenheim Greta Schröder Alexander Granach G.H. Schnell

A Transylvanian vampire named Orlok (Max Schreck) terrorizes Bremen.

Extremely creepy, oppressive horror silent, thanks to Max Schreck's amazingly grotesque central performance and Murnau's disturbing direction. The story is a thinly disguised version of Bram Stoker's *Dracula*, with Bremen standing in for Whitby. Stoker's widow sued successfully to have the film withdrawn from distribution. It is much more cinematic and scary than the 1931 film which Universal eventually made of the novel. There was a sound and colour remake of *Nosferatu* in 1979, starring Klaus Kinski: much too slow, and not in the least frightening.

ANTI:

'Is this overacting, or is it my fault for not entering into the spirit of the story? . . . [Some scenes] are thrilling, but a glimpse of the Count himself brings a smile to the lips. "That's a vampire," one thinks, "and isn't he funny?"' *(Oswell Blakeston, Close-Up, 1929)*

'More of a soporific than a thriller . . . The backgrounds are often quite effective, but most of it seems like cardboard puppets doing all they can to be horrible on papier-mâché settings.' *(Mordaunt Hall, New York Times)*

'Rather crude . . . the production obviously cheap, some of the effects . . . seeming more ridiculous than weird. On the other hand, the film did show Murnau's flair for pictorial effect.' *(Theodore Huff, 1948)*

PRO:

'[It is as if] a chilly draft of doomsday passes through it.' *(Béla Balazs, Der Sichtbare Mensch: Eine Film-Dramaturgie, 1924)*

'There are no gimmicky effects here, no thrusting of wooden stakes into hearts, spurting Technicolor blood. Yet the film is good and creepy. Dramatic use of lighting lends it an uncanny atmosphere.' *(Sunday Express, 1974)*

'One of the most poetic of all horror films. Its power derives partly from Schreck's almost literally subhuman portrait of the Count, resplendent with long ears and fingers and a wizened, skeletal face, partly from the sexual undercurrents coursing through the movie which suggest that the vampire is a threat not only to bourgeois society and its emphasis upon scientific rationality, but also to the very marriage of the Harker couple.' *(Geoff Andrew, Time Out)*

'The greatest of all vampire films.' *(Danny Peary)*

'This first important film of the vampire genre has more spectral atmosphere, more ingenuity, and more imaginative ghoulish ghastliness than any of its successors.' *(Pauline Kael)*

NOTHING SACRED CT: 6 AV: 7.64

1937 US 75/77 C COMEDY

D William A. Wellman ☆
W Ben Hecht Ring Lardner Jr Budd Schulberg from James H. Street's story *Letter to the Editor*

Carole Lombard ☆ Fredric March ☆ Charles Winninger Walter Connolly ☆ Sig Rumann Frank Fay Maxie Rosenbloom

A small-town girl (Carole Lombard) wrongly assumed to be dying of radium poisoning becomes a media celebrity, thanks to a manipulative journalist (Fredric March).

Likeably acerbic, fast-paced satirical comedy which pokes fun at journalists, public sentimentality and small-town America. It was later transformed into a stage musical, *Hazel Flagg* (1953) and a Jerry Lewis-Dean Martin comedy, *Living it Up* (1954), with Lewis in the Lombard role.

'Hit comedy . . . Will be one of the big grossers of the year.' *(Variety)*

'Because it does hold up a mirror, even though a distorting mirror, to a very real world of ballyhoo and cheap sensationalism, the pleasure to be obtained from it is something more than the usual mulish guffaw.' *(Basil Wright, Spectator)*

'This admirable comic situation is developed with verve, resource and irony. O rare Ben Hecht! He has done brilliant work for the cinema before, but he never struck a richer vein than this . . . It will be a long time, I fear, before we see another film so adult and so diverting.' *(P. Galway, New Statesman)*

NOTORIOUS CT: 9 AV: 8.43

1946 US 101 BW THRILLER/ROMANCE

D Alfred Hitchcock ☆
W Ben Hecht ☆ AAN

Cary Grant ☆ Ingrid Bergman ☆ Claude Rains ☆ AAN Louis Calhern Leopoldine Konstantin Reinhold Schunzel

Cary Grant and Ingrid Bergman are out to trap a neo-Nazi in South America.

Hitchcock's sexiest, most romantic thriller, not as highly rated on release as it should have been. Bergman and Grant are just wonderful together, and there is one of the screen's great villains in Claude Rains – splendidly subtle and rounded as Grant's fascist quarry. The outstanding cinematography by Ted Tetzlaff gives a lovely sense of period and place; and Hitchcock's mastery of camera movement is breathtaking. The film contains perhaps the most brilliant crane-shot in Hollywood history – all the way from a wideshot at the top of the stairway in Rains's mansion, down to a close-up of a key in Bergman's hand.

MIXED:

'The story is not notably original . . . Yet in . . . Hitchcock's hands and with the beauty of Bergman, this old material takes on new life.' *(Joan Lester, Reynolds News)*

'If [it] offers nothing new to the high-brow it has everything it needs to delight the million.' *(Campbell Dixon, Daily Telegraph)*

'Alfred Hitchcock gives a well worn subject that extra plausibility and polish we expect of him.' *(Daily Worker)*

'Lacks many of the qualities which made the best of Alfred Hitchcock's movies so good, but it has more than enough good qualities of its own. Hitchcock has always been as good at domestic psychology as at thrillers, and many times here he makes a moment in a party, or a lovers' quarrel, or a mere interior shrewdly exciting in ways that few people in films seem to know how. His great skill in directing women, which boggled in *Spellbound*, is functioning beautifully again: I think that Ingrid Bergman's performance here is the best that I have seen.' *(James Agee, Nation)*

'Great trash, great fun.' *(Pauline Kael, 70s)*

PRO:

'Hitchcock's direction and his cutting constantly provide surprises . . . A tense taut story, beautifully acted.' *(Ewart Hodgson)*

'Magnificent.' *(Sunday Chronicle)*

'Hitchcock has used all his box of tricks to jolt, to unnerve: the distortions, the shadows, the watchful faces of melodrama. In a film consisting so largely of close-ups the burden on the players is heavy, and credit is due to Ingrid Bergman and in a smaller degree Cary Grant for playing which by shades of facial expression alone indicates the emotional undertones of the narrative. But the movement of the camera is overruling; and possible distaste for the elements of Ben Hecht's script is most of the time lost in the interest of watching the rhythm of motion, the sidling or the sudden approaches, the swoops and swerves and horizontal swings.' *(Dilys Powell)*

'Ranks high among the fright operas he has staged in Hollywood.' *(Herb Sterne)*

'A subjective adventure into morbid eroticism and primitive fears.' *(Albert J. LaValley; Focus on Hitchcock, 1972)*

NOTTE DI SAN LORENZO, LA: *see* NIGHT OF THE SHOOTING STARS

NOTTI DI CABIRIA, LE: *see* NIGHTS OF CABIRIA, THE.

NOVECENTO: *see* 1900.

NOW, VOYAGER CT: 8 AV: 7.92

1942 US 117 BW DRAMA/ROMANCE

D Irving Rapper ☆
W Casey Robinson from Olive Higgins Prouty's novel

Bette Davis ☆ AAN Claude Rains ☆ Paul Henreid ☆ Gladys Cooper ☆ AAN John Loder Bonita Granville Charles Drake Ilka Chase

A dowdy spinster (Bette Davis) makes herself over with the help of an understanding psychiatrist (Claude Rains), and finds Love in the form of a married man (Paul Henreid).

Modern audiences may find Henreid resistible, and the script over-talky. The emotional self-indulgence on display – not to mention the blind faith in psychiatry – is enough to make Woody Allen feel queasy. But with great performances from Davis and Gladys Cooper as her domineering mother (plus Max Steiner's Oscar-winning score to ladle on the pathos) this remains a magnificent tearjerker.

ANTI:

'Strained, suffering and as beautiful as the Warner makeup department can manage, Bette takes a South American cruise and encounters both love and lust. From then on Life (that Torquemada!) really applies the heat, and the emotional agony becomes so intense as to threaten not only the sanity of the shadow-protagonists but that of the spectators as well. It is all desperately slow, shatteringly inane and violently verbose, but certain ladies at the preview wept and sniffed copiously, thereby conclusively proving that Time has not dimmed the truth of Phineas T. Barnum's most famous observation. Miss Davis repeats the same higgledy-piggledy performance that has been consistently lauded by press and public alike, while Paul Henreid, no longer content to be a competent actor, bursts forth as a sloe-eyed lover and devotes most of his footage to making febrile googoo eyes in the free French fashion that has made Charles Boyer the toast of matinee audiences.' *(Herb Sterne)*

'If it were better, it might not work at all. This way, it's a crummy classic.' *(Pauline Kael, 1977)*

'A basically soggy script gets by, and how, through the romantic magic of its stars, who were all at their best; and suffering in mink went over very big in wartime.' *(Halliwell)*

MIXED:

'Hysteria and neurosis have found a dependable interpreter in Miss Davis, and she lacks nothing on this occasion that her saucer eyes will not do.' *(Manchester Guardian, 1944)*

'A long-drawn-out well-directed, earnest and slightly unconvincing film, worth visiting for the high level of the acting and some skilfully managed episodes.' *(William Whitebait, New Statesman)*

'This piffle is directed by Rapper with mesmerising skill.' *(Higham & Greenberg, Hollywood in the Forties)*

'Gives Bette Davis a part of the nervous, high-tension type which becomes her; it is a pity that the precision and control of her playing are not paralleled by a greater austerity of form in the telling of the story.' *(Dilys Powell)*

NOZ W WODZIE: *see* KNIFE IN THE WATER.

NUIT AMÉRICAINE, LA: *see* DAY FOR NIGHT.

NUN'S STORY, THE AAN CT: 7 AV: 7.89

1959 US 149 C DRAMA/BIOPIC

D Fred Zinnemann ☆ AAN
W Robert Anderson ☆ AAN from Kathryn C. Hulme's book

Audrey Hepburn ☆ AAN Peter Finch ☆ Edith Evans ☆ Peggy Ashcroft ☆ Dean Jagger Mildred Dunnock Beatrice Straight Patricia Collinge Eva Kotthaus Ruth White

Belgian nun (Audrey Hepburn) goes to Congo as a nurse, meets a fanciable doctor (Peter Finch) and wonders if celibacy is all it's cracked up to be.

A touching, involving drama, based on a true story, and much less sanctimonious than might be imagined. Hepburn gives her role a quiet integrity; the details of a nun's life are well-researched; and the love story is handled tastefully. Franz Planer's photography, Franz Waxman's music and Walter Thompson's editing were all Oscar-nominated.

ANTI:

'A catalogue of [its] imperfections . . . would include the coloured glossiness in which [it] is set, the comeliness of the nuns, the overprecise dignity of their "ceremonial drill", the director's excessive preoccupation with ritual . . . and, finally, the lush, insistent and typical quality of the background music.' *(Manchester Guardian)*

PRO:

'An enthralling, fascinating and a remarkably beautiful film.' *(Derek Monsey, Sunday Express)*

'A film that restores one's faith in an art form and by implication . . . one's faith in human nature . . . I beg you not to miss it. Only a bigoted materialist would deny that this is one of the classics of the screen.' *(Campbell Dixon, Daily Telegraph)*

'A major directorial achievement . . . the best study of the religious life ever made in the American cinema. A masterpiece of semidocumentary and character revelation.' *(Albert Johnson, Film Quarterly)*

'Careful, composed and impressive film with little Hollywood exaggeration.' *(Halliwell)*

NUTTY PROFESSOR, THE CT: 6 AV: 6.00

1963 US 107 C COMEDY

D Jerry Lewis Bill Richmond
W Jerry Lewis

Jerry Lewis Stella Stevens Del Moore Kathleen Freeman Med Flory

A professor of chemistry (Jerry Lewis) falls for a student (Stella Stevens) and transforms himself by means of a potion into a narcissistic singer (played by Jerry Lewis as a parody of his erstwhile comedy partner, Dean Martin).

Generally considered Lewis's best comedy, this variation on the Jekyll and Hyde story contains some very funny sight (and sound) gags; but there are long, boring stretches and far too much repetition. Some French critics construed the film as a satire on masculine stereotypes in American society. It was more likely an attempt by Lewis to reconstitute his successful double-act, this time with him playing both halves.

ANTI:

'Only the truly scavenger Lewis-fan is invited to attend.' *(John Coleman, New Statesman)*

'Every man to his taste. Some like cucumbers and vinegar. I cannot abide them. Others like Jerry Lewis . . . If ever a personality needed changing it is [his].' *(Cecil Wilson, Daily Mail)*

'For all the patience of the camera which dwells lovingly on the comedian's face, laughter is hard to drum up.' *(Eric Shorter, Daily Telegraph)*

'Lewis plays the hapless Julius for childlike pathos, and Buddy for hollow-man Las Vegas loathsomeness; yet in his TV appearances in the years that followed he moved even closer to Buddy Love – even down to singing loudly and off-key, and being aggressively maudlin as he milked the audience for approval.' *(Pauline Kael, 70s)*

MIXED:

'For a few brief sequences the film comes wonderfully to life.' *(The Times)*

'Uneven, at times barely competent . . . [But Lewis's] wildness and skill and invention and charm always leave one still hoping.' *(Financial Times)*

'The first 10 minutes of *The Nutty Professor* provide, even for non-Jerry Lewis fans, one of the funniest Jekyll-Hyde transformation takeoffs on film. Otherwise, this comedy . . . is fitfully funny' *(Judith Crist)*

PRO:

'The comedian's best film since *The Ladies' Man* . . . adventurous avant-garde stuff . . . The film's air of slow-motion delirium is enhanced by its long, expectant silences and by the many close-ups . . . A fantasia on the theme of virility and self-assurance . . . so offbeat and tantalising that one isn't bored for a for a moment, even during the passages which turn out to be dull after all.' *(Raymond Durgnat, Films & Filming)*

'I like [it] . . . The first half is perfect . . . The actual metamorphosis is a *tour de force*.' *(Peter John Dyer, Guardian)*

'Probably Jerry Lewis's best comedy to date, it uses the ingenious twist . . . which presents us Hyde as the more handsome of the two characters to parody the Stevenson theme of the repressed individual and, at the same time, satirise the American matriarchal society and its idolisation of the super-male.' *(NFT Bulletin, 1975)*

'Hindered as much as helped by Cahiers-canonisation, Jerry Lewis is not a recondite Gallic folly but a universal – nay, paramount – comic original.' *(Nigel Andrews, NFT Bulletin, 1984)*

NUOVO CINEMA PARADISO: *see* CINEMA PARADISO.

O LUCKY MAN CT: 6 AV: 6.80

1973 GB 174 C COMEDY/MUSICAL

D Lindsay Anderson
W David Sherwin (songs by Alan Price)

Malcolm McDowell Arthur Lowe ☆
Ralph Richardson ☆ Rachel Roberts Helen Mirren
Mona Washbourne Alan Price Dandy Nichols
Graham Crowden

The progress of a modern pilgrim (Malcolm McDowell).

Rambling comedy with enjoyable musical interludes and mythic pretensions. Some of it is amusingly satirical, but three hours is too long for a series of more-or-less disconnected sketches of variable quality. This is the middle section of an interesting though flawed triptych which begins with *If* . . . and ends with *Britannia Hospital*. All three movies star McDowell as Mick Travis, but his character is hardly consistent from film to film, or even (in this picture) from scene to scene.

PRO:

'An epic look at society.' *(Variety)*

'A very good film . . . a kind of modern *Candide* . . . I don't think the result is wholly pessimistic. The world, it says, is full of crimes and criminals. But charity is possible; after the terrors of atomic research Mick is allowed the respite of the beautiful lyrical passage in the country church. Even happiness is possible; he is finally shocked into reconciliation with life.' *(Dilys Powell)*

ANTI:

'Not even a concoction of satire slapstick, black fantasy and morality tale as wickedly witty as this – and sharply pointed by songs as tunefully composed and sung as those of Alan Price – can justify a three-hour sitting.' *(Cecil Wilson, Daily Mail)*

'An undisciplined . . . shriek of anger at what "They" are doing to "Us", lashing out wildly without purpose. The result is a film that approaches its material not in the manner of a Swift or an Orwell, but as the *Carry On* team might under the temporary influence of surrealism.' *(Phil Hardy, Time Out)*

O THIASSOS: *see* TRAVELLING PLAYERS, THE.

OBCHOD NA KORZE: *see* SHOP ON MAIN STREET, THE.

OCCUPE-TOI D'AMÉLIE: *see* KEEP AN EYE ON AMELIA.

OCTOBER CT: 5 AV: 7.89

(aka *Ten Days that Shook the World, The; Oktyarbr*)

1927 USSR 103/120/164 BW DRAMA/SILENT/ FOREIGN

D Sergei Eisenstein Gregori Alexandrov ☆
W Sergei Eisenstein Gregori Alexandrov based on John Reed's novel

Nikandrov Vladimir Popov Boris Livanov
Red Army soldiers Red Navy sailors
citizens of Leningrad

Bolsheviks overthrow the Kerensky government in 1917.

Revolutionary epic, worth seeing for the big set-pieces (notably the St Petersburg massacre, the destruction of Alexander III's statue and the storming of the Winter Palace) and daring use of montage, but otherwise over-rated. Eisenstein's use of symbolism is heavy-handed, his attempts at satire are crude, and most of the spectacular sequences are concentrated within the first hour. For political reasons, Eisenstein was persuaded to edit Trotsky out of the proceedings – the result is a bit like the 1953 Bolton-Blackpool Cup Final without any footage of Stanley Matthews. Re-released in 1967, with a Shostakovich soundtrack.

PRO:

'A colossal achievement of the Russian cinema.' *(Close-Up)*

'Retains its tremendous strength of direction and in places still remains a magnificent creative achievement . . . A giant among films.' *(Paul Rotha, S & S, 1934)*

'It still makes modern film makers look like babies.' *(Derek Malcolm, Guardian, 1969)*

'Eisenstein's masterpiece.' *(Nina Hibbin, Morning Star, 1969)*

'Showed Eisenstein's innovatory theories of montage which added intellect to a silent cinema dominated by the emotionalism of D.W. Griffith and Chaplin.' *(Brian Case, Time Out, 1989)*

MIXED:

'Clever, but a bore . . . Yet it must be admitted that in the course of the wanderings . . . one is every now and again confronted with a flash that is fired with imagination, and then on other occasions a bit of photography that is as soft and seductive as a Turner study.' *(Mordaunt Hall, New York Times)*

ANTI:

'[A] strangely jagged, uneven torso of a film.' *(Ian Christie, London Film Festival Brochure, 1989)*

'Watching it today can seem like hard work.' *(Geoff Andrews, Time Out)*

OCTOPUSSY: *see BOND* SERIES.

ODD COUPLE, THE

CT: 6 AV: 7.10

1968 US 105 C COMEDY

D Gene Saks
W Neil Simon ☆ AAN from his play

Jack Lemmon ☆ Walter Matthau ☆ John Fiedler Herb Edelman David Sheiner Larry Haines Monica Evans

After unsuccessful marriages, an ill-matched pair of American males try to set up home together.

Lemmon (as the houseproud hypochondriac) is downbeat and real, allowing Walter Matthau (as the slob) the chance to be wilder and funnier, which he gratefully accepts. Neil Simon's gag-packed Broadway comedy didn't need the wide-screen treatment and goes too often for the easy gag, but this is still a very entertaining comedy.

MIXED:

'Both actors go through their usual routines; but as these routines are outstanding by anyone's standards they are well worth re-seeing . . . You may . . . wish [Billy Wilder] had been on hand to spruce up the visual side of things.' *(Eric Rhode, Listener)*

'That both [characters] appear to be latent or unconscious homosexuals is not exactly helpful to the comedy, though Mr Simon skates over this aspect with his usual skill . . . There is an intensity or desperation about Mr Lemmon's performance, a coarseness about Mr Matthau's that for me goes against the grain of the comedy, however funny they are now and then.' *(Patrick Gibbs, Daily Telegraph)*

'Dialogue and performances are impeccable, extremely funny and accurate. A brilliant comedy, in fact; and I laughed a lot despite ungratefully wishing that it would break out of its highly polished shell and become something more.' *(James Price, Spectator)*

PRO:

'Jack Lemmon as the Saran-wrapped, fanatical argument against toilet training turns in his best performance since *The Apartment*, and Walter Matthau eclipses his achievement in *The Fortune Cookie* . . . Paramount has a hit and laughs will ring to the sound of coin.' *(Hollywood Reporter)*

'A Manhattan-slick crackle of wisecracks almost from beginning to end, delivered and directed . . . with masterly timing.' *(David Nathan, Sun)*

'The funniest thing around . . . A gloriously funny performance by Walter Matthau, an almost equally good one by Jack Lemmon.' *(Barry Norman, Daily Mail)*

'Wise, witty, perceptive, and hilarious.' *(Judith Crist)*

ODD MAN OUT

CT: 7 AV: 9.00

(aka *Gang War)*

1947 GB 115 BW THRILLER

D Carol Reed ☆
W F.L. Green R.C. Sherriff from Green's novel

James Mason ☆ Robert Newton Kathleen Ryan Robert Beatty William Hartnell F.J. McCormick Fay Compton Cyril Cusack

A wounded IRA gunman (James Mason) goes on the run in Belfast.

A marvellously atmospheric, well acted chase thriller which shows Reed's mastery of light and sound. Fergus McDonnell's editing was rightly Oscar-nominated, but credit is also due to the Australian cinematographer, Robert Krasker, who shot *Brief Encounter* for David Lean and *Henry V* for Olivier. Unfortunately, the script's arty, allegorical, mystical overtones gradually take over, at the expense of characterization, credibility and pace. It's difficult in the end to understand the point of it all.

PRO:

'Carol Reed, who has more pace than any other director working in this country, has given to the scenes of chase a brilliance of action which dazzles . . . The fast-moving images are in themselves beautiful: erratic shadows spinning along lamp-lit walls, children playing in the shining dark night streets; but amid the poetry of light and shadow, the drama of the tumbling elaborate fights which Mr Reed handles so surely, the central movement is never lost from sight. Sound is used with unusual descriptive effect: the alarm bell, the dog yapping after the wounded man, the musty silence in the air-raid shelter with the children's voices shrilling in the distance and the small hollow thump as the little girl's ball bounces in. But again the whole complex of sound is directed towards a single narrative end: the clock striking the quarters, the ship hooting, delicately remind us of the shortening of time, the impossible margin for escape.' *(Dilys Powell)*

'The best British film since *Brief Encounter*.' *(Roger Manvell, Cinema)*

'Makes Hollywood chatter ridiculous and lifts our art and industry to a pinnacle. At the end there was silence. No clapping. No talking . . . A thousand people got up and walked out . . . Like zombies . . . The women were crying . . . They had seen a very great film . . . the best film that has ever been made in Britain and clearly in the company of the best half-dozen in the world.' *(Paul Holt, Daily Express)*

'One of the best of recent British imports. Here is a

play that is completely free of the distortions and exaggerations of American films, one which devotes itself to dramatic effect and the shadings of characterization rather than to the building up of a star role.' *(Fortnight)*

'One of the best acted, most technically accomplished movies ever made.' *(Philip French, 1984)*

'An imaginative, surrealistic and occasionally slightly overheated thriller that explores one of Reed's favourite themes of a lone protagonist caught in a situation over which he has no control and which he must struggle . . . to overcome . . . One of the rare masterpieces of British cinema.' *(Allan Hunter & Kenny Mathieson, Movie Classics, 1992)*

MIXED:

'It might well have been a great film, for Carol Reed's direction sparkles and the camerawork is brilliant. But it has not been cut ruthlessly enough . . . Mason's part is largely inarticulate.' *(Noel Whitcomb, Daily Mirror)*

'I could willingly have been deprived of some of the passages between Father Tom and the girl (Kathleen Ryan); and one or two other short sequences, notably that wherein Mason, in his delirium, quotes from the New Testament, jarred.' *(Richard Winnington)*

'The early reels are exciting and beautiful – purely in movie terms, they are the best – yet they fail all but entirely to communicate the revolutionary edge that is so well got in F.L. Green's novel; in that respect John Ford's *The Informer* was better . . . In the later reels the film, like the novel, tries for broader and broader allegory and phantasmagoria, but much as I respect this boldness, I don't think it succeeds. The story seems merely to ramify too much, to go on too long, and at its unluckiest to go arty. Most unfortunately the central character, effectively yet monotonously played by James Mason, is given too little remaining life of his own. He has virtually no will or mind or strength left but almost from the beginning is just a football, deflated so far that even its kicking around by the rest of the cast is rather soggy . . . The tone of pity for man is much too close to self-pity.' *(James Agee, Nation)*

OF HUMAN BONDAGE CT: 5 AV: 6.67

1934 US 83 BW DRAMA/ROMANCE

D John Cromwell
W Lester Cohen from W. Somerset Maugham's novel

Leslie Howard ✗ Bette Davis ☆ Frances Dee Reginald Owen Reginald Denny Kay Johnson Alan Hale

A club-footed medical student (Leslie Howard) marries the Cockney waitress he loves (Bette Davis), but she is unfaithful to him.

Creaky drama which is drearily directed and suffers from the fact that Howard's character is a wimp – you find yourself siding with the villain of the piece (Davis), which is not at all what Maugham intended (the central male character is based on Maugham himself). Davis took on a role which had been turned down as too unsympathetic by Katharine Hepburn, Ann Harding and Irene Dunne; and part of the venom in her performance may arise from the fact that she found her co-star arrogant and stand-offish. Although Davis's cockney accent wavers, the power and range of her performance, from youthful trollop to syphilitic wreck, makes this a famous *tour de force*. The film lost $45,000 at the box office and Davis failed to be nominated for an Oscar as Best Actress, but this was the picture which made her reputation and paved the way for future Academy Awards. Both the 1946 and 1964 remakes are inferior.

'Leslie Howard tries hard to mellow his assignment. But somehow he misses at times because the script is too much against him. Perhaps Bette Davis is to blame. She plays her free 'n' easy vamp too well, so that it negates any audience sympathy for Howard.' *(Variety)*

'A totally obtuse concoction, serving only to demonstrate how untalented an actress Bette Davis was before she perfected those camp mannerisms.' *(John Simon, 1967)*

'Static, claustrophobic and uninterestingly acted by Howard.' *(Danny Peary)*

'If the very power of her performance severely unbalances the film, it remains a monstrous exercise in character creation the like of which Hollywood was not to see again until Marlon Brando imported the Method style in the 1950s. Davis reached the same ends as Brando by comparable means.' *(Alexander Walker, 1992)*

'Most people believe that *Of Human Bondage* was my first picture although I had made twenty-one films before it.' *(Bette Davis)*

OF MICE AND MEN AAN CT: 6 AV: 7.60

1939 US 107 BW DRAMA

D Lewis Milestone ☆
W Eugene Solow ✓ from John Steinbeck's novel

Burgess Meredith ☆ Lon Chaney Jr ☆ Betty Field ☆ Charles Bickford Roman Bohnen Bob Steele Noah Beery Jr

Two ranch-hands – one of them (Lon Chaney Jr) simple – try to find work in California during the Depression.

A depressing story is enlivened by three outstanding performances. Milestone directs self-effacingly but with emotional power, greatly assisted by Aaron Copland's Oscar-nominated score. Gary Sinise's 1992 remake is competent but uninspired, and many find

John Malkovich's impersonation of Lenny too actorish.

ANTI:

'We noted but one flaw in Mr Milestone's direction: his refusal to hush the off-screen musicians when Candy's old dog was being taken outside to be shot. A metronome, anything, would have been better than modified Hearts and Flowers.' *(Frank S. Nugent, New York Times)*

PRO:

'Perhaps the biggest compliment one can pay Lewis Milestone is to say that his direction is not noticeable when you see this film for the first time . . . The second time through you notice particularly his imaginative use of sound.' *(Documentary News Letter)*

'Vibrantly sympathetic direction strips development of intrusive detail . . . Many arresting scenes and moments of tension . . . Terrifying climax; tragic finale. Fine acting . . . First-class production values.' *(Today's Cinema)*

'An improvement both on the book and the play, first because the sentimentality . . . is less noticeable in the film, and secondly because the camera, brilliantly handled, gives great authenticity to the general atmosphere.' *(New Statesman)*

'Milestone has used, with positive genius, just those elements special to the screen which will heighten the general tension of the story without destroying its unity . . . An object lesson in good film making.' *(Basil Wright, Spectator)*

'A beautifully directed and moving picture. Lon Chaney Jr gives the film its great moments.' *(MFB)*

OFFICIAL STORY, THE AAN CT: 7 AV: 7.20

(aka *Official Version, The; La Historia Official*)

1985 Argentina 110 C THRILLER/DRAMA/ FOREIGN

D Luis Puenzo ☆
W Luis Puenzo Aída Bortnik ☆

Héctor Alterio Chela Ruiz Hugo Arana Norma Aleandro ☆ Chunchuna Villafañe Patricio Contreras Guillermo Battaglia María-Luisa Robledo Analío Castro ☆

A teacher (Norma Aleandro) becomes more and more disturbed as she suspects the sinister origins of her adopted child (Analio Castro).

An excellent Argentinian thriller about life under the sinister and corrupt regime of General Galtieri. Like the American film *Missing*, it tells a story of an ordinary, middle-class person – superbly portrayed by Aleandro – who becomes politicized. Unlike many other films with a political message and a feminist slant, the unfolding of the narrative seems to spring from character, not contrivance. Though slow by Hollywood standards, it's a spectacular debut from Puenzo.

MIXED:

'A serious, intelligent, well-acted film which fails quite to hold one's attention . . . There is a failure to gather pace and the ending is melodrama.' *(Michael Wigan, Scotsman)*

'If the message is that people, the middle classes too, have to learn through their own experience, it is a poor one – even for a popular film, when the film works so well on every other level.' *(Manny, Spare Rib)*

PRO:

'Towers over everything this week . . . Puenzo has a style devoid of flashy mannerisms . . . The integrity of the acting is exceptional.' *(George Perry, Sunday Times)*

'Outstanding.' *(Richard Barkley, Sunday Express)*

'Measured and oblique.' *(Philip French, Observer)*

'A powerhouse film, all the more shocking for resting its case upon quiet emotion.' *(Chris Peachment, Mail on Sunday)*

'The film's business is not to unwind a plot but to frame a parable about the individual's relationship to totalitarianism. And that is subtly written on the lovely face of Aleandro as she descends from serenity and self-possession to a final, harrowing acknowledgement that her privileged life was based on willed blindness, that her future is as an emotional *desaparecido*. Hers is a performance that one knows will not be forgotten, much as one would like to try to erase it, and all that it stands for, from memory.' (Richard Schickel)

OFFRET: *see* SACRIFICE, THE.

OH, AMELIA!: *see* KEEP AN EYE ON AMELIA.

OH! FOR A MAN: *see* WILL SUCCESS SPOIL ROCK HUNTER?

OH, MR PORTER! CT: 7 AV: 9.13

1937 GB 84 BW COMEDY

D Marcel Varnel ☆
W Marriott Edgar Val Guest J.O.C. Orton ☆ from Frank Launder's story

Will Hay ☆ Moore Marriott ☆ Graham Moffatt ☆ Dave O'Toole Dennis Wyndham

Stationmaster (Will Hay) in the backwoods of Ireland tries to discover why previous occupants of his job have disappeared or gone bonkers.

Enjoyable comic yarn with the three leads on top form. The script is witty, the final chase a classic.

'Here is something entirely British, which can be set

in independent glory over against the vaudeville and slapstick tradition of America . . . Gainsborough Pictures have found the formula for transmuting the magic of Will Hay . . . [to] the screen.' *(Basil Wright , Spectator)*

'The banter is great, the teamwork greater still and the technical presentation expert.' *(Kine Weekly)*

'Riotous comedy in which the Will Hay trio supply slapstick and satire in their inimitable style.' *(Kine Weekly, 1947, on the reissue)*

'Immortal comedy . . . The chase climax, in which they round up some gun-runners, is hilarious.' *(Shipman)*

'A vintage Hay comedy that is almost certainly his best.' *(RAE Pickard, Dictionary of 1000 Best Films, 1971)*

OH, WHAT A LOVELY WAR! CT: 5 AV: 5.90

1969 GB 132 (GB)/144 (US) C MUSICAL/WAR

D Richard Attenborough ✗
W Len Deighton (who removed his name from the credits) from Joan Littlewood and Charles Chilton's stage musical

Ralph Richardson ✓ Meriel Forbes Kenneth More John Clements Paul Daneman Joe Melia Jack Hawkins John Mills Maggie Smith ✓ Laurence Olivier ✓ Edward Fox ✓ John Gielgud ✓ Susannah York Vanessa Redgrave Phyllis Calvert

Men go to their deaths in World War I.

Richard Attenborough's first film as a director is a brash, flashy filming of the Joan Littlewood stage success, and satirizes the British upper classes who sent young men to their deaths at the start of the century. There are good moments including a tremendous last shot, but mainly this is a plod. Some immaculate performances cannot disguise the crudity and over-familiarity of the anti-war message.

PRO:

'Dedicated, exhilarating, shrewd, mocking, funny, emotional, witty, poignant and technically brilliant.' *(Variety)*

'A baronial splendor in which actor Richard Attenborough makes a thrilling directorial début . . . As a hilarious bit of peace propaganda, it is born out of pacifist pride and an obvious contempt for Establishment greed. And it has one of the most gorgeous closing shots I've ever seen in any motion picture, as the surviving female members of a family of war dead dressed in lacy white crinolines walk through a military battleground marked by thousands of white crosses. A helicopter rises from the ground and the camera pans down on the battlefield as a military chorus sings Jerome Kern's "They'll Never Believe Me". It's a scene I'll never forget and *Oh! What a Lovely War* is a movie I intend to see again and again.' *(Rex Reed)*

'We come away chastened and ashamed of having laughed so much at a holocaust so palpably beyond a joke . . . If [the film] all adds up in retrospect to a muddle of satire, protest and seaside-postcard fun that leaves you torn between laughter and tears, it vividly reflects the muddle of war itself and is accordingly a masterpiece.' *(Cecil Wilson, Daily Mail)*

'I found it impossible to restrain my tears.' *(Dilys Powell)*

MIXED:

'A big elaborate, sometimes realistic film whose elephantine physical proportions and often brilliant all-star cast simply overwhelm the material with a surfeit of good intentions . . . A musical entertainment that has grown too big for its puttees.' *(Vincent Canby, New York Times)*

ANTI:

'A naive, sentimental, populist affair, using many (too many) clever devices yet making the same old simplistic statements.' *(John Simon)*

Its heart is surely in the right place, and it makes a conscientious attempt to find the cinematic equivalents of Miss Littlewood's theater piece. But it doesn't work. It doesnt work at all . . . I could weep, for *Oh! What a Lovely War* was one of those experiences I have always wanted to share with as many people as possible. And now it's been ruined. Looking at this monstrosity, will anyone believe in its original greatness? *(Richard Schickel, Life)*

'This musical lampoon is meant to stir your sentiments, evoke nostalgia, and make you react to the obscenity of battles and bloodshed and apparently it does all that for some people . . . Attenborough has a stately, measured approach – just what the 50 musical numbers don't need.' *(Pauline Kael, 1977)*

'An overlong and rarely cinematic musical satire that ladles its anti-war message on by the bucketload.' *(Time Out, 1984)*

'Sir Richard ("I'm-going-to-attack-the-Establishment-fifty-years-after-it's-dead") Attenborough [is guilty of] caricature, a sense of righteous self-satisfaction, and repetition [which] all undermine the impact of the film.' *(Ken Russell, 1993)*

OKLAHOMA! CT: 8 AV: 6.67

1955 US 143 C MUSICAL/WESTERN

D Fred Zinnemann
W Sonya Levien William Ludwig from Richard Rodgers and Oscar Hammerstein's musical

Gordon Macrae Shirley Jones Rod Steiger

Gloria Grahame ☆ Gene Nelson Eddie Albert Charlotte Greenwood

Boys (Gordon Macrae, Gene Nelson) meet girls (Shirley Jones, Gloria Grahame), lose girls, win them back again.

Actually filmed in Arizona, this is probably the only musical in which the villain (Rod Steiger) and comic female juvenile (Gloria Grahame) are more sympathetic than the leading couple (Gordon Macrae and Shirley Jones), who come across as grossly insensitive. However, the parade of Rodgers and Hammerstein songs is of such breathtakingly high quality that one can hardly complain. Robert Surtees's cinematography and the editing by Gene Ruggiero and George Boemler were Oscar-nominated. The score, not surprisingly, won an Academy Award. Performed with verve, this is a classic musical.

ANTI:

'[Nine years after the stage show] the novelty has worn off . . . Between the songs and the flirtations there is too much time . . . to realize how thin the story has become on a wide, wide screen; how dull rather than engagingly homespun the humour seems when stretched.' *(Harold Conway, Daily Sketch)*

'So pleasantly straight-forward on the stage . . . in its picture form it has an air of magniloquence hardly suited to the simple rusticity of its theme. The principal reason for this pomposity is that it was filmed in something called Todd-AO . . . This latest contribution to optical shenanigans involves 64mm film and a curved screen 50 feet wide and 25 ft high. While these proportions are useful for portraying vistas they are rather excessive when the screen is devoted to close-ups. It is quite unnerving to have a face suddenly loom up before you with every pore looking like a crater.' *(John McCarten, New Yorker)*

'He [Zinnemann] was forced to use the cumbersome Todd-AO process for Oklahoma, and either demonstrated a lack of affinity for the musical form or was hampered by the presences of Rodgers and Hammerstein, as well as an uncongenial cast that included Rod Steiger, Gloria Grahame, and Shirley Jones. The zest needed for the piece was missing, pictorially fetching as the film turned out to be in some of its moments. The sound track blared out the tunes too stridently, and as in some of Zinnemann's films one receives the impression that the accompanying musical score is not under his supervision, and is added as underscoring to what is felt might be too delicate for mass consumption.' *(Hollis Alpert, 1962)*

'Zinnemann's literalism coudn't be more inappropriate for this sophisticated hokum.' *(Scheuer)*

MIXED:

'There are times when the songs and dances blend together with a kind of noisy charm.' *(John McCarten, New Yorker)*

'The orchestra, facing melodies played to exhaustion and knowing it, seems to have said, "Well, anyway, we can play them louder than ever before".' *(Fred Majdalany, Daily Mail)*

'This is not a film musical. It is a wide-screen record of the stage show. It is good entertainment . . . It should have been better.' *(Peter Baker, S & S)*

PRO:

'A perfect, beautiful, fresh and melodiously flowing thing, with a superb cast.' *(New York Times)*

'The tunes ring out with undiminished delight. The characters pulsate with spirit. The Agnes De Mille choreography makes the play literally leap.' *(Variety)*

'A visit to [the film] will supply reason enough for the belief that a musical like [this] can occur only once in a very long while.' *(The Times)*

'Only utter nasties will be able to resist the simple pleasures of this 145-minute musical bonanza.' *(Judith Crist)*

OKTYARBR: *see* OCTOBER.

OLD DARK HOUSE, THE CT: 7 AV: 8.33

1932 US 70/74 BW HORROR/COMEDY

D James Whale ☆
W Benn W. Levy R.C. Sherriff from J.B. Priestley's novel *Benighted*

Melvyn Douglas ☆ Charles Laughton ☆ Raymond Massey ☆ Boris Karloff ☆ Ernest Thesiger ☆ Eva Moore ☆ Gloria Stuart Lilian Bond Brember Wills John Dudgeon

Tourists in Wales find shelter in house full of weirdos.

Director Whale's witty, campy sense of humour is ideally suited to this horror comedy, also memorable for Arthur Edeson's spooky cinematography. The plot is not exactly plausible, nor are the characters – but an enthusiastic cast makes the shenanigans go with a swing. William Castle's 1962 remake is nowhere near as enjoyable.

ANTI:

'Somewhat inane.' *(Variety)*

MIXED:

'Not first-rate but I though it much better than *Frankenstein*. The English players are nearly all excellent.' *(Daily Telegraph)*

'There are by no means so many ragged edges as are usual in such adaptations.' *(The Times)*

PRO:

'Like most of its type, this eerie thriller is somewhat

vague and incredible and wholly fantastic; but there is this difference – it is exceedingly cleverly acted and characterized and the direction is quite brilliant.' *(Photoplay)*

'To be warmly recommended. Not only is it really thrilling, but the characterization, the dramatic vigour, the genuine suspense and shock of it are all in the first grade of achievement . . . The only possible criticism of its faults could be that it is so packed with frightfulness as to leave the imagination no further scope.' *(Sunday Times)*

'A confidence trick worked with cynical humour by a brilliant technician.' *(John Baxter, 1968)*

'*A jeu d'esprit* in which comedy of manners is edged into tragedy of horrors, the film never puts a foot wrong.' *(Tom Milne, MFB, 1978)*

OLD MAID, THE

CT: 6 AV: 7.38

1939 US 95 BW DRAMA

D Edmund Goulding ☆
W Casey Robinson from Zoe Akins's play based on Edith Wharton's novel

Bette Davis ☆ Miriam Hopkins ☆ George Brent Jane Bryan Donald Crisp Louise Fazenda Henry Stephenson Jerome Cowan William Lundigan Rand Brooks

An unmarried mother (Bette Davis), whose suitor has died in the American Civil War, hands over her child (who grows up to be Jane Bryan) to her married cousin (Miriam Hopkins), who proceeds to turn her daughter and prospective suitors against her.

Lay in plenty of handkerchiefs for this weepie, based on a novel by Edith Wharton, which offers ample opportunities for dramatic conflict between Misses Davis and Hopkins, every one of which is gratefully seized.

ANTI:

'Stagey, sombre and generally confusing fare. Must aim for the femme trade chiefly.' *(Variety)*

'Bette Davis doesn't have much talent for masochism. When she attempts the sacrificial-mother roles that were meat and potatoes to many a trouper, she builds the character so painstakingly that she loses her flair and turns mealy . . . Full of tight-lipped renunciation, Davis gives what might be called a creditable performance; the picture isn't bad, but it trudges along and never becomes exciting.' *(Pauline Kael, 1977)*

PRO:

'It is better than average, and sticks heroically to its problem, forsaking all delights and filling a whole laundry bag with wet and twisted handkerchiefs.' *(Otis Ferguson)*

OLIVER! AAW

CT: 8 AV: 8.46

1968 GB 153 C MUSICAL

D Carol Reed ☆ AAW
W Vernon Harris AAN from Lionel Bart's musical adapted from Charles Dickens's novel *Oliver Twist*

Ron Moody ☆ AAN Shani Wallis Oliver Reed Harry Secombe Mark Lester Jack Wild ☆ AAN Hugh Griffith Joseph O'Conor Peggy Mount Leonard Rossiter

In Victorian London, an orphan boy (Mark Lester) falls in with a gang of junior thieves.

Ron Moody is a memorable Fagin; and the songs are more rousing, melodic and witty than Bart's detractors are prepared to admit. There's plenty to admire in this film, which is good family entertainment and won six Oscars – three of them for choreography (Onna White), musical direction (John Green) and sound (Shepperton Studio Sound Department). Oswald Morris's cinematography, Phyllis Dalton's costumes and Ralph Kemplen's editing were also nominated. The problem is that it's all more impressive if you haven't read Dickens's book, which works on a much more profound, dark level of social observation.

PRO:

'[A] magnificent picture . . . brilliantly directed.' *(F.H. Samuel, Jewish Chronicle)*

'A nice, big movie musical about which it is hard to say anything of special interest to the reader or even to oneself.' *(John Simon)*

'The sets . . . are delightfully imaginative and the dancing is the sort of energetic jumping-about one expects. What is much, much more, [it] is splendidly acted as well as sung.' *(Ann Pacey, Sun)*

'After seeing [producer] John Woolf's screen adaptation the original [stage musical] now seems in retrospect to have been a beautiful blueprint, a working drawing that has just blossomed into life . . . [The] film is overwhelming in its vitality, impressive in its performances, and thoroughly delightful in its humour.' *(Ian Christie, Daily Express)*

MIXED:

'Not half bad: roughly five-eighths at last count.' *(New Statesman)*

'The best thing about [it] is John Box's production design . . . The most trying thing is a degree of sound amplification.' *(Spectator)*

'Personally I would like to heap a lot of praise on to Sir Carol Reed, Oswald Morris, and John Box. Between them they have ensured that the look of the thing is magnificent . . . The performances are slightly variable in quality.' *(Michael Billington, Illustrated London News)*

'The scenes of brutality do not sit comfortably

alongside the comedy scenes and there are too many longueurs between numbers – but for all that we have a good ethnic rough and tumble and a subtle use of colour which enhances the mood of every scene, be it sunny or sombre. And not a whiff of Hollywood anywhere.' *(Ken Russell, 1993)*

ANTI:

'Lionel Bart's score is lumpy, tired, and not very good.' *(Rex Reed)*

'From *The Third Man* to *Oliver!* is a pretty vertiginous collapse, even for twenty years in the British film industry. Reed is craftsman enough to make an efficient family entertainment out of Lionel Bart's musical, but not artist enough to put back any of Dickens' teeth which Bart had so assiduously drawn.' *(Steve Grant, Time Out)*

OLIVER TWIST — CT: 8 AV: 9.46

1948 GB 105 BW DRAMA

D David Lean ☆
W David Lean Stanley Haynes from Charles Dickens's novel *Oliver Twist*

Robert Newton ☆ Alec Guinness ☆ Kay Walsh Francis L. Sullivan Henry Stephenson Mary Clare John Howard Davies ☆ Josephine Stuart Henry Edwards Ralph Truman Anthony Newley ☆ Diana Dors ☆

In Victorian London, an orphan boy (John Howard Davies) falls in with a gang of junior thieves.

Dark, nightmarish and far more cinematic than Carol Reed's musical version, this film is second only to David Lean's *Great Expectations* as a filming of Dickens. The acting is tremendous throughout. Some may feel that Alec Guinness's portrayal of Fagin is anti-semitic, and the film's American release was deferred until 1951 after protests by Jewish pressure-groups; but Guinness is faithful to the character that Dickens wrote. Some sequences, including the opening storm and the murder of Nancy, have a poetic grandeur; and Lean's style – a mixture of German expressionism and film noir – is wonderfully effective.

ANTI:

'The character of Fagin is grossly exaggerated . . . and [it is no wonder that] many still find the portrayal objectionable.' *(New York Journal-American, 1951, about first unexpurgated showing)*

MIXED:

'*Oliver Twist* suffers, I suspect, from the very care and precision with which it has been made: from its very skill. There is no room in it for a mistake, and none for the magnificent outbursts of rage, grief and passion which are the essence of Dickens. Like its predecessor *Great Expectations* it is always admirable, often beautiful, and sometimes a shade cold.' *(Dilys Powell)*

'As one anticipated, a thoroughly expert piece of movie entertainment. As such I can guarantee it. In any deeper aspect the film profoundly disappoints. *Great Expectations*, a far more uneven film, touched higher levels of poetry and drama. My impression is that Lean has become imprisoned by technique.' *(Richard Winnington)*

PRO:

'Within [its] limits . . . it is a painstaking and faithful version of the original which will be generally enjoyed and appreciated. Alec Guiness . . . is excellent.' *(MFB)*

'It is vastly clever – harsh, ugly, sly, unwholesome, yet curiously appealing . . . Society is indicated as the real villain.' *(Bosley Crowther)*

'An impressive picture, complete with fine acting. Alec Guinness's Fagin is as Dickens painted him – conniving and treacherous.' *(New York Daily News)*

'A brilliant, fascinating movie, no less a classic than the Dickens novel which it brings to life.' *(Time)*

'From the movie's stormy prologue to its climactic rooftop chase, Lean propels Dickens's tale of a crime-buffeted orphan with stylized sequences that connect in electric arcs. He surrounds his limpid, poignant Oliver, John Howard Davies, with a terrifying and delightful rogues' gallery, including Robert Newton as Bill Sikes and a young Anthony Newley as the Artful Dodger. The movie's influence on Carol Reed's great movie musical *Oliver!* is evident when Alec Guinness, a magnificently scurvy Fagin, transforms a pickpocketing lesson into a comic ballet.' *(Michael Sragow)*

OLVIDADOS, LOS:

see YOUNG AND THE DAMNED, THE.

OMEN, THE — CT: 6 AV: 5.33

1976 US 111 C HORROR

D Richard Donner
W David Seltzer

Gregory Peck Lee Remick David Warner Billie Whitelaw Leo McKern Harvey Stevens Patrick Troughton Anthony Nicholls Martin Benson

American diplomat (Gregory Peck) and wife (Lee Remick) raise Anti-Christ.

Disliked to an almost pathological degree by the critics but appreciated by audiences, this is a professionally made, well constructed little chiller with an atmospheric score by Jerry Goldsmith which won an Oscar. There were three sequels, of which only *Damien – Omen II* (1978) is watchable.

PRO:

'Richard Donner's direction is taut. Players all are strong.' *(Variety)*

'Farfetched in subject matter, but not far out in its

handling of it, *The Omen* speaks well of the Devil – and of the virtues of solid commercial craftsmanship.' *(Time)*

'Large scale, large budget and sensational horror opus, among whose set pieces is the justly famous decapitation of David Warner. It is less scary than it might be, possibly due to its starry cast and the leaden acting of [Gregory] Peck but deserves its box office success.' *(Alan Frank)*

ANTI:

'There seems to exist a special kennel in Hollywood where pictures that were artistic dogs but popular successes are crossbred for the delectation of the great unwashed, and the even keener delight of the money men. Possibly the highest stud fees of the moment go to that champion hellhound, *The Exorcist*, and the prize bitch, *Rosemary's Baby*, whose latest whelp, *The Omen*, is certainly all dog from snout to tail . . . Nowhere can you glimpse a hint of subtlety or credibility . . . As for Peck, he worries and suffers as nobly as only a piece of granite can . . . Most annoying, however, is the music by that pretentious hack Jerry Goldsmith, who has cannibalized Stravinsky without crediting him.' *(John Simon)*

'Its horrors are not horrible, its terrors are not terrifying, its violence is ludicrous.' *(Richard Eder, New York Times)*

'A dumb and largely dull movie . . . The latest serving of deviled ham.' *(Jack Kroll, Newsweek)*

'Crude, derivative, heavy-handed . . . There is something sleazy about the whole enterprise partly because of its cold commercial calculation, and partly because of its reliance on excessively gory shock effects . . . The climax of *The Omen* is particularly unsavory.' *(Stephen Farber, New West)*

'Although *The Omen* is pretty beastly, its treatment of The Beast is superficial and silly . . . A pathetic attempt to sound ominous.' *(James M. Martin, Coast)*

'Stick a pin in this nonsensical balloon at any point and the story will deflate.' *(William Wolf, Cue)*

'I did it strictly for the money. I was flat broke . . . I do find it horrifying to find how many people actually believe all this silliness.' *(David Seltzer, author of the original screenplay)*

ON GOLDEN POND AAN CT: 5 AV: 7.14

1981 US 109 C DRAMA

D Mark Rydell ✗ AAN
W Ernest Thompson ✗ AAW from his play

Henry Fonda ☆ AAW Katharine Hepburn ☆ AAW
Jane Fonda ☆ AAN Doug McKeon Dabney Coleman

A grown-up woman (Jane Fonda) comes to terms with the behaviour of her crotchety father (Henry Fonda).

There's something creepy, parasitical about the way the script feeds off the well-known tensions between Fonda *pére et fille*; and this, combined with the chocolate-box cinematography and a willingness to avoid real emotion and settle for sentiment, make this popular and highly acclaimed film impossible to watch without a sense of unease. The acting is fine, of course, but seems to have been wasted on a meretricious screenplay. The film was Oscar-nominated for its music (Dave Grusin), editing (Robert L. Wolfe) and cinematography (Billy Williams).

PRO:

'The unbridled joy of [it] lies in seeing . . . two of America's greatest screen actors, working together for the first time in the twilight of their careers, yet still with all the vigour and virility that marked theirs as exceptional talents.' *(David Castell, Sunday Telegraph)*

'A thoroughly nice film made in rather nasty times . . . I sniff Oscars in the wind.' *(Derek Malcolm, Guardian)*

'A treasure for many reasons, but the best one, I think, is that I could believe it. I could believe in its major characters and their relationships, and in the things they felt for one another, and there were moments when the movie was witness to human growth and change. I left the theater feeling good and warm, and with a certain resolve to try to mend my own relationships and learn to start listening better.' *(Roger Ebert)*

MIXED:

'The performance of Fonda senior is strong and gritty enough to carry [the film] through some cloying contrivances.' *(Geoff Brown, The Times)*

'Everything about [it] has a golden touch . . . Golden syrup? Dangerously near, at times, but very fine performances all round just about prevent any mawkishness.' *(Albert Jacobs, Sunday Mirror)*

'Moments of truth survive some cloying contrivance. Rydell directs on bended knee.' *(S & S)*

ANTI:

'Martin Knelman, the theater critic for Toronto's *Saturday Night* dubbed [the play] the "geriatric *Our Town*." The movie is a lot worse . . . In this movie, love means having to do a back flip.' *(Michael Sragow, Rolling Stone)*

'There really are no sparks.' *(Carlos Clarens, SoHo News)*

'Two of Hollywood's best-loved veterans deserve a far better swansong than this sticky confection.' *(Rod McShane, Time Out)*

'The kind of uplifting twaddle that traffics heavily in rather basic symbols: the gold light on the pond stands for the sunset of life, and so on and on.' *(Pauline Kael)*

ON HER MAJESTY'S SECRET SERVICE:

see BOND SERIES.

ON THE BEACH CT: 4 AV: 5.89

1959 US 134 BW SF/DRAMA

D Stanley Kramer ✗
W John Paxton from Nevil Shute's novel

Gregory Peck Ava Gardner Fred Astaire ☆
Anthony Perkins Donna Anderson John Tate

The last people on earth struggle to survive after Armageddon.

There are good things in this film: Fred Astaire's performance, for one. But its hard to see why this incredibly turgid, cliché-ridden, melodramatic film once garnered the critical acclaim that it did. Some critics may have been reluctant to pen an adverse review, for fear of seeming to be in favour of nuclear war. Increasingly, some have ventured to suggest that the film is not a masterpiece.

PRO:

'It may be that some years from now we can look back and say that *On The Beach* is the movie that saved the world.' *(Linus Pauling)*

'An extraordinary movie . . . the year's most devastating picture, and one of the best.' *(Newsweek)*

'The great merit of this picture, aside from its entertainment qualities, is the fact that it carries a passionate conviction that man is worth saving, after all.' *(Bosley Crowther)*

Never have I been so profoundly frightened by the Cinema's fleeting shadows as I have been by this remarkable piece of propaganda . . . it is horrible, terrifying and shocking.' *(F & F)*

'Pretty disturbing . . . also well acted and extremely well made: the horror of the situation dawns on you quietly and naturally, the process by which humanity is gradually snuffed out is implied with great skill. There is brilliant detail . . . Intermittently exciting and far less glum than you might think.' *(Dilys Powell)*

ANTI:

'Its effect on general audiences, who know they can't do much about the situation anyway, is so blisteringly miserable that it reduces one to a state of feeling "What's the good of anything?" "Why, nothing," the film seems to say.' *(C.A.Lejeune)*

'Lacks depth, shading, above all a thoughtful and intelligent viewpoint . . . The characters remain little more than spokesmen for timid ideas and Salvation Army slogans, their emotions hired from a Hollywood prop room; which is all pretty disturbing in a film about nothing less than the end of the world.' *(Robert Vas)*

'A Hollywood vision of the end of the world . . . A sentimental sort of radiation romance, in which the customers are considerately spared any scenes of realistic horror . . . Aside from its sentimentality, the worst of the films offenses is its unreality.' *(Time)*

'One wonders, for example, at the complete absence of corpses, both in the periscope survey of San Francisco and, later, in the exploration of a San Diego power plant . . . And, although it is difficult to imagine just how ordinary folks would react to the knowledge of certain death in the very near future, it is equally difficult to believe that all would remain as calm and self-possessed as the people seen here . . . There is no looting, no licentiousness, no desperate last-chance fling.' *(Arthur Knight, Saturday Review)*

'Heavy going indeed, as Mr Liberal Conscience himself, Stanley Kramer, wades turgidly through Nevil Shute's story.' *(Geoff Andrew, Time Out)*

'Pompous and trivial at the same time, overwritten and insufficiently tense . . . Kramer makes the end of the world antiseptic.' *(Bill Mitchell, Keep Watching The Skies!)*

'Many of us preferred to watch *The Tingler* and *The Wasp Woman*.' *(Psychotronic Enclopaedia of Film)*

ON THE TOWN CT: 8 AV: 8.69

1949 US 98 C MUSICAL/COMEDY/ROMANCE

D Gene Kelly Stanley Donen ☆
W Adolph Green Betty Comden from Comden, Green and Leonard Bernstein's musical play from Jerome Robbins's ballet *Fancy Free*.

Gene Kelly ☆ Frank Sinatra ☆ Jules Munshin ☆
Vera-Ellen ☆ Betty Garrett ☆ Ann Miller ☆
Tom Dugan Florence Bates Alice Pearce

Three sailors (Gene Kelly, Frank Sinatra, Jules Munshin) go on 24-hour shore leave in New York City.

Although the songs (music by Leonard Bernstein) are not of the highest quality, this ranks as one of the great Musicals by virtue of its energy, high spirits, and the fact that it broke new ground by escaping from the Hollywood sound stage. (Several crucial scenes were shot hastily in a week on location in New York City.) Kelly and Donen work well together as a directorial team – their next film was to be the sublime *Singin' in the Rain*. Vera-Ellen and Ann Miller dance wonderfully, while Jules Munshin and Betty Garrett have the funniest lines. Winner of the Oscar for Best Score.

ANTI:

'Its intrinsic merits suffer from a surfeit of stridency, a lack of individual charm. These three American sailors, singing and dancing and wise-cracking and capering their way round New York, with their respective girls pirouetting about them, are a little too brash and noisy for my English ear.' *(Matthew Norgate)*

'Has an undeserved high reputation . . . Its exuberant love of New York seems forced, and most of the numbers are hearty and uninspired.' *(Pauline Kael)*

MIXED:

'The singing and dancing is excellent and almost endless. The comedy sinks to the low level of poking fun at the personal unloveliness of Miss Florence Bates.' *(Evening Standard)*

'Introduces a new era of musical comedy . . . The only thing wrong with it is that the wit of the songs is not quite equal to their intention, and the music is not memorable; but as a design for a musical it is a model for writers in this medium.' *(Daily Mail)*

PRO:

'The best musical since *Forty-Second Street* . . . *On the Town* is based on a stage piece, but the handling of its theme – twenty-four hours' leave in New York for three exuberant sailors – is wholly cinematic. Everything is imagined in terms of movement; the background, with the camera swinging breathlessly after the players, cutting and dissolving from street to street, rooftop to rooftop, joins in the fun; while in the graceful Fred Astaire-Ginger Rogers pieces of the 1930s the dance was part of the film, here the whole film is dance.' *(Dilys Powell)*

'A film that will be enjoyed more than twice.' *(Lindsay Anderson)*

'So exuberant that it threatens at moments to bounce right off the screen.' *(Time)*

'The speed, the vitality, the flashing colour and design, the tricks of timing by which motion is fitted to music, the wit and invention and superlative technical accomplishment make it a really exhilarating experience.' *(Richard Mallett, Punch)*

ON THE WATERFRONT AAW CT: 10 AV: 9.56

1954 US 108 BW DRAMA

D Elia Kazan ☆ AAW
W Budd Schulberg ☆ AAW from Malcolm Johnson's articles

Marlon Brando ☆ AAW Karl Malden ☆ AAN
Lee J. Cobb ☆ AAN Rod Steiger ☆ AAN Pat Henning
Eva Marie Saint ☆ AAW Leif Erickson
James Westerfield Tony Galento Tami Mauriello

A washed-up ex-boxer (Marlon Brando) has to decide whether to squeal on the racketeers who dominate a dockside union.

Marlon Brando gives his most powerful screen performance, in a magnificent melodrama which updated the 1930s gangster picture, mixed it with Method Acting at its best, and applied it to 1950s union racketeering. Boris Kaufman's cinematography, Richard Day's art direction and Gene Milford's editing won Oscars. Leonard Bernstein's score was only nominated, but it is one of the most dramatically effective in the history of cinema.

ANTI:

'Technically, its trouble was an overabundance of fancy work, calling attention to Kazan's virtuosity, but detracting from the ultimate effect of the picture.' *(Richard Schickel, Movies, 1964)*

'There are a few places where Kazan's dexterity fails completely: moving the union men around as a herd is too staged to be convincing. And even good theater doesn't allow for elements that are tossed in without being thought out (the ships owner, an oddly ambiguous abstraction, possibly cartooned in obeisance to the labor-union audience) or tossed in without being felt (the complacent, smiling faces of the priest and the girl at the end – converted, by a deficiency of artistic sensibility, into pure plaster).' *(Pauline Kael, 1965)*

PRO:

'The kind of entertainment which leaves one with the feeling of having just awakened shaken and soaking from an appalling nightmare . . . Under Kazan's expert direction, the movie was photographed right in the setting it concerns . . . This with the foundations of a soundly gripping story, fine attention to the details of authenticity and the wonderfully full portrayals of each performer, gives it its intense bite of truth.' *(Fortnight)*

'A stark and stirring tale of the reawakening of a man's conscience . . . Under Kazan's deft direction the handpicked cast achieves a peak of picturemaking perfection.' *(Jesse Zunser, Cue)*

'Brando's performance . . . is terrific and wholly admirable . . . you will not find more powerful acting on the screen . . . Here is a great picture for those whose stomachs are not squeamish about squalor and bloodshed.' *(Jympson Harmon, Evening News)*

'A violent film? Yes . . . but only so that its [violence] may be condemned.' *(Roy Nash, Star)*

'Marlon Brando is the Rebel of Hollywood, 1954 model . . . Well I have just seen [his] performance in the last picture he made before suspension . . . and with every enthusiasm I cry: Good Luck to the rebel.' *(Harold Conway, Daily Sketch)*

'This is GREAT – I mean that. So many well-directed movies evoke merely the slick, finicky, pernickety click of the cutting-room scissors that it comes as a relief to be half-stunned by a picture like [this] which appears to have been beaten out magnificently on an anvil.' *(Paul Dehn, News Chronicle)*

'Leaning heavily on sensationalism, [*On the Waterfront*] is a medley of items from the Warner Brothers gangland pictures of the 30s, brought up to date. Many ingredients of the classic pattern are present. Yet, because of the inventive direction of Elia Kazan, the formula becomes fresh . . . The casting of Brando and Steiger as brothers is a stroke of genius, since Steiger, new to movies but familiar on TV, has for years been using many of Brando's mannerisms.' *(Steve Sondheim, Films in Review, 1954)*

'There remains Mr Marlon Brando as the inarticulate, struggling hero, who can somehow contrive to touch us with his simplicity, amuse us with his awkwardness, and unnerve us with his brutishness, almost in one hesitant sentence.' *(Derek Granger, Financial Times)*

'Mr Brando is the only actor in the world who can make unintelligibility sound like poetry. Nor is there any other actor I have seen who at one and the same moment can reach for the stars and wallow in the gutter.' *(Evening Standard)*

'[Of Brando] Within the bounds set by the brutal society of this film and others like it there is no one to touch him.' *(Dilys Powell)*

ONCE UPON A TIME IN AMERICA (DIRECTOR'S CUT): CT: 8 AV: 8.71

ONCE UPON A TIME IN AMERICA CT: 4 AV: 8.00

1984 US 227 (director's cut) 147 (original) C DRAMA

D Sergio Leone ☆
W Leonardo Benvenuti Piero de Bernardi Enrico Medioli Franco Arcalli Franco Ferrini Sergio Leone from Harry Grey (David Aaronson's) novel *The Hoods*

Robert De Niro ☆ James Woods ☆ Elizabeth McGovern ☆ Treat Williams Tuesday Weld Burt Young Danny Aiello William Forsythe Jennifer Connelly ✓

Five decades in the lives of four New York gangsters.

The Jewish answer to *The Godfather* benefits from tremendous performances by De Niro, Woods and (although Pauline Kael disagrees) McGovern. Jennifer Connelly is also impressive as the junior version of McGovern. The narrative is sometimes confusing, even in the superior longer version, scenes are unnecessarily protracted, and the overall point is hard to discern; moreover, the observation seems second-hand – all the action seems to be seen through the filter of other gangster movies. Despite these faults, the evocation of ghetto life and some gorgeously shot set-pieces make this epic gangster movie the most highly, and rightly, acclaimed of Leone's films. The short, American version is incomprehensible; the longer, original cut was released elsewhere in the world. All reviews below are of the long version.

'Can you imagine? Here I am, working all my life, doing good work, asking for that chance to play a lead role with a great actor, and promising that I won't let anybody down. Then Sergio Leone calls me and tells me that I have the role of a lifetime, and I say, wonderful. This will be the role that turns my entire career around. Three weeks before release, they have the assistant editor of *Police Academy* chop it to ribbons. I mean, do you think I was suicidal? It got slaughtered by the critics, as it should have. What chance in hell did the studio think the picture was going to have of pleasing the critics when they've already created the political scandal of interfering with a great artist's film? . . . Let's point out that the film did not get one Oscar nomination. I made a great film and they killed it. So I live with what I live with, and they live with what they live with.' *(James Woods)*

ANTI:

'A botched patchwork of moods, verbal clichés and improbabilities.' *(John Coleman, New Statesman)*

'Unnecessarily long – almost every sequence, even those which begin so well, outstays its welcome.' *(Quentin Falk, Daily Mail)*

MIXED:

'A grand, not to say grandiose, work . . . The social analysis is thin, the psychology often naive. There are moments of grossness. But the breadth of vision sweeps us along, and the eye for small intimate detail holds our attention.' *(Philip French, Observer)*

PRO:

'I don't know if it is a masterpiece, but it is certainly Leone's best movie, and it may well be as good a film as anyone will see this year.' *(Richard Roud, Guardian)*

'We have never before seen so ambitious a recreation of the ghetto streets of the 1920's . . . The film is visually thrilling and dramatically absorbing.' *(David Robinson, The Times)*

'To stupendous effect Leone uses what he remembers of Hollywood gangster movies of the Thirties . . . to evoke a grandiose spectacle of a corrupt American dream.' *(Alexander Walker, Standard)*

'There are moments in this movie so breathtakingly daring, so grand, that they're romantically transcendent. When the grown Noodles impresses Deborah by hiring a Long Island oceanfront restaurant out of season, complete with retinue and band, it's a Jazz Age vignette worthy of Fitzgerald. And the director's feeling for the size of his criminals, and the size of their guilty consciences, makes this movie something more. It's an amazing combination of pulp and Proust: Leone's *Remembrance of Crimes Past*.' *(Michael Sragow, Boston Phoenix, 1985)*

'It is, finally, a heart-breaking story of mutual need. By matching that need with his own need to come to terms with his own cultural memories, Leone has made his most oneric and extraordinary film.' *(Tony Rayns, MFB)*

ONCE UPON A TIME IN THE WEST

CT: 6 AV: 8.13

(aka *C'era Una Volta Il West*)

1969 US 140/165 C WESTERN

D Sergio Leone ☆
W Sergio Leone Sergio Donati

Henry Fonda Claudia Cardinale Jason Robards Jr Charles Bronson Gabriele Ferzetti Keenan Wynn Paolo Stoppa Lionel Stander Jack Elam Woody Strode

Gunmen (led by Henry Fonda) threaten the safety of a lonely woman (Claudia Cardinale).

Leone's lyrical western has achieved classic status over the years, partly thanks to its outstanding Ennio Morricone score. On release, it was panned for being clichéd, boring and ultra-violent. It's more a homage to the Western than to the West; almost every cliché of the genre is present, artily photographed and padded out to inordinate length. Slow to the point of somnolence and with a plot borrowed from *Johnny Guitar* (1953), it is impressive if you dote on atmosphere and don't pine for a gripping narrative.

PRO:

'The irresistible thing about Leone is that his affection for both Westerns and moviemaking is unbounded. He goes for large pictorial compositions and operatic effects at a time when most films are modestly or forlornly shrinking to a size suitable for television. The story itself is rather spare and predictable; what turns it into an epic is Leone's peculiar talent for embellishment. This movie has the longest prelude with a brilliant piece of business between Jack Elam and a fly and the longest coda I've seen; in between it's full of grand ominous entrances and exits, buildups and showdowns.' *(Washington Post)*

'Leone's anthology of all the clichés and stereotypes of the Hollywood Western serves both as a lament for the passing of golden age America, and for the passing of the Western: fable meets economic reality, and fable must therefore die. The story . . . is the least important aspect of this magisterial film.' *(NFT Bulletin, 1984)*

'This masterly Western is a superb study in revenge . . . Henry Fonda is marvellously cast against type as the villain. Leone's unmistakably baroque signature is writ large across the wide screen.' *(NFT Bulletin, 1994)*

MIXED:

'A horrific Western, harbinger of the death of a genre and of a dream – both of them American . . . marred by rococo camerawork, obtrusive symbolism and the desecration of hallowed Fordian ground.' *(Wim Wenders)*

ANTI:

'Tedium in the tumbleweed.' *(Time)*

'Two hours of sonorous nothing.' *(Francis Hope, New Statesman)*

'Continues Leone's love affair with the Western. But what was fairly entertaining in the previous films is now tedious taken seriously. [His] trademarks are stupidly over-indulged.' *(Margaret Hinxman, Sunday Telegraph)*

'A simple-minded, blood-splattered amorality tale that hopefully will be trimmed from its original 165 minutes for telecasting. It's a rehash of the Clint Eastwood Italian Westerns, but it's as vile and violent a slaughter festival as any even Eastwood has to his discredit.' *(Judith Crist)*

'Made in 1966, it seemed to me then very long, lazy and overbearingly mannered. Now, revived, it hasn't improved with age, although the violence doesn't appear so stomach-turning – a sad sign of the changing times.' *(Shaun Usher, Daily Mail, 1982)*

ONE EYED JACKS AAW

CT: 5 AV: 6.50

(aka *One-Eyed Jacks*)

1961 US 141 C WESTERN

D Marlon Brando
W Guy Trosper Calder Willingham from Charles Neider's novel *The Authentic Death of Hendry Jones*

Marlon Brando ● Karl Malden ☆ Katy Jurado ☆ Pina Pellicer Slim Pickens Ben Johnson, Timothy Carey Elisha Cook Jr

An outlaw (Marlon Brando) seeks revenge on a treacherous former friend (Karl Malden).

Marlon Brando directed and starred in this psychological western – which may be one reason why it's much too long and self-indulgent. But Charles Lang Jr's cinematography was rightly Oscar-nominated, and most of the performances (apart from Brando's, which is tiresomely mannered) are fine.

PRO:

'I used to be against Westerns with Mexican hats and Westerns with psychology. I have lately conquered my prejudice against the hats; *One-Eyed Jacks* brings me round to the psychology too. It is not simply that the hero isn't all heroic . . . It is that one feels him to be a genuine outlaw: a young man with experiences and motives which exclude him morally as well as physically from the settled world.' *(Dilys Powell)*

'A highly efficient and consistently lively Western.' *(David Robinson, Financial Times)*

'After a scrappy start the film takes a deliberately slow but far from tedious course . . . Not surprisingly Brando has done a splendid job of directing himself . . . He builds the part from within.' *(Gordon Gow, S & S)*

Combining a violent story of betrayal and vengeance with a sensuous romanticism, and extraordinary visual beauty, the film is distinguished by fine performances (Karl Malden as Brando's betrayer and Katy Jurado as Malden's wife match Brando in interest). The characters are three-dimensional, a depth rare indeed in Westerns, and Brando proves as tantalizing a director as he is an actor. There's a muted ferocity, an intensity, a visual excitement to so much of the film that its lapses into lushness are forgivable.' *(Judith Crist)*

MIXED:

'As a director Mr Brando reveals a fine eye for scenery and colour. The Mexican desert has the strange beauty of a lunar landscape . . . If a theme emerges it is that . . . beautiful beasts can be tamed by women. Had the writing matched the photography and acting, this would have been a fine film . . . Overlong.' *(Patrick Gibbs, Daily Telegraph)*

The big action scenes, in fact, are ingenious and exciting. . . . Director Brando, however, comes off much better than actor Brando, the Method Cowboy, who incessantly mumbles, scratches, blinks, rubs his nose, and sulks. In short, Brando plays the same character he always plays, the only character who seems to interest him, Marlon Brando.' *(Time)*

'A new variant . . . The Brando Western which . . . tries to Bonapartise the whole thing by imposing his own idiosyncratic code and image . . . The tale slumps into inactivity in the midst of action, a fascinating display of Brando versus the Western he's engaged in . . . It's a huge pity; and still in the half-failure there's a great deal to enjoy and admire . . . [Brando's] mere presence evokes power . . . and in . . . Lang's photography, he can claim comparison with the best of Ford . . . Altogether the faults are far out-balanced by the spell-binding.' *(William Whitebait, New Statesman)*

ANTI:

'For far too much of the time, Mr Brando is merely sombre under his sombrero.' *(Alan Dent, Sunday Telegraph)*

'In a well-intentioned programme note . . . or the first film that Marlon Brando has directed, he describes it as a "frontal attack on the temple of clichés". The sad thing about it, on the contrary, is that it buttresses almost every reactionary cliché about the Actors' Studio method that has ever been uttered.' *(Penelope Gilliatt, Observer)*

I don't mind that when Brando talks, I can still only understand half of what he is saying. As an actor, he can mumble. As a director, he definitely cannot. *One-Eyed Jacks* is, at times, one long mumble-jumble.' *(Leonard Mosley, Daily Express)*

For all its ambitiousness and size [it] ends like any other yarn of the Great Outdoors – the bad man shot, the boy and girl together again.' *(Nina Hibbin, Daily Worker)*

ONE FLEW OVER THE CUCKOO'S NEST AAN

CT: 8 AV: 8.75

1975 US 129 C DRAMA

D Milos Forman ☆ AAW

W Lawrence Hauben Bo Goldman ☆ AAW from Ken Kesey's novel and Dale Wasserman's play

Jack Nicholson ☆ AAW Louise Fletcher ☆ AAW William Redfield Michael Berryman Brad Dourif ☆ AAN Peter Brocco Dean R. Brooks Alonzo Brown Scatman Crothers Mwako Cumbuka

Rebel patient (Jack Nicholson) leads a revolt in a mental hospital against a nasty nurse (Louise Fletcher).

It isn't hard to see why this won so many Oscars: Jack Nicholson's performance is hugely charismatic; Czech director Milos Forman skilfully reinterprets Ken Kesey's novel as an allegory about the end of Communism; and it's an important, stirring and prophetic film of it's time. It's much less convincing in its R.D. Laingian view of mental illness as a myth. Haskell Wexler and Jack Nitzsche were Oscar-nominated for their cinematography and music, respectively.

ANTI:

'The excellent Jack Nicholson disappoints as McMurphy; he isn't intrinsically suitable, as Kirk Douglas was in the original stage production. Somehow Nicholson radiates a wise-guy quality, the ability to outsmart through clever trickery, and not (as Douglas did) through being fundamentally right, and strong in that rightness. There is too much of the trickster-comedian about Nicholson; you do not see him as representing some greater salutary principle, only as an operator outwitting others who could as easily embody dumb honesty as cunning oppression . . . Louise Fletcher . . . is a fine, expressive actress, but wrong for Big Nurse . . . Some deep-seated decency and common sense are always too much in evidence . . . There is finally something distasteful about a film . . . in which Big Nurse prods a disturbed young man into suicide. It is one thing to say the Establishment is blind, stupid, and uncaring; another, and irresponsible, to say it is deliberately murderous.' *(John Simon)*

MIXED:

'The film as a whole is warped, sentimental, possibly dangerous; but Nicholson is tremendous . . . Even Kesey didn't go as far as the film script does in its quasi-Laingian implications that mental trouble is a kind of health, in its simplistic (and weary) allegory of the mental hospital as the world with the patients as the People struggling against Authority, the medical staff.' *(Stanley Kauffmann)*

PRO:

'A memorable film. A black comedy that inspires a gut reaction both to the story as it appears on screen and to its deeper relevance as an attack on established order and the bureaucrats who believe it is their god-given right and duty to destroy personal freedom. Milos Forman, too long neglected as a director, creates an atmosphere so totally convincing that every minor incident, however amusing, has relevance and pathos.' *(Marjorie Bilbow, Screen International)*

'It is heartening to know that the moral fable can still be made to work . . . Metaphor notwithstanding, director Milos Forman sticks to his customary realism, so that everything we watch looks inherently true.' *(Gordon Gow, F & F)*

'Whatever the intentions of the original novel, this is more than a film about callousness and the abuse of authority in a mental hospital. It is a political film. Not symbolically political in the sense that it shows an individual taking on the system and suffering a dreadful defeat. I mean political in the sense that it is about power, about ideological tyranny, and that behind its facade are all the Solzhenitsyns who didn't get out. Milos Forman, one of the group of brilliant young directors who flourished in the Dubcek days, did get out; difficult to believe that, directing *One Flew Over the Cuckoo's Nest*, he failed to think of the inmates left behind. For me his film is about Czechoslovakia.' *(Dilys Powell)*

ONE HOUR WITH YOU AAN CT: 6 AV: 7.43

1932 US 84 BW MUSICAL/COMEDY/ROMANCE

D George Cukor Ernst Lubitsch ☆
W Samson Raphaelson from Lothar Schmidt's play *Only a Dream*

Maurice Chevalier ☆ Jeanette MacDonald ☆ Genevieve Tobin ☆ Roland Young ☆ Charles Ruggles George Barbier

An amorous doctor (Maurice Chevalier) has marital problems.

Endearing remake of Lubitsch's silent hit, *The Marriage Circle* (1924). It's no more than a frothy farce, but the performances are charming and Chevalier makes the most of his asides to the audience.

PRO:

'A 100% credit to all concerned.' *(Variety)*

'Mr Lubitsch's nimble mind has been busy not only in the direction of the subject but also in the handling of the script . . . Chevalier is as enjoyable as ever.' *(Mordaunt Hall, New York Times)*

'It has Chevalier. Oh, how it has Chevalier – this gay, naughty, sizzling little farce . . . It races and patters along its risqué, saucy way to snappy lingering music . . . Even better than the silent version.' *(Photoplay)*

MIXED:

'In spite of its tuneful songs and clever detail and technique, it has not half the subtlety of its original nor that rapier-like satire which the great director knows so well how to handle. Its great weakness is its abrupt and rather inconclusive ending.' *(Lionel Collier, Picturegoer)*

ANTI:

'It's really a Lubitsch picture . . . Lubitsch's pictures were brilliant, even if they lacked feeling. He didn't want his comedies to have any feeling. Now, my idea of comedy is that they should always touch you unexpectedly.' *(George Cukor, who walked out during shooting, in protest at producer Lubitsch's interference)*

101 DALMATIANS CT: 9 AV: 7.56

1961 US 79 C CARTOON/COMEDY

D Wolfgang Reitherman Hamilton S. Luske
W Bill Peet from Dodie Smith's novel (music and lyrics by Mel Leven)

Voices: Rod Taylor Cate Bauer Betty Lou Gerson ☆ J. Pat O'Malley Lisa Davis Ben Wright Frederic Worlock

Canine detective force tries to find Dalmatian pups dognapped for their skins in London.

Economics meant that the backgrounds here are less animated than in the very finest Disney cartoons; but compensations include a classic villainess in Cruella de Vil (splendidly voiced by Betty Lou Gerson), good gags, and a story which children and adults alike will find gripping and heartwarming.

MIXED:

'While not as indelibly enchanting or inspired as some of the studio's most unforgettable animated endeavors, this is nonetheless a painstaking creative effort.' *(Variety)*

'Not one of the great Disney classics – it's not in the same league with *Snow White* or *Pinocchio* – but it's passable fun, and will entertain its target family audiences . . . The story seems somewhat perfunctory, the chase scene is not as inventive as the climaxes of other Disney feature cartoons, and the animators never solve the problem of making the puppies seem different from one another.' *(Roger Ebert)*

PRO:

'It has the freshness of the early short colour-cartoons without the savagery which has often disfigured the latest feature-length stories.' *(Dilys Powell)*

'[Disney's] best for a long time . . . a story of considerable charm, equally acceptable for adults and children.' *(Derek Hill, Tribune)*

'The Master's best full-length colour-cartoon ever.' *(Paul Dehn, Daily Herald)*

'Warms the heart, amuses the mind and can be unreservedly recommended.' *(The Times)*

Should please just about everybody but cats . . . The wittiest, most charming, least pretentious cartoon feature Walt Disney has ever made.' *(Time)*

ONE HUNDRED MEN AND A GIRL AAN

CT: 6 AV: 7.22

1937 US 85 BW COMEDY/DRAMA/MUSICAL/FAMILY

D Henry Koster ☆
W Bruce Manning Charles Kenyon James Mulhauser Hans Kraly from Kraly's story AAN

Deanna Durbin ☆ Adolphe Menjou ☆ Leopold Stokowski ☆ Alice Brady ☆ Mischa Auer ☆ Eugene Pallette ☆ Billy Gilbert Alma Kruger Philadelphia Symphony Orchestra ☆

Enthusiastic teenager (Deanna Durbin) persuades famous conductor (Leopold Stokowski) to conduct an orchestra of unemployed musicians.

Most Deanna Durbin musicals have not worn well; this, her third picture, is an exception – despite its implausible, sentimental, old-fashioned plot, it's charming, funny and well acted. Charles Previn won an Oscar for his musical direction; the music is from numerous sources. The following year, after two further hits – *Mad About Music* and *That Certain Age* – the wholesome Miss Durbin won a special Oscar 'for bringing to the screen the spirit and personification of youth'. She was retired from movies by the age of 28, and said in 1959 that, 'just as a Hollywood pin-up represents sex to dissatisfied erotics, so I represented the ideal daughter millions of fathers and mothers wished they had.'

'Smash hit for all the family . . . something new in entertainment.' *(Variety)*

'Aside from its value as entertainment, which is considerable, [it] reveals the cinema at its sunny-sided best . . . Through it all, over the highs and lows of symphony and comedy, Miss Durbin weaves her refreshing course.' *(Frank S. Nugent, New York Times)*

'Useless to pretend that I am tough enough to resist the blandishments of Miss Deanna Durbin . . . A pure fairy tale, but it comes off.' *(P. Galway, Statesman)*

'An original story put over with considerable skill.' *(MFB)*

ONE MILLION YEARS B.C.

CT: 5 AV: 3.89

1966 GB 96/100 C FANTASY/SO BAD

D Don Chaffey
W Michael Carreras

John Richardson ● Raquel Welch ☆ (the star is for the bikini) Robert Brown Percy Herbert Martine Beswick

Rock man (John Richardson) falls for Shell woman (Raquel Welch) in dangerous prehistoric times.

Although it was reviewed with a marked lack of enthusiasm, this remake of 1940's *One Million B.C.* became Hammer Films' most profitable movie. John Richardson is more wooden than rocklike in the lead, and Mario Nascimbene's score is excruciating, but the film retains an eccentric appeal. Raquel Welch (at the peak of physical condition) was such a distracting sight in her fur bikini that many critics failed to notice that the film also contains some of Ray Harryhausen's most impressive stop-motion photography. No one could accuse this film of being historically accurate, with humans and dinosaurs living alongside each other, but what the hell: who would pay to see a Tyrannosaurus Rex in a fur bikini?

PRO:

'Very easy to dismiss the film as a silly spectacle; but Hammer production finesse is much in evidence and Don Chaffey has done a competent job of direction. And it is all hugely enjoyable' *(David Wilson, MFB)*

MIXED:

'Compared to its 1940 predecessor . . . the new grunt-and-groaner isn't as effective with its trick photography . . . Several sequences though are pretty good . . . The best scene has a giant bird dangling Miss Welch over a nest of its gaping younguns while it battles a rival in mid-air. Poor Miss Welch, but a shrewd old bird.' *(Howard Thompson, New York Times)*

'Chaffey directs at a fair clip . . . whatever else changes, the screen's ideas about prehistory remain nasty, brutish and reassuringly nonsensical.' *(Penelope Houston, Spectator)*

ANTI:

'Whether [Raquel Welch] can act . . . remains a moot point because all she is required to do . . . is run around a lot and say "Urgh!" – a word which almost exclusively serves the entire cast.' *(Cecil Wilson, Daily Mail)*

'The only trouble really is . . . Raquel Welch [who] may for all I know be the greatest tragedienne since Duse, but she is lacking in the vital ability for this sort of role, which is to scream and scream and scream again.' *(The Times)*

'Among the silliest, campiest and dullest of the ludicrous caveman genre . . . The dinosaurs created by Ray Harryhausen are impressive, but their sizes in relation to humans seem to fluctuate in different shots.' *(Danny Peary)*

ONE, TWO, THREE

CT: 5 AV: 7.08

1961 US 115 BW COMEDY

D Billy Wilder ☆
W Billy Wilder I.A.L. Diamond from Ferenc Molnar's play

James Cagney ☆ Horst Buchholz Arlene Francis

Pamela Tiffin Lilo Pulver Howard St. John Leon Askin

Coca-Cola executive (James Cagney) tries to sell his product in East Berlin, simultaneously concealing from his boss that his daughter has married a Communist.

Dated Cold War comedy, with bleak surroundings that don't exactly inspire belly-laughs. The satirical targets (American consumer culture, Communist stodginess) are clichéd, the gags are hit-and-miss, and the concessions to sentiment lack conviction. All the same, some one-liners stand out, and the action is conducted at commendable speed. Sample dialogue . . . 'Is everyone in the world corrupt?!' 'I don't know everyone.'

PRO:

'A fast-paced, high-pitched, hard-hitting, lighthearted farce crammed with topical gags and spiced with satirical overtones.' *(Variety)*

'Cagney is priceless . . . I hardly stopped laughing.' *(Bryan Buckingham, News of the World)*

'A sometimes bewildered, often wonderfully funny exercise in nonstop nuttiness.' *(Time)*

'This first-class featherweight farce is a serious achievement.' *(Stanley Kauffmann)*

MIXED:

'A real laugh-getter . . . Cagney shatters the screen in his well-known machine-gun manner, the girls are beautiful, the style is handsome, and the film . . . about three miles too long.' *(Ernest Betts, People)*

ANTI:

'As far as taste is concerned [it] is a film that deserves to be counted out before it gets into the ring . . . But Billy Wilder's jokes have always been more famous than his taste . . . It's sad to see the caustically witty Wilder lowering his aim, widening his style and blunting his brilliance on naive wisecracks and national jokes . . . Sad and – forgive me – beWildering.' *(Alexander Walker, Evening Standard)*

'Divided Berlin is as fundamentally unfunny a subject as, say, smallpox or the hydrogen bomb.' *(Alan Dent, Sunday Telegraph)*

'Really, Mr Wilder! All that stuff [cheap jibes at Soviet life] went out with Pip Squeak and Wilfred and Popski and Bombski.' *(Nina Hibbin, Daily Worker)*

'A film of no usefulness at all. Despite an air of almost hysterical exuberance, it is not even vulgarly funny.' *(Robert Hatch, Nation)*

'The end is a holocaust of clichés with Horst Buchholz irretrievably out of his depth.' *(New Statesman)*

'In Hollywood it is now common to hear Billy Wilder called the world's greatest movie director. This judgment tells us a lot about Hollywood: Wilder hits his effects hard and sure, he's a clever, lively director whose work lacks feeling or passion or grace or beauty or elegance. His eye is on the dollar, or rather on success, on the entertainment values that bring in dollars. But he has never before, except perhaps in a different way in *Ace in the Hole*, exhibited such a brazen contempt for people.' *(Pauline Kael, 1965)*

ONE-EYED JACKS: *see* ONE EYED JACKS.

ONLY ANGELS HAVE WINGS

CT: 6 AV: 8.00

1939 US 121 BW DRAMA/ROMANCE/ACTION/ADVENTURE

D Howard Hawks ☆
W William Rankin (uncredited) Eleanore Griffin (uncredited) Jules Furthman from Hawks's story

Cary Grant ☆ Jean Arthur ☆ Richard Barthelmess ☆ Rita Hayworth ☆ Thomas Mitchell Sig Rumann Victor Kilian John Carroll

Pilots in South America are grounded in a bar.

Talky, set-bound drama – but this is appropriate, since it's about men who find their surroundings claustrophobic and really want to fly. It's a 'man's movie' with most of the familiar tough-guy touches you expect from a Hawks picture, and a couple of feisty women in Arthur and Hayworth. Though it is often called a classic, it's stilted and artificial by modern standards, and requires a measure of tolerance for its lack of action. It received an Oscar nomination for Best Special Effects.

ANTI:

'All these people did the best they could with what they were given – but look at it.' *(Otis Ferguson)*

PRO:

'Hawks had a story to tell, and he has done it inspiringly well.' *(Variety)*

'The splendid performances . . . make this first-rate entertainment.' *(Era)*

'Deftly handled, well characterised and containing some super shots in the way of flying scenes . . . Acting of all is the best, Cary Grant outstanding.' *(Faulkner's Film Review)*

'As important as it is unquestionably box-office . . . Thrilling, intelligent and human.' *(Kine Weekly)*

'Brilliant flying, romantic interest and atmosphere of tension all through.' *(Daily Film Renter)*

'One of the finest of its type yet presented. Outstanding entertainment.' *(Today's Cinema)*

'The definitive Howard Hawks picture. Graced with superlative flying sequences, but dominated by crackling dialogue scenes in which characters trade loving insults, the film boasts a glorious cast.' *(Michael Wilmington, They Went Thataway, 1993)*

ONLY TWO CAN PLAY CT: 7 AV: 6.80

1961 GB 106 BW COMEDY/ROMANCE

D Sidney Gilliat ☆
W Bryan Forbes from Kingsley Amis's novel *That Uncertain Feeling*

Peter Sellers ☆ Mai Zetterling ☆ Virginia Maskell ☆ Richard Attenborough ☆ Raymond Huntley John Le Mesurier Kenneth Griffith ☆

Adventures of an adulterous Welsh librarian (Peter Sellers).

In this mostly successful adaptation of Kingsley Amis's novel, *That Uncertain Feeling*, the edge of the social satire has been blunted, and the tone has been coarsened; but the performances are a joy, and Peter Sellers is at his most restrained and effective.

MIXED:

'Some of the humor is over-earthy and slightly lavatory, and the film never fully decides whether it is supposed to be light comedy, farce or satire. But it remains a cheerful piece of nonsense.' *(Variety)*

'Some of [Forbes's] humour is surely too juvenile and crude . . . Virginia Maskell is admirable . . . Mai Zetterling much less than admirable . . . and Richard Attenborough brilliant . . . Deplorable as this film may be, it would make a puritanical cat laugh.' *(Alan Dent, Sunday Telegraph)*

'The farcical moments in this delightful and serious film, which includes a particularly beautiful performance by Virginia Maskell . . . are mostly tugged into relevance, though I could have done with less of the cow-beset, dashboard-anticry of that car.' *(John Coleman, New Statesman)*

PRO:

'The best comedy I have seen since I started this job.' *(Quentin Crewe, Daily Mail)*

'The most triumphantly and hilariously naughty comedy I can remember . . . You'll miss the laugh of a life-time if you don't see it.' *(Bryan Buckingham, News of the World)*

'Has the funniest script since the heyday of Ealing . . . The real comic triumph . . . is in the dialogue. For the first time that I can think of in the history of British film comedy, a screen marriage is as grown-up and as rich in private jokes as the relationship between Katharine Hepburn and Cary Grant in *Bringing up Baby*. The vocabulary is the one we all use about the house, but we had despaired of ever hearing it in the cinema.' *(Penelope Gilliatt, Observer)*

'A British comedy in which the script is as funny as the acting is a rare find . . . The laugh-lines tumble over each other so thick and fast that you often have to stop yourself chuckling in order to hear what comes next.' *(Nina Hibbin, Daily Worker)*

'Whether faithful to its original or not, the screenplay is uninhibited, irreverent, impudent, funny and frequently witty . . . It is Peter Sellers's playing as the librarian which turns the joke into an occasion.' *(Dilys Powell)*

OPEN CITY CT: 6 AV: 8.30

(aka *Rome – Open City; Roma, Città Aperta*)

1945 Italy 101 BW DRAMA/FOREIGN/WAR

D Roberto Rossellini ☆
W Sergio Amidei Frederico Fellini

Aldo Fabrizi ☆ Anna Magnani ☆ Marcello Pagliero Maria Michi Harry Feist

Italian underground undermines Nazis.

Documentary-style drama which shows Rossellini at his best. Shooting with minimal resources, no sound crew, and in difficult circumstances at the end of the Second World War, he draws powerful performances from his two leading actors. The story is merely functional, the characters are too melodramatic and black-and-white for comfort, and the post-synch dubbing is primitive. Even so, it won the Palme d'Or at Cannes.

MIXED:

'Lacks the depth of characterization, thought, and feeling which might have made it a definitively great film. From there on out I have nothing but admiration for it . . . You will seldom see as pure freshness and vitality in a film, or as little unreality and affectation among the players.' *(James Agee, Nation)*

PRO:

'There have been many resistance films, but none where Nazi vice is so vivid . . . A superb film evolved with courage and emotion and beautifully and realistically acted.' *(MFB)*

'A worthy example of Italian screen art. There are pardonable technical shortcomings, but the acting has a fine nervous energy.' *(Standard)*

'The most moving film I have seen . . . a great human drama, made with tenderness and understanding as well as zeal.' *(Joan Lester, Reynolds News)*

'A great film . . . One actor outshone them all, Aldo Fabrizi.' *(Manchester Guardian)*

'A motion-picture classic. For once the heroic conception has been heroically worked out.' *(Fred Majdalany, Daily Mail)*

'I was moved . . . not so much by the story as by the warm humanity of its approach . . . Magnani's performance . . . is superb.' *(Cyril Ray, Sunday Times)*

'To us who have been accustomed to the slickly manufactured sentiments of Hollywood's studio-made pictures, the hard simplicity and genuine passion of the film lend to its not unfamiliar story the smashing impact of a shocking expos. And its sharp estimation of realities gives it a rare intellectual authority.' *(Bosley Crowther)*

ORCA . . . KILLER WHALE CT: 1 AV: 3.13

1977 US 92 C HORROR/ADVENTURE

D Michael Anderson ●
W Luciano Vincenzoni Sergio Donati ●

Richard Harris ● Charlotte Rampling ●
Will Sampson Keenan Wynn Bo Derek

Shark-hunter (Richard Harris) is called in to hunt a killer whale terrorizing the Newfoundland coast.

Ludicrously inept attempt to cash in on the success of *Jaws* (1975). Harris hams it up. Rampling is always at the ready with boring scientific exposition. It's Will Sampson's thankless task to provide the tribal lore.

MIXED:

'Some fine special effects and underwater camera-work are plowed under in dumb story-telling.' *(Variety)*

ANTI:

'There are more thrills to be found in the average dolphinarium.' *(S & S)*

'A lousier movie may get made one of these months or years, but it will have to wrest the trophy from the dead and icy grasp of *Orca* . . . It is not easy to remember a major commercial filmmaking enterprise that violates so many of the customary concerns for characterization, motivation, narrative coherence, credible dialogue or credibility in any aspect.' *(Charles Champlin, LA Times)*

'For nasty snickers, this movie is as good a dog as any in these dog days . . . Among the screenplay's lush absurdities, my favorite is Charlotte Rampling's invitation to a ghoulish looking Richard Harris, as the ice closes in on them: "Come, let me warm you"; Personally, I'd prefer an iceberg.' *(John Simon)*

'At the end, when the whale has lured Harris north with a come-hither flick of its tail, Miss Rampling is caught on the icefloes, leaping from one to t'other and clad in thigh boots, homespun poncho and a turban, as if she expected David Bailey to surface and photograph her for *Vogue*'s Arctic number.' *(Alexander Walker, Evening Standard)*

'The biggest load of cod imaginable.' *(Phillip Bergson, Sunday Times)*

ORDET CT: 7 AV: 6.75

(aka *Word, The*)

1954 Denmark 126 BW DRAMA/FOREIGN

D Carl Dreyer ☆
W Carl Dreyer from Kaj Munk's play

Henrik Malberg ☆ Emil Hass Christensen
Preben Lerdorff-Rye ✔ Cay Kristiansen ✔
Birgitte Federspiel Ejner Federspiel Ove Rud
Ann Elisabeth Rud Susanne Rud Gerda Nielsen

In a remote farming community, an austerely religious father (Henrik Malberg) forbids one of his three sons (Cay Kristiansen) to marry a woman whose father is of a different persuasion.

Typically sombre, slow, austere exploration by this great director of the eternal conflict between organized religion and personal faith. It's no barrel of laughs and the atmosphere is deliberately claustrophobic; but the dramatic intensity and Dreyer's visual flair make this a masterpiece of European cinema. The miraculous finale is wonderfully uplifting. Devotees of hyperactive, rock promo-style editing may be distressed to learn that the whole film, which lasts 126 minutes, contains only 114 shots. Voted Best Film at the Venice Film Festival.

PRO:

'Told with the luminous sincerity that haloes most of what Dreyer does . . . And he can paint for the ear as well as for the eye.' *(Time)*

'Shares with his earlier masterpieces . . . an underlying concern with the problems of good and evil . . . Watching it becomes in itself virtually an act of faith. It is a picture that one can wholeheartedly admire, but not particularly like.' *(Arthur Knight, Saturday Review)*

'Take a clean hanky and remember that this miracle film was made when Hollywood was churning out *The Song of Bernadette* and *The Robe*, and be grateful that Dreyer has testified to the sort of faith that real people might have felt.' *(Tim Radford, Guardian, 1977, on first UK showing)*

'[The film] gives us Christianity with a human face.' *(Nigel Andrews, Financial Times)*

'Dreyer goes at his own pace; but it's worth staying with him for the luminous images . . . the confident austerity with which he uses his camera and a minimum of cutting, the psychological truth with which the characters are drawn; above all the real and intense passion which is subdued beneath the ordered surfaces of quiet rural life.' *(David Robinson, The Times)*

'It is of awesome dimensions – a film about Christianity made with an intensity that achieves exaltation. It is sombre almost to the point of self-parody, yet Dreyer's ability to communicate is so total that one is utterly absorbed and renewed from whatever viewpoint of belief . . . It is altogether a memorable film by a great artist.' *(Tom Hutchinson, Sunday Telegraph)*

ORDINARY PEOPLE AAW CT: 5 AV: 7.40

1980 US 124 C DRAMA

D Robert Redford ✗ AAW
W Alvin Sargent ✗ AAW from Judith Guest's novel

Donald Sutherland Mary Tyler Moore ☆ AAN Judd Hirsch ☆ AAN Timothy Hutton ☆ AAW M. Emmet Walsh Elizabeth McGovern Dinah Manoff Fredric Lehne James B. Sikking Basil Hoffman

Members of an American family tear themselves apart over the death of a son.

Earnest attempt to lift the lid of bourgeois affluence and reveal the teeming emotions underneath. Understandably praised for its acting (especially that of Timothy Hutton and Mary Tyler Moore, here playing against her sitcom image), it's terribly plodding, the characters lack genuine depth, and the insights smack of soap operatics and psychobabble. Marvin Hamlisch's sanctimonious score doesn't help.

PRO:

'Represents the height of craftsmanship across the board.' *(Variety)*

'Intelligent, perceptive, and deeply moving.' *(Roger Ebert)*

'A remarkable first film! . . . with a first-rate script and superb performances, [Redford has] come up with a powerful and absorbing drama.' *(Alan Frank, Daily Star)*

'About as honest, humorous, intelligent, well written and played as anything I have yet to see devoted to American family angst.' *(John Coleman, New Statesman)*

'An intelligent, sensitive, serious work, unusually made in chronological sequence so that an exceptional company of actors seem to be discovering themselves only minutes ahead of us.' *(Alan Brien, Sunday Times)*

MIXED:

'An out of the ordinary film . . . The denouement is a little too pat . . . the psychological problems are a little too easily tied up. None the less, the film matches the theme: well, clean-cut in a way reminiscent of its eligible director, the photography composed, the editing sharp, the whole percipient.' *(Sue Lermon, Times Higher Educational Supplement)*

'At times Redford's work is so precise and cold that the mother (Mary Tyler Moore) might have directed it. Yet he's very sensitive toward his actors, and gets several outstanding performances.' *(Danny Peary)*

ANTI:

'When is soap-opera not a soap-opera? . . . Redford plays his film perilously close to the lather, and there are times when the suds overflow the bath-edge . . . A worse problem is the movie's "McGuffin" or plot-trigger. The drowning accident is never woven convincingly into the movie's texture.' *(Nigel Andrews, Financial Times)*

'An academic exercise in catharsis: it's earnest, it means to improve people, and it lasts a lifetime . . . The movie is about the harm that repression can do, but the movie is just as repressive and sanitized as the way of life it means to expose, and it backs away from anything messier than standard TV-style psychiatric explanations.' *(Pauline Kael)*

'A stiff sermon masquerading as poignant human drama.' *(Bruce Bawer, American Spectator)*

'Everything remains a bit propaedeutic, a mite primitive, as if someone, instead of creating a work of the imagination, had dramatized a self-help book.' *(John Simon)*

ORFEU NEGRO: *see* BLACK ORPHEUS.

ORPHANS OF THE STORM CT: 6 AV: 6.63

1921 US 125 BW DRAMA/EPIC/SILENT

D D.W. Griffith ☆
W Marquis de Trolignac (pseudonym for D.W. Griffith) from Adolph Ennery's play *Les Deux Orphelines*

Lillian Gish ☆ Dorothy Gish ☆ Joseph Schildkraut Lucille La Verne Morgan Wallace Frank Puglia Creighton Hale

Two orphan girls (Lillian and Dorothy Gish), one of them blind (Dorothy), become separated and caught up in the French Revolution.

The plot is the creakiest melodrama, the narrative rambles on forever, and most of the acting looks terribly overstated; but sumptuous staging, attention to historical detail and some thrilling sequences (especially in the final reel) make this probably the most watchable of Griffith's epics today. And The Gish sisters are very touching.

PRO:

'A delightful piece of characterization it is that Miss Lillian gives throughout the play. Dorothy Gish's portrayal of the blind girl is delicate, interesting and most pathetic . . . The power of the play is in the big pictures of those turbulent times in France . . . and in [Griffith's] scenes of the crowded street, of the battles, the barricades.' *(Walter Brown, The Moving Picture World)*

'Production is so colossal in conception and in execution that one is immensely moved. The thrills are stirring . . . The acting is superb . . . A film not to be missed.' *(Motion Picture Daily)*

'Griffith has come back with a bang . . . He has recreated history as no other living man has done.

And this is his greatest triumph. It is massive, but it is human.' *(Photoplay)*

'There is scarcely a scene or an effect in the entire production that is not beautiful to look upon, and there is scarcely a moment that is not charged with intense dramatic power.' *(Robert Sherwood, Life)*

MIXED:

'Much that is interesting and exciting . . . despite the fact that it is melodrama rather than history.' *(New York Times)*

'Owing mainly to the poverty of their material, the players are on the whole disappointing . . . The staging – by far the finest feature of the production – is quite superb . . . and the detail work is meticulously correct . . . No features of outstanding technical novelty are exhibited by the production which has been made according to the well-known and easily recognisable Griffith formula.' *(Bioscope)*

'Not one of Griffith's greatest; in a way, it seems dated, even for a 1921 movie. (Not in its technique – in its thinking.) But those who saw it as children never forgot the sequence in which Lillian hears the voice of her long-lost blind sister, played by Dorothy Gish. Griffith sequences like this go beyond heart-wringing into some arena of theatrical sublimity.' *(Pauline Kael)*

ORPHEUS CT: 6 AV: 8.67

(aka *Orphée*)

1950 France 112 BW FANTASY/FOREIGN

D Jean Cocteau ☆
W Jean Cocteau from his play

Jean Marais ☆ François Périer ☆ Maria Casarès ☆ Marie Déa Edouard Dermithe Juliette Gréco

A poet (Jean Marius) enters Hell in search of inspiration and his dead wife (Marie Déa).

Poetic, enigmatic film which starts out as realistic but becomes poetic and dreamlike. Some critics have detected overtones of misogyny and anti-fascism, but this is one of those films which means different things to different people. Its air of intellectual pretentiousness and lack of narrative clarity will irritate many, and Marie Déa is boringly anodyne as Eurydice; but few will deny that its images have a haunting power. Maria Casarès, in particular, gives one of the cinema's most memorable impersonations of Death. Georges Auric's score and Nicolas Hayer's cinematography adds to the magical atmosphere. Cocteau's penultimate film, it won Best Film at the Venice Film Festival, and there was a belated sequel, *Le Testament d'Orphée*, in 1959.

'A film of rare value – one which is often as fantastic as a poem.' *(James Monahan)*

'I cannot pretend to know what it all means, and I have a lurking suspicion that Cocteau doesn't know either, but I do know that it sent me out of the theatre quivering with excitement, and more provocatively engaged than I have been by any film for seasons.' *(C.A. Lejeune)*

'An unmatched achievement in the telling of a magical adventure. It reasserts wonder, ritual, the power of illusion and magic, reinterpreting them in a contemporary setting which brings the myth closer, gives it a disturbing edge of reality.' *(Gavin Lambert)*

OSCAR, THE CT: 5 AV: 2.88

1966 US 118 C DRAMA/SO BAD

D Russel Rouse ●
W Harlan Ellison Russel Rouse Clarence Greene ● from Richard Sale's novel

Stephen Boyd ● Elke Sommer ● Eleanor Parker ✓ Joseph Cotten ✓ Ernest Borgnine ✓ Tony Bennett ● Milton Berle Hedda Hopper ● (as herself)

An amoral actor (Stephen Boyd) sleeps and lies his way to the top in Tinseltown.

Splendidly salacious, tremendously tawdry, no-holds-barred exposé of the hell that is Hollywood. Visually, it's well produced; the costumes and art direction were themselves Oscar-nominated. But it's a camp classic, thanks to a script that should have been consigned to the nether regions of Development Hell. Surprisingly, Eleanor Parker (as a nymphomaniac talent scout), Ernest Borgnine (as a detective) and Joseph Cotten (as a producer) manage to turn in respectable performances; the same can not be said of others in the cast.

Sample dialogue . . . (1) Stephen Boyd to Elke Sommer: 'You a tourist or a native?' Sommer: 'Take one from Column A and two from Column B. You get an eggroll either way.' Boyd: 'You make my head hurt with all that poetry.' (2) Studio mogul (Joseph Cotten) to agent (Milton Berle) and talent scout (Eleanor Parker): 'Once in a while, you bring me meat like this. It all has different names: prime rib of Gloria, shoulder cut of Johnny. Meat!' (3) Eleanor Parker in bed with Stephen Boyd: 'I'm not some sort of garbage pail you can slide a lid on and walk away from!'

PRO:

'Clarence Green as producer and Russell Rouse as director . . . make handsome use of the Hollywood background . . . Boyd makes the most of his part, investing it with an audience-hate symbol which he never once compromises. Elke Sommer, as his studio-designer wife who is another of his victims, is chief distaff interest in a well-undertaken portrayal.' *(Variety)*

'The sort of film that only Hollywood could make, and on that level it is preposterously enjoyable.' *(David Wilson)*

ANTI:

'That true movie rarity – a picture that attains a perfection of ineptitude, quite beyond the power of words to describe.' *(Richard Schickel)*

'This film deserves to stand as a classic; a classic to all that is shoddy and second-rate and cliché-ridden, a grim warning to directors and writers on how not to make a film. Joseph Levine, mogul of the mediocre . . . has combined the basic elements into a story so monumentally banal that even the stoutest-hearted audience will find itself hard put to sit through two hours of intelligence-insulting boredom.' *(Richard Davis, S & S)*

'Tony [Bennett] looks like a sad, abandoned bullfrog.' *(Cue)*

'A film that tells you the garbage truths about Hollywood in all those one-syllable movie-magazine clichés. Perfectly awful.' *(Judith Crist)*

'Meant to be hard-hitting, the picture is florid-fancy, and so energetically overacted that it was instantly hailed as a classic of unintentional comedy . . . This picture is a wonder; it's of a lurid badness that has to be experienced.' *(Pauline Kael)*

OSSESSIONE

CT: 6 AV: 7.44

1942 Italy 112 BW ROMANCE/DRAMA/FOREIGN

D Luchino Visconti ☆
W Mario Alicata Antonio Pietrangeli Gianni Puccini Giuseppe de Santis Luchino Visconti om James M. Cain's novel *The Postman Always Rings Twice*

Clara Calamai Massimo Girotti Juan De Landa Elia Marcuzzo Dhia Cristiani Vittorio Duse Michele Riccardini Michele Sakara

Good-looking drifter (Massimo Girotti) has affair with the wife (Clara Calamai) of an innkeeper (Juan De Landa), whom they murder.

This Italian version of *The Postman Always Rings Twice*, filmed by first-time director Luchino Visconti, is more realistic than either its French predecessor (*Le Dernier Tournant*, made in 1939) or the later Lana Turner version of 1945. It shows a good eye for the Italian countryside (the setting is the Po delta) and was hailed as a masterpiece on release. Scheuer's Film Guide calls it 'the first great neo-realist film'. The two central actors lack a certain subtlety and power, however, and the narrative becomes sluggish after the murder.

MIXED:

'There is usually a touch of pity amid all the harshness of Italian film realism. In this film pity has no place.' *(Manchester Guardian)*

'There is some melodrama and some final slackening of interest. But it is amazing how quickly and strongly Visconti has created a whole new manner of film-making . . . It is an important and germinal film.' *(Birmingham Post, 1961, on first commercial showing in UK)*

'Visconti used landscape in a new way . . . integrated into the events being played against [it] . . . The first 40 minutes . . . are by far the best . . . After the crime, things begin to deteriorate.' *(Burgo Partridge, Time & Tide)*

'My reservations are concerned with the pace which I find too deliberate and with the performances . . . which are surely inadequately sustained.' *(Patrick Gibbs, Daily Telegraph)*

'The film is best at wedding character to landscape.' *(John Ardagh, Observer)*

OSTRE SLEDOVANE VLAKY: *see* CLOSELY OBSERVED TRAINS.

OTHER SIDE OF MIDNIGHT, THE

CT: 5 AV: 2.56

(aka *Sidney Sheldon's The Other Side of Midnight*)

1975 US 166 C DRAMA/ROMANCE/SO BAD

D Charles Jarrott ●
W Herman Raucher Daniel Taradash ● from Sidney Sheldon's novel

Marie-France Pisier ● John Beck ● Susan Sarandon Michael Lerner ● Raf Vallone Clu Gulager Christian Marquand

Pausing only to abort herself with a wire coathanger, a young French woman sleeps her way to the top and seeks revenge on the American pilot (John Beck) who impregnated her.

A seemingly never-ending movie adapted from a junk novel, the story is as tasteless as it is implausible – but its sheer awfulness makes it perversely entertaining. Michel Legrand's overblown score perfectly complements a film that wallows in material luxury and emotional squalor. It received an Oscar nomination for Best Costume Design, and was successful enough to generate a sequel, *Memories of Midnight* (1991) – which was not quite as bad and therefore not nearly as much fun.

PRO:

'Undressed or elegantly gowned, Mlle Pisier is a joy to behold and so good an actress that she makes this harpy of a heroine believable, even likeable: and that is no small trick.' *(Felix Barker, Evening News)*

MIXED:

'Totally absurd and I'm ashamed to say I enjoyed every minute of it . . . For an idle night's entertainment, it couldn't be bettered.' *(Alexander Walker, Evening Standard)*

'Hamhanded, obvious, and totally plastic . . . Somehow the script's arrant vulgarity . . . wooden direction and John Beck's mummified acting . . . all contribute to the dreadful watchability of it all.' *(Spectator)*

'This epic of schlock [is] the movie equivalent of a good bad read.' *(Andrew Nickolds, Time Out)*

ANTI:

'The producer, Frank Yablans, is said to be the smartest salesman in the business, and he may have set up the whole thing as a challenge to himself: if you can sell *The Other Side of Midnight*, the Brooklyn Bridge should be child's play.' *(John Simon)*

'After 166 minutes the feeling that one has actually lived through it all is a little too real for comfort.' *(David Badder, MFB)*

'It has no core. The plot is too ridiculous to stand alone, yet the characters have no existence outside it; they are totally subservient to it and in return it rapes them . . . Garbage.' *(Alexander Stuart, F & F)*

'Kitsch prototype is Andy Warhol's favorite film, but will have average viewers alternately laughing at stupidity and climbing the walls. As usual, Sarandon is likable in horrible film. But Pisier, who must speak English, isn't strong enough to carry a lead in such a long picture. Some of her scenes (particularly her love scene with ice cubes) are embarrassingly bad. Worst of all is character actor Michael Lerner, who has the least convincing French accent since Pépé Le Pew.' *(Danny Peary)*

OTTO E MEZZO: *see* 8½.

OUR HOSPITALITY CT: 7 AV: 8.13

1923 US 66 BW COMEDY/SILENT

D Buster Keaton Jack Blystone ☆ **W** Jean Havez Joseph Mitchell Clyde Bruckman

Buster Keaton ☆ Natalie Talmadge Joe Keaton Buster Keaton Jr. Joe Roberts

In 1831, the son of an old Southern family (Buster Keaton) returns to claim his inheritance, and begins dating the daughter (Natalie Talmadge) of a family with whom he is supposed to be feuding.

Keaton's second full-length feature, a classic silent comedy, shows off his appetite for period detail, his love of transportation gags, and his marvellous acrobaticism. It features some of his most famous stunts, including the final waterfall rescue, for which he did not use a double. After the film, he married his leading lady, although they did not live happily ever after.

MIXED:

'A comedy of whims . . . and in many sequences whimsical. It starts rather slowly, but gathers speed with a vengeance toward the last reel . . . This funny film moves along quietly at the outset, but in the end it gets there, and to our mind it is a mixture that is extremely pleasing, as there is no out-and-out slapstick effect.' *(New York Times)*

PRO:

'A novelty mélange of dramatics, low comedy, laughs and thrills . . . one of the best comedies ever produced.' *(Variety)*

'The film is staged throughout as elaborately as a feature and the direction is masterly. A really funny comedy of considerable originality, both in subject matter and in treatment.' *(Bioscope)*

'Perhaps because dry comedy is so much more rare and odd than dry wit, there are people who never much cared for Keaton. Those who do cannot care mildly.' *(James Agee, Life)*

'Shows Keaton in full possession of his mature gifts: as a film-maker he is as assured as a King or a Vidor; and certainly the superior of Chaplin, who at the time that Keaton was making *Our Hospitality* was preparing *The Gold Rush* – a beautiful film, but technically archaic and visually feeble when seen alongside the Keaton film.' *(David Robinson, Buster Keaton, 1969)*

OUT OF AFRICA AAW CT: 4 AV: 7.07

1985 US 150 C DRAMA/ROMANCE

D Sidney Pollack ✗ AAW
W Kurt Luedtke AAW from writings of Isak Dinesen, alias Karen Blixen

Meryl Streep ✗ AAN Robert Redford ●
Klaus Maria Brandauer ☆ AAN Michael Kitchen ✓
Michael Gough Malick Bowens Joseph Thiaka
Suzanna Hamilton Rachel Kempson
Graham Crowden Leslie Phillips Shane Rimmer

Danish woman (Meryl Streep) commits adultery in Kenya.

Critically acclaimed for its scenery and Meryl Streep's portrayal of a 'strong woman' (with an even stronger accent), this must be one of the worst films to have received an Academy Award as Best Picture. Streep is cold, unsympathetic and mannered in the leading role, while Redford's impersonation of an English, upper-class Etonian is surely among the laziest performances ever to win an Oscar nomination. The saving grace is Klaus-Maria Brandauer, who at least doesn't look like a Hollywood actor picnicking in a Safari Park. After he's gone, the film goes downhill – much too slowly, and with little sense of direction. In a poor year, the film won seven Oscars – including awards for photography (David Watkin), art direction (Stephen Grimes) and music (John Barry); it was nominated for three more.

PRO:

'A movie with the courage to be about complex, sweeping locations, and to use the star power of its actors without apology . . . [Pollack] understands the special, somewhat fragile mystique of his star, who has a tendency to seem over-protective of his own image. In the wrong hands, Redford can look narcissistic. This time, he seems to have much to be narcissistic about.' *(Roger Ebert)*

'What the entire cast . . . helps to realize, what Pollack has captured in simple forceful imagery and in the perfect pace of his editing, is something one dared not hope to find in this movie. It is Dinesen's remarkable rhythm.' *(Richard Schickel, Time)*

'Pollack handles it all with assurance and at the same time manages to tackle quite thorny issues with aplomb . . . In one short scene [he] incisively pinpoints all the clashes of values and contradictions inherent in the process of colonisation . . . But finally it is the commitment to perfection in every aspect of the film – the acting, the period, the settings, the photography, and the people – that makes this such a sparkling film.' *(Sally Hibbin, F & F)*

'A tribute to a liberated woman.' *(Virginia Dignam, Morning Star)*

'The film purrs pleasantly along like one of its own big cats.' *(S & S)*

'Strongly visual direction, a script . . . which is timeless and superlative performances . . . result in a little slice of perfection.' *(Mike Coren, Girl About Town)*

MIXED:

'The Sundance Kid Goes to Kenya! . . . Worth watching just for the scenery.' *(Daily Mirror)*

'The real star of the film . . . is Africa. The Kenyan locations have been gloriously photographed . . . Not for ages have there been so many violins hiding behind every tussock, such huge symphony orchestras thundering away behind the wainscoting. It is, however, more than a very superior travelogue . . . Go armed with a spare Kleenex – and possibly something to read in the duller patches, because it does go on for an awfully long time . . . It is, however, the very best Fortnum's molasses, the sort of film Bette Davis once made, only she would have done it in 90 minutes flat.' *(William Russell, Glasgow Herald)*

'Intelligent, beautiful to look upon, honest (did a movie heroine before admit to having syphilis?) and distinguished . . . But after Brandauer has been shunted into the background and Michael Kitchen (as a fellow-hunter) has died we're left with the most boring couple to moon about in Africa since *The Garden of Allah*.' *(Shipman)*

ANTI:

'May well be exactly what you're looking for: a long romantic movie set in exotic landscapes distanced by time . . . with fine performances . . . For me [it is] a sentimental wallow.' *(John Coleman, New Statesman)*

'For all that it may come out of Africa, the film's final destination is not many miles from Disneyland.' *(Chris Peachment, Time Out)*

'[It] has hit the screen. Hit it? Well, not really. More fallen on it from a great height and sploshed all over it.' *(Nigel Andrews, Financial Times)*

'For a film based around travel, adultery, syphilis, war, fights with lions and a plane crash, it's slow. More than that, it's sedate.' *(William Leith, New Musical Express)*

'Adult, cryptic, self-conscious, and unsatisfying . . . The picture squirms around trying to make these people morally acceptable to a modern audience.' *(Pauline Kael)*

'It's a long way to go for a downbeat ending.' *(Variety)*

OUT OF THE PAST CT: 8 AV: 8.45

(aka *Build My Gallows High*)

1947 US 97 BW THRILLER

D Jacques Tourneur ☆
W James M. Cain (uncredited) Frank Fenton (uncredited), Geoffrey Homes from his novel *Build My Gallows High*

Robert Mitchum ☆ Jane Greer ☆ Kirk Douglas ☆ Rhonda Fleming Richard Webb Steve Brodie Virginia Huston Paul Valentine Dickie Moore Ken Niles

Private detective (Robert Mitchum) falls for the girl (Jane Greer) he's chasing on behalf of a gangster (Kirk Douglas).

Tortuous, amoral film noir with sharp dialogue and one of the great, double-crossing femmes fatales in Jane Greer. Nicholas Musuraca's very black black-and-white cinematography is superb, and Tourneur keeps the tension building as Mitchum is pulled ever deeper into the mire. Remade as *Against All Odds* (1984), but this is the classic version.

ANTI:

'[Mitchum's] curious languor, which suggests Bing Crosby supersaturated with barbiturates, becomes a brand of sexual complacency that is not endearing.' *(James Agee, Time)*

'The sum of deceitful complications that occur in [the film] must be reckoned by logarithmic tables, so numerous and involved do they become. The consequence is that the action . . . is likely to leave the napping or unmathematical customer far behind.' *(Bosley Crowther)*

MIXED:

'A thin but well-shot suspense melodrama, kept from collapsing by the suggestiveness and intensity that the director, Jacques Tourneur, pours on. It's empty trash, but you do keep watching it.' *(Pauline Kael)*

PRO:

'Morbid curiosity in the fate of these intriguing

Henry Fonda ☆ Dana Andrews Mary Beth Hughes Anthony Quinn William Eythe Henry Morgan Jane Darwell ✓ Frank Conroy ☆ Matt Briggs Harry Davenport

Cowboy (Henry Fonda) tries to prove that three drifters (Dana Andrews, Anthony Quinn, Henry Morgan) were unjustly lynched.

A western which is normally hailed as a classic, even though it was a box-office flop and received a few severe reviews on release, for the way it self-consciously debunked the Old West, and the Fordian notion of 'frontier spirit'. It makes up in characterization and atmosphere for what it lacks in action – but it's awfully depressing, and wears its didactically liberal, anti-lynching sympathies a little too prominently on its sleeve. Wellman's set-bound, theatrical shooting style has dated badly, and his symbolism is often trite.

MIXED:

'Very firm, respectable and sympathetic. But I still think it suffers from rigor artis.' *(James Agee)*

PRO:

'Realism that is as sharp and cold as a knife.' *(Frank S. Nugent, New York Times)*

'The *Ox-Bow Incident* is a significant moment in our culture.' *(Manny Farber, The New Republic)*

'It's easy to be put off by the studio sets and lighting and by the 40s approach to a "serious" subject, but the director, William Wellman, has made the characters so vivid that after many years people may still recall Frank Conroy as the sadistic Southern major, and the rapid changes of expression of William Eythe, as his son.' *(Pauline Kael)*

'One of the greatest westerns ever . . . a powerful portrait of mob violence that rises to the level of Greek tragedy.' *(Baseline)*

'*The Ox-Bow Incident* didn't make money, but they finally got hold of it in Europe, and it was a great success. One of the great critics of the time in the States – he was the biggest voice of them all – went against the mainstream at that time. He said it had less merit than the smallest B western. I have it in my safe deposit box – it's reading something like that can still turn an artist's insides into knots. But mostly the reaction was favorable. I'm proud of it.' *(William A. Wellman)*

PADRE PADRONE CT: 6 AV: 6.44

(aka *Father and Master*)

1977 Italy 113 C BIOPIC/DRAMA/FOREIGN

D Paolo Taviani Vittorio Taviani ☆
W Paolo Taviani Vittorio Taviani from Gavino Ledda's book

Omero Antonutti ☆ Saverio Marconi
Marcella Michelangeli Fabrizio Forte Marino Cenna

A boy (Saverio Marconi) is pulled out of school by his tyrannical father (Omero Antonutti), beaten and sent to tend sheep in the mountains – but he rebels.

Grim, frightening view of rural life and patriarchal oppression. It's based on a true story, and looks like it – although the Taviani Brothers sometimes descend into melodrama and over-emphatic use of Egisto Macchi's music, to tell us what we should be feeling. Though made in 16mm for Italian television, it found an appreciative audience in the cinema and won the Palme d'Or and International Critics' Prize at Cannes.

MIXED:

'It is filled with stunning images, with surprising and even shocking mixes of visual beauty and savage sounds . . . What bothered me was not the obscenity but its potential for unwanted laughs.' *(Clancy Sigal, Spectator)*

'Completely convincing . . . marred only by occasional lapses from the verissimo style.' *(Patrick Gibbs, Daily Telegraph)*

'A good picture that is racked by its ambition to be a great one.' *(Stanley Kauffmann)*

PRO:

'The film entraps us in a sumptuous world of its own.' *(Claude-Marie Tremois, Télérama)*

'What will overwhelm British filmgoers . . . is the sweep of the imagination displayed . . . Not since the early days of the Soviet cinema have a pair of revolutionary film-makers come so close to embodying on the screen the ideals of heroic humanism.' *(Alan Brien, Sunday Times)*

'It manages to be assertive without being dogmatic, and is a resilient and optimistic challenge to out-worn, out-dated ideas. Should be, must be, seen.' *(Virginia Dignam, Morning Star)*

'This bleak, desperate account . . . is almost unbearable. After thirty minutes I wanted to leave. Ten minutes later I couldn't.' *(Margaret Hinxman, Daily Mail)*

'This splendid film, abounding in originality and energy and surprise and human optimism.' *(David Robinson, The Times)*

'The Taviani Brothers have gone back to the soil broken by Rossellini and De Sica and refertilized it in fresh, surprising ways. Their film, a work of desolate poetry and harsh physical power, is a gritty tribute to the spirit of survival.' *(David Ansen)*

PAISÀ CT: 4 AV: 7.30

(aka *Paisan*)

1946 Italy 90 (US)/115 (Italy) BW DRAMA/WAR/FOREIGN

D Roberto Rossellini ☆
W Roberto Rossellini Federico Fellini Sergio Amidei

William Tubbs Gar Moore Maria Michi
Carmela Sazio Robert van Loon Dots Johnson
Dale Edmonds

Six vignettes from the Second World War, starting with the Allied invasion of Sicily in 1943 and ending with the Italian surrender in 1944.

Rossellini's film is designed to show the resilience of people in wartime; and, like his previous film, *Open City*, it attracted much critical acclaim for its realism. Now, much of it looks sentimental. The shooting and editing is often amateurish, performances are uneven, and much of the dialogue seems poorly improvized. The absence of narrative and dramatic conflict means that the film drags long before its end.

MIXED:

'I see no signs of originality in his [Rossellini's] work: a sickening lack of mental firmness, of fundamental moral aliveness, and of taste; but at his best an extremely vigorous talent for improvisation, for naturalistic poetry, and for giving the illusion of the present tense.' *(James Agee, Nation)*

'It cannot be doubted that [the film] will stand as one of the few great comments on the Second World War to be made by the contemporary cinema . . . Humorous and tragic, [it] fully earns the depleted title "great." Its deficiencies are as obvious as its brilliance . . . [It is] distinctly disparaging in the representation of and comment on the British . . . I take it that Rossellini to gain on the American market was prepared to lose in objectivity.' *(Richard Winnington, News Chronicle)*

'It is no exaggeration to say the [the film], with its warm shifting episodes, gives a greater and more heart-rending sense of the totality of war than any other film . . . For that reason it is unfortunate – though unimportant – that the few references to ourselves should be disobliging.' *(William Whitebait, New Statesman)*

'Often crudely cut, unprofessionally acted and emotionally prejudiced. But it is so deeply felt that I defy you not to be moved.' *(Sunday Chronicle)*

PRO:

'This is not a film anyone truly interested in the cinema can afford to miss . . . Though as touchy as the next one in my national pride, I find nothing to which I can take grave exception . . . Patchy, but brilliant, too, and at times, almost unbearably moving.' *(Reynolds News)*

'The spirit is one of sadness, but not pessimism, of faith, but not of optimism, and of charity which is not sentimental.' *(Manchester Guardian)*

'Not pretty, but it is an emotional experience that is immensely real and moving. And it is warm and humorous and delicate as well as grim.' *(Fortnight)*

'Real and absorbing . . . simple, unglamorized, done with an obvious understanding of human beings and compassion for their suffering.' *(Jane Lockhart, The Rotarian)*

PAJAMA GAME CT: 6 AV: 7.69

1957 US 101 C MUSICAL

D Stanley Donen ☆
W George Abbott Richard Bissell from Bissell's book *Seven and a Half Cents*

Doris Day ☆ Eddie Foy Jr ☆ John Raitt Reta Shaw Carol Haney ☆ Barbara Nichols Thelma Pelish

Workers go on strike in a pajama factory, but their female 'grievance committee chairman' (Doris Day) falls in love with the factory superintendent (John Raitt).

Bob Fosse's choreography is the best thing about this bouncy musical, competently adapted from a Broadway success. Doris Day is delightful, and the cast makes the most of some memorable songs, including 'Hernando's Hideaway', 'Hey, There' and 'Steam Heat'.

MIXED:

'The [novel's] sexiness is much less evident but the humour remains; and most conspicuous are the production's zest, vigour, and efficiency.' *(Manchester Guardian)*

'Though the incidental fun-making may not be a very realistic portrait of labor or management, even the most aggressive bureaucrats on both sides will likely be too diverted to object.' *(Time)*

PRO:

'Highspot of the film is the annual works picnic . . . which sets a new standard in what in Busby [Berkeley]'s day would have been called an "ensemble number".' *(Felix Barker, Evening News)*

'Doris Day . . . certainly keeps things cracking . . . Catchy music, lively dancing and a good lacing of comedy make the film a fruity salad of fun.' *(Ross Shepherd, People)*

'As radiant and gay as the first day of Spring . . . A happy, happy film.' *(Peter Burnup, News of the World)*

'A satisfactory version of the theatre piece . . . Splendidly performed and to my mind immensely enjoyable.' *(Dilys Powell)*

'The first left-wing operetta.' *(Jean-Luc Godard)*

PALM BEACH STORY, THE CT: 6 AV: 8.67

1942 US 88 BW COMEDY

D Preston Sturges ☆
W Preston Sturges ☆

Claudette Colbert ☆ Joel McCrea ☆ Rudy Vallee ☆ Mary Astor Sig Arno ✔ Robert Warwick Torben Meyer Jimmy Conlin William Demarest Jack Norton Robert Greig Roscoe Ates Robert Dudley ☆ Chester Conklin Franklin Pangborn Alan Bridge

Wife (Claudette Colbert) thinks up solution to the money problems of her inventor husband (Joel McCrea). She'll divorce him, find a rich husband and use his money to finance her ex-husband's schemes.

An idiotic screwball premise sparks off a series of improbable encounters with larger-than-life characters – the most engaging of them played by Rudy Vallee (as an amorous millionaire), Mary Astor (as his acerbic, much-married sister) and Sig Arno (as Astor's current boyfriend). None of it is plausible, and the final twist is so ludicrous, it verges on the insulting. But if you don't take any of it seriously, and why should you, there's plenty to enjoy in its energy, sophisticated dialogue and sheer joie de vivre. McCrea and Colbert make an especially charming couple. Sturges clearly intended the film to take people's minds off the Second World War, and it did.

PRO:

'Just as Jean-Baptiste Molière dressed his themes, often of dangerous leverage socially, in acceptable comic surfaces, Preston Sturges, in our time, is making a series of serious, often bitter satires, disguised as slapstick farces.' *(Script)*

'Minus even a hint of the war . . . packed with delightful absurdities.' *(Variety)*

'Surprises and delights as though nothing of the kind had been known before . . . farce and tenderness are combined without a fault.' *(William Whitebait)*

MIXED:

'Despite its lusty laughs, its quite meaningful sarcasms and its lavish inventiveness, it has an over-all weakness that is disturbing in a Preston Sturges movie . . . This time Sturges, who wrote and directed it, simply had too many engaging ideas, with the result that none of them gets quite enough attention.' *(John T. McManus, PM)*

'Sturges's comic invention soars, but the picture is too wild to be sustained.' *(Pauline Kael)*

PANDORA'S BOX CT: 7 AV: 8.25

(aka *Lulu; Die Büchse der Pandora*)

1928 Germany 97/110 BW DRAMA/SILENT/FOREIGN

D G.W. Pabst ☆
W G.W Pabst Laszlo Wajda from Franz Wedekind's plays *Erdgeist* and *Pandora's Box*

Louise Brooks ☆ Fritz Kortner Franz Lederer Gustav Diessl Alice Roberts

Femme fatale (Louise Brooks) wreaks emotional havoc on a doctor (Fritz Kortner), his son (Franz Lederer) and a Lesbian countess (Alice Roberts), before being murdered by Jack the Ripper (Gustav Diessl)

Wedekind's two *Lulu* plays are compressed into a silent classic by German director, G.W. Pabst. It's very episodic and the earliest scenes are the best, but it has a cumulative, sexual power. Louise Brooks's tart who embraces the life-force without caring about morality has to be one of the sexiest performances in the history of cinema. The film has been heavily bowdlerized since its release, and one version even ends up with Lulu and Jack the Ripper repenting their evil ways and joining the Salvation Army! The full version was restored in 1983. It was poorly remade in America as *No Orchids for Lulu* (1962), starring Nadja Tiller.

ANTI:

'For the hundredth time: one should not make films of literature. Especially not of Wedekind. And especially not by G.W. Pabst. The most significant quality of the [his] work . . . is his love for the single scene . . . These sections are not developed one from the other according to their tension, not getting stronger dynamically.' *(A. Kraszna-Krausz, Close-Up)*

'Starts fairly well, but tails out towards the end . . . Development is slow and the gradual descent of the two [lead characters] is devoid of incident . . . A sordid story for characters in which it is impossible to feel sympathy . . . The photography [in the early] sequences is excellent . . . In later sequences, brilliance and sparkle are lacking alike in production and camera-work.' *(Bioscope)*

MIXED:

'Although there are several adroitly directed passages . . . the narrative is seldom interesting. One is not in the least concerned as to what happens to any of the characters whose nonchalance during certain junctures is not a little absurd. It is a disconnected melodramatic effusion in which there is an attempt to depict a thoughtless attractive woman and her unsavory experiences . . . Miss Brooks is attractive and she moves her head and eyes at the proper moment but whether she is endeavoring to express joy, woe, anger or satisfaction is often difficult to decide.' *(Mordaunt Hall, New York Times)*

'Pabst's screen version of the Lulu plays . . . remains one of the great expositions of the cultural myth of the femme fatale . . . a peculiarly pernicious, if flattering, myth.' *(Angela Carter, New Society, 1978)*

PRO:

'The point of the Franz Wedekind plays on which the film is based is that Lulu's destructive sensuality is instinctual, not calculated. To be effective, she must be an innocent. Pabst understood this; flapper Brooks, with her black helmet of bobbed hair and her exuberant freedom of movement, seems a force of nature, not a performer, even during her comic scene when she throws a backstage tantrum. The sexual energy moves in torrents under Pabst's imaginative editing. On the strength of this performance alone, Brooks will be remembered as one of film's great femmes fatales.' *(Jay Carr, 1991)*

PANIC IN THE STREETS CT: 6 AV: 7.40

1950 US 96 BW THRILLER

D Elia Kazan ☆
W Richard Murphy Edward Anhalt Edna Anhalt ✔ from the Anhalts's story AAN

Richard Widmark ☆ Jack Palance (billed as Walter Palance) ☆ Paul Douglas ☆ Zero Mostel ☆ Barbara Bel Geddes

Doctor (Richard Widmark) and detective (Paul Douglas) hunt for everybody who came into contact with a murder victim, who was carrying the pneumonic plague; first and foremost, they need to find the murderers.

A gripping urban thriller with plenty of action, rightly praised for its atmospheric, New Orleans locations. The actors – especially bad guys Palance and Mostel – make the most of some sharp, cynical dialogue. Joe MacDonald makes effective use of deep focus photography, and Alfred Newman contributes one of his most atmospheric scores. The great defect is a domestic sub-plot which adds nothing to the story, and makes the film sag quite badly towards the middle.

MIXED:

'After a splendid and sustained beginning, an irresolute though thrilling middle, and a conventional end, we are sill a great deal more dazzled than disappointed.' *(William Whitebait, New Statesman)*

'A fine hunt-the-gangster chase . . . but . . . the whole appears undisciplined as if for once the brilliant Kazan was not too confident about what he was trying to achieve.' *(Margaret Hinxman, Time & Tide)*

'Sensitive may seem an odd word to apply to

anything which so largely concerns itself with brutality, but this is a sensitive film in that its theme, overclouded at times, is a humane one, and faithfully pursued . . . The film gains nothing by [the two fugitives] being types so exaggerated . . . A more serious defect is that Mr Kazan seems to have interested himself at least as much in the violence and the chases and the shootings as in the hunting down of the disease, which is his real subject.' *(Tribune)*

'The climactic chase is overlong and a little too ingenious . . . It becomes unintentionally funny . . . Some quiet interludes of hero Widmark's home life . . . gain nothing from the mannered acting of Barbara Bel Geddes . . . But moviegoers may be most impressed by nightclub comedian Zero Mostel's straight portrayal of a sniveling grifter, and the striking début of able villain Walter [later Jack] Palance, a onetime prizefighter with a face like a Halloween mask.' *(Time)*

PRO:

'Elia Kazan made most of the picture in New Orleans, and he draws every ounce of atmosphere from his real-life material. The dialogue is handled superlatively – interrupting, interlocking, sounding like real talk. His thugs make you feel as if you'd been locked up overnight in a museum of unnatural history. But at least no breath of the film studio touches the picture.' *(Stephen Watts)*

'Incisiveness in the writing as well as the handing give the characters more depth and surprise than is usual in the genre.' *(Gavin Lambert)*

'Elia Kazan directs this tough and unique story with the speed, imagination and ruthlessness that it needs.' *(Milton Shulman)*

'A model of what an action story should be . . . every department is admirably handled.' *(Richard Mallet, Punch)*

PAPER, THE

CT: 7 AV: 6 (est)

1994 US 82 C COMEDY/DRAMA

D Ron Howard ✓
W David Koepp Stephen Koepp ✓

Michael Keaton ☆ Marisa Tomei ✓ Glenn Close ✓ Randy Quaid ✓ Robert Duvall ☆ Spalding Gray Jason Alexander

A news editor (Michael Keaton) placates his pregnant wife (Marisa Tomei) who wants him to apply for a sedately managerial nine-to-five job on an upmarket New York paper.

A big, bustling blockbuster about a New York tabloid. It's got that *Hill Street Blues*, move-the-camera, smell-the-sweat feel about it; and it piles on the pace and pressure. You end up with the same adrenaline high you get walking the streets of Manhattan for the first time. The domestic side of the film could easily have been a pain, as in *JFK*, where Sissy Spacek kept on moaning at Kevin Costner to stop investigating Kennedy's assassination, and the audience kept wishing she'd give him a break and let him get on with the movie. But the writers have shrewdly woven the wife into the main story: she's a reporter too – albeit on maternity leave – and so can appreciate the enthusiasm which drives him, and help out. Better still, she's played by that truthful and touching actress, Marisa Tomei.

This being a neatly crafted Hollywood screenplay, Keaton's editor boss (Robert Duvall) is An Awful Example Of What May Happen If You Take Your Wife And Family For Granted, and the villain is Glenn Close doing her crazed career-woman again. I would say she's playing a malicious sexist stereotype, but unfortunately I know at least two senior journalists of whom this is a recognizable, even a kindly, caricature.

Holding the elements together is a plot-line about two black youths accused of murdering some tourists. Close assumes they're guilty and wants to picture them on the front page under the headline 'Gotcha!' Keaton smells a rat and wants time to investigate whether they're just scapegoats. This makes for a pretty perfunctory examination of journalistic ethics, and might have had problems sustaining an episode of *Lou Grant*; but really it's an excuse to portray the excitement of a modern newspaper office – and this, the picture does triumphantly. Ron Howard directs with a sure hand, not allowing the black comedy elements to swamp the drama; and the result is a hugely entertaining film, with an array of ensemble acting to rival Howard's own hit, *Parenthood*.

ANTI:

'Having dug up the bones of a cunning old genre, Howard lets the flesh hang like crape. There's beaucoup bustle but not much pulse. The pace is too slow for farce, the characters too cartoony for drama. Whereas *His Girl Friday* ran its gags on the fast track, *The Paper* often slows down to lend its galaxy of star types (Robert Duvall, Jason Alexander) a hint of dimension to their roles. But these subplots aren't much more sophisticated than those in *The Wizard of Oz*: Duvall gets a heart, Close a brain, Keaton courage. Tomei gets a baby – and gets left out.' *(Richard Corliss, Time)*

'A burst of nitty-gritty hustle, laced with sideways sentimentality, to make the audience believe for a couple of hours that it was feeling the pulse of ruthless America while, underneath the ruthlessness, all the pretty standards by which the audience lived were being slyly reaffirmed.' *(Stanley Kauffmann)*

MIXED:

'Was it necessary that everyone turn out to be decent, caring, and committed to truth and/or family? This kind of soft-heartedness ultimately robs

The Paper's skillful cast members of their considerable bite. The exception is Duvall, as an editor trying to reconcile with his daughter after learning that he has cancer. It's hard to imagine any other actor who could convey heartbreak and redemption with such sinewy toughness.' *(Tom Gliatto, People Weekly)*

'Howard rarely slackens his pace long enough for us to brood about the various implausibilities of plot (would even a New York police department lock up a couple of obviously innocent youths to trick tourists into believing the streets were safe for strolling?).' *(Guy Flatley, Cosmopolitan)*

PRO:

'I used to write real news on deadline, and those were some of the happiest days of my life. This movie knows how that feels.' *(Roger Ebert)*

'Cynical, mean-spirited, self-righteous – and exactly on the money. Michael Keaton is perfect . . . Robert Duvall, Glenn Close and Marisa Tomei are charming and chilling as decent folk diseased by the tabloid biz.' *(Rod Lurie, LA Magazine)*

PAPER CHASE, THE

CT: 5 AV: 7.00

1973 US 111 C COMEDY/DRAMA/ROMANCE

D James Bridges
W James Bridges ✗ AAN from John Jay Osborn Jr's novel
Timothy Bottoms Lindsay Wagner
John Houseman ☆ AAW Graham Bickel
James Naughton

Bright Harvard law student (Timothy Bottoms) falls for the daughter (Lindsay Wagner) of his tyrannical professor (John Houseman).

Bottoms isn't an interesting enough rebel to make this movie work as an allegory about the Youth Revolt of the 60s, though that seems to have been the intention. The love story between Bottoms and Wagner is poorly written; her motivation is especially unclear when they drift apart and then come back together. The element that does work is the surrogate father-son relationship between Bottoms and Houseman, which is elegantly scripted and immaculately acted. Houseman's character later formed the basis of a TV series spin-off of the same name.

PRO:

'Has some great performances, literate screenwriting, sensitive direction and handsome production.' *(Variety)*

'Beautifully made, splendidly acted and in its quiet way involves you.' *(Ian Christie, Daily Express)*

'Over all of it presides John Houseman – hooded eyes, pursed lips, more a presence than a Professor, and radiating a quality which, once we recognise it, we realise how seldom it is we see it paraded so entertainingly, so convincingly on the cinema screen. That quality is called intelligence.' *(Alexander Walker, Evening Standard)*

'A worthy film which engages the eye and the brain.' *(Benny Green, Punch)*

'Highly intelligent, witty and anything but dull.' *(Virginia Dignam, Morning Star)*

MIXED:

'Good: Houseman's hammy father-figure performance is one of those once-in-a-lifetime-things . . . Bad: Timothy Bottoms and Lindsay Wagner can't keep up with the challenge . . . The ending is pure cop-out and the subplot . . . is both maudlin and dishonest.' *(Andrew Sarris, Village Voice)*

'Very entertaining, though marred by repetitiousness and a slowing of pace half way through . . . Not a great movie, but watchable, amusing and thoughtful.' *(Hugh Herbert, Guardian)*

'Entertaining, excellently acted and mentally challenging . . . [but] lacks sufficient dramatic structure and clarity of purpose.' *(Felix Barker, Evening News)*

ANTI:

'A slightly unfocused account of conformism and milk-mild rebellion on the campus.' *(S & S)*

'Tries to be thoughtful and provocative, but it has nothing to say.' *(Pauline Kael)*

'Writer-director Bridges seems totally unaware that his ambitious young hero, not the professor, is the villain.' *(Clancy Sigal, Time Out)*

PAPER MOON

CT: 6 AV: 7.50

1973 US 102 C COMEDY

D Peter Bogdanovich ✗
W Alvin Sargent ☆ AAN from Joe David Brown's novel *Addie Pray*

Ryan O'Neal ☆ Tatum O'Neal ☆ AAW
Madeline Kahn ☆ AAN John Hillerman Randy Quaid

Con-man (Ryan O'Neal) and his little daughter (Tatum O'Neal) make a fine pair of criminals in the American midwest during the Depression.

Charming, cheerfully amoral romp which is never original or plausible, but amuses in a Runyonesque way. Laszlo Kovacs's camerawork is excellent. It was later turned into a TV series.

'Tatum O'Neal emerged in *Paper Moon* to enormous applause and an Oscar at seven. She served as a refuge for an America sick to its stomach over the atrocities it had committed and its abysmal defeat by Communist Vietnam as she took them for a stroll through the Depression which now seemed like the good old days. And although she played a shrewd little shrew, she was the most comfortably asexual child actress ever to hit the screen. Just what the Sandman ordered in a decade when child pornography became common knowledge.' *(Julie Burchill, Girls on Film)*

ANTI:

'As [Bogdanovich's] films become cleverer, they grow colder. They're dying from the roots up . . . this one's about the growing bond between . . . cute Shirley Temple and the con-man Paul Muni . . . What am I saying? I mean Ryan O'Neal and his daughter.' *(Gavin Millar, Listener)*

'I've never seen a film that looked so unlike what it was about.' *(Stanley Kauffmann)*

'Claptrap . . . The child is much too clever for her age, and the adult is rather too dumb for a man supposedly living by his wits . . . With *Paper Moon*, Peter Bogdanovich continues his progress into the past. Not a real past that he knew or creatively imagined, but the past of trashy old movies that he religiously lapped up as a buff and now proudly regurgitates as a director. If *The Last Picture Show* was Bogdanovich's *King's Row*, and *What's Up, Doc?* his *Bringing Up Baby, Paper Moon* is, as Vincent Canby correctly diagnosed, his *Little Miss Marker*.' *(John Simon)*

'At its best the film is only mildly amusing, and I'm not sure I could recall a few undeniable highlights if pressed on the point.' *(Gary Arnold)*

PRO:

'So enjoyable, so funny, so touching that I couldn't care less about its morals.' *(Daily Telegraph)*

'It could have been the worst sort of Shirley Temple slush, but instead it is an utterly delightful and entertaining film . . . Ryan O'Neal is excellent . . . Tatum [is] the only American child actor I have seen in the cinema whom I can wholeheartedly endorse.' *(Christopher Hudson, Spectator)*

'Though often delightfully knowing and charming, not to say entertaining, also looks curiously manufactured as well. Two things lift it from the ruck of the current crop of cinematic back-projections – a first-class screenplay . . . and the playing of the young Tatum O'Neal.' *(Derek Malcolm, Guardian)*

'An impressive new actress illuminates the screen . . . She is tough, sensitive, intelligent, completely captivating and just nine years old . . . See [the film] even if you hate children.' *(Ian Christie, Daily Express)*

PARALLAX VIEW, THE CT: 7 AV: 7.08

1974 US 102 C THRILLER

D Alan J. Pakula ☆
W David Giler Lorenzo Semple Jr ✔ from Loren Singer's novel
Warren Beatty ☆ Paula Prentiss ✔ William Daniels Hume Cronyn ☆ Walter McGinn

A journalist (Warren Beatty) investigates a Kennedy-style assassination, which seems to have been followed by the death of a suspicious number of witnesses.

Underestimated on release and unsuccessful with the public (possibly because of the depressing conclusion), but now rightly regarded as a classic conspiracy movie of the 1970s. Suspense-filled, and directed with visual imagination by Alan J. Pakula.

ANTI:

'Leaves us with precisely nothing and that's what's wrong with it . . . The conspiracy theory is carried through at just that level of flash banality Beatty operates on as an actor; great surface, needs depth.' *(Russell Davies, Observer)*

'Could well have a political viewpoint or even a theological one, but its head is filled with wood shavings.' *(Penelope Gilliatt, New Yorker)*

MIXED:

'A partially-successful attempt to take a serious subject – a nationwide network of political guns for hire – and make it commercially palatable to the popcorn trade – via chases, fights, and lots of exterior production elements.' *(Variety)*

'A consistently gripping film that . . . never makes the mistake of tying up the loose ends and offering any specific solution . . . We never discover what Parallax exists to do or who runs it . . . [The film is] not only . . . about paranoia but [is] in itself a deeply paranoid film. This is its strength as a disturbing entertainment, and its weakness as a truly valuable contribution to an understanding of American society.' *(Philip French, S & S)*

PRO:

'*North by Northwest* as imagined by Kafka.' *(Carlos Clarens)*

'Successful on two levels, as a taut engrossing thriller and as a searing political comment . . . Stylish, genuinely scary.' *(Virginia Dignam, Morning Star)*

'Complex in structure, demanding and deserving the closest concentration, this sociological thriller . . . is a very stylish affair . . . A thinking thriller has made its mark.' *(Gordon Gow, F & F)*

'There is no one to call a villain, only an impenetrable superstructure of corrupt power, and Warren's commission is to render the Hollywood hero as an anachronism.' *(NFT Bulletin, 1980)*

PARAPLUIES DE CHERBOURG, LES: *see* UMBRELLAS OF CHERBOURG, THE.

PARENTHOOD

CT: 8 AV: 7.33

1989 US 124 C COMEDY

D Ron Howard ✔
W Lowell Ganz Babaloo Mandel ✔

Steve Martin ☆ Mary Steenburgen ☆
Dianne Wiest ☆ AAN Jason Robards ✔
Rick Moranis ✔ Tom Hulce Martha Plimpton
Keanu Reeves ✔ Harley Jane Kozak ✔
Dennis Dugan Leaf Phoenix Eileen Ryan
Helen Shaw Jason Fisher

A film which casts a sardonic eye over current notions of parenthood, as held by the four grown-up children of feckless Frank (Jason Robards).

Parenthood features the kind of witty dialogue and terrific ensemble acting which you used to have to attend a Woody Allen movie in order to find. The story does contain improbabilities. Steve Martin might pass as 45 in a dim light, but here is supposed to be 35. Not even an actor as fine as Jason Robards can convince us that a man of Frank's advanced years would see the error of his ways so easily. And the plethora of plot-lines mean that some of the endings (notably the resolution of Gil's problems at work) occur much too arbitrarily and abruptly.

Some critics found fault with the sentimental climax; but this is, after all, a comedy – a genre which attracts happy endings, just as dogs attract fleas. Besides, for most of its length the film is refreshingly hard-edged; the children are commendably un-cute; and the movie is courageous enough to convey a sense of how families can destroy, as well as nurture.

The script by Lowell Ganz and Babaloo Mandel is even more entertaining than their other successful collaboration with director Ron Howard, *Splash*, and on the same high level of sophistication as *When Harry Met Sally*. Howard, though not the most visually talented director in the world, is a master of pacing, doesn't fumble a gag, and handles his large and talented cast with aplomb.

ANTI:

'A sprawling comic saga, forever on the brink of saying something meaningful about family life, forever collapsing into detachable comic sketches . . . A stronger controlling hand (with less of a sweet tooth) would have stopped the script dribbling and given it more punch.' *(Geoff Brown, The Times)*

'The one really staggering misstep comes at the very ending, which is set in a maternity ward, and which is so inanely, gratuitously sentimental that it would make Frank Capra wince. It's one of those ending endings, which ties up too many story lines too quickly, too glibly, and too improbably for comfort; and the picture that it offers of perfect family harmony and of difficulties overcome by love and patience contradicts the whole point of the movie – namely, that family life is by its nature fraught with predicaments which have no easy solutions . . . If I ever watch *Parenthood* on videotape, I'll turn the TV off after the charming and funny penultimate sequence (set at a school play), which does all the summing-up required, and which Howard would have been well advised to end with.' *(Bruce Bawer, American Spectator)*

'Did you notice that . . . even the "shitty" father, patriarch Jason Robards, had a lot to say about parenting while his wife, who should have been the matriarch of the clan, had nothing to say about anything throughout the entire film?' *(Kathi Maio)*

'An easygoing, mainly amusing, fundamentally empty comedy-drama that seems designed to be the pilot for a TV series . . . It's riotously funny in spurts, but it also has that congealed gooey centre familiar from too many Hollywood films and you end up wishing that Americans weren't quite so keen on expressing their love for each other. (*Kim Newman, Film Yearbook)*

PRO:

'Ambitious, keenly observed, and often very funny.' *(Variety)*

'Dianne Wiest does high-style comedy in *Parenthood* – the kind of acting that won acclaim for Broadway stars in the Thirties.' *(Pauline Kael)*

'Although occasionally mushy, the film is warm-hearted and funny enough to carry it off.' *(Rose)*

'The best kind of comedy,where we recognize the truth of what's happening even while we're smiling, and where we eventually acknowledge that there is a truth in comedy that serious drama can never quite reach.' *(Roger Ebert)*

PARIS, TEXAS

CT: 4 AV: 6.14

1984 West Germany/France 148 C DRAMA

D Wim Wenders ✗
W Sam Shepard ●

Harry Dean Stanton ☆ Dean Stockwell
Aurore Clément Hunter Carson Nastassja Kinski
Bernhard Wicki

A man (Harry Dean Stanton) tries to reunite his family by winning back the love of his son (Hunter Carson) and wife (Nastassja Kinski).

At first, *Paris Texas* looks and sounds as if it is going to be a great film; and Harry Dean Stanton endows the leading character with an impressive depth and melancholy. Ry Cooder's score is great, as is Robby Muller's cinematography. The pace of the picture is, however, intolerably slow and there comes a point when you realize that the film and its anti-hero aren't getting anywhere and never will. It's flat and arid as the desert landscape. Sam Shepard's screenplay proceeds on the assumption that narrative is a dirty word, and the two-hander scene with Nastassja Kinski at the end is unpardonably protracted. Wenders's direction is, as so often, modishly cool and pretentious. The film won him the British Film Academy Award for Best Director.

PRO:

'Masterpiece is not a word I use freely, but in this instance I use it without hesitation.' *(Clive Hirschhorn, Sunday Express)*

'There's something poetically just about the fact that . . . the great American movie can still be made [by a foreigner] . . . No synopsis can hint at the kind of resonance this film achieves . . . as though the story is literally developing before your eyes . . . A masterpiece about the contemporary American experience.' *(Cynthia Rose, New Musical Express)*

'Reflects the director's persistent fascination with the cultural clash between Europe and America . . . The key scene, and one of the most brilliant in Wenders's films, is the painful confrontation between Travis and Jane though the peepshow mirror.' *(NFT Bulletin)*

'Not the standard attack on American alienation. It seems fascinated by America, by our music, by the size of our cities, and a land so big that a man like the Stanton character might easily get misplaced . . . A defiantly individual film, about loss and loneliness and eccentricity . . . True, deep, and brilliant.' *(Roger Ebert)*

MIXED:

'A departure in style for Wim Wenders . . . the film is rather long but the tension . . . is maintained throughout . . . An unfortunate downbeat ending to a very stimulating film.' *(Sally Hibbin, F & F)*

'This is the most affectionate film from Wenders to date . . . [with] powerful, humorous, loving "moments" . . . But the sense of some larger ache . . . stays unspecified, unspecific.' *(John Coleman, New Statesman)*

ANTI:

'Even Ry Cooder's vivid score cannot prevent this lengthiest of "road" movies from becoming an extremely long haul.' *(Quentin Falk, What's On in London)*

'Begins so beautifully and so laconically that when about three-quarters of the way through it begins to talk more and say less, the great temptation is to yell at it to shut up. If it were a hitchhiker you'd stop the car and tell it to get out . . . Extremely diluted Sam Shepard.' *(Vincent Canby, New York Times)*

'Wenders's unbearably slow pacing and the bleakness of Texas landscape and cityscape overwhelm characters, minimalizing their touching moments and almost depriving the picture of warmth. Even if you're not a romantic, the resolution is unsatisfying.' *(Danny Peary)*

PASQUALINO SETTEBELLEZZE: *see* SEVEN BEAUTIES.

PASSAGE TO INDIA, A AAN CT: 5 AV: 6.86

1984 GB 163 C DRAMA

D David Lean AAN
W David Lean AAN from E.M. Forster's novel

Judy Davis ☆ AAN Alec Guinness ●
Victor Bannerjee ☆ Peggy Ashcroft ☆ AAW
James Fox Nigel Havers Richard Wilson
Antonia Pemberton Michael Culver ● Art Malik
Saeed Jaffrey Clive Swift Roshan Seth

A repressed English spinster (Judy Davis) claims that an Indian (Victor Bannerjee) attempted to rape her in the Malabar caves.

Beautiful, craftsmanlike and (for the most part) wonderfully acted, with some powerful scenes which show director Lean (at 75) somewhere near his best. He downplays E.M. Forster's hatred of colonialism, but adds some inspired touches of his own, such as Miss Quested's visit to a ruined temple, which beautifully illustrates the sexual feelings that lie beneath her repressions. Ernest Day's photography, John Box's art direction and David Lean's editing were all Oscar-nominated – so why is the film so uninvolving? Part of the reason is that we never know for certain what did happen in the caves – but there is something curiously detached about Lean's approach, throughout. Not all the acting convinces: Alec Guinness is sadly miscast, and Michael Culver fights a losing battle with a Scottish accent. And, at two-and-three-quarter hours, the film is overlong; the narrative often seems to plod, and loses momentum altogether after the courtroom climax.

PRO:

'One of the greatest screen adaptations I have ever seen . . . Lean places these characters in one of the most beautiful canvases he has ever drawn (and this is the man who directed *Doctor Zhivago* and *Lawrence of Arabia*). He doesn't see the India of travel posters and lurid postcards, but the India of a Victorian watercolorist like Edward Lear, who placed enigmatic little human figures here and there in spectacular landscapes that never seemed to be quite finished. Lean makes India look like an amazing, beautiful place that an Englishman can never quite put his finger on – which is, of course, the lesson Miss Quested learns in the caves.' *(Roger Ebert)*

'Although it is flawed, some of the film is absolutely and memorably right.' *(William Russell, Glasgow Herald)*

MIXED:

'Inevitably characters and incidents are scrubbed clean of detail . . . When the film behaves like a richly-decorated comedy of manners . . . there is much surface entertainment; when it lurches into

Forster's deeper waters, the passage to India is rough and tedious.' *(Geoff Brown, The Times)*

'David Lean really has a right regal nerve! . . . You can forget Forster . . . [This] is a noisily dramatic highway, embellished with elephants and pomp . . . But I liked it as fabulous, marvellous soap-opera.' *(Tom Hutchinson, Mail on Sunday)*

'If Lean's technique is to simplify and to spell everything out in block letters, this kind of clarity has its own formal strength. It may not be the highest praise to say that a movie is orderly and dignified or that it's like a well-cared-for, beautifully oiled machine, but of its kind this *Passage to India* is awfully good, until the last half hour or so. Having built up to the courtroom drama, Lean isn't able to regain a narrative flow when it's over; the emotional focus is gone, and the concluding scenes wobble all over the place.' *(Pauline Kael)*

PASSENGER 57 CT: 5 AV: 5.00

1992 US 84 C THRILLER/SO BAD

D Kevin Hooks
W David Loughery Dan Gordon

Wesley Snipes Bruce Payne Tom Sizemore Alex Datcher Elizabeth Hurley Robert Hooks

Brave man (Wesley Snipes) foils gang of aerial terrorists.

A fantastically silly thriller full of plot-holes and absurdities. Set in and around an aircraft, with Wesley Snipes in the kind of role normally played by Bruce Willis, it became known to its small but fanatical band of admirers as *Fly Hard*. It can be recommended to anyone in search of a good laugh, since it suffers from almost every disability ever spotted in an action pic:

1. *Rebel Without a Cause* Syndrome. As in *Die Hard*, a lone good guy is up against a gang of highly motivated international terrorists, but the source of their motivation is enjoyably unclear: these terrorists are just out-and-out psychos who enjoy acting intellectually superior and blowing up aircraft. Aren't they all?

2. Man of the People Rule. It is vital that your hero have street credibility, even at the expense of plot credibility. In this movie, our hero is a guy whom an airline has just hired as their Head of Counter-Terrorism, and they don't even give him a first class seat. Instead, they treat him as rudely as possible, even placing him next to the most garrulous old bore on the plane. Any real man of the people would, of course, complain bitterly and get himself upgraded.

3. The Law of the Gratuitous Close-Up. Any unknown subsidiary character who is given a close-up will turn out to be a villain. (See also *The Hunt For Red October*.)

4. The English Disease. You can't make a good, or a bad, action movie without an English actor to play your villain (Alan Rickman in *Die Hard*, Joss Ackland in *Lethal Weapon 2*, Stuart Wilson in *Lethal Weapon 3*, Charles Dance in *The Golden Child*). It doesn't matter that no one can remember the last terrorist who actually came from England: the point is that an inarticulate man of the American people can always outwit a smartass who talks in sentences. In *Passenger 57* we have the bonus of two English villains: Bruce Payne and Elizabeth Hurley. Miss Hurley explains why Americans don't like her accent: 'It makes me sound cold and heartless'. So much for the special relationship.

5. The Unhappy Bunny Principle. Psychotic villainy is always the result of an unhappy childhood (see *Kindergarten Cop*). The tip-off that this is true of *Passenger 57*'s villain comes when he assaults his own lawyer, hissing 'Never mention my childhood' and remarks 'I never had any toys: my father believed they would warp my personal values'.

6. The Curse of the Convenience Store. No hero of a Hollywood action movie can enter a convenience store without an armed robbery taking place within twenty seconds. This will always end with our hero shooting the robber dead, and more broken glass than you would have thought possible.

7. The Flashback Horror. Hollywood heroes have some terrible secret in their past, which causes them to have immobilizing flashbacks at moments of maximum peril. Such flashbacks abruptly cease at the end of the movie, when the hero miraculously conquers his innermost fear.

8. The Surround on One Side Scenario. Law enforcement agencies only ever surround an aircraft, train or bus on one side. This enables a clean getaway and a movie that lasts longer than one hour. Here the vehicle's a plane, but see also *Silver Streak* (train) and *Midnight Run* (bus).

9. Idiot Police-Chief Syndrome. Often resulting in the Surround on One Side Scenario, this means that the powers-that-be immediately jump to the conclusion that our hero is just a troublemaker. (See both *Die Hards*, and the *Lethal Weapon* series) At the end of the movie, the Idiot Cop is either dead, or dead impressed.

10. None But The Brave Deserve The Fair Principle. No American fair is complete without a chase through screaming people and a showdown on a Big Dipper (see also *Slayground, Fear*).

11. The Irrational Chase Postulate. At some point, when on the verge of escape, the villain will decide that getting away is of secondary importance to chasing the hero (often linked, as here, to the None But The Brave Deserve The Fair Principle).

12. The Grudging Respect Announcement. At some point, the villain will always tell the hero that they are two of a kind, even if they patently aren't. (See *In the Line of Fire* and the *Bond* movies, passim).

13. The Steel Underpants Rule. Although we never see them, the hero must wear steel underpants, for kicks in the groin which would incapacitate the rest of us for days leave no visible sign of distress, bar a sharp intake of breath.

14. The After You Clause. Out of some unspoken law of fairness, bad guys only attack the hero one at a time.

15. The Psychic Villain Rule. If the odds are starting to favour the forces for law enforcement, one of the villains will intuitively guess what the good guys are going to do, thus extending the movie by another half hour.

16. The 'He's Mine' Fallacy. Eventually, even the idiot police chief realizes he's in the kind of movie which can be resolved only by the hero beating the villain in hand-to-hand combat. Once the hero has uttered the fateful words 'He's mine', the entire might of US law enforcement is powerless to do anything except let him get on with it.

17. The Big Bang Theory, or The Post-Newtonian Law: The Harder They Are, The Further They Fall. All villains die either by exploding or by falling from a great height. Minor villains may fall from the top of a Big Dipper (see above) or advertising hoarding (*The Last Boy Scout*). For the principal villain, only a fall from a thousand feet will do, (see *The Rocketeer, Die Hard 2, Cliffhanger*) preferably accompanied by a massive explosion.

18. Not Dead, Only Resting Rule. Any villain you haven't actually seen explode or fall from a thousand feet isn't really dead, and will launch an attack on the hero when he's least expecting it. (See *Fatal Attraction, Dead Calm*.)

19. The Law of Sexual Magnetism. The hero may behave like a violent psychopath, but can easily be distinguished from the villain by the fact that every woman but one is attracted to the hero like a bitch on heat. The woman who plays hard to get is, of course, the one with whom he'll end up. The Law of Sexual Magnetism is enforced with even more unsubtlety if the hero's black. (See the films of Eddie Murphy, passim.)

20. The Black Guy in Command Commandment. In order to provide a role-model, at least one senior law-enforcement official shall be black (although the Idiot Police Chief must be white). In big-budget films, he will usually be James Earl Jones; in *Passenger 57*, he's played by the director's father.

PRO:

'So exciting, funny, suspenseful, and packed with great bits that you daren't take your eyes off the screen for a second.' *(Martin & Porter)*

MIXED:

'A reasonably saucy action tale that runs out of gas before landing.' *(Variety)*

'Sure, the movie has holes in it large enough to fly a DC-10 through, but what the hey . . . It has high energy and the kind of crazy intensity that makes you care in spite of yourself.' *(Roger Ebert)*

ANTI:

'A promising *Die Hard* at 40,000 Feet plot turns into a leaden *Raid on Entebbe* kind of thing . . . The only really interesting aspect of [the film] is that its black director has been integrated fully into the moribund Hollywood genre machine.' *(Andrew Pulver, City Limits)*

'A hackneyed action movie that might have given even Van Damme pause.' *(Stephen Amidon, Financial Times)*

'The only clichés missing are bad weather and George Kennedy.' *(Geoff Brown, The Times)*

'About as fresh as an in-flight meal.' *(Lizzie Francke, Guardian)*

'An inflated cartoon of excess without a modicum of charm, wit, or sense.' *(Baseline)*

PASSION, A: *see* PASSION OF ANNA, THE.

PASSION DE JEANNE D'ARC, LA: *see* PASSION OF JOAN OF ARC, THE.

PASSION OF ANNA, THE CT: 5 AV: 7.40

(aka *A Passion; En Passion*)

1969 Sweden 100 C FOREIGN

D Ingmar Bergman ☆
W Ingmar Bergman ☆

Max Von Sydow Liv Ullmann Erland Josephson Bibi Andersson Erik Hell Hjördis Pettersson

A recluse (Max Von Sydow) has his peace disturbed by a crippled widow (Liv Ullmann) who wishes to use his telephone; she involves him in the problems of a married couple (Erland Josephson, Bibi Andersson).

Bergman at his bleakest, coldest, and most humourless. The acting is impressive, and his framing of shots is meticulous; but Bergman's view of human existence is so relentlessly gloomy that it becomes not merely tiresome but unconvincing.

PRO:

'A masterpiece.' *(Penelope Gilliatt)*

'As usual, the acting of Bergman's "repertory company" is magisterial.' *(John Simon)*

'I cannot hope to convey the subtleties, the haunting quality and the deep humanity of this film . . . Another Bergman masterpiece all right.' *(Felix Barker, Evening News)*

'This masterly piece of work may be the film towards which Bergman had been working all his life; it restates the themes of the films immediately preceding it and utilizes some of the same situations, but with greater richness and density.' *(Shipman)*

MIXED:

'Impressive as it is intractable, though on a second viewing it seems to contract even further into itself, to offer less and withhold more.' *(Penelope Houston, Spectator)*

'I reckoned *The Shame* to be his grimmest film ever: *A Passion* turns the screw of despair even tighter.' *(John Coleman, New Statesman)*

'What makes [these characters] seem slightly absurd (as Chekhov's characters, for instance . . . never are) is that their mental agony is out of all proportion to their actual circumstances . . . Their acting is flawless . . . Like the island on which it is set, the film is bleak and barren.' *(Nina Hibbin, Morning Star)*

ANTI:

'I don't doubt that Bergman is perfectly serious about all this as a microcosm of life as he sees it . . . but I find, perhaps by the working of some quite craven, unworthy defence mechanism in my own psyche, cheerfulness keeps breaking through: the manoeuvres of these characters, so tense, so solemn, suddenly become so idiotic, and it then takes some minutes to return to a proper mood of high seriousness.' *(John Russell Taylor, The Times)*

PASSION OF JOAN OF ARC, THE

CT: 6 AV: 9.00

(aka *La Passion de Jeanne d'Arc*)

1928 France 77/85 BW BIOPIC/DRAMA/FOREIGN/SILENT

D Carl Dreyer ☆
W Carl Dreyer

Marie Falconetti ☆ Eugène Silvain Maurice Schutz Michel Simon Antonin Artaud

Joan of Arc (Marie Falconetti) is interrogated before being burned at the stake.

Like *Ordet*, this is a rumination by Dreyer on the inevitable conflict between individual faith and organized religion. Marie Falconetti gives one of the great silent screen performances in this, her only film. It was a critical success but a box-office flop, and it's very hard going, partly because of the need for long title-cards to reveal what the characters are saying. And it's intense: Rudolph Maté's photography concentrates pitilessly on the faces of Joan's judges, who are no oil paintings and wear no make-up. To say that virtually all of the film is shot in close-up makes it sound duller than it is – Dreyer skilfully keeps his camera and Joan's accusers on the move, while she remains motionless at the centre, constricted, penned in by her persecutors. We come to share her sense of claustrophobia, which is another reason why the film is so painful to watch.

ANTI:

'Very little is conveyed to us, especially as such potentially moving sequences as Joan's head being shaved and her burning are intercut with rabble-rousing images.' *(Shipman)*

PRO:

'Just as the rest of us seem determined to do with the very institution of the silent cinema, the French, of all people, come along with one of the grandest of all motion pictures in the perishing tradition. I won't go so far as to say [it] is the greatest photoplay I have ever seen, but, unquestionably, it is one of the four or five indisputable masterpieces of the dying medium; a superb indication of what could be done with the old art form if efforts had really been made to develop it seriously . . . It is not only a magnificent film, but . . . one of the greatest and most significant achievements of 20th century art, no matter what its form.' *(Richard Watts Jr, Film Mercury)*

'Dreyer . . . has engaged in a whole series of interesting experiments [which] . . . can hardly fail to have an effect on the procedure of other directors in England and abroad. [It] is remarkable both in its scheme and its execution . . . He tells this story . . . almost entirely in close-ups . . . The unusual camera angles . . . are an additional point of originality . . . and the fact that the film was made in the open [with] no make-up . . . may suggest a wider flexibility in production methods than has been customary.' *(Film Weekly)*

'Dreyer deserved the highest praise for his marvellous representation of environment; his terrible and strong use of camera angle and camera movement for the close establishment of an intimacy between the characters and the audience that has rarely, if ever, been equalled; and for his splendid subordination of detail in settings and general atmosphere.' *(Paul Rotha & Richard Griffith, The Film Till Now, 1930)*

'The camera angles reveal the power relationships as low-angle shots fill the screen with the threatening forms of the judges.' *(Marsha Kinder & Beverle Houston, 1972)*

'Dreyer was never so much ahead of his time as out of his time. No critic ever described him as "modern." *The Passion of Joan of Arc* seemed backward in its period, not only because it was a silent movie released in the midst of talkies with all the self-consciousness of an "art" film but also because Dreyer's enormous close-ups lacked the structural dynamism of Eisenstein's dialectical montage in *Potemkin* and *October*. *Day of Wrath* struck most critics of its time as too slowly paced for the demands of film art.' *(Andrew Sarris)*

PASSPORT TO PIMLICO CT: 6 AV: 7.58

1949 GB 84 BW COMEDY

D Henry Cornelius ☆
W T.E.B. Clarke ☆ AAN

Margaret Rutherford ☆ Stanley Holloway Basil Radford Naunton Wayne Hermione Baddeley John Slater Raymond Huntley Sidney Tafler Barbara Murray Jane Hylton Paul Dupuis

A district of London discovers that it legally belongs to Burgundy, and announces itself to be free of rationing restrictions.

Lighthearted, generous-spirited Ealing comedy with an ingenious idea, plenty of amusing jokes and character performances, and precious few pretensions to political satire. Margaret Rutherford, as an enthusiastic history scholar, is at her most enchanting.

MIXED:

'It is his [Cornelius's] first job as director. He has done well, but now and again he misses a point; now and again a joke lumbers by, a scene fails to go off with a bang. It is only fair to say that the hesitations come mostly in the opening of the film, before the central situation has ripened; and that he has admirably handled the out-at-elbows London background. Having said this, I will add that had the direction been entirely equal to the script we might have had a film on the level of René Clair, though without Clair's poetry. The satire of *Passport to Pimlico* often reminds one of Clair. It laughs with and at the English, and, by implication, at the brouhaha of international relations.' *(Dilys Powell)*

'British comedy with a fine flavor and wonderful details, though the whimsey is rather self-congratulatory.' *(Pauline Kael)*

PRO:

'The theme is related with a genuine sense of satire and clean, honest comedy.' *(Variety)*

'The first bearably funny native comedy for some time . . . Mr Clarke has mixed reality and fantasy as skilfully as he did in that kindred frolic *Hue and Cry*.' *(Fred Majdalany, Daily Mail)*

'A beautifully satirical piece and for the life of me, I can't recall having enjoyed a comedy so much in years.' *(Evening Standard)*

'Enormously funny, not in spasmodic patches but continuously from beginning to end. I hardly stopped laughing for an hour and a half.' *(A.E. Wilson)*

PATHER PANCHALI: *see APU* TRILOGY.

PATHS OF GLORY CT: 8 AV: 9.33

1957 US 86 BW WAR/DRAMA

D Stanley Kubrick ☆
W Stanley Kubrick Calder Willingham Jim Thompson from Humphrey Cobb's novel

Kirk Douglas ☆ Adolphe Menjou ☆ George Macready ☆ Wayne Morris Richard Anderson Ralph Meeker ☆ Timothy Carey ☆

Three soldiers are unjustly courtmartialled for cowardice during World War I.

Although one-sided and melodramatic, Kubrick's powerful anti-war film contains fine performances, an authentic evocation of trench warfare, many memorable visual moments (such as the condemned men's journey to the stakes where they are to be shot) and a genuine anger at corruption and incompetence among the officer class. The film was critically acclaimed, but a commercial failure. It was banned by the French Government and the US armed forces in Europe.

ANTI:

'Seems dated and makes for grim screen fare.' *(Variety)*

'The general . . . becomes not merely a bad man, but an impossibly bad man and the whole story floats off into the unreality of over-vehemence.' *(Times Educational Supplement)*

'Made twenty years ago . . . [it] might have been greeted as a minor masterpiece. Made today it leaves the spectator often confused and numb, like a moving speech in a dead language . . . The court martial is a farce. No written indictment . . . No witnesses . . . for the defense. No stenographic record.' *(Time)*

MIXED:

'[It] makes for a rather one-sided argument, but the thing has quite a dramatic wallop anyhow.' *(John McCarten, New Yorker)*

'It isn't another *All Quiet*, but it has considerable integrity and there are flashes of brilliance in dialogue and acting.' *(Daily Mirror)*

'Kubrick made the film with savagely ironical brilliance – marred only by the Americanisms at the trial.' *(Harold Convoy, Daily Sketch)*

'I think Kubrick is just a little too brilliant at the moment. When he learns to control his tricks he will be a great director.' *(Anthony Carthew, Daily Herald)*

'The film invites compassion for the herd of soldiers, helpless, wavering between callousness and self-pitying sentimentality. But the invitation is made intellectually, from the outside. And except for a moment or two in the performance of Timothy Carey as a pathetic, bemused prisoner the characters are characters from a novel, not from life; Mr. Kubrick has not been able to inject into figures which are literary and alien from him the rough vitality which so naturally flowed through the inhabitants of the American underworld [in Kubrick's film *The Killing*]. Nevertheless, *Paths of Glory*, in its authority, its piercingness, is an extraordinary film.' *(Dilys Powell)*

'A simple-minded pacifist film, but he gave it nervous rhythm and a sense of urgency.' *(Pauline Kael, 1965)*

PRO:

'A harsh and brutal treatment of some of the less savory aspects of war, the ironically titled *Paths of Glory* is an etched-in-acid story of resounding impact . . . Kubrick utilizes a device of sharp cuts, deliberately violating the time sequences to give an almost frantic tempo . . . that emphasizes the indecent haste of much of the action. It also points up the irony of the savage contrast in the lives of the men and officers as well as their different thinking and morals.' *(James Powers, Hollywood Reporter)*

'Probably the most savage indictment of the military mind the screen has known. It is more than a film – it is an experience. Its attack is so sharp, its comments so bitter that the film's very existence seems something of a miracle . . . [It] indicates just how mealy-mouthed *The Bridge on the River Kwai* was in its attempt at a similar target.' *(Derek Hill, Tribune)*

'A film of brilliance and integrity . . . Its message is timeless . . . The performances are painfully real.' *(Sunday Dispatch)*

'Beautifully performed, staged, photographed, cut and scored.' *(Colin Young)*

'It may be the best movie ever to come out of Hollywood.' *(David Shipman, 1984)*

'Not only one of the strongest anti-war movies ever made, but one of the great films of all time.' *(Judith Crist)*

PATTON AAW — CT: 6 AV: 8.50

(aka *Patton – Lust for Glory*)

1970 US 170 C WAR/BIOPIC

D Franklin J. Schaffner ☆ AAW
W Francis Ford Coppola Edmund H. North ☆ AAW

George C. Scott ☆ AAW Karl Malden Michael Bates Stephen Young Michael Strong Frank Latimore

Life and times of an American military man (George C. Scott).

Entertaining as a conventional war epic, a character study by Scott of a rampant egomaniac, and a debunking of war heroism. Since there was something in it for everyone, it was unsurprisingly a big hit. The co-screenwriter Francis Ford Coppola went on to re-examine much the same themes in *Apocalypse Now*, a darker and more disorganized work.

ANTI:

'I was much better playing Shylock in a Central Park performance' *(George C. Scott quoted in Academy Awards Illustrated)*

MIXED:

'Scott is unsurpassed at portraying a demonically driven man who can, in turn, frighten you out of your skin with a look, a word, the weight of an implication. He also has wit and charm and can make you laugh and rejoice with him . . . But Patton's psyche, motives, background, and private life are not probed, or just barely; no worthy antagonists are pitted against him; the film is devoid of poetry. The people remain two-dimensional, the battle scenes are just proficient battle scenes, the words spoken are prosaic and superficial.' *(John Simon)*

'The film reconstructs the desert battle marvellously . . . For spectacle, this film is as good as most conventional war films . . . Two weaknesses were Karl Malden's flaccid Bradley and Michael Bates' shallow Montgomery.' *(Hugh Lambert, Sunday Press)*

'Though competently handled, this potted history somehow fails to generate any real sense of excitement.' *(Clive Hirschhorn, Sunday Express)*

PRO:

'War is hell, and Patton is one hell of a war picture.' *(Variety)*

'Scott turns the task of believably portraying a basically unbelievable man into a towering achievement. Scott devours the screen in Attila-like mouthfuls. Schaffner . . . has charged it with insight and compassion and the kind of beautifully controlled artistic skill and intelligence seldom found in action films . . . I have never seen battle footage with such light and dimension, or such total regard for space and movement. There will undoubtedly be those who loathe Patton and everything he stood for, but I dare anyone who sees this movie of his life to tell me he was ever a bore. Patton is an absorbing testament to the life of a unique human being and a war movie for people who hate war movies.' *(Rex Reed)*

'In a performance of remarkable authority, George C. Scott has re-created [Patton's] mixture of contradictions.' *(Felix Barker, Evening News)*

'Patton became a mirror through which warring doves and hawks viewed the confirmation of their own deeply emotional beliefs. To the former, General Patton was the Antichrist, who symbolized the gutsy brand of militarism that had led to the Vietnam débâcle. And yet, as an audience, they found it difficult to criticize a film that was so overtly honest. It would be the key to the film's success, for there was no need to embellish or disparage the character of Patton; the paradox of his makeup was obvious from the beginning.' *(Steven Jay Rubin, Combat Films: 1945-1970, 1980)*

PAWNBROKER, THE CT: 6 AV: 7.60

1965 US 114 BW DRAMA/WAR

D Sidney Lumet ☆
W David Friedkin Morton Fine from Edward Lewis Wallant's novel

Rod Steiger ☆ AAN Brock Peters
Geraldine Fitzgerald Jaime Sanchez Thelma Oliver
Juano Hernandez

A New York Jew (Rod Steiger) keeps having flashbacks of life in a concentration camp.

Sharp, uncomfortable portrayal of a Holocaust survivor who has lost his faith in God and human nature, and takes refuge in materialism. Despite some critics' accusations of overacting, Steiger is terrific in his first leading role on screen, though he isn't helped by the fact that his character doesn't really develop; we just get to know him better. One point in its favour is the fact that it alienated almost every minority – Jewish groups because the protagonist was shown to be a Jew interested only in money, black organizations because of the film's portrayal of black gangsterism, the Legion of Decency because at one point Thelma Oliver exposes her breasts. How easily shocked people were in the 60s.

ANTI:

'Not only is [Steiger's] character isolated, the performance is, as well . . . The director, usually so sure with his actors, allows them to be strangely overplayed. All the world's a concentration camp may be the film's conclusion, but it remains very much a stage.' *(Patrick Gibbs, Daily Telegraph)*

'The feeling is all on the surface where it doesn't belong, and the central experience . . . seems unconnected with the theatrical goings on . . . It's a bit as though they're trying to pass off something by Tretchikoff as though it had been painted by Rembrandt.' *(Robert Robinson, Sunday Telegraph)*

MIXED:

'Lumet . . . knows how to create an atmosphere, how to create film . . . [which] for all its impact and importance leaves an impression of glibness and uncertainty of intent.' *(Ann Pacey, Sun)*

'Harshly lit, metallic and very terrifying . . . My one quarrel with this sombre, torturing film is that is shows no dramatic or emotional development in the main character, simply a death's head vision of a broken creature.' *(Felix Barker, Evening News)*

'The film is trite, and you can see the big pushes for powerful effects, yet it isn't negligible. It wrenches audiences, making them fear that they, too, could become like this man. And when events strip off his armor, he doesn't discover a new, warm humanity, he discovers sharper suffering – just what his armor had protected him from.' *(Pauline Kael)*

PRO:

'The surest, cruellest depiction of the Jewish tragedy that I have seen in many years of watching this painful but vulnerable theme being crassly exploited for profit or cheaply debased by sentimentality.' *(Alexander Walker, Evening Standard)*

PEEPING TOM CT: 5 AV: 6.86

1959 GB 101 (US)/109 (full version) C THRILLER/HORROR

D Michael Powell ☆
W Leo Marks

Carl Böhm ☆ Moira Shearer ● Anna Massey
Maxine Audley Esmond Knight Michael Goodliffe
Shirley Ann Field ● Jack Watson Pamela Green ●
(cameo: Michael Powell as the Killer's dad)

Mad, voyeuristic cameraman (Carl Böhm) slaughters women.

Not all that violent by modern standards, but heartily disliked by nearly all contemporary critics for seeming to revel in both the anti-hero's deeds and (even more tastelessly) the terror of his victims. It is fashionable now to say that the initial reaction was mistaken, and to hail the movie as a masterpiece. I'm not so sure that the original critics were entirely wrong: though cleverly made by an obviously talented director, this is a nasty, mean-spirited, somewhat pretentious film about the – rather tenuous – links between voyeurism, sadism, film-making and film-watching; some of the performances are embarrassingly bad. One highly regrettable effect of the critical reception was that Powell, a very distinguished film-maker whose credits included *Black Narcissus, A Matter of Life And Death* and *The Red Shoes*, was shunned by the British film industry, and over the remaining 31 years of his life was able to make only four more (very low-budget) films.

'I was genuinely surprised by the vicious reaction.' *(Michael Powell, 1983)*

ANTI:

'The only really satisfactory way to dispose of *Peeping Tom* would be to shovel it up and flush it swiftly down the nearest sewer. Even then, the stench would remain.' *(Derek Hill, Tribune)*

'The sickest and filthiest film I remember seeing . . . children's terror used as entertainment, atrocious crudity put on the screen for fun. And the main character, and madman murderer, is played all through as hero – handsome, tormented, lovable, a glamorous contrast to the heroine's alternative youths . . . and in the end her romantic sprawl beside the beloved killer is implicitly sickening. *(Isabel Quigly, Spectator)*

'In the last three and half months . . . I have carted my travel-stained carcass to some of the filthiest and most festering slums in Asia. But nothing, nothing, nothing – neither the hopeless leper colonies of East Pakistan, the back streets of Bombay nor the gutters of Calcutta – has left me with such a feeling of nausea and depression as I got this week while sitting through a new British film called *Peeping Tom*. I am a glutton for punishment, and I never walk out of films or plays no matter how malodorous. But I must confess that I almost followed suit when I heard my distinguished colleague Miss Caroline Lejeune say: "I am sickened!" just before she made her indignant exit . . . Mr Michael Powell (who once made such outstanding films as *Black Narcissus* and *A Matter of Life and Death*) produced and directed *Peeping Tom* and I think he ought to be ashamed of himself. The acting is good. The photography is fine. But what is the result as I saw it on the screen? Sadism, sex, and the exploitation of human degradation.' *(Len Mosley, Daily Express)*

'Its a long time since a film disgusted me as much as *Peeping Tom*. . . . This so-called entertainment is directed by Michael Powell, who once made such distinguished films as *A Matter of Life and Death* and *49th Parallel* . . . I don't propose to name the players in this beastly picture.' *(C.A. Lejeune, Observer)*

'Ugh! Obviously, Michael Powell made *Peeping Tom* in order to shock. In one sense he has succeeded. I was shocked to the core to find a director of his standing befouling the screen with such perverted nonsense. It wallows in the diseased urges of a homicidal pervert, and actually romanticises his pornographic brutality. Sparing no tricks, it uses phoney cinema artifice and heavy orchestral music to whip up a debased atmosphere . . . From its slumbering mildly salacious beginning to its appallingly masochistic and depraved climax, it is wholly evil.' *(Nina Hibbin, Daily Worker)*

'Frankly beastly.' *(Financial Times)*

'A thoroughly nasty piece of horror non-comic by the gifted but wayward Michael Powell . . . There has always been a morbid streak in Powell's best films – *Red Shoes* and *Black Narcissus* were two of them – but this time all is morbid, even to the point of photographing Moira Shearer, Anna Massey and Maxine Audley as though he had a grudge against them. The sorry theme has been dolled up in a flurry of trick effects with camera and lighting – another of Mr Powell's infatuations.' *(Fred Majdalany, Daily Mail)*

'A clever but corrupt and empty exercise in shock tactics which displays a nervous fascination with the perversions it illustrates . . . Not only is it drivel, it is crude, unhealthy sensation at its worst. A sad discredit to a fine producer's reputation.' *(Alexander Walker, Evening Standard)*

'Perhaps one would not be so disagreeably affected by this exercise in the lower regions of the psychopathic were it handled in a more bluntly debased fashion. One does not, after all, waste much indignation on the Draculas and Mummies and Stranglers of the last few years; the tongue-chopping and blood-sucking, disgusting as they may be, can often be dismissed as risible. *Peeping Tom* is another matter. It is made by a director of skill and sensibility . . . He did not write *Peeping Tom*; but he cannot wash his hands of responsibility for this essentially vicious film.' *(Dilys Powell)*

PRO:

'Mr Michael Powell, who produces with the finesse one expects of him, works all this up into a sufficiently nasty climax; earlier horrors, one feels as they arrive, are curiously muted but their quietness allows a hard turn of the screw at the end, and the encounter between Maxine Audley, the blind mother, and Mr Carl Böhm in the film's centre reminds us that Mr Powell is a director who knows where he is going; if he makes a thriller, it will thrill.' *(The Times)*

'Heavily censored in most countries . . . Critics and censors, united for once, seemed to find the display of terror more deplorable than actual blood-spilling.' *(Carlos Clarens, An Illustrated History of the Horror Film, 1967)*

'Michael Powell's remarkable film . . . was derived in certain respects from de Sade and anticipated in others the kind of appalling sadistic experiments revealed in the Moors case of 1966.' *(Roger Manvell, New Cinema in Britain, 1969)*

'Perhaps the most notorious British film ever: a startling treatment of voyeurism and the mechanics of cinema, wrapped in the clothes of a lurid psychological thriller. Director Michael Powell once called it a very tender film, a very nice one; hardly, but its fiendish skill and garish imagery haunt the mind long after well-bred films are forgotten.' *(Geoff Brown, Radio Times, 1983)*

'Arguably the most genuinely shocking British film ever made . . . reflects Powell's obsession with the nature and form of film . . . His distinctive use of colour and lighting and the constantly shifting visual surface of the film make it the most stylistically radical of his works, and easily the most controversial.' *(Allan Hunter & Kenny Mathieson, Movie Classics, 1992)*

'A remarkable examination of the psychology of film-making and film viewing, and one of the most disturbing films ever made.' *(Virgin)*

'Is the film as disgusting as the British critics found it? Yes, but it is also very moving, a case study that could have been simply sadistic but emerges (especially because of the Böhm performance) as a tragic record of a destroyed life. Perhaps that's why *Peeping Tom* was so disturbing to its first viewers. It is not distanced into "entertainment" like *Psycho*, but remains unforgivingly as the story of horrible crimes seen straight on.' *(Roger Ebert)*

'I hated the piece and, together with a great many other British critics, said so. Today, I find I am convinced that it is a masterpiece. If in some afterlife conversation is permitted, I shall think it my duty to seek out Michael Powell and apologise. Something more than a change of taste must exist . . . With so gifted a director this can hardly be anything but a frightening movie, but its object is the examination of emotion and not titillation. Interesting that it should be revived now when there has been much concern about the influence of cinema. All the more reason to distinguish between the serious and the merely sensational horror. Reading now what I wrote in 1960 I find that, despite my efforts to express revulsion, nearly everything I said conceals the extraordinary quality of *Peeping Tom*. See it, and spare a moment to respect the camerawork of Otto Heller.' *(Dilys Powell, Sunday Times, 1994)*

PELLE THE CONQUEROR AAW CT: 7 AV: 8.27

(aka *Pelle Erobreren*)

1987 Denmark/Sweden 138/150 C DRAMA/FOREIGN

D Bille August ☆
W Bille August from Martin Andersen Nexo's novel

Max Von Sydow ☆ AAN Pelle Hvenegaard ☆
Erik Paaske Kristina Törnqvists Morten Jorgensen

An illiterate Swedish immigrant worker (Max Von Sydow) and his young son (Pelle Hvenegaard) struggle to survive on an inhospitable Danish farm.

Yet another critical success that was not a hit with the public. *Pelle*'s uncommerciality lies not so much in its length (over two and a half hours) as in its almost total lack of humour. Despite a mildly optimistic ending, the prevailing atmosphere is one of grinding pessimism and repeated blows administered by a sadistic fate. The film also contains one of the most splendidly gloomy lines in Scandinavian cinema: 'Herring, herring, herring! Every single day!' Fortunately, the negativity is offset by the film's unflinching, unsentimental willingness to portray real human emotions, helped by truly remarkable ensemble acting and a magnificent performance by Max Von Sydow.

MIXED:

'August's film comes on at times like an overgrown soap-opera. But handsome photography and rich characterization work their spell, and Von Sydow is the film's lantern-jawed lynchpin.' *(Harlan Kennedy, Film Review)*

PRO:

'Imagine a Scandinavian Dickens novel, brought to the screen with its detail, richness of character, and passion for social reform reimagined in sweeping, urgent visual terms, and you'll have an idea of the epic amplitude of *Pelle*. Grand, deep-breathing, profoundly humanistic, *Pelle* is a magnificent achievement.' *(Jay Carr)*

'An almost perfect example of narrative cinema, lovingly made, full of emotion, sentiment and compassion.' *(Sandy Lieberson, Film Yearbook)*

'One of those rare Foreign Oscar-winners that actually deserves the award.' *(Rose)*

PENNIES FROM HEAVEN CT: 6 AV: 5.58

1981 US 108 C MUSICAL/ROMANCE

D Herbert Ross
W Dennis Potter AAN

Steve Martin ● Bernadette Peters ☆ Christopher Walken ✓ Jessica Harper John McMartin

A fantasizing sheet-music salesman (Steve Martin) refuses to face reality, with tragic results.

This famous flop has been called 'underrated' so often that it's in danger of being overrated. It is relentlessly pessimistic, and not a patch on the original BBC TV series in terms of performances: Steve Martin is especially weak in Bob Hoskins's leading role. However, it has compensating strengths in the form of some dazzling production numbers which explore the callous, almost fascistic side of Busby Berkeley musicals. A fascinating failure.

'I knew *Pennies From Heaven* was a gigantic career mistake, but I loved the thing so much. I loved the language, the writing, the script. I thought it was an original movie done in an original style. I thought it had something to say. I still feel that way. Besides, if I have a career 15 years from now maybe it won't look like such a blunder. A lot of people come up to me now and tell me they saw *Pennies* in film class. That makes an impact. It might have been esoteric when it was released but more and more people are beginning to understand it better. First, they had to get over seeing me in it, then they had to figure out what was going on. There were a lot of humps to get over.' *(Steve Martin)*

ANTI:

'All flash and style and no heart.' *(Roger Ebert)*

'An extravaganza all right, a big color musical [which] is no backstage story – goodness no. It was tough during the Depression, see? . . . This [film] is seedy all right – $10 million worth of seediness.' *(Carlos Clarens, SoHo News)*

'I'd have been much happier if the plot had been

scrapped altogether and there had been nothing but song and dance.' *(Francis Wheen, New Statesman)*

MIXED:

'The picture is not helped by a curiously low key and anonymous performance from Steve Martin . . . though Bernadette Peters is excellent.' *(Charles Spencer, Evening Standard)*

'What the film lacks are the pinpoint sharp performances by Bob Hoskins, Gemma Craven, and Cheryl Campbell . . . Most of all it reminded me how much I miss the great movie musicals that used to roll off the Hollywood assembly line.' *(Margaret Hinxman, Daily Mail)*

'What I love is the audacity of its craftsmen and performers. What I hate is its single-minded, monotonous rendering of the Great Depression and of depression generally.' *(Michael Sragow, Rolling Stone)*

PRO:

'In its own way it is every bit as successful [as the original television series].' *(Madeleine Harmsworth, Sunday Mirror)*

'The dance numbers are funny, amazing, and beautiful all at once; several of them are just about perfection.' *(Pauline Kael)*

'[The screenplay serves] a dual purpose, both recreating the fantasies of the 1930s and exploring the nightmarish underside of those dreams . . . *Pennies From Heaven* is a wonderful film that has gone unrecognized by the audiences of 1981. Its appeal is timeless, however, and some day it will find the audience that it deserves.' *(Don K. Thompson, Magill's Cinema Annual 1982)*

PÉPÉ LE MOKO

CT: 6 AV: 6.86

1936 France 90 BW DRAMA/ROMANCE/FOREIGN

D Julien Duvivier ☆
W Henri Jeanson Julien Duvivier from Roger D'Ashelbé's novel

Jean Gabin ☆ Mireille Balin Marcel Dalio Lucas Gridoux Line Noro Gilbert-Gil Saturnin Fabre Gabriel Gabrio

A Parisian gangster (Jean Gabin) hiding in the Algiers casbah is tempted to his doom by love of a woman (Mireille Balin).

Based on a true story, this is a 30s classic – a beautifully lit, highly romanticized precursor to American film noir, with lots of doom-laden atmosphere and a charismatic performance from Gabin as an existential loner against the system – or, to put it another way, a crook. Duvivier does an exceptionally skilful job of drawing attention away from the anti-hero's criminality, and stressing his loneliness and desperation. Banned during the Second World War by the French authorities who felt it was too depressing and might lower morale.

MIXED:

'Grim but powerful . . . In spite of its ponderous pace, the picture compels interest by its picturesque settings, the appealing central character, and the masterly direction which achieves two tremendous dramatic highlights . . . More than anything, however, it is the direction . . . which gives the picture undeniable force, in spite of its heavy tempo . . . Gabin is both masterful and moving.' *(Film Weekly)*

PRO:

'Duvivier shows himself to have absorbed perfectly, and transmuted, the technique of the American gangster-movie. This tale . . . is based on an evident formula, but developed with considerable dexterity . . . Men of this type do after all live and die, grimly, very much according to formula.' *(Arthur Vesselo, S & S)*

'The very frankness of the picture is the secret of its power and distinction.' *(Bosley Crowther)*

'Strong drama of Algerian underworld. Fine acting, brilliant direction, picturesque and unusual settings . . . Extremely well told, very human in characterisation . . . Pictorially expressive.' *(Kine Weekly)*

'The most brilliant achievement of the French studios in 1936 . . . Direction is superb, action is fast and . . . there is good music, good technical work, and excellent dialogue.' *(Pierre Autre, Motion Picture Herald)*

'Perhaps there have been pictures as exciting on the thriller level . . . but I cannot remember one which has succeeded so admirably in raising the thriller to a poetic level.' *(Graham Greene)*

'One of the most compelling of all French fatalistic screen romances, yet seen by few Americans because it was remade in Hollywood two years later as *Algiers* . . . *Algiers* was so closely copied from *Pépé le Moko* that look-alikes were cast in many of the roles, and some sequences were followed shot by shot. But *Algiers* is glamorous pop that doesn't compare to the original' *(Pauline Kael)*

PER UN PUGNO DI DOLLARI:

see FISTFUL OF DOLLARS, A.

PERSONA

CT: 6 AV: 8.33

1966 Sweden 81/85/90 BW DRAMA/FOREIGN

D Ingmar Bergman ☆
W Ingmar Bergman

Liv Ullmann ☆ Bibi Andersson ☆
Gunnar Björnstrand Margaretha Krook
Jörgen Lindstrom

An actress (Liv Ullmann) who has become a mute is cared for by a nurse (Bibi Andersson); gradually, their identities begin to merge.

Sombre, compelling study of two women, who descend into mental turmoil as their identities compete, then combine – at least that's what most people reckon it's about. Though the ultimate meaning is obscure, this is one of Ingmar Bergman's most haunting creations, with moments of savage sadism and insinuating eroticism. It contains two memorable performances by Liv Ullmann and Bibi Andersson.

PRO:

'The most personal film of a director who perhaps more than any other has made his films a thinly concealed reflection of his own personality.' *(David Wilson, Guardian)*

'To be held at constant imaginative, intellectual and dramatic stretch for 81 minutes is no ordinary pleasure in a cinema – but Bergman's new work manages this and more.' *(Alexander Walker, Evening Standard)*

'Never before on film has the derailed psyche been more penetratingly examined, never before has the drama been played so consistently beneath the surface, yet without the slightest sacrifice in palpable excitement . . . I can only guess at the ultimate meaning. The artist and the ordinary human being need each other, but this is a love-hate, a fight for absolute power over the other. Their complete communion is illusory and painful – only a dream, a nightmare – yet also real enough, perhaps, to mark them both. Life and art batten on each other, art sucking life's blood, life trying to cajole or bully art into submission, into becoming its mirror. The result of the strife is madness, whether feigned or real hardly matters. Relatives, lovers, friends, all who are sucked into this conflict, suffer along with the principal combatants. The end is, at best, a draw. And, with luck, a magnificent film.' *(John Simon)*

'*Persona* has variously been interpreted as an exploration of the role of the artist, as an embodiment of the psychoanalytic process, and as a meditation on Bergman's standard existential themes – reality, life, and death.' *(Baseline)*

MIXED:

'Acted with dazzling perception . . . immaculately shot . . . The timing is masterly and the pressure unrelenting. If one finds the effect suffocating, it's because Bergman's dramatic material seems to exist to be used up rather than explored, as though air were being drained out by all these excruciating turnings of the screw, and none being let in.' *(Penelope Houston, Spectator)*

ANTI:

'Fairly incomprehensible and not especially attractive . . . Bergman's own artistic persona is curiously divided between the clarity of his means, and the obscurity of his intentions.' *(David Robinson, Financial Times)*

'Desperately solemn, if not quite so portentous as Bergman's recent trilogy . . . For about half its length, before it goes off too obviously into fantasy, it is holding. But after that, despite all its appearance of being deep and significant, it is difficult indeed to banish a nagging recollection that the artist . . . may be half visionary, but must also be half charlatan.' *(John Russell Taylor, The Times)*

'More drastically and far less entertainingly than Fellini in *8½*, Bergman may here be seen to be both waving and drowning.' *(John Coleman, New Statesman)*

'I don't trust an inch of it . . . [It] is all structure and no affect. It is a "pretend" film.' *(Robert Robinson, Sunday Telegraph)*

'Although . . . several ideas are lying around, they are not really integral to the film, which is a kind of a ghost story in Bergman's cold, forbidding and baffling style.' *(Nina Hibbin, Morning Star)*

'Reactions have ranged from incomprehension to irritation with what is dismissed as a characteristic piece of self-indulgence on Bergman's part – Bergman talking to himself again.' *(David Wilson, MFB)*

'A puzzling, obsessive film that Bergman seems not so much to have worked out as to have torn from himself.' *(New Yorker, 1977)*

PERSONS UNKNOWN: *see* BIG DEAL ON MADONNA STREET.

PETER PAN CT: 6 AV: 6.83

1953 US 76 C CARTOON/COMEDY/ACTION/ADVENTURE

D Wilfred Jackson Clyde Geronimi Hamilton Luske (supervisor: Ben Sharpsteen)
W Ted Sears Bill Peet based on J.M. Barrie's novel and play

Voices: Bobby Driscoll Kathryn Beaumont Hans Conreid Bill Thompson Heather Angel Paul Collins

Boy who refuses to grow up leads three London children – Wendy, Michael, and John Darling – to Neverland, in order to fight with Captain Hook and his pirates.

Peter's American accent, the over-broad slapstick and Disney-style sentimentality are unlikely to appeal to anyone familiar with the original book, while the stereotypical Indians won't find favour with the politically correct. The story sags, too. Even so, the film has a few magical moments – especially the flying sequences, and all the episodes involving Hook and the ticking crocodile. Disappointingly, the song 'Never Smile at a Crocodile' is not included, though the tune can be heard as part of the underscore.

ANTI:

'Death of a classic.' *(Gavin Lambert, Evening Standard)*

'Disney has made one whale of a mistake. Barrie's play is not for children; but for middle aged people who would like to dream they are children again.' *(Paul Holt, Daily Herald)*

'I don't in the least object to Mr Disney's story being different [from Barrie's]: I only object to its being, on the whole, unfunny, tasteless, vulgar and dull . . . I make this complaint with sincere regret: it is like slapping an old friend.' *(Campbell Dixon, Daily Telegraph)*

'It has spirit and movement but it completely lacks magic. Its sentiment . . . is far more cloying than the original. Only Tinker Bell gives it something. But whatever that is – it definitely is not the fairy innocence that the late Sir J.M. Barrie dreamed up.' *(Leonard Mosley, Daily Express)*

PRO:

'A feature cartoon of enchanting quality.' *(Variety)*

'Disney has cut some of the stickier sentiment in Barrie's play and concentrated on the fantasy and the fun. I shouldn't be surprised if this proves to be his most popular film.' *(Star)*

PETER'S FRIENDS CT: 6 AV: 6.13

1992 GB 101 C DRAMA/COMEDY

D Kenneth Branagh ✗
W Rita Rudner Martin Bergman

Kenneth Branagh Alphonsia Emmanuel ●
Stephen Fry Hugh Laurie ☆ Phyllida Law
Alex Lowe Rita Rudner Tony Slattery ●
Imelda Staunton ☆ Emma Thompson

Friends from a university revue group reassemble at a country house, ten years on.

Cheap and mainly cheerful comedy which sacrifices depth and character development in pursuit of one-line gags and easy sentiment. Odd moments are touching, such as the sing-song around the piano, and a lot of the jokes are funny; but much of it looks and sounds like an over-extended situation comedy. The performances are variable; at least two are embarrassingly dreadful, and Branagh gives one of the least convincing drunk acts in recent memory. As a director, Branagh continues to give the impression that he has yet to find a style of his own.

PRO:

'Well written, beautifully performed and highly entertaining.' *(Derek Malcolm, Guardian)*

'As sad and touching at times as it is funny.' *(Robin Stringer, Evening Standard)*

'If it is not Chekhov it is a good English equivalent. And if it is not *The Big Chill* – well, actually it is better than *The Big Chill* . . . when not corseting itself with overemphatic nostalgia, [it] is lithe with non-didactic charm.' *(Nigel Andrews, Financial Times)*

'If film is basically a voyeuristic medium, then one of the questions that might be asked about *Peter's Friends* is: would we like to be one of these friends and attend such a reunion ourselves? I would. I liked this group better, in fact, than the friends in *The Big Chill*, perhaps because they seem to like each other more, or perhaps just because they're more amusing.' *(Roger Ebert)*

MIXED:

'Sometimes funny, often cloying.' *(Variety)*

'Branagh . . . has now dished up a most curious meal: part Simon Gray, part *The Big Chill*, part brittle American sitcom . . . [and] gives a lazy performance.' *(The Times)*

'[It] really isn't all that bad, if you like wordy, character-driven pieces. It's a well acted, moderately funny, inward-looking TV-sized film . . . [But if you're] not really in the post-Cambridge nostalgia business . . . I'd wait for it to get to TV.' *(Ruth Picardie, City Limits)*

'Less a feature film than a series of witty sketches strung together, it is packed with enough splendid retorts and one-liners to keep you chortling.' *(Rose)*

ANTI:

'The latest piece of flim-flam passed off as film . . . Branagh . . . is unconvincing . . . The script founders badly, falling somewhere between comedy and light drama, and Branagh's flaccid direction, together with an almost entirely miscast cast, sends it packing down the path of self-indulgence . . . The film is most notable for its tacky use of Aids for a cheap and inappropriate, dramatic effect which will probably leave most gay audiences with a severe case of cringe-induced toe-curling.' *(Rose Collis, Gay Times)*

'Awful, with glimpses of wit. The script is hopelessly schematic: one long drawing-room chat in which people dish each other, then leave the room so they can be talked about.' *(Richard Corliss, Time)*

'Kenneth Branagh . . . apart from a dire drunk scene, turns in a winning performance. But . . . [there's a] sentimental ending, when everyone stops bitching as they listen with growing horror to Peter's awful revelation. I wonder if their reactions would have been the same if his incurable disease had been a little less trendy – something like shingles or Alzheimer's. What we end up with is a small-scale TV sitcom made by the 'In' crowd.' *(Ken Russell, 1993)*

PETRIFIED FOREST, THE CT: 6 AV: 7.10

1936 US 83 BW DRAMA

D Archie Mayo ●
W Charles Kenyon Delmer Daves ● from Robert E. Sherwood's play

Humphrey Bogart ☆ Bette Davis ☆
Leslie Howard ✗ Charley Grapewin ✓ Genevieve Tobin Dick Foran Joe Sawyer Porter Hall

Gangster (Humphrey Bogart) holds people hostage in a gas-station café.

This stagey, pretentious melodrama is lifted above mediocrity by two magnificent central performances from Davis and Bogart (the latter of whom had played the role on Broadway). Leslie Howard's style hasn't stood the test of time nearly as well, and he isn't helped by a basically unconvincing character (he's meant to be a disillusioned poet) and an excess of speechifying ('All this evening I've had the feeling of destiny closing in,' 'You're the last great apostle of rugged individualism,' etc). The script is so hellishly long-winded and sluggishly directed at times that it's hard to avoid wishing that Bogart would shoot the lot of them, so we could all go home.

PRO:

'Bogart's study of Duke Mantee, the killer, is a remarkable piece of acting, underlining without exaggeration the animal-like mentality of a professional murderer.' *(Film Weekly)*

'Humphrey Bogart . . . acts with such understanding that one pities the man as much as one detests the crime he commits.' *(Picturegoer)*

'Tender emotional drama . . . Howard is superb.' *(Kine Weekly)*

'Tense melodrama with an arresting and unusual plot . . . A very skilful adaptation . . . It has excitement, tense situations, humour, romance, witty and brilliant dialogue. The direction is in every way admirable . . . Mention must be made of a remarkable performance by Humphrey Bogart.' *(MFB)*

'A notable philosophical gangster drama.' *(Lionel Williams, Evening Standard)*

MIXED:

'Very little movement, but lots of dialogue, some of which is clever, but otherwise too subtle for the average cinemagoer . . . The story is never for one minute convincing.' *(Era)*

'Drama slackens under the weight of Mr Sherwood's half-baked philosophy.' *(Alastair Cooke)*

'There is good dramatic material here, but Mr Sherwood doesn't see his play as certain things happening, but as ideas being expressed, "significant", cosmic ideas.' *(Graham Greene)*

'For a guy who's supposed to be burnt out, Howard sure has a lot of talk in him, and it's fancy and poetic as all getout.' *(Pauline Kael)*

PETULIA CT: 5 AV: 6.91

1968 US 105 C DRAMA

D Richard Lester ✗
W Lawrence B. Marcus from John Haase's novel *Me and the Arch Kook Petulia*

George C. Scott ☆ Julie Christie
Richard Chamberlain Shirley Knight ☆
Joseph Cotten Arthur Hill Kathleen Widdoes
Pippa Scott

Divorced, middle-aged doctor (George C. Scott) falls for married young socialite (Julie Christie).

Dismissed by most critics on release, this bleak commentary on values in the Swinging 60s was not what people expected from the young director who had made the high-spirited *A Hard Day's Night* and *The Knack*. Over the years, it has gained respectability – now, it is in more danger of being overrated. Very much a companion piece to *Darling*, which starred Christie in a similar though less whimsical role, it is unnecessarily flashy (cinematography is by Nicolas Roeg) and the narrative is abstruse. But Scott's central performance is one of his best.

'It's about the inability of people to make contact.' *(Richard Lester)*

PRO:

'People will go to the film prepared to laugh and stay to sniff. For Mr Lester, the arch-clown among comedy directors has come up with a tear-jerker . . . an emotion packed drama of non-communication . . . designed to pack a wallop that isn't funny at all.' *(William Hall, Evening News)*

'I've seen it twice and the second time was more rewarding, always a good sign . . . What lasts are the many insights that make up the composite picture of marriage on the rocks . . . I still can't go all the way with the admirers of Julie Christie, but I liked her far more than I'd expected . . . Released from the strait-jacket of *Dr Kildare*, Richard Chamberlain gives a finely judged portrayal. But best of all is George C. Scott, whose reflective performance is the solid core of a mature and moving film.' *(Margaret Hinxman, Sunday Telegraph)*

'Manages to depict boredom with boring the audience, which puts Lester one up on Michelangelo Antonioni . . . [Lester] has made another one of those pictures about the malaise of our times.' *(R.E. Pincus, After Dark)*

'There is a subtext of powerful feeling under every scene.' *(Penelope Gilliatt)*

'A terrific movie, at once a sad and savage comment on the ways we waste our time, our money and ourselves in upper-middle-class America. It is a subject much trifled with in movies these days, but rarely – if ever – has it been tackled with the ferocious and ultimately purifying energy displayed in this highly moral, yet unmoralistic, film . . . The triumph rightly belongs to Lester . . . He has at last controlled his enormous gift for movie making and placed it in the service of a brilliantly conceived, carefully aimed, splendidly detailed satire.' *(Richard Schickel, Life)*

'Filming in San Francisco in the midst of the summer of love in 1967, [Lester] had an uncanny sense of the impending failure of that ethos. With quick, deft strokes he and screenwriter Lawrence B. Marcus were able to sketch most of the major contradictions of the hip middle-class lifestyle of the late Sixties: spuriously romantic and ultimately artificial . . . *Petulia* is about the death force that pervades and eventually triumphs over the summer of love. Lester and Marcus proved to be right, but in 1968 people didn't want to hear criticism of this sort.' *(James Monaco American Film Now, 1979)*

ANTI:

'A soulless, arbitrary, attitudinizing piece of claptrap.' *(John Simon)*

'Compared with, say, his [Lester's] Beatles frolics it is a strangely serious film and like all his work, it is technically brilliant. But, as a vehicle for Julie Christie, it runs off the rails and with its giddy camerabatics and its twists of time, place and mood it might be said to go from Marienbad to worse . . . When he does stop shaking them up to dwell on a gentle love scene Mr Lester handles it quite poetically, but before the characters can expand or explain themselves off they go on another spree of jump cuts, frenetic flashbacks, frozen shots and over exposures.' *(Cecil Wilson, Daily Mail)*

'Mr Lester has jazzed the whole thing up so relentlessly that substance is swamped by style . . . In spite of the good performances and the vividness of Nicolas Roeg's photography, the film leaves one feeling there is an unresolved conflict between the traditional, romantic story-line and the whizz-bang, trendy directorial style: it's rather like seeing a stately home plastered with psychedelic designs.' *(Michael Billington, The Times)*

'A captivating fan dance but it there really anything behind the feathers?' *(Ian Wright, Guardian)*

PHANTOM LADY

CT: 6 AV: 7.13

1944 US 87 BW THRILLER

D Robert Siodmak ☆
W Bernard C. Schoenfield from William Irish's novel

Franchot Tone Alan Curtis Elisha Cook Jr
Ella Raines Fay Helm Andrew Tombes
Thomas Gomez

An innocent man (Alan Curtis) tries to clear himself, with the help of his secretary (Ella Raines) and an off-duty cop (Thomas Gomez) when he is accused of murdering his wife, but can't seem to track down the woman (Fay Helm) who could give him his alibi.

Above-average suspense thriller of its period, with unusual camera angles, moody lighting and expressionistic overtones. The first-time producer was Joan Harrison, who had served as Hitchcock's assistant for eight years.

ANTI:

'Just a bit of journeyman film-making . . . Now and again as the film is unrolled a jazz band appears playing like half-wits.' *(The Times)*

MIXED:

'Siodmak has done much with an old formula . . . Franchot Tone contributes a fine pathological study. Here is what Carlyle called "trash written with imagination".' *(Manchester Guardian)*

'The late reels of the picture slacken, and the ending, upon which Universal insisted, is half-heartedly done. But this is written as a would-be corrective of too much indiscriminate praise. There is plenty in *Phantom Lady* to enjoy, and to be glad of.' *(James Agee, Nation)*

PRO:

'[Breaks] all the rules and tells a story in terms of cinema . . . [With] the materials which Siodmak uses to construct suspense . . . he escapes banality and gives a tantalising flavour of the old fearless days of the films.' *(Richard Winnington, News Chronicle)*

'Very good American thriller.' *(William Whitebait)*

PHANTOM OF LIBERTY, THE

CT: 5 AV: 7.29

(aka *La Fantôme de la Liberté*)

1974 France 104 C DRAMA/FOREIGN

D Luis Buñuel
W Luis Buñuel Jean-Claude Carrière

Monica Vitti Jean-Claude Brialy Michel Piccoli
Jean Rochefort Adolfo Celi Michel Lonsdale
Adriana Asti Bernard Verley Maxence Malifort
Muni Philippe Brigaud

A series of surreal and not very funny revue sketches.

Somehow, at the age of 75, Buñuel continued to wow the critics with this collection of recycled ideas from his previous films.

PRO:

'Another violently original motion picture . . . Its incidents are all of fantastic coloring and each ends with a surprise, the general effect being that of a collection of Poe fables with O. Henry endings . . . The thing shimmers with a dazzling brilliance. It is Buñuel at his best.' *(Thomas Quinn Curtis, International Herald Tribune)*

The flavour throughout is tragicomic . . . This astonishing, disturbing masterwork veers between lunacy and sanity and shows us the reality of lives that walk voluntarily into the padded cell of convention.' *(Tom Hutchinson)*

'Buñuel remains the miracle of the cinema . . . His bombs are now disguised as custard pies . . . This is Buñuel's most consistently conscious film, quite without elements of the subconscious, of automatism, of surrealism. It is also, incidentally, his funniest film, and the funniest film around.' *(David Robinson, The Times)*

'An entirely characteristic series of small entertainments . . . masquerading as a unit. That one feels it as a kind of whole is more a tribute to the complete confidence with which it proceeds . . . than to the persistence of a running theme or story.' *(John Coleman, New Statesman)*

'The film, like life itself, is a mixture of the surreal, complex, mysterious, grotesque and absurd.' *(Virginia Dignam, Morning Star)*

'Comparatively easy Buñuel – easier anyway than the *Exterminating Angel*, less complex than The *Discreet Charm of the Bourgeoisie*; it is, also, extremely funny.' *(Dilys Powell)*

'Uses his [Buñuel's] usual prejudices and fetishes to play variations on his favorite theme, which might be stated: in a world cast loose of its moorings by freedom, only anarchy is logical . . . The most impressive thing about the movie is the way Buñuel leads us effortlessly from one wacky parable to the next. We ought to be breathless but we aren't because his editing makes everything seem to follow with inevitable logic. It doesn't, of course, but that's freedom's fault: If people want liberty, they shouldn't be expected to count on anything. *The Phantom of Liberty* is a *tour de force*, a triumph by a director confronting almost impossible complications and contradictions and mastering them. It's very funny, all right, but remember: With Buñuel, you only laugh when it hurts.' *(Roger Ebert)*

ANTI:

'A confused ragbag of surrealism, nightmare, Monty Python-type humour and Buñuel's obsessions which are often so private as to be completely baffling . . . If he is trying to convey some profound philosophical message, it didn't get through to me.' *(Ian Christie, Daily Express)*

'The film drifts out of your head before it's over.' *(Pauline Kael)*

PHANTOM OF THE OPERA, THE

CT: 6 AV: 7.36

1925 US 94 BW (2 colour sequences) HORROR/ ROMANCE/SILENT

D Rupert Julian ☆ (chase directed by Edward Sedgwick; other sequences directed by Lon Chaney)

W Raymond Schrock Elliott Clawson from Gaston Leroux's novel

Lon Chaney ☆ Mary Philbin Norman Kerry Snitz Edwards Gibson Gowland Arthur Edmund Carewe

Deformed, crazed musician (Lon Chaney) falls for beautiful opera singer (Mary Philbin).

Easily the finest version of Leroux's story, with a commanding performance by Lon Chaney: probably his best. Director Rupert Julian was replaced in mid-production after arguments with his star, and this may help to explain the vast differences in quality between the big set-pieces and some extremely tedious and undistinguished padding. Dan Hall's art direction is splendid, and its influence can be seen on later film and stage versions. In 1929 Ernst Laemmle directed extra scenes with sound (dialogue by Frank McCormack, recorded by the surviving actors) and the movie was released in 1930 as an 89-minute part-talkie .

ANTI:

'It suffers from dated technique, poor continuity and undistinguished dialogue . . . Mary Philbin and Norman Kerry . . . are both stagey and deliver their words in parrot fashion. Lon Chaney's . . . task is limited to looking as repulsive as possible . . . The rest of the cast have very little to do . . . stilted and slow in tempo . . . Recording is not of the best.' *(Kine Weekly, on the 1930 version)*

MIXED:

'An ambitious production in which there is much to marvel at in the scenic effects . . . The narrative could have been fashioned in a more subtle manner and would then have been more interesting to the few. As it stands it will . . . appeal to everybody.' *(Mordaunt Hall, New York Times)*

'Elaborate and spectacular production, with strongly dramatic situations, masterly direction and sound action . . . It is, perhaps, a pity that adventitious circumstances prevented this film being shown at the period of its production, for it is a stirring story . . . mounted with artistic prodigality . . . and only suffers in comparison with more recent productions by pointing out the great advances made in a few years in technical details of photography and effective realism . . . The music is well-recorded, the voices not quite so successfully.' *(Bioscope, 1930)*

'Tacky yet unforgettable piece of Guignol claptrap . . . The first half is a botch and dreary, but then the mixture of the morbid, the gaudy, the ornate, and the rotted becomes scary and, in a way that may be peculiar to movies, thrilling.' *(Pauline Kael)*

PRO:

'Spook melodrama at its wildest and weirdest, and it is beautifully done . . . Julian's direction . . . is excellent; he has emphasised his pictures rather than his drama, and has thus achieved an optical illusion which could never have been gained by any direct appeal to the intelligence.' *(Robert E. Sherwood, Life)*

'An ambitious spectacle . . . intensely entertaining . . . There is not a ray of sunlight, a spark of tender passion or a real vivid moment of comedy relief in the whole production, and yet, the atmosphere of mystery, the tense coil of suspense, the morbid quality of the story, the lavishness of the whole production is such that we pronounce it excellent screen entertainment.' *(Photoplay)*

'The greatest inducement to nightmare that has yet been screened . . . Not a bad film from a technical viewpoint.' *(Variety)*

'Eric the Phantom proves to be among the simplest and best of Chaney's thousand faces, although almost half the film goes by before he is fully revealed.' *(MFB, 1975)*

The highs are way up there with the best in the tradition of Gothic fantasy: Chaney's best ever phantom, his face scarred to hell by acid, unmasked at the organ by the timorous heroine: the phantom stopping a costume ball when he appears as the Red Death; the phantom shrouded in the most romantic cape ever seen, perched on top of the statue of Apollo to eavesdrop on the lovers. And the sustained crescendo of the end is still unrivalled.' *(Tony Rayns, Time Out)*

PHILADELPHIA CT: 6 AV: 7.00 (est)

1993 US 125 C DRAMA

D Jonathan Demme
W Ron Nyswaner AAN

Tom Hanks ☆ AAW Denzel Washington ☆
Jason Robards Antonio Banderas
Joanne Woodward ✔ Mary Steenburgen

A rising young attorney who is secretly gay, Andy Beckett (Tom Hanks), suddenly loses his job in a top law firm and suspects he has been fired for having Aids. Even in Philadelphia, the city of brotherly love, he can not find a lawyer to help him sue his employers for wrongful dismissal – so he has to settle for a downmarket, black ambulance-chaser (Denzel Washington), who just happens to hate homosexuals.

The story offers a novel way into the subject of Aids; and one of the best things about *Philadelphia* is its avoidance of the expected TV-movie-disease-of-the-week clichés. Scenes which are not in the film include the tear-stained one when our hero learns the awful truth from the doctor ('Sit down, Andy, I have something to tell you'/'Doc, you don't mean . . . ?'); the one where he and his lover break down in self-pity and recriminations ('Why did this have to happen to you/me?'); the moment when he confronts his bigoted parents (commonly known as the 'Why didn't you ever try to understand me, dad?' scenario).

The subject is approached in a more cinematic way: there's a big courtroom showdown (not unlike the one in *A Few Good Men*), and along the way there's the developing relationship between Hanks and Washington – reminiscent of the uneasy respect which grew in *In the Heat of the Night* between Sidney Poitier and Rod Steiger, except that now the man with the prejudices is black.

Demme even manages to convince us – at least for the duration of the movie – that the problem of Aids is a civil rights issue, created by heterosexuals' fear and loathing of gays. The turning point in the relationship between Hanks and Washington comes when the latter sees the Aids patient discriminated against in a library, and identifies with him for the first time.

Perhaps the most original aspect of *Philadelphia* is that the film-makers have given Hanks a trouble-free home life. We are shown a concerned, affectionate longterm lover (Antonio Banderas), and an adoring, supportive family. He even has dewy-eyed Joanne Woodward as his mom. The scenes with his family may be too schmaltzy and good to be true, but they are oddly unexpected. At the very least, they have an educational value, as a kind of instruction manual on how to behave if one of your family catches Aids.

For this is, of course, a didactic film. And it is here that it makes its mistakes. It loads the dice too heavily against Hanks's law firm: would this allegedly hot-shot company rest its defence on only one example of Andy's incompetence? Of course not: they would have found, and if necessary invented, plenty more. And wouldn't they have come up with some convincing explanation of why they had promoted him just a few days before firing him? You bet.

The central civil rights tenet of *Philadelphia* is also unconvincing, because there is one important difference between an Aids-sufferer and someone who is black: being black is not a degenerative disease, nor does it prevent someone from working effectively. You only have to look at Andy to know that he would soon have had to give up his job in any case – another reason why it is unlikely his firm would have bothered to fire him.

The film avoids the issue of whether an Aids-sufferer has duties as well as rights. It's certain that, in any real courtroom showdown, Andy's bosses would have emphasized his moral obligation to tell them he had a debilitating illness. By constantly failing to give the villains their due, the film-makers lessen the movie's plausibility and weaken the dramatic conflict.

The movie is so anxious to avoid alienating its mass audience that it is unduly timid – even misleading – in its suggestion of how Andy caught Aids. The bizarre impression given is that he contracted it simply by entering a gay porno cinema. And, at times, it's needlessly sentimental. The final home movies sequence of Andy as a boy is distressingly conventional Hollywood mawkishness.

Yet the film-makers are to be congratulated for

making a thoughtful, humane movie out of so tricky a subject. It's the kind of movie which never could have pleased everyone – least of all those gay activists who criticized it so immoderately. It strikes me as ridiculous to object, for example, that Andy does not show enough passion towards his lover in public, or that he leads too straight a lifestyle. Many homosexuals, particularly those with professional careers, are like that. Nor was there any reason why the film-makers should have risked alienating a mass audience by making Andy overtly radical or belligerent: it is far more effective that we feel angry on his behalf.

Philadelphia is a timely, decent film of the kind that may broaden a few minds but also tends to date very fast. It is akin to those politely liberal films of the 60s like *To Kill a Mockingbird* or *Guess Who's Coming to Dinner*. It makes an audience that might not naturally sympathise with a gay Aids sufferer, do so. It is a compelling human drama. And – thanks to Tom Hanks's calm, dignified and typically likeable performance – it will probably make you cry.

ANTI:

'Actually what [the film] lacks is not so much the "proper" polemic representation . . . The details are accurate, the tone is lifeless. [Its] problems stem from its form: realism, narrative, naturalism, whatever. Naturalism problematises gay men.' *(John Lyttle, Independent)*

MIXED:

'Too many of the straight characters are either deified . . . or demonised. I give Demme some credit for breaking the Aids taboo . . . and for making a film infinitely more realistic than Home Box Office's toothless *And the Band Played On*. But if he had a higher opinion of his audience, perhaps the director would have given his best and created a movie as sociologically sophisticated as a television series with gay characters – like Roseanne.' *(Frank Rich, Guardian)*

'It is honest as far as it goes. But, by its very nature, it travels along the road to enlightenment only so far and no further . . . There isn't a limp wrist to be seen.' *(Derek Malcolm, Guardian)*

'Features superb performances by Hanks and Washington, but is hampered by its urge to teach lessons in tolerance . . . [It] may not be the most daring possible portrait of Aids in the mid-90s, but the risks it does take should connect the crisis to general audiences in a way they've never felt before.' *(Kevin Lally, Film Journal)*

PRO:

'A powerful drama with outstanding performances from all quarters, both in front of and behind the cameras. The picture pulls off an amazing feat: telling stories about some of the most divisive issues in our society today in an entertaining, uplifting yet thoughtful way . . . The film lacks the usual courtroom drama cliches, such as the triumphant disclosure of startling new evidence or surprise witnesses, and it's all the more powerful for that.' *(Donald Devich, Hollywood Hotline)*

'Actually Hanks is outacted by . . . Washington, who . . . exposes the real point of the picture, the ferocious homophobia still rampant in the US.' *(Hugo Davenport, Daily Telegraph)*

'A major watershed for the gay community.' *(Dale Reynolds, Gay Times)*

'Hanks delivers the performance of his life . . . Often profoundly moving, the movie avoids melodrama as it slowly draws you in . . . and there won't be a dry eye in the house.' *(Marshall Julius, What's On in London)*

'While I was watching it I was crying too much to be analytical – after a decade in which Hollywood failed to look at Aids but managed to unleash dozens of gay and lesbian grotesques into the world's cinemas, the decency of *Philadelphia* is incredibly moving.' *(Howard Schuman, Moving Pictures, BBC-2)*

PHILADELPHIA STORY, THE CT: 9 AV: 9.21

1940 US 112 BW COMEDY/ROMANCE

D George Cukor ☆ AAN
W Donald Ogden Stewart ☆ AAW from Philip Barry's play

Katharine Hepburn ☆ AAN Cary Grant ☆
James Stewart ☆ AAW Ruth Hussey ☆ AAN
Roland Young ☆ John Halliday ☆ Mary Nash ☆
Virginia Weidler ☆ John Howard ☆ Henry Daniell ☆

Reporters from Spy magazine (James Stewart and Ruth Hussey) arrive to cover wedding of society ice-maiden (Katharine Hepburn), who has recently divorced millionaire (Cary Grant) to marry a dull dog (John Howard).

Stylish screwball comedy which later, when turned into a musical by Cole Porter, became *High Society*. This version stays very close to the Broadway play and features incomparable performances by Katharine Hepburn and Cary Grant. James Stewart, rather surprisingly for such a light-weight role, won an Oscar for Best Actor. Stewart thought the award should have gone to Henry Fonda for *The Grapes of Wrath*, and voted for him. There were more visually daring directors than Cukor, but there have been few better at eliciting great performances from actors.

ANTI:

'I just don't believe any of it. Hepburn as Joan of Arc waving her oriflamme and charging the English, nostrils quivering to match her horse's – yes, there is the true Hepburn. I see her again as any of the unpleasanter Aeschylean or Euripidean heroines, sword-struck and flame-consumed. But as a society pet enticing a hard-boiled reporter into a bathing pool and a midnight game of hide-and-seek among the nenuphars – the answer to this one is just plain No.' *(James Agate, Tatler)*

MIXED:

'When the acid tongues are turned on at the beginning and end of the film it's a laugh-provoker from way down. When the discussion gets deep and serious, however, on the extent of Hepburn's stone-like character, the verbiage is necessarily highly abstract and the film slows to a toddle.' *(Variety)*

'Having expended so much care to such effect, they might have considered also that it is only brooks in poems that go on forever without somebody's beginning to yawn, scratch and wonder seriously whether it is the suspense or just his underwear climbing.' *(Otis Ferguson, New Republic)*

'Shiny and unfelt and smart-aleck-commercial as the movie is, it's almost irresistibly entertaining – one of the high spots of M-G-M professionalism. There isn't much real wit in the lines, and there's no feeling of spontaneity, yet the engineering is so astute that the laughs keep coming. This is a paste diamond with more flash and sparkle than a true one.' *(Pauline Kael)*

'The film in which [Hepburn] triumphantly returned to Hollywood after being labelled box-office poison by *Variety* in 1938. Despite the felicities of dialogue and performance on which the work's reputation is based, its project is clearly to subdue and punish Hepburn. She must learn to become a first-class human being, which means, here, condoning and reconciling herself to male sexual exploitativeness.' *(NFT Bulletin, 1984)*

PRO:

'I have no pedestal for Miss Hepburn. She can be wrong. She can be difficult. We have had our arguments. But Miss Hepburn can most sincerely be judged by the almost tearful affection with which the crew regarded her at the completion of *The Philadelphia Story*.' *(George Cukor, Hollywood Reporter)*

'Polished sophisticated comedy . . . Acting brilliant, dialogue smart and atmosphere flawless . . . Katharine Hepburn is a little vague in her character drawing in opening scenes, but once she gets fully into her stride she gives a clever, sensitive and spirited performance . . . The play does not take a flying start . . . but once the salient points are established it arrives at its obvious but . . . hilarious climax through a cleverly engineered sequence of grand comedy situations.' *(Kine Weekly)*

'How that boy [James Stewart] does troupe . . . There are just not enough superlatives sufficiently to appreciate this show.' *(Hollywood Reporter)*

'Cary Grant . . . flourishes under Cukor's direction . . . For once his style of unwounding mockery seems to come out of the character; and though it is partly due to the editing that his glances at his recalcitrant ex-wife are as shrewdly fond as they are, they would never have been thrown at all if it had not been for the atmosphere of trust and intimacy that Cukor palpably creates for his cast.' *(Penelope Gilliatt, 1961)*

'Smart, sophisticated and beautifully played by all concerned, but Hepburn's film from first to last.' *(R.A.E. Pickard, Dictionary of 1000 Best Films, 1971)*

PIANO, THE AAN — CT: 5 AV: 7.25

1993 Australia/France 120 C DRAMA/ROMANCE

D Jane Campion ✗ AAN
W Jane Campion ● AAW

Holly Hunter ☆ AAW Anna Paquin ✗ AAW
Harvey Keitel ✗ Sam Neill Kerry Walker
Genevieve Lemon

Ada (Holly Hunter), a mute since the age of six – for reasons unexplained – has borne an illegitimate daughter, now nine years old (Anna Paquin). This being the 19th century, Ada has been sent off by her father to marry Stewart (Sam Neill), a man she has never met, on the other side of the world in New Zealand. The only ways she can express her feelings are through sign language, and playing the piano. Her new husband has no interest in her piano, and leaves it stranded on the beach where she landed. But a tattooed neighbour, Baines (Harvey Keitel), appreciates the beauty of her piano-playing and buys it. Baines uses it to get Ada into bed with him, paving the way for a romantic triangle, as the husband learns what is going on, through the child.

Though beautifully shot and intensely acted by Holly Hunter, this fashionable feminist fable which won the Palme d'Or at Cannes didn't impress me. Its numerous admirers seem able to disregard its shambolic plot, failure to understand its period, and characters who are inconsistent, unsympathetic and puppetlike caricatures.

Although writer-director Campion goes to great lengths to ensure authenticity of costume, she leaves out scenes crucial to a sense of social authenticity: is it credible that no one would have pointed out a wife's marital obligations – around the house, if not in the marital bed? Everything Ada does, she seems to do for herself, with no thought for her child's welfare. Her sullen attitude has a strong whiff of 70s, women-as-victims, feminism: the underlying notion is that the world owes women a loving. When she does change towards her husband – from hostility to, so far as I could tell, genuine lasciviousness – she does so without rhyme or reason.

But then none of the characters makes sense. At one moment, the little girl hates her new step-father; the next, she is informing to him of her mother's adultery. One moment, Sam Neill's character is consumed by jealousy and hatred, brandishing an axe like Bluebeard; the next, he's reason personified. No sooner has Ada tried to commit suicide than she decides not to. Humans are paradoxical and they do change; but in a drama we're entitled to some clue as to why. In *The Piano*, they just seem like marionettes under the control of a whimsical puppet-mistress – and an absent-minded one. In one scene, Baines tells Ada he's illiterate; a few minutes later, she's sending him a note to tell him she loves him.

The acting, too, is variable. Harvey Keitel seems completely out of his depth: his accent, along with that of the little girl (who incomprehensibly won an Oscar), seems to alter from scene to scene. But the actors have little chance to flesh out characters written in a politically correct shorthand: Ada's husband is cutting down the forest, so he can't be in touch with his emotions; Baines has gone native and wears Maori tattoos, so he must be all right. There were times when I longed for the relative subtlety of male characterization in a Jilly Cooper novel.

Feminists may smile knowingly at the way Ada is punished – it fits in neatly with modern preconceptions that men will countenance no threat to phallic supremacy – and men may marvel at Sam Neill's accuracy with an axe. Film students may admire the clarity – or the crashing obviousness – of the piano and axe symbolism throughout. They may commend the unusual camera viewpoints, and not mind the fact that these are more often gimmicky than revelatory. Even less will they be bothered that the direction gives no impression of space or distance, in a film whose early plot hinges on how far or not Stewart's house is from the beach where Ada lands. Posterity may not be so kind.

'I really wanted to do a love story where you could see the growth from fetishism towards eroticism, and to more of a blend of love and sexuality.' *(Jane Campion)*

PRO:

'Remarkable for its superb performances and Michael Nyman's rapturous score; she [Campion] not only offers something more starkly, strangely beautiful than most costume-dramas, but puts a fresh spin on the traditional love-story. Campion's most entrancing work to date.' *(Geoff Andrew, Time Out)*

'Visually sumptuous and tactile.' *(Variety)*

'A film about silence and expression beyond language . . . It is a virtuoso interpretation of that literary sensibility in a cinematic form.' *(Lizzie Francke, S & S)*

'Every now and then, a movie comes along that restores faith in the visionary power of cinema. *The Piano* . . . is that kind of film. It arrives as a welcome antidote to almost everything that seems to be wrong with the movies. People complain that there are no good stories, that there are no strong roles for women, that there is no eroticism, just sex – no magic, just manipulation. On all counts, *The Piano* serves as an exhilarating exception to the rule . . . Despite its 19th-century setting, *The Piano* seems in tune with the times, resonant with contemporary obsessions ranging from gender confusion to aboriginal rights.' *(Brian D. Johnson, Maclean's)*

'A triumph of dazzling movie art and canny show-biz heart . . . *The Piano*, with startling craft and anguish, asks the question, "How much does love hurt?" The answer is, "Too much". And what is love worth? "Everything".' *(Richard Corliss, Time)*

'Hunter makes this woman – who at first can express her feelings only through music – an almost mythically powerful character, as memorably vivid as one of Thomas Hardy's headstrong, rustic heroines. Like them, she is hounded by destiny, lovers and personal demons, and her drama is acted out against a wild, primal landscape of forest and sea.' *(Tom Gliatto, People Weekly)*

'A romantic melodrama of almost classical grandeur . . . Campion views all her characters with a compassion bordering on grace, a humanity – like her heroine's – as dark, quiet, and enveloping as the ocean.' *(Owen Gleiberman, Entertainment Weekly)*

'The sudden liberation of locked-up libido has seldom been more gloriously rendered than it is by Hunter and Keitel in this exotic, raw-passioned, slightly sick, totally enthralling drama . . . Campion, working from her own superb screenplay, not only delivers what she promises in terms of gothic upheaval, but she does so with such wit, startling perception, resonant imagery, and merciless tension that we are left with no choice but to place her in the front rank of today's filmmakers.' *(Guy Flatley, Cosmopolitan)*

'Sexuality erupts with volcanic fury . . . hypnotic.' *(Bruce Williamson, Playboy)*

'The way the movie develops their relationship, in eroticism and fierce combativeness, is wonderful to watch: The woman is strong as steel and determined to have her way, but the unschooled man surprises her by his tenderness. And Campion's feel for the location, an overgrown wilderness of rain and privation, makes love and all the other aspects of life seem more desperate.' *(Roger Ebert)*

ANTI:

'An overwrought, hollowly symbolic glob of glutinous nonsense. The New Zealand writer-director Jane Campion, who made an appealing film of Janet Frame's autobiography *An Angel at My Table*, here reverts to the thick, self-conscious poeticizing of her first film, *Sweetie* . . . Every moment is upholstered with the suffocating high-mindedness that declines to connect symbols with comprehensible themes. I haven't seen a sillier film about a woman and a piano since John Huston's *The Unforgiven* (1960), a Western in which Lillian Gish had her piano carried out into the front yard so she could play Mozart to pacify attacking Indians.' *(Stanley Kauffmann)*

'Unfortunately – and I know I'm in the minority here, as this film won Best Picture at Cannes – I found it lumbering, decidedly unpleasant and hopelessly pointless.' *(Rod Lurie, LA Magazine)*

'We never find out anything about Ada's background, her first husband, and how Stewart acquired her in marriage. Or why she gave up speaking . . . Why would a welcoming husband abandon his bride's beloved piano, her chief mode of self-expression, when there are enough porters to carry it; and why not at least move it out of the reach of the waves? Later, it is Stewart's less affluent partner, Baines – an Englishman gone native, who sports Maori tattoos on his face – who buys the piano from Stewart, and seems to have no problem hauling it to his homestead. That the piano should play perfectly after what it's been through is one of the film's most resounding lies . . . Jane Campion prides herself on leaving much unexplained. She has every right to be proud: at leaving things unexplained, Miss Campion is a champion . . . Flora's actions consistently make no sense, but she at least has the excuse of being a child. What the adults do would make sense only as the wet dream of an inane woman, which *The Piano*, apparently, is not meant to be.' *(John Simon)*

'Stewart is a thoroughly rigid, shuttered man – the kind who would abandon a large piece of symbolic furniture on the beach. He's so thick, he tries to buy a Maori burial ground with a jar of buttons as his payment. Yet he has the exquisite sensitivity to wait for a mail-order wife to come to his bed. When she does, he also has the spiritual refinement to hear her unvoiced words. Naturally, an experience of such depth and tenderness leads him to violence (his love turns to hate), in the course of which, though a clumsy man, he performs a feat requiring near-miraculous fine-motor control. After that, three more reversals occur without benefit of motivation, whereupon the film reaches as satisfying a happy ending as Zanuck himself might have engineered, or even Louis B. Mayer. In brief, this skeptic thinks *The Piano* is a work of imagination but also of the will – not Ada's will, unfortunately, but Jane Campion's . . . In *The Piano*, Campion's whim is the only law. You can't learn anything about the characters beyond what she chooses to tell you at the moment, because they are mere artifices – like Michael Nyman's music, which is neither convincing as a nineteenth-century imposture nor substantial enough to withstand scrutiny as part of our own era.' *(Stuart Klawans, Nation)*

PICKPOCKET

CT: 5 AV: 7.50

1959 France 75 BW DRAMA/FOREIGN

D Robert Bresson ✗
W Robert Bresson ✗

Martin Lassalle Marika Green Kassagi
Pierre Leymarie Jean Pelegri Pierre Etaix
Dolly Scal

Pickpocket (Martin Lassalle) is redeemed by love of a good woman (Marika Green).

Mildly interesting are the scenes where an old thief (Kassagi) instructs our anti-hero on the art of picking pockets. For most of the time, however, this is a disappointingly dull character-study which fails to place the pickpocket in any social context and doesn't give any convincing reason why he has a change of heart at the end. Bresson here is at his most austere, pseudo-philosophical and inaccessible. Obviously influenced by Dostoievsky's *Crime and Punishment*, he is drawn into questions of Free Will versus Predestination, but conspicuously fails to dramatize his ideas.

PRO:

'From that excellent director Robert Bresson comes a most intriguing and informative lesson . . . on how to pick a wallet, a watch or a handbag.' *(Ivon Adams, Star)*

'Bresson's greatest . . . The treatment is wonderfully spare and the manner, both visual and vocal, is almost stylized . . . A film to be seen, not only by practitioners of petty larceny.' *(Guardian)*

MIXED:

'This is a story which having been fully developed by Dostoievsky and frequently retold by Simenon doesn't really stand repetition. However . . . I like the way the story is told with a minimum of dialogue and a background of the young man's spoken thoughts.' *(John Mortimer, Evening Standard)*

ANTI:

'One long yawn, 75 minutes of pretentious pseudo-psychological drivel . . . [without] the remotest connection with life or reality or what we know of the hidden impulses that lie behind people's actions. Even the visual beauty . . . of his previous films . . . has disappeared here in Bresson's entirely literary obsessions.' *(Garry Broughton, Oxford Opinion)*

'Slow to the point of exasperation. What a pity [the character] wasn't gaoled for good in the first reel.' *(Edward Betts, People)*

'Appalling tedium.' *(Elizabeth Frank, News Chronicle)*

'In rejecting every irrelevant action, in ruthlessly refining away every decoration, Bresson has thrown away the motives as well . . . The central figures stand apart from life. In their sparse exchanges, their calculated movements they communicate not the pure essence of emotion which Bresson intends, but a sort of stageyness.' *(Dilys Powell)*

PICNIC AAN

CT: 4 AV: 7.09

1955 US 115 C DRAMA

D Joshua Logan ✗ AAN
W Daniel Taradash from William Inge's play

William Holden ✗ Kim Novak ● Rosalind Russell ● Susan Strasberg ● ☆ Arthur O'Connell ☆ AAN Cliff Robertson Betty Field Verna Felton Reta Shaw

Arrival of a sexy stranger (William Holden) in a steamy southern town disrupts the lives of three women (Kim Novak, Rosalind Russell and Susan Strasberg).

Big, boring melodrama with performances which range from over-the-top (Russell) to non-existent (Novak). Holden seems ill-at-ease and miscast as a force for sexual liberation, and the script's assumptions about femininity have dated so badly that modern audiences may find it difficult to understand the three women's attitudes, still less sympathize with them. Art director William Flannery and editors Charles Nelson and William A. Lyon won Oscars; George Duning was nominated for his score. Easily the best aspect of the film is James Wong Howe's cinematography.

ANTI:

'Inge . . . deserves a fair hearing. In . . . *Picnic* . . . he doesn't quite get it . . . The dramatic effectiveness of [his] original play is considerably reduced by the star's determination to play a Marlon Brando role after the style of Gary Cooper.' *(Eleanor Wintour, Tribune)*

'Suffers slightly from staginess.' *(Manchester Guardian)*

MIXED:

'Logan lingeringly builds up his effects . . . At times there are gaps of wearisome, wholesome bonhomie and there is a frenzied unreality about some of the final scenes . . . Holden ideally sustains the outward veneer of brash assurance, but the underlying uncertainty sometimes eludes him.' *(Milton Shulman, Sunday Express)*

PRO:

'For me, the picture belongs to Rosalind Russell.' *(Peter Burnup, News of the World)*

'What makes [it] something to shout about? Its beautifully written script . . . superb direction . . . and the first-rate acting.' *(Roy Nash, Star)*

'For the first time in many weeks films-going I liked the people shown in a Hollywood picture.' *(Thomas Spencer, Daily Worker)*

PICTURE OF DORIAN GRAY, THE

CT: 8 AV: 7.50

1945 US 110 BW (final sequence colour) HORROR/DRAMA

D Albert Lewin
W Albert Lewin from Oscar Wildes novel

Hurd Hatfield George Sanders ☆ Donna Reed Angela Lansbury ☆ AAN Peter Lawford Cedric Hardwicke (uncredited narrator)

Corrupt young man (Hurd Hatfield) retains youthful beauty; the portrait in the attic doesn't.

Beautifully staged, reasonably faithful adaptation of Oscar Wilde's novel. It's probably too faithful, since we never really see Dorian commit most of the unspeakable acts which are his downfall – one reason why this film has never achieved the acclaim of that more sensational Victorian novel about split personality, *Dr Jekyll and Mr Hyde* (1932). Critical opinion is split about Hurd Hatfield, who underplays Dorian to the point of immobility; but young Angela Lansbury is touching as the girl whom he jilts, and George Sanders steals the show as the devilish Lord Henry Wotton. Albert Lewin's direction is a shade ponderous, but Harry Stradling's cinematography fully deserved its Oscar.

ANTI:

'Respectful, earnest, and, I am afraid, dead . . . The novel . . . is distinguished, wise and frightening; whereas the movie is just a cultured horror picture, decorated with epigrams and an elaborate moral, and made with a sincere effort at good taste rather than with passion, immediacy or imagination.' *(James Agee, Nation)*

'The sets, grandiose, well aired and streamlined, do much to negate the stifling, patchouli-clotted atmosphere which Wilde managed to make so poisonously inferential in print. Only George Sanders' Lord Henry Wotton has rudiments of the original intent, even though the actor handles the rapier epigrams as though they were a cricket bat, and sedulously avoids any suggestion that he is portraying a Britisher with marked Greek inclinations . . . Hurd Hatfield essays Dorian throughout the entire film with the same lack of facial animation which Clara Kimball Young employed in characterizing those moments of the screen transcription of the Du Maurier novel when Trilby was totally under the spell of the hypnotic prowess of the Svengali of Wilton Lackaye. Further in the direction of novelty, young Hatfield dubiously enhances Dorian, described in the text as "a young man of extraordinary personal beauty" with as unfortunate an affliction of acne as a make-up department has been called upon to conceal.' *(Herb Sterne)*

'The offscreen narration, explaining among other

things what is going on in Gray's mind may be too much for most to grasp.' *(Variety)*

'The growing beastliness of the picture – shown rather incongruously in Technicolor – is horrific, perhaps a little too much for conviction.' *(Picturegoer)*

'[Hatfield] is not active or imaginative enough to be feared. And once sweet Lansbury kills herself, there's no one, including his new love, Donna Reed, that we worry about getting involved with him. Indeed George Sanders, as his "friend" Lord Henry Wotton (Wilde's snobby, erudite stand-in), who encourages and gets a charge out of Gray's insensitivity, comes across as a far more interesting and despicable character.' *(Danny Peary)*

MIXED:

'It has its ludicrous side. Hurd Hatfield's Dorian (who sells his soul to keep his youth) doesn't look fresh; he looks glacéed. And the other characters don't seem to age with the years either, so there's no contrast with him . . . Neither Hatfield, who tries scrupulously hard, nor George Sanders . . . rises above Lewin's chic gothic conception, but as Dorian's victim, gullible Sibyl Vane, the young Angela Lansbury gives her scenes true depth of feeling. This may be her most intuitive and original screen performance. When she sings "Little Yellow Bird" in a pure, sweet voice, the viewer grasps that the man who would destroy this girl really is evil.' *(Pauline Kael)*

PRO:

'One or two passages – the murder of Hallward for instance – are treated with a fine sense of drama and terror. As Dorian, Hurd Hatfield preserves an immobility of face which accords with the stylised story, and epigrams come naturally from George Sanders as Sir Henry Wotton. But I shall remember the film for its astonishing interior sets and the play of figures against an exquisitely baroque ground.' *(Dilys Powell)*

'Loving and practised hands have really improved Wilde's original, cutting down the epigrammatic flow . . . and rooting out all the preciousness which gets in the way of the drama.' *(Richard Winnington)*

'Underrated . . . Its that rare thing: a Hollywoodian literary adaptation that both stays faithful and does justice to its source.' *(Geoff Andrew, Time Out)*

'Note the significant role that objets d'art and curios play in the pictorial composition, with unusual props like the oculist's sign on the sandwich board and a whole host of small details (Dorian briefly examining a book of Beardsley etchings at the beginning of one scene) which are cleverly controlled to produce an overwhelmingly suffocating atmosphere of *Yellow Book* decadence. Symbolism plays a key part in the pictorial composition. The film is laced through with captive butterflies, sinister knives, suggestive toys, and a handsome Egyptian bronze cat that serves as a kind of evil leit-motif.' *(George Aachen)*

PINK PANTHER, THE

CT: 6 AV: 6.77

1963 US 116 C COMEDY

D Blake Edwards
W Maurice Richlin Blake Edwards

Peter Sellers ☆ David Niven Capucine Robert Wagner Claudia Cardinale Colin Gordon Brenda de Banzie

Incompetent Inspector Clouseau (Peter Sellers) tries to prevent the theft of a valuable diamond by a notorious jewel thief.

This first outing for the accident-prone Inspector Clouseau – in what was supposed to be a supporting role – is one of the funniest, despite a mechanical plot and many longueurs when Sellers is off screen. The explanation is simple: Peter Sellers's slapstick in this and its sequel, *A Shot in the Dark*, has the spontaneity and timing of the great silent comedians. David Niven is his usual suave self in the role intended to be the lead, but struggles with some dull dialogue. The cartoon title sequence (by Richard Williams) is excellent. Henry Mancini's title tune was Oscar-nominated.

ANTI:

'A rare near miss . . . The puzzle to me is how an actor with his freedom to pick and choose came to play the unworthy role of a French police inspector with two left feet . . . It all looks very rich and glossy, but I fancy that when Peter Sellers glances back in old age over the film peaks of his prime he will prefer to forget this one.' *(Cecil Wilson, Daily Mail)*

'One's main feeling is that Mr Sellers ought no longer to accept these off-the-peg roles when he can now undoubtedly afford to have them tailored to his particular – and formidable – talents.' *(Thomas Wiseman, Sunday Express)*

'Unfunny.' *(Elliott)*

'Etiolated.' *(Shipman)*

MIXED:

'Some of the episodes in this feather-weight society romp strain to be funny and at all costs . . . A long passage of would-be sophisticated love-talk [between Niven and Capucine] falls very flat. But there are some sublimely funny moments, too, especially when Peter Sellers is around.' *(Nina Hibbin, Daily Worker)*

'Sellers is so superbly funny that Niven, Claudia Cardinale and Capucine are almost completely overshadowed.' *(News of the World)*

'Sellers has created a pratfalling bungler who is one of the most ingratiating and funny fools to have ever come our way. When he's not on screen everything seems wrong with this terribly cute, terribly posh, and terribly attenuated Continental comedy. But at least the sodden interludes will give your ribs a rest until Sellers reappears.' *(Judith Crist)*

'Quite palatable for the uncritical.' *(Halliwell)*

PRO:

'Intensely funny.' *(Variety)*

'Has a performance by Peter Sellers that is one of the most delicate studies in accident-proneness since the silents.' *(Penelope Gilliatt)*

'A comedy with a difference: comedy with grace. Absurd grace, but still grace.' *(Dilys Powell)*

PINKY

CT: 5 AV: 6.38

1949 US 102 BW DRAMA

D Elia Kazan ✗
W Philip Dunne Dudley Nichols ✗ from Cid Ricketts Sumner's novel *Quality*

Jeanne Crain ☆ AAN Ethel Barrymore ☆ AAN
Ethel Waters ☆ AAN William Lundigan
Basil Ruysdael

The fact that a black girl (Jeanne Crain) can pass for white leads to drama in the American south.

Acclaimed 'problem' picture which seemed daring at the time, but now seems excessively timid, especially in its cop-out ending. The three leading performances aren't bad and Miss Crain suffers sympathetically, but Kazan's direction (he replaced John Ford during shooting, and all Ford's material was scrapped) is extremely ponderous. A companion-piece to Kazan Zanuck's equally acclaimed but now dated film about anti-Semitism, *Gentleman's Agreement (1947)*.

PRO:

'With his brilliantly compelling presentation of *Pinky*, Zanuck [producer] again writes motion picture history . . . A devastating indictment of bigotry and prejudice – its fine purpose, however, is accomplished without preachment and without sacrifice of entertainment. It is not necessary to agree with *Pinky* to enjoy it.' *(Hollywood Reporter)*

'Vivid, revealing and emotionally intense. The veteran scriptwriters and Elia Kazan . . . have brought all their talents to . . . cleverly [contriving] it so that each blow and shock [Pinky] receives is soundly transmitted to the audience . . . No genuinely constructive thinking of relationships between blacks and whites is offered. A vivid exposé of certain cruelties and injustices is all it gives . . . with moving and disturbing force. And for this we can be . . . grateful.' *(Bosley Crowther)*

'*Pinky* is an extremely moving piece of work; moving in its acting, its direction and its writing. It is a good film, in fact, not because it has a praiseworthy subject (*Home of the Brave* is unimpeachable in sentiment, yet I find it a dull piece) but because it speaks to us with understanding, pity and indignation of the suffering, the courageous human figure.' *(Dilys Powell)*

'Still remarkable for its sincerity and directness, especially when one considers its date of origin.' *(Virgin)*

MIXED:

'Crain brings proper dignity and sincerity to her role, although she's not always convincing.' *(Variety)*

'The cardinal crippling evasion of *Pinky* lies in the selection of an established white film actress to play the heroine. Thus is the audience insulated against the shock of seeing white and Negro embrace, against any effect of realism. I do not doubt that *Pinky* will leave Negro baiters comfortably purged and as rabid as ever, and I have even less doubts as to its effects on Negroes. As for average audiences; they will come from *Pinky*, touched, entertained and unperturbed by a well made and well acted film drama.' *(Richard Winnington, S & S)*

'The film garnered a little too much praise for its courage; it isn't overwhelmingly courageous . . . At the end Pinky renounces her white fiancée, William Lundigan, thereby sparing 20th Century-Fox no end of awkwardnesses. But the film hasn't been given its due for the tense dramatic sequences and the pressures we're made to feel. *Pinky* is slick and Hollywoodized, but it's also pretty good.' *(Pauline Kael)*

ANTI:

'It has about as much daring as a cheese-mite. It is careful to affront no particular section of the public, to draw no particular conclusion, to outrage no particular code of cinema ethics, to challenge no particular box-office convention.' *(C.A. Lejeune)*

PINOCCHIO

CT: 10 AV: 9.71

1939 US 77 C CARTOON/FAMILY

D Ben Sharpsteen Hamilton Luske ☆
W various (music and lyrics by Leigh Harline, Ned Washington, Paul J. Smith ☆ AAW)

Voices: Dickie Jones Christian Rub
Cliff Edwards ☆ Evelyn Venable Walter Catlett
Frankie Darro

Puppet with ambition of becoming a real live boy embarks upon career as wooden actor.

Stern morality tale about the importance of not lying is transformed into a joyful masterpiece by superbly detailed animation, memorable supporting characters who compensate for the essentially passive hero, and enchanting songs.The score won an Oscar, as did the song 'When You Wish Upon a Star', beautifully performed by Cliff (Ukelele Ike) Edwards, who provides the voice for one of Disney's most endearing creations, Jiminy Cricket. This must be one of the great films of all time – not only is it brilliantly made, it has a universal resonance for every child, who can respond to *Pinocchio*'s view of the world as a frightening but fascinating place to discover.

ANTI:

'It makes an admirable fairy story, and my only trouble is that I just can't spend an evening over a book of fairy stories or in looking at the pictures in a book of fairy stories, even when these have been drawn by Arthur Rackham. And Walt Disney's pictures are not, to my way of thinking, as good as Arthur Rackham's. Nor do I see any particular virtue in the trick of animation once the novelty has worn off . . . Intrinsically, the film of *Pinocchio* possesses less than one-tenth of the invention of *Peter Pan* and none at all of that play's wit.' *(James Agate, Tatler)*

MIXED:

'A compound of imagination and craftsmanship, of beauty and eloquence, which is to be found only in great works of art . . . [but it] lacks the element of surprise and something of the emotional depth [of *Snow White*]. Smaller than its parts . . . One misses the lyrical parts of *Snow White* . . . and also its stronger central idea.' *(Franz Hollering, Nation)*

'To some people the didacticism of the picture may seem a bit overpowering. But how marvellous the invention is throughout! The beginning of the film, it is true, is a little slow. And the setting of the first part of the story, the old woodcarver's house, encourages the quaintness into which Disney sometimes descends rather than the fantasy of which he is so brilliant a master. Geppetto the woodcarver is a stock quaint figure; Disney, who makes his animals such marvellous caricatures of human beings, has not yet found a way to give individuality and life to his human characters . . . But with his central character he has been much more successful than in *Snow White*, for *Pinocchio*, being a puppet, calls for none of the attempts at realism which disfigured much of the first picture. And the second part of the film, when the action moves with growing speed, has a quality of size new in Disney.' *(Dilys Powell)*

'Picture stresses evil figures and results of wrongdoing more vividly and too a greater extent than *Snow White*, and at times somewhat overplays these factors for children. This is minor, however.' *(Variety)*

'A rum old mixture of the excellent and the awful. The story itself has the harsh morality and cruelty of Victorian children's literature, but Disney organises his queasy material with some stunning animation of a monster whale thrashing about and much delightful background detail (the candle-holders and clocks in the toymaker's shop). However, one also has to suffer the cavortings of a cute goldfish called Cleo, and several appearances of an odious fairy. *Pinocchio*, in fact, probably shows Disney's virtues and vices more clearly than any other cartoon.' *(Geoff Brown, Time Out)*

PRO:

'A work that gives you almost every possible kind of pleasure to be got from a motion picture.' *(Richard Mallett, Punch)*

'The limits of the animated cartoon have been blown so wide open that some of the original wonder of pictures has been restored.' *(Otis Ferguson)*

'The best thing Mr Disney has ever done and therefore the best cartoon ever made.' *(Frank S. Nugent, New York Times)*

'A triumph . . . the film is absolutely real. But it is also absolutely fantastic. It is, in fact, genuinely imbued with the atmosphere of a dream. As soon as [it] begins the senses of space, of scale, of time become elastic . . . It is probably the mixture of strict morality with completely unbridled phantasy which makes [the film] . . . so completely engrossing. Apart from the awful fairy . . . and the rather weak figure of the wood-carver, it is crowded with some of Disney's finest characters . . . But it is Jiminy Cricket who steals the film.' *(Basil Wright, Spectator)*

'The best cartoon I have ever seen. It had a good motto behind it "Always distinguish right from wrong" . . . Jiminy Cricket . . . was the funniest character . . . I liked the part where [he] balanced on Monstro's eyelash . . . I think the best song was "When You Wish Upon a Star".' *(Anonymous 11-year-old pupil from Raynes Park County School, Documentary News Letter, 1940)*

'The very pinnacle of [Disney's] finest phase . . . hard, brilliant, satirical wit.' *(Tribune)*

'Not only technically a remarkable improvement on anything [Disney] has provided before, but also an enchanting entertainment . . . irresistible, because of the constant and ever surprising fancifulness . . . Every minute provides some new and ingenious detail, exploring the wonderful elasticity of the medium.' *(New Statesman)*

'[Structurally it] bears a closer relationship to music than it does to drama . . . with stylistic echoes created from movement to movement by having either one or both of the two parts begin with an elaborate camera movement . . . Collodi's *Pinocchio* is a Catholic parable of sin and redemption, with the miscreant son achieving a state of grace, by risking his life to rescue his father. Disney's *Pinocchio* is born into a state of grace, however, and he undergoes no moral transformation in the course of the film . . . [It is] decidedly more Calvinist in tone, filled with an unrelenting sense of predestination . . . *Pinocchio* is the most ravishingly beautiful of animated films, the cartoon raised to a baroque spectacle, as detail is piled on detail.' *(William Paul, Movie, 1977)*

'The beauty of *Pinocchio* is that what happens to

Pinocchio seems plausible to the average kid – unlike what happens, say, to the *Little Mermaid*. Kids may not understand falling in love with a prince, but they understand not listening to your father, and being a bad boy, and running away and getting into real trouble.' *(Roger Ebert)*

PIRATE, THE CT: 5 AV: 7.09

1948 US 102 C MUSICAL/ROMANCE

D Vincente Minnelli ✗
W Albert Hackett Frances Goodrich from S.N. Behrman's play (music and lyrics by Cole Porter

Gene Kelly ✗ Judy Garland ☆ Walter Slezak Gladys Cooper The Nicholas Brothers ☆ Reginald Owen George Zucco

Circus clown (Gene Kelly) impersonates Caribbean pirate to woo romantic girl (Judy Garland) who is about to wed another (Walter Slezak).

A disappointment, especially in view of the talents involved. Kelly is at his most athletic and hard-working, but falls short in the charm department, and the songs – with the exception of 'Be A Clown', featuring the wonderful Nicholas Brothers – don't give the stars the chance to shine at their brightest. Minnelli's production is garish, and the operetta-style plot is plain silly. Oscar-nominated for Best Scoring of a Dramatic Picture.

PRO:

'A rare and happy combination of expert dancing, catchy tunes, and utterly unbelievable plot which manages to achieve pure escapism without becoming either sentimental or corny.' *(Newsweek)*

'Escapist film fare. It's an eye and ear treat of light musical entertainment, garbing its amusing antics, catchy songs and able terping in brilliant color.' *(Variety)*

MIXED:

'Colour worth seeing, and Gene Kelly's very ambitious, painfully misguided performance, by John Barrymore out of the elder Douglas Fairbanks. Judy Garland is good; and Vincente Minnelli's direction gives the whole business bulge and splendour. My sympathies are largely with them, for they're all really trying something – and in musical comedy, whose wonderful possibilities are too seldom realized by "artists", good or bad. Many people admire *The Pirate*, but it seems to me to have the death's-head, culture-cute, "mirthful" grin of the average Shakespearean comic.' *(James Agee)*

'It's fine when Judy Garland is singing or Gene Kelly dancing. The rest is a very tiresome musical romantic story and – shock of shocks – the undistinguished songs are by Cole Porter.' *(Sunday Express)*

'One of the liveliest, loudest, most colorful and generally overpowering musical romps ever to reach the screen. Sparked by Gene Kelly's immense vitality and the most sensational dancing he has done for the movies, *The Pirate* is bursting with vitality. Director Minnelli has created an irresistible spectacle that combines visual opulence with carnival gaiety. It may just be that there is an excess of sound and fury in the production, and that, like an opium dream, it will leave the beholder entranced but exhausted. More likely, though, audiences will applaud the tireless zest of the high-spirited cast and the directorial artistry with which Minnelli puts them through their paces.' *(Herb Sterne, Fortnight)*

ANTI:

'There are signs that one or two thoughts went into its preparation, but to no avail when its ingredients, except for Judy Garland, are all so stale. I cannot recommend it.' *(Time & Tide)*

'An extremely silly and boring costume story . . . that fails to utilise the great dancing talent of Gene Kelly, the charm of Judy Garland, the music of Cole Porter or the directing skill of Vincente Minnelli.' *(Daily Worker)*

'Sounds like the libretto of a third-rate opera painstakingly read aloud.' *(News Chronicle)*

'[Garland, aided by Kelly] does her best to turn the loud and highly Technicolored whimsy . . . into acceptable entertainment; it is small blame to her that she does not come nearer to success.' *(Manchester Guardian)*

'It wasn't the success I hoped it would be. I think one of the reasons was the public didn't want to see Judy as a sophisticate . . . It was 20 years ahead of its time.' *(Arthur Freed, producer)*

PIXOTE CT: 5 AV: 7.69

(aka *Pixote a Lei Do Mais Fraco*)

1980 Brazil 127 C DRAMA/FOREIGN

D Hector Babenco ☆
W Hector Babenco Jorge Duran from José Louzeiro's novel *Infância dos Mortos*

Fernando Ramos da Silva ✔ *Marilia Pera Jorge Juliao Gilberto Moura José Nilson Martin Dos Santos*

10-year-old street urchin (Fernando Ramos da Silva) escapes from a detention centre and becomes involved in drugs and prostitution.

Horribly realistic account of life on the streets of Sao Paolo, enacted mostly by real-life homeless children. The social analysis is far from acute, and dramatically it's rather monotonous and downbeat, but the detailed observation is shocking. The leading actor was shot dead by the police in 1987, before he was out of his teens.

PRO:

'Harsh, truthful, funny and ultimately tragic . . . Babenco creates a naturalistic, almost documentary surface, but there's nothing random about the film . . . produced by an artist fully in control of his terrifying subject.' *(David Denby, New York Magazine)*

'Comes over like *Oliver Twist* re-written by Hubert Selby.' *(Philip French, Observer)*

'One of the very best realistic dramas of modern cinema.' *(Roger Ebert)*

MIXED:

'Smoothly linked, the picaresque adventures described in *Pixote* constitute, at least in its first half, an excoriating critique of the prevailing structures of power wherein official authority and the agents of care are either corrupt or . . . pathetically ineffectual. Regrettably, there are also exploitative elements at work.' *(Jack Babuscio, Gay News)*

'The performances are extraordinary and frightening . . . but [Babenco] seems unable to decide what tone to adopt – deadpan vérité or else a style more artfully dramatic.' *(Mat Snow, New Musical Express)*

'The picture isn't quite great, maybe because you can see it struggling to be, and the end (a lyric, ironic switch on the Vitelloni ending) is awfully portentous . . . But *Pixote* is goód enough to touch greatness; it restores your excitement about the confusing pleasures that movies can give.' *(Pauline Kael)*

ANTI:

'Degenerates into a catalogue of the violent antics of a quartet of boys on the run . . . the kids . . . do their stuff. The director, one suspects, does us.' *(John Coleman)*

'Its aesthetic and moral rewards are minimal . . . and we are left with little more than the perverse thrills and spills of an average exploitation film.' *(Geoff Brown, The Times)*

PLACE FOR LOVERS, A CT: 1 AV: 1.60

1969 US 102 C ROMANCE/DRAMA

D Vittorio De Sica ●
W Peter Baldwin Ennio de Concini Tonino Guerra Julian Halevy Cesare Zavattini

Marcello Mastroianni ● Faye Dunaway ●
Caroline Mortimer Karin Engh Esmerada Ruspoli

Dying US fashion designer (Faye Dunaway) finds late love with Italian engineer (Marcello Mastroianni).

Trashy fatal disease romancer along the lines of the later *Love Story* – but much more boring and pretentious.

'Looks not so much directed as whittled to death.' *(Rex Reed)*

'The luxury of how the rich die! And, oh, the lethargy of it, too! Five scriptwriters have laboured – collectively or consecutively, it's not stated – to do as little as possible in the way of providing a story.' *(Alexander Walker)*

'The most godawful piece of pseudo-romantic slop I've ever seen! . . . Even a director who had made no movies would have a hard time making one as bad as this.' *(Roger Ebert)*

'The worst movie I have seen all year and possibly since 1926. It is endlessly, interminably, paralyzingly, stupefyingly bad . . . I found myself resenting having to commit two hours of my life to this posturing and phony piece of derivative melodramatics. It isn't even an interesting failure.' *(Charles Champlin, LA Times)*

'Woefully inept . . . Marcello Mastroianni displays all the zest of a man summoned up for tax evasion. The five scriptwriters who supposedly worked on the film must have spent enough time at the water-cooler to flood a camel. The only smidgen of plot is that Dunaway makes a late abortive attempt at suicide, something the film successfully achieves after about ten minutes.' *(Time)*

'The one distinction this sickly melodrama has is that it succeeds in making not only Miss Dunaway but Marcello Mastroianni appear to be the worst actress and actor ever to darken the silver screen . . . About as exciting to watch as a game of tiddly-winks.' *(Kathleen Carroll, New York Daily News)*

'A pretentious and overwrought tale . . . unfailingly boring.' *(Stanley Newman, Cue)*

'Interminable.' *(Dean Holzapple, Hollywood Citizen-News)*

'A dismal mess . . . schmaltz.' *(Roger Greenspun, New York Times)*

'Glutinous tearjerker . . . singularly unaffecting.' *(MFB)*

'Marks career low-points for Dunaway, Mastroianni, De Sica.' *(Maltin)*

'A dish of tripe, has Faye Dunaway raging to live before she dies (of costume changes we suspect).' *(Judith Crist)*

PLACE IN THE SUN, A AAN CT: 4 AV: 6.33

1951 US 122 BW DRAMA/ROMANCE

D George Stevens ☆
W Michael Wilson Harry Brown from Theodore Dreiser's novel *An American Tragedy*

Montgomery Clift ✗ AAN Elizabeth Taylor
Shelley Winters ☆ AAN Anne Revere
Keefe Brasselle Raymond Burr

Upwardly mobile young man (Montgomery Clift) makes mill-girl (Shelley Winters) pregnant, but wants to marry rich girl (Elizabeth Taylor).

Turgid, self-important, predictable tale which

became popular with critics and audiences alike in the 1950s. Despite three showy performances by the leads, it's hard to see why, for Dreiser's story has been foolishly updated and de-fanged; and Clift's character becomes incomprehensible in the process. Dreiser's social analysis is turned into just another Hollywood romance.

PRO:

'It is a sizzler.' *(David Lewin, Daily Express)*

'Montgomery Clift, Shelley Winters and Elizabeth Taylor give wonderfully shaded and poignant performances.' *(Variety)*

'For Dreiser's stodgy, repetitious finally unilluminating prose [Stevens] substitutes a strikingly dramatic, often highly original visual style.' *(Karel Reisz, S & S)*

'A work of beauty, tenderness, power and insight . . . a credit to both the motion picture craft and . . . the author's major intentions . . . [Clift's] portrayal, often terse and hesitating, is full, rich, restrained, and above all, generally credible and poignant . . . a believable mama's boy gone wrong. Equally poignant is Shelley Winters . . . never seen to better advantage.' *(Howard Thompson, New York Times)*

MIXED:

'Beautifully produced and directed . . . faultlessly acted, flawlessly photographed. And it left me entirely unmoved.' *(Elspeth Grant, Daily Express)*

'A not ill-written triangle drama. It even has its moments of pathos . . . [The script] fails to expose the rottenness of society and gives no clue to the hero's pitiful weakness and vanity.' *(Freda Cook, Woman Today)*

'Pretty strong stuff . . . lacking the deeper significance that pervaded the book . . . Although frequently absorbing, it is marred by a vague superficiality that causes it to lose any higher significance as drama, and fall somewhere in the area of a romantic triangle that devolves into a murder melodrama.' *(Jess Zunser, Cue)*

'In the end does not amount to much. A sad story of a boy's entanglement, a love affair, a boating accident, a guilty conscience and a murder trial. I shall remember from it some good acting, some beautiful camerawork and some first-rate direction: but the general impression I retain is not of an important event in the cinema, but of an exquisitely polished piece of Hollywood amour.' *(Dilys Powell)*

'George Stevens's most highly respected work is an almost incredibly painstaking movie . . . Perhaps because Stevens's methods here are studied, slow and accumulative (which does suggest a parallel with Dreiser), the work was acclaimed as "realistic" which it most certainly is not. It is full of meaning-charged details, murky psychological overtones, darkening landscapes, the eerie sounds of a loon, and overlapping dissolves designed to affect you emotionally without your conscious awareness. It is mannered enough for a very fancy Gothic murder mystery, while its sleek capitalists and oppressed workers seem to come out of a Depression cartoon.' *(Pauline Kael, 1968)*

ANTI:

'The depressing sordidness and remorseless inevitability in the original have been toned down perhaps too much.' *(Mark Lane, Time & Tide)*

'It was inevitable in condensing Dreiser's huge novel for the screen that something should be lost and almost inevitable that this should be his social criticism and comment. George Eastman's tragedy lies in his aspirations – which Dreiser considered futile, though the film does not – and in their conflict with his Puritanical upbringing. The film conveys this less as an integral part of the story than in sidelights . . . After the first introduction to the Eastmans . . . the implicit social comment is almost neglected.' *(Philip Hope-Wallace, MFB)*

'Most of the book's acid social comment is elided, turning Dreiser's hero's attempts to better himself by latching on to a snobbish society girl into something like starry-eyed romance; what is left is rendered meaningless by being ripped out of period context into a contemporary setting.' *(Tom Milne, Time Out)*

'Overblown, overlong and overpraised.' *(Halliwell)*

PLAN NINE FROM OUTER SPACE

CT: 5 AV: 2.78

(aka *Grave Robbers from Outer Space; Plan 9 from Outer Space*)

1959 US 79 BW SF/HORROR/SO BAD

D Edward D. Wood Jr ●
W Edward D. Wood Jr ●

Bela Lugosi ● (who died four days into production and was replaced by a double who looked nothing like him) Tor Johnson ● Gregory Walcott ● Mona McKinnon ● Vampira ● Lyle Talbot ● Dudley Manlove ●

Aliens raise the dead in their ninth attempt to achieve world domination.

Inept in every department, this is the master-work of the famous bad director, Ed Wood, the most eccentric auteur and cross-dresser in the history of Hollywood. It was a worthy winner of the title Worst Film of All Time in a reader's poll for Harry and Michael Medved's Golden Turkey Awards. The film has a perversely wonderful lead-in announcement by a psychic named Criswell, who was a real-life Los Angeles TV personality: "Greetings, my friends. We are all interested in the future, for that is where you and I are going to spend the rest of our lives. Future events, such as these, will affect you in the future!"

This opening speech culminates in the originally intended title of the movie, *Grave Robbers From*

Outer Space (which, needless to say, was junked in favour of a worse one). The impression is that even the announcer doesn't know what he is doing.

The special effects are among the worst ever: fleecy clouds are visible through spaceship windows; night and day alternate at random from shot to shot; flying saucers are obviously paper plates suspended on string. The sets are equally unimpressive: the ruler of the earth inhabits a tiny office; patio furniture for an outdoor scene is also pressed into service in a bedroom; one tombstone in the cemetery falls over when knocked by a careless foot.

But the tacky production values are as nothing compared to Wood's imperishable dialogue: (1) Man: 'I saw a flying saucer.' Woman: 'Saucer? You mean the kind from up there?' Man: 'Yeah. Or its counterpart.' (2) Colonel (about the aliens): 'There's got to be a reason for their visits.' Captain: 'Visits! That would indicate visitors.' (3) Cop (scratching head with barrel of his gun): 'One thing's sure, Inspector Clay's dead. Murdered. And somebody's responsible.'

PRO:

'Wood is more critical of America's government (which conceals much from the public) and military strategy (that calls for an arms build-up and further nuclear testing) than any other director of the period dared to be. For that reason alone, we should find another, less daring film to wear the World's Worst Film banner. Just kidding.' *(Danny Peary)*

ANTI:

'A routine idea, crudely written, directed and acted, provides just about the weakest SF-cum-horror thriller to come out of Hollywood in years.' *(MFB)*

'Poor . . . Played out with an obvious eye on the type of audience that is not particularly concerned with logic and clamors only for weirdness.' *(Allen M. Widen, Motion Picture Herald)*

'A thriller for the most indulgent. Obviously made on a shoestring, this picture is too naively written, directed and acted to make more than a double biller for the least demanding audiences . . . Some quite smart special effects.' *(Daily Cinema)*

'Gives the appearance of having been slung together by drunk mortuary attendants.' *(Philip Strick, Science Fiction Movies)*

'This grade Z 1956 home movie masquerading as a theatrical film is an unalloyed delight, raising rank amateurism to the level of high comic art.' *(Joe Dante, Castle of Frankenstein)*

'It's not actually the worst film ever made, but its the most entertainingly bad one.' *(Michael Weldon, The Psychotronic Encyclopaedia of Film)*

'So very bad that it exerts a strange fascination. It appears to have been made in somebody's garage.' *(John Brosnan)*

'How bad is it? Give a monkey a camera and it'll make a better picture.' *(Danny Peary)*

PLANES, TRAINS AND AUTOMOBILES

CT: 8 AV: 5.85

1987 US 88/93 C COMEDY

D John Hughes ☆
W John Hughes ✔

Steve Martin ✔ John Candy ✔ Michael McKean Kevin Bacon Dylan Baker Carol Bruce Olivia Burnette Diana Douglas William Windom

An uptight businessman (Steve Martin) is trying to get home for Christmas, but a well-intentioned muddler (John Candy) constantly gets in his way.

Entertainingly farcical air-rail-and-road movie, with Laurel-and-Hardy overtones. Both stars are on top form, as is writer-director John Hughes (although *Home Alone* is his best-known film, this is his funniest). The physical comedy gags are so hilarious that the film's occasional sentimental excesses are easily forgiven. Very underrated on release.

MIXED:

'[The film's message] is laying it on a bit thick, emotionally, but is well prepared in terms of structure; the ending is handled with a bit of schmaltzy tact.' *(Adam Mars-Jones, Independent)*

'The physical gags work well . . . The moral of the story is that comedy is less funny if it means well.' *(Victoria Mather, Daily Telegraph)*

'Has about it the feel of a Preston Sturges movie: madcap comedy with a problematic tone of American social satire . . . Until the soft-centred, sellout climax, John Hughes writes and directs sharply, deftly building-up the situations, interweaving comic strip technique with the more plangent business of finding humour in human foibles . . . an auspicious début by Hughes . . . Such a pity therefore that the movie is let down by a soppy ending . . . He wants to send-up and celebrate at the same time.' *(Martin Sutton, F & F)*

'As usual with Hughes, one extra draft would have cut out the misfire gags and the slushy ending.' *(Winnert)*

PRO:

'Though the protagonists . . . are middle-aged, the road movie format . . . retains a youthful flavour and certainly the realisation betrays no stiffness in the joints . . . The needlesharp camerawork . . . carries this comedy of misadventures to a greater degree than the ingenuity of the script.' *(Tim Pulleine, Guardian)*

'Hughes . . . retains his strength as an actor's director.' *(Ann Totterdell, Financial Times)*

'Has Hughes . . . finally grown up? . . . If you peer too closely, implausibilities loom up; but Hughes' nose for the indignities of modern travel and the skill of the players, keep the film racing along.' *(Geoff Brown, The Times)*

'Much of the film's pleasure lies in the wit of the script and performances . . . The underlying socialism subverts any Reaganite interpretation . . . Another pleasing aspect . . . is its emphasis on the possibilities of male friendship.' *(Janet Hawken, MFB)*

'A funny movie, but also a surprisingly warm and sweet one.' *(Roger Ebert)*

PLANET OF THE APES CT: 7 AV: 6.92

1968 US 112 C SF/DRAMA

D Franklin J. Schaffner☆
W Michael Wilson☆ Rod Serling☆ from Pierre Boulle's novel *Monkey Planet*

Charlton Heston☆ Roddy McDowall Kim Hunter☆ Maurice Evans James Whitmore James Daly Linda Harrison

Astronauts discover a planet dominated by intelligent apes.

Intelligent science fiction with magnificent, Oscar-winning ape make-up by John Chambers, splendid cinematography by Leon Shamroy which makes full use of desolate landscape (borrowed from Arizona and Utah), and a twist ending. Though under-appreciated by most contemporary critics, it did garner a few good reviews. Oscar-nominations went to Jerry Goldsmith for his music, and Morton Haack for his costumes. Box-office success meant that sequels were inevitable. *Beneath The Planet of the Apes* (1969), *Escape From The Planet of the Apes* (1971) are watchable; *Conquest of the Planet of the Apes* (1972) and *Battle For The Planet of the Apes* (1973), much less so.

MIXED:

'It is no good at all, but fun, at moments, to watch.' *(Renata Adler, New York Times)*

'A slick commercial picture, with its elements carefully engineered – pretty girl (who unfortunately doesn't seem to have had acting training), comic relief, thrills, chases – but when expensive Hollywood engineering works, the results can be impressive. This is one of the most entertaining science-fiction fantasies ever to come out of Hollywood.' *(Pauline Kael)*

'Starts and finishes splendidly but suffers from a sag in the middle.' *(Halliwell)*

PRO:

'An ingenious, adventurous, humorous, deliciously spooky example of one of my favorite popular genres, science fiction, it was smartly made and contained a useful moral or two.' *(Richard Schickel, Life)*

'An amazing film. A political-sociological allegory, cast in the mold of futuristic science-fiction, it is an intriguing blend of chilling satire, a sometimes ludicrous juxtaposition of human and ape mores, optimism and pessimism.' *(Variety)*

'This unique film is a curious mixture of drama and science fiction that offers viewers not only a tale that is different but one that holds interest on high pretty much throughout its running time.' *(Motion Picture Exhibitor)*

'Superior SF all the way, and a clever amalgam by Franklin Schaffner of lucid comedy (*The Best Man*) and haunting meetings with the unknown (*The War Lord*).' (S & S)

PLATOON AAW CT: 5 AV: 7.64

1986 US 111/120 C WAR/VIETNAM/RITES-OF-PASSAGE/ANTI-WAR

D Oliver Stone☆ AAW
W Oliver Stone ✗ AAN

Tom Berenger☆ AAN Willem Dafoe☆ AAN Charlie Sheen☆ Forest Whitaker☆ Francesco Quinn John C. McGinley Richard Edison Kevin Dillon Reggie Johnson Keith David Johnny Depp David Neidorf Mark Moses

A young soldier (Charlie Sheen) goes to fight in Vietnam.

Vietnam veteran Oliver Stone's Oscar-winner tries to evoke what being an American soldier in the Vietnam War was really like; it's a worm's eye view, and therefore more frightening than those war movies which reassure us by showing where the enemy is. The documentary effect is diminished by the schematic (good versus bad) characterization and pseudo-poetic, preachy narration which tells us nothing we couldn't have worked out for ourselves. It won Oscars for the sound team (John Wilkinson, Richard Rogers, Charles Grenzback and Simon Kaye) and editor (Claire Simpson), plus a nomination for Robert Richardson's cinematography.

PRO:

'Real enough to hold the attention like a vice.' *(Derek Malcolm, Guardian)*

'If you don't come away . . . feeling bruised and battered – then you're made of pretty strong stuff! . . . It is a movie that could scar your soul.' *(Pauline McLeod, Daily Mirror)*

'A movie like this helps to insure that it will never happen again . . . What *Platoon* does – better than I've ever seen before – is to show what it was like being there. What those men went through.' *(Jane Fonda, actress)*

'Traditional movies impose a sense of order upon combat. Identifying with the soldiers, we feel that if we duck behind this tree or jump into this ditch, we will be safe from the fire that is coming from over there. In *Platoon*, there is the constant fear that any movement offers a fifty-fifty chance between a safe place or an exposed one. Stone sets up his shots to deny us the feeling that combat makes sense.' *(Roger Ebert)*

'The most realistic war film ever made. *Platoon*'s success lies in the mass of detail Stone brings to the screen. He bombards the senses with vivid sights and sounds that have the feel of actual experience. Stone captures the heat, the dampness, the bugs, the jungle rot, and most important, the confusion and fear experienced by the average soldier.' *(Baseline)*

MIXED:

'The novelty of [it] is its suggestion that war is not only hell but hard to follow.' *(Adam Mars-Jones, Independent)*

'Reaches us over-praised and overwrought – but it is certainly overdue . . . Simply as a study of battlefield behaviourism, it's vivid and awesome and awful . . . it has the shock value of obscene graffiti . . . For all its emetic realism, it delivers the same macho message as dozens of American "anti-war" war movies. War makes men out of boys.' *(Alexander Walker, Evening Standard)*

'At best we are given generalised anti-war sentiments, but very little political commentary . . . It is successful as a suspense-filled entertainment. But as a comment on the Vietnam war it leaves a lot unsaid.' *(David E. Morgan, Morning Star)*

'It is not the best film about the horrors of war . . . And it is not Stone's best effort . . . [It] is an expertly directed study in brutalisation.' *(Victoria Mather, Daily Telegraph)*

'Realistic, fascinating and harrowing. Whether you'd want to watch it twice is another matter.' *(Rose)*

ANTI:

'Meant in part as an argument against American involvement in Vietnam – and, by extension, an argument against our involvement in Central America. But what does either of these films [*Platoon* and *Salvador*] really prove? Not a thing. Both of them pretend to be contributing to intellectual discourse upon a significant issue, when all that they actually have to offer is a searing visceral experience that sheds no light on anything.' *(Bruce Bawer, American Spectator)*

'Some may feel that Stone takes too many melodramatic shortcuts, and that there's too much filtered light, too much poetic license, and too damn much romanticized insanity.' *(Pauline Kael)*

PLAY MISTY FOR ME

CT: 9 AV: 7.29

1971 US 102 C THRILLER/HORROR

D Clint Eastwood ✔
W Jo Heims Dean Reisner ✔

Clint Eastwood ☆ Jessica Walter ☆ Donna Mills John Larch Jack Ging

A disc jockey (Clint Eastwood) has a casual affair with a woman (Jessica Walter) who turns out to be insanely possessive.

Director-star Clint Eastwood subverts his own macho image to wonderful effect, in this extremely scary movie: perhaps the best thriller to tap into male paranoia (other hot contenders including *Fatal Attraction, Misery* and *The Beguiled*). Eastwood extracts every ounce of black humour and terror from a situation which many men have experienced on a much lesser scale; the audience both shares his fear and enjoys his discomfiture. Unselfishly, he allows Jessica Walter to dominate, in the outstanding performance of her career. Like Kathy Bates in *Misery*, she adds depth and pathos to a role which could easily have been demeaning. Though generally liked by critics, it found little favour with audiences, who preferred Eastwood in more traditional he-man roles.

ANTI:

'Nothing in Mr Eastwood's career so far suggests that he might be a great director and the opening of the film complete with zooms over the sea and shots into the sun does little to bolster one's confidence. Then suddenly things pick up; the hair on the neck starts to prickle . . . Is this going to be a real shocker? . . . Alas, the answer is no.' *(Gillian Hanson, Evening Standard)*

'Though Jessica Walter is just great as the gal, it's still a schlock shocker.' *(Judith Crist)*

'I like the slightly mocking way [Eastwood] projects himself . . . but when the story suddenly switches to gory melodrama, credibility snaps and everything goes wrong. It's like another film altogether and a poor one at that.' *(Nina Hibbin, Morning Star)*

MIXED:

'[Ventriloquist dummies] Charlie McCarthy and Archie Andrews are just two actors I can think of who show more personality and animation than the boxwood performance of box office pinup Clint Eastwood . . . His every expression is still an actor's nightmare of paralysis of the facial muscles . . . When [he] finally stops fooling about with chocolatebox shots, he comes near to giving his film the sharp edge of *Psycho*.' *(Fergus Cashin, Sun)*

'On an informal Richter scale of movie terror, *Play Misty for Me* registers a few gasps, some frissons and at least one spleen-shaking shudder. A good little scare show, in other words, despite various gaps in logic and probability . . . Eastwood displays a vigorous talent for sequences of violence and tension. He has obviously seen *Psycho* and *Repulsion* more than once, but those are excellent texts and he has learned his lessons passing well.' *(Jay Cocks, Time)*

If Don Siegel had been directing this one can imagine that the accent would have been fairly and squarely on the suspense element: what will happen to the hero ? Will the woman scorned get to his girlfriend before he does? But that is clearly not Mr Eastwood's way as a director. Indeed, the film could be accused of playing down that side of the story too much, building its melodramatic climaxes too slowly and when it comes to the point not letting rip enough. On the other hand, there are corresponding merits. The whole slow build-up of the relationship with the "Misty" lady in the opening sequences is beautifully done, as she gradually goes a little too far, assumes a little too much from a casual one-night encounter, degenerates from an irritation to a nuisance, and from a nuisance to a menace. The whole atmospheric side of the film is also strikingly well done, with its use of the unfamiliar suburban Californian coast, so much so that one can even overlook a couple of lyrical excursions into Lelouch country . . . Altogether, a very promising debut for Clint Eastwood as director.' *(John Russell Taylor, The Times)*

PRO:

Highly enjoyable . . . What gives the film that little bit extra is the utter credibility with which the character of the hysteric is gradually built up . . . Jessica Walter is stunningly good in the role.' *(Tom Milne, Financial Times)*

A surprisingly auspicious directorial debut for Clint Eastwood.' *(Village Voice)*

An inventive and genuinely frightening reworking of *Psycho* . . . an exercise in pure-grain paranoia . . . Eastwood's macho image is cunningly subverted . . . becoming extraordinarily vulnerable in his Carmel beach house, the way women usually are in thrillers. The imagery is at once excessively romantic and sinister, perfectly attuned to the unbalanced minds on view.' *(NFT Bulletin, 1980)*

Not the artistic equal of *Psycho*, but in the business of collecting an audience into the palm of its hand and then squeezing hard, it is supreme.' *(Roger Ebert)*

PLAYER, THE

CT: 8 AV: 8.73

1992 US 123 C COMEDY/ROMANCE

D Robert Altman ☆ AAN

W Michael Tolkin ☆ AAN from his novel

Tim Robbins ☆ Greta Scacchi Fred Ward Whoopi Goldberg Peter Gallagher Dina Merrill Brion James Cynthia Stevenson Vincent D'Onofrio Dean Stockwell Richard E. Grant Sydney Pollack Lyle Lovett (cameos: Harry Belafonte, Karen Black, Gary Busey, Cher, James Coburn, John Cusack, Brad Davis, Peter Falk, Anjelica Huston, Jack Lemmon, Burt Reynolds, Julia Roberts, Susan Sarandon, Bruce Willis and many more)

Griffin Mill (Tim Robbins), a ruthless movie executive, receives death threats from a writer he has offended. In defending himself, Mill kills the wrong writer (Vincent D'Onofrio).

The Player has been praised as the ultimate satire on modern Hollywood, but if it had been all that vicious would it have picked up three Oscar nominations (for direction, script and Geraldine Peroni's editing)? Altman hits the targets at which he can be bothered to aim: the power games, the patronizing attitude of movie executives towards anyone creative, the Hollywood parochialism, the idiocy of trying to 'pitch' a film in under 25 words, the shameless insincerity. But Altman avoids attacking over-powerful agents or inflated star salaries (one reason, perhaps, he could get so many famous actors to appear). He neglects to pillory directorial egos or waste. Nor does he have anything to say about Hollywood's casual use of violence as entertainment.

One reason the film didn't wow the masses was that Altman supplies no one they can 'root for'. Even the angry voices in opposition to our anti-hero are cracked. The English writer (Richard E. Grant) refuses to sell out to Hollywood stars and happy endings, but eventually does just that. The murdered writer who taunts Mill with the words 'I can write, what can you do?' turns out to have no talent. Even Mill's betrayed girlfriend (Dina Merrill) has such a corrupted notion of friendship that she accuses Mill of flaunting his new conquest at a party 'with several hundred of my closest friends'.

What about the anti-hero? Altman handles Griffin Mill beautifully; he skilfully makes us feel just enough sympathy for him, without unduly softening him. Mill really does have an impossible job, fielding 125 phone calls a day and trying to choose 12 ideas per year out of 50,000. He probably does love film and is less insensitive than some. He's even troubled by guilt when he kills the wrong writer. But this is black comedy: we mustn't feel too much for Mill. Otherwise we wouldn't be able to enjoy his discomfiture.

Altman is at his most deadly accurate when he goes beyond Hollywood and satirizes the extent to which audiences (and, by extension, society) love a winner. The 'happy' ending is that Mill gets away with his crime, makes a successful film, upgrades his car from a Range Rover to a Rolls, and gets the girl. The film ends with a David Lynch-style shot of him with his new, pregnant wife outside their new, perfect house with that old American flag fluttering proudly. But, like Woody Allen in his unhappy ending to *Crimes and Misdemeanors*, Altman implies that there is more to life and happiness than not getting caught.

In a twist too far, Altman 'reveals' that *The Player*

itself is a Hollywood film written by the very writer who has been stalking Mill. The death threats were, we are asked to believe, just a writer's way of researching his story-line. This might have been a masterly ending, except that any writer who was merely out to frighten a movie executive would hardly put a lethal rattlesnake in his car and risk going on trial for murder The twist is a clever but unconvincing way of rounding off the film: just the kind of cheap, crowd-pleasing trick which Altman clearly deplores if the audience, rather than a writer or director, demands it.

Other weaknesses? The movie contains at least one star too many. Whoopi Goldberg, amusing though she is, is a distraction as the Pasadena cop who's trailing Mill. And it is hard to care about the love story between Mill and the murdered writer's girl-friend (Greta Scacchi). It may be that Altman is making a deliberate point: that Hollywood makes actresses like Scacchi play thankless roles. I fear, however, that the female character has a more serious purpose and symbolizes Art as Self-Expression (she paints, but has no interest in selling her pictures). The scenes between Robbins and Scacchi are the weakest in the film.

'Right from [its] opening moments . . . [it] grabs the audience by the eyeballs . . . A triumph.' *(Geoff Brown, The Times)*

'Altman [gives] his Hollywood paymasters an off-the-cuff display of cinematic wit – as if to say: "So, you've forgotten how to make good movies. Here's how" . . . [The film] works both as a film-about-film for film cognoscenti and as a clever Hollywood comedy thriller. Robbins is superb.' *(Nick James, City Limits)*

'This is a film that can be enjoyed as a simple exercise in film-buffery . . . yet it is also an astonishing *tour de force* of film-structure.' *(Hugo Davenport, Daily Telegraph)*

'It exposes the greed and ruthlessness of the film world in hilarious fashion and has a twist at the end worthy of a Hitchcock classic. A must for all movie buffs.' *(Karen Hockney, Sun)*

'With breathtaking assurance, it veers from psychological-thriller suspense to goofball comedy to icy satire.' *(Terrence Rafferty, New Yorker)*

'After the savings and loan scandals, after Michael Milken, after junk bonds and stolen pension funds, here is a movie that uses Hollywood as a metaphor for the avarice of the 1980s.' *(Roger Ebert)*

PLOUGHMAN'S LUNCH, THE

CT: 4 AV: 5.78

1983 GB 100/107 C DRAMA

D Richard Eyre ✗
W Ian McEwan ●

Jonathan Pryce Tim Curry Rosemary Harris ✓ Frank Finlay Charlie Dore David De Keyser Nat Jackley Bill Paterson

A young man in the media (Jonathan Pryce) is on the make, and sells out his left-wing ideals.

Thatcher's Britain and the Falklands Spirit are the targets of Richard Eyre's silliest film, all too typical of its era. Jonathan Pryce and Tim Curry play a pair of unlovable journalists, Charlie Dore a repulsive TV production assistant. The only sympathetic character is a kind of anguished Shirley Williams figure, played beautifully by Rosemary Harris. Ostensibly an attack on the cheap cynicism of media people, the film inadvertently turns out to be more patronizing, self-satisfied, cheap and cynical than the people it is attacking. It enjoyed minor popularity among those who frequented some of the trendy locations pictured in the film. The public wisely disregarded the critics' approving notices, and stayed away.

PRO:

'It has a savagery about contemporary life rare enough at any time – but of enormous topicality now. It slices narrow but deep . . . It is a film to come out swinging with an open scalpel and bulging knuckle-dusters, not only at what it sees as the country's manipulated indifference, but at the communicators . . . It is refreshing to find a British film with such heated passions, that sees Tories . . . and Socialists . . . as two sides of the same decayed coin.' *(Tom Hutchinson, Mail on Sunday)*

'It's a plot that could have turned out over-schematic, but Richard Eyre's strong directorial hand shows in delicately ambivalent performances from all players.' *(Variety)*

'Tough and intelligent, with nice observation and twists of detail.' *(Halliwell)*

'A gripping film that honestly explores political morality in the 1980s.' *(Virgin)*

MIXED:

'The film quietly and persuasively suggests that we get, on the whole, precisely the media we deserve . . . Eyre's perceptive first feature . . . works best when it seems most detached from the ironically observed media throng. When it wants to drum home a message, it tends to get silly.' *(Derek Malcolm, Guardian)*

'Brilliantly acrid and enjoyable biased study of the media people who, one way or another, manipulate the thinking of society as cold-bloodedly as any rising politician on the make . . . It has faults. I don't go along with its apparent belief that the media is the refuge of rotters and charlatans . . . But it is a pleasure to see a British film that addresses itself to a theme which is relevant to today and affects us all.' *(Margaret Hinxman, Daily Mail)*

'An interesting attempt to equate personal duplicity with deceit on a national scale . . . It isn't totally convincing but the story has a sharp, contemporary edge to it that strikes home.' *(Ian Christie, Daily Express)*

'There are clichés (the working-class parents) and irrelevancies (the poetry reading), and the central character would be even less convincing with a lesser actor in the role, but since few British movies are aware of the existence of politics this is a *rara avis*.' *(Shipman)*

ANTI:

'Veers wildly in quality, and fails to cast much illumination on either past or present . . . It's all far too literary for its own good (McEwan indulges himself by including portraits of his bookish mates), and these aren't people you love to hate, they're just people you hate.' *(Richard Rayner, Time Out)*

'Too talky and preachy to really work as cinema.' *(Rose)*

POCKETFUL OF MIRACLES CT: 5 AV: 5.10

1961 US 136 C COMEDY

D Frank Capra
W Hal Kanter Harry Tugend Robert Riskin from Damon Runyon's story

Glenn Ford ● Bette Davis ☆ Hope Lange ●
Ann-Margret Peter Falk ☆ Arthur O'Connell ☆
Thomas Mitchell Edward Everett Horton
David Brian Jerome Cowan Mike Mazurki
Sheldon Leonard

Gangster (Glenn Ford) helps an old apple seller (Bette Davis) impersonate a woman of substance to impress her daughter (Ann-Margret, in her screen début) who has returned from abroad.

Frank Capra's last film, a remake of his own *Lady For A Day* (1934), was panned on release for being sentimental, overlong and outmoded. Glenn Ford and Hope Lange are miscast in important roles, and this adds to the feeling of insincerity. However, there is much to enjoy in the Runyonesque supporting performances – Peter Falk is especially amusing as a chauffeur – and Bette Davis is splendid as usual. Though it is slow at times, modern audiences may well find it pleasantly dated and heartwarming.

ANTI:

'The effect is less one of whimsy than of being beaten to death with a toffee apple.' *(Peter John Dyer)*

'Is sweet corn as digestible to today's blasé audiences, especially the teen-agers, as it was a quarter of a century ago?' *(Dick Williams, LA Times)*

'Repetition and a world faced with grimmer problems seem to have been excessively tough competition for this plot.' *(A.H. Weiler, New York Times)*

'The story has enough cracks in it for the syrup to leak through.' *(Playboy)*

'Reveals the ultimate emptiness of Capra's line of thought . . . [He] emerges, not as a humanist, but only as a peddler of sunbeams.' *(Nina Hibbin, Chicago Daily Worker)*

PRO:

'Shows us the way out of our dreary Tennessee Williams-ish rut . . . Pocketful pulls us back into the clean, fresh, upper air . . . Let's stay there.' *(Mike Connolly, Hollywood Reporter)*

'The whole audience, in a mass reaction, started to cheer and sections of the audience rose to the their feet in a tribute that was deafening.' *(Lorraine Gaugin, Hollywood Callboard)*

'Rowdy humor and pardonable sentiment . . . crackling dialogue and competent acting.' *(Wanda Hale, New York Daily News)*

'It is happy news, that after 40 years in movies, Capra's way is as sure as ever.' *(Newsweek)*

'An organ peal of rambunctious humor, the best of the past wrapped up in the best of the present.' *(Paul Beckley, New York Herald Tribune)*

'Warm, sentimental, funny.' *(Doris Arden, Chicago Sun-Times)*

POINT BLANK CT: 6 AV: 6.90

1967 US 92 C THRILLER/GANGSTER

D John Boorman ☆
W Alexander Jacobs David Newhouse Rafe Newhouse from Richard Stark's (pseudonym for Donald E. Westlake) novel *The Hunter*

Lee Marvin Angie Dickinson Keenan Wynn
Carroll O'Conor John Vernon Sharon AcKer

Gangster (Lee Marvin) vows vengeance on former wife (Sharon AcKer) and her mobster boyfriend (John Vernon) after they double-cross and leave him for dead.

Most contemporary critics found it over-violent, flashy, pretentious and needlessly abstruse – and they are not wrong. Boorman's Resnais-like refusal to tell his story in a straightforward narrative does become irksome, especially as he refuses to make it clear whether we really are watching the fragmented memories of a dying man. However, this bleak exercise in 60s film noir has rightly built up a reputation over the years. Boorman has always had a fine visual imagination, and here he and photographer Philip Lathrop make effective use of geometrical shapes and unusual framings to show his anti-hero becoming overpowered by his surroundings. And Lee Marvin gives a tremendous performance as a rugged individualist coming to realize that he is outmoded in modern, corporate America.

ANTI:

'A rapid succession of violent incidents makes very

little sense. Mr Boorman disdains straight storytelling. He puts a top dressing of tricksy cutting and arty photography on a basically empty story.' *(Felix Barker, Evening News)*

MIXED:

'Almost a very good movie, tough, hard, unsentimental . . . The opening is pretentious, style gone mad (or mod), jumpcutting between past and present, fancy camera angles, bits of disintegrating violence, as if the director had suffered a rush of Resnais to the head. But once [he] stops trying to impose an alien style on his material . . . and lets the style rise naturally with the story, the piece becomes a tight, cynical piece of work with everyone ruthlessly double-crossing everyone . . . The best contemporary gangster melodrama we've had in a long time . . . It may not be accurate, but it's believable.' *(Richard Whitehall, LA Free Press)*

'A thriller with Kafka-esque echoes which are the right sort of echoes for thrillers to be transmitting these days . . . The film's tricks are more dazzling than its woebegone plot . . . Boorman . . . is obviously working towards a distinctive style that is rather wasted here.' *(Margaret Hinxman, Sunday Telegraph)*

PRO:

'Extraordinary . . . The torture by household appliances . . . is both funny and frighteningly accurate. Stylistically [it] is more than a little forty-ish, with Wellesian angle shots, unusual locations . . . Boorman is almost too clever . . . The ultimate effect . . . is riveting; the screenplay is intelligent; and the performances are just right . . . [With *Bonnie & Clyde*] the best film of the year: an absolute must.' *(Richard Roud, Guardian)*

'John Boorman . . . shows himself to be a considerable craftsman.' *(Patrick Gibbs, Daily Telegraph)*

'A quite fascinating visual experience . . . Boorman . . . has distinctly proved himself and we'll have to watch for what he comes up with next.' *(Hollis Alpert , Saturday Review of Literature)*

'Boorman's films work best when most anchored in reality and performed by actors of great physical presence. This is why the gangster thriller *Point Blank* with its hard-edged view of Los Angeles and its energetic central performance by an expressionless, constantly active Lee Marvin remains his best picture and is indeed one of the masterpieces of the Sixties.' *(David Robinson, The Times, 1974)*

'When John Boorman's thriller first appeared in 1967, critics praised it but also called it show-offy, even pretentious. Almost a quarter century later, it has the authority of a minor classic. As Walker murders his way up the organization ladder demanding his money, he gradually discovers that crime (and by extension all business) is no longer the province of individuals but of faceless corporations – everybody he meets claims that he has to see somebody higher. Nobody takes responsibility, the organization runs everything, paranoia is king. This idea alone makes *Point Blank* one of the prophetic sixties movies.' *(John Powers)*

'The great US noir of the 60s, which virtually reinvented the genre for Hollywood and introduced a modernist vein to sustain itself . . . A fabulous and vicious allegory for modern corporate America, filmed in a dreamlike, sensuous style, all of which may be the last few seconds of a dying man's thoughts.' *(Elkan Allan, NFT Bulletin)*

'The fragmentation was necessary to give the characters and the situation ambiguity, to suggest another meaning beyond the immediate plot.' *(John Boorman)*

POINT BREAK CT: 5 AV: 4.45

1991 US 122 C ACTION/ADVENTURE/SO BAD

D Kathryn Bigelow
W W. Peter Iliff ●

Patrick Swayze Keanu Reeves ● Gary Busey Lore Petty John McGinley James Le Gros John Philbin

FBI agent (Keanu Reeves) goes in pursuit of bank-robbing surfers. New buddy called Bodhi (Patrick Swayze) introduces him to delights of surfing, sky-diving and getting a great tan.

The ultimate in mindless action flicks, directed with such speed and style that it looks like an advert for testosterone. Director Kathryn Bigelow's obvious admiration for Swayze's torso turns this into a Bodhi body movie. The action sequences are exciting, although there are so many false endings that the movie seems to go on forever. Peter Iliff's screenplay is splendidly banal and shows about as much awareness of FBI procedure as *Fantasia*. Even the dumbest audience will be able to outguess the Feds on this case, and the movie isn't well served by Keanu Reeves, whose attempts to suggest spiritual awakening are risible. He offers two expressions: gormless and unbelievably gormless.

PRO:

'The film is constructed from a series of increasingly outrageous tests to which the director herself has responded with an unflagging zeal . . . Confirmation that Kathryn Bigelow . . . is now one of the finest action directors in the business.' *(Philip Strick, S & S)*

'If it is action sequences you want . . . Bigelow would be hard to beat.' *(Derek Malcolm, Guardian)*

'A frenetic, superbly-edited, no-discernible-reality movie . . . Swayze [is] a man with lovely blonde highlights, a tan that looks like its been polished by *The Antiques Roadshow* and a penchant for talking like a stale fortune cookie . . . [The film] gallops along at an amazing lick, fuelled by some genuinely exhilarating action sequences.' *(Sue Heal, Today)*

'Exhilarating surfing and skydiving, cleverly mixed with a grippingly shot crime story.' *(NFT Bulletin, 1994)*

'You've got to love any suspense movie that asks us to buy Keanu Reeves, player par excellence of clueless dudes, as Johnny Utah, a football supernova whose career was detoured by a busted knee. Considering that Reeves suggests a guy who scored too many tackles without a helmet, that's already pushing it, but Reeves's character is also supposed to have won a law degree and graduated at the top of his class.' *(Margulies & Rebello)*

MIXED:

'A hare-brained wild ride through big surf and bad vibes, *Point Break* acts like a huge, nasty wave, picking up viewers for a few major thrills but ultimately grinding them into the sand via overkill and absurdity. What it lacks is subtlety, logic or any redeeming grace.' *(Variety)*

'Though it's anything but watertight where plotting is concerned, [it] again reveals [Bigelow's] real talents as a director of fast-paced, high-adrenaline action.' *(Janet Maslin, New York Times)*

'The pace is effectively structured . . . There isn't a whole lot to this movie, but it succeeds as an action adventure that is worth the price of admission.' *(James M. Welsh, Films in Review)*

'There are times when the dialogue is a shade comical . . . Plausibility has never been Bigelow's strong suit, and there's precious little to be found here. Even so, there's enough high-octane, heart-racing excitement for a dozen movies.' *(Nigel Floyd, Time Out)*

'Best not to ask what Reeves is doing in the FBI with a gammy leg, or why he goes back to the beach when his cover is blown, or why Swayze chooses to go for the vault on his ultimate raid. Director Kathryn Bigelow patches over script and story deficiencies here by giving us action on land, sea and in the air, including the screen's first freefall fistfight!' *(Quinlan)*

POPEYE — CT: 5 AV: 4.45

1980 US 92/114 C COMEDY/ROMANCE/MUSICAL

D Robert Altman
W Jules Feiffer from E.C. Segar's characters (music and lyrics by Harry Nilsson)

Robin Williams ☆ Shelley Duvall ☆ Ray Walston Paul Dooley Paul L. Smith Linda Hunt

Popeye (Robin Williams), searching for his long-lost father, finds love with Olive Oyl (Shelley Duvall).

Robert Altman's film, an enormous critical and commercial flop, mainly because it confounded everyone's expectations, is now getting a cult reputation. It's a pity that the storyline and songs are boring, and the only action comes at the end. Even so, it looks gorgeous, and the two leading performances make it worth the price of admission. Duvall's rendition of 'He Needs Me' manages to be both funny and touching: it's a magical moment in a movie which could have used more of them.

PRO:

'Popeye was a nice fairy tale with a loving spirit to it, and I think most people – especially movie critics – were expecting a combination of *Superman* and a Busby Berkeley musical . . . In the end, I think that what Altman got was a very gentle fable with music and a lot of heart.' *(Robin Williams)*

'Altman has breathed life into the material, and he hasn't done it by pretending that it's camp, either. He organizes a screenful of activity, so carefully choreographed that it's a delight.' *(Roger Ebert)*

'Inventive, imaginative, funny, and heart-warming.' *(Kenneth Von Gunden, Flights of Fancy, 1989)*

MIXED:

'The picture doesn't come together . . . and much of it is cluttered, squawky, and eerily unfunny. But there are lovely moments – especially when Olive is loping along or singing, and when she and Popeye are gazing adoringly at the foundling Swee' Pea.' *(Pauline Kael)*

ANTI:

'Jules Feiffer's meandering script and Harry Nilsson's lifeless songs reduce an alleged musical comedy to a tuneless bore.' *(Robert Asahina, New Leader)*

'I don't get the point.' *(Dilys Powell)*

'Boring beyond endurance.' *(Archer Winsten, New York Times)*

'The songs and minimal dances are designed for singers who can't sing and dancers who can't dance.' *(David Ansen, Newsweek)*

'Kids may wonder where their Popeye went. This one hates spinach.' *(John Coleman, New Statesman)*

'One of the most grievously miscalculated movies in recent history, claustrophobic in manner, mean in spirit, downright grotesque to look at. *Popeye* will bore children and offend adults who fondly remember the original.' *(Richard Schickel, Time)*

PORT OF SHADOWS — CT: 6 AV: 8.00

(aka *Quai des Brumes)*

1938 France 89/91 BW DRAMA/THRILLER/ FOREIGN

D Marcel Carné ☆
W Jacques Prévert ☆ from Pierre Mac Orlan

Jean Gabin ☆ Michèle Morgan Michel Simon Pierre Brasseur Marcel Pérès Edouard Delmont

Army deserter who has committed a murder (Jean Gabin) tries to run off with teenage girl (Michèle Morgan) but is thwarted by her guardian (Michel Simon).

An archetypal French film of its period, full of moody lovers and romantic pessimism – just the kind of movie which the New Wave tried to get away from. Though much of it looks set-bound and stilted today, it still has tremendous elegance. Gabin is very charismatic.

MIXED:

'The film is nothing more than a lament for the living expressed somberly by a camera greedy for shots of rain and fog, by a writer who has looked at life through gray-tinted glasses, seeing nothing but its drabness, its sordidness and the futility of those who expect anything more of it . . . As a steady diet, of course, it would give us the willies; for a change it's as tonic as a raw Winter's day.' *(Frank S. Nugent, New York Times)*

'[A] charming if unsubstantial piece of atmospherics.' *(William Whitebait, New Statesman & Nation, 1948)*

PRO:

'As a dialogue writer [Prévert] is magnificent . . . Carné has seized the opportunity . . . of establishing that borderline mood of the real and the dreamlike which is an especial perquisite of the cinema.' *(Basil Wright, Spectator)*

'Carné and his camera-man . . . have that sense of rhythm, atmosphere and pictorial composition which is in no way incompatible with the talkies, but has in fact become rarer and rarer since their introduction. Not for some time has the pleasure of the eye been so consistently and delightfully courted throughout a long film . . . The plot is hardly firm enough to support the emotional climax; on the other hand, the acting is superb.' *(P. Galloway, New Statesman)*

'Invites a response similar to that created by dramatic poetry.' *(Roger Manvell)*

'Brilliant . . . a joy.' *(Richard Winnington, News Chronicle)*

'Unity of space, time and action give the film a classic finish.' *(Georges Sadoul)*

PORTIERE DI NOTTE, IL: *see* NIGHT PORTER, THE.

PORTRAIT OF JENNIE

CT: 5 AV: 6.92

(aka *Jennie; Tidal Wave*)

1948 US 86 BW DRAMA/ROMANCE/FANTASY

D William Dieterle ☆
W Peter Berneis Paul Osborn Leonard Bernovici from Robert Nathan's novel

Jennifer Jones ☆ Joseph Cotten ☆ Ethel Barrymore ☆ David Wayne Lillian Gish Henry Hull Florence Bates

An artist is inspired by love of a ghost (Jennifer Jones) to paint his best work.

How about this for a pretentious opening? A voice intones: 'Since the beginning, Man has looked into the awesome reaches of infinity. Out of the shadows of knowledge, and out of a painting that hung on a museum wall comes our story, the truth of which lies not on our screen but in your heart.' Not surprisingly, the story turns out to be silly, sentimental, pretentious old tosh, but it's presented so glossily and acted with such sincerity that it is worth seeing. Joseph August's Oscar-nominated cinematography must be among the most stunning ever; but don't believe anyone who tells you that this is Selznick's masterpiece – *Rebecca* and *Gone with the Wind* are vastly superior. The special effects won an Oscar.

PRO:

'Easily the Selznick masterpiece, rich in superb performances, tasteful direction and superb photography.' *(Motion Picture Herald)*

'One of the most exquisite fantasy films ever made . . . a sensuous evocation of time and timelessness.' *(Cinefantastique)*

'There'll be some who will be confused by time's shuttling back and forth between the worlds of reality and infinity. But the film will have a message of consolation for many.' *(Frankie McKee Robins, McCall's, 1949)*

ANTI:

'Snaring elusive fantasy is difficult under the best of conditions, and Nathan's novelette, left between its book covers, is far more likely to make a lasting impression than it does when transposed into celluloid upon a harshly realistic screen.' *(Cue)*

'At times director William Dieterle succeeds quite well in translating this elusive tale to the screen, and a sort of dreamy, poetic mood is temporarily achieved. But the mood is transitory, for no matter how well Mr Cotten plays his difficult role, he can not for long make it believable; nor can Miss Jones' wraith seem anything but make-believe. Lastly, a tempest of unparalleled fury is unleashed on the screen, completely out of keeping with the fragile nature of the fantasy and serving as a final disenchantment from whatever spell has been created.' *(Fortnight)*

'Though the story may not make sense, the pyrotechnics, joined to the dumbfounded silliness, keep one watching.' *(Pauline Kael, 1976)*

POSEIDON ADVENTURE, THE

CT: 6 AV: 5.58

1972 US 117 C THRILLER/SO BAD

D Ronald Neame ●
W Stirling Silliphant Wendell Mayes ● from Paul Gallico's novel

Shelley Winters ✗ AAN Gene Hackman ✔ Ernest Borgnine Red Buttons Carol Lynley Leslie Nielsen Arthur O'Connell Roddy McDowall Stella Stevens Jack Albertson Pamela Sue Martin

An ocean liner turns upside down, trapping some passengers.

Ludicrous but likeable, this is one of the most enjoyably bad disaster films. You know the ship's going to be in trouble, as soon as you see that Leslie Nielsen is the captain. Neame directs with his usual dullness, as though he hasn't a clue that the script is full of clichés. The movie contains a commendably straight-faced performance from Gene Hackman as a preacher; Shelley Winters was inexplicably Oscar-nominated for a performance which can only be described as wildly camp. The song 'The Morning After' won an Oscar. John Williams's score was more deservedly nominated, as was Harold Stine's cinematography. Sample line . . . (Hackman addressing God): 'What more do you want of us? How much more blood? How many more lives?'

PRO:

'A highly imaginative and lustily-produced meller . . . permits powerful action and building tension.' *(Variety)*

'The underwater scene . . . deserves some special technical award.' *(Fergus Cashin, Sun)*

'Neame directs with a good sense of how and when to tighten the screw.' *(George Melly, Observer)*

'Shameless hokum . . . The trick is it does hold you from start to finish . . . What you might call scorching entertainment!' *(Margaret Hinxman, Sunday Telegraph)*

'A terrific piece of junk.' *(Geoff Andrew, Time Out)*

ANTI:

'Alas, this movie was directed by Ronald Neame who saw his role as that of a traffic cop . . . *The Poseidon* passenger list is a manifest of stereotypes, her cargo clichés.' *(Jay Cocks, Time)*

'Overacting in a gray wig that makes her resemble Miss Piggy's grandmother, Winters performs the most crazed of the film's many madcap surprises. When Hackman is trapped underwater, Winters waddles forward to exclaim, "I was the underwater swimming champ of New York for three years running. Swimming through corridors, and up and down stairwells – I'm the only one here trained to do things like that!" (Honorable mention must be awarded to Stella Stevens, who snaps, "Will you shut up?"). Winters then dives in and saves Hackman, while doing an underwater ballet that is unparalleled in Bad Movie madness; her dress floats up over her head, showing off Winters's mindbending pantyline and buns.' *(Margulies & Rebello)*

'The script is the only cataclysm in this waterlogged Grand Hotel . . . Shelley Winters [is] so enormously fat she goes way beyond the intention to create a warm, sympathetic Jewish character. It's like having a whale tell you you should love her because she's Jewish.' *(Pauline Kael)*

POSTCARDS FROM THE EDGE

CT: 6 AV: 7.23

1990 US 101 C COMEDY

D Mike Nichols
W Carrie Fisher from her book

Meryl Streep Shirley Maclaine ☆ Dennis Quaid Gene Hackman ✔ Richard Dreyfuss Rob Reiner Mary Wickes Conrad Bain Annette Bening ✔ Simon Callow Robin Bartlett Anthony Heald Dana Ivey Oliver Platt Michael Ontkean

Starlet with a drugs problem (Meryl Streep) battles for emotional independence from her alcoholic, fading movie-star mother (Shirley MacLaine).

This under-plotted film may disappoint any who expect it to be as intense or hard-hitting as Carrie Fisher's autobiographical novel about her love-hate relationship with her mother Debbie Reynolds. Nevertheless, the move towards comedy is evidently a conscious decision by Fisher, and to some extent it works. The film neatly avoids the traps of earnestness and self-pity by emphasizing the heroine's gains on the showbiz roundabouts as well as her losses on the personal swings. It may distrust Hollywood phoneyness, but also shows a certain affection for its 'show must go on' mentality.

Many of the film's visual images are witty (with Streep in police costume, for example, as she investigates her latest trauma); and Mike Nichols directs with the same sharp observation that he has showed on comedies from *The Graduate* to *Working Girl*. It also betrays some of his usual faults: glibness, superficiality and a lurking misogyny.

The cast, if not the movie itself, is notable for its depth. Meryl Streep performs wonderfully, insofar as you see every insult and humiliation go right through her. She delivers witty one-liners with style, emotional accuracy and vulnerability: vital for the success of the movie, since she could easily appear an intellectual snob. Just to make Streep's actress rivals even more suicidal, she also displays a singing voice which could easily win her leading parts on Broadway. She is, however, miscast: she doesn't look like Shirley MacLaine's daughter, and there's such maturity and intelligence in Streep's performance that she fails to convince as an emotional Beirut. And lines spoken by other characters about her cellulite and lack of fitness make no sense: she looks in great shape throughout.

No such reservations need apply to Shirley Maclaine's performance, which is as subtle as it is monstrous, hugely funny, and one of the high points of an illustrious acting career. She offers a razor-sharp study of a woman torn between maternal devotion and raw egotism: Claire Rayner one moment, Saddam Hussein the next.

PRO:

'Stripped of her usual mannerisms and fake accents, Meryl Streep tosses off the comedy with ease, and displays touching vulnerability . . . Nichols keeps a tight hand on the caustic patter, the overlapping dialogue and the script's mosaic of incident.' *(Geoff Brown, The Times)*

'Laugh-out-loud funny, with all the right tension relief. Nor is it all candy-floss.' *(David Davies, City Limits)*

'Fisher and Nichols don't attack with cudgels, they tickle with tiger tails . . . [The] script is observant, paranoid, witty . . . never slick . . . Streep is so compelling and MacLaine so subtle that the brittle plot hardly matters.' *(Angus Wolfe Murray, Scotsman Weekend)*

MIXED:

'Virtually every trace of real anxiety has been expunged. Instead, it offers an intelligent, but largely superficial, exploration of the relationship between a larger-than-life showbusiness parent and her clever but emotionally numbed daughter . . . The male characters . . . are largely ciphers.' *(Hugo Davenport, Daily Telegraph)*

'Much of Fisher's dialogue is dry and very funny . . . [Her] intelligence and confidence turn what could be movie brat indulgence into something much sharper, sparkling and involving . . . Despite the serious themes, the film remains essentially lightweight.' *(Colette Maude, Time Out)*

'A movie that never quite knew where it was headed and didn't really care. There is masses to enjoy in watching it roam around, but for God's sake don't try to take it seriously.' *(Anthony Lane, Independent on Sunday)*

ANTI:

'Meryl Streep just about always seems miscast. (She makes a career out of seeming to overcome being miscast.) In *Postcards from the Edge*, she's witty and resourceful, yet every expression is eerily off, not quite human . . . There's a deep jadedness in this picture (and in *Working Girl*) that can pass for sophistication. Nichols appeals to the narcissism of show-biz insiders and to the would-be insider in the rest of us. The assumption of *Postcards* is the assumption of the tabloids: that all any of us really want is to be movie stars, and we despise the ordinary Joes who aren't rich. The movie brings out the part of us that feels bitchily superior to our own lives.' *(Pauline Kael)*

'It is Lowell [Gene Hackman] who delivers the movie's punchline: "Your mother did it to you, and her mother did it to her . . . back to Eve." Here, at last, is the gospel according to the daddy/director: the world is but an endless continuum of women doing damage to their young. The child must reject the mother's power, to survive. Lowell advises Suzanne to say "Fuck it! I start with me." He further counsels her to "grow up" and "leave mother". He assigns no blame to papa. It's a conveniently misogynist view, to say the least, since statistics have long shown us that it is Daddy who is much more likely to abandon, beat, rape, and otherwise maim the lives of his children.' *(Kathi Maio)*

POSTMAN ALWAYS RINGS TWICE, THE

CT: 5 AV: 7.92

1946 US 113 BW THRILLER/ROMANCE

D Tay Garnett ☆
W Harry Ruskin Niven Busch from James M. Cain's novel

Lana Turner John Garfield Cecil Kellaway Hume Cronyn Leon Ames Audrey Totter Alan Reed

Lovers (John Garfield, Lana Turner) murder her husband (Cecil Kellaway), but don't get away with it.

Though often hailed nowadays as a masterpiece of film noir, this is a sanitized version of James M. Cain's novel. It suffers from dull leading characters, and it runs out of steam (and steaminess) long before the end. Still, it is efficiently handled by the director and better than the 1980 remake, with Jack Nicholson and Jessica Lange. It was a big hit. The generally unenthusiastic reviews which it attracted on release had much to do with the fact that it followed hard upon a superior example of its genre, *Double Indemnity*, which had a similar plot, also by Cain.

'It was a real chore to do *Postman* under the Hays Office, but I think I managed to get the sex across.' *(Tay Garnett)*

PRO:

'Strong meat, fascinating entertainment. Not for prudes.' *(People)*

'Garfield and Turner ignite the screen.' *(Maltin)*

'A classic film noir.' *(Quinlan)*

MIXED:

'Garnett handles the emotional scenes with his usual ability, but is too explicit in his staging of the action scenes, which demand a fast pace. Nevertheless, it's an absorbing and frequently exciting picture.' *(Hollywood Review)*

'The charm of [it] is that it's unpredictable. Only charm is the wrong word. It's too sordid to have any . . . You won't be bored and you won't be edified . . . [It's] a thriller that could have had art if it had not preferred to have laundry and Lana.' *(Sunday Graphic)*

'Played by John Garfield and Lana Turner they are a couple of nice nitwits who like swimming more than anything – the most reluctant murderers ever filmed. And as reward for their essential niceness they're allowed to die with an air of noble abnegation and, with the blessing of the prison chaplain, to find love and happiness in death . . . The instruments of the law on the other hand . . . are crooks, double-crossers and cynical sadists . . . Now could this be satire? Or could it?' *(Richard Winnington)*

ANTI:

'Mainly a terrible misfortune from start to finish . . . It looks to have been made in a depth of seriousness incompatible with the material, complicated by a paralysis of fear of the front office. It is, however, very interesting for just those reasons – it is what can happen, especially in Hollywood, if you are forced to try both to eat your cake and have it, and don't realize that it is, after all, only good pumpernickel.' *(James Agee)*

'Bears little of the true mark of Cain. The screen transcription of the novel is less mayhem than moral values, and as an osculatory opera its merits are strictly those of the kiss of death.' *(Herb Sterne)*

'One of the nastiest films I have seen for seasons . . . [Its] real fault . . . is its sentimental smear . . . The result is singularly unwholesome, and there is nothing in the acting, the direction or the dialogue to make me modify my opinions.' *(Observer)*

'Cain's novel, which this film travesties, had a grim sordid ineluctable quality which made it rightly a classic in its genre . . . Garnett has achieved merely the tawdry despite his typically masterful marshalling of overcrowded detail. The crowning falsity is the attempt . . . to whitewash a mean intrigue by suggesting that these two will be reunited in true love in paradise. The basic misconception is carried over into most departments – including the miscasting, mis-costuming and mis-direction of Lana Turner, who remains angelically beautiful and well-groomed throughout.' *(MFB)*

POTEMKIN

CT: 7 AV: 9.83

(aka *Battleship Potemkin; Bronenosets Potemkin*)

1925 USSR 65/75 BW DRAMA/FOREIGN/SILENT

D Sergei Eisenstein ☆
W Sergei Eisenstein

A. Antonov Vladimir Bakski Grigori Alexandrov Mikhail Gomorov

The crew of a battleship mutinies against rotten food, and is joined by the disgruntled civilian population. The revolt is brutally put down by Tsarist troops.

Eisenstein's propaganda film about an incident in the 1905 Russian revolution is one of the most famous movies ever made. It was voted the greatest picture of all time by international panels of critics in 1950 and 1958. Certainly, Eisenstein's use of montage is ground-breaking. The Odessa steps sequence is a masterpiece of editing, and has been much imitated and parodied – by Woody Allen in *Bananas* (1971), Terry Gilliam in *Brazil* (1985), Brian De Palma in *The Untouchables* (1987) and David Zucker in *Naked Gun 33⅓* (1994). However, there is not much in the way of story; and the appearance of documentary objectivity is distinctly questionable, since Eisenstein plays fast and loose with historical facts to suit his political masters.

'Max Reinhardt and Douglas Fairbanks unite in saying that it is great art, the best motion picture either has ever seen . . . Here is epic material, full of pity, terror and truth.' *(Ernestine Evans, Nation)*

'It has no story . . . But it is revolution! Not the anaemic and picaresque dumbshow patented in Hollywood, but a black cosmic flurry . . . Here is a cinematic masterpiece, architectonic, self-conscious, as all art must be. It has movement, tempo, rhythm, compositional beauty. Technically superb, it has no hollow virtuosity. Potemkin and its young director Eisenstein are cinema wise . . . . . [It] is often badly lighted; this may be due to the state of the present print, however. But Eisenstein has a musician's feeling for tempo; his rhythms throughout are amazing, flexible, trenchant, cumulative . . . Potemkin stands alone, a solitary cinema masterpiece.' *(Evelyn Gerstein, New Republic)*

'Eisenstein's silent *Potemkin* galvanized a whole generation of film aesthetes with the revolutionary battle cry of montage! The influential pioneering of America's D.W.Griffith notwithstanding, Russia's Eisenstein and Potemkin became synonymous with an elevation of the editing process to the status of a dynamic stylist imperative.' *(Andrew Sarris)*

'A textbook demonstration of Eisenstein's theoretical and practical approach to montage . . . according to which a film's meaning was created from the series of synthetic collisions between image and subsequent image.' *(Allan Hunter & Kenny Mathieson, Movie Classics 1992)*

'A dynamic early motion picture masterpiece that is a thrilling experience. One of the world's great films.' *(Judith Crist)*

PRÉPAREZ VOS MOUCHOIRS: *see* GET OUT YOUR HANDKERCHIEFS.

PRETTY WOMAN CT: 6 AV: 6.77

1990 US 115/119 C COMEDY/ROMANCE

D Garry Marshall ✔
W J.F. Lawton

Richard Gere ✔ Julia Roberts ☆ AAN
Ralph Bellamy Jason Alexander Laura San Giacomo Hector Elizondo ✔ Alex Hyde-White Elinor Donahue Judith Baldwin Larry Miller

A rich, ruthless tycoon (Richard Gere), known to his female admirers as 'the Wolf of Wall Street', encounters his Red Riding Hood (Julia Roberts), an improbably sweet, unassuming Hollywood hooker. They discover lots in common, notably the fact that they don't allow themselves to become emotionally involved in business. He teaches her class and she shows him there's more in life to strip than assets.

A macho variation on the Svengali-Trilby story, a kind of male chauvinist *Pygmalion*. The central relationship develops in ways which are at once predictable and utterly unrealistic. However, the film is written, directed and performed with such irony and charm that it's no wonder it became the biggest hit of its year. Gere underacts pleasantly; Julia Roberts is glamorous but cute as the tart with a heart; and Laura San Giacomo (the naughty sister in *sex, lies and videotape*) exudes a ruder sex appeal as Miss Roberts's room-mate.

Like director Garry Marshall's previous film, *Beaches*, this is unashamedly a woman's picture, though more a comedy than a weepie. As in most successful romances of the Aids era, there is practically nothing about the pleasures of sex, but a hard-core pornographic emphasis on the joy of shopping. It is also, very obviously, a fantasy.

The most disappointing aspect is that, despite nods in the direction of humanity, its values are resolutely materialistic. In the old days, maidens dreamed of being carried away by knights with white chargers: nowadays, it seems, girls are only carried away by nights out with the right charge-cards.

ANTI:

'Critics have described it as a fairy tale, and I guess it is, if you can imagine the brothers Grimm confabbing poolside at the Beverly Hills Hotel with a gaggle of box-office-obsessed Touchstone execs . . . Sheer balderdash, based on the fantasy that the guests at top-dollar Beverly Hills hotels, and the shoppers at fancy Rodeo Drive emporia, are all tasteful patricians, socialites of the sort that used to be played by Lucile Watson. The truth is quite the opposite: these establishments are patronized largely by gauche, over-paid show-biz types and their dependents, many of whom not only dress but talk and behave very much like cheap hookers. Anyone strolling into a Rodeo Drive boutique clothed the way Vivian is at the beginning of *Pretty Woman* would probably be taken for a rock star and treated like royalty.' *(Bruce Bawer, American Spectator)*

'*Pretty Woman* makes it very clear that money is power, and that all of the money (minus her $3000 dollar salary) still belongs to Edward Lewis. Vivian, unlike Shaw's Eliza, is as powerless in her happy ending as she was in the beginning of the tale. Less powerful, it could be argued.' *(Kathi Maio)*

'An inane, sexist and above all highly unoriginal adaptation of *Pygmalion* . . . [in which] class . . . translates into an American society dictated by wealth. Phonetic hurdles are swapped for shopping problems . . . Like a MacDonald's chocolate shake, it provides instant superficial gratification . . . but leaves a bad taste in your mouth. Verdict: boring and predictably sentimental. I'll leave you to guess the ending.' *(Sue Murphy, Spare Rib)*

'The disturbing thing . . . is that apparently nobody at Disney . . . saw it as anything but a light romantic comedy . . . What's wrong with [it] is that it's an astonishingly self-obvious piece of woman-bashing. Its real message is that money rules, that it can buy anything . . . Its real view is without this rich guy, [Vivian's] nothing . . . If the prostitute trades in her tie-dyed miniskirt for the right cocktail dress, her problems will be solved . . . Only once . . . is there even the hint that the world of the prostitute is filled with anything unpleasant, much less ugly . . . [It's] not so much glamorized as sanitized – no drugs, no disease, no pimps. It's almost as if Disney is packaging a new theme park attraction – Hooker World.' *(Jay Carr, Boston Globe)*

'A re-run of *My Fair Lady* without the wit or songs . . . We watch as Roberts, spilling champagne charm and sweetness all over the Beverly Wilshire furniture, locks acting egos with Richard Gere, who appears to have been novocained shortly before shooting.' *(Harlan Kennedy, Film Yearbook)*

'The first thing you should know about [it] is that it was directed by . . . a man who became famous . . . for doing the impossible – namely lowering the intellectual level of the television sitcom . . . [This] romantic comedy . . . will do nothing to tarnish [his] reputation as a shlockmeister par excellence . . . [It] is the very model of the slick, formulaic contemporary star vehicle, the sort of glossy, diverting, outrageously synthetic picture that nobody involved could possibly take seriously . . . [a] picture whose every last line feels as if it has been test-marketed . . . Next to Marshall, Steven Spielberg is an Italian neo-realist.' *(Bruce Bawer, American Spectator)*

'A moderately risqué film . . . [whose] plot will induce feelings of déjà vu even in those whose parents never read them to sleep.' *(Kevin Jackson, Independent)*

PRO:

'Despite its obvious flaws, Garry Marshall's sentimental pic hits the right emotional targets to shape up as monster hit.' *(Variety)*

'The reason to see *Pretty Woman* is the gal who plays her . . . the first American actress with both Audrey Hepburn's gamine air and Ava Gardner's earthy sexuality – a killer combo.' *(Carrie Rickey, Philadelphia Inquirer)*

'I cannot remember the last time a female performance of verve, charm, and subtlety eclipsed a hyped-up, all-male macho romance.' *(Andrew Sarris, New York Observer)*

'Roberts does an interesting thing; she gives her character an irrepressibly bouncy sense of humor, and then lets her spend the movie trying to repress it. Actresses who can do that *and* look great can have whatever they want in Hollywood. The movie was directed by Garry Marshall, whose films betray an instinctive good nature, and it is about as warmhearted as a movie about two cold realists can possibly be.' *(Roger Ebert)*

'Cinderella in thigh-length boots, a pinch of *Pygmalion* and . . . the glossy air of Eighties corporate greed . . . [It] sounds like a recipe for throwing up in the stalls, but . . . Marshall has crafted a fantasy of verve and charm . . . [bearing] as much relation to ordinary life as the working day of Princess Di, but I forgave its shameless sexism because it pretends to be nothing more than it is – a beautifully crafted, wittily written, gloriously acted exercise in hearts and flowers.' *(Sue Heal, Today)*

'A bland West Coast revamping of the Cinderella story . . . [The film] with its airy dismissal of class barriers and its easy assumption that a shopping trip can make a new woman of you, has – I admit with some embarrassment – a certain seductive appeal. Would Richard and Julia find true love? Frankly, I didn't give a damn. But I did want to know where she bought the jacket she wore in the last scene.' *(Margaret Walters, Listener)*

PRIDE AND PREJUDICE CT: 7 AV: 8.23

1940 US 117 BW DRAMA/ROMANCE

D Robert Z. Leonard
W Aldous Huxley Jane Murfin from Helen Jerome's play based on Jane Austen's novel

Laurence Olivier ☆ Greer Garson ☆ Edmund Gwenn ☆ Mary Boland ☆ Melville Cooper ☆ Edna May Oliver ☆ Karen Morley Frieda Inescort Bruce Lester Edward Ashley Ann Rutherford Maureen O' Sullivan E.E. Clive Marsha Hunt Heather Angel

Female intellectual (Greer Garson) finds love in 18th-century England.

As long as you don't expect the subtlety of Jane Austen's novel and can tolerate the odd Hollywood gaffe, this is a highly polished, very entertaining filming of the classic novel. Laurence Olivier smoulders, Greer Garson is pert, and the art direction (Cedric Gibbons and Paul Groesse) deserved its Oscar.

ANTI:

'The general impression is slightly pedestrian, almost pedantic – as though Hollywood's anxiety not to profane a shrine had led to a fear of liveliness.' *(Basil Wright, Spectator)*

MIXED:

'As the treatment of classics goes, [the film] comes out pretty well . . . Austen's tone has quite or almost gone; but it's rather difficult to think of any filming of her book that would be otherwise.' *(New Statesman)*

'Five thousand pounds a year and unmarried! That's the best piece of news since Waterloo!' The manners of Meryton have, indeed, acquired a certain freedom since Jane Austen described them; for here is Mr Bingley leering agreeably over a sick-room screen at Jane, who ogles back as the doctor examines her uvula. Gatecrashing is, apparently, on the up and up; the invitation to the Netherfield party bears the postscript: "Please bring this invitation with you." . . . Perhaps there is an injustice in singling out the instances in which Hollywood has got the better of Hertfordshire . . . The film is a pleasant enough entertainment, and it remains only to commend the foresight of the character, I forget which, overheard playing a snatch of Mendelssohn.' *(Dilys Powell)*

'Greer Garson is not as intolerably noble as she became later. She's effective and has nice diction, though she's arch and incapable of subtlety, and a viewer can get weary watching that eyebrow that goes up like the gold curtain at the old Met.' *(Pauline Kael)*

PRO:

'The most deliciously pert comedy of old manners, the most crisp and crackling satire in costume that we can remember ever having seen on the screen.' *(Bosley Crowther)*

'Charming . . . astute direction and perfect acting.' *(Daily Film Renter)*

'Brought beautifully to life with delightfully smooth direction, brilliant all-round portrayal and artistic production qualities.' *(The Cinema)*

'Highly entertaining.' *(MFB)*

'A screenplay of point, quality, humanity and wit.' *(Kine Weekly)*

'A virtually perfect adaptation, rich and charming and funny – the best possible answer to anyone who claims that a great novel cannot be made into a first-rate movie. If Olivier can be faulted for occasional overacting in *Wuthering Heights* and *Rebecca*, his performance here is essentially flawless. His pairing with Garson is particularly fortuitous; the two leads play splendidly off each other's wit, and the combination of mutual animosity and attraction between them feels wonderfully real.' *(Bruce Bawer, American Spectator, 1989)*

PRIME OF MISS JEAN BRODIE, THE

CT: 7 AV: 6.92

1969 GB 116 C DRAMA

D Ronald Neame
W Jay Presson Allen from Muriel Spark's novel

Maggie Smith ☆ AAW Robert Stephens
Pamela Franklin ✔ Celia Johnson ☆
Gordon Jackson Jane Carr

Edinburgh schoolmistress (Maggie Smith) wields power for good and ill over her 'gels'.

Maggie Smith is mannered but marvellous as Muriel Spark's anti-heroine. Pamela Franklin is also outstanding as a pupil. Unfortunately, Neame's direction is stodgy at best, and the wider political implications get lost. It is impossibly to take Jean seriously as a force for evil. An even bigger drawback is Rod McKuen's song 'Jean', which unaccountably was nominated for an Oscar.

PRO:

'An hour and 56 minutes of absolute, joyous happiness . . . Maggie Smith, with a face so long and eyes so big that she looks like a beautiful entry for the Oaks, is gorgeous.' *(Fergus Cashin, Daily Sketch)*

'The film abounds in humorous lines.' *(Ian Christie, Daily Express)*

'A haunting, lyrical film with one of the most magnificent screen performances in the history of the medium by Maggie Smith.' *(Rex Reed)*

MIXED:

'A very reputable, painstaking film, adorned with Maggie Smith . . . but otherwise uninspired. The mistake, perhaps, has been in taking it all too seriously.' *(Penelope Mortimer, Observer)*

'It isn't as if the film . . . were a masterpiece or anything of that sort: visually it is quite undistinguished, and Rod McKuen's music is more than slushy . . . Nevertheless, the film is to be recommended for the performances of Maggie Smith and Pamela Franklin.' *(Richard Roud, Guardian)*

'Safe, solid, sound . . . I can hardly believe that I found the result so desperately disappointing. But I did.' *(Margaret Hinxman, Sunday Telegraph)*

ANTI:

'The novel lost a good deal in its stage simplification, and loses still more in its movie reduction of that stage version . . . Ronald Neame's old-hat direction assists the process of vulgarization . . . Maggie Smith is fine in the quieter moments of the part, but much of the time she does a grossly mannered, female-impersonatorish camping-around – which undoubtedly earned her the praises of our most masculine female and feminine male reviewers.' *(John Simon)*

PRISONER OF SHARK ISLAND, THE

CT: 8 AV: 7.14

1936 US 95 BW DRAMA

D John Ford ☆
W Nunnally Johnson ☆

Warner Baxter ☆ Gloria Stuart Joyce Kay
Claude Gillingwater Douglas Wood Harry arey
Paul Fix John Carradine ☆

A doctor (Warner Baxter) innocently sets the injured leg of John Wilkes Booth after he has assassinated President Lincoln – and is unjustly imprisoned as a result.

This 30s classic is ripe for rediscovery. Based on a true story, it is an impressive, involving movie, currently underrated – perhaps because of its view of black people, who instinctively defer to our hero as a 'southern gentleman'. Such depictions may strike modern audiences as outdated and racist, even though they may be historically accurate! Baxter gives one of his finest performances, and has a worthy opponent in John Carradine, playing his sadistic jailer. Its elegantly written by Nunnally Johnson (not, as the *Time Out* guide says, Dudley Nichols) and marvellously directed by John Ford, at the height of his powers.

MIXED:

'For the most part it is an example of those American films of prison life which seem designed to appeal to a special, infantile, and not altogether wholesome taste . . . The prisoner's escape . . . is most painfully exciting and his immediate recapture so contrived that it is almost unbearably distressing.' *(The Times)*

PRO:

'A [convincing] study in brutality . . . Baxter is excellent . . . and there is a striking study in malevolence by John Carradine . . . We shall hear more of [him].' *(Daily Telegraph)*

'A powerful film, rarely false or slow, maintaining the relentless cumulative pressure, the logical falling of one thing into another, until the audience is included in the movement, and carried along with it in some definite emotional life that is peculiar to the art of motion pictures at their best.' *(Otis Ferguson)*

'Baxter . . . puts up a magnificent performance . . . John Carradine steals every scene he appears in . . . a sinister yet understandable characterisation . . . Ford has directed with all his known artistry and force.' *(Era)*

'The story is inherently grim, but such is the dramatic power and poignancy wrapped up in Warner Baxter's brilliant interpretation . . . that it is able to assume the proportions of impressive all-round entertainment . . . A praiseworthy achievement . . . [with] profound psychological significance . . . [and] vital direction.' *(Kine Weekly)*

PRISONER OF ZENDA, THE CT: 8 AV: 9.08

1937 US 101 BW ACTION/ADVENTURE

D John Cromwell ☆
W John L. Balderston Wills Root Donald Ogden Stewart ☆ from Anthony Hope's novel

Ronald Colman ☆ Douglas Fairbanks Jr ☆ Madeleine Carroll David Niven Raymond Massey ☆ Mary Astor C. Aubrey Smith ☆ Byron Foulger Montagu Love

Englishman (Ronald Colman) is asked to impersonate Ruritanian who has been kidnapped just as he is about to be crowned King.

Classic swashbuckler with Colman at his best in a dual role, and Fairbanks and Massey enjoying themselves as the villains. Highlight is a terrific swordfight between Colman and Fairbanks. This is easily the most entertaining version of the novel, although Cromwell's taste for pomp and ceremony slows the action down too much at times. Lyle Wheeler's handsome art direction and Alfred Newman's score were Oscar-nominated.

'Hokum of the 240-carat variety.' *(Variety)*

'The most pleasing film that has come along in ages.' *(New York Times)*

'Forty years after it was written audiences can still be thrilled by the story . . . Director Cromwell knows the value of a colourful plot and exploits to the full its romantic possibilities. The staging is lavish and the settings beautiful.' *(MFB)*

'This is the version that everyone remembers because it succeeds in capturing the very spirit of Ruritania. Selznick believed that the time was ripe for a return to romance but he knew that he had to get the ingredients exactly right and he would not proceed until he had secured Colman for the dual roles of Rassendyll and King Rudolph. It is one of the best swashbucklers ever made.' *(NFT Bulletin , 1974)*

PRIVATE LIFE OF HENRY VIII, THE AAN CT: 9 AV: 8.25

1933 GB 96 BW DRAMA/BIOPIC

D Alexander Korda ☆
W Lajos Biro Arthur Wimperis ☆

Charles Laughton ☆ AAW Merle Oberon Binnie Barnes Elsa Lanchester ☆ Robert Donat Franklin Dyall Miles Mander Wendy Barrie Claud Allister Everley Gregg John Loder

Henry VIII (Charles Laughton) marries . . . and marries.

Alexander Korda's cheerfully muckraking, irreverent, historically inaccurate biopic has achieved classic status – mainly thanks to Laughton's charismatic, Oscar-winning performance, one of the most fondly remembered in cinema. The odd musty joke doesn't spoil the wit of Arthur Wimperis and Lajos Biros's screenplay. Elsa Lanchester, Laughton's real-life wife, is outstanding as the ugly Anne of Cleves, especially in the card-playing scene. It was voted third-best film of the year on the *Film Daily*'s annual poll of US film critics (*Cavalcade* was first, *42nd Street* second). It cost only £60,000 to produce.

ANTI:

'I thought it vulgar.' *(Dilys Powell, 1961)*

PRO:

'Not surprisingly the film is made memorable by Charles Laughton's immensely powerful if provocative portrait . . . In technique the film is the most polished and workmanlike yet produced in this country . . . [and] gives Korda an assured place among the important directors in contemporary cinema.' *(Forsyth Hardy, Cinema Quarterly)*

'A true masterpiece, directed . . . with rare skill and with superb photography . . . Laughton works in his own inimitable humor in a way that's positively delicious . . . It is a great, strong picture.' *(Photoplay)*

'A film of taste, of wit, of good, boisterous humour, as English as a Sussex field. Technically it is first rate.' *(Ernest Betts)*

'A really brilliant if suggestive comedy. Mr Laughton not only reveals his genius as an actor, but also shows himself to be a past master in the art of make-up . . . [He] may be guilty of caricaturing the role, but occasionally truths shine in the midst of the hilarity . . . It is a remarkably well-produced film.' *(Bosley Crowther)*

'Henry VIII and his matrimonial misadventures have always been considered a joke by all but the sober historian, and this film's direction and script deal with him wittily from the popular angle, giving only the barest hints of the other sides of the all-too-efficient tyrant.' *(MFB, 1946)*

'An amazing exploration of the morbid doubts and fears underlying a seemingly virile masculinity.' *(Robert Murphy, Time Out)*

PRIZZI'S HONOR AAN CT: 8 AV: 7.79

1985 US 129 C THRILLER/ROMANCE/COMEDY

D John Huston ☆ AAN
W Richard Condon Janet Roach ☆ AAN from Richard Condon's novel

Jack Nicholson ☆ AAN Kathleen Turner ☆

Robert Loggia William Hickey ☆ AAN
John Randolph Anjelica Huston ☆ AAW
Lee Richardson Michael Lombard

A thick Mafia hit-man (Jack Nicholson) becomes infatuated with a hit-woman (Kathleen Turner), literally a femme fatale.

A triumphant late flowering of director John Huston's talent: this must be the quirkiest gangster film of all time. Its cheerful tastelessness, amorality and lack of pace leaves some people cold, but I loved the acting – especially William Hickey, amusing and chilling as a repellent Mafia boss, and Anjelica Huston, delicious as Nicholson's less than steady girlfriend. Kathleen Turner is appropriately cool and mysterious; and while Nicholson does not entirely convince as an Italian-American, he's very funny.

ANTI:

'A potentially hilarious idea is taken at the pace of a funeral procession with about as many laughs.' *(Rose)*

'Puzzling and unsatisfactory. Takes far too long to get going, is muddled in narrative, and leaves an unpleasant taste.' *(Halliwell)*

MIXED:

'Certainly one of the most curious films to kick off the summer season by an American major.' *(Variety)*

PRO:

'Delivers a high most commonly associated with controlled substances, or with works of art of liberating imagination.' *(Vincent Canby, New York Times)*

'I can't remember when I last saw a black comedy on Italian customs as applied to American ways of life and death that chilled my funny-bone so well ... *The Godfather* had an ersatz sweetness due to [Brando's Corleone] as a lovably, murderous old rogue. *Prizzi's Honour* is bitter stuff by comparison ... Grim, gritty and sometimes gruesome' *(Alexander Walker, Evening Standard)*

'Without doubt one of John Huston's finest films and [it] should be seen by everyone who appreciates witty dialogue, black humour and well-tuned performances ... What marks it out from every other Italian gangster film is the tone; deadpan violence, Machiavellian intrigue and fallible hitmen turn the genre on its head and simultaneously make you laugh and chill the spine.' *(Neil Norman, Hampstead & Highgate Express)*

'As enjoyable a couple of hours in the cinema as you could wish to find ... Huston directs with a gentle pace and simplicity which respect the quality of the writing and the performances, not least from his daughter.' *(Iain Johnstone, Sunday Times)*

'A sustained good joke at the expense of the Mafia.' *(John Coleman, New Statesman)*

'I fell about laughing ... I found it killingly funny.' *(Ian Christie, Daily Express)*

'An adult movie at last! An oasis in the paedo-pic desert!' *(Mat Snow, New Musical Express)*

PRODUCERS, THE   CT: 9 AV: 7.08

1968 US 88 C COMEDY

D Mel Brooks ✓
W Mel Brooks AAW

Zero Mostel ☆ Gene Wilder ☆ AAN Kenneth Mars ✓
Estelle Winwood ✓ Renée Taylor Dick Shawn ●
Christopher Hewett ✓ Andreas Voutsinas ✓

Two theatrical producers (Zero Mostel and Gene Wilder) try to fleece their investors by deliberately over-financing a sure-fire flop musical on the life of Adolf Hitler. Needless to say, their attempt to fail fails.

Critically savaged on release as crude, tasteless and unfunny – and there are certainly a few moments which fit all three descriptions – Mel Brooks's farce stands up today as a comedy classic. The two leading performances have a wild charm, and the production number 'Springtime For Hitler' is an imperishable delight.

ANTI:

'An almost flawless triumph of bad taste, unredeemed by wit or style.' *(Arthur Schlesinger Jr)*

'I am sure Zero Mostel is a brilliant comedian. Everybody tells me so, and I recognize that what he does is done with unrivalled skill. My trouble is that he doesn't make me laugh ... The Hitler-play, designed to show that the Führer was a dear kind fellow, opens with a number ("Spring-time for Hitler and Germany") performed by a chorus in a jack-booted musical-comedy version of Nazi uniform. And now I really don't laugh. The scene turns the stomachs of the audience on the screen, but only until they smell a take-off; it goes on turning mine.' *(Dilys Powell)*

'With every character so grotesque and most of the situations exploited ... with the subtlety of an all-in wrestler, it raised only a few chuckles from me.' *(Ian Christie, Daily Express)*

'Over and over again promising ideas are killed off, either by over-exposure or bad timing.' *(Tom Milne)*

'Dismally unfunny satire except for the play itself, *Springtime for Hitler*, which is neatly put down. This has, however, become a cult film, so that criticism is pointless.' *(Halliwell)*

MIXED:

'A violently mixed bag. Some of it is shoddy and gross and cruel; the rest is funny in an entirely unexpected way. It has the episodic revue quality of so much contemporary comedy ... *Springtime for Hitler* ... is the funniest part.' *(Renata Adler, New York Times)*

'There are clumsinesses in places where comic direction must always be exact; and it drags a bit . . . By and large, though, it is one of the rare films to approach the colour of the classic Hollywood comedy of the 20s and 30s.' *(David Robinson, Financial Times)*

PRO:

'Last night I saw the ultimate film . . . It is the essence of great comedy, combined in a single motion picture.' *(Peter Sellers 1969)*

'Sly, sad, occasionally deadly accurate and frequently in the most outrageous bad taste . . . The English on the whole tend to laugh at how people behave, the Americans at what people are. It is the humour of the psychiatrist's couch and may, I suppose seem macabre to many . . . To my mind, this is by far the funniest picture in London.' *(Penelope Mortimer, Observer)*

'Hilariously tasteless.' *(Tim Pulleine, Orbis, 1984)*

PROSPERO'S BOOKS CT: 3 AV: 6.00

1991 Netherlands/France/Italy 120 C DRAMA/FANTASY

D Peter Greenaway ✗

W Peter Greenaway ● based on Shakespeare's play *The Tempest*

John Gielgud Michael Clark Michel Blanc Roland Josephson Isabelle Pasco Tom Bell Kenneth Cranham

Mariners are washed up on an enchanted island.

Some directors have interpreted *The Tempest* as being about colonialism, or mid-life crisis, or the conflict between nature and civilisation: Peter Greenaway's approach is simply to emphasize the extraordinary affinity between Prospero, Shakespeare and himself. Prospero's isle becomes a nudist colony inhabited by land-locked synchronized swimmers and over-persistent performance artists. The tableaux look like window displays for a chain of sex boutiques. The whole unintentionally comic display of neo-classical kitsch is brought further down to earth by Greenaway's writing, which is as awful as ever: lame interpolations in Civil Service prose jar with some of the finest verse Shakespeare ever wrote, while the humourlessness of Greenaway's direction destroys even the famous drunk scene between Trinculo, Stephano and Caliban.

PRO:

'The film's main pleasures are in spectacle – the technological wizardry of the digital image books . . . or Gielgud's magnificent oration, irascible and fruity as ever . . . realised with unrivalled visual panache.' *(Nick James, City Limits)*

'Whatever its flaws, on an aesthetic and intellectual level this is thrilling cinema.' *(Geoff Andrew, Time Out)*

'The encyclopaedic summum of Greenaway's formal and thematic concerns to date . . . [He] interprets *The Tempest* as the story of a mind reviewing its entire contents . . . If Greenaway seems to be cramming like there's no tomorrow, there is at least a thematic justification. The images come and go, consuming themselves in a flash, just as the books finally combust or erase themselves. The film embodies a desperate awareness of the transitory, immaterial nature of images . . . a conceptual cacography that invites reading all the more energetically for defying it.' *(Jonathan Romney, S & S)*

'A remarkable feast . . . [which] will almost certainly become a benchmark of a kind.' *(Derek Malcolm, Guardian)*

'Greenaway's work, Renaissance though it is in temper, is radically new in cinema. Gielgud's work is radically traditional. They don't blend; they exist, side by side, fully.' *(Stanley Kauffmann)*

'Dazzling . . . Greenaway is true to his star and his Shakespeare, while making it wonderfully cinematic, simultaneously experimental and formally beautiful, both magical and accessible.' *(Winnert)*

ANTI:

'Greenaway floods the screen with erotic pageantry that overwhelms more than clarifies the narrative. A viewer may ogle the naked male and female figures flashing or floating across the screen with only a hint as to what the hell is going on.' *(Bruce Williamson, Playboy)*

'Contemptible . . . pretentious . . . Gielgud's noble voice, tremulous with age, can still send poetic shivers up and down your and my spines, but there are only shudders of horror to be had from Michael Nyman's accompanying music. It all depends on whether you can black out every sight, block out every sound that isn't Gielgud.' *(John Simon)*

'Greenaway is master of the deeply incomprehensible, pretentious British film . . . [He] does indeed have a stunning visual gift. But I just wish he would stop creating cold, clinical movies that place a claustrophobic anally retentive slant on our vision of the world and are not very entertaining besides.' *(Sue Heal, Today)*

'In terms of his audience, Peter Greenaway may be the most indifferent director who's ever lived . . . [The film] has his trademark lushly pictorial look . . . but it also features his rackety music and sound effects, indecipherable acting and droning pacing . . . Greenaway's technique could aptly be described as anti-cinema . . . a painterly, collage-like notion . . . and irredeemably banal.' *(David Noh, Film Journal)*

PROVIDENCE

CT: 4 AV: 5.44

1977 France/Switzerland/GB 107 C DRAMA/FANTASY

D Alain Resnais ✗
W David Mercer ✗

John Gielgud ☆ Dirk Bogarde Ellen Burstyn David Warner ● Elaine Stritch Denis Lawson ●

An ancient, alcoholic writer (John Gielgud) has a series of ideas for his next book during a long, long night of the soul. These amount to a jumbled, nonsensical, sub-Buñuel attack on the bourgeoisie. Somewhere in the back of his mind, terrorists are planting bombs and police are piling up bodies in football stadia. The next morning, the characters from his dreams turn up; and they're members of his family – not at all as Gielgud has depicted them.

Wildly overrated by some critics. One international jury even voted this the greatest film of the 70s. If *Providence* had been written in French, it might have deluded even more English-speaking reviewers into thinking it had depth. However, it was written in a ridiculously florid style of English by the British TV playwright David Mercer; and its dreadfulness, lethargy and suffocating pretentiousness are everywhere apparent. Sample lines: (1) Bogarde, on how he and his wife live, 'In a state of unacknowledged mutual exhaustion, behind which we scream silently.' (2) Gielgud, on dusk: 'How darkness creeps into the blood – darkness, the chill obsidian fingers.'

PRO:

'An unusual visual *tour-de-force* . . . A riveting pic pictorially, offering dense insights into the flights of imagination of a supposedly dying writer.' *(Variety)*

'This is a game (as *Marienbad* was a game), for the novelist and for Resnais, in which the rules are made up as we go along, and often recognized only after being broken and revised. Its a game that tells us a lot about the nature of human aspiration and the ways we delude, flatter, lacerate, rearm, and console ourselves. The characters play it in this movie, and Resnais, very genially, plays it in making this movie. If you think you might enjoy seeing some immensely talented artists taking their pretentious public identities and making artful existential play out of them, get to *Providence* fast.' *(Richard T. Jameson)*

'Resnais creates the steps and sets of a kind of Freudian ballet that is also pure cinema. Past and future dissolved into a totally compelling present tense that can, paradoxically, only be approached through memory and imagination.' *(Jan Dawson, Time Out)*

ANTI:

'The effect of the pearl-gray tones and the swift, smooth cutting is peculiarly fastidious and static; you feel as if the movie, with all its technique and culture, were going to dry up and blow away.' *(Pauline Kael)*

'[David] Warner once again is only a long lump.' *(Stanley Kauffmann)*

'For Resnais himself, it's no longer possible to hope. He's consumed with artiness . . . And under artiness there is always at least a whiff of stupidity.' *(Stanley Kauffmann)*

'Repellent and not too well acted . . . told at undue length and in turgid colour.' *(Halliwell)*

PSYCHO

CT: 9 AV: 9.50

1960 US 109 BW HORROR/THRILLER

D Alfred Hitchcock ☆ AAN
W Joseph Stefano from Robert Bloch's novel

Anthony Perkins ☆ Janet Leigh ☆ AAN Vera Miles John Gavin Martin Balsam John McIntire Simon Oakland

Blonde on the run (Janet Leigh) stops off at wrong motel, and meets a boy (Anthony Perkins) who really loves his mother.

Fun and frolics down at the Bates motel. This is either a movie classic or the product of a sick mind – possibly both. Anyway, it's the mother of all slasher movies, and a masterpiece of horror film-making. Yet it was more comprehensively savaged by the critics than any other film of high quality, except *Peeping Tom*.

The American critics generally commended Hitchcock's technical brilliance but thought it had been misapplied; British critics were almost unanimously hostile. One, C.A. Lejeune of the *Observer*, grew so sick and tired of the whole beastly business that she walked out. On both sides of the Atlantic, critics were needled by Hitchcock's refusal to allow special press screenings, which meant they could not see the film in advance of the general public, and by his refusal to accommodate latecomers into the film, which they felt savoured of a publicity stunt:

'Don't worry if they won't let you in. If you are lucky enough to miss the beginning, you will miss the end and the middle too.' *(Paul Dehn, News Chronicle)*

Others were needled by his insistence that critics not give away any of the plot twists:

'Hitch, old cock, I am so much your admirer that I will not only not give away the end. I will not even give away the beginning and the middle. This is the worst film you have made.' *(Ivon Adams, Star)*

'If you haven't guessed the ending after the first 25 minutes, you're a square. You never read a book. You don't know anything of the facts of life.' *(Leonard Mosley, Daily Express)*

The film also flew in the face of critics' expectations of Hitchcock. It was not one of his cool, glossy thrillers, but a venture into the most violent end of the horror genre. Nowadays, when almost any slasher movie is described as Hitchcockian, it's easy to forget that this was his first horror film and the first of its kind in the commercial mainstream.

It also turned out to be one of the most profitable movies of all time. In return for a $780,000 investment, within 12 months it had returned over 14 million dollars. By the end of 1960, the tide of critical opinion was changing, to keep in line with the film's popular success. America's most influential critic, Bosley Crowther of the *New York Times*, who had described *Psycho* on release as old melodramatics, was having second thoughts by the time of his end-of-year round-up:

Old-fashioned horror melodrama was given a new and frightening look in this bold psychological mystery picture. Sensual and sadistic though it was, it represented expert and sophisticated command of emotional development with cinematic techniques.'

Psycho received four Oscar nominations – for Hitchcock's direction, John L. Russell's photography and the art direction by Joseph Hurley and Robert Clatworthy, though not for George Tomasini's skilful editing, or Bernard Herrmann's brilliant and innovative score. Over the years, *Psycho* has risen hugely in critical esteem – although as late as 1972, the three US film guides still rated it only at 6.33. It has even paved the way for a whole new genre – the slasher movie. Many will doubt whether this influence has been for good.

The film isn't perfect and suffers from a dullish middle half-hour, where Hitchcock is clearly manoeuvring more characters so they can visit the Bates motel. But his use of the camera throughout is masterly:

'Consider the moment in *Psycho* when Norman Bates carries his mother down to the fruit cellar. In literary terms there is almost nothing there: a young man carrying a limp body out of a room and down some stairs. Yet in the film the overhead shot with its complicated camera movement communicates to us precisely that sense of metaphysical vertigo that Hitchcock's subject requires at that moment: a sense of sinking into a quicksand of uncertainties, or into a bottomless pit; communicates it by placing us in a certain position in relation to the action and controlling our movements in relation to the movements of the actors. The cinema has its own methods and its own scope.' *(Robin Wood, Hitchcock's Films, 1965)*

In another famous scene, Norman Bates sits beneath stuffed birds of prey; and it is pleasingly ambiguous whether he is like them, or (because of his position underneath) one of their potential victims. Hitchcock uses parent-child references and imagery throughout to bolster up his main theme of parental oppression; and the climactic exploration of the house turns into a tour of Norman Batess psychotic personality, ending in the fruit cellar, where there lurks the repressed, hidden cause of his behaviour. Perhaps the most unusual aspect of the film is the way it invites us to understand, even empathize with, a disturbed personality.

But it's the shower-scene which everyone remembers from *Psycho* – and not only because its cleverly shot: it is a revolutionary moment in cinematic story-telling, for the way it suddenly, brutally leaves the audience with no one to root for – and makes us transfer our sympathies, naturally enough, to the one character we feel we already know: the villain (who, we gradually realize to our horror, is mad!) It is probably the most brilliant narrative twist in the history of cinema.

ANTI:

'The film is a reflection of a most unpleasant mind, a mean, sadistic little mind.' *(Dwight MacDonald)*

'You better have a pretty strong stomach and be prepared for a couple of grisly shocks.' *(Bosley Crowther)*

'Sicko.' *(Picturegoer)*

'One of the messiest, most nauseating murders ever filmed. At close range, the camera watches every twitch, gurgle, convulsion and haemorrhage in the process by which a living human becomes a corpse . . . A spectacle of stomach-churning horror.' *(Time)*

'One of the most vile and disgusting films ever made. Now look here, Maestro Hitchcock, just what is the game? . . . A sad prostitution of talent.' *(Rene MacColl, Daily Express)*

'[Hitchcock has] scraped the bottom of the psychiatric barrel.' *(Fred Majdalany, Daily Mail)*

'Alfred Hitchcock may try to frighten me to death . . . but I draw the line at being bored to death.' *(Alexander Walker, Evening Standard)*

'Sad to see a really big man make a fool of himself.' *(Sunday Express)*

'Not only the most horrible film Hitchcock has ever made . . . probably the most horrible anybody has made . . . An hour's traffic of depravity ends with a scene so unintentionally comic that it makes Chaplin into Olivier.' *(Jympson Harmon, Evening News)*

'Quite implausible.' *(Guardian)*

'Gothick absurdity.' *(Spectator)*

'*Psycho* is neither so horrifying nor so surprising as might have been expected, and there are scenes and lines of dialogue which inspire the wrong sort of laughter.' *(The Times)*

'This is more miserable than the most miserable peepshow I have ever seen, and far more awful and suggestive than any pornographic film I have ever seen . . . Wholly uninteresting.' *(Clancy Sigal, Time & Tide)*

PRO:

'If the camera, under Hitchcock's direction, tends to

overemphasise a point here and there, well, it's forgivable.' *(Variety)*

'Any exhibitor who fights shy of "Psycho" should be certified.' *(Kine Weekly)*

'As thrillers go, this is a good one . . . It presents real aspects of a real world and then crumbles them slowly as you, transfixed, watch.' *(Archer Winsten, New York Post)*

'[See it three times –] the first time for the sheer terror of the experience; . . . the second time for the macabre comedy inherent in the conception of the film; and the third for all the hidden meanings and symbols lurking beneath the first American movie since *Touch of Evil* to stand in the same creative rank as the great European films.' *(Andrew Sarris, Village Voice)*

'To my relief, this is the felicitous, the mischievous, old-style Old Master Hitchcock. Though you, of course, may say I am loco about *Psycho.*' *(Dilys Powell, Sunday Times)*

'As hair raising as anything I've seen on the screen . . . And I warn you if you've got a queasy stomach stay away . . . The picture is as magnetising as a snake poised to pounce . . . It makes *Frankenstein* seem as dull as noughts and crosses.' *(Margaret Hinxman, Daily Herald)*

'A journey into hell that robs us, at calculated intervals of our guides . . . For the first time in movie history the heroine . . . has actually been murdered . . . and the hero has been demolished: Hitchcock has removed the last line of defense between us and the knife.' *(Kenneth Tynan, Observer, 1968)*

'One of the key works of our age. Its themes are of course not new – obvious forerunners include *Macbeth* and Conrad's *Heart of Darkness* – but the intensity and horror of their treatment and the fact that they are here grounded in sex belong to the age that has witnessed on the one hand the discoveries of Freudian psychology and on the other the Nazi concentration camps.' *(Robin Wood)*

'My main satisfaction is that the film had an effect on the audiences, and I consider that very important. I dont care about the subject-matter; I dont care about the acting; but I do care about the pieces of film and the photography and the sound-track and the technical ingredients that made the audiences scream. I feel it's tremendously satisfying for us to be able to use the cinematic art to achieve something of a mass emotion. And with *Psycho* we most definitely achieved this. It wasn't a message that stirred the audiences, nor was it a great performance or their enjoyment of the novel. They were aroused by pure film.' *(Alfred Hitchcock interviewed by François Truffaut, 1968)*

PUBLIC ENEMY, THE — CT: 6 AV: 8.53

(aka *Enemies of the Public*)

1931 US 84 BW THRILLER

D William A. Wellman ☆
W Harvey Thew from Kubec Glasmon, John Bright and Harvey Thew's story AAN based on Beright's story *Beer and Blood* AAN

James Cagney ☆ Edward Woods Jean Harlow Joan Blondell Beryl Mercer Donald Cook Mae Clarke Leslie Fenton

Slum kids become gangsters (James Cagney, Edward Woods) but find that crime never pays.

Until two days before shooting, Cagney was going to play the good guy, and Woods the anti-hero. Then the roles were reversed, and Wellman's film started Cagney on the road to stardom. The new emphasis on sex, violence and the brutality of the streets turns this into a seminal gangster movie – but time has made it much less shocking and effective. Cagney remains very powerful, but some of the supporting performances are far from great. A few scenes are unpleasantly exploitative and misogynistic (notably the one where Cagney presses a grapefruit into Mae Clarke's face). Far from deglamorizing mobsters (Warner Brothers' stated intention), the film made it look as though being a gangster meant having a hell of a good time.

ANTI:

'Just another gangster film . . . weaker than most in its story, stronger than most in its acting.' *(New York Times)*

PRO:

'A grim and terrible document, with no attempt to soften or humanize the character. Of all racketeer films it is the most brutal and least like movie fiction. For this reason it is the most arresting . . . Cagney . . . triumphs.' *(Norbert Lusk, Picture Play)*

'Roughest, toughest and best of the gang films to date. It's low-brow material given such workmanship as to make it high-brow.' *(Variety)*

'The real power of *The Public Enemy* lies in its vigorous and brutal assault on the nerves and in the stunning acting of James Cagney.' *(James Shelley Hamilton)*

'Cagney was playful and dynamic, and so much more appealing than the characters opposed to him that audiences rooted for him in spite of themselves.' *(Martin Quigley Jr, 1970)*

PUGNI IN TASCA, I: *see* FIST IN HIS POCKET.

PULP FICTION — CT: 10 AV: 8.00 (est)

1994 US 153 C THRILLER/COMEDY

D Quentin Tarantino ☆
W Quentin Tarantino ☆

John Travolta ☆ Bruce Willis ☆ Samuel L.

Jackson ☆ Uma Thurman ☆ Harvey Keitel ✔
Eric Stoltz ✔ Rosanna Arquette ✔
Christopher Walken Maria de Medeiros
Ving Rhames Quentin Tarantino ✔

A boxer (Bruce Willis) is supposed to take a dive in a fight but kills his opponent instead, then tries to escape with his wife (Maria de Medeiros). The other chief protagonists are a pair of hit-men: aging pretty-boy Vincent (John Travolta), rapidly running to seed on a diet of junk food, pop culture and heroin, and his black sidekick (Samuel L. Jackson) who sees himself as an instrument of Biblical vengeance.

Along the way, these two run into a smooth-talking dope dealer (Eric Stoltz) and his wacky wife (Rosanna Arquette, even spacier than in Scorsese's After Hours*). Uma Thurman gives the performance of her life as a gangster-boss's cocaine-addicted spouse – and the world's worst date. And there's a super-cool trouble-shooter (Harvey Keitel, who else?) who has the job of cleaning up after the two hitmen have accidentally blown a man's head off in the back of their car.*

Inevitably, many reviews concentrated on the blood, bad language, drugs and depravity; but the ingredient which lifts this black comedy thriller to greatness is the storytelling. Although the dialogue has the bite of an Elmore Leonard novel or a David Mamet play, it is Quentin Tarantino's sheer delight in spinning a yarn which makes him the Spielberg of splatter.

But whereas Spielberg pictures are about Good versus Evil, Tarantino is interested in the palpable friction between Evil and Much, Much Worse. On display here is the kind of lowlife which makes the underside of a stone look salubrious. There is scarcely a character who is not motivated by greed or self-indulgence. Perhaps the most shocking moment is when a wife bursts into tears of relief at her husband's blood-soaked return; it's virtually the only sign of normal human concern in the whole movie.

Bookending the film is an episode where two petty crooks (Tim Roth and Amanda Plummer) hold up a fast-food joint. The narrative connection between them and the rest of the picture only becomes clear at the end; but their role is morally crucial. For they are young people who, lacking any roots or morality, are contemplating a life of crime. They fancy themselves as a latterday Bonnie and Clyde. The rest of the film charts that descent into a Dante's Inferno which they risk entering. The *denouement* delivers them from the worst consequences of their stupidity, and looks likely to dissuade them from trying anything like it again.

There will be those who argue that *Pulp Fiction* trivialises violence and glamorizes crime; but what clearly fascinates Tarantino is a world where bloodshed can become trivialized, where crime really does confer glamour, where greed and depravity are disguised beneath a veneer of cool professionalism. As surely as Martin Scorsese in *GoodFellas*, Tarantino exposes the banality of evil, but he does so with the clinical detachment of French 'New Wave' film-makers such as Jean-Pierre Melville or the very early Jean-Luc Godard. He – and they – know that you can't hope to understand criminality without appreciating its attractions.

The numerous movie references within *Pulp Fiction* should not be construed as mere Post-Modernist affectation, or showing off for the benefit of critics; they reflect a recognition that films help create the role-models for our society. It was often said of the Kray brothers that they imitated the Hollywood gangsters they had seen (though, of course, they chose to ignore those movies' moral lessons). Tarantino doesn't disguise the fact that Cinema forms part of criminal culture.

When Bruce Willis escapes in a cab from his fatal fight, for instance, the back-projection behind him is black-and-white. This reminds the audience that his story is part of a boxing movie tradition which runs from *Body and Soul* through to *Raging Bull*. At the same time, the colour foreground reveals that this is all taking place very much in the amoral present, with his cab-driver gaining a perverted pleasure from the knowledge that her passenger has just killed a man.

How many times have people said of reality, especially at moments of danger, that it was like being in the movies? Here is the film which, more cleverly than any art-house classic like 8½, explores that symbiotic interaction between movies and life.

The question remains as to whether Tarantino has made a film about desensitization, or has merely made a desensitized film. It is hard to see *Pulp Fiction* without the uneasy feeling that modern audiences may – like the Krays with those old gangster movies – respond to the style, violence and sleaze without perceiving the moral underpinning.

This is not a film for anyone easily offended by bad language, or squeamish about violence. Do see it, however, if you enjoy a cracking story, lively characters, sparkling dialogue and bravura cinematic talent. For once, the Grand Jury at Cannes – under the timely Chairmanship of Clint Eastwood – came to the right decision in awarding *Pulp Fiction* the *Palme d'Or*. For this is the film in which Tarantino fulfils the promise of *Reservoir Dogs* and lifts himself immediately into the class of Scorsese. Not only is this among the best films of the 90s; it is also the most 90s film of the 90s.

'I don't make movies that bring people together.' *(Quentin Tarantino)*

ANTI:

'One cannot help wondering whether the appropriate response to this sort of souped-up trailer-park trash might be to acquire a gun and blow the director's head off. I mean, strictly for laughs, OK? In Tarantino's world, no doubt, it would be a scream. The serious point, however, is not that violence in films is wrong per se, nor that it requires knee-jerk censorship. It's that extremes need a justification beyond being gourmet garbage for jaded gluttons.' *(Hugo Davenport, Daily Telegraph)*

'Undisciplined, and certainly not deep, emotionally or intellectually.' *(Geoff Andrew, Time Out)*

MIXED:

'Hits you like a jolt of adrenaline; at the climax of one of its three episodes it's literally about a jolt of adrenaline. Soon enough you come down off its high, with that druggie feeling of your bones being hollow and your skin encrusted with dirt; but you can't deny that the movie delivers what you paid for, or that it somehow elevates craft and cleverness to the level of art.' *(Stuart Klawans, Nation)*

PRO:

'A spectacularly entertaining piece of pop culture.' *(Variety)*

'Whether or not he is trying to say something that matters about the banality of evil, Tarantino is a masterful cinematic storyteller – and with this rogues' gallery, he will keep you amused, intrigued, grossed out and glued to your seat.' *(Bruce Williamson, Playboy)*

'*Die Hard* with a brain.' *(Richard Corliss, Time)*

PUMPKIN EATER, THE

CT: 6 AV: 6.44

1964 GB 118 BW DRAMA

D Jack Clayton ☆
W Harold Pinter from Penelope Mortimer's novel

Anne Bancroft ☆ AAN Peter Finch ☆
James Mason ☆ Maggie Smith ☆
Cedric Hardwicke ☆ Richard Johnson Eric Porter

A thrice-married mother of eight (Anne Bancroft) discovers that her screenwriter husband (Peter Finch) is unfaithful.

One of the better domestic dramas of the 60s: a harrowing portrait of a marriage in crisis, transparently inspired by Penelope Mortimer's own marital tribulations with her husband, screenwriter John Mortimer. The acting, unfortunately, is much better than the script, which is confused and has a tendency to ramble. Clayton's direction becomes unconscionably arty at times, but he does elicit marvellous performances, especially from Bancroft and Mason.

ANTI:

'A disappointing and ultimately stultifying film analysis of domestic relations, with closeup dissections of Miss Bancroft's sorrows as a woman wallowing in childbearing and self-pity.' *(Judith Crist)*

MIXED:

'Solid, serious, intelligent, stylish. It is also, for the most part, quite dead.' *(The Times)*

'Brilliantly made if basically rather irritating kaleidoscope of vivid scenes about silly people, all quite recognizable as Sixties Londoners; very well acted.' *(Halliwell)*

PRO:

'There never was a film so rawly memorable.' *(Evening Standard)*

'[Anne Bancroft produces] one of the finest pieces of acting ever captured on film.' *(Rex Reed)*

'Has authority and accomplishment of an uncommon sort . . . It is not so much about emotions as about nerves, sensations. Look in it for an interpretation of living and you may well come away chilled. But you won't be disappointed if you take it for what it is: a supremely skilled copy of life.' *(Dilys Powell)*

PURPLE ROSE OF CAIRO, THE

CT: 7 AV: 6.50

1985 US 82 C COMEDY/ROMANCE

D Woody Allen ☆
W Woody Allen ☆

Mia Farrow ☆ Jeff Daniels ☆ Danny Aiello ☆
Dianne Wiest Van Johnson Zoe Caldwell
John Wood Milo O'Shea

A silent screen star (Jeff Daniels) walks out of the screen and into the affections of a film fan (Mia Farrow).

Woody Allen's touching romantic comedy is one of his most technically accomplished, and contains three charming performances from Daniels, Farrow and Aiello. The film explores one of Allen's favourite themes: the difference between dreams and reality. Bitter-sweet, it has a predominantly bitter aftertaste. The British Film Academy voted this Best Picture and Best Original Screenplay, but it failed to get a single Oscar nomination.

ANTI:

'Movie fanatics and incurable Woody Allen buffs are far likelier than anyone else to derive maximum enjoyment.' *(Bruce Williamson, Playboy)*

'Wears thin pretty fast.' *(David Denby, New York)*

'For all its situational goofiness, pic is a tragedy, and it's too bad Allen didn't build up the characters and drama sufficiently to give some weight to his concerns.' *(Variety)*

'It's plain curmudgeonly giving us a fantasy and then denying us an upbeat ending.' *(Rose)*

PRO:

'Slight but charming.' *(Molly Haskell, Vogue)*

'Pure enchantment . . . a sweet, lyrically funny, multi-layered work that again demonstrates Woody is our premier film-maker . . . I'd go so far as to rank it with two acknowledged classics, Luis Buñuel's

Discreet Charm of the Bourgeoisie and Buster Keaton's *Sherlock Jr*, both of which it recalls though in no way imitates.' *(Vincent Canby, New York Times)*

'One of the best movies about movies ever made.' *(Richard Schickel, Time)*

'One of the shrewdest, funniest, most plaintive explorations of movies as dream machine and escape mechanism.' *(Jack Kroll, Newsweek)*

'A sweet film, funny, smart, lovely, sad . . . human.' *(Michael Wilmington, LA Times)*

'The first Woody Allen movie in which a whole batch of actors really interact and spark each other.' *(Pauline Kael)*

'Filled with funny lines, but that doesn't take away from what's ultimately a tragic vision. The final image of Cecilia, robbed of her innocent dreams but not freed from her need for them, can bring an audience to the brink of tears.' *(Douglas Brode, Woody Allen: His Films and Career, 1987)*

'*Stardust Memories* was about a celebrity whose fame prevented people from relating to anything but his image. *Zelig*, the other side of the coin, was about a man whose anonymity was so profound that he could gain an identity only by absorbing one from the people around him. In *Purple Rose*, the movie hero has the first problem, and the woman in the audience has the second, and when they get together, they still don't make one whole person, just two sad halves.' *(Roger Ebert)*

PYGMALION AAN   CT: 8 AV: 9.31

1938 GB 96 BW COMEDY/DRAMA

D Anthony Asquith ☆
W Anatole de Grunwald W.P. Lipscomb Cecil Lewis Ian Walrymple ☆ AAW from George Bernard Shaw's play AAW

Wendy Hiller ☆ AAN Leslie Howard ☆ AAN
Wilfrid Lawson ☆ Scott Sunderland ☆ Marie Lohr ☆
David Tree Esmé Percy Everley Gregg Jean Cadell

Professor of phonetics (Leslie Howard) educates flower-girl (Wendy Hiller) for a bet.

Anthony Asquith's best film suffers less from its staginess than from the fact that, after *My Fair Lady*, one keeps half-expecting the actors to burst into song and feels an unwarranted disappointment when they don't. The leading actors are wonderful – especially Wendy Hiller, who makes a far more convincing flower-girl than Audrey Hepburn. The decision to update the story from the Edwardian era was ill-advised, but doesn't damage the play too badly. It was voted into third place on the *Film Daily* annual poll of US film critics (beaten only by *Goodbye Mr Chips* and *Mr Smith Goes to Washington*) and was Britain's top money-making picture of 1939. *Variety* attributed the original play, somewhat misleadingly, to Shakespeare.

ANTI:

'I don't believe in Mr Shaw's fairy-tales. In other words, I believe in Tinker Bell but not in Eliza Doolittle . . . Nothing can rid man or woman of inherent commonness. Other commonnesses would have betrayed Eliza in real life – commonness of bearing, of manner, of look, of walk, of the way of listening. But let us grant the teller of the fairy story his premises. Suppose any girl of today to be an Eliza abandoned by her Higgins. Would she talk of being thrown back into the gutter? Not on your life. She would realise that the world was open to her – the stage, the screen, the chance to be dance hostess, mannequin, mistress to a rich man, or wife to a poor one. No, readers, I never believed in the play and I don't believe in the film . . . And I don't believe in the fine sentiments at the end. Once a flower-girl, always a flower-girl. Having found a mug in Higgins, Eliza would have played him up good and plenty, and being a woman, she would have made her father look like an amateur at the game of extorting money politely.' *(James Agate, 1944)*

MIXED:

'An excellent, witty and always entertaining picture . . . The fault seems to lie with the script. It not only follows the play too closely, repeating its errors, but even more than the play it stresses the situations of the transformation process at the expense of more important values . . . If the shortcomings of the script are not felt as long as one looks at the screen, we have to thank Wendy Hiller who steals the show . . . Leslie Howard does very intelligently everything a Professor Higgins may do, but one cannot quite believe him. He is too conscious, too slick.' *(Franz Hoellering, Nation)*

'Represents a triumph of Anthony Asquith, whose sincere cinematic sensitivity has been all too neglected by producers in recent years . . . Like the bulk of Shaw's work, there is a completely static and stagy feeling to the story; it depends largely on good acting and on well-timed interplay of dialogue; and worse still, at times it dates horribly – especially as regards . . . Doolittle *pére* . . . by no means helped by Wilfrid Lawson's heavy . . . interpretation . . . But this is minor criticism, for the film is otherwise brilliantly cast.' *(Basil Wright, Spectator)*

'The film follows the original with unusual fidelity. For two-thirds of its course the result is highly diverting . . . The acting is remarkably good . . . It is altogether a capital film, with everything handsome about it, failing only where its inevitable dependence on Shaw's text made failure unavoidable.' *(Peter Galway, New Statesman)*

PRO:

'Live, human entertainment, flawlessly presented and making an obvious appeal to all kinds of audiences.' *(The Cinema)*

'Unfortunately for the sake of his own ego and for the sake of Hollywood's reputation the Sage of

Albion [Shaw] makes good his promise [to show Hollywood barbarians how to make a good picture]. His picture is easily one of the best pictures of this or any other season.' *(Robert Joseph, Hollywood Spectator)*

'The story has been admirably translated in terms of film until the third act, when action is subjugated to dialogue. But since the story and dialogue are by Shaw there is little to complain about! It is brilliantly amusing and remarkably undated.' *(MFB)*

'Preserves the buoyant comedy and agile dialogue of the celebrated play, and it is not a static reproduction of a stage success . . . It is a fluid photoplay, expertly photographed, offering flawless performances.. Perhaps [it] loses effervescence toward the end . . . But I have only one complaint . . . I thought I cracked a couple of ribs . . . [It] gets my nomination as the funniest of the year.' *(Richard Sheridan Ames, Rob Wagner's Script)*

QIU JU DA GUANSI: *see* STORY OF QIU JU, THE.

QUAI DES BRUMES, LE: *see* PORT OF SHADOWS.

QUATRE CENTS COUPS, LES: *see* 400 BLOWS, THE.

QUEEN CHRISTINA CT: 7 AV: 8.69.

1933 US 101 BW DRAMA/ROMANCE/BIOPIC.

D Rouben Mamoulian ☆
W Salka Viertel H.M. Harwood S.N. Behrman ☆

Greta Garbo ☆ John Gilbert Ian Keith Lewis Stone C. Aubrey Smith Reginald Owen Elizabeth Young

In the 17th century, the Queen of Sweden (Greta Garbo) ill-advisedly falls for the Spanish ambassador (John Gilbert).

Romantic tosh, raised well above the average by Garbo, who is beautiful, mysterious, and passionate in the title role. The final, enigmatic shot of her on the prow of the ship is one of the most famous – and romantic – in screen history. Just for the record, the real Queen Christina was a short, fat, ugly lesbian who never bathed and smelled so bad that few of her courtiers ventured within 20 feet of her.

'I want your face to be a blank piece of paper. I want the writing to be done by every member of the audience. I'd like it if you could avoid blinking your eyes, so that you're nothing but a beautiful mask.' *(Director Mamoulian's instructions to Garbo for the final shot)*

ANTI:

'Chief fault with *Christina* is its lethargy. It is slow and oft-times stilted.' *(Variety)*

'*Queen Christina* is a re-writing of history that transcends dramatic license, presenting among other objectionable incidents a bedroom sequence which registers with voluminous and unnecessary detail the fact of a sex affair. The sequence is emphasized and dwelt upon beyond all purposes legitimate to the telling of the story, thereby assuming a pornographic character. Its portrayal of the queen is dangerous because queens have authority, acceptance.' *(Martin Quigley, 1937)*

MIXED:

'Where the film falls down as an historical picture is chiefly in its failure to suggest the cold and rugged Sweden of those rough days when the warrior sons of the Vikings took up the Protestant banner and made such a stir in Europe. Mamoulian's silken direction has a strangely softening effect on the scenes he is depicting, which distorts history far more than mere departures from recorded fact. But the film gives Garbo space – a magnificent space – for the loveliest characterization she has yet offered.' *(James Shelley Hamilton, NBR, 1934)*

PRO:

'Affords Greta Garbo a magnificent range . . . the Queen mischievous and the Queen Embarrassed . . . the Queen in love and loving and the Queen in a moment of great tragedy. It is a great performance.' *(Punch)*

'Though idealized, the film is never empty and very seldom falls into the crudities that might so easily have come from such simplification.' *(The Times)*

'The story may not take history too seriously, but such is the . . . brilliance of its pictorial and histrionic treatment that . . . it can be readily forgiven . . . Brilliant performances by box office's star, fine, dramatic story, outstanding treatment, piquant humour, compelling sentiment, moving irony, spectacular dignified presentation and compelling supporting cast.' *(London Film Club)*

'Brilliantly executed. Magnificent performance by star, fine support, imaginative treatment and superb presentation.' *(Kinematograph Weekly)*

'Garbo, as enchanting as ever, is still enveloped by her unfathomable mystery.' *(Photoplay)*

'An unending series of exceptional scenes.' *(Modern Screen)*

QUEEN OF HEARTS CT: 10 AV: 7.23

1989 GB 112 C DRAMA/FANTASY

D Jon Amiel ✔
W Tony Grisoni ✔

Ian Hawkes ✔ Vittorio Duse ✔ Joseph Long ✔ Anita Zagaria ✔ Eileen Way ✔ Vittorio Amandola ✔ Tat Whalley

The unreliable memoirs of a child (Ian Hawkes) growing up in London's Italian community.

Probably the best film about a boy's childhood, and in my opinion one of the most magical movies ever made. It's a modern myth, a fantastic fairy-tale about the importance of family and forgiveness, movingly written by first-time screenwriter Tony Grisoni, and beautifully directed by Jon Amiel. Italians are here portrayed with the same quirky affection which Scottish villagers received from Bill Forsyth in *Local Hero*.

The film which it most resembles, however, is Frank Capra's 1946 masterpiece, *It's A Wonderful Life*. In both movies, the plot revolves around suicide and miraculous survival. But it is also reminiscent of *The Godfather*, for it is also about that most Italian of emotions, revenge. The villain, Barbariccia (Vittorio Amandola), and our child-hero both attempt acts of revenge; but neither is successful, and it is only when Eddie's father, Danilo, renounces revenge in favour of forgiveness that the story can end.

The film is openly emotional, with an almost operatic feel. The opening, Italian sequence is worthy of Visconti in its over-the-top romanticism and pictorial lushness. Even when the story moves to London, the lighting could have been designed by Zeffirelli; and director Jon Amiel, though Jewish rather than Italian, exhibits a Felliniesque flair for photographing the human face.

At the same time, there is a distinctively British irony and sophistication. Immediately after the picturesque, opening account of how our child-hero's parents escaped certain death, we become aware that the sequence we have just watched is probably not the literal truth. We hear a child's voice narrating the tale, and we realize that the story may have grown in the telling. Uniquely and brilliantly, the film hooks us on the narrative and the characters, yet keeps us subtly distanced at the same time.

Throughout the rest of the film, there are constant visual hints that what we are seeing may not be the literal truth. *Queen of Hearts* has a particular affinity with *The Ladykillers*, in the way Jim Clay's production design creates a fantastical, cinematic landscape in a stylized corner of London. The set – supposedly in the Italian quarter of Clerkenwell – is deliberately and charmingly phoney.

Queen of Hearts draws its visual style mainly from the 1950s; but little anachronisms constantly appear, to remind us that this is not reality, but romance. The Beatles, D-registration cabs, an anti-Aids poster, all lurk around the corner, in the outside world of the present. Such anachronisms are not, as some critics assumed, mistakes. They are central to the movie. The film is a child's unreliable memoirs, not a faithful history; poetic, not literal, truth. One of the messages is that it is folly to try to turn the clock back and recreate the past in the present; and the style of this lovely little picture – a unique mixture of nostalgia and irony – imaginatively reflects its content.

ANTI:

'This would-be British *Moonstruck* suffers from self-conscious direction and an erratic script . . . Director Jon Amiel . . . and screenwriter Tony Grisoni strain for a richly flavorful, picaresque style – Italianate Dickens – in which to tell their rambling story. The wavering technique, ranging from kitchen-sink melodrama to surrealistic interpolations, prevents their movie from being the heartwarming emotional feast intended.' *(David Noh, Film Journal)*

'Whatever did Amiel see in [this] whimsical screenplay?' *(Philip French, Observer)*

'I mean is this *I Remember Mama* or what?' *(Amy Taubin, Village Voice)*

'Odd but ultimately unsatisfactory mix of fantasy and reality, contrasting Italian warmth and British cool to the detriment of both.' *(Halliwell. A review which suggests that Halliwell couldn't possibly have seen it – Ed.)*

MIXED:

'Recapitulates just about every screen cliché of Italian domestic life . . . but does it all so knowingly that the film becomes like a standing family joke on which non-Italian outsiders are being graciously allowed to eavesdrop . . . A film gifted with a funny, distinctive script, an exceptionally strong cast and Amiel's confident direction.' *(Kevin Jackson, Independent)*

'A modest film, but rich in human relationships – their scams, aspirations and myths – and true to the fantastic spirit of the boy narrator. The strong cast (some of the actors unprofessional) makes up for the rough edges. It plays like a mix of Ealing kid's fantasy and a gentle, naive pastiche of *The Godfather*.' *(Wally Hammond, Time Out)*

PRO:

'Captures [the] subtle mixture of reality and fiction most beautifully . . . [and] sensitively highlights the feeling of displacement immigrants often feel when . . . they return to their place of birth.' *(Giulianna Mercorio, Independent)*

'It's *un bellissimo regalo* . . . a real movie with imagination, wit and a pinch of Anglo guile . . . a joy and a delight.' *(Angus Wolfe Murray, Scotsman)*

'A thoroughly disarming, highly unusual little film . . . It's partly an episodic family comedy, but there's also a melodramatic and sometimes magical plot about a vendetta spanning the decades which takes the film into the realm of the bizarre . . . The film's gradual accumulation of nice little moments adds up into an entrancing spell.' *(Kim Newman, Film Yearbook)*

'The kind of movie that grows on you, letting you in on the family jokes and involving you in the family feuds. By the end, you feel good, in a goofy way, and then when you think back over the movie you realize that under the fantasy and the humor there was also a fairly substantial story. A story about what it means to belong to a family.' *(Roger Ebert)*

'A unique blend of comedy, whimsy, romance and magic resulting in a delightful, unforgettable whole. Shamefully overlooked.' *(Rose)*

QUEEN OF OUTER SPACE CT: 5 AV: 3.40

1958 US 80 C SF/SO BAD

D Edward Bernds
W Charles Beaumont from Ben Hecht's story

Eric Fleming ● Paul Birch Dave Willock
Patrick Walz Laurie Mitchell Zsa Zsa Gabor ●

Spacemen discover that Venus is a planet inhabited by sexually frustrated women.

It's the sexism which has helped to make this a cult film. A typical line comes when one spaceman suggests that the scantily clad Venusian women have invented a destructive space-ray, and another replies: 'Oh, come off it! How could a bunch of women invent a gizmo like that? And even if they invented it, how could they aim it? You know how women drivers are!'

Ben Hecht wrote the story as a parody, as did Charles Beaumont the screenplay, but no one seems to have told the director, who made it with deadly seriousness as space opera. 'I think the light parts of it worked, Bernds told an interviewer later, but the melodrama parts were a little heavy for my taste.'.

The acting is dull, rather than bad – although Eric Fleming is a lumbering lead, and Zsa Zsa Gabor (slightly miscast as a Venusian scientist) delivers her lines in a thick, totally unexplained Hungarian accent. The sets (especially the jungle) are laughable; some of the costumes were recycled from a previous picture, *Forbidden Planet*; the special effects (including a ridiculous giant spider) are especially poor and pinched from another picture, *World Without End*. Contemporary reviewers were understandably confused over whether it was intended as parody.

'Ben Schwalb's production is a good-natured attempt to put some honest sex into science fiction and as such it is an attractive production.' *(Variety)*

'An elaborate parody of science fiction and, as such, it is quite good, indeed.' *(Charles Stinson, LA Times)*

'A show that the lowbrows will drool over and the highbrows will chuckle over.' *(Jack Moffitt, Hollywood Reporter)*

'Good-natured hokum . . . Besides the glamour contingent, there's a background of rich colour, flashing dials, push-button devices and weird sound effects . . . professional escapist entertainment for the undemanding.' *(Daily Cinema)*

'A few prigs offended by a girlie leg may not like it, but they'll be a minority.' *(Jack Moffitt, Hollywood Reporter)*

'Very good.' *(Motion Picture Herald)*

'The stylized settings, costumes and effects are pleasantly shot in shiny space-colour. Otherwise, this is an amiable, if rather tame burlesque of science fiction formulae.' *(MFB)*.

'Of all the science fiction films zooming into orbit this one must surely be the pottiest.' *(Picturegoer)*

'Silly, to say the least, but at least some of the laughs were intentional.' *(Maltin)*

'So bad, it's hysterical.' *(Martin & Porter)*

QUEST FOR PEACE, THE: *see* SUPERMAN IV: THE QUEST FOR PEACE.

QUIET MAN, THE AAN CT: 5 AV: 7.93

1952 US 124/129 C COMEDY/DRAMA/ROMANCE

D John Ford ☆ AAW
W Frank S. Nugent Richard Llewellyn (uncredited) AAN from Maurice Walsh's story

John Wayne ☆ Maureen O'Hara ☆
Barry Fitzgerald ☆ Victor McLaglen ☆ AAN
Ward Bond ☆ Mildred Natwick Francis Ford
Arthur Shields.

Boxer (John Wayne) returns to his homeland of Ireland and woos a difficult woman (Maureen O'Hara).

Would you believe, *The Taming of the Shrew* starring John Wayne and Maureen O'Hara, directed by John Ford, and set in a heavily romanticised Irish village? It's hardly a masterpiece, but tolerable on a wet Sunday afternoon, if you can stand the whimsy and the air of unreality, which extends far beyond the patently artificial sets. The cinematography of Winton C. Hoth and Archie Stout won an Academy Award.

ANTI:

'I must [take a trip to Ireland and] see for myself. The Irish cannot possibly be [such] blathering nitwits . . . The whole thing is played out at the bottom of a wishing well in fairyland . . . Label it Fairytale and it is good clean fun. Presume to call it a film about people and it is fantastic.' *(Connery Chappell, Picturegoer)*

'Fearfully Irish and green and hearty.' *(Pauline Kael)*

MIXED:

'This might be the work of any good Hollywood hack.' *(Richard Winnington, News Chronicle)*

'Good-natured and boisterous but overlong. The exterior sets are ghastly.' *(Shipman)*

PRO:

'The sexiest picture ever made.' *(John Ford)*

'The picture kisses the Blarney Stone and brandishes the shillelagh with like glee and vigour . . . Never a dull or superfluous moment.' *(Josh Billings, Kine Weekly)*

'A burst of Irish oddity and whimsy . . . John Ford's feeling for landscape, and for the relation between figures and landscape, has seldom been clearer. *The*

Quiet Man reminds us too how gifted he is in the handling of players.' *(Dilys Powell)*

'As darlin' a picture as we've seen this year . . . [with] dialogue . . . as tuneful as a lark's song. [The film] is not entirely muscular. Mr Ford has gotten superb visual effects . . . [and] has adorned the scene and story with enough airs to make even a poteen-filled tenor reach for High C . . . Mr Ford is in love with Ireland, as is his cast, and they give us a fine, gay time while they're about it.' *(A. H. Weiler, New York Times)*

'The spell of *The Quiet Man* will stay with you. People may say that things are not thus in Ireland, that there a Catholic Priest does not get his flock to cheer an Anglican bishop, that the IRA is not as genial as the representatives of it in this film, that the full-throated ballads sung in the pub are not so heartening, the "Square" Danahers so tractable, the Mary Kates so beautiful, and the Michaeleen Flynns so wise. Such cynicism will be in vain. John Ford has transmuted it all nearer to our heart's desire, and made us happy. We are obliged to him, and grateful for his art, and even for his artifice.' *(Henry Hart, Films in Review, 1952)*

RACHEL, RACHEL AAN CT: 6 AV: 7.25

1968 US 101 C DRAMA

D Paul Newman ☆
W Stewart Stern ☆ AAN from Margaret Laurence's novel *A Jest of God*

Joanne Woodward ☆ AAN Estelle Parsons ☆ AAN James Olson Kate Harrington Donald Moffat Geraldine Fitzgerald Bernard Burrow

Spinster schoolmistress (Joanne Woodward) tires of her smalltown existence.

Paul Newman directed his wife, the talented Joanne Woodward, in this acclaimed drama set in New England. Beautifully acted and neatly scripted, it was a rarity for its time: an intelligent Hollywood film for grown-ups. However, it is talky and turgid at times, and follows much too predictable a course.

PRO:

'It could all very easily degenerate into a woman's weepy; and the fact that it doesn't is due largely to Newman's refusal to treat Manawaka as another *Peyton Place*.' *(Jan Dawson)*

'Joanne Woodward, one of the most underrated and sadly underexposed actresses of this era, deserves a Valentine for a performance of such monumental character and strength it is hard to describe. There are really two Rachels in the film and she plays them both magnificently . . . Newman's direction of his wife is so detailed you not only see the expressions on her face, you also see the motivations behind them.' *(Rex Reed)*

'Appealing and freshly observed.' *(Halliwell)*

MIXED:

'The stuff is plainly that of women's magazines and women's pictures. But with a difference: it is more real, more restrained, more literate . . . The film tends to verge on dullness, but something always saves it. Often it is Miss Woodward: she is one of those rare actresses who can put a basic lack of charm to good advantage by playing it off against a certain pathos which, coming from someone so rough-and-tumble, becomes moving rather than coy.' *(John Simon)*

ANTI:

'What I really thought was that it was a bloody bore.' *(Richard Schickel, correcting his initially more favourable review, in 1972)*

RADIO DAYS CT: 5 AV: 7.29

1987 US 85 C COMEDY/ROMANCE

D Woody Allen ☆
W Woody Allen AAN

Woody Allen Mia Farrow ✔ Seth Green Julie Kavner ✔ Michael Tucker Dianne Wiest ✔ Josh Mostel Wallace Shawn Kenneth Mars Danny Aiello Jeff Daniels Mercedes Ruehl Richard Portnow Tony Roberts Diane Keaton

A child called Joe (Seth Green) grows up during the golden age of radio.

Great cinematography (by Carlo Di Palma), production design (by Santio Loquasto) and art direction (Speed Hopkins); shame about the script, which for some reason was Oscar-nominated, along with the art direction. The screenplay is a shapeless, rambling affair which apes Fellini's *Amarcord*. (Most of Allen's worst films mimic a European model.) Pleasant and unobjectionable, the movie offers a foolishly rosy view of the past, along with a disappointingly sanctimonious view of the present.

PRO:

'One of his most purely entertaining pictures.' *(Variety)*

'Small, sweet and sentimental – a relatively minor film by a major director . . . *Radio Days* is not a story but a rambling personal essay; the anecdotes of which it consists are designed not to advance a plot but to communicate what the word radio means to Woody Allen. For the most part, they do so with considerable charm and wit.' *(Bruce Bawer, American Spectator)*

'Almost plotless but not pointless, this tuneful tribute to golden oldies on the airwaves during America's age of innocence ranks in the collected works of Woody Allen as a trivial pursuit – which makes it approximately twice as funny and meaningful as a magnum opus by anyone else.' *(Bruce Williamson, Playboy)*

'Rather than a personal history or an exercise in nostalgia, it is a meditation on the evanescence of seemingly permanent institutions . . . Somehow, one thinks of Chekhov, and is once again astonished by the complexity and clarity of Woody Allen's vision.' *(Richard Schickel, Time)*

ANTI:

'The film, charming at first, becomes puzzling after half an hour or so of "I remember this, I remember that" vignettes, finally infuriating as we realize there isn't going to be a point . . . The great mystery of *Radio Days* is why Allen insists on telling us yet again everything we already know about him.' *(Terrence Rafferty, Nation)*

'Allen has reduced everyone to harmlessness. It's pure nostalgia – the past sweetened and trivialized.' *(Pauline Kael)*

'Woody Allen is always weakest when nostalgic indulgence leads to caricature and overstatement.' *(Geoff Andrew, Time Out)*

RAGING BULL AAN CT: 8 AV: 8.94

1980 US 119 BW (with colour sequences)
DRAMA/BIOPIC

D Martin Scorsese ☆ AAN
W Paul Schrader Mardi R. Martin based on Jake LaMotta's book with Joseph Carter, Peter Savage

Robert De Niro ☆ AAW Cathy Moriarty ☆ AAN Joe Pesci ☆ AAN Frank Vincent Nicholas Colasanto Theresa Saldana

Life and times of boxing champ Jake LaMotta (Robert De Niro).

A poll of American critics voted this the best film of the 1980s. De Niro certainly gives one of the decade's outstanding performances, and technically the movie is a *tour de force*. Thelma Schoonmaker deservedly won an Oscar for her editing, and Michael Chapman was nominated for his cinematography. The boxing sequences are some of the greatest ever filmed. Yet there are important ingredients missing: there's very little story, and we are left no one to cheer for, or even empathize with. LaMotta is a study in brutish, uncomprehending rage and masculinity; but he (and we) are never allowed any kind of release. The result is an impressive but uninvolving film, a success according to most critics, but never a hit.

PRO:

'A bravura display of cinematic skill.' *(Daily Mail)*

'For honest, impactive film-making of a slice of real life, it deserves high credit.' *(John du Pré, Sunday People)*

'This film does more than make you think about masculinity, it makes you see it – in a way that's relevant to all men, not just Bronx boxers.' *(Judith Williamson, Time Out)*

'Scorsese and Robert De Niro do a fearless job of showing us the precise feelings of their central character.' *(Roger Ebert)*

MIXED:

'Scorsese excels at whipping up an emotional storm but seems unaware that there is any need for quieter, more introspective moments in drama.' *(Variety)*

'Not a pretty film . . . No doubt that Robert De Niro gives a searing performance . . . But . . . [the film] overdoes the rage and I suspect the screenplay contains a little too much bull.' *(Arthur Thirkell, Daily Mirror)*

ANTI:

'The last thing I expected was to be bored. But I was.' *(Madeleine Harmsworth, Sunday Mirror)*

'Brilliantly conceived and thoroughly repellent . . . I'm not as you may think, chicken-hearted about boxing films. But . . . I do find the incessant stream of expletives . . . jarring, not merely because it's offensive but because it seems to me a lazy form of scriptwriting.' *(Margaret Hinxman, Daily Mail)*

'Left me cold . . . Much of the blame must lie with the writers and Scorsese who appear to have forgotten that movies should be entertaining.' *(Alan Frank, Star)*

'There is no continuous story, only an accumulation of "big" scenes . . . The film, though it revels in accurate reconstructions of the Bronx in the Forties, the ring, Mafia lairs, yesteryear's night clubs, and the like, does not have any social statement to make . . . I am thoroughly convinced by Scorsese when he conveys to me . . . what it feels like to be battered senseless; I am even more impressed when he gleans a novel insight: how frayed the ropes of the ring have become from the bodies that have scraped against them – with the implication of what the ropes, which surely fought back, must have done to those bodies. But when Scorsese tries to tell me something about people – assuming he has any ideas on that subject – even the most polished technique amounts to no more than a stammer.' *(John Simon)*

'Scorsese puts his unmediated obsessions on the screen, trying to turn raw, pulp power into art by removing it from the particulars of observation and narrative. He loses the lowlife entertainment values of prizefight films; he aestheticizes pulp and kills it. De Niro put on more than 50 pounds to play the older, drunken LaMotta; he seems a swollen puppet.' *(Pauline Kael)*

'It has no core, no real theme. It's just about a louse.' *(Danny Peary)*

RAIDERS OF THE LOST ARK: *see INDIANA JONES* SERIES.

RAILWAY CHILDREN, THE CT: 9 AV: 7.20

1970 GB 108 C DRAMA/FAMILY

D Lionel Jeffries ☆
W Lionel Jeffries ☆ from E. Nesbit's novel *The Railway Children*

Dinah Sheridan William Mervyn Jenny Agutter ☆ Bernard Cribbins Ian Cuthbertson Gary Warren Sally Thomsett

Three Edwardian children have adventures on a Yorkshire railway line.

Lionel Jeffries's delightful, nostalgic film is lovely to look at, with its backdrop of Yorkshire scenery and railway lines. It's one of those pictures which seems to improve with age. Ideal family viewing, it's guaranteed to have anyone fumbling for a handkerchief.

MIXED:

'You may feel at first that if the picture grows any goody-goodier it will bring on a bilious attack, but unashamedly sentimental though it is, the sentiment is so endearingly honest that you soon yield to it completely.' *(Cecil Wilson, Daily Mail)*

'It may sound feeble, but it is directed and acted with affection and warmth.' *(Dick Richards, Daily Mirror)*

'Miss Nesbit adhered to the all's-well school of story-telling. Like the Swiss Family Robinson, the Railway Children always rise above it, while porters are proud but grateful and old gentlemen are rich and benevolent. Really this view of human nature and behaviour grows winning, at any rate in comparison with the lethal atmosphere of most of the current cinema. Today's children are brought up on war. There are passages in Mr Jeffries' deliberately nostalgic film which may appeal more to sensitive parents than to the bloodthirsty among their offspring. But everybody, I hope, will enjoy the playing . . . In the background the green English countryside comports itself as the landscape of childhood should comport itself. It smiles.' *(Dilys Powell)*

PRO:

'Laughter, tears, sentiment, nostalgia – that's the mixture. Qualities in short supply all year have suddenly come off the ration . . . It's almost a relief to be sent out with affection in your heart, a bit of wonder on your lips, and yes, a trace of a tear you hoped you'd wiped away before the lights went up.' *(Alexander Walker, Evening Standard)*

'A pleasant sense of period and some nice touches of humour. The children . . . are likeable without being precocious.' *(Ian Christie, Daily Express)*

'This nursery classic is given a sunny glow and a dry-eyed tender treatment that stays the right side of sentimentality.' *(Robert Ottaway, Daily Sketch)*

'We can all be believers for the duration of this charming re-creation of the bygone days of the pure in heart and of simple pleasures, charmingly performed.' *(Judith Crist)*

RAIN MAN AAW CT: 6 AV: 7.62

1988 US 133 C DRAMA

D Barry Levinson ☆ AAW
W Ronald Bass Barry Morrow ☆ AAW

Dustin Hoffman ☆ AAW Tom Cruise ☆
Valeria Golino Gerald R. Molen Jack Murdock Michael D. Roberts Ralph Seymour Lucinda Jenney Bonnie Hunt (cameo: Barry Levinson as examining psychiatrist)

A selfish yuppie (Tom Cruise) becomes humanized through a journey across America with his autistic brother (Dustin Hoffman).

Barry Levinson's sensitive, mildly enjoyable road movie is supposedly Princess Diana's favourite film. Its soft-centred approach to mental illness and meandering, unimaginative storyline are offset by the wry humour and brilliant observation of Hoffman's performance. The movie won four Oscars, plus nominations for score (Hans Zimmer), cinematography (John Seale), editing (Stu Linder, Thomas R. Moore) and art direction (Ida Random, Linda DeScenna).

'Why, in 1989, is asexual bonding big business? Could be because we live in an age of moral hygiene, where the West has turned Right and America keeps loosening the buckles on its Bible Belt to contain its swelling piety? *Rain Man* appeals to this constituency because it speaks of strength through friendship, and love without the untidy convulsions of passion.' *(Harlan Kennedy, Film Yearbook)*

ANTI:

'*Rain Man* is Dustin Hoffman humping one note on a piano for two hours and eleven minutes. It's his dream role . . . Autistic means self-involved, and Raymond is withdrawn in his world of obsessive rituals. So Hoffman doesn't have to play off anybody; he gets to act all by himself . . . This whole picture is Hoffman's stunt. It's an acting exercise – working out minuscule variations on his one note. It's no more than an exercise, because Hoffman doesn't challenge us: we're given no reason to change our attitude toward Raymond; we have the same view of him from the beginning of the movie to the end . . . And Cruise as a slimeball is just a sugarpuss in Italian tailoring. He doesn't even use his body in an expressive way. His performance here consists of not smiling too much – so as not to distract his fans from watching Hoffman (this could be called "restraint") Cruise is an actor in the same sense that Robert Taylor was an actor. He's patented: his knowing that a camera is on him produces nothing but fraudulence . . . Autism here is a dramatic gimmick that gives an offbeat tone to a conventional buddy movie . . . And the picture has its effectiveness: people are crying at it. Of course they're crying at it – it's a piece of wet kitsch.' *(Pauline Kael)*

MIXED:

'*Rain Man*'s script is running on empty by the time the brothers reach California. And director Barry Levinson . . . cushions the narrative with too much sentiment. But wonderful performances make it a memorable trip.' *(Brian D. Johnson, Maclean's)*

'Just good enough to make you wish it had been better . . . There are a few subtle observations along the way, such as an implied comparison between Raymond's autism and the behavior of small-town bores and Las Vegas slotmachine players. There are also some observations that are less than subtle, such as the point that Raymond is superior in many ways to his "normal" brother. Even Charlie finally wakes up to that idea, about forty-five minutes after the audience.' *(Stuart Klawans, Nation)*

PRO:

'Director Barry Levinson . . . brings all his skill to bear on a screenplay by Ronald Bass and Barry Morrow, assiduously avoiding the maudlin sentiment and cheap shots that might have made *Rain Man* a tearjerker instead of the fine, intelligent human comedy it turns out to be.' *(Bruce Williamson, Playboy)*

'If fiction is about change, then how can you make a movie about a man who cannot change, whose whole life is anchored and defended by routine? Few actors could get anywhere with this challenge, and fewer still could absorb and even entertain us with their performance, but Hoffman proves again that he almost seems to thrive on impossible acting challenges . . . At the end of *Rain Man*, I felt a certain love for Raymond, the Hoffman character. I don't know quite how Hoffman got me to do it.' *(Roger Ebert)*

RAINING STONES

CT: 8 AV: 7.00 (est)

1993 GB 90 C DRAMA/COMEDY

D Ken Loach ☆
W Jim Allen ☆

Bruce Jones Ricky Tomlinson ☆ Julie Brown Jonathan James Gemma Phoenix Tom Hickey

A hard-working northern man (Bruce Jones), out of work and luck, tries to salvage his paternal pride by buying a new communion dress for his daughter (Gemma Phoenix). He does a bit of petty thieving with his pal (Ricky Tomlinson), meets with disappointment and disaster, and falls ever further into debt.

It's hard to summarize that plot without sounding like the voice of doom. The amazing thing is that Loach and screenwriter Jim Allen (who previously gave us such polemical works as *Hidden Agenda*) tell the story with so much humour and humanity that the film is great fun. The laughs are mainly thanks to Ricky Tomlinson, who showed his comedic flair in *Riff-Raff* (he was the embarrassed nude in the bath): here he's even better, well served by Loach's talent for turning humour into pathos. The potentially clichéd scene where Tomlinson reluctantly accepts money from his daughter is very touching.

The acting generally doesn't look like acting: a tribute not just to the performers, but to Loach's tactic of filming in sequence and never telling the actors what is to happen next. The scene where our hero's wife (Julie Brown) is terrorized by a loan-shark (Jonathan James) is absolutely convincing – and terrifying.

Naturally, there is a social dimension as well; but (unusually for them) Loach and Allen avoid preaching. Their attitude towards the Catholic Church is refreshingly ambivalent, while the bleakness of their social analysis is offset by many tiny examples of humanity and an upbeat, though not unrealistically happy, ending.

Loach seems to have recovered that lightness of touch and generosity of spirit which made his first film, *Kes*, a classic of the 60s. He has also abandoned that nihilism which diminished his otherwise impressive *Riff-Raff*. Loach will never be a great director visually – framing beautiful shots is not where his talent or interest lies – but he is one of the most socially observant film-makers Britain has produced.

MIXED:

'Stresses resilience rather than despair. It has some forced moments and a soft ending, but it also contains a scene of astonishing power and ugliness towards the end.' *(Adam Marsh-Jones, Independent)*

PRO:

'One of [Loach's] best films . . . It's a small film, but pretty perfectly formed . . . funny, sad and pertinent, and the cast is superb.' *(Derek Malcolm, Guardian)*

'The Great Uncompromiser has edged delightfully nearer the mainstream . . . I find it one of the most enjoyable of Loach's later works . . . It is not a move in the wrong direction to shift . . . from neo-realism to magical realism.' *(Tom Hutchinson, Hampstead & Highgate Express)*

'Without a lively, convincing cast, Loach's unadorned style might well appear drab. With these players, the risk never surfaces.' *(Geoff Brown, The Times)*

'One of Loach's long-standing strengths is that, unlike some other political filmmakers, he doesn't offer pat answers. Nor does he set up characters that are straw men to be shot down in predictable fashion . . . The film quietly shines with beautiful moments of recognition.' *(Ed Kelleher, Film Journal)*

RAISE THE RED LANTERN AAN

CT: 6 AV: 8.00

(aka *Dahong Denglong Gaogao Gua*)

1992 China/Hong Kong/Taiwan 126 C DRAMA/FOREIGN

D Zhang Yimou ☆
W Ni Zhen

Gong Li ☆ Ma Jingwu He Caifei Cao Cuifeng Jin Shuyuan Kong Lin

A young woman (Gong Li) becomes, much against her will, the fourth wife of a rich old merchant.

I was very disappointed by this, especially as Zhang Yimou's previous film, *Ju Dou*, was one of my ten favourites of 1991. His trademarks are all here: a period setting, a gorgeous leading actress (Gong Li again), lush colours, a stifled sensuality, a sense of tragically wasted lives. And, pretty clearly, it's another coded attack on the elderly, male, faceless

Chinese establishment. It's worth seeing, especially if you haven't seen any of Yimou's work before, but it doesn't add to anything he hasn't said before, much more effectively. The pace is soporific, and there's something mannered, literary and aetiolated about it, like the worst of Merchant Ivory.

PRO:

'A finely crafted piece of Ming china: delicate, beautifully proportioned, refined and visually exquisite. It is . . . spare and convoluted . . . Zhang imposes a hypnotic mood on his story . . . [a] haunting and unforgettable experience.' *(Toronto Film Festival Programme, 1991)*

'Can no doubt be interpreted in a number of ways – as a cry against the subjection of women in China, as an attack on feudal attitudes, as a formal exercise in storytelling – and yet it works because it is so fascinating simply on the level of melodrama.' *(Roger Ebert)*

'Zhang Yimou . . . is a visual poet . . . The pace is complementary to the style, gentle and hushed, like a blanket of snow. When action breaks, it sounds like thunder and feels like war.' *(Scotsman)*

'Hauntingly resonant . . . Yimou has an exquisite sense of menace, evoking it from such minutiae as the sound of a pair of shears as they cut hair . . . Gong Li . . . perfectly embodies the torment of a spirited woman forced to fight within the boundaries of a social system she knows will ultimately crush her.' *(Stephen Amidon, Financial Times)*

'Certainly one of the best films of this, or any other, year . . . one is utterly, timelessly transported into another fantastical world . . . You watch entranced, almost never wanting this fable to human emotions to end . . . Gong Li breaks your heart as the factious little maid: Her final scene calls up Lillian Gish as the Little Match Girl.' *(David Noh, Film Journal)*

ANTI:

'Clearly, the story offers a bleak analogy with the repressive conservatism and internecine conflicts of Chinese society, but . . . the film seems rather studied and passionless.' *(Geoff Andrew, Time Out)*

RAISIN IN THE SUN, A — CT: 5 AV: 7.22

1961 US 128 BW DRAMA

D Daniel Petrie
W Lorraine Hansberry

Sidney Poitier ☆ Claudia McNeil ☆ Ruby Dee ☆ Diana Sands John Fielder Louis Gossett Jr Ivan Dixon

Members of a black family have different ideas on how to escape from their Chicago slum.

Seven of the cast had already appeared in the Broadway production of this claustrophobic, conventional drama. Its theatrical origins are only too obvious, and the script is talky, and at least half an hour too long. Some critics found Poitier's performance too mannered for the screen, although it looks fine to me – indeed, the piece is powerfully acted throughout. There was a modestly effective, made-for-TV remake in 1988, with Danny Glover excellent in Poitier's role.

PRO:

'A shining example of an interesting play . . . being turned into a film which is much more effective . . . What matters most in the film . . . is Sidney Poitier's superbly relaxed and expressive performance.' *(Alan Dent, Sunday Telegraph)*

'A fine film, a brave, beautiful and dignified film.' *(Felix Barker, Evening News)*

'Wonderfully moving and exciting . . . beautifully acted and told.' *(Ernest Betts, People)*

'Twice the impact of the original Broadway play.' *(Harold Conway, Sunday Dispatch)*

'Brilliant performances by Claudia McNeil, Sidney Poitier, Ruby Dee, and Diana Sands save the story from the taint of soap opera.' *(Judith Crist)*

MIXED:

'Although . . . nothing more than a photographed stage play, it makes an impact with every line . . . thanks to performances which would be praiseworthy coming from players who were pink, blue, green, yellow or, in this film, black to ivory.' *(Leonard Mosley, Daily Express)*

'Poitier . . . is sometimes brilliant, but sometimes flashy and overtheatrical. The best performance comes from Ruby Dee.' *(Nina Hibbin, Daily Worker)*

'Although *A Raisin in the Sun* is a bit long and somewhat verbose, this film remains a strong portrayal of humanity in a lower-class family that is universal in concept.' *(Baseline)*

RAISING ARIZONA — CT: 8 AV: 6.08

1987 US 94 C COMEDY

D Joel Coen ☆
W Ethan Coen Joel Coen ☆

Nicolas Cage ☆ Holly Hunter ☆ Trey Wilson ✔ John Goodman ✔ William Forsythe ✔ Sam McMurray Frances McDormand Randall 'Tex' Cobb M. Emmet Walsh

A luckless petty criminal (Nicolas Cage,) and his cop wife (Holly Hunter) decide to steal one of a tycoon's quintuplets, with entertainingly disastrous results.

The Coen Brothers' quirky, warm-hearted comedy about childlessness is not to everyone's taste, but it's original, well sustained (unlike most other of the Coens' films) and one of the best offbeat movies of the 80s. Cage is deadpan and funny; Hunter is desperate and cute.

ANTI:

'The initial inspiration sags into the worst aspects of

Saturday morning TV – its repetitiousness, banality, and bald sadism. Instead of invention, *Raising Arizona* settles for gags that were stale when the Three Stooges used them. Long before the end, the Coens abandon comedy altogether for a *Mad Max* romp of car chases and explosions and an endless, Capraesque homily that leaves the stunned viewer waiting, in vain, for a punchline.' *(Peter Keough, Chicago Reader)*

'Everyone in *Raising Arizona* talks funny. They all elevate their dialogue to an arch and artificial level that's distracting and unconvincing and slows down the progress of the film. And what *Raising Arizona* needs more than anything else is more velocity. Here's a movie that stretches out every moment for more than it's worth, until even the moments of inspiration seem forced. Since the basic idea of the movie is a good one and there are talented people in the cast, what we have here is a film shot down by its own forced and mannered style.' *(Roger Ebert)*

PRO:

'A glorious comedy . . . Cage makes good use of his sleepy raccoon charm.' *(Adam Mars-Jones, Independent)*

'Who else but two brothers . . . could have such a consistently funny and weird creative vision?' *(Jodie Burke, Premiere)*

'A supersonic, live-action cartoon; an octane fuelled cocktail . . . One almost expects the Keystone Kops to appear over the horizon . . . The screen is chock full of deadpan humour, crazee situations, gags and stunts. The hand-picked players are perfectly cast with Nic Cage giving his most sympathetic performance to date: relaxed, charming, engaging and even noble. [The film's] main strength however is its complete unpredictability . . . [It] does occasionally flag but those are minor quibbles . . . A Road Runner cartoon brought to life.' *(Allan Hunter, Films & Filming)*

'A true original. Its deadpan, off-the-wall humour is established from the start . . . The movie is a weird and wonderful combination of shrewd observation and knockabout farce . . . The Coens juggle cosy sentiment, out-and-out bad taste, slapstick and cool satire. Somehow it all adds up to an idiosyncratically entertaining whole.' *(Margaret Walters, Listener)*

'The Coen Brothers make fun not only of contemporary American manners and morals but of contemporary American film: *Raising Arizona* is full of camera moves and angles that parody the visual clichés of *Friday the Thirteenth* and *Halloween* type movies, as well as of Steven Spielberg. *Raising Arizona* is not a work of genius, by any means, but it is inspired and inventive throughout.' *(Bruce Bawer, American Spectator)*

RAMBO: FIRST BLOOD CT: 6 AV: 4.42

(aka *First Blood*)

1982 US 94 C ACTION/ADVENTURE

D Ted Kotcheff
W Michael Kozoll William Sackheim Sylvester Stallone from David Morrell's book

Sylvester Stallone Richard Crenna Brian Dennehy David Caruso Jack Starrett Michael Talbott

Vietnam veteran (Sylvester Stallone) uses his military skills to avoid arrest at home.

David Morrell's thoughtful book is here simplified and turned into entertaining hokum, with Stallone as a misunderstood mumbler who finds himself at war with the American authorities. Characterization went out of the window in the sequels, *Rambo II* and *Rambo III*: here at least there's some excuse for the violence.

'I certainly never saw [*First Blood*] as any kind of celebration of jingoism. I saw it as a cry from the veteran . . . John Rambo was like a machine that couldn't stop its engine. He was this Frankenstein monster we had created in Vietnam and then brought home.' *(Ted Kotcheff, director)*

ANTI:

'Socially irresponsible . . . there are enough nuts out there without giving them a hero to cheer for.' *(Variety)*

'It's difficult to know where credibility and John Rambo part company. Perhaps it's when he jumps a hundred feet on to some rocks with barely a scratch? Or perhaps it's when he survives the mine cave-in? Or an attack by what looks like the bulk of the State's armed forces? Startlingly violent but occasionally exciting, little of it makes any sense.' *(Rose)*

MIXED:

'The ability of this film . . . to dramatise a social issue is what makes it exhilarating besides the graphic illustration it provides of humanity pushed to extremes.' *(Alexander Walker, Evening Standard)*

'The film isn't pretty . . . but its violence . . . is there for a reason . . . Stallone's strong performance never loses sympathy . . . A quieter movie might have been more persuasive. But then I doubt whether it would have been such a hot box office prospect.' *(Margaret Hinxman, Daily Mail)*

'Shockingly well-photographed and located, a very unpleasant effort.' *(John Coleman, New Statesman)*

RAMBO: FIRST BLOOD PART TWO

CT: 4 AV:4.18

1985 US 95 C ACTION/ADVENTURE

D George Pan Cosmatos
W Sylvester Stallone James Cameron

Sylvester Stallone Richard Crenna Charles Napier Julia Nickson Steven Berkoff Martin Kove

Vietnam veteran Rambo (Sylvester Stallone) rescues former colleagues still held prisoner after the Vietnam War.

Ridiculously macho, horribly jingoistic action adventure. The way the film revels in death and destruction is disgusting, but the violence is of the comic-strip variety and the action sequences are exciting. The sequel, *Rambo III* (1988) had no redeeming characteristics.

'One mounting fireball . . . . risible production, comic book heroics.' *(Variety)*

'Credibility is trained considerably by Rambo's invincibility. At least Superman can be brought down by Kryptonite.' *(Rose)*

'We all care about MIAs, but to present a made-up scenario in which they are alive, living in hellish work-camps run by Vietnamese but controlled by Russian officers in the Vietnamese jungle, is inexcusable and tasteless. Also infuriating is Stallone's revisionist history, which takes the popular Reagan era notion that the Vietnam War was a justified war after all and that our soldiers were all heroes who could have won if only Washington had taken the reins off them.' *(Danny Peary)*

'Vietnam By Numbers For Retards.' *(Julie Burchill, Girls on Film)*

RAN

CT: 7 AV: 8.54

1985 France/Japan 161 C DRAMA/EPIC/FOREIGN

D Akira Kurosawa ☆ AAN
W Akira Kurosawa Hideo Oguni Masato Ide based on Japanese legend and Shakespeare's play *King Lear*

Tatsuya Nakadai Akira Terao Jinpachi Nezu Daisuke Ryu Mieko Harada ☆ Yoshiko Miyazaki

A 16th-century warlord (Tatsuya Nakadai) abdicates from leadership of his clan, divides his property between his three sons, but finds that this arrangement has its problems.

Though ponderous at the outset and with acting that frequently strays into the melodramatic, this develops into a truly spectacular epic, with stunning use of colour and amazing battle scenes. Mieko Harada's performance as a daughter-in-law combining the worst aspects of Goneril, Reagan and Cruella De Vil, is riveting. Kurosawa was at his best when directing another work of Shakespeare, *Throne of Blood* (1957). Here – at the age of 75 – he is very much in tune with Lear's disappointments and frustrations; *Ran* is his last great film. It won an Academy Award for Emi Wada's gorgeous costumes, and nominations for cinematography (Takao Saito) and art direction (Yoshiro Muraki, Shinobu Muraki).

MIXED:

'An epic statement about the pointlessness of war, visually awesome, dramatically stunning. My only reservation is that we are detached from the characters.' *(Michael Wigan, Scotsman)*

'For the first 40 minutes or so, the picture is all preparation, and it seems dead, but then the preparation begins to pay off, and by the end the fastidiousness and the monumental scale of what Kurosawa has undertaken can flood you with admiration.' *(Pauline Kael)*

PRO:

'Prepare to be astonished . . . a towering achievement in any language.' *(People)*

'Not to be missed for its stirring pageantry alone . . . Spectacularly exciting, with stylised violence, as any western, too, but much deeper richer and stranger.' *(Shaun Usher, Daily Mail)*

'A superb technical achievement with performances, photography, costume and design combined with imaginative flair and impact.' *(Virginia Dignam, Morning Star)*

'Dazzling . . . the drama contains enough bitchery, betrayal and bloodshed to fill dozens of episodes of *Dallas* and *Dynasty* and is absolutely riveting.' *(Alan Frank, Star)*

'A visually stunning epic with some of the most beautiful, colorful, breathtaking imagery ever committed to celluloid. *Ran* is also the work of a mature artist in complete control of his medium, who cares not for trend or fashion.' *(Baseline)*

RANDOM HARVEST AAN

CT: 5 AV: 7.20

1942 US 126 BW DRAMA/ROMANCE

D Mervyn Le Roy ☆ AAN
W Claudine West George Froeschel Arthur Wimperis AAN from James Hilton's novel

Ronald Colman ☆ AAN Greer Garson ☆ Susan Peters ☆ AAN Philip Dorn Reginald Owen Henry Travers Margaret Wycherly Bramwell Fletcher Arthur Margetson

After a taxi crash, a shell-shocked World War I veteran (Ronald Colman) forgets he's married to a music-hall singer (Greer Garson); she then goes to work for him as his secretary . . .

Unforgettable amnesia movie. Greer Garson and Ronald Colman play this romantic melodrama for much more than it's worth – the plot is ridiculous and riddled with such obvious contrivances that it's amazing that audiences ever took it seriously. The score (by Herbert Stothart) and art direction (by Cedric Gibbons and Randall Duell) were Oscar-nominated.

PRO:

'One of the truly fine motion pictures of this or any year . . . an emotional experience of rare quality. Rave press notices cannot fail to greet the excellence of its production, direction, performances and craftsmanship, for there can be no fault to find with any phase of the great, enduring love story it stirringly brings to life.' *(Hollywood Reporter)*

'*Random Harvest* . . . is distinguished by (1) a moving love story, (2) the unveiling of Miss Garson's interesting legs.' *(Time)*

'[Miss Garson] is modestly permitted to show off her dimpled knees.' *(New York Times)*

'A less reticent screenplay and unrestrained manipulation could have converted the film into an experience as moist as the Johnstown flood. Fortunately, tact was lavished on the depiction of the amnesia victim of the last war and some importance is granted the count of his bi-world travails through the genuinely consummate performances of Ronald Colman, Greer Garson, and that of a brilliant new star in the Hollywood heavens, Susan Peters.' *(Herb Sterne)*

ANTI:

'I would . . . like to recommend *Random Harvest* to those who can stay interested in Ronald Colman's amnesia for two hours and who could with pleasure eat a bowl of Yardley's shaving soap for breakfast.' *(James Agee, Nation)*

'A strangely empty film . . . its characters are creatures of fortune, not partisans in determining their own fates.' *(Bosley Crowther)*

'There is nothing random about *Random Harvest*. It is shrewdly and meticulously dollar-crafted in every particular . . . It is cast with pearly players in every part. Its pedigreed plot is savoured with just the right mixture of ups and downs, ecstasy and well-bred anguish, implausibility and psyche. And it moves towards its climax with the measured tread and nicely timed emotional bumps of a Hearst Cosmopolitan serial. It is perhaps the clearest example of the year of how a studio possessing lion's shares of movie-making capital and ingratiating talent can mate these two to synthesize a magnificent neuter.' *(John McManus, PM)*

'The only reason to see this hunk of twaddle is the better to savor the memory of the Carol Burnett-Harvey Korman parody, which also was shorter. Mervyn LeRoy, who directed many a big clinker, also gets the blame for this one.' *(Pauline Kael)*

RASHOMON AAW CT: 8 AV: 9.47

(aka *In the Woods*)

1950 Japan 83/90 BW THRILLER/FOREIGN

D Akira Kurosawa ☆
W Akira Kurosawa ☆ from Ryunosuke Akutagawa's story *Inside a Bush*

Toshiro Mifune ☆ Machiko Kyo ☆ Masayuki Mori ☆ Takashi Shimura ☆ Minoru Chiaki Kichijiro Veda

Four witnesses to a rape and a death offer different interpretations of the same events.

A weird and often wonderful thriller, with an original approach to narrative construction and unusually fantastical overtones (one of the four witnesses is a ghost). *Rashomon* was immediately hailed as a masterpiece, winning first prize at the Venice Film Festival, and Best Foreign Film at the Oscars. It now looks slow and repetitive; even so, it is visually striking and beautifully acted. Its reputation has remained high over the years, and led to it being remade in Hollywood twice – as *The Outrage* (1964) and *Iron Maze* (1991). Neither was remotely as effective as the original.

MIXED:

'[The optimistic epilogue] seems an arbitrary afterthought that doesn't fit the story. [The film] has other failings. Its slow pace is deliberate and yet US moviegoers are likely to find much of it draggy . . . and Kurosawa . . . sometimes becomes self-consciously infatuated with the look of his own images. For all that [it] is a novel, stimulating moviegoing experience.' *(Time)*

'Mr Kurosawa describes essentially the same event three times, always approaching it afresh . . . Then [he] makes a mistake: he repeats the story a fourth time. This is decidedly one too many . . . But . . . the total impression [is of] a savage and beautiful film.' *(E. Wintour, Time & Tide)*

'I cannot prostrate myself before [it] with quite the fervour of the Venice Festival judges . . . But it is a fascinating little oddity which makes me want to see more Japanese films.' *(Fred Majdalany, Daily Mail)*

'Honourable *Evening News* gentleman does not like Japanese acting very much. But what he does like is the magnificent use of the camera.' *(Jympson Harmon, Evening News)*

'The introductory and closing sequences are tedious; the woman's whimpering is almost enough to drive one to the nearest exit. Yet the film transcends these discomforts: it has its own perfection.' *(Pauline Kael)*

PRO:

'Sensational news . . . a great [film] . . . one of the two or three films ever made for grown-ups, instead of kiddies 6 to 60 . . . The acting . . . is a reminder of [silent films] at its best and this is no accident. It is part of the design of the film . . . [Kurosawa] knows how difficult it is to live, how necessary to love.' *(Richard Griffith, Saturday Review of Literature)*

'There has never been such a film . . . Do not let its Oriental origin put you off seeing it, for it is that rare event in film – something entirely, excitingly and peculiarly new.' *(Leonard Mosley, Daily Express)*

'The oddest, most starting film I ever saw . . . As a curiosity the film is impressive; as entertainment it is frightening.' *(Paul Holt, Daily Herald)*

'A masterpiece, and a revelation.' *(Gavin Lambert, MFB)*

'A mixture of the mysterious, the legendary and the realistic that sets it apart.' *(Dilys Powell)*

'[Kurosawa] is evidently very much influenced by Western cinema of the Thirties, and perhaps even more by American films than by neo-realism. His admiration for John Ford, Fritz Lang and Chaplin in particular is clear enough. But this is not a passive influence. What matters for him is not just absorbing it; his intention is to use it to transmit back to us an image of Japanese tradition and culture that we can assimilate visually and mentally. He succeeds in dong this so well with *Rashomon* that this film can truly be said to have opened the gates of the West to the Japanese cinema.' *(André Bazan, Cahiers du Cinéma, 1957)*

RAYON VERT, LE: *see* GREEN RAY, THE.

REACH FOR THE SKY   CT: 7 AV: 5.60

1956 GB 123 (US)/135 (GB) BW WAR/DRAMA

D Lewis Gilbert
W Lewis Gilbert from Paul Brickhill's book

Kenneth More ☆ Muriel Pavlow Lyndon Brook Lee Patterson Alexander Knox Dorothy Alison Sydney Tafler Howard Marion Crawford

Adventures of a fighter pilot who flies on despite the loss of his legs.

Based on the true story of Douglas Bader, this is the kind of movie which went out of fashion during the 60s, when it became fashionable to debunk anything and anyone that smacked of military heroism. This is a plodding, conventional war movie in many respects, with undistinguished action sequences, but it's lifted out of the ordinary by Kenneth More's sparky, touchy portrayal of a man whose difficult temperament was probably his salvation. As a character study of an improbable but somehow typical Englishman, the film is always interesting.

ANTI:

'Maudlin, overlong, hero-worshipping stuff, with More waddling pathetically around on artificial legs . . . If you haven't seen this, you're probably the saner for it.' *(Geoff Andrew, Time Out)*

MIXED:

'The legendary story . . . should have made an outstanding film. But [it] . . . is too cumbersome and conventional to achieve real distinction . . . More's skill . . . carries the Bader story . . . Unfortunately, the heroic clichés overlay the drama . . . It's worth seeing all the same for its good touches and for its sincere tribute to human courage.' *(Daily Worker)*

PRO:

'Bader could not have been better served . . . Lewis Gilbert has handled his material with great restraint and avoided any temptation to overemphasize.' *(Manchester Guardian)*

'It stands or falls by whether or not it pays adequate and honest tribute to Bader. I think that it does.' *(Peter Forster, Financial Times)*

'That the story . . . succeeds as well as it does in moving you . . . is due in the greatest measure to Kenneth More,' *(Harold Conway, Daily Sketch)*

'A heart-lifting experience; and entertainment of the choicest kind.' *(Peter Burnup, News of the World)*

'The story has everything, character and action, spectacle, excitement, above all human endurance and determination at their most stirring. It is the kind of subject which the British cinema ought to tackle, the kind which only too often is left to Hollywood . . . It is least successful in what should be exciting action. . . . Sometimes both direction and script strike a little cool; there must, one feels, have been more passion than this in Bader's fight to get back. And yet when all is said and done the film stirs the heart. Its general story is still close enough in time to belong to our own lives. And its particular hero, one gratefully remembers, stands high among those to whom we owe those lives.' *(Dilys Powell)*

REAR WINDOW   CT: 10 AV: 8.82

1954 US 112 BW THRILLER

D Alfred Hitchcock ☆ AAN
W John Michael Hayes ☆ AAN from Cornell Woolrich's novel

James Stewart ☆ Grace Kelly ✓ Raymond Burr ✓ Judith Evelyn Wendell Corey ✓ Thelma Ritter ✓

A photographer (James Stewart) confined to a wheelchair because of a broken leg witnesses what he thinks may be a murder in an apartment opposite, and persuades his girlfriend (Grace Kelly) to help him investigate.

Most of Hitchcock's masterpieces have divided the critics, but this one is admired by virtually everyone. It's one of the most skilful and exciting thrillers ever made, with a heart-stopping climax. The ingenuity of it lies in the way we witness almost every event through the hero's eyes, and piece the evidence together as he does. This places us firmly inside the photographer's head, and yet isn't there something a shade voyeuristic, prurient, even sick, about the way he spies on those around him . . .?

Some critics, notably those coming from a Roman Catholic standpoint, such as Eric Rohmer and Claude Chabrol, have interpreted *Rear Window* as an outright condemnation of the leading character, but that is only part of the truth. His unhealthy curiosity does turn out to be justified – if dangerous. Hitchcock seems to be playing with our guilty enjoyment of his voyeurism, not to mention our own as cinemagoers; as usual, he implies that there is good and bad in all of us.

Other assets include an excellent supporting cast. Grace Kelly gives probably her best – and her sexiest – performance as a glamorous society girl who reveals (like most of the characters in the film) surprising depths to her personality. The subtext of the film movie is the way that Stewart initially (if subconsciously) feels that she is invading his space, but then finds himself falling in love with her. Robert Burks's cinematography and Loren L. Ryder's sound design were rightly Oscar-nominated, but this is above all a masterly exercise in directorial style.

ANTI:

'Miss Lejeune, the critic of *The Observer*, complained . . . that *Rear Window* was a horrible film because the hero spent all of his time peeping out of the window. What's so horrible about that? Sure, he's a snooper, but aren't we all?' *(Alfred Hitchcock, 1966)*

'I was still a working critic the first time I saw *Rear Window*, and I remember writing that the picture was very gloomy, rather pessimistic, and quite evil. But now I don't see it in that light at all; in fact, I feel it has a rather compassionate approach. What Stewart sees from his window is not horrible but simply a display of human weaknesses and people in pursuit of happiness. ' *(François Truffaut, 1966)*

'Back in 1954 when it was made . . . there were mutters of distaste and disappointment at its voyeuristic implications. Thirty years later . . . the only doubt one can have . . . is whether in the final score it really was . . . the very best of Hitchcock. Rate it above *Psycho, Marnie* or *Vertigo?* Let battle commence.' *(Philip Strick, F & F, 1983)*

MIXED:

'Tension is almost non-existent in the first hour and a half of *Rear Window*, but the last twenty minutes are as exciting as anything Hitchcock has ever done. And what *Rear Window* lacks in suspense it more than makes up for in humor. Hitchcock's distinction as a director is not his ability to create suspense, as is commonly supposed. Other directors – Reed, Welles, Wilder – are equally adept with suspense. Hitchcock's brilliance is his wit, and his flawless technique for using that wit to support and counterpoint suspense.' *(Steve Sondheim – yes, that Steve Sondheim , Films in Review, 1954)*

PRO:

'One of Alfred Hitchcock's better thrillers.' *(Variety)*

'Enchants us immediately, and need not be analyzed to death to achieve its place in the Pantheon.' *(Vincent Canby, New York Times)*

'Fascinating and unique . . . Tiptoes at the start, but rapidly quickens as it passes the halfway mark and ends on a screeching note of suspense . . . Intriguing and gripping story, outstanding performance by James Stewart, popular supporting team, flawless atmosphere and showmanlike finale.' *(Josh Billings, Kine Weekly)*

'Whatever happens, I think the release of *Rear Window* will tend to create a united front in film criticism . . . Right from its opening, [it presents] an immediate focus of interest that puts it on a higher plane than the majority of the earlier works . . . beyond the mere entertainment thriller . . . *Rear Window* affords me the satisfaction of greeting the pious blindness of the sceptics with a gentle and compassionate hilarity.' *(Claude Chabrol, Cahiers du Cinéma)*

'Hitchcock had already refined his use of subjective camera – putting the audience in the mind of the characters; in this film he pushes the technique to new heights. As our heroes gibe and quibble over the suspected murder (which we never see), we take refuge in the anonymity and safe distance of Jeff's flattening long lens – until the terrifying moment when Thorwald stares right back. It's an astonishing visual and psychological coup.' *(Michael Sragow, Boston Phoenix, 1983)*

'Hitchcock's most uncompromising attempt to imprison us, not only within a limited space, but within a single consciousness. From the beginning of the film to the end, we are enclosed in the protagonist's apartment, leaving it only when he leaves it (precipitately, through the window!).' *(Robin Wood, Hitchcock's Films Revisited, 1989)*

'Corresponds most closely to the Hitchcockian ethos; it's extremely suspenseful, macabre and technically innovative . . . Much has been written, of course, about Stewart's window being a cinema screen and, indeed, Hitchcock's great movie is a definition and a celebration of cinema itself.' *(Adrian Turner, 27th London Film Festival Booklet, 1983)*

REBECCA AAW CT: 9 AV: 9.46

1940 US BW THRILLER

D Alfred Hitchcock ☆ AAN
W Robert E. Sherwood ☆ Joan Harrison ☆ from Daphne du Maurier's novel

Laurence Olivier ☆ AAN Joan Fontaine ☆ AAN George Sanders ☆ Judith Anderson ☆ AAN Nigel Bruce ☆ Gladys Cooper ☆ Florence Bates ☆ Reginald Denny ☆ C. Aubrey Smith ☆ Melville Cooper Leo G. Carroll Leonard Carey

A young bride (Joan Fontaine) becomes convinced that her husband (Laurence Olivier) is harbouring some dreadful secret about his dead ex-wife.

Daphne du Maurier's romantic melodrama is given the Hollywood treatment with all the trimmings, by one of the great American producers of romance (David O. Selznick, who was also responsible for *Gone with the Wind*) and Britain's master of suspense, Alfred Hitchcock, who clearly revels here in having a big, Hollywood budget for the first time. The result is a fascinating, atmospheric classic, with three memorable performances: by Joan Fontaine as the nameless heroine, Laurence Olivier as her coolly enigmatic husband, and – best of all – Judith Anderson as the housekeeper Mrs Danvers.

Hitchcock added to the latter's mystique by never showing her walking and rarely showing her in motion. Even today, the scene where Fontaine is investigating Rebecca's room and suddenly finds Mrs Danvers beside her can make the most hardened horror fan jump. Recent critics have stressed the psycho-sexual overtones of the piece (especially interesting in view of du Maurier's own lesbian tendencies): were Rebecca and Mrs Danvers lovers? There are no answers in Hitchcock's film, but he gives a few broad hints in that direction; and if you look closely at the 'happy' ending, you may notice that there is no promise of happiness for the central couple. She still doesn't even have a name, or an identity of her own, and her tone of voice is not exactly celebrational!

Rebecca may not be Hitchcock's most personal work, but it is still a fascinating piece, with a mood of Gothic unease that has rarely been surpassed – the film noticeably goes downhill once the central mystery has been solved, but that's really the fault of the original storyline. (Hitchcock did, incidentally, soften the ending of the original novel, by making Rebecca's death an accident, rather than murder.)

George Barnes's cinematography won an Academy Award, but Hitchcock lost the directing Oscar to John Ford, for *The Grapes of Wrath* and, in fact, never did win one. Also nominated were Franz Waxman for his haunting score, Lyle Wheeler for his production design (including the creation of Manderley, the exterior of which was merely a model), editor Hal C. Kern, and Jack Cosgrove and Arthur Johns for their visual effects.

ANTI:

'*Rebecca* is not really a bad picture, but it is a change in stride and not a healthy one. A wispy and overwrought femininity in it somehow. A boudoir.' *(Otis Ferguson)*

'It's not a Hitchcock picture; it's a novelette, really. The story is old-fashioned; there was a whole school of feminine literature at the period; and though I'm not against it, the fact is that the story is lacking in humour.' *(Alfred Hitchcock, 1966)*

'It is not insignificant that the three films Alfred Hitchcock directed for Selznick – *Rebecca, Spellbound, The Paradine Case* – are also Hitchcock's least personal and least interesting American films. *Notorious*, which began as a Selznick project, but which he sold and was not actively involved with as a producer, is, also, significantly, by far the best of that series.' *(Peter Bogdanovich, 1975)*

'Hitchcock's first Hollywood film [is] an expensive production, and one guesses he didn't have much say in the script. In any case, the film fails either to assimilate or to vomit out the indigestible novelettish ingredients of Daphne du Maurier's book, and it suffers further from Olivier's charmless performance, which finally destroys our sympathy with the heroine, doting on such a boor . . . What was Rebecca's crime? Apart from minor mental cruelty to a harmless lunatic, simply that she resisted male definition, asserting her right to define herself and her sexual desires (including an at least implicit lesbian attachment to Mrs Danvers).' *(Robin Wood, Hitchcock's Films Revisited, 1989)*

MIXED:

'The atmosphere menaces; and a sharp climax of fright is reached in the scene where the girl enters the forbidden room, with its great veil of curtains and the sea booming outside: so sharp, indeed, that when in the silence the latch clicks I started in my seat. From this point the film collapses. One might have thought that when blackmail and murder were out Hitchcock's feeling for quick explosive action would show itself. Oddly enough he seems instead to lose interest. Perhaps the exquisite silliness of the story was too much for him. It was, apparently, too much for the cast, who, playing admirably so far, suddenly dwindled to automata . . . Many sequences in the picture are extremely beautiful to look at; unfortunately many others are extremely boring.' *(Dilys Powell)*

'Hitchcock fans will have to put up with a surprising lack of the characteristic Hitchcock improvisations in the way of salty minor personages and humorous interludes, and satisfy themselves with a masterly exhibition of the Hitchcock skill in creating suspense and shock with his action and his camera.' *(NBR)*

'Magnificent romantic-gothic corn, full of Alfred Hitchcock's humor and inventiveness. It features one of Laurence Olivier's rare poor performances; he seems pinched and too calculated – but even when he's uncomfortable in his role he's more fascinating than most actors.' *(Pauline Kael)*

PRO:

'In true Hitchcockian style, we are shown how the power of the dead can affect the living, a theme Hitch successfully explored in his later box office hits *Spellbound, Psycho*, and another marriage of Hitchcock with du Maurier storytelling, *The Birds*.' *(Susan Sackett)*

'An altogether brilliant film, haunting, suspenseful,

handsome and handsomely played.' *(New York Times)*

'Admittedly this story belongs to an artificial world more akin to Victorian melodrama than to the present day, but it is nonetheless holding and interesting, with suspense, dramatic situations and an unexpected and effective climax . . . Hitchcock [creates] successfully an eerie atmosphere. The acting of a practically all-star cast is admirable.' *(MFB)*

'The mood of haunting fear is magnificently contrived, aided of course by Olivier's intense performance and the really fine acting of Miss Fontaine . . . The picture is a strange mixture of mystery, melodrama, scenic effects and pathos.' *(Photoplay)*

'A carefully considered trying out of superior technical resources now at Hitchcock's disposal.' *(George Perry, 1965)*

'Riveting and painful – a tale of fear and class and power.' *(Time Out, 1988)*

REBEL WITHOUT A CAUSE CT: 6 AV: 8.13

1955 US 111 C DRAMA

D Nicholas Ray ☆
W Stewart Stern ☆ from Nicholas Ray's story AAN

James Dean ☆ Natalie Wood ☆ AAN Jim Backus Sal Mineo ☆ AAN Ann Doran Dennis Hopper Corey Allen

Alienated youth (James Dean) rebels against parental upbringing.

Controversial – and critically underrated – because of the way it seemed to condone violence, lionized a disruptive teenager, and portrayed the older generation as caricatures. However, it soon became recognized as a classic of adolescent angst, all the more interesting because it suggested that delinquents could come from prosperous homes too. James Dean's incoherent but sympathetic performance (condemned at first as an imitation of Brando) has a unique status in the history of youth icons. Bizarrely, Warner Brothers wanted the movie to star Tab Hunter and Jayne Mansfield – but Nicholas Ray talked them out of it.

ANTI:

'In the two hours it takes [the film] to exhaust itself, time goes by slowly.' *(John McCarten, New Yorker)*

'Happily the X certificate will keep youngsters out, so they won't know how richly their parents deserve a good spanking. Everything they do is their parents' fault. Even if they haven't got any parents.' *(Sunday Dispatch)*

'I must be a reactionary. I feel a sudden urge to see a gay, charming, socially-unconscious picture of a juvenile delinquent about the size and shape of Miss Grace Kelly.' *(Campbell Dixon, Daily Telegraph)*

MIXED:

'[Ray and Stern] are so obviously men of good will, inspired by such earnest devotion to the cause of youth, that it is a source of regret to me that I cannot admire their film . . . Pretentious and confused though it is, the film's shortcomings are almost submerged in Dean's brilliant portrait.' *(Eleanor Wintour, Tribune)*

'A gloomy story of parental delinquency . . . There's a knife fight, which needs pruning, and a nice performance from Natalie Wood.' *(Reg Whitley, Daily Mirror)*

'Fairly exciting, suspenseful and provocative, if also occasionally far-fetched, melodrama.' *(Variety)*

'Had more emotional resonance for the teen-agers of the time than many much better movies.' *(Pauline Kael)*

PRO:

'[The film] is – like Dean's acting – out of the ordinary.' *(Manchester Guardian)*

'Script and direction still have the power to move and thrill.' *(Winnert)*

'In this powerful study of juvenile violence, Dean is riveting as a teenager groping for love from a society he finds alien and oppressive.' *(Virgin)*

RED BADGE OF COURAGE, THE CT: 6 AV: 7.38

1951 US 69 BW WAR/DRAMA

D John Huston ☆
W John Huston ☆ from Stephen Crane's novel

Audie Murphy ☆ Bill Mauldin Douglas Dick Royal Dano John Dierkes Andy Devine Arthur Hunnicutt

In the American Civil War, a Yankee soldier (Audie Murphy) flees when under fire and believes himself a coward.

Huston's fine, thoughtful war movie fell foul of preview audiences, who found it slow and difficult to understand. MGM shortened and re-edited it, adding a (largely redundant) narration taken word-for-word from the original novel. The finished version won favourable reviews, but failed to find an audience. The film has many strengths – chief among them Huston's World War II documentary style of shooting, which helps to emphasize that this is a film about all wars, not just the American Civil War. He also elicited an excellent performance from Audie Murphy, who was the most decorated American war hero of World War II. Good though his performance was, it contributed to the movie's commercial failure: US audiences would not accept him playing a man frightened of battle. Harold Rosson's camerawork was good enough to have won an Oscar, but failed even to be nominated; the same might be said of Bronislau Kaper's music. There was a competent made-for-TV remake, starring Richard Thomas, in 1974.

PRO:

'[It] will I believe be showing in 10 and 20 years' time with other film classics . . . The film does not attack war so much as show its illogicality and its unchanging aspect.' *(Richard Winnington, News Chronicle)*

'A great film . . . Readers of this column will know that I use the word "great" most sparingly – perhaps once or twice a year. [This] is a great picture. I urge you to pester your local cinema manager to show it.' *(Milton Shulman, Evening Standard)*

'Skilfully directed, imaginatively photographed, and excellently acted.' *(The Times)*

'Scrupulously faithful to the novel, one of the best war films ever made . . . Both the camera and the spoken commentary (taken word for word from the novel) are filled with human understanding.' *(Time)*

'A major achievement that should command admiration for years and years.' *(New York Times)*

'Bids fair to become one of the classic motion pictures.' *(Newsweek)*

MIXED:

'As simple and forthright as a nursery rhyme . . . [Huston's] panoramas of battle are certainly exciting to observe. Nevertheless, the characters who populate [the film] don't seem to have much more depth than a bunch of juveniles in a Beaver Patrol.' *(John McCarten, New Yorker)*

'Two facts are unassailable: It received wonderful reviews and it was a mournful disappointment at the box office . . . It was too simple a story, and how could America's greatest war hero [Audie Murphy] be a coward?' *(Dore Schary)*

RED BALLOON   CT: 6   AV: 8.75

(aka *Le Ballon Rouge*)

1956 France 34/36 C DRAMA/FAMILY/FOREIGN

D Albert Lamorisse ☆
W Albert Lamorisse ☆

Pascal Lamorisse Maurice Le Roux

A lonely boy (Pascal Lamorisse) makes friends with a balloon.

Whimsical and sentimental, but it's also beautifully photographed and a touching metaphor for the freedom and innocence of childhood. A classic short film.

ANTI:

'Lamorisse always makes the same film . . . He refuses to take advantage of the facilities of the studio, he refuses also to clearly define his subject . . . The script, if that's the right word, is only an idea, a point of departure.' *(Jean d'Yvoire, Télérama)*

PRO:

'Thirty minutes of cinema magic – I declare this picture a small masterpiece . . . a work of art . . . a superb poem in colour.' *(Fred Majdalany, Daily Mail)*

'A delightful film that will touch the heart of everyone.' *(News of the World)*

'[It] moved me to laughter and tears . . . [and] will be remembered when many full length pictures are forgotten.' *(Daily Mirror)*

'In 35 touching minutes Lamorisse makes the red balloon live. His film is unlike anything you have seen before and unforgettable.' *(Anthony Carthew, Daily Herald)*

'Officially for children but a special treat for adults too, it's in beautiful color and epitomizes just the kind of offbeat movie gem which is ideal for television.' *(Judith Crist)*

RED DESERT, THE   CT: 4 CT: 6.75

(aka *Il Deserto Rosso*)

1964 Italy/France 116 C DRAMA/FOREIGN

D Michelangelo Antonioni ☆
W Michelangelo Antonioni Tonino Guerra

Monica Vitti ☆ Richard Harris Carlo Chionetti Xenia Valderi Rita Renoir Aldo Grotti

The alienated wife (Monica Vitti) of an electronics engineer (Carlo Chionetti) has an affair with his best friend (Richard Harris).

More terrible, tedious twaddle from Antonioni. It's his first venture into colour, and he uses it intelligently to reflect Vitti's confused emotions; but the absence of a story or human interest becomes wearisome, and the alienated view of industrialism just seems facile. Richard Harris gives every indication of not understanding what the hell is going on, a viewpoint with which many members of the audience will sympathize. Winner of Best Film at Venice.

PRO:

'A key film for its director, and . . . a work of memorable and disquieting beauty.' *(Penelope Houston, Financial Times)*

'Perhaps the most extraordinary and riveting film of Antonioni's career . . . The film is an aesthetic feast, but don't let that distract you from the haunting intricacy of the plot and the performances.' *(David Pirie, Time Out)*

MIXED:

'Even if the film were a shoddy failure instead of a pretentious parable with rewarding moments, it would still be worth while for Miss Vitti.' *(Leonard Mosley, Daily Express)*

'Little happens in the two hours' running time, apart

from Antonioni's favourite and most infuriating habit of making his characters wander endlessly in time and space to no very apparent purpose. The colour is used cleverly and beautifully and . . . adds to the sensuality . . . Antonioni has become suspended in his own vacuum.' *(Ann Pacey, Sun)*

'The beauty is stationary, painterly; and the arresting image precisely arrests and retards the already moribund thrust of the film.' *(John Simon)*

ANTI:

'[The child's toys] are, like so much else in that film, either absurdly or pretentiously symbolic.' *(Patrick Gibbs, Daily Telegraph)*

'Full of implicit Marxism . . . You get the feeling that [Antonioni] started out to make a film about the dwarfing, dehumanising effect of heavy industry on the soul, and then . . . fell in love with the visual largesse offered by factory chimneys and oil refineries and industrial garbage . . . Banquets for the eye are not enough: the mind and heart are hungry too.' *(Kenneth Tynan, Observer)*

'Boredom in Ravenna, and it seeps into the viewer's bones.' *(Pauline Kael, 1984)*

RED DUST

CT: 6 AV: 8.00

1932 US 86 BW DRAMA/ROMANCE/COMEDY

D Victor Fleming ☆
W John Lee Mahin from Wilson Collison's play

Clark Gable ☆ Jean Harlow ☆ Mary Astor Gene Raymond Donald Crisp Tully Marshall Forrester Harvey

Sexual heatwave in the tropics as the macho fireman of a rubber plantation (Clark Gable) is torn between nice married woman (Mary Astor) and a wisecracking prostitute (Jean Harlow).

Harlow's scintillating, sexy performance is the main reason to see this hokey romantic melodrama. Gable's boorish he-man act is less sympathetic now than it must have been in the 1930s, but he's unmistakably a star. Remade, none too well, in 1953 as *Mogambo*, with Ava Gardner and Grace Kelly fighting over Clark Gable, who by this time looked too old and tired to care.

MIXED:

'The dialogue is not especially bright or strong, but some of the lines spoken by . . . Harlow aroused laughter . . . Mr Gable is efficient.' *(Mordaunt Hall, New York Times)*

'Conventional story . . . competent direction secures interesting local atmosphere and offers interesting detail of rubber manufacture processes, but main narration follows beaten track of he-man assault on wifely virtue, husbandly oblivion of marital upset, sexy comicalities of hard-boiled vamp and calculated climax of incredible altruism.' *(Cinema Supplement)*

'Hard-boiled hokum, this, but none the less thoroughly entertaining . . . The frankly sexy story is relieved by bright dialogue and sound characterisation.' *(Lionel Collier, Picturegoer)*

'Astor is OK in the passive virtuous moments but falls down badly on the clinches, sustained only by Gable. As the putteed, unshaven he-man rubber planter, Gable's in his element, sustaining an unsympathetic assignment until it veers about a bit.' *(Variety)*

PRO:

'Lusty and fresh.' *(Pare Lorentz, Vanity Fair)*

'Worth seeing . . . There's a lightness in the direction, a sparkle in the dialogue and a grand punch ending. Jean Harlow gets the most out of every line and all but steals the show.' *(Photoplay)*

RED RIVER

CT: 8 AV: 8.73

1948 US 125/133 BW WESTERN

D Howard Hawks ☆
W Borden Chase Charles Schnee from Borden Chase's story AAN

John Wayne ☆ Montgomery Clift ☆ Joanne Dru Walter Brennan Colleen Gray

An authoritarian cattleman (John Wayne) and his more liberal adopted son (Montgomery Clift) fall out during and after a cattle drive.

Brave American pioneers are sorely beset by hordes of cruel Comanche Indians in this traditional western on a grand scale. Some film textbooks record that this received poor reviews on release, but the truth is that it was received favourably. The view of Indians is far from sympathetic and now looks naive, but this remains an outstanding western of the 40s – and not just because it's full of scenic grandeur and impressive set-pieces, especially the cattle stampede. The relationship between the two protagonists (which owes a lot to *The Mutiny on the Bounty*) is well written and strongly played; Clift's performance won the critical attention, but Wayne is at least as impressive. Christian Nyby's editing was Oscar-nominated; Russell Harlan's photography and Dimitri Tiomkin's score should have been.

MIXED:

'I thought the performance of newcomer Montgomery Clift disappointing . . . Certainly a finely made Western but oxblood is not my cup of tea.' *(News of the World)*

'Ethics apart, the film is worth seeing for its scenery and sweeping movement, the performances of John Wayne, Montgomery Clift (a promising newcomer), and Walter Brennan.' *(Colin Dixon, Daily Telegraph)*

'Mr Hawks . . . has made . . . an excellent film . . . The only blots on the landscape are the two young women. I'm happy to say the Injuns get one of them early on.' *(Graphic)*

'The usual impossible but tremendously exciting

hocus-pocus about brave American pioneers sorely beset by hordes of cruel Comanche Indians as they plod through the arid prairies. Some day – and I mean this – I should like to see an American Indian company make a film depicting those early palefaces filching thousands of square miles of land from the Indians.' *(Evening Standard)*

'The ending of *Red River* has been much criticised. Everything hinges on why Dunson (John Wayne) doesn't shoot at Matthew Garth (Montgomery Clift) at the showdown. Our sympathy, unequivocally with Dunson at the beginning of the film, has been largely transferred to Matthew; the "traditional" ending would have Wayne, the tragic hero of formidable moral stature but fatally flawed, killed (though not by Clift – we are, I think, sure that Matthew won't shoot), but achieving as he dies the clarity that enables him to judge himself and his actions, and leaving Matthew free for life. One feels that Hawks, in rejecting this ending, broke more than the rules of the traditional Western – he broke the rules of classical tragedy as well.' *(Robin Wood, Howard Hawks, 1968)*

PRO:

'[Clift's] a sympathetic personality that invites audience response. Hawks has loaded the film with mass spectacle and earthy scenes. His try for naturalness in dialog between principals comes off well. The staging of physical conflict is deadly, equalling anything yet seen on screen.' *(Variety)*

'The genuine tang of the outdoors . . . Mr Hawks has used real Western scenery for its most vivid and picturesque effects.' *(New York Times)*

'An exceptionally beautiful and exciting western.' *(Dilys Powell)*

'As long as you are not specially allergic to cows, you can hardly fail to wallow happily in *Red River*, a huge, full-blooded cowboy picture full of all the right qualities . . . And for once the boyish fun is singularly free from interference by females. There is one . . . just before the end [who] is caught smartly near the apex of her shoulder strap by an Indian arrow, which passes through the skin and out the other side. This . . . is one practical solution to that shoulder strap trouble which seems to afflict even the slyest of our women friends from time to time.' *(Fred Majdalany, Daily Mail)*

'Superbly made drama of the wide open spaces.' *(Richard Winnington)*

'A magnificent horse opera. The director, Howard Hawks, makes the drive an exciting series of stampedes, Indian battles, and gunfights, with the fight between the two principals, John Wayne as the father and Clift as the stepson, as the ferocious climax. *Red River* is not really so great as its devotees claim (what Western is?) and a lot of it is just terrible, but Clift – in his most aggressively sexual screen performance – is angular and tense and audacious, and the other actors brawl amusingly in the strong-silentman tradition. Russel Harlan's photography makes the rolling plains the true hero: the setting, if not the material, has epic grandeur.' *(Pauline Kael, 1968)*

RED ROCK WEST

CT: 7 AV: 6.20

1993 US 98 C THRILLER/ROMANCE

D John Dahl ✔
W John Dahl Rick Dahl ✔

Nicholas Cage ☆ Dennis Hopper ✔
Lara Flynn Boyle ✔ J.T. Walsh ✔ Timothy Carhart

An innocent stranger (Nicolas Cage) finds himself up to his neck in murder, mayhem and steamy sensuality in a one-horse town.

Nicolas Cage excels in this entertaining low-budget pastiche of a hundred B-movies; but the best thing about it is the ingenious and logical plotting by two film-buff brothers John and Rick Dahl. No matter what Cage does, he simply can't escape. Dennis Hopper reprises previous roles as a psychopathic hit-man, Lara Flynn Boyle is the femme fatale, and the ubiquitous J. T. Walsh covers equally familiar ground as an unprincipled sheriff. It's a film which goes through the motions without over-involving the emotions, but it's well constructed, genuinely gripping – and well worth catching.

ANTI:

'Over-plotted yarn, whose twists begin to work against it.' *(Winnert)*

PRO:

'This is a movie like *Blood Simple* (which it somewhat resembles) or the David Lynch movies, constructed out of passion, murder, revenge and a quirky sense of humor. The plot is incredibly complicated. It is also easy to follow and, eventually, makes perfect sense.' *(Roger Ebert)*

'It's exciting stuff, despite being partly tongue-in-cheek, and the multi-layered plot is full of satisfying twists and turns. Boyle is wonderful in the sort of part Mary Astor used to make her own.' *(Rose)*

RED SHOES THE AAN

CT: 7 AV: 9.21

1948 GB 136 C DRAMA/DANCE

D Michael Powell Emeric Pressburger ☆
W Michael Powell Emeric Pressburger ✗ from their story AAN

Anton Walbrook ☆ Moira Shearer ☆
Marius Goring ● Robert Helpmann Albert Basserman Frederick Ashton Leonide Massine Ludmilla Tcherina Esmond Knight

The life and early death of a ballerina (Moira Shearer).

Powell and Pressburger's film is obviously some kind

of a masterpiece, for its flamboyant use of colour, deep-focus photography, and sensational ballet sequences, beautifully danced by Moira Shearer, Leonide Massine and Robert Helpmann. Anton Walbrook and Shearer play their parts with conviction, and yet . . . the story doesn't add up. We are asked to believe there is some fatal incompatibility between getting married and being a ballerina, and this doesn't convince – especially if you know the personal histories of Pavlova or Fonteyn.

The central dramatic conflict is meant to be between Art and Romance. But Marius Goring here lives down to his unkind nickname of Marius Boring; he is hardly charismatic enough to personify Romance. As Art, Anton Walbrook is a good deal more plausible – but the 14-minute 'Red Shoes Ballet' looks too modern and imaginative to have been choreographed by the stiff, old-fashioned authoritarian whom he impersonates.

Perhaps, as some critics have argued, the plot is a coded version of the homosexual affair between Diaghilev and Nijinsky, with Nijinsky's sex changed for the sake of propriety. Within a heterosexual context, the story becomes increasingly melodramatic and depressing, and there's no plausible reason for the final tragedy. Great production, shame about the plot.

It won Oscars for Art Direction and Set Design (Hein Heckroth, Arthur Lawson), and Best Score (Brian Easdale). Reginald Mills's editing was also nominated. Other important contributions were by Jack Cardiff (cinematography) and Robert Helpmann (choreography).

PRO:

'A prestige film . . . on a handsome scale.' *(The Times)*

'As the leading ballerina and the romantic heroine of the film, Moira Shearer is amazingly accomplished and full of a warm and radiant charm.' *(New York Times)*

'Professional film previews are cold, calculating affairs. But . . . the audience burst into applause in the middle of the show . . . paying tribute to an exciting new blend of ballet and film technique and to a stunning new star . . . [who] can act as well . . . her personality . . . is one of the most entrancing visions the cinema has ever known.' *(Jympson Harmon, Evening News)*

'Opening with acid realism, developing into fantasy and finishing on a note of melodrama . . . a strange mixture. The film is lush and often lovely, but even during its moments of supreme visual beauty the spell it casts is not one of innocent enchantment. I left the cinema . . . with a slightly dazed sense of returning from some strange, exotic nether region.' *(Joan Lester Reynolds News, 1948)*

'Like nothing the British cinema had ever seen: a rhapsody of colour expressionism, reaching delirious heights in the ballet scenes, but never becoming too brash and smothering in its nuances.' *(Tony Rayns, Time Out)*

MIXED:

'Shaped showily rather than tragically; its frequent falsities make the story (as so often in the work of this gifted team) the weakest part of the film. But if one accepts the story, talent becomes a small word for the quality of its handling. Once more an extraordinary audacity informs the screen.' *(Dilys Powell)*

'For the first hour or so . . . you have to be patient . . . Everything very real (though Covent Garden seemed strangely denuded of veg) very pretty and rather dull. And then the film flares into life with a 20-minute ballet sequence that is one of the most enchanting dance sequences ever filmed.' *(Fred Majdalany, Daily Mail)*

'Perhaps Miss Shearer, an attractive 22-year-old redhead, is a little too sweet and starry-eyed to make the tragic Vicky's fate completely credible. Nevertheless, the Covent Garden ballet star proves that she is a promising actress as well as a graceful and appealing dancer.' *(Newsweek)*

'Of historic importance, for it represents the first major attempt at film ballet . . . [It] could have been a masterpiece . . . but the artistic and psychological problems . . . are treated on a very different plane [from the authentic early scenes . . . and the] final suicide is so incredible that one cannot take it seriously . . . The impresario . . . is a pasteboard figure of melodrama.' *(Fernan Hall, New Theatre)*

'Balletomanes will enjoy [it] . . . What of the rest? . . . They too will enjoy the dancing, the bustle, and the colour of back-stage life . . . [but] they will [also] have to sit through the extra two hours of a tame love story.' *(W.A. Wilcox, Evening Standard)*

'The first film to take the world of ballet as its subject, and for all the mushy sentimentality, all the exaggeration and prettifying, it does give some idea of what it is all about . . . In spite of being so corny it still works.' *(John Percival, The Times, 1982)*

'Never was a better film made from a penny plain story so unpersuasively written and performed; the splendour of the production is in the intimate view it gives of life backstage in the ballet world with its larger-than-life characters. The ballet excerpts are very fine, and the colour discreet; the whole film is charged with excitement.' *(Halliwell)*

'Blubbery and self-conscious, but it affects some people passionately . . . Written, produced, and directed by Michael Powell and Emeric Pressburger – master purveyors of high kitsch.' *(Pauline Kael)*

ANTI:

'Irritatingly crude – directed like a dirge, grotesquely acted . . . insistently trite and for far too long.' *(Fortnight)*

'It was a miserable experience.' *(Moira Shearer, 1949)*

RED SORGHUM CT: 8 AV: 8.00

(aka *Hong Gaoliang*)

1987 China 92 C DRAMA/COMEDY/FOREIGN

D Zhang Yimou ☆
W Chen Jian Yu Zhu Wei Mo Yan

Gong Li Jiang Wen Teng Rujun Liu Ji Qian Ming Ji Cunhua Zhai Cunhua

An 18-year-old (Gong Li) is attacked and raped on her way to marry a leprous old man who owns a sorghum wine distillery. She is rescued by a strong, younger man (Jiang Wen) to whom she makes love . . .

Visually stunning debut by Zhang Yimou, whose experience as a cameraman (on, among other pictures, *Yellow Earth*) shows in elegant compositions and breathtaking use of colour. The story rambles, but there is no shortage of incident; and the heroine is so well played by Gong Li that she holds the audience's interest. The tone of the film darkens throughout, and the final scenes of Japanese invasion are harrowing, but there are humorous moments along the way, and the acting has a lot of charm. Winner of the Golden Bear at the Berlin Film Festival.

'This arty, often comic tale of love, death and very good brew possesses a visual power which will leave you stunned like a duck in thunder . . . Boring, it ain't.' *(Harlekin Dane, New Musical Express)*

'A study of strength and vulnerability . . . that confidently passes from humour to tragedy. The photography is stunning.' *(Robin Buss, Times Educational Supplement)*

'Spellbinding . . . The early part of the story . . . wanders somewhat: so did my attention. But the wartime scenes are tense and grisly.' *(Richard Mayne, Sunday Telegraph)*

'In truth the fable plays second fiddle to the fabulous exposition of the director . . . [who] fills his frames with brilliantly burnished images.' *(Iain Johnstone, Sunday Times)*

'A truly epic tale . . . a film and a film-maker to watch.' *(Neil Norman, Evening Standard)*

'A rough proletarian belch of a film, a gleeful assertion of peasant vitality, founded on amoral (but fully justified) acts of transgression.' *(Tony Rayns, MFB)*

'During 1989's fiftieth anniversary of the great 1939 films, a lot of people have wondered: Where are our grand, sweeping visions of the world, our movies that once raised terrific entertainment to the level of art? In China, that's where. Director Zhang Yimou's *Red Sorghum* – funny, funky, lusty, and rip-roaring – turns love and sorrow, peace and war into a story so powerful it virtually boils out of the celluloid. The whole film is a series of surprises, of veils suddenly removed to reveal that life is never what you expect it to be.' *(Kathy Schulz Huffhines)*

REDS AAN CT: 6 AV: 7.07

1981 US 196 C DRAMA/EPIC/ROMANCE/BIOPIC

D Warren Beatty ✗ AAW
W Warren Beatty Trevor Griffiths ✗ AAN

Warren Beatty ✗ AAN Diane Keaton ✗ AAN Edward Herrman Jerzy Kosincki Jack Nicholson ☆ AAN Maureen Stapleton ☆ AAW Paul Sorvino

Life and times of John Reed (Warren Beatty), whose account of the Russian Revolution influenced the world, and who became the only American buried within the Kremlin walls.

Or: how being a revolutionary can improve your sex life. This is a good yarn with impressive crowd scenes; but Warren Beatty and Diane Keaton are too modern, lightweight and Hollywoody as John Reed and Louise Bryant, and their love story as written here makes the one in David Lean's *Dr Zhivago* look deep. Maureen Stapleton (as Emma Goldman), and Jack Nicholson (magnetic as Eugene O'Neill) overshadow them all too easily. The use of real eye-witnesses – such as Henry Miller and Rebecca West – interspersed between the dramatic action does not illuminate the politics of the period as much as one might hope, and the decision not to identify them is irritating. The Oscar-winning cinematography is by Vittorio Storaro; the editing by Dede Allen and Craig McKay was nominated.

PRO:

'The thinking man's *Doctor Zhivago*, told from the other side, of course.' *(Roger Ebert)*

'More than history, it is poetry, the poetry of revolution.' *(Sheila Benson, LA Times)*

'Not since *Lawrence of Arabia* has there been a serious historical movie of this sweep, complexity and intelligence . . . As a director, Beatty's staging and shooting choices are smart, tasteful, even impassioned.' *(Michael Sragow, Rolling Stone)*

'A timely monument to dissent.' *(Paul Taylor, Time Out)*

MIXED:

'Long but absorbing . . . Although not a great emotional experience it is intellectually satisfying and whets the appetite for learning more . . . The performances are uniformly excellent and it is undoubtedly the finest work of both Beatty and his co-star.' *(Ivor Davis, The Times)*

ANTI:

'A courageous and uncompromising attempt to meld a high-level socio-political drama of ideas with an intense love story, but it is ultimately too ponderous . . . The film is also, to its eventual detriment, structured as a Marxist history lesson.' *(Variety)*

'The story of the radical journalist . . . is trivialised by placing the love affair between him and Louise Bryant (irritatingly played by Diane Keaton) at the centre of the stage.' *(Lindsay Mackie, Glasgow Herald)*

'The writers didn't work out a scrutable character for Louise. In the first half, she's presented as a tiresome, pettishly hostile, dissatisfied woman, and the film moves on the messy currents of sexual politics. In the second half, she is made to set off on a (fictitious) dangerous journey to go to Reed, who has been imprisoned in Finland; she makes her way across the icy tundra in scenes that seem to belong to a different picture (something Zhivagoey), and then the film embraces her, because she's doing what a woman is supposed to do – go through any hardship to be with her man. This second half moves more swiftly but with conventional epic situations and very familiar visual rhetoric.' *(Pauline Kael)*

REGLE DU JEU, LA: *see* RULES OF THE GAME, THE.

REMAINS OF THE DAY, THE AAN

CT: 8 AV: 8 (est)

1993 US 138 C DRAMA/ROMANCE/COSTUME

D James Ivory ☆ AAN
W Ruth Prawer Jhabvala ☆ AAN from Kazuo Ishiguro's novel

Anthony Hopkins ☆ AAN Emma Thompson ☆ AAN James Fox ☆ Peter Vaughan ☆ Christopher Reeve Hugh Grant Michael Lonsdale Tim Piggott-Smith

A butler (Anthony Hopkins) is torn three ways: between his love of a housekeeper (Emma Thompson), his loyalty to his father (Peter Vaughan) and his professional duties.

Merchant-Ivory's faithfulness to classics of English literature has always been assiduous to the point of deference, and sometimes to the point of tedium; so they were ideally suited to Kazuo Ishiguro's excellent Booker prize-winning novel about a butler blinkered by a sense of duty to his cultural superiors, and rendered inarticulate when called upon to express passion.

Ever the professional himself, director James Ivory is a master of minutiae; and the workings of a great stately home are depicted in fascinating detail. The strengths of Ishiguro's novel – his narrative structure, the parallels between private and public life, his sympathy for English stuffiness and reserve – have been carefully preserved in Ruth Prawer Jhabvala's screenplay. Though occasionally too schematic and laborious, the film ends up as more touching than either *A Room With A View* or *Howards End*.

The main reason is Anthony Hopkins, who gives one of the greatest performances in the history of cinema. Every detail of posture, nuance of voice, change of expression, evidence of ageing, is subtle, exactly measured, yet apparently spontaneous. He is, as he has to be, heart-breaking.

Emma Thompson is less perfectly cast and not altogether convincing when called upon to act older than her years, but she exudes an appropriately crisp competence, leading to a series of moving emotional breakdowns which confirm her as one of the best actresses of her generation.

There isn't a weak link among the other members of the cast, but outstanding support is given by James Fox and Peter Vaughan as the butler's employer and father, both guilty of thoughtless oppression, yet both sympathetic in different ways.

The Remains of the Day is not easy to watch. It's hard to see the humiliation of the central character, his inability to overcome his limitations, his chilling failure to embrace life, without wanting to step on to the screen, give Hopkins a good shaking, and yell 'Snap out of it!' But that, of course, is a measure of the film's artistic success.

'I can say it's simple now, but it's taken years to distil my work to a more economic form. I suppose I'm pretty adept now at playing these rather still parts.' *(Anthony Hopkins)*

ANTI:

'This is another designer movie . . . that patronizes the past – and, incidentally, badly oversimplifies its politics.' *(James Bowman, American Spectator)*

'Jhabvala is certainly no crude hack, but she has underscored some matters and has altered the tone of the original . . . Both the political element and the personal element are subtly drawn in the book, but Jhabvala italicizes much of the subtlety . . . Stevens's relationship with Miss Kenton is as it was in the book, but the film's treatment of it is more sentimental . . . To Ishiguro's exquisitely poised work, Jhabvala has painted on colors of *Upstairs, Downstairs*.' *(Stanley Kauffmann)*

'Not nearly as melancholy or involving as Kazuo Ishiguro's novel . . . It's all perfectly okay, but run to read the book instead.' *(Lawrence O'Toole, Entertainment Weekly)*

'Thompson is actually somewhat miscast here: She's too vibrant and forceful a presence to play such a fragile blossom.' *(Owen Gleiberman, Entertainment Weekly)*

MIXED:

'It is to Mrs Jhabvala's credit that she has managed to objectify and animate what in the novel is mostly internalized, point-of-view reflection. And, for once, that basically amateurish director, James Ivory, rouses himself to greater professionalism. His chief flaw has been the inability to hit on the right tempos: compartmentalizing scenes into languid talkiness or hectic action, and not finding musical ways for the orchestration and interpenetration of the two. Here, because the nature of the material calls for small, spasmodic outbursts within an overwhelming stasis, Ivory's idiosyncrasy can feel right at home.' *(John Simon)*

PRO:

'Not only a very handsome drama but an involving, compassionately human one . . . Throughout, this cleverly structured film is richly detailed; above all its other claims, however, towers the awesome performance of Anthony Hopkins.' *(Angie Errigo, Today)*

'Hopkins and Thompson deliver understated performances of solid gold – a lesson in how to say a lot with as little as a gesture or a sidelong glance. *Remains of the Day* ranks as another finely cut jewel in the Merchant-Ivory crown.' *(Bruce Williamson, Playboy)*

'An immaculate adaptation, capturing the astringent wit and luxuriously private sense of melancholy that made Ishiguro's novel so affecting.' *(Brian D. Johnson, Maclean's)*

'Thompson is heartbreaking as a woman with much charming girlishness left in her, all gone to waste. In his utter opacity and failure to comprehend, the extraordinary Hopkins, as a butler, is more frightening than even Hannibal Lecter.' *(Joanne Kaufman, People Weekly)*

'The most exquisite, finely acted, meticulously directed, physically gorgeous, historically profound bit of cinema to emerge from the team of Merchant-Ivory . . . For the most part, I detest these ostentatious, tuxedo-crammed, tea-sipping, rain-falling, pretty-diction, Helena Bonham Carter-starring, pseudo epics. I find them boring and overbearing and about as applicable to my own life as some possum in Lower Tibet. And I'm still recommending *Remains* – big-time.' *(Rod Lurie, LA Magazine)*

'As the elderly Stevens waves a final farewell to Miss Kenton – by now the drearily married Mrs Benn – at a rain-swept bus stop, you'll need a drying off, too. But it won't be from the rain.' *(Guy Flatley, Cosmopolitan)*

REMBRANDT CT: 6 AV: 7.80

1936 GB 84 BW BIOPIC/DRAMA

D Alexander Korda
W Lajos Biro June Head Carl Zuckmayer Arthur Whimperis

Charles Laughton ☆ Elsa Lanchester Gertrude Lawrence Edward Chapman Walter Hudd Roger Livesey Herbert Lomas Allan Jeayes Sam Livesey Raymond Huntley John Clements

Life of a debt-ridden artist (Charles Laughton).

What's wrong with this picture? Generally liked by the critics, it flopped with the public. The biggest problem is that Rembrandt seems to have lived primarily for his art. This may be commendable in an artist, but leaves a biopic with precious little by way of dramatic conflict. Also, for rather too much of the film, he seems to be caught in a downward spiral, personally if not professionally – which may be truthful, but adds to the impression of downbeat monotony. Lugubrious though his performance is, Laughton gives one of his best performances, with comparatively few excursions into ham-acting. The art direction by Vincent Korda and chiaroscuro photography by Georges Perinal and Richard Angst are extraordinary achievements.

'It was a resounding commercial failure. Stately, magnificent, but somewhat depressing, *Rembrandt* was simply too much of a *tableau vivant* to interest the average moviegoer . . . The theme of the movie suggested museums and culture, and even so great an actor as Laughton could not overcome that barrier.' *(Michael Korda, Charmed Lives, 1979)*

ANTI:

'Laughton is far from satisfactory . . . The only tragic things in his life are the deaths of his two wives. On neither occasion does Laughton express the overwhelming sorrow the story calls for.' *(Variety)*

'[The film] never was an effective or moving portrait . . . Simply a Study in Laughton, shaggy, shambling, roguish, rolling of eye and, as far as I'm concerned, intolerable.' *(Richard Winnington, News Chronicle, 1949)*

MIXED:

'Laughton had, besides some rather horrid moments of mugging, some of his most conscientious work. Give Mr Laughton fine words to declaim and he scores a bull every time.' *(Jympson Harman, Evening News, 1949)*

'The visual style seems more Vermeer than Rembrandt, but that's closer than most movies about painters get.' *(Pauline Kael, 70s)*

PRO:

'Between the two of them, Charles Laughton and Alexander Korda have produced a great and rich and glowing motion picture.' *(Bosley Crowther)*

'One of the finest films ever produced . . . It is singularly austere. It lacks – which may disconcert the public – any independent dramatic plot, and is based on the assumption that man in the mass is interested in genius in the individual. Possibly the assumption is true. But it has never been proven, for the simple reason that no producer before has thought of putting it to the test. Whatever the box office verdict may be, Rembrandt remains, for me, a very keen recollection of pleasure. It is produced, set, and written with a fastidious feeling for beauty. The pictures shine and glow, the lines ring with music.' *(C.A. Lejeune, Observer)*

'[Laughton] . . . has never bettered the vigour, sense

of character, humour and pathos that he put into the figure of the reckless and debt-ridden Dutch painter.' *(A.E. Wilson, Star, 1949)*

REPULSION

CT: 8 AV: 7.92

1965 GB 104 BW HORROR/THRILLER

D Roman Polanski ☆
W Roman Polanski Gérard Brach

Catherine Deneuve ☆ Ian Hendry ✔ John Fraser ✔ Patrick Wymark Yvonne Furneaux

Young woman (Catherine Deneuve) goes dangerously mad in swinging London.

One of the most frightening films ever made: Polanski takes us inside the mind of a paranoid murderess, and keeps us there. There's little attempt to explain the reason for her mental state: she's sexually repressed (supposedly the root of all evil in the 1960s), but it's unclear whether that is a cause of her crack-up or merely a symptom. Deneuve's chilling performance and Polanski's expressionist camerawork combine to make a film that is ugly and sordid, but also a memorably disturbing portrait of emotional disintegration.

PRO:

'Classy, truly horrific psychological drama.' *(Variety)*

'An unashamedly ugly film, but as a lynx-eyed view of a crumbling mind it is a masterpiece of the macabre.' *(Daily Mail)*

'One of the most terrifying films I have ever seen.' *(Evening Standard)*

MIXED:

'Not a film for the squeamish, I should make clear, or for the moralist, but quite accomplished of its kind.' *(Daily Telegraph)*

'There is no pity for the girl, no human regard. I am aware of no rule insisting that art must feel for its characters; permissible, though, to expect from a work of imagination an attitude towards them not wholly detached. I think it is the absence of such an attitude which makes me wary of this brilliant film.' *(Dilys Powell)*

'The approach is so objective, so external, that the film doesn't raise questions about this foreign girl's estrangement and loneliness, doesn't offer explanations of her madness. It just stays on her – on her hallucinations and her fantasies of being in danger, and on the actual reprisals she takes against anyone who comes her way. It's clinical Grand Guignol, and the camera fondles the horrors: the high spot is a man being slashed in the face with a straight razor – until he's cut to death. (If you're too scared to look you still hear the slashing sounds.) Undeniably skillful and effective, all right – excruciatingly tense and frightening. But is it entertaining? You have to be a hard-core horror-movie lover to enjoy this one.' *(Pauline Kael)*

'Overrated critically, the movie turns out to be a very ordinary melodrama posing as a "realistic" case study of madness and, apart from the horrific set pieces, directed without flair or style.' *(Alan Frank)*

'Whether such a film finally serves any purpose other than to scare people silly remains doubtful, yet in the long tradition of cinematic shockers, *Repulsion* looms as a work of monstrous art.' *(Bruce Williamson)*

RESERVOIR DOGS

CT: 7 AV: 7.30

1992 US 105 C THRILLER

D Quentin Tarantino ☆
W Quentin Tarantino ☆

Harvey Keitel Tim Roth ☆ Christopher Penn Steve Buscemi Lawrence Tierney Michael Madsen ☆ Quentin Tarantino Eddie Bunker

A heist goes wrong, and some robbers try to discover the traitor in their midst.

Quentin Tarantino's first hit is extremely – and dispassionately – violent, but it's undeniably stylish and has an inventively twisted storyline. Harvey Keitel stars, but it's Tim Roth and Michael Madsen who carry off the acting honours. Critics were divided between acclaiming and deploring it. I enjoyed it as a technical exercise, but couldn't see that it had anything to say.

PRO:

'A violent and bloody first feature I wouldn't wish upon anyone's maiden aunt or susceptible uncle. But it is also an extraordinarily impressive début . . . supremely cinematic, which is why its violence is so difficult to handle.' *(Derek Malcolm, Guardian)*

'Essentially, this bloody chamber piece is a heist movie, but [Tarantino] tampers with the chronology and turns it into a post-mortem . . . an ambitious structure, but [he] pulls it off with panache . . . It is also very funny. They may not realise it, but these are post-modernist felons.' *(Anne Billson, Sunday Telegraph)*

'[It] isn't quite *Crime and Punishment* but it is a remarkable achievement for a first film. It is unquestionably an ordeal to sit through, but on the far side of the squirming and flinching there is something almost moral. All right then, yes, rather more Dostoyevskian than we have any right to expect.' *(Adam Mars-Jones, Independent)*

'Jumping from the tension of the moment to revealing flashbacks that precede the crime, *Reservoir Dogs* reduces evil to its essence with classic style and concentration.' *(Bruce Williamson, Playboy)*

'The acting and dialogue fairly fizz with wit and energy. If only film-makers didn't forget how to make tight little thrillers like this once they're given big bucks to spend.' *(Rose)*

Puts a post-modernist spin on the classic Hawksian heme of professionalism. The gangsters keep lefining and redefining the meaning of the term, vhile their actions undercut their words by proving hese addled sociopaths to be anything but professional". In Tarantino's vision, the age of ıeroic competence is as dead as his characters are at he fadeout.' *(Baseline)*

MIXED:

If it's flamboyance you want, head straight for *Reservoir Dogs*, a lurid mélange of crime caper and omoerotic bloodbath . . . Its ho-hum plot about a ank robbery gone wrong is condensed and stylised o an intensity somewhere between classical Greek ragedy and grand opera.' *(David Melville, Gay Times)*

A showy but insubstantial comic opera of violence . . as much a calling card as a movie . . . Though t's impossible not to appreciate the undeniable skill nd élan Tarantino brings to all this, it is also lifficult not to wish *Reservoir Dogs* weren't so leterminedly one-dimensional, so in love with peratic violence at the expense of everything else. The old gangster movies its creator idolizes were etter at balancing things, at adding creditable motional connection and regret to their dead-end roceedings.' *(Kenneth Turan, LA Times)*

Here is the new creed: movies are pictures of stuff appening. And the uglier the stuff, the more, well, inematic the result. Naked aggression is sexy. I hout in your face. I spit in your face. I blow off your ace. I blow up your family. I blow up the city . . . t's *Glengarry Glen Ross* at gunpoint. The talented arantino has devised one bravura sequence in vhich an undercover detective acts out, for the enefit of the duped hoodlums, a fake story about a lose call with the cops; easing from the past tense o the present and then into seductive fantasy, the equence reveals how we all must be performers, cting for our lives. But most of the movie is Actors cting: gifted guys (Harvey Keitel, Tim Roth, Steve Buscemi, Chris Penn) running nattering riffs on amiliar lout themes.' *(Richard Corliss, Time)*

ANTI:

At the end I was left with a kind of despair. Yes, arantino has a sense of dramatic disposition and, vith his imaginative cinematographer Andrzej ekula, he lights and frames every scene as if he vere sculpting it. Yes, the very last moments of the lm quite consciously take the multiple killings and he torrential gore into the edges of satire. What epresses is that a director of Tarantino's cinematic ifts should have chosen this particular film for his ébut . . . It clearly was made just for the sake of its naking, the application of style to sheer slaughter. ndulging the so-called critical fallacy of trying to ecipher an artist's intent, I'd hazard that Tarantino vrote this script because he thought it would be elatively easy to get it financed. Is this to accuse him of cynicism? Well, what god hovers over this film but the classic deity of cynicism?' *(Stanley Kauffmann)*

'Here is the ideal date movie, assuming you're dating a psychopathic sadist with a high tolerance for dillydallying . . . A convoluted, pretentious combination of *Diner* and such crime caper movies as *The Killing* and *The Asphalt Jungle*. Tarantino, though, is no Barry Levinson, Stanley Kubrick or John Huston . . . Tarantino displays little understanding of human behavior in general and criminal behavior in particular. He seems to think, for instance, that your average armed robber-murderer spends his off-duty hours sitting around philosophizing about tipping waitresses, engaging in pompous textual analysis of Madonna songs and playing movie trivia games. As the gang's mastermind, character actor Lawrence Tierney, affecting a how-gruff-I-am voice, seems like a loser in a Broderick Crawford imitation contest. The younger actors who are doing his dirty work all seem fresh off the campus of the James Woods-Willem Dafoe Institute for Acting Surly, Nervous and Disheveled.' *(Ralph Novak, People)*

RETURN OF MARTIN GUERRE, THE

CT: 8 AV: 8.67

(aka *Le Retour de Martin Guerre*)

1982 France 123 C DRAMA/ROMANCE/FOREIGN

D Daniel Vigne ✔
W Jean-Claude Carrière Daniel Vigne

Gérard Depardieu Stéphane Peau Nathalie Baye Bernard-Pierre Donnadieu Sylvie Méda Maurice Barrier Isabelle Sadoyan

In the 16th century, a man (Gérard Depardieu) arrives in a French village claiming to be Martin Guerre and reclaims his wife (Nathalie Baye) after eight years absence. But is he an impostor?

Though a little overlong and lacking in panache, Daniel Vigne's film paints a convincing picture of a suspicious small community, elicits fine leading performances and keeps the audience in suspense to the end. Production values are high, and Anne-Marie Marchand won an Oscar nomination for her costume designs. The story – which is based on a real court-case of the period – was remade (competently, though not brilliantly) by British director Jon Amiel as *Sommersby* (1993), with the period updated to the American Civil War. The Hollywood version does avoid imposing a happy ending and contains a wonderful performance as the wife by Jodie Foster. Unfortunately, it inserts a lot of silly, anachronistic Civil Rights stuff; the original French version remains preferable.

ANTI:

'A plodding, confusing narrative that neither does proper justice to the story nor really teases out the complex historical, moral and psychological issues which it raises.' *(Observer)*

MIXED:

'If Buñuel had made [it] we might have had quite a film. But he didn't . . . Consequently, there are only the merest traces of either irony or imagination in this good-looking, well-acted but rather remorseless plod though the story.' *(Derek Malcolm, Guardian)*

'[The film] lacks only one thing, one little thing which Vigne ought to consider: a style, a rhythm, a visual invention which would allow him to escape from a simple illustration of his formidable subject.' *(Le Nouvel Observateur)*

'The movie's mediaevalism is strictly rent-a-tunic and [the] photography is in the currently overused amber-and-sackcloth style . . . but the tale's the thing. That and the cracking performance of Depardieu.' *(Nigel Andrews, Financial Times)*

PRO:

'Has the kind of shapeliness that one associates more often with fiction than fact . . . Depardieu . . . is superb . . . Almost as good . . . is Nathalie Baye.' *(Vincent Canby, New York Times)*

'Absorbing . . . Vigne's direction brings us a real feeling that this is what medieval France must have looked like.' *(Milton Shulman, Evening Standard)*

'It is rare for a film to excite the eye and the mind at once. [but] . . . Vigne has succeeded . . . It is an original and compelling masterpiece.' *(Michael Wigan, Scotsman)*

RETURN OF THE JEDI: *see* THE *STAR WARS* SERIES.

REVENGE OF THE DEAD: *see* NIGHT OF THE GHOULS.

REVERSAL OF FORTUNE   CT: 6   AV: 7.50

1990 US 111 C DRAMA/THRILLER

D Barbet Schroeder AAN
W Nicholas Kazan AAN from Alan Dershowitz's book

Glenn Close Jeremy Irons ☆ AAW Ron Silver Annabella Sciorra Uta Hagen Fisher Stevens Jack Gilpin Christine Baranski Stephen Mailer Julie Hagerty

Claus von Bülow (Jeremy Irons) is convicted and later acquitted for the 'murder' of his society wife, Sunny (Glenn Close).

Jeremy Irons's witty, ironic performance as Claus von Bülow is worthy of the superlatives it received. He starts out as chilly and dangerous: less a lounge lizard than a club crocodile. He is revealed, gradually, as a man emasculated by wealth, yet retaining a cold dignity and an enviable resilience. By the end, you find yourself almost liking him, despite his abysmal taste in women.

Some aspects of the film don't work. Glenn Close's narration (as Sunny, commentating on the action from within her coma) was presumably intended as an echo of William Holden in *Sunset Boulevard*; but it comes across as arch and uninformative – it looks like a sop to the female star. Attempts to fill us in on the love-life of attorney Alan Dershowitz (Ron Silver) are half-hearted and irrelevant. Not even Silver and a skilful screenplay can make the lawyer terribly likeable: the result is a film which is always emotionally detached.

Even so, the movie is highly entertaining in its portrayal of the kind of upper-class lifestyle which more resembles a deathstyle. It's also praiseworthy for the way it respects its audience: it presents the possibilities fairly, and leaves us to draw our own conclusions.

PRO:

'A classy piece of filmmaking.' *(Variety)*

'Schroeder has made a delightfully funny, irreverent, and immensely entertaining movie out of the sordid von Bülow affair – that real-life murder, suicide, accident, or whatever it was. Some people may find the light touch, the parodic performances, the brio of [the film] offensive. Cluck, cluck. Tsk, tsk. . . . Refreshingly, [it] isn't striving to be either definitive or profound . . . Hilarious social satire.' *(Georgia Brown, Village Voice)*

'Easily survives its fuzzy spots and pulls us into an enthralling mystery.' *(Geoff Brown, The Times)*

'The big revelation is Irons' performance. It's a transfixing study in perfectly observed poise, accent and mannerisms, which coalesce to form a convincingly cool and clipped exterior.' *(Andrew Anthony, City Limits)*

'The deep, mellow drawl that comes out of Irons' von Bülow is . . . the voice of self-satisfaction – of a man who likes his vowel sounds so much he lingers over them. Irons' von Bülow is a pop conception of a decadent aristocrat – a creep so polished and courtly and cynical that he finds the accusation of murder too banal to be seriously addressed.' *(Pauline Kael)*

'The genius of *Reversal of Fortune* is that the story is narrated by Sunny from her sickbed. We hear her voice, wondering aloud at the chain of events caused by that day when she sank into her long sleep. She guides us through the details of the case. She reminisces about the first time she met Claus, about what she felt for him, about how their marriage progressed. She confesses herself as confused as anyone about what happened on her last day of consciousness. "You tell me," she says, and somehow this gives us permission to look at the film in a more genial mood.' *(Roger Ebert)*

MIXED:

'The performances from [Irons and Silver] hit the right pitch within a rather difficult scenario. This is a strange, unsatisfactory mixture of satire and docudrama which engages the mind and leaves the emotions intact.' *(Colette Maude, Time Out)*

'The film's only error is to have given us too little of [the von Bülows'] flashback-recreated home life.' *(Nigel Andrews, Financial Times)*

'A good old rollicking mini-series yarn, cleverly masquerading as an in-depth study . . . dressed up in Gucci shoes and Bond Street underwear . . . An eminently watchable film, but with such a cracking story and both its main stars in marvellous form, it could have been a wonderful one. What we have is a missed opportunity and a cop-out.' *(Sue Heal, Today)*

REVOLUTION CT: 1 AV: 1.88

1985 GB/Norway 121/125 C WAR/DRAMA/ROMANCE

D Hugh Hudson ●
W Robert Dillon ●

Al Pacino ● Donald Sutherland ● Nastassja Kinski ● Joan Plowright Dave King Steven Berkoff

Baddies (British) fight goodies (American). Somewhere in the middle of all this, Al Pacino and Nastassja Kinski play love scenes.

Lavish production values and impressive battle scenes couldn't save this dire film from critical and commercial Armageddon. *Revolution* got the worst reviews of any British film released during the 1980s – which was unfortunate, since the fortunes of its production company, Goldcrest, were riding on its success. But, if you look at the film it's hard to understand how anyone at Goldcrest ever gave such a stupid, confused script the go-ahead. The miscasting of the three lead actors didn't help, and the accents of Pacino and Sutherland were laughable.

'Easily one of the worst movies of the year.' *(LA Daily News)*

'Watching *Revolution* is like visiting a museum – it looks good without really being alive.' *(Variety)*

'Dull and long-winded.' *(Christian Science Monitor)*

'Storyline often appears confused and fractured and its script at times almost laughably one-dimensional.' *(Guardian)*

'Dingily photographed with the compositional eye of an earthworm.' *(Toronto Globe and Mail)*

'A chaotic two-hour, five-minute mess.' *(Time)*

'The most hilariously maladroit historical pageant since *King David* – this movie is nuts.' *(Village Voice)*

'If Al Pacino's accent doesn't put you off, wait till you hear the screams during the ten-minute infected-foot cauterising scene. Not the patient's screams – yours.' *(USA Today)*

'Pacino [is] two centuries too contemporary to be convincing.' *(Maltin)*

'At last, the real reason Britain lost America. We bored them so much they couldn't stand it any more.' *(Rose)*

RICHARD III CT: 8 AV: 8.69

1955 GB 139/161 C DRAMA

D Laurence Olivier
W Laurence Olivier Alan Dent from Shakespeare's play

Laurence Olivier ☆ AAN Claire Bloom Ralph Richardson ☆ Cedric Hardwicke ☆ Stanley Baker Alec Clunes John Gielgud Mary Kerridge Pamela Brown Michael Gough Norman Wooland Helen Hayes Patrick Troughton Clive Morton Andrew Cruickshank

A malevolent hunchback (Laurence Olivier) schemes his way to the English throne, but gets his come-uppance.

This is very obviously filmed theatre and the battle climax is a shade disappointing; but here is one of the great Shakespearean performances of all time – Olivier's treacherous, narcissistic but incredibly charming rogue. And, unlike some other star turns that originated in the theatre, he works magnificently in close-up. For those too young to have seen Olivier in his prime on stage, and who have only seen him hamming it up in screen roles unworthy of his talents, this film should come as a revelation.

ANTI:

'In spite of some valiant snipping, Olivier has not succeeded in cutting away entirely the tangle of genealogical undergrowth that clutters up this play.' *(Milton Shulman, Sunday Express)*

'Larry plays this monster like a cross between Hermione Gingold and the Hunchback of Notre Dame . . . [He] has had to butcher the original play so badly to make it into a film, that when the ghosts of those Richard had murdered appear before him, I expected to see Shakespeare among them!' *(Frank Jackson, Reynolds News)*

'[Olivier's directorial] approach is for the most part tediously staid and conservative, and it becomes almost laughable when it tries to transcend its own timidity in the dramatic sequences.' *(Tony Rayns, Time Out)*

MIXED:

'As director and star, Olivier succeeds with the soliloquies as neither he nor anyone else ever did on film before; they're intimate, yet brazen. If the film were all malevolent crookback Richard, it would be a marvel; unfortunately, he was plagued with quantities of associates and relations, and even when impersonated by Ralph Richardson, John Gielgud,

Cedric Hardwicke, etc, they're a dull lot.' *(Pauline Kael)*

PRO:

'Wherever the play was loose-jointed or ill-fitting, Sir Laurence has been its tinker and its tailor, but never once its butcher . . . We shall certainly never see the piece better acted.' *(Paul Dehn, News Chronicle)*

'The measure of Sir Laurence Olivier's genius for putting Shakespeare's plays on the screen is beautifully and brilliantly exhibited.' *(Bosley Crowther)*

'Once again it is Olivier's achievement that he makes this self-admiring and treacherous murderer entertaining without loss of size and without loss of fascination. Of his stage performance one remembers both how funny it was, and how ferocious. Nothing is lost of those qualities: perhaps something is gained by the intimacy which the cinema permits . . . If I am asked whether this translation from the theatre is good cinema, I shall reply that it is something rarer, good theatre-cinema; that it brings to the theatre the movement, the close look, the attentive comment of the cinema, and to the cinema the depth and intellectual vigour of the theatre.' *(Dilys Powell)*

RIDE THE HIGH COUNTRY CT: 8 AV: 9.00

(aka *Guns in the Afternoon*)

1962 US 94 C WESTERN

D Sam Peckinpah ☆
W N.B. Stone Jr William S. Roberts (latter uncredited) ✔

Joel McCrea ☆ Randolph Scott ☆ Edgar Buchanan Mariette Hartley ✔ James Drury Ronald Starr R. G. Armstrong

Two superannuated lawmen (Joel McCrea, Randolph Scott) have to decide whether to resist criminal temptation when called upon to escort gold from a mining camp to a bank.

A wry, nostalgic tribute to the Old West – surprisingly upbeat and non-violent for a Peckinpah movie. It's a lot of people's favourite western, because of its quirky sense of humour and obvious affection for the main actors (it turned out to be Scott's final film, after a lifetime in the saddle). The screenplay is not startlingly original, but it's been underrated; Stone, the uncredited Roberts and the director find new, more realistic slants on western mythology, without demeaning it. Treasurable scenes include the surreal wedding celebration at the mine (where five men have an eye for the bride), the saloon with its distinctly unalluring madam and whores, and the final shoot-out among the chickens. Lucien Ballard's photography is excellent.

The picture, which was only Peckinpah's second, received good reviews but was underestimated by MGM, who released it as the lower half of a double-bill, supporting far inferior movies, such as *Boys' Night Out* and *The Tartars*. Despite MGM's best efforts to bury it, the film rapidly earned a reputation around the world, winning First Prize at the Cannes Film Festival, the Grand Prize at the Brussels Film Festival (beating Federico Fellini's *8½*), the Silver Goddess from the Mexican Film Festival for Best Foreign Film, and a further prize at the Venice Film Festival. It was named as one of the top films of 1962 by both *Newsweek* and *Film Quarterly*.

MIXED:

'The old saying "you can't make a silk purse out of a sow's ear" rings true for Metro-Goldwyn-Mayer's artistic western . . . It remains a standard story, albeit with an interesting gimmick and some excellent production values.' *(Variety)*

'Seven marks for the film. Eight for Joel McCrea and Mariette Hartley.' *(Ernest Betts, People)*

PRO:

'It was the first time I'd seen a cowpuncher thunder into town on a camel. The first time I'd seen a hired gunman put on spectacles . . . The first time, come to think of it, I'd heard a toilet flushed in a gold-mining community. Who says that Westerns hold no more surprises? [It] is the most likeable, hard-bitten humorous old-time Western so far.' *(Alexander Walker, Evening Standard)*

'Takes a fresh and disillusioned look at the western hero and makes him for the first time a figure of pathos . . . You might call this a western weepie except that it is much better than such a description would suggest.' *(Thomas Wiseman, Sunday Express)*

'Its freshness and quirkiness and laconic high spirits are all its own, or rather Mr Peckinpah's.' *(Isabel Quigly, Spectator)*

'It is a resourceful young director's attempt to create something original within a fairly rigid framework of tradition.' *(New York Herald Tribune)*

'Peckinpah's finest achievement, and one of the best westerns ever made.' *(Danny Peary)*

RIFIFI CT: 6 AV: 8.44

(aka *Du Rififi Chez les Hommes*)

1955 France 116 BW THRILLER/FOREIGN

D Jules Dassin ☆
W Jules Dassin René Wheeler Auguste Le Breton from Le Breton's novel

Jean Servais ☆ Carl Mohner Robert Manuel Marie Sabouret Perlo Vita (Jules Dassin) Magali Noël

Robbers fall out after a heist.

The blacklisted American director Jules Dassin went to France and made this tense thriller with one of the most famous robbery sequences ever – it takes up a sizeable chunk of the film, and there isn't a word of dialogue. Violent and realistic for its time, with memorably sleazy scenes of the Parisian underworld, the film does run out of steam and suspense before the end. It won Dassin Best Director award at the Cannes Film Festival.

MIXED:

'The robbery itself is 30 minutes of brilliant silent suspense. After that it is routine, old-fashioned thuggery.' *(Milton Shulman, Sunday Express)*

'Not quite the piece noir of the underworld that it has been cracked up to be; but it is still . . . fairly engrossing.' *(Derek Granger, Financial Times)*

'Out of the worst crime novel I have ever read, Dassin has made the best crime film I have ever seen . . . Everything in [it] is intelligent . . . The two failures are the female casting and the specially written song, which is execrable.' *(François Truffaut, Cahiers du Cinéma)*

PRO:

'Leave your moral scruples at the pay-box and you'll find this the chilliest antidote to the summer sun the cinema is likely to provide . . . The whole seedy piece is acted and directed . . . so incisively, that every nerve is stretched to the limit.' *(Sunday Graphic)*

'One of the tensest melodramas we have seen . . . for ages.' *(Leonard Mosley, Daily Express)*

'*Rififi* is the granddaddy of a batch of suspense films featuring how to knock over safes or break into banks and museums, but its own chief distinction is its nasty tone.' *(Pauline Kael)*

RIGHT STUFF, THE

CT: 6 AV: 7.43

1983 US 193 C DRAMA

D Philip Kaufman
W Philip Kaufman from Tom Wolfe's book

Sam Shepard ☆ Barbara Hershey Scott Glenn Ed Harris ☆ Dennis Quaid ☆ Fred Ward Kim Stanley Veronica Cartwright Pamela Reed Scott Paulin Charles Frank Lance Henriksen Donald Moffat Peggy Davis Jeff Goldblum Kathy Baker

America trains astronauts.

A box office flop, but a very interesting one: this is a sprawling, disjointed but often brilliant movie about the pioneer days of space travel. It opens with an old-fashioned western hero, test-pilot Chuck Yeager (Sam Shepard), who's a loner; and it closes with new heroes – a highly trained band of team-players.

The Right Stuff is primarily a meditation on the changing nature of heroism. The trouble is that an unfocused screenplay allows actor/playwright Sam Shepard's charismatic performance to turn the first part of the movie into a biography of Chuck Yeager. And Kaufman can't make up his mind about how real, or how cartoon-like, the rest of his characters are. Despite winning performances from many individuals, especially Quaid and Harris, the piece appears emotionally detached from its subject-matter.

MIXED:

'Fine camerawork and amazing stunts compensate for a lot of jingoistic attitudes, guff, blather and hot air.' *(Virginia Dignam, Morning Star)*

'Comic strip banality, fifth form humour and dazzling photographic effects.' *(Richard Barkley, Sunday Express)*

'A bold, confident picture that makes its points with visual flair . . . There are longueurs and odd sticky moments, but at the end Kaufman has fully justified [the] running time.' *(Philip French, Observer)*

'Some of the satire falls flat and the scatalogical humor becomes tiresome, but the picture has remarkable scope; spectacular, nail-biting flying sequences (in jets, in rockets); romance; wit; and an interesting view on the difference between what is heroic and what the public is manipulated into believing is heroic.' *(Danny Peary)*

PRO:

'Kaufman maintains a wise blend of human anxieties, exciting action with the hardware and plenty of wit . . . It's a terrific yarn.' *(Paul Jackson, Western Mail)*

'To those of you, like me, who find the exploration of space about as exciting as watching the window of a tumble dryer, take heart! I approached [the film] as a duty. By the end, it had become a pleasure.' *(Margaret Hinxman, Daily Mail)*

'A gigantic and impressive film.' *(Jenny Rees, Daily Express)*

'An adventure film, a special-effects film, a social commentary, and a satire . . . One of the best recent American movies.' *(Roger Ebert)*

'It's nothing like the straightforward documentary you'd expect, but has some sharp and funny satire mixed in with the exciting aerial footage. Despite its length, *The Right Stuff* is just that.' *(Rose)*

RIO BRAVO

CT: 7 AV: 7.43

1959 US 141 C WESTERN

D Howard Hawks ☆
W Jules Furthman Leigh Brackett

John Wayne ☆ Dean Martin ☆ Ricky Nelson Angie Dickinson Walter Brennan Ward Bond John Russell Pedro Gonzalez Claude Akins Harry Carey Jr Bob Steele

A sheriff (John Wayne) needs help from the local community when bad hombres try to spring one of their number from jail.

High Noon was a liberal western which debunked

the frontier spirit by portraying most pioneers as cowards unwilling to rally round their law-enforcer (Gary Cooper). Hawks wanted this film to show America in a better light. The initial plot premise is the same, but in Hawks's Old West virtually everyone in the community volunteers to help the beleaguered forces of law and order. The problem is that they're mostly too young, old, female, crippled or drunk. Even so, Wayne moulds them into a winning team. Dean Martin gives easily his best performance in pictures, as an alcoholic regaining his self-respect; and the film has many good points, including a terrific score by Dimitri Tiomkin.

Underrated on release, it is now in danger of being overrated. Pop singer Ricky Nelson is a dead weight in the acting department; Angie Dickinson isn't much better; and the pace is over-deliberate. Hawks himself had reservations about the picture, remaking it in 1966 as *El Dorado*, and again in 1970 as *Rio Lobo* – although most critics reckon he never surpassed his original. John Carpenter's *Assault on Precinct 13* (1976) is, to all intents and purposes, an updated remake.

ANTI:

'Starts slowly and gets slower. There are times when John Wayne, who set the trancelike pace, seems to find the exhausting act of speech almost more than he can physically endure.' *(Derek Prouse, Sunday Times)*

'A typical western of this age of the long-winded, large screen. It lasts for 140 minutes and it contains enough inventiveness to make do for about half that time. It is, in fact, a soporific blockbuster.' *(Guardian)*

'A western is, or should be, a simple affair, capable of winding itself up in an hour and a half, but *Rio Bravo* . . . goes on for no less than two hours and 20 minutes. Perhaps this is a subconscious flattery of Mr John Wayne, who is seldom in a hurry over anything and who here, as the sheriff, spends a lot of time walking slowly up and down the street in the company of his deputy.' *(The Times)*

'Hawks has put too many shooting irons in the fire. The picture has not one but three heroes; they divide the sympathies and overpopulate the screen. For another thing, the film lasts almost as long as five TV westerns laid end to end – and it makes about as little consecutive sense.' *(Time)*

PRO:

'Just about as standard western fare as has ever turned up on a Hollywood menu . . . But when brewed by Howard Hawks . . . suddenly everything begins to work. There is excitement, tension, the pleasure of looking at western landscapes and the age-old gratification when the good guys beat the bad.' *(Arthur Knight, Saturday Review of Literature)*

'Don't be put off if you hear that *Rio Bravo* is a western two and a half hours long, because it is so rattlingly good you won't notice the time pass . . . The dialogue is crisp, the action dramatic, and the acting throughout soars into top gear.' *(George Sterling, Evening Standard)*

'*Rio Bravo* is a very long film, but it succeeds in holding our attention completely. Unless you don't care about westerns. As for me, the western (more than the musical) is the only film form where the poetical feelings of America can still find some place. Give him a horse, a wagon, and boundless space, and an American begins to sing. Isn't this the same feeling and nostalgia that drives Kerouac's generation on the road? A man cannot live without poetry.' *(Jonas Mekas, Village Voice, 1959)*

'*Rio Bravo* is a gem. For some strange reason (probably the presence of a pop singer, Ricky Nelson, in the cast) it was not too well reviewed in this country when it was first shown, but it was (deservedly) a great popular success and also achieved great prestige on the Continent . . . Wayne at his most archetypal, Dean Martin at his coolest, and Angie Dickinson at her hottest, *Rio Bravo* is, however, first and last a Howard Hawks film . . . an example of the classical, pre-Welles school of American filmmaking at its most deceptively simple: broad lines, level glances, grand design, elementary emotions.' *(Guardian, 1963)*

'Arguably Hawks's greatest film . . . beautifully acted, wonderfully observed, and scripted with enormous wit and generosity.' *(Geoff Andrew, Time Out)*

RIO GRANDE

CT: 6 AV: 6.50

1950 US 105 BW WESTERN

D John Ford

W James Kevin McGuinness from James Warner Bellah's story

John Wayne ☆ Maureen O'Hara ☆ Ben Johnson Claude Jarman Jr Chill Wills J. Carrol Naish Victor McLaglen

The life of a cavalry colonel (John Wayne) is disrupted by the arrival of his grown-up son (Claude Jarman Jr) and estranged wife (Maureen O' Hara).

Third of John Ford's films about the US cavalry – the others being *Fort Apache* (1948) and *She Wore A Yellow Ribbon* (1949). There are several of the director's familiar flaws, including sentimental Oirishness, some crude attempts at humour and obviously phoney sets; but the action sequences are exciting, the scenery is spectacular, and underlying the clichéd white man-versus-the Indian situation (which has not, needless to say, worn well) there is the sense of men behaving bravely out of notions of honour and duty which have fallen out of fashion in later, more cynical times. Wayne and O'Hara play very well opposite each other.

ANTI:

'An intolerable amount of maternal sentimentality.' *(Guardian)*

'There are occasions . . . when [Wayne] appears to be more afraid of Miss O'Hara than he is of the Indians he is fighting . . . Some of the scenes . . . have a hint of burlesque. When the regimental choir takes over – again, their songs are excellent if out of place – the picture seems to be developing into a musical and the unabashed sentimentality of some episodes . . . heighten this impression.' *(Roy Nunn, Star)*

'Thin . . . too many pauses for song, too many studio sets, and too little plot.' *(Halliwell)*

PRO:

'Filmed outdoor action at its best . . . Wayne is very good and Miss O'Hara gives one of her best performances.' *(Brog, Variety)*

'Wayne is outstanding . . . brilliant camerawork . . . big thrills . . . tender sentiment.' *(Josh Billings, Kine Weekly)*

'Whatever may ail the business, a couple of films like this and a cure should be quickly effected.' *(Cinema)*

'The scenes in which quantities of horses are seen violently in action are (as always) most impressive. Mr Wayne (as always) suggests the very noblest kind of horse not in action.' *(Fred Majdalany, Daily Mail)*

RIVER, THE CT: 6 AV: 6.18

1951 US/India 99 C DRAMA

D Jean Renoir
W Rumer Godden Jean Renoir from Rumer Godden's novel

Nora Swinburne Esmond Knight Arthur Shields Thomas E. Breen ● Patricia Walters ☆ Adrienne Corri Radha ☆

A British family in India is disrupted by the arrival of a neighbouring, crippled American soldier (Thomas E. Breen).

Renoir presents a romanticized but attractive view of life along the Ganges, with lyrical photography by Claude Renoir. There are two main themes – being an outsider, and conquering feelings of self-hatred – but neither is well dramatized. The story is very thin, and further undermined by the miscasting of Thomas E. Breen, who lacks the acting ability to play the man whose attractions create problems for the womenfolk.

PRO:

'A distinctive study of adolescent love, with a philosophy that life flows on just as the river . . . Neither Technicolor nor India ever looked better. Throughout it is ablaze with vivid, contrasting colors. But one never feels the real India and rather suspects that this is a highly glamorized version.' *(Variety)*

'[Renoir] has probably exceeded anything that has gone before . . . a film of real artistry and intelligence [which] helps remind us that the motion picture can be a truly creative art, a great art that makes it possible for us to look deeply into the customs of other lands and the passions of other hearts.' *(Arthur Knight, Saturday Review of Literature)*

'That happy blend of realistic detail and lyric poetry for which Renoir is famous.' *(Campbell Dixon, Daily Telegraph)*

'Some people, accustomed to films edited for dramatic crescendo, dislike the serene flow – so much is going on that they feel nothing happens. There are static patches of dialogue, and some of the casting is questionable, but the theme (outsiders in a culture) meshes perfectly with the director's own position as a moviemaker in India, and visually the film is serenely yet passionately beautiful.' *(Pauline Kael)*

MIXED:

'If, within its artful unity of theme and mood [it] has its trying moments, the film also offers some exceptionally rewarding ones.' *(Time)*

'Atones for a gossamer-like story and some ragged sequences with a deep sincerity and pictorial loveliness . . . that I have seldom seen equalled.' *(Ewart Hodgson, News of the World)*

RIVER'S EDGE CT: 7 AV: 7.08

1987 US 95/100 C DRAMA

D Tim Hunter ☆
W Neal Jimenez ✓

Crispin Glover ✓ Keanu Reeves Ione Skye Leitch Dennis Hopper ☆ Daniel Roebuck Joshua Miller

Teenagers don't know how to react when one of their number (Daniel Roebuck) strangles his girlfriend and leaves her on a riverbank.

Disturbing film, all the more upsetting since it is based on fact. Many critics found its message and darkly humorous tone alienating; but it captures more than any other film the anomie and amorality of youth. Crispin Glover's hyperactive performance in the lead is a matter of taste and the film has rough edges technically, but this is one of those films which stays with you long afterwards.

ANTI:

'Unusually downbeat and depressing youth pic.' *(Variety)*

'The film is sincere and very ambitious. It is also, I think, a dismal failure – a slovenly, lurching mess, and so nakedly pretentious about what it's "saying" that hardly a scene in it plays naturally, fluidly, with the indelible rhythm of life unfolding. There's really no plot. Instead, Jimenez builds an episodic structure meant to mirror the searching, existential emptiness of the kids' lives, as they group off in twos and threes, cruise around the nameless town at night, drink and play video games and battle their divorced parents, return to the scene of the crime, or try to score some pot from the only adult they can stand – a one-legged ex-Sixties biker named Feck (Dennis Hopper) who shares his bombed-out house with a party doll. Hopper plays the same sort of glassy-eyed burnout he did before *Blue Velvet* offered him a chance to give a performance, and the scenes in which he clutches his beloved doll or speaks about the woman he shot in the head for love are so campy-ghastly they seem to knock his status as an actor right back down.' *(Owen Gleiberman, Boston Phoenix)*

'The Americans seem to get upset more easily than we do . . . This summer's shocker has been advertised here as the most controversial film you will see this year. Wrong, but it is the most dislikeable . . . Violence is shown to have superseded emotion as the commonplace reaction to injustice.. [The film] is horrible yet utterly riveting; but its credibility is undermined by the fact that the plot and characters are vacuum packed . . . All in all . . . a nasty piece of work.' *(Victoria Mather, Daily Telegraph)*

MIXED:

'At its best [it] is sombre without being portentous . . . Aiming at a calm examination of disaffected youth, the film can't quite give up the adolescent kicks of melodrama.' *(Adam Mars-Jones, Independent)*

'Relentlessly grungy . . . though not without a certain black humour. It does seem to rather wallow in its fetid air of moral retardation . . . but an eerily convincing variety of lank-haired American teenage actors keeps you watching and the film develops a trance-like logic.' *(Ian Penman, The Face)*

PRO:

'The most disturbing movie I have seen in the nearly nine years I have held this job. Certainly not the best, but the most disturbing . . . As far as real moral interest or complexity goes, this is the only [film about teens] that matters . . . [It] is everyone's nightmare, a cloud of misery wafting out of the familiar confusions and vacancies of American adolescence . . . Some of [it] is sheer bravado and pretty terrible. Yet [its] failures paradoxically make me care about it more.' *(David Denby, New York Magazine)*

'I don't remember ever seeing a film that disturbed me the way this one did. *Blue Velvet* came closest, but one was able to remind oneself, after experiencing its emotionally devastating (and, at the same time, weirdly funny) vision of the heart of small-town darkness, that it was a fiction; with *River's Edge* one has no such consolation. What made these kids this way? The film places a good deal of the blame – and convincingly so – on the values and life-styles that became popular during, and continue to be associated with, the Sixties. For the Sixties mentality, in one way or another, seems to be responsible for the character of the adults who play the most significant roles in these kids' lives . . . *River's Edge* is the most frightening American film to come along in many a year – and it is frightening not because it makes us believe in an implausible tale of horror, but because it opens our eyes to a horror story that happened in our midst, and that – in a very real sense – is all around us still.' *(Bruce Bawer, American Spectator)*

'It would be comforting to think of *River's Edge* as a kind of science fiction, but in fact it's based in part on an actual 1981 incident in Milpitas, California. This is the scariest vision of youth since the alarming Brazilian movie *Pixote*, but there one could point a finger at the appalling poverty that drove kids into crime. Hunter, working from a tough, authentic script by Neal Jimenez, isn't a finger pointer, and he doesn't approach the subject in the "problem-solving" style of TV sociology. *River's Edge* pitches the audience inside this nightmare world of affectless, middle-class kids and lets us watch them wallow their way through moral dilemmas they can only half articulate.' *(David Ansen, Newsweek)*

'May well be the year's most upsetting film. Not because of its violence . . . Not because its language is rough . . . Not because it's visually shocking . . . It is this total rejection of what makes up most teenage movies. They have excess of feelings. This one has none at all. It is about the great void inside the young . . . [It] is a cheerless but important work, a film that fishes for something under the dark surface of today's violent America. A moral backlash, maybe?' *(Alexander Walker, Evening Standard)*

ROAD HOUSE:

see ROADHOUSE.

ROAD, THE:

see LA STRADA.

ROAD WARRIOR, THE:

see MAD MAX II.

ROADHOUSE

CT: 8 AV: 4.10

(aka *Road House*)

1989 US 107 C ACTION/ADVENTURE/COMEDY

D Rowdy Herrington ✔
W David Lee Henry Hilary Henkin

Patrick Swayze ✔ Kelly Lynch Sam Elliott ✔
Ben Gazzara Marshall Teague Julie Michaels
Red West Sunshine Parker Jeff Healey

Dalton (Patrick Swayze), a highly paid, Mercedes-driving bouncer, is hired to bring order to a rough Missouri nightclub, and discovers that both club and town are under the heel of evil Brad Wesley (Ben Gazzara).

This modern western, produced by action-expert Joel Silver, was a disappointment at the box office and slammed by the critics, most of whom seemed not to notice that it was a send-up. It's certainly not for those who attend films for intellectual stimulation.

The parallels with old-fashioned westerns are conscious. 'Hear you're the new marshal in town,' comments Dalton's girlfriend, who is of course beautiful when she removes her glasses, and is even called Doc. 'This town is big enough for both of us,' blusters the baddie after the Magnificent One has demolished the last of his mean *hombres*.

The numerous brawls are so expertly directed by the aptly named Rowdy Herrington, that violence here takes on the quality of ballet. One might prefer to see such talent applied to something more worthwhile; but there is no denying that this is superbly crafted mass entertainment.

ANTI:

'Beware any movie directed by a person whose first name is Rowdy.' *(Bart Mills, Film Yearbook)*

'A star vehicle shackled by a couple of flat tires in the script department. Ill-conceived and unevenly executed.' *(Variety)*

'Ludicrous dialogue sinks this ultimate male fantasy . . . This far-fetched story is in deep trouble from the start . . . Both [writer and director] deserve a nod for reaching a new plateau in excessively graphic violence.' *(Nancy Kolomitz, Film Journal)*

'Walter Hill might have made something of this project, but in Rowdy's hands it is long on posing and short on poise.' *(Philip French, Observer)*

'Really a contemporary western – but . . . honestly [it] isn't fit to be in the same cinema as something like *Rio Bravo*, which I am scared to death some idiot will say it resembles. Even so, I have to say that it is watchably bad.' *(Derek Malcolm, Guardian)*

MIXED:

'A formula action picture with plenty of muscle and very little brain . . . Swayze, unlike many I could name, lends a certain presence and credibility to his role . . . while Kelly Lynch supplies some great legs.' *(James Cameron-Wilson, What's On in London)*

PRO:

'Very nearly a perfect exploitation movie.' *(MFB)*

'Swayze . . . moseys through this unbelievably violent eruption of a movie like Wyatt Earp at the OK Corral . . . Skilfully directed.' *(Sue Heal, Today)*

'Mindless entertainment of the highest order.' *(Nigel Floyd, Time Out)*

'I left the funniest movie I've seen all year smiling and swooning which is the way it should be.' *(Michele Kirsch, New Musical Express)*

'A western in everything but name . . . Connoisseurs of redneck culture will find much to amuse them.' *(Anne Billson, Sunday Correspondent)*

'In its blending of the lurid, the silly and the ambitious, it is pleasantly reminiscent of the populist Roger Corman-produced New World rural action movies (*Fighting Back, The Black Oak Conspiracy, Moving Violation*) of the 1970s . . . After looking dopey in his last few films (*Dirty Dancing, Tiger Warsaw*), Swayze is here in his element as an intellectual action man who has to overcome his trauma-induced inability to rip out a baddie's throat happily emerging in the finale as a complete man who can read poetry with one hand while he kills a redneck villain with the other. . . . By no means unsophisticated, widely misunderstood (of course) by the snotty critics, and cinematic to its last frame, *Road House* is where movies should be headed in the 1990s.' *(Kim Newman, Film Yearbook)*

ROARING TWENTIES, THE CT: 7 AV: 7.85

1939 US 106 BW DRAMA

D Raoul Walsh Anatole Litvak ☆
W Jerry Wald Richard Macaulay Robert Rossen from Mark Hellinger's story

James Cagney ☆ Humphrey Bogart ☆ Priscilla Lane Jeffrey Lynn Gladys George ☆ Frank McHugh Paul Kelly Elizabeth Risdon

A World War I veteran (James Cagney) returns to New York during Prohibition and turns to organized crime.

Raoul Walsh's big, bold, densely plotted gangster film is a classic, thanks mainly to James Cagney's star performance; but there's more sentiment than is good for a gangster movie, the characterization is superficial, and the message – that the Republicans are responsible for the anti-hero's life of crime – is more than a little tendentious. The first-rate supporting cast includes Humphrey Bogart and Gladys George though, so the hackneyed moments are well played and easy to tolerate. The picture ends with one of Hollywood's most memorable climaxes.

PRO:

'James Cagney is, as usual, excellent with his lightning movements and his machine-gun retorts . . . the personification of the self-reliant little tough. Gladys George is first-rate as the night-club hostess, the dialogue is well written, the period is neatly indicated by songs and dresses, and if you want shooting, here it is.' *(Dilys Powell)*

'Cagney . . . is always a superb and witty actor . . . Mr Bogart was, of course, magnificent – always a pleasure to see Mr Bogart pumped full of lead.' *(Graham Greene, Spectator)*

MIXED:

'[The] melodrama has taken on an annoying pretentiousness which neither the theme nor its treatment can justify . . . If it also seems to be good entertainment of its kind (and it is) . . . credit it to James Cagney in another of his assured portrayals.' *(Frank S. Nugent, New York Times)*

'[It] has failed to make the most of a good idea . . .

All very pleasant, but obviously the Twenties can yield a more original story than this.' *(Anthony Bower, New Statesman)*

ROBIN HOOD: *see* ADVENTURES OF ROBIN HOOD, THE (1991).

ROBIN HOOD: PRINCE OF THIEVES

CT: 7 AV: 5.31

1991 US 137/141 C ACTION/ADVENTURE/COMEDY

D Kevin Reynolds
W Pen Densham John Watson

Kevin Costner ● Morgan Freeman ✔
Alan Rickman ☆ Mary Elizabeth Mastrantonio ✔
Christian Slater Sean Connery Geraldine McEwan
Micheal McShane ● Brian Blessed
Michael Wincott Nick Brimble Soo Drouet
Daniel Peacock

A young aristocrat (Kevin Costner) returns from the Crusades to discover that things are not going well at home.

Comic, swashbuckling action-romance in the tradition of *Raiders of the Lost Ark*, and no less enjoyable (though sometimes needlessly violent). It was panned by American critics, who misunderstood it as a failed attempt at serious history – the slang and anachronisms are clearly deliberate.

As Robin, Kevin Costner is a shade wooden and doesn't bother to disguise his American accent, but he does show us a thoughtless young man gaining nobility of soul. As Azeem the Saracen (a new addition to the Merry Men), Morgan Freeman is more than a sop to black audiences: his ironic asides on England and Robin add to the fun. Mary Elizabeth Mastrantonio is an attractively feisty Maid Marian. The mixture of American and British accents is inoffensive, although Micheal McShane as Friar Tuck should have decided on one accent and stuck to it.

The film is stolen, nay plundered, by Alan Rickman's magnificently villainous Sheriff of Nottingham. 'No more merciful beheadings!' he snarls after one Hood outrage, 'and call off Christmas!' He has an equally uncomplicated attitude towards peasant girls. 'You, my room, 10.30 tonight!' he snaps, before turning to another. 'You, 10.45! And bring a friend!' At the climax, he is trying to rape Marian (in church, naturally) when Robin bursts in through the window. 'I can't do this with all that racket!' Rickman complains.

This is a cod-medieval romp on an epic scale – thrillingly photographed, humorously scripted, with the emphasis on sword, sorcery and spectacle. The set-pieces are confidently directed by Kevin Reynolds. The rumour is that Costner insisted on having much of Rickman's footage cut after previews showed the Sheriff was more popular than he was; it would be interesting to see the movie with that material restored. Even in its cut version, it was tremendous fun, and deserved to be a big hit. It received only one Oscar nomination, for Best Song.

ANTI:

'So politically correct that no one has any fun . . . Where's Errol Flynn when we need him?' *(Jami Bernard, New York Post)*

'Murky, unfocused, violent and depressing.' *(Roger Ebert)*

'A mess, a big, long, joyless reconstruction of the legend that comes out firmly for civil rights, feminism, religious freedom and economic opportunity for all . . . If you let a bunch of unskilled carpenters loose in Sherwood Forest, don't be surprised if you wind up with a load of kindling.' *(Vincent Canby, New York Times)*

'[Costner's performance is] one long embarrassment.' *(LA Daily News)*

'[Costner] suggests Dan Quayle with a sword.' *(Mike Clark, USA Today)*

'An abysmal, tedious, contemptible mishmash of ancient and modern.' *(Alexander Walker, Evening Standard)*

'As the Sheriff of Nottingham, Alan Rickman, swaggering through his scenes in sinister black, hissing one-liners and basically acting up a storm, is so theatrically vile that he seems to be in another movie altogether, and one can't help but think that it must be a more entertaining movie than *Robin Hood: Prince of Thieves*.' *(Baseline)*

PRO:

'I can't see what my American counterparts are whingeing about . . . It is indeed true that those of us who fondly remember nice, clean-shaven Richard Greene gambolling through the forest had never envisaged Robin Hood's accent tremulously wavering somewhere between Maidstone and Malibu . . . [but Costner] is lissom and fetching . . . and desperately sincere about feeding all those poor, ragged extras with stick-on-warts . . . [The film] is a jolly entertaining romp . . . Rickman turns what could have become a ho-hum swashing of buckles into a popcorn crunching delight.' *(Sue Heal, Today)*

'Ye olde legend gets a right olde hammering . . . [but] don't give a Friar Tuck about the savaging [it] got from the US critics. This is a really good Hood.' *(Peter Cox, Sun)*

'An old-fashioned, swashbuckling romp in the best traditions of Hollywood hokum.' *(Hugo Davenport, Daily Telegraph)*

'Forget the carping of US critics. Kevin Costner's Robin Hood is right on target as a roller-coaster ride of thrills and laughs.' *(Ian Lyness, Daily Express)*

'If Costner isn't dashing enough to fill Errol Flynn's tights, then Alan Rickman . . . certainly proves he is indeed an excellent Basil Rathbone for the 90's.' *(Kim Newman, Empire)*

'Pantomimes its way into our good graces with pithy action scenes and pretty scenery . . . There are also some important historical discoveries . . . Did you know that Will Scarlet was Robin Hood's long-lost brother? That the Sherwood Forest encampment was a picturesque series of tree houses and overhead walkways just like *The Return of the Jedi*? Or that when Robin Hood pleaded defencelessness after his . . . river-dunking by Little John, the no-nonsense Merry Men cried in unison, "Bollocks!" Cinema can be such an education.' *(Nigel Andrews, Financial Times)*

ROBOCOP CT: 8 AV: 6.38

1987 US 103 C SF/ACTION

D Paul Verhoeven ☆
W Edward Neumeier Michael Miner ✔

Peter Weller ✔ Nancy Allen Ronny Cox Kurtwood Smith Miguel Ferrer Robert DoQui Dan O'Herlihy Leeza Gibbons Ray Wise Felton Perry

Cyborg cop (Peter Weller) combats crime.

Very funny, very violent. Much as Clint Eastwood cleaned up the city in *Dirty Harry*, so does our cyborg hero – half John Wayne, half biscuit-tin – take revenge on the drug-barons who blew him apart as a human. Paul Verhoeven directs the action with panache, and the script is an often witty satire on contemporary values (or the lack of them). The conflict within RoboCop's character between the human and the mechanical is sensitively portrayed by Peter Weller, who creates echoes of other classic monsters from Frankenstein's to King Kong. The initially mixed critical reception reflected reviewers' unease that the audience was being invited to applaud violence. Box-office success and a growing cult reputation among the young have resulted in a major critical re-evaluation – although this did not prevent *RoboCop 2* from receiving much more damning reviews than the original.

ANTI:

'Essentially, it's just a hipper, more bam-bam version of the law-and-order hits of the Seventies . . . The picture keeps telling you that its brutishness is a terrific turn-on, and maybe it is if you're hooked on Wagnerian sci-fi comic books.' *(Pauline Kael)*

MIXED:

'This is no clean-cut morality tale from Gotham City, but a leering bloodbath, crude, contemptuous, and wildly entertaining.' *(Philip Strick, MFB)*

'It's a bleak world they inhabit, one where theres a thin line between lawfulness and lawlessness. Nearly everyone depicted here, anyway, exhibits a certain out-for-number-one mentality, the cop or crook.' *(Daily Variety)*

'While those whose tastes don't include the spectacle of large machines noisily blasting each other are not likely to be enticed by *RoboCop*, this shocked look at the urban future should engage and crank up action fans.' *(Duane Byrge, Hollywood Reporter)*

PRO:

'As tightly worked as a film can be, not a moment or line wasted.' *(Daily Variety)*

'The fine Dutch director Paul Verhoeven tells what could have been another high-tech assault picture with fresh visuals and a refreshing sense of humor, especially about big business.' *(Gene Siskel, Tribune Media Services)*

'Considering that he spends much of the movie hidden behind one kind of makeup device or another, Weller does an impressive job of creating sympathy for his character. He is more "human", indeed, when he is RoboCop than earlier in the movie, when he's an ordinary human being. His plight is appealing, and Nancy Allen is effective as the determined partner who wants to find out what really happened to him.' *(Roger Ebert)*

'A winsome and blood-soaked critique of corporate America.' *(Peter Keough, Boston Phoenix)*

'The greatest science fiction film since *Metropolis*.' *(Ken Russell)*

ROBOCOP 2 CT: 7 AV: 3.90

1990 US 117 C SF/ACTION

D Irvin Kershner ✔
W Frank Miller Walon Green

Peter Weller ✔ Nancy Allen Dan O'Herlihy Belinda Bauer Tom Noonan Gabriel Damon Willard Pugh Felton Perry

The boss of the company which manufactured RoboCop (Daniel O'Herlihy) commissions a deadly, psychopathic cyborg, RoboCop 2, to make him and the human members of the Detroit police force obsolete.

Cartoonish, violent but intelligently ironic view of a future where even muggers get mugged, conveyor-belt TV presenters present appalling news with comforting smiles, and the profit motive rules. The screenplay lacks the elegant, if simplistic, structure of the original; the human relationship between RoboCop and his policewoman partner has been partially sacrificed, in pursuit of action and thrills; and, inevitably, many who enjoyed the first film will find the sequel not as fresh.

But in some respects, its an improvement on the original: funnier, sharper, and more subversive. In the opening shots of the film, for instance, a commercial extols the virtues of an automobile attachment which fries any car thief, with the cheery promise that 'it won't even run down your battery'. Vigilante attitudes, condoned in the first movie, are here ridiculed; and this may account partly for the movie's disappointing box-office performance in the States. An audience which had come to applaud vigilante-style violence found itself invited to question it.

There are good jokes about the willingness of business to make profits out of an environment which it is itself helping to worsen. But liberals don't have things all their own way. In one of the funniest sequences, civic do-gooders argue that RoboCop should behave less aggressively, and re-programme him to act like a progressive primary-school teacher. As a result, he terrorizes someone who is guilty only of smoking, then wags his finger ineffectually at a vicious criminal.

There are echoes of Tom Wolfe's *Bonfire of the Vanities* in the film's beady attitude towards the black mayor of the city, forced by bankruptcy and managerial incompetence to countenance a pact with dope-dealers. When someone objects that his new pals are criminals, he reacts impatiently: 'Why do you have to label people?' Most critics failed to see the joke.

ANTI:

'The level of constant violence, with noisy sound effects, explosions and hundreds of thousands of rounds fired by automatic weaponry, is at first arresting but ultimately numbing and boring.' *(Variety)*

'If you like to stagger away from a film feeling numb and slightly sick, this one's for you.' *(Empire)*

'The action sequences are more violent than ever (I shut my eyes during one especially unpleasant brain surgery sequence, only to find the soundtrack even worse than the visuals).' *(Margaret Walters, Listener)*

'Repugnant sequel . . . [in which] they cut out the human drama . . . [It] is all machine, and it's all vile.' *(Peter Travers, Rolling Stone)*

'The movie's screenplay is a confusion of half-baked and unfinished ideas. The most distracting loose end is the suggestion that Murphy, the cop whose organic matter has been recycled into RoboCop, may still be human after all. He acts as if he is – driving past his house to look longingly at his wife – but then they reprogram him to acknowledge that he is only a machine. The way he says that makes us suspect that he's trying to fool his programmers, but then the whole plot thread is dropped and we never find out if he's really human or not.' *(Roger Ebert)*

MIXED:

'Weller repeats his definitely human robot role with his strutting walk (reminiscent I thought of Fred Astaire) and that sideways slide that really gives the RoboCop a true personality . . . As sequels go, this is rather an enjoyable one.' *(Michael Darvell, What's On in London)*

'Intermittent amusements [mostly] drowned out by its numbing violence and countless explosions.' *(Kevin Johnson, Independent)*

'Not a bad sequel. The script retains a sharp edge of humour and political bite and the special effects are spectacularly impressive. But like a reheated Chinese meal you enjoyed the night before, the same ingredients simply don't taste as good.' *(Sue Heal, Today)*

ROBOT MONSTER CT: 5 AV: 2.40

(aka *Monsters from the Moon*)

1953 US 63 BW SF/HORROR/SO BAD

D Philip Tucker ●
W Wyott Ordung ●

George Nader Claudia Barrett Selena Royle Gregory Moffett John Mylong

Gorilla in diving helmet destroys the population of Earth – except one family.

Endearingly incompetent science fiction which, though not intended to raise laughs, certainly does so. The special effects are hopeless (the only decent footage, of dinosaurs, is from *One Million Years B.C.*). When a robot costume proved too expensive, director Tucker had the less than inspired idea of dressing a man in a gorilla suit and a diving helmet with antennae. The one element of respectability is the score by Elmer Bernstein, but even that is overdramatic and adds to the air of pretentiousness.

The acting is lousy, and the dialogue hilariously inane, especially when the splendidly named screenwriter Ordung attempts to endow the Robot monster with pathos. 'To be like the hu-man!' exclaims the Monster. 'To laugh! Feel! Want! Why are these things not in the plan? I cannot, yet I must. How do you calculate that? At what point on the graph do "must" and "cannot" meet? Yet I must but I cannot!'

The movie was advertised as being in 3D, but turned out not to be. The director fell out with the producers to such an extent that they barred him from seeing the finished film. He proceeded to attempt suicide, but – perhaps inevitably – failed.

'Preposterous.' *(Picture Show)*

'Ancient and hackneyed. . . . Incredible. . . . Dialogue is strictly for the birds. The audience is asked to accept some rather far-fetched situations, even for a fantasy.' *(Hollywood Citizen-News)*

'Loaded with inconsistencies.' *(Hollywood Reporter)*

'Scripting and majority of performances rarely rise to a professional level . . . Of the principals, the less said the better. . . . Phil Tucker's direction (he also draws producer credit) is off.' *(Variety)*

'A crazy, mixed-up movie . . . The seven man cast has to keep pretty busy, especially the not-too-threatening robot, who resembles a gorilla from the neck down . . . Even children may be a little bored by it all. *(LA Times)*

'Incredibly bad . . . Ranks right up there with *Fire Maidens from Outer Space*; or should I have said "right down there".' *(Jerry Neely, Famous Monsters of Filmland)*

'The major attribute of *Robot Monster* is its earnest ludicrousness, or ludicrous earnestness ... Perhaps Tucker did the best he could. Two of his other films, *Dance Hall Racket* (1954) (starring Lenny Bruce, no less) and *The Cape Canaveral Monsters* (1960) are at least as bad as *Robot Monster*; the latter film is considerably worse.' *(Bill Warren, Keep Watching The Skies!)*

'Deficient in all departments, except sheer gall.' *(Alan Frank)*

ROCCO AND HIS BROTHERS CT: 6 AV: 7.11

(aka *Rocco e i Suoi Fratelli*)

1960 Italy/France 180 BW DRAMA/FOREIGN

D Luchino Visconti ☆
W Luchino Visconti Suso Cecchi D'Amico Vasco Pratolini

Alain Delon ● Renato Salvatori ☆ Annie Girardot ☆ Katina Paxinou Roger Hanin Paolo Stoppa Suzy Delair Claudia Cardinale Spiros Focas Rocco Vidolazzi

A country family moves to Milan and finds that the streets aren't paved with gold.

A run-of-the-mill, naturalistic plot is given operatic, over-the-top treatment by a job-lot of actors. Delon is embarrassingly awful; Renato Salvatori and Annie Girardot are excellent. The film won Visconti Best Director at Venice, but shouldn't he have insisted on some consistency of acting style? The exceptional cinematography is by Giuseppe Rotunno.

PRO:

'Milan comes alive on the screen: a masculine city. It is Visconti's birthplace and family home; he knows the cafés, the tall apartment blocks, the roads under snow or rain, the sightseers at the cathedral and the haunters of the back-street boxing-ring. Superficially the film is divided into five episodes, each with the name of one of the boys. But the episodes interlock to create an organic whole: the destiny of simple beings in a complex and corrupting society. It is also a hostile society. The Northerners despise what they regard as the fecklessness and ignorance of the Southerners: the emphasis on the division of Italy is important to Visconti, important in the film.' *(Dilys Powell)*

A fine Italian film to stand alongside the American classic *Grapes of Wrath* ... Delon ... is touchingly pliant and expressive, but it is Renato Salvatori ... [who gives a] raw and restless performance, overpowering and unforgettable.' *(Bosley Crowther)*

MIXED:

All the humanity and all the actuality of this film cannot save it from the romantic melodrama into which it is finally drawn by the violent needs of the story ... The weakness lies in the conception of Rocco himself ... a figure of romance, the dreamer from elsewhere, from fiction ... It is impossible to think of Delon as a tough and skilful boxer ... An imperfect film, but nevertheless one full of life and strength and humanity.' *(Roger Manvell, F & F)*

'Compelling though the subject matter is, the sheer weight of its three-hour duration implies a more profound investigation of relationships and milieu than is finally the case.' *(Derek Prouse, S & S Winter '61)*

'Begins satisfactorily in a vein that was, however, more or less exhausted by 1960; but as it goes on, it becomes more and more the usual Viscontian strident pseudoprofundity devoid of human authenticity and artistic vision.' *(John Simon, 1970)*

ANTI:

'Delon's interpretation is totally unconvincing – a dreamy-eyed mediator, a puppy-fat masochist all silent suffering, guilt complexes and Ganymedean charm.' *(MFB)*

'Has no integrity – artistic or otherwise. Indeed, if this is all Visconti ... can do at this stage of his career he is at the end of his tether. The "script" ... is a jumble of private preconceptions, misconceptions, delusions, rationalisations, and public deceptions ... Almost every sequence runs on too long ... The acting is only so-so ... Delon ... is an inexpressive pretty-boy whose chief appeal will be to the sex perverts who laud Visconti.' *(Henry Hart, Films in Review)*

'Basically soap opera.' *(Shipman)*

ROCKET TO THE MOON: *see* CAT WOMEN OF THE MOON.

ROCKY AAW CT: 8 AV: 8.00

1976 US 119 C DRAMA/ACTION/ROMANCE

D John G. Avildsen ☆ AAW
W Sylvester Stallone AAN

Sylvester Stallone ☆ AAN Burgess Meredith ☆ AAN Talia Shire ☆ AAN Burt Young ☆ AAN Carl Weathers Thayer David

A no-hoper boxer from Philadelphia (Sylvester Stallone) gets a crack at the world title.

A lot of critics patronized this old-fashioned boxing movie, which might have hailed from the Depression era, but was here updated to the depressing 1970s. It's crude and clichéd at times, but the sincerity of the performances, zest of Avildsen's direction and message of hope for the little guy against the system made this a box-office winner and created a superstar.

ANTI:

'I wish I could summon up a little more enthusiasm

for [the film which] . . . has been directed by Avildsen with the staccato power of a boxer hitting a punch-bag . . . I am glad I didn't pay for my ring-side seat.' *(Felix Barker, Evening News)*

'Generally dressed in a traditional thuggish zoot-suit, [Stallone] has been at pains not to look too animated, lest he should inadvertently normalise his big asset: a face that would look well upon a three-toed sloth . . . The film . . . is just a publicity man's extension of the face . . . Improbable Hulk Writes Movie! Amazing Feat of Intellectual Concentration by Hulk! . . . It's as though Frankenstein's creation . . . had turned up at the studios with a new monster-script of his own under his arm.' *(Russell Davies, Observer)*

MIXED:

'[Of Talia Shire] She's a real actress, genuinely touching and funny as an incipient spinster who comes late to sexual life. She's so good, in fact, that she almost gives weight to Mr Stallone's performance, which is the large hole in the center of the film.' *(New York Times)*

'The film has its share of faults. Most of Stallone's characters, for example, are taken straight out of stock . . . But the film moves along too quickly and surefootedly to stumble over such defects . . . and Avildsen's direction preserves exactly the right balance between fact and fable.' *(Nigel Andrews, Financial Times)*

'Based on a number of well-worn clichés, but clichés which are neatly turned on their head and invested with a sly humour which gives them a new twist . . . The urban decay and dereliction is splendidly caught by the stark photography.' *(Virginia Dignam, Morning Star)*

'Stallone . . . is repulsive one moment, noble the next. He's amazing to watch: there's a bull-necked energy in him, smouldering, and in his deep caveman's voice he gives the most surprising, sharp, fresh shadings to his lines. The picture is poorly made, yet its naive, emotional shamelessness is funny and engaging.' *(Pauline Kael)*

PRO:

'A personal triumph for Sylvester Stallone . . . *Rocky* is championship material.' *(Arthur Thirkell, Daily Mirror)*

'A lovely, welcome new kind of film.' *(Kenneth Baily, Sunday People)*

'A pugnacious, charming, grimy, beautiful fairy tale . . . Rocky is the most likeable and unaggressive of punks, and, certainly, an original. Stallone has imagined him with intense, bristling love, and plays him with relaxed affection.' *(John Simon)*

'What makes the movie extraordinary is that it doesn't try to surprise us with an original plot, with twists and complications; it wants to involve us on an elemental, a sometimes savage, level. It's about heroism and realizing your potential, about taking your best shot and sticking by your girl. It sounds not only clichéd but corny – and yet it's not, not a bit, because it really does work on those levels. It involves us emotionally, it makes us commit ourselves: we find, maybe to our surprise after remaining detached during so many movies, that this time we care.' *(Roger Ebert)*

ROCKY HORROR PICTURE SHOW, THE

CT: 5 AV: 5.17

1975 GB 95 (US)/105 (GB) C MUSICAL/ COMEDY/SF

D Jim Sharman
W Jim Sharman Richard O'Brien from O'Brien's musical play

Tim Curry ☆ Susan Sarandon Barry Bostwick Richard O'Brien Patricia Quinn Nell Campbell Charles Gray ☆ Jonathan Adams Peter Hinwood Meatloaf

Straights Brad (Barry Bostwick) and Janet (Susan Sarandon) have the misfortune of having their car break down in Transylvania, close to the castle of notorious transexual Frank N. Furter (Tim Curry).

The camp cult musical. It survived poor reviews and commercial failure to become a hugely profitable cult success, with midnight movie fans indulging in audience participation throughout. Tim Curry and Charles Gray are great fun, but the whole film is very hit-and-miss and disappointingly lacking in genuine wit. There was a truly pathetic sequel, *Shock Treatment* (1982).

PRO:

'There's an underlying quality of tenderness and even innocence in this loving send-up . . . Moves fast and looks slick. Performances are amusing.' *(Kevin Thomas, LA Times)*

'A quite wonderful mixture of spoof horror and sci-fi.' *(Empire)*

MIXED:

'The whole thing about *Rocky Horror* was that the movie played as a backdrop to the stage show by the fans. As for the movie itself, it's no better than it ever was. Viewed on video simply as a movie, without the midnight sideshow, it's cheerful and silly, and kind of sweet, and forgettable.' *(Roger Ebert)*

ANTI:

'Not a very good film, maybe; but the sort of film it sets out to be, combining *Top of the Pops* visuals, Sixties camp, and loose parody of the B-picture horror-movie tradition . . . It needed a lot more poise and style in conception . . . The flabbiness of camp could have acquired a stiffening of satire.' *(David Robinson, The Times)*

'Most damagingly misconceived is the opening

sequence, showing the wedding that inspires Brad and Janet to get engaged, where the crudely signalled hints of parody and American Gothic are both insulting in their obviousness and redundant in the context of what follows. What does follow is a self-consciously slick rendition of the original material, shorn of the song reprises, staged and performed with evident delight in having larger and more lavish sets to move around in.' *(Tony Rayns, MFB)*

'Most of the jokes that might have seemed jolly fun on stage now appear obvious and even flat. The sparkle's gone.' *(Variety)*

ROMA, CITTÀ APERTA: *see* OPEN CITY

ROMAN HOLIDAY AAN CT: 6 AV: 8.15

1953 US 118 BW COMEDY/ROMANCE

D William Wyler ☆ AAN
W Ian McLellan Hunter John Dighton ☆ AAN from McLellan Hunter's story AAW

Gregory Peck ☆ Audrey Hepburn ☆ AAW
Eddie Albert ☆ AAN Hartley Power Harcourt Williams

A European princess (Audrey Hepburn) on an official tour of Rome falls in love with an American reporter (Gregory Peck).

Nowadays, this variation on the Cinderella story may look old-fashioned, ponderous and too much like a travelogue; but in the 1950s it seemed fresh and enchanting, and made the world fall in love with Audrey Hepburn. Peck is less treelike than usual, and turns in one of his most charming performances. Wyler's direction lacks the light touch or the satirical imagination which might have made this a classic, but it's still modestly entertaining. Edith Head won an Academy Award for her costumes; also nominated were Franz Planer and Henri Alekan (photography), Robert Swink (editing) and Hal Pereira and Walter Tyler (art direction).

ANTI:

'While Capra, or in a different way Lubitsch, could have made something wholly enjoyable from it, it would seem that Wyler's technique is now too ponderously inflexible for such lightweight material.' *(MFB)*

'The film moves like a great, smooth, polished, crushing machine, and towards the end, with the farewell scenes of Bradley and the Princess bled to the last reaction shot, it becomes positively oppressive . . . One cannot help feeling that a butterfly has, unintentionally, been broken on the wheel.' *(BFI Bulletin, 1953)*

PRO:

'The part of the princess is a long one, but not rich in acting opportunities . . . The action becoming at times quite extraordinarily slow. But though the quality of the dialogue often fails Miss Hepburn, the camera never does.' *(Daily Telegraph)*

'A delightful fairy story, with the bells of topicality tinkling in a number of the scenes . . . Hepburn . . . is a joy in every scene. Gregory Peck is good too – but who cares about him with Miss Hepburn around?' *(Leonard Mosley, Daily Express)*

'An enchanting fantasy.' *(Paul Dehn, Sunday Chronicle)*

'Most of the world's filmgoers met Audrey Hepburn just about when Peck did in film, the men in the audience tumbling, the women delegating . . . It was the lusciousness of Hepburn's voice and speech, in addition to the accent itself, in addition to the girlish-impish charm of the face, that ravished us.' *(Stanley Kauffmann)*

ROME – OPEN CITY: *see* OPEN CITY.

ROMUALD & JULIETTE CT: 9 AV: 6.43

(aka *Mama There's a Man in Your Bed; Romuald et Juliette*)

1989 France 107/111 C COMEDY/ROMANCE/ FOREIGN

D Coline Serreau ☆
W Coline Serreau ☆

Daniel Auteuil ☆ Firmine Richard ☆ Pierre Vernier ☆ Maxine Leroux Gilles Privat Muriel Combeau Catherine Salviat Sambou Tati

A rich, married white boss (Daniel Auteuil) loses his wife and job, but falls in love with the black, much-divorced office cleaner (Firmine Richard).

A joyful romantic comedy. The sharp social distinctions between the two central characters are delineated with complete realism, but great good humour. Miss Richard is wonderfully natural in her first screen role, and Auteuil proves himself a master of light comic acting. The obvious racist pitfalls are neatly avoided by director Coline Serreau, whose screenplay is notable for images which are as witty as its words.

ANTI:

'There is much droll detail, but the final half hour is pure Hollywood-ish wish fulfilment . . . and though [the film] has all the audience-pleasing qualifications to be ripe for a similar remake [to Serreau's previous film, *Three Men and a Cradle*], it is less likely that the bigwigs will bite this time round; after all these years, miscegenation is still not considered kosher in mainstream movieland.' *(Anne Billson, Sunday Correspondent)*

'The courtship is utterly unbelievable, leaving the viewer awash in sugar-coated circumstances.' *(Scheuer)*

PRO:

'Firmine Richard . . . shows herself in her first acting

role a remarkable natural star.' *(David Robinson, The Times)*

'Funny, charming and kind.' *(Victoria Mather, Daily Telegraph)*

'A fairy tale? Without a doubt. But under Serreau's magic wand – it shoos away the harsher realities – Auteuil and Richard make an improbable attraction an irresistibly witty proposition.' *(Rolling Stone)*

'As comic as it is serious . . . Firmine Richard is sublime . . . Auteuil is completely convincing.' *(Jeff Sawtell, Morning Star)*

'A wickedly funny, cogent love story that reverberates with intrigue and cross-class culture shock . . . A wonderful film, full of richly played comic performances . . . This one is a must.' *(Sue Heal, Today)*

RONDE, LA: see LA RONDE

ROOM AT THE TOP AAN CT: 6 AV: 8.58

1958 GB 117 BW DRAMA

D Jack Clayton ☆ AAN
W Neil Paterson ☆ AAW from John Braine's novel

Laurence Harvey ☆ AAN Simone Signoret ☆ AAW Heather Sears ✓ Donald Wolfit Ambrosine Philpotts Donald Houston Raymond Huntley John Westbrook Allan Cuthbertson Hermione Baddeley ☆ AAN Mary Peach

Long before the days of Yuppies, Joe Lampton (Laurence Harvey) shows how to make it to the top, if you aren't fussy about morality and old-fashioned things like that.

Jack Clayton's landmark film of the 50s seemed terribly daring about sex when it was first released, though that aspect of it has dated. The film improves upon John Braine's novel, thanks to Neil Paterson's intelligent screenplay and Freddie Francis's cinematography, which caught more than any other picture of its period the claustrophobia of a northern provincial town. Simone Signoret won an Academy Award for her moving portrayal of Harvey's older woman. There was an inferior sequel, *Life at the Top* (1965), also starring Laurence Harvey.

MIXED:

'Now and again the overbearingness of the moneyed has a note of caricature; but for the rest one is smoothly made to understand the young accountant's touchiness and his fox-gnaw scheming. Ralph Brinton's sets – the grandiose mansion, the borrowed love-nest with its upright piano and its flossy theatrical photographs – beautifully stress social barriers; and I must not overlook the camerawork, directed by Freddie Francis, and the ferocity of its stare at the scabrous alleys of the town from which Joe Lampton has managed to escape. Subtlety, in fact, is married with an emotional directness not often found in a British film.' *(Dilys Powell)*

'Jack Clayton's first major assignment . . . fell uneasily between an uncompromising exposure of corruption in the relations between Lampton and the rich, cultureless society he aspires to join and a certain novelettishness belonging to an older style in British films . . . Laurence Harvey, Simone Signoret and Heather Sears gave exceptionally good performances.' *(Roger Manvell, New Cinema in Britain, 1969)*

PRO:

'Brilliantly courageous and startlingly outspoken . . . Some of the best acting all round I have seen for a long time.' *(Ivon Adams, Star)*

'The film is much better than the novel . . . More than that, it is one of the bravest and best British films in years . . . directed with glittering honesty . . . and full of fine acting performances.' *(Derek Monsey, Sunday Express)*

'It has strength. It has artistry. It is not imitation-American . . . There is still room at the top for Britain's best.' *(Star)*

'A very pertinent piece of social commentary . . . explains what those Angry Young Men . . . are angry about . . . While I'm throwing bouquets around I should aim one at Mr. Clayton. He's quite a man to have behind a camera.' *(John McCarten, New Yorker)*

'A beautifully constructed, artistically fine picture.' *(New York Herald Tribune)*

'It may be basically cheerless and sombre, but it has a strikingly effective view.' *(New York Times)*

'A well-made drama, serious of theme and development.' *(New York Journal American)*

'A drama of human drives and torments told with maturity and precision.' *(Stanley Kauffmann)*

ROOM WITH A VIEW, A AAN CT: 7 AV: 7.93

1985 GB 115 C DRAMA

D James Ivory ☆ AAN
W Ruth Prawer Jhabvala ☆ AAW from E.M. Forster's novel

Maggie Smith ☆ AAN Denholm Elliott ☆ AAN Helena Bonham Carter Julian Sands Daniel Day-Lewis ☆ Simon Callow Judi Dench ☆ Rosemary Leach ☆ Rupert Graves

An Edwardian young lady (Helena Bonham-Carter) broadens her horizons and loses some inhibitions while travelling in Italy.

Immaculate film of E.M. Forster's novel, a bit slow but not without humour, and deservedly one of Merchant-Ivory's biggest successes. Jenny Beavan and John Bright won Oscars for their costumes, as did Gianna Quaranta and Brian Ackland-Snow for their production design. Tony Pierce-Roberts was Oscar-nominated for his lovely cinematography.

MIXED:

'What we have . . . is a long, slow, lingering, lazy, dreamy look at a slice of Victorian life so vivid and lovely you can smell the roses and feel the rain. But alas, alack and ho hum, very little else . . . It is an earnest, honest and loving examination . . . which will delight a lot of people and bore the pantaloons off the rest.' *(William Marshall, Daily Mirror)*

'The film's plot is a simple and fairly predictable one but there are many rewards along the way . . . Sumptuous to look at.' *(Virginia Dignam, Morning Star)*

'It is a spry and cultured, but profoundly conventional piece of film-making – of the kind one is more used to seeing on television.' *(Alan Hollinghurst, Times Literary Supplement)*

'Bonham Carter lacks the carriage and presence of a trained actress, and Sands, though likeable, is playing Forster's flimsy – almost abstract – dream of a natural, uninhibited lover, and is rather vague. But the movie is well paced, and it never loses its hold on a viewer's affections, because it's so thoroughly inhabited. The actors who circulate around the heroine create a whirring atmosphere – a comic hum . . . Full of allusions to art and literature, the movie is more than a little precious, but it's a piece of charming foolishness.' *(Pauline Kael)*

PRO:

'Quality-starved filmgoers will welcome it.' *(Variety)*

'If you relish gentle humour arising from the interplay of bygone social attitudes, you will undoubtedly be much entertained by the [Merchant-Ivory] team's brilliant adaptation . . . The performances are totally delightful and never teeter into caricature and James Ivory directs . . . with warmth and a sense of fun.' *(Ian Christie, Daily Express)*

'Delightful . . . Much ado about what strikes us as nothing, turned into delicious, colourful fare begging to be wolfed at a sitting . . . I want to see it again just for Denholm Elliott's performance.' *(Shaun Usher, Daily Mail)*

'Colour, music and setting admirably enhance the spirited playing, well serving a timeless original.' *(Phillip Bergson, What's On in London)*

ROSEMARY'S BABY   CT: 8 AV: 8.13

1968 US 137 C HORROR

D Roman Polanski ☆
W Roman Polanski AAN from Ira Levin's thriller ☆

Mia Farrow ☆ John Cassavetes ☆ Ruth Gordon ☆ AAW Sidney Blackmer Maurice Evans Ralph Bellamy Angela Dorian Patsy Kelly Elisha Cook Jr Charles Grodin

A young woman (Mia Farrow) is impregnated by the Devil.

Effective, suspense-filled horror film about demonic possession. Some critics found it cold and sadistic, but Mia Farrow arouses the audience's pity as the pregnant innocent. Polanski expertly creates a feeling of unease (helped by excellent performances) and wisely hints at horrors too horrible to show. His one major error of taste is the scene where we see Farrow raped by the Devil.

ANTI:

'It may not be for the very young, and pregnant women should see it at their own risk.' *(Motion Picture Herald)*

'The film is very proficient, but all the same, what's it for? If it weren't made by Polanski (*Knife in the Water, Cul-de-Sac,* and *Repulsion*), I suppose one mightn't ask the question. A horror film isn't for anything; it's just something to scare yourself with. The trouble is that *Rosemary's Baby* doesn't really scare you much.' *(Penelope Gilliatt)*

'Whoever directed this picture must have been the brilliant Polanski's dopey Doppelganger, if not indeed his Hollywood stand-in . . . The lone authentic bit of horror in the film is Ruth Gordon's performance: a sort of self-serving, nonstop tuneless singsong issuing from a decrepit butterfly that thinks itself the Empress Theodora, it is easily one of the most offensive spectacles of any year and does make *Rosemary's Baby*, whenever it is on view, perhaps not horrifying but certainly disgusting.' *(John Simon)*

'If it lacks some of the book's suspense, put that down to a rasping performance by Ruth Gordon, who plays all parts exactly the same . . . As the witch on the case, she couldn't frighten a cat.' *(Esquire)*

MIXED:

'Glossy schlock about satanists and the devil's child is not as scary as it is uncomfortable to watch. It becomes upsetting seeing Farrow not only look pale due to her unusual pregnancy but feel confused and constantly tormented . . . A big hit that is on some levels quite enjoyable – yet it's really an ugly film.' *(Danny Peary)*

'Conspicuously well made. But it is insufferably silly.' *(Dilys Powell)*

'A pleasant surprise [is] the very real acting ability of Mia Farrow . . . The film's most memorable performance though is turned in by veteran Ruth Gordon . . . dispensing that old Black Magic she knows so well in a voice that sounds like a crow with a cold.' *(Time)*

'The section of *Rosemary's Baby* that's been most publicly controversial – her nightmare of being raped by Satan, which the censor has unjustifiably cut – is actually its least successful . . . The sharpest bit of casting is Mia Farrow. Her curious physical deficiencies are turned into advantages by Polanski who makes the thin, ravaged, angular, listless, anorexia-like appearance that the character presents . . . into a pathetic counterpoint to the supernatural powers operating on her.' *(Alexander Walker, Evening Standard)*

PRO:

'Excellent . . . The film holds attention without explicit violence or gore.' *(Variety)*

'Tension is sustained to a degree surpassing Alfred Hitchcock at his best.' *(Daily Telegraph)*

'Genuinely funny, yet it's also scary, especially for young women: it plays on their paranoid vulnerabilities. The queasy and the grisly are mixed with its entertaining hipness. (It's probably more fun for women who are past their childbearing years.)' *(Pauline Kael)*

'Ira Levin created *Rosemary's Baby* . . . But it was Polanski who endowed it with plastic elegance, visual shape, vocal timing, frightening camera movement and the full acting benefit of high definition performance . . . Levin is the creator and Polanski the artist.' *(Kenneth Tynan, Observer)*

'By far [Polanski's] most satisfying film so far, precisely because it is stylistically polished, restrained and pretty conventional, and because it is a glossy, superficially psychological horror thriller with no noticeable pretensions to be taken as anything more.' *(John Russell Taylor, The Times)*

'Like all good horror films [it] is set in a completely realistic and tangibly normal environment.' *(Sean Brestin, Irish News)*

ROXANNE

CT: 5 AV: 7.00

1987 US 107 C COMEDY/ROMANCE

D Fred Schepisi
W Steve Martin

Steve Martin ☆ Daryl Hannah Rick Rossovich Shelley Duvall John Kapelos Fred Willard Max Alexander Michael J. Pollard Damon Wayans

Man with big nose (Steve Martin) can't summon up the courage to woo beautiful girl (Daryl Hannah).

This variation on *Cyrano de Bergerac* has many sweet and funny moments, and a winning performance from Steve Martin; but Daryl Hannah is anodyne, and the movie seems to go on forever.

PRO:

'One of the most beautiful, elating romantic comedies ever made in this country. It makes you feel mysteriously, unreasonably happy, as if you were watching colors being added to a sunset. The glow from this film stays with you; it has a radiance like no other movie.' *(Peter Rainer, LA Herald Examiner)*

'Comedic acting this good is at least – if not more – difficult than the latest Method interior voyage.' *(Ian Penman, The Face)*

'The main joy is in the old-fashioned sense of caring what becomes of the characters. It's that and the daring ingenuity of the idea, which make this one of the most enjoyable movies I've seen this year . . . By a nose, you might say.' *(Tom Hutchinson, Mail on Sunday)*

'Martin's sense of humour . . . scorns the cheap option of cynicism and is instead life-enhancing and romancing. Marvellous stuff. Go seek it out.' *(Richard Barkley, Sunday Express)*

'The film contains a host of sparkling one-liners, neatly conceived minor characters, sustained comic sequences, dextrous sight gags and bravura routines.' *(Kim Newman, New Musical Express)*

'[Martin] is one of the few American comics who can make body-language funny . . . American comedy is a rarity; an intelligent one, almost unique.' *(Alexander Walker, Evening Standard)*

MIXED:

Schepisi . . . does a professional job of creating a breezy atmosphere, but in the end it's hopelessly sappy stuff.' *(Variety)*

'Martin . . . wants it all: laughs, tears, low comedy, uplift. It doesn't quite happen, partly because the movie begs for poignance like an orphaned puppy, partly because modern plastic surgery makes the plot anachronistic, partly because, even with his cyranose, CD is a darned sight more attractive than his beefy rival. Aaaahh, who cares, as long as Steve Martin gets a chance to strut his physical grace, wrap his mouth around clever dialogue . . . He's so good; his movies will get even better.' *(Richard Corliss, Time)*

'More often amusing than it is hilarious, but it is consistently good-natured and charming; though Daryl Hannah brings less substance to the title role than one might hope (this is another example of a director trying to make an actress look intelligent by putting glasses on her), Steve Martin is wonderfully impressive in a role that requires him to be at once heroic and pathetic, romantic and ridiculous; he handles intimate dialogue, comic patter, and out-and-out slapstick with equal grace and self-possession . . . But what is most special about *Roxanne* is its respect for intelligence, sensitivity, and articulateness. In an era when American movie comedies tend to present us with heroes who are "common men" with a vengeance (ie, inarticulate lunkheads) and with villains whose villainy is defined by their erudition and wit, it is very gratifying to see a movie in which the hero wins his beloved's heart because he can express himself intelligently.' *(Bruce Bawer, American Spectator)*

RUBY GENTRY CT: 5 AV: 4.67

1952 US 82 BW DRAMA/ROMANCE/SO BAD

D King Vidor
W Sylvia Richards ●

Jennifer Jones ● Charlton Heston ● Karl Malden Josephine Hutchinson Tom Tully Bernard Phillips

Tomboy (Jennifer Jones) wreaks emotional and other forms of havoc in the tidewater country of North Carolina.

Unintentionally humorous melodrama, with dire dialogue and two leading actors who are thoroughly miscast.

PRO:

'Jennifer Jones gives a tempestuous performance.' *(Jewish Chronicle)*

'A bold, adult drama laying heavy stress on sex.' *(Variety)*

MIXED:

'All this is supposed to be . . . another *Duel in the Sun*. If that was Lust in the Dust, then this is Sex in the Swamps.' *(Campbell Dixon, Daily Telegraph)*

'To some extent [Vidor] redeems this cheap and rowdy novelette by infusing it with a genuine swampy atmosphere.' *(Peter Parrish, Tribune)*

ANTI:

'There is a quality of tedium that bores from within so to speak, and that quality is evident in abundance and with the persistence of a dentist's drill in this long, draggy, gloomy drama . . . The photography is darkly grim and the acting's not much better.' *(Jesse Zunser, Cue)*

'A good illustration of the fatal American inability to take certain things for granted and to refrain from making a fantastic fuss about them. The American film cannot accept that, in general, it is a good thing for people to marry into their own class and the way it carries on about democracy over this simple proposition has to be seen to be believed.' *(The Times)*

'Quintessential later Vidor: extravagant, weird, monstrous, destructive, as the earlier Vidor was simple, appealing and affirmative. Perhaps no other modern director of note has gone off the rails quite so spectacularly.' *(Gavin Lambert, MFB)*

'Pure lard.' *(Judith Crist)*

'You'll never forget the spectacle of [Jennifer] Jones playing yet another sexy hellcat for Vidor who, after directing her hilariously bad performance in *Duel in the Sun*, really should have known better.' *(Margulies & Rebello)*

'Vidor said he thought Jennifer Jones "very good" in this blazing melodrama, a verdict which must seem bizarre to anyone unfortunate enough to see it . . . Jones and Heston are not the players to suggest uncontrollable passion.' *(Shipman)*

RUE CASES NÈGRES CT: 6 AV: 7.44

(aka *Sugar Cane Alley; Black Shack Alley*)

1983 France 106 C DRAMA/FOREIGN

D Euzhan Palcy ☆
W Euzhan Palcy

Garry Cadenat ☆ Darling Legitimus ☆ Douta Seck Joby Bernabé Francisco Charles Marie-Jo Descas

In Martinique during the 1930s, a woman (Darling Legitimus) sacrifices her life through overwork to ensure that her orphan grandson (Garry Cadenat) has a proper education and can escape the sugar-cane plantation.

Female self-sacrifice is a familiar theme in the movies, but seldom has it been portrayed more movingly than here. The picture is not all gloom and doom by any means; there are many touches of humour. Darling Legitimus won Best Actress at the Venice Film Festival.

'Palcy has created a true little world crawling with life and emotion which excuses her occasional clumsiness.' *(Michel Mardore, Le Nouvel Observateur)*

'Sheerly enjoyable, wonderfully natural.' *(Derek Malcolm, Guardian)*

'With an exceptional child actor . . . and a wonderful old professional . . . Palcy has made a film of infectious verve and charm . . . It's a tough and touching film, and the début of a considerable artist.' *(David Robinson, The Times)*

'Bewitching.' *(Nigel Andrews, Financial Times)*

'Telling a charming success story with barely a trace of excess sentiment is not easy, yet it has been achieved superbly by Euzhan Palcy.' *(Ms London)*

'An unusually assured directorial début . . . the film's sense of time and place is impeccable.' *(William Parente, Scotsman)*

'It captures a youngster's confusing passage into adulthood, his dawning awareness of the world that stretches beyond his poor home village. There's the humiliation of life under the overseer's whip, but there's also the discovery of surprising joys by resilient people.' *(Henry Sheehan)*

RUGGLES OF RED GAP AAN CT: 5 AV: 7.89

1935 US 90 BW COMEDY/WESTERN

D Leo McCarey
W Walter de Leon Harlan Thompson Humphrey Pearson from Harry Leon Wilson's novel

Charles Laughton ☆ Mary Boland ☆ Charles Ruggles ☆, ZaSu Pitts ☆ Roland Young ☆ Leila Hyams James Burke Maude Eburne Lucien Littlefield

An Englishman (Roland Young) loses his deferential valet (Charles Laughton) in a poker game to a rich American couple (Mary Boland and Charles Ruggles), who take him to America. Here, he discovers that all men are created equal.

Fish-out-of-water comedy which is beautifully acted, but oozes sentiment and American self-congratulation in a most unbecoming manner.

PRO:

'The most heart-warming comedy of the season. Ruggles's astonishment and frequent consternation when faced with the rough-and-ready gusto of the 1908 frontier is delightful comedy, but Ruggles's discovery of the democratic spirit, and his development of his own manhood, make for really moving and poignant drama.' *('Argus', Literary Digest)*

'Highly amusing comedy . . . Ernest Torrance and Edward Horton provide the bulk of the many laughs.' *(Photoplay)*

'Fast and furiously funny.' *(Variety)*

ANTI:

'The protracted scenes of clowning in the French capital are quite excruciatingly dull . . . The story I propose to dismiss as one of the worst ever devised, all that part of it in which Ruggles visits America having no relation to an English butler visiting America, and being like nothing on earth except the delirium of a small boy with a sharp attack of influenza and believing himself at the pictures.' *(James Agate, Tatler)*

'A famous comedy which seemed hilarious at the time but can now be seen as mostly composed of flat spots.' *(Halliwell)*

RULES OF THE GAME, THE CT: 8 AV: 9.41

(aka *La Règle du Jeu*)

1939 France 85/113 BW COMEDY/ROMANCE/FOREIGN

D Jean Renoir ☆
W Jean Renoir Carl Koch

Marcel Dalio ☆ Nora Gregor Jean Renoir ✔
Mila Parély Julien Carette Gaston Modot
Roland Toutain Paulette Dubost

A weekend shooting party at a country chateau degenerates into fights, squabbles and amorous intrigues

Half-farcical, half-serious portrait of a decadent aristocracy and a disunited France on the brink of war. The political overtones ensured that it was banned in France before the war as 'too demoralizing', then refused release by Vichy and German authorities. Since it became available in the 50s, international critics have often voted it one of the best films of all time.

Technically, it is remarkable for containing only 337 shots; cameraman Jean Bachelet uses deep focus and a moving camera to transport us from one group of characters to another. Some of the set-pieces, especially the rabbit hunt, are masterly.

Most of all, though, it is notable for its variations in tone, starting off as sunny farce and ending as bleak tragedy. The fact that the actors carry this off is little short of miraculous.

'During the shooting of the film I was torn between my desire to make a comedy of it and the wish to tell a tragic story. The result of this ambivalence was the film as it is.' *(Jean Renoir)*

ANTI:

'An extremely dull description of a weekend in the country . . . Lord knows what M. Renoir had in mind.' *(John McCarten, New Yorker, 1950, first US release)*

'Renoir has combined too many things – the comedy of manners . . . social satire; farce and melodrama . . . Once again [he] has been wanting in self-criticism and the general effect is of a low-spirited charade ending off-key in tragedy.' *(Campbell Dixon, Daily Telegraph, 1951, first British release)*

MIXED:

'A clever but confusing picture . . . by Renoir who . . . became intoxicated with his freedom and just followed his particular whimsy of the day . . . I am not sure it is a successful venture but at any rate it is interesting, original and mad, which in these sombre days, is not a bad thing to be.' *(Virginia Graham, Evening Standard)*

PRO:

'It has stood the years very well indeed, turning from a smart contemporary satire into something near a social document . . . It remains one of Renoir's best films and one of the most devastating commentaries on a society to come from any country.' *(Frank Hauser, Tribune)*

'A witty and sardonic analysis of an irresponsible, though possibly attractive, section of French society . . . [Renoir] is firmly and intellectually satirical to the end, and in an admirably Gallic fashion.' *(Time & Tide)*

'One of the most remarkable French films ever made . . . an undoubted masterpiece.' *(Richard Winnington, News Chronicle)*

'Outwardly this is the story of a house party that comes to an ironic denouement; on another level, it is a tragicomic view of a world in flux, of changing morality and social standards, where heroic- and unheroic-notions of honor are out of date and where those who don't stick to the rules upset the game.' *(Judith Crist)*

'The film's whiff of war is conveyed in a now classic scene in which the aristocrats slaughter birds and rabbits during a shoot – presaging the film's climactic incident of poignantly absurd human sacrifice. Renoir later said he wanted a certain disorder, wanted to tell a light story about a world dancing on a volcano. His indirection, his refusal to become explicit, is the reason the film remains so hauntingly resonant.' *(Jay Carr)*

'Not only a wonderful piece of film-making, not only a great work of humanism and social comedy in a perfect rococo frame, but also an act of historical testimony.' *(Penelope Gilliatt)*

RYAN'S DAUGHTER CT: 5 AV: 5.33

1970 GB 206 C DRAMA/ROMANCE/EPIC

D David Lean
W Robert Bolt

Sarah Miles AAN Robert Mitchum Trevor Howard ☆ John Mills ☆ AAW Christopher Jones Leo McKern Barry Foster

In 1916 Ireland, the wife (Sarah Miles) of a village schoolteacher (Robert Mitchum) falls in love with a British officer (Christopher Jones).

Magnificent Irish scenery, over-the-top romantic performances, and painfully clichéd sexual symbolism (waves crashing, stallions neighing . . .) add up to David Lean's most vulgar film: an emotional wallow of epic proportions, popular with punters but clobbered by the critics. John Mills (unrecognizable) steals the acting honours from Sarah Miles (excitable), Trevor Howard (reliable) and Robert Mitchum (barely awake). Freddie Young's photography is wonderful, though, and the storm sequence is a classic.

MIXED:

'A brilliant enigma, brilliant, because director David Lean achieves to a marked degree the daring and obvious goal of intimate romantic tragedy along the rugged geographical and political landscape of 1916 Ireland; an enigma, because its overlength of perhaps 30 minutes serves to magnify some weaknesses of Robert Bolt's original screenplay, to dissipate the impact of the performances, and to overwhelm outstanding photography and production.' *(Variety)*

'Never dull or boring . . . *Ryan's Daughter* has the best storm [in the history of cinema]: the best, the most splendid, the most terrifying. As always in a David Lean film the acting is finely balanced. A beautiful, impressive, well-staged and well-acted film but not really four hours' worth of drama.' *(Halliwell)*

ANTI:

'Instead of looking like the money it cost to make, the film feels like the time it took to shoot.' *(Alexander Walker)*

'Gush made respectable by millions of dollars tastefully wasted.' *(Pauline Kael)*

'A *folie de grandeur*.' *(Shipman)*

'An awe-inspiringly tedious lump of soggy romanticism . . . banal, predictable, ludicrously overblown, it drags on interminably.' *(Tom Milne, Time Out)*

SABOTAGE

CT: 6 AV: 7.00

(aka *A Woman Alone*)

1936 GB 76 BW THRILLER

D Alfred Hitchcock ☆
W Charles Bennett Ian Hay Helen Simpson E.V.H. Emmett from Joseph Conrad's novel *The Secret Agent*

Oscar Homolka ☆ Sylvia Sidney ☆ John Loder ● Desmond Tester Joyce Barbour Matthew Boulton

A wife (Sylvia Sidney) suspects that her husband, a cinema manager (Oscar Homolka) may be a saboteur.

Tense little thriller which shows many of Hitchcock's talents fully developed; some scenes, such as Homolka's death scene are superbly handled. The main thing he hasn't perfected is his knowledge of audience psychology. He mishandles the flirtatious relationship between the wife and the policeman (poorly played by John Loder, Hitchcock's second choice for the role, after the unavailable Robert Donat). The director also makes the mistake of creating suspense as to whether a small boy carrying a bomb is to be blown up, and then double-crossing the audience by letting the bomb explode and kill him.

ANTI:

Truffaut: 'Making a child die in a picture is a rather ticklish matter: it comes close to an abuse of cinematic power.' Hitchcock: 'I agree with that. It was a grave error on my part.' *(François Truffaut, Hitchcock, 1966)*

MIXED:

'This production is a smart one and executed in a business-like manner from start to finish. But the story, somehow, seems outmoded. Joseph Conrad was never a dramatist, and his novels were dependent altogether upon his genius for descriptive writing. Film play is, therefore, more or less obscure in plot.' *(Variety)*

'London, as you should know by now, is Alfred's favourite star . . . In *Sabotage* London has no rival. Sad words but true . . . Sylvia Sidney was brought from Hollywood . . . and I do not think the journey is justified by the event.' *(Walter Webster, Sunday Pictorial)*

'[Hitchcock has] a robust – and sometimes rude – sense of humour, a fine eye for dramatic irony, and an infallible instinct for suspense . . . I was rather disappointed in Oscar Homolka . . . [But] if all other British films were half as good, we would have no complaints.' *(Daily Mail)*

PRO:

'In the United States it was called *A Woman Alone*, and for once an American title is apt – Mrs Verloc learns just how nightmarish a marriage of compromise can be. The movie deserves to be seen fresh, without having its surprises revealed and then analyzed to death. Hitchcock creates an atmosphere of booby-trapped claustrophobia: the characters release their secret hatreds and ambitions in terrifying spasms and explosions. The killings don't offer audiences the usual cathartic genre thrills; instead, they deepen our identification with Mrs Verloc. This film is as wrenching as it is eruptive. Hitchcock never went further beyond pop than he did in *Sabotage*.' *(Michael Sragow)*

'Each scene knits into the whole as neatly as bits in a jig-saw puzzle . . . The dialogue is first-rate.' *(Evening Standard)*

'[Hitchcock's] best picture . . . Once you accept the initial improbability, you are swept on a rising tide of excitement to a terrific climax . . . Suspense [which] has rarely been equalled on the screen; never, perhaps, surpassed.' *(Daily Telegraph)*

'Definitely a picture you should see.' *(News of the World)*

'A good film [with] a nice shivery touch of suspense at the end.' *(Harry Deans, Sunday Graphic and Sunday News)*

SABOTEUR

CT: 6 AV: 7.50

1942 US 108 BW THRILLER

D Alfred Hitchcock ☆
W Peter Viertel Joan Harrison Dorothy Parker

Robert Cummings Priscilla Lane Otto Kruger Alan Baxter Alma Kruger Norman Lloyd ☆ Murray Alper ✔

An innocent man (Robert Cummings) has to clear his name of being a wartime saboteur.

The leading actors are too lightweight, and the story is messily constructed and unevenly paced, but *Saboteur* is still exciting. It has some typically inspired Hitchcock set-pieces, most memorably a finale on the Statue of Liberty. There's an interesting social dimension, too, in the way all the working-class characters and social outsiders instinctively guess our hero's innocence, while those higher up the social system have crypto-fascist sympathies. Hitchcock returned to the 'innocent manhunt' theme in *North by Northwest* (1959), and got it absolutely right that time.

ANTI:

'Robert Cummings is . . . a competent performer, but he belongs to the light-comedy class of actors. Aside from that, he has an amusing face, so that even when he's in desperate straits, his features don't convey any anguish . . . [Universal] imposed the leading lady on me as a *fait accompli*. She simply wasn't the right type for a Hitchcock picture.' *(Alfred Hitchcock, 1966)*

MIXED:

'Hitchcock stretches credibility to the snapping point . . . but compensates for it by providing us with several taut moments and typical surprises, and in the extravagant finale . . . the plastic values achieved . . . are equal to Hitchcock at his best, which is very good indeed.' *(Herman G. Weinberg, S & S)*

'It's absurd but it grips . . . [The film] just falls below the master's best.' *(William Whitebait, New Statesman)*

PRO:

'The drama of a nation stirred to action, of a people's growing realization of themselves and their responsibilities.' *(Motion Picture Herald)*

'To put it mildly, Mr Hitchcock and his writers have really let themselves go. Melodramatic action is their forte, but they scoff at speed limits this trip . . . As a consequence . . . *Saboteur* is a swift, high-tension film which throws itself forward so rapidly that it permits slight opportunity for looking back. And it hurtles the holes and bumps which plague it with a speed that forcefully tries to cover them up.' *(Bosley Crowther)*

'Action, full-bodied and thrilling . . . sheer entertainment . . . Performances are good, some are so good – Norman Lloyd, Otto Kruger, and Murray Alper – that they scarcely seem to be acting.' *(E.A. Cunningham, Motion Picture Herald)*

'The suspense and thrills in this highly melodramatic story are manifold and the lighting and photography are worthy of special mention. The acting is admirable in every respect . . . Some of the smaller characterisations are specially good.' *(MFB)*

SACRIFICE, THE CT: 4 AV: 6.44

(aka *Offret*)

1986 Sweden/France 145/149 C DRAMA/FOREIGN

D Andrei Tarkovsky ✗
W Andrei Tarkovsky ✗

Erland Josephson Susan Fleetwood
Valérie Mairesse Allan Edwall Gudrún Gisladóttir
Sven Wollter Filippa Franzén

A writer (Erland Josephson) tries to make a pact with God that he will renounce his own life, family and possessions if the Almighty will spare the world from nuclear destruction.

Tarkovsky's last film – he died at the age of only 54 – is called a masterpiece by the critics, a colossal bore by almost everyone else. It is pervaded by a sense of mortality (Tarkovsky knew he had cancer) and encircling gloom. Sven Nykvist's cinematography is always a pleasure, but this writer-director strikes me as more pompous and ponderous, than poetic. Winner of the Special Jury Prize at Cannes.

PRO:

'A work of genius.' *(David Robinson, The Times)*

'The film, superbly shot . . . in muted colours which reflect its content in almost every detail, is both poetry and polemic, and also a salute to the kind of cinema that presupposes imaginative effort on the part of its audiences . . . It is a difficult film . . . [but] one particularly unlikely to be easily forgotten.' *(Derek Malcolm, Guardian)*

'Haunting, harrowing, utterly original and made at the point where art reaches into the profoundest dreams.' *(Nigel Andrews, Financial Times)*

'A profound, elegiac, often obscure film, it loomed above the rest of the [Cannes Festival] entries like a Beethoven symphony at a James Last concert.' *(Iain Johnstone, Sunday Times)*

'Towering over everything else in the [Edinburgh] Film Festival . . . [it] is a film which lives in the memory.' *(William Russell, Glasgow Herald)*

'This beautiful film is less opaque than [Tarkovsky's] others . . . It is a startling, pure film.' *(Ian Bell, Scotsman)*

'Tarkovsky . . . is one of the last surviving poets of the cinema . . . Sad, reflective and elegiac, *The Sacrifice* is a movie of a slowburning potency from which one appears to emerge older and wiser.' *(Neil Norman, The Face)*

'No one else can approach his [Tarkovsky's] sense of the Apocalyptic. His death leaves a gaping hole in the cinema of spiritual quest.' *(Chris Peachment, Time Out)*

MIXED:

'The mixture of Swedish and Russian post-nuclear angst is heavy-going, despite the mastery of the camerawork and some impressive set-pieces.' *(Bergan & Karney)*

SAFETY LAST CT: 8 AV: 8.40

1923 US 70 BW COMEDY/SILENT

D Fred Newmeyer Sam Taylor
W Hal Roach Sam Taylor Tim Whelan

Harold Lloyd ☆ Mildred Davis Noah Young
Bill Strother Westcott B. Clarke Mickey Daniels

Country lad (Harold Lloyd) tries to make fortune in the big, bad city (Los Angeles) and impress girl-friend (Mildred Davis) with how well he's doing.

One of the funniest of all silent comedies, culminating in the amazing sequence where Harold Lloyd climbs a skyscraper and hangs high above the street from the hands of a clock. The rest of the film isn't bad either.

ANTI:

'Harold Lloyd is one of the very few who can be laughed at in the same breath as the mighty Chaplin. So it is annoying to have him spoil it all in his first seven-reel picture by falling back on a succession of cheap spectacularisms for much of its effect.' *(Time)*

MIXED:

'The audience was reduced to a state of gibbering hysteria. Although [the film] was more mechanical than most of Lloyd's pictures, it was certainly a superb mechanism.' *(Robert E. Sherwood)*

PRO:

'Filled with laughs and gasps. When people are not rocking in their seats . . . they will be holding on to the chair arms to keep them down . . . The titles are witty. For instance there is the floorwalker, Lloyd's boss, who "is muscle-bound from patting himself on the back" . . . The original "business" in this picture has every one on the alert.' *(New York Times)*

'This new Harold Lloyd farce will become a classic of its kind, or we will miss our guess. For it is the bespectacled comedian's best effort to date . . . The shrieks of hysteria that greeted Lloyd . . . would convince even a hardened critic – but this reviewer left the showing in a state bordering on collapse, along with the rest . . . Easily one of the big comedies of the year.' *(Frederick James Smith, Photoplay)*

'This month's comedy high-spot and Harold Lloyd's best film to date. Excellent stunts, thrills and humour . . . We heartily recommend this.' *(Pictures & Picturegoer)*

'Harold Lloyd owes his success entirely to his own unique personality, and the neat and effective manner in which he carries out an endless succession of amusing and original tricks . . . The plot . . . is of the slightest.' *(Bioscope)*

'Each new floor is like a new stanza in a poem; and the higher and more horrifying it gets, the funnier it gets . . . Lloyd demonstrates beautifully his ability to do more than merely milk a gag, but to top it . . . He was outstanding even among the master craftsmen at setting up a gag clearly, culminating and getting out of it deftly, and linking it smoothly to the next . . . Few people have equalled him, and nobody has ever beaten him.' *(James Agee, Life, 1949)*

SAIKAKU ICHIDAI ONNA: *see* LIFE OF OHARU.

SALAAM BOMBAY! CT: 7 AV: 7.17

1988 India/France/GB 113 C DRAMA/FOREIGN

D Mira Nair ☆
W Sooni Taraporevala

Shafiq Syed ☆ Raghubir Yadav Nana Patekar Irshad Hasni Aneeta Kanwar Hansa Vithal

A 12-year-old boy (Shafiq Syed) tries to survive on the streets of Bombay.

Grim on the outside, warm on the inside, this is a touching film about Bombay street-life, full of vitality and character. The little boy is delightfully natural; there's none of the coyness or political tub-thumping with which most western film-makers would tackle this potentially grim subject. A promising début by Mira Nair, whose experience as a documentary-maker gives the film the unmistakable ring of truth.

MIXED:

'Nair's conventional shooting style and accessible plot may offend purists who seek a more "authentic" India – but the fact remains that this fluid, engaging movie will correct dominant retro-raj visions and no doubt will prove a bigger draw than even the most popular Satyajit Ray film.' *(Katherine Dieckmann, Village Voice)*

'Miss Nair punches away at the city with all fingers, but the letter she keeps hitting is S for sentimentality . . . Whenever it moves from close-up into long shot, [the film] is magnificent. It gives us a portrait of a city that dwarfs – in every possible sense – the individual characters peopling it.' *(Nigel Andrews, Financial Times)*

'I was instantly impressed by Nair's narrative skill . . . The second time [I saw it] her sentimental streak was more apparent and more annoying, but [it] still convinces as a modest, uplifting movie.' *(Sheila Johnston, Independent)*

PRO:

'Probably the best street movie since *Pixote*, made with heart.' *(Sandy Lieberson, Film Yearbook)*

'It is a tough film, not unlike Babenco's *Pixote*, and an antidote to those many Indian movies which, in avoiding any hint of sexual explicitness have also hidden from sight the extremes of deprivation and exploitation which exist in the major cities of the continent . . . [Nair's] deep concern is poignantly communicated.' *(Mansell Stimpson, What's On in London)*

'Nair has achieved the naked truth . . . [and] made a compelling urban *tour de force*.' *(Victoria Mather, Daily Telegraph)*

'[Nair] clearly possesses a sizeable talent for gently nudging raw material – and raw performers . . . into a convincing fictional framework.' *(Geoff Brown, The Times)*

SALAIRE DE LA PEUR, LE: *see* WAGES OF FEAR.

SALERNO BEACHHEAD: *see* WALK IN THE SUN, A.

SALOME, WHERE SHE DANCED

CT: 5 AV: 3.17

1945 US 90 WESTERN/SO BAD

D Charles Lamont ●
W Laurence Stallings from Michael J. Phillips's story

Yvonne De Carlo Rod Cameron ● Albert Dekker David Bruce Walter Slezak Marjorie Rambeau J. Edward Bromberg Abner Biberman ● John Litel Kurt Katch

An exotic dancer (Yvonne De Carlo) turns spy in the Austro-Prussian War and flees to the Wild West.

Bizarre western, with one of the silliest plots ever committed to celluloid. The film made Yvonne De Carlo a star; she certainly deserved some kind of award for bravery.

PRO:

'An enjoyable hocus-pocus.' *(Daily Mail)*

'Competently produced on a lavish scale and will satisfy those who desire nothing more than a kaleidoscopic display.' *(Ernest Lindgren, MFB)*

'I gratefully salute it as the funniest dead-pan parody I have ever seen.' *(James Agee)*

'I decline absolutely to believe that the way to enjoy [this film] is to think of it as satire. Anyway, it isn't . . . Look at it how you will, it is a feat of imagination . . . There hasn't been such romance around a campfire since *The Sheik*.' *(Time & Tide)*

'Its plot seems born of a hashish nightmare. Audiences must have thought they were watching the wrong film when the opening scenes set them down in the middle of the Franco-Prussian war and the court of Bismarck. By degrees – if not altogether by logic – the film does make its way to the American west, and a kind of rhythm pervades the rest of the film: in every scene one plot complication is resolved while another is set up. At one point, several boatloads of westerners travel out to a Chinese junk to resolve one of these plot complications, but forget their purpose when they witness Yvonne De Carlo (who must have seen them coming) perform an exotic dance before a shrine in the ship's hold. The picture reaches its zenith of nuttiness when introducing a Chinese doctor (Abner Biberman) who speaks English with a Scottish accent.' *(Parish & Pitts, The Great Western Pictures, 1976)*

ANTI:

'Personally I don't regard the lure or the dancing of Miss De Carlo as much above the average.' *(Daily Herald)*

'A ghastly movie: quite funny, but it wasn't intended to be.' *(Brian Garfield, Western Films, 1982)*

'This passed for intentional camp even when it was made.' *(Scheuer)*

SALVADOR

CT: 8 AV: 7.15

1986 US 123 C THRILLER/WAR

D Oliver Stone
W Richard Boyle Oliver Stone ☆ AAN

James Woods ☆ AAN James Belushi ✔ Michael Murphy John Savage Elpidia Carrillo Tony Plana Colby Chester Cynthia Gibb

In 1980, a reporter (James Woods) uncovers American involvement in some nasty deeds abroad.

Narrative structure is not its strong point, nor is political subtlety; but it is by far Oliver Stone's most involving film. Woods is dynamic in the leading role, and given splendid support by Belushi.

ANTI:

'The ultimate message . . . is that America's military presence in places like Vietnam and Central America serves only to make the lives of the local peasantry more miserable and tragic – it's the powerful rich destroying the lives of the helpless poor. (Plainly, Stone is going to spend his life trying to atone for being born rich.) Just as Stone romanticizes Sergeant Elias in *Platoon*, so in *Salvador* he romanticizes a leader of the rebel army who, standing in his tent before a portrait of Marx and Lenin, tells a group of journalists that "the will of the people and the march of history cannot be changed – not even by the norteamericanos!" Outside, members of his happy and noble peasant army sing "*el futuro sera nuestro*" ("the future will be ours").' *(Bruce Bawer, American Spectator)*

MIXED:

'James Woods puts nervous energy and self-mockery into the part, and it is not his fault if the qualities of scrounger, scoopseeker, friend of the common man and sharp political analyst don't quite stick together . . . As an adventure film [it] has plenty of speed, grit and grime . . . but Mr Stone has more on his mind than action . . . he offers an interpretation of history.' *(Walter Goodman, New York Times)*

'No question about it: when James Woods shuts his mouth for a second . . . he's the most interesting actor in America. And [this is] his best film . . . another Oliver Stone masterpiece from the dark side. The team of Woods and Stone is a potent one – not for weak tummies – and each brings out the worst, which is to say the best, in the other . . . A little on the shapeless side, . . . but it deserves a following.' *(Peter Biskind, Premiere)*

'Drama torn from the headlines; it should have stayed there, as few people proved to be interested in paying to see it. One cannot, however, deny its brilliant if superficial technical command.' *(Halliwell)*

PRO:

'As raw, difficult, compelling, unreasonable, reckless and vivid as its protagonist.' *(Variety)*

'At heart . . . [it's] about the unleashing of chaos on the world . . . the moment when the centre falls away . . . a vision of a civilization overturned and it is the film's extraordinary ability to crystallize and sustain that vision without ever losing sight of the essential humanism that is chaos's only antidote which makes it such a powerful and important document . . . Films like [this] don't come along very often; neither do directors like Stone with the conviction and vision to make them. *(George Robert Kimball, F & F)*

SAMSON AND DELILAH CT: 6 AV: 4.91

1949 US 128 C DRAMA/EPIC/SO BAD

D Cecil B. DeMille
W Jesse L. Lasky

Hedy Lamarr Victor Mature Angela Lansbury George Sanders Henry Wilcoxon Olive Deering Fay Holden Russ Tamblyn

Strong man (Victor Mature) suffers unwanted haircut.

Wonderfully silly biblical epic, entertaining because of its blatantly modern attempt to see events in terms of Hollywood stereotypes. Sample line . . . Samson, about to grapple with a big cat: 'I don't need that spear – it's only a young lion.' The film won an Academy Award for its art direction (by Hans Dreier, Walter Tyler, Sam Comer and Ray Moyer) and costume design (Edith Head, Dorothy Jeakins, Elois Jenssen, Gile Steele and Gwen Wakeling). It was nominated for George Barnes's cinematography, Victor Young's music, and its visual effects.

ANTI:

'Perfectly awful.' *(Judith Crist)*

'Absurd biblical hokum, stodgily narrated and directed, monotonously photographed and edited, and notable only for the 30-second destruction of the temple at the end.' *(Halliwell)*

MIXED:

'To ignore so enormous, over-coloured, over-stuffed, flamboyant an "epic" would be almost as absurd as taking it seriously.' *(Richard Mallett, Punch)*

'Perhaps DeMille's survival is due to the fact that he decided in his movie nonage to ally himself with God as his co-maker and get his major scripts from the Bible, which he has always handled with the proprietary air of a gentleman fondling old love letters.' *(New Yorker)*

PRO:

'Even lovers of cinematic art who recognize *Samson and Delilah* as a run-of-DeMille epic should enjoy it as a simple-minded spree. In its way, it is as much fun as a robust, well-organized circus.' *(Time)*

'If ever there was a movie for DeMillions, here it is . . . Victor Mature as Samson is a dashing and dauntless hunk of man . . . Hedy Lamarr as Delilah is a sleek and bejeweled siren whose charms have a strictly occidental and twentieth-century grace and clarity.' *(New York Times)*

'It has everything but subtlety . . . DeMille' s genius for detail is always evident. Even in his gigantic mob scenes there is reason for every movement, every actor. He balances these scenes with quick flashes of individual reactions to the momentary situation. His sense of design is wonderful, he groups and moves people with the artistry of an expert choreographer.' *(Fortnight)*

SAN FRANCISCO AAN CT: 8 AV: 8.17

1936 US 117 BW DRAMA

D W.S. Van Dyke ☆ AAN
W Anita Loos ☆ from Robert Hopkins's story AAN

Clark Gable ☆ Spencer Tracy ☆ AAN Jeanette MacDonald ☆ Jack Holt ☆ Jessie Ralph ☆ Ted Healy Shirley Ross Al Shean Harold Huber

A saloon proprietor (Clark Gable) and a priest (Spencer Tracy) battle over singer (Jeanette MacDonald), while awaiting the 1906 earthquake.

Classy MGM melodrama with interesting characters, three stars on top form, and a splendid special-effects climax which makes up for longueurs in the build-up. It was voted into fourth place on the annual *Film Daily* poll of US film critics, and was MGM's top-grossing picture of the 1930s. Winner of the Academy Award for Best Sound Recording (Douglas Shearer).

ANTI:

'*San Francisco* offers cinemaddicts views of two unusual phenomena: the San Francisco earthquake and Jeanette MacDonald acting with her teeth. Of the two, the latter is the more appalling . . . [The film] makes it plain that the real cause [of the quake] lay in the fact that Clark Gable did not say his prayers at night.' *(Time)*

'Half-baked lyricism.' *(Arthur Vesselo, S & S)*

MIXED:

'From the first rumble . . . the emotional effect of [the earthquake] sequence is as great as the spectacle itself. Clark Gable gives a good performance . . . and if he does not make his conversion convincing, it is hardly his fault. Jeanette MacDonald . . . gives a good performance generally.' *(MFB)*

'Corking cast and super-fine production . . . Lone incongruous note is the remarkable survival of Clark Gable after a whole wall has toppled over on him. His survival is necessary, to complete the picture, but it might have been made easier to believe.' *(Variety)*

PRO:

'During its two-hour course on the Capitol's screen

it manages to encompass most of the virtues of the operatic film, the romantic, the biographical, the dramatic and the documentary. Astonishingly, it serves all of them abundantly well, truly meriting commendation as a near-perfect illustration of the cinema's inherent and acquired ability to absorb and digest other art forms and convert them into its own sinews.' *(Frank S. Nugent, New York Times)*

'Encompasses every form of screen entertainment, and then some. Gargantuan in range, scope, cast and spectacle, and universal in its appeal, it is, in a phrase, one of the box-office certainties of the year.' *(Kine Weekly)*

SANG D'UN POÊTE, LE: *see* BLOOD OF A POET, THE.

SANS TOIT NI LOI: *see* VAGABOND.

SANSHO THE BAILIFF CT: 9 AV: 8.86
(aka *Sansho Dayu*)

1954 Japan 125/130 BW DRAMA/FOREIGN

D Kenji Mizoguchi ☆
W Yahiro Fuji Yoshikata Yoda from Ogai Mori's story

Yoshiaki Hanayagi Kyoko Kagawa Masao Shimizu Kinuyo Tanaka Eitaro Shindo Aritake Kono

A family suffers numerous misfortunes in feudal Japan.

A memorable though depressing portrait of a barbaric society, with special emphasis on the oppression of women, and on man's infinite capacity for cruelty. It's beautiful, lyrical and moving – but also harsh and unsentimental: a genuine masterpiece. The stunning cinematography is by Kazuo Miyagawa.

'The greatest movie I have ever seen.' *(Robin Wood, 1964)*

'Mizoguchi's haunting images create an atmosphere in which the film comes perhaps as close as it can to the pity and terror of classic Greek tragedy . . . [His] extraordinary eye finds just that setting which will give meaning to the dramatic scene to be enacted.' *(Eileen Bowser, Film Quarterly, 1964)*

'There are tiny, unforgettable moments, slight gestures that carry a depth-charge of emotion.' *(John Coleman, New Statesman, 1976)*

'Mizoguchi gives this pathetic tale a quality somewhere between the fatalism of a medieval romance and the catharsis of classical tragedy . . . With Mizoguchi, form and idea, atmosphere and feeling are indivisible. He is a painter by training and his films are assembled out of images of breathtaking exactness . . . The images, the subtle music . . . combine to create a world which irresistibly captures and enfolds the spectator.' *(David Robinson, The Times, 1976)*

'The theme of slavery, exploitation and oppression – especially of women – is almost contemporary and handled with a psychological perception which never allows the melodramatic plot to interpose between the audience and the essential human understanding of the characters.' *(Virginia Dignam, Morning Star)*

'Goes quietly and tenderly about its business which is to move you gradually and deeply.' *(Alexander Walker, Evening Standard)*

'A heartbreaking medieval fable with modern political and psychological overtones . . . the choice (of naming the film after the villain) reflects the director's tragic vision . . . In this fairy tale no one lives happily ever after . . . Terrifying and cathartic, *Sansho the Bailiff* is a morality play without easy moralism.' *(Michael Sragow, New Yorker, 1990)*

'Almost subliminally we come to realize that slavery is equally as corrupting as power.' *(Screen International, 1976)*

SANTA CLAUS CONQUERS THE MARTIANS CT: 5 AV: 2.43
(aka *Santa Claus Defeats the Aliens*)

1964 US 82 C SF/FAMILY/SO BAD

D Nicholas Webster ●
W Glenville Mareth ●

John Call ● Leonard Hicks Vincent Beck ● Victor Stiles Donna Conforti Bill McCutcheon ● Leila Martin Pia Zadora

Martians invade Earth and attempt to kidnap Santa Claus.

Lamentable special effects, a simple-minded story and a barmy (though accurate) title combine to make this a cult classic. The performances are equally absurd. John Call's attempts at Santa-style friendliness are more reminiscent of a neighbourhood child molester. Vincent Beck gives a ludicrous performance as Volgar, Mars's answer to Ming The Merciless. Bill McCutcheon's unlovable performance as the good Martian Dropo suggests that the only good Martian is a dead one. The score is by one Milton Delugg.

'Obvious and square cut as cheese . . . Like a children's television show enlarged on movie house screens. . . . Supplies humor not quite attuned to this planet, anyway.' *(Howard Thompson, New York Times)*

'Overly saccharine and nonsensical. . . . A lobby sign with No One Admitted OVER 16 Years of Age might be appropriate.' *(Boxoffice)*

'Absolutely the worst science-fiction flick ever made, bar none!' *(Jason Thomas and Joe Kane, The Monster Times)*

SANTA SANGRE CT: 4 AV: 5.38

1990 Italy 124 C HORROR/DRAMA/FOREIGN

D Alejandro Jodorowsky ✗
W Robert Leoni Alejandro Jodorowsky Claudio Argento

Axel Jodorowsky Blanca Guerra Guy Stockwell Thelma Tixou Sabrina Dennison Adan Jodorowski

When we first meet our hero, Fenix (played by Axel Jodorowsky, son of the director) he is stark naked on top of a stump in a lunatic asylum, under the mistaken impression that he is an eagle. We witness, in flashback, the family background which has turned Fenix from a promising eight-year-old circus magician into a prominent birdbrain. His mother, Concha, is an unbalanced trapeze artist: his father, Orgo, a sadistic alcoholic knife-thrower (you'd think that alcoholism and sadism would be disadvantages for a knife-thrower, but apparently not). Concha discovers Orgo having it away with a tattooed lady, and sprinkles sulphuric acid over the parts of her husband which are already in flagrante. Orgo responds by hacking off his wife's arms and feeding them to the chickens, slashing his own throat and lying down to become (literally) a dogs' dinner.

More than a decade later, our aquiline Fenix escapes from the asylum, discovers that his henpecked mother is now a vaudeville artist in need of a helping hand, if not two. Though armless, she turns out to be far from harmless, and persuades Fenix to become a mass-murderer of women who exhibit signs of a sexual appetite. Victims range from Mommie Dearest's old adversary, the tattooed lady, to a heavyweight-wrestling transexual. Finally, our hero is redeemed by his ideal woman, a deaf-mute virgin, who offers her own arms to him for amputation: an act which gives him the bright, and long overdue, notion of hurling knives at his mother.

I shall not tire you with an exhaustive list of the other horrors on display. Suffice it to say that an elephant bleeds to death and is torn apart; our young hero is tied up and engraved with a knife until his chest is a mass of blood; the deaf-mute girl is sold as a prostitute by her own mother, sexually assaulted and propositioned by a man who tears off one of his ears as foreplay; and there are heavy hints that our hero is a necrophiliac – though, frankly, this is the least abnormal thing about him.

Grotesquely overrated by some critics on release, it is an international curiosity: made in the English language by a Chilean of Russian parentage, with Italian money, and shot in Mexico by a Spanish production team whose common language was French. Perhaps the best thing about the movie is that no single nation can be blamed for it.

Blood and guts are nothing new in the cinema; and the excessive violence is probably less shocking than the 60-year-old director's shameless plundering of visual ideas from Fellini and Buñuel, and his depressingly crude notions of sexual symbolism (at one point, an enormous snake even emerges from our hero's trousers and starts choking him).

The film is presumably trying to say something uncomplimentary about religious mothers who warp their sons' sexuality. Certainly, the central mother-son relationship makes the one in *Psycho* look relatively healthy. I am not a fan of censorship; but this film's sick sadism, obsession with sexual violence and viciously misogynistic division of women (where necessary with a knife) into madonnas and whores leaves me at a loss to understand how it ever got a certificate.

PRO:

'I like to take reality and put it into an imaginative context and it becomes a masterwork.' *(Alejandro Jodorowsky)*

'An astonishing film . . . A surreal fantasy about violence, revenge and murder.' *(Guardian)*

'A throwback to the golden age, to the days when filmmakers had bold individual visions and were not timidly trying to duplicate the latest mass-market formulas . . . A rush of energy and creative joy.' *(Roger Ebert)*

'With a tapestry of cultural references that embraces the Venus De Milo, Marcel Marceau, Liberace and *Night of the Living Dead*, Jodorowsky's is a strange, violent, but ultimately liberating vision.' *(Nigel Floyd, Time Out)*

'A film that no adventurous moviegoer can afford to miss . . . If Jodorowsky is not yet worthy of inclusion in the pantheon with Buñuel and Hitchcock (the latter can be either credited with or blamed for starting the Oedipal-slasher trend with *Psycho*, 1960), he is, nonetheless, in a class by himself.' *(Baseline)*

ANTI:

'Determinedly shocking, nauseating and – some would say – sacrilegious . . . There is a plot of sorts but it often seems to be a mere pretext for a process of bizarre images that make no . . . literal sense . . . Some may suspect that Jodorowsky is leading them by the nose. No recent cinematic bag of tricks has hoax so plainly written across it.' *(Alan Stanbrook, F & F)*

'Ersatz surrealism for those who can't afford or wouldn't recognize the real thing.' *(Harlan Kennedy, Film Yearbook)*

SATURDAY NIGHT AND SUNDAY MORNING CT: 6 AV: 7.85

1960 GB 89 BW DRAMA

D Karel Reisz ☆
W Alan Sillitoe ☆ from his novel

Albert Finney ☆ Shirley Anne Field

Rachel Roberts ☆ Bryan Pringle
Norman Rossington Hylda Baker

A rebellious factory worker (Albert Finney) has an affair with a married woman (Rachel Roberts) but settles in the end for conventional domesticity.

An important film of its time, marvellously acted by Roberts and Finney, who makes a role that could easily have been a clichéd 'angry young man' intensely sympathetic. Freddie Francis contributes exceptional cinematography. If the film doesn't have the impact it once had, it's because Karel Reisz's direction thumps home all the points with clarity, but no great subtlety; everything is spelt out for us. The influence of the picture can clearly be seen on *Saturday Night Fever* (1977), which is in many respects a New York remake.

PRO:

'In Karel Reisz the tale has a deeply sympathetic director, a man who can face without revulsion the brutality as well as the ferocious good-humour of his subject. And the film is lucky in its interpreters, especially Rachel Roberts, full of a warm, natural vulgarity as the married woman, and Albert Finney, giving all our English actors a lesson in the playing of a young man of the working class. Mr Finney's Arthur Seaton – insolent look, dangerous look – is brilliant.' *(Dilys Powell)*

'Here is a chance for our own new wave.' *(Evening Standard)*

'Beautifully made.' *(Stanley Kauffmann, Film Quarterly)*

'Reisz's main achievement, shared by his writer and his leading actor . . . is the creation of a contemporary backyard-and-factory conscience.' *(Peter John Dyer, S & S)*

'One of the best examples to date of the new British inspiration, one of the most vigorous of recent pictures from any source.' *(New York Herald Tribune)*

'This is an occasion for running up the flags, rolling out the red carpet and giving three rousing cheers. For this film is so good it made me ache with admiration.' *(Margaret Hinxman, Daily Herald)*

MIXED:

'A good, absorbing but not very likeable film.' *(Variety)*

ANTI:

'This study of working-class energies and frustrations has been overdirected [by Karel Reisz]. Everything is held in check; every punch is called and then pulled. When the hero and his cousin are fishing, the caught fish signals the end of the scene; a dog barks for a fade out. The central fairground sequence is like an exercise in cinematography, and the hero's beating is just another mechanical plot necessity.' *(Pauline Kael)*

SATURDAY NIGHT FEVER CT: 7 AV: 6.33

1977 US 119 C MUSICAL/ROMANCE

D John Badham
W Norman Wexler

John Travolta ☆ AAN Karen Lynn Gorney ●
Barry Miller Joseph Cali Paul Pope Bruce Ornstein

A cool Brooklyn dude (John Travolta) is a loser at life, but a winner as a disco dancer.

John Travolta struts his stuff on and off the dance floor in the movie that made his name. Great Bee Gees songs evoke a bygone era, and compensate for unsympathetic male characters, and forgettable females. John Badham's flashy, trashy but entertaining movie was heavily indebted to *Saturday Night, Sunday Morning* (1960); other influences obviously included *Mean Streets* and *Rocky* (whose picture Travolta has on his bedroom wall).

ANTI:

'The clumsy story lurches forward through predictable travail and treacle.' *(Variety)*

MIXED:

'Poppycock . . . What is truly dismaying, though, is the script by Norman Wexler (Joe, Mandingo), which patronizes young and old alike, although the dialogue does have its scattered pungencies. Not even the disco scenes are done with sufficient choreographic abandon – the director, John Badham, opts for mushy sentimentality on the dance floor. But Travolta does give an exceptionally convincing performance, a seamless blend of cockiness and vulnerability. What remains to be seen is whether it is really acting, or merely type-casting.' *(John Simon)*

'The mood, the beat, and the trance rhythm are so purely entertaining, and Travolta is such an original presence, that a viewer spins past the crudeness in the script.' *(Pauline Kael)*

'All the characters seem to have crawled out from under stones. The slick direction, fast editing and exciting dance numbers do something to take away the sour taste.' *(Halliwell)*

PRO:

'John Travolta is – the exact word for this performance – terrific. A flat-stomached, good-hearted, frustrated, vain and clever cockerel. When he hits that dance floor on Saturday night, after six days of obeying his boss, he sheds his chains and becomes a king. When the girls rave about him, we believe it.' *(Stanley Kauffmann)*

'An especially hard-edged case and a very good movie.' *(Roger Ebert)*

'A stylish piece of contemporary anthropology, an urban safari into darkest America, a field study of the mystery cults among the young braves and squaws growing up in North Brooklyn.' *(Alan Brien, Sunday Times)*

SATYRICON CT: 4 AV: 5.33

(aka *Fellini Satyricon*)

1969 Italy/France 129 C DRAMA

D Federico Fellini ***X*** AAN
W Federico Fellini

Martin Potter Hiram Keller Salvo Randone Max Born Alain Cluny Lucia Bose Capucine

A handsome young student (Martin Potter) enters into the pagan spirit of Ancient Rome.

Big, bold, boring, repetitive movie about Ancient Roman debauchery, which Fellini unsurprisingly finds A Bad Thing. The trouble is that he also revels in it, which confuses his message; there's hardly any characterization or plot; and the whole thing is grossly overlength.

PRO:

'It remains a film about images, not about stories. Some shots are as carefully composed as a 17th-century painting . . . And hardly any of this is done artily.' *(Paul Barker, New Society)*

'From Petronius, Fellini has taken a title, names and episodes, a loose picaresque framework, but the preoccupations, emphases, and the peculiar quality of joyless zestfulness are quintessentially his own . . . As the film so slowly unrolls, the impression is of sameness rather than variety: a sameness of excess, of masks and grotesques, entrails and decapitation, blubbery flesh and billowing costumes.' *(Penelope Houston, Spectator)*

'Translates this decadence into visual terms so stunning and fantastic that one can only conclude Fellini is a marvelous madman . . . The film doesn't have a plot [but] . . . the landscape of fantasy doesn't need plots . . . A work of genius.' *(Lorraine Alterman, Rolling Stone)*

'An explosion of madness and perversion, designed like grand opera of the absurd – a homosexual odyssey in which the creatures of Fellini's mind writhe about like sequinned snakes toward some surrealistic damnation of the soul. Every frame is filled with lust, greed, avarice, sacrifice, pain, and human torture . . . There is no point in trying to analyze Satyricon in terms of theme, plot, or character development. Scenes melt into each other without connection or cohesion. It is Cocteau out of Dali, an exercise in mind expansion which is a major requisite for anyone who sincerely cares about movies and the direction in which they are going.' *(Rex Reed)*

MIXED:

'Certainly his technique stupefies us. But his ideas are too confused or too personal to engage us.' *(Michel Capdenac, Lettres Français)*

'For the final half-hour and more bewilderment has set in. Yes, it is boring all right, boring because it is not only long but disconnected, allowing no sympathy for its characters, admitting no development of anything . . . In the cinema, Fellini's *Satyricon* grows wearisome. But in retrospect the film suddenly isn't boring . . . it is a brilliant curiosity.' *(Dilys Powell)*

ANTI:

'Barely satiric and a huge con . . . Part of the gradual decomposition of what once was one of the greatest talents in film history . . . A gimcrack, shopworn nightmare.' *(John Simon)*

'In *La Dolce Vita*, he used the orgies of modern Rome as a parallel to ancient Rome, and now he reverses the analogy to make the same point – that man without a belief in God is a lecherous beast. The film is full of cautionary images of depravity that seem to come out of the imagination of a Catholic schoolboy: an unconscionable number of performers stick out their evil tongues at us, and there are leering cripples, fat freaks with hideous grins, and so on. Fellini draws upon his master-entertainer's feelings for the daydreams of the audience, and many people find this film eerie, spellbinding, and even profound. Essentially, though, it's just a hip version of De Mille's *The Sign of the Cross* (also a photogenic demonstration of the highly dubious proposition that godlessness is lawlessness), and it's less entertaining than DeMille's kitsch – maybe because no one is given a role to play; Fellini is the only star.' *(Pauline Kael)*

SCARAMOUCHE CT: 6 AV: 7.11

1952 US 115 C ACTION/ADVENTURE/FAMILY

D George Sidney
W Ronald Millar George Froeschel from Rafael Sabatini's novel

Stewart Granger Mel Ferrer Eleanor Parker Janet Leigh Henry Wilcoxon Nina Foch Lewis Stone Robert Coote Richard Anderson

At the time of the French Revolution, a young man (Stewart Granger) disguises himself as an actor to avenge the death of a friend.

Entertainingly colourful swashbuckler for the whole family. Handsomely produced and wittily scripted, and featuring some great action scenes – including the longest sword-fight in screen history (six-and-a-half minutes).

ANTI:

'Pic never seems to be quite certain whether it is a costume adventure drama or a satire on one.' *(Variety)*

'Unless I am completely mistaken, *Scaramouche* is not meant to be a comedy. I have sought in vain for a benevolent kind of approach which might make it possible to recommend [it] for any audience above the mental age of twelve.' *(Jympson Harman, Evening News)*

PRO:

'A colourful, rollicking Hollywood cook-up.' *(Leonard Mosley, Daily Express)*

'I like swashbuckling and Stewart Granger swashbuckles finely and takes a few ungainly tumbles and clouts . . . The swordplay is dazzling.' *(Roy Nash, Star)*

'The production is lavish, the direction fine, the flights and fights grand. No trouble or expense has been spared to give you what you want – assuming you do want hokum.' *(Elspeth Grant, Daily Graphic)*

SCARFACE CT: 6 AV: 8.69

(aka *Scarface, The Shame of the Nation*)

1932 US 99 BW THRILLER

D Howard Hawks ☆
W Ben Hecht Seton I. Miller John Lee Mahin W.R.Burnett Fred Pasley from Armitage Traill's novel

Paul Muni ☆ Ann Dvorak ☆ George Raft ☆ Boris Karloff Osgood Perkins Karen Morley Vince Barnett

Life and death of a gangster (Paul Muni).

Seminal gangster movie, startlingly violent in its day, and so close in time to the real events that it might almost be a newsreel. Paul Muni is excellent as a thinly disguised Al Capone. Made in 1930, it was not deemed releasable until two years later, and the feeble, moralizing scene in the publisher's office – not directed by Hawks – was put in as a concession to pressure groups. The film's still exciting, and (very daringly for its period) there's even a hint of incest in Scarface's relationship with his sister (Ann Dvorak).

ANTI:

'A gangster picture which presents heroically the exploits of a criminal, showing him as rich, courageous and cunning against contrasting characteristics on the part of the guardians of the law. It glorifies crime, presents methods of crime and familiarizes the audience with them. Even though the criminal is brought to justice in the final scenes it is an influence against law and order and an incitement to impressionable minds to follow vicious practices.' *(Martin Quigley, Decency in Motion Pictures, 1937)*

MIXED:

'As good as any gangster film that has been made. It is more brutal, more cruel, more wholesale than any of its predecessors, and by that much, means to tell the truth. It is built with more solid craftsmanship, it is better directed and better acted . . . The incidents . . . hang together with the coherence of actual life. The only real troublesome weaknesses in the story are in extraneous moralizing speeches, indubitably thrown in for whatever they might be worth as a lesson. The lesson of such films is never taught by incidental sermons but by the life we see being lived.' *(James Shelley Hamilton, NBR)*

'It has weathered all [the] unfortunate advance hullaballoo very satisfactorily . . . although it is unusually long and has so many killings as it is, you wonder what violence on earth could have been omitted . . . It lacks the brilliance of acting and detail [of] *Public Enemy* and *Little Caesar* . . . Paul Muni plays . . . with talent, especially in the earlier sequences.' *(John Mosher, New Yorker)*

'It is a completely successful film: excellent actors, good photography, irreproachable direction. It is a work of Howard Hawks, auteur of *A Girl in Every Port*, which is in itself a recommendation. But *Scarface* is a documentary and one doesn't become involved with its characters as one did with Bancroft in *Underworld*, Gary Cooper in *City Streets*, and Edmund Lowe in *Club 73*.' *(Michel Vaucaire, Le Crapouillot, 1932)*

PRO:

'Presumably the last of the gangster films . . . It is going to make people sorry that there won't be any more.' *(Variety)*

'The most poignant of the gangster school, with Paul Muni's magnificent playing throughout and the unforgettable moment of George Raft's dying.' *(James Agate, Tatler, 1941)*

'Nobody has matched the vigor of the violence in Howard Hawks's *Scarface* . . . but it was terse, fast – before you had a chance to marvel, it was over.' *(Peter Bogdanovich, 1975)*

'The most striking scene in the movie is unquestionably Boris Karloff's death. He squats down to throw a ball in a game of ninepins and doesn't get up; a rifle shot prostrates him. The camera follows the ball he's thrown as it knocks down all the pins except one that keeps spinning until it finally falls over, the exact symbol of Karloff himself, the last survivor of a rival gang that's been wiped out by Muni. This isn't literature. It may be dance or poetry. It is certainly cinema.' *(François Truffaut)*

SCARLET EMPRESS, THE CT: 6 AV: 7.78

1934 US 109 BW DRAMA/BIOPIC

D Josef von Sternberg
W Manuel Komroff based on the diary of Catherine the Great

Marlene Dietrich ☆ John Lodge ☆ Sam Jaffe ☆ Louise Dresser ● C. Aubrey Smith Gavin Gordon Jameson Thomas

The rise of Catherine the Great (Marlene Dietrich).

This heavily fictionalized biopic is hard going at times, mainly because von Sternberg can't resist piling on more and more period detail; but it is memorable for its opulence, hints of unspeakable decadence, and the ravishing beauty of Marlene Dietrich, who is superbly photographed by Bert Glennon. It was a failure at the box office – at least partly because Paul Czinner's inferior film, *Catherine the Great* (1934), which painted a more appealing, romanticized picture of its heroine, had been released only eight months earlier.

'A relentless excursion into style.' *(Josef von Sternberg)*

ANTI:

'Von Sternberg is a brilliant technician, unexcelled in the art of creating atmosphere. Yet the fact remains that, with the exception of *The Blue Angel* . . . he seems incapable of telling a story, preferring to dissipate his resources on a series of possibly effective but only loosely connected episodes. People say that [the film] is not very good history. I hardly think that matters. The point is that it is not very good cinema.' *(Daily Telegraph)*

'Alas, my poor Marlene! What have they done to Dietrich? . . . In common with millions of others whose taste on the subject is impeccable, I would go miles to see Marlene. I resent all the more her great talents being obscured by a lot of showy photography.' *(Edward Betts, Sunday Express)*

'It is with great difficulty that the actors manage to make themselves seen and heard . . . It is the drawback of the film that as the actors are dwarfed into insignificance there is very little development possible.' *(The Times)*

'Can anyone tell me . . . why Josef von Sternberg . . . has elected to spend . . . a sum in the region of a quarter of a million pounds sterling in evolving such a film nightmare? . . . It provides a continuous exhibition of a gargoyled intelligence, the grotesqueries and protuberances of which resemble the details of a picture by Gustave Doré . . . [It] is rampantly ugly in spite of its magnificence.' *(Sydney W. Carrol, Sunday Times)*

MIXED:

'A ponderous, strangely beautiful, lengthy and frequently wearying production.' *(Mordaunt Hall, New York Times)*

'Von Sternberg becomes so enamoured of the pomp and flash that he subjugates everything else to them. That he succeeds as well as he does is a tribute to his artistic genius and his amazingly vital sense of photogenic values. Marlene Dietrich has never been as beautiful as she is here.' *(Variety)*

'Sometimes clumsy, sometimes pretentious, but . . . interesting . . . Mr von Sternberg approaches all his films with an awful reverence, with enormous solemnity . . . If somebody asked him to make a picture about Little Miss Muffet (with, of course, Miss Dietrich swimming around gorgeously in luscious bowls of curds and whey) I have the uncomfortable feeling that every time Miss Muffet winked you'd be likely as not to hear the Brandenburg Concerto.' *(Alistair Cooke, Listener)*

'The decor and the visual motifs became the stars, and Marlene Dietrich was used as a camera subject instead of as a person. She's photographed behind veils and fishnets, while dwarfs slither about and bells ring and everybody tries to look degenerate. Von Sternberg had a peculiar notion that this showy pomposity proved that film was an art medium. The picture is egocentric and empty of drama, yet it has the fascination (and the tediousness) that bizarre, obsessional movies often have.' *(Pauline Kael)*

SCARLET PIMPERNEL, THE CT: 8 AV: 7.64

1934 GB 85/98 BW ACTION/ADVENTURE

D Harold Young ☆
W Robert E. Sherwood Sam Berman Arthur Wimperis Lajos Biro from Baroness Orczy's novel

Leslie Howard ☆ Merle Oberon ☆ Raymond Massey ☆ Nigel Bruce Bramwell Fletcher Anthony Bushell Joan Gardner Walter Rilla

In the French Revolution, an upper-class Englishman (Leslie Howard) keeps his head while all about him are losing theirs.

The film itself had a troubled history, with the original director (Rowland Brown) fired on the first day of shooting. Producer Alexander Korda himself took over the direction for a time, but – like the movie – everything ended happily. It's a first-rate historical adventure, very lavishly mounted for a British production of its period, and superbly acted. The always slightly effete Leslie Howard is perfectly cast; Raymond Massey makes a hissable villain; and Merle Oberon is gorgeous. The picture is so enjoyable that one can almost overlook its snobbish assumption that aristocrats are noble, while the rest of us need to be kept firmly in our place. Michael Powell and Emeric Pressburger remade it with David Niven as *The Elusive Pimpernel* (1950), but it isn't in the same class.

'Enemies of the screen, who still exist and still maintain for it a vitriolic stream of contempt and abuse, should pay a visit to [this film] to see how many ways the intelligent film director can deal with a certain class of dramatic material with infinitely better results than the stage could possibly provide . . . This old-time and popular favourite . . . becomes under the supervision of Mr Alexander Korda not merely revitalised and renovated, but an excitingly new and splendid revolutionary romance . . . It is unsurpassable.' *(Sydney W. Carrol, Sunday Times)*

'One of the finest, most entertaining historical pictures ever made, in this country or out of it.' *(Sunday Telegraph)*

'Admirable direction . . . [of a] first-rate film . . . Mr

'Raymond Massey was as sinister and sarcastic a Chauvelin as you could wish to see.' *(Punch)*

'Stirring to the pulse and beautiful to the eye . . . Mr Howard is the Pimpernel himself, gallant and resourceful . . . He is an infinite delight even in a cast which is correct down to the smallest roles.' *(Andre Sennwald, New York Times)*

SCARLET STREET

CT: 6 AV: 7.00

1945 US 98/103 BW DRAMA

D Fritz Lang ☆
W Dudley Nichols from George de la Fouchardière's play *La Chienne*

Edward G. Robinson ☆ Joan Bennett ☆
Dan Duryea ☆ Jess Barker Margaret Lindsay
Rosalind Ivan Samuel S. Hinds Arthur Loft

An ineffectual, middle-aged, amateur artist (Edward G. Robinson) becomes obsessed with a prostitute (Joan Bennett) who persuades him to rent her a studio apartment. When she sells his pictures as her own work, he contents himself with painting her toenails. But suddenly the worm turns . . .

Lang's remake of Jean Renoir's *La Chienne* (1931) offers him the chance to reunite the three stars of *The Woman in the Window* (1944) and his excellent cinematographer Milton Krasner. The result is a classic of film noir style, and a cool, sadistic study of a masochist in love. Edward G. Robinson plays one of his most tortured, sensitive roles. The film, though admirable in many respects, suffers dramatically from the fact that the audience may find it hard to sympathize with so passive a hero. It was controversial because, for the first time in a Hollywood movie, a murderer avoided punishment – though not a guilty conscience.

'From *Scarlet Street* on, I wanted to show that the average citizen is not very much better than a criminal.' *(Fritz Lang)*

PRO:

'The director unerringly chooses the right sound and image to assault the spectator's sensibilities.' *(C.A. Lejeune)*

'I can recommend [it].' *(James Agee, Nation)*

'Dan Duryea gives a brilliant performance.' *(Daily Mail)*

MIXED:

'The capacity of a pretty slut to overturn the most solid and respectable existence . . . evidently obsesses Mr Lang, and there is something overly Teutonic indeed . . . in the ponderous treatment of it . . . I can confess to no great weakness for Mr Robinson in his new ersatz-Jannings act. That strange face, like a pike's, was tolerable when the words came rattling out of it as fast and pitiless as the machine-guns among which it flourished. But Mr Robinson in his gently murderous role I find well-nigh intolerable. The picture is, however, well worth seeing if only for the superb performance of Miss Bennett.' *(Tribune)*

'An ambitious melodrama bristling with fine directorial touches and expert acting. Its trouble is its painfully obvious story . . . Audiences will not be in much suspense, but they may stay interested just wondering what the dim-witted, unprincipled characters will think of next . . . The chill look of reality in the sets only emphasizes the two-dimensional unreality of the characters who walk through them.' *(Time)*

'A fine film, honest and done with immense care to detail . . . My only criticism is that the fate of Mr Robinson does not move you as it should.' *(Daily Express)*

'Despite the title and all the lurid implications of the censors' ban [it] is a painfully moral picture, and, in the light of modern candor, rather tame.' *(Bosley Crowther)*

SCENES FROM A MARRIAGE

CT: 6 AV: 7.78

(aka *Scener ur ett Äktenskap*)

1974 Sweden 168 C DRAMA/FOREIGN

D Ingmar Bergman ☆
W Ingmar Bergman ☆

Liv Ullmann ☆ Erland Josephson ☆
Bibi Andersson ☆ Jan Malmsjö Gunnel Lindblom
Anita Wall

A woman (Liv Ullman) re-evaluates her marriage when she discovers that her husband (Erland Josephson) is having an affair with a younger woman (Bibi Andersson).

Gruelling analysis of a troubled modern relationship, wonderfully acted, and starkly photographed by Sven Nykvist. Unfortunately, the narrative rambles, despite having been edited down from a six-part, 300-minute TV series, and at the end of the day – or what seems like a day – the film says nothing new about non-communication.

PRO:

'Bergman has never before made such an exhilarating film about grownup love, with all its twists, rituals, and benedictions. It takes . . . a genius to flood a tragic work with this piercing affection and sense of fun.' *(Penelope Gilliatt, New Yorker)*

'Such a precise work, seemingly so uncomplicated, that it has the impact of one of those laws of physics that are so fundamental you can't understand why it was thousands of years before someone discovered it . . . I find myself slipping into hyperbole here to emphasize the particularity of Bergman's achievement.' *(Vincent Canby, New York Times)*

'The masterly Bergman once again puts the most painful of human relationships on the operating table . . . A terrible and true film.' *(Felix Barker, Evening News)*

'Displays all Bergman's psychological skill and acuity and draws inspired performances from the two principals.' *(Virginia Dignam, Morning Star)*

'By any standards it is a marvellous piece of cinema which leaves you drained, exhausted yet oddly exhilarated.' *(Margaret Hinxman, Daily Mail)*

'One of the truest, most luminous love stories ever made.' *(Roger Ebert)*

MIXED:

'For those who can stand the marathon, the confidences, the despairs and the close-up confabs of sleepless bedmates have a cumulative impressiveness – rather like a ship's foghorn, warning off smaller craft. Cheerless but insistent.' *(Alexander Walker, Evening Standard)*

SCENT OF GREEN PAPAYA AAN

CT: 6 AV: 8.00

(aka *Mui Du Du Xanh; L'Odeur de la Papaye Verte*)

1993 France 104 C DRAMA/FOREIGN

D Tran Anh Hung
W Tran Anh Hung

Lu Man San Tran Nu Yen-Khe Lu Man San Truong Thi Loc Tuo Nguyen Anh Hoa Vyong Hoa Hoi

A 10-year-old Vietnamese maidservant (Lu Man San) grows up in a Saigon household resigned to her subordinate role. As a 20-year-old (Tran Nu Yen-Khe) she is made pregnant by her employer.

This is a movie which many westerners will be unable to watch without feeling frustrated at the heroine's placid acceptance of life, treating the worst and best it has to offer with the same cheerful stoicism. Nor will it appeal to those who believe cinema to be a narrative art: there aren't enough events in the film to fill the average American movie's pre-titles sequence.

Yet it is never boring. Its fluid camerawork and wonderful evocation of Vietnamese life (unbelievably, it was shot in a French studio) amount to a rare and rewarding look at a Buddhist culture. The style, too, is an interesting mixture of east and west: it has the appetite for the texture of everyday life which you can see in Ozu or Satyajit Ray. But the sensuality of the detail compares with the best work of Robert Bresson. And the willingness to move the camera and sensitivity to colour compare with Britain's Peter Greenaway and Terence Davies.

MIXED:

'One is more satisfying in its modesty and because the child playing Mui is perfectly at ease in front of the camera and a joy to watch. Part Two, which develops into a soap opera, I find a bit creepy . . . What bugs me about the second, "grown-up" half [is that] suddenly something delicate and quiet turns into a slightly hysterical Cinderella story.' *(Georgia Brown, Village Voice)*

'Moody, gentle, evocative of lost-world elegance, but oddly uncompelling.' *(Sheridan Morley, Sunday Express)*

PRO:

'So placid and filled with sweetness that watching it is like listening to soothing music . . . It is a placid, interior, contemplative film – not plot-driven, but centered on the growth of the young woman . . . This is a film to cherish.' *(Roger Ebert)*

'Introduces a brilliant, delicate new male sensibility to audiences whose exposure to Vietnam has been derived primarily from war films . . . The outcome will fail to stir up feminist passions, but for those who can manage to withhold judgment, this film offers ample pleasures to the eyes and ears.' *(Liza Bear, Film Journal)*

'The film examines the complex ambiguity surrounding subservience and love: women liberated by love, only to be further enslaved.' *(Pamela Avis, Moving Pictures)*

'A film of intense charm, remarkable tranquillity and ultimate happiness . . . a work of love.' *(Alexander Walker, Evening Standard)*

'Ravishing . . . Tran . . . is a name to be watched.' *(Geoff Brown, The Times)*

'Sensitive, evocative and politically ambivalent.' *(Tom Charity, Time Out)*

SCHINDLER'S LIST AAW

CT: 9 AV: 9.50

1993 US 195 BW (some colour) DRAMA/ WAR

D Steven Spielberg ☆ AAW
W Steven Zaillian ☆ AAW from Thomas Keneally's book *Schindler's Ark* (later renamed *Schindler's List*)

Liam Neeson ☆ AAN Ralph Fiennes ☆ AAN Ben Kingsley ☆ Caroline Goodall ☆ Embeth Davidtz Jonathan Sagalle

A Nazi (Liam Neeson) saves more than 1100 Jews from the Holocaust.

One thing that's often forgotten in times of back-to-basics Puritanism is that flawed people can achieve great things. The hero of Spielberg's film is an inveterate womanizer, an exploiter of slave labour, and a Nazi – yet still a hero. Where Thomas Keneally's Booker prize-winning novel was obliged to describe him with words, Spielberg shows us Schindler through a montage of visual images. He is a hedonistic dandy: his first, dressing-up scene is reminiscent of Richard Gere going to work in *American Gigolo*. He fraternizes with Nazis in a club, like a more corrupt Humphrey Bogart in *Casablanca*. He wheels, deals and threatens, like a Germanic Godfather.

His first act of rescue – when he saves his hapless accountant Itzhak Stern (Ben Kingsley) from a train leaving for a concentration camp – is for selfish, business reasons. 'What if I'd got here five minutes late?' Schindler demands. 'Then where would I be?' But he happens to be riding on a hilltop on March 13th, 1943, when he sees beneath him the brutal clearing of the Cracow ghetto: people being shot, children running for cover. He finds himself sympathizing with a Jewish workforce which he had intended only to exploit. His moment of truth is not accompanied by angst-ridden soul-searching: instead, we see him starting to change through his deeds.

Neeson plays Schindler convincingly as a big man of impulsive appetites and actions, someone whose force of character, bonhomie and ability to turn nasty enabled him to bluff his (and other's) way out of danger. He has an expert foil in Ben Kingsley's more calculating, self-effacing right-hand man. But the most stunning performance comes from another British actor, Ralph Fiennes, as Amon Goeth, the murderous commandant of the Plaszcow forced labour camp. Fiennes plays this monster with such understanding and black humour that he becomes comprehensible and even pitiable – while Schindler's attempts to dupe him with bribes and flattery become doubly scary.

One of the worst side-effects of modern cinema is that it has partly anaesthetized us to scenes of violence; but the casual shootings here – many of them by the demented Goeth – have the immediacy of today's news. Jews are dispatched as casually as pigs being slaughtered. This is how it must have been; and it is horrible to watch.

Yet this is not a depressing picture – so much so that Spielberg was even accused of making a feelgood film out of the Holocaust. It is true that he is eager as always to see light in the darkness: the striking of a match is his opening image. But he is not guilty of prettification, as he was in *Empire of the Sun* and (especially) *The Color Purple*, which lost impact through Spielberg's constant pursuit of the perfect, backlit shot, and his seeming inability to contemplate the uglier sides of life.

Here, he seems a different and far superior director. At no point does he sanitize history, and he achieves a much harder-edged, black-and-white, hand-held style of shooting which (though as perfectly lit as ever) has the rough immediacy of real life.

He is unable to resist one vulgar, Hollywood touch: a schmaltzy, over-theatrical farewell where Schindler breaks down and expresses the wish that he could have saved more Jews. But perhaps Spielberg and screenwriter Steven Zaillian may be allowed one crass scene in three-and-a-quarter hours.

Schindler's List has been called Spielberg's *Citizen Kane*, but in its vitality, style and quality it is more like John Ford's *Grapes of Wrath*. Spielberg gives a similar impression of huge numbers of people on the move: his amazing sense of scale and shot composition (first revealed in his worst ever flop, *1941*) comes into its own with the enormous, hellish set-pieces, such as the exhumation and incineration of massacred Jews; the loading of children on to cattle trucks and the chase by their screaming mothers; the entrance into Auschwitz. Spielberg is not afraid to take us into the heart of darkness, and many of his images are unforgettable.

Most astonishingly of all, he achieves this epic scale without sacrificing any humanity – and without allowing himself to be sidetracked into the easy pathos of soap opera. Some have complained it is impossible to keep track of every individual Jew in the film, but that is one reason why it will bear re-seeing. Their stories are going on in the background, but their behaviour is shown in wonderful detail and variety – and every now and again (there is one staggering moment involving a girl in a red coat) Spielberg brings us face to face with some moment of salvation or personal tragedy.

Schindler's List was bound to win the Best Film Oscar for all sorts of bad reasons – in recompense for the one he should have won for *E.T.*, as a way of saying thank you for the box-office success of *Jurassic Park*, because its portrayal of a wheeler-dealer capitalist with a heart was bound to appeal to voters in Hollywood. But it is a masterpiece – a brilliantly made, richly textured and profoundly moving picture which does more than any other film to illuminate one of the central events of the twentieth century.

ANTI:

'Propaganda with a purpose of asking for sympathy [for Jews] as well as to tarnish the other race.' *(The Malaysian Film Censor Board, in a letter to Universal International Pictures, explaining why Schindler's List was to be banned in Malaysia.)*

'The film never successfully explains what drives Neeson, a Nazi party member, a heretofore unremarkable man and frankly a bit of a cad and a swine, to such a change of mind and heart and to such spectacular acts of heroism. There is almost nothing here about his life before the war. The movie depicts his epiphenomenal moment as the sighting of a little Jewish girl in a scarlet coat (the only gash of color until the coda) in the Cracow ghetto. But that seems thin and pat. Despite admirable intentions and the undeniable splendor of his craft, ultimately what Spielberg has told is the story of the list; he has not told the story of Schindler.' *(Joanne Kaufman, Time)*

'While in the prolonged, lachrymose ending, Schindler reminds his former laborers that they are the heroes, since they have done all the surviving, viewers have just seen three hours of evidence to the contrary. The film is about Schindler's genius, Schindler's survival instincts, and Schindler's centrality to all events. Like Vietnam War movies that have nothing to say about the Vietnamese, this is a Holocaust narrative where Jews, for all the scenes of ghetto liquidation, degradation, and execution, are rather marginal . . . Perhaps more troubling than Spielberg's sense of the Holocaust's heroes is his concept of its villains . . . The Nazi state was created not by psychopaths and drug addicts, but by lawyers, corporate executives, businessmen, professors, even clergymen . . . Spielberg's simplistic view of heroes and villains, his unproblematical approach to a topic that reveals a profound horror by seeing its complexity, is at the root of the film's error. The savagery of Nazism isn't to be located in the whims of a deranged brute, but in assumptions nascent within our entire civilization. Nazism was a manifestation of a political, economic, and philosophical world view that still is implicated deeply in our basic institutions. It is precisely the type of phenomenon that Hollywood is ill-equipped and uninterested in representing.' *(Christopher Sharrett, USA Today)*

PRO:

'I went to see *Schindler's List* . . . I implore every one of you to go see it.' *(President Bill Clinton)*

'What Spielberg achieves in *Schindler's List* is nearly miraculous. It is by far the finest, fullest, dramatic (i.e. nondocumentary) film ever made about the Holocaust. And few American movies since the silent era have had anything approaching this picture's boldness, visual audacity and emotional directness.' *(Terrence Rafferty, New Yorker)*

'By dramatizing the Holocaust with such vividness and scale, Spielberg has helped to pass its lessons on to future generations.' *(Brian D. Johnson, Maclean's)*

'This is no weepy, but a cover-your-face-and-try-to-stop-shaking experience . . . From its dark urgency, *Schindler's List* cries out the undeniably thrilling, empowering promise that one person can make a difference, because one did.' *(Angie Errigo, Empire)*

'Steven Spielberg has succeeded beyond all expectations . . . It is an amazing story, but to make a three-hour black and white film of it, and refrain from romanticizing or sensationalizing the plot, could have been contemplated by few other directors . . . A film that will live in the memory of all who see it.' *(Derek Malcolm, Cosmopolitan)*

'One of the great films in the history of the cinema.' *(Iain Johnstone, Sunday Times)*

'What is most amazing about this film is how completely Spielberg serves his story. The movie is brilliantly acted, written, directed and seen. Individual scenes are masterpieces of art direction, cinematography, special effects, crowd control. Yet Spielberg, the stylist whose films have often gloried in shots we are intended to notice and remember, disappears into his work. Neeson, Kingsley and the other actors are devoid of acting flourishes. There is a single-mindedness to the enterprise that is awesome.' *(Roger Ebert)*

'Masterly . . . Spielberg has not used one trite shot, one cheap tear-jerking assemblage. Tears are evoked, but honorably; his aim was to make a film that gripped us with authenticity . . . Imagination, talent, commitment shine in every frame . . . This film is a welcome astonishment from a director who has given us much boyish esprit, much ingenuity, but little seriousness. His stark, intelligent style here, perfectly controlled, suggests that this may be the start of a new period in Spielberg's prodigious career – Part Two: The Man.' *(Stanley Kauffmann)*

SCHRECKLICHE MÄDCHEN, DAS: *see* NASTY GIRL, THE.

SCIUSCIA: *see* SHOESHINE.

SCROOGE CT: 8 AV: 8.50

(aka *A Christmas Carol*)

1951 GB 86 BW DRAMA/FANTASY

D Brian Desmond Hurst ☆
W Noel Langley from Charles Dickens' novel A *Christmas Carol*

Alastair Sim ☆ Mervyn Johns Kathleen Harrison Jack Warner Hermione Baddeley Michael Hordern, George Cole

Miser (Alastair Sim) is haunted by ghosts on Christmas Eve, and decides to change his ways.

The magnificently quirky Alastair Sim excels in this superior version of the Dickens' Christmas classic. Though beautifully art-directed and faithful to the original novel, it has none of the usual vices of literary adaptations; the plot proceeds at a good pace, and the cast is always sensitive to the original author's intentions.

MIXED:

'Of its sort [it] is a good film.' *(Manchester Guardian)*

'It misses opportunities in such essential bits of bravura as Mr Fezziwig's ball and the Cratchits'

Christmas dinner but [director and writer] contrive the right atmosphere and have dealt most honestly with the author.' *(Jympson Harman, Evening News)*

'On the whole it is a straight-forward job . . . and very useful and welcome it is. If the film lacks some spark of greatness, one of the reasons is Scrooge himself . . . For although he is a very fine and intelligent actor, Alastair Sim never for a moment persuaded me that he was as wicked as he sounded.' *(Thomas Spencer, Daily Worker)*

PRO:

'Mr Sim is an actor who brings great artistry to the big round eye and the gaping mouth . . . [His] miser converted to bounding benevolence is no caricature, but a real man, fierce, funny and sometimes pathetic. this is rich and rare acting, something to be relished like a thick slice of plum pudding.' *(Roy Nash, Star)*

'Makes Scrooge credible at last . . . Few will be disappointed . . . Scrooge as I think Dickens wanted him to be.' *(Milton Shulman, Evening Standard)*

SEA HAWK, THE CT: 6 AV: 8.15

1940 US C ACTION/ADVENTURE

D Michael Curtiz ☆
W Seton I. Miller Howard Koch

Errol Flynn ☆ Flora Robson Brenda Marshall Henry Daniell ☆ Claude Rains Donald Crisp Alan Hale Una O'Connor James Stephenson Gilbert Roland William Lundigan

Elizabeth I (Flora Robson) encourages pirate (Errol Flynn) to acts against Spanish shipping.

Flora Robson is content to repeat her Goodish Queen Bess from *Fire Over England* (1937), while Errol Flynn seems to base what there is of his character on his own previous outings as *Captain Blood* (1935) and *Robin Hood* (1938). The plot is unhistorical as well as formulaic, and there is far too much talk; but when the movie sets out to sea, it's thrilling and lives up to its reputation as a classic swashbuckler. Erich Wolfgang Korngold was Oscar-nominated for his music, Anton Grot for his art direction.

ANTI:

'Little credit can be extended to the over-written script, with long passages of dry and uninteresting dialog, or to the slow-paced, uninspired direction by Michael Curtiz. Errol Flynn fails to generate the fire and dash necessary to put over the role of the buccaneer leader.' *(Variety)*

MIXED:

'The production and photography are in the main good, but on occasions in the sea scenes one feels the unreality of the set. A little more trouble with the dialogue would have been amply repaid as in a film of this nature Americanisms strike a particularly anachronistic note. But the story certainly grips, particularly if you do not bother too much about its impossibilities. ' *(MFB)*

PRO:

'The Brothers Warner have invested the [film] with all the advantages inherent in 16 years of technological advancement [since the 1924 version] and staffed it, off screen as on, with an array of talent such as is seldom assembled for a single production.' *(William R. Weaver, Motion Picture Herald)*

'Aloft there! Clear away on your miz'n braces! Charge your cannon and stand ready to prepare for an attack! For Errol Flynn and his raffish crew . . . are coming about on the starboard quarter . . . Yessir, mates, the Burbank Brothers are really giving us some action this time . . . Of course it is all historically cockeyed, and the amazing exploits of Mr Flynn . . . are quite as incredible as the adventures of Dick Tracy. But Flora Robson makes an interesting Queen Elizabeth . . . there is a lot of brocaded scenery . . . and, of course, there is Brenda Marshall to shed a bit of romantic light.' *(Bosley Crowther)*

SEA OF LOVE CT: 7 AV: 6.77

1989 US 112 C THRILLER/ROMANCE

D Harold Becker ☆
W Richard Price ☆

Al Pacino ☆ Ellen Barkin ☆ John Goodman William Hickey Michael Rooker Richard Jenkins

Someone is murdering Manhattan men who advertise themselves in verse in Lonely Hearts columns. The victims are invariably to be found, naked and shot through the head, with a record called Sea of Love *spinning on the turntable. A tough, lonely cop (Al Pacino) attempts to lay his hands on this over-zealous literary critic by penning an ad himself. Initially single-minded but increasingly singles-minded, Pacino is soon laying hands all over the chief suspect (the sultry Ellen Barkin).*

Those who enjoyed the suspense of *Jagged Edge* or the erotic charge of *Body Heat* could do much worse than submerge themselves in *Sea of Love*. The film falls some way short of excellence. The sub-plot about a delivery boy, intended as a red herring, is more like a dead herring. The title record is revealed eventually (and irksomely) as an irrelevance. The twist in the tale and the motivation of the killer are disappointingly predictable.

However, Richard Price's dialogue is sharp enough to compensate for the deficiencies of his storyline; Harold Becker's direction is his grittiest since *The Onion Field* in 1979; and there is less of the misogyny which has disfigured other recent thrillers in the post-Aids, sexual paranoia genre, notably *Fatal Attraction*.

In the potentially clichéd role of the cop, Al

Pacino has a bantam-weight cockiness befitting the small-arms champion of the New York Police Department (he is presumably also the recipient of its short-legs award), Mr Pacino struts through the picture in great style, and shows unsuspected warmth in his comic scenes. As in *The Big Easy*, Ellen Barkin is both real and real sexy.

MIXED:

'It's all slightly unbelievable, but what the hell, it's entertaining . . . [and] crafted with consummate skill.' *(Jeff Sawtell, Morning Star)*

'The script's complexities are buried too deep, sometimes obscured by the push-me-pull-you aspect of the two stars, and there is a fogginess in the plotting. It is, nonetheless, a smart piece of entertainment, shaded in more subtle tones than the comic book colours of most of its contemporaries. And, yes, damned sexy.' *(Neil Norman, Evening Standard)*

PRO:

'With . . . his first good movie in fourteen years, Al Pacino ends a hellish losing streak . . . [This] low-down, gorgeously lurid thriller can't make up for those career crushers . . . But Pacino is terrific in it: vital, charming, funny, torchy and touching.' *(Peter Travers, Rolling Stone)*

'Taut, racy, sublimely witty . . . [it] crackles with verve and erotic overtones . . . Becker expertly combines a display of gripping, roving camera angles – giving an intelligent thriller lots of bite and substance, combined with the testy flowering of sophisticated romance.' *(Kathryn Bailey, Today)*

'The word Aids is never mentioned in *Sea of Love*, nor is the issue of condoms in sex scenes ever raised, but that doesn't stop the subject from resonating through the movie. The film looks like a mystery – a singularly under-populated mystery with a small cast that features far too few red herrings, and narrative holes that one could drive a small delivery van through. But the mystery – who is the personal ads killer? – is of less interest and importance than the film's love story and its subtext. . . . *Sea of Love* takes its power from the universality of its subtext. Everyone who has not yet found the stability of the couple is out there, on edge, usually looking for love in all the wrong places and finding something else.' *(John Harkness, Film Yearbook)*

SEARCHERS, THE

CT: 8 AV: 9.26

1956 US 119 C WESTERN

D John Ford ☆
W Frank S. Nugent from Alan Le May's novel

John Wayne ☆ Jeffrey Hunter Natalie Wood
Vera Miles Ward Bond John Qualen
Henry Brandon Antonio Moreno

Racist Confederate war veteran (John Wayne) searches for the Indians who murdered his brother and sister-in-law and abducted his niece (Natalie Wood).

Former film critic Frank S. Nugent contributes a memorably dark screenplay to this classic John Ford picture, which received mixed reviews on release but is now generally considered a masterpiece. Ford skilfully switches points-of-view throughout the film, which holds the interest despite its length. Winton Hoch's landscape photography is magnificent, and extends beyond familiar Fordian locations like *Monument Valley*; unfortunately, it is rather wasted on TV.

The aspect which makes this look the most modern of Ford's westerns is its anti-hero, Ethan Edwards. He is a complex, obsessive character, an odd mixture of good and bad, and he's played with absolute conviction by Wayne, in one of his strongest performances. The film received Oscar nominations for Best Score (Max Steiner) and Editing (Jack Murray).

ANTI:

'Disappointing. There is a feeling that it could have been so much more. Overlong and repetitious, there are subtleties in the basically simple story that are not adequately explained. There are, however, some fine vignettes of frontier life.' *(Variety)*

'It's a peculiarly formal and stilted movie, with Ethan framed in a doorway at the opening and the close. You can read a lot into it, but it isn't very enjoyable. The lines are often awkward and the line readings worse, and the film is often static, despite economic, quick editing.' *(Pauline Kael)*

MIXED:

'The beginning [is] . . . the one first rate portion of the picture . . . All is far too quiet on [Ford's] western front.' *(Harold Conway, Daily Sketch)*

'A very good film, but with all its advantages of glorious colour it will not wear as *Stagecoach* has worn . . . Nevertheless, the horseriding is beautiful and thrilling . . . and the final raid on the Indian encampment has you holding on to your seat. The Old Master has not lost all his magic.' *(R.D. Smith, Tribune)*

'The western has come a long way . . . Black-and-white sagebrush . . . with a vague mountain or two in the background won't do nowadays . . . The characters have stopped being black and white too . . . John Ford . . . has probably done as much as any man to elevate the western into a work of art . . . All [his] characters are warm-hearted, human being, bubbling with life . . . One exception . . . is the Comanche chief . . . [whose] motives are not sufficiently explained . . . The film would gain from a stronger drawing of [his] character.' *(Thomas Spencer, Daily Worker)*

PRO:

'Yippee! This is the best western I have seen in ten years . . . It is spectacular. It is rough and tough . . .

[and] never pulls its punches – in its fights or its basic situations.' *(Leonard Mosley, Daily Express)*

'Nobody like Ford for suggesting the feeling of the settlement in the wilderness: the moments of gaiety, the terrible transience of mourning in a country where before the first soil falls on the grave men are already buckling on their guns to hunt the killers. Above all, nobody like Ford for suggesting the idea of what we call home . . . It may seem puzzling that Ford, whose feeling in the western can be warmly sentimental, should allow himself passages of vulgar and brutal horseplay.' *(Dilys Powell)*

'Outwardly a shoot-em-up western, *The Searchers*' complex theme has struck deep chords in the American consciousness, interpreting the white fear of darker races as a sexual fear, and suggesting that America is still uneasily poised half-way between civilization and the wilderness it has so recently conquered.' *(Herbert Kretzmer, Daily Mail, 1979)*

'In modern terms, *The Searchers* is a racist film. Wayne's passionate hatred of the Comanches is portrayed as justifiable and heroic. No effort is made to explain the Indian point of view. Tut tut. Yet the brilliant images composed by the director John Ford may last longer than political westerns which set out to entertain us by siding with the Red Indian.' *(Peter McKay, Evening Standard, 1990)*

'The best western ever made . . . Wayne was never better than as the tormented, potentially murderous Ethan, and John Ford stages heartbreaking moments in the action-packed plot.' *(Empire, 1994)*

'It's a great western and Wayne, who never got enough credit for his performances, is an incredible presence.' *(Jonathan Ross, Flicks)*

'From its opening scene *The Searchers* is unified on a visual and structural level . . . In him [Wayne] are all the qualities that make a western hero – strength, individualism, self-sufficiency, leadership, authority.' *(J.A. Place, The Western Films of John Ford, 1973)*

SEARCHING FOR BOBBY FISCHER

CT: 6 AV: 7. 00

(aka *Innocent Moves*)

1993 US C DRAMA

D Steven Zaillian ✔
W Steven Zaillian ✔

Max Pomeranc ☆ Joe Mantegna ✔ Joan Allen ✔
Ben Kingsley Laurence Fishburne
Robert Stephens David Paymer

Well-meaning, middle-class parents (Joe Mantegna and Joan Allen) discover their son (Max Pomeranc) is a genius at chess.

The directorial début of Steven Zaillian, who wrote the epic *Schindler's List*, is at the other end of the cinematic scale – a minutely detailed analysis of what it means to be a gifted child. Zaillian's script is extremely clever, constantly inverting audience expectations, and neatly avoiding facile moral judgments. The acting throughout is wonderful. This is a lovely, thoughtful, touching little film. Conrad Hall's camerawork, though a trifle too claustrophobic at times for no reason, is mainly excellent, as is the editing. The one fly in the ointment is Hollywood's most pompous composer, James Horner, who has the same effect that he had on another fine film, Edward Zwick's *Glory*, of turning affecting sentiment into clod-hopping schmaltz.

MIXED:

'This film teaches you an awful lot. Sometimes it even feels like an educational film . . . A good film, certainly, but not so good you don't sometimes wish the whole thing was about Fischer, and not Waitzkin who is still only 16.' *(William Leith, Mail on Sunday)*

'Zaillian's film is rather better at dramatising juvenile genius than, say *Little Man Tate* . . . [It] is predictably sentimental, but the chess tournaments that punctuate it are well enough mounted to carry the movie through its sticky patches.' *(Kevin Jackson, Independent)*

'Zaillian's intelligence is matched only by his sweet tooth . . . But Joe Mantegna and Max Pomeranc are excellent and the chess is surprisingly dramatic.' *(Quentin Curtis, Independent on Sunday)*

PRO:

'For the kids who'll make it a hit [it's] *Star Wars* on a chess board . . . For the adults who'll be happy they went, it's two hours of therapy, a battle between the reality principle . . . and the pleasure principle . . . A compelling fable about innocence.' *(Joe Levy, Village Voice)*

'A witty, original, exciting film . . . Often very funny . . . the film captures vividly the pressure of national competition. Best of all it eschews easy moralising for a humane notion of balance between the drive to succeed and a proper respect for the simpler needs of childhood.' *(Hugo Davenport, Daily Telegraph)*

'The movie is one of the best about the incubation of gifted children and is wise enough to do more than hint at what will eventually hatch . . . Conrad Hall's lighting adds visible drama to cerebral suspense.' *(Alexander Walker, Evening Standard)*

SECRET GAME, THE: *see* JEUX INTERDITS.

SECRET GARDEN, THE

CT: 8 AV: 6 (est)

1993 US C DRAMA/FAMILY

D Agnieszka Holland ✔
W Caroline Thompson ✔ from Frances Hodgson Burnett's novel

Kate Maberly ☆ Maggie Smith ☆ Andrew Knott ✔
Heydon Prowse ✔ John Lynch Laura Crossley

A spoiled, selfish young girl, Mary Lennox (Kate Maberly) is orphaned and goes to live in a vast, loveless house on the Yorkshire moors. Here she survives the cold – both physical and emotional.

This book is a natural for the cinema, since its metaphors are so visual: winter turns into spring as the characters' emotions thaw; the dormant garden is a symbol of the children's better nature. No wonder, then, that Hollywood had already filmed the story: the 1949 black and white film simplified and Americanized the characters for the screen, but was memorable for the way it burgeoned into colour for the garden sequences, And there was a lavishly produced, though indifferently acted, BBC production in 1987. But it took a Polish director, an American executive producer (Francis Ford Coppola) and an almost entirely British cast and crew, led by cinematographer Roger Deakins and designer Stuart Craig, to put together this version – and it's a beauty.

I have minor niggles. The continuity is dismayingly amateurish early on – the dirt on Mary Lennox's face rarely stays in one place for two consecutive shots. The director makes too little use of the coldness of the interiors (they are lit, instead, with a kind of autumnal glow which gives them the aura of advertisements for English Heritage). I could certainly have done without the heavenly chorus which swells whenever a plant comes into focus; and the climax is prolonged to the point of irritation. Nevertheless, the American screenwriter Caroline Thompson wrote a magical screenplay for *Edward Scissorhands*, and she's pulled off the same trick again. She has even spotted some largely unnoticed undertones of the original: the quasi-sexual relationship between Mary and Dickon, the extent to which the three children's relationship is an emotional triangle in the making.

Interestingly for a woman screenwriter, she has banished the one benevolent mother-figure of the novel (Mrs Sowerby, mother of Martha the maid) and focused totally on the relationship – or lack of it – between Colin and his father. In doing so, it must be admitted, Thompson is following every recent cinematic precedent. Fatherhood, or the absence of fathers, seems to be the burning cinematic topic of the single-parent 90s.

A few other elements of the novel have been lost. In the original, Mary Lennox's parents die of cholera. The film replaces this with that more cinematic instrument of death, an earthquake. This weakens one of the underlying themes of the novel: fear of contamination. In the film, the servants' wearing of surgical masks when visiting the invalid Colin is laughable: in the book, there is more sense that they may have a point, that Mary Lennox may be meddling in things she doesn't understand.

Another dimension which has been mislaid is one of adult malice: one reason that Colin is treated so poorly in the novel is his doctor's desire that the boy be an invalid. It's no accident that the doctor is Colin's uncle, and stands to inherit the estate if Colin dies.

But these are relatively minor quibbles – and perhaps one should be grateful that so much of the story and spirit of the novel remain intact, and at a length which children will find tolerable.

Stalwartly refusing to be upstaged by children, animals or time-lapse photography, Maggie Smith is predictably wonderful as Mrs Medlock, the Yorkshire housekeeper, normally played (as in the 1949 film by Gladys Cooper) as a forbidding old woman who would have intimidated *Rebecca*'s Mrs Danvers. Maggie Smith offers a much richer, more comic interpretation: here is a woman who is fundamentally well-meaning but medically naive, insensitive, fearful for her job, and a stickler for Victorian ideas of discipline. She is, in her way, endearingly eccentric – and there's a lovely moment towards the end when Martha the maid consoles her, in the movie's one concession to a mother-daughter relationship.

John Lynch, as Colin's absentee father, has little in the way of dialogue, and Ms Holland sensibly takes the opportunity to portray him in more visual terms, as a saturnine, moody mixture of Heathcliff and Dracula, surrounded by snarling mastiffs or, like Bram Stoker's anti-hero, being transported across bleak moorland in a black carriage.

But it's the children you remember. The director has wisely resisted all Hollywood temptation to sweeten them, so their journey from brattishness to openness is all the more realistic and unaffected – and, as a consequence, very affecting. Anyone of any age should enjoy this lovely, lively, often enchanting film – and it's such an effective weepie that it will make even the most hard-hearted of us wish we had shares in Kleenex.

ANTI:

'The body of a famous children's classic is found dead on a boardroom table: that of Warner Brothers. Means: genteel strangulation . . . Determined to avoid Burnett's Victorian sentimentality, [Holland] manages to avoid every other tolerable emotion too.' *(Nigel Andrews, Financial Times)*

MIXED:

'A solid adaptation . . . [which] lacks the edge of [Holland's] two last films and, probably for that reason, has been a great success in America . . . It is sentimental without having the nerve to throw caution to the devil and go all out for high kitsch.' *(Sheila Johnston, Independent)*

PRO:

'Whether together or separately, [Holland and Thompson] strive to do right by Burnett's classic, but they've also changed details to strengthen its force as a girl's own story . . . By playing down the gothic and resisting the temptations of conventional cinematic narrative . . . [Holland] quite simply and very beautifully reveals evil's roots.' *(Georgia Brown, Village Voice)*

'Its excellence is rooted firmly in first-class production design and cinematography . . . Most of all, credit is due to the outstanding quality of a mostly English cast.' *(Hugo Davenport, Daily Telegraph)*

'Everything in the garden – and outside it too – is lovely.' *(Alexander Walker, Evening Standard)*

SECRET OF DR MABUSE, THE: *see* THE *DR MABUSE* SERIES (THE THOUSAND EYES OF DOCTOR MABUSE).

SENGZHENG, LAN: *see* BLUE KITE, THE.

SEPARATE TABLES AAN CT: 5 AV: 7.60

1958 US 98 BW DRAMA

D Delbert Mann
W Terence Rattigan John Gay AAN from Terence Rattigan's play

Burt Lancaster Rita Hayworth David Niven ☆ AAW Deborah Kerr ✗ AAN Wendy Hiller ☆ AAW Gladys Cooper ☆ Cathleen Nesbitt ☆ Felix Aylmer ☆ Rod Taylor Audrey Dalton May Hallatt ☆

Inmates of a Bournemouth boarding house undergo various emotional torments.

Uninspired film of Terence Rattigan's genteel play, with American imports Rita Hayworth and Burt Lancaster miscast and struggling, and the excruciatingly inappropriate Vic Damone crooning over the credits. The noteworthy performances are by the British contingent, especially Niven and Hiller – Deborah Kerr slightly overdoes her repressed spinster. Charles Lang Jr's photography and David Raksin's music were Oscar-nominated.

MIXED:
'The acting goes from brilliant to mediocre . . . Softness where toughness is needed runs through all the direction of this sympathetic but stagy and always slightly remote and incredible film.' *(Isabel Quigly, Spectator)*

PRO:
'This is such a grand array of first-class acting that I find myself judging fine work as just good because there is so much else that is superlative . . . The picture is too talkative, allows too much to happen off stage to be a good movie, and has an ending which is too facile in its solution. But it is a film nobody should miss.' *(Jympson Harman, Evening News)*

'Rattigan has unfolded [the story] with intelligence and compassion and has been helped by admirable casting and playing . . . Niven . . . gives one of the best performances of his career.' *(Fred Majdalany, Daily Mail)*

'Here is a film in which little happens yet is taut with drama, which has scarcely any action, yet moves to disgust and delight, to laughter and to tears. Its people are real, its dialogue deft, its intertwining of characters and interchange of situation brilliantly done.' *(Ivon Adams, Star)*

'A moving, adult film enhanced by brilliant acting.' *(Dick Richards, Daily Mirror)*

SERGEANT PEPPER'S LONELY HEARTS CLUB BAND CT: 1 AV: 1.86

1978 US/West Germany 111 C MUSICAL

D Michael Schultz ●
W Henry Edwards

Peter Frampton ● Barry Gibb ● Robin Gibb ● Maurice Gibb ● George Burns Frankie Howerd Donald Pleasence Paul Nicholas Sandy Farina Alice Cooper Steve Martin Earth, Wind and Fire

A small American town is threatened by wicked capitalists.

A moronic plot fails to pull together indifferent cover-versions of excellent Beatle numbers. The Bee Gees' acting skills are not exactly impressive, either. The critics panned it; audiences stayed away.

'Another of those films which serve as feature-length screen advertising for an album.' *(Variety)*

'This crass moral pantomime is plain embarrassing . . . Somehow Bee Gees Against Capitalism doesn't ring true. It's almost guaranteed to raise a smile.' *(Jennifer Selway, Time Out)*

'The Bee Gees are fresh and lively. Frampton is awful, but since the entire film is camp, and camp camped, awfulness is something to be mined . . . A theaterful of young people at the invitational screening . . . booed the film off the screen.' *(John Skow, Time)*

'To be fair, the movie does show a certain charm in its relentlessly stupid grasp of the obvious. When Frampton sings The Long and Winding Road, for instance, he is walking down a long and winding road. You keep laughing and thinking it can't get any worse. But it does.' *(Charles M. Young, Rolling Stone)*

'Key songs are interpreted with relentless cheerfulness, whatever their burden.' *(Richard Barkley, Sunday Express)*

'Someone has thrown together a ludicrous tale to link some Beatles' oldies.' *(Madeleine Harmsworth, Sunday Mirror)*

'It has been extraordinarily difficult to type a summary of this ridiculous entertainment.' *(Ted Whitehead, Spectator)*

SERGEANT YORK AAN CT: 6 AV: 7.33

1941 US 134 BW WAR/DRAMA

D Howard Hawks ☆ AAN
W Abem Finkel Harry Chandlee Howard Koch John Huston AAN

Gary Cooper ☆ AAW Joan Leslie Walter Brennan ☆ AAN George Tobias David Bruce Stanley Ridges Margaret Wycherly ☆ AAN Dickie Moore Ward Bond

Tennessee backwoodsman (Gary Cooper) receives message from God, becomes World War I hero.

This pro-war propaganda film, based on a somewhat unbelievable true story, was hugely popular in its time – though its lack of subtlety is very evident in retrospect. Cinematographer Sol Polito, art director John Hughes, musical director Max Steiner and editor William Holmes were all Oscar-nominated; but the biggest accolade rightly went to Gary Cooper, whose quiet integrity makes the whole thing work, despite its inordinate length.

PRO:

'An honest, heartening account of simplicity that blossoms as valour, of the struggles, hopes and indomitable courage of plain, everyday people. Presented with lyricism and poetic insight, this study of the marrow of a nation is as engrossing, as encompassing, as anything the screen has presented. Gary Cooper's portrayal of the name part is likely to become legendary . . . Performances, without exception, are genuine and moving.' *(Herb Sterne, Rob Wagner's Script)*

MIXED:

'It's all the flavor of true Americana, the blunt and homely humor of back-woodsmen and the raw integrity peculiar to simple folk . . . [but] the overly glamorized ending . . . jars sharply with the naturalness which has gone before.' *(Bosley Crowther)*

'Parts good, parts very, very bad . . . I came out feeling that Sergeant York would have been better employed felling trees than felling Germans. Hardly the correct attitude of mind to be produced by a patriotic propaganda film.' *(Tribune)*

'I hardly think the effect is any different from that of a parade, with colours and a band; it is stirring and it is too long; there are too many holdups and too many people out of step, and your residue of opinion on the matter is that it will be nice to get home and get your shoes off.' *(Otis Ferguson, New Republic)*

SERPICO CT: 6 AV: 7.23

1973 US 130 C THRILLER

D Sidney Lumet ☆
W Waldo Salt Norman Wexler AAN from Peter Maas's book

Al Pacino ☆ AAN John Randolph Jack Kehoe Biff McGuire Tony Roberts Barbara Eda-Young

An incorruptible policeman (Frank Serpico) tries to expose corruption in the New York police force.

Gripping, authentic but ultimately depressing story, with a script that would be too episodic and repetitive to sustain a movie of this length, were it not for Pacino, who is utterly compelling as the nonconformist cop.

ANTI:

'There's nothing seriously wrong with *Serpico* except that it's unmemorable, and not even terribly interesting while it's going on.' *(Stanley Kauffmann)*

'Gratuitously denigrates the entire police force by seeing its protagonists as either black or white, good or bad. Only Serpico, Blair, and Lombardo are "good"; the other detectives are vengeful, mercenary and vicious. Without excusing their behavior, surely it is not asking too much to wish the movie had presented another side to their characters, made them more fully rounded, complex individuals.' *(Judith M. Kass, Magill's American Film Guide, 1983)*

PRO:

'As enjoyable and engrossing as a film can be without being a work of art.' *(John Simon)*

'It is galvanizing because of Al Pacino's splendid performance in the title role and because of the tremendous intensity that Mr Lumet brings to this sort of subject. The method – sudden contrasts in tempo, lighting, sound level – seems almost crude, but it reflects the quality of Detective Serpico's outrage, which, in our society, comes to look like an obsession bordering on madness.' *(Vincent Canby, New York Times)*

'An excellent general audience film. Pacino dominates the entire film, from his inarticulate idealism as a rookie cop to a knowing, frustrating cynicism as bureaucratized corruption perpetuated itself before his eyes. The inner personal torment is vividly detailed.' *(Variety)*

'In a splendidly energetic performance, he [Pacino] brings vivid life to the dedicated lawman hidden by a hippie beard and a liking for ballet – and thus brings a welcome humanity to a film often steeped in naturalistic savagery.' *(David Sterritt, Christian Science Monitor)*

SERVANT, THE CT: 5 AV: 6.92

1963 GB 116 BW DRAMA

D Joseph Losey
W Harold Pinter from Robin Maugham's novel

Dirk Bogarde ☆ James Fox ☆ Sarah Miles ☆ Wendy Craig Catherine Lacey Richard Vernon

A decadent manservant (Dirk Bogarde) gradually dominates his upper-class master (James Fox).

Pinter, Losey and the leading actors inject plenty of menace into this story, which was presumably intended as some kind of allegory about class in modern British society. The narrative, however, proceeds too slowly and predictably, with one-dimensional characters and irritating delusions of socio-psychological grandeur. In the final half-hour, it runs out of steam completely and resorts to implausible plot contrivances and an anti-climactic orgy in order to bring the proceedings to an end.

PRO:

'To say you can't take your eyes off Mr Bogarde would be to wrong both him and his director, for the role is delicately dovetailed with the rest by editing, visual emphasis, the shapes of movement within the screen. I would rather put it that you are always conscious of him, of the wary look which turns slack or derisive the moment it knows itself unobserved . . . A flawless performance, then, in a masterly film.' *(Dilys Powell)*

'I urge you to see it not only for the fascination of the plot but also because of two brilliant performances by Bogarde and one of the year's most exciting discoveries, Fox.' *(News of the World)*

'On its most meaningful level [it] is acid splashed into the wound of class distinction. But it is best enjoyed simply as a slick, spooky, frequently spellbinding study of corruption.' *(Time Magazine)*

'Highly accomplished . . . Much is owed to Pinter's screenplay . . . [which] resists the temptation to go off into surrealist realms . . . Acting matches writing and direction.' *(Patrick Gibbs)*

'Compelling portrait of power and corruption . . . Black-and-white photography helps focus the attention on the personalities involved and make them stand out in sharp contrast to the background. The characters become deeply etched in the memory, thanks to Losey and his team, including the art direction of Richard MacDonald and the photography of Douglas Slocombe. The cast is faultless, with James Fox as the master and Dirk Bogarde as the manservant giving the performances of their lives. Wendy Craig as the long-suffering girlfriend and Sarah Miles as the scheming maidservant are also at the top of their form. For ensemble acting I doubt if this brilliant quartet has ever been bettered.' *(Ken Russell, 1993)*

MIXED:

'The ear for class is deadly accurate . . . So is the casting, apart from Wendy Craig, who is a very good actress but not quite believable as a posh girl . . . The lines have a wit almost like Wilde's and the whole frosty group looks as though it has been preserved in pickle . . . It is an enormously exciting picture.' *(Penelope Gilliatt, Observer)*

'Backed by some good casting and the most effective and witty camerawork of recent years, [Pinter's screenplay] should have made for outstandingly good film drama. It has, in fact, produced an outstanding film melodrama . . . Some of the sequences have such impact that they deserved to feature in a better, subtler story.' *(Shell Magazine)*

'Moodily suggestive, well acted, but petering out into a trickle of repetitious, unmeaningful nastiness.' *(John Simon)*

SET-UP, THE

CT: 6 AV: 7.50

1949 US 72 BW DRAMA

D Robert Wise ☆
W Art Cohn from Joseph Moncure March's poem

Robert Ryan ☆ Audrey Totter ● George Tobias Alan Baxter Wallace Ford Percy Helton

Boxer (Robert Ryan) refuses gangsters' invitation to 'throw' his last fight.

Classic if predictable film noir about 72 minutes in the life of a boxer, notable for a gutsy central performance by Robert Ryan, and the skill with which Robert Wise directed the whole thing on a shoestring. The film is, however, badly let down by the leading actress.

MIXED:

'The direction is firm, gripping and maintains a deliberate rhythm which is very effective; visually the film is memorable. Its one flaw is an artificial performance . . . by Audrey Totter.' *(MFB)*

'Banality of subject had me blinded for the first few reels to the undoubted brilliance of the treatment.' *(Campbell Dixon, Daily Telegraph)*

'I confess I found this a nasty, greasy film, and hated myself for being so gripped by it . . . Why did this film fascinate me? For its crisp reportage . . . For its cynical observation . . . And for the gory fight itself.' *(Leonard Mosley, Daily Express)*

'[It] succeeds in its honourable intentions and is an excellent example of studio-built realism . . . And the characters . . . including that first-rate actor Robert Ryan and excepting Miss Audrey Totter, ring absolutely true. [She] is socially and histrionically false to the occasion.' *(Richard Winnington, News Chronicle)*

'It's not a great movie, or even a very good one (it's rather mechanical), but it touches one's experience in a way that makes it hard to forget. (Maybe that's why so many movies have imitated it, even though it wasn't a commercial success.)' *(Pauline Kael)*

PRO:

'Compact and suspenseful.' *(Variety)*

'Taut, tense, terrific.' *(Sunday Pictorial)*

'Let me preface a conviction that [this] is the best boxing picture in film history by expressing the further conviction that boxing itself is a detestable affair . . . The film is also, in its minor genre, a work of art.' *(Paul Dehn, Sunday Chronicle)*

SEVEN BEAUTIES AAN CT: 4 AV: 7.56

(aka *Pasqualino Settebellezze*)

1975 Italian 115 C DRAMA/WAR/FOREIGN

D Lina Wertmüller ✗ AAN
W Lina Wertmüller ✗ AAN

Giancarlo Giannini ☆ AAN Fernando Rey
Shirley Stoler Piero di Iorio Elena Fiore Enzo Vitale

Italian crook-turned-army deserter (Giancarlo Giannini) is sent to a German concentration camp.

A very odd film, with a Chaplinesque anti-hero scheming his way to survival in a Felliniesque world (Miss Wertmüller had been Fellini's assistant on *8½*). The leading character is a crook, murderer and rapist, so it is hard to care much about him; all the same, there's something sick about being asked to enjoy his repeated slapstick disasters and sexual humiliations. The critical success of this sadistic piece of grotesquerie strikes me as both baffling and distinctly disturbing.

PRO:

'Miss Wertmüller's *King Kong*, her *Nashville*, her *8½*, her *Navigator*, her *City Lights*.' *(New York Times)*

'The only film this week to deploy images as a language is the dignified *Seven Beauties*: it's real film' *(David Hughes, Sunday Times)*

'A terrifying vision of life and death, pride and degradation, honor and survival . . . intensified by Wertmuller's sense of the comic and the absurd and deepened by her humanity and taste for paradox.' *(Ephraim Katz, The Film Encyclopaedia, 1979)*

'Giannini's scene in the POW camp where he tries to save his life by making love to the gross German commandant, superbly played by Stoler, is one of the most searing scenes in modern cinema.' *(Scheuer)*

MIXED:

'Although Miss Wertmüller's film is stupidly bestrewn with adolescent analisms . . . she has an unusual talent for large-scale tableaux . . . But much too much of the film either plays about wastefully with the demands of the new realism . . . or indulging its star.' *(Russell Davies, Observer)*

'A firecracker of a talent, but one lacking in discipline.' *(David Castell, Sunday Telegraph)*

ANTI:

'Bloated images where something suppler might have worked.' *(John Coleman, New Statesman)*

'Wertmüller has been unable to weld the disparate elements of comedy and cruelty into a coherent whole.' *(Ian Christie, Daily Express)*

'Pasqualino is everybody's dupe – a man who has swallowed all the lies that society hands out. He believes what the Mafia tells him, what Mussolini tells him, what anybody in authority tells him. As Giannini plays him, he's a Chaplinesque Fascist – the Italian Everyman as a pathetic worm. He's the man who never fights back – the one who wheedles and whimpers and crawls through. Wertmüller reactivates the entire comic-opera view of Italians as cowards who will grovel to survive. The picture is full of flashy ideas, cruelty, moist wistfulness, and pious moralizing, and Wertmüller presents it all in a goofy, ebullient mood. The box-office success of this film represents a triumph of insensitivity.' *(Pauline Kael)*

SEVEN BRIDES FOR SEVEN BROTHERS AAN CT: 8 AV: 8.31

1954 US 104 C MUSICAL/WESTERN

D Stanley Donen ☆
W Frances Goodrich Albert Hackett AAN from Stephen Vincent Benet's story *Sobbin' Women* ● (music and lyrics by Johnny Mercer and Gene de Paul ☆)

Howard Keel Jane Powell Jeff Richards
Russ Tamblyn Tommy Rall Howard Petrie
Marc Platt Jacques d'Amboise Matt Mattox

Seven brothers who live in the mountains of Oregon decide to find themselves some brides.

Howard Keel and Jane Powell head a dynamic cast in Hollywood's best danced musical, which also has a serviceable plot and outstanding songs. Adolph Deutsch and Saul Chaplin won Academy Awards for Best Score; also nominated were George Folsey's cinematography and Ralph E. Winters's editing.

Michael Kidd's choreography is so spectacular that Stanley Donen's direction went almost unnoticed, but he does a fine job within the studio-set limitations. By this point in his career he had already directed three of the greatest film musicals of all time – this one, *On the Town* (1949) and *Singin' in the Rain* (1951) – yet he was still only 30 years old.

ANTI:

'It's marred by a holiday family-picture heartiness – the M-G-M back lot Americana gets rather thick.' *(Pauline Kael)*

MIXED:

'The film takes a while to get up speed and is apt to waste too much time being ponderous and facetious about the bedroom aspect of marriage: not offensively, just ponderously. But when it breaks into song and dance, it is fine.' *(Fred Majdalany, Daily Mail)*

'Hardly marked by delicacy of feeling, and I dare say the toughness in itself will one day look old fashioned. But I don't think the gaiety and animal spirits will easily lose their charm. The new film has some entrancing song-and-dance scenes (staged by Michael Kidd); one of them, the set-to-partners at the barn-raising, is as good as anything of its kind I can remember. The songs are nearly all enjoyable (lyrics by Johnny Mercer, music by Gene de Paul). I admit that once or twice I could have wished for more seductive personalities in the leading parts: Howard Keel and Jane Powell sing well, but neither casts over me the spell which, for example, Judy Garland can cast. On the other hand, I have to say that a film of this kind comes off well in CinemaScope.' *(Dilys Powell)*

PRO:

'Magnificently staged, fast-moving and tuneful . . . The dancing is out of this world . . . Who cares if the dialect at times is a bit tricky to follow and the story does not quite keep up its cracking pace? It's still a musical in a million!' *(Reg Whitley, Daily Mirror)*

'Sweet as a fondant.' *(Jympson Harman, Evening News)*

'The chorus line is the real star of the show.' *(Time)*

'The fresh high-spirited humor of the plotting is irresistible; each and every tune is a charmer (on repeated viewings, lend a particular ear to the lovely ballads "Wonderful Day" and "When You're in Love"); and the dancing – particularly a barn-raising and roughhouse sequence – still stands beyond compare.' *(Judith Crist)*

SEVEN CHANCES

CT: 6 AV: 7.33

1925 US 69 BW COMEDY/SILENT

D Buster Keaton
W Clyde Bruckman Jean Havez Joseph A. Mitchell from Roi Cooper Megrue's play

Buster Keaton ☆ Ruth Dwyer, T. Roy Barnes Snitz Edwards Frankie Raymond

In order to claim a seven million dollar inheritance, a young man (Buster Keaton) has to find a girl willing to marry him; this turns out not to be as straightforward as he had hoped.

Not one of Keaton's best, since repetitiousness sets in after his first few tries at matrimony. Fortunately for him and the film's prospects, after a sneak preview suggested the film was going to be a flop, he came up with a famous, and very funny, climax where his flight from an army of pursuing women causes an avalanche.

PRO:

'Delightful.' *(The Stoll Herald)*

'Keaton is a really clever comedian and the absurdity of the situations in which he finds himself is greatly heightened by his expressionless face, very much like that of a torpid tortoise. For clean, irresistible humour and ingenious novelty this film would be difficult to beat.' *(Bioscope)*

ANTI:

'Inclines one's belief in the old adage concerning too many cooks, as although there are quite a number of good twists, some of them have been produced in haste. The ideas did not have time to ripen and are therefore put before the audience in a rather sour state . . . It would have been a stronger comedy were it only half the length.' *(Mordaunt Hall, New York Times)*

SEVEN DAYS TO NOON

CT: 6 AV: 7.43

1950 GB 94 BW THRILLER

D John Boulting ☆
W Frank Harvey Roy Boulting Paul Dehn James Bernard ☆ from Dehn and Bernard's story AAW

Barry Jones ☆ Olive Sloane ☆ Andre Morell ☆ Joan Hickson ☆ Sheila Manahan Hugh Cross Ronald Adam Marie Ney

The scientist (Barry Jones) threatens to blow up London unless his own work on the atom bomb is ended.

The Boulting Brothers' most acclaimed film. The message has dated and the style has often been imitated, so it has lost a lot of the impact it had in 1950, but the Oscar-winning screenplay skilfully creates suspense, and John Boulting's pacy direction make this reliable entertainment.

PRO:

'Tremendously exciting and terrifying . . . This is pure cinema and, in my opinion, the best thriller to be produced in a British film studio in a decade.' *(News of the World)*

'There remains little but praise for . . . the Brothers Boulting, who have illustrated the story with imagination.' *(Daily Telegraph)*

'Olive Sloane . . . acts with a full-blooded liveliness that would blast most of our anaemic contemporary stars off the screen.' *(Sunday Express)*

'Like Alfred Hitchcock and Carol Reed, those other masters of screen melodrama, the Boultings are able to give a new dimension to a thriller by the respect they show for their characters as individuals.' *(Saturday Review of Literature)*

'A film of great tension and excitement with a climax that is reached after breathless suspense.' *(Star)*

'A first rate thriller that does not pretend to a serious message, but yet will leave a query in the mind.' *(Richard Winnington)*

MIXED:

'After the magnificent climax, the end is a little summary, though it makes amends by being most dramatically photographed.' *(Stephen Watts, guesting for regular critic Paul Dehn who co-wrote the screenplay, Sunday Chronicle)*

'Only the Cockney cameos (all pluck and chatter)

deflate the otherwise carefully sustained paranoia.' *(Geoff Andrew, Time Out)*

SEVEN SAMURAI CT: 8 AV: 9.70

(aka *Shichinin No Samurai*)

1954 Japan 141/148/155/161/208 BW ACTION/ ADVENTURE/FOREIGN

D Akira Kurosawa ☆
W Akira Kurosawa Shinobu Hashimoto

Takashi Shimura ☆ Toshiro Mifune ☆ Yoshio Inaba Isao Kimura Seiji Miyaguchi Kuniniri Kodo Minoru Chiaki Daisuke Kato Keiko Tsushima

Seven warriors defend a 16th-century village from bandits.

Kurosawa's period action-movie was the costliest film ever to have been made in Japan. He creates a wonderful atmosphere of suspense and makes clever use of comic relief; the final battle sequences are brilliantly choreographed. The story and style of shooting were clearly influenced by American westerns; later, Hollywood repaid the compliment, re-set the picture in the Old West, and called it *The Magnificent Seven*. (Even later, there was a sci-fi rip-off, *Battle Beyond the Stars*). Kurosawa's characters are, to my western eyes at least, slightly less developed and therefore less moving than the ones in the cowboy version; but this is still a masterpiece. Winner of a Venice Festival Lion, and Oscar-nominated for art direction (Takashi Matsuyama) and costume design (Ezaki Kohei).

MIXED:

'Kurosawa's brilliant new film . . . [in which his] method and personality emerge clearly . . . [He] is striving for . . . a recreation, a bringing to life of the past and the people whose story he is telling. Here, for all the surface conviction of period, the perceptive observation, the raging vitality and the magnificent visual style, the film doesn't quite succeed. One feels each incident is too carefully worked into the texture as a whole . . . These ultimate reservations should not, however, present us from recognizing the film's astonishing qualities . . . and one's final acknowledgement is not of the intrinsic fascination of the material but the wrested skill of the artifice.' *(Tony Richardson, S & S)*

'*Seven Samurai* is long; it is brutal; it is not always easy to follow. But it is magnificent.' *(Dilys Powell)*

PRO:

'So absorbing that one loses count of time . . . Though [its] content is exotic, its form is familiar enough. Kurosawa has mastered Western technique without any sacrifice of national outlook.' *(Screencomber, Shell Magazine)*

'It is as sheer narrative, rich in incisiveness and sharp observation, that it makes its strongest impact . . . It provides a fascinating display of talent, and places its director in the forefront of creative film-makers of his generation.' *(Gavin Lambert, S & S)*

'This, on the surface, is a world of unmitigated action, as epic as any film ever made, and, again on the surface, sheer entertainment. Yet it is also an unquestionable triumph of art.' *(John Simon)*

'Kurosawa's social epic is multi-leveled: it is a stirring entertainment, with action every step of the way; a brilliant historical view of sixteenth-century Japan in the throes of social change; a timeless tale of heroism, of a man who does his best for others in the hope of bettering the world. Kurosawa's story of the seven swordsmen who save poor farmers from bandits has served as plot model for many Hollywood and Italian-made westerns; his, however, is a meaningful film, concerned with individuals rather than stock characters, and his artistry raises his work to classic stature.' *(Judith Crist)*

'Separation is . . . the subject of Kurosawa's *mise-en-scène*. Using both the foreground-background separation of deep-focus shots and the flattening, abstracting effect of telephoto lenses, Kurosawa puts a sense of unbridgeable space in nearly all of his shots. The primary visual motif is one of boundaries: the natural boundaries formed around the village by the mountains, woods, and flooded rice fields, the man-made boundaries of fences, stockades, and doorways. The extreme formality of Kurosawa's compositions also emphasizes the boundaries of the frame; there is only occasionally a sense of off-screen space, as if nothing existed beyond the limits of the camera's eye. The world of *The Seven Samurai* is carefully delineated, compartmentalized; not only are the characters isolated in their separate groups, but in separate spaces.' *(Dave Kehr)*

SEVEN YEAR ITCH, THE CT: 7 AV: 6.92

1955 US 105 C COMEDY/ROMANCE

D Billy Wilder ☆
W Billy Wilder George Axelrod from Axelrod's play

Tom Ewell ☆ Marilyn Monroe ☆ Sonny Tufts Evelyn Keyes Robert Strauss Oscar Homolka Victor Moore Marguerite Chapman

A married man (Tom Ewell), left on his own, contemplates having an affair with the blonde upstairs (Marilyn Monroe).

Two wonderfully skilful leading performances prevent this from being just another filmed stage comedy. Unfortunately, the story relies overmuch on fantasy sequences which don't propel the plot forward; and the whole thing ends in anti-climax, since this is one itch the leading man never gets to scratch. It was rather different in the stage version.

ANTI:

'If only Marilyn Monroe had as much talent as she gets publicity, what an artist she would be. But beyond her figure and a certain roguish charm she robs the screen of little when she leaves it. There is a certain amount of sauciness but not much invention or wit in the script.' *(M. Raymond, Sunday Dispatch)*

'Much overrated, too talky and stagy, only occasionally funny.' *(Danny Peary)*

MIXED:

'In its last third this comedy . . . runs a little shallow and predictable. But the inventions of the first two-thirds are full of gaiety and surprise, the dialogue is lively, and the romantic fantasies with which the hero, a Mitty in his own way, decorates his solitude come successfully to life on the screen. The central character is played by Tom Ewell, who played it on Broadway: he brings a skilled comic technique and an agreeably dry personality to his first major role in the cinema. But the unexpected treat is Marilyn Monroe, whose normal air of not quite understanding her lines is miraculously suited to the character of the girl from upstairs whose outrageousness comes from naiveté. Miss Monroe's performance, as well as Billy Wilder's direction, must be called witty.' *(Dilys Powell)*

PRO:

'Wilder's direction distils the maximum of laughter from fantasy and fact. Marilyn Monroe is incomparable; and Mr Ewell . . . courts comparison only with Hollywood's best.' *(Paul Dehn, News Chronicle)*

'As a simple piece of sexy sightseeing it is the most delightful eyeful of the year – and Marilyn acts better than ever.' *(Donald Zec, Daily Mirror)*

'Very "New Yorkerish" and full of funny and unedifying wisecracks.' *(Philip Hope-Wallace, Manchester Guardian)*

'A good deal better than the play.' *(Reynolds News)*

'Miss Monroe brings a special personality and a certain physical something or other to the film that may not be exactly what the playwright ordered but which definitely conveys an idea. From the moment she steps into the picture, in a garment that drapes her shapely form as though she had been skillfully poured into it, the famous screen star with the silver-blonde tresses and the ingenuously wide-eyed stare emanates one suggestion. And that suggestion rather dominates the film. It is – well, why define it? Miss Monroe clearly plays the title role.' *(Bosley Crowther)*

SEVENTH SEAL, THE CT: 8 AV: 9.46

(aka *Det Sjunde Inseglet*)

1956 Sweden 95 BW FANTASY/DRAMA/FOREIGN

D Ingmar Bergman ☆
W Ingmar Bergman

Max Von Sydow ☆ Bengt Ekerot
Gunnar Björnstrand Bibi Andersson Nils Poppe
Gunnel Lindblom Inga Gill Maud Hansson

A knight returning from the Crusades (Max Von Sydow) tries to persuade Death (Bengt Ekerot), over a game of chess, that there is good in mankind.

Ingmar Bergman at his most original but morbidly portentous, ending the proceedings with a dance of death. A film about fear of the H-bomb? Your guess is as good as mine, but the visual imagery is unforgettable.

PRO:

'A great, gaunt film that grips the heart with bony fingers and does not let go . . . It ravaged me . . . with its terrible beauty . . . [It] excites both the heart and the mind. It is every inch a masterpiece.' *(Philip Oakes, Evening Standard)*

'An impressive and oppressive saga.' *(Ivon Adams, Star)*

'A blazing masterpiece . . . but one defying brief description . . . The allegory fascinates and grips . . . with some of the loveliest girls I have seen on the screen.' *(Harold Conway, Daily Sketch)*

'Although . . . set in medieval Sweden, nothing could be more modern than its author's conception of death as the crucial reality of man's existence . . . Perhaps the first genuinely existential film . . . Unlike Dreyer [Bergman] refuses to reconstruct mystic consolations from the dead past. If modern man must live without the faith which makes death meaningful, he can at least endure life with the aid of certain necessary illusions . . . The various threads of the plot are woven together into the fabric of a town which represents for Bergman many of the evils of society . . . As Death leads his six victims, hand to hand, in the fierce merriment of their last revels, *The Seventh Seal* soars to the heights of imaginative cinema . . . For all its intellectual complexity, [it] is remarkably entertaining.' *(Andrew Sarris, Film Culture)*

'The most extraordinary mixture of beauty and lust and cruelty, Odin-worship and Christian faith, darkness and light.' *(Alan Dent, Illustrated London News)*

'If Ingmar Bergman had lived a hundred years ago he would have been a great novelist. For me he is the greatest figure since sound and *The Seventh Seal* is probably the film he's become most associated with.' *(William Goldman, NFT Bulletin, 1984)*

ANTI:

'For all its exquisite, pastoral photography, lyrically phrased dialogue and earnest acting [it] offers only the sort of surface-beauty which Keats would not have approved of because it has nothing to do with truth . . . Bergman is merely terrible (in the good-old hair-raising sense) without being an enfant.' *(Paul Dehn, News Chronicle)*

'A film about fear of the H-bomb . . . I find it repulsive . . . The magnificent craftsmanship, of course, I admit. But beneath the surface of the high-class, bony morality which has understandably attracted so much admiration there lurks what to me is a dreadful squashy sentimentality, the kind of sentimentality which goes hand in hand with obsession by the dark and the cruel. On the one side the executioners and the hysterical self-indulgers, on the other the naive dreamer, the loving fair-haired wife in a low-necked blouse, the chubby baby. And it goes almost without saying that the dreamer is a strolling player. Innocence in the circus-tent and the caravan; it is the oldest hat in the business.' *(Dilys Powell)*

SEVENTH VEIL, THE

CT: 6 AV: 6.56

1945 GB 94 BW DRAMA/ROMANCE

D Compton Bennett ☆
W Muriel Bat Sydney Box ☆ AAW

James Mason ☆ Ann Todd ☆ Herbert Lom ☆
Albert Lieven Hugh McDermott Yvonne Owen
David Horne Manning Whiley

A suicidally disturbed concert pianist (Ann Todd) is psychoanalysed (by Herbert Lom) and discovers that she is unconsciously in love with her crippled, Svengali-like guardian (James Mason).

The performances are so powerful and intensely felt that the psychological absurdities of this popular melodrama become apparent mainly in retrospect. To modern eyes, there is something more than a little masochistic about a heroine who eventually subjugates herself to the man (Mason) who has treated her worst during the entire picture, but the decision went down well with audiences at the time – indeed, they voted for her to do so at sneak previews when the ending was still uncertain. The film made Mason an international star.

PRO:

'A popular film that does not discard taste and atmosphere.' *(Daily Mail)*

MIXED:

'An example of the intelligent, medium-priced picture made with great technical polish which has represented for Hollywood the middle path between the vulgar and the highbrow.' *(Spectator)*

'An odd, artificial, best sellerish kind of story, with reminiscences of *Trilby* and *Jane Eyre* and all their imitations down to *Rebecca*.' *(Richard Mallett, Punch)*

'A rich, portentous mixture of Beethoven, Chopin, Kitsch and Freud.' *(Pauline Kael, 1968)*

'Maybe, with a few veils stripped away, all of us have a fantasist inside who gobbles up this sadomasochistic sundae, with its culture sauce.' *(Pauline Kael, 70s)*

'Ineffable tripe . . . Enjoyable, sort of.' *(Tom Milne, Time Out)*

SEVENTH VOYAGE OF SINBAD, THE

CT: 6 AV: 6.70

D Nathan Juran
W Kenneth Kolb

Kerwin Mathews Kathryn Grant Torin Thatcher
Richard Eyer Alec Mango Danny Green
Harold Kasket

Sinbad (Kerwin Mathews) searches for roc's (giant two-headed bird) egg to bring cursed shrunken princess (Kathryn Grant) back to normal size.

Enjoyable Arabian Nights fantasy adventure. The plot is juvenile, but Ray Harryhausen's special effects were excellent and innovative for their day. Underrated by critics on release, the film understandably caught the imagination of family audiences.

ANTI:

'I got [a lot of] giggles from [it] which I am sure the makers did not intend . . . It is all done very seriously.' *(Ivon Adams, Star)*

'Some of the most effective trick shots (by a new system called Dynamation) I have seen in films for years.' *(Leonard Mosley, Daily Express)*

'[Dynamation] took five years, they tell us, to perfect and one can't help wondering why, with all that time in hand, the producers didn't find a nicer film to go with the photography.' *(Time & Tide)*

'Resolutely dull.' *(Scheuer)*

MIXED:

'The cute American talk of Kathryn Grant, as the Arabian princess who is reduced to three-inch size by the wicked magician, is the only flaw in a wonderful fantasy which will thrill and intrigue young and old alike.' *(Jympson Harman, Evening News)*

'Perfect screen magic [such] as you have never seen before . . . And if you don't want to thrill, you can always laugh at the Americanisms of the princess.' *(John Balfour, Daily Sketch)*

PRO:

'A brilliant technical achievement which makes the miraculous seem plausible . . . There is superb novelty in addition to magnificent action, spectacle, arresting drama as well as cleverly contrived horror, and while it may well frighten the lives out of very young children it nevertheless spells brilliantly out-of-the-rut hokum entertainment for the masses.' *(CEA Film Report)*

'Sheer delight.' *(Alan Frank)*

SEX, LIES AND VIDEOTAPE

CT: 6 AV: 7.08

1989 US 100 C DRAMA/ROMANCE

D Steven Soderbergh ✗
W Steven Soderbergh ✗ AAN

James Spader ☆ Andie MacDowell ✓ Peter Gallagher ✓ Laura San Giacomo ✓ Ron Vawter

A married couple – one of whom (Andie MacDowell) is frigid, the other of whom (Peter Gallagher) is having an affair with his sister-in-law (Laura San Giacomo) – are visited by the husband's college friend (James Spader) who, the wife is intrigued to learn, likes to videotape women's sexual confessions.

The performances are the thing in this low-budget movie which wowed them all at Cannes, surprisingly winning the Palme d'Or for its first-time writer-director, and the Best Actor award for James Spader. It's an intriguing little story, reminiscent of an Eric Rohmer film in the way the characters talk to disguise their hypocrisies but end up revealing them anyway. It doesn't really get anywhere, but the journey is entertaining and illuminating.

PRO:

'An acerbic exploration of part of the American yuppie generation . . . A visual and aural treat.' *(Brinley Hamer-Jones, Western Mail)*

'It has more intelligence than heart, and is more clever than enlightening. But it is never boring, and there are moments when it reminds us of how sexy the movies used to be, back before they could show everything, and thus had to think about nothing.' *(Roger Ebert)*

MIXED:

'Soderbergh gets away with long, close-up shots of dialogue that in other films might be deemed pretentious, precisely because [the film] is so well written, and, not least, because most of that dialogue centres on everyone's favourite subject – sex . . . With [its] echoes of *Peeping Tom* and its emphasis on the phallic power of the camera, [the film] shows more insight into its male characters than its female ones . . . Overall though, the film is totally compelling.' *(Suzanne Moore, New Statesman & Society)*

'In-people will be obliged to see it. The rest of us could do a lot worse, for in its deadpan, slow-burning, sly way this is a potent social comedy.' *(Shaun Usher, Daily Mail)*

'If you like your movies with brain not brawn [this one] should not be missed.' *(Sue Heal, Today)*

SGT PEPPER'S LONELY HEARTS CLUB BAND: *see* SERGEANT PEPPER'S LONELY HEARTS CLUB BAND)

SHACK OUT ON 101

CT: 5 AV: 6.00

1955 US 80 BW THRILLER/SPY/SO BAD

D Ed Dein ✗
W Ed Dein Mildred Dein ●

Frank Lovejoy Lee Marvin Keenan Wynn Terry Moore Whit Bissell

Waitress (Terry Moore) suspects two of her boy-friends of being Commie spies.

There are colourful characters and right-wing sentiments galore in this amazingly trashy insight into the dining habits of Red saboteurs. Lee Marvin gives his all in the arduous role of a man called, believe it or not, Slob. Bizarrely, the movie was praised on release for its realism.

PRO:

'Since [the Deins] have fashioned dialogue that is occasionally adult and funny and have the services of principals who can accentuate these humorous lines and situations, [the film] . . . avoids the stigma of being a sub-standard spies vs FBI imbroglio.' *(A. H. Weiler, New York Times)*

'Unpretentious yet intriguing espionage melodrama . . . to be taken with a pinch of salt, but Lee Marvin's clever performance . . . gets it over. At once humorous and thrilling, it's definitely worthy of a place on the average double bill.' *(Josh Billings, Kine Weekly)*

'Dialogue is really original and the very capable cast makes the most of it. Direction shows many fresh and imaginative touches . . . Atmospherically helpful is the background score of bop and blues. An unusual and highly entertaining film . . . On the surface, a good fast-moving thriller with off-beat jokes; but there are definite undertones if you care to look for them.' *(Today's Cinema)*

MIXED:

'A brisk but sombre and not altogether edifying spy thriller. The dialogue is over-loaded with would-be wisecracks, yet the film has an unusually distinctive atmosphere for a "B" picture and benefits considerably from [the] camerawork. As a mixture of viciousness and humour, moderately successful.' *(MFB)*

'Worthy of a place in the pantheons of Hollywood trash thanks to its hysterical anti-commie sentiment. What once passed for realism now appears high camp in this drama combining the dangers of dish-pan hands with fear of the Red peril.' *(Winnert)*

SHADOW OF A DOUBT

CT: 10 AV: 8.91

1943 US 108 BW THRILLER

D Alfred Hitchcock ☆
W Thornton Wilder Sally Benson Alma Reville ☆ from Gordon McDonell's story ☆ AAN

Joseph Cotten ☆ Teresa Wright ☆ Hume Cronyn
Macdonald Carey Patricia Collinge Henry Travers
Wallace Ford

A small-town girl (Teresa Wright) suspects her favourite uncle (Joseph Cotten) of being a murderer.

Based on the case of Earle Leonard Nelson, a mass strangler of the 1920s, who became known as the 'Merry Widow Murderer', this is low-key but effective Hitchcock – and one of the director's own favourites. There is much less action than in most of his best movies, but plenty of suspense. Hitchcock and Thornton Wilder – author of that nostalgic piece of Americana, *Our Town* – economically establish a vision of a safe, conservative, boring Middle America, then give us the frisson of seeing it under attack from within.

More than any other Hitchcock film, *Shadow of a Doubt* captures the attractiveness of evil. Joseph Cotten is outstanding, but so is Teresa Wright as the niece who is, to some extent, his soul-mate. Joe Valentine's cinematography is superb. The picture was undervalued by American reviewers on release (for some reason Hitchcock fell out of critical fashion during the 50s), but the British ones liked it well enough.

MIXED:

'In disagreement with most qualified people I think more well than ill of *Shadow of a Doubt*; but I must admit that its skill is soft and that it is distinctly below the standard set by Hitchcock's best English work.' *(James Agee)*

'It's very well worked out in terms of character and it has a sustained grip, but it certainly isn't as much fun as several of his other films'. *(Pauline Kael)*

PRO:

'One of the top spine-tinglers to come from Mr Hitchcock's well-stocked chamber of horrors. It is recommended to those whose blood-pressure can stand being manoeuvered into the higher brackets.' *(Herb Sterne)*

'The essence of such a tale is the solidity and ordinariness of the background against which the strangeness of murder is disclosed. Hitchcock, from long ago a master in this kind of solid plausibility, has, I fancy, learned from Orson Welles the value of the interrupted broken conversation, the dialogue drowned in chatter. I do not think I was mistaken in seeing the Welles influence elsewhere in this admirably made film; in the use of close-ups, the pictorial handling of the solitary figure, and the suggestion of the voice overheard.' *(Dilys Powell)*

'A-quiver with suspense. Nothing much happens but like a nervous girl going down a dark alley, you've got your mouth open ready to scream if necessary.' *(Harris Deans, Sunday Dispatch)*

'The best film Hitchcock has made . . . Good acting . . . good photography, good script. If [it] has a fault it is that Hitchcock is too tender-hearted and shuffles a bit at the end. But it comes off, shuffle and all.' *(New Statesman)*

'Hitchcock's American masterpiece was *Shadow of a Doubt*, a perfect stylistic morsel alongside of which the flourishes of *Citizen Kane* seem pathetic.' *(Georges Sadoul, Histoire d'un art: le cinéma, 1949)*

'His finest film, *Shadow of a Doubt*, derived much of its power from the authenticity of the small town setting. This was one of the rare instances in his career when his locale was integrated thematically with his characters. For the most part, it has been a matter of big stars wandering over strange landscapes in contrived plots.' *(Andrew Sarris, Film Culture, 1955)*

'Crucial to *Shadow of a Doubt* is Hitchcock's commitment to Young Charlie (Teresa Wright) – (that he is also committed, on another level, to her murderous uncle is crucial to the enactment of the dialectic). Her goodness and innocence are revealed as in a certain sense limitations (she has to learn to become aware of the evil her society produces and nourishes), but we are never invited to find them ridiculous. Indeed, it is precisely because they are convincingly realized as genuine and positive that the film is so authentically disturbing.' *(Robin Wood, Hitchcock's Films Revisited, 1989)*

'This is Hitchcock's most penetrating analysis of a murderer – a masterful profile, aided by Cotten's superb performance, of a subtle killer who cannot escape his dark passions, despite a superior intellect.' *(Baseline)*

SHADOW WARRIOR: *see* KAGEMUSHA.

SHADOWLANDS

CT: 9 AV: 8.00 (est)

1993 GB 131 C DRAMA/ROMANCE

D Richard Attenborough ☆
W Nicholson ☆ from his play and TV film

Anthony Hopkins ☆ Debra Winger ☆ AAN
Joseph Mazzello ☆ John Wood Michael Denison
Edward Hardwicke ☆ Peter Firth

Confirmed bachelor (Anthony Hopkins) who is also

a famous author and Oxford academic finds love (Debra Winger) late in life.

Attenborough's opening shots are conventional to the point of cliché: the dreaming spires of Oxford, at their most somnolent. Scattered throughout the film are other familiar images of university life: punts beneath Magdalen Bridge, choral singing on May Morning, donnish dinners at High Table. Stuart Craig's production design lovingly evokes academic life in the 1950s (he was also responsible for the beautiful look of *The Secret Garden*).

But Attenborough is not muted by his milieu, or numbed by nostalgia. For Oxford is also a place where a boy need never grow up, and a don can live his life in a suspended state of emotional detachment. We may have been here before (Michael Palin tackled the same subject comedically in *American Friends*) but Attenborough manages to make the observation seem bright and fresh. He is helped by a number of telling performances from Lewis's fellow-dons, especially John Wood and Michael Denison.

For into this cosy coterie comes a human bombshell: a Jewish Communist poet – and, worse, a woman. Her opening tea-room scene at the Randolph Hotel gives Debra Winger one of the most splendid entrances in movie history, and from then on she actually improves. She could have turned the part into a caricature – especially as the screenplay gives her all the best wisecracks. Instead, she gives a beautiful, multi-layered performance: hurt and lost one moment, the next fighting back against Lewis's unconscious assumption of masculine superiority, one moment ravaged by illness, then delivering a smile that lights up the screen.

She is matched by young Joseph Mazzello as Joy Gresham's son Douglas. Attenborough's forte as a director has always been his ability to draw performances out of people, and this nine-year-old (who also played the boy in *Jurassic Park*) is terrific. Almost without our noticing, the father-son relationship turns out to be as much of a choker as the man-woman one.

But this is, first and foremost, Anthony Hopkins's film. He had a dry run for this role as the bookseller in *84 Charing Cross Road* (where Anne Bancroft, you may recall, stole the show in the role of the loudmouth American). Wonderful though Winger is, there's never any danger that she will do the same.

Under Attenborough's direction for the fifth time, Hopkins takes hold of Lewis like a terrier and worries every last nuance out of him: his genius, religious faith, intellectual rigour, authoritarianism, complacency, fear, awkwardness – in short, his humanity. Because of its complexity and huge emotional range, from intense joy to the most appalling grief, from faith to railing against God, Hopkins's performance is arguably an even greater *tour de force* than his butler in *The Remains of the Day*.

Shadowlands is a lovely, intelligent film which easily surpasses anything Attenborough has given us before – even *Gandhi*. It is as if he has been liberated by a story which does not require him to mount a liberal soapbox, or command us to feel reverence towards a Great Man of Our Time. Ironically, by depicting the frailties of Lewis so clearly and sympathetically, Attenborough has given us by far his most perceptive study of a Great Man yet.

For *Shadowlands* rises above its apparently parochial subject to touch all of us, on a surprisingly profound level. It says that to love someone is the most rewarding emotion you can experience, and that a life without love is – however intelligent, talented, rich or famous you may be – to some extent a life spent in the shadows.

ANTI:

'[It] feels warmed over from reel one . . . I found it to be substantive twaddle, bar the performances . . . [It] promises us a true-life tragedy but gives us only a weepie with a message: one that only the actors emerge from with dignity. Amid the encroaching schmaltz, Winger somehow manages a few strong, acerbic, moving strokes.' *(Nigel Andrews, Financial Times)*

'We're in TV weepie-of-the-week country – *Love Story* with knobs on.' *(Mark Steyn, Spectator)*

'Debra Winger as a single mother dying of cancer – again. Hmmm, how can you go wrong? I'll tell you: None of the wit of *Terms of Endearment* and none of the accessibility . . . If you want to see Hopkins as a stiff, upper-crust Brit, there's at least one better place to do it.' *(Rod Lurie, LA Magazine)*

'Nicholson writes the way Attenborough directs: it's a perfect match. Each looks for the kitschiest approach, the most Hallmark-apt expression of the matter in hand. Since this is the story of a well-known Oxford theologian who goes through a crisis of faith, and a New York Jewish ex-Communist who finds solace in his arms, Nicholson and Attenborough are not exactly hard-up for chances to do their dampest.' *(Stanley Kauffmann)*

'*Shadowlands* may be the most painfully civilized British tearjerker since David Lean's *Brief Encounter*. Unlike that stiff-upper-lip weeper, however, Attenborough's rather poky fable never succeeds in balancing the passions of its two shy lovebirds. Hopkins, once again, proves a master of the mood of inchoate longing. As Lewis, he shows a new vulnerability and warmth, revealing a gaze so tender it caresses everything in its path. Winger's performance, on the other hand, is a problem, in part because her role isn't as well defined. Is Joy meant to be a vibrant vulgarian playfully cajoling Lewis out of his repression, or a home-grown intellectual who first bonds with his mind? Winger, slipping in and out of a vaudeville-Brooklyn accent, plays her as a bit of both, and so the character never quite gels. At the very least, it's a stretch to believe that this woman fell for this man because of the magic of his writing – and if we can't believe that, the very basis of the romance collapses.' *(Owen Gleiberman, Entertainment Weekly)*

PRO:

'Intelligent, moving and beautifully acted. It understands that not everyone falls into love through the avenue of physical desire; that for some, the lust may be for another's mind, for inner beauty.' *(Roger Ebert)*

'Anthony Hopkins is making quite a career out of playing emotionally challenged, tidy-minded Englishmen. In *Howard's End*, he portrayed a starchy financier who held a hand up to his face, as if blocking the sun, whenever feelings threatened to mar his composure. More recently, in *The Remains of the Day*, he played a terminally repressed butler, a man blinkered by decorum and incapable of passion. Painfully beautiful, *Remains* is a romance under glass, a tragedy of manners without a breath of catharsis. Now, in *Shadowlands*, Hopkins performs yet another variation on English constraint. But this time, there is a release. He laughs, he cries – and so do we.' *(Brian D. Johnson, Maclean's)*

'I suppose you could call [it] a very superior weepie. But that would be somehow to denigrate what is a first-class piece of film-making, acted in a way that sometimes takes the breath away. It is the best piece of direction [Attenborough] has ever accomplished . . . An unalloyed triumph.' *(Derek Malcolm, Guardian)*

'Attenborough's best movie for years . . . brimming with aching honesty and sublime dialogue, great globules of universal truth and an intense evocative Fifties' period feel. If you have tears, prepare to shed them now. I did, in torrents.' *(Sue Heal, Today)*

'Enormously rich in humor, drama, local color, and psychological detail. And surprisingly, Richard Attenborough – who, for my money, never made a good movie (only overblown and naive spectaculars or tiresome whimsies) – directed this with remarkable poise, empathy, and finesse . . . *Shadowlands* reports, but does not revel in, harsh realities, even as it unlipsmackingly savors happiness and humor. Every one of its tears, like every one of its laughs, is scrupulously earned, and understatement has never been deployed to better effect.' *(John Simon)*

SHALL WE DANCE

CT: 5 AV: 6.67

1937 US 116/120 BW MUSICAL/ROMANCE

D Mark Sandrich
W Allan Scott Ernest Pagano ● (music and lyrics by George Gershwin, Ira Gershwin ☆)

Fred Astaire ☆ Ginger Rogers ☆
Edward Everett Horton Eric Blore Harriet Hoctor
Jerome Cowan Ketti Gallian Ann Shoemaker

A ballet star (Fred Astaire) has a shipboard romance with a musical-comedy star (Ginger Rogers) and they decide to get married and then divorced in order to persuade everyone that they're not married. Can you make head or tail of that? Me neither.

This appallingly plotted musical contains some of the loveliest songs ever written (including the Oscar-nominated 'They Can't Take That Away From Me') and the dancing is mostly sublime, but the linking material is among the most turgid that Fred and Ginger ever had to wade through. It's well worth watching on video – with one finger poised over the fast-forward button. It opened to almost universally ecstatic reviews.

'One of the best things the screen's premiere dance team has done, a zestful, prancing, sophisticated musical show. It has a grand score . . . a generous leavening of comedy, a plot or so, and forever and ever, the nimble hoofing of a chap with quicksilver in his feet and a young woman who has learned to follow him with assurance.' *(Frank S. Nugent, New York Times)*

'It does not seem to matter that the plots of the Astaire-Rogers musicals should be all according to the same pattern. Variations on a nursery theme do very well for them, and all that does matter is that they should have good songs, dance numbers that fit in easily with the comic situations, Eric Blore and Edward Everett Horton. All these they had in Shall We Dance and that should be enough for anyone.' *(Alan Page, S & S)*

'Even if [Astaire and Rogers] didn't dance in . . . this bubbling fast-moving comedy . . . [it] would be a picture to set the 1938 fashion in musical films . . . The whole thing is de luxe.' *(Photoplay)*

'Highly polished . . . with the stars in excellent form . . . Sandrich has done an excellent job . . . He has made one of the best Astaire-Rogers musicals ever.' *(Film Weekly)*

SHAME OF A NATION, THE: *see* SCARFACE

SHANE AAN

CT: 7 AV: 8.60

1953 US 118 C WESTERN

D George Stevens ☆ AAN
W A. B. Guthrie Jr Jack Sher ☆ AAN from Jack Schaefer's novel

Alan Ladd ☆ Jean Arthur Van Heflin ✔
Jack Palance ☆ AAN Brandon de Wilde ☆ AAN
Ben Johnson Edgar Buchanan Elisha Cook Jr
Emile Meyer John Dierkes

A mysterious outsider (Alan Ladd) helps protect a family of homesteaders.

George Stevens's influential western has a convincing feel for place and period, a splendidly laconic performance from Jack Palance, and a charismatic hero in Alan Ladd (though he does look a bit small to be beating up the baddies quite so easily). At times it is slow and pompous, but it has a mythic grandeur which places it in the top flight of westerns. Loyal Giggs won an Academy Award for his cinematography.

PRO:

'It is Master de Wilde with his bright face, his clear voice and his resolute boyish ways who steals the affections for the audience and clinches *Shane* as a most unusual film.' *(New York Times)*

'What makes *Shane* so good a film is its combination of simplicity and warmth of feeling with grandeur of composition. The human figures with their humble show of courage and loyalty are set against a magnificent panorama of plain and mountain; or sometimes they are composed in groups finely poised for drama. There are beautiful single effects – the man watching a burial, his face reflecting a struggle of conscience; or the mountains which echo the voice of the child calling as Shane rides away. But this is a film not of moments but of continuing excellence in which the characters within the romantic convention strike no false note.' *(Dilys Powell)*

'Stevens managed to infuse a new vitality, a new sense of realism into the time-worn story through the strength and freshness of his visuals.' *(Arthur Knight)*

'*Shane* stands apart from most westerns of recent years – even such superior ones as *Red River, The Gunfighter, High Noon* – mainly by virtue of George Stevens' unromantic and entirely convincing evocation of the period.' *(BFI Bulletin)*

'*Shane* is the original source for many of the clichés of subsequent westerns-clichés that in the original are matters of inspiration, of genius, and of art. Jean Arthur and Van Heflin set the classic mold for frontier parents – humble, hard-working, sweat-stained, and handsome. No frontier lad has surpassed Brandon de Wilde in his curiosity, his open-hearted hero worship, his vulnerability, nor mystery-man exceeded Alan Ladd's close-lipped courage in the face of an innocent boy or a ready-to-blaze six shooter. And no gunman has ever slipped on his shootin' glove with the cruel calm Jack Palance displays in his original gesture.' *(Judith Crist)*

MIXED:

'The western stranger in town consciously turned into Galahad on the range. Superficially, this is a western, but from Shane's knightly costume, from the way his horse canters, from the Agincourt music, it's all too recognizable as an attempt to create a myth. With chivalric purity as his motivation, the enigmatic Shane (Alan Ladd) defeats enemies twice his size – the largest is the Prince of Darkness himself, Jack Palance . . . This George Stevens film is overplanned and uninspired: westerns are better when they're not so self-importantly self-conscious.' *(Pauline Kael, 1975)*

'In my view, Stevens is the most overrated craftsman in American film history, but some of his pictures have been competent entertainments – *Shane,* for example.' *(Stanley Kauffmann, 1966)*

SHANGHAI EXPRESS AAN CT: 6 AV: 8.60

1932 US 84 BW DRAMA

D. Josef von Sternberg ☆
W W Jules Furthman ☆

Marlene Dietrich ☆ Clive Brook ● Warner Oland Anna May Wong Eugene Pallette Lawrence Grant Louise Closser Hale Gustav von Seyffertitz

A prostitute (Marlene Dietrich) meets a former fiancée (Clive Brook) on a Chinese train, and sacrifices what remains of her virtue to save him from uncouth rebels.

Enjoyable old tosh. Another of von Sternberg's star vehicles for Dietrich, who is exquisitely photographed as usual (Lee Garmes's lighting-camerawork won an Oscar). The plot is melodramatic, and not helped by Clive Brook's performance, which would make the average tree look supple. Several characters act with unclear motivation at crucial moments, and the dialogue is wildly uneven – some of it witty, much of it clichéd. It contains two immortal lines, one spoken by Dietrich ('It took more than one man to change my name to Shanghai Lily.'), the other spoken by Warner Oland as the rebel war lord ('The white woman stays with me.').

PRO:

'Don't miss this exciting film.' *(Photoplay)*

'It is by all odds the best picture Josef von Sternberg has directed . . . Dietrich gives an impressive performance. She is languorous but fearless.' *(Mordaunt Hall, New York Times)*

'Von Sternberg was uninterested in a realistic China. He wanted only to evoke China on the screen in deft, brief strokes.' *(Herman G. Weinberg)*

'A limited amount of characters, all meticulously etched, highly atmospheric sets and innumerable striking photographic compositions.' *(Curtis Harrington, 1964)*

MIXED:

'Joe Sternberg is now the great Josef von Sternberg . . . This high argument is staged with stupendous care, stupendous skill and with the air of most stupendous importance. I remember one shot of the [train] pulling into a wayside station . . . [which] is one of the half-dozen greatest shots ever taken, and I would see the film for that alone. It is, however, the only noble moment in the film [which is dominated by Dietrich] . . . For me, seven thousand poses of

Dietrich (or seventy) are Dietrich ad nauseam.' *(John Grierson, Everyman)*

'Good programme picture bolstered by the Dietrich name . . . Excellent camerawork overcomes really hoke melodramatic story.' *(Variety)*

SHANGHAI GESTURE, THE CT: 5 AV: 4.14

1941 US 90 BW DRAMA/SO BAD

D Josef von Sternberg ☆
W Josef von Sternberg Geza Herczeg Karl Vollmöller Jules Furthman from John Colton's play

Ona Munson ☆ Victor Mature Walter Huston Gene Tierney Albert Basserman Phyllis Brooks Maria Ouspenskaya ☆ Eric Blore Ivan Lebedeff Mike Mazurki

In a low Shanghai gambling dive, Madame Gin Sling (Ona Munson) taunts her ex-husband (Walter Huston) with the degree to which their daughter (Gene Tierney) has become degraded.

Tedious, turgid melodrama lifted to the realms of high camp by von Sternberg's visual flamboyance, a hilariously humourless script, and the lurid excesses of his cast. Boris Leven's art direction was Oscar-nominated, as was Richard Hageman's music. Now a cult film, it was not kindly treated by contemporary critics.

ANTI:

'Recently opened nationally to quite as many critical catcalls, lampoonings, derisive comments as any major movie has received . . . Stacked to the rafters with clichés, [it] is lamentably slow and dull . . . It was to be hoped that von Sternberg's . . . comeback would have been . . . a return to . . . vigor and ingenuity . . . Instead he repeats the errors of monotony, formlessness, and arty antics which caused him to lapse into professional limbo.' *(Herb Sterne)*

'So utterly and lavishly pretentious, so persistently opaque and so very badly acted in every lead role but one, that it finally become laughable . . . Victor Mature . . . describes himself as a thoroughbred monster – a description which his performance justifies . . . Only Walter Huston . . . indicates some acquaintance with the art of projecting a character . . . The director was apparently so interested in shooting magnificent scenes that he overlooked the necessity of fitting together a lucid film.' *(Bosley Crowther)*

'An absolutely ridiculous film – the reason that it has a cult following – directed by Josef von Sternberg, who was flat on his back, lying on a cot, during most of the shooting. The extremely weird, overwritten, often dull script by Jules Furthman and others – full of awkward introductions, lectures, people yelling at each other, double entendres – comes across like a clumsy first draft that was filmed only because the next 20 drafts were lost.' *(Danny Peary)*

'Though profitable, it was ridiculed by the critics . . . [This] ludicrous film contained the memorable crane shot, several times repeated, in which the camera hovers over the gambling casino, searching out its febrile and foolish viciousness – an image reminiscent in feeling of Van Gogh's Night Cafe. In view of these achievements, there can be no question of Sternberg's great talent for the medium, nor of the fact that he has a highly individual style entirely invented by himself (though owing something, perhaps, to the German example of the Twenties). The Sternberg problem is a problem of taste, not of ability.' *(Paul Rotha & Richard Griffith, 1949)*

'Hilariously, awesomely terrible.' *(Pauline Kael, 1977)*

MIXED:

'Rather dull and hazy . . . Victor Mature, as the matter-of-fact Arab despoiler of Tierney's honor, provides a standout performance. Huston's abilities are lost in the jumble, while Munson cannot penetrate the mask-like make-up arranged for her characterization.' *(Variety)*

PRO:

'In spite of all the changes necessitated by the Hays Office, seldom have decadence and depravity been better suggested on the screen.' *(Richard Roud, 1966)*

'Von Sternberg uses this tale of the terrible vengeance of a daughter sacrificed to debauchery to paint his most mordant image of depravity and decadence. Furthman's epigrammatic style is well-suited to the baroque, Oriental world created in this film.' *(NFT Bulletin, 1984)*

'Sternberg's last masterpiece, a delirious melodrama of decadence and sexual guilt that uses its Oriental motifs as a cypher for all that is unknown or unknowable . . . Subversive cinema at its most sublime.' *(Tony Rayns, Time Out)*

SHANGHAI SURPRISE CT: 1 AV: 2.00

1986 GB 97 C ACTION/ADVENTURE/ROMANCE

D Jim Goddard ●
W John Kohn Robert Bentley ● from Tony Kenrick's novel *Faraday's Flowers*

Sean Penn ● Madonna ● Paul Freeman Richard Griffiths Clyde Kusatsu ✓ (cameo: George Harrison)

In 1937 China, a missionary (Madonna, not exactly typecast) hires a ne'er-do-well (Madonna's then husband, Sean Penn) to find some opium. Don't ask me why.

The casting of Madonna as a missionary is a clue to the awfulness of this would-be adventure, with no thrills and charmless leading actors (Penn seems to be attempting an impersonation of Razzo Rizzo in

Midnight Cowboy). Presumably they thought they were making a latterday *African Queen*; they weren't. Songs are by executive producer George Harrison, who makes a cameo appearance as a bandleader.

'A silly little trifle which wouldn't even have passed muster as a 1930s programmer.' *(Variety)*

'Heavy-handed manipulation of genre ingredients simply results in vulgar, often embarrassing, kitsch.' *(Steven Goldman, Time Out)*

'The advance word was bad and [the film] more than lives up to it . . . The film is a dull hopelessly muddled mess . . . [which] should head straight into the rent-a-turkey department of video stores.' *(Jim DeBrosse, USA Today)*

'Frankly I've seen more animation in a block of wood . . . Madonna proves she cannot act her way out of a paper bag . . . The lady appears to be reading off an auto cue.' *(Pauline McLeod, Daily Mirror)*

'Moves along at the pace of a water-logged rat negotiating a paddy-field.' *(Quinlan)*

'Makes you long for something lighter and wittier such as a documentary on the Khmer Rouge.' *(Rose)*

SHE DONE HIM WRONG AAN CT: 7 AV: 8.75

1932 US 68 BW COMEDY

D Lowell Sherman

W Mae West Harvey Thew John Bright ☆ from West's play *Diamond Lil*

Mae West ☆ Cary Grant ☆ Owen Moore Gilbert Roland Noah Beery David Landau Rochelle Hudson

In the 1890s, a Bowery saloon-keeper (Mae West) seduces a Salvation Army crusader (Cary Grant) who turns out to be an undercover cop.

A funny film containing some of Mae West's most suggestive one-liners, although there are a few too many halts for musical numbers. As usual, she plays a larger-than-life version of herself – though not that much larger than life: Hollywood legend has it that West spotted the unknown Cary Grant on the Paramount lot, liked what she saw, and told her director Lowell Sherman 'If he can talk, I'll take him'.

ANTI:

'Only alternative to a strong drawing cast, nowadays if a picture wants business, is strong entertainment. This one has neither.' *(Variety)*

MIXED:

'See this amusing picture (heavily cut though it is by the Censor) and you can readily understand why Miss West has been at once an idol of Broadway and the object of attention by the police.' *(Daily Telegraph)*

'The film is not a pleasant one – the reek of the underworld is in every foot of it – but it is, apart from its quite preposterous ending, exceedingly competently made and something more than competently acted.' *(The Times)*

'No lack of wise-cracking comedy or of superficial incident, but general atmosphere and type of characters may not be commended to universal approval. Robust portrayal, uneven direction, convincing period settings, excellent general technique.' *(Today's Cinema Supplement)*

PRO:

'Superb period piece.' *(Graham Greene, Spectator)*

'A hearty and blustering cinematic cartoon . . . Miss West gives a highly amusing performance, which necessarily overshadows the commendable efforts of Cary Grant, Noah Beery [et al] . . . Lowell Sherman's direction is light and fast.' *(Mordaunt Hall, New York Times)*

'The epic has been refined somewhat, ladies and gents, but I am happy to report that Lil or Lou shines with her accustomed brilliance, one of the finest women that ever walked the streets. As an actress Mae West is a refreshing and healthy change from the slinky dopey foreigners and the simpering little home-grown chits to whom we . . . have grown accustomed, but not resigned . . . As for you, Aunt Effie, I think that you'll love it, but won't admit it.' *(Cy Caldwell, New Outlook)*

SHE WORE A YELLOW RIBBON

CT: 7 AV: 8.07

1949 US 103 C WESTERN

D John Ford ☆

W Frank S. Nugent Laurence Stallings from James Warner Bellah's stories

John Wayne ☆ Joanne Dru John Agar Ben Johnson Harry Carey Jr Victor McLaglen Mildred Natwick George O'Brien Arthur Shields

A cavalry officer (John Wayne) on the verge of retirement has to cope with Indians on the warpath.

Wayne gives a splendidly battered, world-weary performance in this, the second of Ford's cavalry westerns – it comes between *Fort Apache* (1948) and *Rio Grande* (1950). The scenery of Monument Valley is among the most magnificent ever on film, and Winton C. Hoch's cinematography won an Oscar. Unfortunately, the story rambles, and there's much too much maudlin sentiment and wearisome low-comedy (mainly from Victor McLaglen).

ANTI:

'Ford's films have lost their discipline tending towards the crude, the overlengthy and the sentimental. Like *Fort Apache*, [this one] . . . with distressing frequency, lapses into sentimentality [and] banality, the humour into tedious horse-play.' *(MFB)*

MIXED:

'All right as long as its characters keep on the move, which they do about half the time. When they pause to indulge in a bit of conversation, though, the sound track gets cluttered up with clichés that must have been intolerable even to Sitting Bull.' *(John McCarten, New Yorker)*

'Like Ford's other large-scale, elegiac westerns of this period, it's not a plain action movie but a pictorial film with slow spots and great set pieces. There's some tedious Irish comedy (Victor McLaglen is around too much) and an irksome pair of lovers – John Agar and Joanne Dru.' *(Pauline Kael)*

PRO:

'In this big Technicolored western Mr Ford has superbly achieved a vast and composite illustration of all the legends of the frontier cavalryman. He has got the bold and dashing courage, the stout masculine sentiment, the grandeur of rear-guard heroism . . . and best of all, he has got the brilliant color and vivid detail . . . His action is crisp and electric. His pictures are bold and beautiful . . . [It's] a dilly of a picture. Yeehooooo!' *(Bosley Crowther)*

'A symphony for the ears and a canvas for the eyes more than a narrative for the mind. The feelings of longing and loss, of a better past than present, and of the dignity of the men who are passing are conveyed through the sounds and scenes of the film, not through the themes of the story.' *(J.A. Place, The Western Films of John Ford, 1973)*

SHERLOCK JR. CT: 8 AV: 8.44

1924 US 45 BW COMEDY/FANTASY/SILENT

D Buster Keaton
W Clyde Bruckman Jean Havez Joseph Mitchell

Buster Keaton ☆ Kathryn McGuire Ward Crane Joseph Keaton Erwin Connolly

A projectionist accused of stealing a watch (Buster Keaton) dreams himself into the movie which is on screen, and becomes a great detective.

Surreal comedy which wastes little time on exposition and sets out on a succession of marvellously inventive sight-gags. The witty special effects are impressive for their time. It's a silent comedy masterpiece which many consider Keaton's best. Its influence can clearly be seen on much later films such as *The Purple Rose of Cairo* and *The Last Action Hero*.

ANTI:

'About as unfunny as a hospital operating room. The picture has all the old hoke in the world in it . . . There are . . . two chases; but neither can for a single second hold a candle to Harold Lloyd. In comparison they appear child's play. There is one piece of business, however, that is worthy of comment. It is the bit where Buster as a motion-picture machine operator in a dream scene walks out of the booth and into the action that he is projecting. That is clever. The rest is bunk.' *(Variety)*

PRO:

'You smile, snigger, chuckle, grin and guffaw . . . This is an extremely good comedy which will give you plenty of amusement, so long as you permit Mr Keaton to glide into his work with his usual deliberation.' *(New York Times)*

'If, a thousand years hence, the cinema were as dead as the Dodo, any archaeologist would be capable of recapturing its essence, simply by having the good fortune to see [this film]. He might even become aware that a little poetry, a sense of humour and the odd touch of genius mean more than all the text-books in the world.' *(Jacques B. Brunius, Cahiers d'Art)*

'If the film cannot be the ideal medium of surrealism, it is nevertheless for the spectator's mind an incomparable field of surrealist activity. The outstanding Sherlock Holmes Jr. analyses this characteristic of the cinema as Pirandello analysed the theatre in *Six Characters in Search of an Author*.' *(René Clair)*

'Delicious and surprising.' *(Gavin Lambert, Sunday Times, 1955)*

'Boiling along on the handlebars of a motorcycle quite unaware that he has lost his driver, Keaton whips through city traffic, breaks up a tug-of-war, gets a shovelful of dirt in the face from each of a long line of Rockette-timed ditch-diggers, approaches a log at high speed which is hinged open by dynamite precisely soon enough to let him through and, hitting an obstruction, leaves the handle-bars like an arrow leaving a bow, whams through the window of a shack in which the heroine is about to be violated, and hits the heavy feet-first, knocking him through the opposite wall. The whole sequence is as clean in motion as the trajectory of a bullet.' *(James Agee, Life, 1949)*

SHICHININ NO SAMURAI: *see* SEVEN SAMURAI.

SHINING, THE CT: 5 AV: 5.54

1980 GB 119/146 C HORROR

D Stanley Kubrick
W Stanley Kubrick Diane Johnson from Stephen King's novel

Jack Nicholson ● Shelley Duvall Danny Lloyd Barry Nelson Scatman Crothers Philip Stone Joe Turkel

Writer (Jack Nicholson) acting as caretaker in Colorado hotel becomes homicidal maniac.

Panned on release as being horrifyingly overacted, lacking in thrills and full of plot-holes, this Kubrick movie is now being reassessed as a profound and stylish study of Oedipal conflict. I'm with the original sceptics.

PRO:

'Seldom in any film has there been such a blénding of the manic and the comic . . . [It] makes previous horror pictures look pale and bloodless.' *(Alexander Walker, Evening Standard)*

'[Kubrick's] unflagging curiosity, capacity for innovation and disconcerting switches of mood and tempo have intensified over the years and are all present . . . It is the texture of uncertainty which makes the most impact.' *(Virginia Dignam, Morning Star)*

MIXED:

'In many ways a remarkable film; its clarity and resourcefulness far exceed the quality of the original plot . . . and it consistently baffles or defies expectation . . . But . . . to present evil as spectacle, to confront horror head-on as Kubrick does, is to render it lifeless and incredible. As a result [he] damages the skilful and original narrative which he has constructed.' *(Peter Ackroyd, Spectator)*

'Although there are some sequences of great power, it is often a case of too much, too soon. Nicholson [is] all hobgoblin leers and grimaces . . . The characters are just not established, while the time-jumbling produces confusion that not even Polanski-like reference to a climactic photography can resolve.' *(Tom Hutchinson, Now)*

ANTI:

'The biggest non-event of the year. It's not even scary.' *(Daily Star)*

'Sorry, Stanley. This time you blew it.' *(Evening News)*

'The story lacks suspense and any atmosphere of evil. Nicholson's performance is hammy enough to leave you rolling in the aisles.' *(Daily Mirror)*

'The crazier Nicholson gets, the more idiotic he looks. Shelley Duvall transforms the warm sympathetic wife of the book into a simpering, semi-retarded hysteric.' *(Variety)*

'As usual, Kubrick exhibits his basic inability to deal with people . . . Key plot developments are left unexplained. Thus after Wendy manages to lock the murderously mad Jack into the larder, we are shown how he gets out. Clearly the ghostly butler did it; but, if so, why doesn't he help Jack with other locked doors? . . . Jack Nicholson hams atrociously from the outset; Shelley Duvall is better but unable to fashion a whole character out of disparate fragments; little Danny Lloyd is as obdurately dour as other child actors are relentlessly cute . . . One thing the film does teach us; stymied creators are a bad lot: if they don't murder their families, which is bad enough, they come up with things like *The Shining*, which is worse.' *(John Simon)*

'Empty and pretentious. Apologists for the auteur theory fought hard to claim the movie as a masterpiece but potential audiences (as usual) knew better. The script abandons just about every element that makes Stephen King's novel so effectively atmospheric and horrific (including any believable explanation for "the shining" itself), replacing it with a banal plot and dialogue to match which might just have passed muster for a run-of-the-mill supernatural second feature.' *(Alan Frank)*

SHINING THROUGH CT: 5 AV: 3.75

1992 US 127 C WAR/THRILLER/ROMANCE/SO BAD

D David Seltzer ●

W David Seltzer Laurie Frank ● from Susan Isaacs's novel

Michael Douglas ● Melanie Griffith ● Liam Neeson Joely Richardson John Gielgud Francis Guinan

A secretary (Melanie Griffith) travels to Nazi Germany as a spy, where she attempts to discover the secrets of Hitler's rocket programme and rescue three of her Jewish relatives.

A mesmerizingly idiotic spy thriller set in modern Hollywood's idea of World War II, in which Germans come out with such memorable lines as *'Mein Gott*, you've got guts'. Melanie Griffith is endearingly inane as the spy, and Michael Douglas raises almost as many unintended chortles, playing her rescuer.

The climactic chase is a masterpiece of inanity, as is Melanie Griffith's voice-over throughout, keeping us abreast of her 'thoughts'. Sample: 'By late October of '41 London was reeling under a hailstorm of German bombs called the Blitz, and life in America was energized with the knowledge of what was inevitable.' Pardon?

Other great lines . . . (1) Griffith to Douglas: 'What's a war for if not to hold on to what we love?' (2) Interviewer to elderly Melanie Griffith: 'Tell me about the war. When did you first become interested in it?' (3) Griffith's voice-over: 'In one leap I landed in the upstairs chambers of the German elite.' (4) Griffith's voice-over: 'I knew it was a Friday we said goodbye because the next day was Saturday.'

PRO:

'The dialogue is crisp, funny and self-knowing, the story well-plotted and the production values first-rate.' *(James Cameron-Wilson, Film Review)*

'A clever and effective homage to the war films of the Forties that manages to re-create their charm and naiveté.' *(Martin & Porter)*

MIXED:

'An old-fashioned women's picture that could pass for a television movie except for its lavish trappings.' *(Variety)*

'Fun, in an extravagant, hopelessly retrograde fashion.' *(Janet Maslin, New York Times)*

ANTI:

'Little more than a big, brassy Hallmark card with a World War II backdrop.' *(Variety)*

'The only exercise Miss G gets in this daft wartime thriller is to run from Potsdam to Berlin one night in high heels and an opera gown. Have you ever tried this? It is, I assure you, impossible. But then, so is everything else in [the film].' *(Nigel Andrews, Financial Times)*

'God knows, you'd have a hard time to dislike a film as stupid as [this]. It belongs to the ancient and great tradition of films so bad they're hilarious . . . Throughout it all, Griffith's little dumb-blonde drawl sounds as if she were taking a reading test and flunking it.' *(Alexander Walker, Evening Standard)*

'An insult to the intelligence . . . a cross between *Working Girl* and *The Cassandra Crossing*.' *(Roger Ebert)*

'One of the funniest bad movies ever. Despite superb production values, the script is so silly and the dialogue so priceless that audiences were shrieking with laughter.' *(Rose)*

SHIP OF FOOLS AAN CT: 5 AV: 7.00

1965 US 150 BW DRAMA

D Stanley Kramer
W Abby Mann ✗ AAN from Katherine Anne Porter's novel

Vivien Leigh ✗ Simone Signoret ☆ AAN Oskar Werner ☆ Heinz Rühmann Jos Ferrer Lee Marvin Elizabeth Ashley Michael Dunn ☆ George Segal José Greco Lilia Scala

An ocean liner in 1933 becomes the setting for various characters to exemplify the reasons for the spread of Nazism.

Banal soap opera, which many critics in 1965 thought powerful and profound. The script is full of lazy, obvious hindsight and heavy-handed irony. One Jewish passenger even gets to say 'There are nearly a million Jews in Germany. What are they going to do? Kill us all?' It won Oscars for cinematography (Ernest Laszlo) and art direction (William Clatworthy).

PRO:

'A film that appeals to the intellect and the emotions . . . All the principals give strong performances.' *(Variety)*

'There is such wealth of reflection upon the human condition, so subtle an orchestration of the elements of love and hate, that it is not fair to tag this with the label of any other film.' *(New York Times)*

'The picture is awash with interesting and believable – even if far from admirable – characters who possess independent vitality and are extremely well acted . . . And director Kramer and scenarist Mann, while they have trouble with a few recalcitrant and labored plot strands, have generally managed to keep the proceedings tidily knit and absorbingly well-paced.' *(Moira Walsh, America, 1965)*

'It's an adult picture with graphic language and important themes, the main one being Nazism.' *(Virgin)*

ANTI:

'This is not Grand Hotel afloat but rather Grand Hotel aground in the shallows of Mr Kramer's imagination.' *(Kenneth Tynan, Observer)*

'The enervation of the long sea voyage hangs heavily over them all. They are too symbolically adrift, with nothing but their dialogue to keep them from going under . . . Mann . . . is a master of the exhaustive sledge-hammer irony and momentous pause, the dialogue that leaves no symbolic stone unturned.' *(Penelope Houston, Financial Times)*

'When you're not being hit over the head with the symbolism, you're being punched in the stomach by would-be inventive camerawork while the music score unremittingly fills our nostrils with acrid exhalations.' *(John Simon)*

'One can enjoy the movie by giggling over its florid swoony trash, such as the doomed lovers – the ship's doctor (Oskar Werner) smiling mistily, and compassionately giving injections and adoring love to La Condesa (Simone Signoret), who has met him too late. (Doctor: 'You're so strange – sometimes you're so bitter, then you're like a child, soft and warm.' La Condesa: 'I'm just a woman.') The international star cast includes Vivien Leigh as an ageing divorcée (this may be her most embarrassing screen performance – she's like a jerky Pinocchio).' *(Pauline Kael)*

SHOESHINE AAW CT: 7 AV: 8.20

(aka *Sciuscia*)

1946 Italy 90/93 BW DRAMA/FOREIGN

D Vittorio De Sica ☆
W Cesare Zavattini Sergio Amidei Adolfo Franci C.G. Viola AAN

Franco Interlenghi Rinaldo Smordoni Anielo Mele Bruno Ortensi Pacifico Astrologo

In Rome, just after the Second World War, two shoeshine boys (Franco Interlenghi, Rinaldo Smordoni) go in for black marketeering, with tragic consequences.

One of the most famous neo-realist dramas, this is a rough-and-ready piece of film-making, primitive by modern standards. Critics of its day rightly hailed it as a gruelling depiction of poverty and a heartfelt denunciation of Italy's brutal penal system. Over and above that, however, it is a very moving, powerful study of how easy it is to lose one's innocence. In the days before Foreign Oscars, it won a special

Academy Award, for 'proving to the world that the creative spirit can triumph over adversity' – which makes the film sound rather more optimistic than it is.

MIXED:

'Not a pretty picture to contemplate nor is it by any means a well-made picture. But [it] mirrors the anguished soul of a starving, disorganized and demoralized nation with such uncompromising realism that the roughness of its composition is overshadowed by its driving, emotional force . . . The English title translations by Herman G. Weinberg preserve the earthy tone of [street] talk . . . Not an entertainment; rather it is a brilliantly executed social document.' *(New York Times)*

PRO:

'One of the few fully alive, fully rational films ever made . . . It is remarkably perceptive and compassionate in its study of authority and of those who embody authority, serve it, and suffer in and under it. It is also the rarest thing in contemporary art – a true tragedy. This tragedy is cross-lighted by pathos, by the youthfulness and innocence of the heroes . . . The film is in no sense a despairing or "defeatist" work, as some people feel it is. I have seldom seen the more ardent and virile of the rational and Christian values more firmly defended, or the effects of their absence or misuse more pitifully and terribly demonstrated.' *(James Agee, Nation)*

'In spite of the fact that [it] will probably break your heart, I must advise you to see this extraordinary Italian film . . . The acting throughout . . . is so real that in many cases it does not seem like acting at all . . . This film is not only powerful as a tract on the evils of juvenile prisons, but it is equally powerful for its picture of post-war Europe.' *(Philip T. Hartung, Commonweal)*

'It is a human documentary, gripping revealing and frightening . . . a film everyone with the welfare of the world's youth at heart must see.' *(Ross Shepherd, People)*

'In handling a camera I feel that I have no peer. But what De Sica can do, that I can't do! I ran his *Shoeshine* again recently and the camera disappeared, the screen disappeared; it was just life.' *(Orson Welles, 1960)*

SHOOT THE PIANO PLAYER CT: 5 AV: 7.75

(aka *Tirez sur le Pigniste; Shoot the Pianist*)

1960 France 80 BW THRILLER/FOREIGN

D François Truffaut
W Marcel Moussy François Truffaut from David Goodis's novel *Down There*

Charles Aznavour ✓ Nicole Berger Marie Dubois Michèle Mercier Albert Rémy Claude Mansard Daniel Boulanger

A bar-room pianist (Charles Aznavour) helps two petty crooks escape from gangsters – an act which leads to the death of his girlfriend (Marie Dubois).

A run-of-the-mill gangster plot keeps getting sidetracked by some amusing visual gags and Charles Aznavour's amusingly hangdog performance. Truffaut's second film, applying New Wave techniques to American film noir, is as anarchic as Dick Lester films were later to be in England. It has a tendency to trivialize human emotions and create caricatures, which would be all very well in a comedy, but then demands that we sympathize with these characters as rounded human beings. Still, there are delights along the way.

'The idea behind *Shoot the Piano Player* was to make a film without a subject, to express all I wanted to about glory, success, downfall, failure, women, and love by means of a detective story. It's a grab-bag.' *(François Truffaut)*

PRO:

'A comedy about melancholia – perhaps the only comedy about melancholia. Truffaut is freely inventive here – a young director willing to try almost anything – and Charlie's encounters with the world are filled with good and bad jokes, bits from old Sacha Guitry films, clowns and thugs, tough kids, songs and fantasy and snow scenes, and homage to the American Grade-B gangster pictures of the 40s and 50s. The film is nihilistic in attitude yet by its wit and good spirits it's totally involved in life and fun. Nothing is clear-cut; the ironies crisscross and bounce.' *(Pauline Kael)*

MIXED:

'Tries to combine farce and tragedy; it fails but is more interesting than most successes.' *(Dwight MacDonald, Esquire)*

'Nuttiness pure and simple . . . surges and swirls through the tangle of solemn intimations in this film until one finds it hard to see or figure what M. Truffaut is about . . . It is a teasing and frequently amusing (or moving) film . . . but it simply does not hang together.' *(Bosley Crowther)*

'Lacks the impact of Truffaut's exceptional first effort, but is good enough to make one look forward to his third.' *(Fred Majdalany, Daily Mail)*

'The film is often funny in a likeable bizarre way . . . and the whole is distinguished by its perky flights of fancy, the assured handling of its players and its air of personal enjoyment . . . Pictorially it is magnificent, revealing Truffaut's brilliant control over his images; emotionally it's a little jejeune.' *(John Gillet, MFB)*

ANTI:

'Suffers from hesitancy . . . Truffaut vacillates

between high-drama and low comedy in [this] vivid little yarn.' *(Jewish Chronicle)*

'The film's quaint pixilated humour is awkwardly interwoven with tragedy and difficult to accept against a background of crime, suicide and murder.' *(Nina Hibbin, Daily Worker)*

SHOOT TO KILL: *see* HUE AND CRY.

SHOOTIST, THE CT: 6 AV: 7.50

1976 US 100 C WESTERN

D Don Siegel ☆
W Miles Hood Swarthout Scott Hale from Glendon Swarthout's novel

John Wayne ☆ Katharine Hepburn James Stewart Ron Howard Bill McKinney Richard Boone Scatman Crothers John Carradine Hugh O'Brian Sheree North Harry Morgan

An old gunfighter (John Wayne) awaits a natural death, but finds that too many people want to shoot him first.

John Wayne's last ride, in which he stars as a dying ex-gunfighter, is too self-consciously mythic, feebly motivated and full of barely reheated clichés (Ron Howard, for instance, gets to re-play the Brandon de Wilde role in *Shane*), but it boasts one of Wayne's most moving performances. Don Siegel directs efficiently, and with the necessary feel for those old John Ford values. Bruce Surtees's photography is especially fine.

PRO:

'Just when it seemed that the western was an endangered species, due for extinction because it had repeated itself too many times, Wayne and Siegel have managed to validate it once more.' *(Arthur Knight)*

'Watching this film is like taking a tour of Hollywood legends.' *(Frank Rich)*

'Without a doubt, *The Shootist* is the finest western of the 1970s and one of the best all-time genre productions. Packed with superb performances, fine pacing and direction and a most literate script, The Shootist is nonetheless dominated by John Wayne in his final and most magnificent screen role.' *(Parish & Pitts, The Great Western Pictures, 1988)*

MIXED:

'This script is absolutely awful . . . Wayne is good. He has always been a good manager and dispenser of his persona. Now, although his nose has gone Fieldsian, he still manages his persona capably, still makes his listening and speaking fit two requirements: what the scene demands and what the audience expects. We know that he knows he's an institution, but it's a fairly well-run one.' *(Stanley Kauffmann)*

ANTI:

'The script . . . is a mechanical demonstration of how greedy and unfeeling the townspeople are, and Don Siegel's directing lacks rhythm – each scene dies a separate death.' *(Pauline Kael)*

One of those relatively few movies whose badness makes one feel genuinely sad. It is the sort of picture that, had it been made in almost any other country – ie any country that can see itself and its people straight rather than through a veil of myth and legend – could have emerged human and moving. Instead, it is superficial, cliché-riddled, and torn apart by conflicting aims of abiding by and debunking or transcending its genre . . . Wayne gives a surprisingly effective performance as Books, a role somewhat more demanding than Rooster Cogburn in *True Grit*, his previous high. If at the age of sixty-nine, after forty-seven years in the movies, Wayne can truly have learned his trade, there is hope for every one of us, no matter how slow a study.' *(John Simon)*

SHOP AROUND THE CORNER, THE CT: 10 AV: 8.40

1940 US 97 BW DRAMA/ROMANCE/COMEDY

D Ernst Lubitsch ☆
W Samson Raphaelson ☆ from Nikolaus Laszlo's play *Parfumerie*

James Stewart ☆ Margaret Sullavan ☆ Frank Morgan ☆ Joseph Schildkraut ✔ Sara Haden Felix Bressart ☆ William Tracy ✔

In a Budapest shop, a senior clerk (James Stewart) and a junior sales girl (Margaret Sullavan) hate each other, become pen-friends, and fall in love.

My nomination for Lubitsch's finest film, and one of the most delightful pictures ever made. The central plot development is predictable from reel one and most of the action takes place in a single set – an indication of the piece's theatrical origins – yet none of this detracts in the slightest.

Sullavan and Stewart had known and worked together since she was a teenager, in the University Players. Here, they are wonderful together, and play everything for real; the narrative assists them by ensuring that every emotional change and subterfuge is fully motivated. There is a marvellous array of supporting actors, whose foibles and failings cover an amazingly wide area of human behaviour. The ambience of a shop is perfectly captured, and there's something endearingly good-hearted, even Dickensian, in the way these flawed people are portrayed.

The three leading actors worked together so successfully that they were reunited immediately for Frank Borzage's *The Mortal Storm*. The film was later turned into the screen musical *In the Good Old Summertime* (1949) and the stage musical *She Loves Me*.

MIXED:

'The quintessential mandragora of escapism . . .

Lubitsch takes a handful of first-class actors and actresses, flings them into a gay and flimsy set, throws in a few misunderstandings, one cad and half a dozen assorted whimsies; beats all up together and disarms your criticism. True, he is becoming almost too arrogant . . . Here, as in *Ninotchka*, the climax is in the wrong place, and the whole film could quite easily be fifteen minutes shorter.' *(Basil Wright, Spectator)*

'Enchantment for those who like marzipan.' *(Shipman)*

PRO:

'MGM has another hit and Lubitsch another triumph . . . There's not a second of the picture's unreeling that you would care to miss.' *(Hollywood Reporter)*

'Admirably played . . . adroitly developed and smartly conceived . . . Lubitsch is at his best.' *(Motion Picture Herald)*

'Lubitsch's direction has supplied deft touches, while the picture has been ideally cast.' *(Film Daily)*

'From beginning to end, aided by the excellent trouping [it] is topnotch in every department . . . Sure to be a box-office hit.' *(Showmen Trade Review)*

'*Ninotchka* appears to have used up [Lubitsch's] supply of hearty comedy for the time at least, but his sense of humor is inexhaustible . . . So there it is and a pretty kettle of bubbling brew it makes under Mr Lubitsch's deft and tender management and with a genial company to play it gently, well this side of farce and well that side of utter seriousness.' *(Frank S. Nugent, New York Times)*

'It has those warm qualities that Lubitsch seems to have discovered within himself of late, not over-sentimentalized and presented with a humorous kindliness. It is romantic in a lively, almost jolly way, and its substance is no newer and more important than that familiar plot about a fellow and a girl who are in love with each other without knowing it . . . The people who did it seem to have enjoyed doing it just as much as their audiences will enjoy seeing it.' *(James Shelley Hamilton, NBR)*

'Close to perfection – one of the most beautifully acted and paced romantic comedies ever made in this country . . . In no other movie has this kind of love-hate been made so convincing.' *(Pauline Kael, 1978)*

'As for human comedy, I think I never was as good as in *The Shop Around the Corner*. Never did I make a picture in which the atmosphere and the characters were truer than in this picture.' *(Ernst Lubitsch)*

SHOP ON MAIN STREET, THE AAW

CT: 6 AV: 7.71

(aka *Obchod Na Korze; Shop on the High Street, The*)

1965 Czechoslovakia 128 BW DRAMA/WAR/FOREIGN

D Ján Kádar Einar Klos
W Ladislav Grosman Ján Kádar Elmar Klos

Ida Kaminská ☆ AAN Josef Króner ☆ Hana Slivková Martin Holly Frantisek Zvarik Helena Zvaríková

In Nazi-occupied Czechoslovakia, an 'Aryan' carpenter (Josef Króner) is placed in charge of a button-shop owned by an old Jewess (Ida Kaminská). His attempts to protect her have tragic consequences.

Touching, sentimental fable with amusing comic moments, and a feeling for place and period. It's nothing particularly original – simply a good story, well told, and brilliantly acted by the two leads.

ANTI:

'Overlong, derivative, ploddingly directed.' *(John Simon)*

PRO:

'Outstanding . . . it is all absolutely credible . . . Klos and Kádar [are] great directors . . . aided by excellent camerawork, at times lyrical, at other almost crackling with the faded sunshine of an aged photograph.' *(Prague News Letter)*

'This treasure of the renascent Czech cinema is still the most moving new film I have seen this year. Beginning in a key of sly, bucolic comedy, it modulates into tragedy so gently that we hardly notice the shift. . . . The direction is by . . . a seamless team whose self-denying respect for the script may well prevent them from ever becoming fashionable. [The] dialogue is subtitled with brilliant succinctness by Lindsay Anderson.' *(Kenneth Tynan, Observer)*

'The best acting in London is now to be seen [in this film] . . . The most striking performance comes from Josef Króner . . . the best thing in a brilliant film.' *(Philip Oakes, Sunday Telegraph)*

'If a film is original, personal, and deeply felt, it doesn't necessarily have to be experimental as well to be any good . . . And in [this one] we are treated to a performance the like of which one has not seen in some time . . . [Króner's] performance . . . has a solidity and a strength on which the whole film is built.' *(Richard Roud, Guardian)*

SHORT CUTS

CT: 9 AV: 9.00 (est)

1993 US 188 C COMEDY/DRAMA

D Robert Altman ☆ AAN
W Robert Altman Frank Barhydt ☆ from Raymond Carver's short stories and poem

Bruce Davison ☆ Andie MacDowell ✔ Jack Lemmon ✔ Tim Robbins ☆ Madeleine Stowe ✔ Frances McDormand ✔ Jennifer Jason Leigh Christopher Penn Annie Ross Lori Singer Lily Tomlin, Tom Waits Matthew Modine Anne Archer Robert Downey Jr

People struggle to exist in modern Los Angeles.

Much of Altman's most acclaimed work (even *M*A*S*H* and *Nashville*) has left me cold. Almost all his stories have been messily structured; beneath his studied quirkiness, he has always had an unpleasant habit of sneering at his own characters. Politically, he has espoused a complacent leftism which seldom amounted to more than mouthing the radical chic of the time. And he often cloaks triviality with pretentiousness.

But in *Short Cuts*, he harnesses his cinematic talents to the insights of the American short-story writer Raymond Carver, interweaving eight of Carvers short stories and one poem, and has come up with some kind of masterpiece.

The plots in this three-and-a-quarter-hour epic (which is not a minute too long) are many and various. Each illustrates some different facet of American life, and they come together to form a coherent image – of people who have forgotten to care about each other; men who have forgotten that life is about more than pursuing their own desires; and people who live their lives at second-hand through TV – which crops up in various guises, as informer, escape route, baby-sitter and anaesthetist.

Carver's stories have been transplanted to Los Angeles, which Altman evidently sees as some kind of hell on earth. But Carver's ironies – like the men who get upset about finding a naked female corpse in the river, because they think she'll interfere with their fishing – remain intact alongside Altman's inventions, such as the night-club singer (Annie Ross) who can croon about emotion but never shows any to her disturbed daughter (Lori Singer).

The great thing is that there's nothing facile or mean-minded about *Short Cuts*. Characters who seemed bad turn out to be redeemable; weaklings turn out to be stronger than you had imagined; apparently fragile relationships (such as the one between waitress Lily Tomlin and chauffeur Tom Waits) prove resilient. This richness of characterization – along with Altman's reputation – help to explain why he has been able to attract an all-star cast.

This is not a polite film. Women scratch their bottoms and utter obscenities; men fart in bed, have their spots squeezed, pull out their penises and pee. This is a film for those who can handle the harsher sides of reality. It's as dark a vision of America as anything that Altman has given us before, in *McCabe and Mrs Miller*, *Nashville* or *The Player*. There is a constant undertow of menace, pollution, a sense of life's injustices, amounting almost to a mass psychosis. But this time, influenced by Carver's original texts, he seems more generous-spirited, less glib and sanctimonious.

ANTI:

'Vulgar, pretentious, voyeuristic, overlong, and, above all, contrived. After that, you can add that Altman has all kinds of technical prowess. But is that adequate compensation for a gross insufficiency of artistry, intellect, and taste?' *(John Simon)*

'Carver's pervasive quality, under his terse style, is compassion . . . In Altman, however, compassion extends only to plainly terrible moments, such as death. Most of the time, unlike Carver, he merely observes, often satirically. In addition, he misses no chance to exploit sex. Sex is very present in Carver, but generally it's treated as a constant unfathomable mystery in otherwise prosaic lives. Altman seizes every sexual moment to move from mystery to flaunting. Often it's not amplification of Carver, it's invention. He gives one of Carver's characters a wife who earns money doing telephone sex while holding a small child on her lap. It's the kind of smirk that Altman knows he can't be reproved for in these liberated times . . . Throughout the film, the feeling grows that these good actors are being grubbily utilized by the director; the object of the film is not empathy but his self-celebration. All the nominal subjects – agony, affection, passion, hate, remorse – are finally congealed by Altman's mechanistic cleverness.' *(Stanley Kauffmann)*

'*Short Cuts* is exactly what you'd expect from a bloated ego who sees his recent coronation as a "genius" as justification for inflicting on us even more artsy-fartsy trash. What am I talking about? I'm talking about a movie that lasts more than three hours. I'm talking about 22 major characters, mostly played by B-level actors who couldn't make it into the latest Woody Allen flick. I'm talking about eight stories (more, if you add subplots), crossing, crisscrossing, meandering and, at the end, having no point whatsoever. I'm talking about taking the stories of the great Raymond Carver and having the audacity to muck with them. I'm talking about Robert Altman.' *(Rod Lurie, LA Magazine)*

'A rambling ensemble piece . . . very long . . . very episodic, very LA and very tedious . . . It is all very unsatisfactory and long-winded. I shouldn't bother if I were you.' *(Sue Heal, Today)*

PRO:

'The most abrasively brilliant movie of this director's long and illustrious career.' *(Bruce Williamson, Playboy)*

'A movie that works a wild and brilliant alchemy on Carver's fiction while blowing out the frontiers of cinema. *Short Cuts* is not only the strongest film of Altman's career, it dissects white middle-class America with greater acuity and vision than any movie in recent years.' *(Brian D. Johnson, Maclean's)*

'Riveting . . . ranks at the top of Robert Altman's work. A large cinematic canvas magnificently painted with unforgettable characters, superbly portrayed. Like it or not (and Altman detractors will carp), this is what movie making is all about.' *(Ed Kelleher, Film Journal)*

'Brilliantly cohesive . . . a parable about the ills of America . . . that grips you like a vice throughout.' *(Derek Malcolm, Guardian)*

'Uses Carver's writing partly to hack away at, and re-shape, the soap opera tradition's spreading empire on the modern screen . . . [Its] brilliance . . . lies in its surgical casualness, at once blithe and precise.' *(Nigel Andrews, Financial Times)*

SHORT FILM ABOUT KILLING, A

CT: 5 AV: 7.25

(aka *Krotki Film O Zabijaniu; Thou Shalt Not Kill*)

1989 Poland 84 C DRAMA/FOREIGN

D Krzysztof Kieślowski ✗
W Krzysztof Piesiewicz Krzysztof Kieślowski

Miroslaw Baka Krzysztof Globisz Jan Tesarz Zbigniew Zapasiewicz

The film is intended to be a powerful indictment of capital punishment, and compares a brutal, senseless murder by a young man (Miroslaw Baka) with his clinical execution by the state.

A Polish art-movie which, though made for TV as one of 'The Dekalog', a ten-part series based on the Ten Commandments, was garlanded with movie awards. It won the Prix du Jury and the International Critics Prize at Cannes, and Best Film at the first European Film Awards in Berlin.

The style of the piece was praised for its originality. To me, it looked like regulation 80s art-house realism: the violence is filmed at excruciating length and with loving attention to the most disgusting physical detail; bright colours have been abolished everywhere by directorial edict; everyone looks agonized throughout (even a young lawyer when he has just passed his bar exams).

The one touch of originality is the director's adoption of a weird visual technique whereby a black cloud obliterates sometimes the right of frame, sometimes the left. Now and again, without any particular reason, it seeps into the top or bottom of frame. I was unable to decide whether this was indicative of creeping melancholia, or defective film stock.

The picture's success is all the more curious, since it fails as drama: it is hard to care about the characters, the pace is funereal, and there is negligible character development. For example, the sensitive young lawyer through whose eyes we see much of the action (Krzysztof Globisz) is agonized about capital punishment from the start, so that witnessing his first execution does no more than prolong his agony, and ours.

To suit his didactic message, Kieślowski emphasizes the visual parallels between senseless murder and judicial execution. The murderer, for example, winds rope around his fingers before garrotting his victim: the hangman winds his rope tightly around a pulley before the execution.

Unfortunately, the director's concentration on such minutiae disguises rather than illuminates the important differences between murder and judicial execution. The hangman tests his equipment in order *not* to cause the victim unnecessary pain: for the murderer, his victim's pain is of no importance. The hangman is committing an act designed (however misguidedly) to safeguard society, and to be both punishment and deterrent. The murderer's killing is anti-social and has no basis in rationality.

Despite its critical reputation, the film struck me as dreary, predictable and stupid: an awful reminder that just because a film is gruelling does not make it powerful, dourness does not guarantee profundity, and the road to bad art is all too often paved with liberal intentions.

'Unforgettable in its condemnation of killing.' *(Halliwell)*

'Astonishingly powerful and shocking.' *(Winnert)*

'Made with a masterly hand that cannot fail to shake any sense of audience complacency.' *(Bergan & Karney)*

SHOT IN THE DARK, A

CT: 8 AV: 7.00

1964 US 101 C COMEDY

D Blake Edwards ☆
W Blake Edwards William Peter Blatty ☆ from Marcel Achard's play (translated by Harry Kurnitz)

Peter Sellers ☆ Herbert Lom ☆ Elke Sommer ☆ Burt Kwouk George Sanders ☆ Tracy Reed Graham Stark ☆ Bryan Forbes

Lovesick inspector (Peter Sellers) tries to show that a maid (Elke Sommer) is innocent of murder.

Easily the funniest and most inventive of the Clouseau pictures, this is the second in the series (the first being *The Pink Panther*) and brings the whole team together for the first time. Sellers shows here why he was the best farceur of his generation. Underrated by the critics, better appreciated by audiences.

ANTI:

'A very flat cocktail with only intermittent taste and sparkle.' *(Michael Thornton, Sunday Express)*

'Someone . . . thought that since . . . Sellers had been so funny . . . in *The Pink Panther*, it would be a good idea to expand the character and build a new film round him. It wasn't.' *(The Times)*

MIXED:

'Has some engaging send-ups of favourite moments of the typical whodunnit. Unlike the typical whodunnit, however, it has very little story development, no trail of clues, and no build-up of tension. It simply relies on endless variations of the falling about joke.' *(Nina Hibbin, Daily Worker)*

'What has happened inevitably is that the gags follow each other so closely that the comedy is impacted. The good and the bad are bonded together like strips of veneer and the join between what's feeble and what's really funny is sometimes the result of brute force rather than inspiration.' *(Philip Oakes, Sunday Telegraph)*

'It has its moments, which mostly include Herbert Lom . . . and it has some very snappy credits.' *(Isabel Quigly, Spectator)*

'Sometimes the narrative is subordinated to individual bits of business and running gags but Sellers's skill as a comedian again is demonstrated.' *(Variety)*

'Mildly funny for those in the mood for pratfalls.' *(Halliwell)*

PRO:

'[Sellers] is funnier [than in the original] . . . This is slapstick carried so far beyond the bounds of farce that it becomes a highly sophisticated game; mere plausibility is abolished . . . Such logic as applies is that of cartoon films.' *(Kenneth Tynan, Observer)*

'Gaspingly hilarious.' *(Maltin)*

SHOW BOAT CT: 7 AV: 8.55

(aka *Showboat*)

1936 US 110 BW MUSICAL/DRAMA

D James Whale
W Oscar Hammerstein II from his musical play (music by Jerome Kern)

Irene Dunne ☆ Allan Jones ☆ Helen Morgan ☆ Paul Robeson ☆ Charles Winninger ☆ Hattie McDaniel ☆ Donald Cook Sammy White

Magnolia Hawks (Irene Dunne), a singer on a Mississippi River showboat, falls for unreliable gambler Gaylord Ravenal (Allan Jones).

British director James Whale, best known for quirky horror films such as *The Bride of Frankenstein*, turns in a glossily produced musical with plenty of pace, though he never solves the problem of a screenplay which leaps about in time too much (greatly diminishing the impact of the final half-hour) and leaves too many plot strands dangling. Even as it is, the cast is magnificent, the racial sub-plot is touching, and the numbers – especially 'Old Man River', 'Can't Help Lovin' Dat Man', and 'Bill' – are, of course, classics.

'Very lavish . . . directed with a fine moneyed smoothness . . . For three-quarters of its length [it] proves good entertainment, sentimental, literary, but oddly appealing.' *(Graham Greene, Spectator)*

'It is a trifle conventional in some of its native American values . . . but it is . . . undoubtedly the film of the year . . . Mr Whale has seized the atmosphere uncommonly well . . . It is Mr Robeson's film, though that opinion carries no disrespect for other performances.' *(G.A. Atkinson, Era)*

'It is of course the music that makes [the film] but James Whale . . . has had the perception to hold to its melodic qualities without losing sight of the cinema's insistent need for action. Here is one of the few musical shows which is not merely a screened concert.' *(Frank S. Nugent)*

SHOW BOAT CT: 6 AV: 6.75

(aka *Showboat*)

1951 US 107 C MUSICAL/DRAMA

D George Sidney
W John Lee Mahin from Oscar Hammerstein II's musical (music by Jerome Kern)

Kathryn Grayson Howard Keel ☆ Ava Gardner (vocals dubbed by Annette Warren) Joe E. Brown ☆ William Warfield Robert Sterling Agnes Moorehead Marge & Gower Champion ✔

Magnolia Hawks (Kathryn Grayson), a singer on a Mississippi River showboat, falls for unreliable gambler Gaylord Ravenal (Howard Keel).

Enjoyable, lavishly produced but pedestrian re-make of the great Kern-Hammerstein musical. On an actor-for-actor comparison, the 1936 version comes out tops; but this version does have the advantage of Charles Rosher's colourful, Oscar-nominated photography. The musical direction, by Conrad Salinger and Adolph Deutsch, was also nominated.

ANTI:

'To halve the tempo and even alter the melodic line of "Can't Help Lovin' Dat Man" is sheer sacrilege, and I can't help hatin' the presumptuous Philistine who did it.' *(Sunday Chronicle)*

MIXED:

'[Keel and Grayson] sing even better than they act . . . and I found the production sufficiently satisfying to forgive the more sugary bits of sentiment.' *(P.L. Mannock, Daily Herald)*

PRO:

'Outstanding.' *(Kine Weekly)*

'Superlative entertainment . . . a gilt-edged investment for showmen.' *(Cinema)*

'A really lovely [remake] which with its touching story and melting melodies should surely charm you to a tear.' *(Daily Graphic)*

'This is her third voyage as a film and the greatest yet.' *(B. Wickstead, Daily Express)*

SHOW PEOPLE CT: 8 AV: 6.75

928 US 80 BW COMEDY/SILENT

King Vidor ☆
W Wanda Tuchock Agnes Christine Johnston, Lawrence Stallings
Marion Davies ☆ William Haines Dell Henderson Paul Ralli Tenen Holtz

n aspiring actress (Marion Davies) tries to be a success in Hollywood.

revelation, at least to those of us whose view of Marion Davies was coloured by Orson Welles's cruelly satirical portrait in *Citizen Kane*. This is an amusing, surprisingly sophisticated silent comedy about Hollywood – the leading character is said to be modelled on Gloria Swanson – which shows Davies to be a fine comic actress. What a tragedy that her lover, W. Randolph Hearst, forced her into serious roles beyond her range. The film has extra historical interest, since it has innumerable stars of the period Charles Chaplin, Douglas Fairbanks, John Gilbert, etc – in cameo roles.

'You have never before seen as many stars in any one picture. Their combined salaries would bankrupt the US mint . . . The story is not new nor startling but Marion and Bill keep you laughing. Don't miss this.' *(Photoplay)*

'I hope it will have the effect of impressing someone with power to make the necessary decision, that Marion Davies should appear in comedies with a touch of human interest in them, and not in pictures in which she is cast on the assumption that she is as great and as versatile an artist as the Hearst papers insist that she is. . . . In light comedy roles I don't know of anyone who can surpass her. Certainly in *Show People* she is delightful . . . [and it] is one of the most entertaining pictures that have come from the Metro lot in a long time.' *(Wilfred Beaton, Film Spectator)*

'A hardy satire on Hollywood life . . . While there are one or two instances here where the fun boils over, most of the time it simmers in a delightful fashion.' *(Mordaunt Hall, New York Times)*

SHOWBOAT: *see* SHOW BOAT.

SIDNEY SHELDON'S THE OTHER SIDE OF MIDNIGHT: *see* OTHER SIDE OF MIDNIGHT, THE.

SILENCE OF THE LAMBS, THE AAW
CT: 9 AV: 8.33

1991 US 120 C THRILLER/HORROR

Jonathan Demme ☆ AAW
Ted Tally ☆ AAW from Thomas Harris's novel
Jodie Foster ☆ AAW Anthony Hopkins ☆ AAW Scott Glenn Ted Levine ✔ Anthony Heald Brooke Smith Diane Baker Kasi Lemmons Roger Corman

Murderous psycho Hannibal Lecter (Anthony Hopkins) helps FBI trainee Clarice Starling (Jodie Foster) track down a serial killer Buffalo Bill (Ted Levine), so named because he skins his female victims.

A terrific, though melodramatic, thriller with a frightening view of humanity – especially men. Jonathan Demme directs with Hitchcockian flair, but less of the old master's voyeurism and misogyny. Jodie Foster and Anthony Hopkins, both on top form, play some of the most memorable scenes in cinema history.

The film was much criticized for glorifying the serial killer. The author of the original, million-selling novel, Thomas Harris, was once a crime reporter and could undoubtedly have written a more realistic mass-murderer than Hannibal Lecter. However, the extent to which Lecter acquired a mythic status – and won Hopkins an Oscar as leading actor when really he was in a supporting role – suggests his decision not to was a shrewd one. Lecter is really a variation on an old cinematic theme: the evil genius, also known as Count Zaroff, Dr Frankenstein and the Phantom of the Opera.

Although Lecter is the most courteous, civilized and intelligent person in the film, he is not so clever that he understands what drives him: the result is that he also has something about him of the noble savage. There are moments when, trussed and restrained, he has the pathos of the Man in the Iron Mask or Frankenstein's Monster. His escape from custody is as ingenious as that of a James Bond, and the audience increasingly feels a sneaking sympathy for him as a free spirit. The film ends with him stalking his old jailer, and few members of the audience will not wish him bon appetit.

Lecter is also the sexiest man in the film. He can recognize the heroine by her walk and the smell of her skin-cream. He draws romantic pictures of her. The moment when she ventures too close and Lecter chooses just to brush one finger across hers is erotically charged, precisely because we (and she) are aware of what he *could* do to her. The film is, in a perverse way, a romance.

The scenes between Hopkins and Foster won Oscars for the actors because they are so well written as love-hate sparring matches, with each punching deep into the other's psyche. The key speech in the film is Hopkins's, where he compares Clarice's childhood failure to save lambs from slaughter, with her feeble attempts as a member of the FBI to fight the dark side of humanity. That such attempts are ultimately doomed is never in doubt, for both Harris's novel and Ted Tally's screenplay are steeped in a sense of original sin.

In the film, however, the sin is specifically masculine. Director Jonathan Demme goes to great lengths to emphasize Clarice Starling's femininity. She is dwarfed physically by the men around her, and patronized or chatted up wherever she goes. Her boss chooses her to approach Lecter because she is young and pretty; and it is only because she is sexually humiliated in his presence that Lecter offers to help. Ironically, she finds the serial killer Buffalo Bill first because of her knowledge of dressmaking.

But Miss Starling, like her ornithological namesake, is also a mimic, in her case of men. When we first see her, she is sweat-stained and on an assault course. She is mechanically adept, and knows how to use a car jack. And she's no wimp: unlike your traditional heroine, she doesn't scream when she discovers the occasional severed head or decomposing corpse.

The reason why a lot of women found this the scariest film since *Psycho* lies in the way the external threats to Clarice reflect the conflict within her (and so many modern women) between masculine ambition and feminine vulnerability. The strength and luminous sincerity of Jodie Foster's performance allows the film-makers to get away with an almost comically extreme paranoia about the male sex.

In style, director Jonathan Demme wisely takes a more populist approach than Michael Mann did in his acclaimed but too self-consciously artistic 1986 flop *Manhunter*, based on Harris's previous million-seller, *Red Dragon*. Demme acknowledges the influence of his old mentor, Roger Corman, by allowing him on screen, briefly, as Head of the FBI. Demme's film – easily his most polished and self-assured – echoes Corman at his best, in its boldness of colour, texture and pace: two hours pass in a flash.

There are times when it is too frenetic: I would have liked more of Starling's relationship with her boss (who is, in the book, a moral counterbalance to Lecter), and more of that FBI procedural detail which makes Harris's novels seem so grounded in reality.

After all the publicity surrounding its release, the film is not as frightening as you might expect, and its view of men is more fashionable than convincing. Still, it is a masterpiece of the horror genre, and explores the dark side of humanity and humanism to an extent very rarely seen in the commercial cinema. The editing (Craig McKay) and sound (Tom Fleischman, Christopher Newman) were Oscar-nominated.

ANTI:

'Demme has finally given up: he's succumbed to the temptations of movie authoritarianism, making a film about domination that seeks itself to dominate its audience. Clarice's compassion is only the alibi; the film's deepest appeal lies in the dream of complete callousness, of irresistible power and perfect freedom from moral constraint, that Lecter represents. Ultimately, the film is a power fantasy barely distinguishable from the crudest Arnold Schwarzenegger or Eddie Murphy vehicle, though aimed at a more knowing, more sophisticated public.' *(Dave Kehr, Chicago Tribune)*

'In the book, Buffalo Bill's systematic skinning of his victims had a gruesome logic: he literally wanted to wear a woman's torso. Here, his taxidermic ambitions have been made somewhat more vague, and so we aren't hit with the full, shocking horror of what Clarice is up against. I got the feeling that Demme didn't want to spend too many scenes exploring the diseased mind of a misogynistic psychopath. Yet artistically speaking, his reticence may have been a mistake. No other pop novelist has gotten as far inside the heads of serial killers as Thomas Harris has. *The Silence of the Lambs* would have been harder to shake off had it been crazier and less moral – less of a feminist outcry over the violence perpetrated against women.' *(Owen Gleiberman, Entertainment Weekly)*

'Overrated. The scenes with the brilliant but dangerous Hopkins burrowing into Foster's mind are compulsive and deeply disturbing. But when Hopkins disappears half-way through, the pic turns into a daft and implausible thriller.' *(Rose)*

MIXED:

'The characterisation is crude, but then Buffalo Bill's pathology, even less developed here than in the novel, only makes metaphoric sense. In his bloody quest for self-actualization, the serial killer is Clarice's nightmare opposite . . . She too is a freak, a woman alone in a man's world. (Demme includes several shots in which she is surrounded by male officers.) Ultimately, what makes *The Silence of the Lambs* so potent is the heroine's inconsolable unhappiness, her solitude and sense of abandonment, the rescue fantasies she nurtures, the defensive posture she's forced to maintain. Not the least of *The Silence of the Lambs*'s reversals is that, although Clarice is the heroine, the movie's final image of freedom does not belong to her.' *(J. Hoberman, Village Voice)*

'The notion of the beauty and the beast is of course, central to horror stories, but watching *The Silence of the Lambs* for the second time, I began to wonder if the author of the original novel, Thomas Harris, had started the project by jotting down a list of the great universal phobias and dreads. Here is a movie involving not only cannibalism and the skinning of people, but also kidnapping, being trapped in the bottom of a well, decomposing corpses, large insects, being lost in the dark, being tracked by someone you cannot see, not being able to get people to believe you, creatures who jump from the shadows' people who know your deepest secrets, doors that slam shut behind you, beheadings, bizarre sexual perversions, and being a short woman in an elevator full of tall men. If the movie were not so well made, indeed, it would be ludicrous.' *(Roger Ebert)*

PRO:

'Deliberately, unabashedly, and uncompromisingly a feminist movie.' *(Amy Taubin, Village Voice)*

'A mesmerizing thriller that will grip audiences from first scene to last.' *(Variety)*

'A sombre masterpiece.' *(S & S)*

'An exceptionally good film, perhaps this fine director's best, in which the horror genre is elevated into the kind of cinema that can at least be argued about as a treatise for its unsettling times.' *(Derek Malcolm, Guardian)*

SILENT RUNNING CT: 6 AV: 7.00

1971 US 89 C SF/DRAMA

D Douglas Trumbull ☆
W Deric Washburn Michael Cimino Steve Bochco

Bruce Dern Cliff Potts Ron Rifkin Jess Vint

Man in outer space (Bruce Dern) tends his garden, to the detriment of human colleagues.

Unduly slow story-telling detracts from this high-quality science fiction film with a green message, set aboard a post-holocaust space station. The star (Bruce Dern), though competent, is upstaged by the special effects and his two cute robots, who – it should be noted – pre-date *Star Wars*.

'The message of *2001: A Space Odyssey* (for which Trumbull did the special effects) was that man needed guidance from beyond; the message of *Silent Running*, symbolically set in the year 2001, is that man (and his creations: the film's robots) must, even at the risk of madness, be his own saviour.' *(Phil Hardy, Time Out)*

PRO:

'The philosophic-mythic-religious dimensions of *2001* were insupportably trite. I much prefer the scaled-down secular, humane perspective expressed in *Silent Running*, but I'm afraid Trumbull's avoidance of the grandiose may be used against him.' *(Washington Post)*

'*Silent Running* isn't, in the last analysis, a very profound movie, nor does it try to be. (If it had, it could have been a pretentious disaster.) It is about a basically uncomplicated man faced with an awesome, but uncomplicated, situation. Given a choice between the lives of his companions and the lives of Earth's last surviving firs and pines, oaks and elms, and creepers and cantaloupes, he decides for the growing things. After all, there are plenty of men. His problem is that, after a while, he begins to miss them.' *(Roger Ebert)*

MIXED:

'The first hour of the film generates a kind of claustrophobic urgency. Thereafter – and this is unusual in the genre – it seems to run out of plot and develops a vein of whimsical charm.' *(Observer)*

'Technically, although the forests do tend to look a bit like the Snowdon birdhouse at the London Zoo, the film is ingenious and occasionally beautiful, but human interest is low.' *(Sunday Times)*

ANTI:

'Trumbull probably had some noble intentions, but I couldn't help feeling that he conceived his space odyssey primarily to show off some neat special effects, and that the story – developed secondarily and rather haphazardly – is therefore not especially effective. Since there is a fundamental fuzziness in his conception, the entire film seems more illogical than ecological.' *(Village Voice)*

SILVERADO CT: 8 AV: 6.00

1985 US 132 C WESTERN

D Lawrence Kasdan ✓
W Lawrence Kasdan Mark Kasdan ✓

Kevin Kline Scott Glenn ☆ Kevin Costner ☆
Danny Glover ✓ Brian Dennehy ✓ Linda Hunt
Jeff Goldblum Rosanna Arquette John Cleese

Pioneers go west in the 1880s.

Underrated western, notable for its witty script, affectionate subversion of the genre's clichés, excitement value, and intelligent performances. Bruce Broughton's music was Oscar-nominated. Stirring stuff, great fun.

ANTI:

'Falls considerably short of the lofty, epic goals it sets for itself. Overlong, overreaching and so top heavy with climaxes that it practically self-destructs in gunfire.' *(Hollywood Reporter)*

'The best westerns are the simplest. And [this] being far from simple is by no means one of the best . . . Whoever needed a psychological motive to draw a gun? . . . It's a rotten script that drops [Cleese] completely out of the film.' *(Alexander Walker, Evening Standard)*

'Its pieces feel rather loosely bolted together; it bears the sort of relation to old westerns that Victor Frankenstein's friend bore to man.' *(Michael Wood, New Society)*

'The atmosphere is arch and uninvolving, and these actors don't seem sure what their characters are meant to be. The film is so opulent it has a nouveau riche aura about it; it's a counterfeit western, without the feel of the memorable ones. The pounding orchestral score is a bad mistake; it tries to inflate the emotions that the movie intended to arouse.' *(Pauline Kael)*

MIXED:

'[Kasdan] sees the west as a place where each character seeks his or her own kind of family, and Kasdan lightens the search with deadpan humor. For a generation of kids to whom the western is a new adventure, there probably will be action and distraction enough to dazzle. Those who need to be deeply stirred by this redoubtable form will still have to wait: *Silverado* is good but not great.' *(Sheila Benson, LA Times)*

'Gripped by a near-fatal self-consciousness . . . as if Kasdan had set out not to make a western but the western, a sort of anthology of the genre's essential elements . . . The trouble is that to accommodate all these, the plot is obliged to ramble about all over the place.' *(Tim Pulleine, F & F)*

PRO:

'Has everything – action and gunplay galore, four tough heroes and several black-hearted villains.' *(Alan Frank, Star)*

'A good smelly western . . . Kasdan has produced a *Clichérado* guaranteed to please all western fans . . . a modern moral western for the Eighties.' *(Colin Booth, The Face)*

'Kasdan's rambling shaggy-dog Western resuscitates the genre with good-natured gall and quiet proficiency . . . It perhaps tries too hard to be all westerns to all audiences . . . But it will do until the old warhorse is really on its feet.' *(Richard Combs, Listener)*

'Dennehy, a great silvery bear, crawls inside this western archetype as if it were an irresistible oversized coat, and wears it with rare style. Basically, that's what *Silverado* does with the long-neglected mantle of the Western.' *(Richard T. Jameson, Film Comment)*

'What does it prove, this movie about a bunch of cowboys held together by honor, this movie about bartender philosophers, evil sheriffs, and young pioneer women with lines like "My beauty will pass someday, but the land will only grow more beautiful." What does it prove? That the western myth is most at home in a setting of innocence.' *(Roger Ebert)*

SINCERELY YOURS CT: 5 AV: 2.00

1955 US 115 C DRAMA/SO BAD

D Gordon Douglas ●
W Irving Wallace ●

Liberace ● Joanne Dru Dorothy Malone Alex Nicol William Demarest Lori Nelson

Concert picnist (Liberace) goes deaf, becomes philanthropist.

Liberace proves that he can't act sincerely, in this hilariously kitsch remake of *The Man Who Played God*, which starred George Arliss.

MIXED:

'This picture will probably make a grand piano full of money for Warner Brothers. It's filled with the corn that is the box office staff of life.' *(Hollywood Reporter)*

ANTI:

'Unintentionally hilarious.' *(LA Times)*

'Drenched in coy bathos to the point of embarrassment.' *(F & F)*

'Given sufficient intoxication, you could find this movie amusing.' *(Saturday Review)*

'A competent set of supporting actors looks on in bewilderment.' *(Winnert)*

'My big try for stardom in the movies, but no one noticed it or me. Maybe I should have worn my candelabra on my head, Carmen Miranda style.' *(Liberace)*

SINGIN' IN THE RAIN CT: 10 AV: 9.90

1952 US 102 C MUSICAL/ROMANCE

D Gene Kelly Stanley Donen ☆
W Adolph Green Betty Comden ☆

Gene Kelly ☆ Donald O'Connor ☆ Debbie Reynolds (singing voice dubbed by Betty Royce; speaking voice dubbed by Jean Hagen) Millard Mitchell ☆ Jean Hagen ☆ AAN Rita Moreno Cyd Charisse ☆ Douglas Fowley ☆

The arrival of talkies presents problems for a star (Jean Hagen), but turns out to be the making of another (Debbie Reynolds).

A revealing example of how critics can only too easily pre-judge films. On release, this received only curmudgeonly reviews; reviewers seemed to assume in advance that it was just another big movie on MGM's conveyor-belt of successful musicals, and judged it to be less innovative than *On the Town* and less serious than *An American in Paris*.

Those points may be true, but they are hardly criticisms of a work which sets out to be neither innovative nor serious – just first-rate musical entertainment. This most tuneful, brilliantly performed, wittily written and sensitively choreographed of all film musicals has now rightly been upgraded to classic status, and scores the highest rating of any musical in this book.

Gene Kelly and Donald O'Connor are both on top form; and the hilarious screenplay by Betty Comden and Adolph Green is worthy of the songs by Nacio Herb Brown and Arthur Freed. Ironically, in view of the film's storyline, Jean Hagen dubbed Debbie Reynolds's speaking voice. Both its Oscar nominees (Lennie Hayton for musical direction and Jean Hagen for Best Supporting Actress) failed to win.

MIXED:

'A big lush musical . . . bound to be popular . . . With just a little wit the film might have ranked high among its kind.' *(Campbell Dixon, Daily Telegraph)*

'The costumes, looking like potato sacks ending a few inches above knobbly knees, are an eyesore, but the music is tuneful and there is attractive dancing by Gene Kelly and Cyd Charisse.' *(Evening Standard)*

'[Kelly's] new picture hasn't the torrential impact of the last [*An American in Paris*] – for one thing, it hasn't the Gershwin score – but it is insidiously easy to enjoy.' *(Daily Mail)*

'I have to say that there are some excellent things in this burlesque of Hollywood at the period of the change from silent to talking films . . . The parody of early talkies would have been funnier if less overdone, but the joke is gay all the same.' *(Dilys Powell)*

'An impudent, offhand comedy . . . At times it reaches the level of first-class satiric burlesque.' *(Bosley Crowther)*

'A merry gambol in the cinematic cornfield . . . Mixed through the corn are ten tuneful, whistleable songs – half a dozen revue numbers – and some first rate ballet.' *(Jesse Zunser, Cue)*

'Much wit and observation . . . Though the whole film is not the high level of the ballets, it is that rare thing, a picture with style.' *(Catherine de la Roche, Picture Post)*

'The script . . . is smoothly constructed, vigorous and satirical . . . Comparisons with *On the Town* are inevitable; like it, the film prefers energy and zip to charm; unlike it the film is diffuse rather than concentrated, a mixture of elements rather than a unified whole. Less completely successful, it provides considerable enjoyment.' *(Penelope Houston, MFB)*

'Nearly as good as *On the Town*, [Kelly's] masterpiece.' *(The Times)*

'Probably the most enjoyable of all American movie musicals . . . The film falters during a too-long love song on a deserted studio stage (later cut from some of the prints) and during a lavish oversize Broadway ballet, but these sequences don't seriously affect one's enjoyment.' *(Pauline Kael, 1975)*

PRO:

'Easily one of the three best musicals of the year; certainly it is the most consistently amusing.' *(News of the World)*

'Gene Kelly and MGM have laid an Easter egg of purest gold.' *(Paul Dehn, Sunday Chronicle)*

'A witty, boisterous musical satire on Hollywood in the Twenties. One of the best screen musicals ever made, noisy, tuneful, directed in great style by Kelly and Donen from a sparkling script by Betty Comden and Adolph Green . . . Jean Hagen's delicious squeaky-voiced silent movie queen was an unexpected additional gem.' *(R.A.E. Pickard, Dictionary of 1000 Best Films)*

'The greatest musical ever made . . . also one of the few musicals where the screenplay . . . is as entertaining as the numbers themselves.' *(NFT Bulletin, 1975)*

'Posterity . . . has placed its reputation beyond the mere arbitrary awarding of statuettes.' *(Allan Hunter & Kenny Mathieson, Movie Classics, 1992)*

'I've made a lot of films that were bigger hits and made a lot more money, but now they look dated. This one, out of all my pictures, has a chance to last.' *(Gene Kelly, 1977)*

SINGLES CT: 10 AV: 6.67

1992 US 99 C ROMANCE/COMEDY

D Cameron Crowe ☆
W Cameron Crowe ☆

Bridget Fonda ✔ Campbell Scott ✔
Kyra Sedgwick ✔ Sheila Kelley Jim True
Matt Dillon ✔ Bill Pullman James Le Gros
Devon Raymond Camilo Gallardo Ally Walker
Eric Stoltz (cameo Tim Burton)

Young people try to find partners in Seattle.

The most underrated film of recent years. This warm, witty, constantly inventive, intricately structured comedy about modern dating seems lightweight and inconsequential on a first viewing, but deepens the more often you see it.

As the central couple in their twenties, Campbell Scott and Kyra Sedgwick are touchingly confused and pompous about their emotions. Bridget Fonda has never been funnier than as the nice but misguided girl trying to make herself attractive to her thick, heavy-metal-playing boyfriend (Matt Dillon, hilariously deadpan).

But the real star is the film's young writer-director Cameron Crowe. Formerly a journalist, he has a fresh eye and pays minute attention to the detail of how real young people live today. His symbolic use of modern technology (such as garage-door openers and answering-machines) is especially witty. Most critics were simply too old to appreciate this one. The soundtrack's great, as well.

ANTI:

'Is *Singles* the most annoying film ever made? No – not by a long shot, in fact. But it says something that one is tempted to pose the question . . . [The film] is depressingly shallow in its attempt to chronicle the lives and loves of a generation . . . Why . . . do characters address their complaints about love and loss directly to the camera? Breaking the fourth wall may be meant to be clever, but when nothing interesting is said it smacks either of inability to figure out any other way to let the characters articulate their self-centred thoughts, or of a desperate need to keep viewers from going out for popcorn.' *(Maitland McDonagh, Film Journal)*

'Never as solid – or as insightful – as you would like it to be . . . a rather uneven script.' *(Maltin)*

'It's mainly the lack of oomph that makes you cool towards it.' *(Winnert)*

MIXED:

'The movie gets nowhere in particular, but the

leading performances are immensely attractive.' *(Philip French, Observer)*

'Witty, perceptive, refreshing . . . There are odd moments of excessive cuteness, but they stand out only because the rest of this warm-hearted, observation film captures the foibles and self-deceptions of love with such admirable nuance.' *(Hugo Davenport, Daily Telegraph)*

'Too many plots competing for one charm franchise . . . However I liked the safe sex party that enjoins guests to come dressed as your favourite contraceptive.' *(Nigel Andrews, Financial Times)*

'Kinda funny and kinda corny and crap. You could go see it. But do twentysomethings go to the movies?' *(Ruth Picardie, City Limits)*

'*Singles* is not a great cutting-edge movie, and parts of it may be too whimsical and disorganized for audiences raised on cause-and-effect plots. But I found myself smiling a lot during the movie, sometimes with amusement, sometimes with recognition. It's easy to like these characters, and care about them.' *(Roger Ebert)*

PRO:

'Entertaining and mostly well-acted.' *(Jeff Salamon, Village Voice)*

'Superbly scripted, cast and scored, pic is a natural for the partner-hunting twentysomething crowd and should easily cross over to thirtysomething singles or couples primed to laugh at the dating syndrome.' *(Variety)*

'Guiding us gently through the rude realities of club culture and the paralysing uncertainties of romance, . . . Crowe reserves ample tender humour for his roundelay of relationships.' *(Colette Maude, Time Out)*

'Wonderfully funny.' *(Rose)*

SINS OF LOLA MONTÈS, THE: *see* LOLA MONTES.

SJUNDE INSEGLET, DET: *see* SEVENTH SEAL, THE.

SKIDOO

CT: 5 AV: 3.33

1968 US 98 C COMEDY/SO BAD

D Otto Preminger ●
W Doran William Cannon

Jackie Gleason ● Carol Channing ● Groucho Marx ● Frankie Avalon ● Fred Clark Michael Constantine Peter Lawford ● Burgess Meredith George Raft Cesar Romero Mickey Rooney John Phillip Law ●

Gangsters are reformed by hippies.

Drivel – a hilariously pathetic attempt by Otto Preminger to cash in on flower power. Harry Nilsson's songs of love and peace plumb new depths of banality . . . Sample lines . . . (1) Hippie: 'You know what I want to be? Nothing, you dig? If you can't dig nothing, you can't dig anything, you dig?' (2) Hardened convict, wondering whether to drop acid: 'Say, maybe if I took some, I wouldn't have to rape people any more!'

'Skidon't.' *(Anonymous)*

'There is a place for this film . . . It's called a dustbin.' *(Ian Christie, Daily Express)*

'In his private life Otto Preminger is the most tasteful of men. Unfortunately, none of that taste seems to turn up in his pictures.' *(Arthur Knight, Saturday Review)*

'I thought Otto Preminger had touched rock bottom with *Hurry Sundown* but this time he is digging well below the substrata.' *(Tom Milne, Observer)*

'Otto Preminger's direction would make an elephant doing the frug look light-toed by comparison.' *(Alexander Walker, Evening Standard)*

'Not my scene at all, man.' *(Cecil Wilson, Daily Mail)*

'[Beneath the surface of] this gaudily coloured and supposedly comic farrago . . . there lurks the message that a diet of LSD may well constitute a workable alternative to the crimes engendered by capitalism.' *(MFB)*

'Unspeakable.' *(Michael Billington, Illustrated London News)*

'Mr Preminger is really in there swinging, and I wouldn't be surprised if he next produced the Timothy Leary Story, a sort of inspirational film along the lines of *The Cardinal*.' *(Dan Wakefield, Atlantic Monthly)*

'Do not – repeat, do not! – miss the psychedelic musical number with dancing garbage cans. We can't swear Preminger slipped his entire cast, crew and studio a massive dose of LSD, but what other possible explanation could there be?' *(Margulies & Rebello)*

'About one in a thousand will have the temperament to like this; everyone else will sit there dumbstruck.' *(Maltin)*

SLEEPER

CT: 6 AV: 7.15

1973 US 88 C COMEDY/SF

D Woody Allen
W Woody Allen Marshall Brickman

Woody Allen Diane Keaton ✔ John Beck Mary Gregory Don Keeler Don McLiam

A wimp (Woody Allen) goes into hospital for an operation on an ulcer and wakes up in a 22nd-century police state.

An uneven movie with some dreary patches, but on

the whole a witty satire on 70s fads, assisted by funny futuristic designs (the costumes are by Joel Schumacher, who later turned to directing movies like *Cousins* and *Falling Down*). Sleeper is most memorable for the largest banana-skin gag ever, Allen's attempts to impersonate a domestic robot, and a wonderfully surreal moment when he kidnaps the world leader's nose.

MIXED:

'Foully paced and insufficiently inventive to overcome the longueurs between jokes, a few of which are good.' *(Shipman)*

'While it fumbles the end, the parade of verbal and visual amusement is pleasant as long as it lasts.' *(Variety)*

PRO:

'The simplest measure of *Sleeper*'s success is perhaps the fact that one recalls it not by quoting Allen's one-liners but by trying to describe – inadequately – his beautifully built visual gags.' *(Richard Schickel, Life)*

'The most stable and sustained of his comedies, with a clean visual style and an elegant design.' *(Pauline Kael)*

'Not only an immensely funny science fiction comedy but also a well crafted, intelligent, even visionary movie.' *(Hollywood Reporter)*

'Not only his most ambitious but also his best . . . the stand-up comedian has at last made an unequivocal transition to the screen.' *(Vincent Canby, New York Times)*

'The two aspects of Allen (character comedy and broad gags) meshed beautifully.' *(David Ehrenstein, LA Herald-Examiner)*

'Allen . . . adds to our cinematic repertoire political and cultural satire, almost as sorely needed as a change in our politics and culture themselves.' *(John Simon)*

'Probably the funniest genre film ever, with Woody Allen's comic invention rarely failing and some inspired slapstick sequences.' *(Alan Frank)*

'Woody's exaggerated, nightmare vision of the LA lifestyle: beautiful, superficial people who think they are deep, who elevate kitsch to the level of high art . . . and immerse themselves in immediate pleasures.' *(Douglas Brode, Woody Allen: His Films and Career, 1987)*

SLEEPLESS IN SEATTLE CT: 9 AV: 7.25

1993 US 104 C COMEDY/ROMANCE

D Nora Ephron ☆
W Nora Ephron David S. Ward Jeff Arch ☆ AAN

Tom Hanks ☆ Meg Ryan ☆ Bill Pullman ✓
Ross Malinger ☆ Rosie O'Donnell ✓
Gaby Hoffmann Rob Reiner

Annie (Meg Ryan) is engaged to formal, well-meaning Walter (Bill Pullman), but she hears on the radio a widower, Sam (Tom Hanks), being interviewed – much against his will – about his wife. More and more, Annie finds herself harbouring the screwball idea of meeting this mystery man, whom the radio station christens Sleepless in Seattle.

Nauseatingly sentimental, hopelessly predictable, a 'women's weepie', Hollywood film-making at its most cynically commercial. *Sleepless in Seattle* was dismissed as all of these by critics. They were wrong: it's one of the great romances of all times, a movie which will be making people laugh and cry fifty years from now.

Any film is a bit sentimental which believes in the possibility of love at first sight – or, in this case, first hearing. But *Sleepless* does not, as so many romances do, ignore painful emotions: Hanks gives a very convincing portrayal of bereavement. The film casts a sceptical eye over the way Hollywood conventionally depicts romance and recognizes some uncomfortable aspects of modern life – notably, that in the age of feminism and Aids dating is difficult, often unrewarding, and potentially lethal.

In some ways, the film is quite subversive, dismissing as a second-best compromise the kind of relationship for which many less fortunate mortals settle – and towards which Annie is heading as the film begins. The movie ends up taking a ruthless stance in favour of the kind of total bonding which Hollywood has always seen as 'real' love, and which Annie feels herself drawn to, much against her common sense.

Nor is the outcome as predictable as its detractors think. Right up to the last moment of suspense – will they or won't they meet on top of the Empire State Building? – there is the possibility of a bitter-sweet ending: with the woman settling for second-best (like Judy Davis in *Husbands and Wives*) or learning to live alone (like Jill Clayburgh in *An Unmarried Woman*), or being kept apart from her lover by fate and geography (as in *Manhattan*). That Ephron chooses to end her film differently is, these days, refreshingly unconventional.

Then there's the accusation that this is a 'woman's weepie'. Well, yes: it's concerned with love and relationships, and most women will love this film.

But men may shed the odd tear too, for at least half the film is seen from a male point of view. Ephron and her male co-writers, David S. Ward and Jeff Arch have brilliantly avoided the flaw in so many 'women's pictures' of portraying the men as cardboard cut-outs. Sam is a living, breathing character, with faults, responsibilities, and a masculine suspicion of 'chick's movies' like this one might have been.

As for the film's supposedly flagrant commercialism, that's wisdom after the event. The premise of the movie was, on the contrary, commercially dangerous: it was about middle-aged people at a time when most moviegoers were below

30, and it went against the format of almost every successful Romantic Comedy: 'boy meets girl, boy and girl hate each other, boy and girl fall in love'. It's unique in motion picture history, in that the two lovers hardly meet, let alone have a developing relationship.

The premise of the film poses a seemingly intractable problem for a film-maker: how to show two people are ideally suited, when they don't even know each other. Ephron's solution is to build up visual and aural connections between the pair – most obviously through songs and common attitudes, more subtly through shared tastes in decor, clothes and colour (notice how both like the identical shade of blue).

In doing this, she is wonderfully served by her designer Jeffrey Townsend and cinematographer, Sven Nykvist. His work for Ingmar Bergman (notably *Cries and Whispers,* and *Fanny and Alexander*) may have brought him more critical kudos; but he's never done better work.

ANTI:

'The entire picture is a collection of nauseating quotations from and references to *An Affair to Remember*, both visual and verbal. And as it wiggles on, it becomes a pre-coitus interruptus of gigantic dimensions. If it has any bearing on reality – which the film proudly and repeatedly denies – Annie could very happily marry Walter, a decent fellow who takes rejection with touching magnanimity. But no, Sleepless and Feckless must finally take each other by the hand to the sound of Jimmy Durante croaking out 'Make Someone Happy', and go off together with eight-year-old Reckless to stop being sleepless – in Seattle, or Baltimore, or Timbuctoo, for all anyone not partial to cutesypoo, but also amazingly smartass, soap operas cares. Perhaps a sequel, Smartass in Smyrna, is indicated.' *(John Simon)*

'Will Sam and Annie find one another – physically and (yawn!) emotionally? Will Trigger stay stuffed?' *(Rob Lurie, LA Magazine)*

'*Sleepless in Seattle*, meet Not Amused in New York . . . *Sleepless* is full of the effortful, let's-be-topical-or-die banter that's the hallmark of a Nora Ephron movie . . . The movie's problems go deeper than the dialogue; its whole premise is flawed. Hanks is never made to seem sufficiently winning, nor Pullman sufficiently outclassed (in fact, he's a sweetheart), to make Ryan's obsession comprehensible. Consequently, the cynically manipulative *Sleepless* must rely on a score of standards such as 'In the Wee Small Hours of the Morning' and 'Stardust' and frequent references to the 50s weeper *An Affair to Remember* to create a sense of romance that would be otherwise lacking – and is still pretty spurious. Hanks's sardonic teddy bear charm is at full throttle, while Ryan keeps twitching her head from side to side as though trying to dislodge water from her ear.' *(Joanne Kaufman, People Weekly)*

'Too smart for its own good. For clever as it is conceptually, it violates the most basic rule of romantic-comedy construction. If boy doesn't meet girl, then the drama of boy losing girl and the final satisfaction of boy getting girl cannot happen. The complications in this movie are all logistical. They are never confrontational, as they so giddily were in the classic comedies of muddled love, the spirit of which co-writer and director Nora Ephron has said she wanted to recapture . . . Mostly, *Sleepless in Seattle* leaves you feeling restless in the audience.' *(Richard Schickel, Time)*

'Unabashedly romantic . . . shameless in its effects . . . More hardened viewers are likely to be somewhat annoyed by yet another film in which kids are wiser and more instinctive than any of the fumbling adults overseeing them.' *(Kevin Lally, Film Journal)*

PRO:

'With its high-concept premise and cloying sound track, *Sleepless* has a dangerously high sugar quotient. But director and co-writer Nora Ephron teases her ingredients into a light, airy confection. And Hanks gives it emotional substance.' *(Brian D. Johnson, Maclean's)*

'Delivers ample warmth and some explosively funny moments.' *(Variety)*

'My advice is, take a twist of lemon to cut the sugar, and sit back and savor the charm of Tom Hanks, who truly is in a league of his own.' *(Guy Flatley, Cosmopolitan)*

'The actors are well-suited to this material. Tom Hanks keeps a certain detached edge to his character, which keeps him from being simply a fall guy. Meg Ryan, who is one of the most likeable actresses around and has a certain ineffable Doris Day innocence, is able to convince us of the magical quality of her sudden love for a radio voice, without letting the device seem like the gimmick it assuredly is. *Sleepless in Seattle* is as ephemeral as a talk show, as contrived as the late show, and yet so warm and gentle I smiled the whole way through.' *(Roger Ebert)*

'Shamelessly slushy stuff it may well be, but you'd have to be hard-hearted indeed to leave the cinema without feeling just that touch gooey inside. A real treat.' *(Mark Salisbury, Empire)*

'One of those magical, all-time-great romantic movies which catch the imagination of millions.' *(Christopher Tookey, Daily Mail)*

SLEUTH

CT: 6 AV: 7.23

1972 GB 138 C THRILLER

D Joseph L. Mankiewicz AAN
W Anthony Shaffer ☆ from his play

Laurence Olivier ☆ AAN Michael Caine ☆ AAN
Alec Cawthorne Margo Channing

Crime writer (Laurence Olivier) devises what he thinks is the perfect murder.

Exquisitely contrived mystery, rather too verbose and theatrical, but very well acted against a background wittily designed by Ken Adam. John Addison's music was Oscar-nominated.

PRO:

'Tastefully designed bauble, spreading charming, perishable joy.' *(John Simon)*

'What Michael Caine lacks in Old Vic background he makes up in new cut self-confidence. His acquired expertise even enables him to pull off the great acting trick which this particular part requires.' *(Felix Barker, Evening News)*

'[The film's] merit . . . is that it not only acknowledges the gulf between [a film and a play] but makes a point and a merit of it, rather than trying to hide it up with patches and plaster . . . A very effective sort of entertainment.' *(David Robinson, Financial Times)*

'A totally engrossing entertainment . . . funny and scary by turns, and always superbly theatrical.' *(Roger Ebert)*

MIXED:

'One of the year's superior entertainments . . . Even those who find its twists and turns predictable (of which I am one) and those who find its moral conclusions contemptible (of which I am also one) admit that their attention never flags and that they are never bored.' *(Stuart Byron)*

'[Olivier and Caine] display an unexpectedly well-matched virtuosity; pirouetting with consummate ease through the innumerable *volte-faces* imposed by their characters' grisly games of cops-and-robbers . . . Yet neither . . . can adequately camouflage the film's formula theatricality.' *(Jan Dawson, Listener)*

'Caine is more personality than performer, has a limited emotional range, and is poor at accents – a particular minus in this part . . . But Caine has a very real charm of his own: an impudent enjoyment of his masculinity, a canny proletarian refusal to be snowed by excessive refinements, and the self-confidence of the plebeian risen by sheer shrewdness, This is good in itself, but even better when pitted against Olivier's consummate artistry. It gives the film an added – perhaps irrelevant, but irresistible – mythic fascination of duel between the great stage actor and the lionized movie-star personality. The film's (and play's) underlying theme – the skills of experienced, crafty age versus the resourcefulness and vigor of youth – is thus couched in histrionic as well as human terms.' *(John Simon)*

SLIGHT CASE OF MURDER, A

CT: 6 AV: 7.50

1938 US 85 BW COMEDY/THRILLER

D Lloyd Bacon ☆
W Earl Baldwin Joseph Schrank from Damon Runyon and Howard Lindsay's play

Edward G. Robinson ☆ Jane Bryan Ruth Donnelly ☆ Willard Parker Allen Jenkins John Litel Harold Huber Edward Brophy Bobby Jordan

At the end of Prohibition, an ex-bootlegger (Edward G. Robinson) discovers that, though he is innocent of murder, his house is full of his rivals' corpses.

Funny, frantic farce, now unjustly forgotten. Robinson parodies some of his former roles, and shows a surprising talent for comedy. Poorly remade as *Stop, You're Killing Me* (1953), starring Broderick Crawford.

MIXED:

'Lloyd Bacon, succeeds in getting giggles out of some of these scenes, but his style is too broad, and the tone of the film is archly childish.' *(Pauline Kael)*

PRO:

'I have written of this film in superlatives before. I have seen it four times and it still seems to have no flaw. It's absolutely national and absolutely universal. Hollywood must hate it a lot.' *(Richard Winnington)*

'A very, very funny film.' *(New Statesman)*

'Nothing funnier has been produced by Hollywood for a long time . . . a mirthful and hilarious whimsy.' *(Variety)*

'Just about the funniest show the new year has produced . . . It goes after its laughs with Rabelaisian gusto.' *(Frank S. Nugent, New York Times)*

'Murder is certainly not taken seriously at the Odeon. There was one corpse, you will remember, in *True Confession*, last year's funniest film: there are four corpses in [this one] and the picture is nearly four times funnier. Where will this mathematical progression end? . . . The complications crazily mount, sentiment never raises its ugly head, a long nose is made at violence and death.' *(Graham Greene, Spectator)*

SMALL CHANGE

CT: 6 AV: 7.64

(aka *L'Argent De Poche*)

1976 France 104 C DRAMA/FOREIGN

D François Truffaut ☆
W François Truffaut Susan Schiffman

Geory Desmouceaux Philippe Goldman Claudio Deluca Franck Deluca Jean-François Stévenin Bruno Staab

Children grow up in a small provincial town.

A cute, somewhat sentimental return to the kind of rites-of-passage movie with which Truffaut made his name, in *The 400 Blows. Small Change* lacks narrative coherence and dramatic focus, but has many good-natured, charming episodes. Perhaps

Truffaut does idealize childhood, but he also shows a rare appreciation of it.

ANTI:

'I'm afraid it irritated me beyond measure. This is the Truffaut I always feared lay behind that avid Hitchcock fan, a rather soft-centred operator belonging to the Renoir tradition.' *(Derek Malcolm, Guardian)*

'He said [it all] memorably and much more convincingly nearly 20 years ago.' *(Patrick Gibbs, Daily Telegraph)*

'Truffaut has little more to offer here than have most kiddie calendars or greeting cards or those old newsreels of children and puppies that made the audience sigh "Aaaah". He simply wants to love children in front of us and to have us admire the way he loves them.' *(Stanley Kauffmann)*

MIXED:

'Unashamedly sentimental but meaningful . . . entertaining but not inconsequential.' *(Virginia Dignam, Morning Star)*

PRO:

'Every character, every episode . . . results in a work unified by freshness.' *(France Soir)*

'Light as thistledown and no plot to speak of [it] is a charming glance at children . . . [and] mainly very funny . . . The screen breathes truth.' *(Molly Plowright, Glasgow Herald)*

'Both an enchanting insight into the world of childhood and an anguished plea for compassion for the adult fraternity . . . Truffaut catches exactly the glum silences and inquisitive chat, the niceness and naughtiness that punctuates the process of growing up.' *(Margaret Hinxman, Daily Mail)*

SMILE

CT: 7 AV: 7.20

1975 US 113 C DRAMA/COMEDY

D Michael Ritchie
W Jerry Belson ☆

Bruce Dern ☆ Barbara Feldon Michael Kidd Geoffrey Lewis Nicholas Pryor Colleen Camp

Teenagers compete for the title Young Miss America.

Cynical but not too patronizing drama, in documentary style, about a beauty pageant. It's over-long and patchy, but still one of the funniest satires on American provincial values and hypocrisies. Bruce Dern is very entertaining as the used-car salesman who has financed the pageant.

MIXED:

'Glib but amusing.' *(Alexander Walker, Evening Standard)*

'It's true that in the early stages, the film gets all too predictable laughs from setting up easy targets and then knocking them down. But Ritchie's too good a director to keep things on this level . . . While it pales in comparison with the likes of *Nashville*, *Smile* is a well-paced and entertaining movie with more to it than its gentle surface suggests.' *(Rob Mackie, Street Life)*

'Good work is expended on a script that only makes us say, "Yes, but I knew that." . . . *Smile*, for all its skills in execution, is really a new kind of middle-of-the-road film, playing it newly safe, plumb in the middle of widely accepted social criticism.' *(Stanley Kauffmann)*

PRO:

'The wittiest and most lethally deadpan picture of small-town life since Milos Forman's *The Fireman's Ball* . . . The film see-saws between tragedy and farce . . . [Its] sly comedy never slips into caricature.' *(Financial Times)*

'Dazzlingly entertaining . . . creative, original . . . written with affection yet never fearing to be devastatingly critical . . . and directed with a keen, observant eye.' *(Clive Hirschhorn, Sunday Express)*

'The theme that runs through Ritchie's movies is that of lost innocence: in *Downhill Racer*, our own Olympic skiers going unclean; in *Prime Cut*, the formerly less spoiled heartland proving more evil than the city; in *The Candidate*, a Lochinvarish liberal politician getting co-opted and morally rumpled; and in *Smile*, fresh high-school girls being turned into pious dissemblers. It is muckraking cinema, not always deep enough, yet often able to say much through quick, throwaway scenes or even, in *Smile*, the furnishings of a house.' *(John Simon)*

SMILES OF A SUMMER NIGHT

CT: 8 AV: 8.50

(aka *Sommarnattens Leende*)

1955 Sweden 105 BW COMEDY/ROMANCE/ FOREIGN

D Ingmar Bergman ☆
W Ingmar Bergman

Gunnar Björnstrand ☆ Eva Dahlbeck Ulla Jacobsson Harriet Andersson Margit Carlquist Naima Wifstrand Jarl Kulle

A lawyer (Gunnar Björnstrand) with marital problems re-meets an old actress flame (Eva Dahlbeck).

Elegant but passionless sex comedy which shows Bergman in uncharacteristically buoyant mood, and contains an excellent performance by Björnstrand. It was later turned into a musical by Stephen Sondheim (*A Little Night Music*) and imitated by Woody Allen (*A Midsummer Night's Sex Comedy*). It is itself influenced by Shakespeare's *A Midsummer Night's Dream*.

MIXED:

'It may not be all that funny, but it is sexy enough in a simple, sweaty way . . . Plainly, director Bergman intended to produce the best French picture ever made in Sweden. But in this at least he failed. A Frenchman would surely have reminded himself . . . that the best way to spoil sex is to talk too much about it.' *(Time)*

'Heavily frolicsome, emphatically sensual, and beautifully photographed in that hygienic, refrigerated style the Swedes are so good at.' *(Lindsay Anderson, New Statesman)*

'Sometimes silly, occasionally moving, often witty and always watchable.' *(Alan Brien, Evening Standard)*

'What the film lacks in sparkle is made up for by most satisfying stylishness.' *(Jympson Harman, Evening News)*

'Audacious and lyrical by turns, with a . . . delicious performance by Ulla Jacobsson . . . Only the whimsies languish sadly for a genuine Parisian touch.' *(Harold Conway, Daily Sketch)*

PRO:

'One of the few classics of carnal comedy: a tragicomic chase and roundelay that raises boudoir farce to elegance and lyric poetry.' *(Pauline Kael)*

SMILING LIEUTENANT, THE AAN

CT: 5 AV: 7.20

1931 US 88 BW COMEDY/ROMANCE/MUSICAL

D Ernst Lubitsch ☆
W Ernest Vajda Samson Raphaelson Ernst Lubitsch from the operetta *A Waltz Dream* (music by Oscar Strauss)

Maurice Chevalier Claudette Colbert
Miriam Hopkins George Barbier Charles Ruggles
Robert Strange

A Viennese soldier (Maurice Chevalier) wins a beautiful, violinist mistress (Claudette Colbert) , but a plain princess (Miriam Hopkins) is determined to marry him.

'The Lubitsch touch' was much acclaimed in the 1930s, but today his escapist musicals have lost much of their impact. This critical and commercial hit of its day is a very dated, mechanically plotted operetta with four undistinguished songs. The morality is questionable, and Colbert's motivation is sketchy; the three stars make it just about watchable.

PRO:

'All the shrewd delights that were promised in *The Love Parade* all realised with an economy and sureness that give it a luster which no other American-made comedy satire has achieved. One must look to *Le Million* to find its peer.' *(Richard Watts, New York Post)*

'Wit and melody swing through [it] . . . Chevalier delivers another of his beguiling portrayals . . . [Lubitsch's] satire permeates this film, whether he is dealing with romance or royalty.' *(Mordaunt Hall, New York Times)*

'Delicious satire . . . Masterly direction . . . Piquant dialogue and amusing songs admirably recorded . . . Lubitsch in his lightest vein and as such provides irresistible entertainment . . . The recording is faultless.' *(Bioscope)*

'A tremendous combination of acting talent, directorial genius, uniting wisdom and movie-making magic lore, have been woven into a thrilling and joyous entertainment.' *(The Astorian)*

MIXED:

'Will delight smart audiences and figures to be liked well enough by the average fan. A good but not a smash picture.' *(Variety)*

'You won't be able to resist the combined charm of the stars, in spite of a slight story in which very little real sympathy is enlisted for any of the characters . . . It is hardly necessary to say that [Chevalier] is excellent and is extremely well supported by Claudette Colbert . . . but I don't think Lubitsch's direction shows the subtlety that used to characterise it.' *(Lionel Collier, Picturegoer)*

SMULTRONSTÄLLET:

see WILD STRAWBERRIES.

SNAKE PIT, THE AAN

CT: 6 AV: 7.64

1948 US 108 BW DRAMA

D Anatole Litvak ✗ AAN
W Frank Partos Millen Brand AAN from Mary Jane Ward's novel

Olivia de Havilland ☆ AAN Leo Genn Mark Stevens, Celeste Holm Glenn Langan Leif Erickson
Beulah Bondi Lee Patrick Natalie Schaefer

A young woman (Olivia de Havilland) undergoes horrific experiences in a mental institution.

Anatole Litvak's direction is dull, and does not build to a sufficiently shattering climax. Still, it's well acted – especially by the lead, who won the New York Critics' Award for her performance – and an important film for its day, the first to plead for more sympathetic treatment of mental illness. Alfred Newman's score was Oscar-nominated.

MIXED:

'The conception is confused, and the approach fundamentally opportunist. Yet it cannot be labelled a failure, redeemed, as it is, and justified, by its central performance.' *(Peter Ericsson)*

'One follows her [the heroine's] progress with interest but without gripping concern: emotional tension is somehow lacking. Probably it is director

Anatole Litvak's fault that the film is not the overwhelming experience it might have been, for the script is lucid, the acting excellent, the photography graphic – but the film does not build.' *(Fortnight)*

'A film of superficial veracity that requires a bigger man than Litvak; a good film with bad things.' *(Herman G. Weinberg)*

PRO:

'Olivia de Havilland, in the role of the unhappy girl, gives a performance that is as exciting to watch as it must have been strenuous to play. It is one of the greatest performances we have ever seen on screen or stage.' *(Hollywood Reporter)*

'A terribly poignant and distressing picture of life in an American mental home, a picture of frightful, hellish darkness. It is an astounding film, and Miss de Havilland gives an astounding performance.' *(Virginia Graham)*

'The film itself belongs to the category of *Lost Weekend*. The choice of subject is sensational, the treatment realistic and sober. Anatole Litvak's direction has given us a brilliant impression of a mad-house – in America, apparently, not unlike a prison-house – and acting of a remarkable order. Miss Olivia de Havilland, playing the heroine, gives a close-up of insanity that is her performance of a lifetime.' *(William Whitebait)*

'There can be no doubt that as a picture of conditions in an overcrowded state asylum in US it is genuinely moving as well as disturbing and it carries complete conviction. It is at once the story of a particular case and a general indictment of a condition of affairs which one hopes does not apply to such institutions in this country.' *(A.E. Wilson)*

SNAPPER, THE

CT: 7 AV: 7.00

1993 GB 91 C COMEDY

D Stephen Frears
W Roddy Doyle ☆

Tina Kellegher ☆ Colm Meaney ☆ Ruth McCabe Pat Laffan Eanna MacLiam

An Irish girl (Tina Kellegher) discovers she's pregnant as a result of a drunken, meaningless, one-off sex-act with the paunchy, middle-aged father of a girlfriend. She can't bring herself to tell anyone, but the humiliating truth will out – as will the baby (the 'snapper' of the title).

The story sounds depressing. Fortunately, comic novelist Roddy Doyle (who co-wrote *The Commitments*), transforms this storyline into an affectionate, often very funny celebration of Irish working-class life. Doyle is a master of detailed observation, and deftly undercuts every moment of drama by making it clear that these characters have their own survival mechanisms: they're too busy, harrassed and downright humorous to have time for soap opera melodramatics.

The writing lacks the wit, the suspense or the narrative twists of the timeless Ealing classics. And as social comedy, it's over-gentle, almost sentimental: it doesn't try to probe beneath the surface, to analyse why the only way these people have of amusing themselves seems to be to get drunk. It's also too intimately shot for comfortable viewing in the cinema. In keeping with the TV medium for which it was created, director Stephen Frears creates a claustrophobic atmosphere with cramped, overcrowded interiors and more close-ups than you'd expect in film comedy.

The great strength of *The Snapper* lies in the two leading performances. By the end, it has turned into a touching, eccentric love story between the pregnant girl and her bumbling, bewildered but benign father (sublimely played by Colm Meaney, who was also the father in *The Commitments*). Such a picture of family life may be cosy, but it isn't unrealistic: a lot of families do cope with adversity without breaking up, or indulging in East Enders-style histrionics. It's good to see a British film which doesn't try to blame its characters' failings on the internal contradictions of post-war capitalism, or the social policy of whatever government it is in power, and takes such a positive view of ordinary people, warts and all. Best of all, the film made me laugh.

'Fans of Alan Parker's raucous film hoping for a *Commitments II* are in for a disappointment . . . Where Parker's film was vibrant, electric, in-our-face, Frears' is intimate and subtle – a touching, witty chamber-piece to Parker's big-screen fiesta.' *(Sophy Kershaw, Time Out)*

'A celebration of life.' *(Gary Leboff, Sun)*

'Exuberant script . . . great performances . . . painstaking comic direction . . . Not a moment was wasted, not the tiniest role overlooked.' *(Lynne Truss, The Times)*

'Very funny and sometimes touching.' *(Hugh Hebert, Guardian)*

'Hits you like a welcome gust of cold air. . . . Frears, who spearheaded the mid-80s renaissance of British filmmaking with *My Beautiful Laundrette*, is a ripe contradiction: an acerbic humanist. The characters in *The Snapper* show an ebullient optimism in the face of comically meager options . . . In *The Snapper*, those two quintessentially British qualities – sweetness and cynicism – prove to be no contradiction at all.' *(Owen Gleiberman, Entertainment Weekly)*

'The director is at his best when jumbling moods and mixing motives, yet keeping everything straight and true. He neither patronizes nor celebrates these lives. He just makes them real. And in the process makes us their loving, laughing, admiring intimates.' *(Richard Schickel, Time)*

'Hilarious and touching, it is the season's most unlikely endorsement of family values.' *(Diane Turbide, Maclean's)*

SNOW WHITE AND THE SEVEN DWARFS

CT: 9 AV: 9.89

1937 US 82 C CARTOON/FAMILY

D David Hand ☆
W Ted Sears Otto Englander Earl Hurd Dorothy Ann Blank Richard Creedon Dick Richard Merrill de Maris Webb Smith from the Grimm Brothers' fairy tale (songs by Frank Churchill and Larry Morey ☆)

Voices: Adriana Caselotti Harry Stockwell Lucille LaVerne ☆ Billy Gilbert Otis Harlan

Pleasant girl with talent for housekeeping shacks up with vertically challenged backwoodsmen, and discovers that diamond miners are a girl's best friend.

Until recently, most of us had seen only old, faded prints of *Snow White and the Seven Dwarfs*; but the wonders of digital technology have resulted in a brand-new version which returns to the original, ravishing colours enjoyed by audiences in 1938. With a cleaned up soundtrack and the benefits of modern speakers and wide-screen projection, this classic looks and sounds better than ever. Walt Disney's first feature-length cartoon is among the most important and innovative films ever made.

Snow White herself (whose movements were based on the Broadway dancer Marge Champion) is a reminder of how tastes in beauty change. There's something quaint about her tiny voice, mincing steps and relentless domesticity. Her plump, rosy cheeks are in marked contrast to The Little Mermaid or the princess in *Aladdin* – both of whom evidently adhere to rigorous diets, bask on California beaches for that all-over tan, and work out with a personal fitness trainer.

The prince, like all such characters in Disney cartoons, is such a drip he makes the male members of the British royal family look marriageable; it's hard to avoid the suspicion that poor Snow White might do herself a favour by staying with the dwarfs, as engaging a bunch of comic characters ever assembled.

The other stars of this movie are the cute animals (many future Disney stars, such as Bambi and Thumper, are visible in the woodland scenes), and the Wicked Queen. She (memorably voiced by Lucille LaVerne) was actually based on a character, 'The Vengeance', whom LaVerne had played in the 1935 film *A Tale of Two Cities*. Miraculously, she is still nasty after all these years we have spent being frightened out of our wits by Joan Collins and Danny La Rue.

And let's not forget the songs. Of the 25 written for the film by Frank Churchill and Larry Morey (and, uncredited, the score composer Leigh Harline), only seven made it into the final cut. 'Someday My Prince Will Come', 'Whistle While You Work' and 'Heigh Ho' have all become all classic melodies; and it's easy to see why *Snow White and the Seven Dwarfs* was the first musical to generate its own soundtrack album.

Snow White now has a period charm and nostalgic appeal for any adult. But it has retained its timeless virtues – tunefulness, tenderness, and a miraculous understanding of young children's dreams. It's not to be missed – a life-enhancing experience for the most jaded modern child.

On release, it won a Special Award from the New York Film Critics; the annual *Film Daily* poll of US film critics voted it Best Picture of 1938; and Disney received a special Oscar at the Academy Awards for 'significant screen innovation'. It was in the shape of Snow White and the dwarfs, and was presented by Shirley Temple. Frank Churchill, Leigh Harline and Paul Smith were nominated for Best Score.

ANTI:

'Less satisfactory than we had hoped. The principal problem is how to treat the human characters . . . Disney has fallen back on conventional notions of prettiness, and the face of Snow White in particular (not altogether unlike Betty Boop) lacks the character and individuality which rightly belongs to the resourceful heroine.' *(New Statesman)*

'The depiction of the human figure is not Walt Disney's forte . . . Disney's draughtsmanship cannot remove Snow White and her friends from the auntish competence of a second-rate picture book.' *(Spectator)*

'Has all the roughness and error of a first try.' *(Observer, 1943)*

'The witch [sic] in *Snow White* probably has caused more children's nightmares than Frankenstein's monster and Godzilla combined.' *(Bill Davidson)*

'Some of Disney's best draughtsmanship is in it, and it added many new creations to his pantheon of folk-characters. But . . . the drawing begins to imitate conventional camerawork and, alas, the directorial clichés of Hollywood story-telling. Disney had begun to try to imitate the real world instead of continuing to create a world of his own.' *(Paul Rotha & Richard Griffith, The Film Till Now, 1949)*

'The best children's folk-stories should be adapted for the screen in a way] that is similar to the original work in imaginative intensity and depth of feeling. This is precisely what *Snow White* failed to draw from Disney and his craftsmen, though in the general excitement over what they were attempting, this was overlooked. Disney, the man who could never bear to look upon animals in zoos or prisoners in jail or other "unpleasant things", was truly incapable of seeing his material in anything but reductive terms . . . Disney lacked the tools, intellectual and artistic, he needed for this task. He could make something his own, all right, but that process nearly always robbed the work at hand of its uniqueness, of its soul, if you will. In its place he put jokes and songs and fright effects, but he always seemed to diminish what he touched. He came always as a conqueror, never as a servant. It is a trait, as many have observed, that many Americans share when they venture into Foreign lands hoping to do good but equipped only with know-how instead of sympathy and respect for alien traditions.' *(Richard Schickel)*

MIXED:

'Even in 1938 critics noticed a tension . . . between the fantastic rendering of the animals and dwarfs and the clumsy, sticky attempts at naturalism in rendering the people.' *(Gerald Mast, A Short History of the Movies, 1971)*

'Features some of Disney's most inventive (the animals of the forest, the wicked queen and the Dwarfs themselves) and banal (Snow White and her cardboard prince) animation.' *(R.A.E. Pickard, Dictionary of 1000 Best Films, 1971)*

PRO:

'Sustained fantasy, the animated cartoon grown up . . . Among the genuine artistic achievements of the country.' *(Otis Ferguson)*

'Delightful, gay and captivating.' *(Frank S. Nugent, New York Times)*

'[Ranks] with the greatest motion pictures of all time.' *(Howard Barnes, New York Herald Tribune)*

'Probably the most lovely example of pure fantasy that has yet been seen on the screen . . . It is difficult to find any flaws in this very lovely film; there is beauty here and tenderness, fantasy and humour and, above all, a perfect understanding of a young child's dreams. The animation is almost perfect, giving . . . the illusion of life . . . To see the film is to see Fairyland.' *(MFB)*

'55 years old and as delightful as ever . . . A work of pioneering innovation and magical, musical entertainment.' *(Geoff Brown, The Times, 1992)*

SOAPDISH — CT: 7 AV: 5.18

1991 US 96 C COMEDY/ROMANCE

D Michael Hoffman
W Robert Harling Andrew Bergman ✓

Sally Field ✓ Kevin Kline ✓ Robert Downey Jr Cathy Moriarty ✓ Whoopi Goldberg ✓ Elisabeth Shue Kathy Najimy Garry Marshall Carrie Fisher

A soap opera queen (Sally Field) finds her position threatened by a rival (Cathy Moriarty).

Malicious performances, a witty script and pacy direction make this funny, even if the targets are a shade obvious, and the story is as mechanical as anything it is attempting to spoof. The screenplay, by Robert (*Steel Magnolias*) Harling and Andrew (*Blazing Saddles*) Bergman is perhaps over-indebted to *Tootsie*, but full of comic observations and pacily directed by Michael Hoffman.

Two of America's finest actors, Sally Field and Kevin Kline, bravely play downmarket parodies of themselves. Field – renowned for lachrymose acting and embarrassing acceptance speeches at the Oscars – plays a temperamental, ageing harridan, showered with hideous awards for crying on camera. Kline plays her bête noir: a vain, greying juvenile with ludicrous pretensions, including an ambition to perform a one-man Hamlet. And those are the likeable characters.

ANTI:

'The private and public dramas are, of course, deliberately contrived, but it proves impossible to maintain the pace without veering towards hysteria . . . Come back *Dynasty* – all is forgiven.' *(Colette Maude, Time Out)*

MIXED:

'For a hilarious half hour or so of simple satire and sexy gags, [it] is a joy . . . The film's snag is that it has a terrific situation but no story to speak of . . . Lively nonsense, though . . . I laughed a lot.' *(Shaun Usher, Daily Mail)*

'Though the comedy doesn't always hit the mark, and Field is not too convincing in the lead, there is enough madness and mayhem here to keep audiences amused . . . On a sad note, Whoopi Goldberg is wasted in a supporting role . . . Oh, dear, she's playing Beulah again, though Field thankfully restrains herself from asking Goldberg to peel her a grape.' *(Stephen Bourne, Gay Times)*

PRO:

'A brilliant parody of the genre – and more . . . The convoluted plot works up to the best screwball climax in ages . . . A treat for the thinking addict.' *(Alexander Walker, Evening Standard)*

'Enormous fun . . . In the best traditions of good farce, [it] shoots from the hip with a dazzling array of camp encounters. And if one line fails there is another swiftly on its heels.' *(Sue Heal, Today)*

SOIL: *see* EARTH.

SOLARIS — CT: 5 AV: 6.50

1972 USSR C BW 165 SF/FOREIGN

D Andrei Tarkovsky
W Andrei Tarkovsky Friedrich Gorenstein ● from Stanislaw Lem's novel

Donatas Banionys Natalya Bondarchuk Vladislav Dvorjetzki Yuri Yarvet

A psychologist (Donatas Banionys) investigates nervous breakdowns and suicides on a distant planet, which appears to be sentient, and discovers that there are some mysteries which even science cannot unravel.

This visually spectacular movie by a hugely acclaimed film-maker is pretty much the Soviet equivalent to *2001: A Space Odyssey*. It won the

Critics' Jury prize at Cannes and has always had its admirers; but the mystical message (which many find incomprehensible) was branded élitist and non-Marxist by the Soviet leadership. The deadly slow narrative and tedious, humourless philosophizing ruin it for most viewers, including this one.

PRO:

'Tarkovsky contrasts Kelvin [the hero]'s revelation with the obstinate pragmatism of scientific and military leaders back on earth. Surrounded, in classic Soviet fashion, with elephantine blowups of Big Brotherly politicians, they view the cryptic footage of the ocean planet. Even with strong evidence that Solaris is impenetrable – its mysteries beyond human grasp – they decide to plunge on. "We have no moral right to discontinue the investigation," they argue. Here is Tarkovsky's pre-glasnost, "space race-at-any-cost" Soviet Union . . . *Solaris* is hardly a propaganda vehicle for state directed research. It is, if anything, an anti-space exploration sci-fi movie.' *(Gerald Peary, Technology Review)*

MIXED:

'Slow-moving and occasionally pretentious, but hypnotic once one adjusts.' *(Maltin)*

'Striking to look at but pretentious and vastly long.' *(Winnert)*

ANTI:

'Kindergarten psychology and inane melodrama . . . a genuinely mind-freezing experience.' *(Tony Rayns, Time Out)*

'Both *2001* and *Solaris* offer intellectual banalities cloaked in cinematic splendour.' *(Phil Hardy, The Film Encyclopaedia: Science Fiction)*

'I fled from *Solaris* after an hour.' *(David Shipman)*

SOLDIER OF ORANGE CT: – AV: 7.80

(aka *Soldaat van Oranje 1940-45*)

1977 Netherlands 165 C WAR/DRAMA/FOREIGN

D Paul Verhoeven
W Paul Verhoeven Gerard Soeteman Kees Holierhoek based on Erik Hazelhof Roelfsema's autobiography

Rutger Hauer ☆ Jeroen Krabbé ☆ Peter Faber Derek de Lint Eddy Habbema Lex van Delden Edward Fox Belinda Meuldijk

During World War II, some students resist the Nazis.

Before Paul Verhoeven went to Hollywood and made movies like *RoboCop, Total Recall* and *Basic Instinct*, he made subtler dramas like this critically acclaimed, commercially successful picture which analyses the different effects which Nazi occupation had on Dutch youth.

'An oddly dislocating experience . . . For the small Dutch film industry, a milestone – the most daring and ambitious cinema production ever attempted.' *(Holland Herald)*

'Jeroen Krabbé . . . is especially fine . . . There's a casual wartime bawdiness coloring the film, and that's convincing, too . . . Verhoeven's direction and Vacano's photography are both calm, unfancy.' *(Donald Barthelme, New Yorker)*

'Superior drama.' *(Maltin)*

'Great performances, with Hauer shining as the young aristocrat who becomes a hero of the resistance.' *(Winnert)*

SOLITI IGNOTI, I: *see* BIG DEAL ON MADONNA STREET.

SOME LIKE IT HOT CT: 10 AV: 9.61

1959 US 122 BW COMEDY/ROMANCE

D Billy Wilder ☆ AAN
W Billy Wilder I.A.L. Diamond ☆ AAN

Jack Lemmon ☆ AAN Tony Curtis ☆ Marilyn Monroe ☆ Joe E. Brown George Raft Pat O' Brien Nehemiah Persoff Joan Shawlee George E. Stone

Two musicians (Jack Lemmon and Tony Curtis) escape from Mobsters by joining a touring all-girl band (including Marilyn Monroe at her most gorgeous and vulnerable).

Funny, frantic, wildly implausible farce. The construction is meticulous, the dialogue is witty, and two amusing drag performances are augmented by Marilyn Monroe at her most stunning – gorgeous, sexy, innocent and vulnerable. Under all the low comedy, there's a surprisingly uninhibited examination of sexual identity. Some critics found the movie anachronistic, vulgar and much too long; most people don't want it to stop, and it's now acquired the status of a classic comedy. Nominated for six Oscars including art direction (by Ted Haworth and Edward G. Goyle) and cinematography (Charles Lang Jr), but it won only one, for costume design (Orry-Kelly).

ANTI:

'No comedy dependent on men impersonating women can make friends and influence laughter for very long, certainly not for two hours.' *(Daily Mail)*

'The film comes near to success, when it does, by virtue of its own unashamed and rollicking vulgarity . . . Perhaps it would justify its determination to make jokes out of sudden death and prolonged female impersonation by claiming that callousness and crudity were the hallmarks of the place and the time.' *(The Times)*

'A queer kettle of fish . . . The hundred-proof flavor of the jazz era is rapidly diluted in a series of watery jokes in which the events and the vernacular of the

1950s are prefigured: groping for improbabilities, the hero-heroine (played by Tony Curtis) says, "Suppose the Dodgers leave Brooklyn!"; a tough cop (Pat O'Brien), waiting for his colleagues to burst into the aforementioned speak-easy, indulges in an atomic-age countdown; "You flipped your wig," Mr Curtis tells his crony Jack Lemmon.' *(Jay Jacobs, Reporter)*

PRO:

'Whistles along at a smart, murderous pace. Mr Curtis, whom one used to think of as simply a haircut, gets better and better.' *(Dilys Powell)*

'Miss Monroe, whose figure simply cannot be overlooked . . . proves to be the epitome of a dumb blonde and a talented comedienne.' *(A. H. Weiler, New York Times)*

'Marilyn does herself proud, giving a performance of such intrinsic quality that you begin to believe she's only being herself and it is herself who fits into that distant period and this picture so well.' *(Archer Winsten, New York Post)*

'A riot from beginning to finish and a polished delight to boot . . . More laughs per reel than for quite some time.' *(George Sterling, Evening Standard)*

'Probably the funniest picture of recent memory. It's a whacky, clever, farcical comedy that starts off like a firecracker and keeps on throwing off lively sparks till the very end . . . Marilyn has never looked better . . . She's a comedienne with that combination of sex appeal and timing that just can't be beat.' *(Variety)*

SOMETHING WILD

CT: 6 AV: 6.50

1986 US 106 C THRILLER/COMEDY

D Jonathan Demme ✔
W E. Max Frye

Jeff Daniels ☆ Melanie Griffith ☆ Ray Liotta ☆ Margaret Colin Tracey Walter Dana Preu Jack Gilpin

A free spirit (Melanie Griffith) leads yuppie (Jeff Daniels) astray.

Jonathan Demme's cult comedy helped make a star out of Melanie Griffith, who's great fun here. The morality of the movie doesn't bear thinking about, and the tone darkens into nightmare at odd moments; but this is one of the more entertaining offbeat movies of the 80s. Ray Liotta makes a splendidly scary movie début.

PRO:

'Conceptually and stylistically compelling.' *(Variety)*

'A sharply observed study of eccentricity combined with a little paranoia and a lot of decency. It is funny, frightening, admirably original and most insidiously, rather touching.' *(Victoria Mather, Daily Telegraph)*

MIXED:

'A messy loveable shaggy dog . . . The script suffers a bit from mange, but for the most part the picture licks your face and begs to play – it's a triumph of velocity and *mise-en-scène* over making [narrative] sense.' *(J. Hoberman, Village Voice)*

'Constantly confounding your expectations of where it's going, possibly because it doesn't know itself, this is still a highly entertaining and blackly amusing film. Griffith is just wonderful.' *(Rose)*

ANTI:

'Illustrates the perils of being one's own producer. A more impartial [one] . . . might have . . . advised [Demme] against the trite and predictable ending that is an anticlimax in a film otherwise so waywardly appealing.' *(David Robinson, The Times)*

'The closing scenes are surprisingly awkward and over-explicit . . . [The film] creaks and strains as it tries to pack away the nightmares and impose the obligatory happy ending. It's a sleek, slick and finally unsatisfying movie.' *(Margaret Walters, Listener)*

'A contemptible film, and the obtuse reviewers who have hailed it unequivocally as a delightfully wacky comedy – a "wonderful offbeat movie", as one of them put it – are contemptible too . . . Patently, Demme and Frye idealize rebellion. But rebellion, to them, has no moral dimension, has nothing to do with self-sacrifice or commitment to a principle, with the right challenging the power of the wrong. Their sensibilities are so fundamentally immature and solipsistic that the only conception that they have of their theme is as follows: being a rebel is fun. Being a rebel means not going to work, means stiffing a coffee shop on a check, means getting a free ride. The definition, needless to say, has its corollaries: stealing and lying and drinking behind the wheel are really neat (so long as you don't physically hurt anybody); the road to happiness is paved with irresponsibility; the worst thing you can do with your life is to hold down a job, especially a good job. It disturbs me profoundly to think of the number of children and teenagers who will be exposed to this movie, and of the number of reviewers who have blithely praised its madcap comedy while managing thoroughly to ignore its moral scuzziness.' *(Bruce Bawer, American Spectator)*

SOMMARNATTENS LEENDE:

see SMILES OF A SUMMER NIGHT.

SON OF FRANKENSTEIN:

see THE *FRANKENSTEIN* SERIES.

SONG OF BERNADETTE, THE AAN

CT: 5 AV: 7.18

1943 US 156 BW DRAMA/BIOPIC

D Henry King AAN
W George Seaton AAN from Franz Werfel's novel

Jennifer Jones ☆ AAW William Eythe
Charles Bickford ☆ AAN Vincent Price Lee J. Cobb
Gladys Cooper ☆ AAN Anne Revere ☆ AAN
Sig Rumann Linda Darnell (as Virgin Mary)

A French peasant girl (Jennifer Jones) has visions of the Virgin Mary and gives a boost to the Lourdes tourist industry.

A profound religious experience for some; deadly Hollywood hokum, for others. I favour the latter view, but the production values and performances make it modestly entertaining, and not as kitschy as one might expect. Arthur Miller's cinematography and Alfred Newman's score won Oscars, as did the art direction of James Basevi and William Darling. Barbara McLean's editing was nominated.

PRO:

'Great spiritual masterpiece . . . Jennifer Jones proves to be the perfect choice for *Bernadette*, and she gives a beautiful, moving performance of rare sincerity . . . It is doubly a remarkable work being her first important screen role.' *(Hollywood Reporter)*

'Absorbing, emotional and dramatic.' *(Variety)*

ANTI:

'Tedious and repetitious; it lingers too fondly over images that lack visual mobility, and it goes in for dialectic discourse that will clutter and fatigue the average mind.' *(New York Times)*

MIXED:

'Unusually well made – within limits. The limits are those of middle-class twentieth-century genteelism . . . Within its limitations, most of *The Song of Bernadette* is reverent, spiritually forthright, dignified. The photography is continuously elegant. Most of the cast (especially Gladys Cooper as a Mistress of Novices) plays with unusual soberness and intensity. As Bernadette, newcomer Jennifer Jones . . . makes one of the most impressive screen debuts in many years.' *(James Agee, Time)*

'The film is, by contemporary standards, tedious and repetitious – but it is reverential, dignified, and relatively tasteful.' *(Judith Crist)*

SONG OF NORWAY

CT: 1 AV: 2.00

1970 US 141 C MUSICAL/BIOPIC

D Andrew L. Stone ●
W Andrew L Stone from the stage musical, book by Davis Boulton (music by Edvard Grieg, lyrics by Bob Wright and Chet Forrest)

Toralv Maurstad Florence Henderson ●
Christina Schollin Frank Poretta Harry Secombe
Edward G. Robinson Robert Morley
Elizabeth Larner Richard Wordsworth

Life of Norwegian composer Edvard Grieg (Toralv Maurstad).

Nice scenery, shame about what's in front of it.

PRO:

'Quite watchable, and the landscapes are certainly splendid.' *(Halliwell)*

ANTI:

'The movie is of an unbelievable badness; it brings back clichés you didn't know you knew – they're practically from the unconscious of moviegoers. You can't get angry at something this stupefying; it seems to have been made by trolls.' *(Pauline Kael)*

'Godawful . . . The musical numbers, when not downright ugly, are ludicrous, containing all the conventions of staging that made *The Sound of Music* so easy to hate. Grieg having apparently lived a life of exemplary dullness, the only issue Stone can trump up for dramatic purposes is his thwarted desire to create an indigenous national music for Norway hardly a matter to keep us on the edge of our chairs. In the ineptitude of his writing, Mr Stone matches the clumsiness of his direction, unconsciously creating a double parody of both the operetta and biographical forms truly an amazing work of unintentional humor.' *(Richard Schickel, Life)*

'Nerve-numbing . . . [Florence Henderson, who plays Grieg's wife, is] the female Peter Frampton for the Geritol generation.' *(Harry & Michael Medved)*

'If he were not dead, Norwegian composer Edvard Grieg would expire upon seeing this insult to his life and career.' *(Martin & Porter)*

SONS AND LOVERS AAN

CT: 6 AV: 7.89

1960 GB 103 BW DRAMA

D Jack Cardiff ☆ AAN
W Gavin Lambert T.E.B. Clarke ☆ AAN from D.H. Lawrence's novel

Dean Stockwell Trevor Howard ☆ AAN
Wendy Hiller ☆ Mary Ure AAN Heather Sears
Donald Pleasance William Lucas
Ernest Thesiger ✔ Rosalie Crutchley ✔

A Nottingham miner's son (Dean Stockwell) has amorous exploits, but remains dominated by his mother (Wendy Hiller).

Stiff, over-literary screen version of D.H. Lawrence's most autobiographical novel. Critics are divided about many of the performances, and Stockwell's efforts to maintain an English accent – though mostly successful – do get in the way of his acting; but Howard and Hiller received almost universal praise, as Stockwell's mother and father. Cinematographer Freddie Francis rightly won an Oscar; Tom Morahan's art direction was nominated.

ANTI:

'Rather listless . . . the story . . . remains lifeless and remote.' *(Frank Lewis, Sunday Dispatch)*

'The artist's fire simply isn't here – the movie is temperate, earnest, episodic. ' *(Pauline Kael)*

MIXED:

'An album of decent Edwardian snapshots.' *(Peter John Dyer)*

'Dean Stockwell does very well except that he is a little short of passion . . . Jack Cardiff has directed . . . with a visual brilliance that is a constant reminder that he used commonly to be accepted as the outstanding cameraman in British films.' *(Fred Majdalany, Daily Mail)*

'The script by Mr Gavin Lambert and Mr T.E.B. Clarke, generally a sound piece of work, is here of little use to [Mr Stockwell] . . . Not a complete success, but it is a film worth making which has been honestly made.' *(The Times)*

'Suffers . . . from a hollow central performance [by] Dean Stockwell, miscast . . . Despite this limitation [it] remains a remarkable film.' *(Derek Hill, Tribune)*

PRO:

'A rare, remarkable and courageous film.' *(Daily Herald)*

'Told by director Jack Cardiff with blazing clarity. The love scene enacted at the watermill is one of the most moving ever filmed.' *(Ivon Adams, Star)*

'A film that fascinates and is superbly photographed.' *(Edward Betts, People)*

'Not merely pictorially beautiful but an all-round triumph.' *(Peter Burnup, News of the World)*

SONS OF THE DESERT CT: 6 AV: 8.67

(aka *Fraternally Yours*)

1934 US 68 BW COMEDY

D William A. Seiter
W Frank Craven Byron Morgan ☆

Stan Laurel ☆ Oliver Hardy ☆ Charlie Chase ☆ Mae Busch Dorothy Christie Lucien Littlefield

Two husbands (Stan Laurel, Oliver Hardy) sneak off to a fraternal convention while telling their wives they are going on a sea cruise; the ship then sinks.

An amusing comic premise – which bears more than a passing resemblance to that of their 1928 two-reeler, *We Faw Down* – is moderately well explored. Neither direction nor screenplay are top-class, but the teamwork of Laurel and Hardy makes this much loved by their devotees.

'Despite the fact that the picture is ten years old, it is still one of Laurel and Hardy's most amusing efforts. The story is slight and the fun hilarious. Particularly good are the scenes with the wives . . . There is a smashing climax, particularly in regard to crockery . . . Laurel and Hardy . . . are ably supported by Mae Busch and Dorothy Christie.' *(Today's Cinema, 1944)*

'Their optimism is indestructible. Their ignorance is truly invincible because it is the angelic armor of perpetual childhood.' *(John McCabe, 1968)*

'They are the most innocent of clowns.' *(David Robinson, S & S)*

'Laurel and Hardy have a special sweetness about them, a gentle politeness . . . Time and again anger, suspicion, greed, lust and revenge come between them . . . Yet the magic of Laurel and Hardy is their love for each other.' *(John Landis, Close-Ups, 1978)*

'I think this film could have used a couple of floozies . . . What I most enjoy . . . is just watching Ollie and Stan move through life at their peculiar pace.' *(Danny Peary, 1988)*

'One of their [Laurel and Hardy's] finest features, with funny jokes, fast handling and the stars perfectly cast.' *(Winnert)*

SORRY, WRONG NUMBER CT: 7 AV: 6.82

1948 US 89 BW THRILLER

D Anatole Litvak ✗
W Lucille Fletcher from her radio play

Barbara Stanwyck ☆ AAN Burt Lancaster Ann Richards Wendell Corey Ed Begley Harold Vermilyea Leif Erickson William Conrad

A neurotic invalid (Barbara Stanwyck) overhears a murder being plotted on a crossed line, and gradually realizes that the death being discussed is her own.

A 30-minute, one-woman radio play has been opened out and expanded; but it's still all about the mounting terror of the heroine. Stanwyck gives a finely judged performance which carries the audience over a few implausibilities. Lancaster doesn't have as much to work with, but acquits himself well as a husband driven to desperate measures. Sol Polito's film noir camerawork adds to the suspense, and Litvak directs with pace if no great inspiration. With Hitchcock in charge, this might have been an all-time-great.

ANTI:

'The director, Anatole Litvak, seems to be defeated by the extravagantly jumbled, shallow script. ' *(Pauline Kael)*

MIXED:

'No doubt there are all sorts of serious-minded reservations to be made about this film. Its characterisation, for instance, is unstable, its tone is one of almost unrelieved unpleasantness, and some of the links in the neat chain of argument are found, on later examination, to be distinctly weak. But the point is that the people who made it . . . have tried to do just one thing – to thrill. This they have triumphantly done.' *(James Monahan)*

'About as exciting a thriller as your nerves will stand. The film is somewhat confused in flashback technique but the suspense is undeniable and it is skilfully heightened by sound effects. Barbara Stanwyck's part is one of constant fear, helplessness and bewilderment.' *(A.E. Wilson)*

PRO:

'Among the most effective suspense films of the year.' *(Fortnight)*

'Litvak . . . knows how to handle a complicated story in a swift, simple way.' *(Time)*

'Calculated to scare the wits out of a spectator.' *(Howard Barnes, New York Herald Tribune)*

'For sheer, unadulterated terror there have been few films in recent years to match the quivering fright of *Sorry, Wrong Number* and few performances to equal the hysteria of a woman doomed.' *(Cue)*

'A classic thriller. The classicism stems from the cool bloodlessness and lack of gore in the creation and depiction of shivering and unrelieved terror.' *(Judith Crist, 60s)*

SOUND OF MUSIC, THE AAW CT: 9 AV: 8.19

1965 US 177 C MUSICAL/ROMANCE/WAR

D Robert Wise AAW
W Ernest Lehman from the musical with book by Howard Lindsay, Russel Crouse (music and lyrics by Richard Rodgers and Oscar Hammerstein II ☆)

Julie Andrews ☆ AAN Christopher Plummer (singing voice dubbed by Bill Lee) Richard Haydn Eleanor Parker Peggy Wood ☆ AAN Anna Lee Marni Nixon Charmain Carr ✓

Naughty nun (Julie Andrews) woos and weds wooden widower (Christopher Plummer); noble nuns help nice newly-weds flee nasty Nazis.

Though she's often accused of being sugary, Julie Andrews turns in a gutsy performance which takes the curse off this musical's more dangerously mawkish moments. Robert Wise and a highly skilled production team (many of whom had collaborated on the more intellectually acceptable West Side Story, four years before) do a terrific job on this movie which unfashionably celebrated childcare and a feminine sense of duty. Its excellent Rodgers and Hammerstein songs, gripping story and life-affirming atmosphere make this a timeless classic, whatever curmudgeonly critics might say (and they did).

The film won five Oscars, including Best Music Score (orchestrated by Irwin Kostal), Film Editing (William Reynolds) and Sound (James P. Corcoran, Fred Hynes). Nominated were cinematographer Ted McCord, art directors Boris Leven, Walter M. Scott and Ruby Levitt, and costume designer Dorothy Jeakins.

ANTI:

'Nuns sing in cloisters. Miss Andrews (who plays Maria) sings in her bedroom. Christopher Plummer sings in self-defence. Most of what they sing is pretty awful. Charmain Carr – agreeably ardent as Plummer's eldest daughter – has a good song about young love, "Sixteen, Going on Seventeen". But the remainder come stodgily from the Rodgers and Hammerstein hymnal with lots of those lines about whiskers on kittens and larks learning how to pray, which fairly reek of high sentiments and tired minds.' *(Philip Oakes)*

'So mechanically engineered and so shrewdly calculated that the background music rises, the already soft focus blurs and melts, and, upon the instant, you can hear all those noses blowing in the theatre. Whom could this operetta offend? Only those of us who, despite the fact that we may respond, loathe being manipulated in this way and are aware of how cheap and ready-made are the responses we are made to feel.' *(Pauline Kael)*

'It has a convent of singing nuns who warble in their wimples, "Sister Mary is not an asset to the abbey." It has a family of seven children, all of different sizes and cuteness and guaranteed to come out with endearing remarks like, "I'm incorrigible – what's incorrigible mean?" It has views of Salzburg that are a pastrycook's fantasy and panoramas of the Austrian Alps that are a mountaineer's paradise. It has lakes with swans on them, and bunches of edelweiss, and lederhosen, and shaving brushes in hat trims and a Tyrolean folk festival.' *(Alexander Walker)*

MIXED:

'Belongs to the sentimental class of musicals; it offers decent feelings, misty tunes and a refuge from the electric guitar. I find it all a bit smothering. But that is a matter of taste, not judgment; the question is whether in its class the film is well done, and I think the answer is yes . . . I wish it well. As long, that is, as I don't have to see it again.' *(Dilys Powell)*

'Difficult to enjoy without the uneasy feeling that one's emotions were being mercilessly manipulated. Yet . . . it was a shrewdly professional piece of work, stunningly presented, and crafted with awesome expertise.' *(Clive Hirschhorn, The Hollywood Musical, 1981)*

'Reactionary shit, about how a woman's true vocation is to look after kids (even if they're not her own), turn curtains into clothes, and stand by her man. But . . . get smashed first, and you'll be singing along with the inescapably memorable tunes.' *(Geoff Andrew, Time Out)*

PRO:

'One of the top musicals to reach the screen . . . a warmly-pulsating, captivating drama . . . magnificently mounted and with a brilliant cast.' *(Variety)*

'*Sound of Music* restores faith in the art of motion pictures . . . Who says you can't buy happiness? As long as Robert Wise's *The Sound of Music* is playing, you can. And that's going to be for a good long time. Don't, however, wait. Don't deprive yourself of the pleasure a moment longer than necessary. Run, do not walk, to the nearest boxoffice.' *(Hollywood Reporter)*

'It's very joyous. It's refreshing and not complicated. A love story, with children and music. That word "joyous" has an awful lot to do with it.' *(Julie Andrews)*

SOUNDER AAN CT: 6 AV: 8.09

1972 US 105 C DRAMA/FAMILY

D Martin Ritt
W Lonnie Elder III ✗ AAN from William H. Armstrong's novel

Paul Winfield ☆ AAN Cicely Tyson ☆ AAN Kevin Hooks Taj Mahal Carmen Matthews James Best

Black sharecroppers in the deep south have a depressing time during the Depression.

Earnest, well-meaning, liberal drama, which makes up in sincerity and fine performances for what it lacks in character depth and narrative surprise.

ANTI:

'What's missing [is] the feeling of bone-edge existence and incipient anger . . . In its desire to be uplifting, [the film] leaves its characters one-dimensional without ensuring that the one dimension is heroic.' *(Verina Glaessner, Time Out)*

MIXED:

'A rare honest movie about people who work the soil under conditions of extreme rigor. *Sounder* is also a rare honest Hollywood movie about blacks, making it virtually unique . . . There are weaknesses, to be sure: Ritt is not a particularly imaginative director, and the screenplay (probably following the novel) does not explore character in depth.' *(John Simon)*

'Neither exciting nor profound, but the director knows the pitfalls – patronage, sentiment, stereotypes – and crests them with ease.' *(Shipman)*

PRO:

'An outstanding film . . . Martin Ritt's masterful direction, an excellent adaptation, and a uniformly terrific cast make this a film which transcends space, race, age and time.' *(Variety)*

'It is pleasant to see a film about black people that depicts them as human beings . . . not ciphers or symbols or fantasy figures but recognisable people with recognisable emotions.' *(Ian Christie, Daily Express)*

'Heartwarming yet unsentimental film . . . [which] triumphs in its faithful period sense.' *(George Melly, Observer)*

'Deeply, emotionally rich . . . Perhaps the first movie about black experiences in America that can stir people of all colors.' *(Pauline Kael)*

SOUTH PACIFIC CT: 8 AV: 5.67

1958 US 151/171 C MUSICAL/ROMANCE/WAR

D Joshua Logan
W Paul Osborn Richard Rodgers Oscar Hammerstein II Joshua Logan (music and lyrics by Rodgers and Hammerstein ☆)

Mitzi Gaynor Rossano Brazzi (dubbed by Giorgio Tozzi) Ray Walston John Kerr (dubbed by Bill Lee) France Nuyen Juanita Hall (dubbed by Muriel Smith) Ken Clark (dubbed by Thurl Ravenscroft) Warren Hsieh (Betty Wand) Candace Lee (Marie Greene)

On a South Pacific Island in 1943, a naval nurse (Mitzi Gaynor) falls for a Frenchman (Rossano Brazzi) who becomes a war hero.

Of the leading artistes, only Mitzi Gaynor was allowed to sing with her own voice – even Juanita Hall, who had played the role on Broadway, was replaced by Muriel Smith, who had played the part in London. It's symptomatic of a musical which feels over-produced and artificial. This is a highly didactic musical which, though publicized as being about wartime love and heroics, is really a tract about racism. But neither the turgid narrative nor the garishly over-dramatic photography can destroy the impact of one of Rodgers and Hammerstein's greatest scores.

It won an Oscar for Best Sound and received nominations for Best Scoring of a Musical Picture (Alfred Newman and Ken Darby) and Best Color Cinematography (Leon Shamroy) – although the distracting use of colour filters is probably the worst aspect of the whole film.

'My interpretation of the South Pacific was like Gauguin painted it. I also wanted to create a change of pace. You have to think of the audience's restlessness watching the same thing for three hours. You have to change the atmosphere. So I shot the musical parts as a fantasy by sliding colored gelatin filters across the lens.' *(Leon Shamroy, Newsweek)*

PRO:

'Compelling entertainment . . . Boffo.' *(Variety)*

'It's HOT STUFF. To see it is one whale of an enchanted evening . . . And to see it is to fall in love

. . . with the ritzy Mitzi Gaynor.' *(Chris Reynolds, Daily Mirror)*

'Todd-AO is . . . an ideal medium for storytelling . . . There is a wonderful presence to the sound . . . Logan has hit on the ingenious idea of using colour rather in the way that a composer underscores a film's drama with music . . . [and he] has made yet another break with Hollywood musical conventions . . . [He] takes virtually . . . whole songs in big close up . . . Genuinely explores a new realm of entertainment . . . For sheer relaxation, enchantment and good humour we have seen nothing like it.' *(Peter Baker, S & S)*

MIXED:

'No question about it: Todd-AO wipes the floor with Cinerama . . . The only point now is, what can it be used for? . . . One answer would be: anything, except *South Pacific*.' *(William Whitebait, New Statesman)*

'If the heroine emerges as a bit of a bigot by today's standards, or de Becque seems a bit of a stick, relax and enjoy those lovely melodies.' *(Judith Crist)*

ANTI:

'About as tastelessly impressive as a ten-ton marshmallow . . . Nevertheless, it will probably run almost as long as it did on Broadway . . . and it seems sure to make yet another bale of kale.' *(Time)*

'If I found less pleasure in [it] than some you can put it down to lack of humour, a tin ear, or a stuffy disposition: but not, please, to insincerity . . . I'll begin by uttering heresy. I find . . . Hammerstein's songs a little tasteless . . . As for the story . . . well, I didn't much care for that either . . . (More heresy) I think Rossano Brazzi is miscast . . . Finally, the film lacks humour.' *(Colin Dixon, Daily Telegraph)*

'Much too long . . . There is indeed much talent to be seen and heard but not enough.' *(Manchester Guardian)*

'The director is in the unenviable position of continually having to offset the embarrassing advantages of his new and expensive technologies. The lumbering cameras tend to remain solidly in one position and there is never any real solution to the impossible problem of achieving an appetising close-up of a leading lady on a 50 foot screen . . . It is difficult to see the advantage of having something on the screen that the theatre was doing very much better six years ago.' *(Times Educational Supplement)*

'Dull.' *(Vanessa Miles, F & F)*

'Disappointing, despite the haunting familiar melodies . . . It lacks the zest and high spirits to carry it along for three hours.' *(Nina Hibbin, Daily Worker)*

SOUTHERN COMFORT CT: 8 AV: 6.23

1981 US 106 C ACTION/ADVENTURE

D Walter Hill ☆
W Michael Kane Walter Hill David Giler

Keith Carradine Powers Boothe Fred Ward Franklyn Seales T.K. Carter Lewis Smith Peter Coyote Les Lannom

National Guardsmen are rude to the local Cajuns and are slaughtered, one by one, in inhospitable Bayou country.

Walter Hill's action thriller is one of the most exciting, atmospheric and stylish films of the 80s. Unfortunately, it also has pretensions as an allegory about US involvement in Vietnam, and Hill is guilty of pursuing this parallel at the expense of characterization – it's hard to care much about the characters as they die.

ANTI:

'Quite what this violent film intends to illustrate, unless it is the speed with which humans can revert to savages, rather escapes me, and I was left with the impression of violence being illustrated for its own sake.' *(Patrick Gibbs, Daily Telegraph)*

'More barbarity than comfort . . . [It leaves] one punch-drunk from a lavish mixture of over-emphasis, incongruity and vituperation.' *(Virginia Dignam, Morning Star)*

'An intellectually muddled, Grade B Deliverance.' *(Maltin)*

MIXED:

'Watchable, even compulsive. The missing dimension [urgency] however, is more noticeable because it is strived for so hard.' *(Derek Malcolm, Guardian)*

PRO:

'As an action director Walter Hill has a dazzling competence. *Southern Comfort* comes across with such immediacy that it had a near-hypnotic hold on me.' *(Pauline Kael)*

'Hill . . . handles his grim subject with an instinctive flair for the unnerving effect.' *(Margaret Hinxman, Daily Mail)*

'Keith Carradine and Les Lannom are outstanding in this impressive study of fear and suspense.' *(Arthur Thirkell, Daily Mirror)*

'Soundly appropriate for America under Reagan with Vietnam not only brought back home but clutched to the xenophobic bosom.' *(Jane Root, The Leveller)*

SOUTHERNER, THE CT: 6 AV: 7.90

1945 US 91 BW DRAMA

D Jean Renoir ☆ AAN
W Jean Renoir from George Sessions Perry's novel *Hold Autumn in Your Hand* (according to some sources, the adaptation was by William Faulkner)

Zachary Scott ☆ Betty Field Beulah Bondi ✗ J. Carrol Naish Percy Kilbride Blanche Yurka Norman Lloyd

A year in the life of a poor family in the American south.

Zachary Scott gives the performance of his career in this slow, elegiac, loosely plotted study of poverty, which is usually reckoned to be Renoir's best American film, and has even been compared with *The Grapes of Wrath*. The rest of the acting is uneven, however, with Beulah Bondi's enthusiastically overacted Granny being very much a matter of taste. The movie was considered ultra-realistic, perhaps because of its pessimism, but Agee was right – it still looks too much like a Hollywood movie. Oscar-nominated for Best Score (Werner Janssen) and Sound (Jack Whitney).

PRO:

'Not since *The Grapes of Wrath* has an American film got so close to the lives of the struggling poor . . . [Renoir] brings something of the French tradition to the handling of it, but the director whom he most recalls is Dovzhenko, the Ukrainian poet of the film, who stands in a magnificent niche all his own. Renoir has a remarkable cameraman to help him visualize the spirit in which he has worked, Lucien Andriot, who has turned out some of the most beautiful photography you will see in many a day.' *(James Shelley Hamilton, New Movies)*

'A rare and rewarding motion picture and a challenge to those agents and elements in our society who believe in full freedom of democratic expression.' *(John T. McManus, PM)*

'I cannot imagine anybody failing to be spellbound by this first successful essay in Franco-American screen collaboration . . . The grief of a mother over her sick child, the helplessness of the husband to comfort her (watch the sensitive acting of Zachary Scott and Betty Field), a fight in a saloon, a fight in the farmyard – these and other sequences have a suggestiveness both intelligent and tender, a sophistication behind the simplicity. I cannot let pass this short review of a fine and beautifully acted film without referring to superb playing of the grandmother by Beulah Bondi. It merits at least a couple of dozen Oscars at current rates.' *(Richard Winnington)*

'You can smell the earth as the plough turns it up; you can sense the winter and the rain and the sunshine.' *(C.A. Lejeune)*

MIXED:

'It may be trenchant realism, but these are times when there is a greater need. Escapism is the word.' *(Variety)*

'One of the most sensitive and beautiful American-made pictures I have seen. . . . [Yet] I saw it with as much regret as pleasure. The heart of this kind of living is work, and the picture should have made the work as immediate to the watcher as to the worker in all its methods, meanings, and emotions. It offers instead, mere token shots of work; and in these, too often, the clothes aren't even sweated. Just as unfortunate and more constantly disappointing, most of the players are . . . screechingly, unbearably wrong. They didn't walk right, stand right, eat right, sound right, or look right, and, as bad or worse, behind the work of each it was clear that the basic understanding and the basic emotional and mental – or merely human – attitudes were wrong, to the point of unintentional insult.' *(James Agee)*

SPARTACUS CT: 9 AV: 7.64

1960 (re-released 1991) US 187/196 (1991) C DRAMA/EPIC

D Stanley Kubrick ☆
W Dalton Trumbo from Howard Fast's novel

Kirk Douglas ☆ Laurence Olivier ☆ Tony Curtis Jean Simmons ✔ Charles Laughton ☆ Peter Ustinov ☆ AAW John Gavin ● Woody Strode ✔

Slave (Kirk Douglas) leads revolt against Roman Empire.

In the original 1960 version, the battle-scenes were grievously mutilated on grounds of taste. Amputated completely was a sequence where Crassus (Laurence Olivier) lived up to his name, and propositioned his slave (Tony Curtis) with a sceneful of salacious suggestions about seafood. These sins of censorship have now been expiated, with Anthony Hopkins's voice deputizing for Olivier (the new scene could, I suppose, be entitled Slyness of the Clams).

Re-viewed in the 90s, the original cracks in the edifice look more colossal than ever. The 'exterior' studio sets appear to have been left over from an amateur production of *Carousel*; Tony Curtis and John Gavin (as Julius Caesar) seem to be modelling for *Thunderbirds*; and the over-emphasis on Kirk Douglas's pulsating pectorals reflects the equally muscular involvement of Mr Douglas as Executive Producer.

It remains, however, a stirring story with marvellously staged set-pieces, an intelligent script by Dalton Trumbo, and memorable supporting performances by Olivier, Laughton and Ustinov, who deserved an Oscar for his cowardly slave-trader. *Spartacus* was brave in its day for having an 'unhappy' ending; now, it's just great popular entertainment, on the grandest possible scale.

It was Oscar-nominated for Best Editing (Robert Lawrence) and Score (Alex North) and won for Best Cinematography (Russell Metty), Art Direction (Alexander Golitzen, Eric Orbom, Russel A. Gausman, Julia Heron), and Costume Design (Bill Thomas, Valles).

ANTI:

'One comes away feeling rather revolted and not at all ennobled.' *(Alan Dent, Illustrated London News)*

'Everything is depicted with a lack of imagination that is truly Marxian . . . Of all the recent king-size spectacles, *Spartacus* is the least moving emotionally.' *(Anne Grayson, Films in Review, 1960)*

'An opulent, uneven, and dawdling film.' *(Judith Crist)*

'Spartacus stands at a divide between earlier epics, where the female characters tended to look like models for hairdressing salons, and later epics that placed more emphasis on historical accuracy. But the hairstyles of the visiting Roman women at the gladiatorial school are laughable, and even Jean Simmons looks too made up and coiffed at times.' *(Roger Ebert, 1990)*

PRO:

'A lot of first-rate professionals have pooled their abilities to make a first-rate circus.' *(Stanley Kauffmann)*

'The individual who emerges above all is director Kubrick. At 31, and with only four other pix behind him . . . Kubrick has out-DeMilled the old master in spectacle, without ever permitting the story or the people who are the core of the drama to become lost in the shuffle. He demonstrates here a technical talent and comprehension of human values.' *(Variety)*

'Olivier brings not only great authority but an exceptional poignancy to the character of Crassus, the urbane, corrupt Roman general and dictator whom the film consistently contrasts with Kirk Douglas's true-blue, unrefined slave general.' *(Bruce Bawer, American Spectator)*

'Long, well-made, downbeat epic with deeper than usual characterizations and several bravura sequences.' *(Halliwell)*

'Probably the best epic about the ancient world ever produced for the screen.' *(Baseline)*

SPEED

CT: 9 AV: 8 (est)

1994 US 115 C ACTION/ADVENTURE

D Jan de Bont ☆
W Graham Yost ☆

Keanu Reeves ☆ Dennis Hopper ☆
Sandra Bullock ☆ Joe Morton Jeff Daniels
Alan Ruck Glenn Plummer

A psychopath (Dennis Hopper) has a grudge against the police, and plants a bomb on a bus, primed to explode if the vehicle goes less than 50 miles per hour.

Director Jan De Bont had worked as cinematographer on one modern classic of the action genre, *Die Hard*, and this is on the same high level; it has enough thrills and humour to satisfy the most jaded sensation-seeker. The plot is implausible but exciting; and one has to respect a screenwriter who can still think of inventive variations on this dangerously hackneyed theme.

Speed is not for the faint-hearted. It is a sweat-inducing, nerve-jangling, rollercoaster-ride that leaves your legs feeling as if they're made of blancmange. *Speed* more than lives up to its name and reputation.

MIXED:

'Once again we of the hard-nosed present are willing to anesthetize the smart-guy skepticism with which (we think) we examine everything and to plunge into fantasy wilder than the *Arabian Nights* – so long as some twentieth-century protocol is observed. The details have to be realistic: a real bus, real streets, real TV and explosives technology. After this nitty-gritty admission fee, fantasy. For instance, the speeding bus hits dozens and dozens of cars, plows through construction sites with workers leaping out of the way and at the LA airport smashes into a large airplane on a runway. In any quasi-realistic accounting of these matters, some hundreds of people would have been killed – to save the dozen or so passengers on the bus. In *Speed* no one is hurt. (They don't even bother to tell us whether anyone was on that plane.) In a film that otherwise doesn't spare the gore – it begins with one man driving a screwdriver into another man's temple, and it ends with a decapitation – the omission of the real results of this bus's foray is straight from never-never land.' *(Stanley Kauffmann)*

PRO:

'The can't-slow-down bus ride is bookended with a pair of thrill sequences, either one of which would provide enough of a plot for most movies . . . The movie has two virtues essential to good pop thrillers. First, it plugs uncomplicatedly into lurking anxieties – in this case the ones we brush aside when we daily surrender ourselves to mass transit in a world where the loonies are everywhere. Second, it is executed with panache and utter conviction.' *(Richard Schickel, Time)*

'Wall-to-wall with action, stunts, special effects and excitement. We've seen this done before, but seldom so well, or at such a high pitch of energy . . . Keanu Reeves . . . is a completely convincing action hero who is as centered and resourceful as a Clint Eastwood or Harrison Ford in similar situations. He and Bullock have good chemistry; they appreciate the humor that is always flickering just beneath the surface of the preposterous plot.' *(Roger Ebert)*

'Like *The Wages of Fear* redone at roller-coaster tempo . . . It's a pleasure to be in the hands of an action filmmaker who respects the audience. De Bont's craftsmanship is so supple that even the triple ending feels justified, like the cataclysmic final stage of a Sega death match. De Bont understands that the best suspense is honest suspense. He wants us to know exactly what it feels like to be on that bus . . . Hopper is the perfect maniacal spark plug for a movie in which a zooming bus becomes a pop metaphor for a world speeding chaotically out of control. Even Hitchcock, I think, would have approved.' *(Owen Gleiberman, Entertainment Weekly)*

SPELLBOUND AAN CT: 7 AV: 7.00

1945 US 82 BW (with one colour shot – of a gunshot – in original theatrical prints) THRILLER

D Alfred Hitchcock ☆ AAN, dream sequence by William Cameron Menzies using designs by Salvador Dali ✔
W Ben Hecht Angus MacPhail from Francis Beeding's novel *The House of Dr Edwardes*

Ingrid Bergman ☆ Gregory Peck Leo G. Carroll ☆ Michael Chekhov ☆ AAN Rhonda Fleming John Emery Norman Lloyd Steven Geray Wallace Ford

A psychoanalyst (Ingrid Bergman) tries to cure an amnesiac patient (Gregory Peck) who also happens to be her boss, and who believes he may have committed a murder.

A fascinating psychological thriller which suffers from the wooden Peck in the leading role, and a plot which never quite delivers the killer punch. As usual with Hitchcock movies, there are enough compensations to make it watchable. Bergman is lovely; Salvador Dali's dream sequences are fascinating; and George Barnes's Oscar-nominated cinematography is extraordinary. Miklos Rozsa's score (which Hitchcock rightly believed to be too schmaltzy) won an Academy Award, while Jack Cosgrove was nominated for his special effects.

MIXED:

'Objections that the romantic elements slow the melodrama can be sustained but they do enrich the whole picture with a warmth and humanness somewhat rare in Hitchcock.' *(Arthur Beach, New Movies)*

'Worth seeing, but hardly more . . . The psychological pretensions cluttered up the murder mystery.' *(James Agee)*

'Bad in its exposition, which is slow and laboured and apparently designed for an audience slower in the uptake than a British audience, good in its latter half, where Hitchcock, after a series of banal passages which might have been directed by pretty well anybody, goes into his chase: and who can chase better? . . . Ingrid Bergman gives, in my opinion, the performance of her career so far.' *(Dilys Powell)*

ANTI:

'Hitchcock's least noteworthy goose-pimple photoplay since *Saboteur*. The "mystery" is cumbersomely wrought, passively developed, and the denouement in which the murderer is revealed is quite as irritatingly pat as though Nick Charles [of the *Thin Man* movies] were the "private eye" involved in the case.' *(Herb Sterne)*

'The hero of the film suffers from amnesia, a guilt complex, split personality and a form of paranoia that not only makes him believe he killed a man but on several occasions gives the impression he intends to commit murder again. With all that the matter with him, his psychiatrist sweetheart, who takes on herself to cure him, snaps him out of it in what appears to be little more than three days.' *(Arthur Beach, New Movies)*

'A disaster. It was fitting that the actress who was once described as a "fine, strong, cow-country maiden" should be cast as a good, solid analyst, dispensing cures with the wholesome simplicity of a mother adding wheat germ to the family diet, but Bergman's apple-cheeked sincerity has rarely been as out of place as in this confection whipped up by jaded chefs.' *(Pauline Kael, 1976)*

'It's just another manhunt picture wrapped up in pseudo-psychoanalysis . . . The whole thing's too complicated, and I found the explanations towards the end very confusing.' *(Alfred Hitchcock, 1966)*

SPIRAL STAIRCASE, THE CT: 8 AV: 8.60

1946 US 83 BW THRILLER/HORROR

D Robert Siodmak ☆
W Mel Dinelli from Ethel Lina White's novel *Some Must Watch* ☆

Dorothy McGuire ☆ George Brent Kent Smith Ethel Barrymore ☆ AAN Rhys Williams Rhonda Fleming Gordon Oliver Sara Allgood James Bell

Mad murderer menaces mansion mute (Dorothy McGuire).

The identity of the murderer does not come as a surprise, but that's the only weakness in this tense, claustrophobic, superbly plotted thriller, directed in the highest Hitchcock style by Robert Siodmak. Dorothy McGuire gives one of the great woman-in-peril performances. Peter Collinson's remake in 1975 showed how difficult it is to make this sort of hokum convincing.

MIXED:

'Overrated . . . Even though she plays it well, I am not impressed by Dorothy McGuire – or anyone else – stunting along through several reels as a suffering mute; nor am I willingly hornswoggled by Ethel Barrymore's unprincipled use of her lighthouse eyes, wonderful as they are. Still, the movie is visually clever.' *(James Agee)*

'One of the undoubted masterpieces of the Gothic mode, even if the happy ending comes more than a shade too pat.' *(Tom Milne, Time Out)*

PRO:

'A shocker, plain and simple.' *(New York Times)*

'The most gripping, spellbinding and intensely thrilling motion picture seen in many, many years.' *(Hollywood Review)*

'Mood and pace are well set, and story grips throughout.' *(Variety)*

'A nice, cosy and well-sustained atmosphere of horror.' *(C.A. Lejeune)*

'A film on the conventional theme of the schizophrenic killer, lifted out of its class by the imaginative quality of its visual design as well as its playing. The murderer feels impelled to destroy what is imperfect: he sees the heroine, who is dumb, as a creature without a mouth; and the audience too, looking over his shoulder at the girl's image in the mirror, sees her face fading away into a blur.' *(Dilys Powell)*

'This little horror classic . . . has all the trappings of the genre – a stormy night and a collection of psychopaths. But the psychopaths are quite presentable people, and this, plus the skillful, swift direction, makes the terror convincing.' *(Pauline Kael)*

SPIRIT OF THE PEOPLE: *see* ABE LINCOLN IN ILLINOIS.

SPLASH! CT: 7 AV: 6.47

1984 US 110 C COMEDY/FANTASY/ROMANCE

D Ron Howard ✔
W Lowell Ganz Babaloo Mandel Bruce Jay Friedman Brian Gazer ☆ AAN

Tom Hanks ☆ Daryl Hannah ✔ Eugene Levy John Candy ☆ Dody Goodman Richard B. Shull Bobby DiCicco Howard Morris

A young man (Tom Hanks) falls for a mermaid (Daryl Hannah).

One of the most charming Hollywood comedies of the 80s, with a witty and ingenious script (ground-breakingly risqué for a Disney film of this period), and funny performances by John Candy and Hanks. Hannah was not called upon to act much, but she looked gorgeous.

ANTI:

'A typically Disney subject trying to be grown up.' *(Kim Newman, MFB)*

'It's too bad the relentlessly conventional minds that made this movie couldn't have made the leap from sitcom to comedy. ' *(Roger Ebert)*

MIXED:

'The picture is frequently on the verge of being more wonderful than it is . . . more lyrical, a little wilder.' *(Pauline Kael)*

'Occasionally funny but far too long.' *(Halliwell)*

PRO:

'Howard's comedies . . . have a comfortably old-fashioned flavor . . . [*Splash!*] accomplishes the improbable with some enchanting underwater sequences, scenes that make credible the thought that Daryl Hannah might really be a mermaid . . . [It] could have been shorter, but it probably couldn't have been much sweeter. Only purists will quibble with the blissfully happy ending.' *(Janet Maslin, New York Times)*

'The comedy surprise of the year . . . a splendid performance from Tom Hanks.' *(Phillip Bergson, What's On in London)*

'Not so silly as it sounds . . . due partly to the amiable performances and partly to [its] comic invention.' *(Patrick Gibbs, Daily Telegraph)*

'There's a kind of streetwise literacy about both the script and the playing . . . A genuinely witty and amusing variant on *Miranda* with fine playing from its principals . . . The best thing the Disney studios have evinced for some time.' *(Derek Malcolm, Guardian)*

SPOORLOOS: *see* VANISHING, THE.

SPY WHO CAME IN FROM THE COLD, THE CT: 5 AV: 7.18

1965 GB 112 BW THRILLER

D Martin Ritt
W Paul Dehn Guy Trosper from John Le Carré's novel

Richard Burton ☆ AAN Claire Bloom Oskar Werner ☆ Peter Van Eyck Sam Wanamaker Rupert Davies Cyril Cusack Michael Hordern Robert Hardy Bernard Lee Beatrix Lehmann George Voskovec

Burned-out spy (Richard Burton) has to masquerade as a drunk on his final assignment.

This bleak, pessimistic story, wonderfully photographed by Oswald Morris, had more realism than spy thriller audiences were prepared for in the Bond-dominated mid-60s, and it wasn't a hit. By this stage in Burton's life, masquerading as a seedy drunk was not exactly difficult; it was a lot harder for him to masquerade as anything else. Even so, this is probably his finest screen performance.

'Achieves solid impact via emphasis on human values, total absence of mechanical spy gimmickry, and perfectly controlled underplaying.' *(Variety)*

'The film makes you believe it could have happened. And that's the remarkable thing.' *(Bosley Crowther)*

'Here for once is a spy film where the plotting is

involved, but never rum . . . Nothing is superfluous . . . Burton abandons the winking nostril and the florid stare, and gathers himself for a performance whose concentration and discretion are a real surprise from an actor whose style on the screen has always looked like an orgy of dispersal . . . but the story is the star.' *(Robert Robinson, Sunday Telegraph)*

'Director Martin Ritt has fashioned a moody and desolate film to match his hero and gives us a stark and embittered portrait of a frozen, perfidious world.' *(Judith Crist)*

SPY WHO LOVED ME, THE: *see BOND* SERIES.

STACHKA: *see* STRIKE.

STADT SUCHT EINEN MÖRDER, EINE: *see* M.

STAGE DOOR AAN CT: 6 AV: 8.20

1937 US 93 BW DRAMA/COMEDY

D Gregory La Cava ☆ AAN
W Morris Ryskind Anthony Veiller ☆ AAN from Edna Ferber and George S. Kaufman's play

Katharine Hepburn ☆ Ginger Rogers ☆ Adolphe Menjou ☆ Andrea Leeds ☆ AAN Ann Miller Gail Patrick Constance Collier Lucille Ball Samuel S. Hinds Jack Carson Franklin Pangborn Eve Arden

A cool debutante (Katharine Hepburn) and a hot-tempered girl from the working-class (Ginger Rogers) have to share a room in a theatrical boarding-house.

An entertainingly bitchy backstage comedy, with the two female leads striking sparks off each other, and Leeds there to add the tragic element. Gregory La Cava incorporated some of his young actresses' own improvisations and ad libs into the final script, which had already been a success on Broadway, with Margaret Sullavan in Hepburn's role. The film is enjoyable entertainment in its own right, but also has a certain sociological interest for modern audiences. And it offers a chance to spot many budding stars, such as Lucille Ball, Ann Miller and Eve Arden at the outset of their careers.

MIXED:

'*Stage Door* is already booked by half a dozen critics as a masterpiece and it is certainly a remarkably directed description of a theatrical boarding house. The fact is there is something theatrical and light weight about the whole business. Here we have the story of youth, ambition, and disillusion in the great city. Evidently someone took it seriously for there is . . . suicide and there are the antics of tragedy. I don't know, but I wouldn't say there was real pity or that the tear was genuine.' *(John Grierson, World Film News)*

PRO:

'Zest and pace and photographic eloquence . . . Wittier than the original, more dramatic than the original, more meaningful than the original, more cogent than the original.' *(Frank S. Nugent, New York Times)*

'Miss Hepburn, for all her supreme technical accomplishment . . . is acted right off the screen by Ginger Rogers whose talent for acting turns out to be as certain as the parade-ground accuracy of her twinkling feet.' *(Spectator)*

'It all makes, for those whose ears can stand the racket and detect the wit that crackles underneath it, a lively setting for Miss Hepburn and Miss Rogers. The latter is certainly the rose within this budding grove.' *(New Statesman)*

'It is a long time since we have seen so much feminine talent so deftly handled.' *(Otis Ferguson)*

'The story is a brilliant pattern of humour, sophistication, aspirations, tragedy and realism. The acting is impeccable; and the film as a whole finely balanced, acidly humorous and intensely human . . . Not to be missed.' *(Film Weekly)*

'One of the flashiest, most entertaining comedies of the 30s, even with its tremolos and touches of heartbreak.' *(Pauline Kael)*

STAGECOACH AAN CT: 9 AV: 9.53

1939 US 99 BW WESTERN

D John Ford ☆ AAN
W Dudley Nichols (Ben Hecht uncredited) from Ernest Haycox's story *Stage to Lordsburg* inspired by Guy de Maupassant's *Boule de Suif*

Claire Trevor ☆ John Wayne ☆ Thomas Mitchell ☆ AAW George Bancroft ☆ Andy Devine, Berton Churchill ☆ Louise Platt John Carradine ☆ Donald Meek ☆ Tim Holt Chris-Pin Martin

A stagecoach travels west, and falls foul of an Indian attack.

A great western, despite its unreconstructed view of Indians as savages. The climactic attack is among the most exciting ever filmed – and is all the more effective because we have come to care about the characters, all of them beautifully written and acted.

Stagecoach made a star of John Wayne, who had been languishing in B-features; it established Monument Valley in Utah as the classic western location; and it made John Ford the foremost director in this genre – prior to this, he had not directed a western for 13 years.

The New York Film Critics voted Ford Best Director; but credit should also go to cinematographer Bert Glennon, art director Alexander Toluboff, and editor Dorothy Spencer, all of them Oscar-nominated. The Academy Award-winning music (by Richard Hegeman, W. Franke Harling, John Leipold, Leo Shuken and Louis Gruenberg) also played an important role in making this film a classic.

ANTI:

'When placed within the context of Ford's body of work and judged by that high standard, the film does not measure up . . . The dramatic contrivance characteristic of *Stagecoach* is rigidly based on the A-B structural scheme – scenes of action alternating with scenes of character interaction until four scenes of each have been played out . . . Everything we know about each character we know for a reason, and the reason exists only for the purpose of the whole script. There is little that is mysterious, ambiguous, complex, or intriguing about any of the characters – each exists primarily as a foil for the others.' *(J.A. Place, The Western Films of John Ford, 1973)*

PRO:

'Acting, direction, conception of the story, musical score – all are excellent . . . Subtle touches . . . raise the film from an ordinary thrilling adventure to something greater . . . The ending tends to be a little slow, but the fact that it is not a complete anti-climax after so exciting and moving a beginning is a great achievement.' *(MFB)*

'A solid and soundly satisfying demonstration of the virtue inherent in the entertainment-for-entertainment's-sake policy of film production . . . Gripping in universal appeal, spectacular in photographic beauty.' *(Motion Picture Herald)*

'Ford is the screen's romantic and in *Stagecoach* he can sing its song to that 19th-century American faith. For at least three quarters of its length [it] is as well-photographed, well-scored, and as well cut as any film made since the coming of sound.' *(J.A. Wilson)*

'A great film – the kind that gets it into the movie history books.' *(A. Jympson Harman, Evening News)*

'One of the most exciting Westerns I have seen for years . . . exciting not simply because it tells a story of a wild journey across the Apache country, but because every point in the story is emphasized by brilliant pictorial effects . . . When the Indians ride out to attack the coach it is as if the desert itself had sprung to life.' *(Dilys Powell)*

'John Ford has swept aside ten years of artifice and talkie compromise and has made a motion picture that sings a song of camera. Mr Ford is not one of your subtle directors, suspending sequences on the wink of an eye or the precisely calculated gleam of a candle in a mirror. He prefers the broadest canvas, the brightest colors, the wildest brush and the boldest possible strokes. He hews to the straight narrative line with the well-reasoned confidence of a man who has seen that narrative succeed before. He takes no shadings from his characters: either they play it straight or they don't play at all. He likes his language simple and he doesn't want too much of it. When his Redskins bite the dust, he expects to hear the thud and see the dirt spurt up. Above all, he likes to have things happen out in the open, where his camera can keep them in view.' *(Frank S. Nugent, New York Times)*

'The coach itself becomes Ford's metaphor for civilized society . . . a machine built by civilized hands . . . The key dramatic conflict is between the humanness of the coach society and the savagery of the Apaches.' *(Gerald Mast, A Short History of the Movies, 1971)*

'The basic western, a template for everything that followed.' *(John Baxter, 1968)*

'Perhaps the most likable of all westerns, and a Grand Hotel-on-wheels movie that has just about everything – adventure, romance, chivalry – and all of it very simple and traditional.' *(Pauline Kael, 1975)*

STAIRWAY TO HEAVEN: *see* A MATTER OF LIFE AND DEATH.

STALAG 17 CT: 8 AV: 8.38

1953 US 119 BW WAR/COMEDY/DRAMA

D Billy Wilder ☆ AAN
W Billy Wilder Edwin Blum ☆ from Donald Bevan and Edmund Trczinski's play

William Holden ☆ AAW Don Taylor Otto Preminger ✔ Robert Strauss ☆ AAN Harvey Lembeck Richard Erdman Peter Graves Neville Brand Sig Rumann

Lusty, boisterous American prisoners-of-war suspect a traitor in their midst; suspicion falls on a loner (William Holden).

A black comedy with melodramatic overtones, *Stalag 17* baffled some British reviewers but was very well received in America, both critically and commercially. William Holden showed a power that hadn't been apparent in his performances before, and was well supported by a fine array of character actors. Otto Preminger is especially memorable as the gloatingly sadistic Kommandant, a role for which many who had been directed by him felt he was ideally suited. Ernest Laszlo's photography and Franz Waxman's score are outstanding.

ANTI:

'About as good as the play. The authors have never made up their minds whether it is a comedy or drama. I could not raise a smile.' *(A. Russell, Reynolds News)*

'Extraordinary and not in the least successful . . . [It] lacks all semblance of reality . . . Every taste is catered for but no palate satisfied, even the moments of tension and excitement having an artificial tang to them. No, this is a film which, unless the feet give out completely in the Haymarket, can well be missed.' *(Virginia Graham, Spectator)*

'It is supposed to be a rough comedy with dramatic moments. I just found it rough.' *(Leonard Mosley, Daily Express)*

'Proves once again that it is more than the Atlantic that divides the United States from Britain. It is a sense of humour.' *(Harry Deans, Sunday Dispatch)*

MIXED:

'There is a certain amount of tension in the play as Billy Wilder presents it. But a play it remains, with creaking stage devices and almost no movement.' *(Thomas Spencer, Daily Worker)*

'There is a great deal of heavy-handed high spirits, an excellent performance from Otto Preminger . . . and a few moments of passable thrills.' *(Sunday Graphic)*

PRO:

'The finest comedy drama out of Hollywood this year. Raucous and tense, heartless and sentimental, always fast-paced, it has already been assigned by critics to places on their lists of the year's best ten movies.' *(Life)*

'A lusty comedy-melodrama, loaded with bold, masculine humor and as much of the original's uninhibited earthiness as good taste and the Production Code will permit.' *(Variety)*

'Both hilarious and deadly serious, a delightful mixture of gags and gallantry, thanks to Billy Wilder's touch in screenplay and direction.' *(Judith Crist)*

STAR! CT: 7 AV: 5.89

(aka *Those Were the Happy Times*)

1968 US 194 C MUSICAL/BIOPIC

D Robert Wise ☆
W William Fairchild

Julie Andrews ✔ Richard Crenna Michael Craig Daniel Massey ☆ AAN Bruce Forsyth Beryl Reid Jenny Agutter

The life of theatrical star Gertrude Lawrence, psychological warts and all.

A rewarding study not just of the star, but of a vanished theatrical era. Julie Andrews is excellent in the musical numbers (rather better than Miss Lawrence used to be, in fact), but struggles in the dramatic scenes. Daniel Massey steals the picture with a remarkable performance as Noel Coward. Despite its many assets, including Michael Kidd's witty choreography, the film was a box office flop (it cost $14 million, and made only 4). Presumably Julie Andrews's public really wanted to see her in another *Sound of Music*. Ernest Laszlo's cinematography, Lennie Hayton's musical direction, Costume Design, Art Direction, Sound and the title song were all Oscar-nominated.

'A big financial failure because Julie Andrews was not playing a governess, she was a real-life woman who drank and swore and had a sex drive. Yet the leading man was her gay friend, and her husbands were minor characters, and she spent all her time quarrelling with them. Mostly, it was about her lavish lifestyle, with marvellous songs thrown in, and lots of close-ups of Julie Andrews in costume. It was a wonderfully tuneful flop.' *(Daniel Massey, co-star)*

'What went wrong with *Star*? . . . It had too many musical numbers and we didn't get Gertie Lawrence's character enough on screen. The numbers were great but there was not enough development of Gertie herself. It was hard to capture her. Too bad, because there was a lot of good work, and I know that Julie was disappointed.' *(Robert Wise, director)*

ANTI:

'Deals in types rather than people, romances rather than loves. It is always at a documentary distance from its subject and her world.' *(Richard Schickel, Life)*

'Julie Andrews fans will certainly rave. Gertrude Lawrence fans will probably cavil. Personally, being not one nor the other, I find that [it] leaves me cold . . . Like Andrews' performance, it is careful, tasteful, mechanically efficient.' *(Tom Milne, Observer)*

'Miss Andrews has many more gifts than Gertie – but she hasn't got the magic.' *(Robert Ottaway, Daily Sketch)*

'Miss Andrews . . . is not at her best . . . There is some sort of clash between her special niceness and innocence and the attitude that the film . . . has toward [Gertrude Lawrence . . . who is] portrayed as a kind of monster, with none of the crispness or glamour or wit that would have given her ambition style.' *(Renata Adler, New York Times)*

'Julie Andrews lacks the insolent confidence and the elusive, magical sophistication that can make mannerisms into style; she's pert and cheerful in some professional way that is finally cheerless. Trying for glamour, she merely coarsens her shining, nice-girl image, becoming a nasty girl guide.' *(Pauline Kael)*

MIXED:

'A fairly straightforward account . . . [which] is most successful when Miss Andrews . . . sings.' *(David Nathan, Sun)*

'Elephantiasis finally ruins this patient, detached, generally likeable recreation of a past theatrical era.' *(Halliwell)*

PRO:

'A pleasing tribute.' *(Variety)*

'A spectacular victory for . . . Wise and Julie Andrews . . . Maybe she's more Julie than Gertie, but she's pure exuberant entertainment and her sense of comedy has never been more usefully – or energetically – employed . . . Really a delectable show!' *(Margaret Hinxman, Sunday Telegraph)*

STAR IS BORN, A AAN CT: 7 AV: 7.64

1937 US 111 C DRAMA/ROMANCE

D William A. Wellman ☆ AAN
W Dorothy Parker Alan Campbell Robert Carson ☆ AAN from William A. Wellman's story AAW based on the film *What Price Hollywood?* (1932)

Janet Gaynor ☆ AAN Fredric March ☆ AAN Adolphe Menjou ☆ Lionel Stander ☆ May Robson Franklin Pangborn Owen Moore Andy Devine

Upwardly mobile starlet (Janet Gaynor) marries downwardly-mobile star (Fredric March).

Janet Gaynor, 31 years old and unflatteringly photographed, looks a little mature to be a starlet, but gives probably her best screen performance. Fredric March also acquits himself well. But Wellman seems uninspired by the story; despite lavish production, this film is no match for the later Cukor version. Even so, it was a big success, and was voted Number 4 on *The Film Daily* annual poll of US film critics. W. Howard Greene won a special Academy Award for his colour cinematography.

PRO:

'A good picture and the first color job that gets close to what screen color must eventually come to: it keeps the thing in its place, underlining the mood and situation of the story rather than dimming everything else out in an iridescent razzle-dazzle.' *(Otis Ferguson)*

'This story which is sometimes bitingly satirical and at other times screamingly funny, shows Hollywood film people as they really are . . . The film is so devastatingly true, so full of beauty and ugliness, that it will shock every film-fan in the world into a new sympathy for the film-famous.' *(Walter Wyndham, Daily Mail)*

'One of those rare ones which everyone will want to see and talk about . . . Disproves the tradition that good pictures can't be made with a Hollywood background.' *(Variety)*

MIXED:

'The detail of the acting "business" is particularly good, and the film is finely directed. The less said about its story of rising and waning star values, and all the vanities and ambitions which are the life stream of Hollywood, the better.' *(John Grierson, World Film News)*

'[Fredric March] is so good that the film is thrown out of balance so far as its title is concerned. At least I found myself more sorry to see the falling star than happy to see the rising star.' *(Seton Margrave, Daily Mail)*

ANTI:

'Peculiarly masochistic and self-congratulatory.' *(Pauline Kael)*

STAR IS BORN, A CT: 10 AV: 9.13

1954 US 154/181 C MUSICAL/ROMANCE

D George Cukor ☆
W Moss Hart

Judy Garland ☆ AAN James Mason ☆ AAN Charles Bickford ✔ Jack Carson ✔ Tommy Noonan Amanda Blake Lucy Marlow

Upwardly mobile starlet (Judy Garland) marries downwardly-mobile star (James Mason).

A myth has grown up that *A Star is Born* was reviewed negatively on release; in reality, the original three-hour version won director Cukor the best American reviews of his career. Despite these, the Warner Brothers sales and exhibition hierarchy insisted on 27 minutes of cuts and destroyed all existing prints and the original negative before it went on general release. They took an axe to the movie, Cukor complained, years later, and he never spoke to the editor, Folmar Blangsted, again.

Even the 154-minute version succeeds as a musical, a tearjerker and a depiction of Hollywood fame. The two central performances proved unspoilable. In 1983, however, film historian Ron Haver reconstructed a 181-minute version approximating to Cukor's original, and that is a masterpiece. The recording-studio proposal scene between Mason and Garland is so charming that it should never have been lost; while the re-inclusion of a cut number 'Lose That Long Face' makes Garland's feelings about the decline of her husband more touching. This is among the most moving of all screen musicals, and one of the best integrations of songs with drama. Musical director Ray Heindorf, art directors Malcolm Bert, Gene Allen and Irene Sharaff, and the song 'The Man That Got Away' (music by Harold Arlen, lyrics by Ira Gershwin) were all Oscar-nominated.

ANTI:

'[Although] Hollywood's Number One Problem Girl . . . will earn cheers . . . for the most astonishing comeback in cinema history . . . the grand-mannered tragedienne just doesn't ring true.' *(Harold Conway, Daily Sketch)*

'The sets are dreadful and Miss Garland is made up in such a startling way that her eyes seem about to take off from their sockets and her lips, which are by nature too prominent, are nearly always a shrill vermilion. In the few moments when she is not painted in this bizarre manner, she looks quite middle-aged, the lower half of her face full and heavy as though she were a lesser member of the

British royal family.' *(Quentin Crisp, Christopher Street, on the longer version, 1983)*

'*A Star Is Born* always seemed to me overlong at two and a half hours, and at three it begins to look not so much slow as totally stopped.' *(Sheridan Morley, The Times, on the longer version, 1983)*

'Wellman's *A Star is Born* is a much better picture because it tells the story more simply and correctly, because really the emphasis should be on the man rather than the girl. It's more his story.' *(James Mason)*

'The numbers add very little except length.' *(Halliwell)*

MIXED:

'It boasts a couple of never-say-die troupers in Judy Garland and James Mason. They manage to make some sense of it here and there.' *(New York Herald Tribune)*

'Mr Cukor's direction gets off to a brilliant start, with a rich confusion involving Norman's semi-drunkenness, but at times it wanders into obviousness and prolixity.' *(The Times)*

'It is the warm, virile, stimulating recovery of Judy Garland that makes the picture one of the finest musical dramas since talkies came in. She sings in a variety of moods with the precision of a great artist And she acts beautifully as well – much better than she has ever done before. Only in her two biggest tragic moments does she find the task just beyond her.' *(Jympson Harman, Evening News)*

'Clever satire of Hollywood, not as sharp as it was in the original, but sharp enough to be stimulating fun.' *(Bosley Crowther)*

'A Garland for Judy . . . Her personality dominates the long, lavish picture . . . But . . . the film itself . . . is no great shakes.' *(Thomas Spencer, Daily Worker)*

'A terrible, fascinating orgy of self-pity and cynicism and mythmaking. Garland's jagged, tremulous performance is nakedly intense . . . George Hoyningen-Huen served as color consultant, and the strikingly sumptuous color design gives the film deep, neurotic, emotional tones.' *(Pauline Kael)*

PRO:

'A socko candidate for anyone's must-see list.' *(Variety)*

'A brilliantly staged, scored and photographed film, worth all the effort.' *(Life)*

'The greatest one-woman show on earth.' *(Look)*

'The entire success of the picture depends on the fact that Judy really has it. One scene ranks with the finest screen acting jobs of all time.' *(Hollywood Reporter)*

'As the loving wife of a chronic drunk she gives the loveliest performance I have ever seen on stage or screen. Judy Garland will naturally get the greater praise, for hers is the sympathetic role. But without Mason's incisive playing there would have been nothing to wring our hearts.' *(Evening Standard)*

'Bigger, broader and better in every way than its hallowed predecessor . . . [it] becomes a stupendous, if somewhat exhausting, achievement. Miss Garland has made this . . . a tremendous personal triumph.. Judy carries the show with her – and is the show . . . [The film] is the essence of showmanship: it has laughs, tears, tunes and triumphs, color and excitement, comedy, drama, slapstick and spectacle.' *(Jesse Zunser, Cue)*

'Maintains a skilful balance between the musical and the tearjerker.' *(Penelope Houston)*

'Fresh, exciting, touching and alive . . . By far the best of all the films about life behind the cameras, the lights, the wind-machines, and the cocktail bars of Hollywood . . . [Garland] displays an extraordinary maturing of her talents . . . Pathos she always had; but today the pathos has deepened, and her acting has a nervous tension which, when I saw the film, held the house silent and tear-stained. And her playing is beautifully contrasted with that of Mr Mason, who as the declining star gives a performance of great charm and authority. *A Star Is Born* is a rocket: going off with a bang and a scream, slowing for a moment at the height of its trajectory while we wonder if it will fail to explode, then bursting in the dark into tearful sparkles. It strikes me as a film which in ten years' time will still be talked of.' *(Dilys Powell)*

'Judy . . . deserves an Oscar.' *(Jympson Harman, Evening News)*

'The biggest robbery since Brinks.' *(Groucho Marx, when Garland lost the Best Actress Oscar to Grace Kelly)*

'[In the 3-hour version] Cukor's film gains mainly from a smoother narrative flow. As a result, Judy Garland's marvellous performance acquires extra dynamism and James Mason's an added depth.' *(Cecil Wilson, Mail on Sunday)*

STAR IS BORN, A — CT: 5 AV: 4.20

1976 US 140 C MUSICAL/SO BAD

D Frank Pierson
W John Gregory Dunne Joan Didion Frank Pierson

Barbra Streisand Kris Kristofferson Paul Mazursky Gary Busey, Oliver Clark Marta Heflin

Remake, ill-advisedly set in the rock world.

Savaged by the critics, but oddly enjoyable if you're in the mood for wallowing in sentiment or giggling at the star's outrageous histrionics – and she certainly can sing. 'Evergreen' won an Oscar; also nominated were Robert Surtees (photography) and Roger Kellaway (music underscoring).

'A bore is starred.' *(Village Voice)*

'Streisand's notion of acting is to bulldoze her way from one end of a line to the other without regard for anyone or anything; you can literally feel her impatience for the other performer to stop talking so she can take over again. If dialogue there is, it is that between a steamroller and the asphalt beneath it . . . And then I realize with a gasp that this Barbra Streisand is in fact beloved above all other female stars by our moviegoing audiences; that this hypertrophic ego and bloated countenance are things people shell out money for as for no other actress; that this progressively more belligerent caterwauling can sell anything concerts, records, movies. And I feel as if our entire society were ready to flush itself down in something even worse than a collective death wish a collective will to live in ugliness and self-debasement.' *(John Simon)*

'The film looks very like an ego-trip for a superstar.' *(Margaret Hinxman)*

'A clear case for the Monopolies Commission.' *(Michael Billington, Illustrated London News)*

'Updating and transposing the story-line from Hollywood to the rock world was a grave mistake; the plot's hackneyed pattern of intertwined careers . . . simply does not suit the unglamorous world of monster open-air concerts, thunderous decibels, drugs and groupies . . . The present script is distinguished only by large amounts of foul language and even larger amounts of addled sentimentality.' *(Geoff Brown, MFB)*

THE *STAR TREK* SERIES

STAR TREK: THE MOTION PICTURE

CT: 4 AV: 4.58

1979 US 132 (143: TV/video versions) C SF/FAMILY/ADVENTURE

D Robert Wise
W Harold Livingstone Gene Roddenberry based on Alan Dean Foster's story

William Shatner Leonard Nimoy DeForest Kelley James Doohan Persis Khambatta George Takei Nichelle Nichols

The Starship Enterprise is taken prematurely out of dry dock to intercept hostile aliens.

Spectacular but ponderous cinema spin-off from the cult TV series. The film divided the critics about evenly between those who admired its special effects and those who found it boring and overlong. Audiences flocked to it, and it grossed more than $56 million. Academy Award nominations went to Jerry Goldsmith (music), Douglas Trumbull, John Dykstra, Richard Yuricich, Robert Swarthe, Dave Stewart and Grant McCune (visual effects), and Harold Michelson, Joe Jennings, Leon Harris, John Vallone, and Linda DeScenna (art direction).

ANTI:

'A long day's journey into ennui.' *(Time)*

'The film is about a century too long and will be best appreciated by those who like colourful lighting displays, loud music and bald women.' *(Daily Mirror)*

MIXED:

'The smart plot and effects go some way towards compensating for the plastic characters and costumes.' *(David Pirie, Time Out)*

'The special effects are marvellous but the mumbo-jumbo that passes for dialogue only adds to the tedium.' *(News of the World)*

PRO:

'One of the screen's finest science-fiction achievements.' *(MFB)*

'An extravaganza of futuristic electronic photo-effects and kaleidoscopic sci-fi wizardry.' *(Sunday People)*

'A superb piece of work . . . It benefits from a clever basic premise, a taut script and excellent special effects, impeccably integrated into the movie without self-congratulation by director Robert Wise.' *(Alan Frank)*

'Includes all of the ingredients the TV show's fans thrive on: the philosophical dilemma wrapped in a scenario of mind control, troubles with the space ship, the dependable and understanding Kirk, the ever-logical Spock, and suspenseful take with twist ending.' *(Variety)*

'A very well-made piece of work, with an interesting premise . . . Some of the early reviews seemed pretty blasé, as if the critics didn't allow themselves to relish the film before racing out to pigeonhole it. My inclination, as I slid down in my seat and the stereo sound surrounded me, was to relax and let the movie give me a good time. I did and it did.' *(Roger Ebert)*

STAR TREK II: THE WRATH OF KHAN

CT: 6 AV: 5.69

1982 US 113 C SF/FAMILY/ADVENTURE

D Nicholas Meyer ☆
W Jack B. Sowards ✔ based on Sowards and Harve Bennett's story

William Shatner Leonard Nimoy DeForest Kelley James Doohan George Takei Walter Koenig Nichelle Nichols Bibi Besch Kirstie Alley Ricardo Montalban

Evil alien (Ricardo Montalban) swears vengeance on Captain Kirk (William Shatner).

Plenty of tongue-in-cheek amusement here, and a great improvement on the first *Star Trek* movie. It also did well at the box office, grossing $46 million.

ANTI:

'The net effect, between embarrassed guffaws, is incredulity: a movie at once post-TV and pre-D.W. Griffith.' *(Paul Taylor, Time Out)*

'A pitiful snack for the eyes with some unappetizing crumbs left over for the mind to chew on.' *(Philip Strick, MFB)*

MIXED:

'A long way from the controlled intelligence of some episodes of the TV series; but more entertaining than the first movie.' *(Halliwell)*

PRO:

'Wonderful dumb fun. The director, Nicholas Meyer, hits just the right amused, slightly self-mocking note . . . Montalban plays his fiery villainy to the hilt, smiling grimly as he does the dirty; his bravado is grandly comic.' *(Pauline Kael)*

'Khan is played as a cauldron of resentment by Ricardo Montalban, and his performance is so strong that he helps illustrate a general principle involving not only *Star Trek* but *Star Wars* and all the epic serials, especially the James Bond movies: each film is only as good as its villain.' *(Roger Ebert)*

'A very satisfying space adventure, closer to the spirit and format of the popular TV series than its big-budget predecessor . . . . Final reel is a classic of emotional manipulation.' *(Variety)*

STAR TREK III: THE SEARCH FOR SPOCK

CT: 4 AV: 5.31

1984 US 105 C SF/FAMILY/ADVENTURE

D Leonard Nimoy ●
W Harve Bennett ●

William Shatner Leonard Nimoy DeForest Kelley James Doohan George Takei Walter Koenig Nichelle Nichols Robin Curtis

The crew of the Enterprise travels to Vulcan to try and bring Spock (Leonard Nimoy) back to life.

A direct chronological sequel to *Star Trek II*, but in terms of quality not in the same universe. The critics were dismissive.

'A morose, darkly unilluminated film with none of the fun usually associated with the series characters. Even more disturbing is the fact the multi-tiered climax of the film – the defeat of the Klingons, the escape from the planet and its destruction – does not come at the film's finale. Instead, the audience is subjected to the tedious ceremony of Spock's resurrection in an incredibly incomprehensible sequence.' *(Parish & Pitts, The Great Science Fiction Pictures II)*

'Too much talk, bad acting and Vulcan mysticism. Not enough action, humour or plot.' *(Rose)*

'Very silly, empty and unamusing.' *(Halliwell)*

'Achingly prosaic.' *(Pauline Kael)*

STAR TREK IV: THE VOYAGE HOME

CT: 6 AV: 6.71

(aka *The Voyage Home*)

1986 US 119 C SF/FAMILY/ADVENTURE

D Leonard Nimoy ☆
W Harve Bennett Steve Meerson Peter Krikes Nicholas Meyer ✓

William Shatner Leonard Nimoy DeForest Kelley James Doohan George Takei Walter Koenig Nichelle Nichols Jane Wyatt Catherine Hicks

Captain Kirk saves Planet Earth in the 23rd century by importing whales from the 20th.

Likeable nonsense with more humour and gentle satire than usual. It grossed over $109 million, and was Oscar-nominated for cinematography (Don Peterman), score (Leonard Rosenman), sound (Terry Porter, Dave Hudson, Mel Metcalfe, Gene S. Cantamessa) and sound effects editing (Mark Mangini).

MIXED:

'It has an irresistibly sure touch, an easy command of its audience . . . It's reminiscent of an old trouper – Chevalier, Hope or Crosby in their later years. Short of wind, it captures us with a wink or a word, a nudge on our mutual memory banks.' *(Michael Wilmington, LA Times)*

'Some of the kidding around is fairly genial.' *(Pauline Kael)*

PRO:

'Warmer, wittier, more socially relevant and truer to its TV origins than prior odysseys.' *(Variety)*

'Easily the most absurd of the *Star Trek* stories – and yet, oddly enough, it is also the best, the funniest, and the most enjoyable in simple human terms. I'm relieved that nothing like restraint or common sense stood in their way.' *(Roger Ebert)*

'Best of the series: it isn't saying much, but at least there are shreds of wit in the script.' *(Halliwell)*

STAR TREK V: THE FINAL FRONTIER

CT: 4 AV: 4.08

1989 US 102/107 C SF/FAMILY/ADVENTURE

D William Shatner ●
W David Loughery ● from William Shatner's story

William Shatner ● Leonard Nimoy DeForest Kelley ● James Doohan ● Walter Koenig, Nichelle Nichols George Takei, David Warner

The Starship Enterprise's quest is for Heaven; but it would have done better to boldly go in search of a decent screenplay.

Tired and tedious, flaccidly directed by William

(Captain Kirk) Shatner. Lieutenant Uhura's dance of the seven veils might pass muster in a glamorous granny competition, but is embarrassing in any other context. Several other members of the cast look and act as though semi-embalmed by a negligent mortician.

'Even diehard Trekkies may be disappointed by *Star Trek V*.' *(Variety)*

'The plot, about a quest for the Ultimate Answer, resembles something that Douglas Adams would have thrown in the bin.' *(Mark Kermode, Time Out)*

'There is no clear line from the beginning of the movie to the end, not much danger, no characters to really care about, little suspense, uninteresting or incomprehensible villains, and a great deal of small-talk and pointless dead ends. Of all of the *Star Trek* movies, this is the worst.' *(Roger Ebert)*

'Jaw-dropping in its ghastliness . . . With a rubbishy script, a cast who are well past their sell-by stardate and some remarkably ugly visuals, this is the least appetizing sci-fi spectacular since *The Black Hole*.' *(Kim Newman, Film Yearbook)*

'If you thought Shatner was a bad actor, wait till you see him direct.' *(Rose)*

STAR TREK VI: THE UNDISCOVERED COUNTRY

CT: 8 AV: 7.33

1991 US 110 C SF/FAMILY/ADVENTURE

D Nicholas Meyer ✔
W Nicholas Meyer Denny Martin Flinn ✔

William Shatner Leonard Nimoy DeForest Kelley James Doohan Walter Koenig Nichelle Nichols George Takei Kim Cattral David Warner Christopher Plummer (cameo Christian Slater)

Captain Kirk (William Shatner) is blamed when persons unknown blast leading Klingons into small red globules.

Best of the *Star Trek* movies, and a fitting finale to the series. As usual, there is a philosophical content: the 'undiscovered country' of the title is not a planet but the future. *Star Trek VI* neatly spoofs the notion that the thawing of a cold war means the end of history. But basically this is a first-rate action movie with impressive special effects, ably directed by Nicholas Meyer (who also directed *Star Trek II*). There are some of the seediest-looking aliens since the bar-room scene in *Star Wars*, and the dialogue and ideas are consistently witty. Even if you're not normally a *Star Trek* fan, you'll enjoy this one. A few critics didn't appreciate that it was any different from some of its less inspired predecessors; most, however, appreciated its strengths.

ANTI:

'A lumbering and self-indulgent picture, dragged down at every turn by the weight of twenty-five years of illogical mediocrity, as if the series, notional science-fiction aspects pre-empted the need for characters, stories or a universe that made any dramatic sense.' *(Kim Newman, S & S)*

'[It is] weighed down by a midsection even flabbier than the long-in-the-tooth cast . . . The murder is a rather tepid mystery and the ice planet to which Kirk and McCoy travel feels like a pale imitation of the *Star Wars* films.' *(Variety)*

'Enterprise crew that looks ever more ready for intergalactic rocking chairs.' *(Janet Maslin, New York Times)*

PRO:

'Hiro Narita's photography is breathtaking, and the script by the director and Denny Martin Flinn is filled with wit and polish.' *(Scheuer)*

'The crew of the Enterprise boldly push their Zimmer frames where no man has pushed them before. Despite looking as if they should be travelling on senior citizen passes, this is one of the best of the bunch . . . A rattling good yarn is enlivened by plenty of thrills, lots of cod Shakespearean references and some delightful deadpan humour.' *(Rose)*

THE *STAR WARS* SERIES

STAR WARS AAN

CT: 9 AV: 8.18

1977 US 121 C SF/ADVENTURE/FAMILY

D George Lucas ☆ AAN
W George Lucas ☆ AAN

Mark Hamill Harrison Ford ☆ Carrie Fisher Alec Guinness AAN Peter Cushing Peter Mayhew (Chewbacca) Anthony Daniels (C-3PO) Kenny Baker (R2-D2) David Prowse (as Darth Vader, with voice redubbed by James Earl Jones).

Young man (Mark Hamill) saves galaxy and princess (Carrie Fisher) with help of assorted humans, aliens and robots.

One of the most profitable movies of all time, *Star Wars* cost $10 million but grossed over $193 million. It was a landmark in cinema – the first big hit to use computer animation; the first successful SF blockbuster since *2001: A Space Odyssey*; and its huge success sparked a revived interest in making films with a strong narrative.

The critics main accusations on release were that *Star Wars* was soulless, characterless and pointless. Many found the film's attempts at mysticism pretentious, despite Alec Guinness's valiant efforts to breathe life into the grand old man Ben Kenobi. Some pointed out George Lucas's cavalier approach to science: the film wrongly suggests you can hear explosions in space, refers to parsec as a unit of time rather than distance, and commits other errors which audiences will have found unimportant. Some criticized it for being a compendium of other people's ideas; others found its eclecticism part of its charm.

Worst aspects are the adequate but colourless performances by Hamill and Fisher, and a few draggy moments with Ben Kenobi. Best aspects are the many enjoyable comic touches in the bar-room scene, the byplay between the robots, and Harrison Ford's wry performance as the guy who doesn't get the girl. John Williams's score is glorious. The shoot-em-up finale excitingly anticipates the growth of computer games in the 80s. Most of all, the film benefits from a well-structured, dynamically paced narrative with a refreshingly straightforward sense of right and wrong.

The orthodoxy expressed by critic Roger Ebert and most others nostalgic for the American cinema of the 70s is that movies like *Star Wars* led to the eclipse of more personal films. But in their way the movies of Lucas, Spielberg and others are just as personally revealing as films where directors are obviously trying to deliver a message. And it was the fillip they gave to more narrative-based film which reinvigorated audience interest in the cinema, and led to the big hits (and good films) of the 1980s and 1990s. It was the work of Lucas and Spielberg in *Star Wars* and the like, which arrested cinemas apparently inexorable decline into being a minority interest. They saved it, in short, from being of interest only to critics.

The film won Oscars for its score (John Williams), art direction (Jonathan Barry, Norman Reynolds, Leslie Dilley, Roger Christian), costume design (John Mollo), sound (Don MacDougall, Ray West, Bob Minkler, Derek Ball), editing (Marcia Lucas, Paul Hirsch, Richard Chew) and visual effects (John Stears, John Dykstra, Richard Edlund, Grant McCune, Robert Blalack).

ANTI:

'O dull new world! . . . It is all as exciting as last year's weather reports . . . It is all trite characters and paltry verbiage, handled adequately by Harrison Ford as a blockade-running starship pilot, uninspiredly by Mark Hamill as Luke Skywalker . . . and wretchedly by Carrie Fisher, who is not even appealing as Princess Leia . . . Sir Alec has a wistful yet weighty dignity of tone and aspect that is all his own; why he should waste it on the likes of Luke, whom he befriends, protects, and bequeaths the Force to, remains the film's one mystery.' *(John Simon)*

'Mr Guinness made a valiant attempt to bestow upon the movie a saintly, El Greco halo, but the story remained paralyzingly monotonous. I longed for its incessant, violent motion to cease.' *(Quentin Crisp, Christopher Street)*

'The parodies of many old movies . . . [are] done without wit or skill.' *(David Shipman)*

MIXED:

'This is Lucas's tribute to *Flash Gordon*, and is now enthralling all those who feel that *Flash Gordon* needs a two-hour, eight million dollar tribute.' *(Stanley Kauffmann)*

'Hollywood began in an amusement arcade, so it's appropriate that it's most profitable film should be as formally enchanting and psychologically sterile as a Gottlieb pinball machine.' *(David Pirie, Time Out)*

'There's no breather in the picture, no lyricism; the only attempt at beauty is in the double sunset. It's enjoyable on its own terms, but it's exhausting too; like taking a pack of kids to the circus. An hour into it, children say that they're ready to see it all over again; that's because it's an assemblage of spare parts – it has no emotional grip . . . Even if you've been entertained, you may feel cheated of some dimension – a sense of wonder, perhaps.' *(Pauline Kael)*

PRO:

'*Star Wars* will undoubtedly emerge as one of the true classics in the genre of science fiction/fantasy films. In any event, it will be thrilling audiences of all ages for a long time to come.' *(Hollywood Reporter)*

'Pure sweet fun all the way . . . [George Lucas] says it's a movie for children – what he means is that he wants to touch the child in all of us.' *(Newsweek)*

'A mind-blowing spectacle that sends the audience off into the wondrously strange world of fantasy and satisfies just about everyone's adolescent craving for a corny old-fashioned adventure movie.' *(New York Times)*

'A blazing science fiction fairy tale that will brighten the faces of filmgoers like a supernova . . . For two hours, viewers will be caught up in pure escapism as a fanciful story unfolds with a whirl of dazzling special effects.' *(Omaha World Herald)*

'This film is visually astonishing, exciting – and most of all – enormous fun. If it's escapism you're after, it's like Christmas cake with a file and rope ladder in it.' *(Daily Express)*

'It is an anthology not so much of actual scenes as of almost subconsciously recalled sensations and sentiments of the film-goer's memory. Maybe it is this more than anything that inspires such fierce loyalty in audiences. People who have already seen the film get snappishly defensive if you have the temerity to say things like "It's very silly, of course": and retort "But it's such fun". And, indeed, it is. *Star Wars* unashamedly restores all those qualities which film-makers and audiences have almost forgotten in their chase after illusory sophistication.' *(The Times)*

'He intended his film, Lucas confesses, for a generation growing up without fairy tales. His target audience was fourteen years and younger . . . It was a celebration, a social affair, a collective dream, and people came again and again, dragging their friends and families with them.' *(Les Keyser, Hollywood in the Seventies)*

'Critics found in it resonances of everything from Isaac Asimov, *Forbidden Planet*, the great science fiction comic strips and serials, *Tarzan, The Wizard of Oz, Sir Gawain and The Green Knight, The Sword in the Stone* to Errol Flynn action films and aerial war movies. And audiences revelled in its excitement, with *Star Wars* winning people over to the genre who had probably never even heard of science fiction . . . Its characters, while based on obvious stereotypes and involved in none-too-original adventures, struck a powerful chord in all those who saw them. They were both credible and likeable (and, in the case of villains Peter Cushing and David Prowse, eminently hissable), and the robots C-3PO and R2-D2 became instantly classic figures, the Laurel and Hardy of the space age.' *(Alan Frank)*

EMPIRE STRIKES BACK, THE

CT: 6 AV: 7.54

1980 US 124 C SF/ADVENTURE/FAMILY

D Irving Kershner
W Leigh Brackett Lawrence Kasdan

Mark Hamill Harrison Ford Carrie Fisher David Prowse Anthony Daniels Peter Mayhew Kenny Baker Frank Oz (as Yoda) Billy Dee Williams Alec Guinness.

Luke Skywalker (Mark Hamill) and his pals take on Darth Vader again.

Visually more polished than its predecessor, this received overwhelmingly favourable reviews (after all, it was obviously going to be a hit) and grossed over $140 million. I loved it the first time I saw it in the cinema.

Once one has admired the monsters and special effects, however, the shortcomings of plot and characterization become obvious. Re-seen (especially on the small screen) the film fails to live up to its tremendous opening sequence, getting bogged down in pretentious mysticism with the appearance of the tiresome Grand Master Yoda; and the characters don't develop in any interesting way. And the movie doesn't so much end as break off. Oscar-nominations went to John Williams (score), Norman Reynolds, Leslie Dilley, Harry Lange, Alan Tomkins and Michael Ford (art direction), Bill Varney, Steve Maslow, Gregg Landaker and Peter Sutton (sound).

ANTI:

'A lifeless copy of *Star Wars* propelled chiefly on the momentum of that earlier film.' *(Cinefantastique)*

'Malodorous offal . . . Stale, limp, desperately stretched out, and pretentious . . . Infantile is the operative word . . . This witless banality is made even less bearable by the nonacting of the principals. Harrison Ford (Han) offers loutishness for charm and becomes the epitome of the interstellar drugstore cowboy. Mark Hamill (Luke) is still the talentless Tom Sawyer of outer space – wide-eyed, narrow-minded, strait-laced. Worst of all is Carrie Fisher, whose Leia is a cosmic Shirley Temple but without the slightest acting ability or vestige of prettiness. Though still very young, she looks, without recourse to special effects, at least fifty – the film's only true, albeit depressing, miracle. It turns out, as part of the movie's barbershop Freudianizing, that Darth Vader is really Luke's father; by the time we get to the next episode, Leia may easily be his mother . . . The program lists five and a half pages of credits; it would take at least twice that space to list the debits.' *(John Simon)*

PRO:

'It is technically even more proficient, has virtually the same ingredients and bursts forth into a world that still seems ripe for its special blend of nostalgically simple story-telling and complicated technology. If George Lucas wants to go on and on . . . there seems no good reason yet why anything should stop him.' *(Guardian)*

'As the successor to *Star Wars* it is every bit as visually astounding, fast-moving, noisy, swashbuckling and unbelievable as its parent.' *(Sunday Telegraph)*

'The impact of *Star Wars* derived considerably from its spectacular and unheralded appearance: the sequel did not have the advantage of surprise and, instead, settles for a strong storyline and plenty of action recalling the heyday of the serials, and, as such, succeeds splendidly both in its own right and as the continuation of the story, of the characters introduced in the first movie. The level of invention and the special effects are as high as ever and, for once, a sequel is as enjoyable and exciting as the original.' *(Alan Frank)*

'By far the most imaginative part of the *Star Wars* trilogy. This middle, bridging film is chained to an unresolved plot and doesn't have the leaping, comic-book hedonism of the 1977 *Star Wars*, but you can feel the love of movie magic that went into its cascading imagery.' *(Pauline Kael)*

RETURN OF THE JEDI

CT: 6 AV: 6.50

1983 US 132 C SF/ADVENTURE/FAMILY

D Richard Marquand
W Lawrence Kasdan George Lucas

Mark Hamill Harrison Ford Carrie Fisher Billy Dee Williams Anthony Daniels Peter Mayhew Kenny Baker Frank Oz Sebastian Shaw Ian McDiarmid David Prowse James Earl Jones Alec Guinness

Continuation of the previous story.

Weakest of the *Star Wars* movies, because of a rambling plot and dull performances. It doesn't help that the most interesting character, Han Solo (played by the series best actor, Harrison Ford) is on the sidelines most of the time. But the memorable aliens, first-class special effects and a few fine action sequences, notably the chase through the woods, make the film just about worth seeing. Oscar nominations went to John Williams (score), Norman Reynolds, Fred Hole, James Schoppe and Michael Ford (art direction), Ben Burtt, Gary Summers, Randy Thom, Tony Dawe (sound), and Ben Burtt again (sound effects).

ANTI:

'An impersonal and rather junky piece of moviemaking . . . In *The Empire Strikes Back*, the three central figures seemed capable of real exhilaration and suffering. Here, they're back to being what they were in the first film – comic-strip characters wandering through a jokey pastiche of the Arthurian legends.' *(Pauline Kael)*

'Only the effects are special.' *(S & S)*

'Doesn't really end the trilogy as much as it brings it to a dead stop. The film . . . is by far the dimmest adventure of the lot. All the members of the old *Star Wars* gang are back doing what they've done before, but this time with a certain evident boredom.' *(New York Times)*

'Unfortunately, it conveys the sense that the machinery has already begun to wear down, and the inventiveness to wear thin . . . There's a kind of desperation about it, a feeling that Lucas and co-writer Lawrence Kasdan are simply trying to figure out what they can do next to amuse the kiddies.' *(Hollywood Reporter)*

'The problem is, fantasy films, to be truly fantastic, require an imaginative range that's beyond the reach of most filmmakers. Lucas has more of a range and a reach than most, but *Return of the Jedi* is his Waterloo. The movie is a demonstration of the limitations of a pop-comic sensibility. There's no imaginative fervor to bind it together for us. It's a myth without a vision.' *(Peter Rainer, LA Herald Examiner)*

'Hamill is not enough of a dramatic actor to carry the plot load here, especially when his partner in so many scenes is really little more than an oversized gas pump, even if splendidly voiced by James Earl Jones.' *(Variety)*

MIXED:

'I admire the exquisite skill and talent which have been poured into these films, while finding the concepts behind these gigantic video games in the sky mindlessly tedious.' *(Margaret Hinxman, Daily Mail)*

PRO:

'Fabulous entertainment for all.' *(Quinlan)*

'We encounter several unforgettable characters, including the evil Jabba the Hutt, who is a cross between a toad and the Cheshire cat; the lovable, cuddly Ewoks, the furry inhabitants of the "forest moon of Endor"; a fearsome desert monster made of sand and teeth; and hateful little ratlike creatures that scurry about the corners of the frame. And there is an admiral for the Alliance who looks like the missing link between Tyrannosaurus Rex and Charles de Gaulle . . . *Return of the Jedi* is fun, magnificent fun. The movie is a complete entertainment, a feast for the eyes and a delight for the fancy. It's a little amazing how Lucas and his associates keep topping themselves.' *(Roger Ebert)*

STARDUST MEMORIES CT: 6 AV: 5.00

1980 US 88 BW COMEDY

D Woody Allen ✔
W Woody Allen

Woody Allen Charlotte Rampling Jessica Harper Marie-Christine Barrault Tony Roberts

A film director (Woody Allen) discovers how much he hates the people who admire him.

Despite Woody Allen's disclaimers, the autobiographical nature of this movie is all too clear; and his tone often slips out of self-analysis and into self-pity. That said, it's an interesting, well-crafted movie, with many a humorous homage to Fellini. One can see why critics might not have warmed to Allen's amusing sideswipes at film buffs and other cinematic parasites. A bilious, misanthropic comedy that's due for re-evaluation. Sample line . . . Allen: 'Me, narcissistic? No, the Greek figure I identify with is Zeus.'

ANTI:

'Is it philistine to wish [Allen's] movies were funnier these days? I don't think so – they would be better movies if they were. Gifted filmmakers should be free to experiment, of course, but there comes a time when you have to realize what your limitations are, and build on your friends.' *(Peter Rainer, LA Herald-Examiner)*

'Its posturing pyrotechnics seem more the symptom of a crisis than its controlled expression.' *(Gilbert Adair, MFB)*

'When Woody Allen discovered Underlying Seriousness in *Annie Hall*, he may have gained the world, but he lost those of us who prefer, even on screen, an honest stand-up comic to a dishonest social commentator, metaphysical seeker, and existential sniveler. *Stardust Memories* merely reaffirms his strategy of having it both ways: self-aggrandizement that tries to pass for self-irony, virulent misanthropy that masquerades as amusement at the human show, artistic pretentiousness that copies major filmmakers while pretending to be good-natured pastiche.' *(John Simon)*

'Satire becomes parasitism. Allen isn't kidding

Fellini or even revering: he's saying that he wishes he were Fellini and by the very act of persistent imitation confesses that he knows he never will be.' *(Stanley Kauffmann)*

'*Stardust Memories* is a deliberate homage to *8½* . . . The major difference between the two films is that Fellini's movie was *about* a director bankrupt of new ideas, while Allen's is a movie *by* a director with no new ideas.' *(Roger Ebert)*

'Woody degrades the people who respond to his work and presents himself as their victim . . . Woody Allen has often been cruel to himself in physical terms – making himself look smaller, scrawnier, ugly. Now, he's doing it to his fans.' *(Pauline Kael)*

'What we have here falls into the category of kvetch.' *(Judith Crist)*

PRO:

'A wonderfully witty exploration of a deeply serious subject.' *(Madeleine Harmsworth, Sunday Mirror)*

'Allen . . . demonstrates it is possible to be both serious and funny at the same time . . . [The film] is occasionally confusing [but] stay with it. It is ultimately rewarding.' *(Ian Christie, Daily Express)*

'[A] sourly funny film.' *(Alexander Walker, Evening Standard)*

'Both more serious and more funny than *Manhattan*, even, and you can't get seriouser or funnier than that.' *(Gavin Millar, Listener)*

'The best film I ever did, really, was *Stardust Memories*. It was my least popular film.' *(Woody Allen)*

STARS LOOK DOWN, THE CT: 6 AV: 7.27

1939 GB 104/110 BW DRAMA

D Carol Reed ☆
W J.B. Williams A.J. Cronin ☆ from Cronin's novel

Michael Redgrave ☆ Margaret Lockwood Emlyn Williams Edward Rigby Nancy Price Allan Jeayes Cecil Parker Linden Travers

Idealistic young man (Michael Redgrave) wants to improve working conditions of the Welsh miners among whom he grew up.

Absorbing drama and a precursor of the kitchen-sink dramas of the 1960s. The pro-nationalization message might have been expressed with greater subtlety, and the domestic scenes between Redgrave and Lockwood smack of melodrama rather than truth, but the mining scenes (many shot on location in Workington) are directed with passion by Carol Reed, who was still only 33. The atmosphere is much more authentic than it was in Hollywood's *How Green Was My Valley* (1941), and Redgrave enriches the film with one of his best performances.

MIXED:

'The fundamental weakness . . . is in the character of the coal-owner – a compound of melodramatic clichés which never add up to anything better than a puppet . . . Aesthetically this film contains some of Reed's best work . . . [and] makes no compromise whatever.' *(Basil Wright, NFT Programme Notes)*

PRO:

'Thoroughly holding entertainment. The settings appear authentic, and the atmosphere . . . has been extraordinarily well caught. Skilful direction and admirable acting.' *(MFB)*

'Would merit laurels alone for a faithful and gripping treatment. But film goes for more; it is a splendid dramatic portrait of those who burrow for the black diamond in England's northland. Direction is of class standing and picture is mounted with exactness of detail and technique.' *(Variety)*

'A very good film – I doubt whether in England we have ever produced a better . . . We are aware of direction which is every bit as good as Pabst's [in *Kameradschaft*].' *(Graham Greene, Spectator)*

STATE OF THE UNION CT: 6 AV: 7.40

(aka *The World and His Wife*)

1948 US 110 BW COMEDY

D Frank Capra ☆
W Anthony Veiller Myles Connolly from Howard Lindsay and Russel Crouse's play

Spencer Tracy ☆ Katharine Hepburn ☆ Adolphe Menjou ☆ Van Johnson ☆ Angela Lansbury ✓ Lewis Stone Raymond Walburn

Backed by an ambitious millionairess (Angela Lansbury), an airplane manufacturer (Spencer Tracy) becomes a Presidential candidate and starts to lose his integrity, but he is brought down to earth by his wife (Katharine Hepburn).

Mildly satirical, political comedy, cleverly constructed and expertly played – although not even Hepburn can do much with the role of Tracy's priggish wife, and some dialogue scenes seem to last for ever. The villains (Menjou and Lansbury) have, and are, the most fun. The corny, populist ending is Capra at his corniest. Needless to say, the cold war references have dated terribly.

PRO:

'A triumphant film, marked all over by Frank Capra's mastery.' *(Howard Barnes, New York Herald Tribune)*

'A truly excellent film.' *(Elspeth Grant, Graphic)*

'Huge fun.' *(Daily Herald)*

MIXED:

'Some very witty lines . . . make up for a great deal of the adolescent political background.' *(Evening Standard)*

'The tritely sentimental end does not quite succeed

in spoiling the rest of the film.' *(Manchester Guardian)*

'Powerfully acted by Tracy and Hepburn. I respect their work in this film so much that it overcame my difficulty in finding out what they were talking about.' *(Evening News)*

'Words, words, words! It's such a talkative tale! The dialogue moves at a rattling pace; the action mainly consists of people sitting down. Yet it has its moments of humour and sincerity.' *(Sunday Dispatch)*

ANTI:

'From as muddled a piece of political fictionalising as you are ever likely to hear, one pristine concept emerges: that Communists and Fascists are equal enemies of any right-thinking American.' *(Daily Worker)*

STAYING ALIVE CT: 5 AV: 3.75

1983 US 96 C MUSICAL/SO BAD

D Sylvester Stallone ●
W Sylvester Stallone Normal Wexler ●

John Travolta Finola Hughes ● Cynthia Rhodes Steve Inwood Julie Bovasso

Rebellious dancer (John Travolta) wants to dance his own steps in Broadway show.

The hilariously naff sequel to *Saturday Night Fever*. Sylvester Stallone's direction is not exactly subtle, and the grotesque choreography for the opening night of the show, called Satan's Alley, ensures the film's immortality in kitsch heaven.

PRO:

'Hugely enjoyable, a great glossy hymn to showbusiness, gorgeously photographed, zippily directed and with its superficial characters all beautiful movers – the emotional charge is slight but it races along with brio.' *(Phillip Bergson, What's On in London)*

MIXED:

'Only the presence of John Travolta turns [the film] from an unqualified disaster into a qualified one . . . [He] is able to radiate warmth and sweetness even under the direst of circumstances, which are certainly the ones in which he finds himself here . . . A sequel with no understanding of what made its predecessor work . . . Clumsy, mean-spirited and amazingly unmusical.' *(Janet Maslin, New York Times)*

'By turns exhilarating and absurd.' *(Nick Roddick, MFB)*

ANTI:

'It's staying awake that's the problem.' *(Paul Jackson, Western Mail)*

'Travolta's *Saturday Night Fever* has now become his Sunday Morning Hangover . . . Directed . . . as though it were by *Rocky* on tiptoe . . . it is a movie so expensively, awesomely bad that you almost feel it had been intended that way.' *(Tom Hutchinson, Mail on Sunday)*

'Ludicrous . . . Stallone doesn't bother much with character, scenes or dialogue. He just puts the newly muscle-plated Travolta in front of the camera, covers him with what looks like an oil slick, and goes for the whambams.' *(Pauline Kael)*

'Opening night of the show, which is called Satan's Alley, is what guarantees *Staying Alive* deserved immortality: an impossibly funny series of overproduced production numbers, it's high-tech camp heaven as Travolta, clad only in Bob Mackie's barely there Centurion outfit, struts and leaps around a set filled with moaning chorus girls in cages, laser beams, and all the dry ice in America. (Out in the audience, [Julie] Bovasso [playing Travolta's Italian mama] crosses herself, but it's too late: Travolta's movie career has definitely gone straight to Hell.) Travolta then spontaneously breaks into a dance of his own creation doing a ooooh-baby, Chippendale's stripper shimmy while being whipped by muscled chorus boys – which, naturally, brings the first-nighters to a screaming, stomping, standing ovation.' *(Margulies & Rebello)*

STEAMBOAT BILL, JR CT: 6 AV: 7.00

1928 US 71 BW COMEDY/SILENT

D Charles Riesner
W Carl Harbaugh Buster Keaton

Buster Keaton ☆ Ernest Torrence Marion Byron Tom McGuire Joseph Keaton

Effete student (Buster Keaton) tries to prove his masculinity to his burly, steamboat captain father (Ernest Torrence).

Not one of Keaton's funniest, despite the famous cyclone finale and a *tour de force* sequence where, by trying on different hats, Keaton transforms himself into other silent movie stars.

ANTI:

'A sorry affair . . . The producer appears to rely chiefly on water and smashing scenery to create fun. It seems longer than it really is, and the end strikes one as being brought about by sheer fatigue . . . Ernest Torrence succeeds in demonstrating his talent in spite of the lethargy of this film. Mr Keaton preserves his stoicism, but while watching this film one feels that one looked rather like Mr Keaton the greater part of the time, which is probably not exactly what Mr Keaton was aiming at.' *(Mordaunt Hall, New York Times)*

PRO:

'Generally when I view a motion picture I peer at it intently and find things in it to make catty remarks about. I laugh at funny things, but I do it sternly and judicially, and keep my eyes peeled for faults the directors commit. When the picture ends I have notes in a little book . . . [But when I saw this film] I never made a blessed note . . . I laughed or giggled all the time the picture was running and that it kept me so amused that I forgot my little book.' *(Welford Beaton, Film Spectator)*

'A pip of a comedy. It's one of Keaton's best.' *(Variety)*

'One of the least known of the Buster Keaton features, yet it possibly ranks right at the top. It is certainly the most bizarrely Freudian of his adventures, dealing with a tiny son's attempt to prove himself to his huge, burly, rejecting father.' *(Pauline Kael)*

STELLA DALLAS CT: 6 AV: 6.73

1937 US 106 BW DRAMA

D King Vidor ☆
W Victor Heerman Sarah Y. Mason from Olive Higgins Prouty's novel

Barbara Stanwyck ☆ AAN Anne Shirley ☆
John Boles Barbara O'Neil Alan Hale
Marjorie Main Tim Holt

Working-class Stella (Barbara Stanwyck) sacrifices her happiness to give her daughter (Anne Shirley) a better life among the middle classes.

Though dated even when it was released (it was a remake of a 1925 silent), this remains one of the classic 'women's films'. It made a star out of Barbara Stanwyck, and still has the power to activate the tear ducts.

MIXED:

'Unashamedly a tear-jerker . . . In spite of theatricalism and over-emotionalised sequences, [Stanwyck] manages to make the role of a woman who sacrifices herself for her daughter a moving and convincing one . . . The story is full of pictorial clichés and the development is definitely mechanical, but its appeal is directed to and will be appreciated by the sentimental.' *(Lionel Collier, Picturegoer)*

'The old emotional pull of the situation is still active, and the good acting of Barbara Stanwyck and Anne Shirley wrings every drop of pathos from it. Effective sob-stuff, most likely to appeal to women . . . The result has enough glaring faults to damn most pictures: the novelettish plot, its crude snobbery and accompanying squalor, the heavy sentimentality and exaggerated character-drawing. But all these will probably prove irrelevant . . . beside the authentic pathos of the situation.' *(Film Weekly)*

'There are things about the story that will not appeal to some men, but no one will be annoyed or offended by it. And the wallop is inescapably there for femmes.' *(Variety)*

PRO:

'Miss Stanwyck is superbly suited for her role, in which enormous vitality must justify crude vulgarity and leave the character sympathetic . . . A major screen achievement.' *(Photoplay)*

'It is without doubt, one of the most satisfactory – say the most – of all the remakes the screen has attempted . . . Miss Stanwyck's portrayal is as courageous as it is fine . . . Miss Shirley is flawless . . . John Boles is his usual colorless self.' *(Frank S. Nugent, New York Times)*

STING, THE AAW CT: 7 AV: 7.25

1973 US 129 C THRILLER/COMEDY

D George Roy Hill ☆ AAW
W David S. Ward ☆ AAW

Paul Newman ☆ Robert Redford ☆ AAN
Robert Shaw ✔ Charles Durning Ray Walston
Eileen Brennan Harold Gould

Two con-men (Robert Redford, Paul Newman) outwit a big-time gangster (Robert Shaw).

Handsomely produced buddy-buddy movie which has worn better than *Butch Cassidy and the Sundance Kid*, starring the same two actors, because there's a better sense of period and a more ingenious plot. It does go on a bit, though.

The biggest hit of its year, *The Sting* was nominated for 10 Oscars and won 7, including awards for Marvin Hamlisch's score (based on Scott Joplin piano rags), William Reynolds's editing, Edith Head's costumes and the art direction of Henry Bumstead and James Payne. The film was also nominated for cinematography (Robert Surtees) and sound (Ronald K. Pierce, Robert Bertrand).

PRO:

'Paul Newman and Robert Redford are superbly reteamed . . . George Roy Hill's outstanding direction of David S. Ward's finely-crafted story of multiple deception and surprise ending will delight both mass and class audiences.' *(Variety)*

'A disciplined, delightful film.' *(Newsweek)*

'Like its heroes, the film succeeds on charm and con. Newman and Redford radiate a charismatic appeal that tilts the movie in their favor.' *(Newsweek)*

'A variation on the old Dr Gillespie – Dr Kildare relationship, with a bit of Laurel and Hardy thrown in. It is also apparently very good box office.' *(New York Times)*

'Directed and played with great verve; the 1936 underworld is re-created with delight; and the victims deserve what they get. You can sit back and enjoy their discomfiture.' *(Dilys Powell)*

'It demonstrates what can happen when a gifted young screenwriter has the good fortune to fall among professionals his second time out.' *(Judith Crist)*

'Works endearingly without a hitch.' *(John Simon)*

MIXED:

'The script . . . is a collection of Damon Runyon hand-me-downs with the flavor gone. This is a visually claustrophobic, mechanically plotted movie that's meant to be a roguishly charming entertainment, and many people probably consider it just that.' *(Pauline Kael)*

'Bright, likeable, but overlong, unconvincingly studio-set and casually developed.' *(Halliwell)*

STOLEN CHILDREN, THE CT: 5 AV: 7.25

(aka *Il Ladro Di Bambini*)

1992 Italy C DRAMA/FOREIGN

D Gianni Amelio ✗
W Gianni Amelio ✗

Enrico Lo Verso ☆ Giuseppe Ieracitano
Valentina Scalici ☆ Florence Darel Marina Golovine

A naive young carabiniere (Enrico Lo Verso) is inexplicably given the job of escorting an 11-year-old prostitute (Valentina Scalici) and her kid brother (Giuseppe Ieracitano) to a children's home, then finds himself accused of kidnapping them.

It is symptomatic of writer-director Gianni Amelio's confused plot that, no sooner have the Italian police accused the hero of kidnapping, they let him go. Throughout, the realism of the direction and performances (the girl is especially good) serves only to expose the poverty of the writing, and how little we end up knowing about any of the characters. Over-enthusiastically voted Film of the Year at the 1992 Felix Awards, the film is uninvolving, turgid and interminable.

PRO:

'Here is a movie with the spontaneity of life; watching it is like living it.' *(Roger Ebert)*

'Shot in a rigorously spare style and brilliantly acted . . . [it] is as restrained as it is powerful . . . A work of uncommon grace, one that brushes at the soul even as it refuses to break the heart.' *(Manohla Dargis, Village Voice)*

'Another film to warm the heart's cockles . . . Amelio knows how to understate . . . [and] never bludgeons us into getting our handkerchiefs out.' *(Geoff Brown, The Times)*

'Marked very much by understatement . . . thought-provoking.' *(Alistair Owen, Time Out)*

MIXED:

'Inspired by a news story, [it] has little of the fast-paced journalistic feel of the neo-realist school.' *(Beth Blosser, Moving Pictures International)*

'A little long and its refusal to over-dramatise at times leaves a certain sense of flatness. But the playing is very natural, the direction totally sympathetic.' *(Derek Malcolm, Guardian)*

'The idea intrigues; the execution is a touch maudlin and more than a touch longwinded.' *(Nigel Andrews, Financial Times)*

STOLEN KISSES AAN CT: 5 AV: 7.13

(aka *Baisers Volés*)

1968 France 91 C COMEDY/ROMANCE/DRAMA/FOREIGN

D François Truffaut
W François Truffaut Bernard Revon Claude de Givray

Jean-Pierre Léaud Delphine Seyrig
Michel Lonsdale Claude Jade Harry-Max
Daniel Ceccaldi Claire Duhamel Catherine Lutz
André Falcon Paul Pavel

An awkward young man (Jean-Pierre Léaud) finds it difficult to find love – or hang on to various jobs, which include being a hotel clerk, a shoe-salesman and a private detective.

Bright but slight, very French romantic comedy which is evocative of René Clair, though it lacks his invention. Your enjoyment may depend upon whether you find the ineffectual anti-hero Antoine Doinel as sympathetic as Truffaut obviously does. This is the third of five films about the same character. Easily the best is the first, *The Four Hundred Blows* (1959), which was followed by an episode in *Love at Twenty* (1962) entitled 'Antoine and Colette' . The series concludes with *Bed and Board* (1970) and *Love On The Run* (1979).

PRO:

'Entirely beguiling . . . The film wears its charm on its sleeve, which is probably as good a place as any to wear it: tender, hilarious, gracefully reticent.' *(Penelope Houston, Spectator)*

'Funny and charming . . . The fun is never forced, the plot ambles along happily without recourse to fancy camera tricks . . . A sweet little picture.' *(Cecil Wilson, Daily Mail)*

'Very slight, very pretty and very welcome.' *(Ann Pacey, Sun)*

'A light-hearted yarn . . . a neat, stylish trifle which makes bright-as-a-button entertainment.' *(Dick Richards, Daily Mirror)*

MIXED:

'An immensely assured piece of film-making and also very fetching in its way. But one wishes one could discover some point of view behind it all, something to point the charm, to make it seem less of an affectionate trifle.' *(Derek Malcolm, Guardian)*

'A magical little film that gives more pleasure than it bears analysis.' *(Alexander Walker, Evening Standard)*

'Charming and likable, but maybe too easily likable. (The tenderness is a little flabby.)' *(Pauline Kael)*

ANTI:

'A weak, watery little trifle.' *(Rex Reed)*

'Too aimless, casual, slight.' *(John Simon)*

STORY OF ADELE H, THE CT: 4 AV: 7.00

(aka *L'Histoire D'Adèle H*)

1975 France 98 C DRAMA/ROMANCE/FOREIGN

D François Truffaut
W François Truffaut Jean Gruault Suzanne Schiffman

Isabelle Adjani ☆ AAN Bruce Robinson Sylvia Marriott Joseph Blatchley Reubin Dorey

A young woman (Isabelle Adjani), the daughter of author Victor Hugo, becomes obsessed with an English lieutenant (Bruce Robinson) who does not return her love.

Odd, unsatisfactory film which pulls in two directions at once. Adjani (though much too young and beautiful for the role) dominates the tale as a woman torn and driven by unrequited passion; but Truffaut adopts a distant, half-mocking style, as if deconstructing old Hollywood romances. And the screenplay, based on real-life diaries, rambles all over the place without ever showing much sign of forward momentum. The object of desire, Bruce Robinson, gave up acting after this and turned to writing and directing, with films such as *The Killing Fields* and *Withnail and I* to his credit.

PRO:

'There are three good reasons to see *The Story of Adele H*. Two of them are familiar: the direction of François Truffaut and the cinematography of Nestor Almendros. The third is a very welcome new reason: the acting of Isabelle Adjani.' *(Stanley Kauffmann)*

'A François Truffaut film to rank with *Shoot the Piano Player, Jules and Jim,* and *The Wild Child* – and perhaps his most passionate work. The picture is damnably intelligent – almost frighteningly so, like some passages in Russian novels which strip the characters bare. And it's deeply, disharmoniously funny – which Truffaut has never been before.' *(Pauline Kael)*

MIXED:

'Oddly quiet and slow-paced . . . yet it is a mesmerising film.' *(Kenneth Baily, Sunday People)*

'Although Truffaut holds our interest, one never becomes involved. The chief mistake . . . is casting Isabelle Adjani . . . It is implausible she would spend her life as a rejected woman.' *(Judith Simons, Daily Express)*

'If he is indifferent to the other players [besides Adele] Truffaut reveals extraordinary care in setting the scene.' *(David Robinson, The Times)*

'It is unfair to blame the cast. The under-direction of the supporting players and the over-direction of the main performer do amount to a kind of style, chilly and clinical though it often is.' *(Alan Brien, Sunday Times)*

'Handsome, morose, compelling and tiresome . . . Truffaut calls it "the autopsy of a passion"; but biopsy would be a better word, a living, malignant hypertrophy projected with a sombre clarity.' *(Eric Korn, New Statesman)*

ANTI:

'For once he [Truffaut] fails to tell us enough . . . Since there is no basic dramatic development . . . it is a story with nothing but middle – and a middling one at that.' *(Eric Shorter, Daily Telegraph)*

'Surprisingly slow and stilted.' *(Halliwell)*

STORY OF DR EHRLICH'S MAGIC BULLET, THE: *see* DOCTOR EHRLICH'S MAGIC BULLET.

STORY OF G.I. JOE, THE CT: 7 AV: 7.38

(aka *GI Joe, War Correspondent; War Correspondent*)

1945 US 109 BW WAR/DRAMA

D William A. Wellman ☆
W Leopold Atlas Guy Endore Philip Stevenson ☆ AAN from Ernie Pyle's book

Burgess Meredith ☆ Robert Mitchum ☆ AAN Freddie Steele Wally Cassell Jimmy Lloyd Jack Reilly William Murphy William Self Dick Rich

A war correspondent (Burgess Meredith) reports the stories of ordinary soldiers at the front line, during World War II.

One of the most authentic combat films of all time, this is based on the front-line dispatches of a war journalist and noticeably avoids false heroics or jingoism – though not always sentimentality. It follows *All Quiet on the Western Front* (1930) and predates *The Big Red One* (1980) and *Platoon* (1986) in offering a worm's eye view of warfare as confusing, dirty and scary. Mitchum's role as Lieutenant Walker made him a star. The score, by Ann Ronell and Louis Applebaum, and the song 'Linda' (music and lyrics by Ann Ronell) were Oscar-nominated.

'The greatest war picture I've ever seen.' *(General Dwight D. Eisenhower)*

'Humorous poignant and tragic, an earnestly human reflection of a stern life and the dignity of man.' *(Thomas M. Pryor, New York Times)*

'Add to authentic story-handling a production that's superb, casting and directing that's perfect, and a sock star supported by a flawless group of artists.' *(Variety)*

'A masterpiece . . . Many things in the film itself move me to tears . . . The first great triumph in the effort to combine "fiction" and "documentary" film. That is, it not only makes most of its fiction look and sound like fact – and far more intimate and expressive fact than it is possible to record on the spot; it also, without ever inflating or even disturbing the factual quality, as Eisenstein used to, gives fact the constant power and meaning beyond its own which most "documentors" – and most imaginative artists as well – totally lack feeling for. I don't insist on the word if you feel it is misleading, but most of this film is good poetry, and some of it is great poetry, and all of its achievements, and even most its failures, are earned in terms purely of moving pictures.' *(James Agee, Nation)*

STORY OF LOUIS PASTEUR, THE AAN

CT: 5 AV: 7.11

1936 US 85 BW BIOPIC/DRAMA

D William Dieterle ☆
W Sheridan Gibney Pierre Collings AAW

Paul Muni ☆ AAW Josephine Hutchinson Anita Louise Donald Woods Fritz Leiber Henry O'Neill Akim Tamiroff Porter Hall Walter Kingsford

A French scientist (Paul Muni) tries to find a cure for anthrax and hydrophobia.

Good, solid biopic with a memorable central performance. It tackled scientific research with a seriousness and accuracy which previous films had not attempted, and was therefore widely acclaimed by critics. It also started a trend and was much imitated; as a result, it no longer looks as fresh or ground-breaking, but somewhat reverential and over-conventional. The flaws which Otis Ferguson spotted on release are much more glaringly obvious today. It was voted Number 2 (after *Mr Deeds Goes To Town*) on the *National Board of Review*'s 1936 list of Best American Pictures.

PRO:

'So great is the honourable contrast between this film and the ordinary clap-trap of the screen that it is hard to praise it with that persuasive operation which alone will ensure it the public it deserves . . . *Pasteur* stands apart.' *(The Times)*

'Brilliant . . . Rich in human interest . . . Spectacular emotional highlights are cleverly worked into the theme . . . Muni is superb.' *(Kine Weekly)*

'It is due to Muni's perfect conception and thoroughly convincing portrayal that the picture hangs so close together and succeeds in maintaining its interest and suspense throughout.' *(Byron James, Era)*

'Something almost approaching reverence for the subject is the quality which enhances the drama.' *(F.S. Jennings)*

'More exciting than any gangster drama.' *(C.A. Lejeune)*

ANTI:

'The producers couldn't avoid some dull stretches of scientific discourse.' *(Variety)*

'The first criticism is that the story is undramatic, that Pasteur's conflict is either against intangible, nonscreenable forces, or against the solemn beards of the Academy, who are too overdrawn, dull, and fatuous for a good fight. And the second criticism is one of overdrawing in general: Pasteur is too good and meek, his wife is too patient and sugary; . . . and the decent sentiment of the family scenes is so invariable as to be tiresome.' *(Otis Ferguson)*

STORY OF MANKIND, THE CT: 5 AV: 2.57

1957 US 100 C EPIC/SO BAD

D Irwin Allen ●
W Irwin Allen Charles Bennet ● from Hendrik van Loon's book

Ronald Colman (as the Spirit of Man) Vincent Price (The Devil) Cedric Hardwicke (The High Judge) Agnes Moorehead (Queen Elizabeth I) Peter Lorre ● (Nero) Virginia Mayo ● (Cleopatra) Harpo Marx (Sir Isaac Newton) Hedy Lamarr ● (Joan of Arc) Francis X. Bushman ● (Moses) Dennis Hopper (Napoleon)

A heavenly High Tribunal reviews the history of man.

One of the most bizarre movies of all time, with some of the worst miscasting ever perpetrated.

'Amateurishly conceived and acted . . . It is my personal observation that if the High Tribunal ever catches the picture, we're goners.' *(Philip K. Sheuer, LA Times)*

'Allen seems unable to decide whether to do a faithful history of man's development into a thinking being, a debate on whether man's good outweighs his evil, or a compilation of historical sagas with some humor dragged in for relief.' *(Variety)*

'It is the kind of pontification that any kid who has ever dozed through a history class has learned to see through.' *(Richard W. Mason, New York Times)*

'Unearthly . . . A poor excuse to use a bunch of available actors in some of the weirdest casting ever committed.' *(Newsweek)*

'In a Warner Brothers picture based dimly – very dimly – on a book by the late Hendrik van Loon, we have a West Coast interpretation of history as it might have been made if one of the Warner Brothers had been around to gas things up a little.' *(New Yorker)*

'Historical dud . . . Poor van Loon is probably standing in his grave and banging on his coffin in protest at the caricature to which his serious work has been reduced here.' *(S.A. Desick, LA Examiner)*

'Sophomoric. . . . The big names parading through this schoolboyish charade are all made to look and sound foolish by the inane dialogue.' *(Jesse Zunser, Cue)*

'We knew during the filming that *The Story of Mankind* was heading downwards; the script was bad to begin with and it worsened with daily changes. I remember one puzzled visitor asking Ronnie Colman, "Is this picture based on a book?", and he replied in that beautiful, soft diction of his, "Yes. But they are using only the notes on the dust jacket".' *(Vincent Price)*

STORY OF QIU JU, THE   CT: 7 AV: 8.20

(aka *Qiuju Da Guansi*)

1993 Hong Kong/China 92 C DRAMA/FOREIGN

D Zhang Yimou ☆
W Liu Heng from Chen Yuanbin's novel

Gong Li ☆ Lei Laosheng Liu Peiqi Yang Liuchun

A discontented peasant woman (Gong Li) goes in search of justice through the Chinese Communist party and judicial system. Whereas in the traditional Hollywood film, such as Mr. Deeds Goes To Town, *her folksy wisdom might be expected to prevail over a corrupt system, she finds only helpfulness and common sense. Her naivety and aggrieved sense of justice makes her see things out of proportion, and her actions have unexpected results.*

A fascinating glimpse of peasant life and of how the Chinese like to think their society operates. It's a humane, likeable film with an almost sentimental sympathy for those saddled with authority. Though made in a near-documentary style, it's as beautiful to look at as any of Zhang Yimou's films, and – however conservative its political message – the gripping story makes it the most accessible of this director's pictures.

MIXED:

'Zhang focuses this potentially sprawling material in two related ways. First, by editing tightly . . . Second, more debatably, he pushes the storyline towards melodrama . . . to provide himself with a rather glib moral conundrum in the closing scenes . . . As ever, [he] is aided considerably by Gong Li.' *(Tony Rayns, S & S)*

PRO:

'Humorously affectionate . . . Although somewhat less spectacular than Zhang's previous works, this latest film is just as visually compelling.' *(John Francis Lane, Screen International)*

'Almost Dickensian – though cinematically it resembles nothing as much as Ken Loach . . . Gong Li . . . gives her least glamorous, most persuasive performance yet.' *(Graham Fuller, Interview)*

'What's fascinating is the way Zhang uses this one small story to open up a much larger picture of China dragging itself into the Western world . . . Gong Li . . . has a strangely enchanting gracefulness.' *(Amanda Lipman, Empire)*

'If a similar story were set in America, it would probably be made more obviously funny, and star someone famous for pluck – Sally Field, for example. Zhang's approach is more understated. Watching the film, we find the humor for ourselves, and along the way we absorb more information about the lives of ordinary people in everyday China than in any other film I've seen.' *(Roger Ebert)*

STORY OF THE LONDON FOG, A: *see* LODGER, THE.

STRADA, LA: *see* LA STRADA.

STRANGE ADVENTURE OF DAVID GRAY, THE: *see* VAMPYR.

STRANGE INCIDENT: *see* OX-BOW INCIDENT, THE.

STRANGER, THE   CT: 6 AV: 6.60

1946 US 95 BW THRILLER

D Orson Welles ☆
W Anthony Veiller John Huston (uncredited) Orson Welles from Victor Trivas and Decla Dunning's story AAN

Edward G. Robinson ✔, Orson Welles ✔, Loretta Young ✔, Philip Merivale, Richard Long, Konstantin Shayne, Byron Keith

A government agent (Edward G. Robinson) searches for a Nazi war criminal (Orson Welles) who has married an American girl (Loretta Young) and settled in a Connecticut village.

Enjoyable thriller in the Hitchcock mode – the film it most resembles in tone and content is *Shadow of a Doubt* (1943). The plot may be mechanical and the characters thin and melodramatic, but Welles keeps up the pace, adds some typical touches, and stages a memorable climax on a clock tower. Welles described this as his 'worst' film; it's certainly his least personal. The film is handsomely photographed by Russell Metty.

ANTI:

'A bloodless, manufactured show.' *(Bosley Crowther)*

'The type of horrendous melodrama that woos and glues pre-puberty listeners to the family radio. . . . Never for a split second can one credit the frenetic events . . . Loretta Young's appearance has begun to belie her surname.' *(Herb Sterne, Rob Wagner's Script)*

'I find it sad that the new Orson Welles film . . .

should be dull. I don't mean that it hasn't a certain physical excitement but that it lacks mental excitement . . . I don't ever remember a film that was quite so sadistic to its heroine.' *(Time & Tide)*

'Welles, like many another bright spirit in Hollywood, has at last had to submit to the demands of the boys who handle the cash.' *(Daily Sketch)*

'A film of confused motivation and clumsy effects.' *(Basil Wright, 1972)*

MIXED:

'Only [its] unnecessary improbabilities . . . preclude it from being rated as one of the best-made thrillers of the past few years . . . It has suspense, excitement, violence and intelligence.' *(Spectator)*

'Why – how – Welles managed to end such an adroit story, with its invocative geography (autumn in New England has never on the screen been so crisp to the touch), by means of a gimmick in the worst Hitchcock taste will be the first question I shall want answered if we ever meet.' *(Vernon Young)*

'If any film can be said to be well written, well acted, exciting, and at the same time disappointing, that film is *The Stranger*.' *(Guardian)*

'Who would want to be cantankerous when the result is as entertaining as this? . . . Though director Welles might have hinted to actor Welles once or twice that he was inclined to overdo the glaring eyes and the other bogy-man tricks.' *(Fred Majdalany, Daily Mail)*

PRO:

'Welles treats each time-honoured situation as if it were something new and startling.' *(Shell Magazine)*

'Both as actor and director, Mr Welles is superb. The film has the sort of cosy intimacy of horror that Alfred Hitchcock can touch off so well in his better moods, with a bold grasp of form that is, as a rule, beyond Mr Hitchcock's art.' *(Observer)*

'As a director, Welles seems to have found himself at last. He never lets up on you.' *(Daily Express)*

'Socko melodrama, spinning an intriguing web of thrills and chills.' *(Variety)*

STRANGER THAN PARADISE

CT: 1 AV: 6.40

1984 US/West Germany 90 BW COMEDY

D Jim Jarmusch ✗
W Jim Jarmusch ●

John Lurie Eszter Balint Richard Edson
Cecilia Stark Danny Rosen Tom Docillo

Two Polish cousins (John Lurie, Eszter Balint) and a friend (Richard Edson) drift around America.

Jim Jarmusch's hip, detached, plotless movies have become more impressive over the years. But this terminally tedious and modish piece of laid-back pseudery is a reminder that Jarmusch had a lot of scope for improvement. Aren't comedies supposed to make you laugh? For some reason this won the Camera d'Or at Cannes, as the best first film of 1984. Glad I didn't have to sit through the runners-up.

PRO:

'A bracingly original avant-garde black comedy . . . Since plot doesn't count for much here, the style takes over, and Jarmusch has made such matters as camera placement, composition (in stunning black and white) and structure count for a lot.' *(Variety)*

'Each frame bespeaks a spiritual bleakness as well as a material one, and a detachment from any culture as such . . . Marginality, for Jarmusch, is a state of mind as well as a social condition: totally amoral, basically harmless, his people cheat, steal and lie with such a perfect sense of entitlement that they appear innocent.' *(Nikki Stiller, The Hudson Review)*

'The acting and performances combine to produce an obliquely effective study of the effect of landscape upon emotion, and the wry, dry humour is often quite delicious.' *(Geoff Andrew, Time Out)*

'It seems to be going nowhere, and knows every step it wants to make. It is a constant, almost kaleidoscopic experience of discovery, and we try to figure out what the film is up to and it just keeps moving steadfastly ahead, fade in, fade out, fade in, fade out, making a mountain out of a molehill.' *(Roger Ebert)*

'Plays a lot like a Woody Allen comedy. It's a silly film for smart people.' *(Martin & Porter)*

MIXED:

'It has an odd, nonchalant charm; it's fun. But it's softhearted fun – shaggy-dog minimalism – and it doesn't have enough ideas (or laughs) for its 90-minute length. It's so hemmed in that it has the feel of a mousy Eastern European comedy.' *(Pauline Kael)*

ANTI:

'I didn't think much of it.' *(Derek Malcolm, Guardian)*

'Has all the pretensions of being significant without ever being more than an art-house oddity designed to appeal to those who patronise ordinary people as interesting social types.' *(Jeff Sawtell, Morning Star, 1994)*

'Deeply soporific . . . Style-buffs may appreciate those shirts, those hats, that awful Fifties architecture; for others, it will be worse than Mogadon.' *(Hugo Davenport, Daily Telegraph, 1994)*

'So cool that it leaves me cold.' *(Anne Billson, Sunday Telegraph, 1994)*

STRANGERS ON A TRAIN CT: 8 AV: 8.93

1951 US 101 BW THRILLER

D Alfred Hitchcock☆
W Raymond Chandler Czenzi Ormonde Whitfield Cook from Patricia Highsmith's novel

Farley Granger Ruth Roman Robert Walker☆ Leo G. Carroll Patricia Hitchcock Laura Elliot Marion Lorne☆ Jonathan Hale Howard St. John John Brown

Psychopath Bruno (Robert Walker) murders wife of unhappily married tennis player Guy (Farley Granger), then expects Guy to return the favor.

One of Hitchcock's best thrillers, with cracking set-pieces mainly disguising the plot contrivances. Let-downs are that Guy is so much less charismatic than Bruno, and leading lady Ruth Roman is such a cold fish it's hard to care if Guy ends up landing her or not. Where Hitchcock is so skilful is in his suggestion that Bruno represents the darker, suppressed side of Guy's personality.

ANTI:

'The film's partial failure can be partly explained . . . in terms of a conflict between the impulse toward the "art" movie . . . and the requirements of popular cinema . . . It would be interesting to know (I have found no documentation) at precisely what stage in the elaboration of the scenario the crucial decision was made: the decision to depart drastically from the narrative line of Patricia Highsmith's novel, wherein Guy does murder Bruno's father. This seems to me absolutely demanded by the narrative logic and characterisation, but it obviously conflicts with certain major requirements of the classical Hollywood film: no "hero", no construction of the heterosexual couple, no happy end.' *(Robin Wood, Hitchcock's Films Revisited, 1989)*

MIXED:

'Full of camera tricks and a good many laughs – not all intentional . . . Some thrills, but verdict Only Fair.' *(People)*

'Once you admit a lunatic to a film the whole thing is likely to go off the rails; and that is where *Strangers on a Train* goes. In particular the ending, with a chase on a merry-go-round taking the place of Hitchcock's favourite rooftop chase, is wildly over-complicated; one feels that the director has been distracted from his job of creating suspense by the fun of handling the trick setting. All the same the film . . . is enjoyable enough for one to wish it were longer . . . *Strangers on a Train* is the best thing Hitchcock has done for a good many years.' *(Dilys Powell)*

'Undoubtedly an improvement on [Hitchcock's] last three or four. If he no longer appears to have the gift for making the excitement seem to spring directly from the plot, even [the] deviously contrived thrills . . . are undeniably thrilling.' *(Margaret Hinxman, Time & Tide)*

'As cunning a fabrication as [Hitchcock] has developed for a long while. The plot . . . is an exceptionally good one . . . If we are left unsatisfied and given too much time to pick apart the fat conjuror's apparatus . . . he still has a trick or two up his sleeve, an illusion in the grand manner.' *(William Whitebait, New Statesman)*

'The film begins to sag when Haines [Granger] fails to develop as a plausible character . . . The bad casting of Farley Granger is not the only lapse; the tempo has diminished and the flaws of logic obtrude . . . [The film] confirms Hitchcock's utter dependence on his script – in this case the best he has had for years – and a basic superficiality which prevents him from developing the psychological conflicts his characters do nothing more than suggest . . . But in spite of its many lapses, the film will certainly be classed a one of the successes of the year. And rightly.' *(Richard Winnington, S & S)*

PRO:

'A first rate film with a novel murder twist . . . [which] under Hitchcock's skilled touch comes off very nicely. The movie murder master tosses in thrills, suspense, comic relief and melodramatic explosions; and there is a lot of excitement.' *(Jesse Zunser, Cue)*

'A gripping, palm-sweating piece of suspense.' *(Variety)*

STRAW DOGS CT: 5 AV: 6.33

1971 GB 118 C THRILLER/HORROR

D Sam Peckinpah
W David Zelag Goodman Sam Peckinpah from Gordon M. Williams's novel *The Siege of Trencher's Farm*

Dustin Hoffman Susan George Peter Vaughan David Warner T.P. McKenna Colin Welland Jim Norton

Bookish mathematician (Dustin Hoffman), terrorized by Cornish peasants, turns nasty.

A highly controversial melodrama which is still unavailable on video in Britain. It is a deeply nasty film – *Home Alone* for psychopaths – taking a lip-smacking delight in violence and rape; the scene where Susan George is forcibly sodomized is deliberately filmed for erotic effect. Almost as distasteful is the long action climax, where we are supposed to applaud the villagers' gory come-uppances. Jerry Fielding's music was Oscar-nominated.

PRO:

'The almost subliminal flashbacks in which Amy sees herself being raped and sodomized are sardonically juxtaposed with shots of the rapists dressed to the nines, and acting as jolly good fellows and pillars of the village community. This is brilliantly horrifying and forcefully makes the picture's main point: under the veneer of civilized behavior and social order there exists a world of untamed and perhaps untamable violence that remains hidden from general view mostly because the general view closes its cowardly, hypocritical eye to it. Hardly a new idea, that, but one Peckinpah infuses with extraordinary new vitality.' *(John Simon)*

'It is hard to imagine that Peckinpah will ever make a better movie . . . The rape sequence is a masterful piece of erotic cinema . . . What [he] does for his hero, he does for us: he puts us in touch with our primal feelings.' *(Paul D. Zimmerman, Newsweek)*

'A magnificent piece of red-raw, meaty entertainment.' *(Edward Betts, People)*

'A brilliant but brutal film that says something important.' *(Stephen Murphy, Secretary of the British Board of Film Censors)*

MIXED:

'The final bloody shoot-out is, without question, fully motivated . . . [and staged] with incredible skill . . . It is tremendous moviemaking, [but] it is also tremendously sickening.' *(Arthur Knight, Saturday Review)*

'One might say that Mr Peckinpah was bringing the outside inside, translating the Sioux or the Apache massacre from the western to an English living-room. But no redskin attack, no paleface revenge I ever saw on the screen was as mindlessly revolting . . . For the first time in my life I felt concern for the future of cinema.' *(Dilys Powell)*

ANTI:

'Ferocious . . . shocking . . . artistic pornography.' *(Joseph Gelmis, Newsday)*

'An orgy of unparalleled violence and nastiness . . . The script relies on shock and violence to tide it over weakness in development, characterization and lack of motivation.' *(Variety)*

'[The rape sequence] is the toughest and most erotic scene in the film . . . and ends with the woman's complete and willing submission . . . [It won't] endear the director to something over half of this country's population.' *(Vincent Canby, New York Times)*

'The worst film of 1971 . . . telling us, wonder of wonders, that evil lurks in the hearts of men . . . and proceeding to show it by way of an incredible and unoriginal realism . . . It is one of a trash series . . . that tells us that violence and/or war are not nice and wallows in the unniceties for hours. We hasten to note that a certain school of young critics . . . has deemed the Peckinpah spew a masterpiece . . . Peckinpah's contempt for intelligence . . . and his obvious preference for the fighter-fornicator . . . is the director's hang-up. What is truly contemptible is the suggestion from his admirers that non-machismo-minded men will get a vicarious release from the desperation of their own days by seeing the bookish worm turn! (All anyone with an IQ of 70-plus can get out of this film is a case of the heaves.)' *(Judith Crist, New York Magazine)*

STRAY DOG

CT: – AV: 8.20

(aka *Nora Inu*)

1949 Japan 122 BW THRILLER/FOREIGN

D Akira Kurosawa
W Ryuzo Kikushima Akira Kurosawa from Kurosawa's novel

Toshiro Mifune ☆ Takashi Shimura Ko Kimura Keiko Awaji Reisaburo Yamamoto Noriko Sengoku

A detective (Toshiro Mifune) descends into the Tokyo underworld in pursuit of his stolen gun.

Over-flashy technique and a ponderous pace detract from this thriller, which is renowned for its atmosphere – Tokyo during a stifling heatwave – and powerful character study of the leading character. Kurosawa shows his slide towards criminality as he loses his sense of right and wrong. Though it was a popular and critical success, Kurosawa did not consider this to be among his finest work.

MIXED:

'While it rambles and rants something awful, which is probably why it has never been shown here before, and thus is not recommended to the general moviegoer, it should entertain the student and tickle a few funny bones . . . It is a conventional crime story loaded with . . . [pre-war Hollywood] clichés . . . But there are also some very vivid and even poetic scenes.' *(Bosley Crowther, 1964)*

PRO:

'If the Japanese cinema enlarges its playing field internationally, I am convinced that Kurosawa will be the first from our country to get the chance. His cinematic language is comprehensible to everyone . . . This film especially appeals to the post-war generation.' *(Shimizu, Cinema Jumpo)*

'A fine blend of US thriller material with Japanese conventions, it's a small classic.' *(Chris Peachment, Time Out)*

'[Seeing] Akira Kurosawa's *Stray Dog* is like seeing *The Bicycle Thief*, the De Sica masterpiece, for the first time. Both films were made in 1949, both deal with the difficult postwar periods of two defeated nations, and both reflect the bold response of two great directors to a new freedom of expression, long suppressed by the police state.' *(Kevin Thomas)*

STREETCAR NAMED DESIRE, A AAN

CT: 6 AV: 9.12

1951 US 122 BW DRAMA

D Elia Kazan ✗
W Tennessee Williams Oscar Saul ☆ AAN from Tennessee Williams's play

Vivien Leigh ☆ AAW Marlon Brando ☆ AAN Kim Hunter ☆ AAW Karl Malden ☆ AAW Rudy Bond Nick Dennis Peg Hillias Wright King Richard Garrick Ann Dere

Neurotic southern belle (Vivien Leigh) has her personality dismantled by her brutish brother-in-law (Marlon Brando).

Tennessee Williams's powerful play, with its stylised dialogue, is brought somewhat theatrically to the screen. Blanche's nymphomania has been toned down, and the homosexuality of her first husband has disappeared altogether, but the film is sexually frank for its day. The critical acclaim which greeted Marlon Brando's electrifying performance as Stanley Kowalski has tended to obscure the fact that the film is mainly notable as a piece of ensemble acting. Vivien Leigh, Kim Hunter and Karl Malden won Academy Awards: Brando had to be satisfied with being nominated – he lost out to Humphrey Bogart, in *The African Queen*.

The film was nominated for Best Cinematography (Harry Stradling) Score (Alex North), Sound Recording (Colonel Nathan Levinson), Costume Design (Lucinda Ballard). Richard Day and George James Hopkins won the Oscars for art direction and set decoration.

ANTI:

'Stops at every possible point along its route to pick up new variations on the theme of human degradation . . . The excellence of some of the acting and writing serves only to emphasize the negative, defeatist and decadent nature of the film.' *(Thomas Spencer, Daily Worker)*

MIXED:

'Brando at times captures strongly the brutality of the young Pole but occasionally he performs unevenly in a portrayal marked by frequent garbling of his dialog.' *(Variety)*

'All the acting is first-class . . . [but] the piece, however superbly executed, remains pointlessly destructive.' *(Dilys Powell)*

PRO:

'One of those rare . . . cinematic miracles: a distinguished motion picture drama which in many respects exceeds even the already considerable merits of its staged progenitor . . . A magnificent example of the cinematic and dramatic arts joined in artistry, enhanced by superb performances and a masterful translation to its new medium.' *(Jesse Zunser, Cue)*

'One of Hollywood's rare attempts to give the whole meaning and scope of the author's vision . . . It contains characters more full and subtle than any yet shown in a Hollywood movie and beyond a few minor points, little has been softened in it.' *(Hollis Alpert, Saturday Review of Literature)*

'The story is still as murky [as the play], the passion as brutal . . . For [which] we have to thank the courage of [Kazan] . . . The acting is very fine.' *(Campbell Dixon, Daily Telegraph)*

'Though the movie has its flaws, it can claim a merit rare in Hollywood films: it is a grown-up, gloves-off drama of real human beings . . . As the hulking, animalistic Kowalski, Marlon Brando fills his scenes with a virile power that gives *Streetcar* its highest voltage.' *(Time)*

'Today I come to the top of the page to give you – Marlon Brando, as the most powerful and disturbing male star to cross the screen since Clark Gable first assaulted our consciousness in *Hell's Divers*.' *(Paul Dehn, Evening Standard)*

'Vivien Leigh gives one of those rare performances that can truly be said to evoke pity and terror. As Blanche DuBois, she looks and acts like a destroyed Dresden shepherdess. No one since the early Lillian Gish and the almost unknown, plaintive *Nadia Sibirskaya of Menilmontant* (1926) has had this quality of hopeless, feminine frailty.' *(Pauline Kael)*

STRICTLY BALLROOM

CT: 10 AV: 7.75

1992 Australia 94 C MUSICAL/COMEDY/ROMANCE

D Baz Luhrmann ☆
W Baz Luhrmann Craig Pearce ☆

Paul Mercurio ✔ Tara Morice ✔ Bill Hunter Barry Otto Pat Thompson Gia Carides Peter Whitford

A rebellious young ballroom dancer (Paul Mercurio) finds a new partner (Tara Morice).

This musical comedy from Australia skilfully reheats such old chestnuts as the Cinderella story, The Ugly Duckling, and the Busby Berkeley musical, and makes them seem fresh again. Paul Mercurio dances beautifully and Tara Morice is funny and touching as his unlikely inamorata. They are well supported by an exuberant cast and an ingenious script which seems conventional and clichéd, yet constantly delights you with unexpected turns. First-time director Baz Luhrmann directs with a flair which brilliantly disguises the film's stage origins; and although there's much campy caricature, everything is done with such affection that it never seems crude or overdone. A magical 'feelgood' movie.

MIXED:

'A noisy, sentimental "feel good" movie which virtually hammers you into the ground with its exuberance . . . Hardly something to write home about in terms of cinematic art. But in its artlessness lies its secret.' *(Derek Malcolm, Guardian)*

'Luhrmann, like many first-time directors, is intoxicated with the possibilities of the camera. He uses too many wide-angle shots, in which the characters look like blowfish mugging for the lens, and too many story lines, until we worry we may have lost track of something, but what works is an exuberance that cannot be faked . . . What's best about the movie is the sense of madness and mania running just beneath its surface. In one sense, the characters care about nothing but ballroom dancing . . . [which] is simply the strategy they use to hold the world at bay. They are profoundly frightened of change, and have created an insular little world, with rigid rules and traditions; here they can be in control, as the larger world goes haywire. Scott's attempt to introduce anarchy – and new dance steps – into their tiny enclave is all the funnier because he, too, cares about nothing but dancing. He doesn't even WANT to be a rebel. But it's in his blood.' *(Roger Ebert)*

'Sacrifices credibility for caricature but despite its rough edges emerges a winner.' *(Maltin)*

PRO:

'Bright, breezy and immensely likable.' *(Variety)*

'This story will warm your heart.' *(David Gritten, Daily Telegraph)*

'One would call the movie camp if it seemed remotely self-conscious about its hyperboles. But it begins as straightfaced baroque, shifts up into rococo and ends as a roaring essay in comical-romantic glitz . . . See and delight.' *(Nigel Andrews, Financial Times)*

'It's wonderful . . . The dancing is fab, the sequins sparkle and numerous rivalries burst out in an explosion of ruffled ostrich feathers. Make this movie a priority.' *(Sue Heal, Today)*

'Luhrmann uses the camera with great economy of style, never straying far from the screenplay's theatrical origins, yet keeping images to the fore . . . Give it a whirl.' *(Nick James, City Limits)*

'One of the freshest, funniest and happiest films to hit the cinema in years. A joy from start to finish.' *(Rose)*

STRIKE

CT: 5 AV: 7.89

(aka *Stachka*)

1924 USSR 73/82 BW DRAMA/FOREIGN

D Sergei Eisenstein ☆
W Sergei Eisenstein

Grigori Alexandrov Maxim Strauch Mikhail Gomarov Alexander Antonov I. Klukvin

Workers and the military clash during a prolonged factory strike, in 1912.

Eisenstein's first feature film is technically remarkable for its age, and contains some striking camerawork (by Edouard Tiss) and editing. Don't expect individual characterization or subtle narrative. The message is crude propaganda: the workers all suffer nobly, while the capitalists are caricatured ogres. The symbolism is as crass and obvious as the use of montage; the most famous sequence intercuts the massacre of the strikers with scenes of a slaughterhouse.

'In *Strike* we see the first revolutionary creation of our cinema.' *(Mikhail Koltsov, Pravda)*

'The style . . . is electric: all swift startle and surprise . . . Eisenstein's . . . wonder, delight, exuberance and tremendous enthusiasm for the medium, makes itself felt in every frame . . . A work of imaginative flourish . . . [which] makes for a wonderfully invigorating sixty-minutes.' *(John Cutts, F & F, 1961)*

'*Strike* stands apart from other films: it hammers the nerves and exalts the spirit as intensely as *Oedipus* or *Lear*, and it goes on so doing as relentlessly.' *(David Sylvester, New Statesman, 1956)*

'Everything in it is young, overflowing with the abundant excitement and imagination of a genius feeling its way and not knowing its powers.' *(Ivor Montagu, S & S, 1956)*

'A raucous, rousing hymn to human dignity and courage.' *(Geoff Andrew, Time Out)*

STRONG MAN, THE

CT: 8 AV: 6.86

1926 US 75 BW COMEDY/SILENT

D Frank Capra ☆
W Frank Capra Arthur Ripley Hal Conklin Robert Eddy

Harry Langdon ☆ Gertrude Astor Tay Garnett Priscilla Bonner William V. Mong

War veteran (Harry Langdon) tries to trace pen-friend.

Harry Langdon's best silent comedy, co-written and directed brilliantly by the young Frank Capra (who, of course, went on to direct talking masterpieces like *It Happened One Night* and *It's a Wonderful Life*).

ANTI:

'Probably one of the poorest pictures that ever supported such excellent comicalities. In the middle it sags to the ground and after a very dreary stretch makes a few floundering efforts to rise, but even the pleasant antics of Mr Langdon fail to revivify it.' *(Oliver Claxton, New Yorker)*

PRO:

'A whale of a comedy production . . . It has a wealth of slapstick, a rough and tumble finish . . . notable in the whole range of screen comedy . . . One of the remarkable things about the picture is the fact that its action and its comedy values are sustained for more than an hour . . . A rich comedy that should take Langdon a step toward the class of stars, whose pictures figure for more than a week's engagement.' *(Rush, Punch Magazine)*

'A grand and glorious laugh from the start to the finish . . . It begins with one laugh overlapping the other. Chuckles are swept into howls. Howls creep into tears – and by that time you're ready to be carried out. And we don't mean maybe! . . . Gertrude Astor is outstanding as a big-blonde-mama vamp.' *(Photoplay)*

'I don't know when I've seen anything more touchingly beautiful than Harry Langdon's performance in this. Probably never.' *(Robert E. Sherwood, Life)*

'[Langdon's] very finest.' *(John Grierson, Artwork, 1931)*

STUD, THE

CT: 5 AV: 2.14

1978 GB 90/95 C DRAMA/ROMANCE

D Quentin Masters ●
W Jackie Collins ● from her novel

Oliver Tobias ● Joan Collins ● Sue Lloyd Mark Burns Doug Fisher Walter Gotell Emma Jacobs

A waiter (Oliver Tobias) sleeps his way to the top, via his boss's nymphomaniac wife (Joan Collins).

Tacky, softcore, hilariously inaccurate portrait of London in the none-too-swinging 70s. Its success paved the way for a sequel, *The Bitch*, which was even more ridiculous – and Collin's Queen Bitch in the TV role *Dynasty*.

PRO:

'Lush nonsense in plush surroundings . . . As self-indulgently enjoyable as lazing in a warm, scented bath with a glass of sweet sherry and one of the more scurrilous Sunday newspapers.' *(Marjorie Bilbow, Screen International)*

ANTI:

'Tobias is short on sensitivity and would-be Lotharios seeking useful tips might be excused for wondering what, apart from rakish good looks, is the secret of his success in persuading so many eligibles into the sack. He, in fact, seems faintly embarrassed about the whole thing.' *(Variety)*

'Watching it is rather like being buried alive in a coffin stuffed with back numbers of *Men Only*.' *(Alan Brien)*

'What might have salvaged the project was a script which attempted to analyse its apparently empty-handed characters' behaviour, but nowhere is one given the slightest inkling of what makes anyone tick.' *(David McGillivray, MFB)*

'The script (by Jackie herself), permeated with an appalling and deeply rooted snobbery, contrives to be completely inaccurate and therefore offensive to every facet of the social structure, in a London that swings like the corpse on the end of a rope.' *(Jennifer Selway, Time Out)*

'A surprise box-office success, richly undeserved.' *(Halliwell)*

STUDENT OF PRAGUE, THE

CT: 6 AV: 8.00

(aka *Der Student von Prag*)

1926 Germany 45/60/113 BW FANTASY/ SILENT/ FOREIGN

D Henrik Galeen
W Henrik Galeen from Hanns Heinz Ewers's novel

Conrad Veidt ☆ Werner Krauss Agnes Esterhazy Ferdinand Von Alten

Student (Conrad Veidt) makes pact with Devil (Werner Krauss) and becomes rich.

The Faust legend revisited. Ponderous but a superior, well-acted example of German expressionism.

'The vivid realization of the fable is a genuine achievement for the screen . . . The acting . . . is of high distinction . . . Herr Werner Krauss . . . has an amazing power of malevolent suggestion, and is, perhaps as fine a piece of acting as the screen can show.' *(The Times)*

'Conrad Veidt gives the finest performance yet seen on the screen.' *(W.A. Mutch, Daily Chronicle)*

'Proves what can be done with the art of the screen by actors of real gifts and experience . . . A most enthralling film!' *(E.A. Baughan, Daily News)*

'Thrilling and beautiful . . . While eerie, it is never horrible.' *(Iris Barry, Daily Mail)*

'In the past eight years I have seen no film to be compared with [it].' *(W. Webster, Sunday Pictorial)*

'An absorbing story of intense human appeal, superbly produced and played . . . [especially] the brilliance of Conrad Veidt . . . It is a film that will satisfy the highbrows and enthral the populace.' *(Bioscope)*

SUGAR CANE ALLEY: *see* RUE CASES NÈGRES.

SULLIVAN'S TRAVELS

CT: 10 AV: 9.83

1941 US 90 BW COMEDY/DRAMA/ROMANCE

D Preston Sturges ☆
W Preston Sturges ☆

Joel McCrea ☆ Veronica Lake ☆ Robert Warwick ☆ William Demarest Franklin Pangborn Porter Hall

Byron Foulger Margaret Hayes Robert Greig Eric Blore Jimmy Conlin ☆

A Hollywood director (Joel McCrea) tires of making mindless entertainment, such as 'Ants in Your Pants of 1939,' in a war-devastated world. He decides to make a movie with social significance, 'O Brother, Where Art Thou?' and conduct some field research into poverty.

Scripted, directed and acted with panache, this is one of the greatest Hollywood comedies. Sturges was always at his best when debunking pomposity and pretentiousness, and here he puts the boot into the 'social cinema' of the 1930s.

The early scenes contain delightful sideswipes at tinseltown superficiality, but the tone rapidly darkens, and the narrative grips. With the help of some clever, but not over-contrived narrative twists, Sturges makes his hero suffer alongside ordinary Americans, and concludes that what most people really want from the movies is escapism, not instruction. Sturges's film thus becomes his personal apologia for peddling escapism – and, by extension, Hollywood's.

Such a film could easily have been glib and cynical, but Sturges blends social melodrama with romantic comedy so skilfully that he manages surreptitiously to say a surprising amount about the state of wartime America, as well as Hollywood.

Preston Sturges on the film: 'The result of an urge, an urge to tell some of my fellow playwrights that they were getting a little too deep-dish and to leave the preaching to the preachers.'

ANTI:

'Though the metropolitan gentry found the film to be "great art", this reporter believes it to be no more than an inept, carelessly manufactured jibe that is no-end dull . . . Sullivan doesn't travel so much as merely wander about. It changes its theatrical attack with a frequency causing suspicion that the photoplay was shot off the cuff. Satire, slapstick, melodrama, romance, and sociology each has an inning, with the net result a patchwork, completely without pattern, in which the colors jar. Fault must be placed with the screenplay, and if director Sturges wishes to invite author Sturges into the alley for a good, sound thrashing, I hereby offer to donate my services as referee.' *(Herb Sterne)*

MIXED:

'Your opinion of the piece may depend partly on how much of a scream you find it to remember, when Sullivan is safe home, that the convicts are still in gaol. Impossible to deny, though, that it is a remarkable film, written as well as directed by Sturges, and ably executed.' *(Dilys Powell)*

'No picture has ever more savagely satirised Hollywood, The distorted values, the essential inhumanity, of the film colony are glaringly highlighted, and the futility of inflated publicity punctured in a cross-country chase which out-Sennetts Sennett. Deflated also are the pretentious directors and writers who yearn to create Art on the movie assembly-line. But what is the issue? . . . [McCrea] comes to the conclusion that the producers were right, that the masses don't want to solve their problems but to forget them in movie escapism. The cynicism of this vindication of the box-office is at the core of Sturges' outlook and has remained characteristic of him ever since.' *(Paul Rotha & Richard Griffith, The Film Till Now, 1949)*

PRO:

'A brilliant fantasy in two keys – slapstick farce and the tragedy of human misery.' *(James Agee)*

'Seems set for an hour of Sturges' wit and slapstick; but the mood changes . . . this development [leading to] a macabre climax . . . [It] is rich in surprise and parody. It has a bit of Chaplin, a bit of Lubitsch and a great deal of Preston Sturges.' *(William Whitebait, New Statesman)*

'A deftly sardonic apologia for Hollywood make-believe.' *(New York Times)*

'A ringingly Shavian denunciation of poverty as a proposed life-style . . . making explicit what had always been implicit in [Sturges's] success-story-oriented Cinderella plots. Not that Sturges was a Pollyanna about the American capitalism system; but the only way to beat it, he implied, was to hang loose, roll with the punches, dance around the ring, and wait for the one opening that can turn a life around from savage frustration to frenzied success.' *(Andrew Sarris, Village Voice, on the reissue)*

'Taken as seriously as it deserves, *Sullivan's Travels*, the story of a conscience-stricken Hollywood director in search of real life anguish, entitles Sturges to be ranked as a great humanist director.' *(Film, 1959)*

SUMMER: *see* GREEN RAY, THE.

SUMMER MADNESS: *see* SUMMERTIME.

SUMMERTIME

CT: 6 AV: 7.50

(aka *Summer Madness*)

1955 US 99 C DRAMA/ROMANCE

D David Lean ☆ AAN
W David Lean H.E. Bates from Arthur Laurents's play *The Time of the Cuckoo*

Katharine Hepburn ☆ AAN Rossano Brazzi Isa Miranda Darren McGavin Mari Aldon Jane Rose MacDonald Parke Gaitano Audiero Andre Morell Jeremy Spenser

An Ohio spinster (Katharine Hepburn), holidaying in Venice, meets a handsome Italian antique-dealer (Rossano Brazzi).

David Lean's least-known film is an early precursor of *Shirley Valentine* – a bitter-sweet romance which threatens at times to become a travelogue full of caricature Italians. However, Jack Hildyard's photography of Venice is stunning; and the drama holds its own, thanks to Hepburn's sensitive, mature and ultimately moving performance.

MIXED:

'A most irritating film. It is brilliantly directed, acted and photographed, it has Katharine Hepburn and Venice, too, and yet I cannot help feeling that my delight in it rests on something basically superficial . . . Hepburn is, by any standards, superb.' *(MFB)*

'With tremendous skill David Lean . . . has made a Cinderella story into what the censors term as "more suitable for adult audiences". By flouting film conventions, he partly disguises the story's implausibility . . . He has allowed one or two film clichés to creep in . . . [including] dialogue which actually contains the line, "I am a man. You are a woman".' *(Felix Barker, Evening News)*

'Promising entertainment – with some reservations. There is a lack of cohesion and some abruptness in plot transition without a too-clear buildup. Lesser characterizations, too, are on the sketchy side.' *(Variety)*

PRO:

'Katharine Hepburn is . . . [so] stylish and delightful and Jack Hildyard has photographed her so beautifully . . . that it hardly matters what [the film] is about. The acting and the travelogue, not the play, are the thing, and they turn a well-contrived piece of glossy romanticism into something sparkling and almost distinguished.' *(Thomas Spencer, Daily Worker)*

'It is three years since [Lean's] last picture. *Summer Madness* proves well worth every year of our wait . . . [He] has seemingly mesmerised Katie Hepburn out of her familiar mannerisms.' *(Harold Conway, Daily Sketch)*

'Wonderful . . . Hepburn has done few things better . . . [It] is that rare thing – an adult film.' *(Daily Herald)*

'The most beautiful tribute to the Venetian scene which has been paid by any film-maker.' *(Manchester Guardian)*

'The eye is endlessly ravished.' *(Dilys Powell)*

SUNA NO ONNA: *see* WOMAN IN THE DUNES.

SUNDAY, BLOODY SUNDAY CT: 6 AV: 6.82

1971 GB 110 C DRAMA/ROMANCE

D John Schlesinger ☆ AAN
W Penelope Gilliatt ☆ AAN

Glenda Jackson ☆ AAN Peter Finch ☆ AAN Murray Head Peggy Ashcroft Maurice Denham Vivian Pickles Frank Windsor Tony Britton

A Jewish doctor (Peter Finch) and a businesswoman (Glenda Jackson) find that they are sharing the same lover (Murray Head).

Civilized, humane, low-key drama about two people trying to make the best of a bad job. It's an antidote to all those Hollywood movies where Love and Desire are everything; here, they seem to be just makeshift ways of warding off loneliness. The trouble is that it's hard to see what either of the two leads see in Head, whose character is superficial and selfish, and there's not enough in the way of dramatic conflict or surprise. It's all a bit lacking in passion – like the characters.

ANTI:

'[Schlesinger] reckons this is a typical slice of English life. God help us!' *(Mark Russell Scarr, People)*

'A classic example of a film running out of control at every moment, while its creators . . . strive for "meaning" with little regard for the simple matters of shot-by-shot consistency, let alone formal unity.' *(Phil Hardy, Time Out)*

MIXED:

'Cleverly constructed and completely engrossing, with a humane appeal to live and let live. But for me it had one major weakness. I found it difficult to accept that two such comparatively worthwhile people could lavish such devotion on this flabby and flat young man.' *(Madeleine Harmsworth, Sunday Mirror)*

PRO:

'A beautiful film so brimful of genius that one hesitates to put into words the delicate plot . . . In a life of watching films, it is the only picture I look forward to seeing a second time.' *(Fergus Cashin, Sun)*

'One of [Schlesinger's] very best films . . . [It] never does the obvious . . . Not to be missed.' *(Derek Malcolm, Guardian)*

'How marvellous it is, for once to see a serious film which is not a problem piece, feels no need to explain itself, and can be called adult because it is by, about and for adults . . . The film's achievement is all the more remarkable when you consider its basic materials . . . Scene by scene the film is a continuing triumph of observation.' *(John Russell Taylor, The Times)*

'It's an unusual film – perhaps a classic. A curious sort of plea on behalf of human frailty – it asks for sympathy for the nonheroes of life who make the best deal they can.' *(Pauline Kael)*

'A warm, compassionate film, conveying the complex textures of everyday experience and with them the unresolved tension between passionate love and more mundane social commitments that distinguishes adult life from adolescence.' *(Jan Dawson, Financial Times)*

'A transitional film embodying a terminal feeling. It was the only major film of the new decade with principal characters drawn from the newly beleaguered middle class . . . The film's characters resemble the capital city they inhabit: apprehensive people undergoing a state of change, uncertain of the next move. It was also the first major film to give a glimpse of the drug scene as a "problem", not a "kick" . . . Luciana Arrighi's production design for the film showed the "Playtime" delights of the Sixties turning into the cast-offs of the Seventies.' *(Alexander Walker)*

SUNDOWNERS, THE AAN CT: 8 AV: 7.90

1960 GB/Australia 133 C DRAMA/WESTERN/FAMILY

D Fred Zinnemann ☆ AAN
W Isobel Lennart ☆ AAN from Jon Cleary's novel

Deborah Kerr ☆ AAN Robert Mitchum ☆ Peter Ustinov ✔ Glynis Johns ☆ AAN Dina Merrill Chips Rafferty ✔ Michael Anderson Jr Lola Brooks Wylie Watson John Meillon

In the 1920s, a poor man (Robert Mitchum) and his family (Deborah Kerr, Michael Anderson Jr) lead more than 1000 sheep overland to Western Australia, with the idea of making enough money to settle down.

Fred Zinnemann's picturesque yarn may be set in Australia, but it's basically a big, family western about pioneering folk. Though very long and sprawling, it's exciting, full of human interest, and exceptionally well acted by Mitchum and Kerr. The supporting actors (especially Peter Ustinov, Glynis Johns and Chips Rafferty) are no less memorable.

ANTI:

'For all Zinnemann's generous attention to character, the hints of longing, despair and indomitable spirit, the overall impression remains of sheer length and repetition and synthetic naturalism.' *(Richard Winnington)*

'It is regrettable that the story of [the film] isn't nearly up to its incidentals . . . [its] dilemma perhaps more suitable for a half-hour Lassie episode.' *(Roger Angell, New Yorker)*

PRO:

'Unquestionably, its major delight is Deborah Kerr's virtuoso performance.' *(Clancy Sigal, Daily Express)*

'Full of bits of life, real bits . . . It is this casualness which counteracts the sentimentality, which gives the film its quality. This and the acting.' *(Derek Monsey, Sunday Express)*

'It makes me want to pack a tent and few billy-cans into an old horse-drawn van and set off at once for the wide open spaces . . . Zinnemann has proved once and for all with this big, colourful, fresh-air film that you can have plenty of excitement and human interest without indulging in violence, bloodshed and neurosis.' *(Nina Hibbin, Daily Worker)*

SUNRISE AAW CT: 6 AV: 8.00

1927 US 117 BW DRAMA/ROMANCE/SILENT

D F.W. Murnau
W Carl Meyer from Hermann Sudermann's novel *A Trip to Tilsitt*

Janet Gaynor ☆ AAW George O'Brien Margaret Livingston Bodil Rosing J. Farrell MacDonald Ralph Sipperly

A siren from the city (Margaret Livingston) seduces a young farmer (George O'Brien) into attempting to drown his wife (Janet Gaynor).

The film was based on a short story, and it shows – there isn't enough narrative, and the last two-thirds are just a lyrical evocation of a couple making up. It's lovely to look at, though, and the hero's spiritual passage from darkness into light is represented in images which are as startling today as they must have been in 1927. Karl Struss and Charles Rosher won Oscars for their expressionist cinematography; Rochas Gliese was nominated for his equally stylized art direction. The film was given a special Oscar, for being 'a unique and artistic picture', but it was more of a critical than a commercial success.

PRO:

'A distinguished contribution to the screen, made in this country, but produced after the best manner of the German school.' *(Variety)*

'A mixture of Russian gloom and Berlin brightness . . . Mr Murnau shows himself to be an artist in camera studies, bringing forth marvellous results from lights, shadows and settings. He also proves himself to be a true story-teller, and, incidentally, here is a narrative wherein the happy ending is welcome.' *(Mordaunt Hall, New York Times)*

'Not since the earliest, simplest moving pictures, when locomotives, fire-engines, and crowds in streets were transposed to the screen artlessly and endearingly, when the entranced eye was rushed through tunnels and over precipices on runaway trains, has there been such joy in motion.' *(Louise Bogan, New Republic)*

'*Sunrise* throughout was built by moods. Lighting, pace, the carriage and movement of actors, and the camera were all applied to create the dominant mood of each sequence.' *(Lewis Jacobs, 1939)*

'Puts pep into pap . . . Simple and intense images of unequalled beauty.' *(Don Macpherson, Time Out)*

MIXED:

'The story is told in a flowing, lyrical German manner that is extraordinarily sensual, yet is perhaps too self-conscious, too fable-like for American audiences.' *(Pauline Kael)*

ANTI:

'*Sunrise* tries very hard and succeeds in providing A Happy Hour for Housemaids. The cinema should be the means of this age to express what this age feels and there is nothing of this age in *Sunrise*. Trying as it sets out to do to be of no place and every place, of all time and no time, it succeeds quite elaborately in repeating the superficialities of every age whilst giving expression to none of the complexities of this.' *(Robert Herring, Close Up)*

SUNSET BOULEVARD AAN CT: 9 AV: 9.39

1950 US 110 BW DRAMA

D Billy Wilder ☆ AAN
W Charles Brackett Billy Wilder D.M. Marshman Jr ☆ AAW

Gloria Swanson ☆ AAN William Holden ☆ AAN
Erich von Stroheim ☆ AAN Fred Clark ☆
Nancy Olson ☆ AAN Jack Webb Lloyd Gough
Cecil B. DeMille ☆ H.B. Warner Anna Q. Nilsson
Buster Keaton Hedda Hopper

An unscrupulous writer (William Holden) inveigles himself into the affections of a legendary Hollywood star (Gloria Swanson).

Billy Wilder's malicious view of the movie business is part black comedy and part Grand Guignol, all of it beautifully shot and acted. Gloria Swanson, in a come-back role, gives one of the great screen performances: melodramatic but subtle, funny yet tragic. The Andrew Lloyd Webber musical is much more sentimental; Wilder leaves the viewer with a nasty taste in his mouth, and means to. Franz Waxman's score won an Academy Award. John F. Seitz's cinematography was Oscar-nominated.

'After nine years of obscurity, I was in the glaring spotlight again, thanks to Billy Wilder and a brilliant script.' *(Gloria Swanson, in her autobiography)*

'You bastard! You have disgraced the industry that made you and fed you! You should be tarred and feathered and run out of Hollywood!' *(MGM chief Louis B. Mayer to Billy Wilder after a private screening)*

ANTI:

'Almost everyone else seems to think [it is] admirable, but [it] strikes me as being the sheerest balderdash. Empty as Gloria Swanson's acting seems to me, I cannot deny that she has not lost her looks or dispute her courage in playing such a part . . . Even so . . . it is . . . downright absurd . . . I cannot understand why the aging star . . . should allow her home to look like a Charles Addams interior . . . von Stroheim seems to . . . be acting the least likely character I have encountered.' *(John Mason Brown, Saturday Review)*

'A pretentious slice of Roquefort . . . [which] substituted snappy photography and dialogue for what could have been a genuinely moving tragedy. It seemed to me that the authors never quite made up their minds whether they were with Miss Desmond or against her. There are moments when they appear to have a healthy cynicism toward Hollywood, past and present, but before the film is over, it is quite evident that they have a pretty unhealthy contempt for aging stars.' *(Philip Hamburger, New Yorker)*

'While I appreciate it I don't altogether like it . . . The bizarre melodrama . . . is worked out in Edgar Allan Poe style . . . but [Brackett and Wilder] appear to be afraid of the monster they created . . . Miss Swanson's performance is so powerful that the film seems weak when she is not on the screen.' *(Jympson Harmon, Evening News)*

'*Sunset Boulevard* sets out to impale some Hollywood values and roast them over some burning bright coals of observation. It further attempts to do so in a style that may best be described as Hollywood Gothic. The style, which is effective if not original, is more successful than the content, for somewhere along the line *Sunset Boulevard* turns into the very sort of goods it attempts to discredit.' *(Fortnight)*

'Where the film disappoints is in its failure to explore the situation once it has been presented; its level remains anecdotal. The pivotal figure of the story is the writer – it is his tragedy – but our knowledge of his motives and his feelings remains superficial. The observation of Norma Desmond is similarly exterior; though it must be admitted that Miss Swanson's exterior is so triumphantly exotic that one's attention is most of the time fully occupied. The second half of the film is taken at the deliberate pace which calls for detailed analytical writing, and equal perception in the direction. These it does not get. The script is not concerned to penetrate; the first half of the climax, where the writer voluntarily exposes his degradation to the girl with whom he has fallen in love, is taken far too lightly; and the last sequence comes across as Grand Guignol rather than serious drama. It is perhaps ungrateful to carp at so brave a venture of originality, but that is apt to be the risk run by brilliance unaccompanied by depth.' *(Lindsay Anderson)*

MIXED:

'The analysis is admirable so far as it goes, which is not quite far enough . . . Excellently observed as [the characters] are, they do not gain enough depth in the second half of the film . . . An increase in intensity . . . could have made it more than a series of brilliant anecdotes . . . There is no doubt, though that [it] is one of the most genuinely original films from Hollywood for some time.' *(Gavin Lambert)*

'She [Swanson] grasps each scene in her violent, over-emotional role like a drug-addict pouncing on a hypodermic full of cocaine. I didn't like *Sunset Boulevard* for its cumulative effect is unpleasant, but I shall go to see it again and again. It is a sanitary inspection of that part of Hollywood we do not often visit – the kitchen behind the brassy front.' *(Leonard Mosley, Daily Express)*

'The picture itself goes from improbability to reality and back again, but Miss Swanson holds it all together.' *(Esquire)*

'It reminds us by its own single deficiency: want of pathos. But a certain clinical detachment in the manner of the piece cannot destroy its claim to be regarded as an exceptionally distinguished work.' *(Dilys Powell)*

PRO:

'I believe the film will be studied years hence when the pundits of the screen set themselves to the task of analyzing the durability and the greatness of the picture.' *(South London Advertiser)*

'That rare blend of pungent writing, expert acting, masterly direction and unobtrusively artistic photography which quickly casts a spell over an audience and holds it enthralled to a shattering climax.' *(New York Times)*

'Miss Swanson's performance takes her at one bound into the class of Boris Karloff and Tod Slaughter.' *(Richard Mallett, Punch)*

'A weird, fascinating motion picture about an art form which, new as it is, is already haunted by ghosts.' *(Otis L. Guernsey Jr, New York Herald Tribune)*

'Hollywood craftsmanship at its smartest and just about at its best, and it is hard to find better craftsmanship than that, at this time, in any art or country. It is also, in terms of movie tradition, a very courageous picture . . . much the most ambitious movie about Hollywood ever done and is the best of several good ones into the bargain.' *(James Agee)*

THE *SUPERMAN* SERIES

SUPERMAN CT: 7 AV: 7.13

1978 GB 143 C SF/ADVENTURE/COMEDY/FAMILY

D Richard Donner
W Mario Puzo David Newman Robert Benton Leslie Newman

Christopher Reeve ☆ Marlon Brando Margot Kidder ✔ Jackie Cooper Glenn Ford Phyllis Thaxter Trevor Howard Gene Hackman Ned Beatty Susannah York Valerie Perrine

A super-hero (Christopher Reeve) grows up in America.

Terrific fun, and an odd but entertaining blending of genres. There's mythological epic: the early scenes on Krypton, though a shade ponderous, are more impressive than the original critics recognized. Then there's a memorably lyrical evocation of rural America as Superman grows up on a farm. It's also a romantic light comedy, with Christopher Reeve charming as Clark Kent bumbling through his courtship of Lois Lane (an underrated, multi-faceted performance by Margot Kidder). And it's a fine action adventure with – on the whole – impressive special effects, plenty of witty ideas and Reeve the archetypal square-jawed hero.

The dodgy moments come when the film descends into broad comedy, with Gene Hackman playing too hard for laughs and dispelling any menace he might otherwise have had. One other blot on the escutcheon: the end credits last a record-breaking (and ridiculous) seven and a half minutes.

The critics, possibly prejudiced by excessive hype and the news that Marlon Brando had been paid an unprecedented three million dollars for a ten-minute performance, were generally cool – and especially critical of the first, Brando-dominated section. There were Oscar nominations for the score (John Williams), editing (Stuart Baird), sound (Gordon K. McCallum, Graham Hartstone, Nicolas LeMessurier, Roy Charman), and it received a Special Achievement Award for its visual effects (Les Bowie, Colin Chilvers, Denys Coop, Roy Field, Derek Meddings, Zoran Perisic).

ANTI:

'Blah. Not only blah but occasionally inexplicable . . . for instance, the entrance to the villain's headquarters seems to be far under Grand Central Terminal in New York but the interior seems to be in the terminal itself.' *(Stanley Kauffmann)*

'Cheesy-looking, and the plotting is so hit or miss that the story never seems to get started . . . It gives the impression of having been made in panic – in fear that its style or too much imagination might endanger its approach to the literal-minded.' *(Pauline Kael)*

'The epitome of supersell.' *(Les Keyser, Hollywood in the Seventies)*

'Long, lugubrious and only patchily entertaining . . . with far too many irrelevant preliminaries and a misguided sense of its own importance.' *(Halliwell)*

MIXED:

'While the special effects may be inconsistent in quality, when they do take off, they soar . . . The same film that boasts this kind of technical mastery also plummets us to the depths of comic book inanity and blatant incongruities.' *(Cinefantastique)*

'*Superman* is good, clean, simple-minded fun, though it's a movie whose limited appeal is built in. There isn't a thought in this film's head that would be out of place on the side of a box of Wheaties.' *(New York Times)*

'What makes [it] the best screen version to date is not the amazing effects, but the exciting acting from the benevolent aliens. Marlon Brando . . . sets the mood perfectly, his awesome presence pervading the rest of the film after his early disappearance . . . The . . . small disappointment . . . is that it is never really possible to believe that a man can fly . . . The suspension of disbelief is often shattered by the stiff-limbed posture of Reeve, necessary for the complicated harness worn in the flying scenes.' *(Stephen Woolley, Orbis)*

PRO:

'Magnify James Bond's extraordinary physical powers while curbing his sex drive and you have the essence of *Superman*, a wonderful, chuckling, preposterously exciting fantasy guaranteed to challenge world box office records this time round, and perhaps with sequels to come.' *(Variety)*

'*Superman* is packed with everything adventure lovers could wish for.' *(Film Review)*

'Not since *Star Wars*, the alltime champ, has there been such an entertaining movie for children of all ages . . . two hours and 15 minutes of pure fun, fancy, and adventure.' *(Time)*

'A surprisingly infectious entertainment, nicely balanced between warmth and wit, intimacy and impressive special effects, comic-strip fantasy and several elements that make the movie eminently eligible for Deep Thinking about rescue fantasies, cherubic messiahs and other pieces of popcorn metaphysics.' *(Jack Kroll, Newsweek)*

'Pure delight, a wondrous combination of all the old-fashioned things we never really get tired of: adventure and romance, heroes and villains, earthshaking special effects, and – you know what else? Wit.' *(Roger Ebert)*

SUPERMAN II CT: 6 AV: 6.54

1980 GB 127 C SF/ADVENTURE/FAMILY

D Richard Lester ☆
W Mario Puzo David Newman Leslie Newman

Christopher Reeve ☆ Terence Stamp ✓
Margot Kidder Ned Beatty Jackie Cooper
Gene Hackman Valerie Perrine Sarah Douglas
Susannah York Jack OHalloran E.G. Marshall

Superman battles against three alien enemies.

Most favourably reviewed of the *Superman* films and an entertaining action-adventure, stylishly directed by Richard Lester. Terence Stamp is an excellent villain, and the action scenes are spectacular. But it lacks the depth and imagination of the first *Superman*, and takes an unconscionably long time to get going.

ANTI:

'There's an underlying cynicism to this sequel that makes it less enjoyable than its predecessor.' *(Cinefantastique)*

'The special effects are highly variable in quality, and the whole film – blown up from 35mm to 70mm for the big-theatre showings – is grainy and bleached and often poorly framed. You're much better off if you see it in 35mm.' *(Pauline Kael)*

MIXED:

'The sequel is all the better for diving straight into the action, but a classic it isn't, even of the comic strip kind.' *(Halliwell)*

PRO:

'The special effects are an eyeful.' *(Glasgow Herald)*

'An outstanding exception to the rule that sequels are rarely as good as the originals. Compared with the first film, this is a good deal more thrilling and a lot more fun.' *(Sun)*

'A success, a stirring sequel to the smash of 79. Whether you will prefer it to the original is like choosing between root beer and Fresca. They're both bubbly, but the flavor is different.' *(Newsweek)*

'I thought the original *Superman* was terrific entertainment – and so I was a little startled to discover that I liked *Superman II* even more.' *(Roger Ebert)*

SUPERMAN III CT: 4 AV: 4.15

1983 GB 120/125 C SF/ADVENTURE/FAMILY

D Richard Lester
W David Newman Leslie Newman

Christopher Reeve ☆ Richard Pryor Jackie Cooper
Robert Vaughn Margot Kidder Annette O'Toole
Annie Ross Pamela Stephenson Marc McClure

A tycoon (Robert Vaughn) bent on world domination uses the talents of a computer genius (Richard Pryor) to try and destroy Superman (Christopher Reeve).

A silly plot allows the comic relief (Richard Pryor) to dominate the man from Krypton to a tiresome extent. There are a few laughs – especially in the opening sequence – but really they belong to a different film. Reeve continues to impress in the title role, but the film as a whole is far from super.

'Sometimes humorous but overwritten and overacted variation on a tired theme.' *(Halliwell)*

'The kind of movie that I feared the original *Superman* would be. It's a cinematic comic book, shallow, silly, filled with stunts and action, without much human interest.' *(Roger Ebert)*

'Supe may be able to save the world, but he's no comedian. An interesting compilation of early 80s paranoias, though.' *(Rose)*

SUPERMAN IV: THE QUEST FOR PEACE

CT: 2 AV: 2.82

(aka *Quest for Peace, The*)

1987 GB 89 C SF/ADVENTURE/FAMILY

D Sidney J. Furie ●
W Lawrence Konner Mark Rosenthal Christopher Reeve ●

Christopher Reeve Gene Hackman Jackie Cooper Marc McClure Jon Cryer Sam Wanamaker Mark Pillow Mariel Hemingway Margot Kidder

Superman (Christopher Reeve) tries to rid the world of nuclear weapons.

Dull dialogue, stodgy direction and idiotic attempts to ram home a political message combine to make this the weakest of the series. The special effects are especially tacky.

'An improvement over *III* but still pretty ordinary, with second-rate special effects.' *(Maltin)*

'You'll believe a superhero can bellyflop. Superman here does his bit for CND (apparently at Reeves' insistence) by reducing the world's stock of nuclear weapons. He should stop wearing his underpants outside his trousers; they're beginning to wear out. Next thing you know he'll be turning them into dusters and showing us that a superhero can do the housework just like any New Man.' *(Rose)*

'As dreary as a summit conference in Belgium.' *(Brian Case, Time Out)*

SUSPICION AAN

CT: 7 AV: 7.33

1941 US 99 BW THRILLER

D Alfred Hitchcock
W Samson Raphaelson Alma Reville Joan Harrison from Frances Iles's novel *Before the Fact*

Joan Fontaine ☆ AAW Cary Grant ☆ Nigel Bruce Cedric Hardwicke May Whitty Isabel Jeans Heather Angel Leo G. Carroll

A wife (Joan Fontaine) suspects her husband (Cary Grant) may be a murderer.

Hitchcock felt that *Suspicion*, like *Rebecca*, was too lavishly produced and didn't look English enough. Another disappointing aspect is the happy ending, which was imposed upon the director by the front office. Even so, this is a gripping thriller, with a tremendous Franz Waxman score (which was Oscar-nominated). The film contains some of Hitchcock's most brilliant images, such as the one where Joan Fontaine stands before a window in a black dress, and looks the way she feels – like a fly caught in a web. But look again – and she may be the spider, fattening herself on suspicions, and her husband may be the fly. Or there's the classic shot where Cary Grant carries a suspicious glass of milk upstairs, and Hitchcock rivets the audience's attention by the simple means of putting a light inside the glass. It's another of those Hitchcock films where the narrative springs naturally from the characters' deepest fears:

'Joan Fontaine, at the outset, is a dowdy, repressed young woman, a colonel's daughter, who has led a sheltered life characterized by the rigid values of respectability and a total ignorance of the outer world. She is irresistibly attracted to the man who represents glamor and reckless, carefree abandon; but he represents also a total rejection of everything her family background and upbringing have stood for: subconsciously, she wants him to be a murderer.' *(Robin Wood, Hitchcock's Films Revisited, 1989)*

ANTI:

'It asks us to imagine that Cary Grant is a charming and well-bred English ne'er-do-well moving in good society. Whereas he isn't anything of the kind, his shoulders have the American campus written all over them, and his manners have obviously been learnt in some *Palais de Danse*. Also he says "fix" when he means "arrange". However, he is likeable enough for us to take him at the film-director's valuation and as I have said so often, a film has got to be got going somehow. Cary falls in love with Joan Fontaine, who is the daughter of General Sir Cedric Hardwicke and Dame May Whitty. These three characters are authentic with the exception of two very small matters. One is that even today young women brought up as ladies do not receive telegrams in the presence of their mothers without revealing their contents. The other is that an English girl, speaking on the telephone, does not use the phrase "thank you for calling me", when she means "thank you for ringing me up". A trifling fee of, say, £5,000 would put any Hollywood director wise on these tiny points. But Mr Alfred Hitchcock is not a Hollywood director but an English director who happens to be in Hollywood. Which just shows how Hollywood's communications corrupt English manners.' *(James Agate, Tatler)*

MIXED:

'There are certainly some good passages in the film. But the story begins with a barely tolerable deliberation (and against a curiously unconvincing background); and somehow the veneer of good society blurs the significant detail for which we look in Hitchcock. Still, an exciting enough piece.' *(Dilys Powell)*

'The fact that Hitchcock throws in a happy end during the last five minutes, like a conjuror explaining his tricks, seems to me a pity; but it spoils the film only in retrospect, and we have already had our thrills.' *(William Whitebait, New Statesman)*

PRO:

'*Suspicion* pretty nearly scared the gray flannel slacks off this reporter. It is a diversion recommended to those who enjoy an intelligent shocker-saga.' *(Herb Sterne)*

'A class production provided with excellence in direction, acting and mounting.' *(Variety)*

SWARM, THE CT: 5 AV: 2.00

1978 US 116 C HORROR/SO BAD

D Irwin Allen ●
W Stirling Silliphant ● from Arthur Herzog's novel

Michael Caine ● Katharine Ross Richard Widmark Richard Chamberlain Olivia de Havilland ● Fred MacMurray Ben Johnson Lee Grant, José Ferrer Patty Duke Astin Bradford Dillman Slim Pickens Henry Fonda Cameron Mitchell

Killer bees invade USA.

It's hard to know which is worse: the ridiculous special effects or the dreary direction. Or perhaps its Olivia de Havilland's southern accent. Some kind of all-time booby prize should go to Stirling Silliphant's screenplay: it's the kind of film in which people are telling each other things they must already know, and the dialogue is of unsurpassed banality. Classic lines include 'They're more virulent than the Australian brown box jellyfish.' (Henry Fonda, playing an immunologist) and 'I'm going to be the first officer in US battle history to get his butt kicked by a mess of bugs!' (Richard Widmark).

Sample dialogue . . . Fred MacMurray: 'Maureen, how long have we known each other? About thirty years? All that time, have you ever heard me beg? Maureen, I'm willing to beg now. I want you to marry me. I know people look at me and think that I'm just the man behind the aspirin counter, but inside I love you.' Olivia de Havilland: 'How lucky I am!'

PRO:

'To judge by some of the critical comments . . . you'd be excused for imagining it must be about the worst movie ever made. In fact, it's quite exciting in its own soppy way . . . [The screenplay] makes an intelligent use of technical jargon and creates some tension . . . The film is a lot of fun . . . [and] succeeds in not being completely laughable . . . [It's] the Bees Knees.' *(Julian Fox, F & F)*

ANTI:

'An atrocity . . . the kind of movie one waits years to avoid.' *(John Kobal, Films)*

'One of those grand catastrophes that make audiences either hoot in derisive surprise or look away in embarrassment.' *(Jay Cocks, Time)*

'This is failure so dismal it goes beyond failure.' *(Hollis Alpert, Saturday Review)*

'The surprise comedy hit of the season.' *(New York Times)*

'Simply the worst film ever made.' *(Alan Brien, Sunday Times)*

'[The bees'] periodic manifestations, peppering the skies with darkness, look as convincing as if the projectionist had dropped iron filings into his machine. Their human opponents – well, the synopsis says they are human – seem to have been picked by a pin out of *Spotlight* or some out-of-date casting album. The longest surviving, Dr Michael Caine, is a world-famous entomologist and tax exile who just happens to be passing; Henry Fonda spends all his not inconsiderable time on-screen in a wheelchair (obviously suffering from total collapse after reading his parts of the screenplay); and there is a fetching little romantic sub-plot involving glum schoolmarm Olivia de Havilland (who sounds as if she's just stumbled off the set of *Gone with the Wind*) and two aging hicks vying for her attention; if you go after a hearty meal, it's likely to fetch your dinner up.' *(Phillip Bergson, Times Educational Supplement)*

'You could pass it all off as a sick joke, except that it cost twelve million dollars, twenty-two million bees, and several years of someone's life.' *(Guardian)*

'The story is of a banality matched only by the woodenness of the acting.' *(Barry Took, Punch)*

'Killer bees periodically interrupt the arch writing, stilted direction and ludicrous acting in Irwin Allen's disappointing and tired non-thriller.' *(Variety)*

'The ultimate in B pictures.' *(Alan Frank)*

SWEET CHARITY CT: 7 AV: 6.67

1969 US 133/149 C MUSICAL/ROMANCE

D Bob Fosse ☆
W Neil Simon based on Fellini's film *Nights of Cabiria* (songs by Cy Coleman and Dorothy Fields ☆)

Shirley MacLaine ✔ Chita Rivera ✔ Ricardo Montalban John McMartin Paula Kelly Stubby Kaye Sammy Davis Jr

The amorous encounters of a dance hall hostess (Shirley MacLaine).

Bob Fosse's début as a choreographer-director is a dynamic affair, enthusiastically performed by Shirley MacLaine as a tart with a heart. Unfairly panned on release, it is very enjoyable if a little long (and the last half-hour is downbeat, for a musical). Highlights include 'Big Spender' and the big rooftop dance number, 'There Must Be Something Better Than This'. Cy Coleman was Oscar-nominated for his musical direction.

ANTI:

'The worst-photographed musical I've ever seen; aside from that it's plain awful. . . . The kind of platinum clinker designed to send audiences flying in the opposite direction, toward the safety of their television sets . . . I like Miss MacLaine, but one thing is certain: she's not touched by a stroke of genius. She is not a great actress, she dances only adequately, and her singing voice is pleasant without any trace of power or presence.' *(Rex Reed)*

'If [it] had been a simply told tart with a heart story it might have made remarkably sweet and charitable entertainment. But done up with the big-time, give-it-all-you've-got, we're-what-the-world's-been-waiting-for treatment, it leaves you shrinking in your seat . . . The characters don't talk: they spout lines at each other, frantic to amuse . . . When the film . . . finally goes over to being an ordinary, honest-to-movieland weepie, it at least builds up a certain charm.' *(Nina Hibbin, Morning Star)*

'Has pretensions to being musical drama . . . This particular form of rot set in on Broadway with *Oklahoma!*, when all of a sudden it was decided that musicals had to have some significance . . . What had really happened was the conquest of musical comedy by operetta . . . Shirley MacLaine, accomplished comedienne and actress though she is, is neither a singer nor a dancer.' *(Richard Roud, Guardian)*

'Shirley MacLaine is certainly sweet as Charity . . . [The film] is slick, amusing even moving while it lasts, but is ultimately to be despised for refusing to be modern at heart. Not all [its] hippies and flower-children . . . can cloak its old-fashioned attitudes.' *(Madeleine Harmsworth, Sunday Mirror)*

'Although Shirley MacLaine tries hard, it's obvious that her dancing isn't up to the demands of the role.' *(Pauline Kael)*

MIXED:

'Comes charging on to the screen with a prepacked reputation which brackets it with *West Side Story* and *Sound of Music*. I wouldn't rate it as high as either, but it's got great pace, colour and excitement and some fine numbers for Shirley MacLaine to put over . . . All the same [she] has to plough through a fantastically silly yarn.' *(Edward Betts, People)*

'Generally pleasing, it passes the time so quickly and divertingly . . . [But] because Bob Fosse does . . . things . . . so very well . . . it would be an insult not to give him less than one's serious attention . . . What is right with [the film] is nearly all the bits and pieces; what is wrong . . . is that it never quite manages to pull them together into a totally convincing whole. Though [its] style . . . is far from stagey . . . I suspect that the ghost of the stage production has proved hard to lay.' *(John Russell Taylor, The Times)*

PRO:

'Fine, overlooked.' *(Maltin)*

'Neglected on release, but it's first class.' *(Winnert)*

SWEET LIFE, THE: *see* LA DOLCE VITA.

SWEET SMELL OF SUCCESS

CT: 7 AV: 8.79

1957 US 96 BW DRAMA

D Alexander Mackendrick ☆
W Clifford Odets Ernest Lehman ☆ from Lehman's short story *Tell Me About It Tomorrow*

Burt Lancaster ☆ Tony Curtis ☆ Susan arrison Martin Milner Sam Levene Barbara Nichols ☆ Jeff Donnell Emile Meyer ☆ Joseph Leon

Unscrupulous press agent (Tony Curtis) aids and abets nefarious schemes of beastly New York columnist (Burt Lancaster).

This magnificently mean, moody movie about the misuse of media power grows more and more timely. It has splendid baddies, with Lancaster wonderfully sinister as 'The Eyes of Broadway', and Curtis giving the performance of his life as his sleazy accolyte. Director Alexander Mackendrick had showed a dark side in films like The *Ladykillers*; here, in the melodrama which was his American début, he shows sublime confidence and mastery of film noir technique. He is helped by Elmer Bernstein and Chico Hamilton's fine jazz score, James Wong Howe's restless camerawork and a terrific script with interestingly stylized dialogue. The one disappointment is that the young lovers, Martin Milner and Susan Harrison, are too anodyne.

The film was a flop, mainly because the mass audience would not accept Curtis as a bad guy. Its lack of success may have coloured Mackendrick's own low estimation of it.

ANTI:

'A piece of absolute hokum and melodrama . . . My worst film.' *(Alexander Mackendrick)*

'If you could believe it, it would be a shocker; but if you could believe it, you would not be going round without an attendant . . . The character Mr Lancaster is really playing is the mad scientist of the side-show horror movies.' *(Robert Hatch, Nation)*

'Slightly arty-crafty . . . [it fails] in the first requisite of any play, which is to bring the characters to life.' *(C.A. Lejeune, Observer)*

PRO:

'So superbly is the thing done, one's skin crawls with credulous horror. The acting is first-rate, in particular Tony Curtis's performance as the lizard who scurries at the crocodile's call. And a dreadful authenticity is given by the feeling of place – the smell, you might say, of New York: the roaring, rushing streets, the glittering nights, the dense, sophisticated discomfort of smart bars and restaurants.' *(Dilys Powell)*

'Few films have maintained such a constant atmosphere of menace . . . The pace is hectic and the jargon and allusions – often obscure enough in themselves – are made still more confusing by an extraordinarily literary style of dialogue . . . But Lancaster, miscast, makes a gallant attempt at the impossibly written part of Hunsecker.' *(MFB)*

'You emerge thankfully to breathe London's carbon monoxide again and rejoin the human race.' *(Campbell Dixon, Daily Telegraph)*

'Curtis, foxy eyes set in a little-boy face, has never done anything better. His performance is something to goggle at.' *(Anthony Carthew, Daily Herald)*

'A high-tension jolt into the rat-eat-rat, rat-tat-tattle world of a monstrous Broadway columnist . . . which could have been offal, is raised to considerable dramatic heights by intense acting, taut direction, superb camerawork . . . and above all, by its whiplash dialogue.' *(Time)*

'Has the cold-blooded excitement of a stroll through the reptile house . . . Venom spurts from every sentence. And the terrified victims are swallowed whole . . . Not for everyone. But I recommend it as a savage and satisfying piece of picture-making.' *(Philip Oakes, Evening Standard)*

'[Captures] better than any film I know the atmosphere of Times Square and big-city journalism.' *(David Denby, New York Magazine, 1985)*

'A sweet slice of perversity, a study of dollar and power worship.' *(Pauline Kael)*

SWING TIME CT: 10 AV: 9.46

1936 US 103 BW MUSICAL/ROMANCE

D George Stevens
W Howard Lindsay Allan Scott from Erwin Gelsey's story (songs by Jerome Kern and Dorothy Fields ☆)

Fred Astaire ☆ Ginger Rogers ☆ Victor Moore Helen Broderick Eric Blore Betty Furness George Metaxa Landers Stevens John Harrington Pierre Watkin

Gambler (Fred Astaire) tries to impress prospective father-in-law (Landers Stevens) by holding down a job in New York.

The talent of Fred Astaire and Ginger Rogers is here combined with a script that is quite amusing and certainly above-average for their movies. But the highlight is the score which includes definitive versions of 'A Fine Romance', 'Pick Yourself Up', 'Never Gonna Dance', 'Bojangles Of Harlem' and the Oscar-winning masterpiece, 'The Way You Look Tonight'. Probably the best Astaire-Rogers musical. Hermes Pan picked up an Oscar nomination for his dance direction of 'Bojangles'.

PRO:

'Smart, modern and impressive in every respect.' *(Variety)*

'Fred Astaire's pleasing personality, his rhythmic grace as a dancer, charm and intelligence as an actor, and proficiency as a singer mark *Swing Time* as highly entertaining picture. He is teamed again with Ginger Rogers, who continues to make progress, but still has some distance to go before her contribution. . . . measures up to that of her partner . . . George Stevens . . . succeeds admirably in pleasantly befuddling our senses until we are indifferent to the weaknesses of the story . . . I know of no law that would be broken if a picture like *Swing Time* were made to appeal to the intellect as well as to the eye. but the eye appeal of *Swing Time* is quite sufficient to make it worth your while.' *(Welford Beaton, Hollywood Spectator)*

'The magnificent "Bojangles of Harlem" [is] one of the most accomplished of all Astaire's dance routines.' *(R.A.E. Pickard, Dictionary of 1000 Best Films, 1972)*

MIXED:

'Made to . . . formula. But this formula is a handicap when it results, as it does here . . . in imposing an empty silly story on an audience impatient to see Fred Astaire and Ginger Rogers dance . . . The virtuosity of Fred Astaire is established and he does not disappoint; his dancing is the finest of its kind. Ginger Rogers is glamorous . . . but her métier is comedy . . . As a dancer she still seems commonplace beside Fred Astaire – lacking technique in footwork and lightness of touch. However tasteless the setting and chorus costumes, there remains the excitement of watching Fred Astaire and this makes the film worth seeing. The dance music . . . is not interesting. The camerawork on the dancefloor is good.' *(MFB)*

'Considered the best all-around Astaire-Rogers musical with first-rate songs from Jerome Kern and Dorothy Fields.' *(Elkan Allan, NFT Bulletin)*

SWINGER, THE CT: 5 AV: 3.25

1966 US 81 C DRAMA/ROMANCE/SO BAD

D George Sidney ●
W Lawrence Roman ●

Ann-Margret ● Tony Franciosa Robert Coote Yvonne Romain Horace MacMahon Nydia Westman

A writer (Ann-Margret) pretends to have a racy past in order to get her writing published.

A cherishably tacky, tasteless artefact from the Swinging 60s. Sample dialogue . . . Ann-Margret (confessing to parents): 'I was in an orgy, I was a stripper, I was a streetwalker, then in a motel a man tried forcibly to seduce me!' Mother: 'There, there, dear. If you think these things are bad, wait till your children grow up.'

PRO:

'A very amusing original screen comedy which satirizes nudie books and magazines . . . hip scripting and good performances.' *(Variety)*

ANTI:

'I started to say . . . [the film] has a good idea but on thinking it over for thirty seconds I can't even give it that . . . The producer has tried to disguise this trash with a lot of splashy production and mechanical trick camera work. But he can't conceal cheapness and lack of talent.' *(Bosley Crowther)*

'Goodwill being customary at this season, I'll make no comment.' *(Patrick Gibbs, Daily Telegraph, 23rd December 1966)*

'I can't think of anyone who could have made . . . this repulsive, leering film.' *(Ian Christie, Daily Express)*

'The nastiest, most vulgar, most inept film of the year . . . [which] is not worthy of further comment.' *(Ann Pacey, Sun)*

'I do not recall seeing a less sexy or less funny sex comedy.' *(David Robinson, Financial Times)*

'Racking the recesses of memory fails to yield a more consistently distasteful film . . . and every adjective is a pitfall that risks lending it some oblique allure.' *(Derek Prouse, Sunday Times)*

'A hectically saucy mixture of lechery, depravity, perversion, voyeurism and girlie magazines . . . A heavy, witless pudding.' *(MFB)*

'It's hard not to love *The Swinger*, since it's proof positive that Elvis Presley didn't star in the worst movies in Hollywood history Ann-Margret did. In fact, *The Swinger* just might be the all-time tackiest major studio movie: the opening voice-over features a narrator who belches not once but three times.' *(Margulies & Rebello)*

'Leering farce with Ann-Margret looking and acting incapable of reading, much less writing a book.' *(Scheuer)*

SYLVIA SCARLETT

CT: 5 AV: 6.00

1935 US 94 BW COMEDY/DRAMA

D George Cukor
W Gladys Unger John Collier Mortimer Offner from Compton Mackenzie's novel

Katharine Hepburn Cary Grant ☆ Edmund Gwenn ☆ Brian Aherne Lennox Pawle Dennie Moore ●

A young woman (Katharine Hepburn) dresses as a man in order to evade the police, then falls in love with an artist (Brian Aherne).

Panned on release, this odd but appealing mixture of romantic drama with screwball comedy has a rambling narrative structure which owes more to Shakespearean plays like *As You Like It*, than to conventional screenwriting. It is an interestingly coded examination of gender reversal (director Cukor was himself homosexual), and part of the reason for its initial lack of success may be that Aherne is evidently attracted to Hepburn while she is dressed as a boy. Cary Grant steals the film as a Cockney criminal.

ANTI:

'A disaster, and the reason it's a success now is that the audience is also a disaster. At least when it was made the audience had sense enough not to go . . . A lot of pictures of mine that people thought bad at the time have since been called "classics", but of those Sylvia Scarlett is the most surprising. I remember going home one night from the studio and writing in my diary, "This picture makes no sense at all and I wonder whether George Cukor is aware of the fact, because I certainly don't know what the hell I'm doing".' *(Katharine Hepburn)*

'A story that's hard to believe. Dubious entertainment for the public.' *(Variety)*

'A sprawling and ineffective essay in dramatic chaos.' *(Richard Watts Jr, New York Herald Tribune)*

'A tragic waste of time and screen talent.' *(Eileen Creelman, New York Sun)*

'Undistinguished, unclear, and ill-mannered. I profess no great love for [the original story] but it was never as footling as the work the studios have made from it . . . Some people would call it picaresque. Personally I'd call it plain bad and go home and play marbles.' *(Observer)*

MIXED:

'Hepburn is somewhat uneven, but occasionally rises near to perfection.' *(Daily Mail)*

'In print Mr Mackenzie unquestionably made the adventures of Sylvia Scarlett more interesting and vital than Sylvia herself . . . Yet [in the film] it is not long before her adventures become monotonous and dull. The reason perhaps lies in the fact that . . . they are taken too seriously . . . [Hepburn] is forced to stand outside the character . . . because there is not enough substance in that skeleton to support the flesh and blood with which it might have been clothed. But at least she makes the bones rattle intelligently.' *(The Times)*

'You may think [Hepburn] overacts badly at times; but you will still find it difficult to resist the charm of her beautiful movements . . . Cary Grant has never before given as fine a performance . . . The only false note in the acting is . . . Dennie Moore, whose idea of a Cockney serving girl, will not be shared by the British filmgoer.' *(Film Weekly)*

'A very entertaining film. Parts of the story are a trifle illogical but the direction, acting and some very delightful photography make it seem almost possible – Katharine Hepburn makes a most attractive boy, but is a little monotonous in some of her rather coy scenes with Brian Aherne . . . Cary Grant is especially good.' *(MFB)*

'It seems to go wrong in a million directions, but it

has unusually affecting qualities.' *(Pauline Kael, 1978)*

PRO:

'A much more polished comedy than most, and consistently engaging.' *(Winston Burden, Brooklyn Daily Eagle)*

'Hepburn's histrionic abilities [are] given full rein in light-hearted crook adventures and [she makes an] appealing transition to femininity when romance enters the field . . . [Her] versatility is run a close second by Cary Grant as the likeable and nonchalant Cockney crook . . . Very good.' *(Era)*

'Very good popular entertainment, a first class booking for the multitude as well as Hepburn fans.' *(Kine Weekly)*

T

TAGEBUCH EINER VERLORENEN, DAS:

see DIARY OF A LOST GIRL.

TAKE THE MONEY AND RUN

CT: 7 AV: 6.00

1969 US 85 C COMEDY

D Woody Allen
W Woody Allen Mickey Rose ✔

Woody Allen ✔ Janet Margolin Marcel Hillaire Lonny Chapman Jacqueline Hyde Louise Lasser

Virgil Starkwell (Woody Allen) tries to become a master criminal.

Woody Allen's comedy about an incompetent's life of crime is structured as a spoof documentary. It's little more than a succession of sketches, but some of these are hilarious – the bank robbery and jail-break especially.

ANTI:

'A limply good-natured little nothing of a comedy, soft as sneakers.' *(Pauline Kael)*

'A few good laughs in an 85-minute film do not a comedy make.' *(Variety)*

MIXED:

'Mr Allen's considerable comic ability needs "springing" from his inadequate writing ability.' *(Anne Sharpley, Evening Standard)*

'Given a decent plot and an accomplished director I am sure [Allen] could make a film that would have the populace falling about with mirth.' *(Ian Christie, Daily Express)*

'One of the most endearing films I've seen for some time, but also one of the messiest.' *(Derek Malcolm, Guardian)*

PRO:

'A fair run of laughs for your money.' *(Frank Cashlin, Sun)*

'Allen has created a frame for his talents that really works – enough discipline to provide point and focus and enough freedom for his comic genius to run amuck.' *(Stanley Newman, Cue)*

'Something very special and eccentric and funny.' *(Vincent Canby, New York Times)*

TAKING OFF

CT: 6 AV: 7.14

1971 US 92 C COMEDY

D Milos Forman ☆
W Milos Forman John Guare Jean-Claude Carrière John Klein

Lynn Carlin ✔ Buck Henry Linnea Heacock Georgia Engel Tony Harvey Audra Lindley Paul Benedict Vincent Schiavelli David Gittler Ike Turner

Two middle-aged parents (Lynn Carlin, Buck Henry) try to lure home their runaway daughter (Linnea Heacock) by getting more on her wavelength.

Forman's first American film is an episodic but often touching and amusing comedy about the generation gap. Youth movies of this period had a tendency to preach; this one is more concerned with wry observation of the generational divide, and as a result it has worn better than most.

ANTI:

'I cannot think offhand of any other movie as gracelessly, smugly, and stupidly antihuman, self-servingly and gloatingly superior to all humanity . . . I consider Milos Forman morally deficient to the utmost degree, and, as usually though not always follows, a worthless imitation of an artist. And I think that the army of his admirers whether critics or audiences, are, at the very least, dupes and fools.' *(John Simon)*

PRO:

'A series of anecdotes. There are anecdotes about marital idiosyncrasies, about runaway teenagers, about aspiring pop singers . . . But the anecdotes are based on observation: they coalesce, they form, when one looks back, a coherent view. Mr Forman has made an extraordinarily successful transition from the Czechoslovak to the American scene.' *(Dilys Powell)*

'At times it is so funny you dare not laugh in case you miss something and as always with Forman often you can't quite laugh because it's so poignant and so interesting.' *(Melvyn Bragg, The Times)*

'Perhaps the most attractive thing about Forman's view of America is that he never seems to have felt it incumbent on him to take a view . . . As always [his] comedy is in his timing, particularly in those moments when everything seems chaotically off balance and his actors lurch about as though someone had shifted the furniture in familiar rooms . . . But the film is at least as funny, and quite as sharp, as anything he has done in Czechoslovakia.' *(Penelope Houston, New Statesman)*

'For the very first time, here's a movie you really feel spans the generation gap like a suspension bridge – its girders are satire but its anchorage is truth.' *(Alexander Walker, Evening Standard)*

'A refreshingly perceptive tragi-comedy about the

xcesses of the affluent American way of life.' *Arthur Thirkell, Daily Mirror)*

It is not . . . an analytic film, but a kind of fable – a ›oem to youth and a lament for the generation that ıas lost it . . . The poetry comes from a series of mages . . . which flow through the story of the ›arents' search for their straying daughter.' *(Nina Iibbin, Morning Star)*

Forman plays on [a] conflict of styles, catching at all he pedantic nuances of American jargon and pop ulture to create a universally recognisable image of nan's unfounded optimism.' *(Jan Dawson, 'inancial Times)*

TALE OF THE FOX CT: 9 AV: 8.00 (est)

.932 France 65 BW PUPPET/COMEDY/FANTASY/ AMILY

) Wladyslaw Starewicz ☆
V Wladyslaw Starewicz

wily fox outwits the rest of the animal kingdom, y means both fair and foul.

Iot many movies have to wait six decades for their British premiere. And even fewer are masterpieces. his animated picture by the long-forgotten Polish vriter-director, Wladyslaw Starewicz, is his only eature-length film, it took him 10 years to prepare nd 18 months to shoot. The plot, though based on a tory by Goethe, is a throwback to Aesop's fables: the vorld created is one where no one is to be trusted. A adger barrister lies on behalf of his client, then etrays him to save his own skin. Even the Lion Čing is a sanctimonious hypocrite, sentencing his nimal subjects to become vegetarians while he and is family remain carnivores.

The film may be set in a feudal never-neverland, ut its subversive attitudes have a 20th-century esonance: Starewicz emigrated from the city where e was brought up, Moscow, in 1918, convinced that is art could never flourish under Communist ictatorship. And his fable of how to survive under a epressive regime won its first French release, ignificantly enough, in 1941 – during the Nazi ccupation of Paris.

The film's Orwellian cynicism extends to the way ıe animals look. The frogs aren't cute and furry, ke Kermit: they look cold and clammy. A number f the animals seem moth-eaten and flea-infested: ne of them (the monkey narrator) has what sounds ke an unpleasant chest cold. Most have seen better ays. All are on the make.

Starewicz is just as anthropomorphic as Disney: is fox hero walks on his hind legs and wears some nappy outfits. But the Pole's tone of no-nonsense ırvivalism is a far cry from Disney's cosy platitudes, hich have dominated film animation for enerations, and not always for good. Underlying tarewicz's humour – some of which is as bizarre nd fantastical as anything in *Fantasia* – is a willingness to tackle the darker sides of life, human and animal nature in the raw.

It is easy to see why Starewicz never enjoyed commercial success. Even modern children might find some of these very uncuddly puppets disturbing, and adults may think its storyline too simple (some of the animals are a little too easily outwitted by Reynard). But in its originality, it's freshness of tone, and technical skill, it's breathtaking. One 3-minute sequence contains 273,000 different puppet scenes.

And it's funny. The darkness of the humour resembles Roald Dahl. The hilarious visual images and high slapstick invention rival Buster Keaton. And, like a drawing by Heath Robinson or Rowland Emett, there are so many ingenious touches and tiny observations that you know it will bear reseeing.

MIXED:

'Starewicz can't be accused of skimping on scale; the cast . . . includes a raven, a minstrel cat . . . tightrope-walking mice, grasshoppers, frog choruses . . . a bear and a cockerel with hen wife and chicks . . . unrivalled even today in terms of their facility for sheer physical articulation. A shame the same can't really be said of [his] none-too-convincing grasp of filmic narrative.' *(Jeremy Clarke, What's On in London, 1993)*

'Even adults feel queasy before [Starewicz's] grotesque oeuvre . . . Shot through with adult satire and whimsy.' *(Geoff Brown, The Times)*

'As finely tuned yet endearingly rickety as a Fabergé wind-up egg.' *(Jonathan Romney, New Statesman & Society)*

PRO:

'Oozes care, rivalling anything done in animation since, it reminds you that all the digital technology and computer wizardry in the world cannot beat a solitary injection of passion and humanity.' *(Stephen Amidon, Financial Times)*

'A virtuoso piece of puppet animation.' *(Alexander Walker, Evening Standard)*

'A blend of delirious East European surrealism . . . and good, all-American custard-pie slapstick . . . Above all, *Fox* impresses for its craftsmanship, its botanist's attention to the detail of fur and feather . . . The passing years have robbed it of none of its capacity to enchant and amuse.' *(Sheila Johnston, Independent)*

TALE OF TWO CITIES, A AAN CT: 6 AV: 8.31

1935 US 120 BW DRAMA

D Jack Conway ☆
W W.P. Lipscomb S.N. Behrman from Charles Dickens's novel

Ronald Colman ☆ Elizabeth Allan Edna May Oliver Blanche Yurka ☆ Reginald Owen Basil Rathbone

Henry B. Walthall ✔ Donald Woods Walter Catlett Fritz Leiber Isabel Jewell ✔ (as the little seamstress)

At the time of the French Revolution, a bored and aimless barrister (Ronald Colman) finds meaning to his life through self-sacrifice.

The best of many screen versions of Dickens's classic. The story has been simplified, not too damagingly, and there are strong performances from Colman and Blanche Yurka (as Madame De Farge). It's on a very grand scale (17,000 extras were reputedly used in one scene) although some of the sets are rather too obviously artificial. Conrad A. Nervig's editing was Oscar-nominated. Val Lewton and Jacques Tourneur were involved in directing the crowd and second-unit scenes.

MIXED:

'This latest version succeeds brilliantly in one aspect of Dickens's story, and fails lamentably in another. So far as Sydney Carton, his character and his relationships are concerned, the film is not only confident and assured, but shrewd . . . and Mr Colman . . . has never acted so well before . . . When the film leaves Carton and turns to the revolution, however, it loses all its assurance . . . The storming of the Bastille is the storming of a cardboard Bastille.' *(The Times)*

'The settings vary in quality, some being palpably backcloths (in a few of the mob scenes likewise the violence is only too plainly artificial). There are some very impressive scenes, in particular, the trial of the aristocrats and the final scene at the guillotine. The photography is excellent.' *(MFB)*

PRO:

'Has . . . that quality which is known to entertainment makers as "heart". At times this picture almost has cardiac trouble . . . There is much sentiment, but not enough to discount the genuine drama and thrills. And if you should be not averse to dropping a tear, then I cannot recommend the picture too highly.' *(Edward Betts, Sunday Express)*

'A screen classic . . . The fall of the Bastille is breathtaking.' *(Variety)*

'Handsomer than any of its predecessors, fuller in detail, deliberately respectful and, particularly in the case of Blanche Yurka's Mme De Farge and Edna May Oliver's Miss Pross, notably acted. I think it is probably a very superior piece of work.' *(Observer)*

'For more than two hours it crowds the screen with beauty and excitement.' *(New York Times)*

'Conway has, I think, directed admirably. He has resisted the temptation . . . to over-act the Dickensian humours, while justly letting his players go all out in the wild revolutionary scenes.' *(Campbell Dixon, Daily Telegraph)*

'History is recreated by magnificent technical work, and against the superb and thrilling backgrounds is developed a mighty plot, the appeal of which is addressed to all classes and all ages . . . Lighting and photography are excellent.' *(Kine Weekly)*

TALK OF THE TOWN, THE AAN

CT: 6 AV: 7.58

1942 US 118 BW COMEDY/ROMANCE/FAMILY

D George Stevens ☆
W Irwin Shaw Sidney Buchman ☆ AAN from Sidney Harmon's story AAN adapted by Dale Van Every

Ronald Colman ✔ Cary Grant ✔ Jean Arthur ✔ Edgar Buchanan Glenda Farrell Charles Dingle Emma Dunn Rex Ingram

An impulsive suspected murderer (Cary Grant) and a staid, legalistic lawyer (Ronald Colman) both fancy the same girl (Jean Arthur).

Screwball comedy with serious overtones, in which a professor on the verge of the Supreme Court learns some home truths about civil liberties. It could have been obvious and earnest, but it's entertaining thanks to a witty script and a delightful cast. Ted Tetzlaff's photography, Frederick Hollander's music, Otto Meyer's editing and art directors Lionel Banks and Rudolph Sternad were all Oscar-nominated.

'I knew it was going to come off all along: it didn't have that element of hazard in it. It was more of an understood flight with a take-off time and an arrival time and not too much headwind.' *(George Stevens)*

PRO:

'A rip-roaring, knock-down-and-drag-out comedy.' *(John T. McManus)*

MIXED:

'Well tuned and witty, at its best when it sticks to the middle ground between farce and melodrama. The chief fault of the script is its excessive length and the fact that a standard lynching mob climax is followed by a prolonged anti-climax.' *(Newsweek)*

'I can't take my lynching so lightly, even in a screwball. Still, I am all for this kind of comedy and for players like Arthur and Grant, who can mug more amusingly than most scriptwriters can write.' *(Manny Farber)*

'Story doesn't give Grant quite enough to do . . . George Stevens's direction is topflight for the most part. Transition from serious or melodramatic to the slap-happy and humorous sometimes is a bit awkward, but in the main it is solid escapist comedy.' *(Variety)*

'Did the authors think they were writing a Shavian comedy of ideas? The ideas are garbled and silly, but the people are so pleasant that the picture manages to be quite amiable and high-spirited.' *(Pauline Kael, 70s)*

TALK RADIO

CT: 6 AV: 6.83

1988 US 109 C DRAMA

D Oliver Stone
W Eric Bogosian Oliver Stone from Eric Bogosian, Ted Savinar's play and Stephen Singular's book *Talked to Death: The Life and Murder of Alan Berg*

Eric Bogosian☆ *Alec Baldwin Ellen Greene Leslie Hope John C. McGinley John Pankow Michael Wincott*✔

Barry Champlain, a combative phone-in host (Eric Bogosian), delights in insulting his bigoted listeners ('Shouldn't you be out burning crosses or molesting children or something?'). Eventually, Champlain is assassinated by one such loony.

The film, based on the murder of real-life radio host Alan Berg, self-consciously takes the lid off a sick America. The screenplay, by Stone and Bogosian, crackles with abrasive one-liners. 'I like you Jews,' says one black caller, patronizingly. 'I like you blacks,' responds Champlain coolly, 'I think everyone should own one.' In the central role of an angry youngish man no longer sure of why he is angry, Bogosian gives a performance which deserved at least an Oscar nomination.

The movie draws an interesting parallel between Champlain's self-destructive motivation, and the more widely destructive social implications of TV and radio programmes which exploit bigotry as entertainment. There is one masterly scene – hilarious and horrible – where Champlain comes face to face with a young fan (Michael Wincott), and doesn't like what he sees.

The romantic sub-plot is disappointingly weak; and, for all his moving of the camera, Stone can't disguise the film's origins as a stage play – it's very reminiscent at times of Stephen Poliakoff's *City Sugar*. Even so, this is Stone's most thoughtful film since *Salvador*, and the most apocalyptic cinematic view of the media since Paddy Chayefsky's *Network*.

PRO:

'Bogosian commands attention in a patented *tour-de-force*.' *(Variety)*

'Bogosian gives a spellbinding performance, mostly solo in his cave-like studio, interacting with the frightening voices of his callers. And those anonymous callers, who represent an entire spectrum of human misery, complacency and monstrousness, finally come to dominate the movie as the camera circles round Barry or moves in on his spitting lips. It's screamingly funny, but also deeply upsetting.' *(Kim Newman, Film Yearbook)*

'Further proof that Stone works best on smaller budgets.' *(Rose)*

ANTI:

'Bogosian is both amusing and mesmerizing – for a while. But well before the end, his character's narcissism and the unrelenting sound of his ranting become unbearable. Bogosian's one-man brilliance needs the acoustic distance of a theatre. Instead, Stone bludgeons the viewer with claustrophobic camera effects, an overwrought sound track and a tawdry romantic subplot.' *(Brian D. Johnson, Maclean's)*

'Eric Bogosian brings new meaning to the word obnoxious . . . Champlain talks endlessly about America – yet his message amounts to little more than a garbled replay of Peter Finch's "I'm mad as hell and I'm not going to take it anymore!" spiel in *Network*. Forget about America, though – Stone and Bogosian don't even have a half-way intelligent take on their central character. "The most important thing," Champlain's ex-wife tells him, "is you've got to start loving yourself!" That's about as deep as this movie goes. Only KGAB's station manager appears to have the picture in focus. "All you are," he tells Champlain, "is a f – g suit salesman with a big mouth." Amen.' *(Bruce Bawer, American Spectator)*

TANK MALLING

CT: 5 AV: 2.40

1988 GB 109 C THRILLER/SO BAD

D James Marcus ●
W James Marcus Mick Southworth ●

Ray Winstone ● Peter Wyngarde ● Jason Connery ● Amanda Donohoe Glen Murphy ● Marsha Hunt ● John Conteh ● Nick Berry ●

Top reporter (Ray Winstone) investigates high-level corruption in British establishment.

Malling may look like a yob but is a top reporter. 'I'm a top reporter,' he says. Tank is also, in the felicitous words of sensuous high-class prostitute Helen (Amanda Donohoe) 'the man they couldn't gag'. This is a pity, since Tank's dialogue is not up to much: 'I'm a reporter, Salina, and I believe wiv every particle of my being that the little people out there deserve to know the troof.'

Pitted against tongue-tied Tank is the Evil Establishment, led by silky-smooth Sir Robert (Peter Wyngarde), who preaches moral revival, but in private life arranges orgies for the upper classes ('More brandy, bishop?'). Other baddies include Cashman (Glen Murphy), alias the Soho Ripper, a sadistic killer with a remarkable talent for slashing tarts – sorry, women – a dozen times or more, then walking out without a speck of blood on him. And there's a Himmler lookalike (Jason Connery), who says terrible things like 'I will drag you to the abyss of despair and throw you in, ha, ha, ha, ha!'

Throughout, writer-director James Marcus's naivety makes the works of Daisy Ashford seem like the last word in sophistication. His inattention to detail would be sad, were it not laughable. The plot has the air of having being scrawled on a succession of beermats, several of which have got lost. Other movies have been as incompetently scripted, crudely directed and badly acted; but, in view of the way

Tank Malling combines all these qualities with grotesque sexism, gratuitous violence and subnormal intelligence, there can be little doubt that this marks a new low in cinema.

PRO:

'For a movie made on a shoestring budget . . . it's a considerable achievement.' *(Suzanne Hill, Sun)*

ANTI:

'A cheaper, nastier film would be hard to find . . . Mindbendingly dull and boring.' *(Marshall Julius, What's On in London)*

'For sheer daftness there's no beating [this film] . . . John Conteh [was] rendered practically speechless by the goings-on around him. Which was lucky for him, really, considering the script.' *(Derek Malcolm, Guardian)*

'Nasty, brutish, and much too long.' *(Sheila Johnston, Independent)*

'A nasty, low-life thriller [which] is not even redeemed by decent acting.' *(Pauline McLeod, Daily Mirror)*

'Oh, dear, one hates to discourage new British initiative . . . but [this] début is a stinker.' *(Shaun Usher, Daily Mail)*

'*Tank Malling* doesn't believe in subtlety where a sledgehammer will do. Characters don't talk, they shout; scenes don't merely evolve, they're telegraphed. The actors do their best (Donohoe in particular), but they're left struggling with impossible stereotypes and hackneyed dialogue.' *(Colette Maude, Time Out)*

'Ray Winstone blunders about like an idiot. Amanda Donohoe gets hysterical without adding to the plot, and Jason Connery is laughable in the change-of-pace role of the evil, yuppie mastermind with slicked-back hair. There are clichés aplenty, embarrassing speeches, gory bits sure to be snipped from the video version and an ending at once depressing, predictable and bathetic. There should be more British films like *Tank Malling*. It might stop Richard Attenborough and David Puttnam being pompous about Britain's great and prestigious film industry.' *(Kim Newman, Film Yearbook)*

'If you want an explanation of the demise of the British film industry, here it is.' *(Rose)*

TARGETS

CT: 5 AV: 7.25

1967 US 90 C THRILLER/HORROR

D Peter Bogdanovich ☆
W Peter Bogdanovich

Boris Karloff ☆ Tim O'Kelly ✔ James Brown Sandy Baron Peter Bogdanovich Nancy Hsueh Arthur Peterson

An ageing horror star (Boris Karloff) confronts a crazed sniper (Tim O'Kelly) at a drive-in movie. As in Joe Dante's *Matinee (1993)*, there's some attempt to investigate the difference between screen horror and the real thing, but the idea isn't thought through. Nor is there enough narrative to sustain a full-length feature. But Karloff gives one of his best performances and first-time director Bogdanovich certainly creates suspense and an exciting finale. Cinematographer Laszlo Kovacs did an excellent, atmospheric job on a low budget; he went on to shoot *Easy Rider, Close Encounters of the Third Kind,* and *Ghostbusters*.

PRO:

'Riveting originality.' *(Alexander Walker, Evening Standard)*

'A work of love, both a hymn to the sort of movies we all grew up with . . . and a serious attempt to come to terms with a particular kind of apparently unmotivated violence in American life . . . A distinguished directional début, and a movingly appropriate farewell to a great star.' *(John Russell Taylor, The Times)*

'A good deal more interesting than most second features you are likely to stumble across and a good many first features too.' *(David Robinson, Financial Times)*

'I urge you to look out for . . . [this] compelling, small-scale film.' *(Margaret Hinxman, Sunday Telegraph)*

'Brilliantly directed, this is a shocker different from anything you have seen.' *(Ernest Betts, People)*

'Really excellent . . . an admirable little picture and I have no doubt that Bogdanovich will make many even better.' *(Penelope Mortimer, Observer)*

MIXED:

'A good programmer, within low budget limitations.' *(Variety)*

'A raw, energetic blend of social comment and movie-buff nostalgia . . . In spots it was crude and cornily *cahier*, and in general there was much too much footage from godawful Roger Corman movies to be of much interest to the general public, but Bogdanovich got a fantastic performance out of Boris Karloff, and Targets will still go down in my book as one of the most exciting movie ideas of the year.' *(Rex Reed)*

TARZAN AND HIS MATE

CT: 7 AV: 7.50

1934 US 105 BW ACTION/ADVENTURE

D Jack Conway Cedric Gibbons
W Howard Emmett Rogers Leon Gordon from James Kevin McGuinness's story and Edgar Rice Burroughs's characters

Johnny Weissmuller Maureen O'Sullivan Neil Hamilton Paul Cavanagh Forrester Harvey William Stack Desmond Roberts Nathan Curry

Tarzan (Johnny Weissmuller) and Jane (Maureen

O'Sullivan) have their domestic bliss in the jungle interrupted by an old flame of Jane's from Mayfair (Neil Hamilton) who tries to get Tarzan to lead him to the elephants' graveyard, so that he and his friends can poach ivory.

Wildly improbable picture of jungle life, with O'Sullivan wearing surprisingly revealing costumes (this was before the Hays code) and assorted beasts behaving in a ludicrously domesticated manner. Usually counted the best *Tarzan* movie, it was the second in the famous series, following *Tarzan The Ape Man* (1932). Weissmuller continued playing the role and beating off all rivals, more-or-less annually, until *Tarzan and the Huntress* (1947).

PRO:

'[Tarzan's language] does not appear to have perceptibly improved since his marriage to the girl from Mayfair . . . No one in his senses can deny that this new exposition of primitive fitness is a brilliant technical job. I have seldom seen more expert camera work or ingenious cutting in any American film.' *(C.A. Lejeune, Observer)*

MIXED:

'The ingenuity and often imagination, which shows itself in the settings, the photography, and many of the incidents . . . make a strange contrast with the extraordinary puerility of the story . . . The conduct of the animals is ludicrously anthropomorphized, and that of the human beings is childishly sentimental.' *(The Times)*

'The monkeys do everything but bake cakes and the very human elephants always seem on the verge of sitting down for a nice, quiet game of chess; yet the picture has a strange sort of power that overcomes the total lack of logic.' *(Variety)*

'Certainly one of the funniest things you'll ever see.' *(Otis Ferguson)*

'Weissmuller is again the ape-man, chivalrous to a fault, though his vocabulary is still limited . . . There are some first-class fights with cannibals . . . Will it surprise the reader to learn that [Tarzan] is invariably victorious?' *(Daily Telegraph)*

ANTI:

'I confess that that love-call of dear old Tarzan, half-way between a gargle and a hiccup, gets on my nerves at times . . . As a story, it is the bunk.' *(Edward Betts, Sunday Express)*

TARZAN, THE APE MAN CT: 5 AV: 2.10

1981 US 112 C ROMANCE/ACTION/ADVENTURE/SO BAD

D John Derek ●
W Tom Rowe Gary Goddard ● based on the characters created by Edgar Rice Burroughs

Bo Derek ● Richard Harris ● John Phillip Law ● Miles O'Keeffe ● Akushula Selaya ● Steven Strong ●

Tarzan (Miles O'Keeffe) is mildly put out when his virginal best friend (Bo Derek) is kidnapped by sex-crazed natives.

Glamorously photographed excuse for director Derek to snap his wife wandering about in the nude. The script and acting are risible in the extreme, with Bo Derek not entirely convincing as a virgin and Richard Harris (as her dad) yelling his head off, in a passable imitation of a town crier. The level of super-sophistication can be gauged by the film's publicity slogan: 'The most exciting pair in the jungle!'

MIXED:

'*The Blue Lagoon* with elephants. Of course it's completely ridiculous, but at the same time it has a certain disarming charm. Sure, it's easy to groan at the secondhand "plot". It's easy to laugh at the clichés and mourn the demotion of Tarzan, who started out in the movies as king of the jungle and now gets fourth billing behind a schoolgirl, an anthropologist, and a wimp. And yet when Tarzan beats his chest and screams and swings to the rescue on a vine, there is something primal happening on the screen. And when Jane and three loyal chimpanzees tenderly bathe the body of the unconscious ape-man, we're getting very close to the reasons why we watch movies, and why there will always be a few movies to reawaken the child within us.' *(Roger Ebert)*

'As inept and silly as all this is, the film is sometimes fun.' *(Jack Babuscio, Gay News)*

'[Bo's] the one who brightens an otherwise boring story from darkest Africa.' *(Alan Frank, Star)*

'The critics are slamming it – so it's bound to make millions.' *(Ivan Waterman, News of the World)*

ANTI:

'This ridiculous remake . . . becomes more ludicrous by the minute.' *(Madeleine Harmsworth, Sunday Mirror)*

'A pretty but virtually actionless cods-up . . . looking about as authentic as those £50 versions of Di's wedding dress.' *(Derek Malcolm, Guardian)*

'Bo Derek's boobs in snail-paced yarn interrupted by bursts of slow-motion.' *(John Coleman New Statesman)*

'Derek's direction is woozy and relies heavily on slow-motion at moments of crisis.' *(Maria Aitken, Daily Mail)*

'To walk around naked and yet be uninteresting is a curious achievement, but one Bo achieves with charmlessness to spare.' *(Quinlan)*

TASTE OF HONEY, A CT: 6 AV: 7.50

1961 GB 100 BW DRAMA/COMEDY

D Tony Richardson ☆
W Shelagh Delaney Tony Richardson from Delaney's play

Rita Tushingham ☆ Murray Melvin ☆ Dora Bryan ☆ Robert Stephens Paul Danquah David Boliver

Unmarried mother (Rita Tushingham) is cared for by male friend (Murray Melvin).

If it weren't for the three central performances, this famous kitchen sink drama would be about as exciting as a superannuated episode of *EastEnders*. Shocking in its day (the father of the girl's child is – horrors! – black; her best friend is gay), it now looks underplotted and unspeakably dreary.

PRO:

'The brilliantly cast company in the picture look, speak and seem to live as though camera and audience were nowhere . . . They make us deeply concerned for them.' *(Paul Dehn, Daily Herald)*

'[Rita Tushingham] looks remarkably like Donald Duck's sister . . . The face is like a relief map of Lancashire . . . [but] she is the girl of the year in one of the films of the year.' *(Leonard Mosley, Daily Express)*

'It has humor, understanding and poignance.' *(Variety)*

'Richardson has achieved an . . . opaque realism, striking a remarkable balance between raw comedy and something deeper and more acrid . . . Dora Bryan . . . is wonderfully funny, while still conveying the essential viciousness which underlies Helen's good-natured carelessness.' *(David Robinson, Financial Times)*

'Richardson [is] the most skilful of our younger directors, if not the best . . . [He] manages a sad end with fireworks, and his pictorial cunning has more or less done the trick.' *(William Whitebait, New Statesman)*

'Tart and lively around the edges and bitter at the core.' *(Peter John Dyer)*

MIXED:

'The plot is still shapeless and inconclusive . . . It is little more than an anecdote . . . and the characters often seem to lack consistency. But there is heart in the telling and an intense realism in the situation.' *(The Times)*

'The best scenes . . . are those between Dora Bryan . . . and Rita Tushingham . . . What [the film] needs is a bit more love, and consequently, a lot more life.' *(Eve Perrick, Daily Mail)*

'The portrait-writing – the ironies, harsh exchanges, violent rebuffs – is brilliant. It is in organisation that the script is weak.' *(Dilys Powell)*

ANTI:

'With no real attempt to place characters in an explicit social or political context, the story becomes reduced to a drab, voyeuristic celebration of ordinariness and poverty. There's no anger, no joy, and ultimately no insight in this film; its shallow reliance on clichés reeks of complacency.' *(Geoff Andrew, Time Out)*

TATTOO CT: 1 AV: 1.88

1981 US 103 C HORROR/THRILLER

D Bob Brooks ●
W Joyce Buñuel ●

Bruce Dern ● Maud Adams ● Leonard Frey Rikke Borge John Getz Peter Iacangelo

Temperamental tattooist (Bruce Dern) abducts, tattoos and rapes a cover girl (Maud Adams).

Psycho meets *The Collector* meets *The Illustrated Man*. This has to be one of the nastiest, most sadistically voyeuristic films of all time. It's a surprise that it wasn't directed by Michael Winner.

'Such is Bob Brooks's direction and Joyce Buñuel's script that the problems of getting the unconscious Adams from her NY highrise apartment to an abandoned house on the New Jersey seashore isn't difficult at all. In one scene, they are in NY. In the next, NJ. Filmmaking is simple.' *(Variety)*

'A sensational package for the Eighties confected from ideas half remembered from other films.' *(Mark Le Fanu, MFB)*

'Despite vague attempts to give tattoos global significance, the result is a peepshow of psychopathology, devoid of insight or even context. See the mad artist kidnap the hysterical girl! See him make her masturbate while he watches through a hole in the door! Roll over Sigmund Freud and tell Bill Reich the bad news.' *(Mike Bygrave, Time Out)*

'The merest glimmer of an interesting idea is lost beneath the welter of ugly images and dangerously disturbing attitudes.' *(Winnert)*

'This sick, repulsive movie was written by Joyce Buñuel; like father-in-law, Luis, she intended to present perverse, controversial material, but director Bob Brooks couldn't give it any artistry.' *(Danny Peary)*

'The most vile, reprehensible, sexist and misogynistic piece of tripe ever released under the guise of a mainstream film.' *(Martin & Porter)*

TAUSEND AUGEN DES DR MABUSE, DIE:

see THE *DOCTOR MABUSE* SERIES (THE THOUSAND EYES OF DOCTOR MABUSE).

TAXI BLUES CT: 5 AV: 7.17

1990 USSR/France 110 C DRAMA/FOREIGN

D Pavel Lounguine ☆
W Pavel Lounguine

Piotr Nikolajevitch Mamonov ✔ Piotr Zaitchenko ✔ Vladimir Kachpur Natalia Koliakanova Hal Singer Elena Saphonova Sergei Gazorov Evgueni Gortchakov

An uneasy relationship develops between an anarchic, Jewish jazz musician (Piotr Nikolajevitch Mamonov) and an old-fashioned, anti-Semitic Moscow cab driver (Piotr Zaitchenko).

The first-time director revels in the seamy, depressing underside of his city, and pulls no punches in his depiction of corruption, alcoholism, sexism and racism. On a quasi-documentary level the film holds a certain interest, since such things were long hidden from the west. Unfortunately, the two central characters, who are well portrayed and obviously intended as symbolic of the intellectual and the worker in Russian society, are so unlikeable that it's hard to care what happens to them. Also, there are few narrative skills on display, and the movie doesn't get anywhere. Even so, it won Lounguine the best director prize at Cannes – where they have always admired film-makers who slag off their own country.

'A dazzling evocation of the dark underside of modern Moscow . . . a wonderfully rich film of *perestroika*.' *(Scott Murray, Cinema Papers)*

'The two main characters, beautifully cast and played . . . act as though they had grown up in the ugly, violent lowlife background against which the story unfolds.' *(Tom Porteous, Screen International)*

'[A] superb tragicomedy . . . a robust and even buoyant film . . . Lounguine displays vast sympathy and affection.' *(Janet Maslin, New York Times)*

'If a society advances from lethargy to hedonism, can it be called progress? . . . Lounguine is anything but a visionary, yet this film seems to be about what happens to a nation as its vision dies . . . Although his début has a hip panache, it shows us a Soviet Union more capable of changes in style than in content.' *(Karen Jaehne, Film Quarterly)*

'It is clear from the energy in the story that Lounguine has been waiting a long time to get his hands on the camera, and his point of view swoops and soars through Moscow like a bird released from its cage. If the story is sometimes hard to take – neither one of the protagonists is very pleasant to be around – the anger and passion of the director are exhilarating.' *(Roger Ebert)*

TAXI DRIVER AAN CT: 9 AV: 8.47

1976 US 114 C THRILLER/DRAMA

D Martin Scorsese ☆
W Paul Schrader

Robert De Niro ☆ AAN Jodie Foster ☆ AAN Cybill Shepherd Peter Boyle ☆ Leonard Harris Harvey Keitel Martin Scorsese

A New York taxi driver (Robert De Niro) goes bonkers.

Critics were very divided on release, but more and more this looks like a classic. It's a frightening picture of urban alienation – and although we don't get to know much about Travis Bickle's past, we certainly understand where he's coming from. De Niro gives an astonishing performance which makes us share many of his feelings, yet keeps us distanced at the same time. The view of New York as Hell is exaggerated and melodramatic, of course, but it's obviously one man's vision; most of the time, we're seeing it though Bickle's paranoid eyes. The one thing that doesn't ring true in any sense is the interest shown in him by Betsy (Cybill Shepherd). Bernard Herrmann's score, his creepiest since *Psycho* (and his last) was rightly Oscar-nominated.

ANTI:

'The first shot is of steam gushing up from a manhole in a Manhattan street. Thus the director, Martin Scorsese, tells us two things: that his film is about the pressures that boil up in a big city today and that the level of his metaphoric invention is low. Nothing in the picture is more subtle, less nudgingly and greasily assumptive, than that opening shot . . . The hero of *Taxi Driver* is a psychotic, nothing more, and his story is a case history, nothing more . . . Jodie Foster as the twelve-year-old is only minimally effective.' *(Stanley Kauffmann)*

'Where Scorsese and Schrader go wrong in [the film] is in attempting to make Travis Bickle in some way politically and socially significant. But he's not. He is an aberration.' *(Vincent Canby, New York Times)*

'Why does Betsy consent to go out for coffee with his obnoxious, importunate fellow? Why, since he is both boring and uncouth, does she go out on a date with him? And why would Travis, who sees her as some ideal, virginal creature, take her to a cheap porno theater, from which – and from him – she runs away disdainfully? Motivation is extremely fuzzy here. Is Betsy a nice girl, genuinely interested in this odd fellow? Or is she a spoiled rich kid, merely playing with Travis? . . . The fact that she is played by the supremely untalented Cybill Shepherd, who here sinks to new depths of unblinking smugness coupled with prefabricated come-hither inflections, adds further layers of needless obscurity . . . [Her] presence is not even a tribute to Scorsese's healthy appetites: having gained weight, most noticeably in the face, she looks like Mussolini in drag.' *(John Simon)*

MIXED:

'As some kind of allegory directly relating to the American experience it suffices, though only just . . . But its proper value lies not in the schematic nature of Paul Schrader's script . . . but in the terrifyingly fluent portrait of unease, frustration and corruption that is up there on the screen.' *(Derek Malcolm, Guardian)*

'Schrader must take much of the praise . . . He makes us see ourselves through a wing-mirror darkly. And if Scorsese's pace sometimes seems too monotonously panic-stricken, who can blame him? The ideas he is projecting are, indeed, frightening ones.' *(Tom Hutchinson, Sunday Telegraph)*

PRO:

'It is a wonderful performance by De Niro, permitting us to see . . . into this ignorant, inarticulate and secret man as his personality disintegrates under stress.' *(David Robinson, The Times)*

'Scorsese . . . is a brilliant director . . . De Niro give a fine and truthful performance . . . and Jodie Foster is splendid.' *(Philip Mackie, Sunday Times)*

'The best movie on the rank this week . . . De Niro's taxi driver is a sinister and inarticulate Walter Mitty . . . There's some extraordinary acting particularly by Jodie.' *(Fergus Cashin, Sun)*

'A brilliant, odd film . . . The killing . . . out-gores anything I've seen . . . the camera rubbing our noses into the congealing blood.' *(Hilary Kingsley, Sunday People)*

'Feverish, horrifyingly funny.' *(Pauline Kael)*

TEENAGE MUTANT NINJA TURTLES

CT: 6 AV: 4.64

1990 US 93 C SF/COMEDY/FAMILY

D Steve Barron
W Todd W. Langen Bobby Herbeck based on comic book characters created by Kevin Eastman and Peter Laird

Judith Hoag Elias Koteas Josh Pais Michelan Sisti Leif Tilden David Forman James Sato

Radioactive mutants and their rat guru battle against the forces of darkness.

Children of all ages ignored those Middle-aged Futile Whinger Critics who argued that this film advocates gang warfare and the ruthless pursuit of pizza, and they were right – it's really just an engaging, rumbustious action movie with silly jokes. The pity is that it's so tackily directed and rips off ideas from every action picture of the previous ten years. The Turtles themselves are pretty indistinguishable, even though they're colour-coded.

Uniting the Turtles with their audience is an uncritical taste for junk-culture: not only do they live surrounded by junk and eat only pizza, their post-literate culture consists of practising martial arts, watching movies and TV, and sorting through the intellectual lumberyard of Trivial Pursuit. Despite the reviews, this became the most successful independent movie of all time. There were two sequels (both awful).

ANTI:

'It is photographed in murky Grungecolor, lacks humour, has unindividualised characters who are as interchangeable as egg boxes, and depends on a monotonous and repetitive resort to violence.' *(Alexander Walker, Evening Standard)*

'It's a very dark film, and one wonders, after seeing it, if young Turtle fans are being denied the brightness and bounciness of an earlier generation of kiddie films.' *(Roger Ebert)*

'Visually rough around the edges, sometimes sluggish in its plotting and marred by overtones of racism in its use of Oriental villains.' *(Variety)*

MIXED:

'Totally dotty . . . You cannot dislike a film so sumptuously daft and so insouciant in its implausibility. At the same time you cannot but wonder at the mental age of modern America, when a movie which redefines the concept of triviality holds an entire generation is its power.' *(Nigel Andrews, Financial Times)*

'I absolutely loved it. Even though [it's] appallingly made . . . It is a wonderfully funny movie that combines endearing characterization, wit and chutzpah . . . This movie is so profoundly daft, it is awesome.' *(Sue Heal, Today)*

PRO:

'What makes [the film] so brilliant are the special effects – and the sheer hilarity of seeing huge Turtles leap around. The script, too, is ribticklingly funny.' *(Sun)*

'The film's success proves that young audiences today have a capacity to take an adventure story seriously and to see it sent up at the same time. Even the title, an adult joke on the idiocy of mix-and-shake genre cocktails, fails to deflate youngsters' enthusiasm with excess derision . . . *Teenage Mutant Ninja Turtles* combines the philosophy of the 1960s – do your own thing, cleave to your own values – with the super-hero action stuff of the 1980s.' *(Harlan Kennedy, Film Yearbook)*

TEENAGERS FROM OUTER SPACE

CT: 3 AV: 1.50

(aka *The Gargon Terror*)

1959 US 87 BW SF

D Tom Graeff
W Tom Graeff ●

David Love ● Dawn Anderson ●

Harvey B. Dunn ● Bryan Grant ● Tom Lockyear ● King Moody Helen Sage

A teenage alien called Derek (David Love) falls for an earth-girl (Dawn Anderson) and beats off fellow-aliens who intend to turn earth into a breeding-ground for their Gargons (giant lobsters).

Graeff does his best with an obviously non-existent budget, but the fact remains that this is a stinker – inanely plotted, ineptly acted and incoherently directed, with virtually non-existent special effects. All we see of the giant lobsters is their shadows. The dialogue is, at best, clichéd. ('Somehow I feel that I've always known you,' simpers the earth-girl.) At worst, it's complete mumbo-jumbo – '42 saturation degrees in 96 volumes,' rasps one invading alien; 'Diagonal adjustment reading resisting structural norms by two point eight zero vernums!' adds another, presumably trying to help.

MIXED:

'Perhaps due to a lower than low budget, the film often is inescapably inept. Lighting is poor, interiors are pallid, the monster is pathetically makeshift. The film is impudently grandiose in its tone and is more likely to elicit shrieks of amusement than horror. But the film is also carefully thought out, concocted of exploitable elements yet different from its many predecessors. While Graeff may not have made a good picture, he has made an interesting one that every now and then smacks of brilliance. Several scenes – eg a sequence of youngsters peering wide-eyed at their first spaceman – are composed of an artistry that marks Graeff as a filmmaker to be heard from.' *(Variety)*

'[Graeff] shows considerable imagination as a cinematographer; there's a nicely-staged and inventively-shot scene in which Thor returns to Gramps's house with gun drawn; the camera moves with confidence and intelligence. Later, as Derek faces down the Gargon, the final camera setup is designed for maximum scary impact, diminished considerably by the fact that the monster is (a) altogether too dark, and (b) a lobster anyway.' *(Bill Warren, Keep Watching The Skies!)*

ANTI:

'The acting ranges from bad to no acting at all . . . Tom Graeff's production constantly struggles to overcome the disadvantage of his own bad direction which, in turn, is gravely handicapped by a script written by himself . . . Now that monkeys have been trained to successfully execute space flight, it is to be hoped that they can be induced to collaborate on an improved science-fiction.' *(Jack Moffitt, Hollywood Reporter)*

'While the story is no more far-fetched than the average science-fiction, its execution is not strong, especially with respect to the performances of an unknown cast . . . also the Gargon is not especially terrifying.' *(Motion Picture Herald)*

'Graeff . . . has unfortunately bitten off more than he can chew . . . The trick effects are variable, the lighting is poor, the script and acting pretty terrible and the grown Gargon itself a feeble piece of monstercraft.' *(MFB)*

'Its plot is rambling; its extreme low budget insures a thoroughly sleazy quality of photography, costume and prop. And though the direction is all right, ninety per cent of the script is either stereotyped action talk or portentous, badly stilted attempts at motivation or romance.' *(Charles Stinson, LA Times)*

TELL ME THAT YOU LOVE ME, JUNIE MOON CT: 2 AV: 5.00

1969 US 113 C DRAMA/COMEDY

D Otto Preminger ●
W Marjorie Kellogg ● from her novel

Liza Minnelli ● Robert Moore ● Ken Howard
Kay Thompson Fred Williamson

An acid-scarred girl (Liza Minnelli), a homosexual paraplegic (Robert Moore) and an introverted epileptic (Ken Howard) set up home together.

Tasteless schmaltz with a glib script and two rotten performances from Minnelli and Moore. Preminger directs with no sensitivity for the material whatever. The critics were, and remain, sharply divided.

PRO:

'Director Otto Preminger tugs determinedly at the heart, and despite the odd slip into sentimentality and plot contrivance gets through to the target.' *(Winnert)*

'Moments of comedy, melodrama, compassion expertly blended by Preminger in one of his best films.' *(Maltin)*

ANTI:

'Just plain repulsive. There are so many technical flaws in it, so many sleazy disregards for coherence, so many holes in the script and so many tired clichés that I haven't the space to list them all. I might add, however, that I've seldom seen more incompetent lighting and cinematography.' *(Rex Reed)*

'Like seeing a venerated senior citizen desperately trying to show he's in love with today by donning see-through clothes.' *(Michael Billington, Illustrated London News)*

'It slushes us with sentimentality to the point past compassion.' *(Judith Crist)*

'Another in the great series of disasters with which Preminger seemed intent on finishing his career . . . Little but a series of Smart Aleck exchanges/platitudes.' *(Phil Hardy, Time Out)*

'10' CT: 3 AV: 4.93

1979 US 122 C COMEDY/ROMANCE

D Blake Edwards ✗
W Blake Edwards

Dudley Moore ✗ Bo Derek Julie Andrews Robert Webber Dee Wallace Sam Jones

Middle-aged lecher (Dudley Moore) makes a fool of himself over attractive young blonde (Bo Derek).

Tacky, tasteless, ugly, sexist sex comedy which was a surprise success commercially, and made stars out of Dudley Moore and Bo Derek. Henry Mancini's score was Oscar-nominated, as was the song 'It's Easy To Say' (music by Mancini, lyrics by Robert Wells).

PRO:

'A shrewdly observed and beautifully executed comedy of manners and morals.' *(Variety)*

'Its humor gets laughs by touching on emotions and yearnings that are very real for us.' *(Roger Ebert)*

'The climactic love scene – in which Moore proves utterly unable to perform when he gets his emancipated dream woman (Derek) to bed – is very funny and represents a real catharsis in the history of Hollywood romance. Dudley Moore became the first actor to turn screen impotence into superstardom.' *(David Pirie, Time Out)*

ANTI:

'The plot is simple and old, which would not matter if Edwards, who wrote as well as directed it, were not simplistic and old-hat . . . A self-indulgent film, this, and one that sacrifices comedic structure to cheap laughs and easy pathos.' *(John Simon)*

'Leering, derivative and over-long.' *(Shipman)*

TEN COMMANDMENTS, THE AAN CT: 8 AV: 7.36

1956 US 219 C DRAMA/EPIC

D Cecil B. DeMille ●
W Aeneas Mackenzie Jesse L. Lasky Jr Jack Gariss Frederic M. Frank

Charlton Heston ☆, Yul Brynner ☆, Edward G. Robinson, Anne Baxter, Nina Foch, Yvonne De Carlo, John Derek, John Carradine, Cedric Hardwicke, Martha Scott, Vincent Price, Debra Paget

The story of Moses (Charlton Heston).

Cecil B. DeMille's last film is a remake of his 1923 epic, and it is among his best work. Some of John Fulton's Oscar-winning visual effects (such as God writing on Moses's tablets of stone) are vulgar, the dialogue is banal, and there is not much characterization; but there is a scale and magnificence about it, and a naive sincerity which is quite touching. Loyal Griggs's photography, the art direction, editing, sound and costumes were all Oscar-nominated. Sample dialogue . . . 'Where are we going, Rachel?' 'Some land flowing with milk and honey.'

ANTI:

'One is compelled to respect the organization of the scenes of spectacle . . . With more private scenes he [DeMille] has greater trouble . . . Beneath the weight of so much narrative the acting is flat; I cannot recall one single trace of observation of character, and the only figure who looks anything like alive is Anne Baxter. With the exception of a few spectacular crowd-scenes the film is visually dull. The details of action are excruciatingly obvious; if a child is seen toddling alone amidst the exodus, one knows with certainty that somebody, Moses probably, is about to carry it. And the whole experience (with an interval) lasts roughly four hours. I am afraid that long before the time was up I was silently imploring Mr DeMille (for a critic, too, can misquote Scripture for his purpose) to let his people go.' *(Dilys Powell)*

'The result of all these stupendous efforts? Something roughly comparable to an eight-foot chorus girl – pretty well put together, but much too big and much too flashy . . . What DeMille has really done is to throw sex and sand into the moviegoers' eyes for almost twice as long as anyone else has ever dared to.' *(Time)*

'I'm sure DeMille could have had any actor he wanted . . . Yet the actors [he] chose with few exceptions are second and third rate . . . Heston . . . looks well and nothing else . . . John Derek and Debra Paget have faces on which neither mind nor heart has left a trace. And how ridiculous Edward G. Robinson and Vincent Price are in Egyptian costumes! . . . The visual representation of supernatural occurrences are inexcusably crude . . . And I cannot understand how Mr DeMille allowed a voice on the sound track to represent the voice of God.' *(Henrietta Lehman, Films in Review)*

'DeMille's monstrous masterpiece . . . Each scene consists of one cliché or other . . . so that for all the millions that have been spent, the heroic is constantly transmuting itself into the commonplace.' *(Times Educational Supplement)*

'There is no reason why a filmmaker should not, if he wishes, shoot the life of Buddha, make an adaptation of the Koran, or present Miss Jayne Mansfield as a Sun Goddess. If, however, he fails to touch his audience with some awareness of the value of human life, some new scope of human existence, then he must not be surprised if we reject his work as spurious.' *(Peter Baker, S & S)*

MIXED:

'The trouble with [Bible epics] is that they make explicit what the Bible is content to leave to the imagination . . . Heston has a cowboy-like virility as the young Moses and a booming authority as the elderly Moses which is about all we can expect under he circumstances.' *(Milton Shulman, Evening ;tandard)*

PRO:

Its theme, its photographic magnificence and the ruly powerful publicity campaign must mean that *'he Ten Commandments* will run on and on.' *Variety)*

The most magnificent and exciting spectacle the creen has ever shown.' *(Raymond Moore, Sunday)ispatch)*

TEN DAYS THAT SHOOK THE WORLD, THE:

see OCTOBER.

TERMINATOR, THE

CT: 6 AV: 7.07

984 US 108 C SF

) James Cameron ☆
W Gale Anne Hurd James Cameron

Arnold Schwarzenegger ✔ Michael Biehn
Linda Hamilton Paul Winfield Lance Henriksen ✔
Rick Rossovich Bess Motta Earl Boen

A cyborg assassin (Arnold Schwarzenegger) is sent rom the future to our present.

ames Cameron's directorial flair, an ingenious story nd some witty comic touches – plus Arnold ;chwarzenegger's laconic, monolithic presence as he killer android – made this low-budget sci-fi hriller first a surprise hit (it grossed over $40 nillion) and then a cult classic. But there's little haracterisation, and the time travel scenario makes o logical sense (not that it did in the sequel, ither). Memorable moments, but to this critic at east, it's over-violent, and far surpassed as ntertainment by *Terminator 2*.

MIXED:

The surprises come thick and fast in this slickly irected sci-fi thriller. True, it is not original in oncept . . . Nevertheless it is highly enjoyable . . . If ou are prepared to leave your thinking cap at home, ou could do worse than lose yourself in this ntertaining dollop of hokum.' *(Curtis Hutchinson, & F)*

Schwarzenegger is about as well suited to movie cting as he would be to ballet, but his presence in the film] is not a deterrent. This is a monster movie nd the monster's role fits [him] just fine . . . Even if he movie had nothing else to recommend it, the heer unlikeliness of [the] mission and the teasing radualness with which its meaning is revealed vould be enough to hold the audience's attention . . A B-movie with flair.' *(Janet Maslin, New York 'imes)*

PRO:

A blazing, cinematic comic book, full of virtuoso noviemaking, terrific momentum, solid erformances and a compelling story.' *(Variety)*

'A bonanza for thinking cultists.' *(Village Voice)*

'It is refreshing in the 80s to find a film in which women are allowed power and control and above all, are not subordinated by the male. At the same time the woman is not sexually objectified, and she is allowed to transcend genre role expectations. From the very first time we see Sarah, we are aware of her strength and independence.' *(Lillian Necakor, CineAction, 1987)*

'[Proves] talent, intelligence and originality can make a positive difference in even the most formula-restricted genres . . . The direction is assured . . . imaginative and often dazzling. The script . . . not only is loaded with wit, clever touches and jolts by the second, but also interjects bright, interesting ideas into the time-traveler-tries-to-alter-history premise.' *(Danny Peary, 1988)*

TERMINATOR 2: JUDGMENT DAY

CT: 9 AV: 7.23

1991 US 135 C SF

D James Cameron ✔
W James Cameron William Wisher ✔

Arnold Schwarzenegger ✔ Linda Hamilton ✔
Edward Furlong ✔ Robert Patrick ✔ Earl Boen
Joe Morton S. Epatha Merkerson

A lumbering, obsolescent cyborg from the future (Arnold Schwarzenegger) is sent back to our present to save an all-important child (Edward Furlong) from a state-of-the-art assassin (Robert Patrick).

James Cameron's best movie, Schwarzenegger's finest two hours, and one of the great science fiction films. Inventive chases, breathtaking stunts and truly special effects co-exist with believable performances, funny jokes and an exciting, though broken-backed, story. It's really two films in one, and there's a stretch in the middle where a whole new plot has to be set up. However, that's no bad thing, since it gives us time for a breather before the final, climactic half-hour.

There is, of course, a measure of hypocrisy in any film which preaches the virtues of peace in so violent a fashion. The movie may poke fun at the machismo of which Schwarzenegger is so endearing an embodiment, but there are less comfortable moments when it endorses the testosterone-crazed ethos which it is pretending to deride. The writers also try to have it both ways when they castigate technology at the same time as celebrating it. Like most action films of its period, it is needlessly violent, but the script is surprisingly intelligent: as a result, the movie even looks good on the small screen.

Reviews of *Terminator 2* ranged from mixed to favourable. Younger critics were noticeably more enthusiastic, but even the film's detractors recognized that it had merits.

ANTI:

'Even if the plotting were defter [it] wouldn't work, because the whole movie is based on the insane conceit that Arnold Schwarzenegger is the underdog.' *(Terrence Rafferty, New Yorker)*

MIXED:

'[The special effects] are fabulous . . . but there are problems. Whereas *T1* (in common parlance) is an acknowledged classic of the genre, *T2* is a classic case of abuse of form (awesome accoutrements) over substance (the less than complete characterizations). It's fascinating but not as much fun as it should be.' *(Bobby Cramer, Films in Review)*

'The story sags midway, but the first hour and the last 30 minutes display an enjoyably relentless bravura.' *(Geoff Andrew, Time Out)*

'This is the big one . . . Fifteen times the cost of the original . . . It is not fifteen times as good . . . the money is up there on the screen, no question . . . This is the sort of movie in which major car crashes are staged in the background . . . One has to applaud Cameron's chutzpah, in describing his film as "an action movie about world peace", even if the anti-war message gets swamped by the sound of automatic gunfire. Whatever its faults, this is deftly the treat of the summer for those who like their movies big and loud.' *(Anne Billson, New Statesman)*

'A humongous, visionary parable that intermittently enthralls and ultimately disappoints. *T2* is half of a terrific movie – the wrong half. For a breathless first hour, the film zips along in a textbook display of plot planting and showmanship. But then it stumbles over its own ambitions before settling for a conventional climax with a long fuse.' *(Richard Corliss, Time)*

'The story . . . is sparse. Some of the action sequences are surprisingly flat, and the narration is cornball fantasy, but Patrick, as the villainous cyborg, is evil incarnate.' *(Scheuer)*

PRO:

'Mr Cameron has made a swift, exciting special effects epic that thoroughly justifies its vast expense and greatly improves upon the first film's potent but rudimentary style.' *(Janet Maslin, New York Times)*

'A top-notch triumph of spectacle over sense, featuring a self-aware performance from Arnie . . . Superbly orchestrated by James Cameron.' *(Kim Newman, Empire)*

'Arnie's lack of acting ability makes him perfect casting as an android and I just love this film on a purely visceral level – on wide screen and with the volume turned right up.' *(Jonathan Ross, Flicks)*

'An entertainment machine as expertly functional as its robotic protagonist . . . The script . . . is both funny and acute . . . The film is also, in its way, in love with militaristic technology.' *(Sean French, Observer)*

'It's fun for a kid, having his own pet Terminator, and that's one of the inspirations in the screenplay . . . Another intriguing screenplay idea is to develop the Terminator's lack of emotions; like Mr Spock in *Star Trek*, he does not understand why humans cry . . . The key element in any action picture, I think, is a good villain. *Terminator* 2 has one, along with an intriguing hero, a fierce heroine, and a young boy who is played by Furlong with guts and energy. The movie responds to criticisms of excessive movie violence by tempering the Terminator's blood lust, but nobody, I think, will complain it doesn't have enough action.' *(Roger Ebert)*

'Equally at home in small-scale skirmishes like one-on-one chases down narrow corridors and complex, bravura effects involving tottering helicopters, exploding buildings, and as many as five different special-effects houses, Cameron flamboyantly underlines, for those who may have forgotten, why the pure adrenaline rush of motion is something motion pictures can't live for very long without.' *(Kenneth Turan, LA Times)*

'A science-fiction film with verve, imagination and even a little wit.' *(Derek Malcolm, Guardian)*

'Here is next-generation cinema, offering sights so startling, so downright impossible, that only dreams or nightmares can match them.' *(Shaun Usher, Daily Mail)*

TERMS OF ENDEARMENT

AAW CT: 6 AV: 7.38

1983 US 132 C DRAMA/COMEDY

D James L. Brooks ✗ AAW
W James L. Brooks ✗ AAW from Larry McMurtry's novel

Shirley MacLaine ☆ AAW Debra Winger ☆ AAN Jack Nicholson ☆ AAW Jeff Daniels ✔ Danny DeVito ✔ John Lithgow ☆ AAN

Ex-astronaut (Jack Nicholson) woos mother (Shirley MacLaine) who smothers her daughter (Debra Winger) until the latter leaves with a husband (Jeff Daniels) who turns out to be unfaithful and she (that's Winger) falls Dreadfully Ill.

This shambolically constructed, over-sentimental study of a wife-daughter relationship is little more than an over-extended sitcom; but it contains funny moments early on and a lot of excellent performances before turning into a *Love Story*-style tearjerker. It's hard to see why it won an Academy Award as best picture, but there's no doubting its entertainment value. It was also nominated for art direction (Polly Platt, Harold Michelson, Tom Pedigo, Anthony Mondell), sound (Donald O. Mitchell, Rick Kline, Kevin O'Connell, Jim

Alexander), score (Michael Gore), and editing (Richard Marks).

PRO:

'There are no bad performances, no slack scenes, no inattention of any kind . . . No comedy since *Annie Hall* or *Manhattan* has so intelligently observed not just the way people live now but what's going on in the back of their minds . . . The best movie of the year.' *(Richard Schickel, Time)*

'Shirley MacLaine looks a mess. Jack Nicholson looks a slob. The film looks a sprawl. So why is [the film] so enjoyable? Why am I still chuckling? . . . The film can land a blow whose very daring is the stuff that makes champions . . . [It] puts the life back into Hollywood.' *(Alexander Walker, Evening Standard)*

'I would have said that [it] was a "woman's film" if it wasn't for my fear of being attacked tooth and unvarnished nail by feminists under the impression that the description is a term of disparagement . . . There is nothing like a terminal illness to bring out the best in screen people, that's what I say. I will go even further. To hell with the consequences – this is a woman's film.' *(Ian Christie, Daily Express)*

'There isn't a thing I would change.' *(Roger Ebert)*

MIXED:

'Under its brittle sophisticated guise this is really the Ultimate-Sitcom-meets-the Ultimate-Soap Opera. But it's also oddly compulsive. Especially when Jack Nicholson is . . . stealing every scene he's in.' *(Nigel Andrews, Financial Times)*

'My reservations . . . stem from the fact that the people and many of the situations in which they find themselves never seem more than clever inventions of the author . . . Yet the acting constantly rises above the soap operatics of the material.' *(Margaret Hinxman)*

'I didn't believe Shirley MacLaine for a moment as Debra Winger's possessive but emotionally inexpressive mama, but I bought it as a premise for the duration of the movie because so many funny situations were built upon it; nor, though his house was full of pictures of Saturn rockets and space capsules, did I believe that Jack Nicholson was an ex-astronaut; nor did I believe in Debra Winger's sudden fatal illness . . . As in a sitcom, the dramatic complications and resolutions in *Terms* seemed not to have been coaxed delicately and sensitively out of the inner truth of the characters and the inner logic of the story, but to have been hammered out over bagels and cream cheese by half a dozen comedy writers. To be sure, Brooks pulled the strings well: I laughed my way through *Terms*, and when Winger died, my eyes teared up, but I left the theater thinking "How phony".' *(Bruce Bawer, American Spectator)*

ANTI:

'The biggest disappointment . . . [Brooks] should have stuck to television, for on the basis of this film he has little talent for making movies.' *(Richard Roud, Guardian)*

'Neither of these super actresses is given much to make sense of . . . There are funny lines and there are hurtful lines and there are philosophical lines; and they are all, quite woefully, crossed.' *(John Coleman, New Statesman)*

'An outsize sitcom and a crassly constructed slice of anti-feminism that contrives to rub liberal amounts of soap in the viewer's eyes.' *(S & S)*

TERRA TREMA, LA: *see* LA TERRA TREMA

TERROR OF TINY TOWN CT: 1 AV: 1.50

1938 US 63 BW MUSICAL/WESTERN

D Sam Newfield ●
W Fred Myton ●

Billy Curtis ● Yvonne Moray ● Little Billy ●
Billy Platt ● Nita Krebs ●

Midget cattlemen have a range war.

Bizarre musical western, badly acted by an all-midget cast. Perhaps the intention was, as in the later *Bugsy Malone*, to satirize a genre by playing out its clichs with undersized performers; but overwhelming incompetence ensured that any such intention is obscured. The production team reunited the following year to make an all-black western, *Harlem on the Prairie*.

ANTI:

'Contrived.' *(Variety)*

'The trouble . . . was that without a few normal-sized folks for contrast, midgets appear much like other people.' *(Time)*

'Inexplicably, a penguin wanders on to the set and overshadows the entire cast.' *(Harry & Michael Medved)*

MIXED:

'Quaint . . . Performed by the first all-midget cast ever to make a feature . . . The hard-riding, two gun boys go buckety-buck on Shetland ponies. The heroine escapes the villain by running under the furniture instead of around it . . . The formula drama has been given pint-sized treatment.' *(Hollywood Reporter)*

PRO:

'The definitive all-midget western.' *(Martin & Porter)*

TESTAMENT CT: 6 AV: 7.00

1983 US 90 C SF/DRAMA

D Lynne Littman
W John Sacret Young from Carol Amen's story *The Last Testament*

Jane Alexander ☆ AAN William Devane Ross Harris Roxana Zal Lukas Haas ✓ Lilia Skala Leon Ames

A suburban mother (Jane Alexander) and her family struggle to survive after the holocaust.

Bleak, gruelling but rewarding: its realism contrasts sharply with the sanitized vision of a better-known but inferior picture, *On the Beach* (1959). Jane Alexander is moving in the leading role.

'After thirty years of learning to live with the Bomb, we still lack ways of conceiving the unthinkable.' *(Sheila Johnston, MFB)*

'Exceptionally powerful.' *(Variety)*

'Gentle, loving, noble, angry and heartrending.' *(John Gill, Time Out)*

'Alexander's performance makes the film possible to watch without unbearable heartbreak, because she is brave and decent in the face of horror. And the last scene, in which she expresses such small optimism as is still possible, is one of the most powerful movie scenes I've ever seen.' *(Roger Ebert)*

TESTAMENT DES DR MABUSE, DAS: *see* THE *DOCTOR MABUSE* SERIES.

TESTAMENT OF DR MABUSE, THE: *see* THE *DOCTOR MABUSE* SERIES.

TEXAS CHAINSAW MASSACRE, THE

CT: 5 AV: 4.90

1974 US 81/87 C HORROR

D Tobe Hooper
W Kim Henkel Tobe Hooper

Marilyn Burns Allen Danziger Paul A. Partain William Vail Terry McMinn

Mad family attacks young people in rural Texas.

One of the most horrific films of all time, and among the most controversial. The suspense generated is considerable, but Hooper goes for overkill when he shows the gore and violence with maximum brutality. It's nasty and meretricious, but undeniably well made. After being denied a BBFC certificate, it was finally awarded an X for London only, by the Greater London Council, in 1976.

'It's a film about meat, about people who are gone beyond dealing with animal meat and rats and dogs and cats. Crazy retarded people going beyond the line between animal and human.' *(Tobe Hooper)*

ANTI:

'It's without any apparent purpose, unless the creation of disgust and fright is a purpose.' *(Roger Ebert)*

'Just a mindless echo of Frankenstein, Grand Guignol, Jekyll and Hyde [et al] . . . The film is neither sickening not thrilling nor artistically interesting.' *(Eric Shorter, Daily Telegraph)*

'If ever a film should be banned this is it.' *(Margaret Hinxman, Daily Mail)*

'An absolute must for all maniacs and blood drinkers in need of a few tips.' *(Benny Green, Punch)*

'The prolonged screams of the girl who escapes, covered of course with blood, aptly reflect my feelings.' *(Patrick Gibbs, Daily Telegraph)*

'Hitler had Wagner to enjoy: modern Londoners get *The Texas Chainsaw Massacre* . . . It really is execrable.' *(Russell Davis, Observer)*

'This is about the sickest carnival of slaughter even seen . . . Why did the Greater London Council let this nightmare through?' *(News of the World)*

MIXED:

'This is enough to bring on instant schizophrenia. On the one hand the subject matter . . . is meretricious tosh. On the other, its judgement of how long the suspense can be sustained in each of its numerous passages of apprehension and its impeccably effective *trompe l'oeil* flourishes that convince you the horrors are actually happening cannot be eschewed as the incidentals of sensationalist trivia, since . . . they are filmic to a degree.' *(Gordon Gow, F & F)*

PRO:

'Without doubt the most frightening and macabre shocker I have ever seen.' *(Felix Barker, Evening News)*

'Annihilation is inevitable, humanity is now completely powerless . . . Uncontrol is emphasized throughout the film . . . This is partly, in conjunction with the film's relentless and unremitting intensity, what gives [it] the authentic quality of nightmare . . . [In this] all-male family . . . woman becomes the ultimate object of the characters' animus . . . Here sexuality is totally perverted from its functions, into sadism, violence and cannibalism . . . [which] represents the ultimate in possessiveness, hence the logical end of human relations under capitalism. The implication is that "liberation" and "permissiveness" . . . are at once inadequate and too late – too feeble, too unaware, and too undirected to withstand the legacy of long repression . . . [The film] achieves the force of authentic art. It is profoundly disturbing and intensely personal.' *(Robin Wood, Hollywood From Vietnam to Reagan, 1986)*

THAT OBSCURE OBJECT OF DESIRE AAN

CT: 5 AV: 7.30

(aka *Cet Obscur Objet Du Désir*)

1977 France/Spain 103 C DRAMA/ROMANCE

D Luis Buñuel ***X***
W Luis Buñuel Jean-Claude Carriere ***X*** AAN from Pierre Louys's novel *La Femme et le Pantin*

Fernando Rey ☆ Carole Bouquet Angela Molina Julien Bertheau André Weber Milena Vukotic

A middle-aged man (Fernando Rey) enjoys being humiliated by his maid-lover (Carole Bouquet and Angela Molina, playing two sides of the same character).

Luis Buñuel's light comedy about masochism is disappointingly heavy going – repetitive and monotonous despite a good performance from Rey. It was Buñuel's last film and contains echoes (or rip-offs) of his former work.

'Filled with small, droll touches, with tiny peculiarities of behavior, with moral anarchy, with a cynicism about human nature that somehow seems, in his [Buñuel's] hands, almost cheerful. His most obvious touch is perhaps his best: to dramatize Conchita's tantalizing elusiveness, he has cast two actresses to play her. So just when poor Mathieu has all but seduced this Conchita, the other emerges from the dressing room.' *(Roger Ebert)*

'Art of the most subversive kind . . . For all the anarchy of Buñuel's vision, there is nothing chaotic about his filmmaking style. At 77 he is in such fluid touch with his medium that he seems incapable of staging an awkward shot. The movie appears to flow directly from his subconscious, just as surrealist art is meant to do.' *(Frank Rich, Time)*

'Buñuel . . . has never been more witty, or more wicked . . . Rey, of course, is perfect in his part, and the absurd violence of the story concealed by the gloss of high living is the essence of Buñuel, the comment of a lifetime on the ridiculous contradictions of how things are today.' *(Molly Plowright, Glasgow Herald)*

'The movie is one of his very best . . . Our ends are so obscure, our means so absurd, Buñuel seems to be saying, that for most of us today it's only a difference in scale between a fly in the Martini and a bomb in the street.' *(Alexander Walker, Evening Standard)*

'Buñuel's films are seldom what they appear to be on the surface and this one, too, has its after-thought surprises, plus superb crystal-clear photography.' *(Douglas Blake, Evening News)*

THAT SINKING FEELING CT: 7 AV: 5.70

1979 GB 82/90/93 C COMEDY

D Bill Forsyth ✓
W Bill Forsyth ✓

Robert Buchanan ✓ John Hughes Billy Greenlees Douglas Sannachan Alan Love John Gordon Sinclair ✓

Unemployed Glaswegian teenagers plan a major robbery.

Charmingly understated comedy about bored Scottish teenagers, wittily written and directed as his screen début by Bill Forsyth (whose next films were to be the classics, *Gregory's Girl* and *Local Hero*). Despite its rough edges, this remains a wonderful example of how to make a movie with minimal resources. Sample line . . . 'There must be something more to life than suicide.'

ANTI:

'There are some pleasing shots of back streets and some mild jokes but much of it is stilted and pretentious.' *(Shipman)*

MIXED:

'Lively and amusing . . . Although scarcely justifying feature length playing time . . . [it] is refreshingly unorthodox.' *(Derek Malcolm, Guardian)*

'Truly wonderful even if the story seems a little preposterous.' *(Girl about Town)*

PRO:

'A fresh, chirpy, cheeky comedy . . . Forsyth has made the most original and most enjoyable Scottish film that I can remember. No one who has been to Glasgow and enjoyed the warmth and wit of its inhabitants could resist its charms.' *(Nicholas Wapshott, Scotsman)*

'Trying to analyse Bill Forsyth's street humour, vigour and irreverent send-up of authority is like nailing jelly to the wall – it eludes one's grasp. but his grasp of the ideas, ideals and outraged dignity of the young unemployed cannot be faulted.' *(Virginia Dignam, Morning Star)*

'The sweet inconsequential gallows farce of Forsyth's first feature . . . announced itself . . . as one of the most agreeable and individual voices to come to the big screen in Britain for ages . . . In feeling and method [he] is closer to that line which stretches back through Truffaut to Renoir and Vigo. The feeling is a wide and all-embracing sympathy which so far has not tipped into sentimentality nor looks likely to.' *(Gavin Millar, Listener)*

'A contemporary fairytale in which just about everybody has a skin problem . . . [It] might be classified as a caper film . . . [but it] doesn't move – it ambles from one moment to the next . . . A gentle film . . . [which] cannot obscure the strength of its intelligence and wit. Mr Forsyth is one of a kind.' *(Vincent Canby, New York Times, on the film's US release, 1984)*

'This delightful comedy . . . showed the way out of the sponsored documentary ghetto, brought in the customers and put a new name on the filmmaking map.' *(NFT Bulletin, 1984)*

THELMA & LOUISE CT: 9 AV: 7.92

1991 US 128 C DRAMA

D Ridley Scott ☆ AAN
W Callie Khouri ☆ AAW

Geena Davis ☆ AAN Susan Sarandon ☆ AAN

Harvey Keitel Michael Madsen Christopher McDonald Stephen Tobolowsky Brad Pitt

Thelma, a downtrodden wife (Geena Davis), and world-weary waitress Louise (Susan Sarandon) go on a weekend which turns sour. Louise shoots a man who tries to rape Thelma, and decides to go on the run to Mexico. Robbed of their money, they hold up a convenience store and are pursued by the FBI.

Ignore the solemn socio-sexual analysts: this is no feminist tract, but an exhilarating female riposte to the buddy-buddy movie. Some of the world's silliest feminists criticized the film for being insufficiently militant: neither Thelma nor Louise displays even a hint of lesbianism, and their first impulse when in trouble is to phone up their men (a perfectly natural reaction, but not one which will endear them to radical feminists). Surprisingly soon after nearly being raped, Thelma picks up a male hitch-hiker and goes to bed with him – not very likely, I admit, but Geena Davis's enthusiasm is enough to make you believe it at the time.

The movie isn't perfect. Like many of its male characters, it sags in the middle; there's something slightly depressing about any film where guns and cars are used to confer independence and strength on the leading characters; and the fate of the truck-driver's tanker smacks of escapist fantasy. But why shouldn't one action movie in ten thousand respond to women's fantasies, rather than men's?

Like most big commercial successes, it contains at least one timely social insight: namely, that feminism can be sexy. Geena Davis transforms herself from submissive child-woman to resilient adult so attractively that she will undoubtedly influence more women to re-evaluate their lives, than the entire works of Andrea Dworkin.

Susan Sarandon has to make a less positive transformation and is lumbered with the only laboured scenes in the film, as she decides whether to accept her boyfriend's clumsy proposal of marriage; but hers too is a performance of taste, intelligence and warmth.

The screenplay, a first-time effort by Callie Khouri, wittily inverts the audience's expectations all the way along, and was the first since *Alien* to harness Ridley Scott's visual talent to an involving story. Scott's flair for using landscape to arouse emotion (a memorable aspect of *Blade Runner* and *Black Rain*) gives the film more than just surface gloss: it lends it a mythic, allegorical clarity. Adrian Biddle's photography was Oscar-nominated, as was Thom Noble's editing.

Some commentators have found the end nihilistic, or a blatant rip-off of *Butch Cassidy*; but for the audience it's inevitable and emotionally satisfying. It contains a central truth about feminism: there is no return to dependency on men, any more than a child can regain innocence.

The whole film is an exhilarating celebration of popular cinema's ability to turn stories of ordinary people into myths with a social resonance; and the final frames are a signal that, whatever the fate of Thelma and Louise themselves, their story will survive. This is more than an entertaining movie: it's a great one.

ANTI:

'Khouri's screenplay . . . is burdened with contrivances. First, the pistol. When Thelma shows Louise her husband's pistol, which she doesn't know how to use, and makes a lame excuse for bringing it on the trip, we know that the gun is somehow going to be used as sure as (let's say) shooting. Then there's the stop for a drink. It's hard to believe that they would do this when they have a long trip ahead of them – especially the hard-headed Louise, who is driving. It's even harder to believe that Thelma would let herself get tipsy so quickly, would so quickly cling to a man who asked her to dance, and would then so easily go outside with him – for a breath of air. (And by this time, it's dark.) . . . Thelma is supposed to be feather-headed, but Khouri piles so much on her that very soon we're aware that contrivance is being passed off as character – to render the pair desperately broke. It's hard to believe that the shrewd Louise could have been friends with anyone as dumb as Thelma is shown to be. Thus, what was meant to be a fated descent into the maelstrom becomes a patent piece of engineering.' *(Stanley Kauffmann)*

'Any movie that went as far out of its way to trash women as this female chauvinist sow of a film does to trash men would be universally, and justifiably, condemned . . . First-time screenwriter Callie Khouri mistakes cruelty for camaraderie . . . But she has some excuse for participating in the man-bashing, being a woman. Director Ridley (*Alien*) 'Scott comes across as a gender quisling.' *(Ralph Novak, People Weekly)*

PRO:

'Working territory new to him, Scott has balanced action, comedy and doomy subtext to create a morally firm yet very entertaining fable that reaches out to an audience far larger than its natural feminist constituency.' *(Richard Schickel, Time)*

'Exuberant, spontaneous and brimful of social comment.' *(Bruce Williamson, Playboy)*

'Does to film images of women what *Dances with Wolves* did to those of Native Americans: take decades of cinematic stereotypes and turn them upside down.' *(Baseline)*

THEM!

CT: 7 AV: 6.92

1954 US 94 BW HORROR/SF

D Gordon Douglas ☆
W Ted Sherdeman Russell Hughes ☆ from George Worthing Yates's story

Edmund Gwenn ☆ James Whitmore Joan Weldon James Arness Onslow Stevens Sean McClory

Ants made huge by atomic radiation infest New Mexico and start spreading . . .

Much imitated monster movie of the 50s, all the more effective for realistic treatment, an eerie score and excellent cinematography (by Sid Hickox). The sensible script builds logically from its fantastic premise, and the romantic sub-plot does not slow the action too much. But it is the direction which makes the film a classic of its genre: the early desert sequences are memorably well shot, as is the climax in the Los Angeles sewers.

This mildly anti-Bomb picture was favourably reviewed, although it was denounced by one magazine, *Twentieth Century*, as an anti-Comunist allegory calling for the extermination of Reds rather than ants. This seems an over-fanciful interpretation.

'Tense, absorbing and, surprisingly enough, somewhat convincing.' *(New York Times)*

'Terrifying newsreel-styled thriller . . . [that] carries considerable conviction.' *(Jesse Zunser, Cue)*

'A well-built example of the neo-monstrous . . . quite persuasively documented . . . The direction is smoothly machined, and the writing decent.' *(MFB)*

'A right little fright of a picture . . . preposterous, but lively and with a fine atmosphere of fact.' *(Newsweek)*

'As persuasively realistic a horror story as one could comfortably imagine.' *(Arthur Knight, Saturday Review)*

'Surrender yourself to its inspiring horrors and you will, in the happiest sense, be ant-agonized.' *(News Chronicle)*

'A shocker. It made the men gasp and the women cry out, because *Them!* makes all the other 'X' certificate thrillers seem as harmless as a Sunday afternoon stroll.' *(Daily Express)*

THESE THREE

CT: 6 AV: 7.80

1936 US 93 BW DRAMA

D William Wyler
W Lillian Hellman from her play *The Children's Hour*

Miriam Hopkins ✓ Merle Oberon ✓ Joel McCrea Catherine Doucet Alma Kruger Bonita Granville ☆ AAN Marcia Mae Jones Carmencita Johnson

A schoolgirl (Bonita Granville) maliciously accuses two teachers (Miriam Hopkins, Merle Oberon) of immoral behaviour.

In the Broadway play, the schoolmistresses' alleged offence was lesbianism. This was deemed too shocking for cinema audiences; but, though bowdlerized, dated and theatrical, the film retains an impact as a study of the effects that scandal can have. The lesbianism was made explicit in Wyler's remake, *The Loudest Whisper* (1962).

PRO:

'Earnestly written, produced, directed and acted . . . Despite its all-round excellence this is the type of profound drama which oft proves to be a questionable attraction . . . [The three stars] are really excellent, but they cannot help it if they are overshadowed by the two children.' *(F.S. Jennings, Era)*

'Lifted from an ordinary plane to compelling heights of sincere emotionalism through brilliant, understanding direction and the cleverness of two unknown juvenile players . . . [Bonita Granville's] amazingly accurate portrait of evil precocity is, in fact, the keystone of the drama . . . The staging is unpretentious, but more than adequate.' *(Kine Weekly)*

'Little short of brilliant . . . An absorbing, tautly written and dramatically vital screenplay . . . One of the finest screen dramas in recent years.' *(Frank S. Nugent, New York Times)*

'There is no individual part of it at which you would cry out genius. Individually, the work of producer, actors, director, is good, sound, sensitive, no more; collectively it is rich and moving.' *(Observer)*

'A picture of personal triumphs . . . for Goldwyn . . . Hellman . . . Wyler . . . [and the actors] . . . Two new little stars have surely been born.' *(Photoplay)*

MIXED:

'The grown-ups are all good but the children are brilliant . . . The film is . . . dramatic, enthralling and moving. The only blemish is the "incidental" music which is both too continuous and too loud.' *(MFB)*

'In spite of the fact that the footage and dialogue are rather excessive, the high level of the acting and the clever direction . . . makes this picture very good and unusual entertainment . . . and in spite of a little sagging of interest at times, it will hold your attention.' *(Lionel Collier, Picturegoer)*

'Has an excellence of production and acting, but a synthetic quality . . . It could have been so much better had it been made with more integrity – had it been less consciously a series of strong dramatic moments, rosily rounded off with a happy ending.' *(John Gammie, Film Weekly)*

THEY LOVED LIFE:

see KANAL.

THEY SHOOT HORSES, DON'T THEY?

CT: 6 AV: 7.43

1969 US 129 C DRAMA

D Sydney Pollack ☆ AAN
W James Poe Robert E. Thompson ☆ AAN from Horace McCoy's novel

Gig Young ☆ AAW Jane Fonda ☆ AAN
Susannah York ☆ AAN Michael Sarrazin Red Buttons ☆ Bonnie Bedelia ☆ Bruce Dern Allyn Ann McLerie ☆

In the Depression, couples take part in a marathon dance contest.

As you might imagine from the subject-matter, the dance is a metaphor for Life, and a pretty depressing one, with Gig Young as a singularly unpleasant God. It's hardly uplifting entertainment, yet the look of the film – with its deliberately sickly colours – and an exceptionally strong cast make this a memorable microcosm of Depression-era America. John Green and Albert Woodbury were Oscar-nominated for their score.

ANTI:

'Weakened by a ludicrous device of flash-forwards, which bewilderingly predict the hero's eventual arrest and trial.' *(David Robinson, Financial Times)*

MIXED:

'I didn't find the picture entirely unsatisfactory. It is, by the very nature of its story, rather monotonous, and the characters, apart from the hideous Rocky [Gig Young], are a little stereotyped . . . I would hardly call it enjoyable, but it is still a movie of some stature.' *(Penelope Mortimer, Observer)*

PRO:

'Drenched me in compassion, left me bitter with anger . . . Pollack puts us through this dance of death until our feet positively ache in sympathy.' *(Robert Ottaway, Daily Sketch)*

'A brilliant job of filmmaking: harrowing in the extreme, yet desperately exciting as well.' *(Margaret Hinxman, Sunday Telegraph)*

'The sleazy dance emporium is recreated in all its tawdriness, the costumes are painfully accurate, the false gaiety enough to make a tin angel weep. Yet through this jiggling morass there runs a thread of life, of gallows humor, of sheer defiant tenacity, toward a paltry but touching heroism . . . Not the least remarkable thing about *They Shoot Horses, Don't They?* is the photography by Philip A. Lathrop. There were considerable problems to contend with. Though shot in color, the film had to have the shoddy look of a godforsaken ballroom jutting out into the Pacific, and Lathrop accordingly underexposed and overdeveloped the film, getting a grainy texture and somber coloration – predominantly purplish brown of an unwholesome, almost macabre quality. And because the camera had to keep whirling along with the dancers, no ground-level lights, only overhead ones, could be used. It all works very well, despite the difficulties, and when Lathrop's camera seems to collide head-on with some of those overhead light beams, the result is not only glaringly realistic, it is almost hallucinatory.' *(John Simon)*

'The movie begins on a note of alienation and spirals down from there. *Horses* provides us no cheap release at the end; and the ending, precisely because it is so obvious, is all the more effective. We knew it was coming. Even the title gave it away. And when it comes, it is effective not because it is a surprise but because it is inevitable. As inevitable as death.' *(Roger Ebert)*

THEY WERE EXPENDABLE CT: 5 AV: 7.80

1945 US 135 BW WAR/DRAMA

D John Ford ☆ Robert Montgomery (the latter was uncredited)
W Frank Wead from William L. White's book

Robert Montgomery ☆ John Wayne Donna Reed
Jack Holt Ward Bond Marshall Thompson
Paul Langton Leon Ames

Motor torpedo boats operate in the Pacific during World War II.

A story of heroic teamwork and courage in defeat, this was an astonishingly downbeat film to be released before the war was won. The biggest weaknesses are an over-episodic and unclear narrative, excessive length and an extraneous romantic sub-plot between John Wayne and Donna Reed (both the characters on whom they were based sued MGM and won). But Robert Montgomery, a naval officer in real life, gives a moving portrayal of the loneliness of leadership – a favourite Fordian theme, to be explored in his later cavalry westerns. This is probably the most artistically shot of all World War II films; Ford's direction and Joseph H. August's cinematography have an expressionistic intensity in the battle and hospital sequences. Ford broke his leg two weeks before the end of shooting, and Montgomery took over.

'The studio-made battle sequences convey a brilliant sense of the terror undergone by the men on their boats – things which must have seemed targets designed especially for drawing enemy-fire to the men themselves.' *(Stephen P. Belcher Jr, NBR)*

'This is one of the fine war movies and a stirring reminder of American gallantry in the early days of disaster . . . The acting is first-rate throughout, but the film is at its documentary best in action, whether the sea-going gadflies are nipping at a Kuma-class cruiser or, in the blackest day of the campaign, whisking General MacArthur to his historic rendezvous off Mindanao.' *(Newsweek)*.

'An exciting and nostalgic story of Navy men who fought in the tiny PT boats in the rear-guard action around the Philippines in the first months of the war. Played stoutly and with plenty of rugged sentiment.' *(Bosley Crowther)*

'For what seems at least half of the dogged, devoted length of *They Were Expendable* all you have to watch is men getting on or off PT boats, and other men watching them do so. But this is made so beautiful and so real that I could not feel one foot of the film was wasted.' *(James Agee)*

THEY WON'T FORGET CT: 5 AV: 7.29

1937 US 94 BW DRAMA

D Mervyn LeRoy ☆
W Robert Rossen Aben Kandel from Ward Greene's novel *Death in the Deep South*

Claude Rains ☆ Gloria Dickson Edward Norris Clinton Rosemond Otto Kruger Allyn Joslyn ☆ Lana Turner Linda Perry Cy Kendall

In 1913, the death of a high-school girl (Lana Turner) in a southern town leads to a lynching.

Though only on screen for a few minutes, Lana Turner made a big impression in this, her first billed appearance on screen, playing a sexy adolescent. The acting honours in this big, social melodrama go, however, to Rains as an ambitious, bigoted attorney who prosecutes a Northerner for murder, simply in order to ease his own path to the governorship. The picture was admired by critics of the day, but it has obvious weaknesses: the baddies are much more entertaining than the good (there's a lovely character performance by Allyn Joslyn as a corrupt reporter), and – although the film is based on real events – there are gaping holes in the plot. But at least the film doesn't cop out at the end.

MIXED:

'Although both plot and treatment have immense vigour and challenging realism, there is too much indictment and not enough straight drama . . . Thematically inconclusive . . . rather like a Hyde Park orator whose eloquence has got the better of him.' *(Film Weekly)*

'Not a pleasant film, nor is it a particularly entertaining one, but it is immensely powerful and gripping. It has an axe to grind and it grinds it so forcefully that the sharp edge cuts right into one.' *(Alan Page, S & S)*

PRO:

'In content and uncompromising treatment this film is just the blood-and-guts sort of thing we've been hollering for.' *(Otis Ferguson)*

'In many ways it is superior to *Fury* and *Black Legion* which have been milled from the same dramatic mine. Not so spectacular, or melodramatic, or strident perhaps, yet it is stronger, more vibrant than they through the quiet intensity of its narrative, the simplicity of Mervyn LeRoy's direction, its integrity of purpose, the even perfection of its cast.' *(Frank S. Nugent, New York Times)*

'Emotional dynamite, artistic cinema and excellent entertainment . . . LeRoy had great daring in producing and directing this celluloid thunderbolt. Don't think of missing it.' *(Photoplay)*

'Handled with superb assurance . . . and the camera unobtrusively illuminates the action at every point . . . A very remarkable film.' *(Liam O'Leary)*

'The end makes no concession to sentimentality . . . This is an adult film.' *(New Statesman)*

'A grim and scathing portrayal of prejudice, intolerance and mob fury in the deep south, [it] progresses with a newsreel objectivity that gives its incidents the reality if not the intensity of Lang's *Fury*. The depiction of Redwine, the terrified Negro janitor who discovers the body of the murdered girl in the school's elevator shaft, is one of the few instances in American films in which the fear and oppression that fill the life of the southern negro is strikingly told.' *(Lewis Jacobs, 1968)*

THIEF OF BAGDAD, THE CT: 7 AV: 6.67

1924 US 135 BW (colour sequences) FANTASY/ FAMILY/ SILENT

D Raoul Walsh ☆
W Lotta Woods Douglas Fairbanks

Douglas Fairbanks ☆ Snitz Edwards Anna May Wong Julanne Johnston Etta Lee Brandon Hurst Sojin

Thief (Douglas Fairbanks) outwits Caliph with magic.

This *Thief* is well worth catching: Douglas Fairbanks excels in the most action-packed and lavish of all silent adventures, imaginatively designed by William Cameron Menzies. The story gallops along, enlivened by special effects which must have seemed very impressive at the time. The new soundtrack is by Carl Davis, based on themes by Rimsky-Korsakov.

PRO:

'A classic in pictures.' *(Variety)*

'An entrancing picture, wholesome and compelling, deliberate and beautiful, a feat of motion picture art which has never been equalled.' *(New York Times)*

'Here is magic. Here is beauty. Here is the answer to cynics who give the motion picture no place in the family of the arts . . . A work of rare genius.' *(James Quirk, Photoplay)*

'[Fairbanks was] arguably the most dashing, athletic and Ariel-like of all screen swashbucklers . . . [He] wrote, performed and produced [the film] intending to create the cinema's most lavish Arabian Nights fantasy. Almost 70 years later it still impresses with its sense of scale and an incident-strewn scenario involving . . . of course, a magic carpet . . . suspended by six wires from a 90-foot crane, to fly over Bagdad . . . The result remains unrivalled with an ingenuity and invention that contemporary advances in special-effects pyrotechnics have done little to diminish.' *(Allan Hunter & Kenny Mathieson, Movie Classics, 1992)*

'Pure excitement . . . charming, fabulous . . . with its

engaging hero, its evil wizard, and its storybook thrills, among those that can be counted: a flying horse, a magic carpet, a Djinn in a bottle, and a deadly, six-armed dancing doll.' *(Carlos Clarens, An Illustrated History of the Horror Film, 1967)*

MIXED:

'One of the best of Doug's costume films. He and his director borrow both the plot devices and the cinematic gimmicks of Fritz Lang's *Destiny* without borrowing any of the German's mysticism. The result is a rather long, empty, and yet entertaining film of adventures and cinematic tricks . . . The film is impressive visually . . . [It] adds up to a slick, pleasant show, but that sum seems less significant than the incisive wit, the cleverness, the insight of the early Doug films.' *(Gerald Mast, A Short History of the Movies, 1971)*

THIEF OF BAGDAD, THE CT: 8 AV: 9.23

1940 GB 106 C FANTASY/FAMILY

D Ludwig Berger Michael Powell Tim Whelan Zoltan Korda William Cameron Menzies Alexander Korda
W Lajos Biro Miles Malleson

Conrad Veidt ☆ Sabu ✔ June Duprez ✔ John Justin ✔ Rex Ingram ✔ Miles Malleson Morton Selten Mary Morris Bruce Winston Hay Petrie

A little thief (Sabu) outwits a wicked Grand Vizier (Conrad Veidt).

Spectacular foray by producer Alexander Korda into the realm of the Arabian Nights; although six directors were used, the film has a remarkable consistency of style. The storyline is episodic and the special effects are primitive by modern standards, but it's entertaining from start to finish. Alexander Korda thought the film flashy and lacking in warmth, but he may just have grown tired of the production difficulties which dogged it (two years in the making, it was shot during the Blitz in England but had to be finished in California).

One of the best aspects is the acting, not always the strongest element in fantasies. Conrad Veidt stole the reviews for his evil Jaffar, but Sabu is charming and June Duprez makes a very attractive princess. The film won Oscars for art direction (Vincent Korda), cinematography (Georges Perinal), and special effects (Lawrence Butler and Jack Whitney). Miklos Rozsa's outstanding score was also nominated.

ANTI:

'The unimpressive story and stagey acting of the cast fail to measure up to the general production qualities.' *(Variety)*

PRO:

'A model of pictorial beauty and without sensationalism provides thrills that can hardly be measured.' *(William Whitebait, New Statesman)*

'Outstanding lavish spectacular Arabian Nights fantasy with every artifice of trick photography and special effects . . . Epoch making film event in terms of technical performance and a rich fairy story entertainment which everyone will clamour to see.' *(Daily Film Renter)*

'Its brilliant technical presentation, marvellous trick camera work and superb colour photography are responsible for a continuous flow of pictorial wonders.' *(Kine Weekly)*

'*The* best fantasy film ever made . . . Every frame of *The Thief of Bagdad* is magical and exciting.' *(Baseline)*

THIN MAN, THE AAN CT: 8 AV: 8.83

1934 US 93 BW THRILLER/COMEDY

D W.S. Van Dyke AAN
W Frances Goodrich Albert Hackett AAN from Dashiell Hammett's novel

William Powell ☆ AAN Myrna Loy ☆ Maureen O'Sullivan Nat Pendleton Minna Gombell Porter Hall Henry Wadsworth William Henry Harold Huber Cesar Romero

Private detective Nick Charles (William Powell), retired and married to the wealthy Nora (Myrna Loy), is coaxed by his wife into finding a missing inventor (Edward Ellis).

William Powell and Myrna Loy were at their stylish best in the first of this popular and much-imitated series of six thrillers, which struck an emotional chord with Depression-weary audiences. Their hedonistic, hard-drinking, extravagant way of life seemed the last word in sophistication. Now, the defects of the film are obvious – overlong exposition and an insubstantial plot – but the two leading performances (three if you include Asta, the wire-haired terrier) still sparkle, as does most of the repartee.

'Every now and then the powers at Metro . . . toss off a thriller that for sheer pace, fun and efficiency leaves all the others standing. [It] is a lovely medley of murders, shrewdly and ironically directed.' *(Observer)*

'Has the unusual merit of combining exciting adventure and genuine comedy.' *(The Times)*

'A joyful melodrama which bursts into comedy and stays there . . . More hilarity than horror . . . First rate entertainment . . . Exceedingly high grade.' *(Daily Express)*

'Brilliantly put over by expert direction and an outstanding cast. Story clever, dialogue smart and humour sophisticated and popular.' *(Kine Weekly)*

'Set a high mark in realism with the ease,

spontaneity, and intimacy of the actors' speeches and the flow of images and talk generally. The camera did not wait on the sound, and the conversation did not seem to be aware of the microphone's presence. The whole scene was maintained at a natural pitch and tone without any "microphone consciousness".' *(Lewis Jacobs, 1939)*

THING, THE CT: 7 AV: 7.10

(aka *The Thing From Another World*)

1951 US 87 BW SF/ HORROR

D Christian Nyby ☆
W Charles Lederer from Don A. Stuart's (pseudonym for John W. Campbell) story *Who Goes There*

Robert Cornthwaite Kenneth Tobey
Margaret Sheridan Bill Self Dewey Martin
James Arness (as The Thing).

An eight-foot alien terrorizes the men of an Arctic polar exploration station.

A popular and critically acclaimed science fiction shocker that rises above B-movie standards because it's humorous, suspense-filled, shot with loads of atmosphere and leaves plenty to the imagination. It's sternly moralistic and with strong Cold War overtones (there is always a sense that Russia is only a few miles away). It has been imitated a little too often since, in films such as *Alien*, so that modern audiences may find it dated.

The accredited director, Christian Nyby, had been Howard Hawks's editor on *Red River*; and some critics (particularly auteurists) have argued that Hawks must have directed most, if not all, of *The Thing* and given Nyby the credit to earn him his union card. The film does bear many Hawksian hallmarks – overlapping dialogue, professionals working together, a leavening of suspense with humour (it contains the immortal sci-fi line: 'An intellectual carrot – the mind boggles!'). However, evidence from the actors suggests that it was indeed Nyby who gave the orders – and Hawks was rarely to be seen around the set.

ANTI:

'The resourcefulness shown in building the plot groundwork is lacking as the yarn gets into full swing. Cast members . . . fail to communicate any real terror as the Thing makes its appearance and its power potential to destroy the world is revealed.' *(Variety)*

'There seems little point in creating a monster of such original characteristics if he is to be allowed only to prowl about the North Pole, waiting to be destroyed by the superior ingenuity of the US Air Force.' *(Penelope Houston)*

PRO:

'Not since Dr Frankenstein wrought his mechanical monster has the screen had such a good time dabbling in science fiction . . . A movie that is generous with thrills and chills and comes up with just enough light, bantering dialogue – the kind of desperate wit which acts as a safety valve under pressing circumstances – so that the film does not appear to take itself too seriously.' *(New York Times)*

'Pseudo-scientific thriller, extremely well produced. In fact, so much so that the more extravagant sequences manage to squeeze some sense of conviction into their basic improbabilities.' *(Picturegoer)*

'One of the greatest science fiction films ever made.' *(Baseline)*

THINGS TO COME CT: 6 AV: 7.64

1936 GB 100 BW SF/DRAMA

D William Cameron Menzies ☆
W H.G. Wells Lajos Biro from Wells's book *The Shape of Things to Come*

Raymond Massey ☆ Edward Chapman
Ralph Richardson Margaretta Scott ●
Cedric Hardwicke ● Maurice Braddell
Sophie Stewart ● Derrick de Marney Ann Todd
Pearl Argyle Kenneth Villiers

H.G. Wells's pessimistic vision of the future, predicting war in 1940, a rocket to the moon and a plague.

Then, an amazing spectacular: now, a fascinating period piece. Tremendous sets, impressive scenes of devastation, a great score by Arthur Bliss (the first ever to be commercially recorded) and a fine central performance by Raymond Massey make this a landmark British film. The grave weaknesses, which have become more apparent over the intervening decades, are stagey, melodramatic acting and a talky, amateurishly constructed script. Lavishly produced by Alexander Korda, it cost over $1.5 million, a huge amount for the time, and eventually made back its money.

ANTI:

'*Things to Come* is based on what is possibly, in our opinion, the worst scenario that has ever been written. It is so bad that it seems to be beyond discussion, and we are quite unable to understand how it got into production.' *(Era)*

MIXED:

'Tremendous, awe-inspiring, challenging, imaginative and technically magnificent – but, viewed in the light of sheer entertainment, far too prolix in its argumentative vision of the future.' *(News Chronicle)*

'Wells, alas, has taken himself a little too seriously. Now and then there is so much talk, yes, and of such an uninteresting kind, that, even before the dullest bits started, some ironical person at the preview greeted the line, "I want you to do, not think," with a loud laugh. When that is said, I must immediately declare that no American picture I have seen, except perhaps *King Kong*, has equalled the technical achievements of *Things to Come*. The awe of it all is over-powering.' *(People)*

'Successful in every department but emotionally. For heart interest Mr Wells hands you an electric switch.' *(Variety)*

'An amazingly ingenious technical accomplishment, even if it does hold out small hope for our race . . . The existence pictured is as joyless as a squeezed grapefruit.' *(Don Herold)*

PRO:

'A leviathan among films . . . a stupendous spectacle, an overwhelming, Dorean, Jules Vernesque, elaborated *Metropolis*, staggering to eye, mind and spirit, the like of which has never been seen and never will be seen again.' *(Sunday Times)*

'Incomparably the greatest technical achievement of filmcraft to date, and in scope and sincerity sets a mark for film producers to aim at for many years to come.' *(Morning Post)*

'Not merely entertainment but a religious ceremony: it purges the mind with terror and with wonder.' *(Inquirer)*

'The greatest British science fiction movie.' *(Alan Frank)*

THIRD MAN, THE CT: 9 AV: 9.74

1949 GB 100 BW THRILLER

D Carol Reed ☆ AAN
W Graham Greene ☆

Joseph Cotten ☆ Orson Welles ☆ Alida Valli ☆ Trevor Howard ☆ Paul Hörbiger Ernst Deutsch Erich Ponto Siegfried Breuer Bernard Lee ☆ Geoffrey Keen Wilfrid Hyde-White

An American writer (Joseph Cotten) arrives in postwar Vienna to find that a friend of his, Harry Lime (Orson Welles), is dead – or is he?

A great film noir thriller: stylish, humorous and elegantly written by Graham Greene – it was his only completely original screenplay. It is slow-paced by comparison with most films in its genre, but has an atmosphere all its own, thanks partly to Robert Krasker's Academy Award-winning black-and-white photography, but also to Anton Karas's haunting zither music. It's a meditation on the nature of friendship and loyalty in a war-weary world.

Carol Reed directs in fine style, and is helped by Oswald Hafenrichter's Oscar-nominated editing. Many critics have noticed Orson Welles's influence on the chiaroscuro photography and unusual camera angles, and he certainly wrote much of his own, ultra-cynical dialogue. Although he is not on screen for long, this is one of his most memorable performances – a study in decadence and evil, hiding behind a smooth exterior.

ANTI:

'It is, I suppose, because Reed's exceptional talent leads one to expect miracles that I feel a shade of disappointment at the reappearance of the familiar trick or the familiar situation. The chase through the sewers, for instance, is far from new – though to be fair it has never been done better, or possibly as well as here. Hitchcock's films are full of the terror of heights, and though in *The Third Man* when hero and villain look down from the giant wheel nobody falls off, I could not help thinking that the situation was secondhand. It was, as a matter of fact, not of Hitchcock but of Orson Welles that I thought – and not simply because he was present as an actor. There are passages in the Reed-Greene film with a touch of the pretentiousness which creeps into the later Welles films . . . To say all this is, I know, to be hypercritical. But *The Third Man* is excellent enough to be judged by severe standards. And because of its excellence I shall not refrain from adding that the intentional deliberation of the cutting is occasionally over-insistent; that the admirably played zither which provides the only musical accompaniment . . . is occasionally distracting; and that Valli, who plays the actress, does not seem to me to have yet justified her reputation.' *(Dilys Powell)*

MIXED:

'What exquisite artful photography Reed gives us to conceal the fact that his script is not going anywhere very special!' *(Daily Compass)*

'There is little in the story that would seem to matter. Whether it was all worth doing with so much care and talent and wit (for there are some good jokes) can only be a minority's murmured query.' *(Cyril Ray)*

'After the incomparably clever scene-setting, which occupies most of the film, the latter part descends almost to the level of merely competent "cops and robbers".' *(James Monahan)*

'The senses are catered for but the emotions are untouched.' *(Joan Lester)*

'*The Third Man* reveals Carol Reed as probably the most brilliant craftsman of the modern cinema (certainly as Britain's best talent) and yet as one who is devoid of the urges that make a really great director. Sensitive and humane and dedicated, he would seem to be enclosed from life with no specially strong feelings about the stories that come his way to film other than that they should be something he can perfect and polish with a craftsman's love.' *(Richard Winnington)*

'*The Third Man*, for all the awesome hoopla it has received, is essentially a first-rate contrivance in the way of melodrama – and that's all. It isn't a penetrating study of any European problem of the day. It doesn't present any "message". It hasn't a point of view. It is just a bang-up melodrama, designed to excite and entertain.' *(Bosley Crowther)*

PRO:

'Within the framework of commercial film-making, the film is exceptional for the quality of its rhythmic structure, achieved by Carol Reed's supple interlacing of effects: the profusion of low-level, tilted, and oblique shots; the short duration of separate images in narrative sequences, the almost exclusive use of the cut (there is very little tracking camera and few dissolves); the sharply selected "off-mike" sounds; and by the urgency of the zither – not an accompaniment merely but a counter-figure that contributes its own special pattern, as every good film score should. These means to fluidity, surprise, and persuasion, combined with the unreal reality of war-stripped Vienna and the incidental locales – a cemetery, a Ferris wheel, the sewers, the wide boulevards – give the whole film a percussive fluency, like a plausibly scripted nightmare.' *(Vernon Young)*

'The most enthralling picture since . . . *Fallen Idol* . . . takes on the quality of a symphonic movement.' *(New York Daily News)*

'The work of a craftsman so skilled that he has earned the right to be judged as an artist.' *(Time)*

'All the glowing advance tidings . . . have been confirmed. Every detail calls for superlative praise.' *(New York World Telegram & Sun)*

'A thriller which uses every trick in the pack to remain thrilling.' *(Eve Perrick, Daily Express)*

'Just enough Orson Welles to please, not saturate . . . With the aid of exceptional camerawork and carefully paced direction, the suspense of the film is well-nigh physically overpowering.' *(Fortnight)*

'*The Third Man*, the best picture shown here this year, reaffirms Carol Reed as our foremost film-maker and one of the best three or four in the world. In essence his films seem no more than melodramas. But to dismiss *The Third Man* as such is equivalent to dismissing *Hamlet* as a play about a moody boy who hates his mother and kills his stepfather. What Carol Reed hangs on this melodramatic framework is something perilously like life, bless its dear old heart – life, whose image in films so seldom bears much resemblance to the original.' *(Fred Majdalany, Daily Mail)*

'I am inclined to use the word genius sparingly but there is no other word that adequately suggests the power, the thrill, the mystery and suspense with which Carol Reed invests Graham Greene's dramatic story of a man-hunt in the underworld of Vienna.' *(A.E. Wilson)*

'The only good picture ever to come out of Britain.' *(Quentin Crisp, Christopher Street, 1980s)*

39 STEPS, THE

CT: 9 AV: 9.69

1935 GB 81/85 BW THRILLER

D Alfred Hitchcock ☆
W Charles Bennett Alma Reville Ian Hay from John Buchan's novel

Madeleine Carroll ☆ Robert Donat ☆
Lucie Mannheim Godfrey Tearle Peggy Ashcroft ☆
John Laurie Helen Haye ☆ Wylie Watson ☆
Frank Cellier Peggy Simpson

A Canadian rancher (Robert Donat) on holiday in London becomes involved in espionage, and is suspected of being a murderer.

One of the great thrillers – exciting, humorous and full of classic sequences. Several ideas which now seem old hat were here used for the first time – such as a woman's scream blending into the whistle of a locomotive. Hitchcock obviously delights in the last-minute escapes, the risqué connotations of a man and a woman spending a night together in handcuffs, and the final set-piece at the London Palladium. Donat and Carroll are realistic in the central roles, and there isn't a weak link in the supporting cast. They make the most of some cleverly written scenes, a few of which are little films in themselves.

Because the political aspect of the espionage is left unclear, the story has dated far less than most other spy thrillers. There were remakes in 1959 and 1978; both are watchable, but the 1978 one is better directed, and the most faithful of all three versions to Buchan's original plot.

'I am out to give the public good, healthy, mental shake-ups. Civilization has become so screening and sheltering that we cannot experience sufficient thrills at first hand. Therefore, to prevent our becoming sluggish and jellified, we have to experience them artificially.' *(Alfred Hitchcock, at the time of the film's release)*

MIXED:

'It's melodrama and at times far-fetched and improbable, but the story twists and spins artfully from one high-powered sequence to another while the entertainment holds like steel cable from start to finish.' *(Variety)*

PRO:

'An exciting film of espionage . . . adapted with complete success, from John Buchan's novel. The atmosphere of adventure and mystery . . . is excellently maintained throughout . . . until . . . Hannay unmasks the spy organization and clears himself of the murder . . . Hitchcock's direction, the speed at which the film moves, and Donat's high-spirited acting get away with [the lucky accidents of plot] . . . The success of the film as a whole is in large part due to Donat's vigorous and full-blooded acting . . . The photography throughout is excellent

. . . but some of the studio outdoor sets are bad because patently studio sets.' *(MFB)*

'A grand mixture of comedy, melodrama and character study . . . I cannot say that Hitchcock has surpassed the standard he set himself in *The Man Who Knew Too Much*. He hasn't. But perhaps that would be too much to expect. It suffices to say that he has made a sure-fire success, an intelligent picture, and a noteworthy addition to the scant gallery of first-rate British films all rolled into one.' *(Evening Standard)*

'One of the fascinating pictures of the year . . . A master of shock and suspense, of cold horror and slyly incongruous wit, [Hitchcock] uses his camera the way a painter uses his brush . . . There is a subtle feeling of menace on the screen all the time in Mr Hitchcock's low-slung, angled use of the camera . . . Robert Donat is excellent . . . The lovely Madeleine Carroll . . . is charming and skillful.' *(Andre Sennwald New York Times)*

'The average British film contains from four to six major stuations and moves at about the pace of a bath-chair. In *The 39 Steps*, there are fourteen major situations, and the pace of the film is like the Flying Scotsman, which is one of its stars.' *(Daily Mail)*

'The "falsely accused man" films typically take the form of what Andrew Britton has termed the "double chase" plot structure: the hero, pursued by the police, pursues the real villain(s). He is always innocent of the crime of which he is accused but (perhaps ambiguously) guilty of something else: at the least, egoism and irresponsibility (*North by Northwest*), at the most of a desire that the crime be committed (*Strangers on a Train*). Somewhere in between lies the attribution of sexual guilt, a concept that has undergone such transformation during our century that a proper understanding of (at least) some of the earlier films has become problematic: today's audiences may have difficulty in grasping that, say, Richard Hannay (in *The 39 Steps*) is to be regarded as "guilty" because he anticipated a night of "illicit" sex with a woman who (after all) picked him up, not the other way around, but the apprehension is crucial to a reading of the film's narrative progress.' *(Robin Wood, Hitchcock's Films Revisited, 1989)*

'One of the three or four best things Hitchcock ever did.' *(Pauline Kael)*

'A grand spy mystery and a harrowing portrait of an innocent man struggling to prove his innocence while the world turns against him, *The 39 Steps* is one of the all-time great thrillers.' *(Baseline)*

THIS GUN FOR HIRE

CT: 7 AV: 7.50

1942 US 81 BW THRILLER

D Frank Tuttle ☆
W Albert Maltz W.R. Burnett from Graham Greene's novel *A Gun for Sale*

Veronica Lake ☆ Robert Preston Laird Cregar ☆ Alan Ladd ☆ Tully Marshall Mikhail Rasumny Pamela Blake

A singer (Veronica Lake) gets tangled up with a professional killer (Alan Ladd) and a fifth-columnist plot.

Suspenseful but depressing melodrama with overtones of film noir. Graham Greene's novel underwent huge changes for the adaptation, with the locale changed to California and the leading character altered from the cop (played by Robert Preston) to Alan Ladd's anti-hero. Ladd and Veronica Lake are understated and outstanding; their scenes have an erotic charge. On the strength of this movie's success, they went on to co-star in *The Glass Key, The Blue Dahlia* and *Saigon*.

'A strong melodramatic story well worked out, and admirably produced with some fine acting . . . The excitement of suspense is well sustained.' *(MFB)*

'There is Veronica Lake, improving on previous performance by showing both eyes instead of one; and there is the plot, a . . . taut affair.' *(William Whitebait, New Statesman)*

'[In comparison with *Saboteur*] *This Gun For Hire* seemed to me the superior film in every way, better acted, better written, better put together.' *(C.A. Lejeune, Observer)*

'Comes pretty high in the melodrama class. It is exciting and ingenious without losing the directness of its plot, fast-moving without disturbing the neat dovetailing of its parts; it has touches of visual imagination – the killer running madly down the long perspective of the bridge – and only rare moments of the sentimentality which Hollywood likes to fancy as psycho-analysis. An actor new, not to films, but to leading parts, Alan Ladd, gives a good performance as the gunman double-crossed by fifth-column big business, and as the cabaret girl caught up in his escape silky Veronica Lake improves and improves.' *(Dilys Powell)*

THIS HAPPY BREED

CT: 6 AV: 7.44

1944 GB 114 C DRAMA

D David Lean ☆
W David Lean Ronald Neame Anthony Havelock-Allan from Noel Coward's play

Robert Newton Celia Johnson ☆ John Mills Kay Walsh ✓ Stanley Holloway ✓ Amy Veness Alison Leggatt Eileen Erskine John Blythe (narrator: Laurence Olivier)

Life and times of a south London family between the wars.

It's episodic, studio-bound and artificial (some of the accents sound as phoney as the sets look); but Celia Johnson as the mater familias remains moving, and Noel Coward's cavalcade of London life remains a fascinating period piece. Its simple patriotism and conservatism (it even defends strike-breaking) have gone out of fashion among film-makers. To encounter them in a post-war British film is almost shocking.

PRO:

'Mr David Lean does splendidly . . . and generally the film is yet another proof of the excellence of the work British studios are now doing.' *(The Times)*

'It would be hard to overpraise the skill, the feeling, and the enhance fidelity of this film . . . [which] puts [Coward] in the front rank of film makers. A minor triumph . . . is the use of Technicolor.' *(William Whitebait, New Statesman & Nation)*

'It is the small detailed life of No 17 that steals the picture . . . To those who believe fervently in the British cinema the three young men who made the picture are a confirmation and a hope.' *(Richard Winnington)*

'The special talent of [this film] is so quiet that it hardly becomes manifest. It appears to record drab, physical facts from the outside, while actually indicating a mute spiritual experience from within . . . Miss Johnson . . . will touch many people in a large, loose way, and move not a few personally and poignantly. This is beautiful acting; the sort of acting that the French have been taught to understand; confessional acting from the inside outwards.' *(C.A. Lejeune, Observer)*

'Miss Johnson's inarticulate portrait of Mum is extraordinary.' *(Manchester Guardian)*

MIXED:

'A brilliant and bewildering piece of work . . . [which] would have been a great film if its total effect had been as brilliantly convincing as most of its separate parts.' *(Edgar Anstey, Spectator)*

'Nearly two hours of the pleasure of recognition, which does not come very far up the scale of aesthetic values.' *(Richard Mallett, Punch)*

ANTI:

'The suburban family in their suburban house are presented with warmth and sympathy; but is the sympathy too resolute? Should not the observation be a trifle less benevolent, the defence of the ordinary man a trifle less condescending? Whatever the knowledge of human behaviour which has gone to the writing of play and film, I find in *This Happy Breed* a tendency, not there in *In Which We Serve*, to stand well away and, however admiringly, point; Coward is here not so much the artist as the patron.' *(Dilys Powell)*

'Phoney from the second shot in the film to the penultimate shot, the first and last being panning shots across rooftops to and from a house in Clapham where most of the action is supposed to take place – I say "supposed" because the intervening scenes are all filmed in the studio. Nothing wrong with that, if the film doesn't look as stagey as the Noel Coward play from which it was adapted. Unfortunately it does, including the garden, glimpsed through the dining-room window, where Frank Gibbons, the head of the family, seems to spend most of his time – apparently with little success because we don't see a single flower in the house for two decades – not even a plastic poppy. Robert Newton plays Frank and, although he doesn't roll his eyes as much as he did as Long John Silver in *Treasure Island*, he is clearly lost without his wooden leg and his parrot. Instead, Celia Johnson, as his long-suffering wife, does the shrieking. Judging by the hard looks Newton gives her, he would prefer acting with the parrot.' *(Ken Russell, 1993)*

THIS IS SPINAL TAP: A DOCUMENTARY BY MARTIN DIBERGI

CT: 10 AV: 7.69

1984 US 82 C MUSICAL/COMEDY

D Rob Reiner ☆
W Christopher Guest Michael McKean Harry Shearer Rob Reiner ✔

Michael McKean ✔ Christopher Guest ✔ Harry Shearer R.J. Parnell Rob Reiner ✔ Bruno Kirby

A movie-brat director (Rob Reiner) shoots a documentary about a British heavy metal band which is falling apart while touring the States.

Wonderful American satire. It seems to have been inspired by Martin Scorsese's portentous 'rockumentary' about The Band's final concert, *The Last Waltz* (1978), but the film goes on to hit out at many other targets. The portrait of a self-destructive British rock band is funny and horribly accurate (even the British accents are spot-on). It features a terrific central performance from Christopher Guest as the angst-ridden 'thinker' of the group. The Stonehenge number is a classic. The script, director and Guest should have been in the running for Oscars, but they weren't even nominated.

MIXED:

'As much a comment on movie style as on rock 'n' roll . . . Indeed there's nothing funnier (and much that's less amusing) than Reiner himself introducing the film as a bearded movie-brat director . . . The picture isn't as clever, nasty or well-sustained as Eric Idle's . . . *Rutles*. But it is intermittently very funny indeed.' *(Philip French, Observer)*

'Cunning satire through and through, though not always terribly funny.' *(Maltin)*

PRO:

'Does embody rock and roll at its most horrible and yet . . . it isn't mean-spirited at all. It's much too affectionate for that . . . there's an in-joke quality to the film . . . However, you need not have heard of a band like Spinal Tap to find its story highly amusing . . . The most appealing thing about [it] . . . is the . . . lack of condescension.' *(Janet Maslin, New York Times)*

'One of the funniest films of the year . . . A very delicate balance between silly overkill and in-jokes for the hip set has been achieved; a must for anyone possessing the ability to laugh.' *(Mike Coren, Girl about Town)*

'[The film] isn't an exaggeration. Would a documentary on Motorhead or Status Quo be less funny?' *(Steve Turner, New Society)*

'Wickedly well-observed . . . Highly recommended.' *(Neil Sinyard, Sunday Telegraph)*

'A deliciously cynical, abrasively witty examination of certain aspects of the heavy rock scene . . . Catch it if you can.' *(Clive Hirschhorn, Sunday Express)*

'It simply, slyly, destroys one level of rock pomposity after another.' *(Roger Ebert)*

THIS SPORTING LIFE CT: 5 AV: 7.18

1963 GB 129/134 BW DRAMA

D Lindsay Anderson ☆
W David Storey from his novel

Richard Harris ☆ AAN Rachel Roberts ☆ AAN
Alan Badel William Hartnell Colin Blakely
Vanda Godsell Arthur Lowe Anne Cunningham
Jack Watson

Miner (Richard Harris) finds success as a rugby player, but his macho tendencies prevent him finding peace of mind.

Lindsay Anderson's first feature film has an aura of documentary realism and is well-acted; and these strengths led to some extravagantly favourable reviews. It doesn't look as impressive today. The two leading characters are irritatingly self-destructive, and their world is so dourly depressing that it's hard to watch, let alone become involved. There's something anti-climactic about the film's message, which is muddled but seems to amount to that good old liberal standby 'Only connect'.

PRO:

'It's hardly pretty but you won't remain detached.' *(Hollis Alpert, Saturday Review)*

'Lucid, realistic stuff, as tough and genuine as the tough rugby star on whom it is centred . . . Harris projects artistic fumbling nuances and in rough gentle and explosive terms the terrible desperation he cannot overcome.' *(A.H. Weiler, New York Times)*

'The fact that [it] happens to be the best feature ever made in this country is perhaps less important than the extraordinary horizons which it suddenly opens up . . . In one sense the film suggests a more muscular Antonioni; in another . . . it recalls Kurosawa . . . But I can think of no comparison which could begin to suggest its overwhelming impact.' *(Derek Hill, Town)*

'A masterpiece, a wonder, a marvel – almost certainly the best British movie since the war.' *(John Leversley, Scene)*

'At the heart of the story is a love affair: the man loves her. But the love-affair fails because neither of the two has the strength to sustain love, or rather to give in to it. The woman – a chilled, stubborn, inward-looking figure superbly played by Rachel Roberts – is afraid: life asks too much. The man, in Richard Harris's splendid fierce glowering portrait, regards life as an act of defiance. You see him, when emotional generosity is demanded of him, folding his arms in a skinflint gesture; he can never, until it is too late, admit dependence on anybody. He is destroyed by his own fault. And his fault is of a size, he himself as a man is of a size to make you recognise, in the images of his final grief and solitude and despair, a tragic hero.' *(Dilys Powell)*

'Mr Harris, a black-haired giant who is a remarkable, young physical blend of Marlon Brando and Trevor Howard, bristles with the ego and impatience of the man aware of his physical superiority. He warms with *naiveté* and childish charm at his success, bellows in befuddlement at the quicker brains and more venal men about him and can but scream with anguish at his final loss.' *(Judith Crist)*

MIXED:

'It suggests all sorts of passion and protest, like a group of demonstrators singing "We Shall Overcome" and leaving it to you to fill in your own set of injustices . . . The film is heavy with multiple meanings that the director doesn't sort out, and even the best sequences are often baffling. The rugby games were said to be a "microcosm of a corrupt society", and you can certainly tell that the movie is meant to be bold and tragic. (It has something of the disturbing brute force of Scorsese's *Raging Bull*.) It's a mixture of the powerful, the inexplicable, and the dislikable.' *(Pauline Kael)*

ANTI:

'A quite unextraordinary film. For the eye of the director, although earnest and talented, is basically banal and sentimental, drawn with magnetic inevitability to visual clichés and predictable images.' *(Isabel Quigly, Spectator)*

'With his mascaraed eyes and charismatic presence, Richard Harris is every inch a cut-price Marlon Brando, whom he appears to be impersonating. But, with her tight-lipped, disapproving glare, shapeless figure and scraped-back hair, Rachel Roberts looks old enough to be his mother – and acts like it . . . The only time she seems to achieve contentment is when she is polishing her dead husband's boots.' (Ken Russell, 1993)

THOSE WERE THE HAPPY TIMES: *see* STAR!

THOU SHALT NOT KILL: *see* SHORT FILM ABOUT KILLING, A.

THOUSAND EYES OF DR MABUSE, THE: *see* THE *DOCTOR MABUSE* SERIES .

THREE BAD MEN IN A HIDDEN FORTRESS: *see* HIDDEN FORTRESS, THE.

THREE BROTHERS CT: 5 AV: 7.43

(aka *Tre Fratelli*)

1980 Italy 113 C DRAMA/FOREIGN

D Francesco Rosi
W Francesco Rosi from A. Platonov's story *The Third Son*

Philippe Noiret Charles Vanel ☆ Michele Placido Vittorio Mezzogiorno Andréa Férreol Maddalena Crippa Sara Tafuri

A judge (Philippe Noiret), teacher (Vittorio Mezzogiorno) and trade unionist (Michele Placido) return to their home village after their mother's death.

Italian state-of-the-nation film which contrasts the confusion of the brothers with the contentment of their father (Charles Vanel). Slow, sombre, and of limited interest to non-Italians. Beautifully shot, though.

'Stronger on atmosphere and feeling than on arguments. And it is at its very considerable best when the camera rather than the script holds sway, disturbing and enlightening at the same time.' *(Derek Malcolm, Guardian)*

'All the principal characters are perceptively played . . . a masterly film that has a rare resonance and beauty.' *(Margaret Hinxman, Daily Mail)*

'Fine performances, lyrical photography and strong interaction between the personal and the political makes [it] a must-see film.' *(Virginia Dignam, Morning Star)*

'Very moving.' *(News of the World)*

'Rosi blends his observations into a meditative, deeply moving portrait of different generations, searching for common bonds.' *(Geoff Brown, The Times)*

'Magical . . . moving, affirmative, unsentimental; it would be inexcusable to miss it.' *(David Castell, Sunday Telegraph)*

THREE CABALLEROS, THE CT: 5 AV: 7.08

1945 US 70 C CARTOON (WITH LIVE ACTION)/ FAMILY

D Norman Ferguson Clyde Geronimi Jack Kinney Bill Roberts Harold Young
W Homer Brightman Ernest Terrazzas Ted Sears Bill Peet and others

Voices: José Olivera Joaquin Garay Fred Shields Sterling Holloway Frank Graham Aurora Miranda Clarence Nash

In a revue format, Donald Duck salutes South America (in keeping with US's 'Good Neighbor' policy).

Pompously arty, shapeless Disney cartoon with an unconvincingly sunny view of South America. But there are moments of technical virtuosity; and modern film guides seem determined to rehabilitate the film as some kind of classic. The music, by Edward Plumb, Paul J. Smith and Charles Wolcott, was Oscar-nominated.

PRO:

'It's a quacker.' *(Quinlan)*

'Spectacular, greatly underrated.' *(Scheuer)*

'The kaleidoscopic sequences and the combination of live action with cartoon remain of absorbing interest.' *(Halliwell)*

MIXED:

'Represents a point at which meet all the paths of this great craftsman's exploration. Technical brilliance can carry him no further . . . [It] is too concerned with Hollywood notions of comedy, dress and dancing. South America, we are encouraged to believe, is very gay and very funny. Bob Hope would be a fit President for any of the republics . . . Yet no one should miss this film. It represents the final development of a medium of artistic expression more flexible than anything we have yet known.' *(Edgar Anstey, Spectator)*

'The story . . . is of the thinnest and is obviously designed as yet another tough masculine American rapprochement to the glamorously feminine beauty of the South American states . . . [The] stories are in the delightful traditional style of Disney . . . The merging of two-dimensional flat-colour animations with the three-dimensional live dancers is technically brilliant, but artistically unsatisfying.' *(Roger Manvell, MFB)*

ANTI:

'Dazzles and numbs the senses without making any tangible sense.' *(Bosley Crowther)*

'A streak of cruelty which I have for years noticed in Walt Disney's productions is now certifiable.' *(James Agee)*

'[Merely] a variety show with the accent on trick

photography and oddities of line and color.' *(Otis L. Guernsey, New York Herald Tribune)*

'Very confused and often boring . . . Donald Duck pursuing glamour girls is disgusting rather than funny.' *(Guardian)*

'[A] loud and bewildered Technicolor yell.' *(Observer)*

THREE COMRADES CT: 5 AV: 7.33

1938 US 98 BW DRAMA

D Frank Borzage
W F. Scott Fitzgerald Edward E. Paramore ☆ from Erich Maria Remarque's novel

Robert Taylor Margaret Sullavan ☆ AAN Franchot Tone ● Robert Young Guy Kibbee Lionel Atwill Henry Hull George Zucco Charley Grapewin Monty Woolley

Three male friends share a love of a young woman dying of TB (Margaret Sullavan).

A curious mixture of good and bad. Best of all is the performance of Margaret Sullavan; she's as wonderful here as she was in the light comedy, *The Shop Around the Corner*, and it's sad that she wasn't in more films worthy of her talent. F. Scott Fitzgerald's screenplay also has its moments; this and *Winter Carnival* are the only movies in which his genius shines through. The bad news is that the plot is poorly structured, the pace is plodding, and US censorship ensured that the central, anti-Nazi message of Remarque's novel was lost. It's also very gloomy.

ANTI:

'There must have been some reason for making this picture, but it certainly isn't in the cause of entertainment.' *(Variety)*

'It's conventional and heavy and false in the M-G-M manner, but with this delicate Fitzgerald feeling rising out of it at times. The movie is still awful; it has a particularly offensive tearjerking score by Franz Waxman.' *(Pauline Kael)*

MIXED:

'A love story, beautifully told and consummately acted, but so drenched in hopelessness and heavy with the aroma of death, of wasted youth in a world of foggy shapes and nameless menaces, that its beauty and strength are often clouded and betrayed.' *(Time)*

'This anti-climax [ie Patricia Hollmann's novel method of suicide] unfortunately greatly weakens the impression of dignity and power of which one is strongly aware at earlier stages of the film.' *(MFB)*

PRO:

'A beautiful and memorable film . . . magnificently directed, eloquently written and admirably played. And in Margaret Sullavan's case, the word "admirably" is sheer understatement. Hers is a shimmering, almost unendurably lovely performance. We ask angrily why she hasn't been seen more often.' *(Frank S. Nugent, New York Times)*

'Emotionally disturbing, the story is one it is impossible to watch unmoved, for it is both an entertainment and an education . . . Margaret Sullavan . . . [gives] a portrayal that is nothing short of a triumph.' *(Today's Cinema)*

'A remarkably high combination of talents has made it all very impressive and moving – good writing, a good man at the camera, good actors, and presiding over them a good director.' *(NBR)*

THREE GODFATHERS CT: 6 AV: 7.10

1948 US 106 C WESTERN

D John Ford
W Laurence Stallings Frank S. Nugent from Peter B. Kyne's story

John Wayne Pedro Armendariz Harry Carey Jr Ward Bond Mildred Natwick Charles Halton Jane Darwell Mae Marsh Guy Kibbee Dorothy Ford

Three outlaws (John Wayne, Pedro Armendariz, Harry Carey Jr) take an orphaned baby to New Jerusalem, Arizona.

It's a much-told story. There are at least six other versions including a 1919 silent by Ford, starring Harry Carey Senior, to whom this film is dedicated. Despite the obvious biblical overtones, it's based on truth. There are times when it's twee and predictable – a cross between *The Nativity Story and Three Men and A Baby*. But if you can swallow the sentimentality, there's a lot to enjoy in the acting and the look of the film.

John Ford takes obvious delight in using Technicolor for the first time; and cinematographer Winton C. Hoch shows his wonderful eye for desert landscape.

ANTI:

'Founders when only halfway through and its laudable intentions are drowned in an orgy of unconvincing sentiment.' *(MFB)*

'Hard to believe but the director is John Ford.' *(Reynolds News)*

MIXED:

'A minor work of a major director . . . I think this is a film that will be too readily despised; there is a lot of quality behind its nonsense.' *(C.A. Lejeune, Observer)*

PRO:

'Many fine, high intensity moments, told with warmth, humour and humanity. The direction is tops and the photography superb.' *(Film Daily)*

'Breath-taking . . . excellent in all departments.' *(Boxoffice)*

Ford, an unqualified artist, lives up to his earned reputation.' *(Motion Picture Herald)*

THREE MUSKETEERS, THE CT: 8 AV: 7.00

(aka *The Queen's Diamonds*)

1973 GB 107 C ACTION/ADVENTURE/COMEDY

D Richard Lester ☆
W George MacDonald Fraser from Alexander Dumas's novel

Oliver Reed Raquel Welch Richard Chamberlain Michael York Frank Finlay Christopher Lee Jean-Pierre Cassel Geraldine Chaplin Simon Ward Faye Dunaway

A country lad (Michael York) wishes to join an élite force within the French army.

Jolly swashbuckler which follows the Dumas novel reasonably closely and captures its thrills, but also finds time for humorous interludes and slapstick. Lester directs with bravura pace, and this is the best version of the much-filmed story – although the 1948 film starring Gene Kelly has its admirers, and the 1994 version is quite a merry romp as well. Lester made a sequel, *The Four Musketeers* (1974), which he shot at the same time and is very watchable, and *The Return of the Musketeers* (1989), which is a sad disappointment.

ANTI:

'It's one dragged-out forced laugh. No sweep, no romance, no convincing chivalric tradition to mock.' *(Stanley Kauffmann)*

'For all Lester's invention, soaring imagination and jokey gimmicks the efforts of [the Musketeers] are stodgy, obvious and juvenile. Their rapiers may flash but their humour remains unsheathed. The swash is decidedly buckled . . . The characters are not so much Three Musketeers as Three Musty Dears, stranded in that no man's land between burlesque and drama . . . Miss Welch . . . is about as flat as the humour.' *(Arthur Thirkell, Daily Mirror)*

PRO:

'Certainly there are one or two duels too many, but the sightgags and funny business are so swiftly paced and the action so mercurial that the eye is bombarded by a continuous succession of spectacular images. Altogether, a wholly engaging escapade memorable for its sheer abundance and vitality.' *(Virginia Dignam, Morning Star)*

'Miraculously enough one of the best things [Lester] has done . . . Marks his complete return to comic form and also hints that Lester has other, hitherto undisclosed, virtues: an accurate and irreverent sense of period, an instinct for narrative, an ability to pace his films.' *(Nigel Andrews, Financial Times)*

'Mr Lester . . . has pulled off a remarkably difficult job, combining slapstick, swashbuckling, and social satire while doing injury to none of the moods.' *(Peter Bogdanovich, New York)*

'Mr Lester doesn't merely like the cinema . . . He likes the extravagant past of the cinema. He has a feeling for the bravado of its action and the gusto with which its often very simple jokes are put over.' *(Dilys Powell, Sunday Times)*

'It is good for once to see a real family film dedicated to nothing more pretentious than making us forget all the miseries of the world for an hour or two.' *(Cecil Wilson, Daily Mail)*

3:10 TO YUMA CT: 6 AV: 7.22

1957 US 92 BW WESTERN/THRILLER

D Delmer Daves
W Halsted Welles from Elmore Leonard's story

Van Heflin ☆ Glenn Ford Felicia Farr Henry Jones Richard Jaeckel Leora Dana ☆ Robert Emhardt Sheridan Comerate George Mitchell

A poor farmer (Van Heflin) has to escort a gunman (Glenn Ford) to the state penitentiary.

An engrossing western which relies on suspense rather than action, strong performances more than violence. Leora Dana is outstanding as the farmer's wife, while Ford and Van Heflin are fine as men secretly envious of the other's life. The excellent cinematography is by Charles Lawton Jr – and though the script is unnecessarily talky, it's based on an Elmore Leonard story, so at least the dialogue is good.

MIXED:

'That the climax fizzles must be laid on doorstep of Halsted Welles, who adapts Elmore Leonard's story quite well until that point.' *(Variety)*

PRO:

'Of its kind this is a class film.' *(Observer)*

'The best western since *High Noon*.' *(Evening Standard)*

'This is the finest acting partnership I have seen in a western for years.' *(Daily Sketch)*

'A vivid, tense and intelligent story about probable people, enhanced by clever, economical writing and supremely efficient direction and playing.' *(Manchester Guardian)*

'It starts where most westerns leave off. Characters actually develop logically and inevitably, tension is credible in terms of the people experiencing it, and there is a breath-taking picture of what a border town looks like.' *(Times Educational Supplement)*

'A good western film, loaded with a suspenseful situation and dusty atmosphere. The opening scene of a stagecoach hold-up is crisply and ruggedly staged and all the incidents of lawmen versus bandits are developed nicely from there.' *(Bosley Crowther)*

THRONE OF BLOOD

CT: 7 AV: 8.33

(aka *Kumonosu Jo*)

1957 Japan 105/109 BW DRAMA/FOREIGN

D Akira Kurosawa ☆
W Hideo Oguni Shinobu Hashimoto Ryuzo Kikushima Akira Kurosawa from Shakespeare's play *Macbeth*

Toshiro Mifune ☆ Isuzu Yamada ☆ Takashi Shimura Minoru Chiaki Akira Kubo Takamaru Sasaki Yoichi Tachikawa Chieko Naniwa

A Samurai warrior (Toshiro Mifune) and his wife (Isuzu Yamada) scheme their way to power, but receive their come-uppance.

A massive film which eye-catchingly re-enacts *Macbeth* in a Samurai setting. Complaints that Kurosawa seems detached from his subject-matter contain an element of truth. Nevertheless, the two central performances leap triumphantly across the language barrier; and the direction (especially of the action sequences and finale) is by a man at the height of his powers and confidence, mingling Noh, Kabuki and western styles to make a unique cinematic experience.

ANTI:

'We label it amusing because lightly is the only way to take this substantially serio-comic rendering of the story of an ambitious Scot into a form that combines characteristics of the Japanese No [sic] theatre and the American western film. Probably Mr Kurosawa . . . did not intend it to be amusing . . . but its odd amalgamation of cultural contrasts hits the occidental funnybone.' *(Bosley Crowther)*

'Its final impression is of a man who storms into a room with an impassioned speech to deliver and then discovers he has forgotten what he came to say.' *(Kenneth Cavander, MFB)*

MIXED:

'Its greatness is in Kurosawa's glorious bad taste; he flings mad, absurd images on the screen. He has the courage to go over the top. Just one effect seems a mistake: when he uses a mechanical device (slowing down the sound) to simulate a witch's voice. (It's too obvious a trick.)' *(Pauline Kael)*

PRO:

'[Kurosawa's] direction is masterly both in the way he has handled his big mass scenes and his individuals who, though remaining human, are still terrifying and strange.' *(Daily Cinema)*

'Kurosawa has . . . developed the [*Macbeth*] story in an atmosphere of immense tension and violence.' *(S & S)*

'Beauty and terror are combined in such a way that audiences can never forget the tragedy that unfolds before their eyes. In *Throne of Blood*, Kurosawa departs from his usual (very western) fluid camera style and fast-paced editing and instead gets his inspiration from the classic Noh theater tradition.' *(Baseline)*

THUNDER ROCK

CT: 7 AV: 7.50

1942 GB 112 BW DRAMA/WAR/FANTASY

D Roy Boulting ☆
W Jeffrey Dell Bernard Miles from Robert Ardrey's play

Michael Redgrave ☆ James Mason ☆ Lilli Palmer ☆ Barbara Mullen ☆ Frederick Valk ☆ Frederick Cooper ☆ Finlay Currie ☆ Sybilla Binder ☆ A.E. Matthews

Disillusioned war correspondent (Michael Redgrave) retires and becomes keeper of a haunted lighthouse, where ghosts reawaken his faith in the common man and lead him to rediscover political commitment.

Anti-isolationist tract for its time, dedicated to proving – somewhat literally – that no man is an island. Its preachiness and theatricality are offset by an array of fine performances, especially from Michael Redgrave and James Mason. An untypically serious and visually imaginative film for the Boulting Brothers.

ANTI:

'I like my ghosts to pine, not whine.' *(Elspeth Grant, Daily Graphic)*

MIXED:

'I was glad of some outspoken virulence against some of the people – those, next to the Nazis, most often blamed – who did most to get the world into this war, until I reflected that even when it was written, around 1940, it came late enough to be safe. To find oneself, and others, approving this sort of intrepid *esprit d'escalier* is not only shaming but frightening.' *(James Agee, Nation)*

'Tastefully photographed and well-acted . . . [but] a compromise between stage and screen, with screen honourably losing.' *(William Whitebait, New Statesman)*

'This ambitious movie is spectacularly handsome (especially the scenes outside the lighthouse); yet the situation is very theatrical – those dead people seem an awfully elaborate contrivance just to reinvigorate the hero.' *(Pauline Kael)*

PRO:

'What a stimulus to thought it is, this good, brave, outspoken unfettered picture.' *(Observer)*

'An unusual theme, well directed and produced with experiments in technique which in the main succeed. The photography and lighting and the acting . . . are most sensitive and effective.' *(MFB)*

'A really intelligent film and more moving in parts

than anything this country's studios have produced before.' *(Manchester Guardian)*

'Boldly imaginative in theme and treatment.' *(Sunday Express)*

'If I thought it wouldn't keep too many people away, I'd call it a work of art.' *(Daily Express)*

'More interesting technically than anything since *Citizen Kane*.' *(Manchester Guardian)*

'Beautifully performed, closer in tone to Powell and Pressburger than to the British mainstream, it's weird and unusually gripping.' *(Geoff Andrew, Time Out)*

THUNDERBALL: *see BOND* SERIES.

TIDAL WAVE: *see* PORTRAIT OF JENNIE.

TIGER BAY CT: 7 AV: 7.18

1959 GB 105 BW THRILLER

D J. Lee Thompson ☆
W John Hawkesworth Shelley Smith ✔ from Noel Calef's novel *Rudolphe et le Revolver*

John Mills ☆ Horst Buchholz ☆ Hayley Mills ☆ Yvonne Mitchell Megs Jenkins Anthony Dawson George Selway Shari George Pastell Marne Maitland

Lonely Cardiff child (Hayley Mills) witnesses a murder and is abducted by the killer (Horst Buchholz).

Suspenseful chase-drama with outstanding performances, especially from 12-year-old Hayley Mills in her first screen role. It made her a star.

'Hayley is not just another child in a picture. She is an actress with terrific talent . . . It's a good story, which works up to an exciting climax.' *(Pearson Phillips, Daily Mail)*

'John Mills is unpunchingly good . . . Buchholz excellent.' *(Isabel Quigly, Spectator)*

'Hayley Mills . . . steals the film from right under the nose of her talented father . . . [This] is a brisk, well-directed film with some slick performances.' *(Dick Richards, Daily Mirror)*

'The film . . . is Hayley's, and whether she is being funny, sly or touching – the child has it almost all her own way.' *(Charles MacLaren, Time & Tide)*

'Basically it is another murderer-on-the-run story. But the wise and lively eye of director J. Lee Thompson makes it a thriller out of the ordinary.' *(Ivon Adams, Star)*

'Hayley Mills . . . responds without self consciousness to direction . . . succeeds not by mere cuteness but by a feeling for timing which enables her to stand up to established players (among them John Mills himself, agreeably wry as the police superintendent). There is a passage in which she describes her accidental view of the murder: deliberately theatrical and self-caricaturing, the re-enactment flowers into ironic comedy. One hopes that her talent, so clear within the limits here imposed, will prove to have range.' *(Dilys Powell)*

TIGHT LITTLE ISLAND: *see* WHISKY GALORE.

TIME AFTER TIME CT: 6 AV: 6.55

1979 US 112 C SF/THRILLER/ROMANCE

D Nicholas Meyer ☆
W Nicholas Meyer ☆ from Karl Alexander and Steven Hayes's story

Malcolm McDowell ☆ David Warner ☆ Mary Steenburgen ☆ Charles Cioffi Kent Williams Laurie Main

H.G. Wells (Malcolm McDowell) chases Jack the Ripper (David Warner) through time and finds love with a 70s women's-libber (Mary Steenburgen).

It's a shade overlong and parts of it are unnecessarily gruesome, but on the whole this is an entertaining, wittily scripted, beautifully acted thriller – along with *Back to the Future* and *Terminator 2*, the most entertaining time travel picture ever made. Miklos Rozsa contributes a fine score, and for once the romantic interest doesn't seem to slow down the plot. It helps, of course, that Mary Steenburgen is enchanting. Meyer also had a hand in the three best films in the *Star Trek* series.

'A bookish joke which comes unstuck: after nearly two hours the tension has evaporated, and all that's left is a curdle of jokes and brutality.' *(Time Out)*

'A clever story, irresistible due to the competence of its cast.' *(Variety)*

'A robust, splendidly detailed entertainment that with its superb craftsmanship accomplishes the rare, if often attempted, feat of mixing romance, comedy and horror.' *(Cinefantastique)*

'Film has enormous wit, terrific suspense, and, best of all, three outstanding lead performances. Warner is memorable as a vicious, intelligent villain; and McDowell and Steenburgen completely charm us as they fall in love (off camera as well as on) – are there other violent pictures that have such a charming couple?' *(Danny Peary)*

TIN DRUM, THE AAW CT: 4 AV: 7.27

(aka *Die Blechtrommel*)

1979 France/West Germany 142 C DRAMA/FOREIGN

D Volker Schlöndorff ☆
W Franz Seltz Volker Schlöndorff Jean-Claude Carrière Günter Grass from Grass's novel

David Bennent ☆ Mario Adorf Angela Winkler ☆ Daniel Olbrychski ☆ Katharina Thalbach Charles Aznavour ☆ Heinz Bennent Andréa Férreol Fritz Haki Mariella Oliveri

German boy (David Bennent), incensed at the behaviour of grown-ups, decides to stop growing at the age of three, and – as the Nazis rise to power – he beats out his frustrations on a drum.

Extraordinary fantasy based on the first two-thirds of Günter Grass's epic novel. 12-year-old Bennent is impressive; there are some memorably grotesque sequences (especially the hero's birth, shot from his point of view); and it makes its point about German – or is it bourgeois? – complacency. But there's a heavy-handedness and repetitiousness which, together with the long running-time, make it heavy going.

PRO:

'What makes it worth seeing? Spectacle, nothing but spectacle . . . Schlöndorff excels at it . . . But the supreme reason to submit to the film's two and a half hours is the actors . . . Angela Winkler alone creates a new German miracle . . . And it's been a long time since we've seen someone like Olbrychski display such strength and intelligence.' *(Michel Mardore, Le Nouvel Observateur)*

'Light-footed and quick witted . . . Schlöndorff has assembled a superb cast of players . . . [A] shrewd and masterly film.' *(Margaret Hinxman, Daily Mail)*

'It is an atmospheric work of art that will be an object of discussion long after you have seen it.' *(William Hall, Evening News)*

'Intelligent and beautifully photographed, it reassures us that some movie makers still have sensitivity and imagination.' *(Judith Simons, Daily Express)*

'I doubt very much if the Cannes Film Festival has been able to offer anything more disturbing, more grotesque yet more compelling, anything more capable of welding you to your seat when all you want to do is rush outside and make sure the real world is still there.' *(Peter Clayton, Sunday Telegraph)*

MIXED:

'The imagery is powerful, bold, somewhat grandiose, occasionally inflatedly obvious, conjuring up an atmosphere of heightened naturalism shot through with flashes of the occult and the uncanny, confidently painted on the screen by [the] cinematography.' *(Alan Brien, Sunday Times)*

'Somewhat lumbering in its humour.' *(Shipman)*

TIREZ SUR LE PIANISTE: *see* SHOOT THE PIANO PLAYER.

TITFIELD THUNDERBOLT, THE

CT: 5 AV: 6.78

1953 GB 84 C COMEDY

D Charles Crichton
W T.E.B. Clarke

Stanley Holloway ☆ George Relph ☆ John Gregson Godfrey Tearle Edie Martin ☆ Naunton Wayne Gabrielle Brune Hugh Griffith Sidney James Jack McGowran Ewan Roberts

Villagers try to save their local railway branch-line by setting up an amateur service.

Full of nostalgia for an England that is lost – where all good chaps pull together for the sake of the village. Douglas Slocombe's shots of the Somerset countryside, trains and traction engines are worth seeing, and it's top entertainment for those who love cosy humour and find comic clergymen hilarious. It's not so good for those who like profound characterization or social realism, and might be torture for anyone who finds English middle-class complacency exasperating.

PRO:

'The most rib-tickling train journey I've ever been on.' *(Ray Nunn, Daily Sketch)*

'A wonderfully warm, wry, gay, disarming, gentle picture about real people.' *(New York Post)*

'Right in the same groove as *Passport to Pimlico* and other such cinematic collector's items.' *(New York Journal American)*

'A romantic comedy, escapist and nostalgic . . . full of fine moments . . . a charming film.' *(The Times)*

'Undervalued on its release in the wake of other Ealing comedies, this now seems among the best of them as well as an immaculate colour production showing the England that is no more; the script has pace, the whole thing is brightly polished and the action works up to a fine climactic frenzy.' *(Halliwell)*

MIXED:

'Ealing Studios do not hit their usually high comedy marks but it will do, and the Somerset scenery is lovely.' *(Jympson Harman, Evening News)*

ANTI:

'I was a little disappointed. The machines were delightful but the human beings failed to live up to them.' *(Fred Majdalany, Daily Mail)*

'A feeble attempt at the brand of whimsy that has characterized previous [Ealing] films.' *(New York Times)*

'The film that marked the beginning of Ealing's decline into whimsy and toothless eccentricity.' *(Tony Rayns, Time Out)*

TO BE OR NOT TO BE CT: 9 AV: 9.20

1942 US 94/99 BW COMEDY/ROMANCE/WAR

D Ernst Lubitsch ☆
W Edwin Justus Mayer ☆ from Ernst Lubitsch and Melchior Lengyel's story

Jack Benny ☆ Carole Lombard ☆ Robert Stack
Stanley Ridges ☆ Felix Bressart ☆ Lionel Atwill
Sig Rumann ☆ Tom Dugan ☆ Charles Halton

An egotistical actor-producer (Jack Benny) and his actress wife (Carole Lombard) cope with the Nazi occupation of Warsaw.

Lombard's untimely death in a plane crash shortly after filming put a dampener on the film on release; and the fact that many people regarded the Nazis as no laughing matter guaranteed mixed reviews. Posterity has raised its reputation – quite rightly, for it's very funny, with two outstanding performances from Benny and Lombard. Werner Heymann's score was Oscar-nominated. Rudolph Maté's cinematography, Vincent Korda's art direction and Edwin Justus Mayer's witty script should have been. Mel Brooks and Anne Bancroft did a moderately amusing but much coarser remake in 1983.

'Why do audiences laugh during *To Be or Not to Be*, and at times very heartily? Aren't they aware of what happened to Poland? Did I try to make them look at the Polish background through those rose-colored glasses? Nothing of the kind. I went out of my way to remind them of the destruction of the Nazi conquest, of the terror regime of the Gestapo . . . Do I minimize their danger because I refrained from the most obvious methods in their characterization? Is whipping and flogging the only way of expressing terrorism? No, the American audience doesn't laugh at those Nazis because they underestimate their menace, but because they are happy to see this new order and its ideology being ridiculed.' *(Ernst Lubitsch, defending his film in a letter to the New York Times)*

ANTI:

'Anti-Nazi, skilful, and I suppose funny. But jokes connected with concentration camps in Poland and the execution of Polish patriots seem to me inexcusable.' *(Roger Manvel, New Statesman)*

'Ernst Lubitsch, who directed, starts off on the wrong foot and never gets his balance; the performers yowl their lines, and the burlesque of the Nazis, who cower before their superior officers, is more crudely gleeful than funny.' *(Pauline Kael)*

MIXED:

'The film had to be witty to obtain our consent to a number of incredible things, which if the wit had ever ceased, we should never have believed. We should not have believed, for instance, that those typical flowers of Hollywood, Jack Benny and Carole Lombard, were Poles. That the Gestapo is so loosely conducted that an actor can wander about bamboozling authority and impersonating at will a Nazi spy and a Gestapo chief familiar to every one. The art of farce does not consist in plunging your characters into monstrous predicaments from which no ingenuity can extricate them. The art of farce consists in the ingenuity with which the farce-maker is able to get his characters out of situations from which, without that ingenuity, they could not be extricated . . . And the art of the master is shown when the successful extrication from one scrape merely serves to plunge the hero into another. Judged by this standard *To Be or Not To Be* is a failure. But it is a failure redeemed by somebody's, and presumably Lubitsch's, wit.' *(James Agate, Tatler)*

'In a sense, the photoplay is a companion piece to *Ninotchka*. The director found a valid target for satire in the shirt-sleeved satellites of Comrade Stalin and their inordinate passion for the commonplace; he now looses vitriol-tipped arrows at Hitler and his Germaniacs. The results are largely amusing, and while the picture is one you surely won't want to miss, its score is somewhat less high than that achieved by its forerunner. The wind that keeps some of the missiles from reaching dead-center is an accent on plot, the slighting of psychological factors. While *Ninotchka* explored the proletarian vitals of the borschtites and disclosed the gnawing amoeba of mediocrity, this contents itself with superficially ridiculing the symptoms of Nazism and bothers not to investigate the virus of the disease.' *(Herb Sterne)*

PRO:

'Absorbing drama with farcical trimmings.' *(Variety)*

'The comedy is hilarious, even when it is hysterically thrilling.' *(Commonweal)*

'As prescribed by the slick Ernst Lubitsch direction, Carole [Lombard] has to let her ham-actor husband steal practically every scene. And some of the scenes of Jack Benny hamming for his life are among Benny's, and Lubitsch's, best.' *(John T. McManus, PM)*

'Like an unmixed cocktail it packs a wallop, and its rating as entertainment is high.' *(Life)*

'Lubitsch's comic genius and corrosive wit are displayed at every turn.' *(John Baxter)*

'The actual business at hand . . . is nothing less than providing a good time at the expense of Nazi myth . . . Lubitsch distinguishes the film's zanier moments with his customary mastery of sly humour and innuendo, and when the story calls for outright melodrama he is more than equal to the occasion.' *(Newsweek)*

'As effective an example of comic propaganda as *The Great Dictator* and far better directed.' *(Charles Higham, 1972)*

'Survives not only as satire but as a glorification of man's indomitable good spirits in the face of disaster

– survives in a way that many more serious and high-toned works about the war do not.' *(Peter Bogdanovich, 1975)*

'In any other medium it would be acknowledged as a classic to rank with *The Alchemist* or *A Modest Proposal*.' *(Peter Barnes)*

TO HAVE AND HAVE NOT CT: 6 AV: 7.42

1944 US 101 BW DRAMA/ROMANCE

D Howard Hawks
W Jules Furthman William Faulkner ☆ from Ernest Hemingway's novel

Humphrey Bogart ☆ Walter Brennan Lauren Bacall ☆ Dolores Moran Hoagy Carmichael Walter Molnar Sheldon Leonard Marcel Dalio

In Martinique, the cynical captain of a charter boat (Humphrey Bogart) is persuaded by young woman (Lauren Bacall) to help the Free French against the Nazis.

Slow, sometimes tedious and a pale imitation of *Casablanca*, this has only the most tangential relationship with Hemingway's story, which was filmed quite faithfully as *The Breaking Point* (1950). It's notable, however, for some sparky dialogue, a typically charismatic Bogart performance and a striking début from Bacall (whose singing voice was dubbed, bizarrely, by Andy Williams). She and Bogie fell in love during shooting, and it shows.

PRO:

'It introduces Bacall in her first picture. She's an arresting personality. She can slink, brother, and no fooling!' *(Variety)*

'Newcomer Lauren Bacall certainly has an individual personality and invites one's interest in her future work but it is Humphrey Bogart who dominates the portrayal and the artistes.' *(Today's Cinema)*

'An unusually happy exhibition of teamwork . . . concentrates on character and atmosphere rather than plot. The best of the picture has no plot at all, but is a leisurely series of mating duels between Humphrey Bogart at his most proficient and the very entertaining, nervy, adolescent new blonde, Lauren Bacall. Whether or not you like the film will depend I believe almost entirely on whether you like Miss Bacall. I am no judge. I can hardly look at her, much less listen to her – she has a voice like a chorus by Kid Ory – without getting caught in a dilemma between a low whistle and a bellylaugh. It has been years since I have seen such amusing pseudo-toughness on the screen.' *(James Agee, Nation)*

ANTI:

'Neither the plot nor the setting is convincing and Humphrey Bogart has an over-familiar task as the toughly sentimental Harry. Lauren Bacall shows such real talent and personality as to maintain interest in a not very interesting film.' *(MFB)*

'Remarkable at least for the ingenuity and industry by which the original story and individualities of Faulkner and Hemingway have been rendered down into Hollywood basic. Miss Bacall is an extract of several stars – Dietrich, Bankhead, Harlow, Lake and Garbo. She is much more handsome than Humphrey Bogart but not nearly as talented.' *(Richard Winnington)*

MIXED:

'Results are above average, especially for those who never saw *Casablanca*, a slightly better edition of the same story.' *(Guardian)*

'On these familiar paths, Bogart moves with his old nonchalant ease, and a pause now and then to take in Miss Bacall: still waters running so deep as to be indistinguishable from stagnation, sulky fire running so hot as to be indistinguishable from a frost. I wouldn't say the film hasn't, in the absence of anything better, its enjoyable moments, but I could use something better.' *(Dilys Powell)*

'Miss Bacall's . . . reading of the single words which are her "lines" has been so coached as to totally erase originality. Her movements at all times indicate that she has an infernal machine secreted somewhere about her person. The studied glances, meant, no doubt to be provocative, only succeed in making one fear that the lady is the victim of a myopia third only to that possessed by Laurette Taylor and Theda Bara.' *(Herb Sterne)*

TO KILL A MOCKING BIRD

AAW CT: 6 AV: 7.71

1962 US 129 BW DRAMA

D Robert Mulligan AAN
W Horton Foote ✗ AAW from Harper Lee's novel

Gregory Peck ☆ AAW Mary Badham ☆ AAN Phillip Alford ✓ John Megna Frank Overton Rosemary Murphy Ruth White Brock Peters ✓ Robert Duvall (narrator: Kim Stanley)

A white lawyer (Gregory Peck) defends a black man (Brock Peters) accused of rape.

Solid, well acted drama which works okay as an evocation of childhood in a southern town (the two kids are especially good). But it's also a Hollywood parable about racial bigotry, which wears its liberal intentions a little too earnestly on its sleeve. Would rednecks really be so easily talked out of their lynch-mob by a little girl? Might they not just have lynched the little girl as well? Russell Harlan's photography and Elmer Bernstein's score were Oscar-nominated, as were Alexander Golitzen, Henry Bumstead, and Oliver Emert for Art Direction and Set Decoration

ANTI:

'When Gregory Peck got the Academy Award for Best Actor for his performance as an upstanding widowed lawyer practising in a small Alabama town in the early 30s, there was a fair amount of derision throughout the country: Peck was better than usual, but in that same virtuously dull way.' *(Pauline Kael)*

'Has nothing very profound to say about the south and its problems. Sometimes, in fact, its side-porch sociology is simply fatuous . . . Peck . . . seems to imagine himself the Abe Lincoln of Alabama.' *(Time)*

'Mulligan's direction is merely solid and academic.' *(Times)*

PRO:

'Peck always seems to do very little acting, but he has the great screen actor's ability to evoke feeling and suggest inner thoughts by his deep sincerity . . . He lifts this leisurely film into the first class.' *(Felix Barker, Evening News)*

'The kind of film that grows on you like a skin.' *(Daily Mail)*

'What the film has – and this is what gives it its maturity and wisdom – is a poetic realism that soars way above the requirements of surface truth . . . There is a contradiction . . . between the child's-eye fantasy of . . . the "haunted house" and the very adult emotions of the courtroom . . . [which] throws the development a bit off balance. But there is so much sincerity and passion in [the] direction, and so little compromise in the script, that the total impact sweeps away all quibble or doubt.' *(Nina Hibbin, Daily Worker)*

'The story may seem slightly sentimental today in its portrayal of race relations, but its stature and lasting substance stem from the beautifully observed relationship between father and children and from the youngsters' perceptions of the enduring human values in the world around them.' *(Judith Crist)*

'I can only say that I am a happy author. They have made my story into a beautiful and moving motion picture. I am very proud and grateful.' *(Harper Lee)*

'My favorite film, without any question.' *(Gregory Peck)*

TO LIVE: *see* IKIRU.

TOKYO STORY CT: 10 AV: 9.67

(aka *Tokyo Monogotari*)

1953 Japan 135 BW DRAMA/FOREIGN

D Yasujiro Ozu ☆
W Yasujiro Ozu, Kogo Noda

Chishu Ryu ☆ Chiyeko Higashiyama ☆
So Yamamura Kuniko Miyake Haruko Sugimura
Nobuo Nakamura Kyoko Kagawa

Two simple, well-meaning Japanese grandparents (Chishu Ryu and Chiyeko Higashiyama) make one last visit to their children and grandchildren in Tokyo and Osaka, and discover that their family has drifted apart, spiritually as well as geographically, and failed to live up to expectations.

Only too often, 'classics' of art-house cinema prove to be overpraised, dated and pretentious. But that is not the case with this masterpiece by one of the greatest Japanese film-makers. In other hands, the story might have been the stuff of satirical black comedy, with barbs at the mercenary, self-centred, younger generation. Ozu takes a more sympathetic and mature approach: he accepts it as a sad but inevitable fact that children do grow away from their parents.

His style of shooting matches this fair-minded attitude. The camera remains slightly distanced and objective, but never cruel or detached: he is merely keen to show that there are at least two sides to virtually every question. And cutaway shots of the environment surrounding the characters emphasize that they do not exist in a vacuum: they are at the mercy of differing social, economic, industrial demands. The result, though leisurely by modern standards, is one of the great cinematic experiences.

MIXED:

'If one has the patience to sit through this marathon, with its quaint customs and queer language, its significance becomes apparent and the story grows on you.' *(Graham Clarke, Kine Weekly)*

'The film lacks both the richness and the melodrama of the best movie on the subject, Make Way For Tomorrow.' *(David Shipman, F & F, 1965)*

PRO:

'Alluring and compelling . . . There can be no doubt at all that Ozu is one of the greatest, most subtle and individual of all artists in the history of cinema . . . [This] if not actually his best film is one of [them] . . . Not, perhaps, everybody's film and yet it is impossible to think that anyone who cares at all for the cinema could totally fail to respond.' *(The Times)*

'No sex, no car chases, (no cars, come to that), no colour and a dwelling insistence on taking a simple story at a snail's pace . . . All the dynamism of [Ozu's] films comes from the craft with which he cuts (never a dissolve or fade) from one tiny scene to the next . . . They unfold like those flower-pellets . . . one used to drop into water.' *(John Coleman, New Statesman)*

'One of the most profoundly rewarding films ever made.' *(Richard Roud, Guardian)*

'There is treasure for everyone in *Tokyo Story* . . . a film that encompasses so much of the viewer's life, that you are convinced that you have been in the presence of someone who knew you very well.' *(Stanley Kauffmann)*

'No artist shows more respect for simple decency or looks on ordinary life with more tenderness.' *(John Powers)*

'Ozu takes a detached and unsensationalist view of a tragic situation. He allows his camera to linger on scenes well after their dramatic point has been achieved, creating an extraordinary, documentary sense of reality. A cinema classic.' *(Paul Sussman, The Big Issue, 1993)*

TOM JONES AAW CT: 8 AV: 8.67

1963 GB 129 C COMEDY/ROMANCE

D Tony Richardson ☆ AAW
W John Osborne ☆ AAW from Henry Fielding's novel

Albert Finney ☆ AAN Susannah York
Hugh Griffith ☆ AAN Edith Evans ☆ AAN
Joan Greenwood Diane Cilento ☆ AAN
George Devine David Tomlinson Joyce
Redman ☆ AAN George A. Cooper

Life and loves of a bawdy lad (Tom Jones).

Sixties permissiveness in 18th-century costume. Great fun, with Albert Finney hugely likeable as the hero. Literary critics may have disapproved (and did); but John Osborne's script succeeded in capturing the rumbustious spirit of Fielding's novel. Richardson's style may be eclectic and messy; but its uninhibited vitality seems very appropriate. Memorable sequences include Finney's sexy eating scene with Joyce Redmond, and a brutal stag-hunting sequence. John Addison's lively score won an Oscar; Ralph Brinton's art direction was nominated.

'I have shot it all as if it were happening today. I am a director of improvisation.' *(Tony Richardson, Life, 1963)*

ANTI:

'Uncertainty, nervousness, muddled method . . . Desperation is writ large over it.' *(Stanley Kauffmann)*

'Much of the time it looks like a home movie, made with sporadic talent by a group with more enthusiasm than discipline.' *(Tom Milne)*

'It is hard to think of a role for which Mr [Hugh] Griffith would not be Too Much, with his piercing glare, his insanely dominant nose, his beetling brows, and cavernous mouth, his overripe diction. Perhaps God.' *(Dwight MacDonald)*

'Please note the title . . . is not . . . Carry On, Tom Jones . . . My main reproach [is that Osborne and Richardson] have milked Fielding's classic in order to make a non-stop, bawdy, rowdy, bosom-waving, backside slipping, upstairs-downstairs, in-my-lady's-chamber – that especially – sex romp . . . It is such a pity that with quite a lot in it to be enjoyed, the film should be sunk by . . . Tony Richardson.' *(Alexander Walker, Evening Standard)*

'It is as though the camera had become a method actor: there are times when you wish you could buy, as on certain juke boxes, five minutes' silence . . . Obviously a film which elicits such lyric ejaculations from the reviewers cannot be all good.' *(John Simon)*

'There is something impersonal about the film's inconsistent weaving of cinematic styles – part romance, part Feydeau bedroom face, part Sennett romp, part gratuitous naturalism with its shots of horsemen's spurs drawing real blood from their abused mounts.' *(Gerald Mast, A Short History of the Movies, 1971)*

PRO:

'Tom Jones is a continually delightful, mercurially rhapsodic, and altogether breath-taking film. There is, in fact, no detail, however small, which does not merit unstinting admiration. *Tom Jones*, an absolute triumph, is the best comedy ever made.' *(Newsweek)*

'Exactly fulfils the author's intention.' *(Nina Hibbin, Daily Worker)*

'Here, at last, is a paean of praise to the stuff of life . . . Stylistically the picture is a mess; but a glorious mess that comes off . . . Why I think *Tom Jones* is so superbly good is because Richardson and his Woodfall colleagues did not make the mistake of assuming that comedies can be cheaply made . . . It is a constant delight to the eye. Romantic? Yes. Richardson is a phony realist; he gets to the truth through rose-tinted spectacles. Which is better than most directors today who can but turn a blind eye to the things that make life tick.' *(Peter Barker, F & F)*

'An uproarious success . . . [What the filmmakers] have done is to treat their original with handsome enjoyment; you feel they truly like the novel. Their *Tom Jones* is far less caustic than Fielding's, a more farcical and less satirical picture of eighteenth-century manners. But Fielding's amused eye is there. And for once the eighteenth-century is there; the players aren't embarrassed by their costumes and don't assume a false elegance . . . The heart of the piece, of course, is Albert Finney's Tom Jones. I cannot believe the hero could be better played: the sense of a solid goodness shining through all the pranks and entanglements.' *(Dilys Powell)*

'Captures Fielding's classic in all the glowing coarseness, robust wit, unadorned venality, forthright hypocrisy, social cruelty, and elegant crudity of an age when acreage made the squire and foppishness the gentleman.' *(Judith Crist)*

TOOTSIE AAN CT: 9 AV: 8.38

1982 US 116 C COMEDY/ROMANCE

D Sydney Pollack ☆ AAN
W Larry Gelbart Murray Schisgal ☆ AAN from Don McGuire's story

Dustin Hoffman ☆ AAN Jessica Lange ☆ AAW Teri
Garr ☆ AAN Dabney Coleman Charles Durning
Bill Murray ✓ Sydney Pollack ✓ George Gaynes
Geena Davis

A desperate actor (Dustin Hoffman) dresses up as a woman to land a part in a TV soap opera, becomes a star, and falls in love with his leading lady (Jessica Lange).

Funny New York comedy which, for once, is urbane as well as urban. Sexism, soap opera and showbiz all come under scrutiny, and the screenplay is full of cracking dialogue. All the acting is superb, none more so than in two small supporting roles by Bill Murray (as Hoffman's room-mate) and Pollack (as Hoffman's agent).

ANTI:

'The film never comes within a thousand miles of confronting its own implications: Hoffman's female impersonation is strictly on the level of Dame Edna Everage, and the script's assumption that "she" would wow female audiences is at best ridiculous, at worst crassly insulting to women.' *(David Pirie, Time Out)*

MIXED:

'Mr Hoffman becomes a woman before our very eyes. Left to its own devices, his face resembles that of a tired mongrel dog. That is why his appeal is universal. When he changes his sex, his features are totally transformed. He tidies up his face and instead of looking out of it as a man does he presents it to the world like a shield, as women do. I thought his walk was slightly ill-judged; the paces are too short for the no-nonsense woman he has decided to impersonate. He should have adopted the Rosalind Russell stride. Everything else is perfect.' *(Quentin Crisp, Christopher Street)*

PRO:

'Brilliant.' *(Victor Davis, Daily Express)*

'Pollack has kept his movie's many ingredients straight and has heated them all up to the right temperature. He's pulled all the stops out of a remarkably lucid and witty script . . . It's an extremely nimble job of directing; [he] mixes sweet and sour flavorings with the deftness of a Chinese chef.' *(Michael Sragow, Rolling Stone)*

'A lulu. Remarkably funny and entirely convincing.' *(Variety)*

'Funny, light, moving and subtle. Pollack prefers melancholy to farce, comedy of manners to sit-com.' *(Le Nouvel Observateur)*

'Although [it] looks like an argument for Women's Lib, while sounding infinitely funnier than any Women's Libbers I know, it seems to be guilty of false if profitable pretences . . . Having thus come out of the critic's closet . . . let me now . . . state that I found almost every minute of *Tootsie* to be rare and intelligent comedy.' *(Alexander Walker, Evening Standard)*

'It is not just the best comedy of the year; it is popular art on the way to becoming cultural artefact.' *(Time)*

TOP GUN

CT: 5 AV: 4.86

1986 US 110 C ACTION/ADVENTURE/WAR/ ROMANCE

D Tony Scott
W Jim Cash Jack Epps Jr

Tom Cruise Kelly McGillis Val Kilmer Anthony Edwards Tom Skerritt Michael Ironside John Stockwell Barry Tubb Rick Rossovich Tim Robbins Clarence Gilyard Jr Whip Hubley James Tolkan Meg Ryan Adrian Pasdar

Fighter pilot (Tom Cruise) proves he's the best, gets the girl (Kelly McGillis).

Popular with the masses, hated by the critics, this glossy action-romancer made Tom Cruise the biggest star in Hollywood. It's an unashamed celebration of American technological know-how and the success ethic – just the thing to pep folks up and help them forget the Vietnam débâcle. The plot is a re-hash of old movies; what's new is the packaging. The flashy, Oscar-nominated editing by Billy Weber and Chris Lebenzon and the catchy Academy Award-winning theme song 'Take My Breath Away' (by Giorgio Moroder and Tom Whitlock) played a big part in the movie's success. Critics took the movie more seriously than audiences, pointing out that it did for killing people what *Flashdance* had done for dancing.

PRO:

'Audiences prepared to go with it will be taken for a thrilling ride in the wild blue yonder.' *(Variety)*

MIXED:

'The story is risible, the direction routine, the underlying ethic highly questionable; but the flying stirs the blood like speed.' *(Chris Peachment, Time Out)*

ANTI:

'Too bad the entire movie wasn't airborne; whenever the story touches down, it falls apart in the hand like thousand-year-old parchment. . . .Cruise doesn't hold the screen like a movie star, although to a portion of the teen audience he certainly passes for a star. He strikes designer-jeans poses, and his blank, fixated stare and teeth-baring smile make him seem as flat and despiritualized as a Sunset Strip billboard portrait . . . The movie never digs into the paradox of warriors whose lives are geared for a war that may never come. That's why the filmmakers cook up a MIG fracas at the end; they can't bear to see all that training go to waste. And so we watch enemy planes being incinerated in the air, video game-style, as the audience applauds each kill.' *(Peter Rainer, LA Herald-Examiner, 1986)*

'A great part of the problem, naturally, is that the script . . . is mediocre and the direction . . . superficial. But the weakest link in the chain is without question the vaingloriously vapid Tom

Cruise. His performance as Maverick is downright ludicrous. He stalks through the movie with a board up his back and a macho snarl frozen on his face. The point of the snarl, apparently, is to make him look more like a man than a boy, but it backfires: He looks more than ever like an adolescent playing a grownup in a junior high school show – an adolescent, I might add, who has absolutely no star quality, no charisma, no presence whatsoever, but whose every move demonstrates that he himself believes quite the opposite to be the case . . . The implicit message throughout appears to be that cruising chicks is more or less like going on a search-and-destroy mission and that war is sexy – that gunning for MIGs, to put it baldly, is a thrilling and manly way of sublimating homoerotic drives . . . This film lionizes ignorance, venerates immaturity, reveres raw, primitive instinct; it strives aggressively – and, alas, manages completely – not to contradict a single inane illusion of the type cherished by the most horrible sort of teenage boy. Certainly the good old USA deserves better.' *(Bruce Bawer, American Spectator)*

'To help him remember his characterisation, maverick pilot Cruise is called Maverick. Although it's fantastic while in the air, albeit a little confusing at times, it's rather more leaden on the ground. McGillis is perhaps not the most convincing flying instructor in the history of the movies.' *(Rose)*

TOP HAT AAN — CT: 10 AV: 9.63

1935 US 93/101 BW MUSICAL/ROMANCE/ COMEDY

D Mark Sandrich
W Dwight Taylor Allan Scott

Fred Astaire ☆ Ginger Rogers ☆
Edward Everett Horton ✔ Helen Broderick
Erik Rhodes ✔ Eric Blore ✔ Lucille Ball
Leonard Mudie Edgar Norton Gino Corrado

An American dancer (Fred Astaire) falls for a young woman (Ginger Rogers), but their romance does not run smoothly.

Astaire and Rogers had already made three films together, but this is the first to be designed around them. She supplies a Broadway-style drive which perfectly balances his more English diffidence. Despite a corny, far-fetched plot, there's a good deal of humour which can still raise a smile; the sets are classics of art deco design; and Irving Berlin's songs combine lyrical simplicity, melodic beauty and structural ingenuity ('Cheek To Cheek' has one of the longest verses in the history of popular music). Above all, Astaire's dancing, acting and singing reveal a grace, originality and charm which – decades later – still make him look a performer of unique, miraculous talent. Oscar-nominated for Best Art Direction (Carroll Clark, Van Nest Polglase), Best Choreography (Hermes Pan), and Best Song for 'Cheek to Cheek'.

MIXED:

'A cheerful song-and-dance affair whirled along at a very proper pace . . . [but with] a thin plot.' *(Daily Telegraph)*

'May not be Mr Astaire's most distinguished vehicle . . . but I doubt whether that will worry anyone seriously.' *(Observer)*

'Has a few surprises in store before it settles down to the customary routine.' *(The Times)*

'Fred Astaire's talking feet are as rapid and fluent as ever and Ginger Rogers follows him well. If only she had more personality in herself she would walk away with the film, but good as she is, she strikes one as being admirably trained rather than a natural actress.' *(MFB)*

PRO:

'The nimble tread of the feet of Fred Astaire has never been nimbler . . . . A good picture and grand entertainment.' *(Sunday Express)*

'This one can't miss and the reasons are three – Fred Astaire, Irving Berlin's 11 songs and sufficient comedy between numbers to hold the film together.' *(Variety)*

'In 25 years, *Top Hat* has lost none of its gaiety and charm.' *(Dilys Powell, 1960)*

'The featherweight scenario of mistaken identity matters less than the way in which Irving Berlin's marvellous tunes and the choreography . . . allow the emotional thrust of the material to be expressed through the production numbers. . . . Typifying sophisticated 1930's cool as their bodies swirled with precise grace across the screen, here was a professional chemistry that would stand the test of time.' *(Allan Hunter & Kenny Mathieson, Movie Classics, 1992)*

TOPKAPI — CT: 6 AV: 7.00

1964 US 119 C COMEDY/THRILLER

D Jules Dassin
W Monja Danischewsky ☆ from Eric Ambler's novel *The Light of Day*

Melina Mercouri Peter Ustinov ☆ AAW
Maximilian Schell Robert Morley ✔ Akim Tamiroff
Gilles Segal Jess Hahn Titos Vandis Ege Ernart
Senih Orkan

Thieves try to rob the Istanbul museum.

Amiable, energetic caper movie which parodies Dassin's previous success, *Rififi*. There's suspense and humour; but it's let down by variable performances. Mercouri, Dassin's wife, seems to be trying a little too hard. Morley and Ustinov, both at their confident best, show the others how it's done.

ANTI:

'Like Mae West, whom she is beginning to resemble

in style, Melina Mercouri leans heavily for her effects on the techniques of the female impersonator . . . [The set-pieces] ought to have been fairly entertaining. I didn't find that they were, however; for my taste, it was all too cute, all too arch.' *(Richard Roud, Guardian)*

MIXED:

'The elaborate robbery it involves seems crude beginner's stuff compared with the way Peter Ustinov steals the whole picture.' *(Cecil Wilson, Daily Mail)*

'Ustinov has probably the meatiest part in the film and one that allows him to use many of the unsubtleties he has at his command.' *(Variety)*

PRO:

'I found the whole thing highly entertaining . . . I even suspect that I would sooner see the film again than re-read my own book . . . I wish I had written the screenplay.' *(Eric Ambler, Daily Express)*

'Mr Dassin keeps his plot bubbling with humor.' *(Saturday Review)*

'A few really nice lines . . . some enticing shots of Istanbul . . . and a thoroughly ingenious and protracted robbery sequence.' *(John Coleman, New Statesman)*

'Ustinov, of whom I expect nothing less than pure genius, almost disappointed me with a just brilliant portrayal . . . An excellent film, perfect entertainment.' *(John Viner, Daily Sketch)*

TOPPER

CT: 6 AV: 7.27

1937 US 98 COMEDY/FANTASY

D Norman Z. McLeod
W Jack Jevne Eric Hatch Eddie Moran from Thorne Smith's novel *The Jovial Ghosts*

Constance Bennett ☆ Cary Grant ☆ Roland Young ☆ AAN Billie Burke ☆ Alan Mowbray ☆ Eugene Pallette Arthur Lake Hedda Hopper Virginia Sale Theodore von Eltz

High-spirited ghosts (Constance Bennett, Cary Grant) transform the life of a meek and mild bank manager (Roland Young).

In a role originally intended for W.C. Fields, Young gives the comedy performance of his life. Just as good in their way are Cary Grant and Constance Bennett, the spirit world's answer to Nick and Nora Charles (of the *Thin Man* series). To a Depression-era audience, the style, sophistication and irresponsibility of the couple was terribly attractive; the characters' appeal has diminished, but the actors' comic timing remains intact. This hugely successful film spawned two inferior sequels, a television series, and a made-for-television remake. Elmer Raguse was Oscar-nominated for Best Sound.

ANTI:

'We honestly regret our inability to shout hurrah for [the film] . . . Mr Young and his fellow players are responsible for whatever success an otherwise completely irresponsible film enjoys.' *(Bosley Crowther, New York Times)*

'Effort to excuse the story's absurdities on the theory that the intent is farce comedy does not entirely excuse the production from severe rebuke. Fact also that the living dead are always facetious may be shocking to sensibilities. Some of the situations and dialog offend conventional good taste.' *(Variety)*

MIXED:

'The rich possibilities of the story are not entirely fulfilled, chiefly because of too much insistence on technical trickery for its own sake. But in spite of this, the film offers very bright entertainment, thanks to the novel plot, the very good acting, and the downright humour . . . The acting is excellent . . . Alan Mowbray . . . acts everyone else off the screen.' *(Film Weekly)*

PRO:

'The film blazes a new trail for the fantasy shown in motion pictures . . . A complete triumph for outstanding screen acting . . . The audience was intrigued and was sent into gales of laughter.' *(MGM suggestions to the press on how the film should be reviewed)*

'Highly amusing . . . and the trick-work is brilliant throughout . . . Roland Young's performance really makes the film . . . It is difficult to discern whether there is a moral in the film . . . but it cleverly gives the impression that there is one.' *(Basil Wright, Spectator)*

'The tempo [is] brisk, the manner swank, the purpose first, last and always, to amuse.' *(Motion Picture Herald)*

'Hurrahs for [the] direction of a grand cast of comedians.' *(Photoplay)*

TORCH SONG

CT: 6 AV: 4.63

1953 US 90 C DRAMA/SO BAD

D Charles Walters ☆
W John Michael Hayes Jan Lustig ● from I.A.R. Wylie's story *Why Should I Cry?*

Joan Crawford ● Michael Wilding Gig Young Marjorie Rambeau Henry Morgan Dorothy Patrick

A temperamental star from Broadway (Joan Crawford) finds love with her blind pianist (Michael Wilding).

Hilariously awful, clichéd melodrama, with Crawford – in her first role in a colour movie – giving a very highly coloured performance indeed. Her singing was dubbed (by India Adams) for all but one number, 'Tenderly'. A must for lovers of showbiz camp. Sample line . . . Crawford to her kept lover: 'You're no good, but you're beautiful.'

PRO:

'Here is Joan Crawford all over the screen, in command, in love and in color.' *(Otis L. Guernsey Jr)*

'For her homecoming after years of wandering, MGM have staged a royal return for Joan Crawford; glossy production, Technicolor, fabulous clothes, and scarcely ever off the screen for ninety minutes . . . For the Crawford addict there is much to enjoy . . . Apart from providing a field day for the Crawford enthusiast [it's] a slickly made film.' *(MFB)*

'Lest my female readers think that the film . . . will appeal to men only, I must add that [MGM] have generously thrown in Michael Wilding [who is so appealing] that every lady member of the audience will want to mother him. Hang it, I actually wanted to father him myself.' *(Paul Dehn, Sunday Chronicle)*

'A silly and conventional film, but there is no denying that of its sort, it is well-made.' *(Isabel Quigly, Manchester Guardian)*

ANTI:

'British fans [of Wilding] should declare war on Hollywood.' *(Reynolds News)*

'Crawford is a stage star who keeps a gigolo, behaves offensively to all her colleagues and thinks caricaturing the Negro people just the thing to give zing to her show . . . Non-stop aggression is not entertainment.' *(Thomas Spencer, Daily Worker)*

'I'm afraid only inclement weather could recommend this foolishness.' *(Derek Granger, Financial Times)*

'The viewer is asked to admire Joan Crawford's legs and her acting, which consists of pushing her mouth into positions meant to suggest suffering. The first is easy; the second impossible. In this misbegotten melodrama with some musical numbers, she finally settles for a blind musician (Michael Wilding). Which, all things considered, is a remarkably sensible decision.' *(Pauline Kael)*

'As unintentionally funny as any that Crawford ever made . . . In the finale Crawford bugs her eyes, makes that mouth, and rips off her wig to reveal orange hair. (Oh, the horror, the horror!) Not even unmasking the Phantom of the Opera or discovering mother's corpse in *Psycho* come close.' *(Margulies & Rebello)*

TOTAL RECALL CT: 8 AV: 6.17

1990 US 109 C SF/ACTION/ADVENTURE

D Paul Verhoeven ✔
W Ronald Shusett Dan O'Bannon Gary Goldman ✔ from Philip K. Dick's story *We Can Remember It For You Wholesale*
Arnold Schwarzenegger ☆ Rachel Ticotin ✔ Sharon Stone ✔ Ronny Cox Michael Ironside Marshall Bell Mel Johnson Jr Roy Brocksmith

A man (Arnold Schwarzenegger) is disturbed by recollections of life on Mars, when he can't recall having been there.

The mechanical and violent – but a top-class action thriller and one of the most successful examples of big-screen science fiction. Director Paul (*RoboCop*) Verhoeven is as subtle as Ken Russell wielding a chainsaw, but directs with pace, and finds time to mock the macho excesses of the genre. He is helped by the amiable persona of his star and an ingeniously plotted script. As usual with most action films, most critics found the violence hard to take, and several pointed out scientific flaws in the storyline.

Oscar-nominated for sound (Nelson Stoll, Michael J. Kohut, Carlos DeLarios, Aaron Rochin) and sound effects editing (Stephen H. Flick), *Total Recall* won an Academy Award for visual effects (Eric Brevig, Rob Bottin, Tim McGovern, Alex Funke).

ANTI:

'How does Arnie cope with the self-doubt and paranoia induced by having had your mind stolen and your reality adjusted? You've guessed it. He blasts his way out of it. This is the most violent film I've seen for a long time, bodies torn apart and corpses riddled with bullet holes every ten seconds. Verhoeven likes splatter. He puts this down to having been in Holland during the German occupation.' *(Suzanne Moore, New Statesman)*

'The movie is wall-to-wall with violence, much of it augmented by special effects. Even in this future world, people haven't been able to improve on the machine gun as a weapon of murder, even though you'd imagine that firearms of all kinds would be outlawed inside an airtight dome. There are indeed several sequences in which characters are sucked outside when the air seal is broken, but that doesn't stop the movie's villains from demonstrating the one inevitable fact of movie marksmanship: bad guys never hit their target, and good guys never miss. Not that it makes the slightest difference, but the science in this movie is laughable throughout.' *(Roger Ebert)*

'While the temptation is just to shrug off *Total Recall* as an excessive but exciting "no brainer", enough intelligence and artistry lie behind the numbing spectacle to also make one regret its heedless contribution to the accelerating brutality of its time.' *(Variety)*

PRO:

'In *Total Recall*, as previously in *Predator, Commando* and *The Terminator*, the clichés are turned on their heads just when you least expect it. For a time Sharon Stone plays a perfect Doris Day wife with a centrefold body, but it turns out she's married to Michael Ironside's relentless villain. The comic relief sidekick turns out to be a traitor, and the real villain of the piece comes as a big surprise. While most other stars are refining their screen persona, only Arnie seems interested in expanding his in new directions, while never failing to deliver what an increasingly loyal audience requires of him.' *(Trevor Willsmer, Film Yearbook)*

'A revolutionary parable, two great female characters, and some colossal special effects. The future doesn't come any better.' *(Tom Charity, Time Out)*

TOTO THE HERO CT: 8 AV: 7.55

(aka *Toto Le Héros*)

1991 Belgium/France/Germany 91 C DRAMA/FOREIGN

D Jaco van Dormael ☆
W Jaco van Dormael

Michel Bouquet ☆ Jo De Backer Thomas Godet Gisela Uhlen Mireille Perrier Sandrine Blancke Peter Böhlke

An embittered old man (Michel Bouquet, looking uncannily like Laurence Olivier) dreams of breaking out of his old people's home and murdering Alfred, his childhood neighbour with whom he believes he was swopped at birth.

A rewarding study of an old man's envy, bitterness and regret. Any similarity to Dennis Potter's *Singing Detective* is far from coincidental: it was seeing the British TV series that encouraged first-time writer-director Jaco Van Dormael to persist with a script which he feared might be too complicated for an audience to grasp.

The complicated structure is not an affectation, however: it very convincingly reflects an old man's thought processes; the jigsaw pieces of reminiscence and fantasy fit together in the end to make sense.

The film is full of allusions to American cinema, from *Vertigo* and *Citizen Kane* through to *Rachel Rachel*, but has its own, distinctively European voice. There are delightfully original touches of humour, as for example in the supermarket scene where Thomas's mother seems to be bleeding from the head, but is then found to be hiding stolen meat under her hat. Or there's the humorous juxtaposition of a couple's love-making with the washing of a corpse. The film's a reminder that Belgium was the home of surrealism.

It could easily have been depressing; but throughout there's an underlying sense of joy and the absurdity of life, exemplified in Charles Trenet's catchy song 'Boum', which crops up now and again at apposite (and inapposite) moments.

MIXED:

'In terms of technique it's an impressive first film, but erratic acting and the sheer burden of its improbable storyline are serious handicaps which even the movie's buoyant stylishness can't offset . . . The film . . . suffers from a lackluster performance by newcomer Jo De Backer . . . The young children . . . are first-rate.' *(Ed Kelleher, Film Journal)*

'The feeling . . . is of a specifically childish omnipotence, and though the structure of the film comes full circle, it would be truer to say that [the film] has never really left the magic bath of infantile emotions.' *(Adam Mars-Jones, Independent)*

'An interesting film, but I would have liked it more, I think, if it had been more bitter and unforgiving; if someone like Buñuel had directed it. It's strange, a comedy about resentment.' *(Roger Ebert)*

PRO:

'At times we might be watching a children's version of . . . *Blue Velvet* . . . We never know till the final fade if it will end in tears or laughter and by then we are too engrossed and delighted to care.' *(Nigel Andrews, Financial Times)*

'Van Dormael . . . manages, through flashback, fantasy and sheer film-making skill to fashion an ironic, funny, truthful and altogether extraordinary parable.' *(Derek Malcolm, Guardian)*

'A fully fledged piece of cinematic art . . . It fizzes with startling images . . . Above all, the film is supremely poignant, truthful and funny.' *(Hugo Davenport, Daily Telegraph)*

'A film so unique it's difficult to explain why it's so wonderful. Extraordinarily witty and inventive and utterly spellbinding.' *(Rose)*

TOUCH OF CLASS, A AAN CT: 5 AV: 5.73

1973 GB 106 C COMEDY/ROMANCE

D Melvin Frank
W Melvin Frank Jack Rose AAN

Glenda Jackson ✗ AAW George Segal ☆ Paul Sorvino ☆ Hildegarde Neil Cec Linder

Married, middle-aged Lothario (George Segal) finds love with sharp-tongued dress designer (Glenda Jackson).

Popular blend of old-fashioned screwball comedy and 60s sexual ethics. Widely regarded as hilarious at the time, it's one of those 'daring' comedies which now looks embarrassingly old-fashioned. Glenda Jackson seems at sea – and quite humourless – during much of it; how she won an Oscar remains a mystery. Segal's underplaying has worn better. The music by John Cameron was Oscar-nominated, along with the song 'All That Love Went To Waste' (music by George Barrie, lyrics by Sammy Cahn).

PRO:

'Sensational.' *(Variety)*

MIXED:

'Brightly performed and quite engaging until it fades into vapid variations on a one-joke theme.' *(S & S)*

'Miss Jackson is a bit on the crude side, as is her wont, yet she is masterly with both comic and pathetic exasperation . . . What makes the actor [George Segal] so likeable despite his lack of versatility (he cannot even get rid of a slight Jewish inflection) and his rather undistinguished looks (his head, for instance, is much too big for his body) is that he falls exactly midway between Robert Redford and Woody Allen, between virile handsomeness and amusingly hangdog schnookiness. If you blink as you look at him, he is dashing enough for women to crave and men to envy him; at a closer look, men can feel comfortable and women motherly.' *(John Simon)*

'Amiable and very physical sex farce with hilarious highlights and a few longueurs between.' *(Halliwell)*

ANTI:

'Machine-tooled junk.' *(William S. Pechter)*

TOUCH OF EVIL CT: 8 AV: 9.38

1958 US 95/114 BW THRILLER

D Orson Welles ☆ Harry Keller (uncredited)
W Orson Welles from Whit Masterson's novel *Badge of Evil*

Charlton Heston Janet Leigh Orson Welles Joseph Calleia Marlene Dietrich Akim Tamiroff Val DeVargas Ray Collins Dennis Weaver Joanna Moore Mort Mills

In a Mexican border town, a narcotics investigator (Charlton Heston) on honeymoon with his wife (Janet Leigh) confronts a corrupt police chief (Orson Welles) over a murder.

Touch of Evil is weak on narrative and characterisation, but strong on noir atmosphere and camera technique (the long opening shot is a classic). Universal Pictures were dissatisfied with Welles's cut, which now no longer exists. They replaced the editor and ordered additional close-ups which were directed by Harry Keller.

Although the film won the international prize at the 1958 Brussels' World Fair, it was panned on release (when it was shown to the critics at all). Over the years, it has come to be regarded as a masterpiece and is now in danger of being overrated. It has the familiar Wellesian weakness of being too clever for its own good; a little more clarity in telling the story would have helped. Russell Metty's photography and Henry Mancini's music, however, are excellent.

'*Touch of Evil* never had a first-run, never had the usual presentation to the press and was not the object of any critical writing in either the weeklies, the reviews or the daily papers. It was considered to be too bad.' *(Orson Welles)*

ANTI:

'The flashy interplay of queer character defeats itself in the end. Far from clear speech and pretentious lighting and photographic effects add to the confusion. In short, Orson Welles . . . overplays his hand . . . Utterly incoherent and unpleasantly smelling of evil, the film will give most men, let alone women, the willies.' *(Kine Weekly)*

'Not one of Welles's successes.' *(Evening Standard)*

'Critics have not been invited to review *Touch of Evil*, the new Orson Welles picture, from which you are free to draw your own conclusions.' *(Observer)*

'As usual, a bizarre film within a film [which Welles] turns into something uncertain and strangely unfamiliar . . . [He] gradually transmutes his story into some abstruse stylistic allegory to which finally no one . . . quite possesses the key.' *(Times Educational Supplement)*

MIXED:

'There is an unpleasant awareness that technical facility is being exploited to gild pure dross – and the suspicion that the dross was chosen because of the opportunities it afforded for virtuoso display . . . Director Welles is much too busy angling his camera at a plethora of marvelously baroque settings, costumes and faces to bother about the original premise of his story . . . [Yet] there is a manic intensity . . . that makes it at once repellent and fascinating.' *(Arthur Knight, Saturday Review)*

'Smacks of brilliance but ultimately flounders in it.' *(Variety)*

'I cannot pretend that Welles's new film is a good one. It is not. It is often laughably bad, often pompously bad. Yet it has virtues. For one thing, it is not dull; and that, in a decade of big-budget, wide-screen, many-starred extravaganzas, is a pleasant surprise. It also makes an attempt – a fruitless one as it turns out – to deal with a serious theme, power and corruption. *Touch of Evil* is pure Orson Welles and impure balderdash, which may be the same thing. It shows, as all Welles's films do, that he is a man who understands the way in which a camera can be used, and that he will sacrifice plot and verisimilitude for an attempt at a consistent mood – in this case an almost tangible sense of corruption. Unfortunately, the line between the corrupt and the comic is a thin one, and Welles keeps slipping over. *Touch of Evil* is not a good movie, but it is a good bad movie, which is more fun to see than the mediocre or even the adequate.' *(Gerald Weales, Reporter)*

'A thriller about a cop who gets his man by framing him, it has the faults we have seen in half a dozen Welles films: the narrative line repeatedly broken, the fluency sliding into confusion. All the same, from the superb opening to the melodrama of the end one feels the presence of one of the cinema's masters . . . The director may exaggerate his own style, but the style is there, and again and again in *Touch of Evil* it gives one a start of delight. The playing – Welles himself, hugely padded and pouched as the cop, Charlton Heston, Joseph Calleia, Akim Tamiroff – has a ferocious edge.' *(Dilys Powell, Sunday Times)*

'May not be best Welles . . . Visually stirring, overemphatic, muddled, rich in urban scenery . . . and enlivened by a fantasy of gross men.' *(William Whitebait, New Statesman)*

PRO:

'Nobody, and we mean, nobody, will nap during *Touch of Evil* . . . Welles's is an obvious but brilliant bag of tricks. Using a superlative camera (manned by Russell Metty) like a black-snake whip, he lashes the action right into the spectator's eye.' *(Howard Thompson, New York Times)*

'For all the tampering that has been done with it, [it] emerges as recognizable Welles, which in itself is a great deal in a time of stupefying banality and meretricious pretensions with which the current American cinema is rife.' *(Herman G. Weinberg, Film Culture, 1959)*

'Despite a highly complex and almost unfathomable plot, this is a visually brilliant film, with Welles in exceptional form.' *(R.A.E. Pickard, 1971)*

'A terrifying, Goyaesque vision of corruption, and probably the most original thriller ever made.' *(Peter Bogdanovich, 1975)*

'Often regarded as film noir's most fraught epitaph, *Touch of Evil*'s aura of nocturnal menace is unremitting, a despairing journey to Hades that is also electrifyingly inventive cinema.' *(NFT Bulletin, 1980)*

TOWERING INFERNO, THE AAN

CT: 7 AV: 5.85

1974 US 165 C ACTION/ADVENTURE

D John Guillermin ☆, Irwin Allen ☆
W Stirling Silliphant from Richard Martin Stern's novel *The Tower* and Thomas M. Scortia and Frank M. Robinson's novel *The Glass Inferno*

Steve McQueen Paul Newman Fred Astaire ☆ AAN Robert Vaughn ✔ William Holden Faye Dunaway Susan Blakely Richard Chamberlain Jennifer Jones

On the night of its opening, the tallest building in the world is consumed by fire.

The most gripping of all disaster movies, with convincing special effects, a delightful supporting performance from Fred Astaire and a splendidly shifty one from Robert (*Man From Uncle*) Vaughn. The two heroes, Steve McQueen and Paul Newman, are less memorable. The film won Oscars for cinematography (Fred Koenecamp, Joseph Biroc) and Best Song ('We May Never Live Like This Again'). Also nominated were the editing (Harold F. Kress, Carl Kress), score (John Williams) and art direction (William Creber).

ANTI:

'Falls engagingly wide of the mark . . . Several generations of blue-eyed charmers act their roles as if each were under a separate bell jar . . . Guillermin drives his film with a kind of efficiency that sidesteps the exploration of any implicit ambiguities . . . Predictably the big star syndrome tends to operate finally to deadly effect . . . [The film] is everything the entertainment industry understands by the term "movie magic": a piece of harmless, resolutely overblown and occasionally effective hokum.' *(Verina Glaessner, MFB)*

'Each scene of someone horribly in flames is presented as a feat for the audience's delectation.' *(New Yorker)*

'The most overproduced glossy swill in "disaster movie" history.' *(Margulies & Rebello)*

MIXED:

'The combination of Grade A spectacle and B-picture characters induces a feeling of sideline detachment.' *(Michael Billington, Illustrated London News)*

'If you must have a conflagration-film this is the hell of a good conflagration, the stunts superbly executed, the illusion of a desperate situation brilliantly achieved. Once or twice I caught myself wondering what D.W. Griffith would have done if such technical resources had been available to him (not that he did badly in the Babylonian sequences of *Intolerance*). Thinking back now I fancy he would have drawn a stronger moral conclusion from disaster. *The Towering Inferno* merely remarks, not very forcibly, that high-rise buildings ought to have better electric wiring and better fire proofing. In the huge spectacle pity is lost; and I am left reflecting that addiction to Great Disaster cinema is lowering to the sensibilities.' *(Dilys Powell)*

PRO:

'You can tell that a disaster film is achieving its purpose if your palms begin to sweat. Mine did . . . The special effects boys have done wonders. So let the sweat flow.' *(Gordon Gow, F & F)*

'[McQueen] is quite exhausted at the end of it all and to tell you the truth – so was I. As one disaster piled on top of another with astonished realism, my heart was seldom out of my mouth.' *(Ian Christie, Daily Express)*

'The real stars are surely the stuntmen, technicians, photographers and all those responsible for the amazing special effects.' *(Virginia Dignam, Morning Star)*

'Carries its weight with such enormous verve and lightness of foot that initial qualms are soon dispelled by the sheer enthusiasm and bravado of the enterprise.' *(Nigel Andrews, Financial Times)*

'The glass tower becomes a combustible symbol of American affluence, built precariously on rotten foundations. *Towering Inferno* senses that beneath the best of everything lurks the worst of everything. And its torrential climax, when a roomful of enormous top-floor water tanks is blown up, can be read as an apocalyptic ritual cleansing of all that is decayed in our society.' *(Paul D. Zimmerman, Newsweek)*

TOYS

CT: 2 AV: 3.3

1992 US 121 C FAMILY/DRAMA

D Barry Levinson ●
W Valerie Curtin Barry Levinson ●

Robin Williams ● Michael Gambon ●
Joan Cusack ● Robin Wright L.L. Cool J
Jack Warden (cameo Donald O'Connor)

A toy factory is taken over by a military-minded manager (Michael Gambon).

Despite some splendid visuals, Barry Levinson's insufferably preachy, twee fairy-tale is to be avoided like the plague. Robin Williams is at his over-ingratiating worst as the defender of all that's good, childlike and pacifist. A film that set out to have an enchanting, childlike innocence ends up as a dispiriting monument to childish pomposity. *Toys* won Oscar nominations for Ferdinando Scarfiotti's art direction, and Albert Wolsky's costumes.

PRO:

'A brave try at something warm-hearted and basically nice, full of generosity of spirit and good humour, and dedicated to joy or innocence.' *(Winnert)*

MIXED:

'Visually brilliant, flashes of extraordinary wit occasionally bubble to the surface, enough for film buffs to enjoy. But for others, this disjointed, rambling mess of a movie will be a big turn-off.' *(Rose)*

ANTI:

'Only a filmmaker of Barry Levinson's clout would have been so indulged as to create such a sprawling, seemingly unsupervised mess. It will be hard to top as the season's major clunker.' *(Variety)*

'There's a reason why the Good Lord in his wisdom did not endow the elephant with a sense of whimsy. A person could get crushed by a large creature's attempts to trip the light fantastic. That's pretty much the way *Toys* leaves you: flattened, bruised and whimpering. Based on a moldering script by director Barry Levinson and Valerie Curtin, *Toys* is informed by a sensibility still more antique: 1960s peacenik.' *(Richard Schickel, Richard Corliss, end of 1992 round-up, Time)*

'A disaster . . . It is quite unlike anything Levinson has done before, and it is sincerely to be hoped that he never does anything like it again.' *(Derek Malcolm, Guardian)*

'Robin Williams behaves like a dimwitted second cousin of a Kafka character. Too smart for the role, he attempts a muted version of his stream-of-consciousness shtick that is grating and unfunny. Joan Cusack opts for a metallic, performance-artist version of Dustin Hoffman's idiot-savant routine from, and comes across like Cher in slow motion. Michael Gambon tries to give a serious performance, but achieves only a hysterical amalgam of Adolf Hitler and Doctor Doom.' *(Baseline)*

'No ordinary bad movie. It was the kind of stuporously wasteful white elephant that made you think a filmmaker had temporarily lost his mind.' *(Owen Gleiberman, Entertainment Weekly, 1994)*

TRADING PLACES

CT: 7 AV: 6.86

1983 US 116 C COMEDY

D John Landis
W Timothy Harris Herschel Weingrod

Dan Aykroyd ☆ Eddie Murphy ☆ Ralph Bellamy ☆
Don Ameche ☆ Denholm Elliott ☆
Jamie Lee Curtis ☆ Kristin Holby Robert Earl Jones
Paul Gleason Frank Oz Bo Diddley
James Belushi Philip Bosco

Two rich brokers (Ralph Bellamy and Don Ameche) lay a wager on whether a black have-not (Eddie Murphy) can change places successfully with a white preppie (Dan Aykroyd).

Starting out as an update on *The Prince and the Pauper*, it develops into a witty satire on yuppiedom and Reaganite ethics. Denholm Elliott all but steals the show as the butler, but the whole film is energetic, well acted, and full of laughs. Murphy was never better.

'Proof positive that the genuine American populist comedy can still attract attention.' *(John Pym, MFB)*

'John Landis' movie confirms what *48 HRS*. suggested: Murphy is the most dynamic new comic talent around, a quicksilver, quick-change artist whose rapport with the audience is instantaneous . . . Murphy is the movie's hottest – and funniest – commodity.' *(Newsweek)*

'The film's pleasures are unequivocal, beginning with the lithe, graceful, uproarious performance of Mr Murphy . . . A terrific career is in store.' *(New York Times)*

'One of the most emotionally satisfying and morally gratifying comedies of recent times . . . *Trading Places* also makes Eddie Murphy a force to be reckoned with . . . [He] demonstrates the powers of invention that signal the arrival of a major comic actor, and possibly a great star. He makes *Trading Places* something more than a good-hearted comedy. He turns it into an event.' *(Time)*

'This is good comedy. It's especially good because it doesn't stop with sitcom manipulations of its idea, and it doesn't go only for the obvious points about racial prejudice in America. Instead, it develops the quirks and peculiarities of its characters, so that they're funny because of who they are. This takes a whole additional level of writing on top of the plot-manipulation we usually get in popular comedies, and it takes good direction, too.' *(Roger Ebert)*

TRAGÉDIE DE LA MINE, LA: *see* KAMERADSCHAFT.

TRANSVESTITE, THE: *see* GLEN OR GLENDA?

TRAUM DES ALLAN GRAY, DER: *see* VAMPYR.

TRAVELLING PLAYERS, THE

CT: 5 AV: 3.50

(aka *O Thiassos*)

1975 Greece 230 C DRAMA/FOREIGN

D Theodor Angelopoulos ✗
W Theodor Angelopoulos ✗

Eva Kotamandiou Petros Zarkadis Maria Vassiliou Statos Pachis Aliki Georgoulis

Travelling actors tour Greece.

How are the mighty forgotten. Much praised on its release in the 70s for its oblique examination of Greek politics (it was made under the infamous Colonels), the film's incongruously low score today is explained by the fact that it has only ever got into one of the major guides (Shipman), which thought little of it. It's scenically beautiful but too long, poetic but completely lacking in narrative drive, and therefore soporific. The troupe turns up again in another Angelopoulos film, *Landscape in the Mist* (1988).

PRO:

'This stylised and intricate film is multi-layered, vivid and powerful . . . Truly a memorable experience.' *(Virginia Dignam, Morning Star)*

'A style pregnant with its own kind of suspense so that at the end of nearly four hours you are left still eager and anxious to be told more.' *(David Robinson, The Times)*

'A major work has the right to be long, and [this] is a major work. You might say it has a kind of grandeur.' *(Dilys Powell, Sunday Times)*

'Vastly ambitious, vastly long . . . To enjoy its wonderfully varied change of rhythms and styles you do not need to know your Greek history . . . The film offers in almost every scene . . . a director in full command of extraordinary material.' *(Alexander Walker, Evening Standard)*

'Not a gentle film . . . Not an easy film. But one utterly engrossing . . . Never for a moment did it seem too long.' *(Felix Barker, Evening News)*

'Perhaps the greatest unseen [in America] film of the Seventies . . . Its plan is epic (Brecht crossed with Aeschylus and Mizoguchi): to reveal the period's political history while focusing on a group of itinerant actors who spend those fourteen years wandering through provinces and cities, performing – in increasingly threadbare circumstances – a popular Greek folk tale, Golfo the Shepherdess.' *(Michael Wilmington)*

MIXED:

'A work of almost painful dignity.' *(Russell Davies, Observer)*

'Extremely slow but ultimately impressive.' *(Bergan & Karney)*

'Will obviously provide problems for people raised on machine-gun cutting techniques. Editing is very restrained, and some takes last up to five minutes, but the stately pace of the film soon becomes compulsive; and the shabby provincial Greece of rusting railway tracks and flaking facades which the slow camera examines is visually beguiling.' *(David Perry, Time Out)*

ANTI:

'The director has no narrative sense and incident follows incident without cumulative effect except that the slow pace and meaningless detail begin to wear down one's patience.' *(Shipman)*

TRE FRATELLI: *see* THREE BROTHERS.

TREASURE OF THE SIERRA MADRE, THE

AAN CT: 7 AV: 8.79

1948 US 126 BW WESTERN/ADVENTURE/ACTION

D John Huston ☆ AAW
W John Huston ✗ AAW from Berwick Traven Torsvan's novel

Humphrey Bogart ☆ Walter Huston ☆ AAW
Tim Holt ✓ Alfonso Bedoya ✓ John Huston
Bruce Bennett Barton MacLane

A gold prospector (Humphrey Bogart) is consumed by greed.

John Huston's highly acclaimed, Oscar-winning action adventure is marred by a poor score, unconvincing sets and some banal dialogue, but is saved by the central performances and a gripping story. Bogart's Fred C. Dobbs, who changes from a drifter to a cold-blooded murderer, is one of his best performances. Walter Huston's acting smells strongly of ham, but is always watchable. Brutal for its time, pessimistic about human nature and a middling performer at the box office (it took some years to recover its costs), the film has proved very influential on later film-makers, especially Sam Peckinpah, whose *The Wild Bunch* (1969) and *Bring me the Head of Alfredo Garcia* (1974) contain conscious allusions to it.

ANTI:

'Besides the hurly-burly of the wide open spaces the film has irony, and it has a theme – namely, the corrupting effect the quest for gold can have on otherwise reasonable men. Unfortunately, the example chosen to demonstrate this is a man so unpleasantly corrupted anyway that nothing is really proved . . . Mr Huston tirelessly uses all the old tricks and mannerisms which go to the making of the screen old gaffer, and the result is a piece of that likeable ham that is sometimes confused with great acting.' *(Fred Majdalany, Daily Mail)*

'If the action were in itself completely engrossing one would, no doubt, overlook the frequent banality of the dialogue and forget the absence of narrative subtlety. But the expedition takes a long time to get under way; and when the three men are in the wilds we have plenty of leisure to let our attention wander: to reflect, for instance, on the unconvincing quality of some of the back projection and sets, and to wish that once in a while somebody would really take Humphrey Bogart and Tim Holt and the enchanting Walter Huston off to the mountains and let them act in natural light against a natural background . . . It is, from John Huston, a disappointment.' *(Dilys Powell)*

MIXED:

'This bitter fable is told with cinematic integrity and considerable skill. True, there is some unnecessary melodrama for which Herr Traven is to blame. Occasionally there is Hollywood hyperbole, as when Mr Huston assembles hundreds of Mexican Indians for an effect Sergei Eisenstein achieved with a few dozen. And Humphrey Bogart is miscast. Mr Bogart can exhibit grace under pressure incomparably, but he cannot successfully be mean. Moreover, his part has atrocious lines.' *(Henry Hart, New Movies)*

PRO:

'The director, Mr John Huston, has invested this film with a cloak of such harsh realism, and has woven the thread of morality so cunningly into its pattern, he has caught with such a relentless eye both the weakness of man and the strength of nature, that it all seems new and exciting.' *(Virginia Graham)*

'One of the best things Hollywood has done since movies learned to talk.' *(Time)*

'A film that will raise Hollywood's prestige to Himalayan heights . . . An immense, dramatic, ironic, masculine film.' *(Daily Graphic)*

'The faces of the men, in close-up or in a group, achieve a kind of formal pattern and always dominate the screen.' *(Peter Ericson)*

'The success of the film depends on Bogart, his face concealed for most of the film behind a facade of whiskers and grime. He plays it perfectly.' *(Sunday Graphic)*

'Would you realise how strong drama can hold the screen absorbingly without a spark of feminine interest and sentiment but with the rugged force of its masculine characters? Then you must see *Treasure of the Sierra Madre* in which both Humphrey Bogart and Walter Huston give the best performances of their careers.' *(A.E. Wilson)*

'I doubt we shall ever see a film more masculine in style; or a truer movie understanding of character and of men; or as good a job on bumming, a bum's life, a city as a bum sees it; or a more beautiful job on a city; or a finer portrait of Mexico and Mexicans (compare it with all the previous fancy-filter stuff for a definitive distinction between poetry and poeticism); or a crueller communication of absolute desolateness in nature and its effect on men (except perhaps in *Greed*); or a much more vivid communication of hardship, labor, and exhaustion (though I wish these had been brutally and meticulously presented rather than skilfully sketched); or more intelligent handling of amateurs and semi-professionals (notably the amazing character who plays Gold-Hat, the bandit leader); or a finer selective eye for location or a richer understanding of how to use it; or scenes of violence or building toward violence more deeply authentic and communicative . . . The camera is always where it ought to be, never imposes on or exploits or overdramatizes its subject, never for an instant shoves beauty or special meaning at you. This is one of the most visually alive and beautiful movies I have ever seen; there is a wonderful flow of fresh air, light, vigour, and liberty through every shot, and a fine athlete's litheness and absolute control and flexibility in every succession and series of shots.' *(James Agee, Nation)*

'John Huston produced a number of great films, but this tale of greed, fear, and murder in Mexico is undoubtedly his finest, a towering masterpiece with Humphrey Bogart simply wonderful as the inimitable Fred C. Dobbs. Bogart, within the space of two hours, undergoes an incredible metamorphosis, changing from a rather personable down-and-outer to a homicidal maniac willing to kill his closest friends.' *(Baseline)*

TREE GROWS IN BROOKLYN, A

CT: 8 AV: 8.40

1945 US 128 BW DRAMA

D Elia Kazan ☆

W Tess Slesinger Frank Davis ☆ AAN from Betty Smith's novel

Peggy Ann Garner ☆ (special AAN as outstanding child actress) James Dunn ☆ AAW Dorothy McGuire ☆ Joan Blondell ☆ Lloyd Nolan ☆ Ted Donaldson James Gleason ✓

The story of an Irish family living in the New York slums at the turn of the century.

Though hailed for its realism, the movie is rather

too clean and art-directed; it looks like the big studio production it was. Even so, it's a pleasant, warm-hearted tearjerker, directed with pace and panache by Elia (*On The Waterfront*) Kazan on his début. Kazan concentrated his attention on the actors, who repaid him with some of their best performances. On the technical side, he was greatly helped by his experienced director of photography, Leon Shamroy, and editor Dorothy Spencer.

MIXED:

'A more interesting and likable movie than most. It concentrates on poverty, on some crucial aspects of early puberty, on domestic relationships, and on life in a big city, which are rarely undertaken on the American screen, with considerable enthusiasm, tenderness, discipline, and intelligence. It even presents and accepts the idea, unpopular enough even in contemporary fiction, that some antagonisms and inadequacies are too deeply rooted to be wholly explicable or curable . . . The tenement sets and city streets of the movie are as lovingly and exhaustively detailed and as solid-looking as any I can remember . . . The characters themselves bother me most . . . The imagination has been used a little too glibly to blow up and trim off the presumptive originals of these characters into very comfortably readable, actable, easily understandable creatures, whose faults and virtues are all tagged or neatly braided.' *(James Agee, Nation)*

PRO:

'An artistically satisfying and emotionally quickening tearjerker.' *(Kine Weekly)*

'Its drabness is softened by a glow of love and hope.' *(Picture Show)*

'As credible and creditable a depiction of American tenement life as has been seen on the talking screen. The Betty Smith novel is transposed with tenderness and restraint by writers Tess Slesinger and Frank Davis, and director Elia Kazan has contoured the characters with considerably more veracity than one has come to expect of "people" in Hollywood pictures . . . Worthy of note is the harrowing realism with which the child-birth sequences are presented. Not since Griffith first exploded the stork myth on the screen two decades ago by showing Anna Moore in the throes of hideous labor in *Way Down East* has a movie so had the courage to announce motherhood as anything but a most beautiful and delightful experience.' *(Herb Sterne)*

'The picture has pace and movement and sustains interest throughout. For the information of the film industry this is accomplished without any "love interest", "glamor girls" or sex of any kind. Kazan goes into minute detail, using his camera to get inside the characters of the individuals, and he tells a maximum amount of story with a minimum of film. Little touches of humor and human understanding, which are the characteristics of a good director, crop up throughout the picture.' *(Frank Ward, NBR, 1947)*

TREE OF WOODEN CLOGS, THE

CT: 6 AV: 8.50

(aka *L' Albero degli Zoccoli*)

1978 Italy 186 C DRAMA/FOREIGN

D Ermanno Olmi ☆
W Ermanno Olmi

Luigi Ornaghi Francesca Moriggi Omar Brignoli Antonio Ferrari Teresa Brescianini Giuseppe Brignoli Carlo Rota

A year in the life of some Lombardy peasants in the 1890s.

When critics start calling a film 'a work of art', it usually means there's nothing much in the way of a story. That's certainly true of this very beautiful evocation of a bygone era – a remarkable achievement in view of the fact that it was shot on 16mm film, and with non-professional actors. But it's almost entirely lacking in dramatic incident, and its Marxist, anti-exploitation message is spelt out at so sluggish a pace that it may test the patience of non-critics.

ANTI:

'The peasants, though not faultless, are seen through such a haze of adoration that Olmi's picture becomes anachronistic in a way, more of an exercise in fifty-year-old sentimentality about the proletariat than a re-creation of 100-year-old peasant life.' *(Stanley Kauffmann)*

MIXED:

'The period is caught with conviction and the peasants viewed with much sympathy; the only weakness for me being the absence of any significant action and the slowness of the pace.' *(Patrick Gibbs, Daily Telegraph)*

'It could go on forever and seems to. Respecting and admiring much, I was irritated by more.' *(John Coleman, New Statesman)*

PRO:

'The miracle is that . . . works of art can still surface, and sometimes reach the height of [this film].' *(David Robinson, The Times)*

'A masterwork.' *(Philip French, Observer)*

'Warm sympathy and precise observation go hand in hand.' *(Virginia Dignam, Morning Star)*

'Long, leisurely and exquisitely photographed.' *(Richard Barkley, Sunday Express)*

'What is truly miraculous about *The Tree of Wooden Clogs* is its fusion of the highest art with the humblest milieu. The utter helplessness of the poor has never been depicted with such unbearable irony, and yet this is not what the picture is about. Olmi shows instead that love is unconditional and that it can flourish blessedly even in the most difficult circumstances.' *(Andrew Sarris)*

'A work of art.' *(Maltin)*

TREMORS CT: 8 AV: 6.64

1989 US 96 C HORROR/COMEDY

D Ron Underwood ✔
W Brent Maddock S.S. Wilson ✔

Kevin Bacon Fred Ward Finn Carter Michael Gross Reba McEntire Bobby Jacoby

A small town is threatened by giant worms.

The best monster movie of the 1980s. While it may not be the scariest, the consistently ingenious plot has more than its share of thrills, the special effects are excellent, and it's enormous fun. Whereas most films in the genre take place in semi-darkness, director Ron Underwood follows the great ant-movie, *Them!* (1954), and lends a sinister dimension to American exteriors in broad daylight. The first corpse we see is of a man who has died of thirst, having been chased up a telegraph pole and stayed there for three days. It's an image which sums up the movie: quirky, funny, yet oddly disturbing.

The movie also departs from convention by allowing its characters to behave normally (in other words, eccentrically), even when confronted by the threat of homicidal, 30-foot long, smelly, subterranean sandworms which can swallow a station-wagon for elevenses. An odious teenage boy is principally interested in being photographed next to one of the monsters' severed tentacles; the Chinese owner of the local store shrewdly buys off its discoverers for 15 bucks; two Rambo-style survivalists use the critters as an excuse to show off their comically enormous arsenal of weapons; while other townspeople just bicker over what they ought to call the monsters. Even the local intellectual – a female seismologist – isn't the infallible authority she is in most monster movies: she can't decide whether the creatures were caused by radiation, were government-built, or came from outer space. The one thing certain, as one character remarks, 'no way are these local boys.'

MIXED:

'*Tremors* has a few clever twists but ultimately can't decide what it wants to be – flat-out funny, which its not, or a scarefest.' *(Variety)*

'Silly, trashy and derivative . . . the suspense is all there, as are all of the stock clichés.' *(Scheuer)*

PRO:

'Shrewdly, unpretentiously written, energetically directed and played with high comic conviction, *Tremors* is bound to become a cult classic. But why wait years to rediscover it?' *(Richard Schickel, Time)*

'Witty, fast and highly enjoyable, this delivers the thrills while at the same time parodying the monster genre. Note, too, the ingenious way in which the Politically Correct 90s heroine is still separated from her jeans.' *(Rose)*

'This is what a monster movie is supposed to be like, and it's terrific.' *(Tom Charity, Time Out)*

'[Its monsters] are large, deadly and best of all, unexplained . . . While not exactly a classic monster movie, [it] is an extremely salutary addition to the genre and should please sci-fi fans. The monsters themselves are pretty convincing and pretty damned ugly, too.' *(Marshall Julius, What's On in London)*

'I have not learned so much valuable natural history since *Godzilla vs The Thing*.' *(Nigel Andrews, Financial Times)*

TRIAL OF BILLY JACK, THE CT: 2 AV: 1.25

1974 US 170 C DRAMA

D Frank Laughlin (though really directed by Tom Laughlin) ●
W Tom Laughlin ●

Tom Laughlin ● Delores Taylor William Wellman Jr Victor Izay Teresa Laughlin

Native American (Tom Laughlin) continues his crusade against white corruption.

A surprise hit in the States, since it is one of the most boring sequels and hypocritical 'peace' films ever made. It does, however, have lingering entertainment value, as the most pretentious movie ever produced by the counter-culture; it's a treasure-trove of idiotic attitudes. Never released in the UK.

'The average American is a sucker for anything described as homemade. Slap that label on candy, cookies, ice cream, canned soups and . . . (the American consumer) will buy it, no matter what it tastes like . . . In at least one respect, *The Trial of Billy Jack* really is home-made . . . The only thing the Laughlins aren't doing is making the popcorn being sold in the theaters.' *(New York Times)*

'Piece of dreck . . . Scales the heights of amateur movie making with out-of-focus photography, sloppy editing, blurred sound track, and horse-opera distortion of historical events . . . Three hours of illustrated mind rot.' *(Gallery)*

'Laughlin's once quiet *Billy Jack* has turned into an unbearably preachy Billy Jerk.' *(John Barbour, Los Angeles)*

'One of the longest, slowest, most pretentious and self-congratulatory ego trips ever put on film.' *(Charles Champlin, LA Times)*

'Movie-western clichés and wretched sentiment . . . padded out with an Ed Sullivan-like grab bag of variety acts. These range from stagy musical numbers that are multiracial equivalents of the grand finales of the old Garland-Rooney pictures to long mumbo-jumbo mystical sequences that only a Khalil Gibran devotee could find riveting.' *(Frank Rich, New Times)*

'Twice as bad as the original 1971 film, and not just because it's an hour longer . . . Scenes of revolting violence and banal blandness alternate against some very handsome scenery with an incoherence that only a mindless twelve-year-old could tolerate.' *(Judith Crist, New York)*

'Unintentionally funny. New Left rhetoric, translated to the screen in the most juvenile manner imaginable . . . Political brainwashing of the most irresponsible kind.' *(Benjamin Stein, Wall Street Journal)*

'More of a trial for me than it was for Billy.' *(Donald J. Mayerson, Cue)*

'I fled the theater . . . They've brought the worst of mass culture together with the worst of the counterculture.' *(Pauline Kael)*

TRISTANA AAN CT: 6 AV: 8.00

1970 Spain/Italy/France 98 (US)/105 C DRAMA

D Luis Buñuel ☆
W Luis Buñuel Julio Alejandro from Benito Perez Galdos's novel

Catherine Deneuve ✔ Fernando Rey ☆
Franco Nero Lola Gaos Antonio Casas
Jesús Fernández Vicente Soler José Calvo
Fernando Cebrián Candida Losada

Hypocritical, womanizing nobleman (Fernando Rey) takes sexual advantage of his ward (Catherine Deneuve), who loves an artist (Franco Nero).

One of Buñuel's most straightforward films, capturing the stifling provincial atmosphere of 20s Toledo and telling his story without unnecessary frills. Bunuel pummels some over-familiar targets – religion and the hypocrisy of the governing classes – and throws in sexism for good measure. Deneuve and Rey breathe life into underwritten roles.

PRO:

'Buñuel at his most majestic.' *(Tom Milne, MFB)*

'The performances he has charmed out of his principals are impeccable.' *(John Russell Taylor, The Times)*

'Despite the extraordinary simplicity and directness of Buñuel's narrative, there remains all the old sense of the relativity of reality – a reality which is always on the margin of the irrational, the subconscious, the surreal.' *(David Robinson, Financial Times)*

'The Deneuve girl is unforgettable in creating this emotional time-bomb.' *(Weston Taylor, News of the World)*

'It is – one can almost write "of course" – a masterpiece.' *(George Melly, Observer)*

ANTI:

'It pretty nearly put me to sleep.' *(Michael Goodwin, Rolling Stone)*

TROPIC OF CANCER CT: 2 AV: 4.50

1970 US 88 C DRAMA/BIOPIC

D Joseph Strick ●
W Joseph Strick Betty Botley ● from Henry Miller's novel ●

Rip Torn James Callahan Ellen Burstyn ✔
David Bauer Laurence Lignères Phil Brown

American writer (Rip Torn) bonks his way round Paris.

One of the worst and most boring writer-directors in cinema meets one of the worst and most boorish novelists, in this monumentally tedious, long-winded journal of sexual escapades in Paris. Presumably because of budgetary considerations, the story (such as it is) has been updated from the 30s, thus removing any social or psychological depth which it might have had. Sample line . . . Henry Miller to latest sexual conquest: 'Oh, Tanya, I make your ovaries incandescent'.

PRO:

'A series of good-natured sexual vignettes and escapades.' *(Scheuer)*

MIXED:

'A trivial but entertaining sex comedy.' *(Pauline Kael)*

'Slapdash but invigorating.' *(Maltin)*

ANTI:

'The cinema here pays unfortunate tribute to literary achievement – by erecting a blank and ugly monument with the work itself firmly interred beneath.' *(Richard Combs, MFB)*

'"A spit in the face of art" is how Henry Miller described this non-book about his life in Paris. Now Joseph Strick has tried but failed to turn it into a movie. Miller was a shiftless bum, a human leech, a wastrel parasite living off the tables and bodies of others. He also took notes that read like scribblings on the urine-stained walls of an asylum toilet . . . The women all look like dead prostitutes from a Transylvanian cemetery. *Tropic of Cancer* is execrable gibberish. The man who wrote it was sick. The people who made it into a movie are whores. The people who pay money to see it are fools.' *(Rex Reed)*

'The director . . . Joseph Strick, has a distinguished record of turning his attention only to genuine works of art and consistently botching them. Genet's *The Balcony* and Joyce's *Ulysses* had to bear the brunt of his highminded amateurishness.' *(John Simon)*

'Miller's overheated prose – intoned, voice-off by Rip

Torn as Miller in the intervals between his breathless sexual encounters – is revealed as a mixture of bad poetry and bad travelogue. Four-letter words and female pubic hair have themselves a field day.' *(Tom Milne, Time Out)*

TROUBLE IN PARADISE CT: 9 AV: 9.22

1932 US 86 BW COMEDY

D Ernst Lubitsch ☆
W Grover Jones Samson Raphaelson ☆ from Laszlo Aladar's play *The Honest Finder*

Miriam Hopkins ☆ Kay Francis ☆
Herbert Marshall ☆ Charles Ruggles ☆
Edward Everett Horton ☆ C. Aubrey Smith
Robert Greig George Humbert

Two jewel-thieves (Herbert Marshall, Miriam Hopkins) hope to rob a widow (Kay Francis).

Glittering comedy, which despite its sophistication takes good care to peer behind the facade of social niceties, revealing that almost everyone in the piece is a cheat. The relationship between Herbert Marshall and Miriam Hopkins was racy for its day, and the double entendres would have fallen foul of the Hays morality code, which was enforced soon afterwards. The film would be worth seeing for Hans Dreier's art deco settings and Travis Banton's costumes alone; but the screenplay is a brilliantly structured farce with sizzling dialogue, and the actors take full advantage. This was Lubitsch's favourite out of all his films, and although I prefer his more homespun, generous-spirited *The Shop around the Corner* (1940), this is faultless of its kind – one of the most sparkling, sophisticated comedies of all time.

ANTI:

'Swell title, poor picture.' *(Variety)*

MIXED:

'One may wish there were more sting, more sarcasm, in Ernst Lubitsch's polished wit, but . . . with all his limitations he seems to be the only direct or in Hollywood who talks the language of adult people and whose suave, subtle humour betrays a keen if cynical mind . . . *Trouble in Paradise* is one of the gossamer creations of [his] narrative art . . . It would be impossible in this brief notice to describe the innumerable touches of wit and of narrative skill with which it is unfolded.' *(Alexander Bakshy)*

PRO:

'A shimmering, engaging piece of work . . . In virtually every scene a lively imagination shines forth.' *(New York Times)*

'A pretty bit of frosting, so well-contrived that you barely mind the fact that there is no cake whatsoever under the tasty puff.' *(Pare Lorentz, Vanity Fair)*

'The Lubitsch magic is in evidence again . . . and thereupon [the film] becomes a thoroughgoing delight.' *(Richard Watts Jr, New York Herald Tribune)*

'The most polished comedy of manners of the American film.' *(Gerald Mast, A Short History of the Movies, 1971)*

TROUBLE WITH HARRY, THE CT: 7 AV: 6.50

1955 US 99 C COMEDY/THRILLER

D Alfred Hitchcock ☆
W John Michael Hayes ✔ from Jack Trevor Story's novel

Edmund Gwenn ☆ Mildred Natwick ☆
Shirley MacLaine ☆ John Forsythe ●
Mildred Dunnock

A corpse poses problems for various people in New England.

A classic macabre comedy which was panned on release for being tasteless. Actually, the tastelessness is part of the fun; and this is the film in which Hitchcock comes closest to Buñuel in his sly mockery of bourgeois society. John Michael Hayes's script starts out as farcical, then deepens into something more disturbing. This is one of the few examples of film noir to make effective use of colour: Robert Burks's Technicolor exteriors of autumnal Vermont are superb, and add to the feeling of decay. Bernard Herrmann's jaunty score, his first for Hitchcock, helps keep the audience pleasantly off-balance throughout. Although John Forsythe is, er, stiff, the rest of the cast is lively enough, with Shirley MacLaine's début (as Harry's widow) especially amusing. The film was one of Hitchcock's favourites, but a rare failure for him at the box office.

ANTI:

'Has, I fear, neither the desperation which makes the predicament of its characters wryly enjoyable nor the urbanity which would make their actions sympathetic . . . Everybody carries on in a manner to describe which I am driven to use a word I generally deny myself: whimsical. And because there is no urgency there is no comedy, nothing matters. Worn out, no doubt, by the archness of the script, the cast, led by Edmund Gwenn, take refuge in extreme deliberation; only Mildred Dunnock and newcomer Shirley MacLaine, escape the general lethargy. The New England scenery, however, flaunts its autumn banners unclouded by this boring little misfire.' *(Dilys Powell)*

'Hitchcock is reluctant to follow the subversive premises of the story through to their outrageous logical conclusion; the dialogue's sexual innuendoes now seem coy and awkward; the male leads are wooden; and the discreet style stranded by that dreaded British restraint so dear to the director.

Now, if Buñuel had made it . . . ' *(Geoff Andrew, Time Out)*

MIXED:

'It would be quite unfair to suggest [it] does not come off. Cast and director handle the comedy with delightful composure and polite mirth, but the situation lacks variety and . . . it palls on one occasion.' *(Jympson Harmon, Evening News)*

PRO:

'I found it in excellent, if eccentric taste . . . Hitchcock leads us through the improbable but absolutely convincing plot.' *(Alan Brien, Evening Standard)*

'Only Alfred Hitchcock would think of making a funny film about a corpse and get away with it.' *(Roy Nash, Star)*

'The most comically outrageous whodunit in living memory . . . beautifully performed . . . There is a stunning new girl star – a crop-headed poppet named Shirley MacLaine, who has a flat, round face and the devilish tranquillity of a highly intelligent cat.' *(Fred Majdalany, Daily Mail)*

TRUE GRIT

CT: 6 AV: 7.23

1969 US 128 C WESTERN/DRAMA/COMEDY

D Henry Hathaway
W Marguerite Roberts from Charles Portis's novel

John Wayne ☆ AAW Kim Darby ☆ Glen Campbell ● Jeremy Slate Robert Duvall ✔ Dennis Hopper ✔ Alfred Ryder

A teenage girl (Kim Darby) shames a clapped-out, hard-drinking, old marshal (John Wayne) to avenge the murder of her father.

Sam Peckinpah told a similar story much better in *Ride the High Country* (1962); but he didn't have John Wayne. Henry Hathaway's film has several serious defects – too slow a pace, a pitiful performance from singer Glen Campbell as a Texas Ranger, and a script that should have been sharper. The villains (Robert Duvall and Dennis Hopper) are good, though, and Wayne is near his best, half-mocking his own image in the role that won him an overdue Oscar.

'An amusing, unassuming western, antiheroic with a vengeance.' *(John Simon)*

'The first time I have ever seen the movies use John Wayne intelligently . . . There are other likable things in *True Grit*: sturdy, no-nonsense direction by Henry Hathaway; a script with a wonderful regard for details such as a boarding-house that makes cowboys check in their spurs before sitting down to chicken and dumplings (the table legs are scratched enough already); judges who eat peppermints in court to settle their stomachs before a hanging; dialogue like "I was raised Episcopal"/"I figured you for some kinda kneeler"; and beautiful, sensitive color photography by Lucien Ballard . . . But most of the credit for making *True Grit* more than just a routine western programmer belongs to Kim Darby, one of the few young actresses in American movies today worth building a movie around.' *(Rex Reed)*

'Kim Darby makes an extraordinary impression of matter-of-fact, undecorated charm combined with the vengeful temper and the ultimate indifference to human life which were surely characteristic of the pioneering west. One can say that this is a rather old-fashioned film – old-fashioned title, old-fashioned rough humour; no psychological interpolations; none of the careful sadism which has become a feature of up-to-date Westerns; simply the ferocity, kill or be killed, of a society perilously in the making.' *(Dilys Powell)*

'Readers may remember it as a book about a girl, but it's a film about John Wayne.' *(Stanley Kauffmann)*

'Hathaway is seventy years old and has been making action films since 1933, so he knows instinctively, it seems, when he may invoke our laughter at the conventions of the western, when he must retain his seriousness about them. But perhaps the most important element in the film's triumph is John Wayne. He has discovered what's funny about the character he has always played (one has observed him working toward this knowledge in several recent movies), and now he gives us a rich double vision of it. He is himself, and he is himself playing himself – an exuberant put-on that seems to delight him as much as it does us.' *(Richard Schickel)*

'Wayne steals the film in the role of tough, colorful Rooster Cogburn.' *(William Wolf, Cue)*

'*True Grit* is not the western to end all westerns. But it's sure as straight-shootin' a western as ever was to celebrate all westerns and the west that was and the American dreams of self-reliance, resourcefulness, gumption, git-up-and-go – and grit. It's a josh and a joy, irreverent but never disrespectful, a fairy tale which, like all fairy tales, we can believe or not, and would rather.' *(LA Times)*

TRUE LIES

CT: 8 AV: 6 (est)

1994 US 135 C ACTION/ADVENTURE

D James Cameron ✔
W James Cameron ✔ based on Claude Zidi, Simon Michael and Didier Kaminka's screenplay

Arnold Schwarzenegger ✔ Jamie Lee Curtis ✔ Tom Arnold ✔ Bill Paxton Tia Carrere Art Malik Eliza Dushku Grant Heslov

American spy (Arnold Schwarzenegger) terrorizes terrorists and his wife (Jamie Lee Curtis).

True Lies is, as every schoolboy used to know, an oxymoron. Its star, Arnold Schwarzenegger, though built like an ox, is anything but a moron. Hollywood's most likeable monster – the Abominable Showman – is back in harness with the writer-director of his *Terminator* films, James Cameron; they're both on top form. Spectacularly silly, exhilaratingly explosive, it proves that nothing succeeds like excess.

This is the kind of movie where terrorists have access to billions of pounds of weaponry, yet not one of them can shoot straight. Hero Harry Trasker is so impervious to bullets that he makes *RoboCop* seem sissy, so cool he makes James Bond look educationally subnormal: at some point during Harry's glittering career as a one-man army, he has found time off to learn six languages fluently, take a degree in nuclear physics and become an expert dancer of the tango – although we have to take these terpsichorean skills on trust. Director Cameron never dares to show us Arnold's feet and his face in the same shot, except at the end, when Jamie Lee Curtis throws herself about a bit, while hubby exhibits all the grace and manoeuvrability of a Giant Redwood. There's something endearing about a multi-million dollar action-movie whose least convincing stunt is its hero pretending he can dance.

Otherwise, the least plausible aspect of the film is its central gimmick, which is that Harry's wife (who is accustomed to waiting patiently at home, Penelope to his Ulysses) thinks he's a boring computer-salesman, and pines for a more adventurous life. This idea is all that remains of the tiny French movie on which *True Lies* is based – Claude Zidi's *La Totale!* (1992). Despite an enjoyable (and sexy) light comedy performance by Jamie Lee Curtis, this domestic sub-plot fails to convince, not so much because of Arnold's limitations as a comedy actor, as because his physique is not exactly that of the average computer-salesman.

There's also something disturbing about the way he indulges in illegal wire-tapping merely to test the fidelity of his wife. He misuses federal resources to victimize the used-car salesman creep (Bill Paxton) who's out to seduce her with promises of a more exciting existence. True, Schwarzenegger's character gets a kind of comeuppance when his wife whacks him over the head with a telephone, but a man of Arnie's size has to watch out or he can easily come across as a bully. Feminists, Civil Rights activists, Muslim fundamentalists and used-car salesmen will all find something in this film to upset them.

But this darker side is the thing that makes *True Lies* so interesting. In this movie, Schwarzenegger gets to play the principal villain, as well as the hero. Like his Arab fundamentalist adversary, he has no sense of moral perspective, applying the same obsessive determination to his personal life that he does to saving the world. Harry's no saint. He's lied to his wife throughout 15 years of marriage; he's not a good father to his teenage daughter; when he thinks his wife is deceiving him, he becomes as jealous as Othello, and as devious as Iago. And he thinks nothing of using terrorist tactics in his private life as well as his career.

Some critics seized on all this as if it were a hidden flaw that only they have spotted. But the film-makers brandish this paradox before us. Hence the oxymoronic title – one man's truth is another man's lie; one country's terrorist is another land's freedom-fighter. The middle, romantic comedy section of the movie isn't padding. It is central to the main theme, which shows Harry (and, by implication, American foreign policy) in terms of patriarchy and challenged virility.

Now that the moral certainties of the Cold War have collapsed, the spy movie needed to find not only new villains, but also a different kind of post-Bond hero, a red-blooded heterosexual who would flirt with women but not wish to bed them, an intelligent man who could still wear the kind of moral blinkers which would allow him to function as a professional assassin.

'Have you ever . . . killed anyone?' Arnold's wife asks him, finally rumbling him as a spy. 'Yeah,' he says poker-faced, 'But they were all BAD.' The great thing about Schwarzenegger is that he can play such lines straight, while happy to leave others to poke fun at his machismo. Many of the best lines fall to his fellow-spy (Tom Arnold), who reckons he knows what has gone wrong with Arnie's marriage – 'You're just not,' he quips, 'in touch with your feminine side.'

And that is really why a lot of intellectuals won't like *True Lies*. Behind its jocular tone, its assumptions are profoundly masculine, sincerely right-wing – hold on to what's yours, protect your interests, and fight back with every means at your disposal, fair or foul. Whether in the field of international politics or domestic relationships, Harry Tasker is the 90s' answer to Dirty Harry. It's hard to see how he would fit in with a wimpish Clinton administration, still less the Clinton approach to personal relationships, but perhaps this paradox could form the basis of the inevitable sequel.

Schwarzenegger's action-movies have always explored serious topics ranging from fear of technology *(Terminator 2)* to child abuse *(Kindergarten Cop)*. Here, apart from the dark-light dichotomy within the hero, there is a half-submerged subtext about the way couples can lose emotional contact with each other through concentration on careers or parenthood. Unfortunately, the movie's solution seems a shade simplistic: apparently the important thing is to discover things you enjoy in common, like humiliating used-car salesmen or blowing up terrorists.

But I wouldn't wish to make *True Lies* sound nasty or pretentious, still less a failure. First and foremost, it's a romp – a hugely enjoyable romp. After the comparative failure of *The Last Action Hero*, it's a triumphant comeback by Big Arnie, who here takes Hollywood giantism to agreeably outrageous extremes. If you don't come out of this picture wearing a silly, incredulous grin, then maybe action blockbusters just aren't your scene.

'I liked the comedy potential of the lies, the facades,

the allegory of relationships. For me, this movie is about the unknowability of people. And I loved the potential of Arnold playing the spy role. Arnold lives in a strange, dialectic world. On one hand, he's a family man; on the other, he's a superstar, which means that so much is expected of him.' *(James Cameron)*

'During the interrogation, she [Harry's wife] says her life is boring. She needs excitement, to be at risk. My character realizes he hasn't given her the life she wanted, so he starts giving her the excitement right there. She was begging for it.' *(Arnold Schwarzenegger)*

ANTI:

'It's in three very distinct parts, the middle one – marital comedy stuff – involving an alarming drop in dramatic tension . . . Some will say it's harmless fun, but . . . Helen is dim enough to be duped by both husband and slimeball suitor; moreover for the sin of even letting herself *consider* an adventure away from hubby, Harry – still persisting in his own deceit as he acts incognito – punishes Helen by humiliating, manhandling, imprisoning and interrogating her, before tricking her into doing a strip for a shady stranger played by himself . . . This is woman not only as man's possession, but as a Galatea-like creation to be leered at. Post-modern pastiche or unthinking misogyny? . . . I'd bet on the latter.' *(Geoff Andrew, Time Out)*

'A loud misfire. It rarely brings its potent themes to life. And it seems not to realize that Harry is less a hero than a wife-abusing goon . . . Will audiences have fun at *True Lies*? Count on it. They will giggle at the embarrassment of Paxton's character, who is punished by having to pee in his pants – twice. They will savor the spectacle of the delightful Curtis screaming in inane fear more often than any other actress since Fay Wray in *King Kong*. They will enjoy the lavishing and squandering of talent by Hollywood's shrewdest showman. No question, you get a lot of movie for your $7.50. It's just not the right movie.' *(Richard Corliss, Time)*

MIXED:

'*True Lies* has a lot of . . . laugh-out-loud moments when the violence is so cartoonish we don't take it seriously, and yet are amazed at its inventiveness and audacity. Schwarzenegger has found himself in a lot of unlikely situations in his action-packed career, and *True Lies* seems determined to raise the ante – to go over the top with outlandish and extravagant special effects scenes . . . [It] doesn't rank as high as *Terminator 2* and *Total Recall* among Schwarzenegger's action epics for a couple of reasons: the unconvincing interlude where the hero suspects adultery, and the perfunctory nature of the plot. Both earlier titles had tighter, more absorbing stories. But on the basis of stunts, special effects and pure action, it delivers sensationally.' *(Roger Ebert)*

TRULY, MADLY, DEEPLY CT: 7 AV: 6.67

(aka *Cello*)

1990 GB C DRAMA/ROMANCE/FANTASY

D Anthony Minghella
W Anthony Minghella

Juliet Stevenson ☆ Alan Rickman Bill Paterson Michael Maloney Jenny Howe Christopher Rozycki

A North London woman (Juliet Stevenson), whose lover (Alan Rickman) has died, can't get over him, and wishes he would come back. Miraculously he does. She finds herself torn between living with a ghost – which has its inconveniences – and finding a new love, in the form of a sensitive social worker and amateur conjuror (Michael Maloney).

Like many British TV writers, Minghella is good at irony at the expense of his characters' foibles; but he also has the very un-English and much more cinematic ability to portray raw emotion – from the depths of grief to the heights of joy. At both ends of this emotional spectrum, he is wonderfully served by Juliet Stevenson, whose complex reactions to bereavement show up the sanitized acting of Demi Moore in *Ghost*: this performance should have earned Miss Stevenson an Oscar nomination. She is given able support by Alan Rickman (at his most Eeyore-like) and Michael Maloney (a more than passable Piglet).

Most people love it, but some people really hate it. It's a superior TV play rather than madly cinematic. Even on a miserly £600,000 budget, the continuity between shots (as regards time, lighting and weather) should have been better. Minghella doesn't move the camera much, and his visual symbolism (mainly involving clouds) is mechanical, clichéd and – because its meaning is unclear – pretentious. There are moments of unbearable cuteness; and Michael Maloney and Miss Stevenson play such Hampsteady goody-goodies (he's an art therapist for the mentally handicapped, she helps immigrants to speak English) that some may find them smug rather than appealing.

Still, anyone who enjoyed *Manhattan* and *Annie Hall*, or who admired Whit Stillman's *Metropolitan*, should see this. It's a witty, civilized chamber-piece which manages, in a deceptively lightweight way, to say a lot about how people cope with losing a loved one.

ANTI:

'Strays into sentimentality and is nearly rescued by Juliet Stevenson's superb performance . . . [It] starts out as a refreshing original, then gets sabotaged by its own cuteness.' *(Ed Kelleher, Film Journal)*

'My Cannes notice . . . called the film "unwatchable". That has to be untrue since I watched it . . . The film has been eulogised in America and no movie with Alan Rickman can be all bad . . . But despite the big emotional themes Minghella tilts at, from bereavement to life-rebuilding, the keynote remains cosiness.' *(Nigel Andrews, Financial Times)*

'Predictably, the critics loved it – truly, madly and very deeply. They praised the performance of Juliet Stevenson, as the necrophiliac, to the skies. Aye. there's the rub! That's what it was – a performance – a word often associated with seals balancing balls on their noses. What they do is clever, but you couldn't call it acting. There were several occasions when I almost expected Ms Stevenson to pat herself on the back for being so clever. Every blink of an eye, tilt of the chin, twitch of the nose seemed choreographed to the demands of the script. I didn't catch one moment of honest emotion. The ghost of Alan Rickman was far more real. Even so, I don't buy it. Reality and fantasy seldom mix. It all left me as cold as a dead man's dick.' *(Ken Russell, 1993)*

MIXED:

'A funny and thoroughly absorbing movie, yet there's more than things that go rumpy-pumpy in the night to disturb us here . . . Occasionally irritating ickiness aside, Minghella's first feature has wit . . . File under beautifully modulated ensemble piece.' *(Nick James, City Limits)*

'Beautifully acted . . . Has arch moments, but in the main stays matter-of-fact.' *(Shaun Usher, Daily Mail)*

PRO:

'Its special distinction is not just the solidity and humanity of its ghosts, but its very European sentiment and use of pure fantasy.' *(Hugh Hebert, Guardian)*

'This is one of those films that splits the sexes, with the distaff side generally thinking it witty, romantic and deserving of a good weep while many males reckon it sloppy tripe. Whichever camp you're in, there are some splendid moments to treasure in this British version of *Ghost*, which looks better on the small screen for which it was originally intended.' *(Rose)*

TSVET GRANATA: *see* COLOUR OF POMEGRANATES, THE.

TUNES OF GLORY CT: 6 AV: 7.91

1960 GB 106 C DRAMA

D Ronald Neame
W James Kennaway ✗ AAN from his novel

Alec Guinness ☆ John Mills ☆ Dennis Price Susannah York John Fraser Allan Cuthbertson Kay Walsh John MacKenzie Gordon Jackson Duncan Macrae

A disciplinarian (John Mills) takes over a regiment from an old hand (Alec Guinness), who's allegedly losing his grip.

Stirring, well acted personal battle with two juicy parts for the leading actors. It won Mills the best actor award at the Venice Film Festival. Neame's plodding direction doesn't add anything, though, and Arthur Ibbetson's cinematography isn't up to the level of his work on *The Angry Silence* or *The Railway Children*. Kennaway's screenplay begins strongly, then loses its way in the final half-hour, with a twist too far.

PRO:

'A storming performance by Guinness, one of the best things he has ever done.' *(Fred Majdalany, Daily Mail)*

'A film which has life in it.' *(Dilys Powell)*

MIXED:

'Even without [Guinness and Mills] this would not be a bad film . . . The story has, however, a big dramatic weakness: its final tragedy is really not prepared for by what precedes it.' *(Guardian)*

'The script . . . manoeuvres skilfully, developing the situations out of the characters. Until the denouement, that is, when the film lurches into high old melodrama.' *(David Robinson, The Times)*

'One doesn't want to carp at high-grade entertainment, because if this film isn't another *Paths of Glory* – what film is? – it's a pleasant change from *Kwai* and the years that the stiff upper lips have eaten.' *(John Morgan, New Statesman)*

'The story needs a large swallow. But Neame's sensitive direction exactly captures the humours and tensions.' *(Frank Lewis, Sunday Dispatch)*

TURN OF THE SCREW, THE: *see* THE INNOCENTS.

12 ANGRY MEN CT: 9 AV: 8.87

1957 US 95 BW DRAMA

D Sidney Lumet ☆
W Reginald Rose ☆ from his television play

Henry Fonda ☆ Lee J. Cobb ☆ Ed Begley ☆ E.G. Marshall ☆ Jack Warden ☆ Martin Balsam ☆ Jack Klugman ☆ George Voskovec ☆ Robert Webber ☆ Edward Binns ☆ Joseph Sweeney ☆ John Fiedler ☆

Jury-room melodrama, with Henry Fonda winning round 11 jurors to his view of a seemingly open-and-shut case.

It wasn't a hit with a public, who may have distrusted its bleeding-heart liberal assumptions; but the critics rightly admired this accomplished directorial début by Sidney Lumet, who went on to make films such as *Dog Day Afternoon* and *Network* – but nothing better than this. It's neat, gripping and much imitated, with a faultless ensemble cast.

ANTI:

'The argument is too hard to sustain and the end of the film lapsing into near pathos makes other directors appear double wise who stick to the things the cinema has always done well.' *(Times Educational Supplement)*

MIXED:

'A film which with outstanding success uses the enclosed scene . . . The writing is remarkable for the skill with which it turns to advantage the restrictions imposed by the form of the plot. And the film is splendidly played . . . Only in the last passages does the entry of that old transatlantic bore father-and-son-trouble admit a false touch of hysteria. For the rest *12 Angry Men* holds the attention unquestioning.' *(Dilys Powell)*

PRO:

'A tense, taut claustrophobic piece of work . . . exciting, serious-minded and brilliantly acted.' *(The Times)*

'I veritably believe it will prove to be not only the picture of the year but many other years. It's a remarkable piece of moviecraft . . . What gives it significance and majesty is the sense of warm compassion that inspires each one of its 95 minutes.' *(Peter Burnup, News of the World)*

'One of the tightest, tensest and most absorbing films of the year . . . the tension never slackens. Henry Fonda gives the performance of his career.' *(Leonard Mosley, Daily Express)*

'A dozen brilliant character studies in a script of extraordinary perception and vitality . . . Not once does the powerful accent break down the illusion of [the jury's] everyday ordinariness.' *(Morning Herald)*

'An unusual, gripping and worthwhile film.' *(Frank Jackson, Reynolds News)*

'Works up quite a lot of ingenious suspense as it analyzes its various characters . . . The clashing motivation to keep this group in turmoil have been neatly worked out . . . and Mr Lumet has managed to avoid monotony . . . Practically everybody on hand is commendable.' *(John McCarten, New Yorker)*

'A penetrating, shocking dissection of the hearts and minds of men who obviously are something less than gods. It makes for taut, absorbing, compelling drama . . . Henry Fonda gives his most forceful portrayal in years.' *(A.H. Weiler, New York Times)*

'These pictures may lose money, but they have inspired applause from those who still think freely and for themselves. These pictures have gone beyond Hollywood formulas and ingredients, and will affect strongly the future of American motion pictures.' *(John Cassavettes, Film Culture, 1959)*

'One of the most revered examples of the genre . . . [it] established [Lumet's] concerns with the workings of the judicial system and fondness for central characters whose actions are dictated by conscience regardless of the personal consequences.' *(Allan Hunter & Kenny Mathieson, Movie Classics 1992)*

TWELVE O'CLOCK HIGH AAN CT: 7 AV: 7.69

1949 US 132 BW WAR

D Henry King ☆
W Sy Bartlett Beirne Lay Jr from their novel

Gregory Peck ☆ AAN Hugh Marlowe ✔
Gary Merrill ✔ Dean Jagger ☆ AAW Millard Mitchell
Robert Arthur

A US officer in Britain (Gary Merrill) is replaced for becoming too emotionally involved with the pilots he is sending over to bomb Germany; his replacement (Gregory Peck) doesn't find the job any easier.

Probably the best picture about the pressures which war imposes on those at the top – although the underrated *Sink The Bismarck!* (1960) comes close. Leon Shamroy's photography is at its best in the aerial sequences, and Henry King's sensitive direction draws fine performances from the leading actors. Modern audiences may find much of the drama run of the mill (it's often been imitated, in movies such as *Memphis Belle*), but the film's anti-heroic, realistic approach to warfare was unusual so soon after a war.

MIXED:

'A top-flight drama, polished and performed to the nth degree . . . [But] all war pictures are beginning to be stamped with a familiarity that cries for a new character and story set-up.' *(Variety)*

PRO:

'There hasn't yet been . . . [a war picture] from Hollywood which could compare in rugged realism and punch to *Twelve O'Clock High*, a top-flight drama.' *(Bosley Crowther)*.

'The best war film since the fighting stopped.' *(Daily Mirror)*

'A denial of the schoolboy sentimentality which falsely sweetens so much of the cinema of war; the figures in the story are heroes indeed, but there are . . . no heroics. As a result our understanding of danger becomes much more acute.' *(Dilys Powell)*

TWENTIETH CENTURY CT: 7 AV: 7.82

1934 US 91 BW COMEDY

D Howard Hawks ☆
W Charles MacArthur Ben Hecht ☆ from their play from Charles Bruce Milholland's play *Napoleon on Broadway*

John Barrymore ☆ Carole Lombard ☆
Roscoe Karns ✔ Walter Connolly ✔ Ralph Forbes
Dale Fuller Etienne Girardot ☆

Egotistical producer Oscar Jaffe (John Barrymore) takes advantage of a lengthy train journey to woo the shopgirl (Carole Lombard) whom he made into a Broadway star.

Top-notch screwball comedy which, though never a hit with the public (it's very New Yorker-sophisticated), gave Barrymore his funniest role. Some of the wisecracks in the script have dated, but Hawks's pacy direction and lively performances more than compensate. Later turned into a hit Broadway musical, *On the Twentieth Century*.

ANTI:

'Oh, no, the nineteenth, surely.' *(Time)*

MIXED:

'Probably too smart for general consumption.' *(Variety)*

'I don't say that this is more than farce, or that Jaffe is not largely a caricature, but it is good farce, and Jaffe is a good caricature.' *(Punch)*

PRO:

'Shows an extraordinary combination of technical talents, the whole thing moving quickly and even naturally from one incredible situation to another without any loose joints. Great fun.' *(MFB)*

'Superb satire of theatrical temperament and [a] neat way of telling a story.' *(Observer)*

'Barrymore's performance is a grand piece of burlesque, rich in mockery, full of frenzy.' *(Sunday Express)*

'In the role of Jaffe, John Barrymore fits as wholly and smoothly as a banana in a skin.' *(John Barrymore)*

'The first comedy in which sexually attractive, sophisticated stars indulged in their own slapstick instead of delegating it to their inferiors.' *(Andrew Sarris, 1963)*

'The film not only takes place on a train, it moves like one too.' *(Geoff Brown, Time Out)*

20,000 LEAGUES UNDER THE SEA

CT: 7 AV: 7.25

1954 US 127 C SF/ACTION/ADVENTURE/FAMILY

D Richard Fleischer ✔
W Earl Felton from Jules Verne's novel

Kirk Douglas James Mason ☆ Paul Lukas Peter Lorre ✔ Robert J. Wilke Carlton Young Ted de Corsia

Victorian scientists are kidnapped at sea by Captain Nemo (James Mason) and his submarine.

Most critics recognized this immediately as one of the best live-action Disney adventures (it was the first put out by the Disney offshoot, Buena Vista); it is one of those rare family films which don't patronize their adult audience. Kirk Douglas's performance strikes some as charismatic, others (including me) as tiresomely narcissistic; but there's no question that James Mason makes a superb Captain Nemo. The submarine is a lovely piece of set design, with luxurious Victorian interiors; Academy Awards went to John Meehan and Emile Kuri for best art direction and set decoration. Even the most blasé child should be enthralled by the fight with the giant squid (the visual effects team also won an Oscar). Elmo Williams was also nominated for his film editing.

MIXED:

'Only the setting and the peculiar cast distinguish this ponderous production from the average third-rate adventure story.' *(F & F)*

PRO:

'A very special kind of picture-making, combining photographic ingenuity, imaginative story-telling and fiscal daring.' *(Variety)*

'Fun for all ages.' *(Newsweek)*

'As fabulous and fantastic as anything he [Disney] has ever done in cartoons.' *(New York Times)*

'The production abounds in belly laughs and spine-tingling thrills, set forward with an all-important air of plausibility.' *(Jack Moffitt, Hollywood Reporter)*

'A marvellous combination of a good script, excellent performances – especially Mason's Nemo – and stunning art direction and special effects, both winning Oscars.' *(Alan Frank)*

TWENTY-FOUR HOUR LOVE AFFAIR: *see* HIROSHIMA MON AMOUR.

TWO MOON JUNCTION

CT: 5 AV: 3.00

1988 US 104 C DRAMA/ROMANCE/SO BAD

D Zalman King ●
W Zalman King from Zalman King MacGregor Douglas's story

Sherilyn Fenn ● Richard Tyson ● Louise Fletcher ● Burl Ives Kristy McNichol Martin Hewitt Juanita Moore Don Galloway Millie Perkins

A virginal but voyeuristic southern belle (Sherilyn Fenn) appears destined for an aristocratic marriage. However, when a carnival comes to town, she finds herself strangely affected by a muscle-bound ride attendant (Richard Tyson), or possibly his big dipper. In no time at all, she is trying to have her beefcake and eat it.

A film which was lavishly publicized as pushing back the frontiers of sensuality. It is, in fact, the most flaccid soft porn imaginable; the only original aspect, the southern setting, is wasted; and the dialogue puts the rot back into erotica. British audiences may particularly enjoy the unintended double entendre when our heroine's lot of rough meets her the night before her marriage, produces a puppy from between his legs, and murmurs 'I was thinking about giving you one for your wedding present'.

'A bad hick version of *Last Tango in Paris*.' *(Variety)*

'Sex-mad director King could lay claim to being the postmodern Russ Meyer – except that he actually seems to take his crackpot oeuvre seriously . . . Louise Fletcher [is] terrifying in a wig that looks as if it's made of Dream Whip.' *(Margulies & Rebello)*

'A classic example of the Zalman King recipe at work: glitzy camerawork, camp performances, blatant Freudian symbolism and just enough plot to reassure viewers they're not watching out-and-out porn. Deadly.' *(Rose)*

'Sick-making.' *(Suzy Feay, Time Out)*

'Really dumb.' *(Scheuer)*

'Slice of poseurs porno . . . Its a slow, draggy, stately, downright tedious little movie. Fenn and Tyson are one-star acting talents trapped in five-star bodies, and their nipples are more expressive than their faces.' *(Kim Newman, Film Yearbook)*

2001: A SPACE ODYSSEY CT: 7 AV: 9.25

1968 GB 141/149 C SF

D Stanley Kubrick ☆
W Stanley Kubrick Arthur C. Clarke from Clarke's story *The Sentinel*

Gary Lockwood Keir Dullea William Sylvester Leonard Rossiter Robert Beatty Daniel Richter Douglas Rain (voice of HAL).

The story of mankind, from apeman to spaceman.

2001 has maintained its reputation as a classic because, more than any other science fiction movie, it evokes the grandeur of space. Unfortunately, the ending looks more like a 60s acid trip than anything else and dates the film badly. And the small screen accentuates the absence of plot.

One reason why *2001* elicits very mixed reactions is that, like *Blade Runner*, it visualizes a tediously dehumanized future, in which people are less human than machines. HAL, the spaceship computer, is the nearest the film has to a fully developed character.

Contemporary critics were mostly enthusiastic, though vague about what the film actually meant. A few found it turgid and pretentious, however, and such doubts have persisted. The best way to enjoy the film is to slip the logical parts of ones mind into neutral and abandon yourself to the experience; the film has always had a following among junkies.

In 1968, Stanley Kubrick explained why he made the film and noticeably fought shy of philosophical or allegorical analysis: 'I tried to create a visual experience, one that bypasses verbalized pigeonholing and directly penetrates the subconscious with an emotional and philosophical content . . . I intended the film to be an intensely subjective experience that reaches the viewer at an inner level of consciousness, just as music does.'

Not surprisingly, the special effects won an Academy Award. The art direction (Tony Masters, Harry Lange and Ernie Archer) was nominated. Peter Hyams made an underrated sequel, *2010* (1984), which is worth seeing for its special effects.

PRO:

'Some sort of great film, and an unforgettable endeavor.' *(Penelope Gilliatt)*

'One of the few giant movies that one wouldn't want an inch smaller. Marvellously ingenious, tantalising and intelligent, as well as having the irresistible allure of a space age motor show.' *(S & S)*

'The most impressive part of this picture is the collection of superbly made machines Stanley Kubrick has got together and the visions of space he has dreamed up.' *(People)*

'A parable of a future toward which metaphysical dread and mordant amusement trip side by side . . . I have never seen the death of the mind rendered more profoundly or poetically . . . *2001* is concerned ultimately with the inner fears of Kubrick's mind as it contemplates infinity and eternity . . . There is absolutely nowhere we can go to escape ourselves.' *(Andrew Sarris)*

'Every moment of the lens has a surprising yet slow lift and lilt to it . . . Big as it is, the screen is but a slit through which to comprehend immensities that always escape the frame. The film is haunted by imminences always outside, left and right, above and beneath, its depth of field – imminences which make even the most complete local information look arbitrary in face of the scope now opened up.' *(Max Kozloff, Film Culture, 1970)*

'*2001* deals everywhere in dispersal, boundlessness, mystery – concepts which the stupendous battery of special effects projects with an astronomical and scientific precision that shades ultimately into metaphysics and philosophy.' *(Alexander Walker, Stanley Kubrick Directs, 1971)*

MIXED:

'I shrink from the cold pitiless worlds into whose light Kubrick leads us . . . [but] the film with its ranging imagination and its superb execution (laurels, surely, for British technicians) is an adventure not to be missed.' *(Dilys Powell)*

'Big, beautiful, but plodding and confusing.' *(Variety)*

'Kubrick dares to move at an ultra-slow pace to create his very special atmosphere. This he overdoes with repetition, as if unable to edit the visually fabulous sequences. Nevertheless, in total it is a brilliantly conceived cosmic adventure.' *(William Wolf, Cue)*

'The ponderous, blurry appeal of the picture may be in its mystical vision of a graceful world of space, controlled by superior, godlike minds . . . It says that man is just a tiny nothing on the stairway to paradise; something better (ie non-human) is coming, and it's all out of your hands.' *(Pauline Kael)*

ANTI:

'Either an exercise in transcendental meditation or a bloody bore, depending on your point of view.' *(Richard Schickel, Life)*

'The slab, of course, is never explained, leaving *2001*, for all its lively visual and mechanical spectacle, a kind of space-*Spartacus* and, more pretentious still, a shaggy god story.' *(John Simon)*

'Has he [Kubrick] gone to all this trouble . . . to tell us that life goes on from tomb to womb, that there's something, or someone, out there who's going to outlast us all, and that there's a star in heaven for every baby born? And even if this were not too banal to bear repetition, should its repetition be in technical terms all-too-familiar to watchers of a number of television series, with techniques more effectively used in various Expo films?' *(Judith Crist)*

'A film in which infinite care, intelligence, patience, imagination and Cinerama have been devoted to what looks like the apotheosis of the fantasy of a precocious, early nineteen-fifties boy . . . The movie is so completely absorbed in its own problems, its use of color and space, its fanatical devotion to science fiction detail, that it is somewhere between hypnotic and immensely boring.' *(Renata Adler, New York Times)*

'Incredibly ponderous and languid. For producer-director Stanley Kubrick plays with his model hardware like a child with a construction set – and I was on the outside not allowed in.' *(Daily Sketch)*

'One feels that this most deliberate of artists has lost control over his materials. It is morally pretentious, intellectually obscure, and inordinately long . . . [Kubrick] has succumbed to technological fetishism. One noticed the first symptoms in *Dr Strangelove*. In *2001* he has gone mad over electronic artefacts – flashing dials, rotating wheels, computer consoles, space stations. Alas, the technical detail is not only overwhelming but unclear. Obsession continues to outrun explanation, and this reviewer, at least, could not understand a good deal of what was going on.' *(Arthur Schlesinger Jr, Vogue)*

'Process became more important than plot. The tedium was the message.' *(Joseph Gelmis, The Film Director as Superstar, 1970)*

'A special effects movie in search of a plot.' *(Alan Frank)*

'Pretty half-baked. Quite how the general theme fits in with the central drama of the astronauts battle with the arrogant computer HAL, who tries to take over their mission, is unclear; while the final farrago of light-show psychedelia is simply so much pap.' *(Geoff Andrew, Time Out)*

TWO WOMEN

CT: 5 AV: 7.89

(aka *La Ciociara*)

1961 Italy/France 110 BW WAR/FOREIGN

D Vittorio De Sica
W Cesare Zavattini Vittoria De Sica from Alberto Moravia's novel

Sophia Loren ☆ AAW Jean-Paul Belmondo
Eleanora Brown Raf Vallone Renato Salvatori
Carlo Ninchi Andrea Checchi Pupella Maggio

An Italian mother (Sophia Loren) and her daughter (Eleanora Brown) are raped by Allied Moroccan soldiers during WW2.

Originally, the idea was for Sophia Loren to play the daughter; but Anna Magnani flatly refused to play Loren's mother. Redesigned as an old-fashioned, melodramatic star vehicle for Loren, the film won her the first ever Oscar for a non-American actress in a foreign-language film. Too bad that all the characters around her are so grievously under-written.

PRO:

'Loren is a fine Italian ham, but unfortunately most US directors can't see the prosciutto for the melon. De Sica knows better . . . [Here she] makes a superlative tigress. Cunning, selfish, sensual, ferocious and above all female, she leaps on her passions and tears them to spectacular tatters.' *(Time Magazine)*

'Belmondo . . . is so good as the sensitive, awkward-limbed youth that for a few minutes I did not realise I was seeing the same actor [from] *Breathless*.' *(Alexander Walker, Evening Standard)*

'A great film . . . touched by truth, great beauty, and poetry.' *(Felix Barker, Evening News)*

MIXED:

'Perhaps the trouble is there is too much of De Sica, he is too prolific, too undiscriminating . . . [The film] is a fair example of this dissipation of emotional energy. Not that [it] is a bad film . . . But the director's passionate care has gone.' *(Isabel Quigly, Spectator)*

'It remains difficult to determine exactly what [De Sica's] purpose is [in making the film at all] . . . At least [his] direction suits Miss Loren . . . by no means an Anna Magnani, yet something of Magnani's own fire, scorn and temperament are here.' *(The Times)*

UGETSU MONOGATARI CT: – AV: 8.42

(aka *Ugetsu; Tales of the Pale and Silvery Moon after Rain*)

1953 Japan 94 BW FANTASY/FOREIGN

D Kenji Mizoguchi ☆
W Matsutaro Kawaguchi Yoshikata Yoda from tales by Akinari Ueda and Guy de Maupassant

Machiko Kyo Masayuki Mori Kenuyo Tanaka Sakae Ozawa Mirsuko Mito Sugisaku Aoyama

Peasant potter (Masayuki Mori) and brother-in-law (Sakae Ozawa) yield to carnal temptations in the city, whereupon their wives are punished for their husbands' sins.

This beautiful, enigmatic, grindingly slow film made a big impression in the 50s; and many critics continue to regard it as a masterpiece. Its feminist theme (that women suffer through trying to indulge their menfolk) is unusual for its time and country of origin. Oscar-nominated for best costume design (Tadaoto Kainoscho).

PRO:

'One of the most beautiful films in the world.' *(Alexandre Astruc, Cahiers du Cinéma)*

'[An] authentic masterpiece [which poses] the question – what is reality?' *(Arthur Knight, The Liveliest Art, 1957)*

'Deservedly praised . . . One of the director's best films and one of the most perfect in the history of Japanese cinema . . . As a period film it was most unusual, fitting into no category at all, self-sufficient, nearly allegorical and a film experience both beautiful and disturbing.' *(Joseph Anderson & Donald Richie, The Japanese Film, 1982)*

'The most remarkable feature of the film to western audiences is the way in which it combines elements of everyday realism with fantasy and the supernatural. The transitions . . . are seamless rather than disruptive . . . It reflects Mizoguchi's own shift from the radical political standpoint of his earlier films towards a much more emphatic interest in aestheticism and spirituality . . . While some critics have found fault with the movement away from his more ideologically committed works, the film remains widely regarded as a master work.' *(Allan Hunter & Kenny Mathieson, Movie Classics, 1992)*

'A haunting, beautifully shot film. Among the scenes that stick in the memory are the spooky boat ride across the mist-shrouded water and Mori's strange homecoming.' *(Danny Peary)*

'Mizoguchi's unique establishment of atmosphere by means of long shot, long takes, sublimely graceful and unobtrusive camera movement, is everywhere evident . . . Ravishingly composed, evocatively beautiful.' *(Rod McShane, Time Out)*

MIXED:

'There are films I should like to like better, and Ugetsu Monogatari is one of them.' *(Dilys Powell)*

'Will be hard for American audiences to understand . . . for both the theme and the style of exposition . . . have a strangely obscure, inferential, almost studiously perplexing quality . . . [which gives it] a sort of eerie charm . . . If you have patience . . . you'll get flavor from this weird, exotic stew.' *(Bosley Crowther)*

'This subtle, violent yet magical film is one of the most amazing of the Japanese movies that played American art houses after the international success of *Rashomon* in 1951. The director, Kenji Mizoguchi, handles the narrative in two styles: barbaric sequences dealing with greed and civil war that seem realistic except that the characters are deliberately animalistic and are symbolically acting out the bestial side of man; and highly stylized sequences dealing with the aesthetic, luxurious, and romantic modes of life. The film is upsetting and unspeakably cruel at times, and then so suggestive and haunting that its confounding. Heavy going in spots, but with marvelous passages that are worth a bit of patience.' *(Pauline Kael)*

ANTI:

'Achieved the remarkable distinction of coming into fourth place [in the magazine's Ten Best Films of all Time]. Frankly, I simply fail to understand why . . . There are, of course, some isolated visually beautiful shots: what Japanese film hasn't. But overall I found the direction turgid to the point of boredom and the acting on the level of good hokum.' *(Paul Rotha, S & S, 1962)*

UKIGUSA: *see* FLOATING WEEDS.

ULTIMO TANGO A PARIGI: *see* LAST TANGO IN PARIS.

UMBERTO D. CT: 6 AV: 8.80

1969 Italy 89 BW DRAMA/FOREIGN

D Vittorio De Sica ☆
W Cesare Zavattini ☆ AAN from his story

Carlo Battisti Maria Pia Casilio Lina Gennari Alberto Albani Barbieri Elena Rea Ileana Simova Memmo Carotenuto

A pensioner (Carlo Battisti) reduced to penury chooses between begging and killing himself.

In *Shoeshine*, De Sica attacked Italy for not taking more care of its youth; here, he lashes out on behalf of the elderly. It's a moving but profoundly pessimistic analysis of old age, showing – as De Sica put it, 'the indifference of society towards suffering. They are a word in favour of the poor and unhappy'. Though the film is powerful and realistic, the leading actor is a non-professional and it shows; and the doom and gloom become overpowering. The film is the last of De Sica's 'neo-realist' period.

'No other medium of expression has the cinema's original and innate capacity for showing things in what we might call their "dailiness".' *(Cesare Zavattini, writer)*

PRO:

'Of works of art so instantly appealing and, I am sure, durable, the cinema has known few. I doubt whether De Sica will ever again quite reach this pinnacle.' *(William Whitebait, New Statesman)*

'A brilliant study.' *(Roy Nash, Star)*

'An abiding picture . . . one of the most outstanding moving pictures of our time.' *(C.A. Lejeune, Observer)*

'The best film De Sica has made.' *(Dilys Powell, Sunday Times)*

'A great piece of movie-making . . . handling the problem of lonely, impoverished old age with great understanding, bounteous compassion and no sentimentality.' *(Jympson Harman, Evening News)*

MIXED:

'All "neo-realist" directors who use non-actors are playing roulette, not always successfully – De Sica succeeded with non-actors in *The Bicycle Thief*; but *Umberto D.*, which ought to have been a masterpiece, is not because the old man in the title role is inadequate.' *(Stanley Kauffmann, 1979)*

UMBRELLAS OF CHERBOURG, THE AAN

CT: 6 AV: 7.50

(aka *Les Parapluies De Cherbourg*)

1964 France/West Germany 92 C MUSICAL/ ROMANCE/FOREIGN

D Jacques Demy
W Jacques Demy AAN (songs by Jacques Demy, Michel Legrand AAN)

Catherine Deneuve Nino Castelnuovo Anne Vernon Ellen Farner Marc Michel Mireille Perrey

A shop-girl (Catherine Deneuve) falls in love with a service station attendant (Nino Castelnuovo), but he is called up for military service.

Sickly-sweet musical with a tinkly Michel Legrand score and entirely sung dialogue. Jean Rabier's pretty-pretty cinematography is not to all tastes, and Demy seems determined to make Hollywood movies like *The Sound of Music* look hard-edged. Many people adore it, however; it's ruthlessly professional at jerking the tears; and it was voted best film at Cannes. It was Oscar-nominated for best song ('I Will Wait for You'). Legrand received two further nominations for composition and scoring.

PRO:

'The first opera film . . . which comes off completely both as opera and as film.' *(John Russell Taylor, The Times)*

'I can't think of a better Christmas treat for adults.' *(Richard Roud, Guardian)*

'A film which gives the impression of having been made with joy.' *(Dilys Powell)*

'Poetic neo-realism.' *(Georges Sadoul)*

'Never has an Esso station looked so romantic.' *(Chris Peachment, Time Out)*

MIXED:

'The film delights the eye, but it gives the mind very little to feed upon.' *(Time)*

'A slender plot but dazzlingly embroidered.' *(Isabel Quigly, Spectator)*

ANTI:

'A thumping bore.' *(Rex Reed)*

'We are told that in Paris the opening night audience wept and the critics were ecstatic. It would have made a little more sense the other way round.' *(John Simon)*

'Anything may be perfect of its kind, even a lollipop [and this] is a lollipop to lick them all: or rather, for all to lick . . . [with] no lyricism but mechanised sweetness . . . Undeniably, every line of the script is sung; and if M. Legrand were a Mozart, a Weill or a Leonard Bernstein, this might have some artistic significance. As he isn't, it hasn't.' *(Kenneth Tynan, Observer)*

UN CHIEN ANDALOU

CT: 5 AV: 7.29

(aka *An Andalusian Dog*)

1928 France 17/24 BW DRAMA/SILENT/FOREIGN

D Luis Buñuel ☆
W Luis Buñuel Salvador Dali

Simone Mareuil Pierre Batcheff Jaime Miravilles Salvador Dali Luis Buñuel

What plot?

Director Luis Buñuel's first film, which he co-wrote with surrealist artist Salvador Dali, was one of the most shocking films of its time, but is now more of a curiosity. It is not hard to imagine the impact on 1928 audiences of the opening shot, which is of a razor cutting a woman's eye. The rest of this 17-minute film sums up much of what is best and worst about Buñuel: his wild, macabre imagination on the one hand, his infantile desire to shock on the other.

'NOTHING in the film symbolises ANYTHING.' *(Luis Buñuel)*

ANTI:

'I defy any qualified authority to detect the slightest artistic merit [in] its crop of utterly obscene, repugnant, and tawdry episodes. Country, family, religion, are dragged through the mire.' *(Richard-Pierre Bodin, Le Figaro)*

'Utterly unsuitable for showing to general audiences; the latter would not only find it completely incomprehensible, but would probably be revolted by many of its images.' *(Oxford University Film Society Report, 1953)*

PRO:

'Forcefully and intelligently constructed. From the beginning of the first shot real warmth, at once brutal and admirable, emanates from the chosen images and remains throughout the whole performance . . . A complete cinematic intelligence.' *(Jean Lenauer, Close Up)*

'It is never the plot of [a surrealist] film that should receive attention, but rather the wealth of innuendo . . . Buñuel and Dali are the first to attempt using the film as a medium for metaphor and ideology.' *(Julien Levy, Surrealism, Black Sun Press, 1936)*

'[The film] remains a unique effort to exalt total love as I conceive it to be . . . Love in all that it can mean to two human beings . . . has never been shown with such freedom and quiet audacity.' *(André Breton, L'Amour Fou, 1937)*

'A work of major importance in every respect.' *(Jean Vigo)*

'I am convinced that [it] is unique and unparalleled.' *(Henry Miller)*

'The musical track added by Buñuel in 1960 . . . enormously enhances the film's effect, stressing the sharp changes of mood. What first strikes one is the modernity of the language and impact . . . [and] the extent to which it is Buñuel's film, full of his characteristic humour and insolence . . . With *L'Age d'Or* it remains the most important manifestation of surrealism in the cinema.' *(MFB, 1968)*

UN COEUR EN HIVER: *see* HEART IN WINTER, A.

UN DIMANCHE À LA CAMPAGNE: *see* SUNDAY IN THE COUNTRY.

UN GRAND AMOUR DE BEETHOVEN: *see* ABEL GANCE'S BEETHOVEN.

UN HOMME ÉCHAPPÉ: *see* MAN ESCAPED, A.

UN HOMME ET UNE FEMME: *see* MAN AND A WOMAN, A.

UNBEARABLE LIGHTNESS OF BEING, THE

CT: 5 AV: 6.83

1987 US 172 C DRAMA/ROMANCE

D Philip Kaufman ✗
W Jean-Claude Carrière Philip Kaufman ✗ AAN from Milan Kundera's novel

Daniel Day-Lewis ☆ Juliette Binoche ☆ Lena Olin ☆ Erland Josephson Daniel Olbrychski Derek de Lint

During the Prague Spring of 1968, a young doctor (Daniel Day-Lewis) enjoys a life of sexual freedom with his lover (Lena Olin). As Soviet tanks roll in and he meets a less out-going woman (Juliette Binoche), he changes into a more sombre citizen.

Sven Nykvist's Oscar-nominated cinematography and three terrific performances can't disguise the rambling nature of the screenplay – which starts off as lively but loses its way, and threatens to become comatose in the second half. Gone is most of the philosophizing of Kundera's novel, to be replaced by sexy, nude frolics featuring two of Europe's most gorgeous actresses. Even so, it's hard to care about these characters, and there's a meaningless 'shock' ending; fate strikes, seemingly for no other reason than to put us out of our misery. Known to its detractors as The Unbearable Boredom of Seeing.

PRO:

'Richly satisfying.' *(Variety)*

'A film that puts relationships within the context of the world, or maybe puts the world within the context of relationships . . . Phil Kaufman, most famous for the misunderstood *The Right Stuff*, directs with great feeling.' *(Martin Sutton, F & F)*

'A fascinating film . . . Daniel Day-Lewis gives a quiet, subtle performance . . . [The film's] astute attentions to detail . . . are so brilliantly choreographed that its few shortcomings are overcome.' *(Jon Silberg, American Film)*

'The film builds inexorably, thanks to a cast that could not be bettered . . . Erotically and politically charged, this film speaks eloquently of love in the shadow of oppression. Kundera's voice is heard.' *(Peter Travers, People Weekly)*

'It's a prankish sex comedy that treats modern political events with a delicate – yet almost sly – sense of tragedy. It's touching in sophisticated ways that you don't expect from an American director.' *(Pauline Kael)*

'It's faithful to the novel as it exists in the mind of a reader, rather than to a novel considered as some form of autonomous entity, or to a notion of the author's intent . . . The movie's most interesting character is Philip Kaufman . . . [His] directness . . . links him to Tomas . . . [who] examines [women] and makes love to them at the same time. That, in a way, is what Kaufman does to Kundera's novel – he strips it so he can know and love it better.' *(Terrence Rafferty, S & S)*

ANTI:

'Of course the book had to be compressed – the picture runs almost three hours anyway – but Kaufman and Carrière have done their compressing less with an eye to condensing the original than to transforming it into a well-behaved film with good conventional narrative manners . . . What we are left with is just a story, not particularly enthralling in itself.' *(Stanley Kauffmann)*

'It takes an unappetizing mixture of arrogance and folly to make a film out of Milan Kundera's *The Unbearable Lightness of Being*, a book about as suited for cinematic treatment as, say, Sartre's *Words*. What the director, Philip Kaufman, and his co-scenarist, the ubiquitous Jean-Claude Carrière, have contrived is, you might say, the movie version of the jacket copy.' *(John Simon)*

'Alternatively droll, earnest and aimlessly trashy [it] has no style to speak of . . . It's David Lean for intellectuals, an egghead *Dr Zhivago* . . . Ideas are introduced with portentous pauses and bracketed by admiring reaction shots. Kaufman is never matter-of-fact when he might be picturesque.' *(J. Hoberman, Village Voice)*

'Unbearable's the word for this elephantine but much-praised adaptation. Despite the impeccable acting, it goes on for so long the Russians could get their invasion over and done with before the end credits roll.' *(Rose)*

UNDER FIRE

CT: 8 AV: 7.27

1983 US 127 C THRILLER/WAR/ROMANCE

D Roger Spottiswoode ☆
W Ron Shelton Clayton Frohman

Nick Nolte ☆ Ed Harris ☆ Gene Hackman ☆ Joanna Cassidy ☆ Alma Martinez Jean-Louis Trintignant ✔ Richard Masur Renèe Enriquez

Journalists come under fire in Nicaragua.

An American political thriller with a fashionably left-wing message, not dissimilar to that of *The Year of Living Dangerously* (1982) and *Salvador* (1986). Maybe the view of Central American politics is naive, but there's a strong sense of reality, the action is exciting, the acting is very good, and this is easily Spottiswoode's best film. Even the central romance feels possible, not dragged in to supply love interest. Jerry Goldsmith's score was Oscar-nominated.

ANTI:

'As duplicitous as it is busy . . . One wishes it would state its sympathies openly . . . But [it] ends up as a movie too pleased with its own intellectual bravado.' *(Richard Schickel)*

'The film's didactic drift is often specious and it ends with a let's-all-have-a-revolution tableau that should be chopped up and used for Free World firewood.' *(Nigel Andrews, Financial Times)*

PRO:

'Extraordinary because it not only thinks in images, it also thinks about images . . . Few things are explained . . . yet everything is made clear . . . It's certainly the first great picture of the year.' *(Andy Gill, New Musical Express)*

'Excellent performances all round.' *(Virginia Dignam, Morning Star)*

'A complex, genuinely thrilling drama of commitment, the mercenary mentality and the tortuous ironies of history.' *(S & S)*

UNE PARTIE DE CAMPAGNE

CT: 8 AV: 8.75

(aka *A Day in the Country*)

1936 (released 1946) France 40/45 BW ROMANCE/COMEDY/FOREIGN

D Jean Renoir ☆
W Jean Renoir from Guy de Maupassant's story

Sylvie Bataille Georges Darnoul Jeanne Marken Paul Temps Georges Saint-Saens

A 19th-century Parisian family picnics in the country, and the daughter has a brief love affair.

Though this is an unfinished masterpiece, it is only a few scenes short of the one-hour film which Renoir intended it to be. (A rainy summer in 1936 led to a postponement of shooting.) It makes perfect sense with two additional titles, added in 1946, and the film has been delighting audiences ever since with its mixture of wit and sensuality. It's a lyrical, romantic vision of rural France, full of nostalgia for lost love. The look of the piece is indebted to the impressionists.

MIXED:

'Two of the minor parts are overplayed, the sub-titles weigh heavy, but nothing can tarnish the intense lyrical simplicity underlaid with an aching irony and made almost unbearable by the yearning musical score of Kosma. This is everybody's lost love.' *(Richard Winnington)*

'The director puts plenty of feeling into his pastoral atmosphere, and his love scenes catch fire. However, the script is poorly constructed, much of the comedy seems forced, and the picture's mooning romanticism finally cloys.' *(The Times, 1950)*

PRO:

'It seems Renoir has been well inspired by his father, the great painter, who also in his youth painted the banks of the Seine . . . Jean Renoir's populist empathy allows him to express himself with consummate emotion . . . and he is well served in this by his cinematographer and composer.' *(Georges Charensel, France Soir)*

'An all-but-perfect film, and one can trick oneself into believing that had it been finished it would have been even better than all-but-perfect.' *(Manchester Guardian)*

'All the wit and disillusionment of the story on which it is based.' *(MFB)*

'Moved one as great literature can do, adding that something further, that greater extension of experience which the cinema . . . so seldom leaves as a permanent part of our memory.' *(Patricia Hutchins, S & S, 1947)*

UNFAITHFUL WIFE, THE: *see* LA FEMME INFIDÈLE

UNFAITHFULLY YOURS CT: 8 AV: 7.45

1948 US 105 BW COMEDY/ROMANCE

D Preston Sturges ☆
W Preston Sturges

Rex Harrison ☆ Linda Darnell ☆
Barbara Lawrence ✔ Rudy Vallee ☆ Kurt Kreuger
Lionel Stander Edgar Kennedy Alan Bridge

A conductor (Rex Harrison) who believes his wife (Linda Darnell) is unfaithful plots revenge during a concert.

Preston Sturges's last film in Hollywood is a black comedy which received mixed reviews on release and was a commercial flop. However, Rex Harrison is very funny as the anti-hero, whose character is based on Sir Thomas Beecham; and Sturges very skilfully sets his fantasies to Rossini, Wagner and Tchaikowsky. The film is a unique mixture of high art and low comedy. Howard Zieff directed an uninspired remake starring Dudley Moore in 1984.

'The Fox advertising department tried to sell it as some sort of murder mystery . . . Consequently, it never hit its mark. I suppose it was a flawed picture, but the ad campaign destroyed any chances it might have had.' *(Barbara Lawrence, actress)*

ANTI:

'Misses that stamp of originality which marked the scripting and direction of Preston Sturges's previous films. The fabric of stale ideas and antique gags out of which this pic was spun is just barely hidden by its glossy production casting. The yarn is too slight to carry the long running time . . . Stylization of the fantasies would have given these sequences that comic energy which is lacking.' *(Variety)*

MIXED:

'A little too wordy, its slapstick a little too prolonged, the film nevertheless has moments of Sturges at his funniest.' *(New Movies)*

PRO:

'It does sound like a difficult theme for comedy hijinks. But it is Sturges' particular talent to blend sophisticated comedy with pratfalls. He is gifted with the rare ability to conceive a witty idea, develop it into a literate screenplay, stage it with insane slapstick – yet make it retain its incisive, witty point. Dialogue, comic business, sound (which Sturges uses more imaginatively than any other movie-maker except Disney) make this movie a superlative treat. And the performances are sheer delight.' *(Fortnight)*

'It is a characteristic piece of Sturges fantasy, this story of extravagant jealousy that combines comedy, music and mock-melodrama with a touch of imagination in technique. Rex Harrison, alternating between bouts of Othello-like passion, cynical humour, fatuous sentiment and comic despair, gives full rein to extravagance and the result is capital fun which Linda Darnell adorns with dusky beauty and an understandable air of bewilderment.' *(A.E. Wilson)*

'An acid and fantastic comedy generally underestimated and neglected here.' *(BFI Bulletin, 1949)*

'Harrison discovers more ways of tripping over a telephone cable than one can count, and his efforts to falsify evidence through a recalcitrant tape recorder are as funny as anything thought up by Clair in *À Nous La Liberté* or by Chaplin in *Modern Times*.' *(Basil Wright, 1972)*

'There are so many great lines and situations in this movie that writers and directors have been stealing from it for years, just as they've been stealing from Sturges's other work, but no one has ever come close to the wild-man devilry of the best Preston Sturges comedies.' *(Pauline Kael)*

UNFORGIVEN, THE CT: 5 AV: 6.22

1960 US 120 C WESTERN

D John Huston
W Ben Maddow from Alan Le May's novel

Audrey Hepburn Burt Lancaster Lillian Gish ☆
Charles Bickford ✔ Audie Murphy ✔ Doug McClure John Saxon Joseph Wiseman Albert Salmi

A foundling (Audrey Hepburn) rumoured to be Indian becomes the centre of racial tensions in the Texas Panhandle.

Confusing, ponderous and overblown, Huston's picture has acquired a cult reputation since it was released to many a critical catcall; and it scores surprisingly highly in most modern film guides. There are great moments (and lovely performances by Lillian Gish, Charles Bickford and Audie Murphy), but the two leads are miscast and this is far from a great western.

PRO:

'Gish and Bickford are outstanding in stellar-cast story, with rousing Indian attack climax.' *(Maltin)*

'Huston's career probably hit its critical nadir with this hysterical western with racial overtones . . . but if it's viewed in the context of this subgenre of the Forties [the racial western], the film becomes a satisfying and stimulating work.' *(Scheuer)*

MIXED:

'Huston is at the top of his form as an entertainer in the grandstand manner. Unfortunately, he has tried to be more than an entertainer. *The Unforgiven* is designed and executed as a heroic poem, a sort of cow-country Cid. Its pace is slow and noble . . . But the legend, like most synthetic folklore, fails to come alive. How could it when the sod hut looks like a page from *House and Home*, when the back country heroine has an elocution-school accent, when the cowpunching hero has clean, executive hands?' *(Time)*

'*The Unforgiven* isn't an important picture, but it's the best Huston has directed in some time.' *(Films in Review)*

'A disappointment . . . Still there is . . . Lillian Gish who, after forty years, remains one of the most economical and accomplished screen actresses.' *(David Robinson, The Times)*

ANTI:

'How much strain can a director's reputation take? Of late, John Huston seems to have been trying to find out. I think he has carried the experiment too far with *The Unforgiven* . . . a work of profound phoniness, part adult western – I prefer Tom Mix – part that *Oklahoma!* kind of folksy Americana. it is limp as drama, every situation is built up until it soggily collapses, even the final Indian attack is tedious: can this be the man who gave us *The Maltese Falcon* and *Beat the Devil?*' *(Dwight MacDonald)*

'It has become almost a ghoulish task to comment on a new John Huston picture. The latest is . . . ludicrous . . . a hodgepodge of crudely stitched sententiousness and lame story-conference inspiration . . . The direction shows a now-pathetic flash or two of old Huston quality, but for the most part it is feeble and disconcerted. That Huston could not get a good performance out of Lancaster cannot be held against him, but he has achieved what no other director has done: he has got a bad performance out of lovely, miscast Audrey Hepburn.' *(Stanley Kauffmann)*

'A mess. Its story is rambling and unlikely. It casts Miss Hepburn as . . . an Indian foundling [whom] Burt Lancaster calls . . . "You squaw – you red nigger!" . . . And all the time little Audrey is looking so pathetic and appealing that I doubt if even Dr Verwoerd himself would have had the heart to show her the back door . . . I was bored by this film and irritated by it, too.' *(Len Mosley, Daily Express)*

'If not wholly void, it is at least conspicuously null.' *(Fred Majdalany, Daily Mail)*

'What seems likely is that the [filmmakers] failed to think through the implications of their themes. They had ideas but lacked a point of view . . . Nor does John Huston's direction do anything to strengthen the point of view. The reasons for the Texas settlers' unremitting hatred for the Indians are muffled; and Joseph Wiseman, the vengeful saddle-tramp who reveals the secret of the girl's shameful origins, remains a man of mystery throughout.' *(Saturday Review)*

'Some of my pictures I don't care for, but *The Unforgiven* is the only one I actually dislike. Despite some good performances, the overall tone is bombastic and over-inflated. Everybody in it is larger than life. I watched it on television one night recently, and after about half a reel I had to turn the damned thing off. I couldn't bear it.' *(John Huston)*

UNFORGIVEN AAW   CT: 8 AV: 8.00

1992 US 127/131 C WESTERN

D Clint Eastwood ☆ AAW
W David Webb Peoples ☆ AAN

Clint Eastwood ☆ AAN Gene Hackman ☆ AAW
Morgan Freeman ☆ Richard Harris ☆
Jaimz Woolvett Saul Rubinek Frances Fisher
Anna Thomson David Mucci Rob Campbell
Anthony James

An old gunfighter (Clint Eastwood) is reluctantly brought out of retirement to avenge the disfigurement of a prostitute. His chief adversaries are a corrupt sheriff (Gene Hackman) and a British assassin (Richard Harris).

The storyline is deceptively slight, contains logical flaws and 'politically correct' anachronisms – surely someone in the Old West would have mentioned the fact that Morgan Freeman is black? – and it leaves some people disappointed. Nevertheless, this is one of Eastwood's best films, and covers two of his favourite subjects: masculinity under threat, and the nature of heroism. Seldom has violence been shot in such a dark, mythic, alluring way: this reflects the central theme, which is the corrupting nature of violence. Eastwood rightly got most of the credit for directing this impressive western which finally won him respectability and a best film Oscar – but hes helped by Jack N. Green's Oscar-nominated photography, Joel Cox's sharp editing (which won an Academy Award), and a dream supporting cast. Also nominated were the art direction and sound.

PRO:

'The movie's grizzled male ensemble, its gradual build, and its juxtaposition of brutality and sardonic humor testify to its disdain for box-office conventions.' *(Michael Sragow, New Yorker)*

'A tense, hard-edged, superbly dramatic yarn that is also an exceedingly intelligent meditation on the west, its myths and its heroes.' *(Variety)*

A classic western.' *(Iain Johnstone, Sunday Times)*

An exceedingly clever meditation on the West, its myths and heroes.' *(Variety)*

Eastwood's direction has never been better, giving a grand aura to the wide screen, with artful use of light and darkness by [the] photographer . . . Freeman . . . [is] by far the warmest presence in the movie . . . *Unforgiven* is not just a solid western but one of the year's most intelligent and provocative dramas.' *(Kevin Lally, Film Journal)*

What is so infernally smart about this movie is the way Clint weaves a modern, adult disquisition on the moral ambiguity of the Old West into an edge-of-your-seat vengeance splatterfest with only the seams he wants you to see showing . . . Clint may be dour, taciturn and alarmingly aged, but his humour is as keen as a hunting knife and blacker than a hangman's heart.' *(Steven Keane, City Limits)*

A clever mixture of almost all the anti-westerns you have ever seen.' *(Clancy Sigal, Guardian)*

Despite its bleakness, the film remains richly rewarding, peppered with the sort of memorable one-liners for which Eastwood is famous . . . Just don't expect the good guys to ride off into the sunset.' *(Stephen Amidon, Financial Times)*

For Clint Eastwood, one of the most intelligent and self-aware of filmmakers, *Unforgiven* may have been a reaction to the rising tide of meaningless violence in films and on television. In a way, this is a movie about how, when you kill someone, they're really dead.' *(Roger Ebert)*

A full-scale, systematic act of contrition, a repudiation and dismantling of the whole legendary, masculine character type of which, for this generation, Eastwood himself had become the leading icon.' *(Richard Grenier, Commentary)*

Eastwood has taken the best of Sergio Leone's operatic style and merged it with a contemporary moral vision. Shooting up the classic western, Eastwood picks off the heroic clichés one by one: the gunfight in the boulders, the campfire at night, the showdown in the saloon. But he resurrects the visual romance, with magnificent images that cut from shadow-rich interiors to bright, breathtaking Alberta skies. Eloquent and expansive, *Unforgiven* is arguably the best film of Eastwood's career – a movie that could well serve as the last word on the western.' *(Brian D. Johnson, Maclean's)*

ANTI:

If Clint Eastwood represents America in *Unforgiven*, then America is a drunk who can't stay on the wagon, a killer who can't resist one last murder. Among this figures other attributes: he idealizes women but apparently can't live with them; loves children but abandons them to fend for themselves . . . That's the America Eastwood seems to represent – either stuck in a posture of rigid moralism or else descending into a frenzy of total war.' *(Stuart Klawans, Nation)*

'Frequently bogs down in self-doubt . . . While Eastwood dedicates the film to Sergio Leone and Don Siegel, his early directors, he doesn't seem to have learned all that much from them. If their action films had been this plodding, nobody would ever have heard of Clint Eastwood outside of television's *Rawhide*.' *(Ralph Novak, People Weekly)*

'Eastwood's really disturbing flaw as director is his acceptance of David Webb Peoples's defective screenplay. The two cowboys ticketed for slaughter are not both guilty: the innocent one even tried to stop the knifer. After the price is set on their heads, they just hang around their ranch waiting to be shot at. (The marshall lamely covers this plot lapse by saying they'd probably rather stay with their friends.) . . . After Munny [Eastwood's character] kills the first cowboy, neither the marshall nor the victim's friends ride after him. After the Kid kills the second one under Munny's direction, again no pursuit. Instead the killers pose picturesquely on a hillock outside of town waiting for the reward money. For good reason, Munny later rides into town to confront the marshall and though he is earlier shown to have lost his marksmanship, he now kills five men in a saloon full of armed opponents. When he rides off, again no one at all pursues him – and no ever does, apparently, because our last view shows him back at home in Kansas. And the symbolism! Some critics have helpfully pointed out the significance of Munny's name. With almost equal subtlety, the Kid is short-sighted, both literally and figuratively . . . When Munny rides out of Big Whiskey near the end, there's an American flag in the corner of the frame for no perceptible reason other than to give film journals something to analyse. The whole heavy symbology of the film seems laid on to draw admiring attention to itself . . . At the last, we're left with a film that tries to doll up a conventional genre with hints of depth.' *(Stanley Kaufmann)*

UNINVITED, THE

CT: 7 AV: 7.70

1944 US 98 BW HORROR

D Lewis Allen ☆
W Dodie Smith Frank Partos from Dorothy McArdle's novel *Uneasy Freehold* ☆

Ray Milland Ruth Hussey Gail Russell ☆
Donald Crisp Cornelia Otis Skinner
Dorothy Stickney Barbara Everest Alan Napier

Ghost terrorizes couple who buy house on Cornish coast.

One of the cinema's great ghost stories, all the better for leaving much to the audiences imagination. The screenplay adeptly mixes in humorous relief, without in the least diminishing some truly terrifying sequences. The outstanding,

Oscar-nominated cinematography is by Charles Lang.

MIXED:

'Gail Russell never could act worth a damn, but she had an eerie luster, and she's lovely as the mysterious young girl who helps in the exorcism. The picture was popular, though it doesn't come anywhere near fulfilling one's initial hopes that it will be a first-rate ghost movie.' *(Pauline Kael)*

PRO:

'A pretty skilful flesh-creeper.' *(Dilys Powell)*

'*The Uninvited*, through an adroit counterpointing, syncopating, and cumulation of the natural and the super-natural, turns a mediocre story and a lot of shabby clichés into an unusually good scare-picture. It seems to me harder to get a fright than a laugh, and I experienced thirty-five first-class jolts, not to mention a well-calculated texture of minor frissons.' *(James Agee, Nation)*

'Proceed at your own risk, we warn you, if you are at all afraid of the dark . . . It sets out to give you the shivers – and will do so, if you're readily disposed.' *(New York Times)*

'Allen's direction tightens the screws of tension to genuinely frightening effect, aided by an intense performance from Russell as the girl who believes herself haunted by the malevolent ghost of her mother, and by beautiful camerawork in the noir style from Charles Lang. The real strength of the film, though, is its atypical stance part way between psychology and the supernatural, achieving a disturbingly serious effect.' *(Geoff Andrew, Time Out)*

UNMARRIED WOMAN, AN AAN

CT: 4 AV: 7.33

1978 US 124 C DRAMA/ROMANCE/COMEDY

D Paul Mazursky ✗
W Paul Mazursky ✗ AAN

Jill Clayburgh ✗ AAN Michael Murphy Alan Bates Cliff Gorman Pat Quinn Kelly Bishop

A New Yorker (Jill Clayburgh) is deserted by her husband (Michael Murphy) and has to rebuild her life.

Paul Mazursky's shallow script and glib direction combine with unattractive performances and watered-down feminism to make this late-70s period-piece. At the time, it seemed frank and truthful.

PRO:

'I've been reviewing movies for a long time now without ever feeling the need to use dumb lines like "You'll laugh – you'll cry" But I did cry, and I did laugh.' *(Roger Ebert)*

'Miss Clayburgh gives us something as gradual and miraculous as the opening of a flower followed through all its stages by a nature documentary.' *(John Simon)*

'Perceptive and penetrating.' *(Quinlan)*

MIXED:

'Buoyant, enormously friendly . . . What may be disappointing to those who love Mazursky's earlier work is that in trying to identify with Erica and tell the story from a woman's point of view, he shies away from having her look foolish; in crucial parts, he suppresses his sense of satire, and the picture becomes virtuous.' *(Pauline Kael)*

ANTI:

'Seems to have been commissioned by *New York* magazine. Want to know what's in? Everything from lunching places to emotional crises? Don't miss it. *An Unmarried Woman* can also be seen as a cooked-up response to the demand for more pictures about women. That cry reached its peak about two years ago, just about the time that *Woman* must have been planned. The picture makes us feel that a product has been manufactured for a market: considered as carefully, packaged as smartly, as a new deodorant . . . This picture carries a buried insult to its ostensible subject. Finally, the picture says that what a woman really needs is a man . . . [Clayburgh] is only a slick mannequin, seemingly made of chrome. I have the feeling that if you flicked her with your finger, she would ping . . . As the husband, Michael Murphy is again like good wallpaper, not jarring, just not visible. Cliff Gorman, as the one-night stand, is just as grating as he was in *Chapter Two* on Broadway. Alan Bates is between planes.' *(Stanley Kauffmann)*

'It was hailed as a groundbreaking feminist film, but, considering that the women's movement had been going strong for a good eight years, it was long overdue and daring only by Hollywood standards.' *(Danny Peary)*

UNTOUCHABLES, THE

CT: 7 AV: 7.79

1987 US 119 C THRILLER

D Brian De Palma ☆
W David Mamet

Kevin Costner Sean Connery AAW Charles Martin Smith Andy Garcia Robert De Niro Richard Bradford Jack Kehoe Brad Sullivan Billy Drago Patricia Clarkson

Treasury agent Eliot Ness (Kevin Costner) takes on Chicago gangster Al Capone (Robert De Niro).

Pacy and popular. The opening shot is a great one, and De Palma's update of Eisenstein's Odessa Steps sequence (from *Potemkin*) is pretty good as well; but too much of the picture seems to be second hand, a tribute to old gangster movies rather than an examination of real events – it could almost be a film by Peter Bogdanovich. Mamet's dialogue is anonymous and so is much of De Palma's direction (though there is some of that extreme brutality which is his hallmark). The performances don't extend beyond putting flesh on the sterotypes; Connery is the only one who gives the impression that he might have existed before the movie began. It's appropriate that the film was Oscar-nominated for its incidental pleasures: Ennio Morricone's score, the art direction by Patrizia Von Brandenstein and Hal Gausman, and Marilyn Vance-Straker's costumes.

PRO:

'Beautifully crafted . . . De Palma has brought his sure and skilled hand to a worthy enterprise.' *(Variety)*

MIXED:

'Like an attempt to visualize the public's collective dream of Chicago gangsters; our movie-fed imagination of the past is enlarged and given a new vividness. De Palma is a showman here . . . It's not a great movie; it's too banal, too morally comfortable – the script is too obvious. But it's a great audience movie – a wonderful potboiler. It's a rouser.' *(Pauline Kael)*

'This is a gangster picture so there is violence, and it is a De Palma picture so the violence is vivid. But there is nothing like the exuberant gore (limbs sliced off by chainsaws, women pierced by electric drills, for example) that has in the past won Mr De Palma as many detractors as admirers. Fans may miss his wild cackle, the darkly absurdist tilt on the world that distinguished most of his work. But *The Untouchables* lets him show that he isn't just a brilliant sicko. Now he has also made a big, absorbing crowd pleaser.' *(Julie Salamon, Wall Street Journal)*

'There are so many distracting camera movements . . . that after a while one wants to scream, "Enough already!" Similarly, the musical score (by Ennio Morricone) is often excessively dramatic and several of the performances (notably De Niro's) are almost ludicrously overdrawn – all of which is, of course, in the classic De Palma tradition. Even Costner, in his magnificently minimalistic performance as Ness, comes dangerously close to excess – ie, to overdoing his underplaying. Nor has De Palma grown tired of perpetrating his famous homages to great directors and films of the past. Given a choice between creating an original, realistic sequence and contriving a derivative one with an immediately recognizable filmic antecedent, he'll do the latter every time . . . But I was very pleasantly surprised by the degree to which *The Untouchables* held up in spite of this cinemacentric sensibility. For the truth is that, despite its superficiality and cynicism, this film is wonderfully entertaining.' *(Bruce Bawer, American Spectator)*

ANTI:

'A movie about an era when law enforcement resembled gang warfare, but the movie seems more interested in the era than in the war. *The Untouchables* has great costumes, great sets, great cars, great guns, great locations, and a few shots that absolutely capture the Prohibition Era. But it does not have a great script, great performances, or great direction. The script is by David Mamet, the playwright, but it could have been by anybody. It doesn't have the Mamet touch, the conversational rhythms that carry a meaning beyond words. It also lacks any particular point of view about the material, and, in fact, lacks the dynamic tension of many gangster movies written by less talented writers. Everything seems cut and dried, twice-told, preordained.' *(Roger Ebert)*

UNVANQUISHED, THE: *see APU* TRILOGY: APARAJITTO.

USUAL UNIDENTIFIED THIEVES, THE: *see* BIG DEAL ON MADONNA STREET, THE.

V

VACANCES DE MONSIEUR HULOT, LES:

see MONSIEUR HULOT'S HOLIDAY.

VAGABOND CT: 7 AV: 7.89

(aka *Vagabonde; Sans Toit Ni Loi*)

1986 France 105 C DRAMA/FOREIGN

D Agnès Varda ☆
W Agnès Varda

Sandrine Bonnaire ☆ Macha Méril Stéphane Freiss Laurence Cortadellas Marthe Jarnias Yolande Moreau Joël Fosse

The last few weeks in the life of an 18-year-old drifter (Sandrine Bonnaire).

Depressing film, in the fake-documentary style, about a girl who acts as a mirror to other people's prejudices and failings. Given the enigmatic, opaque nature of her character, Sandrine Bonnaire works wonders in making her realistic, and fully deserved her French César award. Varda paints a memorable picture of a chilly, uncaring world; but her anti-heroine is so irritatingly passive and self-destructive that she never acquires the tragic dimension which might have made this a great film, as opposed to an interesting and unusual one.

MIXED:

'Another grim piece.' *(Patrick Gibbs)*

'A depressing fable, perhaps, but Miss Varda tells it with unsentimental compassion . . . Bonnaire . . . gives a performance of truth and conviction.' *(John Gillett, Economist)*

'The purity and boldness of Varda's approach may call Robert Bresson to mind, and it's perfectly evident why this film won the Golden Lion at the 1985 Venice Film Festival; it's the work of a visual artist. But we see the closed-off girl strictly from the outside, and this factual, objective view isn't enough. Varda's flat-out approach excludes the uses of the imagination – both hers and ours.' *(Pauline Kael)*

PRO:

'The film centres on the extraordinary performance of Sandrine Bonnaire.' *(David Robinson, The Times)*

'A very moving, spare and eloquent film – the best this director has achieved for years.' *(Derek Malcolm, Guardian)*

'Visually very beautiful in a still, Vermeer-like way.' *(Cynthia Kee, Observer)*

'Varda creates a symbolic journey that is never pompous, programmatic or predictable.' *(Nigel Andrews)*

'What a film this is. Like so many of the greatest films, it tells us a very specific story, strong and unadorned, about a very particular person. Because it is so much her own story and does not seem to symbolize anything – because the director has no parables, only information – it is only many days after the end of the film that we reflect that the story of the vagabond could also be the story of our lives. For how many have truly known us, although many have shared our time?' *(Roger Ebert)*

'Through this tough, memorable film, Ms Varda reaches for our humanity with a force that very few movies can muster.' *(Julie Salamon, Wall Street Journal)*

VALLEY OF THE DOLLS CT: 6 AV: 2.40

1967 US 123 C DRAMA/SO BAD

D Mark Robson ●
W Helen Deutsch Dorothy Kingsley ● from Jacqueline Susann's novel

Patty Duke ● Barbara Parkins ● Sharon Tate Susan Hayward Paul Burke ● Martin Milner Tony Scotti Charles Drake Lee Grant Richard Dreyfuss (cameo: Jacqueline Susann, as a reporter)

Three young hopefuls (Patty Duke, Barbara Parkins, Sharon Tate) try to make it in a corrupt Hollywood.

A high-point in Hollywood kitsch, Somehow, Susan Hayward (a late replacement for Judy Garland) and Sharon Tate (as a porno star with cancer) retain some trace of dignity; but for the most part, this is an engagingly dreadful exploitation movie. John Williams's score was Oscar-nominated.

'What a howl! . . . *Valley of the Dolls*, one of the most stupefyingly clumsy films ever made by alleged professionals, has no more sense of its own ludicrousness than a village idiot stumbling in manure.' *(Joseph Morgenstern, Newsweek)*

'An unbelievably hackneyed and mawkish mishmash of backstage plots and *Peyton Place* adumbrations . . . All a fairly respectful admirer of movies can do is laugh at it and turn away.' *(Bosley Crowther)*

'Think of a showbiz cliché and *Valley of the Dolls* has it.' *(MFB)*

'A thoroughly maladroit soap opera, whose innumerable iridescent suds are blown up ten times bigger than life and therefore become, even when they are meant to be tragic, laughable.' *(Brendan Gill, New Yorker)*

'The story is about girls who take all sorts of pills, but *Valley of the Dolls* offers only bromides . . . Viewers are also not likely to feel anything – except numbness – after ingesting this film.' *(Time)*

'What kind of pills do you have to take to sit through a film like this?' *(Cue)*

'A skilfully deceptive imitation of a real drama . . . On a closer look the characters turn out to be images that have almost nothing to do with people.' *(Christian Science Monitor)*

'For out and out trash, few films have surpassed [it] . . . The movie lacks smut but compensates by being badly acted, badly plotted, and sleazily made, with a cheapjack production underlying the near-idiot level of the script.' *(Judith Crist, New York Herald Tribune)*

'Ineptitude, inadequacy, and downright dishonesty characterize every aspect of this . . . production.' *(Arthur Knight, Saturday Review)*

'The Mount Everest of Bad Movies About Show Biz . . . When Hayward and Duke square off for a wig-pulling fight in the ladies' room, *Valley of the Dolls* soars into Bad Movie Heaven.' *(Margulies & Rebello)*

VAMPYR CT: 6 AV: 7.00

(aka *Vampyr ou Étrange Aventure de David Gray; Der Traum des Allan Gray; The Strange Adventure of David Gray; Castle of Doom*)

1931 France/Germany 65 BW HORROR/SILENT/FOREIGN

D Carl Dreyer ☆
W Christen Jul Carl Dreyer from Sheridan le Fanus's novel *Carmilla*

Julian West (pseudonym for Baron Nicolas de Gunsberg, who financed the film) Sybille Schmitz Maurice Schutz Jan Hieronimko Henriette Gérard

A young man (Julian West) suspects that he is threatened by vampires, and dreams his own death.

Although there is insufficient plot to sustain its length, and modern audiences expect more shocks, the stunning camerawork by Rudolph Maté and Louis Née makes this a masterpiece of the silent era – and the use of a subjective camera predates John Carpenter's *Halloween* by almost half a century. The film builds up horror through creating unease in the audience, and the sequence where the hero dreams of being buried alive is terrifying. Dreyer is best known for his sombre meditations on faith and salvation; and – beneath the horror film trappings – this is all about his favourite themes.

ANTI:

'Although in many ways it was one of the worst films I have ever attended, there were some scenes in it that gripped with a brutal directness . . . It was a peculiarly irritating picture. The scenario was so bad that the author had to excuse it by pretending it was a dream. It was merely a tritely developed, muddled treatment of the old vampire theme . . . and then the photography was always underexposed, evidently with the idea of its being ghostly. It succeeded only in looking muddy.' *(C. Hooper Trask, New York Times)*

PRO:

'A worthy successor to Murnau's *Nosferatu*. It is bathed in an atmosphere whose magic only the cinema could express.' *(Lotte Eisner)*

'Dreyer somehow manages to imply horrors: evil wafts off the screen like a chill of bad breath.' *(John Coleman, New Statesman, 1976)*

'Makes our contemporary explicit Draculas look like an advertisement for false teeth.' *(Dilys Powell, 1976)*

'Taken frame by frame there is an eerie beauty about it that is positively staggering.' *(Guardian, 1976)*

'Not so much a horror film as an eerie mood piece, a dream, the visualization of the conflict between the heart and the brain for the soul.' *(Danny Peary)*

'Most vampire movies are so silly that this film by Carl Dreyer – a great vampire film – hardly belongs to the genre. Dreyer preys upon our subconscious fears. Dread and obsession are the film's substance, and its mood is evocative, dreamy, spectral.' *(Pauline Kael)*

'*Vampyr* never achieved the vogue of such inferior horror films as James Whale's *Frankenstein* and Tod Browning's *Dracula*.' *(Andrew Sarris)*

VANGELO SECONDO MATTEO, IL: *see* GOSPEL ACCORDING TO SAINT MATTHEW, THE.

VANISHING, THE CT: 10 AV: 7.58

(aka *Spoorloos*)

1988 Netherlands 100 C HORROR/THRILLER/FOREIGN

D George Sluizer ☆
W Tim Krabbé from his novel *The Golden Egg*

Bernard-Pierre Donnadieu ☆ Gene Bervoets ☆ Johanna Ter Steege ☆ Gwen Eckhaus Bernadette Le Saché Tania Latarjet

A young Dutch couple, Saskia (Johanna Ter Steege) and Rex (Gene Bervoets), who are driving to the south of France on holiday, stop at a service station, and Saskia disappears without trace. Three years later, Rex – taunted by postcards from Saskia's kidnapper – is still trying to find out what happened to her, via an expensive poster campaign and appeals on television. Eventually, Rex and the villain come face to face.

George Sluizer's first version of his frightening thriller is far superior to his own American re-make, which lost everything that was unusual and truly scary from the original.

It is not a whodunit. The cinema audience is never in doubt as to the identity of the kidnapper: an apparently ordinary, middle-aged family man, whom we see preparing for the kidnapping with obsessive precision but no great competence. The questions which remain unanswered until the end are: why did he do it? and what exactly did he do? Although the film might have gained from being tightened by ten minutes, the story is always absorbing.

As Hitchcock appreciated, one of the most important things in a thriller is to establish the underlying normality of the protagonists. Sluizer is wonderfully served by all his principals. Johanna Ter Steege is delightful as Saskia, every centimetre the girl next door. Gene Bervoets is a complex, flawed hero (early on in the picture he leaves Saskia alone in a tunnel: a petty cruelty which finds an echo in the eventual denouement). Bernard-Pierre Donnadieu is no less complicated a villain: capable of good acts as well as bad, curious to know the extent of his capacities.

Even more skilfully than *Psycho* or *Blue Velvet*, *The Vanishing* plays with the familiar conventions of the thriller, to reveal the sickness, perversity and horror which can lie below the surface of normal life. It is one of the outstanding, and grimmest, thrillers of the 80s.

ANTI:

'Although critics said that this Dutch thriller was in the Hitchcockian vein, the master would never have waited until the final minutes of a film before injecting any tension or excitement. In many ways the Hollywood remake is a little better.' *(Rose)*

PRO:

'A real nail-biter: a clean, logical nightmare with a fantastically absorbing plot . . . and the appalling, horrific climax will haunt your mind long after this film is over.' *(Michael Wilmington, LA Times)*

'A first-class suspenseful mystery.' *(New Musical Express)*

'This finely crafted thriller crackles with a chilling, malevolent air and gave even this old film warrior an uneasy night.' *(Sue Heal, Today)*

'Here is a scorpion of a psychological suspense film – its venomous power to disturb concentrated in a sting in the tail, represented by the final, horrific minutes.' *(Shaun Usher, Daily Mail)*

'With a script that breaks many of the supposed rules of thriller writing, but has enough character perception and insight into what keeps an audience watching to end up totally engrossing.' *(James Park, Film Yearbook)*

'A consistently bewildering and surprising thriller, chillingly unsentimental and expertly constructed.' *(Kim Newman, MFB)*

'Through some fiendish alchemy, *The Vanishing* manages to scare people out of their wits more effectively than a legion of better-known horror films.' *(Virgin)*

VERDICT, THE AAN — CT: 6 AV: 7.47

1982 US 128 C DRAMA

D Sidney Lumet ☆AAN
W David Mamet ☆AAN from Barry Reed's novel

Paul Newman ☆AAN James Mason ☆AAN Charlotte Rampling Jack Warden Milo O'Shea Lindsay Crouse Edward Binns Wesley Addy Julie Bovasso Roxanne Hart

Alcoholic attorney (Paul Newman) sues a hospital for malpractice.

Too slow to be an effective thriller, Sidney Lumet's film works well as a character-driven courtroom drama. It draws terrific performances from Paul Newman and James Mason as legal sparring partners. David Mamet's script is (despite holes in the plot and a hokey romantic subplot) highly intelligent. True, the ending is contrived, but what do you expect from a courtroom drama?

PRO:

'Hard to fault, being intelligent, morally interested, good-looking . . . and gripping. Newman gives the kind of performance which should win him an Oscar.' *(Lindsay Mackie, Glasgow Herald)*

'Some reviewers have found *The Verdict* a little slow-moving, maybe because it doesn't always hum along on the thriller level. But if you bring empathy to the movie, if you allow yourself to think about what Frank Galvin is going through, there's not a moment of this movie that's not absorbing.' *(Roger Ebert)*

'Newman . . . makes you care more about the lawyer than the verdict – and that's what the story is about.' *(David Castell, Sunday Telegraph)*

MIXED:

'[The film] scarcely needs the irrelevance of a love affair . . . That it gets it is one of the film's flaws. But the verdict on the rest, and on Newman, is that they are quite obviously guilty – of being prime suspects in Oscar stealing.' *(Tom Hutchinson, Mail on Sunday)*

'[Lumet] is an intelligent director but not a forceful one . . . It is a rather portentous movie, too, groaning and stretching for significance, constantly asking us to believe there is more in it than meets the eye. There is less, I suspect.' *(Michael Wood, New Society)*

ANTI:

'Newman gives us an actor's gymnastics exercise, It's quirky, resourceful, protean, fun, and almost totally unbelievable from start to finish . . . Occasionally the sheer helter-skelter of histrionic grace-notes are enough to give the film an illusion of movement and meaning . . . But sooner or later a whopping plot-contrivance comes along to punch a hole in the fabric of credibility . . . And the trial itself seems to have been choreographed by the Deus Ex Machina Company for Surprise Revelations, Last-minute Witnesses and Lump-in-the-Throat Summing-up Speeches.' *(Nigel Andrews, Financial Times)*

'It's a Frank Capra setup given art-film treatment. (There's plenty of drizzle and brown gloom.) Newman plays his role for all it has got, making himself look soft and heavier, and even a little jowly, but it's a tired old show-business view of "a good man". In its own sombre, inflated terms, the picture is effective, but it's dragged out so self-importantly that you have time to recognize what a hopelessly naive, incompetent, and untrustworthy lawyer the hero is.' *(Pauline Kael)*

VERTIGO

CT: 9 AV: 8.72

1958 US 128 BW THRILLER

D Alfred Hitchcock ☆
W Alec Coppel Samuel Taylor from Pierre Boileau and Thomas Narcejac's novel *D'Entre les Morts*

James Stewart ☆ Kim Novak
Barbara Bel Geddes ✓ Tom Helmore Henry Jones
Raymond Bailey

A detective (James Stewart) who's afraid of heights falls for a woman he's protecting (Kim Novak), only for her to fall (apparently) to her death. He suffers an emotional breakdown, then sees a woman who is her double . . .

An extraordinary, dreamlike thriller with a memorably bleak view of human nature, *Vertigo* received some of the most boneheaded reviews in critical history. Far from a conventional whodunit, it is a searching examination of emotional manipulation and dependency; and, though slow at the start, it's a masterpiece.

It resembles Hitchcock's other most unjustly maligned movie, *Psycho*, in that it makes us empathize with the central character (here played by James Stewart), then abruptly detaches us. Unlike Janet Leigh in *Psycho*, Stewart doesn't die; but as soon as we know something he doesn't (that Judy and Madeleine are identical), we begin to watch him with new eyes. Unnervingly, we both empathize with his obsession but remain detached from him – much the same ambiguity of response that we feel for Anthony Perkins in *Psycho*.

The film received Oscar nominations for best art direction (Hal Pereira, Henry Bumstead, Sam Comer, Frank McKelvy) and sound (George Dutton); but Robert Burks's outstanding photography and Bernard Herrmann's music might also have been recognized. Hitchcock failed even to be nominated for best director, but this is one of the great directorial *tours de force*.

ANTI:

'Alfred Hitchcock, who produced and directed the thing, has never before indulged in such far-fetched nonsense.' *(John McCarten, New Yorker)*

'Technical facility is being exploited to gild pure dross . . . [The film] pursues its theme of false identity with such plodding persistence that by the time the climactic cat is let out of the bag, the audience has long since had kittens.' *(Arthur Knight, Saturday Review)*

'The old master has turned out another Hitchcock-and-bull story, in which the mystery is not so much who done it as who cares.' *(Time)*

'The trouble, I think, is that the ideas which Hitchcock pioneered have since been made commonplace by imitation: great close-ups of an eye, or half an eye, or the corner of a quivering mouth, or a hand holding a pistol, or hair-raising chases up high places. All this amusing Hitch-poppycock is no longer exclusive to him.' *(Daily Mail)*

'Tricksy . . . *Vertigo* has its moments, all right, but between them stretches a lot of wasted time.' *(Philip Oakes, Evening Standard)*

'A film in which character and theme are unimportant, and which therefore relies heavily on plot interest. Unfortunately in this case, the plot is an involved one.' *(MFB)*

MIXED:

'The plot is a brilliant box of devilish tricks. And yet the film disappoints. It seems too long, too elaborately designed; the narration of this kind of criminal intrigue sags under such luscious treatment; it needs the touch of the harsh and squalid. As the mysterious quarry Kim Novak makes one of her more lifelike appearances.' *(Dilys Powell)*

'A complex tale with supernatural overtones . . . What is apparently seen may not be what actually happened at all. The feeling of vertigo is communicated in the music, in the overemphatic titles . . . and in a sequence which visualizes the delirium suffered by the detective. Hitchcock uses a highly elaborate and oddly leisurely style in telling this unlikely tale.' *(Gerald D. MacDonald, Library Journal)*

'*Vertigo* would be pretty preposterous if it weren't for Hitchcock.' *(Isabel Quigly, Spectator)*

'Brilliant but despicably cynical view of human obsession.' *(Geoff Andrew, Time Out)*

PRO:

'A good old-fashioned brew of sock, suspense and surprise . . . A most handsomely furnished film.' *(Peter Burnup, News of the World)*

'It entertains and is admirably photographed.' *(The Times)*

'Hitchcock in vintage form.' *(Frank Jackson, Reynolds News)*

'Hitchcock pulls a major mystery and a bit of a miracle out of his capacious bag.' *(Harold Conway, Daily Sketch)*

'The mechanisms and motivations of the male power drive are subjected to the most ruthless and uncompromising critique.' *(Robin Wood, Hollywood from Vietnam to Reagan, 1986)*

'Of all Hitchcock's films the one nearest to perfection. Indeed, its profundity is inseparable from the perfection of form: it is a perfect organism, each character, each sequence, each image, illuminating each other. Form and technique here become the perfect expression of concerns both deep and universal.' *(Robin Wood, Hitchcock's Films Revisited, 1989)*

'In *Vertigo*, Hitchcock reveals himself to his audience, embodying, in Stewart's character, his own obsessions and desire to make women over.' *(Baseline)*

VICTIM

CT: 5 AV: 7.10

1961 GB 100 BW THRILLER

D Basil Dearden
W Janet Green John McCormick

Dirk Bogarde ☆ Sylvia Syms Dennis Price ✓ Anthony Nicholls Peter Copley Norman Bird Peter McEnery ✓ Donald Churchill Derren Nesbitt Charles Lloyd Pack ✓

A bisexual barrister (Dirk Bogarde) risks his reputation by trying to track down blackmailers who murdered his lover (Peter McEnery).

A well acted but mechanically plotted whodunit which was widely praised on release for its sympathetic treatment of homosexuality. Audiences now may wonder why Bogarde's heterosexual relationship (with Sylvia Syms) had to be depicted as so much more meaningful than his homosexual one. Even so, the film was thought so shocking that it was refused the Seal of the Motion Picture Association of America.

ANTI:

'[Its] argument against a cruel and unnecessary persecution is hardly advanced by [the] script, which is more concerned with hoodwinking audiences about the identity of the principal blackmailer than with any serious inquiry into the issues.' *(Derek Hill, Financial Times)*

'Judged purely as a "whodunnit" it is a bit creaky in the joints.' *(Guardian)*

'One must admire the sheer acrobatic skill displayed . . . in walking the tightrope between holier-than-thou hypocrisy and dirtier-than-thou offensiveness.' *(Thomas Wiseman, Sunday Express)*

MIXED:

'I could have done without the melodramatic tingle that occasionally afflicts [the film] . . . And I could certainly have done without those moments when the characters plead the homosexual case . . . and not always convincingly. For all that I applaud *Victim*. It is a good film. Good as a fast-paced thriller. Overwhelmingly good as an acting triumph for Bogarde.' *(Alexander Walker, Evening Standard)*

PRO:

'[The film] has a neat plot, deft direction . . . and the sort of glum good manners one expects of the British in these trying situations.' *(Time)*

'A very efficient and crisply edited thriller.' *(Sunday Telegraph)*

'It takes a stand, has a point of view, says something. And what it says is that English law on homosexuality offers special opportunities to the blackmailer . . . As the successful barrister who must confess his own homosexuality if he is to trap the blackmailers, Dirk Bogarde gives the commanding performance one has long expected from him. With a fine control of gesture and tone he conveys both the suffering of the man condemned by nature and the resolve of the man bent on sacrifice.' *(Dilys Powell)*

VIE ET RIEN D'AUTRE, LA:

see LIFE AND NOTHING BUT.

VIEW TO A KILL, A:

see BOND SERIES.

VINCENT, FRANÇOIS, PAUL AND THE OTHERS

CT:6 AV: 7.67

(aka *Vincent, François, Paul et Les Autres*)

1974 France 118 C DRAMA/FOREIGN

D Claude Sautet
W Jean-Louis Dabadie Claude Neron Claude Sautet

Yves Montand ☆ Michel Piccoli ☆ Serge Reggiani ☆ Gérard Depardieu ☆ Stéphane Audran ☆ Marie Dubois Antonella Lualdi Umberto Orsini Catherine Allégret Ludmilla Mikael

Middle-class, middle-aged Parisians have a collective midlife crisis.

You have only to read the cast list of Claude Sautet's film to know you're in for a feast of acting, and anyone acquainted with this director's work will also be able to anticipate that it will look beautiful. However, the story is weak and the characterization disappointingly superficial. It's not bad – just disappointing in view of the talents involved.

PRO:

'The acting is astonishing . . . everyone is perfect.' *(Jean-Louis Bory, Le Nouvel Observateur)*

MIXED:

'Sautet and Dabadie have rather neglected the women's roles . . . [but] Sautet has used Montant and Depardieu in a particularly pleasing way. One feels an ingratiating personal and professional closeness in the way these two actors play a scene together . . . as if an unofficial yet elemental rite were taking place.' *(Gary Arnold, Washington Post)*

'Undeservedly neglected . . . The director, Claude Sautet, is a wizard at juggling and balancing the complex *Dinner at Eight* situation, and he's got the control and refinement of a master – the film may be too impersonally crafted, but it moves rhythmically, as if it were a melancholy, romantic tune.' *(Pauline Kael)*

'A paradigm of all that is best and worst about the work of Claude Sautet. It looks very good, boasts clever performances and chronicles middle-class Parisian lifestyle with deft accuracy, but it is overwhelmed by its superficial perfection and the powerful glamour of its all-star cast. The real issues of pain, fear and failure are thus left to lie buried in the hollow at its centre.' *(Bergan & Karney)*

VIRGIN SPRING, THE AAW CT: 4 AV: 7.00

(aka *Jungfraukällan*)

1959 Sweden 87 BW DRAMA/FOREIGN

D Ingmar Bergman ☆
W Ulla Isaksson from *Töres Dotter i Vänge* (14th century ballad)

Max Von Sydow Brigitta Pettersson
Brigitta Valberg Gunnel Lindblom Axel Düberg
Tor Isedal

In mediaeval Sweden, a spoiled 15-year-old girl (Brigitta Pettersson) is raped and murdered; whereupon her father and mother (Max Von Sydow, Brigitta Valberg) exact a brutal revenge.

Lyrical one moment, horrific the next, this is one of director Ingmar Bergman's most visual, atmospheric films – partly thanks to his new cameraman, Sven Nykvist, a master of his craft. The point of the story remains obscure, however, and it has a relentlessly gloomy view of human nature. In addition to winning the International Critics' Prize at Cannes, it won the Best Foreign Film Oscar and was also nominated for Marik Vos's costume design.

PRO:

'Outstanding . . . [The film] should put Bergman back where he belongs, among the very few, that is, who can take a script and turn it into a poem . . . The tension never slackens and the beauty seldom fails.' *(The Times)*

'Bergman once again shows his absolute mastery of his craft.' *(Felix Barker, Evening News)*

'Beauty, and vivid, brutal realism stand out sharply against each other.' *(Alexander Walker, Evening Standard)*

'Stark and rather lovely filming of a medieval legend, with heavy symbolism and a strong pictorial sense.' *(Halliwell)*

MIXED:

'There's tremendous talent in Mr Bergman's work, and something else besides, but it's not for me.' *(Burgo Partridge, Time & Tide)*

'Superbly made, of course, but so what?' *(Derek Hill, Tribune)*

ANTI:

'Bergman has converted a stark and simple medieval folk ballad into a complicated evocation of guilt and expiation, cluttered with symbolic mumbo-jumbo.' *(Nina Hibbin, Daily Worker)*

'When I first saw the film I thought it merely nauseous. At a second view I find it generally tedious, occasionally absurd, and always retrograde.' *(Dilys Powell)*

VIRIDIANA CT: 5 AV: 8.45

1961 Spain/Mexico 91 BW DRAMA/COMEDY/FOREIGN

D Luis Buñuel
W Luis Buñuel Julio Alejandro from Buñuel's story

Silvia Pinal Francisco Rabal Fernando Rey
Margarita Lozano Victoria Zinny Teresa Rabal
José Calvo Joaquin Roa Luis Heredia
José Manuel Martin

A wealthy nobleman (Fernando Rey) attempts to rape a novice nun (Silvia Pinal), who reminds him of his dead wife. He then commits suicide out of remorse; inheriting his estate alongside his more pragmatic bastard son (Francisco Rabal), the idealistic girl decides to use it to benefit the poor – but her good intentions are ridiculed by the beggars she is attempting to save.

Buñuel's anti-clerical parable is one of his most acclaimed films, and it's undeniably well made. But like much of his output, it's a nasty piece of work, concerned with emphasizing all that is most ungrateful, cruel and insensitive in human nature. The climax is an orgiastic parody of the Last Supper. Once considered sacrilegious, it now looks more like a juvenile attempt to shock. It won the Palme d'Or at the Cannes Film Festival, whereupon it was immediately condemned by the Vatican and banned by Franco's government in Spain, which had (in what one can only imagine to be a moment of mental aberration) commissioned it.

PRO:

'Yes, the satire is certainly savage in this wonderfully conceived and executed [parody of the Last Supper], yet the implicit protest . . . has an eloquence and force that gives it a kind of poetic beauty. Whether palatable or not must depend on the strength both of your stomach and your religion.' *(Patrick Gibbs, Daily Telegraph)*

'[The film's] painful frankness and wild fury are transcended by the blazing honesty and humanism; and, too, by the author's sheer artistry. Buñuel still makes films – and great films – with the precise assurance of a countrywoman making an apple pie. This is a great film, the masterpiece of one of the world's outstanding living artists.' *(David Robinson, Financial Times)*

'All that is best in Buñuel's work finds expression in *Viridiana*.' *(Robin Grove-White, Isis)*

'One of the cinema's few major philosophical works.' *(Robert Vas)*

'A superb film . . . Buñuel goes far beyond attacking professional religion and the practices of celibacy and self-mortification. He assaults the very basis of a creed which he sees as upholding a callous and decaying society. The Christian myths are savagely parodied. A band of the maimed, the halt and the blind, recipients of Viridiana's charity, drunkenly re-enact the Last Supper and after it fall to coupling behind the sofa, while a repulsive outcast puts on the veil and crown of the Bride and, scattering the feathers of the murdered Dove, joins in dancing to the Hallelujah Chorus. This is not the simple derisive reaction against the forms of religion which many inquiring minds go through in early life (and from which many permanently adolescent minds never emerge). It is the expression of a hatred which has developed, which has matured. For Buñuel the Church is anti-life.' *(Dilys Powell)*

ANTI:

'Incomprehensible.' *(Pauline Kael)*

'Buñuel has all the hatred: what he lacks is the necessary antidote – love.' *(Isabel Quigly, Spectator)*

VISKINGAR OCH ROP: *see* CRIES AND WHISPERS.

VIVA VILLA! AAN CT: 5 AV: 7.44

1934 US 110/115 BW BIOPIC/ACTION/WESTERN

D Jack Conway, Howard Hawks (uncredited, since he was replaced half-way through shooting)
W Ben Hecht AAN from Edgcumb Pinchon, O.B. Stade's book

Wallace Beery ☆ Fay Wray Stuart Erwin
Leo Carrillo ✔ Donald Cook George E. Stone
Joseph Schildkraut ✔ Henry B. Walthall
Katherine DeMille

A Mexican bandit (Wallace Beery) becomes a hero of his people, and ultimately President.

A true story forms the basis of this highly fictional, episodic western which looks primitive by modern standards, but is full of exciting action sequences. Highlights are Beery's dynamic performance, which survives a wobbly accent, and the superb cinematography of James Wong Howe. It was hugely popular, ranked 7th in the *Film Daily* annual poll of US film critics, and Oscar-nominated for best sound (Douglas Shearer).

PRO:

'A colourful and at times exciting procession with a good job of work by Wallace Beery.' *(MFB)*

MIXED:

'Strong bo fodder . . . handicapped a bit by its abnormal masculine appeal.' *(Variety)*

'As history it naturally won't do . . . Instead we have a dashing, expertly fashioned movie, full of galloping and shooting, rough love-making and sudden death.' *(Daily Telegraph)*

'As a spectacle and an excitement this is very satisfactory . . . The plot has many ups and downs and most of the characters are at once definite and wildly romantic . . . Beery shows his remarkable powers.' *(The Times)*

'A good, lusty, commercial film which will make money beyond its artistic merits, because it shouts very loud and rather stirringly the half-truths that people love to hear.' *(C.A. Lejeune, Observer)*

ANTI:

'A glorified horse opera . . . badly edited and clumsily constructed. A high pitch of dramatic excitement is reached much before the middle. The rest is anti-climax. The spectators excitement is incited by the purely physical impact of the furious riding and war sequences, by the frequent sadism, and the lively musical score.' *(Irving Lerner, New Masses)*

VIVA ZAPATA! CT: 6 AV: 7.92

1952 US 113 BW DRAMA/BIOPIC/WAR

D Elia Kazan
W John Steinbeck ☆AAN from Edgcumb Pichon's novel *Zapata the Unconquered*

Marlon Brando ☆AAN Jean Peters
Anthony Quinn ☆ AAW Joseph Wiseman Arnold Moss Alan Reed Harold Gordon Lou Gilbert
Mildred Dunnock Frank Silvera ☆ Margo

A Mexican bandit (Marlon Brando) leads a revolution.

A curious mixture of political drama (with the unsurprising message that power corrupts) and a straightforward action movie. The film grinds to a halt too often to make room for histrionics by Brando or Quinn, and a predictable whitewash job is done on a man who was in reality a brutal killer, but even so this stands out as one of the more intelligent and enjoyable biopics turned out by Hollywood. Alex North's music and the art direction of Lyle Wheeler and Leland Fuller were Oscar-nominated.

ANTI:

'Undoubtedly there is great drama in Zapata's life. But this picture fails to exploit it. The film is flashy and episodic, uneven in its pacing, superficial in its story and sporadic in its dramatics . . . Brando . . . continues to act in his monotoned, stony-faced style, and his blank expression doesn't help the drama much.' *(Jesse Zunser, Cue)*

'Comes out as a disjointed western, too wordy for those solely concerned with the horses and the shooting and too distorted for those interested in its more lofty aspirations . . . Mr Brando has still to prove he is good at something other than being Mr Brando.' *(Milton Shulman, Evening Standard)*

'The voice and the manner of this Zapata are those of the dumb-ox of *Streetcar* . . . Is it the only kind of part Brando can play?' *(Margaret Hinxman, Evening News)*

'Hard, cruel, curiously unemotional . . . Kazan's direction strives for a personal intimacy but neither he nor the John Steinbeck scripting achieves this in enough measure.' *(Variety)*

MIXED:

'Strange, exotic and exciting . . . The last ten minutes . . . are memorable cinema. Viva the players, too . . . [Brando's] is a performance of impressively controlled power . . . Big scenes shake with drama, even though others are sad or soggy.' *(Leonard Mosley, Daily Express)*

'This is not one of the slick, illiterate tracts we have come to expect as Hollywood's contribution to the discussion of politics and revolution. But neither is it another *Grapes of Wrath*. It is well worth seeing . . . But in the end, confused and repetitive, it fails.' *(Thomas Spencer, Daily Worker)*

'Elia Kazan's direction of Steinbeck's salute to the revolutionary impulse is not always effective. Kazan is very clever in delineating small, highly dramatic and melodramatic situations. His forte is not the larger, the abstract themes, and in this film he often evades the subtler, and sometimes the more important, scenes . . . .But Kazan is very able whenever the drama involves action.' *(Henry Hart, Films in Review, 1952)*

PRO:

'The [film's] strength is in Kazan's direction backed by [the] magnificent unromantic photography . . . And Marlon Brando . . . Brando conveys power, which, in the cinema, can transcend acting.' *(Richard Winnington, News Chronicle)*

'The best film I have seen this year . . . a fascinating study of a man, a savagely beautiful evocation of a background, a superb piece of all-round film-making . . . [Brando gives] a performance of slow-combustion power ranging from sullen peasant cunning to tigerish ferocity.' *(Fred Majdalany, Daily Mail)*

VOINA I MIR: *see* WAR AND PEACE.

VON RYAN'S EXPRESS CT: 7 AV: 7.20

1965 US 117 C WAR/ACTION/ADVENTURE

D Mark Robson ☆
W Wendell Mayes Joseph Landon ✓ from David Westheimer's novel

Frank Sinatra ☆ Trevor Howard ☆ Raffaella Carrà Brad Dexter Sergio Fantoni ☆ John Leyton Edward Mulhare Wolfgang Preiss James Brolin John Van Dreelen

American colonel Frank Sinatra leads a mass escape of 600 American and British prisoners-of-war.

Well-crafted World War II chase-adventure, none too realistic but very entertaining in the way it mixes humour and suspense.

MIXED:

'Comforting fiction . . . in its complete predictability . . . It is a businesslike escape story.' *(David Robinson, Financial Times)*

'Robson directs the actors the way a signalman would direct his rolling-stock.' *(Alexander Walker, Evening Standard)*

'We've seen it all, or nearly all, before . . . All the same, Mark Robson, after an uncertain beginning, directs an exciting melodramatic story . . . The Alps are magnificent.' *(Ian Wright, Guardian)*

PRO:

'The prevailing tone is high adventure . . . and everything clicks along with the gathering momentum of the train itself.' *(Arthur Knight, Saturday Review)*

'Wherever you bite this exciting wartime thriller, you sink your teeth into good red meat.' *(Felix Barker, Evening News)*

'As entertainment, it works . . . Intelligently done, good to look at, and often exciting, and Trevor Howard is first-rate.' *(Richard Mallett, Punch)*

VOYAGE HOME, THE: *see* STAR TREK VI: THE VOYAGE HOME.

VREDEN'S DAG: *see* DAY OF WRATH.

WAGES OF FEAR CT: 9 AV: 9.09

(aka *Le Salaire De La Peur*)

1953 France/Italy 105/140/155 BW THRILLER/ FOREIGN

D Henri-Georges Clouzot ☆
W Henri-Georges Clouzot from Georges Arnaud's novel

Yves Montand ☆ Charles Vanel ☆ Véra Clouzot Folco Lulli ☆ Peter van Eyck ☆ William Tubbs Dario Moreno Jo Dest Antonio Centa Luis de Lima

Yves Montand and Charles Vanel are two of four truckers ferrying nitro-glycerine through many sorts of nastiness.

The opening shot makes the point clear enough: it's a world in which humans are like frantic beetles, teased by an uncaring God and struggling for individual survival. It's also a harshly capitalistic, America-dominated world; and early US prints were trimmed of such offending passages as the one where the American boss who hires the drivers says 'They don't belong to a union, and they don't have any relatives, so if anything happens, no one will come around causing trouble.'

Clouzot takes care to establish his characters in the first hour, and some may find this part of the film laboured. However, the preparation pays dividends in the final two-thirds, when *Wages of Fear* turns into one of the most suspense-filled movies ever made. The film was awarded the Palme d'Or at Cannes. The American remake, *Sorcerer* (1977), is far inferior.

MIXED:

'Though quite a thriller, [it] would not seem to merit a festival award.' *(Bosley Crowther)*

'As skilful as, in its preoccupation with violence and its unrelieved pessimism, it is unlikeable.' *(Penelope Houston, S & S)*

'The characters . . . have no size, and at the end one is left without pity for them and without terror of the forces which have overwhelmed them. One respects and admires the strength of Clouzot's style and the vigour of his imagination – an imagination, I may say, which by its creation of cruelties and horrors left a mark on critics usually impassive enough. And after that one simply doesn't care, and not all the fine acting of Yves Montand, Folco Lulli, Peter van Eyck and Charles Vanel, especially Charles Vanel, can make one care.' *(Dilys Powell)*

'One of the most evil [pictures] ever made, and yet, curiously, one that uses the approach of religion. [It] seeks out epiphanies at the cold-blooded level of the swamp . . . where deity is first experienced – as despair . . . The actors try hard, but [it] is not a drama of character; Clouzot is much more interested in ideas than people. He is saying the world is sick unto death . . . The evil in all this is that [he] does not seem to care what happens to human consciousness . . . He takes instead a cruel pleasure in all violent dissolution. Clouzot and his kind are cultural atavists arrested in the savage stage.' *(Derek Granger, Financial Times)*

'An acrid, guilty, bitter piece . . . but . . . an exercise in dramatic tension rarely equalled . . . Clouzot's long-drawn reliance on physical suspense . . . makes the film . . . seem somewhat arbitrary and contrived.' *(Time)*

'A long film, maybe a bit overlong . . . Possesses a cunning craftsmanship which means it doesn't drag . . . Not a great film, but a commanding one.' *(Tim Pulleine, F & F, 1986)*

PRO:

'*Wages of Fear* . . . is now being hailed by Parisians as a truly great French film. It is certainly a great cinematic thriller.' *(New Yorker)*

'Clouzot may be neither the most talented nor the maker of the most likeable films but he is perhaps the most significant and certainly the toughest . . . [This] is probably his best film to date . . . No nice film, but . . . very powerful and well made and very well worth seeing.' *(Manchester Guardian)*

'Narrative suspense so appallingly good that it leaves the spectator literally exhausted . . . A bitter film.. the atmosphere of oppressive despair and heartbreak . . . is the more terrible for being totally unsentimental.' *(Fred Majdalany, Time & Tide)*

'In terms of sheer construction and vigorous narration the film is a masterpiece; its tension, relieved only by a few necessary touches of humour, is utterly unrelenting.' *(Roy Armes, French Cinema Since 1946, 1966)*

'It has some claim to be the greatest suspense thriller of all time; it is the suspense not of mystery but of Damocles's sword.' *(Basil Wright, 1972)*

WAGON MASTER CT: 7 AV: 6.80

(aka *Wagonmaster*)

1950 US 86 C WESTERN

D John Ford ☆
W Frank S. Nugent Patrick Ford ☆

Ben Johnson ☆ Joanne Dru Harry Carey Jr ✓ Ward Bond ✓ Charles Kemper Alan Mowbray

An odd assortment of people, including a convoy of Mormons, travels west in pioneering days.

No film illustrates better Ford's vision of America as a collection of nationalities, religions and interests coming together to form a common civilization. The plot is episodic, the characters are simple, and there's no John Wayne; but the film has an epic sweep which makes it one of the great westerns. The fine camerawork is by Bert Glennon. The movie inspired the long-running TV series, *Wagon Train*.

'A good outdoor action film, done in the best John Ford manner. That means careful character development and movement, spiced with high spots of action, good drama and leavening comedy moments.' *(Variety)*

'Under Ford's leadership . . . a trip well worth the taking.' *(New York Times)*

'*Wagonmaster* is the nearest any director has come to an avant-garde western . . . The feel of the period, the poetry of space and of endeavour, is splendidly communicated.' *(Lindsay Anderson, S & S)*

'It can be argued that *Wagonmaster* is John Ford's greatest film. Ford does not waste any time over the subtleties of characterization and twists of plot. He strokes boldly across the canvas of the American past as he concentrates on the evocative images of a folk tradition of free adventure and compelling adaptability. There are no moral shadings. His villains are evil incarnate – whining, wheedling and uselessly destructive. The hero destroys them in the end as he would destroy a snake.' *(Andrew Sarris, Confessions of a Cultist, 1970)*

'The emotional quality of *Wagonmaster* is like that of *Rio Grande* (1950) and *She Wore a Yellow Ribbon* (1949) – very rich in gentle, nostalgic emotion, underscored by comedy, and not disturbed by a disruption in the eventual integration of all emotional elements into the whole. This deceptively unpretentious film is in many ways the high point of Ford's westerns. Ford's optimism and pessimism are in perfect balance. The darker side of his vision gives an emotional depth lacking in earlier films like *Stagecoach* (1939) and *Drums along the Mohawk* (1939), but the optimism prevails and renders this film essentially undisturbing and only gentle in its nostalgia, not bitter like the later films.' *(J.A. Place, The Western Films of John Ford, 1973)*

'What emerges at the end is nothing less than a view of life itself, the view of a poet.' *(Patrick Gibbs, 1965)*

'Along with *The Fugitive* (1947) and *The Sun Shines Bright* (1953), I think *Wagonmaster* came closest to being what I had wanted to achieve.' *(John Ford)*

WAIT UNTIL DARK — CT: 6 AV: 6.82

1967 US 108 C THRILLER

D Terence Young
W Robert Carrington Jane Howard Carrington from Frederick Knott's play

Audrey Hepburn ☆ AAN Alan Arkin ☆ Richard Crenna Efrem Zimbalist Jr Jack Weston Samantha Jones Julie Herrod Frank O'Brien Gary Morgan Jean Del Val

A blind women (Audrey Hepburn) is terrorized by three crooks (Alan Arkin, Richard Crenna, Jack Weston) who believe she has heroin in her New York apartment.

Tense, influential thriller where Hepburn memorably turns the tables on the villains by killing the lights and rendering them as blind as she is.

ANTI:

'Sometimes a tiresome play suffers a sea-change on its way to the screen and turns into something thoroughly enjoyable. Not, so unfortunately, [this] thriller . . . Terence Young directed efficiently with no great flair.' *(John Russell Taylor, The Times)*

MIXED:

'To give [it] its due [the film] scares you just as much as it is meant to . . . The people who contrived this melodrama have played some dirty, sloppy tricks that may evoke our adrenalin but rarely our respect.' *(Joseph Morgenstern, Newsweek)*

'If you were to take it apart and examine it carefully, the plot . . . would shrivel under your gaze into a little heap of melodramatic mud . . . [but the film] succeeds in holding.' *(Ann Pacey, Sun)*

'Part of the film is absorbing and terrifying. But it strangely fails to achieve a really daunting climax . . . I recommend it as an ice-cube for a hot day.' *(Robert Ottaway, Daily Sketch)*

PRO:

'An ingeniously plotted, heart-poundingly suspenseful thriller that will pulverise every nerve in your body.' *(Clive Hirschhorn, Sunday Express)*

'Three of the meanest scoundrels for some time menace Audrey Hepburn . . . and what they do will make you jump out of your seat at least once.' *(David York, Sunday Mirror)*

'Mr Young's film does well. The ingenious narrative persuades; the shocks are smartly contrived.' *(Dilys Powell, Sunday Times)*

WALK IN THE SUN, A — CT: 6 AV: 8.00

(aka *Salerno Beachhead*)

1945 US 117 BW WAR/DRAMA

D Lewis Milestone ☆
W Robert Rossen from Harry Brown's story

Dana Andrews ☆ Richard Conte ☆ John Ireland George Tyne Lloyd Bridges Sterling Holloway Herbert Rudley

In 1943, an infantry platoon lands at Salerno and fights its way six miles inland.

Powerful, well acted war film which was successful at the box office and favourably reviewed. But it's not on the level of Milestone's previous war epic, *All*

Quiet on the Western Front (1930), and it hasn't dated well. The problem lies in Rossen's script – though literate, intelligent and ironic, it's also literary, verbose and pseudo-philosophical. The action sequences are exciting, though, and its principal innovation – the use of a ballad as a narration device – proved influential on later films, such as *High Noon* (1952).

PRO:

'A swiftly overpowering piece of work.' *(Bosley Crowther)*

'Concerned with the individual rather than the battlefield, the film is finely perceptive, exciting, and very moving.' *(Penelope Houston)*

'A notable war film, if not the most notable war film to come from America.' *(Richard Winnington)*

'After nearly two hours one is sorry when it ends.' *(Richard Mallett, Punch)*

MIXED:

'The greatest weakness in *A Walk in the Sun* is its dialogue. It is intelligent dialogue, and at times even brilliant. But there is too much of it.' *(Milton Shulman)*

'Comes nearer than any film I have seen to giving a reasonably accurate impression of a platoon in action . . . The film has faults. The talk of the men is too self-consciously "literary". There are those monotonous repetitions of phrases common to all authors who base their style on Hemingway. There are one or two cases of military poetic licence: bridges, for instance, are not blown by having hand grenades thrown at them. But taking it all in all, the film presents (in American terms) in a much more truthful and imaginative way than I can previously recall, the particular and universal nature of life in an infantry battle.' *(Fred Majdalany)*

ANTI:

'Much of the film is worked out with very unusual vitality and care – much of which, unfortunately, is related more nearly to ballet than to warfare. But mainly, I think, it is an embarrassing movie. The dialogue seems as unreal as it is expert. Most of the characters – as distinct from the men who play them – are as unreal and literary as the dialogue. The aesthetic and literary and pseudo-democratic preoccupations are so strong that at times all sense of plain reality drops out of the picture. At the end, for instance, with their farmhouse captured, various featured players are shown completing the gags which tag their characters – chomping an apple, notching a rifle-stock, and so on – while, so far as the camera lets you know, their wounded comrades are still writhing unattended in the courtyard.' *(James Agee, Nation)*

WALKABOUT

CT: 6 AV: 7.44

1970 Australia 100 C DRAMA/ADVENTURE

D Nicolas Roeg ☆
W Edward Bond from James Vance Marshall's play

Jenny Agutter Lucien John David Gulpilil John Meillon Peter Carver John Illingsworth Barry Donnelly Noelene Brown Carlo Manchini

A girl and her younger brother (Jenny Agutter and Lucien John) are left marooned in the Australian outback when their father (John Meillon) kills himself. The girl finds herself attracted to an aborigine (David Gulpilil) who befriends them.

Nicolas Roeg's first solo attempt at direction (after his co-directed *Performance*) is stylish and vivid. As always in his films, the meaning is conveyed through visuals, rather than words. Trees, animals and radio all carry symbolic significance. But his attempt to draw links between the aborigine boy and Christ seem self-conscious and forced, while the noble savage versus evil civilization motif is obvious and schematic.

PRO:

'Exciting and sad.' *(Quinlan)*

'A parable of biblical density.' *(John Izod, The Films of Nicolas Roeg, 1992)*

MIXED:

'[Roeg] has sometimes been carried away by the pleasures of his medium: too many flash-backs, too many elegantly dissolving landscapes. But the film is rich enough, especially at a second look, to make you forget the flaws. You are left with the impression of a fresh, powerful and humane imagination.' *(Dilys Powell)*

'The shimmering light and colour, the conflict of cultures, and the emergence of semi-mystic sexual forces in the desert landscape make this as Roegian a film as *The Man Who Fell To Earth* or *Bad Timing*. Only the rather cute casting of Jenny Agutter as an English Rose and some implausibly romantic moments detract.' *(Chris Auty, Time Out)*

'There's . . . a tendency (unfortunate, probably) to read *Walkabout* as a catch-all of symbols and metaphors, in which the noble savage and his natural life are tested and found superior to civilization and cities. The movie does, indeed, make this comparison several times. Hundreds of miles from help, the girl turns on her portable radio to hear a philosopher observe: "It is now possible to state that 'that is' is." Well, this isn't exactly helpful, and so we laugh.' *(Roger Ebert)*

ANTI:

'A tepid artistic effort . . . Roeg's bag is photography, but pretty pictures alone cannot sustain – and, in fact, inhibit – this fragile and forced screen adaptation . . . In an effort to pump up the plot,

Roeg resorts to ad nauseam inserts of insects, reptiles and assorted wild beasts, in varying stages of life and decay.' *(Variety)*

'A hysterical indictment of civilization and science, full of weird photographic effects, maniacal crosscutting and chronology jumbling (his favorite devices), making sure that the story became all but impossible to follow.' *(John Simon)*

WAR AND PEACE AAW CT: 6 AV: 8.40

(aka *Voina i Mir*)

1967 US SR 373/507 C WAR/EPIC/FOREIGN

D Sergei Bondarchuk ☆
W Sergei Bondarchuk Vasili Solovyov from Leo Tolstoy's novel

Ludmila Savelyeva Sergei Bondarchuk Vyacheslav Tikhonov Anastasia Vertinskaya Vasily Lanovoi Irina Skobotseva

Two Russian families react to the invasion of their country by Napoleon.

Second-rate dubbing detracts from this long, lavish and faithful adaptation of Tolstoy's classic. But the set-pieces are among the most spectacular ever. King Vidor's 1956 version, starring Audrey Hepburn and Henry Fonda, has many faults (mainly of omission) but is probably more enjoyable for an English-speaking audience.

PRO:

'Without doubt, one of the greatest films ever made, a cinematic superspectacular that is not only the finest epic film of our time but also a great and noble translation of a literary masterpiece. Though Bondarchuk is obviously master of the panoramic (you have not seen or even imagined anything like his forty-minute battle of Borodino, staged with 120,000 men and 800 horses, or the looting and burning of Moscow or the fairy-tale ballrooms and grandeurs of that city's pre-1812 elegance), it is the human vignettes and the leading characters that emerge triumphant.' *(Judith Crist)*

'The film's frequent lapses into grandiloquence and its reliance on the dissolve don't detract from the stunning use of overhead tracking shots, split-screen techniques and the subjective camera.' *(Bergan & Karney)*

ANTI:

'Spectacle apart, Bondarchuk's version of Tolstoy falls into the category of respectable mediocrity, and matters aren't helped by the loud American voices with which everyone speaks in this much-edited and dubbed version.' *(Geoff Brown, Time Out)*

'The New York Film Critics' Circle recently picked *War and Peace* best foreign picture of the year. Ratings, it would seem, are needed less by films than by film critics. Any critic . . . who voted for *War and Peace* should be given a rating of R, meaning "to be admitted to films with adult pretensions only in the company of an adult guardian who can explain to the critic the difference between pretension and achievement".' *(John Simon)*

WAR CORRESPONDENT: *see* STORY OF G.I. JOE, THE.

WAR OF THE ROSES, THE CT: 7 AV: 6.69

1989 US 116 C DRAMA/COMEDY/ROMANCE

D Danny DeVito ✔
W Michael Leeson from Warren Adler's novel

Michael Douglas ☆ Kathleen Turner ✔ Danny DeVito Marianne Sagebrecht Sean Astin Heather Fairfield G.D. Spradlin Trenton Teigen Bethany McKinney

Oliver Rose (Michael Douglas) is a handsome, thrusting lawyer with a beautiful, supportive wife, Barbara (Kathleen Turner). Suddenly, she wishes he were dead.

One of the surprise hits of 1989. Though publicized as a comedy, it is more disturbing than funny, as it scrutinizes the microscopic bacteria which lie dormant in any relationship, and watches – with surgical detachment – as they evolve into a terminal disease. Couples should see this, if only as a terrible example.

Michael Douglas plays the husband as a blinkered male chauvinist, but wins you over with his realization that he is still in love with his wife, no matter what she does to him. Kathleen Turner's transformation from supine spouse to feline fury is delicate, inexorable, yet oddly likeable.

Danny DeVito's direction is as deft as it is psychologically ruthless. The only cop-out – a mistaken concession, I suspect, to appalled preview audiences – is a two-second shot which suggests that Barbara hasn't quite had the courage of her convictions, and turned Oliver's dog into pooch paté.

PRO:

'Though over the top, [the film] manages to tickle the funny bone as well as touch a nerve. It also resonates with the uncomfortable shock of recognition.' *(Clive Hirschhorn, Sunday Express)*

'Marriage guidance counsellors could do worse than mount special screenings of this film.' *(Nigella Lawson, Sunday Times)*

'A comedy so black it makes Billy Wilder look like Walt Disney.' *(Trevor Willsmer, Film Review)*

'The ballsiest comedy to come out of Hollywood in years.' *(Scheuer)*

MIXED:

'The battle of the sexes escalates to new levels of viciousness . . . DeVito . . . delivers an even bleaker vision of domestic discord his second time out. Maybe too bleak: Douglas and Turner go at each other with all the ferocity of two cartoon characters but with less dimension than, say, Bugs Bunny and Daffy Duck . . . Turner begins well, but midway adopts an icy facade that seldom thaws.' *(Kevin Lally, The Film Journal)*

'As satiric comedy on yuppie materialism, this very black comedy scores a bull's-eye – for about an hour. Then, having made its point, it continues for nearly an hour more as the couple grows increasingly vicious and irrational . . . Some people loved this film (the star performances are perfect) so obviously it's a matter of taste. DeVito's odd point of view and wild camera angles are an asset throughout.' *(Maltin)*

'Rancorous comedy, sometimes amusing but too mean-spirited for many laughs.' *(Halliwell)*

'In its later stages, it achieves a level of silliness even Stan and Ollie wouldn't have dared attempt but, without a sympathetic character to latch onto, it leaves us detached from the proceedings.' *(Rose)*

ANTI:

'The idea runs into the ground. When entertainment depends on the next obscene act of revenge, humour has sickened into a state of voyeuristic decay.' *(Angus Wolfe Murray, Scotsman)*

WATERDANCE, THE CT: 8 AV: 7.30

1991 US 107 C DRAMA/ROMANCE

D Neal Jimenez ✔ Michael Steinberg
W Neal Jimenez

Eric Stoltz ☆ Helen Hunt ✔ William Forsythe ☆ Wesley Snipes ☆ Elizabeth Pena

A writer (Eric Stoltz) and his married girlfriend (Helen Hunt) come to terms with his being confined to a wheelchair. Meanwhile, a black sexist (Wesley Snipes) and a racist biker (William Forsythe) get on each other's nerves.

One of the most thoughtful dramas of 1992, this disappeared from cinemas undeservedly soon, because audiences thought – wrongly – that the subject might be depressing. *The Waterdance* is one of the best acted, most truthful, and therefore most moving, films ever about disability: it was written and co-directed by Neal Jimenez, who became wheelchair-bound himself after an accident. It's the work of an extremely able man.

ANTI:

'Oh dear. Sometimes when you pour your experiences into something, they spill over and require much mopping up by non-responsible parties; in this case the audience . . . Long before curtain-time the film has withdrawn into a narcotic buddyism.' *(Nigel Andrews, Financial Times)*

'At best [it] is a compendium of negative virtues . . . The script is weakest at male-female confrontations.' *(Michael Sragow, New Yorker)*

MIXED:

'Its ensemble nature is both its strongest asset and its weakness . . . [The movie] cannot quite bring itself to resist the balm of male bonding, so that at worst it comes perilously close to something like a buddy movie on wheels. Even then, the script, direction and performances are all right on the nose. It's frank and funny with it.' *(Tom Charity, Time Out)*

PRO:

'Jimenez is relentless about avoiding sentimentality or condescension, and the refreshing difference distinguishes this film from its run of worthy predecessors . . . [His] bracing candor lifts [the film] far above the merely uplifting . . . The pathos invoked is not for the unfortunate condition of these wounded bodies, but for the inescapably wounded condition of the human soul . . . This is a wise and witty script, directed with a keen eye, cut sharply and acted with dash.' *(Myron Meisel, Film Journal)*

'Delineated with perception and generosity, skirting the pitfalls of sentimental excess. The film's real achievement, however, is in the depiction of Garcia's relationship with his married lover . . . A small but skilfully crafted film.' *(Hugo Davenport, Daily Telegraph)*

'What sounds like a prescription for 90 minutes of gut-wrenching worthiness actually emerges as one of the year's most witty, intelligent and incisive comedies.' *(Mark Kermode, New Musical Express)*

'Honest, unsentimental, deeply moving, often extremely funny.' *(Philip French, Observer)*

'Films are so often about big, dumb conflicts and predictable conclusions. *The Waterdance* is about the everyday process of continuing one's life under a tragically altered set of circumstances. It considers what life is, and under what conditions it is worth living. After all the cheap sentiment that's been brought to this subject over the years, it is exhilarating and challenging to see a movie that knows exactly what it's talking about, and looks you straight in the eye.' *(Roger Ebert)*

'A smashing success if great performances and a deftly told, thoroughly absorbing tale mean anything.' *(Variety)*

WAY AHEAD, THE CT: 8 AV: 7.33

(aka *The Immortal Battalion*)

1944 GB 91 US/116 BW WAR/DRAMA

D Carol Reed ☆
W Eric Ambler Peter Ustinov ☆ from Ambler's story

David Niven ☆ Stanley Holloway ☆ Raymond Huntley William Hartnell ☆ James Donald John Laurie Peter Ustinov Trevor Howard

An officer (David Niven) trains a platoon of raw recruits, which finds itself in battle all too soon.

Carol Reed's initially humorous, ultimately moving drama was intended to be a wartime training film; it turned out much superior to that, and is one of the best movies about ordinary men being transformed into an effective fighting force. Richard Lester's scornful parody of it, *How I Won The War* (1967) has, ironically, aged less well.

'It is a beautiful portrait of the Army and of the ordinary citizen. Please accept my most sincere congratulations and thanks.' *(Private letter from Jack Beddington, head of Films Division, Ministry of Information to Carol Reed)*

'Technique apart, perhaps the greatest merit of this film is the fidelity of its characterisations, both of the individuals and of the homes and community from which they come.' *(MFB)*

'A pretty skilled piece of movie-making . . . it scarcely puts a foot down wrong.' *(C.A. Lejeune, New York Times)*

'Brilliantly and humorously handled by Carol Reed.' *(Manchester Guardian)*

'To be admired and recommended for its direction, its writing and its playing . . . In spite of the lively dialogue of the first half of the film . . . it was not until the second half and embarkation for service overseas that *The Way Ahead* seemed to me to show its real quality. Carol Reed, though he works successfully in the semi-documentary technique of the early sequences, is at his best when he can use his rare talent for speed, for split-second timing and the creation of emotional suspense.' *(Dilys Powell)*

WAY OUT WEST

CT: 8 AV: 8.82

1936 US 66 BW COMEDY/WESTERN

D James Horn ☆
W Charles Rogers Felix Adler James Parrott from Jack Jevne and Charles Rogers's story

Stan Laurel ☆ Oliver Hardy ☆ James Finlayson ✓ Sharon Lynne Stanley Fields Rosina Lawrence James Mason James C. Morton Frank Mills David Pepper

Laurel and Hardy deliver the deed for a gold mine to the daughter (Rosina Lawrence) of a dead prospector.

Laurel and Hardy in their most celebrated movie, a spoof of B-westerns featuring some of their greatest slapstick routines and their rendition of 'The Trail of the Lonesome Pine'. James Finlayson is a splendid parody villain. Marvin Hatley's score was Oscar-nominated.

ANTI:

'Manner in which this comedy falters and stumbles along is probably due both to formula direction and scripting . . . There's too much driving home of gags.' *(Variety)*

MIXED:

'Very much the usual Laurel and Hardy style, with the usual elaborate Laurel and Hardy gags and a considerable amount of broad slapstick. There is little that can be said to break new ground; but Laurel and Hardy fans will find the film quite up to scratch . . . Much of the humour [is] long-drawn and a trifle mechanical . . . [The film] contains grotesque and terrifying elements not suitable for children.' *(MFB)*

'The plot is somewhat thin in texture, but a number of original gags are nevertheless introduced, and these mingle with the evergreen in a manner that makes for much hearty laughter . . . Laurel and Hardy extend their repertoire by adding singing and dancing to their crazy fooling and are resourceful enough to cloak occasional flat spots in the development . . . The film may be a two-reeler masquerading as a full length feature, but the enlargement is fully justified.' *(Kine Weekly)*

'The slight story is simply an excuse for the comedians to put over a generous sample of their typical comedy. The fooling is amusing enough, but more use could have been made of the setting . . . There is all the usual Laurel nonsense and the Hardy exasperation . . . But in spite of these good things, one feels that there is something lacking. the fooling, laughable though most of it is, just isn't sufficiently strong enough to carry such a sketchy story . . . The supporting cast have little to do.' *(Film Weekly)*

PRO:

'[It] has all the exhilarating tonic of the unashamedly absurd; one comes away feeling years younger and practically kittenish.' *(Paul Jacobs, Hollywood Spectator)*

'[It] is not only one of their most perfect films, but ranks with the best screen comedy anywhere.' *(David Robinson, S & S, 1954)*

'The film is leisurely in the best sense: you adjust to a different rhythm and come out feeling relaxed as if you'd had a vacation.' *(Pauline Kael, 1980)*

'With the possible exception of *Sons of the Desert, Way Out West* must rank as the best of all the Laurel & Hardy features . . . .(It) is 100-proof undiluted Laurel & Hardy, and one of their best showcase vehicles.' *(William K. Everson; The Films of Laurel and Hardy, 1967)*

WAY TO THE STARS, THE CT: 6 AV: 7.63

(aka *Johnny in the Clouds*)

1945 GB 109 BW WAR/DRAMA

D Anthony Asquith ☆
W Terence Rattigan Anatole de Grunwald ☆ from Terence Rattigan and Richard Sherman's story based on John Pudney's poem.

John Mills ☆ Rosamund John ☆ Michael Redgrave ☆ Douglass Montgomery ☆ Basil Radford Stanley Holloway Joyce Carey Renee Asherson Trevor Howard Jean Simmons

World War II, as seen by the inhabitants of a hotel near a British airfield.

A war film with practically no battle footage, this deals with two themes: the way wartime affects romance, and the impact of American forces on Britain. It's a humorous, humane comedy-drama which always holds the attention and ends up extremely touching. Some of the stiff-upper-lip attitudes may strike modern audiences as laughable. However, most critics who lived through World War II were agreed that it evokes very effectively the atmosphere that existed during wartime.

ANTI:

'It has dated badly in its genteelly romantic view of the hazards and heartbreaks, and in its cosy cementing of Anglo-American relations.' *(Tom Milne, Time Out)*

MIXED:

'My only criticism is that the British social distinctions between officers and men are too sharp. It is a fine achievement and first-rate entertainment.' *(Daily Herald)*

'The reticences of [the] theme are admirably conveyed and the subtleties of the script are sensitively enlarged by [the] direction . . . It is a film that moved me at times, and yet I find it difficult to be enthusiastic about it. Its tameness, however . . . deserves better than the sensationalism that usually clouds this theme.' *(New Statesman)*

'Does not quite match the achievement of *In Which We Serve* or *The Way Ahead*, but comes close to both . . . Most memorable is Asquith's creation of a group of typical British and American flying men.' *(Edgar Anstey, Spectator)*

PRO:

'Flawlessly observed . . . The love passages have all the poignancy of unexpressed emotion . . . A moving film . . . which somehow catches the rhythm of war and the baffled courage of men.' *(Richard Winnington, News Chronicle)*

'Mr Rattigan is . . . at the very peak of the second rank of craftsmen . . . Redgrave plays with great sensitivity . . . But it is Mr Douglass Montgomery . . . who bears the palm from this picture . . . [and] steals it from the competition.' *(Daily Mail)*

'Sensitive and intelligent . . . It is not perfect – but it has, as so many films have not, a close relation to reality.' *(Elspeth Grant, Daily Sketch)*

'Not for a long time have I seen a film so satisfying, so memorable, or so successful in evoking the precise mood and atmosphere of the recent past.' *(Richard Mallett, Punch)*

'British emotional understatement has become a cliché in the British cinema, and it would have been easy to overdo the offhandedness in this tale of battle and heroism. Anthony Asquith has achieved a delicate balance of timing throughout the stumbling, clipped speeches of the characters in emotional sequences, the easy, rapid flow of talk and laughter in the intervals of hilarity combine to evoke with scarcely a false touch the atmosphere of wartime. The life of an RAF camp, or come to that the life of an RAF flyer, has, I feel sure, some flavour not to be apprehended by the ordinary civilian. Whether or not *The Way to the Stars* holds that flavour I am not qualified to judge; I can only say that now, at this end of a moment in history, the piece is to the ordinary civilian inexpressibly moving.' *(Dilys Powell)*

'Humour, humanity and not a sign of mawkishness.' *(Basil Wright, 1972)*

WEDDING BANQUET, THE

CT: 7 AV: 7.00 (est)

1993 US 107 C ROMANCE/COMEDY

D Ang Lee ☆
W Ang Lee ☆

Winston Chao May Chin Sihung Lung Ah-Leh Gua Mitchell Lichtenstein

A gay Taiwanese businessman (Winston Chao) living in New York can't bring himself to reveal his sexuality to his conservative parents. He undergoes a marriage of convenience to placate them and get his bride (May Chin) a work permit.

Ang Lee's second film is a romantic comedy which entertainingly explores the comic possibilities of this situation, without forfeiting sympathy for any of his characters, or duplicating scenes from other movies (not even *Green Card*, which started from a similar premise).

The acting lacks depth, the story is sweet rather than moving, and there's a reluctance to broach the not entirely irrelevant subject of Aids – which gives the film a dated air. Even so, this is an enjoyable experience. It's especially refreshing to see a film which treats homosexuality neither as something to be aggressively proud of, nor as a problem, but merely as a fact of life.

MIXED:

'[A] gentle, very appealing comedy of errors . . . It has such a warm and fuzzy countenance, it jumps up and licks your face . . . One of [its] charms is that it isn't wholly predictable . . . and while many of the choices are formulaic, enough are mild surprises . . . Some gays may resent the lightness, the sweetness, the plugs for family values.' *(Georgia Brown, Village Voice)*

PRO:

'The surface is pure situation comedy . . . Although the patterned plot is unrealistically neat, Ang Lee . . . digs deep into the characters' feelings, and avoids easy laughs about sexual orientation.' *(Geoff Brown, The Times)*

'The film is relatively weightless but it is subtly enough characterised and well enough played to be a comedy of modern manners that works well.' *(Derek Malcolm, Guardian)*

'A delight. Never patronising . . . Lee contrives to combine comedy both subtle and raucous . . . There's genuine pain and confusion amid the jokes . . . True, Winston Chao's Wai-Tung is initially rather stilted, but the rest of the cast . . . give excellent performances, while the script is admirably matter-of-fact in its unsentimental depiction of the threatened gay relationship.' *(Geoff Andrew, Time Out)*

'[Along with *Sleepless in Seattle*] two of the best romantic comedies in recent memory. There is enough sour wit and credible cross-accident to make any last-reel handkerchief-reaching feel well earned.' *(Nigel Andrews, Financial Times)*

'The first half is a hoot . . . The second half becomes really touching.' *(Angie Errigo, Today)*

WEDDING MARCH, THE   CT: – AV: 7.71

1928 US 196 BW DRAMA/ROMANCE/SILENT

D Erich von Stroheim ☆
W Henry Carr Erich von Stroheim

Erich Von Stroheim Fay Wray ZaSu Pitts Matthew Betz Maude George

In pre-World War I Vienna, a prince (Erich von Stroheim) sacrifices his love for a penniless musician (Fay Wray) to marry a crippled heiress (ZaSu Pitts).

Von Stroheim's pessimistic view of human nature is fully expressed, as is his keen interest in sex; but the film survives only in mutilated form. Its sequel, *The Honeymoon*, is believed lost.

PRO:

'A pitilessly authentic portrait of decadent Imperialist Austria.' *(Georges Sadoul)*

'A most ambitious picture, as vast in emotional scope as *The Birth of a Nation* is vast in physical scope. Its greatness rests in the fact that it is ambitious without being heavy, serious without being dull, at once deeply felt and expressed in effective cinematic terms.' *(Dwight Macdonald, 1933)*

'Survives as a mutilated masterpiece . . . Marvellously detailed portrait of the corruption of society in general, rich and poor. Nevertheless, it is the love scenes, played beneath shimmering apple blossoms in lyrical soft focus, that stick in the memory.' *(Geoff Andrew, Time Out)*

MIXED:

'A ponderous slow moving production and some beautiful photography telling a very familiar story.' *(Variety)*

'There is in places too much of the von Stroheim realism and also there is an unevenness in story apparently caused in the cutting of the picture to prescribed feature length. For the mature audience.' *(NBR)*

ANTI:

'The slowness, heaviness, mindlessness of this temple of unnaturalness through which man passes as through a forest of clichés beggars description.' *(John Simon, 1967)*

'Incredibly overblown and long beyond belief.' *(Martin & Porter)*

WEE WILLIE WINKIE   CT: 6 AV: 6.22

1937 US 77/99/103 BW ACTION/ADVENTURE/FAMILY

D John Ford
W Ernest Pascal Julien Josephson from Rudyard Kipling's story

Shirley Temple ☆ Victor McLaglen
C. Aubrey Smith June Lane Michael Whalen Cesar Romero Constance Collier Douglas Scott

A loveable scamp (Shirley Temple) and her widowed mother (June Lang) go to live at a British Army outpost in India; here, the little girl works her way into the affections of her colonel grandfather (C. Aubrey Smith), a kindly sergeant (Victor McLaglen) and even a rebel leader (Cesar Romero).

Hilariously naive action-adventure, with Shirley Temple able to bring two warring sides together simply by being nice. (This must be the film which inspired her to take up a diplomatic career in later life.) John Ford – very much a 'man's man' and an Irish patriot – was an odd choice to direct this sugary confection celebrating British imperialism; and it cannot be said to be one of his most personal films. However, it's entertaining enough in a mindless way, and deserved its Oscar nomination for art direction (William S. Darling, David Hall).

It also has importance in the history of criticism, since Graham Greene's taboo-breaking review about the sexual allure of Shirley Temple caused an outcry. Britain's Lord Chief Justice declared it 'a gross outrage' and libellous. The offending passage now seems mild – especially in view of Miss Temple's later revelations of how she was pursued by paedophile movie executives all the time she was a child star:

'Infancy with her [Shirley Temple] is a disguise, her appeal is more secret and more adult. Already two years ago, she was a fancy little piece . . . In *Captain January*, she wore trousers with the mature suggestiveness of a Dietrich: her neat and well-developed rump twisted in the tap dance: her eyes had a sidelong searching coquetry. Now in *Wee Willie Winkie*, wearing short kilts, she is a complete totsy.' *(Graham Greene, Night & Day)*

ANTI:

'Will add another clean-up to her cycle, but those knees are losing their contour . . . A pretentiously produced melodrama.' *(Variety)*

MIXED:

'Sophisticated filmgoers will find a good deal to smile at. Bizarre but entertaining – if you don't take it too seriously . . . Your reaction will depend entirely upon the mood in which you see it. Admirers of Kipling will undoubtedly find it just too much.' *(Film Weekly)*

'It isn't, we are very much afraid, an entirely credible story . . . Of course, Mistress Temple is just as cute as she can be. She looks simply ravishing, in her brief little kilts . . . Miss Temple will get us all if we don't watch out.' *(Frank S. Nugent, New York Times)*

PRO:

'No longer is [Shirley Temple] just a cute youngster, possessed of remarkable talents . . . She handles [this dramatic role] in a masterly fashion . . . Ford has wrapped all [the film's elements] together into a piece of film merchandise in a convincing, believable way.' *(Gus McCarthy, Motion Picture Herald)*

'Shirley Temple . . . proves in this splendid little picture that she isn't through just because she is no longer a precocious baby . . . A "must see".' *(Photoplay)*

WEEKEND CT: 5 AV: 7.82

(aka *Week-End; Le Weekend*)

1967 France 103 C DRAMA/FOREIGN

D Jean-Luc Godard ✗
W Jean-Luc Godard

Mireille Darc Jean Yanne Jean-Pierre Kalfon
Valerie Lagrange Jean-Pierre Léaud

Two lovers (Mireille Darc and Jean Yanne) set off in their car to murder the man's father for his money, only to fall foul of traffic accidents and a bizarre collection of strangers, including a gang of cannibalistic terrorists.

In keeping with the film's hostility to bourgeois materialism, Godard conscientiously flouts the conventions of popular film-making: his hero and heroine behave repellently from the start, and the director's lack of sympathy for his characters is the opposite of Capra-esque. Even some dustmen from the third world, who announce their hatred of bourgeois society in terms of which Godard would presumably have approved, are presented in as deliberately boring a fashion as possible.

The film works principally as a demonstration of directorial perversity. At times it's as amateurish as a home movie, at other times it's a *tour de force*. Godard's 10-minute tracking shot of a French traffic jam remains a tiny masterpiece.

Weekend is far from the devastating satire on materialism which some film historians claim it to be. It's an experiment in style which ends up going nowhere. It was in this film that Godard broke free from the constraints of conventional film-making, only to find himself in a void where he never rediscovered his talents. It's a fascinating, over-acclaimed failure.

PRO:

'A savage Swiftian satire.' *(Tom Milne, Time Out)*

MIXED:

'Repulsive but brilliant.' *(Dilys Powell)*

'As long as Godard stays with cars as the symbol of bourgeois materialism, the barbarity of these bourgeois – their greed and the self-love they project onto their possessions – is exact and funny. The picture goes much further – sometimes majestically, sometimes with surreal details that suggest an affinity between Godard and Buñuel, sometimes with methods and ideas that miss, badly. There are extraordinary passages, such as a bourgeois wife's erotic confession and a long virtuoso sequence of tracking shots of cars stalled on the highway, with the motorists pressing down with all their might on their car horns, which sound triumphant, like trumpets in Purcell. Though deeply flawed, this film has more depth than any of Godard's earlier work. It's his vision of hell and it ranks with the greatest.' *(Pauline Kael)*

'Whenever Godard is at his most stimulating, he gives up and takes to childish tricks, aiming potshots at the bourgeoisie.' *(Shipman)*

ANTI:

'Socially irresponsible, cinematically useless, politically simple-minded, and artistically banal. Worse, it was boring.' *(Rex Reed)*

'The picture peters out once the guerillas turn up.' *(Danny Peary)*

WENT THE DAY WELL? CT: 7 AV: 7.00

(aka *Forty-Eight Hours*)

1942 GB 92 BW WAR/DRAMA

D Alberto Cavalcanti ☆
W Angus MacPhail John Dighton Diana Morgan from Graham Greene's story

Leslie Banks Elizabeth Allan Frank Lawton Basil Sydney Valerie Taylor

German paratroopers attempt to take over an English village.

Though clearly designed to be wartime propaganda, this is a film which missed its moment. By the time it was released, Britain was thinking more of invading than being invaded. But it still stands up as an exciting, sinister melodrama, portraying how the English might have behaved under Nazi occupation. Like many other Ealing films, it's principally a celebration of British resilience; and its critical stock has risen over the years.

'The public enjoyed its pathos and its exceptional violence . . . The critics, led by Miss Lejeune, literally pulled us to pieces.' *(Alberto Cavalcanti)*

ANTI:

'Any display of hate, except in the hands of an expert director and artist, is to be avoided, since high passions without high performance are less likely to lead to conviction than laughter . . . The nearer a plot sticks to life at this tense moment of our fortunes, the nearer it gets to drama. The most patriotic film can lose nothing by the exercise of a little talent and taste.' *(C.A. Lejeune)*

'The invasion of this country is not a theme to be treated frivolously.' *(Evening Standard)*

'[Has] all the appearance of having been made with one eye on the clock and the other on a copy of the *Boys' Own Paper*.' *(Documentary News Letter)*

'Fair average, thick-ear fiction for the unsophisticated masses.' *(Kine Weekly)*

'Candidate only for the most transparent and fantastic type of penny dreadful fiction.' *(Motion Picture Herald)*

MIXED:

'The villager types are the sort of entomologically observed, remarkably lifelike, charming dolls which not only Greene but Coward and Waugh so often create instead of characters . . . Well written and directed and beautifully played, these characters are not to be scorned . . . There is poetic force in this puppetry though it lacks complexity and depth . . . And at moments, when the invaders prowlingly approach through the placid gardens of the barricaded manor in the neat morning light, the film has the sinister, freezing beauty of an Auden prophecy come true.' *(James Agee, Nation)*

'A mixture of friendly human nature and walking nightmare . . . It understates its message, it is beautifully but not too beautifully done . . . Cavalcanti has opened our eyes to reality, even if we may feel that this particular reality is past.' *(William Whitebait, New Statesman)*

PRO:

'For once the English people are shown as capable of individual and concerted resourcefulness in a fight and not merely steady in disaster. But the essential virtue of the film is its expression of an English tradition: the tradition of the rural community, self-contained, living intensely inside its own customs and laws, still drawing strength from the past, still adding its own experience to the common store of village history . . . At last, it seems, we are learning to make films with our own native material.' *(Dilys Powell)*

WEST SIDE STORY AAW CT: 10 AV: 8.60

1961 US 155 C MUSICAL/ROMANCE

D Robert Wise Jerome Robbins ☆ AAW
W Ernest Lehman ☆ AAW from Arthur Laurents's play conceived by Jerome Robbins from Shakespeare's play *Romeo and Juliet* (music by Leonard Bernstein ☆, lyrics by Stephen Sondheim)

Natalie Wood ☆ (dubbed by Marni Nixon) Richard Beymer ● (dubbed by Jim Bryant) Russ Tamblyn ☆ Rita Moreno ☆ AAW (dubbed by Betty Wand) George Chakiris ☆ AAW Simon Oakland Bill Bramley Tucker Smith Tony Mordente Eliot Feld

In New York, a white American Romeo (Richard Beymer) falls for a Puerto Rican Juliet (Natalie Wood).

One of the great film musicals, despite an odd mixture of stylized and realistic sets, and a stiff leading performance by Richard Beymer, who never looks as if he would be seen dead in a street gang. Natalie Wood has difficulty holding her accent, but is still very touching.

Most critics blame the ultra-conventional nature of the non-choreographed numbers on Wise – who took over directing from Robbins, when the latter's perfectionism threatened to take the picture over budget. Jerome Robbins's choreography of the production numbers is unsurpassed, as is Leonard Bernstein's score. Stephen Sondheim's lyrics are far from his best – soppy in the romantic numbers, tongue-twisting in 'America', and too sophisticated for Maria's character in 'I Feel Pretty'; but 'Gee Officer Krupke' is a masterpiece. Full of faults it may be, but there are few films that I've re-watched as often, or with so much enjoyment.

The film's 10 Oscars included awards to Daniel Fapp's cinematography, Boris Leven's art direction, Victor Gangelin's set decoration, Irene Sharaff's costume design, Thomas Stanford's film editing, the musical scoring by Johnny Green, Sid Ramin, Irwin Kostal, and associate producer Saul Chaplin, the sound by the Todd-AO company and the Samuel Goldwyn sound department, with a special honorary Oscar to Robbins for 'his brilliant achievements in the art of choreography on film in *West Side Story*.'

ANTI:

'They seem like real people. But they are not real people. Every so often they burst into co-ordinated song, and more important, dance, and we become instantly aware that these are not hooligans, but stage performers . . . On the screen the effect is schizophrenic and worrying.' *(Burgo Partridge, Time & Tide)*

'There is something gripping and hopeful about the way [the aerial shots of New York's stone canyons] unroll at the beginning . . . until the screen is alive with cunningly edited, tumultuous movement. It's a bore when this checks for the plot to be furthered in dialogue, and more of a bore when one realizes that these stops and starts are to be part of the fabric of the film.' *(John Coleman, New Statesman)*

'Doesn't ever quite fulfil the promise of those first few minutes and it suffers from the occupational complaint of almost all "big" pictures – agglomeration, the inability to throw anything out.' *(Isabel Quigly, Spectator)*

'The impressive, widely admired opening shots of New York from the air overload the story with values and importance – technological and sociological. And the dance movements are so sudden and huge, so portentously "alive" they're always near the explosion point. Consider the feat: first you take Shakespeare's *Romeo and Juliet* and remove all that cumbersome poetry; then you make the Montagues and Capulets modern by turning them into rival street gangs of native-born and Puerto Ricans. (You get rid of the parents, of course; America is a young country – and who wants to be bothered by the squabbles of older people?) . . . The irony of this hyped-up, slam-bang production is that those involved apparently don't really believe that beauty and romance can be expressed in modern rhythms, because whenever their Romeo and Juliet enter the scene, the dialogue becomes painfully old-fashioned and mawkish, the dancing turns to simpering, sickly romantic ballet, and sugary old stars hover in the sky.' *(Pauline Kael)*

'It's a melange of fantasy and reality and doesn't always work. The sets were obvious sets, and the streets were obvious streets, thus jarring the senses somewhat. They might have done better had they remained with one style rather than attempting to blend them.' *(Baseline)*

PRO:

'What makes this exuberantly savage American musical unique is that it seems to slap down all it has got in its opening minutes . . . Then it triumphantly trumps it . . . . [It] brings the musical back to town.' *(Alexander Walker, Evening Standard)*

'To call this a musical or a song-and-dance film would be to mock it . . . [Natalie Wood's] is surely the most painfully lovely performance of the year. The rest of the film matches her sensitive skill.' *(Leonard Mosley, Daily Express)*

'Bought a new dimension to movie musicals both in its social content and in its cinematic techniques. The brilliance of the dances and the design of the production are the chief distinctions of this film, marked by a near-hurricane energy in its direction.' *(Judith Crist)*

'A work of art. It is most unusual when a work of art also captures the popular imagination, but in the case of this drama-musical ballet, popularity and art danced arm in arm through the teeming city streets, the gymnasium, the tenements.' *(Paul Michael, The Academy Awards: A Pictorial History, 1978)*

WESTWORLD

CT: 8 AV: 6.75

1973 US 89 C SF/WESTERN

D Michael Crichton ☆
W Michael Crichton ☆

Richard Benjamin ☆ Yul Brynner ☆ James Brolin Norman Bartold Alan Oppenheimer

An urban wimp of the near future (Richard Benjamin) fantasizes about being a cowboy, and a holiday to Westworld provides him with the opportunity to live out his fantasy and shoot android bad guys, at no risk to himself. Unfortunately, one android (Yul Brynner) begins stalking him in earnest.

The picture satirizes modern man's search for vicarious experience, in a way that's clever, funny and gripping, despite a low budget. Brynner, revelling in his own inexpressiveness, was never more suitably cast. It's an exciting science fiction, and its notion of an implacable android had a big influence on later movies, such as *The Terminator*. The sequel, *Futureworld* (1976), wasn't bad either; and Crichton recycled his idea of a theme park that goes out of control, in his novel and screenplay *Jurassic Park* (1993).

MIXED:

'The idea is ingenious, and the film might have been marvellous: it isn't, quite (it has the skimped TV-movie look of a too-tight budget), but it's reasonably entertaining.' *(Pauline Kael)*

'Unusual and amusing but under-produced melodrama with slipshod story development and continuity, atoned for by memorable moments and underlying excitement.' (Halliwell)

PRO:

'Combines solid entertainment, chilling topicality, and superbly intelligent serio-comic story values.' *(Variety)*

'A rare entertainment. Exciting both emotionally and intellectually, it holds wide appeal for a broad spectrum of filmgoers ranging from the action and sci-fans to the youth audience and the more discriminating . . . The futuristic trappings look plausibly familiar and Gene Polito's cinematography is first-rate.' *(Film Bulletin)*

'Great stuff.' *(Tom Milne, Time Out)*

WHAT A MAN: *see* NEVER GIVE A SUCKER AN EVEN BREAK.

WHAT EVER HAPPENED TO BABY JANE?: *see* WHATEVER HAPPENED TO BABY JANE?

WHAT'S NEW PUSSYCAT? CT: 6 AV: 4.70

1965 US/France 108 C COMEDY/ROMANCE

D Clive Donner
W Woody Allen

Peter O'Toole Peter Sellers Woody Allen Romy Schneider Ursula Andress Capucine Paula Prentiss

Mad psychiatrist (Peter Sellers) becomes jealous of client (Peter O'Toole) whom women find irresistible.

A monument to 60s permissiveness. It seemed fresh and anarchic to me when I saw it at fifteen. Today, it looks sexist and hit-and-miss, but it's still enjoyable for Peter Sellers's mad psychiatrist, Woody Allen (on his screen début) as an unsuccessful wooer, and Peter O'Toole as Paris's flustered answer to Warren Beatty. Allen's screenplay contains many of the ideas which he explored more fully in later films: the charming Romy Schneider is in many ways a forerunner of Annie Hall. Burt Bacharach and Hal David's theme song was Oscar-nominated, and the film was a big hit despite critical condemnation.

ANTI:

'The madder the pace set by the director, the more the would-be comedy creaks, and eventually it collapses into a yawning pit of boredom.' *(Hollis Alpert, Saturday Review)*

'A shrieking, reeking conglomeration of dirty jokes, dreary camp and blatant ambi-sexuality wrapped around a tediously plotting plot and stale comedy routines.' *(Judith Crist)*

'No one in his right mind would have written this excuse for a script.' *(Bosley Crowther)*

'Unfortunately for all concerned, to make something enjoyably dirty a lot of taste is required.' *(John Simon)*

'Has all the pace, wit, thrills, inventiveness and sheer high-spirits of a Bank Holiday traffic jam . . . As I walked away from the smoking gun I wondered what had got on my nerves most, and I'm almost certain it was the performance of Peter O'Toole . . . Woody Allen's script makes fun of sex, marriage and psychiatrists with a blurry inexactness . . . A spoiled farce, a mirror for egregiousness, the film sells everything short, but chiefly the cast.' *(Robert Robinson, Sunday Telegraph)*

'An extended, overblown snigger . . . Fearful deceit. By maintaining a pose that it is smiling at the dilemmas caused by sexual instability, it in fact cocks a nasty cynical eye at them.' *(Stuart Douglas, Daily Worker)*

'I loathe everyone and everything concerned with it and they all loathe me . . . They butchered my script. They wrenched it into a commercial package . . . I couldn't go to see it for a year.' *(Woody Allen, 1970)*

PRO:

'A wild and wonderful romantic farce.' *(James Powers, Hollywood Reporter)*

'The best picture of the year thus far and by far the funniest comedy . . . I suggest that the reviewers who have been barking at *Pussycat* drop into a movie theatre where the picture is playing before live people rather than projection room zombies and then clock the laughs.' *(Andrew Sarris, Village Voice)*

'The wildest, wackiest comedy to come along in memory . . . a madcap mixture of farce, fantasy, slapstick . . . [with a] highly imaginative screenplay by Woody Allen.' *(George H. Jackson, LA Herald-Examiner)*

'A post-TW3 picture, homing in . . . on a new life style, where it's freely conceded that sex is just about as obsessive as Grandfather Freud said it was, that everyone's love-happy at heart, that since nuttiness is inevitable we might as well relax and enjoy it, and that, in a world gone grey with routine and flannel, the hunt for pleasure is an ebullition of the soul. It's a world of shamelessness and not simply about sex . . . What can you lose, the film asks . . . by being . . . a nutty [psychiatrist who] . . . pursues his female patients as fanatically as Harpo . . . With so many assorted goodies what's surprising is not that the film's extremely pleasant, but that it isn't more.' *(Raymond Durgnat, S & S)*

'The entire film attests to the remarkable impact of movies: the way in which ordinary lives often become aborted attempts to live up to those patterns schematized by the "lives" glimpsed in films. "Shall I get dressed?" Carol asks Michael while stepping out of her shower, "or is it foreign movie time?" The idea of the sexual act performed not as an original and spontaneous meeting of mates but as an attempt to capture in the flesh those idealized onscreen couplings is basic to the film's – and Allen's – viewpoint.' *(Douglas Brode, Woody Allen: His Films and Career, 1987)*

WHAT'S UP, DOC? CT: 2 AV: 5.83

1972 US 94 C COMEDY/ROMANCE

D Peter Bogdanovitch ✗
W Buck Henry David Newman

Ryan O'Neal ● Barbra Streisand Kenneth Mars Austin Pendleton Madeline Kahn Mabel Albertson

An absent-minded musicologist (Ryan O'Neal) finds

his orderly life disrupted by a scatty New Yorker (Barbra Streisand).

Tedious farce which met with astonishing box office success. America's notorious autourist, Bogdanovich imitates other screwball comedies (especially *Bringing Up Baby*) and freely plunders gags from his betters, but never ties them to credible characters or a logical plot. Ryan O'Neal appears to be attempting an impersonation of Cary Grant and is dismally unfunny. Barbra Streisand works hard, but is signally lacking in the requisite charm.

PRO:

'Terrific. This picture is a total smash. The script and cast are excellent; the direction and comedy staging are outstanding; and there are literally reels of pure, unadulterated and sustaining laughs . . . Mature audiences haven't seen a new film like this in a generation . . . The Warner Bros release has nothing in sight but money, by the carload.' *(Variety)*

'Great.' *(Barry Norman)*

MIXED:

'Miss Streisand is very funny. The film is very funny. And Mr Bogdanovich has made it all the funnier by his use of what are often deliberate quotations from the cinema of the past sixty years . . . I admit that a close acquaintance with the cinema does help. But it isn't necessary; without it you can still settle down to laugh. I wish only that Mr O'Neal himself showed a gift for being or looking funny.' *(Dilys Powell)*

ANTI:

'Freely borrows from the best screen comedy down the ages but has no discernible style of its own.' *(Michael Billington, Illustrated London News)*

'Remains obstinately the blueprint for a funny film rather than a film which in itself makes one laugh a lot . . . There is something very dry and mechanical about it.' *(David Robinson, The Times)*

'Miss Streisand looks like a cross between an aardvark and an albino rat surmounted by a platinum-coated horse bun. Though she has good eyes and a nice complexion, the rest of her is a veritable anthology of disaster areas. Her speaking voice seems to have graduated with top honors from the Brooklyn Conservatory of Yentaism, and her acting consists entirely of fishily thrusting out her lips, sounding like a cabbie bellyaching at break-neck speed, and throwing her weight around. Even her singing has become mannerism-infested, and a brief attempt at a Bogart impersonation may be the film's involuntary comic high spot. Miss Streisand is to our histrionic aesthetics what the Vietnam war is to our politics.' *(John Simon)*

'Ryan O'Neal is so stiff and clumsy that he can't even manage a part requiring him to be stiff and clumsy . . . [It's a] comedy made by a man who has seen a lot of movies, knows all the mechanics, and has absolutely no sense of humour. Seeing it is like shaking hands with a joker holding a joy buzzer: the effect is both presumptuous and unpleasant.' *(Jay Cocks)*

WHATEVER HAPPENED TO BABY JANE?

CT: 8 AV: 7.15

1962 US 133 BW THRILLER/HORROR

D Robert Aldrich ✔
W Lukas Heller from Henry Farrell's novel

Bette Davis ☆ AAN Joan Crawford ☆ Victor Buono ☆ AAN Anna Lee

Sibling rivalry is taken to hideous extremes by two elderly sisters (Bette Davis and Joan Crawford).

Splendid Hollywood Gothic shocker. The plot takes too long to get going and runs out of steam long before the actresses do – but there are quite a few scary moments, and it's great, campy fun with both stars leaving teeth-marks on the scenery. Ernest Haller's stylish cinematography won him an Oscar nomination.

'The best time I ever had with Joan Crawford was when I pushed her down the stairs in *Whatever Happened To Baby Jane?' (Bette Davis)*

'Working with [Bette] Davis was my greatest challenge ever, and I mean that kindly. Bette likes to scream and yell and I just sit and knit. During *Whatever Happened To Baby Jane?* I knitted a scarf from Hollywood to Malibu.' *(Joan Crawford)*

ANTI:

'It goes on and on, in a light much dimmer than necessary, and the climax, when it belatedly arrives, is a bungled, languid mingling of pursuers and pursued.' *(New Yorker)*

'It's so whorishly concerned to please in one way or the other . . . that it begins to jar quite early on . . . The whole is so thoughtlessly dispensed as to leave a bad taste in the mouth.' *(John Coleman, New Statesman)*

'Once the basic situation is stated . . . there is virtually no development, just a series of scenes of Bette being ever more beastly to Joan. And in between . . . Aldrich lets his film go flat.' *(Richard Roud, Guardian)*

'This kind of horror film, if it is to succeed in the modern cinema, needs a quite different form of treatment from that given by [Aldrich] . . . A heavy-handed and drawn-out piece of Grand Guignol . . . unconvincing alike in story and situation and unpleasantly over-acted . . . Bette Davis . . . gives . . . a completely out-moded and garish performance, though in fairness it is only right to point out that it is a garish and outmoded kind of character to have to play.' *(Roger Manville, F and F)*

'Because of its overkill *Baby Jane* is *Sunset Boulevard* without the sophistication or the heart.

Aldrich doesn't pity the two old-time movie stars . . . he gloats on their tragedy and loneliness. This isn't to say that *Baby Jane* is worthless – it's a key Crawford film and she relishes the opportunity, but it's cruel and grotesque.' *(NFT Bulletin)*

MIXED:

'Once the inept, draggy start is passed, the films pace builds with ever-growing force.' *(Variety)*

'Nobody – at least nobody in their right mind – could reasonably claim that [this] was a consistently well-directed film . . . And yet, in its curious Gothic way, the film works marvellously, though mainly as a field day for its actors . . . It is really Bette Davis's film . . . [She is] magnificent. Genuinely magnificent . . . and in Victor Buono she has found a fitting partner . . . It is all vastly enjoyable and, at the end, oddly moving.' *(Tom Milne, MFB)*

PRO:

'A thoroughly enterprising piece of movieland hokum. And it's put over by two of the most dazzling experts in movieland hokum that Hollywood has never known.' *(Nina Hibbin, Daily Worker)*

'For suspense, excitement, macabre atmosphere, gruesome incident, and sheer marvellous acting, [it] far outdoes anything which I have seen in years.' *(Rene MacColl, Daily Express)*

'An enjoyably macabre horror comic.' *(Daily Herald)*

'It's just the sort of film you should take your favourite ghoulfriend to see. For besides these two vintage actresses Frankenstein looks like a church choir-boy.' *(People)*

'The film's real centre of interest is its *Sunset Boulevard*-style acerbity about Hollywood.' *(Tony Rayns, Time Out)*

'This landmark in personality-disorder horror films is often regarded as a camp classic; and it is hard not to smile a bit while Bette Davis is brutally mistreating her off-screen nemesis, Joan Crawford (especially today when we have knowledge that Crawford was a child abuser).' *(Danny Peary)*

WHEN DINOSAURS RULED THE EARTH

CT: 6 AV: 4.56

1970 GB 96 US/100 (GB) C FANTASY/SO BAD

D Val Guest
W Val Guest ● from a treatment by J.G. Ballard

Victoria Vetri ● Robin Hawdon ● Patrick Allen
Drewe Henley Imogen Hassall

Beautiful cavewoman (Victoria Vetri) is ostracized for being blonde.

Enjoyably terrible movie which contains only 27 words of dialogue, all of them incomprehensible. A sequel to *One Million Years B.C.*, this stars *Playboy*'s 1968 Playmate of the Year, Angela Dorian, here wisely masquerading under a false name. Sample line . . . 'N yde krasta m'kan neecro redak'.

ANTI:

'Despite pretensions to . . . "science-fact", this is very much the old mixture as before, with the girls running round in fetching little bikini creations, and everybody enunciating the "prehistoric" language in impeccable drama school manner. Monsters, cyclones and tidal waves are all tolerably well done, but remain totally artificial and unexciting.' *(MFB)*

'This is life at the "dawn of history" comic book style. Sun worshipping tribes decked out in Club Mediterranée gear react with dismay and violence to the first appearance of the moon . . . The inane story, heavily padded with ponderous ritual, barely holds the attention.' *(Margaret Tarrat, F & F)*

'I'm very proud that my first screen credit was for what is, without doubt, the worst film ever made.' *(J.G. Ballard)*

MIXED:

'One of those simple sci-fi prehistoric films which do no harm. Normally, they're taken either dead seriously or as send-ups. This one quite deftly combines the two angles . . . There are a lot of very nubile, scantily-clad dames.' *(Variety)*

'The plot is rather more complicated than seems altogether wise, especially as it is far from easy to tell the many male characters apart. However, as spectacle the film is wholly successful . . . Action packed hokum lavishly supplied with super monsters, lovely girls and brawny bewhiskered men.' *(Marjorie Bilbow, Today's Cinema)*

'As a piece of technology it's bad – the print quality, the matching and the process work are all shoddy, even for what one assumes was an extremely frugal budget. And as entertainment, it's not much either. But when a movie is this bad it's somehow rather comforting . . . Absorbing, in a simple-minded way, but it does go on, so that after a while, one begins paying a lot of attention to certain tertiary details – like the fact that Miss Vetri has very nice breasts, and that they're constantly in danger of falling out of her scanty costume, or that dinosaurs when they die, all seem to sound like jets taxiing to a stop. The details are not much, but then one has to settle for what there is.' *(Craig Fisher, Hollywood Reporter)*

'My reaction upon viewing the film was mixed; elation for its being the finest film of its type to date; and disappointment for its being still quite worthless . . . [It] is the first of its sub-genre to achieve the look and feel of the epic . . . The film's unique achievement, however, is in the manner in which the effects scenes are used . . . A minor triumph in its own very narrow field.' *(Frederick S. Clarke, Cinefantastique)*

'Dotty but perversely endearing variation on the

theme of the good old days with a very variable line in prehistoric monsters.' *(Alan Frank)*

WHEN HARRY MET SALLY . . .

CT: 8 AV: 7.58

1989 US 95 C COMEDY/ROMANCE

D Rob Reiner
W Nora Ephron

Billy Crystal Meg Ryan ✔ Carrie Fisher Bruno Kirby Steven Ford Lisa Jane Persky Michelle Nicastro Harley Jane Kozak

Sally (Meg Ryan) hates Harry (Billy Crystal) at first sight. Over the course of 10 years, she changes her opinion.

Though over-indebted to Woody Allen, Nora Ephron's romantic comedy lacks Allen's pretensions and has a sparkle all its own thanks to Meg Ryan and Billy Crystal. Director Rob Reiner's visual wit skilfully augments the word-play. The aim of the movie is merely to entertain, and the ending is always predictable; but, in a deceptively easygoing way, the film pinpoints some uncomfortable differences between male and female sexuality.

ANTI:

'Could a woman really have created such an odious romantic hero? It seems incredible. Yet think about it for a minute, and it begins to make sense: any woman who married Carl Bernstein would find Harry Burns appealing . . . Why does Reiner imitate Woody Allen so slavishly? Partly, I'm sure, for the same reason that Allen, in his weaker films (eg, *Interiors*), goes overboard emulating Bergman; he admires the man's work. But one also has the feeling that Reiner, so comfortable in the realm of storybook fantasy, farce, and boyhood, is ill at ease in the territory of this film – adult romance – and, like a smart but un-self-confident kid copying a book report out of an encyclopedia, felt a need to lean strongly on a recognized authority.' *(Bruce Bawer, American Spectator)*

'A pale imitation of *Annie Hall* ten years on. Boasting what has to be the longest meeting-cute in movie history – twelve years – *When Harry Met Sally* . . . is little more than a very smart, classy and funny romantic comedy of manners and social ritual that breaks no new ground but provides an ideal dating movie.' *(Trevor Willsmer, Film Yearbook)*

MIXED:

'Reiner's confident direction has coaxed warmly convincing performances . . . The only complaint is that the inevitable outcome is telegraphed way before the end.' *(Mike Naughton, Morning Star)*

'Wonderful, sparkling entertainment, but I left none the wiser as to whether mixed-sex friendships are really *coitus interruptus* in heavy disguise.' *(Sue Heal, Today)*

'The best Woody Allen film in years . . . it's hard to accept that this isn't just parody . . . [The film] will ultimately seduce you.' *(Dylan Jones, The Face)*

PRO:

'A zippy romantic comedy . . . Emotional navel-gazing is indulged in with gusto and humour . . . Reiner . . . oils the wheels of this pacey rendezvous with considerable panache and not a little tenderness. Make a date.' *(John Mulholland, Evening Standard)*

'Good entertainment and women will love it. But don't dismiss it, fellas – if you don't like the plot, you'll love Meg Ryan at her sexiest . . . Harry up and see it!' *(Suzanne Hill, Sun)*

'Ephron's script snaps, crackles and pops, never soggy . . . It's an outstanding comedy because so much of the fiction has truth's offbeat, incongruous ring . . . I defy all but terminal grouches to experience this film without laughing a lot and willing a happy ending for its fallible characters.' *(Shaun Usher, Daily Mail)*

'Hilarious examination of the age-old question: can men and women be friends as well as lovers? Extraordinarily witty and wise, everything about this movie is spot on. The actors are perfect for their roles, the direction is unobtrusive and the mix between humour, sentiment and plot is just right.' *(Rose)*

WHEN TIME RAN OUT . . .

CT: 5 AV: 2.00

(aka *Earth's Final Fury*)

1980 US 121/144 C ACTION/ADVENTURE/SO BAD

D James Goldstone ●
W Carl Foreman Stirling Silliphant ● from Max Morgan Witt's novel *The Day The World Ended*

Paul Newman Jacqueline Bisset ● William Holden ● Edward Albert Burgess Meredith Valentina Cortesa Red Buttons Alex Carras Ernest Borgnine James Franciscus

A volcano threatens to erupt on a south sea island.

Critical opinion is divided as to whether this or *The Swarm* (1978) is the worst disaster movie of all time. Both were made by Irwin Allen – and this was certainly the bigger financial disaster. Made for $22 million, it took less than $2 million at the box office. One of the worst actresses of all time, Jacqueline (*Wild Orchid*) Bisset, gives another of her memorable performances.

'Disaster movies don't come any more disastrous than this.' *(Tom Milne, MFB)*

'[A] penny-dreadful harlequinade . . . The special effects are terrible and the dialogue largely worse . . . On and up the script and characterisation go into an empyrean of ever more cerulean absurdity.' *(Nigel Andrews, Financial Times)*

'If you can keep a straight face for more than a

minute during [the film] you must be made of stone.' *(Arthur Thirkell, Daily Mirror)*

'I could be funny about it. But I don't feel funny. Just angry at this waste of money and talent on tripe.' *(Margaret Hinxman, Daily Mail)*

'What could have persuaded so many established, not to say ageing, stars to take part in an idiot farce like this? Could it really have been for the money?' *(Molly Plowright, Glasgow Herald)*

'Almost unbelievable that this idiotic pile of clichés could be written by esteemed Foreman and Silliphant (responsible respectively for *The Guns of Navarone* and *In The Heat of The Night*).' *(Winnert)*

'*When Ideas Ran Out*, or, *The Blubbering Inferno*: Irwin Allen's shameless rehash of all his disaster-movie clichés is a monumental bore that even a volcanic eruption cannot save.' *(Maltin)*

'Time never seems to run out as we wait and wait for a volcano to erupt and put the all-star cast out of its misery.' *(Martin & Porter)*

WHERE THE BOYS ARE '84 CT: 1 AV: 2.00

1984 US 91/97 C DRAMA/ROMANCE

D Hy Averback ●
W Stu Krieger Jeff Burkhart ● Lisa Hartman Russell Todd Lorna Luft Lynn-Holly Johnson Russel Todd Howard McGillin Louise Sorel Alana Stewart

Four girls go to Fort Lauderdale in search of boys.

Tacky remake of a reasonably charming original, made in 1960. Sample line . . . 'All you need is a bikini and a diaphragm.' Producer Allen Carr was also responsible for another all-time turkey, *Can't Stop The Music* (1980).

'A travesty . . . insufferably coy.' *(Tom Milne, MFB)*

'No one's going to make any claims for the original . . . but at least it had a certain innocence . . . The new [film] which is dumb, vulgar, and mostly humorless . . . has no such nostalgic charm . . . [The] four predatory coeds . . . say things like "Check out those hamstrings!" . . . The music is resoundingly mediocre . . . The trailer wasn't better than the film, but it was shorter.' *(Janet Maslin, New York Times)*

'Sillier than the 1960 version, and not much more modern.' *(David Robinson, The Times)*

'The performances in the 1960 film version . . . gave it a charm this new one entirely lacks.' *(Philip French, Observer)*

'A depressing portrait of rich, young and stupid Americans . . . There is no style, charm, originality or genuine humour anywhere in [it] . . . Fun, sun, sand and sex are not enough as a basis for a film.' *(Phillip Bergson, What's On in London)*

'The sight of girls going ape and getting their socks off is ultimately no more uplifting than that of the usual pimply youths doing the same thing.' *(Anne Billson, Time Out)*

'Has all the appeal of an oil slick.' *(Maltin)*

'About as enjoyable as getting damp sand in your underwear.' *(Rose)*

WHISKY GALORE CT: 6 AV: 8.67

(aka *Tight Little Island*)

1949 GB 82 BW COMEDY

D Alexander Mackendrick ☆
W Compton Mackenzie Angus MacPhail from Mackenzie's novel

Basil Radford Joan Greenwood Jean Cadell Gordon Jackson James Robertson Justice Wylie Watson John Gregson Morland Graham Duncan Macrae Catherine Lacey Bruce Seton Henry Mollinson A.E. Matthews Compton Mackenzie (as Captain Buncher)

Scottish islanders discover a cargo of shipwrecked whisky.

Amusing, anarchic Ealing comedy which spoofs resistance movies of its period, and (in its opening moments) the British documentary tradition that created Robert Flaherty's *Man of Aran* and John Grierson's *Drifters*. It has memorable characters, plenty of comic observation and gallons of charm. Some recent critics have interpreted it as a satire on colonialism, with Waggett (Basil Radford) as the imperialist. The same basic notion of an outsider outwitted by shrewd islanders was reworked – as a horror story – in *The Wicker Man* (1973), then more benevolently in *Local Hero* (1983).

PRO:

'Has not the richness of comic invention of *Passport To Pimlico*, but it will do; it has ideas, it has character, and it has a background which by charm and truth sharpens the gaiety of the central joke.' *(Dilys Powell)*

'What lifts *Tight Little Island* above its own high mark of insular drollery . . . is its mastery of the visual gag. For lightness, comic movement and inventive detail, these sequences are worthy of René Clair.' *(Time)*

'One of the best laughs of this or any year.' *(New York Herald Tribune)*

'A most satisfactory comedy.' *(Fred Majdalany, Daily Mail)*

'One of those all-too-few British comedies that critics have a right to rave about . . . Laughs galore.' *(W.A. Wilcox, Evening Standard)*

'Brilliantly witty and fantastic, but wholly plausible.' *(Sunday Chronicle)*

'Rollicking fun with a Gaelic tang.' *(A.E. Wilson)*

WHISTLE DOWN THE WIND CT: 7 AV: 7.22

1961 GB 98 BW DRAMA/FAMILY

D Bryan Forbes ☆
W Keith Waterhouse Willis Hall ☆ from Mary Hayley Bell's novel

Hayley Mills ☆ Bernard Lee Alan Bates ☆ Diane Holgate Alan Barnes Norman Bird Diane Clare

Three Lancashire children think they have found Jesus Christ, although in fact he's a murderer on the run (Alan Bates).

Bryan Forbes's directorial début is most touching, with outstanding performances from Alan Bates and Hayley Mills (the original story is by her mother). The film is at its best in the opening half-hour, however, and becomes less convincing as adults intrude and the Christ parallels are explored to the full.

ANTI:

'Bryan Forbes adrift on a substantial raft of talent, way out of sight of land . . . It is exasperating to see qualities of this order lavished upon so hollow a theme.' *(Derek Hill, Financial Times)*

MIXED:

'When the three children leak their secret to others . . . the story loses both its conviction and its pace. A good film, though, with heart and pathos.' *(Leonard Mosley, Daily Express)*

'A poor film irritatingly marred by good features. These features are so good, however, that they almost rescue the piece from the embarrassments of its plot . . . It is maddening to see such a regiment of talent go to waste on such inadequate material.' *(Jonathan Miller, New Statesman)*

'Done with a kind of grubby lyricism borrowed from *Jeux Interdits*, the early scenes are quite effective . . . But as the parable (and the parallels) extend towards a scene in which the killer is apprehended and adopts the posture of crucifixion as he is searched, it all becomes more than faintly embarrassing.' *(Tom Milne, Time Out)*

PRO:

'An exceptionally capable first film.' *(The Times)*

'Mr Forbes has handled story and children with the greatest sensitivity, the maudlin is always avoided, and any false religious intensity is dispelled by shafts of humour.' *(Felix Barker, Evening News)*

'Forbes, brilliantly directing his first feature, rides a knife edge between excessive caution and sentimentality.' *(Paul Dehn, Daily Herald)*

'Takes a modern, sentimental-religious subject and treats it with care, taste, sincerity, imagination and good humor.' *(Variety)*

WHITE HEAT CT: 8 AV: 9.31

1949 US 114 BW DRAMA/

D Raoul Walsh ☆
W Ivan Goff Ben Roberts from Virginia Kellogg's story AAN

James Cagney ☆ Margaret Wycherly ☆ Edmond O'Brien Virginia Mayo Steve Cochran John Archer

The life and death of a mother-dominated gangster (James Cagney).

Cagney was never better than in this gangster classic, underrated and even vilified on release for its brutality. Now the violence looks almost tame. The finale, when psychotic gangster Cagney commits suicide to join Ma in gangster heaven, is one of the great moments in cinema.

ANTI:

'The most gruesome aggregation of brutalities ever presented under the guise of entertainment.' *(Cue)*

'Here is death by bullet and death by boiling steam. A member of the gang holding up a train has his face scalded off; a prisoner who has failed in an attempt to drop a large metal pulley on an acquaintance is crammed in the luggage-holder of a car and shot when he begs to be let out; a rival tumbles downstairs full of bullets; Mr Cagney himself is blown to bits in an explosion at the plant he is trying to rob. There was a time when a single murder would content the cinema. Today death by the dozen is the entertainment of the people.' *(Dilys Powell)*

'A gangster film of the day before yesterday . . . [which] occasionally tears itself away from its preoccupation with violence to illustrate, in [a] documentary manner the scientific aids the police use in detection.' *(The Times)*

'Crime still don't pay, you see – and movies don't change much, either.' *(Graphic)*

MIXED:

'No one can accuse it of needing more grue. It is one of the toughest and finest [pictures] of its kind . . . My fear is that much as millions everywhere will enjoy [it] as a hard-boiled thriller-diller, no one will enjoy it more than our enemies. The America it depicts is the America they would like to believe is every American's daily living.' *(John Mason Brown, Saturday Review of Literature)*

'The film is not remarkable and it is too long but for Cagney's sake it is interesting.' *(Daily Mail)*

'Vivid, lively, well-acted, but somehow too much like seeing a revival.' *(Reynolds News)*

'Not a pleasant film . . . The planning is as ingenious as the execution is ruthless . . . Walsh directs this sort of thing as few can.' *(Campbell Dixon, Daily Telegraph)*

PRO:

'A wild and exciting picture of mayhem and madness.' *(Life)*

'Takes the successful cops and robbers formula of the 30s, adds psychopathic complexes and scientific sleuthing . . . brings back James Cagney as the tough guy . . . and proves again crime never, never pays, except at the box office.' *(Fortnight)*

'A return to the Cagney of old, Cagney at his best, cast as a ruthless, brutal gangster leader in a picture so dramatically-compelling that it will be one of Warners' top grossers of the year.' *(Daily Variety)*

'Cagney – the most satisfying screen gangster who ever blasted his way to the electric chair.' *(Paul Dehn, Sunday Chronicle)*

'Look at Cagney – everything he does is big – and yet it's never for a moment unbelievable, because it's real. It's true. He's a great movie actor and his performances are in no way modulated for the camera – he never scaled anything down. He was different from most of the great stars in that he often played villains . . . He could express ambiguities in a character even if they were not written into the script. He was also innately sympathetic. *White Heat* particularly has a subversive duality because of this . . . He was one of a kind.' *(Peter Bogdanovich, Picture Shows, 1975)*

'The blistering savagery, unpredictability and childlike qualities of this animalistic man are expertly conveyed by Cagney in an emotional *tour de force*.' *(Allan Hunter & Kenny Mathieson, 1992)*

'Among the best films made in this country, and one with much to tell us about the kind of country – its marriages, family life, and corrupting aspirations – in which it was made.' *(William S. Pechter, 1967)*

WHITE PALACE CT: 8 AV: 6.09

1990 US 103 C DRAMA/ROMANCE

D Luis Mandoki ☆
W Ted Tally Alvin Sargent ✔ from Glenn Savan's novel

Susan Sarandon ☆ James Spader ☆
Jason Alexander Kathy Bates Eileen Brennan Steven Hill

A 27-year-old yuppie (James Spader) leading a sanitized, passionless existence meets the 43-year-old cashier (Susan Sarandon) at his local burger joint. He falls head-over-meals in lust, but is too embarrassed to let his friends meet her.

Immaculately scripted and acted, with Sarandon giving a performance which should have won her an Oscar nomination. By turns raddled and beautiful, aggressive and vulnerable, sluttish and dignified, she is enchanting. Like *Pretty Woman*, this is a modern fairytale of a Prince Charming rescuing a lower-class damsel in distress – but by the end it is pleasingly uncertain who is rescuing whom. The final, happy ending (introduced on the insistence of preview audiences) was a mistake, though.

ANTI:

'Screenwriters Ted Tally and Alvin Sargent spend so much time showing us *Odd Couple* contrasts in the house-keeping habits of the two lovers (he's a neat-freak, she's a total slob), that they never get to the more important issues. And the big break-up at Thanksgiving dinner never makes a lot of sense. Nora over-reacts in a situation she knew ahead of time would be difficult, and Max does nothing to make things easier for her. As for Max's family, each is a stereotype of an upper-class Jew, and their group portrait creates a cumulative impression that's unmistakably anti-semitic. The film's view of Nora comes dangerously close to elitism, too. Although she is braver, stronger, sexier, and more honest than Max (so much so that you wonder why she'd waste herself on this guy), there is much in her portrayal that reinforces the negative stereotype that poor women are sexpot slatterns. It is easy to view Nora as earthy, because she is one step up from dirt. But since Mr Spader is forced to play yet another of his stereotypically tight-assed yuppies, one shouldn't take Nora's character too much to heart, I suppose. It's stock characters all around. And a ludicrous ending, to boot.' *(Kathi Maio)*

MIXED:

'Glenn Savan's novel offered a stronger exploration of Reaganism and consumerism, but overall he's well-served by this intelligent, involving adaptation . . . Acting honours go to Sarandon, who brings off a complex depiction of vulgarity, defiance and vulnerability.' *(Colette Maude, Time Out)*

'There is something chilling about a movie that gives you the blowjob but shies away from the small talk. Still [the film] is well worth seeing . . . Mandoki virtually never misses . . . His tempo is sure, and so is his respect for his characters.' *(Gary Giddins, Village Voice)*

'Starts out as a steamy slice of erotic life only to end up a soggy May–December romance . . . Sarandon is superb.' *(Stephen Amidon, Financial Times)*

'The essential spark between [Spader and Sarandon] is missing . . . Told without prurience, [the film] is still rather enjoyable in a downbeat sort of way.' *(Neil Norman, Evening Standard)*

'The film barrels along on the energy of [the] performances . . . but the impossible romance is achieved at the expense of too many details of their lives and an absurd wish-fulfilment ending.' *(Sheila Johnston, Independent)*

PRO:

'One of the best films of its kind since *The Graduate*.' *(Variety)*

'A delightful, marvellously played, poignant drama

that is one of the best screen romances of the past five years.' *(Sue Heal, Today)*

'Nora has all the best lines and Susan Sarandon leaps on them with gusto. She's magnificent at the defence mechanisms, laughing to stop crying, joking to hide fear, lusting after life to stop thinking about death . . . while Spader allows Max no depth to his conversion and little understanding of his irrational rationality.' *(Angus Wolfe Murray, Scotsman Weekend)*

'Believable, touching, sexy and quite special.' *(Winnert)*

WHO FRAMED ROGER RABBIT

CT: 10 AV: 8.47

1988 US 103 C COMEDY/CARTOON & LIVE-ACTION/FAMILY

D Robert Zemeckis ☆
W Jeffrey Price Peter S. Seaman

Bob Hoskins ☆ AAN Christopher Lloyd
Joanna Cassidy Stubby Kaye Alan Tilvern
Voices: Charles Fleischer ✓ Kathleen Turner ✓
Amy Irving ✓ Lou Hirsch Mel Blanc ✓
Frank Sinatra

A private detective (Bob Hoskins) helps a cartoon rabbit to escape a murder rap.

Stunningly animated by Richard Williams (who received a special Academy Award) and pacily directed by Robert Zemeckis, this is a perfect integration of cartoon and live action. It's also among the funniest comedies of all time – and Hoskins gives a terrific performance under the circumstances (most of the time he was having to act on his own).

Other notable contributions are from Charles Fleischer, who provides the voice of Roger Rabbit. The seductive Jessica's spoken voice is Kathleen Turner's, while her singing voice belongs to Amy Irving. Special commendation should also go to executive producer Steven Spielberg who successfully negotiated the use of cartoon characters from different studios.

Not surprisingly, the film won Oscars for visual effects (Ken Ralston, Richard Williams, Edward Jones, George Gibbs), sound effects editing (Charles L. Campbell, Louis L. Edermann), and film editing (Arthur Schmidt). It was nominated for Cinematography (Dean Cundey), art direction/set decoration (Elliot Scott, Peter Howitt), and sound (Robert Knudson, John Boyd, Don Digirolamo, Tony Dawe).

ANTI:

'I find *Who Framed Roger Rabbit* a deplorable development in the possibilities of animation – and a melancholy waste of the gifts of one of our most gifted actors.' *(Dilys Powell)*

'Not all the gags . . . have the limber wit of the cartoons that inspired them. Nor do the human actors add much . . . Something got lost in the move from storyboard to screen, and in the stretch from seven minutes (the typical cartoon length) to 103.' *(Richard Corliss, Time)*

'Loud and excessive.' *(Virgin)*

MIXED:

'Magical [but] the main plot line . . . bogs down in the middle.' *(Scheuer)*

'. . . Or *Who Rogered Jessica Rabbit*, as some wags had it. Despite the presence of the sexiest cartoon character ever in Jessica Rabbit, it's mainly worth watching to admire the technical achievement, rather than the lacklustre story.' *(Rose)*

PRO:

'It's a breakthrough technical achievement that borrows liberally from our collective cinematic past and fuses it all into an accomplished original work – part zany cartoon, part serious detective story.' *(Richard Natale, Movieline)*

'The real stars are the animators, who have pulled off the technically amazing feat of having humans and Toons seem as if they're interacting with one another. It is clear from how well the imagery syncs that a lot of painstaking work went into this production – and clearly a lot of money.' *(Daily Variety)*

'A blazing, rollicking animation live action feature. Technically terrific and narratively engaging.' *(Hollywood Reporter)*

'All ages will thrill to the pure enchantment of the visuals. There's Hoskins joyriding through LA in a cartoon cab, Daffy and Donald Duck uniting for a piano duet and a knockout finale featuring the starry likes of Mickey Mouse, Goofy, Porky Pig, Snow White, Bambi and Dumbo. Your eyeballs have no choice but to go boinnnnng.' *(People)*

'Sheer, enchanted entertainment from the first frame to the last – a joyous, giddy, goofy celebration of the kind of fun you can have with a movie camera . . . The movie is filled with throwaway gags, inside jokes, one-liners, and little pokes at the screen images of its cartoon characters. It is also oddly convincing, not only because of the craft of the filmmakers, but also because Hoskins and the other live actors have found the right note for their interaction with the Toons. Instead of overreacting or playing up their emotions cartoon-style, Hoskins and the others adopt a flat, realistic, matter-of-fact posture toward the Toons. They act as if they've been talking to animated rabbits for years.' *(Roger Ebert)*

'The closest thing I've ever seen to a perfect piece of film entertainment. Not only is it wonderful, it reminds you what the word wonder really means: it excites wonder, astonishes you, causes you to marvel . . . You have to see it at least three times: the first time to gasp in amazement at the technical achievement and, after fifteen minutes or so, to forget the technical achievement entirely and fall into a glorious, childlike belief in the whole magnificent illusion (and laugh at the jokes); the second time to follow the Byzantine suspense plot more carefully, to note that virtually everything in the second half of the film is foreshadowed in the first half, and to recognize how wonderfully organized and tightly plotted it is (and laugh at the jokes); the third time to look closely at all that technical stuff and drive yourself crazy trying to figure out how the hell they did it (and laugh at the jokes).' *(Bruce Bawer, American Spectator)*

'Supremely entertaining – especially for adults.' *(Brian Case, Time Out)*

WHO'S AFRAID OF VIRGINIA WOOLF? AAN

CT: 7 AV: 8.08

1966 US 129 BW DRAMA

D Mike Nichols ☆ AAN
W Ernest Lehman ☆ AAN from Edward Albee's play
Elizabeth Taylor ☆ AAW Richard Burton ☆ AAN
George Segal ☆ AAN Sandy Dennis ☆ AAW

A college professor (Richard Burton) and his wife (Elizabeth Taylor) fall out in front of a couple (George Segal and Sandy Dennis) whom they have invited home for a nightcap.

Elizabeth Taylor and Richard Burton go howlingly, entertainingly over the top in Edward Albee's coruscating drama about the horrors of a failing marriage. Mike Nichols directs with claustrophobic intensity, and brings out the underlying black comedy. The shock value of the four-letter words is not what it was, and it's far from pleasant viewing; but the performances remain riveting.

Academy Awards went to Richard Sylbert and George James Hopkins for art direction; Irene Sharaff for costumes; and Haskell Wexler cinematography (Wexler replaced Harry Stradling during production). Other nominations included best sound (George R. Groves), score (Alex North), and editing (Sam O'Steen).

ANTI:

'The weakness of the film is that it does not understand that what is wrong with Martha is that she is a nobody.' *(Anne Laurence, Morning Star)*

MIXED:

'There is not much that is original in Mr Nichols's camerawork, no sense of the personality that we got in his stage direction. In fact, the direction is weakest when he gets a bit arty: electric signs flashing behind heads or tilted shots from below to show passion and abandon (both of them hallmarks of the college cinema virtuoso). But he has minimized the stage feeling, and he has given the film an insistent presence, good phrasing and a nervous drive. It sags towards the end, but this is because the third act of the play sags.' *(Stanley Kauffmann, New York Times)*

'Even in its bitterest moments, the invective can be fiendishly, blisteringly funny, but towards the end the strain of soberly watching a drunken free-for-all becomes too much. Nevertheless, it is a brave, bulldozing, trail-blazing film and I shall gratefully, if unlovingly, remember it all my life.' *(Cecil Wilson, Daily Mail)*

'The movie itself, with Mike Nichols making his directorial début in film, was undoubtedly overpraised simply because it was not a Doris-Day-domestic-fracas bowdlerization of the text; it retained many of Albee's expletives, and was even more explicit than the play in that it visualized adultery, albeit in silhouette.' *(Judith Crist)*

'As a film of a play, fair to middling; as a milestone in cinematic permissiveness, very important; as an entertainment, sensational for those in the mood.' *(Halliwell)*

PRO:

'Here is a real terror. Out of the screen step our own innermost fears . . . Sordid? Did I hear you murmur Sordid, madam? Oh, most certainly. But it is also a film of quite unprecedented power . . . and it gives Burton a chance for his best performance since *Look Back In Anger* and Miss Taylor her best ever . . . . One of the most disturbing films of all time.' *(Felix Barker, Evening News)*

'The laughs come thick and fast . . . almost throughout, as the bitter game is played through to its finish . . . As a superlative sweet and sour entertainment . . . its merits are undeniable.' *(The Times)*

'[Taylor] is nothing less than brilliant.' *(Kate Cameron, New York Daily News)*

'Not so much a film as a permutation of a husband and wife's A to Z alphabet of lust, hatred and brutality towards each other . . . Repulsive or not, [Taylor's] performance astonished me. For the first time, in my eyes, she proved herself to be an actress of top quality.' *(Weston Taylor, Sunday Express)*

'Miss Taylor, who has proven she can act in response to sensitive direction, earned every penny of her reported million plus. Her characterization is at once sensual, spiteful, cynical, pitiable, loathsome, lustful and tender . . . The projection of three-dimensional reality requires talent which sustains the interest; the talent is here. Burton . . . delivers a smash portrayal. He evokes sympathy during the public degradations to which is wife subjects him, and his outrage, as well as his deliberate vengeance, are totally believable.' *(Variety)*

'A magnificent triumph of determined audacity.' *(Bosley Crowther)*

WICKER MAN, THE

CT: 7 AV: 6.90

1973 GB 86/95/103 C THRILLER/HORROR

D Robin Hardy
W Anthony Shaffer

Edward Woodward ☆ Christopher Lee ✔
Diane Cilento Britt Ekland Ingrid Pitt
Lindsay Kemp Russell Waters Aubrey Morris

Policeman (Edward Woodward) investigates disappearance of girl on sinister Scottish island.

A cult classic. Originally publicized as a horror film, this is really an erotic thriller about paganism and repression. Despite uninspired direction by Robin Hardy, the nasty ending still works powerfully, as indeed does the whole film – thanks to an excellent script by Anthony (*Sleuth*) Shaffer, which is in some respects a nightmarish re-working of *Whisky Galore* (1948). Avoid all but the 103-minute version.

ANTI:

'The trouble is that the film . . . doesn't make [the] situation acceptable either as reality or fantasy.' *(Patrick Gibbs, Daily Telegraph)*

'Hardy's real trouble . . . is his inability to posit anything but bluntly literal images . . . [He] industriously shows us pagan artefacts when he should be suggesting atavistic fears.' *(Tom Allen, Village Voice)*

MIXED:

'Fascinating ingredients that do not quite blend . . . It is the kind of film that desperately needs the transforming hand of a good director . . . but in Robin Hardy's hands it remains raw material . . . [This] offbeat and exotic story has become . . . an erratic and ultimately forgettable little thriller.' *(Nigel Andrews, Financial Times)*

'The story turns into a barbarous joke too horrible for pleasure, but one must admire the playing.' *(Sunday Times)*

PRO:

'A weird, disturbing story . . . filmed with style and a genuine sense of what is horrific.' *(Margaret Hinxman, Sunday Telegraph)*

'Superb, unclassifiable thriller.' *(Cinefantastique)*

'A fascinating mixture of horror, sex and pseudo-religion which makes for potent terror and gives Lee one of his finest roles.' *(Alan Frank)*

'Genuinely disturbing . . . [It lingers] in the mind, long after more polished horror movies have faded from memory.' *(Ken Russell, 1993)*

WILD AT HEART

CT: 5 AV: 5.75

1990 US 127 C THRILLER/ROMANCE

D David Lynch ✗
W David Lynch from Barry Gifford's novel

Nicolas Cage Laura Dern Diane Ladd ☆ ✗ AAN
Willem Dafoe Isabella Rossellini
Harry Dean Stanton Crispin Glover J.E. Freeman
W. Morgan Sheppard Sherilyn Fenn

Young lovers Sailor and Lula (Nicolas Cage and Laura Dern) go on the run from Lula's murderous mom (Diane Ladd, auditioning belatedly for the lead in Mommie Dearest*). On their way across the States, they are pursued by mom's wimpish boyfriend (Harry Dean Stanton, underacting to the point of invisibility) and various hired killers, notably Bobby Peru (Willem Dafoe with overlarge teeth and underdeveloped motivation).*

The message is not so very different from that of Lynch's previous, more impressive success, *Blue Velvet*: that just below the surface of America, there is sadism, necrophilia, mayhem, madness and murder. But whereas *Blue Velvet* established normality and then subverted it, *Wild At Heart* offers such a distorted, vacuous version of reality from the start that it's never convincing, and rapidly becomes a bore.

Blue Velvet explored the dark side of sexuality in a way which was sensuous but disturbing; in *Wild at Heart*, Lynch falls into the trap of voyeurism himself. The sex scenes between Sailor and Lula are straightforward soft porn. The scene where Lula invites rape has no foundation in her character.

Lynch's use of colour is often inspired, and his use of sound is always entertainingly bizarre – a legacy of his background in animation, where all sound is artificial and dubbed on afterwards. And there are a few funny jokes, albeit of an extremely sick nature.

But Lynch's usual faults are in abundance. Some of the sound effects and close-ups are just pretentious and repetitive; the actors don't appear to have been directed at all; and the continuity errors are glaring (a town which is empty of cars one moment is jammed with them a second later). The narrative structure is – even for a road movie – self-indulgent and shambolic. The film won the Palme d'Or at Cannes.

PRO:

'Funny, scary, and brilliantly cinematic.' *(Geoff Andrew, Time Out)*

'Joltingly violent, wickedly funny and rivetingly erotic.' *(Variety)*

'Lynch's special angle on the world is sometimes repellent but often smashingly effective. One roadside sequence, in which Sailor and Lula encounter the staggering victim of a car accident – played by Sherilyn Fenn, Audrey in *Twin Peaks* – resonates with a ghostly, poetic terror. Lynch's gorgeously lurid style is superbly complemented by the photography of Frederick Elmes, who worked with Lynch on *Eraserhead*, *Dune*, and *Blue Velvet*, and by the eerily evocative score of the *Twin Peaks* maestro Angelo Badalamenti.' *(Peter Travers, Rolling Stone)*

MIXED:

'This picture is packed with so much deranged energy, so many bravura images, that it's hard not to be seduced by the sick wonder of it all.' *(Richard Corliss, Time)*

'A trifle disappointing . . . It's not that Lynch isn't a virtuoso filmmaker, but this piece of American gothic . . . does not in the end quite add up . . . But no one could complain that it isn't a real film, born of the imagination like no other . . . There are marvellous performances.' *(Derek Malcolm, Guardian)*

'A semi-deranged road movie . . . It is fast, furious and colourfully scripted. It is structurally a total mess.' *(Nigel Andrews, Financial Times)*

'Lynch seems to be in schoolboyish collusion with an audience that expects to be shocked.' *(Margaret Walters, Listener)*

ANTI:

'From the opening scene of *Wild at Heart*, David Lynch crosses the line between art and obscenity. A white man beats a black man to a literal pulp – blood oozes, bones crack, body crumples . . . Lynch's paean to Fifties values in *Wild at Heart* shows exactly where his heart is: deep in the darkness of a lily-white paranoid America.' *(Armond White, City Sun)*

'A real contender for bad-taste movie of the year . . . And the rock score matches the mood – heavy, man, heavy . . . Take a sick bag.' *(Peter Cox, Sun)*

'There is something repulsive and manipulative about it, and even its best scenes have the flavor of a kid in the schoolyard, trying to show you pictures you don't feel like looking at.' *(Roger Ebert)*

'Much of it makes no sense and is just plain pretentious and tedious. Don't look too hard for the plot or you'll strain your eyes.' *(Rose)*

'As lurid, bizarre, absurd, erotic, sick and perverse as any film you are likely to see this year. Every character seems to have stepped freshly minted from a nightmare . . . [It] is a suburban grotesque, warped American gothic; a surreal joy ride through hell.' *(Evening Standard Magazine)*

WILD BUNCH, THE

CT: 8 AV: 8.63

1969 US 134/142/145 C WESTERN

D Sam Peckinpah ☆

W Walon Green Roy N. Sickner Sam Peckinpah ☆ AAN

William Holden ☆ Ernest Borgnine ☆ Robert Ryan ☆ Edmond O'Brien Warren Oates Jaime Sanchez

Texas outlaws whose way of life belongs to the 19th century find themselves butchered in the 20th.

One of the most controversial films of all time, with critics divided over whether the use of violence was justified or meretricious. I think it's one of Sam Peckinpah's finest achievements: an exciting, atmospheric, *fin de siècle* western clearly designed (unlike other Peckinpah films, such as *Straw Dogs*) to show that violence doesn't pay. The brutality and bloodshed were considered excessive for its day; by modern standards, they are relatively tame. A more serious criticism is that the story could have been clearer. Lucien Ballard's cinematography is stunning. Jerry Fielding's score was Oscar-nominated.

ANTI:

'Peckinpah has stated that he made [the film] as a protest against violence . . . Who the hell does he think he's kidding? . . . There is nothing in [it] except the savagery itself . . . perversely . . . imaginatively conceived and beautifully shot. Well, "nothing" is a bit unfair, perhaps. There is a [very ordinary] story.' *(Nina Hibbin, Morning Star)*

'Phony, pretentious piece of throat-slashing slobber . . . which goes around announcing good anti-violent intentions while exploiting and glorifying violence to the happy jungle of box-office coins . . . But the violence is not what I object to as much as the obvious glorification of violence as titillation. Peckinpah's philosophy of life appears to be that the world is totally corrupt, that there is no decency or morality left in society, and therefore the best thing to do is blow everyone's head off and have a great time doing it. He's a man to be pitied, not admired.' *(Rex Reed)*

'An unsurpassed orgy of blood and butchery that sickened many in the audience . . . Hollywood has gone too far this time.' *(William Hall, Evening News)*

'I would prefer to believe that Sam Peckinpah was sincere when he stated that he wanted to make a picture so strong, so stomach-churning, so detailed in its catalogue of horrors that all the glamour, all the attraction of violence for its own sake would promptly disappear. I think he is wrong, but I very much doubt that anyone who was not totally honest in his wrongheadedness could ever come up with a picture as wholly revolting as this . . . Every member of *The Wild Bunch* is so thoroughly hateful and corrupt as to richly deserve the fate that Peckinpah has in store for him – but I suspect that Peckinpah feels that so does all mankind.' *(Arthur Knight, Saturday Review)*

'Peckinpah's westerns excel in style, atmosphere and action, but invariably lose their story line in the blood and dust. In this one the plot is hardly any more obscure even when the Mexicans break into their native tongue.' *(Cecil Wilson, Daily Mail)*

'We watch endless violence to assure us that violence is not good.' *(Judith Crist, 1976)*

MIXED:

'Even in its currently mutilated version . . . [it] is too long, the plot too lumpy, the acting wildly uneven, and the continuity too often suspended for effects of pretty pictorialism. The director is apparently unable to do more than one thing at a time within a single shot. Hence, the film lurches wastefully back and forth between brutal realism and sentimental liberalism. The editing, crudely old-fashioned much of the time, seldom misses an opportunity to cop out on a cynical action shot of one character with a remorseful reaction shot of another. Still *The Wild Bunch* is one of the few American films of recent memory that doesn't seem to have been concocted by a market research computer.' *(Andrew Sarris, Village Voice)*

'The bloody deaths are voluptuous, frightening, beautiful. Pouring new wine into the bottle of the western, Peckinpah explodes the bottle; his story is too simple for this imagist epic.' *(Pauline Kael)*

PRO:

'A fascinating movie.' *(Vincent Canby, New York Times)*

'A nerve-racking film, grim in its instance but optimistic in its message . . . And any nausea I felt – and I did – was in a good cause.' *(Robert Ottaway, Daily Sketch)*

'Not easy to forget, beautifully acted . . . superbly mounted and fondly photographed.' *(Derek Malcolm, Guardian)*

'After this the west will never be quite the same again . . . Peckinpah is already a name to place up there at the top, alongside Thomas Ince and John Ford.' *(Tom Milne, Observer)*

'One of the year's best.' *(Time)*

'An extraordinary accomplishment . . . .a highly personal vision of what man is and how he relates to his world.' *(LA Herald-Examiner)*

'A magnificent western. Not a romantic western in the John Ford manner; ferocious rather, in the manner of Elizabethan drama; it is a tale of men who destroy themselves . . . pitiless murderers, though Peckinpah now and then allows a hint of decent feelings long overlaid; but no matter how often and with what insistence the film emphasizes their criminal progress one can't help sympathizing with them. Detach yourself from the heroic myth of the west and you have to recognize that morally there is nothing to be said in their favour. Nevertheless, in their end there is a kind of grandeur. It may contradict the central theme of a film ostensibly concerned to portray the squalors of violence. But the contradiction creates what is finally the tragic mood of *The Wild Bunch*.' *(Dilys Powell)*

'It is difficult to fault Mr Peckinpah. He is depicting, quite deliberately, a violent era and a society attuned to violence in which no one, not even children, can remain totally innocent. To do this, he needs to show violence; but he never broods on it, never sensationalizes it, and certainly never milks it for some kind of sadistic kick.' *(John Russell Taylor, The Times)*

'A western that enlarged the form aesthetically, thematically, demonically.' *(Stanley Kauffmann, 1972)*

'One of the most moving elegies for a vanished age ever created within the genre.' *(Time Out, 1984)*

WILD CHILD, THE

CT: 6 AV: 7.22

(aka *L'Enfant Sauvage*)

1969 France 85/90 C DRAMA/FOREIGN

D François Truffaut
W François Truffaut Jean Gruault from Jean-Marc Gaspard Itard's *Memoire et Rapport sur Victor de L'Aveyron*

Jean-Pierre Cargol François Truffaut Jean Daste Françoise Seigner Paul Ville Claude Miller Annie Miller

In 1797, a doctor (François Truffaut) tries to civilize a boy who has been living wild in the forest.

Truffaut was raised in an orphanage, and his affinity for the outcast child is obvious in many of his films – none more so than in this reconstruction of a true story from a doctor's diaries. Truffaut also succeeds in his intellectual purpose, which is to be ironic about scientific detachment, to show the limitations of rationalism. But the tone is muted, and there isn't enough narrative excitement, so that the picture ends up as far less satisfying than films such as *The Miracle Worker* (1962) or *The Elephant Man* (1980).

PRO:

'A hauntingly strange film and in some ways very beautiful. Not for all tastes, but if you go for this kind of thing you'll never forget it.' *(Molly Plowright, Glasgow Herald)*

'No one but Truffaut could possible have made this picture . . . [He] has made a wonderful film about the spirit of the Romantic Age.' *(Penelope Gilliatt, New Yorker)*

'Tells Victor's story with compassion and dignity. It makes no modern comment and comes to no modern conclusions.' *(Madeleine Harmsworth, Sunday Mirror)*

'Superb . . . Here [a distant period] is austerely depicted and to achieve the correct emphasis Truffaut goes back to the silent screen techniques of Griffith.' *(Margaret Hinxman, Sunday Telegraph)*

'What gives the film its special quality is the point at which Truffaut has chosen to end it – the moment when the boy gives crude proof of his human essence by showing that he can tell the difference between right and wrong.' *(Nina Hibbin, Morning Star)*

MIXED:

'Respecting the spirit of [Itard's] text, Truffaut invents little, contenting himself with translating or showing what is suggested or recounted in the book. It is this respect which gives the film both its value and its limitations . . . Within its limits, it is an excellent document and not a work of art.' *(Mireille Amiel, Cinema)*

ANTI:

'A rather dull film.' *(Dilys Powell, Sunday Times)*

WILD FLIGHT, THE *see* HIDDEN FORTRESS, THE.

WILD ONE, THE CT: 6 AV: 6.90

1954 US 79 BW DRAMA

D Laslo Benedek
W John Paxton from Frank Rooney's story

Marlon Brando Mary Murphy Robert Keith Lee Marvin Jay C. Flippen Peggy Maley Hugh Sanders Ray Teal John Brown Will Wright

An outlaw motorcycle gang under its leather-jacketed leader (Marlon Brando) terrorizes a town.

Inspired by events in Hollister, California, during 1947, this movie aroused controversy on several counts. The depiction of the local townsfolk's greed and hypocrisy (and their implicit fascism) was deemed anti-American by the US censors, who demanded cuts; while the British censors felt that the whole film glamorized juvenile delinquency and might incite young people to riot, and banned it until 1968.

Now, of course, it looks tame; and the ending – where Brando is tamed by a nice, sympathetic girl (Mary Murphy) – is pat and unconvincing. Still, the nature of the bikers' revolt is sensibly left unclear, and this gives the film a timeless appeal, while Brando is at his most charismatic. Its historical importance, as both the first biker movie and the first 'youth picture', makes it worth a look. Sample line . . . Woman: 'What are you rebelling against?' Brando: 'What have you got?'

'There was no glorification of violence. We simply showed that this was the first indication that a whole set of people were going to divorce themselves from society and set up their own standards.' *(Stanley Kramer, producer)*

'I think it was a failure. We started out to do something worthwhile, to explain the psychology of the hipster. But somewhere along the way we went off the track. The result was that instead of finding out why young people tend to bunch into groups that seek expression in violence, all that we did was show the violence.' *(Marlon Brando)*

ANTI:

'I think young people are quite bad enough; we don't want them to get any worse. This film would give them quite the wrong sort of stimulant. That is what I think about it and I would not pass it. It is not right to excite young people to have a row and go against authority. It is a dangerous form of excitement. Also it is a bad film, there is no story, and the repetition of fighting and brutality is monotonous.' *(Novelist Ursula Bloom, Evening Standard)*

'The censorship ban gave the film an aura of significance it never deserved.' *(Margaret Hinxman, 1968)*

'A strangely purposeless film. I think the main reason . . . is that [it] is a directorless film . . . Its point of view is too generalised.' *(Paul Mayersberg, New Society, 1968)*

'I am tempted to call it, by contemporary standard of slaughter, *The Mild One*.' *(Cecil Wilson, Daily Mail, 1968)*

'To a generation caught up in the metaphysics of *Bonnie and Clyde*, it's Desperate Dan in a leather jacket. They'll fall asleep.' *(Paul Pickering, Sunday Express, 1968)*

MIXED:

'Splendidly made: superb handling of the mob of vicious boys, brilliantly contrived tension as, to the accompaniment of the drumming engines, the temper of the gang rises and crowd insolence turns ugly. And Brando as the leader gives another extraordinary performance in the manner of *On the Waterfront* . . . [Yet] *The Wild One* has been refused even an X certificate; in the view of the censor it should not be seen at all. . . .I am bound to say I think the Board was absolutely right . . . There are films which at a particular time and in a particular setting can be dangerous. *The Wild One* with its exciting rhythm, its adolescent arrogance and the inventiveness of its destruction seems to me to be one of them.' *(Dilys Powell)*

'Violence is the keynote of this drama, violence in mind and body . . . almost documentary in technique . . . Its basic weakness is that as it nears its end it veers away from the objective and takes sides . . . It is nevertheless, well worth seeing. The cast is excellent.' *(Jesse Zunser, Cue)*

'Let it be seen. It is so far removed from anything that could possibly happen in this country that it borders on farce.' *(John Watney, Sunday Dispatch)*

'Still looks tolerably good, thanks chiefly to some edgy dialogue and the performances of Brando and Lee Marvin . . . Sadly studio-bound, though.' *(Tom Milne, Observer, 1968)*

PRO:

'The picture neither condones violence nor takes it for granted, and the censor's attitude seems due less to a fear that the majority might be shocked than that the minority inclined to hooliganism might be further corrupted. . . . The film goes a long way around to make the point that violence breeds violence, and in doing so loses its own way, taking refuge in some conventional melodramatics and an uncertain and equivocal ending. There remain though the general tone, appalled but unsensational . . . and the central fact of Brando's performance.' *(Penelope Houston, Spectator)*

'A powerful, blazing picture – and though Brando does not give one of his best performances, the tale the film tells is profoundly disturbing.' *(Sunday Express, 1959)*

'Stands up well . . . Brando, as you'd expect, has some terrific scenes . . . [He] is always exciting to watch. I recommend it.' *(Ernest Betts, People, 1968)*

WILD ORCHID CT: 5 AV: 2.20

1989 US 103/107 C DRAMA/ROMANCE/SO BAD

D Zalman King ●
W Patricia Louisianna Knop Zalman King ●

Mickey Rourke ● Jacqueline Bisset ●
Carre Otis ● Assumpta Serna Bruce Greenwood
Jens Peter Oleg Vidov

An international lawyer (Carre Otis) becomes the love-slave of a mumbling idiot (Mickey Rourke).

This movie contains so much soft-focus photography that it might more properly be called *Love-in-a-Mist*. It is writer-director Zalman King's seedy sequel to *9½ Weeks* and *Two Moon Junction*, movies which did so much to put the rot back into erotica.

Mr King's sensual imagery is as depressingly detumescent as ever (waves crash, motorbikes throb, waterpipes spurt), and his dialogue is not so much sexually depraved as intellectually deprived. Connoisseurs of unintentional ambiguity will relish the moment when its male star Mickey Rourke, playing a hero who might most charitably be described as a greasy, brain-damaged voyeur, has to mumble: 'I'm not very good at being touched.'

The heroine Emily (Carre Otis) is meant to be an international lawyer with five languages, though she's only too obviously an international model with no acting ability. Bisset is no less laughable, with an accent which globe-trots from Seattle to Surbiton and back again.

Other great lines . . . (1) Jacqueline Bisset: 'I'm not used to men in masks biting my neck.' (2) Mickey Rourke: 'I had a father for a while. When he disappeared, I barely spoke for years. I stayed in the third grade for a long time.'

A sequel followed, in 1992, *Wild Orchid II: Two Shades Of Blue* – of which the less said the better.

PRO:

'Shamefully enjoyable.' *(Winnert)*

ANTI:

'Despite a good-humoured performance from Jacqueline Bisset as Otis's calm and beautiful boss, and a genuinely erotic cameo by the magnificent Assumpta Serna as a frustrated wife liberated on the back seat of a limo, there aren't 9½ minutes of fun or feeling to be had in this risible celebration of the stars' untrammelled narcissism.' *(Graham Fuller, Film Yearbook)*

'There are some erotic films that give sex a bad name. They don't make it disgusting or perverting or anything lip-wetting like that. They just make it dull. This is the unforgivable sin and [this film] commits it.' *(Derek Malcolm, Guardian)*

'Bisset's bitchy executive is so overwritten she makes Joan Collins look like an ingenue.' *(David Robinson, The Times)*

'The psychology owes more to Bob Guccione than Sigmund Freud. Hard to say what is worst in this film . . . the dreadful acting (Mickey Rourke stands out, playing his character like the Phantom of the Opera on tranquillizers), the script, by turns risible and offensive in its depiction of women, or the cliché-ridden direction. Take your choice, but don't pay the money.' *(Hugo Davenport, Daily Telegraph)*

'What doesn't work is the hold Rourke is supposed to have over Otis. Looking pudgy and puffy-faced, with a little gold earring, he is anything but an appetising sex object.' *(Variety)*

'The film's central male performance – which struck this observer, at least, as having all the animal magnetism of a dead dog – is tragic confirmation that Mickey Rourke's head needs examining. Who can say whether nature or vanity has played a cruel trick on him, but he has acquired high cheekbones precipitately and rather late in life, so that he now looks like Michael Jackson trying to turn himself into Mount Rushmore. Meanwhile, the cheeks below have gained that stretched, latex sheen hitherto seen only on cinematic aliens whose heads are about to explode.' *(Christopher Tookey, Sunday Telegraph)*

'This is a staggeringly awful and offensive film . . . Rourke looks most bizarre, as if his facial skin has been pulled taut and secured by a bulldog clip at the back of his unnaturally tanned head, giving him the appearance of a young and very startled chipmunk . . . It would all be laughable tosh that wouldn't excite the inhabitants of a monastery were it not for the thinly-veiled premise that . . . women are all grasping sexual predators who open their legs like revolving doors to get their wicked way with men . . . I don't know whether it is . . . King . . . or . . . Rourke who has been so horribly frightened by my own sex. I strongly suggest they take it up with their mothers and spare us any future dire cinematic efforts.' *(Sue Heal, Today)*

'The much ballyhooed climactic sex scene is about as erotic as earwax.' *(Scheuer)*

During the decades between the rather boring bonking you might try this quiz. Whoever told Otis he could act? Why is Rourke such a deep shade of orange? And when was the last time Bisset was in a decent film?' *(Rose)*

WILD STRAWBERRIES CT: 8 AV: 9.07

(aka *Smultronstället*)

1957 Sweden 93 BW DRAMA/FOREIGN

D Ingmar Bergman ☆
W Ingmar Bergman ☆ AAN

Victor Sjöström ☆ Bibi Andersson Ingrid Thulin Gunnar Björnstrand Julian Kindahl Folke Sundquist Naima Wifstrand

An old professor (Victor Sjöström) looks back on his life as he travels to accept an honorary degree.

Woody Allen changed the sex of the protagonist and re-used the central idea as the basis of his film, *Another Woman*; but it can't really compare in quality with Bergman's original masterpiece – a profound piece of writing, beautifully performed by 78-year-old Sjöström (himself a marvellous director). The picture is an arrestingly cruel vision of life's disappointments, all the more effective for having a warmth and affection often absent from Bergman's work. Winner of Best Film at the Berlin Festival.

MIXED:

'This strange dreamlike allegorical piece . . . dwells . . . on pain and darkness and the neurotic scream, and the sunny patches are limited. But although the first third commands attention, in the end it amounts to little, as though Mr Bergman himself had lost interest in his conclusion.' *(Glasgow Herald)*

'Weakest in its obsession of character, the fault lying in the script rather than the acting . . . I find it hard to reconcile Bergman's inspired imagery with such immature obsession of human nature.' *(Edinburgh Evening News)*

'A very uneven film . . . with peculiarly unconvincing flashbacks and overexplicit dialogue . . . One can try to forget the irritations: the incredibly callow representatives of youth, the "cold" rigid son (Gunnar Björnstrand), the disappointingly vacuous parts assigned Bibi Andersson as the two Saras, the expendable role of Naima Wifstrand as the ancient mother.' *(Pauline Kael)*

PRO:

'His use of light and shade is consistently good . . . [Sjöström's] acting is subtle, sensitive and credible from first to last.' *(Neville Garden, Evening Dispatch)*

'Dream sequences in films are usually silly and irrelevant, tiresome, unrewarding interruptions of the action and since *Wild Strawberries* . . . consists for, say, a quarter of the time of dreams while another equally substantial proportion is devoted to reconstructions of the past which have a dreamlike quality, it would seem to follow that the film is an untidy piece of work lacking rhythm and unity. Nothing, however, could be further from the truth.' *(The Times)*

'One bite is not enough to appreciate its entire subtle flavour.' *(John Waterman, Evening Standard)*

'The work of a man obsessed by cruelty, especially spiritual cruelty, trying to find some resolution.' *(Kenneth Cavander, MFB)*

'A mature masterwork . . . An early road movie, this benefits from extraordinarily moving performances and an intricate challenging script. Among Bergman's most deeply affecting works, balancing Swedish chill with a deep humanity. *(Empire, 1994)*

WILD TARGET CT: 10 AV: 8.00 (est)

(aka *Cible Émouvante*)

1993 France 87 C COMEDY/THRILLER/FOREIGN

D Pierre Salvadori ☆
W Pierre Salvadori ☆

Jean Rochefort ☆ Marie Trintignant ☆ Guillaume Depardieu ✓, Patachou ☆ Charlie Nelson Wladimir Tordanoff Serge Riaboukine Philippe Girard

Victor Meynard (Jean Rochefort) is a model of bourgeois respectability, with his regimental bearing, meticulous suiting, and passion for order. His hobbies are bonsai gardening and teaching himself English – which he does at every conceivable opportunity, even when killing people. For Victor is a professional hit-man. He has been trained for the job from his cradle by his Maman (Patachou). Emotionally stunted and mother-dominated to a degree unseen since Anthony Perkins in Psycho, *he lives a life free of emotional relationships.*

Childless himself, he seizes on a young man unfortunate enough to witness one of his hits (Guillaume Depardieu, son of Gérard), and decides to train him as his successor – a process which he estimates will take 14 years. Since the only alternative is to be murdered, the young man agrees. Their first victim turns out to be a beautiful art-forger (Marie Trintignant). For the first time in his life, Victor can't bring himself to kill. Gradually, he comes to suspect that he may not be the repressed gay which he and his mother have always assumed him to be, but a 'normal' heterosexual.

Black comedy of the highest quality – an entrancing, riotously amusing, brilliantly-crafted piece of entertainment. The film has the symmetry of the best Alan Ayckbourn, the anarchic bawdiness of Joe Orton, yet it also manages to be distinctively French. It is, like all the best caper movies, a work of soaring fancy – but there's a degree of psychological truth and social observation which keeps it tethered to the ground. Thus, the second-most expensive hit-man in France is motivated by professional jealousy of Victor, who dares to overcharge even more outrageously. A Parisian Mr Big inspires terror in others not by disclosing details of his career as a gangster, but by revealing that he prepared for it with 10 years as an estate agent.

In the lead, Jean Rochefort is a joy. He handles the physical comedy with a deftness reminiscent of the great silent comedians. Even the way he walks is funny; he has the stiff-backed, determined dignity of a military man being catapulted with invisible rotten eggs. Rochefort has proved himself a great screen actor before (notably in Bertrand Tavernier's *The Clockmaker of Saint-Paul*, and Patrice Leconte's *The Hairdresser's Husband*). Here, at last, he has a script which explores his unique talents to the full.

The film isn't entirely original. The romantic aspect is reminiscent of *The Accidental Tourist*, with a middle-aged man (there it was William Hurt) being taught to unbend by a free-spirited younger woman. And the apprenticeship theme has something in common with Bill Forsyth's *Breaking In*, where another old criminal (Burt Reynolds) also passed on the secrets of his trade. But this film is funnier and more ingenious than either.

It is, unbelievably, the first by writer-director Pierre Salvadori; it's utterly assured, beautifully shot, and structurally perfect. The pace lets up a little when the protagonists leave Paris for Victor's country chateau, but only because we need a breather before the grand finale, which has been described accurately as '*Reservoir Dogs* shot by Jacques Tati'.

MIXED:

'This situation comedy is fine, but the film's bid for pathos fails, amid sideswipes at sexual manners only the French will ken. But it ends with a scene of such ridiculous symmetricality that you'll forgive it.' *(Wally Hammond, Time Out)*

PRO:

'A sweet, hilarious black comedy.' *(James Cameron-Wilson, Film Review)*

'The funniest film in London . . . not to be missed.' *(Alexander Walker, Evening Standard)*

'One of the best comedies I have seen for years.' *(Sue Heal, Today)*

'The funniest movie to have arrived in London this year.' *(Philip French, Observer)*

'A joy from start to finish.' *(Rachel Simpson, Daily Express)*

WILL SUCCESS SPOIL ROCK HUNTER?

CT: 6 AV: 6.67

(aka *Oh! For a Man!*)

1957 US 95 C COMEDY

D Frank Tashlin ☆
W Frank Tashlin from George Axelrod's play

Jayne Mansfield ✓ Tony Randall ☆ Betsy Drake ✓ Joan Blondell John Williams Henry Jones Groucho Marx

A timid advertising executive (Tony Randall) becomes famous as the world's greatest lover.

A fast-moving, cartoon-like satire on business, advertising, sex, TV and Jayne Mansfield (here playing a dumber version of herself). Tony Randall gives the performance of his life. Jean-Luc Godard had it on his 'Best 10' list, but don't hold that against it.

MIXED:

'Scores some cracking bullseyes at the expense of commercial television . . . The moral of it all is, you will not be surprised to learn, that success is "just the art of being happy." . . . To reach this unexceptionable, hackneyed moral is like taking a thousand-mile trip in search of beauty only to land up at Euston Station. But at least the journey is fun most of the way.' *(Frank Jackson, Reynolds News)*

'Some good jokes . . . though repetition and exaggeration take the edge off.' *(Dilys Powell, Sunday Times)*

'A joke's a joke, Stanley Lupino used to say, but you can't laugh all night. I find I can no longer summon up the dutiful smirk that is expected when yet another actress blessed with *haute gonflage* is paraded before us as though that simple fact were all . . . Must we go on about it? Jayne Mansfield seems primarily charged with seeing that we [must]. A pity because there is a genuine comedy talent there.' *(Fred Majdalany, Time & Tide)*

PRO:

'Here at last Jayne arrives as a genuine comedienne whose talents match her measurements . . . This film . . . contrives to be immensely funny about very little.' *(Ross Shepherd, The People)*

'The best thing about it is a newcomer called Tony Randall, who make a chirruping attractive arrival.' *(Isabel Quigly, Spectator)*

'It pricks the balloons of Big Business with the crude delight of a schoolboy drawing teacher on the blackboard.' *(Edward Goring, Daily Mail)*

WINCHESTER '73

CT: 6 AV: 7.09

1950 US 92 BW WESTERN

D Anthony Mann ☆
W Robert L. Richards

James Stewart ☆ Shelley Winters Dan Duryea ☆

Stephen McNally ☆ Millard Mitchell Charles Drake John McIntire Will Geer Jay C. Flippen Rock Hudson Tony Curtis

Western hero (James Stewart) is driven to the point of madness by his need to avenge the death of his father and recover a stolen rifle.

Both a rousing adventure story, and a superior psychological western in which the landscapes (beautifully photographed by William Daniels) illustrate the mood of the protagonists. Stewart's complicated, neurotic performance brought him renewed popularity with the public and launched him on two further collaborations with director Anthony Mann, *Bend of the River* (1952) and *The Far Country* (1954).

MIXED:

'[The film] has two great assets: a good idea and a good actor; but disappointingly fails to make the most of either . . . [The idea] provides an excellent framework for a picture, but unhappily the producers have neglected to provide a picture for the framework.' *(C.A. Lejeune, Observer)*

'The only gleam of intelligence to be seen is in a first-class performance by villainous Stephen McNally.' *(Daily Worker)*

'The dramatic exploitation of an inanimate object . . . seems to have frightened or exhausted the makers of this film; they have shied away from it to the safe, uncomplicated emphasis of ordinary shootings, hold-ups, and chases on horseback.' *(Manchester Guardian)*

PRO:

'Thanks to writing, direction and acting of unusual quality, [it] is one of the best things of its kind for years . . . James Stewart . . . gives his best performance for years.' *(Campbell Dixon, Daily Telegraph)*

'If you keep your eye on the gun, you are liable to lose track of the characters; if you keep your eye on the characters, you are liable to lose track of the gun. Recommended unreservedly to the swivel-eyed.' *(Paul Dehn, Sunday Chronicle)*

WIND, THE

CT: 8 AV: 8.80

1927 US 74 BW DRAMA/SILENT

D Victor Sjöström ☆
W Frances Marion from Dorothy Scarborough's novel

Lillian Gish ☆ Lars Hanson Montagu Love Dorothy Cummings

Virginian virgin (Lillian Gish) travels to Texas and finds herself up to her neck in hatred, rape and murder.

Great, melodramatic silent, notable for Lillian Gish's immensely sympathetic leading performance.

ANTI:

'Everything about the picture breathes quality. Yet it flops dismally . . . Lifeless; and unentertaining.' *(Variety)*

PRO:

'Unrelieved by the ghost of a smile . . . gloomy and even morbid, *The Wind*, Lillian Gish's final picture for Metro-Goldwyn, is nevertheless a fine and dignified achievement. Its lack of lightness will stand in the way of its success with many, but the enjoyment of the few – presuming that serious moviegoers are in the minority – is assured.' *(Picture Play, 1929)*

'So penetrating is the atmosphere that one can almost feel the wind itself and taste the endless dust.' *(Georges Sadoul)*

'One of the finest achievements among silent American films.' *(Lewis Jacobs)*

'Achieves a level of emotional intensity that few films have ever matched.' *(Scheuer)*

'Sjöström directs with immaculate attention to psychological detail, while making perfectly credible the film's transition from low-key naturalistic comedy of manners to full-blown hysterical melodrama . . . Erotic, beautiful, astonishing.' *(Geoff Andrew, Time Out)*

WINDOW, THE

CT: 6 AV: 7.57

1949 US 73 BW THRILLER

D Ted Tetzlaff
W Mel Dinelli from Cornell Woolrich's novelette *The Boy Cried Murder*

Barbara Hale Bobby Driscoll ☆ (AAW as 'outstanding juvenile actor) Arthur Kennedy Paul Stewart Ruth Roman Anthony Ross Richard Benedict Jim Nolan Ken Terrell Lee Phelps

A boy (Bobby Driscoll) witnesses a murder but can't make anyone believe him.

If the story has echoes of *Rear Window*, that's hardly surprising because Cornell Woolrich wrote them both. Ted Tetzlaff is not as imaginative as Hitchcock, but he had obviously learned a lot from being Hitchcock's cinematographer on *Notorious* three years before. He turns in a very suspenseful, atmospheric thriller, with Driscoll outstanding in the lead. Frederick Knudtson's editing was Oscar-nominated.

MIXED:

'Although Tetzlaff's direction is not always as restrained as might be desired, there is no denying that his contribution looms large, for he has not permitted any of several increasingly harrowing incidents to spoil the full crushing force of the picture's climax.' *(New York Times)*

PRO:

'Logical, well-shaped, cohesive, admirably acted, beautifully photographed and cut to a nicety.' *(Richard Winnington)*

'Starts rather slowly, but has a terrific impact once it gets started and never lets up until the fadeout . . . Very good.' *(Charles J. Lazarus, Motion Picture Herald)*

'Without the footage and star value of a great many other productions of its kind, this thriller . . . reveals how much can be achieved with a genuinely original story and an enterprising and intelligent director . . . Bobby Driscoll gives an appealing and remarkably realistic performance.' *(Today's Cinema)*

'Much of the credit for this well-presented and wholly absorbing film is undoubtedly due to the splendid acting of young Bobby Driscoll.' *(MFB)*

'This taut, tense story . . . is a "must" on any film-lover's list. . . . Tetzlaff takes the pattern of the fire escapes, scores of them, all lancing the screen with diagonals, for both his opening and closing shots . . . [The climax] is something new in thrills, a fitting nightmare culmination to a nightmare story . . . Sorrow, not shock is [its] trump card.' *(R.H. Alder, Amateur Cine World)*

'Why *The Window* has not been rated as a first feature for West End showing is one of those mysteries which now and again surprise those engaged in film-sampling. There is more virtue – more life, excitement, interest and genuine feeling – in this obviously economically-made picture than in an average half-dozen star-laden offerings. All praise to the Academy for coming to the rescue and providing the opportunity for reviewing it. There are no star names attached to it, it is true, though it creates a new young star in 12-year-old Bobby Driscoll.' *(A.E. Wilson)*

WINGS OF DESIRE CT: 5 AV: 7.90

(aka *Der Himmel über Berlin*)

1987 France/West Germany 130 C DRAMA/FANTASY/FOREIGN

D Wim Wenders ✗
W Wim Wenders Peter Handke ✗

Bruno Ganz Solveig Dommartin ● Otto Sander Curt Bois, Peter Falk

Two angels (Bruno Ganz, Otto Sander) keep watch over Berlin and become involved in the lives of a poet (Curt Bois), a film star (Peter Falk, playing himself) and a trapeze artist (Solveig Dommartin).

Wenders's most celebrated film is memorable for Henri Alekan's beautiful cinematography, but for little else. As usual in this vastly overrated writer-director's films, there are glaring weaknesses in casting and narrative. A potentially interesting story is sabotaged by the stolid, uncharismatic non-acting of Solveig Dommartin (who we are supposed to believe would convince Bruno Ganz that he should give up immortality) and a plot which asks us to swallow the notion that Peter Falk is a fallen angel. The film won Wenders the best director prize at Cannes, and spawned a belated and inferior sequel, *Faraway So Close* (1993).

PRO:

'A near-masterpiece, a movie whose sublime black-and-white images of phlegmatic angels peering into human souls announced that, even if the New German Cinema was dead, its moody metaphysical branch was very much alive and well.' *(Stephen Schiff)*

'It's not only the loveliest, most delicate, most original angel movie ever made; it's the kind of metaphysical love story that makes love itself seem daring and miraculous, pushing up from beneath bleak tons of ruin.' *(Jay Carr)*

'A visual poem about the walls that exist in our world – those that separate fiction from reality, heaven from earth, history from the present, those who observe from those who feel, East Berlin from West Berlin (before the tumultuous 1990 removal of the Berlin Wall), black and white from color, angels from mortals.' *(Baseline)*

MIXED:

'*Wings of Desire* has a visual fascination but no animating force – that's part of why it's being acclaimed as art.' *(Pauline Kael)*

WINSLOW BOY, THE CT: 8 AV: 7.92

1948 GB 117 BW DRAMA

D Anthony Asquith ☆
W Terence Rattigan Anthony Asquith Anatole de Grunwald from Rattigan's play

Robert Donat ☆ Margaret Leighton ☆ Cedric Hardwicke ☆ Basil Radford Frank Lawton ☆ Kathleen Harrison Francis L. Sullivan Marie Lohr Jack Watling Neil North ✔ Wilfrid Hyde-White

A barrister (Robert Donat) defends a young naval cadet (Neil North) expelled from college for stealing a postal order.

Terence Rattigan's deftly constructed drama, based on a true story, is expertly directed by Anthony Asquith with a good sense of period and pace. At the head of a strong cast, Robert Donat gives one of his finest performances. Hardwicke, normally a dry actor, is moving as the father ready to sacrifice everything to prove his son's innocence.

MIXED:

'It is too long and would benefit from some judicious cutting . . . [but] this is quite definitely a film to see and enjoy.' *(MFB)*

PRO:

'The play could scarcely have been better adapted.

The film has a script of which the sensible, credible, and, on occasion, stirring dialogue makes one remember with a start how very rare it is for a film's dialogue to have even one of those qualities. It has a superb cast.' *(Manchester Guardian)*

'Should be seen not only because it is a sincere and moving piece of filmcraft, but because it will remind you that British justice is a right which must constantly be fought for.' *(Evening Standard)*

'Mr Donat makes a magnificent come-back in one of the best British films for months . . . Equally impressive is Sir Cedric . . . My compliments [to Asquith] on a fine job of direction.' *(Daily Herald)*

'Outstanding.' *(New York Journal American)*

'As long as there's an England, there will be films like [this] and that's all right by me . . . In the midst of his highly experienced elders, Neil North is properly unobtrusive as the boy.' *(John McCarten, New Yorker)*

'Only a clod could see this film without excitement, laughter and some slight moisture about the eyes.' *(Daily Telegraph)*

WITCHFINDER GENERAL CT: 5 AV: 5.89

(aka *The Conqueror Worm*)

1968 GB 87 C HORROR

D Michael Reeves ✗
W Michael Reeves Tom Baker from Ronald Bassett's novel

Vincent Price ☆ Rupert Davies Ian Ogilvy Patrick Wymark Hilary Dwyer Wilfrid Brambell

17th-century witchfinder (Vincent Price) uses job for his own sadistic and sexual purposes.

A cult movie, and certainly the best work of its writer-director (who died young). Vincent Price gives one of his most menacing performances. The critics on release were less than kind to it, and they had a point: there is something gloatingly misogynistic about Reeves's treatment of violence to women; the young hero (Ian Ogilvy) is boring; and the pacing is not all it might be.

PRO:

'With the artwork . . . and the superb camerawork . . . the film carries us magically back into the 17th century . . . Vincent Price damps down his habitual villainy . . . Patrick Wymark makes a stab at Cromwell (and misses).' *(Felix Barker, Evening News)*

'Reeves . . . is a very good director. He has a sharp sense of pace, a sophisticated eye for possible absurdity that is pleasing . . . Above all, he has that vital gift in a filmmaker, the instinctive ability to make anything he trains his camera on look interesting.' *(John Russell Taylor, The Times)*

'It does have real style and presence.' *(Observer)*

'Extremely bloody and gruesome, the violence is, in fact, integral to the story and not gratuitous. Nevertheless, it was condemned on all sides on its release. Superbly photographed, the film is notable for Reeves's direction and for the fact that, for once, Price played it absolutely straight, giving a chillingly believable performance. Inexplicably, the title was changed for its American release where the publicity attempted to imply a connection (not there) with Edgar Allan Poe.' *(Alan Frank)*

MIXED:

'Excessively and gratuitously sadistic, with lashings of blood and the camera lingering with relish over rape, hangings and assorted mutilations. Fine, if you like that kind of thing.' *(S & S)*

'Features any number of attractive young aspiring stars who seem to have been cast . . . mainly for their ability to scream . . . Vincent Price has a good time.' *(Renata Adler, New York Times)*

'The film is less concerned with narrative than with exploiting every opportunity for gratuitous sadism.' *(David Wilson, Guardian)*

'An exercise in sadistic extravagance, all the more repugnant for being ably directed . . . and decently acted.' *(Margaret Hinxman, Sunday Telegraph)*

WITHNAIL & I CT: 6 AV: 6.23

1987 GB 108 C COMEDY

D Bruce Robinson ☆
W Bruce Robinson

Richard E. Grant ☆ Paul McGann Richard Griffiths ☆ Ralph Brown Michael Elphick

Two out-of-work actors (Richard E. Grant, Paul McGann) scrape an existence in Camden and Cumbria.

Turgid, rambling comedy saved by Grant's charismatic performance and some hilarious moments; it captures better than any other movie what it was like to be young in the 60s. Richard Griffiths is memorably offbeat as gay Uncle Monty.

ANTI:

'Ineffably patronising, tedious and unconvincing . . . It has a frenzied-camp air of exaggeration . . . Maybe I don't like British overacting.' *(Ian Penman, The Face)*

PRO:

'At its best, *Withnail* is civilized Cheech and Chong.' *(J. Hoberman, Village Voice)*

'[McGann, Grant and Griffiths] are a triple treat . . . certainly one of the most original works on display.' *(Iain Johnstone, Sunday Times)*

'Robinson has made a memorable début that verifies that his directorial talents are as rich and ingenious as his writing abilities.' *(Hollywood Reporter)*

'The script is terribly funny . . . Grant could become a bit of a cult.' *(Maggie Alderson, Evening Standard Magazine)*

'A quirky invention.' *(John Marriott, Daily Mail)*

'Wickedly witty, acid-sharp.' *(Pauline McCleod, Daily Mirror)*

'Beautifully scripted, indecent, honest, and truthful, it's a true original.' *(Wally Hammond, Time Out)*

'A comedy, but a grimly serious one. Nothing is played for laughs. The humor arises from poverty, desperation, and bone-numbing cold. It is not the portrait of two colorful, lovable characters, but of two comrades in emotional shipwreck. The movie is rigorously dyspeptic, and that's why I liked it. It doesn't go for the easy laughs or sentimentalized poverty, but finds its humor in the unforgiving study of selfish human nature.' *(Roger Ebert)*

WITNESS AAN CT: 8 AV: 8.29

1985 US 112 C THRILLER/ROMANCE

D Peter Weir ☆ AAN
W Earl W. Wallace William Kelley
Pamela Wallace ☆ AAW

Harrison Ford ☆ AAN Kelly McGillis ✔
Josef Sommer Lukas Haas ✔ Jan Rubes
Alexander Godunov Danny Glover Brent Jennings
Patti LuPone Viggo Mortensen

A cop (Harrison Ford) has to protect a small boy (Lukas Haas) who has witnessed a murder. The boy and his mother (Kelly McGillis) are members of the American Amish community, who choose to live in an approximation to the 18th century.

Dirty Harry meets Mother Teresa. One of the best romantic thrillers, and the film which showed doubters that Harrison Ford really could act. The raising of the barn is one of the great scenes of modern cinema – as is the love scene between Ford and McGillis. Thom Noble's editing won an Oscar; and the film narrowly missed out on others, for photography (John (Seale), music (Maurice Jarre) and art direction (Stan Jolley, John Anderson). Australian director Peter Weir's first film set in America offers a bleak, foreigner's eye view of a violent prevailing culture, and the non-availing attempts of a peaceful sub-culture to survive within it. Kelly McGillis and Alexander Godunov appear in the same roles for one scene in Rob Reiner's film *North* (1994).

ANTI:

'*Witness* is at times a gentle, affecting story of star-crossed lovers limited within the fascinating Amish community. Too often, however, this fragile romance is crushed by a thoroughly absurd shoot-em-up, like ketchup poured over a delicate Pennsylvanian Dutch dinner.' *(Variety)*

'The movie seems to take its view of the Amish from a quaint dreamland, a Brigadoon of tall golden wheat, and to take its squalid, hyped-up view of life in Philadelphia from prolonged exposure to TV cop shows . . . The picture is like something dug up from the earliest days of movies; it has a bland, seductive lyricism, and one familiar, "mythic" scene after another . . . McGillis shifts uneasily between the heroic naturalness of Liv Ullmann and the dimpled simpering of the young Esther Williams.' *(Pauline Kael)*

'*Witness* is still a more engaging thriller than most, even if its ballyhooed "freshness" is a bit smelly around the edges. And to give credit where it is due, they have forced some new twists to an old saw.' *(Rex Reed, New York Post)*

'Entertaining film is marred by jarring shifts in tone, especially towards the end.' *(Maltin)*

PRO:

'Peter Weir's *Witness* is a remarkable film – both an exciting thriller and a beautifully directed meditation on violence . . . From the beginning of American movie history . . . audiences have trusted the man who uses his violent skill righteously . . . In *Witness* the code of the man of violence is once again questioned and criticized: John Book, surrounded by peace lovers, looks a little foolish, and when he acts violently he goes too far. Yet such is the pull of righteous violence . . . ' *(David Denby, New York Magazine)*

'It is precisely the business of *Witness*, which is one of the most originally conceived and gracefully made suspense dramas of recent years, to work into edgy juxtaposition the representatives of two subcultures (the Amish and the police) that ordinarily are mutually exclusive.' *(Richard Schickel, Time)*

'The beauty of *Witness*, a delicately woven, wide-eyed thriller set in Amish country, is that it views the familiar macho cop-movie rituals from a child's perspective, and from that vantage they look strange and disquieting . . . At *Witness*'s bucolic pace, we have time to contemplate his [Harrison Ford] knobbly nose and soft, rounded chin. This ain't such a tough guy. When he isn't squinting like a hardened man of battle, Ford's eyes go goo-goo and his manner sheepish – he's the movie's other little boy.' *(David Edelstein, Village Voice)*

'Three terrific movies in one: an exciting cop thriller, a touching romance, and a fascinating screen study of a modern-day clash of cultures.' *(Martin & Porter)*

WITNESS FOR THE PROSECUTION AAN CT: 6 AV: 8.36

1957 US 114 BW THRILLER

D Billy Wilder AAN
W Billy Wilder Harry Kurnitz ☆ from Agatha Christie's play

Charles Laughton ☆ AAN Tyrone Power ✗
Marlene Dietrich ✗ Elsa Lanchester ☆ AAN

A convalescing QC (Charles Laughton) takes on a murder case against medical advice.

The plot is a classic (though an alternative suspect might have been a good idea); and the film is worth seeing, if only for its outrageous denouement. Laughton is outstanding, and Dietrich is fine when being austere and Germanic. But when called upon to do other things vital to the plot, Dietrich is hopeless, and Tyrone Power's performance throughout – inexplicably praised by some reviewers – is so hammy that it calls attention to the staginess of the script and direction. Oscar nominations went to Daniel Mandell for his editing, and Gordon Sawyer for best sound.

MIXED:

'Because the Laughtons are amusing people [the film] is often very funny . . . But it isn't quite the sharp, dry melodrama that Mrs Christie fashioned for the stage . . . [and] will leave more people less interested in who done it, than amused by that Charles Laughton, he's a scream.' *(John McCarten, Time & Tide)*

'How nice to see . . . that benevolent old pachyderm Charles Laughton trumpeting through the undergrowth . . . Mrs Christie may be devilish deep at spinning plots, but in the delineation of character she spins about as deeply as the dull, comic-strip weavers of Bayeux . . . It is not Miss Dietrich's fault that . . . [when singing] she is ill-served by the lyrics. But it is her fault that, at the film's climax, she proves technically quite incapable of masquerading as – oh, pish! I can't divulge that either.' *(Paul Dehn, News Chronicle)*

'Inane yet moderately entertaining.' *(Pauline Kael)*

PRO:

'A witty script, a good story, and the triple stardom . . . Bang on top for entertainment . . . [which] gives Laughton such a fat part he looks slim by comparison.' *(People)*

'My advice is to get along to this film as soon as you can. I repeat – it's magnificent!' *(Peter Burnup, News of the World)*

'Ingeniously contrived . . . At a period when the cinema, in order to stir even the most languid interest, has to throw the Thing from the blue lagoon into boiling bitumen, [this] manages to be exciting with no bashing about at all.' *(Dilys Powell, Sunday Times)*

'Wilder has given [Laughton] every opportunity to pull off all the dramatic tricks.' *(Moore Raymond, Sunday Dispatch)*

'A courtroom meller played engagingly and building evenly to a surprising and arousing, albeit tricked-up, climax.' *(Variety)*

'There is no courtroom drama more enjoyable . . . The most fun comes from trying to work out if the obvious overacting by the defendant and witnesses is being done by the actors or by the characters they're portraying.' *(Danny Peary)*

WIZARD OF OZ, THE AAN   CT: 8 AV: 9.56

1939 US 102 C MUSICAL/FANTASY
D Victor Fleming ☆ (finished, uncredited, by King Vidor)

W Noel Langley Florence Ryerson
Edgar Allan Woolfe from Frank L. Baum's book
(songs by Harold Arlen and E.Y. Harburg ☆)

Judy Garland ☆ (AAW 'for her outstanding performance as a screen juvenile in *The Wizard of Oz* and *Babes in Arms*) Frank Morgan ☆ Ray Bolger ☆
Jack Haley ☆ Bert Lahr ☆ Margaret Hamilton ☆
Billie Burke Charley Grapewin Clara Blandick

Unhappy girl (Judy Garland) travels and makes new friends but discovers there's no place like home.

Classic family musical which was slagged off on release for having an overage heroine, garish sets and heavy-handed direction (though it still managed to reach Number 7 on the 1939 *Film Daily* poll of US film critics). Audiences either believed the hostile reviews or were not in the mood for fantasy, for it did disappointing business; not until a re-release in 1948 did it turn a profit. It was TV that made people appreciate the film's finest qualities. The musical highlight is Judy Garland singing the Oscar-winning 'Somewhere Over The Rainbow', a song that studio executives wanted to cut out. The art direction by Cedric Gibbons and William A. Horning and visual effects by A. Arnold Gillespie and Douglas Shearer were Oscar-nominated.

'The Sydney trade paper *The Film Weekly* which reviewed just about every feature released in Australia didn't bother to review *The Wizard of Oz* at all – because it was considered of such peripheral interest to exhibitors. The movie was booked almost solely into kiddies' matinees – and even there it fared poorly.' *(John Howard Reid)*

ANTI:

'I sat cringing before *Oz* which displays no trace of imagination, good taste or ingenuity . . . The vulgarity of which I was conscious all through the film is difficult to analyze.' *(New Yorker)*

'Intended to hit the same audience as *Snow White*, and won't fail for lack of trying. It has dwarfs, music, Technicolor, freaks, characters, and Judy Garland. It can't be expected to have a sense of humor as well – and as for the light touch of fantasy, it weighs like a pound of fruitcake soaking wet . . . Any kid tall enough to reach up to a ticket window will be found at the *Tarzan* film down the street. The story of course has some lovely and wild ideas – men of straw and tin, a cowardly lion, a wizard who isn't a very good wizard – but the picture doesn't know what to do with them, except to be painfully literal and elaborate about everything.' *(Otis Ferguson)*

MIXED:

'Cleverly and sometimes brilliantly devised and amusingly acted . . . occasionally witty, frequently imaginative, and only for short periods dull . . . Judy Garland, as the competent heroine, is flagrantly too old for her shoes. The settings have been stylised, though not enough.' *(Dilys Powell)*

'I don't see why children shouldn't like it, but for adults there isn't very much except Bert Lahr.' *(Richard Mallett, Punch)*

'The morality [in the book] seems a little crude and the fancy material – Fairy Queen and witches . . . Munchkins [et al] – rattles like dry goods . . . But if we regard this picture as a pantomime, it has good moments: the songs are charming, the Technicolor no more dreadful than the illustrations to most children's books . . . and the tornado is very fine indeed . . . Miss Judy Garland . . . would have won one's heart for a whole winter season twenty years ago, and Miss Margaret Hamilton . . . can compete successfully with a Disney drawing. The whole picture is incredibly lavish, and there's a lot of pleasure to be got these days from watching money spent on other things than war.' *(Graham Greene, Spectator)*

PRO:

'There's an audience for it wherever there's a projection machine and a screen.' *(Variety)*

'Not since *Snow White* has anything quite so fantastic succeeded quite so well.' *(Frank S. Nugent, New York Times)*

'A film of irresistible charm.' *(Seton Margrave, Daily Mail)*

'One of Hollywood's most beguiling fantasies. No one factor can explain a phenomenon that is the product of many elements: the vibrant use of colour, the delightful Munchkins, the memorable art direction, effects and musical score, and the unforgettable performances from all the cast.' *(Allan Hunter & Kenny Mathieson, Movie Classics, 1992)*

WOLF MAN, THE CT: 7 AV: 7.00

1941 US 71 BW HORROR

D George Waggner
W Curt Siodmak

Lon Chaney Jr ☆ Claude Rains Warren William Bela Lugosi Maria Ouspenskaya ☆ Ralph Bellamy Patric Knowles Evelyn Ankers Fay Helm

Dog bites man (Lon Chaney Jr).

The Welsh settings arent terribly convincing, and the special effects are primitive, compared to later werewolf pictures; but a good cast and Joseph Valentine's atmospheric cinematography make the most of a thin story. The result is one of the three great werewolf movies, along with Terence Fisher's *The Curse of the Werewolf* (1961) and John Landis's *An American Werewolf in London* (1981). It is also the film which made Lon Chaney Jr a horror star. The success of the movie resulted in Chaney's werewolf character being used to beef up Universal's *Frankenstein* series.

ANTI:

'Perhaps in deference to a Grade-B budget it has tried to make a little go a long way, and it has concealed most of that little in a deep layer of fog.' *(New York Times)*

MIXED:

'A compactly-knit tale of its kind, with good direction and performances by an above par assemblage of players, but dubious entertainment.' *(Variety)*

PRO:

'Fantastic melodramatic hokum well put over for those with a bent for the macabre.' *(Picturegoer)*

'Ranks behind only *Bride of Frankenstein* on Universal's horror parade. Intelligent, literate, fatalistic.' *(Danny Peary)*

'One of the finest horror films ever made.' *(Maltin)*

WOMAN ALONE, A: *see* SABOTAGE.

WOMAN IN THE DUNES AAN CT: 5 AV: 7.63

(aka *Woman of the Dunes; Suna No Onna*)

1964 Japanese 123 BW DRAMA/FOREIGN

D Hiroshi Teshigahara ☆ AAN
W Kobo Abe from his novel

Eiji Okada Kyoko Kishida Koji Mitsui Hiroko Ito Sen Yano Ginzo Sekigushi Kiyohiko Ichiha

Entomologist (Eiji Okada) is forced to cohabit with a mysterious, inarticulate widow (Kyoko Kishida) who lives in a sand-pit; finally, when he has the opportunity to escape, he finds he doesn't want to.

Grindingly slow, symbolic melodrama. It has style and beauty, but the meaning – if any – is very obscure. If it's an allegory about monogamy, it's a very depressing one.

PRO:

'Certainly a film of a deliberate, strange, individual beauty. But, too, I think its makers are trying to make a social and philosophical point which seems to have particular and radical significance in Japanese life.' *(David Robinson, Financial Times)*

'Teasingly opaque, broodingly erotic.' *(MFB)*

'Erotic Zen.' *(Philip Oakes, Sunday Telegraph)*

MIXED:

'Although the restricted setting results in an occasional longueur, and some of the multi-layered symbolism seems a bit strained, the style is formidably brilliant.' *(Peter John Dyer, Guardian)*

'Kyoko Kishida . . . succeeds in being often touchingly attractive. Some were bored and irritated, but I found the atmosphere of the whole thing mysteriously compelling.' *(Richard Mallett, Punch)*

'A powerfully peculiar film, and one is hypnotised, and sometimes lulled, by the interplay of flesh and landscape . . . Some of it is slow, some of it comes near to parodying itself . . . but it lingers in the mind, or rather in the senses, grainy and disturbing.' *(Isabel Quigly, Spectator)*

ANTI:

'[This] heavily symbolic drama is art-film with a vengeance . . . Aiming at profundity [Teshigahara] achieves only pretentiousness.' *(Films)*

WOMAN IN THE WINDOW, THE

CT: 8 AV: 7.60

1944 US 95/99 BW THRILLER

D Fritz Lang ☆
W Nunnally Johnson ☆ from J.H. Wallis's novel *Once Off Guard*

Edward G. Robinson ☆ Joan Bennett ✓
Raymond Massey ☆ Edmund Breon Dan Duryea ☆
Thomas Jackson Arthur Loft Dorothy Peterson
Frank Dawson Carol Cameron

A middle-aged, married college professor (Edward G. Robinson) has an innocent flirtation with a beautiful woman (Joan Bennett); but it leads to him killing a man and finding the forces of law and order closing in on him.

Highly entertaining film noir graced by four memorable performances, a witty script and Milton Krasner's moody photography. The weakest aspect is the (rather clichéd) trick ending. Oscar-nominated for best score (Hugo Friedhofer, Arthur Lange).

'I don't say a man must never go out for cocktails with a charming girl, but I say "Always be on guard". That picture followed to a perfectly logical conclusion the events that can follow even one second of being off guard.' *(Fritz Lang, 1945)*

ANTI:

'A thriller in the new tradition of *Double Indemnity* and *Laura*, it fails to reach the standard of either because it lacks the courage of its murderous conclusions to an extent only fully revealed by a disappointing ending . . . Lang gives us only a few characteristically sinister moments.' *(New Statesman)*

MIXED:

'Fritz Lang has done a stylish piece of direction which I enjoyed so much that I forgive the unforgivable trick ending . . . If a dozen Hollywood films in a year were as accomplished as this one, the level of our entertainment would be raised considerably.' *(Spectator)*

'Although subtlety falls away piecemeal into polished melodrama with a smart ending . . . the film maintains a steady tension.' *(Richard Winnington)*

'A good bit of craftsmanship on the theme of unpremeditated murder and tallyho, with a nicely judged use of realistic detail . . . But if one asks in what direction this director, who began with such decision, is travelling, the answer is Nowhere; and if one asks what this director, who spoke once such horrible half-truths, is saying, the answer is Nothing.' *(Dilys Powell)*

PRO:

'That old master Nunnally Johnson has done it again! . . . It's a winner . . . as full of suspense as a dark street, with plenty of surprises lurking around its dark corners . . . It bears the hallmark of good dialogue, crisp humor, and excellent characterization.' *(Margaret Sylvester, Life)*

'The story is built up with relentless realism . . . with all the chilling suspense of which Fritz Lang is master . . . A thriller you shouldn't miss.' *(Daily Telegraph)*

'The whole film, mainly because of its fine photography, effective cutting, and Fritz Lang direction, is like a bad dream.' *(Philip T. Hartung, The Comonweal)*

'Nunnally Johnson has provided a script that is literate, slightly tinged with sophistication, and topped off with penetrating satirical thrusts at radio advertising and newsreel coverage of crime stories.' *(New York Times)*

'On the level of murder melodrama – which is all to the good so far as audiences are concerned because it will not disturb them with the kind of deeper meanings that made *M* so much more than a mere murder story and a man hunt. But it is a perfect specimen of its kind, and a very good kind, too.' *(James Shelley Hamilton, NBR)*

'It has a swift, svelte brilliance. It's so good you don't have time to think how good it is.' *(Time & Tide)*

WOMAN OF THE DUNES: *see* WOMAN IN THE DUNES.

WOMAN OF THE YEAR

CT: 6 AV: 8.18

1941 US 114 BW COMEDY/ROMANCE

D George Stevens ✗
W Ring Lardner Jr Michael Kanin ☆ AAW

Spencer Tracy ☆ Katharine Hepburn ☆ AAN
Fay Bainter Reginald Owen William Bendix
Dan Tobin Minor Watson Roscoe Karns

A sports journalist (Spencer Tracy) marries a writer on international affairs (Katharine Hepburn), but he resents the time she gives her career.

Wisecracking comedy about the war between the sexes, starring Spencer Tracy and Katharine Hepburn (in their first film together) as journalism's answer to Beatrice and Benedick. It has delightful moments, but runs out of steam before the end. The denouement, where she decides to become a good housewife and cook him breakfast, is unlikely to please feminists.

PRO:

'For the first time in months this critical spectator feels like tossing his old hat into the air and weaving a joyous snake dance over the typewriter keys in celebration of [this film] which brought sunshine and glee . . . in spite of the weather . . . The jolliest screen comedy that's come along since *The Lady Eve* – a cheering, delightful combination of tongue-tip wit and smooth romance . . . It's as warming as a Manhattan cocktail and as juicy as a porterhouse steak.' *(Bosley Crowther)*

'Dialog is of the best and many episodes rich in amusement on their own behalf figure in the continuity . . . [Both Mankiewicz and Stevens] are entitled to take bows.' *(William R. Weaver, Motion Picture Herald)*

'Tracy gives another fine character-portrayal . . . Dramatically this film achieves a sincerity and breadth of characterisation which is unusual in such an ordinary theme . . . An excellent film.' *(MFB)*

'Between them, they have enough charm to keep any ball rolling.' *(William Whitebait, New Statesman)*

MIXED:

'Within its conventional limits it has all the fluid drive, all the stream-lining, all the super-charging which only Hollywood knows how to give; and if one comes away with no particular impression beyond that of a flashing bit of who-cares, it has at least been a pleasure to watch the technical command of the two principal performers.' *(Dilys Powell, Sunday Times)*

'The chemistry is great, but the plot and the tone are wobbly . . . The comedy goes sour whenever the movie scores points against her [Hepburn], and the slapstick resolution has an air of desperation.' *(Pauline Kael)*

ANTI:

'Somehow or another, this department is unable to flagellate itself to the pitch of enthusiasm about *Woman of the Year* achieved by the New York scribes and the audiences which jampacked the Music Hall for weeks on end. To me the most amusing thing about the venture is that Kit Hepburn read the original script and considered it such a novelty that she prevailed upon the studio to buy it for her use. If the star and the executives got around to seeing movies, instead of just acting in and producing them, they would have realized that the piece, in substance, has already been filmed twice within a twelvemonth as *You Belong to Me* and *Appointment for Love*.' *(Herb Sterne)*

'Director George Stevens lets it get out of hand completely with minutes on end devoted to a few, tired situation gags. Picture runs 114 minutes and frequently seems every moment of that.' *(Variety)*

WOMEN, THE

CT: 8 AV: 8.64

1939 US 132 BW (with colour sequence)
COMEDY/DRAMA

D George Cukor ☆
W Anita Loos Jane Murfin from Clare Boothe Luce's play

Norma Shearer Joan Crawford ☆ Rosalind Russell ☆ Mary Boland ☆ Joan Fontaine Paulette Goddard Florence Nash Virginia Weidler Lucille Watson Phyllis Povah

A wealthy woman (Norma Shearer) discovers that her husband is having an affair with a shopgirl (Joan Crawford).

Clare Booth Luce's bitchy play is handsomely mounted by George Cukor with a 135-strong, all-woman cast. Shearer has the most sympathetic and least rewarding role; the film affords wonderful opportunities to the other leading actresses, who spit out the repartee with relish. Sample line – Joan Crawford: 'There's a name for you ladies, but it's not used in high society outside of kennels.'

ANTI:

'Whether you go or not depends on whether you can stand Miss Shearer with tears flowing steadily in all directions at once, and such an endless damn back fence of cats.' *(Otis Ferguson)*

'This clinical study of the domestic problems of the idle rich, which was hilarious on stage, hasn't transferred very well to the screen – in large measure because of the heavy direction of George Cukor, who doesn't seem to know a laugh-line from the kitchen sink, and the acting of "Norma Shearer", who plays the leading, or sweet wife, role, and is so lovely and so tragic that you expect the tumbrils to roll any moment over the cobblestones for her or Romeo to come traipsing down to her tomb with a drawn sword.' *(Gordon Sager, TAC)*

MIXED:

'Adapted . . . with passable success . . . It cannot be Norma Shearer's fault that Mary Haines is one of the most exasperating characters ever seen on the screen. Although the film is less caustic and pointed than the play, it still manages to be extremely amusing entertainment.' *(New Statesman)*

'It confirms rich men's worst suspicions and fantasies of what women want (money) and what they're like when they're together (clawing beasties).' *(Pauline Kael)*

PRO:

'It's a field day for the gals to romp intimately in panties, scanties and gorgeous gowns . . . Smash hit of solid proportions for extended runs and heavy profit . . . A strong woman entry but still has plenty of spicy lines and situations for the men.' *(Variety)*

'Satirical comedy-drama, a merciless if superficial exposure of the lives of a few decadent, well-to-do women . . . put over with smart and sophisticated dialogue, bristling with wisecracks, by an all-star cast . . . The settings are the last word in opulence and the technical presentation is impeccable.' *(MFB)*

'So marvelous that we believe every Hollywood studio should make at least one thoroughly nasty picture a year.' *(New York Times)*

'Rosalind Russell and Paulette Goddard prove conclusively that sarcasm is the highest form of humour – and that men are totally superfluous to a good Thirties film. No men appear here; they are dished about, stolen, spurned and shared but they are never actively needed. The only men an actress needed in the Thirties were Cukor to direct her films, Adrian to design her clothes, and someone who looked sweet in uniform to drive her car.' *(Julie Burchill, Girls on Film, 1986)*

WOMEN IN LOVE

CT: 5 AV: 7.21

1969 GB 130 C DRAMA/ROMANCE

D Ken Russell ***X*** AAN
W Larry Kramer ***X*** AAN from D.H. Lawrence's novel

Alan Bates Oliver Reed Glenda Jackson ☆ AAW
Jennie Linden Eleanor Bron Alan Webb
Vladek Sheybal Catherine Willmer Sarah Nicholls
Sharon Gurney

An artist (Glenda Jackson) and a teacher (Jennie Linden) get laid during the 1920s.

A typically annoying film by Ken Russell with hugely pretentious moments and little grasp of story-telling. The point of D.H. Lawrence's novel gets lost in all the naked running through wheatfields and nude wrestling in flickering firelight. Billy Williams's good-looking photography was Oscar-nominated. Larry Kramer's screenplay fails to impose a cinematic structure on some recalcitrant material, and unwisely keeps some of Lawrence's worst dialogue intact. Sample line . . . Glenda Jackson to Oliver Reed: 'How are your thighs? Are they strong? Because I want to drown in hot, physical, naked flesh.'

PRO:

'A dazzling feat of film-making . . . [Russell] has this genius for immersing himself in the subject, making it alive and new and popularly accessible.' *(Margaret Hinxman, Sunday Telegraph)*

'I, myself, consider the objection [to making a film of a novel] rather priggish . . . The criterion is simply that if a thing is worth doing, it must be done well. And [this] most certainly is.' *(Penelope Mortimer, Observer)*

'Directed with style and punch . . . Episodic but challenging and holding.' *(Variety)*

MIXED:

'Whoever had the idea of bringing D.H. Lawrence and Ken Russell together, it was a stroke of something like genius. . . . The result is ludicrous, but really rather likeable.' *(John Russell Taylor, The Times)*

'Apart from being a beautiful film to look at it is finely acted . . . Why then, is [it] so difficult to like while being easy to admire? I found it oppressive, heavy, unhealthy. This is not a criticism of Ken Russell's direction. It must be a lack of affinity in me with Lawrence.' *(Madeleine Harmsworth, Sunday Mirror)*

ANTI:

'Worse books have made good films before now: what a pity [this] isn't one of them.' *(Richard Roud, Guardian)*

'A profound betrayal [of Lawrence's novel] . . . As Gudrun, Glenda Jackson gives the most interesting performance of the film, but is, alas, almost frighteningly plain. Her features are heavy and somehow malevolent in their irregularity; her body is like a block of uncarved stone except for her much-revealed breasts, shaped like collapsing gourds; and her thick arms and legs might as well be those of the West African fetish that figures so prominently in the novel but is cut from the film. Even her line-reading is rather too slow and mannered, but at least it is intelligent and arresting.' *(John Simon)*

'Glenda Jackson has a face to launch a thousand dredgers.' *(Jack de Manio, BBC Radio)*

'I had forgotten what a pretentious bore D.H. Lawrence was until I saw the film . . . so dull that the director has had to introduce three sex-acts of unparalleled lubricity to stop the audience going to sleep.' *(Lord Annan, Evening News)*

'Bold and erotic and filled with D.H.Lawrence's passionate search for sexual fulfillment and love expressed as aesthetic masochism, but there is little humanity in it and a great deal of hysteria . . . Although Russell is certainly an impressive show-off of a director, none of it ever comes to much more than a lot of horny perspiration. They should take all the pretentious dialogue off the soundtrack and call it *Women in Heat*.' *(Rex Reed)*

WOMEN ON THE VERGE OF A NERVOUS BREAKDOWN AAN CT: 4 AV: 6.23

(aka *Mujeres al Borde de un Ataque de Nervios*)

1988 Spain 88/98 C COMEDY/ROMANCE/ FOREIGN

D Pedro Almodóvar ✗
W Pedro Almodóvar ✗

Carmen Maura ✗ Antonio Banderas Julieta Serrano Maria Barranco Rossy de Palma Guillermo Montesinos Kiti Manver

A moody actress (Carmen Maura), distracted by the desertion of her lover, becomes farcically entangled in her own and others' emotional problems.

Laboured, unfunny and curiously offensive. Although the film poses as a feminist comedy, it reinforces the Latin macho view of men as the centre of women's lives, and women as emotional cripples. A creaky boulevard comedy in trendy wrappings; the plot is nonsensical, and the characterization thin. Best aspect is the colourful design, which has a camp, tacky flamboyance. It was named best foreign film by the US industry's National Board of Review and by critics' associations in New York City and Los Angeles. It also won prizes at the Toronto and Venice Film Festivals. Very overrated.

PRO:

'Extravagantly stylish.' *(Tim Clark, Time Out)*

'Plays like an old Doris Day sex comedy recycled by a disciple of Buñuel and Fellini . . . An ebullient and saucy knockabout farce.' *(Bruce Williamson, Playboy)*

'A wild, wanton, wickedly witty farce . . . There's only one thing to do about this invigorating movie joyride: hop on.' *(Peter Travers, People Weekly)*

'Generalissimo Franco kept the lid on for thirty-six years; he died in 1975, and Pedro Almodóvar is part of what jumped out of the box. The most original pop writer-director of the Eighties, he's Godard with a human face – a happy face. *Women on the Verge* is serenely unbalanced – a hallucinogenic Feydeau play.' *(Pauline Kael)*

'The sort of film that British critics just can't deal with. The pace is too fast, the plot too much motivated by a sense of fun and the "messages" lie concealed too far beneath a bubbling surface . . . Watching *Women on the Verge* makes you realize just how lifeless and formulaic other film comedy has become. You'd have to go a long way back to find anything so fresh, so zippy, so observant of peoples tics and habits. For once, when you laugh, you're laughing at life rather than plot construction or clever-clever dialogue.' *(James Park, Film Yearbook)*

MIXED:

'With his satirical touch and playful use of coincidence, Almodóvar seems to have inherited the surrealist mantle from Luis Buñuel . . . But Buñuel, who died in 1983, was rebelling against a more repressive regime. And Almodóvar lacks his profound insights into the follies of church, state and capitalism. Although he clearly has things to say about freedom and alienation, his strength is style. Almodóvar makes a fetish of decor and fashion. Caressing surfaces, his camera moves with stealth and wit through a self-contained world of synthetic images. Underlying the movie's random lunacy is a fastidious attention to detail, right down to Pepa's espresso-pot earrings: Almodóvar had them specially designed for the movie . . . Almodóvar has gone out of his way to dazzle and divert the audience.' *(Brian D. Johnson, Maclean's)*

ANTI:

'The best to be said . . . is that Almodóvar makes a good interior decorator.' *(Mark Finch, MFB)*

'All surface gloss without a jot of depth, with all the female characters being shown as poor creatures unhinged by their attraction to worthless men. A great disappointment despite the rave reviews it received from many critics upon release.' *(Elliot)*

'Overrated. Marred by a handful of extraordinary coincidences and is nowhere near as funny as it thinks it is.' *(Rose)*

WORD, THE: *see* ORDET.

WORKING GIRL AAN CT: 7 AV: 7.54

1988 US 113 C COMEDY/ROMANCE

D Mike Nichols ☆ AAN
W Kevin Wade

Melanie Griffith ☆ AAN Harrison Ford Sigourney Weaver ☆ AAN Joan Cusack ☆ AAN Alec Baldwin Philip Bosco Nora Dunn Oliver Platt James Lally Kevin Spacey Robert Easton Olympia Dukakis

An upwardly mobile secretary (Melanie Griffith) outwits her obstructive boss (Sigourney Weaver), succeeds in business by really trying, and gets her man (Harrison Ford).

Director Mike Nichols made *The Graduate* one of the archetypal comedies of the 60s. Here, he made the quintessential comedy of the 80s. Melanie Griffith is the yuppie dream made flesh. Few critics of the time noticed the overtones of social snobbery, or that our heroine's business tactics put at risk not only the reputation of the company that employs her, but also the career of the unwitting boyfriend. It's somehow appropriate that one of the 80s' most successful comedies should have celebrated corporate in-fighting, unscrupulous business tactics and unthinking selfishness. Still, there's a lot to enjoy in the cleverly contrived plot and the performances. Griffith won the rave reviews, but

Weaver clearly relished her role as the queen bitch, and Joan Cusack also stands out as Griffith's cheerfully vulgar best friend. The only Oscar it won was for best song with 'Let The River Run' (by Carly Simon).

ANTI:

'The film's class values seem rather confused, to say the least. Consider this: in the tried-and-true tradition of Hollywood moviemaking, Tess and her lower-middle-class girlfriends are (without apparent exception) good and decent folks; the upper-middle-class types in the executive suites are almost entirely rotten. The only problem with Tess's life (aside from the fact that her boyfriend is a creep) is that her home, wardrobe, and neighborhood are pretty tacky – but that's not even a problem, really, because she doesn't know they're tacky. By her own standards, then, Tess's life doesn't seem to be missing anything important. Yet she wants nothing more than to escape from the world she knows and to move up into the world of these Ivy League snobs whom she despises – and we're supposed to cheer for her. Why? . . . Are we supposed to laugh condescendingly at these people or identify with them?' *(Bruce Bawer, American Spectator)*

'*Working Girl*, the most recent "hit romantic comedy", is really about women trying to make it in the business world (by tearing down other women). The romantic relationship between Melanie Griffith and Harrison Ford is given short shrift. A wise decision, since it makes even less sense than the rest of the film, and as a sexual chemistry experiment it doesn't sizzle, it fizzles . . . Some of those male critics who liked *Working Girl* saw it as a throwback to the career-women comedies of the 40s. Which comedies are those? *Working Girl* is nothing like any of the classics I remember. Try to picture Katherine Hepburn or Rosalind Russell playing one of their career parts as this kind of bimbo. Maybe you can. I can't. They had more respect for themselves and the women they played.' *(Kathi Maio)*

'We're supposed to be cheered by watching Tess become part of the establishment: she makes it into the world of mergers and acquisitions. Her victory is certified when she's ensconced in a cubicle high up in a skyscraper; on the soundtrack, Carly Simon and a women's choir sing exultantly. No, there's no irony – only fatuity. Lest we get the wrong idea, the picture makes it clear that the victory is only for a sweet, feminine girl like Tess – not for anybody forceful or butch. The villain is Tess's sneaky, upper-crust boss, played by Sigourney Weaver: she doesn't just try to steal Tess's big, career-making radio-network idea; she's also unwomanly. At first, Weaver is a confident, entertaining cartoon of moneyed egomania; she's a genuinely game actress, eager to be funny. But then the picture demeans her, by making her a ludicrous witch who can't hang on to her guy or her job (it even demeans her in small, gross ways: when she's in the hospital, doctors try to look under her nightie) . . . This Cinderella story seems to have been concocted by people at the top of the skyscraper who have no fellow-feeling for losers.' *(Pauline Kael)*

PRO:

'The plot of *Working Girl* is put together like clockwork. It carries you along while you're watching it, but reconstruct it later and you'll see the craftsmanship.' *(Roger Ebert)*

'Enjoyable largely due to the fun of watching scrappy, sexy, unpredictable Melanie Griffith rise from Staten Island secretary to Wall Street whiz.' *(Variety)*

'A treat.' *(Brian Case, Time Out)*

'Just sit back and enjoy one of the funniest, sharpest and liveliest fairy tales of the decade.' *(Rose)*

WORLD ACCORDING TO GARP, THE

CT: 5 AV: 6.23

1982 US 126 C DRAMA

D George Roy Hill
W Steve Tesich ● from John Irving's novel

Robin Williams Mary Beth Hurt ☆ Glenn Close ☆ AAN John Lithgow ☆ AAN Hume Cronyn Jessica Tandy Swoosie Kurtz Amanda Plummer (cameos John Irving George Roy Hill)

The life and times of a New England writer (Robin Williams) and his mother (Glenn Close).

Generally good performances can't compensate for a shambolic narrative structure, and irritating pretentiousness. It seems to be trying to say something about the meaning of life, but heaven knows what it is. Robin Williams doesn't seem to. Maybe it's clearer if you've read the novel.

PRO:

'Has taste, intelligence, craft and numerous other virtues going for it.' *(Variety)*

'The vein of romantic fatalism that Mr Hill mined in *Slaughterhouse Five* surfaces naturally in [this] confident, footsure delight of a film.' *(David Castell, Sunday Telegraph)*

'This is as beautiful as film gets . . . The film's chief symbol of chaos-at-the-ready is the car. This is appropriate, because the climactic accident of the film involves two cars. I have already mentioned the car (in the script, a hearse) that almost hits Garp when he is chasing after Helen with his first story. There is also the pickup that speeds dangerously through Garp's neighborhood. There is Garp's car, which, pulled over to the side of the road to allow Garp to play around with the babysitter (Sabrina Lee Moore), looms in the darkness . . . Later, Garp, in bed with Helen, suggests that they move away because there are "crazy drivers everywhere".

Ironically, the crazy driver who will be partly to blame for his family tragedy is Garp himself, whose unorthodox way of entering a driveway makes possible the accident that kills Walt. Of course, cars make possible Michael's seduction of Helen: he fixes her car so it won't start, then offers her a ride in his. (Perhaps, indeed, the school where Garp will die is called Steering because that word reminds us of cars, the instruments of death.)' *(Bruce Bawer, American Spectator)*

MIXED:

'Individual passages are quite felicitous, but their going together is not smooth. The same is true of the direction.' *(Freda Bruce Lockheart, Catholic Herald)*

'This misjudged movie steadily compiles a hit-list of suspects as to what it is really about . . . Much is slackly funny enough to carry a loose script. Lots looks like padding. Some of it, here and there, takes off into the bad-lands of truth. The actors never fail it. It fails itself . . . I feel mean not mentioning its robust humour.' *(David Hughes, Sunday Times)*

ANTI:

'In the book, Garp was a natural storyteller; the movie Garp, however, is just a nice, athletic American . . . [who] doesn't have anything interesting to say. How could he create a "world"? Robin Williams is completely at sea . . . [and] has become as cute as a leprechaun . . . Hill traffics in disaster without passion or anguish or black-comedy exuberance and his picture feels weightless, repressed and empty.' *(David Denby, New York Magazine)*

'Declamatory and strident . . . strung out to insupportable lengths, has no plot and is generally shapeless and aimless.' *(Michael Wigan, Scotsman)*

'When the movie was over, all I could find to ask myself was: what the hell was all that about?' *(Roger Ebert)*

'Rather like watching a puppy chasing its own tail: engaging, touching, but pointless.' *(Margaret Hinxman, Daily Mail)*

WORLD AND HIS WIFE, THE: *see* STATE OF THE UNION.

WORLD OF APU, THE: *see APU* TRILOGY: WORLD OF APU, THE.

WRITTEN ON THE WIND CT: 6 AV: 6.73

1956 US 99 C DRAMA

D Douglas Sirk ☆
W George Zuckerman from Robert Wilder's novel

Lauren Bacall Robert Stack ☆ AAN Dorothy Malone ☆ AAW Rock Hudson Robert Keith Grant Williams

A secretary (Lauren Bacall) marries her boss (Robert Stack) and becomes part of a Texas oil-owning family.

If you thought *Dallas* was over the top, get a load of this. It's often called cult director Douglas Sirk's masterpiece – but his overblown, melodramatic style is often ludicrous, and any serious criticisms of American family life are lost through overstatement.

PRO:

'Tip top scripting from the Robert Wilder novel, dramatically deft direction by Douglas Sirk, and sock performances by the cast give the story development a follow-through.' *(Variety)*

'Stack . . . gives a strong study in hysteria.' *(Campbell Dixon, Daily Telegraph)*

'Hollywood moonshine of the slickest vintage. A streamlined piece of magazine fiction, mounted with a superb physical gloss, the melodrama seems at times almost to be parodying the King Vidor type of exercise in love hate . . . A viscous musical background swamps every dramatic crisis, whilst a nasal choral group chant their way through the credits.' *(MFB)*

'The ultimate in lush melodrama . . . Douglas Sirk's finest directorial achievement, and one of the most notable critiques of the American family ever made . . . Some critics have seen his sumptuous visual style, full of parody and cliché, as a kind of Brechtian distancing that calls attention to the artificiality of the film medium, in turn commenting on the hollowness of middle-class American life.' *(Virgin)*

'A conspicuously fierce critique of American society, the disintegrating middle class . . . The acting is dynamite, the melodrama is compulsive, the photography, lighting and design share a bold disregard for realism.' *(Tony Rayns, Time Out)*

'Meticulously filmed, utterly sublime, here's the GIANT of Bad Movies We Love.' *(Margulies & Rebello)*

ANTI:

'A far-fetched tale.' *(Ross Shepherd, People)*

'I've often had to protest at the libelling of Africans in films. Now I protest at this anti-white prejudice: we aren't all as greedy, selfish or oafish as these films would have one think . . . As far as I could see [the dignified coloured butler] and his wife are about the only decent, reasonably sane and likeable characters in the whole film. Rock Hudson, Lauren Bacall (poor girl), Robert Stack and Dorothy Malone represent the master race.' *(Thomas Spencer, Daily Worker)*

'Turgid material this, straight from a glossy magazine. It's what we used to call servant-girl's stuff, so it should go down well with today's wives of all classes.' *(Jympson Harman, Evening News)*

'A howling gust of melodrama which seemed to me

to take a terrible time to blow over.' *(Roy Nash, Star)*

WRONG KIND OF GIRL, THE: *see* BUS STOP.

WUTHERING HEIGHTS CT: 8 AV: 8.31

1939 US 104 BW DRAMA/ROMANCE

D William Wyler ☆
W Ben Hecht Charles MacArthur from Emily Brontë's novel

Merle Oberon Laurence Olivier David Niven Donald Crisp Flora Robson Hugh Williams Geraldine Fitzgerald Leo G. Carroll Cecil Humphreys Miles Mander

The daughter of a respectable middle-class family (Merle Oberon) chooses to marry the lord of the manor (David Niven) rather than the stableboy (Laurence Olivier) she really loves.

William Wyler's solid, respectful version of the Brontë classic only reaches chapter 17 and loses most of the sexual passion, replacing it with High Romance; but the actors perform with gusto, and this remains the best (though hardly definitive) version. It's said to have been producer Sam Goldwyn's favourite of all his films, and it's notable for its lavish but atmospheric production (art director James Basevi and composer Alfred Newman were Oscar-nominated). The best aspect remains Gregg Toland's Academy Award-winning camerawork. It was voted 4th best film of the year in the *Film Daily's* annual poll of US film critics.

ANTI:

'How much better they would have made [it] in France. They know there how to shoot sexual passion; but in this Californian-constructed Yorkshire . . . sex is cellophaned; there is no egotism, no obsession . . . Mr Olivier's nervous, breaking voice belongs to balconies and Verona and romantic love . . . Miss Merle Oberon cannot help making [Cathy] a very normal girl . . . A lot of reverence has gone into a picture which should be coarse as a sewer . . . The whole picture is keepsake stuff.' *(Graham Greene, Spectator)*

'For a few moments it seems as though [the film] were going to do justice to the dark power of the novel . . . But when [the ghost] did come, she came in the guise of Miss Merle Oberon and a more unfortunate piece of casting could scarcely be imagined. This is a girl nurtured not by Ellen Deane but by Roedean . . . Everything is much too grand . . . But the real trouble is the dullness, flatness and reverence that pervade the entire narrative . . . The dialogue is limp and modern . . . The film is hopelessly polite and banal. Wuthering Depths, I'm afraid.' *(New Statesman)*

'Mr Olivier acts best when he acts least.' *(James Agate, Tatler)*

MIXED:

'Sombre, dramatic tragedy productionally fine, but with limited appeal.' *(Variety)*

PRO:

'A strong and sombre film poetically written as the novel not always was, sinister and wild as it was meant to be, far more compact dramatically than Miss Brontë had made it.' *(Richard Mallett, Punch)*

'One of the most distinguished pictures of the year.' *(Frank S. Nugent, New York Times)*

'Among the best pictures made anywhere.' *(Otis Ferguson)*

'Tastefully brought to the screen with the perfect cast.' *(Scheuer)*

X, Y AND ZEE: *see* ZEE AND CO.

XANADU CT: 4 AV: 3.60

1980 US 88 C MUSICAL/FANTASY

D Robert Greenwald
W Richard Christian Danus Marc Reid Rubel Michael Kane ● (songs by Jeff Lynne and John Farrar)

Olivia Newton-John ● Gene Kelly Michael Beck James Sloyan Dimitra Arliss Katie Hanley Fred McCarren Ren Woods Sandahl Bergman (heavenly voices: Wilfrid Hyde-White Coral Browne)

A muse (Olivia Newton-John) comes to life, none too amusingly.

Musical fantasy was tried several times in the 40s, notably in *Yolanda and the Thief* (1945), *Down To Earth* (1947) and *One Touch of Venus* (1948). The appearance of an obviously toupéed Gene Kelly in this movie only adds to the sense of déjà vu. The horrendous script and lyrics and Miss Newton-John's lack of screen charisma were savaged by the critics; but it's all quite colourful, and some of the music is lively. Two of the songs ('Magic' and 'Xanadu') were top ten hits in America, and the soundtrack album was in the charts for 14 weeks, rising to number 4 position.

ANTI:

'An experience so vacuous it's almost frightening . . . . An unashamed showcase for Livvy's "talents". As the film grinds from one epic production routine to another, it becomes painfully clear that she can't deliver a line (the script, full of gnomic punchlines, is admittedly abysmal), hold a note (the Jeff Lynne/John Farrar songs are lowest common denominator) or step *à pas de deux* (despite the helping hand of Gene Kelly, who can still cut it on the dance floor).' *(Ian Birch, Time Out)*

'Truly a stupendously bad film whose only salvage is the music.' *(Variety)*

'A Forties musical submerged by contemporary tat.' *(Guardian)*

'A mushy and limp musical fantasy, so insubstantial it evaporates before our eyes . . . [though] it's not as bad as *Can't Stop the Music*.' *(Roger Ebert)*

'Tries to offer something for everyone, but its eclecticism seems motivated less by nostalgia or generosity towards the past than by the absence of any new material. Pastiche can often be a compliment, but here it is simply cruel to Gene Kelly when the resemblance of two show-girls, across a generation, is used to remind us of the splendid *Cover Girl*.' *(Jill Forbes, MFB)*

'The entertainment value is akin to watching war newsreel while someone shines a bright light in your eye.' *(Philip J. Kaplan, 1983)*

MIXED:

'The famous Astaire description – "Can't act, can't sing, can dance a little" is all too pertinent to her [Newton-John's] performance here. Fortunately production designer John Corso and director Robert Greenwald demonstrate great flair for colour, composition and movement, with the result that *Xanadu* is as dazzling to the eye as any of the vintage Hollywood musicals.' *(Quinlan)*

'I thought the musical numbers were great, but the dialogue left something to be desired. I knew that while we were shooting, but there wasn't much I could do. Then they changed the whole story midway through production, and that didn't help. Although *Xanadu* didn't do well in this country [the US], it was very successful abroad.' *(Olivia Newton-John)*

YANKEE DOODLE DANDY AAN

CT: 8 AV: 8.71

1942 US 126 BW MUSICAL/BIOPIC

D Michael Curtiz ☆ AAN
W Robert Buckner Edmund Joseph from Robert Buckner's story AAN

James Cagney ☆ AAW Joan Leslie
Walter Huston ☆ AAN Richard Whorf
George Tobias Irene Manning Rosemary De Camp
Jeanne Cagney S.Z. Sakall George Barbier

The life of one of America's most famous and patriotic showmen, George M. Cohan.

A must for musical lovers and proof that James Cagney was one of the great, idiosyncratic dancers of his day. It's a shame he didn't make more musicals, but there weren't many roles as suited as this one to his brand of dynamism. Production values are terrific, and the film works wonderfully as a series of parades and production numbers, all expertly shot by James Wong Howe. Needless to say, the story bears virtually no relation to Cohan's real life; and the domestic scenes carry little conviction, even by the standards of a Hollywood biopic. George Amy's editing was Oscar-nominated; Ray Heindorf and Heinz Roemheld won for best score, and Nathan Levinson won for best sound.

PRO:

[The patriotism] is enough to send movie audiences straight off to battle . . . Possibly the most genial screen biography ever made.' *(Time)*

'Two hours of delightful entertainment – a feast of music sprinkled with mirth; a story of a family which has earned for itself a lasting place in the history of the American theatre. Jimmie Cagney, as George M. Cohan, gives a magnificent performance, and the acting support given him by all the other members of the long cast leaves no room for criticism.' *(Welford Beaton, Hollywood Spectator)*

'Captivating entertainment.' *(Seton Margrave, Daily Mail)*

MIXED:

'Full of songs, dances, choruses, back-cloths, patriotism, and James Cagney, who gives a performance of terrific vivacity but less persuasion. The flag-waving, since it is American and not British, can be stomached, and the whole production has a bounce and flounce which, in a kind of sickened way, one cannot but admire.' *(Dilys Powell)*

'Cagney doesn't merely imitate or impersonate Cohan; he really gets under the man's Thespian skin, evaluates his attributes as an entertainer and supplies a trenchant commentary on the actor's footlights salesmanship . . . While George Cohan remains behind footlights, *Yankee Doodle Dandy* is authoritative; whenever he leaves by the stage door the fictional meanderings become agonizing to those who like a bit of authenticity in their entertainment.' *(Herb Sterne)*

YEAR OF LIVING DANGEROUSLY, THE

CT: 5 AV: 7.07

1982 Australia 114 C THRILLER

D Peter Weir ☆
W David Williamson Peter Weir C.J. Koch from Koch's novel

Mel Gibson Sigourney Weaver Linda Hunt ☆ AAW
Michael Murphy Bill Kerr Noel Ferrier

In Indonesia in 1965, Australian journalist (Mel Gibson) goes in pursuit of a good story and an attractive military attaché at the British embassy (Sigourney Weaver).

Peter Weir's typically good-looking film, set in Indonesia in 1965, is about a likeable guy who's apolitical – until he has an uncomfortably close encounter with Sukarno's dictatorship. The left-wing politics are superficial and the Gibson-Weaver relationship is ultra-conventional; but Weir's evocation of Third World anarchy makes it all worthwhile. So does actress Linda Hunt, who won an Oscar playing the half-Chinese, half-Australian cameraman who befriends Mel. She deserved it for speaking some pretty pious sentiments without blushing, and giving the film more realism than its directionless screenplay deserved.

PRO:

'Ambitious and compelling . . . Weaver and Gibson give their finest screen performances so far.' *(Michael Sragow, Rolling Stone)*

'A quite extraordinary film . . . one of the most hypnotic and brilliant films of the year . . . The major factor in creating the depths of the film and its shadowed canvas is the acting of Linda Hunt.' *(Lindsay Mackie, Glasgow Herald)*

'Good as [Weaver and Gibson] may be, they are – it's hard to avoid the word – dwarfed by Linda Hunt.' *(Nigel Willmott, Tribune)*

'Weir has an extraordinary sense of spectacle, and the march on the American embassy, the food riots, the scene of martial law at the palace, and the trip to the airport are some of the best scenes of Third World politics in a contemporary fiction film. Weir has succeeded in bringing the remote and alien near and in making the seemingly inexplicable at least partly understandable. "The west no longer has answers", Kumar explains to Guy at the end of the film, and *The Year of Living Dangerously* is a complex and visually stunning confirmation of that assertion.' *(Stuart Y. McDougas, Magill's Cinema Annual, 1984)*

MIXED:

'Perhaps it is a too-literary contrivance, but the acting is fine and the love story affecting.' *(Tom Hutchinson, Mail on Sunday)*

'I was held by it and had a very good time, though I didn't believe any of it. And I was held despite my aversion to its gusts of wind about destiny, truth versus appearance and so on.' *(Pauline Kael)*

'A sophisticated attempt at a contemporary *Casablanca*. (It) has Mel Gibson and Sigourney Weaver caught up in a romance as steamy as its exotic Indonesian locale – the time is the toppling of Sukarno. It offers a tragic perception of East-West relations, and it has Weir's unusual bold, sensual style. All these elements don't mesh quite as stunningly as they did in Weir's *The Last Wave*, but it is a worthy film all the same. Part of the problem is that Weir never seemed to decide whether the film belongs to the lovers or to Linda Hunt.' *(Kevin Thomas, Los Angeles Times)*

'Freshly observed but ultimately pointless.' *(Halliwell)*

ANTI:

'The film is fogged by silly melodrama and travelogue atmospherics, and tends, like its hero to keep forgetting its whereabouts.' *(Nigel Andrews, Financial Times)*

YEARLING, THE AAN CT: 8 AV: 7.30

1946 US 134/94 C DRAMA/FAMILY

D Clarence Brown ☆ AAW
W Paul Osborn from Marjorie Kinnan Rawlings's novel

Gregory Peck ☆ AAN Jane Wyman ☆ AAN Claude Jarman Jr ☆ (special AAN as outstanding child actor) Chill Wills Clem Bevans Margaret Wycherly Henry Travers Forrest Tucker Donn Gift Dan White

An 11-year-old boy (Claude Jarman Jr) persuades his impoverished parents to let him look after an orphaned fawn.

A classic boy-and-his-pet weepie, underplayed effectively by all concerned. Clarence Brown already had a reputation for family films, after *National Velvet* (1944); and this is on the same high level. It won Oscars for cinematography (Charles Rosher, Leonard Smith Arthur Arling) and art direction (Cedric Gibbons, Paul Groesse, Edwin B. Wills). Editor Harold Kress was nominated.

'An emotional experience seldom equalled in the theatre.' *(Jack D. Grant, Hollywood Reporter)*

'A thorough and earnest regional study, a strong tale of a simple, forthright, pioneering people. Technically, it is one of the finest films ever produced.' *(Fortnight)*

'Drenched though it is with tearful sentiment, it is acted with rare perfection. It has the air of being very close to nature and it is charged with beauty.' *(A.E. Wilson)*

'Excellent family film for four-handkerchief patrons.' *(Halliwell)*

'Heart-wrenching.' *(Scheuer)*

YELLOW SKY CT: 6 AV: 7.00

1948 US 98 BW WESTERN

D William A. Wellman ☆
W Lamar Trotti ☆ from W.R. Burnett's novel

Gregory Peck Anne Baxter Richard Widmark Robert Arthur John Russell Harry Morgan James Barton Charles Kemper Robert Adler Victor Kilian

Bankrobbers on the run (including Gregory Peck) discover a ghost town containing a gold prospector (James Barton) and his granddaughter (Anne Baxter).

If the plot sounds vaguely familiar, that's because it's our old pal *The Tempest* again – later transformed into science fiction (for *Forbidden Planet*) and technological ego-trip (in *Prospero's Books*). Here, it provides the structure for a superior western. The role of Caliban, incidentally, is shared between some renegade Apache Indians.

The film is better at the beginning – when everyone seems motivated by greed or lust – than later on, when the pace slows and Peck becomes too much of a goodie-goodie to be credible. However, Wellman's atmospheric direction (making effective use of natural sound) and Joseph MacDonald's stark photography make it something special. Lamar Trotti's screenplay is one that could usefully be studied by aspiring screenwriters; it makes minimal use of dialogue, yet won an award from America's Writers' Guild as the best written American western of the year. There was an inferior remake, *The Jackals* (1967), set in South Africa.

ANTI:

'[Western] seem to have grown slower and slower and *Yellow Sky* is, in parts, practically stationary . . . [Everything] is expected and unremarkable.' *(Daily Worker)*

'The appearance of Anne Baxter as the only woman in the west has an enfeebling influence on the grip as well as the characters of the plot and *Yellow Sky* is a goner from the instant when one bandit looks at [her] and shaves off his beard.' *(C.A. Lejeune, Observer)*

'From the very first reel there's talk of the bloodthirsty Apaches . . . After one hour and 10 minutes they put in an appearance and one hopes for some excitement – but I rather think they must have had a better offer from a rival studio, for the next minute they are all riding off again.' *(Elspeth Grant, Graphic)*

'Joe MacDonald's brilliant high-key camerawork – especially in the salt flat scenes, hard and white and clear – made something visually compelling out of trite situations, poor scripting and worse acting.' *(Charles Higham & Joel Greenberg, Hollywood in the Forties, 1968)*

PRO:

'If it is fightin', shootin' and not too much talkin' films you like, this is better than average.' *(Leonard Mosley, Daily Express)*

'Plenty of tense excitement and atmosphere . . . Baxter is excellent. Widmark is subdued.' *(Sunday Pictorial)*

'Here is good meaty drama of a high order. I thoroughly enjoyed it and recommend it.' *(Sunday Dispatch)*

'Peck is one of those agreeable bandits who need only a shave and the influence of a good woman to turn them into thoroughly decent citizens with the prospect of a happy and blameless future. This rousing western drama, with its vistas of arid deserts, its bold, bad men lusting for gold, and not caring much how they get it, its hold-ups and its shootings, has all in it that you expect – and more.' *(A.E. Wilson)*

'Beautifully cast and characterised, this is one of Wellman's best films.' *(Tom Milne, Time Out)*

YELLOW SUBMARINE

CT: 8 AV: 7.55

1968 GB C CARTOON/MUSICAL/FAMILY

D George Dunning ☆
W Lee Minoff Al Brodax Erich Segal Jack Mendelsohn from Minoff's story from Lennon and McCartney's song (music and lyrics by Lennon and McCartney ☆ George Harrison, additional music by George Martin)

Paul McCartney John Lennon Ringo Starr George Harrison
Voices: John Clive (John) Geoffrey Hughes (Paul) Peter Batten (George) Paul Angelis (Ringo) Dick Emery Lance Percival

Blue Meanies attack the happy kingdom of Pepperland.

Though the sappy 'All You Need Is Love' message has dated, this remains a classic cartoon – a high-spirited romp with a uniquely surreal visual style, an onslaught of visual puns, and a great soundtrack. Highlights include 'Lucy in the Sky with Diamonds' and 'Eleanor Rigby'. The appearance of the real Beatles at the end is an anti-climax.

ANTI:

'The basic trouble with the film is it tries to exaggerate [the Beatles] into quirky characters . . . But a cartoon world demands creatures larger than life, and the Beatles, mainly reduced to muttering dreadful puns on the soundtrack, are no bigger than their voices or their instruments.' *(Robert Ottaway, Daily Sketch)*

'Hard to watch for non-addicts.' *(Halliwell)*

MIXED:

'A kaleidoscopic, psychedelic trip which is highly enjoyable while the creators' collective imaginations hold out. When they flag, which is about three-quarters of the way through, the sub sinks.' *(David Nathan, Sun)*

'A lively, jazzy jest which may leave many people cold, but will certainly be a surefire hit with the younger set.' *(Dick Richards, Daily Mirror)*

'At last the Beatles have found their film form. The secret seems to be to keep them off screen . . . Their [brief] appearance is not very funny. But the film itself is.' *(Eric Shorter, Daily Telegraph)*

PRO:

'I must confess I really enjoyed it.' *(John Russell Taylor, The Times)*

'Here are all the ingredients of a novel entertainment . . . Unlike Disney the film makes no concession to sentiment. Characters are mostly matter-of-fact, grotesque and anti-heroic.' *(Variety)*

'[It] brings a new dimension to cartoon film entertainment. With a witty blend of madly imaginative animation . . . it propels you on a psychedelic trip . . . It is a fantastic achievement . . . [and] a step forward in animation techniques.' *(Nina Hibbin, Morning Star)*

'Fun, and an animated feature that holds the interest of adults of all ages (I don't think there are children of any age left) is not to be sneezed at. Visually, every conceivable style is thrown in pell-mell: there is art nouveau and psychedelic, op and pop, dada and surrealist. Hieronymus Bosch and just plain bosh. Why does it work? Because of its reckless generosity . . . The sight gags and sound gags interbreed, until the film stretches before and behind us like a vast punorama . . . Too sappily good-natured, too commercial, too lacking in the old Beatle rebelliousness – these charges have been brought against *Yellow Submarine* with some justification. But this, too, is finally not unmoving. The mixture of naiveté and cynicism, of coziness and exploitation, is the portrait of the authors as not quite so young men and explains where all those flower children have gone.' *(John Simon)*

'Good-natured, full of verbal-visual jokes, and surprisingly entertaining.' *(Pauline Kael)*

YEUX SANS VISAGE, LES: *see* EYES WITHOUT A FACE

see EYES WITHOUT A FACE

YOJIMBO CT: 8 AV: 8.60

1961 Japan 110 BW ACTION/ADVENTURE/ COMEDY/FOREIGN

D Akira Kurosawa ☆
W Akira Kurosawa Ryuzo Kikushima Hideo Oguni

Toshiro Mifune ☆ Eijiro Tono Seizaburo Kawazu Isazu Yamada Hiroshi Tachikawa

A resourceful samurai warrior named Sanjuro (Toshiro Mifune) teaches two warring factions a brutal lesson.

Amusing, highly entertaining western in oriental dress. Kurosawa was obviously inspired by those westerns in which a lone gunslinger comes to town, but here he puts a spin on the tradition where the hero fights on behalf of good versus bad, order versus chaos. Kurosawa's anti-hero is a self-interested cynic and the two factions in town are as bad as each other; therefore, he has to destroy everyone. The movie was influential on all spaghetti westerns, but especially *A Fistful of Dollars*, which is virtually a remake. The sequel, *Sanjuro* (1962) is also worth seeing.

MIXED:

'One can mildly enjoy it as a rather leisurely adventure . . . But from Kurosawa one expects more than a likeable pastiche.' *(Dilys Powell, Sunday Times, on first British release, 1970)*

'No masterpiece but the film is made with Kurosawa's usual flair for atmosphere and tongue-in-cheek melodramatics.' *(Derek Malcolm, Guardian, 1970)*

'Certainly it is not *Rashomon* or even *Seven Samurai*. But what a pleasure, all the same! What zest! What authority!' *(Margaret Hinxman, Sunday Telegraph, 1970)*

PRO:

'Kurosawa has, in effect, taken a familiar tale of violence and made from it a magnificent ironic parable . . . helped, too, by Toshiro Mifune . . . His Sanjuro is a virtuoso blend of confidence, high humor, and agile theatricality . . . [He] won the best actor award at last year's Venice Festival, and no wonder.' *(Hollis Alpert, Saturday Review)*

'In a movie that is both a wow of a show and masterpiece of misanthropy, Kurosawa emerges as a bone-cracking satirist who with red-toothed glee chews out his century as no dramatist has done since Bertold Brecht.' *(Time)*

'[Its Japanese style savagery] serves to demonstrate that screen violence cannot be condemned in the abstract; it depends on the why and the how . . . Beneath its satire on death dealing westerns and their Oriental counterparts the easters, lie Kurosawa's strong, warm, characteristic humanism and feeling for life . . . Mifune is magnificent.' *(Nina Hibbin, Morning Star, 1970)*

'One of the rare Japanese movies that is both great and funny to American audiences.' *(Pauline Kael)*

YOL: THE WAY CT: 8 AV: 7.56

1982 Switzerland 114 C DRAMA/FOREIGN

D Serif Goren (under supervision of Yilmaz Guney, then in prison)
W Yilmaz Guney ☆

Tarik Akan Halil Ergun Necmettin Cobanoglu ☆ Serif Sezer Meral Orhousoy Semra Ucar Hikmet Celik

Five prisoners are given a week's parole and find that the society outside is no less of a prison.

Grim, gruelling stuff. 'Yol' means the road of life, and Guney's angry, political drama suggests that the Turkish authorities and his countrymen's patriarchal culture are dedicated to putting up roadblocks on the way to happiness. The most moving passage comes when a Kurd (Necmettin Cobanoglu) returns home to find his village destroyed by the Turkish army; but none of the episodes is a barrel of laughs. The film could not be directed by Guney, since he was in prison (for shooting a judge, though his supporters would say that it was for his left-wing beliefs); he edited it after his escape in 1981. Winner of the Palme d'Or at Cannes.

MIXED:

'The film is grindingly depressing and therefore hard to watch until we become caught up in the characters' destinies . . . The final lesson of Guney's film is how effectively social codes break apart the closest ties and basic human instincts.' *(Mary Harron, Times Educational Supplement)*

'[Guney and Goren] cram an already laden film with sweeping landscapes, vivid country colour and music . . . There is more, perhaps, than Europeanised eyes and ears can take in at one visit, but that is hardly a fault. It is a powerful, chastening experience.' *(John Coleman, New Statesman)*

PRO:

'A shattering experience, yet, as a monument to human endurance, not finally a depressing one . . . A film of controlled anger, powerful feeling and shrewd intelligence, it compels us to re-examine our sense of social responsibility.' *(Philip French, Observer)*

'Remarkable.' *(Arthur Thirkell, Daily Mirror)*

'*Yol* is no heavy tract. It drives forward with impassioned urgency . . . [and] convincingly dramatises the idea of our common humanity.' *(Mat Snow, New Musical Express)*

'Confirms Guney as a radical director of

international status.' *(Virginia Dignam, Morning Star)*

YOU CAN'T SLEEP HERE: *see* I WAS A MALE WAR BRIDE.

YOU CAN'T TAKE IT WITH YOU AAW CT: 5 AV: 7.50

1938 US 127 BW COMEDY

D Frank Capra ☆ AAW
W Robert Riskin AAN from George S. Kaufman and Moss Hart's play

Jean Arthur Lionel Barrymore James Stewart Edward Arnold Mischa Auer Ann Miller Spring Byington ☆ AAN Harry Davenport ☆ Donald Meek ✓

An eccentric family (under patriarch Lionel Barrymore) pursues individual happiness in a mansion which a stuffy banker (Edward Arnold) wishes to pull down. The daughter of the family (Jean Arthur) is in love with the banker's son (James Stewart).

The Capra comedy which has aged least well. Robert Riskin's rewrite turned the Broadway play's celebration of individual eccentricities into a sanctimonious attack on big business. The whimsical sentimentality would be hard to bear, even without the homely philosophizing. There's far too much dialogue, and the anti-capitalist message is trite (the only reason the family can afford to live so anarchically is because they are rich). Fortunately, the performances are appealing and Capra choreographs the mayhem with some style. It was the second best picture of 1938 (*Snow White* was first), according to the *Film Daily* poll of US film critics. Joseph Walker's cinematography, Gene Havlick's editing and John Livadary's sound were Oscar-nominated.

PRO:

'A grand picture, which will disappoint only the most superficial admirers of the play . . . [and] jumps smack into the list of the year's best.' *(Frank S. Nugent, New York Times)*

'[Its] moral sticks out a mile . . . The Bad Life of Wall Street is brilliantly debunked . . . but the Good Life turns out to be hardly less nerve-racking . . . No actor on the screen today manages to appear more unconscious of script, camera and director than Mr Stewart.' *(P. Galway, New Statesman)*

'Capra's direction is leisurely and meticulous, but he knows the effect he wants to get and get them he brilliantly does . . . His handling of the cast, too is quite masterly.' *(MFB)*

'Wholly American, wholesome, homespun, human, appealing, and touching in turn.' *(Variety)*

'Shangri-La in a frame house.' *(Otis Ferguson)*

'At least the best thing Capra has ever done, this is everything you could want from a motion picture . . . [It] will send you forth loving your fellow man – but you will be weak with laughter.' *(Photoplay)*

'Created a sensation in Hollywood, influencing other directors to a surprising degree. There was no "production value", meaning glamour and lavish decor and elegant dresses, in this study of a lower-middle-class family, each of whose members was characterized by fads and hobbies that made them twice as natural as most screen people. The informality of Capra's approach, the serene curiosity with which he looked at his countrymen, the simplicity of sentiment, were something new and refreshing.' *(Egon Larsen, Spotlight on Films, 1950)*

YOU ONLY LIVE TWICE: *see BOND* SERIES.

YOUNG AND THE DAMNED, THE CT: 8 AV: 8.20

(aka *Los Olvidados*)

1950 Mexico 88 BW DRAMA/FOREIGN

D Luis Buñuel ☆
W Luis Buñuel Luis Alcoriza

Stella Inda Alfonso Mejia Roberto Cobo Jesús Navarro Miguel Inclán Alma Fuentas Francisco Jambrina

In the slums of Mexico City, an innocent boy (Alfonso Mejia) is corrupted by juvenile delinquents.

Perhaps the one film by Luis Buñuel that qualifies as 'great'. It's relentlessly depressing; but, unlike most of the director's attacks on the bourgeoisie, church and authorities, it is genuinely subversive. He takes here a genre which has always suffered from fatuous complacency and still does – the liberal 'social problem' picture – and lays the blame not on the government, 'society' or any one economic system, but on the human nature which creates such things. Far more disastrous than these characters' material poverty is their moral poverty. An inspired mixture of dream sequences and documentary realism (the superb camerawork is by Gabriel Figueroa), the film was made in only 21 days and won Buñuel best director at Cannes.

'For several months I toured the slums . . . I came to know these people and much of what I saw went unchanged into the film.' *(Luis Buñuel)*

ANTI:

'A work of art must inspire as well as shock and contribute to our understanding as well as to our knowledge of the ghastlier facts of life.' *(Thomas Spencer, Daily Worker)*

'Its very proficiency and excellent photography tend to glamorize its subject.' *(Halliwell)*

MIXED:

'Retailed with a fluid power of composition and a

microscopic care for detail . . . [Buñuel's] protest has no anger, warmth or pity, and I found myself coolly admiring the art and style of a film that left me more or less emotionally unaffected.' *(Richard Winnington, News Chronicle)*

'Life in the lower depths, heartbreaking and dreadful. I shall not put *Los Olvidados* among the films I have most enjoyed; but I am far from sure that it should not go among the monuments of the cinema.' *(Dilys Powell)*

'[Buñuel's direction] leaves you almost numb with its chilly message of harsh futility.' *(Milton Shulman, Evening Standard)*

PRO:

'Paints a terrible picture of the degrading effects of poverty and squalor . . . Though Buñuel has been accused of sensationalism, his presentation of his story completely eschews the shock-effect . . . [He] charges his film with a poetic quality which lifts it far above the level of brilliantly realistic reportage.' *(MFB)*

'Kills the other films I've seen this week stone dead. It is a fine, brave picture.' *(Sunday Chronicle)*

'Its characters and backgrounds are rooted in a determined and unsentimental realism.' *(The Times)*

'A film that probably won't let you sleep nights – but which you can't afford to miss.' *(Hollis Alpert, Saturday Review)*

'A film that lashes the mind like a red-hot iron and leaves one's conscience no opportunity for rest.' *(André Bazin)*

'Buñuel doesn't treat his characters as ideas but as morally responsible human beings; there is little of the familiar American-movie cant that makes everyone responsible for juvenile crimes except the juveniles. There's no pathos in this film; it's a squalid tragedy that causes the viewer to feel a moral terror. Buñuel, whose early work fascinated Freud, creates scenes that shock one psychologically. Among them here is the mother-meat dream – perhaps the greatest of all movie dream sequences; it is disturbing long after the lacerations of the more realistic material have healed.' *(Pauline Kael)*

'A masterfully brutal portrait of slum youths in Mexico City. In this harshly fatalistic film, Buñuel explores a world of savage cruelty – the meanest character is a blind beggar, a great believer in law and order – that includes but transcends all sociological categories. In the tradition of Freud and the surrealists, Buñuel saw his people less as victims of their environment than as pawns of their own murderous and sado-masochistic fantasy lives. In later films he learned to take this with grim amusement and, finally, with serene detachment. His fascination with ugliness and violence was almost stereotypically Spanish.' *(Morris Dickstein)*

'Devastating and unforgettable.' *(Judith Crist)*

YOUNG EINSTEIN

CT: 6 AV: 4.10

1988 Australia 91 C COMEDY

D Yahoo Serious
W Yahoo Serious David Roach ✔

Yahoo Serious ✔ (real name: Greg Pead)
Odile Le Clezio John Howard Peewee Wilson
Su Cruickshank

Albert Einstein (Yahoo Serious), a simple, Tasmanian apple-farmer, discovers the theory of relativity, splits the atom, invents the surfboard and rock 'n' roll, and still finds time to fall in love with Marie Curie (Odile Le Clezio).

Funny, underrated Australian comedy, with inventive sight gags. The story is a celebration of individualism, and a good-natured parody of solemn historical films about geniuses. The film starts hilariously, sags in the middle, and picks up again when Einstein is consigned to an asylum, along with other genius inventors like Ernest Rutherford and Brian Aspirin. There is a memorable climax involving the Wright Brothers, Charles Darwin (plus beagle), and an over-excited radio commentary by Marconi. The film scores over many would-be zany comedies by being beautifully shot, in the style of David Lean. Some critics sat through the whole thing straightfaced; but I laughed a lot.

ANTI:

'Manages to be innocuous and appalling at the same time.' *(MFB)*

'Probably only someone biffed over the head with a jar of Fosters just before the screening would find the movie as hilarious as it aims to be.' *(Nigel Andrews, Financial Times)*

'Yahoo Serious is no Paul Hogan.' *(Bart Mills, Film Yearbook)*

MIXED:

'A rip-roaring but half serious comedy . . . Serious himself is clearly a lively talent and a half. But this début film has as many drawbacks as virtues and survives on its set pieces rather than as an entity.' *(Derek Malcolm, Guardian)*

'Follows old Hollywood biopic traditions in its slight dramatic liberties . . . [Serious's] style in absurdist parody is more artless than Mel Brooks or Monty Python. [It] is, however, a stylish and well-made film.' *(David Robinson, The Times)*

'The jokes are copious, hit and miss, and very broad.' *(Sheila Johnston, Independent)*

PRO:

'Seriously funny.' *(Sun)*

YOUNG FRANKENSTEIN CT: 6 AV: 7.33

1974 US 80 BW COMEDY/HORROR/SF

D Mel Brooks ✓
W Gene Wilder Mel Brooks ☆ AAN

Gene Wilder ✓ Peter Boyle ☆ Madeline Kahn Marty Feldman ● Teri Garr Gene Hackman (unrecognizable as a blind hermit)

Frankenstein's grandson (Gene Wilder) carries on where grandad left off.

After a blood-curdlingly corny first quarter of an hour, much too dependent on unfunny mugging by Marty Feldman, this turns into Mel Brooks's most accomplished parody, with uncharacteristically stylish direction from Brooks, excellent monochrome cinematography by Gerald Hirschfeld and witty art direction by Dale Hennesy. The jokes are hit-and-miss, but the sketches involving the little girl, hermit, and the singing of 'Putting on the Ritz' work beautifully. The targets are *Frankenstein* (1931) and its first sequel, *The Bride of Frankenstein* (which was itself a parody of the genre). Brooks rented the original laboratory set for greater authenticity. The most favourably reviewed of all Brooks's films.

ANTI:

'By and large, a rather pitiful parody . . . with characters and plot resorting to juvenile mugging . . . For a really delightful parody, James Whale's own *Bride of Frankenstein* is far better value.' *(Geoff Andrew, Time Out)*

MIXED:

'Brooks's best-directed film (which is to say passable) . . . *Young Frankenstein* is like a sketch from the old Sid Caesar show, for which Brooks wrote, spun out ten times as long. Ten times too long.' *(Stanley Kauffmann)*

PRO:

'Much superior to Mel Brooks's earlier features.' *(John Simon)*

'Although patchy as all Mel Brooks' films are, it is on balance hilariously funny. But oddly, it is also true in its looney fashion to Mary Shelley's novel. There comes a point when you have to treat a legend with respect. Brooks and Wilder understand that.' *(Margaret Hinxman, Daily Mail)*

'Brooks' most sustained piece of moviemaking – the laughs never let up.' *(Pauline Kael)*

'It looks right, which makes it funnier. And then, paradoxically, it works on a couple of levels: first as comedy, and then as a weirdly touching story in its own right. A lot of the credit for that goes to the performances of Gene Wilder, as young Frankenstein, and Peter Boyle as the monster.' *(Roger Ebert)*

'The only Mel Brooks film that almost everyone likes.' *(Danny Peary)*

YOUNG IN HEART, THE CT: 6 AV: 7.13

1938 US 90 BW COMEDY/ROMANCE

D Richard Wallace ☆
W Paul Osborn Charles Bennett ☆ from I.A.R. Wylie's novel *The Gay Bandit*

Douglas Fairbanks Jr ☆ Janet Gaynor ☆ Roaland Young ☆ Billie Burke ☆ Minnie Dupree ☆ Paulette Goddard ☆ Richard Carlson Henry Stephenson

A family of confidence tricksters plans to fleece an old lady (Minnie Dupree), but instead they are 'corrupted' by her goodness.

Sentimental comedy, with a polished, witty script and sweet performances. The crooks are too good to be true, but thoroughly enjoyable. Leon Shamroy's photography and Franz Waxman's score were Oscar-nominated.

PRO:

'The story is charmingly unfolded in a leisurely manner. The direction is sympathetic and sensitive; the dialogue crisp and witty . . . The teamwork of the leading players is a joy to watch . . . The staging is ornate but not unpleasing, and the sepia-tinting of the photography is effective.' *(MFB)*

'So different, so novel that the finesse of its human, humorous amusement is likely to go unappreciated unless showmen resort to aggressive business building.' *(Today's Cinema)*

'Sentimental drama, vastly touching and entertaining . . . has everything to ensure box office success.' *(Variety)*

MIXED:

'Contains many amusing scenes and has the virtue of bringing Paulette Goddard back to the screen; but its scheme is too tidy and predictable and the family a shade too likeable: we miss in it the salutary bite of true satire.' *(New Statesmen)*

'The title is slightly sickening, and the movie does have a mushy messagey side, but . . . [it] has some good, bright moments.' *(Pauline Kael)*

YOUNG MR. LINCOLN CT: 6 AV: 7.55

1939 US 100 BW DRAMA/BIOPIC

D John Ford ☆
W Lamar Trotti ☆ AAN

Henry Fonda ☆ Alice Brady ☆ Marjorie Weaver Arleen Whelan Eddie Collins Pauline Moore Richard Cromwell

A young lawyer (Henry Fonda) prevents a lynching and proves a young man innocent of murder.

John Ford was perhaps the greatest exponent of the western myth, and here he turns his talents to fictionalizing the early life of a historical figure.

Ford and his screenwriter Trotti depict Lincoln as a moderator and unifier (the early date, 1837, enables them to avoid all mention of his part in the American Civil War which split the nation). They are also free to omit the process of learning the law and becoming a politician; this Lincoln is born a leader and is intuitively good – he even has a personal hot-line to God. What a good thing he happens to be a Democrat, rather than a fascist. Fortunately, Henry Fonda endows this saintly figure with awkwardness and humanity. The small-town atmosphere is lovingly conveyed. And the closing courtroom drama is played so well that its essentially B-movie contrivances are easily overlooked.

'For me it was like playing Jesus Christ.' *(Henry Fonda)*

MIXED:

'A dignified saga of early Lincolniana, paced rather slowly . . . Lack of romance interest is one of the prime factors which deter the film from interpreting itself into big box office.' *(Variety)*

PRO:

'Its source is a womb of popular and national spirit. This could account for its unity, its artistry, its genuine beauty.' *(Sergei Eisenstein)*

'Its simple good faith and understanding are an expression of the country's best life that says as much as forty epics.' *(Otis Ferguson)*

'Period details are lovingly sketched in – a log splitting contest, a tug of war, a tar barrel rolling match.' *(Charles Higham)*

'In spite of the excitements of a murder, a near-lynching and a crackerjack trial, it remains a character study.' *(New York Sun)*

'Never one to cut for shock effect or to create an artificial sense of surprise or excitement, Ford's film demonstrates functional editing at its best – precise, unobtrusive and sure.' *(Arthur Knight, The Liveliest Art)*

'One of John Ford's most memorable films, and not at all the tedious bummer that the title might suggest.' *(Pauline Kael, 70s)*

YOUNG SCARFACE: *see* BRIGHTON ROCK.

YOUNGBLOOD HAWKE   CT: 5 AV: 3.43

1964 US 137 BW DRAMA/SO BAD

D Delmer Daves ●
W Delmer Daves ● from Herman Wouk's novel

James Franciscus ● Genevieve Page Suzanne Pleshette Eva Gabor Mary Astor ☆ Lee Bowman Edward Andrews John Emery Don Porter

A southern truck-driver (James Franciscus) becomes the darling of the New York literary scene.

A camp masterpiece, with clichés galore, classic bad dialogue, a dire leading performance from Franciscus, and a risibly naive view of literary life. Improbable though it is, it's loosely based on the real-life experiences of novelist Herman Wouk.

Sample lines . . . Married temptress (Genevieve Page): (1) 'What shall I call you, Youngie or Bloody?' (2) 'When I'm with you, everything seems new again. It's sharp, and good, and food tastes better, and colours seem more intense, and oh, I love you, Bloody.'

MIXED:

'Delmer Daves has an inimitable way with soap operas and he almost brings [this] off. But not quite. The more massive absurdities . . . are splendidly enjoyable . . . but these scenes don't mix at all well with the keenly satirical observations of socialites [et al] . . . In between times, interminable footage . . . slows the whole thing down disastrously . . . Both art direction and photography give the film a pleasant visual texture, however, and the acting. . . . is excellent.' *(Tom Milne, MFB)*

'Apart from insensitive direction, a ludicrous script, inept casting and a goggle-eyed approach to literature, luxury living and love, it isn't bad.' *(Nina Hibbin, Daily Worker)*

ANTI:

'All the sound, fury and color of [the] novel have been reduced almost to a round zero in the movie version . . . [which] is a triumphantly bloodless mirage of entertainment stretched out for more than two and a half hours . . . Mr Wouk's story . . . has become as thin and glossy as wax paper.' *(Howard Thompson, New York Times)*

'Trite story . . . so unconvincing that Mr Daves would have been well advised to play it for laughs.' *(Ian Wright, Guardian)*

'A giggle a minute.' *(John Coleman, New Statesman)*

'Hilariously details the heartbreak of success in the New York literary game . . . As written and directed by Delmer Daves, *Youngblood Hawke* seems the work of someone who has never even read a book.' *(Margulies & Rebello)*

'The portrait of Manhattan's literary set is enough to give the girls on the *Squeedunk High Gazette* the giggles.' *(Judith Crist)*

Z

Z AAW AAN

CT: 7 AV: 8.69

1968 France/Algeria 125 C DRAMA/FOREIGN

D Constantin Costa-Gavras AAN
W Constantin Costa-Gavras Jorge Semprun ☆ AAN from Vassili Vassilikos's novel

Yves Montand Jean-Louis Trintignant ☆
Irene Papas Jacques Perrin Charles Denner
François Périer Pierre Dux Julien Guiomar

A magistrate (Jean-Louis Trintignant) investigates the death of a left-wing politician (Yves Montand) in an unnamed Mediterranean country.

Suspense-packed political thriller. Although the target is clearly the Colonels' regime in Greece, the film works today because it might apply to any totalitarian regime. It's talky and simplistic, but well acted and convincing in its paranoia. Director Costa-Gavras went on to make other fine political thrillers including *Missing* and *Music Box*, but this is certainly one of his best. It not only won the Oscar for best foreign film, it was even deemed worthy of nomination as best film. Françoise Bonnot won an Academy Award for her editing.

MIXED:

'Certainly, the complex political issues involved are simplified – but as a general statement on the mechanics of political corruption *Z* has rarely been equalled and never surpassed.' *(Clive Hirschhorn, Sunday Express)*

'Talky film praised more for its topicality than cinematics is nonetheless gripping; good acting.' *(Maltin)*

PRO:

'Converted and unconverted alike will be riveted to their seats by the impact of this finest foreign language film of the year, a fiercely passionate, coolly detailed story of political assassination and of the death of virtue.' *(Judith Crist)*

'Taut, humane, intelligently constructed, sharply executed.' *(John Simon)*

'Not only a fine social protest, but exciting movie-making.' *(Scheuer)*

ZANDALEE

CT: 5 AV: 2.75

1991 US 100 C ROMANCE/DRAMA/SO BAD

D Sam Pillsbury ●
W Mari Kornhauser ●

Nicolas Cage ● Judge Reinhold ●
Erika Anderson ● Joe Pantoliano Viveca Lindfors
Marisa Tomei Zach Galligan Steve Buscemi

In New Orleans, two men (Judge Reinhold, Nicolas Cage) fight for the same woman (Erika Anderson).

Excruciatingly pretentious American attempt to make a soft porn art-house movie. In the absence of a more exotic setting, New Orleans is pressed into erotic service, as in Paul Schrader's *Cat People*, to provide ironwork as overwrought as the characters. These correspond to the miserable triangle in *Lady Chatterley's Lover*: the impotent husband (Judge Reinhold), the frustrated wife (Erika Anderson) and the earthy philanderer (Nicolas Cage). Mix in a little Ken Russellesque nonsense about the link between artistic inspiration and free love, plus a Norman Mailer-chauvinist relish for sodomy, and there you have it. And, frankly, you're welcome to it.

Sample lines . . . Impotent husband (Judge Reinhold) to wife (Erika Anderson): 'I'm just paralyzed – a paraplegic of the soul.' Cage to Anderson : (1) 'Without creativity, without life, then you are truly unable to go straight up the devil's ass, look him right in the face, smile, and survive.' (2) 'We're inevitable. I want to shake you naked and eat you alive, Zandalee!'

Sample dialogue . . . (1) Cage: 'Why'd you marry him?' Anderson: 'He was a poet.' Cage (sticking hand down her jogging shorts): 'Isn't this poetry?' (2) Anderson: 'I can't be what you want me to be.' Cage: 'Yes, you can. Roll over on your stomach.'

'The plot is daft, the dialogue worse.' *(Nigel Floyd, Time Out)*

'Ill-written, pretentious trash.' *(Philip French, Observer)*

'From bedroom to bayou we follow . . . our minds boggling that this ill-kempt farrago was directed by the talented . . . Pillsbury.' *(Nigel Andrews, Financial Times)*

'Has the disconcerting air of an *Emmanuelle* film scripted by an aspiring D.H. Lawrence . . . [The film] founders on pretentious dialogue and on inadequate character development.' *(Hugo Davenport, Daily Telegraph)*

'Some of the most coldly explicit sex scenes I have witnessed . . . [It's] a clinical exercise in soft porn dressed up as a tale of complex personal relationships. I longed for someone to come along and throw a bucket of cold water over the lot of them. Dreadful stuff.' *(Sue Heal, Today)*

'Despite gratuitous nudity being the film's *raison d'être*, watching leaves fall would be still more fun than wading through this tripe.' *(Rose)*

'Shamefully unsexy' *(Winnert)*

'It's quite a while before it sinks in fully that this movie isn't an *Airplane* or *Hot Shots*-style send-up of such trash classics as *9½ Weeks* and *Wild Orchid*, but just utterly deadpan, unintentionally funny moviemaking.' *(Margulies & Rebello)*

ZEE & CO CT: 5 AV: 3.57
(aka *X, Y & Zee*)

1971 GB 109 C DRAMA/SO BAD

D Brian Hutton ●
W Edna O'Brien ●

Michael Caine ● Elizabeth Taylor ● Susannah York ● Margaret Leighton ● John Standing

A husband (Michael Caine) and wife (Elizabeth Taylor) bicker; she has an affair with his mistress (Susannah York).

Trashy but perversely entertaining sex melodrama. Action-director Hutton directs with zero taste and sensitivity.

Sample lines . . . (1) Elizabeth Taylor: 'I sat next to a man at dinner one night who said you haven't lived until you've seen a woman breast-feed twins. Evidently his wife would lie sprawled on the bed, a tit in either direction, and it was just fantastic.' (2) Michael Caine about Susannah York: 'She sees beauty in everything – especially shit!'

PRO:

'Not in years have three people more deserved the star billing they get in this *Love Story* for adults. Elizabeth Taylor and Susannah York both turn in performances that fully capture the excellently conceived characters of Edna O'Brien's original screenplay. Michael Caine keeps up beautifully with the pace set by his femme co-stars.' *(Variety)*

'Basically the old story of a human triangle . . . given pep by fierce dialogue and Miss Taylor's vitriolic performance . . . The film is worth seeing for [her] alone.' *(Madeleine Harmsworth, Sunday Mirror)*

MIXED:

'It thinks in its juicy examination of marriage on the rocks that it is being incredibly smart and worldly. Actually it arrives at the stage of being ridiculous . . . without ever passing within hailing distance of the sublime. I quite enjoyed it, however, since there's nothing like an overt piece of pseudery to make one feel all lilywhite and uncompromised.' *(Derek Malcolm, Guardian)*

ANTI:

'Reading Edna O'Brien's published screenplay would, I'm sure, be a far finer experience.' *(Alexander Walker, Evening Standard)*

'Clearly had every intention of being very sophisticated indeed . . . Any plausibility [it] may have had is pretty soon shattered by the truly awful structure and dialogue which scorns practically no movie cliché.' *(David Robinson, Financial Times)*

'A phoney little adventure in trendy-land . . . Caine commutes between [York and Taylor] as if in a hypnotic trance . . . The women . . . act their heads off to no avail. For [the] script is a load of smart-talk wrapped in mush and life, to . . . Hutton, is evidently one long telly commercial.' *(Nina Hibbin, Morning Star)*

'Miss Taylor seems to have set her mind on giving scrapping lessons to fishwives . . . Hutton . . . tends to stage a family fracas as though it . . . had to compete with a Force 8 gale.' *(Penelope Houston)*

'A slice-of-jet-set-life nightmare far beyond the dreams of the piggiest male chauvinist . . . The distinction of this film is that its characters are repulsive, its style vulgar, its situations beyond belief and its dialogue moronic.' *(Judith Crist)*

'Taylor-York love scene ranks high in the annals of poor taste.' *(Maltin)*

'One of those follies that everyone involved (especially writer Edna O'Brien) must look back on with cringing embarrassment . . . The real highpoint is the sight of Margaret Leighton in a see-thru blouse with a pet faggot in tow.' *(Tony Rayns, Time Out)*

ZELIG CT: 5 AV: 6.40

1983 US 79 BW C COMEDY

D Woody Allen ☆
W Woody Allen

Woody Allen Mia Farrow John Buckwalter Marvin Chatinover

Woody Allen's fake biography of a human chameleon (Woody Allen) who hob-nobs with the great and the not-so-good of the 20th century.

Allen is in muted as well as mutated form. Although the way live action is combined with documentary footage is technically wonderful, this is a one-joke movie and (as several film guides point out in identical words) 'more clever than funny'. There is something disturbing and haunting about this figure of Zelig, who rises to celebrity by being all things to all men; but ultimately Allen seems unsure of what he is trying to say. Though praised by many of those who hated his *Stardust Memories* for being misanthropic, this musing on the nature of fame is at least equally jaundiced. Gordon Willis's cinematography and Santo Loquasto's costume design were Oscar nominated; surprisingly, the visual effects (by John Caglione Jr, Joel Hynick, Stuart Robinson and Richard Greenberg) were overlooked.

PRO:

'*Citizen Kane* miraculously transformed into side-splitting comedy.' *(New York Times)*

'By astounding technical wizardry [Allen] is seamlessly matched into authentic documentary footage with Hitler and Marion Davies. Allen at his peak – sharply funny, socially relevant, totally original.' *(NFT Bulletin)*

'The skill is so clever as to approach brilliance.' *(Stanley Kauffmann)*

'The technical brilliance of *Zelig* . . . is the manufacturing of documentary pastiche more detailed and accurate than any we have ever seen done in the cinema . . . The precise meaning of the allegory remains obscure; or shall we say complex, multifarious . . . It has something to do . . . with the redemption that may be brought about through love . . . [Allen's] films have the right degree of personality and impersonality. They are brilliantly marshalled and directed. He is a genius and an enthusiast – surely one of the most important current artists of the cinema.' *(Mark Le Fanu, F & F)*

'The movie's wit never flags . . . As important as the humor and quite unexpected, considering the high quotient of satire and parody, is the film's generosity of spirit.' *(Vincent Canby, New York Times)*

'A brilliant cinematic collage that is pure magic, and allows Woody to satirize all sorts of things, from nostalgia, psychoanalysis and the American Dream to critics, himself and much more . . . His Zelig is a romantic who desperately wants the supreme cocktail of realism mixed with glory – the Great Gatsby as schlemiel.' *(Jack Kroll, Newsweek)*

'Consistently funny, though more academic than boulevardier.' *(Variety)*

MIXED:

'The movie is a technical masterpiece, but in artistic and comic terms, only pretty good.' *(Roger Ebert)*

'We can all admire the brilliance and economy with which it is made. But is it funny enough? I take leave to doubt it.' *(Derek Malcolm, Guardian)*

'A film with too much cleverness for its own good.' *(John Simon)*

ZEMLYA: *see* EARTH.

ZERO FOR CONDUCT CT: 5 AV: 8.20

(aka *Zéro de Conduite*)

1933 France 45/47 BW DRAMA/FOREIGN

D Jean Vigo ☆
W Jean Vigo

Jean Dasté Louis Léfèvre le nain Delphin Robert Le Flem Louis de Gonzague-Frick Gilbert Pluchon Gérard de Bédarieux Constantin Goldstein-Kehler

School children rebel against the petty restrictions of their teachers.

This hugely acclaimed surrealist picture by the short-lived Jean Vigo (1905-1934) was once thought so subversive that the French government banned it soon after release, on the grounds that it might lead to social unrest. Rereleased in 1945, it soon acquired a reputation for its set-pieces (notably a pillow-fight that looks suspiciously like the one in Abel Gance's *Napoléon*) and idealization of youthful iconoclasm. It remains famous as the anarchic inspiration behind Lindsay Anderson's *If . . .*; but the truth is that its satire is crude, its story-telling perfunctory, and the performances (mostly by non-professionals) pretty awful.

PRO:

'Witty, intelligent, vital and original. It has already been condemned as highbrow. For it gives you a startling picture of a community of boys, savage, ritualistic and remote from the normally levelled adult eye and understanding. And it gives you a boy's eye view of the masters, too, with all their deficiencies, absurdities, madnesses and indecencies thrown into necessary caricature. It gathers lucidity with each viewing.' *(Richard Winnington)*

'One of the most visually eloquent and adventurous movies I have seen . . . The spirit of this film, its fierceness and gaiety, the total absence of well-constructed "constructive" diagnosis and prescription, the enormous liberating force of its quasi-nihilism, its humor, directness, kindliness, criminality, and guile, form for me as satisfying a revolutionary expression as I know.' *(James Agee, Nation)*

'A celebration of the pure freedom of children's imaginations, a stirring expression of resistance to the forces of authority and order – to anything that would impose discipline on the diverse, unruly energy of play. *Zero for Conduct* isn't constructed like an ordinary movie; Vigo evidently considered the discipline of narrative a form of repression, too, and his indifference to it has a lot to do with why *Zero for Conduct* still seems, fifty-seven years later, like one of the few truly subversive movies ever made.' *(Terrence Rafferty)*

'An ode to fierce joy, ending with kids on a roof reaching for the sky, a lyrical finale that celebrates the liberating genius of childhood and offers this director's vision of how we all should try to live.' *(John Powers)*

MIXED:

'A clear forerunner of *If . . .* and one of the most famous of surrealist films, though it pales beside Buñuel and is chiefly valuable for being funny.' *(Halliwell)*

ZOMBIES: *see* DAWN OF THE DEAD.

ZULU CT: 7 AV: 7.23

1964 GB 138 C WAR/ACTION/ADVENTURE/EPIC

D Cy Endfield
W John Prebble Cy Endfield

Stanley Baker ☆ Jack Hawkins ☆ Ulla Jacobsson

James Booth Michael Caine ✓ Nigel Green ☆ Glynn Edwards Ivor Emmanuel Paul Daneman

Outnumbered British soldiers take on the Zulu hordes at Rorke's Drift.

Epic action movie set in 1879, very faithful to the real historical events, with an exciting climax that takes up about half the running-time. Michael Caine was cast against type as an upper-class officer, but gave one of his better performances, alongside the ever-reliable Stanley Baker and Jack Hawkins.

Not surprisingly, the film was popular with the public, but critically underrated. Imperialistic heroics were extremely unfashionable with the intelligentsia during the 60s, as was any depiction of black people as enemies rather than victims or social problems. A few decades on, this movie deserves to be recognized for what it is – a rip-roaring action film with strong performances and a terrific story to tell.

MIXED:

'*Zulu* arrives armed to the teeth to make a killing at the box office, and it deserves to do so, but is it ungracious to regret that all the screen shows us nearly all the time is another kind of killing?' *(Alexander Walker, Evening Standard)*

'Mr Endfield now and then rises to his visual opportunity . . . For a film that's largely taken up with killing, it strikes me as decidedly unbloodthirsty.' *(Isabel Quigly, Spectator)*

'[The] direction . . . adroitly pieces together the grim jig-saw puzzle of war and mingles little *Journey's End* touches of shy self stock-taking and backs-to-the-wall kinship with the din and the odd dignity of death. Sometimes the drama is too theatrical to ring true.' *(Cecil Wilson, Daily Mail)*

ANTI:

'Once the carnage is over, there's a general sort of feeling that the Zulus are jolly fine chaps (for savages). The one point that is never even hinted at is that the land belonged to the Zulus and the British had no business to be there at all.' *(Nina Hibbin, Daily Worker)*

'Oh, how slow it all is . . . The Zulus look terribly embarrassed as they are put through their paces, but then, so does Jack Hawkins . . . This is the kind of film where nobody ever seems to have given any real thought to what the characters do and say.' *(Richard Roud, Guardian)*

'This overdose of gore and clichés is strictly for kiddies with cast-iron stomachs.' *(Judith Crist)*